The *Enhanced* Guide for Occupational Exploration

Descriptions for the 2,500 Most Important Jobs

Compiled by Marilyn Maze and Donald Mayall
With introductory materials by J. Michael Farr

Based on information from the U.S. Department of Labor,
Department of Commerce, Census Bureau, Ciasa, Inc.,
and other sources

Publisher/Editor: J. Michael Farr
Project Director: Spring Dawn Reader
Production Editor: Sara Hall
Cover Design: Al Smith
Interior Design: Spring Dawn Reader
Proofreader: Michelle R. Head

The *Enhanced* Guide for Occupational Exploration—*Descriptions for the 2,500 Most Important Jobs*

©1991, JIST Works Inc., Indianapolis, IN

Disclaimer of liability: The authors and publisher have been careful to obtain reliable and accurate information in this work but can accept no responsibility for any omissions or errors in fact nor for any decisions made or actions taken as a result of the information provided. As in all things, we humbly suggest that you accept your own judgement regarding career and life decisions as the ultimate human authority.

JIST Works, Inc.
720 North Park Avenue
Indianapolis, IN 46202-3431
Phone: (317) 264-3720 • FAX: (317) 264-3709

Library of Congress Catologing-in-Publication Data
Maze, Marilyn.
   The enhanced guide for occupational exploration : descriptions for
the 2,500 most important jobs / compiled by Marilyn Maze and
Donald Mayall with introductory materials by J. Micahel Farr.
      p.   cm.
   Based on information from the U.S. Department of Labor and other sources.
   Includes index.
   ISBN 0-942784-76-6 : $29.95
   1. Vocational interests—United States. 2. Vocational guidance—United States.
3. Job descriptions. 4. United States—Occupations. I. Mayall, Donald, 1932- .
II. United States. Dept. of Labor. III. Title.
HF5382.M37   1991
331.7'02'0973—dc20
                                                             91-8830
                                                               CIP

ISBN: 0-942784-76-6

About This Book

This book represents the first time that such a wide variety of data on all the major occupations has been assembled in one place. The fact that it was done without government funding is noteworthy, although it would not have been possible without access to the computerized data files of the U.S. Department of Labor and other government sources. In that sense, it is the result of positive collaboration between the public and private sectors.

Just as computer access to various data bases have made this book possible, many other jobs have been affected by recent changes in technology and changed so dramatically that their old descriptions are no longer valid. During the same time, new technologies have created new job titles while others have been eliminated.

The data in this book is based on the latest computer data bases updated every month by the U.S. Department of Labor and other sources. In fact, this book contains data and codification systems that have never before been published and that reflect the most recent changes available from various sources. This includes all the new and revised job descriptions as published by the Department of Labor in the supplements to the *Dictionary of Occupational Titles* as well as additional changes that will not be available from any other published source until the revision of the *Dictionary of Occupational Titles* itself. For this reason, this book will not be outdated for some time. We hope that you find it helpful.

About RAVE

The information in this book is based on a database of occupational information that has been constructed for use in career assessment by Ciasa, Inc., a corporation located in Berkeley, California. The title of the computer program that uses the database is Realistic Assessment of Vocational Alternatives (RAVE). In preparing this book, a special set of 2,500 occupations were selected from the RAVE database and special data categories were coded for them.

RAVE is designed to search for appropriate occupations. To use the program, a job seeker selects the attributes which best describe them from the ones listed in this book. Then the computer finds the occupations which match best. This client profile can be based on transferable skills for people, with prior work experience, or on personal assessment. For more information about RAVE, contact The Vocational Resource at 1-800-888-0258 or 1-415-644-2771.

Table of Contents

All 2,500 job descriptions in this book are listed within one of 12 major interest areas defined by the U.S. Department of Labor and used in the original *Guide for Occupational Exploration*. Brief definitions of each of these interest areas are found on this page. Be sure to read them in order to get an idea of the basic structure used throughout this book.

Within each of the 12 major interest areas, there are increasingly specific groupings of related jobs. This list provides a summary listing of these categories and allows you to quickly identify clusters of jobs with similar characteristics for further exploration.

This is a summary list of the codes used in the job descriptions throughout this book. Use it as a "quick" reference source when interpreting the codes.

This chapter provides information on how this book was developed and how to use it. Sections include: Who should use this book; How the book is organized; Interest Areas; Work Groups; Subgroups; Tips for finding a particular job or cluster; A sample occupational description; Brief review of the elements of a job description and its codes; Which jobs have been included; Occupations that are not included; Sources of data used in this book; Tips for using the book without counselor assistance .

Provides a more detailed review of the sources and interpretation of the occupational descriptions and the codes that are provided for each. Sections include: The Narrative Section of the Occupational Description; Detailed Descriptions of the Data Categories and Codes; Industry Designation; The DOT Code Number; Definitions of Data, People, and Things Skills; The OES Code; The GED Code; The SVP Code; Academic Codes (Ed and Eng); The Work Field Code; The MPSMS Code; Aptitudes Codes; Temperaments Codes; Stress Related Codes; Physical Requirements Codes; Work Environment Codes; Salary Codes; Outlook Codes.

OCCUPATIONAL DESCRIPTIONS

This is the major component of this book. It provides descriptions of 2,500 jobs organized within increasingly specific clusters of related jobs. The occupations are arranged in numerical order, with each cluster of related jobs listed within the numeric sections that follow. In addition to the descriptions themselves, there is a narrative section at the beginning of each major cluster of jobs that describes what these jobs have in common. These brief narratives allow you to gain an overview of each job cluster before looking more closely at specific jobs listed within each. It provides an effective method for exploring career alternatives in a simple and efficient manner.

Following are the titles of the 12 major occupational interest areas into which each of the 2,500 jobs are organized along with the numeric section of the book where these jobs begin. The Definitions of Interest Factors on page IX and The Summary Listing of Interest Groups, Work Groups and Subgroups, beginning on page X, will provide you additional details on how the jobs in this book are organized.

©1991, JIST Works, Inc. • Indianapolis, IN

An Introduction

The *Enhanced Guide for Occupational Exploration* (hereafter often referred to as the Enhanced *GOE* or *EGOE*) is a significant new resource for job seekers, career changers, and vocational counselors. Containing 2,500 occupational descriptions, it covers over 95 percent of all workers in the U.S. economy. Its cross-referencing systems allow you to find jobs by skills, interests, education required, industry, and many other criteria.

Based on information provided by the U.S. Department of Labor, the Census Bureau, and other reliable sources, this book has been carefully researched and compiled to provide useful information. Some of the information provided is not available in any other published source and the variety of information provided on each occupation has never been gathered together in one book before. Each occupational description and related information code is based on the latest data provided by the U.S. Department of Labor's computerized database and other sources rather than the older information sources typically provided.

To understand the importance of this book, it is useful to know its predecessors. The original *Guide for Occupational Exploration* (often referred to as the *GOE* throughout this work) was published by the U.S. Department of Labor in 1979. A second edition with significant improvements, by Drs. Thomas Harrington and Arthur O'Shea, was published by another source in the mid-1980s. Each of these books organized over 12,000 occupations into logical clusters and provided a number of ways to cross-reference them. Designed to help job seekers, career changers, students and others explore career alternatives, these are also widely used by vocational counselors.

The earlier editions of the GOE were — and are — very helpful. They allow users to access the huge variety of occupational choices in a rational and useful way. But both books have limitations caused by the huge number of occupations being listed. The first limitation is that neither edition contains descriptions of the jobs it lists. The 12,000 jobs are simply listed by title. To find descriptions of a job, you have to refer to another U.S. Department of Labor Publication, the Dictionary of Occupational Titles (often called the DOT or D.O.T.). This approach is understandable since the original GOE was over 700 pages and providing even brief descriptions for each occupation would have made it an unmanageable 2,000 pages or so.

The second major limitation of the *GOE* is that, for many people, there are too many occupations listed. Many are highly specialized occupations and have very few people employed in them. In fact, fewer than 5 percent of the workforce are employed in 10,000 of the over 12,000 occupations listed. Since the *GOE* does not differentiate the more important occupations from the less, this made the book difficult for many to use.

The third limitation of the *GOE* is that many people want specific information that is not available in either the *GOE* or in the *DOT* it cross-references. For example, most individuals would want to know how much training is required for a specific job and its salary range. Vocational counselors and individuals also need information on a variety of other measures such as work field codes, temperaments, or stress and physical requirements codes. Yet the information is not available in the *GOE* without reference to a variety of other governmental and other information sources. In some cases, the information is not readily available at all.

This book, *The Enhanced Guide for Occupational Exploration*, (*EGOE*) was designed to correct the three major limitations of the original and second edition of the original *GOE*. A careful analysis of over 12,000 occupations was conducted to identify the 2,500 jobs included in this book. Few people would be interested in the occupations that have been excluded as they employ very few people or are highly specialized.

viii The Enhanced GOE

Each of these 2,500 selected jobs has a narrative description as well as substantial additional information. The authors used sophisticated computer techniques to develop the descriptions of jobs included in this book. The data was obtained from a variety of published and unpublished sources and includes information for each occupation that had previously been available only by combing through a variety of reference books. In some cases, information has been included that has not been previously published at all. Additional details on selection criteria and sources of data are provided in the first two chapters.

The 2,500 occupations selected for this book are arranged in the same useful clusters found in the original *GOE*. A series of indices is also provided in this book to cross-reference the various jobs listed in a variety of helpful ways.

The original *GOE* and its second edition will remain useful career reference tools for years to come. For cross-referencing obscure occupations, they will remain the books of choice. For most people, however, we think that this *"Enhanced GOE"* will be more useful.

Definitions of Interest Factors

The U.S. Department of Labor has divided all jobs into one of 12 major groupings based on interests. Brief definitions of these 12 Interest Factors are explained below. These are the same groupings used in the original *Guide for Occupational Exploration* and are frequently used in other career information systems.

One way to approach career exploration or job seeking is to look for the interest groups that you like best or in which you have previous experience or training. These groups then define the clusters of jobs worthy of additional exploration.

Look over the brief descriptions that follow. They are the same 12 groupings provided in the Table of Contents of this book.

The 12 Interest Factors

1. **Artistic**: Interest in creative expression of feelings or ideas.
2. **Scientific**: Interest in discovering, collecting, and analyzing information about the natural world and in applying scientific research findings to problems in medicine, life sciences, and natural sciences.
3. **Plants and Animals**: Interest in activities involving plants and animals, usually in an outdoor setting.
4. **Protective**: Interest in the use of authority to protect people and property.
5. **Mechanical**: Interest in applying mechanical principles to practical situations, using machines, hand tools, or techniques.
6. **Industrial**: Interest in repetitive, concrete, organized activities in a factory setting.
7. **Business Detail**: Interest in organized, clearly defined activities requiring accuracy and attention to detail, primarily in an office setting.
8. **Selling**: Interest in bringing others to a point of view through personal persuasion, using sales and promotion techniques.
9. **Accommodating**: Interest in catering to the wishes of others, usually on a one-to-one basis.
10. **Humanitarian**: Interest in helping others with their mental, spiritual, social, physical, or vocational needs.
11. **Leading-Influencing**: Interest in leading and influencing others through activities involving high-level verbal or numerical abilities.
12. **Physical Performing**: Interest in physical activities performed before an audience.

©1991, JIST Works, Inc. • Indianapolis, IN

Summary List of Interest Areas, Work Groups, and Subgroups

The 12 major interest factors are further divided into 66 work groups and 348 subgroups. This structure is presented in the summary table that follows with the 12 interest areas in large capital letters, the 66 work groups in bold letters and their 348 related subgroups organized under each work group. Each of the increasingly specific interest areas, work groups, and subgroups have brief narratives at the beginning of their respective sections providing an overview of the jobs in that cluster. Job descriptions with similar characteristics are arranged within these clusters.

Because each of the 2,500 jobs in this book are organized within increasingly specific clusters of related jobs, any job is easy to find in the numerical sequence of its GOE number. These numbers are also provided in various indices of this book. One way to use this book is to identify one or more of the 12 major interest factors, then look for work groups and subgroups within these that are of particular interest. Jobs listed in these clusters should then be studied more carefully.

Summary List of Interest Areas, Work Groups, and Subgroups

01 Artistic

01.01 Literary Arts
01.01-01 Editing
01.01-02 Creative Writing
01.01-03 Critiquing

01.02 Visual Arts
01.02-01 Instructing and Appraising
01.02-02 Studio Art
01.02-03 Commercial Art

01.03 Performing Arts: Drama
01.03-01 Instructing and Directing
01.03-02 Performing
01.03-03 Narrating and Announcing

01.04 Performing Arts: Music
01.04-01 Instructing and Directing
01.04-02 Composing and Arranging
01.04-03 Vocal Performing
01.04-04 Instrumental Performing

01.05 Performing Arts: Dance
01.05-01 Instructing and Choreography
01.05-02 Performing

01.06 Craft Arts
01.06-01 Graphic Arts and Related Crafts
01.06-02 Arts and Crafts
01.06-03 Hand Lettering, Painting, and Decorating

01.07 Elemental Arts
01.07-01 Psychic Science
01.07-02 Announcing
01.07-03 Entertaining

01.08 Modeling
01.08-01 Personal Appearance

02 Scientific

02.01 Physical Sciences
02.01-01 Theoretical Research
02.01-02 Technology

02.02 Life Sciences
02.02-01 Animal Specialization
02.02-02 Plant Specialization
02.02-03 Plant and Animal Specialization
02.02-04 Food Research

02.03 Medical Sciences
02.03-01 Medicine and Surgery
02.03-02 Dentistry
02.03-03 Veterinary Medicine
02.03-04 Health Specialties

02.04 Laboratory Technology
02.04-01 Physical Sciences
02.04-02 Life Sciences

03 Plants and Animals

03.01 Managerial Work: Plants and Animals
03.01-01 Farming
03.01-02 Specialty Breeding
03.01-03 Specialty Cropping
03.01-04 Forestry and Logging

03.02 General Supervision: Plants and Animals
03.02-01 Farming
03.02-02 Forestry and Logging
03.02-03 Nursery and Groundskeeping
03.02-04 Services

03.03 Animal Training and Service
03.03-01 Animal Training
03.03-02 Animal Service

03.04 Elemental Work: Plants and Animals
03.04-01 Farming
03.04-02 Forestry and Logging
03.04-03 Hunting and Fishing
03.04-04 Nursery and Groundskeeping
03.04-05 Services

04 Protective

04.01 Safety and Law Enforcement
04.01-01 Managing
04.01-02 Investigating

04.02 Security Services
04.02-01 Detention
04.02-02 Property and People
04.02-03 Law and Order
04.02-04 Emergency Responding

05 Mechanical

05.01 Engineering
05.01-01 Research
05.01-02 Environmental Protection
05.01-03 Systems Design
05.01-04 Testing and Quality Control
05.01-05 Sales Engineering
05.01-06 Work Planning and Utilization
05.01-07 Design
05.01-08 General Engineering

05.02 Managerial Work: Mechanical
05.02-01 Systems
05.02-02 Maintenance and Construction
05.02-03 Processing and Manufacturing
05.02-04 Communications
05.02-05 Mining, Logging, and Petroleum Production
05.02-06 Services
05.02-07 Materials Handling

05.03 Engineering Technology
05.03-01 Surveying
05.03-02 Drafting
05.03-03 Expediting and Coordinating
05.03-04 Petroleum
05.03-05 Electrical-Electronic
05.03-06 Industrial and Safety
05.03-07 Mechanical
05.03-08 Environmental Control
05.03-09 Packaging and Storing

05.04 Air and Water Vehicle Operation
05.04-01 Air
05.04-02 Water

05.05 Craft Technology
05.05-01 Masonry, Stone, and Brick Work
05.05-02 Construction and Maintenance
05.05-03 Plumbing and Pipefitting

Summary List of Interest Areas, Work Groups, and Subgroups

	Marking, Labeling, and Ticketing
06.04-38	Wrapping and Packing
06.04-39	Cleaning
06.04-40	Loading, Moving, Hoisting, and Conveying

07 Business Detail

07.01	**Administrative Detail**
07.01-01	Interviewing
07.01-02	Administration
07.01-03	Secretarial Work
07.01-04	Financial Work
07.01-05	Certifying
07.01-06	Investigating
07.01-07	Test Administration
07.02	**Mathematical Detail**
07.02-01	Bookkeeping and Auditing
07.02-02	Accounting
07.02-03	Statistical Reporting and Analysis
07.02-04	Billing and Rate Computation
07.02-05	Payroll and Timekeeping
07.03	**Financial Detail**
07.03-01	Paying and Receiving
07.04	**Oral Communication**
07.04-01	Interviewing
07.04-02	Order, Complaint, and Claims Handling
07.04-03	Registration
07.04-04	Reception and Information Giving
07.04-05	Information Transmitting and Receiving
07.04-06	Switchboard Services
07.05	**Records Processing**
07.05-01	Coordinating and Scheduling
07.05-02	Record Verification and Proofing
07.05-03	Record Preparation and Maintenance
07.05-04	Routing and Distribution
07.06	**Clerical Machine Operation**
07.06-01	Computer Operation
07.06-02	Keyboard Machine Operation
07.07	**Clerical Handling**
07.07-01	Filing
07.07-02	Sorting and Distribution
07.07-03	General Clerical Work

08 Selling

08.01	**Sales Technology**
08.01-01	Technical Sales
08.01-02	Intangible Sales
08.01-03	General Clerical Work
08.02	**General Sales**
08.02-01	Wholesale
08.02-02	Retail
08.02-03	Wholesale and Retail
08.02-04	Real Estate
08.02-05	Demonstration and Sales
08.02-06	Services
08.02-07	Driving-Selling
08.02-08	Soliciting-Selling

08.03	**Vending**
08.03-01	Peddling and Hawking
08.03-02	Promoting

09 Accommodating

09.01	**Hospitality Services**
09.01-01	Social and Recreational Activities
09.01-02	Guide Services
09.01-03	Food Services
09.01-04	Safety and Comfort Services
09.02	**Barber and Beauty Services**
09.02-01	Cosmetology
09.02-02	Barbering
09.03	**Passenger Services**
09.03-01	Group Transportation
09.03-02	Individual Transportation
09.03-03	Instruction and Supervision
09.04	**Customer Services**
09.04-01	Food Services
09.04-02	Sales Services
09.05	**Attendant Services**
09.05-01	Physical Conditioning
09.05-02	Food Services
09.05-03	Portering and Baggage Services
09.05-04	Doorkeeping Services
09.05-05	Card and Game Room Services
09.05-06	Individualized Services
09.05-07	General Wardrobe Services
09.05-08	Ticket Taking, Ushering

10 Humanitarian

10.01	**Social Services**
10.01-01	Religious
10.01-02	Counseling and Social Work
10.02	**Nursing, Therapy and Specialized Teaching Services**
10.02-01	Nursing
10.02-02	Therapy and Rehabilitation
10.02-03	Specialized Teaching
10.03	**Child and Adult Care**
10.03-01	Data Collection
10.03-02	Patient Care
10.03-03	Care of Others

11 Leading-Persuading

11.01	**Mathematics and Statistics**
11.01-01	Data Processing Design
11.01-02	Data Analysis
11.02	**Educational and Library Services**
11.02-01	Teaching and Instructing, General
11.02-02	Vocational and Industrial Teaching
11.02-03	Teaching, Home Economics, Agriculture, and Related
11.02-04	Library Services
11.03	**Social Research**
11.03-01	Psychological
11.03-02	Sociological
11.03-03	Historical

11.03-04	Occupational
11.03-05	Economic
11.04	**Law**
11.04-01	Justice Administration
11.04-02	Legal Practice
11.04-03	Abstracting, Document Preparation
11.05	**Business Administration**
11.05-01	Management Services: Non-Government
11.05-02	Administrative Specialization
11.05-03	Management Services: Government
11.05-04	Sales and Purchasing Management
11.06	**Finance**
11.06-01	Accounting and Auditing
11.06-02	Records Systems Analysis
11.06-03	Risk and Profit Analysis
11.06-04	Brokering
11.06-05	Budget and Financial Control
11.07	**Services Administration**
11.07-01	Social Services
11.07-02	Health and Safety Services
11.07-03	Educational Services
11.07-04	Recreational Services
11.08	**Communications**
11.08-01	Editing
11.08-02	Writing
11.08-03	Writing and Broadcasting
11.08-04	Translating and Interpreting
11.09	**Promotion**
11.09-01	Sales
11.09-02	Funds and Membership Solicitation
11.09-03	Public Relations
11.10	**Regulations Enforcement**
11.10-01	Finance
11.10-02	Individual Rights
11.10-03	Health and Safety
11.10-04	Immigration and Customs
11.10-05	Company Policy
11.11	**Business Management**
11.11-01	Lodging
11.11-02	Recreation and Amusement
11.11-03	Transportation
11.11-04	Services
11.11-05	Wholesale-Retail
11.12	**Contracts and Claims**
11.12-01	Claims Settlement
11.12-02	Rental and Leasing
11.12-03	Booking
11.12-04	Procurement Negotiations

12 Physical Performing

12.01	**Sports**
12.02-01	Coaching and Instructing
12.02-02	Officiating
12.02-03	Performing
12.02	**Physical Feats**
12.02-01	Performing

Summary List of Codes Used in This Book

As you start reading the actual job descriptions beginning on page 31, it may help to return to these pages which contain a quick reference guide to interpret the occupational codes used. More thorough descriptions of these codes are explained in chapter 2.

The GOE Number: Refers to the unique job classification system used in the *Guide for Occupational Exploration*. This six digit number categorizes occupations into 12 basic categories based on "interest" factors.

The DOT Number: Consists of nine digits. The first three numbers refer to the occupational classification system used by the *Dictionary of Occupation Titles*. The fourth through sixth digit refer to skills required for the job relative to data, people and things, while the last three numbers further categorize each job within an occupational group. Because knowing what skills each job requires is useful, the fourth through sixth digit of the DOT number is interpreted below.

DOT Code, 4th Digit = Data (high = 0, low = 6)

0 = Synthesizing
1 = Coordinating
2 = Analyzing
3 = Compiling

4 = Computing
5 = Copying
6 = Comparing

DOT Code, 5th Digit = People (high = 0, low = 8)

0 = Mentoring
1 = Negotiating
2 = Instructing
3 = Supervising
4 = Diverting

5 = Persuading
6 = Speaking-Signaling
7 = Serving
8 = Taking Instruction-Helping

DOT Code, 6th Digit = Things (high = 0, low = 7)

0 = Setting Up
1 = Precision Working
2 = Operating-Controlling
3 = Driving-Operating

4 = Manipulating
5 = Tending
6 = Feeding-Offbearing
7 = Handling

The OES Code: Explains the Office of Employment Statistics category in which the occupation belongs. Helpful for looking up the occupations in government reports.

The GED Code: Refers to general educational development required for the job. There are six levels in each of the following areas: Reasoning (R), Math (M), and Language (L). The higher the number, the more complex the skill required to do that job.

The SVP Code: Stands for "Specific Vocational Preparation" and refers to the time in years, months or days required to demonstrate standard proficiency in a job.

Academic Codes: (Ed and Eng): Refer to the educational degrees required and knowledge and proficiency in the English language.

Ed Codes:
M = Master's degree or above
B = Bachelor's degree
A = Associate degree or apprenticeship
H = High school diploma or GED
N = No diploma

Eng Codes:
G = Understanding English grammar
S = Simple communication in English
N = No communication in English

The Work Field Code: A three digit code that refers to groups of occupations clustered together based on similar techniques, related skills and overall socioeconomic objectives. For a full listing of these codes and corresponding categories refer to appendix H.

The MPSMS Code: This three digit code classifies jobs by materials, products, subject matter and services. Appendix G lists the specific job categories.

The Aptitudes Codes: Refers to aptitudes required in specific areas measured on a rating scale (high = 1 to low = 5), relative to the total population.

G = General Learning Ability
V = Verbal Ability
N = Numerical Aptitude
S = Spatial
P = Form Perception
Q = Clerical Perception

K = Motor Coordination
F = Finger Dexterity
M = Manual Dexterity
E = Eye-Hand-Foot Coordination
C = Color Discrimination

The Temperaments Code: Defined as adaptability requirements placed on workers.

D = Directing or supervising others
F = Judging based on feelings or esthetics
I = Influencing or persuading others
J = Judging based on experiences
M = Making decisions based on facts
P = Working with people

R = Doing repetitive work
S = Working quickly or with concentration
T = Doing precise work, to close tolerances
V = Changing tasks often, varied duties.

The Stress Related Code: Some occupations are coded for stress related factors. The stress categories are:

E = Using emotional control
T = Tolerating repetition

A = Accepting responsibility
S = Sustaining attention

The Physical Requirements Code: The codes refer to physical requirements of a particular job. There are four major categories which are further broken down to more specific demands.

V = Vision Needed
   G = Normal vision needed
   L = Limited vision needed
   N = No vision needed
H = Hearing Needed
   G = Normal hearing needed
   L = Limited hearing needed
   N = No hearing needed
L = Lifting Needed
   V = Very heavy
   H = Heavy

M = Medium
L = Light
S = Sedentary (very light)
Other Physical Requirements
   W – Walking and\or mobility needed
   C = Climbing and\or balancing needed
   S = Stooping, kneeling, crouching, and\or crawling needed
   H = Handling, fingering, feeling, and\or reaching needed

The Work Environment Code: These codes provide information on the types of work environments found in a given job.

I = Inside
O = Outside
B = Both
C = Extremes of cold
H = Extremes of heat

W = Wet and\or humid
N = Noise and\or vibration
R = Hazards
F = Fumes

The Salary Code: Occupations are assigned to one of five salary categories based on expected starting salary (high = 5, low = 1).

1 = Lowest, below $11,000 per year

2 = Moderately low, $11,000 to $14,999 per year

3 = Mid-range, $15,000 to $19,999 per year

4 = Moderately high $20,000 to $27,999 per year

5 = Highest, $28,000 per year and above

The Outlook Code: Occupations were assigned to one of five employment outlook categories based on the average length of time it takes before finding employment in this field (low = 1, high = 5).

1 = Lowest - can take over a year

2 = Moderately low - can take a few months to a year

3 = Mid-range - can be found in a few months

4 = Moderately high - can be found in a couple of weeks

5 = Highest - employment can be found quickly

Chapter 1
How to Use This Book

This chapter provides background information on how *The Enhanced Guide for Occupational Exploration* was developed and how it can best be used. The next chapter, chapter 2, provides additional information on interpreting the occupational codes used in each occupational description.

Note: At various times throughout this book we use the words "occupation" and "job" interchangeably. Some argue that the two words have different meanings but, for our purposes, they will mean the same thing.

Who Should Use This Book

The Enhanced Guide for Occupational Exploration (EGOE) was created to serve the needs of two primary groups of people. The first group includes persons trying to explore career alternatives or find a job. The second group consists of vocational counselors, business people, and other professionals needing access to the specialized information provided in this book.

Few people are able to identify the "best" jobs for them from among the many thousands of job titles that exist. They have difficulty relating their interests, skills, potentials, experiences, and preferences to appropriate occupations. For them, this book offers a well-organized and thorough guide to finding various occupations that most closely match their criteria.

Vocational counselors and other professionals also need access to information about occupations to assist their clients in making good career decisions, to classify jobs for documentation purposes, or to obtain technical information on various occupational characteristics and requirements.

For both groups, this book will help. By providing descriptions for the jobs that an overwhelming majority of the people actually work in, it becomes a unique and valuable resource. The use of a simple and logical clustering of related jobs allows a novice to access one or more of the 2,500 jobs in an orderly and easy-to-understand manner. The addition of technical data and codes from a variety of previously hard-to-obtain sources provides information of great value to novices and professional vocational counselors alike. And the various appendices provide additional information and ways to access the many listed jobs that can prove to be invaluable to many.

How the Book Is Organized

The major portion of the book consists of detailed descriptions of 2,500 occupations. To provide a helpful way to find and explore career alternatives, they are grouped into increasingly specific clusters of related occupations. The basic organizational structure consists of 12 major interest areas, 66 work groups, and 348 subgroups of related occupations. This is the same structure developed by the U.S. Department of Labor and used in the original *Guide for Occupational Exploration*. It is a very useful structure for finding clusters of related occupations.

There are also several appendices at the end of this book. These allow you to look up the 2,500 listed jobs in a variety of helpful ways. The appendices also provide useful information regarding the classification of occupations. This technical information will be of particular interest to vocational counselors and other professionals, though some job seekers may also find it of interest. Look at the Table of Contents at the beginning of this book for a list of the appendices and brief descriptions of their content.

Interest Areas

If you have not yet read the sections of this book titled "Definitions of Interest Factors" and "Summary List of Interest Factors, Work Groups and Subgroups," please look up their location in the Table of Contents and refer to them to best understand what follows.

All 2,500 of the jobs listed in the *EGOE* are listed within one of 12 major occupational categories called interest areas. These 12 interest areas correspond to the major occupational interest factors identified in research conducted by the Division of Testing in the U.S. Employment Service. The interest areas are identified by the first two digits used in the six digit numerical *GOE* code system applied to each occupation described in this book. For example, the first two digits of the *GOE* number 01.01.01 refer to the "Artistic" interest area, one of the 12 major interest areas.

Work Groups

Each major interest area is further divided into 66 work groups. Within each work group, the jobs are the same general type of work and require the same general capabilities of the worker. Each group has its own unique four digit code and title. For example in numbering 01.01.01, the first two digits refer to the "Artistic" interest area, while the second two digits refer to the "Literary Arts" work group. The number of work groups within each interest area varies from two to five.

Subgroups

Within each work group, jobs are further divided into 348 subgroups to make it easier to distinguish among similar jobs. Each subgroup has its own unique six digit code and title, as in the example 01.01.01, where the last two digits refer to the subgroup titled "Creative Writing."

Specific occupations or jobs are then listed under this subgroup. Because of the number of jobs within some of the larger subgroups, a further clustering of jobs within industries is made, for example, aircraft manufacturing, iron and steel, and motion picture. Within the same category designation, jobs are listed alphabetically. If a job has more than one industry designation, it is listed under that which occurs first alphabetically.

Tips for Finding a Particular Job or Job Cluster

The grouping of descriptions by increasingly specific groups of occupations makes it quite easy to find a specific job by beginning with the major interest area within which it would be found. Use the Table of Contents to identify the major interest areas or find the more specific work group or subgroup on pages x through xiii. You can also look up the specific title in the alphabetical listing in Appendix A or you can use another appendix to look up occupations in a variety of other useful ways.

A Sample Occupational Description

Each of the 2,500 occupational descriptions found in this book provides a substantial amount of useful information. Because of the large numbers of descriptions, the authors had to either eliminate useful information or use codes to conserve space. Some of the coded information is of use to professional career counselors while others would be of interest to a person considering career options or looking for a job.

To help you understand how each occupational description is organized, below is a sample job description along with a brief analysis of what each section of the description means. Comments on each of the numbered sections are provided following the sample description. While most components of each occupational description are readily understood, you will need to familiarize yourself with the coding system for those codes you are most interested in. Additional details on the interpretation of the various codes used are provided in the next chapter and in several appendices.

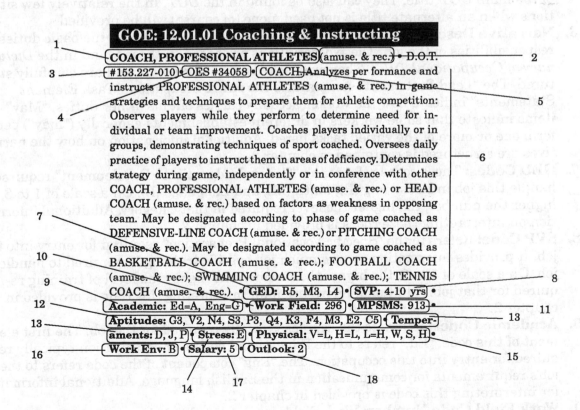

GOE: 12.01.01 Coaching & Instructing

COACH, PROFESSIONAL ATHLETES (amuse. & rec.) • D.O.T. #153.227-010 • OES #34058 • COACH, Analyzes performance and instructs PROFESSIONAL ATHLETES (amuse. & rec.) in game strategies and techniques to prepare them for athletic competition: Observes players while they perform to determine need for individual or team improvement. Coaches players individually or in groups, demonstrating techniques of sport coached. Oversees daily practice of players to instruct them in areas of deficiency. Determines strategy during game, independently or in conference with other COACH, PROFESSIONAL ATHLETES (amuse. & rec.) or HEAD COACH (amuse. & rec.) based on factors as weakness in opposing team. May be designated according to phase of game coached as DEFENSIVE-LINE COACH (amuse. & rec.) or PITCHING COACH (amuse. & rec.). May be designated according to game coached as BASKETBALL COACH (amuse. & rec.); FOOTBALL COACH (amuse. & rec.); SWIMMING COACH (amuse. & rec.); TENNIS COACH (amuse. & rec.). • **GED:** R5, M3, L4 • **SVP:** 4-10 yrs • **Academic:** Ed=A, Eng=G • **Work Field:** 296 • **MPSMS:** 913 • **Aptitudes:** G3, V2, N4, S3, P3, Q4, K3, F4, M3, E2, C5 • **Temperaments:** D, J, P • **Stress:** E • **Physical:** V=L, H=L, L=H, W, S, H • **Work Env:** B • **Salary:** 5 • **Outlook:** 2

Brief Review of the Elements of a Job Description

Below are brief definitions of the various components contained in each job description. Additional details on interpreting each component will be provided later in this chapter.

1. **Occupational (or "job") Title:** This is the formal name of the occupation as provided by the U.S. Department of Labor. It is the same title as listed in the *Dictionary of Occupational Titles (DOT)* or, for newer titles, in the Department of Labor's computer database.

2. **Industry Designation:** This is the industry in which the occupation is most commonly found. Additional details are provided in chapter 2 and appendix B provides several listings of the industries, their abbreviations as used in this book, and their code numbers.

3. *DOT* **Code Number:** This is the code number assigned to this occupational title by the U.S. Department of Labor in its publication titled the *Dictionary of Occupational Titles*. This number provides important information about each job and it also allows you to cross-reference the job in a variety of other career information systems. We will provide more information on elements of the *DOT* number in the next chapter.

4. **OES Code Number:** The Office of Employment Statistics (OES) coding system is widely used in government publications. This code can help you cross-reference to other occupational information sources. Additional information on the OES codes are provided in chapter 2 and appendix F provides a listing of the codes and their related occupations.

5. **Alternate Titles:** Following the OES code and title you will typically see one or more additional titles in all capital letters. These titles are used by some employers instead of the main *DOT* title. They can also be found in the *DOT*. In the relatively few situations when an alternate title is not used, none (of course) will be provided.

6. **Narrative Description:** This brief narrative description outlines the basic duties and responsibilities of the job. These descriptions are based on those found in the *Dictionary of Occupational Titles*. They are packed with information and are carefully structured. The "Lead Statement" summarizes the entire occupation. "Task Element Statements" indicate how the worker actually carries out his or her duties. "May" items indicate that some workers in different establishments generally ("may") perform one or more of the varied tasks listed. Additional information on how the narratives are structured is contained in chapter 2.

7. **GED Codes:** These codes refer to the "General Educational Development" required to handle this job in Reasoning (R), Math (M), and Language (L). On a scale of 1 to 6, the higher the number, the higher the level required in that category. Additional information on interpreting these codes is provided in chapter 2.

8. **SVP Code:** Refers to the "Specific Vocational Preparation" required for entry into the job. It provides information on how much job-specific training is required to handle the job. On a scale of 1 to 9, the higher the number, the higher the level of training required for that job. Additional information for interpreting this code is provided in chapter 2.

9. **Academic Codes:** Refers to the degrees typically required for the job. The first element of this code, "Ed," refers to the Educational degree or certification typically required for entry into this occupation. The "Eng" component of the code refers to the job's requirements for communication in the English language. Additional information for interpreting this code is provided in chapter 2.

10. **Work Field Code Number:** Work Fields are intended to help you find jobs that use the skills you enjoy using. Look through the list in appendix H and pick the ones you want to use in your work. These skills are sometimes called "specific content skills" because they are used only in specific types of jobs. For example, if "knitting" is one of

your skills, you could find jobs that use that skill. But many jobs do no use it. It is "specific" to a certain group of jobs. Many people learn these skills through on-the-job training. If you change jobs, you may need to learn new specific content skills for your new job.

11. **MPSMS Code Number:** The letters refer to "Materials, Products, Subject Matter, and Services." The codes tell you what materials, products, subject matter or services are used or provided in the job. Additional information for interpreting these codes is provided in chapter 2. Appendix G provides a complete listing of the MPSMS code numbers and their related meanings.

12. **Aptitudes:** These codes refer to various work-related aptitudes: General Learning Ability (G), Verbal Ability (V), Numerical Aptitude (N), Spatial (S), Form Perception (P), Clerical Perception (Q), Motor Coordination (K), Finger Dexterity (F), Manual Dexterity (M), Eye-Hand-Foot Coordination (E) and Color Discrimination (C). On a scale of 1 to 5, the lower the number, the higher the level required for the job in each of the categories provided. Additional information for interpreting these codes is provided in chapter 2.

13. **Temperaments:** These letter codes indicate that a particular personality characteristic is required of the worker for this job. These codes are described in chapter 2.

14. **Stress:** These codes refer to stress-related demands such as using emotional control and accepting responsibility. Note that stress factors will be listed only for jobs where they are present at significant levels. In many jobs, there will be no stress factors listed and this category will not be shown for these jobs. This is not an error on our part. Additional information for interpreting these codes is provided in chapter 2.

15. **Physical:** These codes refer to job requirements for Vision (V), Hearing (H), Lifting (L), and other physical requirements. Additional information for interpreting these codes is provided in chapter 2.

16. **Work Environment:** These codes provide information on the types of work environments that are typically found or that must be endured for each job. Additional information for interpreting these codes is provided in chapter 2.

17. **Salary:** The salary code provides information on the average salary range to be expected for the job. On a scale of 1 to 5, the higher the number, the higher the salary. Additional information for interpreting these codes is provided in chapter 2.

18. **Outlook:** This code indicates how long it takes, on average, to find this type of job. It provides a measure of how much the job is in demand. On a scale of 1 to 5, the lower the number, the longer it takes (on average) to obtain this type of job. Additional information for interpreting these codes is provided in chapter 2.

As you can see, there is a substantial amount of information provided for each occupation described in this book. The use of codes allows us to provide all of this information in a compact and useful format.

Which Jobs Are Included

The *EGOE* uses standard job titles that are defined by the U.S. Department of Labor and listed in the *Dictionary of Occupational Titles*. As anyone who has ever tried to use the *DOT* knows it has a great many job titles—over 20,000. Many are unfamiliar and even curious-sounding to most readers. This is because the *DOT* attempts to describe the entire work world throughout the United States. It thus includes jobs which are held by only a few people; are limited to a single industry or geographic location; or are only available through occupation-specific internal promotion ladders. For the vast majority of people entering the labor market or considering an occupational change, these jobs are not realistic alternatives.

To overcome this shortcoming, the 2,500 most important occupations have been selected from the *DOT* for inclusion in the *EGOE*. These occupations represent over 95 percent of the jobs in which people actually work. As a group, they offer realistic alternatives for those entering the job market, recent graduates from training or educational programs, job changers, and job seekers. The criteria for jobs included are:

1. **There is a significant labor market for the job.** Many of the occupations in the *DOT* are very rare, with very few people who actually work in these jobs. Some of the jobs have always been small while others have been shrinking since they were studied. For example, how many people today work in ice plants, manufacturing ice? There are 10 separate occupations in the *DOT* for people who manufacture ice. At one time, this was a major industry, but today it is very small and highly mechanized. These and other jobs in which fewer than 200 people are employed—and are shrinking or found only in limited locations—have been excluded from this book.

2. **The occupation is an "access point" for people who have been working in other fields or are just starting to work.** Some jobs can only be reached by promotion from within an establishment or by highly specific training, education or experience. This book does not include many of these jobs. If you are planning a significant occupational change, you need to know which occupations are "access points" since these are the jobs offering the most opportunity for initial entry into a field and eventual promotion. It is important to understand the difference between "access points" and "entry-level" occupations. Entry-level jobs can be done by people who are just starting their work life, with very little training or experience. Although significant numbers of the occupations in this book are entry-level (that is, they can be obtained by a person with little specialized education or training), many do require job-related training and/or experience and some require substantial preparation. But these jobs do not necessarily require experience in the same company or organization, and may not need to be in the same industry. Instead, these jobs are access points, jobs where a person with the necessary training or experience can get an initial job with an organization.

This book contains virtually all of the titles commonly regarded as "career fields" and described in the *Occupational Outlook Handbook* (a standard career reference book published by the U.S. Department of Labor and often referred to as the *OOH*) and other career exploration publications. All of the traditional professional pursuits — engineering, law, science, health, teaching, business, and the arts — are represented. Also included are all apprenticeable trades and technical fields that require any kind of specialized training or certificate program. All clerical and service jobs for which there are significant labor markets are also included as are the more common sales jobs. Entry-level jobs are included for every industrial category of national significance.

Occupations That Are Not Included

Not included in this book are many upper-level specialties in the professions which normally require becoming competent in a related lower-level profession. Thus "physician" is included but not cardiologist, anesthesiologist, or some other medical specialties. Most high-level, highly specialized positions in administration and management are also excluded as are highly specialized sales titles such as sewing machine salesperson or veterinarian supplies sales representative. Also not included are many specialized supervisory jobs and other jobs that can be obtained only by promotion from lower-level jobs where skills are learned on-the-job.

Some people may be concerned about the occupations which have been omitted. It is always tempting to think that something exciting may be found if a larger set of occupations is explored. One way of looking at the occupations which have been omitted is to study the industries in which these occupations are found.

The graph on the following page is based on the book *Projections 2000*, (DOL, 1988). It shows the percentage of workers in various industries, both in 1986 (black bars) and projected to 2000 (striped bars). The industry clusters used here are a combination of Standard Industrial Classification (SIC) clusters and the industry categories used in the *DOT*. Specifically, "Professional and Kindred" and "Clerical" are *DOT* industry categories, even though they are actually occupational clusters, not "industries." Therefore the workers in these areas are counted twice in this table, once in their actual industry and again in these clusters.

Looking at the first graph, we can see that the industries of Manufacturing, Retail Trade, Services, Government, Professional and Kindred, and Clerical are major areas of employment, with significant growth in Services and significant decline in Manufacturing.

The next graph shows the percentage of titles in the *DOT* using the same categories. This graph differs from the other only in that titles in Professional and Kindred and Clerical are not counted twice and another cross-industry category, "Any Industry," has been added. Since this clustering is based on the *DOT* industry classification system and considers only the most significant industry for each occupation, each title is counted exactly once. The black bar shows the percentages in each cluster that are listed in this book and the striped bar shows the percentages of titles in the *DOT*.

Looking at the same graph, we can see that, in the *DOT*, manufacturing job titles are seriously over-represented. Over 60 percent of the titles in the *DOT* are in manufacturing, yet manufacturing employs only 17 percent of the workers and is declining. Therefore, occupations in this industry cluster were carefully scrutinized before including them in this book and only the occupations which are found in significant numbers are included. Thus the percentage of titles in the Manufacturing area included in this book is only 25 percent, a much more realistic number.

Of course, it was not possible to correct all of the imbalances by careful selection since the occupations in this book are a subset of the *DOT*. For example, Retail Trade is a major employer (16 percent of the labor force) but has only 1.4 percent of the titles in the *DOT*. Even by including most of the titles for this industry, Retail Trade is proportionally under-represented in this book. Perhaps there are many workers in this industry with the same occupational title (i.e. salesperson), so the number of titles is small although most types of jobs in retail are covered by descriptions in this book.

Sources of Data Used in This Book

A variety of sources have been used to obtain the information provided for each job listed in this book. The primary sources include the U.S. Department of Labor, the U.S. Census Bureau, and various other sources compiled by Ciasa, Inc., a corporation specializing in labor market information located in Berkeley, California. This section provides a brief overview of the sources of information used. More detailed information will be provided in the next chapter.

The U.S. Department of Labor

The U.S. Department of Labor (DOL) is an agency of the federal government. For many years it has collected and analyzed labor market information and is considered to be the most authoritative — and sometimes only — source of key information on jobs and labor market data.

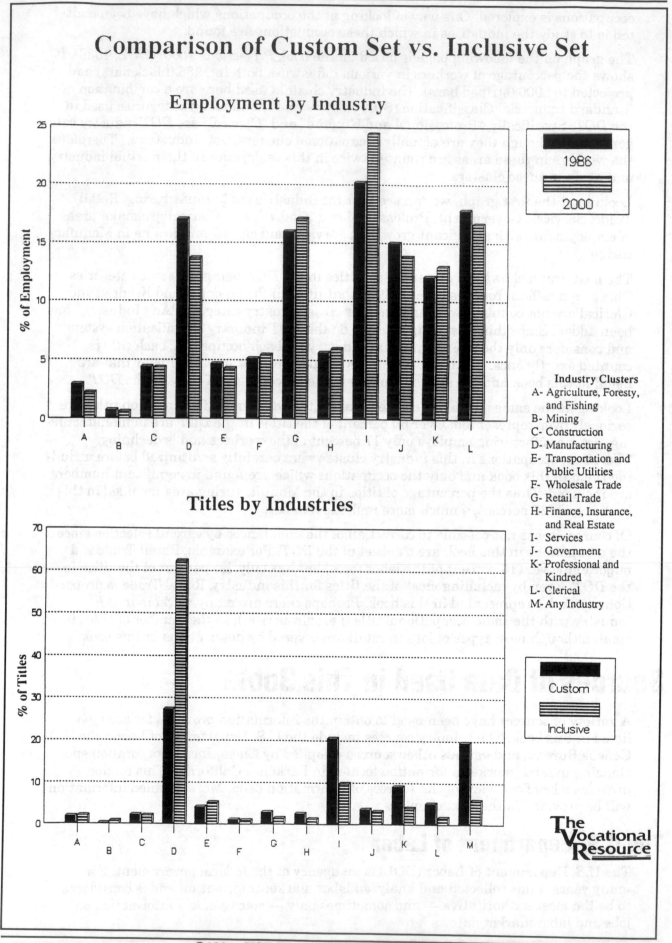

Comparison of Custom Set vs. Inclusive Set

Employment by Industry

% of Employment

1986

2000

Industry Clusters
A- Agriculture, Foresty, and Fishing
B- Mining
C- Construction
D- Manufacturing
E- Transportation and Public Utilities
F- Wholesale Trade
G- Retail Trade
H- Finance, Insurance, and Real Estate
I- Services
J- Government
K- Professional and Kindred
L- Clerical
M- Any Industry

Titles by Industries

% of Titles

Custom

Inclusive

The Vocational Resource

The DOL has compiled a large amount of information about occupations, including descriptions and "Worker Traits" of people who are successful working in each. It has published parts of this data but not all of it. The books published by the federal government are not updated frequently, so they often do not have the latest information. The most accurate and up-to-date source for this information is a computer database which is published and maintained by the DOL. This database is the source of much of the data in this book.

Some of the information in the DOL database has been published by the U.S. Government and is available in any Government Printing Office bookstore. In 1977, the fourth edition of the *Dictionary of Occupational Titles (DOT)* was published containing 12,099 occupations with titles, industries, and definitions. Supplements to the *DOT* were published in 1982 and 1986, with the 1986 supplement containing the information published in the earlier supplement. These supplements contain descriptions of newly created occupations as well as revisions of old descriptions. This is confusing since it is necessary to look in two books to be sure you are using the most accurate data. We have merged this information, for the first time, into one book.

The narrative descriptions for each of the 2,500 jobs in this book are based on those published in the *DOT* and updated periodically. The descriptions include all the definitions, titles, alternate titles, and industry titles. The DOL updates this database of occupations every 2 months. The information in this book is the newest information available at the time of the publication of this book in 1991. In addition to the narrative descriptions, a substantial amount of additional information is also provided for each of the listed jobs. This data was also obtained from current DOL databases and may differ from the format used in older data sources published by the DOL.

The Guide for Occupational Exploration (GOE) was originally published in 1979 to help students and career changers find occupations more easily. In 1981 the DOL published a book called *Selected Characteristics of Occupations* defined in the *Dictionary of Occupational Titles*. That book contains *GOE* numbers, Physical Demands, Environmental Conditions, General Educational Development (GED), Specific Vocational Preparation (SVP) and Standard Occupational Classification (SOC) codes for each occupation. Many of the traits have been revised since that book was published and the latest revisions are included in this volume.

Other Worker Traits have not been published in any government publication, including Aptitudes, Temperaments, Work Fields, MPSMS (Materials, Products, Subject Matter, and Services), and OES (Office of Employment Statistics) codes. Private sources have published these code numbers as lists provided by a computer. For the first time, this book provides this information in a useful printed format by combining them along with each occupational description.

Instructions for analyzing jobs and explanations of the coding used in the 1977 edition of the *DOT* was published in the *Handbook for Analyzing Jobs* in 1972. Some of this information is still useful but many of the coding systems, like Work Fields and MPSMS, have been revised and have not been republished by the government. This volume includes accurate, updated descriptions of all of the coding systems used in this volume.

In summary, this volume brings together for the first time many information elements which have been scattered in a bewildering array of books, printed in various years, and now sadly out of date. In this one volume you will find all of the information which the DOL has painstakingly collected for 40 years, in a format which can readily be used by people who need this information.

Other Sources of Data

In addition to the information provided by the Department of Labor, this book contains information which has been developed by the authors and is not published anywhere else. The authors are founders of Ciasa, Inc., a company located in Berkeley, California. Under Ciasa's name, the authors created and coded the proprietary categories of Education, English Proficiency, Vision, Hearing, Mobility, and the four stress factors. These codes are provided for each job listed in this book. To construct these measures, they used a variety of DOL and other governmental sources including:

- *The Dictionary of Occupational Titles*
- *The Occupational Outlook Handbook*
- *The Guide for Occupational Exploration*
- *The Handbook for Analyzing Jobs*
- *Projections of Employment* (DOL, 1990)
- *Projections 2000* (DOL, 1988)
- *Standard Occupational Classification Manual* (U.S. Department of Commerce, 1977)
- *Standard Industrial Classification Manual* (Office of Management and Budget, 1987)

The OES (Office of Employment Statistics) codes provided in this book were obtained from the U.S. Census Bureau. The OES codification system changed just before the census in 1990 and the new codes are included here. Until now, the only source for these codes had been the DOL database, available through the National Crosswalk Service Center in Des Moines, Iowa.

In addition, the authors incorporated information from want ads, private industry surveys (like those done by Chambers of Commerce, etc.) and placement statistics from schools and colleges. These combined government and private sources were interpreted by Donald Mayall, an expert labor market analyst. It is his 40 years of expertise on which most of the coding is actually based.

Perhaps the most useful additions are indicators for Salary and Outlook. Each occupation has a Salary indicator, on a scale from 1 to 5, to let you know approximately how much you could expect to earn on that job. And each occupation has an Outlook indicator to give you an estimate of how hard or easy it will be to find a job in this field. Other special information about the academic, physical, and stress-related demands of the occupations have also been included.

Tips for Using the Book by Individuals without Counselor Assistance

The Enhanced Guide for Occupational Exploration is a unique and valuable book for vocational counselors as it provides the most often wanted information for most jobs in one location. It is also arranged in such a way to make it a useful tool for exploring career and job search alternatives for individuals as well.

If you need help in deciding what kind of work you should choose, you can use *The Enhanced Guide for Occupational Exploration* to help you plan your career, identify jobs you qualify for, consider jobs requiring additional training or education, or move up within your organization or field. Your task is to find not just any job, but one you can do well and that will be satisfying to you.

To find the right kind of job for you, you need two types of information:

1. **Information about yourself.** You need to know the kind of work you would like to do and whether you are able to do such work. If you can't do it now, can you learn to do it through an educational or training program?

2. **Information about occupations that sound interesting to you.** What does the worker do on such jobs? What knowledge and skills must the worker have? What training is required?

The Enhanced Guide for Occupational Exploration helps you locate and learn about occupations that relate to your interests and abilities. When you use it properly, you will be better prepared to plan your career or seek employment. You will learn about many jobs, including some you never knew existed.

The Enhanced Guide for Occupational Exploration clusters occupations into major interest areas and work groups within each major interest area. These work groups are then further divided into subgroups of similar jobs, with specific jobs then listed within each subgroup.

A rational and easy-to-use system of code numbers allows jobs to be organized and found within this book. This system was developed by the U.S. Department of Labor and used in the original *GOE* and was retained for this book because of its practical value. Rather than trying to explore the impossibly large world of job options, this book allows you to identify those areas of work in which you have the strongest interest and, within the interest areas, those work groups that are most closely related to your interests, skills, aptitudes, education, training, and physical abilities.

Step 1. Think About Your Interests

What kind of work would you most like to do? Did you know that all jobs have been organized into groups according to the interests of the workers?

Some workers like to help others. Some would rather work with their hands or tools. Others prefer artistic work, or writing, selling, clerical or other types of work. *The Enhanced Guide For Occupational Exploration* uses a system developed by the U.S. Department of Labor to organize all its jobs into 12 areas based on the interest of workers. Each of these 12 interest areas has been given a name, a code number, and a brief description. In order to learn more about the relationship of your interests to occupations, turn to the "Definitions of Interest Factors" on page ix and read the titles and descriptions of each interest area and select one or more that you would like to explore.

Step 2. Select One or More Work Groups to Explore

In order to know what work groups to explore, you need to decide whether you would find satisfaction in work activities such as those required by occupations in the group. To do this, turn to the "Summary List of Interest Areas, Work Groups, and Subgroups" on pages x-xiii of this book. Under each major interest area, notice that there are various clusters of jobs listed in bold letters. These are called work groups. Listed beneath each of these are even more specific subgroups of similar occupations.

As you identify work groups that you would like to learn more about, note the numbers listed next to each. You can use these numbers to learn more about each of these work groups. Simply look for the narrative descriptions for each in the Occupational Descriptions section of this book. All descriptions are in numerical order within each interest area and work group. Each work group has a brief narrative description of the types of jobs within that group at the beginning of that numerical grouping. You can also find descriptions for each of the subgroups using the numbers provided in a similar way.

Many of the jobs listed in the interest areas you have selected may require knowledge and skills that you do not have or would have difficulty acquiring. There should be some occupations, however, that fit your interests and that you can do or can learn to do.

The groups that require the most experience, education or training are usually listed first among the work groups in most interest areas. The last work groups in a work area are often open to workers with little formal education. As you make your selections of work groups from the first interest area, follow the same process for any other areas you selected in Step 1.

Step 3. Explore the Work Groups You Selected

To explore a work group, look up its description and read it very carefully. As you read about a group, you may discover that it is not what you thought it would be and that you are not interested in it. Or you may find that the training or other requirements are more difficult than you want. As you discover this, drop this group from further consideration and go on to the next group.

In some cases, you could consider jobs that require substantial training or education as a long-term objective. Don't eliminate such a job if it is one you are very interested in. You may need to consider other jobs while you return or continue on to school, gain experience, or get additional training.

Step 4. Explore Subgroups and Specific Occupations

Once you have learned more about the work groups and subgroups you are interested in, you can then look at the job descriptions that are listed within each category. Each work group contains occupations that have been organized into subgroups. Each subgroup is identified by a six digit code and a title, plus a list of all the occupations assigned to it.

After you have studied a work group description and decided that you are interested in considering it further, you should examine its subgroups to see if one or more of them appears to match your interests and qualifications better than the others. The various subgroups are also listed on pages x through xiii of this book. Look over these subgroups carefully. Since the job descriptions in this book are arranged in order of their *GOE* numbers, the numbers accompanying the various subgroups will tell you where to find these jobs described.

Look over the job descriptions within that subgroup carefully and give particular attention to any that appear to most closely match your interests and qualifications.

Step 5. Create a Plan of Action

Once you have identified groups of jobs that you are interested in, you need to decide what to do next. Perhaps you can qualify for some of these with your present qualifications, while others will require additional training, education, or experience.

Your next step may be clear to you. Perhaps your exploration has identified some jobs that you will begin looking for right away, using your present qualifications. Or some other plan is obvious to you. But if you are still not sure about what you want to do, you can probably be helped by a vocational counselor or by a course or program designed for people who want assistance in career planning.

If you are currently enrolled in school (or have been in the past), check with them for career planning assistance as these services are often available to graduates. Most areas also have government-funded programs that provide these services, as do local colleges and Universities. Look in the *Yellow Pages* of the phone book under Vocational or Career Counseling or ask your librarian for help in locating these resources.

Because the descriptions in this book are brief, you may want additional information on one or more of them before you make a decision on what to do. Longer descriptions for 250 of the most popular jobs can be found in the *Occupational Outlook Handbook*. This is a book published by the U.S. Department of Labor and available in most libraries and schools. Your librarian will also be able to help you find additional books, journals, magazine articles and other information on many jobs. The library will also have a variety of books to help you find sources of training or education for many occupations.

You should also consider visiting with people who have the kind of jobs you are interested in to obtain first-hand information. School or vocational counselors will often be able to provide you with additional information on resources for deciding on job or training objectives as well. For important decisions such as career planning, it is difficult to have too much information.

Where the Jobs Are

The labor market has changed rapidly over the last decade and is projected to continue to change in the years to come. In some cases the changes have been dramatic, yet many people are not fully aware of how these changes affect them. For example, there are far more women in the workforce today and they tend to stay in for longer periods of time. And there are many millions of new workers that have been absorbed into the labor force. Many factors have also affected the types of jobs and the training required to handle them.

Jobs are constantly changing. Companies go out of business and new ones start. Plants close down and relocate in countries with lower salaries. New technology makes old ways of doing things obsolete.

While the labor force has expanded, the number of manufacturing jobs has actually declined. Many relatively unskilled people have lost these jobs as a result and have had a difficult time finding replacement jobs that pay as well. But many new manufacturing jobs have also been created, though they often require more training and education than the manufacturing jobs that have been lost.

Virtually all of the increase in our new jobs have been in the "Service" economy in sectors such as medicine, business services, and technical, professional and managerial jobs. Many of these jobs pay good wages but also require special training and advanced education.

Not all of the new jobs in the service sector require special training, but those that do not typically pay lower wages. For example, entry-level jobs in transportation, hotels, restaurants, entertainment, amusement parks, and recreation do not typically pay well. In some areas, there is a shortage of workers who are willing to work for low wages, so older people, those with little education or education deficits, persons that don't speak English well, and persons with disabilities are finding jobs more easily. For some people who work hard and accept responsibility in these jobs, it is possible to move up into jobs which pay well, or to start their own business.

Also included in the service industry are medical services such as hospitals, clinics, homes for the elderly, and drug rehabilitation centers. Medical and social services are growing rapidly because modern medicine is able to keep people alive longer and because of improvements in medical services. Jobs in this industry range from janitors and orderlies to nurses and counselors to doctors and hospital administrators. This industry offers a variety of salaries, training requirements, and responsibility levels.

Business services of all kinds are another service sector that is growing rapidly. These jobs include banking, accounting, insurance, and data processing. Many of the new jobs in business require using a computer or professional skills. Many of these jobs require good academic skills and special training and pay quite well. People who can type accurately and use English well can usually find clerical jobs quite easily. Clerical salaries are typically lower than in manufacturing but there is opportunity for moving up and good skills are rewarded with higher salaries.

Another area of rapid growth is in retail trade. The number of stores is growing fast. Clerks, salespeople, and managers are needed for these businesses. Starting salaries tend to be low. People who work hard and accept responsibility for their department or other employees may be promoted fairly quickly into jobs with good salaries.

For people who want higher salaries, opportunities are good for managers, technicians, and information processors. People who are dependable, willing to work long hours, and able to convince others to work hard, are always in demand for promotion to management positions. People who can understand machines (computers, sophisticated measurement devices, office machines, telephones, etc.) and design, program, or repair them can earn excellent wages. People who have the ability to read and understand information, to recognize and summarize important information, and to write or speak clearly can find a variety of jobs, from trainers to technical writers to graphic artists. All of these areas are growing quickly.

It seems clear that people in today's labor market can benefit from special training more than ever before. There is a clear relationship between earnings and the amount of training and education you have. Career planning has become an essential survival skill in the new economy. This book can help you explore career alternatives that use your existing skills and experiences to their best effect. It can help you identify jobs that use the skills you already have or to help you more clearly define a long-term objective to prepare for a career that you are particularly interested in.

Chapter 2
Detailed Information on the Narrative/Codes Used in the Occupational Descriptions

This chapter provides more detailed information on interpreting the various codes provided in each of the 2,500 job descriptions in *The Enhanced Guide for Occupational Exploration*. Some of the codes may be of limited use to some people but of great importance to others. For this reason, pay relatively more attention to those coded categories that are of particular interest or value to you.

We have attempted to provide a nontechnical review of the structure, terms, and codes used in this book. We hope that this is enough to satisfy most users. To obtain a more technical understanding of the many complex issues incorporated into the various classification and codification systems covered will require additional reading. We refer the reader to additional sources of this technical information as appropriate. Most users of this book will not need to refer to these references as this section should provide you with a working knowledge sufficient for most purposes.

It will be helpful to refer to a sample occupational description as you read the following material. An annotated sample description is on page 3 of this book, although any description found in this book will have similar elements.

The Narrative Section of the Occupational Descriptions

The narrative section of each job description in this book is based on the descriptions used in the *Dictionary of Occupational Titles* (*DOT*), published by the U.S. Department of Labor. This section reviews the narrative section only, with other elements covered later in this chapter.

The Lead Statement: Each narrative description opens with a "Lead Statement" as the first sentence following the alternative titles (if any) and is followed by a colon (:). This lead statement summarizes the entire occupation. It offers essential information:

- worker actions
- the objective or purpose of worker actions
- machines, tools, equipment, or work aids used by the worker
- materials used, products made, subject matter dealt with, or services rendered
- instructions followed or judgments made

Task Element Statements: Following the lead statement are task element statements indicating the specific tasks the worker performs to accomplish the overall job purpose described in the lead statement. These statements indicate how the worker actually carries out his or her duties.

"May" Items: Many definitions contain one or more sentences beginning with the word "May." They describe duties required of workers in this occupation in some establishments but not in others. The word "May" does NOT indicate that a worker will sometimes perform this task but rather that some workers in different establishments generally perform one or more of the varied tasks listed.

Should you wish to know more about how the narrative descriptions are devised, you can find additional details in the *Dictionary of Occupational Titles*.

Detailed Descriptions of the Data Categories and Codes

This section describes the non-narrative component of each job description. This will provide sufficient information to satisfy most users of this book in interpreting the occupational descriptions. If you wish to obtain additional and far more detailed information on the source and meanings of the codes used in classifying jobs, you will need to refer to other reference materials. Many of the codes are described in more detail in the *Handbook for Analyzing Jobs* published by the U.S. Department of Labor. This and other references will be mentioned as appropriate.

You should also note that, while every precaution has been taken to assure the accuracy of the data used in this book, some errors may exist. Local conditions may vary substantially from the national information used in the descriptions. There are also often significant differences in the duties and requirements for jobs with the same titles found in different organizations. For these and other reasons the occupational descriptions, and the data they contain, should only be considered as guidelines in making any decision. The information in the rest of this chapter will help you interpret the data categories and codes used in each occupational description.

Industry Designation:

Following the occupational title in each description is an industry name in parenthesis. Think of this as part of the title. You will sometimes see the same title used in more than one occupation and with different definitions. This is not an error since different industries often require different tasks, even though using the same job title.

We decided to include abbreviated industry names in the occupational descriptions rather than use less readily understood numeric codes. Each occupation has up to four industries listed, indicating the industries where the occupation is most often (but not always) found. The industry designation system is the same as that used in the *DOT* and other Department of Labor publications. In cases where an occupation is found in many industries, the industry is assigned a cross-industry designation. For example, clerical occupations are found in most industries, so a broad "Clerical" designation is used for these jobs. Other cross-industry designations include "Professional and Kindred" and " Industry," and others.

In appendix B you will find two lists of industries. The first list provides an alphabetical listing of industries along with their related abbreviations used in this book. The second list organizes each industry within clusters of related industries and provides the DOL industry designation code for use in cross-referencing other career information systems.

The *DOT* Code Number:

The U.S. Department of Labor (DOL) has done extensive research into the types of jobs in the U.S. economy. They have described over 12,000 different jobs and identified over 20,000 job titles (the difference in numbers is because some of the jobs have alternative names). Several classification systems have been used to organize these jobs into some rational order. One of the systems used by the DOL provides for a unique number assigned to each job. This number is called the *DOT* number because it is the major classification system used in the *Dictionary of Occupational Titles (DOT)*, published by the Department of Labor. The *DOT* number is a standard number for cross-referencing jobs in most career information systems.

Besides this use, the number also provides substantial information on the occupation it refers to. Each *DOT* number consists of nine digits such as 132.037-022 (for the job titled "Editor, Publications"). The first three numbers refer to that occupation's major occupational category (the first digit), division (the second digit), and group (the third digit). Because this classification system is not followed in *The Enhanced Guide for Occupational Exploration*, we have not provided additional details on this part of the *DOT* code number. Details are described in the *DOT* itself.

The *DOT* number's fourth through sixth digit refer to skills required for the job in relation to data, people and things. Because of the value of this information, we have provided additional information here to help you interpret the meaning of this part of the *DOT* code number.

The last three numbers are simply a unique number given to each job within a group and are assigned sequentially.

Definitions of Data, People, and Things Skills

The middle three digits of the *DOT* number refer to the highest level of skill required in that job in relation to data, people and to things. The lower the number, the higher the level of skill required. By analyzing these numbers, you can determine the highest level of skill required for each of the jobs listed in this book.

Knowing what skills the job requires is useful information. It can help identify jobs that require the skills you already have or want to develop. Appendix E arranges the 2,500 jobs described in this book into various combinations of skills required to do that job. This can be very helpful, especially if you are looking for jobs in unfamiliar fields requiring skills you have used in the past. Following are the definitions for the various skills and their related numbers as used in the *DOT* numbering system.

Data (high = 0, low = 6)

This refers to the fourth digit in the *DOT* code number.

- **0 = Synthesizing:** Putting ideas and facts together in new ways to explain how things work. Developing new ideas and theories.
- **1 = Coordinating:** Organizing things. Planning projects. Deciding in which order things must be done. Checking to be sure the steps are done on time and correctly.
- **2 = Analyzing:** Studying information to find out what it means. Deciding what could be done to solve a problem.
- **3 = Compiling:** Collecting, arranging or combining facts about data, people, or things and reporting the results.

4 = **Computing:** Using arithmetic. Reporting the results or following instructions based on the results.

5 = **Copying:** Writing, listing, or entering numbers or letters exactly as seen.

6 = **Comparing:** Deciding if data, people, or things are alike or different. Using rules to decide how different they are.

People (high = 0, low = 8)

This refers the fifth digit in the *DOT* code number.

0 = **Mentoring:** Helping people deal with problems. May give legal, scientific, clinical, spiritual, or other professional advice.

1 = **Negotiating:** Talking over ideas, information, and opinions with others until all agree on solutions.

2 = **Instructing:** Teaching people (or animals) by explaining, showing, or watching them practice. Giving advice on a topic that you know a great deal about.

3 = **Supervising:** Directing workers by giving orders and explaining duties. Making sure they do the work on time. Helping everyone work together.

4 = **Diverting:** Amusing others. Saying or doing things that people find interesting. May work on a stage, radio, TV or movie.

5 = **Persuading:** Winning others over to a product, service, or point of view.

6 = **Speaking-Signaling:** Talking or making motions so people can understand you and getting an answer from them. Telling people what to do in a way that they understand.

7 = **Serving:** Helping people or animals. Carrying out their wants or wishes right away.

8 = **Taking Instructions-Helping:** Doing what you are told. Following orders without deciding if they are right or wrong.

Things (high = 0, low = 7)

This refers to the sixth digit in the *DOT* code number.

0 = **Setting Up:** Changing parts on machines so they can do different tasks. Fixing them if they break down. Knowing how to operate several different machines.

1 = **Precision Working:** Being responsible for making things that fit exact rules or standards. Deciding which tools or materials to use to make them correctly.

2 = **Operating-Controlling:** Starting, stopping, and watching machines or equipment to be sure they are doing the right thing. Watching gages, dials, etc. and changing valves or controls as needed.

3 = **Driving-Operating:** Steering or guiding machines or tools. Estimating distance, speed, and direction.

4 = **Manipulating:** Moving, guiding, placing, or working things using your body or tools. Selecting tools, objects, or materials.

5 = **Tending:** Starting, stopping, and watching machines work. Watching timers or gages. Making changes based on rules.

6 = **Feeding-Offbearing:** Filling up or emptying machines which are running automatically or run by other workers.

7 = **Handling:** Moving or carrying things.

The OES Code:

Every 10 years a census is conducted to count the citizens in the United States. One of the questions on the census form asks for the occupation of each citizen. The data reported on this form is cataloged into about 500 categories by the Office of Employment Statistics (OES). There is no accurate way to know how many people work in each of the thousands of occupations in the *DOT*. We only know, accurately, how many people work in each of the 500 OES categories.

This code number explains in which OES category the occupation belongs. You can use it to find information about the size of the occupation and salaries in government reports. These reports are updated annually (or more often) by the branch of your state government which serves unemployed people. In general, these agencies are called employment security offices, but in each state they have a different name. If you ask at these offices, you can obtain current information about salaries and outlook for the OES occupational groups. Refer to appendix F for a complete list of the OES codes in numerical order along with their related occupational category.

The GED Code:

The GED code refers to education of a general nature which does not have a specific occupational objective. Ordinarily, such education is obtained in elementary school, high school, or college, but it can also be obtained through self-study and experience. The codes used in the occupational descriptions refer to the "General Educational Development" required to handle this job in Reasoning (R), Math (M) and Language (L). Additional information on this code system can be found in the *Handbook for Analyzing Jobs*. Use the following information to interpret the numeric codes used for each of these three major categories.

Reasoning Development (high = 6, low = 1)

Level 6: Using abstract concepts, symbols (formulas, musical notes, etc.), and scientific theories to solve problems.

Level 5: Defining problems, collecting data, and drawing conclusions about all kinds of problems.

Level 4: Interpreting instructions. Using logic to solve concrete problems.

Level 3: Using common sense while following instructions. Solving problems by trying solutions that have worked before.

Level 2: Following detailed instructions. Choosing the right solution to problems based on rules.

Level 1: Following one- or two-step instructions. Dealing with problems when they fit simple rules.

Mathematical Development (high = 6, low = 1)

Level 6: Using advanced calculus, modern algebra, or statistics.

Level 5: Using linear algebra, calculus, or statistics.

Level 4: Using algebra, geometry, or shop math.

Level 3: Using business math, simple algebra, or simple geometry.

Level 2: Multiplying, dividing, using fractions, or reading graphs.

Level 1: Adding, subtracting, making change, or measuring.

Language Development (high = 6, low = 1)

Level 6:   Creating literature or technical reports, or teaching or supervising those who do.

Level 5:   Understanding and enjoying literature or poetry, or making speeches.

Level 4:   Reading novels or manuals, writing summaries or business letters, or speaking before an audience as part of a group.

Level 3:   Reading novels or rules, writing reports with proper grammar, or speaking correctly in public.

Level 2:   Reading instructions and using the dictionary, writing with proper punctuation, or speaking clearly.

Level 1:   Reading up to 2,500 words, printing simple sentences, or speaking using normal correct order.

The SVP Code:

SVP stands for "Specific Vocational Preparation" and refers to the time required to learn the techniques, acquire the information, and develop the facility needed for average performance in a specific job. The training may be acquired in a school, on the job, military, institutional, or vocational environment. Additional information on this code system can be found in the *Handbook for Analyzing Jobs.*

The SVP code is a bit confusing for most people. It does not indicate how many years it will take you to reach the job. Instead, it tells you how long you would have to train if you were to receive the training without pausing to work. Since many jobs can only be reached by on-the-job experience (managers, for example) it is hard to determine how much time it would take for the training if you never stopped to work. Consider, for example, the difference between a two-year associate's degree and an apprenticeship. It is generally assumed that one year of college is equal to two years of apprenticeship, since apprentices spend a lot of time working between the learning experiences.

Use the SVP coding system to compare the amount of training needed by two different jobs. You should be more careful in using it to determine how much education is required. Some of your prior training may help you to qualify for the job faster. Or you may need to slow down and practice the skills you are learning before you complete the training. So these codes may not apply directly to you. But they will help you to determine which jobs require a lot of training and which jobs can be entered with very little training.

The SVP codes used in this book are as follows:

Specific Vocational Preparation (SVP) (high = 9, low = 1)

9 =   Over 10 years
8 =   Over 4 years up to 10 years
7 =   Over 2 years up to 4 years
6 =   Over 1 year up to 2 years
5 =   Over 6 months up to 1 year
4 =   Over 3 months up to 6 months
3 =   Over 30 days up to 3 months
2 =   Beyond a short demonstration up to 30 days
1 =   Short demonstration only

Academic Codes (Ed and Eng):

The "Ed" Code:

The academic code has two components. The first component, "Ed," refers to the educational degree or certification typically required for entry into this occupation. In some fields the educational requirements are clearly defined, while in others they are ambiguous. For example, a movie producer usually has a college education, but a talented individual without this education would be accepted into this field. Thus the minimum education level for this occupation is much lower than the average education level. The Education Code indicates the minimum education accepted for entry into this type of work. If you do not have the educational background necessary for a particular job, and lack the time, preparation, ability, temperament, or other resources needed to get that education, then this job will not be available to you.

There is no single satisfactory source of data on the educational requirements of occupations. In many cases the education required is a direct function of the level of difficulty and complexity of the work and is closely related to the General Educational Development (GED) factors in the *DOT* database. In other cases, educational attainment such as receipt of a high school diploma, college degree, or completion of an apprenticeship or certificate program are often used as screening criteria in government agencies and large private enterprises, and there is no close relationship between educational attainment and complexity of the job.

Educational Codes used in this book are based upon data in the *Occupational Outlook Handbook* (published by the DOL), newspaper want ads, civil service job announcements, and similar sources for all occupations where such information was available. The remaining occupations were then coded based upon GED levels. Adjustments to this coding were made for occupations in which screening requirements were known to be a significant factor such as apprenticeable skilled trades, white-collar clerical jobs in certain industries, health and social service jobs, and technical jobs in fields with certificate training programs.

The "Ed" Codes used in this book are as follows:

M = Master's degree or above: A Master of Arts, Master of Science, Ph.D., Ed.D., MD, DDS, or other similar professional degree based upon collegiate education beyond the bachelor's degree, is required.
B = Bachelor's degree: A Bachelor of Arts or a Bachelor of Science or similar four-year college degree is required.
A = Associate degree or apprenticeship: An Associate of Arts or Sciences or completion of a certificate program at a post-secondary collegiate institution or completion of a formal apprenticeship program is required.
H = High school diploma or GED: A high school diploma or the equivalent is required. Post-secondary or technical school courses of less than two years duration may also be required.
N = No diploma: While a high school diploma is very useful in getting any job, some occupations do not actually require a high school diploma or GED.

The "Eng" Code:

The "Eng" code is another characteristic that is coded within the academic code section of each job description.

Many jobs require knowledge of and proficiency in the English language. For example, you must be fluent in English to answer correspondence, understand instructions, contracts, or specifications written in English. You must be fluent in English to respond to inquiries from the public, or to explain things to others where English is normally spoken. In some jobs there is no substantial need for English proficiency. These are situations where work routines can be picked up through observation, instructions are available in other languages, or co-workers are available to translate instructions.

The occupations in this book were coded on the level of English Proficiency required by using the DOL database indicators on levels of Language Development, the relationship with the People Worker Function, the Dealing with People temperament, and the description of the occupation.

The "Eng" Codes used are as follows:

G = Understanding English Grammar: Knows English grammar and vocabulary of over 5,000 words; can understand and communicate using nontechnical written or spoken English. Examples include most professional, clerical, and sales representative jobs.

S = Simple Communication in English: Knows enough English words and phrases to respond to simple communications in English from co-workers or the public. Examples include sales clerk, taxi driver, and carpenters with limited amounts of public contact.

N = No Communication in English: While speaking English is always useful in getting a job, there are some jobs which have no requirements for English proficiency at either of the two previous levels.

The Work Field Code:

This is a numeric code referring to groups of occupations clustered together based on similar technology, related skills, and overall socioeconomic objective. Although every job requires many different skills, the skills within a work field tend to be quite specific and relate very closely to the occupation. They are usually not easily "transferable" to other work fields and are often used only in a small number of occupations.

There are 100 work fields and all the jobs in the economy have been classified into one or more of them. Each work field has a title, definition, and three digit code number. The work fields are also organized into groups on the basis of similar overall objectives. Additional information on this code system can be found in the *Handbook for Analyzing Jobs*.

The work fields are arranged numerically in appendix H. Should you be familiar with the codes used in the *Handbook for Analyzing Jobs*, you may note that the list in appendix H differs in some respects. This is not an error. The codes provided there are newer revisions now used by the U.S. Department of Labor but have been previously unpublished in this form. They are relatively easily cross-referenced to the old codes should you need to do that.

Materials, Products, Subject Matter, and Services (MPSMS) Code:

This category answers the question "What do you do it with?" They include (a) basic materials being processed, such as fabric, metal, or wood; (b) final products being made, such as automobiles or baskets; (c) data, when being dealt with or applied, such as insurance or physics; and (d) services, such as barbering or dentistry.

The system of codes are derived from the *Standard Classification Manual*, (*SCM*) published by the U.S. Department of Commerce. It consists of 580 categories organized into 55 groups, each designated by a three digit code. A code ending in 9 designates a "Not Elsewhere Classified" (N.E.C.) category. Additional information on this code system can be found in the *Handbook for Analyzing Jobs*.

The MPSMS code list is provided in appendix G and contains a complete listing of the 580 MPSMS codes in numerical order. This is an updated list of codes and will have some differences from the older codes listed in the *Handbook for Analyzing Jobs*. This updated version is also unpublished elsewhere, though it reflects the codes now used by the U.S. Government.

The Aptitudes Code:

This code refers to aptitudes required in General Learning (G), Verbal Ability (V), Numerical Aptitude (N), Spatial (S), Form Perception (P), Clerical Perception (Q), Motor Coordination (K), Finger Dexterity (F), Manual Dexterity (M), Eye-Hand-Foot Coordination (E) and Color Discrimination (C).

Aptitudes are defined as the specific capacities or abilities required of an individual in order to facilitate the learning of some task or job duty. Aptitudes are often measured through the administration of tests such as the GATB (General Aptitude Test Battery), administered under the direction of the U.S. Employment Service. Various studies have been conducted to determine the level of aptitudes to assure success in various jobs. Additional information on this code system can be found in the *Handbook for Analyzing Jobs*.

Following is information needed to interpret this code in the occupational descriptions.

The following scale applies to all aptitudes:

Aptitude Codes (high = 1, low = 5)

1 = The top 10 percent of the population. This segment of the population possesses an extremely high degree of the aptitude.
2 = The highest third exclusive of the top 10 percent of the population. This segment of the population possesses an above average or high degree of the aptitude.
3 = The middle third of the population. This segment of the population possesses a medium degree of the aptitude, ranging from slightly below to slightly above average.
4 = The lowest third exclusive of the bottom 10 percent of the population. This segment of the population possesses a below average or low degree of the aptitude.
5 = The lowest 10 percent of the population. This segment of the population possesses a negligible degree of the aptitude.

Definitions of the Aptitudes

G = **General Learning Ability:** Catching on to things quickly. Understanding instructions easily. Reasoning and making judgments. (Closely related to doing well in school.)
V = **Verbal Ability:** Understanding the meaning of words and using them effectively. Understanding what others say to you. Knowing how to use grammar and write properly.
N = **Numerical Aptitude:** Understanding numbers and doing arithmetic quickly and accurately.
S = **Spatial:** Understanding drawings or visualizing plans. (Used in such tasks as blueprint reading and in solving geometry problems.)
P = **Form Perception:** Seeing slight differences in shapes and objects. Noticing differences in shapes, widths, or lengths.
Q = **Clerical Perception:** Proof-reading — finding errors in words or numbers quickly.
K = **Motor Coordination:** Moving quickly and accurately when you see something happen.
F = **Finger Dexterity:** Moving fingers and working with small things quickly and accurately.
M = **Manual Dexterity:** Moving hands quickly and accurately. Placing and turning things.
E = **Eye-Hand-Foot Coordination:** Moving hands and feet accurately when you see something happen.

C = **Color Discrimination:** Seeing slight differences in colors or shades. Knowing when colors match or contrast.

The Temperaments Code:

Temperaments are defined as the adaptability requirements placed on the worker by specific types of job-worker situations. Often described as "personality requirements," many employers specify which of these traits they do or do not want in a person they hire. They are often predictors of employee success in the job since many job failures are more the result of an inability to adjust to a work situation than to an inability to do the required tasks.

The occupational descriptions include one or more of the following letter codes if that temperament is important to have in the occupation described. If one or more of the codes are missing from a given occupational description, that temperament is not considered as important to have for that occupation.

D = **Directing or Supervising Others:** Taking responsibility for telling others what to do or planning their tasks (not your own work). Making rules and decisions that others must follow.

F = **Judging Based on Feelings or Esthetics:** Creating art or criticizing the art of others. Using imagination and creativity.

I = **Influencing or Persuading Others:** Convincing people. Getting them to do the things you want them to do.

J = **Judging Based on Experiences:** Making decisions based on what you see, hear, smell, or touch.

M = **Making Decisions Based on Facts:** Using charts, tables, books, or other facts to decide what to do.

P = **Working with People:** Working together with others or helping them (more than just giving or receiving instructions).

R = **Doing Repetitive Work:** Doing the same task or following the same steps over again many times each day.

S = **Working Quickly or with Concentration:** Working under stress caused by emergencies, danger, or criticism. Working very fast or concentrating very hard.

T = **Doing Precise Work, to Close Tolerances:** Being very precise in making things, doing arithmetic, recording data, or inspecting things.

V = **Changing Tasks Often, Varied Duties:** Being able to change tasks quickly. Doing many different types of work during a day.

The Stress Related Code:

A remarkable array of health conditions have been attributed to stresses associated with working. Heart attacks, stroke, chronic back pain, alcoholism, fatigue, depression, and suicide all have been blamed on problems arising in the workplace. These phenomenon are not unique to the workplace, of course. Interpersonal relationships, adverse economic, political, or environmental conditions can also be stressful.

The term "burn-out" is sometimes used to describe a syndrome in which people who have been successfully performing a job, then begin experiencing one or more of these symptoms and feel they can no longer stay on the job. Occupations in which burn-out is frequent include police, bus drivers, social workers, firefighters, guards, and school teachers.

A variety of factors have been cited as causes of stress on the job, ranging from constant exposure to danger, to tedium, to sexual harassment. Some of these factors, such as constant exposure to danger, are associated with specific occupations. Others, like sexual harassment, cannot be associated with specific occupations. Four major job-specific factors appear as a common thread in many research studies. They are: emotional control, tedium, responsibility, and sustained attention.

In coding occupations for these factors, a variety of DOL worker traits were used to identify possible problem occupations. Then each definition was read by a panel of experts. These experts made the determination, for each occupation, whether or not to code it for the stress-related factor. The worker traits used in coding these traits are listed for your information, but the actual coding of these traits may be different than the DOL category on which they were based.

Note that many jobs will not have any stress factor indicated for that job. In these cases, the stress category will not appear for that job. This is not an error or omission on our part, just a way to avoid including meaningless listings. When the stress category is included for a job, it will only list those codes where a particular stress code is a factor. For example, many jobs will list only one or two stress factors and few will list more than three.

E = Using emotional control: Psychologists in examining the burn-out phenomenon among health professionals and workers in bureaucracies, have concluded that all work with people involves some degree of stress. This is particularly the case where the work requires maintaining control over the expression of feelings of anger or grief. Jobs require Emotional Control when you are dealing with people and must continually exercise control over the expression of feelings such as anger or grief toward others, or where you are others are continually expressing these feelings toward you. Occupations coded for this trait often require the People Temperament and a significant, high score on the People Function (indicated by the fifth digit in the *DOT* number). Examples of include counselors, nurses, tellers, and receptionists.

T = Tolerating repetition: Another factor identified by a number of researchers is tedium (meaning drudgery or boredom). Tedium is most common when doing a repetitive task, receiving little encouragement or praise, and being unable to alter the work to make it more pleasant. Typical examples of this type of work include production jobs in factories and clerical jobs in large, bureaucratic organizations or typing pools. Typical occupations include word processors, shirt pressers, and drill-press operators. The DOL Temperament of Repetition was considered in coding this trait.

A = Accepting responsibility: Yet another source of stress that has received much attention is that found among workers who hold responsibility for making decisions under conditions of uncertainty which affect the safety or welfare of other people or property. Examples here are physicians, lawyers, securities traders and various kinds of managers. Responsibility refers to situations requiring the worker to make decisions under conditions of uncertainty which involve the safety or security of other persons or property. The DOL Temperament of "Directing or Supervising Others" was considered in coding this trait.

S = Sustaining attention: The DOL, in defining the temperament "Performance Under Stress," identifies emergencies or dangerous situations, working with speed and sustained attention or where danger or tension is a regular, consistent part of the job as stress sources. Other research has shown working under hazardous conditions (a DOL Work Environment category) to be stressful. Sustained attention refers to situations where there is tension caused by the requirements of continuous attentiveness, exposure to danger or pressure to maintain work speed. Airline pilots, grocery checkers, and police officers all have this characteristic.

The Physical Requirements Code:

These codes refer to job requirements for vision, hearing, lifting, and other physical demands of a particular job.

Vision Needed (V)

Some form of visual ability is required by a significant portion of jobs in the labor market. In consequence, the relatively small numbers of individuals with severe vision impairments are faced with significant limitations on work opportunities. The DOL worker traits include a code for vision, but this does not, unfortunately, provide a satisfactory basis for identifying jobs that cannot be performed by the blind or visually impaired.

The *Handbook for Analyzing Jobs* explains that six different factors were considered by the DOL analysts in coding occupations on the vision factor. They are:

a) **Far Acuity:** Clarity of vision at 20 feet or more
b) **Near Acuity:** Clarity of vision at 20 inches or less
c) **Depth of Perception:** Ability to judge distance and space relationships
d) **Field of Vision:** The area that can be seen to the right or left and above and below while eyes are focused on a fixed point
e) **Accommodation:** Adjustment of the eye to bring an object into sharp focus
f) **Color Vision:** Ability to distinguish colors

There is, however, no direct indication of which of these factors are involved in a given occupation. It can only be inferred by reading the job description.

A second and more important drawback with the DOL coding is that the code is used only where vision is important, not simply required. For example, vision is not coded for the occupation of tractor driver, although that is clearly not a reasonable occupational choice for a blind person. To remedy this, a new coding scheme is used in this book. These are the levels of vision needed:

G = Normal Vision Needed (with or without correction): The work requires either far or near acuity or both. Examples of jobs requiring near acuity include dentists, drafters, machinists, clerical, and other jobs that involve reading handwriting or examining documents or other material closely. Examples of occupations requiring far acuity include firefighters, border guards, and any job involved in driving a vehicle.

L = Limited Vision Needed (either distant objects or written documents): The work cannot be done by a non-sighted or legally blind person but could be done by a person with limited vision. Jobs with this requirement may involve reading printed material such as reports, letters or invoices as in the case of many professional, sales and clerical fields. Or they may require sight to locate and recognize objects or persons, typical of much service and craft work.

N = No Vision Needed (could be blind): This work does not require vision or the work could be done with assistive devices or the help of an aide.

Hearing Needed (H)

Persons with deafness or speech impairments also face labor market restrictions although not as many as the blind. The DOL, in analyzing occupations, considered two hearing-related dimensions. They are:

a) **Talking:** Expressing or exchanging ideas by means of the spoken word

b) **Hearing:** Perceiving the nature of sounds by ear

In coding jobs for worker traits, the DOL followed the same procedure as for vision and identified those occupations for which talking or speaking are important, not those for which it is required. This book identifies those occupations that could not be done by persons with hearing impairments. The levels of hearing impairment are:

G = Normal Hearing Needed: To do this work you must discriminate among similar sounds, as in carrying on conversations over an ordinary telephone or in listening to sounds of a defective engine. Examples of jobs which require normal hearing include reporters, police officers, auto mechanics, and piano technicians.

L = Limited Hearing Needed (problem with similar sounds): While the work cannot be done by a deaf or non-speaking person, it could be done by a person who does not hear as well as normal. These jobs require the ability to hear sounds or engage in spoken conversation. Examples include teachers, administrators, supervisors, sales and service employees who must communicate with the public or co-workers by speaking.

N = No Hearing Needed (could be deaf): This work does not require that you hear. It could be done by a person who has severe hearing loss.

Lifting Needed (L)

Many occupations require the ability to raise or lower objects. Back injuries and other physical conditions may prevent such activities and thus eliminate these occupations from consideration by people with such impairments. The DOL database categorizes jobs in terms of strength requirements. This concept includes walking and other dimensions of movement in addition to lifting. In this book the occupations have been recoded to reflect lifting requirements alone. The levels of lifting identified by the DOL were used, but the issue of walking and moving around was removed and dealt with as a separate issue. The levels of lifting are:

V = Very heavy: Could require lifting over 100 pounds. Examples include furniture movers and professional weight lifters.

H = Heavy: Requires lifting 100 pounds maximum with frequent lifting and/or carrying objects weighing up to 50 pounds. Examples include pastry chef, pipefitter, and materials handler.

M = Medium: Requires lifting 50 pounds maximum with frequent lifting and/or carrying objects weighing up to 25 lbs. Veterinarians, sales route drivers, and dinner cooks must do this much lifting.

L = Light: Requires lifting 20 pounds maximum with frequent lifting and/or carrying objects weighing up to 20 pounds. Fast food workers, library assistants, and most sales and benchwork jobs require this much lifting.

S = Sedentary (Very Light): Requires lifting 10 pounds maximum and/or carrying objects such as ledgers and small tools. Examples include bookkeepers and telephone operators.

Other Physical Requirements

Codes in the physical categories that follow will only appear with occupations where these factors are important. In some cases, none of these codes will appear if a particular job does not require any of them. In other cases, one or two of these codes will appear. This is not an error or omission on our part, just an attempt to avoid providing unnecessary information.

W = Walking and/or Mobility Needed: Being able to walk is a requirement of many jobs, especially those involved with other physical activities such as lifting, carrying, or crawling. This restriction eliminates people in wheelchairs or those who have a hard time walking. This physical demand is not directly reported by the DOL. In most cases, occupations coded as Medium or heavier in Lifting also require mobility, and occupations coded as Sedentary do not require mobility. But occupations coded as Light may require either mobility or lifting 20 pounds. These occupations were coded for mobility by reading the descriptions carefully. The Walking and/or Mobility Needed Code was selected only if walking was required as an essential function of the job. For example, surveyors, nurses, and most sales representatives must be able to walk and move around on uneven surfaces.

C = Climbing and/or Balancing Needed: On some jobs, not only must you move around, but you must be able to ascend and descend stairs or ladders, scaffolding, ramps or poles. Balancing and the ability to steady yourself and keep from falling may also be required. The data for this item comes directly from the DOL.

S = Stooping, Kneeling, Crouching, and/or Crawling Needed: The DOL identifies another movement category which includes four separate activities. They are: Stooping (bending the body downward and forward by bending the spine at the waist); Kneeling (bending legs at the knees to come to rest on one or both knees); Crouching (bending the body downward and forward by bending legs and spine); and Crawling (moving about on hands and knees or hands and feet). The data for this item comes directly from the DOL.

H = Handling, Fingering, Feeling, and/or Reaching Needed: Most jobs involve some use of the arms and hands. DOL has grouped four separate activities under this heading. They are: Reaching (extending the hands or arms in any direction); Handling (seizing, holding, grasping, turning, or otherwise working with the hand or hands); Fingering (picking, pinching, or otherwise working with fingers); and Feeling (perceiving attributes of objects such as size, shape, temperature, or texture by means of receptors in skin, particularly those of fingertips).

The Work Environment Code:

These codes provide information on the types of work environments that are found in a given job and must be accepted by the worker. The data for these categories comes directly from the DOL.

The codes used are as follows:

Inside/Outside

One of the following codes will always appear in each job description:

I =   Inside: Protection from weather conditions but not necessarily from temperature changes. Includes occupations like pilots and truck drivers in which the worker is sheltered from the weather.

O = Outside: No effective protection from weather.

B = Both: Work is done inside and outside in approximately equal amounts.

Other Work Environment Codes

These codes will appear in a job description only when it is found to be typically required in the job.

C = Extremes of Cold: DOL considered two elements in determining this requirement. They are: Extremes of Cold (temperature sufficiently low to cause marked bodily discomfort); and Temperature Changes (variations in temperature which accompany extreme cold are sufficiently marked and abrupt to cause marked bodily reaction).

H = Extremes of Heat: The criteria used for identifying occupations associated with high temperatures parallel those used for low temperature extremes. They are: Extremes of Heat (temperature sufficiently high to cause marked bodily discomfort); and Temperature Changes (variations in temperature which accompany extreme heat are sufficiently marked and abrupt to cause marked bodily reaction).

W = Wet and/or Humid: Two types of situations were considered by DOL in identifying occupations in this category. They were: Wet (contact with water or other liquids); and Humid (atmospheric conditions with moisture content sufficiently high to cause marked bodily discomfort).

N = Noise and/or Vibration: DOL marked this condition present if there was sufficient noise, exceeding 80 decibels, constant or intermittent, to cause marked distraction or possible hearing loss, or if there was sufficient vibration to cause bodily harm, if endured day after day.

R = Hazards: Hazards includes conditions in which there is danger to life, health, or the risk of bodily injury. This category includes a variety of physical hazards, such as proximity to moving mechanical parts, electrical shock, working on scaffolding and high places, exposure to burns and radiant energy, exposure to explosives, toxic chemicals, and biological agents.

F = Fumes, Odors, Dust: Occupations were identified by DOL if any of the following atmospheric conditions were present to a degree or length of time sufficient to cause marked discomfort or possible bodily injury to a worker.

Fumes: Solid particles generated by condensation from a gaseous state.

Odors: Noxious nontoxic smells.

Dusts: Solid particles by handling, crushing, grinding, rapid impact, detonation, or decrepitation of materials such as rock, ore, metal, coal, wood, and grain.

Mists: Suspended liquid droplets generated by condensation from the gaseous to the liquid state or by breaking up a liquid into a dispersed state.

Gases: Normally formless fluids which occupy the space of enclosure and which can be changed to the liquid or solid state only by the combined effect of increased pressure and decreased temperature.

Poor Ventilation: Insufficient or excessive movement of air causing a feeling of suffocation or exposure to drafts.

The Salary Code:

Occupations were assigned into one of five pay ranges based on the expected starting salary for a qualified worker. These codes are based on data in the *Occupational Outlook Handbook*, numerous wage and salary surveys, want ads, and many other sources. They reflect salaries as of June, 1990. Please note that these are starting salaries for workers with training but no experience. In some cases wages increase rapidly with experience. In other cases, wages change little as the worker stays longer in the job.

Salary Code (low = 1, high = 5)

1 = Lowest = Below $11,000 per year

2 = Moderately Low = $11,000 to $14,999 per year

3 = Mid-Range = $15,000 to $19,999 per year

4 = Moderately High = $20,000 to $27,999 per year

5 = Highest = $28,000 per year and above

The Outlook Code:

Occupations were assigned to one of five employment outlook categories based upon the length of time that a qualified but inexperienced job seeker could expect to spend before finding employment in the specified field. This data is based on national averages. The time you spend looking for a job will depend on conditions in your community including when you are looking, your skills, and how well you are able to impress possible employers. It is also important to note that higher-paying jobs and those requiring advanced education or credentials typically take longer to find but are often more stable.

These codes are based on the *Occupational Outlook Handbook, Projections of Employment* (DOL, 1990), educational program completion statistics, want ads, and many other data sources. Due to the delay in compiling data, the projections used here are about one year old at the time this book was published. Generally, this data does not change rapidly from year to year and should provide useful guidelines for years to come.

Outlook Code (low = 1, high = 5)

1 = Lowest = Finding employment can take over a year
2 = Moderately Low = Finding employment can take from a few months to a year
3 = Mid Range = Employment can be found within a few months
4 = Moderately High = Employment can be found within a couple of weeks
5 = Highest = In many areas, employment can be found quickly

Artistic 01

An interest in creative expression of feelings or ideas. You can satisfy this interest in several of the creative or performing arts fields. You may enjoy literature. Perhaps writing or editing would appeal to you. You may prefer to work in the performing arts. You could direct or perform in drama, music, or dance. You may enjoy the visual arts. You could become a critic in painting, sculpture, or ceramics. You may want to use your hands to create or decorate products. Or you may prefer to model clothes or develop acts for entertainment.

01.01 Literary Arts

Workers in this group write, edit, or direct the publication of prose or poetry. They find employment on newspapers or magazines, in radio and television studios, and in the theater and motion picture industries. Some writers are self-employed and sell stories, plays, and other forms of literary composition to publishers.

✔ **What kind of work would you do?**
Your work activities would depend upon your specific job. For example, you might:

- write plays or scripts for movies.
- write short stories, poems, or novels.
- edit the work of creative writers.
- write dialogue for television programs.
- write reviews of literature, musical performances, and other artistic work.
- select writers and subject matter for television productions.

✔ **What skills and abilities do you need for this kind of work?**
To do this kind of work, you must be able to:

- present personal views or interpretations relating to such subjects as politics, social conditions, religion, or plays or other writings.
- deal with various kinds of people.
- make decisions based on personal judgment.
- influence the opinion of people through words.

✔ **How do you know if you would like or could learn to do this kind of work?**
The following questions may give you clues about yourself as you consider this group of jobs.

- Have you written a book review for a class? Do you enjoy others reading your interpretations?
- Have you written an original story? Can you create original characters or situations that interest and entertain others?
- Have you developed publicity posters for a garage sale, fund drive, or community activity? Can you select words that spark people's curiosity and interest?
- Have you written poems for an English class or for poetry contests? Do you enjoy expressing personal thoughts and feelings in this type of writing?
- Have you written for or edited a school newspaper, union bulletin, or company newsletter? Can you edit and improve the writing of others?
- Have you told ghost stories around a campfire or other setting? Were they interesting and entertaining to others?

✔ **How can you prepare for and enter this kind of work?**

Occupations in this group usually require education and/or training extending from two to over ten years, depending upon the specific kind of work. Experience in writing is usually required for employment. Writing for weekly or monthly newspapers or magazines can be helpful in getting jobs with large newspapers or advertising agencies. Employers often require samples of published writing. Editing jobs usually require several years experience as a writer.

Courses in English grammar and composition, as well as literature, are basic high school subjects. Community colleges and universities offer programs that prepare people for this kind of work. Courses in journalism, English, and creative writing provide necessary skills. Some occupations require proficiency in one or more foreign languages; while others require a knowledge of political science, art, drama, or other subjects. For example, a person wishing to become a critic must have in-depth knowledge of the subject to be criticized, art, music, or the like. This knowledge can be acquired through courses at colleges or universities; specialized schools, such as art institutes, or performing arts little theaters or playhouses.

Self-employed or free-lance writers sometimes use literary agents to help them find publishers. These agents may help the writer prepare material for publication. Publishers occasionally hire experienced free-lance writers to write about a particular subject.

✔ **What else should you consider about these jobs?**

Most new workers in writing occupations start with routine assignments such as writing headlines. Only in establishments where few writers are employed is the newcomer given creative writing assignments.

Some jobs are available for part-time workers. Free-lance writers sometimes prepare advertising copy or serve as local correspondents for daily newspapers.

If you think you would like to do this kind of work, look at the job descriptions listed below.

GOE: 01.01.01 Editing, Literary Arts

CONTINUITY DIRECTOR (radio & tv broad.) • D.O.T. #132.037-010 • OES #34002 • EDITOR, CONTINUITY AND SCRIPT. Coordinates activities of continuity department of radio or television station: Assigns duties to staff and freelance writers. Supervises staff writers preparing program continuity and scripts for broadcasting, and edits material to insure conformance with company policy, laws, and regulations. May be responsible for nonmusical copyright material. May supervise administrative research workers and employees receiving and examining program ideas and scripts suggested by public for station or network presentation. • GED: R5, M2, L5 • SVP: 4-10 yrs • Academic: Ed=A, Eng=S • Work Field: 261 • MPSMS: 863 • Aptitudes: G2, V1, N3, S4, P4, Q3, K4, F4, M4, E5, C5 • Temperaments: D, J, M, P • Physical: V=N, H=L, L=S • Work Env: I • Salary: 5 • Outlook: 3

EDITOR, FILM (motion pic.) • D.O.T. #962.264-010 • OES #34032 • FILM CUTTER. Edits motion picture film, television video tape, and sound tracks: Evaluates and selects scenes in terms of dramatic and entertainment value and story continuity. Trims film segments to specified lengths and reassembles segments in sequence that presents story with maximum effect. Reviews assembled film on screen and makes corrections. Confers with supervisory personnel and others concerning filming of scenes. May specialize in particular field of film editing, such as feature, news, sound, sound effects, or music. • GED: R5, M2, L4 • SVP: 4-10 yrs • Academic: Ed=A, Eng=G • Work Field: 261 • MPSMS: 911 • Aptitudes: G2, V2, N3, S3, P2, Q4, K4, F3, M3, E5, C3 • Temperaments: F, J, T • Physical: V=L, H=N, L=S, H • Work Env: I • Salary: 5 • Outlook: 1

EDITOR, PUBLICATIONS (print. & pub.) • D.O.T. #132.037-022 • OES #34002 • Formulates policy; plans, coordinates, and directs editorial activities; and supervises workers who assist in selecting and preparing material for publication in magazines, trade journals, house organs, and related publications: Confers with executives, department heads, and editorial staff to formulate policy, coordinate department activities, establish production schedules, solve publication problems, and discuss makeup plans and organizational changes. Determines theme of issue and gathers related material. Writes or assigns staff members or freelance writers to write articles, reports, editorials, reviews, and other material. Reads and evaluates material submitted for publication consideration. Secures graphic material from picture sources and assigns artists and photographers to produce pictures and illustrations. Assigns staff member, or personally interviews individuals and attends gatherings, to obtain items for publication, verify facts, and clarify information. Assigns research and other editorial duties to assistants. Organizes material, plans overall and individual page layouts, and selects type. Marks dummy pages to indicate position and size of printed and graphic material. Reviews final proofs and approves or makes changes. Reviews and evaluates work of staff members and makes recommendations and changes. May perform related editorial duties listed under EDITORIAL ASSISTANT (print. & pub.). May direct activities of production, circulation, or promotion personnel. May prepare news or public relations releases, special brochures, and similar materials. May be designated according to type of publication worked on as COMMUNICATIONS MANAGER (print. & pub.); EDITOR, FARM JOURNAL (print. & pub.); EDITOR, HOUSE ORGAN (print. & pub.); EDITOR, MAGAZINE (print. & pub.); EDITOR, TRADE JOURNAL (print. & pub.); INDUSTRIAL EDITOR (print. & pub.). • GED: R6, M3, L6 • SVP: 4-10 yrs • Academic: Ed=B, Eng=G • Work Field: 261, 264, 295 • MPSMS: 480 • Aptitudes: G1, V1, N3, S3, P3, Q3, K3, F4, M4, E5, C5 • Temperaments: D, F, I, J, P • Stress: E, A • Physical: V=L, H=L, L=S • Work Env: I •

Salary: 5 • **Outlook:** 1

PRODUCER (motion pic.) • D.O.T. #187.167-174 • OES #34056 • Coordinates activities of personnel engaged in writing, directing, editing, and producing motion pictures: Reviews synopses and scripts and directs adaptation for screen. Determines treatment and scope of proposed productions and establishes departmental operating budgets. Selects principal members of cast and key production staff members. Reviews filmed scenes of each day's shooting, orders retakes, and approves final editing of filmed productions. Conducts meetings with DIRECTOR, MOTION PICTURE (motion pic.), SCREEN WRITER (motion pic.; radio & tv broad.), and other staff members to discuss production progress and results. • **GED:** R6, M5, L6 • **SVP:** 4-10 yrs • **Academic:** Ed=B, Eng=G • **Work Field:** 295, 297 • **MPSMS:** 754 • **Aptitudes:** G1, V2, N2, S2, P4, Q4, K4, F4, M4, E5, C5 • **Temperaments:** D, J, P • **Stress:** E, A • **Physical:** V=N, H=L, L=S • **Work Env:** I • **Salary:** 5 • **Outlook:** 3

GOE: 01.01.02 Creative Writing

COPY WRITER (profess. & kin.) • D.O.T. #131.067-014 • OES #34002 • Writes advertising copy for use by publication or broadcast media to promote sale of goods and services: Consults with sales media, and marketing representatives to obtain information on product or service and discuss style and length of advertising copy. Obtains additional back ground and current development information through research and interview. Reviews advertising trends, consumer surveys, and other data regarding marketing of specific and related goods and services to formulate presentation approach. Writes preliminary draft of copy and sends to supervisor for approval. Corrects and revises copy as necessary. May write articles, bulletins, sales letters, speeches, and other related informative and promotional material. • **GED:** R5, M2, L5 • **SVP:** 2-4 yrs • **Academic:** Ed=A, Eng=S • **Work Field:** 261 • **MPSMS:** 896 • **Aptitudes:** G2, V1, N3, S4, P3, Q3, K3, F4, M4, E5, C5 • **Temperaments:** F, I, J, M, P • **Physical:** V=N, H=N, L=S, H • **Work Env:** I • **Salary:** 4 • **Outlook:** 3

EDITORIAL WRITER (print. & pub.) • D.O.T. #131.067-022 • OES #34002 • Writes comments on topics of reader interest to stimulate or mold public opinion, in accordance with viewpoints and policies of publication: Prepares as signed or unassigned articles from knowledge of topic and editorial position of publication, supplemented by additional study and research. Submits and discusses copy with editor for approval. May specialize in one or more fields, such as international affairs, fiscal matters, or na-tional or local politics. May participate in conferences of editorial policy committee to recommend topics and position to be taken by publication on specific public issues. • **GED:** R5, M3, L5 • **SVP:** 4-10 yrs • **Academic:** Ed=A, Eng=S • **Work Field:** 261 • **MPSMS:** 480 • **Aptitudes:** G1, V1, N3, S4, P3, Q3, K3, F4, M4, E5, C5 • **Temperaments:** F, I, J, P, V • **Physical:** V=N, H=L, L=S • **Work Env:** I • **Salary:** 5 • **Out look:** 3

SCREEN WRITER (motion pic.) • D.O.T. #131.087-018 • OES #34002 • SCENARIO WRITER; SCRIPT WRITER. Writes scripts for motion pictures or television: Selects subject and theme for script based on personal interests or assignment. Conducts research to obtain accurate factual background information and authentic detail. Writes plot outline, narrative synopsis, or treatment and submits for approval. Confers with PRODUCER (motion pic.) or PRODUCER (radio & tv broad.) and DIRECTOR, MOTION PICTURE (motion pic.) or DIRECTOR, TELEVISION (radio & tv broad.) regarding script development, revisions, and other changes. Writes one or more drafts of script. May work in collaboration with other writers. May adapt books or plays into scripts for use in television or motion picture production. May write continuity or comedy routines. May specialize in particular type of script or writing. • **GED:** R6, M2, L6 • **SVP:** 2-4 yrs • **Academic:** Ed=H, Eng=G • **Work Field:** 261 • **MPSMS:** 754 • **Aptitudes:** G1, V1, N4, S4, P4, Q4, K4, F4, M4, E5, C5 • **Temperaments:** F, J, M, P • **Physical:** V=N, H=N, L=S, H • **Work Env:** I • **Salary:** 5 • **Outlook:** 1

WRITER, PROSE, FICTION AND NONFICTION (profess. & kin.) • D.O.T. #131.067-046 • OES #34002 • WRITER. Writes original prose material for publication: Selects subject matter based on personal interest or receives specific assignment from publisher. Conducts research and makes notes to retain ideas, develop factual information, and obtain authentic detail. Organizes material and plans arrangement or outline. Develops factors, such as theme, plot, order, characterization, and story line. Writes draft of manuscript. Reviews, revises, and corrects it and submits material for publication. Confers with publisher's representative regarding manuscript changes. May specialize in one or more styles or types of writing, such as descriptive or critical interpretations or analyses, essays, magazine articles, short stories, novels, and biographies. • **GED:** R6, M3, L6 • **SVP:** 4-10 yrs • **Academic:** Ed=H, Eng=G • **Work Field:** 261 • **MPSMS:** 757 • **Aptitudes:** G1, V1, N3, S4, P4, Q4, K4, F4, M4, E5, C5 • **Temperaments:** F, J • **Physical:** V=N, H=N, L=S, H • **Work Env:** I • **Salary:** 3 • **Outlook:** 1

01.02 Visual Arts

Workers in this group create original works of art or do commercial art work, using such techniques as drawing, painting, photographing, and sculpturing to express or interpret ideas or to illustrate various written materials. Some visual artists design products, settings, or graphics (such as advertisements or book covers), and oversee the work of other artists or craftsmen who produce or install them. Others teach art, or appraise or restore paintings and other fine art objects. Advertising agencies, printing and publishing firms, television and motion picture studios, museums and restoration laboratories employ visual artists. They also work for manufacturers and in retail and wholesale trade. Many are self-employed, operating their own commercial art studios or doing free-lance work.

✔ **What kind of work would you do?**

Your work activities would depend upon your specific job. For example, you might:

- paint or sketch portraits, landscapes, or other subjects in oils, watercolors, or charcoals.

- design and supervise the construction of scenery for plays.
- plan the arrangement of advertising materials for a department store.

- examine oil paintings to determine the need for restoration, and use scientific and artistic techniques to restore them to their original appearance.
- design and cut original patterns for women's clothing.

- sculpture a statue or other work of art.
- draw accurate and precise pictures of diseased body organs to illustrate articles in medical journals.
- photograph subjects to prepare a photo story.

✔ What skills and abilities do you need for this kind of work?

To do this kind of work, you must be able to:

- understand and apply artistic principles and techniques.
- visualize how the final product will look from rough sketches or work drawings.
- use paint brushes, pens, charcoal, or sculpturing tools skillfully, to produce accurate plans for displays or scenery, illustrations for written materials, or original works of art.

- choose the most appropriate equipment to express an idea or create a particular effect.
- tell whether a work of art is the 'real thing' or a fake by examining it and using various chemical tests, knowledge of art history, and familiarity with the characteristics of the style of various artists.

✔ How do you know if you would like or could learn to do this kind of work?

The following questions may give you clues about yourselves as you consider this group of jobs.

- Have you taken courses in drawing or sketching? Were any of your works selected for display or entry in competition?
- Have you helped paint scenery for amateur plays? Can you select the proper color combinations to achieve a desired effect?

- Have you taken photographs of family, friends, or activities? Do you think they were of good quality and pleasing to the eye?
- Have you viewed art galleries and shows? Do you try to judge the quality of paintings or sculptures?
- Have you worked with modeling clay? Do you enjoy creating original designs in clay?

✔ How can you prepare for and enter this kind of work?

Occupations in this group usually require education and/or training extending from two years up to and over ten years, depending upon the specific kind of work. A common method of preparation is to obtain a four-year degree with a major in fine arts or commercial art. Some artists earn a two- or three-year certificate at an art institute. Programs include the study of art history and critique as well as instruction in techniques.

Small advertising agencies, department stores, and photography studios sometimes hire workers with vocational school or junior college background. These workers are assigned tasks according to their ability. They are usually provided on-the-job training to improve their skills.

Industrial designing jobs require artistic and engineering skills to make scale drawings and to illustrate technical information. Jobs in restoring and appraising art objects usually require a background in art history, chemistry, and similar subjects.

Free-lance visual artists usually have experience as illustrators, designers, art restorers, or photographers. These workers must be well-known for their work and have contact with potential buyers. Samples of their work are used to show their skills to customers.

Administrative and supervisory jobs in the visual arts require extensive experience in the field.

✔ What else should you consider about these jobs?

Most visual artists depend upon some sort of commercial art or design work for financial security. Few can afford to be artists with no regular income.

People who can use a variety of techniques and art media have more opportunities for employment than those who specialize in one area.

If you think you would like to do this kind of work, look at the job titles listed below.

GOE: 01.02.01 Instructing & Appraising, Visual Arts

APPRAISER, ART (profess. & kin.) • D.O.T. #191.287-014 • OES #49999 • Examines works of art, such as paintings, sculpture, and antiques, to determine their authenticity and value: Examines work for color values, style of brush stroke, esthetic correctness, and other characteristics, to establish art period or identify artist. Judges authenticity and value, based on knowledge of art history, materials employed, techniques of individual artists, and current market. May illuminate work with quartz light to determine whether discoloration is present. May X-ray painting and perform chemical tests on paint sample to detect forgery or to authenticate work. May specialize in particular categories of art or in specific types of artistic articles appraised. • **GED:** R5, M4, L4 • **SVP:** 4-10 yrs • **Academic:** Ed=A, Eng=G • **Work Field:** 211 • **MPSMS:** 751, 759 • **Aptitudes:** G2, V2, N4, S3, P2, Q4, K4, F4, M4, E4, C1 • **Temperaments:** J, M, T • **Physical:** V=G, H=N, L=S • **Work Env:** I • **Salary:** 5 • **Outlook:** 2

GOE: 01.02.02 Studio Art

QUICK SKETCH ARTIST (amuse. & rec.) • D.O.T. #149.041-010 • OES #34035 • Sketches likeness of customers: Poses subject to accentuate most pleasing features and draws likeness, using pencil, charcoal, pastels, or other medium. May draw sketch from photograph. May only draw exaggerated likenesses and be designated CARICATURIST (amuse. & rec.). May be identified according to medium worked in. • **GED:** R5, M1, L3 • **SVP:** 1-2 yrs • **Academic:** Ed=A, Eng=G • **Work Field:** 262 • **MPSMS:** 752 • **Aptitudes:** G2, V3, N4, S2, P2, Q4, K2, F2, M2, E5, C2 • **Temperaments:** F, J • **Physical:** V=L, H=N, L=S, H • **Work Env:** B • **Salary:** 2 • **Outlook:** 1

GOE: 01.02.03 Commercial Art

ART DIRECTOR (motion pic.) • D.O.T. #142.031-010 • OES #34038 • Formulates design concepts, selects locations and settings, and directs and coordinates set design, construction, and erection activities to produce sets for motion picture and television productions: Reads script and confers with heads of production and direction to establish budget, schedules, and determine setting requirements. Conducts research and co sults experts to establish architectural styles which accurately depict given periods and locations. Conducts search for appropriate locations and constructed sets. Assigns assistants and staff members to complete design ideas and prepare sketches, illustrations, and detailed drawings of sets. Estimates construction costs and presents plans and estimates for approval. Directs and coordinates set construction, erection, and decoration activities to insure that they conform to design, budget, and schedule requirements. May make rough drawings of design concepts. May formulate design concepts for costumes, makeup, photographic effects, titles, and related production items. • **GED:** R5, M3, L5 • **SVP:** 4-10 yrs • **Academic:** Ed=B, Eng=S • **Work Field:** 264 • **MPSMS:** 889, 911 • **Aptitudes:** G1, V2, N3, S2, P2, Q4, K2, F2, M3, E5, C2 • **Temperaments:** D, F, J • **Stress:** A • **Physical:** V=G, H=G, L=S • **Work Env:** I • **Salary:** 5 • **Outlook:** 1

ART DIRECTOR (profess. & kin.) • D.O.T. #141.031-010 • OES #34035 • Formulates concepts and supervises workers engaged in executing layout designs for art work and copy to be presented by visual communications media, such as magazines, books, newspapers, television, posters, and packaging: Reviews illustrative material and confers with client or individual responsible for presentation regarding budget, background information, objectives, presentation approaches, styles, techniques, and related production factors. Formulates basic layout design concept and conducts research to select and secure suitable illustrative material, or conceives and assigns production of material and detail to artists and photographers. Assigns and directs staff members to develop design concepts into art layouts and prepare layouts for printing. Reviews, approves, and presents final layouts to client or department head for approval. May perform duties of GRAPHIC DESIGNER (profess. & kin.) to design art layouts. May mark up, paste up, and finish layouts to prepare layouts for printing. May draw illustrations. May prepare detailed story board showing sequence and timing of story development when producing material for television. May specialize in particular field, media, or type of layout. • **GED:** R5, M3, L5 • **SVP:** 4-10 yrs • **Academic:** Ed=A, Eng=G • **Work Field:** 264 • **MPSMS:** 752 • **Aptitudes:** G2, V2, N3, S2, P2, Q3, K3, F3, M3, E5, C2 • **Temperaments:** D, F, I, J, P • **Stress:** E • **Physical:** V=L, H=L, L=S, H • **Work Env:** I • **Salary:** 5 • **Outlook:** 2

AUDIOVISUAL PRODUCTION SPECIALIST (profess. & kin.) • D.O.T. #149.061-010 • OES #31508 • INSTRUCTIONAL TECHNOLOGY SPECIALIST. Plans and produces audio, visual, and audiovisual material for communication, information, training, and learning purposes: Develops production ideas based on assignment or generates own ideas based on objectives and person al interest. Conducts research or utilizes knowledge and training to determine format, approach, content, level, and media which will be most effective, meet objectives, and remain within budget restrictions. Plans and develops, or directs assistants to develop, preproduction ideas into outlines, scripts, continuity, story boards, and graphics. Executes rough and finished graphics and graphic designs or directs assistants to execute them. Locates and secures settings, properties, effects, and other production necessities. Directs and coordinates activities of assistants and other production personnel during production. May review, evaluate, and direct changes and modifications to material produced independently by other personnel. May set up, adjust, and operate equipment, such as cameras, sound mixers, and recorders during production. May present narration or announcements. May construct and position in place properties, sets, lighting equipment, and other environmental effects. May develop manuals, texts, work books, or related materials for use in conjunction with production materials. May conduct training sessions on selection, use, and design of audiovisual materials and operation of presentation equipment. May perform duties listed under DIRECTOR, INSTRUCTIONAL MATERIAL (education). • **GED:** R6, M4, L5 • **SVP:** 2-4 yrs • **Academic:** Ed=B, Eng=S • **Work Field:** 201, 261, 264 • **MPSMS:** 750, 860 • **Aptitudes:** G1, V2, N2, S2, P2, Q2, K2, F2, M3, E5, C2 • **Temperaments:** D, F, J, P, V • **Physical:** V=G, H=L, L=S, H • **Work Env:** I • **Salary:** 4 • **Outlook:** 3

CLOTHES DESIGNER (profess. & kin.) • D.O.T. #142.061-018 • OES #34038 • FASHION DESIGNER. Designs men's women's, and children's garments, shoes, and handbags: Analyzes trends and predictions, confers with sales and management executives, compares leather, fabrics, and other apparel materials, and integrates findings with personal interests, tastes, and knowledge of design to create new apparel designs. Sketches rough and detailed drawings of apparel and writes specifications describing factors, such as color scheme, construction, and type of material to be used. Confers with and coordinates activities of workers who draw and cut patterns and construct garments to fabricate sample garment. Examines sample garment on and off model and modifies or alters design as necessary to achieve desired effect. May draw garment or shoe pattern, using measuring and drawing instruments. May cut pattern. May construct sample, using standard sewing equipment. May arrange for showing of sample garments at sales meetings or fashion shows. May attend fashion and fabric shows to observe new fashions and materials. May be identified according to specific group designed for as men, women, or children; and areas of specialization, such as sportswear, coats, dresses, suits, lingerie, or swimwear. May design custom garments for clients and be designated CUSTOM GARMENT DESIGNER (ret. tr.). May conduct research and design authentic period, country, or social class costumes to be worn by motion picture, television, concert, stage, and other media performers and be designated COSTUME DESIGNER (profess. & kin.). Workers who perform similar duties to design, copy, or modify clothing accessories are designated according to article designed such as HANDBAG DESIGNER (leather prod.); HAT DESIGNER (hat & cap); and SHOE DESIGNER (boot & shoe). • **GED:** R5, M3, L5 • **SVP:** 2-4 yrs • **Academic:** Ed=A, Eng=G • **Work Field:** 264 • **MPSMS:** 440, 522, 524 • **Aptitudes:** G2, V2, N3, S2, P2, Q3, K3, F2, M3, E5, C2 • **Temperaments:** F, J, T, V • **Physical:** V=L, H=N, L=S, W, H • **Work Env:** I • **Salary:** 4 • **Outlook:** 1

COMMERCIAL DESIGNER (profess. & kin.) • D.O.T. #141.081-014 • OES #34038 • Creates and designs graphic material for use as ornamentation, illustration, advertising, or cosmetic on manufactured materials and packaging: Receives assignment from customer or supervisor. Studies traditional, period, and contemporary design styles and motifs to obtain perspective. Reviews marketing trends and preferences of target and related markets. Integrates findings with personal interests, knowledge of design, and limitations presented by methods and materials. Creates, draws, modifies, and changes design to achieve desired effect. Confers with customer or supervisor regarding approval or desired changes to design. May be required to have specialized knowledge of material designed. May prepare original artwork and design model. May perform related duties, such as fabricating silk screens, drawing full size patterns, or cutting stencils. May work with specific items, such as signs, packaging, wallpaper, ceramics, tile, glassware, monograms, crests, emblems, or embroidery. See INDUSTRIAL DESIGNER (profess. & kin.) for workers who design both product form and associated graphic materials. • **GED:** R5, M3, L4 • **SVP:** 2-4 yrs • **Academic:** Ed=A, Eng=S • **Work Field:** 262, 264 • **MPSMS:** 752, 889 • **Aptitudes:** G2, V2, N3, S2, P2, Q3, K3, F2, M3, E5, C2 • **Temperaments:** F, J • **Physical:** V=G, H=L, L=S, H • **Work Env:** I • **Salary:** 4 • **Outlook:** 3

DIRECTOR OF PHOTOGRAPHY (motion pic.) • D.O.T. #143.062-010 • OES #34026 • CAMERA OPERATOR, FIRST; CAMERA OPERATOR, HEAD; CINEMATOGRAPHER. Plans, directs, and coordinates motion picture filming: Confers with DIRECTOR, MOTION PICTURE (motion pic.) regarding interpretation of scene and desired effects. Observes set or location and reviews drawings and other information relating to natural or artificial conditions to determine filming and lighting requirements. Reads charts and computes ratios to determine required lighting, film, shutter angles, filter factors, camera distance, depth of field and focus, angles of view, and other variables to produce desired effects. Confers with ELECTRICIAN, CHIEF (motion pic.) to establish lighting requirements. Selects cameras, accessories, equipment, and film stock, utilizing knowledge of filming techniques, filming requirements, and computations. Instructs camera operators regarding camera setup, angles, distances, movement, and other variables and signals cues for starting and stopping film ing. Surveys set or location for potential problems, observes effects of lighting, measures lighting levels, and coordinates necessary changes prior to filming. Views film after processing and makes adjustments, as necessary, to achieve desired effects. May direct television productions which utilize electronic cam eras. May specialize in special effects and be designated DIRECTOR OF PHOTOGRAPHY, SPECIAL EFFECTS (motion pic.; radio & tv broad.). • **GED:** R5, M4, L4 • **SVP:** 4-10 yrs • **Academic:** Ed=B, Eng=S • **Work Field:** 201 • **MPSMS:** 753, 911 • **Aptitudes:** G2, V2, N2, S2, P2, Q4, K4, F4, M4, E5, C1 • **Temperaments:** D, F, J, T, V • **Physical:** V=G, H=L,

L=S • **Work Env:** B • **Salary:** 5 • **Outlook:** 1

DISPLAY DESIGNER (profess. & kin.) • D.O.T. #142.051-010 • OES #34038 • DISPLAY AND BANNER DESIGNER; FLAG DECORATOR AND DESIGNER. Designs displays, using paper, cloth, plastic, and other material to decorate streets, fair grounds, buildings, and other places for celebrations, fairs, and special occasions: Confers with client regarding budget, theme, materials, colors, emblem styles, and related factors. Plans display and sketches rough design for client's approval. Selects stock decorations or directs construction according to design concepts. May construct decorations. May direct and supervise workers who put up decorations. May design, draw, paint, or sketch backgrounds and fixtures made of wood, cardboard, paper, plaster, canvas, or other material for use in windows or interior displays and be designated DISPLAY ARTIST (profess. & kin.). May specialize in designing outdoor displays and be designated DISPLAY DESIGNER, OUTSIDE (profess. & kin.). • **GED:** R5, M3, L4 • **SVP:** 2-4 yrs • **Academic:** Ed=A, Eng=G • **Work Field:** 262, 264 • **MPSMS:** 752, 889 • **Aptitudes:** G2, V3, N3, S2, P2, Q4, K3, F2, M3, E4, C2 • **Temperaments:** F, J • **Physical:** V=L, H=N, L=L, W, H • **Work Env:** B • **Salary:** 4 • **Outlook:** 3

DISPLAYER, MERCHANDISE (ret. tr.) • D.O.T. #298.081-010 • OES #34044 • DECORATOR, STORE; DISPLAY TRIMMER. Displays merchandise, such as clothes, accessories, and furniture, in windows, showcases, and on sales floor of retail store to attract attention of prospective customers: Originates display ideas or follows suggestions or schedule of MANAGER, DISPLAY (ret. tr.) and constructs or assembles prefabricated display properties from wood, fabric, glass, paper, and plastic, using handtools. Arranges properties, mannequins, furniture, merchandise, and backdrop according to prearranged plan or own ideas. Places price and descriptive signs on backdrop, fixtures, merchandise, or floor. May dress mannequins for use in displays and be designated MODEL DRESSER (ret. tr.). May be designated according to area trimmed or decorated as SHOWCASE TRIMMER (ret. tr.); WINDOW DRESSER (ret. tr.). • **GED:** R4, M3, L3 • **SVP:** 1-2 yrs • **Academic:** Ed=H, Eng=S • **Work Field:** 264 • **MPSMS:** 889 • **Aptitudes:** G2, V3, N3, S2, P2, Q4, K4, F4, M3, E4, C2 • **Temperaments:** F, I, J • **Physical:** V=G, H=N, L=M, W, S, H • **Work Env:** I • **Salary:** 4 • **Outlook:** 3

EXHIBIT DESIGNER (museum) • D.O.T. #142.061-058 • OES #34038 • Plans, designs, and oversees construction and installation of permanent and temporary exhibits and displays: Confers with administrative, curatorial, and exhibit staff members to determine theme, content, interpretive or informational purpose, and planned location of exhibit, to discuss budget, promotion, and time limitations, and to plan production schedule for fabrication and installation of exhibit components. Prepares preliminary drawings of proposed exhibit, including detailed construction, layout, and special effect diagrams and material specifications, for final drawing rendition by other personnel, basing design and specifications on knowledge of artistic and technical concepts, principles, and techniques. Submits plan for approval, and adapts plan as needed to serve intended purpose or to conform to budget or fabrication restrictions. Oversees preparation of artwork and construction of exhibit components to ensure intended interpretation of concepts and conformance to structural and material specifications. Arranges for acquisition of specimens or graphics or building of exhibit structures by outside contractors as needed to complete exhibit. Inspects installed exhibit for conformance to specifications and satisfactory operation of special effects components. Oversees placement of collection objects or informational materials in exhibit framework. • **GED:** R5, M4, L5 • **SVP:** 2-4 yrs • **Academic:** Ed=A, Eng=S • **Work Field:** 264, 295 • **MPSMS:** 889, 931, 933 • **Aptitudes:** G2, V2, N3, S2, P2, Q3, K3, F3, M4, E5, C2 • **Temperaments:** D, F, J, P • **Stress:** A • **Physical:** V=G, H=N, L=S, H • **Work Env:** I • **Salary:** 4 • **Outlook:** 2

FASHION ARTIST (ret. tr.) • D.O.T. #141.061-014 • OES #34035 • Draws or paints apparel and accessory illustrations for newspaper or related advertisements: Positions garment, accessory, or model to accentuate desired sales features. Renders drawing of garment or accessory, complementary articles, and background, using various art media and materials. May use models, props, and settings to accentuate subject materials. May draw lettering. •

GED: R5, M2, L4 • **SVP:** 2-4 yrs • **Academic:** Ed=A, Eng=S • **Work Field:** 262 • **MPSMS:** 752 • **Aptitudes:** G2, V2, N3, S2, P1, Q3, K2, F1, M2, E5, C2 • **Temperaments:** F, J • **Physical:** V=G, H=N, L=S, H • **Work Env:** I • **Salary:** 4 • **Outlook:** 1

FLORAL DESIGNER (ret. tr.) • D.O.T. #142.081-010 • OES #34038 • FLORIST. Designs and fashions live, cut, dried, and artificial floral and foliar arrangements for events, such as holidays, anniversaries, weddings, balls, and funerals: Confers with client regarding price and type of ar rangement desired. Plans arrangement according to client's requirements and costs, utilizing knowledge of design and properties of materials, or selects appropriate standard design pattern. Selects flora and foliage necessary for arrangement. Trims material and arranges bouquets, sprays, wreaths, dish gardens, terrariums, and other items, using wire, pins, floral tape, foam, trimmers, cutters, shapers, and other materials and tools. May decorate buildings, halls, churches, or other facilities where events are planned. May pack and wrap completed arrangements. May estimate costs and price arrangements. May conduct classes or demonstrations. May instruct and direct other workers. May arrange according to standard designs or under instruction of designer and be designated FLORAL ARRANGER (ret. tr.). • **GED:** R4, M3, L3 • **SVP:** 1-2 yrs • **Academic:** Ed=H, Eng=S • **Work Field:** 264 • **MPSMS:** 310, 889 • **Aptitudes:** G3, V3, N3, S3, P2, Q3, K3, F2, M2, E5, C2 • **Temperaments:** F, J • **Physical:** V=L, H=N, L=L, H • **Work Env:** I, C, W • **Salary:** 3 • **Outlook:** 2

FURNITURE DESIGNER (furn.) • D.O.T. #142.061-022 • OES #34038 • Designs furniture for manufacture, according to knowledge of design trends, offerings of competition, production costs, capability of production facilities, and characteristics of company's market: Confers with production, design, and sales personnel to obtain design suggestions and customer orders. Evaluates orders and proposals to determine feasibility of producing item. Sketches freehand design of article. Obtains approval from customer, design committee, or authorized company officials, and originates scale or full size drawing, using drawing instruments. Prepares itemized production requirements to produce item. Traces drawing on material for use in production of blueprints, using drawing instruments. Prepares or directs preparation of blueprints containing manufacturing specifications, such as dimensions, kind of wood, and upholstery fabrics to be used in manufacturing article. Attends staff conference with plant personnel to explain and resolve production requirements. May design and prepare detailed drawings of jigs, fixtures, forms, or tools required to be used in production. May plan modifications for completed furniture to conform to changes in design trends and increase customer acceptance. May design custom pieces or styles according to specific period or country. May build or oversee construction of models or prototypes. May design fixtures and equipment, such as counters and display cases, and be designated FIXTURE DESIGNER (furn.). • **GED:** R5, M4, L4 • **SVP:** 2-4 yrs • **Academic:** Ed=A, Eng=G • **Work Field:** 264 • **MPSMS:** 460 • **Aptitudes:** G2, V3, N2, S2, P2, Q3, K3, F2, M3, E5, C2 • **Temperaments:** F, J, M, T • **Physical:** V=L, H=N, L=S, H • **Work Env:** I • **Salary:** 4 • **Outlook:** 2

GRAPHIC DESIGNER (profess. & kin.) • D.O.T. #141.061-018 • OES #34035 • LAYOUT ARTIST. Designs art and copy layouts for material to be presented by visual communications media, such as books, magazines, newspapers, television, and packaging: Studies illustrations and photographs to plan presentation of material, product, or service. Determines size and arrangement of illustrative material and copy, selects style and size of type, and arranges layout based upon available space, knowledge of layout principles, and esthetic design concepts. Draws sample of finished layout and presents to ART DIRECTOR (profess. & kin.) for approval. Prepares notes and instructions for workers who assemble and prepare final layouts for printing. Reviews final layout and suggests improvements as needed. May prepare illustrations or rough sketches of material according to instructions of client or supervisor. May prepare series of drawings to illustrate sequence and timing of story development for television production. May mark up, pasteup, and assemble final layouts to prepare layouts for printer. May specialize in particular field, medium, or type of layout. • **GED:** R5, M3, L4 • **SVP:** 2-4 yrs • **Academic:** Ed=A, Eng=G • **Work Field:** 264 • **MPSMS:** 752, 860, 896 • **Aptitudes:**

G2, V2, N3, S2, P2, Q3, K3, F3, M3, E5, C2 • **Temperaments:** F, J • **Physical:** V=G, H=N, L=S, H • **Work Env:** I • **Salary:** 4 • **Outlook:** 2

ILLUSTRATOR (profess. & kin.) • D.O.T. #141.061-022 • OES #34035 • ARTIST; COMMERCIAL ARTIST; GRAPHIC ARTIST. Draws or paints illustrations for use by various media to explain or adorn printed or spoken word: Studies layouts, sketches of proposed illustrations, and related materials to become familiar with assignment. Determines style, technique, and medium best suited to produce desired effects and conform with reproduction requirements, or receives specific instructions regarding these variables. Formulates concept and renders illustration and detail from models, sketches, memory, and imagination. Discusses illustration at various stages of completion and makes changes as necessary. May select type, draw lettering, layout material, or perform related duties. May be identified according to specific style, technique, medium, subject material or combination of variables. May draw or paint graphic material and lettering to be used for title, background, screen advertising, commercial logo, and other visual layouts for motion picture production and television programing, and be designated TITLE ARTIST (motion pic.; radio & tv broad.). • **GED:** R5, M2, L4 • **SVP:** 2-4 yrs • **Academic:** Ed=A, Eng=S • **Work Field:** 262 • **MPSMS:** 752 • **Aptitudes:** G2, V2, N3, S1, P1, Q3, K2, F1, M2, E5, C1 • **Temperaments:** F, J • **Physical:** V=G, H=L, L=S, H • **Work Env:** I • **Salary:** 4 • **Outlook:** 3

INDUSTRIAL DESIGNER (profess. & kin.) • D.O.T. #142.061-026 • OES #34038 • Originates and develops ideas to design the form of manufactured products: Reads publications, attends showings, and consults with engineering, marketing, production, and sales representatives to establish design concepts. Evaluates design ideas based on factors such as appealing appearance, design-function relationships, serviceability, materials and methods engineering, application, budget, price, production costs, methods of production, market characteristics, and client specifications. Integrates findings and concepts and sketches design ideas. Presents design to client or design committee and discusses need for modification and change. May design product packaging and graphics for advertising. May build simulated model, using hand and power tools and various materials. May prepare illustrations. May prepare or coordinate preparation of working drawings from sketches and design specifications. May design products for custom applications. May be required to have specialized product knowledge. Usually specializes in specific product or type of product including, but not limited to hard ware, motor vehicle exteriors and interiors, scientific instruments, industrial equipment, luggage, jewelry, housewares, toys, or novelties and is designated accordingly. • **GED:** R5, M4, L4 • **SVP:** 2-4 yrs • **Academic:** Ed=B, Eng=G • **Work Field:** 264 • **MPSMS:** 700, 759, 889 • **Aptitudes:** G2, V2, N3, S2, P2, Q3, K3, F2, M3, E5, C2 • **Temperaments:** F, J, P • **Physical:** V=G, H=N, L=S, H • **Work Env:** I • **Salary:** 4 • **Outlook:** 2

INTERIOR DESIGNER (profess. & kin.) • D.O.T. #142.051-014 • OES #34041 • Plans, designs, and furnishes interior environments of residential, commercial, and industrial buildings: Confers with client to determine architectural preferences, purpose and function of environment, budget, types of construction, equipment to be installed, and other factors which affect planning interior environments. Integrates findings with knowledge of interior design and formulates environmental plan to be practical, esthetic, and conducive to intended purposes, such as raising productivity, selling merchandise, or improving life style of occupants. Advises client on interior design factors, such as space planning, layout and utilization of furnishings and equipment, color schemes, and color coordination. Renders design ideas in form of paste ups, drawings, or illustrations, estimates material requirements and costs, and presents design to client for approval. Selects or designs and purchases furnishings, art works, and accessories. Subcontracts fabrication, installation, and arrangement of carpeting, fixtures, accessories, draperies, paint and wall coverings, art work, furniture, and related items. May plan and design interior environments for boats, planes, buses, trains, and other enclosed spaces. May specialize in particular field, style, or phase of interior design. May specialize in decorative aspects of interior design and be designated INTERIOR DECORATOR (profess. & kin.). • **GED:** R5, M3, L4 • **SVP:** 2-4 yrs • **Academic:** Ed=A, Eng=G • **Work Field:** 264 • **MPSMS:** 889 • **Aptitudes:** G2, V2, N3, S2, P2, Q3, K3, F2, M3, E5, C2 • **Temperaments:** D, F, I, J, P • **Stress:** E • **Physical:** V=G, H=L, L=L, H • **Work Env:** I • **Salary:** 4 • **Outlook:** 1

MANAGER, DISPLAY (ret. tr.) • D.O.T. #142.031-014 • OES #34038 • Develops advertising displays for window or interior use and supervises and coordinates activities of workers engaged in laying out and assembling displays: Consults with advertising and sales officials to ascertain type of merchandise to be featured and time and place for each display. Develops layout and selects theme, colors, and props to be used. Oversees requisitioning and construction of decorative props from such materials as wood, plastics, paper, and glass. Plans lighting arrangement and selects coloring medium. May design store fixtures. May prepare sketches or floor plans of proposed displays. May develop merchandise displays at special exhibits, such as trade shows. • **GED:** R5, M3, L4 • **SVP:** 2-4 yrs • **Academic:** Ed=A, Eng=S • **Work Field:** 264, 292 • **MPSMS:** 889 • **Aptitudes:** G2, V2, N3, S2, P2, Q4, K3, F4, M4, E5, C2 • **Temperaments:** D, F, J, P, V • **Physical:** V=G, H=N, L=L, H • **Work Env:** I • **Salary:** 4 • **Outlook:** 3

OPTICAL-EFFECTS-CAMERA OPERATOR (motion pic.) • D.O.T. #143.260-010 • OES #34026 • Sets up and operates optical printers and related equipment to produce fades, dissolves, superimpositions, and other optical effects required in motion pictures, applying knowledge of optical effects printing and photography: Reads work order and count sheet to ascertain optical effects specifications and location of subject material on original photography film. Analyzes specifications to determine work procedures, sequence of operations, and machine setup, using knowledge of optical effects techniques and procedures. Loads camera of optical effects printer with magazine of unexposed film stock. Mounts original photography film in transport and masking mechanism of optical-printer projector and moves film into designated position for optical effect, using counter and film markings to determine placement. Adjusts camera position, lens position, mask opening, lens aperture, focus, shutter angle, film transport speed, and related controls, using precision measuring instruments and knowledge of optical effects techniques to determine settings. Selects designated color and neutral density filters and mounts in filter holder to control light and intensity. Sets controls in automatic or manual mode, moves control to start camera, and observes printer operation and footage counter during filming. Adjusts controls during filming operation when operating in manual mode, and stops camera when designated counter reading is observed. Moves controls to rewind camera film and original photography film and repeats select portions or entire operation number of times necessary to produce designated effect. Sets up and operates animation and matte cameras and related equipment to photograph artwork, such as titles and painted mattes. Sets up and operates single pass optical printers when enlarging or reducing film or performing related operations. Sets up and operates subtitle camera and related equipment to photograph film subtitles. Examines frames of film exposed with different combinations of color filters (wedges) to select optimum color balance based on experience and judgment. • **GED:** R4, M3, L3 • **SVP:** 2-4 yrs • **Academic:** Ed=H, Eng=G • **Work Field:** 201 • **MPSMS:** 753, 911 • **Aptitudes:** G2, V3, N3, S3, P3, Q3, K3, F3, M3, E4, C2 • **Temperaments:** J, T • **Physical:** V=G, H=N, L=L, W, H • **Work Env:** I • **Salary:** 4 • **Outlook:** 3

PACKAGE DESIGNER (profess. & kin.) • D.O.T. #142.081-018 • OES #34038 • Designs containers for products, such as foods, beverages, toiletries, cigarettes, and medicines: Confers with representatives of engineering, marketing, management, and other departments to determine packaging requirements and type of product market. Sketches design of container for specific product, considering factors, such as convenience in handling and storing, distinctiveness for identification by consumer, and simplicity to minimize production costs. Renders design, including exterior markings and labels, using paints and brushes. Typically fabricates model in paper, wood, glass, plastic, or metal, depending on material to be used in package. Makes changes or modifications required by approving authority. • **GED:** R5, M3, L4 • **SVP:** 2-4

yrs • **Academic:** Ed=A, Eng=G • **Work Field:** 264 • **MPSMS:** 752, 889 • **Aptitudes:** G2, V2, N3, S2, P2, Q3, K3, F2, M3, E5, C2 • **Temperaments:** F, J • **Physical:** V=L, H=N, L=S, H • **Work Env:** I • **Salary:** 4 • **Outlook:** 2

PHOTOGRAPHER, MOTION PICTURE (profess. & kin.) • D.O.T. #143.062-022 • OES #34026 • Photographs various subjects and subject material using motion picture cameras and equipment and utilizing knowledge of motion picture techniques, limitations, and advantages to photograph scenes: Resolves problems presented by motion picture exposure control, subject and camera movement, changes in subject distance during filming, and related variables. May set up and operate dollies, cranes, camera mounting heads, power zooms, and related motion picture equipment and accessories. May maintain or repair equipment and accessories. May specialize in particular subject mate rial or field, such as medical, scientific, news, or commercial, and be designated accordingly. May photograph action on motion picture sets and locations and be designated CAMERA OPERATOR, SECOND (motion pic.; radio & tv broad.) or photograph special effects and be designated CAMERA OPERATOR, SPECIAL EFFECTS (motion pic.; radio & tv broad.). May specialize in operation of television cameras and be designated CAMERA OPERATOR, TELEVISION (radio & tv broad.). • **GED:** R4, M3, L4 • **SVP:** 2-4 yrs • **Academic:** Ed=H, Eng=S • **Work Field:** 201 • **MPSMS:** 753, 911 • **Aptitudes:** G2, V3, N3, S2, P2, Q4, K3, F3, M3, E5, C2 • **Temperaments:** F, J, P, T • **Physical:** V=G, H=L, L=L, W, H • **Work Env:** B • **Salary:** 4 • **Outlook:** 2

PHOTOGRAPHER, STILL (profess. & kin.) • D.O.T. #143.062-030 • OES #34023 • COMMERCIAL PHOTOGRAPHER. Photographs subjects using still cameras, color or black-and-white film, and a variety of photographic accessories: Selects and assembles equipment according to subject material, anticipated conditions, and knowledge of function and limitations of various types of cameras, lenses, films, and accessories. Views subject and setting and plans composition, camera position, and camera angle to produce desired effect. Arranges subject material, poses subject, or maneuvers into position to take candid photo. Estimates or measures light level, using light meter or creates artificial lighting with flash units, lights, and lighting equipment. Adjusts lens aperture and shutter speed based on combination of factors, such as lighting, depth of field, subject motion, and film speed. Determines subject to lens distance, using tape measure, range finder, ground glass, or reflex viewing system to adjust focus. Positions camera and trips shutter to expose film. May calculate variables, such as exposure time, exposure interval, filter effect, and color temperature using tables, standard formulas, and mechanical or electronic measuring instruments. May make adjustments to camera, lens, or equipment to compensate for factors, such as distorted perspective and parallax. May be required to have detailed knowledge of use and characteristics of various types of film, including specialty films, such as infrared. May design, build, arrange, or secure properties and settings to be used as background for subject material. May direct activities of other workers. May mix chemicals, process film and photographic paper, and make contact and enlarged prints. May spot and retouch prints and negatives. May conceive and plan photographic sequence for effective presentation. May specialize in particular type of photography, such as illustrative, fashion, architectural, or portrait and be designated accordingly. • **GED:** R4, M3, L4 • **SVP:** 2-4 yrs • **Academic:** Ed=H, Eng=S • **Work Field:** 201 • **MPSMS:** 896 • **Aptitudes:** G2, V3, N3, S2, P2, Q4, K3, F3, M3, E5, C2 • **Temperaments:** F, J, P, T • **Stress:** E • **Physical:** V=G, H=N, L=S, H • **Work Env:** B • **Salary:** 4 • **Outlook:** 1

PHOTOJOURNALIST (print. & pub.) • D.O.T. #143.062-034 • OES #34023 • PHOTOGRAPHER, NEWS. Photographs newsworthy events, locations, people, or other illustrative or educational material for use in publications or telecasts, using still cameras: Travels to assigned location and takes pictures. Develops negatives and prints film. Submits negatives and pictures to editorial personnel. Usually specializes in one phase of photography, as news, sports, special features, or as freelance photographer. • **GED:** R4, M2, L4 • **SVP:** 2-4 yrs • **Academic:** Ed=H, Eng=G • **Work Field:** 201, 202 • **MPSMS:** 480, 753 • **Aptitudes:** G3, V3, N3, S2, P2, Q3, K3, F3, M3, E5, C5 • **Temperaments:** F, J, P, T • **Stress:** E

• **Physical:** V=G, H=L, L=L, W, H • **Work Env:** B • **Salary:** 4 • **Outlook:** 2

POLICE ARTIST (gov. ser.) • D.O.T. #141.061-034 • OES #34035 • FORENSIC ARTIST. Sketches likenesses of criminal suspects, according to descriptions of victims and witnesses, and prepares schematic drawings depicting scenes of crimes: Interviews crime victims and witnesses to obtain descriptive information concerning physical build, sex, nationality, facial features, and related characteristics of unidentified suspect. Prepares series of simple line drawings conforming to description of suspect and presents drawings to informant for selection of sketch that most resembles suspect. Questions in formant to obtain additional descriptive information and draws and verifies details of features to improve resemblance of conception to recollection of informant. Measures distances and sketches layout of crime scene, or develops sketches from photographs and measurements taken at scene of crime by other police personnel to prepare schematic drawing of scene of crime. • **GED:** R5, M3, L4 • **SVP:** 2-4 yrs • **Academic:** Ed=A, Eng=G • **Work Field:** 262 • **MPSMS:** 759, 951 • **Aptitudes:** G2, V2, N3, S2, P2, Q3, K2, F2, M2, E5, C3 • **Temperaments:** J, P, T • **Stress:** E • **Physical:** V=G, H=L, L=S, H • **Work Env:** I • **Salary:** 4 • **Outlook:** 3

SET DECORATOR (motion pic.) • D.O.T. #142.061-042 • OES #34038 • Selects decorations and coordinates activities of workers who decorate sets for motion picture or television production: Reads script to determine decoration requirements. Selects furniture, draperies, pictures, lamps, and rugs for decorative quality and appearance on film. Gives directions to GRIP (motion pic.; radio & tv broad.) in placing items on set. Examines dressed sets to insure that props and scenery do not interfere with movements of cast or view of camera. • **GED:** R5, M2, L4 • **SVP:** 4-10 yrs • **Academic:** Ed=A, Eng=G • **Work Field:** 264 • **MPSMS:** 759 • **Aptitudes:** G2, V2, N3, S2, P2, Q4, K4, F4, M4, E5, C1 • **Temperaments:** D, F, J, P • **Physical:** V=L, H=N, L=S, W • **Work Env:** I • **Salary:** 4 • **Outlook:** 1

SET DESIGNER (amuse. & rec.) • D.O.T. #142.061-050 • OES #34038 • SCENIC DESIGNER; THEATRICAL-SCENIC DESIGNER. Designs sets for theatrical productions: Confers with play's director regarding interpretation and set requirements. Conducts research to determine appropriate architectural and furnishing styles. Integrates requirements, interpretation, research, design concepts, and practical considerations regarding factors, such as mobility, interchangeability, and budget to plan sets. Renders drawing or illustration of design concept, estimates costs, and presents drawing for approval. Prepares working drawings of floor plan, front elevation, scenery, and properties to be constructed. Prepares charts to indicate where items, such as curtains and borders are to be hung. Oversees building of sets, furniture, and properties. May build scale models from cardboard, plaster, or sponge. May design stage lighting to achieve dramatic or decorative effects. • **GED:** R5, M3, L4 • **SVP:** 4-10 yrs • **Academic:** Ed=A, Eng=G • **Work Field:** 264 • **MPSMS:** 701, 912 • **Aptitudes:** G2, V2, N3, S1, P2, Q4, K2, F2, M3, E5, C2 • **Temperaments:** D, F, J, P, T • **Physical:** V=L, H=N, L=L, H • **Work Env:** I • **Salary:** 5 • **Outlook:** 1

SET DESIGNER (motion pic.) • D.O.T. #142.061-046 • OES #34038 • Designs motion picture sets and scenic effects and prepares scale drawings for use in construction, modification, or alternation: Confers with ART DIRECTOR (motion pic.; radio & TV broad.) and reviews illustrations to determine set requirements and discuss preliminary design ideas. Integrates requirements and concepts to conceive set design. Performs duties of DRAFTER (profess. & kin.) to prepare rough and scale working drawings of set. Presents drawings for approval and makes changes and corrections as directed. May design miniature motion picture sets used in filming backgrounds, titles, and special effects and be designated MINIATURE SET DESIGNER (motion pic.; radio & tv broad.). • **GED:** R5, M3, L4 • **SVP:** 4-10 yrs • **Academic:** Ed=A, Eng=G • **Work Field:** 242, 264 • **MPSMS:** 911 • **Aptitudes:** G2, V2, N3, S2, P2, Q4, K2, F2, M3, E5, C2 • **Temperaments:** F, M, T • **Physical:** V=L, H=N, L=S, H • **Work Env:** I • **Salary:** 5 • **Outlook:** 1

TELEVISION TECHNICIAN (radio & tv broad.) • D.O.T. #194.062-010 • OES #34028 • Performs combination of duties to record and transmit broadcasts, working as member of limited-staff television station: Operates studio and mini-television (portable, shoulder-mounted) cameras [CAMERA OPERATOR, TELEVISION (radio & tv broad.) 143.062-022]. Controls console to regulate transmission of television scenes [VIDEO OPERATOR (radio & tv broad.) 194.282-010]. Produces educational and training films and video tapes [COMMUNICATIONS TECHNICIAN (education) 962.362-010]. Sets up and controls lights [LIGHT TECHNICIAN (motion pic.; radio & tv broad.) 962.362-014], microphones and microphone booms [MICROPHONE-BOOM OPERATOR (motion pic.; radio & tv broad.) 962.384-010], and recording equipment [RECORDIST (motion pic.) 962.382-010]. May perform duties of other related occupations depending upon specific production needs of individual airwave or closed-circuit station where workers must be able to set up and operate most or all equipment due to limited size of staff. • **GED:** R5, M4, L5 • **SVP:** 2-4 yrs • **Academic:** Ed=A, Eng=G • **Work Field:** 201, 281 • **MPSMS:** 864 • **Aptitudes:** G2, V2, N3, S2, P2, Q3, K3, F3, M3, E4, C3 • **Temperaments:** F, J, P, T, V • **Stress:** E • **Physical:** V=G, II=G, L=M, W, S, II • **Work Env:** I • **Salary:** 4 • **Out look:** 2

01.03 Performing Arts: Drama

Workers in this group produce, direct, and perform in dramatic productions and similar forms of entertainment. They also tech acting, choose performers for particular roles, and perform other 'behind-the-scenes' work to make productions run smoothly. They are employed by motion picture, television, and radio studios, and by stock companies, theaters and other places where plays or floor shows are presented. Schools and colleges hire performing artists both to teach drama and to produce and direct student productions. Full time employment in this field is found at educational institutions, at studios which have staff announcers, disc jockeys, and regularly scheduled 'talk shows' or dramatic presentations. However, most performing artists are not permanently employed, and must audition for roles in both short-term and long-run productions.

✔ **What kind of work would you do?**
Your work activities would depend upon your specific job. For example, you might:

- do a pantomime, using only body movements and facial expressions.
- instruct students in the basic techniques of acting.
- direct actors and other workers involved in a play or motion picture.

- select, announce, and play popular records at a radio station.
- perform a comic monologue on a television variety show or in a night club.

✔ **What skills and abilities do you need for this kind of work?**
To do this kind of work, you must be able to:

- perform before an audience with poise and self-confidence.
- interpret roles, and express ideas and emotions through body motions, facial expressions, and voice inflections.
- understand the ideas that the author of a script is trying to get across, and demonstrate to others methods of moving or speaking to convey these ideas to an audience.

- speak clearly and loudly.
- memorize dialogue and respond to cues promptly.
- maintain physical and mental energy through long hours of rehearsal and performance.

✔ **How do you know if you would like or could learn to do this kind of work?**
The following questions may give you clues about yourself as you consider this group of jobs.

- Have you performed in a play? Do you enjoy performing before an audience?
- Have you spoken on radio or television? Are you able to control your voice and is it pleasing when electronically amplified?

- Have you memorized a long passage? Can you recite from memory before an audience?

✔ **How can you prepare for and enter this kind of work?**

Occupations in this group usually require education and/or training extending from one year to over ten years, depending upon the specific kind of work. Because of the strong competition for jobs, workers in this group must have both training and experience. Initial training and experience are available in speech classes, debate programs, and school or community plays. Four-year degrees and advanced study in drama or communications provide additional training. Courses in speech, pantomime, directing, and acting are a part of these programs. Colleges also provide opportunities for experience in acting, announcing, and directing. Special acting schools offer professional training in the dramatic arts.

Experience in numerous productions is very important, including both amateur and paid jobs. Dinner theaters, summer theaters, repertory groups, and local radio and television stations provide valuable experiences.

Jobs in directing require extensive acting experience or experience in directing amateur productions. Dramatic coaching and college level teaching usually require advanced degrees in dramatics. Professional experience in acting, directing, or play production is also helpful. Teachers of high school courses in drama, speech, or communications must meet specific educational and licensing requirements.

✔ **What else should you consider about these jobs?**

Dramatic artists are often required to meet demanding work schedules. These schedules may require early or late hours for rehearsals and performances. Memorizing sessions require individual study. In addition, frequent travel may be necessary.

Work assignments sometimes depend upon an individual's voice or physical appearance. Distinctive features are assets which are in much demand.

If you think you would like to do this kind of work, look at the job titles listed below.

GOE: 01.03.01 Instructing & Directing, Drama

DIRECTOR, MOTION PICTURE (motion pic.) • D.O.T. #159.067-010 • OES #34056 • Reads and interprets script, conducts rehearsals, and directs activities of cast and technical crew for motion picture film: Confers with ART DIRECTOR (motion pic.; radio & tv broad.) to insure that music, sets, scenic effects, and costumes conform to script interpretation. Confers with DIRECTOR OF PHOTOGRAPHY (motion pic.) to explain details of scene to be photographed and to consider utilization of miniatures, stock film, inserts, transparencies, backgrounds, or trick shots. Schedules sequences of scenes to be filmed for each day of shooting, grouping scenes together according to set and cast of characters. Rehearses cast and suggests changes, using knowledge of acting, voice, and movement to elicit best possible performance. Informs technicians of scenery, lights, props, and other equipment desired. Approves scenery, costumes, choreography, and music. Directs cast, DIRECTOR OF PHOTOGRAPHY (motion pic.; radio & tv broad.), and other technicians during rehearsals and final filming. May audition and select cast. May cut and edit film. May direct film on set in studio or on location. May direct film for television. • GED: R5, M4, L5 • SVP: 4-10 yrs • Academic: Ed=A, Eng=G • Work Field: 295 • MPSMS: 911 • Aptitudes: G1, V2, N3, S3, P3, Q3, K4, F4, M4, E5, C5 • Temperaments: D, J, P, V • Stress: E, A • Physical: V=L, H=L, L=S • Work Env: B • Salary: 5 • Outlook: 1

PRODUCER (amuse. & rec.) • D.O.T. #187.167-178 • OES #34056 • Selects play for stage performance, arranges finances, and coordinates play production activities: Reads manuscripts and selects play on basis of plot, timeliness, and quality of writing. Sells shares to investors to finance production. Hires DIRECTOR, STAGE (amuse. & rec.); MANAGER, STAGE (amuse. & rec.), cast, and crew. Formulates business management policies and coordinates production schedules. Suggests or approves changes in script and staging. Arbitrates personnel disputes. May direct production of play [DIRECTOR, STAGE (amuse. & rec.)]. May produce shows for special occasions, such as fund-raising events or testimonial banquets. • GED: R5, M4, L5 • SVP: 2-4 yrs • Academic: Ed=B, Eng=S • Work Field: 295, 297 • MPSMS: 754 • Aptitudes: G2, V2, N3, S4, P2, Q4, K4, F4, M4, E5, C4 • Temperaments: D, J, P, V • Stress: A • Physical: V=L, H=L, L=L • Work Env: I • Salary: 5 • Outlook: 1

PRODUCER (radio & tv broad.) • D.O.T. #159.117-010 • OES #34056 • Plans and coordinates various aspects of radio and television programs: Interviews and selects SCREEN WRITERS (motion pic.; radio & tv broad.) and cast principals from staff members or outside talent. Obtains costumes, props, music, and other equipment or personnel to complete production. Outlines program to be produced to SCREEN WRITERS (motion pic.; radio & tv broad.) and evaluates finished script. Suggests changes in script to meet management or other require ments. Coordinates audio work, scenes, music, timing, camera work, and script. Gives instructions to staff to schedule and conduct rehearsals and develop and coordinate details to obtain desired production. Reviews production to insure objectives are attained. May represent television network acting as liaison to independent producer of television series produced for network broadcast. May review budget and expenditures for programs for conformance to budgetary restrictions. May be designated according to media as RADIO PRODUCER (radio & tv broad.) or TELEVISION PRODUCER (radio & tv broad.). • GED: R6, M4, L6 • SVP: 4-10 yrs • Academic: Ed=B, Eng=S • Work Field: 295 • MPSMS: 863 • Aptitudes: G1, V1, N3, S4, P3, Q4, K4, F4, M4, E5, C5 • Temperaments: D, J, P, V • Stress: A • Physical: V=G, H=G, L=L • Work Env: I • Salary: 5 • Outlook: 1

GOE: 01.03.02 Performing, Drama

CLOWN (amuse. & rec.) • D.O.T. #159.047-010 • OES #34056 • Dresses in comical costume and makeup and performs original or stock comedy routines to entertain audience. • GED: R4, M2, L3 • SVP: 1-2 yrs • Academic: Ed=N, Eng=N • Work Field: 297 • MPSMS: 919 • Aptitudes: G3, V3, N4, S3, P4, Q5, K2, F3, M2, E2, C4 • Temperaments: I, J, P, T • Stress: E • Physical: V=L, H=L, L=L, W, C, S, H • Work Env: B • Salary: 2 • Outlook: 1

COMEDIAN (amuse. & rec.) • D.O.T. #159.047-014 • OES #34056 • COMIC. Attempts to make audience laugh by telling jokes, delivering comic lines, singing humorous songs, performing comedy dances or walks, or facial contortions, wearing funny costumes, or resorting to any similar device to amuse audience. May do impersonations [IMPERSONATOR (amuse. & rec.)]. • GED: R5, M2, L4 • SVP: 6 mos-1 yr • Academic: Ed=N, Eng=G • Work Field: 297 • MPSMS: 919 • Aptitudes: G3, V2, N4, S3, P4, Q4, K3, F4, M4, E5, C5 • Temperaments: F, P, V • Stress: E • Physical: V=N, H=L, L=S • Work Env: I • Salary: 3 • Outlook: 1

INTERPRETER, DEAF (profess. & kin.) • D.O.T. #137.267-014 • OES #39999 • TRANSLATOR, DEAF. Provides translation between spoken and manual (sign language) communication: Translates spoken material into sign language for under standing of deaf. Interprets sign language of deaf into oral or written language for hearing individuals or others not conversant in sign language. May translate television news and other broad casts for deaf viewers. • GED: R4, M3, L4 • SVP: 6 mos-1 yr • Academic: Ed=H, Eng=G • Work Field: 282 • MPSMS: 869 • Aptitudes: G3, V2, N4, S4, P3, Q3, K2, F3, M3, E5, C5 • Temperaments: J, P • Stress: E • Physical: V=L, H=L, L=S • Work Env: I • Salary: 3 • Outlook: 4

MAGICIAN (amuse. & rec.) • D.O.T. #159.041-010 • OES #34056 • Performs original and stock tricks of illusion and sleight of hand to entertain and mystify audience, using props, such as illusion boxes, scarf, cards, rabbit, and jewelry. May include participant from audience in act to remove personal valuables, such as wallets or jewelry, without participant's knowledge. • GED: R4, M3, L4 • SVP: 1-2 yrs • Academic: Ed=N, Eng=G • Work Field: 297 • MPSMS: 919 • Aptitudes: G3, V3, N4, S3, P3, Q4, K2, F2, M2, E5, C4 • Temperaments: D, F, J, T • Physical: V=L, H=L, L=L, W, H • Work Env: I • Salary: 3 • Outlook: 1

MIME (amuse. & rec.) • D.O.T. #159.047-022 • OES #34056 • PANTOMIMIST. Presents serious, humorous, or burlesqued interpretations of emotions, dramatic actions, and various situations through body movements, facial expressions and gestures. • GED: R5, M2, L3 • SVP: 2-4 yrs • Academic: Ed=N, Eng=N • Work Field: 297 • MPSMS: 754 • Aptitudes: G2, V3, N4, S2, P2, Q5, K3, F4, M4, E2, C4 • Temperaments: D, F, J, P • Stress: E • Physical: V=N, H=N, L=L, W, H • Work Env: I • Salary: 2 • Outlook: 1

PUPPETEER (amuse. & rec.) • D.O.T. #159.041-014 • OES #34056 • Originates puppet shows, designs and constructs puppets and moves controls of puppets to animate them for entertainment of audience: Writes or adapts script for use in puppet theater.

Sketches designs for puppets based on script. Constructs hand, string, rod, and shadow puppets from materials, such as wood, papier-mache, styrofoam, and wires, using handtools and machine tools. Sews clothing for puppets by hand or machine. Animates puppets, using string, wire, rod, fingers or hands from position above, below, or at level with stage. Talks or sings during performance to give illusion of voice to puppets. • **GED:** R5, M3, L5 • **SVP:** 4-10 yrs • **Academic:** Ed=N, Eng=G • **Work Field:** 102, 297 • **MPSMS:** 919 • **Aptitudes:** G2, V2, N3, S1, P2, Q4, K1, F2, M2, E3, C1 • **Temperaments:** F, J, P • **Stress:** E • **Physical:** V=L, H=L, L=L, W, H • **Work Env:** I • **Salary:** 3 • **Outlook:** 1

GOE: 01.03.03 Narrating & Announcing

ANNOUNCER (radio & tv broad.) • D.O.T. #159.147-010 • OES #34017 • Announces radio and television programs to audience: Memorizes script, reads, or ad-libs to identify station, introduce and close shows, and announce station breaks, commercials, or public service information. Cues worker to transmit program from network central station or other pick-up points according to schedule. Reads news flashes to keep audience informed of important happenings. May rewrite news bulletin from wire service teletype to fit specific time slot. May describe public event such as parade or convention. May interview guest such as sport or other public personality and moderate panel or discussion show to entertain audience. May keep daily program log. In small stations may perform additional duties, such as operating control console or radio transmitter [TRANSMITTER OPERATOR (radio & tv broad.)], selling time, or writing advertising copy. May be designated according to media as RADIO ANNOUNCER (radio & tv broad.) or TELEVISION ANNOUNCER (radio & tv broad.). When announcing program of local interest may be designated LOCAL ANNOUNCER (radio & tv broad.). When announcing program for transmission over network and affiliated stations may be designated NETWORK ANNOUNCER (radio & tv broad.). May announce in foreign language for international broadcast and be designated ANNOUNCER, INTERNATIONAL BROADCAST (radio & tv broad.). May describe sporting event during game from direct observation or announce sports news received at station for radio or television broadcasting and be designated SPORTS ANNOUNCER (radio & tv broad.). • **GED:** R5, M3, L4 • **SVP:** 1-2 yrs • **Academic:** Ed=A, Eng=G • **Work Field:** 282, 297 • **MPSMS:** 863 • **Aptitudes:** G2, V2, N3, S4, P4, Q3, K4, F4, M4, E5, C5 • **Temperaments:** P, T, V • **Stress:** E • **Physical:** V=G, H=G, L=S

• **Work Env:** I • **Salary:** 3 • **Outlook:** 1

DISK JOCKEY (radio & tv broad.) • D.O.T. #159.147-014 • OES #34017 • Announces radio program of musical selections: Selects phonograph or tape recording to be played based on program specialty and knowledge of audience taste. Comments on music and other matters of interest to audience, such as weather, time, or traffic conditions. May interview music personalities. May specialize in one type of music, such as classical, pop, rock, or country and western. May be designated COMBINATION OPERATOR (radio & tv broad.) when operating transmitter or control console. • **GED:** R5, M3, L5 • **SVP:** 6 mos-1 yr • **Academic:** Ed=A, Eng=S • **Work Field:** 282, 297 • **MPSMS:** 863 • **Aptitudes:** G2, V2, N3, S4, P4, Q3, K4, F4, M4, E5, C5 • **Temperaments:** P, V • **Physical:** V=N, H=G, L=L • **Work Env:** I • **Salary:** 3 • **Outlook:** 1

NARRATOR (motion pic.) • D.O.T. #150.147-010 • OES #34056 1• MOTION-PICTURE COMMENTATOR. Makes explanatory comments to accompany action parts of motion picture: Reads from script and speaks into microphone as film is being projected, timing comments to fit action portrayed. May write script. • **GED:** R5, M2, L5 • **SVP:** 6 mos-1 yr • **Academic:** Ed=A, Eng=G • **Work Field:** 297 • **MPSMS:** 911 • **Aptitudes:** G2, V2, N3, S4, P4, Q4, K4, F4, M4, E5, C5 • **Temperaments:** F, J, P, V • **Stress:** E • **Physical:** V=N, H=L, L=S • **Work Env:** I • **Salary:** 4 • **Outlook:** 3

PROGRAM COORDINATOR (amuse. & rec.) • D.O.T. #139.167-010 • OES #34056 • Coordinates activities of amusement park educational department to present educational scripts during animal performances: Reviews educational materials to gather information for scripts. Confers with animal trainer to verify format of performance, and writes script to coincide with performance, or reviews scripts prepared by department researchers for suggested changes in format. Prepares brochures containing information, such as time of performances, theme of performances, and map of park facilities. Reads reservation log to determine information, such as name of visiting groups, size of groups, and time of arrival. Greets visitors, passes out brochures, answers questions, and escorts visitors to site of performance. May introduce trainer to audience and present memorized script during performance over speaker system and be designated NARRATOR (amuse. & rec.). • **GED:** R4, M2, L4 • **SVP:** 4-10 yrs • **Academic:** Ed=H, Eng=G • **Work Field:** 261, 295 • **MPSMS:** 931 • **Aptitudes:** G2, V2, N3, S4, P4, Q2, K4, F4, M4, E5, C5 • **Temperaments:** D, I, J, P • **Stress:** E • **Physical:** V=N, H=N, L=S, H • **Work Env:** I • **Salary:** 4 • **Outlook:** 2

01.04 Performing Arts: Music

Workers in this group sing or play instruments, teach, or direct vocal or instrumental music. They compose, arrange, or orchestrate musical compositions, and plan the presentation of concerts. They work for motion picture studios, television and radio networks or local stations, recording studios, night clubs, and other places where musical entertainment is provided regularly. They may be employed by orchestras, bands, or choral groups which give scheduled performances or are hired for special events. Composers, arrangers, and orchestrators work for music publishing companies and firms in the recording and entertainment fields. Schools and colleges hire musicians to teach and direct vocal and instrumental music. Many musicians are self-employed, and like all performing artists, must audition for parts in musical productions or for employment with an orchestra or other performing group.

✔ **What kind of work would you do?**
Your work activities would depend upon your specific job. For example, you might:

- direct a choir, orchestra, or band.
- sing in a professional choir.
- play a musical instrument in a band.
- sing several solos in a concert.

- prepare the musical score for all instruments in an orchestra.
- compose an original music number.
- select and arrange a program of music.
- give private voice or instrument lessons.

✔ **What skills and abilities do you need for this kind of work?**
To do this kind of work, you must be able to:

- spend long hours developing and perfecting your talent, and, even after becoming extremely skilled, continue to practice daily.
- perform before an audience with poise and self-assurance.
- recognize and follow music symbols and oral or written instructions for interpreting music properly.

- understand the qualities of various musical instruments and consider these in orchestrating or arranging compositions to create desired effects.
- apply standard musical theories and techniques to direct performances of vocal or instrumental groups.
- use your hands and fingers skillfully to play an instrument.

✔ **How do you know if you would like or could learn to do this kind of work?**
The following questions may give you clues about yourself as you consider this group of jobs.

- Have you sung in school choruses or church choirs? Does your voice blend well with others? Do you enjoy singing in public?
- Have you had lessons in singing or playing a musical instrument? Have you played in a school band or orchestra? Can you read music?

- Have you composed a song or music for an instrument? Did others enjoy it?
- Have you sung or played with a rock or country group?

✔ **How can you prepare for an enter this kind of work?**
Occupations in this group usually require education and/or training extending from two years to over ten years, depending upon the specific kind of work. Professional instrumental musicians usually receive initial training while in elementary school. They continue studying throughout most of their working life. Several hours of practice each day is a continuing requirement for the development and maintenance of the needed skills.

Professional vocal musicians usually start formal training in high school or whenever their voices mature. School music groups and programs provide good initial training. Daily individual or group practice is a continuing requirement for vocal musicians.

Although some persons with fine natural singing voices or self-developed skill in playing an instrument may find work—or even achieve great success—in popular rock, country, or jazz music, they are the rare exceptions. Study in college, at a music conservatory, or with private teachers is recommended for people who want to become professional musicians. Courses in music theory, composition, and conducting are required in addition to technical instruction. Arrangers, composers, and conductors need extensive training in these subjects.

Membership in a musical group is considered valuable experience and preparation for musicians. This experience is also helpful for people studying for solo performances.

Employment as a professional musician is usually dependent upon the skill and experience of the individual. Teachers in public schools and colleges are required to meet specific educational and licensing requirements.

✔ **What else should you consider about these jobs?**
Vocal musicians sometimes have a shorter working life than instrumentalists. Voice quality may change with age or the personal singing style may become outdated. Singers who can also dance or act may have more job opportunities.

Some instrumentalists are required to have the ability to play several different instruments.

If you think you would like to do this kind of work, look at the job titles listed below.

GOE: 01.04.01 Instructing & Directing, Music

TEACHER, MUSIC (educ.) • D.O.T. #152.021-010 • OES #31317 • INSTRUCTOR, MUSIC; PROFESSOR, MUSIC. Teaches individuals or groups instrumental or vocal music in public or private school: Plans daily classroom work based on teaching outline prepared for course of study to meet curriculum requirements. Evaluates student's interests, aptitudes, temperament, and individual characteristics to determine suitable instrument for beginner. Instructs students in music theory, harmony, score and sight reading, composition, music appreciation, and provides individual or group vocal and instrumental lessons using technical knowledge, aesthetic appreciation, and appropriate teaching techniques. Conducts orchestra rehearsals and coaches members in their individual orchestra parts. Instructs and trains choral groups in fundamentals of musicianship and ensemble singing. Leads orchestra and choral groups in regular and special perform ances for school programs, community activities, concerts, and festivals. May be designated as TEACHER, INSTRUMENTAL (education); TEACHER, VOCAL (education). • GED: R5, M2, L5 • SVP: 4-10 yrs • Academic: Ed=A, Eng=G • Work Field: 296 • MPSMS: 756, 931 • Aptitudes: G2, V2, N3, S4, P3, Q3, K2, F2, M2, E5, C5 • Temperaments: D, F, J, P • Stress: E • Physical: V=L, H=L, L=S, H • Work Env: I • Salary: 3 • Outlook: 1

GOE: 01.04.02 Composing & Arranging

COPYIST (any ind.) • D.O.T. #152.267-010 • OES #34047 • Transcribes musical parts onto staff paper from score written by ARRANGER (profess. & kin.) or ORCHESTRATOR (profess. & kin.) for each instrument or voice, utilizing knowledge of music notation and experience and background in music. May transpose score to different key. • GED: R5, M3, L5 • SVP: 2-4 yrs • Academic: Ed=H, Eng=G • Work Field: 263 • MPSMS: 756 • Aptitudes: G2, V2, N3, S4, P3, Q3, K4, F3, M3, E5, C4 • Temperaments: M, T • Physical: V=L, H=N, L=S, H • Work Env: I • Salary: 3 • Outlook: 2

PROMPTER (amuse. & rec.) • D.O.T. #152.367-010 • OES #34047 • Prompts performers in operatic productions: Marks copy of vocal score to note cues. Observes CONDUCTOR, ORCHESTRA (profess. & kin.) and follows vocal score to time cues accurately. Speaks or sings in language required by opera prompt performers. • GED: R4, M3, L4 • SVP: 2-4 yrs • Academic: Ed=H, Eng=G • Work Field: 282 • MPSMS: 754, 756 • Aptitudes: G3, V2, N3, S5, P3, Q2, K4, F4, M4, E4, C5 • Temperaments: J, M, P, T • Stress: E • Physical: V=L, H=L, L=S, H • Work Env: I • Salary: 3 • Outlook: 1

GOE: 01.04.03 Vocal Performing

SINGER (amuse. & rec.) • D.O.T. #152.047-022 • OES #34047 • Sings as soloist or member of vocal ensemble: Interprets music using knowledge of harmony, melody, rhythm, and voice production to present characterization or to achieve individual style of vocal delivery. Sings following printed text and musical notation or memorizes score. May sing a cappella or with musical accompaniment. May watch CHORAL DIRECTOR (profess. & kin.) or CONDUCTOR, ORCHESTRA (profess. & kin.) for directions and cues. May be known according to voice range as soprano, contralto, tenor, baritone, or bass. May specialize in one type of music, such as opera, lieder, choral, gospel, folk, or country and western and be identified according to specialty. • GED: R4, M3, L4 • SVP: 4-10 yrs • Academic: Ed=H, Eng=S • Work Field: 297 • MPSMS: 756, 919 • Aptitudes: G2, V2, N3, S4, P4, Q3, K4, F4, M4, E5, C5 • Temperaments: F, J, P • Stress: E • Physical: V=N, H=L, L=S • Work Env: I • Salary: 4 • Outlook: 1

GOE: 01.04.04 Instrumental Performing

MUSICIAN, INSTRUMENTAL (amuse. & rec.) • D.O.T. #152.041-010 • OES #34051 • Plays musical instrument as soloist or as member of musical group, such as orchestra or band, to entertain audience: Studies and rehearses music to learn and interpret score. Plays from memory or by following score. May transpose music to play in alternate key. May improvise. May compose. May play instrument to signal activity, such as flag raising, post time, or arrival of dignitaries at sporting or other events. May be designated according to instrument played as CALLIOPE PLAYER (amuse. & rec.); DRUMMER (amuse. & rec.); HARPIST (amuse. & rec.); ORGANIST (amuse. & rec.); PIANIST (amuse. & rec.); VIOLINIST (amuse. & rec.). May accompany soloist or anoth er MUSICIAN, INSTRUMENTAL (amuse. & rec.) and be designated ACCOMPANIST (amuse. & rec.). • GED: R5, M3, L3 • SVP: 4-10 yrs • Academic: Ed=N, Eng=S • Work Field: 297 • MPSMS: 756 • Aptitudes: G2, V2, N3, S4, P3, Q2, K2, F2, M2, E3, C4 • Temperaments: F, J • Physical: V=N, H=G, L=S, H • Work Env: B, N • Salary: 1 • Outlook: 1

01.05 Performing Arts: Dance

Workers in this group compose, perform, or teach dance routines or techniques. Performing dancers and composers (choreographers) work for motion picture and television studios, nightclubs and theaters, and other places where this kind of entertainment is regularly presented. Dance teachers are employed by schools and studios. Although some dancers work full-time as performers or teachers, most must audition for both chorus and solo work in theatrical productions of all kinds. Many dancers are self-employed as teachers who give private lessons to children and adults, specializing in ballroom or ballet instruction.

✔ **What kind of work would you do?**
Your work activities would depend upon your specific job. For example, you might:

- perform a dance routine as a member of a chorus line.
- create dance routines for a musical show.
- perform a solo dance in a variety show.
- teach people to dance.
- direct a troupe of dancers.

✔ **What skills and abilities do you need for this kind of work?**
To do this kind of work, you must be able to:

- memorize and follow instructions for dance routines.
- move with grace and rhythm, coordinating your body movements to music, and with the movements of other dancers.
- keep in excellent physical condition by exercising and performing dance routines regularly.

- perform before an audience with poise and self-confidence.
- express emotions, such as joy, sorrow, or excitement, by the way you move your arms, legs, and body.
- understand all of the basic dance steps and the way they relate to various kinds of music, to devise routines for musical comedy dance sequences.

✔ **How do you know if you would like or could learn to do this kind of work?**
The following questions may give you clues about yourself as you consider this group of jobs.

- Have you participated in ballroom or social dancing? Do you like to learn new dances? Do you learn dance steps rapidly?
- Have you taken lessons in ballet or tap dancing? Were you able to learn different dance routines?

- Have you done free style or interpretive dancing? Do you like this kind of expression? Can you move your body and limbs gracefully?

✔ **How can you prepare for and enter this kind of work?**
Occupations in this group usually require education and/or training extending from one year to over ten years, depending upon the specific kind of work. Initial training in dance is often provided in physical education or music classes in elementary and high schools. However, instruction in a dance studio is usually needed to develop the skills. This instruction often starts at the preschool age and continues after employment as a dancer. Daily practice is a continuing requirement to develop and maintain the physical condition and techniques needed.

Liberal arts colleges, dance academies, and theater arts schools offer two- to four-year programs in dancing techniques, interpretation, and the history of dance. Many dance schools cooperate with professional ballet and interpretive dance companies to provide experience as well as instruction.

Some people find jobs as ballroom dancing instructors or part-time entertainers after taking dancing instructions. They usually have a natural aptitude and an attractive appearance. Intensive preparation is needed to be hired as a ballet or interpretive dancer, as a chorus dancer in musical comedies, or in television or other media. Dancers must audition for jobs with permanent resident or touring companies. Becoming a choreographer requires extensive performing experience as well as a thorough knowledge of dance.

Private dancing teachers must be able to demonstrate the techniques of many different types of dancing. Teachers in public schools and colleges are required to meet specific educational and licensing requirements.

✔ **What else should you consider about these jobs?**
Strong feet, ankles, and legs are essential for professional dancers. Most people cannot make dancing a lifetime occupation because of the strenuous physical demands of dancing. Teaching is too strenuous for some dancers nearing retirement age. Few dancers, other than well-known performers, are hired for show work after the age of thirty.

Performing jobs may be found in most metropolitan areas as well as areas where there are musical shows, nightclubs or other settings.

If you think you would like to do this kind of work, look at the job titles listed below.

GOE: 01.05.01 Instructing & Choreography, Dance

CHOREOGRAPHER (amuse. & rec.) • D.O.T. #151.027-010 • OES #34053 • DIRECTOR, DANCE. Creates and teaches original dances for ballet, musical or revue to be performed for stage, television, motion picture or nightclub production: Composes dance designed to suggest story, interpret emotion or enliven show coordinating dance with music. Instructs performers at rehearsals to achieve desired effect. May audition performers for specific parts. May direct and stage presentation. • GED: R5, M3, L5 • SVP: 4-10 yrs • Academic: Ed=A, Eng=G • Work Field: 263 • MPSMS: 755, 919 • Aptitudes: G2, V2, N3, S3, P3, Q4, K4, F4, M3, E2, C3 • Temperaments: D, F, J, P, V • Stress: E • Physical: V=N, H=L, L=L, W • Work Env: I • Salary: 5 • Outlook: 1

INSTRUCTOR, DANCING (educ.) • D.O.T. #151.027-014 • OES #31317 • PROFESSOR, DANCE; TEACHER, DANCING. Instructs pupils in ballet, ballroom, tap, and other forms of dancing: Observes students to determine physical and artistic qualifications and limitations and plans programs to meet students' needs and aspirations. Explains and demonstrates techniques and methods of regulating movements of body to musical or rhythmic accompaniment. Drills pupils in execution of dance steps. May teach history of dance. May teach theory and practice of dance notation. May choreograph and direct dance performance. May be designated according to style of dancing taught as INSTRUCTOR, BALLROOM DANCING (education); INSTRUCTOR, TAP DANCING (education); TEACHER, BALLET (education). May be employed by ballet company to train corps de ballet, and be designated as BALLET MASTER/MISTRESS (education). • GED: R5, M2, L5 • SVP: 2-4 yrs • Academic: Ed=A, Eng=S • Work Field: 296 • MPSMS: 755 • Aptitudes: G2, V2, N4, S2, P4, Q4, K2, F3, M3, E2, C5 • Temperaments: D, F, P, T • Stress: E • Physical: V=G, H=G, L=H, W, C, H • Work Env: I • Salary: 4 • Outlook: 3

GOE: 01.05.02 Performing, Dance

DANCER (amuse. & rec.) • D.O.T. #151.047-010 • OES #34053 • Dances alone, with partner, or in group to entertain audience: Performs classical, modern, or acrobatic dances, coordinating body movements to musical accompaniment. Rehearses dance movements developed by CHOREOGRAPHER (amuse. & rec.). May choreograph own dance. May sing and provide other forms of entertainment. May specialize in particular style of dancing and be designated according to specialty as ACROBATIC DANCER (amuse. & rec.); BALLET DANCER (amuse. & rec.); BALLROOM DANCER (amuse. & rec.); BELLY DANCER (amuse. & rec.); CHORUS DANCER (amuse. & rec.); INTERPRETATIVE DANCER (amuse. & rec.); STRIP-TEASE DANCER (amuse. & rec.); TAP DANCER (amuse. & rec.). • GED: R4, M2, L4 • SVP: 2-4 yrs • Academic: Ed=H, Eng=G • Work Field: 297 • MPSMS: 755, 919 • Aptitudes: G2, V3, N3, S2, P3, Q4, K2, F3, M3, E1, C4 • Temperaments: F, J, T • Physical: V=L, H=N, L=H, W, C, S, H • Work Env: I • Salary: 1 • Outlook: 1

01.06 Craft Arts

Workers in this group apply artistic techniques, fabricate, decorate or repair a variety of products, and reproduce photographs and graphics or printed materials. They use engraving and etching precision equipment, knives and chisels, paint brushes and power tools to work wood, stone, clay, metal, and gemstones, or embellish objects made from all these materials. They are employed by manufacturing firms, printing and publishing companies, and motion picture and television studios. They also work for advertising agencies and other firms which provide specialized services, museums, and retail stores. Some craft artists are self-employed, selling items they have made, or providing their services on a free-lance basis to businesses and individuals.

✔ What kind of work would you do?
Your work activities would depend upon your specific job. For example, you might:

- carve designs and lettering on wooden blocks or rollers for printing greeting cards.
- engrave designs and names on athletic trophies.
- paint designs and letters on posters with an airbrush.
- retouch photographs to highlight features of subjects.
- hand letter documents, such as diplomas and charters, using pen and ink.
- use special tools and techniques to clean and prepare fossils for a museum display.

✔ What skills and abilities do you need for this kind of work?
To do this kind of work, you must be able to:

- apply artistic skills, such as painting, drawing, or modeling, in practical ways.
- select the tools, materials, and methods which are best for each purpose.
- picture the way the finished product should look from drawings prepared by a designer.

- take pride in turning out work that appears attractive and meets the standards set by a customer or your supervisor.

- use your eyes, hands, and fingers skillfully to guide knives, pens, brushes, and modeling tools precisely.
- look at an object and notice tiny flaws which should removed or repaired.

✔ **How do you know if you would like or could learn to do this kind of work?**

The following questions may give you clues about yourself as you consider this group of jobs.

- Have you made your own jewelry? Do you enjoy working with your hands and making things?
- Have you made or decorated clay pottery?
- Have you completed a paint-by-number picture? Did you have a steady hand?

- Have you used a wood-burning tool to etch a preprinted design? Do you like to use tools of this kind?
- Have you decorated a cake for a birthday or other event? Did you create your own designs?

✔ **How can you prepare for and enter this kind of work?**

Occupations in this group usually require education and/or training extending from one year to over ten years, depending upon the specific kind of work. Courses in industrial art, drafting, art, or craft work may provide initial preparation. More specific training is needed for some jobs depending on the industry, process, or product involved.

Vocational high schools, technical schools, and junior colleges offer training in lettering, engraving, or etching. Trade unions and employers sometimes cooperate to offer apprenticeship training.

Training in the conservation and restoration of art objects and artifacts is given at a number of colleges, and lasts from six months to two years. This is usually followed by a year or two of on-the-job training as an intern or assistant, working under the direction of a skilled craftsman in a museum or conservation laboratory.

Some employers hire workers on the basis of manual skill, experience, and learning ability. Workers are given on-the-job training to develop the knowledge and skills they need. Many of these jobs are specialized crafts, which require two or more years of training and experience.

Hand decorating jobs do not require formal training. Art courses, drafting, or mechanical drawing classes at the high school or junior college level are helpful. Most employers provide six months to one year of on-the-job training to teach the proper techniques.

✔ **What else should you consider about these jobs?**

Opportunities for workers to express their own creativity vary among the jobs in this group. People who are interested in art, but prefer working under specific instructions rather than strictly on their own, will find many job possibilities here. Although these workers use art and craft tools and materials, and produce work that is artistic in nature, they do not have to spend as much time or money in training as they would to prepare for other jobs in the visual arts.

Workers with skill and experience sometimes open their own businesses. Some do free-lance or contract work.

If you think you would like to do this kind of work, look at the job titles listed below.

GOE: 01.06.01 Graphic Arts & Related Crafts

ADVERTISING-SPACE CLERK (print. & pub.) • D.O.T. #247.387-018 • OES #53908 • SPACE CLERK. Measures and draws outlines of advertising space on dummy newspaper copy and compiles and records identifying data on dummy copy and other worksheets used as guides for production workers: Computes total inches of advertising and news copy for next day's edition, using adding machine, and reads chart to determine required number of newspaper pages. Measures and draws outlines of advertisements in sizes specified onto dummy copy sheets, using pencil and ruler and arranging advertisements on each sheet so that competitive ones do not appear on same page and balance is attained. Records name of advertiser and dimensions of advertisement within ruled outlines and date and page number on each sheet. Extracts data from dummy copy and other sources and records onto lineage break down sheets (production worksheets). Delivers dummy copy and lineage breakdown sheets to designated production and administrative personnel for review and use. • **GED:** R3, M3, L3 • **SVP:** 6 mos-1 yr • **Academic:** Ed=N, Eng=G • **Work Field:** 231, 232, 242 • **MPSMS:** 480, 898 • **Aptitudes:** G3, V3, N3, S4, P4, Q3, K3, F3, M3, E5, C4 • **Temperaments:** T • **Physical:** V=L, H=N, L=S, H • **Work Env:** I • **Salary:** 2 • **Outlook:** 3

ENGRAVER, HAND, HARD METALS (engraving) • D.O.T. #704.381-026 • OES #89128 • Lays out and cuts lettering and designs on surfaces of hard metal for hobs, dies, and molds or plates used to imprint designs on paper, metal, plastic, or porcelain products, following sketches and blue prints, and using engraving tools: Computes dimensions of lettering and design, and marks or scribes layout lines on workpiece, using drawing tools, such as straightedge, compass, and scriber. Positions workpiece in vise and cuts designs in surface of work piece or trims precut designs, using gravers, punches, files, hammer, and shaped chisels. Sharpens and forms cutting edge of gravers on cutter grinder [TOOL-GRINDER OPERATOR (mach. shop)]. May sketch original design for customer. May enlarge or reduce reproduction of pattern according to size of article to be made. May brush surface of metal with acidproof paint to prevent corro sion. May be designated according to type of imprinting device engraved as STENCIL MAKER (engraving). • **GED:** R4, M3, L3 • **SVP:** 4-10 yrs • **Academic:** Ed=N, Eng=S • **Work Field:** 183 • **MPSMS:** 617 • **Aptitudes:** G3, V3, N3, S2, P2, Q4, K2, F2, M2, E5, C5 • **Temperaments:** J, M, T • **Physical:** V=G, H=N, L=M, W, H • **Work Env:** I • **Salary:** 5 • **Outlook:** 2

ENGRAVER, HAND, SOFT METALS (engraving) • D.O.T. #704.381-030 • OES #89128 • CARVER; DECORATOR. Engraves lettering and ornamental designs on soft metal articles, such as silverware, trophies, aluminum or plastic eyeglass frames, and jewelry articles, according to sketches, diagrams, photographs, or sample workpieces, using engraver's handtools: Lays out design or lettering to be engraved on object by brushing chalklike powder or solution on item and sketching design in powder, locating reference points, and marking outline of design on item, using scribers or gravers, or by imprinting design on surface of item, using inked rubber stamp, and marking outline, using scribers. Mounts piece in chuck and affixes chuck in jeweler's ball (rotating vise) or mounts piece directly in jeweler's ball. Cuts design in workpiece, using chisel-like engraving tools. May sketch original designs. May be designated according to kind of product engraved as ENGRAVER, FLATWARE (engraving); ENGRAVER, JEWELRY (engraving); ENGRAVER, OPTICAL FRAMES (engrav ing); or according to specialty as ENGRAVER, LETTERING (engrav ing); ENGRAVER, ORNAMENTAL DESIGN (engraving). • **GED:** R3, M2, L2 • **SVP:** 2-4 yrs • **Academic:** Ed=N, Eng=N • **Work Field:** 183 • **MPSMS:** 605, 611, 612 • **Aptitudes:** G3, V3, N4, S2, P2, Q4, K3, F2, M2, E5, C5 • **Temperaments:** M, T • **Physical:** V=G, H=N, L=S, H • **Work Env:** I • **Salary:** 4 • **Outlook:** 2

ENGRAVER, PICTURE (print. & pub.) • D.O.T. #979.281-018 • OES #89128 • Engraves metal dies to represent portraits, landscapes, figures, and ornamental engravings used to make plates to print bonds, stamps, currency, diplomas, and other paper documents, following models and oral instructions: Traces model of drawing on gelatin sheet, using magnifying glasses and graver. Makes wax impression of tracing, transfers tracing to polished metal die, and stains design with weak acid solution. Engraves or etches lines, dots, and dashes in specified depths, widths, spacings, and directions to portray features, such as drapery, foliage, or flesh by either one or combination of following methods: (1) Draws design through transparent, acid-resistant background on metal plate, using tempered steel point, and washes design with acid that etches lines and other markings in metal surface to produce representations of images, such as wood, stone, foliage, and sky. (2) Cuts or carves lines of design in surface of metal die, using graver. Repeats cuts to obtain required depth for portrayal of images, such as flesh, hair, drapery, and clothing. Makes proof of

engraved design, examines proof print, and reworks engraving as required. May engrave lettering on plates and be designated ENGRAVER, LETTER (print. & pub.). • **GED:** R4, M3, L3 • **SVP:** 4-10 yrs • **Academic:** Ed=A, Eng=S • **Work Field:** 182, 183 • **MPSMS:** 567 • **Aptitudes:** G3, V3, N3, S2, P2, Q3, K2, F2, M3, E5, C4 • **Temperaments:** J, M, T • **Physical:** V=G, H=N, L=L, H • **Work Env:** I • **Salary:** 5 • **Outlook:** 2

ETCHER (engraving) • D.O.T. #704.684-010 • OES #93951 • Etches designs, lettering, and figures on processed plates of brass, steel, copper, zinc, magnesium, or plastic: Mixes acid solution according to formula, and pours mixture into etching tank. Places plate on rack in etching tank, sets tank timing controls, and starts machine that sprays plate with corrosive solution. Removes plate periodically, and measures depth to which metal has been etched, using gage. Inspects plate to insure that design is not undercut. Washes plate to remove etching powder and protective ink. May brush etching powder on surface of plate to prevent undercutting of reproduction. • **GED:** R3, M2, L2 • **SVP:** 1-2 yrs • **Academic:** Ed=N, Eng=N • **Work Field:** 182 • **MPSMS:** 556 • **Aptitudes:** G3, V4, N4, S3, P2, Q4, K4, F4, M3, E5, C5 • **Temperaments:** M, T • **Physical:** V=G, H=N, L=L, H • **Work Env:** I • **Salary:** 4 • **Outlook:** 2

PHOTOENGRAVER (print. & pub.) • D.O.T. #971.381-022 • OES #89712 • ENGRAVING OPERATOR; PHOTOLITH OPERATOR. Photographs copy, develops negatives, and prepares photosensitized metal plates, such as copper, zinc, aluminum, and magnesium for use in printing, using photography and developing equipment and engravers' handtools: Positions copy on copy board of darkroom camera and exposes film to copy. Fastens scoured metal plate to whirling machine table or suspension hooks, pours photosensitizing solution on plate, and starts machine which rotates plate to distribute and dry solution evenly over plate surface. Exposes negative and plate to bright light in vacuum type printing frame to transfer image onto plate. Rolls ink onto exposed plate and washes unexposed and unfixed emulsion from plate, using running water and cotton pad to expose bare metal. Places developed plate in acid bath or etching machine to erode unprotected metal to specified depth. Mounts etched plates on wood blocks, using hammer and nails or on metal base, using thermosetting adhesive to raise printing surface type to speci fied height. Removes excess metal from nonprinting areas of cut, using routing machine [ROUTER (print. & pub.)]. Cuts mortises in mounted plates, using power drill and jigsaw, for insertion of type or other cuts. Modifies and repairs finished plates, using engravers' handtools, etching brush, and acid. May be designated according to type of plate made as PLATEMAKER, ZINC (print. & pub.). • **GED:** R4, M3, L3 • **SVP:** 4-10 yrs • **Academic:** Ed=A, Eng=S • **Work Field:** 191 • **MPSMS:** 752 • **Aptitudes:** G3, V3, N3, S3, P2, Q4, K3, F3, M3, E5, C3 • **Temperaments:** M, T • **Physical:** V=G, H=N, L=L, H • **Work Env:** I • **Salary:** 5 • **Outlook:** 1

SILK-SCREEN CUTTER (any ind.) • D.O.T. #979.681-022 • OES #89908 • FILM CUTTER; SILK-SCREEN MARKER; STENCIL CUTTER. Cuts stencils by hand for use in silk-screen printing: Superimposes transparent gelatinous film or shellacked onionskin paper on design or lettering to be reproduced, and cuts outline of design, using knife. Irons stencil on silk or fine copper mesh screen to transfer film or shellac onto screen. Cuts additional stencils for each color to be printed in design. May draw design directly on screen and fill in surfaces around design with glue, lacquer, or paper. May print designs [SCREEN PRINTER (any ind.)]. May cut stencils for use in making computer circuit plug boards and be designated SILK-SCREEN-LAYOUT DRAFTER (any ind.). • **GED:** R3, M1, L2 • **SVP:** 6 mos-1 yr • **Academic:** Ed=N, Eng=N • **Work Field:** 191 • **MPSMS:** 567 • **Aptitudes:** G3, V3, N4, S3, P3, Q4, K3, F2, M3, E5, C4 • **Temperaments:** M, T • **Physical:** V=L, H=N, L=L, H • **Work Env:** I • **Salary:** 2 • **Outlook:** 3

GOE: 01.06.02 Arts & Crafts

BOW MAKER, CUSTOM (sports equip.) • D.O.T. #732.381-010 • OES #89999 • Selects, laminates, shapes, and finishes woods, plastics, and metals to make archery bows: Selects materials from stock according to customer's specifications, and preshapes parts, using handtools and power tools. Applies specified adhesives between parts. Assembles parts and places assembled bows in glue press to cure. Heats bows in steam box until pliable and clamps bows on form to shape curves and recurves. Trims and smooths bows, using handtools and sandpaper. Stains, paints, and varnishes bows according to specifications. May apply decals to bows. May rework or repair damaged bow and be designated BOW REPAIRER, CUSTOM (sports equip.). May make arrows, using die cutter to cut feathers used on arrows. • **GED:** R4, M2, L2 • **SVP:** 2-4 yrs • **Academic:** Ed=N, Eng=N • **Work Field:** 102 • **MPSMS:** 616 • **Aptitudes:** G3, V4, N3, S2, P2, Q4, K3, F3, M3, E4, C4 • **Temperaments:** M, T • **Physical:** V=L, H=N, L=L, H • **Work Env:** I, R • **Salary:** 3 • **Out look:** 3

CLAY MODELER (any ind.) • D.O.T. #779.281-010 • OES #89908 • Molds full-sized or scale models of products, such as automobiles, automobile parts, television sets, radios, washers, refrigerators, caskets, or boats from clay following artist's sketches or from verbal instructions: Builds rough lumber form to fit around model or centers preformed lath-covered wood frame on grid platform. Kneads clay into slots between laths so clay will adhere to frame. Molds clay by hand to approximate shape. Pulls sheet aluminum forming tool over surface of clay to shape areas that have constant cross sections. Shapes sculptured surfaces, using various types of sculptor's tools and scrapers. Verifies uniformity and smoothness of curved surfaces with splines and sweeps. Scrapes clay from high areas and builds up and smooths low areas to attain desired shape. Cuts cardboard templates for use as guides to shape symmetrical sections. Takes measurements from completed half of model and duplicates them on unfinished half to make both sides symmetrical. Covers bumpers, lights, door handles, and other parts with aluminum foil to simulate chrome or colored glass. • **GED:** R4, M3, L4 • **SVP:** 2-4 yrs • **Academic:** Ed=N, Eng=S • **Work Field:** 136 • **MPSMS:** 539 • **Aptitudes:** G2, V3, N3, S2, P2, Q4, K3, F2, M2, E5, C4 • **Temperaments:** J, M, T, V • **Physical:** V=L, H=N, L=L, H • **Work Env:** I • **Salary:** 4 • **Outlook:** 2

CONSERVATION TECHNICIAN (museum) • D.O.T. #102.261-010 • OES #31511 • Repairs and cleans art objects, such as pottery, statuary, etchings, or tapestries, to restore art objects' natural appearance: Studies descriptive information on object or conducts standard chemical and physical tests to determine such factors as age, composition, and original appearance, and plans methods or procedures for restoring object. Cleans object or broken pieces, using such methods as scraping and applying solvents to metal objects; washing statuary, using soap solutions; or cleaning and polishing furniture and silver objects. Repairs objects, using glue or solder, to assemble broken pieces, buffing assembled object where repaired, or repainting faded or incomplete designs with paint of same chemical composition and color in order to restore original appearance. Notifies superior when problem of restoration requires outside experts. Fabricates or repairs picture frames for paintings, using hand tools and power tools and machines. Mounts pictures in frames. • **GED:** R4, M4, L4 • **SVP:** 1-2 yrs • **Academic:** Ed=H, Eng=S • **Work Field:** 102 • **MPSMS:** 969 • **Aptitudes:** G2, V2, N3, S2, P2, Q3, K2, F2, M2, E4, C1 • **Temperaments:** J, M, T, V • **Physical:** V=G, H=N, L=M, H • **Work Env:** I • **Salary:** 4 • **Outlook:** 3

CONSERVATOR, ARTIFACTS (profess. & kin.) • D.O.T. #055.381-010 • OES #27199 • PRESERVATIONIST. Cleans, restores, and preserves archeological specimens and historical artifacts according to accepted chemical and physical techniques and training in archeological science: Cleans and repairs or reinforces specimens, such as weapons, mummified remains, and pottery, using handtools and prescribed chemical agents. Restores artifacts by polishing, joining together broken fragments, or other procedures, using handtools, power tools, and acid, chemical, or electrolytic corrosion-removal baths. Treats specimens to prevent or minimize deterioration, according to accepted procedures. Records treatment of each artifact. Prepares reports of activities. May plan and conduct research to improve methods of restoring and preserving specimen. • **GED:** R4, M4, L4 • **SVP:** 1-2 yrs • **Academic:** Ed=H, Eng=S • **Work Field:** 031, 102 • **MPSMS:** 745 • **Aptitudes:** G3, V3, N3, S2, P3, Q3, K3, F3, M3, E5, C4 • **Temperaments:** J, M, V • **Physical:** V=L, H=N, L=L, H • **Work Env:** I • **Salary:** 4 • **Outlook:** 1

DECORATOR (any ind.) • D.O.T. #298.381-010 • OES #34044 • COMMERCIAL DECORATOR. Prepares and installs decorations and displays from blueprints or drawings for trade and industrial shows, expositions, festivals, and other special events: Cuts out designs on cardboard, hard board, and plywood, according to motif of event. Constructs portable installations according to specifications, using woodworking power tools. Installs booths, exhibits, displays, carpets, and drapes, as guided by floor plan of building. Arranges installations, furniture, and other accessories in position shown in prepared sketch. Installs decorations, such as flags, banners, festive lights, and bunting, on or in building, street, exhibit halls, and booths, to achieve special effects [DECORATOR, STREET AND BUILDING (any ind.)]. Assembles and installs prefabricated parts to reconstruct traveling exhibits from sketch submitted by client, using hand tools. • **GED:** R4, M4, L3 • **SVP:** 2-4 yrs • **Academic:** Ed=N, Eng=G • **Work Field:** 102 • **MPSMS:** 889 • **Aptitudes:** G2, V3, N3, S2, P3, Q3, K3, F3, M3, E4, C3 • **Tempera ments:** M, T • **Physical:** V=L, H=N, L=L, S, H • **Work Env:** I • **Salary:** 4 • **Outlook:** 3

DISPLAY MAKER (signs) • D.O.T. #739.361-010 • OES #89908 • EXPERIMENTAL-DISPLAY BUILDER; MODEL MAKER. Designs, fabricates, assembles, or installs displays, exhibits, and models of point-of-sale displays: Designs displays or exhibits from pictures or sketches, or according to verbal instructions from customer. Lays out, cuts, shapes, and finishes wood, plastic, plexiglass, sheet metal, and hardboard parts of displays, using woodworking machines, metal machines, and handtools, according to drawings or blueprints. Cuts glass to specified shape with glasscutter. Assembles parts with nails, screws, bolts, and glue, using handtools. Confers with designer, customer, or salesperson regarding refinements, additions, and adjust ments. May disassemble display to make working drawings for production run and to produce estimates for accounting and sales departments. Reassembles and sends to prospective customer. May wire display for illumination, audio, or video. May travel and set up display on designated site. May specialize in making diorama models and be designated DIORAMA MODEL-MAKER (signs). • **GED:** R4, M4, L3 • **SVP:** 2-4 yrs • **Academic:** Ed=N, Eng=S • **Work Field:** 102 • **MPSMS:** 896 • **Aptitudes:** G3, V3, N4, S3, P2, Q4, K3, F3, M3, E5, C3 • **Temperaments:** J, M, T • **Physical:** V=L, H=N, L=M, W, H • **Work Env:** I • **Salary:** 4 • **Outlook:** 3

DISTRESSER (furn.) • D.O.T. #763.687-018 • OES #98999 • Marks surface of furniture with crayon or strikes surface with rough edged object, such as chain, broken bottle, or rock, to distress (simulate antique) furniture finish: Reads work ticket to ascertain items to be distressed or receives oral instructions from supervisor. Swings chain against surface of furniture to cause dents in surface. Taps surface with wooden hammer containing protruding nails to produce pattern of holes in surface. Scrapes pointed end of metal rod across surface to produce random scratches. Marks surface with crayon to produce desired antique finish. • **GED:** R2, M1, L2 • **SVP:** 30 days-3 mos • **Academic:** Ed=N, Eng=N • **Work Field:** 134, 262 • **MPSMS:** 460 • **Aptitudes:** G4, V4, N5, S4, P4, Q5, K4, F4, M3, E5, C4 • **Temperaments:** R • **Stress:** T • **Physical:** V=L, H=N, L=L, H • **Work Env:** I • **Salary:** 2 • **Outlook:** 2

EXHIBIT BUILDER (museum) • D.O.T. #739.261-010 • OES #89908 • EXHIBITION SPECIALIST; EXHIBIT TECHNICIAN; MUSEUM CRAFT WORKER. Constructs and installs museum exhibit structures, electric wiring, and fixtures of materials, such as wood, plywood, and fiberglass, using handtools and power tools: Studies sketches or scale drawings for temporary or permanent display or exhibit structures, such as framework, fixtures, booths, or cabinets to determine type, amount, and cost of material needed. Confers with exhibit planning and art personnel to discuss structural feasibility of plans and to suggest alternate methods of displaying objects in exhibit. Cuts, assembles, and fastens parts to construct framework, panels, shelves, and other exhibit components of specified materials, using handtools and power tools. Sprays or brushes paint, enamel, varnish, or other finish on structures, or creates special effects by applying finish with cloth, sponge, or fingers to prepare structure for addition of fittings. Mounts fittings and fixtures, such as shelves, panelboards, and shadowboxes to framework, using hand tools or adhesives. Installs electrical wiring, fixtures, apparatus, audiovisual components, or control equipment in framework, according to design specifications. Installs or affixes murals, photographs, mounted legend materials, and graphics in framework or on fixtures. Assembles, installs, or arranges structures in exhibit galleries working with maintenance and installation personnel. Tests electrical, electronic, and mechanical components of exhibit structure to verify operation. May maintain inventory of building materials, tools, and equipment, and order supplies as needed for construction of exhibit fixtures. May assign duties to and supervise work of carpentry, electrical, and other craftworkers engaged in constructing and installing exhibit components. May assist in placement of display accessories and collection objects or specimens. May be designated according to speciality as EXHIBIT CARPENTER (museum) or EXHIBIT ELECTRICIAN (museum) or job location as PLANETARIUM SKY SHOW TECHNICIAN (museum) or SCIENCE CENTER DISPLAY BUILDER (museum). • **GED:** R4, M4, L4 • **SVP:** 2-4 yrs • **Academic:** Ed=N, Eng=S • **Work Field:** 102, 111 • **MPSMS:** 360 • **Aptitudes:** G3, V3, N3, S2, P2, Q4, K3, F3, M2, E5, C4 • **Temperaments:** J, T, V • **Physical:** V=L, H=N, L=M, W, H • **Work Env:** I • **Salary:** 4 • **Outlook:** 3

JEWELER (jewelry) • D.O.T. #700.281-010 • OES #89123 • BENCH WORKER; JEWELRY JOBBER; JEWELRY REPAIRER. Fabricates and repairs jewelry articles, such as rings, brooches, pendants, bracelets, and lockets: Forms model of article from wax or metal, using carving tools. Places wax model in casting ring, and pours plaster into ring to form mold. Inserts plaster mold in furnace to melt wax. Casts metal model from plaster mold. Forms mold of sand or rubber from metal model for casting jewelry. Pours molten metal into mold, or operates centrifugal casting machine to cast article [CENTRIFUGAL-CASTING-MACHINE OPERATOR (jewelry)]. Cuts, saws, files, and polishes article, using hand tools and polishing wheel. Solders pieces of jewelry together, using soldering torch or iron. Enlarges or reduces size of rings by sawing through band, adding or removing metal, and soldering ends together. Repairs broken clasps, pins, rings, and other jewelry by soldering or replacing broken parts. Reshapes and restyles old jewelry, following designs or instructions, using handtools and machines, such as jeweler's lathe and drill. Smooths soldered joints and rough spots, using hand file and emery paper. May be designated according to metals fashioned as GOLDSMITH (jewelry); PLATINUMSMITH (jewelry); SILVERSMITH (jewelry). • **GED:** R4, M3, L3 • **SVP:** 2-4 yrs • **Academic:** Ed=H, Eng=S • **Work Field:** 057 • **MPSMS:** 611 • **Aptitudes:** G3, V3, N3, S2, P2, Q4, K3, F2, M3, E5, C5 • **Temperaments:** M, T, V • **Physical:** V=G, H=N, L=S, H • **Work Env:** I • **Salary:** 4 • **Outlook:** 3

MAKE-UP ARTIST (amuse. & rec.) • D.O.T. #333.071-010 • OES #68005 • Studies production require ments, such as character, period, setting, and situation, and applies makeup to performers to alter their appearance to accord with their roles: Examines sketches, photographs, and plaster models in period files to obtain an image of character to be depicted. Confers with stage and motion picture officials and performer to determine alterations to be made and makeup to be used. Designs prostheses of rubber or plastic and requisitions cosmetics and makeup materials, such as wigs, beards, rouge, powder, and grease paint. Applies prostheses, cosmetics, and makeup to change such physical characteristics of performer as facial features, skin texture, bodily contours, and dimensions and to produce effect appropriate to depict character and situation. May make drawings or models based upon independent research to augment period files. • **GED:** R4, M3, L3 • **SVP:** 2-4 yrs • **Academic:** Ed=N, Eng=S • **Work Field:** 264, 291 • **MPSMS:** 909 • **Aptitudes:** G2, V2, N3, S3, P2, Q4, K3, F3, M3, E5, C2 • **Temperaments:** F, J, P, V • **Stress:** E • **Physical:** V=L, H=N, L=L, H • **Work Env:** I • **Salary:** 3 • **Outlook:** 3

MODEL MAKER 1 (any ind.) • D.O.T. #777.261-010 • OES #89908 • Constructs scale model of objects: Builds and molds models, using clay, metal, wood, fiberglass, other substance, depending on industry for which model is constructed, such as ship and boat building or automobile manufacturing. • **GED:** R5, M3, L3 • **SVP:** 2-4 yrs • **Academic:** Ed=N, Eng=S • **Work Field:** 102 • **MPSMS:** 619 • **Aptitudes:** G2, V3, N3, S2, P2, Q4, K3, F2, M2, E5, C4 • **Temperaments:** F, J, M • **Physical:** V=G, H=N, L=S, H • **Work Env:** I • **Salary:** 4 • **Outlook:** 2

MOLD MAKER 1 (jewelry) • D.O.T. #700.381-034 • OES #89126 • CHASER. Finishes, alters, and repairs metal molds used to cast jewelry articles and trophy figurines, using hand carving and engraving tools: Cuts design in mold and files, grinds, and shapes points, surfaces, and contours. Fits halves of molds together to determine if they close tightly. Drills holes in mold to allow gases to escape during casting. Reshapes pouring funnels of molds to facilitate flow of molten metal. Drills holes in mold and attaches handles, using drill press and screwdriver. Forms sample castings in mold and measures casting to verify dimensions. May grind, sharpen, and make tools. • **GED:** R4, M3, L3 • **SVP:** 4-10 yrs • **Academic:** Ed=N, Eng=S • **Work Field:** 183 • **MPSMS:** 611 • **Aptitudes:** G3, V3, N3, S3, P3, Q4, K3, F3, M3, E5, C5 • **Temperaments:** M, T, V • **Physical:** V=L, H=N, L=L, H • **Work Env:** I • **Salary:** 4 • **Outlook:** 2

MORTUARY BEAUTICIAN (per. ser.) • D.O.T. #339.361-010 • OES #68005 • EMBALMER ASSISTANT; FUNERAL-HOME ATTENDANT. Prepares embalmed bodies for interment: Manicures nails, using files and nail polish, and performs other grooming tasks, such as arching and plucking eyebrows and removing facial hair, using depilatory cream and tweezers. Shampoos, waves, presses, curls, brushes, and combs hair, and applies cosmetics on face to restore natural appearance, following photograph of deceased, or verbal or written description obtained from family. Dresses and arranges body in casket. May select casket or burial dress, arrange floral displays, and prepare obituary notices. May record personal effects delivered with body and information about deceased. May wash and dry bodies, using germicidal soap and towels or hot air drier. May reshape or reconstruct damaged or disfigured areas of body, using such materials as cotton or foam rubber. • **GED:** R3, M2, L2 • **SVP:** 1-2 yrs • **Academic:** Ed=N, Eng=N • **Work Field:** 291 • **MPSMS:** 909 • **Aptitudes:** G3, V3, N4, S3, P3, Q4, K3, F3, M3, E5, C3 • **Temperaments:** M, T, V • **Physical:** V=L, H=N, L=M, W, H • **Work Env:** I, R • **Salary:** 4 • **Outlook:** 3

MUSEUM TECHNICIAN (museum) • D.O.T. #102.381-010 • OES #31511 • MUSEUM PREPARATOR. Prepares specimens for museum collections and exhibits: Cleans rock matrix from fossil specimens, using electric drills, awls, dental tools, chisels, and mallets. Brushes preservatives, such as plaster, resin, hardeners, and shellac on specimens. Molds and restores skeletal parts of fossil animals, using modeling clays and special molding and casting techniques. Constructs skeletal mounts of fossil animals, using tools, such as drill presses, pipe threaders, welding and soldering apparatus, and carpenter's tools. Constructs duplicate specimens, using plaster, glue, latex, and plastiflex-molding techniques. Reassembles fragmented artifacts, and fabricates substitute pieces. Maintains museum files. Cleans, catalogs, labels, and stores specimens. May in stall, arrange, and exhibit materials. • **GED:** R4, M3, L4 • **SVP:** 2-4 yrs • **Academic:** Ed=H, Eng=G • **Work Field:** 102 • **MPSMS:** 750 • **Aptitudes:** G3, V3, N4, S2, P2, Q4, K4, F2, M2, E3, C3 • **Temperaments:** J, M, V • **Physical:** V=N, H=N, L=M, W, C, S, H • **Work Env:** I, N, R • **Salary:** 3 • **Outlook:** 3

PICTURE FRAMER (framing) • D.O.T. #739.684-146 • OES #93956 • FITTER. Frames pictures in custom-made or stock frames: Mounts picture on backing, using glue. Cuts mounted picture to fit frame, using papercutter or powersaw. Cuts glass to fit frame, using glass-cutting tool. Cleans glass and places it in upturned frame. Places picture on top of glass. Cuts piece of cardboard to fit frame, and places it on back of picture. Pushes or taps brads into frame or uses stapler to staple picture in place. Glues paper cover to back of frame. Attaches screw eyes and wire to frame, using handtools or staple gun. May frame oil paintings that do not require glass fronts or paper covers. May repair and redecorate old or broken frames. • **GED:** R3, M1, L1 • **SVP:** 6 mos-1 yr • **Academic:** Ed=N, Eng=N • **Work Field:** 102 • **MPSMS:** 457 • **Aptitudes:** G3, V3, N4, S3, P4, Q4, K3, F3, M3, E5, C5 • **Temperaments:** T, V • **Physical:** V=L, H=N, L=L, H • **Work Env:** I • **Salary:** 3 • **Outlook:** 4

PROP MAKER (amuse. & rec.) • D.O.T. #962.281-010 • OES #87102 • Fabricates and assembles props, miniatures, and sets for motion pictures and theatrical productions from a variety of materials, using handtools and woodworking and metalworking machines and equipment: Analyzes sketches, blue prints, and verbal instructions to determine type props and other materials needed and equipment required. Measures and marks cutting lines on material, using work aids, such as jigs and fixtures, micrometers, calipers, and templates. Fabricates parts, using machinery such as drill press, metal and wood lathes, power saws, router, and milling machine. Assembles parts into props, miniatures, and sets, using handtools and equipment, such as screwdrivers, wrenches, hammers, and welding apparatus. Rigs and controls moving or functioning elements of sets that depict action. • **GED:** R4, M4, L4 • **SVP:** 2-4 yrs • **Academic:** Ed=N, Eng=S • **Work Field:** 102, 121 • **MPSMS:** 754, 911 • **Aptitudes:** G3, V3, N3, S2, P2, Q4, K3, F2, M2, E4, C3 • **Temperaments:** M, S, T, V • **Stress:** S • **Physical:** V=L, H=N, L=M, W, H • **Work Env:** B, R • **Salary:** 4 • **Outlook:** 2

REPAIRER, ART OBJECTS (any ind.) • D.O.T. #779.381-018 • OES #85999 • Repairs and restores objects of art, such as figurines and vases made of antique or fine porcelain, glass, or semiprecious stone: Fits together broken or otherwise marred pieces with wires and glue or other adhesive. Refinishes surfaces with lacquer or paint. Restores decorative patterns by repainting blemished lines or creating new designs. • **GED:** R4, M3, L3 • **SVP:** 2-4 yrs • **Academic:** Ed=N, Eng=S • **Work Field:** 102 • **MPSMS:** 759 • **Aptitudes:** G3, V3, N4, S2, P2, Q4, K4, F2, M2, E5, C3 • **Temperaments:** J, T, V • **Physical:** V=L, H=N, L=S, H • **Work Env:** I • **Salary:** 4 • **Outlook:** 2

RESTORER, CERAMIC (museum) • D.O.T. #102.361-014 • OES #31511 • Cleans, preserves, restores, and repairs objects made of glass, porcelain, china, fired clay, and other ceramic materials: Coats excavated objects with surface-active agents to loosen adhering mud or clay and washes objects with clear water. Places cleaned objects in dilute hydrochloric acid or other solution to remove remaining deposits of lime or chalk, basing choice of solution on knowledge of physical and chemical structure of objects and destructive qualities of solvents. Cleans glass, porcelain, or similar objects by such methods as soaking objects in lukewarm water with ammonia added, wiping gilded or enameled objects with solvent-saturated swab, or rubbing objects with paste cleanser. Rubs objects with jewelers' rouge or other mild cleanser, soaks objects in distilled water with bleach or solvent added, or applies paste or liquid solvent, such as magnesium silicate or acetone, basing choice of method and material on age, condition, and chemical structure of objects, to remove stains from objects. Recommends preservation measures, such as control of temperature, humidity, and exposure to light, to curatorial and building maintenance staff to prevent damage to or deterioration of object. Impregnates surfaces with diluted synthetic lacquers to reduce porosity of material to increase durability of ancient earthenware. Restores or simulates original appearance of objects by such methods as polishing surfaces to restore translucency, removing crackled glaze and applying soluble synthetic coating, grinding or cutting out chipped edges and repolishing surfaces, or applying matt paints, gold leaf, or other coating to object, basing methods and materials used on knowledge of original craft and condition of objects. Repairs broken objects, employing such techniques as bonding edges together with adhesive, inserting dowel pins in sections and cementing together, or affixing adhesive coated strips to inner portions of broken objects. Replaces missing sections of objects by constructing wire frames of missing sections, shaping plasticene or other materials over frames, affixing modeled sections to objects with dowels or adhesive, and painting attached sections to reproduce original appearance. Constructs replicas of archaeological artifacts or historically significant ceramic ware, basing construction design on size, curvature, and thickness of excavated shards or pieces of objects available and knowledge of techniques and designs characteristic of period. • **GED:** R5, M5, L5 • **SVP:** 2-4 yrs • **Academic:** Ed=A, Eng=S • **Work Field:** 031, 102, 251 • **MPSMS:** 530 • **Aptitudes:** G2, V2, N2, S2, P2, Q4, K2, F2, M3, E5, C2 • **Temperaments:** J, T • **Physical:** V=L, H=N, L=L, H • **Work Env:** I • **Salary:** 3 • **Outlook:** 3

SAMPLE MAKER 1 (jewelry) • D.O.T. #700.381-046 • OES #89123 • CRAFTER. Fabricates sample jewelry articles, according to drawings or instructions: Cuts and shapes metal into findings II, using metal cutting and carving tools. Arranges metal findings into specified design, softens findings by heating with gas torch, and shapes findings, using hammer and die. Solders pieces together, and smooths rough surfaces, using wooden mallet, files, or

polishing wheel. Attaches decorative trimmings, such as wax flowers, enamel motifs, and stones. • **GED:** R3, M2, L2 • **SVP:** 2-4 yrs • **Academic:** Ed=N, Eng=N • **Work Field:** 102 • **MPSMS:** 611 • **Aptitudes:** G3, V3, N4, S2, P2, Q4, K2, F2, M3, E5, C3 • **Temperaments:** M, T, V • **Physical:** V=L, H=N, L=L, H • **Work Env:** I • **Salary:** 3 • **Outlook:** 2

SILVERSMITH (silverware) • D.O.T. #700.281-022 • OES #89123 • Assembles and repairs silverware, such as coffee pots, tea sets, and trays: Anneals workpiece in gas oven for prescribed time to soften metal for reworking. Wires parts, such as legs, spouts, and handles, to body to prepare unit for soldering. Solders parts together and fills in holes and cracks with silver solder, using gas torch. Hammers out deformations and levels and sets bottoms, using dollies, hammers, and tracing punches. Shapes and straightens damaged legs, lids, and spouts with pliers. Restores dented embossing on articles, using hammers and punches. Pierces and cuts open design in ornamentation, using hand drill and scroll saw. Glues plastic separators to handles of coffee and teapots. May operate lathe to form articles of silver ware out of silver or plated sheet, according to sketches. May hammer metal into shape and solder seams to make handles and spouts. May work with metals other than silver, such as pewter, brass, chromium, and nickel. • **GED:** R4, M2, L3 • **SVP:** 2-4 yrs • **Academic:** Ed=N, Eng=S • **Work Field:** 102 • **MPSMS:** 612 • **Aptitudes:** G3, V4, N4, S2, P2, Q4, K3, F2, M2, E5, C5 • **Temperaments:** J, T, V • **Physical:** V=L, H=N, L=L, H • **Work Env:** I, H • **Salary:** 4 • **Outlook:** 2

STONE CARVER (stonework) • D.O.T. #771.281-014 • OES #89905 • HAND CARVER; SCULPTOR. Carves designs and figures in full and bas-relief on stone, employing knowledge of stone-carving techniques and sense of artistry to produce carving consistent with designer's plans: Analyzes artistic objects or graphic materials, such as models, sketches, or blueprints; visualizes finished product; and plans carving technique. Lays out figures or designs on stone surface by freehand sketching, marking over tracing paper, and transferring dimensions from sketches or blueprints, using rule, straightedge, square, compass, calipers, and chalk, or scriber. Selects chisels and pneumatic tools and determines sequence of their use according to intricacy of design or figure. Roughs out design freehand or by chipping along marks on stone, using mallet and chisel or pneumatic tool. Shapes, trims, or touches up roughed out design with appropriate tool to finish carving. Periodically compares carving with sketches, blueprints, or model and verifies dimensions of carving, using calipers, rule, straightedge, and square. Moves fingers over surface of carving to verify smoothness of finish. May smooth surface of carving with rubbing stone. May be designated according to type of work as MONUMENT CARVER (stonework); or according to kind of stone carved as GRANITE CARVER (stone work); MARBLE CARVER (stonework). • **GED:** R4, M4, L4 • **SVP:** 4-10 yrs • **Academic:** Ed=N, Eng=S • **Work Field:** 052, 264 • **MPSMS:** 537, 759 • **Aptitudes:** G2, V3, N2, S2, P2, Q3, K2, F2, M2, E5, C5 • **Temperaments:** F, J, T • **Physical:** V=L, H=N, L=M, W, S, H • **Work Env:** I, N • **Salary:** 5 • **Outlook:** 1

WIG DRESSER (hairwork) • D.O.T. #332.361-010 • OES #68005 • HAIRDRESSER. Dresses wigs and hair pieces according to instructions, samples, sketches, or photographs: Attaches wig or hair piece onto model head, using hammer and tacks or pins. Combs and sets hair, using barber and beautician equipment. Arranges hair according to instructions, pictures, or photographs, using brush and comb. Sprays hair with lacquer to keep hair in place. May cut wigs and hair pieces to specified length and style, using scissors or razor. May wash and dry hair pieces. • **GED:** R3, M2, L2 • **SVP:** 1-2 yrs • **Academic:** Ed=N, Eng=S • **Work Field:** 264, 291 • **MPSMS:** 619, 904 • **Aptitudes:** G3, V3, N4, S3, P2, Q4, K3, F3, M3, E5, C3 • **Temperaments:** J, P, T, V • **Physical:** V=L, H=N, L=L, H • **Work Env:** I • **Salary:** 3 • **Outlook:** 3

GOE: 01.06.03 Hand Lettering, Painting & Decorating

GIFT WRAPPER (ret. tr.) • D.O.T. #299.364-014 • OES #49999 • WRAPPER. Wraps and decorates customer's purchases with gift-wrapping paper, ribbons, bows, and tape in retail store. May collect money and make change for gift-wrapping service. May assist customer to select appropriate wrapping materials. • **GED:** R3, M2, L1 • **SVP:** 30 days-3 mos • **Academic:** Ed=N, Eng=N • **Work Field:** 041, 292 • **MPSMS:** 881 • **Aptitudes:** G4, V4, N4, S3, P4, Q4, K4, F3, M4, E5, C4 • **Temperaments:** P, R • **Stress:** T • **Physical:** V=N, H=N, L=L, H • **Work Env:** I • **Salary:** 1 • **Outlook:** 3

GILDER (any ind.) • D.O.T. #749.381-010 • OES #89911 • GOLD CHARMER; GOLD-LEAF GILDER; METAL-LEAF GILDER; METAL-LEAF LAYER. Covers surfaces of items, such as books, furniture, harps, and signs, with metal leaf, such as aluminum, gold, or silver, to decorate them, using brushes, T-shaped handtool, and hands: Brushes sizing (thin glue) on sections of items which are to be covered with leaf (gilded), according to design. Transfers leaf from supply book onto pallet. Rubs camel-hair brush in hair to electrify brush and picks up leaf with brush, or picks up leaf with T-shaped, felt-edged tool, and lays leaf over sizing; or presses sheets or ribbons of leaf onto sizing by hand. Smooths leaf over surface and removes excess, using brush. Rubs leaf with polished burnishing agate, cotton pad, or gloved hand to polish leaf or simulate worn metal finish. May brush or spray protective lacquer coat over gilded surface. • **GED:** R3, M1, L1 • **SVP:** 1-2 yrs • **Academic:** Ed=N, Eng=N • **Work Field:** 092 • **MPSMS:** 559 • **Aptitudes:** G3, V4, N4, S3, P2, Q4, K3, F2, M2, E5, C2 • **Temperaments:** J, T • **Physical:** V=L, H=N, L=L, H • **Work Env:** I • **Salary:** 4 • **Outlook:** 2

PAINTER, AIRBRUSH (any ind.) • D.O.T. #741.684-018 • OES #93947 • Coats, decorates, glazes, retouches, or tints articles, such as fishing lures, toys, dolls, pottery, artificial flowers, greeting cards, and household appliances, using airbrush: Stirs or shakes coating liquid and thinner to mix solution to specified consistency. Pours solution into airbrush container, couples airbrush to airhose, and starts compressor or opens valve on compressed-air line. Turns adjusting sleeve on nozzle of airbrush to regulate spray pattern to size of workpiece or area to be sprayed. Presses button on airbrush to spray coating over workpiece, or to spray specified designs and decorations on workpiece, spraying freehand or using stencils, masks, screens, and tape. Cleans airbrush nozzle and hose with solvent. May be designated according to article sprayed as BAIT PAINTER (sports equip.). • **GED:** R3, M1, L1 • **SVP:** 6 mos-1 yr • **Academic:** Ed=N, Eng=N • **Work Field:** 153, 262 • **MPSMS:** 485, 535, 610 • **Aptitudes:** G3, V4, N4, S3, P3, Q4, K3, F3, M3, E5, C3 • **Temperaments:** M, T • **Physical:** V=L, H=N, L=L, H • **Work Env:** I • **Salary:** 3 • **Outlook:** 2

PAINTER, HAND (any ind.) • D.O.T. #970.381-022 • OES #89911 • ARTIST; DECORATOR; FILLER-IN TINTER. Paints decorative freehand designs on objects, such as pottery, cigarette cases, and lampshades, using hand brushes: Sketches design, using pencil or permanent ink. Grinds colors on pottery tile, using palette knife, to mix colors and oils to desired consistency. Paints freehand or within sketched design, using mixed colors, or applies pure colors, one over another, to produce desired shade, allowing time for drying between applications. May stipple (create designs by dabbing dots on ware). May trace design prior to painting or sketch guidelines for decals and be designated SKETCH LINER (pottery & porc.). • **GED:** R4, M2, L3 • **SVP:** 2-4 yrs • **Academic:** Ed=N, Eng=G • **Work Field:** 262 • **MPSMS:** 889 • **Aptitudes:** G3, V4, N4, S2, P2, Q5, K4, F2, M4, E5, C2 • **Temperaments:** F, J, T • **Physical:** V=L, H=N, L=S, H • **Work Env:** I • **Salary:** 3 • **Outlook:** 2

PAINTER, SIGN (any ind.) • D.O.T. #970.381-026 • OES #89911 • LETTERER. Designs, lays out, and paints letters and designs to create signs, using measuring and drawing instruments, brushes, and handtools: Reads work orders to determine type of sign specified, work procedures, and materials required. Sketches design on paper, using drawing instruments, such as angles, rulers, and shading pencils. Lays out design on plastic, silk, or tin to prepare stencil, or on paper to draw pounce I pattern, using measuring and drawing instruments. Sketches or follows pattern to draw design or lettering onto objects, such as billboards and trucks, using stencils and measuring and drawing instruments. Brushes paint, lacquer, enamel, or japan over stencil, or paints details, background, and shading to fill in out lines or sketch of sign, using paintbrush or airbrush. When painting window signs, draws outline of sign on outside window, using chalk, or dusts pounce pattern

to mark outline and paints inside of window following drawing or outline, using brush. When making gold or silver leaf signs, forms sign by either of following methods: (1) Paints sign, positions leaf over fresh paint, and removes excess leaf, after sign has dried, using cotton swab and knife blade; (2) Paints inside of window with watersize (glue), applies leaf, and paints sign in reverse on back of leaf, using paintbrush or airbrush. May cut out letters and apply background coating to construct and prepare signs, using tinning shears. May project layout image on paper and trace outline of design, using projector and electric needle. May specialize in maintenance of signs along railroad right-of-way and be called PAINTER, SIGN, MAINTENANCE (r. r. trans.). • **GED:** R4, M3, L3 • **SVP:** 2-4 yrs • **Academic:** Ed=H, Eng=G • **Work Field:** 262 • **MPSMS:** 889 • **Aptitudes:** G3, V3, N3, S3, P2, Q4, K3, F2, M2, E3, C2 • **Temperaments:** J, M, T • **Physical:** V=G, H=N, L=L, W, C, H • **Work Env:** B, R • **Salary:** 4 • **Outlook:** 2

SIGN WRITER, HAND (any ind.) • D.O.T. #970.281-022 • OES #89911 • CARD WRITER, HAND; SHOW-CARD WRITER. Writes, paints, or prints signs or showcards used for display or other purposes, using brushes. May cut out letters and signs for display purposes from wallboard or cardboard, by hand or machines, such as electrically powered jigsaw or bandsaw. • **GED:** R4, M3, L3 • **SVP:** 6 mos-1 yr • **Academic:** Ed=N, Eng=G • **Work Field:** 262 • **MPSMS:** 889 • **Aptitudes:** G3, V3, N4, S3, P3, Q3, K3, F3, M3, E5, C2 • **Temperaments:** J, T • **Physical:** V=L, H=N, L=S, H • **Work Env:** I • **Salary:** 3 • **Outlook:** 2

SPOTTER, PHOTOGRAPHIC (photofinish.) • D.O.T. #970.381-034 • OES #89914 • Covers or spots out imperfections on photographic prints, using gloved finger, brush, or pencil: Positions print under viewing light or on illuminated table and examines print to detect defects, such as surface blemishes, dust spots, and uneven margins. Selects premixed paint or mixes paint, using color charts, when repairing color prints. Applies paint to defective area of color print, using gloved finger or artists' brush. Shades light areas on black-and-white prints, using pencil. Rubs surface of photograph with cloth to remove debris and reduce gloss. Trims edges of print to enhance appearance, using scissors or paper cutter. Places prints in customer bag and records number per bag or mounts print in specified frame. May retouch film negatives and be called NEGATIVE SPOTTER. • **GED:** R3, M2, L1 • **SVP:** 6 mos-1 yr • **Academic:** Ed=N, Eng=N • **Work Field:** 262 • **MPSMS:** 867 • **Aptitudes:** G3, V4, N4, S4, P2, Q4, K3, F2, M4, E5, C2 • **Temperaments:** J, T • **Physical:** V=G, H=N, L=S, H • **Work Env:** I • **Salary:** 1 • **Outlook:** 4

STRIPER, HAND (any ind.) • D.O.T. #740.484-010 • OES #93947 • Paints stripes, letters, or decorative edges on bicycle frames, motorcycle fenders and tanks, utensils, or other stamped products, using handbrushes and enamel or lacquer. Marks area to be stamped, lettered, or decorated, using rule or template. Mixes paint and matches colors according to specifications, or uses prepared paints. • **GED:** R3, M2, L2 • **SVP:** 1-2 yrs • **Academic:** Ed=N, Eng=N • **Work Field:** 262 • **MPSMS:** 556, 595 • **Aptitudes:** G3, V4, N4, S4, P3, Q4, K3, F3, M3, E5, C3 • **Temperaments:** R, T • **Stress:** T • **Physical:** V=L, H=N, L=L, H • **Work Env:** I • **Salary:** 4 • **Outlook:** 2

TYPE COPYIST (mach. mfg.) • D.O.T. #970.381-042 • OES #89911 • Draws and cuts out type characters of plastic, such as letters, numbers, and logos for use in manufacturing phototypesetting type disks, using drawing and cutting instruments: Searches reference sources to determine availability of characters in type style specified on orders. Reproduces reference copies of new characters required to obtain working copies, using automatic film developer. Places tracing paper over working copies, and traces and draws new characters, using pencil and triangle. Measures width, thickness, and spacing of characters, using optical and other measuring instruments, and pencils in or erases markings of characters as necessary to arrive at specified size and spacing requirements. Places tracing paper with finalized characters in light box, positions plastic sheets over light box, and cuts plastic following character outlines on tracing paper to obtain plastic characters, using cutting tools and metal guides. Records identity of characters on card for filing with reference source and routes characters for further processing. • **GED:** R4, M3, L3 • **SVP:** 2-4 yrs • **Academic:** Ed=H, Eng=G • **Work Field:** 262 • **MPSMS:**

752 • Aptitudes: G3, V3, N3, S3, P2, Q2, K2, F2, M3, E5, C4 •   I • Salary: 3 • Outlook: 3
Temperaments: J, T • Physical: V=L, H=N, L=S, H • Work Env:

01.07 Elemental Arts

Workers in this group entertain or divert people by announcing features or performing acts at carnivals or amusement parks, or by conducting person-to-person consultations with people to predict their future or tell them other things about themselves. They work with traveling carnivals or circuses, or at permanently located amusement parks. Some are self-employed, conducting interviews in their homes or giving consultations by mail.

✔ **What kind of work would you do?**
Your work activities would depend upon your specific job. For example, you might:

- introduce circus acts and signal the start and finish of each act.
- shout show attractions to the passing public.
- analyze handwriting to determine personal characteristics.
- guess weight of people at an amusement park or carnival.

✔ **What skills and abilities do you need for this kind of work?**
To do this kind of work, you must be able to:

- attract the attention of others by speaking, gesturing or shouting.
- be at ease when appearing before an audience.
- speak clearly, using easily understood terms, and offering your information with sincerity when dealing with clients on a person-to-person basis.
- learn and apply the specialized techniques needed for such feats as fire-eating, snake charming, or sword-swallowing.

✔ **How do you know if you would like or could learn to do this kind of work?**
The following questions may give you clues about yourself as you consider this group of jobs.

- Have you played Santa Claus? Have you worn a costume as a mascot? Did you enjoy doing this type of activity?
- Have you played games involving reading the minds of others? Do you feel you have psychic powers?
- Have you performed card tricks for friends? Do you enjoy amusing others?
- Have you worked at a school or community fair or carnival? Were you able to get people to play the games or watch the shows?

✔ **How can you prepare for and enter this kind of work?**
Occupations in this group usually require education and/or training extending from a short demonstration to over six months, depending upon the specific kind of work. Many of these jobs require only brief training for workers to become familiar with the work setting and tasks. Greater training and practice in areas such as astrology, numerology, or graphology are necessary for some jobs. Other jobs, such as ring conductor in a circus, require related work experience. Some workers are hired if they fit a specific costume. Some people develop the necessary skills through practicing their hobbies such as snake handling, or telling fortunes.

✔ **What else should you consider about these jobs?**
Many of these jobs are seasonal or temporary with few chances for promotion. Jobs with circuses and other amusement shows require frequent travel.

If you think you would like to do this kind of work, look at the job titles listed below.

©1991, JIST Works, Inc. • Indianapolis, IN

GOE: 01.07.01 Psychic Science

GRAPHOLOGIST (amuse. & rec.) • D.O.T. #159.247-018 • OES #34056 • Analyses handwriting to appraise personal characteristics: Obtains handwriting specimen to observe overall appearance of writing and detailed formation of letters. Measures height of letters and slant of writing, using calibrated templates. Observes individual writing strokes to determine unique or distinguishing characteristics which categorize subject. Interprets findings according to theories of handwriting analysis. May use psychogram to plot writing characteristics. • **GED:** R3, M3, L3 • **SVP:** 3-6 mos • **Academic:** Ed=N, Eng=G • **Work Field:** 297 • **MPSMS:** 910 • **Aptitudes:** G3, V3, N4, S4, P2, Q4, K4, F4, M4, E5, C5 • **Temperaments:** F, J, P • **Stress:** E • **Physical:** V=L, H=L, L=S • **Work Env:** I • **Salary:** 3 • **Outlook:** 1

GOE: 01.07.02 Announcing

ANNOUNCER (amuse. & rec.) • D.O.T. #159.347-010 • OES #34021 • PUBLIC-ADDRESS ANNOUNCER. Announces information of interest to patrons of sporting and other entertainment events, using public address system: Announces program and substitutions or other changes to patrons. Informs patrons of coming events or emergency calls. May observe sporting event to make running commentary, such as play-by-play description or explanation of official decisions. May speak extemporaneously to audience on items of interest, such as background and past record of players. May read prepared script to describe acts or tricks during performance. May furnish information concerning play to SCOREBOARD OPERATOR (amuse. & rec.). • **GED:** R4, M2, L4 • **SVP:** 1-2 yrs • **Academic:** Ed=H, Eng=G • **Work Field:** 282, 297 • **MPSMS:** 914, 919 • **Aptitudes:** G2, V2, N4, S3, P4, Q3, K4, F4, M4, E5, C4 • **Temperaments:** M, P • **Stress:** E • **Physical:** V=N, H=L, L=S • **Work Env:** I • **Salary:** 3 • **Outlook:** 2

GOE: 01.07.03 Entertaining

AMUSEMENT PARK ENTERTAINER (amuse. & rec.) • D.O.T. #159.647-010 • OES #34056 • Entertains audience in amusement park by exhibiting special skills. Designated according to specialty act performed as FIRE EATER (amuse. & rec.); HYPNOTIST (amuse. & rec.); ORGAN GRINDER (amuse. & rec.); PHRENOLOGIST (amuse. & rec.); PHYSIOGNOMIST (amuse. & rec.); SNAKE CHARMER (amuse. & rec.); SWORD SWALLOWER (amuse. & rec.). May be designated SIDE-SHOW ENTERTAINER (amuse. & rec.). May entertain in nightclubs and similar establishments. May entertain for live variety show or for television production. • **GED:** R2, M2, L2 • **SVP:** 2-30 days • **Academic:** Ed=N, Eng=G • **Work Field:** 297 • **MPSMS:** 919 • **Aptitudes:** G3, V3, N4, S4, P4, Q5, K4, F4, M4, E5, C5 • **Temperaments:** F, P • **Stress:** E • **Physical:** V=N, H=L, L=S, W, H • **Work Env:** B • **Salary:** 3 • **Outlook:** 1

01.08 Modeling

Workers in this group appear before a camera or live audience in non-speaking capacities. They stand in for actors and take part in crowd scenes in television or motion picture productions. They show clothing, hair styles, and other products, appear in fashion shows and other public or private product exhibitions, and pose for artists and photographers. They work for manufacturers, or wholesale, and retail establishments. Some are employed by motion picture and television studios, nightclubs, and other entertainment facilities. Modeling instructors work for public or private schools. Many of these workers are self-employed, or obtain job assignments through model agencies or unions which represent persons in the entertainment industry.

✔ **What kind of work would you do?**
Your work activities would depend upon your specific job. For example, you might:

- model clothing for a designer or department store.
- pose for a photographer or an artist.
- stand in place for a movie star so cameras can be adjusted.

- parade across a stage to display costumes as background for a chorus line.

✔ **What skills and abilities do you need for this kind of work?**
To do this kind of work, you must be able to:

- follow directions for movements and poses to express certain emotions or convey various visual impressions.
- appear before an audience with poise and self-assurance.

- stand, sit, walk, or pose in front of an audience, photographer, or artist for long periods of time.

✔ **How do you know if you would like or could learn to do this kind of work?**
The following questions may give you clues about yourself as you consider this group of jobs.

- Have you modeled for an artist or photographer? Can you hold a pose for a half-hour or longer?

- Have you modeled clothes in a fashion show? Do you enjoy appearing before groups?

✔ **How can you prepare for and enter this kind of work?**

Occupations in this group usually require education and/or training extending from a short demonstration to over six months, depending upon the specific kind of work. Training for many of these jobs is usually brief and given on the job. Modeling schools offer courses in graceful movement and personal grooming.

Workers are often hired because of their appearance or size. Workers may be under contract to a booking agency or may obtain work on their own.

Models may work only part-time until the quality of their work is recognized. Workers in this group often hold other jobs.

✔ **What else should you consider about these jobs?**

Many of these jobs are short-term or seasonal and offer little opportunity for advancement. A few models may be in constant demand and earn large salaries.

If you think you would like to do this kind of work, look at the job title listed below.

GOE: 01.08.01 Personal Appearance, Modeling

MODEL, ARTISTS' (any ind.) • D.O.T. #961.667-010 • OES #49032 • Poses as subject for paintings, sculptures, and other types of art for translation into plastic or pictorial values by PAINTER (profess. & kin.) or SCULPTOR (profess. & kin.). • **GED:** R3, M1, L1 • **SVP:** 30 days-3 mos • **Academic:** Ed=N, Eng=N • **Work Field:** 291 • **MPSMS:** 750 • **Aptitudes:** G3, V4, N5, S4, P5, Q5, K4, F4, M4, E4, C4 • **Temperaments:** F, P • **Stress:** E • **Physical:** V=N, H=N, L=S, H • **Work Env:** I • **Salary:** 2 • **Outlook:** 1

Scientific 02

An interest in discovering, collecting, and analyzing information about the natural world and applying scientific research findings to problems in medicine, the life sciences, and the natural sciences.

You can satisfy this interest by working with the knowledge and processes of the sciences. You may enjoy researching and developing new knowledge in mathematics. Perhaps solving problems in the physical or life sciences would appeal to you. You may wish to study medicine and help humans or animals. You could work as a practitioner in the health field. You may want to work with scientific equipment and procedures. You could seek a job in research or testing laboratories.

02.01 Physical Sciences

Workers in this group are concerned mostly with non-living things, such as chemicals, rocks, metals, mathematics, movements of the earth and the stars, etc. They conduct scientific studies and perform other activities requiring a knowledge of math, physics, or chemistry. Some workers investigate, discover, and test new theories. Some look for ways to develop new or improved materials or processes for use in production and construction. Others do research in such fields as geology, astronomy, oceanography, and computer science. Workers base their conclusions on information that can be measured or proved. Industries, government agencies, or large universities employ most of these workers in their research facilities.

✔ **What kind of work would you do?**
Your work activities would depend upon your specific job. For example, you might:

- study (aerial) photographs for indications of possible oil or gas deposits.
- examine rock formations to develop theories about the earth and its history.
- use information about wind, temperature, humidity, and land formations to predict weather.
- help solve environmental problems such as pollution.
- develop chemical formulas for making fine perfumes.
- conduct experiments to develop new metals.
- gather and interpret information about movements in the earth.
- use advanced math to solve very complex problems.

✔ **What skills and abilities do you need for this kind of work?**
To do this kind of work, you must be able to:

- use logic or scientific thinking to deal with many different kinds of problems.
- make decisions based on information that can be measured or verified.
- understand and express complex, technical, and scientific information.
- recognize textures, colors, shapes, and sizes.
- make decisions using your own judgments.
- gather and interpret data about earth movements.
- use non-verbal symbols (such as numbers) to express ideas or solve problems.

The above statements may not apply to every job in this group.

✔ **How do you know if you would like or could learn to do this kind of work?**
The following questions may give you clues about yourself as you consider this group of jobs.

- Have you taken courses in earth science or space science?
- Have you read articles or stories about scientific expeditions? Do you understand scientific terminology?
- Have you collected rocks or minerals as a hobby? Can you recognize differences in ores or mineral deposits?

- Have you watched television weather shows? Do you understand the terms and symbols used?
- Have you owned a chemistry set or microscope? Do you enjoy testing new ideas with this type of equipment?

✔ **How can you prepare for and enter this kind of work?**
Occupations in this group usually require education and/or training extending from four years to over ten years, depending upon the specific kind of work. A bachelor's degree with a major in mathematics or a specific physical science is the minimum requirement for entrance into this type of work. Graduate degrees are needed for most research work or college teaching. A master's degree may qualify an individual for work in laboratory teaching or applied research in a college, university, or industrial setting. Advanced studies or a Ph.D. are usually required for work in basic research. Important courses include algebra, geometry, advanced math, physics, and earth and space science. Chemistry and technical writing courses are helpful and in some cases required.

✔ **What else should you consider about these jobs?**
Physical scientists may be required to work irregular hours to meet research deadlines or to study phenomena. Frequent relocation or travel to remote areas may be required. Workers should keep informed of developments in their field by attending seminars, reading professional journals, and being active in professional organizations.

If you think you would like to do this kind of work, look at the job titles listed below.

GOE: 02.01.01 Theoretical Research, Physical Sciences

CHEMIST (profess. & kin.) • D.O.T. #022.061-010 • OES #24105 • Conducts research, analysis, synthesis, and experimentation on liquid, solid and gaseous materials, substances, and compounds for purposes of product and process development, quality control, quantitative and qualitative analysis, improvement of analytical techniques, methodologies and procedures, and application of new products and instrumentation: Devises new equipment, and develops formulas, processes, techniques, and methods for solution of technical problems. Analyzes organic and inorganic compounds to determine chemical and physical properties, utilizing techniques, such as chromatography, spectroscopy and spectrophotometry. Induces changes in composition of substances by introduction of heat, light, energy, and chemical catalysts. Conducts research on products, such as paints, coatings, plastics, rubber, glass, textiles, metals, resins, adhesives, leather, dyes, detergents, or petroleum. Conducts research into relationship between molecular, chemical, and physical properties of substances and compounds. Confers with scientists and engineers regarding research of solutions to problems, and prepares technical reports for management. Prepares standards and specifications for processes, facilities, products, and tests. May be designated according to specialty in chemistry as CHEMIST, ANALYTICAL (profess. & kin.); CHEMIST, INORGANIC (profess. & kin.); CHEMIST, ORGANIC (profess. & kin.); CHEMIST, PHYSICAL (profess. & kin.). May specialize in environmental problems [CHEMIST, POLLUTION CONTROL (profess. & kin.)]. • GED: R6, M6, L5 • SVP: 4-10 yrs • Academic: Ed=B, Eng=G • Work Field: 211, 251 • MPSMS: 723, 729 • Aptitudes: G1, V1, N1, S2, P2, Q2, K3, F3, M3, E5, C3 • Temperaments: D, M, T, V • Physical: V=N, H=N, L=S, H • Work Env: I • Salary: 5 • Outlook: 3

COMPUTER-APPLICATIONS ENGINEER (profess. & kin.) • D.O.T. #020.062-010 • OES #22127 • Formulates mathematical models of systems, and sets up and controls analog or hybrid computer system to solve scientific and engineering problems: Consults with originator of problem to determine sources and methods of data collection and methods of determining values of variables, or examines and studies physical models, graphic representations, and verbal descriptions of problem to apply knowledge of scientific discipline and define problem. Prepares mathematical model of problem, and draws data-flow chart to indicate mathematical steps required in solving problem. Computes voltage and time scales to convert mathematical equation into computer equation to obtain potentiometer settings. Draws computer-circuit diagrams to indicate connections between components and their values, and wires patchboard onto computer. Observes behavior of variables on output devices, such as plotters, recorders, digital voltmeters, oscilloscopes, digital displays and readouts, to obtain solution of problem. Prepares technical report for originator, describing step by step solution of problem. Develops new techniques for solving problems, and prepares articles for publication in scientific journals. • GED: R6, M6, L6 • SVP: 4-10 yrs • Academic: Ed=B, Eng=G • Work Field: 244, 251 • MPSMS: 700, 710, 723 • Aptitudes: G1, V1, N1, S1, P2, Q2, K4, F4, M4, E5, C5 • Temperaments: D, M, V • Stress: A • Physical: V=L, H=L, L=S • Work Env: I • Salary: 5 • Outlook: 5

GEOGRAPHER (profess. & kin.) • D.O.T. #029.067-010 • OES #24199 • Studies nature and use of areas of earth's surface, relating and interpreting interactions of physical and cultural phenomena: Conducts research on physical and climatic aspects of area or region, making direct observation of landforms, climates, soils, plants, and animals within area under study and incorporating available knowledge from related scientific fields, such as physics, geology, oceanography, meteorology, and biology. Studies human activities within given area, such as ethnic distribution, economic activity, and political organization. Acts as adviser or consultant to governments and international organizations on subjects, such as economic exploitation of regions and determination of ethnic and natural boundaries between nations or administrative areas. May use surveying equipment or meteorological instruments. May construct and interpret maps, graphs, and diagrams. May specialize in particular branch of cultural geography, such as economic, political, urban, social, or historical geography. • **GED:** R6, M6, L6 • **SVP:** 2-4 yrs • **Academic:** Ed=M, Eng=G • **Work Field:** 251 • **MPSMS:** 729 • **Aptitudes:** G1, V1, N2, S3, P3, Q4, K4, F4, M4, E5, C4 • **Temperaments:** D, J, M, V • **Physical:** V=N, H=N, L=S, H • **Work Env:** B, C, H, W • **Salary:** 4 • **Outlook:** 2

GEOLOGIST (profess. & kin.) • D.O.T. #024.061-018 • OES #24111 • Studies composition, structure, and history of earth's crust: Examines rocks, minerals, and fossil remains to identify and determine sequence of processes affecting development of earth. Applies knowledge of chemistry, physics, biology, and mathematics to explain these phenomena and to help locate mineral, geothermal, and petroleum deposits and under ground water resources. Studies ocean bottom. Applies geological knowledge to engineering problems encountered in construction projects, such as dams, tunnels, and large buildings. Studies fossil plants and animals to determine their evolutionary sequence and age. Prepares geologic reports and maps, interprets research data, and recommends further study or action. May specialize in area of study and be designated GEOMORPHOLOGIST (profess. & kin.); OCEANOGRAPHER, GEOLOGICAL (profess. & kin.); PHOTOGEOLOGIST (profess. & kin.). May conduct or participate in environmental studies and prepare environmental reports. Workers applying principles of rock and soil mechanics for engineering projects may be designated GEOLOGICAL ENGINEER (profess. & kin.). Workers applying all branches of geologic knowledge to conditions that affect planning, design, construction, operation and safety to engineering projects may be designated ENGINEERING GEOLOGIST (profess. & kin.). • **GED:** R6, M6, L6 • **SVP:** 4-10 yrs • **Academic:** Ed=B, Eng=G • **Work Field:** 251 • **MPSMS:** 725 • **Aptitudes:** G1, V1, N1, S2, P2, Q3, K3, F4, M3, E4, C3 • **Temperaments:** J, M, T, V • **Physical:** V=N, H=N, L=S, W, C, S, H • **Work Env:** B • **Salary:** 5 • **Outlook:** 3

GEOPHYSICIST (profess. & kin.) • D.O.T. #024.061 030 • OES #24111 • Studies physical aspects of earth, including its atmosphere and hydrosphere: Investigates and measures seismic, gravitational, electrical, thermal, and magnetic forces affecting earth, utilizing principles of physics, mathematics, and chemistry. Analyzes data obtained to compute shape of earth, estimate composition and structure of earth's interior, determine flow pattern of ocean tides and currents, study physical properties of atmosphere, and help locate petroleum and mineral deposits. Investigates origin and activity of glaciers, volcanoes, and earthquakes. Compiles data to prepare navigational charts and maps, predict atmospheric conditions, prepare environmental reports, and establish water supply and flood-control programs. May study specific aspect of geophysics and be designated GEOMAGNETICIAN (profess. & kin.); GLACIOLOGIST (profess.& kin.); OCEANOGRAPHER, PHYSICAL (profess. & kin.); TECTONOPHYSICIST (profess. & kin.); VOLCANOLOGIST (profess. & kin.). • **GED:** R6, M5, L5 • **SVP:** 4-10 yrs • **Academic:** Ed=B, Eng=G • **Work Field:** 251 • **MPSMS:** 725 • **Aptitudes:** G1, V1, N1, S2, P2, Q3, K3, F4, M3, E4, C4 • **Temperaments:** D, J, M, T, V • **Physical:** V=L, H=N, L=S, W, H • **Work Env:** B • **Salary:** 5 • **Outlook:** 1

HYDROLOGIST (profess. & kin.) • D.O.T. #024.061-034 • OES #24111 • Studies distribution, disposition, and development of waters of land areas, including form and intensity of precipitation, and modes of return to ocean and atmosphere: Maps and charts water flow and disposition of sediment. Measures changes in water volume due to evaporation and melting of snow. Studies storm occurrences and nature and movement of glaciers, and determines rate of ground absorption and ultimate disposition of water. Evaluates data obtained in reference to such problems as flood and drought forecasting, soil and water conservation programs, and planning water supply, water power, flood control, drainage, irrigation, crop production, and inland navigation projects. • **GED:** R6, M6, L6 • **SVP:** 4-10 yrs • **Academic:** Ed=B, Eng=G • **Work Field:** 251 • **MPSMS:** 725 • **Aptitudes:** G1, V1, N1, S2, P3, Q3, K3, F3, M3, E4, C4 • **Temperaments:** D, J, M, T, V • **Physical:** V=L, H=N, L=S, W, H • **Work Env:** B • **Salary:** 5 • **Outlook:** 2

MATHEMATICIAN (profess. & kin.) • D.O.T. #020.067-014 • OES #25319 • Conducts research in fundamental mathematics and in application of mathematical techniques to science, management, and other fields, and solves or directs solutions to problems in various fields by mathematical methods: Conducts research in such branches of mathematics as algebra, geometry, number theory, logic, and topology, and studies and tests hypotheses and alternative theories. Conceives and develops ideas for application of mathematics to wide variety of fields including science, engineering, military planning, electronics data processing, and management. Applies mathematics or mathematical methods to solution of problems in research, development, production, logistics, and other functional areas, utilizing knowledge of subject or field to which applied, such as physics, engineering, astronomy, biology, economics, business and industrial management, or cryptography. Performs computations, applies methods of numerical analysis, and operates or directs operation of desk calculators and mechanical and electronic computation machines, analyzers, and plotters in solving problems in support of mathematical, scientific, or industrial research activity. Acts as advisor or consultant to research personnel concerning mathematical methods and applications. May be designated according to function as MATHEMATICIAN, APPLIED (profess. & kin.); MATHEMATICIAN, RESEARCH (profess. & kin.). • **GED:** R6, M6, L6 • **SVP:** 4-10 yrs • **Academic:** Ed=M, Eng=G • **Work Field:** 251 • **MPSMS:** 721 • **Aptitudes:** G1, V2, N1, S1, P4, Q4, K4, F4, M4, E5, C5 • **Temperaments:** D, J, M, T • **Physical:** V=N, H=N, L=S, H • **Work Env:** I • **Salary:** 5 • **Outlook:** 3

METEOROLOGIST (profess. & kin.) • D.O.T. #025.062-010 • OES #24108 • Analyzes and interprets meteorological data gathered by surface and upper-air stations, satellites, and radar to prepare reports and forecasts for public and other users: Studies and interprets synoptic reports, maps, photographs, and prognostic charts to predict long and short range weather conditions. Issues weather information to media and other users over teletype machine or telephone. Prepares special forecasts and briefings for those involved in air and sea transportation, agriculture, fire prevention, and air-pollution control. Issues hurricane and severe storm warnings. May direct forecasting services at weather station. May conduct basic or applied research in meteorology. May establish and staff observation stations. • **GED:** R5, M5, L5 • **SVP:** 2-4 yrs • **Academic:** Ed=A, Eng=G • **Work Field:** 251 • **MPSMS:** 725 • **Aptitudes:** G2, V2, N2, S2, P2, Q2, K4, F4, M3, E5, C4 • **Temperaments:** D, J, M • **Physical:** V=L, H=L, L=L • **Work Env:** I • **Salary:** 4 • **Outlook:** 3

MINERALOGIST (profess. & kin.) • D.O.T. #024.061-038 • OES #24111 • Examines, analyzes, and classifies minerals, gems, and precious stones: Isolates specimen from ore, rocks, or matrices. Makes microscopic examination to determine shape, surface markings, and other physical characteristics. Performs physical and chemical tests and makes X-ray examinations to determine composition of specimen and type of crystalline structure. Identifies and classifies samples. Develops data and theories on mode of origin, occurrence, and possible uses of minerals. • **GED:** R6, M6, L6 • **SVP:** 4-10 yrs • **Academic:** Ed=B, Eng=G • **Work Field:** 251 • **MPSMS:** 725 • **Aptitudes:** G1, V1, N2, S2, P3, Q3, K3, F3, M3, E4, C3 • **Temperaments:** D, J, M, T • **Physical:** V=L, H=N, L=S, W, H • **Work Env:** B • **Salary:** 5 • **Outlook:** 2

PETROLOGIST (profess. & kin.) • D.O.T. #024.061-046 • OES #24111 • Investigates composition, structure, and history of rock masses forming earth's crust. Applies findings to such fields of investigation as causes of formations, breaking down and weathering, chemical composition and forms of deposition of sedimentary rocks, methods of eruption, and origin and causes of metamorphosis. • **GED:** R6, M6, L5 • **SVP:** 4-10 yrs • **Academic:** Ed=B, Eng=G • **Work Field:** 251 • **MPSMS:** 725 • **Aptitudes:** G1, V1, N2, S2, P3, Q3, K3, F3, M3, E4, C3 • **Temperaments:** D, J, M, T • **Physical:** V=L, H=N, L=S, W, H • **Work Env:** B • **Salary:** 5 • **Outlook:** 3

PHYSICIST (profess. & kin.) • D.O.T. #023.061-014 • OES #24102 • Conducts research into phases of physical phenomena, develops theories and laws on basis of observation and experiments, and devises methods to apply laws and theories of physics to industry, medicine, and other fields: Performs experiments with masers, lasers, cyclotrons, betatrons, telescopes, mass spectrometers, electron microscopes, and other equipment to observe structure and properties of matter, transformation and propagation of energy, relationships between matter and energy, and other physical phenomena. Describes and expresses observations and conclusions in mathematical terms. Devises procedures for physical testing of materials. Conducts instrumental analyses to determine physical properties of materials. May specialize in one or more branches of physics and be designated as PHYSICIST, ACOUSTICS (profess. & kin.); PHYSICIST, ASTROPHYSICS (profess. & kin.); PHYSICIST, ATOMIC, ELECTRONIC AND MOLECULAR (profess. & kin.); PHYSICIST, CRYOGENICS (profess. & kin.); PHYSICIST, ELECTRICITY AND MAGNETISM (profess. & kin.); PHYSICIST, FLUIDS (profess. & kin.). Additional titles: PHYSICIST, LIGHT AND OPTICS (profess. & kin.); PHYSICIST, NUCLEAR (profess. & kin.); PHYSICIST, PLASMA (profess. & kin.); PHYSICIST, SOLID EARTH (profess. & kin.); PHYSICIST, SOLID STATE (profess. & kin.); PHYSICIST, THERMODYNAMICS (profess. & kin.). • **GED:** R6, M6, L6 • **SVP:** 4-10 yrs • **Academic:** Ed=M, Eng=G • **Work Field:** 251 • **MPSMS:** 724 • **Aptitudes:** G1, V1, N1, S1, P1, Q3, K3, F3, M3, E5, C2 • **Temperaments:** J, M, T • **Physical:** V=N, H=N, L=S, H • **Work Env:** I • **Salary:** 5 • **Outlook:** 2

SEISMOLOGIST (profess. & kin.) • D.O.T. #024.061-050 • OES #24111 • Studies and interprets seismic data to locate earthquakes and earthquake faults: Reviews, analyzes, and interprets data from seismographs and geophysical instruments. Establishes existence and activity of faults, and direction, motion, and stress of earth movements before, during, and after earthquakes. Conducts research on seismic forces affecting deformative movements of earth. May issue maps or reports indicating areas of seismic risk to existing or proposed construction or development. • **GED:** R6, M6, L6 • **SVP:** 4-10 yrs • **Academic:** Ed=B, Eng=G • **Work Field:** 251 • **MPSMS:** 725 • **Aptitudes:** G1, V1, N1, S2, P3, Q3, K3, F3, M3, E4, C3 • **Temperaments:** D, M, T, V • **Physical:** V=L, H=N, L=S, W, H • **Work Env:** B • **Salary:** 5 • **Outlook:** 2

GOE: 02.01.02 Technology

ENVIRONMENTAL ANALYST (profess. & kin.) • D.O.T. #029.081-010 • OES #24199 • ENVIRONMENTAL SCIENTIST. Conducts research studies to develop theories or methods of abating or controlling sources of environmental pollutants, utilizing knowledge of principles and concepts of various scientific and engineering disciplines: Determines data collection methods to be employed in research projects and surveys. Plans and develops research models, using knowledge of mathematical, statistical, and physical science concepts and approaches. Identifies and analyzes sources of pollution to determine their effects. Collects and synthesizes data derived from pollution emission measurements, atmospheric monitoring, meteorological and mineralogical information, and soil or water samples. Prepares graphs, charts, and statistical models from synthesized data, using knowledge of mathematical, statistical, and engineering analysis techniques. Analyzes data to assess pollution problems, establish standards, and develop approaches for control of pollution. May be designated according to aspect of environment in which engaged as AIR POLLUTION ANALYST (profess. & kin.); SOILS ANALYST (profess. & kin.); WATER QUALITY ANALYST (profess. & kin.). • **GED:** R6, M6, L6 • **SVP:** 4-10 yrs • **Academic:** Ed=B, Eng=G • **Work Field:** 244, 251 • **MPSMS:** 719 • **Aptitudes:** G1, V1, N1, S2, P2, Q3, K3, F3, M3, E4, C4 • **Temperaments:** D, M, T • **Physical:** V=L, H=N, L=S, W, H • **Work Env:** I • **Salary:** 5 •

Outlook: 3

GEOLOGIST, PETROLEUM (petrol. production) • D.O.T. #024.061-022 • OES #24111 • Explores and charts stratigraphic arrangement and structure of earth to locate gas and oil deposits: Studies well logs, analyzes cores and cuttings from well drillings, and interprets data obtained by electrical or radioactive well logging and other subsurface surveys to identify earth strata. Examines aerial photographs, evaluates results of geophysical prospecting, and prepares surface and subsurface maps and diagrams depicting stratigraphic arrangement and composition of earth and probable deposits of gas and oil. Recommends acquisition, retention, or release of property leases or contracts. Estimates oil reserves in proven or prospective fields, and consults with PETROLEUM ENGINEERS (petrol. production) concerning drilling and production methods. May direct drilling of shallow exploratory wells. • **GED:** R6, M6, L5 • **SVP:** 4-10 yrs • **Academic:** Ed=B, Eng=G • **Work Field:** 251 • **MPSMS:** 725 • **Aptitudes:** G1, V1, N2, S1, P2, Q3, K4, F3, M4, E5, C5 • **Temperaments:** J, M, P, T, V • **Physical:** V=L, H=N, L=S, W, C, S, H • **Work Env:** B, C, H, W • **Salary:** 5 • **Outlook:** 3

MATERIALS SCIENTIST (profess. & kin.) • D.O.T. #029.081-014 • OES #24199 • Conducts scientific studies for understanding, characterizing and developing materials leading to potential uses for the benefit of science and emerging technologies: Conducts programs for studying structures and properties of various materials, such as metals, alloys, ceramics, semiconductors and polymers to obtain research data. Plans experimental laboratory production of materials having special characteristics to confirm feasibility of processes and techniques for potential users. Prepares reports of materials studies for information of other scientists and requestors. May guide technical staff engaged in developing materials for specific use in projected product or device. • **GED:** R6, M6, L5 • **SVP:** 2-4 yrs • **Academic:** Ed=B, Eng=S • **Work Field:** 251 • **MPSMS:** 722, 723, 724 • **Aptitudes:** G1, V1, N1, S1, P1, Q2, K3, F3, M3, E4, C3 • **Temperaments:** J, M, V • **Physical:** V=L, H=N, L=S, H • **Work Env:** I • **Salary:** 4 • **Outlook:** 4

METALLURGIST, PHYSICAL (profess. & kin.) • D.O.T. #011.061-022 • OES #22105 • Investigates and conducts experiments concerned with physical characteristics, properties, and processing of metals to develop new alloys, applications, and methods of commercially fabricating products from metals: Conducts microscopic, X-ray, X-ray diffraction, and spectroscopic studies of metals and alloys, such as steel, cast iron, and nonferrous alloys, to determine their physical characteristics, such as crystal structure, dispersion of alloy particles through basic metal, and presence of impurities, fractures, and other defects in metal samples. Develops melting, hot-working, cold-working, and heat-treating processes to obtain desired characteristics, such as ductility, malleability, elongation ability, durability, and hardness. Tests alloys in tension, compression, impact, bending, or fatigue devices to study physical characteristics for manufacturing purposes or determine compliance with manufacturing specifications and standards. Consults with engineers and officials to develop methods of manufacturing alloys at minimum costs. May specialize in particular area of physical metallurgy, such as development of improved techniques and materials, for use in production of pressed metallic-powder products. • **GED:** R6, M6, L6 • **SVP:** 4-10 yrs • **Academic:** Ed=B, Eng=G • **Work Field:** 244, 251 • **MPSMS:** 708, 711, 723 • **Aptitudes:** G1, V1, N1, S2, P3, Q3, K3, F3, M3, E4, C3 • **Temperaments:** D, M, T, V • **Physical:** V=L, H=N, L=L, H • **Work Env:** I • **Salary:** 5 • **Outlook:** 3

PROJECT MANAGER, ENVIRONMENTAL RESEARCH (profess. & kin.) • D.O.T. #029.167-014 • OES #13017 • Plans, directs, and coordinates activities of staff involved in developing procedures, equipment, and techniques to solve pollution problems, using scientific research methods: Schedules and as signs duties to staff research scientists and engineers based on evaluation of their knowledge of specific disciplines. Confers with project scientists and research engineers to formulate research plan, coordinate project activities, and establish reporting procedures. Prepares environmental research project feasibility and progress reports. Coordinates activities of research personnel conducting successive phases of problem analysis, solution proposals, and testing. Reviews technical aspects of project to assist staff and assess productivity of lines of research. Reviews project operations to insure coordination of efforts and timely submission of reports. Analyzes reports to evaluate program effectiveness and budgetary needs. Approves expenditures necessary for completion of project. Coordinates planning, testing, and operating phases to complete project. Confers with local regulatory agencies to discover local environmental quality standards, industrial practices, and new developments in pollution abatement. May provide technical assistance to agencies conducting related environmental studies. • **GED:** R5, M5, L5 • **SVP:** 4-10 yrs • **Academic:** Ed=A, Eng=S • **Work Field:** 244, 251 • **MPSMS:** 719, 729 • **Aptitudes:** G2, V2, N2, S3, P3, Q3, K4, F4, M4, E5, C5 • **Temperaments:** D, J, M, P, V • **Physical:** V=N, H=L, L=L, H • **Work Env:** I • **Salary:** 5 • **Outlook:** 4

02.02 Life Sciences

Workers in this group are concerned mostly with living things such as plants and animals. They conduct research and do experiments to expand man's knowledge of living things. Some may work on problems related to how the environment affects plant and animal life. Others may study causes of disease and ways to control disease. These workers are usually employed in the research facilities of hospitals, government agencies, industries, or universities.

✔ What kind of work would you do?
Your work activities would depend upon your specific job. For example, you might:

- prepare slides and use microscopes to study cells and cell structure.
- examine animals and specimens to study the effect of drugs on living tissue.
- study the origin and classification of plants or animals.
- conduct research to develop improved ways to process food.
- conduct experiments with growing bacteria to develop new information about diseases.
- conduct experiments by breeding animals or plants to study characteristics passed from parents to offspring.

✔ What skills and abilities do you need for this kind of work?
To do this kind of work, you must be able to:

- use logic and scientific methods to study living things.
- understand and use instructions that use work numbers, diagrams, or chemical formulas.
- learn and use knowledge about how living things function, how plants and animals are classified, and how to use laboratory and scientific equipment.
- recognize differences in size, form, shape, color, and textures.
- use eyes, hands, and fingers easily and accurately.
- do a lot of different things and change what you are doing frequently.
- make decisions using your own judgment.
- make decisions based on information that can be measured or verified.
- do things which require you to be very careful and accurate.

✔ How do you know if you would like or could learn to do this kind of work?
The following questions may give you clues about yourself as you consider this group of jobs.

- Have you studied plants in a garden, forest, or laboratory setting? Can you recognize and identify different types of plants?
- Have you been a member of a scouting or environmental protection group? Do you take part in efforts to preserve forests, parks, or campgrounds?
- Have you taken courses in biology or zoology? Do you enjoy conducting experiments which involve plants and animals?
- Have you participated in a project or hobby which involved breeding, caring for, or studying plant life?

✔ **How can you prepare for and enter this kind of work?**

Occupations in this group usually require education and/or training extending from four years to over ten years, depending upon the specific kind of work. Important academic courses include algebra, geometry, advanced math, chemistry, biological sciences. Technical writing or composition courses are helpful. A bachelor's degree with a major in biology or another life science is generally required. Graduate degrees are needed for most research work or for college teaching. A master's degree may qualify an individual for laboratory teaching. Advanced studies or a Ph.D. are usually required for work in basic research.

✔ **What else should you consider about these jobs?**

Some courses and some jobs require workers to cut up or handle tissue and waste products of humans and animals. Some jobs require living or working in remote areas such as forests or deserts.

It is important that life scientists keep informed of developments in their field by attending seminars, reading professional books and magazines, or being active in professional organizations.

If you think you would like to do this kind of work, look at the job titles listed below.

GOE: 02.02.01 Animal Specialization, Life Sciences

ANIMAL BREEDER (profess. & kin.) • D.O.T. #041.061-014 • OES #24305 • Develops systems of breeding desirable characteristics, such as improvement in strength, maturity rate, disease resistance, and meat quality, into economically important animals: Determines generic composition of animal populations, and heritability of traits, utilizing principles of genetics. Crossbreeds animals within existing strains, or crosses strains to obtain new combinations of desirable characteristics. Selects progeny having desired strains of both parents, and continues process until acceptable result is obtained. • GED: R6, M6, L6 • SVP: 4-10 yrs • Academic: Ed=A, Eng=S • Work Field: 251 • MPSMS: 732 • Aptitudes: G1, V1, N2, S3, P3, Q4, K3, F3, M4, E4, C5 • Temperaments: D, M, T, V • Physical: V=L, H=N, L=L, W, H • Work Env: I • Salary: 4 • Outlook: 3

ANIMAL SCIENTIST (profess. & kin.) • D.O.T. #040.061-014 • OES #24305 • Conducts research in selection, breeding, feeding, management, and marketing of beef and dual-purpose cattle, horses, mules, sheep, dogs, goats, and pet animals: Develops improved practices in feeding, housing, sanitation, and parasite and disease control. Controls breeding practices to improve strains of animals. May specialize in animal nutritional research and be designated ANIMAL NUTRITIONIST (profess. & kin.). May be designated according to animal specality. • GED: R6, M6, L6 • SVP: 4-10 yrs • Academic: Ed=B, Eng=G • Work Field: 251 • MPSMS: 731 • Aptitudes: G1, V1, N2, S2, P2, Q3, K3, F2, M2, E5, C4 • Temperaments: D, M, T, V • Physical: V=L, H=N, L=M, W, H • Work Env: B • Salary: 4 • Outlook: 3

BIOMEDICAL ENGINEER (profess. & kin.) • D.O.T. #019.061-010 • OES #22199 • Conducts research into biological aspects of humans or other animals to develop new theories and facts, or test, prove, or modify known theories of life systems, and to design life-support apparatus, utilizing principles of engineering and bio-behavioral sciences: Plans and conducts research concerning behavioral, biological, psychological, or other life systems. Studies engineering aspects of bio-behavioral systems of humans, utilizing knowledge of electrical, mechanical, chemical, or other engineering principles and knowledge of human anatomy and physiology. Develops mathematical models to simulate human bio-behavioral systems in order to obtain data for measuring or controlling life processes, utilizing knowledge of computer, graphics, and other related technologies. Designs and develops instruments and devices, such as artificial organs, cardiac pacemakers, or ultrasonic imaging devices, capable of assisting medical or other health-care personnel in observing, repairing, or treating physical ailments or deformities, using knowledge of materials compatible with body tissues, energy exchanges within the body, and instrumentation capable of measuring and controlling body functions. May specialize in design and development of biomedical equipment used by medical facilities and be known as CLINICAL ENGINEER (profess. & kin.). • GED: R6, M6, L5 • SVP: 4-10 yrs • Academic: Ed=B, Eng=G • Work Field: 244, 251 • MPSMS: 700, 710 • Aptitudes: G1, V1, N1, S1, P2, Q2, K3, F3, M3, E5, C3 • Temperaments: D, M, T • Physical: V=L, H=N, L=S, H • Work Env: I • Salary: 5 • Outlook: 3

DAIRY SCIENTIST (profess. & kin.) • D.O.T. #040.061-018 • OES #24305 • Conducts research in selection, breeding, feeding, and management of dairy cattle: Studies feed requirements of dairy animals and nutritive value of feed materials. Carries out experiments to determine effects of different kinds of feed and environmental conditions on quantity, quality, and nutritive value of milk produced. Develops improved practices in care and management of dairy herds and use of improved buildings and equipment. Studies physiology of reproduction and lactation, and carries out breeding programs to improve dairy breeds [ANIMAL BREEDER (agric.)]. May be designated according to specialty as DAIRY-MANAGEMENT SPECIALIST (profess. & kin.); DAIRY-NUTRITION SPECIALIST (profess. & kin.). • GED: R6, M6, L6 • SVP: 4-10 yrs • Academic: Ed=B, Eng=S • Work Field: 251 • MPSMS: 731 • Aptitudes: G1, V1, N2, S3, P3, Q4, K2, F2, M2, E4, C5 • Temperaments: D, M, T • Physical: V=L, H=N, L=L, H • Work Env: I • Salary: 5 • Outlook: 3

ENVIRONMENTAL EPIDEMIOLOGIST (gov. ser.) • D.O.T. #041.167-010 • OES #24311 • Plans, directs, and conducts studies concerned with incidence of disease in industrial settings and effects of industrial chemicals on health: Confers with industry representatives to select occupational groups for study and to arrange for collection of data concerning work history of individuals and disease concentration and mortality rates among groups. Plans methods of conducting epidemiological studies and provides detailed specifications for collecting data to personnel participating in studies. Develops codes to facilitate computer input of demographic and epidemiological data for use by data processing personnel engaged in programming epidemiological statistics. Compares statistics on causes of death among members of selected working populations with those among general population, using life-table analyses. Analyzes data collected to determine probable effects of work settings and activities on disease and mortality rates, using valid statistical techniques and knowledge of epidemiology. Presents data in designated statistical format to illustrate common patterns among workers in selected occupations. Initiates and maintains contacts with statistical and data processing managers in other agencies to maintain access to epidemiological source materials. Evaluates materials from all sources for addition to or amendment of epidemiological data bank. Plans and directs activities of clerical and statistical personnel engaged in tabulation and analysis of epidemiological information to ensure accomplishment of objectives. • **GED:** R6, M6, L5 • **SVP:** 4-10 yrs • **Academic:** Ed=B, Eng=S • **Work Field:** 251 • **MPSMS:** 732, 925 • **Aptitudes:** G1, V2, N1, S2, P2, Q1, K3, F3, M3, E5, C2 • **Temperaments:** D, J, T • **Physical:** V=N, H=L, L=L • **Work Env:** I • **Salary:** 5 • **Outlook:** 4

HISTOPATHOLOGIST (medical ser.) • D.O.T. #041.061-054 • OES #24311 • HISTOLOGIST. Studies human or animal tissue to provide data on body functions or cause and progress of disease: Trains and oversees laboratory personnel in preparing tissue sections or prepares tissue sections from surgical and diagnostic cases and autopsies. Examines tissue under microscope to detect characteristics of cell structure indicative of disease and writes diagnostic reports. Devises and directs use of special stains and methods for isolating, identifying, and studying function, morphology, and pathology of obscure or difficult-to-identify cells, tissues, and connecting fibers. May conduct autopsies to select tissue specimens for study. May engage in research to develop techniques for diagnosing and identifying pathological conditions. May study anatomy of body tissues, formation of organs, and related problems to obtain data on body functions. • **GED:** R6, M6, L6 • **SVP:** 4-10 yrs • **Academic:** Ed=M, Eng=G • **Work Field:** 211, 251 • **MPSMS:** 732, 925 • **Aptitudes:** G1, V1, N3, S1, P1, Q4, K3, F2, M2, E5, C2 • **Temperaments:** D, J, M, T • **Physical:** V=L, H=N, L=S, H • **Work Env:** I • **Salary:** 5 • **Outlook:** 3

MEDICAL PHYSICIST (profess. & kin.) • D.O.T. #079.021-014 • OES #24311 • Applies knowledge and methodology of science of physics to all aspects of medicine, to address problems related to diagnosis and treatment of human disease: Advises and consults with PHYSICIANS (medical ser.) in such applications as use of ionizing radiation in diagnosis, therapy, treatment planning with externally delivered radiation as well as use of internally implanted radioactive sources; complete subject of X-ray equipment, calibration, and dosimetry; medical uses of ultrasound and infrared; bioelectrical investigation of brain and heart; mathematical analysis and applications of computers in medicine; formulation of radiation protection guides and procedures specific to hospital environment; development of instrumentation for improved patient care and clinical service. Plans, directs, conducts, and participates in supporting programs to insure effective and safe use of radiation and radionuclides in human beings by PHYSICIAN (medical ser.) specialist. Teaches principles of medical physics to PHYSICIANS (medical ser.), residents, graduate students, medical students, and technologists by means of lectures, problem solving, and laboratory sessions. Directs and participates in investigations of biophysical techniques associated with any branch of medicine. Conducts research in development of diagnostic and remedial procedures and develops instrumentation for specific medical applications. Acts as consultant to education, medical research, and other professional groups and organizations. • **GED:** R6, M6, L6 • **SVP:** 4-10 yrs • **Academic:** Ed=M, Eng=G • **Work Field:** 251, 293 • **MPSMS:** 729, 732 • **Aptitudes:** G1, V1, N2, S2, P4, Q4, K4, F4, M4, E5, C5 • **Temperaments:** D, M, P • **Stress:** E, A • **Physical:** V=L, H=L, L=S, H • **Work Env:** I • **Salary:** 5 • **Outlook:** 3

PARASITOLOGIST (profess. & kin.) • D.O.T. #041.061-070 • OES #24311 • Studies characteristics, habits, and life cycles of animal parasites, such as protozoans, tapeworms, roundworms, flukes, and other parasitic organisms, to determine manner in which they attack human beings and animals and effects produced: Investigates modes of transmission from host to host. Develops methods and agents to combat parasites. May specialize in study of one variety of parasite, such as animal parasites that attack man, and be designated MEDICAL PARASITOLOGIST (profess. & kin.); of parasitic worms and be designated HELMINTHOLOGIST (profess. & kin.); of one celled free living and parasitic organisms and be designated PROTOZOOLOGIST (profess. &

kin.). • **GED:** R6, M6, L6 • **SVP:** 4-10 yrs • **Academic:** Ed=B, Eng=G • **Work Field:** 251 • **MPSMS:** 732 • **Aptitudes:** G1, V1, N2, S2, P2, Q3, K4, F3, M3, E5, C4 • **Temperaments:** D, M, T • **Physical:** V=L, H=N, L=S, H • **Work Env:** I • **Salary:** 4 • **Outlook:** 3

PHARMACOLOGIST (profess. & kin.) • D.O.T. #041.061-074 • OES #24311 • Studies effects of drugs, gases, dusts, and other materials on tissue and physiological processes of animals and human beings: Experiments with animals, such as rats, guinea pigs, and mice, to determine reactions of drugs and other substances on functioning of organs and tissues, noting effects on circulation, respiration, digestion, or other vital processes. Standardizes drug dosages or methods of immunizing against industrial diseases by correlating results of animal experiments with results obtained from clinical experimentation on human beings. Investigates preventative methods and remedies for diseases, such as silicosis and lead, mercury, and ammonia poisoning. Analyzes food preservatives and colorings, vermin poisons, and other materials to determine toxic or nontoxic properties. Standardizes procedures for manufacture of drugs and medicinal compounds. • **GED:** R6, M6, L6 • **SVP:** 4-10 yrs • **Academic:** Ed=B, Eng=S • **Work Field:** 251 • **MPSMS:** 732 • **Aptitudes:** G1, V2, N1, S1, P2, Q3, K3, F2, M3, E5, C3 • **Temperaments:** M, T • **Physical:** V=G, H=N, L=L, H • **Work Env:** I • **Salary:** 5 • **Outlook:** 4

ZOOLOGIST (profess. & kin.) • D.O.T. #041.061-090 • OES #24308 • Studies origin, interrelationships, classification, life histories, habits, life processes, diseases, relation to environment, growth and development, genetics, and distribution of animals: Studies animals in natural habitat and collects specimens for laboratory study. Dissects and examines specimens under microscope and uses chemicals and various types of scientific equipment to carry out experimental studies. Prepares collections of preserved specimens or microscopic slides for such purposes as identification of species, study of species development, and study of animal diseases. May raise specimens for experimental purposes. May specialize in one aspect of animal study, such as functioning of animal as an organism, or development of organism from egg to embryo stage. May specialize in study of reptiles, frogs, and salamanders and be designated HERPETOLOGIST (profess. & kin.); of fish and fishlike forms and be designated ICHTHYOLOGIST (profess. & kin.); of sponges, jelly fish and protozoa and be designated INVERTEBRATE ZOOLOGIST (profess. & kin.). of birds and be designated as ORNITHOLOGIST (profess. & kin.); of mammals and be designated as MAMMALOGIST (profess. & kin.). May study animals for purposes of identification and classification and be designated ANIMAL TAXONOMIST (profess. & kin.); or study effects of environment on animals and be designated ANIMAL ECOLOGIST (profess. & kin.). • **GED:** R6, M6, L6 • **SVP:** 4-10 yrs • **Academic:** Ed=B, Eng=G • **Work Field:** 251 • **MPSMS:** 732 • **Aptitudes:** G1, V1, N2, S2, P2, Q4, K2, F2, M2, E5, C3 • **Temperaments:** J, M, V • **Physical:** V=L, H=N, L=S, W, C, S, H • **Work Env:** B • **Salary:** 4 • **Outlook:** 3

GOE: 02.02.02 Plant Specialization

AGRONOMIST (profess. & kin.) • D.O.T. #040.061-010 • OES #24305 • CROP-RESEARCH SCIENTIST; CROP SCIENTIST. Conducts experiments or investigations in field-crop problems and develops new methods of growing crops to secure more efficient production, higher yield, and improved quality: Plans and carries out breeding studies at experiment stations or farms to develop and improve varieties of field crops, such as cotton, tobacco, or cereal with respect to characteristics, such as yield, quality, adaptation to specific soils or climates, and resistance to diseases and pests [PLANT BREEDER (profess. & kin.)]. Studies crop production to discover best methods of planting, cultivation, harvesting, and effects of various climatic conditions on crops. Develops methods for control of noxious weeds, crop diseases, and insect pests [PLANT PATHOLOGIST (profess. & kin.)]. May specialize in specific field crop, group of field crops, or specific agronomic problem. • **GED:** R6, M6, L6 • **SVP:** 4-10 yrs • **Academic:** Ed=B, Eng=G • **Work Field:** 251 • **MPSMS:** 731 • **Aptitudes:** G1, V1, N2, S4, P4, Q3, K4, F3, M3, E4, C4 • **Temperaments:** D, J, M • **Physical:** V=N, H=N, L=S, H • **Work Env:** B • **Salary:** 4 • **Outlook:** 2

BOTANIST (profess. & kin.) • D.O.T. #041.061-038 • OES #24308 • Studies development and life processes, physiology, heredity, environment, distribution, anatomy, morphology, and economic value of plants for application in such fields as agronomy, forestry, horticulture, and pharmacology: Studies behavior of chromosomes and reproduction, internal and external structures, and examines mechanics and biochemistry of plants and plant cells, using microscopes, staining techniques, and scientific equipment. Investigates environment and plant communities and effect of rainfall, temperature, climate, soil, and elevation on plant growth from seed to mature plants. Identifies and classifies plants. May conduct environmental studies and prepare reports. May be designated according to field of specialization as PLANT ECOLOGIST (profess. & kin.); PLANT TAXONOMIST (profess. & kin.). • **GED:** R6, M6, L6 • **SVP:** 4-10 yrs • **Academic:** Ed=B, Eng=G • **Work Field:** 251 • **MPSMS:** 732 • **Aptitudes:** G1, V1, N2, S1, P1, Q3, K3, F3, M4, E4, C3 • **Temperaments:** D, M, T • **Physical:** V=L, H=N, L=S, S, H • **Work Env:** B • **Salary:** 4 • **Outlook:** 3

FOREST ECOLOGIST (profess. & kin.) • D.O.T. #040.061-030 • OES #24302 • Conducts research in environ mental factors affecting forests: Carries out studies to determine what conditions account for prevalence of different varieties of trees. Studies classification, life history, light and soil requirements, and resistance to disease and insects of different species. Investigates adaptability of different species to new environmental conditions, such as changes in soil type, climate, and altitude. • **GED:** R6, M6, L6 • **SVP:** 4-10 yrs • **Academic:** Ed=B, Eng=S • **Work Field:** 251 • **MPSMS:** 319, 731 • **Aptitudes:** G1, V1, N2, S3, P3, Q4, K4, F3, M3, E5, C4 • **Temperaments:** D, M, T • **Physical:** V=G, H=N, L=L, W, H • **Work Env:** B • **Salary:** 5 • **Outlook:** 3

HORTICULTURIST (profess. & kin.) • D.O.T. #040.061-038 • OES #24305 • Conducts experiments and investigations on problems of breeding, production, storage, processing, and transit of fruits, nuts, berries, vegetables, flowers, bushes, and trees: Experiments to develop new or improved varieties having higher yield, quality, nutritional value, resistance to disease, or adaptability to climates, soils, uses, or processes. Determines best methods of planting, spraying, cultivating, and harvesting. May specialize in research, breeding, production, or shipping and storage of fruits, nuts, berries, vegetables, ornamental plants, or other horticultural products and be identified according to specialty. • **GED:** R6, M6, L6 • **SVP:** 4-10 yrs • **Academic:** Ed=B, Eng=G • **Work Field:** 251 • **MPSMS:** 731 • **Aptitudes:** G1, V1, N2, S3, P3, Q3, K4, F3, M3, E5, C4 • **Temperaments:** D, M, T • **Physical:** V=N, H=N, L=S, S, H • **Work Env:** B • **Salary:** 4 • **Outlook:** 2

PLANT BREEDER (profess. & kin.) • D.O.T. #041.061-082 • OES #24305 • Plans and carries out breeding studies to develop and improve varieties of crops: Improves specific characteristics, such as yield, size, quality, maturity, and resistance to frost, drought, disease and insect pests in plants, utilizing principles of genetics and knowledge of plant growth. Develops variety and selects most desirable plants for crossing. Breeds plants, using methods such as inbreeding, cross breeding, backcrossing, outcrossing, mutating, or interspecific hybridization and selection. Selects progeny having desired characteristics and continues breeding and selection process to reach desired objectives. • **GED:** R6, M6, L6 • **SVP:** 4-10 yrs • **Academic:** Ed=B, Eng=S • **Work Field:** 251 • **MPSMS:** 732 • **Aptitudes:** G1, V1, N2, S3, P3, Q4, K3, F3, M4, E5, C4 • **Temperaments:** D, M, T • **Physical:** V=G, H=N, L=L, H • **Work Env:** I • **Salary:** 5 • **Outlook:** 3

PLANT PATHOLOGIST (profess. & kin.) • D.O.T. #041.061-086 • OES #24308 • Conducts research in nature, cause, and control of plant diseases and decay of plant products: Studies and compares healthy and diseased plants to determine symptoms of diseased condition. Inoculates healthy plants with culture of suspected agents taken from diseased plants and studies effects to determine agents responsible for disease. Isolates disease-causing agent, studies habits and life cycle, and devises methods of destroying or controlling agent [MICROBIOLOGIST (profess. & kin.)]. Tests possible control measures under laboratory and field conditions for comparative effectiveness, practi cality, and economy. Investigates comparative susceptibility of different varieties of plants and develops varieties immune to disease [PLANT BREEDER (profess. & kin.)]. Studies rates of spread and intensity of disease under different conditions of soil, climate, and geography, and predicts outbreaks of plant diseases. Determines kinds of plants and insects that harbor or transmit disease. Studies losses from deterioration of perishable plant products in transit or storage and develops practices to prevent or reduce losses. Determines presence of disease producing agents in seed stocks to reduce losses from seed borne diseases. May specialize in type of plant affected, such as cereal crops, fruit, or forest trees, or by type of disease, such as bacterial, virus, fungus, mycoplasma, or nematode. May inspect flower and vegetable seeds and flowering bulbs for diseases, infections, and insect injuries. • **GED:** R6, M6, L6 • **SVP:** 4-10 yrs • **Academic:** Ed=B, Eng=G • **Work Field:** 251 • **MPSMS:** 732 • **Aptitudes:** G1, V1, N2, S2, P2, Q3, K4, F2, M2, E5, C3 • **Temperaments:** D, M, T • **Physical:** V=L, H=N, L=S, H • **Work Env:** B • **Salary:** 4 • **Outlook:** 3

RANGE MANAGER (profess. & kin.) • D.O.T. #040.061-046 • OES #24302 • RANGE-MANAGEMENT SPECIALIST. Conducts research in range problems to provide sustained production of forage, livestock, and wildlife: Studies range lands to determine best grazing seasons and number and kind of livestock that can be most profitably grazed. Plans and directs construction and maintenance of range improvements, such as fencing, corrals, reservoirs for stock watering, and structures for soil-erosion control. Develops improved practices for range reseeding. Studies forage plants and their growth requirements to determine varieties best suited to particular range. Develops methods for controlling poisonous plants, and for protecting range from fire and rodent damage. May specialize in particular area and be designated as RANGE CONSERVATIONIST (profess. & kin.). • **GED:** R6, M6, L6 • **SVP:** 4-10 yrs • **Academic:** Ed=B, Eng=G • **Work Field:** 251 • **MPSMS:** 310, 731 • **Aptitudes:** G1, V1, N2, S2, P2, Q3, K3, F3, M3, E4, C4 • **Temperaments:** J, M, T, V • **Stress:** A • **Physical:** V=L, H=L, L=L, W, H • **Work Env:** B • **Salary:** 4 • **Outlook:** 3

SILVICULTURIST (profess. & kin.) • D.O.T. #040.061-050 • OES #24302 • Establishes and cares for forest stands: Manages tree nurseries and thins forests to encourage natural growth of sprouts or seedlings of desired varieties. Conducts research in such problems of forest propagation and culture as tree growth rate, effects of thinning on forest yield, duration of seed viability, and effects of fire and animal grazing on growth, seed production, and germination of different species. Develops techniques for measuring and identifying trees. • **GED:** R5, M5, L5 • **SVP:** 2-4 yrs • **Academic:** Ed=A, Eng=G • **Work Field:** 251 • **MPSMS:** 310, 731 • **Aptitudes:** G1, V1, N2, S3, P3, Q4, K3, F2, M2, E5, C4 • **Temperaments:** D, M, T • **Physical:** V=L, H=N, L=L, W, H • **Work Env:** B • **Salary:** 4 • **Outlook:** 3

SOIL CONSERVATIONIST (profess. & kin.) • D.O.T. #040.061-054 • OES #24302 • Plans and develops coordinated practices for soil erosion control, moisture conservation, and sound land use: Conducts surveys and investigations on rural or urban planning, agriculture, construction, forestry, or mining on measures needed to maintain or restore proper soil management. Plans soil management practices, such as crop rotation, reforestation, permanent vegetation, contour plowing, or terracing as related to soil and water conservation. Prepares soil conservation plans in cooperation with state, county, or local government, farmers, foresters, miners, or urban planners to provide for use and treatment of land according to needs and capability. Applies principles of two or more specialized fields of science, such as agronomy, soil science, forestry, or agriculture to achieve objectives of conservation. May develop or participate in environmental studies. • **GED:** R6, M6, L6 • **SVP:** 4-10 yrs • **Academic:** Ed=B, Eng=G • **Work Field:** 251 • **MPSMS:** 731 • **Aptitudes:** G1, V1, N2, S2, P2, Q4, K3, F3, M3, E5, C4 • **Temperaments:** D, J, M, P • **Physical:** V=L, H=N, L=S, W • **Work Env:** B • **Salary:** 4 • **Outlook:** 3

SOIL SCIENTIST (profess. & kin.) • D.O.T. #040.061-058 • OES #24305 • Studies soil characteristics and maps soil types, and investigates responses of soils to known management practices to determine use capabilities of soils and effects of alternative practices on soil productivity: Classifies soils according to standard types. Conducts experiments on farms or experimental stations to determine best soil types for different plants. Performs chemical analysis on micro-organism content of soil to determine microbial reactions and chemical and mineralogical relationship to plant growth. Investigates responses of specific soil types to tillage, fertilization, nutrient transformations, crop rotation, environmental consequences, water, gas or heat flow, industrial waste control and other soil management practices. Advises interested persons on rural or urban land use. May specialize in one or more types of activities relative to soil management and productivity and be designated SOIL FERTILITY EXPERT (profess. & kin.). • **GED:** R6, M6, L6 • **SVP:** 4-10 yrs • **Academic:** Ed=B, Eng=S • **Work Field:** 251 • **MPSMS:** 731 • **Aptitudes:** G1, V1, N2, S3, P3, Q4, K4, F3, M3, E5, C3 • **Temperaments:** D, M, T • **Physical:** V=G, H=N, L=L, H • **Work Env:** B • **Salary:** 5 • **Outlook:** 3

SOIL-CONSERVATION TECHNICIAN (profess. & kin.) • D.O.T. #040.261-010 • OES #24302 • Provides technical assistance to land users in planning and applying soil and water conservation practices, utilizing basic engineering and surveying tools, instruments, and techniques and knowledge of agricultural and related sciences, such as agronomy, soil conservation, and hydrology: Analyzes conservation problems of land and discusses alternative solutions to problems with land users. Advises land users in developing plans for conservation practices, such as conservation cropping systems, woodlands management, pasture planning, and engineering systems, based on cost estimates of different practices, needs of land users, maintenance requirements, and life expectancy of practices. Computes design specification for particular practices to be installed, using survey and field information technical guides, engineering field manuals, and calculator. Submits copy of engineering design specifications to land users for implementation by land user or contractor. Surveys property to mark locations and measurements, using surveying instruments. Monitors projects during and after construction to ensure projects conform to design specifications. Periodically revisits land users to view implemented land use practices and plans. • **GED:** R5, M4, L4 • **SVP:** 2-4 yrs • **Academic:** Ed=A, Eng=S • **Work Field:** 243, 244 • **MPSMS:** 716, 731 • **Aptitudes:** G2, V2, N2, S2, P2, Q2, K2, F3, M3, E3, C4 • **Temperaments:** J, P, T, V • **Physical:** V=L, H=N, L=L, W, H • **Work Env:** I • **Salary:** 4 • **Outlook:** 3

WOOD TECHNOLOGIST (profess. & kin.) • D.O.T. #040.061-062 • OES #24302 • Conducts research to determine composition, properties, behavior, utilization, development, treatments, and processing methods of wood and wood products: Analyzes physical, chemical, and biological properties of wood. Studies methods of curing wood to determine best and most economical procedure. Develops and improves methods of seasoning, preservation, and treating wood with substances to increase resistance to wear, fire, fungi, insects, and marine borers. Conducts tests to determine ability of wood adhesives to with stand water, oil penetration, temperature extremes, and stability, strength, hardness and crystallinity of wood under variety of conditions. Evaluates and improves effectiveness of industrial equipment and production processes. Investigates processes for converting wood into commodities, such as alcohol, veneer, plywood, wood plastics, and other uses. Determines best type of wood for specific application, and investigates methods of turning waste wood materials into useful products. May specialize in research, quality control, marketing and sales, materials engineering, management or administration, manufacturing, production, or process development. • **GED:** R6, M5, L5 • **SVP:** 4-10 yrs • **Academic:** Ed=B, Eng=S • **Work Field:** 251 • **MPSMS:** 459, 739 • **Aptitudes:** G1, V1, N2, S3, P3, Q4, K4, F3, M3, E4, C4 • **Temperaments:** D, M, T • **Physical:** V=N, H=N, L=S, H • **Work Env:** I • **Salary:** 4 • **Outlook:** 2

GOE: 02.02.03 Plant & Animal Specialization

BIOCHEMIST (profess. & kin.) • D.O.T. #041.061-026 • OES #24308 • CHEMIST, BIOLOGICAL. Studies chemical processes of living organisms: Conducts research to determine action of foods, drugs, serums, hormones, and other substances on tissues and vital processes of living organisms. Isolates, analyzes, and identifies hormones, vitamins, allergens, minerals, and enzymes and determines effects on body functions. Examines chemical aspects of formation of antibodies, and conducts research into chemistry of cells and blood corpuscles. Studies chemistry of living processes, such as mechanisms of development of normal and abnormal cells,

breathing and digestion, and of living energy changes, such as growth, aging, and death. May specialize in particular area or field of work, and be designated CHEMIST, CLINICAL (profess. & kin.); CHEMIST, ENZYMES (profess. & kin.); CHEMIST, PROTEINS (profess. & kin.); CHEMIST, STEROIDS (profess. & kin.). May clean, purify, refine, and other wise prepare pharmaceutical compounds for commercial distribution, develop new drugs and medications, and be designated CHEMIST, PHARMACEUTICAL (profess. & kin.). • **GED:** R6, M6, L6 • **SVP:** 4-10 yrs • **Academic:** Ed=B, Eng=G • **Work Field:** 251 • **MPSMS:** 732 • **Aptitudes:** G1, V2, N1, S2, P2, Q2, K3, F3, M3, E5, C3 • **Temperaments:** M, T • **Physical:** V=L, H=N, L=S, H • **Work Env:** I • **Salary:** 5 • **Outlook:** 4

BIOLOGIST (profess. & kin.) • D.O.T. #041.061-030 • OES #24308 • Studies origin, relationship, development, anatomy, functions, and other basic principles of plant and animal life. May specialize in research centering around particular plant, animal, or aspect of biology. May collect and analyze biological data to determine environmental effects of present and potential use of land and water areas. May prepare environmental impact reports. May teach. • **GED:** R6, M6, L6 • **SVP:** 4-10 yrs • **Academic:** Ed=B, Eng=G • **Work Field:** 251 • **MPSMS:** 732 • **Aptitudes:** G1, V1, N1, S1, P2, Q3, K3, F3, M3, E4, C3 • **Temperaments:** M, T • **Physical:** V=N, H=N, L=S, H • **Work Env:** B • **Salary:** 3 • **Outlook:** 3

BIOPHYSICIST (profess. & kin.) • D.O.T. #041.061-034 • OES #24308 • Studies physical principles of living cells and organisms, their electrical and mechanical energy, and related phenomena: Conducts research to investigate dynamics in such areas as seeing and hearing; the transmission of electrical impulses along nerves and muscles, and damage to cells and tissues caused by X-rays and nuclear particles; manner in which characteristics of plants and animals are carried forward through successive generations; and absorption of light by chlorophyll in photosynthesis or by pigments of eye involved in vision. Analyzes functions of electronic and human brains, such as transfer of information into brain from outside (learning), transfer and manipulation of information within brain (thinking), and storage of information (memory). Studies spatial configuration of submicroscopic molecules, such as proteins, using X-ray and electron microscope. May specialize in one activity, such as use of radiation and nuclear particles for treating cancer or use of atomic isotopes to discover transformation of substances in cells. • **GED:** R6, M6, L6 • **SVP:** 4-10 yrs • **Academic:** Ed=B, Eng=S • **Work Field:** 251 • **MPSMS:** 732 • **Aptitudes:** G1, V1, N1, S1, P1, Q3, K3, F3, M3, E5, C2 • **Temperaments:** J, M, T • **Physical:** V=G, H=N, L=L, H • **Work Env:** I • **Salary:** 5 • **Outlook:** 4

MICROBIOLOGIST (profess. & kin.) • D.O.T. #041.061-058 • OES #24308 • BACTERIOLOGIST. Studies growth, structure, development, and general characteristics of bacteria and other micro-organisms: Isolates and makes cultures of significant bacteria or other micro-organisms in prescribed or standard inhibitory media, controlling factors, such as moisture, aeration, temperature, and nutrition. Identifies micro-organisms by microscopic examination of physiological, morphological, and cultural characteristics. Observes action of micro-organisms upon living tissues of plants, higher animals, and other micro-organisms and on dead organic matter. Makes chemical analyses of substances, such as acids, alcohols, and enzymes produced by bacteria and other micro-organisms on organic matter. May specialize in study of viruses and rickettsiae and be designated VIROLOGIST (profess. & kin.). May specialize in particular material or product field and be designated BACTERIOLOGIST, DAIRY (profess. & kin.); BACTERIOLOGIST, FISHERY (profess. & kin.); BACTERIOLOGIST, FOOD (profess. & kin.); BACTERIOLOGIST, INDUSTRIAL (profess. & kin.); BACTERIOLOGIST, MEDICAL (profess. & kin.); BACTERIOLOGIST, PHARMACEUTICAL (profess. & kin.); or BACTERIOLOGIST, SOIL (profess. & kin.). • **GED:** R6, M6, L6 • **SVP:** 4-10 yrs • **Academic:** Ed=B, Eng=G • **Work Field:** 251 • **MPSMS:** 732 • **Aptitudes:** G1, V1, N2, S2, P2, Q3, K4, F3, M3, E5, C4 • **Temperaments:** D, M, T • **Physical:** V=L, H=N, L=S, H • **Work Env:** I • **Salary:** 4 • **Outlook:** 4

PHYSIOLOGIST (profess. & kin.) • D.O.T. #041.061-078 • OES #24308 • Conducts research on cellular structure and organ-system functions of plants and animals: Studies growth, respiration, circulation, excretion, movement, reproduction, and other functions of plants and animals under normal and abnormal conditions. Performs experiments to determine effects of internal and external environmental factors on life processes and functions, using microscope, X-ray equipment, spectroscope, and other equipment. Studies glands and their relationship to bodily functions. May specialize in physiology of particular body area, function, or system. May specialize in physiology of animals and be designated ANIMAL PHYSIOLOGIST (profess. & kin.); of plants and be designated PLANT PHYSIOLOGIST (profess. & kin.); of human organisms and be designated MEDICAL PHYSIOLOGIST (medical ser.). • **GED:** R6, M6, L6 • **SVP:** 4-10 yrs • **Academic:** Ed=B, Eng=S • **Work Field:** 251 • **MPSMS:** 732 • **Aptitudes:** G1, V2, N1, S1, P1, Q3, K2, F2, M2, E5, C3 • **Temperaments:** D, M, T • **Physical:** V=G, H=N, L=L, H • **Work Env:** I • **Salary:** 5 • **Outlook:** 2

GOE: 02.02.04 Food Research

CHEMIST, FOOD (profess. & kin.) • D.O.T. #022.061-014 • OES #24105 • Conducts research and analysis concerning chemistry of foods to develop and improve foods and beverages: Experiments with natural and synthetic materials or byproducts to develop new foods, additives, preservatives, antiadulteration agents, and related products. Studies effects of various methods of processing, preservation, and packaging on composition and properties of foods, such as color, texture, aroma, taste, shelf life, and nutritive content. Tests food and beverage samples, such as starch, sugar, cereals, beer, canned and dehydrated food products, meats, vegetables, dairy foods, and other products to ensure compliance with food laws, and standards of quality and purity. May perform, or supervise workers performing, quality control tests in food processing, canning, freezing, brewing or distilling. May specialize in particular food or process. • **GED:** R6, M5, L5 • **SVP:** 2-4 yrs • **Academic:** Ed=B, Eng=S • **Work Field:** 251 • **MPSMS:** 732 • **Aptitudes:** G1, V2, N1, S3, P2, Q3, K3, F3, M3, E5, C3 • **Temperaments:** D, J, M, T • **Physical:** V=L, H=N, L=L, H • **Work Env:** I • **Salary:** 4 • **Outlook:** 3

DAIRY TECHNOLOGIST (profess. & kin.) • D.O.T. #040.061-022 • OES #24502 • DAIRY-MANUFACTURING TECHNOLOGIST; DAIRY-PRODUCTS TECHNOLOGIST. Applies principles of bacteriology, chemistry, physics, engineering, and economics to develop new and improved methods in production, preservation, and utilization of milk, cheese, ice cream, and other dairy products: Conducts experiments in such problems as preventing bacterial increase in milk during handling and processing, improving pasteurization methods, and designing better packaging materials, dairy equipment, or supplies. May specialize according to product, as ice cream or cheese, or according to functional activity, as sanitation research or storage problems. • **GED:** R6, M6, L6 • **SVP:** 4-10 yrs • **Academic:** Ed=B, Eng=S • **Work Field:** 251 • **MPSMS:** 383 • **Aptitudes:** G1, V1, N2, S3, P3, Q3, K4, F2, M2, E4, C3 • **Temperaments:** D, M • **Physical:** V=L, H=N, L=L, W, H • **Work Env:** I • **Salary:** 4 • **Outlook:** 2

FOOD TECHNOLOGIST (profess. & kin.) • D.O.T. #041.081-010 • OES #24305 • FOOD SCIENTIST. Applies scientific and engineering principles in research, development, production technology, quality control, packaging, processing, and utilization of foods: Conducts basic research, and new product research and development of foods. Develops new and improved methods and systems for food processing, production, quality control, packaging, and distribution. Studies methods to improve quality of foods, such as flavor, color, texture, nutritional value, convenience, or physical, chemical, and microbiological composition of foods. Develops food standards, safety and sanitary regulations, and waste management and water supply specifications. Tests new products in test kitchen and develops specific processing methods in laboratory pilot plant, and confers with process engineers, flavor experts, and packaging and marketing specialists to resolve problems. May specialize in one phase of food technology, such as product development, quality control, or production inspection, technical writing, teaching, or consulting. May specialize in particular branch of food technology, such as cereal grains, meat and poultry, fats and oils, seafood, animal foods, beverages, dairy products, flavors, sugars and starches, stabilizers, preservatives, colors, and nutritional additives, and be identified according to branch of food technology. • **GED:** R6, M5, L4 • **SVP:** 2-4 yrs • **Academic:** Ed=B, Eng=G • **Work Field:** 211, 251 • **MPSMS:** 380, 390, 395 • **Aptitudes:** G1, V2, N2, S2, P2, Q2, K3, F2, M3, E5, C3 • **Temperaments:** M, T, V • **Physical:** V=L, H=N, L=S, H • **Work Env:** I • **Salary:** 4 • **Outlook:** 3

02.03 Medical Sciences

Workers in this group are involved in the prevention, diagnosis, and treatment of human and animal diseases, disorders, or injuries. It is common to specialize in specific kinds of illnesses, or special areas or organs of the body. Workers who prefer to be more general may become general practitioners, family practitioners, or may learn to deal with groups of related medical problems. A wide variety of work environments is available to medical workers ranging from large city hospitals and clinics, to home offices in rural areas, to field clinics in the military or in underdeveloped countries.

✔ **What kind of work would you do?**
Your work activities would depend upon your specific job. For example, you might:

- perform surgery to correct deformities, repair injuries, or remove diseased organs.
- diagnose and treat diseases of the ear, nose, and throat.
- examine patients to determine causes of speech defects.

- remove teeth and perform other mouth surgery.
- diagnose and treat mental illnesses.
- oversee all medical activities of a hospital.
- examine and treat patients for all physical problems, referring them to specialists when necessary.

✔ **What skills and abilities do you need for this kind of work?**
To do this kind of work, you must be able to:

- use logic and scientific thinking to diagnose and treat human or animal injuries and illnesses.
- deal with people or animals when they are in pain or under stress.
- stay calm and keep your head in emergencies.
- use eyes, hands, and fingers with great skill and accuracy.

- deal both with things that are known and obvious and with things which frequently are not easy to recognize or understand.
- make important decisions using your own judgment.
- make decisions based on information you can measure or verify.

✔ **How do you know if you would like or could learn to do this kind of work?**

The following questions may give you clues about yourself as you consider this group of jobs.

- Have you taken courses in biology, physiology, or anatomy? Can you understand scientific concepts?
- Have you had any training in first-aid techniques? Have you treated an accident victim? Can you work well with people in emotionally upsetting situations?
- Have you dissected an animal? Can you skillfully handle small instruments such as scalpels, syringes, or tweezers?

- Have you watched medical shows on television? Do you enjoy these programs? Can you understand the technical terms used?
- Have you been a medical corpsman in the armed services? Did you learn techniques and terminology that would be helpful in medical school?

✔ **How can you prepare for and enter this kind of work?**

Occupations in this group usually require education and/or training extending from four years to over ten years, depending upon the specific kind of work. Academic courses helpful in preparing for the medical sciences are: algebra, geometry, advanced math, chemistry, biological sciences, English, and Latin. Two to four years of undergraduate study followed by four years of advanced study is considered the minimum preparation. Most doctors serve a one- or two-year internship in an approved hospital after graduation from medical school.

Some physicians spend several additional years in study and training as a resident or intern to specialize. Dentists who specialize, teach, or perform research must have post-graduate courses or complete a residency in a hospital or clinic. Medical doctors, dentists, and veterinarians must have a license to practice.

✔ **What else should you consider about these jobs?**

The training time and cost involved are significant. Workers must adjust to irregular hours, weekend and holiday work, and 24-hour on-call duties.

Workers should update their knowledge and professional skills through periodic courses and continuous study.

If you think you would like to do this kind of work, look at the job titles listed below.

GOE: 02.03.01 Medicine & Surgery

GENERAL PRACTITIONER (medical ser.) • D.O.T. #070.101-022 • OES #32102 • PHYSICIAN, GENERAL PRACTICE. Attends to variety of medical cases in general practice: Examines patients, utilizing stethoscope, sphygmomanometer, and other instruments. Orders or executes various tests, analyses, and X-rays to provide information on patient's condition. Analyzes reports and findings of tests and of examination, and diagnoses condition. Administers or prescribes treatments and drugs. Inoculates and vaccinates patients to immunize them from communicable diseases. Promotes health by advising patients concerning diet, hygiene, and methods for prevention of disease. Provides prenatal care to pregnant women, delivers babies, and provides postnatal care to mother and infant [OBSTETRICIAN (medical ser.)]. Reports births, deaths, and diseases to governmental authorities. May make house and emergency calls to attend to patients unable to visit office or clinic. May conduct physical examinations of insurance company applicants to determine health and risk involved in insuring applicant. May provide care for passengers and crew aboard ship and be designated SURGEON (medical ser.) II.
• **GED:** R6, M5, L6 • **SVP:** 4-10 yrs • **Academic:** Ed=M, Eng=G

• **Work Field:** 294 • **MPSMS:** 929 • **Aptitudes:** G1, V1, N1, S1, P1, Q2, K2, F1, M2, E4, C3 • **Temperaments:** D, J, M, P • **Stress:** E, A • **Physical:** V=G, H=G, L=S, H • **Work Env:** I • **Salary:** 5 • **Outlook:** 3

PODIATRIST (medical ser.) • D.O.T. #079.101-022 • OES #32111 • CHIROPODIST; FOOT SPECIALIST. Diagnoses and treats diseases and deformities of human foot: Diagnoses foot ailments, such as tumors, ulcers, fractures, skin or nail diseases, and congenital or acquired deformities, utilizing diagnostic aids, such as urinalysis, blood tests, and X-ray analysis. Treats deformities, such as flat or weak feet and foot imbalance, by mechanical and electrical methods, such as whirl pool or paraffin baths and short wave and low voltage currents. Treats conditions, such as corns, calluses, ingrowing nails, tumors, shortened tendons, bunions, cysts, and abscesses by surgical methods, including suturing, medications, and adminis tration of local anesthetics. Prescribes drugs. Does not perform foot amputations. Corrects deformities by means of plaster casts and strappings. Makes and fits prosthetic appliances. Prescribes corrective footwear. Advises patients concerning continued treat ment of disorders and proper foot care to prevent recurrence. Refers patients to PHYSICIAN (medical ser.) when symptoms observed in feet and legs indicate systemic disorders, such as arthritis, heart disease, diabetes, or kidney trouble. May treat bone, muscle, and joint disorders and be designated PODIATRIST, ORTHOPEDIC (medical ser.); childrens' foot diseases and be designated PODOPEDIATRICIAN (medical ser.), or perform surgery and be designated PODIATRIC SURGEON (medical ser.). • **GED:** R5, M4, L5 • **SVP:** 2-4 yrs • **Academic:** Ed=B, Eng=G • **Work Field:** 294 • **MPSMS:** 929 • **Aptitudes:** G2, V3, N3, S3, P3, Q4, K4, F3, M3, E5, C5 • **Temperaments:** J, M, P • **Stress:** E • **Physical:** V=G, H=L, L=S, H • **Work Env:** I • **Salary:** 5 • **Outlook:** 4

GOE: 02.03.02 Dentistry

DENTIST (medical ser.) • D.O.T. #072.101-010 • OES #32105 • DENTAL SURGEON. Diagnoses and treats diseases, injuries, and malformations of teeth and gums, and related oral structures: Examines patient to determine nature of condition, utilizing X-rays, mouth mirrors, explorers, and other diagnostic procedures and instruments. Cleans, fills, extracts, and replaces teeth, using rotary and hand instruments, dental appliances, medications, and surgical implements. • **GED:** R6, M5, L5 • **SVP:** 4-10 yrs • **Academic:** Ed=M, Eng=G • **Work Field:** 294 • **MPSMS:** 922 • **Aptitudes:** G1, V2, N1, S1, P1, Q3, K4, F2, M2, E4, C4 • **Temperaments:** M, P, V • **Stress:** E, A • **Physical:** V=G, H=N, L=S, H • **Work Env:** I • **Salary:** 5 • **Outlook:** 4

GOE: 02.03.03 Veterinary Medicine

ANIMAL HEALTH TECHNICIAN (medical ser.) • D.O.T. #079.361-014 • OES #32999 • Assists veterinary staff to diagnose and treat animals for injury and illness, applying knowledge of veterinary medical assisting procedures and techniques and following directions of veterinary staff: Soothes and quiets patients prior to examination or treatment and restrains patients during examination and treatment to facilitate procedures. Measures and records patient temperature, pulse rate, and respiration as directed. Applies bandages, dressings, and splints, and administers oxygen and oral and injected medications as prescribed. Administers treatments, cleans teeth, removes sutures, and inserts catheters, endotracheal tubes, and related devices as instructed. Draws patient blood and collects specimens as directed. Gathers and positions surgical packs and related instruments and materials for use by veterinary staff during surgery. Administers prescribed pre-anesthetic drugs to patient, and washes, shaves, and applies antiseptic solution to surgical site to prepare patient for surgery. Monitors patient's vital signs and reflexes during and after surgery and informs veterinary staff of changes. Observes patients in hospital to monitor eating and elimination and to detect abnormal conditions. Conducts tests and microscopic examinations of specimens, following standard test and examination procedures and using various laboratory equipment and materials. Dispenses prescribed drugs, maintains prescription records, and inventories supplies of drugs, instruments, and related items. Cleans and

sterilizes instruments and materials and maintains equipment and machines. Sets up and operates radiological equipment to conduct x-ray examinations of patients, utilizing knowledge of radiological techniques and procedures. • **GED:** R4, M3, L4 • **SVP:** 1-2 yrs • **Academic:** Ed=H, Eng=G • **Work Field:** 294 • **MPSMS:** 929 • **Aptitudes:** G2, V2, N4, S4, P3, Q2, K3, F3, M3, E5, C3 • **Temperaments:** P, T, V • **Stress:** E • **Physical:** V=L, H=L, L=M, W, H • **Work Env:** I • **Salary:** 4 • **Outlook:** 4

VETERINARIAN (medical ser.) • D.O.T. #073.101-010 • OES #32114 • DOCTOR, VETERINARY MEDICINE. Diagnoses and treats diseases and disorders of animals: Determines nature of disease or injury and treats animal surgically or medically. Tests dairy herds for tuberculosis and brucellosis, and inoculates animals against diseases, such as hog cholera and rabies. Performs autopsies to determine causes of death. Inspects animals intended for human consumption, before and after slaughtering. Advises on care and breeding of animals. Engages in general practice, treating various animal species, or specializes, restricting practice to dogs, cats, and other pets, or to single species, such as cattle, horses, or poultry. May engage in particular function, such as research and development, consultation, administration, teaching, technical writing, sale or production of commercial products, or rendition of technical services for commercial firms. May specialize in investigation, prevention, and control of animal diseases communicable to man through direct contact, insects, food, or contamination of environment, and be designated VETERINARIAN, PUBLIC HEALTH (gov. ser.). May specialize in diagnosis and treatment of animal diseases, using roentgen rays and radioactive substances, and be designated VETERINARY RADIOLOGIST (medical ser.). • **GED:** R5, M4, L5 • **SVP:** 4-10 yrs • **Academic:** Ed=M, Eng=G • **Work Field:** 294 • **MPSMS:** 929 • **Aptitudes:** G1, V1, N2, S1, P1, Q3, K2, F2, M1, E5, C4 • **Temperaments:** M, P, T, V • **Stress:** E • **Physical:** V=G, H=L, L=M, W, H • **Work Env:** B • **Salary:** 5 • **Outlook:** 4

GOE: 02.03.04 Health Specialties

ACUPUNCTURIST (medical ser.) • D.O.T. #079.271-010 • OES #32199 • Administers specific therapeutic treatment of symptoms and disorders amenable to acupuncture procedures, as specifically indicated by supervising PHYSICIAN (medical ser.): Reviews patient's medical history, physical findings, and diagnosis made by PHYSICIAN (medical ser.) to ascertain symptoms or disorder to be treated. Selects needles of various lengths, according to location of insertion. Inserts needles at locations of body known to be efficacious to certain disorders, utilizing knowledge of acupuncture points and their functions. Leaves needles in patient for specific length of time, according to symptom or disorder treated, and removes needles. Burns bark of mugwort tree in small strainer to administer moxibustion treatment. Covers insertion area with cloth and rubs strainer over cloth to impart heat and assist in relieving patient's symptoms. • **GED:** R5, M4, L5 • **SVP:** 1-2 yrs • **Academic:** Ed=A, Eng=G • **Work Field:** 294 • **MPSMS:** 929 • **Aptitudes:** G2, V2, N3, S2, P2, Q3, K2, F3, M3, E5, C3 • **Temperaments:** J, M • **Physical:** V=L, H=L, L=L, W, H • **Work Env:** I • **Salary:** 4 • **Outlook:** 3

AUDIOLOGIST (profess. & kin.) • D.O.T. #076.101-010 • OES #32314 • Specializes in diagnostic evaluation of hearing, prevention, habilitative and rehabilitative services for auditory problems, and research related to hearing and attendant disorders: Determines range, nature, and degree of hearing function related to patient's auditory efficiency (communication needs), using electro-acoustic instrumentation, such as pure-tone and speech audiometers, and acoustic impedance equipment. Coordinates audiometric results with other diagnostic data, such as educational, medical, social, and behavioral information. Differentiates between organic and nonorganic hearing disabilities through evaluation of total response pattern and use of acoustic tests, such as Stenger and electrodermal audiometry. Plans, directs, conducts, or participates in conservation, habilitative and rehabilitative programs including hearing aid selection and orientation, counseling, guidance, auditory training, speech reading, language habilitation, and speech conservation. May conduct research in physiology, pathology, biophysics, and psychophysics of auditory systems. May design and develop clinical and research procedures and apparatus. May act as consultant to educational, medical, and other professional groups. May teach art and science of audiology and direct scientific projects. May specialize in fields, such as industrial audiology, geriatric audiology, pediatric audiology, and research audiology. See SPEECH PATHOLOGIST (profess. & kin.) for one who specializes in diagnosis and treatment of speech and language problems. • **GED:** R5, M4, L5 • **SVP:** 2-4 yrs • **Academic:** Ed=M, Eng=G • **Work Field:** 251, 294 • **MPSMS:** 732, 929 • **Aptitudes:** G1, V1, N2, S3, P2, Q3, K3, F3, M3, E5, C4 • **Temperaments:** D, J, M, P • **Stress:** E • **Physical:** V=G, H=G, L=S, H • **Work Env:** I • **Salary:** 4 • **Outlook:** 4

CHIROPRACTOR (medical ser.) • D.O.T. #079.101-010 • OES #32113 • CHIROPRACTIC; DOCTOR, CHIROPRACTIC. Adjusts spinal column and other articulations of body to prevent disease and correct abnormalities of human body believed to be caused by interference with nervous system: Examines patient to determine nature and extent of disorder, using X-ray machine, electrocardiograph, otoscope, proctoscope, and other instruments and equipment. Manipulates spine or other involved area. May utilize supplementary measures, such as exercise, rest, water, light, heat, and nutritional therapy. • **GED:** R5, M4, L5 • **SVP:** 2-4 yrs • **Academic:** Ed=B, Eng=G • **Work Field:** 294 • **MPSMS:** 923 • **Aptitudes:** G2, V2, N3, S2, P2, Q4, K2, F2, M2, E4, C4 • **Temperaments:** D, J, M, P • **Stress:** E, A • **Physical:** V=L, H=G, L=M, W, H • **Work Env:** I • **Salary:** 4 • **Outlook:** 3

OPTOMETRIST (profess. & kin.) • D.O.T. #079.101-018 • OES #32108 • Examines eyes to determine visual efficiency and performance, diseases, or other abnormalities by means of instrumentation and observation, and prescribes corrective procedures: Conserves, improves, and corrects vision through use of lenses, prisms, vision therapy, visual training, and control of visual environment. Examines patients for visual pathology or ocular manifestations of systemic disease, and refers those with pathological conditions to medical practitioner for further diagnosis and treatment. May specialize in treatment of children with learning problems, vision of aged, rehabilitation of partially sighted, or environmental vision. May specialize in vision training, vision therapy, vision development, contact lenses, or low vision aids. May conduct research, instruct in college or university, act as consultant, or work in public health field. • **GED:** R5, M5, L5 • **SVP:** 2-4 yrs • **Academic:** Ed=B, Eng=G • **Work Field:** 294 • **MPSMS:** 929 • **Aptitudes:** G2, V2, N2, S2, P2, Q4, K3, F3, M3, E5, C3 • **Temperaments:** M, P • **Stress:** E • **Physical:** V=G, H=L, L=S, H • **Work Env:** I • **Salary:** 4 • **Outlook:** 4

RADIATION-THERAPY TECHNOLOGIST (medical ser.) • D.O.T. #078.361-034 • OES #32914 • Operates radiation therapy equipment to treat patients with prescribed doses of ionizing radiation: Positions patient under equipment to expose necessary areas to treatment and adjusts equipment according to instructions. Calculates exposure time and intensity required, using mechanical and electronic regulating controls. Turns controls to operate and adjust equipment and regulate application. Observes dials to monitor duration and intensity of treatment. Prepares and maintains records for review by medical staff. • **GED:** R5, M4, L4 • **SVP:** 1-2 yrs • **Academic:** Ed=A, Eng=S • **Work Field:** 294 • **MPSMS:** 925 • **Aptitudes:** G3, V3, N4, S4, P4, Q3, K4, F4, M4, E5, C4 • **Temperaments:** D, P, T • **Stress:** E • **Physical:** V=L, H=N, L=L, W, H • **Work Env:** I, R • **Salary:** 4 • **Outlook:** 3

SPEECH PATHOLOGIST (profess. & kin.) • D.O.T. #076.107-010 • OES #32314 • SPEECH CLINICIAN; SPEECH THERAPIST. Specializes in diagnosis and treatment of speech and language problems, and engages in scientific study of human communication: Diagnoses and evaluates speech and language competencies of individuals, including assessment of speech and language skills as related to educational, medical, social, and psychological factors. Plans, directs, or conducts habilitative and rehabilitative treatment programs to restore communicative efficiency of individuals with communication problems of organic and nonorganic etiology. Provides counseling and guidance to speech and language handicapped individuals. May act as consultant to educational, medical, and other professional groups. May teach scientific principles of human communication. May direct scientific projects investigating biophysical and biosocial phenomena associated with voice, speech, and language. May conduct research to develop

diagnostic and remedial techniques or design apparatus. See AUDIOLOGIST (profess. & kin.) for one who specializes in diagnosis of, and provision of rehabilitative services for, auditory problems. • **GED:** R6, M5, L6 • **SVP:** 2-4 yrs • **Academic:** Ed=M, Eng=G • **Work Field:** 251, 294 • **MPSMS:** 749, 929 • **Aptitudes:** G1, V1, N3, S3, P2, Q3, K3, F3, M3, E5, C4 • **Temperaments:** J, P • **Stress:** E • **Physical:** V=N, H=G, L=S, H • **Work Env:** I • **Salary:** 4 • **Outlook:** 4

GOE: 02.04.01 Physical Sciences

ASSAYER (profess. & kin.) • D.O.T. #022.281-010 • OES #24505 • Tests ores and minerals and analyzes results to determine value and properties of components, using spectrographic analysis, chemical solutions, and chemical or laboratory equipment, such as furnaces, beakers, graduates, pipettes, and crucibles: Separates metals or other components from dross materials by solution, flotation, or other liquid processes, or by dry methods, such as application of heat to form slags of lead, borax, and other impurities. Weighs residues on balance scale to determine proportion of pure gold, silver, platinum, or other metals or components. May specialize in testing and analyzing precious metals and be designated GOLD-AND-SILVER ASSAYER (profess. & kin.). • **GED:** R5, M5, L4 • **SVP:** 2-4 yrs • **Academic:** Ed=A, Eng=S • **Work Field:** 211 • **MPSMS:** 350 • **Aptitudes:** G2, V2, N3, S2, P3, Q3, K3, F3, M3, E5, C3 • **Temperaments:** M, T • **Physical:** V=L, H=N, L=L, H • **Work Env:** I • **Salary:** 4 • **Outlook:** 2

BALLISTICS EXPERT, FORENSIC (gov. ser.) • D.O.T. #199.267-010 • OES #24599 • FIREARMS EXPERT. Examines and tests firearms, spent bullets, and related evidence in criminal cases to develop facts useful in apprehension and prosecution of suspects: Examines bullets, bullet fragments, cartridge clips, firearms, and related evidence found at scene of crime or in possession of suspect to identify make and caliber of weapon. Test-fires weapons allegedly used to facilitate microscopic comparison of bullets from test weapon with those discovered at scene of crime. Determines, from knowledge of ballistics theory and standard test procedures, probable angle and distance from which crime weapon was fired, revealing origin of shot. Prepares reports of findings and testifies at inquests, trials, and other hearings to facilitate prosecution or exoneration of suspects on basis of determinations. May perform standardized tests on other articles of evidence, using chemical agents, physical-testing equipment, measuring instruments, and prescribed procedure, to determine relationship of evidence to suspect and to crime. May order and maintain departmental weapons and related equipment. May be designated by rank as LIEUTENANT, BALLISTICS (gov. ser.). • **GED:** R5, M5, L5 • **SVP:** 2-4 yrs • **Academic:** Ed=A, Eng=G • **Work Field:** 211 • **MPSMS:** 373 • **Aptitudes:** G2, V2, N2, S2, P2, Q3, K3, F3, M3, E5, C3 • **Temperaments:** J, M, V • **Physical:** V=L, H=L, L=L, W, H • **Work Env:** I, N • **Salary:** 4 • **Outlook:** 2

CALIBRATION LABORATORY TECHNICIAN (aircraft-aerospace mfg.) • D.O.T. #019.281-010 • OES #22505 • STANDARDS LABORATORY TECHNICIAN. Tests, calibrates, and repairs electrical, mechanical, and electronic measuring and indicating instruments for conformance to established standards, and assists engineering personnel in development of calibration standards: Plans sequence of testing and calibration procedures for instruments, using blueprints, schematic drawings, and other data. Sets up standardized laboratory equipment to test and measure accuracy of other instruments which are used to record voltage, heat, magnetic resistance, and other factors. Disassembles recording systems and instrumentation, using handtools, and inspects parts for defects. Measures parts for conformity with specifications, using micrometers, calipers, and other precision instruments. Repairs or replaces parts, such as jewels, and electronic units, using jeweler's lathe, files, soldering iron, and other tools. Reassembles and adjusts instrument to calibration standard. Devises formulas to solve problems in measurements and calibrations. Writes procedures and practical guides under direction of engineers to minimize calibration time and maintain precision accuracy of instruments, measuring devices, and recording equipment. • **GED:** R5, M5, L4 • **SVP:** 2-4 yrs • **Academic:** Ed=A, Eng=S • **Work Field:** 111, 211 • **MPSMS:** 601, 602 • **Aptitudes:** G2, V3, N2, S2, P2, Q4, K3, F2, M2, E5, C4 • **Temperaments:** M, T, V •

Physical: V=L, H=N, L=L, S, H • **Work Env:** B, R • **Salary:** 4 • **Outlook:** 4

CHEMICAL-LABORATORY TECHNICIAN (profess. & kin.) • D.O.T. #022.261-010 • OES #24505 • Conducts chemical and physical laboratory tests and makes qualitative and quantitative analyses of materials, liquids, and gases for purposes, such as research, development of new products and materials, processing and production methods, quality control, maintenance of health and safety standards, criminology, environmental, and others involving experimental, theoretical or practical application of chemistry and related sciences: Sets up laboratory equipment and instrumentation required for tests, research or process control. Analyzes products, such as food, drugs, plastics, dyes, paints, detergents, paper, petroleum, and other products, to determine strength, stability, purity, and other characteristics of chemical content. Tests ores, minerals, gases, pollutants, and other materials and substances, such as carbon, tungsten, nitrogen, iron, gold, or nickel. Prepares chemical solutions for use in processing materials, such as textiles, detergents, paper, felt, and fertilizers, following standardized formulas or experimental procedures. May work with radioactive and biological materials, radiochemical procedures, emission spectrometry, and other techniques. • **GED:** R5, M4, L3 • **SVP:** 2-4 yrs • **Academic:** Ed=A, Eng=S • **Work Field:** 147 • **MPSMS:** 722, 723, 724 • **Aptitudes:** G2, V2, N3, S3, P2, Q3, K3, F3, M3, E5, C4 • **Temperaments:** M, T • **Physical:** V=L, H=N, L=L, H • **Work Env:** I • **Salary:** 4 • **Outlook:** 3

CRIMINALIST (profess. & kin.) • D.O.T. #029.281-010 • OES #24599 • CRIME LABORATORY ANALYST; POLICE CHEMIST. Applies scientific principles to analysis, identification, and classification of mechanical devices, chemical and physical substances, materials, liquids, or other physical evidence related to criminology, law enforcement, or investigative work: Searches for, collects, photographs, and preserves evidence. Performs variety of analytical examinations, utilizing chemistry, physics, mechanics, and other sciences. Analyzes items, such as paint, glass, printed matter, paper, ink, fabric, dust, dirt, gases, or other substances, using spectroscope, microscope, infrared and ultraviolet light, microphotography, gas chromatograph, or other recording, measuring, or testing instruments. Identifies hair, skin, tissue, blood, bones, or human organs. Examines and classifies explosives, firearms, bullets, shells, and other weapons. Interprets laboratory findings relative to drugs, poisons, narcotics, alcohol, or other compounds ingested or injected into body. Reconstructs crime scene, preserving marks or impressions made by shoes, tires, or other objects by plaster or moulage casts. Prepares reports or presentations of findings, methods, and techniques used to support conclusions, and prepares results for court or other formal hearings. May testify as expert witness on evidence or crime laboratory techniques. Confers with experts in such specialties as ballistics, fingerprinting, handwriting, documents, electronics, metallurgy, biochemistry, medicine, or others. • **GED:** R5, M4, L5 • **SVP:** 2-4 yrs • **Academic:** Ed=A, Eng=G • **Work Field:** 251, 271 • **MPSMS:** 722, 723, 724 • **Aptitudes:** G1, V1, N1, S2, P2, Q2, K4, F4, M4, E5, C2 • **Temperaments:** M, P, T, V • **Physical:** V=L, H=L, L=L, S, H • **Work Env:** B • **Salary:** 4 • **Outlook:** 3

DECONTAMINATOR (any ind.) • D.O.T. #199.384-010 • OES #39999 • Decontaminates radioactive materials and equipment, using chemical solutions, and sandblasting machine: Reads contamination level, using radiation meter, and sorts contaminated items by size and radiation level, following specifications. Weighs out and mixes chemical solutions in tank according to prescribed formula, and heats solution, using steam hose. Immerses objects, such as pipes, motors, valves, hose, and containers, in solution for specified time, using hoist. Places smaller objects in sandblasting machine, using manipulators or protective gloves, and starts machine to remove greater proportion of contamination and reduce immersion time. Places hot (radioactive) waste, such as sweepings and broken sample bottles, into disposal containers to be processed for land or sea burial. Cleans objects having radiation count under specified amount, using cloth, soap, solvents, wire brush, and buffing wheel. Records type of material and equipment decontaminated and method used. May accompany coffins of waste to disposal area. May monitor radiation-exposed equipment, plant and hospital areas, and materials, using radiation-detector measuring instruments, such as portable gamma survey meter, Geiger counter, and alpha-beta-gamma survey meter. May determine method of decontamination according to size and nature of equipment, and degree of contamination. • **GED:** R3, M3, L3 • **SVP:** 1-2 yrs • **Academic:** Ed=N, Eng=G • **Work Field:** 031, 211 • **MPSMS:** 929 • **Aptitudes:** G3, V3, N4, S4, P4, Q4, K4, F4, M3, E5, C5 • **Temperaments:** M, V • **Physical:** V=L, H=N, L=M, W, H • **Work Env:** I, W, R • **Salary:** 4 • **Outlook:** 3

FILM LABORATORY TECHNICIAN 1 (motion pic.) • D.O.T. #976.381-010 • OES #89914 • Evaluates motion picture film to determine characteristics, such as sensitivity to light, density, and exposure time required for printing, using sensitometer, densitometer, and timer lights: Threads film strip through sensitometer, exposes film to light, and reads gages to determine film's sensitivity to light. Threads film strip through densitometer and exposes film to light to determine density of film. Computes amount of light intensity needed to compensate for density of film, using standardized formulas. Exposes film strip to progressively timed lights to compare effects of various exposure times. Examines developed film strip to determine optimal exposure time and light intensity required for printing. Records test data and routes to FILM DEVELOPER (motion pic.; photofinish.) and FILM PRINTER (motion pic.). May be designated according to specialty as DENSITOMETRIST (motion pic.); SENSITOMETRIST (motion pic.); TIMER (motion pic.). • **GED:** R4, M4, L4 • **SVP:** 2-4 yrs • **Academic:** Ed=N, Eng=S • **Work Field:** 202, 211, 231 • **MPSMS:** 911 • **Aptitudes:** G2, V3, N2, S3, P2, Q3, K3, F3, M3, E5, C2 • **Temperaments:** J, M, T • **Physical:** V=G, H=N, L=L, H • **Work Env:** I • **Salary:** 4 • **Outlook:** 4

FINGERPRINT CLASSIFIER (gov. ser.) • D.O.T. #375.387-010 • OES #39999 • FINGERPRINT EXPERT. Classifies fingerprints and compares fingerprints of unknown persons or suspects with fingerprint records to determine if prints were involved in previous crimes: Classifies record cards containing fingerprints of crime suspects according to specified grouping, and compares fingerprints with others in file to determine if prisoner has criminal record or if he is wanted for other crimes. Examines fingerprint evidence left at scene of crime, classifies prints, and endeavors to identify person. May fingerprint prisoner, using ink pad. May transfer residual fingerprints from objects, such as weapons or drinking glasses, to record cards, using standard technique. May keep files of criminals and suspects, containing such information as photographs, habits, and modus operandi of crimes with which individual has been connected. • **GED:** R4, M2, L3 • **SVP:** 1-2 yrs • **Academic:** Ed=H, Eng=G • **Work Field:** 231, 271 • **MPSMS:** 951 • **Aptitudes:** G3, V4, N4, S2, P2, Q3, K4, F4, M4, E5, C5 • **Temperaments:** M, T • **Physical:** V=G, H=N, L=S • **Work Env:** I • **Salary:** 3 • **Outlook:** 3

GEOLOGICAL AIDE (petrol. production) • D.O.T. #024.267-010 • OES #24511 • Examines and compiles geological information to provide technical data to GEOLOGIST, PETROLEUM (petrol. production) 024.061-022, using surface and subsurface maps, oil and gas well activity reports, and sand and core analysis studies: Studies geological reports to extract well data and posts data to maps and logs. Draws subsurface formation contours on charts to lay out and prepare geological cross section charts. Compiles information regarding well tests, completions, and formation tops to prepare oil or gas well records. Records net sand and sand percentage counts and calculates isopachous values to compile sand analysis data. Studies directional logs and surveys to calculate and plot formation tops. Reads well activity reports and records key well locations in drilling activity book. Assembles and distributes prepared charts, maps, and reports to geologist requesting material. Maintains file record systems and geological library. Attends SCOUT (petrol. production) 010.267-010 meeting to compile information on well activity. Contacts competitors to acquire oil and gas samples from wells. Operates computer terminal for input and retrieval of geological data. • **GED:** R5, M5, L5 • **SVP:** 4-10 yrs • **Academic:** Ed=A, Eng=S • **Work Field:** 251 • **MPSMS:** 725 • **Aptitudes:** G2, V2, N1, S2, P2, Q2, K3, F3, M4, E5, C5 • **Temperaments:** I, P, V • **Physical:** V=L, H=N, L=L, W, H • **Work Env:** I • **Salary:** 5 • **Outlook:** 1

HOT-CELL TECHNICIAN (profess. & kin.) • D.O.T. #015.362-018 • OES #24508 • IRRADIATION TECHNICIAN. Operates

©1991, JIST Works, Inc. • Indianapolis, IN

remote-controlled equipment in hot cell to conduct metallurgical and chemical tests on radioactive materials: Controls slave manipulators from outside cell to remove metal or chemical materials from shielded containers inside hot cell and places on bench or equipment work station. Tests chemical or metallurgical properties of materials according to standardized procedures, and observes reaction through cell window. Sets up and operates machines to cut, lap, and polish test pieces, following blueprints, X-ray negatives, and sketches. Tests physical properties, using equipment, such as tensile tester, hardness tester, metallographic unit, micrometer, and gages. Immerses test sample in chemical compound to prepare for testing. Places irradiated nuclear fuel materials in environmental chamber to test reaction to temperature changes. Records results of tests for further analysis by engineers, scientists, or customers. Places specimen in shielded container for removal from cell, using manipulators. Participates in cleaning and decontamination of cell during maintenance shutdown. May devise adapters and fixtures for use in hot cell operations. • **GED:** R4, M3, L4 • **SVP:** 2-4 yrs • **Academic:** Ed=H, Eng=S • **Work Field:** 211, 251 • **MPSMS:** 715 • **Aptitudes:** G3, V3, N3, S2, P2, Q4, K2, F2, M2, E4, C4 • **Temperaments:** M, T, V • **Physical:** V=L, H=N, L=L, W, H • **Work Env:** I, R • **Salary:** 4 • **Outlook:** 2

HYDROGRAPHER (waterworks) • D.O.T. #025.264-010 • OES #24599 • Analyzes hydrographic data to determine trends in movement and utilization of water: Reads meters and gages to measure waterflow and pressure in streams, conduits, and pipelines, and records data. Measures water level in lakes, reservoirs, and tanks. Calculates seepage and evaporation rates for dams and reservoirs. Measures depth of water in wells and test holes to determine ground water level. Measures snow characteristics to evaluate water yield from snow runoff. Prepares graphs and charts to illustrate water patterns. Positions sluice gates to direct water onto spreading grounds. Installs, calibrates, and maintains metering instruments. Recommends locations for metering stations and instrument placement. • **GED:** R4, M4, L4 • **SVP:** 1-2 yrs • **Academic:** Ed=H, Eng=G • **Work Field:** 232, 251 • **MPSMS:** 725 • **Aptitudes:** G3, V3, N2, S3, P2, Q2, K5, F3, M3, E3, C5 • **Temperaments:** J, M • **Physical:** V=L, H=N, L=M, W, H • **Work Env:** O • **Salary:** 4 • **Outlook:** 3

LABORATORY ASSISTANT (light, heat, & power) • D.O.T. #029.361-018 • OES #24599 • LABORATORY TECHNICIAN. Performs standardized physical and chemical tests on materials and supplies used throughout power system to insure compliance with specifications: Tests water used in boilers of steam generating plant for alkalinity and silica and phosphate content, using colorimeter and spectrophotometer. Notifies POWER-PLANT OPERATOR (light, heat, & power) or AUXILIARY-EQUIPMENT OPERATOR (light, heat, & power) of amount of chemical additives required to bring water to prescribed level of purity. Tests coal to determine B.T.U. content by burning coal samples in colorimeter. Tests oil used in circuit breakers for dielectric strength by placing sample of oil in ceramic cup positioned between two electrodes, and measuring current conducted by oil, using ohmmeter. Ascertains heat resisting qualities of insulating paints and varnishes by coating pieces of sheet metal with paint and varnish and subjecting them to high temperatures. May determine viscosity index of lubricating oils, using viscosimeter. May inspect rubber protective equipment, such as aprons, gloves, and blankets for flaws. • **GED:** R5, M5, L5 • **SVP:** 1-2 yrs • **Academic:** Ed=A, Eng=S • **Work Field:** 211 • **MPSMS:** 722, 723, 724 • **Aptitudes:** G2, V2, N3, S3, P2, Q4, K3, F2, M3, E4, C3 • **Temperaments:** M, T, V • **Physical:** V=L, H=N, L=L, H • **Work Env:** I • **Salary:** 4 • **Outlook:** 3

LABORATORY ASSISTANT (petrol. production) • D.O.T. #024.381-010 • OES #24511 • ANALYST, GEOCHEMICAL PROSPECTING; CORE ANALYST; LABORATORY TESTER. Tests sand, shale, and other earth materials to determine petroleum and mineral content and physical characteristics: Performs routine chemical or physical tests of earth samples in field or laboratory to determine content of hydrocarbon or other minerals indicating presence of petroleum and mineral deposits. Tests core samples brought up during well drilling to determine permeability and porosity of sample, fluid content of sand and shale, salinity of drilling mud, and other conditions affecting oil well drilling oper-

ations. • **GED:** R4, M4, L3 • **SVP:** 6 mos-1 yr • **Academic:** Ed=H, Eng=S • **Work Field:** 211 • **MPSMS:** 340 • **Aptitudes:** G2, V2, N2, S3, P3, Q4, K3, F2, M3, E5, C5 • **Temperaments:** M, T • **Physical:** V=G, H=N, L=L, H • **Work Env:** I • **Salary:** 3 • **Outlook:** 3

LABORATORY ASSISTANT (textile) • D.O.T. #029.381-014 • OES #24599 • LABORATORY TESTER. Performs standardized laboratory tests to verify chemical characteristics or composition of textile fibers, yarns, and products, and materials used in processing textiles: Tests oil and soap products to determine fitness for use in cloth and yarn finishing processes. Tests dyed goods for stripping (removing dye). Tests grey (greige) goods to determine if goods are of specified quality for dyeing, printing, and finishing. Verifies dye formulas used to develop or match colors by dyeing samples of cloth, yarn, or textile fibers, and determines fastness of dyes, using laboratory equipment. Tests raw stock for moisture content with meter-equipped probe. Verifies efficiency of scouring process by testing wool samples to determine percentage of natural greases removed, using scales, solvents, and ovens. Measures tear strength and wet and dry tensile strength, using tensile-testing equipment. Determines color value by subjecting material to lights. Visually inspects yarns and finished materials. May classify finished product according to quality and estimate amount of mending required. • **GED:** R4, M3, L3 • **SVP:** 6 mos-1 yr • **Academic:** Ed=H, Eng=S • **Work Field:** 211 • **MPSMS:** 410, 420 • **Aptitudes:** G3, V3, N3, S3, P2, Q3, K3, F4, M3, E5, C2 • **Temperaments:** M, T, V • **Physical:** V=G, H=L, L=L, H • **Work Env:** I • **Salary:** 3 • **Outlook:** 3

LABORATORY ASSISTANT, METALLURGICAL (iron & steel) • D.O.T. #011.281-010 • OES #22599 • METALLURGICAL ANALYST; METALLURGICAL INSPECTOR. Analyzes data obtained from investigation of physical and chemical properties of metals, or processes used in recovering metals from their ores to select method, standards, and procedures of examination and testing and conducts tests: Analyzes operating records and test reports, or by personal observation and investigation, determines conformance to established procedures, methods, and standards. Conducts physical, chemical, and process examinations, using metallurgical equipment and instruments for routine, special, and experimental investigations. Writes report indicating deviations from specifications and recommends corrective measures for approval. • **GED:** R4, M4, L4 • **SVP:** 2-4 yrs • **Academic:** Ed=A, Eng=S • **Work Field:** 211 • **MPSMS:** 540 • **Aptitudes:** G3, V3, N3, S3, P4, Q3, K4, F3, M3, E5, C5 • **Temperaments:** M, T, V • **Physical:** V=G, H=L, L=L, H • **Work Env:** I • **Salary:** 4 • **Outlook:** 4

LABORATORY SUPERVISOR (profess. & kin.) • D.O.T. #022.137-010 • OES #24105 • Supervises and coordinates activities of personnel engaged in performing chemical and physical tests required for quality control of processes and products: Assigns duties to personnel. Trains new employees. Confers with workers to resolve testing problems. Directs and advises personnel in special test procedures to analyze components and physical properties of materials. Compiles test information required to determine operating efficiency of process or equipment. Reviews laboratory test reports and operating records to diagnose malfunctions. Confers with scientists or engineers to develop nonstandard tests and conduct analyses. • **GED:** R5, M5, L5 • **SVP:** 2-4 yrs • **Academic:** Ed=A, Eng=S • **Work Field:** 211 • **MPSMS:** 722, 723, 724 • **Aptitudes:** G2, V2, N2, S3, P3, Q3, K4, F4, M4, E4, C3 • **Temperaments:** D, M, P, T, V • **Stress:** A • **Physical:** V=N, H=L, L=L • **Work Env:** B • **Salary:** 4 • **Outlook:** 3

LABORATORY TECHNICIAN (auto. mfg.) • D.O.T. #019.381-010 • OES #22599 • Tests soundproofing materials used in automobiles: Operates oscillator, oscilloscope, amplifier, noisemeter, and level recorder to measure sound transmission, absorption, and deadening qualities of materials, such as fiber glass, pressed board felts, and plastics. Prepares and fabricates materials for sample soundproofing components to be evaluated in test automobiles. Records test data. • **GED:** R4, M4, L4 • **SVP:** 6 mos-1 yr • **Academic:** Ed=H, Eng=S • **Work Field:** 211 • **MPSMS:** 591 • **Aptitudes:** G3, V3, N3, S3, P5, Q3, K3, F4, M3, E5, C5 • **Temperaments:** M • **Physical:** V=L, H=N, L=L, H • **Work Env:** I • **Salary:** 3 • **Outlook:** 4

LABORATORY TESTER (any ind.) • D.O.T. #029.261-010 • OES #24505 • Performs laboratory tests according to prescribed standards to determine chemical and physical characteristics or composition of solid, liquid, or gaseous materials and substances for purposes such as quality control, process control, product development, or determining conformity to specifications: Sets up, adjusts and operates laboratory equipment and instrumentation, such as microscopes, centrifuge, agitators, viscosimeter, chemical balance scales, spectrophotometer, colorimeter, and other equipment. Tests liquids and materials used as ingredients in adhesives, cement, propellants, lubricants, refractories, synthetic rubber, plastics, paint, paper, cloth, and other products for such qualities as purity, stability, viscosity, density, absorption, burning rate, and melting or flash point. Tests solutions used in processes, such as anodizing, waterproofing, cleaning, bleaching, and pickling, for chemical strength, specific gravity, or other specification. Tests materials for presence and content of elements or substances, such as hydrocarbons, manganese, natural grease, tungsten, sulfur, cyanide, ash, or dust, or other impurities. Tests samples of manufactured products to verify conformity to specifications. Records test results on standardized forms and writes test reports describing procedures used. May prepare graphs and charts. Cleans and sterilizes laboratory equipment. May prepare chemical solutions according to standard formulas. May add chemicals or raw materials to process solutions or product batches to correct deviations from specifications. May be designated according to product tested as CEMENT TESTER (cement); GAS TESTER (chem.; light, heat, & power; pipe lines); PAINT-AND-VARNISH TECHNICIAN (paint & varn.); SOILS TESTER (profess. & kin.); TESTER, AMMONIA SHIPPING (comp. & liquified gases). For testing of food products see FOOD TESTER (any ind.). • **GED:** R4, M4, L3 • **SVP:** 6 mos-1 yr • **Academic:** Ed=H, Eng=S • **Work Field:** 211 • **MPSMS:** 722, 723, 724 • **Aptitudes:** G3, V3, N3, S3, P2, Q3, K3, F3, M3, E4, C3 • **Temperaments:** J, M, T • **Physical:** V=L, H=N, L=L, H • **Work Env:** I • **Salary:** 3 • **Outlook:** 4

LABORATORY TESTER (synthetic fibers) • D.O.T. #022.281-018 • OES #24505 • Examines, measures, photographs, and tests synthetic fiber samples to facilitate quality control of forming, treating, and texturing processes, performing any combination of following tasks: Dips several twisted threads in melted wax and directs stream of cold water over threads to congeal wax. Slices threads crosswise, using microtome. Dissolves wax, using solvent, and positions thread sample on microscope slide. Inserts slide in microscope and photographs sample, using standard microphotographic equipment and techniques. Develops, prints, and labels photographs. Analyzes photographs to determine whether structure and other characteristics of thread meet plant standards. Determines tensile strength of thread samples, using device that draws material between two jaws until breakage occurs. Measures cross-sectional area of thread samples, using planimeter. Immerses samples in water, corrosives, or cleaning agents to detect shrinkage or damage. Places thread samples in dye bath to evaluate permeability of dye and exposes samples to controlled light source to ascertain fade resistance. Prepares and submits reports of findings to production personnel to facilitate quality control of product. • **GED:** R4, M3, L3 • **SVP:** 1-2 yrs • **Academic:** Ed=H, Eng=S • **Work Field:** 211 • **MPSMS:** 414 • **Aptitudes:** G2, V2, N2, S2, P2, Q3, K4, F3, M3, E5, C2 • **Temperaments:** M, T • **Physical:** V=G, H=N, L=L, H • **Work Env:** I • **Salary:** 4 • **Outlook:** 4

METALLURGICAL TECHNICIAN (profess. & kin.) • D.O.T. #011.261-010 • OES #22599 • METALLURGICAL-LABORATORY ASSISTANT; METALLURGICAL TESTER; PHYSICAL-LABORATORY ASSISTANT. Examines and tests metal samples to determine their physical properties, under direction of METALLOGRAPHER (profess. & kin.): Conducts routine microscopic examinations of metals and alloys to determine their crystal structure, porosity, homogeneity, and other characteristics. Polishes or etches metal specimens and photographs samples, using photomicroscope, or directs photography technical personnel to take, develop, and mount photomicrographs. Examines metal and alloy samples with X-ray, gamma-ray, and magnetic-flux equipment to detect internal fractures, impurities, and similar defects in metals. Tests samples in pressure devices, hot-acid baths, and other apparatus to determine strength, hardness, elasticity, toughness, or

other properties of metal. • **GED:** R4, M4, L4 • **SVP:** 1-2 yrs • **Academic:** Ed=A, Eng=S • **Work Field:** 211 • **MPSMS:** 350, 540 • **Aptitudes:** G3, V3, N3, S3, P3, Q3, K3, F3, M3, E4, C3 • **Temperaments:** M, T • **Physical:** V=L, H=N, L=L, H • **Work Env:** I • **Salary:** 4 • **Outlook:** 4

PHARMACIST (profess. & kin.) • D.O.T. #074.161-010 • OES #32517 • DRUGGIST; REGISTERED PHARMACIST. Compounds and dispenses medications, following prescriptions issued by PHYSICIAN (medical ser.); DENTIST (medical ser.); or other authorized medical practitioner: Weighs, measures, and mixes drugs and other medicinal compounds, and fills bottles or capsules with correct quantity and composition of preparation. Dispenses nonprescription medication to public. Advises self-diagnosing and self-medicating patients, or provides information on potential drug interactions, potential adverse drug reactions, and elements of patient's history which might bear on prescribing decision when in advisory capacity to PHYSICIAN (medical ser.). Advises patient regarding storage for prescription medication. Assures that patient understands prescribed instructions. Answers patient's questions regarding prescription medication. Stores and preserves biologicals, vaccines, serums, and other drugs subject to deterioration, utilizing refrigeration and other methods. Orders and maintains supply of drugs, chemicals, and other pharmaceutical stock. Insures specified quantity and potency of materials for medical use. May act as consultant to civic groups and health practitioners on matters pertaining to pharmacy. May assay medications to determine identity, purity, and strength. May instruct INTERNS (medical ser.) and other medical personnel on matters pertaining to pharmacy, or teach in college of pharmacy. May work in particular area and be designated PHARMACIST, COMMUNITY (profess. & kin.); PHARMACIST, HOSPITAL (profess. & kin.). • **GED:** R5, M5, L5 • **SVP:** 2-4 yrs • **Academic:** Ed=M, Eng=G • **Work Field:** 147 • **MPSMS:** 493 • **Aptitudes:** G1, V2, N2, S4, P2, Q3, K4, F2, M3, E5, C2 • **Temperaments:** M, T • **Physical:** V=G, H=N, L=S, H • **Work Env:** I • **Salary:** 5 • **Outlook:** 3

PHARMACIST ASSISTANT (military ser.) • D.O.T. #074.381-010 • OES #32999 • Mixes and dispenses prescribed medicines and pharmaceutical preparations in absence of or under supervision of PHARMACIST (profess. & kin.): Compounds preparations according to prescriptions issued by medical, dental, or veterinary officers. Pours, weighs, or measures dosages and grinds, heats, filters, or dissolves and mixes liquid or soluble drugs and chemicals. Procures, stores, and issues pharmaceutical materials and supplies. Maintains files and records and submits required pharmacy reports. • **GED:** R4, M4, L3 • **SVP:** 1-2 yrs • **Academic:** Ed=H, Eng=S • **Work Field:** 142, 143, 221 • **MPSMS:** 493 • **Aptitudes:** G2, V2, N3, S4, P3, Q4, K3, F3, M4, E5, C3 • **Temperaments:** M, T • **Physical:** V=G, H=N, L=L, H • **Work Env:** I • **Salary:** 4 • **Outlook:** 4

PHOTO-OPTICS TECHNICIAN (profess. & kin.) • D.O.T. #029.280-010 • OES #24599 • Sets up and operates photo-optical instrumentation to record and photograph data for scientific and engineering projects: Operates and calibrates photo-optical equipment according to formalized procedures, maintenance manuals, and schematic diagrams. Operates test equipment and performs analysis of data for engineering and scientific personnel. May install and calibrate optical and photographic data collection equipment in missiles, aircraft, weaponry, weather or communication satellites, underwater devices, or other installations. May evaluate adequacy of data obtained to determine need for future changes in instrumentation. May modify existing equipment and participate in planning and testing modified equipment and instrumentation procedures. • **GED:** R5, M4, L3 • **SVP:** 1-2 yrs • **Academic:** Ed=A, Eng=S • **Work Field:** 201 • **MPSMS:** 601, 602, 609 • **Aptitudes:** G2, V2, N3, S2, P2, Q4, K3, F3, M3, E5, C4 • **Temperaments:** M, T • **Physical:** V=L, H=N, L=L, H • **Work Env:** I • **Salary:** 4 • **Outlook:** 3

PHOTOGRAPHER, SCIENTIFIC (profess. & kin.) • D.O.T. #143.062-026 • OES #34023 • Photographs variety of subject material to illustrate or record scientific data or phenomena, utilizing knowledge of scientific procedures and photographic technology and techniques: Plans methods and procedures for photographing subject material and setup of equipment required, such as microscopes, telescopes, infrared or ultraviolet lighting, and

X-ray. Sets up and positions camera for photographing material or subject. Trips shutter to expose film. May prepare microscope slides. May make photographic copies of fragile documents and other material. May engage in research to develop new photographic procedures, methods, and materials. May process film and photographic paper to produce transparencies, prints, slides, and motion picture film. Usually specializes in specific field, such as chemistry, biology, medicine, metallurgy, physiology, astronomy, aerodynamics, ballistics, or engineering and is designated accordingly. • **GED:** R4, M3, L4 • **SVP:** 2-4 yrs • **Academic:** Ed=H, Eng=S • **Work Field:** 201 • **MPSMS:** 723, 724, 730 • **Aptitudes:** G2, V3, N3, S2, P2, Q4, K3, F3, M3, E5, C2 • **Temperaments:** J, T, V • **Physical:** V=G, H=N, L=L, W, H • **Work Env:** I • **Salary:** 4 • **Outlook:** 3

QUALITY-CONTROL TECHNICIAN (profess. & kin.) • D.O.T. #012.261-014 • OES #22599 • Tests and inspects products at various stages of production process and compiles and evaluates statistical data to determine and maintain quality and reliability of products: Interprets engineering drawings, schematic diagrams, or formulas to arrive at specified quality and reliability standards. Selects products for tests at specified stages in production process, and tests for items, such as dimensions, performance, and mechanical, electrical, or chemical characteristics. Sets up and performs destructive and nondestructive tests on materials, parts, or products to measure performance, life, or material characteristics. Records test data, using statistical quality control procedures and prepares data in graph or chart form. Evaluates data and writes summaries to validate or show deviations from existing standards. Suggests in written or oral form, modifications of existing quality or production standards to achieve optimum quality within limits of equipment capability. May specialize in any of following areas of quality-control engineering as design, incoming material, process control, product evaluation, inventory control, product reliability, research and development, and administrative application. • **GED:** R5, M5, L4 • **SVP:** 2-4 yrs • **Academic:** Ed=A, Eng=G • **Work Field:** 211, 244 • **MPSMS:** 712 • **Aptitudes:** G2, V2, N2, S2, P2, Q3, K3, F3, M3, E5, C4 • **Temperaments:** M, T, V • **Physical:** V=L, H=N, L=L, W, H • **Work Env:** I • **Salary:** 4 • **Outlook:** 4

RADIOISOTOPE-PRODUCTION OPERATOR (profess. & kin.) • D.O.T. #015.362-022 • OES #24508 • ISOTOPE-PRODUCTION TECHNICIAN. Controls laboratory compounding equipment en closed in protective hot cell to prepare radioisotopes and other radioactive materials for use as tracers for biological, biomedical, physiological, and industrial purposes according to written procedures: Places specified amounts of chemicals into container to be irradiated at nuclear reactor or with other irradiation equipment. Secures vacuum pump head to outlet valve on special container to replace air with inert gas, and routes container to irradiation facility. Receives irradiated chemicals delivered in shielded cell. Moves manipulator to open container and transfer irradiated contents into glass vessel. Opens pneumatic valves or uses manipulators to add specified types and quantities of chemical reagents into glass vessel to produce radioactive product. Controls manipulators to pour liquids required to perform standard chemical analyses involving titration and filtration. With draws radioactive sample for transport to chemical laboratory for analysis. Fills shipping container inside cell with prescribed quantity of radioisotope material for shipment pending sample approval. • **GED:** R4, M3, L4 • **SVP:** 1-2 yrs • **Academic:** Ed=H, Eng=S • **Work Field:** 147 • **MPSMS:** 490, 715 • **Aptitudes:** G3, V3, N3, S3, P3, Q4, K3, F3, M3, E3, C4 • **Temperaments:** M, T • **Physical:** V=L, H=N, L=L, W, H • **Work Env:** I, R • **Salary:** 4 • **Outlook:** 2

RADIOPHARMACIST (medical ser.) • D.O.T. #074.161-014 • OES #32517 • Prepares and dispenses radio active pharmaceuticals used for patient diagnosis and therapy, applying principles and practices of pharmacy and radiochemistry: Receives radiopharmaceutical prescription from PHYSICIAN (medical ser.) and reviews prescription to determine suitability of radio pharmaceutical for intended use. Verifies that specified radioactive substance and reagent will give desired results in examination or treatment procedures, utilizing knowledge of radiopharmaceutical preparation and principles of drug biodistribution. Calculates volume of radioactive pharmaceutical required to provide patient with de-sired level of radioactivity at prescribed time, according to established rates of radioisotope decay. Compounds radioactive substances and reagents to prepare radio pharmaceutical, following radiopharmacy laboratory procedures. Assays prepared radiopharmaceutical, using measuring and analysis instruments and equipment, such as ionization chamber, pulse-height analyzer, and radioisotope dose calibrator, to verify rate of drug disintegration and to ensure that patient receives required dose. Consults with PHYSICIAN (medical ser.) following patient treatment or procedure to review and evaluate quality and effectiveness of radiopharmaceutical. Conducts research to develop or improve radiopharmaceuticals. Prepares reports for regulatory agencies to obtain approval for testing and use of new radiopharmaceuticals. Maintains control records for receipt, storage, preparation, and disposal of radioactive nuclei. Occasionally conducts training for students and medical professionals concerning radiopharmacy use, characteristics, and compounding procedures. • **GED:** R6, M5, L5 • **SVP:** 2-4 yrs • **Academic:** Ed=B, Eng=G • **Work Field:** 147 • **MPSMS:** 484, 732 • **Aptitudes:** G1, V1, N2, S2, P1, Q2, K2, F2, M3, E5, C4 • **Temperaments:** J, T • **Physical:** V=L, H=N, L=L, H • **Work Env:** I, R • **Salary:** 4 • **Outlook:** 3

REACTOR OPERATOR, TEST-AND-RESEARCH (profess. & kin.) • D.O.T. #015.362-026 • OES #24508 • Controls operation of nuclear reactor to create fissionable materials used for research purposes, study structure of atoms, and determine properties of materials: Positions fuel elements (uranium) and object to be irradiated in position in reactor core, using slave manipulators. Installs instrumentation leads in core to measure operating temperature and pressure in reactor working from mockups, blueprints, and wiring and instrumentation diagrams. Activates reactor and inserts object to be irradiated into rabbit (pneumatic) tube, beam hole, or irradiation tunnel according to size of object and nature of experiment. Monitors instruments at console and reactor panels to control chain reaction, following directions of nuclear experimenters. Calculates applicable limits of operating factors, such as temperature and pressure, using standard formulas, and adjusts controls to maintain operating conditions, such as power level, airflow and waterflow, temperature, and radiation and neutron levels in reactor within operating limits. Records data, such as type of material irradiated, exposure time, pile atmospheric conditions, and position of control rods in core. Disassembles reactor parts, such as core plug (shield) and control rods, using crane and handtools. Lifts spent fuel elements and irradiated objects from core, using extension tool, and drops them through chute into canal for recovery of fissionable material. May work as member of team and alternate between operating reactor controls and monitoring instruments, gages, and other recording devices in control room. • **GED:** R4, M4, L4 • **SVP:** 2-4 yrs • **Academic:** Ed=H, Eng=S • **Work Field:** 251 • **MPSMS:** 715 • **Aptitudes:** G3, V3, N3, S3, P3, Q3, K3, F3, M3, E4, C4 • **Temperaments:** M, T, V • **Physical:** V=L, H=L, L=L, H • **Work Env:** I, R • **Salary:** 4 • **Outlook:** 2

SCANNER (profess. & kin.) • D.O.T. #015.384-010 • OES #24508 • Compiles lists of events (collisions of atomic nuclei) from photographs of bubble chamber, cloud chamber, or other particle detector, and operates machine to record characteristics of events on magnetic tape or punchcards: Observes projected photographs to locate particle tracks, locate and count events indicated by tracks, and identify nature of observed events. Receives instructions from scientist directing project as to specific events that are important in experiment, and identifies such events from among other "pseudoevents". Turns cranks to move projector and locates point on track under crosshairs of eyepiece. Presses button to record coordinates of point on tape or punchcard. Repeats process to record successive stages of tracks resulting from each event to provide information for scientists to identify particles. May use microscope fitted with scales and protractors to scan photographic emulsions previously exposed to direct radiation and to compute direction, angle, length, curvature, density, and depth of tracks from standard formulas. • **GED:** R4, M3, L4 • **SVP:** 1-2 yrs • **Academic:** Ed=H, Eng=G • **Work Field:** 211, 232 • **MPSMS:** 715 • **Aptitudes:** 1G3, V3, N3, S2, P2, Q3, K3, F4, M4, E5, C5 • **Temperaments:** J, M, T • **Physical:** V=L, H=N, L=S, H • **Work Env:** I • **Salary:** 4 • **Outlook:** 2

SPECTROSCOPIST (profess. & kin.) • D.O.T. #011.281-014 •

OES #22599 • SPECTROGRAPHER; SPECTROGRAPHIC ANALYST. Conducts spectrographic examinations of metal and mineral samples under established procedures, using spectrograph, spectrometer, densitometer, and other measuring instruments: Analyzes densitometer or spectrometer readings to measure density ratio of specific elements in sample. Computes percentage composition of sample by comparing intensity ratio with standard charts. Investigates deviations from standard, performing further examinations by other spectrographic procedures and methods to establish degree of conformance to standard. Records quantitative determination, procedure, and standard applied for each sample examined. • GED: R4, M4, L4 • SVP: 2-4 yrs • Academic: Ed=A, Eng=S • Work Field: 211 • MPSMS: 708, 711 • Aptitudes: G2, V3, N2, S2, P3, Q4, K3, F3, M3, E5, C3 • Temperaments: M, T • Physical: V=L, H=N, L=L, H • Work Env: I • Salary: 4 • Outlook: 3

TESTER (petrol. refin.) • D.O.T. #029.261-022 • OES #24511 • CRUDE TESTER; GAS ANALYST; LABORATORY INSPECTOR; LABORATORY TECHNICIAN; LABORATORY TESTER; OIL TESTER. Tests and analyzes samples of crude oil and petroleum products during processing stages, using laboratory apparatus, testing equipment, and following standard test procedures to determine physical and chemical properties and insure products meet quality control standards: Tests samples of crude and blended oils, gases, asphalts, and pressure distillates to determine characteristics, such as boiling, vapor, freeze, condensation, flash and aniline points, viscosity, specific gravity, penetration, doctor solution, distillation, and corrosion, using test and laboratory equipment, such as hydrometers, fractionators, distillation apparatus, and analytical scales. Analyzes content of products to determine presence of gases, such as propane, iso-butane, butane, iso-pentane, and ethene. Determines hydrocarbon composition of gasolines, blending stocks and gases, using fractional distillation equipment, gas chromatography, and mass spectrometer. Operates fractionation column to separate crude oil into oils with different boiling points to determine their properties. Analyzes composition of products to determine quantitative presence of gum, sulfur, aromatics, olefins, water, and sediment. Compares color of liquid product with charts to determine processing factors measurable by color. May test air and water samples to detect industrial pollutants. • GED: R4, M4, L3 • SVP: 1-2 yrs • Academic: Ed=H, Eng=S • Work Field: 211 • MPSMS: 501 • Aptitudes: G2, V3, N2, S3, P3, Q4, K4, F3, M3, E4, C3 • Temperaments: M, T • Physical: V=L, H=N, L=L, H • Work Env: I, R • Salary: 4 • Outlook: 3

TESTER (profess. & kin.) • D.O.T. #011.361-010 • OES #22599 • PHYSICAL TESTER; TESTING-MACHINE OPERATOR. Measures tensile strength, hardness, ductility, or other physical properties of metal specimens, following a prescribed series of operations on various types of testing machines: (1) Determines tensile strength on tension-testing machines. Measures dimensions of specimen with scales and micrometers and records measurements. Screws or clamps specimen in holders on machine. Clamps extensometer onto specimen and connects wire from extensometer to automatic stress-strain recorder. Turns handwheels or moves levers to apply tension to specimen at specified rate. Notes reading of indicator dial on control panel of machine or observes stress-strain curve (curve obtained by plotting applied tension against resultant elongation) being drawn by recorder to determine yield point and tensile strength of specimen. Removes pieces of broken specimen from machine, fits them together, and measures the amount of elongation. Makes simple calculations of values, such as unit tensile strength and percentage elongation, using tables. Records readings and calculations on special forms. (2) Measures hardness of specimens [HARDNESS INSPECTOR (heat treat.)]. (3) Measures ductility of sheet-metal specimens in sheet-metal testing machine. May test specimens for plasticity and compression. May specialize in testing iron or steel sheets for ductility and be designated SHEET TESTER (iron & steel). • GED: R4, M4, L3 • SVP: 6 mos-1 yr • Academic: Ed=A, Eng=S • Work Field: 211 • MPSMS: 540 • Aptitudes: G3, V3, N3, S3, P3, Q3, K3, F3, M3, E4, C4 • Temperaments: M, T • Physical: V=L, H=N, L=L, W, H • Work Env: I • Salary: 3 • Outlook: 3

ULTRASOUND TECHNOLOGIST (medical ser.) • D.O.T. #078.364-010 • OES #32999 • Operates ultrasound diagnostic equipment to produce two-dimensional ultrasonic pattern and positive pictures of internal organs, for use by professional personnel in diagnosis of disease, study of malfunction of organs, and prenatal examination of fetus and placenta: Selects equipment for use in ultrasound setup according to specifications of examination. Explains process to patient, and instructs and assists patient in assuming physical position for required exposure to ultrasonic waves. Adjusts equipment controls according to specific orders and part of body to be examined. Moves transducer by hand or by manipulation of remote control device and observes sound wave display screen to note ultrasonic pattern produced. Activates equipment which automatically produces visual image of internal organs from ultrasonic pattern, or which produces continuing recorder strip printout of ultrasonic pattern. Photographs visual image of organs shown on display module, or removes recorder strip printout from machine when specified time for recording has elapsed, to obtain permanent record of internal examination. Attaches identification tag to photographs or recorder printouts to insure maintenance of records. Discusses test results with department supervisor or professional personnel to determine whether additional ultrasound examination is required, and repeats process as needed to secure desired results. • GED: R5, M4, L4 • SVP: 2-4 yrs • Academic: Ed=A, Eng=S • Work Field: 294 • MPSMS: 925 • Aptitudes: G3, V3, N3, S2, P2, Q3, K3, F3, M3, E5, C3 • Temperaments: M, P, T • Stress: E • Physical: V=L, H=L, L=L, W, H • Work Env: I • Salary: 4 • Outlook: 4

WEATHER OBSERVER (profess. & kin.) • D.O.T. #025.267-014 • OES #24599 • METEOROLOGICAL TECHNICIAN. Observes and records weather conditions for use in forecasting: Periodically observes general weather, sky and visibility conditions, and reads weather instruments including thermometers, barometers, and hygrometers to ascertain elements, such as temperature, barometric pressure, humidity, wind velocity, and precipitation. Transmits and receives weather data from other stations over teletype machine. May collect upper-air data on temperature, humidity, and winds, using weather balloon and radiosonde equipment. May conduct pilot briefings. • GED: R4, M4, L4 • SVP: 1-2 yrs • Academic: Ed=H, Eng=S • Work Field: 232, 251 • MPSMS: 725 • Aptitudes: G3, V3, N2, S3, P2, Q2, K5, F4, M5, E5, C5 • Temperaments: J, M • Physical: V=L, H=N, L=L • Work Env: I • Salary: 4 • Outlook: 1

02.04 Laboratory Technology

Workers in this group use special laboratory techniques and equipment to perform tests in the fields of chemistry, biology, or physics. They record information that results from their experiments and tests. They help scientists, medical doctors, researchers, and engineers in their work. Hospitals, government agencies, universities, and private industries employ these workers in their laboratories and research facilities.

✔ **What kind of work would you do?**
Your work activities would depend upon your specific job. For example, you might:

©1991, JIST Works, Inc. • Indianapolis, IN

- set up and operate laboratory equipment to conduct chemical and physical tests on metal ores.
- prepare slides and use microscopes to identify diseases in an organ removed by surgery.
- measure rainfall and riverflow, record findings, and prepare a summary report of conditions.

- set up equipment to test fire a gun to gather evidence for a criminal investigation.
- prepare compounds and package prescription drugs.
- conduct tests on samples from oil drilling operations.

✔ **What skills and abilities do you need for this kind of work?**

To do this kind of work, you must be able to:

- understand and use scientific and technical language and symbols.
- recognize slight differences in the shape, color, or texture of things.
- follow technical instructions which may be verbal, in writing, or in the form of charts or drawings.

- do work that requires being very precise or accurate.
- use eyes, hands, and fingers to operate delicate and sensitive equipment.
- use measurable and verifiable information for making decisions or judgments.

✔ **How do you know if you would like or could learn to do this kind of work?**

The following questions may give you clues about yourself as you consider this group of jobs.

- Have you used test tubes, microscopes, or other laboratory instruments? Do you enjoy working with scientific equipment?
- Have you read scientific or technical manuals or journals? Can you understand the language and symbols used?
- Have you collected rocks? Can you recognize different minerals that are present?

- Have you had algebra or geometry courses? Can you read and understand charts and graphs?
- Have you repaired or assembled a precision device such as a radio or clock? Did it work properly afterwards?
- Have you had military experience collecting water samples, or conducting blood tests? Do you enjoy this type of work?

✔ **How can you prepare for and enter this kind of work?**

Occupations in this group usually require education and/or training extending from one year to over ten years, depending upon the specific kind of work. Most of these jobs are entry positions requiring workers to have a two-to four-year degree. Some workers may move into laboratory or testing work from production areas. On-the-job training is sometimes available to applicants who have appropriate skills or work related experience. Some jobs are offered to those who have taken scientific or technical courses in high school or a post-high school program. Courses in chemistry, physical science, or life science will be helpful.

✔ **What else should you consider about these jobs?**

Many medical and technical facilities operate on a 24-hour schedule. Some employees must work at night or at varying hours throughout the week.

If you think you would like to do this kind of work, look at the job titles listed below.

GOE: 02.04.02 Life Sciences

BIOLOGICAL AIDE (agric.) • D.O.T. #049.384-010 • OES #24502 • Assists research workers in experiments in biology, bacteriology, plant pathology, mycology, and related agricultural sciences: Sets up laboratory and field equipment, performs routine tests, and keeps records of plant growth, experimental plots, greenhouse activity, use of insecticides, beehives, and other agricultural experimentation. Cleans and maintains field and laboratory equipment. • GED: R3, M3, L3 • SVP: 1-2 yrs • Academic:

Ed=H, Eng=S • **Work Field:** 002, 003, 251 • **MPSMS:** 300, 310 • **Aptitudes:** G3, V3, N4, S3, P3, Q4, K3, F4, M3, E4, C5 • **Temperaments:** R • **Physical:** V=L, H=L, L=M, W, H • **Work Env:** B • **Salary:** 4 • **Outlook:** 3

BIOLOGY SPECIMEN TECHNICIAN (profess. & kin.) • D.O.T. #041.381-010 • OES #24502 • Prepares and embeds in plastic, biological specimens of plant and animal life for use as instructional aids: Selects plant or animal specimen in preserved or dried state. Dissects animal and cleans all matter from skeletal structures. Prepares slices or cross sections of small animals, embryos, or cross sections of animal organs, such as glands, kidneys, hearts, or eyes. Selects, trims, and stains a variety of stalks, flowers, and leaves to show plant structure and systems. Selects different stains to clearly indicate support structure, circulatory system, or other feature of plant or animal. Assembles and positions components of specimen in mold, using pins and holding devices. Mixes polylite plastic or other material and completes embedding by varied molding techniques. Works with plants, animals, mollusks, insects, and other classes of plants and animals. Identifies type and age of specimen, date of preparation, and type of embedding material used. May operate incubator to grow chicken eggs for embryo specimens. May prepare ecological kits which demonstrate polluting conditions in water, soil, or air. • **GED:** R4, M3, L3 • **SVP:** 2-4 yrs • **Academic:** Ed=H, Eng=S • **Work Field:** 136, 152 • **MPSMS:** 732 • **Aptitudes:** G3, V3, N4, S2, P2, Q4, K2, F2, M2, E5, C3 • **Temperaments:** J, M, R, T • **Physical:** V=G, H=N, L=S, H • **Work Env:** I • **Salary:** 4 • **Outlook:** 3

BIOMEDICAL EQUIPMENT TECHNICIAN (profess. & kin.) • D.O.T. #019.261-010 • OES #85908 • BIOMEDICAL ELECTRONICS TECHNICIAN; BIOMEDICAL ENGINEERING TECHNICIAN. Repairs, calibrates, and maintains medical equipment and instrumentation used in health-care delivery field: Inspects and installs medical and related technical equipment in medical and research facilities for use by physicians, nurses, scientists, or engineers involved in researching, monitoring, diagnosing, and treating physical ailments or dysfunctions. Services various equipment and apparatus, such as patient monitors, electrocardiographs, blood-gas analyzers, X-ray units, defibrillators, electrosurgical units, anesthesia apparatus, pacemakers, blood-pressure transducers, spirometers, sterilizers, diathermy equipment, in-house television systems, patient-care computers, and other related technical paraphernalia. Repairs, calibrates, and maintains equipment, using handtools, power tools, measuring devices, and knowledge of manufacturers' manuals, troubleshooting techniques, and preventive-maintenance schedules. Safety-tests medical equipment and health-care facility's structural environment to insure patient and staff safety from electrical or mechanical hazards. Consults with medical or research staff to ascertain that equipment functions properly and safely, utilizing knowledge of electronics, medical terminology, human anatomy and physiology, chemistry, and physics. May demonstrate and explain correct operation of equipment to medical personnel. May modify or develop instruments or devices, under supervision of medical or engineering staff. May work as salesperson or service technician for equipment manufacturers or their sales representatives. • **GED:** R4, M4, L4 • **SVP:** 1-2 yrs • **Academic:** Ed=H, Eng=S • **Work Field:** 111 • **MPSMS:** 580 • **Aptitudes:** G3, V3, N3, S2, P2, Q3, K3, F3, M3, E5, C3 • **Temperaments:** M, T • **Physical:** V=L, H=N, L=L, W, H • **Work Env:** I • **Salary:** 4 • **Outlook:** 3

CEPHALOMETRIC ANALYST (medical ser.) • D.O.T. #078.384-010 • OES #32999 • CEPHALOMETRIC TECHNICIAN; CEPHALOMETRIC TRACER; TRACER. Traces head X-rays and illustrates cosmetic result of proposed orthodontic treatment: Traces frontal and lateral head X-rays onto transparent paper, using template, compass, protractor, and knowledge of cranial-facial skeletal structure. Traces lower teeth from occlusal X-ray or photograph to locate key points defining true curve of lower dental arch. Records cephalometric measurements to prepare data for computer analysis, using electronic data recording equipment. Compiles data from tracings and computer plot sheets to illustrate results of proposed surgery or other orthodontic treatment. • **GED:** R4, M4, L4 • **SVP:** 1-2 yrs • **Academic:** Ed=H, Eng=S • **Work Field:** 242, 282 • **MPSMS:** 922 • **Aptitudes:** G3, V3, N3, S3, P3, Q4, K3, F3, M3, E5, C4 • **Temperaments:** M, T • **Physical:** V=L,

H=N, L=S, H • **Work Env:** I • **Salary:** 4 • **Outlook:** 3

CHEMISTRY TECHNOLOGIST (medical ser.) • D.O.T. #078.261-010 • OES #32902 • MEDICAL TECHNOLOGIST, CHEMISTRY; TECHNOLOGIST, BIOCHEMISTRY. Performs qualitative and quantitative chemical analyses of body fluids and exudates, following manual instructions, to provide information used in diagnosing and treating diseases: Tests body specimens, such as urine, blood, spinal fluid, and gastric juices, for presence and quantity of metabolic substances and byproducts, such as sugar, albumin, and acetone bodies; and for various chemicals, drugs, and poisons. Prepares solutions used in chemical analysis. Calibrates and maintains spectrophotometers, colorimeters, flame photometers, and other equipment used in quantitative and qualitative analysis. • **GED:** R5, M4, L5 • **SVP:** 2-4 yrs • **Academic:** Ed=B, Eng=G • **Work Field:** 294 • **MPSMS:** 925 • **Aptitudes:** G2, V2, N3, S3, P3, Q4, K3, F2, M3, E4, C3 • **Temperaments:** M, T, V • **Physical:** V=L, H=N, L=L, H • **Work Env:** I • **Salary:** 4 • **Outlook:** 3

CYTOTECHNOLOGIST (medical ser.) • D.O.T. #078.281-010 • OES #32902 • Stains, mounts, and studies cells of human body to determine pathological condition: Examines specimen, and diagnoses nature and extent of disease or cellular damage. Executes variety of laboratory tests and analyses to confirm findings. Reports information to PATHOLOGIST (medical ser.). • **GED:** R5, M4, L5 • **SVP:** 1-2 yrs • **Academic:** Ed=A, Eng=S • **Work Field:** 211 • **MPSMS:** 925 • **Aptitudes:** G2, V3, N3, S1, P1, Q3, K4, F1, M2, E4, C3 • **Temperaments:** M, T, V • **Physical:** V=L, H=N, L=L, H • **Work Env:** I • **Salary:** 4 • **Outlook:** 4

EMBALMER (per. ser.) • D.O.T. #338.371-014 • OES #39014 • Prepares bodies for interment in conformity with legal requirements: Washes and dries body, using germicidal soap and towels or hot air drier. Inserts convex celluloid or cotton between eyeball and eyelid to prevent slipping and sinking of eyelid. Presses diaphragm to evacuate air from lungs. May join lips, using needle and thread or wire. Packs body orifices with cotton saturated with embalming fluid to prevent escape of gases or waste matter. Makes incision in arm or thigh, using scalpel, inserts pump tubes into artery, and starts pump that drains blood from circulatory system and replaces blood with embalming fluid. Incises stomach and abdominal walls and probes internal organs, such as bladder and liver, using trocar to withdraw blood and waste matter from organs. Attaches trocar to pump-tube, starts pump, and repeats probing to force embalming fluid into organs. Closes incisions, using needle and suture. Reshapes or reconstructs disfigured or maimed bodies, using materials, such as clay, cotton, plaster of paris, and wax. Applies cosmetics to impart lifelike appearance. Dresses body and places body in casket. May arrange funeral details, such as type of casket or burial dress and place of interment [DIRECTOR, FUNERAL (per. ser.)]. May maintain records, such as itemized list of clothing or valuables delivered with body and names of persons embalmed. • **GED:** R4, M4, L4 • **SVP:** 2-4 yrs • **Academic:** Ed=H, Eng=S • **Work Field:** 291 • **MPSMS:** 909 • **Aptitudes:** G2, V3, N3, S3, P2, Q4, K3, F2, M3, E5, C3 • **Temperaments:** J, M, T, V • **Physical:** V=L, H=N, L=H, W, S, H • **Work Env:** I, R • **Salary:** 4 • **Outlook:** 3

FOOD TESTER (any ind.) • D.O.T. #029.361-014 • OES #24505 • Performs standardized tests to determine quantity or quality of physical or chemical properties of food or beverage products, or to insure compliance with company or government quality standards: Conducts standardized tests of foods or beverages, packaged, canned, frozen or specialty food products, and additives and preservatives for flavor, color, texture, nutritional, or other factors, using incubator, auto clave, ovens, balance scales, refractometer, or other equipment. Tests flavoring and spice products for moisture, oil content, coloring, and pungency, using spectrophotometer, stereomicroscope, and ovens. Tests production samples of foods for compliance with standards, using luminatron, pH meter, distillation equipment, and balance scales. Refers to prepared tables or computes such factors as moisture, salt content, sediment, or solubility. Smells samples of food for odors or tastes for prescribed flavor. Observes sample smear, sediment disk, or agar sample through microscope to identify bacterial or extraneous matter. Compares test results with standards and records results. May mix ingredients to make reagents. May operate calculating machine to compute percentages of ingredients in finished product. May use special methods or equipment to test certain foods. May be identified according to quality or product tested. • **GED:** R5, M5, L4 • **SVP:** 6 mos-1 yr • **Academic:** Ed=A, Eng=S • **Work Field:** 211 • **MPSMS:** 380, 390 • **Aptitudes:** G3, V3, N3, S3, P3, Q3, K3, F3, M3, E5, C3 • **Temperaments:** M, T • **Physical:** V=L, H=N, L=L, H • **Work Env:** I • **Salary:** 3 • **Outlook:** 2

HERBARIUM WORKER (profess. & kin.) • D.O.T. #041.384-010 • OES #24502 • Fumigates, presses, and mounts plant specimens, and maintains collection records of herbarium maintained by botanical garden, museum, or other institution: Records identification information concerning incoming plants. Places specimens in fumigation cabinet and turns valves to release toxic fumes that destroy insects, fungus, or parasites adhering to specimens. Arranges specimens between sheets of unsized paper so that upper and under portions of leaves, blossoms, and other components are visible, and pads paper with layers of felt and newsprint to protect specimens and form stacks. Places specified number of stacks in pressing frame and writes identification information on top layer of paper on each stack. Secures frame around stacks by tightening frame section with screws, fastening with leather straps, or tying with twine, to compress stacks and press and dry specimens in desired configuration. Mounts dried specimens on heavy paper, using glue, adhesive strips, or needle and thread, taking care to prevent distortion or breakage of specimens. Writes identification information on papers and inserts mounted specimens in labeled envelopes or folders. Files folders in drawers or cabinets according to standard botanical classification system. Maintains card files of specimens in herbarium collection and records of acquisitions, loans, exchanges, or sales of specimens. • **GED:** R4, M3, L4 • **SVP:** 6 mos-1 yr • **Academic:** Ed=H, Eng=S • **Work Field:** 031, 063, 231 • **MPSMS:** 310, 732, 969 • **Aptitudes:** G3, V3, N4, S3, P2, Q3, K3, F3, M3, E5, C4 • **Temperaments:** J, T, V • **Physical:** V=L, H=N, L=L, H • **Work Env:** I • **Salary:** 3 • **Outlook:** 2

IMMUNOHEMATOLOGIST (medical ser.) • D.O.T. #078.221-010 • OES #32999 • Performs immunohematology tests, recommends blood problem solutions to doctors, and serves blood bank and community as consultant and instructor: Visually analyzes blood in specimen tubes to determine temperature and speed of centrifuge for starting hematology tests. Centrifuges blood specimen to separate red cells from serum and examines separated cells to detect presence of antibodies. Interprets evidence observed to devise experiments and suggest techniques that will resolve patient's blood problems. Combines known and unknown serums with red cells in test tubes and selects reagents, such as albumin, protolytic enzymes, and anti-human globulin, for individual tests to enhance and make visible reactions of agglutination and hemolysis. Processes various combinations in centrifuge and examines resulting samples under microscope to identify evidence of agglutination or hemolysis. Repeats and varies tests until normal suspension of reagents, serum, and red cells is attained. Writes blood specifications to meet patient's need, on basis of test results, and applies knowledge of blood classification system to locate donor's blood. Performs hematology tests on donor's blood to confirm matching blood types. Requisitions and sends blood to supply patient's need, and prepares written report to inform physician of test results and of required volume of blood to administer. Forwards copy of report to furnish data input for computer files. Studies worksheets to evaluate completeness of hematology tests and reads labels of related specimen tubes to identify known patients. Instructs MEDICAL-LABORATORY TECHNICIANS (medical ser.) 078.381-014 in classroom, in work situations, and over telephone to teach techniques of microscopic identification of precipitation, agglutination, or hemolysis in blood that leads to resolutions of problems. Writes notes on worksheets of MEDICAL-LABORATORY TECHNICIANS (medical ser.) 078.381-014 to suggest possible solutions for specific problems and returns worksheets and specimens to aid personnel in blood bank reference library. • **GED:** R5, M3, L5 • **SVP:** 4-10 yrs • **Academic:** Ed=B, Eng=G • **Work Field:** 211, 294 • **MPSMS:** 925 • **Aptitudes:** G2, V2, N3, S1, P1, Q3, K2, F2, M2, E5, C2 • **Temperaments:** J, P, T • **Stress:** E • **Physical:** V=L, H=N, L=S, S, H • **Work Env:** I • **Salary:** 5 • **Outlook:** 4

LABORATORY ASSISTANT, BLOOD AND PLASMA (drug prep. & related) • D.O.T. #078.687-010 • OES #32905 • Performs routine laboratory tasks related to processing whole blood and blood components: Centrifuges whole blood to produce various components including packed red cells, platelet concentrate, washed red cells, and plasma. Examines blood stock at designated intervals to confirm that all units are in satisfactory condition. Observes thermostats on storage units to confirm that temperature remains constant at designated temperature. Inspects blood units returned from hospitals to determine whether plasma can be salvaged and if so refers to plasma salvage unit. Confirms that sedimentation has occurred, that color is normal, and that containers are in satisfactory condition. Cleans and maintains laboratory equipment, supplies, and laboratory. Performs related clerical duties including updating statistical records, labeling tubes, and scheduling processing runs. • **GED:** R3, M3, L3 • **SVP:** 1-2 yrs • **Academic:** Ed=H, Eng=S • **Work Field:** 211 • **MPSMS:** 493 • **Aptitudes:** G3, V3, N3, S4, P4, Q3, K3, F3, M3, E4, C3 • **Temperaments:** J, R, T • **Stress:** T • **Physical:** V=L, H=N, L=L, W, H • **Work Env:** I • **Salary:** 4 • **Outlook:** 3

LABORATORY ASSISTANT, CULTURE MEDIA (drug prep. & related) • D.O.T. #559.384-010 • OES #24502 • LABORATORY AIDE; TECHNICAL ASSISTANT. Prepares culture media used to develop vaccines and toxoids or to conduct chemical, microscopic, and bacteriologic tests: Measures and weighs ingredients, such as food source, chemicals, preservatives, and vitamins, to prepare growth medium, using scales, graduated flasks, syringes, pipettes, and standard formulas. Adjusts controls of equipment, such as pumps, filters, steam kettles, and autoclaves, to obtain uniform consistency of sterile medium. Removes sample of medium from batch and tests sample for consistency, potency, and sterility, according to standardized procedures. Pours medium or adjusts controls on automatic equipment that dispenses medium into containers, such as petridishes, test tubes, or storage drums. Seals containers and prepares and affixes identification labels to containers. Maintains production and test records. May order supplies. May mix ingredients to prepare stains used in tests. • **GED:** R3, M3, L3 • **SVP:** 6 mos-1 yr • **Academic:** Ed=N, Eng=S • **Work Field:** 147 • **MPSMS:** 493 • **Aptitudes:** G3, V3, N3, S3, P3, Q3, K3, F3, M3, E5, C4 • **Temperaments:** J, T, V • **Physical:** V=G, H=N, L=L, W, H • **Work Env:** I • **Salary:** 3 • **Outlook:** 4

LABORATORY TECHNICIAN, VETERINARY (medical ser.) • D.O.T. #073.361-010 • OES #32905 • Prepares vaccines, biologicals, and serums for prevention of animal diseases: Inoculates embryo chicks, broths, or other bacteriological media with organisms. Incubates bacteria for specified period and prepares vaccines and serums by standard laboratory methods. Tests vaccines for sterility and virus inactivity and bottles them. Examines meat and dairy products to determine if products meet standards of quality and purity. Prepares standard volumetric solutions and reagents used in testing. • **GED:** R5, M4, L4 • **SVP:** 1-2 yrs • **Academic:** Ed=A, Eng=S • **Work Field:** 147, 294 • **MPSMS:** 929 • **Aptitudes:** G3, V3, N3, S3, P3, Q4, K3, F2, M3, E5, C4 • **Temperaments:** M, T, V • **Physical:** V=L, H=N, L=L, H • **Work Env:** I • **Salary:** 4 • **Outlook:** 2

MEDICAL TECHNOLOGIST (medical ser.) • D.O.T. #078.361-014 • OES #32902 • Performs chemical, microscopic, serologic, hematologic, immunohematologic, parasitic, and bacteriologic tests to provide data for use in treatment and diagnosis of disease: Receives specimens for laboratory, or obtains such body materials as urine, blood, pus, and tissue directly from patient, and makes quantitative and qualitative chemical analyses. Cultivates, isolates, and identifies pathogenic bacteria, parasites, and other microorganisms. Cuts, stains, and mounts tissue sections for study by PATHOLOGIST (medical ser.). Performs blood tests for transfusions, studies morphology of blood. Groups or types blood and crossmatches that of donor and recipient to ascertain compatibility. Engages in medical research to further control and cure disease. May calibrate and use equipment designed to measure glandular and other bodily activity [NUCLEAR MEDICAL TECHNOLOGIST (medical ser.)]. May take electrocardiograms. May train and supervise MEDICAL-LABORATORY TECHNICIAN (medical ser.) and student MEDICAL TECHNOLOGISTS (medical ser.). May be designated according to field of specialization as BLOOD-BANK TECHNOLOGIST (medical ser.); HEMATOLOGY TECH-

NOLOGIST (medical ser.); SEROLOGY TECHNOLOGIST (medical ser.). • **GED:** R5, M4, L5 • **SVP:** 2-4 yrs • **Academic:** Ed=B, Eng=S • **Work Field:** 294 • **MPSMS:** 925 • **Aptitudes:** G2, V2, N2, S3, P2, Q3, K2, F2, M3, E5, C3 • **Temperaments:** M, T • **Physical:** V=G, H=N, L=S, H • **Work Env:** I • **Salary:** 4 • **Outlook:** 4

MEDICAL-LABORATORY ASSISTANT (medical ser.) • D.O.T. #078.381-010 • OES #32905 • Performs routine tests in medical laboratory under supervision of MEDICAL TECHNOLOGIST (medical ser.) or other qualified individual, utilizing prescribed procedures, in urinalysis, hematology, serology, and bacteriology. May perform routine tests in chemistry. • **GED:** R4, M4, L4 • **SVP:** 3-6 mos • **Academic:** Ed=H, Eng=S • **Work Field:** 211 • **MPSMS:** 925 • **Aptitudes:** G3, V3, N3, S3, P3, Q4, K3, F3, M3, E5, C3 • **Temperaments:** M, T, V • **Physical:** V=N, H=N, L=L, H • **Work Env:** I • **Salary:** 3 • **Outlook:** 4

MEDICAL-LABORATORY TECHNICIAN (medical ser.) • D.O.T. #078.381-014 • OES #32905 • MEDICAL TECHNICIAN. Performs routine tests in medical laboratory for use in treatment and diagnosis of disease: Prepares tissue samples for PATHOLOGIST (medical ser.). Takes blood samples. Executes such laboratory tests as urinalysis and blood counts. Makes quantitative and qualitative chemical and biological analyses of body specimens, under supervision of MEDICAL TECHNOLOGIST (medical ser.) or laboratory director. May be designated according to field of specialization as BLOOD-BANK TECHNICIAN (medical ser.); CYTOTECH NICIAN (medical ser.); HEMATOLOGY TECHNICIAN (medical ser.); SEROLOGY TECHNICIAN (medical ser.); TISSUE TECHNICIAN (medical ser.). • **GED:** R5, M4, L5 • **SVP:** 6 mos-1 yr • **Academic:** Ed=A, Eng=S • **Work Field:** 211 • **MPSMS:** 925 • **Aptitudes:** G2, V3, N3, S3, P3, Q4, K3, F3, M3, E5, C3 • **Temperaments:** M, T, V • **Physical:** V=G, H=N, L=S, W, H • **Work Env:** I • **Salary:** 3 • **Outlook:** 4

MICROBIOLOGY TECHNOLOGIST (drug prep. & related) • D.O.T. #078.261-014 • OES #32902 • MEDICAL TECHNOLOGIST, BACTERIOLOGY. Cultivates, isolates, and assists in identifying bacteria and other micro-organisms, and performs various bacteriological, mycological, virological, and parasitological tests: Receives human or animal body materials from autopsy or diagnostic cases, or collects specimens directly from patients, under supervision of laboratory director. Examines materials for evidence of disease or parasites. Makes parasitological tests of specimens concentrated or inoculated on culture media. • **GED:** R5, M4, L5 • **SVP:** 1-2 yrs • **Academic:** Ed=B, Eng=G • **Work Field:** 294 • **MPSMS:** 925 • **Aptitudes:** G2, V2, N2, S3, P2, Q3, K2, F2, M3, E5, C3 • **Temperaments:** M, T, V • **Physical:** V=G, H=N, L=L, H • **Work Env:** I • **Salary:** 4 • **Outlook:** 4

MORGUE ATTENDANT (medical ser.) • D.O.T. #355.667-010 • OES #66005 • Prepares bodies, specimens of human organs, and morgue room to assist PATHOLOGIST (medical ser.) in postmortem examinations: Places body in compartment tray of refrigerator or on autopsy table, using portable hoist and stretcher. Lays out surgical instruments and laboratory supplies for postmortem examinations. Washes table, storage trays, and instruments, sharpens knives, and replaces soiled linens. Records identifying information for morgue file. Releases body to authorized person. May close post mortem incisions, using surgical needle and cord. May fill cranium with plaster. May feed, water, and clean quarters for animals used in medical research. May prepare preserving solutions according to formulas. May preserve specimens and stain slides. May photograph specimens. • **GED:** R3, M2, L2 • **SVP:** 3-6 mos • **Academic:** Ed=N, Eng=N • **Work Field:** 031, 291 • **MPSMS:** 929 • **Aptitudes:** G3, V4, N4, S4, P3, Q4, K3, F3, M3, E4, C5 • **Temperaments:** R • **Physical:** V=N, H=N, L=M, W, H • **Work Env:** I, W • **Salary:** 3 • **Outlook:** 3

PHLEBOTOMIST (medical ser.) • D.O.T. #079.364-022 • OES #66099 • Draws blood from patients or donors in hospital, blood bank, or similar facility for analysis or other medical purposes: Assembles equipment, such as tourniquet, needles, blood collection devices, gauze, cotton, and alcohol on worktray, according to requirements for specified tests or procedures. Verifies or records identity of patient or donor and converses with patient or donor to allay fear of procedure. Applies tourniquet to arm, locates accessible vein, swabs puncture area with disinfectant, and inserts needle into vein to draw blood into collection tube or bag. Withdraws needle, applies treatment to puncture site, and labels and stores blood container for subsequent processing. May prick finger to draw blood. May conduct interviews, take vital signs, and draw and test blood samples to screen donors at blood bank. • **GED:** R4, M2, L4 • **SVP:** 30 days-3 mos • **Academic:** Ed=H, Eng=G • **Work Field:** 294 • **MPSMS:** 929 • **Aptitudes:** G3, V3, N4, S3, P3, Q3, K2, F2, M2, E5, C4 • **Temperaments:** J, P • **Stress:** E • **Physical:** V=L, H=L, L=L, H • **Work Env:** I • **Salary:** 3 • **Outlook:** 4

POLYGRAPH EXAMINER (profess. & kin.) • D.O.T. #199.267-026 • OES #39999 • LIE-DETECTION EXAMINER. Interrogates and screens individuals to detect deception or to verify truthfulness, using polygraph equipment and standard polygraph techniques: Attaches apparatus to individual to measure and record changes in respiration, blood pressure, and electrical resistance of skin as result of perspiration changes. Evaluates reactions to questions of a non-emotional nature. Interprets and diagnoses individual's emotional responses to key questions recorded on graph. Visits morgues, examines scene of crime, or contacts other sources, when assigned to criminal case, to gather information for use in interrogating suspects, witnesses, and other persons. Appears in court as witness on matters relating to polygraph examinations, according to formalized procedures. Prepares reports and keeps records on polygraph examinations. May instruct classes in polygraph interrogation techniques, methods, and uses. When analyzing voice stress charted on moving tape by needle of recording device for deception or truthfulness verifi cation, may be designated PSYCHOLOGICAL STRESS EVALUATOR (pro fess. & kin.). • **GED:** R5, M3, L5 • **SVP:** 6 mos-1 yr • **Academic:** Ed=H, Eng=G • **Work Field:** 211, 271 • **MPSMS:** 951 • **Aptitudes:** G2, V1, N4, S3, P2, Q2, K3, F4, M3, E5, C4 • **Temperaments:** J, M, P, T • **Stress:** E • **Physical:** V=G, H=G, L=L, H • **Work Env:** I • **Salary:** 4 • **Outlook:** 2

PUBLIC-HEALTH MICROBIOLOGIST (gov. ser.) • D.O.T. #041.261-010 • OES #24311 • Conducts experiments to detect presence of harmful or pathogenic bacteria in water, food supply, or general environment of community and to control or eliminate sources of possible pollution or contagion: Makes periodic laboratory counts of bacteria in water supply. Analyzes samples of sewage for harmful micro-organisms and for rate of sludge purification by aerobic bacteria. Examines milk, shell fish, and other food items for micro-organisms constituting menace to public health. Cooperates with hospitals and clinical laboratories in identifying micro-organisms taken from diseased persons to determine presence of bacteria causing contagious or epidemic diseases. May inoculate members of community against contagious diseases. • **GED:** R6, M6, L6 • **SVP:** 2-4 yrs • **Academic:** Ed=B, Eng=G • **Work Field:** 211 • **MPSMS:** 732, 929 • **Aptitudes:** G1, V1, N2, S2, P2, Q3, K3, F2, M2, E5, C4 • **Temperaments:** M, P, T • **Physical:** V=L, H=N, L=S, H • **Work Env:** I • **Salary:** 4 • **Outlook:** 4

TISSUE TECHNOLOGIST (medical ser.) • D.O.T. #078.361-030 • OES #32902 • MEDICAL TECHNOLOGIST, HISTOLOGY; HISTOPATHOLOGY TECHNOLOGIST. Cuts, stains, mounts, and prepares tissues for examination by PATHOLOGIST (medical ser.): Prepares specimen for immediate analysis by freezing. Decalcifies bone specimens. Prepares and maintains paraffin, reagents, and other solutions and stains, according to standard formulas. May assist PATHOLOGIST (medical ser.) in autopsy. • **GED:** R5, M4, L5 • **SVP:** 1-2 yrs • **Academic:** Ed=A, Eng=S • **Work Field:** 294 • **MPSMS:** 925 • **Aptitudes:** G2, V2, N2, S3, P3, Q3, K3, F1, M1, E4, C2 • **Temperaments:** M, T, V • **Physical:** V=L, H=N, L=L, H • **Work Env:** I • **Salary:** 4 • **Outlook:** 3

TOXICOLOGIST (drug prep. & related) • D.O.T. #022.081-010 • OES #24308 • Conducts research on toxic effects of cosmetic products and ingredients on laboratory animals for manufacturer of cosmetics: Applies cosmetic ingredient or cosmetic being developed to exposed shaved skin area of test animal and observes and examines skin periodically for possible development of abnormalities, inflammation, or irritation. Injects ingredient into test animal, using hypodermic needle and syringe, and periodically observes animal for signs of toxicity. Injects antidotes to determine which antidote best neutralizes toxic effects. Tests and analyzes blood samples for presence of toxic conditions, using microscope and laboratory test equipment. Dissects dead animals, using surgical instruments, and examines organs to determine effects of cosmetic ingredients being tested. Prepares formal reports of test results. • **GED:** R5, M4, L5 • **SVP:** 4-10 yrs • **Academic:** Ed=M, Eng=G • **Work Field:** 251 • **MPSMS:** 732 • **Aptitudes:** G2, V2, N3, S3, P2, Q3, K3, F3, M3, E5, C4 • **Temperaments:** J, T • **Physical:** V=L, H=N, L=S, H • **Work Env:** I • **Salary:** 5 • **Outlook:** 2

VECTOR CONTROL ASSISTANT (gov. ser.) • D.O.T. #049.364-014 • OES #24502 • Assists public health staff in activities concerned with identification, prevention, and control of vectors (disease- carrying insects and rodents): Carries and sets up field equipment to be used in surveys of number and type of vectors in area. Sets traps and cuts through brush and weeds to obtain specimens of vector population for use in laboratory tests, using sweep. Prepares, mounts, and stores specimens, following instructions of supervisor. Prepares reports of field surveys and laboratory tests based upon information obtained from personnel involved in specific activities, for use in planning and carrying out projects for prevention and control of vectors. • **GED:** R4, M2, L3 • **SVP:** 6 mos-1 yr • **Academic:** Ed=H, Eng=G • **Work Field:** 211 • **MPSMS:** 920 • **Aptitudes:** G3, V3, N3, S3, P3, Q3, K4, F3, M3, E3, C4 • **Temperaments:** J • **Physical:** V=L, H=N, L=L, W, H • **Work Env:** I • **Salary:** 3 • **Outlook:** 3

Plants and Animals 03

An interest in activities to do with plants and animals, usually in an outdoor setting.

You can satisfy this interest by working in farming, forestry, fishing, and related fields. You may like doing physical work outdoors, such as working on a farm. You may enjoy animals. Perhaps training or taking care of animals would appeal to you. You may have management ability. You could own, operate, or manage farms or related business or services.

03.01 Managerial Work: Plants and Animals

Workers in this group operate or manage farming, fishing, forestry, and horticultural service business of many kinds. Some of them breed specialty plants and animals. Others provide services to increase production or beautify land areas. Many of them work in rural or woodland areas, on farms, ranches, and forest preserves. Others find employment with commercial nurseries, landscaping firms, business services, or government agencies located in large and small communities all over the country. Many are self-employed, operating their own large or small businesses.

✔ **What kind of work would you do?**
Your work activities would depend upon your specific job. For example, you might:

- plan and oversee the sales and shipment of farm crops or animals.
- arrange for the purchase of seed, livestock, fertilizer, feed, and other supplies.
- advise poultry farmers on ways to improve the quality of their products.
- breed earthworms and sell them as bait, or to companies that produce fish food or soil conditioners.
- study market trends to plan the type and quantity of crops to plant.
- plan and direct projects for cutting timber and replanting forests.

✔ **What skills and abilities do you need for this kind of work?**
To do this kind of work, you must be able to:

- understand and apply procedures related to a particular kind of activity in a practical way, such as rotating crops so that farm soil will stay fertile, treating trees with the right chemicals to prevent the spread of disease, or feeding cattle to produce beef of prime quality.
- plan an entire activity and see that it is carried out.
- keep accurate financial and production records.
- get along well with other people in many different work situations, such as overseeing their activities or negotiating with them for the purchase of materials or the sale of products.
- spend much of your time outdoors in all kinds of weather, overseeing or participating in the work being done.

✔ **How do you know if you would like or could learn to do this kind of work?**
The following questions may give you clues about yourself as you consider this group of jobs.

- Have you raised plants or animals as a hobby? Would you like to take courses to help you expand your hobby?
- Have you been a leader in scouting or any other outdoor group? Do you enjoy planning and directing activities?

- Have you been a member of FFA or 4-H? Did you complete any projects which required planning, budgeting, and record keeping?

✔ **How can you prepare for and enter this kind of work?**

Occupations in this group usually require education and/or training extending from one year to over ten years, depending upon the specific kind of work. Most of the jobs in this group are open only to people with work experience. Growing up on a farm is good initial preparation for many of these jobs. Formal training for management jobs is available at the high school and post-high school levels. For example, vocational agriculture courses are offered in many high schools with similar courses available to adults at night and on weekends. Programs such as agribusiness, animal husbandry, forest management, and small business management are provided by many colleges and technical schools. Each state has at least one college which offers four or five year programs in related fields.

Workers with training in management and farm experience qualify for jobs with cooperative groups, corporations, and large farm owners. Some workers form companies which contract to provide farm services.

Courses in horticulture, gardening, or turf management provide preparation for jobs in nurseries, tree services, and landscaping firms.

✔ **What else should you consider about these jobs?**

Federal loans are available to qualified people who wish to start their own businesses. Most of these businesses are small and hire few people.

If you think you would like to do this kind of work, look at the job titles listed below.

GOE: 03.01.01 Farming, Managerial

FARMER, FIELD CROP (agric.) • D.O.T. #404.161-010 • OES #79999 • Plants, cultivates, and harvests specialty crops, such as alfalfa, cotton, hops, peanuts, mint, sugarcane, and tobacco, applying knowledge of growth characteristics of individual crop, and soil, climate, and market conditions: Determines number and kind of employees to be hired, acreage to be tilled, and varieties and quantities of plants to be grown. Selects and purchases plant stock and farm machinery, implements, and supplies. Decides when and how to plant, cultivate, and irrigate plants and harvest crops, applying knowledge of plant culture. Attaches farm implements, such as plow, disc, and seed drill to tractor and drives tractor in fields to till soil and plant and cultivate crops. Drives and operates farm machinery to spray fertilizers, herbicides, and pesticides and haul harvested crops. Hires, assigns duties to, and oversees activities of farm workers. Demonstrates and explains farm work techniques and safety regulations to new workers. Maintains employee and financial records. Arranges with buyers for sale and shipment of crop. May install irrigation system(s) and irrigate fields. May set poles and string wires and twine on poles to form trellises. May lubricate, adjust, and make minor repairs on farm machinery, implements, and equipment, using mechanic's handtools and work aids. May plant seeds in cold-frame bed and cover bed with cloth or glass to protect seedlings from weather. May transplant seedlings in rows, by hand or using transplanter machine. May grade and package crop for marketing. May be designated according to crop grown as COTTON GROWER (agric.); GINSENG FARMER (agric.); HAY FARMER (agric.); HOP GROWER (agric.); PEANUT FARMER (agric.); SUGARCANE PLANTER (agric.); TOBACCO GROWER (agric.). • **GED:** R4, M4, L4 • **SVP:** 2-4 yrs • **Academic:** Ed=H, Eng=S • **Work Field:** 002, 003 • **MPSMS:** 300 • **Aptitudes:** G2, V3, N3, S2, P3, Q3, K4, F4, M4, E4, C4 • **Temperaments:** D, J, M, V • **Physical:** V=L, H=N, L=M, W, S, H • **Work Env:** O, W, N, R • **Salary:** 4 • **Outlook:** 1

FARMER, GENERAL (agric.) • D.O.T. #421.161-010 • OES #79999 • Raises both crops and livestock: Determines kinds and amounts of crops to be grown and livestock to be bred, according to market conditions, weather, and size and location of farm. Selects and purchases seed, fertilizer, farm machinery, livestock, and feed, and assumes responsibility for sale of crop and livestock products. Hires and directs workers engaged in planting, cultivating, and harvesting crops, such as corn, peas, potatoes, strawberries, apples, peanuts, and tobacco, and to raise livestock, such as cattle, sheep, swine, horses, and poultry. Performs various duties of farm workers, depending on size and nature of farm, including setting up and operating farm machinery. • **GED:** R4, M4, L4 • **SVP:** 2-4 yrs • **Academic:** Ed=H, Eng=S • **Work Field:** 002, 003 • **MPSMS:** 300, 320 • **Aptitudes:** G2, V3, N3, S2, P3, Q3, K4, F4, M4, E4, C4 • **Temperaments:** D, J, M, V • **Physical:** V=L, H=N, L=H, W, C, S, H • **Work Env:** B, R • **Salary:** 4 • **Outlook:** 1

FARMER, VINE-FRUIT CROPS (agric.) • D.O.T. #403.161-014 • OES #79999 • BERRY GROWER. Plants and cultivates fruit bushes and vines and harvests crops, such as grapes, cranberries, and strawberries, applying knowledge of growth characteristics of specific varieties and soil, climate, and market conditions: Determines varieties and quantities of plants to be grown, acreage to be tilled, and employees to be hired. Selects and purchases plant stock and farm machines, implements, and supplies. Decides when and how to plant, bud, graft, prune, sucker, cultivate and irrigate plants, and harvest crop, based on knowledge of vine-crop culture. Attaches farm implements, such as harrow and ditcher, to tractor and drives tractor in fields to till soil. Drives and operates farm machinery to spray fertilizers, herbicides, and pesticides and haul fruit boxes. Hires, assigns duties to, and oversees activities of seasonal workers engaged in tilling and irrigating soil; pruning plants; and harvesting and marketing crop. Demonstrates and explains farm work techniques and safety regulations. Maintains employee and financial records. Makes arrangements with buyers for sale and shipment of crop. May make arrangements with

AIRPLANE PILOT (agric.) to spray and dust fertilizers and pesticides on planted acreage. May install irrigation system(s) and irrigate fields. May set poles, string wires on poles to form trellises, and tie vines and canes to trellis wires. May prune vines and canes to size and shape growth. May lubricate, adjust, and make minor repairs on farm machinery, implements, and equipment, using oilcan, grease gun, and handtools, such as hammer and wrench. May be designated according to crop grown, as BLUEBERRY GROWER (agric.); CRANBERRY GROWER (agric.); GRAPE GROWER (agric.); RASPBERRY GROWER (agric.); STRAWBERRY GROWER (agric.). • **GED:** R4, M4, L4 • **SVP:** 2-4 yrs • **Academic:** Ed=H, Eng=S • **Work Field:** 002, 003 • **MPSMS:** 300 • **Aptitudes:** G3, V3, N3, S3, P3, Q4, K3, F4, M3, E4, C4 • **Temperaments:** D, J, M, V • **Physical:** V=L, H=N, L=H, W, S, H • **Work Env:** O, W, N, R • **Salary:** 4 • **Outlook:** 3

GENERAL MANAGER, FARM (agric.) • D.O.T. #180.167-018 • OES #79999 • Manages farm concerned with raising, harvesting, packing, and marketing farm products for corporations, cooperatives, and other owners: Analyzes market conditions to determine acreage allocations. Negotiates with bank officials to obtain credit from bank. Purchases farm machinery and equipment and supplies, such as tractors, seed, fertilizer, and chemicals. Hires and discharges personnel. Prepares financial and other management reports. Supervises office personnel engaged in preparing payrolls and keeping records. Visits orchards and fields to inspect and estimate maturity dates of crops. Confers with purchasers, and determines when and under what conditions to sell crops, marine life, or forest products. May be designated according to type of crop. • **GED:** R5, M4, L4 • **SVP:** 4-10 yrs • **Academic:** Ed=A, Eng=S • **Work Field:** 002, 003 • **MPSMS:** 300, 310, 320 • **Aptitudes:** G2, V2, N2, S3, P3, Q3, K4, F4, M4, E5, C5 • **Temperaments:** D, I, J, P, V • **Stress:** A • **Physical:** V=G, H=L, L=L • **Work Env:** B • **Salary:** 5 • **Outlook:** 3

GROUP LEADER (agric.) • D.O.T. #180.167-022 • OES #72002 • CREW BOSS; CREW LEADER; ROW BOSS. Coordinates activities of group of FARMWORKERS, GENERAL (agric.) I engaged in planting, cultivating, and harvesting diversified crops: Recruits members for group. Locates jobs for group and accompanies group on job. May be required to hold state registration certificate. Performs other duties as described under SUPERVISOR (any ind.). • **GED:** R3, M2, L2 • **SVP:** 2-4 yrs • **Academic:** Ed=N, Eng=N • **Work Field:** 002, 003 • **MPSMS:** 300 • **Aptitudes:** G3, V3, N4, S4, P4, Q4, K4, F4, M3, E4, C4 • **Temperaments:** D, M, P, V • **Stress:** A • **Physical:** V=G, H=G, L=L, S, H • **Work Env:** O • **Salary:** 4 • **Outlook:** 4

MANAGER, DAIRY FARM (agric.) • D.O.T. #180.167-026 • OES #79999 • Manages dairy farm: Plans, develops, and implements policies, procedures, and practices for operation of dairy farm to insure compliance with company's or owner's standards for farm production, propagation of herd, and regulations of regulatory agencies. Directs and coordinates, through subordinate supervisory personnel, farm activities, such as breeding and rearing livestock, feeding and milking of cows, storage of milk, and sterilizing and maintaining facilities and equipment. Reviews breeding and milk production records to determine bulls and cows that are unproductive and should be sold. Inspects facilities and equipment to insure compliance with sanitation standards, and to determine maintenance and repair requirements. Authorizes, requisitions, or purchases supplies and equipment, such as feed, disinfective and sanitation chemicals, and replacements for defective equipment. Secures services of VETERINARIAN (medical ser.) for treatment of herd or when cows are calving. Prepares farm activity reports for evaluation by management or owner. May direct and coordinate activities concerned with planting, growing, harvesting, and storage of feed forage crops. May directly supervise dairy workers on small farms. • **GED:** R4, M3, L3 • **SVP:** 4-10 yrs • **Academic:** Ed=H, Eng=S • **Work Field:** 295 • **MPSMS:** 383 • **Aptitudes:** G2, V3, N3, S3, P3, Q3, K4, F4, M4, E4, C4 • **Temperaments:** D, J, P • **Stress:** A • **Physical:** V=G, H=L, L=L, S, H • **Work Env:** B • **Salary:** 5 • **Outlook:** 3

MIGRANT LEADER (agric.) • D.O.T. #180.167-050 • OES #72002 • CREW LEADER; FARM-CREW LEADER. Contracts seasonal farm employment of MIGRANT WORKERS (agric.): Consults employment agencies to locate work and confers with FARMERS (agric.) to obtain suitable contracts for crew. Recruits and organizes crew and furnishes transportation to worksite. Schedules en-route rest stops that afford shelters, benches or beds, cooking facilities, fuel and water, and adequate toilet and sanitary provisions. Confers with employer and community officials at site of employment to insure availability of living quarters for families and single individuals, educational and recreational facilities, medical care, and day care for children. Supplies farm implements and machinery to crew and directs them in methods of cultivation, harvesting, and packaging of crop. Prepares payroll and production records. May provide initial financing of trips and advance funds to workers during idle periods. May be required to hold State registration certificate. Performs other duties as described under SUPERVISOR (any ind.). • **GED:** R3, M2, L2 • **SVP:** 2-4 yrs • **Academic:** Ed=N, Eng=N • **Work Field:** 002, 003 • **MPSMS:** 300 • **Aptitudes:** G3, V3, N3, S4, P4, Q3, K4, F4, M4, E4, C4 • **Temperaments:** D, M, P, V • **Stress:** A • **Physical:** V=L, H=L, L=L, S, H • **Work Env:** O • **Salary:** 4 • **Outlook:** 3

GOE: 03.01.02 Specialty Breeding

BEEKEEPER (agric.) • D.O.T. #413.161-010 • OES #79999 • APIARIST; BEE FARMER; BEE RAISER; BEE RANCHER; HONEY PRODUCER. Raises bees to produce honey and pollinate crops: Assembles beehives, using handtools. Arranges with sellers for purchases of honeybee colonies. Inserts honeycomb of bees into beehive or inducts wild swarming bees into hive of prepared honeycomb frames. Places screen plug in hive entrance to confine bees and sets hive in orchard, clover field, or near other source of nectar and pollen. Forces bees from hive, using smoke pot or by placing carbolic acid soaked pad over hive to inspect hive and to harvest honeycombs. Scrapes out parasites, such as wax moth larvae, and removes vermin, such as birds and mice. Collects royal jelly from queen bee cells for sale as base for cosmetics and as health food. Destroys superfluous queen bee cells to prevent division of colony by swarming. Destroys diseased bee colonies, using cyanide gas. Burns hive of diseased bee colony or sterilizes hive, using caustic soda solution. Uncaps harvested honeycombs and extracts honey. Arranges with buyers for sale of honey. May cultivate bees to produce bee colonies and queen bees for sale and be designated as BEE PRODUCER (agric.); QUEEN PRODUCER (agric.). • **GED:** R3, M3, L3 • **SVP:** 2-4 yrs • **Academic:** Ed=N, Eng=S • **Work Field:** 002, 003 • **MPSMS:** 329 • **Aptitudes:** G3, V3, N3, S3, P3, Q4, F4, M3, E4, C4 • **Temperaments:** M, V • **Physical:** V=N, H=N, L=H, W, S, H • **Work Env:** O, R • **Salary:** 2 • **Outlook:** 2

FISH FARMER (fish.) • D.O.T. #446.161-010 • OES #79999 • Spawns and raises fish for commercial purposes: Strips eggs from female fish and places eggs in moist pans. Adds milt stripped from male fish to fertilize eggs. Fills hatchery trays with fertilized eggs and places trays in incubation troughs. Turns valves and places baffles in troughs to adjust volume, depth, velocity, and temperature of water. Transfers fingerlings to rearing ponds. Feeds high protein foods or cereal with vitamins and minerals to fingerlings to induce growth to size desired for commercial use. Arranges with buyers for sale of fish. Removes fish from pond, using dip net. Counts and weighs fish. Loads fish into tank truck, or dresses and packs in ice for shipment. May perform standard tests on water samples to determine oxygen content. May be designated according to kind of fish raised, as TROUT FARMER (fish.). • **GED:** R4, M1, L2 • **SVP:** 1-2 yrs • **Academic:** Ed=H, Eng=N • **Work Field:** 002, 003 • **MPSMS:** 331 • **Aptitudes:** G3, V3, N4, S4, P3, Q4, K4, F3, M3, E4, C4 • **Temperaments:** D, M • **Physical:** V=L, H=N, L=M, W, C, S, H • **Work Env:** O, W • **Salary:** 3 • **Outlook:** 2

SHELLFISH GROWER (fish.) • D.O.T. #446.161-014 • OES #79999 • OYSTER CULTURIST. Cultivates and harvests beds of shellfish, such as clams and oysters: Lays out and stakes tide flats (ground beneath shallow water near shoreline). Piles up stone, poles, and mud, using farm tractor and hand implements to make dikes to control water drainage at low tide. Removes debris by hand and levels soil with tractor and harrow. Sows spat by hand or with shovel or sets out strings or baskets of shells onto which spat attaches. Covers seeded area with mixture of sand and broken shells or transfers seeded strings or baskets to growing area. Rigs net or star mop (mop of heavy rope yarn) and drags it over bed behind power boat to entangle and remove shell fish predators, such as crabs and starfish. Walks about bed at low tide, and scoops or digs shellfish and piles them onto barge or mud sled, using pitchfork or shovel. Packs shellfish, according to market specifications, in containers and returns small ones to bed. Poles barge to wharf at high tide or pulls it, using boat. Drags mud sled from bed, using tractor. May pour oil around bed and spread oil-treated sand over bed with shovel to form chemical barrier to shellfish predators. May reach from boat with rake-tongs and grope for shellfish by moving handles to open and close tongs. May supervise workers who cultivate and harvest bed. May negotiate with buyers for sale of crop. May be designated according to type of shellfish grown as CLAM GROWER (fish.); OYSTER GROWER (fish.). • **GED:** R4, M1, L2 • **SVP:** 1-2 yrs • **Academic:** Ed=H, Eng=N • **Work Field:** 002, 003 • **MPSMS:** 332 • **Aptitudes:** G3, V3, N4, S4, P4, Q4, K3, F3, M3, E3, C5 • **Temperaments:** D, V • **Physical:** V=N, H=N, L=M, W, C, S, H • **Work Env:** O, W • **Salary:** 3 • **Outlook:** 2

GOE: 03.01.03 Specialty Cropping

LANDSCAPE CONTRACTOR (const.) • D.O.T. #182.167-014 • OES #15017 • Contracts to landscape grounds of houses, industrial plants, other buildings, or areas around highways: Confers with prospective client, studies landscape designs or drawings, and bills of materials to ascertain scope of landscaping work required, such as installation of lighting or sprinkler systems, erection of fences, concrete work, and types of trees, shrubs, or ornamental plants specified. Inspects grounds or area to determine equipment requirements for grading, tilling, or replacing top soil, and labor requirements to install sprinkler or lighting system, build fences, or perform concreting and planting work. Calculates labor, equipment, material, and overhead costs to determine minimum estimate or bid which will provide for margin of profit. Prepares and submits estimate for client or bid to industrial concern or governmental agency. Prepares contract for client to sign or signs contract if successful bidder. Plans landscaping functions and sequences of work at various sites to obtain optimum utilization of work force and equipment. Directs and coordinates, through subordinate supervisory personnel, activities of workers engaged in performing landscaping functions in contractual agreement. Purchases and insures that materials are on site as needed. Inspects work at sites for compliance with terms and specifications of contract. May personally supervise workers. May participate in performing landscaping functions. May be required to possess state license as landscape contractor. May subcontract electrical installation or concrete work if not equipped to provide those services. • **GED:** R4, M4, L4 • **SVP:** 4-10 yrs • **Academic:** Ed=H, Eng=S • **Work Field:** 295 • **MPSMS:** 719 • **Aptitudes:** G3, V3, N2, S3, P3, Q3, K4, F4, M4, E5, C3 • **Temperaments:** D, J, P, V • **Stress:** A • **Physical:** V=G, H=L, L=L • **Work Env:** B • **Salary:** 5 • **Outlook:** 3

MANAGER, NURSERY (agric.) • D.O.T. #180.167-042 • OES #79999 • Manages nursery to grow horticultural plants, such as trees, shrubs, flowers, ornamental plants, or vegetables for sale to trade or retail customers: Determines type and quantity of horticultural plants to be grown, considering such factors as whether plants will be grown under controlled conditions in hothouse or greenhouse or under natural weather conditions in field, and market demand or conditions, utilizing knowledge of plant germination, growing habits of plants, soil conditions, plant nutrients, and disease control requirements. Selects and purchases seed, plant nutrients, and disease control chemicals according to type of horticultural plants and conditions under which plants will be grown. Directs and coordinates, through subordinate supervisory personnel, activities of workers engaged in planting of seed, raising, feeding, and controlling growth and disease of plants, and transplanting, potting, or cutting plants for marketing. Coordinates clerical, record keeping, accounting, and marketing activities. May purchase nursery stock for resale and sell gardening accessories, such as sprays, garden implements, and plant nutrients and be known as MANAGER, RETAIL NURSERY (agric.; ret. tr.). May grow horticultural plants under controlled conditions hydroponically and be known as MANAGER, HYDROPONICS NURSERY (agric.). • **GED:** R4, M4, L4 • **SVP:** 2-4 yrs • **Academic:** Ed=H, Eng=S • **Work Field:** 003, 292, 295 • **MPSMS:** 310 • **Aptitudes:** G2, V3, N3, S4, P3, Q4, K4, F4, M3, E4, C3 • **Temperaments:** D, J, P, V • **Stress:** A • **Physical:** V=G, H=L, L=L, H • **Work Env:** B • **Salary:** 4 • **Outlook:** 3

GOE: 03.01.04 Forestry & Logging, Managerial

FORESTER (profess. & kin.) • D.O.T. #040.061-034 • OES #24302 • Manages and develops forest lands and their resources for economic and recreational purposes: Plans and directs projects in forestation and reforestation. Maps forest areas, estimates standing timber and future growth, and manages timber sales. Plans cutting programs to assure continuous production of timber. Conducts research in methods of cutting and removing timber with minimum waste and damage, and methods of processing wood for various uses. Directs suppression of forest fires and conducts fire-prevention programs. Plans campsites and recreation centers, and directs construction and maintenance of cabins, fences, telephone lines, and roads. Assists in planning and carrying out projects for control of floods, soil erosion, tree diseases, and insect pests in forests [ENTOMOLOGIST (profess. & kin.); PLANT PATHOLOGIST (profess. & kin.); SOIL CONSERVATIONIST (profess. & kin.)]. Advises on forestry problems and conducts educational programs on care of forests. May participate in environmental studies and prepare variety of environmental reports. May be designated according to specialty as CONSULTING FORESTER (profess. & kin.); FOREST EXAMINER (profess. & kin.); FOREST RANGER (profess. & kin.); FOREST RECREATIONIST (profess. & kin.); FOREST SUPERVISOR (profess. & kin.); RESEARCH FORESTER (profess. & kin.); TIMBER-MANAGEMENT SPECIALIST (profess. & kin.). • **GED:** R5, M5, L5 • **SVP:** 4-10 yrs • **Academic:** Ed=B, Eng=G • **Work Field:** 251, 295 • **MPSMS:** 731 • **Aptitudes:** G1, V1, N3, S3, P3, Q4, K4, F4, M4, E5, C4 • **Temperaments:** D, P, V • **Physical:** V=G, H=N, L=S, W • **Work Env:** B • **Salary:** 5 • **Outlook:** 1

LOGGING-OPERATIONS INSPECTOR (forestry) • D.O.T. #168.267-070 • OES #21911 • Inspects contract logging operations to ensure adherence to contract provisions and safety laws and to prevent loss of timber through breakage and damage to residual stand: Examines logging area for utilization practices, slash disposal, sanitation, observance of boundaries, and safety precautions. Issues remedial instructions for violations of contract agreement and fire and safety regulations, and prepares report of logging method, efficiency, and progress. May initiate bid requests and negotiate terms of contracts with logging contractors. • **GED:** R5, M3, L4 • **SVP:** 2-4 yrs • **Academic:** Ed=A, Eng=S • **Work Field:** 211 • **MPSMS:** 712 • **Aptitudes:** G2, V2, N3, S3, P4, Q3, K4, F4, M4, E5, C5 • **Temperaments:** J, M, P • **Physical:** V=G, H=L, L=L, W • **Work Env:** I • **Salary:** 4 • **Outlook:** 3

03.02 General Supervision: Plants and Animals

Workers in this group supervise others, and often work right along with them, on farms or ranches, fish hatcheries or forests, plant nurseries or parks. Most of them work in rural or forest locations, but some jobs are located in city or suburban areas. Some of these workers travel throughout an area to inspect or treat croplands for insects or disease, or supervise workers performing agricultural or lawn care services.

✔ What kind of work would you do?

Your work activities would depend upon your specific job. For example, you might:

- supervise workers in planting, cultivating, and harvesting all farm crops.
- supervise workers in milking, breeding, and caring for dairy cows.
- supervise workers in planting, cultivating, harvesting, and packing seedling forest trees.

- supervise workers in incubating eggs and caring for fish in a state hatchery.
- inspect fields for presence of insects or plant disease.
- coordinate activities of crew of workers engaged in caring for park grounds.

✔ What skills and abilities do you need for this kind of work?

To do this kind of work, you must be able to:

- get a clear picture of the work to be done during a specific time period, as explained to you by the manager of the business, and pass this information along clearly to the workers you supervise.
- assign duties to workers according to your judgment of their capabilities, and the amount of work to be done.

- demonstrate the use of tools and equipment to other workers, and show them ways of doing their jobs more efficiently.
- organize details and use basic arithmetic to keep time and production records for the workers you supervise, or prepare reports of areas you inspect.
- work outdoors in all kinds of weather, sometimes performing tasks that require strenuous activities.

✔ How do you know if you would like or could learn to do this kind of work?

The following questions may give you clues about yourself as you consider this group of jobs.

- Have you been in charge of a scout troop or other group during a clean-up campaign? Did the members follow your directions?
- Have you been a member of FFA or 4-H? Did you have a project related to farming, fishing, or forestry?

- Have you worked a whole day mowing lawns, cutting weeds, or picking fruit? Could you do this type of work every day? Are you interested in supervising this type of work?
- Have you had military experience as a work detail leader? Did you like being responsible for getting the work done?

✔ How can you prepare for and enter this kind of work?

Occupations in this group usually require education and/or training extending from one year to over ten years, depending upon the specific kind of work. Most workers must have related work experience. They must know about the tools, processes, and methods used by the workers they supervise. This involves having practical knowledge of wide variety of tasks.

Almost all workers in this group start out in routine jobs in the same or similar work location. They are promoted to these jobs after showing that they have leadership ability and are thoroughly familiar with the work.

Vocational and technical courses in agriculture, forestry, or related fields provide a helpful background for some of these jobs.

✔ What else should you consider about these jobs?

Workers in this group may help to do many of the physical tasks they supervise. These workers are exposed to all types of weather conditions as well as natural hazards as storms, fires, and extremes of temperatures.

If you think you would like to do this kind of work, look at the job title listed below.

GOE: 03.02.02 Forestry & Logging, Supervision

FORESTER AIDE (forestry) • D.O.T. #452.364-010 • OES #79002 • **FOREST TECHNICIAN.** Compiles data pertaining to size, content, condition, and other characteristics of forest tracts, under direction of FORESTER (profess. & kin.); and leads workers in forest propagation, fire prevention and suppression, and facilities maintenance: Traverses forest in designated pattern to gather basic forest data, such as topographical features, species and population of trees, wood units available for harvest, disease and insect damage, tree seedling mortality, and conditions constituting fire danger. Marks trees of specified species, condition, and size for thinning or logging. Collects and records data from instruments, such as raingage, thermometer, stream-flow recorder, and soil moisture gage. Holds stadia rod, clears survey line, measures distances, records survey data, and performs related duties to assist in surveying property lines, timber sale boundaries, and road and recreation sites. Trains and leads conservation workers in seasonal activities, such as planting tree seedlings, collecting seed-cones, suppressing fires, cleaning and maintaining recreational facilities, and clearing fire breaks and access roads. Gives instructions to visitors of forest, and enforces camping, vehicle use, fire building, sanita tion, and other forest regulations. • **GED:** R4, M3, L3 • **SVP:** 1-2 yrs • **Academic:** Ed=H, Eng=S • **Work Field:** 243, 293 • **MPSMS:** 313 • **Aptitudes:** G3, V3, N3, S3, P3, Q4, K3, F3, M3, E3, C3 • **Temperaments:** M, P, V • **Stress:** E • **Physical:** V=G, H=N, L=M, W, C, S, H • **Work Env:** O • **Salary:** 4 • **Outlook:** 2

03.03 Animal Training and Service

Workers in this group take care of animals of many kinds, and train them for a variety of purposes. They work in pet shops, testing laboratories, animal shelters, and veterinarians' offices. Some are employed by zoos, aquariums, circuses, and at other places where animals are exhibited or used in entertainment acts. Others work for animal training or obedience schools, or in stables or kennels maintained by individuals or such facilities as race tracks or riding academies. These workers are not employed on farms, ranches, or other places where animals are raised as crops.

✔ **What kind of work would you do?**
Your work activities would depend upon your specific job. For example, you might:

- train and condition horses for racing.
- train animals to obey commands, compete in shows, or perform tricks.
- feed, water, and care for mice, guinea pigs, monkeys, and other animals in a hospital or research laboratory.
- feed, exercise, and groom horses to protect their health and improve their appearance.
- bathe and groom pets for their owners.
- control aquarium water temperature and acidity and meet other needs of aquatic life.

✔ **What skills and abilities do you need for this kind of work?**
To do this kind of work, you must be able to:

- understand the habits and physical needs of the animals you care for, and think of each of them on an individual basis.
- keep calm during emergencies.
- observe the animals you care for to notice changes in their appearance, appetite, or behavior, which might mean that they are sick.
- stay very patient while going over and over the same routines with animals, to train them to perform or to respond to commands.
- use your hands and fingers skillfully to perform such tasks as trimming the nails of dogs and cats without hurting them, fastening shoes to horses' hooves, or helping a veterinarian give shots to sick animals.
- do the hard physical work needed to keep stables and other animal quarters clean, using equipment such as shovels, pitchforks, rakes, mops, and high-pressure hoses.

✔ **How do you know if you would like or could learn to do this kind of work?**
The following questions may give you clues about yourself as you consider this group of jobs.

- Have you raised or cared for an animal? Do you enjoy the responsibility of caring for an animal?
- Have you had military experience training animals? Were you patient with the animal when you had to repeat commands many times? Did the animals learn what you were teaching?

- Have you taken care of a sick or an injured animal? Can you tell if an animal is getting sick or getting better by the way it looks or acts?
- Have you had a hobby raising small animals or fish? Did you use eyedroppers, strainers or other tools to feed, treat, or care for them?

✔ **How can you prepare for and enter this kind of work?**

Occupations in this group usually require education and/or training extending from a short demonstration to over four years, depending upon the specific kind of work. Most beginning workers are given a few simple duties. More responsibility is added as these workers gain experience. Some high schools, vocational schools, and junior colleges have courses in animal care. These courses cover the housing and feeding of animals, basic zoology and anatomy, and methods of treating sick or injured animals.

Some of these jobs require special skills. For instance, workers who train or exercise horses must know how to ride, and those who work for aquariums must know how to swim.

Jobs which involve training guide dogs, saddle horses, or animal performers are given to workers who have at least six months experience in the care of animals.

✔ **What else should you consider about these jobs?**

Expansion in testing of food and drugs by government agencies will increase the need for people to care for laboratory animals. An increase in the number of household pets will create jobs for animal groomers, veterinary hospital helpers, and other pet-care workers.

If you think you would like to do this kind of work, look at the job titles listed below.

GOE: 03.03.01 Animal Training

ANIMAL TRAINER (amuse. & rec.) • D.O.T. #159.224-010 • OES #34056 • Trains animals to obey commands, compete in shows, or perform tricks to entertain audience: Evaluates animal to determine temperament, ability, and aptitude for training. Conducts training program to develop desired behavior. May organize format of show. May conduct show. May cue or signal animal during performance. May rehearse animal according to script for motion picture or television film or stage or circus program. May train guard dog to protect property. May teach guide dog and master to function as team. May feed, exercise, and give general care to animal. Trainers are identified according to specific animal trained. May be designated HEAD ANIMAL TRAINER (amuse. & rec.) or SENIOR ANIMAL TRAINER (amuse. & rec.) when directing activities of other workers. • **GED:** R4, M3, L4 • **SVP:** 1-2 yrs • **Academic:** Ed=N, Eng=N • **Work Field:** 296, 297 • **MPSMS:** 919 • **Aptitudes:** G3, V3, N4, S3, P4, Q4, K3, F4, M3, E3, C5 • **Temperaments:** D, J, P, S • **Stress:** E, S • **Physical:** V=L, H=L, L=L, W, S, H • **Work Env:** B, W, R • **Salary:** 3 • **Outlook:** 2

EXERCISER, HORSE (amuse. & rec.) • D.O.T. #153.674-010 • OES #34058 • Rides racehorses to exercise and condition them for racing: Rides racehorse during workout and training races, following specific instructions of training personnel. Informs training personnel of horses temperament, peculiarities, and physical condition as demonstrated during exercise so that training plans can be modified to prepare horse for racing. • **GED:** R2, M1, L1 • **SVP:** 30 days-3 mos • **Academic:** Ed=N, Eng=N • **Work Field:** 291 • **MPSMS:** 329 • **Aptitudes:** G4, V4, N4, S4, P4, Q5, K3, F4, M3, E4, C4 • **Temperaments:** F, J • **Physical:** V=L, H=N, L=M, W, C, S, H • **Work Env:** O, R • **Salary:** 2 • **Outlook:** 2

GOE: 03.03.02 Animal Service

ANIMAL CARETAKER (any ind.) • D.O.T. #410.674-010 • OES #79017 • ANIMAL ATTENDANT; FARMWORKER, ANIMAL. Performs any combination of the following duties to attend animals, such as mice, canaries, guinea pigs, mink, dogs, and monkeys, on farms and in facilities, such as kennels, pounds, hospitals, and laboratories: Feeds and waters animals according to schedules. Cleans and disinfects cages, pens, and yards and sterilizes laboratory equipment and surgical instruments. Examines animals for signs of illness and treats them according to instructions. Transfers animals between quarters. Adjusts controls to regulate temperature and humidity of animals' quarters. Records information according to instructions, such as genealogy, diet, weight, medications, food intake, and license number. Anesthetizes, inoculates, shaves, bathes, clips, and grooms animals. Repairs cages, pens, or fenced yards. May kill and skin animals, such as fox and rabbit, and pack pelts in crates. May be designated according to place worked, such as DOG-POUND ATTENDANT (gov. ser.); FARMWORKER, FUR (agric.); HELPER, ANIMAL LABORATORY (drug. prep. & rel. prod.); KENNEL ATTENDANT (agric.); PET SHOP ATTENDANT (ret. tr.); VETERINARY-HOSPITAL ATTENDANT (medical ser.). • **GED:** R2, M1, L1 • **SVP:** 3-6 mos • **Academic:** Ed=N, Eng=N • **Work Field:** 003, 291, 294 • **MPSMS:** 329 • **Aptitudes:** G3, V3, N4, S4, P4, Q4, K3, F3, M3, E5, C4 • **Temperaments:** T, V • **Physical:** V=L, H=N, L=M, W, H • **Work Env:** I, R • **Salary:** 3 • **Outlook:** 3

ANIMAL KEEPER (amuse. & rec.) • D.O.T. #412.674-010 • OES #79017 • ANIMAL CARETAKER; MENAGERIE CARETAKER; ZOO CARETAKER. Feeds, waters, and cleans quarters of animals and birds in zoo, circus, or menagerie: Observes animals to detect illnesses and injuries. Treats minor injuries or ailments, and reports serious illnesses and injuries to ANIMAL KEEPER, HEAD (amuse. & rec.). Transfers animals or birds from one cage or pen to another. May prepare food. May bathe and groom animals. May answer questions of visitors concerning animals or birds. May be designated according to animal cared for as BEAR KEEPER (amuse. & rec.); BIRD KEEPER (amuse. & rec.); CAT KEEPER (amuse. & rec.); DEER KEEPER (amuse. & rec.); ELEPHANT KEEPER (amuse. & rec.); MAMMAL KEEPER (amuse. & rec.); MONKEY KEEPER (amuse. & rec.); REPTILE KEEPER (amuse. & rec.). • **GED:** R3, M2, L2 • **SVP:** 3-6 mos • **Academic:** Ed=N, Eng=S • **Work Field:** 291 • **MPSMS:** 329 • **Aptitudes:** G3, V4, N4, S4, P4, Q5, K3, F3, M3, E4, C5 • **Temperaments:** M, V • **Physical:** V=L, H=N, L=M, W, S, H • **Work Env:** B, R • **Salary:** 3 • **Outlook:** 3

ANIMAL-RIDE ATTENDANT (amuse. & rec.) • **D.O.T.** #349.674-010 • OES #68014 • Assists patrons to mount and ride animals, collects payment for ride, and attends animals in amusement facility: Selects animal to be ridden on basis of size and age of patron. Accepts payment for ride. Assists patron to mount and ride animal, performing tasks, such as lifting child into saddle, explaining safe riding techniques, leading animal, and observing patron to detect uneasiness or handling difficulty. Attends animals, performing tasks, such as harnessing, saddling, feeding, watering, grooming, observing symptoms of illness, and cleaning stable. May be designated according to type of animal ridden as PONY-RIDE ATTENDANT (amuse. & rec.). • **GED:** R3, M1, L2 • **SVP:** 2-30 days • **Academic:** Ed=N, Eng=S • **Work Field:** 291 • **MPSMS:** 329, 919 • **Aptitudes:** G3, V4, N4, S4, P4, Q4, K3, F4, M3, E3, C5 • **Temperaments:** J, P, R • **Stress:** E • **Physical:** V=L, H=L, L=H, W, S, H • **Work Env:** O • **Salary:** 2 • **Outlook:** 2

AQUARIST (amuse. & rec.) • D.O.T. #449.674-010 • OES #79017 • AQUARIUM TANK ATTENDANT. Attends fish and other aquatic life in aquarium exhibits: Prepares food and feeds fish according to schedule. Cleans tanks and removes algae from tank windows. Attends to aquatic plants and decorations in displays. Collects and compares water samples to color-coded chart for acid analysis and monitors thermometers to ascertain water temperature. Adjusts thermostat and adds chemicals to water to maintain specified water conditions. Observes fish to detect disease and injuries, reports condition to supervisor, and treats fish according to instructions. May fire sedation gun and assist crew expedition members in collection of aquatic life. • **GED:** R3, M2, L2 • **SVP:** 3-6 mos • **Academic:** Ed=N, Eng=S • **Work Field:** 031, 291 • **MPSMS:** 329 • **Aptitudes:** G3, V3, N4, S3, P3, Q4, K3, F3, M3, E4, C4 • **Temperaments:** M, V • **Physical:** V=L, H=N, L=L, W, S, H • **Work Env:** B, W • **Salary:** 3 • **Outlook:** 2

DOG BATHER (per. ser.) • D.O.T. #418.677-010 • OES #79017 • Bathes dogs in preparation for grooming: Combs and cuts out heavy mats from dog's coat, using barber shears and steel comb. Brushes fur to remove dead skin, using dog brush. Draws bath water and regulates temperature. Washes dog, using perfumed soap or shampoo and handbrush and repeats process until dog is clean. Dries dog, using towel and electric drier. Cleans animals' quarters. May trim and shape dog's coat and clip toenails, using scissors and clippers. • **GED:** R3, M2, L2 • **SVP:** 2-30 days • **Academic:** Ed=N, Eng=N • **Work Field:** 291 • **MPSMS:** 329, 904 • **Aptitudes:** G3, V4, N4, S3, P3, Q4, K3, F3, M3, E4, C4 • **Temperaments:** P, T • **Stress:** E • **Physical:** V=N, H=N, L=L, W, H • **Work Env:** I • **Salary:** 2 • **Outlook:** 2

DOG GROOMER (per. ser.) • D.O.T. #418.674-010 • OES #79017 • DOG BEAUTICIAN; DOG-HAIR CLIPPER. Combs, clips, trims, and shapes dogs' coats to groom dogs, using knowledge of canine characteristics and grooming techniques and styles: Reads written or receives oral instructions to determine clipping pattern desired. Places dog on grooming table and fits grooming collar on dog to hold animal to table. Studies proportions of dog to determine most appropriate cutting pattern to achieve desired style. Clips dog's hair according to determined pattern, using electric clippers, comb, and barber's shears. Combs and shapes dog's coat. Talks to dog or uses other techniques to calm animal. • **GED:** R3, M2, L3 • **SVP:** 3-6 mos • **Academic:** Ed=N, Eng=S • **Work Field:** 291 • **MPSMS:** 329, 904 • **Aptitudes:** G3, V4, N4, S3, P3, Q4, K2, F3, M3, E4, C4 • **Temperaments:** J, P • **Stress:** E • **Physical:** V=L, H=N, L=M, W, H • **Work Env:** I, R • **Salary:** 2 • **Outlook:** 1

HORSESHOER (agric.) • D.O.T. #418.381-010 • OES #79017 • PLATER. Selects aluminum and steel shoes (plates) and fits, shapes, and nails shoes to animals' hooves: Removes worn or defective shoe from hoof, using nail snippers and pincers. Examines hoof to detect bruises and cracks and to determine trimming required. Trims and shapes hoof, using knife and snippers. Measures hoof, using calipers and steel tape. Selects aluminum or steel shoe from stock, according to hoof measurements and animal usage. Places leather pad, sponge, or oakum-pine tar mixture on bruised or cracked hoof for protection. Shapes shoe to fit hoof, using swage, forge, and hammer. Nails shoe to hoof and files hoof flush with shoe. May forge steel bar into shoe. May drive shop truck to worksite. • **GED:** R3, M2, L2 • **SVP:** 1-2 yrs • **Academic:** Ed=N, Eng=N • **Work Field:** 291 • **MPSMS:** 969 • **Aptitudes:** G3, V4, N4, S3, P3, Q5, K3, F3, M2, E5, C4 • **Temperaments:** M, T • **Physical:** V=L, H=N, L=M, W, S, H • **Work Env:** I, R • **Salary:** 3 • **Outlook:** 2

STABLE ATTENDANT (any ind.) • D.O.T. #410.674-022 • OES #79017 • BARNWORKER, GROOM. Cares for horses and mules to protect their health and improve their appearance: Waters animals and measures, mixes and apportions feed and feed supplements according to feeding instructions. Washes, brushes, trims and curries animals' coats to clean and improve their appearance. Inspects animals for disease, illness, and injury and treats animals according to instructions. Cleans animals' quarters and replenishes bedding. Exercises animals. Unloads and stores feed and supplies. May whitewash stables, using brush. May clean saddles and bridles. May saddle animals. May shoe animals. May be designated according to animal cared for, such as HORSE TENDER (any ind.); MULE TENDER (any ind.); STALLION KEEPER (agric.). • **GED:** R2, M1, L1 • **SVP:** 2-30 days • **Academic:** Ed=N, Eng=N • **Work Field:** 002, 003, 291 • **MPSMS:** 329 • **Aptitudes:** G4, V4, N4, S4, P4, Q4, K4, F4, M3, E4, C5 • **Temperaments:** M, V • **Physical:** V=N, H=N, L=H, W, H • **Work Env:** I • **Salary:** 2 • **Outlook:** 2

03.04 Elemental Work: Plants and Animals

Workers in this group perform active physical tasks, usually in an outdoor, non-industrial setting. They work with their hands, use various kinds of tools and equipment, or operate machinery. They find employment on farms or ranches, at logging camps or fish hatcheries, in forests or game preserves, or with commercial fishing businesses where they may work onshore or in fishing boats. In urban areas, they work in parks, gardens, or nurseries, or for businesses that provide horticultural or agricultural services.

✔ **What kind of work would you do?**
Your work activities would depend upon your specific job. For example, you might:

- operate farm machinery to plant, cultivate, harvest, and store grain crops.
- use shovels, hoes, and shears to plant, cultivate, and prune fruit trees.

- walk, stoop, crawl, or sit between rows of hops, peanuts or tobacco to harvest the crop.

- use an auger or ax to cut a tap in trees to collect sap.
- use an ax and chainsaw to clear a path for trees to be felled.

- set and haul in large commercial fishing nets by hand or using a winch.

✔ **What skills and abilities do you need for this kind of work?**
To do this kind of work, you must be able to:

- work outside for long periods of time and in all kinds of weather, performing tasks that require physical strength and endurance.
- work quickly and skillfully with your hands, to do such things as picking fruit or vegetables, sawing or sorting logs, or operating tractors or lawn mowers.

- follow instructions exactly.
- adjust to doing the same kind of work all day long, with little opportunity for diversion, or perform a variety of different tasks on the same day, as they are needed to carry out the activities of the business.

✔ **How do you know if you would like or could learn to do this kind of work?**
The following questions may give you clues about yourself as you consider this group of jobs.

- Have you worked a whole day mowing lawns, cutting weeds, or picking fruit? Could you do this type of work every day?
- Have you used rakes, shovels, saws, or other tools? Do you like to work with your hands?

- Have you been a member of FFA or 4-H? Did you have a project related to farming, fishing, or forestry?
- Do you like to camp, fish, or hunt? Would you like a full-time job doing these activities?

✔ **How can you prepare for and enter this kind of work?**
Occupations in this group usually require education and/or training extending from a short demonstration to over three months, depending upon the specific kind of work. Prior training is not required for most jobs in this group. Training is usually given by the employer when workers are hired or when their duties are changed. Most employers require job applicants to be in good physical condition, and commercial fisheries hire only persons who can swim for jobs on fishing boats. To be eligible for jobs in local, state or national parks, or with other government agencies, applicants must take and pass Civil Service examinations. Some vocational high schools offer courses in general farming, farm animal care, and equipment operation, and a few participate in work/study projects. This kind of training can help you get jobs of this kind, since employers don't have to spend as much time training you after employment.

Many vocational schools and training programs offer related courses.

✔ **What else should you consider about these jobs?**
Jobs in this group may involve frequent bending and crouching. Machines and equipment may reduce the amount of heavy physical work. However, these labor-savers may also lead to fewer job openings.

Many of these jobs require long hours of hard work at certain times of the year, such as when planting or harvesting crops. Sometimes extra workers are hired for a short period of time to help in these busy seasons. Persons wanting full-time work need to look for other jobs in the off-season. Some workers in this group must face hazards such as storms, forest fires, and extreme temperatures.

If you think you would like to do this kind of work, look at the job titles listed below.

GOE: 03.04.01 Farming, Elemental

CHRISTMAS-TREE FARM WORKER (forestry) • D.O.T. #451.687-010 • OES #79002 • Plants, cultivates, and harvests evergreen trees on Christmas-tree farm: Removes brush, ferns, and other growth from planting area, using mattock and brush-hook. Plants seedlings, using mattock or dibble [TREE PLANTER (forestry)]. Scatters fertilizer pellets over planted areas by hand. Shears tops and limb tips from trees, using machete and pruning shears, to control growth, increase limb density, and improve shape. Selects trees for cutting according to markings or size, specie, and grade, and fells trees, using ax or chainsaw. Drags cut trees from cutting area, and loads trees onto trucks. May be designated according to seasonal task performed. • **GED**: R1, M1, L1 • **SVP**: 2-30 days • **Academic**: Ed=N, Eng=N • **Work Field**: 002, 003 • **MPSMS**: 312, 313, 319 • **Aptitudes**: G4, V5, N5, S4, P4, Q5, K4, F4, M3, E3, C5 • **Temperaments**: R • **Physical**: V=L, H=N, L=H, W, S, H • **Work Env**: O, W, N • **Salary**: 2 • **Outlook**: 2

FARMWORKER, FRUIT 1 (agric.) • D.O.T. #403.683-010 • OES #79021 • Drives and operates farm machinery to plant, cultivate, spray, and harvest fruit and nut crops, such as apples, oranges, strawberries, and pecans: Attaches farm implements, such as plow, planter, fertilizer applicator, and harvester to tractor and drives tractor in fields to prepare soil and plant, fertilize, and harvest crops. Mixes chemical ingredients and sprays trees, vines, and grounds with solutions to control insects, fungus and weed growth, and diseases. Removes excess growth from trees and vines to improve fruit quality, using pruning saws and clippers. Irrigates soil, using portable-pipe or ditch system. Picks fruit during harvest. Drives truck or tractor to transport materials, supplies, workers, and products. Makes adjustments and minor repairs to farm machinery. May thin blossoms, runners, and immature fruit to obtain better-quality fruit. May select, cut, and graft stock-wood (scion) onto tree stem or trunk to propagate fruit and nut trees. May spray trees in spring to loosen and remove surplus fruit, and in fall to prevent early dropping and discoloration of fruit. May prop limbs to prevent them from breaking under weight of fruit. May start fans that circulate air or light smudge pots or torches to prevent frost damage. May be identified with work being performed, such as picking, plowing, and spraying; or according to crop worked such as cherries, cranberries, lemons, or walnuts. • **GED**: R3, M2, L3 • **SVP**: 6 mos-1 yr • **Academic**: Ed=N, Eng=S • **Work Field**: 002, 003 • **MPSMS**: 300 • **Aptitudes**: G3, V4, N4, S3, P3, Q5, K3, F4, M3, E3, C5 • **Temperaments**: T, V • **Physical**: V=L, H=N, L=M, W, C, S, H • **Work Env**: O, W, N, R • **Salary**: 2 • **Outlook**: 4

FARMWORKER, GENERAL 1 (agric.) • D.O.T. #421.683-010 • OES #79999 • HIRED WORKER. Drives trucks and tractors and performs variety of animal and crop raising duties as directed on general farm: Plows, harrows, and fertilizes soil, and cultivates, sprays, and harvests crops, using variety of tractor-drawn machinery [FARM-MACHINE OPERATOR (agric.)]. Cares for livestock and poultry, observing general condition and administering simple medications to animals and fowls. Hauls feed to livestock during grass shortage and winter months. Operates, repairs, and maintains farm implements and mechanical equipment, such as tractors, gang plows, ensilage cutters, hay balers, cottonpickers, and milking machines. Repairs farm buildings, fences, and other structures. May irrigate crops. May haul livestock and products to market [TRUCK DRIVER, HEAVY (any ind.); TRUCK DRIVER, LIGHT (any ind.)]. Usually works year-round and may oversee casual and seasonal help during planting and harvesting. • **GED**: R3, M2, L3 • **SVP**: 6 mos-1 yr • **Academic**: Ed=N, Eng=S • **Work Field**: 002, 003 • **MPSMS**: 300, 320 • **Aptitudes**: G3, V4, N4, S4, P4, Q4, K3, F3, M3, E4, C4 • **Temperaments**: M, T, V • **Physical**: V=L, H=N, L=H, W, C, S, H • **Work Env**: O, N, R • **Salary**: 2 • **Outlook**: 5

FARMWORKER, GENERAL 2 (agric.) • D.O.T. #421.687-010 • OES #79999 • CHORE TENDER; FARM LABORER. Performs variety of manual, animal-and-crop-raising tasks on general farm under close supervision: Feeds and waters cattle, poultry, and pets. Cleans barns, stables, pens, and kennels, using rake, shovel, water, and other cleaning materials. Digs seedlings, such as tobacco plants, strawberries, tomatoes, and orchard trees, using hoe, and transplants them by hand. Shovels earth to clear irrigation ditches and opens sluice gates to irrigate crops. Cleans plows, combines,

and tractors, using scraper and broom. Picks, cuts, or pulls fruits and vegetables to harvest crop. Stacks loose hay, using pitchfork, or pitches hay into automatic baling machine. Stacks bales of hay and bucks them onto wagon or truck, using handhook. • **GED**: R2, M1, L1 • **SVP**: 2-30 days • **Academic**: Ed=N, Eng=N • **Work Field**: 002, 003 • **MPSMS**: 300, 320 • **Aptitudes**: G4, V4, N5, S4, P4, Q5, K4, F4, M3, E4, C5 • **Temperaments**: R • **Stress**: T • **Physical**: V=L, H=N, L=H, W, C, S, H • **Work Env**: O • **Salary**: 2 • **Outlook**: 5

FARMWORKER, LIVESTOCK (agric.) • D.O.T. #410.664-010 • OES #79999 • LABORER, LIVESTOCK; RANCH HAND, LIVESTOCK. Performs any combination of the following tasks to attend livestock, such as cattle, sheep, swine, and goats on a farm or ranch: Mixes feed and additives, fills feed troughs with feed, and waters livestock. Herds livestock to pasture for grazing. Examines animals to detect diseases and injuries. Vaccinates animals by placing vaccine in drinking water or feed, or using syringes and hypodermic needles. Applies medications to cuts and bruises, sprays livestock with insecticide, and herds them into insecticide bath. Confines livestock in stalls, washes and clips them to prepare them for calving, and assists VETERINARIAN (medical ser.) in delivery of offspring. Binds or clamps testes or surgically removes testes to castrate livestock. Clips identifying notches or symbols on animal or brands animal, using branding iron, to indicate ownership. Clamps metal rings into nostrils of livestock to permit easier handling and prevent rooting. Docks lambs, using hand snips. Cleans livestock stalls and sheds, using disinfectant solutions, brushes, and shovels. Grooms, clips, and trims animals for exhibition. May maintain ranch buildings and equipment. May plant, cultivate, and harvest feed grain for stock. May maintain breeding, feeding, and cost records. May shear sheep. • **GED**: R3, M3, L3 • **SVP**: 3-6 mos • **Academic**: Ed=N, Eng=S • **Work Field**: 002, 003 • **MPSMS**: 320 • **Aptitudes**: G4, V4, N4, S4, P4, Q4, K3, F4, M3, E5, C4 • **Temperaments**: V • **Physical**: V=L, H=N, L=H, W, S, H • **Work Env**: B, R • **Salary**: 2 • **Outlook**: 5

FARMWORKER, VEGETABLE 2 (agric.) • D.O.T. #402.687-010 • OES #79999 • GARDEN WORKER; LABORER, VEGETABLE FARM; VEGETABLE WORKER. Plants, cultivates, and harvests vegetables, working as crewmember: Dumps seed into hopper of planter towed by tractor. Rides on planter and brushes debris from seed spouts that discharge seeds into plowed furrow. Plants roots and bulbs, using hoe or trowel. Covers plants with sheet or caps of treated cloth or paper to protect plants from weather. Weeds and thins blocks of plants, using hoe or spoon-shaped tool. Transplants seedlings, using hand transplanter or by placing seedlings in rotating planting wheel while riding on power-drawn transplanter. Sets bean poles and strings them with wire or twine. Closes and ties leaves over heads of cauliflower and other cabbage and cabbagelike plants. Picks, cuts, pulls, or lifts crops to harvest them. Ties vegetables in bunches and removes tops from root crops. Pitches vine crops into viner (pea or bean shelling machine), using pitchfork or electric fork and boom, and cleans up spilled vines. May participate in irrigation activities. May be identified with work assigned, such as blocking, cutting, and stringing, or with crop raised, such as asparagus, beans, and celery. • **GED**: R1, M1, L1 • **SVP**: 2-30 days • **Academic**: Ed=N, Eng=N • **Work Field**: 002, 003 • **MPSMS**: 303 • **Aptitudes**: G4, V4, N4, S4, P4, Q4, K3, F3, M3, E4, C4 • **Temperaments**: R • **Stress**: T • **Physical**: V=N, H=N, L=M, W, C, S, H • **Work Env**: O, N • **Salary**: 2 • **Outlook**: 3

LIVESTOCK-YARD ATTENDANT (any ind.) • D.O.T. #410.674-018 • OES #79999 • Performs any combination of the following tasks to bed, feed, water, load, weigh, mark, and segregate livestock: Feeds grains, hay, and prepared feed and waters livestock according to schedule. Opens gates and drives livestock to scales, pens, trucks, railcars, and holding and slaughtering areas according to instructions, using electric prod and whip. Weighs animals and records weight. Segregates animals according to weight, age, color, and physical condition. Marks livestock to identify ownership and grade, using brands, tags, paint, or tattoos. Cleans ramps, scales, trucks, railcars, and pens, using hose, fork, shovel, and rake. Scatters new bedding material, such as sawdust and straw, in pens, railcars, and trucks. May vaccinate, apply liniment, drench, isolate, and mark animals to effect disease control program. May make routine repairs and perform general maintenance duties in stockyard. • **GED:** R3, M2, L2 • **SVP:** 2-30 days • **Academic:** Ed=N, Eng=N • **Work Field:** 002, 003 • **MPSMS:** 320 • **Aptitudes:** G3, V4, N3, S4, P3, Q4, K3, F4, M3, E4, C4 • **Temperaments:** R, S • **Stress:** S • **Physical:** V=L, H=N, L=H, W, C, S, H • **Work Env:** B, W, R • **Salary:** 2 • **Outlook:** 2

SORTER, AGRICULTURAL PRODUCE (agric.) • D.O.T. #529.687-186 • OES #79011 • SORTER, FOOD PRODUCTS. Sorts agricultural produce, such as bulbs, fruits, nuts, and vegetables: Segregates produce on conveyor belt or table, working as crew member, according to grade, color, and size, and places produce in containers or on designated conveyors. Discards cull (inferior or defective) items and foreign matter. Bunches, ties, and trims produce, such as asparagus, carrots, celery, and radishes. Picks out choice produce to be used as cappers (top layers on marketing containers). Packs produce in boxes, barrels, baskets, or crates for storage or shipment [PACKER, AGRICULTURAL PRODUCE (agric.; whole. tr.)]. May be designated according to work performed as APPLE SORTER (agric.; can. & preserv.; whole. tr.); ASPARAGUS GRADER AND BUNCHER (agric.); CAPPER PICKER (agric.; whole. tr.); CITRUS-FRUIT-PACKING GRADER (agric.; whole. tr.); CULL GRADER (agric.; whole. tr.); POTATO GRADER (agric.; whole. tr.). Additional titles: ASPARAGUS SORTER (agric.; can. & preserv.; whole. tr.); BANANA GRADER (agric.; whole. tr.); BULB SORTER (agric.); CHERRY SORTER (agric.; can. & preserv.; whole. tr.); CRANBERRY SORTER (agric.; whole. tr.); FIG SORTER (agric.; can. & preserv.; whole. tr.); FLOWER GRADER (agric.); FRUIT SORTER (agric.; can. & preserv.; whole. tr.); HOP SORTER (agric.); NUT SORTER (agric.); PEACH SORTER (agric.; can. & preserv.; whole. tr.); POTATO SORTER (agric.; whole. tr.); SEED SORTER (agric.); TOMATO GRADER (whole. tr.); VEGETABLE SORTER (agric.; can. & preserv.; whole. tr.). • **GED:** R1, M1, L1 • **SVP:** 2-30 days • **Academic:** Ed=N, Eng=N • **Work Field:** 211 • **MPSMS:** 300, 311, 314 • **Aptitudes:** G4, V4, N4, S4, P4, Q5, K4, F4, M3, E5, C4 • **Temperaments:** R • **Stress:** T • **Physical:** V=L, H=N, L=L, H • **Work Env:** I, W • **Salary:** 3 • **Outlook:** 3

GOE: 03.04.02 Forestry & Logging, Elemental

BUCKER (logging) • D.O.T. #454.684-010 • OES #73002 • Saws felled trees into lengths: Places supporting limbs or poles under felled tree to avoid splitting underside and to prevent log from rolling. Cuts previously marked tree into logs, using power chainsaw and ax. Drives wedges into cut behind saw blade to prevent binding saw. May cut limbs from felled trees. May mark felled tree for cutting into log lengths to obtain maximum value [LOG MARKER (logging)]. • **GED:** R2, M1, L1 • **SVP:** 30 days-3 mos • **Academic:** Ed=N, Eng=N • **Work Field:** 004 • **MPSMS:** 452 • **Aptitudes:** G4, V4, N5, S3, P4, Q5, K3, F4, M3, E3, C5 • **Temperaments:** R • **Physical:** V=L, H=N, L=H, W, C, S, H • **Work Env:** O, N, R • **Salary:** 5 • **Outlook:** 4

CHAINSAW OPERATOR (logging) • D.O.T. #454.687-010 • OES #73002 • Trims limbs, tops, and roots from trees, and saws logs to predetermined lengths, using chainsaw, preparatory to removal from forest or processing into wood products. May measure and mark logs for sawing. May be designated according to activity performed as LIMBER (logging). For related classifications involving judgment in determining cutting techniques, see BUCKER (logging); FALLER (logging) II; and TREE CUTTER (agric.; logging). • **GED:** R2, M1, L1 • **SVP:** 2-30 days • **Academic:** Ed=N, Eng=N • **Work Field:** 056 • **MPSMS:** 452 • **Aptitudes:** G4, V4, N4, S3, P4, Q5, K4, F4, M3, E4, C5 • **Temperaments:** R • **Physical:** V=L, H=N, L=H, W, S, H • **Work Env:** O, N, R • **Salary:** 4 • **Outlook:** 4

FALLER 2 (logging) • D.O.T. #454.684-014 • OES #73002 • STUMPER-FELLER. Fells trees, applying specified cutting procedures to control direction of fall: Clears brush from work area and escape route, and cuts saplings and other trees from falling path, using ax and chainsaw. Saws or chops undercut in bole of tree to fix designated direction of fall, using chainsaw and ax, and saws opposite side (back cut) to fell tree. Drives wedges behind saw with mall to tip tree and prevent binding of saw. May cut limbs from tree. May cut tree into log lengths. May tag trees in unsafe condition with high visibility ribbon. Workers are classified as

FALLER (logging) I where adherence to standards of minimum tree damage are of prime importance and considerable judgment is exercised in determining cutting techniques. • **GED:** R2, M1, L1 • **SVP:** 30 days-3 mos • **Academic:** Ed=N, Eng=N • **Work Field:** 004 • **MPSMS:** 452 • **Aptitudes:** G4, V4, N5, S3, P4, Q5, K3, F4, M3, E4, C5 • **Temperaments:** R • **Physical:** V=L, H=N, L=H, W, S, H • **Work Env:** O, N, R • **Salary:** 5 • **Outlook:** 4

FOREST WORKER (forestry) • D.O.T. #452.687-010 • OES #79002 • Performs variety of tasks to reforest and protect timber tracts and maintain forest facilities, such as roads and campsites: Plants tree seedlings in specified pattern, using mattock, planting hoe, or dibble. Cuts out diseased, weak, or undesirable trees, and prunes limbs of young trees to deter knot growth, using handsaw, powersaw, and pruning tools. Fells trees, clears brush from fire breaks, and extinguishes flames and embers to suppress forest fires, using chainsaw, shovel, and engine-driven or hand pumps. Clears and piles brush, limbs, and other debris from roadsides, fire trails, and camping areas, using ax, mattock, or brush hook. Sprays or injects trees, brush, and weeds with herbicides, using hand or powered sprayers or tree injector tool. Erects signs and fences, using posthole digger, shovel, tamper, or other handtools. Replenishes firewood and other supplies, and cleans kitchens, restrooms, and campsites or recreational facilities. Holds measuring tape or survey rod, carries and sets stakes, clears brush from sighting line, and performs related tasks to assist forest survey crew. • **GED:** R2, M1, L1 • **SVP:** 2-30 days • **Academic:** Ed=N, Eng=N • **Work Field:** 002, 003, 293 • **MPSMS:** 313 • **Aptitudes:** G4, V4, N4, S3, P4, Q5, K3, F4, M3, E4, C4 • **Temperaments:** V • **Physical:** V=L, H=N, L=H, W, C, S, H • **Work Env:** O • **Salary:** 3 • **Outlook:** 3

FOREST-FIRE FIGHTER (forestry) • D.O.T. #452.687-014 • OES #63008 • FIRE CREW WORKER; SMOKE EATER. Suppresses forest fires, working alone or as member of crew: Fells trees, cuts and clears brush, digs trenches, and extinguishes flames and embers to contain or suppress fire, using ax, chainsaw, shovel, and hand-or engine-driven water pumps. Patrols burned area after fire to watch for hot spots that may restart fire. When leading and directing fire-fighting activities of a crew of workers, may be designated SUPPRESSION-CREW LEADER (forestry). • **GED:** R2, M1, L1 • **SVP:** 2-30 days • **Academic:** Ed=N, Eng=N • **Work Field:** 293 • **MPSMS:** 313, 951 • **Aptitudes:** G4, V4, N5, S3, P3, Q5, K3, F4, M3, E3, C4 • **Temperaments:** R, S • **Stress:** S • **Physical:** V=L, H=N, L=H, W, C, S, H • **Work Env:** O, H, N, R • **Salary:** 3 • **Outlook:** 3

LOGGER, ALL-ROUND (logging) • D.O.T. #454.684-018 • OES #73002 • Harvests timber trees, performing a combination of the following tasks: Fells trees in specified direction, removes limbs and top, and measures and cuts tree into log lengths, using chainsaw, wedges, and ax. Secures cables to logs and drives tractor or horses to skid logs to landing. Loads logs onto trucks by hand or using winch. May drive truck to haul logs to mill. • **GED:** R2, M1, L1 • **SVP:** 3-6 mos • **Academic:** Ed=N, Eng=N • **Work Field:** 004 • **MPSMS:** 452 • **Aptitudes:** G4, V4, N4, S3, P4, Q5, K3, F4, M3, E4, C5 • **Temperaments:** R • **Physical:** V=L, H=N, L=H, W, C, S, H • **Work Env:** O, N, R • **Salary:** 5 • **Outlook:** 4

GOE: 03.04.03 Hunting & Fishing

DECKHAND, FISHING VESSEL (fish.) • D.O.T. #449.667-010 • OES #79999 • Performs any combination of following duties aboard fishing vessel: Stands lookout, steering, and engine-room watches. Attaches nets, slings, hooks, and other lifting devices to cables, booms, and hoists. Loads equipment and supplies aboard vessel by hand or using hoisting equipment. Signals other workers to move, hoist, and position loads. Rows boats and dinghies and operates skiffs to transport fishers, divers, and sponge hookers and to tow and position nets. Attaches accessories, such as floats, weights, and markers to nets and lines. Pulls and guides nets and lines onto vessel. Removes fish from nets and hooks. Sorts and cleans marine life and returns undesirable and illegal catch to sea. Places catch in containers and stows in hold and covers with salt and ice. Washes deck, conveyors, knives and other equipment, using brush, detergent, and water. Lubricates, adjusts, and makes minor repairs to engines and equipment. Secures and removes vessel's docking lines to and from docks and other vessels. May be designated according to type of vessel worked as DECKHAND, CLAM DREDGE (fish.); DECK HAND, CRAB BOAT (fish.);

DECKHAND, OYSTER DREDGE (fish.); DECK HAND, SHRIMP BOAT (fish.); DECKHAND, SPONGE BOAT (fish.); DECK HAND, TUNA BOAT (fish.). • **GED:** R2, M1, L1 • **SVP:** 30 days-3 mos • **Academic:** Ed=N, Eng=N • **Work Field:** 001 • **MPSMS:** 330 • **Aptitudes:** G4, V4, N4, S3, P4, Q5, K3, F4, M3, E3, C4 • **Temperaments:** T, V • **Physical:** V=L, H=N, L=H, W, S, H • **Work Env:** O, W, R • **Salary:** 3 • **Outlook:** 2

FISH HATCHERY WORKER (fish.) • D.O.T. #446.684-010 • OES #79999 • FISH HATCHERY ASSISTANT; FISH HATCHERY ATTENDANT. Performs any combination of the following tasks to trap and spawn game fish, incubate eggs, and rear fry in fish hatchery: Secures net on both banks of river to divert fish to holding pond. Catches ripened fish from holding pond with hand net and squeezes or slits bellies of female fish to release eggs in pail. Squeezes bellies of male fish to force milt over eggs, and stirs with rubber-gloved hand to fertilize eggs. Fills hatchery trays with fertilized eggs and places trays in incubation troughs. Turns valves and places baffles in troughs to adjust volume, depth, velocity, and temperature of water. Inspects eggs and picks out dead, infertile, and off-color eggs, using suction syringe. Sorts fish according to size, coloring, and species and transfers fingerlings to rearing ponds or tanks, using buckets or tank truck. Scatters food over surface of water by hand or activates blower that automatically scatters food over water to feed fish. Observes appearance and actions of developing fish to detect diseases, and adds medications to food and water as instructed by superior. Transfers mature fish to rivers and lakes, using tank truck. Records field data and prepares reports of hatchery activities. Drains and cleans ponds and troughs, using brushes, chemicals, and water. Makes minor repairs to hatchery equipment, paints buildings, and maintains grounds. May spawn and rear food fish or tropical and exotic fish for commercial use. May mark migrating fish with liquid nitrogen, using hand-operated branding device. • **GED:** R3, M1, L2 • **SVP:** 6 mos-1 yr • **Academic:** Ed=N, Eng=N • **Work Field:** 002, 003 • **MPSMS:** 331 • **Aptitudes:** G3, V4, N4, S3, P4, Q4, K3, F3, M3, E4, C3 • **Temperaments:** M, T, V • **Physical:** V=L, H=N, L=M, W, C, S, H • **Work Env:** B, W, R • **Salary:** 3 • **Outlook:** 2

FISHER, DIVING (fish.) • D.O.T. #443.664-010 • OES #79999 • Gathers or harvests marine life, such as sponges, abalone, pearl oysters, and geoducks from sea bottom, wearing wet suit and scuba gear, or diving suit with air line extending to surface: Climbs overboard or is lowered into water from boat by lifeline. Picks up pearl oysters; tears sponges from sea bottom; pries abalone from rocks, using bar; and flushes geoducks from sand, using air gun connected to air compressor on boat. Places catch in bag or basket and tugs on line to have catch pulled to boat, or surfaces and empties catch on boat or in container. Signals other workers to extend or retract air lines. May monitor air lines and operate air compressor as alternating member of diving crew. May be designated according to quarry sought as ABALONE DIVER (fish.); GEODUCK DIVER (fish.); PEARL DIVER (fish.); SPONGE DIVER (fish.). • **GED:** R3, M2, L2 • **SVP:** 3-6 mos • **Academic:** Ed=N, Eng=N • **Work Field:** 001 • **MPSMS:** 332, 339 • **Aptitudes:** G3, V4, N4, S3, P3, Q4, K4, F4, M3, E3, C4 • **Temperaments:** J, S • **Stress:** S • **Physical:** V=L, H=N, L=H, W, C, S, H • **Work Env:** O, W, R • **Salary:** 3 • **Outlook:** 2

FISHER, LINE (fish.) • D.O.T. #442.684-010 • OES #79999 • FISHER. Catches fish and other marine life with hooks and lines, working alone or as member of crew: Lays out line and attaches hooks, bait, sinkers, and various anchors, floats, and swivels, depending on quarry sought. Puts line in water, and holds, anchors, or trolls (tows) line to catch fish. Hauls line onto boat deck or ashore by hand, reel, or winch, and removes catch. Stows catch in hold or boxes and packs catch in ice. May hit fish with club to stun it before removing it from hook. May fish with gaff to assist in hauling fish from water. May slit fish, remove viscera, and wash cavity to clean fish for storage. May steer vessel in fishing area. When fishing with line held in hand, is designated as FISHER, HAND LINE (fish.). When fishing with fixed line equipped with hooks hung at intervals on line, is designated according to whether line is trawl (anchored in water at both ends) as FISHER, TRAWL LINE (fish.), or trot (reaching across stream or from one bank) as FISHER, TROT LINE (fish.). When fishing with line that is trolled is designated as FISHER, TROLL LINE (fish.). • **GED:** R2, M1, L1 • **SVP:** 30

days-3 mos • **Academic:** Ed=N, Eng=N • **Work Field:** 001 • **MPSMS:** 330 • **Aptitudes:** G4, V4, N4, S4, P4, Q5, K3, F4, M3, E4, C5 • **Temperaments:** R • **Physical:** V=L, H=N, L=M, W, C, S, H • **Work Env:** O, W, R • **Salary:** 3 • **Outlook:** 2

FISHER, NET (fish.) • D.O.T. #441.684-010 • OES #79999 • Catches finfish, shellfish, and other marine life alone or as crew member on shore or aboard fishing vessel, using equipment such as dip, diver, gill, hoop, lampara, pound, trap, reef, trammel, and trawl nets; purse seine; and haul, drag, or beach seine: Inserts and attaches hoops, rods, poles, ropes, floats, weights, beam runners, otter boards, and cables to form, reinforce, position, set, tow, and anchor net. Attaches flags and lights to buoys to identify net location. Puts net into water and anchors or tows net according to kind of net used, location of fishing area, and method of fishing. Hauls net to boat or ashore manually and using winch. Empties catch from net, using dip net, brail, buckets, hydraulic pump, and conveyor, and by lifting net, using block and tackle, and dumping catch. Stows catch in hold and containers, or transfers catch to base ship or buy boat. Fishing with some types of nets may be illegal in some states. May ride in skiff and hold end of net, as base ship discharges net, to surround school of fish or to pull net ends and trap fish. May sort and clean fish. May repair fishing nets and gear. May act as lookout or observe instruments to sight schools of fish. May be designated according to kind of net used as FISHER, DIP NET (fish.); FISHER, DIVER NET (fish.); FISHER, GILL NET (fish.); FISHER, HOOP NET (fish.). Additional titles: FISHER, HAUL, DRAG, OR BEACH SEINE (fish.); FISHER, LAMPARA NET (fish.); FISHER, POUND NET OR TRAP (fish.); FISHER, PURSE SEINE (fish.); FISHER, REEF NET (fish.); FISHER, TRAMMEL NET (fish.); FISHER, TRAWL NET (fish.). • **GED:** R2, M1, L1 • **SVP:** 3-6 mos • **Academic:** Ed=N, Eng=N • **Work Field:** 001 • **MPSMS:** 330 • **Aptitudes:** G3, V4, N4, S4, P4, Q5, K4, F4, M4, E3, C5 • **Temperaments:** R • **Stress:** T • **Physical:** V=L, H=N, L=H, W, C, S, H • **Work Env:** O, W, R • **Salary:** 4 • **Outlook:** 3

SHELLFISH DREDGE OPERATOR (fish.) • D.O.T. #446.663-010 • OES #79999 • SHELLFISH HARVESTER. Drives and operates mechanical or hydraulic dredge to cultivate, transplant, and harvest marine life, such as oysters, clams, and sea grass: Steers dredge to designated area, using navigational aids, such as compass and landmarks, and knowledge of tides, or is towed by other vessel. Fastens water pressure hoses, lifting and towing cables, and dredge baskets to dredge, using handtools. Primes pumps and adjusts angle of water jets and conveyor, to prepare for dredging. Activates dredge engine and lowers dredge baskets or hydraulic dredger to sea bottom, using hoisting boom and winch. Activates hydraulic dredge impeller pumps and conveyor and drags hydraulic dredger or dredge baskets along sea bottom to scoop or flush shellfish from beds. Inspects contents dumped from dredges onto deck to determine depth of cut into sea bottom, and adjusts water pressure or angle of basket blade to attain depth of cut desired. Observes flow of shellfish on conveyor and stops conveyor to prevent or clear jamming. Observes and listens to operation of equipment to detect malfunction and makes adjustments and minor repairs to correct operational defects. Attaches cutting blades or harrows to dredge and lowers to specified distance above or on sea bottom and steers dredge in diminishing circles to cultivate shellfish beds or cut sea grass. May record date, harvest area, and yield in log book. May direct helpers in sorting of clams. May be designated according to type of dredge operated, as HYDRAULIC DREDGE OPERATOR (fish.); SELF-PROPELLED DREDGE OPERATOR (fish.); or kind of shellfish harvested, as CLAM DREDGE OPERATOR (fish.); OYSTER DREDGE OPERATOR (fish.). • **GED:** R3, M2, L2 • **SVP:** 6 mos-1 yr • **Academic:** Ed=N, Eng=N • **Work Field:** 002, 003 • **MPSMS:** 332 • **Aptitudes:** G3, V4, N4, S3, P3, Q5, K3, F4, M3, E4, C5 • **Temperaments:** M, R, T • **Physical:** V=L, H=N, L=H, W, C, S, H • **Work Env:** B, W, N, R • **Salary:** 3 • **Outlook:** 2

SKIFF OPERATOR (fish.) • D.O.T. #441.683-010 • OES #79999 • Operates seiner skiff to hold one end of purse seine in place while purse seiner circles school of fish to set net. Holds purse seine away from ship during pursing and brailing operations. May splash water with pole, on opposite side of school away from purse seiner, to prevent fish from escaping as fish are encircled by purse seine. May locate schools of fish sighted by other fishers. • **GED:** R3, M1, L2 •

SVP: 3-6 mos • **Academic:** Ed=N, Eng=N • **Work Field:** 001 • MPSMS: 331 • **Aptitudes:** G3, V4, N4, S3, P4, Q5, K4, F4, M3, E3, C5 • **Temperaments:** S • **Stress:** S • **Physical:** V=L, H=N, L=H, W, C, S, H • **Work Env:** O, W, R • **Salary:** 2 • **Outlook:** 2

GOE: 03.04.04 Nursery & Groundskeeping, Elemental

CEMETERY WORKER (real estate) • D.O.T. #406.684-010 • OES #79014 • Prepares graves and maintains cemetery grounds: Locates grave site according to section, lot, and plot numbers and marks off area to be excavated. Removes sod from gravesite, using shovel. Digs grave to specified depth, using pick and shovel or back-hoe. Places concrete slabs on bottom and around sides of grave to line it. Positions casket-lowering device on grave, covers dirt pile and sod with artificial grass carpet, erects canopy, and arranges folding chairs to prepare site for burial service. Builds wooden forms for concrete slabs, using hammer, saw, and nails. Sets grave marker (tomb stone) in concrete on gravesite, using shovel and trowel. Mows grass with hand or power mower. Prunes shrubs and plants flowers and shrubs on grave and removes debris from grave. May open and close mausoleum vaults, using handtools. • **GED:** R3, M1, L2 • **SVP:** 6 mos-1 yr • **Academic:** Ed=N, Eng=N • **Work Field:** 003, 102 • MPSMS: 310 • **Aptitudes:** G3, V4, N4, S4, P4, Q4, K4, F4, M3, E4, C5 • **Temperaments:** M, T, V • **Physical:** V=L, H=N, L=H, W, S, H • **Work Env:** O • **Salary:** 4 • **Outlook:** 2

GREENSKEEPER 1 (any ind.) • D.O.T. #406.137-010 • OES #72002 • GREENSKEEPER, HEAD. Supervises and coordinates activities of workers engaged in preserving grounds and turf of golf course in playing condition: Confers with SUPERINTENDENT, GREENS (amuse. & rec.) to plan and review work projects. Determines work priority and assigns workers to specific tasks, such as fertilizing, irrigating, seeding, mowing, raking, and spraying. Mixes and prepares recommended spray and dust solutions. Performs other duties as described under SUPERVISOR (any ind.). May direct and assist workers engaged in maintenance and repair of mechanical equipment. May assist workers to perform more critical duties. • **GED:** R4, M3, L3 • **SVP:** 1-2 yrs • **Academic:** Ed=H, Eng=S • **Work Field:** 003 • MPSMS: 310 • **Aptitudes:** G3, V3, N3, S3, P3, Q4, K4, F4, M4, E4, C4 • **Temperaments:** D, M, P, V • **Physical:** V=L, H=N, L=H, W, C, S, H • **Work Env:** O, R • **Salary:** 3 • **Outlook:** 3

GREENSKEEPER 2 (any ind.) • D.O.T. #406.683-010 • OES #79014 • LABORER, GOLF COURSE. Performs any combination of the following duties, as directed by GREENSKEEPER (any ind.) I, to maintain grounds and turf of golf course in playing condition: Operates tractor, using specific attachments, to till, cultivate, and grade new turf areas, to apply prescribed amounts of lime, fertilizer, insecticide, and fungicide, and to mow rough and fairway areas at designated cut, exercising care not to injure turf or shrubs. Cuts turf on green and tee areas, using hand mower and power mower. Connects hose and sprinkler systems at designated points on course to irrigate turf. Digs and rakes ground to prepare new greens, grades and cleans traps, and repairs roadbeds, using shovels, rakes, spades, and other tools. May plant, trim, and spray trees and shrubs. • **GED:** R2, M1, L2 • **SVP:** 30 days-3 mos • **Academic:** Ed=N, Eng=N • **Work Field:** 003 • MPSMS: 310 • **Aptitudes:** G4, V4, N4, S3, P4, Q5, K3, F4, M3, E3, C4 • **Temperaments:** R, T • **Physical:** V=L, H=N, L=M, W, C, S, H • **Work Env:** O, R • **Salary:** 2 • **Outlook:** 2

GROUNDSKEEPER, INDUSTRIAL-COMMERCIAL (any ind.) • D.O.T. #406.684-014 • OES #79014 • CARETAKER, GROUNDS; GARDENER; YARD LABORER. Maintains grounds of industrial, commercial, or public property, performing combination of following tasks: Cuts lawns, using hand mower or power mower. Trims and edges around walks, flower beds, and walls, using clippers and edging tools. Prunes shrubs and trees to shape and improve growth, using shears. Sprays lawn, shrubs, and trees with fertilizer or insecticide. Rakes and burns leaves and cleans or sweeps up litter, using spiked stick or broom. Shovels snow from walks and driveways. Spreads salt on public passage ways. Plants grass, flowers, trees, and shrubs. Waters lawn and shrubs during dry periods, using hose or by activating fixed or portable sprinkler system. Repairs fences, gates, walls, and walks, using carpentry and masonry tools. Paints fences and outbuildings. Cleans out drainage ditches and culverts, using shovel and rake. Depending on size and nature of employing establishment, uses tractor equipped with attachments, such as mowers, lime-or fertilizer-spreaders, and lawn roller. May perform variety of laboring duties, common to type of employing establishment, when yard work is completed. • **GED:** R2, M1, L2 • **SVP:** 30 days-3 mos • **Academic:** Ed=N, Eng=N • **Work Field:** 003, 102 • MPSMS: 310, 909 • **Aptitudes:** G3, V4, N4, S3, P3, Q4, K4, F4, M3, E4, C5 • **Temperaments:** R, T • **Stress:** T • **Physical:** V=L, H=N, L=M, W, C, S, H • **Work Env:** O, N • **Salary:** 3 • **Outlook:** 3

GROUNDSKEEPER, PARKS AND GROUNDS (gov. ser.) • D.O.T. #406.687-010 • OES #79014 • PARK WORKER. Keeps grounds of city, State, or national park and playgrounds clean and repairs buildings and equipment: Mows lawns, using hand mower or power-driven lawnmower. Grubs and weeds around bushes, trees, and flower beds and trims hedges. Picks up and burns or carts away paper and rubbish. Repairs and paints benches, tables, guardrails, and assists in repair of roads, walks, buildings, and mechanical equipment, using handtools. Cleans comfort stations and other buildings. May live on site and be designated CAMP GROUND CARETAKER (gov. ser.). • **GED:** R2, M1, L2 • **SVP:** 2-30 days • **Academic:** Ed=N, Eng=N • **Work Field:** 003, 031 • MPSMS: 310, 360 • **Aptitudes:** G4, V4, N5, S4, P4, Q5, K4, F4, M4, E4, C4 • **Temperaments:** R, T • **Physical:** V=L, H=N, L=M, W, C, S, H • **Work Env:** O, N • **Salary:** 2 • **Outlook:** 2

HORTICULTURAL WORKER 2 (agric.) • D.O.T. #405.687-014 • OES #79005 • Performs any combination of following duties concerned with preparing soil and growth media, cultivating, and otherwise participating in horticultural activities under close supervision on acreage, in nursery, or in environmentally-controlled structure, such as greenhouse and shed: Hauls and spreads topsoil, fertilizer, peat moss, and other materials to condition land. Digs, rakes, and screens soil and fills cold frames and hot beds to prepare them for planting. Fills growing tanks with water. Plants, sprays, weeds, and waters plants, shrubs, and trees. Sows grass seed and plants plugs of sod and cuts, rolls, and stacks sod. Prepares scion and ties buds to assist worker budding roses. Traps and poisons pests, such as moles, gophers, and mice. Plants shrubs and plants in containers. Ties, bunches, wraps, and packs flowers, plants, shrubs, and trees to fill orders. Moves containerized shrubs and trees, using wheelbarrow. Digs up shrubs and trees and wraps their roots with burlap. May be designated according to employing establishment as GRASS-FARM LABORER (agric.); GREENHOUSE LABORER (agric.); NURSERY LABORER (agric.); ROSE-FARM LABORER (agric.); or according to horticultural specialty as BEAN-SPROUT LABORER (agric.); MUSHROOM LABORER (agric.). • **GED:** R2, M1, L1 • **SVP:** 2-30 days • **Academic:** Ed=N, Eng=N • **Work Field:** 003 • MPSMS: 310 • **Aptitudes:** G4, V4, N5, S4, P4, Q5, K4, F4, M3, E4, C4 • **Temperaments:** R • **Stress:** T • **Physical:** V=L, H=N, L=H, W, S, H • **Work Env:** O • **Salary:** 1 • **Outlook:** 3

LABORER, LANDSCAPE (agric.) • D.O.T. #408.687-014 • OES #79014 • Moves soil, equipment, and materials, digs holes, and performs related duties to assist LANDSCAPE GARDENER (agric.) in landscaping grounds: Digs holes and trenches with pick and shovel. Plants and waters sod and shrubbery. Mixes and pours cement for garden borders and mows lawns. Places stone and plants flowers in garden areas. Hauls topsoil in wheelbarrow and spreads and levels soil, using rake. • **GED:** R2, M2, L2 • **SVP:** 2-30 days • **Academic:** Ed=N, Eng=N • **Work Field:** 003 • MPSMS: 969 • **Aptitudes:** G4, V4, N4, S4, P4, Q5, K4, F4, M3, E4, C4 • **Temperaments:** T, V • **Physical:** V=L, H=N, L=H, W, S, H • **Work Env:** O, N, R • **Salary:** 3 • **Outlook:** 3

LAWN-SERVICE WORKER (agric.) • D.O.T. #408.684-010 • OES #79014 • Cultivates lawns, using power aerator and thatcher and chemicals according to specifications: Lifts dead leaves and grass from between growing grass and soil, using thatcher. Pierces soil to make holes for fertilizer and water, using aerator. Presses aerator fork into soil and pulls rake through grass to cultivate areas not accessible to machines. Distributes granulated fertilizers, pesticides, and fungicides on lawn, using spreader. Records services rendered, materials used, and charges assessed on specified form. Transports thatcher, aerator, tools, and materials to and from job site, using truck with hydraulic lift-gate. May care for athletic field turf and be designated ATHLETIC TURF WORKER (amuse. & rec.). • **GED:** R3, M2, L2 • **SVP:** 3-6 mos • **Academic:** Ed=N, Eng=N • **Work Field:** 003 • **MPSMS:** 969 • **Aptitudes:** G3, V4, N4, S3, P4, Q4, K3, F4, M3, E4, C4 • **Temperaments:** T • **Physical:** V=L, H=N, L=H, W, H • **Work Env:** O, N • **Salary:** 2 • **Outlook:** 2

GOE: 03.04.05 Services, Plants & Animals, Elemental

DOG CATCHER (gov. ser.) • D.O.T. #379.673-010 • OES #63099 • DOG WARDEN. Captures and impounds unlicensed, stray, and uncontrolled animals: Snares animal with net, rope, or device. Cages or secures animal in truck. Drives truck to shelter. Removes animal from truck to shelter cage or other enclosure. Supplies food, water, and personal care to detained animals. Investigates complaints of animal bite cases. Destroys rabid animals as directed. Examines dog licenses for validity and issues warnings or summonses to delinquent owners. May destroy unclaimed animals, using gun, or by gas or electrocution. May examine captured animals for injuries and deliver injured animals to VETERINARIAN (medical ser.) for medical treatment. May maintain file of number of animals impounded and disposition of each. May enforce regulations concerning treatment of domestic animals and be designated HUMANE OFFICER (gov. ser.). • **GED:** R3, M1, L2 • **SVP:** 30 days-3 mos • **Academic:** Ed=N, Eng=G • **Work Field:** 291, 293 • **MPSMS:** 329, 959 • **Aptitudes:** G4, V4, N4, S4, P4, Q4, K3, F4, M3, E3, C5 • **Temperaments:** P, S, V • **Stress:** E, S • **Physical:** V=L, H=N, L=M, W, H • **Work Env:** B, R • **Salary:** 2 • **Outlook:** 2

PLANT-CARE WORKER (agric.) • D.O.T. #408.364-010 • OES #79005 • INTERIOR HORTICULTURIST; PLANT TENDER. Cares for ornamental plants on various customer premises, applying knowledge of horticultural requirements, and using items such as insecticides, fertilizers, and gardening tools: Reads work orders and supply requisitions to determine job requirements, and confers with supervisor to clarify work procedures. Loads plants and supplies onto truck in order of scheduled stops, using hand truck. Drives truck to premises and carries needed supplies to work area. Examines plants and soil to determine moisture level, using water sensor gauge, and waters plants according to requirements of species, using hose and watering can. Sponges plant leaves to apply moisture and remove dust. Observes plants under magnifying glass to detect insects and disease, and consults plant care books or confers with supervisor to identify problems and determine treatments. Selects and applies specified chemical solutions to feed plants, kill insects, and treat diseases, using hose or mist-sprayer. Transplants rootbound plants into larger containers. Pinches and prunes stems and leaves to remove dead and diseased leaves, to shape plants, and to induce growth, using shears. Removes diseased and dying plants from premises and replaces them with healthy plants. Informs customer of plant care needs. Enters record of actions taken at each stop in route book and prepares requisitions for materials needed on subsequent visit. Returns diseased, dying, and unused plants and supplies to employer premises. • **GED:** R3, M2, L3 • **SVP:** 30 days-3 mos • **Academic:** Ed=N, Eng=S • **Work Field:** 003 • **MPSMS:** 310 • **Aptitudes:** G3, V3, N4, S4, P3, Q3, K4, F3, M3, E4, C3 • **Temperaments:** J, T • **Physical:** V=L, H=N, L=M, W, H • **Work Env:** I • **Salary:** 1 • **Outlook:** 3

TREE TRIMMER (light, heat, & power) • D.O.T. #408.664-010 • OES #73099 • TREE TRIMMER, LINE CLEARANCE; TREE-TRIMMING-LINE TECHNICIAN. Trims trees to clear right-of-way for communications lines and electric powerlines to minimize storm and short-circuit hazards: Climbs trees to reach branches interfering with wires and transmission towers, using climbing equipment. Prunes treetops, using saws or pruning shears. Repairs trees damaged by storm or lightning by trimming jagged stumps and painting them to prevent bleeding of sap. Removes broken limbs from wires, using hooked extension pole. Fells trees interfering with power service, using chainsaw (portable power-saw). May work from bucket of extended truck boom to reach limbs. • **GED:** R3, M2, L2 • **SVP:** 3-6 mos • **Academic:** Ed=N, Eng=N • **Work Field:** 054, 056 • **MPSMS:** 312, 313, 319 • **Aptitudes:** G3, V4, N5, S3, P4, Q5, K4, F4, M3, E2, C5 • **Temperaments:** R, S • **Stress:** T, S • **Physical:** V=L, H=N, L=H, W, C, H • **Work Env:** O, R • **Salary:** 4 • **Outlook:** 3

Protective 04

An interest in using authority to protect people and property. You can satisfy this interest by working in law enforcement, fire fighting, and related fields. You may enjoy mental challenge and intrigue. You could investigate crimes or fires. You may prefer to fight fires and respond to other emergencies. Or may want more routine work. Perhaps a job in guarding or patrolling would appeal to you. You may have management ability. You could seek a leadership position in law enforcement and the protective services.

04.01 Safety and Law Enforcement

Workers in this group are in charge of enforcing laws and regulations. Some investigate crimes, while others supervise workers who stop or arrest lawbreakers. Others make inspections to be sure that the laws are not broken. Most jobs are found in the Federal, State, or local governments, such as the Police and Fire Departments. Some are found in private businesses, such as factories, stores, and similar places.

✔ **What kind of work would you do?**
Your work activities would depend upon your specific job. For example, you might:

- set procedures, prepare work schedules, and assign duties for jailers.
- direct and coordinate daily activities of a police force.
- direct and coordinate activities of a fire department.
- hire, assign, and supervise store detectives.
- investigate and arrest persons suspected of the illegal sale or use of drugs.

- patrol an assigned area in a vehicle or on foot and issue tickets, investigate disturbances, render first aid, and arrest suspects.
- patrol an assigned area to observe hunting and fishing activities and warn or arrest persons violating fish and game laws.

✔ **What skills and abilities do you need for this kind of work?**
To do this kind of work, you must be able to:

- work with laws and regulations, sometimes written in legal language.
- use practical thinking to conduct or supervise investigations.
- supervise other workers.
- plan the work of a department or activity.
- deal with various kinds of people.

- work under pressure or in the face of danger.
- patrol an assigned area to observe hunting and fishing activities and warn or arrest persons violating fish and game laws.
- keep physically fit.
- use guns, fire-fighting equipment, and other safety devices.

✔ **How do you know if you would like or could learn to do this kind of work?**
The following questions may give you clues about yourself as you consider this group of jobs.

- Have you had courses in government, civics, or criminology? Did you find these subjects interesting?
- Have you been a member of a volunteer fire department or emergency rescue squad? Were you given training for this work?
- Have you watched detective television shows? Do you read detective stories? Do you try to solve mysteries?

- Have you been an officer of a school safety patrol? Do you like being responsible for the work of others?
- Have you used a gun for hunting or in target practice? Are you a good shot?
- Have you spoken at a civic or community organization? Do you like work that requires frequent public speaking?
- Have you been a military officer?

✔ How can you prepare for and enter this kind of work?

Occupations in this group usually require education and/or training extending from one to over ten years, depending upon the specific kind of work. Local civil service regulations usually control the selection of police officers. People who want to do this kind of work must meet certain requirements. They must be U. S. citizens and be within certain height and weight ranges. In addition, they may be required to take written, oral, and physical examinations. The physical examinations often include tests of physical strength and the ability to move quickly and easily. To work in these jobs, persons should have the physical condition to use firearms or work on dangerous missions. Personal investigations are made of all applicants.

Most police departments prefer to hire people who have a high school education or its equal. However, some departments hire people if they have worked in related activities, such as guarding or volunteer police work.

Jobs with federal law enforcement agencies usually require a college degree. For example, to be hired as customs enforcement officer, a degree or three years of related work experience is required. FBI Special Agents are required to have a degree in law or accounting. Accounting degrees should be coupled with at least one year of related work experience.

Most management or supervisory jobs in this group are filled from within the ranks. Promotions are usually based on written examinations and job performance and are usually subject to civil service laws.

✔ What else should you consider about these jobs?

Most workers in these jobs are on call any time their services are needed. They may work overtime during emergencies. Many of these jobs expose workers to great physical danger.

If you think you would like to do this kind of work, look at the job titles listed below.

GOE: 04.01.01 Managing Safety & Law Enforcement

DEPUTY, COURT (gov. ser.) • D.O.T. #377.137-018 • OES #61005 • Supervises and coordinates activities of court peace officers engaged in providing security and maintaining order within individual courtrooms and throughout court house: Tours and inspects duty stations of BAILIFF (gov. ser.) to ensure compliance with regulation job duties and correct appearance. Patrols courthouse to quell disturbances and to keep order. Trains newly appointed officers in performance of job duties. Communicates with COURT CLERKS (gov. ser.) to identify day's court calendar. Prepares and schedules work assignments of court officers, and issues daily duty assignments. Prepares jury's meal vouchers for court official assigned to escort jurors to restaurant. Secures lodging facilities and transportation for jurors deliberating lengthy trials. Prepares and submits activity and time reports to SHERIFF, DEPUTY, CHIEF (gov. ser.). May witness name selection list of prospective jurors to insure impartiality. May perform duties of

BAILIFF (gov. ser.). • **GED:** R3, M2, L3 • **SVP:** 1-2 yrs • **Academic:** Ed=H, Eng=G • **Work Field:** 293, 295 • **MPSMS:** 951 • **Aptitudes:** G3, V3, N4, S4, P4, Q4, K3, F4, M4, E5, C5 • **Temperaments:** D, P, V • **Stress:** E • **Physical:** V=L, H=N, L=L, W • **Work Env:** I • **Salary:** 4 • **Outlook:** 3

HARBOR MASTER (gov. ser.) • D.O.T. #375.167-026 • OES #19005 • PORT WARDEN. Directs and coordinates activities of harbor police force to insure enforcement of laws, regulations, and policies governing navigable waters and property under jurisdiction of municipality or port district: Confers with officials, such as port authorities, Coast Guard officers, and members of city council to establish policies, define responsibilities, and determine operating requirements. Issues general instructions and outline of departmental policies regarding water-traffic control, public safety, theft prevention, and apprehension of law violators to subordinate officers and confers with them to determine operating procedures. Authorizes or approves departmental expenditures, personnel actions, and department's participation or assistance in activities not regularly assigned. Prepares periodic activity reports and annual budget. May evaluate work performance of captain and crew of

---

ship. May direct rescue operations from patrol launch after major disaster, such as ship collision or downed aircraft. • **GED:** R5, M3, L4 • **SVP:** 4-10 yrs • **Academic:** Ed=H, Eng=G • **Work Field:** 295 • **MPSMS:** 854, 951 • **Aptitudes:** G2, V2, N3, S4, P4, Q4, K4, F4, M4, E5, C5 • **Temperaments:** D, J, M, P, V • **Stress:** E • **Physical:** V=N, H=L, L=S • **Work Env:** I • **Salary:** 5 • **Outlook:** 2

GOE: 04.01.02 Investigating, Enforcement

CUSTOMS PATROL OFFICER (gov. ser.) • D.O.T. #168.167-010 • OES #63011 • Conducts surveillance, inspection and patrol by foot, vehicle, boat or aircraft at as signed points of entry into the United States to prohibit smuggled merchandise and contraband, and to detect violations of Customs and related laws: Inspects vessels, aircraft, and vehicles at docking, landing, crossing, and entry points. Establishes working rapport with local residents, law enforcement agencies, and businesses. Observes activity and regularity of vessels, planes, cargo, and storage arrangements in assigned area. Gathers and evaluates information from informers and other sources. Locates and apprehends customs violators. Assists in developing and testing new enforcement techniques and equipment. Develops intelligence information and forwards data for use by U.S. Customs Service. Testifies in courts of law against customs violators. • **GED:** R5, M3, L4 • **SVP:** 4-10 yrs • **Academic:** Ed=A, Eng=G • **Work Field:** 271 • **MPSMS:** 953 • **Aptitudes:** G3, V3, N3, S3, P3, Q3, K3, F4, M3, E3, C4 • **Temperaments:** J, M, P, S, V • **Stress:** E, S • **Physical:** V=L, H=L, L=L, W, C, S, H • **Work Env:** B, R • **Salary:** 4 • **Outlook:** 1

FIRE WARDEN (forestry) • D.O.T. #452.167-010 • OES #63005 • Administers fire prevention programs and enforces governmental fire regulations throughout assigned forest and logging areas: Inspects logging areas and forest tracts for fire hazards, such as accumulated wastes, hazardous storage or mishandling of fuels and solvents, defective engine exhaust systems, and unshielded electrical equipment. Examines and inventories water supplies and firefighting equipment, such as axes, firehoses, pumps, buckets, and chemical fire extinguishers to determine condition, amount, adequacy, and placement of materials with respect to governmental regulations and company rules. Prepares reports of conditions observed, issues directives and instructions for correcting violations, and reinspects areas to verify compliance. Directs maintenance and repair of firefighting tools and equipment and requisitions new equipment and materials to replace expended, lost, and broken items or add to inventory as required. Restricts public access and recreational use of forest lands during critical fire season. Gives directions to crew section on fireline during forest fire. May direct FIRE RANGERS (forestry). • **GED:** R5, M3, L3 • **SVP:** 2-4 yrs • **Academic:** Ed=A, Eng=G • **Work Field:** 293 • **MPSMS:** 313 • **Aptitudes:** G2, V2, N3, S4, P4, Q4, K4, F4, M4, E4, C4 • **Temperaments:** D, M, P, V • **Stress:** E • **Physical:** V=L, H=L, L=L, W, C, S, H • **Work Env:** O, H, N, R • **Salary:** 4 • **Outlook:** 3

FISH AND GAME WARDEN (gov. ser.) • D.O.T. #379.167-010 • OES #63041 • CONSERVATION OFFICER; GAME AND FISH PROTECTOR; GAME WARDEN; GUARD, RANGE. Patrols assigned area to prevent game law violations, investigate reports of damage to crops and property by wildlife, and compile biological data: Travels through area by car, boat, airplane, horse, and on foot to observe persons engaged in taking fish and game, to ensure method and equipment used are lawful, and to apprehend violators. Investigates reports of fish and game law violations and issues warnings or citations. Serves warrants, makes arrests, and prepares and presents evidence in court actions. Seizes equipment used in fish and game law violations and arranges for disposition of fish and game illegally taken or possessed. Collects and reports information on condition of fish and wildlife in their habitat, availability of game food and cover, and suspected pollution of waterways. Investigates hunting accidents and files reports of findings. Addresses schools and civic groups to disseminate information and promote public relations. May enlist aid of sporting groups in such programs as lake and stream rehabilitation, and game habitat improvement. May assist in promoting hunter safety

training by arranging for materials and instructors. May be designated according to specialty as FISH PROTECTOR (gov. ser.); GAME PROTECTOR (gov. ser.); or according to assigned patrol, as FISH-AND-GAME WARDEN, MARINE PATROL (gov. ser.). • **GED:** R4, M3, L4 • **SVP:** 1-2 yrs • **Academic:** Ed=H, Eng=G • **Work Field:** 293 • **MPSMS:** 959 • **Aptitudes:** G2, V2, N3, S4, P4, Q4, K4, F4, M4, E4, C4 • **Temperaments:** J, M, P, S • **Stress:** E, S • **Physical:** V=G, H=L, L=M, W, S, H • **Work Env:** O, R • **Salary:** 4 • **Outlook:** 2

INVESTIGATOR (light, heat, & power) • D.O.T. #376.367-022 • OES #63035 • Investigates persons suspected of securing services through fraud or error: Makes personal calls on individuals in question and tactfully attempts to secure evidence or personal admission that individual being investigated owes for previous service, or obtains pertinent data to show that suspicion was unwarranted. • **GED:** R3, M2, L3 • **SVP:** 1-2 yrs • **Academic:** Ed=N, Eng=G • **Work Field:** 271 • **MPSMS:** 969 • **Aptitudes:** G3, V3, N4, S4, P4, Q4, K4, F4, M4, E5, C5 • **Temperaments:** J, P • **Stress:** E • **Physical:** V=G, H=L, L=S, W • **Work Env:** I • **Salary:** 4 • **Outlook:** 3

POLICE OFFICER 1 (gov. ser.) • D.O.T. #375.263-014 • OES #63014 • PATROL OFFICER; TRAFFIC OFFICER. Patrols assigned beat on foot, using motorcycle or patrol car, or on horseback to control traffic, prevent crime or disturbance of peace, and arrest violators: Familiarizes self with beat and with persons living in area. Notes suspicious persons and establishments and reports to superior officer. Reports hazards. Disperses unruly crowds at public gatherings. Renders first aid at accidents and investigates causes and results of accident. Directs and reroutes traffic around fire or other disruption. Inspects public establishments requiring licenses to insure compliance with rules and regulations. Warns or arrests persons violating animal ordinances. Issues tickets to traffic violators. Registers at police call boxes at specified interval or time. Writes and files daily activity report with superior officer. May drive patrol wagon or police ambulance. May notify public works department of location of abandoned vehicles to tow away. May accompany parking meter personnel to protect money collected. May be designated according to assigned duty as AIRPORT SAFETY AND SECURITY OFFICER (gov. ser.); DANCE-HALL INSPECTOR (gov. ser.); TRAFFIC POLICE OFFICER (gov. ser.); or according to equipment used as AMBULANCE DRIVER (gov. ser.); MOTORCYCLE POLICE OFFICER (gov. ser.); MOUNTED POLICE OFFICER (gov. ser.). Additional titles: EMERGENCY-DETAIL DRIVER (gov. ser.); PATROL DRIVER (gov. ser.); POOL-HALL INSPECTOR (gov. ser.); RADIO POLICE OFFICER (gov. ser.); SHOW INSPECTOR (gov. ser.). • **GED:** R4, M2, L3 • **SVP:** 1-2 yrs • **Academic:** Ed=H, Eng=G • **Work Field:** 271, 293 • **MPSMS:** 951 • **Aptitudes:** G3, V3, N4, S3, P3, Q3, K3, F4, M3, E3, C4 • **Temperaments:** J, P, S, V • **Stress:** E, S • **Physical:** V=C, H=L, L=M, W, H • **Work Env:** B, R • **Salary:** 4 • **Outlook:** 2

POLICE OFFICER III (gov. ser.) • D.O.T. #375.267-038 • OES #63014 • Conducts investigations to locate, arrest, and return fugitives, persons wanted for non-payment of support payments and unemployment insurance compensation fraud, and to locate missing persons: Reviews files and criminal records to develop possible leads, such as previous addresses and aliases. Contacts employers, neighbors, relatives, law enforcement agencies, and other persons to locate person sought. Obtains necessary legal documents, such as warrants or extradition papers, to bring about return of fugitive. Serves warrants and makes arrests to return persons sought. Examines medical and dental X-rays, fingerprints, and other information to identify bodies held in morgue. Completes reports to document information acquired and actions taken. Testifies in court to present evidence regarding cases. • **GED:** R4, M2, L3 • **SVP:** 2-4 yrs • **Academic:** Ed=H, Eng=G • **Work Field:** 271, 293 • **MPSMS:** 951 • **Aptitudes:** G3, V3, N4, S4, P4, Q3, K3, F3, M3, E5, C5 • **Temperaments:** J, P, S • **Stress:** E, S • **Physical:** V=G, H=L, L=M, W • **Work Env:** I, R • **Salary:** 5 • **Outlook:** 3

SHERIFF, DEPUTY (gov. ser.) • D.O.T. #377.263-010 • OES #63032 • Maintains law and order and serves legal processes of courts: Patrols assigned area to enforce laws, investigate crimes, and arrest violators. Drives vehicle through assigned area, observing traffic violations and issuing citations. Assumes control at traffic accidents to maintain traffic flow, assist accident victims, and investigate causes of accidents. Investigates illegal or suspicious activities of persons, quells disturbances, and arrests law violators. Locates and takes persons into custody on arrest warrants. Transports or escorts prisoners between courtrooms, prison, and medical facilities. Serves subpoenas and summonses [PROCESS SERVER (bus. ser.)] and keeps record of dispositions. Keeps order in courtroom [BAILIFF (gov. ser.)]. May operate radio to deliver instructions to patrol units. May assist in dragging river to locate bodies. • **GED:** R3, M2, L3 • **SVP:** 6 mos-1 yr • **Academic:** Ed=H, Eng=G • **Work Field:** 271, 293 • **MPSMS:** 951 • **Aptitudes:** G3, V3, N4, S4, P3, Q3, K3, F4, M3, E3, C5 • **Temperaments:** J, P, S • **Stress:** E, S • **Physical:** V=L, H=L, L=M, W, H • **Work Env:** B, R • **Salary:** 4 • **Outlook:** 3

SPECIAL AGENT (gov. ser.) • D.O.T. #375.167-042 • OES #63028 • CRIMINAL INVESTIGATOR. Investigates alleged or suspected criminal violations of Federal, or State, or local laws to determine if evidence is sufficient to recommend prosecution: Analyzes charge, complaint or allegation of law violation to identify issues involved and types of evidence needed. Assists in determining scope, timing, and direction of investigation. Develops and uses informants to get leads to information. Obtains evidence or establishes facts by interviewing, observing, and interrogating suspects and witnesses and analyzing records. Examines records to detect links in a chain of evidence or information. Uses cameras and photostatic machines to record evidence and documents. Verifies information obtained to establish accuracy and authenticity of facts and evidence. Maintains surveillances and performs undercover assignments. Presents findings in clear, logical, impartial, and properly documented reports. Reports critical information to and coordinates activities with other offices or agencies when applicable. Testifies before grand juries. Serves subpoenas or other official papers. May lead or coordinate work of other SPECIAL AGENTS. May obtain and use search and arrest warrants. May serve on full-time, detail, or rotational protection assignments. May carry firearms and make arrests. May be designated according to agency worked for, as SPECIAL AGENT, FBI (gov. ser.), SPECIAL AGENT, IRS (gov. ser.), SPECIAL AGENT, SECRET SERVICE (gov. ser.). • **GED:** R5, M5, L5 • **SVP:** 2-4 yrs • **Academic:** Ed=A, Eng=G • **Work Field:** 271, 293 • **MPSMS:** 951, 959 • **Aptitudes:** G2, V2, N2, S2, P3, Q3, K3, F4, M4, E3, C4 • **Temperaments:** J, M, P, S, V • **Stress:** E, S • **Physical:** V=L, H=L, L=M, W, C, S, H • **Work Env:** B, R • **Salary:** 4 • **Outlook:** 2

04.02 Security Services

Workers in this group protect people and animals from injury or danger. They enforce laws, investigate suspicious persons or acts, prevent crime, and fight fires. Some of the jobs are found in Federal, State, or local governments. Some workers are hired by railroads, hotels, lumber yards, industrial plants, and amusement establishments. Some work on their own, acting as bodyguards, or private detectives.

✔ **What kind of work would you do?**
Your work activities would depend upon your specific job. For example, you might:

• guard money and valuables being transported by an armored car.
• patrol a section of an international border to detect persons attempting to enter the country illegally.
• move among customers in a place of entertainment to preserve order and protect property.
• guard inmates and direct their activities in a penal institution.
• respond to alarms to fight fires, render first aid, and protect property.

✔ **What skills and abilities do you need for this kind of work?**
To do this kind of work, you must be able to:

• learn and apply rules and procedures which are sometimes hard to understand.
• use reason and judgment in dealing with all kinds of people in different ways.
• think clearly and react quickly in emergencies.
• keep physically fit.
• use guns and safety equipment skillfully.
• make conclusions based on facts and also on your personal judgment.

✔ **How do you know if you would like or could learn to do this kind of work?**
The following questions may give you clues about yourself as you consider this group of jobs.

• Have you been a member of a school safety patrol? Did you like enforcing safety rules?
• Have you used a gun for hunting or target practice? Are you a good shot?
• Have you worked as a camp counselor or other group leader? Do you like helping people?

- Have you been a member of a volunteer fire or rescue squad? Can you stay calm in emergencies?
- Have you taken a first aid course? Can you treat injuries quickly and skillfully?
- Have you been a member of a military police force or rescue team?

✔ **How can you prepare for and enter this kind of work?**

Occupations in this group usually require education and/or training extending from thirty days to over two years, depending upon the specific kind of work. People with experience in the military, local, or state police are often preferred. Some employers want people with a high school education or its equal.

People interested in these jobs must have character references and no police record. Some employers require a demonstration of skill in using firearms. Written and physical tests also may be required.

✔ **What else should you consider about these jobs?**

Some of these jobs involve night work. People often work alone, with no help nearby in case of accident or injury. In some jobs, they take turns working daytime, weekend, and holiday hours. There is always a danger of bodily injury by lawbreakers.

Workers are often required to have special insurance to protect the employer against dishonesty. They may also be fingerprinted.

If you think you would like to do this kind of work, look at the job titles listed below.

GOE: 04.02.01 Detention Services

CORRECTION OFFICER (gov. ser.) • D.O.T. #372.667-018 • OES #63017 • GUARD. Guards inmates in penal institution in accordance with established policies, regulations, and procedures: Observes conduct and behavior of inmates to prevent disturbances and escapes. Inspects locks, window bars, grills, doors, and gates for tampering. Searches inmates and cells for contraband articles. Guards and directs inmates during work assignments. Patrols assigned areas for evidence of forbidden activities, infraction of rules, and unsatisfactory attitude or adjustment of prisoners. Reports observations to superior. Employs weapons or force to maintain discipline and order among prisoners, if necessary. May escort inmates to and from visiting room, medical office, and religious services. May guard entrance of jail to screen visitors. May prepare written report concerning incidences of inmate disturbances or injuries. May be designated according to institution as CORRECTION OFFICER, CITY OR COUNTY JAIL (gov. ser.); CORRECTION OFFICER, PENITENTIARY (gov. ser.); CORRECTION OFFICER, REFORMATORY (gov. ser.). May guard prisoners in transit between jail, courtroom, prison, or other point, traveling by automobile or public transportation and be designated GUARD, DEPUTY (gov. ser.). • **GED:** R3, M2, L2 • **SVP:** 3-6 mos • **Academic:** Ed=H, Eng=G • **Work Field:** 293 • **MPSMS:** 951 • **Aptitudes:** G3, V3, N4, S4, P3, Q4, K3, F4, M3, E5, C5 • **Temperaments:** J, P, S • **Stress:** E, S • **Physical:** V=G, H=G, L=M, W, H • **Work Env:** I, R • **Salary:** 4 • **Outlook:** 3

GUARD, IMMIGRATION (gov. ser.) • D.O.T. #372.567-014 • OES #63017 • Guards aliens held by immigration service pending further investigation before being released or deported: Takes into custody and delivers aliens to designated jail, juvenile detention facility, hospital, court, claim's office, immigration facility, or other areas to transact business. Escorts aliens departing or arriving by airplane, train, car, ship, or bus. Prepares and maintains records relating to detention, release, transportation of alien, and completes application for travel documents. May prepare related correspond ence. May be required to travel throughout nation and foreign countries. • **GED:** R3, M2, L3 • **SVP:** 3-6 mos • **Academic:** Ed=N, Eng=G • **Work Field:** 231, 293 • **MPSMS:** 959 • **Aptitudes:** G3, V3, N4, S4, P4, Q4, K3, F4, M3, E4, C5 • **Temperaments:** P, S • **Stress:** E, S • **Physical:** V=N, H=L, L=M, W, H • **Work Env:** B, R • **Salary:** 3 • **Outlook:** 3

JAILER (gov. ser.) • D.O.T. #372.367-014 • OES #63017 • JAIL KEEPER; TURNKEY. Guards prisoners in precinct station house or municipal jail, assuming responsibility for all needs of prisoner during detention: Locks prisoner in cell after searching for weapons, valuables, or drugs. Serves meals to prisoner and provides or obtains medical aid if needed. May prepare arrest records identifying prisoner and charge as signed. May question prisoner to elicit information helpful in solving crime. May prepare meals for self and prisoner. May distribute commissary items purchased by inmates, such as candy, snacks, cigarettes, and toilet articles, and record payment on voucher. In small communities, may perform duties of SHERIFF, DEPUTY (gov. ser.) or POLICE OFFICER (gov. ser.) I when not engaged in guard duties. • **GED:** R3, M2, L2 • **SVP:** 3-6 mos • **Academic:** Ed=N, Eng=G • **Work Field:** 293 • **MPSMS:** 951, 959 • **Aptitudes:** G3, V3, N4, S4, P3, Q4, K3, F4, M3, E5, C5 • **Temperaments:** J, M, P, S • **Stress:** E, S • **Physical:** V=L, H=L, L=L, W, H • **Work Env:** I, R • **Salary:** 3 • **Outlook:** 2

GOE: 04.02.02 Property & People

AIRLINE SECURITY REPRESENTATIVE (air trans.) • D.O.T. #372.667-010 • OES #63047 • CUSTOMER SECURITY CLERK; FLIGHT SECURITY SPECIALIST; SCREENING REPRESENTATIVE. Screens passengers and visitors for weapons, explosives, or other forbidden articles to prevent articles from being carried into restricted area of air terminal, performing any combination of the following tasks: Greets individuals desiring to enter re stricted area and informs them that they must be screened prior to entry. Asks individual to empty contents of pockets into tray. Examines contents of tray for forbidden articles and directs individual to pass through metal-detecting device. Asks individual to remove metal articles from person if metal detector signals presence of metal, or uses handheld metal detector to locate metal item on person. Places carry-on baggage or other containers onto X-ray device, actuates device controls, and monitors screen to detect forbidden articles. Requests owner to open baggage or containers when X-ray shows questionable contents. Returns baggage and tray contents to individual if no forbidden articles are detected. Notifies GUARD, SECURITY (any ind.) if forbidden articles are discovered or detector equipment indicates further search is needed. May turn on power and make adjustments to equipment. May perform duties of GUARD, SECURITY (any ind.). May screen boarding passengers against Federal Aviation Administration approved profile of aircraft hijackers. May make reports. • **GED:** R2, M1, L2 • **SVP:** 2-30 days • **Academic:** Ed=N, Eng=G • **Work Field:** 293 • **MPSMS:** 855 • **Aptitudes:** G4, V4, N4, S3, P3, Q4, K4, F4, M4, E5, C5 • **Temperaments:** P, R • **Stress:** E • **Physical:** V=L, H=L, L=L, W, H • **Work Env:** I, R • **Salary:** 2 • **Outlook:** 3

ARMORED-CAR GUARD (bus. ser.) • D.O.T. #372.567-010 • OES #63047 • ARMORED-CAR MESSENGER. Guards armored car enroute to business establishments to pick up or deliver money and valuables: Collects moneybags, receipts, daily guide sheet, and schedule from VAULT WORKER (bus. ser.). Guards money and valuables in transit to prevent theft. Records information, such as number of items received, destination, contents of packages, and delivery time at scheduled stops, on daily guide sheet. Deposits moneybags, receipts, daily guide sheet, change box, and money with cashiering department. • **GED:** R3, M2, L2 • **SVP:** 30 days-3 mos • **Academic:** Ed=N, Eng=S • **Work Field:** 293 • **MPSMS:** 951 • **Aptitudes:** G3, V3, N3, S4, P3, Q3, K3, F4, M4, E5, C5 • **Temperaments:** P, R, S • **Stress:** E, S • **Physical:** V=L, H=N, L=M, W, H • **Work Env:** I, H, R • **Salary:** 2 • **Outlook:** 3

ARMORED-CAR GUARD AND DRIVER (bus. ser.) • D.O.T. #372.563-010 • OES #63047 • ARMORED-CAR MESSENGER. Drives armored van to transport money and valuables, and guards money and valuables during transit: Loads and carries bags of cash, coin, and other valuables into and from armored van at protective service building, bank, or customer establishment. Drives armored van along established routes to transport valuables to destination. Guards bags of money and valuables during receipt and transfer to ensure safe delivery. Issues and receives receipts from customers to verify transfer of valuables. May drive truck along established route and collect coins from parking meters. • **GED:** R3, M2, L2 • **SVP:** 30 days-3 mos • **Academic:** Ed=N, Eng=S • **Work Field:** 011, 013, 293 • **MPSMS:** 899 • **Aptitudes:** G3, V4, N3, S3, P4, Q3, K3, F4, M3, E3, C5 • **Temperaments:** P, R, S • **Stress:** S • **Physical:** V=G, H=N, L=M, W, H • **Work Env:** I, R • **Salary:** 2 • **Outlook:** 3

BODYGUARD (per. ser.) • D.O.T. #372.667-014 • OES #63047 • Escorts individuals to protect them from bodily injury, kidnapping, or invasion of privacy. May perform other duties, such as receiving and transcribing dictation or driving motor vehicle to transport individuals to disguise purpose of employment. • **GED:** R2, M1, L2 • **SVP:** 30 days-3 mos • **Academic:** Ed=N, Eng=S • **Work Field:** 293 • **MPSMS:** 909 • **Aptitudes:** G3, V3, N4, S4, P4, Q4, K3, F4, M3, E4, C5 • **Temperaments:** J, P, S • **Stress:** E, S • **Physical:** V=L, H=L, L=L, W, H • **Work Env:** B • **Salary:** 2 • **Outlook:** 2

DETECTIVE 1 (any ind.) • D.O.T. #376.367-014 • OES #63035 • INVESTIGATOR. Protects property of business establishment by detecting vandalism, thievery, shoplifting, or dishonesty among employees or patrons, performing any combination of following duties: Conducts investigations on own initiative or on request of management. Stakes out company grounds to apprehend suspects in illegal acts. Questions suspects and apprehends culprits. Files complaints against suspects and testifies in court as witness. Writes case reports. Alerts other retail establishments when person of known criminal character is observed in store. May be designated according to type of establishment as STORE DETECTIVE (ret. tr.). • **GED:** R3, M2, L3 • **SVP:** 3-6 mos • **Academic:** Ed=N, Eng=G • **Work Field:** 271, 293 • **MPSMS:** 969 • **Aptitudes:** G3, V3, N4, S4, P4, Q4, K3, F4, M4, E5, C5 • **Temperaments:** J, P, S • **Stress:** E, S • **Physical:** V=G, H=L, L=S, W • **Work Env:** I • **Salary:** 4 • **Outlook:** 2

FIRE RANGER (forestry) • D.O.T. #452.367-014 • OES #63005 • Patrols assigned area of forest to locate and report fires and hazardous conditions and to insure compliance with fire regulations by travelers and campers: Hikes or drives to vista points to scan for fires and unusual or dangerous conditions. Reports findings and receives and relays emergency calls, using telephone or two-way radio. Visits camping sites to inspect activities of campers and ensure compliance with forest use and fire regulations. Gives instructions regarding sanitation, fire, and related forest regulations. Extinguishes smaller fires with portable extinguisher, shovel, and ax. Serves as crew leader for larger fires. Renders assistance or first aid to lost or injured persons. Participates in search for lost travelers or campers. • **GED:** R3, M2, L3 • **SVP:**

3-6 mos • **Academic:** Ed=N, Eng=G • **Work Field:** 293 • **MPSMS:** 313 • **Aptitudes:** G3, V3, N4, S3, P4, Q4, K4, F4, M4, E3, C4 • **Temperaments:** J, P, S, V • **Stress:** S • **Physical:** V=L, H=L, L=M, W, C, S, H • **Work Env:** O • **Salary:** 3 • **Outlook:** 3

GATE TENDER (any ind.) • D.O.T. #372.667-030 • OES #63047 • GATEKEEPER; GUARD; WATCH GUARD, GATE. Guards entrance gate of industrial plant and grounds, warehouse, or other property to control traffic to and from buildings and grounds: Opens gate to allow entrance or exit of employees, truckers, and authorized visitors. Checks credentials or approved roster before admitting anyone. Issues passes at own discretion or on instructions from superiors. Directs visitors and truckers to various parts of grounds or buildings. Inspects outgoing traffic to prevent unauthorized removal of company property or products. May record number of trucks or other carriers entering and leaving. May perform maintenance duties, such as mowing lawns and sweeping gate areas. May require permits from employees for tools or materials taken from premises. May supervise use of time clocks for recording arrival and departure of employees [TIME KEEPER (clerical)]. May answer telephone and transfer calls when switchboard is closed. When stationed at entrance to restricted area, such as explosives shed or research laboratory, may be designated CONTROLLED-AREA CHECKER (any ind.). • **GED:** R3, M2, L2 • **SVP:** 30 days-3 mos • **Academic:** Ed=N, Eng=S • **Work Field:** 293 • **MPSMS:** 951 • **Aptitudes:** G3, V3, N4, S4, P4, Q4, K4, F4, M4, E5, C4 • **Temperaments:** P, R • **Stress:** E • **Physical:** V=L, H=L, L=L, W • **Work Env:** B • **Salary:** 2 • **Outlook:** 2

GUARD, SECURITY (any ind.) • D.O.T. #372.667-034 • OES #63047 • PATROL GUARD; SPECIAL POLICE OFFICER; WATCHGUARD. Guards industrial or commercial property against fire, theft, vandalism, and illegal entry, performing any combination of the following duties: Patrols, periodically, buildings and grounds of industrial plant or commercial establishment, docks, logging camp area, or worksite. Examines doors, windows, and gates to determine that they are secure. Warns violators of rule infractions, such as loitering, smoking, or carrying forbidden articles, and apprehends or expels miscreants. Inspects equipment and machinery to ascertain if tampering has occurred. Watches for and reports irregularities, such as fire hazards, leaking water pipes, and security doors left unlocked. Observes departing personnel to guard against theft of company property. Sounds alarm or calls police or fire department by telephone in case of fire or presence of unauthorized persons. Permits authorized persons to enter property. May register at watch stations to record time of inspection trips. May record data, such as property damage, unusual occurrences, and malfunctioning of machinery or equipment, for use of supervisory staff. May perform janitorial duties and set thermostatic controls to maintain specified temperature in buildings or cold storage rooms. May tend furnace or boiler. May be deputized to arrest trespassers. May regulate vehicle and pedestrian traffic at plant entrance to maintain orderly flow. May patrol site with guard dog on leash. May watch for fires and be designated as FIRE PATROLLER (logging). May be designated according to shift worked as DAY GUARD (any ind.); area guarded as DOCK GUARD (any ind.); WAREHOUSE GUARD (any ind.); or property guarded as POWDER GUARD (const.). May be designated according to establishment guarded as GROUNDS GUARD, ARBORETUM (any ind.); GUARD, MUSEUM (museum); WATCHGUARD, RACE TRACK (amuse. & rec.); or duty station as COIN-VAULT GUARD (any ind.). May be designated as GUARD, CONVOY (any ind.) when accompanying or leading truck convoy carrying valuable shipments. Additional titles: ARMED GUARD (r.r. trans.); CAMP GUARD (any ind.); DECK GUARD (fish.; water trans.); NIGHT GUARD (any ind.); PARK GUARD (amuse. & rec.). • **GED:** R3, M1, L2 • **SVP:** 30 days-3 mos • **Academic:** Ed=N, Eng=S • **Work Field:** 293 • **MPSMS:** 969 • **Aptitudes:** G3, V4, N3, S4, P4, Q4, K4, F4, M4, E5, C5 • **Temperaments:** P, R, S • **Stress:** E, T, S • **Physical:** V=G, H=G, L=S, W • **Work Env:** B, R • **Salary:** 2 • **Outlook:** 2

PARKING ENFORCEMENT OFFICER (gov. ser.) • D.O.T. #375.587-010 • OES #63021 • PARKING ENFORCEMENT AGENT. Patrols assigned area, such as public parking lot or section of city, to issue tickets to overtime parking violators. Winds parking meter clocks. Surrenders ticket book at end of shift to supervisor to facilitate preparation of violation records. May report missing traffic signals or signs to superior at end of shift. May chalk tires of vehicles parked in unmetered spaces, record time, and return at specified intervals to ticket vehicles remaining in spaces illegally. May collect coins deposited in meters. When patrolling metered spaces, may be known as METER ATTENDANT (gov. ser.). • **GED:** R2, M1, L2 • **SVP:** 2-30 days • **Academic:** Ed=N, Eng=N • **Work Field:** 231, 293 • **MPSMS:** 959 • **Aptitudes:** G4, V4, N4, S4, P4, Q4, K4, F4, M4, E5, C4 • **Temperaments:** P, R • **Physical:** V=L, H=N, L=L, W, H • **Work Env:** O • **Salary:** 2 • **Outlook:** 3

SECURITY CONSULTANT (bus. ser.) • D.O.T. #189.167-054 • OES #63035 • Plans, directs, and oversees implementation of comprehensive security systems for protection of individuals and homes, and business, commercial, and industrial organizations, and investigates various crimes against client: Inspects premises to determine security needs. Studies physical conditions, observes activities, and confers with client's staff to obtain data regarding internal operations. Analyzes compiled data and plans and directs installation of electronic security systems, such as closed circuit surveillance, entry controls, burglar alarms, ultrasonic motion detectors, electric eyes, and outdoor perimeter and microwave alarms. Directs installation and checks operation of electronic security equipment. Plans and directs personal security and safety of individual, family, or group for contracted period. Provides bulletproof limousine and bodyguards to ensure client protection during trips and outings. Suggests wearing bulletproof vest when appropriate. Plans and reviews client travel itinerary, mode of transportation, and accommodations. Travels with client and directs security operations. Investigates crimes committed against client, such as fraud, robbery, arson, and patent infringement. Reviews personnel records of client staff and conducts background investigation of selected members to obtain personal histories, character refer ences, and financial status. Conducts or directs surveillance of suspects and premises to apprehend culprits. Notifies client of security weaknesses and implements procedures for handling, storing, safekeeping, and destroying classified materials. Reports criminal information to authorities and testifies in court. • **GED:** R5, M3, L5 • **SVP:** 2-4 yrs • **Academic:** Ed=A, Eng=G • **Work Field:** 271, 293 • **MPSMS:** 951 • **Aptitudes:** G2, V3, N3, S2, P4, Q3, K4, F4, M4, E5, C5 • **Temperaments:** D, I, P, S, V • **Stress:** E, A, S • **Physical:** V=L, H=L, L=L, W • **Work Env:** I • **Salary:** 4 • **Outlook:** 3

GOE: 04.02.03 Law & Order

BAILIFF (gov. ser.) • D.O.T. #377.667-010 • OES #63023 • COURT OFFICER. Maintains order in court room during trial and guards jury from outside contact: Checks courtroom for security and cleanliness. Assures availability of sundry supplies for use of JUDGE (gov. ser.). Enforces courtroom rules of behavior and warns persons not to smoke or disturb court procedure. Collects and retains unauthorized firearms from persons entering courtroom. Stops people from entering courtroom while JUDGE (gov. ser.) charges jury. Provides jury escort to restaurant and other areas outside of courtroom to prevent jury contact with public. Guards lodging of sequestered jury. Reports need for police or medical assistance to sheriff's office. May advise attorneys of dress required of witnesses. May announce entrance of JUDGE (gov. ser.). • **GED:** R2, M1, L2 • **SVP:** 30 days-3 mos • **Academic:** Ed=H, Eng=G • **Work Field:** 291, 293 • **MPSMS:** 951 • **Aptitudes:** G3, V3, N4, S4, P4, Q4, K4, F4, M4, E5, C5 • **Temperaments:** P, S, V • **Stress:** E, S • **Physical:** V=L, H=L, L=L, W • **Work Env:** I • **Salary:** 2 • **Outlook:** 2

BEACH LIFEGUARD (amuse. & rec.) • D.O.T. #379.364-014 • OES #63099 • Patrols public beach area to monitor activities of swimmers and prevent illegal conduct: Observes activities in assigned area on foot, in vehicle, or from tower or headquarters building with binoculars to detect hazard ous conditions, such as swimmers in distress, disturbances, or safety infractions. Cautions people against use of unsafe beach areas or illegal conduct, such as drinking or fighting, using megaphone. Rescues distressed persons from ocean or adjacent cliffs, using rescue techniques and equipment. Examines injured individuals, administers first aid, and monitors vital signs, utilizing training, antiseptics, bandages,

and instruments, such as stethoscope and sphygmomanometer. Administers artificial respiration, utilizing cardiopulmonary or mouth-to-mouth methods, or oxygen, to revive persons. Compiles emergency and medical treatment report forms and maintains daily information on weather and beach conditions. Occasionally operates switchboard or two-way radio system to maintain contact and coordinate activities between emergency rescue units. • **GED:** R3, M2, L2 • **SVP:** 3-6 mos • **Academic:** Ed=N, Eng=S • **Work Field:** 293 • **MPSMS:** 914 • **Aptitudes:** G3, V3, N4, S3, P4, Q4, K3, F3, M3, E3, C4 • **Temperaments:** J, P, S • **Stress:** E, S • **Physical:** V=G, H=L, L=V, W, C, H • **Work Env:** I, R • **Salary:** 3 • **Outlook:** 3

BORDER GUARD (gov. ser.) • D.O.T. #375.363-010 • OES #63014 • BORDER PATROL AGENT. Patrols on foot, by motor vehicle, power boat, or aircraft along border or seacoast of United States to detect persons attempting to enter country illegally. Apprehends and detains illegal entrants for subsequent action by immigration authorities. May question agricultural workers near border to identify and apprehend illegal aliens. May report evidence of smuggling observed on patrol to customs authorities. • **GED:** R3, M2, L3 • **SVP:** 6 mos-1 yr • **Academic:** Ed=N, Eng=G • **Work Field:** 293 • **MPSMS:** 959 • **Aptitudes:** G3, V3, N4, S4, P3, Q4, K3, F4, M4, E4, C5 • **Temperaments:** J, P, S • **Stress:** E, S • **Physical:** V=G, H=L, L=M, W • **Work Env:** B, R • **Salary:** 3 • **Outlook:** 3

BOUNCER (amuse. & rec.) • D.O.T. #376.667-010 • OES #63047 • HOUSE DETECTIVE. Patrols place of entertainment to preserve order among patrons and protect property: Circulates among patrons to prevent improper dancing, skating, or similar activities, and to detect persons annoying other patrons or damaging furnishings of establishment. Warns patrons guilty of infractions and evicts them tactfully from premises if they become unruly or ejects them by force if necessary. Calls police if unable to quell disturbance. May be designated according to type of establishment patrolled as FUN-HOUSE ATTENDANT (amuse. & rec.); GUARD, DANCE HALL (amuse. & rec.); ICE GUARD, SKATING RINK (amuse. & rec.). • **GED:** R2, M1, L2 • **SVP:** 30 days-3 mos • **Academic:** Ed=N, Eng=S • **Work Field:** 293 • **MPSMS:** 910 • **Aptitudes:** G3, V3, N4, S4, P4, Q5, K4, F4, M4, E4, C5 • **Temperaments:** J, P, S • **Stress:** E, S • **Physical:** V=L, H=N, L=L, W • **Work Env:** I • **Salary:** 2 • **Outlook:** 3

CHAPERON (per. ser.) • D.O.T. #359.667-010 • OES #69999 • Accompanies minors on trips to educational institutions, public functions, or recreational activities such as dances, concerts, or sports events, to provide adult supervision in absence of parents. Follows parents' instructions regarding minors' activities and imposes limitations and restrictions to ensure their safety, well-being, and conformance to specified behavior standards. May plan freetime activities. May arrange for transportation, tickets, and meals. • **GED:** R3, M2, L2 • **SVP:** 2-30 days • **Academic:** Ed=N, Eng=S • **Work Field:** 291 • **MPSMS:** 942 • **Aptitudes:** G3, V3, N4, S4, P4, Q4, K4, F4, M4, E5, C5 • **Temperaments:** P, V • **Stress:** E • **Physical:** V=L, H=L, L=L, W • **Work Env:** I • **Salary:** 2 • **Outlook:** 2

PARK RANGER (gov. ser.) • D.O.T. #169.167-042 • OES #21911 • RANGER. Enforces laws, regulations, and policies in State or national park: Registers vehicles and visitors, collects fees, and issues parking and use permits. Provides information pertaining to park use, safety requirements, and points of interest. Directs traffic, investigates accidents, and patrols area to prevent fires, vandalism, and theft. Cautions, evicts, or apprehends violators of laws and regulations. Directs or participates in first aid and rescue activities. May supervise workers engaged in construction and maintenance of park facilities and enforces standards of cleanliness and sanitation. May compile specified park-use statistics, keep records, and prepare reports of area activities. May train and supervise park workers and concession attendants. May specialize in snow safety and avalanche control and be designated SNOW RANGER (gov. ser.). • **GED:** R4, M3, L4 • **SVP:** 2-4 yrs • **Academic:** Ed=B, Eng=G • **Work Field:** 282, 293 • **MPSMS:** 959 • **Aptitudes:** G3, V3, N3, S3, P2, Q4, K3, F4, M3, E2, C4 • **Temperaments:** J, M, P, S, V • **Stress:** E, S • **Physical:** V=G, H=L, L=S, W, C, H • **Work Env:** O, R • **Salary:** 4 • **Outlook:** 1

REPOSSESSOR (clerical) • D.O.T. #241.367-022 • OES #53508

• Locates debtors and solicits payment for delinquent accounts and removes merchandise for nonpayment of account. May initiate repossession proceedings. May drive truck to return merchandise to creditor. May locate, enter, and start vehicle being repossessed, using special tools, if key cannot be obtained from debtor, and return vehicle to creditor. May be designated according to merchandise repossessed as AUTOMOBILE REPOSSESSOR (clerical). • **GED:** R3, M2, L2 • **SVP:** 30 days-3 mos • **Academic:** Ed=N, Eng=C • **Work Field:** 271 • **MPSMS:** 894 • **Aptitudes:** G3, V4, N4, S4, P3, Q4, K4, F4, M4, E3, C4 • **Temperaments:** P • **Physical:** V=L, H=N, L=M, W, H • **Work Env:** B • **Salary:** 3 • **Outlook:** 4

SURVEILLANCE-SYSTEM MONITOR (gov. ser.) • D.O.T. #379.367-010 • OES #63099 • Monitors premises of public transportation terminals to detect crimes or disturbances, using closed circuit television monitors, and notifies authorities by telephone of need for corrective action: Observes television screens that transmit in sequence views of transportation facility sites. Pushes hold button to maintain surveillance of location where incident is developing, and telephones police or other designated agency to notify authorities of location of disruptive activity. Adjusts monitor controls when required to improve reception, and notifies repair service of equipment malfunctions. • **GED:** R3, M1, L3 • **SVP:** 2-30 days • **Academic:** Ed=N, Eng=S • **Work Field:** 281, 293 • **MPSMS:** 951 • **Aptitudes:** G3, V3, N4, S4, P4, Q4, K4, F4, M4, E5, C5 • **Temperaments:** P, R • **Stress:** E, T • **Physical:** V=L, H=N, L=S • **Work Env:** I • **Salary:** 2 • **Outlook:** 3

GOE: 04.02.04 Emergency Responding

ALARM INVESTIGATOR (bus. ser.) • D.O.T. #376.367-010 • OES #63035 • ARMED GUARD; INVESTIGATOR OPERATOR; SECURITY AGENT. Investigates source of alarm and trouble signals on subscribers' premises, as recorded in central station of electrical protective signaling system: Drives radio-equipped car to subscriber's establishment, and locates source of alarm. Investigates disturbances, such as unlawful intrusion, fires, and property damage. Apprehends unauthorized persons found on property, using armed force if necessary, and releases them to custody of authorities. Contacts supervisor by radio or telephone to report irregularities and obtain further instructions. Adjusts and repairs subscriber's signaling equipment to restore service, using handtools. Coordinates activities with police and fire departments during alarms. Writes investigation and automobile usage reports. • **GED:** R3, M1, L3 • **SVP:** 30 days-3 mos • **Academic:** Ed=N, Eng=G • **Work Field:** 293 • **MPSMS:** 969 • **Aptitudes:** G3, V3, N4, S3, P3, Q4, K3, F4, M3, E4, C4 • **Temperaments:** P, S • **Stress:** E, S • **Physical:** V=L, H=L, L=L, W, H • **Work Env:** I, R

• **Salary:** 2 • **Outlook:** 3

FIRE FIGHTER (any ind.) • D.O.T. #373.364-010 • OES #63008 • Controls and extinguishes fires, protects life and property, and maintains equipment as volunteer or employee of city, township, or industrial plant: Responds to fire alarms and other emergency calls. Selects hose nozzle, depending on type of fire, and directs stream of water or chemicals onto fire. Positions and climbs ladders to gain access to upper levels of buildings or to assist individuals from burning structures. Creates openings in buildings for ventilation or entrance, using ax, chisel, crowbar, electric saw, core cutter, and other power equipment. Protects property from water and smoke by use of waterproof salvage covers, smoke ejectors, and deodorants. Administers first aid and artificial respiration to injured persons and those overcome by fire and smoke. Communicates with superior during fire, using portable two-way radio. Inspects buildings for fire hazards and compliance with fire prevention ordinances. Performs assigned duties in maintaining apparatus, quarters, buildings, equipment, grounds, and hydrants. Participates in drills, demonstrations, and courses in hydraulics, pump operation and maintenance, and firefighting techniques. May fill fire extinguishers in institutions or industrial plants. May issue forms to building owners listing fire regulation violations to be corrected. May drive and operate firefighting vehicles and equipment. May be assigned duty in marine division of fire department and be designated FIREFIGHTER, MARINE (any ind.). • **GED:** R4, M2, L3 • **SVP:** 1-2 yrs • **Academic:** Ed=H, Eng=G • **Work Field:** 293 • **MPSMS:** 951 • **Aptitudes:** G3, V3, N4, S2, P4, Q4, K3, F4, M2, E2, C3 • **Temperaments:** J, S, V • **Stress:** S • **Physical:** V=G, H=G, L=V, W, C, S, H • **Work Env:** B, H, W, N, R • **Salary:** 4 • **Outlook:** 2

SMOKE JUMPER (forestry) • D.O.T. #452.364-014 • OES #63008 • Parachutes from airplane into forest inaccessible by ground to suppress forest fires: Jumps from airplane near scene of fire, pulls rip cord when clear of plane, and pulls shroud lines to guide direction of fall toward clear landing area. Orients self in relation to fire, using compass and map, and collects supplies and equipment dropped by parachute. Ascertains best method for attacking fire and communicates plan to airplane or base camp with two-way radio. Fells trees, digs trenches, and extinguishes flames and embers to suppress fire, using ax, chainsaw, shovel, and hand or engine-driven water or chemical pumps. May pack parachutes [PARACHUTE RIGGER (air trans.)]. • **GED:** R3, M2, L2 • **SVP:** 1-2 yrs • **Academic:** Ed=N, Eng=N • **Work Field:** 293 • **MPSMS:** 313 • **Aptitudes:** G3, V3, N4, S2, P3, Q3, K2, F4, M2, E2, C3 • **Temperaments:** J, S, V • **Stress:** S • **Physical:** V=L, H=L, L=V, W, C, S, H • **Work Env:** B, H, W, N, R • **Salary:** 4 • **Outlook:** 4

Mechanical 05

An interest in applying mechanical principles to practical situations using machine, hand tools, or techniques. You can satisfy this interest in a variety of jobs ranging from routine to complex professional positions. You may enjoy working with ideas about things (objects). You could seek a job in engineering or in a related technical field. You may prefer to deal directly with things. You could find a job in the crafts or trades, building, making or repairing objects. You may like to drive or to operate vehicles and special equipment. You may prefer routine or physical work in setting other than factories. Perhaps work in mining or construction would appeal to you.

05.01 Engineering

Workers in this group plan, design, and direct the construction or development of buildings, bridges, roads, airports, dams, sewage systems, air-conditioning systems, mining machinery, and other structures and equipment. They also develop processes and/or techniques for generating and transmitting electrical power, manufacturing chemicals, extracting metals from ore, and controlling the quality of products being made. Workers specialize in one or more kinds of engineering, such as civil, electrical, mechanical, mining, and safety. Some are hired by industrial plants, petroleum and mining companies, research laboratories, and construction companies. Others find employment with Federal, State, and local governments. Some have their own engineering firms, and accept work from various individuals or companies.

✔ **What kind of work would you do?**
Your work activities would depend upon your specific job. For example, you might:

- establish computational methods and computer input data to analyze problems in aircraft design.
- apply knowledge of properties of various materials to the development of electronic and electrical circuits.
- design facilities and equipment for an electrical distribution system.
- use computers to conduct technical research to solve construction problems in designing airport structures.
- conduct research to develop new and improved chemical manufacturing processes.
- analyze technical and cost factors to plan methods to recover oil and gas.
- apply knowledge of the properties of metals to develop improved welding techniques, procedures, and equipment.
- analyze manpower and equipment usage to improve efficiency of industrial operations.

✔ **What skills and abilities do you need for this kind of work?**
To do this kind of work, you must be able to:

- use high level mathematics.
- understand principles of chemistry, geology, physics, and related sciences.
- solve problems, using facts and personal judgment.
- work on different projects and with changing situations.
- deal with various kinds of people.

©1991, JIST Works, Inc. • Indianapolis, IN

✔ **How do you know if you would like or could learn to do this kind of work?**

The following questions may give you clues about yourself as you consider this group of jobs.

- Have you read mechanical or automotive design magazines? Do you enjoy and understand the technical articles?
- Have you taken courses in algebra, geometry, and advanced math? Can you solve practical problems using math?
- Have you built a model airplane, automobile, or bridge? Can you look at a blueprint or drawing and visualize the final structure?

- Have you taken physics courses? Do you like to study energy and matter?
- Have you built or repaired a radio, television, or amplifier? Do you understand electrical or electronic terms and drawings?
- Have you served in an engineering section of the armed forces?

✔ **How can you prepare for and enter this kind of work?**

Occupations in this group usually require education and/or training extending from four years to over ten years, depending upon the specific kind of work. Engineers whose work affects life, health, or property, or who serve the public must be licensed. A degree from an accredited engineering school, four years of related experience, and the passing of a state examination are common requirements for a license.

A bachelor's degree in engineering is usually required for entering this type of work. College graduates trained in one of the natural sciences or mathematics may qualify for a few beginning jobs. Experienced technicians with some engineering education may be advanced to engineering jobs.

Most engineering schools require an average or above average high school record in mathematics, physics, chemistry, and English for admission. Other courses such as history and social studies are helpful in gaining an understanding of fields related to engineering.

A typical four-year curriculum includes two years of study in the basic sciences, such as mathematics, physics, chemistry, introductory engineering, social sciences, and English. The last two years are devoted to specialized engineering courses.

Several engineering schools have agreements with liberal arts colleges to allow students to spend three years in the college and two years in the engineering school. A bachelor's degree is then granted by each. Some engineering schools offer a five or six year cooperative work-study program in which the students alternate periods in school with employment in related jobs. This permits students to earn a part of their tuition costs and get on-the-job experience as they learn.

✔ **What else should you consider about these jobs?**

Many engineers work under quiet conditions in modern offices and research laboratories. Others work in mines, factories, at construction sites, or at outdoor locations.

If you think you would like to do this kind of work, look at the job titles listed below.

GOE: 05.01.01 Research, Engineering

AERODYNAMIST (aircraft-aerospace mfg.) • D.O.T. #002.061-010 • OES #22102 • AERODYNAMICIST; AERODYNAMICS ENGINEER; AEROPHYSICS ENGINEER. Plans and conducts analysis of aerodynamic, thermodynamic, aerothermodynamic, and aerophysics concepts, systems, and designs to resolve problems and determine suitability and application to aircraft, space vehicle, surface effect vehicles, missiles, space probes, and related systems: Establishes computational methods, and computer input data for analyzing problems. Analyzes designs and develops configurations to insure satisfactory static and dynamic stability and control characteristics for completed vehicle. Initiates and assists in formulating and evaluating laboratory, flight, and wind tunnel test programs, and prepares reports and conclusions for other engineering and design personnel. Coordinates activities of model design group and model shop to assure required configuration of wind tunnel models. Prepares air load data on vehicle to conform to aerodynamic requirements. May prepare reports on results of analyses such as flight performance validation, aircraft configuration, trade studies, and aircraft certification. May confer with customer on performance problems during operational life of vehicle. May specialize in analysis of ther modynamic effects and be designated THERMODYNAMICS ENGINEER (aircraft-aerospace mfg.). • **GED:** R6, M6, L6 • **SVP:** 4-10 yrs • **Academic:** Ed=B, Eng=S • **Work Field:** 244 • **MPSMS:** 702 • **Aptitudes:** G1, V1, N1, S1, P2, Q3, K3, F3, M3, E5, C5 • **Temperaments:** D, J, M, T, V • **Physical:** V=L, H=N, L=S, H • **Work Env:** I • **Salary:** 5 • **Outlook:** 3

AERONAUTICAL-RESEARCH ENGINEER (aircraft-aerospace mfg.) • D.O.T. #002.061-026 • OES #22102 • Conducts research in field of aeronautics performing duties as described under RESEARCH ENGINEER (profess. & kin.). • **GED:** R6, M6, L6 • **SVP:** 4-10 yrs • **Academic:** Ed=B, Eng=G • **Work Field:** 244, 251 • **MPSMS:** 702 • **Aptitudes:** G1, V1, N1, S1, P3, Q3, K3, F3, M3, E4, C3 • **Temperaments:** D, J, M, T, V • **Physical:** V=L, H=N, L=L • **Work Env:** I • **Salary:** 5 • **Outlook:** 4

CHEMICAL RESEARCH ENGINEER (profess. & kin.) • D.O.T. #008.061-022 • OES #22114 • Conducts research on chemical processes and equipment performing duties as described under RESEARCH ENGINEER (profess. & kin.). • **GED:** R5, M5, L5 • **SVP:** 4-10 yrs • **Academic:** Ed=B, Eng=G • **Work Field:** 244, 251 • **MPSMS:** 707 • **Aptitudes:** G2, V2, N2, S2, P2, Q3, K4, F4, M4, E4, C4 • **Temperaments:** D, J, M, P • **Physical:** V=L, H=N, L=S, H • **Work Env:** I • **Salary:** 5 • **Outlook:** 4

ELECTRICAL TECHNICIAN (profess. & kin.) • D.O.T. #003.161-010 • OES #22505 • ELECTRICAL-LABORATORY TECHNICIAN. Applies electrical theory and related knowledge to test and modify developmental or operational electrical machinery and electrical control equipment and circuitry in industrial or commercial plants and laboratories: Assembles and tests experimental motor-control devices, switch panels, transformers, generator windings, solenoids, and other electrical equipment and components according to engineering data and knowledge of electrical principles. Modifies electrical prototypes to correct functional deviations under direction of ELECTRICAL ENGINEER (profess. & kin.). Diagnoses cause of electrical or mechanical malfunction or failure of operational equipment and performs preventative and corrective maintenance. Develops wiring diagrams, layout drawings, and engineering specifications for system or equipment modifications or expansion, and directs personnel performing routine installation and maintenance duties. Plans, directs, and records periodic electrical testing, and recommends or initiates modification or replacement of equipment which fails to meet acceptable operating standards. • **GED:** R4, M4, L4 • **SVP:** 2-4 yrs • **Academic:** Ed=H, Eng=S • **Work Field:** 111, 244 • **MPSMS:** 580, 703 • **Aptitudes:** G2, V2, N2, S2, P2, Q3, K2, F2, M2, E4, C4 • **Temperaments:** J, M, T, V • **Physical:** V=L, H=N, L=L, W, H • **Work Env:** I • **Salary:** 4 • **Outlook:** 3

ELECTRONICS TECHNICIAN (profess. & kin.) • D.O.T. #003.161-014 • OES #22505 • Applies electronic theory, principles of electrical circuits, electrical testing procedures, engineering mathematics, physics, and related knowledge to lay out, build, test, troubleshoot, repair, and modify developmental and production electronic equipment, such as computers, missile-control instrumentation, and machine tool numerical controls: Discusses layout and assembly problems with ELECTRONICS ENGINEER (profess. & kin.) and draws sketches to clarify design details and functional criteria of electronic units. Assembles experimental circuitry (breadboard) or complete proto type model according to engineering instructions, technical manuals, and knowledge of electronic systems and components and their functions. Recommends changes in circuitry or installation specifications to simplify assembly and maintenance. Sets up standard test apparatus or contrives test equipment and circuitry, and conducts functional, operational, environmental, and life tests to evaluate performance and reliability of prototype or production model. Analyzes and interprets test data. Adjusts, calibrates, alines, and modifies circuitry and components and records effects on unit performance. Writes technical reports and develops charts, graphs, and schematics to describe and illustrate systems operating characteristics, malfunctions, deviations from design specifications, and functional limitations for consideration by professional engineering personnel in broader determinations affecting systems design and laboratory procedures. May operate bench lathes, drills, and other machine tools to fabricate nonprocurable items, such as coils, terminal boards, and chassis. May check out newly installed equipment in air planes, ships, and structures to evaluate system performance under actual operating conditions. May instruct and supervise lower grade technical personnel. May be designated according to specialization in electronic applications as COMPUTER-LABORATORY TECHNICIAN (profess. & kin.); DEVELOPMENT-INSTRUMENTATION TECHNICIAN (profess. & kin.); ELECTRONIC-COMMUNICATIONS TECHNICIAN (profess. & kin.); ELECTRONIC TECHNICIAN, NUCLEAR REACTOR (profess. & kin.); ENGINEERING-DEVELOPMENT TECHNICIAN (aircraft-aerospace mfg.); SYSTEMS-TESTING-LABORATORY TECHNICIAN (profess. & kin.). • **GED:** R5, M5, L4 • **SVP:** 2-4 yrs • **Academic:** Ed=A, Eng=G • **Work Field:** 111, 211, 244 • **MPSMS:** 703 • **Aptitudes:** G2, V2, N2, S2, P2, Q3, K2, F2, M2, E4, C4 • **Temperaments:** J, M, T, V • **Physical:** V=L, H=N, L=S, H • **Work Env:** I • **Salary:** 4 • **Outlook:** 5

FOUNDRY METALLURGIST (foundry) • D.O.T. #011.061-010 • OES #22105 • FOUNDRY TECHNICIAN. Conducts research to develop and improve methods of sand molding, melting, alloying, and pouring of metals: Makes experimental sand molds, and tests sand for permeability, strength, and chemical composition. Calculates quantity of alloying metals required. Melts alloys and pours metals under controlled conditions to make castings. Performs physical and radiographic tests and evaluates data to develop improved alloys and foundry techniques. • **GED:** R5, M5, L5 • **SVP:** 4-10 yrs • **Academic:** Ed=A, Eng=G • **Work Field:** 244, 251 • **MPSMS:** 708, 711, 723 • **Aptitudes:** G1, V1, N1, S2, P3, Q3, K3, F3, M3, E4, C3 • **Temperaments:** D, M, T, V • **Physical:** V=L, H=N, L=L, H • **Work Env:** I • **Salary:** 5 • **Outlook:** 4

INSTRUMENTATION TECHNICIAN (profess. & kin.) • D.O.T. #003.261-010 • OES #22505 • Devises, sets up, and operates electronic instrumentation and related electromechanical or electrohydraulic apparatus involved in operational and environmental testing of mechanical, structural, or electrical equipment, and translates test data for subsequent use by engineering personnel in making engineering design and evaluation decisions: Selects, installs, calibrates, and checks out sensing, telemetering, and recording instrumentation and circuitry, and develops specifications for nonstandard apparatus according to engineering data, characteristics of equipment under test, and capabilities of procurable test apparatus. Sketches and builds or modifies jigs, fixtures, instruments, and related apparatus, and verifies dimensional and functional acceptability of devices fabricated by craft or technical personnel. Performs preventative and corrective maintenance of test apparatus and peripheral equipment. Directs technical personnel in installation of object in test chamber or other test facility. Operates test apparatus during test cycle to produce, regulate, and record effects of actual or simulated conditions, such as vibration, stress, temperature, humidity, pressure, altitude, and acceleration. Mathematically reduces test data to usable form, and prepares graphs and written reports to translate test results into meaningful terms, such as speed-temperature-horsepower ratios. May plan complete test program. May be designated according to equipment tested as ROCKET-CONTROL TECHNICIAN (profess. & kin.), or according to nature of test as ENVIRONMENTAL-RESEARCH-TEST TECHNICIAN (pro fess. & kin.). • **GED:** R5, M5, L4 • **SVP:** 2-4 yrs • **Academic:** Ed=B, Eng=S • **Work Field:** 244, 251 • **MPSMS:** 700, 710 • **Aptitudes:** G2, V2, N2, S2, P2, Q3, K2, F2, M2, E4, C4 • **Temperaments:** J, M, T, V • **Physical:** V=L, H=N, L=L, H • **Work Env:** I, R • **Salary:** 4 • **Outlook:** 4

LASER TECHNICIAN (electronics) • D.O.T. #019.181-010 • OES #24599 • Constructs and tests prototype laser devices, applying theory and principles of laser engineering and electronic circuits: Reviews project instructions such as assembly layout and sketches with engineering personnel to clarify specifications of device. Interprets detail requirements, such as dimensions and functional requirements for workers engaged in grinding mirror blanks, coating mirror surfaces, machining metal parts, or blowing glass resonator units. Installs and alines mirrors in laser body, using precision instruments. Turns controls of vacuum pump and gas transfer equipment to purge, evacuate, and fill laser body with specified volume and pressure of gases, such as helium and neon. Assembles completed laser body in chassis, and installs tubing and wiring to connect valves, regulators, dials and switches. Sets up precision electronic and optical instruments to test device, utilizing specified electrical or optical inputs. Analyzes test data and reports results to engineering personnel. • **GED:** R5, M4, L4 • **SVP:** 2-4 yrs • **Academic:** Ed=A, Eng=S • **Work Field:** 211, 244 • **MPSMS:** 601, 609, 703 • **Aptitudes:** G2, V2, N2, S2, P2, Q3, K2, F2, M2, E4, C4 • **Temperaments:** J, M, T, V • **Physical:** V=G, H=N, L=S, H • **Work Env:** I • **Salary:** 4 • **Outlook:** 4

MECHANICAL-ENGINEERING TECHNICIAN (profess. & kin.) • D.O.T. #007.161-026 • OES #22511 • ENGINEERING TECHNICIAN; EXPERIMENTAL TECHNICIAN; LABORATORY-DEVELOPMENT TECHNICIAN; MECHANICAL TECHNICIAN. Develops and tests machinery and equipment, applying knowledge of mechanical engineering technology, under direction of engineering and scientific staff: Reviews project instructions and blueprints to ascertain test specifications, procedures, objectives, test equipment, nature of technical problem, and possible solutions, such as part redesign, substitution of material or parts, or rearrangement of parts or subassemblies. Drafts detail drawing or sketch for drafting room completion or to request parts fabrication by machine, sheet metal or wood shops. Devises, fabricates, and assembles new or modified mechanical components or assemblies for products, such as industrial equipment and machinery, power equipment, servosystems, machine tools, and measuring instruments. Sets up and conducts tests of complete units and components under operational conditions to investigate design proposals for improving equipment performance or other factors, or to obtain data for development, standardization, and quality control. Analyzes indicated and calculated test results in relation to design or rated specifications and test objectives, and modifies or adjusts equipment to meet specifications. Records test procedures and results, numerical and graphical data, and recommendations for changes in product or test method. • **GED:** R5, M4, L4 • **SVP:** 2-4 yrs • **Academic:** Ed=A, Eng=S • **Work Field:** 121, 244 • **MPSMS:** 567, 590 • **Aptitudes:** G2, V2, N3, S2, P2, Q4, K3, F3, M3, E5, C4 • **Temperaments:** M, T • **Physical:** V=G, H=N, L=S, H • **Work Env:** I • **Salary:** 4 • **Outlook:** 4

NUCLEAR-DECONTAMINATION RESEARCH SPE-CIAL-IST (profess. & kin.) • D.O.T. #008.061-030 • OES #22117 • Conducts research into problems of decontaminating radioactive equipment and work areas in nuclear plants, laboratories, and other facilities: Examines and tests machinery and equipment to determine type and cause of radioactive contamination, using electron microscope, Geiger counter, and scintillation counter. Develops new decontamination processes, using knowledge of nuclear chemistry. Invents and constructs models of equipment to achieve specific objectives in decontamination processes, devising ways to minimize radiation risk to operative personnel. Devises wash and leach procedures and designs electropolishing equipment to clean and decontaminate metals. Invents regenerative-dilute decontamination process to reduce volume of radioactive liquid waste generated from wash and leach procedures. Prepares technical report to explain research and development of improved techniques and equipment for decontamination of radioactive equipment and work areas. • **GED: R6, M6, L6** • SVP: **4-10 yrs** • Academic: **Ed=A, Eng=G** • Work Field: 244, 251 • MPSMS: **706, 723** • Aptitudes: G1, V1, N1, S1, P1, Q1, K3, F3, M4, E4, C4 • Temperaments: **D, J, T, V** • Physical: V=L, H=L, L=L, W, H • Work Env: **I** • Salary: **5** • Outlook: 3

OPTOMECHANICAL TECHNICIAN (optical goods) • D.O.T. #007.161-030 • OES #22511 • Applies engineering theory and practical knowledge, under direction of engineering staff, to build and test prototype optomechanical devices to be used in such equipment as aerial cameras, gun sights, and telescopes: Reviews project instructions, and preliminary specifications to identify and plan requirements for parts fabrication, purchase, assembly, and test. Prepares sketches and writes work orders and purchase requests for items to be furnished by others, and follows up delivery. Designs, builds, or modifies fixtures used to assemble parts. Lays out cutting lines for machining, using drafting tools. Assembles and adjusts parts and related electrical units of prototype to prepare for test. Sets up prototype and test apparatus, such as control console, collimator, recording equipment, and cables in accordance with specifications. Operates controls of test apparatus

and prototype to observe and record test results. Computes test data on laboratory forms for engineers. Confers in technical meetings, recommending design and material changes to reduce cost and lead time. May be assigned as group leader to coordinate work of technicians, model makers, and others assigned to assist. • **GED:** R5, M4, L4 • **SVP:** 4-10 yrs • **Academic:** Ed=A, Eng=S • **Work Field:** 121, 211, 244 • **MPSMS:** 603, 606 • **Aptitudes:** G2, V2, N2, S2, P2, Q3, K3, F2, M2, E4, C4 • **Temperaments:** J, M, T • **Physical:** V=L, H=N, L=L, H • **Work Env:** I • **Salary:** 5 • **Outlook:** 3

TECHNICIAN, SEMICONDUCTOR DEVELOPMENT (profess. & kin.) • D.O.T. #003.161-018 • OES #22505 • Tests developmental semiconductor devices or sample production units, and evaluates test equipment to develop data for engineering evaluation of new designs or special production yield study, applying knowledge of electronic theory and test equipment operating principles: Designs basic circuitry and prepares rough sketches for design documentation as directed by engineers, using drafting instruments and computer-aided design (CAD) system. Evaluates, calibrates, and tests new equipment circuits and fixtures, using testing equipment, such as oscilloscopes, logic and test probes, and calibrators. Builds and modifies electronic components, using handtools and power tools. Assists engineers in development of testing techniques and laboratory equipment. Assists with equipment maintenance. Liaises between test project sites to ensure orderly flow of information and materials. May supervise other technicians in unit. • **GED:** R5, M5, L4 • **SVP:** 4-10 yrs • **Academic:** Ed=B, Eng=G • **Work Field:** 211, 244 • **MPSMS:** 587, 703 • **Aptitudes:** G2, V2, N2, S2, P2, Q3, K2, F2, M2, E4, C4 • **Temperaments:** J, T, V • **Physical:** V=L, H=N, L=S, H • **Work Env:** I, R, F • **Salary:** 5 • **Outlook:** 5

WELDING TECHNICIAN (profess. & kin.) • D.O.T. #011.261-014 • OES #22599 • Conducts experiments and tests and evaluates data to assist welding engineering personnel in development and application of new or improved welding equipment; welding techniques, procedures, and practices; and specifications for material heat treating: Assists engineering personnel in testing and evaluating welding equipment, metals, and alloys. Evaluates data and conducts experiments to develop application of new equipment or improved techniques, procedures, or practices. Recommends adoption of new developments and applications to engineering personnel and demonstrates practicability of recommendations. Inspects welded joints and conducts tests to ensure welds meet company standards, national code requirements, and customer job specifications. Records inspection and test results and prepares and submits reports to welding engineering personnel. Conducts certification tests for qualification of personnel with national code requirements. • **GED:** R4, M3, L3 • **SVP:** 4-10 yrs • **Academic:** Ed=H, Eng=S • **Work Field:** 211, 244 • **MPSMS:** 871 • **Aptitudes:** G3, V3, N3, S3, P2, Q3, K2, F3, M3, E5, C4 • **Temperaments:** M, T • **Physical:** V=G, H=N, L=L, H • **Work Env:** I • **Salary:** 5 • **Outlook:** 4

GOE: 05.01.02 Environmental Protection

HEALTH PHYSICIST (profess. & kin.) • D.O.T. #079.021-010 • OES #24311 • Devises and directs research, training, and monitoring programs to protect plant and laboratory personnel from radiation hazards: Conducts research to develop inspection standards, radiation exposure limits for personnel, safe work methods, and decontamination procedures, and tests surrounding areas to insure that radiation is not in excess of permissible standards. Develops criteria for design and modification of health physics equipment, such as detectors and counters, to improve radiation protection. Assists in developing standards of permissible concentrations of radioisotopes in liquids and gases. Directs testing and monitoring of equipment and recording of personnel and plant area radiation exposure data. Requests bioassay samples from individuals believed to be exposed. Consults with scientific personnel regarding new experiments to determine that equipment or plant design conforms to health physics standards for protection of personnel. Conducts research pertaining to potential environmental impact of proposed atomic energy related industrial development to determine qualifications for licensing. Requisitions and maintains inventory of instruments. Instructs personnel in principles and regulations related to radiation hazards. Assigns film badges and dosimeters to personnel, and recommends changes in assignment for health reasons. Advises public authorities on methods of dealing with radiation hazards, and procedures to be followed in radiation incidents, and assists in civil defense planning. • **GED:** R6, M5, L5 • **SVP:** 4-10 yrs • **Academic:** Ed=M, Eng=G • **Work Field:** 251, 293 • **MPSMS:** 732 • **Aptitudes:** G1, V1, N2, S2, P4, Q4, K4, F4, M4, E5, C4 • **Temperaments:** D, M, P • **Stress:** E, A • **Physical:** V=L, H=L, L=S • **Work Env:** I, R • **Salary:** 5 • **Outlook:** 3

INDUSTRIAL-HEALTH ENGINEER (profess. & kin.) • D.O.T. #012.167-034 • OES #22132 • INDUSTRIAL HYGIENE ENGINEER. Plans and coordinates private or government industrial health program requiring application of engineering principles and technology to analyze and control conditions contributing to occupational hazards and diseases: Conducts plant or area surveys to determine safe limits of exposure to materials or conditions, such as temperatures, noise, dusts, fumes, vapors, mists, gases, solvents, and radiation which are known or suspected of being real or potential detriments to health, and implements or recommends control measures. Directs workers engaged in field and laboratory verification of compliance with health regulations. Provides technical guidance to management, labor organizations, government agencies, and civic groups regarding health-related problems, such as stream and air pollution and correct use of protective clothing or accessories. • **GED:** R5, M5, L5 • **SVP:** 2-4 yrs • **Academic:** Ed=B, Eng=G • **Work Field:** 244, 295 • **MPSMS:** 712 • **Aptitudes:** G1, V1, N1, S2, P3, Q3, K4, F4, M4, E5, C3 • **Temperaments:** D, J, M, P, T • **Physical:** V=N, H=L, L=S • **Work Env:** B • **Salary:** 5 • **Outlook:** 4

NUCLEAR-CRITICALITY SAFETY ENGINEER (profess. & kin.) • D.O.T. #015.067-010 • OES #22117 • Conducts research and analyzes and evaluates proposed and existing methods of transportation, handling, and storage of nuclear fuel to preclude accidental nuclear reaction at nuclear facilities: Reviews and evaluates fuel transfer and storage plans received from nuclear plants. Studies reports of nuclear fuel characteristics to determine potential or inherent problems. Reads blue prints of proposed storage facilities and visits storage sites to determine adequacy of storage plans. Forecasts nuclear fuel criticality (point at which nuclear chain reaction becomes self-sustaining), given various factors which may exist in fuel handling and storage, using knowledge of nuclear physics, calculator, and computer terminal. Determines potential hazards and accident conditions which may exist in fuel handling and storage and recommends preventive measures. Summarizes findings and writes reports. Confers with project officials to resolve situations where hazard is beyond acceptable levels. Prepares proposal reports for handling and storage of fuels to be submitted to government review board. Studies existing procedures and recommends changes or additions to guidelines and controls to ensure prevention of self-sustaining nuclear chain reaction. • **GED:** R6, M6, L5 • **SVP:** 4-10 yrs • **Academic:** Ed=B, Eng=G • **Work Field:** 244, 251 • **MPSMS:** 715 • **Aptitudes:** G1, V1, N1, S1, P2, Q2, K3, F3, M4, E5, C5 • **Temperaments:** J, T, V • **Physical:** V=L, H=L, L=L, W, H • **Work Env:** I, R, F • **Salary:** 5 • **Outlook:** 2

POLLUTION-CONTROL ENGINEER (profess. & kin.) • D.O.T. #019.081-018 • OES #22199 • Plans and conducts engineering studies to analyze and evaluate pollution problems, methods of pollution control, and methods of testing pollution sources to determine physiochemical nature and concentration of contaminants: Reviews data collected by POLLUTION-CONTROL TECHNICIAN (profess. & kin.) from pollution emission sources. Performs engineering calculations to determine pollution emissions from various industrial sources and to evaluate effectiveness of pollution control equipment. Reviews compliance schedules and inspection reports to insure compliance with pollution control regulations. Recommends issuance or denial of permits for industries to construct or operate facilities. Advises enforcement personnel of noncompliance or unsatisfactory compliance with regulations. Develops or modifies techniques for monitoring pollution. Calibrates and adjusts pollution control monitors to insure accurate functioning of instruments. May be designated according to specialty as AIR-POLLUTION ENGINEER (profess. & kin.);

NOISE-ABATEMENT ENGINEER (profess. & kin.) and WATER QUALITY-CONTROL ENGINEER (profess. & kin.). • **GED:** R6, M6, L6 • **SVP:** 4-10 yrs • **Academic:** Ed=B, Eng=G • **Work Field:** 211, 244 • **MPSMS:** 706, 707 • **Aptitudes:** G1, V1, N1, S2, P2, Q4, K4, F4, M2, E5, C4 • **Temperaments:** D, M, T, V • **Physical:** V=L, H=N, L=S, W, H • **Work Env:** B • **Salary:** 5 • **Outlook:** 3

PRODUCT-SAFETY ENGINEER (profess. & kin.) • D.O.T. #012.061-010 • OES #22132 • Develops and conducts tests to evaluate product safety levels and recommends measures to reduce or eliminate hazards: Establishes procedures for detection and elimination of physical and chemical hazards and avoidance of potential toxic effects and other product hazards. Investigates causes of accidents, injuries, and illnesses resulting from product usage and develops solutions. Evaluates potential health hazards or damage which could result from misuse of products and applies engineering principles and product standards to improve safety. May participate in preparation of product usage and precautionary label instructions. • **GED:** R6, M6, L6 • **SVP:** 4-10 yrs • **Academic:** Ed=B, Eng=G • **Work Field:** 244 • **MPSMS:** 712 • **Aptitudes:** G2, V2, N2, S2, P3, Q3, K3, F3, M3, E3, C3 • **Temperaments:** D, M, P, V • **Physical:** V=L, H=N, L=S, H • **Work Env:** I • **Salary:** 5 • **Outlook:** 4

RADIATION-PROTECTION ENGINEER (gov. ser.) • D.O.T. #015.137-010 • OES #22117 • Supervises and coordinates activities of workers engaged in monitoring radiation levels in water and detecting corrosion of equipment used to produce nuclear energy for generation of power: Evaluates data concerning chemical analysis of water in primary and supportive plant systems to determine compliance with regulations governing radiation content and corrosion control. Investigates problems concerning excessive radiation or corrosion of equipment, applying knowledge of radiation protection techniques and principles of chemistry and engineering to correct conditions. Confers with other supervisory personnel, representatives of equipment manufacturing firms, and regulatory agency staff members to discuss problems and develop plans for safe and efficient monitoring program. Supervises workers who test and analyze water samples and monitor operation of processing system. Prepares reports of environmental monitoring operation and radioactive waste release and shipment activities for review by administrative personnel and submission to regulatory agency. • **GED:** R5, M4, L5 • **SVP:** 4-10 yrs • **Academic:** Ed=B, Eng=G • **Work Field:** 021, 244 • **MPSMS:** 715, 871 • **Aptitudes:** G2, V2, N2, S2, P2, Q2, K3, F4, M4, E5, C5 • **Temperaments:** D, P, V • **Stress:** E, A • **Physical:** V=L, H=L, L=S, W • **Work Env:** I • **Salary:** 5 • **Outlook:** 2

RESOURCE-RECOVERY ENGINEER (gov. ser.) • D.O.T. #019.167-018 • OES #22121 • Plans and participates in activities concerned with study, development, and inspection of solid-waste resource recovery systems and marketability of solid-waste recovery products: Conducts studies of chemical and mechanical solid-waste recovery processes and system designs to evaluate efficiency and cost-effectiveness of proposed operations. Inspects solid-waste resource recovery facilities to determine compliance with regulations governing construction and use. Collects data on resource recovery systems and analyzes alternate plans to determine most feasible systems for specific solid-waste recovery purposes. Prepares recommendations for development of resource recovery programs, based on analysis of alternate plans and knowledge of physical properties of various solid-waste materials. Confers with design engineers, management personnel, and others concerned with recovery of solid-waste resources to discuss problems and provide technical advice. Coordinates activities of workers engaged in study of potential markets for reclaimable materials. Lectures civic and professional organizations and provides information about practices to media representatives to promote interest and participation in solid-waste recovery practices. • **GED:** R6, M6, L5 • **SVP:** 4-10 yrs • **Academic:** Ed=B, Eng=S • **Work Field:** 244, 271 • **MPSMS:** 719 • **Aptitudes:** G1, V2, N1, S1, P2, Q1, K3, F3, M3, E5, C4 • **Temperaments:** J, P, T • **Physical:** V=L, H=L, L=S, H • **Work Env:** I • **Salary:** 5 • **Outlook:** 4

SAFETY ENGINEER (profess. & kin.) • D.O.T. #012.061-014 • OES #22132 • Develops and implements safety program to prevent or correct unsafe environmental working conditions, utilizing knowledge of industrial processes, mechanics, chemistry, psychology, and industrial health and safety laws: Examines plans and specifications for new machinery and equipment to ascertain if all safety precautions have been included. Determines amount of weight that can be placed on plant floor with safety. Inspects machinery to determine places where danger of injury exists. Designs, builds, and installs, or directs installation of guards on machinery, belts, and conveyors. Inspects premises for fire hazards and adequacy of fire protection and inspects firefighting equipment. Studies each accident to minimize recurrence. Educates workers to dangers existing in plant through safety-first campaign. May conduct safety and first-aid classes or train first-aid instructors. • **GED:** R6, M6, L6 • **SVP:** 4-10 yrs • **Academic:** Ed=B, Eng=S • **Work Field:** 244 • **MPSMS:** 712 • **Aptitudes:** G2, V2, N2, S2, P3, Q3, K3, F3, M3, E3, C4 • **Temperaments:** D, J, M, P, V • **Stress:** A • **Physical:** V=G, H=L, L=L, W, H • **Work Env:** I • **Salary:** 5 • **Outlook:** 4

SAFETY ENGINEER, MINES (mining) • D.O.T. #010.061-026 • OES #22108 • DIRECTOR, SAFETY. Inspects underground or open-pit mining areas and trains mine personnel to ensurance compliance with state and Federal laws and accepted mining practices designed to prevent mine accidents: Inspects mine workings to detect unsafe timbers, cribbing, roof bolts, electric wiring, elevators, explosives storage, equipment, and working conditions. Examines walls and roof surfaces for evidence of strata faults indicating cave-in or rock slide hazards. Tests air to detect concentrations of toxic gases and explosive dusts, using safety lamp, methane detector, carbon monoxide register, and anemometer. Recommends alteration or installation of ventilation shafts, partitions, or equipment to remedy inadequate air circulation of air-conditioning. Applies principles of mining engineering and human engineering to design protective equipment and safety devices for mine machinery. Gives instructions to mine personnel in safe working practices and first aid, and strives to promote and maintain safety-mindedness of workers. Investigates explosions, fires, and accidents and reports causes and recommen dations for remedial action to insurance companies, mine manage ment, and state authorities. May lead rescue activities during emergencies and maintain rescue equipment. • **GED:** R5, M5, L5 • **SVP:** 4-10 yrs • **Academic:** Ed=A, Eng=G • **MPSMS:** 708, 711, 712 • **Aptitudes:** G2, V2, N2, S2, P2, Q3, K4, F4, M4, E4, C4 • **Temperaments:** I, J, M, P, V • **Physical:** V=L, H=L, L=S, W, C, S, H • **Work Env:** B, W, R • **Salary:** 5 • **Outlook:** 3

SAFETY MANAGER (profess. & kin.) • D.O.T. #012.167-058 • OES #13017 • Plans, implements, and coordinates program to reduce or eliminate occupational injuries, illnesses, deaths, and financial losses: Identifies and appraises conditions which could produce accidents and financial losses and evaluates potential extent of injuries resulting from accidents. Conducts or directs research studies to identify hazards and evaluate loss producing potential of given system, operation or process. Develops accident prevention and loss control systems and programs for incorporation into operational policies of organization. Coordinates safety activities of unit managers to ensure implementation of safety activities throughout organization. Compiles, analyzes, and interprets statistical data related to exposure factors concerning occupational illnesses and accidents and prepares reports for information of personnel concerned. Maintains liaison with outside organizations, such as fire departments, mutual aid societies, and rescue teams to assure information exchange and mutual assistance. Devises methods to evaluate safety program and conducts or directs evaluations. Evaluates technical and scientific publications concerned with safety management and participates in activities of related professional organizations to update knowledge of safety program developments. • **GED:** R6, M6, L6 • **SVP:** 4-10 yrs • **Academic:** Ed=B, Eng=G • **Work Field:** 244, 295 • **MPSMS:** 712 • **Aptitudes:** G2, V2, N2, S3, P3, Q3, K3, F3, M3, E3, C4 • **Temperaments:** D, M, P, V • **Stress:** E, A • **Physical:** V=L, H=L, L=S, W, H • **Work Env:** I • **Salary:** 5 • **Outlook:** 3

GOE: 05.01.03 Systems Design

CABLE ENGINEER, OUTSIDE PLANT (tel. & tel.) • D.O.T. #003.167-010 • OES #22126 • Plans, directs, and coordinates activities concerned with laying and repairing submarine telecommunication cables: Devises plans for laying cable lines, taking into consideration ocean currents and ocean depths. Determines where and how cables should be laid and decides such matters as where to place buoys, where to cut cable, what grapnel to use, what length of rope to use for a given depth, what type of cable to use, and what route to follow. Keeps charts and records to show depth and location of all cables laid. Analyzes test figures made when cable fault occurs to determine exact location of cable break. Oversees work of locating and repairing damaged cables. • **GED:** R5, M5, L5 • **SVP:** 4-10 yrs • **Academic:** Ed=A, Eng=G • **Work Field:** 244 • **MPSMS:** 586, 703 • **Aptitudes:** G2, V2, N2, S2, P2, Q3, K3, F3, M3, E4, C3 • **Temperaments:** D, M, T, V • **Physical:** V=L, H=N, L=L, H • **Work Env:** B • **Salary:** 5 • **Outlook:** 4

CENTRAL-OFFICE EQUIPMENT ENGINEER (tel. & tel.) • D.O.T. #003.187-010 • OES #22126 • Directs implementation of planning schedule for installation of central office toll or local switching facilities, or interoffice transmission facilities equipment, such as radio, TV, camera, and repeaters: Reviews planning schedule or equipment request and data on projected traffic to determine quantities of specific types of equipment required. Plans arrangement of equipment, prepares cost estimates for equipment and installation, and submits data to management for authorization approval. Prepares drawings and equipment specifications for installation. Monitors installation activities to solve any problems concerning arrangement or specifications. Assigns equipment and installation expenditures to specific program or project accounts. Closes out installation authorization when equipment has been tested and put in service. • **GED:** R6, M6, L6 • **SVP:** 4-10 yrs • **Academic:** Ed=B, Eng=G • **Work Field:** 244 • **MPSMS:** 586 • **Aptitudes:** G1, V1, N1, S2, P3, Q3, K4, F4, M4, E5, C5 • **Temperaments:** M, T, V • **Physical:** V=L, H=N, L=S, H • **Work Env:** I • **Salary:** 5 • **Outlook:** 5

COMMERCIAL ENGINEER (radio & tv broad.) • D.O.T. #003.187-014 • OES #22126 • TRAFFIC ENGINEER. Plans use of wire facilities connecting stations comprising a network to cover changing conditions and requirements: Evaluates technical capabilities of wire facilities, according to availability and range, to obtain most effective method of transmission. Reviews network program schedule to be linked to network stations, and projects use of wire facilities. Subdivides wire facilities linking network stations for simultaneous broadcasting of different programs to stations. Tests facilities prior to broadcast time to determine readiness of transmission line. May prepare engineering estimates of equipment installations or modification of existing equipment. • **GED:** R5, M5, L5 • **SVP:** 2-4 yrs • **Academic:** Ed=B, Eng=S • **Work Field:** 244 • **MPSMS:** 863 • **Aptitudes:** G2, V2, N1, S2, P2, Q3, K4, F4, M4, E5, C5 • **Temperaments:** M, T • **Physical:** V=L, H=N, L=S, H • **Work Env:** I • **Salary:** 4 • **Outlook:** 4

ELECTRICAL ENGINEER, POWER SYSTEM (light, heat, & power) • D.O.T. #003.167-018 • OES #22126 • POWER ENGINEER. Designs power system facilities and equipment and coordinates construction, operation, and maintenance of electric power generating, receiving, and distribution stations, transmission lines, and distribution systems and equipment: Designs and plans layout of generating plants, transmission and distribution lines, and receiving and distribution stations. Directs preparation of, or prepares drawings and specific type of equipment and materials to be used, in construction and equipment installation. Estimates labor, material, construction, and equipment costs. Inspects completed installations for conformance with design and equipment specifications and safety standards. Observes operation of installation for conformance with operational standards. Coordinates operation and maintenance activities to ensure optimum utilization of power system facilities and meet customer demands for electrical energy. May compile power rates and direct others in evaluating properties and developing utilities in new territories. May be designated according to type of engineering functions, as ENGINEER, DESIGN-AND-CONSTRUCTION (light, heat, & power); ENGINEER, OPERATIONS-AND-MAINTENANCE (light, heat, & power). • **GED:** R6, M6, L6 • **SVP:** 4-10 yrs • **Academic:** Ed=B, Eng=G • **Work Field:** 244 • **MPSMS:** 871 • **Aptitudes:** G1, V1, N1, S1, P2, Q3, K3, F3, M3, E4, C4 • **Temperaments:** D, J, M, P, V • **Physical:** V=L, H=N, L=L, H • **Work Env:** I • **Salary:** 5 • **Outlook:** 4

HYDRAULIC ENGINEER (profess. & kin.) • D.O.T. #005.061-

018 • OES #22121 • HYDROLOGIC ENGINEER. Designs and directs construction of power and other hydraulic engineering projects for control and use of water: Computes and estimates rates of waterflow. Specifies type and size of equipment, such as conduits, pumps, turbines, pressure valves, and surge tanks, used in transporting water and converting water power into electricity. Directs, through subordinate supervisors, activities of workers engaged in dredging, digging cutoffs, placing jetties, and constructing levees to stabilize streams or open water ways. Designs and coordinates construction of artificial canals, conduits, and mains to transport and distribute water; and plans reservoirs, pressure valves, and booster stations to obtain proper water pressure at all levels. Frequently builds laboratory models to study construction and flow problems. • **GED:** R5, M5, L5 • **SVP:** 2-4 yrs • **Academic:** Ed=B, Eng=G • **Work Field:** 244 • **MPSMS:** 704, 725 • **Aptitudes:** G2, V2, N2, S2, P2, Q2, K3, F3, M3, E5, C4 • **Temperaments:** D, M, T, V • **Physical:** V=L, H=N, L=S, H • **Work Env:** B • **Salary:** 4 • **Outlook:** 4

ILLUMINATING ENGINEER (profess. & kin.) • D.O.T. #003.061-046 • OES #22126 • Designs and directs installation of illuminating equipment and systems for buildings, plants, streets, stadia, tunnels, and outdoor displays: Studies lighting requirements of client to determine lighting equipment and arrangement of lamps that will provide optimum illumination with economy of installation and operation. Designs lamps of required light intensity and output, light control reflectors and lenses, and lamp arrangement required to meet illuminating standards. Plans and prepares drawings for installation of lighting system in accordance with client's specifications and municipal codes. Directs installation of system to insure conformance with engineering specifications and compliance with electrical codes. May be designated according to type or location of illumination system designed and installed, such as BUILDING-ILLUMINATING ENGINEER (profess. & kin.); INDUSTRIAL-ILLUMINATING ENGINEER (profess. & kin.); OUTDOOR-ILLUMINATING ENGINEER (profess. & kin.). • **GED:** R5, M5, L5 • **SVP:** 4-10 yrs • **Academic:** Ed=B, Eng=G • **Work Field:** 244 • **MPSMS:** 703, 871 • **Aptitudes:** G1, V1, N1, S2, P2, Q3, K3, F3, M3, E5, C4 • **Temperaments:** D, M, T • **Physical:** V=L, H=N, L=S, H • **Work Env:** I • **Salary:** 5 • **Outlook:** 4

MARINE ENGINEER (profess. & kin.) • D.O.T. #014.061-014 • OES #22138 • Designs and oversees installation and repair of marine powerplants, propulsion systems, heating and ventilating systems, and other mechanical and electrical equipment in ships, docks, and marine facilities: Studies drawings and specifications and performs complex calculations to conceive equipment and systems designed to meet requirements of marine craft or facility. Oversees and evaluates operation of equipment during acceptance testing and shakedown cruises. May specialize in design of equipment, such as boilers, steam-driven reciprocating engines, heat exchangers, fire-control and communication systems, electric power systems, or piping and related fittings and valves. • **GED:** R6, M5, L5 • **SVP:** 4-10 yrs • **Academic:** Ed=B, Eng=G • **Work Field:** 244 • **MPSMS:** 714 • **Aptitudes:** G1, V1, N1, S1, P2, Q3, K4, F3, M3, E4, C3 • **Temperaments:** D, M, T, V • **Physical:** V=L, H=N, L=S, H • **Work Env:** B • **Salary:** 5 • **Outlook:** 3

NUCLEAR ENGINEER (profess. & kin.) • D.O.T. #015.061-014 • OES #22117 • Conducts research into problems of nuclear energy systems; designs and develops nuclear equipment; and monitors testing, operation, and maintenance of nuclear reactors: Plans and conducts nuclear research to discover facts or to test, prove, or modify known nuclear theories concerning release, control, and utilization of nuclear energy. Evaluates findings to develop new concepts of thermonuclear analysis and new uses of radioactive processes. Plans, designs, and develops nuclear equipment such as reactor cores, radiation shielding, and associated instrumentation and control mechanisms. Studies nuclear fuel cycle to define most economical uses of nuclear material and safest means of waste products disposal. Monitors nuclear tests and examines operations of facilities which process or utilize radioactive or fissionable material, to ensure efficient functioning and conformance with safety specifications, regulations, and laws. Prepares technical reports, utilizing knowledge obtained during research and development activities and inspectional functions. May direct operating

and maintenance activities of operational nuclear facility. • **GED:** R6, M6, L5 • **SVP:** 4-10 yrs • **Academic:** Ed=B, Eng=S • **Work Field:** 244, 251 • **MPSMS:** 715 • **Aptitudes:** G1, V1, N1, S2, P3, Q3, K3, F3, M3, E5, C5 • **Temperaments:** D, M, T • **Stress:** A • **Physical:** V=L, H=L, L=S, H • **Work Env:** I • **Salary:** 5 • **Outlook:** 2

POWER-DISTRIBUTION ENGINEER (light, heat, & power) • D.O.T. #003.167-046 • OES #22126 • ELECTRIC-DISTRIBUTION ENGINEER. Plans construction and coordinates operation of facilities for transmitting power from distribution points to consumers: Lays out substations and overhead and underground lines in urban and rural areas. Prepares specifications and estimates costs. Makes complex electrical computations to determine type and arrangement of circuits and size, type and number of pieces of equipment, such as transformers, circuit breakers, switches, and lightning arresters. Computes sag and stress for specifications on wire and cable. Plans layout of pole lines and underground cable and solves problems, such as determining height, location, spacing, guying, and insulating of poles. May be designated according to specialization as OVERHEAD-DISTRBUTION ENGINEER (light, heat, & power); RURAL-SERVICE ENGINEER (light, heat, & power); SUBSTATION ENGINEER (light, heat, & power); UNDERGROUND-DISTRIBUTION ENGINEER (light, heat, & power). • **GED:** R5, M5, L5 • **SVP:** 4-10 yrs • **Academic:** Ed=B, Eng=G • **Work Field:** 244 • **MPSMS:** 871 • **Aptitudes:** G1, V1, N1, S1, P2, Q3, K2, F2, M3, E5, C5 • **Temperaments:** M, T • **Physical:** V=L, H=N, L=S, H • **Work Env:** I • **Salary:** 5 • **Outlook:** 4

POWER-TRANSMISSION ENGINEER (light, heat, & power) • D.O.T. #003.167-050 • OES #22126 • ELECTRICAL-TRANSMISSION ENGINEER; TRANSMISSION-AND-COORDINATION ENGINEER; TRANSMISSION-LINE ENGINEER. Lays out plans and estimates costs for constructing transmission lines (high-tension facilities for carrying power from source to distributing points): Visits proposed construction site and selects best and shortest route to avoid interference with telephone or other lines. Submits data on proposed route to right-of-way department for obtaining necessary easements. Arranges for aerial, topographical, and other surveys to be made to obtain pertinent data for planning lines. Devises steel and wood supporting structures for cables and draws sketch showing their location. Performs detailed engineering calculations to draw up construction specifications, such as cable sag, pole strength, and necessary grounding. Estimates labor, material, and construction costs, and draws up specifications for purchase of materials and equipment. Keeps informed on new developments in electric power transmission. Assists various departments of power company on problems involving transmission-line operation and maintenance. Inspects completed installation. Does not usually plan facilities for distributing power to consumers [POWER-DISTRIBUTION ENGINEER (light, heat, & power)]. • **GED:** R5, M5, L5 • **SVP:** 4-10 yrs • **Academic:** Ed=B, Eng=G • **Work Field:** 244 • **MPSMS:** 703, 871 • **Aptitudes:** G1, V1, N1, S2, P2, Q3, K3, F3, M3, E4, C4 • **Temperaments:** D, M, P, V • **Physical:** V=L, H=N, L=L, H • **Work Env:** I • **Salary:** 5 • **Outlook:** 4

SANITARY ENGINEER (profess. & kin.) • D.O.T. #005.061-030 • OES #22121 • PUBLIC-HEALTH ENGINEER. Designs and directs construction and operation of hygienic projects such as waterworks, sewage, garbage and trash disposal plants, drainage systems, and insect and rodent control projects: Plans development of watersheds and directs building of aqueducts, filtration plants, and storage and distribution systems for water supply. Directs swamp drainage, insect spraying, and design of insect-proof buildings. Plans and directs workers in building and operation of sewage-disposal plants. Designs and controls operation of incinerators, sanitary fills, and garbage-reduction plants to dispose of garbage and other refuse. Advises industrial plants in disposal of obnoxious gases, oils, greases, and other chemicals. Inspects and regulates sanitary condition of public places, such as markets, parks, and camps. May plan and direct operation of water treatment plant to soften and purify water for human consumption or industrial use and be known as WATER-TREATMENT-PLANT ENGINEER (profess. & kin.). • **GED:** R5, M5, L5 • **SVP:** 4-10 yrs • **Academic:** Ed=B, Eng=G • **Work Field:** 244 • **MPSMS:** 704 •

Aptitudes: G1, V1, N1, S2, P2, Q2, K4, F3, M3, E4, C4 • Temperaments: D, M, T, V • Physical: V=L, H=N, L=S, H • Work Env: B • Salary: 5 • Outlook: 3

SYSTEMS ENGINEER, ELECTRONIC DATA PROCESSING (profess. & kin.) • D.O.T. #003.167-062 • OES #22127 • COMPUTER SYSTEMS ENGINEER; METHODS ANALYST, ELECTRONIC DATA PROCESSING; INFORMATION PROCESSING ENGINEER. Analyzes data-processing requirements to determine electronic data-processing system that will provide system capabilities required for projects or workloads, and plans layout of new system installation or modification of existing system, utilizing knowledge of electronics and data-processing principles and equipment: Confers with data-processing and project managerial personnel to obtain data on limitations and capabilities of existing system and capabilities required for data-processing projects and workload proposed. Analyzes data to determine, recommend, and plan layout for type of computer and peripheral equipment, or modifications to existing equipment and system, that will provide capability for proposed project or workload, efficient operation, and effective use of allotted space. May specify power supply requirements and configuration. May recommend purchase of equipment to control dust, temperature, and humidity in area of system installation. May specialize in one area of system application or in one type or make of equipment. May represent consulting firm or equipment manufacturer. • GED: R6, M5, L5 • SVP: 4-10 yrs • Academic: Ed=B, Eng=G • Work Field: 244 • MPSMS: 571 • Aptitudes: G1, V1, N1, S1, P3, Q3, K4, F4, M4, E4, C5 • Temperaments: J, M • Physical: V=N, H=N, L=S • Work Env: I • Salary: 5 • Outlook: 5

WASTE-MANAGEMENT ENGINEER, RADIOACTIVE MATERIALS (profess. & kin.) • D.O.T. #005.061-042 • OES #22121 • Designs, implements, and tests systems and procedures to reduce volume and dispose of nuclear waste materials and contaminated objects: Identifies objects contaminated by exposure to radiation, such as trash, workers' clothing, and discarded tools and equipment. Analyzes samples of sludge and liquid effluents resulting from operation of nuclear reactors to determine level of radioactivity in substances and potential for retention of radioactivity, using radioactivity counters and chemical and electronic analyzers. Refers to State and Federal regulations and technical manuals to determine disposal method recommended for prevention of leakage or absorption of radioactive waste. Compares costs of transporting waste to designated nuclear waste disposal sites and reducing volume of waste and storing waste on plant site. Confers with equipment manufacturers' representatives and plant technical and management personnel to discuss alternatives and to choose most suitable plan on basis of safety, efficiency, and cost-effectiveness. Designs and draws plans for systems to reduce volume of waste by solidification, compaction, or incineration. Oversees construction, testing, and implementation of waste disposal systems, and resolves operational problems. Develops plans for modification of operating procedures to reduce volume and radioactive level of effluents, and writes manuals to instruct workers in changes in work procedures. Advises management on selection of lands suitable for use as nuclear waste disposal sites and on establishment of effective safety, operating, and closure procedures. • GED: R5, M5, L5 • SVP: 4-10 yrs • Academic: Ed=B, Eng=G • Work Field: 244, 251 • MPSMS: 704, 723 • Aptitudes: G1, V2, N1, S1, P2, Q3, K3, F3, M3, E5, C4 • Temperaments: D, J, T • Physical: V=L, H=N, L=S, H • Work Env: I, R • Salary: 5 • Outlook: 3

GOE: 05.01.04 Testing & Quality Control

AERONAUTICAL TEST ENGINEER (aircraft-aerospace mfg.) • D.O.T. #002.061-018 • OES #22102 • Performs testing activities on aerospace/aircraft products performing duties as described under TEST ENGINEER (profess. & kin.). • GED: R5, M5, L5 • SVP: 4-10 yrs • Academic: Ed=B, Eng=G • Work Field: 244 • MPSMS: 702 • Aptitudes: G2, V2, N2, S2, P3, Q3, K3, F3, M3, E4, C4 • Temperaments: D, M, T, V • Physical: V=L, H=N, L=L, H • Work Env: I • Salary: 5 • Outlook: 4

AIR ANALYST (profess. & kin.) • D.O.T. #012.261-010 • OES #24599 • AIR TESTER. Analyzes samples of air in industrial establishments or other work areas to determine amount of suspended foreign particles and effectiveness of control methods, using dust collectors: Starts dust collector apparatus that draws air through machine and precipitates dust on tubes, plates, electrodes, or in flasks. Weighs or otherwise determines amount of collected particles, such as lead, rock, or coal dust. Compares weight or count of particles with volume of air passed through machine, and computes percentage of concentration per cubic foot of air tested, using mathematical and chemical formulas. Prepares summary of findings for submission to appropriate department. May recommend remedial measures. • GED: R5, M5, L4 • SVP: 6 mos-1 yr • Academic: Ed=A, Eng=S • Work Field: 211 • MPSMS: 573 • Aptitudes: G2, V3, N2, S3, P3, Q3, K3, F3, M3, E4, C3 • Temperaments: M, T • Physical: V=L, H=L, L=L, W, H • Work Env: I • Salary: 3 • Outlook: 4

CHEMICAL-TEST ENGINEER (profess. & kin.) • D.O.T. #008.061-026 • OES #22114 • Conducts tests on chemicals, fuels, and processes performing duties as described under TEST ENGINEER (profess. & kin.). • GED: R5, M5, L5 • SVP: 4-10 yrs • Academic: Ed=A, Eng=G • Work Field: 211, 244 • MPSMS: 500, 510 • Aptitudes: G2, V2, N2, S2, P3, Q3, K3, F3, M3, E5, C4 • Temperaments: D, M, T, V • Physical: V=L, H=N, L=S, W, H • Work Env: I • Salary: 5 • Outlook: 3

ELECTRICAL TEST ENGINEER (profess. & kin.) • D.O.T. #003.061-014 • OES #22126 • Conducts tests on electrical equipment and systems performing duties as described under TEST ENGINEER (profess. & kin.). • GED: R5, M5, L5 • SVP: 4-10 yrs • Academic: Ed=B, Eng=S • Work Field: 211, 244 • MPSMS: 580, 703 • Aptitudes: G2, V2, N2, S2, P3, Q3, K3, F3, M3, E4, C3 • Temperaments: D, M, T, V • Physical: V=L, H=N, L=L, H • Work Env: B • Salary: 5 • Outlook: 4

FIELD-SERVICE ENGINEER (aircraft-aerospace mfg.) • D.O.T. #002.167-014 • OES #22102 • Investigates performance reports of company manufactured aircraft, space vehicles, missiles or related systems and recommends design changes to eliminate causes of operational or service difficulties: Inspects malfunctioning vehicle to determine cause and required repairs or rework. Writes instructions for and expedites repair work. Performs pre-flight inspections of repaired vehicle to ensure work is completed according to specifications. Analyzes performance reports from customers and field representatives and recommends design or systems changes. May prepare service hand books and bulletins based on field investigations, engineering changes, and overall knowledge of product. May take photographs, or make sketches or drawings, to illustrate faulty equipment, repair or design change, or other recommendations regarding maintenance logistics, engineering design, or systems configuration. • GED: R5, M5, L5 • SVP: 4-10 yrs • Academic: Ed=B, Eng=G • Work Field: 244 • MPSMS: 702 • Aptitudes: G1, V1, N1, S1, P3, Q3, K3, F3, M3, E5, C4 • Temperaments: M, T, V • Physical: V=N, H=L, L=L, W, H • Work Env: I • Salary: 5 • Outlook: 4

METALLOGRAPHER (profess. & kin.) • D.O.T. #011.061-014 • OES #22105 • Conducts microscopic, macro scopic, and other tests and investigations on samples of metals and alloys for purposes as metallurgical control over products or use in developing new or improved grades and types of metals, alloys, or production methods: Directs laboratory personnel in preparing of samples, such as polishing or etching, and designates area of sample where microscopic or macroscopic examination is to be made. Studies photomicrographs and performs microscopic examinations on samples to determine metal characteristics, such as crystal structure, porosity, and homogeniety. Interprets findings and prepares drawings, charts, and graphs for inclusion in reports for reference or instruction purposes, and writes reports regarding findings, conclusions, and recommendations. Coordinates and participates in performing special tests, such as end-quench hardenability, bend and tensile, and grain size tests. • GED: R5, M5, L5 • SVP: 4-10 yrs • Academic: Ed=A, Eng=G • Work Field: 211, 244 • MPSMS: 708, 711, 723 • Aptitudes: G1, V1, N1, S2, P3, Q3, K3, F3, M3, E4, C3 • Temperaments: D, M, T, V • Physical: V=L, H=N, L=S, H • Work Env: I • Salary: 5 • Outlook: 4

METROLOGIST (profess. & kin.) • D.O.T. #012.067-010 • OES #22128 • Develops and evaluates calibration systems that measure characteristics of objects, substances, or phenomena, such as length, mass, time, temperature, electric current, luminous intensity, and derived units of physical or chemical measure: Identifies magnitude of error sources contributing to uncertainty of results to determine reliability of measurement process in quantative terms. Redesigns or adjusts measurement capability to minimize errors. Develops calibration methods and techniques based on principles of measurement science, technical analysis of measurement problems, and accuracy and precision requirements. Directs engineering, quality, and laboratory personnel in design, manufacture, evaluation, and calibration of measurement standards, instruments, and test systems to insure selection of approved instrumentation. Advises others on methods of resolving measurement problems and exchanges information with other metrology personnel through participation in government and industrial standardization committees and professional societies. • **GED:** R6, M6, L6 • **SVP:** 4-10 yrs • **Academic:** Ed=B, Eng=G • **Work Field:** 244 • **MPSMS:** 719 • **Aptitudes:** G2, V2, N1, S2, P2, Q2, K3, F3, M3, E5, C3 • **Temperaments:** D, M, T • **Physical:** V=L, H=N, L=S, H • **Work Env:** I • **Salary:** 5 • **Outlook:** 4

QUALITY-CONTROL ENGINEER (profess. & kin.) • D.O.T. #012.167-054 • OES #22128 • Plans and directs activities concerned with development, application, and maintenance of quality standards for processing materials into partially finished or finished material or product: Develops and initiates methods and procedures for inspection, testing, and evaluation. Devises sampling procedures, designs forms for recording, evaluating, and reporting quality and reliability data, and writes instructions on use of forms. Establishes program to evaluate precision and accuracy of production and processing equipment and testing, measurement, and analytical facilities. Develops and implements methods and procedures for disposition and devises methods to assess cost and responsibility of discrepant material. Directs workers engaged in measuring and testing product and tabulating quality and reliability data. Compiles and writes training material and conducts training sessions on quality control activities. May specialize in any of following areas of quality-control engineering as design, incoming material, process control, product evaluation, inventory control, product reliability, research and development, and administrative application. Usually required to have an engineering degree, such as chemical, mechanical, or electrical engineering which is related to technology of the product evaluated. • **GED:** R6, M6, L6 • **SVP:** 4-10 yrs • **Academic:** Ed=B, Eng=G • **Work Field:** 244 • **MPSMS:** 712 • **Aptitudes:** G1, V1, N1, S2, P2, Q3, K3, F3, M3, E4, C3 • **Temperaments:** J, M, T • **Physical:** V=L, H=N, L=S • **Work Env:** I • **Salary:** 5 • **Outlook:** 5

RELIABILITY ENGINEER (profess. & kin.) • D.O.T. #019.061-026 • OES #22199 • Analyzes preliminary engineering-design concepts of major product, such as aircraft, naval vessel, or electronic communication or control system to recommend design or test methods for attaining customer-specified operational reliability, using knowledge of reliability engineering and other technologies: Analyzes preliminary plans and develops reliability engineering program to achieve customer reliability objectives. Analyzes projected product utilization and calculates cumulative effect on final system reliability of individual part reliabilities. Drafts failure mode and effect analysis sheets or formulates mathematical models, using computer-aided engineering equipment, to identify units posing excessive failure risks and support proposed changes in design. Enters data to simulate electrical inputs, transient conditions, temperature, stress, and other factors to develop computer models, and analyzes and adjusts design to predict and improve system reliability. Advises and confers with engineers in design review meetings to give reliability findings and recommendations. Determines units requiring environmental testing and specifies minimum number of samples to obtain statistically valid data. Reviews subcontractors' proposals for reliability program and submits evaluation for decision. Reviews engineering specifications and drawings, proposing design modifications to improve reliability within cost and other performance requirements. Observes conduct of tests at supplier, plant, or field locations to evaluate reliability factors, such as numbers and causes of unit failures. Monitors failure data generated by customer using product to ascertain potential requirement for product improvement. • **GED:** R6, M6, L5 • **SVP:** 4-10 yrs • **Academic:** Ed=B, Eng=G • **Work Field:** 244 • **MPSMS:** 719 • **Aptitudes:** G1, V1, N1, S2, P2, Q3, K3, F3, M3, E5, C4 • **Temperaments:** D, J, T, V • **Physical:** V=L, H=N, L=S, H • **Work Env:** I • **Salary:** 5 •

Outlook: 4

RESEARCH MECHANIC (aircraft-aerospace mfg.) • D.O.T. #002.280-010 • OES #22599 • LABORATORY TEST MECHANIC; TEST ANALYST, AIRCRAFT. Sets up and operates equipment to test metal aircraft structural, hydraulic, and pneumatic parts, assemblies, and mechanisms, according to standard procedures, to discover faults of design and fabrication: Installs units, such as rib assemblies, struts, landing gears, valves, ducts, universal joints, gears, and motors, in testing equipment and machines, and connects wiring, tubing, couplings, and power sources, using handtools. Operates test equipment and machines to determine factors, such as stress, strain, pressures, turbulences, velocities, flow of fuel, oil and air, wear, and usability of installed units, under conditions of heat, cold, high speeds, torque, and load. Measures induced variations from normal with precision instruments, such as micrometers, verniers, calipers, manometers, pressure gages, flowmeters, strain gages, and dynamometers, and records results for analysis by engineering department. May develop devices, such as flat patterns, contour templates, and forming blocks, using handtools and machine tools, to make mechanical, sheet metal, and plumbing parts and assemblies for experimental test projects. • **GED:** R4, M4, L3 • **SVP:** 2-4 yrs • **Academic:** Ed=H, Eng=G • **Work Field:** 102, 121, 211 • **MPSMS:** 592 • **Aptitudes:** G3, V3, N2, S2, P2, Q3, K3, F3, M3, E5, C5 • **Temperaments:** M, T, V • **Physical:** V=L, H=N, L=L, H • **Work Env:** I • **Salary:** 4 • **Outlook:** 4

STRESS ANALYST (aircraft-aerospace mfg.) • D.O.T. #002.061-030 • OES #22102 • Conducts stress analyses on designs of experimental, prototype, or production aircraft, space vehicles, surface effect vehicles, missiles, and related components to evaluate ability to withstand stresses imposed during flight or ground operations: Analyzes ability of structural components to withstand stresses imposed by load, speed, temperature, performance requirements, and ground tests. Studies preliminary specifications and design requirements to determine strength and bending characteristics of parts, assemblies, and total air frame. Consults with design personnel regarding results of, and need for, additional analysis, testing, or design modifications. May prepare mathematical model of stress problem, or devise other methods of computer analysis or simulation to assist in stress analysis. • **GED:** R5, M5, L5 • **SVP:** 4-10 yrs • **Academic:** Ed=B, Eng=S • **Work Field:** 244 • **MPSMS:** 702 • **Aptitudes:** G1, V1, N1, S2, P2, Q3, K2, F2, M3, E5, C4 • **Temperaments:** J, M, T, V • **Physical:** V=L, H=N, L=S • **Work Env:** I • **Salary:** 5 • **Outlook:** 3

STRESS ANALYST (profess. & kin.) • D.O.T. #007.061-042 • OES #22135 • Conducts stress analyses on engineering designs for electronic components, systems, and products, using mathematical formulas and computer-aided engineering (CAE) systems: Analyzes engineering designs, schematics, and customer specifications to determine stress requirements on product. Formulates mathematical model or three-dimensional computer graphic model of product, using calculator or CAE system. Analyzes ability of product to withstand stress imposed by conditions such as temperature, loads, motion, and vibration, using mathematical formulas and computer simulation. Builds product model of wood or other material, performs physical stress tests on model, and evaluates test results. Consults with ELECTRONICS-DESIGN ENGINEER (profess. & kin.) 003.061-034 to recommend design modifications of product based on results of stress analyses. Prepares stress analysis reports. • **GED:** R6, M6, L5 • **SVP:** 4-10 yrs • **Academic:** Ed=B, Eng=G • **Work Field:** 233, 244 • **MPSMS:** 703 • **Aptitudes:** G1, V1, N1, S1, P2, Q1, K4, F3, M4, E5, C5 • **Temperaments:** J, P, T • **Physical:** V=L, H=N, L=S, H • **Work Env:** I • **Salary:** 5 • **Outlook:** 4

TEST ENGINEER, NUCLEAR EQUIPMENT (profess. & kin.) • D.O.T. #015.061-022 • OES #22117 • Conducts tests on nuclear machinery and equipment performing duties as described under TEST ENGINEER (profess. & kin.). • **GED:** R5, M5, L5 • **SVP:** 4-10 yrs • **Academic:** Ed=B, Eng=S • **Work Field:** 211, 244 • **MPSMS:** 715 • **Aptitudes:** G2, V2, N2, S2, P3, Q3, K3, F3, M3, E4, C4 • **Temperaments:** D, M, P • **Stress:** A • **Physical:** V=L, H=N, L=L, W, H • **Work Env:** I • **Salary:** 5 • **Outlook:** 3

TEST TECHNICIAN (profess. & kin.) • D.O.T. #019.161-014 • OES #22599 • Prepares specifications for fabrication, assembly, and installation of apparatus and control instrumentation used to test experimental or prototype mechanical, electrical, electro-mechanical, hydromechanical, or structural products, and conducts tests and records results, utilizing engineering principles and test technology: Confers with engineering personnel to resolve fabrication problems relating to specifications, and to review test plans, such as types and cycles of tests, conditions under which tests are to be conducted, and duration of tests. Fabricates precision parts for test apparatus, using metal working machines, such as lathes, milling machines, and welding equipment, or interprets specifications for workers fabricating parts. Examines parts for conformance with dimensional specifications, using precision measuring instruments. Coordinates and participates in installing unit or system to be tested in test fixtures, connecting valves, pumps, hydraulic, mechanical or electrical controls, cabling, tubing, power source, and indicating instruments. Activates controls to apply electrical, hydraulic, pneumatic, or mechanical power and subject test item to successive steps in test cycle. Monitors controls and instruments and records test data for engineer's use. May recommend changes in test methods or equipment for engineering review. Workers are classified according to engineering specialty or type of product tested. • **GED:** R5, M4, L4 • **SVP:** 2-4 yrs • **Academic:** Ed=A, Eng=G • **Work Field:** 111, 211, 244 • **MPSMS:** 568, 580, 590 • **Aptitudes:** G2, V2, N2, S2, P2, Q3, K2, F2, M2, E4, C4 • **Temperaments:** M, T, V • **Physical:** V=L, H=N, L=L, H • **Work Env:** I • **Salary:** 4 • **Outlook:** 3

TEST-ENGINE EVALUATOR (petrol. refin.) • D.O.T. #010.261-026 • OES #22599 • RESEARCH-TEST-ENGINE EVALUATOR. Collects and assists in evaluation of data obtained in testing petroleum fuels and lubricants under simulated operating conditions: Inspects engines after test runs have been made by TEST-ENGINE OPERATOR (petrol. refin.), for wear, deposits, and defective parts, using microscope and precision weighing and measuring devices to obtain accurate data. Records findings and assists in analyzing data. Assists in dismantling and reassembling engines during test runs. May obtain and analyze samples of engine-exhaust gas. • **GED:** R4, M4, L4 • **SVP:** 2-4 yrs • **Academic:** Ed=H, Eng=S • **Work Field:** 211 • **MPSMS:** 501 • **Aptitudes:** G3, V3, N3, S3, P2, Q4, K3, F3, M3, E4, C4 • **Temperaments:** M, T • **Physical:** V=L, H=L, L=M, H • **Work Env:** I • **Salary:** 4 • **Outlook:** 4

GOE: 05.01.05 Sales Engineering

SALES ENGINEER, AERONAUTICAL PRODUCTS (aircraft-aerospace mfg.) • D.O.T. #002.151-010 • OES #49002 • Sells aeronautical products and provides customers with technical engineering services as described under SALES ENGINEER (profess. & kin.). • **GED:** R5, M5, L5 • **SVP:** 4-10 yrs • **Academic:** Ed=B, Eng=G • **Work Field:** 244, 292 • **MPSMS:** 702 • **Aptitudes:** G2, V2, N3, S3, P3, Q2, K3, F3, M4, E4, C4 • **Temperaments:** D, I, M, P • **Stress:** E • **Physical:** V=L, H=L, L=L, H • **Work Env:** B, N • **Salary:** 5 • **Outlook:** 4

SALES-ENGINEER, ELECTRONICS PRODUCTS AND SYSTEMS (profess. & kin.) • D.O.T. #003.151-014 • OES #49002 • Sells electronic products and systems and provides technical services to clients performing duties as described under SALES ENGINEER (profess. & kin.). • **GED:** R5, M5, L5 • **SVP:** 4-10 yrs • **Academic:** Ed=A, Eng=G • **Work Field:** 244, 292 • **MPSMS:** 585, 586, 587 • **Aptitudes:** G2, V2, N2, S3, P3, Q3, K4, F4, M4, E4, C3 • **Temperaments:** D, I, M, T • **Physical:** V=L, H=L, L=L, W, H • **Work Env:** B • **Salary:** 5 • **Outlook:** 4

GOE: 05.01.06 Work Planning & Utilization

CONFIGURATION MANAGEMENT ANALYST (profess. & kin.) • D.O.T. #012.167-010 • OES #22128 • Analyzes proposed changes of product design to determine effect on overall system, and coordinates recording of modifications for management control: Confers with manufacturer or customer representatives to establish change-reporting procedure, and prepares directives for change authorization and documentation by company and subcontractor personnel. Analyzes proposed part-design changes and exhibits to prepare report of effect on overall product for management action, using knowledge of engineering, manufacturing, and procurement activities. Confers with department managers to obtain additional information or to interpret policies and procedures for reporting changes in product design. Audits subcontractor's inspection or technical documents preparation procedure to verify compliance with contract requirements. Coordinates activities of personnel preparing manual or automated records of part-design change documents and first-article configuration inspection. • **GED:** R5, M4, L5 • **SVP:** 4-10 yrs • **Academic:** Ed=B, Eng=S • **Work Field:** 211, 282 • **MPSMS:** 700, 710 • **Aptitudes:** G2, V2, N2, S3, P3, Q2, K4, F4, M4, E5, C5 • **Temperaments:** D, M, T, V • **Physical:** V=G, H=L, L=L • **Work Env:** I • **Salary:** 5 • **Outlook:** 4

COST-ANALYSIS ENGINEER (aircraft-aerospace mfg.) • D.O.T. #002.167-010 • OES #22102 • VALUE ENGINEER. Coordinates analysis of aircraft or aerospace vehicle designs to effect maximum utilization of materials, methods, and processes in meeting cost objectives and quality specifications: Examines parts and components to ascertain purpose, cost, and value, utilizing knowledge of product design and budgetary considerations. Recommends changes in product design to effect greatest economy in production methods and material costs. Suggests policies regarding use of forgings, castings, die-formed parts, machining operations, assembly, fabrication, and welding. Submits reports to assist in developing budget for value-engineering activities. Confers with representatives of tooling and production departments to advise in coordination of overall design. • **GED:** R6, M5, L6 • **SVP:** 2-4 yrs • **Academic:** Ed=B, Eng=G • **Work Field:** 244 • **MPSMS:** 712 • **Aptitudes:** G2, V2, N2, S1, P2, Q3, K4, F4, M4, E4, C4 • **Temperaments:** D, M, P • **Physical:** V=N, H=N, L=S, H • **Work Env:** I • **Salary:** 4 • **Outlook:** 4

DOCUMENTATION ENGINEER (profess. & kin.) • D.O.T. #012.167-078 • OES #22128 • Plans, directs, and coordinates preparation of project documentation, such as engineering drawings, production specifications and schedules, and contract modifications, to ensure customer contract requirements are met: Reviews contract to determine documentation required for each phase of project, applying knowledge of engineering and manufacturing processes. Schedules due dates for drawings, specifications, software, technical manuals, and other documents. Monitors status of project to ensure documentation is submitted according to schedule. Reviews and verifies project documents for completeness, format, and compliance to contract requirements. Submits project documentation to management for approval, and transmits approved documents to customer. Confers with engineers, managers, customers, and others to discuss project, prepare documents, or modify contract schedules. • **GED:** R5, M5, L5 • **SVP:** 4-10 yrs • **Academic:** Ed=A, Eng=S • **Work Field:** 244 • **MPSMS:** 712 • **Aptitudes:** G1, V1, N1, S1, P2, Q1, K4, F4, M4, E5, C5 • **Temperaments:** J, P, T • **Physical:** V=L, H=L, L=L • **Work Env:** I • **Salary:** 5 • **Outlook:** 5

FACILITIES PLANNER (any ind.) • D.O.T. #019.261-018 • OES #39999 • OFFICE-PLANNING REPRESENTATIVE. Plans utilization of space and facilities for government agency or unit or business establishment consistent with requirements of organizational efficiency and available facilities and funds: Inspects buildings and office areas to evaluate suitability for occupancy, considering such factors as air circulation, lighting, location, and size. Measures or directs workers engaged in measurement of facilities to determine total square footage available for occupancy. Computes square footage available for each member of staff to determine whether minimum space restrictions can be met. Draws design layout, showing location of furniture, equipment, doorways, electrical and telephone outlets, and other facilities. May review real estate contracts for compliance with government specifications and suitability for occupancy of employing agency. May direct workers engaged in moving furniture and equipment and preparing facilities for occupancy. • **GED:** R5, M5, L5 • **SVP:** 2-4 yrs • **Academic:** Ed=A, Eng=G • **Work Field:** 211, 242 • **MPSMS:** 719 • **Aptitudes:** G2, V2, N2, S2, P3, Q3, K3, F2, M3, E5, C3 • **Temperaments:** D, J, M • **Physical:** V=L, H=N, L=S, W, H • **Work Env:** I • **Salary:** 4 • **Outlook:** 3

FACTORY LAY-OUT ENGINEER (profess. & kin.) • D.O.T.

#012.167-018 • OES #22128 • **PLANNING ENGINEER**. Plans layout of complete departments of industrial plant or commercial establishment to provide maximum possible operating efficiency: Measures and studies available floor space and draws plan of floor space to scale, using drafting tools. Studies sequence of operations to be performed and flow of materials. Studies and measures machines, conveyors, benches, furnaces, and other equipment. Coordinates all available knowledge and information into a finished scale drawing, showing most efficient location for each piece of equipment and necessary working area around each. • **GED:** R5, M5, L5 • **SVP:** 4-10 yrs • **Academic:** Ed=B, Eng=G • **Work Field:** 244 • **MPSMS:** 712 • **Aptitudes:** G2, V2, N2, S2, P2, Q3, K3, F3, M3, E5, C5 • **Temperaments:** D, M, T • **Physical:** V=L, H=N, L=S, H • **Work Env:** I • **Salary:** 5 • **Outlook:** 4

INDUSTRIAL ENGINEER (profess. & kin.) • D.O.T. #012.167-030 • OES #22128 • Plans utilization of production facilities and personnel to improve efficiency of operations in industrial establishment: Studies functional statements, organization charts, and project information to determine functions and responsibilities of various workers and work units. Identifies areas of overlap in duties and responsibilities. Establishes work measurement programs and makes sample observations of work to develop standards of manpower utilization. Analyzes utilization of manpower and machines in units and develops work simplification programs in areas, such as work distribution, work count, process flow, economy of worker motions, and layout of unit. Plans space layout of units to attain objectives of work measurement and simplification studies. May prepare recommendations for reorganization of units and job duties to increase efficiency and eliminate excess processing steps and labor costs and be known as EFFICIENCY ENGINEER (profess. & kin.). • **GED:** R5, M5, L5 • **SVP:** 2-4 yrs • **Academic:** Ed=B, Eng=G • **Work Field:** 244 • **MPSMS:** 712 • **Aptitudes:** G1, V1, N1, S2, P3, Q3, K3, F3, M3, E5, C5 • **Temperaments:** D, M, T, V • **Physical:** V=N, H=N, L=S • **Work Env:** I • **Salary:** 5 • **Outlook:** 4

LAND SURVEYOR (profess. & kin.) • D.O.T. #018.167-018 • OES #22311 • Plans, organizes, and directs work of one or more survey parties engaged in surveying Earth's surface to determine precise location and measurements of points, elevations, lines, areas, and contours for construction, mapmaking, land division, titles, mining or other purposes: Researches previous survey evidence, maps, deeds, physical evidence, and other records to obtain data needed for surveys. Develops new data from photogrammetric records. Determines methods and procedures for establishing or reestablishing survey control. Keeps accurate notes, records, and sketches to describe and certify work performed. Coordinates findings with work of engineering and architectural personnel, clients, and others concerned with project. Assumes legal responsibility for work and is licensed by State. • **GED:** R5, M5, L4 • **SVP:** 2-4 yrs • **Academic:** Ed=A, Eng=G • **Work Field:** 243 • **MPSMS:** 716 • **Aptitudes:** G2, V3, N2, S2, P2, Q3, K3, F3, M3, E3, C3 • **Temperaments:** D, M, T • **Physical:** V=G, H=N, L=S, W, C, H • **Work Env:** O • **Salary:** 5 • **Outlook:** 4

MANAGEMENT ANALYST (profess. & kin.) • D.O.T. #161.167-010 • OES #21905 • SYSTEMS ANALYST. Analyzes business or operating procedures to devise most efficient methods of accomplishing work: Plans study of work problems and procedures, such as organizational change, communications, information flow, integrated production methods, inventory control, or cost analysis. Gathers and organizes information on problem or procedures including present operating procedures. Analyzes data gathered, develops information and considers all available solutions or alternate methods of proceeding. Organizes and documents findings of studies and prepares recommendations for implementation of new systems, procedures or organizational changes. Confers with personnel concerned to assure smooth functioning of newly implemented systems or procedure. May install new systems and train personnel in application. May conduct operational effectiveness reviews to ensure functional or project systems are applied as designed and functioning satisfactorily. May develop or update functional or operating manuals outlining established methods of performing work in accordance with organizational policy. • **GED:** R5, M5, L5 • **SVP:** 2-4 yrs • **Academic:** Ed=B, Eng=G • **Work Field:** 232 • **MPSMS:** 890 • **Aptitudes:** G2, V2, N2, S3, P3, Q2, K4, F4, M4, E4, C5 • **Temper-**

aments: J, M, P • **Stress:** E • **Physical:** V=L, H=L, L=S • **Work Env:** I • **Salary:** 4 • **Outlook:** 3

MANUFACTURING ENGINEER (profess. & kin.) • D.O.T. #012.167-042 • OES #22128 • Directs and coordinates manufacturing processes in industrial plant: Determines space requirements for various functions and plans or improves production methods including layout, production flow, tooling and production equipment, material, fabrication, assembly methods, and manpower requirements. Communicates with planning and design staffs concerning product design and tooling to assure efficient production methods. Estimates production times and determines optimum staffing for production schedules. Applies statistical methods to estimate future manufacturing requirements and potential. Approves or arranges approval for expenditures. Reports to management on manufacturing capacities, production schedules, and problems to facilitate decision-making. • **GED:** R5, M5, L5 • **SVP:** 4-10 yrs • **Academic:** Ed=B, Eng=G • **Work Field:** 244 • **MPSMS:** 706 • **Aptitudes:** G1, V1, N2, S1, P2, Q3, K4, F4, M4, E5, C5 • **Temperaments:** D, M, T • **Physical:** V=L, H=N, L=S • **Work Env:** I • **Salary:** 5 • **Outlook:** 4

MATERIALS ENGINEER (profess. & kin.) • D.O.T. #019.061-014 • OES #22105 • Evaluates technical and economic factors, recommending engineering and manufacturing actions for attainment of design objectives of process or product by applying knowledge of material science and related technologies: Reviews plans for new product and factors, such as strength, weight, and cost to submit material selection recommendations insuring attainment of design objectives. Plans and implements laboratory operations to develop material and fabrication procedures for new materials to fulfill product cost and performance standards. Confers with producers of materials, such as metals, ceramics, or polymers during investigation and evaluation of materials suitable for specific product applications. Reviews product failure data and interprets laboratory tests and analyses to establish or rule out material and process causes. • **GED:** R5, M5, L5 • **SVP:** 4-10 yrs • **Academic:** Ed=B, Eng=G • **Work Field:** 244 • **MPSMS:** 700, 710 • **Aptitudes:** G2, V2, N2, S2, P2, Q3, K3, F3, M3, E5, C4 • **Temperaments:** D, M, T, V • **Physical:** V=L, H=N, L=S, H • **Work Env:** I • **Salary:** 5 • **Outlook:** 3

METALLURGIST, EXTRACTIVE (profess. & kin.) • D.O.T. #011.061-018 • OES #22105 • METALLURGIST, PROCESS. Originates, controls, and develops flotation, smelting, electrolytic, and other processes used in winning metals from their ores, for producing iron and steel, or for refining gold, silver, zinc, copper, and other metals: Studies ore reduction problems to determine most efficient methods of producing metals commercially. Controls temperature adjustments, charge mixtures, and other variables in blast-furnace operations and steel-melting furnaces to obtain pig iron and steel of specified metallurgical characteristics and qualities. Investigates methods of improving metallurgical processes, as in the reduction of alumina by electrolytic methods to produce aluminum, the distillation of molten ore to purify zinc, or selective oxidation methods to extract lead, nickel, mercury, and other nonferrous metals from their ores. • **GED:** R6, M6, L6 • **SVP:** 4-10 yrs • **Academic:** Ed=B, Eng=G • **Work Field:** 244, 251 • **MPSMS:** 708, 711, 723 • **Aptitudes:** G1, V1, N1, S2, P3, Q3, K3, F3, M3, E4, C3 • **Temperaments:** D, M, T, V • **Physical:** V=G, H=N, L=S, H • **Work Env:** I • **Salary:** 5 • **Outlook:** 4

MINING ENGINEER (mining) • D.O.T. #010.061-014 • OES #22108 • Determines location and plans extraction of coal, metallic ores, nonmetallic minerals, and building materials, such as stone or gravel: Conducts or collaborates in geological exploration to determine location, size, accessibility, and estimated value of deposit. Determines most effective and economical method or combination of methods of extraction according to depth of overburden and character of deposit and surrounding strata. Plans location and development of shafts, tunnels, and chambers. Plans height and placement of excavation benches (levels) and type and capacity of excavation and haulage equipment, such as power shovels and trucks for open pit or strip mining. Devises methods and locations for storing and replacing excavated soils to reclaim mining sites. Lays out and directs construction and operation of access roads, water, power supply, drainage, ventilation, rail and conveyor systems, and materials separating, cleaning, grading, and reduction

facilities. Plans and coordinates utilization of manpower and equipment consistent with efficiency and safety. May apply knowledge of mining engineering to solve problems concerned with environment [ENVIRONMENTAL ENGINEER (profess. & kin.)].
• **GED:** R5, M5, L5 • **SVP:** 4-10 yrs • **Academic:** Ed=B, Eng=G • **Work Field:** 244 • **MPSMS:** 708, 711 • **Aptitudes:** G2, V2, N2, S2, P3, Q3, K3, F3, M3, E5, C5 • **Temperaments:** D, M, T, V • **Physical:** V=N, H=N, L=S, H • **Work Env:** B, W, R • **Salary:** 5 • **Outlook:** 2

PREVENTIVE MAINTENANCE COORDINATOR (any ind.) • D.O.T. #169.167-074 • OES #21905 • Plans and coordinates schedule of preventive maintenance for equipment, machinery, tools, and/or buildings: Reviews manufacturers' service manuals, own establishment's usage schedules, and records of maintenance problems to determine optimum frequency of preventive maintenance. Studies production and operation schedules and confers with other staff and with maintenance supervisors to determine when planned maintenance will least interfere with operation of establishment. Estimates costs of personnel, parts, and supplies to be used during scheduled maintenance. Maintains records of planned and completed maintenance. May develop and coordinate plans for reconstruction and/or installation of new equipment, machinery, and/or buildings. May direct and coordinate activities of subordinate staff, such as MAINTENANCE DATA ANALYST (military ser.) 221.367-038. May direct and coordinate activities of maintenance workers. • **GED:** R4, M3, L3 • **SVP:** 2-4 yrs • **Academic:** Ed=H, Eng=S • **Work Field:** 271, 295 • **MPSMS:** 893 • **Aptitudes:** G2, V2, N2, S3, P3, Q3, K5, F5, M4, E5, C5 • **Temperaments:** D, J, T, V • **Stress:** A • **Physical:** V=L, H=L, L=L • **Work Env:** I • **Salary:** 4 • **Outlook:** 3

PRODUCTION ENGINEER (profess. & kin.) • D.O.T. #012.167-046 • OES #22128 • Plans and coordinates production procedures in an industrial plant: Directs production departments. Regulates and coordinates functions of office and shop. Introduces more efficient production line methods. Initiates and directs other procedures to increase company output. • **GED:** R5, M5, L5 • **SVP:** 2-4 yrs • **Academic:** Ed=A, Eng=S • **Work Field:** 244 • **MPSMS:** 712 • **Aptitudes:** G2, V2, N2, S3, P2, Q3, K3, F3, M3, E4, C4 • **Temperaments:** D, M, T, V • **Stress:** A • **Physical:** V=L, H=L, L=S • **Work Env:** I • **Salary:** 4 • **Outlook:** 4

PRODUCTION PLANNER (profess. & kin.) • D.O.T. #012.167-050 • OES #22128 • PLANNER, CHIEF; PLANNING SUPERVISOR; PROCESS PLANNER; PRODUCTION-PLANNING SUPERVISOR; PRODUCTION SCHEDULER; SCHEDULER; TOOL-AND-PRODUCTION PLANNER. Plans and prepares production schedules for manufacture of industrial or commercial products: Draws up master schedule to establish sequence and lead time of each operation to meet shipping dates according to sales forecasts or customer orders. Analyzes production specifications and plant capacity data and performs mathematical calculations to determine manufacturing processes, tools, and manpower requirements. Plans and schedules workflow for each department and operation according to previously established manufacturing sequences and lead times. Plans sequence of fabrication, assembly, installation, and other manufacturing operations for guidance of production workers. Confers with department supervisors to determine status of assigned projects. Expedites operations that delay schedules and alters schedules to meet unforeseen conditions. Prepares production reports. May prepare lists of required materials, tools, and equipment. May prepare purchase orders to obtain materials, tools, and equipment. • **GED:** R5, M5, L5 • **SVP:** 2-4 yrs • **Academic:** Ed=B, Eng=G • **Work Field:** 244 • **MPSMS:** 712 • **Aptitudes:** G2, V2, N2, S2, P3, Q3, K4, F4, M4, E5, C5 • **Temperaments:** D, M, V • **Physical:** V=L, H=L, L=S • **Work Env:** I • **Salary:** 4 • **Outlook:** 4

STANDARDS ENGINEER (profess. & kin.) • D.O.T. #012.061-018 • OES #22128 • Establishes engineering and technical limitations and applications for items, materials, processes, methods, designs, and engineering practices for use by designers of machines and equipment, such as aircraft, automobiles, and space vehicles: Communicates with management of industrial organization to maintain knowledge of current and proposed projects in order to develop appropriate standards for design and production of new items. Evaluates data in scientific journals, suppliers' catalogs, government standards documents, and other sources of information on materials, processes, and parts to update knowledge of available resources. Prepares specification sheets and standard drawings designating parts and materials acceptable for specific uses, using knowledge of primary engineering discipline and relates disciplines. Examines all factors involved to confirm that standards will result in most economic use of material and labor consistent with safety and durability of final product. Reviews standards prepared with other departmental specialists to assure consistency with existing standards and those in other specialized disciplines. Communicates with user personnel to confirm knowledge of standards and cooperation of various project groups. Follows established procedures for retention of data developed to assure optimum storage and retrieval by manual or automated methods. • **GED:** R5, M5, L5 • **SVP:** 4-10 yrs • **Academic:** Ed=B, Eng=G • **Work Field:** 244 • **MPSMS:** 719 • **Aptitudes:** G1, V1, N1, S1, P2, Q3, K3, F4, M4, E5, C3 • **Temperaments:** J, M, T, V • **Physical:** V=L, H=L, L=S, W, H • **Work Env:** I • **Salary:** 5 • **Outlook:** 4

TIME-STUDY ENGINEER (profess. & kin.) • D.O.T. #012.167-070 • OES #22128 • EFFICIENCY EXPERT; MANAGER, PRODUCTION; METHODS-AND-PROCEDURES ANALYST; PRODUCTION ENGINEER; PRODUCTION EXPERT; TIME-STUDY ANALYST; WORK-MEASUREMENT ENGINEER. Develops work measurement procedures and directs time-and-motion studies to promote efficient and economical utilization of personnel and facilities: Directs or conducts observation and analysis of personnel and work procedures to determine time- and-motion requirements of job duties. Analyzes work study data and equipment specifications to establish time and production standards. Applies mathematical analysis to determine validity and reliability of sampling and work study statistics. Applies principles of industrial engineering and applied psychology to evaluate work methods proposals and to develop recommendations to management affecting work methods, wage rates, and budget decisions. Trains INDUSTRIAL ENGINEERING TECHNICIAN (profess. & kin.) in time-and-motion study principles and techniques. • **GED:** R5, M5, L5 • **SVP:** 4-10 yrs • **Academic:** Ed=B, Eng=G • **Work Field:** 244 • **MPSMS:** 712 • **Aptitudes:** G1, V1, N1, S2, P2, Q3, K4, F4, M4, E5, C4 • **Temperaments:** D, J, M, T • **Physical:** V=L, H=N, L=S, W • **Work Env:** I • **Salary:** 5 • **Outlook:** 3

TOOL PLANNER (any ind.) • D.O.T. #012.167-074 • OES #22128 • PROCESSOR. Analyzes blueprints or prototype parts to determine tools, fixtures, and equipment needed for manufacture and plans sequence of operations for fabrication and assembly of products, such as aircraft assemblies, automobile parts, cutting tools, or ball bearings: Studies engineering blueprints, drawings, models, and other specifications to obtain data on proposed part. Applies knowledge of functions and processes of various departments and capacities of machines and equipment to determine tool requirements and establish sequence of operations to fabricate and assemble parts. Lists operations to be performed on routing card or paper, indicates machines, cutting tools, fixtures, and other equipment to be used, and estimates times needed to perform each operation. May prepare reports for PRODUCTION PLANNER (profess. & kin.) in scheduling work for entire plant. May plan tool and operation sequences for only one department. May specify type of material to be used in construction of tools. • **GED:** R5, M5, L5 • **SVP:** 4-10 yrs • **Academic:** Ed=A, Eng=G • **Work Field:** 244 • **MPSMS:** 712 • **Aptitudes:** G2, V2, N2, S2, P3, Q3, K4, F4, M4, E5, C5 • **Temperaments:** D, M • **Physical:** V=L, H=N, L=S, H • **Work Env:** I • **Salary:** 5 • **Outlook:** 4

TOOL PROGRAMER, NUMERICAL CONTROL (any ind.) • D.O.T. #007.167-018 • OES #25111 • COMPUTER-PROGRAMER, NUMERICAL MACHINE TOOL; TOOL-AND-PRODUCTION PLANNER, NUMERICAL CONTROL; TOOL PROGRAMER, AUTOMATIC; TOOL PROGRAMER, TAPE. Plans numerical control tape program to control contour-path machining of metal parts on automatic machine tools by means of magnetic or perforated tape: Analyzes part drawings, sketches, and design data to determine dimension and configuration of cuts, selecting cutting tools, and machine speeds and feeds, according to knowledge of machine shop processes. Determines reference points and direction of machine cutting paths. Computes angular and linear dimensions, radii, and curvatures, and outlines sequence of operations required to machine part. Prepares geometric layout on graph paper to show location of reference points and direction of cutting paths, using drafting instruments. Writes instruction sheets and cutter lists to guide setup and operation of machine. Writes program sheet of machine instructions in symbolic language to encode control tape for regulating tool movement along planned cutting path. Compares encoded tape with original program sheet to assure accuracy of machine instructions. Revises program to eliminate instruction errors or omissions. Observes operation of machine on trial run to prove taped instructions. May program numerical control tape for point-to-point and straight-cut machining operations and be designated accordingly. • **GED:** R5, M4, L4 • **SVP:** 4-10 yrs • **Academic:** Ed=A, Eng=S • **Work Field:** 241, 244 • **MPSMS:** 566, 706 • **Aptitudes:** G2, V3, N2, S2, P2, Q3, K4, F4, M4, E5, C5 • **Temperaments:** D, M, T • **Physical:** V=G, H=N, L=S • **Work Env:** I • **Salary:** 4 • **Outlook:** 4

TOOL PROGRAMMER, NUMERICAL CONTROL (electronics) • D.O.T. #609.262-010 • OES #25111 • PROGRAMMER OPERATOR, NUMERICAL CONTROL; SOFT TOOLING TECHNICIAN. Operates optical programming (digitizing) equipment to generate numerical control (NC) tape program used to control NC machine tools that drill, mill, rout, or notch printed circuit boards (PCBs): Analyzes drawings, specifications and phototool (photographic film copy of printed circuit pattern) to determine program input data, such as hole sizes, tool sizes, reference points, and direction of machine cutting paths, and calculates data, such as starting point coordinates (location), size of panels or boards, and number of boards per panel. Draws machine tool paths on phototool, using colored markers, and following guidelines for tool speed and efficiency, to prepare phototool for use as tool programming aid. Aligns and secures phototool on reference table of optical programmer. Observes enlarger scope of programmer that projects image of circuit board pattern from phototool. Moves reference table, following previously marked paths to align phototool circuit pattern holes with reference marks on enlarger scope. Depresses pedal or pushes button of programmer to enter coordinates of hole locations into program memory. Repeats process for each hole location on phototool to enter NC machine instructions, such as hole locations, machine paths, and reference points. Keys in additional instructions, such as tool size, machine feed and speed rates, and starting point coordinates, basing entries on specifications, calculations, and knowledge of machine capabilities and programming techniques. Types commands on keyboard to generate NC tape. Observes trial run of NC machine to verify tape program accuracy. Revises NC tape program to eliminate instruction errors. May operate NC machine tools on production basis. • **GED:** R3, M3, L3 • **SVP:** 6 mos-1 yr • **Academic:** Ed=A, Eng=S • **Work Field:** 111, 233 • **MPSMS:** 706 • **Aptitudes:** G3, V3, N3, S2, P2, Q2, K3, F3, M3, E4, C4 • **Temperaments:** J, T, V • **Physical:** V=L, H=N, L=S, H • **Work Env:** I • **Salary:** 3 • **Outlook:** 4

UTILIZATION ENGINEER (light, heat, & power) • D.O.T. #007.061-034 • OES #22135 • Solves engineering problems concerned with industrial utilization of gas as source of power: Studies industrial processes to determine where and how application of gas fuel-consuming equipment can be made. Designs equipment to meet process requirements. Examines gas-powered equipment after installation to insure proper functioning. Investigates equipment failures and difficulties and diagnoses faulty operation. Corrects or makes recommendations to maintenance crew to correct faults. Conducts safety, breakdown, and other engineering tests on gas fuel-consuming equipment to ascertain efficiency and safety of design and construction. May solve problems concerned with other gas-consuming equipment, such as air-conditioning and heating. • **GED:** R5, M5, L5 • **SVP:** 4-10 yrs • **Academic:** Ed=B, Eng=S • **Work Field:** 244 • **MPSMS:** 706 • **Aptitudes:** G2, V2, N2, S2, P2, Q3, K4, F4, M4, E5, C4 • **Temperaments:** D, J, M, T, V • **Physical:** V=G, H=N, L=S • **Work Env:** I • **Salary:** 5 • **Outlook:** 3

GOE: 05.01.07 Design

AERONAUTICAL ENGINEER (profess. & kin.) • D.O.T. #002.061-014 • OES #22102 • Designs, develops, and tests aircraft, space vehicles, surface effect vehicles, and missiles, applying engineering principles and techniques: Designs and develops commercial, military, executive, general aviation or special purpose aircraft; space vehicles, satellites, missiles, scientific probes; or other related hardware or systems. Tests models, prototypes, subassemblies, or production vehicles to study and evaluate operational characteristics and effects of stress imposed during actual or simulated flight conditions. May specialize in design and development of structural components, such as wings, fuselage, rib assemblies, landing gear, or operational control systems. May specialize in analytical programs concerned with ground or flight testing, or development of acoustic, thermodynamic or propulsion systems. May assist in planning technical phases of air transportation systems or other aspects of flight operations, maintenance or logistics. • **GED:** R6, M6, L6 • **SVP:** 4-10 yrs • **Academic:** Ed=B, Eng=G • **Work Field:** 244 • **MPSMS:** 702 • **Aptitudes:** G1, V1, N1, S1, P3, Q3, K3, F3, M3, E5, C5 • **Temperaments:** D, J, M, T, V • **Physical:** V=L, H=N, L=S, H • **Work Env:** B • **Salary:** 5 • **Outlook:** 4

AERONAUTICAL-DESIGN ENGINEER (aircraft-aerospace mfg.) • D.O.T. #002.061-022 • OES #22102 • Develops basic design concepts used in design, development, and production of aeronautical/aerospace products and systems performing duties as described under DESIGN ENGINEER, PRODUCTS (profess. & kin.). • **GED:** R5, M5, L5 • **SVP:** 4-10 yrs • **Academic:** Ed=B, Eng=G • **Work Field:** 244, 251 • **MPSMS:** 702 • **Aptitudes:** G2, V2, N2, S2, P2, Q2, K3, F3, M3, E4, C4 • **Temperaments:** J, M, T, V • **Physical:** V=L, H=N, L=S, H • **Work Env:** I • **Salary:** 5 • **Outlook:** 4

AGRICULTURAL-ENGINEERING TECHNICIAN (profess. & kin.) • D.O.T. #013.161-010 • OES #22599 • Prepares original layout and completes detailed drawings of agricultural machinery and equipment, such as farm machinery, irrigation, power, and electrification systems, soil and water conservation equipment and agricultural harvesting and processing equipment: Applies biological and engineering knowledge, design principles and theories to insure compliance with company policy, and an end product which will perform as required. Maintains working knowledge of functions, operations, and maintenance of various types of equipment and materials used in the industry to assure appropriate utilization. • **GED:** R5, M5, L4 • **SVP:** 2-4 yrs • **Academic:** Ed=A, Eng=S • **Work Field:** 244 • **MPSMS:** 713 • **Aptitudes:** G2, V3, N2, S2, P2, Q3, K3, F3, M3, E5, C4 • **Temperaments:** M, T • **Physical:** V=L, H=N, L=S, H • **Work Env:** I • **Salary:** 4 • **Outlook:** 3

AIRPORT ENGINEER (profess. & kin.) • D.O.T. #005.061-010 • OES #22121 • Plans and lays out airports and landing fields and directs construction work involved in leveling fields, laying out and surfacing runways, and providing drainage: Designs runways based on weight and size of aircraft and prepares material and construction specifications. Directs or participates in surveying to lay out installations and establish reference points, grades, and elevations to guide construction. Estimates costs to provide basis for payments to contractor. Observes progress of construction to insure workmanship is in conformity with specifications and advises SUPERINTENDENT, CONSTRUCTION (const.) regarding necessary corrections. May serve as agent or employee of contractor and study plans and specifications to recommend special equipment or procedures to reduce time and cost of construction. May schedule delivery of materials, analyze costs, and provide technical advice in solution of construction problems. • **GED:** R5, M5, L5 • **SVP:** 4-10 yrs • **Academic:** Ed=B, Eng=G • **Work Field:** 244 • **MPSMS:** 704 • **Aptitudes:** G2, V2, N2, S2, P2, Q2, K3, F3, M3, E4, C3 • **Temperaments:** D, M, T, V • **Physical:** V=L, H=N, L=S, H • **Work Env:** B • **Salary:** 5 • **Outlook:** 4

ARCHITECT (profess. & kin.) • D.O.T. #001.061-010 • OES #22302 • Provides professional services in research, development, design, construction, alteration, or repair of real property, such as private residences, office buildings, theaters, public buildings, or factories: Consults with client to determine functional and spatial requirements and prepares information regarding design, specifications, materials, equipment, estimated costs, and building time. Plans layout of project and integrates engineering elements into unified design. Prepares scale and full size drawings and contract documents for building contractors. Furnishes sample recommendations and shop drawing reviews to client. Assists client in obtaining bids and awarding construction contracts. Supervises administration of construction contracts and conducts periodic onsite observation of work in progress. May prepare operating and maintenance manuals, studies, and reports. • **GED:** R6, M6, L6 • **SVP:** 4-10 yrs • **Academic:** Ed=M, Eng=G • **Work Field:** 244 • **MPSMS:** 701 • **Aptitudes:** G1, V2, N1, S1, P1, Q3, K4, F3, M3, E5, C3 • **Temperaments:** I, J, P • **Physical:** V=G, H=N, L=S, H • **Work Env:** I • **Salary:** 5 • **Outlook:** 1

ARCHITECT, MARINE (profess. & kin.) • D.O.T. #001.061-014 • OES #22305 • ARCHITECT, NAVAL; NAVAL DESIGNER. Designs and oversees construction and repair of marine craft and floating structures, such as ships, barges, tugs, dredges, submarines, torpedoes, floats, and buoys: Studies design proposals and specifications to establish basic characteristics of craft, such as size, weight, speed, propulsion, armament, cargo, displacement, draft, crew and passenger complements, and fresh or salt water service. Oversees construction and testing of prototype in model basin and develops sectional and waterline curves of hull to establish center of gravity, ideal hull form, and buoyancy and stability data. Designs complete hull and super structure according to specifications and test data, in conformity with standards of safety, efficiency, and economy. Designs layout of craft interior including cargo space, passenger compartments, ladder wells, and elevators. Confers with MARINE ENGINEERS (profess. & kin.) to establish arrangement of boiler room equipment and propulsion machinery, heating and ventilating systems, refrigeration equipment, piping, and other functional equipment. Evaluates performance of craft during dock and sea trials to determine design changes and conformance with national and international standards. • **GED:** R6, M6, L6 • **SVP:** Over 10 yrs • **Academic:** Ed=B, Eng=G • **Work Field:** 244 • **MPSMS:** 714 • **Aptitudes:** G1, V1, N1, S1, P2, Q2, K2, F3, M3, E5, C4 • **Temperaments:** D, M, T, V • **Physical:** V=L, H=N, L=L, H • **Work Env:** I • **Salary:** 5 • **Outlook:** 2

CERAMIC DESIGN ENGINEER (profess. & kin.) • D.O.T. #006.061-010 • OES #22105 • Designs ceramics manufacturing equipment and products performing duties as de scribed under DESIGN ENGINEER, FACILITIES (profess. & kin.); DESIGN ENGINEER, PRODUCTS (profess. & kin.). • **GED:** R5, M5, L5 • **SVP:** 4-10 yrs • **Academic:** Ed=A, Eng=G • **Work Field:** 244 • **MPSMS:** 742, 743 • **Aptitudes:** G2, V2, N2, S2, P3, Q4, K4, F4, M4, E4, C3 • **Temperaments:** D, M, T • **Physical:** V=L, H=N, L=S, H • **Work Env:** I • **Salary:** 5 • **Outlook:** 4

CERAMIC ENGINEER (profess. & kin.) • D.O.T. #006.061-014 • OES #22105 • Conducts research, designs machinery, develops processing techniques, and directs technical work concerned with manufacture of ceramic products: Directs testing of physical, chemical, and heat-resisting properties of materials, such as clays and silicas. Analyzes results of test to determine combinations of materials which will improve quality of products. Conducts research into methods of processing, forming, and firing of clays to develop new ceramic products, such as ceramic machine tools, refractories for space vehicles, and for use in glass and steel furnaces. Designs equipment and apparatus for forming, firing, and handling products. Coordinates testing activities of finished products for characteristics, such as texture, color, durability, glazing, and refractory properties. May specialize in one branch of ceramic production, such as brick, glass, crockery, tile, pipe, or refractories. May specialize in developing heat-resistant and corrosion-resistant materials for use in aerospace, electronics, and nuclear energy fields. nuclear energy field. • **GED:** R6, M6, L6 • **SVP:** 4-10 yrs • **Academic:** Ed=B, Eng=G • **Work Field:** 244, 251 • **MPSMS:** 705 • **Aptitudes:** G1, V1, N1, S1, P2, Q1, K4, F3, M4, E5, C3 • **Temperaments:** D, M, T, V • **Physical:** V=L, H=N, L=S, H • **Work Env:** I, R • **Salary:** 5 • **Outlook:** 4

CHEMICAL DESIGN ENGINEER, PROCESSES (profess. & kin.) • D.O.T. #008.061-014 • OES #22114 • Designs equipment and processes to produce chemical changes in elements and compounds performing duties as described under DESIGN ENGINEER, FACILITIES (profess. & kin.). • **GED:** R5, M5, L5 • **SVP:** 4-10 yrs • **Academic:** Ed=B, Eng=G • **Work Field:** 147, 244 • **MPSMS:** 707 • **Aptitudes:** G2, V2, N2, S2, P3, Q3, K3, F3, M3, E5, C4 • **Temperaments:** D, M, T • **Physical:** V=L, H=N, L=S, H • **Work Env:** I • **Salary:** 5 • **Outlook:** 4

CHEMICAL ENGINEER (profess. & kin.) • D.O.T. #008.061-018

• OES #22114 • Designs equipment and develops processes for manufacturing chemicals and related products utilizing principles and technology of chemistry, physics, mathematics, engineering and related physical and natural sciences: Conducts research to develop new and improved chemical manufacturing processes. Designs, plans layout, and oversees workers engaged in constructing, controlling, and improving equipment to carry out chemical processes on commercial scale. Analyzes operating procedures and equipment and machinery functions to reduce processing time and cost. Designs equipment to control movement, storage, and packaging of solids, liquids, and gases. Designs and plans measurement and control systems for chemical plants based on data collected in laboratory experiments and pilot plant operations. Determines most effective arrangement of unit operations such as mixing, grinding, crushing, heat transfer, size reduction, hydrogenation, distillation, purification, oxidation, polymerization, evaporation, and fermentation, exercising judgement to compromise between process requirements, economic evaluation, operator effectiveness, and physical and health hazards. Directs activities of workers who operate and control such equipment as condensers, absorption and evaporation towers, kilns, pumps, stills, valves, tanks, boilers, compressors, grinders, pipelines, electro-magnets, and centrifuges to effect required chemical or physical change. Performs tests and takes measurements throughout stages of production to determine degree of control over variables such as temperature, density, specific gravity, and pressure. May apply principles of chemical engineering to solve environmental problems. May apply principles of chemical engineering to solve bio-medical problems. May develop electro-chemical processes to generate electric currents, using controlled chemical reactions or to produce chemical changes, using electric currents. May specialize in heat transfer and energy conversion, petrochemicals and fuels, materials handling, pharmaceuticals, foods, forest products, or products such as plastics, detergents, rubber, or synthetic textiles. May be designated according to area of specialization. • **GED:** R6, M6, L6 • **SVP:** 4-10 yrs • **Academic:** Ed=B, Eng=G • **Work Field:** 244, 251 • **MPSMS:** 707 • **Aptitudes:** G1, V1, N1, S2, P3, Q3, K3, F3, M3, E5, C4 • **Temperaments:** D, J, M, T, V • **Physical:** V=N, H=N, L=S, H • **Work Env:** B • **Salary:** 5 • **Outlook:** 4

CIVIL ENGINEER (profess. & kin.) • D.O.T. #005.061-014 • OES #22121 • Plans, designs, and directs construction and maintenance of structures and facilities, such as roads, railroads, airports, bridges, harbors, channels, dams, irrigation projects, pipelines, powerplants, water and sewage systems, and waste disposal units. May perform technical research and utilize computers as aids in developing solutions to engineering problems. May be designated according to specialty or product. May perform exclusively in environmental engineering specialty as described under ENVIRONMENTAL ENGINEER (profess. & kin.). • **GED:** R5, M5, L5 • **SVP:** 4-10 yrs • **Academic:** Ed=B, Eng=G • **Work Field:** 244 • **MPSMS:** 704 • **Aptitudes:** G2, V2, N2, S2, P2, Q2, K3, F3, M3, E4, C3 • **Temperaments:** D, M, T, V • **Physical:** V=L, H=N, L=S, H • **Work Env:** B • **Salary:** 5 • **Outlook:** 4

ELECTRICAL-DESIGN ENGINEER (profess. & kin.) • D.O.T. #003.061-018 • OES #22126 • Designs electrical equipment and products performing duties as described under DESIGN ENGINEER, PRODUCTS (profess. & kin.); DESIGN ENGINEER, FACILITIES (profess. & kin.). • **GED:** R5, M5, L5 • **SVP:** 4-10 yrs • **Academic:** Ed=B, Eng=S • **Work Field:** 244 • **MPSMS:** 871 • **Aptitudes:** G2, V2, N2, S2, P2, Q3, K3, F3, M3, E4, C4 • **Temperaments:** J, M, P, T, V • **Physical:** V=L, H=N, L=L, H • **Work Env:** I • **Salary:** 5 • **Outlook:** 4

ELECTRO-OPTICAL ENGINEER (profess. & kin.) • D.O.T. #023.061-010 • OES #24102 • Conducts research, and plans development and design of gas and solid state lasers, masers, infrared, and other light emitting and light sensitive devices: Designs electronic circuitry and optical components with specific characteristics to fit within specified mechanical limits and to perform according to specifications. Designs suitable mounts for optics and power supply systems. Incorporates methods for maintenance and repair of components, and designs and develops test instrumentation and test procedures. Confers with engineering and technical personnel regarding fabrication and testing of prototype systems, and modifies design as required. May conduct application analysis to determine commercial, industrial, scientific, medical, military, or other use for electro-optical devices. May assist with development of manufacturing, assembly, and fabrication processes. • **GED:** R6, M6, L6 • **SVP:** 4-10 yrs • **Academic:** Ed=B, Eng=S • **Work Field:** 244 • **MPSMS:** 587, 609, 703 • **Aptitudes:** G1, V1, N1, S1, P2, Q2, K4, F4, M4, E5, C4 • **Temperaments:** D, M, T, V • **Physical:** V=N, H=L, L=S, H • **Work Env:** I • **Salary:** 5 • **Outlook:** 4

ELECTRONICS-DESIGN ENGINEER (profess. & kin.) • D.O.T. #003.061-034 • OES #22126 • Designs and develops electronics equipment performing duties as described under DESIGN ENGINEER, PRODUCTS (profess. & kin.). • **GED:** R5, M5, L5 • **SVP:** 4-10 yrs • **Academic:** Ed=B, Eng=S • **Work Field:** 244, 251 • **MPSMS:** 580, 703 • **Aptitudes:** G2, V2, N2, S2, P2, Q3, K3, F3, M3, E4, C3 • **Temperaments:** J, M, T, V • **Physical:** V=L, H=N, L=L, H • **Work Env:** I • **Salary:** 5 • **Outlook:** 4

LANDSCAPE ARCHITECT (profess. & kin.) • D.O.T. #001.061-018 • OES #22308 • COMMUNITY PLANNER; ENVIRON MENTAL PLANNER; LAND PLANNER; SITE PLANNER. Plans and designs development of land areas for projects, such as parks and other recreational facilities, airports, highways, and parkways, hospitals, schools, land subdivisions, and commercial, industrial, and residential sites: Confers with clients, engineering personnel, and ARCHITECTS (profess. & kin.) on overall program. Compiles and analyzes data on such site conditions as geographic location; soil, vegetation, and rock features; drainage; and location of structures for preparation of environmental impact report and development of landscaping plans. Prepares site plans, working drawings, specifications, and cost estimates for land development, showing ground contours, vegetation, locations of structures, and such facilities as roads, walks, parking areas, fences, walls, and utilities, coordinating arrangement of existing and proposed land features and structures. Inspects construction work in progress to insure compliance with landscape specifications, to approve quality of materials and work, and to advise client and construction personnel on landscape features. May be designated according to project as HIGHWAY-LANDSCAPE ARCHITECT (profess. & kin.); PARK-LANDSCAPE ARCHITECT (profess. & kin.). • **GED:** R5, M5, L5 • **SVP:** 4-10 yrs • **Academic:** Ed=B, Eng=G • **Work Field:** 264 • **MPSMS:** 719 • **Aptitudes:** G1, V1, N2, S1, P2, Q2, K3, F3, M3, E4, C3 • **Temperaments:** D, F, J • **Physical:** V=G, H=N, L=S • **Work Env:** B • **Salary:** 5 • **Outlook:** 1

OPTICAL ENGINEER (profess. & kin.) • D.O.T. #019.061-018 • OES #22199 • OPTICAL DESIGNER. Designs optical systems with specific characteristics to fit within specified physical limits of precision optical instruments, such as still-and motion-picture cameras, lens systems, telescopes, and viewing and display devices: Determines specifications for operations and makes adjustments to calibrate and obtain specified operational performance. Determines proper operation of optical system and makes adjustments to perfect system. Designs mounts for components to hold them in proper planes in relation to each other and instrument in which they will be used. Designs inspection instruments to test optical systems for defects, such as aberrations and deviations. May work with electrical and mechanical engineering staff to develop overall design of optical system. • **GED:** R6, M5, L5 • **SVP:** 4-10 yrs • **Academic:** Ed=B, Eng=G • **Work Field:** 244 • **MPSMS:** 606 • **Aptitudes:** G2, V2, N2, S1, P2, Q2, K4, F4, M4, E5, C5 • **Temperaments:** D, M, T • **Physical:** V=L, H=N, L=S • **Work Env:** I • **Salary:** 5 • **Outlook:** 3

TOOL DESIGNER (profess. & kin.) • D.O.T. #007.061-026 • OES #22135 • DEVELOPMENT MECHANIC; GENER AL-AND-SPECIAL TOOLS INVESTIGATOR AND PLANNER; MACHINE-TOOL-AND-DIE TECHNICIAN; TOOL-AND-EQUIPMENT DESIGN SPECIALIST. Designs broaches, milling-machine cutters, drills, and other single-or multiple-edged cutting tools, and related jigs, dies, and fixtures for production or experimental use in metalworking machines: Studies specifications and confers with engineering and shop personnel to resolve design problems related to material characteristics, dimensional tolerances, service requirements, manufacturing procedures, and costs of tool. Applies algebraic and geometric formulas and standard tool engineering data to develop tool configuration. Selects standard items, such as bushings and tool bits for incorporation into tool design. Draws

preliminary sketches and prepares layout and detail drawings. Modifies tool designs according to trial or production service data to improve tool life or performance. May be designated according to type of tool designed as GAGE DESIGNER (profess. & kin.); SMALL-TOOL DESIGNER (profess. & kin.). • **GED:** R5, M5, L5 • **SVP:** 4-10 yrs • **Academic:** Ed=A, Eng=G • **Work Field:** 244 • **MPSMS:** 706 • **Aptitudes:** G2, V2, N2, S2, P2, Q3, K3, F3, M3, E5, C4 • **Temperaments:** J, M, T, V • **Physical:** V=L, H=N, L=S, H • **Work Env:** I • **Salary:** 5 • **Outlook:** 3

GOE: 05.01.08 General Engineering

AGRICULTURAL ENGINEER (profess. & kin.) • D.O.T. #013.061-010 • OES #22123 • Applies engineering technology and knowledge of biological sciences to agricultural problems concerned with power and machinery, electrification, structures, soil and water conservation, and processing of agricultural products: Develops criteria for design, manufacture, or construction of equipment, structures, and facilities. Designs and uses sensing, measuring, and recording devices and instrumentation to study such problems as effects of temperature, humidity, and light, on plants or animals, or relative effectiveness of different methods of applying insecticides. Designs and directs manufacture of equipment for land tillage and fertilization, plant and animal disease and insect control, and for harvesting or moving commodities. Designs and supervises erection of structures for crop storage, animal shelter, and human dwelling, including light, heat, air-conditioning, water supply, and waste disposal. Plans and directs construction of rural electric-power distribution systems, and irrigation, drainage, and flood-control systems for soil and water conservation. Designs and supervises installation of equipment and instruments used to evaluate and process farm products, and to automate agricultural operations. May conduct radio and television educational programs to provide assistance to farmers, local groups, and related farm cooperatives. Workers are usually designated according to area of specialty or product. • **GED:** R5, M5, L5 • **SVP:** 4-10 yrs • **Academic:** Ed=B, Eng=G • **Work Field:** 244 • **MPSMS:** 713 • **Aptitudes:** G1, V1, N1, S2, P3, Q3, K3, F3, M3, E3, C3 • **Temperaments:** D, M, P, T, V • **Physical:** V=N, H=N, L=S, H • **Work Env:** B • **Salary:** 5 • **Outlook:** 3

AUTOMOTIVE ENGINEER (auto. mfg.) • D.O.T. #007.061-010 • OES #22135 • Develops improved or new designs for automotive structural members, motors, transmissions, and associated automotive equipment or modifies existing equipment on production vehicles, and directs building, modification, and testing of vehicle: Conducts experiments and tests on existing designs and equipment to obtain data on function of and performance of equipment. Analyzes data to develop new designs for motors, chassis, and other related mechanical, hydraulic, and electro-mechanical components and systems in automotive equipment. Designs components and systems to improve economy and safety of operation, control of emissions, and operational performance at optimum costs. Directs and coordinates building, or modification of, automotive equipment or vehicle to insure conformance with engineering design. Directs testing activities on components and equipment under designated conditions to ensure operational performance meets design specifications. Alters or modifies design to obtain specified functional and operational performance. May assist DRAFTER, AUTOMOTIVE DESIGN (auto. mfg.) in developing structural design for auto-body. May conduct research studies to develop new concepts in automotive engineering field. • **GED:** R5, M5, L5 • **SVP:** 4-10 yrs • **Academic:** Ed=B, Eng=G • **Work Field:** 244 • **MPSMS:** 706 • **Aptitudes:** G2, V2, N2, S2, P2, Q3, K3, F3, M3, E5, C3 • **Temperaments:** D, J, M, T • **Physical:** V=L, H=N, L=S, H • **Work Env:** I • **Salary:** 5 • **Outlook:** 3

CHEMICAL-ENGINEERING TECHNICIAN (profess. & kin.) • D.O.T. #008.261-010 • OES #22599 • Applies chemical engineering principles and technical skills to assist CHEMICAL ENGINEER (profess. & kin.) in developing, improving, and testing chemical-plant processes, products, and equipment: Prepares charts, sketches, diagrams, flow charts, and compiles and records engineering data to clarify design details or functional criteria of chemical processing and physical operation units. Participates in fabricating, installing, and modifying equipment to insure that critical standards are met. Tests developmental equipment and formulates standard operating procedures. Tests processing equipment and instruments to observe and record operating characteristics and performance of specified design or process. Observes chemical or physical operation processes and recommends modification or change. Observes and confers with equipment operators to insure specified techniques are used. Writes technical reports and submits finding to CHEMICAL ENGINEER (profess. & kin.). Performs preventive and corrective maintenance of chemical processing equipment. May prepare chemical solutions for use in processing materials, such as synthetic textiles, detergents, and fertilizers following formula. May set up test apparatus. May instruct or direct activities of technical personnel. May assist in developing and testing prototype processing systems and be designated CHEMICAL-ENGINEERING TECHNICIAN, PROTO-TYPE-DEVELOPMENT (profess. & kin.). May assist in development of pilot-plant units and be designated PILOT-PLANT RE-SEARCH-TECHNICIAN (petrol. refin.). • **GED:** R5, M5, L5 • **SVP:** 4-10 yrs • **Academic:** Ed=A, Eng=S • **Work Field:** 244 • **MPSMS:** 707 • **Aptitudes:** G2, V2, N2, S2, P2, Q3, K2, F2, M2, E3, C4 • **Temperaments:** M, T • **Physical:** V=L, H=N, L=L, W, H • **Work Env:** B • **Salary:** 5 • **Outlook:** 3

CUSTOMER-EQUIPMENT ENGINEER (tel. & tel.) • D.O.T. #003.187-018 • OES #22126 • SERVICES ENGINEER. Directs activities concerned with selection and installation of telephone facilities and special equipment on customer's premises to meet customer's communication requirements: Reviews sales order to ascertain extent of telephone facilities and equipment required. Inspects customer premises to ascertain space available for installation of equipment and to determine type and quantity of designated equipment that can be installed to provide specific communication facilities. Prepares floor plan of equipment arrangement for customer or architect approval. Prepares cost estimate for equipment and installation and submits data to management for authorization to proceed with job. Orders equipment, prepares installation specifications, and monitors progress of installation to ensure facilities are ready on specified date. Prepares all job related paper work and closes out work authorization when equipment is in service. • **GED:** R5, M5, L5 • **SVP:** 4-10 yrs • **Academic:** Ed=A, Eng=S • **Work Field:** 244 • **MPSMS:** 861 • **Aptitudes:** G2, V2, N2, S2, P2, Q4, K4, F4, M4, E5, C5 • **Temperaments:** D, M, V • **Stress:** A • **Physical:** V=G, H=N, L=L, W, H • **Work Env:** I • **Salary:** 5 • **Outlook:** 4

ELECTRICAL ENGINEER (profess. & kin.) • D.O.T. #003.061-010 • OES #22126 • Conducts research and development activities concerned with design, manufacture, and testing of electrical components, equipment, and systems; applications of equipment to new uses; and manufacture, construction, and installation of electrical equipment, facilities, and systems: Designs electrical components of equipment, and equipment, used in generation of electric power or products and systems utilizing electrical energy for commercial, domestic, and industrial purposes [DESIGN ENGINEER, FACILITIES (profess. & kin.); DESIGN ENGINEER, PRODUCTS (profess. & kin.)]. Designs and directs activities of engineering personnel engaged in fabrication of test control apparatus and equipment, and in establishment of methods, procedures, and conditions for testing equipment [TEST ENGINEER (profess. & kin.)]. Develops applications of controls, instruments, and systems to new commercial, domestic, and industrial uses. Directs activities concerned with manufacture, construction, installation, and operational testing to ensure conformance of equipment and systems with functional specifications and customer requirements. May direct and coordinate operation, maintenance, and repair activities of field installations of equipment and systems. May specialize in application of electrical principles and technology to specific areas of discipline, such as electrical energy generation, transmission, and distribution systems, instrumentation, control, and protective devices; products as appliances, generators, transformers, relays, switches, motors, and electro-mechanical devices, or area of work as manufacture, applications, construction, or installation. • **GED:** R5, M5, L5 • **SVP:** 4-10 yrs • **Academic:** Ed=B, Eng=G • **Work Field:** 244 • **MPSMS:** 703, 871 • **Aptitudes:** G2, V2, N2, S2, P3, Q3, K3, F3, M3, E3, C3 • **Temperaments:** D, M, T, V • **Physical:** V=L, H=N, L=S, H • **Work Env:** B • **Salary:** 5 • **Outlook:** 5

ELECTRONICS ENGINEER (profess. & kin.) • D.O.T. #003.061-030 • OES #22126 • Conducts research and development activities concerned with design, manufacture, and testing of electronic components, products, and systems, and in development of applications of products to commercial, industrial, medical, military, and scientific uses: Designs electrical circuits, electronic components, and integrated systems, using ferroelectric, nonlinear, dielectric, phosphor, photo-conductive, and thermoelectric properties of materials [DESIGN ENGINEER, PRODUCTS (profess. & kin.)]. Designs and directs engineering personnel in fabrication of test control apparatus and equipment, and determines procedures for testing products [TEST ENGINEER (profess. & kin.)]. Develops new applications of electrical and dielectric properties of metallic and non-metallic materials used in components, and in application of components to products or systems. May direct field operation and maintenance activities of electronic installations. May evaluate operational systems and recommend design modifications to eliminate causes of malfunctions or changes in system requirements. May specialize in development of electronic principles and technology in fields, such as telecommunications, telemetery, aerospace guidance, missile propulsion control, counter-measures, acoustics, nucleonic instrumentation, industrial controls and measurements, high-frequency heating, laboratory techniques, computers, electronic data processing and reduction, teaching aids and techniques, radiation detection, encephalography, electron optics, and bio-medical research. • **GED:** R5, M5, L5 • **SVP:** 4-10 yrs • **Academic:** Ed=B, Eng=G • **Work Field:** 244, 251 • **MPSMS:** 580, 703 • **Aptitudes:** G2, V2, N2, S2, P2, Q3, K3, F3, M3, E4, C2 • **Temperaments:** J, M, T, V • **Physical:** V=L, H=N, L=S, H • **Work Env:** I • **Salary:** 5 • **Outlook:** 5

ENGINEER, SOILS (profess. & kin.) • D.O.T. #024.161-010 • OES #24111 • Studies and analyzes surface and subsurface soils to determine characteristics for construction, development, or land planning: Inspects proposed construction site, and sets up test equipment and drilling machinery to obtain data and soil and rock samples. Analyzes data and soil samples through field and laboratory analysis, to determine type, classification, characteristics, and stability of soil. Computes bearing weights, prepares maps, charts, and reports of test results. May make recommendations regarding foundation design, slope angles, grading or building heights. May participate in environmental studies and prepare environmental impact reports. • **GED:** R6, M5, L6 • **SVP:** 2-4 yrs • **Academic:** Ed=B, Eng=G • **Work Field:** 244 • **MPSMS:** 704 • **Aptitudes:** G1, V1, N1, S2, P3, Q3, K3, F3, M3, E3, C3 • **Temperaments:** D, M, T, V • **Physical:** V=L, H=N, L=S, W, H • **Work Env:** B • **Salary:** 4 • **Outlook:** 3

MECHANICAL ENGINEER (profess. & kin.) • D.O.T. #007.061-014 • OES #22135 • Plans and designs mechanical or electromechanical products or systems, and directs and coordinates operation and repair activities: Designs products or systems, such as instruments, controls, engines, machines, and mechanical, thermal, hydraulic, or heat transfer systems, utilizing and applying knowledge of engineering principles [DESIGN ENGINEER, PRODUCTS (profess. & kin.)]. Plans and directs engineering personnel in fabrication of test control apparatus, and equipment, and development of methods and procedures for testing products or systems [TEST ENGINEER (profess. & kin.)]. Directs and coordinates construction and installation activities to insure conformance of products and systems with engineering design and customer specifications. Coordinates operation, maintenance, and repair activities to obtain optimum utilization of machines and systems. May evaluate field installations and recommend design modifications to eliminate malfunctions or changes in machine or system function. May specialize in one specific field of mechanical engineering discipline, such as heat transfer, hydraulics, electromechanics, controls and instrumentation, nuclear systems, tooling, air-conditioning and refrigeration; or in types of products, as machines, propulsion systems, machinery and mechanical equipment; or in type of work performed as steam or gas generation and distribution, steam plant engineering or system planning. • **GED:** R5, M5, L5 • **SVP:** 4-10 yrs • **Academic:** Ed=B, Eng=G • **Work Field:** 244 • **MPSMS:** 706 • **Aptitudes:** G2, V2, N2, S2, P3, Q3, K3, F3, M3, E5, C5 • **Temperaments:** D, J, M, T, V • **Physical:** V=L, H=N, L=S, H • **Work Env:** B • **Salary:** 5 • **Outlook:** 4

PETROLEUM ENGINEER (petrol. production) • D.O.T.

#010.061-018 • OES #22111 • Analyzes technical and cost factors to plan methods to recover maximum oil and gas in oil-field operations, utilizing knowledge of petroleum engineering and related technologies: Examines map of subsurface oil and gas reservoir locations to recommend placement of wells to maximize economical production from reservoir. Evaluates probable well production rate during natural or stimulated-flow production phases. Recommends supplementary processes to enhance recovery involving stimulation of flow by use of processes, such as pressurizing or heating in subsurface regions. Analyzes recommendations of reservoir engineering specialist for placement of well in oil field. Develops well drilling plan for management approval, specifying factors including drilling time, number of special operations, such as directional drilling, and testing, and material requirements and costs including well casing and drilling muds. Provides technical consultation during drilling operations to resolve problems such as bore directional change, unsatisfactory drilling rate or invasion of subsurface water in well bore. Advises substitution of drilling mud compounds or tool bits to improve drilling conditions. Inspects well to determine that final casing and tubing installations are completed. Plans oil and gas field recovery containers, piping, and treatment vessels to receive, remove contaminants, and separate oil and gas products flowing from well. Monitors production rate of gas or oil from established wells and plans rework process to correct well production, such as repacking of well bore and additional perforation of subsurface sands adjacent to well bottom. May apply knowledge of petroleum engineering to solve problems concerned with environment [ENVIRONMENTAL ENGINEER (profess. & kin.)]. May be designated according to specialty as DEVELOPMENT ENGINEER, GEOTHERMAL OPERATIONS (profess. & kin.); DRILLING ENGINEER (petrol. production); PRODUCTION ENGINEER (petrol. production); RESERVOIR ENGINEER (petrol. production). • GED: R5, M5, L5 • SVP: 4-10 yrs • Academic: Ed=B, Eng=G • Work Field: 244 • MPSMS: 872 • Aptitudes: G1, V1, N1, S1, P2, Q3, K3, F3, M3, E5, C5 • Temperaments: D, M, T, V • Physical: V=N, H=N, L=S, H • Work Env: I • Salary: 5 • Outlook: 4

PLANT ENGINEER (profess. & kin.) • D.O.T. #007.167- 014 • OES #13017 • FACTORY ENGINEER; SUPERINTENDENT, MECHANICAL. Directs and coordinates, through engineering and supervisory personnel, activities concerned with design, construction, and maintenance of equipment and machinery in industrial plant: Establishes standards and policies for pollution control, testing, operating procedure, inspection, and maintenance of equipment in accordance with engineering principles and safety regulations, and oversees directly or through subordinates maintenance of plant buildings. Coordinates resurveys, new designs, and maintenance schedules with operating requirements. Prepares bid sheets and contracts for construction and facilities acquisition. Tests newly installed machines and equipment to insure fulfillment of contract specifications. • GED: R5, M5, L5 • SVP: 4-10 yrs • Academic: Ed=A, Eng=G • Work Field: 244 • MPSMS: 706 • Aptitudes: G1, V1, N1, S1, P3, Q4, K4, F4, M4, E5, C5 • Temperaments: D, J, M • Physical: V=L, H=N, L=S, W, H • Work Env: I • Salary: 5 • Outlook: 4

PROJECT ENGINEER (profess. & kin.) • D.O.T. #019.167-014 • OES #13017 • CHIEF ENGINEER. Directs, coordinates, and exercises functional authority for planning, organization, control, integration, and completion of, engineering project within area of assigned responsibility: Plans and formulates engineering program and organizes project staff according to project requirements. Assigns project personnel to specific phases or aspects of project, such as technical studies, product design, preparation of specifications and technical plans, and product testing, in accordance with engineering disciplines of staff. Reviews product design for compliance with engineering principles, company standards, and customer contract specifications. Coordinates activities concerned with technical developments, scheduling, and resolving engineering design and test problems. Directs integration of technical activities and products. Evaluates and approves design changes, specifications, and drawing releases. Controls expenditures within limitations of project budget. Prepares interim and completion project reports. • GED: R5, M5, L5 • SVP: 4-10 yrs • Academic:

Ed=A, Eng=G • Work Field: 244, 295 • MPSMS: 700, 710 • Aptitudes: G2, V2, N2, S2, P3, Q3, K3, F3, M3, E4, C5 • Temperaments: D, M, P • Stress: E, A • Physical: V=L, H=L, L=S, W, H • Work Env: I • Salary: 5 • Outlook: 4

STRUCTURAL ENGINEER (const.) • D.O.T. #005.061-034 • OES #22121 • Directs or participates in planning, designing, or reviewing plans for erection of structures requiring stress analysis: Designs structure to meet estimated load requirements, computing size, shape, strength, and type of structural members, or performs structural analysis of plans and structures prepared by private engineers. May inspect existing projects and recommend repair and replacement of defective members or rebuilding of entire structure. • GED: R5, M5, L5 • SVP: 4-10 yrs • Academic: Ed=B, Eng=G • Work Field: 244 • MPSMS: 361, 704 • Aptitudes: G2, V2, N2, S2, P2, Q2, K3, F3, M3, E3, C3 • Temperaments: M, T, V • Physical: V=L, H=N, L=S, H • Work Env: B • Salary: 5 • Outlook: 4

TRANSPORTATION ENGINEER (profess. & kin.) • D.O.T. #005.061-038 • OES #22121 • Develops plans for surface transportation projects according to established engineering standards and state or federal construction policy: Prepares plans, estimates, and specifications to design transportation facilities. Plans alterations and modifications of existing streets, highways, and freeways to improve traffic flow. Prepares deeds, property descriptions, and right-of-way maps. Performs field engineering calculations to compensate for change orders and contract estimates. May prepare and present public reports of environmental analysis statements and other transportation information. May specialize in particular phase of work, such as making surveys, improving signs or lighting, preparing plans, or directing and coordinating construction or maintenance activities. May be designated HIGHWAY ENGINEER (gov. ser.). May specialize in studying vehicular and pedestrian traffic conditions and be designated TRAFFIC ENGINEER (gov. ser.). May plan, organize, and direct work in transportation studies to plan surface systems and be designated TRANSPORTATION PLANNING ENGINEER (gov. ser.). • GED: R5, M5, L5 • SVP: 4-10 yrs • Academic: Ed=B, Eng=G • Work Field: 244 • MPSMS: 362, 704 • Aptitudes: G2, V2, N2, S2, P2, Q2, K3, F3, M3, E5, C3 • Temperaments: D, M, T, V • Physical: V=L, H=N, L=S, H • Work Env: B • Salary: 5 • Outlook: 4

WELDING ENGINEER (profess. & kin.) • D.O.T. #011.061-026 • OES #22105 • Develops welding techniques, procedures, and application of welding equipment to problems involving fabrication of metals, utilizing knowledge of production specifications, properties and characteristics of metals and metal alloys, and engineering principles: Conducts research and development investigations to develop and test new fabrication processes and procedures, improve existing or develop new welding equipment, develop new or modify current welding methods, techniques, and procedures, discover new patterns of welding phenomena, or to correlate and substantiate hypotheses. Prepares technical reports as result of research and development and preventive maintenance investigations. Establishes welding procedures to guide production and welding personnel relating to specification restrictions, material processes, pre-and-post heating requirements which involve use of complex alloys, unusual fabrication methods, welding of critical joints, and complex postheating requirements. Evaluates new developments in welding field for possible application to current welding problems or production processes. Directs and coordinates technical personnel in performing inspections to insure workers' compliance with established welding procedures, restrictions, and standards; in testing welds for conformance with national code requirements; or testing welding personnel for certification. Contacts personnel of other agencies, engineering personnel, or clients to exchange ideas, information, or offer technical advice concerning welding matters. May perform experimental welding to evaluate new equipment, techniques, and materials. • GED: R5, M5, L5 • SVP: 4-10 yrs • Academic: Ed=A, Eng=G • Work Field: 244, 251 • MPSMS: 566, 708, 711 • Aptitudes: G1, V1, N1, S2, P2, Q3, K3, F3, M3, E5, C4 • Temperaments: D, J, M, T, V • Physical: V=L, H=N, L=L, H • Work Env: I • Salary: 5 • Outlook: 3

05.02 Managerial Work: Mechanical

Workers in this group manage industrial plants or systems where technical work is being performed. Jobs are found in oil fields, power plants, transportation companies, radio and television networks, and telephone and related communications systems.

✔ **What kind of work would you do?**
Your work activities would depend upon your specific job. For example, you might:

- direct operations of a major generating plant of an electrical power system.
- coordinate engineering, construction, operation, and maintenance activities of a cross-country pipeline.
- direct studies of an existing communications system for a transportation firm and analyze results to plan equipment replacement.
- direct workers who repair and maintain motor transportation equipment to insure safe and efficient operation.
- analyze machine and tool requisitions to determine whether to make tools in the plant or purchase them.
- inspect landfill sites and operations to plan with supervisory personnel the most efficient way to utilize available space.

✔ **What skills and abilities do you need for this kind of work?**
To do this kind of work, you must be able to:

- understand technologies required in the work you are directing.
- plan and direct the work of others, either directly or through lower level supervisors.
- work with a variety of situations.
- solve problems, using facts and personal judgment.
- react quickly in emergency situations and make decisions that may involve a great amount of money or the safety of others.
- work with different kinds of people.

✔ **How do you know if you would like or could learn to do this kind of work?**
The following questions may give you clues about yourself as you consider this group of jobs.

- Have you taken courses in advanced mathematics? Can you understand and work with mathematical concepts?
- Have you taken a physics course? Can you understand and work with the principles of matter and energy?
- Have you collected rocks or minerals as a hobby? Can you identify them?
- Have you owned a chemistry set or microscope? Do you enjoy testing new ideas?
- Have you served in an engineering section of the armed forces?

✔ **How can you prepare for and enter this kind of work?**
Occupations in this group usually require education and/or training extending from two years to over ten years, depending upon the specific kind of work. College level courses in both management and technical fields are usually required. Most jobs require supervisory experience. Some industries, such as public utilities, offer on-the-job training in management techniques. Seminars in principles of electronic data processing are often a part of this training.

✔ **What else should you consider about these jobs?**
Workers in these jobs must make policy decisions as well as operational decisions. These decisions must conform to the overall company policy and must be made quickly. These workers may have to work overtime without additional pay. However, they often receive benefits such as bonuses, stock options, and profit sharing plans.

Although they spend much of their time in an office doing paper work, they frequently tour work sites. While visiting these sites they observe operation, monitor progress, detect possible problems, and give directions to workers.

These workers are usually specialists and can transfer only to another firm in the same or a related industry.

If you think you would like to do this kind of work, look at the job titles listed below.

GOE: 05.02.02 Maintenance & Construction, Managerial

SUPERINTENDENT, BUILDING (any ind.) • D.O.T. #187.167-190 • OES #15011 • BUILDING-SERVICE SUPERVISOR; MANAGER, BUILDING. Directs activities of workers engaged in operating and maintaining facilities and equipment in buildings such as apartment houses or office buildings: Inspects facilities and equipment to determine need and extent of service, equipment required, and type and number of operation and maintenance personnel needed. Hires, trains, and supervises building service personnel. Assigns workers to duties such as maintenance, repair, or renovation and obtains bids for additional work from outside contractors. Directs contracted projects to verify adherence to specifications. Purchases building and maintenance supplies, machinery, equipment, and furniture. Plans and administers building department budget. Compiles records of labor and material cost for operating building and issues cost reports to owner or managing agents. May prepare construction specifications or plans, obtaining advice from engineering consultants, assemble and analyze contract bids, and submit bids and recommendations to superiors for action. • **GED:** R4, M4, L4 • **SVP:** 2-4 yrs • **Academic:** Ed=N, Eng=G • **Work Field:** 295 • **MPSMS:** 900 • **Aptitudes:** G2, V3, N2, S2, P3, Q3, K4, F4, M4, E5, C4 • **Temperaments:** D, M, P, V • **Stress:** E • **Physical:** V=N, H=L, L=L, W • **Work Env:** I • **Salary:** 2 • **Outlook:** 2

SUPERINTENDENT, CONSTRUCTION (const.) • D.O.T. #182.167-026 • OES #15017 • SUPERINTENDENT, JOB. Directs activities of workers concerned with construction of buildings, dams, highways, pipelines, or other construction projects: Studies specifications to plan procedures for construction on basis of starting and completion times and staffing requirements for each phase of construction, based on knowledge of available tools and equipment and various building methods. Assembles members of organization (supervisory, clerical, engineering, and other workers) at start of project. Orders procurement of tools and materials to be delivered at specified times to conform to work schedules. Confers with and directs supervisory personnel and subcontractors engaged in planning and executing work procedures, interpreting specifications, and coordinating various phases of construction to prevent delays. Confers with supervisory personnel and labor representatives to resolve complaints and grievances within work force. Confers with supervisory and engineering personnel and inspectors and suppliers of tools and materials to resolve construction problems and improve construction methods. Inspects work in progress to insure that workmanship conforms to specifications and that construction schedules are adhered to. Prepares, or receives from subordinates, reports on progress, materials used and costs, and adjusts work schedules as indicated by reports. May direct workers concerned with major maintenance or reconditioning projects for existing installations. Workers are usually designated according to type of project, work, or construction activity directed. • **GED:** R5, M5, L4 • **SVP:** 4-10 yrs • **Academic:** Ed=N, Eng=G • **Work Field:** 101, 295 • **MPSMS:** 360 • **Aptitudes:** G2, V3, N2, S2, P3, Q3, K4, F4, M4, E4, C5 • **Temperaments:** D, P, V • **Stress:** E, A • **Physical:** V=L, H=L, L=S, W • **Work Env:** B • **Salary:** 5 • **Outlook:** 1

GOE: 05.02.03 Processing & Manufacturing, Managerial

BREWING DIRECTOR (beer prod.) • D.O.T. #183.167-010 •

OES #15014 • BREWING SUPERINTENDENT. Develops new or modifies existing brewing formulas and processing techniques and coordinates, through subordinate supervisors, brewing, fermenting, lagering, and malting departments of a brewery: Devises brewing formulas and processes or works in conjunction with research personnel to develop or modify formulas and processes. Directs and coordinates activities of departments to control processing, according to formula specifications. Confers with technical and administrative personnel to resolve formula and process problems. Reviews and analyzes production orders to determine brewing schedules and manpower requirements. Tests and inspects beer, grain, malt, wort, and yeast, using saccharimeter, hydrometer, and other test equipment and correlates results with quality control analyses. Advises and recommends to management methods and procedures for selecting, installing, and maintaining equipment. Reviews and resolves personnel actions. Prepares and submits production reports. May confer with worker's representatives to resolve grievances. • **GED:** R5, M4, L4 • **SVP:** 4-10 yrs • **Academic:** Ed=A, Eng=S • **Work Field:** 146 • **MPSMS:** 395 • **Aptitudes:** G2, V2, N2, S3, P3, Q3, K4, F4, M4, E5, C3 • **Temperaments:** D, J, P, T • **Stress:** A • **Physical:** V=L, H=L, L=L, H • **Work Env:** I • **Salary:** 5 • **Outlook:** 1

DIRECTOR, QUALITY CONTROL (profess. & kin.) • D.O.T. #012.167-014 • OES #22128 • QUALITY-CONTROL SUPERVISOR. Plans and coordinates quality-control program designed to ensure continuous production of products consistent with established standards: Formulates and maintains quality-control objectives and supervises workers engaged in plant functions, such as inspection and testing to insure continuous quality control over materials and production facilities. Develops and analyzes statistical data and specifications to indicate present product standards and establish proposed quality and reliability expectancy of finished product. Formulates and coordinates product quality objectives with production procedures to obtain economic optimum product reliability. Plans, promotes, and organizes quality and reliability training activities. May investigate and adjust customer complaints regarding quality. • **GED:** R6, M6, L6 • **SVP:** 4-10 yrs • **Academic:** Ed=B, Eng=S • **Work Field:** 244 • **MPSMS:** 712 • **Aptitudes:** G1, V1, N2, S2, P3, Q3, K4, F4, M4, E5, C3 • **Temperaments:** D, M, P • **Stress:** A • **Physical:** V=L, H=L, L=S • **Work Env:** I • **Salary:** 5 • **Outlook:** 4

MANAGER, FOOD PROCESSING PLANT (can. & preserv.) • D.O.T. #183.167-026 • OES #15014 • Directs and coordinates activities of food processing plant: Contacts buyers or growers to arrange for purchasing or harvesting and delivery of agricultural products, seafoods, meat, or other raw materials to plant for processing. Directs, through subordinate supervisory personnel, workers engaged in processing, canning, freezing, storing, and shipping food products. Directs and coordinates activities concerned with dismantling, moving, installing, or repairing of machines and equipment. Approves plant payroll and payments for purchased materials or products. Estimates quantities of foods for processing required and orders foods, materials, supplies, and equipment needed. Hires, transfers, and discharges employees. May provide suppliers with transportation to expedite delivery of purchased products or supplies to plant. May arrange for freezing of packaged products by other food processing plants. May negotiate with suppliers or growers prices to be paid for purchases. • **GED:** R5, M4, L4 • **SVP:** 4-10 yrs • **Academic:** Ed=A, Eng=S • **Work Field:** 295 • **MPSMS:** 300, 320, 330 • **Aptitudes:** G2, V2, N3, S3, P3, Q3, K4, F4, M4, E5, C4 • **Temperaments:** D, J, P, V • **Stress:** A • **Physical:** V=G, H=L, L=L • **Work Env:** I • **Salary:** 5 • **Outlook:** 1

PRODUCTION SUPERINTENDENT (any ind.) • D.O.T. #183.117-014 • OES #15014 • MANAGER, FACTORY; MANAGER, GENERAL; MANAGER, PLANT; MANAGER, PRODUCTION; PLANT SUPERVISOR; SUPERINTENDENT, FACTORY; SUPERINTENDENT, GENERAL; SUPERINTENDENT, MILL; SUPERINTENDENT, PLANT; SUPERINTENDENT, PRODUCTION; SUPERINTENDENT, SHOP. Directs and coordinates, through subordinate supervisory personnel, activities concerned with production of company product(s), utilizing knowledge of product technology, production methods and procedures, and capabilities of machines and equipment: Confers with management personnel to establish production and quality control standards, develop budget and cost controls, and to obtain data regarding types, quantities, specifications, and delivery dates of products ordered. Plans and directs production activities and establishes production priorities for products in keeping with effective operations and cost factors. Coordinates production activities with procurement, maintenance, and quality control activities to obtain optimum production and utilization of manpower, machines, and equipment. Reviews and analyzes production, quality control, maintenance, and operational reports to determine causes of nonconformity with product specifications, or operating or production problems. Develops and implements operating methods and procedures designed to eliminate operating problems and improve product quality. Revises production schedules and priorities as result of equipment failure or operating problems. Consults with engineering personnel relative to modification of machines and equipment in order to improve production and quality of products. Conducts hearings to resolve or effect settlement of grievances and for wards for management-union negotiations unresolved grievances. Supervises subordinates directly in plants having no GENERAL SUPERVISOR (any ind.). PRODUCTION SUPERINTENDENTS (any ind.) are usually designated according to product produced, or by type of plant, industry or activity. • **GED:** R5, M4, L4 • **SVP:** 4-10 yrs • **Academic:** Ed=H, Eng=G • **Work Field:** 295 • **MPSMS:** 712 • **Aptitudes:** G2, V2, N3, S3, P3, Q3, K4, F4, M4, E5, C5 • **Temperaments:** D, J, P, V • **Stress:** E, A • **Physical:** V=N, H=L, L=S, W • **Work Env:** I • **Salary:** 5 • **Outlook:** 1

QUALITY-CONTROL COORDINATOR (drug prep. & related) • D.O.T. #168.167-066 • OES #21911 • Coordinates activities of workers engaged in testing and evaluating ethical and proprietary pharmaceuticals in order to control quality of manufacture and to ensure compliance with legal standards: Participates with management personnel in establishing procedures for testing drugs and related products, applying knowledge of controlled production, sampling techniques, testing procedures, and statistical analysis. Assigns subordinates to specific testing functions. Reviews laboratory reports of test batches. Recommends full-scale production of batches meeting company or consumer specifications and complying with Federal purity standards. Orders destruction of substandard batches, as authorized by supervisor. Directs and coordinates investigation of complaints concerning defective products. Recommends response to complaints, considering test reports, production records, legal standards, and complaint validity. Reviews legislative developments to determine changes in legal requirements and probable effects on company's manufacturing activities. Directs retention of data and preparation of documents for use by self or other company personnel during inquiries concerning suspect products. • **GED:** R4, M4, L4 • **SVP:** 1-2 yrs • **Academic:** Ed=A, Eng=S • **Work Field:** 211, 295 • **MPSMS:** 493 • **Aptitudes:** G2, V2, N2, S3, P4, Q3, K4, F4, M4, E5, C4 • **Temperaments:** D, M, P, T • **Stress:** A • **Physical:** V=N, H=L, L=S • **Work Env:** I • **Salary:** 4 • **Outlook:** 3

WINE MAKER (wine prod.) • D.O.T. #183.161-014 • OES #15014

• ENOLOGIST. Directs and coordinates all activities of winery concerned with production of wine: Contracts with growers to provide fruit for processing or cooperates with HORTICULTURIST (profess. & kin.) of company vineyard in grape production. Examines grape samples to ascertain presence and extent of such factors as sugar and acid content, and ripeness. Orders grapes picked when analysis indicates they are at degree of ripeness desired. Coordinates processes and directs workers concerned with testing and crushing grapes, fermenting juice, fortifying, clarifying, aging, and finishing of wine, including cooling, filtering, and bottling. Blends wines according to formulas or knowledge and experience in wine making. May develop new processes to improve product. When processing champagne may be designated as CHAMPAGNE MAKER (vinous liquors). When processing wine into vinegar is designated as VINEGAR MAKER (vinous liquors). • **GED:** R5, M3, L4 • **SVP:** 4-10 yrs • **Academic:** Ed=A, Eng=S • **Work Field:** 146 • **MPSMS:** 395 • **Aptitudes:** G2, V3, N2, S2, P2, Q3, K3, F3, M3, E4, C3 • **Temperaments:** D, J, M, P • **Stress:** E, A • **Physical:** V=L, H=N, L=L, W • **Work Env:** I, W • **Salary:** 5 • **Outlook:** 1

GOE: 05.02.06 Services, Mechanical, Managerial

APPLIANCE-SERVICE SUPERVISOR (light, heat, & power) • D.O.T. #187.167-010 • OES #81002 • ELECTRICAL-APPLIANCE SERVICE SUPERVISOR; MERCHANDISE SUPERVISOR; UTILIZATION SUPERVISOR. Coordinates activities of merchandise-servicing department of gas or electric appliance distributors: Supervises, trains, and assigns duties to workers engaged in servicing appliances, pricing, and disposition of returned merchandise and excess repair parts. Develops company policies and procedures regarding servicing of appliances and disposition of defective parts. Consults manufacturers to obtain advice on unusual service problems and to obtain service instructions and parts catalogs. May write instructions on care and use of appliances for distribution to public. • **GED:** R4, M4, L4 • **SVP:** 2-4 yrs • **Academic:** Ed=H, Eng=S • **Work Field:** 295 • **MPSMS:** 880 • **Aptitudes:** G2, V2, N3, S2, P3, Q3, K4, F4, M4, E5, C4 • **Temperaments:** D, M, P, V • **Stress:** A • **Physical:** V=L, H=L, L=L • **Work Env:** I • **Salary:** 4 • **Outlook:** 2

GOE: 05.02.07 Materials Handling, Managerial

MANAGER, MARINA DRY DOCK (amuse. & rec.) • D.O.T. #187.167-226 • OES #19999 • Directs and coordinates dry docking activities at marina: Administers affairs of department, such as planning and coordinating work schedules, assigning storage crib for each boat, and maintaining department budget. Directs workers in maintenance of boats and trailers, such as painting or washing boats, lubricating and repairing motors, and retrofitting trailers and cars with lights and turn signals. Monitors fuel dock operation to ensure services to patrons. Operates, or supervises workers operating, equipment to lift boats from water and transport and dry dock boats, using crane or forklift. Hires, orients, and trains personnel in job duties, safety practices, employer policy, and performance requirements. • **GED:** R4, M3, L3 • **SVP:** 1-2 yrs • **Academic:** Ed=H, Eng=G • **Work Field:** 295 • **MPSMS:** 593, 854 • **Aptitudes:** G2, V2, N3, S3, P4, Q3, K3, F4, M2, E3, C5 • **Temperaments:** D, J, P, V • **Stress:** E, A • **Physical:** V=L, H=L, L=H, W, H • **Work Env:** I, N • **Salary:** 4 • **Outlook:** 3

05.03 Engineering Technology

Workers in this group collect, record, and coordinate technical information in such activities as surveying, drafting, petroleum production, communications control, and materials scheduling. Workers find jobs in construction, factories, engineering and architectural firms, airports, and research laboratories.

✔ **What kind of work would you do?**

Your work activities would depend upon your specific job. For example, you might:

- use astronomical observations, complex computations, and other techniques to compile data for preparing geodetic maps and charts.
- organize and direct the work of surveying parties to determine precise location and measurement points.
- use drafting instruments to prepare detailed drawings and blueprints for manufacturing electronic equipment.
- prepare detailed working drawings of mechanical devices showing dimensions, tolerances, and other engineering data.

- analyze survey data, source maps, and other records to draw detailed maps to scale.
- provide meteorological, navigational, and other technical information to pilots.
- direct activities of workers who set up seismographic recording instruments and gather data about oil-bearing rock layers.

✔ **What skills and abilities do you need for this kind of work?**

To do this kind of work, you must be able to:

- use geometry and other kinds of higher mathematics.
- use clear language to write technical reports.
- perform detail work with great accuracy.
- use fingers skillfully when making drawings.
- make finger and hand movements correspond with seeing to operate equipment, adjust instruments, use pen to make sketches, or use measuring tools.

- make decisions quickly according to both personal judgment and facts.
- direct activities of workers who set up seismographic recording instruments and gather data about oil-bearing rock layers.
- perform under stress in emergency situations.

✔ **How do you know if you would like or could learn to do this kind of work?**

The following questions may give you clues about yourself as you consider this group of jobs.

- Have you taken courses in mechanical drawing? Do you enjoy this type of activity?
- Have you taken courses in geometry and advanced math? Do you like math studies?
- Have you made models of airplanes or cars following detailed plans? Can you follow such instructions easily?

- Have you taken courses in physics or chemistry? Can you work with formulas?
- Have you served in an engineering unit in the armed forces? Did you like the work involved?

✔ **How can you prepare for and enter this kind of work?**

Occupations in this group usually require education and/or training extending from two years to over ten years, depending upon the specific kind of work. The most common way of preparing for this kind of work is through related post high school courses, on-the-job training, and work experience.

Many technical and vocational schools, and community colleges offer programs in surveying. With some classroom instruction in surveying, beginners can start as instrument workers. After gaining experience, they may advance to supervisory positions, and may later apply for positions as registered surveyors. Advancement may be based on written examinations as well as experience. High school graduates with no formal training usually start by assisting instrument workers.

Basic preparation for jobs in drafting include high school level courses in mathematics, physical sciences, industrial arts and mechanical drawing. Technical school courses in structural design and layout provide the knowledge and skills needed for advanced drafting jobs. A three- to four-year apprenticeship program is another method for entering drafting work. This program offers workers the advantages of classroom instruction and on-the-job training while they earn regular wages.

College courses in business administration or industrial engineering provide the most common preparation for jobs in production and material coordination. People with a high school education and work experience in a production firm may be admitted to on-the-job training programs. High school studies should include commercial courses, industrial arts, and bookkeeping or accounting. English courses are also important because they develop oral and written communications skills.

Technicians usually begin work as trainees in routine jobs under close supervision of an experienced technician or engineer. As they again experience, they move up to jobs requiring less supervision. With additional training and experience, technicians may advance to supervisory or professional engineering positions.

✔ **What else should you consider about these jobs?**

Surveyors usually have a 40-hour work week. They sometimes work longer hours during the summer months. Most surveying work is done outdoors in all types of weather. However, workers usually prepare reports, and draw maps in an office setting. Surveyors are exposed to hazards from moving machinery and falling objects on construction projects. There is danger from passing cars when surveying on or near highways. Some surveying work requires traveling to distant job sites or camping out at the site.

Drafters may have to buy some of their own equipment. However, most companies supply them with the equipment they need. They generally work in comfortable, well-lighted, air conditioned offices. They sometimes visit work sites such as factories or construction projects. At times they may work under pressure to meet deadlines.

If you think you would like this kind of work, look at the job titles listed below.

GOE: 05.03.01 Surveying

NAVIGATOR (air trans.) • D.O.T. #196.167-014 • OES #97702 • AERIAL NAVIGATOR; AIRPLANE NAVIGATOR. Locates position and directs course of airplane on international flights, using navigational aids, such as charts, maps, sextant, and slide rule: Establishes position of airplane by use of navigation instruments and charts, celestial observation, or dead reckoning. Directs deviations from course required by weather conditions, such as wind drifts and forecasted atmospheric changes. Utilizes navigation aids, such as radio beams and beacons, when available. Keeps log of flight. Must be licensed by Federal Aviation Administration. • **GED:** R5, M5, L4 • **SVP:** 1-2 yrs • **Academic:** Ed=A, Eng=G • **Work Field:** 243 • **MPSMS:** 719 • **Aptitudes:** G2, V3, N2, S2, P2, Q2, K3, F4, M3, E4, C4 • **Temperaments:** M, S, T, V • **Stress:** S • **Physical:** V=G, H=N, L=S, W, H • **Work Env:** I, N • **Salary:** 5 • **Outlook:** 3

PHOTOGRAMMETRIC ENGINEER (profess. & kin.) • D.O.T. #018.167-026 • OES #22311 • Plans, coordinates, and directs activities of workers concerned with conducting aerial surveys and preparing topographic materials from aerial photographs and other data: Analyzes survey objectives and specifications, utilizing knowledge of survey uses, such as municipal and ecological planning, property and utility mapping, and petroleum and mineral exploration. Selects most appropriate and economical survey methods, using knowledge of capabilities of aerial photography and applications of remote sensing (imagery through electronic scanning). Estimates cost of survey. Advises customers and department supervisors regarding flights for aerial photography and plans for ground surveys designed to establish base lines, elevations, and other geodetic measurements. Prepares charts and tables for aerial navigation, to specify flight path, altitude, and airspeed of camera-carrying aircraft. Computes geodetic measurements and interprets survey data from ground or aerial photographs or remote-sensing images to determine position, shape, and elevation of geomorphic and topographic features. Conducts research in surveying and mapping methods and procedures, using knowledge of techniques of photogrammetric map compilation, electronic data processing, and flight and control planning. May direct one or more phases of technical operations concerned with preparing survey proposals, negotiating with clients, scheduling activities, conducting surveys, processing data, reviewing work quality, and training and assigning person nel. • **GED:** R6, M6, L5 • **SVP:** 4-10 yrs • **Academic:** Ed=B, Eng=S • **Work Field:** 243,

244 • **MPSMS:** 716, 719 • **Aptitudes:** G2, V2, N2, S1, P1, Q2, K3, F3, M3, E5, C3 • **Temperaments:** D, M, P, T, V • **Physical:** V=L, H=L, L=S, H • **Work Env:** I • **Salary:** 5 • **Outlook:** 4

SURVEYOR ASSISTANT, INSTRUMENTS (profess. & kin.) • D.O.T. #018.167-034 • OES #22521 • Obtains data pertaining to angles, elevations, points, and coutours used for construction, map making, mining, or other purposes, using ali dade, level, transit, plane table, Theodolite, electronic distance measuring equipment, and other surveying instruments. Compiles notes, sketches, and records of data obtained and work performed. Directs work of subordinate members of survey team. Performs other duties relating to surveying work as directed by CHIEF OF PARTY (profess. & kin.). • **GED:** R5, M5, L4 • **SVP:** 2-4 yrs • **Academic:** Ed=A, Eng=S • **Work Field:** 243 • **MPSMS:** 716 • **Aptitudes:** G2, V3, N2, S2, P2, Q3, K3, F3, M3, E3, C3 • **Temperaments:** D, M, T • **Physical:** V=L, H=N, L=L, W, H • **Work Env:** O • **Salary:** 4 • **Outlook:** 3

GOE: 05.03.02 Drafting

AUTO-DESIGN CHECKER (auto. mfg.) • D.O.T. #017.261-010 • OES #22511 • CHECKER, PRODUCT DESIGN. Examines detail, layout, and master drawings of either auto-body or chassis parts, assemblies, and systems, for practicality of design, accuracy of mathematical calculations, dimensional accuracy, projection, and conformity to specifications and shop standards. Applies knowledge of auto-body and chassis design, methods of manufacture and assembly, and drafting techniques and procedures. Discusses necessary changes with appropriate staff members and coordinates corrections. • **GED:** R5, M4, L4 • **SVP:** 4-10 yrs • **Academic:** Ed=A, Eng=S • **Work Field:** 242 • **MPSMS:** 706 • **Aptitudes:** G2, V2, N2, S1, P2, Q2, K2, F3, M3, E5, C4 • **Temperaments:** M, T • **Physical:** V=G, H=L, L=L • **Work Env:** I • **Salary:** 5 • **Outlook:** 3

CIVIL ENGINEERING TECHNICIAN (profess. & kin.) • D.O.T. #005.261-014 • OES #22502 • Assists CIVIL ENGINEER (profess. & kin.) 005.061-014 in application of principles, methods, and techniques of civil engineering technology: Reviews project specifications and confers with CIVIL ENGINEER (profess. & kin.) 005.061-014 concerning assistance required, such as plan preparation, acceptance testing, evaluation of field conditions, design changes, and reports. Conducts materials testing and analysis, using tools and equipment and applying engineering knowledge necessary to conduct tests. Prepares reports detailing tests conducted and results. Surveys project sites to obtain and analyze topographical details of sites, using maps and surveying equipment. Drafts detailed dimensional drawings, such as those needed for highway plans, structural steel fabrication, and water control projects, performing duties as described under DRAFTER (profess. & kin.) Master Title. Calculates dimensions, profile specifications, and quantities of materials such as steel, concrete, and asphalt, using calculator. Inspects construction site to determine conformance of site to design specifications. • **GED:** R4, M4, L4 • **SVP:** 2-4 yrs • **Academic:** Ed=H, Eng=S • **Work Field:** 242, 243, 244 • **MPSMS:** 704 • **Aptitudes:** G2, V2, N2, S2, P2, Q2, K2, F2, M3, E5, C4 • **Temperaments:** J, T, V • **Physical:** V=L, H=N, L=S, W, H • **Work Env:** I • **Salary:** 4 • **Outlook:** 4

CONTROLS DESIGNER (profess. & kin.) • D.O.T. #003.261-014 • OES #22514 • CONTROLS PROJECT ENGINEER. Designs and drafts systems of electrical, hydraulic, and pneumatic controls for machines and equipment, such as arc welders, robots, conveyors, and programmable logic controllers, applying knowledge of electricity, electronics, hydraulics, and pneumatics: Discusses project with SUPERVISOR (any ind.) Master Title and APPLICATIONS ENGINEER, MANUFACTURING (profess. & kin.) 007.061-038 to review functions of machines and equipment. Designs and drafts arrangement of linkage of conductors, relays, and other components of electrical, electronic, hydraulic, pneumatic, and lubrication devices, using drafting tools, and applying knowledge of electrical engineering and drafting [DRAFTER (profess. & kin.) Master Title]. Diagrams logic system for functions such as sequence and timing control. Designs and drafts diagrams of cable connection for robots, robot end-of-arm tool, robot controller, and other machines. Illustrates and describes installation and maintenance details, such as where bearings should be lubricated, types

of lubrication, and which parts are lubricated automatically and manually. Confers with ASSEMBLER AND WIRER, INDUSTRIAL EQUIPMENT (elec. equip.; mach. mfg.) 826.361-010 to resolve problems regarding building of controls systems. Reviews schematics with customer's representatives to answer questions during installation of robot systems. Observes gauges during trial run of programmed machine and equipment operation to verify that electrical signals in system conform to specifications. May design controls for energy conversion or other industrial plant monitoring systems. May use computer and software programs to produce design drawings and be designated CONTROLS DESIGNER, COMPUTER-ASSISTED (profess. & kin.). • **GED:** R5, M4, L4 • **SVP:** 4-10 yrs • **Academic:** Ed=B, Eng=G • **Work Field:** 242, 244, 264 • **MPSMS:** 719 • **Aptitudes:** G2, V2, N2, S2, P2, Q1, K2, F3, M3, E5, C5 • **Temperaments:** J, T • **Physical:** V=L, H=N, L=S, H • **Work Env:** I • **Salary:** 5 • **Outlook:** 4

DESIGN DRAFTER, ELECTROMECHANISMS (profess. & kin.) • D.O.T. #017.261-014 • OES #22514 • Drafts designs of electromechanical equipment such as aircraft engine subassemblies, electronic optical-character-recognition and related data-processing systems, gyroscopes, rocket engine control systems, automatic materials handling and processing machinery, or bio-medical equipment: Confers with engineers and other drafters to interpret design concepts, determine nature and type of required detailed working drawings, and coordinate work with others. Drafts detail and assembly drawings performing duties described under DRAFTER (profess. & kin.). Compiles data, computes quantities, determines materials needed, and prepares cost estimates. • **GED:** R5, M5, L4 • **SVP:** 2-4 yrs • **Academic:** Ed=A, Eng=S • **Work Field:** 242, 244 • **MPSMS:** 703, 706 • **Aptitudes:** G2, V3, N2, S2, P2, Q3, K2, F2, M3, E5, C4 • **Temperaments:** M, T • **Physical:** V=G, H=N, L=S, H • **Work Env:** I • **Salary:** 4 • **Outlook:** 3

DESIGN TECHNICIAN, COMPUTER-AIDED (electronics) • D.O.T. #003.362-010 • OES #22599 • DIGITIZER. Operates computer-aided design (CAD) system and peripheral equipment to resize or modify integrated circuit designs (artwork) and to generate computer tape of artwork for use in producing mask plates used in manufacturing integrated circuits: Reviews work order and procedural manuals to determine critical dimensions of design. Calculates figures to convert design dimensions to resizing dimensions specified for subsequent production processes, using conversion chart and calculator. Locates file relating to specified design projection data base library and loads program into computer. Enters specified commands into computer, using keyboard, to retrieve design information from file and display design on CAD equipment display screen. Types commands on key board to enter resizing specifications into computer. Confers with engineering and design staff to determine design modifications and enters editing information into computer. Keys in specified information, using keyboard connected to on-line or off-line peripheral equipment (plotter), to produce graphic representation (hard copy) of design for review and approval by engineering and design staff. Enters specified information into computer, using keyboard, to generate computer tape of approved design. • **GED:** R3, M3, L3 • **SVP:** 6 mos-1 yr • **Academic:** Ed=H, Eng=S • **Work Field:** 233, 264 • **MPSMS:** 703 • **Aptitudes:** G2, V3, N3, S2, P2, Q2, K2, F3, M3, E5, C5 • **Temperaments:** J, T • **Physical:** V=L, H=N, L=S, H • **Work Env:** I • **Salary:** 4 • **Outlook:** 4

DETAILER (profess. & kin.) • D.O.T. #017.261-018 • OES #22514 • Drafts detailed drawings of parts of machines or structures from rough or general design drawings: Shows dimensions, material to be used, and other information necessary to make detailed drawing clear and complete. Makes tracing of finished drawing on semi-transparent paper from which blueprints can be made. Performs other duties as described under DRAFTER (profess. & kin.). May specialize in preparing detail drawings for specific type of machine, structure, or product. • **GED:** R4, M4, L4 • **SVP:** 2-4 yrs • **Academic:** Ed=H, Eng=S • **Work Field:** 242 • **MPSMS:** 700, 710 • **Aptitudes:** G2, V2, N2, S2, P2, Q3, K3, F2, M2, E5, C5 • **Temperaments:** M, V • **Physical:** V=G, H=N, L=S, H • **Work Env:** I • **Salary:** 4 • **Outlook:** 3

DRAFTER, AERONAUTICAL (profess. & kin.) • D.O.T. #002.261-010 • OES #22514 • Performs duties of DRAFTER (profess. & kin.), specializing in drafting engineering drawings of developmental or production airplanes and missiles and ancillary equipment, including launch mechanisms and scale models of prototype aircraft, as planned by AERONAUTICAL ENGINEER (profess. & kin.). • **GED:** R5, M5, L4 • **SVP:** 2-4 yrs • **Academic:** Ed=A, Eng=S • **Work Field:** 242 • **MPSMS:** 702 • **Aptitudes:** G2, V3, N2, S2, P2, Q2, K2, F2, M3, E5, C4 • **Temperaments:** M, T • **Physical:** V=G, H=N, L=S, H • **Work Env:** I • **Salary:** 4 • **Outlook:** 3

DRAFTER, ARCHITECTURAL (profess. & kin.) • D.O.T. #001.261-010 • OES #22514 • Performs duties of DRAFTER (profess. & kin.) by drawing artistic architectural and structural features of any class of buildings and like structures: Delineates designs and details, using drawing instruments. Confirms compliance with building codes. May specialize in planning architectural details according to structural materials used as DRAFTER, TILE AND MARBLE (profess. & kin.). • **GED:** R4, M4, L3 • **SVP:** 2-4 yrs • **Academic:** Ed=H, Eng=S • **Work Field:** 242 • **MPSMS:** 701 • **Aptitudes:** G2, V3, N2, S2, P2, Q2, K2, F2, M2, E5, C4 • **Temperaments:** M, T • **Physical:** V=G, H=N, L=S, H • **Work Env:** I • **Salary:** 4 • **Outlook:** 3

DRAFTER, ASSISTANT (profess. & kin.) • D.O.T. #017.281-018 • OES #22514 • Copies plans and drawings prepared by DRAFTER (profess. & kin.) by tracing them with ink and pencil on transparent paper or cloth spread over drawings, using triangle, T-square, compass, pens, and other drafting instruments. Makes simple sketches or drawings under close supervision. • **GED:** R4, M4, L3 • **SVP:** 2-4 yrs • **Academic:** Ed=H, Eng=S • **Work Field:** 242 • **MPSMS:** 700, 710 • **Aptitudes:** G3, V4, N3, S3, P3, Q3, K3, F3, M3, E5, C4 • **Temperaments:** M, T • **Physical:** V=G, H=N, L=S, H • **Work Env:** I • **Salary:** 3 • **Outlook:** 2

DRAFTER, AUTOMOTIVE DESIGN (auto. mfg.) • D.O.T. #017.281-022 • OES #22514 • Designs and drafts working layouts and master drawings of automotive vehicle components, assemblies, and systems from specifications, sketches, models, prototype and/or verbal instructions, applying knowledge of automotive vehicle design, engineering principles, manufacturing processes and limitations, and drafting techniques and procedures, using drafting instruments and work aids: Analyzes specifications, sketches, engineering drawings, ideas and related design data to determine critical factors affecting design of components based on knowledge of previous designs and manufacturing processes and limitations. Draws rough sketches and performs mathematical computations to develop design and work out detailed specifications of components. Applies knowledge of mathematical formulas and physical laws and uses slide rule or digital calculator to make calculations. Performs preliminary and advanced work in development of working layouts and final master drawings adequate for detailing parts and units of design. Makes revisions to size, shape and arrangement of parts to create practical design. Confers with AUTOMOTIVE ENGINEER (auto. mfg.) and others on staff to resolve design problems. Specializes in design of specific type of body or chassis components, assemblies or systems such as door panels, chassis frame and supports, or braking system. • **GED:** R5, M4, L4 • **SVP:** 2-4 yrs • **Academic:** Ed=A, Eng=S • **Work Field:** 242, 244 • **MPSMS:** 706 • **Aptitudes:** G2, V2, N2, S1, P2, Q2, K2, F3, M3, E5, C4 • **Temperaments:** M, T • **Physical:** V=G, H=N, L=S, H • **Work Env:** I • **Salary:** 4 • **Outlook:** 3

DRAFTER, CARTOGRAPHIC (profess. & kin.) • D.O.T. #018.261-010 • OES #22311 • MAP MAKER; MAPPER. Draws maps of geographical areas to show natural and constructed features, political boundaries, and other features, performing duties described under DRAFTER (profess. & kin.): Analyzes survey data, source maps and photographs, computer or automated mapping products, and other records to determine location and names of features. Studies legal records to establish boundaries of properties, and local, national, and international areas of political, economic, social, or other significance. Geological and topographical maps are drawn by DRAFTER, GEOLOGICAL (petrol. production) and DRAFTER, TOPOGRAPHICAL (profess. & kin.). • **GED:** R4, M4, L3 • **SVP:** 2-4 yrs • **Academic:** Ed=H, Eng=S • **Work Field:** 242 • **MPSMS:** 716 • **Aptitudes:** G2, V3, N2, S2, P2, Q2, K2, F2, M3, E5, C3 • **Temperaments:** M, T • **Physical:** V=G, H=N, L=S, H • **Work Env:** I • **Salary:** 4 • **Outlook:** 3

DRAFTER, CIVIL (profess. & kin.) • D.O.T. #005.281-010 • OES

#22514 • DRAFTER, CIVIL ENGINEERING; DRAFTER, CONSTRUCTION; DRAFTER, ENGINEERING. Drafts detailed construction drawings, topographical profiles, and related maps and specification sheets used in planning and construction of highways, river and harbor improvements, flood control, drainage, and other civil engineering projects, performing duties as de scribed under DRAFTER (profess. & kin.): Plots maps and charts showing profiles and cross-sections, indicating relation of topographical contours and elevations to buildings, retaining walls, tunnels, overhead powerlines, and other structures. Drafts detailed drawings of structures and installations such as roads, culverts, fresh water supply and sewage disposal systems, dikes, wharfs, and breakwaters. Computes volume of tonnage of excavations and fills and prepares graphs and hauling diagrams used in earthmoving operations. May accompany survey crew in field to locate grading markers or to collect data required for revision of construction drawings. May be designated according to type of construction as DRAFTER, REINFORCED CONCRETE (profess. & kin.); DRAFTER, WATER AND SEWAGE (profess. & kin.). • **GED:** R5, M5, L4 • **SVP:** 2-4 yrs • **Academic:** Ed=A, Eng=S • **Work Field:** 242 • **MPSMS:** 704, 716 • **Aptitudes:** G2, V3, N2, S2, P2, Q3, K3, F3, M3, E5, C4 • **Temperaments:** M, T • **Physical:** V=G, H=N, L=S, H • **Work Env:** I • **Salary:** 4 • **Outlook:** 3

DRAFTER, COMMERCIAL (profess. & kin.) • D.O.T. #017.261-026 • OES #22514 • Performs general duties of DRAFTER (profess. & kin.) in all-round drafting, such as laying out location of buildings, planning of arrangements in offices, large rooms, store buildings, and factories, and drawing of charts, forms, and records. Paints and washes colored drawings when required. • **GED:** R5, M5, L4 • **SVP:** 1-2 yrs • **Academic:** Ed=A, Eng=S • **Work Field:** 242 • **MPSMS:** 700, 710 • **Aptitudes:** G2, V3, N2, S2, P2, Q3, K2, F2, M3, E5, C3 • **Temperaments:** M, T • **Physical:** V=G, H=N, L=S, H • **Work Env:** I • **Salary:** 4 • **Outlook:** 3

DRAFTER, ELECTRICAL (profess. & kin.) • D.O.T. #003.281-010 • OES #22514 • Drafts electrical equipment working drawings and wiring diagrams used by construction crews and repairmen who erect, install, and repair electrical equipment and wiring in communications centers, power plants, industrial establishments, commercial or domestic buildings, or electrical distribution systems, performing duties as described under DRAFTER (profess. & kin.) Master Title. May use computer-assisted drafting (CAD) equipment and software and be designated DRAFTER (CAD), ELECTRICAL (profess. & kin.). May prepare detail cable layout and diagrams for cable installation and be designated ELECTRIC-CABLE DIAGRAMMER (elec. equip.). • **GED:** R5, M5, L4 • **SVP:** 2-4 yrs • **Academic:** Ed=A, Eng=S • **Work Field:** 242 • **MPSMS:** 703 • **Aptitudes:** G2, V3, N2, S2, P2, Q2, K4, F3, M4, E5, C4 • **Temperaments:** J, T • **Physical:** V=G, H=N, L=S, H • **Work Env:** I • **Salary:** 4 • **Outlook:** 4

DRAFTER, ELECTRONIC (profess. & kin.) • D.O.T. #003.281-014 • OES #22514 • DRAFTER, ELECTRO-MECHANICAL. Drafts detailed drawings, such as wiring diagrams, layout drawings, mechanical detail drawings, and drawings of intermediate and final assemblies, used in manufacture, assembly, installation, and repair of printed circuit boards and electronic components and equipment: Examines electronic schematics and supporting documents received from design engineering department to verify specifications, such as dimensions and tolerances. Computes drafting specifications to determine data, such as configuration dimensions, using calculator. Prepares final detail drawings of components and equipment [DRAFTER (profess. & kin.) Master Title]. May use computer-assisted drafting (CAD) equipment and software and be designated DRAFTER (CAD), ELECTRONIC (profess. & kin.). • **GED:** R5, M5, L4 • **SVP:** 2-4 yrs • **Academic:** Ed=A, Eng=S • **Work Field:** 242 • **MPSMS:** 703 • **Aptitudes:** G2, V3, N2, S2, P2, Q2, K4, F3, M4, E5, C4 • **Temperaments:** J, T • **Physical:** V=G, H=N, L=S, H • **Work Env:** I • **Salary:** 4 • **Outlook:** 4

DRAFTER, GEOLOGICAL (petrol. production) • D.O.T. #010.281-014 • OES #22514 • Draws maps, diagrams, profiles, cross sections, directional surveys, and subsurface formations to represent geological or geophysical stratigraphy and locations of gas and oil deposits, performing duties as described under DRAFTER (profess. & kin.): Correlates and interprets data obtained from topographical surveys, well logs, or geophysical prospecting reports, utilizing special symbols to denote geological and geophysical formations or oilfield installations. May finish drawings in mediums and according to specifications required for reproduction by blueprinting, photographing, or other duplication methods. • **GED:** R5, M5, L5 • **SVP:** 1-2 yrs • **Academic:** Ed=A, Eng=S • **Work Field:** 242 • **MPSMS:** 872 • **Aptitudes:** G2, V3, N2, S1, P2, Q2, K2, F3, M3, E5, C5 • **Temperaments:** M, T, V • **Physical:** V=G, H=N, L=S, H • **Work Env:** I • **Salary:** 4 • **Outlook:** 2

DRAFTER, GEOPHYSICAL (petrol. production) • D.O.T. #010.281-018 • OES #22514 • Draws subsurface contours in rock formations from data obtained by geophysical prospecting party. Plots maps and diagrams from computations based on recordings of seismograph, gravity meter, magnetometer, and other petroleum prospecting instruments and from prospecting and surveying field notes. Performs other duties as described under DRAFTER (profess. & kin.). May be designated according to method of prospecting as DRAFTER, SEISMOGRAPH (petrol. production). • **GED:** R5, M5, L5 • **SVP:** 2-4 yrs • **Academic:** Ed=A, Eng=S • **Work Field:** 242 • **MPSMS:** 872 • **Aptitudes:** G2, V3, N2, S1, P2, Q3, K2, F3, M2, E5, C5 • **Temperaments:** M, T, V • **Physical:** V=G, H=N, L=L, H • **Work Env:** I • **Salary:** 4 • **Outlook:** 4

DRAFTER, LANDSCAPE (profess. & kin.) • D.O.T. #001.261-014 • OES #22514 • Prepares detailed scale drawings and tracings from rough sketches or other data provided by LANDSCAPE ARCHITECT (profess. & kin.) performing duties described under DRAFTER (profess. & kin.). May prepare separate detailed site plan, grading and drainage plan, lighting plan, paving plan, irrigation plan, planting plan, and drawings and detail of garden structures. May build models of proposed landscape construction and prepare colored drawings for presentation to client. • **GED:** R4, M4, L3 • **SVP:** 2-4 yrs • **Academic:** Ed=H, Eng=S • **Work Field:** 242 • **MPSMS:** 719 • **Aptitudes:** G2, V3, N2, S2, P2, Q2, K2, F2, M3, E5, C3 • **Temperaments:** M, T • **Physical:** V=G, H=N, L=S, H • **Work Env:** I • **Salary:** 4 • **Outlook:** 3

DRAFTER, MARINE (profess. & kin.) • D.O.T. #014.281-010 • OES #22514 • Draws structural and mechanical features of ships, docks, and other marine structures and equipment, performing duties of DRAFTER (profess. & kin.). Works from general design drawings and notes made by ARCHITECT, MARINE (profess. & kin.) or MARINE ENGINEER (profess. & kin.). • **GED:** R5, M5, L4 • **SVP:** 2-4 yrs • **Academic:** Ed=A, Eng=S • **Work Field:** 242 • **MPSMS:** 714 • **Aptitudes:** G2, V3, N2, S2, P2, Q3, K2, F2, M3, E5, C4 • **Temperaments:** M, T • **Physical:** V=G, H=N, L=S, H • **Work Env:** I • **Salary:** 4 • **Outlook:** 2

DRAFTER, MECHANICAL (profess. & kin.) • D.O.T. #007.281-010 • OES #22514 • DRAFTER, ENGINEERING. Drafts detailed working drawings of machinery and mechanical devices, indicating dimensions and tolerances, fasteners and joining requirements, and other engineering data. Drafts multiple-view assembly and subassembly drawings as required for manufacture and repair of mechanisms. Performs other duties as described under DRAFTER (profess. & kin.). • **GED:** R5, M5, L5 • **SVP:** 2-4 yrs • **Academic:** Ed=A, Eng=S • **Work Field:** 242 • **MPSMS:** 706 • **Aptitudes:** G2, V3, N2, S2, P2, Q3, K2, F2, M3, E5, C4 • **Temperaments:** M, T • **Physical:** V=G, H=N, L=S, H • **Work Env:** I • **Salary:** 4 • **Outlook:** 3

DRAFTER, STRUCTURAL (profess. & kin.) • D.O.T. #005.281-014 • OES #22514 • Performs duties of DRAFTER (profess. & kin.) by drawing plans and details for structures employing structural reinforcing steel, concrete, masonry, wood, and other structural materials. Produces plans and details of foundations, building frame, floor and roof framing and other structural elements. • **GED:** R5, M5, L4 • **SVP:** 2-4 yrs • **Academic:** Ed=A, Eng=S • **Work Field:** 242 • **MPSMS:** 704 • **Aptitudes:** G2, V3, N2, S2, P2, Q2, K2, F2, M3, E5, C4 • **Temperaments:** M, T • **Physical:** V=G, H=N, L=S, H • **Work Env:** I • **Salary:** 4 • **Outlook:** 3

DRAFTER, TOPOGRAPHICAL (profess. & kin.) • D.O.T. #018.261-014 • OES #22521 • PHOTO-CARTOGRAPHER. Draws and corrects topographical maps from source data, such as surveying notes, aerial photographs, or other maps. Performs other duties as described under DRAFTER (profess. & kin.). May accompany survey crew in field to compile original survey data or to establish

location of natural or constructed landmarks. • **GED:** R5, M5, L5 • **SVP:** 2-4 yrs • **Academic:** Ed=A, Eng=S • **Work Field:** 242 • **MPSMS:** 716 • **Aptitudes:** G2, V2, N2, S2, P2, Q3, K2, F2, M2, E5, C4 • **Temperaments:** M, T • **Physical:** V=G, H=N, L=S, H • **Work Env:** I • **Salary:** 4 • **Outlook:** 4

DRAWINGS CHECKER, ENGINEERING (profess. & kin.) • D.O.T. #007.267-010 • OES #22135 • Examines engineering drawings of military and commercial parts, assemblies, and installations to detect errors in design documents: Compares figures and lines on production drawing or diagram with production layout, examining angles, dimensions, bend allowances, and tolerances for accuracy. Determines practicality of design, material selection, available tooling, and fabrication process, applying knowledge of drafting and manufacturing methods. Confers with design personnel to resolve drawing and design discrepancies. May specialize in checking specific types of designs, such as mechanical assemblies, microelectronic circuitry, or fluid-flow systems. • **GED:** R4, M4, L4 • **SVP:** 1-2 yrs • **Academic:** Ed=H, Eng=S • **Work Field:** 244 • **MPSMS:** 559, 587, 592 • **Aptitudes:** G2, V2, N2, S1, P2, Q2, K2, F2, M3, E5, C5 • **Temperaments:** J, T • **Physical:** V=G, H=N, L=S, H • **Work Env:** I • **Salary:** 4 • **Outlook:** 3

EDITOR, MAP (profess. & kin.) • D.O.T. #018.261-018 • OES #22521 • Verifies accuracy and completeness of topographical maps from aerial photographs and specifications: Views photographs and other reference materials, such as old maps and records and examines corresponding area of map to verify correct identification of specified topographical features and accuracy of contour lines. Verifies correct location and accuracy of scaled distances between control points and reference lines. Examines reference materials to detect omission of topographical features, poor register, or other defects in photography or draftsmanship. Marks errors and makes corrections, such as numbering grid lines or lettering names of rivers or towns. • **GED:** R4, M4, L4 • **SVP:** 2-4 yrs • **Academic:** Ed=A, Eng=S • **Work Field:** 211, 242 • **MPSMS:** 716 • **Aptitudes:** G2, V2, N2, S2, P2, Q3, K3, F3, M3, E5, C3 • **Temperaments:** M, T • **Physical:** V=G, H=N, L=L, H • **Work Env:** I • **Salary:** 4 • **Outlook:** 4

ENGINEERING ASSISTANT, MECHANICAL EQUIPMENT (profess. & kin.) • D.O.T. #007.161-018 • OES #22514 • DRAFTER; LAY-OUT DRAFTER; MECHANICAL DESIGN TECHNICIAN. Develops detailed design drawings and related specifications of mechanical equipment, according to engineering sketches and design proposal specifications: Analyzes engineering sketches, specifications, and related data and drawings to determine design factors, such as size, shape, and arrangement of parts. Sketches rough layout of machine and computes angles, weights, surface areas, dimensions, radii, clearances, tolerances, leverages, and location of holes. Computes magnitude, direction, and point of application of tension, compression, and bending forces and develops geometric shape of machine parts to accommodate operating loads. Drafts detailed multiview drawings of machine and subassemblies, including specifications concerning gear ratios, bearing loads, and direction of moving parts, using engineering data and standard references. Compiles and analyzes test data to determine effect of design on machine in relation to factors, such as temperature, pressures, speed, horsepower, and fuel consumption. Modifies machine design to correct operating deficiencies or to reduce production problems. May specialize in specific type of machine, such as air-cooled internal combustion engines, diesel engines, or machine tools. • **GED:** R5, M5, L5 • **SVP:** 2-4 yrs • **Academic:** Ed=A, Eng=S • **Work Field:** 242, 244 • **MPSMS:** 706 • **Aptitudes:** G2, V2, N2, S2, P2, Q2, K2, F2, M2, E5, C4 • **Temperaments:** M, T • **Physical:** V=L, H=N, L=S, H • **Work Env:** I • **Salary:** 4 • **Outlook:** 3

ESTIMATOR (profess. & kin.) • D.O.T. #160.267-018 • OES #21902 • COST ESTIMATOR; PRODUCTION ESTIMATOR. Prepares cost estimates for manufacturing of products, construction projects, or services requested to aid management in bidding on or determining price of product or service: Compiles list of type of materials, tool or fixture, or equipment requirements, utilizing knowledge of products to be manufactured, services to be performed, or type of structure to be built, using blueprints and specifications. Itemizes tools, fixtures, or equipment to be manufactured by company or purchased from outside sources. Computes cost estimates for materials, purchased equipment, subcontracted work, production activities and requirements, and labor. May conduct special studies to develop and establish standard hour and related cost data or effect cost reductions. May consult with personnel of other departments relating to cost problems. May specialize according to particular service performed, type of product produced, or phase of work in which involved, as tool and fixture costs, production costs, construction costs, or material costs. • **GED:** R4, M3, L4 • **SVP:** 2-4 yrs • **Academic:** Ed=A, Eng=G • **Work Field:** 232 • **MPSMS:** 899 • **Aptitudes:** G2, V3, N2, S3, P3, Q3, K4, F4, M4, E5, C5 • **Temperaments:** J, M, T • **Physical:** V=L, H=N, L=S • **Work Env:** I • **Salary:** 4 • **Outlook:** 4

ESTIMATOR AND DRAFTER (light, heat, & power) • D.O.T. #019.261-014 • OES #22517 • DETAIL AND LAY-OUT DRAFTER; DISTRIBUTION ESTIMATOR; LAY-OUT AND DETAIL DRAFTER. Draws up specifications and instructions for installation of voltage transformers, overhead or underground cables, and related electrical equipment used to conduct electrical energy from transmission lines or high-voltage distribution lines to consumers: Studies work order to determine type of service, such as lighting or power, demanded by installation. Visits site of proposed installation and draws rough sketch of location. Takes measurements, such as street dimensions, distances to be spanned by wire and cable, or space available in existing buildings and underground vaults which affect installation and arrangement of equipment. Estimates materials, equipment, and incidentals needed for installation. Draws master sketch showing relation of proposed installation to existing facilities. Makes other drawings, such as pertaining to wiring connections or cross sections of underground cables, as required for instructions to installation crew. Consults POWER-DISTRIBUTION ENGINEER (light, heat, & power) on difficulties encountered. May draft sketches to scale [DRAFTER, ELECTRICAL (profess. & kin.)]. May estimate labor and material costs, using pricelists and records on previous projects. May inspect completed installation of electrical equipment and related building circuitry to verify conformance with specifications. May perform duties of LAND SURVEYOR (profess. & kin.) and prepare specifications and diagrams for installation of gas distribution pipes owned by gas-electric utility. • **GED:** R5, M5, L5 • **SVP:** 2-4 yrs • **Academic:** Ed=A, Eng=S • **Work Field:** 242, 244 • **MPSMS:** 581 • **Aptitudes:** G2, V2, N2, S2, P2, Q3, K3, F3, M3, E5, C5 • **Temperaments:** M • **Physical:** V=G, H=N, L=L, W, H • **Work Env:** B • **Salary:** 4 • **Outlook:** 4

FIRE-PROTECTION ENGINEERING TECHNICIAN (profess. & kin.) • D.O.T. #019.261-026 • OES #22599 • Designs and drafts plans and estimates costs for installation of fire protection systems for facilities and structures, applying knowledge of drafting, physical science, engineering principles, and fire protection codes: Analyzes blueprints and specifications prepared by ARCHITECT (profess. & kin.) 001.061-010 to determine dimensions of system to meet fire protection codes. Determines design and size of system components, using calculator or computer. Drafts detailed drawing of system to ensure conformance to specifications and applicable codes. May negotiate relocation of system components with SUPERINTENDENT, CONSTRUCTION (const.) 182.167-026 to resolve conflicts of co-location with other systems. May inspect fire-damaged structures to detect malfunctions. May specialize in one type of fire protection system, such as foam, water, dry chemical, or vaporous gas or specialize in one type of establishment, such as construction, insurance, or government. • **GED:** R4, M4, L4 • **SVP:** 2-4 yrs • **Academic:** Ed=H, Eng=S • **Work Field:** 242, 244 • **MPSMS:** 719 • **Aptitudes:** G2, V2, N2, S2, P2, Q2, K2, F3, M3, E3, C4 • **Temperaments:** J, T • **Physical:** V=G, H=N, L=L, W, C, H • **Work Env:** I • **Salary:** 4 • **Outlook:** 3

INTEGRATED CIRCUIT LAYOUT DESIGNER (profess. & kin.) • D.O.T. #003.261-018 • OES #22514 • MASK DESIGNER. Designs layout for integrated circuits (IC), according to engineering specifications, using computer-assisted design (CAD) equipment and software, and utilizing knowledge of electronics, drafting, and IC design rules (standard IC manufacturing process requirements): Reviews and analyzes engineering design schematics and supporting documents, such as logic diagrams and design rules to plan layout of IC. Confers with engineering staff to resolve design details or problems. Enters engineering specifications into computer memory of CAD equipment and composes configurations on equipment display screen of IC logic elements (basic components of integrated circuit, such as resistors and transistors) for all IC layers, using keyboard, digitizing work aids (light pen or digitizing tablet), and engineering design schematics, and applying knowledge of design rules, programmed CAD functions, and electronics. Compares logic element configuration on equipment display screen with engineering schematics and redesigns or modifies logic elements, as needed, using digitizing work aids (light pen or digitizing tablet), keyboard, and programmed CAD functions. Lays out, redesigns, and modifies arrangement and interconnections of logic elements for each layer of integrated circuit, using digitizing work aids (light pen or digitizing tablet), keyboard and programmed CAD functions listed on display screen. Keys in specified commands, using CAD equipment keyboard, to test final IC layout for errors in design rules, using design rule software package. May generate copy of logic element design, using plotter to verify that logic element design copy meets design requirements and for use in laying out IC layer design for Very Large Scale (VLS) integrated circuits. May generate tape of final layout design for use in producing photo masks for each layer of IC, using CAD equipment. May program CAD equipment to change CAD functions listed on display screen, using keyboard. May be designated according to complexity of IC designed, such as IC DESIGNER, CUSTOM (profess. & kin.); IC DESIGNER, GATE ARRAYS (profess. & kin.); IC DESIGNER, STANDARD CELLS (profess. & kin.). • **GED:** R4, M4, L4 • **SVP:** 4-10 yrs • **Academic:** Ed=A, Eng=G • **Work Field:** 242, 244, 264 • **MPSMS:** 703 • **Aptitudes:** G2, V2, N2, S2, P2, Q2, K2, F3, M3, E5, C4 • **Temperaments:** J, T • **Physical:** V=L, H=N, L=S, H • **Work Env:** I • **Salary:** 5 • **Outlook:** 5

PHOTOGRAMMETRIST (profess. & kin.) • D.O.T. #018.261-026 • OES #22311 • CARTOGRAPHIC TECHNICIAN. Analyzes source data and prepares mosaic prints, contour maps, profile sheets, and related cartographic materials requiring technical mastery of photogrammetric techniques and principles: Prepares original maps, charts, and drawings, from aerial photographs, and survey data and applies standard mathematical formulas and photogrammetric techniques to identify, scale, and orient geodetic points, elevations, and other planimetric or topographic features and cartographic detail. Graphically delineates aerial photographic detail, such as control points, hydrography, topography, and cultural features, using precision stereoplotting apparatus or drafting instruments. Revises existing maps and charts and corrects maps in various stages of compilation. May prepare rubber, plastic, or plaster three-dimensional relief models. • **GED:** R4, M4, L4 • **SVP:** 2-4 yrs • **Academic:** Ed=H, Eng=S • **Work Field:** 242, 243 • **MPSMS:** 716 • **Aptitudes:** G2, V3, N2, S2, P2, Q2, K2, F2, M2, E3, C3 • **Temperaments:** M, T • **Physical:** V=G, H=N, L=S, H • **Work Env:** I • **Salary:** 4 • **Outlook:** 3

PRINTED CIRCUIT DESIGNER (profess. & kin.) • D.O.T. #003.261-022 • OES #22514 • Designs and drafts layout for printed circuit boards (PCBs), according to engineering specifications, utilizing knowledge of electronics, drafting, and PCB design rules (standard design requirements): Reviews and analyzes engineering design schematics and supporting documents to plan layout of PCB components and printed circuitry. Confers with engineering staff to resolve design details or problems. Drafts detailed drawings [DRAFTER (profess. & kin.) Master Title] and composes representation of design components and circuitry on clear mylar sheets (master layout), using press-on adhesive symbols and drafting tools and equipment. Examines and verifies master layout for electrical and mechanical accuracy. May verify accuracy of film reproductions of master layout. May prepare copies of drawings for use in PCB fabrication, using blueprint machine or diazo print machine. May generate computer tape of design for use in photo plotting design onto film, using digitizing equipment. May design and draft layout for multilayered PCBs. May use computer-assisted design equipment and software to design PCBs and be designated PRINTED CIRCUIT DESIGNER, COMPUTER-ASSISTED (profess. & kin.). • **GED:** R4, M4, L4 • **SVP:** 2-4 yrs • **Academic:** Ed=A, Eng=G • **Work Field:** 242, 244, 264 • **MPSMS:** 703 • **Aptitudes:** G2, V2, N2, S2, P2, Q2, K2, F2, M3, E5, C4 • **Temperaments:** J, T • **Physical:** V=L, H=N, L=S, H • **Work Env:** I • **Salary:** 4 • **Outlook:** 5

SPECIFICATION WRITER (profess. & kin.) • D.O.T. #019.267-010 • OES #22599 • Interprets architectural or engineering plans and prepares material lists and specifications to be used as standards by plant employees or contracting personnel in material processing or in manufacturing or construction activities: Analyzes plans and diagrams, or observes and makes notes on material processing, to determine material and material processing specifications, or specifications for manufacturing or construction activities. Writes technical descriptions specifying material qualities and properties, utilizing knowledge of material standards, industrial processes, and manufacturing procedures. May draw rough sketches or arrange for finished drawings or photographs to illustrate specified materials or assembly sequence. Workers usually specialize and are designated according to engineering specialization, product, or process. • **GED:** R5, M4, L4 • **SVP:** 2-4 yrs • **Academic:** Ed=A, Eng=G • **Work Field:** 244 • **MPSMS:** 700, 710 • **Aptitudes:** G2, V2, N2, S2, P2, Q2, K5, F5, M5, E5, C5 • **Temperaments:** M, T • **Physical:** V=L, H=L, L=S • **Work Env:** I • **Salary:** 4 • **Outlook:** 4

TAPER, PRINTED CIRCUIT LAYOUT (electronics) • D.O.T. #017.684-010 • OES #93999 • Places (tapes) adhesive symbols and precision tape on sheets of mylar in conformance with preliminary drawing of printed circuit board (PCB) to produce master layout: Places, aligns, and secures preliminary drawing of PCB and successive layers of transparent sheets of mylar on lighted drafting table, using register bar. Selects specified symbols and width of tape to indicate peak voltage potential. Cuts tape and places tape and adhesive symbols on specified sheets of mylar to outline board size, to indicate connector pads, placement of various components, and to trace circuitry of PCB as indicated on underlying preliminary drawing, using utility knife, precision grid, and straightedge. Places specified adhesive identification and reference numbers on master layout. Reproduces blueprint copy of master layout, using print machine. Inspects copy to verify accuracy. • **GED:** R2, M2, L2 • **SVP:** 2-30 days • **Academic:** Ed=N, Eng=N • **Work Field:** 264 • **MPSMS:** 703 • **Aptitudes:** G4, V4, N4, S3, P4, Q3, K4, F2, M3, E5, C5 • **Temperaments:** T • **Physical:** V=L, H=N, L=S, H • **Work Env:** I • **Salary:** 2 • **Outlook:** 3

TECHNICAL ILLUSTRATOR (profess. & kin.) • D.O.T. #017.281-034 • OES #22514 • ENGINEERING ILLUSTRATOR; PRODUCTION ILLUSTRATOR. Lays out and draws illustrations for reproduction in reference works, brochures, and technical manuals dealing with assembly, installation, operation, maintenance, and repair of machines, tools, and equipment: Prepares drawings from blueprints, designs, mockups, and photoprints by methods and techniques suited to specified reproduction process or final use, such as blueprint, photo-offset, and projection transparencies, using drafting and optical equipment. Lays out and draws schematic, perspective, orthographic, or oblique-angle views to depict function, relationship, and assembly-sequence of parts and assemblies, such as gears, engines, and instruments. Shades or colors drawing to emphasize details or to eliminate undesired background, using ink, crayon, airbrush, and overlays. Pastes in structions and comments in position on drawing. May draw cartoons and caricatures to illustrate operation, maintenance, and safety manuals and posters. • **GED:** R5, M5, L4 • **SVP:** 2-4 yrs • **Academic:** Ed=A, Eng=S • **Work Field:** 242 • **MPSMS:** 752 • **Aptitudes:** G2, V3, N2, S2, P2, Q3, K3, F2, M3, E5, C3 • **Temperaments:** M, T • **Physical:** V=G, H=N, L=S, H • **Work Env:** I • **Salary:** 3 • **Outlook:** 2

GOE: 05.03.03 Expediting & Coordinating

AIR-TRAFFIC-CONTROL SPECIALIST, STATION (gov. ser.) • D.O.T. #193.162-014 • OES #39002 • Receives and transmits flight plans, meteorological, navigational, and other information in air traffic control station to perform preflight and emergency service for airplane pilots: Accepts flight plans from pilots in person or by telephone and reviews them for completeness. Routes plans for operating under instrument flight rules to control center and for operating under visual flight rules to station in vicinity of destination airport, using radio, teletype, radiotelephone, radiotelegraph, telephone, or interphone. Provides meteorological, naviga-

tional, and other information to pilots during flight, using radio. Relays traffic control and other instructions concerned with aircraft safety to pilots. Radios such information as identifying landmarks, beacons, and available landing fields to pilots in flight. Maintains file of plans for operating under visual flight rules until completion of flight, and contacts facilities along route of flight to secure information on overdue aircraft. Reports lost aircraft to control center for rescue or local emergency services. Monitors such radio aids to navigation as range stations, fan markers, and voice communication facilities, and notifies air personnel of availability of these facilities. Maintains written records of messages transmitted and received. • **GED:** R4, M3, L4 • **SVP:** 2-4 yrs • **Academic:** Ed=H, Eng=G • **Work Field:** 281, 282 • **MPSMS:** 860 • **Aptitudes:** G2, V3, N3, S4, P4, Q3, K4, F3, M3, E5, C4 • **Temperaments:** J, P, V • **Stress:** E • **Physical:** V=G, H=G, L=S, H • **Work Env:** I • **Salary:** 4 • **Outlook:** 3

AIR-TRAFFIC-CONTROL SPECIALIST, TOWER (gov. ser.) • D.O.T. #193.162-018 • OES #39002 • AIRPORT-CONTROL OPERATOR; CONTROL-TOWER-RADIO OPERATOR; FLIGHT-CONTROL-TOWER OPERATOR. Controls air traffic on and within vicinity of airport according to established procedures and policies to prevent collisions and to minimize delays arising from traffic congestion: Answers radio calls from arriving and departing aircraft and issues such landing and take-off instructions and information as runway to use, wind velocity and direction, visibility, tax iing instructions, and pertinent data on other aircraft operating in vicinity. Transfers control of departing flights to and accepts control of arriving flights from air traffic control center, using telephone or interphone. Alerts airport emergency crew and other designated personnel by radio or telephone when airplanes are having flight difficulties. Pushes buttons or pulls switches to control airport floodlights and boundary, runway, and hazard lights. Scans control panel to ascertain that lights are functioning. Operates radio and monitors radarscope to control aircraft operating in vicinity of airport. Receives cross-country flight plans and transmits them to air traffic control center. Signals aircraft flying under visual flight rules, using electric signal light or flags. May control cross-runway traffic by radio directions to guards or maintenance vehicles. May keep written record of messages received from aircraft. May control traffic within designated sector of airspace between centers and beyond airport control tower area and be designated as AIR-TRAFFIC-CONTROL SPECIALIST, CENTER (gov. ser.). • **GED:** R4, M3, L4 • **SVP:** 4-10 yrs • **Academic:** Ed=H, Eng=S • **Work Field:** 281, 282 • **MPSMS:** 855 • **Aptitudes:** G2, V3, N3, S3, P3, Q3, K4, F3, M3, E5, C3 • **Temperaments:** J, S, V • **Stress:** S • **Physical:** V=G, H=G, L=L, H • **Work Env:** I • **Salary:** 5 • **Outlook:** 4

DISPATCHER (air trans.) • D.O.T. #912.167-010 • OES #39002 • AIRPLANE DISPATCHER; HELICOPTER DISPATCHER. Authorizes, regulates, and controls commercial airline flights according to government and company regulations to expedite and ensure safety of flight: Analyzes and evaluates meteorological information, such as speed and direction of winds, visibility, and presence of storms, to determine potential safety of flight and desirable route. Computes amount of fuel needed according to type of aircraft, distance of flight, weather conditions, and fuel regulations prescribed by Federal Aviation Agency. Prepares flight plan containing information, such as maximum allowable gross takeoff and landing weights, weather, and landing field conditions. Signs authorization to release flight for takeoff. Delays or cancels flight if unsafe conditions prevail. Studies weather and pilot's position reports and terrain maps to evaluate progress of flight. Recommends flight plan alterations, such as changing course or altitude, cancelling stops, or taking extra fuel. Prepares log of flights, delays and cancellations, and lists reasons for changes in schedules or flight plans. Must be licensed by Federal Aviation Administration. • **GED:** R5, M4, L4 • **SVP:** 4-10 yrs • **Academic:** Ed=N, Eng=G • **Work Field:** 211, 231, 281 • **MPSMS:** 855 • **Aptitudes:** G2, V2, N2, S4, P3, Q2, K4, F4, M4, E5, C3 • **Temperaments:** D, M, P, S • **Stress:** E, A, S • **Physical:** V=L, H=G, L=S, H • **Work Env:** I • **Salary:** 4 • **Outlook:** 3

MATERIAL SCHEDULER (aircraft-aerospace mfg.) • D.O.T. #012.187-010 • OES #22128 • MATERIAL PLANNER; MATERIAL-RELEASE ANALYST. Develops and analyzes lists of raw material, purchased parts, and equipment, needed in manufacture of airplanes and guided missiles: Estimates from engineering drawings and blueprints total amounts required and converts requirements into orders of conventional sizes and quantities, taking into consideration present inventories, unavoidable waste, and kind of material. Schedules deliveries based on production forecasts, market conditions, material substitutions, storage and handling facilities, and maintenance requirements. Reviews material lists for conformance to company standard practices in regard to parts and materials used. Prepares or authorizes requisitions to purchasing department. Estimates need to reorder supplies due to rejections and engineering changes during manufacture. • **GED:** R5, M5, L5 • **SVP:** 2-4 yrs • **Academic:** Ed=A, Eng=G • **Work Field:** 232 • **MPSMS:** 898 • **Aptitudes:** G2, V2, N2, S3, P3, Q3, K4, F4, M4, E5, C4 • **Temperaments:** M, T • **Physical:** V=L, H=L, L=S • **Work Env:** I • **Salary:** 4 • **Outlook:** 4

GOE: 05.03.04 Petroleum Engin. Tech.

FIELD ENGINEER, SPECIALIST (petrol. production) • D.O.T. #010.261-010 • OES #22599 • Collects fluid samples from oil-or gas-bearing formations and analyzes sample to determine potential productivity of formation: Moves controls on panel to fire charge into formation and to operate hydraulic mechanism which thrusts and seals probe into perforation. Analyzes fluid in sample to determine potential productivity of formation. • **GED:** R4, M4, L4 • **SVP:** 2-4 yrs • **Academic:** Ed=H, Eng=G • **Work Field:** 244 • **MPSMS:** 872 • **Aptitudes:** G2, V3, N2, S3, P2, Q3, K4, F3, M4, E5, C4 • **Temperaments:** J, M • **Physical:** V=L, H=L, L=L, H • **Work Env:** B, R • **Salary:** 4 • **Outlook:** 2

GOE: 05.03.05 Elect. Engineering Technology

FIELD ENGINEER (radio & tv broad.) • D.O.T. #193.262-018 • OES #34028 • FIELD TECHNICIAN. Installs and operates portable field transmission equipment to broadcast programs or events originating at points distant from studio: Determines availability of telephone wire facilities for use in making connections between microphone, amplifier, telephone line, and auxiliary power supply to relay broadcast to master control. Sets up, tests, and operates microwave transmitter to broadcast program in absence of telephone wire system. Conducts broadcast from field. Must be licensed by Federal Government. May perform duties of RECORDING ENGINEER (phonograph; radio & tv broad.); ANNOUNCER (radio & tv broad.) in field. May be designated as MICROWAVE ENGINEER (radio & tv broad.) when restricted to operating microwave transmitter. • **GED:** R5, M4, L5 • **SVP:** 2-4 yrs • **Academic:** Ed=A, Eng=S • **Work Field:** 281 • **MPSMS:** 860 • **Aptitudes:** G2, V2, N3, S3, P2, Q3, K3, F3, M3, E5, C3 • **Temperaments:** M, T, V • **Physical:** V=G, H=N, L=S, H • **Work Env:** B • **Salary:** 4 • **Outlook:** 4

RADIOGRAPHER (any ind.) • D.O.T. #199.361-010 • OES #39999 • INDUSTRIAL X-RAY OPERATOR. Radiographs metal, plastics, concrete, or other materials, such as castings, sample parts, pipes, and structural members for flaws, cracks, or presence of foreign materials, utilizing knowledge of radiography equipment, techniques, and procedures: Alines object on stand between source of X-rays and film or plate; or alines source of gamma rays, such as cobalt or iridium isotope and film or plate on opposite sides of object, manually or using hand or electric truck, chain hoist, or crane. Masks peripheral areas with lead shields. Selects type of radiation source and type of film, and applies standard mathematical formulas to determine exposure distance and time, considering size, mobility, and strength of radiation sources in relation to density and mobility of object. Verifies radiation intensities, using radiation meters. Adjusts controls of X-ray equipment on console or exposes source of radioactivity to take radiograph. Removes and develops film or plate. Monitors working area, using survey meters, to protect personnel area. May replace radioactive isotope source in containers by manipulating tongs from behind protective lead shield. Marks defects appearing on film and assists in analyzing findings. May specialize in X-ray work and be designated X-RAY TECHNICIAN (any ind.). • **GED:** R4, M4, L4 • **SVP:** 6 mos-1 yr • **Academic:** Ed=A, Eng=G • **Work Field:** 201, 211 •

MPSMS: 360, 540 • **Aptitudes:** G3, V3, N3, S3, P3, Q4, K3, F3, M3, E4, C3 • **Temperaments:** M, T • **Physical:** V=G, H=N, L=S, W, H • **Work Env:** I, R • **Salary:** 4 • **Outlook:** 4

RADIOTELEPHONE OPERATOR (any ind.) • D.O.T. #193.262-034 • OES #39008 • PHONE-CIRCUIT OPERATOR; RADIOPHONE OPERATOR; RADIOTELEPHONE-TECHNICAL OPERATOR. Operates and keeps in repair radiotelephone transmitter and receiving equipment for commercial communication: Throws switches to cut in power to stages of transmitter. Cuts in antennas and connects transmitting and receiving equipment into telephone system. Turns controls to adjust voice volume and modulation, and to set transmitter on specified frequency. Conducts routine tests and repairs transmitting equipment, using electronic testing equipment, handtools, and power tools, to maintain communication system in operative condition. Must hold Radiotelephone Operator's License issued by Federal Communications Commission. • **GED:** R4, M3, L4 • **SVP:** 2-4 yrs • **Academic:** Ed=H, Eng=G • **Work Field:** 281 • **MPSMS:** 860 • **Aptitudes:** G3, V3, N3, S2, P2, Q3, K3, F3, M3, E5, C5 • **Temperaments:** P, T, V • **Stress:** E • **Physical:** V=N, H=G, L=S, H • **Work Env:** I • **Salary:** 4 • **Outlook:** 3

TRANSMITTER OPERATOR (radio & tv broad.) • D.O.T. #193.262-038 • OES #34028 • TRANSMITTER ENGINEER. Operates and maintains radio transmitter to broadcast radio and television programs: Moves switches to cut in power to units and stages of transmitter. Monitors lights on console panel to ascertain that components are operative and that transmitter is ready to emit signal. Turns controls to set transmitter on FM, AM, or TV frequency assigned by Federal Communications Commission. Monitors signal emission and spurious radiations outside of licensed transmission frequency to insure signal is not infringing on frequencies assigned other stations. Notifies broadcast studio when ready to transmit. Observes indicators and adjusts controls to maintain constant sound modulation and ensure that transmitted signal is sharp and clear. Maintains log of programs transmitted as required by the Federal Communications Commission. Tests components of malfunctioning transmitter to diagnose trouble, using test equipment, such as oscilloscope, voltmeters, and ammeters. Disassembles and repairs equipment, using handtools [RADIO MECHANIC (any ind.)]. May operate microwave transmitter and receiver to receive or send programs to or from other broadcast stations. Must possess First Class Radio-Telephone License issued by Federal Communications Commission. • **GED:** R4, M4, L4 • **SVP:** 2-4 yrs • **Academic:** Ed=A, Eng=G • **Work Field:** 281 • **MPSMS:** 860, 863 • **Aptitudes:** G2, V2, N3, S3, P2, Q4, K3, F2, M3, E5, C3 • **Temperaments:** J, M, T • **Physical:** V=N, H=G, L=S, H • **Work Env:** I • **Salary:** 3 • **Outlook:** 1

VIDEO OPERATOR (radio & tv broad.) • D.O.T. #194.282-010 • OES #34028 • CAMERA-CONTROL OPERATOR; COLOR-TELEVISION-CONSOLE MONITOR; VIDEO ENGINEER. Controls video console to regulate transmission of television scenes including test patterns and filmed and live black-and-white or color tele cast: Views action on television monitor and sets switches and observes dials on console to control framing, contrast, brilliance, color balance, and fidelity of image being transmitted. Moves switches to change scenes being televised in separate studios fading one scene into the next as specified by script. Monitors on-the-air programs to ensure technical quality of broadcast. Previews program to be used next to determine that signal is functioning and that program will be ready at required time. Maintains log on studio to transmitter microwave link. • **GED:** R5, M4, L5 • **SVP:** 2-4 yrs • **Academic:** Ed=H, Eng=G • **Work Field:** 281 • **MPSMS:** 863 • **Aptitudes:** G2, V2, N3, S3, P2, Q4, K3, F3, M3, E5, C2 • **Temperaments:** J, M, T • **Physical:** V=G, H=G, L=S, H • **Work Env:** I • **Salary:** 4 • **Outlook:** 1

GOE: 05.03.06 Industrial & Safety

BUILDING INSPECTOR (insurance) • D.O.T. #168.267-010 • OES #21908 • Inspects buildings to determine fire insurance rates: Examines building for type of construction, condition of roof, and fireproofing. Determines risk represented by adjoining buildings, by nature of business, and building contents. Determines availability of fireplugs and firefighting equipment. Completes inspection report. May compute insurance rate. • **GED:** R4, M3, L4 • **SVP:**

2-4 yrs • **Academic:** Ed=A, Eng=G • **Work Field:** 211 • **MPSMS:** 361, 895 • **Aptitudes:** G2, V2, N3, S3, P4, Q2, K4, F4, M4, E4, C4 • **Temperaments:** J, M, P, T • **Stress:** E • **Physical:** V=G, H=N, L=S, W, C • **Work Env:** B • **Salary:** 4 • **Outlook:** 1

CODE INSPECTOR (gov. ser.) • D.O.T. #168.367-018 • OES #21911 • Inspects existing residential buildings and dwelling units, visually, to determine compliance with city ordinance standards and explains ordinance requirements to concerned personnel: Obtains permission from owners and tenants to enter dwellings. Visually examines all areas to determine compliance with ordinance standards for heating, lighting, ventilating, and plumbing installations. Measures dwelling units and rooms to determine compliance with ordinance space requirements, using tape measure. Inspects premises for overall cleanliness, adequate disposal of garbage and rubbish, and for signs of vermin infestation. Prepares forms and letters advising property owners and tenants of possible violations and time allowed for correcting deficiencies. Consults file of violation reports and revisits dwellings at periodic intervals to verify correction of violations by property owners and tenants. Explains requirements of housing standards ordinance to property owners, building contractors, and other interested parties. • **GED:** R3, M2, L3 • **SVP:** 6 mos-1 yr • **Academic:** Ed=N, Eng=G • **Work Field:** 211 • **MPSMS:** 953 • **Aptitudes:** G3, V3, N4, S3, P2, Q3, K4, F4, M4, E5, C5 • **Temperaments:** P, T • **Stress:** E • **Physical:** V=G, H=L, L=S, W • **Work Env:** I • **Salary:** 3 • **Outlook:** 2

CONSTRUCTION INSPECTOR (const.) • D.O.T. #182.267-010 • OES #21908 • Inspects and oversees construction of bridges, buildings, dams, highways, and other types of construction work to ensure that procedures and materials comply with plans and specifications: Measures distances to verify accuracy of dimensions of structural installations and layouts. Verifies levels, alinement, and elevation of installations, using surveyor's level and transit. Observes work in progress to ensure that procedures followed and materials used conform to specifications. Prepares samples of unapproved materials for laboratory testing. Examines workmanship of finished installations for conformity to standard and approves installation. Interprets blueprints and specifications for CONTRACTOR (const.) and discusses deviations from specified construction procedures to insure compliance with regulations governing construction. Records quantities of materials received or used during specified periods. Maintains daily log of construction and inspection activities and compares progress reports. Computes monthly estimates of work completed and approves payment for contractors. Prepares sketches of construction installations that deviate from blueprints and reports such changes for incorporation on master blueprints. May be designated according to structure or material inspected as BUILDING-CONSTRUCTION INSPECTOR (const.); DITCH INSPECTOR (const.); HIGHWAY INSPECTOR (const.); MASONRY INSPECTOR (const.); REINFORCED-CONCRETE INSPECTOR (const.); ROD INSPECTOR (const.). Additional titles: PIPE-LINE INSPECTOR (const.); STRUCTURAL-STEEL INSPECTOR (const.); TUNNEL-HEADING INSPECTOR (const.). • **GED:** R4, M4, L3 • **SVP:** 1-2 yrs • **Academic:** Ed=H, Eng=S • **Work Field:** 211, 243 • **MPSMS:** 360 • **Aptitudes:** G2, V3, N2, S2, P3, Q4, K4, F4, M4, E2, C5 • **Temperaments:** J, M, T, V • **Physical:** V=G, H=L, L=L, W, C, S, H • **Work Env:** B, N, R • **Salary:** 4 • **Outlook:** 3

FLIGHT ENGINEER (air trans.) • D.O.T. #621.261-018 • OES #97702 • FLIGHT MECHANIC. Makes preflight, inflight, and postflight inspections, adjustments, and minor repairs to ensure safe and efficient operation of aircraft: Inspects aircraft prior to takeoff for defects, such as fuel or oil leaks and malfunctions in electrical, hydraulic, or pressurization systems according to preflight checklist. Verifies passenger and cargo distribution and amount of fuel to insure that weight and balance specifications are met. Monitors control panel to verify aircraft performance, and regulates engine speed according to instructions of AIRPLANE PILOT, COMMERCIAL (air trans.). Makes inflight repairs, such as replacing fuses, adjusting instruments, and freeing jammed flight control cables, using handtools, or takes emergency measures to compensate for failure of equipment, such as autopilot, wing heaters, and electrical and hydraulic systems. Monitors fuel gages and computes rate of fuel consumption. Keeps log of fuel consumption and engine performance. Records malfunctions which were not corrected during flight and reports needed repairs to ground maintenance personnel. May perform repairs upon completion of flight. Must be licensed by Federal Aviation Administration. May be required to be licensed AIRFRAME-AND-POWER-PLANT MECHANIC (aircraft-aerospace mfg.; air trans.) or AIRPLANE PILOT, COMMERCIAL (air trans.). • **GED:** R4, M4, L4 • **SVP:** 2-4 yrs • **Academic:** Ed=H, Eng=G • **Work Field:** 111, 121 • **MPSMS:** 592 • **Aptitudes:** G2, V2, N2, S3, P3, Q2, K3, F3, M3, E4, C4 • **Temperaments:** M, S, T, V • **Stress:** S • **Physical:** V=L, H=L, L=L, W, S, H • **Work Env:** I, N • **Salary:** 4 • **Outlook:** 3

INDUSTRIAL ENGINEERING TECHNICIAN (profess. & kin.) • D.O.T. #012.267-010 • OES #22508 • Studies and records time, motion, methods, and speed involved in performance of maintenance, production, clerical, and other worker operations to establish standard production rate and to improve efficiency: Prepares charts, graphs, and diagrams to illustrate workflow, routing, floor layouts, material handling, and machine utilization. Observes workers operating equipment or performing tasks to determine time involved and fatigue rate, using stop watch, motion-picture camera, electrical recorder, and similar equipment. Recommends revision of methods of operation or material handling, alterations in equipment layout, or other changes to increase production or improve standards. Aids in planning work assignments in accordance with worker performance, machine capacity, production schedules, and anticipated delays. May be designated according to type of studies analyzed as METHODS-STUDY ANALYST (profess. & kin.); MOTION-STUDY ANALYST (profess. & kin.); PACE ANALYST (profess. & kin.); TIME-STUDY ANALYST (profess. & kin.). • **GED:** R5, M5, L4 • **SVP:** 2-4 yrs • **Academic:** Ed=A, Eng=G • **Work Field:** 244 • **MPSMS:** 712 • **Aptitudes:** G2, V2, N2, S2, P2, Q3, K4, F3, M4, E5, C4 • **Temperaments:** D, J, M • **Physical:** V=L, H=L, L=S, H • **Work Env:** I • **Salary:** 4 • **Outlook:** 3

INSPECTOR, AIR-CARRIER (gov. ser.) • D.O.T. #168.264-010 • OES #21911 • AVIATION-SAFETY OFFICER; OPERATIONS INSPECTOR. Inspects aircraft and maintenance base facilities to assure conformance with federal safety and qualifications standards: Examines aircraft maintenance record and flight log to determine if service checks, maintenance checks, and overhauls were performed at intervals prescribed. Inspects landing gear, tires, and exterior of fuselage, wings, and engine for evidence of damage or corrosion and recommends repair. Examines access plates and doors for security. Inspects new, repaired, or modified aircraft, according to checklist, to determine structural and mechanical airworthiness, using handtools and test instruments. Starts aircraft and observes gages, meters, and other instruments to detect evidence of malfunction. Examines electrical systems and accompanies flight crew on proving flight to test instruments. Inventories spare parts to determine whether stock meets requirements. Analyzes training programs to assure competency of persons operating, installing, and repairing equipment. Informs airline officials of deficiencies. Prepares report of inspection to document findings. Approves or disapproves issuance of certificate of airworthiness. Conducts examinations to test theoretical and practical knowledge of construction, maintenance, repair, and trouble diagnosis for Aircraft Mechanics License candidates. Investigates air accidents to determine whether cause was due to structural or mechanical malfunction. Required to have Federal aviation rating for type of aircraft inspected and pass Federal aviation medical certification. May be designated according to specialty as AIR-CARRIER ELECTRONICS INSPECTOR (gov. ser.); AIR-CARRIER MAINTENANCE INSPECTOR (gov. ser.). • **GED:** R5, M5, L4 • **SVP:** 2-4 yrs • **Academic:** Ed=A, Eng=S • **Work Field:** 211 • **MPSMS:** 586, 592 • **Aptitudes:** G2, V3, N2, S2, P2, Q3, K3, F3, M2, E4, C4 • **Temperaments:** J, M • **Physical:** V=G, H=L, L=L, W, S, H • **Work Env:** I, N, R • **Salary:** 4 • **Outlook:** 3

INSPECTOR, BUILDING (gov. ser.) • D.O.T. #168.167-030 • OES #21908 • Inspects new and existing buildings and structures to enforce conformance to building, grading, and zoning laws and approved plans, specifications, and standards: Inspects residential, commercial, industrial, and other buildings during and after construction to ensure that components such as footings, floor framing, completed framing, chimneys, and stairways meet provisions of building, grading, zoning, and safety laws and approved plans, specifications, and standards. Observes conditions and issues notices for corrections to persons responsible for conformance. Obtains evidence and prepares reports concerning violations which have not been corrected. Interprets legal requirements and recommends compliance procedures to contractors, craftworkers, and owners. Keeps inspection records and prepares reports for use by administrative or judicial authorities. May conduct surveys of existing buildings to determine lack of proper maintenance, housing violations, or hazardous conditions. May review request for and issue building permits. May specialize in inspecting multi-family residences, temporary structures, buildings to be moved, or building appendages, such as chimneys, signs, swimming pools, retaining walls, and excavations and fills. May specialize in inspecting single-family residences for enforcement of full range of building, zoning, grading, and mechanical codes, including electrical, plumbing, heating and refrigeration, ventilating, and air-conditioning regulations, and be designated RESIDENTIAL BUILDING INSPECTOR (gov. ser.). • **GED:** R5, M4, L4 • **SVP:** 2-4 yrs • **Academic:** Ed=N, Eng=G • **Work Field:** 211, 271 • **MPSMS:** 361, 959 • **Aptitudes:** G2, V2, N2, S2, P3, Q3, K4, F4, M4, E3, C4 • **Temperaments:** J, M, P, T • **Stress:** E • **Physical:** V=G, H=N, L=S, W, C, S • **Work Env:** B • **Salary:** 4 • **Outlook:** 3

INSPECTOR, INDUSTRIAL WASTE (gov. ser.) • D.O.T. #168.267-054 • OES #21911 • Inspects industrial and commercial waste disposal facilities and investigates source of pollutants in municipal sewage and storm-drainage system to insure conformance with ordinance and permit requirements: Visits establishments to determine possession of industrial waste permits and to inspect waste treatment facilities, such as floor drains, sand traps, settling and neutralizing tanks, and grease removal equipment for conformance with regulations. Extracts samples of waste from sewers, storm drains, and water courses for laboratory tests. Conducts field tests for acidity, alkalinity, and other characteristics to determine if discharged wastes will cause water pollution or deterioration of sewerage facilities. Inspects sewers and storm drains to determine presence of explosive gases, using gas-analysis equipment. Reviews plans of proposed waste-treatment facilities and inspects construction to insure conformance with ordinances. Issues citations to apparent violators of sanitation code or water-quality regulations. Compiles written reports of investigations and findings, and actions taken or recommended. May enforce ordinances concerned with commercial hauling and disposal of contents from cesspools and septic tanks into sewers. May inspect water wells for contamination and conformance with legal construction standards, and order closing of unsanitary or unsafe wells. • **GED:** R5, M4, L5 • **SVP:** 1-2 yrs • **Academic:** Ed=A, Eng=S • **Work Field:** 211 • **MPSMS:** 874 • **Aptitudes:** G2, V2, N3, S3, P3, Q3, K4, F4, M3, E4, C3 • **Temperaments:** M, P, V • **Physical:** V=G, H=L, L=M, W, C, S, H • **Work Env:** B, W • **Salary:** 4 • **Outlook:** 3

INSPECTOR, QUALITY ASSURANCE (gov. ser.) • D.O.T. #168.287-014 • OES #21911 • PROCUREMENT INSPECTOR. Inspects products manufactured or processed by private companies for government use to ensure compliance with contract specifications: Examines company's records to secure such information as size and weight of product and results of quality tests. Inspects product to determine compliance with order specifications, company's quality control system for compliance with legal requirements, and shipping and packing facilities for conformity to specified standards. Submits samples of product to government laboratory for testing as indicated by department procedures. Stamps mark of approval or rejection on product and writes report of examinations. May specialize in lumber, machinery, petroleum products, paper products, electronic equipment, furniture, or other specific product or group of related products. • **GED:** R5, M5, L5 • **SVP:** 2-4 yrs • **Academic:** Ed=A, Eng=S • **Work Field:** 211 • **MPSMS:** 959 • **Aptitudes:** G2, V2, N2, S3, P2, Q3, K4, F4, M4, E5, C3 • **Temperaments:** J, M, T • **Physical:** V=G, H=N, L=L, W, H • **Work Env:** I • **Salary:** 4 • **Outlook:** 3

INSPECTOR, RAILROAD (gov. ser.) • D.O.T. #168.287-018 • OES #21911 • Examines railroad equipment and systems to verify compliance with Federal safety regulations: Inspects railroad locomotives, engines, and cars to ensure adherence to safety standards governing condition of mechanical, structural, electrical, pneumatic, and hydraulic elements or systems, using blueprints, schematic diagrams, gages, handtools, and test equipment. Tests railroad signals to determine warning light responses to commands from dispatcher or tripswitches, using simulator. Inspects roadbeds to detect damaged, worn, or defective equipment, such as rails, ties, bolts, fishplates, or switches. Inspects condition and movement of railroad cars containing flammable or explosive materials to insure safe loading, switching, and transport. Reviews records, operating practices, and accident history to verify compliance with safety regulations. Issues citations to railroad employees of condition or equipment found in violation of standards. Investigates accidents and inspects wreckage to determine causes. Prepares inspection reports for use by administrative or judicial authorities. • **GED:** R4, M3, L4 • **SVP:** 2-4 yrs • **Academic:** Ed=H, Eng=S • **Work Field:** 121, 211 • **MPSMS:** 594, 851 • **Aptitudes:** G3, V3, N3, S2, P3, Q3, K3, F3, M3, E3, C3 • **Temperaments:** M, T • **Physical:** V=G, H=L, L=M, W, C, S, H • **Work Env:** B, N, R • **Salary:** 4 • **Outlook:** 3

MARINE SURVEYOR (profess. & kin.) • D.O.T. #014.167-010 • OES #22138 • SHIP SURVEYOR. Surveys marine vessels and watercraft, such as ships, boats, tankers, and dredges, to ascertain condition of hull, machinery, equipment, and equipage, and to determine repairs required for vessel to meet requirements for insuring: Examines underwater section of hull while ship is drydocked to ascertain conditions that indicate repairs are required. Takes readings on tailshaft and tailshaft bearings. Inspects condition of propellers, rudders, and sea valves. Inspects above waterline section of ship, such as hatchways, freeing ports, ventilators, bulkheads, fittings, and attachments, for compliance with operating standards, and compliance with standards for protection of crew. Observes operating tests on machinery and equipment and inspects opened up machinery for interior condition. Observes testing of cargo gear for compliance with testing standards and issues or endorses certificate for gear tested. Prepares reports on types of surveys conducted, recommended actions and repairs, or conditions remedied. Submits report to client. • **GED:** R5, M4, L4 • **SVP:** 4- 10 yrs • **Academic:** Ed=A, Eng=G • **Work Field:** 211 • **MPSMS:** 593 • **Aptitudes:** G2, V2, N2, S3, P3, Q4, K4, F4, M3, E4, C5 • **Temperaments:** J, M, T • **Physical:** V=L, H=L, L=L, W, C, S, H • **Work Env:** B • **Salary:** 5 • **Outlook:** 2

PLAN CHECKER (gov. ser.) • D.O.T. #168.267-102 • OES #21908 • Examines commercial and private building plans and inspects construction sites to ensure compliance with building code regulations: Reviews building plans for completeness and accuracy. Examines individual plan components to ensure that all code mandated items are included. Calculates footage between building components, such as doors, windows, and parking areas and amount of area occupied by components to ensure compliance with code. Notes instances of noncompliance on plans and correction sheet and suggests modifications to bring plans into compliance. Approves and signs plans meeting code requirements. Inspects building sites and buildings to ensure construction follows plans. Submits reports detailing items of noncompliance to builder for correction. Provides code information to individuals planning buildings. Issues occupancy certificates to building owners when completed buildings are in compliance with codes. Tours jurisdictional area to detect unapproved or noncompliance construction. Proposes studies to improve or update building codes. Testifies at appeal hearings regarding buildings alleged to be not in compliance with codes. • **GED:** R4, M4, L4 • **SVP:** 2-4 yrs • **Academic:** Ed=H, Eng=G • **Work Field:** 211, 271 • **MPSMS:** 953 • **Aptitudes:** G3, V2, N2, S2, P2, Q2, K4, F4, M4, E4, C5 • **Temperaments:** P, T • **Physical:** V=L, H=N, L=S, H • **Work Env:** I • **Salary:** 3 • **Outlook:** 2

SUPERVISOR, VENDOR QUALITY (any ind.) • D.O.T. #012.167-062 • OES #13017 • CHIEF, VENDOR QUALITY. Directs and coordinates quality inspection of parts, components, and materials produced by subcontractors and vendors, and surveillance of subcontractors manufacturing processes: Directs sampling inspection, and testing of received parts, components, and materials to determine conformance to standards. Conducts periodic and special surveys of subcontractors facilities and manufacturing processes to determine adequacy and capability of quality control and ability to comply with complete quality specifications. Reviews quality problems with engineering personnel and directs action required to correct defects. Prepares periodic and special reports concerning departmental activities, problems, subcontractor's quality system, schedules, and rejected items. Aids in organizational planning by participating in departmental conferences. • **GED:** R5, M5, L5 • **SVP:** 2-4 yrs • **Academic:** Ed=A, Eng=S • **Work Field:** 211 • **MPSMS:** 470, 568, 580 • **Aptitudes:** G2, V2, N2, S3, P4, Q4, K3, F3, M3, E5, C5 • **Temperaments:** D, J, M, P • **Physical:** V=N, H=N, L=S • **Work Env:** I • **Salary:** 4 • **Outlook:** 4

GOE: 05.03.07 Mechanical, Engineering Technology

HEAT-TRANSFER TECHNICIAN (profess. & kin.) • D.O.T. #007.181-010 • OES #22511 • Plans requirements for fabricating, installing, testing, and servicing climate control and heat transfer assemblies and systems to assist engineering personnel, utilizing knowledge of heat transfer technology and engineering methods: Calculates required capacities for equipment units of proposed system to obtain specified performance and submits data to engineering personnel for approval. Studies supplier catalogs and technical data to recommend equipment unit selections for system. Prepares unit design layouts and detail drawings for fabricating parts and assembling system. Estimates cost factors, such as labor and material for purchased and fabricated parts, and costs for assembling, testing and installing in customer's premises. Fabricates non-standard parts for system, using metalworking machinery and assembles system, using hand tools and power tools. Installs test fixtures, apparatus, and controls and conducts operational tests under specified conditions. Analyzes test data and prepares report for evaluation by engineering personnel. Installs system in customer premises and tests operational performance for compliance with contract specifications and applicable codes. Diagnoses special service problems of systems under service contract and writes instructions for service or repair personnel. May be designated according to specialty as AIR-CONDITIONING TECHNICIAN (profess. & kin.); HEATING TECHNICIAN (profess. & kin.); REFRIGERATING TECHNICIAN (profess. & kin.). • **GED:** R5, M5, L5 • **SVP:** 2-4 yrs • **Academic:** Ed=A, Eng=S • **Work Field:** 211, 244 • **MPSMS:** 553, 573, 706 • **Aptitudes:** G2, V2, N2, S2, P2, Q3, K2, F2, M2, E4, C5 • **Temperaments:** J, M, T, V • **Physical:** V=L, H=N, L=L, H • **Work Env:** B • **Salary:** 4 • **Outlook:** 3

SOLAR-ENERGY-SYSTEMS DESIGNER (profess. & kin.) • D.O.T. #007.161-038 • OES #22135 • Designs solar domestic hot water and space heating systems for new and existing structures, applying knowledge of energy requirements of structure, local climatological conditions, solar technology, and thermodynamics: Estimates energy requirements of new or existing structures, based on analysis of utility bills of structure, calculations of thermal efficiency of structure, and prevailing climatological conditions. Determines type of solar system, such as water, glycol, or silicone, which functions most efficiently under prevailing climatological conditions. Calculates onsite heat generating capacity of different solar panels to determine optimum size and type of panels which meet structure's energy requirements. Arranges location of solar system components, such as panel, pumps, and storage tanks, to minimize length and number of direction changes in pipes and reconstruction of existing structures. Studies engineering tables to determine size of pipes and pumps required to maintain specified flow rate through solar panels. Specifies types of electrical controls, such as differential thermostat, temperature sensors, and solenoid valves, compatible with other system components, using knowledge of control systems. Completes parts list, specifying components of system. Draws wiring, piping, and other diagrams, using drafting tools. May inspect structures to compile data used in solar system design, such as structure's angle of alignment with sun and temperature of incoming cold water. May inspect construction of system to ensure adherence to design specifications. • **GED:** R5, M4, L4 • **SVP:** 6 mos-1 yr • **Academic:** Ed=A, Eng=G • **Work Field:** 242, 244 • **MPSMS:** 553, 706 • **Aptitudes:** G2, V2, N2, S2, P2, Q2, K2, F3, M4, E5, C4 • **Temperaments:** J, T, V • **Physical:** V=L, H=N, L=S, H • **Work Env:** I • **Salary:** 3 • **Outlook:** 3

TEST TECHNICIAN (agric. equip.) • D.O.T. #019.261-022 • OES #22599 • Tests experimental and production agricultural equipment, such as tractors and power mowers and components to evaluate their performance, using test equipment and recording instruments: Reads data sheet denoting operating specification for unit or component and type of evaluation required. Tests unit for conformance with operating requirements, such as resistance to vibration, specified horsepower, and tensile strength and hardness of parts, using test equipment, such as bend-fatigue machine, dynamometer, strength tester, hardness tester, analytical balance, and electronic recorder. Records data from dial readings and graphs and computes values, such as horse-power and tensile strength, using algebraic formulas. Operates unit to evaluate attachment performance, such as depth of tillage or harvesting capabilities for different types of crops. Draws sketches and describes test procedures and results in test data log. • **GED:** R4, M4, L4 • **SVP:** 1-2 yrs • **Academic:** Ed=A, Eng=S • **Work Field:** 211 • **MPSMS:** 562 • **Aptitudes:** G3, V3, N3, S3, P3, Q3, K3, F3, M3, E5, C4 • **Temperaments:** M, T • **Physical:** V=L, H=L, L=L, W, H • **Work Env:** B, R • **Salary:** 4 • **Outlook:** 4

GOE: 05.03.08 Environmental Control Engineering Technology

ENGINEERING TECHNICIAN (profess. & kin.) • D.O.T. #005.261-010 • OES #22502 • Conducts surveys and studies and inspects existing water and wastewater treatment systems and those under construction to ensure that pollution control requirements are met: Reviews plans and specifications for details concerning construction or repair of sewage systems, sewage and water treatment facilities, and water supply systems for conformance to pollution control requirements. Reviews information, such as size of unit, capacities, length of pipe, reinforcements, unit locations, and other data to ensure adherence to requirements. Conducts stream surveys and comprehensive basin studies to gather data. Sets up and maintains water monitoring equipment to obtain samples, flow measurements, and other data. Tabulates data and prepares sketches, diagrams, and graphs for evaluation by engineering staff. Inspects existing systems and construction, in progress and upon completion, to ensure pollution control requirements are met. Performs various other duties, such as filing plans and other documents, answering inquiries, and assisting engineering personnel, or assisting and training personnel operating equipment. • **GED:** R4, M4, L4 • **SVP:** 2-4 yrs • **Academic:** Ed=H, Eng=S • **Work Field:** 244 • **MPSMS:** 704 • **Aptitudes:** G2, V2, N2, S2, P2, Q3, K3, F3, M3, E5, C4 • **Temperaments:** J, T • **Physical:** V=L, H=N, L=S, H • **Work Env:** I • **Salary:** 4 • **Outlook:** 3

POLLUTION-CONTROL TECHNICIAN (profess. & kin.) • D.O.T. #029.261-014 • OES #24599 • ENVIRONMENTAL TECHNICIAN. Conducts tests and field investigations to obtain data for use by environmental, engineering, and scientific personnel in determining sources and methods of controlling pollutants in air, water, and soil, utilizing knowledge of agriculture, chemistry, meteorology, and engineering principles and applied technologies: Conducts chemical and physical laboratory and field tests according to prescribed standards to determine characteristics or composition of solid, liquid, or gaseous materials and substances, using pH meter, chemicals, autoclaves, centrifuge, spectrophotometer, microscope, analytical instrumentation, and chemical laboratory equipment. Collects samples of gases from smokestacks, and collects other air samples and meteorological data to assist in evaluation of atmospheric pollutants. Collects water samples from streams and lakes, or raw, semiprocessed or processed water, industrial waste water, or water from other sources to assess pollution problem. Collects soil, silt, or mud to determine chemical composition and nature of pollutants. Prepares sample for testing, records data, and prepares summaries and charts for review. Sets monitoring equipment to provide flow of information. Installs, operates, and performs routine maintenance on gas and fluid flow systems, chemical reaction systems, mechanical equipment, and other test instrumentation. May operate fixed or mobile monitoring or data collection station. May conduct bacteriological or other tests related to research in environmental or pollution control activity. May collect and analyze engine exhaust emissions to determine type and amount of pollutants, and be designated EN-GINE EMISSION TECHNICIAN (profess. & kin.). May specialize in one phase or type of environmental pollution or protection and be identified according to specialty. • **GED:** R4, M4, L4 • **SVP:** 1-2 yrs • **Academic:** Ed=A, Eng=S • **Work Field:** 211, 251 • **MPSMS:** 723, 729 • **Aptitudes:** G3, V3, N3, S4, P3, Q3, K4, F4, M4, E5, C3 • **Temperaments:** M, T • **Physical:** V=L, H=L, L=L, W, H • **Work Env:** B • **Salary:** 4 • **Outlook:** 4

GOE: 05.03.09 Packaging & Storing, Engin. Tech.

FINE ARTS PACKER (museum) • D.O.T. #102.367-010 • OES #39999 • ART PREPARATOR. Specifies types of packing materials, crating, containerization, and special handling procedures for shipping or storing art objects, scientific specimens, and historical artifacts to minimize damage and deterioration: Confers with curatorial personnel regarding status of museum projects and proposed shipping or transfer dates of exhibitions. Develops methods and procedures for packing or containerization of art objects, according to weight and characteristics of shipment. Selects protective or preservative materials, such as excelsior, chemical agents, or moistureproof wrapping, to protect shipment against vibration, moisture, impact, or other hazards. Designs special crates, modules, brackets, and traveling frames to meet insurance and museum shipping specifications. Shapes and contours internal support modules, based on size and type of paintings, sculptures, bronzes, glass, and other art objects. Directs workers engaged in moving art objects from receiving or storage areas to galleries of museum, in packing shipments, or in rigging sculptures for installation of exhibition. Inspects incoming shipment to detect damages for insurance purposes. Keeps records and documents of incoming and outgoing shipments, or location of traveling exhibitions and loan materials. Prepares and attaches written or pictorial instructions for unpacking, storage, or for exhibition of contents of shipment. May specify type of carrier, such as barge, train, or messenger according to cost considerations and nature of shipment. • **GED:** R4, M3, L3 • **SVP:** 2-4 yrs • **Academic:** Ed=H, Eng=S • **Work Field:** 041 • **MPSMS:** 969 • **Aptitudes:** G2, V2, N3, S2, P4, Q4, K4, F4, M5, E5, C4 • **Temperaments:** D, J, M, P • **Physical:** V=L, H=N, L=M, W, H • **Work Env:** I • **Salary:** 2 • **Outlook:** 3

PACKAGING ENGINEER (profess. & kin.) • D.O.T. #019.187-010 • OES #22199 • Plans and directs activities concerned with design and development of protective packaging containers: Analyzes engineering drawings and specifications of product to determine physical characteristics of item, special-handling and safety requirements, and type of materials required for container. Consults with establishment's purchasing and production departments to determine costs and feasibility of producing proposed packaging. Develops or directs development of sketches, specifications, samples, and written analyses of proposed packaging in order to present design for approval. May confer with customers or sales representatives to draw up contracts. May advise employer or customers on efficient packing procedures, innovations in packaging materials, and utilization of sealing and fastening devices. • **GED:** R5, M4, L5 • **SVP:** 2-4 yrs • **Academic:** Ed=B, Eng=S • **Work Field:** 244 • **MPSMS:** 475, 492, 559 • **Aptitudes:** G3, V3, N3, S2, P2, Q3, K3, F3, M3, E5, C3 • **Temperaments:** D, M, P, T • **Physical:** V=G, H=L, L=S, H • **Work Env:** I • **Salary:** 4 • **Outlook:** 4

05.04 Air and Water Vehicle Operation

Workers in this group pilot airplanes or ships, or supervise others who do. Some instruct other persons in flying. Most of these workers are hired by shipping companies and commercial airlines. Some find jobs piloting planes or ships for private companies or for individuals.

✔ What kind of work would you do?

Your work activities would depend upon your specific job. For example, you might:

- study load weight, fuel supply, weather conditions, and flight route to plan for a safe commercial plane flight.
- pilot a new airplane through stalls, dives, glides, rolls, and turns to test design and safety factors.
- use knowledge of local winds, weather, tides, and currents to pilot a ship through a harbor or strait.
- use charts, plotting sheets, compass, and sextant to plan and direct course of a ship.

✔ What skills and abilities do you need for this kind of work?

To do this kind of work, you must be able to:

- understand and use techniques and procedures for controlling the airplane or vessel.
- use judgment and make decisions that affect the lives of passengers on board.
- react quickly in emergencies.
- direct the crew on board.
- see readings on instrument panels clearly.
- use hand, feet, and eyes at the same time to control the ship or airplane.
- deal with different kinds of people.

✔ How do you know if you would like or could learn to do this kind of work?

The following questions may give you clues about yourself as you consider this group of jobs.

- Have you read airplane or boat magazines? Do you understand and enjoy technical articles?
- Have you built or operated a model airplane? Could you read and follow the instructions?

- Have you been a member of a Civil Air Patrol unit? Have you had flight or ground training?
- Have you operated a citizen's band radio? Do you understand and use the common code words?

- Have you driven in a bicycle rodeo, car rally, or other vehicle obstacle course? Did you receive a good score?
- Have you owned or operated a pleasure boat? Have you taken a Coast Guard safety training course?

✔ **How can you prepare for and enter this kind of work?**

Occupations in this group usually require education and/or training extending from two years to over ten years, depending upon the specific kind of work. Flight training may be obtained in the military or in FAA approved civilian flight schools. A high school education or its equal is the minimum requirement for acceptance.

Most major airlines have their own programs to provide additional specialized training before assigning pilots to service. Some airlines require a pilot to have two years of college. Many prefer college graduates. Before becoming an airline pilot, a person must have 1,500 hours of flying time.

Ship captains advance through several officer ranks. The beginning rank is that of third mate. Most third mate positions are earned by completing a training course at a marine academy.

Some marine trade unions offer programs to train seamen to become third mates. These trainees must be U.S. citizens and be approved by the U.S. Public Health Service for vision and general health. They must also pass Coast Guard tests on navigation, freight handling, and deck operations.

✔ **What else should you consider about these jobs?**

Pilots are often under mental stress and must always be alert and ready to make decisions quickly. Airlines have flights at all hours of the day and night. Pilots may be away from home frequently. Ship officers are usually away from home for long periods. Workers in this group face the possibility of injury through fires, collisions, and other disasters.

If you think you would like to do this kind of work, look at the job titles listed below.

GOE: 05.04.01 Air Vehicle Operation

AIRPLANE PILOT (agric.) • D.O.T. #196.263-010 • OES #97702 • AERIAL-APPLICATOR PILOT; AGRICULTURAL-AIRCRAFT PILOT; AIRCRAFT PILOT; AIRPLANE PILOT, CROP DUSTING. Pilots airplane or helicopter, at low altitudes, over agricultural fields to dust or spray fields with seeds, fertilizers, or pesticides: Flies over field together with FARMER (agric.) to become acquainted with obstacles or hazards, such as air turbulences, hedgerows, and hills peculiar to particular field. Arranges for warning signals to be posted. Notifies FARMERS (aric.) to move livestock from property over which harmful material may drift. Signals AIRPLANE-PILOT HELPER (agric.) to load aircraft. Observes field markers and flag waved by AIRPLANE-PILOT HELPER (agric.) on ground to prevent overlaps of application and ensure complete coverage. May specialize in application of pesticides and be designated as PEST-CONTROL PILOT (agric.). • **GED:** R5, M4, L5 • **SVP:** 1-2 yrs • **Academic:** Ed=A, Eng=S • **Work Field:** 293 • **MPSMS:** 300 • **Aptitudes:** G2, V2, N2, S2, P2, Q3, K2, F3, M3, E2, C4 • **Temperaments:** J, M, S, T • **Stress:** A, S • **Physical:** V=G, H=G, L=L, H • **Work Env:** I, N, R • **Salary:** 4 • **Outlook:** 1

AIRPLANE PILOT, COMMERCIAL (air trans.) • D.O.T. #196.263-014 • OES #97702 • COMMERCIAL PILOT; PILOT. Pilots airplane to transport passengers, mail, or freight, or for other commercial purposes: Reviews ship's papers to ascertain factors, such as load weight, fuel supply, weather conditions, and flight route and schedule. Orders changes in fuel supply, load, route, or schedule to insure safety of flight. Reads gages to verify that oil, hydraulic fluid, fuel quantities, and cabin pressure are at prescribed levels prior to starting engines. Starts engines and taxies airplane to runway. Sets brakes, and accelerates engines to verify operational readiness of components, such as superchargers, carburetor-heaters, and controls. Contacts control tower by radio to obtain takeoff clearance and instructions. Releases brakes and moves throttles and hand and foot controls to take off and control airplane in flight. Pilots airplane to destination adhering to flight plan and regulations and procedures of Federal Government, company, and airport. Logs information, such as time in flight, altitude flown, and fuel consumed. Must hold Commercial Pilot's Certificate issued by Federal Aviation Administration. May instruct students or pilots in operation of aircraft. May be designated according to Federal license held as TRANSPORT PILOT (air trans.), or type of commercial activity engaged in as AIRLINE PILOT (air trans.) or CORPORATE PILOT (air trans.). When piloting airplane over pipelines, train tracks, and communications systems to detect and radio location and nature of damage is designated AIRPLANE-PATROL PILOT (bus. ser.). When in command of aircraft and crew is designated as AIRPLANE CAPTAIN (air trans.), or when second in command is designated AIRPLANE FIRST-OFFICER (air trans.) or COPILOT (air trans.). • **GED:** R5, M5, L5 • **SVP:** 2-4 yrs • **Academic:** Ed=A, Eng=G • **Work Field:** 013 • **MPSMS:** 855 • **Aptitudes:** G2, V2, N2, S2, P2, Q3, K2, F3, M3, E3, C4 • **Temperaments:** J, M, S, V • **Stress:** A, S • **Physical:** V=G, H=G, L=S, W, H • **Work Env:** I, N, R • **Salary:** 5 • **Outlook:** 3

INSTRUCTOR, FLYING 2 (educ.) • D.O.T. #097.227-010 • OES #31317 • Instructs student pilots in flight procedures and techniques and in ground school courses: Develops and prepares course outlines, study materials, and instructional procedures for students enrolled in basic, advanced, or instrument ground school. Lectures on various subjects, such as aircraft construction, Federal aviation regulations, and radio navigation. Demonstrates operation of various aircraft components and instruments, and techniques for controlling aircraft during maneuvers, such as taxiing, takeoff, and landing, using synthetic instrument trainers. Observes student's actions during training flights to ensure assimilation of classroom instruction and to comply with Federal aviation regulations. Tests and evaluates students' progress, using written and performance tests and oral interviews. May teach advanced, basic, or instrument courses and be designated as GROUND INSTRUCTOR, ADVANCED (education); GROUND INSTRUCTOR, BASIC (education); GROUND INSTRUCTOR, INSTRUMENT (education). Must be certified by Federal Aviation Administration. • **GED:** R4, M4, L3 • **SVP:** 1-2 yrs • **Academic:** Ed=A, Eng=G • **Work Field:** 296 • **MPSMS:** 855 • **Aptitudes:** G2, V3, N3, S2, P2, Q2, K4, F4, M3, E3, C4 • **Temperaments:** D, I, J, M • **Stress:** A • **Physical:** V=G, H=L, L=S, W, H • **Work Env:** I • **Salary:** 4 • **Outlook:** 2

GOE: 05.04.02 Water Vehicle Operation

MATE, SHIP (water trans.) • D.O.T. #197.133-022 • OES #97505 • SHIP OFFICER. Supervises and coordinates activities of crew aboard ship: Inspects holds of ship during loading to insure that cargo is stowed according to specifications. Examines cargo-handling gear and lifesaving equipment and orders crew to repair or replace defective gear and equipment. Supervises crew engaged in cleaning and maintaining decks, superstructure, and bridge of ship. Stands watch during specified periods and determines geographical position of ship, upon request of MASTER, SHIP (water trans.), using loran and azimuths of celestial bodies. Assumes command of ship in event MASTER, SHIP (water trans.) becomes incapacitated. May be required to hold license issued by U.S. Coast Guard, depending on waters navigated and tonnage of ship. When more than one MATE, SHIP (water trans.) is required, may be designated MATE, CHIEF (water trans.) (usually on vessels inspected by U.S. Coast Guard); MATE, FIRST (water trans.) (usually on uninspected vessels) or MATE, FOURTH (water trans.); MATE, SECOND (water trans.); MATE, THIRD (water trans.). May remain in port to relieve another MATE, SHIP (water trans.) who desires to go ashore while ship is in port and be designated as MATE, RELIEF (water trans.). • **GED:** R4, M4, L4 • **SVP:** 2-4 yrs • **Academic:** Ed=A, Eng=G • **Work Field:** 013 • **MPSMS:** 854 • **Aptitudes:** G3, V3, N3, S2, P2, Q3, K3, F2, M3, E3, C4 • **Temperaments:** D, M, P, T • **Stress:** E, A • **Physical:** V=G, H=L, L=S, W, C, S, H • **Work Env:** I, R • **Salary:** 5 • **Outlook:** 3

PILOT, SHIP (water trans.) • D.O.T. #197.133-026 • OES #97508 • Commands ships to steer them into and out of harbors, estuaries, straits, and sounds, and on rivers, lakes, and bays: Directs course and speed of ship on basis of specialized knowledge of local winds, weather, tides, and current. Orders worker at helm to steer ship, and navigates ship to avoid reefs, outlying shoals, and other hazards to shipping, utilizing aids to navigation, such as lighthouses and buoys. Signals TUGBOAT CAPTAIN (water trans.) to berth and unberth ship. Must be licensed by U.S. Coast Guard with limitations indicating class and tonnage of vessels for which license is valid and route and waters that may be piloted. May be designated according to vessel commanded as PILOT, STEAM YACHT (water trans.); PILOT, TANK VESSEL (water trans.). • **GED:** R4, M4, L3 • **SVP:** 4-10 yrs • **Academic:** Ed=H, Eng=S • **Work Field:** 013 • **MPSMS:** 854 • **Aptitudes:** G2, V1, N2, S2, P4, Q3, K3, F4, M3, E3, C4 • **Temperaments:** D, J, M, P, S • **Stress:** A, S • **Physical:** V=G, H=L, L=L, C, H • **Work Env:** B, W • **Salary:** 5 • **Outlook:** 1

05.05 Craft Technology

Workers in this group perform highly skilled hand and/or machine work requiring special techniques, training, and experience. Work occurs in a variety of non-factory settings. Some workers own their own shops.

✔ **What kind of work would you do?**

Your work activities would depend upon your specific job. For example, you might:

- study blueprints and specifications for setting up a machine that shapes metal bolts and screws.
- lay out, drill, turn, grind, and fit metal castings to make patterns for use in a foundry.
- use knowledge of tool design, shop mathematics, metal properties, and machining procedures to make or repair machine tools.
- use handtools, precision-measuring instruments, and machine tools to repair diesel engines.
- use grinders, planers, millers, and handtools to repair or modify rifles and handguns.
- follow blueprints and use handtools and power tools to assemble or repair boilers and tanks in an industrial plant.
- lay brick or cement blocks to build a wall.

- follow blueprints and plans to measure, cut, fit, and nail wooden parts for a structure.
- set up and operate a variety of woodworking machines to make or repair cabinets and fine furniture.
- repair and maintain generators, alternators, motors, and communications systems aboard a ship.
- set up, adjust, and operate a printing press in a publishing company.
- adjust pipes and mechanisms in an organ to correct tone, pitch, or mechanical problems.
- make casts and prepare and fit artificial limbs.
- cut, shape, and polish precious gems and stones.
- develop designs and make tailored suits and coats for men.

- plan menus, order supplies, and oversee food preparation for a large motel.

✔ **What skills and abilities do you need for this kind of work?**
To do this kind of work, you must be able to:

- skillfully use handtools or machines needed for your work.
- read blueprints and drawings of items to be made or repaired.
- measure, cut, or otherwise work on materials or objects with great preciseness.

- use arithmetic and shop geometry to figure amounts of materials needed, dimensions to be followed, and cost of materials.
- picture what the finished product will look like.
- accept responsibility for the accuracy of the work as it is turned out.

✔ **How do you know if you would like or could learn to do this kind of work?**
The following questions may give you clues about yourself as you consider this group of jobs.

- Have you had hobbies such as model building which required assembling parts in a certain manner? Are you able to follow detailed instructions accurately?
- Have you read magazines or trade papers about mechanics? Are you able to understand mechanical details?

- Have you repaired an extension cord or lamp? Can you figure out how things work without looking at directions?
- Have you made minor repairs to a house? Do you enjoy working with your hands?

✔ **How can you prepare for and enter this kind of work?**
Occupations in this group usually require education and/or training extending from two years to over ten years, depending upon the specific kind of work. A four-year formal apprenticeship is the best way to become a general machinist. Training includes the learning of proper machine speeds and feeds, and the operation of various machine tools. Apprentices are also trained in the use of handtools and assembly procedures. They study blueprint reading, shop mathematics, shop practices, and mechanical drawing. High school or vocational school courses in industrial mathematics, physics, machine shop, and mechanical drawing are very useful. Some machinists learn their trade without serving an apprenticeship.

Many mechanics and repairers acquire their skills by working with experienced workers for several years or through apprenticeship training. Some get basic training or increase their skills in vocational and technical schools or by taking correspondence courses. Experience in the armed forces may also help workers gain entry into occupations in this group.

Many high schools and vocational schools offer basic mechanics courses in cooperation with local employers. The programs last from two to three years. Courses in mathematics, physics, electronics, blueprint reading, and machine shop are helpful.

Most automobile mechanics learn their skills on the job. They usually start as helpers, lubrication workers, or gasoline station attendants. However, there are formal training programs available. Three to four years experience is required to become a general automobile mechanic. Experienced mechanics may advance to shop supervisors or service managers. Many mechanics open their own repair shops or gasoline service stations.

Formal apprenticeship training lasting three to four years is the best way to acquire the skills required in the construction trades. Apprentices generally must be at least 18 years of age, and in good physical condition. A high school or a vocational school education is desirable and should include courses in mathematics, mechanical drawing, carpentry, and electricity.

Although apprenticeship is the best way to train for these occupations, many people acquire construction skills by working as laborers and helpers and observing skilled workers. Some acquire skills by attending vocational or trade schools or by taking correspondence school courses.

Craft workers, such as electricians, are required to have a license to work in some localities. They must pass an examination to demonstrate a broad knowledge of the job and of state and local regulations.

✔ What else should you consider about these jobs?

Many of these workers are required to follow strict safety regulations. Machine workers must wear safety glasses and other protective devices. Construction workers are usually required to wear hard hats and sometimes safety straps and shoes.

Many people prefer construction work because it permits them to be outdoors. However, the weather and seasons sometimes affect the availability of work.

Many workers are required to furnish their own handtools.

If you think you would like to do this kind of work, look at the job titles listed below.

GOE: 05.05.01 Masonry, Stone & Brick Work, Craft Tech.

BRICKLAYER (const.) • D.O.T. #861.381-018 • OES #87302 • Lays building materials, such as brick, structural tile, and concrete cinder, glass, gypsum, and terra cotta block (except stone) to construct or repair walls, partitions, arches, sewers, and other structures: Measures distance from reference points and marks guidelines on working surface to lay out work. Spreads soft bed (layer) of mortar that serves as base and binder for block, using trowel. Applies mortar to end of block and positions block in mortar bed. Taps block with trowel to level, aline, and embed in mortar, allowing specified thickness of joint. Removes excess mortar from face of block, using trowel. Finishes mortar between brick with pointing tool or trowel. Breaks bricks to fit spaces too small for whole brick, using edge of trowel or brick hammer. Determines vertical and horizontal alinement of courses, using plumb bob, gageline (tightly stretched cord), and level. Fastens brick or terra cotta veneer to face of structures, with tie wires embedded in mortar between bricks, or in anchor holes in veneer brick. May weld metal parts to steel structural members. May apply plaster to walls and ceiling, using trowel, to complete repair work [PLASTERER (const.)]. May be designated according to material used as CINDER-BLOCK MASON (const.); CONCRETE-BLOCK MASON (const.); TERRA-COTTA MASON (const.); or work performed as BRICKLAYER, MAINTENANCE (any ind.). When specializing in construction of specified structures is designated according to specialty as BRICKLAYER, SEWER (const.); CHIMNEY BUILDER, BRICK (const.). Additional titles: BLOCK SETTER, GYPSUM (const.); HOLLOW-TILE-PARTITION ERECTOR (const.); PLASTER-BLOCK LAYER (const.); SILO ERECTOR (const.). • GED: R4, M3, L3 • SVP: 4-10 yrs • Academic: Ed=H, Eng=S • Work Field: 091 • MPSMS: 360 • Aptitudes: G3, V3, N3, S3, P3, Q4, K3, F3, M3, E3, C4 • Temperaments: M, T • Physical: V=G, H=N, L=M, W, C, S, H • Work Env: B, R • Salary: 5 • Outlook: 4

CEMENT MASON (const.) • D.O.T. #844.364-010 • OES #87311 • CEMENT FINISHER; CEMENT PAVER; CONCRETE FINISHER; CONCRETE FLOATER. Smooths and finishes surfaces of poured concrete floors, walls, sidewalks, or curbs to specified textures, using handtools or power tools, including floats, trowels, and screeds: Spreads concrete to specified depth and workable consistency, using float to bring water to surface and produce soft topping. Levels, smooths, and shapes surfaces of freshly poured concrete, using straightedge and float or power screed. Finishes concrete surfaces, using power trowel, or wets and rubs concrete with abrasive stone to impart finish. Removes rough or defective spots from concrete surfaces, using power grinder or chisel and hammer and patches holes with fresh concrete or epoxy compound. Molds expansion joints and edges, using edging tools, jointers, and straightedge. May sprinkle colored stone chips, powdered steel, or coloring powder on concrete to produce prescribed finish. May produce rough concrete surface, using broom. May mix cement, using hoe or concrete-mixing machine. May direct subgrade work, mixing of concrete, and setting of forms, performing duties as described under GROUP LEADER (any ind.). May specialize in finishing steps and stairways and be designated as STEP FINISHER (const.). May break up and repair old concrete surfaces, using pneumatic tools and be designated CEMENT MASON, MAINTENANCE (any ind.). May spread premixed cement over deck, inner surfaces, joints, and crevices of ships and be designated CEMENTER (ship & boat bldg. & rep.). • GED: R4, M3, L3 • SVP: 2-4 yrs • Academic: Ed=H, Eng=S • Work Field: 102 • MPSMS: 360, 536 • Aptitudes: G3, V4, N4, S3, P3, Q4, K3, F4, M3, E4, C4 • Temperaments: M, T • Physical: V=L, H=N, L=M, W, C, S, H • Work Env: B, W, R • Salary: 5 • Outlook: 3

MARBLE FINISHER (const.) • D.O.T. #861.664-010 • OES #98311 • MARBLE HELPER; MARBLE MASON HELPER; MARBLE MECHANIC HELPER; MARBLE SETTER HELPER. Supplies and mixes construction materials for MARBLE SETTER (const.) 861.381-030, applies grout, and cleans installed marble: Moves marble installation materials, tools, machines, and work devices to work areas. Mixes mortar, plaster, and grout, as required, following standard formulas and using manual or machine mixing methods. Moves mixed mortar or plaster to installation area, manually or using wheelbarrow. Selects marble slab for installation, following numbered sequence or drawings. Drills holes and chisels channels in edges of marble slabs to install metal wall anchors, using power drill and chisel. Bends wires to form metal anchors, using pliers, inserts anchors into drilled holes of marble slab, and secures anchors in place with wooden stake and plaster. Moves marble slabs to installation site, using dolly, hoist, or portable crane. Fills marble joints and surface imperfections with grout, using grouting trowel or spatula, and removes excess grout, using wet sponge. Grinds and polishes marble, using abrasives, chemicals, and manual or machine grinding and polishing techniques. Cleans installed marble surfaces, work and storage areas, installation tools, machinery, and work aids, using water and cleaning agents. Stores marble, installation materials, tools, machinery, and related items. May modify mixing, material moving, grouting, polishing, and cleaning methods and procedures, according to type of installation or materials. May repair and fill chipped, cracked, or broken marble pieces, using torch, spatula, and heat sensitive adhesive and filler. May secure marble anchors to studding, using pliers, and cover ends of anchors with plaster to secure anchors in place. May assist MARBLE SETTER (const.) 861.381-030 to saw and position marble. May erect scaffolding and related installation structures. • **GED:** R2, M1, L1 • **SVP:** 6 mos-1 yr • **Academic:** Ed=N, Eng=N • **Work Field:** 011, 102, 143 • **MPSMS:** 361 • **Aptitudes:** G4, V4, N4, S3, P3, Q4, K3, F3, M3, E4, C4 • **Temperaments:** J, R • **Stress:** T • **Physical:** V=L, H=N, L=V, W, C, S, H • **Work Env:** I, R, F • **Salary:** 4 • **Outlook:** 1

STONECUTTER, HAND (stonework) • D.O.T. #771.381-014 • OES #89905 • CHISEL WORKER; STONE DRESSER; STONEWORKER. Cuts, shapes, and finishes rough blocks of building or monumental stone according to diagrams or patterns: Traces around pattern or transfers dimensions from diagrams to stone, using rule, straightedge, compass, square, and chalk or scriber. Selects surfacing tools according to finish specified or step in finishing process. Chips fragments of stone away from marks on stone, working surface of stone down to specified finish. Verifies progress of finishing to ensure adherence to specifications, using straightedge, level, plumb, and square. May dress surface of stone with bushhammer. May cut decorative designs in stone surface. May cut moldings or grooves in stone that cannot be reached by machine. May drill holes in stone. May be designated according to product as BUILDING STONECUTTER (stonework); CURBING STONECUTTER (stonework); MONUMENT STONECUTTER (stonework). • **GED:** R4, M3, L3 • **SVP:** 2-4 yrs • **Academic:** Ed=N, Eng=S • **Work Field:** 052 • **MPSMS:** 537 • **Aptitudes:** G3, V4, N4, S2, P2, Q4, K3, F3, M2, E5, C5 • **Temperaments:** J, M, T • **Physical:** V=L, H=N, L=M, W, H • **Work Env:** B, N, R • **Salary:** 4 • **Outlook:** 1

TERRAZZO FINISHER (const.) • D.O.T. #861.664-014 • OES #98319 • TERRAZZO HELPER; TERRAZZO MECHANIC HELPER; TERRAZZO WORKER HELPER. Supplies and mixes construction materials for TERRAZZO WORKER (const.) 861.381-046, applies grout, and finishes surface of installed terrazzo: Moves terrazzo installation materials, tools, machines, and work devices to work areas, manually or using wheelbarrow. Measures designated amounts of ingredients for terrazzo or grout, using graduated containers and scale, following standard formulas and specifications, and loads portable mixer, using shovel. Mixes materials according to experience and requests from TERRAZZO WORKER (const.) 861.381-046, and dumps mixed materials that form base or top surface of terrazzo into prepared installation site, using wheelbarrow. Applies curing agent to installed terrazzo to promote even curing, using brush or sprayer. Grinds surface of cured terrazzo, using power grinders, to smooth terrazzo and prepare for grout ing. Spreads grout across terrazzo to fill surface imperfections, using trowel. Fine grinds and polishes surface of terrazzo, when grout has set, using power grinders. Washes surface of polished terrazzo, using cleaner and water, and applies sealer, according to manufacturer's specifications, using brush. Installs grinding stones in power grinders, using handtools. Cleans installation site, mixing and storage areas, tools, machines, and equipment, using water and various cleaning devices. Stores terrazzo installation materials, machines, tools, and equipment. May modify mixing, grouting, grinding, and cleaning procedures according to type of installation or material used. May assist TERRAZZO WORKER (const.) 861.381-046 to position and secure moisture membrane and wire mesh prior to pouring base materials for terrazzo installation. May spread marble chips or other material over fresh terrazzo surface and press into terrazzo, using roller. May cut divider and joint strips to size as directed. May assist TERRAZZO WORKER (const.) 861.381-046 to lay terrazzo. May cut grooves in terrazzo stairs, using power grinder, and fill grooves with nonskid material. • **GED:** R2, M1, L2 • **SVP:** 6 mos-1 yr •

Academic: Ed=N, Eng=N • **Work Field:** 011, 102, 143 • **MPSMS:** 361 • **Aptitudes:** G4, V4, N4, S4, P3, Q4, K3, F4, M3, E3, C4 • **Temperaments:** J, R • **Stress:** T • **Physical:** V=L, H=N, L=V, W, S, H • **Work Env:** I, W, N, R, F • **Salary:** 4 • **Outlook:** 1

TERRAZZO WORKER (const.) • D.O.T. #861.381-046 • OES #87311 • ARTIFICIAL-MARBLE WORKER; FLOOR GRINDER. Applies cement, sand, pigment, and marble chips to floors, stair ways, and cabinet fixtures to attain durable and decorative surfacing according to specifications and drawings: Spreads roofing paper on surface of foundation. Spreads mixture of sand, cement, and water over surface with trowel to form terrazzo base. Cuts metal division strips and presses them into terrazzo base so that top edges form desired design or pattern and define level of finished floor surface. Spreads mixture of marble chips, cement, pigment, and water over terrazzo base to form finished surface, using float and trowel. Scatters marble chips over finished surface. Pushes roller over surface to imbed chips. Allows surface to dry, and pushes electric-powered surfacing machine over floor to grind and polish terrazzo surface. Grinds curved surfaces and areas inaccessible to surfacing machine, such as stair ways and cabinet tops, with portable hand grinder. May precast terrazzo blocks in wooden forms. May perform finishing operations only and be designated as TERRAZZO FINISHER (const.) or TERRAZZO POLISHER (const.). • **GED:** R4, M2, L3 • **SVP:** 2-4 yrs • **Academic:** Ed=H, Eng=S • **Work Field:** 091, 095 • **MPSMS:** 361 • **Aptitudes:** G3, V4, N4, S3, P3, Q4, K3, F3, M3, E4, C4 • **Temperaments:** M, T, V • **Physical:** V=L, H=N, L=M, W, S, H • **Work Env:** B, W, N • **Salary:** 4 • **Outlook:** 1

TILE FINISHER (const.) • D.O.T. #861.664-018 • OES #98311 • TILE MECHANIC HELPER; TILE SETTER HELPER. Supplies and mixes construction materials for TILE SETTER (const.) 861.381-054, applies grout, and cleans installed tile: Moves tiles, tilesetting tools, and work devices from storage area to installation site manually or using wheelbarrow. Mixes mortar and grout according to standard formulas and request from TILE SETTER (const.) 861.381-054, using bucket, waterhose, spatula, and portable mixer. Supplies TILE SETTER (const.) 861.381-054 with mortar, using wheelbarrow and shovel. Applies grout between joints of installed tile, using grouting trowel. Removes excess grout from tile joints with wet sponge and scrapes corners and crevices with trowel. Wipes surface of tile after grout has set to remove grout residue and polish tile, using nonabrasive materials. Cleans installation site, mixing and storage areas, and installation machines, tools, and equipment, using water and various cleaning tools. Stores tile setting materials, machines, tools, and equipment. May apply calk, sealers, acid, steam, or related agents to calk, seal, or clean installed tile, using various application devices and equipment. May modify mixing, grouting, grinding, and cleaning procedures according to type of installation or material used. May assist TILE SETTER (const.) 861.381-054 to position and secure metal lath, wire mesh, or felt paper prior to installation of tile. May cut marked tiles to size, using power saw or tile cutter. • **GED:** R2, M1, L2 • **SVP:** 6 mos-1 yr • **Academic:** Ed=N, Eng=N • **Work Field:** 102, 143 • **MPSMS:** 361 • **Aptitudes:** G4, V4, N4, S4, P4, Q4, K3, F4, M3, E4, C4 • **Temperaments:** R, T • **Stress:** T • **Physical:** V=L, H=N, L=V, W, S, H • **Work Env:** I, R • **Salary:** 3 • **Outlook:** 3

TILE SETTER (const.) • D.O.T. #861.381-054 • OES #87308 • TILE FITTER; TILE LAYER; TILE MASON. Applies tile to walls, floors, ceilings, and promenade roof decks, following design specifications: Examines blueprints, measures and marks surfaces to be covered, and lays out work. Measures and cuts metal lath to size for walls and ceilings with tin snips. Tacks lath to wall and ceiling surfaces with staple gun or hammer. Spreads plaster base over lath with trowel and levels plaster to specified thickness, using screed. Spreads concrete on subfloor with trowel and levels it with screed. Spreads mastic or other adhesive base on roof deck, using serrated spreader to form base for promenade tile. Cuts and shapes tile with tile cutters and biters. Positions tile and taps it with trowel handle to affix tile to plaster or adhesive base. May be designated according to type of work done as ROOF-PROMENADE-TILE SETTER (const.). • **GED:** R4, M3, L3 • **SVP:** 2-4 yrs • **Academic:** Ed=H, Eng=S • **Work Field:** 092 • **MPSMS:** 361 • **Aptitudes:** G3, V4, N4, S3, P3, Q4, K3, F3, M3, E5, C4 • **Temperaments:** M, T •

Physical: V=G, H=N, L=M, W, S, H • **Work Env:** I • **Salary:** 4 • **Outlook:** 2

GOE: 05.05.02 Construction & Maintenance

BOAT REPAIRER (ship bldg. & rep.) • D.O.T. #807.361-014 • OES #85999 • Repairs wooden and fiberglass boats according to blueprints and customer specifications, using handtools and power tools: Confers with customer or supervisory personnel and reads blueprints to determine repairs needed and plan sequence of operations. Examines boat to determine location and extent of defect. Cuts out defective area, using powersaw, drills, and handtools. Measures and records dimensions of defective area and lays out dimension lines and reference points on materials, using rules, straightedge, squares, and scribing instruments. Sets up and operates saws, joiners, planers, and shapers to fabricate repair parts. Positions and fits repair part in boat and secures part to boat, using caulking gun, adhesive, or carpenter's handtools. Cuts fiberglass material to specified size and patches defective surfaces [BOAT PATCHER, PLASTIC (ship & boat bldg. & rep.)]. Smooths repaired surfaces, using power sander. Installs fittings and equipment according to customer specifications, using handtools and portable power tools. Hand brushes or sprays paint or other finishing solution on repaired areas and waxes and buffs area to specified finish. • **GED:** R4, M3, L3 • **SVP:** 2-4 yrs • **Academic:** Ed=N, Eng=S • **Work Field:** 102 • **MPSMS:** 593 • **Aptitudes:** G3, V3, N3, S3, P2, Q4, K3, F3, M3, E4, C4 • **Temperaments:** J, M, T • **Physical:** V=L, H=N, L=M, W, C, S, H • **Work Env:** I, R • **Salary:** 4 • **Outlook:** 3

BOATBUILDER, WOOD (ship bldg. & rep.) • D.O.T. #860.381-018 • OES #87102 • Fabricates, repairs, or modifies wooden boats, liferafts, and pontoons, according to blueprints, using handtools, power tools, and measuring instruments: Lays out full-scale outline of boat on mold-loft floor, using crayon, scales, and protractor, following blueprints and table of offsets. Establishes dimensional reference points on layout and makes templates of parts. Scribes dimensional lines on lumber, following templates. Cuts and forms parts, such as keel, ribs, and sidings, using carpenter's handtools and power tools [MACHINIST, WOOD (woodworking)]. Assembles shell of boat by forming steam-softened sidings on mold, removing mold, and securing sidings to keel, or by securing ribs to keel and covering ribs with planking. Builds and installs structures, such as pilot house, cabin, rudder, and foundations for machinery, shafting, and propellor supports, and installs preformed decking, masts, booms, and ladders, according to blueprints, using handtools, power tools, scale, calipers, and gages. May calk seams [WOOD CALKER (ship & boat bldg. & rep.)]. May specialize in fabricating particular part of boat and be designated BULKHEAD CARPENTER (ship & boat bldg. & rep.); BULWARK CARPENTER (ship & boat bldg. & rep.); HULL BUILDER (ship & boat bldg. & rep.); KEEL ASSEMBLER (ship & boat bldg. & rep.). • **GED:** R4, M4, L4 • **SVP:** 2-4 yrs • **Academic:** Ed=N, Eng=S • **Work Field:** 102 • **MPSMS:** 593 • **Aptitudes:** G3, V3, N3, S2, P3, Q4, K3, F3, M3, E5, C5 • **Temperaments:** M, T • **Physical:** V=L, H=N, L=M, W, C, S, H • **Work Env:** B, N • **Salary:** 5 • **Outlook:** 3

CARPENTER (const.) • D.O.T. #860.381-022 • OES #87102 • Constructs, erects, installs, and repairs structures and fixtures of wood, plywood, and wallboard, using carpenter's handtools and power tools, and conforming to local building codes: Studies blueprints, sketches, or building plans for information pertaining to type of material required, such as lumber or fiberboard, and dimensions of structure or fixture to be fabricated. Selects specified type of lumber or other materials. Prepares layout, using rule, framing square, and calipers. Marks cutting and assembly lines on materials, using pencil, chalk, and marking gage. Shapes materials to prescribed measurements, using saws, chisels, and planes. Assembles cut and shaped materials and fastens them together with nails, dowel pins, or glue. Verifies trueness of structure with plumb bob and carpenter's level. Erects framework for structures and lays subflooring. Builds stairs and lays out and installs partitions and cabinet work. Covers subfloor with building paper to keep out moisture and lays hardwood, parquet, and wood-strip-block floors by nailing floors to subfloor or cementing them to mastic or

asphalt base. Applies shock-absorbing, sound-deadening, and decorative paneling to ceilings and walls. Fits and installs prefabricated window frames, doors, doorframes, weather stripping, interior and exterior trim, and finish hardware, such as locks, letterdrops, and kick plates. Constructs forms and chutes for pouring concrete. Erects scaffolding and ladders for assembling structures above ground level. May weld metal parts to steel structural members. When specializing in particular phase of carpentry is designated according to specialty as COMBINATION-WINDOW INSTALLER (const.); LAY-OUT CARPENTER (const.). When specializing in finish carpentry, such as installing interior and exterior trim, building stairs, and laying hardwood floors is designated FINISH CARPENTER (const.). When erecting frame buildings and performing general carpentry work in residential construction is designated HOUSE CARPENTER (const.). May remove and replace sections of structures prior to and after installation of insulating materials and be designated BUILDING-INSULATING CARPENTER (const.; ret. tr.). May perform carpentry work in construction of walk-in freezers and environmental test chambers and be designated CARPENTER, REFRIGERATOR (refrigerat. equip.). Additional titles: DOOR HANGER (const.); FINISHED-HARDWARE ERECTOR (const.); GARAGE-DOOR HANGER (const.); HARDWOOD-FLOOR INSTALLER (const.); JALOUSIE INSTALLER (const.); STAIR BUILDER (const.); TRIM SETTER (const.); WEATHER STRIPPER (const.); WOOD-SASH-AND-FRAME CARPENTER (const.); WOOD-STRIP-BLOCK FLOOR INSTALLER (const.). • **GED:** R4, M3, L3 • **SVP:** 2-4 yrs • **Academic:** Ed=H, Eng=S • **Work Field:** 102 • **MPSMS:** 360, 450 • **Aptitudes:** G3, V3, N3, S3, P3, Q4, K3, F3, M3, E3, C4 • **Temperaments:** M, T, V • **Physical:** V=G, H=N, L=M, W, C, S, H • **Work Env:** B, N, R • **Salary:** 5 • **Outlook:** 3

CARPENTER, MAINTENANCE (any ind.) • D.O.T. #860.281-010 • OES #87102 • CARPENTER, REPAIR; CARPENTRY RE-PAIRER. Constructs and repairs structural woodwork and equipment in an establishment, working from blueprints, drawings, or oral instructions: Builds, repairs, and installs counters, cabinets, benches, partitions, floors, doors, building framework, and trim, using carpenter's handtools and power tools. Installs glass in windows, doors, and partitions. Replaces damaged ceiling tile, floor tile, and sheet plastic wall coverings. May build cabinets and other wooden equipment in carpenter shop, using woodworking machines, such as powersaws, shaper, and jointer [CABINETMAKER (woodworking)]. May install window shades, venetian blinds, curtain rods, and wall fans for tenants. May be designated according to place at which work is performed as CARPENTER, MINE (mining & quarrying); or according to specific items made or maintained as FLUME MAKER (mining & quarrying); FRAME MAKER (leather mfg.); MEAT-CUTTING-BLOCK REPAIRER (any ind.). • **GED:** R4, M3, L3 • **SVP:** 2-4 yrs • **Academic:** Ed=H, Eng=S • **Work Field:** 102 • **MPSMS:** 361, 450 • **Aptitudes:** G3, V3, N3, S2, P3, Q4, K3, F3, M3, E4, C4 • **Temperaments:** M, T, V • **Physical:** V=G, H=N, L=M, W, C, S, H • **Work Env:** I, W, N, R • **Salary:** 4 • **Outlook:** 3

CARPENTER, ROUGH (const.) • D.O.T. #860.381-042 • OES #87102 • BRACER. Builds rough wooden structures, such as concrete forms, scaffolds, tunnel and sewer supports, and temporary frame shelters, according to sketches, blueprints, or oral instructions: Examines specifications to determine dimensions of structure. Measures boards, timbers, or plywood, using square, measuring tape, and ruler, and marks cutting lines on materials, using pencil and scriber. Saws boards and plywood panels to required sizes. Nails cleats (braces) across boards to construct concrete-supporting forms. Braces forms in place with timbers, tie rods, and anchor bolts, for use in building concrete piers, footings, and walls. Erects chutes for pouring concrete. Cuts and assembles timbers to build trestles and cofferdams. Builds falsework to temporarily strengthen, protect, or disguise buildings undergoing construction. Erects scaffolding for buildings and ship structures and installs ladders, handrails, walkways, platforms, and gangways. Installs door and window bucks (rough frames in which finished frames are inserted) in designated positions in building framework, and braces them with boards nailed to framework. Installs subflooring in buildings. Nails plaster grounds (wood or metal strips) to studding to provide guide for PLASTERER (const.). Fits and nails sheathing (first covering of boards) on outer walls and roofs of buildings. Builds sleds from logs and timbers for use in hauling camp buildings and machinery through wooded areas. When specializing in particular phase of rough carpentry, is designated according to specialty as CARPENTER, CRADLE AND DOLLY (ship & boat bldg. & rep.); DOCK BUILDER (const.); FALSEWORK BUILDER (const.); SCAFFOLD BUILDER (const.; ship & boat bldg. & rep.); SHEATHER (const.); TIMBER SETTER (const.). When building and repairing timber structures which support sawmill machinery is designated as CONSTRUCTION MILLWRIGHT (sawmill), and when performing rough carpentry work above ground on sewer or tunnel projects, is designated as SURFACE CARPENTER (const.). • **GED:** R4, M4, L2 • **SVP:** 2-4 yrs • **Academic:** Ed=H, Eng=N • **Work Field:** 102 • **MPSMS:** 360 • **Aptitudes:** G3, V4, N3, S3, P3, Q4, K3, F3, M3, E3, C5 • **Temperaments:** M, T • **Physical:** V=L, H=N, L=H, W, C, S, H • **Work Env:** B, R • **Salary:** 4 • **Outlook:** 3

CUSTOM VAN INSTALLER (auto. mfg.) • D.O.T. #860.381-074 • OES #85999 • Constructs cabinets and installs paneling, windows, insulation, carpeting, and appliances to outfit custom van trucks according to customer orders and specifications: Measures interior of van to determine area to be modified and to draw diagram. Selects, lays out, saws, sands, glues, nails, and staples paneling and cabinet sections to fabricate parts for walls, cabinets, and supports. Studies diagrams and blueprints and measures and marks locations to route wiring and place outlets. Installs wiring and outlets by drilling holes, pulling wiring through holes, securing wiring, positioning outlets, and connecting wiring to outlets, using drills, routers, clips, clamps, screwdriver, and knife. Installs precut windows by cutting holes in frame with flame torch, filing area to remove burns and scratches, fitting window gaskets and seals over edges of openings, and mounting windows in gaskets. Washes interior of van to remove rust and dirt. Spreads adhesive on walls, using brush and glue gun, and positions fiberglass insulation in place. Glues or tacks block supports onto frame and secures paneling and cabinet sections in place, using screws and bolts. Positions refrigerator in prescribed location and connects electrical leads to power source. Measures and cuts carpet to size, using rule, knife, or scissors. Positions carpet over walls and floor and fastens carpet in place. Measures, cuts, positions, and screws molding around cabinets and between ceiling and wall sections. • **GED:** R4, M3, L3 • **SVP:** 6 mos-1 yr • **Academic:** Ed=H, Eng=S • **Work Field:** 102, 111 • **MPSMS:** 591 • **Aptitudes:** G3, V3, N3, S3, P3, Q4, K3, F3, M3, E4, C4 • **Temperaments:** J, T • **Physical:** V=L, H=N, L=M, W, S, H • **Work Env:** I • **Salary:** 4 • **Outlook:** 4

MARINE-SERVICES TECHNICIAN (ship bldg. & rep.) • D.O.T. #806.261-026 • OES #85116 • Repairs and maintains boats and similar vessels in marine service facility: Examines repair or installation orders, drawings, and vessel, utilizing knowledge based on past experience to determine extent of repairs required or modifications necessary for installation of equipment, accessories, and hardware. Consults with supervisor regarding installation or repair problems, sequence of operations, and time required to complete repair or installation. Removes vessels from water, using movable lift crane or marine railway. Positions and secures blocking at bottom and sides of vessels according to size, weight, and weight distribution of vessels, using fasteners, handtools, and power tools. Removes flaked paint, barnacles, and encrusted debris from hulls of vessel, using scrapers, scrubbers, power washers, and sandblast equipment. Removes damaged or rotted sections from wooden or fiberglass vessels, using drill, saw, and handtools. Fabricates and installs wooden replacement parts, using drawings, measuring instruments, work aids, handtools, power tools, and woodworking machine and equipment, such as saws, drill press, shaper, planer, and steam cabinet. Calks wooden hulls with cotton to prevent leaks. Grinds and sands edges around removed fiberglass sections. Mixes fiberglass bonding resin and catalyst, cuts fiberglass cloth to size, and impregnates cloth with mixture. Positions layers of impregnated cloth over damaged area, and smooths area to match contour of hull, using rollers, squeegee, and power sander. Mixes and applies paint or gel coat to boats with hand and spray equipment, utilizing knowledge of color mixing, matching techniques, and application procedures. Tests engine, transmission, rigging, propeller, navigational, and related systems to diagnose malfunctions, using various measuring instruments. Replaces or repairs defective components, or fabricates new com-

ponents. Installs and tests steering gear, sanitation and refrigeration systems, cabinetry, electrical systems and accessories, hardware, trim, and related components, following manufacturer instructions and drawings. • **GED:** R4, M3, L3 • **SVP:** 2-4 yrs • **Academic:** Ed=H, Eng=S • **Work Field:** 102, 121 • **MPSMS:** 593 • **Aptitudes:** G3, V3, N3, S2, P3, Q4, K3, F3, M2, E2, C2 • **Temperaments:** J, T, V • **Physical:** V=G, H=N, L=H, W, C, S, H • **Work Env:** I, R, F • **Salary:** 4 • **Outlook:** 3

SHIPWRIGHT (ship bldg. & rep.) • D.O.T. #860.381-058 • OES #87102 • CARPENTER, SHIP; WOODWORKER. Constructs or repairs ships, following blueprints or ship's plans: Sights, plots, and marks reference points and lines on building dock or shipway to maintain alinement of vessel during construction or repair, using transit, plumb bob, tapes, and levels. Builds keel and bilge blocks, cradles, and shoring for supporting ships in drydock, marine railways, shipways, or building docks, using woodworking handtools and power tools. Positions and secures blocking and other structures on dock platform, according to ship's blueprints. Alines vessel over blocks [DOCK HAND (ship & boat bldg. & rep.)]. Establishes reference points and lines on ship's hull for locating machinery and other equipment, in accordance with ship's alinement and shape. Fabricates and installs furring pieces, aprons, uprights, and other wood framing in ship. Shapes, finishes, and installs wooden spars, masts, and cargo and boat booms. Trims wooden frames and other timbers, using broadax and adz. Spikes or bolts metal fittings, plates, and bulkheads to wooden parts of ship, using brace and bits, augers, mauls, and wrenches. • **GED:** R4, M4, L3 • **SVP:** 4-10 yrs • **Academic:** Ed=A, Eng=S • **Work Field:** 102 • **MPSMS:** 593 • **Aptitudes:** G3, V3, N3, S3, P3, Q4, K3, F3, M2, E3, C4 • **Temperaments:** M, T, V • **Physical:** V=L, H=N, L=M, W, C, S, H • **Work Env:** O, N, R • **Salary:** 5 • **Outlook:** 2

SUPERINTENDENT, MAINTENANCE (any ind.) • D.O.T. #189.167-046 • OES #15014 • Directs and coordinates, through subordinate supervisory personnel, activities of workers engaged in repair, maintenance, and installation of machines, tools, and equipment, and in maintenance of buildings, grounds, and utility systems of mill, industrial plant, or other establishment: Reviews job orders to determine work priorities. Schedules repair, maintenance, and installation of machines, tools, and equipment to ensure continuous production operations. Coordinates activities of workers fabricating or modifying machines, tools, or equipment to manufacture new products or improve existing products. Directs maintenance activities on utility systems to provide continuous supply of heat, steam, electric power, gas, or air required for operations. Develops preventive maintenance program in conjunction with engineering and maintenance staff. Reviews production, quality control, and maintenance reports and statistics to plan and modify maintenance activities. Inspects operating machines and equipment for conformance with operational standards. Plans, develops, and implements new methods and procedures designed to improve operations, minimize operating costs, and effect greater utilization of labor and materials. Reviews new product plans and discusses equipment needs and modifications with design engineers. Requisitions tools, equipment, and supplies required for operations. Directs training and indoctrination of workers to improve work performance and acquaint workers with company policies and procedures. Confers with management, engineering, and quality control personnel to resolve maintenance problems and recommend measures to improve operations and conditions of machines and equipment. May confer with workers' representatives to resolve grievances. May perform supervisory functions in establishments where subordinate supervisory personnel are not utilized. May prepare department budget and monitor expenditure of funds in budget. • **GED:** R5, M5, L5 • **SVP:** 4-10 yrs • **Academic:** Ed=H, Eng=G • **Work Field:** 295 • **MPSMS:** 893 • **Aptitudes:** G2, V2, N2, S2, P2, Q2, K4, F4, M4, E4, C4 • **Temperaments:** D, J, P, V • **Stress:** E, A • **Physical:** V=L, H=L, L=L, W • **Work Env:** I • **Salary:** 4 • **Outlook:** 1

GOE: 05.05.03 Plumbing & Pipefitting

OIL-BURNER-SERVICER-AND-INSTALLER (any ind.) • D.O.T. #862.281-018 • OES #85902 • Installs and services automatic oil burners in furnaces in homes and commercial establishments, using handtools and pipe-threading tools: Assembles and positions oil-storage tank between furnace and wall of building. Drills holes in wall and affixes oil inlet and outlet pipes from storage tank through holes to outside of building. Removes ashpit and grate bars from furnace and installs burner in opening. Seals space around burner with plaster. Connects pipe to storage tank and burner to convey oil. Installs thermostatic control and damper in chimney. Observes color and height of flame and volume of smoke emitted to determine causes of faulty operation. Examines flue draft, using draftstat, and changes balance weight to adjust damper. May install and service automatic coal stokers. • **GED:** R3, M1, L2 • **SVP:** 2-4 yrs • **Academic:** Ed=N, Eng=S • **Work Field:** 102 • **MPSMS:** 553 • **Aptitudes:** G3, V3, N4, S3, P3, Q4, K4, F3, M3, E5, C3 • **Temperaments:** M, T • **Physical:** V=L, H=N, L=M, W, S, H • **Work Env:** I • **Salary:** 4 • **Outlook:** 3

PIPE FITTER (any ind.) • D.O.T. #862.281-022 • OES #87502 • PLUMBER, PIPE FITTING. Lays out, assembles, installs, and maintains pipe systems, pipe supports, and related hydraulic and pneumatic equipment for steam, hot water, heating, cooling, lubricating, sprinkling, and industrial production and processing systems, applying knowledge of system operation, and following blueprints: Selects type and size of pipe, and related materials and equipment, such as supports, hangers, and hydraulic cylinders, according to specifications. Inspects worksite to determine presence of obstructions and to ascertain that holes cut for pipes will not cause structural weakness. Plans installation or repair to avoid obstructions and to avoid interfering with activities of other workers. Cuts pipe, using saws, pipe cutter, hammer and chisel, cutting torch, and pipe cutting machine. Threads pipe, using pipe threading machine. Bends pipe, using pipe bending tools and pipe bending machine. Assembles and installs variety of metal and non-metal pipes, tubes, and fittings, including iron, steel, copper, and plastic. Connects pipes, using threaded, calked, soldered, brazed, fused, or cemented joints, and handtools. Secures pipes to structure with brackets, clamps, and hangers, using handtools and power tools. Installs and maintains hydraulic and pneumatic components of machines and equipment, such as pumps and cylinders, using handtools. Installs and maintains refrigeration and air-conditioning systems, including compressors, pumps, meters, pneumatic and hydraulic controls, and piping, using handtools and power tools, and following specifications and blueprints. Increases pressure in pipe system and observes connected pressure gauge to test system for leaks. May weld pipe supports to structural steel members. May observe production machines in assigned area of manufacturing facility to detect machinery malfunctions. May operate machinery to verify repair. May modify programs of automated machinery, such as robots and conveyors, to change motion and speed of machine, using teach pendant, control panel, or keyboard and display screen of robot controller and programmable controller. When installing piping systems that must withstand high pressure, may be designated STEAM FITTER (const.). May be designated according to type of system installed as PIPE FITTER, AMMONIA (const.); PIPE FITTER, FIRE-SPRINKLER SYSTEMS (const.); PIPE FITTER, GAS PIPE (const.); or type of piping used as PIPE FITTER, PLASTIC PIPE (const.); PIPE FITTER, SOFT COPPER (const.). Additional titles: AIRDOX FITTER (mining & quarrying); FREIGHT-AIR-BRAKE FITTER (loco. & car bldg. & rep.); INSTRUMENT FITTER (const.); MAINTAINER, SEWER-AND-WATERWORKS (const.); PIPE FITTER, MAINTENANCE (any ind.); PIPE FITTER, WELDING (const.); PNEUMATIC-TUBE FITTER (const.) SPRINKLER-AND-IRRIGATION-SYSTEM INSTALLER (const.); TUYERE FITTER (iron & steel). • **GED:** R4, M3, L3 • **SVP:** 2-4 yrs • **Academic:** Ed=A, Eng=S • **Work Field:** 102, 121 • **MPSMS:** 559 • **Aptitudes:** G3, V3, N3, S3, P3, Q4, K3, F3, M3, E4, C4 • **Temperaments:** J, T • **Physical:** V=L, H=N, L=H, W, C, S, H • **Work Env:** I, R • **Salary:** 5 • **Outlook:** 4

PLUMBER (const.) • D.O.T. #862.381-030 • OES #87502 • Assembles, installs, and repairs pipes, fittings, and fixtures of heating, water, and drainage systems, according to specifications and plumbing codes: Studies building plans and working drawings to determine work aids required and sequence of installations. Inspects structure to ascertain obstructions to be avoided to prevent weakening of structure resulting from installation of pipe. Locates and marks position of pipe and pipe connections and passage holes for pipes in walls and floors, using ruler, spirit level, and plumb bob. Cuts openings in walls and floors to accommodate pipe and pipe fittings, using handtools and power tools. Cuts and threads pipe, using pipe cutters, cutting torch, and pipe-threading machine. Bends pipe to required angle by use of pipe-bending machine or by placing pipe over block and bending it by hand. Assembles and installs valves, pipe fittings, and pipes composed of metals, such as iron, steel, brass, and lead, and nonmetals, such as glass, vitrified clay, and plastic, using handtools and power tools. Joins pipes by use of screws, bolts, fittings, solder, plastic solvent, and calks joints. Fills pipe system with water or air and reads pressure gages to determine whether system is leaking. Installs and repairs plumbing fixtures, such as sinks, commodes, bathtubs, water heaters, hot water tanks, garbage disposal units, dishwashers, and water softeners. Repairs and maintains plumbing, by replacing washers in leaky faucets, mending burst pipes, and opening clogged drains. May weld holding fixtures to steel structural members. When specializing in maintenance and repair of heating, water, and drainage systems in industrial or commercial establishments is designated PLUMBER, MAINTENANCE (any ind.). • **GED:** R4, M3, L3 • **SVP:** 2-4 yrs • **Academic:** Ed=H, Eng=S • **Work Field:** 102 • **MPSMS:** 364 • **Aptitudes:** G3, V3, N3, S3, P3, Q4, K3, F3, M2, E4, C4 • **Temperaments:** M, T, V • **Physical:** V=G, H=N, L=H, W, C, S, H • **Work Env:** B, R • **Salary:** 5 • **Outlook:** 4

GOE: 05.05.04 Painting, Plastering & Paper. Craft Tech.

DRY-WALL APPLICATOR (const.) • D.O.T. #842.381-010 • OES #87108 • DRY-WALL INSTALLATIONS MECHANIC; DRY-WALL INSTALLER; GYPSUM DRY-WALL SYSTEMS INSTALLER. Plans gypsum drywall installations, erects metal framing and furring channels for fastening drywalls, and installs drywall to cover walls, ceilings, soffits, shafts, and movable partitions in residential, commercial, and industrial buildings: Reads blueprints and other specifications to determine method of installation, work procedures, and material, tool, and work aid requirements. Lays out reference lines and points for use in computing location and position of metal framing and furring channels and marks position for erecting metalwork, using chalkline. Measures, marks, and cuts metal runners, studs, and furring channels to specified size, using tape measure, straightedge and hand and portable power cutting tools. Secures metal framing to walls and furring channels to ceilings, using hand and portable power tools. Measures and marks cutting lines on drywall, using square, tape measure, and marking devices. Scribes cutting lines on drywall, using straightedge and utility knife and breaks board along cut lines. Fits and fastens board into specified position on wall, using screws or adhesive. Cuts openings into board for electrical outlets, vents or fixtures, using keyhole saw or other cutting tools. Measures, cuts, assembles and installs metal framing and decorative trim for windows, doorways, and vents. Fits, alines, and hangs doors and installs hardware, such as locks and kickplates [CARPENTER (const.)]. • **GED:** R4, M4, L3 • **SVP:** 2-4 yrs • **Academic:** Ed=H, Eng=S • **Work Field:** 102, 241 • **MPSMS:** 361, 536, 550 • **Aptitudes:** G3, V3, N2, S3, P3, Q4, K3, F3, M3, E3, C3 • **Temperaments:** D, M, T • **Physical:** V=L, H=N, L=V, W, C, S, H • **Work Env:** I, N, R • **Salary:** 5 • **Outlook:** 3

PAPERHANGER (const.) • D.O.T. #841.381-010 • OES #87402 • Covers interior walls and ceilings of rooms with decorative wallpaper or fabric, using handtools: Measures walls and ceiling to compute number and length of strips required to cover surface. Sets up pasteboard and erects scaffolding. Marks vertical guideline on wall to aline first strip, using plumb bob and chalkline. Smooths rough spots on walls and ceilings, using sandpaper. Fills holes and cracks with plaster, using trowel. Removes paint, varnish, and grease from surfaces, using paint remover and water soda solution. Applies acetic acid to damp plaster to prevent lime from bleeding through paper. Applies sizing (thin glue) to waterproof porous surfaces, using brush, roller, or pasting machine. Measures and cuts strips from roll of wallpaper or fabric, using shears or razor. Mixes paste to desired consistency and brushes paste on back of wallpaper or fabric, using paste brush. Trims selvage (rough edge) from strips, using straightedge and trimming knife. Places paste-coated strips on wall or ceiling to match adjacent edges of figured strips, and smooths strips with dry brush or felt-covered roller to remove wrinkles and bubbles. Smooths joints with seam roller and trims excess material at ceiling and baseboard, using knife. Removes old paper, using water, steam machine, or chemical remover and scraper. May apply paint to interior or exterior surface of buildings [PAINTER (const.)]. • **GED:** R4, M2, L2 • **SVP:** 2-4 yrs • **Academic:** Ed=H, Eng=N • **Work Field:** 102 • **MPSMS:** 361 • **Aptitudes:** G3, V3, N3, S3, P3, Q4, K3, F3, M2, E4, C3 • **Temperaments:** J, M, T • **Physical:** V=G, H=N, L=M, W, C, S, H • **Work Env:** I, R • **Salary:** 4 • **Outlook:** 2

PLASTERER (const.) • **D.O.T.** #842.361-018 • **OES** #87317 • Applies coats of plaster to interior walls, ceilings, and partitions of buildings, to produce finished surface, according to blueprints, architect's drawings, or oral instructions, using handtools and portable power tools: Directs workers to mix plaster to desired consistency and to erect scaffolds. Spreads plaster over lath or masonry base, using trowel, and smooths plaster with darby and float to attain uniform thickness. Applies scratch, brown, or finish coats of plaster to wood, metal, or board lath successively. Roughens undercoat with scratcher (wire or metal scraper) to provide bond for succeeding coats of plaster. Creates decorative textures in finish coat by marking surface of coat with brush and trowel or by spattering it with small stones [STUCCO MASON (const.)]. May install lathing [LATHER (const.)]. May mix mortar. May install guide wires on exterior surface of buildings to indicate thickness of plaster to be applied. May install precast ornamental plaster pieces by applying mortar to back of pieces and pressing pieces into place on wall or ceiling and be designated as ORNAMENTAL-PLASTER STICKER (const.). May specialize in applying finish or rough coats of plaster and be designated as PLASTERER, FINISH (const.); PLASTERER, ROUGH (const.). May apply plaster with spray gun and be designated as PLASTERER, SPRAY GUN (const.). May perform maintenance work only and be designated PLASTERER, MAINTENANCE (const.). • **GED:** R4, M2, L3 • **SVP:** 2-4 yrs • **Academic:** Ed=H, Eng=S • **Work Field:** 091, 095 • **MPSMS:** 361, 536 • **Aptitudes:** G3, V3, N4, S4, P3, Q4, K4, F3, M3, E3, C3 • **Temperaments:** J, M, T • **Physical:** V=L, H=N, L=M, W, C, S, H • **Work Env:** B, W, R • **Salary:** 5 • **Outlook:** 2

GOE: 05.05.05 Elect. Systems Installation & Repair

ANTENNA INSTALLER, SATELLITE COMMUNICATIONS (any ind.) • **D.O.T.** #823.261-022 • **OES** #85599 • Installs, tests, and repairs antennas and related equipment that receive communication satellite signals, following specifications and using handtools and test instruments: Reviews installation specifications, building permit, manufacturer's instructions, and government ordinances to determine installation site for antenna. Measures distance from landmarks to identify exact site location. Visually inspects installation site to identify obstructions, such as trees or buildings, that could distort or block microwave signals from satellite. Discusses site location and construction requirements with customer. Digs hole for footing to support antenna base, using gasoline-powered auger, posthole digger, or shovel. Assembles and installs prefabricated form in hole to cast concrete base, using handtools, plumbrule, and level, following specifications. Mixes, pours, and finishes concrete, using concrete mixer, trowel, and float. Inserts pedestal mounting bolts in wet concrete. Digs trench and lays underground cable to connect antenna base to source of power in customer's building. Attaches antenna base to footing after concrete dries, using handtools. Assembles and attaches electronic and structural components of antenna, with co-worker, applying knowledge of electronics and electricity, following installation guidelines, and using handtools. Attaches antenna to base, using nuts, bolts, and handtools. Climbs ladder to install antenna when area is inaccessible from ground. Orients antenna to direction and altitude of communication satellite, using surveying instruments and following charts of satellite position. Solders connections to electronic controls, using soldering gun and wire cutters. Connects antenna and television set to signal converter control box, using handtools. Tests installed system for conformance to specifications, using test equipment, such as multimeters and oscilloscope. Observes picture on television screen to evaluate reception. Instructs customer in use of equipment. Replaces or repairs defective parts, using handtools and test equipment. May construct

pole or roof mounts for antenna base, using carpenter's tools. May reinforce roof of building to provide secure installation site, using carpenter's tools. May install antennas and related equipment to receive satellite signals for such purposes as telephone, telex, facsimile, data, or radio communication. • **GED:** R3, M3, L3 • **SVP:** 1-2 yrs • **Academic:** Ed=N, Eng=S • **Work Field:** 091, 111 • **MPSMS:** 587 • **Aptitudes:** G3, V3, N3, S2, P3, Q3, K3, F3, M3, E3, C5 • **Temperaments:** J, T, V • **Physical:** V=L, H=L, L=M, W, C, S, H • **Work Env:** I • **Salary:** 4 • **Outlook:** 4

AUTOMATED EQUIPMENT ENGINEER-TECHNICIAN (mach. mfg.) • **D.O.T.** #638.261-010 • **OES** #85123 • ENGINEER, AUTOMATED EQUIPMENT; TECHNICIAN, AUTOMATED EQUIPMENT. Installs machinery and equipment used to emboss, die-cut, score, fold, and transfer paper or cardboard stock to form box blanks, knock-down advertising displays, and similar products: Confers with customer's engineering staff to determine layout of equipment, to resolve problems of machine design, and to avoid construction problems in plant. Arranges machine parts according to sequence of assembly and effective use of floor space. Directs workers in positioning equipment, following floor plans and manufacturer's instructions. Assembles and installs electrical and electromechanical components and systems, using handtools, electrical testing instruments, soldering irons, and wiring diagrams. Operates equipment through trial run to verify setup. Adjusts controls and setup of machine for specified type, thickness, and size of stock to be processed, for prescribed sequence of operating stages, and to ensure maximum efficiency. Instructs equipment operators and engineering and maintenance personnel regarding setup, operation, and maintenance of equipment. Repairs and services equipment, following preventive maintenance schedule or upon customer's request. May modify previously installed equipment to insure compatibility with new units, or install safety devices or attachments to old equipment. May confer with customer's engineers to determine effective methods of programing work for machine processing. • **GED:** R4, M4, L4 • **SVP:** 2-4 yrs • **Academic:** Ed=H, Eng=S • **Work Field:** 111 • **MPSMS:** 567 • **Aptitudes:** G2, V3, N2, S3, P2, Q3, K2, F2, M3, E4, C3 • **Temperaments:** M, P, T, V • **Physical:** V=G, H=N, L=M, W, S, H • **Work Env:** I • **Salary:** 4 • **Outlook:** 3

AUTOMATIC-EQUIPMENT TECHNICIAN (tel. & tel.) • **D.O.T.** #822.281-010 • **OES** #85508 • TECHNICIAN, AUTOMATIC; TELEGRAPH-EQUIPMENT MAINTAINER. Analyzes defects in and repairs manual and automatic telegraphic transmitting and receiving apparatus, such as teletypewriters, facsimile-recording devices, and switching equipment: Tests and adjusts equipment, using testing devices, such as signal generators and ohmmeters, following blueprints and wiring diagrams, and using handtools. Tests and regulates telegraph repeaters [TESTING-AND-REGULATING TECHNICIAN (tel. & tel.)]. When repairing and maintaining equipment in branch offices, may be designated OPERATIONS TECHNICIAN (tel. & tel.). May be designated according to type of equipment maintained or repaired as PRINTER MAINTAINER (tel. & tel.); TELEGRAPHIC-TYPE-WRITER REPAIRER (tel. & tel.). • **GED:** R4, M4, L3 • **SVP:** 2-4 yrs • **Academic:** Ed=A, Eng=S • **Work Field:** 111 • **MPSMS:** 586 • **Aptitudes:** G3, V3, N3, S3, P3, Q4, K4, F3, M3, E5, C4 • **Temperaments:** M, T, V • **Physical:** V=L, H=N, L=M, W, C, S, H • **Work Env:** I, N • **Salary:** 4 • **Outlook:** 2

CABLE INSTALLER-REPAIRER (light, heat, & power) • **D.O.T.** #821.361-010 • **OES** #85723 • ELECTRICIAN, UNDERGROUND. Installs and repairs underground conduit and cable systems used to conduct electrical energy between substations and consumers: Installs and repairs conduits following blueprints. Pulls cables through ducts [CABLE PULLER (const.; light, heat, & power)]. Splices cables together or to overhead transmission line, customer service line, or street light line [CABLE SPLICER (const.; light, heat, & power; tel. & tel.)]. Installs and repairs transformers, fuse boxes, bus bars, relays, and other electrical equipment in manhole and underground substations [UNDERGROUND REPAIRER (light, heat, & power)] according to wiring diagrams and specifications. Reinsulates or replaces worn cables and wires. Tests electric cables and equipment wiring to detect broken circuits or incorrect connections, using test lamp, volt meter, ammeter, and thermocouple indicator. • **GED:** R4, M4, L3

• **SVP:** 4-10 yrs • **Academic:** Ed=H, Eng=S • **Work Field:** 111 • **MPSMS:** 581, 585 • **Aptitudes:** G3, V3, N3, S2, P2, Q2, K3, F3, M3, E3, C4 • **Temperaments:** M, S, T, V • **Stress:** S • **Physical:** V=G, H=N, L=M, W, C, S, H • **Work Env:** O, R • **Salary:** 4 • **Outlook:** 3

CABLE SPLICER (const.) • D.O.T. #829.361-010 • OES #85723 • ELECTRICIAN, CABLE-SPLICING; SPLICER. Splices overhead, underground, or submarine multiple-conductor cables used in telephone and telegraph communication and electric-power transmission systems: Climbs utility poles or towers, utilizes truck-mounted lift bucket, or descends into sewers and underground vaults where cables are located. Cuts lead sheath from installed cable to gain access to defective cable connections, using hacksaw. Cuts and peels lead sheath and insulation from newly-installed cables and conductors preparatory to splicing. Tests (traces or phases-out) each conductor to identify corresponding conductors in adjoining cable sections, according to electrical diagrams and specifications, to prevent incorrect connections between individual communication circuits or electric power circuits, using testlamp or bell system. Cleans, tins, and splices corresponding conductors by twisting ends together or by joining ends with metal clips and soldering each connection. Covers conductors with insulating or fireproofing materials. Fits lead sleeve around cable joint and wipes molten lead into joints between sleeve and cable sheath to produce moisture-proof joint. Fills completed sleeve with insulating oil. May work on energized circuits to avoid interruption of service. May locate and repair leaks in pressurized cable. May work on board marine craft when splicing underwater cable and be designated JOINTER, SUBMARINE CABLE (light, heat, & power; tel. & tel.). • **GED:** R4, M3, L3 • **SVP:** 2-4 yrs • **Academic:** Ed=N, Eng=S • **Work Field:** 111 • **MPSMS:** 580 • **Aptitudes:** G3, V3, N3, S3, P2, Q3, K3, F2, M3, E3, C3 • **Temperaments:** M, T • **Physical:** V=L, H=N, L=L, W, C, S, H • **Work Env:** B, R • **Salary:** 4 • **Outlook:** 3

CABLE SUPERVISOR (tel. & tel.) • D.O.T. #184.161-010 • OES #15023 • Directs and coordinates, through subordinate supervisory personnel, activities of workers engaged in installation, maintenance, and repair of underground, buried, aerial, or submarine telephone carrier cables in plant district: Reviews proposed construction plans and schematic drawings to insure that proposals are compatible with existing equipment and that plans adhere to specifications. Inspects construction sites and installations to insure service deadlines are being met. Directs and coordinates testing and inspecting of plant equipment for operational performance. Prepares budget, determines work force requirements, and establishes production schedules to meet service loads. • **GED:** R4, M2, L4 • **SVP:** 4-10 yrs • **Academic:** Ed=H, Eng=S • **Work Field:** 111, 211 • **MPSMS:** 586 • **Aptitudes:** G2, V3, N3, S3, P3, Q4, K4, F4, M4, E5, C4 • **Temperaments:** D, M, P • **Stress:** A • **Physical:** V=G, H=L, L=L • **Work Env:** B • **Salary:** 5 • **Outlook:** 2

CABLE TESTER (tel. & tel.) • D.O.T. #822.361-010 • OES #83002 • Tests insulated wires in aerial, underground, or submarine multiple-conductor cables to determine continuity, insulation, and correctness of cable loading, using standard testing procedures and impedance, resistance, and frequency oscillating meters. Listens for sound of escaping insulating gas from hole in cable sheathing to locate defects in cable. Determines continuity, insulation, capacity imbalance, and cable loading, using meters, such as capacity and resistance bridges. Prepares report identifying location and cause of malfunctions. May drive motor vehicle along route of cable, climb poles, and ride in cable car from pole to pole on cable strand to perform tests. May direct CABLE SPLICER (const.; light, heat, & power; tel. & tel.) in correction of malfunction. • **GED:** R4, M3, L3 • **SVP:** 2-4 yrs • **Academic:** Ed=H, Eng=S • **Work Field:** 111 • **MPSMS:** 586 • **Aptitudes:** G3, V3, N3, S3, P3, Q4, K4, F3, M4, E3, C4 • **Temperaments:** M, T, V • **Physical:** V=G, H=G, L=M, W, C, S, H • **Work Env:** B, R • **Salary:** 3 • **Outlook:** 3

CENTRAL-OFFICE REPAIRER (tel. & tel.) • D.O.T. #822.281-014 • OES #85502 • CENTRAL-OFFICE MAINTAINER. Tests, analyzes defects, and repairs telephone circuits and equipment in central office of telephone company, using test meters and handtools: Locates electrical, electronic, and mechanical failures in telephone switching equipment, using milliammeter boxes, schematic drawings, computer printouts, or trouble tickets. Installs, repairs, and adjusts equipment, such as switches, relays, and amplifiers, using handtools. Removes connections on wire distributing frames and solders or splices wires to terminal lugs, following diagrams [FRAME WIRER (tel. & tel.)]. May maintain telephone switching equipment at private establishments, such as hotels and office buildings [PRIVATE-BRANCH-EXCHANGE REPAIRER (tel. & tel.)]. May diagnose, isolate, and clear electrical faults in circuit [TROUBLE LOCATOR, TEST DESK (tel. & tel.)]. When servicing equipment for intercommunity telephone lines is designated TOLL REPAIRER, CENTRAL OFFICE (tel. & tel.). • **GED:** R4, M3, L3 • **SVP:** 2-4 yrs • **Academic:** Ed=H, Eng=S • **Work Field:** 111 • **MPSMS:** 586 • **Aptitudes:** G3, V3, N3, S3, P3, Q3, K3, F2, M2, E3, C4 • **Temperaments:** M, T, V • **Physical:** V=G, H=G, L=L, W, C, S, H • **Work Env:** I • **Salary:** 4 • **Outlook:** 3

ELECTRIC-METER INSTALLER 1 (light, heat, & power) • D.O.T. #821.361-014 • OES #85911 • Installs, disconnects, removes, and reconnects electric power meters used to record current consumption of residential, commercial, and industrial customers: Splices and connects covered insulated cable to bus bar in pull box or on switchboard. Mounts meter, and other electric equipment for high load installations, such as time clocks, transformers, and circuit breakers, on racks or wall, using electrician handtools. Installs and connects cable from pull box to meter socket or transformer. Attaches color-coded wires from current transformer to test blocks and from test blocks to meter terminals for testing purposes. Tests meter for current flow and recording of current consumption. Disconnects and seals meter on cut-off order or removes seal and reconnects meter on cut-in orders. Removes, replaces, and reconnects meters when current consumption is too high for existing installation. Installs temporary service meter for recording current consumption during construction. Splices and connects jumper cables from current transformer onto bus bar on switchboard to provide temporary power for customer during change of meter and cables or when customer's service equipment is defective. Records meter and installation data on meter cards, work orders, and field service orders. Locates, diagnoses, and clears electrical trouble on customers' premises. Performs minor repairs and changes faulty or incorrect wiring on customers' premises. May be designated according to specialty as METER INSTALLER-AND-REMOVER (light, heat, & power). • **GED:** R4, M4, L3 • **SVP:** 2-4 yrs • **Academic:** Ed=N, Eng=S • **Work Field:** 111 • **MPSMS:** 581 • **Aptitudes:** G3, V3, N3, S3, P3, Q3, K3, F3, M3, E4, C4 • **Temperaments:** M, P, T • **Physical:** V=L, H=N, L=L, W, H • **Work Env:** B • **Salary:** 4 • **Outlook:** 3

ELECTRICIAN (any ind.) • D.O.T. #824.261-010 • OES #87202 • WIRER. Plans layout, installs, and repairs wiring, electrical fixtures, apparatus, and control equipment: Plans new or modified installations to minimize waste of materials, provide access for future maintenance, and avoid unsightly, hazardous, and unreliable wiring, consistent with specifications and local electrical codes. Prepares sketches showing location of wiring and equipment, or follows diagrams or blueprints, ensuring that concealed wiring is installed before completion of future walls, ceilings, and flooring. Measures, cuts, bends, threads, assembles, and installs electrical conduit, using such tools as hacksaw, pipe threader, and conduit bender. Pulls wiring through conduit, assisted by ELECTRICIAN HELPER (any ind.). Splices wires by stripping insulation from terminal leads with knife or pliers, twisting or soldering wires together, and applying tape or terminal caps. Connects wiring to lighting fixtures and power equipment, using handtools. Installs control and distribution apparatus, such as switches, relays, and circuit-breaker panels, fastening in place with screws or bolts, using handtools and power tools. Connects power cables to equipment, such as electric range or motor, and installs grounding leads. Tests continuity of circuit to ensure electrical compatibility and safety of components, using testing instruments, such as ohmmeter, battery and buzzer, and oscilloscope. Observes functioning of installed equipment or system to detect hazards and need for adjustments, relocation, or replacement. May repair faulty equipment or systems [ELECTRICAL REPAIRER (any ind.)]. May be required to hold license. May cut and weld steel structural members, using flame-cutting and welding equipment. May be designated according to work location as MINE ELECTRICIAN (mining & quarrying). • **GED:** R4, M4, L3 • **SVP:** 2-4 yrs •

Academic: Ed=H, Eng=S • **Work Field:** 111 • **MPSMS:** 580 • **Aptitudes:** G2, V3, N2, S2, P2, Q4, K3, F3, M3, E4, C4 • **Temperaments:** J, M, T, V • **Physical:** V=G, H=N, L=M, W, C, S, H • **Work Env:** B, R • **Salary:** 5 • **Outlook:** 4

ELECTRICIAN, MAINTENANCE (any ind.) • D.O.T. #829.261-018 • OES #87202 • ELECTRICAL REPAIRER. Installs and repairs electrical apparatus and electrical and electronic components of industrial machinery and equipment, using hand tools, power tools, and electrical and electronic test equipment, such as multimeter and oscilloscope and following electrical code, manuals, specifications, schematic diagrams, and blueprints: Installs power supply wiring and conduit for newly-in stalled machines and equipment, such as robots, conveyors, and programmable controllers, using handtools and voltage tester and following electrical code and blueprints. Connects power supply wires to machines and equipment, and connects cables and wires between machines and equipment, using handtools and test equipment and following manuals, schematic diagrams, and blueprints. Diagnoses and replaces damaged or broken wires and cables and malfunctioning electrical apparatus, such as transformers, mo tors, and lighting fixtures, using test equipment and handtools. Tests malfunctioning machinery, such as robots and conveyors, using test equipment, and discusses malfunction with production workers, supervisors, or other maintenance workers, such as MACHINE REPAIRER, MAINTENANCE (any ind.) 638.261-030 and TOOL MAKER, MAINTENANCE (mach. shop) 601.280-042, to diagnose malfunction. Replaces faulty electrical components of machines, such as relays, switches, motors, and position sensing devices, using handtools. May diagnose and replace faulty electronic components, such as printed circuit boards, in equipment such as robot controllers and programmable controllers, using test equipment and following manuals, specifications, and schematic diagrams. May push buttons and press keys on robot controller, teach pendant, and programmable controller to program automated machinery, such as robots, to operate automated machinery, to test for malfunctions, and to verify repairs. May install wiring, conduit, and electrical apparatus in new building [ELECTRICIAN (any ind.) 824.261-010]. May plan layout of wiring. May replace electric motor bearings and rewire motors. May test and repair printed circuit boards [ELECTRONICS TESTER (electronics) I 726.281-014]. May dress or replace spot welding electrodes. May diagnose and replace faulty mechanical, hydraulic, and pneumatic components of machines. May install end-of-arm tools on robots. May be required to hold electrician's license. May be designated according to equipment repaired as CIRCUIT-BREAKER MECHANIC (light, heat, & power); ELECTRICIAN, CRANE MAINTENANCE (any ind.); ELECTRICIAN, RECTIFIER MAINTENANCE (light, heat, & power); SALVAGE REPAIRER (light, heat, & power) I; TIME CLOCK REPAIRER (elec. equip.); TRANSFORMER-COIL WINDER (light, heat, & power); or according to work location as ELECTRICIAN, MACHINE SHOP (mach. shop); ELECTRICIAN, REFINERY (petrol. refin.); UNDERGROUND REPAIRER (light, heat, & power). Additional titles: WATCH ELECTRICIAN (tel. & tel.); WIRER, MAINTENANCE (light, heat, & power). • **GED:** R4, M4, L4 • **SVP:** 4-10 yrs • **Academic:** Ed=H, Eng=S • **Work Field:** 111 • **MPSMS:** 560, 570, 580 • **Aptitudes:** G2, V3, N2, S2, P2, Q3, K3, F3, M2, E3, C4 • **Temperaments:** J, T • **Physical:** V=G, H=N, L=M, W, S, H • **Work Env:** I, R • **Salary:** 4 • **Outlook:** 4

ELECTRICIAN, POWERHOUSE (light, heat, & power) • D.O.T. #820.261-014 • OES #85721 • Repairs and maintains electrical equipment in generating station or powerhouse: Tests defective equipment to determine cause of malfunction or failure, using voltmeters, ammeters, and related electrical testing apparatus. Notifies plant personnel of necessary equipment downtime requiring changes from normal generating and transmission equipment operation to maintain uninterrupted service. Repairs and replaces equipment, such as relays, switches, supervisory controls, and indicating and recording instruments. Tests and repairs switchboard and equipment circuitry, interpreting wiring diagrams to trace and connect numerous wires carrying current for independent functions. Cleans and repairs brushes, commutators, windings, and bearings of generators, motors, and converters. May test and maintain transmission equipment, performing such duties as oiling circuit breakers and transformers [ELECTRICIAN, SUBSTATION (light, heat, & power)]. • **GED:** R4, M4, L3 • **SVP:** 4-10 yrs • **Academic:** Ed=N,

Eng=S • **Work Field:** 111 • **MPSMS:** 580 • **Aptitudes:** G2, V3, N3, S2, P2, Q4, K3, F3, M2, E3, C4 • **Temperaments:** M, T, V • **Physical:** V=L, H=N, L=M, W, C, S, H • **Work Env:** B, R • **Salary:** 5 • **Outlook:** 2

ELECTRONICS ASSEMBLER, DEVELOPMENTAL (electronics) • D.O.T. #726.261-010 • OES #22505 • Assembles, modifies, tests and adjusts prototype or custom electronic parts, systems, and apparatus applying knowledge of various assembly techniques: Reads blueprints, wiring diagrams, process sheets, assembly and schematic drawings and receives verbal instruction regarding work to be done. Aligns and joins parts, such as leads, coils, wires, tabs, and terminals into housing, using hand and power tools, soldering iron, brazing fixture and welding head. Routes and laces cables [CABLE MAKER (electronics; elec. equip.)]. Installs components and parts, such as switches, coils, transformers, relays, transistors, and semiconductor circuits on chassis, circuit boards, panels, and other units, using power tools, handtools, and various soldering and welding equipment and techniques, such as thermocompression bonding, wave soldering or resistance welding. Routes and attaches wires and connectors to form circuitry and connect assembly with power supply sources, switch panels, or junction boxes. Attaches hardware and seals assembly, using rivets, screws, hand and power tools, resistance welder or thermocompression bonding. Examines parts to ensure that they are free from defects, such as pinholes or chips, Test-operates unit for specified functioning, to locate defects, measure performance and determine need for adjustment, using ohmmeter, oscilloscope, signal generator, and other electronic test instruments. Replaces defective components and wiring, using handtools and soldering iron. Calibrates unit according to specification. Enters required information to complete records, logs, and other report forms. May determine wiring and cabling proce dure to improve assembly methods for production workers. May assemble experimental circuits to prove engineering design. May assemble prototype microelectronic units, using binocular microscope. May repair defective units rejected by inspection or test personnel [PRODUCTION REPAIRER (electronics)]. May be designated ELECTRONICS ASSEMBLER, PROTOTYPE (electronics). May be designated according to specialty as FILTER ASSEMBLER, PROTOTYPE (electronics); INTEGRATED-CIRCUIT ASSEMBLER, PROTOTYPE (electronics); POTENTIOMETER ASSEMBLER, PROTOTYPE (electronics); SYSTEMS ASSEM BLER, PROTOTYPE (electronics); TRANSFORMER ASSEMBLER, PROTOTYPE (electronics). • **GED:** R4, M4, L4 • **SVP:** 2-4 yrs • **Academic:** Ed=N, Eng=S • **Work Field:** 111 • **MPSMS:** 580 • **Aptitudes:** G3, V3, N3, S3, P3, Q4, K3, F3, M3, E5, C3 • **Temperaments:** M, T • **Physical:** V=L, H=N, L=L, H • **Work Env:** I • **Salary:** 4 • **Outlook:** 3

ELEVATOR REPAIRER (any ind.) • D.O.T. #825.281-030 • OES #85932 • ELECTRICIAN, ELEVATOR-MAINTENANCE; ELEVATOR MECHANIC; ELEVATOR-REPAIR MECHANIC; MAINTENANCE MECHANIC, ELEVATORS. Repairs and maintains elevators, escalators, and dumb-waiters to meet safety regulations and building codes, using handtools, power tools, test lamps, ammeters, voltmeters, and other testing devices: Locates and determines causes of trouble in brakes, motors, switches, and signal and control systems, using test lamps, ammeters, and voltmeters. Disassembles defective units and repairs or replaces parts, such as locks, gears, cables, electric wiring, and faulty safety devices, using handtools. Installs push-button controls and other devices to modernize elevators. Lubricates bearings and other parts to minimize friction. • **GED:** R4, M3, L3 • **SVP:** 2-4 yrs • **Academic:** Ed=A, Eng=S • **Work Field:** 111, 121 • **MPSMS:** 565 • **Aptitudes:** G3, V3, N3, S2, P3, Q4, K4, F3, M2, E4, C4 • **Temperaments:** M, T • **Physical:** V=L, H=N, L=M, W, S, H • **Work Env:** I, R • **Salary:** 5 • **Outlook:** 5

FIELD ENGINEER (electronics) • D.O.T. #828.261-014 • OES #85717 • FIELD-SERVICE REPRESENTATIVE; FIELD-TECHNICAL REPRESENTATIVE; TECHNICAL REPRESENTATIVE. Installs and repairs electronic equipment, such as computer, radar, missile-control, and communication systems, in field installations: Consults with customer to plan layout of equipment. Directs workers to install equipment according to manufacturer's specifications. Operates system to demonstrate equipment and to train workers in service and repair techniques, using standard test instruments and handtools. Analyzes malfunctions in operational equipment and interprets maintenance manuals, using knowledge of equipment and electronics, to train workers in repair procedures. Consults with manufacturer's engineering personnel to determine solutions to unusual problems in system operation and maintenance. May instruct workers in electronic theory. May supervise workers in testing, tuning, and adjusting equipment to obtain optimum operating conditions. May install and maintain equipment for customers. • **GED:** R4, M4, L4 • **SVP:** 2-4 yrs • **Academic:** Ed=H, Eng=S • **Work Field:** 111 • **MPSMS:** 586 • **Aptitudes:** G2, V2, N2, S2, P2, Q4, K3, F3, M3, E5, C3 • **Temperaments:** D, M, P, T, V • **Physical:** V=G, H=G, L=S, W, H • **Work Env:** B • **Salary:** 4 • **Outlook:** 4

FURNACE INSTALLER (light, heat, & power) • D.O.T. #862.361-010 • OES #85902 • Installs and regulates gas-burner units in building-heating furnaces to convert furnaces from wood, coal, or oil to gas: Directs helper to prepare furnace for installation of gas burner unit. Lays brick foundation [BRICKLAYER (const.)] in furnace ashpit and positions heating unit on foundation. Draws sketch of pipes and fittings required to connect gas burner to gas supply. Measures, cuts, threads, bends, and installs pipe between burner and gas supply with assistance of helper, using pipefitters' tools. Installs thermostat in heated area and makes wiring connections between building terminal box, switchbox, burner motor, and thermostat [ELECTRICIAN (any ind.)]. Ignites gas burner and adjusts gas-flow and air-supply control valves until observation of gas flame indicates correct combustion. • **GED:** R4, M2, L3 • **SVP:** 2-4 yrs • **Academic:** Ed=A, Eng=S • **Work Field:** 102, 111 • **MPSMS:** 553, 602 • **Aptitudes:** G3, V3, N3, S3, P3, Q4, K3, F3, M2, E5, C4 • **Temperaments:** M, T, V • **Physical:** V=L, H=N, L=M, W, S, H • **Work Env:** I, R • **Salary:** 5 • **Outlook:** 4

LINE ERECTOR (const.) • D.O.T. #821.361-018 • OES #85723 • Erects, maintains, and repairs wood poles and prefabricated light-duty metal towers, cable, and related equipment to construct transmission and distribution powerlines used to conduct electrical energy between generating stations, substations, and consumers: Directs and assists GROUND HELPERS (light, heat, & power; tel. & tel.) in attaching crossarms, insulators, lightning arresters, switches, wire conductors, and auxiliary equipment to poles preparatory to erection, as in structed by LINE SUPERVISOR (light, heat, & power), and assists in erection of poles or towers and adjustment of guy wires. Climbs erected poles or towers and installs equipment, such as transformers, which are ordinarily installed after poles are erected. Strings wire conductors between erected poles with assistance of GROUND HELPERS (light, heat, & power; tel. & tel.) and adjusts slack in conductors to compensate for contraction and elongation of conductors due to temperature variations, using winch. Splices, solders, and insulates conductors and related wiring to join sections of powerline, and to connect transformers and electrical accessories. May trim trees and brush prior to new construction, during repair of damaged lines, or as part of routine maintenance [TREE TRIMMER (light, heat, & power; tel. & tel.)]. • **GED:** R4, M3, L3 • **SVP:** 2-4 yrs • **Academic:** Ed=N, Eng=S • **Work Field:** 102, 111 • **MPSMS:** 581 • **Aptitudes:** G3, V3, N4, S3, P3, Q4, K2, F3, M2, E2, C4 • **Temperaments:** M, S, T • **Stress:** S • **Physical:** V=L, H=N, L=H, W, C, S, H • **Work Env:** O, R • **Salary:** 4 • **Outlook:** 3

LINE MAINTAINER (any ind.) • D.O.T. #821.261-014 • OES #85723 • Installs, maintains, and repairs telephone and telegraph and electrical powerlines between installations of industrial plant: Directs workers in setting poles. Climbs poles and installs hardware, lightning arresters, telephone repeaters, telephone and telegraph wires, and other equipment [LINE INSTALLER-REPAIRER (tel. & tel.)]. Installs electrical power cables and auxiliary equipment [LINE ERECTOR (const.; light, heat, & power)]. Makes repairs and replacements to maintain lines. May be designated according to area of operations as LINE MAINTAINER, DISTRICT (any ind.). • **GED:** R4, M3, L3 • **SVP:** 2-4 yrs • **Academic:** Ed=N, Eng=S • **Work Field:** 111 • **MPSMS:** 586 • **Aptitudes:** G3, V3, N4, S3, P3, Q4, K3, F3, M3, E3, C4 • **Temperaments:** M, T • **Physical:** V=L, H=N, L=M, W, H • **Work Env:** O, R • **Salary:** 4 • **Outlook:** 3

LINE REPAIRER (light, heat, & power) • D.O.T. #821.361-026 •

OES #85723 • HIKER; LINE SERVICER. Repairs and replaces transmission and distribution powerlines between generating stations, substations, and consumers, requiring use of precautionary work methods and safety equipment due to electrical hazards present when working on or near energized conductors and electrical accessories: Opens switches or clamps grounding device to energized equipment to deenergize lines or accessories as directed by LINE SUPERVISOR (light, heat, & power). Climbs poles or rides in bucket attached to truck-mounted boom to remove broken or defective wires. Secures new wires to crossarm insulators and splices wire to adjoining sections of line to complete circuit. Transfers wires from defective poles to poles erected by GROUND HELPERS (light, heat, & power; tel. & tel.). Installs pole hardware and such auxiliary equipment as transformers, lightning arresters, switches, fuses, and insulators, using handtools. Suspends insulated ladders and platforms from pole crossarms and covers energized lines with rubber mats to facilitate safe handling of high-voltage lines without interrupting service by power shutoff, and uses long insulated poles (hot sticks) fitted with mechanically or hydraulically operated grasping and crimping tools. May service streetlight systems [STREET-LIGHT SERVICER (light, heat, & power)]. May patrol powerlines [ELECTRIC POWER LINE EXAMINER (light, heat, & power)]. Qualifications of workers in this classification include work experience in terms of maximum voltage of powerlines repaired, such as 120-240 volt secondary circuits, 2,300-4,000 volt distribution lines, or 138 kilo volt transmission lines. Powerline repairers experienced in repair of energized or deenergized conductors suspended from electrically conductive metal towers, commonly one-hundred feet or more above ground, may be designated LINE REPAIRER, TOWER (light, heat, & power). • **GED:** R4, M4, L4 • **SVP:** 2-4 yrs • **Academic:** Ed=H, Eng=S • **Work Field:** 102, 111 • **MPSMS:** 581 • **Aptitudes:** G3, V3, N4, S3, P3, Q4, K2, F3, M2, E2, C4 • **Temperaments:** M, S, T, V • **Stress:** S • **Physical:** V=G, H=N, L=H, W, C, S, H • **Work Env:** O, R • **Salary:** 5 • **Outlook:** 3

MAINTENANCE MECHANIC, TELEPHONE (any ind.) • D.O.T. #822.281-018 • OES #85726 • ELECTRICIAN, TELEPHONE. Installs, tests, and repairs communication equipment, such as public address and intercommunication systems, wired burglar alarms, switchboards, telegraphs, telephones, and related apparatus, including coin collectors, telephone booths, and switching keys, using schematic diagrams, testing devices, and handtools: Installs equipment according to layout plans and connects units with inside and outside service wires. Maintains equipment and analyzes operational malfunctioning with testing devices, such as oscilloscopes, generators, meters, and electric bridges to locate and diagnose nature of defect, and ascertain repairs to be made. Examines mechanism and disassembles components to replace, clean, adjust or repair parts, wires, switches, relays, circuits, or signaling units, using handtools. Operates and tests equipment to ensure elimination of malfunction. May climb poles to install or repair outside service lines. May repair cables, lay out plans for new equipment, and estimate material required. • **GED:** R4, M4, L3 • **SVP:** 2-4 yrs • **Academic:** Ed=H, Eng=S • **Work Field:** 111 • **MPSMS:** 586 • **Aptitudes:** G3, V3, N3, S3, P2, Q4, K3, F3, M3, E3, C3 • **Temperaments:** M, T • **Physical:** V=L, H=N, L=L, W, S, H • **Work Env:** I • **Salary:** 4 • **Outlook:** 4

PRIVATE-BRANCH-EXCHANGE REPAIRER (tel. & tel.) • D.O.T. #822.281-022 • OES #85502 • PBX REPAIRER; TELEPHONE REPAIRER. Analyzes and repairs defects in communication equipment, such as telephone switchboards, teletypewriters, and mobile radiophones on customers' premises: Tests equipment to locate malfunctions, using circuit diagrams, polar probes, meters, and telephone test set. Isolates and analyzes malfunction to determine method of repair, according to knowledge of equipment and test readings. Repairs or replaces defective equipment, using handtools, soldering iron, or wire wrap gun. Retests equipment to verify completeness of repair. May install equipment [PRIVATE-BRANCH-EXCHANGE INSTALLER (tel. & tel.)]. • **GED:** R4, M2, L3 • **SVP:** 2-4 yrs • **Academic:** Ed=H, Eng=S • **Work Field:** 111 • **MPSMS:** 586 • **Aptitudes:** G3, V3, N4, S3, P3, Q4, K3, F3, M3, E4, C4 • **Temperaments:** M, T, V • **Physical:** V=G, H=G, L=M, W, S, H • **Work Env:** I • **Salary:** 4 • **Outlook:** 3

PROTECTIVE-SIGNAL INSTALLER (bus. ser.) • D.O.T.

#822.361-018 • OES #87202 • BURGLAR-ALARM INSTALLER; INSTALLER. Installs electrical protective signaling systems used to notify central office of fire, burglary, or other irregularities on subscribers' premises: Installs wires, conduits, and signaling units, following blueprints of electrical layouts and building plans, and using handtools, power tools and soldering iron. May repair signaling systems [PROTECTIVE-SIGNAL REPAIRER (bus. ser.)]. Usually is required to possess identification card issued by local authorities. • **GED:** R4, M3, L2 • **SVP:** 2-4 yrs • **Academic:** Ed=H, Eng=S • **Work Field:** 111 • **MPSMS:** 586 • **Aptitudes:** G3, V3, N3, S3, P2, Q3, K4, F3, M3, E4, C4 • **Temperaments:** M, T • **Physical:** V=L, H=L, L=M, W, C, S, H • **Work Env:** I, R • **Salary:** 4 • **Outlook:** 4

PROTECTIVE-SIGNAL REPAIRER (bus. ser.) • D.O.T. #822.361-022 • OES #87202 • BURGLAR-ALARM INSTALLER AND SERVICER. Inspects, repairs, and replaces electrical protective-signaling systems, such as burglar alarms: Examines signaling installation to insure sound connections and unbroken insulation. Tests circuits, following wiring specifications, using electrical testing devices, such as ohmmeter or voltmeter. Tightens loose connections and disconnects and replaces defective parts and wiring, using electricians' handtools. Adjusts controls to test operation of signaling units on subscriber premises and transmission of signals to central station and police and fire departments. Recommends new installation or modification of existing equipment to meet subscriber needs. May install equipment [PROTECTIVE-SIGNAL INSTALLER (bus. ser.)]. Usually is required to possess identification card issued by local authorities. • **GED:** R4, M3, L3 • **SVP:** 2-4 yrs • **Academic:** Ed=H, Eng=S • **Work Field:** 111 • **MPSMS:** 586 • **Aptitudes:** G3, V3, N3, S3, P2, Q4, K4, F3, M2, E4, C4 • **Temperaments:** M, T, V • **Physical:** V=G, H=G, L=M, W, C, S, H • **Work Env:** I, R • **Salary:** 4 • **Outlook:** 4

STATION INSTALLER-AND-REPAIRER (tel. & tel.) • D.O.T. #822.261-022 • OES #85726 • Installs, maintains, and repairs telephone station equipment, such as telephones, coin collectors, telephone booths, and switching-key equipment: Inspects subscriber premises to determine method of installation. Climbs pole to attach outside (drop) wires. Assembles telephone equipment, mounts brackets, and connects wire leads, using hand tools and following installation diagrams or work order. Tests newly installed equipment and repairs or replaces faulty equipment, using test telephone and other testing devices. May be designated according to specific task performed as STATION INSTALLER (tel. & tel.); STATION REPAIRER (tel. & tel.). May maintain telephones, lines, and equipment in primarily small rural areas and be designated SECTION MAINTAINER (tel. & tel.). • **GED:** R4, M4, L3 • **SVP:** 2-4 yrs • **Academic:** Ed=H, Eng=S • **Work Field:** 111 • **MPSMS:** 586 • **Aptitudes:** G3, V3, N3, S3, P3, Q4, K3, F3, M3, E3, C4 • **Temperaments:** M, P, T, V • **Physical:** V=G, H=G, L=L, W, C, S, H • **Work Env:** B • **Sal ary:** 4 • **Outlook:** 3

STREET-LIGHT SERVICER (light, heat, & power) • D.O.T. #824.381-010 • OES #87202 • STREET-LIGHT REPAIRER. Maintains and repairs mercury-vapor, fluorescent, electric-arc, or incandescent street lights and traffic signals: Climbs ladder or stands in tower-truck bucket to reach lamp. Tests circuits and electric components to locate grounded wires, broken connections, or defective current-control mechanisms, using electrical testing instruments. Replaces blown fuses and bulbs, faulty transformers, photoelectric timers, electrodes, and wires, using electricians' handtools. See LINE REPAIRER (light, heat, & power), and TROUBLE SHOOTER (light, heat, & power) II for classification of workers also qualified to work on high-voltage powerlines. May install and repair traffic signals only and be designated TRAFFIC-SIGNAL REPAIRER (light, heat, & power). • **GED:** R4, M3, L3 • **SVP:** 2-4 yrs • **Academic:** Ed=N, Eng=S • **Work Field:** 111 • **MPSMS:** 584 • **Aptitudes:** G3, V3, N4, S3, P3, Q4, K3, F3, M3, E3, C4 • **Temperaments:** M, T • **Physical:** V=L, H=N, L=M, W, C, H • **Work Env:** O, R • **Salary:** 4 • **Outlook:** 2

TOWER ERECTOR (const.) • D.O.T. #821.361-038 • OES #85723 • Erects structural steel, wood, or aluminum transmission towers and installs electric cables and auxiliary equipment to construct transmission and high-voltage distribution powerlines between generating stations and substations: Repairs and performs scheduled maintenance on towers, cables, and auxiliary equipment. Frequently works more than one hundred feet above ground when erecting upper portion of towers, and when installing insulators, cables, and electrical accessories on completed towers. May trim trees and remove brush along right-of-way [TREE TRIMMER (light, heat, & power; tel. & tel.)]. • **GED:** R4, M3, L2 • **SVP:** 2-4 yrs • **Academic:** Ed=N, Eng=N • **Work Field:** 101, 111 • **MPSMS:** 554, 581 • **Aptitudes:** G3, V3, N4, S3, P3, Q4, K2, F3, M2, E2, C4 • **Temperaments:** M, S, T • **Stress:** S • **Physical:** V=L, H=N, L=H, W, C, S, H • **Work Env:** O, R • **Salary:** 4 • **Outlook:** 3

WIND-GENERATING-ELECTRIC-POWER INSTALLER (const.) • D.O.T. #821.381-018 • OES #85714 • Assembles, installs, and maintains electrical and mechanical parts, such as alternators, generators, and rotors of electric power generating windmills, according to production specifications, using tools and equipment: Assembles and adjusts alternator components according to production specifications, using handtools, drill presses, grinders, and micrometers. Welds steel supports to alternator for mounting on windmill tower, using welding equipment. Crates alternator for shipment to installation site. Attaches cables to alternator and pulls lever to activate truck-mounted hoist to position alternator on windmill tower. Secures alternator to tower structure, using bolts and wrenches. Attaches electric cables, windmill motor, and rotor to alternator, according to schematic, using handtools. Replaces bent or defective parts of windmill and lubricates machinery to service equipment, using handtools, oilcan, and grease gun. • **GED:** R4, M3, L3 • **SVP:** 4-10 yrs • **Academic:** Ed=N, Eng=S • **Work Field:** 111 • **MPSMS:** 871 • **Aptitudes:** G3, V3, N3, S2, P3, Q4, K3, F3, M3, E5, C4 • **Temperaments:** S, T • **Stress:** S • **Physical:** V=L, H=N, L=H, W, C, S, H • **Work Env:** I, R • **Salary:** 4 • **Outlook:** 3

GOE: 05.05.06 Metal Fabrication & Repair

AIRCRAFT BODY REPAIRER (aircraft-aerospace mfg.) • D.O.T. #807.261-010 • OES #85323 • Repairs sheet and extruded metal structural parts of aircraft and missiles according to design specifications, using handtools and power tools and metal working machinery: Reads design specifications or examines sample parts to determine fabrication procedures and machines and tools required. Removes rivets and other fasteners to facilitate removal of defective part, using power drill and punch, or cuts out defective part, using power shears, hacksaw, and file. Locates and marks dimension and reference lines on defective or replacement part, using templates, scribes, compass, and steel rule. Sets up and operates metal fabricating machines, such as saws, brakes, shears, drill press, and grinders to repair defective part or fabricate new part. Reinstalls repaired or replacement parts for subsequent riveting or welding, using clamps and wrenches. Confers with other workers to expedite heat treating, anodizing, or other specified processing of repair parts. May signal crane operator to fit and aline heavy parts. May stretch skin and panel sheets to remove surface tension, using sheet metal hand forming tools. • **GED:** R4, M3, L3 • **SVP:** 2-4 yrs • **Academic:** Ed=N, Eng=S • **Work Field:** 102 • **MPSMS:** 592 • **Aptitudes:** G3, V3, N3, S2, P2, Q4, K3, F4, M3, E4, C5 • **Temperaments:** J, M, T • **Physical:** V=L, H=N, L=M, W, H • **Work Env:** I, N • **Salary:** 4 • **Outlook:** 3

ARC CUTTER (welding) • D.O.T. #816.364-010 • OES #93914 • ARC-AIR OPERATOR; BURN-OUT-SCARFING OPERATOR. Cuts, trims, or scarfs metal objects to dimensions, contour, or bevel specified by blueprints, work order, or layout, using arc-cutting equipment: Positions workpiece onto table or into fixture or with jib or crane. Selects carbon or metal-coated carbon electrode, gas nozzle, electric current, and gas pressure, according to thickness and type of metal, data on charts, or record of previous runs. Inserts electrode and gas nozzle into holder and connects hose from holder to compressed gas supply. Connects cables from power source to electrode and workpiece or fixture, to obtain desired polarity. Turns knobs to select amperage. Turns lever to adjust jet of gas to blow away molten metal. Strikes arc and guides electrode along lines to cut (melt) through metal. May cut off chips or sprues and burn out cracks and holes. May use holder having two electrodes. May cut without using gas jet. May use nonconsumable tungsten electrode and gases, such as helium or carbon dioxide, and be designated ARC CUTTER, GAS-TUNGSTEN ARC (welding). May use plasma-arc cutting torch and gases, such as nitrogen and carbon dioxide, and be designated ARC CUTTER, PLASMA ARC (welding). • **GED:** R3, M3, L3 • **SVP:** 6 mos-1 yr • **Academic:** Ed=N, Eng=S • **Work Field:** 082 • **MPSMS:** 540 • **Aptitudes:** G4, V4, N4, S3, P3, Q4, K3, F3, M3, E5, C3 • **Temperaments:** M, T • **Physical:** V=L, H=N, L=M, W, S, H • **Work Env:** I, N, R • **Salary:** 3 • **Outlook:** 3

AUTOMOBILE-BODY REPAIRER (auto. ser.) • D.O.T. #807.381-010 • OES #85305 • AUTOMOBILE-BODY WORKER; BODY-LINE FINISHER; BODY REPAIRER, BUS; DENT REMOVER; DOOR REPAIRER, BUS; METAL BUMPER; METAL SHRINKER; METAL WORKER; TOUCH-UP FINISHER, METAL. Repairs damaged bodies and body parts of automotive vehicles, such as automobiles, buses, and light trucks according to repair manuals, using handtools and power tools: Examines damaged vehicles and estimates cost of repairs [SHOP ESTIMATOR (auto. ser.)]. Removes upholstery, accessories, electrical and hydraulic window-and-seat-operating equipment, and trim to gain access to vehicle body and fenders. Positions dolly block against surface of dented area and beats opposite surface to remove dents, using hammer. Fills depressions with solder or other plastic material. Removes damaged fenders, panels, and grills, using wrenches and cutting torch, and bolts or welds replacement parts in position, using wrenches or welding equipment. Straightens bent frames, using hydraulic jack and pulling device. Files, grinds, and sands repaired surfaces, using power tools and hand tools. Refinishes repaired surface, using paint spray gun and sander. Aims headlights, alines wheels, and bleeds hydraulic brake system. May paint surfaces after performing body repairs and be designated AUTOMOBILE-BODY REPAIRER, COMBINATION (auto. ser.). May repair or replace defective mechanical parts [AUTOMO BILE MECHANIC (auto. ser.)]. • **GED:** R4, M3, L4 • **SVP:** 2-4 yrs • **Academic:** Ed=H, Eng=S • **Work Field:** 102 • **MPSMS:** 591 • **Aptitudes:** G3, V3, N3, S2, P2, Q4, K3, F3, M3, E5, C4 • **Temperaments:** M, T, V • **Physical:** V=G, H=N, L=M, W, S, H • **Work Env:** I, N • **Salary:** 3 • **Outlook:** 3

BLACKSMITH (forging) • D.O.T. #610.381-010 • OES #85999 • ANVIL SMITH. Forges and repairs variety of metal articles, such as tongs, edged tools, hooks, chains, machine and structural components, and agricultural implements as specified by work orders, diagrams, or sample parts: Heats metal stock in blacksmith's forge or furnace [HEATER (forging)]. Hammers stock into specified size and shape on blacksmith's anvil or positions stock on anvil of power-hammer and depresses pedal to hammer stock with varying force and rapidity. Forge-welds metal parts by heating and hammering them together. Devises jigs and fixtures, forges special handtools, such as hammers or chisels, and sets up form blocks. Tempers or anneals forged articles [HEAT TREATER (heat treat.) I]. May record type of repair or fabrication of tools or machine components performed during work shift to maintain daily activity report and records. May cut, assemble, and weld metal parts, using arc or acetylene welding equipment [WELDER, COMBINATION (welding)]. May repair farm machinery and be designated as BLACKSMITH, FARM (agric.). May be designated according to articles forged as TOOL-DRESSER (forging); SPECIAL-TRACKWORK BLACKSMITH (r.r. trans.). • **GED:** R4, M3, L2 • **SVP:** 2-4 yrs • **Academic:** Ed=N, Eng=N • **Work Field:** 134 • **MPSMS:** 556, 567 • **Aptitudes:** G3, V3, N3, S2, P3, Q4, K3, F3, M3, E4, C3 • **Temperaments:** M, T, V • **Physical:** V=L, H=N, L=H, W, H • **Work Env:** I, H, N, R • **Salary:** 4 • **Outlook:** 2

BOILERHOUSE MECHANIC (any ind.) • D.O.T. #805.361-010 • OES #89135 • BOILER MECHANIC; HEATING-EQUIPMENT REPAIRER; STATION MECHANIC. Maintains and repairs stationary steam boilers and boilerhouse auxiliaries, using handtools and portable power tools: Cleans or directs other workers to clean boilers and auxiliary equipment, using scrapers, wire brush and cleaning solvent. Inspects and repairs boiler fittings, such as safety valves, regulators, automatic-control mechanisms, and water columns, and auxiliary machines, such as pumps, draft fans, stokers, and burners. Replaces damaged boiler tubes and plates [BOILERMAKER (boilermaking) I]. Repairs or replaces high-pressure piping, using powersaw, gas torch, threading die, and welding equip-

ment. May patch boiler insulation with cement. May paint surface of equipment, using brush. May perform water pressure test by pumping water into system to determine location of leaks. May remove and replace defective firebrick, using hammer and chisel. May operate lathe and milling machine to repair or make parts, such as valve stems and pump shafts. • **GED:** R4, M3, L3 • **SVP:** 2-4 yrs • **Academic:** Ed=N, Eng=S • **Work Field:** 102, 121 • **MPSMS:** 554 • **Aptitudes:** G3, V3, N3, S3, P3, Q4, K3, F3, M2, E5, C5 • **Temperaments:** M, T, V • **Physical:** V=L, H=N, L=M, W, C, S, H • **Work Env:** I, H, N • **Salary:** 4 • **Outlook:** 2

BOILERMAKER 1 (boilermaking) • D.O.T. #805.261-014 • OES #89135 • BOILERMAKER, ASSEMBLY AND ERECTION. Assembles, analyzes defects in, and repairs boilers, pressure vessels, tanks, and vats in the field, following blue prints and using handtools and portable power tools and equipment: Locates and marks reference points for columns or plates on foundation, using master straightedge, squares, transit, and measuring tape, and applying knowledge of geometry. Attaches rigging or signals crane operator to lift parts to specified position. Alines structures or plate sections to assemble boiler frame, tanks, or vats, using plumb bobs, levels, wedges, dogs, or turnbuckles. Hammers, flame-cuts, files, or grinds irregular edges of sections or structural parts to facilitate fitting edges together. Bolts or arc-welds structures and sections together. Positions drums and headers into supports and bolts or welds supports to frame. Alines water tubes and connects and expands ends to drums and headers, using tube expander. Bells, beads with power hammer, or welds tube ends to ensure leakproof joints. Bolts or welds casing sections, uptakes, stacks, baffles, and such fabricated parts as chutes, air heaters, fan stands, feeding tube, catwalks, ladders, coal hoppers, and safety hatch to frame, using wrench. Installs manholes, handholes, valves, gages, and feedwater connection in drums to complete assembly of water tube boilers. Assists in testing assembled vessels by pumping water or gas under specified pressure into vessel and observing instruments for evidence of leakage. Repairs boilers or tanks in field by unbolting or flame cutting defective sections or tubes, straightening plates, using torch or jacks, installing new tubes, fitting and welding new sections and replacing worn lugs on bolts. May rivet and calk sections of vessels, using pneumatic riveting and calking hammers. May line firebox with refractory brick and asbestos rope and blocks [BRICKLAYER, FIREBRICK AND REFRACTORY TILE (const.)]. May fabricate such parts as stacks, uptakes, and chutes, to adapt boiler to premises in which it is installed [BOILERMAKER (boilermaking) II]. • **GED:** R4, M4, L3 • **SVP:** 2-4 yrs • **Academic:** Ed=H, Eng=S • **Work Field:** 102 • **MPSMS:** 554 • **Aptitudes:** G3, V3, N3, S2, P3, Q4, K3, F3, M3, E5, C5 • **Temperaments:** M, T, V • **Physical:** V=G, H=N, L=H, W, C, S, H • **Work Env:** B, N, R • **Salary:** 3 • **Outlook:** 2

CONDUIT MECHANIC (const.) • D.O.T. #869.361-010 • OES #87899 • DUCT LAYER. Builds and repairs concrete underground vaults and manholes, and installs ducts to provide installation and maintenance facilities for underground power cables: Installs sheeting, shoring, and bracing for excavation. Builds wooden forms and erects steel reinforcing for concrete vaults and manholes. Directs workers engaged in pouring concrete into forms, and removes forms after concrete has set. Installs brackets and braces, and cuts apertures required for installation of electric equipment and ducts. Lays drainpipe and connects it to sewer system. Forces air through ducts to test for obstructions, using air compressor. Demolishes or trims vaults and manholes, using pneumatic tools, working in close proximity to high-voltage electric cables and equipment. Cuts and lays tile or fiber ducts, using portable powersaw and grinder, and brickmason's handtools. Cuts, threads, bends, and installs metal conduit. May lay precast concrete ducts. • **GED:** R3, M3, L3 • **SVP:** 2-4 yrs • **Academic:** Ed=N, Eng=S • **Work Field:** 102 • **MPSMS:** 369 • **Aptitudes:** G3, V3, N3, S3, P3, Q4, K3, F3, M3, E4, C5 • **Temperaments:** M, T • **Physical:** V=L, H=N, L=H, W, C, S, H • **Work Env:** O, N, R • **Salary:** 4 • **Outlook:** 3

ELEVATOR CONSTRUCTOR (const.) • D.O.T. #825.361-010 • OES #85932 • ELEVATOR BUILDER; ELEVATOR ERECTOR; ELEVATOR INSTALLER; ELEVATOR MECHANIC. Assembles and installs electric and hydraulic freight and passenger elevators, escalators, and dumbwaiters, determining layout and electrical connections from blueprints: Studies blueprints and lays out location of framework, counterbalance rails, motor pump, cylinder, and plunger foundations. Drills holes in concrete or structural steel members with portable electric drill. Secures anchor bolts or welds brackets to support rails and framework, and verifies alinement with plumb bob and level. Cuts prefabricated sections of framework, rails, and other elevator components to specified dimensions, using acetylene torch, power saw, and disc grinder. Installs cables, counterweights, pumps, motor foundations, escalator drives, guide rails, elevator cars, and control panels, using handtools. Connects electrical wiring to control panels and electric motors. Installs safety and control devices. Positions electric motor and equipment on top of elevator shaft, using hoists and cable slings. May be designated according to type of equipment installed as ELEVATOR CONSTRUCTOR, ELECTRIC (const.); ELEVATOR CONSTRUCTOR, HYDRAULIC (const.); ESCALATOR CONSTRUCTOR (const.). • **GED:** R4, M3, L3 • **SVP:** 2-4 yrs • **Academic:** Ed=H, Eng=S • **Work Field:** 111 • **MPSMS:** 565 • **Aptitudes:** G3, V3, N3, S2, P3, Q4, K3, F3, M3, E4, C4 • **Temperaments:** M, T, V • **Physical:** V=G, H=N, L=H, W, C, S, H • **Work Env:** I, N, R • **Salary:** 5 • **Outlook:** 5

FITTER 1 (any ind.) • D.O.T. #801.261-014 • OES #93108 • JIG FITTER. Lays out, positions, alines, and fits together fabricated parts of structural metal products in shop, according to blueprint and layout specifications, pre paratory to welding or riveting: Plans sequence of operation, applying knowledge of geometry, effects of heat, and allowances for weld shrinkage, machining, and thickness of metal. Sets up face block, jigs and fixtures. Locates and marks centerlines and reference points onto floor or face block and transposes them to workpiece, using tape, chains, plumb bob, and squares. Moves parts into position, manually or by hoist or crane. Alines parts, using jack, turnbuckles, wedges, drift pins, pry bars, and hammer. Removes high spots and cuts bevels, using hand files, port able grinders, and cutting torch. Gives directions to WELDER, ARC (welding) to build up low spots or short pieces with weld. Straightens warped or bent parts, using sledge, hand torch, straightening press, or bulldozer. Positions or tightens braces, jacks, clamps, ropes, or bolt straps, or bolts parts in positions for welding or riveting. May use transit to locate reference points and erect ladders and scaffolding to fit together large assemblies. May tack weld and be designated FITTER-TACKER (any ind.). • **GED:** R4, M4, L2 • **SVP:** 2-4 yrs • **Academic:** Ed=N, Eng=N • **Work Field:** 102 • **MPSMS:** 554, 594 • **Aptitudes:** G3, V3, N3, S2, P3, Q4, K4, F4, M3, E3, C4 • **Temperaments:** M, T • **Physical:** V=L, H=L, L=H, W, C, S, H • **Work Env:** I, N, R • **Salary:** 4 • **Outlook:** 2

FORMER, HAND (any ind.) • D.O.T. #619.361-010 • OES #89199 • Bends and straightens cold and hot metal plates, bars, structural shapes, and weldments to angles, curves, or flanges as specified by drawings, layouts, and templates, using form blocks, fixtures forming bars, sledge, power hammer and portable grinders: Lays out reference points onto workpiece and form blocks, using tape, compass, radius bar and applying knowledge of geometry, effects of heat, and physical properties of metal. Sets up and bolts or clamps fixtures, dies, and forming bars to form block to outline specified contour. Heats metal, using furnace or hand torch. Lifts, positions, alines, and clamps or bolts workpiece to form block of fixture, using tongs or hoist. Bends workpiece, using bar or by hammering with sledge or mallet. Straightens out warps or bumps by hammering against face block or by heating with hand torch. Chips, trims, and grinds edges to specified contour, using chipping hammer and portable and stand grinder. Verifies size of workpiece, using ruler or template. May operate hand-powered machines, such as roll, brake, or bender. May be designated by product formed as TOOL BENDER, HAND (any ind.). • **GED:** R4, M3, L3 • **SVP:** 2-4 yrs • **Academic:** Ed=N, Eng=S • **Work Field:** 134 • **MPSMS:** 554, 592 • **Aptitudes:** G3, V4, N3, S3, P3, Q4, K4, F4, M3, E5, C5 • **Temperaments:** M, T, V • **Physical:** V=L, H=N, L=M, W, S, H • **Work Env:** I, W, N, R • **Salary:** 4 • **Outlook:** 2

METAL FABRICATOR (any ind.) • D.O.T. #619.360-014 • OES #91714 • Fabricates and assembles structural metal products, such as framework or shells for machinery, ovens, tanks, stacks, and metal parts for buildings and bridges according to job order or blueprints: Develops layout and plans sequence of operations, applying knowledge of trigonometry, stock allowances for thickness, machine and welding shrinkage, and physical properties of

metal. Locates and marks bending and cutting lines onto workpiece. Sets up and operates fabricating machines, such as brakes, rolls, shears, flame cutters, and drill presses [MACHINE OPERATOR (any ind.) I]. Hammers, chips, and grinds workpiece to cut, bend, and straighten metal. Preheats workpieces, using hand torch or furnace. Positions, alines, fits, and welds together parts [WELDER-FITTER (welding)]. Designs and constructs templates and fixtures. Verifies conformance of work piece to specifications, using square, ruler, and measuring tape. May fabricate and assemble sheet metal products. May set up and operate machine tools associated with fabricating shops, such as radial drill press, end mill, and edge planer. May be designated according to product fabricated as ORNAMENTAL-METAL WORKER (struct. & ornam. metalwork). • **GED:** R4, M4, L3 • **SVP:** 2-4 yrs • **Academic:** Ed=H, Eng=S • **Work Field:** 102 • **MPSMS:** 554, 594 • **Aptitudes:** G3, V3, N3, S2, P3, Q4, K3, F3, M2, E4, C4 • **Temperaments:** M, T, V • **Physical:** V=L, H=N, L=H, W, S, H • **Work Env:** I, N, R • **Salary:** 4 • **Outlook:** 3

MILLWRIGHT (any ind.) • D.O.T. #638.281-018 • OES #85123 • Installs machinery and equipment according to layout plans, blueprints, and other drawings in industrial establishment, using hoists, lift trucks, handtools, and power tools: Reads blueprints and schematic drawings to determine work procedures. Dismantles machines, using hammers, wrenches, crow bars, and other handtools. Moves machinery and equipment, using hoists, dollies, rollers, and trucks. Assembles and installs equipment, such as shafting, conveyors, and tram rails, using handtools and power tools. Constructs foundation for machines, using handtools and building materials, such as wood, cement, and steel. Aligns machines and equipment, using hoists, jacks, hand tools, squares, rules, micrometers, and plumb bobs. Assembles machines and bolts, welds, rivets, or otherwise fastens them to foundation or other structures, using handtools and power tools. May operate engine lathe to grind, file, and turn machine parts to dimensional specifications. May repair and lubricate machines and equipment. May install robot and modify its program, using teach pendant. May perform installation and maintenance work as part of a team of skilled trades workers. • **GED:** R4, M3, L3 • **SVP:** 2-4 yrs • **Academic:** Ed-A, Eng-S • **Work Field:** 102, 121 • **MPSMS:** 550, 560, 580 • **Aptitudes:** G2, V3, N3, S2, P3, Q4, K3, F3, M2, E3, C5 • **Temperaments:** J, T, V • **Physical:** V=G, H=N, L=H, W, C, S, H • **Work Env:** I, N, R • **Salary:** 5 • **Outlook:** 3

ORNAMENTAL-METAL WORKER (fabric. metal prod. nec) • D.O.T. #619.260-008 • OES #89199 • ART-METAL WORKER. Sets up and operates variety of machines and equipment to fabricate ornamental metal products, such as light fixtures, church statuary, lamps, plaques, and metal artwork, following sketches, artistic and architectural drawings, models, written descriptions, and photographs: Interprets data to select materials, lay out reference points, and develop sequence of operations. Operates metal fabricating machines, such as shears, saws, brakes, bending machines, and punch and forming presses, to cut stock to size and bend stock to shape. Heats pieces in forge to working temperature, as indicated by color. Bends, twists, and hammers hot or cold workpieces to achieve specified shape and ornamental imprints, using jigs, scroll iron, twisting fork, vise, and selected peening hammers. Operates machine tools to turn, drill, and mill metal to specified dimensions. Hammers and peens sheets of metal to form designs, such as flowers or leaves. Chases castings to finish metal statuary and plaques. Welds, forge welds, brazes, solders, rivets, or bolts components together to assemble workpiece. Grinds, buffs, and polishes surface to desired finish. Fabricates or forges special jigs, tools, and peening hammers. May sculpture plaster patterns for ornamental castings. May hand paint finished items. May install finished product. May specialize in fabricating religious artwork and be known as ECCLESIASTICAL-ART-METAL WORKER (fabric. metal prod., n.e.c.; silverware). • **GED:** R4, M3, L3 • **SVP:** 4-10 yrs • **Academic:** Ed=N, Eng=S • **Work Field:** 102 • **MPSMS:** 554 • **Aptitudes:** G3, V3, N3, S2, P2, Q4, K3, F3, M2, E5, C4 • **Temperaments:** M, T, V • **Physical:** V=L, H=N, L=M, W, S, H • **Work Env:** I, N, R • **Salary:** 5 • **Outlook:** 2

RIGGER (ship bldg. & rep.) • D.O.T. #806.261-014 • OES #85935 • ERECTOR; LOFT RIGGER; OUTSIDE RIGGER. Fabricates, installs, and repairs rigging and weight-handling gear on ships and attaches hoists and pulling gear to rigging to lift, move, and position machinery, equipment, structural parts, and other heavy loads aboard ship: Forms slings and towing bridles by looping and splicing cable or by crimping metal sleeve around cable end and body of cable, using crimping tool. Splices and ties rope to form nets, ladders, and other rigging. Installs hooks, swivels, and turnbuckles in rigging. Reeves lines through blocks and pulleys. Sews canvas or leather covers on rigging at friction points, using sail twine and sailmaker's palm and needle. Selects and attaches gear, braces, and cushions, according to weight and distribution of load, availability of hoisting machinery, and presence of obstacles, such as ship's structural members and jutting buildings, which might interfere with maneu verability of incorrectly rigged hoisting gear. Signals workers operating cranes or other equipment to move load. Installs beam clamps, pad eyes, gallows frames, and other supporting structures for rigging gear. Controls movement of heavy equipment through narrow openings or in confined spaces, using jacks, pulley blocks, chainfalls, and rollers. Lays out and handles lines, snubs lines on cleats or bollards, or hauls in lines with cap stans to assist SHIPWRIGHT (ship & boat bldg. & rep.) in ship drydocking operations. Installs or repairs ship's rigging, such as mast or antenna rigs, small boat handling gear, and winch or windlass rigging. Installs masts, booms, yardarms, and gaffs, working aloft as required. Rigs and hangs scaffolds and stages that require blocks and pulleys. • **GED:** R4, M2, L2 • **SVP:** 2-4 yrs • **Academic:** Ed=N, Eng=N • **Work Field:** 102, 121 • **MPSMS:** 593 • **Aptitudes:** G3, V3, N3, S2, P3, Q4, K3, F3, M2, E2, C5 • **Temperaments:** M, T, V • **Physical:** V=L, H=N, L=H, W, C, S, H • **Work Env:** B, R • **Salary:** 4 • **Outlook:** 2

SAFE-AND-VAULT SERVICE MECHANIC (bus. ser.) • D.O.T. #869.381-022 • OES #85923 • SAFE REPAIRER; VAULT MECHANIC. Installs and repairs safes and vault doors in banks and other establishments: Installs vault doors and deposit boxes in banks, according to blueprints, using equipment, such as powered drills, taps and dies, and truck crane and dolly. Removes, repairs, adjusts, and reinstalls safes, vault doors, vault compartments, hinges, and other vault and safe equipment, using hand tools and other machines and equipment, such as lathes, drill presses, and welding and acetylene cutting apparatus. Tests and repairs locks and locking devices [LOCKSMITH (any ind.)]. Removes interior and exterior finishes and sprays on new finishes. • **GED:** R3, M3, L3 • **SVP:** 2-4 yrs • **Academic:** Ed=N, Eng=S • **Work Field:** 082, 102 • **MPSMS:** 559 • **Aptitudes:** G3, V3, N3, S3, P3, Q4, K3, F3, M3, E4, C5 • **Temperaments:** M, T, V • **Physical:** V=L, H=N, L=H, W, S, H • **Work Env:** I • **Salary:** 4 • **Outlook:** 3

SHEET-METAL WORKER (any ind.) • D.O.T. #804.281-010 • OES #89132 • SHEET-METAL MECHANIC. Fabricates, assembles, installs, and repairs sheet metal products and equipment, such as control boxes, drainpipes, ventilators, and furnace casings, according to job order or blueprints: Selects gage and type of sheet metal according to product being fabricated and knowledge of metal. Locates and marks dimension and reference lines on metal sheet [SHEET-METAL LAY-OUT WORKER (any ind.)]. Sets up and operates fabricating machines, such as shears, brakes, bending rolls, and punch and drill presses to cut, bend, and straighten sheet metal. Shapes metal over anvils, blocks, or forms, using hammer. Sets up and operates soldering and welding equipment to join together sheet metal parts. Smooths seams, joints, or burred surfaces, using files and portable grinder or buffer. Installs assemblies in plant or worksite according to blueprint specifications, using handtools and portable power tools. Inspects assemblies and installation for conformance with specifications, using measuring instruments, such as calipers, scales, and micrometer. May be designated according to type of metal used as COPPERSMITH (any ind.); TINSMITH (any ind.); or according to type of activity as FABRICATOR, SPECIAL ITEMS (any ind.); MODEL MAKER, SHEET METAL (any ind.); PRODUCT-DEVELOPMENT WORKER (any ind.); ROOFER, METAL (const.); SHEET-METAL INSTALLER (any ind.); SHEET-METAL WORKER, MAINTENANCE (any ind.); SHOP MECHANIC (any ind.). • **GED:** R4, M4, L3 • **SVP:** 2-4 yrs • **Academic:** Ed=H, Eng=S • **Work Field:** 102 • **MPSMS:** 554 • **Aptitudes:** G3, V3, N3, S2, P3, Q4, K3, F3, M3, E4, C4 • **Temperaments:** M, T, V • **Physical:** V=G, H=N, L=M, W, C, S, H • **Work Env:** B, N, R • **Salary:** 5 • **Outlook:** 3

SHIPFITTER (ship bldg. & rep.) • D.O.T. #806.381-046 • OES #89121 • FITTER. Lays out and fabricates metal structural parts, such as plates, bulkheads, and frames, and braces them in position within hull of ship for riveting or welding: Lays out position of parts on metal, working from blueprints or templates and using scribe and handtools. Locates and marks reference lines, such as center, buttock, and frame lines. Positions parts in hull of ship, assisted by RIGGER (ship & boat bldg. & rep.). Alines parts in relation to each other, using jacks, turnbuckles, clips, wedges, and mauls. Marks location of holes to be drilled and installs temporary fasteners to hold part in place for welding or riveting. Installs packing, gaskets, liners, and structural accessories and members, such as doors, hatches, brackets, and clips. May prepare molds and templates for fabrication of nonstandard parts. May tack weld clips and brackets in place prior to permanent welding. May roll, bend, flange, cut, and shape plates, beams, and other heavy metal parts, using shop machinery, such as plate rolls, presses, bending brakes, and joggle machines. • **GED:** R4, M3, L2 • **SVP:** 4-10 yrs • **Academic:** Ed=N, Eng=N • **Work Field:** 102 • **MPSMS:** 593 • **Aptitudes:** G3, V3, N3, S2, P3, Q4, K2, F3, M2, E3, C5 • **Temperaments:** M, T • **Physical:** V=L, H=N, L=H, W, C, S, H • **Work Env:** O, N, R • **Salary:** 5 • **Outlook:** 1

SIGN ERECTOR 1 (signs) • D.O.T. #869.381-026 • OES #89999 • SIGN HANGER. Erects preassembled illuminated signs on buildings or other structures, according to sketches, drawings, or blueprints: Measures location for sign and marks points where holes for expansion shields are to be drilled, using measuring tape and chalk. Drills holes, using star drill. Drives expansion shield into hole with hammer, and secures lag bolts in shield, using wrench. Attaches hanging pole for sign to building front with lag bolts, and secures pole with guy wires attached from pole to lag bolts. Secures cornice hook on roof, rigs block and tackle, and hoists sign into position, or operates hydraulic boom to position sign. Secures sign to hanging pole with hooks. Makes electrical connections to power source and tests sign for correct operation. May prewire sign before in stalling. May use welding equipment when installing sign. May mount plastic signs with adhesives. May fabricate signs according to specifications and be designated SIGN MAKER (signs). • **GED:** R4, M2, L3 • **SVP:** 2-4 yrs • **Academic:** Ed=N, Eng=G • **Work Field:** 102 • **MPSMS:** 559 • **Aptitudes:** G3, V4, N3, S3, P3, Q4, K4, F4, M3, E3, C5 • **Temperaments:** M, V • **Physical:** V=L, H=N, L=M, W, C, S, H • **Work Env:** O, R • **Salary:** 4 • **Outlook:** 3

STRUCTURAL-STEEL WORKER (const.) • D.O.T. #801.361-014 • OES #87814 • BRIDGE WORKER; HOUSESMITH; IRON ERECTOR; IRONWORKER; STEEL ERECTOR; STRUCTURAL-IRON ERECTOR; STRUCTURAL-IRON WORKER; STRUCTURAL-STEEL ERECTOR. Performs any combination of following duties to raise, place, and unite girders, columns, and other structural-steel members to form completed structures or structure frameworks, working as member of crew: Sets up hoisting equipment for raising and placing structural-steel members. Fastens steel members to cable of hoist, using chain, cable, or rope. Signals worker operating hoisting equipment to lift and place steel member. Guides member, using tab line (rope) or rides on member in order to guide it into position. Pulls, pushes, or pries steel members into approximate position while member is supported by hoisting device. Forces members into final position, using turnbuckles, crowbars, jacks, and handtools. Alines rivet holes in member with corresponding holes in previously placed member by driving drift pins or handle of wrench through holes. Verifies vertical and horizontal alinement of members, using plumb bob and level. Bolts alined members to keep them in position until they can be permanently riveted, bolted, or welded in place. Catches hot rivets tossed by RIVET HEATER (heat treat.) in bucket and inserts rivets in holes, using tongs. Bucks (holds) rivets while RIVETER, PNEUMATIC (any ind.) uses airhammer to form heads on rivets. Cuts and welds steel members to make alterations, using oxyacetylene welding equipment. May specialize in erecting or repairing specific types of structures and be designated accordingly, as BRIDGE-MAINTENANCE WORKER (const.); CHIMNEY BUILDER, REINFORCED CONCRETE (const.); SCAFFOLD BUILDER, METAL (const.); STRUCTURAL-STEEL-EQUIPMENT ERECTOR (const.). • **GED:** R3, M2, L3 • **SVP:** 2-4 yrs • **Academic:** Ed=N, Eng=S • **Work Field:** 102 • **MPSMS:** 360 •

Aptitudes: G3, V3, N3, S2, P3, Q4, K3, F3, M3, E2, C5 • **Temperaments:** M, S, T • **Stress:** S • **Physical:** V=G, H=N, L=H, W, C, S, H • **Work Env:** O, N, R • **Salary:** 5 • **Outlook:** 4

WELDER, ARC (welding) • D.O.T. #810.384-014 • OES #93914 • Welds together metal components of such products as pipelines, automobiles, boilers, ships, aircraft, and mobile homes, as specified by layout, blueprints, diagram, work order, welding procedures, or oral instructions, using electric arc-welding equipment: Obtains specified electrode and inserts into portable holder or threads consumable electrode wire through portable welding gun. Connects cables from welding unit to obtain amperage, voltage, slope, and pulse, as specified by WELDING ENGINEER (profess. & kin.) or WELDING TECHNICIAN (profess. & kin.). Starts power supply to produce electric current. Strikes (forms) arc which generates heat to melt and deposit metal from electrode to workpiece and join edges of workpiece. Manually guides electrode or gun along weld line, maintaining length of arc and speed of movement to form specified depth of fusion and bead, as judged from color of metal, sound of weld, and size of molten puddle. Welds in flat, horizontal, vertical, or overhead positions. Examines weld for bead size and other specifications. May manually apply filler rod to supply weld metal. May clean or degrease weld joint or workpiece, using wire brush, portable grinder, or chemical bath. May repair broken or cracked parts and fill holes. May prepare broken parts for welding by grooving or scarfing surfaces. May chip off excess weld, slag, spatter, using hand scraper or power chipper. May preheat workpiece, using hand torch or heating furnace. May position and clamp workpieces together or assemble them in jig or fixture. May tack assemblies together. May cut metal plates or structural shapes [ARC CUTTER (welding)]. May be designated according to type of equipment used as WELDER, CARBON ARC (welding); WELDER, FLUX-CORED ARC (welding); WELDER, GAS-METAL ARC (welding); WELDER, GAS-TUNGSTEN ARC (welding); WELDER, HAND, SUBMERGED ARC (welding); WELDER, PLASMA ARC (welding); WELDER, SHIELDED-METAL ARC (welding). May be designated according to product welded as WELDER, BOILERMAKER (boilermaking). Important variations include types of metals welded, subprocesses used, trade name of equipment used, worksite (inplant, job shop, construction site, shipyard), method of application (manual, semiautomatic), high-production or custom, level of ambidexterity required, type of joints welded (seam, spot, butt). May be required to pass employer performance tests or standard tests to meet certification standards of governmental agencies or professional and technical associations. • **GED:** R4, M4, L3 • **SVP:** 6 mos-1 yr • **Academic:** Ed=H, Eng=S • **Work Field:** 081, 082 • **MPSMS:** 540, 554, 591 • **Aptitudes:** G3, V4, N3, S3, P4, Q3, K3, F3, M3, E5, C4 • **Temperaments:** M, T • **Physical:** V=G, H=N, L=H, W, S, H • **Work Env:** B, N, R • **Salary:** 4 • **Outlook:** 4

WELDER, COMBINATION (welding) • D.O.T. #819.384-010 • OES #93914 • Welds metal components together to fabricate or repair products, such as machine parts, plant equipment, mobile homes, motors, and generators, according to layouts, blueprints, or work orders, using brazing and variety of arc and gas welding equipment: Welds metal parts together, using both gas welding [WELDER, GAS (welding)] or brazing [BRAZER, ASSEMBLER (welding)] and any combination of arc welding processes [WELDER, ARC (welding)]. Performs related tasks, such as thermal cutting and grinding. Repairs broken or cracked parts, fills holes, and increases size of metal parts. Positions and clamps together components of fabricated metal products preparatory to welding. May locate and repair cracks in industrial engine cylinder heads, using inspection equipment and gas torch, and be designated REPAIRER, CYLINDER HEADS (welding). May perform repairs only, and be designated WELDER, REPAIR (welding). May be required to pass employer performance tests or standard tests to meet certification standards of governmental agencies or professional and technical associations. • **GED:** R4, M3, L3 • **SVP:** 1-2 yrs • **Academic:** Ed=H, Eng=S • **Work Field:** 081, 102 • **MPSMS:** 550 • **Aptitudes:** G3, V4, N3, S3, P3, Q4, K3, F3, M3, E5, C4 • **Temperaments:** M, T • **Physical:** V=G, H=N, L=M, W, C, S, H • **Work Env:** B, H, R • **Salary:** 3 • **Outlook:** 4

WELDER, EXPERIMENTAL (welding) • D.O.T. #819.281-022 • OES #93914 • Analyzes engineering data and welds experimental parts and assemblies to determine most effective welding processes, using various welding techniques and equipment: Analyzes engineering drawings and specifications to plan welding operations where procedural information is unavailable. Lays out parts and assemblies according to specifications. Develops templates and other work aids to hold and aline parts. Determines type of welding to be used, such as metallic arc, inert gas, electrode, and oven treatment, applying knowledge of metals to be joined, contours and angles to be formed, and specified stress tolerances. Welds components in flat, vertical, or overhead positions, and adjusts amperage, voltage, and speed during joining to assure required weld deposit. Inspects grooves, angles, gap allowances, and related aspects of assembly to insure conformance to specifications, using micrometer, caliper, and related precision measuring instruments. Observes hydrostatic, X-ray, dimension tolerance, and other tests on welded surfaces to evaluate quality of weld and conformance to production require ments. • **GED:** R4, M4, L3 • **SVP:** 4-10 yrs • **Academic:** Ed=N, Eng=S • **Work Field:** 081, 241 • **MPSMS:** 379 • **Aptitudes:** G3, V3, N3, S3, P2, Q4, K3, F3, M3, E4, C4 • **Temperaments:** J, M, T • **Physical:** V=L, H=N, L=L, W, H • **Work Env:** I, R • **Salary:** 5 • **Outlook:** 3

WELDER, GAS (welding) • D.O.T. #811.684-014 • OES #93914 • Welds metal parts, using gas welding equipment as specified by layout, welding diagram, or work order: Positions parts in jigs or fixtures on bench or floor, or clamps parts together along layout marks. Selects torch, torch tip, filler rod and flux, according to welding chart specifications or type and thickness of metal. Connects regulator valves and hoses to oxygen and fuel gas cylinders, and welding torch. Turns regulator valves to activate flow of gases, lights torch and adjusts gas mixture and pressure, to obtain desired flame, based on knowledge of gas-welding techniques. Holds torch at proper angle to metal and guides along weld joint, applying filler rod to molten area to form weld. Examines weld for bead size and other specifications. Repairs broken or cracked metal objects, fills holes, and builds up metal parts. May apply flux to workpiece instead of filler rod. May preheat workpiece in furnace or with torch. May layout, position and tack weld workpieces. May weld along vertical or overhead weld lines. May scarf or groove weld prior to applying filler metal, using gas welding equipment. May chip or grind off excess weld, slag, or spatter [GRINDER-CHIPPER (any ind.) II]. May clean or degrease parts, using wire brush, portable grinder, or chemical bath. May cut metal plates or structural shapes using gas torch. May be designated according to type of gases used such as WELDER, ACETYLENE (welding); WELDER, OXYACETYLENE (welding); WELDER, OXYHYDRO-GEN (welding). Important variations include type of metals welded, products, subprocesses, trade name of equipment, worksite (inplant, job shop, construction site, shipyard), high-production or custom, level of ambidexterity required or type of joints welded (seam, spot, butt). May be required to pass employer performance tests or standard tests to meet certification standards of governmental agencies or professional and technical associations. • **GED:** R3, M3, L3 • **SVP:** 6 mos-1 yr • **Academic:** Ed=N, Eng=S • **Work Field:** 081 • **MPSMS:** 550, 591 • **Aptitudes:** G3, V4, N3, S3, P3, Q4, K3, F3, M3, E5, C4 • **Temperaments:** M, T • **Physical:** V=G, H=N, L=M, W, S, H • **Work Env:** B, N, R • **Salary:** 4 • **Outlook:** 3

WELDER-ASSEMBLER (mach. mfg.) • D.O.T. #819.381-010 • OES #93914 • Assembles and tack-welds steel frames and other component parts of machinery and equipment in preparation for final welding: Measures and marks locations for metal components on assembly table, following blueprints. Lifts and positions components on assembly table, using electric crane, jacks, and shims. Verifies position of metal components in assembly, using straightedge, combination square, calipers, and rule. Clamps metal components to assembly table for welding. Removes rough spots from castings, using portable powered grinder and hand file, to fit and assemble parts. Tack-welds parts in preparation for final welding. Moves assembly to storage area, using electric crane. • **GED:** R3, M3, L2 • **SVP:** 1-2 yrs • **Academic:** Ed=N, Eng=N • **Work Field:** 081, 102 • **MPSMS:** 564 • **Aptitudes:** G3, V4, N3, S3, P3, Q4, K3, F4, M3, E5, C5 • **Temperaments:** M, T • **Physical:** V=L, H=N, L=M, W, S, H • **Work Env:** I, N, R • **Salary:** 4 • **Outlook:** 3

WELDER-FITTER (welding) • D.O.T. #819.361-010 • OES

#93914 • Lays out, fits, and welds fabricated, cast, and forged components to assemble structural forms, such as machinery frames, tanks, pressure vessels, furnace shells, and building and bridge parts, according to blueprints and knowledge of welding and metallurgy: Selects equipment and plans layout, assembly, and welding, applying knowledge of geometry, physical properties of metal machining weld skrinkage, and welding techniques. Lays out, positions, alines, and fits components together. Bolts, clamps, and tack-welds parts to secure in position for welding [WELDER, TACK (welding)]. Sets up equipment and welds parts, using arc, gas-shielded arc, submerged arc, or gas welding equipment [WELDER, COMBINATION (welding)]. May assemble parts by bolting and riveting. May repair products by dismantling, straightening, reshaping, and reassembling parts, using cutting torch, straightening press, and handtools, and be designated WELDER, STRUCTURAL REPAIR (welding). May specialize in using one welding process and be designated WELDER-FITTER, ARC (welding); WELDER-FITTER, GAS (welding). May specialize in fitting and welding components of metal tools, dies, and fixtures and be designated WELDER, TOOL AND DIE (welding). • **GED:** R4, M3, L3 • **SVP:** 2-4 yrs • **Academic:** Ed=H, Eng=S • **Work Field:** 081, 102 • **MPSMS:** 550 • **Aptitudes:** G3, V3, N3, S2, P2, Q4, K3, F3, M2, E4, C4 • **Temperaments:** M, T • **Physical:** V=G, H=N, L=M, W, C, S, H • **Work Env:** B, N, R • **Salary:** 4 • **Outlook:** 4

GOE: 05.05.07 Machining

DIE SINKER (mach. shop) • D.O.T. #601.280-022 • OES #89102 • FORGING-DIE SINKER. Lays out, machines, and finishes impression cavities in die blocks to produce forging dies, following blueprints and applying knowledge of diesinking: Analyzes blueprint of part or die and plans sequence of operations. Measures and marks die block to lay out designs of cavities. Sets up and operates variety of machine tools, such as shaper, vertical turret lathe, and engine lathe to machine cavities in die block [TOOL-MACHINE SET-UP OPERATOR (mach. shop)]. Obtains specified dimensions, contours, and finish of die cavities, using tools, such as power grinder, scrapers, files, and emery cloth. Inspects die cavities, using templates and measuring instruments, such as calipers, micrometers, and height gages to verify conformance to specifications. May develop die design from blueprint of part, using knowledge of machining and forging processes. May make templates to verify dimensions of cavities [TEMPLATE MAKER, EXTRUSION DIE (mach. shop)]. May make and in spect sample lead or plaster cast of part to verify fit of die members and basic shape of part. May repair forging dies and be designated DIE REPAIRER, FORGING (mach. shop). May set up and operate machines to plane surfaces and edges of forging dies and be known as EDGER MACHINE SETTER (mach. shop). • **GED:** R4, M3, L3 • **SVP:** 2-4 yrs • **Academic:** Ed=H, Eng=S • **Work Field:** 057, 241 • **MPSMS:** 566 • **Aptitudes:** G3, V3, N3, S2, P3, Q4, K3, F3, M3, E5, C5 • **Temperaments:** M, T • **Physical:** V=L, H=N, L=M, W, H • **Work Env:** I, N • **Salary:** 5 • **Outlook:** 4

GUNSMITH (any ind.) • D.O.T. #632.281-010 • OES #85999 • REPAIRER. Repairs and modifies firearms to blueprint and customer specifications, using handtools and machines, such as grinders, planers, and millers: Fits action and barrel into stock and alines parts. Installs parts, such as metallic or optical sights, pistol grips, recoil pads, and decorative pieces of firearms, using screws and handtools. Rebores barrels on boring machine to enlarge caliber of bore. Operates broaching machine to cut rifling in barrel of small arms. Installs choke device on shotguns to control shot pattern. Operates machine to grind and polish metal parts. Immerses metal parts in bluing salt bath to impart rust resistant surface and blue color to metal. Fires firearms with proof loads to determine strength characteristics, correct alinement, and assembly of piece. Fabri cates wooden stock for guns according to customer specifications. Refinishes wooden stocks for rifles and shotguns by hand sanding and rubbing with special finishing oil and quick-drying lacquer. May lay out plans on paper and calculate bullet-flight arcs, sight positions, and other details to design new guns. • **GED:** R4, M3, L3 • **SVP:** 4-10 yrs • **Academic:** Ed=N, Eng=S • **Work Field:** 121 • **MPSMS:** 373 • **Aptitudes:** G2, V3, N3, S2, P2, Q4, K3, F2, M2, E5, C3 • **Temperaments:** M, T, V • **Physical:** V=L, H=N, L=L, H • **Work Env:** I • **Salary:** 4 •

Outlook: 2

MACHINIST (mach. shop) • D.O.T. #600.280-022 • OES #89108 • MACHINIST, ALL-AROUND; MACHINIST, FIRST CLASS; MACHINIST, GENERAL; MACHINIST, PRECISION. Sets up and operates machine tools, and fits and assembles parts to make or repair metal parts, mechanisms, tools, or machines, applying knowledge of mechanics, shop mathematics, metal properties, and layout and machining procedures: Studies specifications, such as blueprint, sketch, damaged part, or description of part to be replaced, to determine dimensions and tolerances of piece to be machined, sequence of operations, and tools, materials, and machines required. Measures, marks, and scribes dimensions and reference points to lay out stock for machining [LAY-OUT WORKER (mach. shop)]. Sets up and operates metal-removing machines, such as lathe, milling machine, shaper, or grinder, to machine parts to specifications. Verifies conformance of workpiece to specifi cations, using measuring instruments [TOOL-MACHINE SET-UP OPERA TOR (mach. shop)]. Positions and secures workpiece in holding device, such as chuck or collet, or on surface plate or worktable with such devices as vises, V-blocks, and angle plates, and uses handtools, such as files, scrapers, and wrenches, to fit and assemble parts to assemblies or mechanisms. Verifies dimensions and alinement with measuring instruments, such as micrometers, height gages, and gage blocks. May operate mechanism or machine, observe operation, or test with inspection equipment, to diagnose malfunction of machine or to test repaired machine. May perform flame cutting and arc or gas welding operations, when required. May develop specifications from general description and draw or sketch product to be made. • **GED:** R4, M4, L3 • **SVP:** 2-4 yrs • **Academic:** Ed=A, Eng=S • **Work Field:** 057, 121 • **MPSMS:** 550, 567 • **Aptitudes:** G3, V3, N3, S2, P2, Q4, K3, F2, M2, E5, C4 • **Temperaments:** M, T, V • **Physical:** V=G, H=N, L=M, W, S, H • **Work Env:** I, N • **Salary:** 5 • **Outlook:** 3

MAINTENANCE MACHINIST (any ind.) • D.O.T. #600.280-042 • OES #89108 • MACHINE REPAIRER; SHOP MECHANIC; MACHINIST. Sets up and operates variety of machine tools, and fits and assembles parts to fabricate or repair machine tools and maintain industrial machines, applying knowledge of mechanics, shop mathematics, metal properties, layout, and machining procedures: Observes and listens to operating machines or equipment to diagnose malfunction and determine need for adjustment or repair. Studies blueprint, sketch, machine part, or specifications to determine type and dimensions of metal stock required. Measures, marks, and scribes dimensions and reference points on metal stock surfaces, using such measuring and marking devices as calibrated ruler, micrometer, caliper, and scriber [LAY-OUT WORKER (mach. shop)]. Dismantles machine or equipment, using handtools, such as wrench and screwdriver, to examine parts for defect or to remove defective part. Substitutes new part or repairs or reproduces part from various kinds of metal stock, using handtools, such as scraper, file, and drill, and machine tools, such as lathe, milling machine, shaper, borer, and grinder [MACHINIST (mach. shop)]. Assembles and starts machine to verify correction of malfunction. Maintains and lubricates machine tools and equipment, using handtools, ladder, and lubricants. May weld broken structural parts, using arc or gas welding equipment. May repair or replace faulty wiring, switches, or relays. May be designated according to type of equipment repaired as MACHINIST, CONSTRUCTION EQUIPMENT (any ind.). • **GED:** R4, M4, L3 • **SVP:** 2-4 yrs • **Academic:** Ed=H, Eng=S • **Work Field:** 057, 121 • **MPSMS:** 567, 568 • **Aptitudes:** G3, V3, N3, S2, P2, Q4, K3, F3, M3, E5, C5 • **Temperaments:** M, T, V • **Physical:** V=L, H=L, L=M, W, H • **Work Env:** I • **Salary:** 4 • **Outlook:** 4

PATTERNMAKER, METAL (foundry) • D.O.T. #600.280-050 • OES #89114 • Lays out, mills, drills, turns, grinds, fits, and assembles castings and parts to make metal foundry patterns, core boxes, and match plates, using handtools and machine tools, and analyzing specifications, according to knowledge of patternmaking methods: Studies blueprint of part to be cast, computes dimensions, and plans sequence of operations. Measures, marks, and scribes layout on castings [LAY-OUT WORKER (mach. shop)]. Sets up and operates machine tools, such as milling machines, lathes, drill presses, and grinders, to machine castings to specifications [TOOL-MACHINE SET-UP OPERATOR (mach. shop)]. Assembles pattern, using handtools, and bolts, screws, or other fasteners. Cleans and hand finishes workpiece, using emery cloth, files, scrapers, and powered hand grinders. Verifies conformance of machined pattern to blueprint specifications, using templates and measuring instruments, such as scale, calipers, and micrometers. May make templates for layout and inspection [TEMPLATE MAKER (any ind.)]. May operate welding equipment in assembling pattern [WELDER, COMBINATION (welding)]. • GED: R4, M4, L3 • SVP: 4-10 yrs • Academic: Ed=A, Eng=S • Work Field: 057 • MPSMS: 540, 567 • Aptitudes: G3, V3, N3, S2, P2, Q4, K3, F3, M3, E5, C4 • Temperaments: M, T, V • Physical: V=G, H=N, L=M, W, H • Work Env: I • Salary: 4 • Outlook: 4

SAW FILER (any ind.) • D.O.T. #701.381-014 • OES #89111 • FILER. Repairs bandsaw, handsaw, and circular saw blades according to customer's or manufacturer's specifications, using handtools, machine tools, and welding equipment: Examines saw for defects. Cuts broken teeth from saw, using power shear [SHEAR OPERATOR (any ind.) I]. Forms teeth on saw blade by beveling joints on grinder and welding or brazing them together. Brazes or welds cracks in saw blades. Straightens twists and kinks in blades, using straightening press, and hammers out dents in blade on metal table. Adjusts cutting width of teeth, using swage or special pliers. Computes number and angle of teeth to produce specified cut. Clamps blade in saw-filing machine and turns handwheel to adjust distance between teeth, angle of bevel, and depth of cut of file or abrasive wheel. Starts machine that automatically grinds and files saw teeth. May be designated according to type of saw sharpened as BAND-SAW FILER (any ind.); CIRCULAR-SAW FILER (any ind.). • GED: R3, M3, L3 • SVP: 1-2 yrs • Academic: Ed=N, Eng=S • Work Field: 121 • MPSMS: 552 • Aptitudes: G3, V3, N3, S3, P3, Q4, K3, F3, M3, E4, C5 • Temperaments: M, T • Physical: V=L, H=N, L=M, W, H • Work Env: I, N • Salary: 4 • Outlook: 1

TEMPLATE MAKER (any ind.) • D.O.T. #601.381-038 • OES #89114 • Designs and fabricates templates of wood, paper, sheet metal, and plastic used for laying out reference points and dimensions on metal plates, sheets, tubes, and structural shapes for fabricating, welding, and assembling into structural metal products or dies: Plans and develops layout as outlined on blueprints or work orders, applying knowledge of trigonometry, product design, effects of heat, and allowances for curvature and thickness of metal. Lays out design onto template material, using instruments, such as compass, protractor, dividers, and rule, and marks shape and reference points with scribe, pencil, chalk, and punch. Operates metal or woodworking machines, such as bandsaw, drill press, jointer, punch press, and power handtools, and uses handtools, such as shears, files, and hammer to fabricate templates. Nails, glues, screws, solders, or welds together component parts to assemble templates. Marks job numbers, file codes, dimensions, and layout and fabricating instructions onto templates. Repairs and reworks templates. May make jigs and fixtures for fabricating machine operations [TOOL MAKER, BENCH (mach. shop)]. May be designated according to metal fabricated as TEMPLATE MAKER, SHEET METAL (any ind.); TEMPLATE MAKER, STRUCTURAL STEEL (any ind.); or according to knowledge of product design as BOILERMAKER LAYER-OUT (boilermaking; ship & boat bldg. & rep.); TEMPLATE MAKER, AIRCRAFT (aircraft-aerospace mfg.); TEMPLATE MAKER, SHIPBUILDING (ship & boat bldg. & rep.). • GED: R4, M3, L3 • SVP: 2-4 yrs • Academic: Ed=H, Eng=S • Work Field: 102, 241 • MPSMS: 566 • Aptitudes: G3, V3, N3, S2, P3, Q4, K3, F3, M3, E5, C5 • Temperaments: M, T • Physical: V=L, H=N, L=M, W, H • Work Env: I, N • Salary: 5 • Outlook: 4

TOOL GRINDER 1 (any ind.) • D.O.T. #701.381-018 • OES #89111 • CUTLERY GRINDER; TOOL SHARPENER. Sharpens shears, scissors, hair clippers, surgical instruments, cleavers, and other fine-edged cutting tools, using whetstone and grinding and polishing wheels: Holds cutting edge of tool against rotating wheel or clamps tool in holder or carriage to steady it during sharpening process. Sharpens surgical instruments and razors, using fine-grained grinding wheels, and hones them on whetstone. May sharpen handsaws. May brush heated mixture of glue and grit onto worn grinding wheels to rebuild them. May specialize in sharpening barbers' tools and be designated BARBER-TOOL SHARP-

ENER (any ind.). May specialize in sharpening shears and scissors and be designated SCISSORS GRINDER (any ind.). May specialize in sharpening tools and implements in homes and business establishments and be designated GRINDER (any ind.) III. • GED: R3, M2, L2 • SVP: 1-2 yrs • Academic: Ed=N, Eng=N • Work Field: 051 • MPSMS: 552 • Aptitudes: G3, V4, N4, S3, P3, Q4, K3, F3, M3, E5, C5 • Temperaments: M, T • Physical: V=L, H=N, L=L, H • Work Env: I, N • Salary: 4 • Outlook: 2

TOOL-AND-DIE MAKER (mach. shop) • D.O.T. #601.280-046 • OES #89102 • Analyzes specifications, lays out metal stock, sets up and operates machine tools, and fits and assembles parts to make and repair metalworking dies, cutting tools, jigs and fixtures, gages, and machinists' handtools, applying knowledge of tool and die designs and construction, shop mathematics, metal properties, and layout, machining, and assembly procedures: Studies specifications, such as blueprints, sketches, models, or descriptions, and visualizes product. Computes dimensions and plans layout and assembly operations. Measures, marks, and scribes metal stock for machining [LAY-OUT WORKER (mach. shop)]. Sets up and operates machine tools, such as lathe, milling machine, shaper, and grinder, to machine parts, and verifies conformance of machined parts to specifications [TOOL-MACHINE SET-UP OPERATOR (mach. shop)]. Lifts machined parts manually or using hoist, and positions and holds them on surface plate or worktable, using devices, such as vises, V-blocks, and angle plates. Smooths flat and contoured surfaces, using scrapers, abrasive stones, and power grinders, and fits and assembles parts into assemblies or mechanisms. Verifies dimensions, alinements, and clearances, using measuring instruments, such as dial indicators, gage blocks, thickness gages, and micrometers. Dowels and bolts parts together, using handtools, such as hammers and wrenches. May connect wiring and hydraulic lines to install electric and hydraulic components. May heattreat tools or parts [HEAT TREATER (heat treat.) II]. May examine standard or previously used tools or dies and decide on modifications to be made. May develop specifications from general descriptions and make drawing or sketch of product. May specialize in repair work and be designated TOOL-AND-DIE REPAIRER (mach. shop). • GED: R4, M4, L4 • SVP: 2-4 yrs • Academic: Ed–A, Eng–S • Work Field: 057, 121, 241 • MPSMS: 566 • Aptitudes: G3, V3, N3, S2, P2, Q4, K3, F2, M2, E5, C5 • Temperaments: M, T, V • Physical: V=G, H=N, L=M, W, H • Work Env: I, N • Salary: 5 • Outlook: 4

TOOL-MACHINE SET-UP OPERATOR (mach. shop) • D.O.T. #601.280-054 • OES #91505 • MACHINE-TOOL OPERATOR, GENERAL; MACHINIST; SET-UP-OPERATOR, TOOL. Sets up and operates variety of machine tools, such as radial drill press, lathes, milling machines, shapers, and grinders, to machine metal work pieces, such as patterns and machine, tool, or die parts, usually on custom basis, analyzing specifications, and determining tooling by applying knowledge of metal properties, machining, and shop mathematics: Studies blueprint or layout on workpiece to visualize machining required, and plans sequence of operations. Selects method of holding workpiece. Lifts workpiece manually or using hoist, and positions and secures it to holding device, such as machine table, chuck, centers, or fixture, using wrenches and aids, such as shims, parallel blocks, planter gages, and clamps. Verifies workpiece position, using instruments, such as surface gages, height gages, and dial indicator. Selects feed rate, cutting speed, depth of cut, and cutting tool (bar tool, rotary cutter, or abrasive wheel) for each operation, according to knowledge of metal properties, machining, and shop mathematics. Positions and secures tool in toolholder (chuck, collet, or toolpost). Moves controls to position tool and workpiece in relation to each other, and to set feeds, speeds, and depth of cut. Starts machine, turns handwheel to feed tool in workpiece or vice versa, and engages automatic feeding device. Turns valve handle to start flow of coolant against tool and workpiece. Observes operation and regulates tool position and action. Verifies conformance of machined workpiece to specifications, using instruments, such as micrometers, gages, and gage blocks. May measure, mark, and scribe workpiece to lay out for machining [LAY-OUT WORKER (mach. shop)]. May devise ways of clamping work pieces and make special jigs and fixtures as needed. May work on nonmetallic materials. May operate bench grinder or cutter grinding machine to sharpen tools [TOOL-GRINDER OPERATOR (mach. shop)]. • GED: R4, M4, L3 • SVP:

2-4 yrs • **Academic:** Ed=H, Eng=S • **Work Field:** 057, 121 • **MPSMS:** 540, 566 • **Aptitudes:** G3, V3, N3, S2, P2, Q4, K3, F3, M3, E5, C5 • **Temperaments:** M, T • **Physical:** V=G, H=N, L=M, W, H • **Work Env:** I • **Salary:** 4 • **Outlook:** 3

GOE: 05.05.08 Woodworking

CABINETMAKER (woodworking) • D.O.T. #660.280-010 • OES #89311 • Sets up and operates variety of wood working machines and uses various handtools to fabricate and repair wooden cabinets and high-grade furniture: Studies blue prints or drawings of articles to be constructed or repaired, and plans sequence of cutting or shaping operations to be performed. Marks outline or dimensions of parts on paper or lumber stock, according to blueprint or drawing specifications. Matches materials for color, grain, or texture. Sets up and operates woodworking machines, such as power saws, jointer, mortiser, tenoner, molder, and shaper, to cut and shape parts from woodstock. Trims component parts of joints to insure snug fit, using handtools, such as planes, chisels, or wood files. Bores holes for insertion of screws or dowels by hand or using boring machine. Glues, fits, and clamps parts and subassemblies together to form complete unit, using clamps or clamping machine. Drives nails or other fasteners into joints at designated places to reinforce joints. Sands and scrapes surfaces and joints of articles to prepare articles for finishing. May repair high-grade articles of furniture. May dip, brush, or spray assemblied articles with protective or decorative materials, such as stain, varnish, or paint. May install hardware, such as hinges, catches, and drawer pulls. May repair furniture, equipment, and fixtures and be designated as CABINETMAKER, MAINTENANCE (woodworking). May be designated according to products made as PIANO-CASE MAKER (musical inst.). May cut, shape, and assemble wooden parts to construct frames for refrigeration equipment and be designated as REFRIGERATOR CABINETMAKER (refrigerat. equip.). • **GED:** R4, M4, L3 • **SVP:** 1-2 yrs • **Academic:** Ed=H, Eng=S • **Work Field:** 102 • **MPSMS:** 450, 460 • **Aptitudes:** G3, V3, N3, S3, P3, Q3, K3, F3, M3, E4, C4 • **Temperaments:** J, M, T, V • **Physical:** V=G, H=N, L=M, W, H • **Work Env:** I • **Salary:** 5 • **Outlook:** 3

FURNITURE FINISHER (woodworking) • D.O.T. #763.381-010 • OES #89314 • COATER; FURNITURE REFINISHER; RECOATER; REFINISHER; WOOD FINISHER. Finishes or refinishes damaged, worn, or used furniture or new high-grade furniture to specified color or finish, utilizing knowledge of wood properties, finishes, and furniture styling: Disassembles article, masks areas adjacent to areas being finished, or removes accessories such as knobs and hinges, using handtools, to prepare article for finishing. Removes old finish from surfaces, using steel wool, sandpaper, or solvent and putty knife. Removes excess solvent with cloth immersed in paint thinner or sal soda. Applies plastic-putty, wood putty, or lacquer-stick to surface, using spatula or knife, to fill nicks, depressions, holes, and cracks. Smooths surface for finishing, using sandpaper or power sander. Selects finish ingredients and mixes them by hand or machine to obtain specified color or shade or to match existing finish. Brushes or sprays successive coats of stain, varnish, shellac, lacquer, or paint on workpiece. Grains wood or paints wood trim, using graining roller, comb, sponge, or brush. Polishes and waxes finished surfaces. May restore wood to natural color, using bleaching acid and neutralizer. May spread graining ink over metal portions of surfaces with cheesecloth to simulate wood-grainlike finish. May finish piano and organ cases and be designated PIANO-AND-ORGAN REFINISHER (woodworking). May finish mirror and picture frames and be designated according to type of finish applied as POWDER GILDER (mirror & pic. frames); WHITENER (mirror & pic. frames). May finish television receiver cabinets and be designated TELEVISION-CABINET FINISHER (woodworking). May finish wooden parts of custom-made firearms and be designated FINISHER, SPECIAL STOCKS (firearms). May stain and finish surfaces of new furniture pieces to simulate antiques, bringing out highlights and shadings by rubbing surfaces with abrasives or cloth, and be designated ANTIQUER (furn.). • **GED:** R4, M2, L2 • **SVP:** 2-4 yrs • **Academic:** Ed=H, Eng=N • **Work Field:** 051, 153 • **MPSMS:** 460 • **Aptitudes:** G3, V4, N4, S4, P2, Q4, K3, F4, M3, E5, C3 • **Temperaments:** J, T • **Physical:** V=L, H=N, L=S, W, S, H • **Work Env:** I • **Salary:** 2 • **Outlook:** 2

FURNITURE RESTORER (museum) • D.O.T. #763.380-010 • OES #89314 • FURNISHINGS CONSERVATOR. Restores and preserves historical furniture in collection of museum or similar institution, using variety of handtools and power tools and applying knowledge of antique fabrics and wood furniture: Examines furnishings to determine type of material, extent of deterioration or damage, or date of construction to verify authenticity and plan restoration. Sets up and operates variety of wood working machines to fabricate, repair, reinforce, and replace parts of furniture. Cuts, shapes, and attaches parts according to blueprints or drawings, using handtools. Matches materials for color, grain, and texture. Strips old finish from furnishings, using solvents and abrasives. Fills cracks, depressions, and other blemishes, using plastic wood or lacquer stick. Treats warped or stained surfaces to restore original contour and color. Glues or replaces veneer sections. Smooths surfaces, using power sander or abrasive material. Washes or bleaches furniture surfaces to prepare surface for application of finish. Selects coatings, such as stain, lacquer, or varnish according to type wood, and brushes or sprays material onto surface to protect surface and produce desired appearance. Polishes, sprays, or waxes finished pieces. Removes damaged or deteriorated coverings from upholstered furniture. Repairs, reinforces, or replaces components, such as springs, webbing, and padding. Selects fabric for new covering, using knowledge of period and style of furniture or following instructions of CURATOR (museum) 102.017-010. Tacks, sews, glues, or staples covering to furniture frame to attach upholstery. Refurbishes leather coverings of furnishings, using softeners, solvents, adhesives, stains, or polishes. Replaces damaged coverings with leather pieces of appropriate color, grain, and weight. Stencils, gilds, embosses, or paints designs or borders on restored pieces to reproduce original appearance. May advise curatorial staff on environmental conditions necessary for preservation of furnishings in exhibit and storage areas. May fabricate replicas of period furniture for use in exhibits. May be designated according to specialty as FINISH SPECIALIST (museum) or UPHOLSTERY RESTORER (museum). • **GED:** R4, M3, L4 • **SVP:** 1-2 yrs • **Academic:** Ed=N, Eng=S • **Work Field:** 102, 153 • **MPSMS:** 460 • **Aptitudes:** G3, V3, N3, S3, P3, Q4, K3, F3, M2, E5, C3 • **Temperaments:** J, T, V • **Physical:** V=L, H=N, L=L, W, H • **Work Env:** I, N, F • **Salary:** 4 • **Outlook:** 2

LOFT WORKER (ship bldg. & rep.) • D.O.T. #661.281-010 • OES #89302 • MOLD LOFT WORKER. Lays out lines of ship to full scale on mold-loft floor and constructs templates and molds to be used as patterns and guides for layout and fabrication of various structural parts of ships: Lays out full-scale portions of ship's plan, working from blueprints and tables of offsets. Marks frame lines and other reference lines on loft floor with marking instrument. Measures dimensions between lines and prepares table of offsets. Compares prepared tables with tables on blueprints. Constructs template, using knowledge of geometric construction, and handtools and woodworking machines, such as crosscut, rip, and bandsaws. Marks templates with identifying data and instructions, such as number of pieces to be made, type, and weight of stock, and location for installation. Constructs full scale wood mockups of ship's parts and sections for use as guide in shaping or positioning parts. May construct wooden plug mold parts, such as hulls, decks, and cabins of fiberglass boats and be designated PLUG BUILDER (ship & boat bldg. & rep.). • **GED:** R4, M4, L3 • **SVP:** 2-4 yrs • **Academic:** Ed=N, Eng=S • **Work Field:** 102, 241 • **MPSMS:** 593 • **Aptitudes:** G3, V3, N3, S2, P3, Q4, K3, F3, M3, E5, C5 • **Temperaments:** M, T • **Physical:** V=L, H=N, L=L, W, S, H • **Work Env:** I • **Salary:** 5 • **Outlook:** 2

GOE: 05.05.09 Mechanical Work, Craft Technology

AIR-CONDITIONING INSTALLER-SERVICER, WINDOW UNIT (any ind.) • D.O.T. #637.261-010 • OES #85711 • Installs, services, and repairs air-conditioning units, ranging from 1/2 to 2 tons capacity, in private residences and small business establishments: Examines unit visually for defective parts, or listens to machine in operation, utilizing knowledge of mechanical, electrical, and refrigeration theory, to determine cause of malfunction. Dismantles whole or part of machine, as indicated by type of malfunction, and repairs or replaces such parts as switches, relays, fan motors, thermostats, and other components, using handtools and power tools. Replaces filters, lubricates unit, and adjusts controls. Reassembles machine, making necessary adjustments to insure efficient operation. May estimate cost of repairs or adjustments. May remove machines from customer's premises for major repairs or overhaul in shop, or for return to manufacturer for extensive repairs. May repair sealed refrigeration units of machines. • **GED:** R4, M3, L3 • **SVP:** 4-10 yrs • **Academic:** Ed=H, Eng=S • **Work Field:** 111, 121 • **MPSMS:** 573 • **Aptitudes:** G3, V3, N3, S2, P3, Q4, K3, F3, M3, E4, C5 • **Temperaments:** M, T • **Physical:** V=G, H=N, L=H, W, C, S, H • **Work Env:** I • **Salary:** 4 • **Outlook:** 3

AIR-CONDITIONING MECHANIC (auto. ser.) • D.O.T. #620.281-010 • OES #85302 • AUTOMOBILE-REFRIGERATION MECHANIC. Installs and repairs automotive air-conditioning units: Bolts compressor to engine block and installs driving pulley on front end of crankshaft. Places fan belt on pulleys, adjusts tension, and tightens bolts. Bolts evaporator unit under dashboard or in trunk. Welds or bolts mounting brackets to automobile frame. Drills holes through interior panels, threads hoses through holes and connects hoses to compressor, evaporator, and cool-air outlet. Fills compressor with refrigerant and starts unit. Measures compressor pressure to determine efficiency of compressor, using gage. Listens to operating unit for indications of malfunction. Removes faulty units from vehicles, disassembles them, and replaces worn and broken parts and fluid in unit. Makes electrical connections as required. May specialize in installation of automotive air-conditioning units and be designated AUTOMOTIVE AIR-CONDITIONER INSTALLER (auto. ser.). • **GED:** R3, M2, L3 • **SVP:** 1-2 yrs • **Academic:** Ed=N, Eng=S • **Work Field:** 121 • **MPSMS:** 591 • **Aptitudes:** G3, V3, N3, S2, P3, Q4, K3, F3, M3, E5, C5 • **Temperaments:** M, T, V • **Physical:** V=G, H=G, L=M, W, S, H • **Work Env:** I • **Salary:** 4 • **Outlook:** 4

AIRFRAME-AND-POWER-PLANT MECHANIC (aircraft-aerospace mfg.) • D.O.T. #621.281-014 • OES #85323 • AIRCRAFT MECHANIC; AIRPLANE MECHANIC. Services, repairs, and overhauls aircraft and aircraft engines to ensure airworthiness: Repairs, replaces, and assembles parts, such as wings, fuselage, tail assembly, landing gear, control cables, propeller assembly, and fuel and oil tanks, using tools, such as power shears, sheet metal breaker, arc and acetylene welding equipment, rivet gun, and air or electric drills to rebuild or replace airframe or its components. Consults manufacturers' manuals and airline's maintenance manual for specifications and to determine feasibility of repair or replacement according to malfunction. Examines engines for cracked cylinders and oil leaks and listens to detect sounds of malfunctioning, such as sticking or burnt valves. Inspects turbine blades to detect cracks or breaks. Tests engine operation, using testing equipment, such as ignition analyzer, compression checker, distributor timer, and ammeter to locate source of malfunction. Replaces or repairs worn or damaged components, such as carburetors, superchargers, and magnetos, using hand tools, gages and testing equipment. Removes engine from aircraft, using hoist or forklift truck. Disassembles and inspects parts for wear, warping, or other defects. Repairs or replaces defective engine parts and reassembles and installs engine in aircraft. Adjusts and repairs electrical wiring system and aircraft accessories and instruments. Inspects, services, and repairs pneumatic and hydraulic systems. Performs miscellaneous duties to service aircraft, including flushing crankcase, cleaning screens, greasing moving parts, and checking brakes. May be required to be licensed by Federal Aviation Administration. May service engines and airframe components at line station making repairs, short of overhaul, required to keep aircraft in safe operating condition and be designated AIRFRAME-AND-POWER-PLANT MECHANIC, LINE SERVICE (air trans.). May specialize in engine repair and be designated as AIRCRAFT-ENGINE ASSEMBLER (air trans.); AIRCRAFT-ENGINE-CYLINDER MECHANIC (air trans.); AIRCRAFT-ENGINE DISMANTLER (aircraft-aerospace mfg.; air trans.); AIRCRAFT-ENGINE INSTALLER (air trans.); AIRCRAFT-ENGINE MECHANIC (air trans.); AIRCRAFT-ENGINE MECHANIC, OVERHAUL (aircraft-aerospace mfg.; air trans.). Additional Titles: CARBURETOR MECHANIC (air trans.); HELICOPTER MECHANIC (aircraft-aerospace mfg.; air trans.); HYDRAULIC TESTER (air trans.); IGNITION SPECIALIST (air trans.); INSTRUMENT REPAIRER (aircraft-aerospace mfg.; air trans.); SUPERCHARGER MECHANIC (aircraft-aerospace mfg.; air trans.). • **GED:** R4, M4, L4 • **SVP:** 2-4 yrs • **Academic:** Ed=A, Eng=S • **Work Field:** 121 • **MPSMS:** 592 • **Aptitudes:** G3, V3, N3, S2, P2, Q4, K3, F3, M2, E4, C5 • **Temperaments:** M, T, V • **Physical:** V=G, H=G, L=M, W, S, H • **Work Env:** B, N, R • **Salary:** 4 • **Outlook:** 2

AUTOMOBILE MECHANIC (auto. ser.) • D.O.T. #620.261-010 • OES #85302 • GARAGE MECHANIC. Repairs and overhauls automobiles, buses, trucks, and other automotive vehicles: Examines vehicle and discusses with customer or AUTOMOBILE-REPAIR-SERVICE ESTIMATOR (auto. ser.); AUTOMOBILE TESTER (auto. ser.); or BUS INSPECTOR (auto. ser.) nature and extent of damage or malfunction. Plans work procedure, using charts, technical manuals, and experience. Raises vehicle, using hydraulic jack or hoist, to gain access to mechanical units bolted to underside of vehicle. Removes unit, such as engine, transmission, or differential, using wrenches and hoist. Disassembles unit and inspects parts for wear, using micrometers, calipers, and thickness gages. Repairs or replaces parts, such as pistons, rods, gears, valves, and bearings, using mechanic's handtools. Overhauls or replaces carburetors, blowers, generators, distributors, starters, and pumps. Rebuilds parts, such as crankshafts and cylinder blocks, using lathes, shapers, drill presses, and welding equipment. Rewires ignition system, lights, and instrument panel. Relines and adjusts brakes, alines front end, repairs or replaces shock absorbers, and solders leaks in radiator. Mends damaged body and fenders by hammering out or filling in dents and welding broken parts. Replaces and adjusts headlights, and installs and repairs accessories, such as radios, heaters, mirrors, and windshield wipers. May be designated according to specialty as AUTOMOBILE MECHANIC, MOTOR (auto. ser.); BUS MECHANIC (auto. ser.); DIFFERENTIAL REPAIRER (auto. ser.); ENGINE-REPAIR MECHANIC, BUS (auto. ser.); FOREIGN-CAR MECHANIC (auto. ser.); TRUCK MECHANIC (auto. ser.). When working in service station may be designated AUTOMOBILE-SERVICE-STATION MECHANIC (auto. ser.). Additional titles: COMPRESSOR MECHANIC, BUS (auto. ser.); DRIVE-SHAFT-AND-STEERING-POST REPAIRER (auto. ser.); ENGINE-HEAD REPAIRER (auto. ser.); MOTOR ASSEMBLER (auto. ser.). • **GED:** R4, M3, L3 • **SVP:** 2-4 yrs • **Academic:** Ed=H, Eng=S • **Work Field:** 111, 121 • **MPSMS:** 591 • **Aptitudes:** G3, V3, N4, S2, P3, Q4, K3, F3, M2, E4, C4 • **Temperaments:** J, M, T, V • **Physical:** V=G, H=G, L=M, W, S, H • **Work Env:** I, N • **Salary:** 5 • **Outlook:** 4

AUTOMOBILE-SERVICE-STATION MECHANIC (auto. ser.) • D.O.T. #620.261-030 • OES #85302 • Repairs and services vehicles of service station customers through performance of any of following tasks: Examines vehicles and confers with customers to determine malfunction and repairs desired. Refers customer with major vehicle repairs to garage. Removes and replaces parts of ignition system, such as spark plugs, points, coil, or alternator to complete tune-up or replace malfunctioning part of system, using mechanic's handtools, gauges, and test meters. Turns adjustment screws of carburetor to set idle speed of engine, using screwdriver. Replaces defective chassis parts, such as shock absorbers, balljoint suspension, brakeshoes, and wheel bearings. Services vehicles [AUTOMOBILE-SERVICE-STATION ATTENDANT (auto ser.) 915.467-010]. • **GED:** R3, M2, L3 • **SVP:** 6 mos- 1 yr • **Academic:** Ed=N, Eng=S • **Work Field:** 121, 292 • **MPSMS:** 591, 961 • **Aptitudes:** G3, V3, N3, S2, P3, Q4, K3, F3, M3, E5, C5 • **Temperaments:** J, T • **Physical:** V=L, H=L, L=M, W, S, H • **Work Env:** I • **Salary:** 3 • **Outlook:** 4

AUTOMOTIVE-COOLING-SYSTEM DIAGNOSTIC TECHNICIAN (auto. ser.) • D.O.T. #620.261-034 • OES #85302 • Inspects and tests automotive cooling systems to diagnose malfunctions and estimates cost of repairs: Questions customer and examines cooling system, hoses, and connections to determine nature and extent of malfunctions. Tests and analyzes electrical, vacuum, pressure, and related functions of system components to locate cause of malfunctions, using vacuum tester, pressure tester, voltmeter, and other specialized test equipment and handtools. Compiles estimate of system repair costs and secures customer approval to perform repairs. Occasionally assists AUTOMOBILE-RADIATOR MECHANIC (auto. ser.) 620.381-010 in repair of cooling system components, using mechanic's handtools. Computes parts and labor charges and routes customer bill to office. • **GED:** R4, M3, L3 • **SVP:** 2-4 yrs • **Academic:** Ed=N, Eng=S • **Work Field:** 121, 212 • **MPSMS:** 591 • **Aptitudes:** G2, V3, N3, S3, P3, Q3, K3, F4, M3, E5, C4 • **Temperaments:** J, T • **Physical:** V=L, H=L, L=M, W, S, H • **Work Env:** I • **Salary:** 4 • **Outlook:** 4

AUTOMOTIVE-MAINTENANCE-EQUIPMENT SERVICER (any ind.) • D.O.T. #620.281-018 • OES #85119 • AUTOMOTIVE-MAINTENANCE-EQUIPMENT REPAIRER; EQUIPMENT-SERVICE ENGINEER; PUMP-AND-TANK SERVICER. Adjusts and repairs automotive repairing, servicing, and testing equipment, using handtools and power tools: Disassembles defective equipment, such as gasoline pumps, air compressors, and dynamometers. Replaces defective parts, using pipe fitting and welding tools. Reassembles, adjusts, and tests repaired equipment. May be required to register with government agency to adjust meters and gages of fuel and oil pumps serving public. May install new equipment. May specialize in repairing gasoline pumps, lubrication equipment, air compressors, or other type of automotive service equipment. • **GED:** R4, M3, L3 • **SVP:** 2-4 yrs • **Academic:** Ed=H, Eng=S • **Work Field:** 111, 121 • **MPSMS:** 568 • **Aptitudes:** G3, V3, N3, S2, P3, Q4, K3, F3, M2, E5, C4 • **Temperaments:** M, T, V • **Physical:** V=G, H=L, L=M, W, S, H • **Work Env:** I, N • **Salary:** 4 • **Outlook:** 3

CASH-REGISTER SERVICER (any ind.) • D.O.T. #633.281-010 • OES #85926 • CASH-REGISTER REPAIRER. Tests and repairs cash registers, using handtools, power tools, and circuit test meters: Examines mechanical assemblies, such as printing mechanisms, counters, and keyboards, for worn or damaged parts, using precision gages. Replaces defective parts, or reshapes parts on bench lathe or grinder. Tests electrical control units, wiring, and motors, using circuit test equipment. Replaces defective electrical parts, using handtools and welding and soldering equipment. Cleans and oils moving parts. May service adding machines [OFFICE-MACHINE SERVICER (any ind.)]. • **GED:** R4, M3, L3 • **SVP:** 2-4 yrs • **Academic:** Ed=H, Eng=S • **Work Field:** 111, 121 • **MPSMS:** 571 • **Aptitudes:** G3, V3, N3, S3, P3, Q3, K3, F3, M2, E5, C5 • **Temperaments:** M, T, V • **Physical:** V=L, H=N, L=M, W, H • **Work Env:** I • **Salary:** 4 • **Outlook:** 2

CONSTRUCTION-EQUIPMENT MECHANIC (const.) • D.O.T. #620.261-022 • OES #85314 • HEAVY-EQUIPMENT MECHANIC. Analyzes malfunctions and repairs, rebuilds, and maintains construction equipment, such as cranes, power shovels, scrapers, paving machines, motor graders, trench-digging machines, conveyors, bulldozers, dredges, pumps, compressors and pneumatic tools: Operates and inspects machines or equipment to diagnose defects. Dismantles and reassembles equipment, using hoists and handtools. Examines parts for damage or excessive wear, using micrometers and gages. Replaces defective engines and subassemblies, such as transmissions. Tests overhauled equipment to ensure operating efficiency. Welds broken parts and structural members. May direct workers engaged in cleaning parts and assisting with assembly and disassembly of equipment. May repair, adjust, and maintain mining machinery, such as stripping and loading shovels, drilling and cutting machines, and continuous mining machines and be designated MINE-MACHINERY MECHANIC (mining & quarrying). • **GED:** R3, M3, L3 • **SVP:** 2-4 yrs • **Academic:** Ed=N, Eng=S • **Work Field:** 121 • **MPSMS:** 563 • **Aptitudes:** G3, V3, N3, S3, P3, Q4, K3, F3, M3, E4, C5 • **Temperaments:** M, T, V • **Physical:** V=G, H=G, L=M, W, S, H • **Work Env:** B, N • **Salary:** 4 • **Outlook:** 4

DIESEL MECHANIC (any ind.) • D.O.T. #625.281-010 • OES #85311 • Repairs and maintains diesel engines used to power machines, such as buses, ships, trucks, railroad trains, electric generators, and construction machinery, using handtools, precision-measuring instruments, and machine tools: Diagnoses trouble, disassembles engines, and examines parts for defects and excessive wear. Reconditions and replaces parts, such as pistons, bearings, gears, valves, and bushings, using engine lathes, boring machines, handtools, and precision-measuring instruments. May weld and cut parts, using arc-welding and flame cutting equipment. May be designated according to type of diesel engine or equipment repaired as DIESEL-ENGINE MECHANIC, AUTO-MOBILE (auto. ser.); DIESEL-ENGINE MECHANIC, BUS (auto. ser.); DIESEL-ENGINE MECHANIC, MARINE (ship & boat bldg. & rep.); DIESEL-ENGINE MECHANIC, TRUCK (auto. ser.); DIESEL-MECHANIC, CONSTRUCTION (const.); DIESEL-MECHANIC, FARM (agric. equip.); LOCOMOTIVE REPAIRER, DIESEL (loco. & car bldg. & rep.). • **GED:** R4, M3, L3 • **SVP:** 2-4 yrs • **Academic:** Ed=H, Eng=S • **Work Field:** 121 • **MPSMS:** 568 • **Aptitudes:** G3, V3, N3, S3, P3, Q4, K3, F3, M2, E4, C4 • **Temperaments:** M, T, V • **Physical:** V=G, H=G, L=H, W, S, H • **Work Env:** I, N • **Salary:** 4 • **Outlook:** 4

ENVIRONMENTAL-CONTROL-SYSTEM INSTALLER-SERVICER (any ind.) • D.O.T. #637.261-014 • OES #85902 • AIR-CONDITIONING MECHANIC; HEATING-AND-AIR-CONDITIONING MECHANIC; HEATING MECHANIC. Installs, services, and repairs environmental-control systems in residences, department stores, office buildings, and commercial establishments, utilizing knowledge of refrigeration theory, pipefitting, and structural layout: Mounts compressor and condenser units on platform or floor, using hand tools, following blueprints or engineering specifications. Fabricates, assembles, and installs ductwork and chassis parts, using portable metalworking tools and welding equipment [DUCT INSTALLER (const.; mfd. bldgs.)]. Installs evaporator unit in chassis or in air-duct system, using handtools. Cuts and bends tubing to correct length and shape, using cutting and bending equipment and tools. Cuts and threads pipe, using machine-threading or hand-threading equipment. Joins tubing or pipes to various refrigerating units by means of sleeves, couplings, or unions, and solders joints, using torch, forming complete circuit for refrigerant [PIPE FITTER (const.)]. Installs expansion and discharge valves in circuit. Connects motors, compressors, temperature controls, humidity controls, and circulating-ventilation fans to control panels and connects control panels to power source [ELECTRICIAN (any ind.)]. Installs air and water filters in completed installation. Injects small amount of refrigerant into compressor to test systems, and adds freon gas to build up prescribed operating pressure. Observes pressure and vacuum gages and adjusts controls to insure proper operation. Tests joints and connections for gas leaks, using gages or soap-and-water solution. Wraps pipes in insulation batting and secures them in place with cement or wire bands. Replaces defective breaker controls, thermostats, switch es, fuses, and electrical wiring to repair installed units, using electrician's handtools and test equipment. May install, repair, and service air conditioners, ranging from fifteen to twenty tons cooling capacity, in warehouses and small factory buildings and be designated AIR-CONDITIONING MECHANIC, INDUSTRIAL (any ind.). • **GED:** R4, M3, L3 • **SVP:** 4-10 yrs • **Academic:** Ed=H, Eng=S • **Work Field:** 111, 121 • **MPSMS:** 573 • **Aptitudes:** G3, V3, N3, S2, P3, Q4, K3, F3, M3, E4, C5 • **Temperaments:** M, T, V • **Physical:** V=G, H=N, L=M, W, C, S, H • **Work Env:** B, N, R • **Salary:** 5 • **Outlook:** 3

EXPERIMENTAL MECHANIC 2 (aircraft-aerospace mfg.) • D.O.T. #621.281-022 • OES #85323 • EXPERIMENTAL AIRCRAFT AND ENGINE MECHANIC, FIELD AND HANGAR; MECHANIC, ENGINEERING RESEARCH. Inspects, tests, modifies and installs mechanical and electrical equipment on new and experimental aircraft according to specifications: Installs engines, de-icing equipment, landing gear assemblies, ejection seats, and other mechanical equipment, following blueprints and sketches and using hand tools. Modifies aircraft components and relocates standard accessories to permit installation of test items, such as recorders, inverters, oscillographs, pressure pickups, strain gauges, transducers and timing devices, following sketches and blueprints and using handtools. Installs, performs operational tests, and repairs or adjusts flight controls, airframe and control surfaces, electrical motors, limit switches, thermocouples, instruments, solenoids and turboregulators, following specifications and using handtools. Removes engine from aircraft and installs it in test apparatus, using chain hoist. Connects wiring and fuel lines to engine, using handtools. Starts engine and observes meter readings to verify specified oil pressure, temperature, and compression. Determines magnitude of stresses in engine parts, using strain gauge. Disassembles and inspects engine to detect evidence of wear and causes of mechanical failure, using handtools and measuring instruments, such as micrometers and calipers. Removes and repairs wings and control surfaces and electrical, plumbing, pneumatic, hydraulic, and fuel systems, using handtools. Removes, cleans, and installs inspection doors, baffles, spark plugs, cowling, ducts, and hatches, using cleaning compounds, rags, and handtools. May assemble experimental engines, filing and adjusting parts according to specifications. May specialize in testing and modifying spacecraft systems and be designated EXPERIMENTAL MECHANIC, SPACECRAFT (aircraft-aerospace mfg.). • **GED:** R4, M3, L4 • **SVP:** 2-4 yrs • **Academic:** Ed=A, Eng=S • **Work Field:** 121, 211 • **MPSMS:** 592 • **Aptitudes:** G3, V3, N3, S3, P3, Q4, K4, F3, M3, E5, C5 • **Temperaments:** M, T, V • **Physical:** V=L, H=N, L=M, W, H • **Work Env:** I, N • **Salary:** 4 • **Outlook:** 3

FARM-EQUIPMENT MECHANIC 1 (agric. equip.) • **D.O.T.** #624.281-010 • **OES** #85321 • FARM MECHANIC. Maintains, repairs, and overhauls farm machinery, equipment, and vehicles, such as tractors, harvesters, pumps, tilling equipment, trucks, and other mechanized, electrically powered, or motor-driven equipment, on farms or in farm-equipment repair shops: Examines and listens to machines, motors, gasoline and diesel engines, and equipment for operational defects and dismantles defective units, using handtools. Repairs or replaces defective parts, using handtools and machine tools, such as drill press, lathe, milling machine, woodworking machines, welding equipment, grinders, and saws. Reassembles, adjusts, and lubricates machines and equipment to ensure efficient operation. May install and repair wiring and motors to maintain farm electrical system. May install and repair plumbing systems on farm. May construct and repair buildings and other farm structures. May assemble and erect new farm machinery and equipment. May be designated according to equipment maintained as VINER MECHANIC (agric. equip.). • **GED:** R4, M3, L3 • **SVP:** 2-4 yrs • **Academic:** Ed=H, Eng=S • **Work Field:** 121 • **MPSMS:** 562 • **Aptitudes:** G3, V3, N3, S3, P3, Q4, K3, F3, M2, E4, C4 • **Temperaments:** M, T, V • **Physical:** V=G, H=G, L=M, W, C, S, H • **Work Env:** B, N, R • **Salary:** 4 • **Outlook:** 3

FIELD SERVICE TECHNICIAN (mach. mfg.) • **D.O.T.** #638.261-026 • **OES** #85123 • ROBOT TECHNICIAN. Installs, programs, and repairs robots and related equipment, such as programmable controllers, robot controllers, end-of-arm tools, conveyors, and parts orienters, applying knowledge of electronics, electrical circuits, mechanics, pneumatics, hydraulics, and programming, using power tools, handtools, and testing instruments and following manuals, schematic diagrams, and blueprints: Reviews work order and related manuals, blueprints, and schematic diagrams to determine tasks to be performed and tools, equipment, and parts needed for installation of repair assignment. Discusses assignment with customer's representative and inspects installation site to verify that electrical supply wires, conduit, switches, and circuit breakers are installed according to specifications. Positions and secures robot and related equipment to floor, assisted by customer's staff, using crane, handtools, and power tools and following manuals and blueprints, or inspects installation site to ensure that robot has been installed according to specifications. Attaches electrical wires to robot controller and programmable controller and connects cables between robot, robot controller, programmable controller, and hydraulic power unit, using handtools. Connects hoses between hydraulic power unit and robot, using handtools. Verifies that electrical power is reaching robot and that voltage is as specified, using testing instruments. Pushes buttons, flips switches, and moves levers to start robot and related equipment to verify that operation is as specified. Programs robot to perform specified tasks, applying knowledge of programming language, using teach pendant and keyboard or control panel on robot controller. Modifies program to refine movement of robot, using teach pendant. Observes and listens to robot and related equipment to detect malfunction and repairs or replaces defective parts, using hand tools and power tools [MAINTENANCE MECHANIC (any ind.) 638.281-014]. Tests electrical components, such as wiring, switches, and relays, using testing instruments, and replaces faulty components, using handtools. Locates and replaces faulty printed circuit boards in robot controller, applying knowledge of circuit board function, using computer display screen on robot controller and following schematic diagram. May train customer's staff in operation of robot and related equipment. May install electric or pneumatic end-of-arm tools on robot. May repair faulty printed circuit boards. • **GED:** R4, M4, L4 • **SVP:** 2-4 yrs • **Academic:** Ed=A, Eng=G • **Work Field:** 111, 121 • **MPSMS:** 560, 570, 580 • **Aptitudes:** G2, V2, N2, S2, P2, Q2, K3, F3, M2, E5, C4 • **Temperaments:** J, P, T • **Physical:** V=L, H=N, L=H, W, H • **Work Env:** I, R • **Salary:** 4 • **Outlook:** 2

FLIGHT-TEST SHOP MECHANIC (aircraft-aerospace mfg.) • **D.O.T.** #621.381-010 • **OES** #85323 • EXPERIMENTAL AIRCRAFT AND ENGINE ELECTRICIAN, FIELD AND HANGER; TEST-STRUCTURES MECHANIC. Plans, lays out, fabricates, overhauls, and shop-tests special mechanical, electrical, pneumatic or hydraulic testing equipment, and experimental parts and assemblies for aircraft and space vehicles, following drawings, sketches, and written and verbal instructions, using handtools and machine tools: Determines operations required to construct, repair, or overhaul parts or assemblies. Develops, fabricates, and assembles such special devices as thermocouples, motor brushes and shafts, camera equipment, strain gages, pressure indicators, radio boxes, instrument glasses, and similar equipment used in flight tests, static tests and other purposes. May select materials to be used in construction, repair, or overhaul of parts or assemblies. May modify and adapt available equipment or parts. May examine air craft or space vehicles to determine method of attachment or installation of equipment or method of construction for proper functioning in airplane or vehicle. May install or assist other workers in installing devices. May construct special tools, equipment, build mockups of special aircraft or spacecraft systems and equipment, and weld parts and assemblies. May specialize in working on mechanical electrical, pneumatic or hydraulic test equipment. • **GED:** R4, M3, L3 • **SVP:** 2-4 yrs • **Academic:** Ed=A, Eng=S • **Work Field:** 121 • **MPSMS:** 592 • **Aptitudes:** G3, V3, N3, S3, P3, Q4, K4, F3, M3, E5, C4 • **Temperaments:** M, T, V • **Physical:** V=L, H=N, L=M, W, H • **Work Env:** I, N • **Salary:** 4 • **Outlook:** 3

FUEL-INJECTION SERVICER (any ind.) • **D.O.T.** #625.281-022 • **OES** #85302 • Rebuilds, tests, and calibrates fuel injection units as used on diesel engines, railroad locomotives, trucks, construction equipment, tractors, and power plants: Studies repair order and disassembles unit to determine cause of malfunction. Refinishes defective parts, using lapping machine to grind and smooth nozzle point and seat. Replaces parts which cannot be refinished. Assembles and calibrates injection pumps, using test equipment. Assembles and tests nozzle assemblies, using test equipment. • **GED:** R4, M4, L4 • **SVP:** 1-2 yrs • **Academic:** Ed=N, Eng=S • **Work Field:** 121 • **MPSMS:** 567 • **Aptitudes:** G3, V4, N4, S3, P3, Q4, K4, F3, M3, E5, C5 • **Temperaments:** M, R • **Stress:** T • **Physical:** V=L, H=N, L=M, W, H • **Work Env:** I, N • **Salary:** 3 • **Outlook:** 3

FUEL-SYSTEM-MAINTENANCE WORKER (any ind.) • **D.O.T.** #638.381-010 • **OES** #85900 • GAS-PIT SPECIALIST. Installs, maintains, repairs, and adjusts pumps, control valves and meters, strainers and filters, water separators, and pipe lines of liquid fuel systems for airfields: Makes periodic in spections of units to detect and correct leakage, corrosion, faulty fittings, and malfunction of mechanical units, meters, and gages, such as fuel hydrants, tank pits, distribution lines, storage tanks, turbines, pumps, and control rooms. Inspects electrical wiring, switches, and controls for safe operating condition, grounding, and adjustment. Repairs, replaces, and adjusts malfunctioning equipment to restore operating condition specified in regulations and repair manuals. Disassembles, ad justs, alines, and calibrates gages and meters. Cleans storage tanks, removes and installs old or new equipment, such as meter and filter installations, pipe systems, pit covers, and vents to modify existing installations. • **GED:** R3, M3, L3 • **SVP:** 2-4 yrs • **Academic:** Ed=N, Eng=S • **Work Field:** 121 • **MPSMS:** 567 • **Aptitudes:** G3, V4, N3, S3, P2, Q4, K3, F3, M3, E4, C4 • **Temperaments:** M, T • **Physical:** V=L, H=N, L=H, W, S, H • **Work Env:** B, R • **Salary:** 4 • **Outlook:** 3

FURNACE INSTALLER-AND-REPAIRER, HOT AIR (any ind.) • **D.O.T.** #869.281-010 • **OES** #85902 • FURNACE WORKER; HEATING WORKER. Installs and repairs hot-air furnaces, stoves, and similar equipment in accordance with diagrams and other specifications, using handtools and pipe-threading tools: Constructs foundation of concrete or other noncombustible material. Assembles and positions heating units in accordance with diagrams, using handtools. Cuts holes in floors and walls to form air-duct outlets. Installs air ducts, smoke pipes, blowers, and stokers, following blueprints of building and using handtools. Installs fuel pipes, using dies, pipe cutters, and pipe wrenches. Wraps insulating asbestos around air ducts. Connects and adjusts timers and thermostats. Inspects inoperative heating units to locate causes of trouble. Disassembles heating unit and replaces or repairs defective parts, using handtools. Cuts, bends, and crimps sheet metal to repair furnace and stove casing and pipes, using crimpers, files, snips, handbrakes, and sheet metal hammers. Reassembles and starts heating unit to test operation. • GED: R4, M3, L3 • SVP: 2-4 yrs • Academic: Ed=H, Eng=S • Work Field: 102 • MPSMS: 553 • Aptitudes: G3, V3, N3, S3, P3, Q4, K3, F3, M3, E4, C4 • Temperaments: M, T, V • Physical: V=L, H=N, L=M, W, S, H • Work Env: I • Salary: 5 • Outlook: 3

GAS-ENGINE REPAIRER (any ind.) • D.O.T. #625.281-026 • OES #85328 • Repairs and maintains gas-driven, internal-combustion engines that power electric generators, compressors, and similar equipment, using handtools and precision-measuring devices: Reads operating reports and diagnoses causes of trouble. Disassembles engines and adjusts or replaces parts, using handtools. Verifies clearances and adjustments, using precision-measuring devices. Reassembles engines and listens to engines in action to detect operational difficulties. May repair air or gas compressors. • GED: R3, M3, L3 • SVP: 1-2 yrs • Academic: Ed=N, Eng=S • Work Field: 121 • MPSMS: 561 • Aptitudes: G3, V3, N3, S3, P3, Q4, K3, F3, M2, E5, C5 • Temperaments: M, T • Physical: V=L, H=L, L=M, W, S, H • Work Env: I, N • Salary: 4 • Outlook: 3

GAS-WELDING-EQUIPMENT MECHANIC (any ind.) • D.O.T. #626.381-014 • OES #85119 • APPARATUS-REPAIR MECHANIC. Repairs acetylene gas welding equipment, using hand tools and metalworking machines: Disassembles parts, such as worn hose, torch tips, torch valves, pressure gages and regulators. Examines parts and repairs usable ones, using hand files and metalworking machines, such as lathes, drill presses, and grinding wheels. Replaces defective parts with new or rebuilt ones, using handtools. • GED: R3, M3, L3 • SVP: 2-4 yrs • Academic: Ed=N, Eng=S • Work Field: 121 • MPSMS: 566 • Aptitudes: G3, V3, N3, S3, P3, Q4, K4, F3, M2, E5, C5 • Temperaments: M, T, V • Physical: V=L, H=N, L=L, W, H • Work Env: I, N • Salary: 4 • Outlook: 3

LOCKSMITH (any ind.) • D.O.T. #709.281-010 • OES #85923 • LOCK EXPERT. Repairs and opens locks, makes keys, and changes lock combinations, using handtools and special equipment: Disassembles locks, such as padlocks, safe locks, and door locks, and repairs or replaces worn tumblers, springs, and other parts. Shortens tumblers, using file, and inserts new or repaired tumblers into lock to change combination. Cuts new or duplicate keys, using keycutting machine. Moves lockpick in cylinder to open door locks without keys. Opens safe locks by listening to lock sounds or by drilling. May keep records of company locks and keys. • GED: R4, M3, L3 • SVP: 1-2 yrs • Academic: Ed=N, Eng=G • Work Field: 121 • MPSMS: 552 • Aptitudes: G3, V3, N3, S3, P2, Q4, K3, F3, M2, E5, C5 • Temperaments: M, T • Physical: V=L, H=G, L=L, W, S, H • Work Env: I • Salary: 4 • Outlook: 3

MACHINE BUILDER (mach. mfg.) • D.O.T. #600.281-022 • OES #93105 • ASSEMBLER, SPECIAL MACHINE; BENCH HAND; FITTER; MACHINIST, BENCH; VISE HAND. Fits and assembles components according to assembly blueprints, manuals, engineering memos, sketches, and knowledge of machine construction to construct, rebuild, and repair machines and equipment, using handtools and power tools: Analyzes assembly blueprint and specifications manual, and plans machine building operations. Verifies conformance of parts to stock list and blueprints, using measuring instruments, such as calipers, gages, and micrometers. Lays out hole locations and drills and taps holes in parts for assembly. Alines components for assembly, manually or with hoist, and bolts, screws, dowels, welds, or rivets parts together, using handtools, rivet gun, and welding equipment, or arranges for assembly by welder and electrician. Brushes blue pigment on parts and mates them to detect high spots on surfaces. Removes high spots, and smooths surfaces, using chisels, scrapers, files, and powered hand

grinder [SCRAPER, HAND (mach. shop)]. Verifies alinement and tolerances of moving parts, using measuring instruments, such as dial indicators and thickness gages. Tests operation of assembly by hand. Assembles, sets up, and operates machine to verify functioning, machine capabilities, and conformance to customer's specifications. May form and fasten piping, fixtures, and attachments required to service machine with air, water, and oil. May install wiring and electrical components to specifications. May work as member of team on limited part of fabrication process. May set up and operate metalworking machines to shape parts [TOOL-MACHINE SET-UP OPERATOR (mach. shop)]. May be designated according to type of machine or machine component as FIXTURE BUILDER (mach. mfg.). • GED: R4, M4, L3 • SVP: 2-4 yrs • Academic: Ed=H, Eng=S • Work Field: 121 • MPSMS: 566 • Aptitudes: G3, V3, N3, S2, P3, Q4, K3, F3, M3, E5, C5 • Temperaments: M, T, V • Physical: V=L, H=N, L=M, W, H • Work Env: I • Salary: 4 • Outlook: 3

MACHINERY ERECTOR (engine & turbine) • D.O.T. #638.261-014 • OES #85123 • ERECTOR; HEAVY-MACHINERY ASSEMBLER. Erects and tests machinery and heavy equipment, such as hydraulic turbines, turbine wheels, jaw stone crushers, industrial surface condensers, flaking machines, valves, and mine hoists, according to blueprints and specifications, using hand tools, heating equipment, and measuring instruments: Positions steel beams to support bedplates of machines and equipment. Levels bedplate and establishes centerline, using straightedge, levels, and transit. Signals BRIDGE-OR-GANTRY-CRANE OPERATOR (any ind.) to lower basic assembly unit, such as shaft, shaft casing, frame, or housing unit, to bedplate and alines unit to center line. Lays out mounting holes, using measuring instruments and drills holes with power drill. Bolts parts, such as side and deck plates, jaw plates, and journals, to basic assembly unit. Attaches moving parts and subassemblies, such as shafts, rollers, flywheels, runners (water wheels), valves, gates, bearings, and bearing supports, to basic assembly unit, using handtools and power tools. Shrink-fits bushings, sleeves, rings, liners, gears, and wheels to specified items, using portable gas heating equipment. Inserts shims, adjusts tension on nuts and bolts, or positions parts, using handtools and measuring instruments to set specified clearances between moving and stationary parts. Connects power unit to machines, or steam piping to equipment, and tests unit to evaluate its mechanical operation. Replaces defective parts of machine or adjusts clearances and alinement of moving parts. Dismantles machinery and equipment for shipment to installation site. • GED: R4, M4, L4 • SVP: 4-10 yrs • Academic: Ed=N, Eng=S • Work Field: 121 • MPSMS: 561, 564 • Aptitudes: G3, V3, N3, S2, P3, Q4, K3, F3, M2, E4, C5 • Temperaments: D, M, T, V • Physical: V=L, H=N, L=H, W, C, S, H • Work Env: I, N • Salary: 5 • Outlook: 3

MAIL-PROCESSING-EQUIPMENT MECHANIC (gov. ser.) • D.O.T. #633.261-014 • OES #85926 • Repairs and maintains mail-processing equipment, such as letter-canceling machines, letter-facing-and-canceling machines, mail-sorting machines, and conveyor systems, following blueprints and schematic diagrams, using handtools, power tools, and electrical testing instruments: Inspects machine to locate causes of trouble, using ammeters, ohmmeters, relay testers, and other testing instruments. Dismantles machine, using handtools and power tools. Repairs wiring circuits and replaces parts, such as relays, resistors, condensers, and rheostats in electrical systems, using handtools. Repairs and replaces parts, such as gears and bearings in mechanical systems, using handtools. Reassembles and starts machines to test performances. Dismantles conveyor systems, using handtools. Repairs or replaces defective parts and reassembles conveyors. May repair hydraulic and pneumatic systems. • GED: R4, M3, L3 • SVP: 1-2 yrs • Academic: Ed=N, Eng=S • Work Field: 111, 121 • MPSMS: 565, 567 • Aptitudes: G3, V3, N3, S3, P2, Q4, K3, F3, M2, E5, C3 • Temperaments: M, T, V • Physical: V=L, H=N, L=M, W, H • Work Env: I • Salary: 4 • Outlook: 2

MAINTENANCE MECHANIC (any ind.) • D.O.T. #638.281-014 • OES #85119 • FIXER; MACHINE-MAINTENANCE SERVICER; MACHINE OVERHAULER; MACHINE REPAIRER; MECHANICAL ADJUSTER; REPAIR MECHANIC; TOOL-AND-MACHINE MAINTAINER. Repairs and maintains, in accordance with diagrams, sketches, operation manuals, and manufacturer's specifications, machinery and mechanical equipment, such as engines, motors, pneumatic tools, convey or systems, and production machines and equipment, using hand tools, power tools, and precision-measuring and testing instruments: Observes mechanical devices in operation and listens to their sounds to locate causes of trouble. Dismantles devices to gain access to and remove defective parts, using hoists, cranes, handtools, and power tools. Examines form and texture of parts to detect imperfections. Inspects used parts to determine changes in dimensional requirements, using rules, calipers, micrometers, and other measuring instruments. Adjusts functional parts of devices and control instruments, using handtools, levels, plumb bobs, and straightedges. Repairs or replaces defective parts, using hand tools and power tools. Installs special functional and structural parts in devices, using handtools. Starts devices to test their performance. Lubricates and cleans parts. May set up and operate lathe, drill press, grinder, and other metalworking tools to make and repair parts. May initiate purchase order for parts and machines. May repair electrical equipment. May be designated according to machine repaired, as CARTON-FORMING-MACHINE ADJUSTER (any ind.); MACHINE ADJUSTER (tobacco); MAINTENANCE MECHANIC, RECORD PROCESSING EQUIPMENT (phonograph). • GED: **R4, M3, L3** • SVP: **2-4 yrs** • Academic: **Ed=H, Eng=S** • Work Field: **121** • MPSMS: **567, 568** • Aptitudes: **G3, V3, N3, S2, P2, Q4, K3, F3, M2, E4, C4** • Temperaments: **M, T, V** • Physical: **V=G, H=L, L=H, W, C, S, H** • Work Env: **B, W, N, R** • Salary: **4** • Outlook: **4**

MAINTENANCE REPAIRER, INDUSTRIAL (any ind.) • D.O.T. #899.261-014 • OES #85132 • MAINTENANCE ASSOCIATE; PLANT-MAINTENANCE WORKER; UTILITY REPAIRER. Installs, maintains, and repairs machinery, equipment, physical structures, and pipe and electrical systems in commercial or industrial establishments, using handtools, power tools, hoist, crane, and testing instruments, and following specifications, blueprints, manuals, and schematic diagrams: Visually inspects and tests machinery and equipment, using electrical and electronic test equipment. Listens for unusual sounds, and talks with supervisors, production workers, or maintenance workers to detect and diagnose malfunctions. Dismantles defective machines and equipment and installs new or repaired parts, following specifications and blueprints and using precision-measuring instruments and handtools [MACHINE REPAIRER, MAINTENANCE (any ind.) 638.261-030]. Cleans and lubricates shafts, bearings, gears, and other parts of machinery, using rags, brushes, and grease gun. Installs and repairs electrical apparatus, such as transformers and wiring, and electrical and electronic components of machinery and equipment [ELECTRICIAN, MAINTENANCE (any ind.) 829.261-018]. Lays out, assembles, installs, and maintains pipe systems and related hydraulic and pneumatic equipment, and repairs and replaces gauges, valves, pressure regulators, and related equipment [PIPE FITTER (any ind.) 862.281-022]. Makes and repairs counters, benches, partitions, and other wooden structures. Repairs and maintains physical structure of establishment [MAINTENANCE REPAIRER, BUILDING (any ind.) 899.381-010]. May install machinery and equipment according to blueprints and other specifications [MILLWRIGHT (any ind.) 638.281-018]. May install, program, or repair automated machinery and equipment, such as robots or programmable controllers. May set up and operate machine tools, such as lathe, grinder, and milling machine to repair or fabricate machine parts, jigs and fixtures, and tools. May operate welding equipment to join metal parts used to repair or fabricate equipment. • GED: **R4, M4, L4** • SVP: **4-10 yrs** • Academic: **Ed=N, Eng=S** • Work Field: **111, 121** • MPSMS: **560, 570, 580** • Aptitudes: **G2, V3, N2, S2, P2, Q3, K3, F3, M2, E5, C4** • Temperaments: **J, T, V** • Physical: **V=L, H=N, L=H, W, S, H** • Work Env: **I, R** • Salary: **5** • Outlook: **4**

MANAGER, MARINE SERVICE (ship bldg. & rep.) • D.O.T. #187.167-130 • OES #81002 • Directs activities of boat-repair service, according to knowledge of maintenance needs of small craft and marine safety requirements: Confers with owner or crew of vessel to obtain maintenance history and details concerning condition of craft. Observes and listens to vessel in operation to detect unsafe or malfunctioning equipment and leaks or other flaws in hull and superstructure. Performs tests on vessel and equipment, using gages and other standard testing devices. Estimates cost of repairs according to familiarity with labor and materials requirements or fee schedule. Directs and coordinates activities of workers engaged in repairing, painting, and otherwise restoring vessels to seaworthy condition. May repair vessels, assisted by other workers. • GED: **R4, M3, L3** • SVP: **4-10 yrs** • Academic: **Ed=H, Eng=S** • Work Field: **102, 121** • MPSMS: **593** • Aptitudes: **G2, V3, N3, S2, P2, Q4, K4, F4, M3, E4, C4** • Temperaments: **D, J, M, P, V** • Stress: **A** • Physical: **V=L, H=G, L=L, C, H** • Work Env: **B, W, N** • Salary: **5** • Outlook: **2**

MECHANIC, INDUSTRIAL TRUCK (any ind.) • D.O.T. #620.281-050 • OES #85311 • TRUCK REPAIRER. Repairs and maintains electric, diesel, and gasoline industrial trucks, following manuals, and using handtools, power tools, and knowledge of electrical, power transmission, brake, and other automotive systems: Reads job order and observes and listens to truck in operation to determine malfunction and to plan work procedures. Installs new ignition systems, alines front wheels, changes or recharges batteries, and replaces transmissions and other parts, using handtools. Overhauls gas or diesel engines, using mechanic's handtools, welding equipment, standard charts, and hoists. Examines protective guards, loose bolts, and specified safety devices on trucks, and makes adjustments, using handtools. Lubricates moving parts and drives repaired truck to verify conformance to specifications. May fabricate special lifting or towing attachments, hydraulic systems, shields, or other devices according to blueprints or schematic drawings. • GED: **R4, M3, L3** • SVP: **2-4 yrs** • Academic: **Ed=N, Eng=S** • Work Field: **121** • MPSMS: **565** • Aptitudes: **G3, V3, N3, S2, P3, Q4, K3, F3, M2, E4, C5** • Temperaments: **M, T, V** • Physical: **V=L, H=L, L=M, W, S, H** • Work Env: **I** • Salary: **4** • Outlook: **4**

OFFICE-MACHINE SERVICER (any ind.) • D.O.T. #633.281-018 • OES #85926 • BUSINESS-MACHINE MECHANIC; OFFICE-EQUIPMENT MECHANIC; OFFICE-MACHINE INSPECTOR. Repairs and services office machines, such as adding, accounting, and calculating machines, and typewriters, using handtools, power tools, micrometers, and welding equipment: Operates machines to test moving parts and to listen to sounds of machines to locate causes of trouble. Disassembles machine and examines parts, such as gears, guides, rollers, and pinions for wear and defects, using micrometers. Repairs, adjusts, or replaces parts, using hand tools, power tools, and soldering and welding equipment. Cleans and oils moving parts. May give instructions in operation and care of machines to machine operators. May assemble new machines. May be designated according to machine repaired or serviced as ACCOUNTING-MACHINE SERVICER (any ind.); ADDING-MACHINE SERVICER (any ind.); CALCULATING-MACHINE SERVICER (any ind.); DUPLICATING-MACHINE SERVICER (any ind.); TYPEWRITER SERVICER (any ind.). • GED: **R4, M3, L3** • SVP: **2-4 yrs** • Academic: **Ed=H, Eng=G** • Work Field: **111, 121** • MPSMS: **571** • Aptitudes: **G3, V3, N3, S2, P3, Q4, K3, F3, M2, E5, C5** • Temperaments: **M, T** • Physical: **V=G, H=L, L=L, W, H** • Work Env: **I** • Salary: **4** • Outlook: **4**

PARTS SALVAGER (any ind.) • D.O.T. #638.281-026 • OES #85999 • Repairs salvable mechanical parts of machines and equipment: Dismantles machinery, equipment, and parts, using handtools, such as hacksaws, files, reamers, wrenches and screwdrivers. Inspects parts to determine salvageability or method of repairing or reworking parts. Sets up and operates metalworking tools, such as engine lathes, milling, drilling, grinding, polishing, and buffing machines to repair parts. Files, taps, reams, bends, and straightens, or uses other methods to recondition parts, using handtools. Verifies dimensions and tolerances, using blueprints, scale, and precision-measuring instruments. May reassemble parts, using handtools and power tools. May direct cleaning, storing, and issuing of reclaimed parts, and packing of usable materials, such as metal sweepings. May arrange for sale of scrap. • GED: **R4, M3, L3** • SVP: **2-4 yrs** • Academic: **Ed=N, Eng=S** • Work Field: **121** • MPSMS: **567** • Aptitudes: **G3, V3, N3, S3, P3, Q4, K3, F3, M2, E5, C5** • Temperaments: **M, T, V** • Physical: **V=L, H=N, L=M, W, H** • Work Env: **I, N** • Salary: **3** • Outlook: **3**

PNEUMATIC-TOOL REPAIRER (any ind.) • D.O.T. #630.281-010 • OES #85119 • AIR-MOTOR REPAIRER; DRILL DOCTOR. Repairs pneumatic tools and air motors, such as pneumatic hammers, chisels, and reamers, using mechanic's tools: Starts motor or tool and listens to sound to locate cause of trouble. Disassembles motor and repairs or replaces defective gears, pistons, connecting rods, and other parts, using taps, files, reamers, wrenches, and other handtools. • **GED:** R4, M3, L3 • **SVP:** 2-4 yrs • **Academic:** Ed=N, Eng=S • **Work Field:** 121 • **MPSMS:** 566 • **Aptitudes:** G3, V3, N3, S3, P3, Q4, K3, F3, M2, E4, C5 • **Temperaments:** M, T • **Physical:** V=L, H=N, L=M, W, H • **Work Env:** I, N • **Salary:** 4 • **Outlook:** 3

POWER-SAW MECHANIC (any ind.) • D.O.T. #625.281-030 • OES #85328 • CHAIN-SAW MECHANIC. Repairs and maintains portable saws powered by internal combustion engines, following manufacturer's repair manuals and using hand tools. Disassembles engine and replaces defective parts, such as piston rings, bearings, and timing mechanism. Cleans or replaces fuel lines and adjusts carburetors. Replaces broken links in chain saw or installs new chain. Replaces rotary or reciprocating blades in other saws as indicated. • **GED:** R3, M3, L3 • **SVP:** 1-2 yrs • **Academic:** Ed=N, Eng=S • **Work Field:** 121 • **MPSMS:** 567 • **Aptitudes:** G3, V3, N3, S3, P3, Q4, K3, F3, M2, E5, C5 • **Temperaments:** M, T • **Physical:** V=L, H=N, L=M, W, H • **Work Env:** I • **Salary:** 4 • **Outlook:** 2

POWERHOUSE MECHANIC (light, heat, & power) • D.O.T. #631.261-014 • OES #85118 • STATION MECHANIC. Installs, adjusts, maintains, and repairs electrical and mechanical equipment and parts in power-generating station: Installs equipment. Dismantles and overhauls equipment [MILLWRIGHT (any ind.); BOILERMAKER (boilermaking) I]. Dismantles and repairs auxiliary equipment, such as pumps, compressors, and pipe systems [MAINTENANCE REPAIRER, FACTORY OR MILL (any ind.)]. Assists in conducting acceptance and performance tests on new or existing equipment. Fabricates special tools, rigging equipment, and replacement parts for equipment. May install wiring between machinery, switchboards, and control panels [WIRER, MAINTENANCE (light, heat, & power)]. May be designated according to type of plant in which maintenance is performed as DIESEL-POWERPLANT MECHANIC (light, heat, & power); GAS-TURBINE-POWERPLANT MECHANIC (light, heat, & power); GEOTHERMAL-POWERPLANT MECHANIC (light, heat, & power); NUCLEAR-POWERPLANT MECHANIC (light, heat, & power); STEAM-GENERATING-POWERPLANT MECHANIC (light, heat, & power). • **GED:** R4, M3, L3 • **SVP:** 4-10 yrs • **Academic:** Ed=H, Eng=S • **Work Field:** 111, 121 • **MPSMS:** 568 • **Aptitudes:** G2, V3, N3, S2, P2, Q3, K3, F3, M3, E3, C4 • **Temperaments:** M, T, V • **Physical:** V=L, H=N, L=H, W, C, S, H • **Work Env:** I, N, R • **Salary:** 5 • **Outlook:** 2

PUMP SERVICER (any ind.) • D.O.T. #630.281-018 • OES #85119 • PUMP REPAIRER. Repairs pumps and pump power units, such as centrifugal and plunger-type pumps, and diesel-engine, gasoline-engine, and electric-motor power units, using hoists and handtools: Diagnoses trouble in pumps. Disman tles pumps and repairs or replaces defective parts, using hand tools. Reseats and grinds valves. Tests performances of repaired pumps. May wire motor to switchboard and install fuse box. May be designated according to type of pump repaired as WATER-PUMP SERVICER (any ind.). • **GED:** R3, M3, L3 • **SVP:** 2-4 yrs • **Academic:** Ed=N, Eng=S • **Work Field:** 111, 121 • **MPSMS:** 568 • **Aptitudes:** G3, V3, N3, S3, P3, Q4, K3, F3, M2, E5, C4 • **Temperaments:** M, T • **Physical:** V=G, H=L, L=M, W, S, H • **Work Env:** B • **Salary:** 4 • **Outlook:** 2

REFRIGERATION MECHANIC (any ind.) • D.O.T. #637.261-026 • OES #85902 • Installs and repairs industrial and commercial refrigerating systems according to blue prints and engineering specifications, using knowledge of refrigeration, structural layout, and function and design of components: Lays out reference points for installation of structural and functional components, using measuring instruments, such as tape, transit, plumb bob, levels, and square. Drills holes and installs mounting brackets and hangers into floor and walls of building. Lifts and alines components into position, using hoist or block and tackle. Screws, bolts, rivets, welds, and brazes parts to assemble structural and functional components, such as motors, controls, switches, gages, wiring harnesses, valves, pumps, compressors, condensors, cores, and pipes. Cuts, threads, and connects pipe to functional components and water or power system of premises [PIPE FITTER (const.)].

Pumps specified gas or fluid into system. Starts system, observes operation, reads gages and instruments, and adjusts mechanisms, such as valves, controls, and pumps to control level of fluid, pressure, and temperature in system. Dismantles malfunctioning systems and tests components, using electrical, mechanical, and pneumatic testing equipment. Replaces or adjusts defective or worn parts to repair systems. May insulate shells and cabinets of systems. May install wiring to connect components to electric power source. May specialize in installing systems and be designated REFRIGERATION-SYSTEM INSTALLER (any ind.). • **GED:** R4, M3, L3 • **SVP:** 4-10 yrs • **Academic:** Ed=H, Eng=S • **Work Field:** 102, 121 • **MPSMS:** 573 • **Aptitudes:** G3, V3, N3, S2, P3, Q4, K3, F3, M3, E4, C5 • **Temperaments:** M, T • **Physical:** V=G, H=N, L=H, W, C, S, H • **Work Env:** I, C, N, R • **Salary:** 4 • **Outlook:** 3

REFRIGERATION MECHANIC (refrig. equip.) • D.O.T. #827.361-014 • OES #85902 • Fabricates and assembles components of refrigeration systems for environmental test equipment according to blueprints or schematic drawings and knowledge of refrigeration systems, using handtools, powered tools and welding equipment: Reads blueprints or schematic drawings to determine location, size, capacity, and type of components, such as compressor, condenser, expansion tank, valves, and tubing or piping needed to build refrigeration system. Mounts compressor, condenser, and other components in specified locations on frame, using handtools and arc or acetylene welding equipment. Cuts, bends, and brazes specified tubing to inlets and outlets of components to form liquid and suction lines of refrigeration system, using knowledge of metal properties. Installs expansion and control valves, using acetylene torch and wrenches. Adjusts valves according to specifications. Removes air from system and charges system with specified amount and type of refrigerant [GAS CHARGER (refrigerat. equip.)]. Tests lines, components, and connections for leaks with leak detector which indicates presence of refrigerant [GAS-LEAK TESTER (refrigerat. equip.)]. Attaches thermocouples to various points of refrigeration system and test-operates equipment to evaluate functioning and cooling capacity of system. Records pressure and temperature readings from gages and temperature potentiometer during test run. Compares reading with specifications to evaluate performance of system, and adjusts or replaces parts as indicated. May fabricate and assemble structural portions of test equipment. May assemble and mount electrical wiring circuits, controls, and recording devices. May fabricate and assemble cascade and multiple stage refrigeration systems. • **GED:** R4, M3, L3 • **SVP:** 2-4 yrs • **Academic:** Ed=N, Eng=S • **Work Field:** 111, 121 • **MPSMS:** 573 • **Aptitudes:** G3, V3, N3, S3, P3, Q4, K3, F3, M3, E5, C5 • **Temperaments:** M, T, V • **Physical:** V=N, H=L, L=H, W, C, S, H • **Work Env:** I • **Salary:** 4 • **Outlook:** 3

ROCKET-ENGINE-COMPONENT MECHANIC (aircraft-aerospace mfg.) • D.O.T. #621.281-030 • OES #85928 • Assembles and tests pneumatic, hydraulic, and mechanical components of rocket engines, such as turbo pumps, generators, and valves, according to specifications, using handtools and precision test instruments: Positions parts in jigs and holding fixtures to facilitate assembly. Fits and assembles interrelating precision parts, using handtools. Inspects configuration and dimensions of assemblies, using instruments, such as optical flats, micrometers, calipers, dial indicators, and monolight instruments. Tests assemblies to determine conditions, such as internal leakage, pressure differentials, and cycles of operation, using gages, meters, and chemicals. Conducts functional tests to determine mechanical performance. Analyzes malfunctions to determine their causes, and repairs, adjusts, synchronizes, and calibrates assemblies. • **GED:** R4, M4, L4 • **SVP:** 2-4 yrs • **Academic:** Ed=A, Eng=S • **Work Field:** 121 • **MPSMS:** 592 • **Aptitudes:** G3, V2, N3, S2, P2, Q4, K3, F3, M2, E3, C3 • **Temperaments:** M, T • **Physical:** V=L, H=N, L=L, W, H • **Work Env:** I • **Salary:** 4 • **Outlook:** 3

SMALL-ENGINE MECHANIC (any ind.) • D.O.T. #625.281-034 • OES #85328 • Repairs fractional-horsepower gasoline engines used to power lawnmowers, garden tractors, and similar machines, using handtools: Locates causes of trouble, dismantles engines, using handtools, and examines parts for defects. Replaces or repairs parts, such as rings and bearings, using handtools. Cleans and adjusts carburetor and magneto. Starts repaired engines and listens to sounds to test performance. Replaces engines on machine. May be designated according to type of engine repaired as LAWNMOWER MECHANIC (any ind.). • **GED:** R3, M3, L3 • **SVP:** 1-2 yrs • **Academic:** Ed=N, Eng=S • **Work Field:** 121 • **MPSMS:** 561 • **Aptitudes:** G3, V3, N4, S3, P3, Q4, K3, F4, M2, E5, C5 • **Temperaments:** M, R, T • **Stress:** T • **Physical:** V=L, H=L, L=M, W, H • **Work Env:** B • **Salary:** 4 • **Outlook:** 3

SOLAR-ENERGY-SYSTEM INSTALLER (any ind.) • D.O.T. #637.261-030 • OES #85902 • Installs and repairs solar-energy systems designed to collect, store, and circulate solar-heated water or other medium for residential, commercial, or industrial use: Locates and marks position of collectors, holding tank, and distribution system on structure, according to specifications and blueprints. Cuts holes in roof, walls, and ceiling to install equipment and plumbing, using power saws and drills. Installs supports and brackets to anchor solar collectors and holding tank, using carpenter's handtools. Cuts, threads, and fits plumbing according to specifications for connecting circulation system, using plumber's handtools. Lays out and connects electrical wiring between controls and pumps according to wiring diagram and knowledge of standard industry practice, using electrician's handtools. Tests electrical circuits and components for continuity, using electrical test equipment. Tests plumbing for leaks, using pressure gauge. Pushes control buttons to activate pumps and observes system to detect malfunctions. Repairs or replaces defective equipment. • **GED:** R4, M4, L4 • **SVP:** 2-4 yrs • **Academic:** Ed=N, Eng=S • **Work Field:** 102, 111 • **MPSMS:** 364 • **Aptitudes:** G3, V4, N3, S2, P2, Q3, K3, F3, M3, E4, C5 • **Temperaments:** J, T • **Physical:** V=L, H=N, L=H, W, H • **Work Env:** I • **Salary:** 4 • **Outlook:** 3

TRACTOR MECHANIC (auto. ser.) • D.O.T. #620.281-058 • OES #85311 • Diagnoses mechanical failures of and repairs tractors and tractor components according to manuals, factory specifications, and knowledge of engine performances, using handtools, power tools, and testing instruments: Attaches compression, ignition, and timing test instruments to certain parts of tractor, using clamps and handtools. Starts engine dials and reads meters and gages of testing equipment to diagnose engine malfunction. Removes and disassembles engine, transmission, and clutches, using hoists, jacks, and mechanic's handtools. Inspects parts for damage, and verifies dimensions and clearances of parts for conformance to factory specifications, using gages, such as calipers, and micrometers. Replaces or repairs worn or damaged parts. Grinds valves, relines and adjusts brakes, tightens body bolts, alines wheels, and tunes engine. May weld defective body or frame parts. • **GED:** R4, M3, L3 • **SVP:** 2-4 yrs • **Academic:** Ed=H, Eng=S • **Work Field:** 121 • **MPSMS:** 565 • **Aptitudes:** G3, V3, N3, S2, P3, Q4, K3, F3, M2, E4, C4 • **Temperaments:** M, T, V • **Physical:** V=G, H=G, L=M, W, S, H • **Work Env:** I, W • **Salary:** 4 • **Outlook:** 3

TUNE-UP MECHANIC (auto. ser.) • D.O.T. #620.281-066 • OES #85302 • Tunes automotive vehicle engines to ensure efficient operation: Removes spark plugs, using socket wrench, and tests them, using spark-plug tester. Cleans electrodes in sandblasting machine, sets spark gap with feeler gage, and replaces or installs new plugs. Inspects distributor breaker points for wear and pits, using feeler gage, and replaces or resets points. Observes ignition timing, using timing light, and adjusts timing, using handtools. Adjusts carburetor needle setting, using handtools, and verifies adjustment, using instruments, such as fuel analyzer, vacuum gage, oscilloscope, and tachometer. Sets valve tappets, using feeler gage or dial indicator. Replaces defective coils, condensers, and electrical connectors. Removes and cleans carburetor and fuel pump. Examines battery and connections and electrical charging and starting circuit. Adjusts, and repairs fan belt, and fuel and water pumps. May tune engine while vehicle runs on rollers connected to dynamometer and be designated as DYNAMOMETER TUNER (auto. ser.). • **GED:** R4, M3, L3 • **SVP:** 2-4 yrs • **Academic:** Ed=H, Eng=S • **Work Field:** 121 • **MPSMS:** 591 • **Aptitudes:** G3, V3, N3, S2, P2, Q4, K3, F2, M3, E5, C4 • **Temperaments:** J, M, T, V • **Physical:** V=L, H=G, L=S, W, S, H • **Work Env:** I, N • **Salary:** 4 • **Outlook:** 3

GOE: 05.05.10 Elect. Equipment Repair

AUDIO-VIDEO REPAIRER (any ind.) • D.O.T. #729.281-010 • OES #85708 • AUDIOVISUAL-AIDS TECHNICIAN. Installs and repairs audio-video equipment, such as tape recorders, public address systems, slide and motion picture projectors, and record players, using handtools, soldering iron, and special testing equipment. Inspects equipment for defects and repairs or replaces parts. Returns equipment to shop for more complicated repairs. • **GED:** R4, M3, L3 • **SVP:** 1-2 yrs • **Academic:** Ed=H, Eng=S • **Work Field:** 111 • **MPSMS:** 585 • **Aptitudes:** G3, V4, N4, S3, P3, Q4, K4, F3, M3, E5, C4 • **Temperaments:** M, T • **Physical:** V=G, H=G, L=L, H • **Work Env:** I • **Salary:** 3 • **Outlook:** 4

AVIONICS TECHNICIAN (aircraft-aerospace mfg.) • D.O.T. #823.281-010 • OES #85514 • AIRPLANE-RADIO TESTER; RADIO-AND-ELECTRICAL MECHANIC; RADIO-EQUIPMENT INSTALLER; RADIO-MAINTENANCE REPAIRER. Inspects, tests, adjusts, and repairs aircraft communication, navigation, and flight control systems: Tests and replaces defective instruments, such as microphones, headsets, dopplers, selcall, transceivers, transponders, and autopilots, using electricians' tools, circuit analyzers, oscilloscopes, and other testing devices. Calibrates installed or repaired equipment to prescribed specifications. Signs overhaul documents for equipment replaced or repaired. Adjusts frequencies of radio sets by signaling ground station and turning setscrews. Required to hold Radiotelephone License issued by Federal Communications Commission or Federal Aviation Agency. • **GED:** R4, M4, L4 • **SVP:** 1-2 yrs • **Academic:** Ed=A, Eng=S • **Work Field:** 111 • **MPSMS:** 586, 587 • **Aptitudes:** G3, V3, N3, S2, P2, Q4, K3, F3, M2, E4, C4 • **Temperaments:** M, T, V • **Physical:** V=L, H=N, L=L, S, H • **Work Env:** I • **Salary:** 4 • **Outlook:** 4

ELECTRIC-METER REPAIRER (light, heat, & power) • D.O.T. #729.281-014 • OES #85911 • METER REPAIRER. Inspects, adjusts, and repairs electric meters used for recording electric current consumption: Disassembles defective meters, using handtools. Examines parts of meter for wear and detects warped or bent parts, using straightedge. Soaks electric parts in chemical solutions to clean parts. Removes dirt from other parts, using brushes, sandpaper, and soap and water. Reassembles meter, using new or repaired parts. Turns setscrews or makes other adjustments required to bring meter accuracy within prescribed limits. May test meters for accuracy [ELECTRIC-METER TESTER (light, heat, & power)] or for correctness of assembly and dielectric strength, using testing apparatus. May repair demand register mechanism of demand meters. May repair such electric components as instrument transformers and relays. May install meters. • **GED:** R4, M2, L3 • **SVP:** 2-4 yrs • **Academic:** Ed=N, Eng=S • **Work Field:** 111 • **MPSMS:** 581 • **Aptitudes:** G3, V3, N3, S3, P2, Q4, K3, F2, M3, E5, C4 • **Temperaments:** M, T • **Physical:** V=L, H=N, L=L, W, H • **Work Env:** I • **Salary:** 4 • **Outlook:** 4

ELECTRIC-METER TESTER (light, heat, & power) • D.O.T. #821.381-010 • OES #83002 • METER TESTER. Tests accuracy of meters used for recording electric current consumption and makes necessary adjustments: (1) Connects meter to standard (specially calibrated electric meter mechanism) and adjusts standard's dials to meter being tested. Pushes switch and allows needle on standard to revolve specified number of turns or for clocked period. Compares meter and standard calibrated dials to ascertain accuracy of meter. (2) Connects testing instruments, such as wattmeter, voltmeter, and ammeter, across coils of meter and allows load to pass through meter for clocked period. Computes watt-hours of current consumed, using instrument readings and time factor. Compares watt-hour computations with dial on tested meter to determine meter accuracy. Adjusts meters by loosening or tightening screws, using screwdriver. Inspects wiring of installed meters for improper connections or diversions of current. May make minor repairs and recommend meter removal for major repair. May clean mechanism with solution and small brush. May calculate inaccurate meter variations from standard. May set up auxiliary equipment to route current around installed meter during testing to avoid interruption to service. Does not perform tests on inaccurate meters to diagnose malfunctioning if inaccuracy cannot be corrected by screw adjustment [INSIDE-METER TESTER (light, heat, & power)]. May be designated according to types of meters tested as METER TESTER, DEMAND METERS (light, heat, & power); METER TESTER, POLYPHASE (light, heat, & power); METER TESTER, PRIMARY (light, heat, & power); METER TESTER, SINGLE PHASE (light, heat, & power). • **GED:** R4, M4, L3 • **SVP:** 2-4 yrs • **Academic:** Ed=N, Eng=S • **Work Field:** 111 • **MPSMS:** 581 • **Aptitudes:** G3, V3, N3, S3, P2, Q3, K3, F3, M3, E4, C4 • **Temperaments:** M, T • **Physical:** V=L, H=N, L=L, W, II • **Work Env:** I • **Salary:** 4 • **Outlook:** 3

ELECTRIC-MOTOR REPAIRER (any ind.) • D.O.T. #721.281-018 • OES #85714 • Repairs electric motors, generators, and equipment, such as starting devices and switches, following schematic drawings, and using hand tools, coil-winding machines, power tools, and test equipment: Disassembles and removes armature, stator, or rotor from housing. Examines coil connections for broken or defective wiring. Tests coils, armature, stator, rotor, and field coils for continuity, shorts, and grounds and insulation resistance, using test lamp, ammeter, and ohmmeter. Cuts out or removes defective coils and removes insulation from core slots. Cuts and forms insulation and inserts insulation into armature, rotor, or stator slots. Rewinds coils on core while in slots manually or makes replacement coils, using coil winding machine. Installs and aligns prewound coils in slots, using hammer drift or mallet. Replaces defective coil leads and solders connections of coils in specified sequence. Examines bearings, shafts, and other moving parts for excessive wear or defects. Refaces commutators and machines parts to specified tolerances, using machine tools. Assembles and tests motor for specified performance. May be designated according to size of motor repaired as FRACTIONAL-HORSEPOWER MOTOR REPAIRER (any ind.); equipment repaired as DYNAMOTOR REPAIRER (any ind.); or part repaired as ARMATURE STRAIGHTENER (elec. equip.); COIL-CONNECTOR REPAIRER (elec equip.); COMMUTATOR REPAIRER (any ind.); FIELD-COIL REPAIRER (elec. equip.); STATOR REPAIRER (any ind.). • **GED:** R4, M3, L3 • **SVP:** 2-4 yrs • **Academic:** Ed=H, Eng=S • **Work Field:** 111 • **MPSMS:** 582 • **Aptitudes:** G3, V3, N3, S3, P2, Q4, K3, F3, M2, E5, C4 • **Temperaments:** M, T • **Physical:** V=G, H=N, L=M, W, H • **Work Env:** I • **Salary:** 4 • **Outlook:** 3

ELECTRICAL-APPLIANCE SERVICER (any ind.) • D.O.T. #827.261-010 • OES #85711 • APPLIANCE-SERVICE REPRESENTATIVE. Installs, services, and repairs stoves, refrigerators, dishwashing machines, and other electrical household or commercial appliances, using handtools, test equipment, and following wiring diagrams and manufacturer's specifications: Connects appliance to power source and test meters, such as wattmeter, ammeter, or voltmeter. Observes readings on meters and graphic recorders. Examines appliance during operating cycle to detect excess vibration, overheating, fluid leaks, and loose parts. Disassembles appliance and examines mechanical and electrical parts. Traces electrical circuits, following diagram, and locates shorts and grounds, using ohmmeter. Calibrates timers, thermostats, and adjusts contact points. Cleans and washes parts, using wire brush, buffer, and solvent, to remove carbon, grease, and dust. Replaces worn or defective parts, such as switches, pumps, bearings, transmissions, belts, gears, blowers, and defective wiring. Repairs and adjusts appliance motors. Reassembles appliance, adjusts pulleys, and lubricates moving parts, using handtools and lubricating equipment. May be known according to appliance repaired as CLOTHES-DRIER REPAIRER (any ind.); COFFEE-MAKER SERVICER (any ind.); DISHWASHING-MACHINE REPAIRER (any ind.); ELECTRIC-RANGE SERVICER (any ind.); ELECTRIC-REFRIGERATOR SERVICER (any ind.); WASHING-MACHINE SERVICER (any ind.). • **GED:** R4, M3, L3 • **SVP:** 2-4 yrs • **Academic:** Ed=N, Eng=S • **Work Field:** 111 • **MPSMS:** 583 • **Aptitudes:** G3, V3, N3, S3, P3, Q4, K3, F3, M2, E5, C4 • **Temperaments:** M, T, V • **Physical:** V=L, H=N, L=M, W, S, H • **Work Env:** I • **Salary:** 4 • **Outlook:** 3

ELECTRICAL-INSTRUMENT REPAIRER (any ind.) • D.O.T. #729.281-026 • OES #85905 • INSTRUMENT MAKER; INSTRUMENT REPAIRER. Repairs, calibrates, and tests instruments, such as voltmeters, ammeters, resistance bridges, galvanometers, temperature bridges, and temperature controlling and recording gages and instruments, using jewelers' tools, electricians' tools, handtools, and measuring instruments: Tests instruments for resistance, voltage, and other characteristics, using potentiometer, voltage divider, and other testing devices. Disassembles instruments, using handtools, and examines parts for defects. Measures, cuts, and fits glass for meters and instruments, using glass cutter. Repairs or replaces defective parts of instruments, using handtools, soldering equipment, grinders, calipers, micrometers, and dividers. Reassembles instruments, following circuit diagrams and using jewelers' tools. Tests new and repaired instruments, using test board. May operate lathe and drill press to make replacement parts. May plan, construct, and assemble test panels for experimental and production testing. May keep records on repair and calibration of instruments. May rebuild induction cores for electric furnaces. May install, repair, and adjust electronically controlled dynamometers and be known as DYNAMOMETER REPAIRER (elec. equip.). • **GED:** R4, M3, L3 • **SVP:** 1-2 yrs • **Academic:** Ed=N, Eng=S • **Work Field:** 111 • **MPSMS:** 581, 602 • **Aptitudes:** G2, V3, N2, S2, P2, Q3, K3, F3, M2, E5, C3 • **Temperaments:** M, T • **Physical:** V=L, H=N, L=L, H • **Work Env:** I • **Salary:** 4 • **Outlook:** 3

ELECTRICIAN, AUTOMOTIVE (auto. ser.) • D.O.T. #825.281-022 • OES #85728 • Repairs and overhauls electrical systems in automotive vehicles, such as automobiles, buses, and trucks: Confers with customer to determine nature of electrical malfunction. Determines malfunction of electrical system by visual inspection and by use of testing devices, such as oscilloscope, voltmeter, and ammeter. Adjusts ignition timing and measures and adjusts distributor breaker-point gaps, using dwell meter or thickness gage. Tests and repairs starters, generators, and distributors. Repairs or replaces defective wiring in ignition, lighting, air-conditioning, and safety control systems, using electrician's handtools. Rebuilds electrical units, such as starters, generators, and door controls. May estimate cost of repairs based on parts and labor charges. May be designated according to specialty as ELECTRICAL REPAIRER, INTERNAL COMBUSTION ENGINES (auto. ser.; engine & turbine); ELECTRICAL-UNIT REBUILDER (auto. ser.); ELECTRICIAN, BUS (auto. ser.); IGNITION-AND-CARBURETOR MECHANIC (auto. ser.); WINDSHIELD-WIPER REPAIRER (auto. ser.). • **GED:** R4, M3, L3 • **SVP:** 2-4 yrs • **Academic:** Ed=H, Eng=S • **Work Field:** 111 • **MPSMS:** 591 • **Aptitudes:** G3, V3, N3, S3, P2, Q5, K3, F3, M3, E5, C4 • **Temperaments:** M, T, V • **Physical:** V=G, H=N, L=L, W, S, H • **Work Env:** I • **Salary:** 4 • **Outlook:** 4

ELECTRONICS MECHANIC (any ind.) • D.O.T. #828.281-010 • OES #85705 • COMMUNICATION TECHNICIAN; ELECTRONICS-EQUIPMENT MECHANIC; ELECTRONICS SPECIALIST; ELECTRONICS-SYSTEM MECHANIC; ELECTRONICS TECHNICIAN. Repairs electronic equipment, such as computers, industrial controls, radar systems, telemetering and missile control systems, transmitters, antennas, and servomechanisms, following blueprints and manufacturers' specifications, and using handtools and test instruments: Tests faulty equipment and applies knowledge of functional operation of electronic units and systems to diagnose cause of malfunction. Tests electronic components and circuits to locate defects, using oscilloscopes, signal generators, ammeters, and voltmeters. Replaces defective components and wiring and adjusts mechanical parts, using handtools and soldering iron. Alines, adjusts, and calibrates equipment according to specifications. Calibrates testing instruments. Maintains records of repairs, calibrations, and tests. May install equipment in industrial or military establishments and in aircraft and missiles. May operate equipment, such as communication equipment and missile control systems in ground and flight tests, and be required to hold license from governmental agency. May be designated according to type of equipment repaired as CUSTOMER-ENGINEERING SPECIALIST (office mach.); ELECTRONICS MECHANIC, COMPUTER (any ind.); RADAR MECHANIC (any ind.); VOTING MACHINE REPAIRER (gov. Ser.). • **GED:** R4, M4, L4 • **SVP:** 2-4 yrs

yrs • **Academic:** Ed=H, Eng=S • **Work Field:** 111 • **MPSMS:** 580 • **Aptitudes:** G2, V3, N3, S2, P2, Q4, K3, F2, M2, E5, C3 • **Temperaments:** M, T, V • **Physical:** V=G, H=L, L=S, W, H • **Work Env:** I • **Salary:** 4 • **Outlook:** 4

INSTRUMENT MECHANIC (any ind.) • D.O.T. #710.281-026 • OES #85905 • INSTRUMENT-MAINTENANCE MECHANIC. Installs, repairs, maintains, and adjusts indicating, recording, telemetering, and controlling instruments used to measure and control variables, such as pressure, flow, temperature, motion, force, and chemical composition, using handtools and precision instruments: Disassembles malfunctioning instruments, and examines and tests mechanism and circuitry for defects. Troubleshoots equipment in or out of control system and replaces or repairs defective parts. Reassembles instrument and tests assembly for conformance with specifications, using instruments, such as potentiometer, resistance bridge, manometer, and pressure gage. Inspects instruments periodically and makes minor calibration adjustments to ensure functioning within specified standards. May adjust and repair final control mechanisms, such as automatically controlled valves or positioners. May calibrate instruments according to established standards. May be designated according to type of instrument repaired as AIRCRAFT INSTRUMENT REPAIRER (air trans.); METER SERVICER (any ind.); PANEL-INSTRUMENT REPAIRER (any ind.); RADIOLOGICAL INSTRUMENT TECHNICIAN (gov. ser.); X-RAY-CONTROL-EQUIPMENT REPAIRER (any ind.). May perform duties as described under GROUP LEADER (any ind.). • **GED:** R4, M3, L4 • **SVP:** 2-4 yrs • **Academic:** Ed=N, Eng=S • **Work Field:** 111, 121 • **MPSMS:** 602 • **Aptitudes:** G3, V3, N3, S3, P3, Q3, K3, F3, M2, E5, C4 • **Temperaments:** M, T • **Physical:** V=G, H=N, L=L, W, C, S, H • **Work Env:** I, R • **Salary:** 4 • **Outlook:** 3

INSTRUMENT-MAKER AND REPAIRER (petrol. production) • D.O.T. #600.280-014 • OES #89105 • Sets up and operates machine tools to remodel electrical and electronic instruments used in electrical logging, gun perforating, sub-surface surveying, and other oil, gas, or borehole prospecting, testing and servicing operations, following engineering orders and specifications and applying knowledge of electronics, mechanics, metal properties, shop mathematics, and machining procedures: Measures, marks, and scribes dimensions of parts to be made on metal or plastic stock, using layout tools, such as rule, square, or scribe [LAY-OUT WORKER (mach. shop)]. Machines parts to specifications, using machine tools, such as lathes, drill presses, and grinders [MACHINIST (mach. shop)]. Assembles fabricated mechanical parts and such purchased parts as pulleys, springs, and dials, using bolts, screws, tweezers, wrenches, and screwdrivers [INSTRUMENT MAKER (any ind.)]. Installs electrical and electronic parts, such as sockets, switches, and rheostats, in chassis. Connects circuit components, such as tubes, coils, and switches, using wire strippers and soldering iron and following circuit diagrams. Tests instruments to determine conformance to specifications, using equipment, such as voltmeters and ohmmeters. May be designated according to product remodeled or repaired. • **GED:** R4, M4, L2 • **SVP:** 2-4 yrs • **Academic:** Ed=H, Eng=N • **Work Field:** 057, 111, 121 • **MPSMS:** 580, 602 • **Aptitudes:** G3, V3, N3, S2, P3, Q4, K3, F2, M3, E5, C5 • **Temperaments:** M, T, V • **Physical:** V=L, H=N, L=S, H • **Work Env:** I • **Salary:** 4 • **Outlook:** 3

METEOROLOGICAL-EQUIPMENT REPAIRER (any ind.) • D.O.T. #823.281-018 • OES #85905 • ELECTRONICS TECHNICIAN. Installs, maintains, and repairs electronic, mercurial, aneroid, and other types of weather-station equipment, using handtools and electronic testing instruments: Tests meteorological instruments for compliance with printed specifications and schematic diagrams, using voltmeters, oscilloscopes, tube testers, and other test instruments. Replaces defective parts, using handtools and soldering iron. Inspects barometers, thermographs, and hydrographs, including recording mechanisms, and repairs, adjusts, or replaces defective parts. Calibrates graphs and other recording devices. Installs radar and two-way radio systems to detect and communicate weather signals. Adjusts and repairs masts, supporting structures, clearance lights, control panels, control cabling and wiring, and other electrical and mechanical devices and equipment, using handtools. • **GED:** R4, M3, L3 • **SVP:** 2-4 yrs • **Academic:** Ed=H, Eng=S • **Work Field:** 111, 121

• **MPSMS:** 586, 602 • **Aptitudes:** G3, V3, N2, S2, P2, Q3, K3, F3, M2, E5, C3 • **Temperaments:** M, T, V • **Physical:** V=L, H=N, L=M, W, H • **Work Env:** B • **Salary:** 4 • **Outlook:** 2

PINSETTER ADJUSTER, AUTOMATIC (sports equip.) • D.O.T. #829.381-010 • OES #85999 • Inspects and adjusts automatic pinsetters, following blueprints, using hand tools and gages: Inspects pinsetter for defects and missing components following blueprint parts list. Mounts components or returns machine to assembly department for reworking. Rolls pinsetter to test bay and connects drive mechanism and power source. Adjusts microswitches, spring tension, traverse or circuit stops, cams, and other control mechanisms to specified settings, using handtools. Operates pinsetters to detect malfunctioning. Measures and regulates height and sweep of rake, using fixed gage and handtools. Runs machine through complete cycle and inspects for pinsetting accuracy. Tests automatic shutoffs by running undersized pins through mechanism. Examines and adjusts each pin and pickup scissor to correct malfunctions. • **GED:** R4, M3, L3 • **SVP:** 1-2 yrs • **Academic:** Ed=N, Eng=S • **Work Field:** 111 • **MPSMS:** 616 • **Aptitudes:** G3, V3, N3, S3, P4, Q4, K4, F3, M3, E4, C5 • **Temperaments:** M, T • **Physical:** V=L, H=N, L=M, W, S, H • **Work Env:** I • **Salary:** 4 • **Outlook:** 3

PUBLIC-ADDRESS SERVICER (any ind.) • D.O.T. #823.261-010 • OES #85599 • ELECTRONIC-SOUND TECHNICIAN; PUBLIC-ADDRESS-SYSTEM OPERATOR. Installs and repairs sound-amplifying systems used at public and private assemblages, using handtools and electronic test meters: Positions loudspeakers on posts or other supports. Strings cable from loudspeakers to amplifiers. Places microphones in position near speaker, orchestra, or other attraction, and plugs microphone wires into amplifiers. Switches on installation. Listens to sound output and adjusts volume controls or repositions microphones. Tests and repairs equipment in shop, using handtools, soldering iron, and electronic test meters. May test and repair sound recorders, radio and television receivers, and other electronic equipment. May drive sound truck. May install and repair mobile sound-amplifying system in truck and be designated as SOUND-TRUCK OPERATOR (any ind.). • **GED:** R4, M3, L2 • **SVP:** 2-4 yrs • **Academic:** Ed=N, Eng=G • **Work Field:** 111 • **MPSMS:** 585 • **Aptitudes:** G3, V3, N3, S3, P3, Q4, K3, F3, M3, E4, C3 • **Temperaments:** J, M, T • **Physical:** V=L, H=L, L=M, W, C, H • **Work Env:** B • **Salary:** 4 • **Outlook:** 2

RADIO MECHANIC (any ind.) • D.O.T. #823.261-018 • OES #85514 • Tests and repairs radio transmitting and receiving equipment in accordance with diagrams and manufacturer's specifications, using handtools and electrical measuring instruments: Examines equipment for damaged components and loose or broken connections and wires. Replaces defective components and parts, such as tubes, condensers, transformers, resistors, and generators, using handtools. Solders or tightens loose connections and cleans and lubricates motor generators. Tests equipment for factors such as power output, frequency power, noise level, audio quality, and dial calibration, using oscilloscopes, radio frequency and watt meters, ammeters, voltmeters, and tube testers. Tests batteries with hydrometer and ammeter and charges batteries. Inserts plugs into receptacles and bolts or screws leads to terminals to connect radios and equipment to power source, using handtools. Turns setscrews to adjust receivers for sensitivity and transmitters for maximum output. Required to have Federal Communications Commission Radiotelephone Operator's license. May install, test, adjust, modify, and repair intercommunication systems. May specialize in testing and repairing radio transmitting and receiving equipment in motor vehicles and commercial and governmental establishments and be designated as RADIO MECHANIC, GROUND INSTALLATION (any ind.). • **GED:** R4, M3, L3 • **SVP:** 2-4 yrs • **Academic:** Ed=H, Eng=S • **Work Field:** 111 • **MPSMS:** 586 • **Aptitudes:** G3, V3, N3, S3, P2, Q4, K3, F3, M2, E5, C3 • **Temperaments:** M, T, V • **Physical:** V=L, H=N, L=L, H • **Work Env:** I • **Salary:** 4 • **Outlook:** 2

GOE: 05.05.11 Sci., Med. & Tech. Equip. Fabrication & Repair

ARTIFICIAL-PLASTIC-EYE MAKER (optical goods) • D.O.T.

#713.261-014 • OES #89917 • OCULARIST; PLASTIC-EYE TECHNICIAN. Fabricates artificial plastic eyes according to specifications and fits eyes into customer's eye sockets, using precision handtools, measuring instruments, molding devices, and bench fabricating machines: Measures customer's eye socket, using calipers, and measures natural eye to determine size and location of pupil and iris, using scale. Records data on examination card. Selects stock artificial eye approximating size and shape of customer's socket and inserts eye into socket. Fills eye area and questions customer to ascertain that eye fit is comfortable. Applies plastic as required to build up and shape stock eye to conform to customer's eye socket. Examines customer's natural eye to determine iris coloring, eye white shading, and number of eye white veins and records information on examination card. Selects samples of iris, pupil, and white to match eye. Positions artificial eye stock in plaster of paris to prepare mold for casting plastic eye. Pours plastic into mold to form artificial eye. Measures molded eye to determine position for pupil and iris, using rule. Positions and presses pupil and iris into place. Immerses eye in boiling water to set plastic. Paints iris and white of artificial eye to produce color of customer's natural eye according to information recorded on examination card. Draws veins on white of eye, using colored pencil or scratches grooves into eye to represent veins and fills grooves with pigment. Immerses eye in clear plastic solution to produce glassy finish. Examines eye for irregularities in shape and removes irregularities, using dental grinding machine. Polishes eye, using pumice and electric buffing wheel. Fits customer with artificial eye and compares artificial eye with natural eye to insure centering of iris and pupils and matching of colors. May fit patients with ready-to-wear plastic eyes of standard sizes and colors. May fabricate implants (plastic and mesh devices fitted in eye socket for retention of eye muscles) and conformers (plastic disks placed in eye socket to maintain socket shape prior to fitting of artificial eye), using standard molds and grinding and polishing machines. • **GED:** R4, M3, L4 • **SVP:** 4-10 yrs • **Academic:** Ed=H, Eng=S • **Work Field:** 102, 136 • **MPSMS:** 604 • **Aptitudes:** G3, V3, N3, S2, P2, Q4, K2, F2, M3, E5, C2 • **Temperaments:** J, M, P, T • **Physical:** V=L, H=N, L=L, H • **Work Env:** I • **Salary:** 4 • **Outlook:** 2

BIOMEDICAL EQUIPMENT TECHNICIAN (inst. & app.) • D.O.T. #719.261-010 • OES #85908 • Inspects, maintains, repairs, calibrates, and modifies electronic, electrical, mechanical, hydraulic, and pneumatic equipment and instruments used in medical therapy, diagnosis, according to schematic and verbal instructions, using handtools and machine tools: Inspects and tests equipment and apparatus, such as blood-gas analyzers, spectrophotometers, radiation monitors, and microscopes, to insure specified functional qualities according to blueprints and written specifications. Examines and tests equipment to determine cause of malfunction or inaccuracy, using manufacturers's schematics, maintenance manuals, and standard and specialized test instruments, such as oscilloscopes and pressure gages. Disassembles equipment to locate malfunctioning components and repairs or replaces defective parts, such as circuit amplifiers, tubes, rotors, bellows, and motors, using handtools or portable power tools. Reassembles equipment and adjusts and calibrates precision components to insure specified operation, using testing and calibrating instrument. Notifies manufacturer or distributor of incorrectable equipment malfunction to arrange for repair by service personnel. Modifies equipment as directed by supervisory personnel performing such duties as adding to or changing original components to meet specific therapeutic or diagnostic requirements. May specialize in repair and maintenance of specific types of bio-medical equipment, such as that used in radiology, nuclear medicine or patient monitoring operations. May train and direct other BIO-MEDICAL EQUIPMENT TECHNICIANS (inst. & app.; medical ser.); with less experience. May maintain inventory of supplies and parts and reorder items as needed. May install, modify, and test airborne bio-medical instrumentation and be designated VEHICLE INSTRUMENTATION TECHNICIAN (inst. & app.). • **GED:** R5, M5, L3 • **SVP:** 2-4 yrs • **Academic:** Ed=A, Eng=S • **Work Field:** 111 • **MPSMS:** 601, 924 • **Aptitudes:** G3, V3, N1, S1, P3, Q3, K3, F1, M3, E2, C3 • **Temperaments:** J, M, T, V • **Physical:** V=L, H=N, L=M, W, S, H • **Work Env:** I • **Salary:** 4 • **Outlook:** 4

CAMERA REPAIRER (photo. apparatus) • D.O.T. #714.281-014

• OES #85914 • Repairs and adjusts cameras, using specialized tools and test devices: Disassembles camera, using handtools. Tests and alines diaphragm, lens mounts, and film transport to minimize optical distortion, using precision gages. Adjusts range and view finders, using fixed focusing target. Calibrates operation of shutter, diaphragm, and lens carriers with dial settings, using electronic or stroboscopic timing instruments. Fabricates or modifies parts, using bench lathe, grinder, and drill press. • **GED:** R4, M4, L4 • **SVP:** 4-10 yrs • **Academic:** Ed=N, Eng=S • **Work Field:** 121 • **MPSMS:** 606 • **Aptitudes:** G3, V3, N3, S2, P2, Q3, K3, F2, M2, E5, C5 • **Temperaments:** M, T, V • **Physical:** V=L, H=N, L=S, H • **Work Env:** I • **Salary:** 4 • **Outlook:** 3

DENTAL CERAMIST (medical ser.) • D.O.T. #712.281-010 • OES #89921 • CERAMICS TECHNICIAN; CERAMIST. Applies layers of porcelain paste or acrylic resins over metal framework to form dental prosthesis, such as crowns, bridges, and tooth facings, according to DENTIST'S (medical ser.) prescription, using spatula, brushes, and baking oven: Mixes porcelain paste or acrylic resins to color of natural teeth according to prescription. Applies mixture over metal framework, using brushes and spatula. Brushes excess mixture from denture and places denture in oven to harden. Removes denture from furnace, brushes on additional layer of mixture, and shapes mixture to contour of denture, using spatula. Repeats mixture-application process and baking until denture conforms to specifications. Verifies accuracy of tooth dimensions and occlusion of teeth, using micrometer and articulator. May solder metal clasps, positioners, and hooks to removable orthodontic appliances. • **GED:** R3, M3, L3 • **SVP:** 1-2 yrs • **Academic:** Ed=N, Eng=S • **Work Field:** 133, 136 • **MPSMS:** 604, 925 • **Aptitudes:** G3, V3, N3, S2, P2, Q4, K3, F2, M3, E4, C2 • **Temperaments:** J, M, T • **Physical:** V=G, H=N, L=S, H • **Work Env:** I • **Salary:** 3 • **Outlook:** 2

DENTAL CERAMIST ASSISTANT (medical ser.) • D.O.T. #712.664-010 • OES #98999 • PORCELAIN FINISHER; PORCELAIN WAXER. Performs any combination of following tasks to assist DENTAL CERAMIST (medical ser.) in molding dental prostheses, such as crowns, bridges, and tooth facings: Brushes liquid separating solution on tip of tooth die and covers die with wax sheet. Invests wax impressions in plaster molds, and inserts mold in furnace to melt wax. Positions mold in casting machine to cast metal framework. Removes metal framework from mold, using sand blasting equipment or hammer. Smooths rough spots from framework, using abrasive grinding wheel. May mix porcelain or acrylic resin solution to match color of natural teeth, under direction of DENTAL CERAMIST (medical ser.). May fill wax impression of tooth with graphite solution, plate impression in electroplating machine, remove die from machine, and apply acrylic resin to base of die, using spatula, to fabricate copper dies for dentures. • **GED:** R3, M2, L3 • **SVP:** 1-2 yrs • **Academic:** Ed=N, Eng=S • **Work Field:** 102 • **MPSMS:** 604, 925 • **Aptitudes:** G3, V3, N4, S3, P3, Q4, K3, F3, M3, E5, C2 • **Temperaments:** M, T • **Physical:** V=L, H=N, L=S, H • **Work Env:** I • **Salary:** 4 • **Outlook:** 3

DENTAL-LABORATORY TECHNICIAN (medical ser.) • D.O.T. #712.381-018 • OES #89921 • DENTAL TECHNICIAN. Fabricates and repairs full and partial dentures according to DENTIST'S (medical ser.) prescription, using handtools, molding equipment, and bench fabricating machines: Reads prescription and examines models and impressions to determine type of denture to be made or repaired, applying knowledge of oral anatomy and restoration procedures. Positions teeth in wax model in specified plane of occlusal harmony. Molds wax around base of teeth and verifies accuracy of occlusion, using articulator. Molds wax over denture setup to form contours of gums, using knives and spatula. Routes workpiece to DENTAL CERAMIST (medical ser.) for casting. Removes plastic particles and excess plastic from surfaces of cast dentures, using bench lathe equipped with grinding and buffing wheels. Casts plaster models of dentures to be repaired. Selects and mounts replacement teeth in model to match color and shape of natural or adjacent teeth, using color chart and tooth illustrations. Casts plastic reproductions of gums, using acrylics and molding equipment. Fills cracks and separations in dentures with plastic, using knives and spatula. Rebuilds denture linings to duplicate original thickness, contour, and color according to specifications, using plastic. Cures denture plastic in pressure pot or oven. Tests repaired dentures for accuracy of occlusion, using articulator. Polishes metal, plastic, and porce lain surfaces to specified finish, using grinding and buffing wheels. Bends and solders gold and platinum wire to construct wire frames for dentures, using soldering gun and handtools. May fabricate denture wire, using centrifugal casting machine. May confer with DENTIST (medical ser.) to resolve problems in design and setup of dentures. May be designated according to type denture fabricated as DENTAL TECHNICIAN, CROWN AND BRIDGE (medical ser.); DENTAL TECHNICIAN, METAL (medical ser.). • **GED:** R4, M3, L4 • **SVP:** 4-10 yrs • **Academic:** Ed=H, Eng=S • **Work Field:** 102 • **MPSMS:** 604, 925 • **Aptitudes:** G3, V3, N3, S2, P2, Q4, K3, F2, M3, E4, C3 • **Temperaments:** J, M, T, V • **Physical:** V=G, H=N, L=L, H • **Work Env:** I • **Salary:** 3 • **Outlook:** 4

DENTAL-LABORATORY-TECHNICIAN APPRENTICE (medical ser.) • D.O.T. #712.381-022 • OES #89921 • DENTAL-TECHNICIAN APPRENTICE. Performs duties as described under APPRENTICE (any ind.). • **GED:** R4, M3, L4 • **SVP:** 4-10 yrs • **Academic:** Ed=H, Eng=S • **Work Field:** 102 • **MPSMS:** 604, 925 • **Aptitudes:** G3, V3, N3, S2, P2, Q4, K3, F2, M3, E4, C3 • **Temperaments:** J, M, T, V • **Physical:** V=L, H=N, L=L, H • **Work Env:** I • **Salary:** 3 • **Outlook:** 3

DENTURE-MODEL MAKER (medical ser.) • D.O.T. #712.681-014 • OES #93956 • Forms plaster, metal, plastic, or rubber models and molds from dental impressions and wax models of dentures and dental appliances, using casting equipment and handtools: Mixes specified amounts of special plaster and water or other model-making ingredients, by hand or electric mixer-vibrator, to form compound used for models and molds. Pours mixture into impressions to form models for upper and lower dentures. Melts pieces of gold, silver, or other metal, using gas torch, and casts inlays, crowns, and pontics for fixed bridges, using centrifugal casting machine. Packs plastic mixture or composition rubber strips in molds to cast orthodontic appliances, such as tooth positioners, mouthguards, and retainers. Positions models in articulator and verifies occlusions. Packs plaster or other denture-making ingredient around wax model of denture to form model or matrix for casting denture. Places mold in boiling water to melt wax from cast model. Scrapes remaining wax from model, using knife, and washes model in soapy solution to remove dirt and foreign matter. • **GED:** R3, M2, L3 • **SVP:** 6 mos-1 yr • **Academic:** Ed=N, Eng=S • **Work Field:** 132 • **MPSMS:** 604, 925 • **Aptitudes:** G3, V3, N4, S3, P3, Q4, K3, F3, M3, E5, C4 • **Temperaments:** M, T • **Physical:** V=L, H=N, L=L, H • **Work Env:** I • **Salary:** 3 • **Outlook:** 2

ELECTROMECHANICAL TECHNICIAN (inst. & app.) • D.O.T. #710.281-018 • OES #93111 • Fabricates, tests, analyzes, and adjusts precision electromechanical instruments, such as temperature probes, gyroscope units, telemetering systems, altimeters, and aerodynamic probes, following blueprints and sketches, using handtools, metalworking machines, and measuring and testing instruments: Operates metalworking machines, such as bench lathe, milling machine, punch press, and drill press, to fabricate housings, fittings, jigs and fixtures, and verifies dimensions, using micrometer and calipers. Assembles wires, insulation, and electrical components, such as resistors and capacitors, following method layouts, using fixtures, binocular microscope, soldering tools, tweezers, and handtools. Installs electrical assemblies and hardware in housing, using handtools and soldering equipment. Tests assembled instruments for circuit continuity and operational reliability, using multimeter, oscilloscope, oscillator, vacuum tube voltmeter, and bridge. Analyzes test results and repairs or adjusts instruments according to analysis. Records test results and writes report on fabrication techniques used. May calibrate instrument dials according to established standards. May specialize in assembly of prototype instruments and be designated as DEVELOPMENT TECHNICIAN (inst. & app.), or in assembly of production instruments and be designated as FABRICATION TECHNICIAN (inst. & app.). • **GED:** R4, M4, L4 • **SVP:** 2-4 yrs • **Academic:** Ed=H, Eng=S • **Work Field:** 111 • **MPSMS:** 602 • **Aptitudes:** G2, V3, N2, S2, P3, Q4, K3, F3, M2, E5, C4 • **Temperaments:** M, T, V • **Physical:** V=G, H=N, L=S, H • **Work Env:** I • **Salary:** 4 • **Outlook:** 4

ELECTROMEDICAL-EQUIPMENT REPAIRER (any ind.) •

D.O.T. #729.281-030 • OES #85908 • ELECTROMEDICAL SERVICE ENGINEER. Tests and repairs electromedical equipment, such as electrocardiographs, electroencephlographs, sterilizers, operating room lamps and tables, and diathermy machines, following schematic diagrams and using handtools and test meters: Tests electrical circuits and components to locate shorts, faulty connections, and defective parts, using test meters. Solders loose connections and replaces defective parts, such as tubes, transformers, resistors, condensors, and switches, using hand tools and soldering iron. Disassembles equipment and repairs or replaces faulty mechanical parts, such as control lever mechanisms and water impellers. Adjusts and repairs stylus, graph, and other recording mechanisms. May replace X-ray tubes. May be designated according to type of machine or equipment repaired as DIATHERMY-EQUIPMENT REPAIRER (any ind.); ELECTROCARDIOGRAPH REPAIRER (any ind.). • **GED:** R4, M3, L3 • **SVP:** 1-2 yrs • **Academic:** Ed=N, Eng=S • **Work Field:** 111 • **MPSMS:** 589, 604 • **Aptitudes:** G3, V3, N3, S3, P2, Q4, K3, F3, M2, E5, C3 • **Temperaments:** M, T, V • **Physical:** V=L, H=N, L=M, W, H • **Work Env:** I • **Salary:** 4 • **Outlook:** 4

EXPERIMENTAL ASSEMBLER (any ind.) • D.O.T. #739.381-026 • OES #89999 • Assembles, inspects, tests, and adjusts a variety of optical, electrical, and mechanical devices on pilot run basis to improve assembly methods and to discover and correct deficiencies in materials, specifications, and equipment prior to production runs: Reads and interprets blueprints, diagrams, schematics, and narrative instructions to determine required parts and tools and lays out workbench to provide assembly arrangement. Assembles up to 100 units or components of optical, electrical, or mechanical devices, such as slide projectors, plastic tape dispensers, duplicating machines, and ribbon-bow-making machines, using power tools and handtools. Inspects, tests, and adjusts assembled devices for specified functioning, using light meter, ammeter, voltmeter, stopwatch, rulers, feeler gages, spring tension tester, torque tester, and depth micrometer. • **GED:** R4, M4, L4 • **SVP:** 1-2 yrs • **Academic:** Ed=N, Eng=S • **Work Field:** 111 • **MPSMS:** 601, 602, 609 • **Aptitudes:** G3, V3, N3, S3, P2, Q4, K3, F3, M3, E4, C4 • **Temperaments:** M, T, V • **Physical:** V=L, H=N, L=M, W, H • **Work Env:** I • **Salary:** 3 • **Outlook:** 3

FINISHER, DENTURE (medical ser.) • D.O.T. #712.681-018 • OES #93956 • METAL FINISHER; POLISHER. Polishes, cleans, and adjusts dentures and dental appliances to obtain specified finish, using handtools, polishing wheels, and cleaning equipment: Removes mold from flask, using ejector press, and breaks investment from denture, using hammer and chipping tool. Holds denture against polishing machine attachments, such as burs, acrylic trimmers, felt cones, and brush wheels to remove plaster particles, excess plastic from facial, lingual, and palatal surfaces, and to debur and remove flashing from metal surfaces. Removes excess plastic from between teeth, using sharp pointed tool. Fills chipped or low spots in surfaces of plastic areas with acrylic resins, using brush. Repairs and adjusts metal framework of dentures, using soldering iron, welding equipment, drills, and handtools. Holds denture against buffing wheel to obtain natural lustrous finish. Verifies occlusion of dentures, using articulator. Places finished denture in ultrasonic cleaning vessel to remove plastic particles and polishing compound. • **GED:** R3, M2, L3 • **SVP:** 6 mos-1 yr • **Academic:** Ed=N, Eng=S • **Work Field:** 031, 051, 102 • **MPSMS:** 604, 925 • **Aptitudes:** G3, V3, N4, S3, P3, Q4, K3, F3, M3, E5, C4 • **Temperaments:** M, T • **Physical:** V=L, H=N, L=L, H • **Work Env:** I • **Salary:** 3 • **Outlook:** 2

FIRE-CONTROL MECHANIC (gov. ser.) • D.O.T. #632.261-014 • OES #85999 • FIRE-CONTROL TECHNICIAN. Services mechanical, electronic, and optical equipment controlling naval guns, following blueprints and diagrams and using handtools and testing devices: Inspects and cleans optical equipment, installing new eyepieces as necessary. Adjusts and lubricates gyroscope. Repairs and replaces parts of motors and remote control equipment, communications equipment, and electronic equipment, using handtools and standard test equipment. Participates in bore-sighting and alining guns. Tests wiring circuits, following blueprints and diagrams. • **GED:** R4, M3, L3 • **SVP:** 1-2 yrs • **Academic:** Ed=H, Eng=S • **Work Field:** 111 • **MPSMS:** 370 • **Aptitudes:** G2, V3, N2, S2, P2, Q4, K3, F2, M3, E4, C4 • **Temperaments:** J, M, T •

Physical: V=L, H=N, L=M, W, C, S, H • **Work Env:** B • **Salary:** 4 • **Outlook:** 3

INSTRUMENT MAKER (any ind.) • D.O.T. #600.280-010 • OES #89105 • MECHANICAL TECHNICIAN; PARTS MECHANIC; PRECISION-INSTRUMENT AND TOOL MAKER; PRECISION-MECHANICAL-INSTRUMENT MAKER. Fabricates, modifies, or repairs mechanical instruments or mechanical assemblies of electrical or electronic instruments, such as chronometric timing devices, barographs, thermostats, seismographs, and servomechanisms, applying knowledge of mechanics, metal properties, shop mathematics, and machining procedures and using machine tools, welding and heat-treating equipment, precision measuring instruments, and hand tools: Measures, marks, and scribes stock, such as silver, nickel, platinum, steel, ivory, and plastic, following blueprints and engineering sketches, and using square, rule, and scribe to lay out workpiece for machining [LAY-OUT WORKER (mach. shop)]. Sets up and operates machine tools, such as lathes, drill presses, punch presses, milling machines, grinders, brakes, and lapping and polishing machines to machine parts to specifications [MACHINIST (mach. shop)]. Anneals and tempers metal parts [HEAT TREATER (heat treat.) I]. Assembles parts in jig and brazes or welds. Fits and installs precision components, such as timing devices, springs, balance mechanisms, and gear trains in housing, using jeweler's lathe, tweezers, loupe, and handtools. Verifies dimensions of parts and installation of components, using measuring instruments, such as micrometer, calipers, and electronic gages. Coats assembled instrument with protective finish, such as lacquer or enamel, using spray gun. May install wiring and electrical components to specifications. May set up and operate machines to fabricate dies for punch presses [DIE MAKER, BENCH, STAMPING (mach. shop)]. May be designated according to product assembled. • **GED:** R4, M4, L3 • **SVP:** 2-4 yrs • **Academic:** Ed=H, Eng=S • **Work Field:** 057, 121 • **MPSMS:** 566, 580, 609 • **Aptitudes:** G3, V3, N3, S2, P2, Q4, K3, F3, M2, E5, C5 • **Temperaments:** M, T, V • **Physical:** V=L, H=N, L=M, W, H • **Work Env:** I • **Salary:** 4 • **Outlook:** 3

INSTRUMENT REPAIRER (any ind.) • D.O.T. #710.261-010 • OES #85905 • Repairs and calibrates speed ometers and other automotive gages and meters, using handtools and test equipment: Confers with customer to determine nature of malfunction. Inspects components, connections, and drive mechanisms to detect defects. Removes instrument from vehicle and disassembles, cleans, and inspects instrument to determine which parts are defective. Replaces worn and defective parts, using handtools. Tests and calibrates instruments, using mechanical and electronic devices, such as voltmeters, pressure generators, and speedometer tester. Installs instruments in vehicle, using hand tools. Computes speedometer drive ratio changes for modified vehicles. Maintains stock and parts inventory. May operate jeweler's lathe and other machines to fabricate instrument parts. May repair automotive clocks [WATCH REPAIRER (clock & watch)]. • **GED:** R4, M3, L4 • **SVP:** 4-10 yrs • **Academic:** Ed=N, Eng=S • **Work Field:** 111, 121 • **MPSMS:** 602 • **Aptitudes:** G3, V3, N3, S2, P2, Q3, K3, F2, M2, E5, C4 • **Temperaments:** M, P, T • **Physical:** V=L, H=L, L=L, W, S, H • **Work Env:** B • **Salary:** 4 • **Outlook:** 3

LENS MOUNTER 2 (optical goods) • D.O.T. #713.681-010 • OES #89917 • Mounts prescription eyeglass lenses in metal, plastic, or combination frames, using handtools: Examines eyeglass prescription to determine style, color, and size of frame. Inspects lenses to detect flaws, such as pits, chips, and scratches. Holds and turns lenses against grinding wheel to remove flaws. Assembles eyeglass frame and attaches ornaments, shields, nose pads, and temple pieces, using pliers and screwdrivers. Drills holes in lenses for mounting on rimless frames, using diamond drill. Immerses plastic frame rims in hot salt solution to soften rims or stretches rims, using hot, metal cone. Inserts and alines lenses in frame. Verifies frame dimensions and alinement of lenses, using protractor, ruler, and straightedge. Turns lenses in frame to correct alinement, using padded pliers. Immerses plastic frames in cold water to set plastic around lenses. Tightens screws to hold lenses in metal frames. Examines lenses under polarized light to detect stress caused by overtightening screws and adjusts screws as necessary. Heats plastic frame bridge and bends frame according to prescription specifications, using fingers and handtools. Immerses plastic

frames in dye for specified period to color frames. Solders broken metal bridges and replaces damaged temples to repair frames, using soldering iron and handtools. Cleans and polishes finished eyeglasses, using cloth and solvent. May be designated according to type frame mounted as METAL-FRAME INSERTER (optical goods); PLASTIC FRAME INSERTER (optical goods); or according to part assembled as TRIM MOUNTER (optical goods) II. • **GED:** R3, M2, L3 • **SVP:** 1-2 yrs • **Academic:** Ed=N, Eng=S • **Work Field:** 102 • **MPSMS:** 605 • **Aptitudes:** G3, V4, N4, S3, P3, Q4, K3, F3, M3, E5, C4 • **Temperaments:** M, T • **Physical:** V=L, H=N, L=M, H • **Work Env:** I • **Salary:** 3 • **Outlook:** 3

OPTICIAN (optical goods) • D.O.T. #716.280-008 • OES #89917 • FLAT OPTICAL ELEMENT MAKER; OPTICAL MODEL MAKER AND TESTER; PRECISION LENS TECHNICIAN. Sets up and operates machine tools to fabricate optical elements and systems, applying knowledge of layout and machining techniques and procedures, shop mathematics, and properties of optical and abrasive materials: Studies work order, blueprints, and sketches to formulate machining plans and sequences. Measures and marks dimensions and reference points to lay out stock for machining. Selects premixed compounds or mixes grinding, polishing, and holding compounds according to formula. Mounts workpiece on holding fixture, using adhesive, friction, or vacuum. Mounts and secures workpiece and tooling in machines. Operates machines, such as saws, lathes, grinders, milling machines, generators, polishers, and edgers to fabricate optics, fixtures, tools, and mountings of specified sizes and shapes. Grinds and polishes optics, using handtools, as required. Measures and tests optics, using precision measuring and testing instruments. May develop specifications and drawings from verbal description. May perform experimental work and research to develop new production methods and procedures applying shop mathematics and knowledge of production techniques. May train and direct other workers. • **GED:** R4, M4, L4 • **SVP:** 4-10 yrs • **Academic:** Ed=H, Eng=S • **Work Field:** 102 • **MPSMS:** 603 • **Aptitudes:** G3, V3, N3, S2, P2, Q4, K3, F3, M2, E5, C4 • **Temperaments:** M, T, V • **Physical:** V=L, H=N, L=L, H • **Work Env:** I • **Salary:** 4 • **Outlook:** 3

OPTICIAN (optical goods) • D.O.T. #716.280-014 • OES #89917 • OPTICAL MECHANIC. Sets up and operates machines to grind eyeglass lenses to prescription specifications and assembles lenses in frames: Reads lens and frame specifications from prescription. Selects lens blanks from stock. Sets up and operates machines, such as generator, polisher, edger, and hardener, to fabricate lenses to specifications. Mounts lenses in metal, plastic, or rimless frames. Inspects mounted lenses for conformance to specifications [INSPECTOR, EYEGLASS (optical goods)]. Examines broken lenses to identify original lens prescription, using power determining and optical centering instruments. • **GED:** R4, M4, L4 • **SVP:** 4-10 yrs • **Academic:** Ed=A, Eng=S • **Work Field:** 102 • **MPSMS:** 605 • **Aptitudes:** G3, V3, N3, S2, P2, Q4, K3, F3, M2, E5, C4 • **Temperaments:** M, T, V • **Physical:** V=L, H=N, L=L, H • **Work Env:** I • **Salary:** 4 • **Outlook:** 3

OPTICIAN, DISPENSING 1 (ret. tr.) • D.O.T. #713.361-014 • OES #89917 • Designs, fits, and adapts lenses and frames, utilizing written optical prescription: Analyzes prescription in conjunction with client's vocational and avocational visual requirements. Recommends specific lenses for safety and efficiency. Assists client in selecting frames according to style and color, coordinating frames with facial and eye measurements and optical prescription. Measures client's bridge and eye size, temple length, vertex distance, pupillary distance, and optical centers of eyes, using millimeter rule and light reflex pupilometer. Prepares work order and instructions for grinding lenses and fabricating spectacles. Verifies exactness of finished lens spectacles. Adjusts frames and lens position to fit client by heating and shaping plastic and bending metal frames, using pliers and hands. Instructs client on adapting and wearing spectacles and procedures for their care. Sells optical goods, such as binoculars, plano sunglasses, magnifying glasses, and low vision aids. May fit contact lenses only and be designated OPTICIAN, CONTACT-LENS DISPENSING (ret. tr.) I. • **GED:** R4, M4, L4 • **SVP:** 2-4 yrs • **Academic:** Ed=A, Eng=S • **Work Field:** 051, 061, 292 • **MPSMS:** 605, 881 • **Aptitudes:** G2, V2, N3, S3, P3, Q4, K3, F3, M3, E5, C4 • **Temperaments:** J, M, P, T • **Stress:** E • **Physical:** V=L, H=L, L=L, W, H • **Work Env:** I

Salary: 4 • **Outlook:** 4

ORTHODONTIC TECHNICIAN (medical ser.) • D.O.T. #712.381-030 • OES #89921 • Constructs and repairs appliances for straightening teeth according to ORTHODONTIST'S (medical ser.) prescription: Shapes, grinds, polishes, carves, and assembles metal and plastic appliances, such as retainers, tooth bands, and positioners, using spatula, pliers, soldering torch, and electric grinders and polishers. Tests appliance for conformance to specifications, using articulator. • **GED:** R4, M3, L4 • **SVP:** 1-2 yrs • **Academic:** Ed=H, Eng=S • **Work Field:** 102 • **MPSMS:** 604, 925 • **Aptitudes:** G3, V3, N3, S2, P2, Q4, K3, F2, M3, E5, C5 • **Temperaments:** J, M, T • **Physical:** V=L, H=N, L=S, H • **Work Env:** I • **Salary:** 4 • **Outlook:** 3

ORTHOTICS ASSISTANT (per. protect. & med. device) • D.O.T. #078.361-022 • OES #32999 • Assists ORTHOTIST (per. protect. & med. dev.) in providing care to patients with disabling conditions of limbs and spine by fabricating and fitting devices known as orthoses: Under guidance of and in consultation with ORTHOTIST (per. protect. & med. dev.), makes assigned casts, measurements, model modifications, and layouts. Performs fitting, including static and dynamic alinements. Evaluates orthoses on patient to ensure fit, function, cosmesis, and workmanship. Repairs and maintains orthoses. May be responsible for performance of other personnel. May perform functions of PROSTHETICS ASSISTANT (per. protect. & med. dev.) and be designated ORTHOTICS-PROSTHETICS ASSISTANT (per. protect. & med. dev.). • **GED:** R4, M4, L4 • **SVP:** 2-4 yrs • **Academic:** Ed=H, Eng=S • **Work Field:** 102, 294 • **MPSMS:** 604 • **Aptitudes:** G2, V3, N3, S2, P2, Q4, K4, F3, M3, E4, C4 • **Temperaments:** J, P, T • **Stress:** E • **Physical:** V=L, H=N, L=M, H • **Work Env:** I • **Salary:** 4 • **Outlook:** 3

ORTHOTICS TECHNICIAN (per. protect. & med. device) • D.O.T. #712.381-034 • OES #89923 • Fabricates, fits, repairs, and maintains orthoses (orthotic devices, such as braces and surgical supports), according to specifications and under guidance of ORTHOTIST (per. protect. & med. dev.) or ORTHOTICS ASSISTANT (per. protect. & med. dev.): Bends, forms, welds, and saws metal brace structural components to conform to measurements, using hammers, anvils, welding equipment, and saws. Drills and taps holes for rivets, and rivets components together. Shapes plastic and metal around cast of patient's torso or limbs. Covers and pads metal or plastic brace structures, using layers of rubber, felt, plastic, and leather. May also perform functions of PROSTHETICS TECHNICIAN (per. protect. & med. dev.) and be designated ORTHOTICS-PROSTHETICS TECHNICIAN (per. protect. & med. dev.). • **GED:** R4, M3, L4 • **SVP:** 1-2 yrs • **Academic:** Ed=H, Eng=S • **Work Field:** 102 • **MPSMS:** 604 • **Aptitudes:** G3, V3, N3, S3, P3, Q3, K3, F2, M2, E4, C4 • **Temperaments:** J, P, T • **Physical:** V=L, H=N, L=M, W, H • **Work Env:** I • **Salary:** 4 • **Outlook:** 3

ORTHOTIST (per. protect. & med. device) • D.O.T. #078.261-018 • OES #32999 • Provides care to patients with disabling conditions of limbs and spine by fitting and preparing devices known as orthoses, under direction of and in consultation with PHYSICIAN (medical ser.): Assists in formulation of specifications for orthoses. Examines and evaluates patient's orthotic needs in relation to disease entity and functional loss. Formulates design of orthosis. Selects materials, making cast measurements, model modifications, and layouts. Performs fitting, including static and dynamic alinements. Evaluates orthosis on patient and makes adjustments to assure fit, function, cosmesis, and quality of work. Instructs patient in orthosis use. Maintains patient records. May supervise ORTHOTICS ASSISTANTS (per. protect. & med. dev.) and other support personnel. May supervise laboratory activities relating to development of orthoses. May lecture and demonstrate to colleagues and other professionals concerned with orthotics. May participate in research. May perform functions of PROSTHETIST (per. protect. & med. dev.) and be designated ORTHOTIST-PROSTHETIST (per. protect. & med. dev.). • **GED:** R5, M4, L4 • **SVP:** 4-10 yrs • **Academic:** Ed=B, Eng=G • **Work Field:** 102, 294 • **MPSMS:** 604 • **Aptitudes:** G2, V3, N3, S2, P2, Q4, K2, F3, M3, E4, C4 • **Temperaments:** J, P, T • **Stress:** E • **Physical:** V=L, H=N, L=M, H • **Work Env:** I • **Salary:** 4 • **Outlook:** 4

PACKER, DENTURE (medical ser.) • D.O.T. #712.684-034 • OES #93944 • MOLDER. Packs plastic material in molds to form base for full or partial dentures: Mixes specified amounts of plastic powder and chemical solution, using spatula. Packs mixture around base of exposed artificial teeth and into cavities of mold sections. Positions sheet of plastic or wax paper or foil over bottom of mold to permit separation of mold from denture. Fits top section of mold over bottom and places assembly in press. Starts press that forces sections together and compresses mixture around teeth to form reproduction of gums. Removes model from press and trims excess plastic from mold, using knife. Submerges mold in hot water for specified time to cure plastic. • **GED:** R3, M2, L3 • **SVP:** 6 mos-1 yr • **Academic:** Ed=N, Eng=S • **Work Field:** 132 • **MPSMS:** 604, 925 • **Aptitudes:** G3, V4, N4, S3, P3, Q5, K4, F3, M3, E5, C4 • **Temperaments:** M, T • **Physical:** V=L, H=N, L=L, H • **Work Env:** I • **Salary:** 3 • **Outlook:** 2

PROSTHETICS ASSISTANT (per. protect. & med. device) • D.O.T. #078.361-026 • OES #32999 • Assists PROSTHETIST (per. protect. & med. dev.) in providing care to patients with partial or total absence of limb by fabricating and fitting devices known as prostheses: Under direction of PROSTHETIST (per. protect. & med. dev.) makes assigned casts, measurements, and model modifications. Performs fitting, including static and dynamic alinements. Evaluates prosthesis on patient to ensure fit, function, cosmesis, and quality of work. Repairs and maintains prostheses. May be responsible for performance of other personnel. May also perform functions of ORTHOTICS ASSISTANT (per. protect. & med. dev.) [ORTHOTICS-PROSTHETICS ASSISTANT (per. protect. & med. dev.)]. • **GED:** R4, M4, L4 • **SVP:** 2-4 yrs • **Academic:** Ed=H, Eng=S • **Work Field:** 102, 294 • **MPSMS:** 604 • **Aptitudes:** G2, V3, N3, S2, P2, Q4, K4, F3, M3, E4, C4 • **Temperaments:** J, P, T • **Stress:** E • **Physical:** V=L, H=N, L=M, H • **Work Env:** I • **Salary:** 4 • **Outlook:** 3

PROSTHETICS TECHNICIAN (per. protect. & med. device) • D.O.T. #712.381-038 • OES #89923 • RESTORATION TECHNICIAN. Fabricates, fits, maintains, and repairs artificial limbs, plastic cosmetic appliances, and other prosthetic devices, according to prescription specifications and under guidance of PROSTHETIST (per. protect. & med. dev.) or PROSTHETICS ASSISTANT (per. protect. & med. dev.): Reads specifications to determine type of prosthesis to be fabricated and materials and tools required. Lays out and marks dimensions of parts, using precision measuring instruments and templates. Saws, carves, cuts, and grinds wood, plastic, metal, or fabric to fabricate parts, using rotary sawing and cutting machines and hand cutting tools. Drills and taps holes for rivets and screws, using drill press. Glues, welds, bolts, sews, and rivets parts together to form prostheses, such as artificial limbs. Makes wax or plastic impression of patient's amputated area, prepares mold from impression, and pours molten plastic into mold to form cosmetic appliances, such as artificial ear, nose, or hand. Assembles layers of padding over prosthesis and fits and attaches outer covering, such as leather, sheet plastic, or fiberglass, over device, using sewing machine, rivet gun, and handtools. Mixes pigments according to formula to duplicate skin coloring of patient and applies pigments to outer covering of prosthesis. Polishes finished device, using grinding and buffing wheels. Tests prostheses for freedom of movement, alinement of parts, and biomechanical stability, using plumbline, goniometer, and alinement fixtures. May harness prosthesis to patient's stump, applying knowledge of functional anatomy. May instruct patient in use of prosthesis. May also perform functions of ORTHOTICS TECHNICIAN (per. protect. & med. dev.); [ORTHOTICS-PROSTHETICS TECHNICIAN (per. protect. & med. dev.)]. • **GED:** R4, M4, L4 • **SVP:** 1-2 yrs • **Academic:** Ed=H, Eng=S • **Work Field:** 102, 121 • **MPSMS:** 604 • **Aptitudes:** G2, V3, N3, S2, P2, Q4, K3, F2, M2, E4, C3 • **Temperaments:** M, T, V • **Physical:** V=L, H=N, L=M, W, H • **Work Env:** I • **Salary:** 4 • **Outlook:** 3

PROSTHETIST (per. protect. & med. device) • D.O.T. #078.261-022 • OES #32999 • Provides care to patients with partial or total absence of limb by planning fabrication of, writing specifications for, and fitting devices known as prothesis under guidance of and in consultation with PHYSICIAN (medical ser.): Assists PHYSICIAN (medical ser.) in formulation of prescription. Examines and evaluates patient's prosthetic needs in relation to disease entity and functional loss. Formulates design of prosthesis and selects materials and components. Makes casts, measurements, and model modifications. Performs fitting, including static and dynamic alinements. Evaluates prosthesis on patient and makes adjustments to assure fit, function, comfort, and workmanship. Instructs patient in prosthesis use. Maintains patient records. May supervise PROSTHETICS ASSISTANTS (per. protect. & med. dev.) and other personnel. May supervise laboratory activities relating to development of prosthesis. May lecture and demonstrate to colleagues and other professionals concerned with practice of prosthetics. May participate in research. May also perform functions of ORTHOTIST (per. protect. & med. dev.)[ORTHOTIST-PROSTHETIST (per. protect. & med. dev.)]. • **GED:** R5, M4, L4 • **SVP:** 4-10 yrs • **Academic:** Ed=B, Eng=G • **Work Field:** 102, 294 • **MPSMS:** 604 • **Aptitudes:** G2, V3, N3, S2, P2, Q4, K4, F3, M3, E4, C4 • **Temperaments:** J, P, T • **Stress:** E • **Physical:** V=L, H=N, L=M, H • **Work Env:** I • **Salary:** 4 • **Outlook:** 4

RADIOLOGICAL-EQUIPMENT SPECIALIST (medical ser.) • D.O.T. #719.261-014 • OES #85908 • RADIOLOGIC ELECTRONIC SPECIALIST. Tests, repairs, installs, calibrates, and modifies radiological and related equipment used in medical diagnosis and therapy, applying technical knowledge of electronic, radiological, and mechanical systems, and using manuals, test equipment, measuring instruments, handtools, and power tools: Confers with supervisor, manufacturers' representatives, equipment operators, and other workers to discuss and establish work priorities, resolve equipment related problems, and plan installation, modification, and repair procedures. Inspects and tests malfunctioning equipment to determine cause of malfunction, following learned procedures and repair manual instructions, using specialized test and analysis instruments and manufacturers' specifications. Disassembles malfunctioning equipment and removes, replaces, or repairs defective components, and readjusts components to manufacturers' specifications, using handtools, power tools, and measuring instruments. Installs and assembles radiological equipment in designated areas, following installation and assembly manuals, using handtools, power tools, and heavy equipment moving devices, and utilizing knowledge of equipment installation and assembly techniques. Tests and calibrates equipment at regular or required intervals, using test and measuring instruments and handtools to maintain manufacturers' operational specifications. Selects, devises, designs, and installs mechanical or structural hardware, using tools and utilizing knowledge of mechanics and structures to resolve special equipment operation problems and expand application capabilities. Writes narrative reports of work activities to maintain history of equipment repairs and modifications. Fabricates modification hardware, using machine and power tools, handtools, and related equipment. Demonstrates operational procedures for new or modified equipment to users. May work for manufacturer and specialize in particular line of equipment. • **GED:** R5, M5, L5 • **SVP:** 2-4 yrs • **Academic:** Ed=A, Eng=S • **Work Field:** 111, 121 • **MPSMS:** 589 • **Aptitudes:** G2, V2, N2, S2, P2, Q3, K2, F2, M2, E2, C3 • **Temperaments:** J, P, T • **Physical:** V=L, H=L, L=H, W, S, H • **Work Env:** I, R • **Salary:** 4 • **Outlook:** 4

SCIENTIFIC GLASS BLOWER (glass prod.) • D.O.T. #006.261-010 • OES #22599 • GLASS TECHNICIAN; GLASS TECHNOLOGIST. Fabricates, modifies, and repairs experimental and laboratory glass products, using variety of machines and tools, and provides technical advice to scientific and engineering staff on function, properties, and proposed design of products, applying knowledge of glass technology: Confers with scientific or engineering personnel to exchange information and suggest design modifications regarding proposed glass apparatus, such as distillation and high-vacuum systems. Cuts glass tubing of specified type, using cutting tools, such as glass saw and hot-wire cutter. Heats glass tubing until pliable, using gas torch, and blows, bends, and shapes tubing to specified form, using blowhose, handtools, and manual pressure. Performs finishing operations to fabricate glass product or section, using machines and equipment, such as lapping and polishing wheels, spot-welding and sandblasting machines, internal-plating equipment, and drill press. Measures products to verify dimensions, using opticalscanner, micrometers, and calipers, and examines glass coloration for degree of internal stress, using polariscope, to determine annealing requirements. Anneals products, using annealing oven. Joins and seals subassemblies to assemble finished product, using gas torch, handtools, and vacuum

pump. May operate special equipment, such as radio-frequency-fusing machine, to bond glass to metal, quartz, and ceramic materials. May identify glass of unknown composition by heating with gas torch and evaluating curvature, bondability, and color characteristics. May direct and train GLASS BLOWERS, LABORATORY APPARATUS (glass prod.; inst. & app.). May design fixtures for use in production of prototype glass products and prepare sketches for machine-shop personnel. May prepare cost estimates for prototype glass products. May requisition or recommend purchase of materials, tools, and equipment. May specialize in specific types of glass scientific apparatus and have knowledge of effects of special environments on glass, such as radioactivity, vacuums, gasses, chemicals, and electricity. • **GED:** R4, M4, L4 • **SVP:** 4-10 yrs • **Academic:** Ed=H, Eng=S • **Work Field:** 102, 133 • **MPSMS:** 531 • **Aptitudes:** G2, V2, N2, S2, P2, Q3, K2, F2, M2, E5, C2 • **Temperaments:** J, M, P, T • **Physical:** V=L, H=N, L=L, H • **Work Env:** I, R • **Salary:** 5 • **Outlook:** 3

GOE: 05.05.12 Musical Instrument Fabrication & Repair

ACCORDION REPAIRER (any ind.) • D.O.T. #730.281-014 • OES #85921 • Repairs and tunes accordions and concertinas, using handtools: Disassembles instrument and parts, such as base and treble mechanisms, bellows, reed blocks, and manuals (keyboards), using handtools. Moves parts, observing their action to detect defects. Files, realines, and adjusts parts, using handtools. Recovers bellows with sateen and cloth. Glues leather on corners of bellows. Operates woodworking machines and uses handtools to make wood replacement parts. Repairs cracks in celluloid. Solders or removes and replaces defective metal parts. Reassembles instrument and plays notes and chords to determine accuracy of repair. May tune accordion or concertina reeds [ACCORDION TUNER (any ind.)]. May repair electronic accordions, using electronic testing equipment to determine defects and to verify repairs. • **GED:** R4, M3, L3 • **SVP:** 2-4 yrs • **Academic:** Ed=N, Eng=S • **Work Field:** 121 • **MPSMS:** 614 • **Aptitudes:** G3, V3, N4, S2, P3, Q5, K3, F3, M2, E5, C4 • **Temperaments:** J, M, T • **Physical:** V=N, H=G, L=M, W, H • **Work Env:** I • **Salary:** 4 • **Outlook:** 1

ELECTRIC-ORGAN INSPECTOR AND REPAIRER (musical inst.) • D.O.T. #730.281-018 • OES #85708 • Inspects and repairs electric and electronic organs: Plays organ to determine nature of malfunction. Studies circuit diagrams and performs standard tests to locate mechanical, electrical or electronic difficulties. Replaces defective components and wiring and adjusts mechanical parts, using soldering equipment and handtools. Alines, adjusts, and calibrates equipment according to specifications, following circuit diagrams and using alinement tools, handtools, and test equipment. • **GED:** R4, M3, L4 • **SVP:** 1-2 yrs • **Academic:** Ed=N, Eng=S • **Work Field:** 111, 211 • **MPSMS:** 614 • **Aptitudes:** G3, V4, N3, S4, P4, Q4, K4, F3, M3, E3, C4 • **Temperaments:** J, T • **Physical:** V=N, H=G, L=L, H • **Work Env:** I • **Salary:** 4 • **Outlook:** 1

ELECTRONIC-ORGAN TECHNICIAN (any ind.) • D.O.T. #828.261-010 • OES #85708 • ELECTRIC-ORGAN TECHNICIAN. Installs, tests, adjusts, and repairs electronic organs, pianos, or related musical instruments, using circuit diagrams, service manuals, and standard test equipment: Places speakers along wall or in sound chambers, or mounts speakers on wall. Wires speakers to console. Tunes or adjusts instruments and amplification systems, using electronic test equipment and hand tools. May be designated according to specialized function as ELECTRONIC-ORGAN INSTALLER (any ind.); ELECTRONIC-PIANO INSTALLER (any ind.); ORGAN TUNER, ELECTRONIC (any ind.). • **GED:** R4, M3, L3 • **SVP:** 1-2 yrs • **Academic:** Ed=N, Eng=S • **Work Field:** 111 • **MPSMS:** 614 • **Aptitudes:** G2, V3, N3, S2, P3, Q4, K4, F3, M3, E4, C4 • **Temperaments:** J, M, T • **Physical:** V=L, H=L, L=L, W, S, H • **Work Env:** I, N • **Salary:** 4 • **Outlook:** 3

FRETTED-INSTRUMENT MAKER, HAND (musical inst.) • D.O.T. #730.281-022 • OES #89999 • Constructs fretted musical instruments, such as banjos, guitars, and mando lins, by hand, applying knowledge of wood properties and instrument design and construction. May construct bowed instruments [VIOLIN

MAKER, HAND (musical inst.)]. May repair bowed instruments [VIOLIN REPAIRER (any ind.)]. May repair fretted instruments [FRETTED-INSTRUMENT REPAIRER (any ind.)]. May be designated according to instrument made as GUITAR MAKER, HAND (musical inst.). • **GED:** R4, M3, L4 • **SVP:** 4-10 yrs • **Academic:** Ed=N, Eng=S • **Work Field:** 102 • **MPSMS:** 614 • **Aptitudes:** G3, V3, N3, S2, P2, Q4, K3, F2, M2, E5, C4 • **Temperaments:** J, M, T • **Physical:** V=L, H=G, L=L, H • **Work Env:** I • **Salary:** 5 • **Outlook:** 1

FRETTED-INSTRUMENT REPAIRER (any ind.) • D.O.T. #730.281-026 • OES #85921 • Repairs fretted musical instruments, such as banjos, guitars, mandolins, and ukuleles, using handtools: Inspects and plays instrument to determine defects. Disassembles instrument, using handtools. Removes, replaces, and dresses (levels) frets, using handtools. Fits wood and metal replacement parts. Reassembles and strings instrument. Adjusts truss rod and bridge to position neck and strings. Plays notes and chords and adjusts string tension to tune instrument. Replaces skin or plastic heads of banjos. Tests and replaces tubes, replaces defective parts, and solders new parts and loose connections on amplifiers, reverberation units, and pickups of electrically amplified instruments. May repair wood bodies or carve wood replacement parts. May be designated according to instrument repaired as GUITAR REPAIRER (any ind.). • **GED:** R4, M3, L3 • **SVP:** 1-2 yrs • **Academic:** Ed=H, Eng=S • **Work Field:** 102, 111 • **MPSMS:** 614 • **Aptitudes:** G2, V3, N3, S2, P2, Q4, K3, F2, M3, E5, C4 • **Temperaments:** J, M, T • **Physical:** V=N, H=G, L=M, H • **Work Env:** I • **Salary:** 2 • **Outlook:** 2

PERCUSSION-INSTRUMENT REPAIRER (any ind.) • D.O.T. #730.381-042 • OES #85921 • Repairs percussion instruments, such as drums, cymbals, and xylophones: Removes drum tension rod screws and rods by hand or using drum key. Lifts rim hoop from drum shell and cuts drumhead from hoop. Cuts new drum head from animal skin, using scissors. Soaks skin in water until it becomes pliable. Stretches skin over rim hoop and tucks it around and under hoop, using hand-tucking tool. Reclamps rim hoop onto drum shell to allow drumhead to dry and become taut. Cuts out section around break in drum shells, and cuts new piece to fit, using powersaw and handtools. Glues and clamps new piece in place. Removes dents in tympani, using steel-hitting block. Operates drill press or hand power drill to drill hole at inside end of crack in cymbal, gong, or similar instruments, to prevent advance of crack, and cuts out section around crack, using shears or grinding wheel. Repairs bass drum and tympani foot-mechanisms, and replaces percussion-instrument hardware, such as tension rods and rim hoops, and xylophone and marimba bars and wheels as needed, using handtools. Performs other duties, such as sanding, painting, and cleaning drum shells, and regluing simulated pearl onto shells. May solder or weld frames of mallet instruments and metal drum parts. May lay out and shape laminated wood, and apply decorative trim to fabricate drum shells, using handtools, machine tools, blueprints, and shop drawings and be designated DRUM-SHELL MAKER (musical inst.). • **GED:** R3, M2, L2 • **SVP:** 1-2 yrs • **Academic:** Ed=N, Eng=N • **Work Field:** 102, 121 • **MPSMS:** 614, 881 • **Aptitudes:** G3, V4, N4, S3, P3, Q4, K3, F2, M3, E3, C5 • **Temperaments:** M, T, V • **Physical:** V=N, H=L, L=M, H • **Work Env:** I, N • **Salary:** 4 • **Outlook:** 1

PIANO TECHNICIAN (any ind.) • D.O.T. #730.281-038 • OES #85921 • Repairs, refinishes, and tunes pianos, using specialized tools and gages: Tests components, such as keyboard, pedals, and action assembly, using special tools and gages. Levels keys by inserting paper shims. Detaches action mechanism and replaces faulty, worn, or broken parts, such as hammers, shanks, and joint connections. Alines hammers and turns screws to adjust striking action of keys [PIANO REGULATOR-INSPECTOR (musical inst.)]. Replaces broken or missing strings [PIANO STRINGER (musical inst.)]. Tunes strings, using tuning hammer and fork [PIANO TUNER (any ind.)]. Examines wooden parts for splits, warps, and other defects. Repairs, replaces, resurfaces, and refinishes wooden parts. • **GED:** R3, M2, L2 • **SVP:** 2-4 yrs • **Academic:** Ed=N, Eng=N • **Aptitudes:** G3, V3, N2, S3, P3, Q4, K3, F3, M2, E4, C5 • **Temperaments:** J, M, T, V • **Physical:** V=N, H=G, L=M, W, S, H • **Work Env:** I • **Salary:** 3 • **Outlook:** 3

PIANO TUNER (any ind.) • D.O.T. #730.361-010 • OES #85921 • TONAL REGULATOR; TUNER. Tunes pianos in private and public establishments, using tuning fork and tuning hammer: Removes board from front of piano to expose strings. Places strips of felt or rubber between strings nearest to string to be tested to mute them. Strikes middle C and compares pitch with that of standard tuning fork. Turns string pin with tuning hammer to adjust tension on string until pitch of string and tuning fork correspond. Tunes remaining notes (strings) by comparing them with middle C and each other. May make initial adjustment of piano strings in factory [CHIP TUNER (musical inst.)]. • **GED:** R3, M2, L3 • **SVP:** 6 mos-1 yr • **Academic:** Ed=N, Eng=S • **Work Field:** 121 • **MPSMS:** 614 • **Aptitudes:** G3, V3, N4, S3, P3, Q4, K3, F3, M3, E5, C5 • **Temperaments:** J, T • **Physical:** V=N, H=G, L=S, W, S, H • **Work Env:** I • **Salary:** 2 • **Outlook:** 3

PIPE-ORGAN INSTALLER (musical inst.) • D.O.T. #730.381-046 • OES #93197 • ORGAN INSTALLER. Assembles and installs components of electrically or mechanically controlled pipe organs, using handtools and following blueprints: Installs and wires components, such as air chests, console, blowers, and airducts, using handtools. Mounts pipes above air chest in predetermined pattern. Secures pipes in wooden racks and fastens racks to chest, using dowels and screws. May tune, maintain, and repair organs [PIPE-ORGAN TUNER AND REPAIRER (any ind.)]. May voice pipes [ORGAN-PIPE VOICER (musical inst.)]. • **GED:** R4, M3, L3 • **SVP:** 2-4 yrs • **Academic:** Ed=N, Eng=S • **Work Field:** 111, 121 • **MPSMS:** 614 • **Aptitudes:** G3, V3, N3, S2, P3, Q4, K3, F3, M3, E5, C5 • **Temperaments:** M, T, V • **Physical:** V=L, H=N, L=M, W, C, S, H • **Work Env:** I, R • **Salary:** 4 • **Outlook:** 1

PIPE-ORGAN TUNER AND REPAIRER (any ind.) • D.O.T. #730.361-014 • OES #85921 • Tunes and services pipe organs: Directs helper to depress organ console key and strikes tuning fork to sound A above middle C. Adjusts pitch of organ A pipes to conform with pitch of tuning fork and adjusts pitch of other pipes with references to pitch of other pipes with reference to pitch of tuned pipes by any combination of following methods: (1) Raises or lowers tuning slides and stoppers of metal and wooden pipes. (2) Rolls or unrolls curled strips of metal across tuning holes of metal pipes. (3) Pinches or spreads metal lips that protrude from mouths of metal pipes. Flares or closes metal pipes, using cone-shaped tool. Cleans pipes, using vacuum cleaner, and repairs or replaces worn parts of pipes, console, bellows, and blower, using handtools and power tools, such as pliers and electric sander. May assemble and install new pipe organs in buildings, such as churches and theatres [PIPE-ORGAN INSTALLER (musical inst.)]. • **GED:** R4, M3, L3 • **SVP:** 4-10 yrs • **Academic:** Ed=N, Eng=S • **Work Field:** 111, 121 • **MPSMS:** 614 • **Aptitudes:** G3, V4, N4, S3, P3, Q4, K4, F3, M3, E4, C5 • **Temperaments:** J, M, T • **Physical:** V=L, H=G, L=M, W, C, S, H • **Work Env:** I, N • **Salary:** 5 • **Outlook:** 1

VIOLIN MAKER, HAND (musical inst.) • D.O.T. #730.281-046 • OES #89999 • Constructs bowed musical instruments, such as violins, cellos, and violas, using hand tools: Selects wood according to type, grain, and seasoning. Lays out parts to be cut, using templates. Saws, carves, and shapes instrument parts, using handtools. Glues parts together, using jigs, forms, and clamps. Finishes surface with stain and varnish. Strings instrument. Plays instrument to evaluate tonal quality. Relocates bridge and sounding post, or shaves wood from bottom of instrument to improve tone. May repair bowed instruments [VIOLIN REPAIRER (any ind.)]. May construct fretted instruments [FRETTED-INSTRUMENT MAKER, HAND (musical inst.)]. May repair fretted instruments [FRETTED-INSTRUMENT REPAIRER (any ind.)]. May rebuild and restore bowed instruments and be designated as VIOLIN RESTORER (musical inst.). • **GED:** R4, M3, L3 • **SVP:** 4-10 yrs • **Academic:** Ed=N, Eng=S • **Work Field:** 102 • **MPSMS:** 614 • **Aptitudes:** G3, V3, N3, S2, P2, Q4, K3, F2, M2, E5, C3 • **Temperaments:** J, M, T • **Physical:** V=L, H=G, L=L, H • **Work Env:** I • **Salary:** 5 • **Outlook:** 1

WIND-INSTRUMENT REPAIRER (any ind.) • D.O.T. #730.281-054 • OES #85921 • Repairs, cleans, and alters brass-wind and woodwind musical instruments: Inspects instrument, moves mechanical parts, or plays scale to determine defects. Unscrews and removes rod pins, keys, pistons, and other parts. Removes soldered parts, using gas torch. Reshapes parts, using handtools. Removes dents, using mallet or burnishing tool. Fills cracks in wood instruments by (1) inserting pinning wire into crack and covering wire with filler, (2) operating lathe to cut groove around crack, applying filler, and clamping retaining band into groove, using hand-operated press. Solders patches over cracks in brass instruments, using silver solder, and files patched area to contour of instrument. Resolders parts, using silver or soft solder. Operates lathe to cut off end of metal tubing, or solders attachments onto tubing to improve instrument's tone or intonation. Washes metal in lacquer-stripping solution and cyanide solution to remove lacquer coating and tarnish. Removes burs from instrument valves, using scraping tool. Laps valves and pistons so they move freely. Heats key cups to melt shellac and removes pads. Polishes instruments, using rag and polishing compound, buffing wheel, or burnishing tool. Glues new pads and cork pieces on key cups, using hot shellac. Bends and cuts replacement springs and screws them into place. May be designated according to type of instrument repaired as BRASS-WIND-INSTRUMENT REPAIRER (any ind.); WOODWIND-INSTRUMENT REPAIRER (any ind.). • **GED:** R4, M2, L2 • **SVP:** 2-4 yrs • **Academic:** Ed=N, Eng=N • **Work Field:** 121 • **MPSMS:** 614, 881 • **Aptitudes:** G3, V3, N4, S3, P3, Q4, K3, F2, M2, E5, C5 • **Temperaments:** J, M, T, V • **Physical:** V=N, H=G, L=M, H • **Work Env:** I • **Salary:** 4 • **Outlook:** 2

GOE: 05.05.13 Printing

ASSISTANT-PRESS OPERATOR (print. & pub.) • D.O.T. #651.585-010 • OES #92543 • FLEXOGRAPHIC-PRESS HELPER; OFFSET-PRESS-OPERATOR HELPER; WEB-PRESS-OPERATOR ASSISTANT. Performs any combination of following duties to assist printing press operator to make ready, operate, and maintain roll-fed (web) or sheet-fed, single-or-multi-color flatbed, cylinder, offset, flexographic, or web press: Assists press operator to install paper packing sheets on impression (back-up) cylinder, fasten reinforcing bars to metal printing plates and offset blankets, and install plates and blankets on press cylinders, using handtools and power tools. Adjusts machine parts, such as feed and delivery mechanisms, suction grippers, guides, feed wheels, jogging device, tapes, and cams as directed by press operator, using handtools. Lifts and positions roll of paper in feed mechanism, using chain hoist, or positions skid of unprinted sheets on feed device, using handtruck or electric lift-truck. Removes loaded skid of printed material from stacking mechanism, using handtruck, and replaces with empty skid. Fills fountains with ink paste, using spatula. Tends press in absence of press operator. Observes mechanical operation and indicating gages, such as ammeter and air pressure gages to insure that specified operating levels are maintained and makes specified adjustments or notifies press operator when malfunction occurs. Assists in lubrication of press, using grease gun and oilcan. Assists press operator to remove and replace worn rollers and adjust pressure between rollers, using handtools. Cleans ink and distributing rollers, ink fountains, and printing type, using cleaning solvent, brush, and rags. Cleans press and work area, using vacuum cleaner, brush, and airhose. Keeps daily time, production, and material usage reports. May assist in exposing and developing printing plates. May regulate temperature of gas-fired drying units. May be required to serve apprenticeship. • **GED:** R3, M2, L2 • **SVP:** 1-2 yrs • **Academic:** Ed=N, Eng=N • **Work Field:** 191 • **MPSMS:** 567 • **Aptitudes:** G3, V4, N3, S3, P3, Q4, K3, F3, M3, E5, C4 • **Temperaments:** M, T • **Physical:** V=G, H=N, L=M, W, S, H • **Work Env:** I, N • **Salary:** 3 • **Outlook:** 2

COMPOSITOR (print. & pub.) • D.O.T. #973.381-010 • OES #89702 • TYPESETTER; TYPOGRAPHER. Sets type by hand and machine, and assembles type and cuts in a galley, for printing articles, headings, and other printed matter, determining type size, style, and compositional pattern from work order: Measures copy with line gage to determine length of line. Sets composing stick to line length indicated on line gage. Selects type from type case and sets it in compositional sequence, reading from copy. Inserts spacers between words or units to balance and justify lines. Transfers type from stick to galley when setup is complete. Inserts leads, slugs, or lines of quads between lines to adjust length of setup. Prepares proof copy of setup, using proof press. Examines proof for errors, corrects setup, and forwards it to imposing stone or bank.

Cleans type after use and distributes it to specified boxes in type case. May set type to print copy that is unaccompanied by specifications, using knowledge of composition and printing processes. May be designated as JOB COMPOSITOR (print. & pub.) when setting type in commercial printing establishments or AD COMPOSITOR (print. & pub.) when assembling type and cuts for display advertisements. • **GED:** R4, M2, L3 • **SVP:** 4-10 yrs • **Academic:** Ed=A, Eng=G • **Work Field:** 191 • **MPSMS:** 480, 567 • **Aptitudes:** G2, V3, N3, S3, P2, Q2, K3, F2, M3, E5, C5 • **Temperaments:** M, T • **Physical:** V=G, H=N, L=L, H • **Work Env:** I • **Salary:** 5 • **Outlook:** 1

CYLINDER-PRESS OPERATOR (print. & pub.) • D.O.T. #651.362-010 • OES #92515 • FLATBED-PRESS OPERATOR; PRESS OPERATOR. Makes ready and operates cylinder-type printing press: Verifies size, color, and type of paper and color of ink from job order. Cleans inking rollers with solvent and replaces them in press, using handtools. Adjusts controls to regulate volume of ink. Packs impression cylinder with tissue or folio. Adjusts delivery tapes, and positions and locks form (type setup or plate) on bed or cylinder of press. Directs CYLINDER- PRESS FEEDER (print. & pub.) in adjustment of feed guides, grip pers, and elevator, or hand-feeding press. Starts press and runs off proofsheet. Examines proof to determine off-level areas, variation in ink volume, register slippage, indications of off setting, and color register. Adjusts press controls, inking fountains, and automatic feeders, and repacks cylinder with overlay to equalize off-level areas as required. May register forms and mix colors. May make overlay for half-tone shades. May operate cylinder press equipped with cutting attachment or may replace type dies with cutting dies to cut or shape paper or paperboard. May operate more than one press. May be designated according to kind of material printed as CHECK IMPRINTER (print. & pub.); ENVELOPE-PRESS OPERATOR (print. & pub.) I; LABEL-PRESS OPERATOR (print. & pub.) I; size of press as PONY-CYLINDER-PRESS OPERATOR (print. & pub.). Important variations may be indicated by trade names of machine used. • **GED:** R4, M3, L3 • **SVP:** 2-4 yrs • **Academic:** Ed=N, Eng=S • **Work Field:** 191 • **MPSMS:** 567 • **Aptitudes:** G3, V3, N3, S3, P2, Q4, K3, F3, M3, E5, C3 • **Temperaments:** M, T, V • **Physical:** V=L, H=N, L=M, W, H • **Work Env:** I, N • **Salary:** 4 • **Outlook:** 2

ELECTROTYPER (print. & pub.) • D.O.T. #974.381-010 • OES #89799 • Fabricates and finishes duplicate electrotype printing plates, according to specifications, using handtools, electroplating equipment, and metal casting, trimming, and forming machines: Forms plastic mold of composed type and cuts, using sheet-molding fiber and hydraulic press. Sprays mold with silver solution and immerses mold in plating tank. Separates mold from plated shell and fills back of shell with molten lead to form plate, using pouring ladle or casting machine. Removes excess metal from edges and back of plate, using power shear and milling machines. Examines plate to detect imperfect formation of halftone dots, lines, and type, using magnifier, and corrects defects, using engraver's hand tools, punches, and hammer. Mounts finished plates on wood or metal blocks for flatbed presses or curves plate for cylinder presses, using hammer, nails, bonding press, or plate-curving machine. Removes excess metal from nonprinting areas of plate surface, using radial or cylindrical routing machine. May operate proof press to obtain proof of plate reproduction and registration. May revise plates to customer's specifications. May be known according to task performed as ELECTROTYPE CASTER (print. & pub.); ELECTROTYPE MOLDER (print. & pub.). • **GED:** R4, M3, L3 • **SVP:** 4-10 yrs • **Academic:** Ed=A, Eng=G • **Work Field:** 191 • **MPSMS:** 480, 567 • **Aptitudes:** G3, V3, N3, S3, P2, Q4, K3, F3, M4, C3 • **Temperaments:** M, T • **Physical:** V=G, H=N, L=M, W, H • **Work Env:** I, W, R • **Salary:** 5 • **Outlook:** 1

JOB PRINTER (print. & pub.) • D.O.T. #973.381-018 • OES #89705 • COUNTRY PRINTER; PRINTER. Sets type according to copy and operates cylinder or automatic platen press to print complete job order: Selects type from type case and inserts in printer's stick to reproduce material in copy. Inserts spacers between words and leads between lines. Slides type from stick into galley. Removes assembled type from galley and places type on composing stone. Places chase over type, inserts quoins, and locks chase to hold type. Lays form (type in locked chase) on bed of proof press, inks type, fastens sheet of paper to press roller, and pulls roller over form to make proof copy. Reads proof for errors and clarity of impression. Corrects errors by resetting type and improves impression by tapping face of type with hammer. Positions form (type in locked chase) on bed of press and tightens clamps, using wrench. Fills ink fountain and moves lever to adjust flow of ink. Sets feed guides according to size and thickness of paper. Runs proofsheet through press and examines sheet for clarity of impression. Pushes button to start press, examines printed sheets, and adjusts press when printing is defective. Cleans ink rollers at end of run. • **GED:** R4, M2, L3 • **SVP:** 4-10 yrs • **Academic:** Ed=A, Eng=G • **Work Field:** 191 • **MPSMS:** 480, 567 • **Aptitudes:** G2, V3, N3, S3, P3, Q3, K3, F2, M3, E4, C3 • **Temperaments:** M, T, V • **Physical:** V=G, H=N, L=M, W, H • **Work Env:** I, N • **Salary:** 5 • **Outlook:** 3

OFFSET-PRESS OPERATOR 1 (print. & pub.) • D.O.T. #651.482-010 • OES #92512 • LITHOGRAPHIC-PRESS OPERATOR. Makes ready and operates offset printing press to print single and multicolor copy from lithographic plates, examining job order to determine press operating time, quantity to be printed, and stock specifications: Washes plate to remove protective gum coating. Builds up back of plate with sheets of folio to raise plate to printing level. Installs plate with backing on plate cylinder and locks in position, using handtools. Applies folio to blanket cylinder to build up to diameter of plate cylinder. Fills ink fountains. Adjusts space between blanket and impression cylinders according to thickness of paper stock. Adjusts controls to regulate moisture delivery to plate cylinder. Operates press to secure proof copy. Examines proof and adjusts press controls to obtain specific color registration. Starts press and completes production run. Removes and cleans plate and cylinders at end of run. • **GED:** R4, M2, L3 • **SVP:** 2-4 yrs • **Academic:** Ed=N, Eng=S • **Work Field:** 191 • **MPSMS:** 567 • **Aptitudes:** G3, V3, N3, S3, P2, Q4, K3, F3, M3, E5, C3 • **Temperaments:** M, T, V • **Physical:** V=G, H=N, L=L, H • **Work Env:** I, N • **Salary:** 4 • **Outlook:** 2

ROTOGRAVURE-PRESS OPERATOR (print. & pub.) • D.O.T. #651.362-026 • OES #92519 • Makes ready and operates rotary-type press that prints illustrative and other subject matter by rotogravure process: Installs engraved copper printing cylinder in press, using handtools. Adjusts doctor (wiper) blade to remove excess ink from surface of printing cylinder. Threads web (roll) of paper or other printing stock through press, adjusting guides and tension bars. Sets focus of electronic scanners on guideline of paper (for multicolor printing) to automatically control color registration. Regulates temperature in web-drying chambers and adjusts automatic cutter at discharge end of press. Inspects material being printed, during production run, and adjusts press as required to produce printed matter to specifications. Directs workers in feeding and unloading press, replenishing ink supply in fountains, cleaning equipment, and other press operations. May operate press equipped to print, cut, and crease paper goods. • **GED:** R3, M2, L2 • **SVP:** 2-4 yrs • **Academic:** Ed=N, Eng=N • **Work Field:** 191 • **MPSMS:** 567 • **Aptitudes:** G3, V3, N3, S3, P2, Q4, K3, F3, M3, E5, C3 • **Temperaments:** M, T, V • **Physical:** V=L, H=N, L=M, W, H • **Work Env:** I, N • **Salary:** 4 • **Outlook:** 2

STEREOTYPER (print. & pub.) • D.O.T. #974.382-014 • OES #89799 • Operates machines to press face of composed type and plates into wood-fiber mat to form stereotype casting mold, pour molten metal into mold, and finish castings by cutting, shaving, and trimming to form plates for printing: Drills matching holes in series of mounted color plates to be duplicated and inserts pilot pins in base to register all plates to key plate for mat molding. Lays sheet of mat paper on form or plates, covers with molding blanket and protective sheet, and pushes to self-feeding rollers of mat-rolling machine or into cavity of hydraulic press. Adjusts time, temperature, and pressure controls to form and dry mold. Cuts and pastes pieces of paper felt or cardboard in large non-printing areas of mat to prevent collapse during casting of plate. Alines and notches mats of series with key color mat (mold), using matching machine with monocolor magnifier attachment. Alines notices with pins of trimming machine and pushes lever to trim three edges of mat simultaneously. Lays mat on casting box platen and arranges steel bars on three sides of mat to confine molten type metal. Pours metal into casting box by hand or operates on auto-

matic stereo type plate-casting machine. Trims plates to specified size [PLATE FINISHER (print. & pub.)]. Coats curved plates with nickel [PLATER (electroplating)]. May register series of color plates and mats by transparent acetate overlay process. May be designated according to task performed as STEREOTYPE CASTER (print. & pub.); STEREOTYPE MOLDER (print. & pub.). • **GED:** R4, M2, L2 • **SVP:** 4-10 yrs • **Academic:** Ed=A, Eng=N • **Work Field:** 191 • **MPSMS:** 567 • **Aptitudes:** G3, V3, N3, S3, P3, Q4, K3, F3, M2, E5, C5 • **Temperaments:** M, T • **Physical:** V=G, H=N, L=M, W, H • **Work Env:** I • **Salary:** 5 • **Outlook:** 1

WEB-PRESS OPERATOR (print. & pub.) • D.O.T. #651.362-030 • OES #92515 • Makes ready and operates multiunit, web-fed rotary press to print newspapers, books, and periodicals according to written specifications: Locks printing plates on printing cylinder and threads loose end of paper supply roll (web) through and around rollers to cutter and folder. Adjusts compensators to guide paper over rollers and cylinders. Inspects printed sheets visually after registration or position printing and readjusts guides and controls to rectify spacing errors. Adjusts feed controls to rotate cylinder into position where plate locking mechanism is accessible. Unlocks plates and replaces with make-over plates according to directions marked on plate regarding location and time of printing. Rethreads paper through press if web breaks (press stops automatically if web breaks) and readjusts tension rollers. Operates pasting device to splice end of new paper roll to depleted roll. Inspects printed material visually during production and readjusts controls to correct irregular ink distribution, faulty cuts or folds. Replaces cutting blades, worn or damaged ink rolls, and fills ink wells. Cleans, inspects, and lubricates moving parts of press. May supervise and instruct apprentices. May load supply rolls of paper in press at beginning and during run. May be designated TENSION REGULATOR (print. & pub.) when installing paper rolls in press and adjusting controls to regulate tension of paper; or COLOR-CONTROL OPERATOR (print. & pub.) when adjusting ink controls to secure specified color registration. May operate press from central control console. • **GED:** R4, M3, L3 • **SVP:** 2-4 yrs • **Academic:** Ed=N, Eng=S • **Work Field:** 191 • **MPSMS:** 567 • **Aptitudes:** G3, V3, N3, S3, P3, Q4, K4, F3, M3, E4, C4 • **Temperaments:** M, T • **Physical:** V=L, H=N, L=M, W, H • **Work Env:** I, N • **Salary:** 4 • **Outlook:** 2

GOE: 05.05.14 Gem Cutting & Finishing

STONE SETTER (jewelry) • D.O.T. #700.381-054 • OES #89126 • JEWELRY SETTER. Sets precious, semiprecious, or ornamental stones in rings, earrings, bracelets, brooches, metal optical frames, and other jeweled items, using handtools: Places item in vise. Cuts and files setting to accommodate stones, using files, chisels, and hand or electric drills. Positions stone in setting and fixes in place by pressing prongs around stone, by raising retaining metal ridge around stone, or by tapping edges of setting with setting tool and hammer, forcing metal against stone. Smooths edges, using emery file and pointed steel tool. Examines union of stone and setting, using magnifying glass. May drill holes in settings preparatory to setting stones in piece. May replace stones in rings. May be designated according to stone set as DIAMOND SETTER (jewelry) or according to item worked on as STONE SETTER, METAL OPTICAL FRAMES (optical goods). • **GED:** R3, M2, L2 • **SVP:** 2-4 yrs • **Academic:** Ed=N, Eng=N • **Work Field:** 061 • **MPSMS:** 605, 611 • **Aptitudes:** G3, V3, N3, S2, P2, Q4, K2, F2, M3, E5, C5 • **Temperaments:** M, T, V • **Physical:** V=L, H=N, L=L, H • **Work Env:** I • **Salary:** 3 • **Outlook:** 2

GOE: 05.05.15 Custom Sewing, Tailoring & Upholstering

ALTERATION TAILOR (garment) • D.O.T. #785.261-010 • OES #89505 • ALTERER; BUSHELER. Alters clothing to fit individual customers or repairs defective garments, following alteration or repair tags or marks on garments: Examines tag or garment to ascertain necessary alterations. Removes stitches from garment, using ripper or razor blade. Shortens or lengthens sleeves and legs, expands or narrows waist and chest, raises or lowers collar, and inserts or eliminates padding in shoulders while maintaining drape and proportions of garment. Trims excess material, using scissors. Resews garment, using needle and thread or sewing machine. Repairs or replaces defective garment parts, such as pockets, pocket flaps, and coat linings. May fit garments on customer to determine required alterations [GARMENT FITTER (ret. tr.)]. May press garment, using hand iron [PRESSER, HAND (any ind.)] or pressing machine [PRESSER, MACHINE (any ind.)]. May be designated according to type of garment altered or repaired as TAILOR, MEN'S READY-TO-WEAR (ret. tr.); TAILOR, WOMEN'S-GARMENT ALTERATION (ret. tr.); or according to garment part altered or repaired as PANTS BUSHELER (ret. tr.); VEST BUSHELER (ret. tr.). • **GED:** R4, M3, L3 • **SVP:** 2-4 yrs • **Academic:** Ed=N, Eng=S • **Work Field:** 171 • **MPSMS:** 440 • **Aptitudes:** G3, V3, N3, S2, P3, Q4, K3, F2, M3, E4, C3 • **Temperaments:** J, M, T • **Physical:** V=L, H=N, L=L, H • **Work Env:** I, N • **Salary:** 4 • **Outlook:** 3

AUTOMOBILE UPHOLSTERER (auto. ser.) • D.O.T. #780.381-010 • OES #89508 • Repairs or replaces upholstery in automobiles, buses, and trucks: Removes old upholstery from seats and door panels of vehicle. Measures new padding and covering materials, and cuts them to required dimensions, using knife or shears. Adjusts or replaces seat springs and ties them in place. Sews covering material together, using sewing machine. Fits covering to seat frame and secures it with glue and tacks. Repairs or replaces convertible tops. Refurbishes interiors of streetcars and buses by replacing cushions, drapes, and floor coverings. May be designated according to specialty as BODY TRIMMER (auto. ser.); BUS UPHOLSTERER (auto. ser.); TOP INSTALLER (auto. ser.). • **GED:** R3, M2, L3 • **SVP:** 1-2 yrs • **Academic:** Ed=N, Eng=S • **Work Field:** 101 • **MPSMS:** 591 • **Aptitudes:** G3, V3, N3, S3, P3, Q4, K3, F3, M3, E4, C4 • **Temperaments:** M, T, V • **Physical:** V=L, H=N, L=M, W, S, H • **Work Env:** I • **Salary:** 3 • **Outlook:** 2

BOOKBINDER (print. & pub.) • D.O.T. #977.381-010 • OES #89721 • BOOKMAKER. Cuts, sews, and glues components to bind books, using sewing machine, handpress, and handcutter: Folds printed sheets to form signatures (sections) and gathers signatures into numerical order. Sews signatures together to form book body, using sewing machine. Compresses sewed signatures to reduce book to required thickness, using handpress or smashing machine. Trims edges of book to size, using handcutter. Inserts book body in device that forms back edge of book into convex shape and produces grooves to facilitate attachment of cover. Applies glue to back of book and attaches cloth backing and head band. Applies color to edges of signatures, using brush, pad, or atomizer. Cuts binder board to specified cover size using board shears or handcutter. Cuts cover material, such as leather or cloth, to specified size and fits and glues material to binder board. Glues outside end sheet to cover. Places bound book in press that exerts pressure on cover until glue dries. May imprint cover with gold lettering or designs, using stamping machine. May rebind damaged or worn books. • **GED:** R3, M2, L2 • **SVP:** 2-4 yrs • **Academic:** Ed=N, Eng=N • **Work Field:** 102 • **MPSMS:** 486 • **Aptitudes:** G3, V3, N4, S3, P3, Q4, K3, F3, M2, E4, C3 • **Temperaments:** M, T, V • **Physical:** V=L, H=N, L=L, H • **Work Env:** I • **Salary:** 3 • **Outlook:** 2

CUSTOM TAILOR (garment) • D.O.T. #785.261-014 • OES #89505 • MADE-TO-MEASURE TAILOR; TAILOR. Develops designs and makes tailored garments, such as suits, topcoats, overcoats, and other dress clothing, applying principles of garment design, construction, and styling: Confers with customer to determine type of material and garment style desired. Measures customer for size and records measurements for use in preparing patterns and making garment. Develops designs for garments or copies existing designs. Draws individual pattern for garment or alters standard pattern to fit customer's measurements. Outlines patterns of garment parts on fabric and cuts fabric along outlines, using scissors. Assembles garments, sewing padding to coat fronts, lapels, and collars to give them shape and joining garment parts with basting stitches, using needle and thread or sewing machine. Fits basted garment on customer and marks areas requiring alterations. Alters garment and joins parts, using needle and thread or sewing machine. Sews buttons and buttonholes to finish garment. May press garment [PRESSER, HAND (any ind.); PRESSER, MACHINE (any ind.)]. May supervise activities of other workers in tailoring shop. May specialize in making garments and be designated accordingly as COAT TAILOR (garment).

May perform specific tasks in tailor shop and be designated as COAT FITTER (garment); TRY-ON BASTER (garment). • **GED:** R4, M3, L3 • **SVP:** 4-10 yrs • **Academic:** Ed=N, Eng=S • **Work Field:** 171, 264 • **MPSMS:** 440 • **Aptitudes:** G2, V2, N3, S2, P3, Q4, K2, F2, M3, E4, C3 • **Temperaments:** J, M, T • **Physical:** V=L, H=N, L=L, H • **Work Env:** I, N • **Salary:** 5 • **Outlook:** 4

DRESSMAKER (any ind.) • D.O.T. #785.361-010 • OES #89505 • Makes women's garments, such as dresses, coats, and suits, according to customer specifications and measurements: Discusses with customer type of material, pattern, or style to be used in making garment. Measures customer to determine modification from pattern, using tape measure. Positions and pins pattern sections, such as collar, sleeve, or waist, on fabric, and cuts fabric with scissors following pattern edge. Pins or bastes together fabric parts in preparation for final sewing. Sews fabric parts by hand or operates single-needle sewing machine that joins fabric parts to form garment. Sews felling stitch in hem of garment by hand to conceal thread. Presses garment, using hand iron, to smooth seams and remove wrinkles [PRESSER, HAND (any ind.)]. May draft standard pattern according to measurements of customer and adapt pattern to obtain specified style. May make garment according to picture furnished by customer. • **GED:** R3, M3, L3 • **SVP:** 2-4 yrs • **Academic:** Ed=N, Eng=S • **Work Field:** 171 • **MPSMS:** 440, 909 • **Aptitudes:** G3, V3, N4, S3, P3, Q4, K3, F3, M3, E4, C3 • **Temperaments:** M, T, V • **Physical:** V=G, H=N, L=S, H • **Work Env:** I • **Salary:** 3 • **Outlook:** 3

FURNITURE UPHOLSTERER (any ind.) • D.O.T. #780.381-018 • OES #89508 • UPHOLSTERER. Repairs and rebuilds upholstered furniture, using handtools and knowledge of fabrics and upholstery methods: Removes covering, webbing, and padding from seat, arms, back, and sides of workpiece, using tack puller, chisel, and mallet. Removes defective springs by cutting cords or wires that hold them in place. Replaces webbing and springs or reties springs [SPRINGER (furn.)]. Measures and cuts new covering material [UPHOLSTERY CUTTER, MACHINE (furn.)]. Installs material on inside of arms, back, and seat, and over outside back and arms of wooden frame. Tacks or sews ornamental trim, such as braid and buttons, to cover or frame [UPHOLSTERY TRIMMER (furn.)]. May operate sewing machine to seam cushions and join various sections of covering material. May repair wooden frame of workpiece. May refinish wooden surfaces [FURNITURE FINISHER (woodworking)]. May upholster cornices and be designated CORNICE UPHOLSTERER (any ind.). May repair seats, carpets, curtains, mattresses, and window shades of railroad coaches and sleeping cars and be designated UPHOLSTERER (r.r. trans.). • **GED:** R4, M3, L3 • **SVP:** 2-4 yrs • **Academic:** Ed=N, Eng=S • **Work Field:** 101 • **MPSMS:** 460 • **Aptitudes:** G3, V3, N3, S2, P2, Q4, K3, F3, M2, E5, C3 • **Temperaments:** M, T • **Physical:** V=L, H=N, L=M, W, S, H • **Work Env:** I • **Salary:** 2 • **Outlook:** 3

FURRIER (fur goods) • D.O.T. #783.261-010 • OES #89599 • FUR REPAIRER; FUR TAILOR. Designs, makes, alters, restyles, and repairs fur garments, applying principles of fur garment construction and styling. May purchase pelts required to make garment. May estimate cost of making, repairing, or restyling garment. May sell furs [SALESPERSON, FURS (ret. tr.)]. • **GED:** R4, M3, L3 • **SVP:** 4-10 yrs • **Academic:** Ed=N, Eng=S • **Work Field:** 171, 264 • **MPSMS:** 447 • **Aptitudes:** G2, V2, N3, S2, P3, Q4, K2, F3, M3, E4, C3 • **Temperaments:** J, M, T • **Physical:** V=L, H=N, L=L, H • **Work Env:** I, N • **Salary:** 5 • **Outlook:** 2

RUG REPAIRER (clean., dye., & press.) • D.O.T. #782.381-018 • OES #89599 • Repairs and remodels rugs and carpets: Cuts patch from corner or edge of defective rug, or from carpet material or another rug of similar color and pattern for use in repair of damaged rug. Darns holes in rug-backing by hand, using cross-stitch to sew fibers together. Selects matching rug fibers and stitches them to rug-backing with needle and thread to reburl (reweave) damaged area and restore nap (pile). Patches rug by stitching edges of rug and patch together with carpet stitch. Remodels rugs by cutting to required size and shape, using hand shears. Binds edges of rugs by operating serging machine, or sews edges of rug or carpet, using needle and thread. • **GED:** R3, M2, L3 • **SVP:** 1-2 yrs • **Academic:** Ed=N, Eng=S • **Work Field:** 171 • **MPSMS:** 431 • **Aptitudes:** G3, V4, N3, S3, P3, Q4, K3, F2, M3,

E4, C3 • **Temperaments:** M, T, V • **Physical:** V=L, H=N, L=M, W, S, H • **Work Env:** I • **Salary:** 4 • **Outlook:** 2

SHOE REPAIRER (per. ser.) • D.O.T. #365.361-014 • OES #89511 • COBBLER; SHOEMAKER. Repairs or refinishes shoes, following customer specifications, or according to nature of damage, or type of shoe: Positions shoe on last and pulls and cuts off sole or heel with pincers and knife. Starts machine and holds welt against rotating sanding wheel or rubs with sandpaper to bevel and roughen welt for attachment of new sole. Selects blank or cuts sole or heel piece to approximate size from material, using knife. Brushes cement on new sole or heel piece and on shoe welt and shoe heel. Positions sole over shoe welt or heel piece on shoe heel and pounds, using machine or hammer, so piece adheres to shoe; drives nails around sole or heel edge into shoe; or guides shoe and sole under needle of sewing machine to fasten sole to shoe. Trims sole or heel edge to shape of shoe with knife. Holds and turns shoe sole or heel against revolving abrasive wheel to smooth edge and remove excess material. Brushes edge with stain or polish and holds against revolving buffing wheels to polish edge. Nails heel and toe cleats to shoe. Restitches ripped portions or sews patches over holes in shoe uppers by hand or machine. Dampens portion of shoe and inserts and twists adjustable stretcher in shoes or pull portion of moistened shoe back and forth over warm iron to stretch shoe. May build up portions of shoes by nailing, stapling, or stitching additional material to shoe sole to add height or make other specified alterations to orthopedic shoes. May repair belts, luggage, purses, and other products made of materials, such as canvas, leather, and plastic. May quote charges, receive articles, and collect payment for repairs [SERVICE-ESTABLISHMENT ATTENDANT (clean., dye., & press.; laund.; per. ser.)]. • **GED:** R3, M2, L1 • **SVP:** 2-4 yrs • **Academic:** Ed=N, Eng=N • **Work Field:** 102 • **MPSMS:** 961 • **Aptitudes:** G3, V3, N4, S3, P3, Q4, K3, F3, M2, E3, C4 • **Temperaments:** M, T • **Physical:** V=L, H=N, L=S, H • **Work Env:** I • **Salary:** 2 • **Outlook:** 3

SHOP TAILOR (garment) • D.O.T. #785.361-022 • OES #89505 • Performs specialized hand and machine sewing operations in manufacture of made-to-measure or ready-to-wear clothing, applying knowledge of garment construction and fabrics: Trims and shapes edges of garment parts preparatory to sewing and cuts excess material from seam edges, using shears or knife. Fits collar facing to underfacing, trims edge of undercollar with shears, and sews undercollar to collar. Bastes collar or sleeves to coat body and sews collar or sleeves to coat with permanent stitches. Stitches shoulder padding, coat facing, and lining together at armhole. Bastes and sews canvas material in various coat parts, such as undercollar, shoulder, and front edge. Joins shoulder padding to coat with basting stitches. May sew on buttons and make buttonholes to finish suits. May be designated according to tasks performed or garments sewn as COAT BASTER (garment; ret. tr.); COAT PADDER (garment; ret. tr.); COLLAR SETTER (garment; ret. tr.); LAPEL PADDER (garment; ret. tr.); SLEEVE TAILOR (garment; ret. tr.); SUIT FINISHER (garment; ret. tr.); Additional titles: TOP-COLLAR MAKER (garment; ret. tr.); UNDERCOLLAR BASTER (garment; ret. tr.); UNDERCOLLAR MAKER (garment; ret. tr.); VEST TAILOR (garment; ret. tr.). • **GED:** R4, M3, L3 • **SVP:** 2-4 yrs • **Academic:** Ed=N, Eng=N • **Work Field:** 171 • **MPSMS:** 440 • **Aptitudes:** G3, V3, N3, S3, P3, Q4, K3, F3, M3, E4, C3 • **Temperaments:** J, M, T • **Physical:** V=G, H=N, L=S, H • **Work Env:** I, N • **Salary:** 3 • **Outlook:** 3

GOE: 05.05.17 Food Preparation, Craft Technology

ANALYST, FOOD AND BEVERAGE (hotel & rest.) • D.O.T. #310.267-010 • OES #39999 • RESEARCH WORKER, KITCHEN. Examines food samples and food service records and other data to determine sales appeal and cost of preparing and serving meals and beverages in establishments, such as restaurants and cafeterias or for chain of food establishments: Tastes food samples to determine palatability and customer appeal. Estimates number of servings obtainable from standard and original recipes and unit cost of preparation. Converts recipes for use in quantity preparation. Studies reservation lists and previous records and forecasts customer traffic and number of servings required for specified

period of time. May investigate complaints relative to faulty cooking or quality of ingredients. May plan menus. May specialize in industrial-employee food service or cafeteria food service. May supervise FOOD-AND-BEVERAGE CONTROLLER (hotel & rest.) and kitchen employees. • **GED:** R5, M4, L4 • **SVP:** 4-10 yrs • **Academic:** Ed=A, Eng=G • **Work Field:** 211, 251 • **MPSMS:** 903 • **Aptitudes:** G2, V2, N2, S3, P3, Q3, K3, F3, M3, E5, C3 • **Temperaments:** D, M, P, T • **Physical:** V=N, H=N, L=S, H • **Work Env:** I • **Salary:** 3 • **Outlook:** 3

CAKE DECORATOR (bake. prod.) • D.O.T. #524.381-010 • OES #89899 • PASTRY DECORATOR. Decorates cakes and pastries with designs, using icing bag or handmade paper cone: Trims uneven surfaces of cake or cuts and shapes cake to required size, using knife. Spreads icing between layers and on surfaces of cake, using spatula. Tints white icing with food coloring. Inserts die of specific design into tip of bag or paper cone and fills bag or cone with colored icing. Squeezes bag to eject icing while moving bag with free-arm writing motions to form design on cake. Forms decorations on flower nail and transfers decorations to cake, using spatula. May mix icing. • **GED:** R3, M2, L2 • **SVP:** 1-2 yrs • **Academic:** Ed=N, Eng=N • **Work Field:** 146 • **MPSMS:** 384 • **Aptitudes:** G3, V4, N4, S4, P3, Q4, K3, F3, M3, E5, C3 • **Temperaments:** F, J • **Physical:** V=L, H=N, L=L, H • **Work Env:** I • **Salary:** 2 • **Outlook:** 2

CHEF (hotel & rest.) • D.O.T. #313.131-014 • OES #61099 • COOK, CHIEF; KITCHEN CHEF. Supervises, coordinates, and participates in activities of cooks and other kitchen personnel engaged in preparing and cooking foods in hotel restaurant, cafeteria, or other establishment: Estimates food consumption, and requisitions or purchases foodstuffs. Receives and checks foodstuffs and supplies for quality and quantity. Selects and develops recipes. Supervises personnel engaged in preparing, cooking, and serving meats, sauces, vegetables, soups, and other foods. Cooks or otherwise prepares food according to recipe [COOK (hotel & rest.)]. Cuts, trims, and bones meats and poultry for cooking. Portions cooked foods, or gives instructions as to size of portions and methods of garnishing. Carves meat. May employ, train, and discharge workers. May maintain time and payroll records. May plan menus. Usually found in small establishments not employing a number of skilled specialists. See EXECUTIVE CHEF (hotel & rest.) when worker's duties are typically limited to supervising kitchen staff, planning menus, and purchasing foodstuffs. May be designated according to cuisine specialty as CHEF, FRENCH (hotel & rest.); CHEF, GERMAN (hotel & rest.); CHEF, ITALIAN (hotel & rest.); or according to food specialty as CHEF, BROILER OR FRY (hotel & rest.); CHEF, SAUCIER (hotel & rest.). May supervise workers preparing food for banquets and be designated BANQUET CHEF (hotel & rest.). • **GED:** R4, M4, L4 • **SVP:** 2-4 yrs • **Academic:** Ed=H, Eng=N • **Work Field:** 146 • **MPSMS:** 903 • **Aptitudes:** G3, V3, N3, S4, P3, Q3, K3, F4, M3, E5, C4 • **Temperaments:** D, J, P, V • **Stress:** E • **Physical:** V=G, H=N, L=M, W, H • **Work Env:** I, H • **Salary:** 4 • **Outlook:** 4

CHEF DE FROID (hotel & rest.) • D.O.T. #313.281-010 • OES #65026 • Designs and prepares decorated foods and artistic food arrangements for buffets in formal restaurants: Confers with EXECUTIVE CHEF (hotel & rest.) and SOUS CHEF (hotel & rest.) and reviews advance menus to determine amount and type of food to be served and decor to be carried out. Prepares foods, such as hors d'oeuvres, cold whole salmon, roast suckling pig, casseroles, and fancy aspics, according to recipe and decorates them following customer's specifications, designated color scheme, or theme, using colorful fruit, vegetables, and relishes. Molds butter into artistic forms, such as dancing girls or animals. Sculptures blocks of ice, using chisels and ice picks. Carves meats in patron's presence employing showmanship. May prepare cold meats, casseroles, and other foods during slack periods [GARDE MANGER (hotel & rest.)]. • **GED:** R4, M3, L3 • **SVP:** 2-4 yrs • **Academic:** Ed=N, Eng=S • **Work Field:** 146 • **MPSMS:** 903 • **Aptitudes:** G3, V3, N3, S2, P2, Q3, K2, F2, M3, E5, C3 • **Temperaments:** F, J, M, V • **Physical:** V=L, H=N, L=M, W, H • **Work Env:** I, C, H • **Salary:** 4 • **Outlook:** 4

COOK (hotel & rest.) • D.O.T. #313.361-014 • OES #65026 • COOK, RESTAURANT. Prepares, seasons, and cooks soups, meats, vegetables, desserts, and other foodstuffs for consumption in hotels and restaurants: Reads menu to estimate food requirements and orders food from supplier or procures it from storage. Adjusts thermostat controls to regulate temperature of ovens, broilers, grills, roasters, and steam kettles. Measures and mixes ingredients according to recipe, using variety of kitchen utensils and equipment, such as blenders, mixers, grinders, slicers, and tenderizers, to prepare soups, salads, gravies, desserts, sauces, and casseroles. Bakes, roasts, broils, and steams meats, fish, vegetables, and other foods. Adds seasoning to foods during mixing or cooking, according to personal judgment and experience. Observes and tests food being cooked by tasting, smelling, and piercing with fork to determine that it is cooked. Carves meats, portions food on serving plates, adds gravies, sauces, and garnishes servings to fill orders. May supervise other cooks and kitchen employees. May wash, peel, cut, and shred vegetables and fruits to prepare them for use. May butcher chickens, fish, and shellfish. May cut, trim, and bone meat prior to cooking. May bake bread, rolls, cakes, and pastry [BAKER (hotel & rest.)]. May price items on menu. Usually found in establishments having only a few employees. May be designated according to meal cooked or shift worked as COOK, DINNER (hotel & rest.); COOK, MORNING (hotel & rest.); or according to food item prepared as COOK, ROAST (hotel & rest.); or according to method of cooking as COOK, BROILER (hotel & rest.). May substitute for and relieve or assist other cooks during emergencies or rush periods and be designated COOK, RELIEF (hotel & rest.). May prepare and cook meals for institutionalized patients requiring special diets and be designated as FOOD-SERVICE WORKER (hotel & rest.). Additional titles: COOK, DESSERT (hotel & rest.); COOK, FRY (hotel & rest.); COOK, NIGHT (hotel & rest.); COOK, SAUCE (hotel & rest.); COOK, SOUP (hotel & rest.); COOK, SPECIAL DIET (hotel & rest.); COOK, VEGETABLE (hotel & rest.). • **GED:** R4, M3, L3 • **SVP:** 2-4 yrs • **Academic:** Ed=H, Eng=S • **Work Field:** 146 • **MPSMS:** 903 • **Aptitudes:** G3, V3, N3, S4, P3, Q3, K4, F4, M3, E5, C4 • **Temperaments:** J, T, V • **Physical:** V=G, H=N, L=M, W, H • **Work Env:** I • **Salary:** 4 • **Outlook:** 4

DIETETIC TECHNICIAN (profess. & kin.) • D.O.T. #077.121-010 • OES #32523 • Provides services in assigned areas of food service management, teaches principles of food and nutrition, and provides dietary counseling, under direction of DIETITIAN (profess. & kin.): Plans menus based on established guidelines. Standardizes recipes and tests new products for use in facility. Supervises food production and service. Selects, schedules, and conducts orientation and in-service education programs. Develops job specifications, job descriptions, and work schedules. Assists in implementing established cost control procedures. Obtains and evaluates dietary histories of individuals to plan nutritional programs. Guides individuals and families in food selection, preparation, and menu planning, based upon nutritional needs. Assists in referrals for continuity of patient care. • **GED:** R5, M4, L5 • **SVP:** 4-10 yrs • **Academic:** Ed=A, Eng=G • **Work Field:** 282, 296 • **MPSMS:** 903 • **Aptitudes:** G2, V3, N3, S3, P3, Q3, K4, F4, M3, E5, C4 • **Temperaments:** D, M, P, V • **Stress:** E • **Physical:** V=L, H=L, L=L • **Work Env:** I • **Salary:** 4 • **Outlook:** 3

DIETITIAN, CLINICAL (profess. & kin.) • D.O.T. #077.127-014

• OES #32521 • DIETITIAN, THERAPEUTIC. Plans and directs preparation and service of diets prescribed by PHYSICIAN (medical ser.): Consults medical, nursing, and social service staffs concerning problems affecting patients' food habits and needs. Formulates menus for therapeutic diets based on indicated physiologic and psychologic needs of patients and integrates them with basic institutional menus. Inspects meals served for conformance to prescribed diets and standards of palatability and appearance. Instructs individuals and their families on nutritional principles, dietary plans, food selection, and preparation. May engage in research. May teach nutrition and diet therapy to DIETETIC INTERNS (profess. & kin.), medical and nursing staff, and students [DIETITIAN, TEACHING (profess. & kin.)]. • **GED:** R5, M4, L5 • **SVP:** 2-4 yrs • **Academic:** Ed=B, Eng=G • **Work Field:** 295 • **MPSMS:** 924 • **Aptitudes:** G2, V2, N3, S3, P3, Q3, K4, F4, M4, E5, C4 • **Temperaments:** D, J, M, P • **Stress:** E • **Physical:** V=L, H=L, L=S • **Work Env:** I • **Salary:** 4 • **Outlook:** 4

SOUS CHEF (hotel & rest.) • D.O.T. #313.131-026 • OES #61099 • CHEF ASSISTANT; CHEF, UNDER; EXECUTIVE-CHEF ASSISTANT; SUPERVISING-CHEF ASSISTANT. Supervises and coordinates activities of COOKS (hotel & rest.) and other workers engaged in preparing and cooking foodstuffs: Observes workers engaged in preparing, portioning, and garnishing foods to insure that methods of cooking and garnishing and sizes of portions are as prescribed. Gives instructions to cooking personnel in fine points of cooking. Cooks and carves meats, and prepares dishes, such as sauces, during rush periods and for banquets and other social functions. Assumes responsibility for kitchen in absence of EXECUTIVE CHEF (hotel & rest.). In establishments not employing an EXECUTIVE CHEF (hotel & rest.), may be designated SUPERVISING CHEF (hotel & rest.). • **GED:** R4, M3, L3 • **SVP:** 4-10 yrs • **Academic:** Ed=N, Eng=S • **Work Field:** 146, 295 • **MPSMS:** 903 • **Aptitudes:** G3, V3, N3, S4, P3, Q3, K3, F4, M3, E5, C4 • **Temperaments:** D, J, M, P, V • **Stress:** E • **Physical:** V=L, H=L, L=M, W, H • **Work Env:** I, H • **Salary:** 5 • **Outlook:** 4

TESTER, FOOD PRODUCTS (any ind.) • D.O.T. #199.251-010 • OES #39999 • CONSULTANT; DIRECTOR OF CONSUMER SERVICES; NUTRITION CONSULTANT. Develops, tests, and promotes various types of food products: Selects recipes from conventional cookbooks, or develops new recipes for company food products. Prepares and cooks food according to recipe to test quality and standardize procedures and ingredients. Evaluates prepared item as to texture, appearance, flavor, and nutritional value. Records amount and kinds of ingredients and various test results. Suggests new products, product improvements, and promotions for company use or for resale to dealers, manufacturers, or other users. Presents food items at demonstration functions to promote desired qualities, nutritional values, and related characteristics. Samples shipments to verify weights, measures, coding data, and other evaluations for product control. Answers consumer mail. • **GED:** R4, M3, L4 • **SVP:** 1-2 yrs • **Academic:** Ed=H, Eng=S • **Work Field:** 146, 211, 292 • **MPSMS:** 380, 390, 395 • **Aptitudes:** G3, V2, N3, S4, P3, Q3, K4, F4, M2, E5, C4 • **Temperaments:** I, J, M, P, T • **Stress:** E • **Physical:** V=L, H=L, L=L, H • **Work Env:** I • **Salary:** 4 • **Outlook:** 2

05.06 Systems Operation

Workers in this group operate and maintain equipment in an overall system, or a section of a system, for such purposes as generating and distributing electricity; treating and providing water to customers; pumping oil from oilfields to storage tanks; making ice in an ice plant; and providing telephone service to users. These jobs are found in utility companies, refineries, construction projects, large apartment houses and industrial establishments, and with city and county governments.

✔ **What kind of work would you do?**
Your work activities would depend upon your specific job. For example, you might:

- coordinate activities of power-line crews and workers in generating stations and substations to ensure adequate production and distribution of power.
- watch panelboard and adjust throttle and valves to regulate turbines which generate electricity.

- operate and maintain steam engines, air compressors, generators, motors, and steam boilers to provide heat and power to a building complex.
- study gas supplies and customer demands to coordinate flow of natural gas through pipes.

✔ **What skills and abilities do you need for this kind of work?**
To do this kind of work, you must be able to:

- learn the functioning of the overall system, as well as the part you are involved in.
- use judgment and make decisions to keep the system operating.

- remain calm in the face of emergencies.
- use arithmetic.
- direct the work of others.
- use eyes, hands, and fingers to operate or adjust equipment.

✔ **How do you know if you would like or could learn to do this kind of work?**
The following questions may give you clues about yourself as you consider this group of jobs.

- Have you taken shop or mechanical drawing courses? Do you enjoy working with machines?
- Have you taken courses that required you to solve problems by using mathematical formulas?
- Have you taken physics courses? Do you understand the principles of electricity?

- Have you operated a model train layout? Can you spot and correct malfunctions?
- Have you subscribed to or read on a regular basis magazines about mechanics?
- Have you worked in electricity, electronics, or mechanics in the armed forces?

✔ **How can you prepare for and enter this kind of work?**
Occupations in this group usually require education and/or training extending from one year to over ten years, depending upon the specific kind of work. Operators of systems which transmit oil or natural gas usually start as helpers. High school and vocational school courses in machine shop, mechanical drawing, mathematics, and physics are helpful.

Water and sewage treatment plants are usually government operated and jobs usually require civil service examinations.

Workers who operate boilers usually enter through apprenticeship programs lasting up to four years. It is also possible to become an operator after several years of experience as an assistant. However, this type of preparation usually takes longer. Some states require operators of various types of equipment to have licenses.

Operators of generating or distributing systems for electricity usually start as manual workers. They advance as they become experienced. One to four years of experience is usually required to develop the necessary knowledge and skills. Some cities and states require licenses for these workers.

Workers in atomic-powered plants must have special training. Some of them must be licensed by appropriate nuclear regulatory commissions or authorities.

✔ **What else should you consider about these jobs?**
Many systems are operated 24 hours a day and require one or more operators to be on duty at all times. Work hours often include weekends and holidays. Sometimes shift work is required.

Operators of boilers are sometimes exposed to high temperatures, dust, dirt, and fumes. They may have to crawl inside boilers and work in cramped spaces to inspect, clean, or repair interiors.

If you think you would like to do this kind of work, look at the job titles listed below.

GOE: 05.06.01 Electricity Generation & Transmission

CABLE MAINTAINER (light, heat, & power) • D.O.T. #952.464-010 • OES #85928 • Maintains pressure in oil-filled and gas-filled cables used to transmit high-voltage electricity: Computes amount of oil or gas required for given section of cable, using standard specifications. Pumps oil or gas into cable until specified pressure is attained. Installs relay (regulating devices) used to control pressure inside cables. Attaches temporary reservoirs to ends of cable to maintain pressure during installation of cable. Tests cables with manual pressure gages. Reports cable sheath defects and joint failure for repair. • **GED:** R3, M3, L3 • **SVP:** 6 mos-1 yr • **Academic:** Ed=N, Eng=S • **Work Field:** 014, 111 • **MPSMS:** 871 • **Aptitudes:** G3, V3, N3, S3, P4, Q4, K4, F3, M3, E4, C4 • **Temperaments:** M, T • **Physical:** V=L, H=N, L=L, W, C, S, H • **Work Env:** O, W, R • **Salary:** 4 • **Outlook:** 3

GAS-ENGINE OPERATOR (any ind.) • D.O.T. #950.382-018 • OES #95032 • Operates stationary internal-combustion engines, using natural gas for fuel, to supply power for equipment, such as electrical generators and air or gas compressors: Starts auxiliary air compressor and turns compressed air and fuel valves to start engine. Observes gages and meters and adjusts controls to regulate ignition, governor, lubrication and cooling systems, and load distribution between engines. Observes operation of equipment, such as generators or compressors to detect malfunctions. May specialize in engines designed for specific processes and be designated GAS-ENGINE OPERATOR, COMPRESSORS (any ind.); GAS-ENGINE OPERATOR, GENERATORS (any ind.). • **GED:** R3, M2, L2 • **SVP:** 1-2 yrs • **Academic:** Ed=N, Eng=N • **Work Field:** 021 • **MPSMS:** 871 • **Aptitudes:** G3, V3, N3, S4, P4, Q3, K4, F4, M3, E5, C5 • **Temperaments:** M, T • **Physical:** V=L, H=N, L=M, W, C, H • **Work Env:** I, W, N, R • **Salary:** 4 • **Outlook:** 3

HYDROELECTRIC-STATION OPERATOR (light, heat, & power) • D.O.T. #952.362-018 • OES #95021 • Controls electrical generating units and related mechanical and hydraulic equipment at hydroelectric-generating station: Operates switch board and manually-operated controls to control water wheels, generators, and auxiliary hydroelectric-generating station equipment and distribute power output among generating units, according to power demands [SWITCHBOARD OPERATOR (light, heat, & power)]. Operates feeder switchboard to control distribution of electric power over feeder circuits between generating station and substations [FEEDER-SWITCHBOARD OPERATOR (light, heat, & power)]. Records control-board meter and gage readings, inspects operating equipment, and notifies HYDROELECTRIC-STATION OPERATOR, CHIEF (light, heat, & power) of conditions indicating abnormal equipment operation. May perform minor maintenance on equipment, such as replacing generator brushes, cleaning insulators, and lubricating machines. • **GED:** R4, M3, L3 • **SVP:** 2-4 yrs • **Academic:** Ed=H, Eng=S • **Work Field:** 021 • **MPSMS:** 871 • **Aptitudes:** G3, V3, N3, S4, P4, Q3, K4, F3, M3, E5, C4 • **Temperaments:** M, R, T • **Stress:** T • **Physical:** V=G, H=N, L=S, W, H • **Work Env:** I, N, R • **Salary:** 4 • **Outlook:** 3

LOAD DISPATCHER (light, heat, & power) • D.O.T. #952.167-014 • OES #95028 • DISPATCHER, ELECTRIC POWER; POWER DISPATCHER; SYSTEM DISPATCHER; SYSTEM OPERATOR. Coordinates activities of personnel engaged in operating generating stations, substations, and lines of electric power system or electrified railway system to insure adequate production and distribution of electricity to meet power demands: In smaller system, calculates load estimates according to corrected weather and consumer-demand records and notifies SWITCHBOARD OPERATOR (light, heat, & power) at generating stations of electric power required to meet fluctuating demands; or in larger systems receives load schedule for various generating stations from POWER-PLANT OPERATOR (light, heat, & power). Monitors control board showing operating condition of lines and equipment throughout system and makes adjustments or directs workers to make adjustments as conditions warrant. Directs SUBSTATION OPERATOR (light, heat, & power) and other workers to deenergize malfunctioning circuits or adjusts switches to ensure safety of maintenance crew and avoid interruptions of service during repairs. Notifies maintenance crew of location and deenergization of troubled sector, and verifies that workers are clear of repaired equipment before directing energization of circuit. Contacts other utilities by telephone to arrange exchange of power according to existing contracts or in an emergency and coordinates tie-in with other systems. Compiles operational records. May operate console of computer which is programed to automatically perform load-control functions. May calculate discharge rate of water in reservoirs utilizing reports of rain, river flow, and water level in reservoirs, and directs setting of watergates at hydroelectric plant to coordinate water flow and power generation with irrigation and flood control requirements. May compute bills for power delivered to interconnected utilities. May be responsible for section of system and be designated LOAD DISPATCHER, LOCAL (light, heat, & power). • **GED:** R4, M3, L3 • **SVP:** 4-10 yrs • **Academic:** Ed=N, Eng=S • **Work Field:** 021 • **MPSMS:** 871 • **Aptitudes:** G3, V3, N3, S3, P3, Q3, K3, F4, M3, E5, C4 • **Temperaments:** D, M, P • **Stress:** E • **Physical:** V=L, H=G, L=L, H • **Work Env:** I • **Salary:** 4 • **Outlook:** 3

POWER-REACTOR OPERATOR (light, heat, & power) • D.O.T. #952.362-022 • OES #95026 • REACTOR OPERATOR; NUCLEAR PLANT CONTROL OPERATOR. Controls nuclear reactor that produces steam for generation of electric power and coordinates operation of auxiliary equipment: Adjusts controls, under supervision, to start and shut down reactor and to regulate flux level, reactor period, coolant temperature, and rate of flow, control rod positions, and other control elements that affect power level within reactor, following standard instructions and prescribed practices. Dispatches orders and instructions to plant personnel through radiotelephone or intercommunication system to coordinate operation of such auxiliary equipment as pumps, compressors, switchgears, and water-treatment systems. May assist in preparing, transferring, loading, and unloading nuclear fuel elements. May be required to hold Nuclear Reactor Operator's license. May be required to hold Radiotelephone Operator's license. May control dual purpose reactors that produce plutonium and steam. May control operation of auxiliary equipment, such as turbines and generators [SWITCHBOARD OPERATOR (light, heat, & power); TURBINE OPERATOR (light, heat, & power)]. • **GED:** R4, M3, L3 • **SVP:** 2-4 yrs • **Academic:** Ed=H, Eng=S • **Work Field:** 021 • **MPSMS:** 871 • **Aptitudes:** G2, V2, N3, S3, P3, Q3, K3, F4, M3, E4, C4 • **Temperaments:** M, S, T, V • **Stress:** S • **Physical:** V=L, H=G, L=M, W, H • **Work Env:** I • **Salary:** 5 • **Outlook:** 2

SUBSTATION OPERATOR (light, heat, & power) • D.O.T. #952.362-026 • OES #95028 • POWER-SWITCHBOARD OPERATOR; RECEIVING-DISTRIBUTION-STATION OPERATOR. Controls equipment, such as current converters, voltage transformers, and circuit breakers, that regulate flow of electricity through substation of electric power system and over distribution lines to consumers: Records readings of switchboard instruments to compile data concerning quantities of electric power used for substation operation and amounts distributed from station. Communicates with LOAD DISPATCHER (light, heat, & power) to report amount of electricity received into substation, and to receive switching instructions. Observes switchboard instruments to detect indications of line disturbances, such as grounded, shorted, or open circuits. Pulls circuit breaker switch or pushes buttons to interrupt flow of current in disturbed line preparatory to repair, and to connect alternate circuit to carry load of deenergized lines. Records temperature of transformers at specified intervals. May inspect equipment, such as transformers, pumps, fans, batteries, and circuit breakers to detect defects. May calculate average and peak load conditions from electric recording instrument data and compile periodic report of load variations for system planning purposes. May locate and replace defective fuses and switches, using test lamp and handtools. May be designated according to primary function of substation as SUBSTATION OPERATOR, CONVERSION (light, heat, & power); SUBSTATION OPERATOR, DISTRIBUTION (light, heat, & power; r.r. trans.); SUBSTATION OPERATOR, TRANSFORMING (light, heat, & power). May operate auxiliary generators and be designated SUBSTATION OPERATOR, GENERATION (light, heat, & power). May control several remote-controlled substations from central station switchboard and be designated SUBSTATION OPERATOR, AUTOMATIC (light, heat, & power). • **GED:** R4, M3, L3 • **SVP:** 2-4 yrs • **Academic:** Ed=H, Eng=S • **Work Field:** 021 • **MPSMS:** 871 • **Aptitudes:** G3, V3, N3, S4, P3, Q3, K4, F4, M3, E4, C4 • **Temperaments:** M, T • **Physical:** V=L, H=N, L=L, W, H • **Work Env:** I, N, R • **Salary:** 4 • **Outlook:** 3

TURBINE OPERATOR (light, heat, & power) • D.O.T. #952.362-042 • OES #95021 • TURBOGENERATOR OPERATOR. Controls steam-driven turbogenerators in electric or nuclear power generating station: Starts or signals AUXILIARY-EQUIPMENT OPERATOR (light, heat, & power) to start turbines and boiler auxiliary units. Adjusts throttle and vacuum-breaker valve to engage governor that regulates speed of turbines and notifies SWITCHBOARD OPERATOR (light, heat, & power) that turbine-driven generators can be synchronized with auxiliary units. Monitors panelboard to control operations of turbines to detect equipment malfunctions. Stops turbines when malfunctions occur, following operating instructions. Records instrument readings at specified intervals. May perform minor maintenance or equipment, using handtools. When controlling operation by remote control may be designated as CENTRAL-CONTROL-ROOM OPERATOR (light, heat, & power). • **GED:** R4, M3, L3 • **SVP:** 2-4 yrs • **Academic:** Ed=H, Eng=S • **Work Field:** 021 • **MPSMS:** 871 • **Aptitudes:** G3, V3, N3, S3, P3, Q3, K3, F4, M3, E5, C4 • **Temperaments:** M, T • **Physical:** V=L, H=N, L=L, W, H • **Work Env:** I, N • **Salary:** 4 • **Outlook:** 3

GOE: 05.06.02 Stationary Engineering

AIR-COMPRESSOR OPERATOR (any ind.) • D.O.T. #950.685-010 • OES #92998 • COMPRESSOR ENGINEER; COMPRESSOR OPERATOR. Tends air compressors driven by steam, electric, or gasoline powered units, to generate and supply compressed air for operation of pneumatic tools, hoists, and air lances: Starts power unit to build up specified pressure in compressor. Adjusts controls or sets automatic controls to maintain continuous air supply to pneumatic tools or equipment. Observes temperature and pressure gages and adjusts controls accordingly. Lubricates and cleans equipment. May connect pipelines from compressor to pneumatic tools or equipment. May repair low pressure steam boilers that furnish power for air compressor units by disassembling unit of boiler and replacing damaged parts, using handtools. May be designated according to type of equipment operated as AIR-COMPRESSOR OPERATOR, STATIONARY (any ind.); COMPRESSOR OPERATOR, PORTABLE (any ind.). • **GED:** R3, M2, L2 • **SVP:** 6 mos-1 yr • **Academic:** Ed=N, Eng=N • **Work Field:** 021 • **MPSMS:** 573 • **Aptitudes:** G3, V4, N4, S4, P4, Q4, K4, F4, M3, E5, C5 • **Temperaments:** M, T • **Physical:** V=L, H=N, L=M, W, H • **Work Env:** B, N • **Salary:** 3 • **Outlook:** 3

BOILER OPERATOR (any ind.) • D.O.T. #950.382-010 • OES #95032 • BOILERHOUSE OPERATOR; CONTROL-ROOM OPERATOR; FIRER, BOILER; STEAM-POWER-PLANT OPERATOR. Operates automatically fired boilers to generate steam that supplies heat or power for buildings or industrial processes: Lights gas-or oil-fed burners, using torch. Starts pulverizer and stoker to grind and feed coal into furnace of boiler. Observes pressure, temperature, and draft meters on panel to verify specified operation of automatic combustion control systems, feed water regulators, stoker, pulverizer, and burners. Turns valves and adjusts controls to set specified fuel feed, draft openings, water level, and steam pressure of boiler. Observes boiler and auxiliary units to detect malfunctions and makes repairs, such as changing burn ers and tightening pipes and fittings. May test and treat boiler feed water, using specified chemicals. May maintain log of meter and gage readings and record data, such as water test results and quantity of fuel consumed. May be designated according to fuel burned, type of boilers, or class of license required. • **GED:** R4, M3, L3 • **SVP:** 2-4 yrs • **Academic:** Ed=N, Eng=S • **Work Field:** 021 • **MPSMS:** 875 • **Aptitudes:** G3, V3, N3, S3, P4, Q3, K4, F4, M3, E5, C4 • **Temperaments:** M, T • **Physical:** V=L, H=N, L=M, W, C, H • **Work Env:** I, H, N, R • **Salary:** 4 • **Outlook:** 3

ENGINEER (water trans.) • D.O.T. #197.130-010 • OES #97521 • MARINE ENGINEER; MECHANIC, MARINE ENGINE. Supervises and coordinates activities of crew engaged in operating and maintaining propulsion engines and other engines, boilers, deck machinery, and electrical, refrigeration, and sanitary equipment aboard ship: Inspects engines and other equipment and orders crew to repair or replace defective parts. Starts engines to propel ship and regulates engines and power transmission to control speed of ship. Stands engine-room watch during specified periods, observing that required water levels are maintained in boilers, condensers, and evaporators, load on generators is within acceptable limits, and oil and grease cups are kept full. Repairs machinery, using handtools and power tools. Maintains engineering log and bell book (orders for changes in speed and direction of ship). May be required to hold appropriate U. S. Coast Guard license, depending upon tonnage of ship, type of engines, and means of transmitting power to propeller shaft. When more than one ENGINEER (water trans.) is required, may be desig nated as ENGINEER, CHIEF (water trans.); ENGINEER, FIRST ASSISTANT (water trans.); ENGINEER, SECOND ASSISTANT (water trans.); ENGINEER, THIRD ASSISTANT (water trans.). May be designated according to ship assigned as BARGE ENGINEER (water trans.); CANNERY-TENDER ENGINEER (water trans.); ENGINEER, FISHING VESSEL (water trans.); TUGBOAT ENGINEER (water trans.). May be designated as CADET ENGINEER (water trans.) when in training. • **GED:** R4, M3, L3 • **SVP:** 4-10 yrs • **Academic:** Ed=H, Eng=G • **Work Field:** 021 • **MPSMS:** 870 • **Aptitudes:** G3, V3, N3, S2, P3, Q3, K3, F4, M3, E4, C4 • **Temperaments:** D, J, M, P, T • **Stress:** E • **Physical:** V=L, H=L, L=M, W, C, S, H • **Work Env:** I, H, W, R • **Salary:** 5 • **Outlook:** 2

FUEL ATTENDANT (any ind.) • D.O.T. #953.362-010 • OES #95005 • Controls equipment to regulate flow and pressure of gas from mains to fuel feedlines of gas-fired boilers, furnaces, kilns, soaking pits, smelters, and related steam-generating or heating equipment in such establishments as power plants, steel mills, pottery works, chemical plants, and petroleum refining facilities: Opens valve on feedlines to supply adequate gas for fuel when boilers are to be put in operation and to maintain standard pressure on gaslines. Closes valve to reduce gas pressure when increase in gas consumption by boilers causes pressure to rise. Observes, records, and reports flow and pressure gage readings on gas mains and fuel feedlines. • **GED:** R3, M2, L2 • **SVP:** 6 mos-1 yr • **Academic:** Ed=N, Eng=N • **Work Field:** 021 • **MPSMS:** 872 • **Aptitudes:** G3, V4, N4, S4, P3, Q3, K3, F4, M4, E4, C4 • **Temperaments:** M, T • **Physical:** V=L, H=N, L=L, H • **Work Env:** I • **Salary:** 3 • **Outlook:** 3

GAS-COMPRESSOR OPERATOR (any ind.) • D.O.T. #950.382-014 • OES #97921 • GAS-LIFT ENGINEER. Operates steam or internal combustion engines to transmit, compress, or recover gases, such as butane, nitrogen, hydrogen, and natural gas in various production processes: Moves controls and turns valves to start compressor engines, pumps, and auxiliary equipment. Monitors meters, gages, and recording instrument charts to insure specified temperature, pressure, and flow of gas through system. Observes operation of equipment to detect malfunctions. Records instrument readings and operational changes in operating log. May operate purification tanks (scrubbers) to purify air or by-product gases. May tend pumps to mix specified amounts of acids and caustics with water for use in purifying gases. May perform minor repairs on equipment, using handtools. May conduct chemical tests to determine sulphur or moisture content in gas. May be designated according to type of gas compressed or recovered as BUTADIENE-COMPRESSOR OPERATOR (chem.); BUTANE-

COMPRESSOR OPERATOR (petrol. refin.); ETHYLENE-COMPRESSOR OPERATOR (chem.). May operate equipment to control transmission of natural gas through pipelines and be designated COMPRESSOR-STATION ENGINEER (pipe lines). • **GED:** R4, M3, L3 • **SVP:** 2-4 yrs • **Academic:** Ed=N, Eng=S • **Work Field:** 021 • **MPSMS:** 872 • **Aptitudes:** G3, V3, N3, S4, P4, Q3, K4, F4, M3, E5, C5 • **Temperaments:** M, T • **Physical:** V=L, H=N, L=M, W, C, H • **Work Env:** I, N, R • **Salary:** 4 • **Outlook:** 3

REFRIGERATING ENGINEER (any ind.) • D.O.T. #950.362-014 • OES #95032 • COOLING-SYSTEM OPERATOR; OPERATING ENGINEER; STATIONARY ENGINEER, REFRIGERATION. Operates freon, carbon-dioxide, or ammonia gas-cooling systems to refrigerate rooms in establishments, such as slaughtering and meat packing plants and dairies, to air-condition buildings, or to provide refrigeration for industrial processes: Opens valves on equipment, such as compressors, pumps, and condensers to prepare system for operation and starts equipment and auxiliary machinery. Observes temperature, pressure and ampere readings for system and equipment and adjusts controls or overrides automatic controls to obtain specified operation of equipment. Records temperature, pressure, and other readings on logsheet at specified intervals. Measures density of brine, using hydrometer, and adds calcium chloride to lower temperature to specified degree. Connects hose from supply tank to compressor to replace coolant. Makes periodic inspection of equipment and system to observe operating condition and need for repair or adjustment. Adjusts controls to isolate and clear broken lines for repair or shuts down equipment. May repack pumps and compressors, clean condensers, and replace worn or defective parts using hand and power tools. When operating refrigeration or air conditioning equipment aboard ship may be known as REEFER ENGINEER (water trans.) and must have endorsement on Merchant Mariner's document as Refrigerating Engineer. • **GED:** R4, M3, L3 • **SVP:** 2-4 yrs • **Academic:** Ed=N, Eng=S • **Work Field:** 021 • **MPSMS:** 573 • **Aptitudes:** G3, V3, N3, S3, P4, Q3, K4, F4, M3, E4, C4 • **Temperaments:** M, T • **Physical:** V=L, H=N, L=M, W, C, H • **Work Env:** I, W, N, R • **Salary:** 4 • **Outlook:** 3

STATIONARY ENGINEER (any ind.) • D.O.T. #950.382-026 • OES #95032 • MAINTENANCE ENGINEER; OPERATING ENGINEER; POWER-PLANT OPERATOR; WATCH ENGINEER. Operates and maintains stationary engines and mechanical equipment, such as steam engines, air compressors, generators, motors, turbines, and steam boilers to provide utilities, such as light, heat, or power for buildings and industrial processes: Reads meters and gages or automatic recording devices at specified intervals to verify operating conditions. Records data, such as temperature of equipment, hours of operation, fuel consumed, temperature or pressure, water levels, analysis of flue gases, voltage load and generator balance. Adjusts manual controls or overrides automatic controls to bring equipment into recommended or prescribed operating ranges, switch to back-up equipment or systems, or to shut down equipment. Visually inspects equipment at periodic intervals to detect malfunctions or need for repair, adjustment or lubrication. Maintains equipment by tightening fittings, repacking bearings, replacing packing glands, gaskets, valves, recorders, and gages, and cleaning or replacing burners or other components, using hand and power tools. May be required to hold license issued by State or municipality, restricting equipment operated to specified types and sizes. May oil and lubricate equipment [OILER (any ind.)]. May perform water titration tests and pour chemical additives, such as water softeners, into treatment tank to prevent scale build-up and to clean boiler lines. May record operation and maintenance actions taken during shift in operators logbook. May specialize in equipment designed for industrial processes and be designated ACID-CONCENTRATION- PLANT-EQUIPMENT ENGINEER (any ind.); AIR-COMPRESSOR-STATION ENGINEER (any ind.); DIESEL-ENGINE OPERATOR, STATIONARY (any ind.); WATER-PUMPING-STATION ENGINEER (any ind.). • **GED:** R4, M4, L3 • **SVP:** 2-4 yrs • **Academic:** Ed=H, Eng=S • **Work Field:** 021 • **MPSMS:** 870 • **Aptitudes:** G3, V3, N3, S3, P4, Q3, K4, F4, M3, E5, C4 • **Temperaments:** M, T, V • **Physical:** V=G, H=N, L=M, W, C, H • **Work Env:** I, H, W, N, R • **Salary:** 5 • **Outlook:** 2

GOE: 05.06.03 Oil, Gas & Water Distribution

PUMP-STATION OPERATOR, WATERWORKS (waterworks) • D.O.T. #954.382-010 • OES #95002 • PUMPING-PLANT OPERATOR; WATER-PLANT-PUMP OPERATOR. Operates pumping equipment to transfer raw water to treatment plant, or distribute processed water to residential, commercial, and industrial establishments: Turns valves, pulls levers, and flips switches to operate and control turbine-or motor-driven pumps that transfer water from reservoir to treatment plant, or to transfer processed water to consumer establishments. Reads flowmeters and gages to regulate equipment according to water consumption and demand. Inspects equipment to detect malfunctions, such as pump leaks or worn bearings. Repairs and lubricates equipment, using handtools. Records data, such as utilization of equipment, power consumption, and water output in log. May operate equipment to treat and process raw water [WATER-TREATMENT-PLANT OPERATOR (waterworks)]. May test water for chlorine content, alkalinity, acidity, or turbidity to determine potability of water, following color analysis standards. May operate hydroelectric equipment to generate power. • **GED:** R3, M2, L3 • **SVP:** 6 mos-1 yr • **Academic:** Ed=N, Eng=S • **Work Field:** 014 • **MPSMS:** 873 • **Aptitudes:** G3, V4, N4, S3, P3, Q4, K4, F3, M3, E5, C4 • **Temperaments:** M, T • **Physical:** V=L, H=N, L=L, H • **Work Env:** I, N • **Salary:** 3 • **Outlook:** 3

PUMPER (any ind.) • D.O.T. #914.682-010 • OES #97953 • CIRCULATOR; PUMP-MACHINE OPERATOR; PUMP OPERATOR; PUMP RUNNER; PUMP TENDER; SIPHONER. Operates power-driven pumps that transfer liquids, semiliquids, gases, or powdered materials, performing any combination of following duties: Observes pressure gages and flowmeters, and adjusts valves to regulate speed of pumps and control pressure and rate of flow of materials. Transfers materials to and from storage tanks, processing tanks, trucks, railroad cars, ships, canals, and mines. Pumps crude oil from wells. Maintains pumps and lines by replacing filters and gaskets, tightening connections, and adjusting pumps, using handtools. May transfer liquids by siphoning. May connect pipelines between pumps and containers or storage tanks being filled or emptied. May collect samples of materials for laboratory analysis. May determine density of liquids, using hydrometer. May record quantity of item pumped. May inventory contents of storage tank, using calibrated rod, or by reading mercury gage and tank charts. Usually receives verbal or written orders from superior as to amount to be pumped and is not responsible for mixing or processing. May be designated according to material pumped or area of work, typical of which are ACID PUMPER (chem.); GLYCOL-SERVICE OPERATOR (synthetic fibers); IRRIGATING-PUMP OPERATOR (agric.); TAILINGS-DAM PUMPER (ore dress., smelt., & refin.); YARD PUMPER (any ind.). • **GED:** R3, M2, L3 • **SVP:** 6 mos-1 yr • **Academic:** Ed=N, Eng=S • **Work Field:** 014 • **MPSMS:** 568 • **Aptitudes:** G3, V3, N3, S3, P4, Q4, K3, F4, M3, E5, C5 • **Temperaments:** M, T • **Physical:** V=L, H=N, L=M, W, C, S, H • **Work Env:** B, W, N, R • **Salary:** 3 • **Outlook:** 3

GOE: 05.06.04 Processing Systems Operation

WATER-TREATMENT-PLANT OPERATOR (waterworks) • D.O.T. #954.382-014 • OES #95002 • FILTER OPERATOR; PURIFYING-PLANT OPERATOR; WATER-CONTROL-STATION ENGINEER; WATER FILTERER; WATER PURIFIER. Controls treatment plant machines and equipment to purify and clarify water for human consumption and for industrial use: Operates and controls electric motors, pumps, and valves to regulate flow of raw water into treating plant. Dumps specified amounts of chemicals, such as chlorine, ammonia, and lime into water or adjusts automatic devices that admit specified amounts of chemicals into tanks to disinfect, deodorize, and clarify water. Starts agitators to mix chemicals and allows impurities to settle to bottom of tank. Turns valves to regulate water through filter beds to remove impurities. Pumps purified water into water mains. Monitors panelboard and adjusts controls to regulate flow rates, loss of head pressure and water elevation and distribution of water. Cleans tanks and filter beds, using backwashing (reverse flow of water). Repairs and lubricates machines and equipment, using handtools and power tools. Tests water samples to determine acidity, color, and impurities, using colorimeter, turbidimeter, and conductivity meter. Dumps chemicals such as alum into tanks to coagulate impurities and to reduce acidity. Records data, such as residual content of chemicals, water turbidity, and water pressure. May operate portable water-purification plant to supply drinking water. May purify waste water from plant preparatory to pumping water into rivers and streams or city mains [WASTEWATER-TREAT MENT-PLANT OPERATOR (sanitary ser.)]. • **GED:** R3, M3, L3 • **SVP:** 6 mos-1 yr • **Academic:** Ed=H, Eng=S • **Work Field:** 014, 145, 147 • **MPSMS:** 873 • **Aptitudes:** G3, V4, N3, S4, P3, Q3, K4, F4, M3, E5, C4 • **Temperaments:** M, T • **Physical:** V=L, H=N, L=M, W, H • **Work Env:** B, W, N, R • **Salary:** 3 • **Outlook:** 2

05.07 Quality Control

Workers in this group inspect and/or test materials and products to be sure they meet standards. The work is carried out in a non-factory setting, and includes such activities as grading logs at a lumber yard, inspecting bridges to be sure they are safe; inspecting gas lines for leaks, and grading gravel for use in building roads. Jobs may be found with construction companies, sawmills, petroleum refineries, and utility companies.

✔ What kind of work would you do?
Your work activities would depend upon your specific job. For example, you might:

- inspect automobiles to see that they meet state safety laws.
- patrol oil or gas pipeline to locate and repair leaks.
- inspect boilers and pipes to locate leaks and identify needed repairs.

- check pressures, gages, and structures to certify the readiness of an airplane for flight.
- inspect crude and refined petroleum before and after transfer from terminal tanks to ship tanks.
- measure and examine logs to determine grade according to specifications.

✔ What skills and abilities do you need for this kind of work?
To do this kind of work, you must be able to:

- learn about the product, materials, or structure you are inspecting or testing.
- keep records and make reports.
- use measuring and testing equipment.

- use specifications, blueprints, and written directions to make decisions about the quality of the object or material you are inspecting.

✔ How do you know if you would like or could learn to do this kind of work?
The following questions may give you clues about yourself as you consider this group of jobs.

- Have you had courses in mechanical drawing or drafting? Can you read blueprints and diagrams?
- Have you inspected cars, appliances, or furniture for surface defects? Do you notice small details?

- Have you taken industrial arts or vocational courses? Can you use rulers, micrometers, scales, and other measuring devices?
- Have you had military experience inspecting equipment or materials? Did you like the work?

✔ How can you prepare for and enter this kind of work?

Occupations in this group usually require education and/or training extending from six months to over ten years, depending upon the specific kind of work. Some jobs in this group are open only to those who are familiar with the materials, processes, or products involved. These workers often get the necessary experience as unskilled workers in the same setting. Other jobs require the ability to read blueprints or specifications. High school or vocational courses in machine shop, mechanical drawing, or blueprint reading are helpful in developing these skills. A few jobs require experience as a skilled worker to develop the knowledge needed to judge quality. Most workers receive on-the-job training in order to learn procedures or to learn how to use measuring or testing equipment.

✔ What else should you consider about these jobs?

Working conditions for inspectors are similar to those for other workers at the site.

If you think you would like to do this kind of work, look at the job titles listed below.

GOE: 05.07.01 Structural Quality Control

CAR INSPECTOR (r.r. car blgd. & rep.) • D.O.T. #910.667-010 • OES #83008 • RAILROAD-CAR INSPECTOR. Inspects railroad cars or streetcars at terminals for damage, such as broken windows, jammed doors, defective locks, worn or damaged seats, and malfunctioning restroom facilities. Notifies train dispatcher if damage requires car to be moved to shop for repair. May make minor repairs. • GED: R3, M2, L3 • SVP: 3-6 mos • Academic: Ed=N, Eng=S • Work Field: 211 • MPSMS: 594 • Aptitudes: G4, V4, N4, S4, P3, Q4, K4, F4, M3, E5, C5 • Temperaments: R, T • Stress: T • Physical: V=L, H=N, L=L, W • Work Env: B, N • Salary: 4 • Outlook: 2

LINE WALKER (petrol. production) • D.O.T. #869.564-010 • OES #83005 • LINE RIDER. Patrols oil and gas pipelines and communication systems on foot, horseback, or in automobile to locate and repair leaks, breaks, washouts, and damaged utility wires and poles: Inspects pipelines to detect evidence of leaks, such as oil stains, odors, and dead vegetation. Repairs small leaks, using calking tools, hammers, clamps, and wrenches. Reports large leaks and washouts to district office. Inspects telephone and telegraph wires to locate broken insulators, wires and fallen poles, and reports findings. Inspects operation of automatic drip bleeder on gaslines to detect malfunctions, such as clogged valves, and adjusts or repairs valves, using handtools. Installs and replaces warning signs along road and water crossings. Prepares inspection reports. • GED: R3, M2, L3 • SVP: 3-6 mos • Academic: Ed=N, Eng=S • Work Field: 121, 293 • MPSMS: 599, 879 • Aptitudes: G3, V4, N4, S4, P3, Q4, K3, F4, M3, E4, C4 • Temperaments: R, T • Stress: T • Physical: V=L, H=G, L=L, W, H • Work Env: O • Salary: 4 • Outlook: 3

NONDESTRUCTIVE TESTER (bus. ser.) • D.O.T. #011.261-018 • OES #22105 • Conducts radiographic, penetrant, ultrasonic, and magnetic particle tests on metal parts in commercial testing laboratory to determine if parts meet nondestructive specifications: Reviews test orders to determine type of tests requested, test procedures to follow, and part acceptability criteria. Applies agents, such as cleaners, penetrants, developers, and couplant (light oil which acts as medium), to parts, or heats parts in oven, to prepare parts for testing. Determines test equipment settings according to type of metal, thickness, distance from test equipment, and related variables, using standard formulas. Calibrates test equipment, such as magnetic particle, X-ray, and ultrasonic contact machines, to standard settings, following manual instructions. Sets up equipment to perform tests, and conducts tests on parts, following procedures established for specified tests performed. Examines surface-treated materials when conducting penetrant and magnetic particle tests to locate and identify flaws, cracks, and related defects, using black light. Moves transducer probe across part when conducting ultrasonic tests and observes

CRT (cathode ray tube) screen to detect and locate discontinuities in metal structure [ULTRASONIC TESTER (bus. ser.) 709.281-018]. Examines film when conducting radiographic tests to locate structural or welding flaws. Marks tested parts to indicate areas where flaws were detected. Evaluates test results against designated standards, utilizing knowledge of metals and testing experience. Prepares reports outlining findings and conclusions. May perform similar tests on parts or structures composed of materials other than metals. • GED: R4, M3, L3 • SVP: 1-2 yrs • Academic: Ed=A, Eng=S • Work Field: 211 • MPSMS: 969 • Aptitudes: G3, V3, N3, S3, P3, Q3, K3, F3, M4, E4, C3 • Temperaments: J, T, V • Physical: V=L, H=N, L=H, W, S, H • Work Env: I, H, W, R, F • Salary: 4 • Outlook: 5

SEWER-LINE PHOTO-INSPECTOR (sanitary ser.) • D.O.T. #851.362-010 • OES #34023 • Operates camera to photograph inside of sewer lines to conduct inspection and determine need for repairs: Locates line sections to be photographed, using map. Determines setup procedures. Floats rope used to pull camera to adjacent manhole to thread sewer lines. Directs workers in setting up cable stands over manholes. Loads camera with film and inspects battery of camera. Depresses button on camera to photograph small blackboard giving location of manhole, manhole number, data, and weather conditions for future reference. Attaches pulling cable to camera and instructs workers to position camera in sewer line and to turn cable stand handles that enable camera to move inside pipe. Snaps pictures at designated intervals until camera reaches downstream manhole. Detaches camera from cable, rewinds cable into reel, and disassembles equipment. Removes film and batteries from camera and sends film to be developed. Confers with supervisor to discuss condition of sewer lines as indicated in developed photographs. Drives pickup truck to haul crew and equipment. Services, adjusts, and makes minor repairs to camera, equipment, and attachments. Communicates with supervisor, using radio telephone. Gives directions to workers in efficient and safe use of camera and equipment, work methods, and safety precautions. Prepares daily report listing lines photographed. • GED: R3, M2, L2 • SVP: 6 mos-1 yr • Academic: Ed=N, Eng=N • Work Field: 201, 211 • MPSMS: 364 • Aptitudes: G3, V3, N4, S3, P3, Q4, K4, F3, M3, E4, C4 • Temperaments: J, T • Physical: V=G, H=N, L=M, W, C, S, H • Work Env: I, W, F • Salary: 4 • Outlook: 3

SHOP ESTIMATOR (auto. ser.) • D.O.T. #807.267-010 • OES #85305 • Estimates cost of repairing damaged automobile and truck bodies, on basis of visual inspection of vehicle and familiarity with standard parts, costs, and labor rates: Examines damaged vehicle for dents, scratches, broken glass, and other areas requiring repair, replacement, or repainting. Sights along fenders to detect frame damage, or positions vehicle in frame-alining rig that indicates location and extent of misalinement. Examines interior for evidence of fire or water damage to upholstery and appointments. Determines feasibility of repair or replacement of parts, such as bumpers, fenders, and doors, according to familiarity with relative costs and extent of damage. Computes cost of replacement parts and labor to restore vehicle to condition specified by customer, using standard labor and parts cost manuals. Enters itemized estimate on job order card or estimate form and explains estimate to customer. May estimate cost of mechanical, electrical, or other repairs where shop performs both body work and mechanical servicing of vehicles [AUTOMOBILE-REPAIR-SERVICE ESTIMATOR (auto. ser.)]. May estimate cost of repainting, converting vehicles to special purposes, or customizing undamaged vehicles, depending on specialty of shop. • **GED:** R4, M3, L3 • **SVP:** 1-2 yrs • **Academic:** Ed=H, Eng=S • **Work Field:** 211 • **MPSMS:** 591 • **Aptitudes:** G3, V3, N3, S3, P3, Q3, K4, F4, M4, E5, C4 • **Temperaments:** J, M • **Physical:** V=L, H=N, L=L, S, H • **Work Env:** I, N • **Salary:** 4 • **Outlook:** 3

ULTRASONIC TESTER (bus. ser.) • D.O.T. #709.281-018 • OES #83002 • Conducts ultrasonic tests on fabricated metal parts or products in commercial testing laboratory to identify discontinuities: Reviews work orders, test procedure sheets, and product acceptance criteria to determine test specifications. Attaches specified crystal probe transducer to ultrasound test device and moves switch to actuate device. Sprays couplant (light oil which acts as medium) over calibration plate, moves transducer over drilled holes of plate, and observes CRT (cathode ray tube) screen to detect specified discontinuity patterns as transducer passes over plate. Turns dials of ultrasonic device to adjust device to test settings, following screen reading and applying knowledge of ultrasonic testing procedures. Applies couplant to metal part to be tested, moves transducer across part, and observes CRT screen to detect patterns that indicate cracks, inclusions, or porosity. Marks defective areas of part and prepares report of test findings. May use forklift to move parts to or from work station. • **GED:** R4, M3, L3 • **SVP:** 1-2 yrs • **Academic:** Ed=N, Eng=S • **Work Field:** 211 • **MPSMS:** 969 • **Aptitudes:** G3, V3, N3, S3, P3, Q3, K3, F3, M4, E5, C5 • **Temperaments:** J, T • **Physical:** V=L, H=N, L=M, W, H • **Work Env:** I • **Salary:** 4 • **Outlook:** 4

GOE: 05.07.02 Mechanical Quality Control

AIRPLANE INSPECTOR (air trans.) • D.O.T. #621.261- 010 • OES #83002 • AIRPLANE-AND-ENGINE INSPECTOR. Examines airframe, engines, and operating equipment to ensure that repairs are made according to specifications, and certifies airworthiness of aircraft: Tests tightness of airframe connections with handtools and employs flashlight and mirror to inspect fit of parts. Signals AIRFRAME-AND-POWER-PLANT MECHANIC (aircraft-aerospace mfg.; air trans.) to start engine and manipulate aircraft controls. Collects data, such as engine revolutions per minute and fuel and oil pressures, to evaluate engine performance, using tachometer and pressure gages. Examines assembly, installation, and adjustment of ailerons and rudders to ensure that workmanship and materials conform with Civil Air Regulations, company specifications, and manual procedures. Determines accuracy of installation of components in power plant and hydraulic system with protractor, micrometer, calipers, and gage to insure that specified tolerances are met. Signs inspection tag to approve unit, or records reasons for rejecting unit. Logs inspections performed on aircraft. Must hold Airframe and Power Plant Mechanic's License, and Inspection Authorization, issued by Federal Aviation Administration. May prepare dismantling schedules for airplanes to be overhauled. May service, repair, and replace airframe components, engines, and operating equipment [AIRFRAME-AND-POWER-PLANT MECHANIC (aircraft-aerospace mfg.; air trans.)]. • **GED:** R4, M4, L4 • **SVP:** 4-10 yrs • **Academic:** Ed=H, Eng=S • **Work Field:** 121 • **MPSMS:** 592 • **Aptitudes:** G2, V3, N3, S2, P2, Q4, K3, F3, M3, E4, C4 • **Temperaments:** J, M, T • **Physical:** V=G, H=N, L=L, W, C, S, H • **Work Env:** B, N • **Salary:** 5 • **Outlook:** 3

GOE: 05.07.03 Electrical Quality Control

ELEVATOR EXAMINER-AND-ADJUSTER (any ind.) • D.O.T. #825.261-014 • OES #85932 • ELEVATOR INSPECTOR. Inspects and adjusts installed freight and passenger elevators and escalators to meet factory specifications and safety codes, using handtools and measuring instruments: Inspects door installations for plumbness, lap, and working action. Adjusts mechanism of doors, using handtools. Inspects car hoistway and mechanical installations for alinement and clearance. Tests power consumption and line voltage changes of motors and motor-generator sets under no-load and full-load conditions to detect overload factors, using tachometer, voltmeter, and ammeter. Adjusts counter weights and regulates controls to compensate for power overload. Inspects wiring connections and control panel hookups, and adjusts switches to meet specifications for gap and timing. Tests and adjusts safety controls, such as brakes and governors. Turns valve or pushes switches to adjust pump pressures, fluid levels, and power supply on hydraulic units of elevators. Operates elevator to determine power demands at various car speeds. May compile service reports to verify conformance of each unit to prescribed standards. • **GED:** R4, M3, L3 • **SVP:** 4-10 yrs • **Academic:** Ed=N, Eng=S • **Work Field:** 111, 211 • **MPSMS:** 565 • **Aptitudes:** G2, V3, N3, S2, P2, Q4, K3, F3, M2, E3, C4 • **Temperaments:** M, T, V • **Physical:** V=L, H=N, L=L, W, C, S, H • **Work Env:** I, R • **Salary:** 5 • **Outlook:** 3

05.08 Land and Water Vehicle Operation

Workers in this group drive large or small trucks, delivery vans, or locomotives, to move materials or deliver products. Some drive ambulances; others operate small boats. Most of these jobs are found with trucking companies, railroads and water transportation companies. Wholesale and retail companies hire delivery drivers; ambulance drivers are hired by hospitals, fire departments, and other establishments concerned with moving the sick or injured.

✔ **What kind of work would you do?**
Your work activities would depend upon your specific job. For example, you might:

- drive a truck to pick up and deliver materials or products.
- drive a bus or locomotive engine to designated stations within a garage or storage yard.
- inspect a truck to see that it is loaded properly and in good running condition.
- operate a locomotive engine for a freight train.
- complete trip logs and other reports to show materials hauled and deliveries made.
- obtain signed receipts from customers for freight delivered.

- operate and maintain a motorboat to deliver passengers or supplies.

✔ **What skills and abilities do you need for this kind of work?**
To do this kind of work, you must be able to:

- understand traffic laws.
- move eyes, hands, and feet together to control the movement of the vehicle.
- use arithmetic to collect money, make change, and total receipts.
- drive vehicle for long periods with few stops.

✔ **How do you know if you would like or could learn to do this kind of work?**
The following questions may give you clues about yourself as you consider this group of jobs.

- Have you read automotive, trucking, or railroad magazines regularly? Do you enjoy reading this type of material?
- Have you driven in heavy traffic? Does it bother you to do so?

✔ **How can you prepare for and enter this kind of work?**
Occupations in this group usually require education and/or training extending from thirty days to over one year, depending on the specific kind of work. High school driver education courses and private driving schools are helpful. Truck driving courses are offered by some private vocational employers may require drivers to pass a physical. A good driving record is also necessary.

Requirements for local drivers vary with the type of vehicle driven and the employer's business. New drivers may train by riding with an experienced driver, but more training may be offered if a special type of truck is used. Requirements are similar for long-haul truckers. Some firms give classes on general duties, operating and loading procedures, and company rules and records.

The U.S. Department of Transportation sets standards for interstate trucking. Long-distance truckers must pass a written exam on the Motor Carrier Safety Regulations. They will drive on the job. Many firms have height and weight limits for their drivers. Others only hire those with long-distance experience.

Railroads prefer that engineer helpers have a high school education or equivalency. Elgibility for promotion is based on knowledge of locomotive equipment and opertions and passing tests.

✔ **What else should you consider about these jobs?**
Some jobs require you to work evenings, nights, on-call, weekends and holidays. In addition, long-distance haulers often spend many nights away from home. Some truck drivers must load and unload their own trucks.

Although advancement in trucking is limited, some drivers become supervisors or managers and many of these workers are self- employed.

If you think you would like to do this kind of work, look at the job titles listed below.

GOE: 05.08.01 Truck Driving

DUMP-TRUCK DRIVER (any ind.) • D.O.T. #902.683-010 • OES #97102 • Drives truck equipped with dump body to transport and dump loose materials, such as sand, gravel, crushed rock, coal, or bituminous paving materials: Pulls levers or turns crank to tilt body and dump contents. Moves hand and foot controls to jerk truck forward and backward to loosen and dump material adhering to body. May load truck by hand or by operating mechanical loader. May be designated according to type of material hauled as COAL HAULER (any ind.); DUST-TRUCK DRIVER (any ind.); MUD TRUCKER (coke prod.). May be designated according to type of equipment driven for off-highway projects as DUMP-TRUCK DRIVER, OFF-HIGHWAY (any ind.). • **GED:** R3, M1, L1 • **SVP:** 2-30 days • **Academic:** Ed=N, Eng=N • **Work Field:** 013 • **MPSMS:** 859 • **Aptitudes:** G3, V4, N4, S3, P4, Q4, K3, F4, M3, E3, C4 • **Temperaments:** R • **Stress:** T • **Physical:** V=L, H=N, L=M, W, H • **Work Env:** B • **Salary:** 4 • **Outlook:** 4

MILK DRIVER (dairy prod.) • D.O.T. #905.483-010 • OES #97102 • MILK HAULER. Drives insulated tank truck to transport bulk milk between farms, dairies, and commercial establishments: Examines milk to detect sediment or stale odor, and takes sample for laboratory analysis. Observes level gage of storage tank and computes and records weight of milk in tank. Connects hose and turns valves to pump milk into truck. Washes truck. May clean and sterilize tank. May load and drive refrigerated van to haul cans of milk. • **GED:** R3, M2, L2 • **SVP:** 30 days-3 mos • **Academic:** Ed=N, Eng=S • **Work Field:** 013, 231 • **MPSMS:** 383 • **Aptitudes:** G3, V4, N3, S3, P3, Q4, K3, F4, M3, E3, C4 • **Temperaments:** R • **Stress:** T • **Physical:** V=G, H=N, L=M, W, C, H • **Work Env:** I • **Salary:** 4 • **Outlook:** 3

TRACTOR-TRAILER-TRUCK DRIVER (any ind.) • D.O.T. #904.383-010 • OES #97102 • TRAILER-TRUCK DRIVER. Drives gasoline or diesel-powered tractor-trailer combination, usually long distances, to transport and deliver products, live stock, or materials in liquid, loose, or packaged form: Drives truck to destination, applying knowledge of commercial driving regulations and skill in maneuvering vehicle in difficult situations, such as narrow passageways. Inspects truck for defects before and after trips and submits report indicating truck condition. Maintains driver log according to I.C.C. regulations. May assist workers in loading and unloading truck. May transport new automobiles or trucks from manufacturers or rail terminals to dealers and be designated TRANSPORT DRIVER (motor trans.). May drive tractor with two trailers hitched in tandem and be designated DOUBLE-BOTTOM DRIVER (any ind.). May drive tractor-trailer combination to deliver poles for utility and construction companies and be designated POLE-TRUCK DRIVER (const.; light, heat, & power; tel. & tel.). May work as member of two-man team driving tractor with sleeper bunk behind cab and be designated LONG-HAUL-SLEEPER DRIVER (any ind.). May drive tractor-trailer combination to deliver or spray water and be designated WATER-TRUCK DRIVER (const.; petrol. production) I. • **GED:** R3, M2, L3 • **SVP:** 3-6 mos • **Academic:** Ed=N, Eng=S • **Work Field:** 013 • **MPSMS:** 859 • **Aptitudes:** G3, V4, N4, S2, P3, Q3, K3, F4, M3, E3, C4 • **Temperaments:** R • **Stress:** T • **Physical:** V=G, H=N, L=M, W, S, H • **Work Env:** B, N • **Salary:** 5 • **Outlook:** 3

TRUCK DRIVER, HEAVY (any ind.) • D.O.T. #905.663-014 • OES #97102 • Drives truck with capacity of more than 3 tons, performing duties similar to those of TRUCK DRIVER, LIGHT (any ind.): May position blocks and tie rope around items to secure cargo during transit. When driving truck equipped for specific purposes, such as fighting fires, digging holes, and installing and repairing utility company lines, may be designated FIRE-TRUCK DRIVER (petrol. production); HOLE-DIGGER-TRUCK DRIVER (const.; light, heat, & power; tel. & tel.); TOWER-TRUCK DRIVER (light, heat, & power; tel. & tel.). When specializing in making deliveries may be designated DELIVERY-TRUCK DRIVER, HEAVY (any ind.). May be designated according to type of truck driven as TRUCK DRIVER, FLATBED (logging). May be designated according to kind of cargo transported as WATER HAULER (logging). • **GED:** R3, M2, L2 • **SVP:** 3-6 mos • **Academic:** Ed=N, Eng=S • **Work Field:** 013 • **MPSMS:** 859 • **Aptitudes:** G3, V4, N4, S3, P4, Q5, K3, F4, M3, E3, C4 • **Temperaments:** R • **Stress:** T • **Physical:** V=G, H=N, L=M, W, S, H • **Work Env:** B, N • **Salary:** 3 • **Outlook:** 4

TRUCK DRIVER, LIGHT (any ind.) • D.O.T. #906.683-022 • OES #97105 • Drives truck with capacity under 3 tons to transport materials in liquid or packaged form and personnel to and from specified destinations, such as railroad stations, plants, residences, offices, or within industrial yards: Verifies load against shipping papers. Drives truck to destination, applying knowledge of commercial driving regulations and roads in area. Prepares receipts for load picked up. Collects payment for goods delivered and for delivery charges. May maintain truck log according to state and federal regulations. May maintain telephone or radio contact with supervisor to receive delivery instructions. May drive truck equipped with public address system through city streets to broadcast announcements over system for advertising or publicity purposes. May load and unload truck. May inspect truck equipment and supplies, such as tires, lights, brakes, gas, oil, and water. May perform emergency roadside repairs, such as changing tires, installing light bulbs, fuses, tire chains, and spark plugs. May be designated according to type of activity as CREW-TRUCK DRIVER (any ind.); INSECT SPRAYER, MOBILE UNIT (gov. ser.); MAIL-TRUCK DRIVER (any ind.); MOTOR-VEHICLE-ESCORT DRIVER (bus. ser.); PICK-UP DRIVER (motor trans.); SERVICE-PARTS DRIVER (auto. ser.); SPRINKLER-TRUCK DRIVER (any

ind.). • **GED:** R3, M2, L2 • **SVP:** 30 days-3 mos • **Academic:** Ed=N, Eng=N • **Work Field:** 013 • **MPSMS:** 859 • **Aptitudes:** G3, V4, N4, S3, P4, Q5, K3, F4, M3, E3, C4 • **Temperaments:** R • **Stress:** T • **Physical:** V=G, H=N, L=M, W, S, H • **Work Env:** B • **Salary:** 3 • **Outlook:** 3

GOE: 05.08.02 Rail Vehicle Operation

FIRER, LOCOMOTIVE (r.r. trans.) • D.O.T. #910.363-010 • OES #97311 • ASSISTANT ENGINEER. Monitors locomotive instruments and watches for dragging equipment, obstacles on right-of-way, and train signals during run: Inventories supplies, such as fuel, water, and sand, to insure safe, efficient operation during run. Inspects locomotive to detect damaged or worn parts. Observes oil, temperature, and pressure gages on dashboard to ascertain if engine is operating safely and efficiently. Observes track from left side of locomotive to detect obstructions on tracks. Observes train signals along route and verifies their meaning for LOCOMOTIVE ENGINEER (r.r. trans.). Observes train as it goes around curves to detect dragging equip ment and smoking journal boxes. Observes signals from workers in rear of train and relays information to LOCOMOTIVE ENGINEER (r.r. trans.). Signals YARD COUPLER (r.r. trans.) to set handbrakes on cars and to throw track switches when switching cars from train at way stations. Operates locomotive during emergency. May start diesel engine to warm engine before run. May be designated ac cording to kind of locomotive as FIRER, DIESEL LOCOMOTIVE (r.r. trans.); FIRER, ELECTRIC LOCOMOTIVE (r.r. trans.); or according to type of traffic as ROAD-FREIGHT FIRER (r.r. trans.); ROAD-PASSENGER FIRER (r.r. trans.). • **GED:** R4, M2, L3 • **SVP:** 1-2 yrs • **Academic:** Ed=N, Eng=S • **Work Field:** 013 • **MPSMS:** 594, 851 • **Aptitudes:** G3, V3, N4, S3, P3, Q4, K3, F4, M3, E4, C4 • **Temperaments:** M • **Physical:** V=L, H=G, L=L, W, H • **Work Env:** I, N • **Salary:** 5 • **Out look:** 1

LOCOMOTIVE ENGINEER (r.r. trans.) • D.O.T. #910.363- 014 • OES #97305 • Drives electric, diesel-electric, or gas-turbine-electric locomotive, interpreting train orders, train signals, and railroad rules and regulations, to transport passengers or freight: Inspects locomotive before run to verify specified fuel, sand, water, and other supplies. Synchronizes watch with that of CONDUCTOR, PASSENGER CAR (r.r. trans.) or CONDUCTOR, ROAD FREIGHT (r.r. trans.) to ensure departure time from station or terminal is in accordance with time schedule. Receives starting signal from CONDUCTOR, PASSENGER CAR (r.r. trans.) or CONDUCTOR, ROAD FREIGHT (r.r. trans.) and moves controls, such as throttle and airbrakes to drive locomotive. Interprets train orders, train signals, and railroad rules and regulations to drive locomotive, following safety regulations and time schedule. Calls out train signals to FIRER, LOCOMOTIVE (r.r. trans.) for verification of meaning to avoid errors in interpretation. Confers with CONDUCTOR, ROAD FREIGHT (r.r. trans.) or traffic control center personnel via radiophone to issue or receive information or instructions concerning stops, delays, or oncoming trains. Observes track to detect obstructions. Inspects locomotive after run to detect damaged or defective equipment. Prepares reports to explain accidents, unscheduled stops, or delays. May lubricate moving parts of locomotive. May drive diesel-electric rail-detector car to transport rail-flaw-detecting machine over railroad and be designated as RAIL-FLAW-DETECTOR-CAR OPERATOR (r.r. trans.). May be designated according to type of locomotive driven as LOCOMOTIVE ENGINEER, DIESEL (r.r. trans.); LOCOMOTIVE ENGINEER, ELECTRIC (r.r. trans.); or according to type of traffic assigned as ROAD ENGINEER, FREIGHT (r.r. trans.) or ROAD ENGINEER, PASSENGER (r.r. trans.). • **GED:** R4, M2, L3 • **SVP:** 2-4 yrs • **Academic:** Ed=H, Eng=G • **Work Field:** 013 • **MPSMS:** 594, 851 • **Aptitudes:** G3, V3, N4, S3, P3, Q3, K3, F4, M3, E4, C4 • **Temperaments:** D, J, M, V • **Stress:** A • **Physical:** V=G, H=G, L=S, W, H • **Work Env:** I, N • **Salary:** 5 • **Outlook:** 1

TRACKMOBILE OPERATOR (any ind.) • D.O.T. #919.683-026 • OES #97399 • Operates trackmobile to transport railcars or trailers to designated station areas: Drives trackmobile onto track and alines steel wheels with rails. Moves lever that activates hydraulic device to raise rubber tires allowing steel wheels of vehicle to rest onto rails. Moves levers to couple trailers or railcars. Drives trackmobile to move rail cars or trailers to specified areas, such as weighing, loading, and cleaning. • **GED:** R2, M1, L2 • **SVP:** 30 days-3 mos • **Academic:** Ed=N, Eng=N • **Work Field:** 013 • **MPSMS:** 859 • **Aptitudes:** G3, V4, N4, S3, P4, Q4, K3, F4, M3, E3, C5 • **Temperaments:** R, T • **Stress:** T • **Physical:** V=G, H=N, L=M, W, H • **Work Env:** I • **Salary:** 3 • **Outlook:** 3

GOE: 05.08.03 Services Requiring Driving

AMBULANCE DRIVER (medical ser.) • D.O.T. #913.683-010 • OES #66023 • Drives ambulance to transport sick, injured, or convalescent persons: Places patients on stretcher and loads stretcher into ambulance, usually with help of AMBULANCE ATTENDANT (medical ser.). Takes sick or injured persons to hospital, or convalescents to destination, using knowledge and skill in driving to avoid sudden motions detrimental to patients. Changes soiled linen on stretcher. Administers first aid as needed. May shackle violent patients. May report facts concerning accident or emergency to hospital personnel or law enforcement officials. • **GED:** R3, M2, L2 • **SVP:** 3-6 mos • **Academic:** Ed=N, Eng=S • **Work Field:** 013, 294 • **MPSMS:** 929 • **Aptitudes:** G3, V4, N4, S3, P4, Q4, K3, F4, M3, E3, C4 • **Temperaments:** P, S • **Stress:** S • **Physical:** V=G, H=N, L=V, W, H • **Work Env:** I, N, R • **Salary:** 3 • **Outlook:** 3

CHAUFFEUR, FUNERAL CAR (per. ser.) • D.O.T. #359.673-014 • OES #97114 • FUNERAL DRIVER. Drives mortuary vehicles, such as hearses and limousines: Drives hearse to transport bodies to mortuary for embalming and from mortuary to place of funeral service or interment. Helps PALLBEARERS (per. ser.) to move casket from mortuary into hearse and from hearse to destination. Arranges flowers in hearse. Drives limousine in funeral procession, following prearranged schedule, to transport mourners. Assists passengers entering or leaving limousine. May clean vehicles prior to funeral. May dust furniture and sweep floors in mortuary. May be designated according to type of vehicle driven as FUNERAL-LIMOUSINE DRIVER (per. ser.); HEARSE DRIVER (per. ser.). • **GED:** R2, M1, L2 • **SVP:** 3-6 mos • **Academic:** Ed=N, Eng=N • **Work Field:** 013 • **MPSMS:** 909 • **Aptitudes:** G3, V4, N4, S3, P4, Q5, K3, F4, M3, E3, C3 • **Temperaments:** R, T • **Physical:** V=L, H=N, L=V, W, H • **Work Env:** I • **Salary:** 3 • **Outlook:** 2

CONCRETE-MIXING-TRUCK DRIVER (const.) • D.O.T. #900.683-010 • OES #97102 • BATCH-MIXING-TRUCK DRIVER; MOTO-MIX OPERATOR; READY-MIX-TRUCK DRIVER; TRANSIT-MIX OPERATOR. Drives truck equipped with auxiliary concrete mixer to deliver concrete mix to job sites: Drives truck under loading hopper to receive sand, gravel, cements, and water and starts mixer. Drives truck to location for unloading. Moves levers on truck to release concrete down truck chute into wheelbarrow or other conveying container or directly into area to be poured with concrete. Cleans truck after delivery to prevent concrete from hardening in mixer and on truck, using waterhose and hoe. May spray surfaces of truck with protective compound to prevent adhering of concrete. • **GED:** R3, M1, L1 • **SVP:** 2-4 yrs • **Academic:** Ed=N, Eng=N • **Work Field:** 013, 031 • **MPSMS:** 536 • **Aptitudes:** G3, V4, N4, S3, P4, Q4, K3, F4, M3, E3, C4 • **Temperaments:** R • **Stress:** T • **Physical:** V=G, H=N, L=M, W, H • **Work Env:** I • **Salary:** 5 • **Outlook:** 2

DELIVERER, CAR RENTAL (auto. ser.) • D.O.T. #919.663-010 • OES #97114 • WASHER DRIVER. Delivers rental cars to customers, and services them prior to delivery: Sweeps out and vacuum cleans interior of rental automobile. Washes windows and exterior of automobile, using water and other cleansing compounds and cloth. Regulates tire pressure and adds gasoline and oil. Adds water to battery and radiator. Delivers automobile to customer at specified pickup point. Collects rental payment and deposit from customer; and observes that customer reads and signs rental contract. May deliver new or used automobiles to customer from automobile dealership. • **GED:** R2, M2, L2 • **SVP:** 30 days-3 mos • **Academic:** Ed=N, Eng=S • **Work Field:** 013, 031 • **MPSMS:** 859 • **Aptitudes:** G4, V4, N4, S3, P4, Q4, K3, F4, M3, E3, C4 • **Temperaments:** R • **Stress:** T • **Physical:** V=G, H=L, L=L, W, H • **Work Env:** I • **Salary:** 3 • **Outlook:** 3

HEALTH-EQUIPMENT SERVICER (medical ser.) • D.O.T. #359.363-010 • OES #66099 • Delivers, installs, demonstrates, and maintains rental medical equipment, such as respirator, oxygen equipment, hospital beds, and wheelchairs, for use in private residences: Loads medical equipment on truck and delivers equipment to renter's or patient's residence. Unloads, installs, and sets up equipment, using handtools. Inspects and maintains rental oxygen equipment, performing such tasks as inspecting hoses and water traps to detect leaks and condensation; observing gauges of oxygen analyzer, pressure gauges, and other monitoring equipment to determine pressure and oxygen content of air output of compressors and concentrators; and changing filters. Maintains record on oxygen equipment by hours of usage to determine need for maintenance. • **GED:** R3, M2, L3 • **SVP:** 6 mos-1 yr • **Academic:** Ed=N, Eng=S • **Work Field:** 013, 121 • **MPSMS:** 929 • **Aptitudes:** G3, V3, N4, S4, P4, Q4, K3, F3, M3, E4, C4 • **Temperaments:** J, T • **Physical:** V=L, H=N, L=V, W, H • **Work Env:** I, R • **Salary:** 3 • **Outlook:** 3

LOT ATTENDANT (ret. tr.) • D.O.T. #915.583-010 • OES #97808 • Verifies receipt of new cars delivered to dealer and parks cars in new car lot in orderly manner: Compares serial numbers of incoming cars against invoice. Inspects cars to detect damage and to verify presence of accessories listed on invoice, such as spare tires and radio and stereo equipment. Records description of damages and lists missing items on delivery receipt. Parks new cars in assigned area according to model. Assigns stock control numbers to cars, and catalogs and stores keys. Reparks cars, following sales, to maximize use of space and maintain lot in order. Delivers sold cars to new car preparation department. Services cars in storage to protect tires, battery, and finish against deterioration. • **GED:** R3, M2, L3 • **SVP:** 30 days-3 mos • **Academic:** Ed=N, Eng=S • **Work Field:** 013, 231 • **MPSMS:** 961 • **Aptitudes:** G3, V3, N4, S4, P3, Q3, K3, F4, M3, E3, C4 • **Temperaments:** R, T • **Physical:** V=L, H=N, L=L, W, H • **Work Env:** I • **Salary:** 2 • **Outlook:** 3

NEWSPAPER-DELIVERY DRIVER (whole. tr.) • D.O.T. #292.363-010 • OES #97117 • Drives truck or automobile over prescribed route to delivery newspapers to wholesale or retail newspaper dealers, or to bus, airline, or express stations for shipment: Loads newspapers onto vehicle. Reviews list of dealers, customers, or station drops for change in deliveries. Drives truck or automobile over prescribed route on city streets or rural roads. Delivers newspapers to dealers or individual subscribers at their homes or place of business, or to bus, airline, or express station for shipment. Keeps records of deliveries made. Collects receipts for deliveries to newsdealers. May pick up unsold newspapers and credit newsdealer's account. May collect payment for newspaper deliveries from customers. May keep records pertaining to driving expenses, such as mileage, oil, and gasoline. May stock newspapers in street sales rack, and collect coins from rack coin boxes. May distribute sales promotion material to customers with newspaper deliveries. May be designated according to publication delivered as MAGAZINE-DELIVERY DRIVER (whole. tr.). • **GED:** R3, M2, L2 • **SVP:** 3-6 mos • **Academic:** Ed=N, Eng=S • **Work Field:** 013, 292 • **MPSMS:** 889, 899 • **Aptitudes:** G3, V4, N4, S4, P4, Q3, K4, F4, M4, E3, C5 • **Temperaments:** P • **Physical:** V=L, H=N, L=M, W, H • **Work Env:** B • **Salary:** 2 • **Outlook:** 3

TELEPHONE-DIRECTORY-DISTRIBUTOR DRIVER (bus. ser.) • D.O.T. #906.683-018 • OES #97105 • Drives automobile or truck to transport telephone directories from central storage facilities to distribution area: Loads vehicle with assigned number of books and drives to distribution district, parking vehicle in convenient or centralized location. Distributes books to TELEPHONE-DIRECTORY DELIVERERS (bus. ser.) for delivery to residences and business establishments indicated on address lists. May transport TELEPHONE-DIRECTORY DELIVERERS (bus. ser.) to distribution area. May deliver telephone directories, on foot, after parking vehicle. • **GED:** R2, M1, L2 • **SVP:** 30 days-3 mos • **Academic:** Ed=N, Eng=N • **Work Field:** 011, 013 • **MPSMS:** 480, 859 • **Aptitudes:** G4, V4, N4, S3, P4, Q4, K3, F4, M3, E3, C4 • **Temperaments:** R • **Stress:** T • **Physical:** V=G, H=N, L=L, W, H • **Work Env:** B • **Salary:** 2 • **Outlook:** 4

TOW-TRUCK OPERATOR (auto. ser.) • D.O.T. #919.663-026 • OES #97102 • TOW-CAR DRIVER; WRECKER OPERATOR. Drives tow-truck to move motor vehicles damaged by accident, stalled, or ticketed by police for traffic violation: Receives call or is dispatched to location by repair garage, automobile association, or police department by radio or telephone. Attaches antisway bar to vehicle by means of cable, chains, or other grappling devices, and hoists one end of vehicle, using hand or powered winch, to tow vehicle to repair garage or to police department's impounding area. May make minor repairs to vehicles along highway, such as replacing spark plugs, batteries, and light bulbs, and connecting loose wires. May perform other duties when not engaged in towing, such as AUTOMOBILE-SERVICE-STATION ATTENDANT (auto. ser.); TIRE REPAIRER (auto. ser.). May dismantle vehicles to salvage parts, using such hand tools as wrenches, pry bar, and hacksaws [AUTOMOBILE WRECKER (whole. tr.)]. May remove, bend, or cut parts of damaged vehicles preparatory to towing. • **GED:** R2, M1, L2 • **SVP:** 30 days-3 mos • **Academic:** Ed=N, Eng=S • **Work Field:** 011, 013 • **MPSMS:** 961 • **Aptitudes:** G3, V4, N4, S3, P4, Q4, K3, F4, M3, E3, C4 • **Temperaments:** J • **Physical:** V=G, H=L, L=M, W, S, H • **Work Env:** B, N • **Salary:** 3 • **Outlook:** 3

GOE: 05.08.04 Boat Operation

DECKHAND (water trans.) • D.O.T. #911.687-022 • OES #97517 • Performs any combination of following duties aboard watercraft, such as dredges, ferryboats, scows, and river boats: Handles lines to moor vessel to wharves, tie up vessel to another vessel, or rig towing lines. Sweeps and washes decks, using broom, brushes, mops, and firehose. Lowers and mans lifeboat in case of emergencies. Stands steering watches or lookout watches while underway. Moves controls or turns hand wheels to raise or lower passenger or vehicle landing ramps or kelp-cutter mechanism. Inserts blocks under wheels of vehicles to prevent them from moving on ferryboats. Loads or unloads material from barges, scows, and dredges. Paints lifeboats, decks, and superstructure of vessel, using brush. Lubricates machinery and equipment. Splices and repairs cables and ropes, using handtools. Examines cables that holds vessels in tow and tightens cables to ensure vessels are snug. May tour decks during watch to caution passengers engaged in unsafe practices, and ensures departure of passengers at end of voyage. Deckhands are designated according to type of craft as BARGE HAND (water trans.); DREDGE DECKHAND (water trans.); FERRYBOAT DECKHAND (water trans.); PILOT-BOAT DECKHAND (water trans.); SCOW DECKHAND (water trans.); TUGBOAT DECK-HAND (water trans.). • **GED:** R2, M1, L1 • **SVP:** 3-6 mos • **Academic:** Ed=N, Eng=N • **Work Field:** 013, 031, 153 • **MPSMS:** 854 • **Aptitudes:** G3, V3, N4, S3, P4, Q5, K4, F4, M3, E3, C4 • **Temperaments:** M, V • **Physical:** V=L, H=N, L=H, W, C, S, H • **Work Env:** B, W, N, R • **Salary:** 4 • **Outlook:** 2

MOTORBOAT OPERATOR (any ind.) • D.O.T. #911.663-010 • OES #97511 • Operates motor-driven boat to carry passengers and freight, take depth soundings in turning basin, serve as liaison between ships, ship to shore, harbor and beach area patrol, or tow, push, or guide other boats, barges, logs, or rafts: Casts off securing lines and starts motor. Starts boat and steers boat with helm or tiller. Maintains equipment, such as range markers, fire extinguishers, boat fenders, lines, pumps, and fittings. Services motor by changing oil and lubricating parts. Cleans boat and repairs hull and superstructure, using handtools, paint, and brushes. May tune up, overhaul, or replace engine. May give directions for loading and seating in boat. May be designated according to type of boat operated as BOAT TENDER (logging); BOOMBOAT OPERATOR (logging); CHARTER-BOAT OPERATOR (amuse. & rec.); SIGHT-SEEING-BOAT OPERATOR (water trans.); and WATER-TAXI DRIVER (water trans.), or operate motor-driven boat to haul fish or other marine life from offshore fishing vessel to buyer and be designated RUN-BOAT OPERATOR (water trans.). • **GED:** R3, M2, L3 • **SVP:** 6 mos-1 yr • **Academic:** Ed=N, Eng=S • **Work Field:** 013 • **MPSMS:** 854 • **Aptitudes:** G3, V4, N4, S3, P3, Q4, K3, F4, M3, E3, C4 • **Temperaments:** M, P, V • **Physical:** V=G, H=N, L=M, W, H • **Work Env:** I • **Salary:** 3 • **Outlook:** 2

05.09 Material Control

Workers in this group receive, store, and/or ship materials and products. Some estimate and order the quantities and kinds of materials needed. Others regulate and control the flow of materials to places in the plant where they are to be used. Most have to keep records. Jobs are found in institutions, industrial plants, and Government agencies.

✔ What kind of work would you do?

Your work activities would depend upon your specific job. For example, you might:

- weigh truck loaded with cotton and compute weight and gin charges.
- count, sort, or weigh articles in a shipment to check accuracy of invoices or requisitions.
- verify inventory records of a department store against the actual count of items.
- fill out receiving tickets on incoming items or complete delivery tickets on outgoing items.
- receive, store, and issue tools, dies, and equipment in a factory.
- store and issue sports equipment for a professional athletic team.
- check the progress of an order in a factory and write a report.

✔ What skills and abilities do you need for this kind of work?

To do this kind of work, you must be able to:

- use arithmetic to keep records, take inventory, estimate quantities, or schedule the flow of materials through the plant.
- avoid errors in recordkeeping.
- use hands and fingers to measure, handle, store, or move large and small items.
- reach to place materials on shelves higher than your head.
- see small print and figures in catalogs, on shipping tickets, and on invoices.

✔ **How do you know if you would like or could learn to do this kind of work?**

The following questions may give you clues about yourself as you consider this group of jobs.

- Have you taken industrial arts or vocational courses? Did you learn how to issue, store, and care for tools?
- Have you been an equipment manager for a sports team? Were you responsible for issuing and maintaining the equipment?

- Have you mailed or sent packages by freight? Can you compute freight or postal rates accurately?
- Have you been a stock clerk in the military service? Did you enjoy this type of work?

✔ **How can you prepare for and enter this kind of work?**

Occupations in this group usually require education and/or training extending from a short demonstration to over two years, depending upon the specific kind of work. Evidence of basic reading, writing, and mathematics skills are usually required by employers. On-the-job training is provided to teach workers the procedures involved in each particular job. Complex tasks involving judgment or responsibility are assigned as workers become experienced.

Jobs involving tools and machines often require a knowledge of the use and care of such equipment. One year of shop experience is sometimes required.

✔ **What else should you consider about these jobs?**

Many jobs in this group require workers to be on their feet most of the work day. Most of the work is done indoors. However, different working conditions are sometimes present on loading platforms, storage yards, or cold storage rooms.

Workers who move heavy objects have to use care to avoid body strain or injury.

If you think you would like to do this kind of work, look at the job titles listed on the following pages.

GOE: 05.09.01 Shipping, Receiving, & Stock Checking

CARGO AGENT (air trans.) • D.O.T. #248.367-018 • OES #58011 • AIR-FREIGHT AGENT; CUSTOMER SERVICE AGENT. Routes inbound and outbound air freight shipments to their destinations: Takes telephone orders from customers and arranges for pickup of freight and delivery to loading platform. Assembles cargo according to destination. Weighs items and determines cost, using rate book. Itemizes charges, prepares freight bills, accepts payments and issues refunds. Prepares manifest to accompany shipments. Notifies shippers of delays in departure of shipment. Unloads inbound freight and notifies consignees on arrival of shipments and arranges for delivery to consignees. May force conditioned air into interior of plane for passenger comfort prior to departure, using mobile aircraft-air-conditioning-unit. • **GED:** R3, M3, L3 • **SVP:** 6 mos-1 yr • **Academic:** Ed=N, Eng=G • **Work Field:** 013, 221 • **MPSMS:** 855 • **Aptitudes:** G3, V3, N3, S3, P4, Q3, K3, F3, M3, E4, C4 • **Temperaments:** M, P, V • **Stress:** E • **Physical:** V=N, H=L, L=M, W, H • **Work Env:** I • **Salary:** 3 • **Outlook:** 3

CUSTODIAN, ATHLETIC EQUIPMENT (amuse. & rec.) • D.O.T. #969.367-010 • OES #58023 • MANAGER, EQUIPMENT. Keeps stock of new and used athletic supplies, such as balls, gloves, bats, shoes, and uniforms, and issues supplies to players. Keeps record of supplies in stock and supplies issued to players. Informs officials when additional supplies are needed. Inspects supplies in stock to detect those requiring repair or cleaning. Repairs torn or damaged supplies or sends supplies out for repair. Issues new or clean supplies to players in exchange for supplies that are worn or dirty. Packs and unpacks supplies for road trips and ensures that arrangements are made for transportation. Accompanies players

on trips. Modifies protective supplies, such as adding additional arch supports to shoes, padding uniforms and helmets, or preparing slings for insured players, under specific direction from INSTRUCTOR, SPORTS (amuse. & rec.; education) or ATHLETIC TRAINER (amuse & rec.). May prepare budget estimate for supplies. May purchase supplies. May wash soiled uniforms and other supplies in automatic washing machine or may arrange to have supplies laundered. • **GED:** R3, M2, L2 • **SVP:** 6 mos-1 yr • **Academic:** Ed=N, Eng=S • **Work Field:** 221 • **MPSMS:** 914 • **Aptitudes:** G3, V3, N3, S4, P4, Q3, K3, F3, M3, E5, C4 • **Temperaments:** P, T, V • **Physical:** V=N, H=N, L=M, W, H • **Work Env:** I • **Salary:** 3 • **Outlook:** 2

INVENTORY CLERK (clerical) • D.O.T. #222.387-026 • OES #58023 • Compiles records of amount, kind, and value of merchandise, material, or stock on hand in establishment or department of establishment: Counts stock, material, or merchandise on hand and posts totals to inventory records. Compares inventories taken by other workers with office records or computes figures from sales, equipment, shipping, production, purchase, or stock records to obtain current theoretical inventory. Verifies clerical computations against physical count of stock and adjusts errors in computation or count, or investigates and reports reasons for discrepancies. Compiles information on receipt or disbursement of goods and computes inventory balance, price, and costs. Prepares reports of inventory balance, prices, and shortages. May list depleted items. May recommend survey of broken or unusable items. May operate typewriter, adding machine, or calculating machine. May update and maintain inventory records, using computer terminal. May be designated according to item inventoried as EQUIPMENT-INVENTORY CLERK (aircraft-aerospace mfg.); PROPERTY-AND-EQUIPMENT CLERK (petrol. refin.) or type of inventory as INVENTORY CLERK, PERPETUAL (clerical); INVENTORY

CLERK, PHYSICAL (clerical) or work location as **INVENTORY CLERK, STOCKROOM** (clerical). • **GED:** R3, M3, L3 • **SVP:** 3-6 mos • **Academic:** Ed=N, Eng=S • **Work Field:** 221 • **MPSMS:** 587, 898 • **Aptitudes:** G3, V3, N3, S4, P4, Q2, K4, F4, M4, E5, C4 • **Temperaments:** R, T • **Stress:** T • **Physical:** V=L, H=N, L=L, H • **Work Env:** I • **Salary:** 2 • **Outlook:** 3

LABORATORY CLERK (clerical) • D.O.T. #222.587-026 • OES #58099 • Keeps records of chemicals, apparatus, and samples, such as coal, ash, and oil, received for testing in control laboratory. Weighs and prepares for shipment chemical supplies furnished by laboratory. Cleans glassware and other laboratory apparatus, and salvages sample bottles or containers for reuse. Returns unused chemicals to designated cabinets and cleans work area, using mop. • **GED:** R3, M2, L2 • **SVP:** 30 days-3 mos • **Academic:** Ed=N, Eng=S • **Work Field:** 212, 221 • **MPSMS:** 891 • **Aptitudes:** G3, V3, N3, S4, P4, Q3, K4, F4, M4, E5, C5 • **Temperaments:** R • **Stress:** T • **Physical:** V=L, H=N, L=L, H • **Work Env:** I • **Salary:** 2 • **Outlook:** 3

LABORER, STORES (any ind.) • D.O.T. #922.687-058 • OES #98999 • ORDER PICKER; PARTS PICKER; STOCK SELECTOR; WAREHOUSE WORKER. Performs any combination of following tasks to receive, store, and distribute material, tools, equipment, and products within establishments: Reads production schedule, customer order, work order, shipping order or requisition to determine items to be moved, gathered, or distributed. Conveys materials and items from receiving or production areas to storage or to other designated areas by hand, handtruck, or electric handtruck. Sorts and places materials or items on racks, shelves, or in bins according to predetermined sequence, such as size, type, style, color, or product code. Sorts and stores perishable goods in refrigerated rooms. Fills requisitions, work orders, or requests for materials, tools, or other stock items and distributes items to production workers or assembly line. Assembles customer orders from stock and places orders on pallets or shelves, or conveys orders to packing station or shipping department. Marks materials with identifying information, using stencil, crayon, or other marking device. Opens bales, crates, and other containers, using handtools. Records amounts of materials or items received or distributed. Weighs or counts items for distribution within plant to ensure conformance to company standards. Arranges stock parts in specified sequence for assembly by other workers. May prepare parcels for mailing. May maintain inventory records. May restock aircraft commissary supplies, such as linens, glasses, emergency kits, and beverages and be designated COMMISSARY AGENT (air trans.). May be known according to specific duty performed as CLOTH-BIN PACKER (textile); COOLER WORKER (dairy prod.); ORDER FILLER (any ind.); PRODUCE CLERK (ret. tr.) II; TOOL CHASER (any ind.). • **GED:** R2, M2, L2 • **SVP:** 2-30 days • **Academic:** Ed=N, Eng=N • **Work Field:** 221 • **MPSMS:** 898 • **Aptitudes:** G4, V4, N4, S4, P4, Q4, K4, F4, M3, E4, C4 • **Temperaments:** R • **Stress:** T • **Physical:** V=L, H=N, L=M, W, H • **Work Env:** I • **Salary:** 3 • **Outlook:** 3

LINEN-ROOM ATTENDANT (hotel & rest.) • D.O.T. #222.387-030 • OES #58023 • LINEN CHECKER; LINEN CLERK; LINEN-EXCHANGE ATTENDANT; UNIFORM ATTENDANT. Stores, issues, and inventories bed and table linen and uniforms to maintain supply in establishments, such as hotels, hospitals, and clinics: Segregates, counts, and records number of items of soiled linen and uniforms, and places items in containers for transmittal to laundry. Examines laundered items to ensure cleanliness and serviceability. Stamps items with identifying marks. Stores laundered items on shelves, after verifying numbers and types of items. Counts and records amounts of linens and uniforms to fill requisition, placing orders on carts for delivery. Conducts monthly and yearly inventories to identify items for replacement. May mend torn articles with needle and thread or sewing machine or send articles to SEWER, LINEN ROOM (hotel & rest.). • **GED:** R3, M2, L2 • **SVP:** 30 days-3 mos • **Academic:** Ed=N, Eng=N • **Work Field:** 221 • **MPSMS:** 898, 900 • **Aptitudes:** G3, V4, N3, S4, P4, Q3, K4, F4, M3, E5, C4 • **Temperaments:** J, M • **Physical:** V=N, H=N, L=L, H • **Work Env:** I • **Salary:** 2 • **Outlook:** 3

MAILER (print. & pub.) • D.O.T. #222.587-030 • OES #57302 • Mails or dispatches newspapers, periodicals, envelopes, cartons, or other bulk printed matter by performing any combination of following duties: Wraps or bundles printed matter by hand or using tying machine. Addresses bundle or wrapped printed matter by hand or stamps, tags, or labels them according to mailing lists and dispatching orders, using stencils and stamping machine. Sorts bundles according to zip code and places bundles to be mailed in specified mail bags. Stacks bundles for shipment and loads and unloads bundles onto and from trucks and conveyors. Files and corrects stencils. Counts and records number of bundles and copies handled. May keep card record distribution file of units mailed or dispatched to subscribers and dealers. • **GED:** R2, M2, L2 • **SVP:** 30 days-3 mos • **Academic:** Ed=N, Eng=S • **Work Field:** 231 • **MPSMS:** 899 • **Aptitudes:** G3, V4, N3, S4, P4, Q3, K3, F3, M3, E5, C5 • **Temperaments:** R • **Stress:** T • **Physical:** V=L, H=N, L=L, H • **Work Env:** I • **Salary:** 2 • **Outlook:** 3

MEAT CLERK (ret. tr.) • D.O.T. #222.684-010 • OES #58023 • Receives, stores, and grinds meats in retail establishment: Unloads fresh, cured, and boxed meats and poultry from delivery truck and transports them to storage room on conveyor and with handtruck. Counts and weighs incoming articles and compares results against invoice. Examines meats in storage and rotates meats to avoid aging. Cuts meat into small pieces suitable for grinding, and grinds for use as hamburgers, meat loaf, and sausage, using powered grinding machine. Cleans grinder, meat containers, and storage room with water hose and broom. May take meat orders from customers. • **GED:** R2, M1, L1 • **SVP:** 2-30 days • **Academic:** Ed=N, Eng=G • **Work Field:** 146, 221 • **MPSMS:** 382 • **Aptitudes:** G4, V4, N4, S4, P4, Q4, K3, F3, M3, E5, C4 • **Temperaments:** R, T • **Physical:** V=L, H=N, L=M, W, H • **Work Env:** I • **Salary:** 2 • **Outlook:** 4

ORDER FILLER (ret. tr.) • D.O.T. #222.487-014 • OES #58026 • Fills customers' mail and telephone orders and marks price of merchandise on order form: Reads order to ascertain catalog number, size, color, and quantity of merchandise. Obtains merchandise from bins or shelves. Computes price of each group of items. Places merchandise on conveyor leading to wrapping area. • **GED:** R3, M2, L2 • **SVP:** 30 days-3 mos • **Academic:** Ed=N, Eng=N • **Work Field:** 221 • **MPSMS:** 880 • **Aptitudes:** G3, V3, N3, S5, P3, Q3, K4, F4, M3, E5, C4 • **Temperaments:** R • **Physical:** V=G, H=N, L=L, W, H • **Work Env:** I • **Salary:** 2 • **Outlook:** 4

PARTS CLERK (clerical) • D.O.T. #222.367-042 • OES #58023 • SHOP CLERK; SPARE-PARTS CLERK. Receives, stores, and issues spare and replacement parts, equipment, and expendable items used in repair or maintenance shop. May take inventory of parts and equipment and maintain inventory records. May drive truck to pick up incoming stock or to pick up and deliver parts to units in other buildings or locations. May sell auto parts to customers. May be designated according to type of parts issued as PARTS CLERK, AUTOMOBILE REPAIR (clerical); PARTS CLERK, PLANT MAINTENANCE (clerical). • **GED:** R3, M2, L2 • **SVP:** 6 mos-1 yr • **Academic:** Ed=N, Eng=S • **Work Field:** 221 • **MPSMS:** 898 • **Aptitudes:** G3, V3, N3, S3, P3, Q3, K4, F4, M3, E5, C4 • **Temperaments:** R, T • **Stress:** T • **Physical:** V=L, H=N, L=H, W, C, S, H • **Work Env:** I • **Salary:** 2 • **Outlook:** 3

PARTS-ORDER-AND-STOCK CLERK (clerical) • D.O.T. #249.367-058 • OES #58023 • PURCHASER, AUTOMOTIVE PARTS. Purchases, stores, and issues spare parts for motor vehicles or industrial equipment: Obtains purchase order number from purchasing department and assigns identifying number. Reads shop manuals to ascertain type and specification of part. Visits, telephones, telegraphs, or contacts vendors by mail to order parts. Compares invoices against requisitions to verify quality and quantity of merchandise received. Stores purchased parts in storeroom bins and issues parts to workers upon request. Keeps records of parts received and issued, and inventories parts in storeroom periodically. May record repair time expended by mechanics. May requisition parts from central parts department for national organization. • **GED:** R3, M2, L2 • **SVP:** 6 mos-1 yr • **Academic:** Ed=N, Eng=S • **Work Field:** 221 • **MPSMS:** 898 • **Aptitudes:** G3, V3, N3, S4, P4, Q3, K4, F4, M4, E5, C5 • **Temperaments:** R, T • **Stress:** T • **Physical:** V=N, H=L, L=L, H • **Work Env:** I • **Salary:** 3 • **Outlook:** 3

PHARMACY HELPER (medical ser.) • D.O.T. #074.387-010 • OES #66026 • PHARMACY CLERK. Assists PHARMACIST (profess. & kin.) by performing following duties: Mixes pharmaceutical preparations under direction of PHARMACIST (profess. & kin.). Prepares inventory and orders supplies to maintain stock levels. Receives and places supplies in stock. Labels drugs, chemicals, and other pharmaceutical preparations as directed by PHARMACIST (profess. & kin.). Delivers drug orders and runs errands. Cleans equipment and work areas in pharmacy. Washes and sterilizes bottles, beakers, and other glassware according to prescribed methods. Computes charges for drugs and engages in other functions designated by and under supervision of PHARMACIST (profess. & kin.). • **GED:** R3, M2, L3 • **SVP:** 30 days-3 mos • **Academic:** Ed=N, Eng=S • **Work Field:** 031, 147, 221 • **MPSMS:** 493 • **Aptitudes:** G3, V3, N3, S4, P3, Q3, K4, F3, M3, E4, C3 • **Temperaments:** R, T • **Physical:** V=L, H=N, L=L, W, H • **Work Env:** I, W • **Salary:** 2 • **Outlook:** 3

PRODUCTION TECHNICIAN, SEMICONDUCTOR PROCESSING EQUIPMENT (electronics) • D.O.T. #590.384-014 • OES #85128 • Cleans and maintains wafer processing machines and equipment and mixes chemical solutions, following production specifications: Reads work orders and specifications to determine machines and equipment requiring replenishment of chemical solutions. Measures and mixes chemical solutions, using graduated beakers and funnels. Pours chemical solutions into wafer processing machine tanks to replenish machine supplies. Cleans furnace accessories, such as quartz tubes and stainless steel tubing, using chemical solutions. Removes broken quartzware and wafers from furnace and vacuums interior of furnace. Cleans processing machines and equipment, using cleaning solvent and cloth. Removes and replaces empty machine and equipment gas tanks. Measures furnace temperatures, using thermal rod or thermocouple, and turns knobs on furnace control panel to adjust temperature. May re-stock storage shelves and work station with supplies, such as chemicals, alcohol, and rubber gloves. May maintain log records of machine and equipment processing readings. • **GED:** R3, M2, L2 • **SVP:** 6 mos-1 yr • **Academic:** Ed=N, Eng=N • **Work Field:** 031, 143, 221 • **MPSMS:** 491, 567 • **Aptitudes:** G3, V3, N3, S4, P3, Q3, K3, F4, M3, E5, C5 • **Temperaments:** T, V • **Physical:** V=L, H=N, L=V, W, S, H • **Work Env:** I, R, F • **Salary:** 3 • **Outlook:** 4

SHIPPING AND RECEIVING CLERK (clerical) • D.O.T. #222.387-050 • OES #58028 • Verifies and keeps records on incoming and outgoing shipments and prepares items for shipment: Compares identifying information and counts, weighs, or measures items of incoming and outgoing shipments to verify against bills of lading, invoices, orders, or other records. Determines method of shipment, utilizing knowledge of shipping procedures, routes, and rates. Assembles wooden or cardboard containers or selects preassembled containers. Inserts items in containers, using spacers, fillers, and protective padding. Nails covers on wooden crates and binds containers with metal tape, using strapping machine. Stamps, stencils, or glues identifying information and shipping instructions onto crates or containers. Posts weights, shipping charges and affixes postage. Unpacks and examines incoming shipments, rejects damaged items, records shortages, and corresponds with shipper to rectify damages and shortages. Routes items to departments. May operate tier-lift truck or use handtruck to move, convey, or hoist shipments from shipping-and-receiving platform to storage or work area. May direct others in preparing outgoing and receiving incoming shipments. May perform only shipping or receiving activities and be known as SHIPPING CLERK (clerical) or RECEIVING CLERK (clerical). May be designated according to specialty as FREIGHT CLERK (clerical); RESHIPPING CLERK (clerical). May receive damaged or defective goods returned to establishment and be designated RETURNED-GOODS RECEIVING CLERK (clerical). May receive unsold products returned by DRIVER, SALES ROUTE (ret. tr.; whole. tr.) and be designated ROUTE RETURNER (clerical). • **GED:** R3, M3, L2 • **SVP:** 6 mos-1 yr • **Academic:** Ed=N, Eng=S • **Work Field:** 221 • **MPSMS:** 898 • **Aptitudes:** G3, V3, N3, S3, P3, Q3, K4, F4, M3, E5, C5 • **Temperaments:** M, T, V • **Physical:** V=L, H=N, L=M, W, H • **Work Env:** I • **Salary:** 3 • **Outlook:** 3

SHIPPING CHECKER (clerical) • D.O.T. #222.687-030 • OES #58028 • LOADING CHECKER; ORDER CHECKER; PACKING CHECKER. Verifies quantity, quality, labeling, and addressing of products and items of merchandise ready for shipment at manufacturing or commercial establishment: Counts, weighs, measures, or examines packaging and contents of items for conformance to company specifications. Affixes postage on packages, using postal meter. Compares items packed with customer's order and other identifying data. May keep records on number of baskets of tobacco sold and removed from auction warehouse and be designated TOBACCO-CHECKOUT CLERK (whole. tr.). May oversee crew of workers engaged in loading and bracing material in railroad cars or trucks. • **GED:** R3, M3, L2 • **SVP:** 3-6 mos • **Academic:** Ed=N, Eng=S • **Work Field:** 221 • **MPSMS:** 898 • **Aptitudes:** G3, V3, N3, S3, P3, Q3, K3, F4, M4, E5, C4 • **Temperaments:** M, T • **Physical:** V=L, H=N, L=L, W, H • **Work Env:** I • **Salary:** 2 • **Outlook:** 3

SHIPPING-AND-RECEIVING WEIGHER (clerical) • D.O.T. #222.367-058 • OES #58017 • WEIGHT RECORDER. Weighs and records weight of filled containers, cargo of loaded vehicles, or rolls of materials, such as cotton, sugarcane, paper, cloth, plastic, and tobacco, to keep receiving and shipping records: Reads scale dial to ascertain weight and records weight on ticket, product, or material; or subtracts tare from gross weight to obtain net weight of product or material; or inserts ticket into automatic scale recorder that prints weight on ticket. May convey objects to scale, using handtruck, and lift objects onto scale. May record information on weight ticket, such as grade and yardage. May be designated according to item weighed as CLOTH WEIGHER (knit goods); GARMENT WEIGHER (knit goods); ROLL WEIGHER (paper & pulp; paper goods; plastics mat.); TOBACCO WEIGHER (clerical). May signal YARD ENGINEER (r.r. trans.) to move cars on and off scale and be designated as SCALER (r.r. trans.). May weigh only incoming or outgoing materials or products and be designated as RECEIVING WEIGHER (clerical); SHIPPING WEIGHER (clerical). • **GED:** R3, M2, L2 • **SVP:** 2-30 days • **Academic:** Ed=N, Eng=S • **Work Field:** 212 • **MPSMS:** 898 • **Aptitudes:** G3, V4, N3, S4, P4, Q3, K3, F3, M4, E5, C5 • **Temperaments:** M, T • **Physical:** V=L, H=N, L=L, H • **Work Env:** I • **Salary:** 2 • **Outlook:** 3

STOCK CLERK, SELF-SERVICE STORE (ret. tr.) • D.O.T. #299.367-014 • OES #49021 • Performs any combination of following duties in self-service store: Marks order form to order merchandise based on available shelf space, merchandise on hand, customer demand, or advertised specials. Periodically counts merchandise to take inventory or examines shelves to identify which items need to be reordered or replenished. Unpacks cartons and crates of merchandise, checking invoice against items received. Stamps or attaches prices on merchandise or changes price tags, referring to pricelist. Stocks shelves with new or transferred merchandise. Sets up advertising signs and displays merchandise on shelves, counters, or tables to attract customers and promote sales. Cleans display cases, shelves, and aisles. May itemize and total customer's selection at check out counter, using cash register, and make change or charge purchases. May pack customers purchases in bags or cartons. May carry packages to customer's automobile. May be designated according to type of merchandise handled as BAKED-GOODS STOCK CLERK (ret. tr.); DELI CATESSEN-GOODS STOCK CLERK (ret. tr.); DISCOUNT-VARIETY-STORE STOCK CLERK (ret. tr.); GROCERY-GOODS STOCK CLERK (ret. tr.); LIQUOR-STORE STOCK CLERK (ret. tr.); MEAT STOCK CLERK (ret. tr.); PHARMACY STOCK CLERK (ret. tr.); PRODUCE STOCK CLERK (ret. tr.); or type of store worked in as SUPERMARKET STOCK CLERK (ret. tr.). • **GED:** R3, M2, L2 • **SVP:** 3-6 mos • **Academic:** Ed=N, Eng=S • **Work Field:** 221, 292 • **MPSMS:** 881 • **Aptitudes:** G3, V4, N4, S3, P3, Q3, K3, F4, M3, E4, C4 • **Temperaments:** M, V • **Physical:** V=L, H=N, L=M, W, S, H • **Work Env:** I • **Salary:** 2 • **Outlook:** 3

SUPPLY CLERK (per. ser.) • D.O.T. #339.687-010 • OES #58023 • DISPENSARY ATTENDANT; STOREKEEPER. Dispenses supplies in beauty parlor or barber shop: Counts, sorts, issues, and collects articles, such as towels, drapes, combs, brushes, curlers, and nets. Washes combs and brushes in antiseptic soap solution and places them in sterilizing cabinet. Dilutes concentrated shampoo, rinses, and waving solutions with water according to instructions. Dissolves cake soap in water to make shampoo. Assembles materials, solutions, and equipment specified for individual treatment, such as facial, permanent wave, and manicure. Maintains perpetual supply inventory and lists items needed to replace stock. Sweeps floor and tidies rooms. • **GED:** R2, M2, L1 • **SVP:** 30 days-3 mos • **Academic:** Ed=N, Eng=N • **Work Field:** 031, 221 • **MPSMS:** 904 • **Aptitudes:** G4, V4, N4, S4, P4, Q4, K4, F4, M4, E5, C4 • **Temperaments:** V • **Physical:** V=N, H=N, L=L, W, H • **Work Env:** I, W • **Salary:** 2 • **Outlook:** 2

TIRE ADJUSTER (ret. tr.) • D.O.T. #241.367-034 • OES #53123 • Examines defective tires and tubes returned by customers to determine allowance due on replacement: Visually and tactually examines tire to determine if defect resulted from faulty construction or curing. Measures tread depth, using tread depth gage, to determine remaining tire life. Prorates allowances based on tread wear, warranty provisions, and knowledge of tire characteristics. Explains basis for allowance to customer, sales representative, or distributor. May train new workers. • **GED:** R3, M3, L2 • **SVP:** 30 days-3 mos • **Academic:** Ed=N, Eng=G • **Work Field:** 211, 292 • **MPSMS:** 511 • **Aptitudes:** G3, V3, N3, S3, P3, Q4, K4, F4, M4, E5, C5 • **Temperaments:** M, P • **Physical:** V=L, H=L, L=M, W, S, H • **Work Env:** I • **Salary:** 2 • **Outlook:** 3

TOOL-CRIB ATTENDANT (clerical) • D.O.T. #222.367-062 • OES #58023 • TOOL CLERK. Receives, stores, and issues handtools, machine tools, dies, and equipment, such as measuring devices, in industrial establishment: Keeps records of tools issued to and returned by workers. Searches for lost or misplaced tools. Prepares periodic inventory or keeps perpetual inventory and requisitions stock as needed. Unpacks and stores new equipment. Visually inspects tools or measures with micrometer for wear or defects and reports damaged and worn-out equipment to superiors. May coat tools with grease or other preservative, using brush or spray gun. May make minor tool repairs. May carry or deliver tools by handtruck to workers. May attach identification tags or engrave identifying information on tools and equipment, using electric marking tool. May be designated according to item stored as DIE-STORAGE CLERK (clerical). • **GED:** R3, M2, L2 • **SVP:** 6 mos-1 yr • **Academic:** Ed=N, Eng=S • **Work Field:** 221 • **MPSMS:** 898 • **Aptitudes:** G3, V3, N3, S4, P3, Q4, K4, F4, M3, E5, C5 • **Temperaments:** M, T • **Physical:** V=N, H=N, L=L, W, S, H • **Work Env:** I • **Salary:** 2 • **Outlook:** 3

GOE: 05.09.02 Estimating, Scheduling & Record Keeping

DRAPERY AND UPHOLSTERY ESTIMATOR (ret. tr.) • D.O.T. #299.387-010 • OES #49999 • Estimates price of making and installing household accessories, such as draperies, slipcovers, window shades, and furniture upholstery: Computes cost of fabric and hardware, according to measurements, work specifications, and type of fabric to be used, using calculator. Itemizes cost of labor in making and installing goods. Records total price on sales check or contract. May contact customer to obtain additional information about order. May confer with ARCHITECTS (profess. & kin.) and interior decorators to obtain additional information when computing estimates for commercial orders. May take measurements for draperies, upholstery, slipcovers, or shades in customer's home [DRAPERY AND UPHOLSTERY MEASURER (ret. tr.)]. May specialize in estimating price of specific type of household accessory and be designated as DRAPERY ESTIMATOR (ret. tr.); UPHOLSTERY ESTIMATOR (ret. tr.). • **GED:** R3, M3, L2 • **SVP:** 6 mos-1 yr • **Academic:** Ed=N, Eng=N • **Work Field:** 211, 232 • **MPSMS:** 439, 881 • **Aptitudes:** G3, V3, N3, S3, P3, Q3, K4, F4, M4, E5, C4 • **Temperaments:** M, T • **Physical:** V=G, H=G, L=S, W, H • **Work Env:** I • **Salary:** 3 • **Outlook:** 3

ESTIMATOR, PRINTING (print. & pub.) • D.O.T. #221.367-014 • OES #21902 • Estimates labor and material costs of printing and binding books, pamphlets, periodicals, and other printed matter, based on specifications outlined on sales order or submitted by prospective customer: Examines specifications, including sketches or sample layouts, and calculates unit and job-lot production costs, using labor and material pricing schedules, and considering such factors as size and number of sheets or pages, paper stock requirements, and binding operations. Confers with department heads or production personnel to develop or confirm information regarding various cost elements. May estimate cost of mailing finished printed matter if specified on order. May estimate labor and material cost of specific phase of printing, such as plate making, and be designated according to specialty as ESTIMATOR, PRINTING-PLATE-MAKING (print. & pub.). • **GED:** R4, M3, L3 • **SVP:** 1-2 yrs • **Academic:** Ed=H, Eng=G • **Work Field:** 232 • **MPSMS:** 480, 898 • **Aptitudes:** G2, V3, N2, S3, P3, Q2, K4, F4, M4, E5, C4 • **Temperaments:** J, M, P, T • **Physical:** V=L, H=N, L=S, H • **Work Env:** I • **Salary:** 3 • **Outlook:** 3

EVALUATOR (nonprofit org.) • D.O.T. #249.367-034 • OES #55344 • Estimates market value of items donated to vocational rehabilitation organization and prepares and mails tax receipts to donors: Sorts collection receipts by type of items donated. Estimates market value of items, using standard formula, and totals amount donated. Prepares tax receipt and mails to donor. • **GED:** R4, M2, L2 • **SVP:** 3-6 mos • **Academic:** Ed=H, Eng=G • **Work Field:** 211, 231 • **MPSMS:** 891 • **Aptitudes:** G3, V3, N3, S5, P5, Q2, K4, F4, M4, E5, C5 • **Temperaments:** M • **Physical:** V=L, H=N, L=L • **Work Env:** I • **Salary:** 3 • **Outlook:** 3

JOB TRACER (clerical) • D.O.T. #221.387-034 • OES #58008 • JOB CHECKER; JOB SPOTTER; PROGRESS CLERK. Locates and determines progress of job orders in various stages of production, such as fabrication, assembly, and inspection, and compiles reports used by scheduling and production personnel. • **GED:** R3, M2, L3 • **SVP:** 3-6 mos • **Academic:** Ed=N, Eng=S • **Work Field:** 231 • **MPSMS:** 898 • **Aptitudes:** G3, V3, N3, S4, P4, Q3, K4, F4, M4, E5, C4 • **Temperaments:** R • **Stress:** T • **Physical:** V=N, H=N, L=L, H • **Work Env:** I • **Salary:** 2 • **Outlook:** 3

LAUNDRY CLERK (clerical) • D.O.T. #221.387-038 • OES #58099 • FLOOR CLERK. Compiles and maintains work-production records of each employee for use in payroll and efficiency records. Frequently performs other clerical duties, such as recording weights of laundry bundles. May convert count of each type of garment to production points achieved, following prepared charts or verbal instructions. • **GED:** R3, M2, L3 • **SVP:** 30 days-3 mos • **Academic:** Ed=N, Eng=S • **Work Field:** 231 • **MPSMS:** 898 • **Aptitudes:** G3, V4, N3, S4, P4, Q3, K4, F4, M4, E5, C4 • **Temperaments:** R, T • **Stress:** T • **Physical:** V=N, H=N, L=L, H • **Work Env:** I • **Salary:** 2 • **Outlook:** 3

MATERIAL COORDINATOR (clerical) • D.O.T. #221.167-014 • OES #58008 • COORDINATOR, MATERIAL CONTROL; EXPEDITER; MATERIAL CONTROL EXPEDITER; PRODUCTION CONTROL WORKER; SCHEDULER; STOCK CHASER; STOCK RUSTLER. Coordinates and expedites flow of material, parts, and assemblies within or between departments in accordance with production and shipping schedules or department supervisors' priorities: Reviews production schedules and confers with department supervisors to determine material required or overdue and to locate material. Requisitions material and establishes delivery sequences to departments according to job order priorities and anticipated availability of material. Arranges for in-plant transfer of materials to meet production schedules. Arranges with department supervisors for repair and assembly of material and its transportation to various departments. Examines material delivered to production departments to verify if type specified. May monitor and control movement of material and parts along conveyor system, using remote-control panelboard. May compute amount of material needed for specific job orders, applying knowledge of product and manufacturing processes and using adding machine. May compile report of quantity and type of material on hand. May move or transport material from one department to another, using handtruck or industrial truck. May compile perpetual production records in order to locate material in process of production, using manual or computerized system. May maintain employee records. • **GED:** R4, M3, L4 • **SVP:** 1-2 yrs • **Academic:** Ed=H, Eng=G • **Work Field:** 221 • **MPSMS:** 898 • **Aptitudes:** G3, V3, N3, S4, P3, Q3, K4, F4, M4, E5, C4 • **Temperaments:** J, P, T, V • **Stress:** E • **Physical:** V=L, H=L, L=S, H • **Work Env:** I • **Salary:** 3 • **Outlook:** 3

MATERIAL EXPEDITER (clerical) • D.O.T. #221.367-042 • OES #58008 • EXPEDITER; STOCK CHASER. Locates and moves materials and parts between work areas of plant to expedite processing of goods, according to predetermined schedules and priorities, and keeps related records: Reviews production schedules, inventory reports, and work orders to determine types, quantities, and availability of required materi al and priorities of customer orders. Confers with department supervisors to determine materials overdue and to inform them of location, availability, and condition of materials. Locates and moves materials to specified production areas, using cart or handtruck. Records quantity and type of materials distributed and on hand. May direct INDUSTRIAL-TRUCK OPERATOR (any ind.) 921.683-050 or MATERIAL HANDLER (any ind.) 929.687-030 to expedite move ment of materials between storage and production areas. May compare work ticket specifications with material at work stations to verify appropriateness of material in use. May prepare worker production records and timecards. May update and maintain inventory records, using computer terminal. **GED:** R3, M3, L3 • **SVP:** 3-6 mos • **Academic:** Ed=N, Eng=G • **Work Field:** 221 • **MPSMS:** 587, 898 • **Aptitudes:** G3, V3, N3, S4, P4, Q3, K4, F4, M4, E5, C4 • **Temperaments:** P, T, V • **Stress:** E • **Physical:** V=L, H=L, L=M, H • **Work Env:** I • **Salary:** 3 • **Outlook:** 3

ORDER DETAILER (clerical) • D.O.T. #221.387-046 • OES #58008 • JOB-ORDER CLERK; TICKETER; WORK-ORDER CLERK; WORK-ORDER DETAILER. Compiles, from customer's order and other specifications, detailed worksheets or tickets for use in plant as guides in assembly or manufacture of products: Compares customer purchase order with specifications to determine method and materials needed. Enters on worksheet data, such as quantity, quality, type, and size of material, piecework wage rate, proposed production rate, and expected completion date. Obtains assembly instructions, blueprints, and tracings from files and attaches to worksheet. May keep inventory of stock on hand and requisition needed material and supplies. May compute data for workticket, such as quantity of material and production and piecework rates, using adding machine or calculator. May prepare worksheets pertaining to cloth printing and mixing of printing colors and be designated FORMULA CHECKER (tex. prod., n.e.c.; textile). May prepare worksheets and order steel stock for rolling mill and be designated PROVIDER (iron & steel). May prepare work order and allocate silicon crystalingots that meet customer specifications for use in manufacturing semiconductor wafers and be designated ALLOCATIONS CLERK (electronics). May compile process specification sheets and prepare and issue materials for use in semiconductor crystal growing and be designated PRODUCTION MATERIAL COORDINATOR (electronics). • **GED:** R3, M3, L3 • **SVP:** 3-6 mos • **Academic:** Ed=N, Eng=S • **Work Field:** 231 • **MPSMS:** 587 • **Aptitudes:** G3, V3, N3, S4, P4, Q2, K4, F4, M4, E5, C4 • **Temperaments:** R, T • **Stress:** T • **Physical:** V=L, H=N, L=L, H • **Work Env:** I • **Salary:** 2 • **Outlook:** 3

PRESCRIPTION CLERK, LENS-AND-FRAMES (optical goods) • D.O.T. #222.367-050 • OES #58023 • Selects lens blanks and frames for production of eyeglasses, according to prescription specifications, and keeps stock inventory at specified level: Reads prescription to determine specifications, such as lens power and base curve and frame style and color. Selects lens blanks and frames from stock and routes them with prescription to production section. Requisitions lens blanks and eyeglass frames and communicates by letter and telephone with suppliers to keep stock at specified level. May work with only lenses or frames and be designated accordingly as PRESCRIPTION CLERK, FRAMES (optical goods); PRESCRIPTION CLERK, LENSES (optical goods). • **GED:** R3, M2, L2 • **SVP:** 6 mos-1 yr • **Academic:** Ed=N, Eng=G • **Work Field:** 221 • **MPSMS:** 605, 898 • **Aptitudes:** G3, V3, N3, S4, P3, Q3, K4, F4, M3, E5, C4 • **Temperaments:** M, T • **Physical:** V=L, H=N, L=L, H • **Work Env:** I • **Salary:** 2 • **Outlook:** 3

PRODUCTION COORDINATOR (clerical) • D.O.T. #221.167-018 • OES #58008 • PRODUCTION CONTROLLER; PRODUCTION EXPEDITER; PRODUCTION SCHEDULER; PROGRESS CLERK; SCHEDULE CLERK; SCHEDULER. Schedules and coordinates flow of work within or between departments of manufacturing plant to expedite production: Reviews master production schedule and work orders, establishes priorities for specific customer orders, and revises schedule according to work order specifications, established priorities, and availability or capability of workers, parts, material, machines, and equipment. Reschedules identical processes to eliminate duplicate machine setups. Distrib-

utes work orders to departments denoting number, type, and proposed completion date of units to be produced. Confers with department supervisors to determine progress of work and to provide information on changes in processing methods received from methods or engineering departments. Compiles reports on progress of work and machine, tool, and equipment failures to inform production planning department of production delays. May expedite material [MATERIAL COORDINATOR (clerical)]. May keep inventory of material in department. May expedite production of spare parts and establish delivery dates for spare-parts orders and be designated SPARES SCHEDULER (clerical). May coordinate and expedite work in automobile repair and service establishment from control tower, using public address system, and be designated as WORK COORDINATOR, TOWER CONTROL (auto. ser.). • **GED:** R4, M3, L4 • **SVP:** 1-2 yrs • **Academic:** Ed=H, Eng=G • **Work Field:** 295 • **MPSMS:** 898 • **Aptitudes:** G2, V2, N3, S3, P3, Q3, K4, F4, M4, E5, C4 • **Temperaments:** D, J, M, P, T • **Stress:** E, A • **Physical:** V=N, H=L, L=S • **Work Env:** I • **Salary:** 3 • **Outlook:** 3

SALES CORRESPONDENT (clerical) • D.O.T. #221.367-062 • OES #55317 • Compiles data pertinent to manufacture of special products for customers: Reads correspondence from customers to determine needs of customer not met by standard products. Confers with engineering department to ascertain feasibility of designing special equipment. Confers with production personnel to determine feasibility of fabrication and to obtain estimate of cost and production time. Corresponds with customer to inform of production progress and costs. May specialize in correspondence dealing with customer service agreements and be designated as SERVICE CORRESPONDENT (clerical). • **GED:** R4, M2, L4 • **SVP:** 1-2 yrs • **Academic:** Ed=H, Eng=G • **Work Field:** 231, 244 • **MPSMS:** 898 • **Aptitudes:** G2, V2, N3, S3, P3, Q3, K4, F4, M4, E5, C5 • **Temperaments:** M, P, V • **Stress:** E • **Physical:** V=L, H=N, L=L • **Work Env:** I • **Salary:** 3 • **Outlook:** 3

STOCK CLERK (clerical) • D.O.T. #222.387-058 • OES #58023 • STOCK CHECKER; STOCKROOM CLERK; STOREKEEPER; STOREROOM CLERK; STOREROOM KEEPER; STORES CLERK; SUPPLY CLERK; SUPPLY-ROOM CLERK. Receives, stores, and issues equipment, material, supplies, merchandise, foodstuffs, or tools, and compiles stock records in stockroom, warehouse, or storage yard: Counts, sorts, or weighs incoming articles to verify receipt of items on requisition or invoices. Examines stock to verify conformance to specifications. Stores articles in bins, on floor, or on shelves, according to identifying information, such as style, size, or type of material. Fills orders or issues supplies from stock. Prepares periodic, special, or perpetual inventory of stock. Requisitions articles to fill incoming orders. Compiles reports on use of stock handling equipment, adjustments of inventory counts and stock records, spoilage of or damage to stock, location changes, and refusal of shipments. May mark identifying codes, figures, or letters on articles. May distribute stock among production workers, keeping records of material issued. May make adjustments or repairs to articles carried in stock. May determine methods of storage, identification, and stock location, considering temperature, humidity, height and weight limits, turnover, floor loading capacities, and required space. May cut stock to size to fill order. May move or transport material or supplies to other departments, using hand or industrial truck. May be designated according to material, equipment, or product stored as CAMERA-STOREROOM CLERK (motion pic.); OIL-HOUSE ATTENDANT (clerical); WIRE STOCKKEEPER (wirework); or work location as WINE-CELLAR STOCK CLERK (hotel & rest.); or stage in manufacture of material or goods as FINISHED-GOODS STOCK CLERK (clerical); or container in which goods are stored as DRUM-STOCK CLERK (cleri cal). Additional titles: CUSTODIAN, BLOOD BANK (medical ser.); FOOD-STOREROOM CLERK (hotel & rest.); HOGSHEAD-STOCK CLERK (tobacco); MATERIAL STOCKKEEPER, YARD (petrol. production); MOLD PICKER (rubber goods); PAINT STOCKER (aircraft-aerospace mfg.); PATTERN-ROOM ATTENDANT (found.); PRINTING-PLATE CLERK (print. & pub.); SACK KEEPER (clerical); TEMPLATE-STORAGE CLERK (clerical); REFRIGERATOR-ROOM CLERK (clerical). May receive, store, and sort unserviceable equipment and supplies for sale, disposal or reclamation and be known as SALVAGE CLERK (clerical). • **GED:** R3, M3, L2 • **SVP:** 3-6 mos • **Academic:** Ed=N, Eng=S • **Work Field:** 221 • **MPSMS:** 898 • **Aptitudes:** G3, V3, N3, S3, P3, Q2, K4, F4, M3, E5, C4 • **Temperaments:** M, T • **Physical:** V=N, H=N, L=H, W, S, H • **Work Env:** I • **Salary:** 3 • **Outlook:** 3

GOE: 05.09.03 Verifying, Recording & Marking

CHECKER, DUMP GROUNDS (bus. ser.) • D.O.T. #219.367-010 • OES #58099 • Estimates size of load on truck entering dump grounds. Collects fees based on size of load and type of material dumped. Keeps record of truckloads and money received. Directs truck drivers to designated dumping areas. May weigh truck, using scale, to determine amount of load. • **GED:** R3, M3, L2 • **SVP:** 30 days-3 mos • **Academic:** Ed=N, Eng=S • **Work Field:** 211, 232 • **MPSMS:** 874, 899 • **Aptitudes:** G4, V4, N3, S3, P4, Q3, K4, F4, M4, E5, C5 • **Temperaments:** J, T • **Physical:** V=L, H=N, L=L, H • **Work Env:** B • **Salary:** 3 • **Outlook:** 2

INDUSTRIAL-ORDER CLERK (clerical) • D.O.T. #221.367-022 • OES #58028 • Verifies completion of industrial orders and conformance of product to specifications: Compares blueprints with contract or order to ascertain that product meets engineering specifications. Communicates with customer and delivery personnel to verify delivery of product. Fills out completion slip after order is filled. May route products not meeting specifications to production units for correction. • **GED:** R4, M3, L4 • **SVP:** 3-6 mos • **Academic:** Ed=N, Eng=S • **Work Field:** 221 • **MPSMS:** 898 • **Aptitudes:** G3, V3, N3, S3, P3, Q3, K3, F3, M3, E5, C5 • **Temperaments:** P, T • **Physical:** V=L, H=N, L=S, H • **Work Env:** I • **Salary:** 3 • **Outlook:** 3

MARKER (ret. tr.) • D.O.T. #209.587-034 • OES #58021 • MARKING CLERK; MERCHANDISE MARKER; PRICE MARKER; TICKET MAKER. Marks and attaches price tickets to articles of merchandise to record price and identifying information: Marks selling price by hand on boxes containing merchandise, or on price tickets. Ties, glues, sews, or staples price ticket to each article. Presses lever or plunger of mechanism that pins, pastes, ties, or staples ticket to article. May record number and types of articles marked and pack them in boxes. May compare printed price tickets with entries on purchase order to verify accuracy and notify supervisor of discrepancies. If worker prints information on tickets, using ticket-printing machine, see TICKETER (any ind.) or TICKET PRINTER AND TAGGER (garment). • **GED:** R2, M1, L1 • **SVP:** 2-30 days • **Academic:** Ed=N, Eng=N • **Work Field:** 231 • **MPSMS:** 881, 882 • **Aptitudes:** G4, V4, N4, S4, P4, Q3, K4, F3, M4, E5, C5 • **Temperaments:** R, T • **Stress:** T • **Physical:** V=L, H=N, L=L, W, H • **Work Env:** I • **Salary:** 2 • **Outlook:** 3

MATERIAL CLERK (clerical) • D.O.T. #222.387-034 • OES #58023 • MATERIAL CHECKER; STOCK EDITOR; STOCK-RECORD CLERK; STORES-AUDITOR CLERK. Compiles records concerned with quantity, cost, and type of material received, stored, and issued in department or establishment or on job, and requisitions needed supplies: Verifies material received against requisitions, shipping notices, or invoices, to determine irregularities in order. Inspects articles and rejects defective ones. Prepares inventory or keeps perpetual inventory records [INVENTORY CLERK (clerical)]. Prepares requisitions for procurement of material and supplies. May be designated according to location of goods as WAREHOUSE-RECORD CLERK (clerical). • **GED:** R3, M3, L2 • **SVP:** 6 mos-1 yr • **Academic:** Ed=N, Eng=N • **Work Field:** 221 • **MPSMS:** 898 • **Aptitudes:** G3, V3, N3, S4, P3, Q2, K4, F4, M4, E5, C5 • **Temperaments:** M, T • **Physical:** V=N, H=N, L=L, H • **Work Env:** I • **Salary:** 2 • **Outlook:** 3

METER READER (light, heat, & power) • D.O.T. #209.567-010 • OES #58014 • Reads electric, gas, water, or steam consumption meters and records volume used by residential and commercial consumers: Walks or drives truck over established route and takes readings of meter dials. Inspects meters and connections for defects, damage, and unauthorized connections. Indicates irregularities on forms for necessary action by servicing department. Verifies readings to locate abnormal consumption and records reasons for fluctuations. Turns service off for nonpayment of charges in vacant premises, or on for new occupants. Collects bills in arrears. Returns route book to business office for billing purposes. May be designated according to type of meter read as ELECTRIC-METER READER (light, heat, & power); GAS-METER READER (light, heat, & power); STEAM-METER READER (light, heat, & power); WATER-METER READER (waterworks). • **GED:** R3, M2, L2 • **SVP:** 3-6 mos • **Academic:** Ed=N, Eng=N • **Work Field:** 231 • **MPSMS:** 871 • **Aptitudes:** G3, V3, N3, S4, P4, Q3, K5, F5, M5, E5, C5 • **Temperaments:** R, T • **Physical:** V=L, H=N, L=S, W, C • **Work Env:** O • **Salary:** 3 • **Outlook:** 3

ORDER CALLER (clerical) • D.O.T. #209.667-014 • OES #58099 • CALLER; CALL-OUT CLERK; ORDER-DESK CALLER. Reads items listed on order sheets to LABORER, STORES (any ind.) who gathers and assembles items or to BILLING TYPIST (clerical) who prepares bills for items. Indicates on order sheets items located and items that are not available. May read items to CHECKER (clerical) I who examines articles prior to shipping. May be designated by kind of data called out to other worker, as WEIGHT CALLER (clerical); YARDAGE CALLER (textile). • **GED:** R2, M1, L2 • **SVP:** 2-30 days • **Academic:** Ed=N, Eng=G • **Work Field:** 221 • **MPSMS:** 880, 898 • **Aptitudes:** G4, V4, N4, S4, P4, Q4, K4, F4, M4, E5, C5 • **Temperaments:** R • **Stress:** T • **Physical:** V=L, H=L, L=S • **Work Env:** I • **Salary:** 2 • **Outlook:** 3

RECEIVING CHECKER (clerical) • D.O.T. #222.687-018 • OES #58017 • CHECKING CLERK; ORDER CHECKER; RECEIVING INSPECTOR; UNLOADING CHECKER. Counts, measures or weighs to verify contents of shipments against bills of lading, invoices, or storage receipts. May examine articles for defects and sort articles according to extent of defect. May attach identification data onto article. May record factors causing goods to be returned. May unload and unpack incoming shipments. • **GED:** R3, M2, L3 • **SVP:** 30 days-3 mos • **Academic:** Ed=N, Eng=S • **Work Field:** 221 • **MPSMS:** 898 • **Aptitudes:** G3, V3, N4, S4, P3, Q3, K4, F4, M3, E5, C5 • **Temperaments:** R, T • **Stress:** T • **Physical:** V=L, H=N, L=M, W, S, H • **Work Env:** I • **Salary:** 2 • **Outlook:** 3

SORTER-PRICER (nonprofit org.) • D.O.T. #222.387-054 • OES #58028 • PRICER-SORTER. Sorts used merchandise received from donors and appraises, prices, wraps, packs, and allocates merchandise for resale in retail outlets of nonprofit organization and maintains related records. Discards unsalable items or sets them aside for salvage or repair. May make minor repairs on damaged merchandise. May be designated according to merchandise sorted as BOOK SORTER (nonprofit organ.); CLOTHING SORTER (nonprofit organ.); JEWELRY SORTER (nonprofit organ.); WARES SORTER (nonprofit organ.). • **GED:** R3, M2, L2 • **SVP:** 6 mos-1 yr • **Academic:** Ed=N, Eng=S • **Work Field:** 211, 221 • **MPSMS:** 898 • **Aptitudes:** G3, V3, N3, S4, P4, Q3, K4, F4, M4, E5, C5 • **Temperaments:** J, M, V • **Physical:** V=L, H=N, L=L, H • **Work Env:** I • **Salary:** 2 • **Outlook:** 3

TURBINE ATTENDANT (light, heat, & power) • D.O.T. #952.567-010 • OES #83005 • Records meter and instrument readings, such as oil and steam temperature and pressure of hydro-electric turbines and related generators that produce electricity. Notifies STATIONARY-ENGINEER SUPERVISOR (any ind.) when recording instruments indicate machine malfunctions. Cleans and lubricates equipment. • **GED:** R3, M2, L3 • **SVP:** 3-6 mos • **Academic:** Ed=N, Eng=S • **Work Field:** 231 • **MPSMS:** 871 • **Aptitudes:** G3, V4, N3, S4, P3, Q3, K4, F4, M3, E5, C4 • **Temperaments:** M, T • **Physical:** V=L, H=N, L=L, W, H • **Work Env:** I, N • **Salary:** 3 • **Outlook:** 3

05.10 Crafts

Workers in this group use hands and handtools skillfully to fabricate, process, install, and/or repair materials, products, and/or structural parts. They follow established procedures and techniques. The jobs are not found in factories, but are in repair shops, garages, wholesale and retail stores, and hotels. Some are found on construction projects, and others with utilities, such as telephone and power systems.

✔ **What kind of work would you do?**
Your work activities would depend upon your specific job. For example, you might:

- take apart household appliances to replace defective parts.
- repair and adjust gas or electric appliances in homes.
- install venetian blinds in commercial establishments.
- repair and adjust radios and television sets.
- plan, set, and shoot explosive charges in mining or oil well drilling.

- operate equipment to regulate volume and quality of sound recordings in a motion picture studio.
- repair, adjust, or replace parts in office machines.
- prepare and cook soups, meats, vegetables, desserts, and other foods in a restaurant.
- install mufflers on automobiles and trucks.
- install air conditioning units in homes.

✔ **What skills and abilities do you need for this kind of work?**
To do this kind of work, you must be able to:

- understand and use blueprints, sketches, drawings, and other kinds of specifications.
- use hands, arms, and fingers.
- work to precise measurements.
- visualize how finished product will look, or how a system operates.

- use arithmetic to measure, compute amount of materials to use, and to inspect product to be sure it conforms to requirements.
- lift and move materials and products.
- climb and balance self.
- work outdoors in all kinds of weather.
- stay calm in face of emergency or danger.

✔ **How do you know if you would like or could learn to do this kind of work?**
The following questions may give you clues about yourself as you consider this group of jobs.

- Have you repaired things that were broken? Can you locate and fix the defective parts?
- Have you cooked or baked? Can you measure and mix ingredients according to recipes?
- Have you repaired or installed parts on an automobile? Can you work skillfully with handtools?

- Have you taken courses in industrial arts or electronics? Can you understand repair instructions and schematic diagrams?
- Have you had military experience involving repair of mechanical or electrical equipment?

✔ How can you prepare for and enter this kind of work?

Occupations in this group usually require education and/or training extending from three months to over four years, depending upon the specific kind of work. The education and training required for jobs involving equipment repair varies according to the type of equipment. Some jobs only require on-the-job training. However, repairers of electronic equipment and business machines must have special training and experience. High schools and vocational schools offer courses in electricity, electronics, mathematics, or blueprint reading.

A few companies provide extensive training to prepare workers for some repair jobs. Correspondence courses in such fields as electricity and electronics are often helpful. Apprenticeships are available.

Many cooks begin as kitchen helpers to get the needed experience and on-the-job training. High school or post-high school training in food preparation is helpful. Training programs are also offered by the armed services, private schools, and some large hotels and restaurants. Apprenticeships are available. It takes several years of training and experience to become a head cook or chef in a large restaurant.

✔ What else should you consider about these jobs?

Working conditions for equipment repairers vary according to the type of equipment. Some jobs require repairs and adjustments to be made in the customer's office or home. Others require that repairs be made in a repair shop setting. Sometimes workers must work in narrow spaces and in uncomfortable positions. Dirt, dust, and grease sometimes create unpleasant conditions.

Working conditions for cooks depend upon the size of the establishment. Many kitchens are well-lighted, well-equipped, and properly ventilated. However, heavy lifting, oven and range heat, and long hours of standing and walking are common to these jobs.

If you think you would like to do this kind of work, look at the job titles listed below.

GOE: 05.10.01 Structural Crafts

ARCH-SUPPORT TECHNICIAN (per. protect. & med. device) • D.O.T. #712.381-010 • OES #89923 • Fabricates steel arch support to fit patient's foot, according to medical prescription: Receives plaster cast of foot from PROSTHETIST (per. protect. & med. dev.) or PODIATRIST (medical ser.). Places protection cloth into cast and fills cast with plaster to mold model of patient's foot. Removes hardened model from cast and traces model outline on paper to use as pattern in cutting support. Selects stainless steel sheet of prescribed thickness and cuts sheet to specified dimensions, using shears, guided by pattern. Hammers steel into prescribed contours to form support and places support against plaster model to determine accuracy of fit. Splits support into front and back pieces when indicated according to prescription, using shears. Polishes support, using abrasive wheel. Glues leather to bottom of arch support to protect shoe, and rivets additional leather across top edge for foot comfort, using riveting tool. • **GED:** R3, M2, L2 • **SVP:** 6 mos-1 yr • **Academic:** Ed=N, Eng=N • **Work Field:** 102 • **MPSMS:** 604 • **Aptitudes:** G3, V4, N4, S3, P3, Q4, K3, F3, M3, E5, C5 • **Temperaments:** M, T • **Physical:** V=L, H=N, L=L, H • **Work Env:** I • **Salary:** 3 • **Outlook:** 2

BOAT RIGGER (ret. tr.) • D.O.T. #806.464-010 • OES #93956 • BOAT ACCESSORIES INSTALLER; OUTBOARD-MOTORBOAT RIGGER. Installs accessories in outboard or inboard motorboats: Drills holes, attaches brackets, and installs accessories, such as lights, batteries, ignition switches, fuel tanks, and guide pulleys, using handtools and power tools. May change propellors and adjust motors to obtain maximum performance. May install outboard and inboard motors and controls, using hand tools. May load boats on trailers and make deliveries to customers. • **GED:** R3, M2, L1 • **SVP:** 3-6 mos • **Academic:** Ed=N, Eng=N • **Work Field:** 102 • **MPSMS:** 593 • **Aptitudes:** G3, V4, N4, S3, P3, Q4, K4, F4, M3,

E5, C4 • **Temperaments:** M, T • **Physical:** V=L, H=N, L=M, W, H • **Work Env:** B • **Salary:** 3 • **Outlook:** 1

BUILDING CLEANER (any ind.) • D.O.T. #891.684-022 • OES #87899 • Cleans brick, stone, or metal exterior of structures, using cleaning agents, such as sand, acid solution, and steam: Cleans limited section of surface to determine strength of cleaning agents needed to prepare desired surface finish. Erects swinging scaffold, positions ladders, or assembles metal scaffolding to facilitate cleaning of structures. Pours specified portions and type of cleaning agents into hoppers or tanks of truck-mounted pumping equipment, and turns valves of equipment to produce steam and pump cleaning agents through hoses. Presses levers of spray nozzles to regulate flow of cleaning agent over structure surface. Cleans excessively stained surface areas, using brushes and cleaning compound. Sprays concrete floor to etch surface for cleaning and applies filler compound to seal floor surface. Cleans exterior surfaces of vehicles, using high pressure hoses and cleaning solutions. Cleans rugs on premise of customer, using chemicals, handbrushes, or portable scrubbing machine. Replaces worn parts of cleaning equipment and maintains equipment, using handtools. • **GED:** R3, M2, L2 • **SVP:** 3-6 mos • **Academic:** Ed=N, Eng=N • **Work Field:** 031 • **MPSMS:** 360 • **Aptitudes:** G3, V4, N4, S3, P3, Q4, K3, F3, M3, E4, C4 • **Temperaments:** R, T • **Stress:** T • **Physical:** V=L, H=N, L=H, W, C, S, H • **Work Env:** I, R, F • **Salary:** 3 • **Outlook:** 3

CARPET CUTTER (ret. tr.) • D.O.T. #929.381-010 • OES #93932 • Measures, marks, and cuts carpeting and linoleum, using measuring and marking devices and knife, or cutting machine, to get maximum number of usable pieces from standard sized rolls, following floor dimensions or diagrams. May be designated according to type of floor covering cut as LINOLEUM CUTTER (ret. tr.). • **GED:** R3, M2, L2 • **SVP:** 6 mos-1 yr • **Academic:** Ed=N, Eng=N • **Work Field:** 054, 241 • **MPSMS:** 431 • **Aptitudes:** G3, V4, N3,

S3, P3, Q4, K3, F3, M3, E5, C3 • Temperaments: M, T • Physical: V=L, H=N, L=H, W, S, H • Work Env: I • Salary: 3 • Outlook: 3

CARPET LAYER (ret. tr.) • D.O.T. #864.381-010 • OES #87602 • Lays carpet and rugs: Measures and cuts carpeting to size according to floor sketches, using carpet knife. Sews sections of carpeting together by hand. Cuts and trims carpet to fit along wall edges, openings, and projections. May lay linoleum. • GED: R3, M2, L2 • SVP: 2-4 yrs • Academic: Ed=N, Eng=S • Work Field: 092 • MPSMS: 431 • Aptitudes: G3, V3, N3, S3, P3, Q4, K3, F3, M3, E5, C3 • Temperaments: M, T • Physical: V=L, H=N, L=H, W, S, H • Work Env: I • Salary: 5 • Outlook: 3

CARPET-LAYER HELPER (ret. tr.) • D.O.T. #864.687-010 • OES #98319 • Assists CARPET LAYER (ret. tr.) to lay carpeting on floors and stairs by performing any combination of the following duties: Stretches and tacks carpeting to floors. Cuts rug padding to specified size and tacks it in place on floor, using hammer. Trims carpeting to fit around openings, using knife. Nails metal treads across door openings to hold carpet in place. Performs other duties as described under HELPER (any ind.). • GED: R2, M1, L2 • SVP: 30 days-3 mos • Academic: Ed=N, Eng=N • Work Field: 092 • MPSMS: 431 • Aptitudes: G4, V4, N4, S4, P3, Q4, K4, F4, M3, E5, C4 • Temperaments: R • Stress: T • Physical: V=L, H=N, L=H, W, S, H • Work Env: I • Salary: 4 • Outlook: 3

CASTING REPAIRER (any ind.) • D.O.T. #619.281-010 • OES #85999 • Repairs broken or cracked castings and forgings, using special cold process requiring no welding: Calculates factors, such as size, depth, and position of fracture, and tensile strength and distribution of stress and strain in material. Employs combination of holding and locking devices to make repair, using airhammers, air drills, air grinders, punches, and strippers to insert holding and locking devices in casting and to smooth finish. May fabricate special angle heads for airhammer, air grinder, and air drill, using blacksmith tools and anvil. • GED: R3, M3, L3 • SVP: 1-2 yrs • Academic: Ed=N, Eng=S • Work Field: 102 • MPSMS: 542, 556 • Aptitudes: G3, V3, N3, S3, P3, Q4, K4, F4, M3, E5, C5 • Temperaments: M, T, V • Physical: V=L, H=N, L=M, W, H • Work Env: I • Salary: 4 • Outlook: 2

DIVER (any ind.) • D.O.T. #899.261-010 • OES #85999 • SUBMARINE WORKER. Works below surface of water, using scuba gear (self-contained underwater breathing apparatus) or in diving suit with airline extending to surface to inspect, repair, remove, and install equipment and structures: Descends into water with aid of DIVER HELPER (any ind.), and communicates with surface by signal line or telephone. Inspects docks, and bottoms and propellers of ships. Repairs vessels below waterline, replacing missing or leaking rivets with bolts. Calks leaks in ships or caissons. Guides placement of pilings for structures, such as docks, bridges, cofferdams, and oil drilling platforms. Lays, inspects, and repairs underwater pipelines, cables, and sewers, using handtools. Cuts and welds steel, using oxyacetylene cutting torch and arc-welding equipment, utilizing air balloon device for working underwater. Cleans debris from intake and discharge strainers. Removes obstructions from marine railway or launching ways with pneumatic and power handtools. Levels rails by driving wedges beneath track with maul or sledge hammer. Removes launching cradles and sliding ways from keels of newly launched vessels, using power and handtools. Places rigging around sunken objects and hooks rigging to crane lines. Rigs explosives for underwater demolitions. Searches for lost, missing, or sunken objects, such as bodies, torpedoes, sunken vessels, and equipment. Places recording instruments below surface of water preparatory to underwater tests or experiments. May set sheet pilings for cofferdams. May drill holes in rock for blasting purposes at bottom of lake or harbor and be designated as MARINE DRILLER (const.). May work in flooded mines. May use armored diving equipment for dangerous missions. May photograph underwater structures or marine life. May place sandbags around pipelines or base of cofferdam to provide structural support. • GED: R4, M3, L3 • SVP: 2-4 yrs • Academic: Ed=N, Eng=S • Work Field: 005, 102 • MPSMS: 365, 593 • Aptitudes: G3, V3, N3, S2, P3, Q4, K3, F3, M3, E2, C5 • Temperaments: S, T, V • Stress: S • Physical: V=L, H=N, L=H, W, S, H • Work Env: O, C, W, R • Salary: 4 • Outlook: 2

DRAPERY HANGER (ret. tr.) • D.O.T. #869.484-014 • OES

#87899 • **INSTALLATION WORKER, DRAPERIES; INSTALLER.** Installs draperies in customers' homes: Measures area to be covered, and delivers finished draperies to customers' homes. Screws and bolts brackets and hangers onto wall, using handtools. Hangs and arranges draperies to enhance appearance of room. May install window shades and venetian blinds. • GED: R3, M2, L2 • SVP: 6 mos-1 yr • Academic: Ed=N, Eng=S • Work Field: 102 • MPSMS: 439 • Aptitudes: G3, V4, N3, S3, P4, Q4, K3, F4, M3, E5, C5 • Temperaments: R, T • Stress: T • Physical: V=L, H=N, L=M, W, H • Work Env: I • Salary: 3 • Outlook: 3

DRY-WALL APPLICATOR (const.) • D.O.T. #842.681-010 • OES #87108 • **DRY-WALL NAILER; SHEETROCK INSTALLER.** Installs plasterboard or other wallboard to ceiling and interior walls of building, using handtools and portable power tools: Installs horizontal and verticle metal studs for attachment of wallboard on interior walls, using handtools. Cuts angle iron and channel iron to specified size, using hacksaw, and suspends angle iron grid and channel iron from ceiling, using wire. Scribes measurements on wallboard, using straightedge and tape measure, and cuts wallboard to size, using hacksaw. Cuts out openings for electrical and other outlets, using hawk-bill knife and hammer. Nails wallboard to wall and ceiling supports, using hammer. Trims rough edges from wallboard to maintain even joints, using knife. Nails prefabricated metal pieces around windows and doors and between dissimilar materials to protect drywall edges. • GED: R3, M2, L2 • SVP: 1-2 yrs • Academic: Ed=N, Eng=N • Work Field: 102 • MPSMS: 361, 455, 536 • Aptitudes: G3, V4, N4, S3, P4, Q4, K3, F3, M3, E4, C5 • Temperaments: M, T • Physical: V=G, H=N, L=M, W, C, S, H • Work Env: I, R • Salary: 5 • Outlook: 3

FENCE ERECTOR (const.) • D.O.T. #869.684-022 • OES #87817 • **IRONWORKER, WIRE-FENCE ERECTOR; WIRE-FENCE BUILDER.** Erects and repairs metal and wooden fences and fence gates around industrial establishments, residences, or farms, using power tools and handtools: Lays out fence line, using tape measure, and marks positions for postholes. Digs postholes with spade, posthole digger, or power-driven auger. Blasts rock formations with dynamite to facilitate digging of postholes. Sets metal or wooden post in upright position in posthole. Mixes concrete by hand or by use of cement mixer. Pours concrete around base of post or tamps soil into posthole to embed post. Alines posts, using line or by sighting along edges of posts. Verifies vertical alinement of posts with plumb bob or spirit level. Attaches fence-rail support to post, using hammer and pliers. Cuts metal tubing, using pipe cutter and inserts tubing through rail supports. Completes top fence rail of metal fence by connecting tube sections by use of metal sleeves. Attaches rails or tension wire along bottoms of posts to form fencing frame. Stretches wire, wire mesh, or chain link fencing between posts and attaches fencing to frame. Assembles gate and fastens it in position, using handtools. Saws required lengths of lumber to make rails for wooden fence. Nails top and bottom rails to fence posts, or inserts them in slots on posts. Nails pointed slats to rails to construct picket fence. Erects alternate panel, basket weave, and louvered fences. May weld metal parts together, using portable gas welding equipment. May be designated according to material used as METAL-FENCE ERECTOR (const.); WIRE-FENCE ERECTOR (const.); WOODEN-FENCE ERECTOR (const.), or according to specific duty performed as FENCE-GATE ASSEMBLER (const.); FENCE SETTER (const.); FENCE STRETCHER (const.). • GED: R3, M2, L2 • SVP: 6 mos-1 yr • Academic: Ed=N, Eng=N • Work Field: 102 • MPSMS: 369 • Aptitudes: G3, V4, N4, S3, P3, Q4, K3, F3, M3, E4, C4 • Temperaments: R, T • Stress: T • Physical: V=L, H=N, L=H, W, S, H • Work Env: O, N • Salary: 3 • Outlook: 3

FIXTURE REPAIRER-FABRICATOR (any ind.) • D.O.T. #630.384-010 • OES #85119 • Fabricates and repairs fixtures, rods, baskets, and hooks used to suspend articles in plating, cleansing, and painting vats, using handtools and portable power tools: Cuts metal stock to size, using handsaws or powersaws and forming machines and following working sketches. Bends metal, using vise or hammer. Drills and taps holes, using portable power drill. Bolts or screws parts together, using wrenches and screwdrivers. May braze, solder, or weld parts together. • GED: R3, M2, L2 • SVP: 6 mos-1 yr • Academic: Ed=N, Eng=N • Work Field: 102 • MPSMS: 550 • Aptitudes: G3, V3, N4, S3, P3, Q4, K4, F3, M3,

E5, C5 • **Temperaments:** M, T • **Physical:** V=L, H=N, L=M, W, H • **Work Env:** I, N • **Salary:** 4 • **Outlook:** 2

FLOOR LAYER (const.) • D.O.T. #864.481-010 • OES #87605 • FLOOR COVERER; FLOOR-COVERING-TILE LAYER. Applies blocks, strips, or sheets of shock-absorbing, sound-deadening, or decorative covering to floors, walls, and cabinets: Disconnects and removes obstacles, such as appliances and light fixtures. Sweeps, scrapes, sands, or chips dirt and irregularities from base surfaces, and fills cracks with putty, plaster, or cement grout to form smooth, clean foundation. Measures and cuts covering materials, such as rubber, linoleum or cork tile, and foundation material, such as felt, according to blueprints and sketches, using rule, straightedge, linoleum knife, and snips. Spreads adhesive cement over floor to cement foundation material to floor for sound-deadening, and to prevent covering from wearing at board joints. Lays out center-lines, guidelines, and borderlines on foundation with chalkline and dividers. Spreads cement on foundation material with serrated trowel. Lays covering on cement, following guidelines, to keep tile courses straight and butts edges of blocks to match patterns and execute designs. Joins sections of sheet covering by overlapping adjoining edges and cutting through both layers with knife to form tight joint. Rolls finished floor to smooth it and press cement into base and covering. May soften area of floor covering with butane torch to fit materials around irregular surfaces. May lay carpet [CARPET LAYER (ret. tr.)]. May be designated according to type of floor laid as ASPHALT-TILE-FLOOR LAYER (const.; ret. tr.); CORK-TILE- FLOOR LAYER (const.; ret. tr.); LINOLEUM-FLOOR LAYER (const.; ret. tr.); LINOLEUM LAYER (const.; ret. tr.); LINOLEUM-TILE-FLOOR LAYER (const.; ret. tr.); RUBBER-TILE-FLOOR LAYER (const.; ret. tr.). • **GED:** R3, M2, L2 • **SVP:** 1-2 yrs • **Academic:** Ed=N, Eng=S • **Work Field:** 092 • **MPSMS:** 361 • **Aptitudes:** G3, V3, N3, S3, P3, Q4, K3, F3, M3, E4, C4 • **Temperaments:** T, V • **Physical:** V=L, H=N, L=M, W, S, H • **Work Env:** I • **Salary:** 5 • **Outlook:** 3

FRAME REPAIRER (furn.) • D.O.T. #763.681-010 • OES #85999 • Repairs frames of sofas and chairs damaged during upholstering in furniture plant: Removes upholstery, burlap, or webbing to expose splits or breaks in frames. Glues and secures splits with screws, dowels, or nails, using hand tools. Cuts out or chisels away broken parts of frames, using handsaw, portable powersaw, or hammer and wood chisel. Cuts replacement parts to fit adjacent parts of frames and glues and dowels replacement parts to frames. • **GED:** R3, M3, L2 • **SVP:** 1-2 yrs • **Academic:** Ed=N, Eng=N • **Work Field:** 101 • **MPSMS:** 462 • **Aptitudes:** G3, V4, N4, S3, P3, Q4, K3, F3, M3, E5, C5 • **Temperaments:** J, T • **Physical:** V=L, H=N, L=H, W, S, H • **Work Env:** I • **Salary:** 4 • **Outlook:** 2

FRONT-END MECHANIC (auto. ser.) • D.O.T. #620.281-038 • OES #85302 • ALINEMENT MECHANIC; AXLE-AND-FRAME MECHANIC; CHASSIS MECHANIC; WHEEL-ALINEMENT ME-CHANIC. Alines wheels, axles, frames, torsion bars, and steering mechanisms of automotive vehicles, such as automobiles, buses, and trucks: Drives automotive vehicle onto wheel alinement rack and tests vehicle for faulty wheel alinement, bent axle, worn ball joints, and bent steering rods, using alinement-testing machine. Straightens axle and steering rods and adjusts shims, tie rods, and joining pins to aline wheels, or installs new parts, using handtools. Places wheel on balancing machine to determine where counter-weights must be added to balance wheel. Hammers counter weights onto rim of wheel. Installs shock absorbers. Straightens frame, using hydraulic jack, chassis aliner, and acetylene torch. • **GED:** R3, M3, L3 • **SVP:** 1-2 yrs • **Academic:** Ed=N, Eng=S • **Work Field:** 121 • **MPSMS:** 591 • **Aptitudes:** G3, V3, N4, S3, P3, Q4, K3, F3, M3, E4, C5 • **Temperaments:** M, T, V • **Physical:** V=L, H=N, L=L, W, S, H • **Work Env:** I • **Salary:** 4 • **Outlook:** 4

FURNITURE ASSEMBLER-AND-INSTALLER (ret. tr.) • D.O.T. #739.684-082 • OES #93999 • Uncrates, assembles, installs, and repairs furniture and office equipment in customers' homes or offices: Uncrates and assembles items, using hand tools. Repairs and paints dents and scratches in metal or wood. Cleans, repairs, and replaces safe and file drawers, locks, catches, and slides. May repair or replace damaged vinyl or fabric upholstery material, using handtools, patching, needle, and thread. • **GED:** R3, M2, L1 • **SVP:** 3-6 mos • **Academic:** Ed=N, Eng=N • **Work Field:** 102 • **MPSMS:** 460 • **Aptitudes:** G3, V4, N4, S3, P3, Q4,

K3, F4, M3, E4, C4 • **Temperaments:** M, T, V • **Physical:** V=L, H=N, L=H, W, H • **Work Env:** I • **Salary:** 2 • **Outlook:** 2

GLASS INSTALLER (auto. ser.) • D.O.T. #865.684-010 • OES #85305 • AUTO-GLASS WORKER; GLAZIER; WINDSHIELD INSTALLER. Replaces broken or pitted windshields and window glass in motor vehicles: Removes broken glass by unscrewing frame, using handtools. Cuts flat safety glass according to specified pattern, using glasscutter. Smooths cut edge of glass by holding against abrasive belt. Applies moisture proofing compound along cut edges and installs glass in vehicle. Weather proofs window or windshield and prevents it from rattling by installing rubber channeling strips around sides of glass. Installs precut replacement glass to replace curved windows. May replace or adjust parts in window-raising mechanism. • **GED:** R3, M1, L2 • **SVP:** 3-6 mos • **Academic:** Ed=N, Eng=S • **Work Field:** 102 • **MPSMS:** 531 • **Aptitudes:** G3, V4, N4, S3, P3, Q4, K3, F3, M3, E5, C5 • **Temperaments:** R, T • **Stress:** T • **Physical:** V=G, H=N, L=M, W, H • **Work Env:** I • **Salary:** 4 • **Outlook:** 3

GLAZIER (const.) • D.O.T. #865.381-010 • OES #87811 • GLASS SETTER; GLASSWORKER; GLAZIER, PLATE GLASS. Installs glass in windows, skylights, store fronts, and display cases, or on surfaces, such as building fronts, interior walls, ceilings, and tabletops: Marks outline or pattern on glass, and cuts glass, using glasscutter. Breaks off excess glass by hand or with notched tool. Fastens glass panes into wood sash with glazier's points, and spreads and smooths putty around edge of panes with knife to seal joints. Installs mirrors or structural glass on building fronts, walls, ceilings, or tables, using mastic, screws, or decorative molding. Bolts metal hinges, handles, locks, and other hardware to prefab-ricated glass doors. Sets glass doors into frame and fits hinges. May install metal window and door frames into which glass panels are to be fitted. May press plastic adhesive film to glass or spray glass with tinting solution to prevent light glare. May install stained glass windows. May assemble and install metal-framed glass enclosures for showers and be designated as SHOWER-ENCLO-SURE INSTALLER (const.). May be designated according to type of glass installed as GLAZIER, STRUCTURAL GLASS (const.); PLATE-GLASS INSTALLER (const.). • **GED:** R3, M2, L2 • **SVP:** 2-4 yrs • **Academic:** Ed=N, Eng=N • **Work Field:** 102 • **MPSMS:** 360, 460 • **Aptitudes:** G3, V4, N4, S3, P3, Q4, K3, F3, M3, E4, C5 • **Temperaments:** M, T, V • **Physical:** V=G, H=N, L=M, W, C, S, H • **Work Env:** B, N, R • **Salary:** 5 • **Outlook:** 3

GRIP (amuse. & rec.) • D.O.T. #962.684-014 • OES #85999 • Erects sets and moves scenery on stage for theatrical productions on stage and television studio, using handtools and power tools and equipment: Ties sets upright with lash lines. Hooks stage brace onto set and adjusts brace to straighten and support set. Connects lines to overhead steel work to support hanging units, using handtools and power tools. Fits and hangs painted backdrops and curtains. Inserts weights as specified to counter-balance hanging units. Changes scenery between acts or scenes according to script. • **GED:** R3, M2, L2 • **SVP:** 6 mos-1 yr • **Academic:** Ed=N, Eng=N • **Work Field:** 102 • **MPSMS:** 863, 912 • **Aptitudes:** G3, V4, N4, S2, P4, Q4, K3, F4, M3, E2, C4 • **Temperaments:** T, V • **Physical:** V=L, H=N, L=V, W, C, S, H • **Work Env:** B, R • **Salary:** 4 • **Outlook:** 2

INSULATION WORKER (const.) • D.O.T. #863.364-014 • OES #87802 • Applies insulating material to exposed surfaces of struc-tures, such as air ducts, hot and cold pipes, storage tanks, and cold storage rooms: Reads blueprints and selects required insulation material (in sheet, tubular, or roll form), such as fiberglass, foam rubber, styrofoam, cork, or urethane, based on material's heat retain-ing or excluding characteristics. Brushes adhesives on or attaches metal adhesive-backed pins to flat surfaces as necessary to facilitate application of insulation material. Measures and cuts insulation material to specified size and shape for covering flat or round surfaces, using tape measure, knife, or scissors. Fits, wraps, or attaches required insulation material around or to structure, follow-ing blueprint specifications. Covers or seals insulation with pre-formed plastic covers, canvas strips, sealant, or tape to secure insu-lation to structure, according to type of insulation used and structure covered, using staple gun, trowel, paintbrush, or calking gun. • **GED:** R3, M2, L3 • **SVP:** 1-2 yrs • **Academic:** Ed=N, Eng=S • **Work Field:** 092 • **MPSMS:** 361 • **Aptitudes:** G3, V4, N4, S3, P3, Q4,

K3, F3, M3, E4, C5 • Temperaments: J • Physical: V=L, H=N, L=M, W, S, H • Work Env: I, R, F • Salary: 5 • Outlook: 3

LATHER (const.) • D.O.T. #842.361-010 • OES #87114 • Fastens wooden, metal, or rockboard lath to walls, ceilings, and partitions of buildings to provide supporting base for plaster, fireproofing, or acoustical material, using handtools and portable power tools: Erects horizontal metal framework to which laths are fastened, using nails, bolts, and studgun. Drills holes in floor and ceiling, using portable electric tool, and drives ends of wooden or metal studs into holes to provide anchor for furring or rockboard lath. Wires horizontal strips to furring to stiffen framework. Cuts lath to fit openings and projections, using handtools or portable power tools. Wires, nails, clips, or staples lath to framework, ceiling joists, and flat concrete surfaces. Bends metal lath to fit corners, or attaches preformed corner reinforcements. Wires plasterer's channels to overhead structural framework to provide support for plaster or acoustical ceiling tile. May install metal casings around openings, metal window stools, and metal trim and plaster grounds (wood or metal strips) nailed to studding to provide guide for PLASTERER (const.). May weld metal frame supports to steel structural members. May be designated according to type of lath applied as METAL LATHER (const.); ROCKBOARD LATHER (const.); WOOD LATHER (const.); or according to task performed as METAL FURRER (const.). • GED: R3, M2, L2 • SVP: 1-2 yrs • Academic: Ed=N, Eng=N • Work Field: 102 • MPSMS: 361 • Aptitudes: G3, V3, N4, S3, P3, Q4, K3, F3, M3, E4, C5 • Temperaments: M, T • Physical: V=L, H=N, L=M, W, C, S, H • Work Env: I, R • Salary: 5 • Outlook: 2

LUGGAGE REPAIRER (any ind.) • D.O.T. #365.361-010 • OES #89511 • HAND LUGGAGE REPAIRER. Repairs and renovates worn or damaged luggage made of leather, fiber, and other materials: Sews rips by hand or machine, inserts and repairs linings, and replaces locks, catches, straps, buckles, corner protectors, and other parts to repair all types of hand luggage. Repairs and reconditions trunks and other heavy luggage, constructing and gluing together frame, cutting and bending fiberboard pieces together, and riveting on locks, catches, corner protectors, and other parts. May construct leather articles, such as purses, wallets, and briefcases, ordered specially by customers. May specialize in repairing trunks and other heavy luggage and be designated TRUNK REPAIRER (any ind.). • GED: R3, M2, L2 • SVP: 1-2 yrs • Academic: Ed=N, Eng=N • Work Field: 102, 171 • MPSMS: 524, 525 • Aptitudes: G3, V4, N4, S3, P3, Q4, K3, F3, M3, E4, C4 • Temperaments: M, T • Physical: V=L, H=N, L=M, H • Work Env: I • Salary: 2 • Outlook: 3

MAINTENANCE REPAIRER, BUILDING (any ind.) • D.O.T. #899.381-010 • OES #85132 • BUILDING REPAIRER. Repairs and maintains physical structures of commercial and industrial establishments, such as factories, office buildings, apartment houses, and logging and mining constructions, using handtools and power tools: Replaces defective electrical switches and other fixtures. Paints structures, and repairs woodwork with carpenters' tools. Repairs plumbing fixtures. Repairs plaster and lays brick. Builds sheds and other outbuildings. • GED: R4, M3, L3 • SVP: 2-4 yrs • Academic: Ed=H, Eng=S • Work Field: 102 • MPSMS: 360 • Aptitudes: G3, V3, N3, S2, P2, Q4, K3, F3, M2, E4, C4 • Temperaments: T, V • Physical: V=L, H=N, L=M, W, C, S, H • Work Env: B, N • Salary: 4 • Outlook: 3

MUFFLER INSTALLER (auto. ser.) • D.O.T. #807.664-010 • OES #85302 • Replaces defective mufflers and pipes on automobiles, buses, trucks, and other automotive vehicles according to factory or customer specifications, using handtools and power tools: Removes defective muffler, using hacksaw, wrenches, air-powered tools, or acetylene torch. Selects replacement muffler according to automotive vehicle model and customer's preference. Bolts or tack welds new muffler in place. Bends and shapes tailpipe sections according to customer specifications, using pipe-bending machine. Welds tailpipe sections to muffler or exhaust pipe, using arc welding equipment. Alines muffler and tailpipe within frame and bolts hangers to frame to secure muffler. • GED: R3, M2, L2 • SVP: 3-6 mos • Academic: Ed=N, Eng=N • Work Field: 102 • MPSMS: 591 • Aptitudes: G3, V4, N4, S3, P4, Q4, K3, F3, M3, E5, C5 • Temperaments: M, T • Physical: V=G, H=N, L=M, W, H • Work Env: I • Salary: 3 • Outlook: 3

PUMP INSTALLER (any ind.) • D.O.T. #630.684-018 • OES #85999 • Installs and adjusts electric, gasoline, and diesel-driven pumps and blowers, using handtools, power tools, and diagrams: Cuts and threads pipes, ducts, and fittings, using handtools and power tools. Levels and bolts down pump. Connects ducts and drive couplings, and alines them to minimize friction, using handtools and gages. Oils and greases moving parts, and adjusts valves to prevent overloading. May recommend repair or adjustment of driving mechanism to improve operation of pumps. • GED: R3, M2, L3 • SVP: 6 mos-1 yr • Academic: Ed=N, Eng=S • Work Field: 121 • MPSMS: 568 • Aptitudes: G3, V3, N3, S3, P3, Q4, K3, F3, M3, E5, C5 • Temperaments: R, T • Stress: T • Physical: V=L, H=N, L=H, W, S, H • Work Env: B • Salary: 4 • Outlook: 3

REPAIRER (furn.) • D.O.T. #709.684-062 • OES #85999 • SALVAGE WORKER. Repairs or replaces damaged metal furniture parts, using handtools and power tools: Welds cracks, using acetylene torch. Files, scrapes, or sands parts to remove dirt, paint, or rust. Melts solder into holes and cracks. Grinds solder until smooth and flush with surrounding metal, using portable grinder. Bends or hammers dented or twisted parts to original shape. Replaces inoperative furniture parts. May reassemble metal furniture. • GED: R3, M1, L2 • SVP: 6 mos-1 yr • Academic: Ed=N, Eng=N • Work Field: 102 • MPSMS: 466 • Aptitudes: G3, V4, N4, S3, P3, Q5, K3, F3, M3, E5, C5 • Temperaments: R, T • Stress: T • Physical: V=L, H=N, L=L, W, S, H • Work Env: I • Salary: 3 • Outlook: 3

ROOFER (const.) • D.O.T. #866.381-010 • OES #87808 • Covers roofs with roofing materials, other than sheet metal, such as composition shingles or sheets, wood shingles, or asphalt and gravel, to waterproof roofs: Cuts roofing paper to size, using knife, and nails or staples it to roof in overlapping strips to form base for roofing materials. Alines roofing material with edge of roof, and overlaps successive layers, gaging distance of overlap with chalkline, gage on shingling hatchet, or by lines on shingles. Fastens composition shingles or sheets to roof, with asphalt, cement, or nails. Punches holes in slate, tile, terra cotta, or wooden shingles, using punch and hammer. Cuts strips of flashing and fits them into angles formed by walls, vents, and intersecting roof surfaces. When applying asphalt or tar and gravel to roof, mops or pours hot asphalt or tar onto roof base. Applies alternate layers of hot asphalt or tar and roofing paper until roof covering is as specified. Applies gravel or pebbles over top layer, using rake or stiff-bristled broom. May construct and attach prefabricated roof sections to rafters [CARPENTER (const.)]. May attach shingles to exterior walls and apply roofing paper and tar to shower pans, decks, and promenades to waterproof surfaces. When specializing in one type of roofing materials is designated according to specialty as ALUMINUM-SHINGLE ROOFER (const.); ASBESTOS-SHINGLE ROOFER (const.); ASPHALT, TAR, AND GRAVEL ROOFER (const.); COMPOSITION ROOFER (const.); ROOFER, GYPSUM (const.); SLATE ROOFER (const.); TILE-AND-TERRA-COTTA ROOFER (const.); WOOD-SHINGLE ROOFER (const.). • GED: R3, M2, L2 • SVP: 2-4 yrs • Academic: Ed=N, Eng=N • Work Field: 092 • MPSMS: 361 • Aptitudes: G3, V4, N3, S3, P3, Q4, K3, F3, M3, E3, C5 • Temperaments: M, T • Physical: V=G, H=N, L=M, W, C, S, H • Work Env: O, R • Salary: 5 • Outlook: 3

ROUSTABOUT (petrol. production) • D.O.T. #869.684-046 • OES #87921 • CONNECTION WORKER; GANG WORKER; ROUGHNECK. Assembles and repairs oilfield machinery and equipment, using handtools and power tools: Digs holes, sets forms, and mixes and pours concrete into forms, to make foundations for wood or steel derricks, using posthole digger, hand tools, and wheelbarrow. Bolts or nails together wood or steel framework to erect derrick. Dismantles and assembles boilers and steam engine parts, using handtools and power tools. Bolts together pump and engine parts. Connects tanks and flow lines, using wrenches. Unscrews or tightens pipe, casing, tubing, and pump rods, using hand and power wrenches and tongs. • GED: R3, M1, L2 • SVP: 6 mos-1 yr • Academic: Ed=N, Eng=N • Work Field: 102 • MPSMS: 564 • Aptitudes: G3, V4, N4, S3, P4, Q4, K3, F3, M3, E5, C5 • Temperaments: R, T • Stress: T • Physical: V=L, H=N, L=H, W, H • Work Env: O, R • Salary: 5 • Outlook: 3

SERVICE REPRESENTATIVE (light, heat, & power) • D.O.T.

#959.574-010 • OES #85928 • Discontinues or connects service to consumer's establishment, following written or oral instructions: Locates curb cock (valve)at customer's establishment and turns valve to shut off or permit flow of gas or water, using handtools. Records meter readings [METER READER (light, heat, & power; waterworks)]. Investigates consumer complaints of high service cost. Inspects meters, valves, and pipes to detect defects, such as leaks or malfunctioning meters, using testing equipment. Tightens pipe connections to prevent leaks, using wrench. Recommends necessary repairs to consumer. May collect delinquent accounts. May install meters [WATER-METER INSTALLER (waterworks); GAS-METER INSTALLER(light, heat, & power)]. • **GED:** R3, M2, L2 • **SVP:** 30 days-3 mos • **Academic:** Ed=N, Eng=G • **Work Field:** 014 • **MPSMS:** 870 • **Aptitudes:** G3, V4, N4, S4, P3, Q4, K4, F4, M3, E5, C5 • **Temperaments:** M, T • **Physical:** V=L, H=G, L=M, W, S, H • **Work Env:** B, W • **Salary:** 3 • **Outlook:** 3

SEWER-LINE REPAIRER, TELE-GROUT (sanitary ser.) • D.O.T. #851.262-010 • OES #83002 • Operates mobile television and chemical sealing units to conduct internal inspection of sewer lines and to seal defects for prevention of water infiltration: Locates line sections to be inspected, using map, and determines setup procedures. Turns knobs to activate television equipment for video viewing. Adjusts TV camera and monitors controls for optimal clarity and contrast. Locates and identifies infiltration points and sewer defects to determine extent of sewer line damage. Prepares description of each sewer defect, and records pertinent data, including exact location of defect. Photographs screen picture of serious or unusual irregularities, using camera. Determines chemical composition of sealing compound based on type of sealing activity necessary to seal defects, and oversees preparation of compound. Turns control knobs of sealing unit to inflate packer to desired pressure, to air test infiltration point, to determine volume of needed sealing compound, and to pump correct amount of sealing chemicals. Turns air release valve to deflate packer after allowing specified time for sealing compound to set. Communicates with workers, using intercom system, and confers with supervisors to discuss condition of sewer lines, based on television inspection. Services, adjusts, and makes minor repairs to equipment and attachments. Gives directions to workers in efficient and safe use of television and grout, in work methods, and safety precautions. Drives television and grout unit truck. • **GED:** R4, M3, L2 • **SVP:** 2-4 yrs • **Academic:** Ed=N, Eng=N • **Work Field:** 094, 211 • **MPSMS:** 364 • **Aptitudes:** G3, V3, N3, S3, P3, Q4, K4, F3, M3, E5, C4 • **Temperaments:** D, J • **Physical:** V=L, H=N, L=L, W, C, S, H • **Work Env:** I, W, F • **Salary:** 4 • **Outlook:** 3

SIDER (const.) • D.O.T. #863.684-014 • OES #87899 • SIDING APPLICATOR. Applies asbestos, aluminum, pulpwood fiber, plastic panels, brick veneer, or porcelainized metal siding to building exteriors to provide decorative or insulating surfaces: Attaches tar paper, building paper, or other material to building surface, using nails or adhesive cement to provide insulating base. Fastens wood or metal laths to surface, using screws or nails. Fits and fastens siding material to laths, using rule, measuring tape, handtools, power tools, nails, screws, or bolts. Cuts and trims material to shape when fitting siding around windows or corners, using knife, shears, or portable powersaw. Waterproofs surface by filling joints or cracks with calking compound, using putty knife, trowel, or calking gun. May apply precut siding or may cut material to size and shape at worksite. May attach siding to surface of building, using adhesive cement. May attach siding by interlocking pieces through tabs provided at edges, following sequence indicated by numbers printed on reverse of each piece. May specialize in type of siding applied and be designated ALUMINUM-SIDING INSTALLER (const.; ret. tr.); ASBESTOS-SIDING INSTALLER (const.; ret. tr.); CONCRETE-PANEL INSTALLER (const.; ret. tr.); ORNAMENTAL-BRICK INSTALLER (const.; ret. tr.); PLASTIC-PANEL INSTALLER (const.; ret. tr.); PORCELAIN-ENAMEL INSTALLER (const.; ret. tr.). • **GED:** R3, M2, L2 • **SVP:** 3-6 mos • **Academic:** Ed=N, Eng=N • **Work Field:** 102 • **MPSMS:** 459, 538, 554 • **Aptitudes:** G3, V4, N3, S4, P3, Q4, K3, F3, M3, E3, C5 • **Temperaments:** R, T • **Stress:** T • **Physical:** V=L, H=N, L=M, W, C, S, H • **Work Env:** O, R • **Salary:** 4 • **Outlook:** 3

SIGN ERECTOR 2 (signs) • D.O.T. #869.684-054 • OES #87899 • Erects, assembles, and maintains roadside signs and billboards at designated locations, using handtools and power tools: Digs hole with post hole digger or shovel. Places wood or metal post in hole. Fills hole with cement and tamps cement to hold post in vertical position. Operates airhammer to drive channel-metal post into ground. Bolts, screws, or nails plywood or metal sign panels to sign post or frame, using hand tools. Replaces worn and damaged signs. Repaints rusted signs. May erect metal sign support structure over highways. May operate banding machine to band signs on utility poles. May dismantle and number signs sections for transfer and reassembly at new locations and be designated ADVERTISING-DISPLAY ROTATOR (bus. ser.). • **GED:** R3, M2, L2 • **SVP:** 30 days-3 mos • **Academic:** Ed=N, Eng=N • **Work Field:** 102 • **MPSMS:** 559 • **Aptitudes:** G3, V4, N4, S3, P4, Q4, K3, F3, M3, E4, C5 • **Temperaments:** R • **Stress:** T • **Physical:** V=L, H=N, L=H, W, C, S, H • **Work Env:** O, R • **Salary:** 5 • **Outlook:** 3

SWIMMING POOL INSTALLER-AND-SERVICER (const.) • D.O.T. #869.463-010 • OES #87899 • Performs any combination of following tasks in constructing, installing, and servicing swimming pools at commercial and residential sites: Plots length and width of pool site, according to specifications, and marks corners of site, using stakes and sledge hammer. Confers with customer to ensure that pool location and dimensions meet customer's demands. Operates backhoe to dig, shape, and grade walls of in-ground pool. Assembles and aligns wall panel sections, using nuts, bolts, electric air gun, and transit. Pours premixed concrete mixture between dirt wall and wall panels to establish footing (foundation base) to anchor bottoms of wall panels and cross braces. Dumps and spreads gravel into hollow foundation to form drain field, using wheelbarrow, shovel, and rake. Digs trenches, spreads gravel, and lays drain tiles uphill of pool site to divert ground water. Lays out and connects pipe lines for water inlets, return valves, and filters, using hand tools. Snaps coping section to inside upper edge of wall panels around pool circumference to secure liner edge and protect pool users. Mixes prescribed amounts of cement, sand, and water, and pours mixture into foundation. Spreads and smooths mixture evenly throughout foundation, using trowel, and allows mixture to set. Assembles heater parts, connects gas, oil, or electric lines, and starts heater to verify working order of unit. Installs liner into pool, starts pump to fill pool with water, and installs return valves. Builds concrete deck around pool. Lays out and assembles prefabricated parts of above-ground pool, installs liner, connects plumbing lines, starts pump, and checks pool for leaks. Maintains and repairs pool and equipment, advises customers, and sells chemicals to prevent pool-water problems. • **GED:** R4, M4, L4 • **SVP:** 4-10 yrs • **Academic:** Ed=N, Eng=S • **Work Field:** 007, 102 • **MPSMS:** 369 • **Aptitudes:** G3, V3, N3, S3, P2, Q4, K3, F4, M3, E3, C5 • **Temperaments:** T, V • **Physical:** V=L, H=N, L=V, W, S, H • **Work Env:** I, W • **Salary:** 5 • **Outlook:** 3

TAPER (const.) • D.O.T. #842.664-010 • OES #87111 • DRY-WALL FINISHER; FINISHER, WALLBOARD AND PLASTER BOARD; SHEETROCK TAPER; TAPER AND BEDDER; TAPER AND FLOATER. Seals joints between plasterboard or other wallboards to prepare wall surface for painting or papering: Mixes sealing compound by hand or with portable electric mixer, and spreads compound over joints between boards, using trowel, broadknife, or spatula. Presses paper tape over joint to embed tape into compound and seal joint or tapes joint, using mechanical applicator that spreads compound and embeds tape in one operation. Spreads and smooths cementing material over tape, using trowel or floating machine to blend joint with wall surface. Sands rough spots after cement has dried. Fills cracks and holes in walls and ceiling with sealing compound. May install metal molding at corners in lieu of sealant and tape. May apply texturing compound and primer to walls and ceiling preparatory to final finishing, using brushes, roller, or spray gun. • **GED:** R3, M2, L2 • **SVP:** 6 mos-1 yr • **Academic:** Ed=N, Eng=N • **Work Field:** 102, 143 • **MPSMS:** 361, 455, 604 • **Aptitudes:** G3, V4, N4, S4, P3, Q4, K3, F3, M3, E4, C4 • **Temperaments:** M, T • **Physical:** V=G, H=N, L=M, W, C, S, H • **Work Env:** I, N, R • **Salary:** 5 • **Outlook:** 3

TEMPLATE MAKER, TRACK (any ind.) • D.O.T. #809.484-014 • OES #93999 • Fabricates and assembles track templates for flame-cutting machines from aluminum bar stock and precut plywood board, using handtools and measuring instruments: Positions and tacks or staples template layout onto specified template board, using hammer or staple gun, or draws specified radial shapes onto board, using compass. Measures and cuts aluminum bars to specified length, using hand shears or saw. Bends bar to contour of template design, using hand roll and handtools. Tacks bent bars to template board along layout lines or pattern, using hammer. Changes track sections of template on flame-cutting machine when used for more than one job. Dismantles track templates and straightens bar for reuse, using straightening roll [STRAIGHTENING-ROLL OPERATOR (any ind.)]. • **GED:** R3, M2, L1 • **SVP:** 30 days-3 mos • **Academic:** Ed=N, Eng=N • **Work Field:** 102 • **MPSMS:** 554 • **Aptitudes:** G3, V4, N4, S3, P4, Q4, K3, F4, M3, E5, C5 • **Temperaments:** M, T • **Physical:** V=L, H=N, L=L, W, H • **Work Env:** I, R • **Salary:** 2 • **Outlook:** 2

TILE SETTER HELPER (const.) • D.O.T. #869.664-014 • OES #87402 • Performs any combination of following duties on construction projects, usually working in utility capacity, by transferring from one task to another where demands require worker with varied experience and ability to work without close supervision: Measures distances from grade stakes, drives stakes, and stretches tight line. Bolts, nails, alines, and blocks up under forms. Signals operators of construction equipment to facilitate alinement, movement, and adjustment of machinery to conform to grade specifications. Levels earth to fine grade specifications, using pick and shovel. Mixes concrete, using portable mixer. Smooths and finishes freshly poured cement or concrete, using float, trowel, or screed. Positions, joins, alines, and seals pipe sections. Erects scaffolding, shoring, and braces. Mops, brushes, or spreads paints or bituminous compounds over surfaces for protection. Sprays materials such as water, sand, steam, vinyl, paint, or stucco through hose to clean, coat, or seal surfaces. Applies calking compounds by hand or with calking gun to seal crevices. Grinds, sands, or polishes surfaces, such as concrete, marble, terrazzo, or wood flooring, using abrasive tools or machines. Performs variety of tasks involving dextrous use of hands and tools, such as demolishing buildings, sawing lumber, dismantling forms, removing projections from concrete, mounting pipe hangers, and cutting and attaching insulating material. May be designated according to duties performed as BATTERBOARD SETTER (const.); BILLBOARD-ERECTOR HELPER (const.); BRICKLAYER, PAVING BRICK (const.); BUILDING CLEANER, SANDBLASTER (const.); BUILDING CLEANER, STEAM (const.); CALKER (const.). Additional titles: CARPENTER HELPER, MAINTENANCE (const.); CEMENT MASON, HIGHWAYS AND STREETS (const.); CEMENT SPRAYER, NOZZLE (conc. prod.; const.); CONCRETE-WALL-GRINDER OPERATOR (const.); CORRUGATED-SHEET-MATERIAL SHEETER (const.); CRADLE PLACER (const.); DAMPPROOFER (const.); DRAIN LAYER (const.); DUCT INSTALLER (const.; mfd. bldgs.); FINE GRADER (const.); FITTER (const.; pipe lines); FLOOR FINISHER (const.); FLOOR-SANDING-MACHINE OPERATOR (const.); FORM-BUILDER HELPER (const.); FORM SETTER, METAL ROAD-FORMS (const.); FORM SETTER, STEEL FORMS (const.); FORM SETTER, STEEL-PAN FORMS (const.); FOUNDATION-DRILL-OPERATOR HELPER (const.); GLAZIER HELPER (const.); GROUND WIRER (const.); HOLDER, PILE DRIVING (const.); HYDRANT-AND-VALVE SETTER (const.); INSULATION INSTALLER (const.); INSULATION WORKER (const.); JOIST SETTER, ADJUSTABLE STEEL (const.); LABORER, ADJUSTABLE STEEL JOIST (const.); LABORER, CARPENTRY (const.); LABORER, CARPENTRY, DOCK (const.); LAYER-OUT, PLATE GLASS (const.); LIGHTNING-ROD ERECTOR (const.); MARBLE-SETTER HELPER (const.); ORNAMENTAL-IRON-WORKER HELPER (const.); PAINTER, ROUGH (const.); PAINTER, STRUCTURAL STEEL (const.); PAINT-STRIPPING-MACHINE OPERATOR (const.); PERMASTONE DRESSER (const.); PILE-DRIVING SETTER (const.); PIPE CALKER (const.); PIPE LAYER (const.); PIPE-LINE WORKER (const.); PLUMBER HELPER (const.); POINTER, CALKER, AND CLEANER (const.); PUMP-ERECTOR HELPER (const.); RECEIVER SETTER (const.); ROOFER, VINYL COATING (const.); SEAT INSTALLER (const.); SEPTIC-TANK SERVICER (const.); SEWER TAPPER (const.); SHORER (const.); STONE POLISHER (const.); TAPPING-MACHINE OPERATOR (const.); TERRAZZO-WORKER HELPER (const.); TILE SETTER HELPER (const.); TUCK POINTER (const.); WATERPROOFER (const.); WELL-DRILL-OPERATOR HELPER, CABLE TOOL (const.); WELL-DRILL-OPERATOR HELPER, ROTARY DRILL (const.); WRECKER (const.). • **GED:** R3, M3, L3 • **SVP:** 3-6 mos • **Academic:** Ed=N, Eng=S • **Work Field:** 102 • **MPSMS:** 360 • **Aptitudes:** G3, V4, N4, S3, P3, Q4, K3, F3, M3, E4, C5 • **Temperaments:** M, T • **Physical:** V=L, H=N, L=H, W, C, S, H • **Work Env:** B, N, R • **Salary:** 5 • **Outlook:** 3

TORCH-STRAIGHTENER-AND HEATER (any ind.) • D.O.T. #709.684-086 • OES #93914 • STRAIGHTENER, TORCH. Straightens metal plates, weldments, and structural shapes or preheats them preparatory to welding or bending, using torch: Selects torch tip from data charts according to thickness, area, and temperature of metal to heat. Screws tip on torch and connects hoses from torch to tanks of oxygen and fuel gas, such as acetylene. Turns levers to activate flow of gas, lights flame, and adjusts mixture to obtain desired size and color of flame. Holds or guides flame along surface of workpiece to heat and expand metal, to achieve specified straightness, or until color indicates sufficient heating for welding or machine straightening or bending. Measures workpiece with straightedge or template to ensure conformance with specifications. May hammer out bulges and bends. May place workpiece into heating furnace for specified period of time, using jib of crane. • **GED:** R3, M2, L2 • **SVP:** 3-6 mos • **Academic:** Ed=N, Eng=N • **Work Field:** 102, 133 • **MPSMS:** 540, 550 • **Aptitudes:** G4, V4, N4, S4, P3, Q5, K4, F4, M4, E5, C3 • **Temperaments:** M, T • **Physical:** V=L, H=N, L=H, W, S, H • **Work Env:** I, H, N, R • **Salary:** 3 • **Outlook:** 2

UMBRELLA REPAIRER (any ind.) • D.O.T. #369.684-018 • OES #93999 • Repairs defective umbrellas, using handtools: Replaces parts of umbrella frames, such as springs, ribs, shanks, and handles, using handtools. Sews umbrella cover to frame [UMBRELLA TIPPER, HAND (umbrella)]. May repair wheels and casters on beds, carts, and similar rolling equipment [WHEEL-AND-CASTER REPAIRER (any ind.)]. • **GED:** R2, M1, L2 • **SVP:** 3-6 mos • **Academic:** Ed=N, Eng=N • **Work Field:** 102 • **MPSMS:** 619 • **Aptitudes:** G3, V4, N4, S4, P3, Q4, K4, F3, M3, E5, C5 • **Temperaments:** M, T • **Physical:** V=N, H=N, L=L, H • **Work Env:** I • **Salary:** 2 • **Outlook:** 1

WATER-SOFTENER SERVICER-AND-INSTALLER (bus. ser.) • D.O.T. #862.684-034 • OES #87502 • Delivers, installs, and reconditions water-softener tanks: Connects hoses of portable regenerating equipment to water-softener tank, and opens valves and sets dials to activate equipment that automatically regenerates water-softener chemical (zeolite) with brine and chlorine to restore its water-softener qualities. Tests chemical for acidity, iron content, and hardness, using test kit. Attaches pipes and rubber hoses to tank, fills tank with water, and inspects it for leaks and worn parts. Cuts, threads, and replaces pipes, control valves, and couplings, using wrenches, pipe cutters, and threaders. Examines water pipes to determine connections to be made and pipe and pipe fittings required. Installs pipes and seals connections, using gas flame and solder stick, and inspects connections for leaks. • **GED:** R3, M2, L2 • **SVP:** 3-6 mos • **Academic:** Ed=N, Eng=S • **Work Field:** 102 • **MPSMS:** 550 • **Aptitudes:** G3, V3, N4, S3, P3, Q4, K3, F4, M3, E5, C5 • **Temperaments:** R, T • **Stress:** T • **Physical:** V=L, H=N, L=H, W, H • **Work Env:** I, W • **Salary:** 3 • **Outlook:** 3

WELDER, TACK (welding) • D.O.T. #810.684-010 • OES #93914 • TACKER. Welds short beads at points specified by layout, welding diagram, or by FITTER (any ind.) I, along overlapping edges of metal parts to hold parts in place for final welding. Performs tasks of FITTER HELPER (any ind.). May tack-weld, using hand, submerged, or gas-shielded arc welding equipment. May tack-weld, using portable spotwelding gun [WELDER, GUN (welding). • **GED:** R3, M2, L2 • **SVP:** 6 mos-1 yr • **Academic:** Ed=N, Eng=N • **Work Field:** 081 • **MPSMS:** 540, 554, 591 • **Aptitudes:** G3, V4, N4, S4, P4, Q4, K3, F3, M3, E5, C4 • **Temperaments:** R, T • **Stress:** T • **Physical:** V=L, H=N, L=H, W, S, H • **Work Env:** B, N, R • **Salary:** 3 • **Outlook:** 3

GOE: 05.10.02 Mechanical Crafts

AUTOMOBILE-ACCESSORIES INSTALLER (auto. ser.) • D.O.T. #806.684-038 • OES #85302 • Installs automobile accessories, such as heaters, radios, antennas, safety seat belts, seat covers, or special clamps, and mirrors: Drills and taps holes, assembles and fits accessories to automobile, and tightens bolts and clamps. May be designated according to specialty as RADIO INSTALLER, AUTOMOBILE (auto. ser.). • **GED:** R2, M1, L2 • **SVP:** 3-6 mos • **Academic:** Ed=N, Eng=N • **Work Field:** 102, 121 • **MPSMS:** 591 • **Aptitudes:** G3, V4, N4, S3, P3, Q4, K3, F3, M3, E5, C4 • **Temperaments:** M, T, V • **Physical:** V=L, H=N, L=M, W, S, H • **Work Env:** I • **Salary:** 3 • **Outlook:** 3

AUTOMOBILE-RADIATOR MECHANIC (auto. ser.) • D.O.T. #620.381-010 • OES #85302 • AUTOMOBILE MECHANIC, RADIATOR; RADIATOR REPAIRER. Repairs cooling systems and fuel tanks in automobiles, buses, trucks, and other automotive vehicles: Pumps water or compressed air through radiator to test it for obstructions or leaks. Flushes radiator with cleaning compound to remove obstructions, such as rust or mineral deposits. Removes radiator core from automobile and cleans it, using rods or boiling water and solvent, or combination of boil out and rod out. Solders leaks in core or tanks, using soldering iron or acetylene torch. Disassembles, repairs, or replaces defective water pump. Replaces faulty thermostats and leaky head gaskets. Installs new cores, hoses, and pumps. Cleans, tests, and repairs fuel tanks. • **GED:** R3, M2, L3 • **SVP:** 1-2 yrs • **Academic:** Ed=N, Eng=N • **Work Field:** 031, 121 • **MPSMS:** 591 • **Aptitudes:** G4, V4, N4, S2, P3, Q4, K3, F3, M3, E5, C5 • **Temperaments:** M, T, V • **Physical:** V=G, H=N, L=M, W, S, H • **Work Env:** I • **Salary:** 4 • **Outlook:** 3

AUTOMOBILE-SERVICE-STATION ATTENDANT (auto. ser.) • D.O.T. #915.467-010 • OES #97805 • FILLING-STATION ATTENDANT; GAS-STATION ATTENDANT; GAS TENDER; SERVICE-STATION ATTENDANT. Services automobiles, buses, trucks, and other automotive vehicles with fuel, lubricants, and accessories: Fills fuel tank of vehicles with gasoline or diesel fuel to level specified by customer. Observes level of oil in crankcase and amount of water in radiator, and adds required amounts of oil and water. Adds necessary amount of water to battery, and washes windshield of vehicle. Lubricates vehicle and changes motor oil [LUBRICATION SERVICER (auto. ser.)]. Replaces accessories, such as oil filter, air filter, windshield wiper blades, and fan belt. Installs antifreeze and changes spark plugs. Repairs or replaces tires [TIRE REPAIRER (auto. ser.)]. Replaces lights, and washes and waxes vehicle. Collects cash from customer for purchases and makes change or charges purchases, using customer-charge plate. May adjust brakes [BRAKE ADJUSTER (auto. ser.)]. May sell batteries and automobile accessories usually found in service stations. May assist in arranging displays, taking inventories, and making daily reports. • **GED:** R3, M2, L2 • **SVP:** 30 days-3 mos • **Academic:** Ed=N, Eng=S • **Work Field:** 292 • **MPSMS:** 961 • **Aptitudes:** G3, V3, N3, S4, P3, Q4, K4, F4, M3, E5, C5 • **Temperaments:** P, V • **Stress:** E • **Physical:** V=L, H=L, L=M, W, S, H • **Work Env:** B • **Salary:** 2 • **Outlook:** 3

BICYCLE REPAIRER (any ind.) • D.O.T. #639.681-010 • OES #85951 • BICYCLE MECHANIC; CYCLE REPAIRER. Repairs and services bicycles, using power tools and handtools: Tightens and loosens spokes to aline wheels. Disassembles axle to repair coaster brakes and to adjust and replace defective parts, using handtools. Adjusts cables or replaces worn or damaged parts to repair handbrakes. Installs and adjusts speed and gear mechanisms. Shapes replacement parts, using bench grinder. Installs, repairs, and replaces equipment or accessories, such as handle bars, stands, lights, and seats. Paints bicycle frame, using spray gun or brush. Rubs tubes with scraper and places patch over hole to repair tube. May weld broken or cracked frame together, using oxyacetylene torch and welding rods. May assemble and sell new bicycles and accessories. • **GED:** R3, M2, L3 • **SVP:** 3-6 mos • **Academic:** Ed=N, Eng=S • **Work Field:** 121 • **MPSMS:** 595 • **Aptitudes:** G3, V4, N4, S3, P3, Q4, K3, F3, M3, E5, C3 • **Temperaments:** R, T • **Stress:** T • **Physical:** V=G, H=N, L=M, W, H • **Work Env:** I • **Salary:** 3 • **Outlook:** 4

BRAKE REPAIRER (auto. ser.) • D.O.T. #620.281-026 • OES #85302 • BRAKE MECHANIC; BRAKE-REPAIR MECHANIC; BRAKESHOE REPAIRER. Repairs and overhauls brake systems in automobiles, buses, trucks, and other automotive vehicles: Pushes handle of hydraulic jack or pushes hoist control to raise vehicle axle. Removes wheels, using wrenches, wheel puller, and sledge hammer. Replaces defective brakeshoe units or attaches

new linings to brakeshoes. Measures brakedrum to determine amount of wear, using feeler gage. Inserts vacuum gage into power-brake cylinder, starts engine, and reads gage to detect brake-line leaks. Repairs or replaces leaky brake cylinders. Repairs or replaces defective air compressor in airbrake systems. Replaces wheel on axle and adjusts drumshoe clearance, using wrench. Fills master brake cylinder with brake fluid, pumps brake pedal, or uses pressure tank, and opens valves on hydraulic brake system to bleed air from brake lines. Closes valves and refills master brake cylinder. May be designated according to specialty as BRAKE REPAIRER, AIR (auto. ser.); BRAKE REPAIRER, HYDRAULIC (auto. ser.); BRAKE REPAIRER, BUS (auto. ser.). • **GED:** R3, M3, L3 • **SVP:** 1-2 yrs • **Academic:** Ed=N, Eng=S • **Work Field:** 121 • **MPSMS:** 591 • **Aptitudes:** G3, V3, N3, S3, P3, Q4, K3, F3, M3, E5, C5 • **Temperaments:** M, T, V • **Physical:** V=G, H=N, L=M, W, S, H • **Work Env:** I, N • **Salary:** 4 • **Outlook:** 3

CARBURETOR MECHANIC (auto. ser.) • D.O.T. #620.281-034 • OES #85302 • CARBURETOR REPAIRER. Repairs and adjusts motor vehicle carburetors: Disassembles carburetors and gasoline filter units, using handtools. Examines parts for defects and tests needle valves with wire gages and flowmeter. Cleans parts in solvents to remove dirt and gum deposits. Repairs or replaces defective parts. Reassembles carburetor and gasoline filter, and installs them in vehicle. Starts engine and turns adjustment screw to regulate flow of air and gasoline through carburetor, using testing equipment. May operate drill press, lathe, and other power tools to retap jets, ream throttle bodies and chokes, and machine seating surfaces of carburetor housings. May install and repair mechanical devices that convert conventional systems to use of other fuels [VEHICLE-FUEL-SYSTEMS CONVERTER (auto. ser.). • **GED:** R3, M2, L3 • **SVP:** 2-4 yrs • **Academic:** Ed=N, Eng=S • **Work Field:** 121 • **MPSMS:** 591 • **Aptitudes:** G3, V4, N4, S3, P2, Q4, K4, F3, M3, E5, C5 • **Temperaments:** M, T • **Physical:** V=L, H=N, L=L, H • **Work Env:** I • **Salary:** 4 • **Outlook:** 4

COIN-MACHINE-SERVICE REPAIRER (coin mach.) • D.O.T. #639.281-014 • OES #85947 • VENDING-MACHINE REPAIRER. Installs, services, adjusts, and repairs vending, amusement, and other coin-operated machines placed in establishments on concession basis: Assembles machines following specifications, using handtools and power tools. Fills machines with ingredients or products and tests ice making, refrigeration, carbonation, evaporation, dispensing, electrical, and coin-handling systems. Examines defective machines to determine causes of malfunctions. Adjusts and repairs machines, replacing worn or defective electrical or mechanical parts, using handtools, such as screwdrivers, hammers, and pliers. May collect coins from machine and make settlements with concessionaires. May replenish vending machines with gum, candy, or other articles. May be designated according to type of machine serviced as JUKE-BOX SERVICER (bus. ser.); PINBALL-MACHINE REPAIRER (bus. ser.). • **GED:** R3, M3, L3 • **SVP:** 6 mos-1 yr • **Academic:** Ed=N, Eng=S • **Work Field:** 111 • **MPSMS:** 572 • **Aptitudes:** G3, V4, N4, S3, P3, Q4, K3, F3, M3, E5, C5 • **Temperaments:** M, T, V • **Physical:** V=G, H=N, L=M, W, S, H • **Work Env:** I • **Salary:** 4 • **Outlook:** 4

CONVEYOR-MAINTENANCE MECHANIC (any ind.) • D.O.T. #630.381-010 • OES #85119 • Repairs and adjusts conveyor systems, using handtools: Installs belts in machinery, tightens bolts, adjusts tension rolls, straightens parts, alines rollers, and replaces defective parts. May install conveyor systems. • **GED:** R3, M3, L3 • **SVP:** 1-2 yrs • **Academic:** Ed=N, Eng=S • **Work Field:** 121 • **MPSMS:** 565 • **Aptitudes:** G3, V4, N4, S3, P3, Q5, K4, F4, M2, E4, C5 • **Temperaments:** M, T • **Physical:** V=L, H=N, L=M, W, S, H • **Work Env:** I, N • **Salary:** 4 • **Outlook:** 2

DOOR-CLOSER MECHANIC (any ind.) • D.O.T. #630.381-014 • OES #85928 • Repairs, services, and installs hydraulic door closers, using machines and handtools: Disassembles closers, using handtools and vise. Immerses parts in solution of caustic soda and water to clean parts. Removes encrusted dirt and rust, using electric rotary wire brush and grinding wheel. Replaces worn or broken parts. Fabricates parts, using lathes, drill presses, shaping and milling machines, and precision measuring instruments, such as micrometers, calipers, and scales. Welds cracked closer casings, using acetylene torch. Fills oil chamber and packs spindle with leather washers. Paints finished door closer. • **GED:** R3, M3, L3 • **SVP:** 2-4 yrs • **Academic:** Ed=N, Eng=S • **Work Field:** 121 • **MPSMS:** 559 • **Aptitudes:** G3, V3, N3, S3, P2, Q4, K3, F3, M3, E4, C4 • **Temperaments:** M, T, V • **Physical:** V=L, H=N, L=L, H • **Work Env:** I • **Salary:** 4 • **Outlook:** 2

GAS-APPLIANCE SERVICER (any ind.) • D.O.T. #637.261-018 • OES #85944 • APPLIANCE SERVICER; CUSTOMER SERVICER. Installs and repairs gasmeters, regulators, ranges, heaters, and refrigerators in customer's establishment, using manometer, voltmeter, handtools, and pipe-threading tools: Measures, cuts, and threads pipe and connects it to feeder line and equipment or appliance, using rule, pipe cutter, threader, and wrench. Tests and examines pipelines and equipment to locate leaks and faulty pipe connections and to determine pressure and flow of gas, using manometer, voltmeter, combustible gas indicator, and soap lather. Dismantles meters and regulators, and replaces defective pipes, thermocouples, thermostats, valves, and indicator spindles, using handtools. May assemble new or reconditioned appliances. May collect for monthly bills or overdue payments. May be designated according to appliance serviced as GAS-REFRIGERATOR SERVICER (any ind.); GAS-STOVE SERVICER (any ind.). • **GED:** R4, M3, L3 • **SVP:** 2-4 yrs • **Academic:** Ed=N, Eng=S • **Work Field:** 121 • **MPSMS:** 553, 602 • **Aptitudes:** G3, V3, N3, S3, P3, Q4, K4, F3, M3, E4, C4 • **Temperaments:** M, T, V • **Physical:** V=L, H=N, L=M, W, S, H • **Work Env:** B • **Salary:** 4 • **Outlook:** 2

LUBRICATION-EQUIPMENT SERVICER (any ind.) • D.O.T. #630.381-022 • OES #85119 • Repairs and adjusts hand-or power-operated equipment used to lubricate automobiles, trucks, and industrial equipment, using handtools: Dismantles equipment, such as grease guns, air lines, and lubricating pumps. Examines parts for breaks, wear, and dirt. Replaces defective parts. Cleans and assembles equipment. • **GED:** R3, M2, L2 • **SVP:** 1-2 yrs • **Academic:** Ed=N, Eng=N • **Work Field:** 121 • **MPSMS:** 568 • **Aptitudes:** G3, V4, N4, S3, P3, Q4, K3, F4, M3, E4, C5 • **Temperaments:** M, T • **Physical:** V=L, H=N, L=M, W, H • **Work Env:** I • **Salary:** 4 • **Outlook:** 2

MANAGER, CUSTOMER SERVICES (bus. ser.) • D.O.T. #187.167-082 • OES #19999 • Directs and coordinates customer service activities of establishment to install, service, maintain, and repair durable goods, such as machines, equipment, major appliances, or other items sold, leased, or rented with service contract or warranty: Reviews customer requests for service to ascertain cause for service request, type of malfunction, and customer address. Determines manhours, number of personnel, and parts and equipment required for service call, utilizing knowledge of product, typical malfunctions, and service procedures and practices. Prepares schedules for service personnel, assigns personnel to routes or to specific repair and maintenance work according to workers' knowledge, experience, and repair capabilities on specific types of products. Arranges for transportation of machines and equipment to customer's location for installation or from customer's location to shop for repairs that cannot be performed on premises. Keeps records of work hours and parts utilized, and work performed for each service call. Requisitions replacement parts and supplies. May contact service personnel over radio-telephone to obtain or give information and directions regarding service or installation activities. Workers are designated according to type of customer service managed or product serviced. • **GED:** R4, M4, L4 • **SVP:** 4-10 yrs • **Academic:** Ed=H, Eng=S • **Work Field:** 111, 121 • **MPSMS:** 568, 571, 580 • **Aptitudes:** G3, V3, N3, S3, P3, Q3, K4, F4, M4, E5, C5 • **Temperaments:** D, J, P • **Stress:** A • **Physical:** V=L, H=G, L=L, H • **Work Env:** I • **Salary:** 5 • **Outlook:** 3

MECHANIC, AIRCRAFT ACCESSORIES (aircraft-aerospace mfg.) • D.O.T. #621.381-014 • OES #85323 • MECHANIC, ACCESSORY REWORK-AND-REPAIR. Repairs, assembles, and tests aircraft accessories, such as power brake units, auxiliary electric motors, carburetors, spark ignitors, valves, and hydramatic and vacuum pumps, using handtools and testing devices, and following shop orders and manufacturer's specifications: Disassembles unit, using hand or power wrenches and screwdrivers. Cleans parts, using cleaning solutions, and polishing and lapping compounds. Measures parts to determine wear, using micrometers and dial indicators. Replaces defective parts and reassembles units. Tests units for conformance to specifications

under simulated operating conditions, using equipment, such as voltmeters and hydraulic testing equipment. • **GED:** R3, M3, L3 • **SVP:** 1-2 yrs • **Academic:** Ed=N, Eng=S • **Work Field:** 111, 121 • **MPSMS:** 592 • **Aptitudes:** G3, V4, N3, S3, P3, Q4, K3, F3, M2, E5, C5 • **Temperaments:** M, T, V • **Physical:** V=G, H=N, L=M, W, H • **Work Env:** I • **Salary:** 4 • **Outlook:** 2

MEDICAL-EQUIPMENT REPAIRER (per. protect. & med. device) • D.O.T. #639.281-022 • OES #85999 • DURABLE MEDICAL EQUIPMENT REPAIRER; WHEELCHAIR REPAIRER. Repairs medical equipment, such as manual or powered wheelchairs, hospital beds, and suction equipment, using knowledge of equipment function and handtools: Test operates and examines malfunctioning equipment to determine cause of malfunction. Disassembles and inspects equipment to locate defective components, such as motors, valves, and electrical controls, using test instruments and handtools. Replaces defective parts, and solders, tightens, and aligns parts which have become loose or out of adjustment, using handtools and soldering iron. Cleans, lubricates, and polishes equipment components to restore surface, using solvent, polish, rags, and grease gun. Test operates unit to ensure equipment functions according to manufacturer's specifications. Occasionally installs modified parts, such as respirator equipment or foot rest, onto wheel chairs, according to customer specification, and fills parts orders from customers. • **GED:** R3, M2, L3 • **SVP:** 6 mos-1 yr • **Academic:** Ed=N, Eng=S • **Work Field:** 111, 121 • **MPSMS:** 604 • **Aptitudes:** G3, V4, N4, S3, P4, Q4, K4, F3, M3, E5, C5 • **Temperaments:** J, T • **Physical:** V=L, H=N, L=H, W, S, H • **Work Env:** I • **Salary:** 4 • **Outlook:** 3

METER REPAIRER (any ind.) • D.O.T. #710.281-034 • OES #85928 • Disassembles, cleans, adjusts, repairs, and tests oil, gas, and water meters, using handtools and testing equipment: Connects meter to testing apparatus. Turns valve to permit specified quantity of oil, gas, or water to pass through meter under varying pressure to test meter for leaks and accuracy of recording. Disassembles meter, removing gear train and disk assembly, using handtools. Removes plant growth, rust, and scale from internal housing and parts, using wire brush, electric buffer, and acid. Repairs or replaces warped or broken disks and gears, and grinds and straightens parts to specified tolerance to fit parts to meter, using grinding machine and hydraulic press. Reassembles and tests meter. Tests large capacity meters in industrial plants to determine accuracy of operation. Records materials used and meters repaired. May install meters [WATER-METER INSTALLER (waterworks)]. May read meters [METER READER (light, heat, & power; waterworks)]. • **GED:** R4, M2, L3 • **SVP:** 6 mos-1 yr • **Academic:** Ed=N, Eng=S • **Work Field:** 121 • **MPSMS:** 602 • **Aptitudes:** G3, V3, N3, S3, P3, Q4, K3, F3, M3, E5, C5 • **Temperaments:** M, T • **Physical:** V=L, H=N, L=M, W, S, H • **Work Env:** B, W, N • **Salary:** 4 • **Outlook:** 3

NEW-CAR GET-READY MECHANIC (auto. ser.) • D.O.T. #806.361-026 • OES #85302 • CAR CHECKER; MAKE-READY MECHANIC. Inspects and services new automobiles on delivery to dealer or customer and makes minor repairs or adjustments to place vehicle in salable condition, using handtools, portable power tools, and specification sheets: Inspects vehicle for obvious damage and missing major components. Records discrepancies and signs acceptance slip for each vehicle delivered. Inspects vehicle for loose or misalined trim, doors, hardware, and other items, and corrects defects, using handtools. Starts engine and drives automobile to test steering, brakes, transmission, and engine operation. Activates power equipment, such as electric windows, seats, radio, horn, lights, and directional signals to ensure specified operating standards. Washes car and vacuums interior. Inspects surfaces to detect minor chips or scratches in paint and touches up imperfections, using brush applicator and factory-supplied matching paint. Installs optional equipment specified by customer or dealer, such as outside mirrors, rugs, and seat covers, using handtools. Installs standard components, such as hubcaps and wiper blades, using handtools. Pours antifreeze into radiator according to seasonal requirements. Polishes car to remove preservative coating and road film accumulated during transit. May spray undercoating material on vehicle, using spray gun. May tune engine, using mechanics' tools and test equipment. May install or repair major mechanical, hydraulic, or electromechanical equipment, such as radios, air-conditioners, power steering units, and power brakes, using mechanics' hand tools. • **GED:** R3, M2, L2 • **SVP:** 1-2 yrs • **Academic:** Ed=N, Eng=N • **Work Field:** 111, 121 • **MPSMS:** 591 • **Aptitudes:** G3, V3, N4, S3, P3, Q4, K3, F4, M3, E3, C4 • **Temperaments:** M, T • **Physical:** V=L, H=N, L=M, W, S, H • **Work Env:** B • **Salary:** 4 • **Outlook:** 4

PNEUMATIC-TUBE REPAIRER (any ind.) • D.O.T. #630.281-014 • OES #85119 • Repairs and maintains pneumatic-tube carrier system, using handtools and precision-measuring instruments: Locates sources of trouble. Repairs and installs parts, using handtools. • **GED:** R3, M3, L3 • **SVP:** 1-2 yrs • **Academic:** Ed=N, Eng=S • **Work Field:** 121 • **MPSMS:** 565 • **Aptitudes:** G3, V3, N3, S3, P3, Q4, K3, F3, M2, E5, C5 • **Temperaments:** M, T • **Physical:** V=L, H=N, L=M, W, H • **Work Env:** I • **Salary:** 3 • **Outlook:** 3

RIDE OPERATOR (amuse. & rec.) • D.O.T. #342.663-010 • OES #68014 • AMUSEMENT-EQUIPMENT OPERATOR. Operates or informs patrons how to operate mechanical riding devices furnished by amusement parks, carnivals, or similar places of entertainment: (1) Informs patron to fasten belt, bar, or other safety device. Moves controls to start and stop equipment, such as roller coaster, merry-go-round, and ferris wheel. (2) Gives directions to patrons, usually over microphone, regarding safety and operation of such rides as midget autos and speed boats. Turns on current to permit operation of ride by patron and turns off current after allotted time. (3) Drives vehicles, such as trains, on which persons ride, guiding and controlling their speed. Adds to or removes equipment, according to amount of patronage. Oils, refuels, adjusts, and repairs device. Tests equipment daily before opening ride to patrons. May notify patron of expiration of period for which fee was paid to use device. May observe patrons boarding vehicle to insure that they are safely seated without being overcrowded, and that safety belts or bars are secure. May collect tickets or cash fares from patrons. May space rides operated in cars or sections to avoid danger of collisions. May be designated according to equipment operated as FERRIS-WHEEL OPERATOR (amuse. & rec.); MERRY-GO-ROUND OPERATOR (amuse. & rec.); RAILROAD OPERATOR (amuse. & rec.); ROLLER-COASTER OPERATOR (amuse. & rec.). Additional titles: AUTO-SPEEDWAY OPERATOR (amuse. & rec.); FLUME-RIDE OPERATOR (amuse. & rec.); MONORAIL OPERATOR (amuse. & rec.); SPEEDBOAT OPERATOR (amuse. & rec.); SWING-RIDE OPERATOR (amuse. & rec.); TRAIN OPERATOR (amuse. & rec.); WHIP OPERATOR (amuse. & rec.). • **GED:** R3, M2, L2 • **SVP:** 30 days-3 mos • **Academic:** Ed=N, Eng=S • **Work Field:** 291 • **MPSMS:** 919 • **Aptitudes:** G3, V4, N4, S4, P4, Q4, K3, F4, M3, E4, C5 • **Temperaments:** P, R • **Stress:** E, T • **Physical:** V=L, H=N, L=S, W, H • **Work Env:** B • **Salary:** 1 • **Outlook:** 3

SERVICE MANAGER (auto. ser.) • D.O.T. #185.167-058 • OES #81002 • Coordinates activities of workers in one or more service departments of automobile accessories sales-service establishment: Directs activities of workers, such as TIRE REPAIRER (auto. ser.) and BRAKE REPAIRER (auto. ser.). Assists sales personnel in adjusting customers' service complaints. Hires, transfers, and discharges workers. Directs activities of workers engaged in testing new equipment and recommends purchase or rejection of equipment. Determines work standards and evaluates workers' performance. May handle claims regarding defective factory workmanship. May determine need and cost of automobile repair [AUTOMOBILE-REPAIR-SERVICE ESTIMATOR (auto. ser.)]. • **GED:** R4, M3, L4 • **SVP:** 1-2 yrs • **Academic:** Ed=N, Eng=G • **Work Field:** 111, 121 • **MPSMS:** 590 • **Aptitudes:** G2, V2, N3, S4, P4, Q3, K4, F4, M4, E5, C5 • **Temperaments:** D, J, P, V • **Stress:** E, A • **Physical:** V=N, H=L, L=S, W, H • **Work Env:** I • **Salary:** 4 • **Outlook:** 2

SERVICE MANAGER (ret. tr.) • D.O.T. #185.164-010 • OES #81002 • Coordinates activities of service department in lawnmower sales and service establishment: Directs activities of workers through supervisory staff. Discusses with supervisory staff methods of assembling and repairing lawnmowers to ensure compliance with prescribed procedures. Interviews and hires workers. Maintains time and production records. Answers questions and discusses complaints with customers regarding services as specified in equipment warranty agreement. Assembles and

tests operation of new lawnmowers to prepare mowers for sales floor, following assembly and test procedures and using hand tools. • **GED:** R4, M3, L3 • **SVP:** 2-4 yrs • **Academic:** Ed=H, Eng=S • **Work Field:** 121, 295 • **MPSMS:** 552 • **Aptitudes:** G3, V3, N3, S3, P3, Q4, K3, F3, M3, E4, C5 • **Temperaments:** D, P, T, V • **Stress:** A • **Physical:** V=L, H=L, L=H, W, H • **Work Env:** I • **Salary:** 4 • **Outlook:** 1

SEWING-MACHINE REPAIRER (any ind.) • D.O.T. #639.281-018 • OES #85113 • SEWING-MACHINE ADJUSTER. Repairs and adjusts sewing machines in homes and sewing depart ments of industrial establishments, using handtools: Turns screws and nuts to adjust machine parts. Regulates length of stroke of needle and horizontal movement of feeding mechanism under needle. Dismantles machines and replaces or repairs broken or worn parts, using handtools. Inspects machines, shafts, and belts. Repairs broken transmission belts. Installs attachments on machines. Initiates orders for new machines or parts. May operate machine tools, such as lathes and drill presses, to make new parts. May be designated according to location in which employed as FITTING-ROOM MAINTENANCE MECHANIC (boot & shoe). • **GED:** R3, M3, L3 • **SVP:** 2-4 yrs • **Academic:** Ed=N, Eng=S • **Work Field:** 121 • **MPSMS:** 583 • **Aptitudes:** G3, V3, N3, S3, P3, Q4, K3, F3, M2, E5, C5 • **Temperaments:** M, T • **Physical:** V=L, H=N, L=M, W, S, H • **Work Env:** I, N • **Salary:** 4 • **Outlook:** 2

THERMOSTAT REPAIRER (inst. & app.) • D.O.T. #710.381-050 • OES #85928 • FIELD RETURN REPAIRER; PRODUCTION REPAIRER. Repairs defective thermostats used in refrigeration, air-conditioning, and heating equipment following specifications: Disassembles and examines thermostats to locate and remove defective parts, using screwdriver and handtools. Replaces defective parts, such as bellows, range spring, and toggle switch, and reassembles thermostat according to blueprint or code book, using cam press and handtools. Measures tolerances of assembled parts, using micrometer and calipers. Repairs leaks in valve seats or bellows of automotive heater thermostats, using soft solder, flux, and acetelyene torch. Examines thermostat for defects, such as loose screws and dents. Writes repair ticket to identify thermostat and places repaired thermostats in tote boxes. Calibrates thermostat for specified temperature or pressure settings [FLOAT-TANK CALIBRATOR (inst. & app.); THERMOSTAT CALIBRATOR (inst. & app.)]. • **GED:** R3, M2, L2 • **SVP:** 6 mos-1 yr • **Academic:** Ed=N, Eng=N • **Work Field:** 121 • **MPSMS:** 602 • **Aptitudes:** G3, V4, N4, S3, P3, Q4, K3, F3, M3, E4, C5 • **Temperaments:** M, T • **Physical:** V=G, H=N, L=M, W, H • **Work Env:** I • **Salary:** 4 • **Outlook:** 3

GOE: 05.10.03 Elect. Crafts

APPLIANCE REPAIRER (elec. equip.) • D.O.T. #723.584-010 • OES #85711 • Repairs portable, household electrical appliances, such as fans, heaters, vacuum cleaners, toasters, and flatirons, on assembly line: Refers to inspector's checklist, or defect-symbol marked on appliance, to identify defective or malfunctioning part. Disassembles appliance to remove defective part, using power screwdrivers, soldering iron, and handtools. Installs new part, and reassembles appliance. Records nature of repair in log or on mechanical counting device. Maintains stock of replacement parts. May determine repair re quirements by connecting appliance to power source or examining parts for defects while disassembling. May file or bend parts to remove burs, or to improve alinement and fit. May hold appliance against buffing or polishing wheel to remove scratches from metal surfaces. May touch up paint defects, using brush or spray gun. May be designated according to part repaired as HEATING-ELEMENT REPAIRER (elec. equip); or appliance repaired as ELECTRIC-FRYING-PAN REPAIRER (elec. equip.); FOOD-MIXER REPAIRER (elec. equip.); TOASTER-ELEMENT REPAIRER (elec. equip.); VACUUM-CLEANER REPAIRER (elec. equip.). • **Academic:** Ed=N, Eng=N • **Work Field:** 111 • **MPSMS:** 583 • **Aptitudes:** G3, V4, N4, S3, P3, Q4, K3, F4, M3, E5, C4 • **Temperaments:** J, M, T • **Physical:** V=L, H=N, L=M, H • **Work Env:** I • **Salary:** 3 • **Outlook:** 3

AUTOMATIC-DOOR MECHANIC (const.) • D.O.T. #829.281-010 • OES #85928 • Installs, services, and repairs opening and closing mechanisms of automatic doors used in self-service grocery stores and similar establishments: Bores and cuts holes in flooring, using handtools and power tools. Sets in and secures floor treadle for activating mechanism and connects hydraulic powerpack and electrical panelboard to treadle. Covers treadle with carpeting and screws or nails down chrome strips around edges. Tests system by stepping on treadle. Repairs nonoperating systems, using handtools, blueprints, and schematic diagrams. May install frames and door units, using cutting tools and handtools. May install systems actuated by electronic-eye mechanism. • **GED:** R3, M2, L2 • **SVP:** 1-2 yrs • **Academic:** Ed=N, Eng=N • **Work Field:** 111 • **MPSMS:** 580 • **Aptitudes:** G3, V3, N2, S2, P3, Q4, K3, F3, M3, E4, C5 • **Temperaments:** M, T, V • **Physical:** V=L, H=N, L=M, W, S, H • **Work Env:** B • **Salary:** 4 • **Outlook:** 3

BATTERY REPAIRER (any ind.) • D.O.T. #727.381-014 • OES #85714 • Repairs and recharges electric-storage batteries: Melts sealing compound on cover, using gas torch. Loosens compound from sides of case, using putty knife. Removes and disassembles cells and inspects parts to detect defects. Replaces defective parts, fuses lead parts, using oxyacetylene torch, reassembles battery, and pours hot seal (tar compound) over cover. Fills cells with acid solution and determines specific gravity of solution, using hydrometer and thermometer. Adds acid or water to obtain specified concentration. Attaches leads from charger to battery posts and starts charger. Reads meters and adjusts rheostat to control flow of current through battery. May repair battery-charging equipment. • **GED:** R3, M2, L2 • **SVP:** 1-2 yrs • **Academic:** Ed=N, Eng=N • **Work Field:** 111 • **MPSMS:** 589 • **Aptitudes:** G3, V4, N4, S3, P2, Q4, K3, F3, M3, E5, C4 • **Temperaments:** M, T • **Physical:** V=L, H=N, L=M, W, H • **Work Env:** I • **Salary:** 4 • **Outlook:** 2

ELECTRIC-GOLF-CART REPAIRER (amuse. & rec.) • D.O.T. #620.261-026 • OES #85714 • GOLF-CART MECHANIC. Repairs and maintains electric golf carts at golf course or in automotive repair shop, using handtools and electrical testing devices: Determines type of repairs required by reading work orders, talking to cart operator, or test-driving cart. Tests operational performance of motor, using voltmeter, ammeter, and wattmeter. Dismantles motor and repairs or replaces defective parts, such as brushes, armatures, and commutator, using wrenches, pliers, and screwdrivers. Rewires electrical systems, and repairs or replaces electrical accessories, such as horn and headlights. Tests and recharges or replaces batteries. Lubricates moving parts and adjusts brakes and belts. May perform structural repairs to body of cart, seats, and fabric tops. May record parts used and labor time on work order. • **GED:** R3, M2, L3 • **SVP:** 6 mos-1 yr • **Academic:** Ed=N, Eng=S • **Work Field:** 111, 121 • **MPSMS:** 582 • **Aptitudes:** G3, V3, N3, S3, P2, Q4, K3, F3, M2, E5, C4 • **Temperaments:** M, T, V • **Physical:** V=L, H=N, L=M, W, H • **Work Env:** I • **Salary:** 3 • **Outlook:** 4

ELECTRIC-TOOL REPAIRER (any ind.) • D.O.T. #729.281-022 • OES #85711 • POWER-TOOL REPAIRER. Repairs electrical handtools and bench tools, such as drills, saws, grinders, and sanders, using lathe, circuit testers, handtools, and power tools: Tests motors, switches, and wiring for grounds, shorts, and loose connections, using electrical circuit testers. Turns motor commutators, using bench lathe. Repairs or replaces defective electrical parts, using handtools, power tools, and soldering and welding equipment. Inspects parts, such as mechanical gears, bearings, and bushings, for wear and damage, and repairs or replaces parts. • **GED:** R4, M3, L3 • **SVP:** 1-2 yrs • **Academic:** Ed=N, Eng=S • **Work Field:** 111 • **MPSMS:** 566, 567 • **Aptitudes:** G3, V3, N3, S3, P3, Q4, K3, F3, M2, E5, C4 • **Temperaments:** M, T • **Physical:** V=L, H=N, L=L, H • **Work Env:** I • **Salary:** 4 • **Outlook:** 3

ELECTRICAL-APPLIANCE REPAIRER (any ind.) • D.O.T. #723.381-010 • OES #85711 • Repairs electrical appliances, such as toasters, cookers, percolators, lamps, and irons, using handtools and electrical testing instruments: Examines appliance for mechanical defects and disassembles appliance. Tests wiring for broken or short circuits, using voltmeters, ohmmeter, and other circuit testers. Replaces defective wiring and parts, such as toaster elements and percolator coils, using handtools, soldering iron, and spot-welding equipment. May compute charges for labor and materials. May assist ELECTRICAL-APPLIANCE SERVICER (any ind.) in repairing such appliances as refrigerators and stoves. •

GED: R4, M2, L3 • **SVP:** 1-2 yrs • **Academic:** Ed=N, Eng=S • **Work Field:** 111 • **MPSMS:** 583 • **Aptitudes:** G3, V4, N4, S3, P3, Q4, K3, F3, M3, E5, C4 • **Temperaments:** M, T • **Physical:** V=L, H=N, L=L, W, H • **Work Env:** I • **Salary:** 4 • **Outlook:** 4

LIGHT TECHNICIAN (motion pic.) • D.O.T. #962.362-014 • OES #39999 • SET ELECTRICIAN, ASSISTANT CHIEF; OPERATOR, LIGHTS. Sets up and controls lighting equipment for television broadcast or motion picture production: Confers with directors and studies script to determine lighting effects required. Sets up spot, flood, incandescent, and mercury vapor lights, reflectors, and other equipment. Switches lights on during broadcast, following script or instructions from directors. Makes minor repairs, such as replacing broken cables on equipment. May perform duties as described under GROUP LEADER (any ind.). • **GED:** R4, M2, L3 • **SVP:** 2-4 yrs • **Academic:** Ed=N, Eng=S • **Work Field:** 111 • **MPSMS:** 863 • **Aptitudes:** G3, V3, N3, S3, P3, Q4, K3, F3, M3, E5, C3 • **Temperaments:** J, M, T • **Physical:** V=L, H=N, L=L, W, H • **Work Env:** I • **Salary:** 4 • **Outlook:** 2

PRODUCTION REPAIRER (electronics) • D.O.T. #726.381-014 • OES #85514 • REWORK OPERATOR. Repairs rejected electronic equipment, such as radio and television receivers, radio transmitters, radar units, amplifiers, and related antenna and cable assemblies, according to product specifications, manufacturing instructions and diagrams, using hand tools and soldering iron: Reads inspection tag and examines unit to locate defects, such as broken wires, burned-out components, or scratches on cabinet. Removes broken wires from units, using soldering iron and pliers. Cuts new wires to specified lengths with wire cutters, or obtains precut wires and solders them to specified terminals. Reroutes and solders color-coded wires to terminals, following wiring diagram. Repairs defectively soldered joints, using soldering iron. Removes defective components, such as resistors, transformers, capacitors, and connectors from chassis, and installs new components, using soldering iron and handtools. Brushes touch-up paint over cabinet or case, and protective varnish on exposed wiring. • **GED:** R3, M2, L2 • **SVP:** 1-2 yrs • **Academic:** Ed=N, Eng=N • **Work Field:** 111 • **MPSMS:** 585, 586 • **Aptitudes:** G3, V4, N4, S3, P3, Q4, K3, F3, M3, E5, C3 • **Temperaments:** M, T • **Physical:** V=L, H=N, L=L, W, H • **Work Env:** I • **Salary:** 4 • **Outlook:** 3

SOUND CONTROLLER (amuse. & rec.) • D.O.T. #194.262-014 • OES #22599 • Operates sound-mixing board to control output of voices, music, and previously taped sound effects during stage performances: Analyzes script of dialog, music, and sound effects as applied to particular scene to determine sound requirements. Confers with producing personnel concerning microphone placement, special sound effects, cues, and acoustical characteristics of theater. Locates sound-mixing board backstage or in theater control room. Arranges microphones in theater to achieve best sound pickup. Moves control to turn microphones on or off and adjusts volume, fader, and mixer controls to blend output of individual microphones. Listens to overall effect on monitor loudspeaker and observes dials on control panel to verify suitability of sounds. May modify design of sound equipment used. May operate record and electrical transcription turntables to supply musical selections and other sound material. • **GED:** R4, M4, L3 • **SVP:** 2-4 yrs • **Academic:** Ed=H, Eng=G • **Work Field:** 281 • **MPSMS:** 586 • **Aptitudes:** G2, V2, N3, S3, P3, Q3, K3, F3, M3, E4, C5 • **Temperaments:** J, M, T, V • **Physical:** V=N, H=G, L=S, H • **Work Env:** I • **Salary:** 4 • **Outlook:** 2

TAPE-RECORDER REPAIRER (any ind.) • D.O.T. #720.281-014 • OES #85708 • Tests, repairs, and adjusts tape-recording machines, following schematic diagrams and manufacturer's specifications, using handtools and electronic testing instruments: Disassembles machine and replaces worn parts, such as sprocket wheels, drive belts, electrical switches, and guide rollers, using handtools. Records voice and listens to playbacks to detect distortion in sound. Tests circuits, using instruments, such as voltmeters, oscilloscopes, audiogenerators, and distortion meters. Replaces defective resistors, condensers, and tubes. Solders loose connections. Tests operation of repaired recorder. • **GED:** R4, M3, L2 • **SVP:** 2-4 yrs • **Academic:** Ed=N, Eng=N • **Work Field:** 111 • **MPSMS:** 585 • **Aptitudes:** G3, V3, N3, S2, P2, Q4, K3, F3, M2, E5, C3 • **Temperaments:** M, T • **Physical:** V=L, H=G, L=M, W, H • **Work Env:** I • **Salary:** 4 • **Outlook:** 4

TELEVISION INSTALLER (any ind.) • D.O.T. #823.361-010 • OES #85708 • Installs and adjusts television receivers and antennas, using handtools: Selects antenna according to type of set and location of transmitting station. Bolts crossarms and dipole elements in position to assemble antenna. Secures antenna in place with bracket and guy wires, observing insurance codes and local ordinances to protect installation from lightning and other hazards. Drills and waterproofs holes in building to make passages for transmission line. Connects line between receiver and antenna and fastens line in place. Tunes receiver on all channels and adjusts screws to obtain desired density, linearity, focus, and size of picture. Orients antenna and installs reflector to obtain optimum signal reception. • **GED:** R3, M3, L3 • **SVP:** 1-2 yrs • **Academic:** Ed=N, Eng=S • **Work Field:** 111 • **MPSMS:** 585 • **Aptitudes:** G3, V3, N4, S3, P3, Q4, K4, F3, M3, E4, C5 • **Temperaments:** M, R, T • **Stress:** T • **Physical:** V=L, H=N, L=M, W, C, S, H • **Work Env:** B, R • **Salary:** 4 • **Out look:** 2

TELEVISION-AND-RADIO REPAIRER (any ind.) • D.O.T. #720.281-018 • OES #85708 • TELEVISION REPAIRER. Repairs and adjusts radios and television receivers, using hand tools and electronic testing instruments: Tunes receiver on all channels and observes audio and video characteristics to locate source of trouble. Adjusts controls to obtain desired density, linearity, focus, and size of picture. Examines chassis for defects. Tests voltages and resistances of circuits to isolate defect, following schematic diagram and using voltmeter, oscilloscope, signal generator, and other electronic testing instruments. Tests and changes tubes. Solders loose connections and repairs or replaces defective parts, using handtools and soldering iron. Repairs radios and other audio equipment [RADIO REPAIR ER (any ind.)]. May install television sets [TELEVISION INSTALLER (any ind.)]. • **GED:** R4, M3, L2 • **SVP:** 2-4 yrs • **Academic:** Ed=H, Eng=N • **Work Field:** 111 • **MPSMS:** 585 • **Aptitudes:** G3, V3, N3, S2, P2, Q4, K3, F3, M2, E5, C4 • **Temperaments:** M, T, V • **Physical:** V=G, H=N, L=M, W, H • **Work Env:** I • **Salary:** 3 • **Outlook:** 3

TELEVISION-CABLE INSTALLER (any ind.) • D.O.T. #821.281-010 • OES #85702 • Installs CATV (community antenna television distribution cables) on customers' premises: Measures television signal strength at utility pole, using electronic test equipment. Computes impedance of wire from pole to house to determine additional resistance needed for reducing signal to desired level. Installs terminal boxes and strings lead-in wires, using electrician's tools. Connects television set to antenna system and evaluates incoming signal. Adjusts and repairs antenna system to ensure optimum reception. • **GED:** R4, M4, L3 • **SVP:** 6 mos-1 yr • **Academic:** Ed=N, Eng=S • **Work Field:** 111 • **MPSMS:** 586 • **Aptitudes:** G3, V3, N3, S2, P3, Q4, K3, F3, M3, E4, C4 • **Temperaments:** M • **Physical:** V=L, H=N, L=M, W, C, H • **Work Env:** O, R • **Salary:** 3 • **Outlook:** 4

TRANSFORMER REPAIRER (any ind.) • D.O.T. #724.381-018 • OES #85714 • Cleans and repairs distribution, streetlight, and instrument transformers: Disassembles transformers, using handtools, and opens valve to drain oil. Boils metal transformer case and cover in chemical solution to remove grease, rinses with hose, and dries with cloth to remove dirt and oil. Reassembles transformer, replacing worn or defec tive parts, using handtools. Solders input and output wires in position and pours compound in transformer-case terminal openings to seal out moisture. Pours oil into transformer until coils are submerged. • **GED:** R3, M2, L2 • **SVP:** 2-4 yrs • **Academic:** Ed=N, Eng=N • **Work Field:** 111 • **MPSMS:** 581 • **Aptitudes:** G3, V3, N3, S3, P3, Q4, K3, F4, M3, E5, C4 • **Temperaments:** M, T • **Physical:** V=L, H=N, L=M, W, H • **Work Env:** I • **Salary:** 4 • **Outlook:** 3

VACUUM CLEANER REPAIRER (any ind.) • D.O.T. #723.381-014 • OES #85711 • Repairs and adjusts vacuum cleaners, using handtools: Observes ammeter reading and listens to sound of cleaner motor to detect cause of faulty operation. Repairs, adjusts, or replaces defective brushes, belts, fans, control switches, extension cords, electric motors, or other mechanical ar electrical parts, using handtools. Lubricates cleaner parts, using grease gun. May sell and demonstrate vacuum cleaners. • **GED:** R3, M2, L2 • **SVP:** 1-2 yrs • **Academic:** Ed=N, Eng=N • **Work Field:** 111, 121 • **MPSMS:** 583 • **Aptitudes:** G3, V3, N3, S3, P3, Q4, K3, F3, M2, E5, C4 • **Temperaments:** J, M, T • **Physical:** V=L, H=N, L=M,

H • **Work Env:** I • **Salary:** 4 • **Outlook:** 3

GOE: 05.10.04
Structural-Mechanical-Electrical Crafts

AIR-CONDITIONING INSTALLER, DOMESTIC (any ind.) • D.O.T. #827.464-010 • OES #85711 • AIR-CONDITIONING-WINDOW-BOX INSTALLER. Installs window-or central-air-conditioning units in private residences and small business establish ments: Inspects existing wiring, fuses, or circuit-breaker panels on customer's premises to insure adequate power supply for oper ating air conditioner. Measures window, transom, or other existing openings for air-conditioning unit, using measuring tape or rule, or cuts opening through wall, using mallet and cold-chisel. Assembles and positions support brackets in place, using screws, clamps, or other braces, and handtools and power tools. Fills space between window support and edge of opening with calking compound and filler board. Places air conditioner on support frame and secures unit in position, leveling unit with screws, clips, and bolts. Starts unit, adjusts controls, and listens for excessive noise or sounds indicating malfunction. May give in structions to customer regarding operation and care of unit. May change filters, lubricate machine, replace fan motor or fan belt, and make minor adjustments. May specialize in installation of central units and be designated CENTRAL-AIR-CONDITIONING INSTALL ER (any ind.). • **GED:** R3, M3, L3 • **SVP:** 3-6 mos • **Academic:** Ed=N, Eng=S • **Work Field:** 111, 121 • **MPSMS:** 573 • **Aptitudes:** G3, V4, N4, S3, P3, Q4, K3, F3, M3, E4, C5 • **Temperaments:** J, M, T • **Physical:** V=L, H=L, L=H, W, C, H • **Work Env:** B • **Salary:** 4 • **Outlook:** 4

AIRPORT ATTENDANT (air trans.) • D.O.T. #912.364-010 • OES #67099 • Performs any combination of following duties in maintenance of small airports and in servicing aircraft: Periodically inspects buildings and hangars to detect fire hazards and violations of airport regulations. Examines firefighting equipment to detect malfunctions and fills depleted fire extinguishers. Performs necessary minor repairs to fire trucks and tractors. Fills light bombs with kerosene and positions bombs on landing field to illuminate danger areas. Cleans, fills, and lights smokepots used to indicate wind direction, and repairs or replaces windsock and other wind indicating devices. Replaces defective bulbs or burnt-out fuses in lighting equipment, such as landing lights and boundary lights. Fills holes and levels low places and bumps in runways and taxiing areas. Cuts grass on airport grounds [LABORER, AIRPORT MAINTE NANCE (air trans.)]. Patrols airfield to ensure security of aircraft and facilities. Verifies and reports specified amount of gasoline and oil supplies. Blocks and stakes down airplanes. Records airport data, such as number of planes stored in hangars, plane landings and departures, and number of passengers carried on planes. May wash and clean cabins and exterior surfaces of airplanes. May fill airplane tanks with gasoline and oil [LINE-SERVICE ATTENDANT (air trans.)]. May be required to possess Red Cross first-aid certificate to render emergency treatment to victims. • **GED:** R3, M2, L3 • **SVP:** 6 mos-1 yr • **Academic:** Ed=N, Eng=S • **Work Field:** 111 • **MPSMS:** 855 • **Aptitudes:** G3, V3, N4, S3, P3, Q3, K3, F4, M3, E4, C4 • **Temperaments:** J, V • **Physical:** V=L, H=N, L=M, W, H • **Work Env:** B, N • **Salary:** 3 • **Outlook:** 3

DOLL REPAIRER (any ind.) • D.O.T. #731.684-014 • OES #85999 • Repairs damaged dolls: Examines doll to determine extent of damage and repairs needed. Disassembles doll to remove damaged parts. Repairs or replaces parts and reassembles doll. Repaints dolls, retouches lips, and cheeks, using paint and brush. Replaces eyelashes and hair, using glue. May package or otherwise prepare repaired doll for shipment or stor age. • **GED:** R2, M1, L1 • **SVP:** 30 days-3 mos • **Academic:** Ed=N, Eng=N • **Work Field:** 102 • **MPSMS:** 615 • **Aptitudes:** G4, V4, N4, S3, P3, Q4, K4, F3, M3, E5, C3 • **Temperaments:** R, T • **Stress:** T • **Physical:** V=L, H=N, L=L, H • **Work Env:** I • **Salary:** 3 • **Outlook:** 2

EQUIPMENT INSTALLER (any ind.) • D.O.T. #828.381-010 • OES #85728 • Installs electronic control panels and related mechanical or electrical equipment, such as motor generator units, battery chargers, utility reels, and darkroom equipment, in panel trucks following blueprint specifi cations: Measures distances with rule to lay out work in body of truck. Drills holes and bolts metal framework and supports in place, using electric drill and wrenches. Cuts, drills, and fits brackets, supports, covers, and fixtures from metal sheet, strap or bar stock, using metal cutting saws, drill press, grinders, and files. Bolts and screws control panels and assembled operating units to framework. Connects electrical wiring and cables, using electricians' handtools. Installs lighting fixtures, out lets, switches, wall boxes, and terminal boards. • **GED:** R4, M3, L3 • **SVP:** 2-4 yrs • **Academic:** Ed=N, Eng=S • **Work Field:** 111, 121 • **MPSMS:** 596 • **Aptitudes:** G3, V3, N3, S3, P3, Q4, K4, F3, M3, E4, C4 • **Temperaments:** M, T, V • **Physical:** V=L, H=N, L=M, W, S, H • **Work Env:** O, R • **Salary:** 4 • **Outlook:** 3

EVAPORATIVE-COOLER INSTALLER (any ind.) • D.O.T. #637.381-010 • OES #85902 • COOLER SERVICER. Repairs and installs cooling units to draw air over moistened pads, using handtools and portable power tools: Disassembles, cleans, and oils parts. Replaces motor bearings, alines pulleys on motor and blower shafts, and tightens slack in drive belts. Replaces defective wiring. Holds tachometer against revolving centers of blowers and motors to verify specified revolutions per minute. Bolts cooler to window or platform adjacent to window, following layout lines. Cuts and installs plywood or building board to fit vacant window space. Installs electrical outlets and thermostat or humidistat controls. Cuts and connects tubing to cooler and water source. Adjusts rate of water flow. May install cooler on roof and assemble prefabricated sheet metal ducts in attic. • **GED:** R3, M3, L3 • **SVP:** 1-2 yrs • **Academic:** Ed=N, Eng=S • **Work Field:** 102, 111 • **MPSMS:** 568 • **Aptitudes:** G3, V3, N4, S3, P3, Q4, K3, F3, M2, E3, C5 • **Temperaments:** R, T • **Stress:** T • **Physical:** V=L, H=N, L=M, W, C, S, H • **Work Env:** B • **Salary:** 4 • **Outlook:** 3

FIRE-EXTINGUISHER REPAIRER (any ind.) • D.O.T. #709.384-010 • OES #85999 • Repairs and tests fire extinguishers in repair shops and in establishments, such as factories, homes, garages, and office buildings, using handtools and hydrostatic test equipment: Dismantles extinguisher and examines tubings, horns, head gaskets, cutter discs, and other parts for defects. Replaces worn or damaged parts, using handtools. Cleans extinguishers and recharges them with materials, such as soda water and sulfuric acid, carbon tetrachloride, nitrogen, or patented solutions. Tests extinguishers for conformity with legal specifications, using hydrostatic test equipment. May install cabinets and brackets to hold extinguishers. May sell fire extinguishers. • **GED:** R3, M2, L2 • **SVP:** 30 days-3 mos • **Academic:** Ed=N, Eng=N • **Work Field:** 121 • **MPSMS:** 969 • **Aptitudes:** G3, V3, N4, S3, P3, Q4, K4, F4, M3, E5, C5 • **Temperaments:** T • **Physical:** V=L, H=N, L=M, W, S, H • **Work Env:** I • **Salary:** 2 • **Outlook:** 3

HOUSEHOLD-APPLIANCE INSTALLER (any ind.) • D.O.T. #827.661-010 • OES #85711 • Installs household appliances, such as refrigerators, washing machines, stoves, and related appliances, in mobile homes or customers' homes, using handtools: Levels refrigerators and adjusts doors. Connects water pipes to washing machines, using plumbing tools. Observes complete cycle of automatic washers and dryers and makes adjustments. Lights and adjusts pilot lights on gas stoves and examines valves and burners for gas leakage and specified flame. May assemble and install prefabricated kitchen cabinets in conjunction with appliances. May stain or finish cabinets. • **GED:** R3, M3, L3 • **SVP:** 1-2 yrs • **Academic:** Ed=N, Eng=S • **Work Field:** 121 • **MPSMS:** 583 • **Aptitudes:** G3, V4, N4, S3, P4, Q4, K3, F4, M3, E4, C4 • **Temperaments:** R, T • **Stress:** T • **Physical:** V=N, H=N, L=H, W, C, S, H • **Work Env:** I • **Salary:** 4 • **Outlook:** 3

MANAGER, CAMP (const.) • D.O.T. #187.167-066 • OES #15026 • Directs and coordinates activities of workers concerned with preparing and maintaining buildings and facilities in residential construction or logging camp: Coordinates through subordinate personnel or personally directs workers engaged in preparing and maintaining such camp facilities as dining halls and barracks used by resident laborers. Directs activities of food service workers. Schedules purchase and deliv ery of food supplies. Enforces safety and sanitation regulations. • **GED:** R4, M3, L3 • **SVP:** 1-2 yrs • **Academic:** Ed=H, Eng=S • **Work Field:** 291 • **MPSMS:** 900 • **Aptitudes:** G3, V3, N3, S3, P3, Q3, K4, F4, M4, E4, C5 • **Temperaments:** D, J, V • **Stress:** A • **Physical:** V=G, H=L, L=L, H

Work Env: B • **Salary:** 4 • **Outlook:** 3

PINSETTER MECHANIC, AUTOMATIC (any ind.) • D.O.T. #638.261-022 • OES #85999 • BOWLING-PIN-MACHINE MECHANIC. Adjusts and repairs automatic pinsetting bowling machines, following maintenance manuals, schematics, and knowledge of equipment, using handtools, power tools, and testing equipment: Observes operation of machine to determine nature and cause of malfunction. Tests relays, solenoids, transformers, electric motors, and wiring for defects, using continuity tester, ammeter, and voltmeter. Disassembles and replaces or repairs mechanical and electrical components or parts, such as bearings, coils, armatures, and wiring, using handtools. Cleans and lubricates machine. Instructs assistants in locating and repairing minor defects. Directs workers or participates in reconditioning and painting bowling pins. Maintains perpetual inventory of and orders replacements for spare parts. • **GED:** R3, M2, L2 • **SVP:** 3-6 mos • **Academic:** Ed=N, Eng=N • **Work Field:** 111, 121 • **MPSMS:** 616 • **Aptitudes:** G3, V3, N4, S3, P3, Q4, K3, F3, M3, E4, C4 • **Temperaments:** M, T, V • **Physical:** V=L, H=N, L=M, W, C, S, H • **Work Env:** I • **Salary:** 3 • **Outlook:** 3

POLISHING-WHEEL SETTER (any ind.) • D.O.T. #776.684-014 • OES #85128 • WHEEL SETTER. Replaces worn abrasive surface on leather or felt polishing wheels, canvas belts, and metal or fiber disks, and balances wheels: Immerses wheel or disk in solution to soften glue. Mounts wheel on electrically-driven, pedestal-mounted spindle, using wrench, and holds pumice stone against rotating wheel to remove compacted abrasive. Rubs fingers over wheel surface to detect abrasive fragments. Brushes binding agent on wheel or disk. Rolls wheel in tray of abrasive powder or sprinkles powder over disk to cover surface with abrasive. Pounds wheel or disk with wooden block to force abrasive into binding agent. Centers wheel on static bal ancer to locate placement for lead weight to balance wheel. Removes lead weight from heavy side of wheel or nails counter weight to opposite side to balance wheel. • **GED:** R2, M1, L2 • **SVP:** 30 days-3 mos • **Academic:** Ed=N, Eng=N • **Work Field:** 102 • **MPSMS:** 538 • **Aptitudes:** G4, V4, N5, S4, P3, Q4, K4, F4, M3, E5, C5 • **Temperaments:** J, R • **Stress:** T • **Physical:** V=L, H=N, L=M, W, H • **Work Env:** I, N • **Salary:** 2 • **Outlook:** 2

SPORTS-EQUIPMENT REPAIRER (any ind.) • D.O.T. #732.684-122 • OES #85999 • Repairs and replaces sporting and athletic equipment, such as fishing tackle, tennis rackets, or archery equipment: Restrings tennis rackets with animal gut or synthetic string. Replaces defective parts of fishing tackle, such as reels and rods. Replaces metal points on arrow shafts. Refinishes surfaces of sporting and athletic equipment with lacquer or paint. May carve wooden parts for sporting and athletic equipment, using handtools and powered woodworking tools. May make new gun stocks and pistol grips. May reglue and rewind bamboo sections of fly rods. May rewind shafts of bows and ar rows. May be designated according to type of sporting or athletic equipment repaired as ARCHERY-EQUIPMENT REPAIRER (any ind.); FISHING-TACKLE REPAIRER (any ind.); FOOTBALL-PAD REPAIRER (any ind.); TENNIS-RACKET REPAIRER (any ind.). • **GED:** R3, M2, L2 • **SVP:** 3-6 mos • **Academic:** Ed=N, Eng=N • **Work Field:** 102 • **MPSMS:** 616 • **Aptitudes:** G3, V4, N4, S3, P3, Q4, K3, F3, M3, E5, C5 • **Temperaments:** R, T • **Stress:** T • **Physical:** V=L, H=N, L=L, W, H • **Work Env:** I • **Salary:** 3 • **Outlook:** 3

SWIMMING-POOL SERVICER (any ind.) • D.O.T. #891.684-018 • OES #85999 • MAINTENANCE WORKER, SWIMMING POOL; POOL SERVICER. Cleans, adjusts, and performs minor repairs to swimming pools and auxiliary equipment: Removes leaves and other debris from surface of water, using net. Cleans bottom and sides of pool, using such aids as underwater vacuum cleaner, hose, brush, detergent, acid solution, and sander. Inspects and replaces loose or damaged tile. Cleans and repairs filter system. Adjusts and performs minor repairs to heating and pumping equipment, using mechanic's handtools. Dumps chemicals, in prescribed amounts, to purify water in pool. Prepares service report of materials used and work performed. • **GED:** R3, M1, L2 • **SVP:** 3-6 mos • **Academic:** Ed=N, Eng=S • **Work Field:** 031, 121 • **MPSMS:** 364, 568 • **Aptitudes:** G3, V4, N4, S3, P3, Q4, K3, F4, M3, E4, C4 • **Temperaments:** R, T • **Stress:** T • **Physical:** V=L, H=N, L=M, W, C, S, H • **Work Env:** B, W • **Salary:** 4 •

Outlook: 3

USED-CAR RENOVATOR (ret. tr.) • D.O.T. #620.684-034 • OES #85305 • USED-CAR CONDITIONER. Renovates used cars for resale at used car lot: Inspects cars for noticeable defects, such as dents, scratches, torn upholstery, and poor mechanical operation. Hammers out dents. Polishes scratches and retouches with enamel. Sews rips and tears in upholstery. Cleans and vacuums interiors. Washes and polishes exteriors. Replaces missing or defective small parts. Performs minor mechanical repairs and adjustments. May inspect cars for compliance with state safety regulations. • **GED:** R3, M2, L2 • **SVP:** 3-6 mos • **Academic:** Ed=N, Eng=N • **Work Field:** 121 • **MPSMS:** 591 • **Aptitudes:** G3, V4, N4, S3, P3, Q4, K4, F3, M3, E4, C4 • **Temperaments:** J, T, V • **Physical:** V=G, H=L, L=M, W, H • **Work Env:** B • **Salary:** 3 • **Outlook:** 3

GOE: 05.10.05 Reproduction Crafts

AUDIO OPERATOR (radio & tv broad.) • D.O.T. #194.262-010 • OES #34028 • AUDIO ENGINEER; AUDIO TECHNICIAN; SOUND ENGINEER; STUDIO ENGINEER, AUDIO CONTROL. Controls audio equipment to regulate volume level and quality of sound during television broadcasts, according to script and instructions of DIRECTOR, TECHNICAL (radio & tv broad.): Directs worker in placing microphones in locations that ensure quality of sound reproduction. Cuts microphones in, and blends output of individu al microphones by adjusting volume, fader, and mixer controls. Monitors audio signals by earphone, loudspeaker, and by observing dials on control panel to verify quality of sound reproduction. Sets keys, switches, and dials to synchronize sound with picture presentation. Obtains tapes, records, and themes from library according to program schedule. Operates turntables and tape recording machines to reproduce music and appropriate audio sounds for specific programs. May direct adjustment of acoustical curtains and blinds within studio. • **GED:** R4, M4, L3 • **SVP:** 2-4 yrs • **Academic:** Ed=H, Eng=S • **Work Field:** 281 • **MPSMS:** 863 • **Aptitudes:** G3, V3, N3, S3, P3, Q4, K2, F3, M3, E5, C4 • **Temperaments:** J, M, T • **Physical:** V=L, H=G, L=L, H • **Work Env:** I • **Salary:** 4 • **Outlook:** 3

AUDIOVISUAL TECHNICIAN (any ind.) • D.O.T. #960.382-010 • OES #92905 • AUDIOVISUAL-EQUIPMENT OPERA TOR; PROJECTIONIST. Operates audiovisual or sound-reproducing equipment to provide or complement educational or public service programs offered by institutions, such as museums, zoos, or libraries: Operates motion picture projecting equipment to show films in auditorium or lecture hall for entertainment or enlight enment of visitors to institution. Operates film, slide, video, audio tape, or turntable equipment to project or produce still or moving pictures, background music, oral commentary, or sound effects to illustrate, clarify, or enhance impact of presentation by TEACHER (museum) 099.227-038. Coordinates equipment operation with material presented, according to notations in script or instructions of speaker. Maintains equipment in working condition. Makes minor adjustments and repairs to equipment, and notifies maintenance personnel when correction of major malfunction is required. Positions, installs, and connects equipment, such as microphones, amplifiers, and lights. • **GED:** R4, M3, L3 • **SVP:** 30 days-3 mos • **Academic:** Ed=N, Eng=G • **Work Field:** 281 • **MPSMS:** 910, 939 • **Aptitudes:** G3, V3, N4, S3, P3, Q4, K3, F3, M3, E5, C4 • **Temperaments:** J, T • **Physical:** V=L, H=L, L=M, W, H • **Work Env:** I • **Salary:** 2 • **Outlook:** 3

BLUEPRINTING-MACHINE OPERATOR (any ind.) • D.O.T. #979.682-014 • OES #92545 • AMMONIA-PRINT OPERATOR; BLUE-LINE OPERATOR; BLUEPRINT MAKER; WHITEPRINT-ING-MACHINE OPERATOR. Operates machine to make copies (blueprints) of printed material, such as documents or drawings: Examines negative of original for translucency. Selects sensitized paper according to color of line specified and positions original over paper. Moves controls to regulate light intensity and exposure time, according to translucency of original and type of sensitized paper. Slides original and sensitized paper into printer to expose and develop print. Examines finished print for specified color, intensity, and sharpness of line. Pushes button to supply machine with ammonia or manually pours ammonia into printer. May cover origi nal negative with translucent sensitized paper and color filter

to prepare autopostive (negative) of original. May be designated according to trade name of printer operated. • **GED:** R3, M1, L1 • **SVP:** 6 mos-1 yr • **Academic:** Ed=N, Eng=N • **Work Field:** 202 • **MPSMS:** 606 • **Aptitudes:** G3, V4, N4, S4, P3, Q4, K3, F4, M3, E5, C5 • **Temperaments:** R, T • **Stress:** T • **Physical:** V=L, H=N, L=L, H • **Work Env:** I • **Salary:** 2 • **Outlook:** 2

COLOR-PRINTER OPERATOR (photofinish.) • D.O.T. #976.382-014 • OES #92908 • Controls equipment to produce color prints from negatives: Reads customer instruction to determine processing requirement. Loads roll or magazine of printing paper into color printing equipment. Examines color negative to determine equipment control settings for production of prints meeting acceptable color-fidelity standards. Sets controls in accordance with examination, loads negative into machine, and starts machine to produce specified number of prints. Removes printed photographic paper from machine and places paper in film bag for further processing or in developing machine. Inspects finished prints for defects, such as dust and smudges, and removes defects, using brush, cloth, and cleaning fluid. Inserts processed negatives and prints into envelope for return to customer. May perform duties as described under GROUP LEADER (any ind.). • **GED:** R3, M2, L2 • **SVP:** 30 days-3 mos • **Academic:** Ed=N, Eng=N • **Work Field:** 202 • **MPSMS:** 867 • **Aptitudes:** G3, V3, N3, S3, P3, Q4, K4, F4, M3, E5, C2 • **Temperaments:** J, M, T • **Physical:** V=L, H=N, L=L, H • **Work Env:** I • **Salary:** 3 • **Outlook:** 4

DEVELOPER (photofinish.) • D.O.T. #976.681-010 • OES #89914 • DARKROOM WORKER; DOPER; HAND DEVELOPER. Develops exposed photographic film or sensitized paper in series of chemical and water baths to produce negative or positive prints: Mixes developing and fixing solutions, following formula. Immerses exposed film or photographic paper in developer solution to bring out latent image. Immerses negative or paper in stop-bath to arrest developer action, in hyposolution to fix image, and in water to remove chemicals. Dries prints or negatives, using sponge or squeegee, or places them in mechanical air drier. May produce color photographs, negatives, and slides, using color reproduction processes and be designated COLOR LABORATORY TECHNI-CIAN (photofinish.). May perform duties described under GROUP LEADER (any ind.). • **GED:** R3, M2, L2 • **SVP:** 3-6 mos • **Academic:** Ed=N, Eng=N • **Work Field:** 202 • **MPSMS:** 867 • **Aptitudes:** G3, V4, N3, S3, P3, Q4, K3, F3, M3, E5, C4 • **Temperaments:** J, M, T • **Physical:** V=G, H=N, L=S, H • **Work Env:** I, W • **Salary:** 3 • **Outlook:** 4

DUPLICATING-MACHINE OPERATOR 1 (clerical) • D.O.T. #207.682-010 • OES #56005 • Operates machine to reproduce data or ruled forms on paper from type in flat impression bed or plates on revolving cylinder: Selects type or em bossed plate and positions type or plate on cylinder or flat bed of machine. Loads paper in feed tray and makes adjustments to parts, such as inking rolls or ribbon and feeding mechanism. Starts machine which automatically pushes sheets under revolving cylinder or against flat impression bed of type where paper is printed. May keep record of number of copies made. Important variations may be indicated by trade name of machines used. • **GED:** R3, M2, L1 • **SVP:** 3-6 mos • **Academic:** Ed=N, Eng=N • **Work Field:** 191 • **MPSMS:** 891 • **Aptitudes:** G3, V3, N4, S3, P3, Q3, K3, F3, M3, E5, C5 • **Temperaments:** M, T • **Physical:** V=N, H=N, L=L, H • **Work Env:** I • **Salary:** 2 • **Outlook:** 2

ENGRAVER, MACHINE 1 (engraving) • D.O.T. #704.682-010 • OES #93951 • Operates pantograph engraving machine to engrave letters and figures on products, such as badges, fraternal emblems, pendants, and thermometers: Inserts specified letters and figures into pattern frame. Positions and secures workpiece in machine holding fixture and sets stylus at beginning of pattern. Depresses pedal to lower cutting tool onto workpiece. Engraves designs on workpiece by moving stylus around pattern causing cutting tool to duplicate motion on workpiece. Removes workpiece and places in tray. • **GED:** R3, M2, L2 • **SVP:** 30 days-3 mos • **Academic:** Ed=N, Eng=N • **Work Field:** 183 • **MPSMS:** 556, 610 • **Aptitudes:** G4, V4, N4, S4, P3, Q4, K3, F3, M3, E5, C5 • **Temperaments:** R • **Stress:** T • **Physical:** V=L, H=N, L=S, H • **Work Env:** I • **Salary:** 2 • **Outlook:** 2

ENGRAVING-PRESS OPERATOR (print. & pub.) • D.O.T. #651.382-010 • OES #92519 • DIE-STAMPING-PRESS OPERA-

TOR. Makes ready and operates press to engrave decorative designs or lettering on announcements, greeting and business cards, letterheads, and related items, following operating proce dures outlined on job order: Installs appropriate die and inking rollers on ram, using wrench. Cuts out and fastens paper template to bed of press to maintain flatness of finished cards or sheets. Inserts and adjusts roll of wiping paper that automatically cleans die between impressions. Thins ink to desired consistency and fills ink fountain. Starts press to obtain proof copy. Examines proof and adjusts press and ink fountain to obtain uniform indentation and color registration. Starts press and feeds cards or sheets to be engraved onto bed of press. • **GED:** R4, M2, L3 • **SVP:** 2-4 yrs • **Academic:** Ed=N, Eng=S • **Work Field:** 192 • **MPSMS:** 567 • **Aptitudes:** G3, V3, N4, S3, P3, Q3, K3, F3, M3, E4, C3 • **Temperaments:** M, R, T • **Stress:** T • **Physical:** V=L, H=N, L=L, H • **Work Env:** I, R • **Salary:** 4 • **Outlook:** 2

EQUIPMENT MONITOR, PHOTOTYPESETTING (print. & pub.) • D.O.T. #650.682-010 • OES #92541 • Monitors and controls electronic computer system used in phototypesetting: Sets control switches on optical character reader, computer, or phototypesetter. Inserts command codes to integrate and operate equipment according to data requirements specified in mark-up instructions. Selects and loads input and output units with materials for operating equipment. Moves switches to clear system and start operation of equipment. Observes equipment and control panels on consoles for error lights, messages, and machine stoppage or faulty output. Notifies superior of errors or equipment stoppage. • **GED:** R3, M1, L2 • **SVP:** 3-6 mos • **Academic:** Ed=N, Eng=N • **Work Field:** 191 • **MPSMS:** 480 • **Aptitudes:** G3, V4, N4, S4, P4, Q3, K3, F3, M4, E5, C5 • **Temperaments:** M, T • **Physical:** V=L, H=N, L=L, H • **Work Env:** I • **Salary:** 3 • **Outlook:** 2

FILM DEVELOPER (motion pic.) • D.O.T. #976.382-018 • OES #92908 • DEVELOPER OPERATOR. Operates machine to develop still or motion-picture film: Pulls reel of motion-picture film or rack of film strips through trapdoor into darkroom. Examines film to determine type processing required, utilizing knowledge of film developing techniques. Feels edges of film to detect tears and repairs film, using hand stapler. Mounts film in guide slot of developing machine according to length of time required for processing and pulls lever to lower film into processing position. Flips switch to start machine that trans ports film through series of solutions and into drying cabinet to develop and dry film. Observes film passing through machine to determine density of image and adjusts machine controls to shorten or lengthen path of film through solutions according to obser vations. May be designated according to type film developed as NEGATIVE DEVELOPER (motion pic,; photofinish.); POSITIVE DEVELOPER (motion pic.; photofinish.). • **GED:** R3, M1, L1 • **SVP:** 1-2 yrs • **Academic:** Ed=N, Eng=N • **Work Field:** 202 • **MPSMS:** 867, 911 • **Aptitudes:** G3, V4, N4, S4, P3, Q4, K3, F3, M3, E5, C5 • **Temperaments:** J, T • **Physical:** V=N, H=N, L=L, H • **Work Env:** I, W, R • **Salary:** 3 • **Outlook:** 4

FILM LABORATORY TECHNICIAN (motion pic.) • D.O.T. #976.684-014 • OES #92908 • Performs one or a combination of the following tasks to process motion picture film: Mixes specified chemicals according to formula to prepare solutions for use in processing film. Cuts and arranges film and splices film together according to written instructions or edited test print, using splicer. Compares film with edited print to detect irregularities in detail and color. Projects film on screen to detect defects in printing and developing, such as blurs, scratches, and perforations, using motion picture projector. Approves film for release, rejects defective film, or routes film to specified department for further processing. May be designated according to specialty as FILM INSPECTOR (motion pic.); FILM SPLICER (motion pic.). • **GED:** R3, M2, L2 • **SVP:** 30 days-3 mos • **Academic:** Ed=N, Eng=N • **Work Field:** 054, 062, 143 • **MPSMS:** 911 • **Aptitudes:** G3, V4, N4, S4, P3, Q4, K4, F3, M3, E5, C4 • **Temperaments:** J, M, T • **Physical:** V=L, H=N, L=L, H • **Work Env:** I • **Salary:** 2 • **Outlook:** 2

MICROFICHE DUPLICATOR (bus. ser.) • D.O.T. #976.381-014 • OES #89914 • Prepares microfiche duplicates of microfilm, using contact printer and developing machine: Cuts roll of exposed microfilm to specified lengths, using paper cutter. Alines film strips in lighted vacuum box and tapes strip together to assemble master print. Inserts master print and sensitized paper into vacuum frame of printer, set timer, and activates printer to transfer image from master print to paper, producing microfiche print. Feeds print into machine that develops and fixes image by heat-ammonia process [BLUEPRINTING-MACHINE OPERATOR (any ind.)]. Positions print on lighted table and exam ines print to detect imperfections, using magnifier. Affixes identification label to microfiche print. • **GED:** R4, M2, L2 • **SVP:** 1-2 yrs • **Academic:** Ed=N, Eng=N • **Work Field:** 201, 202 • **MPSMS:** 890 • **Aptitudes:** G3, V3, N3, S2, P2, Q4, K3, F3, M3, E4, C5 • **Temperaments:** M, T • **Physical:** V=G, H=N, L=L, H • **Work Env:** I, W, R • **Salary:** 4 • **Outlook:** 3

MICROFILM PROCESSOR (bus. ser.) • D.O.T. #976.385-010 • OES #92908 • Tends machine that automatically processes microfilm and examines processed film to ensure that quality of microfiche meets established standards: Loads film into magazine of camera under darkroom conditions, attaches magazine to camera, and splices end of film to leader in machine to facilitate threading film, using splicing tape. Flips switches and turns valves to activate machine components and functions, such as blower, squeegee, water flow into processor, and rate of processing chemical replenishment. Monitors machine warning lights to detect processing malfunctions, such as break in film or leader, and takes action to correct malfunction, using knowledge of machine operation. Records film processing information, such as film type, developing speed, and rate of chemical replenishment to maintain film log. Examines processed film to ensure numerical order and clarity of microfiche, using film winder, light table, and magnifier. Marks defective microfiche section of film and lists identifying number of sections on identification sheet to indicate refilming required. Measures optical density of random film section to ensure standard processing, using densitometer. Places film on cutter, aligns markings on cutter and film, and moves cutting instrument across film to separate indi vidual microfiche sections of film. Discards defective microfiche and places acceptable microfiche in envelope for further processing. Mixes processing chemicals to maintain supply, following specified formula, using mixing machine. Processes sample film and measures density of film to enable MICROFILM-CAMERA OPERATOR (bus. ser.) 976.682-022 to determine exposure settings for new batches of film. • **GED:** R3, M2, L2 • **SVP:** 2-30 days • **Academic:** Ed=N, Eng=N • **Work Field:** 202, 212 • **MPSMS:** 897 • **Aptitudes:** G3, V4, N4, S3, P3, Q4, K4, F3, M3, E5, C5 • **Temperaments:** T • **Physical:** V=L, H=N, L=L, H • **Work Env:** I • **Salary:** 2 • **Outlook:** 2

MOTION-PICTURE PROJECTIONIST (amuse. & rec.) • D.O.T. #960.362-010 • OES #92905 • AUDIOVISUAL EQUIPMENT OPERATOR; PROCESS PROJECTIONIST; PROJECTIONIST; THEATER PROJECTIONIST. Sets up and operates motion picture projection and sound-reproducing equipment to produce coordinated effects on screen: Inserts film into top magazine reel of projector. Threads film through picture aperture of projector, around pressure rollers, sprocket wheels, and sound drum or magnetic sound pickup on film, and onto spool that automatically takes up film slack. Regulates projection light and adjusts sound-reproducing equipment. Monitors operation of machines and transfers operation from one machine to another without interrupting flow of action on screen. Rewinds broken end of film onto reels by hand to minimize loss of time. Inspects and rewinds projected films for another showing. Repairs faulty sections of film. Operates stereopticon (magic lantern) or other special-effects equipment to project picture slides on screen. Cleans lenses, oils equipment, and makes minor repairs and adjustments. • **GED:** R4, M2, L2 • **SVP:** 1-2 yrs • **Academic:** Ed=N, Eng=N • **Work Field:** 281 • **MPSMS:** 911 • **Aptitudes:** G3, V3, N3, S3, P3, Q4, K3, F3, M3, E5, C3 • **Temperaments:** J, M, T • **Physical:** V=L, H=L, L=M, H • **Work Env:** I • **Salary:** 4 • **Outlook:** 1

OFFSET-DUPLICATING-MACHINE OPERATOR (clerical) • D.O.T. #207.682-018 • OES #56005 • Operates offset-duplicating machine to reproduce single or multicolor copies of charts, schedules, bulletins, and related matter, according to oral instructions or layout and stock specifications on job order: Installs sensitized metal printing plate or master copy of plastic-coated paper around press cylinder of machine and locks plate or master copy into position, using handtools. Turns hand wheel and ink fountain screws to regulate ink flow. Selects paper stock to be printed according to color, size, thickness, and quantity specified, stacks paper on feed table, and positions spring guide on side of paper stack. Turns elevator crank to raise feed table to paper height. Sets dial controls to adjust speed and feed of machine according to weight of paper. Starts machine that automatically reproduces copy by offset process. Cleans and files master copy or plate. Cleans and oils machine. May prepare printing plates. May operate stencil-process or spirit-duplicating machines and photocopy equipment. Important variations may be indicated by trade names of machines used. • **GED:** R3, M2, L1 • **SVP:** 6 mos-1 yr • **Academic:** Ed=N, Eng=N • **Work Field:** 191 • **MPSMS:** 891 • **Aptitudes:** G3, V4, N3, S4, P3, Q4, K3, F3, M3, E5, C4 • **Temperaments:** R, T • **Stress:** T • **Physical:** V=L, H=N, L=M, H • **Work Env:** I • **Salary:** 3 • **Outlook:** 2

PHOTOCOMPOSING-MACHINE OPERATOR (print. & pub.) • D.O.T. #650.582-018 • OES #92541 • TYPESETTER. Sets up and operates photocomposing machine to transfer data from perforated or magnetic tape into print on film or photographic paper, using either of following methods: (1) Loads roll of film or paper in machine magazine. Secures roll of perforated tape on machine reel and threads end of tape through machine feed rollers. Selects type font according to size and face of type specified and positions it on photographic unit. Turns dials to adjust line spacing and light intensity according to size and face of type. Starts machine that automatically prints type onto film or paper according to coded signal on tape. Removes finished copy from magazine for development. (2) Places reel of magnetic tape onto feed spindle of phototypesetting unit. Depresses keys to enter command codes, such as size and style of type, width and length of column, and to activate computer to produce phototype setting film, phototypesetting paper, or copy of tape. Removes and stacks finished copies from photocopy printing unit. Removes printing unit from machine, drains chemical solution, washes unit, and refills unit with specified developing solution. • **GED:** R3, M1, L1 • **SVP:** 1-2 yrs • **Academic:** Ed=N, Eng=N • **Work Field:** 191, 202 • **MPSMS:** 606 • **Aptitudes:** G3, V3, N4, S3, P3, Q4, K3, F3, M3, E5, C4 • **Temperaments:** R, T • **Stress:** T • **Physical:** V=G, H=N, L=L, H • **Work Env:** I • **Salary:** 4 • **Outlook:** 2

PHOTOGRAPH FINISHER (photofinish.) • D.O.T. #976.487-010 • OES #93999 • PRINT FINISHER. Performs any combination of the following tasks to dry, trim, and mount photographic prints: Places washed print on conveyor leading to heated rotating cylinder that dries and flattens print. Trims print edges, using paper cutter or scissors. Inserts print in specified frame or mounts print on material, such as paper, cardboard, or fabric, using cement or hand-operated press. Inserts print and corresponding negative in customer envelope. Computes price of order, according to size and number of prints, and marks price on customer envelope. May cut film lengthwise to separate individual print rolls, using slitting machine. • **GED:** R2, M1, L1 • **SVP:** 2-30 days • **Academic:** Ed=N, Eng=N • **Work Field:** 054, 061, 063 • **MPSMS:** 867 • **Aptitudes:** G4, V4, N3, S4, P4, Q4, K4, F3, M3, E5, C4 • **Temperaments:** R • **Stress:** T • **Physical:** V=N, H=N, L=L, H • **Work Env:** I • **Salary:** 3 • **Outlook:** 4

PHOTOGRAPHIC-PLATE MAKER (electronics) • D.O.T. #714.381-018 • OES #89718 • PHOTOGRAPHIC-PROCESS ATTENDANT. Prepares photographic plates used to print pattern of aperture masks on sensitized steel: Examines unexposed plate to detect foreign particles or emulsion flaws. Transfers image from master plate to unexposed plate by means of contact exposure and immerses plate in series of chemical and water baths to develop image on plate [DEVELOPER (photofinish.)]. Examines plate over light box in darkroom to detect flaws and verify conformity of pattern with master plate. Measures dot size and center distance, using calibrated microscope, and examines master and production plates for dot damage. Repairs defective plates by filling in missing dots, using photographic touch-up tool and ink. Installs and alines plates in printing chase for DISPLAY-SCREEN FABRICATOR (electronics). Prepares developing solutions, following formula. • **GED:** R4, M3, L3 • **SVP:** 1-2 yrs • **Academic:** Ed=H, Eng=S • **Work Field:** 202 • **MPSMS:** 567 • **Aptitudes:** G3, V3, N3, S3, P2, Q5, K4, F3, M3, E5, C4 • **Temperaments:** M, T • **Physical:** V=G, H=N, L=S, W, H • **Work Env:** I • **Salary:** 2 • **Outlook:** 3

PROJECTION PRINTER (photofinish.) • D.O.T. #976.381-018 • OES #89914 • PHOTOGRAPH ENLARGER; PROJECTION-CAMERA OPERATOR. Produces enlarged or reduced photographic prints from original negative or positive, using projection printer: Sorts order according to type, size, and processing requirements. Examines negative for contrast to determine grade of sensitized paper required for print. Places sensitized paper on easel and adjusts sliding arms of easel to outline specified area on paper, or threads paper through guides onto takeup spool and secures with tape. Places negative in holder and slides holder beneath light. Raises or lowers carriage of printer to focus image within outlined area on paper. Selects lens assembly according to size and type of negative to be printed and positions lens in holder. Adjusts lens opening, sets exposure timer, and starts machine. Varies contrast by shading darker image areas with hand or sheet of paper (dodging). Develops exposed paper [DEVELOPER (photofinish.)]. Examines developed prints to detect color deficiencies, scratches, and dust specks and retouches print to remove defects, using paints, pencils, brush, and cloth. Computes customer charges and maintains production record. • **GED:** R3, M2, L2 • **SVP:** 2-4 yrs • **Academic:** Ed=N, Eng=N • **Work Field:** 202 • **MPSMS:** 867 • **Aptitudes:** G3, V3, N3, S3, P3, Q4, K3, F3, M3, E5, C3 • **Temperaments:** J, T • **Physical:** V=G, H=N, L=L, H • **Work Env:** I • **Salary:** 3 • **Outlook:** 4

RECORDING ENGINEER (phonograph) • D.O.T. #194.362-010 • OES #22599 • SOUND RECORDING TECHNICIAN. Operates disk or tape recording machine to record music, dialog, or sound effects of phonograph recording sessions, radio broadcasts, television shows, training courses, or conferences, or to transfer transcribed material to sound-recording medium: Threads tape through recording device or places blank disk on turntable. Moves lever to regulate speed of turntable. Places cutting stylus on record. Examines grooves during cutting by stylus to determine if grooves are level, using microscope. Turns knobs on cutting arm to shift or adjust weight of stylus and cause grooves to be cut evenly. Starts recording machine and moves switches to open microphone and tune in live or recorded programs. Listens through earphone to detect imperfections of recording machines or extraneous noises emanating from recording studio or production stage. Observes dials, mounted on machine, to insure that volume level and intensity remain within specified limits. Removes filled reel or completed recordings from machine and attaches identifying labels. Keeps record of recordings in log book. May service and repair recording machines and allied equipment. May be designated according to type of machine used as DISK-RECORDING-MACHINE OPERATOR (phonograph; radio & tv broad.); TAPE-RECORDING-MACHINE OPERATOR (phonograph; radio & tv broad.); When transcribing to disk used in production of phonograph records, may be designated DUBBING-MACHINE OPERATOR (phonograph). When recording live television programs in monochrome or color on magnetic tape is designated VIDEOTAPE-RECORDING ENGINEER (radio & tv broad.). • **GED:** R3, M3, L3 • **SVP:** 2-4 yrs • **Academic:** Ed=A, Eng=G • **Work Field:** 281 • **MPSMS:** 869 • **Aptitudes:** G3, V3, N3, S3, P4, Q4, K3, F4, M3, E5, C5 • **Temperaments:** M, T • **Physical:** V=N, H=G, L=S, H • **Work Env:** I • **Salary:** 3 • **Outlook:** 1

RECORDIST (motion pic.) • D.O.T. #962.382-010 • OES #22599 • Controls equipment to record sound originating on motion-picture set, using magnetic film, optical film, and acetate disk recording equipment: Tests and sets up recording mechanism according to specifications. Starts recorder and synchronizes sound with film. Observes operation to ensure that sound is properly recorded. May be designated according to equipment used as DISK RECORDIST (motion pic.); FILM RECORDIST (motion pic.). • **GED:** R3, M2, L2 • **SVP:** 1-2 yrs • **Academic:** Ed=N, Eng=G • **Work Field:** 281 • **MPSMS:** 911 • **Aptitudes:** G3, V3, N3, S4, P3, Q4, K4, F3, M3, E5, C5 • **Temperaments:** J, M, T • **Physical:** V=N, H=G, L=L, H • **Work Env:** B • **Salary:** 4 • **Outlook:** 2

REPRODUCTION TECHNICIAN (any ind.) • D.O.T. #976.361-010 • OES #89914 • COPY-CAMERA OPERATOR; PHOTOLITH OPERATOR; VACUUM-FRAME OPERATOR. Duplicates printed material on sensitized paper, cloth, or film according to customer specifications, using photographic equipment and handtools: Reads work order and confers with supervisor to determine processes, techniques, equipment, and materials required. Places original on sensitized material in vacuum frame. Mounts camera on tripod or stand and loads prescribed type and size film in camera. Sets camera controls to regulate exposure time according to line density of original and type of sensitized material. Activates camera to expose sensitized material, imprinting original on material. Develops exposed material [DEVELOPER (photofinish.)]. Examines developed reprint for defects, such as broken lines, spots, and blurs, and touches up defects, using chemicals, inks, brushes, and pens. May enlarge reprints [PROJECTION PRINTER (photofinish.)] May reprint original in sections and piece sections together. • **GED:** R4, M2, L2 • **SVP:** 1-2 yrs • **Academic:** Ed=N, Eng=N • **Work Field:** 201, 202 • **MPSMS:** 867 • **Aptitudes:** G3, V3, N3, S2, P2, Q4, K3, F3, M3, E4, C2 • **Temperaments:** M, T • **Physical:** V=G, H=N, L=L, H • **Work Env:** I, W, R • **Salary:** 4 • **Outlook:** 2

RERECORDING MIXER (motion pic.) • D.O.T. #194.362-014 • OES #22599 • Operates console to synchronize and equalize prerecorded dialog, music, and sound effects with action of motion picture film: Reads script and dupe sheets of film and tape or video tape to learn sequence of speaking parts, music, and sound effects to be synchronized and integrated in film or tape or video tape. Informs DUBBING-MACHINE OPERATOR (motion pic.; radio & tv broad.) to load sound tracks onto dubbing machine and MOTION-PICTURE PROJECTIONIST (amuse. & rec.; motion pic.) to place film in projector. Operates console to control starting and stopping of projector and dubbing machine. Observes film or video tape projected onto screen, listens to sound over loud speakers, and turns knobs on panel of console to balance intensity and volume. Informs MOTION-PICTURE PROJECTION IST (amuse. & rec.; motion pic.) to project film onto screen. Observes projection and listens to determine that sound is synchronized and equalized with action on film. • **GED:** R4, M4, L4 • **SVP:** 2-4 yrs • **Academic:** Ed=H, Eng=S • **Work Field:** 281 • **MPSMS:** 586, 911 • **Aptitudes:** G3, V3, N3, S3, P5, Q5, K3, F3, M3, E5, C5 • **Temperaments:** J, M, T, V • **Physical:** V=L, H=G, L=S, H • **Work Env:** I • **Salary:** 4 • **Outlook:** 3

SCREEN MAKER, PHOTOGRAPHIC PROCESS (any ind.) • D.O.T. #979.384-010 • OES #89914 • Fabricates stencils for screen printing, using knowledge of photochemical processing and equipment: Coats screen with photosensitive emulsion, using brush. Places and secures artwork and screen in frame of vacuum printer. Adjusts printer controls and activates printer to transfer image onto screen and form stencil. Washes unexposed emulsion from screen, using water and hose. Hangs screen in rack or places screen in oven to dry. May fabricate stencil by adhering film with specified image to screen, using vacuum frame. May insert screen in frame, using handtools and tension meters [PRINTING SCREEN ASSEMBLER (electronics) 979.684-042]. May measure and mixingredients used in photochemical process, according to standard formulas. May scrub screen for reuse, using solvents, brush, and hose, in sink. May pour ink or other printing material onto screen and move squeegee across screen to test screen or to screen print objects [SCREEN PRINTER (any ind.) 979.684-034]. • **GED:** R3, M2, L2 • **SVP:** 3-6 mos • **Academic:** Ed=H, Eng=N • **Work Field:** 201, 202 • **MPSMS:** 567 • **Aptitudes:** G3, V4, N4, S4, P3, Q4, K3, F4, M3, E5, C3 • **Temperaments:** R, T • **Stress:** T • **Physical:** V=L, H=N, L=M, W, H • **Work Env:** I • **Salary:** 3 • **Outlook:** 3

SOUND MIXER (motion pic.) • D.O.T. #194.262-018 • OES #22599 • MIXER OPERATOR; MUSIC MIXER; STUDIO ENGINEER; STUDIO TECHNICIAN. Operates console to regulate volume level and quality of sound during filming of motion picture, phonograph recording session, or television and radio productions: Determines acoustics of recording studio and adjusts controls to specified levels. Directs installation of microphones and amplifiers for use in sound pickup. Turns knobs and dials on console while recording to cut microphones in and out and blend output of individual microphones so that balance is obtained between music, dialog, and sound effects. Instructs performers to project voices for pickup by microphones. Tests machines and equipment, using electronic testing equipment, such as ohm and voltage meters, to detect defects. May copy and edit recordings. May repair and replace audio amplifier parts. • **GED:** R4, M4, L3 • **SVP:** 2-4 yrs

• **Academic:** Ed=H, Eng=G • **Work Field:** 281 • **MPSMS:** 586, 911 • **Aptitudes:** G2, V2, N3, S3, P3, Q4, K3, F3, M3, E5, C5 • **Temperaments:** J, M, T, V • **Physical:** V=N, H=G, L=S, H • **Work Env:** I • **Salary:** 4 • **Outlook:** 2

TAKE-DOWN SORTER (photofinish.) • D.O.T. #976.665-010 • OES #92908 • Sorts and examines processed photographic film, repairs defective film, and tends drying cabinet that dries film: Flips switch to activate exhaust fan of drier, reads temperature gage, and adjusts heat controls to maintain specified temperature in drier. Notifies supervisor or darkroom personnel concerning need for machine adjustments or solution changes if excessive amounts of film damage occurs. Monitors drying operation to detect dirty, twisted, or torn film in drier and removes defective film from drier. Washes film in negative cleaner to clean, soften, and straighten film and mends torn film, using tape, sealing solution, and scissors. Feels surface of film in drier to determine dryness and removes film from drier when completely dry. Examines film for clearness of image to determine printability and matches numbered label attached to film with number on customer envelope to avoid missorts. Sorts film into bins or attaches to hooks according to size and type processing required. May compute customer charges using pricelist. • **GED:** R3, M1, L1 • **SVP:** 30 days-3 mos • **Academic:** Ed=N, Eng=N • **Work Field:** 202, 211 • **MPSMS:** 867 • **Aptitudes:** G3, V4, N4, S3, P3, Q3, K3, F3, M3, E5, C3 • **Temperaments:** J, T • **Physical:** V=L, H=N, L=L, H • **Work Env:** I • **Salary:** 1 • **Outlook:** 2

TAPE TRANSFERRER (phonograph) • D.O.T. #194.382-014 • OES #22599 • TAPE DUPLICATOR. Operates machines to reproduce tape recordings from master tapes (original tape recording): Consults charts to determine amount of tape needed, considering running time of master tape. Positions master tape in master-reproducing machine and mounts blank tape on spindle of tape-recording machine. Threads tapes through machines. Interconnects and starts machines to record selection on blank tape. Stops machines and reverses tape in recording machine to record second selection on reverse side of tape. Operates recording machine to play back reproduced recording to test quality of reproduced sound. • **GED:** R3, M3, L3 • **SVP:** 6 mos-1 yr • **Academic:** Ed=N, Eng=S • **Work Field:** 281 • **MPSMS:** 585, 869 • **Aptitudes:** G3, V3, N4, S4, P3, Q3, K3, F3, M3, E5, C5 • **Temperaments:** M, R, T • **Stress:** T • **Physical:** V=N, H=G, L=S, H • **Work Env:** I • **Salary:** 3 • **Outlook:** 2

TYPESETTING-MACHINE TENDER (print. & pub.) • D.O.T. #650.685-010 • OES #92541 • TELETYPESETTER MONITOR. Tends and adjusts one or more linecasting machines, equipped with tape converter unit, to produce type composition automatically: Positions spool of punched tape on machine reel. Threads end of tape through feed mechanism of converter unit. Turns control to start unit that sets type automatically as directed by coded signal on punched tape. Transfers lines of type, with copy, to composing or bank table for taking of proof. Adds new pigs of type metal to melting pot to replenish supply. Observes operation of machine to detect malfunction of keyboard, matrix circulation mechanism, tape feeding mechanism or other machine mechanisms, and adjusts their mechanical components, using handtools, or depresses keys on keyboard to clear jamming. Periodically cleans matrices, magazine, and molds. May replace worn parts, such as code bars, keys, and spacebands, using handtools and power tools. • **GED:** R3, M1, L2 • **SVP:** 3-6 mos • **Academic:** Ed=N, Eng=N • **Work Field:** 191 • **MPSMS:** 567 • **Aptitudes:** G3, V4, N4, S3, P3, Q4, K4, F4, M3, E5, C5 • **Temperaments:** R, T • **Stress:** T • **Physical:** V=L, H=N, L=L, H • **Work Env:** I, N • **Salary:** 3 • **Outlook:** 2

GOE: 05.10.06 Blasting

BLASTER (any ind.) • D.O.T. #859.261-010 • OES #87905 • FIRER; SHOOTER. Assembles, plants, and detonates charges of industrial explosives to loosen earth, rock, stumps, or to demolish structures to facilitate removal: Examines mass, composition, structure, and location of object to be blasted, estimates amount and determines kind of explosive to be used, and marks location of charge holes for drilling. Assembles primer (blasting cap and fuse or electric squib and booster charge) and places primer with main charge in hole or near object to be blasted. Covers charge with mud, sand, clay, or other material and tamps firm to improve detonation and confine force of blast. Signals to clear area of personnel and equipment. Lights fuse or connects wires from charge to battery or detonator to detonate charge. May operate jackhammer, hand drill, or electric drill to bore holes for charges. May climb cliffs or banks to plant explosive charge, using ropes and safety harness, and be designated HIGH SCALER (const.). May set and detonate explosive charges to improve flow of water into wells and be designated SHOOTER, WATER WELL (const.). • **GED:** R4, M4, L4 • **SVP:** 2-4 yrs • **Academic:** Ed=H, Eng=S • **Work Field:** 005 • **MPSMS:** 360 • **Aptitudes:** G3, V3, N3, S3, P3, Q4, K3, F3, M3, E3, C4 • **Temperaments:** J, S • **Stress:** S • **Physical:** V=L, H=N, L=H, W, C, S, H • **Work Env:** B, N, R • **Salary:** 5 • **Outlook:** 3

GOE: 05.10.07 Painting, Dyeing & Coating Crafts

PAINTER (const.) • D.O.T. #840.381-010 • OES #87402 • Applies coats of paint, varnish, stain, enamel, or lacquer to decorate and protect interior or exterior surfaces, trimmings, and fixtures of buildings, and other structures: Smooths surfaces, using sandpaper, brushes, or steel wool and removes old paint from surfaces, using paint remover, scraper, wire brush, or blowtorch to prepare surfaces for painting. Fills nail holes, cracks, and joints with putty, plaster, or other filler. Selects premixed paints, or mixes required portions of pigment, oil, and thinning and drying substances to prepare paint that matches specified colors. Paints surfaces, using brushes, spray gun, or paint rollers. Simulates wood grain, marble, brick, or tile effects. Applies paint with cloth, brush, sponge, or fingers to create special effects. Erects scaffolding or sets up ladders to perform tasks above ground level. May be designated according to type of work performed as PAINTER, INTERIOR FINISH (const.); PAINTER, MAINTENANCE (any ind.); or according to type of material used as CALCIMINER (const.); VARNISHER (const.). May also hang wallpaper and fabrics [PAPER-HANGER (const.) 841.381-010]. • **GED:** R3, M2, L2 • **SVP:** 2-4 yrs • **Academic:** Ed=N, Eng=N • **Work Field:** 102 • **MPSMS:** 360, 495 • **Aptitudes:** G3, V3, N3, S4, P3, Q5, K3, F3, M3, E4, C2 • **Temperaments:** J, T • **Physical:** V=G, H=N, L=M, W, C, S, H • **Work Env:** I, R, F • **Salary:** 4 • **Outlook:** 3

PAINTER, SPRAY 1 (any ind.) • D.O.T. #741.684-026 • OES #93947 • SPRAY-GUN OPERATOR. Sprays surfaces of machines, manufactured products, or working area with protective or decorative material, such as paint, enamel, glaze, gel-coat, or lacquer, using spray gun: Cleans grease and dirt from product, using materials, such as lacquer thinner, turpentine, soap, and water. Applies masking tape over parts and areas that are not to be coated [MASKER (any ind.)]. Fills cavities and dents with putty to attain smooth surface. Selects and mixes coating liquid to produce desired color, according to specifications, using paddle or mechanical mixer. Pours coating liquid into spray container and connects gun to airhose, using wrenches. Turns sprayer valves and nozzle to regulate width and pressure of spray, according to knowledge of painting technique. Pulls trigger and directs spray onto work surface to apply prime or finish coat. Coats areas inaccessible to hand sprayer, using brush. Cleans spraying equipment and brushes with solvent. May heat and spray wax onto products after they are tested. May use acid, wire brush, or steel wool to remove rust from metal. May paint designs on rug surfaces for decorative purposes or for use as guidelines in carving rugs, using spray gun and stencil, and be designated as STENCILER (carpet & rug). May be designated according to article sprayed as HAT SPRAYER (hat & cap); PAINTER, ORDNANCE (firearms); SPRAYER, RAIL-ROAD CAR (loco. & car bldg. & rep.; r.r. trans.); or according to material used as GEL-COAT SPRAYER (ship & boat bldg. & rep.; sports equip.); PORCELAIN-ENAMEL SPRAYER (any ind.). Additional Titles: CERAMIC SPRAYER (brick & tile; pottery & porc.); ENAMELER (pottery & porc.); ENAMEL SPRAYER (any ind.) I; GLAZE SPRAYER (auto. mfg.); LACQUER SPRAYER (any ind.) I; PAINTER, INSIGNIA (aircraft-aerospace mfg.; auto. mfg.); PANEL FINISHER (paint & varn.); PRIMER SPRAYER (aircraft-aerospace mfg.; auto. mfg.); SPRAYER, AUTO PARTS (auto. mfg.); THINNER SPRAYER (auto. mfg.); UNDERCOAT SPRAYER (aircraft-aerospace mfg.; auto. mfg.). • **GED:** R3, M2, L2 • **SVP:** 6 mos-1 yr • **Academic:** Ed=N, Eng=N • **Work Field:** 153 • **MPSMS:** 495 • **Aptitudes:** G3, V4, N4, S4, P3, Q4, K3, F3, M3,

E4, C3 • **Temperaments:** R, T • **Stress:** T • **Physical:** V=L, H=N, L=M, W, H • **Work Env:** I • **Salary:** 3 • **Outlook:** 2

PAINTER, TOUCH-UP (any ind.) • D.O.T. #749.684-038 • OES #93947 • FINAL-TOUCH-UP PAINTER; FINISH REPAIRER; SPOT SPRAYER. Brushes or sprays paint to cover scratches, chips, or repairs in painted finish of items, such as refrigerator cabinets, washing machines, or automobile bodies: Cleans and prepares surface for painting, using water, solvent, and scraper. Applies thin, even coat of finish material, such as paint or lacquer, to sanded area, using spray gun. Sprays lacquer or thinner material over finish coats to blend in spots and eliminate halo around repair. Paints chipped spots with brush. Compares color of paint supply with color chart and workpiece and remixes it to match standard colors. Maintains spray painting equipment. May mark identifying code on workpiece to indicate destination for further processing. • **GED:** R3, M1, L1 • **SVP:** 3-6 mos • **Academic:** Ed=N, Eng=N • **Work Field:** 153 • **MPSMS:** 495 • **Aptitudes:** G3, V4, N4, S4, P3, Q4, K3, F4, M3, E5, C2 • **Temperaments:** M, T • **Physical:** V=L, H=N, L=M, W, H • **Work Env:** I • **Salary:** 3 • **Outlook:** 2

GOE: 05.10.08 Food Preparation, Crafts

BAKER (hotel & rest.) • D.O.T. #313.381-010 • OES #65021 • BAKER, BREAD; BREAD MAKER; OVEN TENDER. Prepares bread, rolls, muffins, and biscuits according to recipe: Checks production schedule to determine variety and quantity of goods to bake. Measures ingredients, using measuring cups and spoons. Mixes ingredients to form dough or batter by hand or using electric mixer. Cuts dough into uniform portions with knife or divider. Molds dough into loaves or desired shapes. Places shaped dough in greased or floured pans. Spreads or sprinkles topping, such as jelly, cinnamon, and poppy seeds on specialties. Places pans of dough in proof box to rise. Inserts pans of raised dough in oven to bake, using peel. Adjusts drafts or thermostatic controls to regulate oven temperature. Removes baked goods from oven and places on cooling rack. May bake pies, cakes, cookies, and other pastries [COOK, PASTRY (hotel & rest.)]. May be desig nated according to specialty baked as BAKER, BISCUIT (hotel & rest.); HOT-BREAD BAKER (hotel & rest.); ROLLS BAKER (hotel & rest.); or according to shift worked, as NIGHT BAKER (hotel & rest.). • **GED:** R3, M2, L2 • **SVP:** 1-2 yrs • **Academic:** Ed=N, Eng=N • **Work Field:** 146 • **MPSMS:** 384 • **Aptitudes:** G3, V4, N4, S3, P3, Q4, K3, F4, M3, E5, C4 • **Temperaments:** J, T • **Physical:** V=L, H=N, L=M, W, H • **Work Env:** I, H • **Salary:** 4 • **Outlook:** 4

BAKER, HEAD (hotel & rest.) • D.O.T. #313.131- 010 • OES #61099 • BAKER, BREAD, CHIEF; BAKER CHEF. Supervises and coordinates activities of personnel in bread-baking department: Plans production according to daily require ments. Requisitions supplies and equipment. Maintains production records. • **GED:** R4, M3, L3 • **SVP:** 2-4 yrs • **Academic:** Ed=N, Eng=S • **Work Field:** 146 • **MPSMS:** 384 • **Aptitudes:** G3, V4, N3, S3, P3, Q3, K4, F4, M2, E5, C4 • **Temperaments:** D, M, T • **Physical:** V=L, H=N, L=L, W, H • **Work Env:** I, H • **Salary:** 4 • **Outlook:** 3

BAKER, PIZZA (hotel & rest.) • D.O.T. #313.381-014 • OES #65032 • Prepares and bakes pizza pies: Measures ingredients, such as flour, water, and yeast, using measuring cup, spoon, and scale. Dumps specified ingredients into pan or bowl of mixing machine preparatory to mixing. Starts machine and observes operation until ingredients are mixed to desired consistency. Stops machine and dumps dough into proof box to allow dough to rise. Kneads fermented dough. Cuts out and weighs amount of dough required to produce pizza pies of desired thickness. Shapes dough sections into balls or mounds and sprinkles each section with flour to prevent crust forming until used. Greases pan. Stretches or spreads dough mixture to size of pan. Places dough in pan and adds olive oil and tomato puree, tomato sauce, mozzarella cheese, meat, or other garnish on surface of dough, according to kind of pizza ordered. Sets thermostatic controls and inserts pizza into heated oven to bake for specified time. Removes product from oven and observes color to determine when pizza is done. • **GED:** R3, M2, L1 • **SVP:** 6 mos-1 yr • **Academic:** Ed=N, Eng=N • **Work Field:** 146 • **MPSMS:** 903 • **Aptitudes:** G3, V4, N4, S4, P3, Q4, K4, F4, M3, E5, C4 • **Temperaments:** J, M • **Physical:** V=L, H=N, L=M, W, H • **Work Env:** I • **Salary:** 2 • **Outlook:** 3

BUTCHER, MEAT (hotel & rest.) • D.O.T. #316.681-010 • OES #65023 • BUTCHER; MEAT CUTTER. Cuts, trims, bones, ties, and grinds meats, using butcher's cutlery and powered equipment, such as electric grinder and bandsaw, to portion and prepare meat in cooking form: Cuts, trims, and bones carcass sections or prime cuts, using knives, meat saw, cleaver, and bandsaw, to reduce to cooking cuts, such as roasts, steaks, chops, stew cubes, and grinding meat. Cuts and weighs steaks and chops for individual servings. Tends electric grinder to grind meat. Shapes and ties roasts. May estimate requirements and requisition or order meat supply. May receive, inspect, and store meat upon delivery. May record quantity of meat received and issued to cooks. May clean fowl and fish [BUTCHER, CHICKEN AND FISH (hotel & rest.)]. May oversee other butchers and be designated BUTCHER, HEAD (hotel & rest.). • **GED:** R3, M2, L2 • **SVP:** 1-2 yrs • **Academic:** Ed=N, Eng=N • **Work Field:** 034 • **MPSMS:** 382, 903 • **Aptitudes:** G3, V4, N4, S3, P3, Q4, K3, F3, M2, E5, C4 • **Temperaments:** J, M, T, V • **Physical:** V=L, H=N, L=H, W, H • **Work Env:** I, C, R • **Salary:** 4 • **Outlook:** 3

CARVER (hotel & rest.) • D.O.T. #316.661-010 • OES #65038 • DISPLAY CARVER; EXHIBITION CARVER; MEAT CARVER. Carves individual portions from roasts and poultry to obtain maximum number of meat portions, using carving knives and meat-slicing machines: Disjoints roasts and poultry. Slices uniform portions of meat and places sliced meat in steamtable container, or arranges individual portions on plate. Ladles gravy over food and garnishes plate. Removes shells from seafood and bones fish, using forks. May weigh sliced meat to ensure that portions are uniform. May serve food from steamtable. May serve customers [WAITER/WAITRESS, FORMAL (hotel & rest.)]. • **GED:** R3, M2, L2 • **SVP:** 3-6 mos • **Academic:** Ed=N, Eng=N • **Work Field:** 146 • **MPSMS:** 903 • **Aptitudes:** G3, V4, N4, S4, P3, Q4, K3, F4, M3, E5, C4 • **Temperaments:** R, T • **Stress:** T • **Physical:** V=L, H=N, L=L, W, H • **Work Env:** I, H, R • **Salary:** 3 • **Outlook:** 3

COOK (any ind.) • D.O.T. #315.361-010 • OES #65028 • COOK, MESS. Prepares and cooks family-style meals for crews or residents and employees of institutions: Cooks foodstuffs in quantities according to menu and number of persons to be served. Washes dishes. Bakes breads and pastry [BAKER (hotel & rest.)]. Cuts meat [BUTCHER, MEAT (hotel & rest.)]. Plans menu taking advantage of foods in season and local availability. May serve meals. May order supplies and keep records and accounts. May direct activities of one or more workers who assist in preparing and serving meals. May be designated according to work location as COOK, CAMP (any ind.); COOK, INSTITUTION (any ind.); COOK, RANCH (agric.); COOK, SHIP (water trans.). • **GED:** R3, M2, L2 • **SVP:** 1-2 yrs • **Academic:** Ed=N, Eng=N • **Work Field:** 146 • **MPSMS:** 903 • **Aptitudes:** G3, V4, N3, S4, P3, Q3, K3, F4, M3, E5, C4 • **Temperaments:** J, T, V • **Physical:** V=L, H=N, L=M, W, H • **Work Env:** I, W • **Salary:** 4 • **Outlook:** 2

COOK (dom. ser.) • D.O.T. #305.281-010 • OES #00000 • Plans menus and cooks meals, in private home, according to recipes or tastes of employer: Peels, washes, trims, and prepares vegetables and meats for cooking. Cooks vegetables and bakes breads and pastries. Boils, broils, fries, and roasts meats. Plans menus and orders foodstuffs. Cleans kitchen and cooking utensils. May serve meals. May perform seasonal cooking duties, such as preserving and canning fruits and vegetables, and making jellies. May prepare fancy dishes and pastries. May prepare food for special diets. May specialize in preparing and serving dinner for employed, retired, or other persons and be designated FAMILY-DINNER SERVICE SPECIALIST (dom. ser.). • **GED:** R3, M2, L2 • **SVP:** 1-2 yrs • **Academic:** Ed=N, Eng=N • **Work Field:** 146 • **MPSMS:** 903 • **Aptitudes:** G3, V3, N4, S4, P3, Q4, K4, F4, M3, E5, C4 • **Temperaments:** J, V • **Physical:** V=N, H=N, L=L, W, H • **Work Env:** I • **Salary:** 1 • **Outlook:** 4

COOK, BARBECUE (hotel & rest.) • D.O.T. #313.381-022 • OES #65026 • Prepares, seasons, and barbe cues pork, beef, chicken, and other types of meat: Builds fire in pit below spit, using hickory wood or other fuel to obtain bed of live coals, or regulates gas or electric heat. Secures meat on spit which is slowly turned by hand or electric motor to cook meat uniformly. Seasons meat and bastes it frequently during roasting. May kill and dress animals or fowls or purchase meat from vendors. When cooking whole pigs, may be

designated as COOK, ROAST PIG (hotel & rest.). • **GED:** R3, M2, L2 • **SVP:** 6 mos-1 yr • **Academic:** Ed=N, Eng=N • **Work Field:** 146 • **MPSMS:** 903 • **Aptitudes:** G3, V4, N4, S4, P3, Q5, K4, F4, M3, E5, C4 • **Temperaments:** J, V • **Physical:** V=L, H=N, L=M, W, S, H • **Work Env:** I, H • **Salary:** 3 • **Outlook:** 4

COOK, PASTRY (hotel & rest.) • D.O.T. #313.381-026 • OES #65021 • BAKER, CAKE; BAKER, PASTRY; CAKE MAKER. Prepares and bakes cakes, cookies, pies, puddings, or desserts, according to recipe: Measures ingredients, using meas uring cups and spoons. Mixes ingredients to form dough or batter, using electric mixer or beats and stirs ingredients by hand. Shapes dough for cookies, pies, and fancy pastries, using pie dough roller and cookie cutters or by hand. Places shaped dough portions in greased or floured pans and inserts them in oven, using peel. Adjusts drafts or thermostatic controls to regulate oven temperatures. Prepares and cooks ingredients for pie fillings, puddings, custards, or other desserts. Pours filling into pie shells and tops filling with meringue or cream. Mixes ingredients to make icings. Decorates cakes and pastries [CAKE DECORA TOR (bake. prod.)]. Blends colors for icings and for shaped sugar ornaments and statuaries. May specialize in preparing one or more types of pastry or dessert when employed in large establishment. • **GED:** R4, M3, L3 • **SVP:** 2-4 yrs • **Academic:** Ed=N, Eng=S • **Work Field:** 146 • **MPSMS:** 384 • **Aptitudes:** G3, V3, N4, S3, P3, Q4, K3, F4, M2, E5, C4 • **Temperaments:** F, J, T • **Physical:** V=L, H=N, L=M, W, H • **Work Env:** I, H, R • **Salary:** 4 • **Outlook:** 4

COOK, SHORT ORDER 1 (hotel & rest.) • D.O.T. #313.361-022 • OES #65035 • Prepares and cooks to order foods requiring only short preparation time. May carve meats and fill orders from steamtable. May prepare sandwiches [SANDWICH MAKER (hotel & rest.)]. May prepare salads. May prepare beverages [COFFEE MAKER (hotel & rest.)]. May serve meals to patrons over counter. May be designated according to type of food prepared as HAMBURGER-FRY COOK (hotel & rest.). When cooking is limited to frying foods on grill, may be designated as COOK, GRIDDLE (hotel & rest.). • **GED:** R3, M2, L3 • **SVP:** 3-6 mos • **Academic:** Ed=N, Eng=S • **Work Field:** 146 • **MPSMS:** 903 • **Aptitudes:** G3, V4, N4, S4, P3, Q4, K4, F4, M3, E5, C4 • **Temperaments:** F, J, T • **Physical:** V=L, H=N, L=M, W, S, H • **Work Env:** I, H, W, R • **Salary:** 3 • **Outlook:** 4

COOK, SHORT ORDER 2 (hotel & rest.) • D.O.T. #313.671-010 • OES #65035 • Prepares food and serves restaurant patrons at counters or tables: Takes order from customer and cooks foods requiring short preparation time. Completes order from steamtable and serves customer. Accepts payment or writes charge slip. Carves meats, makes sandwiches, and brews coffee. Usually found in small establishments, such as lunch counters and snack bars. • **GED:** R3, M2, L3 • **SVP:** 30 days-3 mos • **Academic:** Ed=N, Eng=S • **Work Field:** 146 • **MPSMS:** 903 • **Aptitudes:** G3, V3, N4, S4, P3, Q4, K4, F4, M3, E5, C4 • **Temperaments:** P, R • **Stress:** E • **Physical:** V=L, H=L, L=L, W, H • **Work Env:** I • **Salary:** 2 • **Outlook:** 4

COOK, SPECIALTY (hotel & rest.) • D.O.T. #313.361-026 • OES #65032 • Prepares specialty foods, such as fish and chips, tacos, and pasties (Cornish meat pies) according to recipe and specific methods applicable to type of cookery. May serve orders to customers at window or counter. May prepare and serve beverages, such as coffee, clam nectar, and fountain drinks. May be required to exercise showmanship in preparation of food, such as flipping pancakes in air to turn or tossing pizza dough in air to lighten texture. May be designated according to food item prepared as COOK, FISH AND CHIPS (hotel & rest.). • **GED:** R3, M2, L2 • **SVP:** 6 mos-1 yr • **Academic:** Ed=N, Eng=N • **Work Field:** 146 • **MPSMS:** 903 • **Aptitudes:** G3, V4, N4, S4, P3, Q4, K3, F3, M3, E5, C4 • **Temperaments:** M, T • **Physical:** V=L, H=N, L=M, W, H • **Work Env:** I, H • **Salary:** 3 • **Outlook:** 4

FORMULA-ROOM WORKER (dairy prod.) • D.O.T. #520.487-014 • OES #66099 • Prepares, bottles, and sterilizes infant formulas: Weighs or measures and mixes specified quantities of ingredients, such as evaporated, condensed, or powdered milk, food supplements, sugar product, soy product, and prepared meat base, using scales, graduated measures, spoons, and electric blender. Computes number of calories per fluid ounce of formula from information on labels of lingredients, and records information on gummed label and places on bottles. Pours formula into bottles, seals with nipple, protector cap and collar, and places in autoclave for prescribed length of time to sterilize, or affixes hermetically-sealed protector caps and places in commercial retort for sterilization and cooling. Removes sterilized bottles from autoclave and stores in refrigerator or removes bottles from retort after cooling process and packages for delivery. Washes and sterilizes empty bottles, and unused nipples and caps. May be known according to specific duties performed as FORMULA BOTTLER (dairy prod.; medical ser.), or FORMULA MAKER (dairy prod.; medical ser.). • **GED:** R2, M2, L2 • **SVP:** 30 days-3 mos • **Academic:** Ed=N, Eng=N • **Work Field:** 031, 146 • **MPSMS:** 903, 929 • **Aptitudes:** G4, V4, N3, S4, P4, Q4, K4, F4, M3, E5, C5 • **Temperaments:** R, T • **Stress:** T • **Physical:** V=L, H=N, L=L, H • **Work Env:** I • **Salary:** 3 • **Outlook:** 2

GARDE MANGER (hotel & rest.) • D.O.T. #313.361-034 • OES #65026 • COLD-MEAT CHEF; COOK, COLD MEAT. Prepares such dishes as meat loaves and salads, utilizing leftover meats, seafoods, and poultry: Consults with supervisory staff to determine dishes that will use greatest amount of left overs. Prepares appetizers, relishes, and hors d'oeuvres. Chops, dices, and grinds meats and vegetables. Slices cold meats and cheese. Arranges and garnishes cold meat dishes. Prepares cold meat sandwiches. Mixes and prepares cold sauces, meat glazes, jellies, salad dressings, and stuffings. May supervise pantry workers. May follow recipes to prepare foods. • **GED:** R3, M2, L2 • **SVP:** 2-4 yrs • **Academic:** Ed=N, Eng=N • **Work Field:** 146 • **MPSMS:** 903 • **Aptitudes:** G3, V4, N4, S4, P3, Q4, K3, F4, M3, E5, C4 • **Temperaments:** J, P, V • **Physical:** V=L, H=N, L=L, H • **Work Env:** I • **Salary:** 4 • **Outlook:** 3

MEAT CUTTER (ret. tr.) • D.O.T. #316.684-018 • OES #65023 • BUTCHER; SALESPERSON, MEATS. Cuts and trims meat to size for display or as ordered by customer, using handtools and power equipment, such as grinder, cubing machine, and powersaw. Cleans and cuts fish and poultry. May shape, lace, and tie meat cuts by hand, using boning knife, skewer, and twine to form roasts. May place meat in cardboard containers to be wrapped by other workers. May place meat on trays in display counter. May wrap and weigh meat for customers and collect money for sales. May inspect and grade meats and be designated MEAT INSPECTOR (ret. tr.; whole. tr.). • **GED:** R3, M2, L3 • **SVP:** 1-2 yrs • **Academic:** Ed=N, Eng=S • **Work Field:** 034 • **MPSMS:** 382, 881, 882 • **Aptitudes:** G3, V4, N4, S3, P3, Q4, K3, F3, M2, E5, C4 • **Temperaments:** J, M, T • **Physical:** V=G, H=N, L=M, W, H • **Work Env:** I, C, R • **Salary:** 4 • **Outlook:** 3

PANTRY GOODS MAKER (hotel & rest.) • D.O.T. #317.684-014 • OES #65038 • Prepares salads, appetizers, sandwich fillings, and other cold dishes: Washes, peels, slices, and mixes vegetables, fruits, or other ingredients for salads, cold plates, and garnishes. Carves and slices meats and cheese. Portions and arranges food on serving dishes. Prepares fruit or seafood cocktails and hors d'oeuvres. Measures and mixes ingredients to make salad dressings, cocktail sauces, gelatin salads, cold desserts, and waffles, following recipes. Makes sandwiches to order [SANDWICH MAKER (hotel & rest.)]. Brews tea and coffee [COFFEE MAKER (hotel & rest.)]. Prepares breakfast and dessert fruits, such as melons, grapefruit, and bananas. Portions fruit sauces and juices. Serves food to waiters/waitresses as requested. When specializing in making salads, may be known as SALAD MAKER (hotel & rest.). • **GED:** R3, M2, L3 • **SVP:** 30 days-3 mos • **Academic:** Ed=N, Eng=S • **Work Field:** 146 • **MPSMS:** 903 • **Aptitudes:** G3, V4, N4, S4, P3, Q4, K3, F3, M3, E5, C5 • **Temperaments:** R, T • **Stress:** T • **Physical:** V=L, H=N, L=L, W, H • **Work Env:** I, N, R • **Salary:** 2 • **Outlook:** 3

PASTRY CHEF (hotel & rest.) • D.O.T. #313.131-022 • OES #61099 • Supervises and coordinates activities of COOKS (hotel & rest.) engaged in preparation of desserts, pastries, confections, and ice cream: Plans production for pastry department, according to menu or special requirements. Supplies recipes for, and suggests methods and procedures to pastry workers. Fashions table and pastry decorations, such as statuaries and ornaments, from sugar paste and icings, using cream bag, spatula, and various decorating tools. Requisitions supplies and equipment. Maintains production records. May participate in preparing desserts. • **GED:** R4, M3,

L3 • **SVP:** 4-10 yrs • **Academic:** Ed=N, Eng=S • **Work Field:** 146 • **MPSMS:** 903 • **Aptitudes:** G3, V3, N3, S3, P3, Q3, K3, F3, M2, E5, C3 • **Temperaments:** D, F, J, P • **Stress:** E • **Physical:** V=L, H=N, L=L, W, H • **Work Env:** I, H • **Salary:** 5 • **Outlook:** 4

PIE MAKER (hotel & rest.) • D.O.T. #313.361-038 • OES #65021 • BAKER, PIE; COOK, PASTRY; COOK, PIE; PIE CHEF. Mixes ingredients and bakes pies, tarts, and cobblers, according to recipes: Weighs and measures ingredients, using measuring cup and spoons. Mixes ingredients by hand or with electric mixer to form piecrust dough. Rolls and shapes dough, using rolling pin. Places portions of rolled dough in piepans and trims overlapping edges with knife. Cuts, peels, and prepares fruit for pie fillings. Mixes and cooks ingredients for fillings, such as creams and custards. Pours fillings into pie shells. Covers filling with top crust or spreads topping, such as cream or meringue over filling. Places pie in oven to bake. Adjusts drafts or thermostatic controls to regulate oven temperatures. Usually found in a restaurant or cafeteria where no COOK, PASTRY (hotel & rest.) is employed, and need not be able to bake other desserts or pastries as opposed to COOK, PASTRY (hotel & rest.). • **GED:** R3, M2, L2 • **SVP:** 1-2 yrs • **Academic:** Ed=N, Eng=N • **Work Field:** 146 • **MPSMS:** 384, 903 • **Aptitudes:** G3, V4, N4, S4, P3, Q4, K3, F3, M2, E5, C4 • **Temperaments:** J, T • **Physical:** V=L, H=N, L=L, W, H • **Work Env:** I • **Salary:** 4 • **Outlook:** 2

SALAD MAKER (water trans.) • D.O.T. #317.384-010 • OES #65038 • Prepares salads, fruits, melons, and gelatin desserts: Cleans vegetables, fruits, and berries for salads, relishes, and gelatin desserts. Mixes ingredients for green salads, fruit salads, and potato salad. Prepares relish plates of green onions, celery, radishes, and olives. Prepares dressings, such as Thousand Island, French, and Roquefort, to be served on green salads. Peels, cleans, and cuts fruits, to be served for breakfast or compotes. Prepares cold sandwiches and cheeses. Requisitions supplies daily. • **GED:** R3, M2, L3 • **SVP:** 6 mos-1 yr • **Academic:** Ed=N, Eng=S • **Work Field:** 146 • **MPSMS:** 903 • **Aptitudes:** G3, V4, N4, S4, P4, Q4, K3, F3, M3, E5, C4 • **Temperaments:** R • **Stress:** T • **Physical:** V=L, H=N, L=L, W, H • **Work Env:** I • **Salary:** 2 • **Outlook:** 3

GOE: 05.10.09 Environmental Crafts

EXTERMINATOR (any ind.) • D.O.T. #389.684-010 • OES #67008 • PEST CONTROL WORKER; VERMIN EXTERMINATOR. Sprays chemical solutions or toxic gases and sets mechanical traps to kill pests that infest buildings and surrounding areas: Fumigates rooms and buildings, using toxic gases. Sprays chemical solutions or dusts powders in rooms and work areas. Places poisonous paste or bait and mechanical traps where pests are present. May clean areas that harbor pests, using rakes, brooms, shovels, and mops preparatory to fumigating. May be required to hold State license. May be designated according to type of pest eliminated as RODENT EXTERMINATOR (any ind.). • **GED:** R3, M2, L2 • **SVP:** 6 mos-1 yr • **Academic:** Ed=N, Eng=N • **Work Field:** 293 • **MPSMS:** 962 • **Aptitudes:** G4, V4, N4, S4, P4, Q4, K4, F4, M4, E5, C5 • **Temperaments:** J, V • **Physical:** V=L, H=N, L=L, W, H • **Work Env:** I • **Salary:** 3 • **Outlook:** 3

EXTERMINATOR, TERMITE (bus. ser.) • D.O.T. #383.364-010 • OES #67008 • TERMITE TREATER. Treats termite-infested and fungus-damaged wood in buildings: Studies report and diagram of infested area prepared by SALES AGENT, PEST CONTROL SERVICE (bus. ser.) to determine sequence of operations. Examines building to determine means of reaching infested areas. Cuts openings in building to gain access to infested areas, using handtools and power tools, such as electric drills, pneumatic hammers, saws, and chisels. Inserts nozzle into holes and opens compressed air valve of treating unit to force termicide into holes. Sprays pesticide under and around building, using pressure spray gun. Bores holes in concrete around buildings and injects termicide to impregnate ground. Keeps record of work performed. May direct EXTERMINATOR HELPER, TERMITE (bus. ser.). May replace damaged wood in sills, flooring, or walls, using carpenters' tools. May pour concrete or lay concrete blocks to raise height of foundation or isolate wood from contact with earth to prevent reinfestation. • **GED:** R3, M2, L2 • **SVP:** 1-2 yrs • **Academic:** Ed=N, Eng=N • **Work Field:** 293 • **MPSMS:** 962 • **Aptitudes:** G3, V4, N3, S3, P3, Q3, K3, F3, M3, E4, C5 • **Temperaments:** D, J, V •

Physical: V=L, H=N, L=H, W, C, S, H • **Work Env:** B, N • **Salary:** 3 • **Outlook:** 3

FUMIGATOR (bus. ser.) • D.O.T. #383.361-010 • OES #67008 • Releases poisonous gas and sets traps in buildings to kill dry-wood termites, beetles, vermin, and other pests, using cylinders of compressed gas and mechanical traps: Inspects infested building to identify pests causing damage and to determine treatment necessary. Examines porosity of walls and roof, based on knowledge of construction techniques, to determine method of sealing house. Measures inside dimensions of rooms with rule, and calculates volume of fumigant required and cost to owner. Tapes vents. Climbs ladder, pulls tarpaulins over building, and fastens edges of tarpaulins with clamps to make building airtight. Posts warning signs and padlocks doors. Turns valve on cylinder to discharge gas into building through hose. Holds halide lamp near seams of tarpaulins and building vents to detect leaking fumigant. Sprays or dusts chemicals in rooms or work areas and sets mechanical traps to destroy pests. May fumigate clothing and house furnishing in vaults at business establishment. • **GED:** R4, M3, L3 • **SVP:** 6 mos-1 yr • **Academic:** Ed=N, Eng=S • **Work Field:** 293 • **MPSMS:** 962 • **Aptitudes:** G3, V3, N3, S3, P4, Q3, K4, F4, M3, E4, C4 • **Temperaments:** M, P, V • **Physical:** V=L, H=N, L=H, W, C, S, H • **Work Env:** B, R • **Salary:** 3 • **Outlook:** 3

05.11 Equipment Operation

Workers in this group operate heavy machines and equipment to dig, dredge, hoist, or move substances and materials. They also operate machines to pave roads. These jobs are found at mining, logging, and construction sites; docks; receiving and shipping areas of industrial plants; and large storage buildings and warehouses.

✔ **What kind of work would you do?**
Your work activities would depend upon your specific job. For example, you might:

- set up and operate a horizontal earth-boring machine.
- operate a long-wall mining machine in a coal mine.
- operate a portable drilling rig to prospect for oil.
- pump cement through a pipeline to a construction site.
- drive an asphalt spreader on a highway construction site.
- operate a bulldozer to grade a lawn for a new home.
- operate a crane to hoist materials and equipment into place at a building construction site.

✔ **What skills and abilities do you need for this kind of work?**
To do this kind of work, you must be able to:

- operate equipment according to work orders, signals, and oral instructions.
- withstand the jolting and vibration of heavy equipment.
- work outdoors in all kinds of weather.
- move eyes, hands, and feet together to control movement of equipment.
- estimate distances.

✔ **How do you know if you would like or could learn to do this kind of work?**
The following questions may give you clues about yourself as you consider this group of jobs.

- Have you driven a car, motorcycle, or other motorized vehicle? Can you react quickly and safely to sudden dangerous situations?
- Have you taken shop classes or had a home workshop where you operated machines? Do you enjoy this type of activity?
- Have you operated a tractor on a farm?
- Have you operated construction equipment in the armed forces?

✔ **How can you prepare for and enter this kind of work?**
Occupations in this group usually require education and/or training extending from thirty days to over two years, depending upon the specific kind of work. Many workers learn to operate equipment by on-the-job training. However, the best way to prepare for these jobs is to complete a three-year apprenticeship. Apprentices are supervised by experienced workers. They progress from these simple tasks to mechanical operations, such as lifting light loads with a crane. They also receive classroom instruction, which may include engine operation and repair, cable splicing, hydraulics, welding, and safety.

To qualify for an apprenticeship program, workers must be U. S. citizens and have a high school or vocational school diploma, or its equal. Applicants must also pass a physical fitness examination.

Shorter training courses are offered by the manufacturers of heavy equipment and by the armed services. High school and vocational courses in driver education and automobile mechanics are especially helpful.

Workers with leadership abilities may advance to supervisors. Some workers start their own construction companies, equipment rental agencies, or equipment maintenance firms.

Some machine tenders are promoted from manual jobs within a company. Others with machine shop classes are hired immediately after high school graduation. Additional skills are learned on the job.

✔ What else should you consider about these jobs?

For most jobs in this group, work hours and pay rates are dependent upon local union scales.

Machinery and equipment operators and drivers often work outside under noisy and dusty conditions. They must be alert in order to keep machines under control. Those who drive machines on public streets and roads must have state motor vehicle operator licenses. Work in the construction industry is seasonal in some regions of the country.

Some workers operate one type of equipment and change employers from project to project. People who can operate a variety of machines and equipment or who have special skills usually have more job opportunities. Training in operating new machinery may be provided by employers or through union programs.

If you think you would like to do this kind of work, look at the job titles listed below.

GOE: 05.11.01 Construction

ASPHALT-PAVING-MACHINE OPERATOR (const.) • D.O.T. #853.663-010 • OES #87708 • ASPHALT-SPREADER OPERATOR; BITUMINOUS-PAVING-MACHINE OPERATOR; BLACKTOP-PAVER OPERATOR; BLACKTOP SPREADER; MECHANICAL-SPREADER OPERATOR; PAVING-MACHINE OPERATOR, ASPHALT OR BITUMINOUS. Operates machine that spreads and levels hot-mix bituminous paving material on subgrade of highways and streets: Bolts extensions to screed to adjust width, using wrenches. Lights burners to heat screed. Starts engine and controls paving machine to push dump truck and maintain constant flow of asphalt into hopper. Observes distribution of paving material along screed and controls direction of screed to eliminate voids at curbs and joints. Turns valves to regulate temperature of asphalt flowing from hopper when asphalt begins to harden on screed. • **GED:** R3, M1, L1 • **SVP:** 6 mos-1 yr • **Academic:** Ed=N, Eng=N • **Work Field:** 091, 095 • **MPSMS:** 362 • **Aptitudes:** G3, V4, N5, S3, P3, Q5, K3, F4, M3, E3, C5 • **Temperaments:** M, T • **Physical:** V=G, H=N, L=M, W, S, H • **Work Env:** O, N • **Salary:** 5 • **Outlook:** 3

BULLDOZER OPERATOR 1 (any ind.) • D.O.T. #850.683-010 • OES #97938 • GRADER OPERATOR. Operates tractor equipped with concave blade attached across front to gouge out, level, and distribute earth and to push trees and rocks from land preparatory to constructing roads and buildings or planting crops or in mining, quarrying, and lumbering operations: Fastens attachments to tractor with clevis or wedge-pin hitches. Connects hydraulic hoses, belts, mechanical linkage, or power takeoff shaft to tractor to provide power to raise, lower, or tilt attachment. Moves levers to control tool bars, carriers, and disks. Moves levers and depresses pedals to maneuver tractor and raise, lower, and tilt attachment to clear right-of-way. Feels lever and listens for stalling action of engine to estimate depth of cut. Drives bulldozer in successive passes over terrain to raise or lower terrain to specified grade. May grease, oil, and repair tractor. When required to work to close tolerances, may be designated FINE-GRADE-BULLDOZER OPERATOR (any ind.). When operating bulldozer to loosen soil, may be designated SCARIFIER OPERATOR (any ind.). May be designated according to type of tractor operated as CRAWLER-TRACTOR OPERATOR (any ind.), or attachment added as ANGLEDOZER OPERATOR (any ind.). May operate bulldozer to scrape surface clay to determine existence and types of clay deposits or to gather clay into piles preparatory to removal to brick and tile manufacturing plant and be designated SCRAPER OPERATOR (mining & quarrying). • **GED:** R3, M1, L2 • **SVP:** 6 mos-1 yr • **Academic:** Ed=N, Eng=N • **Work Field:** 011 • **MPSMS:** 340, 350, 360 • **Aptitudes:** G3, V4, N4, S3, P3, Q5, K3, F3, M3, E3, C5 • **Temperaments:** J, T • **Physical:** V=L, H=N, L=H, W, C, S, H • **Work Env:** O, R • **Salary:** 5 • **Outlook:** 4

POWER-SHOVEL OPERATOR (any ind.) • D.O.T. #850.683-030 • OES #97923 • Operates power-driven machine, equipped with movable shovel, to excavate or move coal, dirt, rock, sand, and other materials: Pushes levers and depresses pedals to move machine, to lower and push shovel into material, and to lift, swing, and dump contents of shovel into truck, car, or onto conveyor, hopper, or stockpile. May tend mining machinery, such as pulverizer. May be designated according to type of power unit as DIESEL-POWER-SHOVEL OPERATOR (any ind.); ELECTRIC-POWER-SHOVEL OPERATOR (any ind.); GASOLINE-POWER-SHOVEL OPERATOR (any ind.). May operate power shovel equipped with duck-bill scoop and be designated DUCK-BILL OPERATOR (mining & quarrying). May operate power shovel which digs by pulling dipper toward machine and be designated BACK-HOE OPERATOR (any ind.). May operate power shovel on which excavating bucket runs outward along horizontal boom to dig into materials and be designated SKIMMER-SCOOP OPERATOR (any ind.). May operate power shovel designed to be converted to crane, skimmer scoop, backhoe, or dragline and be designated CONVERTIBLE-POWER-SHOVEL OPERATOR (any ind.). • **GED:** R3, M1, L1 • **SVP:** 6 mos-1 yr • **Academic:** Ed=N, Eng=N

• **Work Field:** 011 • **MPSMS:** 340, 350 • **Aptitudes:** G3, V4, N4, S3, P4, Q5, K3, F4, M3, E3, C5 • **Temperaments:** R, T • **Stress:** T • **Physical:** V=G, H=N, L=M, W, H • **Work Env:** B, N • **Salary:** 5 • **Out look:** 4

ROAD-ROLLER OPERATOR (const.) • D.O.T. #859.683-030 • OES #87708 • ROLLER OPERATOR; ROLLER, PNEUMATIC; ROLL OPERATOR. Drives heavy rolling machine (road roller) to compact earth fills, subgrades, flexible base, and bituminous surface to grade specifications preparatory to construction of highways, streets, and runways: Moves levers, depresses pedals, turns handwheels, and pushes throttle to control and guide machine. Drives machine in successive overlapping passes over surface to be compacted. Determines speed and direction of machine, based on knowledge of compressibility of material under changing temperatures, so that ridges are not formed by excessive pressure. Pushes hand roller and pounds surfaces, using hand tamp, or guides portable power roller over areas not accessible to road roller. May be designated according to surface rolled as ROAD-ROLLER OPERATOR, HOT MIX (const.); SUBGRADE-ROLLER OPERATOR (const.); or according to source of power used as DIESEL-ROLLER OPERATOR (const.); GAS-ROLLER OPERATOR (const.). • **GED:** R2, M1, L1 • **SVP:** 30 days-3 mos • **Academic:** Ed=N, Eng=N • **Work Field:** 091, 095 • **MPSMS:** 362 • **Aptitudes:** G3, V4, N5, S4, P3, Q5, K3, F4, M3, E3, C5 • **Temperaments:** J, T • **Physical:** V=G, H=N, L=L, W, H • **Work Env:** O, N • **Salary:** 5 • **Outlook:** 3

ROCK-DRILL OPERATOR 1 (const.) • D.O.T. #850.683-034 • OES #87902 • Drives and operates tractor-mounted rock drilling machine to drill explosive-charge holes through hard materials to facilitate blasting operations: Moves lever to set out-rigger jacks to level machine. Verifies level of machine, using spirit level. Inserts steel drill or rock bit into chuck. Moves levers to start, stop, and control drilling speed of machine. Drills holes and observes depth gage on drill stem to verify depth of hole specified by BLASTER (any ind.). May be designated according to type of machine operated as RECIPROCATing-DRILL OPERATOR (any ind.); ROTARY-ROCK-DRILLING-MACHINE OPERATOR (any ind.). • **GED:** R3, M2, L2 • **SVP:** 6 mos-1 yr • **Academic:** Ed=N, Eng=N • **Work Field:** 005 • **MPSMS:** 360 • **Aptitudes:** G3, V4, N4, S3, P3, Q4, K3, F3, M3, E4, C5 • **Temperaments:** J, M, T • **Physical:** V=L, H=N, L=L, W, S, H • **Work Env:** O, N, R • **Salary:** 5 • **Outlook:** 3

SEPTIC-TANK INSTALLER (const.) • D.O.T. #851.663-010 • OES #97923 • Operates back-hoe (trench-excavating machine) to dig trenches for installation of septic tanks and drain lines for sewage disposal system: Reads blue prints to determine location of septic tank and drainpipes. Operates back-hoe to dig and refill trenches for septic tank and tile drainpipes and to transfer crushed rock or gravel to provide drainage base for pipes. Lowers septic tank into excavation, using back-hoe as hoist. Directs workers engaged in spreading crushed rock and gravel, in laying tile drainpipe, and in connecting drainpipes to branch sewers. May verify levels of rock or gravel, base, and tile drainpipe, using surveyor's or carpenter's level. • **GED:** R3, M2, L2 • **SVP:** 3-6 mos • **Academic:** Ed=N, Eng=N • **Work Field:** 013, 102 • **MPSMS:** 364 • **Aptitudes:** G3, V4, N4, S3, P3, Q4, K3, F4, M3, E3, C5 • **Temperaments:** J, T • **Physical:** V=L, H=N, L=M, W, S, H • **Work Env:** O, N, R • **Salary:** 4 • **Outlook:** 3

STREET-SWEEPER OPERATOR (gov. ser.) • D.O.T. #919.683-022 • OES #97199 • TRACTOR-SWEEPER DRIVER. Drives sweeping machine that cleans streets of trash and other accumulations: Fills water tank of machine from hydrant. Drives sweeper along street near curb. Moves controls to activate rotary brushes and water spray so that machine automatically picks up dust and trash from paved street and deposits it in dirt trap at rear of machine. Pulls lever to dump refuse in piles at curb for removal. May be employed by industrial plant, shopping center, or other establishment to drive modified sweeper through parking lots, factory aisles, or along private roads, and be designated POWER-SWEEPER OPERATOR (any ind.). May drive machine that sucks leaves into vacuum chamber and be designated LEAF-SUCKER OPERATOR (gov. ser.). May drive vehicle equipped with rotating brushes to remove sand and litter from newly constructed highways and be designated SWEEPER OPERATOR, HIGHWAYS

(const.). • **GED:** R2, M1, L1 • **SVP:** 30 days-3 mos • **Academic:** Ed=N, Eng=N • **Work Field:** 031 • **MPSMS:** 362 • **Aptitudes:** G4, V4, N4, S3, P4, Q5, K3, F4, M4, E4, C5 • **Temperaments:** R • **Stress:** T • **Physical:** V=G, H=N, L=L, W, H • **Work Env:** B • **Salary:** 3 • **Outlook:** 3

GOE: 05.11.02 Mining & Quarrying

CORE-DRILL OPERATOR (any ind.) • D.O.T. #930.682-010 • OES #87902 • SHOT-CORE-DRILL OPERATOR; TEST BORER; TEST-HOLE DRILLER; WASH DRILLER. Sets up and operates drilling equipment to obtain solid core samples of strata for analyzing geological characteristics of ground, nature of ore, or strength of foundation material: Drives or guides truck-mounted drilling equipment onto metal or wood foundation, or assembles equipment in position. Connects powerlines to equipment. Attaches diamond churn, alloy, or percussion bit to drill rod, and fastens rod in machine, using wrench or other handtools. Starts power unit. Moves clutch and throttle to control rotation and feed of drill bit into ground. Couples additional lengths of drill rod as bit advances. Withdraws drill rod from hole after specified depth has been reached and extracts core from hollow barrel located behind drilling bit. Records depths from which core samples are taken. Lubricates machine, using grease gun, and replaces parts, such as worn winch cables. May replace diamonds in bit as they become worn, chipped, or lost, where diamond drill is used [DIAMOND MOUNTER (mach. tool & access.)]. May operate water pump to pump water down borehole to cool drill bit. May be designated according to type of drill used as DIAMOND DRILLER (any ind.). • **GED:** R3, M2, L2 • **SVP:** 1-2 yrs • **Academic:** Ed=N, Eng=N • **Work Field:** 005 • **MPSMS:** 340, 350, 369 • **Aptitudes:** G3, V4, N4, S4, P3, Q4, K3, F4, M3, E4, C5 • **Temperaments:** R, T • **Stress:** T • **Physical:** V=L, H=N, L=M, W, H • **Work Env:** B, N, R • **Salary:** 5 • **Outlook:** 1

PLANT OPERATOR (concrete prod.) • D.O.T. #570.682-014 • OES #95099 • Operates concrete, asphalt, or sand and gravel plant to batch, crush, or segregate materials used in construction: Moves controls on panelboard or control board to heat, dry, and mix ingredients, such as asphalt, sand, stone, and naphtha to produce asphalt paving materials, to weigh and mix aggregate, cement, and water to produce concrete, or to control feeding, crushing, and sifting machinery in sand and gravel plant. Observes gages, dials, and operation of machinery to insure conformance to processing specifications. May repair machinery, using handtools, power tools, and welding equipment. May be designated according to type of plant operated as ASPHALT- PLANT OPERATOR (const.); CONCRETE-BATCH-PLANT OPERATOR (conc. prod.; const.); SAND-AND-GRAVEL-PLANT OPERATOR (const.); or according to machine function as CRUSHER OPERATOR (conc. prod.; const.). • **GED:** R3, M2, L2 • **SVP:** 3-6 mos • **Academic:** Ed=N, Eng=N • **Work Field:** 141, 143, 212 • **MPSMS:** 340, 502, 536 • **Aptitudes:** G3, V4, N4, S4, P4, Q4, K3, F4, M3, E4, C5 • **Temperaments:** M, T • **Physical:** V=L, H=N, L=M, W, H • **Work Env:** B, N • **Salary:** 3 • **Outlook:** 3

GOE: 05.11.03 Drilling & Oil Exploration

ROTARY DRILLER (petrol. production) • D.O.T. #930.382-026 • OES #87911 • CORE DRILLER; DRILLER; WELL DRILLER. Operates gasoline, diesel, electric, or steam draw works to drill oil or gas wells: Observes pressure gage and moves throttles and levers to control speed of rotary table which rotates string of tools in borehole, and to regulate pressure of tools at bottom of borehole. Connects sections of drill pipe, using handtools and powered wrenches and tongs. Selects and changes drill bits according to nature of strata, using hand tools. Pushes levers and brake pedals to control draw works which lowers and raises drill pipe and casing into and out of well. Examines operation of slush pumps to ensure circulation and consistency of mud (drilling fluid) in well. Examines drillings or core samples from bottom of well to determine nature of strata. Fishes for and recovers lost or broken bits, casing and drill pipes from well, using special tools attached to end of drill pipe or cable. Keeps record of footage drilled, location and nature of strata penetrated, and materials used. Caps well or turns valves to regulate outflow of oil from well. Repairs or replaces defective parts of machinery, using handtools. May lower and explode charge in borehole to start flow of oil from well. May specialize in drilling underwater wells from barge-mounted derricks or drilling platforms and be designated as ROTARY DRILLER, MARINE OPERATIONS (petrol. production). • **GED:** R3, M2, L2 • **SVP:** 1-2 yrs • **Academic:** Ed=N, Eng=N • **Work Field:** 005 • **MPSMS:** 342 • **Aptitudes:** G3, V3, N3, S3, P3, Q4, K3, F3, M3, E3, C4 • **Temperaments:** M, T, V • **Physical:** V=L, H=N, L=M, W, S, H • **Work Env:** O, N, R • **Salary:** 5 • **Outlook:** 1

GOE: 05.11.04 Materials Handling, Equipment Opererator

BRIDGE-OR-GANTRY-CRANE OPERATOR (any ind.) • D.O.T. #921.663-010 • OES #97944 • CRANE OPERATOR, CAB; OVERHEAD-CRANE OPERATOR; TRAVELING-CRANE OPERATOR. Operates electrically-powered bridge crane (bridge mounted on overhead rails) or gantry crane (bridge mounted on towers which move along floor-mounted rails) consisting of operator's cab and movable hoist mechanism mounted on bridge to lift, move, and position loads, such as machinery, equipment, products, and solid or bulk material, using hoisting attachments, such as hook, sling, elec tromagnet, clamshell, or bucket: Moves pedals and levers to regulate speed and direction of crane and hoist movement in response to signals from worker on floor. Observes load hookup and determines safety of load. Transfers supplies to initial production points, moves materials between machines or equipment in main production flow or subsidiary operations, charges (in serts) materials, such as molten metal andingots into furnaces and machines, transfers scrap and waste to storage piles or railroad cars, and aids in placing parts, such as rollers, shafts, or motors in machines and equipment. Cleans and lubri cates crane and performs routine maintenance on crane and hoisting mechanism. Inspects crane for defective parts and notifies supervisor of mechanical or electrical malfunctions. May control operation of crane from floor by pushing buttons on handheld control box suspended from crane, or using portable radio transmitter. May operate crane with control cab and projecting boom traveling on rails mounted on one wall of building and be designated WALL-CRANE OPERATOR (found.). May be designated according to type of crane operated as BRIDGE CRANE OPERATOR (any ind.); GANTRY CRANE OPERATOR (any ind.); TOWER-WHIRLER OPERATOR (any ind.); or material handled as CINDER-CRANE OPERATOR (found.; iron & steel) I; SCRAP-CRANE OPERATOR (iron & steel) I, or operation performed as CHARGING-CRANE OPERATOR (found.; iron & steel) I; HOT-METAL-CRANE OPERATOR (found.; iron & steel; ore dress., smelt., & refin.) I; INGOT STRIPPER (iron & steel) I. • **GED:** R3, M1, L2 • **SVP:** 6 mos-1 yr • **Academic:** Ed=N, Eng=N • **Work Field:** 011 • **MPSMS:** 565 • **Aptitudes:** G3, V4, N4, S3, P4, Q5, K3, F4, M3, E3, C5 • **Temperaments:** R, T • **Stress:** T • **Physical:** V=L, H=N, L=L, H • **Work Env:** I, N • **Salary:** 4 • **Outlook:** 3

CONVEYOR OPERATOR (any ind.) • D.O.T. #921.683-026 • OES #97951 • Controls conveyor system or conveyors that transfer materials by belt, auger, or bucket conveyors, or pneumatic conveyors to load or unload vehicles, railcars, and ships, or move materials or products to and from stockpiles, processes, or departments, or from underground workings to vehicles or stockpiles: Starts conveyor and loads or directs other workers to load conveyor, or adjusts chute or gate or positions pipe into bin or stockpile to permit material to flow onto conveyor. Moves controls to regulate rate of movement and routing of materials or products according to signals or knowledge of process by switching and reversing conveyors, moving deflector bars or gates at intersecting points, or opening and closing chute gates. Dislodges jammed materials or products, using pole, bar, or other handtools or by hand. Observes moving materials or products for obvious defects and operation of equipment for malfunction. Lubricates parts. May adjust conveyor scales and cutoffs to sort and deposit specified kinds and amounts of materials or containers at process, storage, or shipping areas. May collect samples of materials for analysis. May join sections of conveyor frames at temporary working areas and connect power units. May operate scoop to load materials onto conveyor. May clean materials from under conveyor to prevent jamming and damage. May clean working area. May record data, such as material moved, weight, and operating condition of equipment. May be designated according to product moved as COAL-CONVEYOR OPERATOR (any ind.); GRAIN DISTRIBUTOR (grain & feed mill.), or according to type of equipment as GRAIN-ELEVATOR OPERATOR (grain & feed mill.); SCREEN OPERATOR (cement); SUCTION OPERATOR (agric.), or according to quantity moved as BULK-LOADER OPERATOR (water trans.). • **GED:** R3, M1, L2 • **SVP:** 3-6 mos • **Academic:** Ed=N, Eng=N • **Work Field:** 011 • **MPSMS:** 565 • **Aptitudes:** G3, V4, N4, S3, P4, Q4, K4, F4, M3, E4, C4 • **Temperaments:** M, T • **Physical:** V=L, H=N, L=H, W, H • **Work Env:** B, N • **Salary:** 3 • **Outlook:** 2

DERRICK OPERATOR (any ind.) • D.O.T. #921.663-022 • OES #97944 • CRANE OPERATOR. Operates electric-, diesel-, gasoline-, or steam-powered guy-derrick or stiff-leg derrick (mast supported by fixed legs or tripod), to move products, equipment, or materials to and from quarries, storage areas, and processes, or to load and unload trucks or railroad cars: Pushes and pulls levers and depresses pedals to raise, lower, and rotate boom and to raise and lower load line in response to signals. May inspect and lubricate cables, pulleys, guides, and drums. May be known according to material moved as LOG-YARD DERRICK OPERATOR (sawmill); or equipment controlled as STIFF-LEG DERRICK OPERATOR (wood preserving). • **GED:** R3, M1, L1 • **SVP:** 3-6 mos • **Academic:** Ed=N, Eng=N • **Work Field:** 011 • **MPSMS:** 565 • **Aptitudes:** G3, V4, N4, S3, P4, Q5, K3, F4, M3, E3, C5 • **Temperaments:** R, T • **Stress:** T • **Physical:** V=L, H=N, L=M, W, H • **Work Env:** B, N • **Salary:** 4 • **Outlook:** 3

DINKEY OPERATOR (any ind.) • D.O.T. #919.663-014 • OES #97308 • LARRY-CAR OPERATOR; TRAMMER. Controls dinkey engine powered by electric, gasoline, steam, compressed air, or diesel engine to transport and shunt cars at industrial establishment or mine: Controls movement of dinkey that transports coal, rock, timber, slag, or supplies by moving power controls and brake levers. Signals BRAKE HOLDER (any ind.) by hand or whistle to couple cars. Positions cars for loading or unloading according to signals of DUMPER (any ind.). Inspects engine at beginning and end of shift. May move levers to open or tilt cars to dump materials. May throw switches and couple cars. May fuel and lubricate engine. May inspect track for defects and assist in repairing track and installing additional rails and ties. May be designated according to kind of power used as DINKEY OPERATOR, COMPRESSED AIR (any ind.), according to work area as DINKEY OPERATOR, MINE (mining & quarrying) or material hauled as DINKEY OPERATOR, SLAG (ore dress., smelt., & refin.); DINKEY OPERATOR, SLATE (mining & quarrying). May operate flatcar equipped with derrick and be designated as DERRICK-CAR OPERATOR (r.r. trans.). May operate railcar to transport personnel and equipment in area of logging camp and be designated as RAIL-CAR OPERATOR (logging). • **GED:** R3, M2, L2 • **SVP:** 3-6 mos • **Academic:** Ed=N, Eng=N • **Work Field:** 013 • **MPSMS:** 851 • **Aptitudes:** G3, V4, N4, S3, P3, Q4, K3, F4, M3, E3, C4 • **Temperaments:** R • **Stress:** T • **Physical:** V=L, H=N, L=L, H • **Work Env:** B, N, R • **Salary:** 3 • **Outlook:** 3

DRAGLINE OPERATOR (any ind.) • D.O.T. #850.683-018 • OES #97926 • Operates power-driven crane equipped with dragline bucket, suspended from boom by cable to excavate or move sand, gravel, clay, mud, coal, or other materials: Drives machine to worksite. Moves hand levers and depresses pedals to rotate crane on chassis and position boom above excavation point, to raise and lower boom, to lower bucket to material, to drag bucket toward crane to excavate or move material, to place bucket over unloading point, and to tilt bucket to release material. May direct workers engaged in placing blocks and out riggers to prevent capsizing of machine when lifting heavy loads. May be designated according to type of chassis or power unit as CRAWLER-DRAGLINE OPERATOR (any ind.); DIESEL-DRAGLINE OPERATOR (any ind.); ELECTRIC-DRAGLINE OPERATOR (any ind.); GASOLINE-DRAGLINE OPERATOR (any ind.); or material excavated as CLAY HOISTER (cement); WALKING-DRAGLINE OPERATOR (any ind.). • **GED:** R3, M2, L2 • **SVP:** 6 mos-1 yr • **Academic:** Ed=N, Eng=N • **Work Field:** 011 • **MPSMS:** 340, 360 • **Aptitudes:** G3, V4, N4, S3, P4, Q5, K3, F4, M3, E3, C5 • **Temperaments:** J, T • **Physical:** V=L, H=N, L=M, W, H • **Work Env:** O, N • **Salary:** 5 • **Outlook:** 4

DUMP OPERATOR (any ind.) • D.O.T. #921.685-038 • OES #97989 • CAR-DUMPER OPERATOR; TIPPLE WORKER. Tends mechanical or electrical dumping equipment to dump materials, such as grain, raw materials, coal, or ore, from mine cars, railroad cars, or trucks into bins or onto conveyor for storage, reloading, or further processing, by either of the following methods: (1) Observes that car or truck is spotted accurately on bed of rotary dump. Moves controls to secure clamps over couplings that hold car while being tipped. Starts motor or pulls lever that tips car and dumps contents. Releases clamps to remove car. (2) Opens bottom or side doors of car or truck spotted over gravity dump. Moves controls to lower car shakeout device into car and to start vibration that loosens remaining coal or ore. May hook winch cables to cars to draw them onto dumping bed. May couple and uncouple cars. May be required to maintain records of unloading operations. May be designated according to type of equipment tended as CAR-SHAKE-OUT OPERATOR (cement; mining & quarrying); ROTARY-DUMP OPERATOR (coke prod.; mining & quarrying); or according to material unloaded as GRAIN UNLOADER, MACHINE (grain & feed mill.). • GED: R2, M1, L1 • SVP: 30 days-3 mos • Academic: Ed=N, Eng=N • Work Field: 011 • MPSMS: 340, 350, 381 • Aptitudes: G4, V4, N4, S3, P4, Q4, K3, F4, M3, E4, C5 • Temperaments: R • Stress: T • Physical: V=L, H=N, L=L, H • Work Env: B, N • Salary: 2 • Outlook: 3

FRONT-END LOADER OPERATOR (any ind.) • D.O.T. #921.683-042 • OES #97947 • LOADER OPERATOR; WHEEL LOADER OPERATOR. Operates straight or articulated rubber-tired tractor-type vehicle equipped with front-mounted hydraulically-powered bucket or scoop to lift and transport bulk materials to and from storage or processing areas, to feed conveyors, hoppers, or chutes, and to load trucks or railcars: Starts engine, shifts gears, presses pedals, and turns steering wheel to operate loader. Moves levers to lower and tilt bucket and drives front-end loader forward to force bucket into bulk material. Moves levers to raise and tilt bucket when filled, drives vehicle to worksite, and moves levers to dump material. Performs routine maintenance on loader, such as lubricating, fueling, and cleaning. • GED: R2, M1, L1 • SVP: 30 days-3 mos • Academic: Ed=N, Eng=N • Work Field: 011, 013 • MPSMS: 565 • Aptitudes: G3, V4, N4, S3, P4, Q4, K3, F3, M3, E3, C5 • Temperaments: R, T • Stress: T • Physical: V=L, H=N, L=M, W, H • Work Env: B, N • Salary: 2 • Outlook: 3

HOISTING ENGINEER (any ind.) • D.O.T. #921.663-030 • OES #97941 • HOISTING-MACHINE OPERATOR. Operates compressed air, diesel, electric, gasoline, or steam drum hoists to control movement of cableways, cages, derricks, draglines, loaders, railcars, or skips to move men and materials for construction, logging, mining, sawmill, and other industrial operations: Starts hoist engine and moves hand and foot levers to wind or unwind cable on drum. Moves brake lever and throttle to stop, start, and regulate speed of drum in response to hand, bell, telephone, loudspeaker, or whistle signals or by observing dial indicator or marks on cable. May fire boiler on steam hoist. May operate hoist with more than one drum. May repair, maintain, and adjust equipment. May be designated according to equipment controlled as CABLE-WAY OPERATOR (any ind.); CAGE OPERATOR (any ind.); GIN-POLE OPERATOR (const.); INCLINED-RAILWAY OPERATOR (any ind.); SKIP-HOIST OPERATOR (any ind.). May transfer logs from trucks to railroad cars and be designated TRANSFER ENGINEER (logging). • GED: R3, M1, L1 • SVP: 3-6 mos • Academic: Ed=N, Eng=N • Work Field: 011 • MPSMS: 586 • Aptitudes: G3, V4, N4, S3, P4, Q5, K3, F4, M3, E3, C4 • Temperaments: R, T • Stress: T • Physical: V=L, H=N, L=M, W, H • Work Env: B, N, R • Salary: 4 • Outlook: 3

RIGGER (any ind.) • D.O.T. #921.260-010 • OES #85935 • CRANE RIGGER; HOOK TENDER; SLINGER; YARD RIGGER. Assembles rigging to lift and move equipment or material in manufacturing plant, shipyard, or on construction project: Selects cables, ropes, pulleys, winches, blocks, and sheaves, according to weight and size of load to be moved. Attaches pulley and blocks to fixed overhead structures, such as beams, ceilings, and gin pole booms, with bolts and clamps. Attaches load with grappling devices, such as loops, wires, ropes, and chains, to crane hook. Gives directions to BRIDGE-OR-GANTRY-CRANE OPERATOR (any ind.) or HOISTING ENGINEER (any ind.) engaged in hoisting and

moving loads to insure safety of workers and material handled, using hand signals, loudspeaker, or telephone. Sets up, braces, and rigs hoisting equipment, using handtools and power wrenches. Splices rope and wire cables to make or repair slings and tackle. May direct workers engaged in hoisting of machinery and equipment into ships and be designated MACHINERY ERECTOR (ship & boat bldg. & rep.). When hoisting and moving construction machinery onto truck beds, may be designated MACHINE MOVER (const.). • GED: R4, M2, L2 • SVP: 1-2 yrs • Academic: Ed=N, Eng=N • Work Field: 011 • MPSMS: 565 • Aptitudes: G3, V3, N4, S3, P3, Q4, K4, F3, M3, E4, C5 • Temperaments: T, V • Physical: V=L, H=N, L=H, W, C, S, H • Work Env: B, N, R • Salary: 5 • Outlook: 3

STEVEDORE 1 (water trans.) • D.O.T. #911.663-014 • OES #97902 • Operates material-handling equipment, such as power winch, grain trimmer, crane, and lift truck, to transfer cargo into or from hold of ship and about dock area: Operates crane or winch to load or unload cargo, such as automobiles, crates, scrap, and steel beams, using hook, magnet, or sling attached in accordance with signals from other workers. Moves controls to start flow of grain from spouts of grain trimmer, stopping flow and repositioning spout over each hatch when previous hatch is filled. Drives lift truck along dock or aboard ship to transfer bulk items, such as lumber, pallet-mounted machinery, and crated products within range of winch. Drives tractor to transfer loaded trailers from warehouse to dockside. May position and fasten hose lines to ships' cargo tanks when loading or unloading liquid cargo, such as animal fats, vegetable oils, molasses, or chemicals. May perform variety of manual duties, such as lashing and shoring cargo aboard ship, attaching slings, hooks, or other lifting devices to winch for loading or unloading, and signaling other workers to move, raise, or lower cargo. May direct activities of cargo gang consisting of STEVEDORE (water trans.) II. May be designated according to equipment operated as LIFT-TRUCK OPERATOR (water trans.); TRACTOR OPERATOR (water trans.); WINCH OPERATOR (water trans.). • GED: R3, M2, L2 • SVP: 6 mos-1 yr • Academic: Ed=N, Eng=N • Work Field: 011 • MPSMS: 854 • Aptitudes: G3, V4, N4, S3, P4, Q4, K3, F4, M3, E3, C5 • Temperaments: J, M, R • Stress: T • Physical: V=L, H=N, L=M, W, H • Work Env: O • Salary: 5 • Outlook: 2

TRACTOR OPERATOR (any ind.) • D.O.T. #929.683-014 • OES #97947 • Drives gasoline or diesel powered tractor to move materials, draw implements, tow trailers, pull out objects imbedded in ground, or pull cable of winch to raise, lower, or load heavy material or equipment: Fastens attachments, such as graders, plows, and rollers, to tractor with hitchpins. Releases brake, shifts gears, and depresses accelerator or moves throttle to control forward and backward movement of machine. Steers tractor by turning steering wheel and depressing brake pedals. May lubricate and repair tractor and attachments. May be designated according to type of power utilized as DIESEL-TRACTOR OPERATOR (any ind.); GASOLINE-TRACTOR OPERATOR (any ind.); TRACTOR OPERATOR, BATTERY (mining & quarrying). May operate tractor mounted with wide spread pneumatic or metallic treads to transport materials over marshes or swamps and be designated MARSH-BUGGY OPERATOR (const.). • GED: R3, M1, L1 • SVP: 30 days-3 mos • Academic: Ed=N, Eng=N • Work Field: 011, 013 • MPSMS: 562 • Aptitudes: G3, V4, N4, S3, P4, Q4, K3, F4, M3, E3, C5 • Temperaments: R, T • Stress: T • Physical: V=G, H=N, L=M, W, C, H • Work Env: B, N • Salary: 4 • Outlook: 2

TRACTOR-CRANE OPERATOR (any ind.) • D.O.T. #921.663-058 • OES #97944 • CRAWLER-CRANE OPERATOR; TRACTOR-CRANE ENGINEER. Operates diesel-, gasoline-, or electric-powered crane mounted on crawler treads to lift and move material and objects: Starts engine and drives crane to worksite, steering crane by moving levers and pressing pedals that control motion of crawler treads. Pushes and pulls levers and presses pedals in response to hand signals to rotate crane on chassis and raise and lower crane boom and loadline. May lubricate motor and moving parts of crane. May be designated according to attachment as CLAMSHELL OPERATOR (any ind.) I; DEMOLITION-CRANE OPERATOR (any ind.) I; ELECTROMAGNET-CRANE OPERATOR (any ind.) I; ORANGE-PEEL OPERATOR (any ind.) I. • GED: R3, M1, L1 • SVP: 3-6 mos • Academic: Ed=N, Eng=N •

Work Field: 011 • MPSMS: 563 • Aptitudes: G3, V4, N4, S3, P4, Q4, K3, F4, M3, E3, C5 • Temperaments: R, T • Stress: T • Physical: V=L, H=N, L=M, W, H • Work Env: I, N • Salary: 4 • Outlook: 3

TRUCK-CRANE OPERATOR (any ind.) • D.O.T. #921.663-062 • OES #97944 • MOBILE-CRANE OPERATOR. Operates gasoline-or diesel-powered crane mounted on specially constructed truck chassis to lift and move materials and objects: Drives truck to worksite and directs activities of LABORER, HOISTING (any ind.) in placing blocks and outriggers to prevent capsizing when lifting heavy loads. Starts crane engine. Moves levers and pedals to rotate crane on chassis, to raise and lower crane boom, and to raise and lower loadline. May operate crane according to signals from helper. May bolt boom sections together to extend or modify boom for pile driving or high lifting. May be designated according to type of power used as DIESEL-TRUCK-CRANE OPERATOR (any ind.); GASOLINE-TRUCK-CRANE OPERATOR (any ind.); or according to attachment as CLAMSHELL OPERATOR (any ind.) II; DEMOLITION-CRANE OPERATOR (any ind.) II; ELEC-TROMAGNET-CRANE OPERATOR (any ind.) II; ORANGE-PEEL OPERATOR (any ind.) II. • GED: R3, M1, L1 • SVP: 6 mos-1 yr • Academic: Ed=N, Eng=N • Work Field: 011 • MPSMS: 563, 565 • Aptitudes: G3, V4, N4, S3, P4, Q5, K3, F4, M3, E3, C5 • Temperaments: R, T • Stress: T • Physical: V=L, H=N, L=M, W, C, H • Work Env: B, N • Salary: 4 • Outlook: 3

05.12 Elemental Work: Mechanical

Workers in this group perform a variety of unskilled tasks, such as moving materials, cleaning work areas, operating simple machines, or helping skilled workers. These jobs are found in a variety of non-factory settings.

✔ What kind of work would you do?
Your work activities would depend upon your specific job. For example, you might:

- dump barrels of oil into tanks and take samples to the refinery.
- position cables around logs in a logging camp and signal for winch to move them.
- clean filters, tanks, and wallways at a sewage-disposal plant.
- lubricate moving parts of vehicles such as automobiles, buses, and trucks.
- use a shovel to remove excess dirt from a ditch or excavation.
- use brooms, vacuums, and shovels to clean working areas in a factory.
- carry brick and mortar to masons constructing a wall.

✔ What skills and abilities do you need for this kind of work?
To do this kind of work, you must be able to:

- use hands to lift, carry, or pull objects that may be heavy.
- understand simple instructions.
- work outdoors in all kinds of weather.
- learn simple procedures and techniques.
- perform routine work or the same task over and over again.

✔ How do you know if you would like or could learn to do this kind of work?
The following questions may give you clues about yourself as you consider this group of jobs.

- Have you done work of a physical nature? Do you like to do this type of work?
- Have you been responsible for cleaning a house or garage? Do you take pride in maintaining an orderly work area?
- Have you helped someone move household goods? Can you lift and carry heavy objects?

✔ How can you prepare for and enter this kind of work?
Occupations in this group usually require education and/or training extending from a short demonstration to over three months, depending upon the specific kind of work. This kind of work requires only a brief explanation of job duties. The most important hiring consideration is usually the physical ability of the applicant. Many of these jobs are available through union hiring halls.

✔ What else should you consider about these jobs?
Weather conditions can cause periods of unemployment for construction workers. Others usually work a 40-hour week all year.

Workers are often required to wear safety clothing to protect themselves from common job hazards such as falling objects, extreme temperature levels, or exposure to dangerous chemicals. Employers often provide classes or on-the-job training about safety. Work locations are often checked by government inspectors to ensure that conditions are safe.

With additional training, workers in this group may qualify for machine tending or operating jobs. Workers with a high school education or its equal may qualify for apprenticeship programs leading to more skilled jobs, especially in construction. Those with leadership ability can advance to supervisory jobs.

If you think you would like to do this kind of work, look at the job titles listed below.

GOE: 05.12.02 Mining, Quarrying, Drilling, Elemental

SURVEYOR HELPER (any ind.) • D.O.T. #869.567-010 • OES #98319 • Performs any of following duties to assist in surveying land: Holds level or stadia rod at designated points to assist in determining elevations and laying out stakes for mapmaking, construction, mining, land, and other surveys. Calls out reading or writes station number and reading in note book. Marks points of measurement with elevation, station number, or other identifying mark. Measures distance between survey points, using steel or cloth tape or surveyor's chain. Marks measuring points with keel (marking crayon), paint sticks, scratches, tacks, or stakes. Places stakes at designated points and drives them into ground at specified elevation, using hammer or hatchet. Cuts and clears brush and trees from line of survey, using brush hook, knife, ax, or other cutting tools. May perform duties as directed by LAND SURVEYOR (profess. & kin.) or SURVEYOR ASSISTANT, INSTRUMENTS (profess. & kin.). May perform one operation and be designated accordingly as BRUSH CLEARER, SURVEYING (any ind.); STAKER, SURVEYING (any ind.); SURVEYOR HELPER, CHAIN (any ind.); SURVEYOR HELPER, ROD (any ind.). • **GED:** R3, M1, L2 • **SVP:** 3-6 mos • **Academic:** Ed=N, Eng=N • **Work Field:** 031, 243 • **MPSMS:** 310, 360 • **Aptitudes:** G4, V4, N4, S4, P4, Q4, K4, F4, M3, E4, C5 • **Temperaments:** R, T • **Stress:** T • **Physical:** V=L, H=N, L=M, W, S, H • **Work Env:** O • **Salary:** 3 • **Outlook:** 2

GOE: 05.12.03 Loading & Moving, Mechanical

ABLE SEAMAN (water trans.) • D.O.T. #911.364-010 • OES #97514 • ABLE-BODIED SEAMAN. Performs following tasks on board ship to watch for obstructions in vessel's path and to maintain equipment and structures: Stands watch at bow or on wing of bridge to look for obstructions in path of vessel. Measures depth of water in shallow or unfamiliar waters, using leadline, and telephones or shouts information to bridge. Turns wheel on bridge or uses emergency steering apparatus to steer vessel as directed by MATE, SHIP (water trans.). Breaks out, rigs, overhauls, and stows cargo-handling gear, stationary rigging, and running gear. Overhauls lifeboats and lifeboat gear and lowers or raises lifeboats with winch or falls. Paints and chips rust on deck or superstructure of ship. Must hold certificate issued by U. S. Government. When working aboard vessels carrying liquid cargoes, must hold tanker operator's certificate. May stow or remove cargo from ship's hold STEVEDORE (water trans.) II]. May be concerned with only one phase of duties, as maintenance of ship's gear and decks or watch duties, and be known as DECKHAND, MAINTENANCE (water trans.); WATCHSTANDER (water trans.). • **GED:** R3, M2, L2 • **SVP:** 6 mos-1 yr • **Academic:** Ed=N, Eng=N • **Work Field:** 013 • **MPSMS:** 854 • **Aptitudes:** G3, V4, N4, S3, P3, Q4, K3, F3, M3, E2, C4 • **Temperaments:** M, T, V • **Physical:** V=L, H=N, L=H, W, C, H • **Work Env:** O, R • **Salary:** 4 • **Outlook:** 2

BAGGAGE HANDLER (r.r. trans.) • D.O.T. #910.687-010 • OES #98999 • Loads and stores baggage on passenger train: Inspects tags on baggage to insure that baggage is routed to designated train. Loads baggage in car according to destination recorded on tags, placing baggage to be unloaded last in rear of car. Unloads baggage from train onto trailers at destination. • **GED:** R2, M1, L1 • **SVP:** 2-30 days • **Academic:** Ed=N, Eng=N • **Work Field:** 011 • **MPSMS:** 851 • **Aptitudes:** G4, V4, N4, S3, P4, Q4, K3, F4, M3, E3, C5 • **Temperaments:** R • **Stress:** T • **Physical:** V=L, H=N, L=H, W, C, S, H • **Work Env:** I • **Salary:** 4 • **Outlook:** 2

BARGE CAPTAIN (water trans.) • D.O.T. #911.137-010 • OES #97502 • SCOW CAPTAIN. Supervises and coordinates activities of workers on towed barge that transports cargo on lakes, bays, sounds, and rivers: Directs workers engaged in loading and unloading barge to ensure that cargo is loaded according to balancing specifications. Inspects barge to ensure that craft is seaworthy. Signals TUGBOAT CAPTAIN (water trans.) to tow barge to destination. Logs barge's movements and ports-of-call. Steers barge when it has steering equipment. • **GED:** R4, M3, L3 • **SVP:** 1-2 yrs • **Academic:** Ed=N, Eng=S • **Work Field:** 011, 013 • **MPSMS:** 854 • **Aptitudes:** G3, V3, N4, S3, P3, Q4, K4, F4, M3, E4, C5 • **Temperaments:** D, J, M • **Stress:** A • **Physical:** V=G, H=G, L=M, W, H • **Work Env:** B • **Salary:** 4 • **Outlook:** 2

BRAKE HOLDER (any ind.) • D.O.T. #932.664-010 • OES #97317 • CAR RIDER; COUPLER; DUKEY RIDER; GANG RIDER; NIPPER; PATCHER; ROPE RIDER; SET RIDER; SWAMPER; TAIL-END RIDER; TRAILER; TRAIN CONDUCTOR; TRIP RIDER; TUB RIDER. Throws switches and couples, or attaches to cable, cars being hauled by locomotive or hoisted by cable or chain in mines, quarries, or industrial plants: Uncouples loaded cars at their destination or uncouples and distributes empty cars to sidings or to loading areas. Moves switches to route cars and signals DINKEY OPERATOR (any ind.) to start or stop cars. May open and close ventilation doors in mines. May open or close chute gates to load or unload cars. May crush oversize rock or ore on grizzly to prevent clogging, using sledge hammer. May remove and tag ore samples for laboratory analysis. May be designated according to type of hauling machine as DINKEY-OPERATOR HELPER (any ind.). • **GED:** R2, M1, L1 • **SVP:** 30 days-3 mos • **Academic:** Ed=N, Eng=N • **Work Field:** 013 • **MPSMS:** 851 • **Aptitudes:** G4, V4, N4, S4, P4, Q4, K4, F4, M3, E5, C5 • **Temperaments:** R • **Stress:** T • **Physical:** V=L, H=N, L=M, W, S, H • **Work Env:** B • **Salary:** 4 • **Outlook:** 2

CONSTRUCTION WORKER 2 (const.) • D.O.T. #869.687-026 • OES #98316 • (const.); SLICER (const.); SQUEEGEE FINISHER (const.); STAIN REMOVER (const.); STONE-AND-CONCRETE WASHER (const.); STONEMASON HELPER (const.); STONE UNLOADER (const.); STRUCTURAL-STEEL-WORKER HELPER (const.); SUBGRADE TESTER (const.); TRACK LAYER (const.); TRACK-REPAIRER HELPER (const.); TRENCH TRIMMER, FINE (const.); WALLPAPER REMOVER, STEAM (const.); WALL WASHER (const.); WATERPROOFER HELPER (const.); WELL DIGGER (const.); WELL-DIGGER HELPER (const.); WHITE WASHER (const.). • **GED:** R2, M1, L1 • **SVP:** 2-30 days • **Academic:** Ed=N, Eng=N • **Work Field:** 011, 102 • **MPSMS:** 360 • **Aptitudes:** G4, V4, N4, S4, P4, Q5, K4, F4, M3, E4, C5 • **Temperaments:** R • **Stress:** T • **Physical:** V=L, H=N, L=V, W, C, S, H • **Work Env:** O, N, R • **Salary:** 4 • **Outlook:** 3

DOLLY PUSHER (radio & tv broad.) • D.O.T. #962.687-010 • OES #98999 • ASSISTANT CAMERA OPERATOR. Pushes television camera dolly around studio, as directed by CAMERA OPERATOR, TELEVISION, to follow action of scene being broadcast. •

GED: R2, M1, L1 • SVP: 2-30 days • **Academic:** Ed=N, Eng=N • **Work Field:** 011 • **MPSMS:** 863 • **Aptitudes:** G4, V4, N5, S4, P4, Q5, K3, F4, M3, E4, C5 • **Temperaments:** R • **Stress:** T • **Physical:** V=L, H=N, L=V, W, H • **Work Env:** I • **Salary:** 4 • **Outlook:** 2

DUMPER (any ind.) • D.O.T. #921.667-018 • OES #97989 • BULK LOADER. Dumps materials, such as coal, chemicals, flue dust, grain, ore, sugar, and salt, into and from railway cars, trucks, or other vehicles, according to specific instructions: Positions and blocks vehicles by signaling LOCOMOTIVE ENGINEER (r.r. trans.) or TRUCK DRIVER, HEAVY (any ind.), or by using winch and car jack or powered tractor to spot cars and set brakes. Positions spout, chute, and conveyor over or into car, truck, bin, or storage pile and opens slide in spout or chute to start flow of material into or from vehicles, positions vehicle over storage bin and opens air valve, side door, or car hopper door, starts conveyors, airveyors, or elevators, and adjusts dampers to feed materials to specified bin. May use power scoop to pull grain from car into receiving chute. May collect grain sample, using probe. May drive truck onto ramp, secure it with blocks, and attach hook from electric hoist to front end of trailer or truck and push button to activate hoist, or move lever of hydraulic lift to elevate front end of truck as tailgate is opened to dump material. May vibrate hopper to facilitate flow into slurry pit, using airhammer. May open solvent tank valve and start pump to wash and transfer residue of materials to saturator and other tanks. May observe pressure gages and adjust valves to maintain specified pumping pressure. May record car identifying information, such as weight and volume of material loaded and number of cars dumped or filled. May be designated according to kind of vehicle unloaded as CAR DUMPER (any ind.); according to kind of material unloaded as GRAIN UNLOADER (grain & feed mill.); or according to type of equipment used as SPOUT POSITIONER (any ind.); WINCHER (any ind.). • GED: R2, M1, L1 • SVP: 2-30 days • **Academic:** Ed=N, Eng=N • **Work Field:** 011, 014 • **MPSMS:** 565, 568 • **Aptitudes:** G4, V4, N4, S3, P4, Q5, K3, F4, M3, E4, C4 • **Temperaments:** R • **Stress:** T • **Physical:** V=L, H=N, L=H, W, C, H • **Work Env:** B, N, R • **Salary:** 4 • **Outlook:** 2

ETCHER HELPER, HAND (print. & pub.) • D.O.T. #971.687-010 • OES #98999 • Assists ETCHER, HAND (print. & pub.) in etching designs on copper printing rollers: Trucks rollers from storage area to etching room. Inserts mandrel through roller and screws collar onto mandrel to hold roller in position. Assists ETCHER, HAND (print. & pub.) in lifting rollers onto machine brackets and in transferring rollers from one vat to another. Turns crank on mandrel to rotate rollers in rinsing and etching vats. Cleans solvent and acid-resistant coating from etched rollers by rubbing with sawdust or using absorbent cloth. Removes mandrel from etched rollers and trucks rollers to mending bench. Drains vats of spent etching solutions and performs other duties as described under HELPER (any ind.) • GED: R2, M1, L1 • SVP: 2-30 days • **Academic:** Ed=N, Eng=N • **Work Field:** 182 • **MPSMS:** 567 • **Aptitudes:** G4, V4, N5, S4, P4, Q5, K3, F4, M3, E5, C5 • **Temperaments:** R • **Stress:** T • **Physical:** V=G, H=N, L=H, W, S, H • **Work Env:** I • **Salary:** 3 • **Outlook:** 2

GARBAGE COLLECTOR (motor trans.) • D.O.T. #909.687-010 • OES #98705 • Collects refuse on designated route within municipality and dumps refuse from containers onto truck. May be designated according to refuse collected as TRASH COLLECTOR (motor trans.). May drive truck [GARBAGE COLLECTOR DRIVER (motor trans.)]. May start hoisting device that raises refuse bin attached to rear of truck and dumps contents into opening in enclosed truck body. • GED: R1, M1, L1 • SVP: 1 day • **Academic:** Ed=N, Eng=N • **Work Field:** 011 • **MPSMS:** 874 • **Aptitudes:** G4, V4, N5, S4, P4, Q5, K4, F4, M3, E4, C5 • **Temperaments:** R • **Stress:** T • **Physical:** V=L, H=N, L=V, W, S, H • **Work Env:** O • **Salary:** 5 • **Outlook:** 2

INSTALLER (museum) • D.O.T. #922.687-050 • OES #98799 • Moves, installs, and stores paintings, statuary, and other art objects in art museum: Places protective pads on handtruck platform and lifts paintings, statuary, or other art objects onto handtruck and places protective pads between and around objects to insure against damage. Pushes handtruck from shipping-receiving area to storage or display gallery as directed by supervisor. Places

objects to be stored in designated sections of storage area. Removes objects to be displayed from handtruck, hangs paintings, and positions statuary and other objects in cabinets or on stands as directed. Dismantles exhibit components, as directed, and moves art objects, cabinets, and other display items to storage area. Moves designated objects from storage area to shipping room. • GED: R2, M1, L1 • SVP: 2-30 days • **Academic:** Ed=N, Eng=N • **Work Field:** 011 • **MPSMS:** 969 • **Aptitudes:** G4, V4, N5, S3, P4, Q5, K3, F4, M3, E4, C5 • **Temperaments:** R • **Stress:** T • **Physical:** V=L, H=N, L=H, W, C, H • **Work Env:** I • **Salary:** 2 • **Outlook:** 3

LABORER (petrol. production) • D.O.T. #939.687-018 • OES #98999 • ROUSTABOUT. Performs any combination of following tasks in and about oilfields and pipe lines, using handtools: Digs trenches for building foundations or for drainage around oil wells, storage tanks, and other installations. Fills excavations with dirt, using shovels. Loads and unloads trucks by hand or using handtrucks. Mixes concrete, using hoe and shovel. Carries concrete and tamps it into building forms. Bails spilled oil into buckets and barrels. Cleans and performs routine adjustments to machinery, using handtools, solvent, and rags. Cuts down trees and brush around oilfield installations to reduce fire hazard or clear way for roads. Rolls and segregates pipe sections on racks in material yard to position pipes for testing. Connects pipe ends and hydraulic hose, using wrenches. Paints oil storage tanks, pumping units, and auxiliary equipment, using brush or spray painting equipment. May clean and service motor vehicles and auxiliary equipment. • GED: R1, M1, L1 • SVP: 1 day • **Academic:** Ed=N, Eng=N • **Work Field:** 011, 143, 153 • **MPSMS:** 342 • **Aptitudes:** G4, V4, N4, S4, P4, Q5, K3, F4, M3, E4, C4 • **Temperaments:** R • **Stress:** T • **Physical:** V=L, H=N, L=V, W, C, S, H • **Work Env:** O, W, N, R • **Salary:** 5 • **Outlook:** 1

LABORER, PETROLEUM REFINERY (petrol. refin.) • D.O.T. #549.687-018 • OES #98999 • PROCESS HELPER. Performs any combination of following tasks in refinery: Digs ditches, builds dikes and levees, and fills holes with earth, rock, sand, and asphalt gravels, using pick and shovel. Smooths ground surfaces and roadways, using hand tamper. Cleans refining equipment. Removes debris from roadways and work areas, and sprays and hoes weeds. Shovels sand and gravel off vehicles and dumps or shovels cement and sand into mixers. Mixes and pours cement and transports cement to forms with wheelbarrow. Unloads materials, such as tools, equipment, sacks of cement, sand, catalyst, salt, and lime, and oil barrels from freight cars and trucks, manually or with handtruck; and stacks barrels and sacks for storage. Uncrates equipment and parts, such as fractionating or treating towers and bubble trays, using pry bar and hammer; and installs bubble caps, using wrenches. Rips open sacks and dumps chemicals and catalysts into mixing, treating, or storage tanks. Dopes pipelines to prevent corrosion, using doping pot and tar. Changes hoist cables, and rigs chain hoists, rope blocks, power winches, and gin poles used to move or raise equipment. Skims oil from cooling water in water boxes. May be designated according to section of refinery in which work is performed as LABORER, FILTER PLANT (petrol. refin.). • GED: R2, M1, L1 • SVP: 30 days-3 mos • **Academic:** Ed=N, Eng=N • **Work Field:** 011, 031 • **MPSMS:** 501 • **Aptitudes:** G4, V4, N4, S4, P4, Q5, K4, F4, M3, E5, C5 • **Temperaments:** R • **Stress:** T • **Physical:** V=L, H=N, L=H, W, C, S, H • **Work Env:** O, N, R • **Salary:** 3 • **Outlook:** 2

LABORER, SHIPYARD (ship bldg. & rep.) • D.O.T. #809.687-022 • OES #98999 • Performs following tasks in shipyards: Loads vehicles, using handtruck or dolly. Washes trucks and other vehicles. Cleans ships, piers, drydocks, and other working areas, using broom and water hose. Opens shipping crates, using hammer and pinchbar. Sorts lumber, metals, and other scrap materials. Collects and burns trash. Mixes and pours cement on inner bottoms of ships and around joints on decks to prepare surfaces for tile or to make joints watertight. Removes paint and scale from ships' metal surfaces, using hand or powered wire brushes. Conveys materials and tools to worksite. • GED: R2, M1, L1 • SVP: 2-30 days • **Academic:** Ed=N, Eng=N • **Work Field:** 011, 102 • **MPSMS:** 593 • **Aptitudes:** G4, V4, N5, S4, P4, Q5, K4, F4, M4, E5, C5 • **Temperaments:** R • **Stress:** T • **Physical:** V=L, H=N, L=H, W, S, H • **Work Env:** O • **Salary:** 2 • **Outlook:** 1

MATERIAL HANDLER (any ind.) • D.O.T. #929.687-030 • OES #98799 • DISTRIBUTOR; FLOOR WORKER; LINE SUPPLY; LOADER AND UNLOADER; SERVICER; STACKER; UTILITY WORKER. Loads, unloads, and moves materials within or near plant, yard, or worksite, performing any combination of the following duties: Reads work order or follows oral instructions to ascertain mate rials or containers to be moved. Opens containers, using steel cutters, crowbar, clawhammer, or other handtools. Loads and unloads materials onto or from pallets, trays, racks, and shelves by hand. Loads materials into vehicles and installs strapping, bracing, or padding to prevent shifting or damage in transit, using handtools. Conveys materials to or from storage or work sites to designated area, using handtruck, electric dolly, wheel barrow, or other device. Secures lifting attachments to materials and conveys load to destination, using hand-operated crane or hoist, or signals crane or hoisting operators to move load to destination [LABORER, HOISTING (any ind.)]. Counts, weighs, and records number of units of materials moved or handled on daily production sheet. Attaches identifying tags or labels to materials or marks information on cases, bales, or other containers. Loads truck for INDUSTRIAL-TRUCK OPERATOR (any ind.). Stacks or assembles materials into bundles and bands bundles together, using banding machine and clincher. Clamps sections of portable conveyor together or places conveyor sections on blocks or boxes to facilitate movement of materials or products. Removes samples of materials, labels with identifying information, and takes samples to laboratory for analysis [LABORATORY-SAMPLE CARRIER (any ind.)]. Lifts heavy objects by hand or using power hoist, and cleans work area, machines, and equipment, using broom, rags, and cleaning compounds to assist machine operators. Makes simple adjustments or repairs, such as realining belts or replacing rollers, using handtools. Assembles crates to contain products, such as machines or vehicles, using handtools and precut lumber. Shovels loose materials such as sand, gravel, metals, plastics, or chemicals into machine hoppers or into vehicles and containers, such as wheelbarrows, scrap truck, or barrels. May occasionally operate industrial truck or electric hoist to assist in loading or moving materials and products. May be designated according to material handled as FILLING HAULER, WEAVING (tex tile); according to method of conveying materials as LUGGER (agric.); according to machine or equipment loaded or unloaded as BLUNGER LOADER (pottery & porc.); VEHICLE UNLOADER (any ind.); or according to work station as OUTSIDE TRUCKER (any ind.); PLATFORM LOADER (any ind.). Additional titles: BALE PILER (textile); BATCH TRUCKER (rubber tire & tube); BOBBIN HANDLER (textile); CAR LOADER (any ind.); CLOTH HAULER (textile); COAL PASSER (any ind.); COMPRESS TRUCKER (agric.); HOGSHEAD DUMPER (tobacco); KILN-CAR UNLOADER (brick & tile); LABORER, YARD (any ind.); LOADER (any ind.) II; LUMBER-YARD WORKER (woodworking); MERCHANDISE CARRIER (any ind.); MOLD MOVER (sports equip.); OVEN STRIPPER (any ind.); OVEN UNLOADER (any ind.); PACKAGING-MACHINE-SUPPLIES DISTRIBUTOR (tobacco); SLAB PICKER (sawmill); POWDER TRUCKER (ammunition; explosives); RACK CARRIER (paper goods); RACKER (any ind.); RETORT LOADER (wood distil. & char.); ROPER (agric.); ROVING STOCK HANDLER (textile); SCRAP WHEELER (mach. shop); SEGREGATOR (agric.; whole. tr.); SUGAR TRUCKER (corn prod.); TIRE TRUCKER (rubber tire & tube); TRUCKER, HAND (any ind.). • GED: R2, M1, L1 • SVP: 30 days-3 mos • Academic: Ed=N, Eng=N • Work Field: 011 • MPSMS: 898 • Aptitudes: G4, V4, N4, S4, P4, Q4, K4, F4, M4, E4, C4 • Temperaments: R • Stress: T • Physical: V=L, H=N, L=V, W, C, S, H • Work Env: B, C, H, W, N, R • Salary: 5 • Outlook: 2

PRESS BUCKER (any ind.) • D.O.T. #920.686-042 • OES #98502 • Removes pressed bales of material, such as cotton, hay, wastepaper, waste metals, and rags from baling machine, using hook. May push bales to storage area, using hand truck. When removing pressed bales of materials by shoving steel band through press platen, is designated BAND SHOVER, PRESS (agric.). • GED: R1, M1, L1 • SVP: 1 day • Academic: Ed=N, Eng=N • Work Field: 011 • MPSMS: 414, 470, 549 • Aptitudes: G4, V4, N5, S4, P4, Q5, K4, F4, M3, E5, C5 • Temperaments: R • Stress: T • Physical: V=N, H=N, L=H, W, H • Work Env: I • Salary: 2 • Outlook: 3

RECORDING STUDIO SET-UP WORKER (phonograph) • D.O.T. #962.664-014 • OES #98799 • Arranges sound recording equipment in studio preparatory to recording session following work order specifications: Reads work order to determine position of equipment and arranges equipment, such as consoles, isolation booths, microphones, tape machines, amplifiers, music stands, and musical instruments, by hand or using handtrucks and dollies. Connects equipment electrical lines to outlets according to session and returns items to storage. Maintains storage area and assists in maintaining tape library. • GED: R3, M1, L1 • SVP: 3-6 mos • Academic: Ed=N, Eng=N • Work Field: 011, 061 • MPSMS: 869 • Aptitudes: G3, V4, N4, S4, P4, Q3, K3, F4, M3, E5, C5 • Temperaments: R, T • Stress: T • Physical: V=L, H=N, L=M, W, S, H • Work Env: I • Salary: 3 • Outlook: 2

WASTE-DISPOSAL ATTENDANT (any ind.) • D.O.T. #955.383-010 • OES #97989 • Disposes of radioactive equipment and wastes, performing any combination of the following duties: Loads contaminated equipment and lead pigs of waste material onto truck, using forklift. Drives truck to storage area and removes load. Shovels specified quantities of ingredients into and tends concrete mixer. Pours or shovels concrete into forms to make disposal coffins (containers). Lifts contaminated equipment or wastes from lead pigs and places them in coffin, using stainless steel rods. Pours concrete into coffin to encase waste. Loads coffins onto truck, using forklift, and transports them to burial ground or arranges for burial at sea. Records amount and type of equipment and waste disposed. May accompany coffins for burial at sea. May clean contaminated equipment for reuse by operating sand blasters, filtering pumps and steam cleaners, or by scrubbing with detergents or solvents. Workers must follow prescribed safety procedures and Federal laws regu lating waste disposal. • GED: R3, M2, L2 • SVP: 6 mos-1 yr • Academic: Ed=N, Eng=N • Work Field: 011, 013 • MPSMS: 491, 530, 540 • Aptitudes: G3, V4, N4, S3, P3, Q4, K3, F4, M3, E3, C4 • Temperaments: S, T, V • Stress: S • Physical: V=L, H=N, L=H, W, S, H • Work Env: B, R • Salary: 3 • Outlook: 3

YARD LABORER (paper & pulp) • D.O.T. #922.687-102 • OES #98999 • Moves and stores material and maintains yard and grounds of paper and pulp plant by performing any combination of the following tasks: Shovels wood chips, pulpwood, sulfur, and limerock into trucks or onto conveyors. Cleans chips or bark from conveyors; bark, leaves, and twigs from water canal, and burns refuse. Removes driftwood from canal, using hoist. May load waste paper from paper machines into carts. May stack bundles of woodpulp and dump pulp and waste paper into beaters. May dig ditches and install pipelines from railroad tank cars to facilitate unloading of chemicals used in paper manufacture. • GED: R1, M1, L1 • SVP: 1 day • Academic: Ed=N, Eng=N • Work Field: 011, 031 • MPSMS: 450, 470 • Aptitudes: G4, V4, N5, S4, P4, Q5, K4, F4, M3, E5, C5 • Temperaments: R • Stress: T • Physical: V=L, H=N, L=H, W, C, S, H • Work Env: B, R • Salary: 3 • Out look: 3

GOE: 05.12.04 Hoising, Conveying

BOOM-CONVEYOR OPERATOR (any ind.) • D.O.T. #921.683-014 • OES #97951 • LOADER-HEAD OPERATOR; STACKER ATTENDANT. Controls boom conveyors to move materials, such as coal, ore, and gravel, to and from railroad cars or processing station, and storage piles: Starts specified boom conveyor and conveyor belts, and adjusts height, swing, and extension of boom according to size of storage pile or position of car. Opens side gates of railroad cars or gates of processing station to dump material onto conveyor that carries it to storage pile. Positions boom conveyor over railroad car and starts flow of materials from plant or storage pile to load car. Regulates conveyor speed to prevent spilling or weight variations among cars. Observes gages and lights on control panel to detect malfunctions of conveyor system. Diverts materials to storage bins or notifies plant or tipple operator to stop supply of materials during emergency. Lubricates machine, using grease gun and oilcan. May drive mobile boom conveyor to designated work area. May be known as STACKER OPERATOR (any ind.). • GED: R2, M1, L1 • SVP: 30 days-3 mos • Academic: Ed=N, Eng=N • Work Field: 011 • MPSMS: 340, 350 • Aptitudes: G3, V4, N4, S3, P4, Q4, K3, F4, M3, E5, C5 • Temperaments: M, T •

Physical: V=L, H=N, L=L, H • **Work Env:** B, N • **Salary:** 4 • **Outlook:** 3

CHOKE SETTER (logging) • D.O.T. #921.687-014 • OES #73005 • Fastens choker cables around logs for yarding from cutting area to landing: Pulls choker cables from tractor winch or main-line of yarding machine, passes ball (one end) under and around log, and secures end to bell (sliding fastener) to form noose. May clear brush and earth from under log, using ax and shovel. May assist RIGGING SLINGER (logging) in installing and dismantling rigging of high lead or similar yarding system. May be designated as CAT HOOKER (logging) in tractor yarding. • **GED:** R1, M1, L1 • **SVP:** 2-30 days • **Academic:** Ed=N, Eng=N • **Work Field:** 011 • **MPSMS:** 452 • **Aptitudes:** G4, V4, N5, S4, P4, Q5, K3, F4, M3, E3, C5 • **Temperaments:** R, S • **Stress:** T, S • **Physical:** V=L, H=L, L=V, W, C, S, H • **Work Env:** O, N, R • **Salary:** 4 • **Outlook:** 3

CONVEYOR-SYSTEM DISPATCHER (any ind.) • D.O.T. #921.662-018 • OES #97951 • CONVEYOR CONSOLE OPERATOR. Operates console to control automated conveyor system that receives, sorts, distributes, and conveys bulk or packaged materials or products to and from loading dock and storage area, and between departments or processes: Reads production and delivery schedules and confers with supervisor to determine sorting and routing procedures. Presses buttons and turns dials to start conveyor system and regulate speed of conveyors. Observes materials or products moving on conveyors, or observes lights on control panel to monitor flow and operation of system. Moves switches or pushes buttons to route order to designated areas and to raise, lower, and aline conveyor with specific adjoining conveyors. Contacts work stations by telephone or intercom to request movement of order or to notify work stations of shipment enroute and approximate delivery time. Stops equipment to clear jams. Informs supervisor of equipment malfunction. May operate elevator system in conjunction with conveyor system. May weigh trucks and railroad cars before and after loading or read scale that continually weighs product on conveyor to ascertain when specified tonnage has been loaded, and record weight on loading ticket. • **GED:** R3, M1, L2 • **SVP:** 30 days-3 mos • **Academic:** Ed=N, Eng=S • **Work Field:** 011, 145 • **MPSMS:** 565 • **Aptitudes:** G3, V3, N4, S4, P4, Q3, K3, F4, M4, E5, C5 • **Temperaments:** R, T • **Stress:** T • **Physical:** V=N, H=G, L=M, W, H • **Work Env:** I • **Salary:** 4 • **Outlook:** 3

ELEVATOR OPERATOR, FREIGHT (any ind.) • D.O.T. #921.683-038 • OES #67011 • ELEVATOR OPERATOR, SERVICE. Operates elevator to transport materials and equipment between floors of an industrial or commercial establishment: Moves control levers, or pushes buttons to control movement of elevator. Opens and closes safety gate and door of elevator at each floor where stop is made. May load and unload elevator. May transport freight from elevator to designated area, using handtruck. May transport passengers. • **GED:** R2, M1, L1 • **SVP:** 2-30 days • **Academic:** Ed=N, Eng=N • **Work Field:** 011 • **MPSMS:** 969 • **Aptitudes:** G4, V4, N4, S4, P4, Q4, K4, F4, M4, E4, C5 • **Temperaments:** R • **Stress:** T • **Physical:** V=L, H=N, L=H, W, H • **Work Env:** I • **Salary:** 2 • **Outlook:** 3

GRIP (motion pic.) • D.O.T. #962.687-022 • OES #98799 • PROPERTY HANDLER. Performs any combination of following tasks in motion picture or television studio or set location: Moves control levers and wheels to guide cranes, booms, and dollies that move cameras and other equipment. Sews canvas and other materials to make and repair tents, tarps, scrims, and backings, using sewing machine. Erects canvas covers to protect camera from rain on location. Cuts gelatin and fiberglass light diffusers to fit metal frame of camera and inserts diffusers into frame. Rigs and dismantles frames, scaffolding, backdrops, prefabricated dressing rooms, camera platforms, and tents for set in studio or on location, using carpenter's handtools. May be designated according to department assigned as CONSTRUCTION GRIP (motion pic.); PRODUCTION GRIP (motion pic.); SEWING ROOM GRIP (motion pic.). • **GED:** R2, M1, L2 • **SVP:** 6 mos-1 yr • **Academic:** Ed=N, Eng=N • **Work Field:** 011, 102, 171 • **MPSMS:** 911 • **Aptitudes:** G3, V3, N4, S3, P3, Q4, K3, F3, M3, E3, C4 • **Temperaments:** V • **Physical:** V=L, H=N, L=H, W, C, S, H • **Work Env:** I, R • **Salary:** 3 • **Outlook:** 2

LABORER, CONCRETE-MIXING PLANT (const.) • D.O.T. #579.665-014 • OES #98799 • CONCRETE-MIXER-OPERATOR

HELPER; LABORER, MIXING PLANT; MACHINE HELPER; MIXER HELPER; MIXER TENDER; MIXING-PLANT DUMPER. Performs any combination of following duties in concrete mixing plant: Verifies amount of aggregate in storage bins by visual inspection, and turns swivel head to direct aggregate into specified bin. Tends electrically powered conveyor or pneumatic pump to hoist cement from feeder hopper, railroad car, or transport truck into storage container, such as cement silo. Loosens locking pin, using hammer to dump cement from cars into storage hopper, prodding cement with pole through trapdoor in car until car is empty. Positions trucks, cars, or buckets under spouts of concrete mixers, batching plants, or hoppers, using hand signals, and moving levers or handwheels to discharge concrete into trucks, cars, or buckets. May haul cement from storage in bulk or bags, emptying, cleaning, and bundling empty bags. May be designated according to duties performed as AGGREGATE-CONVEYOR OPERATOR (const.); BAG SHAKER (const.); CEMENT CAR DUMPER (const.); CEMENT-CONVEYOR OPERATOR (const.); CEMENT HANDLER (const.); CEMENT-SACK BREAKER (const.). Additional Titles: CONCRETE-BUCKET LOADER (const.); CONCRETE-BUCKET UNLOADER (const.); CONCRETE-CONVEYOR OPERATOR (const.); CONCRETE-HOPPER OPERATOR (const.); CONCRETE-MIXER LOADER, TRUCK MOUNTED (const.); CONVEYOR TENDER, CONCRETE-MIXING PLANT (const.); DUMPER, CENTRAL-CONCRETE-MIXING PLANT (const.); LOFT WORKER, CONCRETE-MIXING PLANT (const.). • **GED:** R2, M1, L1 • **SVP:** 2-30 days • **Academic:** Ed=N, Eng=N • **Work Field:** 011 • **MPSMS:** 536 • **Aptitudes:** G4, V4, N5, S4, P4, Q5, K4, F4, M4, E4, C5 • **Temperaments:** R • **Stress:** T • **Physical:** V=L, H=N, L=H, W, C, S, H • **Work Env:** O, N • **Salary:** 2 • **Outlook:** 3

LABORER, HOISTING (any ind.) • D.O.T. #921.667-022 • OES #98799 • CRANE FOLLOWER; CRANE HOOKER; HITCHER; HOOKER; OILER; SIGNALER. Assists workers engaged in operating derricks, cranes, power shovels, or other hoisting machines used to lift and move machinery, equipment, or materials, such as concrete, castings, structural steel, stone slabs, mill rolls, scrap metal, pipe, dirt, and logs, performing any combination of the following duties: Couples and uncouples railroad cars and throws railroad track switches. Affixes hook, bucket, electromagnet, or demolition ball to crane, or affixes rope, cable, chain, sling, or other grappling equipment or attachments to object being lifted or to lifting mechanism. Places blocking, out-riggers, or screw-jacks in position to hold crane or shovel upright when lifting heavy loads. Places supports in position to receive load. Signals operator, vocally or with hand signals, to guide operator in lifting and moving loads when view from crane or shovel cab is obstructed. Pushes or pulls load as it is lowered, until it is deposited in desired place. Secures load to trucks or railcars, using ropes, chains, or bands. Lubricates moving parts of crane or shovel with grease gun or oilcan. May install extension sections to boom, using pins and cotter keys, or nuts and bolts. May lay track or timber runways on which tread-wheeled machines move. May drive truck-mounted crane from one work location to another. May be designated according to equipment used, attachments made, or area worked in as CONCRETE-BUCKET HOOKER (const.); FLOOR WORKER, TRANSFER BAY (nonfer. metal alloys); LOCOMOTIVE-CRANE-OPERATOR HELPER (any ind.); LOG HOOKER (sawmill; veneer & plywood); MAGNET PLACER (iron & steel); PIT-WORKER, POWER SHOVEL (any ind.); POWER-SHOVEL-OPERATOR HELPER (any ind.); TRUCK-CRANE-OPERATOR HELPER (any ind.). Performs other duties as described under HELPER (any ind.). • **GED:** R2, M1, L1 • **SVP:** 30 days-3 mos • **Academic:** Ed=N, Eng=N • **Work Field:** 011 • **MPSMS:** 565 • **Aptitudes:** G4, V4, N5, S4, P4, Q5, K4, F4, M3, E3, C5 • **Temperaments:** R • **Stress:** T • **Physical:** V=L, H=N, L=M, W, C, S, H • **Work Env:** B, N, R • **Salary:** 4 • **Outlook:** 4

LABORER, POWERHOUSE (light, heat, & power) • D.O.T. #952.665-010 • OES #98999 • Performs any combination of following duties in powerplants, such as electrical power companies, industrial plants, and central heating plants: Assists in control and maintenance of coal conveying equipment, using handtools and lubricating equipment. Shovels coal spillage onto conveyors. Takes samples of coal and carries samples to laboratory for analysis. Loads trucks or rail cars with fly ash from dust collectors, using suction hose. Starts and stops pumps, opens and closes floodgates, and adjusts valves of ash sluice system. Sweeps, washes, cleans, and paints buildings, floors, and equipment. Assists in inspection, maintenance, and repair of rail tracks, ties, and roadbeds, using shovels, picks, sledge hammers, jacks, and cutting torches. Maintains roads, lawns, shrubs, and flowers, using power mowers and gardener's handtools. Operates, loads, and unloads trucks to transport personnel and equipment. Keeps logs on equipment and materials and submits production reports to supervisor. • **GED:** R2, M1, L1 • **SVP:** 30 days-3 mos • **Academic:** Ed=N, Eng=N • **Work Field:** 003, 011, 031 • **MPSMS:** 870 • **Aptitudes:** G4, V4, N4, S4, P4, Q4, K4, F4, M3, E4, C4 • **Temperaments:** V • **Physical:** V=L, H=N, L=H, W, C, S, H • **Work Env:** B, N, R • **Salary:** 4 • **Outlook:** 3

GOE: 05.12.05 Braking, Switching, & Coupling

BRAKE COUPLER, ROAD FREIGHT (r.r. trans.) • D.O.T. #910.367-010 • OES #97317 • Performs any combination of following duties, working as member of train crew: Inspects couplings and airhoses to ensure that they are securely fastened. Inspects journal boxes to ensure that they are lubricated. Inspects handbrakes on cars to insure that they are released before run begins. Walks on top of cars and peers down between them to inspect couplings, airhoses, and journal boxes. Sets warning signals, such as flares, flags, lanterns, or torpe does in front of and at rear of train during emergency stops to warn oncoming trains. Climbs ladder to top of car and turns brakewheel to set car brakes or rides atop car to control its speed when it is shunted. Pulls or pushes track switch to reroute cars during breakup at way stations. Signals LOCOMOTIVE ENGINEER (r.r. trans.) to start or stop train when coupling or uncoupling cars. Rides in cab of engine or cupola of caboose to observe signals from other crew members. Makes minor repairs to couplings, airhoses, and journal boxes. Reports to CONDUCTOR, ROAD FREIGHT (r.r. trans.) any equipment requiring major repairs. • **GED:** R3, M2, L3 • **SVP:** 3-6 mos • **Academic:** Ed=N, Eng=S • **Work Field:** 013 • **MPSMS:** 851 • **Aptitudes:** G3, V3, N4, S3, P2, Q4, K3, F4, M3, E3, C4 • **Temperaments:** M, V • **Physical:** V=L, H=N, L=M, W, C, S, H • **Work Env:** B, R • **Salary:** 4 • **Outlook:** 1

SWITCH TENDER (r.r. trans.) • D.O.T. #910.667-026 • OES #97317 • Throws track switches within yard of railroad, industrial plant, quarry, construction project, or similar location to switch cars for loading, unloading, making up, and breaking up of trains: Receives oral or written instructions from CONDUCTOR, YARD (r.r. trans.), YARD COUPLER (r.r. trans.) or YARD MANAGER (r.r. trans.). Observes arm or lantern signal from YARD COUPLER (r.r. trans.) and relays information to HOSTLER (r.r. trans.) or throws track switch to facilitate shunting of cars to different locations in yard. May couple and uncouple cars for makeup and breakup of trains. May ride atop cars that have been shunted and turn handwheel to control speed of car or stop it at specified position. May wave arm or lantern to signal YARD ENGINEER (r.r. trans.) to start or stop engine. • **GED:** R2, M1, L2 • **SVP:** 2-30 days • **Academic:** Ed=N, Eng=N • **Work Field:** 013 • **MPSMS:** 851 • **Aptitudes:** G4, V4, N4, S4, P4, Q4, K3, F4, M3, E4, C4 • **Temperaments:** M • **Physical:** V=L, H=N, L=M, W, H • **Work Env:** O, N • **Salary:** 4 • **Outlook:** 1

GOE: 05.12.06 Pumping, Elemental

AIRPORT UTILITY WORKER (air trans.) • D.O.T. #912.663-010 • OES #97899 • Services aircraft, working as member of crew, performing any combination of following tasks: Directs incoming and outgoing aircraft near terminal area to assist pilot's maneuvering of aircraft, using visual hand or light signals. Operates service vehicles to replenish fuel, water, and waste system chemicals and to remove liquid waste. Cleans exterior or interior of aircraft, using portable platform, ladders, brushes, rags, waterhose, and vacuum. Positions and removes boarding platform to unload or load aircraft passengers. Unloads and loads luggage and cargo from aircraft, using tow truck with luggage carts. Traces lost baggage for customers and prepares lost baggage claims. • **GED:** R3, M2, L3 • **SVP:** 3-6 mos • **Academic:** Ed=N, Eng=S •

Work Field: 013, 014, 031 • **MPSMS:** 855 • **Aptitudes:** G3, V3, N3, S2, P3, Q3, K3, F4, M3, E3, C4 • **Temperaments:** T, V • **Physical:** V=L, H=N, L=H, W, C, H • **Work Env:** I, N, R • **Salary:** 3 • **Outlook:** 3

BOAT LOADER 1 (water trans.) • D.O.T. #911.364-014 • OES #97989 • DOCK HAND; PIER HAND; WHARF HAND; WHARF OPERATOR; WHARF TENDER. Connects hose couplings to enable liquid cargo, such as petroleum, gasoline, heating oil, sulfuric acid, and alum liquor, to be pumped from and into barges and tankers: Reads timetable to determine name of ship, location of pier, and number and types of hoses to be connected. Climbs aboard ship and lowers measuring tape and thermometer into each tank to measure depth and temperature of liquid cargo to be unloaded. Positions coupling of pier hose next to valve of ship, using winch and boom, and connects coupling to valve, using wrench. Attaches ground wire to hose to prevent explosion caused by static electricity generated when liquid cargo flows through hose. Opens valve to allow flow of cargo through hose and signals worker aboard ship to start pumps to unload cargo. Signals worker aboard ship to pump ballast from cargo tanks in order to prepare transfer of cargo onto ship. Signals worker on shore to pump liquid cargo onto ship. May be designated according to water vessel loaded as BARGE LOADER (water trans.). • **GED:** R2, M2, L2 • **SVP:** 30 days-3 mos • **Academic:** Ed=N, Eng=N • **Work Field:** 014 • **MPSMS:** 854 • **Aptitudes:** G3, V4, N4, S3, P3, Q4, K3, F3, M3, E4, C5 • **Temperaments:** M • **Physical:** V=L, H=N, L=M, W, C, S, H • **Work Env:** O, R • **Salary:** 5 • **Outlook:** 2

LINE-SERVICE ATTENDANT (air trans.) • D.O.T. #912.687-010 • OES #98799 • Services aircraft prior to flight according to specifications: Fills fuel and oil tanks and examines tires for specified air pressure. Adds water and other cooling agents as required to batteries and liquid-cooled engine radiators. Fills landing gear struts with hydraulic fluid. May clean exterior and interior of aircraft. May load and unload containers of food, beverages, and dishes for in-flight meal services. May deice aircraft wings and assemblies, using glycol mixture. May assist mechanics in repair of aircraft. • **GED:** R3, M2, L2 • **SVP:** 2-30 days • **Academic:** Ed=N, Eng=N • **Work Field:** 041 • **MPSMS:** 855 • **Aptitudes:** G3, V4, N4, S4, P4, Q4, K3, F4, M3, E4, C5 • **Temperaments:** M • **Physical:** V=L, H=N, L=M, W, C, H • **Work Env:** O, N • **Salary:** 3 • **Outlook:** 3

WATER TENDER (any ind.) • D.O.T. #599.685-122 • OES #92998 • Tends pumps that maintain level of water in boilers: Reads boiler gages to ascertain need for water. Opens valves and starts boiler-feed water pumps to supply water, or adjusts controls to start pumps automatically when water level reaches specified point. Observes operation of pumps to detect malfunctions. Tests water to determine suitability for boiler use or obtains sample for laboratory analysis. Adds specified chemical to condition boiler water. May clean boilers. May tend evaporator to purify water. • **GED:** R2, M2, L2 • **SVP:** 3-6 mos • **Academic:** Ed=N, Eng=N • **Work Field:** 014 • **MPSMS:** 875 • **Aptitudes:** G4, V4, N4, S4, P3, Q3, K4, F4, M3, E5, C5 • **Temperaments:** R • **Stress:** T • **Physical:** V=L, H=N, L=L, W, H • **Work Env:** I, N, R • **Salary:** 2 • **Outlook:** 2

GOE: 05.12.08 Lubricating

GARAGE SERVICER, INDUSTRIAL (any ind.) • D.O.T. #915.687-014 • OES #97805 • Services trucks, buses, automobiles, and other automotive equipment used in industrial or commercial establishments: Inspects equipment to ascertain gasoline, oil, and water requirements. Tests batteries and tires. Changes oil and lubricates automotive equipment [LUBRICATion SERVICER (auto. ser.) 915.687-018]. May keep record of gas and oil supplied to each vehicle and gasoline and oil supplies in storage tanks. • **GED:** R2, M1, L1 • **SVP:** 30 days-3 mos • **Academic:** Ed=N, Eng=N • **Work Field:** 033 • **MPSMS:** 591 • **Aptitudes:** G3, V4, N4, S4, P4, Q4, K4, F4, M3, E5, C5 • **Temperaments:** R • **Stress:** T • **Physical:** V=L, H=N, L=M, W, S, H • **Work Env:** I, F • **Salary:** 2 • **Outlook:** 3

LUBRICATION SERVICER (auto. ser.) • D.O.T. #915.687-018 • OES #97805 • GREASER; LUBRICATION TECHNICIAN; OILER. Lubricates moving parts of automotive vehicles, such as automobiles, buses, and trucks: Injects grease into units, such as springs, universal joints, and steering knuckles, using hand or compressed-air powered grease gun. Inspects fluid level of steering gear, power steering reservoir, transmission, differential, rear axle housings, and shackles. Checks air pressure of tires. Lubricates moving parts with specified lubricants. Drains oil from crankcase and refills crankcase with required amount of oil. Sprays leaf springs with lubricant, using spray gun. Adds water to radiator and battery. Replaces oil and air filters. May sell lubrication and safety inspection services and maintain related records on regular customers, following up periodically with telephone, mail, or personal reminders. • **GED:** R2, M1, L1 • **SVP:** 3-6 mos • **Academic:** Ed=N, Eng=N • **Work Field:** 033 • **MPSMS:** 961 • **Aptitudes:** G3, V4, N4, S4, P4, Q4, K3, F4, M3, E5, C5 • **Temperaments:** M, T • **Physical:** V=L, H=N, L=M, W, S, H • **Work Env:** I • **Salary:** 3 • **Outlook:** 3

MARINE OILER (water trans.) • D.O.T. #911.584-010 • OES #97517 • OILER; STRIKER. Oils and greases moving parts, such as gears, shafts, and bearings, of engines and auxiliary equipment used to propel maritime vessels: Examines machinery for specified pressure and flow of lubricants. Fills oilcups on machinery with grease and lubricating oil, according to machinery lubrication instructions. Reads pressure and temperature gages and records data in engineering log. Assists ENGINEER (water trans.) in overhauling and adjusting machinery. May lubricate deck machinery when vessel is unloading cargo. • **GED:** R3, M2, L2 • **SVP:** 3-6 mos • **Academic:** Ed=N, Eng=N • **Work Field:** 033 • **MPSMS:** 568 • **Aptitudes:** G4, V4, N4, S4, P3, Q4, K3, F3, M3, E5, C5 • **Temperaments:** M • **Physical:** V=L, H=N, L=M, W, H • **Work Env:** I, N • **Salary:** 4 • **Outlook:** 2

OILER (any ind.) • D.O.T. #699.687-018 • OES #85128 • BOILER-ROOM HELPER; GREASER; GREASER AND OILER; HOSTLER; LUBRICATOR; MACHINE HOSTLER; OILER AND GREASER. Oils and greases moving parts of friction surfaces of mechanical equipment, such as shaft and motor bearings, sprockets, drive chains, gears, and pulleys, according to specified procedures and oral instructions: Fills container, such as oilcan, grease gun, or tank of lubrication truck with specified lubricant. Squirts or pours oil on moving parts and friction surfaces, or into holes, oil cups, or reservoirs. Turns oil cup valves to regulate flow of oil to moving parts. Forces grease into bearings with grease-gun, smears grease on friction surfaces, or packs grease cups by hand. Fills wells and sumps of lubricating systems with oil. Reports machinery defects or malfunctions to supervisor. May clean machines, sweep floors, and transport stock. May be specified according to type of machine or equipment lubricated. May tend machine that automatically oils parts. • **GED:** R2, M1, L1 • **SVP:** 30 days-3 mos • **Academic:** Ed=N, Eng=N • **Work Field:** 033 • **MPSMS:** 567, 568 • **Aptitudes:** G4, V4, N5, S4, P4, Q5, K4, F3, M3, E5, C5 • **Temperaments:** R • **Physical:** V=L, H=N, L=M, W, S, H • **Work Env:** I, N • **Salary:** 2 • **Outlook:** 3

GOE: 05.12.11 Welding

THERMAL CUTTER, HAND 2 (welding) • D.O.T. #816.684-010 • OES #93914 • SALVAGE CUTTER; SCRAP BURNER; SCRAP CUTTER. Dismantles metal assemblies, such as automobiles, machines, building girders, and pipelines, or cuts scrap metal to size for shipping, using thermal-cutting equipment, such as flame-cutting torch or plasma-arc equipment: Connects hoses from hand torch to cylinders of oxygen and fuel gas, or turns knobs to adjust settings of arc-cutting equipment. Turns handle to open gas valve to specified pressure. Lights torch and adjusts flow of oxygen to obtain desired mixture, as indicated by color and size of flame. Directs flame on workpiece to heat it to oxidizing temperature, as indicated by color of metal. Squeezes lever or trigger to release additional jet of oxygen which cuts path through metal. Guides flame or arc across workpiece and observes cutting action to judge speed of movement. May change cutting tips or adjust gas pressure or arc-welding equipment to cut metal of different types and thickness. May climb ladders or work on scaffolds to disassemble structures. • **GED:** R2, M1, L1 • **SVP:** 2-30 days • **Academic:** Ed=N, Eng=N • **Work Field:** 082 • **MPSMS:** 540 • **Aptitudes:** G4, V4, N5, S4, P4, Q5, K4, F4, M3, E4, C3 • **Temperaments:** R • **Stress:** T • **Physical:** V=L, H=N, L=H, W, C, S, H • **Work Env:**

B, N, R • **Salary:** 2 • **Outlook:** 3

GOE: 05.12.12 Structural Work, Elemental

AUTOMOBILE-BODY-REPAIRER HELPER (auto. ser.) • D.O.T. #807.687-010 • OES #98102 • Performs duties as described under HELPER (any ind.). • **GED:** R2, M1, L1 • **SVP:** 2-30 days • **Academic:** Ed=N, Eng=N • **Work Field:** 102 • **MPSMS:** 591 • **Aptitudes:** G4, V4, N5, S4, P3, Q5, K4, F4, M3, E5, C5 • **Temperaments:** R • **Stress:** T • **Physical:** V=L, H=N, L=M, W, S, H • **Work Env:** I, N • **Salary:** 3 • **Outlook:** 3

BILLPOSTER (any ind.) • D.O.T. #299.667-010 • OES #98999 • SIGN POSTER. Places posters and banners in prominent places to advertise entertainment, political event, or product: Secures permission from owner to place posters and banners on private property. Displays posters in windows of stores, restaurants, and other public places. Fastens banners and posters to fences, poles, and sides of buildings, using paste, twine, tacks and hammer, hand staplers, and ladders. • **GED:** R2, M1, L2 • **SVP:** 2-30 days • **Academic:** Ed=N, Eng=N • **Work Field:** 062, 063, 072 • **MPSMS:** 896 • **Aptitudes:** G4, V4, N4, S4, P4, Q5, K4, F4, M3, E4, C5 • **Temperaments:** R • **Stress:** T • **Physical:** V=N, H=N, L=M, W, C, H • **Work Env:** O • **Salary:** 2 • **Outlook:** 3

DECORATOR, STREET AND BUILDING (any ind.) • D.O.T. #899.687-010 • OES #87899 • Installs decorations, such as flags, lights, and bunting, on streets, on or in buildings, halls, and booths for events, such as parades, conventions, and festivals: Strings and connects electric wiring and lights. Hangs decorations in streets and in or on buildings and structures, using wire, rope, and handtools, working from ladders or elevated truck platforms. Constructs framework to support displays, using woodworking machines and handtools. May build and decorate parade floats and be designated FLOAT BUILDER (any ind.). • **GED:** R2, M1, L1 • **SVP:** 3-6 mos • **Academic:** Ed=N, Eng=N • **Work Field:** 102 • **MPSMS:** 360 • **Aptitudes:** G4, V4, N4, S4, P4, Q4, K3, F3, M3, E5, C4 • **Temperaments:** R, T • **Stress:** T • **Physical:** V=L, H=N, L=V, W, C, S, H • **Work Env:** B, R • **Salary:** 3 • **Outlook:** 3

HIGHWAY-MAINTENANCE WORKER (gov. ser.) • D.O.T. #899.684-014 • OES #87711 • HIGHWAY WORKER. Maintains highways, municipal and rural roads, and rights-of-way in safe condition, performing combination of following duties: Erects and repairs guardrails, highway markers, and snow fences, using handtools and nails, and power tools. Dumps, spreads, and tamps asphalt, using pneumatic tamper to patch broken or eroded pavement. Drives truck [TRUCK DRIVER, HEAVY (any ind.)] to transport crew and equipment to worksite. May drive snow-removal equipment, consisting of truck or tractor equipped with adjustable snowplow and blower unit and be designated SNOW-PLOW OPERATOR, TRUCK (gov. ser.) or SNOW-PLOW TRACTOR OPERATOR (gov. ser.). May drive tractor with mower attachment to cut grass around airfield runways. • **GED:** R3, M1, L2 • **SVP:** 30 days-3 mos • **Academic:** Ed=N, Eng=N • **Work Field:** 091, 095, 102 • **MPSMS:** 362 • **Aptitudes:** G3, V4, N4, S4, P4, Q4, K4, F4, M4, E4, C5 • **Temperaments:** R, T • **Stress:** T • **Physical:** V=L, H=N, L=M, W, S, H • **Work Env:** O, R • **Salary:** 5 • **Outlook:** 2

PIPE-FITTER HELPER (const.) • D.O.T. #862.684-022 • OES #98315 • FITTER HELPER. Assists PIPE FITTER (const.) to assemble and install piping for air, ammonia, gas, and water systems: Cuts or drills holes in walls to permit passage of pipes, using pneumatic drill. Selects specified type and size of pipe. Mounts pipe hangers and brackets on walls and ceiling to hold pipe. Assists PIPE FITTER (const.) to install valves, couplings, and other fittings. May disassemble and remove damaged or worn pipe. Performs other duties as described under HELPER (any ind.). May assist in installation of high-pressure piping and be designated STEAM-FITTER HELPER (const.). May assist in installation of gas burner to convert furnaces from wood, coal, or oil and be designated FURNACE INSTALLER HELPER (light, heat, & power). • **GED:** R2, M1, L2 • **SVP:** 30 days-3 mos • **Academic:** Ed=N, Eng=N • **Work Field:** 102 • **MPSMS:** 364 • **Aptitudes:** G4, V4, N4, S3, P3, Q4, K4, F4, M3, E4, C5 • **Temperaments:** R, T • **Stress:** T • **Physical:** V=L, H=N, L=H, W, C, S, H • **Work**

Env: B, N • **Salary: 2** • **Outlook: 2**
SEWER-LINE REPAIRER (sanitary ser.) • D.O.T. #869.664-018
• OES #87511 • Repairs and maintains municipal storm and
sanitary sewer lines, performing any combination of following
tasks: Inspects manholes to locate stoppage. Runs cleaning rods
through rod guide, fits front end of rod with auger, using wrench,
and lowers guide into position. Thrusts rods into invert and advances them until auger reaches obstruction. Rotates rods manually with turning pin, or attaches end of rod to portable power
rodder to rotate rods. Pulls lever and depresses pedal of machine
to advance cleaning tool to encounter obstruction and to rotate
cable or rods until obstacle is broken. Retracts rods to drag out
obstructions, such as roots, grease, and other deposits. Cleans and
repairs catch basins, manholes, culverts, and storm drains, using
handtools. Lays brick to raise manhole walls to prescribed street
level, using masonry tools. Measures distance of excavation site,
using tape measure, and marks outline of area to be trenched
according to direction of supervisor. Breaks asphalt and other
pavement, using airhammer, pick, and shovel. Cuts damaged
section of pipe with cutters and removes broken section from ditch.
Replaces broken pipes and reconnects pipe sections, using pipe
sleeve. Inspects joints to ensure tightness and seal before backfill-
ing. Packs backfilled excavation, using air and gasoline tamper.
Taps mainline sewers to install sewer saddles. Replaces manhole
covers. Updates sewer maps and manhole charting. Drives pickup
trucks to haul crew, materials, and equipment. Services, adjusts,
and makes minor repairs to equipment, machines, and attachments. Communicates with supervisor and other workers, using
radio telephone. Pre pares records showing actions taken, manpower and equipment utilization, and disposition of material.
Requisitions tools and equipment. Operates sewer cleaning equipment including power rodder, high velocity water jet, sewer flusher,
bucket machine, wayne ball, and vac-all. Cleans and disinfects
domestic basements and other areas flooded as a result of sewer
stoppages. May lead workers in large repair and construction crew
and direct other workers in efficient and safe use of machines, work
methods, and safety procedures. • **GED:** R3, M2, L2 • **SVP:** 1-2
yrs • **Academic:** Ed=N, Eng=N • **Work Field:** 031, 102 •
MPSMS: 369 • **Aptitudes:** G3, V3, N3, S2, P3, Q4, K3, F3, M3,
E4, C4 • **Temperaments:** R, T, V • **Stress:** T • **Physical:** V=L,
H=N, L=H, W, C, S, H • **Work Env:** I, W, R, F • **Salary:** 4 •
Outlook: 3
SEWER-PIPE CLEANER (bus. ser.) • D.O.T. #899.664-014 •
OES #87511 • ELECTRIC-SEWER-CLEANING-MACHINE OP-
ERATOR. Removes roots, debris, and other refuse from clogged
sewerlines and drains, using portable electric sewer cleaning machine, and repairs breaks in underground piping: Positions or
disassembles sewer trap machine at sewer or drain outlet. Removes drain cover, using wrench. Installs rotary knives on flexible
cable, mounted on reel of machine, according to diameter of pipe
to be cleaned. Starts machine to feed revolving cable into opening,
stopping machine and changing knives as necessary to conform to
diameter or contour of pipe. Withdraws cable to deposit accumulated residue removed from pipe in containers for disposal. Observes residue for evidence of mud, indicating broken sewerline.
Measures distance from sewer opening to suspected break, using
plumbers' snake, tapeline, or by estimating position of cutting head
within sewer. Notifies coworkers to dig out ruptured line or digs
out shallow sewers, using shovel. Removes and replaces broken tile
section or pipe, using calking compound and cement to form
watertight joint. Replaces or directs replacement of earth. Replaces
dull knives and performs repairs on machine, using handtools.
May estimate cost of service to customer. May clean sewage collection points and sanitary lines in streets and sewage plants. • **GED:**
R3, M1, L2 • **SVP:** 30 days-3 mos • **Academic:** Ed=N, Eng=N •
Work Field: 031, 102 • **MPSMS:** 364 • **Aptitudes:** G3, V4, N4,
S2, P3, Q4, K3, F4, M3, E5, C5 • **Temperaments:** R, T • **Stress:**
T • **Physical:** V=L, H=N, L=M, W, S, H • **Work Env:** B, W •
Salary: 3 • **Outlook:** 3
TRACK REPAIRER (r.r. trans.) • D.O.T. #910.682-010 • OES
#87714 • SECTION-GANG WORKER. Operates railroad track
maintenance equipment, such as portable grinder, spike puller,
spike driver, and tieadzer to grind ends of rails, remove old spikes,
drive new spikes, cutties to fit fishplates, and perform related

maintenance, working as member of crew: Operates single-or
multiple-head spike puller to pull old spikes from tie. Raises rail,
using hydraulic jack, to facilitate removal of old tie and installation
of new tie. Operates tie-adzing machine to cut portion of tie so that
tie plate can be inserted to hold rail. Drills holes through rails, tie
plates, and fish plates for insertion of bolts and spike, using power
drill. Operates single-or multiple-head spike driving machine to
drive spike into tie and secure rail. Operates track-wrench machine to tighten or loosen bolts at joints that hold ends of rails
together. Operates rail saw to cut rails to specified lengths. Operates portable grinder to grind worn ends of rails. Sprays ties, fish
plates, and joints with oil to protect them from weather. May paint
railroad signs, such as speed limits and gate-crossing warnings.
May oversee workers and act as section leader. • **GED:** R3, M2, L2
• **SVP:** 3-6 mos • **Academic:** Ed=N, Eng=N • **Work Field:** 102 •
MPSMS: 367 • **Aptitudes:** G3, V4, N4, S3, P4, Q4, K3, F4, M3,
E4, C5 • **Temperaments:** M, T, V • **Physical:** V=L, H=N, L=H,
W, S, H • **Work Env:** O, N • **Sal ary:** 4 • **Outlook:** 3

WINDOW REPAIRER (any ind.) • D.O.T. #899.684-042 • OES
#85999 • Repairs and adjusts metal and wooden casement win-
dows, storm windows and doors, and jalousies, using handtools and
portable power tools: Repairs or replaces locks, hinges, and cranks.
Realines windows and screens to fit casements. Oils moving parts
of sections. May cut and install glass. May paint windows, using
brush or spray equipment. • **GED:** R2, M1, L1 • **SVP:** 3-6 mos •
Academic: Ed=N, Eng=N • **Work Field:** 102 • **MPSMS:** 452, 554
• **Aptitudes:** G3, V4, N4, S4, P3, Q4, K4, F4, M3, E5, C5 •
Temperaments: R, T • **Stress:** T • **Physical:** V=L, H=N, L=M,
W, S, H • **Work Env:** I • **Salary:** 3 • **Outlook:** 3

GOE: 05.12.13 Cutting & Finishing

KEY CUTTER (any ind.) • D.O.T. #709.684-050 • OES #92198 •
KEY MAKER; KEYSMITH; KEY WORKER. Cuts notches in key
blanks to duplicate notches of original key, using key-duplicating
machine: Selects key blank according to size, shape, or code number of original key. Positions original key and blank in vises on
carriage of machine and against guides. Turns thumbscrews to
secure key and blank in vises. Starts cutting disk of machine.
Pushes and pulls horizontally moving carriage of machine to slide
notched edge of original key against stationary guide on machine
and to move key blank against cutting disk, duplicating notches of
original key in bit of blank. Turns thumb screws and removes keys
from vises. Presses and holds duplicated key against revolving wire
wheel to remove burs from key. Positions one key atop the other to
compare notches of keys. May collect payment from customer and
make change. May sell key holders or related novelty items. •
GED: R2, M2, L2 • **SVP:** 2-30 days • **Academic:** Ed=N, Eng=N
• **Work Field:** 055 • **MPSMS:** 552 • **Aptitudes:** G4, V4, N4, S3,
P3, Q4, K3, F4, M3, E5, C5 • **Temperaments:** R, T • **Stress:** T •
Physical: V=L, H=N, L=L, H • **Work Env:** I, N • **Salary:** 2 •
Outlook: 3

GOE: 05.12.14 Painting, Caulking & Coating, Elemental

ASPHALT-DISTRIBUTOR TENDER (const.) • D.O.T.
#853.665-010 • OES #87899 • OIL-DISTRIBUTOR TENDER.
Tends bituminous distributor on rear of road-oiling truck that
sprays tar, asphalt, road oils, and emulsions over highways,
streets, and parking areas: Snaps or screws on spray bars to attain
re quired width of spray. Turns valve to regulate flow of material
at specified rate. Moves levers to adjust height of spray bar from
road surfaces. Signals ROAD-OILING-TRUCK DRIVER (const.)
or ASPHALT-PAVING-MACHINE OPERATOR (const.) to start
and stop truck or paving machine. Observes distribution of material over road surface to ensure uniform distribution. Turns handwheels to set angle and depth of screed. Verifies depth specifications of compacted asphalt, using depth gage. Monitors flow gages,
tachometer, and temperature gage. Oils and lubricates equipment.
• **GED:** R2, M2, L1 • **SVP:** 2-30 days • **Aca demic:** Ed=N, Eng=N
• **Work Field:** 091, 095, 153 • **MPSMS:** 362 • **Aptitudes:** G4, V4,
N4, S4, P3, Q4, K3, F4, M3, E5, C5 • **Temperaments:** R, T •
Stress: T • **Physical:** V=L, H=N, L=L, W, H • **Work Env:** O, N,
R • **Salary:** 4 • **Outlook:** 3

BILLPOSTER (bus. ser.) • D.O.T. #841.684-010 • OES #98999 • Attaches advertising posters on surfaces, such as walls and billboards, using handtools: Removes old poster, using scraping tool. Mixes paste-powder with water to form paste. Smears paste on wall or billboard surface, using brush. Alines poster sections on billboard and smooths sections, using long-handled brush. Staples or tacks posters on fences, walls, or poles. Climbs ladder to work from deck at bottom of elevated billboard. May work from scaffolding. • **GED:** R2, M1, L1 • **SVP:** 2-30 days • **Academic:** Ed=N, Eng=N • **Work Field:** 063 • **MPSMS:** 896 • **Aptitudes:** G4, V4, N5, S3, P3, Q4, K3, F4, M3, E4, C4 • **Temperaments:** R, T • **Stress:** T • **Physical:** V=L, H=N, L=L, W, C, S, H • **Work Env:** O, R • **Salary:** 2 • **Outlook:** 3

SHOE DYER (per. ser.) • D.O.T. #364.684-014 • OES #93999 • SHOE TINTER. Dyes or tints shoes for customers of shoe repair or shoe shining shops: Inserts shoetree or stuffs paper into shoe to stiffen shoe upper, forming smooth working surface on shoe. Cleans shoes with acetone, alcohol, water, or other solutions to remove dirt, dye, and grease, using brushes, cloths, and sponges. Selects prepared dye or mixes dyes to match shade specified by instructions or color chart. Applies coat of dye or tint onto shoe upper, using spray gun or swab. Ignites dye on shoe to drive dye into leather. • **GED:** R2, M2, L1 • **SVP:** 30 days-3 mos • **Academic:** Ed=N, Eng=N • **Work Field:** 152 • **MPSMS:** 961 • **Aptitudes:** G4, V4, N4, S5, P3, Q4, K4, F3, M3, E5, C2 • **Temperaments:** J, R, T • **Stress:** T • **Physical:** V=L, H=N, L=L, H • **Work Env:** I • **Salary:** 2 • **Outlook:** 2

STEEL-PLATE CALKER (any ind.) • D.O.T. #843.684-010 • OES #93999 • CALKER. Calks seams between plates of boilers, tanks, pressure vessels, or ships to make them watertight: Connects airhose to calking hammer and inserts calking chisel in hammer socket. Positions chisel on edge of seam and presses trigger of hammer to pound edge of overlapping plate into surface of adjoining plate to seal seam. May use hand calking tool to close seams. • **GED:** R2, M1, L1 • **SVP:** 3-6 mos • **Academic:** Ed=N, Eng=N • **Work Field:** 094 • **MPSMS:** 554, 593 • **Aptitudes:** G4, V4, N5, S4, P4, Q5, K3, F4, M3, E4, C5 • **Temperaments:** R • **Stress:** T • **Physical:** V=L, H=N, L=M, W, C, S, H • **Work Env:** B, N • **Salary:** 3 • **Outlook:** 2

STOVE REFINISHER (any ind.) • D.O.T. #749.684-046 • OES #93947 • Cleans, removes rust, polishes, and enamels used stoves and ranges: Dips stove or range shell and fittings into caustic solution which removes dirt and grease, using block and tackle. Transfers dipped article to drying oven. Removes rust from parts, using power-driven rotary wire buffer, and polishes brightwork surfaces on polishing wheel. Dips parts or article in enamel vat, using hoist, and transfers article to drying oven for prescribed time. May similarly refinish other articles, such as refrigerator cabinets, washing machines, and clothes driers. • **GED:** R2, M1, L1 • **SVP:** 30 days-3 mos • **Academic:** Ed=N, Eng=N • **Work Field:** 031, 051, 151 • **MPSMS:** 583 • **Aptitudes:** G4, V4, N4, S3, P3, Q4, K3, F4, M3, E5, C4 • **Temperaments:** R, T • **Stress:** T • **Physical:** V=L, H=N, L=H, W, S, H • **Work Env:** I • **Salary:** 3 • **Outlook:** 2

UNDERCOATER (auto. ser.) • D.O.T. #843.684-014 • OES #93947 • RUST PROOFER. Sprays protective compound onto chassis and underbody of automobiles and trucks to minimize rust and corrosion and to eliminate noise: Drives vehicle onto overhead rack. Removes headlights and other accessories, using handtools. Steam cleans or pressure washes underside of vehicle preparatory to application of protective compound. Drills holes for interior spraying as required, using electric drill. Sprays specified areas of vehicle, using spray gun. Inserts plastic plugs to reseal holes subsequent to spraying. Replaces accesso ries and removes overspray and excess seepage from body seams and joints, using cloth and solvents. May mask painted or chromed surfaces to prevent exposure to undercoating spray, using tape. May spray firewall, underside of hood, and interior of trunk compartment. • **GED:** R2, M1, L1 • **SVP:** 30 days-3 mos • **Academic:** Ed=N, Eng=N • **Work Field:** 031, 153 • **MPSMS:** 499, 961 • **Aptitudes:** G4, V4, N5, S3, P3, Q5, K4, F4, M3, E4, C5 • **Temperaments:** R, T • **Stress:** T • **Physical:** V=L, H=N, L=L, W, S, H • **Work Env:** I • **Salary:** 4 • **Outlook:** 2

GOE: 05.12.15 Mechanical Work, Elemental

AUTOMOBILE WRECKER (whole. tr.) • D.O.T. #620.684-010 • OES #85999 • WRECKING MECHANIC. Salvages usable parts from wrecked cars and trucks in auto salvage yard: Dismantles vehicles, using handtools, bolt cutters, and oxyacetylene torch. Cleans parts, using solvents and brush, or vapor-degreasing machine, and stores parts in bins according to condition and part number. Sorts, piles, and loads scrap on railroad cars or trucks. May drive tow-truck. May sell automobile glass, tires, and parts. • **GED:** R3, M2, L2 • **SVP:** 3-6 mos • **Academic:** Ed=N, Eng=N • **Work Field:** 121, 211 • **MPSMS:** 591 • **Aptitudes:** G4, V4, N4, S4, P4, Q4, K3, F3, M3, E5, C5 • **Temperaments:** V • **Physical:** V=L, H=N, L=H, W, C, S • **Work Env:** B • **Salary:** 3 • **Outlook:** 3

BELT REPAIRER (any ind.) • D.O.T. #630.684-014 • OES #85128 • Repairs and replaces canvas, leather, or rubber belts used to drive machinery and convey materials: Examines belts for defects and cuts out defective sections, using knife. Cuts strip of unused belting material, using knife. Clamps metal fasteners to ends of belt, using pincers, or splices ends of belt, using splicing machine. Positions repaired belt on pulleys. Applies dressing compound to belt to prevent slippage. May patch and sew defective areas of belts, using needle and thread. May specialize in repairing conveyor belts and be designated CONVEYOR-BELT REPAIRER (any ind.). • **GED:** R2, M1, L1 • **SVP:** 3-6 mos • **Academic:** Ed=N, Eng=N • **Work Field:** 121 • **MPSMS:** 568 • **Aptitudes:** G4, V4, N4, S4, P4, Q4, K4, F4, M3, E5, C5 • **Temperaments:** R, T • **Stress:** T • **Physical:** V=L, H=N, L=L, S, H • **Work Env:** I, N • **Salary:** 3 • **Outlook:** 2

ROLLER-SKATE REPAIRER (any ind.) • D.O.T. #732.684-102 • OES #85999 • Repairs roller skates by disassembling skates, and cleaning and replacing bearings, wheels, and other worn parts, using handtools and power tools. May repair attached shoes and leather straps. • **GED:** R2, M2, L1 • **SVP:** 3-6 mos • **Academic:** Ed=N, Eng=N • **Work Field:** 121 • **MPSMS:** 616 • **Aptitudes:** G4, V4, N4, S4, P4, Q4, K4, F3, M3, E5, C5 • **Temperaments:** R, T • **Stress:** T • **Physical:** V=L, H=N, L=L, H • **Work Env:** I • **Salary:** 3 • **Outlook:** 2

TIRE REPAIRER (auto. ser.) • D.O.T. #915.684-010 • OES #85953 • TIRE-AND-TUBE REPAIRER; TIRE-AND-TUBE SERVICER; TIRE FIXER; TIRE SERVICER. Repairs damaged tires of automobiles, buses, trucks, and other automotive vehicles: Raises vehicle, using hydraulic jack, and unbolts wheel, using lug wrench. Removes wheel from vehicle by hand or, when repairing giant tires of heavy equipment, by use of power hoist. Locates puncture in tubeless tire by visual inspection or by immersing inflated tire in water bath and observing air bubbles emerging from puncture. Seals puncture in tubeless tire by inserting adhesive material and expanding rubber plug into puncture, using handtools. Separates tubed tire from wheel, using rubber mallet and metal bar or mechanical tire changer. Removes inner tube from tire and inspects tire casing for defects, such as holes and tears. Glues boot (tire patch) over rupture in tire casing, using rubber cement. Inflates inner tube and immerses it in water to locate leak. Buffs defective area of inner tube, using scraper, and patches tube with adhesive rubber patch or seals rubber patch to tube, using hot vulcanizing plate. Reassembles tire onto wheel, and places wheel on balancing machine to determine counterweights required to balance wheel. Hammers required counter weights onto rim of wheel. Cleans sides of white wall tires and remounts wheel onto vehicle. Responds to emergency calls to make repairs or replacements of damaged tires at customer's home or on road. May be designated according to specialty as GIANT-TIRE REPAIRER (auto. ser.); TIRE CHANGER (auto. ser.); TIRE CHANGER, AIRCRAFT (air trans.); TIRE CHANGER, ROAD SERVICE (auto. ser.). • **GED:** R2, M1, L1 • **SVP:** 30 days-3 mos • **Academic:** Ed=N, Eng=N • **Work Field:** 121 • **MPSMS:** 511 • **Aptitudes:** G4, V4, N4, S3, P3, Q4, K3, F4, M3, E4, C5 • **Temperaments:** M • **Physical:** V=L, H=N, L=H, W, S, H • **Work Env:** I • **Salary:** 3 • **Outlook:** 3

GOE: 05.12.16 Electrical Work, Elemental

ANTENNA INSTALLER (any ind.) • D.O.T. #823.684-010 • OES #87899 • Installs antennas for radio or television receiving sets: Sets up wooden or metal mast and secures in place with guy wires and base plate, using handtools. Attaches single dipole antenna to mast for FM radio reception or antenna composed of several directors plus dipole antenna and reflector for television reception. Positions antenna with direc tors toward station transmitters or toward reflection point to obtain optimum signal. Attaches lead-in wire to dipole antenna and other end to set. May install lightning arrester on lead-in wire. • **GED:** R3, M2, L2 • **SVP:** 3-6 mos • **Academic:** Ed=N, Eng=N • **Work Field:** 111 • **MPSMS:** 584 • **Aptitudes:** G3, V4, N5, S3, P3, Q5, K3, F3, M3, E2, C4 • **Temperaments:** R, T • **Stress:** T • **Physical:** V=L, H=N, L=M, W, C, S, H • **Work Env:** O, R • **Salary:** 4 • **Out look:** 2

CABLE PULLER (const.) • D.O.T. #829.684-018 • OES #93999 • CABLE PLACER; CABLE RIGGER. Pulls lead-sheathed electrical cables for electric power systems through ducts: Pushes long, flexible, steel ribbon (fish tape) or rods through duct. Attaches wire to rod or fish tape and pulls wire through duct. Attaches wire to cable and pulls cable through duct by hand or using winch. May pull ball or mandrel through duct to ensure clear passage for cable. • **GED:** R2, M1, L1 • **SVP:** 3-6 mos • **Academic:** Ed=N, Eng=N • **Work Field:** 011, 111 • **MPSMS:** 544, 557, 871 • **Aptitudes:** G4, V4, N5, S4, P4, Q5, K4, F4, M3, E3, C5 • **Temperaments:** R • **Stress:** T • **Physical:** V=L, H=N, L=H, W, C, S, H • **Work Env:** B • **Sal ary:** 4 • **Outlook:** 3

ELECTRICAL-APPLIANCE PREPARER (any ind.) • D.O.T. #827.584-010 • OES #93956 • UNCRATER. Assembles and tests electrical appliances, such as ranges, refrigerators, and washing machines, to prepare appliance for delivery and installation, using handtools and test lamp: Uncrates appliances, using pry bar, wire cutters, and nail puller. Assembles appliance parts, using screws and handtools. Connects appliance to electric current to test performance. Locates faulty circuits with test lamp. Solders and wraps wires with friction tape to repair insulation. Washes and polishes appliances. Examines exterior of appliance for chips, scratches, and dents. Keeps records of appliances received, assembled, and delivered. May be designated according to type of appliance assembled and tested as DISHWASHER PREPARER (any ind.); ELECTRIC-RANGE PREPARER (any ind.); ELECTRIC-REFRIGERATOR PREPARER (any ind.); WASHER-DRIER PREPARER (any ind.). • **GED:** R2, M2, L2 • **SVP:** 30 days-3 mos • **Academic:** Ed=N, Eng=N • **Work Field:** 061, 211 • **MPSMS:** 583 • **Aptitudes:** G3, V4, N4, S4, P4, Q4, K4, F4, M3, E5, C4 • **Temperaments:** R, T • **Stress:** T • **Physical:** V=N, H=N, L=H, W, S, H • **Work Env:** I • **Salary:** 4 • **Outlook:** 3

LIGHTING-EQUIPMENT OPERATOR (amuse. & rec.) • D.O.T. #962.381-014 • OES #39999 • ELECTRICIAN, FRONT. Controls lighting equipment, such as floodlamps, strip lights, and spotlights from projection room and front or backstage areas of theater to cast spotlight on stage performers: Places spotlights in specified locations in theater and connects wiring for lighting. Moves spotlight to follow movements of performers with beam of light, according to instructions on prepared cue sheet. Turns color wheel, causing light to be diffused through varicol ored gelatin disks to change color of light. Cleans and adjusts light, replacing carbons or bulbs as needed. May insert varicolored gelatin sheets in frame to assemble color wheel. • **GED:** R4, M2, L3 • **SVP:** 1-2 yrs • **Academic:** Ed=N, Eng=S • **Work Field:** 111 • **MPSMS:** 912 • **Aptitudes:** G3, V3, N4, S3, P3, Q4, K3, F3, M3, E4, C3 • **Temperaments:** M, T • **Physical:** V=L, H=N, L=L, S, H • **Work Env:** I • **Salary:** 4 • **Outlook:** 2

GOE: 05.12.17 Food Preparation, Elemental

COFFEE MAKER (hotel & rest.) • D.O.T. #317.684-010 • OES #65038 • COFFEE-URN ATTENDANT. Brews coffee, tea, and chocolate, using coffee urns, drip or vacuum coffee makers, teapots, drink mixers, and other kitchen equipment. Performs various duties to assist in filling customers' orders, such as cooking hot cakes and waffles, boiling eggs, and making toast [PANTRY GOODS MAKER (hotel & rest.)]. Cleans and polishes utensils and equipment used in food and beverage preparation. May serve coffee. May prepare and issue iced beverages, such as coffee, tea, and fountain or bottled drinks, to be served by COUNTER ATTENDANT, LUNCHROOM OR COFFEE SHOP (hotel & rest.). • **GED:** R2, M1, L1 • **SVP:** 2-30 days • **Academic:** Ed=N, Eng=N • **Work Field:** 146 • **MPSMS:** 903 • **Aptitudes:** G4, V4, N4, S4, P4, Q4, K3, F4, M3, E5, C4 • **Temperaments:** R, T • **Stress:** T • **Physical:** V=L, H=N, L=M, W, H • **Work Env:** I, R • **Salary:** 2 • **Outlook:** 3

COOK HELPER (hotel & rest.) • D.O.T. #317.687- 010 • OES #65038 • Assists workers engaged in preparing foods for hotels, restaurants, or ready-to-serve packages by performing any combination of the following tasks: Washes, peels, cuts, and seeds vegetables and fruits. Cleans, cuts, and grinds meats, poultry, and seafood. Dips food items in crumbs, flour, and batter to bread them. Stirs and strains soups and sauces. Weighs and measures designated ingredients. Carries pans, kettles, and trays of food to and from work stations, stove, and refrigerator. Stores foods in designated areas, utilizing knowledge of temperature requirements and food spoilage. Cleans work areas, equipment and utensils, segregates and removes garbage, and steam-cleans or hoses garbage containers [KITCHEN HELPER (hotel & rest.)]. Distributes supplies, utensils, and portable equipment, using handtruck. May be designated according to worker assisted as COOK HELPER, BROILER OR FRY (hotel & rest.); COOK HELPER, DESSERT (hotel & rest.); COOK HELPER, VEGETABLE (hotel & rest.); PANTRY GOODS MAKER HELPER (hotel & rest.). Performs other duties as described under HELPER (any ind.). • **GED:** R2, M1, L1 • **SVP:** 2-30 days • **Academic:** Ed=N, Eng=N • **Work Field:** 031, 146 • **MPSMS:** 903 • **Aptitudes:** G4, V4, N4, S4, P4, Q4, K4, F4, M3, E5, C4 • **Temperaments:** R • **Stress:** T • **Physical:** V=L, H=N, L=M, W, H • **Work Env:** I • **Salary:** 2 • **Outlook:** 4

DELI CUTTER-SLICER (ret. tr.) • D.O.T. #316.684-014 • OES #65038 • Cuts delicatessen meats and cheeses, using slicing machine, knives, or other cutters: Places meat or cheese on cutting board and cuts slices to designated thickness, using knives or other hand cutters. Positions and clamps meat or cheese on carriage of slicing machine. Adjusts knob to set machine for desired thickness. Presses button to start motor that moves carriage past rotary blade that slices meats and cheeses. Stacks cut pieces on tray or platter, separating portions with paper. May weigh and wrap sliced foods and affix sticker showing price and weight. • **GED:** R2, M2, L1 • **SVP:** 2-30 days • **Academic:** Ed=N, Eng=N • **Work Field:** 054 • **MPSMS:** 382, 383, 881 • **Aptitudes:** G4, V4, N4, S4, P3, Q4, K3, F3, M3, E5, C4 • **Temperaments:** R, T • **Stress:** T • **Physical:** V=L, H=N, L=L, W, H • **Work Env:** I, R • **Salary:** 2 • **Outlook:** 4

FOOD ASSEMBLER, KITCHEN (hotel & rest.) • D.O.T. #319.484-010 • OES #65038 • DINING-SERVICE WORKER; FOOD ASSEMBLER, COMMISSARY KITCHEN; FOOD-TRAY ASSEMBLER; SUPPLY SERVICE WORKER; TRAY SETTER. Prepares meal trays in commissary kitchen for inflight service of airlines, multiunit restaurant chains, industrial caterers, or educational, hospital, and similar institutions, performing any combination of following duties: Reads charts to determine amount and kind of foods and supplies to be packaged. Fills individual serving cartons with portions of various foods and condiments, such as cream, jams, and sauces, by hand or using automatic filling machine. Portions and garnishes hot cooked foods, such as meat and vegetables, into individual serving dishes. Stores dishes of hot food on shelves of portable electric warming cabinet or food cart for stowing aboard airplane or transfer to restaurant or cafeteria dining unit. Removes pans of portioned salads, desserts, rolls, cream, and other cold food items from refrigerator or pantry, and places at appropriate stations of tray assembly counter to facilitate loading meal trays. Places food items, silverware, and dishes in depression of compartmented food tray passing on conveyor belt. Examines filled tray for completeness and appearance, and stores completed trays in refrigerated storage cabinets to be transported to airplane, dining room, or cafeteria. May be designated according to type of food assembled as APPETIZER PACKER (hotel & rest.); CASSEROLE PREPARER (hotel & rest.); COLD-FOOD PACKER (hotel & rest.); HOT-FOOD

PACKER (hotel & rest.). • **GED:** R2, M2, L1 • **SVP:** 30 days-3 mos • **Academic:** Ed=N, Eng=N • **Work Field:** 146 • **MPSMS:** 903 • **Aptitudes:** G4, V4, N4, S4, P3, Q4, K3, F3, M3, E5, C4 • **Temperaments:** R, T • **Stress:** T • **Physical:** V=N, H=N, L=S, W, H • **Work Env:** I • **Salary:** 1 • **Outlook:** 4

SANDWICH MAKER (hotel & rest.) • D.O.T. #317.684-018 • OES #65038 • SANDWICH-COUNTER ATTENDANT. Prepares sandwiches to individual order of customers: Slices cold meats and cheese by hand or machine. Cuts bread and sandwich buns and toasts them on grill or in electric toaster, when requested. Butters bread and places meat or filling and garnish, such as chopped or sliced onion and lettuce, between bread slices. Prepares garnishes for sandwiches, such as sliced tomatoes and pickles. May cook, mix, and season ingredients to make dressings, fillings, and spreads. May fry hamburgers, bacon, steaks, and eggs for hot sandwiches. • **GED:** R2, M1, L1 • **SVP:** 2-30 days • **Academic:** Ed=N, Eng=N • **Work Field:** 146 • **MPSMS:** 903 • **Aptitudes:** G4, V4, N4, S4, P4, Q5, K3, F3, M3, E5, C5 • **Temperaments:** R, T • **Stress:** T • **Physical:** V=N, H=N, L=M, W, H • **Work Env:** I • **Salary:** 1 • **Outlook:** 4

GOE: 05.12.18 Cleaning & Maintenance, Mechanical

ATTENDANT, CAMPGROUND (amuse. & rec.) • D.O.T. #329.683-010 • OES #67099 • CAMPGROUND HAND. Performs general maintenance on facilities and grounds at recreational camp or park: Operates riding lawn mower to mow grass. Checks buildings and furnishings, repairs minor damage, using handtools, and reports major repair needs to DIRECTOR, CAMP (social ser.). Replaces light bulbs. Carries and places supplies in storage areas. Cleans swimming pool, using vacuum cleaner and scrub brushes. Measures and pours chemicals into pool water to maintain chemical balance. Performs minor repairs to dock, and keeps lakefront swimming area clean and free from hazards. Drives truck to pick up trash and garbage and deliver to central area. • **GED:** R2, M1, L1 • **SVP:** 2-30 days • **Academic:** Ed=N, Eng=N • **Work Field:** 003, 013, 031 • **MPSMS:** 969 • **Aptitudes:** G4, V4, N4, S4, P4, Q5, K4, F4, M3, E4, C5 • **Temperaments:** V • **Physical:** V=L, H=N, L=M, W, C, S, H • **Work Env:** O • **Salary:** 2 • **Outlook:** 2

AUTOMOBILE DETAILER (auto. ser.) • D.O.T. #915.687-034 • OES #98905 • Cleans and refurbishes new and used automobiles, performing any combination of following duties: Washes vehicle exterior to clean cars, using cleaning solution, water, cloths, and brushes. Applies wax to auto body, and wipes or buffs surfaces to protect surfaces and preserve shine, using cloth or buffing machine. Vacuums interiors of vehicles to remove loose dirt and debris, using vacuum cleaner. Cleans upholstery, rugs, and other surfaces, using cleaning agents, applicators, and cleaning devices. Applies revitalizers and preservatives to vinyl or leather surfaces, and treats fabrics with spot and stain resistant chemicals to preserve and protect interior components. Cleans engine and engine compartment with steam cleaning equipment and various cleaning agents to remove grease and grime. Applies special purpose cleaners to remove foreign materials which do not respond to normal cleaning procedures, utilizing experience and following recommendations of product manufacturer. Paints engine components and related parts, using spray gun or aerosol can and masking material. Applies paint to chipped body surfaces of vehicle, using container of touchup paint. Applies dyes and reconditioning chemical to vinyl tops of vehicle to restore color and condition. • **GED:** R2, M1, L1 • **SVP:** 2-30 days • **Academic:** Ed=N, Eng=N • **Work Field:** 031 • **MPSMS:** 960 • **Aptitudes:** G4, V4, N4, S5, P4, Q5, K4, F4, M4, E5, C4 • **Temperaments:** R • **Stress:** T • **Physical:** V=L, H=N, L=M, W, S, H • **Work Env:** I, N, F • **Salary:** 3 • **Outlook:** 4

BARTENDER HELPER (hotel & rest.) • D.O.T. #312.687-010 • OES #65014 • BAR PORTER; BAR RUNNER. Cleans bar and equipment, and replenishes bar supplies, such as liquor, fruit, ice, and dishes: Stocks refrigerating units with wines and bottled beer. Replaces empty beer kegs with full ones. Slices and pits fruit used to garnish drinks. Washes glasses, bar, and equipment, and polishes bar fixtures. Mops floors. Removes empty bottles and trash. May mix and prepare flavors for mixed drinks. • **GED:** R2, M1, L1

• **SVP:** 2-30 days • **Academic:** Ed=N, Eng=N • **Work Field:** 011, 031 • **MPSMS:** 903 • **Aptitudes:** G4, V4, N4, S4, P4, Q4, K4, F4, M4, E4, C5 • **Temperaments:** R • **Physical:** V=N, H=N, L=M, W, S, H • **Work Env:** I • **Salary:** 1 • **Outlook:** 3

CARETAKER (dom. ser.) • D.O.T. #301.687-010 • OES #00000 • ODD-JOB WORKER. Performs any combination of the following duties in keeping private home clean and in good condition: Cleans and dusts furnishings, hallways, and lavatories. Beats and vacuums rugs and scrubs them with cleaning solutions. Washes windows and waxes and polishes floors. Removes and hangs draperies. Cleans and oils furnace. Shovels coal into furnace and removes ashes. Replaces light switches and repairs broken screens, latches, or doors. Paints exterior structures, such as fences, garages, and sheds. May drive family car. May mow and rake lawn. May groom and exercise pets. When duties are confined to upkeep of house, may be designated as HOUSE WORKER (dom. ser.). • **GED:** R2, M1, L2 • **SVP:** 2-30 days • **Academic:** Ed=N, Eng=N • **Work Field:** 031 • **MPSMS:** 901, 909 • **Aptitudes:** G4, V4, N4, S4, P4, Q5, K4, F4, M3, E4, C5 • **Temperaments:** V • **Physical:** V=L, H=N, L=M, W, C, S, H • **Work Env:** B • **Salary:** 1 • **Outlook:** 3

CENTRAL-SUPPLY WORKER (medical ser.) • D.O.T. #381.687-010 • OES #58023 • CENTRAL-SUPPLY AIDE. Cleans, sterilizes, and assembles hospital equipment, supplies, and instruments according to prescribed procedures and techniques performing any combination of following tasks: Scrubs and washes surgical instruments, containers, and syringes and equipment, such as aspirators, croupettes, and oxygen suppliers. Sterilizes instruments, equipment, surgical linens, and supplies, such as surgical packs, treatment trays, and syringes, using autoclave, water sterilizer, or antiseptic solutions. Prepares packs of supplies and instruments, and dressing and treatment trays, according to designated lists or codes, and wraps, labels, and seals packs. Sharpens hypodermic needles, using hone or abrasive wheel, and matches syringe barrels and plungers, according to size, trade names, or serial number. Stores prepared articles and supplies in designated areas. May fill requisitions, write charges, and inventory supplies. May prepare solutions according to prescribed formula. May be assigned to such hospital rooms as surgery and delivery rooms. May be required to hold Practical Nurse license. • **GED:** R2, M1, L2 • **SVP:** 30 days-3 mos • **Academic:** Ed=H, Eng=N • **Work Field:** 031, 221 • **MPSMS:** 604, 924 • **Aptitudes:** G4, V4, N4, S4, P4, Q4, K4, F3, M3, E5, C4 • **Temperaments:** T, V • **Physical:** V=L, H=N, L=L, W, H • **Work Env:** I • **Salary:** 2 • **Outlook:** 3

CHANGE-HOUSE ATTENDANT (any ind.) • D.O.T. #358.687-010 • OES #67005 • DRY BOSS; DRY JANITOR; SHOWER ROOM ATTENDANT. Maintains building, such as locker room of golf club, change house of mining camp, or shower facilities of industrial plant, in which patrons or workers shower and change clothes: Sweeps floor and scrubs shower stalls, using broom, brushes, and soap and water. Opens windows to control ventilation or adjusts controls of automatic heating, cooling, or dehumidifying unit to maintain healthful and comfortable conditions. May fire boiler to heat water for bathing or heating facility. May place contaminated work clothes in vacuum chamber for removal of toxic chemical dust. May requisition and issue supplies, such as soap, towels, and protective clothing. • **GED:** R2, M1, L2 • **SVP:** 2-30 days • **Academic:** Ed=N, Eng=S • **Work Field:** 031 • **MPSMS:** 905 • **Aptitudes:** G4, V4, N4, S4, P4, Q4, K4, F4, M3, E4, C5 • **Temperaments:** R • **Stress:** T • **Physical:** V=N, H=N, L=M, W, H • **Work Env:** I, W • **Salary:** 2 • **Outlook:** 2

CHIMNEY SWEEP (any ind.) • D.O.T. #891.687-010 • OES #67005 • CHIMNEY CLEANER; CLEANING OPERATOR. Cleans soot from chimneys: Removes pipe connecting furnace to flue, using handtools. Cleans soot from chimney pit, using vacuum cleaner that automatically discharges into receptacle mounted on truck. Cleans connecting pipes with brush, replaces pipe, and seals joints with cement. Closes fireplace openings and other outlets to clean chimney from above. Lowers weighted bag down flue, withdraws bag which expands and scrapes soot from lining of chimney. Empties bag and inspects interior of chimney to ensure completion of cleaning process, using reflecting light of mirror. May make oral or written reports to request services of CHIMNEY REPAIRER (bus. ser.). May brush interior of chimney, boilers, and furnaces. • **GED:** R2, M1, L1 • **SVP:** 30 days-3 mos • **Academic:** Ed=N,

Eng=N • **Work Field:** 031 • **MPSMS:** 553 • **Aptitudes:** G3, V4, N4, S3, P3, Q4, K3, F3, M3, E5, C5 • **Temperaments:** R • **Stress:** T • **Physical:** V=L, H=N, L=M, W, C, S, H • **Work Env:** B • **Salary:** 3 • **Outlook:** 3

CLEANER 2 (any ind.) • D.O.T. #919.687-014 • OES #98905 • Cleans interiors and exteriors of transportation vehicles, such as airplanes, automobiles, buses, rail road cars, and streetcars: Cleans interior of vehicle, using broom, cloth, mop, vacuum cleaner, and whisk broom. Cleans win dows with water, cleansing compounds, and cloth or chamois. Replenishes sanitary supplies in vehicle compartments. Removes dust, grease, and oil from exterior surfaces of vehicles, using steam-cleaning equipment, or by spraying or washing vehicles, using spraying equipment, brush or sponge. May polish exterior of vehicle. May fumigate interior of vehicle, using fumigating gases or sprays. May be designated according to type of vehicle cleaned as AIRPLANE CLEANER (air trans.); AUTOMOBILE WASHER (auto. ser.); BUS CLEANER (auto. ser.); CAR CLEANER (r.r. trans.); COACH CLEAN ER (r.r. trans.); TRUCK WASHER (dairy prod.). When cleaning aircraft interiors may be designated CABIN-SERVICE AGENT (air trans.). • **GED:** R2, M1, L1 • **SVP:** 1 day • **Academic:** Ed=N, Eng=N • **Work Field:** 031 • **MPSMS:** 960 • **Aptitudes:** G4, V4, N4, S4, P4, Q5, K4, F4, M3, E5, C5 • **Temperaments:** R • **Stress:** T • **Physical:** V=L, H=N, L=M, W, S, H • **Work Env:** B, W • **Salary:** 3 • **Out look:** 3

CLEANER, COMMERCIAL OR INSTITUTIONAL (any ind.) • D.O.T. #381.687-014 • OES #67005 • CHAR WORKER; CLEAN-UP WORKER; HOUSEKEEPER; JANITOR; LABORER, BUILD-ING MAINTENANCE; MOPPER; PORTER; SCRUBBER; SWEEPER. Keeps premises of office building, apartment house, or other commercial or institutional building in clean and orderly condition: Cleans and polishes lighting fixtures, marble surfaces, and trim and performs duties described in CLEANER (any ind.) I. May cut and trim grass, and shovel snow, using power equipment or handtools. May deliver messages. May transport small equipment or tools between departments. May set up tables and chairs in auditorium or hall. May be designated according to duties performed as HALL CLEANER (hotel & rest.); LIGHT-FIXTURE CLEANER (any ind.); MARBLE CLEANER (any ind.); METAL POLISHER (any ind.); PAINT CLEANER (any ind.); or according to equipment used as SCRUBBING-MACHINE OPERATOR (any ind.). • **GED:** R1, M1, L1 • **SVP:** 2-30 days • **Academic:** Ed=N, Eng=N • **Work Field:** 031 • **MPSMS:** 905 • **Aptitudes:** G4, V4, N5, S4, P4, Q5, K4, F4, M3, E4, C5 • **Temperaments:** R • **Stress:** T • **Physical:** V=L, H=N, L=H, W, C, S, H • **Work Env:** I • **Salary:** 3 • **Outlook:** 3

CLEANER, HOSPITAL (medical ser.) • D.O.T. #323.687-010 • OES #67002 • Cleans hospital wards, rooms, baths, laboratories, offices and halls: Washes bedframes, brushes mattresses, and remakes beds after dismissal of patients. Keeps utility and storage rooms in neat and orderly condition. Distributes laundered articles and linens in wards. Replaces soiled drapes and cubicle curtains in wards. Performs other duties as described under CLEANER (any ind.) I Master Title. May serve patients' meals and remove trays and dishes. May disinfect and sterilize equipment and supplies, such as rubber gloves, syringes, and test tubes, using germicides and sterilizing equip ment. • **GED:** R2, M1, L2 • **SVP:** 2-30 days • **Academic:** Ed=N, Eng=N • **Work Field:** 031 • **MPSMS:** 905 • **Aptitudes:** G4, V4, N5, S4, P4, Q4, K4, F4, M3, E4, C5 • **Temperaments:** R • **Stress:** T • **Physical:** V=L, H=N, L=M, W, S, H • **Work Env:** I, W • **Salary:** 2 • **Out look:** 4

CLEANER, HOUSEKEEPING (any ind.) • D.O.T. #323.687-014 • OES #67002 • Cleans rooms and halls in such commercial establishments as hotels, restaurants, clubs, beauty parlors, and dormitories performing any combination of the following duties: Sorts, counts, folds, marks, or carries linens. Makes beds. Checks wraps and renders personal assistance to patrons. Moves furniture, hangs drapes, and rolls carpets. Performs other duties as described under CLEANER (any ind.) I. May be designated according to type of establishment as BEAUTY PARLOR CLEANER (per. ser.); MOTEL CLEANER (hotel & rest.); or according to area cleaned as SLEEPING ROOM CLEANER (hotel & rest.). • **GED:** R2, M1, L2 • **SVP:** 2-30 days • **Aca demic:** Ed=N, Eng=N • **Work Field:** 031 • **MPSMS:** 905 • **Aptitudes:** G4, V4, N4, S4, P4, Q4,

K4, F4, M3, E4, C5 • **Temperaments:** R, V • **Stress:** T • **Physical:** V=L, H=N, L=M, W, C, S, H • **Work Env:** I • **Salary:** 1 • **Outlook:** 3

CLEANER, INDUSTRIAL (any ind.) • D.O.T. #381.687-018 • OES #67005 • CLEAN-UP WORKER; JANITOR; SANITOR; SCRUBBER; SWEEPER; TRASH COLLECTOR; VACUUM CLEANER; WASTE COLLECTOR. Keeps working areas in production departments of industrial establishment in clean and orderly condition, performing any combination of the following duties: Transports raw materials and semi-finished products or supplies between departments or buildings to supply machine tenders or operators with materials for processing, using handtruck. Arranges boxes, material, and handtrucks or other industrial equipment in neat and orderly manner. Cleans lint, dust, oil, and grease from machines, overhead pipes and conveyors, using brushes, airhoses, or steam cleaner. Cleans screens and filters. Scrubs processing tanks and vats. Hoses down floors to clean and applies floor drier. Picks up reusable scrap for salvage and stores in containers. Performs other duties as described under CLEANER (any ind.) I. May burn waste and clean incinerator. May pick up refuse from plant grounds and maintain area by cutting grass or shoveling snow. May operate industrial truck to transport materials within plant. May start pumps to force cleaning solution through production machinery, piping, or vats. May start pumps that lubricates machines. May be designated according to area cleaned as ALLEY CLEANER (textile); CASTING-AND-LOCKER-ROOM SERVICER (plastics mat.); ENGINE-ROOM CLEANER (any ind.); OVERHEAD CLEANER (any ind.). Additional titles: CAN-FILLING-ROOM SWEEPER (malt liquors); CEILING CLEANER (any ind.); CLEAN-UP WORKER, SPRAY ROOM (inst. & app.); FLOOR CLEANER (any ind.). • **GED:** R2, M1, L2 • **SVP:** 2-30 days • **Academic:** Ed=N, Eng=N • **Work Field:** 031 • **MPSMS:** 905 • **Aptitudes:** G4, V4, N5, S4, P4, Q5, K4, F4, M3, E4, C5 • **Temperaments:** R • **Stress:** T • **Physical:** V=L, H=N, L=H, W, S, H • **Work Env:** I • **Salary:** 3 • **Outlook:** 3

CLEANER, LABORATORY EQUIPMENT (any ind.) • D.O.T. #381.687-022 • OES #67005 • EQUIPMENT WASHER; LABORA-TORY AID; LABORATORY ASSISTANT; LABORATORY HELPER; LABORER, LABORATORY; TESTER HELPER. Cleans laboratory equipment, such as glassware, metal instruments, sinks, tables, and test panels, using solvents, brushes, and rags: Mixes water and detergents or acids in container to prepare cleaning solution according to specifications. Washes, rinses, and dries glassware and instruments, using water, acetone bath, and cloth or hot-air drier. Scrubs walls, floors, shelves, tables, and sinks, using cleaning solution and brush. May sterilize glassware and instruments, using autoclave. May fill tubes and bottles with specified solutions and apply identification labels. May label and file microscope slides. May arrange specimens and samples on trays to be placed in incubators and refrigerators. May deliver supplies and laboratory specimens to designated work areas, using handtruck. May tend still that supplies laboratory with distilled water. May clean glassware only and be designated GLASS WASHER, LABORATORY (any ind.). • **GED:** R2, M2, L1 • **SVP:** 2-30 days • **Academic:** Ed=N, Eng=N • **Work Field:** 031 • **MPSMS:** 601 • **Aptitudes:** G4, V4, N4, S4, P4, Q4, K4, F4, M3, E5, C3 • **Temperaments:** R, V • **Stress:** T • **Physical:** V=L, H=N, L=M, W, S, H • **Work Env:** I, W • **Salary:** 3 • **Out look:** 3

CLEANER, SIGNS (signs) • D.O.T. #739.687-062 • OES #98905 • Cleans and polishes electrical and outdoor signs and letters: Washes glass, plastic, and painted signs and letters with cleaning agent and water, cleaning compound, or acid solution and cloth or brush to remove dirt, stains, and other foreign matter. Dries surfaces, using cloth, chamois, or squeegee. Rubs metal signs and letters with cleaning agent to remove dirt and corrosion, and polishes with clean cloth. • **GED:** R2, M1, L1 • **SVP:** 2-30 days • **Aca demic:** Ed=N, Eng=N • **Work Field:** 031 • **MPSMS:** 969 • **Aptitudes:** G4, V4, N5, S4, P4, Q5, K4, F4, M3, E2, C5 • **Temperaments:** R • **Stress:** T • **Physical:** V=L, H=N, L=M, W, C, S, H • **Work Env:** B, R • **Salary:** 2 • **Out look:** 3

CLEANER, WINDOW (any ind.) • D.O.T. #389.687-014 • OES #67005 • WINDOW WASHER. Cleans windows, glass partitions, mirrors, and other glass surfaces of building interior or exterior, using pail of soapy water or other cleaner, sponge, and squeegee.

Crawls through window from inside and hooks safety belt to brackets for support, sets and climbs ladder to reach second or third story, or uses bosun's chair, swing stage, or other scaffolding lowered from roof to reach outside windows, or stands to reach first floor or inside windows. • **GED:** R1, M1, L1 • **SVP:** 2-30 days • **Aca demic:** Ed=N, Eng=N • **Work Field:** 031 • **MPSMS:** 905 • **Aptitudes:** G4, V4, N4, S4, P4, Q5, K3, F4, M3, E3, C5 • **Temperaments:** R, S • **Stress:** T, S • **Physical:** V=L, H=N, L=M, W, C, S, H • **Work Env:** B, W, R • **Salary:** 4 • **Outlook:** 4

FURNACE CLEANER (any ind.) • D.O.T. #891.687-014 • OES #98905 • Cleans fire pots, ducts, vents, registers, air chambers, and filter screens of domestic furnaces: Scrapes soot and ash from fire pot and smoke chambers, using scraper and wire brush. Cleans filter screens, using solvent. Removes dust-clogged air filters and places clean filters into brackets. Brushes and washes dust from air chamber and ducts, using wire or fiber brush. Removes loose soot, ash, and dust, using hand scoop and portable vacuum cleaner. Examines seams of furnace section for defects, such as cracks, and reports defects to customer or furnace repairer. May extract dust from ducts and jackets, using vacuum equipment. May tighten nuts, bolts, and screws on furnace, using handtools. • **GED:** R2, M1, L1 • **SVP:** 2-30 days • **Academic:** Ed=N, Eng=N • **Work Field:** 031 • **MPSMS:** 553 • **Aptitudes:** G4, V4, N4, S4, P4, Q5, K4, F4, M4, E4, C5 • **Temperaments:** R • **Stress:** T • **Physical:** V=L, H=N, L=M, W, S, H • **Work Env:** I, N • **Sal ary:** 3 • **Outlook:** 2

GOLF-RANGE ATTENDANT (amuse. & rec.) • D.O.T. #341.683-010 • OES #68014 • Performs combination of the following duties at golf driving range: Picks up golf balls by hand or drives vehicle equipped with trailer that automatically picks up balls as vehicle moves over fairway. Starts revolving tumbler filled with soapy water and immerses golf balls to remove dirt, grass stain, and club marks. Removes and rinses washed balls. Applies liquid cleaner to head and shank of golf clubs and buffs with steel wool. Replaces golf balls and clubs in racks for use by driving range patrons. May perform minor maintenance on benches, using handtools. • **GED:** R2, M1, L2 • **SVP:** 2-30 days • **Academic:** Ed=N, Eng=N • **Work Field:** 013, 031 • **MPSMS:** 616, 914 • **Aptitudes:** G4, V4, N5, S4, P4, Q5, K3, F4, M3, E4, C5 • **Temperaments:** R • **Physical:** V=L, H=N, L=M, W, S, H • **Work Env:** O • **Salary:** 2 • **Outlook:** 2

HOUSEKEEPER (hotel & rest.) • D.O.T. #321.137-010 • OES #61008 • FLOOR HOUSEKEEPER. Supervises work activities of cleaning personnel to ensure clean, orderly, attractive rooms in hotels, hospitals, and similar establishments: Assigns workers their duties, and inspects work for conformance to prescribed standards of cleanliness. Inventories stock to ensure adequate supplies. Issues supplies and equipment to workers. Investigates complaints regarding housekeeping service and equipment, and takes corrective action. Examines rooms, halls, and lobbies to determine need for remodeling, and makes recommendations to management. May screen applicants, train new employ ees, and recommend dismissals, transfers, and promotions. May record data concerning work assignments and personnel actions, and keep time records. May record data and prepare reports concerning room occupancy, payroll expenses, and department expenses. • **GED:** R3, M2, L3 • **SVP:** 1-2 yrs • **Academic:** Ed=N, Eng=S • **Work Field:** 031 • **MPSMS:** 901 • **Aptitudes:** G3, V3, N4, S3, P3, Q3, K4, F4, M3, E4, C4 • **Temperaments:** D, M, P, V • **Stress:** E • **Physical:** V=L, H=N, L=M, W, H • **Work Env:** I • **Salary:** 2 • **Outlook:** 4

JANITOR (any ind.) • D.O.T. #382.664-010 • OES #67005 • MAINTENANCE ENGINEER; SUPERINTENDENT, BUILDING. Keeps hotel, office building, apartment house, or similar building in clean and orderly condition and tends furnace, air conditioner, and boiler to provide heat, cool air, and hot water for tenants, performing any combination of following duties: Sweeps and mops or scrubs hallways and stairs. Regulates flow of fuel into automatic furnace or shovels coal into hand-fired furnace. Empties tenants' trash and garbage containers. Maintains building, performing minor and routine painting, plumbing, electrical wiring, and other related maintenance activities, using hand tools. Replaces air conditioner filters. Cautions tenants regarding complaints about excessive noise, disorderly conduct, or misuse of property. Notifies management concerning need for major repairs or additions to lighting, heating, and ventilating equipment.

Cleans snow and debris from sidewalk. Mows lawn, trims shrubbery, and cultivates flowers, using handtools and power tools. Posts signs to advertise vacancies and shows empty apartments to prospective tenants. May reside on property and be designated MANAGER, RESIDENT (any ind.). • **GED:** R3, M2, L3 • **SVP:** 30 days-3 mos • **Academic:** Ed=N, Eng=S • **Work Field:** 021, 031 • **MPSMS:** 905 • **Aptitudes:** G3, V4, N3, S3, P4, Q4, K4, F4, M3, E4, C4 • **Temperaments:** T, V • **Physical:** V=L, H=N, L=M, W, S, H • **Work Env:** B • **Salary:** 2 • **Outlook:** 3

KITCHEN HELPER (hotel & rest.) • D.O.T. #318.687-010 • OES #65038 • COOKEE; COOK HELPER; KITCHEN HAND; KITCHEN PORTER; KITCHEN RUNNER. Performs any combination of the following duties to maintain kitchen work areas and restaurant equipment and utensils in clean and orderly condition: Sweeps and mops floors. Washes worktables, walls, refrigerators, and meat blocks. Segregates and removes trash and garbage and places it in designated containers. Steam-cleans or hoses-out garbage cans. Sorts bottles, and breaks disposable ones in bot tle-crushing machine. Washes pots, pans, and trays by hand. Scrapes food from dirty dishes and washes them by hand or places them in racks or on conveyor to dishwashing machine. Polishes silver, using burnishing-machine tumbler, chemical dip, buffing wheel, and hand cloth. Holds inverted glasses over revolving brushes to clean inside surfaces. Transfers supplies and equipment between storage and work areas by hand or by use of hand truck. Sets up banquet tables. Washes and peels vegetables, using knife or peeling machine. May be known according to task performed as DISHWASHER, HAND (hotel & rest.); DISHWASHER, MACHINE (hotel & rest.); GARBAGE PORTER (hotel & rest.); POTWASHER (hotel & rest.); SILVERWARE WASHER (hotel & rest.). • **GED:** R2, M1, L1 • **SVP:** 2-30 days • **Academic:** Ed=N, Eng=N • **Work Field:** 031 • **MPSMS:** 903 • **Aptitudes:** G4, V4, N5, S4, P4, Q5, K4, F4, M4, E4, C4 • **Temperaments:** R • **Stress:** T • **Physical:** V=N, H=N, L=M, W, H • **Work Env:** I, H, W, R • **Salary:** 1 • **Outlook:** 4

LAUNDRY WORKER 1 (any ind.) • D.O.T. #361.684-014 • OES #92726 • CAMP-LAUNDRY OPERATOR; COMPANY LAUNDRY WORKER. Washes and irons wearing apparel, sheets, blankets, and other linens and clothes used by employees of logging, construction, mining, or other camp, or washes uniforms, aprons, and towels in establishments supplying employees with these linens. Uses equipment usually found in household or in small laundry. • **GED:** R2, M1, L1 • **SVP:** 2-30 days • **Academic:** Ed=N, Eng=N • **Work Field:** 031, 032 • **MPSMS:** 420, 440 • **Aptitudes:** G4, V4, N4, S4, P4, Q4, K3, F3, M3, E4, C4 • **Temperaments:** J, V • **Physical:** V=N, H=N, L=M, W, H • **Work Env:** I, W • **Salary:** 2 • **Outlook:** 2

LIGHT-FIXTURE SERVICER (any ind.) • D.O.T. #389.687-018 • OES #67099 • FIXTURE RELAMPER; FLUORESCENT LAMP REPLACER; LIGHT-BULB REPLACER; LIGHT CLEANER. Replaces electric light fixture parts, such as bulbs, fluorescent tubes, and starters. Repairs fixture parts, such as switches and sockets, using handtools. Cleans fixtures and lamps, using soap, water and rags. Requisitions and keeps supply of bulbs, tubes, and replacement parts. • **GED:** R1, M1, L1 • **SVP:** 2-30 days • **Academic:** Ed=N, Eng=N • **Work Field:** 031, 111 • **MPSMS:** 909 • **Aptitudes:** G4, V4, N5, S4, P4, Q5, K4, F4, M4, E3, C5 • **Temperaments:** R • **Stress:** T • **Physical:** V=L, H=N, L=M, W, C, H • **Work Env:** I, R • **Sal ary:** 2 • **Outlook:** 2

ORDINARY SEAMAN (water trans.) • D.O.T. #911.687-030 • OES #97517 • Stands deck department watches and performs variety of duties to preserve painted surfaces of ship and to maintain lines, running gear, and cargo-handling gear in safe operating condition: Watches from bow of ship or wing of bridge for obstructions in path of ship. Turns wheel while ob serving compass to steer and maintain ship on course. Mops or washes down deck, using hose to remove oil, dirt, and debris. Chips and cleans rust spots from deck, superstructure, and sides of ship, using hand or air chipping hammer and wire brush. Paints chipped area. Splices wire rope, using marlinespike, wirecutters, and twine. • **GED:** R3, M1, L1 • **SVP:** 3-6 mos • **Academic:** Ed=N, Eng=N • **Work Field:** 013, 031 • **MPSMS:** 854 • **Aptitudes:** G3, V4, N4, S3, P4, Q4, K3, F4, M3, E3, C4 • **Temperaments:** J, M, V • **Physical:** V=L, H=N, L=M, W, C, H • **Work Env:** O, W, R • **Salary:** 4 • **Outlook:** 3

PRINT-SHOP HELPER (print. & pub.) • D.O.T. #979.684-026 • OES #98999 • Assists workers engaged in setting type, operating printing presses, and making plates, performing any combination of following duties: Moves material and supplies to and from various work areas. Assists in making ready and adjusting presses for production runs. Keeps presses supplied with paper stock. Cleans presses, printing plates, and type setups after use. Covers dampening rolls with wool or felt. Counts stacks, and wraps finished printed material. Cleans electrotype shells prior to casting, and removes excess metal from edges or backs of cast printing plates, using metal trimming and shaving machines. Trims stereotype matrices to size and drys them between steam or flame-heated plates. Immerses cast plates in copper and chrome plating solutions. Nails wooden blocks to backs of prepared plates to bring plates to printing level. May set type by hand following copy. May be designated according to work involved as ELECTROTYPER HELPER (print. & pub.); PHOTOENGRAVING HELPER (print. & pub.); STEREOTYPER HELPER (print. & pub.). Performs other duties as described under HELPER (any ind.). • **GED:** R2, M1, L1 • **SVP:** 30 days-3 mos • **Academic:** Ed=N, Eng=N • **Work Field:** 191 • **MPSMS:** 480, 567 • **Aptitudes:** G4, V4, N4, S4, P3, Q4, K3, F3, M3, E4, C5 • **Temperaments:** R • **Stress:** T • **Physical:** V=N, H=N, L=M, W, H • **Work Env:** I, N • **Salary:** 1 • **Outlook:** 2

SANDBLASTER (any ind.) • D.O.T. #503.687-010 • OES #98905 • Directs blast of abrasive-laden compressed air or water from nozzle against metal or hard-composition objects to remove adhering scale, sand, paint, grease, tar, rust, and dirt, and to impart even finish: Shovels abrasives, such as sand, grit, or shot of specified grade into machine hopper. Applies masking materials to protect designated areas from abrasive action. Dons protective equipment, such as helmet, suit, gloves, or hood to protect body from injury, and turns on air supply. Sandblasts parts to required finish. (1) Cleans large parts, using nozzle. Loads large parts on racks within enclosed room, using hoist. Turns valves to regulate pressure and mixture of abrasive and fluid flowing through nozzle. Directs nozzle manually over surfaces of parts for specified interval. (2) Cleans small parts in tumbling barrel. Loads small parts into barrel manually. Starts tumbler and turns valves to direct and regulate abrasive-laden fluid over tumbling parts. Stops action and removes parts. (3) Cleans small parts in abrasive cabinet. Loads small parts into cabinet and closes door. Starts pump and turns valves to regulate abrasive fluid pressure. Inserts arms through glove-fitted cabinet openings, and manipulates parts under nozzle to clean surfaces. May be designated by type of abrasive material used, such as SHOTBLASTER (any ind.), or type of enclosure worked in, such as CABINET-ABRASIVE SANDBLASTER (any ind.). May set up portable equipment at location of work. May examine finished objects to ensure conformance to specifications. • **GED:** R2, M2, L1 • **SVP:** 2-30 days • **Academic:** Ed=N, Eng=N • **Work Field:** 051 • **MPSMS:** 530, 540, 590 • **Aptitudes:** G4, V4, N4, S4, P3, Q5, K3, F4, M3, E5, C5 • **Temperaments:** R, T • **Stress:** T • **Physical:** V=L, H=N, L=M, W, H • **Work Env:** I, N • **Salary:** 4 • **Outlook:** 3

SEWAGE-DISPOSAL WORKER (sanitary ser.) • D.O.T. #955.687-010 • OES #98905 • Cleans and maintains equipment in sewage disposal plant to facilitate flow and treatment of sewage: Cleans filter screens, processing tanks, and walkways, using hose, brushes, and chemical solutions. Cleans precipitates, such as grit, sludge, trash, and muck from sump, catch basin and grit chamber, using shovel, rake, and hand pump. Lubricates equipment, such as pumps and valves. Opens and closes gates and valves according to gage readings or warning lights on equipment. Collects samples of decontaminated refuse for testing. May conduct test on sewage sample, using colorimeter. May maintain grounds and outbuildings [GROUNDSKEEPER, INDUSTRIAL-COMMERCIAL (any ind.)]. May be designated according to equipment cleaned as CATCH-BASIN CLEANER (sanitary ser.). • **GED:** R2, M1, L1 • **SVP:** 2-30 days • **Academic:** Ed=H, Eng=N • **Work Field:** 031 • **MPSMS:** 874 • **Aptitudes:** G4, V4, N4, S4, P4, Q5, K4, F4, M3, E5, C5 • **Temperaments:** R • **Stress:** T • **Physical:** V=L, H=N, L=H, W, S, H • **Work Env:** B, W, N • **Salary:** 3 • **Outlook:** 2

STEAM CLEANER (auto. ser.) • D.O.T. #915.687-026 • OES #98905 • AUTOMOBILE WASHER, STEAM. Cleans engines, bodies, and chassis of automotive vehicles, using high pressure steam hose and detergent solution: Starts boiler to generate steam. Sprays steam and detergent solution over vehicle chassis, engine, or parts, to remove dirt and grease. Lowers engine or chassis parts into tank of detergent solution, by hand or by use of hoist, to clean inaccessible surfaces. Scrapes off adherent grime and grease, using wire brush or putty knife. May spray vehicle body with steam and caustic compound to remove paint. May clean forging dies and be designated STEAM-CLEAN- MACHINE OPERATOR (forging). • **GED:** R2, M1, L1 • **SVP:** 2-30 days • **Academic:** Ed=N, Eng=N • **Work Field:** 031 • **MPSMS:** 961 • **Aptitudes:** G4, V4, N4, S4, P4, Q4, K4, F4, M3, E5, C5 • **Temperaments:** R • **Stress:** T • **Physical:** V=L, H=N, L=M, W, S, H • **Work Env:** O, W, N • **Salary:** 3 • **Outlook:** 3

STREET CLEANER (gov. ser.) • D.O.T. #955.687-018 • OES #98999 • STREET SWEEPER. Sweeps refuse from municipal streets, gutters, and sidewalks into pile and shovels refuse into movable container that is pushed from place to place. May pick up paper and similar rubbish from lawns, flower beds, or highway median strips, using spike-tipped stick. • **GED:** R1, M1, L1 • **SVP:** 1 day • **Academic:** Ed=N, Eng=N • **Work Field:** 031 • **MPSMS:** 959 • **Aptitudes:** G4, V4, N5, S4, P4, Q5, K4, F4, M4, E4, C5 • **Temperaments:** R • **Physical:** V=L, H=N, L=L, W, S, H • **Work Env:** O, R • **Salary:** 3 • **Outlook:** 2

SUPERVISOR, CENTRAL SUPPLY (medical ser.) • D.O.T. #079.164-010 • OES #51002 • Directs activities of personnel in hospital central supply room to furnish sterile and nonsterile supplies and equipment for use in care and treatment of patients: Supervises workers engaged in cleaning, assembling, and packing of linens, gowns, dressings, gloves, treatment trays, instruments, and related items; preparation of solutions; arrangement of stock; and requisitioning, issuing, controlling, and charging of supplies and equipment. Instructs personnel in use of sterilizing equipment and water distillation apparatus, setting up standardized treatment trays, and maintaining equipment of central supply room. Establishes standards of work performance and methods of operation for department. Ensures that aseptic techniques are employed by personnel in preparing and handling sterile items. • **GED:** R4, M4, L4 • **SVP:** 1-2 yrs • **Academic:** Ed=H, Eng=S • **Work Field:** 221 • **MPSMS:** 924 • **Aptitudes:** G2, V3, N3, S3, P3, Q3, K3, F3, M3, E4, C4 • **Temperaments:** D, P, T, V • **Physical:** V=N, H=N, L=L, H • **Work Env:** I • **Salary:** 4 • **Outlook:** 4

SWEEPER-CLEANER, INDUSTRIAL (any ind.) • D.O.T. #389.683-010 • OES #67005 • CLEANER OPERATOR; POWER-CLEANER OPERATOR; VACUUM-CLEANER OPERATOR. Drives industrial vacuum cleaner through designated areas, such as factory aisles and warehouses, to collect scrap, dirt, and other refuse. Empties trash collecting box or bag at end of each shift. May sift refuse to recover usable materials, such as screws, metal scrap, or machine parts. May clean machine, using rags and vacuum cleaner. May refuel machine and lubricate parts. May hand sweep areas inaccessible to machine and pick up scrap. • **GED:** R1, M1, L1 • **SVP:** 2-30 days • **Academic:** Ed=N, Eng=N • **Work Field:** 031 • **MPSMS:** 905 • **Aptitudes:** G4, V4, N5, S3, P4, Q5, K3, F4, M3, E3, C5 • **Temperaments:** R • **Stress:** T • **Physical:** V=L, H=N, L=M, W, S, H • **Work Env:** I • **Salary:** 2 • **Outlook:** 2

TANK CLEANER (any ind.) • D.O.T. #891.687-022 • OES #98905 • Cleans interiors of boilers, storage tanks, industrial processing tanks, kilns, and tank and refrigerator railroad cars to remove emulsion and incrustations, using shovels, squeegees, brooms, scrapers, hoses, water, and solvents: Drains tank, connects hose to water or steam lines, and sprays walls, roof, and bottom of tank to flush residue, such as oil, acid, grease, and sludge through tank openings. Scrapes and scrubs walls, using detergents, solvents, scrapers, and brushes to remove incrustations, scale, or deposits of coke or catalyst. Sweeps up debris and shovels sludge into buckets or wheelbarrows or down chutes. Removes chemical residues and other liquids from tank bottoms with squeegees or pump and suction hoses. May dry tanks with wood shavings or portable air-drying equipment. May test gas content of tanks. May add specified chemicals to industrial tanks to maintain and replenish tank processing solutions. May be designated according to type of tank cleaned as ACID-TANK CLEANER (petrol. refin.); BOILER CLEANER (any ind.); PLATING-TANK CLEANER (electronics); TANK-CAR CLEANER (petrol. refin.). • **GED:** R2, M1, L1 • **SVP:**

30 days-3 mos • **Academic:** Ed=N, Eng=N • **Work Field:** 031 • **MPSMS:** 568 • **Aptitudes:** G4, V4, N4, S4, P3, Q5, K4, F4, M3, E5, C5 • **Temperaments:** R • **Stress:** T • **Physical:** V=N, H=N, L=H, W, C, S, H • **Work Env:** I, W, R • **Salary:** 3 • **Outlook:** 3

TUBE CLEANER (any ind.) • D.O.T. #891.687-030 • OES #98905 • Cleans scale from inside of tubes that are used in boilers, kilns, and stills to circulate hot air or water: Removes plugs or assemblies from tube ends, using handtools. Pushes compressed-air rotary scraper or wire brush through tubes to scrape scales from interior surfaces. Flushes or blows out loosened deposits, using water or airhose. May inspect tubes by drawing electric light through them. May be designated according to type of tube cleaned as BOILER-TUBE REAMER (any ind.); EVAPORATOR REPAIRER (chem.); FLUE CLEANER (any ind.); STILL CLEANER, TUBE (petrol. refin.); TAR HEAT-EXCHANGER CLEANER (petrol. refin.). May steam clean outside of boiler tubes and be designated BOILER-TUBE BLOWER (any ind.). • **GED:** R2, M1, L1 • **SVP:** 2-30 days • **Academic:** Ed=N, Eng=N • **Work Field:** 031 • **MPSMS:** 550 • **Aptitudes:** G4, V4, N5, S4, P4, Q5, K3, F4, M3, E5, C5 • **Temperaments:** R • **Stress:** T • **Physical:** V=L, H=N, L=M, W, C, S, H • **Work Env:** I, H, W, N, R • **Salary:** 2 • **Outlook:** 3

VENETIAN-BLIND CLEANER AND REPAIRER (any ind.) • D.O.T. #739.687-198 • OES #67005 • Cleans and repairs venetian blinds, using handtools: Dusts and washes blinds, using cloth, vacuum, brush, water and detergent. Hangs blinds on rack to dry. Examines blinds to detect defective or worn parts, such as cord, tape, or slats, and replaces parts, using handtools. May install blinds. May assemble blinds. • **GED:** R2, M1, L1 • **SVP:** 2-30 days • **Aca demic:** Ed=N, Eng=N • **Work Field:** 031, 061 • **MPSMS:** 469 • **Aptitudes:** G4, V4, N4, S4, P4, Q4, K4, F4, M4, E5, C5 • **Temperaments:** R • **Stress:** T • **Physical:** V=L, H=N, L=M, W, H • **Work Env:** I, W • **Salary:** 3 • **Outlook:** 2

GOE: 05.12.19 Reproduction Services

ADDRESSING-MACHINE OPERATOR (clerical) • D.O.T. #208.582-010 • OES #56008 • Operates machine to print addresses, code numbers, and similar information on items, such as envelopes, accounting forms, packages, and advertising literature: Positions plates, stencils, or tapes in machine magazine and places articles to be addressed into loading rack. Starts machine that automatically feeds plates, stencils, or tapes through mechanism. Adjusts flow of ink and guides to fit size of paper and sets stops and selectors so that only certain plates will be printed, using wrench and pliers. Maintains plate file and operates embossing machine or typewriter to make corrections, additions, and changes on plates. May type statistical lists of plate files and correspondence concerning addressing jobs. • **GED:** R3, M2, L2 • **SVP:** 3-6 mos • **Academic:** Ed=N, Eng=N • **Work Field:** 191 • **MPSMS:** 891 • **Aptitudes:** G3, V3, N4, S3, P4, Q4, K4, F4, M4, E5, C5 • **Temperaments:** R • **Stress:** T • **Physical:** V=N, H=N, L=L, H • **Work Env:** I • **Salary:** 2 • **Outlook:** 2

AUXILIARY-EQUIPMENT OPERATOR, DATA PROCESSING (clerical) • D.O.T. #213.685-010 • OES #56014 • Tends one or more of the following office machines that sort, assemble, separate, convert, or reproduce computer input or output data in electronic data-processing establishment or department: Tends sorting machine that automatically groups cards or other materials in numerical or alphabetical sequence according to any classification punched in materials [SORTING-MACHINE OPERATOR (clerical)]. Tends reproducer that automatically punches information from one set of punched source cards into another set of cards. Tends interpreting machine that translates alphabetical or numerical data from punched holes in card or tape to printed matter on same or different card or tape, or onto printout sheet. Tends collator that merges two or more sets of input or output cards into one set of given sequence or verifies uniformity of information printed on two or more sets of cards. Tends bursting and decollating equipment that removes carbons from printout sheets and separates sheets [BURSTING-MACHINE TENDER (clerical)]. Performs other clerical duties as assigned by SUPERVISOR, COMPUTER OPERATIONS (clerical), or SUPERVISOR, MACHINE RECORDS UNIT (clerical), to facilitate operation of department. May be designated by specialization of machine tended as COLLATOR OPERATOR, DATA PROCESSING (clerical); INTERPRETER OPERATOR, DATA PROCESSING (clerical); REPRODUCER OPERATOR, DATA PROCESSING (clerical). • **GED:** R2, M1, L1 • **SVP:** 30 days-3 mos • **Academic:** Ed=N, Eng=N • **Work Field:** 231 • **MPSMS:** 890 • **Aptitudes:** G3, V3, N4, S4, P3, Q4, K3, F4, M3, E5, C5 • **Temperaments:** R, T • **Stress:** T • **Physical:** V=L, H=N, L=L, H • **Work Env:** I • **Salary:** 3 • **Outlook:** 3

BOOK REPAIRER (any ind.) • D.O.T. #977.684-010 • OES #85999 • BOOK MENDER. Repairs damaged or worn books for resale or reuse, using handtools: Erases disfigurations from pages. Cuts damaged pages, linings, or covers from book body, using knife. Trims pages, using knife or paper cutter. Positions and pastes repaired or new pages, linings, or covers to book body. Clamps book in press for specified time to bondedges. May operate sewing machine to sew pages into book body. May imprint or emboss lettering on cover, using stamping machine. • **GED:** R2, M1, L1 • **SVP:** 30 days-3 mos • **Academic:** Ed=N, Eng=N • **Work Field:** 102 • **MPSMS:** 486 • **Aptitudes:** G3, V4, N4, S3, P3, Q4, K3, F3, M3, E5, C4 • **Temperaments:** M, T • **Physical:** V=L, H=N, L=L, H • **Work Env:** I • **Salary:** 2 • **Outlook:** 2

BRAILLE-DUPLICATING-MACHINE OPERATOR (print. & pub.) • D.O.T. #207.685-010 • OES #56005 • BRAILLE-THERMOFORM OPERATOR. Tends equipment to reproduce braille-embossed pages, using one of following methods: (1) Places master page on screen bed. Places roll of treated paper on stand. Threads paper through equipment and locks paper in clamping frame. Pulls heat unit over clamping frame. Depresses pedal or handle to lower clamping frame onto screen bed and to create vacuum that forms braille impressions. Pushes heat unit from bed. Releases pedal or handle to raise clamping frame, and releases catch on frame to draw reproduced copy through equipment. Repeats process to make required number of copies. Cuts copies apart, using scissors. Writes identifying information, such as page number or title, on each copy. (2) Positions master page on screen bed. Places sheet of heat-sensitive plastic paper over page and lowers clamping frame to lock page into position on bed. Pulls heat unit over clamping frame to activate vacuum pump trip-lever. Holds heat unit over frame to form braille impressions. Pushes heat unit from bed to release vacuum. Raises frame to release individual copy. Repeats process to make required number of copies. Most workers in this occupation are blind. • **GED:** R2, M1, L2 • **SVP:** 2-30 days • **Academic:** Ed=N, Eng=N • **Work Field:** 192 • **MPSMS:** 567 • **Aptitudes:** G4, V4, N4, S4, P4, Q4, K4, F4, M3, E5, C5 • **Temperaments:** R • **Stress:** T • **Physical:** V=N, H=N, L=M, H • **Work Env:** I • **Salary:** 2 • **Outlook:** 2

BURSTING-MACHINE TENDER (clerical) • D.O.T. #217.685-010 • OES #56099 • Tends machine that separates, trims, and addresses accounting notices and receipt forms: Turns knobs to adjust machine to address and separate forms for mailing and for retention as office copies. Turns roller to position pins that grip continuous forms. Starts machine. Examines emerging forms for correct printing, trimming, and separation. Packs stacked forms into boxes and labels boxes for mailing. Changes machine ribbon. • **GED:** R2, M1, L1 • **SVP:** 2-30 days • **Academic:** Ed=N, Eng=N • **Work Field:** 191 • **MPSMS:** 898 • **Aptitudes:** G4, V4, N4, S4, P3, Q4, K3, F4, M3, E5, C5 • **Temperaments:** R, T • **Stress:** T • **Physical:** V=N, H=N, L=L, H • **Work Env:** I • **Salary:** 2 • **Outlook:** 2

COIN WRAPPER (clerical) • D.O.T. #217.686-010 • OES #56099 • Feeds coins into machine that counts, sorts, and wraps coins of various denominations: Lifts bags of coins and dumps them into hopper of machine. Places rolls of counted coins into bags for distribution. Keeps records of total money processed. May insert fittings on coin channels of machine to sort coins according to denominations. May move money to and from cages and vaults, using handtruck. • **GED:** R2, M1, L1 • **SVP:** 2-30 days • **Academic:** Ed=N, Eng=N • **Work Field:** 041, 232 • **MPSMS:** 899 • **Aptitudes:** G4, V4, N4, S4, P4, Q4, K4, F4, M4, E5, C4 • **Temperaments:** R, T • **Stress:** T • **Physical:** V=N, H=N, L=H, W, H • **Work Env:** I • **Salary:** 2 • **Outlook:** 3

COIN-MACHINE OPERATOR (finan. inst.) • D.O.T. #217.585-010 • OES #56099 • COIN-COUNTER-AND-WRAPPER; COIN TELLER. Sorts, counts, and wraps coins, using various machines: Sorts coins according to denomination, using coin-separating machine. Removes counterfeit and mutilated coins. Feeds coins into hopper of counting machine that counts and bags them. Removes, seals, and weighs bags of counted coins. Wraps coins, using coin-wrapping machine, and places rolls of coins into bags for distribution. Records machine totals, shortages or overages, and kind and value of coins removed from circulation. Verifies totals against deposit slips and prepares coins for shipment. May sort, count, and wrap paper money by hand or machine. • **GED:** R3, M2, L1 • **SVP:** 30 days-3 mos • **Academic:** Ed=N, Eng=N • **Work Field:** 041, 212, 232 • **MPSMS:** 899 • **Aptitudes:** G3, V4, N3, S4, P4, Q3, K3, F3, M3, E5, C4 • **Temperaments:** R, T • **Stress:** T • **Physical:** V=L, H=N, L=H, W, H • **Work Env:** I, N • **Salary:** 2 • **Outlook:** 3

COLLATOR OPERATOR (clerical) • D.O.T. #208.685-010 • OES #56099 • Tends machine that assembles pages of printed material in numerical sequence: Adjusts control that regulates stroke of paper pusher, according to size of paper. Places pages to be assembled in holding trays. Starts machine. Removes assembled pages from machine. • **GED:** R2, M1, L1 • **SVP:** 2-30 days • **Academic:** Ed=N, Eng=N • **Work Field:** 231 • **MPSMS:** 898 • **Aptitudes:** G4, V4, N4, S4, P4, Q3, K4, F4, M3, E5, C5 • **Temperaments:** R • **Stress:** T • **Physical:** V=N, H=N, L=L, W, H • **Work Env:** I • **Salary:** 2 • **Outlook:** 2

CURRENCY SORTER (finan. inst.) • D.O.T. #217.485-010 • OES #56099 • CURRENCY-MACHINE OPERATOR. Sorts and counts paper money, using automatic currency-counting machine. Examines money to detect and sort out counterfeit, mutilated, and worn bills. Requisitions replacements. Sorts bills according to denomination or Federal Reserve District number, and inserts them into open slot of machine to be automatically grouped and counted. Verifies totals registered on machine against amount of deposit reported by member bank or depositor, using adding machine, and posts shortage or overage to account. Bundles and wraps counted money to be placed in vault. May sort, count, and wrap coins [COIN WRAPPER (clerical)]. • **GED:** R3, M3, L2 • **SVP:** 3-6 mos • **Academic:** Ed=N, Eng=N • **Work Field:** 232 • **MPSMS:** 894 • **Aptitudes:** G3, V4, N3, S4, P3, Q3, K3, F3, M3, E5, C4 • **Temperaments:** J, T • **Physical:** V=L, H=N, L=L, H • **Work Env:** I • **Salary:** 2 • **Outlook:** 3

FOLDING-MACHINE OPERATOR (clerical) • D.O.T. #208.685-014 • OES #56008 • FOLDER OPERATOR. Tends machine that folds advertising literature, forms, letters, or other paper sheets: Turns indicator knobs to adjust folding rollers, side guides, and stops, according to specified size and number of folds. Starts machine and feeds paper sheets between folding rollers. Removes folded sheets. May place folded sheets into envelopes preparatory to mailing. • **GED:** R2, M1, L1 • **SVP:** 2-30 days • **Academic:** Ed=N, Eng=N • **Work Field:** 062 • **MPSMS:** 891 • **Aptitudes:** G4, V4, N4, S4, P4, Q4, K3, F4, M3, E5, C5 • **Temperaments:** R • **Stress:** T • **Physical:** V=N, H=N, L=L, W, H • **Work Env:** I • **Salary:** 2 • **Outlook:** 2

INSERTING-MACHINE OPERATOR (clerical) • D.O.T. #208.685-018 • OES #56008 • Tends machine that inserts printed matter, such as letters or booklets into folders or envelopes: Stacks quantities of inserts and covers into machine feedboxes and turns setscrews to adjust feeder mechanisms, according to thickness of material. Starts machine and replenishes feedboxes with inserts and covers. • **GED:** R2, M1, L2 • **SVP:** 2-30 days • **Academic:** Ed=N, Eng=N • **Work Field:** 062 • **MPSMS:** 891 • **Aptitudes:** G4, V4, N4, S4, P4, Q4, K3, F4, M3, E5, C5 • **Temperaments:** R

• **Stress:** T • **Physical:** V=N, H=N, L=L, H • **Work Env:** I • **Salary:** 2 • **Outlook:** 2

MICROFILM MOUNTER (clerical) • D.O.T. #208.685-022 • OES #56099 • Tends machine that automatically mounts developed microfilm onto cards for filing purposes: Inserts roll of microfilm into machine. Fills hopper with presorted cards. Pours specified amount of adhesive solution into hopper to coat cards. Starts machine and observes coating of cards with adhesive solution and mounting of film onto cards. • **GED:** R2, M1, L1 • **SVP:** 2-30 days • **Academic:** Ed=N, Eng=N • **Work Field:** 063 • **MPSMS:** 891 • **Aptitudes:** G4, V4, N4, S4, P4, Q4, K4, F4, M4, E5, C4 • **Temperaments:** R, T • **Stress:** T • **Physical:** V=L, H=N, L=L, H • **Work Env:** I • **Salary:** 2 • **Outlook:** 2

PHOTOCOPYING-MACHINE OPERATOR (clerical) • D.O.T. #207.685-014 • OES #56005 • Tends duplicating machine to reproduce handwritten or typewritten matter: Places original copy on glass plate in machine. Places blank paper on loading tray. Sets control switch for number of copies. Presses button to start machine which transfers image of original copy onto blank paper by photographic and static electricity process. May clean and repair machine. May receive payment for duplicate copies. Important variables may be indicated by trade name of machine tended. • **GED:** R2, M1, L1 • **SVP:** 2-30 days • **Academic:** Ed=N, Eng=N • **Work Field:** 201 • **MPSMS:** 891 • **Aptitudes:** G4, V4, N4, S4, P3, Q4, K3, F4, M3, E5, C5 • **Temperaments:** R • **Stress:** T • **Physical:** V=N, H=N, L=L, H • **Work Env:** I • **Salary:** 2 • **Outlook:** 2

PHOTOGRAPHIC-MACHINE OPERATOR (clerical) • D.O.T. #207.685-018 • OES #56005 • MICROPHOTOGRAPHER. Tends equipment that photographs original documents and records, such as deeds, bills, statements, vouchers, and checks: Loads equipment with reel of film. Feeds records to be photographed into feed rolls that carry material past camera lens to be photographed, or positions records on table beneath camera lens. May adjust camera focus and exposure settings to accommodate size of record and degree of clarity desired. May tend equipment which encases roll film in cartridges or mounts fiche (single frame of film) on aperture card. Important variables are trade names of equipment tended. • **GED:** R3, M2, L2 • **SVP:** 30 days-3 mos • **Academic:** Ed=N, Eng=N • **Work Field:** 201 • **MPSMS:** 891 • **Aptitudes:** G3, V3, N4, S4, P4, Q4, K3, F4, M3, E5, C4 • **Temperaments:** R • **Stress:** T • **Physical:** V=N, H=N, L=L, H • **Work Env:** I • **Salary:** 2 • **Outlook:** 2

GOE: 05.12.20 Signalling

CROSSING TENDER (any ind.) • D.O.T. #371.667-010 • OES #63044 • Guards railroad crossing to warn motorists and pedestrians of approaching trains: Consults train schedules and listens for approaching trains from watchtower. Presses button to flash warning signal lights. Presses control button to lower crossing gates until train passes, and raises gate when crossing is clear. May wave flags, signs, or lanterns in emergencies. • **GED:** R2, M2, L2 • **SVP:** 30 days-3 mos • **Academic:** Ed=N, Eng=N • **Work Field:** 293 • **MPSMS:** 851 • **Aptitudes:** G3, V4, N4, S3, P3, Q4, K4, F4, M4, E5, C4 • **Temperaments:** R • **Physical:** V=L, H=N, L=S, H • **Work Env:** I • **Salary:** 1 • **Outlook:** 2

Industrial 06

An interest in repetitive, concrete, organized activities in a factory setting. You can satisfy this interest by working in one of many industries that manufacture goods on a mass production basis. You may enjoy manual work—using your hands or handtools. Perhaps you prefer to operate or take care of machines. You may like to inspect, sort, count, or weigh products. Using your training and experience to set up machines or supervise other workers may appeal to you.

06.01 Production Technology

Workers in this group use their skill and knowledge of machines and processes to perform one or more demanding or complex activities. Some set up machines for others to operate or set up and perform a variety of machine operations on their own. Some do precision handwork; some supervise or instruct others in the use of machines, processes to be carried out, and the techniques to be used.

✔ **What kind of work would you do?**
Your work activities would depend upon your specific job. For example, you might:

- set up a textile weaving loom to produce specified patterns in cloth.
- use precision measuring devices to inspect watch parts to determine defects in the production process.
- set up a group of production machines and check them to ensure they are operating correctly.
- supervise salvage operations in a factory.
- assemble precision optical instruments.
- inspect electronic systems by following blueprints and diagrams.

✔ **What skills and abilities do you need for this kind of work?**
To do this kind of work, you must be able to:

- read and understand blueprints and diagrams in order to set up and adjust machines and equipment.
- use eyes, hands, and fingers to do precision assembly work or to operate precision instruments.
- use math skills to plan schedules and keep production records.
- detect small differences in shape, size, and texture of products.
- explain how to operate a machine to other workers.
- direct and organize the work of others.
- inspect electronic systems by following blueprints and diagrams.
- pay strict attention to set standards and guidelines.

The above statements may not apply to every job in this group.

✔ **How do you know if you would like or could learn to do this kind of work?**
The following questions may give you clues about yourself as you consider this group of jobs.

- Have you taken industrial arts or machine shop courses? Do you like to set up machines according to written standards?
- Have you taken general or applied maintenance courses? Do you like projects which use math skills such as measuring?

- Have you assembled a bicycle or toy by following drawings or written instructions? Did you have a fairly easy time doing it?
- Have you held a summer or part-time job where mechanical equipment was used? Do you enjoy working in this type of surroundings?

- Have you been in charge of a group project? Do you like to assume the responsibility for getting a project completed?

✔ How can you prepare for and enter this kind of work?

Occupations in this group usually require education and/or training extending from one year to over ten years, depending upon the specific kind of work. Many of the jobs in this group require shop courses. Some may require math classes. Some jobs have formal apprenticeship programs. Others require on-the-job training.

Supervisory positions are usually filled by promoting workers with seniority and skill. Other jobs, such as inspecting, may be advancement positions for machine operators.

✔ What else should you consider about these jobs?

Overtime or night and shift work may be required on some jobs. Some workers are paid hourly wages. Other workers are paid according to the number of pieces they produce.

Workers are exposed to different types of factory conditions. Most plants are well-lighted and ventilated. However, working around machinery may be hazardous or noisy, and safety procedures must be followed.

If you think you would like to do this kind of work, look at the job titles listed on the following pages.

GOE: 06.01.01 Supervision & Instruction, Production Technology

COOK, MEXICAN FOOD (food prep. nec) • D.O.T. #526.134-010 • OES #81008 • Supervises and coordinates activities of workers engaged in preparing, cooking, portioning, and packaging ready-to-serve Mexican food specialties, such as chili, tamales, enchiladas, and tacos (seasoned chili beans wrapped in tortillas): Requisitions ingredients, such as meat, olives, chili, garlic, and spices from storeroom. Directs activities of workers engaged in feeding and tending grinding and mixing machines, rolling, cutting, and baking tortillas, and stirring and tending food in cooking vessels. Tastes foods to determine that they meet seasoning specifications. Supervises workers engaged in portioning and packaging foods. Frequently performs duties of workers supervised. May be designated according to food cooked as COOK, CHILI (food prep., n.e.c.); COOK, ENCHILADA (food prep., n.e.c.); COOK, TACO (food prep., n.e.c.); COOK, TAMALE (food prep., n.e.c.); COOK, TORTILLA (food prep., n.e.c.). • **GED:** R4, M2, L3 • **SVP:** 2-4 yrs • **Academic:** Ed=N, Eng=S • **Work Field:** 146 • **MPSMS:** 399 • **Aptitudes:** G3, V3, N4, S4, P4, Q4, K3, F3, M3, E5, C5 • **Temperaments:** D, J, T, V • **Physical:** V=L, H=N, L=M, W, H • **Work Env:** I • **Salary:** 3 • **Outlook:** 3

GOE: 06.01.02 Machine Set-up

FIRESETTER (elec. equip.) • D.O.T. #692.360-018 • OES #92997 • FIRESETTER, AUTOMATIC MACHINE; STEM-MAKING MACHINE ADJUSTER; TUBULATING MACHINE ADJUSTER. Sets up and maintains battery of machines that make flares and stems, seal stems to bulbs, or seal exhaust tubing to bulbs and cut excess tubing in manufacture of electron tubes and light bulbs: Installs and adjusts specified types and sizes of machine parts, such as cutter, revolving heads, bulb loader, tubing loader, burners, and etching stamp, using handtools. Lights burners and adjusts gas, air, oxygen, and hydrogen valves to attain specified cone, color, and density of flames. Starts machine and dumps bulbs, tubing, or other glass parts into hoppers that automatically feed them into heads of rotating turret. Operates machine through trial run to ensure accuracy of setup, making necessary adjustments. Adjusts air-brake regulator to attain pressure required to control precise stopping of turret at processing locations. Observes processing operations and inspects sample items for quality of cutting, sealing, and punching. Readjusts valves and machine parts to achieve specified standard of product. Examines etching on tube for cleanliness and definition and readjusts bolts or set screws to aline stamp. Replaces and cleans faulty machine parts, using handtools, and lubricates machine. May be designated according to type of product as FIRESETTER, CATHODE RAY (electronics); FIRESETTER, ELECTRON TUBE (electronics); FIRESETTER, INCANDESCENT BULB (elec. equip.). • **GED:** R4, M3, L3 • **SVP:** 1-2 yrs • **Academic:** Ed=N, Eng=S • **Work Field:** 082, 111 • **MPSMS:** 587 • **Aptitudes:** G3, V3, N3, S3, P2, Q4, K3, F3, M3, E5, C4 • **Temperaments:** J, M • **Physical:** V=L, H=N, L=M, W, H • **Work Env:** I, N, R • **Salary:** 4 • **Outlook:** 2

KNITTER MECHANIC (knit goods) • D.O.T. #685.360-010 • OES #92702 • PATTERN-AND-CHAIN MAKER. Builds metal chains, consisting of multisize pattern plates, or installs pattern tapes that control operation of Jacquard, Jacquard loom, link-and-link flat knitting machines and sets up machines to produce specified design in knitted fabric: Obtains specifications for new knitting pattern from supervisor. Studies number, type, and arrangement of stitches in sample and determines arrangement of pattern plates on chains, employing knowledge of machine operation. Connects plates to form chain. Studies sample to determine which perforations in pattern plates are to be covered to produce specified knit and informs JACQUARD-PLATE MAKER (knit goods). Installs chains and pattern plates in machine and makes trial run to determine if knitting meets specifications. May make minor repairs to knitting machines. • **GED:** R4, M3, L3 • **SVP:** 2-4 yrs • **Academic:** Ed=N, Eng=S • **Work Field:** 061, 165 • **MPSMS:** 424, 567 • **Aptitudes:** G3, V3, N3, S2, P2, Q4, K3, F3, M2, E5, C4 • **Temperaments:** M, T • **Physical:** V=L, H=N, L=M, W, H • **Work Env:** I • **Salary:** 4 • **Outlook:** 2

KNITTING-MACHINE FIXER (hosiery) • D.O.T. #689.280-014 • OES #92702 • Sets up, adjusts, and repairs knitting machines to knit hose, garments, and cloth according to specifications, using knowledge of machine function: Inserts cams, links, buttons, or needle jacks in pattern chain to set up machine to knit hose, garment, or cloth according to pattern design chart. Observes operation of machine and examines knitted material to detect defects. Turns setscrews and handwheels to adjust machine parts, such as gears and cams, and to synchronize yarn carriers, needles, dividers, and sinkers. Repairs and replaces machine parts, using handtools. Alines and straightens needles, sinkers, and dividers, using pliers. May clean and oil machines. • **GED**: R4, M3, L3 • **SVP**: 2-4 yrs • **Academic**: Ed=N, Eng=S • **Work Field**: 121, 165 • **MPSMS**: 420, 567 • **Aptitudes**: G3, V3, N3, S2, P2, Q4, K2, F2, M3, E5, C4 • **Temperaments**: M, T, V • **Physical**: V=L, H=N, L=M, W, S, H • **Work Env**: I, N • **Salary**: 4 • **Outlook**: 2

LOOM FIXER (asbestos prod.) • D.O.T. #683.260-018 • OES #92702 • FIXER; LOOM REPAIRER. Sets up, adjusts, and repairs looms to weave cloth of specified quality and design, using knowledge of loom function and weaving, diagrams, and manuals: Inspects loom or woven cloth to determine adjustments or repairs needed. Repairs or replaces defective parts, such as harness straps and shuttles, and adjusts tension and timing of parts, using handtools. Levels and alines parts, such as shuttle boxes, race plates, and reeds, to prevent excessive wear, using straightedge, level, and square. May change setup of loom to weave different pattern or different type yarn [LOOM CHANGER (textile)]. May be designated according to type of loom serviced as DOBBY-LOOM FIXER (textile); JACQUARD-LOOM FIXER (textile); NARROW-FABRIC-LOOM FIXER (narrow fabrics); RAPIER-INSERTION LOOM FIXER (textile); and WATER-JET LOOM FIXER (textile). • **GED**: R4, M3, L4 • **SVP**: 2-4 yrs • **Academic**: Ed=N, Eng=S • **Work Field**: 121, 164 • **MPSMS**: 420, 567 • **Aptitudes**: G3, V4, N4, S3, P2, Q4, K3, F3, M3, E5, C4 • **Temperaments**: J, M, T • **Physical**: V=L, H=N, L=M, W, S, H • **Work Env**: I, N • **Salary**: 4 • **Outlook**: 2

MACHINE SETTER (any ind.) • D.O.T. #616.360-022 • OES #91505 • Sets up various metal fabricating machines, such as brakes, shears, punch presses, bending and straightening machines, to cut, bend, and straighten metal as specified by layout, work order blueprints, and templates: Positions, alines, and bolts dies, blades, bedplates, cushion pins, and stops, using shims and measuring tools, such as squares, straightedges, rules, micrometers, gages, feelers, templates, and handtools. Adjusts flow of lubricants, pressure and depth of stroke, or feed of material, applying knowledge of thickness and properties of metal or according to standard specifications. Makes trial runs and measures workpiece for conformance to specifications. Instructs operator in special handling techniques. Clears jams and corrects malfunction of machines. Reports need for machine repairs to supervisor. Dismantles setups. May sharpen shear blades, drills, or cutting tools. May set up drill presses, flame cutting, and welding machines. May set up automatic or multipurpose machines. May specialize in setup of single type of machine and be designated accordingly as BRAKE MACHINE SETTER (any ind.). May set up machines common to sheet metal operations and be designated MACHINE SETTER, SHEET METAL (any ind.). • **GED**: R4, M3, L3 • **SVP**: 1-2 yrs • **Academic**: Ed=N, Eng=S • **Work Field**: 054, 102 • **MPSMS**: 554 • **Aptitudes**: G3, V3, N3, S2, P3, Q4, K3, F3, M2, E4, C5 • **Temperaments**: M, T, V • **Physical**: V=L, H=L, L=M, W, S, H • **Work Env**: I, N, R • **Salary**: 4 • **Outlook**: 2

PRINT CONTROLLER (photofinish.) • D.O.T. #976.360-010 • OES #92997 • Sets up and adjusts photographic print developing equipment according to density, color, and size of prints: Positions film in densitometer, reads dials, and records findings on plot sheet to locate defects in density and color balance. Confers with SUPERVISOR, QUALITY CONTROL (photofinish.) to determine adjustments required to bring print machine into balance. Runs test film strip through print machine to evaluate machine exposure. Removes cover from control panel of print machine to gain access to control shafts and adjustment knobs, using wrench. Plugs electric timer into printer to determine time elapsed during printing operation. Starts equipment, observes timer, and adjusts shafts and knobs to attain specified process settings, using handtools.

Locks control shafts of printer into position subsequent to final adjustment to prevent shifting in color or density balance during printing. Keeps record of adjustments made for departmental use. • **GED**: R4, M3, L2 • **SVP**: 1-2 yrs • **Academic**: Ed=A, Eng=N • **Work Field**: 202, 211 • **MPSMS**: 867 • **Aptitudes**: G3, V3, N3, S3, P3, Q3, K3, F3, M3, E5, C3 • **Temperaments**: M, T • **Physical**: V=G, H=L, L=L, S, H • **Work Env**: I, N • **Salary**: 4 • **Outlook**: 2

SETTER, AUTOMATIC-SPINNING LATHE (any ind.) • D.O.T. #604.360-010 • OES #91105 • Sets up automatic spinning lathe to spin (form) shaped articles from sheet or plate metal as specified by blueprints and computed from data charts: Bolts specified spinning chuck to headstock spindle and follow block to tailstock, using handtools or power tools. Positions, alines, and bolts specified circular forming tool on hydraulic carriage according to diameter and thickness of metal disk, using such measuring tools as calipers, micrometers, and verniers. Turns control knobs to set speed of lathe and feed speed of carriage according to chart. Makes trial run and measures dimensions of first piece for conformance to blueprint specifications. May set up automatic spinning lathe equipped with special forming tools to shape, trim or form knurls or beads on workpiece and be designated as SETTER, AUTOMATIC-SPINNING-AND-BEADING-LATHE (any ind.). • **GED**: R4, M3, L3 • **SVP**: 1-2 yrs • **Academic**: Ed=N, Eng=S • **Work Field**: 055, 057 • **MPSMS**: 550, 554 • **Aptitudes**: G3, V3, N3, S2, P3, Q4, K3, F3, M3, E5, C5 • **Temperaments**: M, T • **Physical**: V=L, H=N, L=M, W, H • **Work Env**: I • **Salary**: 4 • **Outlook**: 3

GOE: 06.01.03 Machine Set-up & Operation

LATHE OPERATOR, NUMERICAL CONTROL (mach. shop) • D.O.T. #604.362-010 • OES #91502 • Sets up and operates numerically-controlled horizontal lathe to perform machining operations, such as turning, boring, facing, and threading parts, such as castings, forgings, and bar stock: Reads process sheets, blueprints, and sketches of part to determine machining to be done, dimensional specifications, setup, and operating requirements. Inserts beginning point of tape in reading head of control unit. Mounts workpiece between centers, in chuck, or to face plate, manually or using hoist. Selects and installs preset tooling in tool posts, turrets or indexing heads, and automatic-tool-change magazine, in sequence specified on process sheet. Depresses buttons, toggles, or sets tape and starts machining operation. Observes numerical displays on control panel and compares with data on process sheet to verify dimensional adjustments, feed rates, and speeds of machining cuts. Turns dials and switches to override tape control and correct machine performance, applying practical knowledge of lathe operation. Inspects first-run piece and spot-checks succeeding pieces for conformance to specifications, using micrometers and precision dial gages. Studies job packet and organizes materials for next run during automatic tape-controlled cycles to shorten changeover time. May set tools before positioning them in lathe, using precision gages and instruments. May set up and operate another machine tool during tape-controlled machining cycles. May machine nonmetallic materials. May be designated by type of lathe operated as ENGINE LATHE OPERATOR, NUMERICAL CONTROL (mach. shop); TURRET LATHE OPERATOR, NUMERICAL CONTROL (mach. shop). • **GED**: R4, M3, L3 • **SVP**: 1-2 yrs • **Academic**: Ed=H, Eng=S • **Work Field**: 053, 055, 057 • **MPSMS**: 540 • **Aptitudes**: G3, V3, N3, S2, P2, Q4, K3, F3, M3, E5, C5 • **Temperaments**: M, T • **Physical**: V=G, H=N, L=M, H • **Work Env**: I, N • **Salary**: 4 • **Outlook**: 4

MACHINE OPERATOR 1 (any ind.) • D.O.T. #616.360-018 • OES #91714 • FABRICATING-MACHINE OPERATOR. Sets up and operates metal fabricating machines, such as brakes, rolls, shears, saws, and heavy-duty presses to cut, bend, straighten, and form metal plates, sheets, and structural shapes as specified by blueprints, layout, and templates: Selects, positions, and clamps dies, blades, cutters, and fixtures into machine, using rule, square, shims, template, built-in gages, and handtools. Positions and clamps stops, guides, and turntables. Turns handwheels to set pressure and depth of ram stroke, adjustment rolls, and speed of machine. Locates and marks bending or cutting lines and reference points onto workpiece, using rule, compass, straightedge, or by tracing from templates. Positions workpiece manually or by hoist against stops and guides or alines layout marks with dies or cutting blades. Starts machine. Repositions workpiece and may change dies for multiple or successive passes. Inspects work, using rule, gages, and templates. May set up and operate sheet-metal fabricating machines only and be designated SHEET-METAL-FABRICATING-MACHINE OPERATOR (any ind.). • **GED:** R4, M3, L3 • **SVP:** 1-2 yrs • **Academic:** Ed=H, Eng=S • **Work Field:** 057 • **MPSMS:** 554 • **Aptitudes:** G3, V4, N3, S3, P3, Q4, K3, F3, M3, E4, C5 • **Temperaments:** M, T • **Physical:** V=G, H=N, L=M, W, S, H • **Work Env:** I, N, R • **Salary:** 4 • **Outlook:** 3

MACHINE SET-UP OPERATOR (elec. equip.) • D.O.T. #600.380-018 • OES #91505 • MACHINE OPERATOR, ALL AROUND; MACHINE OPERATOR, GENERAL; MACHINIST. Sets up and operates two or more types of machine tools, such as lathes, milling machines, boring machines, and grinders, to machine metal work pieces according to specifications, tooling instructions, and standard charts, applying knowledge of machining methods: Reads blueprint or job order for product specifications, such as dimensions and tolerances, and tooling instructions, such as fixtures, feed rates, cutting speeds, depth of cut, and cutting tools to be used. Positions and secures workpiece to holding device, machine table, chuck, centers, or fixture, using clamps and wrenches. Positions and secures tool in toolholder (chuck, collet, or toolpost). Moves controls to position tool and workpiece in relation to each other, and to set specified feeds, speeds, and depth of cut. Starts machine, turns handwheel to feed tool to workpiece or vice versa, and engages feed. Turns valve handle to direct flow of coolant or cutting oil against tool and workpiece. Observes operation, and verifies conformance of machined work piece to specifications, using measuring instruments, such as fixed gages, calipers, and micrometers. May set up fixtures or feeding device. May operate bench grinder to sharpen tools. May machine nonmetallic materials. May also set up and operate machines and equipment other than machine tools, such as welding machines and flame-cutting equipment. May have experience with particular material, products, precision level, or size, type or trade name of machine and be designated accordingly, as BARREL REAMER-RIFLER, SPECIAL (firearms); SPECIAL-BARREL PROCESSOR (firearms). • **GED:** R4, M4, L3 • **SVP:** 1-2 yrs • **Academic:** Ed=H, Eng=S • **Work Field:** 057 • **MPSMS:** 540, 567, 568 • **Aptitudes:** G3, V3, N3, S3, P3, Q4, K3, F3, M3, E5, C5 • **Temperaments:** M, T, V • **Physical:** V=G, H=N, L=M, W, H • **Work Env:** I • **Salary:** 4 • **Outlook:** 3

MICROELECTRONICS TECHNICIAN (electronics) • D.O.T. #590.362-022 • OES #92902 • Operates variety of semiconductor processing, testing, and assembly equipment to assist engineering staff in development and fabrication of prototype, custom- designed, electronic circuitry chips in research laboratory, using knowledge of microelectronic processing equipment, procedures, and specifications: Operates equipment to convert integrated circuit layout designs into working photo masks; clean, coat, bake, align, expose, develop, and cure photoresist on wafers; grow layers of dielectric, metal, and semiconductor material on masked areas of wafers; clean, etch, or remove materials on areas not covered by photoresist; and implant chemicals to selective areas of wafer substrate to alter substrate electrical characteristics. Operates various test equipment to verify product conformance to processing and company specifications. Operates equipment to assemble, dice, clean, mount, bond, and package integrated circuit devices. May perform some assembly and packaging operations manually. May assist in interpretation and evaluation of processing data and in preparation of related reports. May assist in technical writing of semiconductor processing specifications. • **GED:** R4, M4, L3 • **SVP:** 1-2 yrs • **Academic:** Ed=H, Eng=S • **Work Field:** 147, 182, 212 • **MPSMS:** 587 • **Aptitudes:** G3, V3, N3, S3, P3, Q2, K3, F3, M3, E4, C4 • **Temperaments:** J, T, V • **Physical:** V=L, H=N, L=L, H • **Work Env:** I, H, R, F • **Salary:** 4 • **Outlook:** 4

PRINTER 2 (print. & pub.) • D.O.T. #651.380-010 • OES #92512 • Sets up and operates printing presses, plate-making equipment, and paper-cutting, drilling and folding machines, to print and produce items, such as decorative box wrappers, direct-mail advertising pieces, office forms, menus, and weekly house organ in business or industrial establishment: Duplicates negative on photographically sensitized metal plates, using exposure frame. Sponges exposed plates with chemical solutions to develop image and washes plate, using water and sponge. Sets metal type in chase by hand. Mounts lithographic plate on cylinder of offset printing press and mounts type on cylinder of cylinder press or flatbed letterpress. Loads stock in feeder magazine of press. Turns screws to adjust paper feed guides. Fills ink and moisture reservoirs and starts press to print sample sheet. Examines sample sheet to determine printing defects, such as off-level areas, variations in ink volume, register slippage, indications of offsetting, and color register. Adjusts press controls, inking fountains, and automatic feeders, and repacks cylinder overlay to equalize off-level areas as required. Operates press to print production run. Sets up and operates power shear to cut sheets of paper or cardboard to specified dimensions. Operates paper-drilling machine to punch or drill holes in printed paper. Operates automatic sheet folder to fold printed sheets or multi-page items. Places cardboard sheet on top of specified number of office forms and spreads glue along one edge of stock to make pads. Maintains and repairs presses and machines, using handtools. May operate vertical process camera to produce paper offset printing plates by photo-direct method. May repair office addressing, duplicating, and mailing equipment operated by other workers. • **GED:** R4, M3, L3 • **SVP:** 4-10 yrs • **Academic:** Ed=N, Eng=G • **Work Field:** 063, 191 • **MPSMS:** 567 • **Aptitudes:** G3, V3, N3, S3, P2, Q3, K3, F3, M3, E5, C4 • **Temperaments:** M, T, V • **Physical:** V=L, H=N, L=M, W, H • **Work Env:** I, N, R • **Salary:** 5 • **Outlook:** 2

REFINERY OPERATOR (petrol. refin.) • D.O.T. #549.260-010 • OES #95014 • Analyzes specifications and controls continuous operation of petroleum refining and processing units to produce products, such as gasoline, kerosene, and fuel and lubricating oils, by such methods as distillation, absorption, extraction, adsorption, thermal and catalytic cracking and reforming, polymerization, isomerization, coking, vis breaking, and alkylation: Reads processing schedules, operating logs, test results of oil samples, and laboratory recommendations to determine changes in equipment controls required to produce specified quantity and quality of product. Moves and sets controls, such as knobs, valves, switches, levers, and index arms, on control panels to control process variables, such as flows, temperatures, pressures, vacuum, time, catalyst, and chemicals, by automatic regulation and remote control of processing units, such as heaters, furnaces, compressors, exchangers, reactors, quenchers, stabilizers, fractionators, rechargers, absorbers, strippers, debutanizers, stills, and towers [CONTROL-PANEL OPERATOR (petrol. refin.)]. Moves controls to regulate valves, pumps, compressors, and auxiliary equipment to direct flow of product. Reads temperature and pressure gages and flowmeters, records readings, and compiles operating records. Determines malfunctioning units by observing control instruments, such as meters and gages, or by automatic warning signals, such as lights and sounding of horns. Inspects equipment to determine location and nature of malfunction, such as leaks, breakages, and faulty valves. Determines need for schedules and performs repair and maintenance of equipment. Patrols unit to verify safe and efficient operating conditions. May sample liquids and gases [SAMPLER (petrol. refin.)], and test products for chemical characteristics and color [TESTER (petrol. refin.)]. May inspect and adjust furnaces, heaters, and damper controls. May lubricate equipment. May clean interior of processing units by circulating chemicals and solvents through them. May treat products [TREATER (petrol. refin.)]. May control activities of several processing units operated in conjunction. May be designated according to process involved or plant operated as ABSORPTION PLANT OPERATOR (petrol. refin.); PURIFICATION OPERATOR (petrol. refin.); REFINERY OPERATOR, CRACKING UNIT (petrol. refin.); REFINERY OPERATOR, POLYMERIZATION PLANT (petrol. refin.); REFINERY OPERATOR, REFORMING UNIT (petrol. refin.); REFINERY OPERATOR, VISBREAKING (petrol. refin.). Additional titles: REFINERY OPERATOR, ALKYLATION (pe trol. refin.); REFINERY OPERATOR, COKING (petrol. refin.); REFINERY OPERATOR, CRUDE UNIT (petrol. refin.); REFINERY OPERATOR, GAS PLANT (petrol. refin.); REFINERY OPERATOR, LIGHT-ENDS RECOVERY (petrol. refin.); REFINERY OPERATOR, VAPOR RECOVERY UNIT (petrol. refin.). • **GED:** R4,

M3, L3 • **SVP:** 4-10 yrs • **Academic:** Ed=H, Eng=S • **Work Field:** 147 • **MPSMS:** 500 • **Aptitudes:** G2, V3, N3, S3, P3, Q4, K4, F4, M3, E5, C4 • **Temperaments:** M, S, T, V • **Stress:** S • **Physical:** V=L, H=N, L=L, W, C, S, H • **Work Env:** B, N, R • **Salary:** 5 • **Outlook:** 2

ROLLING ATTENDANT (iron & steel) • D.O.T. #613.662-010 • OES #95099 • Controls equipment from central console to operate rolling mill which reduces steel into products of specified size, shape, and gage: Selects prepunched schedule cards for section to be rolled according to specifications and feeds into card reader. Activates card reader memory bank (push-button) which reads and interprets schedule card information and stores data in storage unit for response to electronic signal in rolling cycle. Sets selector switches of console for automatic operation of electronic equipment, roll stands, and auxiliary equipment. Moves console controls to advance steel from approach table to mill entry table and through complete rolling cycle automatically, to reduce steel products to specified shape, size, and gage. Observes, from control pulpit, rolling irregularities in ingot, such as pipe, split end, or heat loss, and notifies other worker through intercom system to shear defective parts. Observes rolling operations, dial and colored light indicators, and other gages, and manipulates control levers and switches to adjust roll draft, alinement, or mill speed to correct rolling and tolerance deviations or drift. Stops automated mill and changes to manual control operations on breakdown or failure of electronic or mill equipment. Assists mill crew in setup, roll change, maintenance, and adjustment of mill and auxiliary equipment during manual operation of rolling mill. May make adjustments or minor repairs to electronic control equipment or devices. May move electrical control levers in pulpit to operate mill tables, scale breakers, and broadsiding mill screw down when mill operates under manual control. • **GED:** R4, M3, L3 • **SVP:** 1-2 yrs • **Academic:** Ed=N, Eng=S • **Work Field:** 135 • **MPSMS:** 541 • **Aptitudes:** G3, V3, N3, S3, P3, Q3, K2, F2, M3, E4, C4 • **Temperaments:** M, T, V • **Physical:** V=L, H=N, L=L, H • **Work Env:** I, H, N, R • **Salary:** 4 • **Outlook:** 2

GOE: 06.01.04 Precision Hand Work

ASSEMBLER (inst. & app.) • D.O.T. #710.681-010 • OES #93956 • Assembles instruments and devices, such as control valves, electric motors, relays, thermostats, barometers, compasses, tachometers, oil pressure and water temperature gages, hygrometers, thermometers, rheostats, and gyroscopes, using soldering iron, jewelers handtools, tweezers, alinement mirrors, binocular microscope, eye loupe, and other handtools and work aids: Inspects component parts to insure quality of materials, using binocular microscope and eye loupe. Assembles component parts of instrument or device according to diagrams or written and oral instructions, using soldering iron, handtools, and hydraulic press. Inspects and tests assembled article for assembly defects, using gages, and test instruments, such as ohmmeters and voltmeters. May be designated according to product assembled as COUNTER ASSEMBLER (inst. & app.); ODOMETER ASSEMBLER (inst. & app.); PEDOMETER ASSEMBLER (inst. & app.); SPEEDOMETER ASSEMBLER (inst. & app.); TACHOMETER ASSEMBLER (inst. & app.); THERMOSTAT ASSEMBLER (inst. & app.); VALVE ASSEMBLER (inst. & app.). • **GED:** R3, M2, L2 • **SVP:** 6 mos-1 yr • **Academic:** Ed=N, Eng=N • **Work Field:** 111, 121 • **MPSMS:** 602 • **Aptitudes:** G3, V4, N4, S3, P3, Q4, K3, F3, M3, E5, C4 • **Temperaments:** M, T • **Physical:** V=L, H=N, L=L, H • **Work Env:** I • **Salary:** 3 • **Outlook:** 3

BENCH HAND (jewelry) • D.O.T. #735.381-010 • OES #89126 • BENCH WORKER. Cuts out, files, and solders parts for jewelry articles, such as bracelets, brooches, emblems, and rings, performing any combination of following tasks: Cuts out parts, using powersaw or handsaw. Shapes, trims, and smooths parts, using files. Joins parts together, using solder and torch. May bend ring settings and brooch clasps, using pliers. May assemble finished parts of jewelry articles. • **GED:** R3, M2, L1 • **SVP:** 1-2 yrs • **Academic:** Ed=N, Eng=N • **Work Field:** 102 • **MPSMS:** 611 • **Aptitudes:** G3, V4, N4, S3, P2, Q4, K3, F3, M3, E5, C5 • **Temperaments:** M, T, V • **Physical:** V=L, H=N, L=L, H • **Work Env:** I • **Salary:** 4 • **Outlook:** 3

CANVAS WORKER (canvas goods) • D.O.T. #739.381-010 • OES

#89599 • Lays out canvas, plastic, rubber, and other materials and fabricates and assembles material into sails, awnings, tents, and tarpaulins: Lays out full scale drawings on sail loft floor, according to blueprints or sketches, using chalk. Cuts pattern from paper according to full scale drawing. Marks outline on material with crayon. Cuts material with shears or power cutter. Sews sections of material together on power sewing machine. Installs grommets, metal fittings, and fasteners by machine. When hand-sewing grommets, measures and marks off grommet holes on material, punches holes, using mallet, punch, and hardwood block, and sews galvanized iron ring to edge of hole, using sailmaker's palm and sail twine. Splices, inserts, and hems manila or wire rope in edges to relieve strain or sews rope at points where sail is attached to boom or mast. Secures rope or cable to finished article. Wraps and sews parts of rope or wire that are subject to chafing. Installs and adjusts completed product on shipboard. Examines completed sails for conformance to specifications. May make awning frames [AWNING-FRAME MAKER (canvas goods)]. May be designated according to type of product made as AWNING MAKER (canvas goods); SAILMAKER (canvas goods; ship & boat bldg. & rep.); TENTMAKER (canvas goods). • **GED:** R4, M3, L2 • **SVP:** 2-4 yrs • **Academic:** Ed=N, Eng=N • **Work Field:** 171 • **MPSMS:** 436 • **Aptitudes:** G3, V4, N3, S3, P3, Q4, K3, F3, M3, E5, C5 • **Temperaments:** M, T, V • **Physical:** V=L, H=N, L=M, W, C, S, H • **Work Env:** B • **Salary:** 4 • **Outlook:** 2

CHEESEMAKER (dairy prod.) • D.O.T. #529.361-018 • OES #89808 • CHEESE COOKER. Cooks milk and specified ingredients to make cheese, according to formula: Pasteurizes and separates milk to obtain prescribed butterfat content. Turns valves to fill vat with milk and heat milk to specified temperature. Dumps measured amounts of dye and starter into milk. Starts agitator to mix ingredients. Tests sample of milk for acidity and allows agitator to mix ingredients until specified level of acidity is reached. Dumps and mixes measured amount of rennet into milk. Stops agitator to allow milk to coagulate into curd. Pulls curd knives through curd or separates curd with hand scoop to release whey. Observes thermometer, adjusts steam valve, and starts agitator to stir and cook curd at prescribed temperature for specified time. Squeezes and stretches sample of curd with fingers and extends cooking time to achieve desired firmness or texture. Gives directions to CHEESEMAKER HELPER (dairy prod.) or other workers to make curd, drain whey from curd, add ingredients, such as seasonings, or mold, pack, cut, pile, mill, dump, and press curd into specified shapes. Directs other workers who immerse cheese in brine or roll cheese in dry salt, pierce or smear cheese with cultured wash to develop mold growth, and place or turn cheese blocks on shelves to cure cheese. Tastes, smells, feels, and observes sample plug of cheese for quality. Records amounts of ingredients used, test results, and time cycles. Makes variations in time cycles and ingredients used for succeeding batches. Dumps specified culture into milk or whey in pasteurizer to make bulk starter. May be required to hold state cheesemaker's license. • **GED:** R4, M3, L4 • **SVP:** 2-4 yrs • **Academic:** Ed=H, Eng=S • **Work Field:** 146 • **MPSMS:** 383 • **Aptitudes:** G3, V3, N3, S4, P3, Q4, K4, F4, M3, E5, C4 • **Temperaments:** D, J, M, T • **Physical:** V=L, H=N, L=L, W, H • **Work Env:** I, W • **Salary:** 4 • **Outlook:** 3

COREMAKER (foundry) • D.O.T. #518.381-014 • OES #89902 • COREMAKER, EXPERIMENTAL. Makes sand cores used in molds to form holes or hollows in metal castings: Cleans core box with blast of compressed air. Dusts parting sand over inside of core box to facilitate removal of finished core. Partially fills core box with sand by pulling cord that releases sand from overhead chute or by using hands or shovel. Compacts sand in core box, using hands, hand rammer, and air rammer. Bends reinforcing wires by hand, and inserts them in sand. Fills core box and rams sand in tightly. Inverts core box onto metal plate, and lifts box from sand core. Patches cracked or chipped places on core and smooths core surfaces, using spoon and trowel. May bake cores to harden them. May assemble cores. May work at bench making small cores and be designated COREMAKER, BENCH (found.); or make large cores on floor of foundry and be designated CORE MAKER, FLOOR (found.). • **GED:** R3, M2, L2 • **SVP:** 6 mos-1 yr • **Academic:** Ed=N, Eng=N • **Work Field:** 136 • **MPSMS:** 567 • **Aptitudes:** G3, V3, N4, S3, P3, Q4, K3, F3, M3, E5, C5 • **Temperaments:** M, R, T • **Stress:** T • **Physical:** V=L, H=N, L=M, W, S, H • **Work Env:** I, N • **Salary:** 4 • **Outlook:** 2

ELECTRIC-MOTOR-CONTROL ASSEMBLER (elec. equip.) • D.O.T. #721.381-014 • OES #93114 • Assembles electric motor control units, such as transmitters, relays, switches, voltage controls, and starters and mounts unit on panel according to drawings and specifications, using handtools and power tools: Cleans parts, using liquid cleaner, airhose, and cloth. Assembles units, using handtools pneumatic nut runners, power press, and torque wrenches. Lays out and drills mounting holes and mounts units to panel, using scribers, rule, dividers, drill press, portable power drill, reamer, screwdrivers, and wrenches. Adjusts and aligns parts to maintain specified airgap, contact wipe, dimensions, and part movement, using feeler gages and micrometers. Solders electric wire connections and secures spring guides, setscrews and spring post to units, using soldering iron and acetylene torch. Tests electrical circuits for resistance, current and potential difference, using instruments, such as ohmmeter, ammeter, and voltmeter. May be designated according to control assembled as TRANSMITTER ASSEMBLER (elec. equip.); VOLTAGE-REGULATOR ASSEMBLER (elec. equip.). May also operate sheet metal forming machines to fabricate housing for synchro-units and be designated as SYNCHRO-UNIT ASSEMBLER (elec. equip.) • **GED:** R4, M3, L2 • **SVP:** 1-2 yrs • **Academic:** Ed=H, Eng=N • **Work Field:** 111 • **MPSMS:** 581, 582 • **Aptitudes:** G3, V4, N3, S3, P2, Q4, K3, F3, M3, E4, C4 • **Temperaments:** M, T • **Physical:** V=G, H=N, L=M, W, S, H • **Work Env:** I • **Salary:** 2 • **Outlook:** 3

FINAL ASSEMBLER (office mach.) • D.O.T. #706.381-018 • OES #93111 • Assembles, installs, and adjusts variety of electromechanical units, such as feed drives, control key assemblies, and printing units, on new and rebuilt punched card office machines according to blueprints and written specifications, using handtools, assembly fixtures, and test devices: Reads blueprints to determine position of unit and component parts. Positions components in assembly fixture. Assembles unit and mounts it on office machine frame, using screwdrivers and wrenches. Starts machine and adjusts unit for specified clearances and time cycles, using fixed gages, test lights, and handtools. Inspects machine to verify that optional equipment changes have been made according to customer order. May operate electric hoist to position unit on office machine frame. • **GED:** R3, M2, L3 • **SVP:** 1-2 yrs • **Academic:** Ed=N, Eng=S • **Work Field:** 121 • **MPSMS:** 571 • **Aptitudes:** G3, V3, N3, S3, P3, Q4, K3, F3, M3, E5, C4 • **Temperaments:** M, T • **Physical:** V=L, H=N, L=M, W, H • **Work Env:** I • **Salary:** 3 • **Outlook:** 2

GLASS BLOWER (glass mfg.) • D.O.T. #772.681-010 • OES #89905 • BLOWER; GAFFER. Shapes gather (gob of molten glass) into glassware by blowing through blowpipe: Receives blowpipe from GATHERER (glass mfg.) and examines gather (gob of molten glass) on blowpipe for imperfections, utilizing knowledge of molten glass characteristics. Blows through pipe to inflate gather while rotating pipe to prevent sagging and to obtain desired shape, or blows and rotates gather in mold or on board to obtain final shape. May dip end of blowpipe into molten glass to collect gather on head of pipe. May strike neck of finished article to separate article from blow pipe. May pull gather with tongs to aid in shaping. May use compressed air to inflate gather. May be designated according to article blown as BOTTLE BLOWER (glass mfg.). • **GED:** R3, M2, L2 • **SVP:** 2-4 yrs • **Academic:** Ed=N, Eng=N • **Work Field:** 136 • **MPSMS:** 531 • **Aptitudes:** G3, V4, N4, S3, P3, Q4, K3, F3, M3, E4, C4 • **Temperaments:** J, R, T • **Stress:** T • **Physical:** V=L, H=N, L=L, W, S, H • **Work Env:** I, H, N • **Salary:** 4 • **Outlook:** 1

GOLDBEATER (gold leaf & foil) • D.O.T. #700.381-018 • OES #89126 • Beats gold strips into gold leaf, using hammers, for use in decorating products, such as books, furniture, and signs: Cuts gold strip into one inch squares and interlaminates squares with leaves of cutch (packet of vellum sheets). Hammers cutch to reduce thickness and expand area of squares to form gold sheets of specified dimensions. Cuts sheets into quarters and interlaminates quartered sheets with leaves of shoder (packet of skins). Hammers shoder to form gold leaf of specified dimensions. • **GED:** R3, M2, L2 • **SVP:** 1-2 yrs • **Academic:** Ed=N, Eng=N • **Work Field:** 134 • **MPSMS:** 559 • **Aptitudes:** G3, V4, N4, S3, P3, Q4, K3, F4, M3, E5, C5 • **Temperaments:** M, T • **Physical:** V=L, H=N, L=M, H • **Work Env:** I, N • **Salary:** 4 • **Out look:** 2

LENS POLISHER, HAND (optical goods) • D.O.T. #716.681-018

• OES #89917 • Hand polishes optical elements, such as lenses, prisms, and optical flats, to finish element or remove defects, using jeweler's rouge, polishing cloth or device, precision measuring instruments, and jeweler's lathe: Examines surface of element to detect defects, such as stains and scratches, and measures element to determine amount of finish required, using precision measuring instruments. Rubs rouge onto chamois, using jeweler's rouge stick, or onto polishing device mounted on workbench, using sponge. Rubs chamois over surface of element or oscillates element against polishing device to remove defects from element. Mounts element on spindle of jeweler's lathe, starts lathe, and holds rouge-coated chamois against element to finish element. Verifies dimensions of finished element, using precision measuring instruments and examines elements to ensure all defects have been corrected, using magnifying glass. Cleans finished elements, using lens cleaning solution, cloth, and paper. • **GED:** R3, M2, L2 • **SVP:** 6 mos-1 yr • **Academic:** Ed=N, Eng=N • **Work Field:** 051 • **MPSMS:** 603 • **Aptitudes:** G3, V3, N3, S3, P2, Q4, K3, F3, M3, E5, C4 • **Temperaments:** J, M, T • **Physical:** V=L, H=N, L=L, H • **Work Env:** I • **Salary:** 3 • **Outlook:** 3

MOLDER (foundry) • D.O.T. #518.361-010 • OES #89902 • EXPERIMENTAL MOLDER; SAND MOLDER. Forms sand molds for production of metal castings, using handtools, power tools, patterns or match plates, and flasks, and applying knowledge of variables, such as metal characteristics, molding sand, contours of patterns, and pouring procedures: Positions drag half of pattern and flask on follow board. Sprinkles or sprays parting agent on pattern and flask and positions reinforcing wire in flask. Sifts sand over pattern, using riddle and presses sand around contours of pattern. Shovels sand into flask and packs it in place, using hand ramming tools or pneumatic hammer. Turns drag over and positions cope half of pattern and flask on drag. Repeats molding operation to make cope. Lifts cope from drag and removes pattern. Cuts runner and sprue hole into mold and repairs damaged impressions, using molder's handtools, such as slick, trowel, spoon, and sprue cutter. Positions specified cores in drag and reassembles cope and drag. Signals BRIDGE-OR-GANTRY-CRANE OPERATOR (any ind.) to move and position large flasks, patterns, and bottom boards, or moves them, using chain hoist. Pours molten metal into mold, using ladle, or tells POURER, METAL (found.) to fill mold. May form and assemble slab cores around pattern to reinforce mold, using handtools and glue. May harden molds by blowing carbon dioxide gas on them or by injecting gas into molds. May form small molds on bench and be designated MOLDER, BENCH (conc. prod.; found.) or form large molds on floor and be designated MOLDER, FLOOR (found.). • **GED:** R4, M3, L3 • **SVP:** 2-4 yrs • **Academic:** Ed=N, Eng=S • **Work Field:** 136 • **MPSMS:** 567 • **Aptitudes:** G3, V3, N3, S3, P3, Q4, K3, F3, M3, E5, C5 • **Temperaments:** M, T • **Physical:** V=L, H=N, L=M, W, H • **Work Env:** I, N • **Salary:** 4 • **Outlook:** 2

RING MAKER (jewelry) • D.O.T. #700.381-042 • OES #89123 • Fabricates rings by any of following methods: (1) Casts rings, using molds of rubber, plaster, wax, sand, and metal. (2) Cuts out ring blanks from flat metal and shapes blanks into ring bands. (3) Ties or twists gold or silver wires together and bends to form rings. Removes gates, solders ends, and files rings to remove excess metal. Cleans and polishes rings by immersing in metal cleaning or acid solution. May set stones in rings. • **GED:** R3, M2, L2 • **SVP:** 2-4 yrs • **Academic:** Ed=N, Eng=N • **Work Field:** 102, 132 • **MPSMS:** 611 • **Aptitudes:** G3, V3, N4, S3, P3, Q4, K3, F3, M3, E5, C4 • **Temperaments:** M, T, V • **Physical:** V=L, H=N, L=L, H • **Work Env:** I • **Salary:** 4 • **Outlook:** 2

SKIN FITTER (aircraft-aerospace mfg.) • D.O.T. #806.381-054 • OES #93102 • AIRCRAFT-METAL WORKER; AIR CRAFT-SHEET-METAL MECHANIC; FUSELAGE-COVERING FITTER; SKINNER; SPECIALIST, SHEET METAL. Fits sheet metal coverings to fuselage bulkheads and other sections of aircraft and fastens sheet metal in position preparatory to welding or riveting, using handtools and metal fabricating machinery: Trims edges of preformed sheet to ensure flush fit, using rasp. Drills rivet holes through sheets and flanges of bulkheads, using electric drill. Cuts, bends, and trims sheet metal airfoil parts to shape, using metal-fabricating machinery and handtools. Fits sheet metal parts to aircraft framework, using self-tapping screws or C-clamps. Cuts away damaged areas of skin, using metal snips and attaches patch flush with adjoining skin, using rivet gun. May perform duties as described under GROUP LEADER (any ind.). • **GED:** R3, M2, L2 • **SVP:** 2-4 yrs • **Academic:** Ed=N, Eng=N • **Work Field:** 102 • **MPSMS:** 592 • **Aptitudes:** G3, V4, N4, S3, P3, Q4, K3, F3, M3, E5, C4 • **Temperaments:** M, T • **Physical:** V=L, H=N, L=M, W, H • **Work Env:** I, N • **Salary:** 4 • **Outlook:** 1

SOLDERER (jewelry) • D.O.T. #700.381-050 • OES #89126 • Solders together parts of new or broken jewelry, using gas torch and solder: Selects type of solder to be used and lays parts on asbestos board. Lights torch and applies solder and flux to article as needed. Immerses article in water to cool. • **GED:** R3, M2, L3 • **SVP:** 6 mos-1 yr • **Academic:** Ed=N, Eng=S • **Work Field:** 083 • **MPSMS:** 611 • **Aptitudes:** G3, V4, N4, S3, P3, Q4, K3, F3, M3, E5, C4 • **Temperaments:** M, T • **Physical:** V=L, H=N, L=S, H • **Work Env:** I • **Salary:** 3 • **Outlook:** 2

TRANSFORMER ASSEMBLER (elec. equip.) • D.O.T. #820.381-014 • OES #93114 • Connects coils to terminals and builds up supporting structure of power transformers, according to wiring and structural diagrams: Wraps insulation around coil and secures with adhesive tape. Drives fiber wedges between coil and core, using mallet to hold coil around leg of transformer core. Crimps leads to magnet (coil) wire, using hand or hydraulic crimper and tapes connections. Crimps tags to lead wires to conform with wiring diagram. Assembles support structure, clamping angles, terminals, tanks, or cabinet panels, using gas or electric welding equipment, welding jigs tie bolts, nut runner, drill press, and power drill. Brazes coil leads to specified tanks of terminal strip. May fabricate coils and assemble component parts to build electric power, distribution, or specialty transformers according to blueprints and wiring or structural diagrams. Winds copper wire around jig, fixture, or spindle to form primary coil. Fabricates secondary coil on copper plate of specified thickness, using drill, calipers, and bandsaw. May be designated according to type of transformer assembled as DISTRIBUTION-TRANSFORMER ASSEMBLER (elec. equip.); POWER-TRANSFORMER ASSEMBLER (elec. equip.); SPECIALTY-TRANSFORMER ASSEMBLER (elec. equip.); or by type of core used as HYPERCIL-CORE-TRANSFORMER ASSEMBLER (elec. equip.). • **GED:** R4, M4, L3 • **SVP:** 1-2 yrs • **Academic:** Ed=N, Eng=S • **Work Field:** 111 • **MPSMS:** 581 • **Aptitudes:** G3, V3, N3, S3, P2, Q4, K3, F3, M3, E5, C4 • **Temperaments:** M, T, V • **Physical:** V=L, H=N, L=M, W, H • **Work Env:** I • **Salary:** 4 • **Outlook:** 2

TUBE ASSEMBLER, ELECTRON (electronics) • D.O.T. #725.384-010 • OES #93956 • Performs any one or combination of duties to fabricate parts and assemble custom or production electron tubes: Reads work orders, receives verbal instructions, and follows drawings and sample assemblies relating to assembly duties to be performed. Winds wire around grid core or mandrel, using manual or automatic winding machines to form filaments, grids, and heaters. Stretches and presses wound grid cores to shape and cuts to size, using manual or power tools. Forms parts such as grids, stems, and leads, using special purpose automatic machines. Coats designated parts with specified materials which change their conductive properties or produce an effect such as fluorescence, using automatic or manually operated spray equipment. Positions parts such as grids, spacers, plates, caps, shield, stems, targets, getters (chemical solution), heaters, and radiators in specified relationships to each other. Mounts parts in holding fixtures and bonds together using a variety of welding and brazing techniques and equipment, such as spot welders and brazing ovens. Fills bases or top caps of designated tubes with adhesive and attaches to glass bulbs and metal shells. Places assembled tube in automatic equipment to remove impurities, create vacuum, and seal tube. Stamps or etches identifying information on tube and tube parts, using automatic or manually operated printing or etching equipment. Polishes designated parts and assemblies, using buffing wheel. Brushes designated tubes with aquadag (carbon paint) to provide electrostatic shield for tube elements. Tends oven to cure adhesives, inks, and coatings. May tend machine which seals lead wires in glass beads to form stems. May fit cooler jackets on tubes. May assemble small parts under magnifying device. May disassemble, reclaim, rework, or modify parts or assemblies. May perform in-process testing, using electronic test

equipment, to ensure assembly procedures have been completed according to specifications. May make minor adjustments to machinery and power tools, and change dies and guides to maintain manufacturing standards. May tend automatic electronic ageing equipment to stabilize electrical characteristics of finished tubes. May remove tungsten filament coils from mandrels by dissolving in acid bath. May be designated according to duties performed as AGER (electronics); BASE BRANDER (electronics); BULB CARBONIZER (electronics); CATHODE-COATER OPERATOR (electronics); EXHAUST OPERATOR (electronics); FILAMENT DISSOLVER (electronics). Additional titles: BASE FILLER, AUTOMATIC (electronics); BASE FILLER, HAND (electronics); CAGE-AND-DOME-PAD ASSEMBLER (electronics); CATHODE-TAB WELDER (electronics); FILAMENT MAKER (electronics); FILLING-MACHINE OPERATOR (electronics); FLARE BEADER (electronics); GETTER WELDER (electronics); GRID-LEAD FORMER (electronics); GRID OPERATOR (electronics); GRID TRIMMER (electronics); GUN ASSEMBLER (electronics); HEATER LOADER (electronics); MOUNTER (electronics); PARTIAL STEMMER (electronics); ROTARY-PUMP OPERATOR (electronics); STEM-LEAD FORMER (electronics); STEM MAKER (electronics); TOP-CAP FILLER (electronics); TUBE FINISHER (electronics); TUBE LAMINATOR (electronics). • **GED:** R2, M2, L2 • **SVP:** 2-30 days • **Academic:** Ed=N, Eng=N • **Work Field:** 111 • **MPSMS:** 587 • **Aptitudes:** G4, V4, N4, S4, P4, Q4, K3, F3, M3, E5, C5 • **Temperaments:** R, T • **Stress:** T • **Physical:** V=L, H=N, L=L, H • **Work Env:** I • **Salary:** 3 • **Outlook:** 2

GOE: 06.01.05 Inspection, Prod. Tech.

ELECTRONICS INSPECTOR I (electronics) • D.O.T. #726.381-010 • OES #83002 • QUALITY CONTROL INSPECTOR; SYSTEMS INSPECTOR. Inspects electronic assemblies, subassemblies, and parts for compliance with specifications following blue prints, drawings, and production and inspection manuals, using one or combination of following methods: Examines layout and installation of wiring, cables, subassemblies, hardware, and components to detect assembly errors. Compares assembly with parts list to detect missing hardware. Examines joints, using magnifying glass and mirror, and pulls wires and cables to locate soldering defects. Examines alignment of parts and measures parts for conformance with specified dimensions, using precision-measuring instruments, such as micrometers, vernier calipers and gauges. Twists dials, shafts, and gears to verify freedom of movement. Traces cables and harness assemblies, following cable print, to verify routing of wires to specified connections and conformance of cable lacing and insulation with manufacturing standards. Measures plated areas for uniformity and thickness, using micrometers or dial indicators. Verifies location of bolt and rivet holes, using templates, check fixtures, and measuring instruments. Examines parts to locate surface defects, such as chips, scratches, and pinholes. Records inspection data, such as serial number, type and percent of defects, and rework required. May stamp inspected equipment to indicate acceptance. May resolder broken connections. May perform functional and operational tests, using electronic test equipment, such as frequency meters, oscilloscope, and signal generator [ELECTRONICS TESTER (electronics) I 726.281-014]. May inspect and lay out optic axis of raw quartz crystals, using optical inspection equipment and be designated INSPECTOR, RAW QUARTZ (electronics). May inspect parts at random and be designated CHECK INSPECTOR (electronics). May inspect units on assembly line and be designated FINAL INSPECTOR (electronics) or IN-PROCESS INSPECTOR (electronics). May be designated according to kind of unit inspected as INSPECTOR, SUBASSEMBLIES (electronics) or INSPECTOR, TUBES (electronics). • **GED:** R4, M4, L4 • **SVP:** 1-2 yrs • **Academic:** Ed=H, Eng=S • **Work Field:** 211 • **MPSMS:** 587, 589 • **Aptitudes:** G3, V3, N3, S3, P3, Q3, K3, F2, M2, E5, C3 • **Temperaments:** J, T • **Physical:** V=G, H=N, L=L, H • **Work Env:** I • **Salary:** 3 • **Outlook:** 4

ELECTRONICS TESTER I (electronics) • D.O.T. #726.281-014 • OES #83002 • QUALITY-CONTROL-ASSEMBLY-TEST TECHNICIAN; TECHNICIAN, TEST SYSTEMS; TESTER, SYSTEMS; TEST TECHNICIAN; TROUBLE SHOOTER. Performs a variety of electronic, mechanical, and electromechanical tests on electronic systems, subassemblies, and parts to ensure unit functions according to specifications or to determine cause of unit failure, using full range of electronic test instruments: Reads test schedule, work orders, test manuals, performance specifications, wiring diagrams, and schematics to ascertain testing procedure and equipment to be used. Performs functional tests of systems, subassemblies, and parts under specified environmental conditions, such as temperature change, vibration, pressure, and humidity, using devices such as temperature cabinets, shake-test machines, and centrifuges. Calibrates test instruments according to specifications. Connects unit to be tested to equipment, such as signal generator, frequency meter, or spectrum analyzer. Reads dials that indicate electronic characteristics, such as voltage, frequency, distortion, inductance, and capacitance. Compares results with specifications and records test data or plots test results on graph. Traces circuits of defective units, using knowledge of electronic theory and electronic test equipment to locate defects, such as shorts or faulty components. Replaces defective wiring and components, using handtools and soldering iron, or records defects on tag attached to unit and returns it to production department for repair. May write computer programs to control semiconductor device and electronic component test equipment prior to testing, utilizing knowledge of programming techniques, electronics, test equipment, and testing specifications. May examine switches, dials, and other hardware for conformance to specifications. May verify dimensions of pins, shafts, and other mechanical parts, using calipers, vernier gauges, and micrometers. May operate x-ray equipment to verify internal assembly and alignment of part according to specifications. May calibrate unit to obtain specified dial reading of characteristics, such as frequency or inductance. May devise test equipment setup to evaluate performance and operation of nonstandard or customer returned units. May be designated according to unit tested as MEMORY-UNIT TEST TECHNICIAN (electronics); TELEVISION-RECEIVER ANALYZER (electronics); TRANSMITTER TESTER (electronics); TUBE-TEST TECHNICIAN (electronics). • **GED:** R4, M4, L3 • **SVP:** 2-4 yrs • **Academic:** Ed=H, Eng=S • **Work Field:** 111, 211 • **MPSMS:** 586, 587 • **Aptitudes:** G2, V3, N3, S2, P3, Q3, K3, F3, M3, E5, C3 • **Temperaments:** J, T • **Physical:** V=G, H=N, L=L, H • **Work Env:** I • **Salary:** 4 • **Outlook:** 4

INSPECTOR, ASSEMBLIES AND INSTALLATIONS (aircraft- aerospace mfg.) • D.O.T. #806.281-022 • OES #83002 • Inspects assemblies, such as wings, body sections, flap, bonded structure, and tail assemblies, joining of subassemblies into major structures, and complete aircraft for adherence to sequence of operation and for correctness of assembly, according to blue prints, drawings, and production and inspection manuals: Examines cables for kinks, cracks, and loose connections. Inspects alinement of parts, using templates, check jigs, and sight levels. Verifies location, size, shape, reaming, and countersinking of bolt and rivet holes, using ball gages, templates, and calipers. Inspects assembly of mechanical equipment, such as landing gear struts and wing flap and rudder actuators, for tolerance of fit, using micrometers, calipers, and verniers. Examines installation of engines, mechanical equipment, plumbing lines and tanks, wiring shields, and brackets in subassemblies and aircraft structures to verify location and fastening and to determine surface defects, such as scratches and cracks. Examines fit and seal of windows and doors and installation of bulkheads, seats, instrument panels, and decorative panels. Examines installation of floor and wall coverings and upholstery to verify color, quality, and fit of material. Writes inspection reports. May examine metal parts to detect internal fractures, holes, and other imperfections, using X-ray equipment. May set up and control test equipment, such as sensing and telemetering apparatus, to produce and measure effects of vibration, stress, humidity, and pressure on assemblies. May inspect packaging of assemblies prior to shipment to ensure conformity to specifications. May be designated according to assemblies inspected as ENGINE INSTALLATION INSPECTOR (aircraft-aerospace mfg.); INSPECTOR, FINAL ASSEMBLY (aircraft-aerospace mfg.); INSPECTOR, SUBASSEMBLY (aircraft- aerospace mfg.); UPHOLSTERY-AND-TRIM INSPECTOR (aircraft- aerospace mfg.), or according to specialization as INSPECTOR, EXPERIMENTAL (air craft-aerospace mfg.). • **GED:** R4, M3, L2 • **SVP:** 2-4 yrs • **Academic:** Ed=H, Eng=N • **Work Field:** 211 • **MPSMS:** 592 • **Aptitudes:** G3, V3, N3, S2, P2, Q3, K3, F3, M3, E5, C4 • **Temperaments:** M, T • **Physical:** V=G, H=N, L=L, W, C, S, H • **Work Env:** I, N • **Salary:** 4 • **Outlook:** 4

INSPECTOR, METAL FABRICATING (any ind.) • D.O.T. #619.261-010 • OES #83002 • PLATE-AND-WELD INSPECTOR; PLATE-SHOP INSPECTOR; STRUCTURAL INSPECTOR. Inspects materials received, finished products, and work in process of fabrication into metal products to ensure conformance with work orders and diagrammatic and template specifications: Measures center lines and reference points to verify initial and assembly layout and machine setup, using layout plate, templates, squares, straightedge, feelers, tape, transit, and plumblines. Verifies physical properties and size of materials, such as plates, sheets, structural shapes, castings, forgings, dies, fixtures, and work produced by fabricating machines, using magnaflux machine, surface plate, hardness testing equipment, gages, and micrometers. Verifies hole size, using pluggage. Examines finished products for rough edges, cracks, and appearance. Marks parts for acceptance or rejection. Makes reports to suggest changes in dies, fixtures, and materials used. Reports inspection results. Makes sketches and recommends procedure for special salvage or scrapping operations. May inspect material for internal defects, using X-ray and ultrasonic test equipment. May specialize in single phase of inspection and be designated accordingly as LAY-OUT INSPECTOR (any ind.); MACHINE-OPERATIONS INSPECTOR (any ind.); TEMPLATE INSPECTOR (any ind.). • **GED:** R4, M4, L4 • **SVP:** 2-4 yrs • **Academic:** Ed=N, Eng=S • **Work Field:** 102, 211 • **MPSMS:** 550 • **Aptitudes:** G3, V3, N3, S3, P3, Q3, K3, F3, M3, E4, C5 • **Temperaments:** M, T • **Physical:** V=G, H=N, L=L, W, C, S, H • **Work Env:** I, N, R • **Salary:** 4 • **Outlook:** 2

RETICLE INSPECTOR (electronics) • D.O.T. #719.361-010 • OES #83002 • Inspects and measures master reticle patterns and masks and etched or coated processed parts, such as metal sheets, optical lenses, and crystal, silicone, or sapphire wafers to ensure conformance to product specifications and quality control standards, using binocular microscope: Reads specification sheets to determine specified reticle graduations or measurements. Positions pattern, mask, or processed part on illuminated stage of binocular microscope. Examines workpiece at varying powers of magnification to determine quality of workmanship and to detect defects, such as pinholes, cracks, and defective coating or etching. Turns controls on microscope to aline reticles in microscope lens with reticles on workpiece and reads measurements indicated on optical lens or vernier scale on knobs and controls of microscope. Compares measurement readings with specification chart readings to verify dimensional specifications of workpiece. Maintains inspection records and routes defective workpieces for repair or salvage. Notifies supervisory personnel of substandard quality control. May be designated according to type workpiece inspected as RETICLE INSPECTOR, COATED PARTS (electronics; inst. & app.; optical goods); RETICLE INSPECTOR, ETCHED PARTS (electronics; inst. & app.; optical goods); RETICLE INSPECTOR, PATTERNS AND MASKS (electronics; inst. & app.; optical goods). • **GED:** R4, M3, L3 • **SVP:** 2-4 yrs • **Academic:** Ed=N, Eng=S • **Work Field:** 211 • **MPSMS:** 587, 601, 609 • **Aptitudes:** G3, V3, N3, S2, P2, Q4, K3, F3, M3, E5, C5 • **Temperaments:** M, T • **Physical:** V=G, H=N, L=L, H • **Work Env:** I • **Salary:** 4 • **Outlook:** 4

TEST TECHNICIAN, SEMICONDUCTOR PROCESSING EQUIPMENT (electronics) • D.O.T. #590.262-014 • OES #92902 • Operates machines and equipment used in production of semiconductor wafers, such as alignment equipment, automatic developer, and diffusion furnaces, and tests processed wafers to evaluate performance of machines and equipment: Operates machines and equipment to process test wafer. Inspects and measures test wafer, using electronic measuring equipment and microscope, to determine that machines and equipment are processing wafers according to company specifications. Records test results in logbooks. Discusses production problems with workers. Analyzes test results, using engineering specifications and calculator, and writes report on equipment repair or re-calibration recommendations and on operator procedure violations. • **GED:** R4, M3, L4 • **SVP:** 2-4 yrs • **Academic:** Ed=H, Eng=S • **Work Field:** 147, 212 • **MPSMS:** 587 • **Aptitudes:** 2G2, V2, N3, S3, P3, Q2, K2, F3, M3, E5, C5 • **Temperaments:** J, T, V • **Physical:** V=G, H=N, L=L, H • **Work Env:** I, R • **Salary:** 4 •

Outlook: 4

X-RAY-EQUIPMENT TESTER (any ind.) • D.O.T. #729.281-046 • OES #83002 • X-RAY CONSULTANT; X-RAY EQUIPMENT SER-VICER; X-RAY SERVICE ENGINEER. Tests X-ray machines and accessory equipment to locate defects, using voltmeter and laboratory testing instruments: Compares readings on X-ray control meter and timer with measurements taken with standard instruments during machine operation to verify or adjust meter and timer calibra-tion. Tests performance of transformer and measures voltages, using voltmeter, and compares results with standard graphs. May plan layouts of X-ray departments and install equipment. • **GED:** R4, M3, L3 • **SVP:** 1-2 yrs • **Academic:** Ed=N, Eng=S • **Work Field:** 211 • **MPSMS:** 589 • **Aptitudes:** G2, V3, N2, S3, P2, Q3, K4, F3, M3, E5, C4 • **Temperaments:** J, V • **Physical:** V=L, H=N, L=L, W, H • **Work Env:** I, R • **Salary:** 4 • **Outlook:** 3

06.02 Production Work

Workers in this group perform skilled hand and/or machine work to make products in a factory setting.

✔ **What kind of work would you do?**

Your work activities would depend upon your specific job. For example, you might:

- control vacuum pan boilers to crystallize liquid sugar.
- set up and operate machines that make paper products.
- thread nuts and bolts by operating a tapping machine.
- tend a series of coating machines to make artificial leather or oilcloth.
- split animal hides into layers by operating a machine which rolls and cuts leather to specified thicknesses.
- determine amount of fabric to be used for garment patterns and supervise marking and cutting activities.
- use power screw drivers to install automobile doors.

✔ **What skills and abilities do you need for this kind of work?**

To do this kind of work, you must be able to:

- read and follow instructions to set up and adjust machines and equipment.
- use eyes, hands, and fingers to adjust controls on machines, manipulate hand tools, or assemble products.
- use math skills for measuring, computing, or recordkeeping.
- detect differences in the shape, size, and texture of various items.
- pay strict attention to set standards and guidelines.
- direct the work of others.

The above statements may not apply to every job in this group.

✔ **How do you know if you would like or could learn to do this kind of work?**

The following questions may give you clues about yourself as you consider this group of jobs.

- Have you taken industrial arts or machine shop courses? Do you like to operate machines?
- Have you taken general or applied mathematics courses? Do you like projects which use math skills such as measuring?
- Have you assembled a bicycle or toy by following drawings or written instructions? Was it fairly easy for you to do?
- Have you held a summer or part-time job where mechanical equipment was used? Do you enjoy working around mechanical equipment?

✔ **How can you prepare for and enter this kind of work?**

Occupations in this group usually require education and/or training extending from three months to over four years, depending upon the specific kind of work. Machine shop courses are helpful for most jobs in this group. General or applied mathematics courses may also be helpful for some jobs. Apprenticeship programs are available for some jobs. However, most workers are trained on the job. Several jobs in this group can be attained by promotion from a helper's position.

Supervisory jobs are usually given to workers with seniority and skill.

✔ **What else should you consider about these jobs?**

Workers in this group usually follow established work procedures and their activities seldom change from day to day.

Overtime or night and shift work may be required. Workers may advance to higher level jobs as supervisors and inspectors.

Workers are exposed to different types of factory conditions. Most plants are well-lighted and ventilated. However, working around machinery may be hazardous or noisy, and safety procedures must be followed.

If you think you would like to do this kind of work, look at the job titles listed on the following pages.

GOE: 06.02.01 Supervision, Production Work

TOOL GRINDER 2 (any ind.) • D.O.T. #603.664-010 • OES #91117 • TOOL SHARPENER. Sharpens and smooths cutting edge of tools, such as axes, chisels, drills, picks, and straight cutting blades, using abrasive wheel: Presses button to start abrasive wheel. Positions and holds cutting edge of tool against machine guide and abrasive wheel to sharpen and smooth tool edge. Immerses tool in oil to cool edge. Repositions and holds tool edge against guide and abrasive wheel to further sharpen and smooth edge. May heat tools and immerse them in brine, oil, or water to harden them. May remove burs from ground edges of tools, using whetstone. May sharpen and reduce diameter of circular cutting blades. May be designated according to kind of tool sharpened as AX SHARPENER (any ind.); CHISEL GRINDER (any ind.); KNIFE AND SPUR GRINDER (excelsior); KNIFE GRINDER (any ind.). • **GED:** R2, M1, L1 • **SVP:** 30 days-3 mos • **Academic:** Ed=N, Eng=N • **Work Field:** 051 • **MPSMS:** 552 • **Aptitudes:** G4, V4, N5, S4, P3, Q5, K4, F4, M3, E5, C5 • **Temperaments:** R, T • **Stress:** T • **Physical:** V=L, H=N, L=M, W, H • **Work Env:** I, H, N • **Salary:** 2 • **Outlook:** 3

GOE: 06.02.02 Machine Work, Metal & Plastics, Skilled

BRAKE OPERATOR 2 (any ind.) • D.O.T. #619.685-026 • OES #91321 • PRESS-BRAKE OPERATOR. Tends power brake that bends, punches, forms, rolls, arcs, or straightens metal sheets, plates, and bars: Positions work manually or with crane against stops, or alines layout marks to dies. Brushes oil on dies and workpiece. Starts machine to lower ram and shape workpiece. Tightens die nuts to prevent movement of die, using wrenches. Inspects work for conformance to specifications, using rule, square, or templates. Cleans scale or scrap from die with airhose or brush. May depress pedal to lower ram and shape work piece. May tend furnace to preheat metal to specified temperatures before bending. May be designated according to material shaped as BRAKE OPERATOR, SHEET METAL (any ind.) II. • **GED:** R3, M2, L2 • **SVP:** 3-6 mos • **Academic:** Ed=N, Eng=N • **Work Field:** 134 • **MPSMS:** 554 • **Aptitudes:** G3, V4, N4, S3, P4, Q5, K3, F4, M3, E4, C5 • **Temperaments:** R, T • **Stress:** T • **Physical:** V=L, H=N, L=M, W, H • **Work Env:** I, N • **Salary:** 3 • **Outlook:** 2

CRIMPING-MACHINE OPERATOR (any ind.) • D.O.T. #616.682-022 • OES #92197 • Sets up and operates machine to crimp wire to specified shape: Bolts specified crimping wheels into machine jaws, using wrench. Threads end of coiled wire through straightening and feed rollers into wire shaping machine. Starts machine and crimps sample wire of specified type. Measures sample, using micrometers and gages, and changes crimping wheels or adjusts tension of machine until crimp meets specifications. May place shaped wire in rack. May be designated according to product worked on as ZIG-ZAG-SPRING-MACHINE OPERATOR (wirework). • **GED:** R3, M2, L2 • **SVP:** 6 mos-1 yr • **Academic:** Ed=N, Eng=N • **Work Field:** 134 • **MPSMS:** 557 • **Aptitudes:** G3, V4, N4, S4, P3, Q4, K3, F4, M3, E5, C5 • **Temperaments:** M, T • **Physical:** V=L, H=N, L=L, W, H • **Work Env:** I • **Salary:** 4 • **Outlook:** 2

DROP-HAMMER OPERATOR (forging) • D.O.T. #610.462-010 • OES #91317 • BLACKSMITH, HAMMER OPERATOR; BLACKSMITH, MACHINE. Sets up and operates closed-die drophammer to forge metal parts, following work order specifications and using measuring instruments and handtools: Informs HEATER (forging) of specified quantity and temperature of workpieces to be forged. Alines and bolts specified dies to ram and anvil of machine, using scale, rule, square, feelers, shims, and hand tools. Positions workpiece on lower die and presses pedal causing ram to strike metal repeatedly forcing it to shape of die impressions. Moves workpiece through series of dies to attain progressively finer detail. May operate drophammer to form experimental or developmental parts, planning work procedures and tooling in absence of detailed instructions. May turn knobs to regulate speed and feed of conveyor that automatically brings heated stock from furnace, places it on anvil, and carries off finished work piece. May forge unheated metal. May set stops or turn handles to set specified striking force of ram. May trim flash from finished forging. May operate hammer to compress finished forgings to specified tolerances and be designated [RESTRIKE-HAMMER OPERATOR (forging)]. May be designated according to type of hammer operated as BOARD-DROP-HAMMER OPERATOR (forging); STEAM-HAMMER OPERATOR (forging). May set up and operate horizontal or vertical hammer consisting of two opposing rams which strike metal simultaneously and be designated IMPACT-HAMMER OPERATOR (forging). • **GED:** R3, M2, L2 • **SVP:** 1-2 yrs • **Academic:** Ed=N, Eng=N • **Work Field:** 134 • **MPSMS:** 542 • **Aptitudes:** G3, V4, N4, S3, P3, Q4, K3, F4, M3, E4, C4 • **Temperaments:** M, T • **Physical:** V=L, H=N, L=H, W, S, H • **Work Env:** I, C, H, N, R • **Salary:** 4 • **Outlook:** 2

HEATER (forging) • D.O.T. #619.682-022 • OES #91938 • FURNACE OPERATOR; FURNACE TENDER; HAMMER HEATER; HEATER, FURNACE; SLUG-FURNACE OPERATOR. Controls oil, gas, or electrical furnace to heat stock, such as billets, bars, plates and rods, preparatory to forging, following work order specifications: Reads dials and gages, and turns knobs to regulate flow of fuel or electric current to verify and maintain specified temperature within furnace. Positions stock in furnace, using tongs or chain hoist. Observes color of metal or reads pyrometer to determine when stock reaches forging temperature. Pulls stock from furnace and delivers it to forging press or hammer, using tongs or chain hoist. Usually works as member of hammer, press, or upsetter crew. May place heated workpiece on conveyor for transporting to work area. May turn knobs to synchronize speed of feed and takeoff conveyors of automatic furnace. • **GED:** R3, M2, L2 • **SVP:** 3-6 mos • **Academic:** Ed=N, Eng=N • **Work Field:** 133 • **MPSMS:** 556 • **Aptitudes:** G3, V4, N4, S4, P3, Q4, K3, F4, M3, E5, C4 • **Temperaments:** M, T • **Physical:** V=L, H=N, L=H, W, S, H • **Work Env:** I, H, N, R • **Salary:** 3 • **Outlook:** 2

LASER-BEAM-TRIM OPERATOR (electronics) • D.O.T.

#726.682-010 • OES #92944 • Operates computer controlled laser-trim system to trim excess material from electronic components: Reads production sheet to determine specific operation code and depresses keys on console control of computer to input code for particular operation. Inserts electronic component into vacuum chuck of laser-trim system, using tweezers, and depresses prescribed sequence of console buttons to actuate laser beam that automatically trims excess metal and glass from component. Observes light indicator on control panel to determine whether each component meets required specifications. Removes trimmed component from chuck and examines component under microscope for completeness of trim. • **GED:** R4, M3, L3 • **SVP:** 3-6 mos • **Academic:** Ed=N, Eng=S • **Work Field:** 051 • **MPSMS:** 587 • **Aptitudes:** G3, V3, N4, S3, P4, Q4, K3, F2, M2, E5, C4 • **Temperaments:** R, T • **Stress:** T • **Physical:** V=L, H=N, L=S, W, H • **Work Env:** I • **Salary:** 4 • **Outlook:** 3

LATHE HAND (jewelry) • D.O.T. #700.682-014 • OES #91117 • SAWYER. Operates bench lathe to saw, mill, bur, or bevel metal stock or parts used to make jewelry findings II: Secures stock in guide or jig, starts lathe, and moves stock against cutting tool. May manipulate stock against cutting tool without use of guide or jig. • **GED:** R3, M1, L2 • **SVP:** 1-2 yrs • **Academic:** Ed=N, Eng=N • **Work Field:** 057 • **MPSMS:** 611 • **Aptitudes:** G3, V4, N4, S3, P3, Q4, K3, F3, M3, E5, C5 • **Temperaments:** M, T • **Physical:** V=L, H=N, L=L, H • **Work Env:** I • **Salary:** 3 • **Outlook:** 2

NUMERICAL-CONTROL-MACHINE OPERATOR (mach. shop) • D.O.T. #609.662-010 • OES #91502 • Sets up and operates multi-purpose numerically-controlled machine to perform any combination of machining operations, such as milling, drilling, reaming, or broaching metal workpieces to specifications: Reviews set-up sheet and specifications to determine sequence of set-up operations and dimensions of finished workpiece. Bolts fixture to machine bed, using wrench. Positions metal stock in fixture according to setup instructions, using rule and calipers, and secures workpiece in place, using clamps or bolts. Assembles cutting tools in toolholders and positions tools in machine spindles according to directions, using machinists' handtools, or inserts cutting tools in specified machine magazines. Places control tape or punch card in reader of control console. Turns dials to index cutting tool to specified set point. Turns switches to operating position, and starts machine. Changes cutting tools and location of clamps, and repositions metal stock on fixture as directed by set up instructions. Observes machine operation and verifies accuracy of machined workpiece against blueprints or engineering drawings by measuring cuts with micrometers, dial indicators, and gages. Notifies supervisor of discrepancies. May adjust machine feed and speed and change cutters to machine parts according to specifications when automatic programming is faulty or if machine malfunctions. • **GED:** R3, M3, L3 • **SVP:** 6 mos-1 yr • **Academic:** Ed=A, Eng=S • **Work Field:** 057 • **MPSMS:** 540 • **Aptitudes:** G3, V4, N3, S3, P3, Q4, K3, F3, M4, E5, C5 • **Temperaments:** M, T • **Physical:** V=L, H=N, L=M, W, H • **Work Env:** I, N • **Salary:** 3 • **Outlook:** 4

POLISHING-MACHINE OPERATOR (any ind.) • D.O.T. #603.682-026 • OES #91114 • Sets up and operates belt sanding machine to polish flat metal surfaces, such as small arms parts and metal strips: Pushes button to lower drive wheel and installs abrasive belt of specified grit, using wrenches. Places metal part on conveyor belt and turns knobs to raise conveyor and bring workpiece into contact with polishing belt. Turns valves to regulate flow of coolant onto polishing belt and starts machine. Examines first run part to determine conformance of finish to specifications and adjusts height of conveyor as indicated to achieve specified finish. Replaces worn polishing belts, fills coolant tank, and cleans collection tank, using handtools, to maintain machine in operating condition. • **GED:** R3, M2, L2 • **SVP:** 3-6 mos • **Academic:** Ed=N, Eng=N • **Work Field:** 051 • **MPSMS:** 373 • **Aptitudes:** G3, V4, N4, S4, P3, Q5, K4, F4, M3, E5, C5 • **Temperaments:** M, T • **Physical:** V=N, H=N, L=M, W, H • **Work Env:** I, W • **Salary:** 3 • **Outlook:** 3

PRESS OPERATOR (fabric. plastic prod.) • D.O.T. #690.682-062 • OES #92198 • PLATE WORKER. Operates hydraulic press to emboss, laminate, or draw plastic sheets: Clamps sheet to overhead rack and pushes rack into oven to soften sheet for forming. Bolts dies or plates to bed of press and adjusts length of travel of ram arm, using handtools. Positions softened sheet or layers of sheets on press bed and lowers pressure plate to hold sheets in place. Moves controls to lower ram that draws sheet through open die to specified shape, embosses sheet with specified design, or compresses layers of sheets to form laminated plastic board. Turns valves to regulate flow of water or steam through dies or plates to maintain specified forming temperature of plastic. Trims plastic, using shears, powersaw, or knife. May be designated according to operation performed as LAMINATING-PRESS OPERATOR (fabric. plastics prod.); STRAIGHTENING-PRESS OPERATOR (fabric. plastics prod.). • **GED:** R3, M2, L2 • **SVP:** 3-6 mos • **Academic:** Ed=N, Eng=N • **Work Field:** 134, 192 • **MPSMS:** 519 • **Aptitudes:** G4, V4, N4, S4, P3, Q4, K3, F4, M3, E5, C5 • **Temperaments:** R, T • **Stress:** T • **Physical:** V=L, H=N, L=H, W, H • **Work Env:** I, H, R • **Salary:** 3 • **Outlook:** 2

PRESS OPERATOR, HEAVY DUTY (any ind.) • D.O.T. #617.260-010 • OES #91305 • BENDING-PRESS OPERATOR; HYDRAULIC-PRESS OPERATOR; TOGGLE-PRESS OPERATOR. Sets up and operates heavy-duty power press to bend, form, stretch, and straighten metal plates, metal extrusions, formed sheet metal, structural shapes, forgings, and weldments as specified by blue prints, layout, and templates: Plans sequence of operations, applying knowledge of physical properties of metal. Measures and sights along workpiece, using tape, rule, straightedge, and transit to mark reference lines. Selects and positions flat, V-block, radius, or special purpose die sets into ram and bed of machine, using jib or crane. Alines and bolts dies to ram and bed of machine, using gages, templates, feelers, shims, and wrenches. Turns handwheel, or levers to set depth and pressure of ram stroke. Preheats workpiece in furnace, using hand torch. Lifts and positions workpiece between dies of machine, using jib or crane and sledge. Starts machine to lower ram which bends or straightens workpiece between dies. Repositions workpiece and changes dies when making multiple or successive passes. Hand forms or finishes workpiece, using hand sledge and anvil. Grinds out burs and sharp edges, using portable grinder. Inspects and marks job number on finished workpiece. May bend or straighten cold metal. May set dies to punch and blank heavy metal. May operate horizontal power press to bend or straighten long pieces of bar stock or structural shapes. May operate press equipped with two or more rams to bend angles or flanges or bend to radius by successive passes; or operate multiple acting hydraulic press to perform deep progressive and reverse draw operations of sheet metal. May be designated according to type press operated as BULLDOZER OPERATOR (any ind.) II; STRETCH-PRESS OPERATOR (any ind.); or according to shape product produced as DISHING-MACHINE OPERATOR (any ind.). • **GED:** R3, M2, L2 • **SVP:** 2-4 yrs • **Academic:** Ed=N, Eng=N • **Work Field:** 133, 134 • **MPSMS:** 554, 566, 594 • **Aptitudes:** G3, V4, N3, S3, P3, Q4, K4, F4, M3, E4, C3 • **Temperaments:** M, T • **Physical:** V=L, H=N, L=H, W, S, H • **Work Env:** I, N, R • **Salary:** 4 • **Outlook:** 2

PUNCH-PRESS OPERATOR 3 (any ind.) • D.O.T. #615.682-014 • OES #91321 • Operates power press equipped with punch to notch or punch metal or plastic plates, sheets, or structural shapes: Positions, alines, and clamps specified punch and die set into ram and bed of machine, using feelers, gages, shims, rule, or template. Turns handwheel or installs shims to set depth of stroke. Lifts workpiece onto machine bed or roller table, manually or by using jib or crane. Positions layout marks on workpiece between punch and die. Positions and clamps guide stops to run successive pieces. Starts ram to drive punch through workpiece. May operate machine equipped with two or more punch and die sets. May trace layout marks or workpiece from template. May be designated according to function of machine as NOTCHING-PRESS OPERATOR (any ind.). • **GED:** R3, M2, L2 • **SVP:** 3-6 mos • **Academic:** Ed=N, Eng=N • **Work Field:** 134 • **MPSMS:** 541, 554 • **Aptitudes:** G3, V4, N4, S3, P3, Q4, K4, F4, M3, E4, C5 • **Temperaments:** R, T • **Stress:** T • **Physical:** V=L, H=N, L=H, W, H • **Work Env:** I, N, R • **Salary:** 4 • **Outlook:** 2

RIVETER, HYDRAULIC (any ind.) • D.O.T. #800.662-010 • OES #92198 • BULL RIVETER; HYDRAULIC-BULL-RIVETER OPERATOR; MULTIPLE-PRESSURE-RIVETER OPERATOR. Operates hydraulic riveting machine to rivet steel plate sections together: Selects dies according to size of rivet and type of head to be formed and installs dies in machine, using wrench. Signals RIVETER HELPER (any ind.) to hoist plates into position, line up rivet holes with rivet die, insert hot rivets in holes, and hold metal bar or die against rivet head. Starts machine and adjusts valve to regulate pressure according to size of rivet. Moves lever to force piston and die against rivet shank to form head. May operate portable machine and be designated as RIVETER, PORTABLE MACHINE (any ind.). • GED: R3, M1, L1 • SVP: 6 mos-1 yr • Academic: Ed=N, Eng=N • Work Field: 073 • MPSMS: 590 • Aptitudes: G3, V4, N4, S3, P3, Q4, K3, F3, M3, E3, C5 • Temperaments: M, T • Physical: V=G, H=N, L=M, W, C, H • Work Env: I, N, R • Salary: 5 • Outlook: 4

RIVETING-MACHINE OPERATOR 1 (any ind.) • D.O.T. #699.482-010 • OES #92197 • Sets up and operates riveting machine to rivet together parts fabricated from materials, such as sheet metal and plastic, according to work orders and specifications: Positions, alines, and bolts specified dies over anvil and ram of machine and positions fixtures in machine bed, using micrometer, rule, gage, shims, and wrenches. Installs cam and spring in anvil to synchronize action or clinching post of lower die with action of ram and with rivet feed agitator or lever when setting up semiautomatic machines which position rivets over anvil. Turns knobs and sets screws to adjust depth and pressure limit of ram stroke. Alines holes of workpieces and inserts shanks of rivets into holes or onto anvil of machine. Positions rivets or holes in workpieces over anvil or against fixtures. Depresses pedal to lower ram that spreads rivet shank to clinch workpieces. Fills hopper with rivets when operating semiautomatic machines. May set up machines equipped with several rams, or with turret to punch and dimple rivet holes and to reposition workpiece after each operation. • GED: R3, M2, L3 • SVP: 6 mos-1 yr • Academic: Ed=N, Eng=S • Work Field: 073 • MPSMS: 580, 590 • Aptitudes: G3, V3, N3, S3, P3, Q4, K4, F3, M3, E4, C5 • Temperaments: M, R, T • Stress: T • Physical: V=L, H=N, L=M, W, S, H • Work Env: I • Salary: 3 • Outlook: 2

SHEAR OPERATOR 1 (any ind.) • D.O.T. #615.482-034 • OES #91308 • PLATE-SHEAR OPERATOR; POWER-SHEAR OPERATOR. Sets up and operates power shear to cut metal objects, such as plates, sheets, slabs, billets, or bars to specified dimensions and angle: Turns handwheels to adjust rake (angle) and pressure of blade. Positions and clamps stops and side guides to set length and angle of cut, using rule, built-in gages, or template. Lifts workpiece manually or by hoist or crane to machine bed or roller table and positions it against side guide and end stops. Starts machine which clamps workpiece and lowers blade to cut metal. Lays out cutting lines on metal, using rule, square, or template when shearing single pieces. May tilt bed, blade, or install fixtures to shear, bevel, or trim fabricated items. May set up and operate shear on production line in which shear is fed by conveyor, such as automobile frame line or rolling mill. May operate portable shear to cut sheet metal. May inspect work, using tape, compass, gage, template, or micrometer to verify dimensions. May be designated by type of shear as GATE-SHEAR OPERATOR (any ind.) II or by application of shear as SQUARE-SHEAR OPERATOR (any ind.) I; STAPLE-SHEAR OPERATOR (nail). May operate shear that automatically shears to uniform length metal sheets, plates, or structural shapes fed into machine by continuous coil or conveyor and be designated as SHEAR OPERATOR, AUTOMATIC (any ind.) I. • GED: R3, M2, L2 • SVP: 3-6 mos • Academic: Ed=N, Eng=N • Work Field: 054 • MPSMS: 554, 594 • Aptitudes: G3, V4, N4, S4, P4, Q4, K3, F4, M3, E4, C5 • Temperaments: R, T • Stress: T • Physical: V=L, H=N, L=H, W, H • Work Env: I, N, R • Salary: 4 • Outlook: 3

SPINNER, HAND (any ind.) • D.O.T. #619.362-018 • OES #91105 • SPINNING-LATHE OPERATOR. Sets up and operates spinning lathe to spin (form) shaped articles from sheet or plate metal, using blueprints and knowledge of physical properties of metal: Bolts specified spinning chuck to headstock spindle and follow block to tailstock, using handtools or power tools. Clamps metal disk to chuck by turning handwheel that forces follow block against disk. Secures steady rest fixture on cross-slide. Starts machine and coats outside of rotating disk with spinning compound. Positions, holds, and moves long-handled compound lever tool against disk, using steady rest as fulcrum point, to apply required pressure to form disk over and into shape of spinning chuck. Varies amount and location of pressure on disk according to type of metal, shape of spinning chuck, speed of lathe, and temperature and thickness of metal disk. Replaces steady rest with bar tool attachment, turns handwheel to set bar tool and cut off excess metal from workpiece. Verifies dimension of finished article with steel rule and diameter tape. May form wood spinning chucks by turning on lathe. • GED: R4, M3, L3 • SVP: 2-4 yrs • Academic: Ed=N, Eng=S • Work Field: 134 • MPSMS: 550 • Aptitudes: G3, V3, N3, S2, P2, Q4, K3, F4, M3, E4, C4 • Temperaments: M, T • Physical: V=L, H=N, L=M, W, H • Work Env: I, N • Salary: 4 • Outlook: 2

SPINNER, HYDRAULIC (any ind.) • D.O.T. #619.362-022 • OES #91105 • SPINNING-LATHE-OPERATOR, HYDRAULIC. Sets up and operates spinning lathe equipped with hydraulically controlled forming tools to spin (form) shaped articles from sheet or plate metal, compiling specifications from blueprints and knowledge of physical properties of metal: Lifts specified spinning chuck to machine spindle, manually or with power hoist, and bolts chuck in place, using handtools or power tools. Clamps metal disk to spinning chuck. Starts machine and coats rotating disk with spinning compound. Turns valve to set pressure applied to disk according to type of metal, shape of spinning chuck, speed of lathe, and thickness of metal disk. Moves feed pump levers that hydraulically control pressure applied by forming tool, reads pressure gages to determine amount of pressure applied, and guides tool against disk to form disk over and into shape of spinning chuck. Resets position of forming tool on steady rest to form disk into shape. Replaces forming tool with cutting tool to trim excess metal from shaped part. Verifies dimension of finished article with verniers. • GED: R4, M3, L3 • SVP: 1-2 yrs • Academic: Ed=N, Eng=S • Work Field: 134 • MPSMS: 550 • Aptitudes: G3, V3, N3, S3, P3, Q4, K3, F4, M3, E4, C4 • Temperaments: M, T • Physical: V=L, H=N, L=H, W, H • Work Env: I, N • Salary: 4 • Outlook: 2

STRAIGHTENING-PRESS OPERATOR (any ind.) • D.O.T. #617.482-026 • OES #91321 • STRAIGHTENER. Operates power press equipped with pressure blocks or dies to straighten warped or bent metal objects, such as plates, structural castings, shapes, forgings, and shafts to specified dimensions: Examines workpiece to locate defects, using such devices as straightedge, deflection gage, template, and square. Positions and locks specified pressure blocks, or die, into ram of machine, or positions shims under high spots of workpiece. Lifts and positions workpiece into bed of machine manually or using jib or crane. Starts ram which presses out bent or high spots of work piece. Reexamines and repositions workpiece, changing shims for each pass until workpiece conforms with specifications. May turn levers or handwheels to adjust depth and pressure of ram. May preheat metal, using heating furnace or hand torch and clean dies between pressings, using compressed air, oil, and brush. May tend machine equipped with preset dies to bend metal to specified shapes. May grind rough edges from finished workpiece, using portable hand grinder. May be designated according to part straightened as BARREL STRAIGHTENER (firearms) II; CRANKSHAFT STRAIGHTENER (auto. mfg.); GEAR STRAIGHTENER (auto. mfg.); or according to type press operated as GAG-PRESS STRAIGHTENER (iron & steel). • GED: R3, M2, L1 • SVP: 6 mos-1 yr • Academic: Ed=N, Eng=N • Work Field: 134 • MPSMS: 554, 594 • Aptitudes: G3, V4, N4, S3, P3, Q5, K3, F3, M3, E4, C5 • Temperaments: M, T • Physical: V=L, H=N, L=M, W, S, H • Work Env: I, N, R • Salary: 4 • Outlook: 2

STRAIGHTENING-ROLL OPERATOR (any ind.) • D.O.T. #613.462-022 • OES #91321 • STRAIGHTENING-MACHINE OPERATOR. Operates rolling machine to straighten warped or bent metal plates, bars, or sheets: Threads workpiece between rolls of machine manually or with crane. Turns handwheels or nuts to adjust tension between one or more sets of alined drive and adjustment rolls. Pulls lever to move workpiece through rolls of machine. Hammers or pries workpiece into alinement, using hammer or pry bar. Examines work for straightness, using straightedge and plumb bob. Inserts shims under bulges and repeats process to straighten workpiece to specifications. May be designated by product straightened as BAR-STRAIGHTENING-MACHINE OPERATOR (any ind.); PLATE ROLLER (any ind.); WIRE-STRAIGHTENING-MACHINE OPERATOR (any ind.). • GED: R3, M1, L1 • SVP: 3-6 mos • Academic: Ed=N, Eng=N • Work Field: 135 •

MPSMS: 554 • **Aptitudes:** G3, V4, N4, S3, P4, Q4, K3, F3, M3, E4, C5 • **Temperaments:** M, T • **Physical:** V=L, H=N, L=M, W, S, H • **Work Env:** I, N • **Salary:** 4 • **Outlook:** 2

GOE: 06.02.03 Machine Work, Wood, Skilled

CUT-OFF-SAW OPERATOR (woodworking) • D.O.T. #667.682-022 • OES #92308 • CROSS-CUT-SAW OPERATOR; TRIMMER OPERATOR. Operates one or more single-or multiple-blade circular saws to cut wood and wood products to specified lengths: Adjusts and secures ends and backstops on saw table, using wrench, or bolts saws to shaft and turns handwheels to space saws and stops, according to specified length of stock. Starts saw and places material to be cut on conveyor belt, drums, or feed chain that feeds stock into saws, or positions workpiece against end stop and under saw, syncronizing action with automatically descending blade, or pushes material on table and (1) pulls lever to swing saw through material, (2) pushes moveable table past saw, (3) depresses treadle to raise saw through slot in machine table, or (4) tilts table for angle cut and presses pedal to move saw through workpiece to cut stock, depending on type of saw used. Replaces dull or damaged saw blades and lubricates machine, using wrench and grease gun. May examine material prior to cutting to determine what cuts will remove defects and produce maximum footage. May verify dimensions of stock cut and accuracy of cuts, using rule and square. May be designated according to type of saw used as DOUBLE-CUT-OFF-SAW OPERATOR (woodworking); DRUM-SAW OPERATOR (plan. mill); SWINGING-CUT-OFF-SAW OPERATOR (woodworking); TABLE-CUT-OFF-SAW OPERATOR (woodworking); TILTING-SAW OPERATOR (woodworking); TREADLE-CUT-OFF-SAW OPERATOR (woodworking). Additional titles: EQUALIZING-SAW OPERATOR (woodworking); MULTIPLE-CUT-OFF-SAW OPERATOR (veneer & plywood; wood. box); TIMBER CUTTER (mining & quarrying). • **GED:** R3, M2, L2 • **SVP:** 3-6 mos • **Academic:** Ed=N, Eng=N • **Work Field:** 056 • **MPSMS:** 450 • **Aptitudes:** G3, V4, N4, S3, P4, Q4, K3, F4, M3, E4, C5 • **Temperaments:** R, T • **Stress:** T • **Physical:** V=L, H=N, L=M, W, H • **Work Env:** I, N, R • **Salary:** 5 • **Outlook:** 2

HEAD SAWYER (sawmill) • D.O.T. #667.662-010 • OES #92305 • BAND-LOG-MILL-AND-CARRIAGE OPERATOR; BAND-SAW-MILL OPERATOR. Operates head saw and feed carriage to saw logs into cants or boards: Starts mechanical loader arms that place log on carriage. Sets dogs and adjusts carriage blocks to aline log for sawing. Activates carriage that moves log against saw blade. Starts saw to cut log. Observes exposed face of log after first cut to determine grade and size of next cut and adjusts setting of carriage blocks. Starts mechanical log turner that turns log over on carriage for subsequent cuts. May change saw blades. May be designated according to type of saw operated as BAND-HEAD-SAW OPERATOR (sawmill); CIRCULAR-HEAD-SAW OPERATOR (sawmill). • **GED:** R3, M2, L1 • **SVP:** 2-4 yrs • **Academic:** Ed=N, Eng=N • **Work Field:** 056 • **MPSMS:** 452 • **Aptitudes:** G3, V4, N4, S3, P3, Q5, K2, F3, M3, E3, C3 • **Temperaments:** J, M, T • **Physical:** V=L, H=N, L=L, W, H • **Work Env:** I, N, R • **Salary:** 5 • **Outlook:** 2

NAILING-MACHINE OPERATOR (any ind.) • D.O.T. #669.682-058 • OES #92311 • BOX MAKER; NAILER, MACHINE. Sets up and operates machines to drive nails into boards to fasten wood assemblies, such as boxes, furniture frames, crates, and pallets, and to nail lids on boxes: Spaces nail chucks and rails according to specifications and turns setscrews to fasten chucks to rails. Turns wheel to raise or lower table according to size of pieces to be nailed. Fills hopper with nails. Fastens or adjusts stops and jigs on machine table to facilitate positioning of material to be nailed. Starts machine, positions boards on table under chucks, and depresses pedal to drive nails into boards. May move levers to control nail feed and turn knobs to position nail setting heads. May be designated according to part nailed as BOTTOM NAILER (wood. box); CLEAT NAILER (wood. box); FRAME NAILER (wood. box); STRAP NAILER (wood. box); or according to type of machine as LIDDING-MACHINE OPERATOR (any ind.). • **GED:** R2, M1, L1 • **SVP:** 3-6 mos • **Academic:** Ed=N, Eng=N • **Work Field:** 072 • **MPSMS:** 450 • **Aptitudes:** G4, V4, N4, S4, P3, Q5, K3, F4, M3, E4, C5 • **Temperaments:** R, T • **Stress:** T • **Physical:** V=L,

H=N, L=M, W, H • **Work Env:** I, N, R • **Salary:** 3 • **Outlook:** 2

TIMBER-SIZER OPERATOR (planing mill) • D.O.T. #665.482-018 • OES #92314 • PLANER OPERATOR. Operates planing machine to surface planks and timbers and reduce stock to specified dimensions: Installs cutting heads on machine drive spindles and adjusts blade exposure according to specified depth of cut, using wrenches and gages. Adjusts feed roll tension and positions fences that guide stock between cutterheads. Starts machine, exhaust blower, and conveyors, and slides timber against guide to aline timber on feed rolls. Verifies dimensions of sized stock, using gage or rule. • **GED:** R3, M2, L1 • **SVP:** 3-6 mos • **Academic:** Ed=N, Eng=N • **Work Field:** 055 • **MPSMS:** 452 • **Aptitudes:** G3, V4, N3, S3, P3, Q4, K3, F4, M3, E4, C5 • **Temperaments:** M, T • **Physical:** V=L, H=N, L=M, W, H • **Work Env:** B, N, R • **Salary:** 5 • **Outlook:** 2

GOE: 06.02.04 Machine Work, Paper, Skilled

BOX-FOLDING-MACHINE OPERATOR (paper goods) • D.O.T. #649.682-010 • OES #92997 • Sets up and operates machine to fold corrugated paperboard box blanks and to glue, stitch (staple), or tape edges to form boxes. Installs feed bars and adjusts guide assembly and folding mechanism according to box blank dimensions and work order specifications, using handtools. Fills glue reservoir, loads automatic stapler, or threads gummed tape through applicator. Stacks box blanks in feed mechanism, starts machine, and observes automatic feeding and folding of box blanks and gluing, stapling, or taping of edges to detect machine malfunction. Inspects sample completed box to verify conformance to work order specifications and adjusts machine controls to correct variations. May be designated according to type of machine used as FOLDER-GLUER OPERATOR (paper goods); FOLDER-STITCHER OPERATOR (paper goods); FOLDER-TAPER OPERATOR (paper goods). • **GED:** R3, M2, L2 • **SVP:** 3-6 mos • **Academic:** Ed=N, Eng=N • **Work Field:** 062, 063 • **MPSMS:** 475 • **Aptitudes:** G3, V4, N3, S3, P3, Q4, K3, F4, M3, E5, C5 • **Temperaments:** M, T • **Physical:** V=L, H=N, L=H, W, H • **Work Env:** I, N • **Salary:** 3 • **Outlook:** 3

GOE: 06.02.05 Machine Work, Leather & Fabrics, Skilled

BINDER (any ind.) • D.O.T. #787.682-010 • OES #92721 • BINDING-END STITCHER; BINDING-MACHINE OPERATOR; TAPER. Operates sewing machine equipped with folding attachment to sew binding material over edges or seams of articles, such as camping equipment, linens, parachutes, gloves and mittens, or hats and caps, to reinforce, prevent raveling, and give finished appearance: Places roll of binding on holder and draws end through folding attachment. Positions edge of article between folds of binding material and guides article and material under needle. Performs duties as described under SEWING-MACHINE OPERATOR, REGULAR EQUIPMENT (any ind.). When binding blankets, folds binding material at end of seam to form corners and sews over folded corner. When binding fitted sheets, matches curved edges of sheet and guides edges under needle to form sheet corners. May operate sewing machine equipped with shirring mechanism to gather binding as binding is attached to article. May be designated according to article or part bound as BAND-LINING BANDER (hat & cap); BLANKET BINDER (house furn.); EAR-FLAP BINDER (hat & cap); FITTED-SHEET BINDER (house furn.); FLAP-LINING BINDER (hat & cap); HELMET BINDER (hat & cap). Additional titles: PARACHUTE TAPER (tex. prod., n.e.c.); POT-HOLDER BINDER (house furn.); SCREEN-VENT BINDER (hat & cap); SOFT-HAT BINDER (hat & cap). May bind rug samples and be designated SAMPLE PROCESSOR (carpet & rug). • **GED:** R3, M1, L1 • **SVP:** 3-6 mos • **Academic:** Ed=N, Eng=N • **Work Field:** 171 • **MPSMS:** 420, 439, 446 • **Aptitudes:** G4, V4, N4, S4, P3, Q5, K3, F3, M3, E4, C4 • **Temperaments:** R, T • **Stress:** T • **Physical:** V=G, H=N, L=S, H • **Work Env:** I, N • **Salary:** 2 • **Outlook:** 3

CARPET SEWER (carpet & rug) • D.O.T. #787.682-014 • OES #92721 • FRINGE-BINDER OPERATOR; LENO SEWER; SEW-

ING-MACHINE OPERATOR, CARPET AND RUGS. Operates sewing machine to join carpet sections or braided yarn strips to form rug and finish edges, performing any combination of following duties: Joins sections of carpeting to form rug of desired size or continuous length (runner). Sews decorative trimmings on rugs, borders on runners, or binding to prevent edges from raveling. Operates sewing machine that loops yarn into fringe and stitches fringe to edge of rug. Joins braided strips of yarn to form round or oval rug of desired size. Joins widths of leno cloth used on backing of rugs. May join sections of carpet together, using seaming tape and liquid cement. Performs other duties as described under SEWING-MACHINE OPERATOR, REGULAR EQUIPMENT (any ind.). • **GED:** R3, M2, L2 • **SVP:** 30 days-3 mos • **Academic:** Ed=N, Eng=N • **Work Field:** 171 • **MPSMS:** 431, 439 • **Aptitudes:** G3, V4, N4, S4, P3, Q4, K3, F3, M3, E4, C4 • **Temperaments:** M, R, T • **Stress:** T • **Physical:** V=L, H=N, L=M, W, S, H • **Work Env:** I • **Salary:** 2 • **Outlook:** 2

FELTING-MACHINE OPERATOR (felt goods) • D.O.T. #586.662-010 • OES #92998 • HARDENING-MACHINE OPERATOR; LAY-UP PRESSER. Operates felting machine to attach reinforcing burlap to felt strips or to compress several layers of felt by means of heat and pressure: Suspends roll of burlap and two bats of felt over conveyor belt. Starts conveyor and unrolls felt strips, with burlap strip between felt strips, onto conveyor. Opens steam valves or water sprays to moisten felt passing through steam chamber or beneath sprays. Stops conveyor when bed of hydraulic press is covered by felt strip. Opens steam valves to heat press bed. Starts oscillating hydraulic ram that compresses felt. Laps end of felt bat to ends of other bats to form continuous strip. Plucks foreign matter from felt surfaces with tweezers and spreads loose felt over thin spots to produce uniform products. Straightens layers of stock on press bed to remove wrinkled stock. • **GED:** R3, M2, L3 • **SVP:** 3-6 mos • **Academic:** Ed=N, Eng=S • **Work Field:** 133, 134 • **MPSMS:** 439 • **Aptitudes:** G3, V4, N4, S4, P3, Q4, K4, F4, M3, E5, C5 • **Temperaments:** R, T • **Stress:** T • **Physical:** V=L, H=N, L=M, W, H • **Work Env:** I, N • **Salary:** 3 • **Outlook:** 2

HAT-AND-CAP SEWER (hat & cap) • D.O.T. #784.682-014 • OES #92717 • Operates sewing machine to join, decorate, or reinforce hat or cap parts or finished article: Guides parts under machine needle to form crown, sides, brim, sweatband, or visor, or to join parts together to fabricate article. May join reeding onto hat parts to reinforce them and be designated BRIM-WELT-SEWING-MACHINE OPERATOR (hat & cap); CAP SIZER (hat & cap); LEATHER FITTER (hat & cap); REEDING-MACHINE OPERATOR (hat & cap); WIRE-MACHINE OPERATOR (hat & cap). May be designated according to part sewn as CHIN-STRAP SEWER (hat & cap). Additional titles: BRIM STITCHER (hat & cap) II; LABEL SEWER (hat & cap); LINING MAKER (hat & cap); RIBBON-SWEATBAND OPERATOR (hat & cap); STRAW-HAT-MACHINE OPERATOR (hat & cap); TIP MAKER (hat & cap); TOP STITCHER (hat & cap). Performs duties as described under SEWING-MACHINE OPERATOR, REGULAR EQUIPMENT (any ind.). • **GED:** R3, M1, L1 • **SVP:** 30 days-3 mos • **Academic:** Ed=N, Eng=N • **Work Field:** 171 • **MPSMS:** 446, 449 • **Aptitudes:** G4, V4, N4, S4, P3, Q5, K3, F3, M3, E4, C4 • **Temperaments:** R, T • **Stress:** T • **Physical:** V=L, H=N, L=L, H • **Work Env:** I • **Salary:** 2 • **Outlook:** 2

HEMMER (any ind.) • D.O.T. #787.682-026 • OES #92721 • PLAIN-GOODS HEMMER. Operates sewing machine equipped with folding attachment to hem articles, such as curtains and draperies, gloves and mittens, sheets, towels, and pillowcases: Guides edge of material through folding attachment and under machine needle. Inserts and sews labels into hem. May reinforce hem by backstitching at ends of seam. May fold hem manually. When operating machine to hem curtains and draperies to form rod inserts, is designated HEADER (house furn.). May be designated according to article or part hemmed as PILLOWCASE SEWER (house furn.); SHEET SEWER (house furn.); TOWEL SEWER (house furn.); WINDOW-SHADE-CLOTH SEWER (window shade & fix.); WRIST HEMMER (glove & mit.). Performs duties as described under SEWING-MACHINE OPERATOR, REGULAR EQUIPMENT (any ind.). • **GED:** R3, M1, L1 • **SVP:** 3-6 mos • **Academic:** Ed=N, Eng=N • **Work Field:** 171 • **MPSMS:** 420, 430, 449 • **Aptitudes:** G4, V4, N4, S4, P3, Q5, K3,

F3, M3, E4, C4 • **Temperaments:** R, T • **Stress:** T • **Physical:** V=L, H=N, L=L, H • **Work Env:** I, N • **Salary:** 3 • **Outlook:** 2

MENDER (any ind.) • D.O.T. #787.682-030 • OES #85956 • Operates sewing machine to repair defects, such as tears and holes in garments, linens, curtains, draperies, and blankets: Patches, darns, or reweaves holes or tears in garments, curtains, or linens, and resews ripped seams. Sews fringe, tassels, and ruffles onto drapes and curtains. Sews buttons and trimming on garments after they have been cleaned. Operates sewing machine to restitch or replace binding ribbon on edge of blankets. May cut curtains to specified measurements and hem edges. May shorten or lengthen hems to alter size of garments. May replace pockets in coats or trousers. May sew identifying labels and emblems on uniforms, linens, or diapers for linen supply or diaper service. May repair defective stitching on articles. May be designated according to type of article sewn as SEWER, LINEN ROOM (hotel & rest.) or machine used as DARNING-MACHINE OPERATOR (any ind.). May examine lace webbing for defects and be designated EXAMINER-MENDER (tex. prod., n.e.c.). Performs duties as described under SEWING-MACHINE OPERATOR, REGULAR EQUIPMENT (any ind.). • **GED:** R3, M1, L2 • **SVP:** 3-6 mos • **Academic:** Ed=N, Eng=N • **Work Field:** 171 • **MPSMS:** 420, 440 • **Aptitudes:** G3, V4, N4, S4, P3, Q5, K3, F3, M3, E4, C4 • **Temperaments:** R, T • **Stress:** T • **Physical:** V=L, H=N, L=L, H • **Work Env:** I • **Salary:** 3 • **Outlook:** 2

SEWING-MACHINE OPERATOR (any ind.) • D.O.T. #787.682-046 • OES #92721 • Operates sewing machine to join, gather, hem, reinforce, or decorate articles. Performs duties as described under SEWING-MACHINE OPERATOR, REGULAR EQUIPMENT (any ind.). • **GED:** R3, M2, L2 • **SVP:** 6 mos-1 yr • **Academic:** Ed=N, Eng=N • **Work Field:** 171 • **MPSMS:** 420, 440, 604 • **Aptitudes:** G4, V4, N4, S3, P3, Q5, K3, F3, M3, E4, C4 • **Temperaments:** R, T • **Stress:** T • **Physical:** V=G, H=N, L=S, H • **Work Env:** I • **Salary:** 1 • **Outlook:** 3

SEWING-MACHINE OPERATOR (leather prod.) • D.O.T. #783.682-014 • OES #92721 • Operates sewing machine to join parts of leather products, such as suitcases, handbags, and wallets. May operate machine equipped with shirring attachment. May operate machine equipped with wrapping and folding attachment to join parts of handbag handles and be designated HANDLE SEWER (leather prod.). May cut thread, using blade attached to machine or scissors. May oil machine and change needles. When joining or decorating handbag parts with decorative stitches is designated FANCY SEWER (leather prod.). May be designated according to parts joined as APPLIQUE SEWER (leather prod.); LINING-PARTS SEWER (leather prod.); or according to article assembled and sewed as BRIEFCASE SEWER (leather prod.); HANDBAG FINISHER (leather prod.). Performs duties as described under SEWING-MACHINE OPERATOR, REGULAR EQUIPMENT (any ind.). • **GED:** R3, M1, L1 • **SVP:** 3-6 mos • **Academic:** Ed=N, Eng=N • **Work Field:** 171 • **MPSMS:** 520 • **Aptitudes:** G4, V4, N4, S4, P3, Q5, K3, F3, M3, E4, C4 • **Temperaments:** R, T • **Stress:** T • **Physical:** V=L, H=N, L=M, W, H • **Work Env:** I, N • **Salary:** 3 • **Outlook:** 3

STITCHER, STANDARD MACHINE (boot & shoe) • D.O.T. #690.682-082 • OES #92723 • CLOSER; FITTER; JOINER; MAKER; SEAMER; SEWER; STAYER; STITCHER; STITCHING-MACHINE OPERATOR. Operates single, double, or multiple-needle stitching machine to join or decorate shoe parts, or to reinforce edges: Selects spool of thread or prewound bobbin, places it on spindle or looper, and draws thread through guides and needles. Alines parts and presses knee control or pedal to raise presser foot or roller. Positions parts under needle and lowers presser foot or roller. Starts machine and guides parts under needle, following seams, edges, or markings, or moves edges of part against guide. When operating double or multiple-needle machine, may turn set screw on needle bar and position one or more needles as specified. May cut and trim excess material with scissors or knife. May be designated according to shoe parts stitched as BACK-SEAM STITCHER (boot & shoe); BOX-TOE STITCHER (boot & shoe). May be designated according to machine operated as FLATBED STITCHER (boot & shoe); ZIG-ZAG STITCHER (boot & shoe). May be designated according to number of needles in machine operated as DOUBLE-NEEDLE STITCHER (boot & shoe); MULTIPLE-

NEEDLE STITCHER (boot & shoe); SINGLE-NEEDLE STITCHER (boot & shoe). Additional titles: BACKSTAY STITCHER (boot & shoe); BARRER AND TACKER (boot & shoe); BINDING STITCHER (boot & shoe); BUCKLE SEWER, MACHINE (boot & shoe); CALIFORNIA SEAMER (boot & shoe); COUNTER-POCKET SEWER (boot & shoe); COVER MAKER (boot & shoe); CUT-OUT STITCHER (boot & shoe); EDGE STITCHER (boot & shoe); FANCY STITCHER (boot & shoe); FLARE STITCHER (boot & shoe); GORE INSERTER (boot & shoe); INSOLE TAPE STITCHER, UCO (boot & shoe); LABEL STITCHER (boot & shoe); LINING CLOSER (boot & shoe); LINING STITCHER (boot & shoe); LINING-STRAP CLOSER (boot & shoe); LINING VAMPER (boot & shoe); NEVERSLIP STITCHER (boot & shoe); POSTBED STITCHER (boot & shoe); QUARTER-LINING STITCHER (boot & shoe); RAND SEWER (boot & shoe); SADDLE STITCHER (boot & shoe); SADDLE-LINING STITCHER (boot & shoe); SEAM-STAY STITCHER (boot & shoe); SHANK STITCHER (boot & shoe); SOCK-LINING STITCHER (boot & shoe); STITCHER, UTILITY (boot & shoe); STRAP STITCHER (boot & shoe); TAPE STITCHER (boot & shoe); TIP STITCHER (boot & shoe); TOE-LINING CLOSER (boot & shoe); TONGUE AND QUARTER STITCHER (boot & shoe); TONGUE-LINING STITCHER (boot & shoe); TONGUE STITCHER (boot & shoe); TOP STITCHER (boot & shoe); UNDERLAY STITCHER (boot & shoe); UPPER STITCHER (boot & shoe); VAMP STITCHER (boot & shoe); WELTING STITCHER, FRONT (boot & shoe); WRAPPER STITCHER (boot & shoe). • **GED:** R3, M2, L2 • **SVP:** 3-6 mos • **Academic:** Ed=N, Eng=N • **Work Field:** 171 • **MPSMS:** 522 • **Aptitudes:** G4, V4, N4, S3, P3, Q4, K3, F3, M3, E4, C4 • **Temperaments:** R, T • **Stress:** T • **Physical:** V=G, H=N, L=L, H • **Work Env:** I, N • **Salary:** 1 • **Outlook:** 4

TRIMMER, MACHINE (garment) • D.O.T. #781.682-010 • OES #92705 • Operates sewing machine equipped with cutting blade attachment to trim excess fabric from material or article. Depresses pedal to start machine, moves hand and foot controls, and guides material or articles under blade to trim excess fabric and facilitate subsequent operation. May be designated by type of article or material trimmed as COLLAR TRIMMER (garment; knit goods); BRASSIERE-CUP-MOLD CUTTER (garment). • **GED:** R2, M1, L1 • **SVP:** 2-30 days • **Academic:** Ed=N, Eng=N • **Work Field:** 054 • **MPSMS:** 420 • **Aptitudes:** G4, V4, N4, S4, P3, Q5, K3, F4, M3, E4, C5 • **Temperaments:** R, T • **Stress:** T • **Physical:** V=G, H=N, L=S, H • **Work Env:** I, N • **Salary:** 2 • **Outlook:** 3

ZIPPER SETTER (any ind.) • D.O.T. #787.682-086 • OES #92721 • Operates sewing machine equipped with guides that prevent needle from contacting metal to sew slide fasteners in openings or on parts of articles, such as mattresses, blankets, cushions, upholsteries, sleeping bags and other camping equipment, and quilt covers: Places roll of zippers on holder, or selects zipper of specified length, and draws end of zipper through guides. Cuts zippers from roll after sewing, using scissors. Attaches zipper slide to zipper and opens zipper before sewing stops on each end of zipper opening. When sewing zippers on plastic material, operates machine equipped with folding attachment to sew binding material over seam. Performs duties as described under SEWING-MACHINE OPERATOR, REGULAR EQUIPMENT (any ind.). • **GED:** R3, M1, L1 • **SVP:** 3-6 mos • **Academic:** Ed=N, Eng=N • **Work Field:** 171 • **MPSMS:** 420, 439 • **Aptitudes:** G4, V4, N4, S4, P3, Q5, K3, F3, M3, E4, C5 • **Temperaments:** R, T • **Stress:** T • **Physical:** V=L, H=N, L=L, H • **Work Env:** I • **Salary:** 3 • **Outlook:** 2

GOE: 06.02.06 Machine Work, Textiles, Skilled

CARPET WEAVER (carpet & rug) • D.O.T. #683.682-010 • OES #92705 • Operates one or more looms equipped with pile-wire mechanism to weave carpeting: Moves lever to open shed and inserts specified number of pile wires through shed in sequence to produce pile. Forces cop of filling into shuttle, using mallet, and inserts shuttle into loom. Places wax in holder to lubricate pile wires as wires enter and are with drawn from shed. Starts loom and observes weaving to detect exhausted filling packages, mispicks, and irregular cutting of pile. Replaces exhausted filling,

inserts pile wires into missed loops, and replaces dull cutting blades. May be designated according to type of carpet woven as VELVET WEAVER (carpet & rug). • **GED:** R3, M1, L2 • **SVP:** 3-6 mos • **Academic:** Ed=N, Eng=N • **Work Field:** 431 • **Aptitudes:** G3, V4, N4, S3, P3, Q4, K3, F3, M3, E5, C4 • **Temperaments:** R, T • **Stress:** T • **Physical:** V=L, H=N, L=L, W, S, H • **Work Env:** I, N • **Salary:** 3 • **Outlook:** 2

SEAMLESS-HOSIERY KNITTER (hosiery) • D.O.T. #684.685-010 • OES #92705 • KNITTER; KNITTING-MACHINE OPERATOR, AUTOMATIC; KNITTING-MACHINE OPERATOR, SEAMLESS HOSIERY; SOCK-KNITTING-MACHINE OPERATOR. Tends circular knitting machines with automatic pattern controls that knit seamless hose: Places yarn spools on creel; threads and starts machine. Observes operation of machines and notifies KNITTING-MACHINE FIXER (hosiery; knit goods) of any malfunction. Removes knitted hose from machines. Pulls hose over inspection form or over hand to examine for defects, such as holes, runs, or picks. Classifies hose according to specifications into grades, such as first quality, rejects, and mends. Counts, bundles, ties, and labels each grade of hose. May clip loose threads, using scissors. May measure overall length of hose, using scale on inspection form. May mark defective portion of hose for HOSIERY MENDER (hosiery), using crayon. May be designated according to type of hose knitted as SOCK KNITTER (hosiery). • **GED:** R3, M1, L1 • **SVP:** 30 days-3 mos • **Academic:** Ed=N, Eng=N • **Work Field:** 165 • **MPSMS:** 446 • **Aptitudes:** G3, V4, N4, S3, P3, Q4, K3, F4, M3, E5, C4 • **Temperaments:** R, T • **Stress:** T • **Physical:** V=L, H=N, L=L, S, H • **Work Env:** I • **Salary:** 2 • **Outlook:** 2

WEAVER (asbestos prod.) • D.O.T. #683.682-038 • OES #92705 • LOOM OPERATOR; WEAVER, BROADLOOM. Operates battery of looms to weave yarn into cloth: Observes cloth being woven to detect weaving defects. Removes defects in cloth by cutting and pulling out filling. Adjusts pattern chain to resume weaving. Examines looms to determine cause of loom stoppage, such as warp, filling, harness breaks, or mechanical defects. Ties piece of yarn to broken end and threads yarn through drop wires, heddle eyes, and reed dents to repair warp breaks, using hook. Pulls out broken filling and pushes shuttle through shed to insert new pick I and repair filling breaks. Notifies LOOM FIXER (asbestos prod.; narrow fabrics; textile) of mechanical defects. Marks or cuts cloth when sufficient yardage has been woven and notifies CLOTH DOFFER (textile). May place quills or bobbins in battery or magazine of loom [BATTERY LOADER (textile)]. May replace empty bobbins in shuttle with full ones on nonautomatic looms [SHUTTLE HAND (textile)]. May tend winding units attached to looms that wind filling onto quills [LOOM-WINDER TENDER (textile)]. May be designated according to type of loom operated as WEAVER, DOBBY LOOM (textile). When weaving samples, is known as SAMPLE WEAVER (textile). • **GED:** R3, M1, L2 • **SVP:** 6 mos-1 yr • **Academic:** Ed=N, Eng=N • **Work Field:** 164 • **MPSMS:** 420 • **Aptitudes:** G3, V4, N4, S3, P3, Q4, K3, F3, M3, E5, C4 • **Temperaments:** R, T • **Stress:** T • **Physical:** V=L, H=N, L=L, W, S, H • **Work Env:** I, N • **Salary:** 4 • **Outlook:** 2

GOE: 06.02.08 Machine Work, Stone, Clay & Glass, Skilled

EYEGLASS-LENS CUTTER (optical goods) • D.O.T. #716.682-010 • OES #92941 • LENS CUTTER. Sets up and operates bench-mounted cutting machine to cut eyeglass lenses to specified size and shape: Selects metal pattern according to prescription specifications and mounts pattern in spring clamp of cutting machine. Sets control dial for specified lens diameter plus allowance for edge grinding. Alines center and axis marks on lens with markings on pad of cutting machine and lowers cushioned pressure arm of machine which holds lens in position. Lowers cutting arm over lens and turns crank which rotates lens under cutting wheel to determine if machine settings are correct. Presses cutting arm down to hold cutting wheel against lens and turns crank to cut lens. Removes lens from machine and chips excess material from lens edges, using chipping pliers. Routes cut lenses to edging department. • **GED:** R3, M2, L2 • **SVP:** 30 days-3 mos • **Academic:** Ed=N, Eng=N • **Work Field:** 054 • **MPSMS:** 605 • **Aptitudes:** G3, V4, N4, S3, P3, Q5, K3, F3, M3, E5, C5 • **Temper-**

aments: R, T • **Stress:** T • **Physical:** V=L, H=N, L=L, H • **Work Env:** I • **Salary:** 3 • **Outlook:** 3

POTTERY-MACHINE OPERATOR (pottery & porc.) • D.O.T. #774.382-010 • OES #92998 • JIGGER OPERATOR; POT MAKER. Operates pugmill, jigger machine, and drying chamber, that form, dry, and finish ceramic ware, such as bowls, cups, plates, and saucers: Adjusts and sets controls of pugmill that mixes, extrudes, cuts, and deposits clay charges in or over molds as specified. Installs shaping tool in head of jiggering unit, using handtools. Sets controls to regulate temperature of drying chamber. Installs trimming tools and abrasives on arms of ware-finishing unit, using handtools. Starts machine unit and conveyors and observes lights and gages on panelboard to verify operational efficiency. Examines finished ware for defects and measures dimensions, using rule and thickness gage. Adjusts pressures, temperatures, and trimming tool settings as required. May operate jigger machine only and be designated POTTER (pottery & porc.). May form urns and planters, using jolly and be designated JOLLIER (pottery & porc.). • **GED:** R3, M2, L2 • **SVP:** 6 mos-1 yr • **Academic:** Ed=N, Eng=N • **Work Field:** 136, 141 • **MPSMS:** 535 • **Aptitudes:** G3, V4, N4, S3, P3, Q4, K3, F3, M3, E4, C4 • **Temperaments:** M, R, T • **Stress:** T • **Physical:** V=L, H=N, L=M, W, H • **Work Env:** I, N • **Salary:** 3 • **Outlook:** 2

PRECISION-LENS GRINDER (optical goods) • D.O.T. #716.382-018 • OES #89917 • LENS GRINDER; OPTICAL TECHNICIAN. Sets up and operates grinding and polishing machines to make lenses, optical flats, and other precision optical elements for optical instruments and ophthalmic goods, such as telescopes, microscopes, aerial cameras, military optical systems, and eyeglasses or for use as standards: Operates machine to rough-grind blanks of optical glass to approximate size and shape or manually positions and turns blanks against grinding wheel or lap I. Blocks optical element in plaster or other compound. Mounts blocked element in machine and operates machine to oscillate and rotate element against abrasive to fine-grind element to final size and shape. Periodically stops machine to inspect and measure elements for accuracy and degree of completion. Polishes surfaces, using lens-polishing machine [PRECISION-LENS POLISHER (optical goods)]. May cement lens elements together to obtain corrected lens assemblies. May mount optical elements in holders or adapters for use in instruments. May be designated according to type lens ground as EYEGLASS-LENS GRINDER (optical goods); INSTRUMENT-LENS GRINDER (optical goods); MULTIFOCAL-BUTTON GRINDER (optical goods). • **GED:** R4, M3, L4 • **SVP:** 2-4 yrs • **Academic:** Ed=N, Eng=S • **Work Field:** 051 • **MPSMS:** 603, 605 • **Aptitudes:** G3, V3, N3, S2, P3, Q4, K2, F3, M3, E5, C5 • **Temperaments:** M, T • **Physical:** V=L, H=N, L=L, H • **Work Env:** I • **Salary:** 4 • **Outlook:** 3

PRECISION-LENS POLISHER (optical goods) • D.O.T. #716.682-018 • OES #89917 • Operates polishing machines to polish ophthalmic lenses or optical elements, such as lenses, prisms, and flats for use as contact or eyeglass lenses or in precision optical instruments: Mounts optical element on holding tool, using tape or cement. Selects lap I, according to size of optical element and applies pitch or other adhesive to polishing face of lap. Presses optical element into adhesive to form polishing surface. Mounts holding tool on polishing machine spindle and positions lap and element assembly over tool. Applies abrasive or positions abrasive flow nozzle over element and starts machine that polishes element. Observes polishing operation and periodically stops machine to rinse element with water and to test element for conformance to specifications, using test lens, monochromatic light, microscope, and power determining and optical centering instruments. May guide polishing lap manually over element. May mix adhesive according to formula. May be designated according to type lens polished as CONTACT-LENS POLISHER (optical goods). • **GED:** R3, M2, L2 • **SVP:** 2-4 yrs • **Academic:** Ed=N, Eng=N • **Work Field:** 051 • **MPSMS:** 603, 605 • **Aptitudes:** G3, V3, N3, S3, P2, Q4, K3, F3, M3, E5, C5 • **Temperaments:** M, T • **Physical:** V=L, H=N, L=L, H • **Work Env:** I • **Salary:** 3 • **Outlook:** 3

GOE: 06.02.09 Machine Work, Assorted Materials, Skilled

BROOM STITCHER (brush & broom) • D.O.T. #692.682-022 • OES #92998 • Operates machine to stitch twine through broom fibers to strengthen and shape body of broom: Inserts and tightens jaws in vise that holds broom for stitching. Attaches ratchet and turns lever to set number, rows, and length of stitches. Inserts and clamps brush end of broom in vise. Cuts specified length of twine for each course, using knife. Wraps twine around broom and pulls one end between fibers, using hook, and threads other end through needle. Pushes vise into stitcher and starts machine to stitch fibers. May buckle leather strap around broom to hold it during stitching. • **GED:** R3, M2, L2 • **SVP:** 3-6 mos • **Academic:** Ed=N, Eng=N • **Work Field:** 102, 171 • **MPSMS:** 619 • **Aptitudes:** G3, V4, N4, S3, P3, Q4, K3, F3, M3, E4, C4 • **Temperaments:** R, T • **Stress:** T • **Physical:** V=N, H=N, L=M, H • **Work Env:** I • **Salary:** 2 • **Outlook:** 2

CLOTH PRINTER (any ind.) • D.O.T. #652.382-010 • OES #92522 • PRINTER; PRINTING-MACHINE OPERATOR. Sets up and operates machine to print designs on materials, such as cloth, fiberglass, plastics sheeting, coated felt, or oilcloth: Turns handwheel to set pressure on printing rollers, according to specifications. Turns screws to aline register marks on printing rollers with register marks on machine, using allen wrench. Sharpens doctor, using file and oilstone, and verifies evenness of blade, using straightedge. Alines doctor against printing roller, using handtools. Dips color from tubs into color boxes to supply printing rollers. Scans cloth leaving machine for printing defects, such as smudges, variations in color shades, and designs that are out of register (alinement). Realines printing rollers and adjusts position of blanket or back-grey cloth to absorb excess color from printing rollers. Records yardage of cloth printed. Coordinates printing activities with workers who feed and doff machine and aid in setting up and cleaning machine. May notify COLORIST (profess. & kin.) when color shade varies from specifications. May mix own colors. May mount printing rollers on machine for change of pattern [PRINTING-ROLLER HANDLER (textile)]. May position knives specified distance from edge of plastics material to trim excess material from edges. When printing samples of new patterns and novelty designs is designated as NOVELTY-PRINTING-MACHINE OPERATOR (textile) or PROOFING-MACHINE OPERATOR (print. & pub.). May set up and operate cloth printing machine utilizing caustic soda paste instead of color paste to print designs on cloth which shrink to form plisse, and be designated PLISSE-MACHINE OPERATOR (textile). • **GED:** R4, M1, L3 • **SVP:** 2-4 yrs • **Academic:** Ed=N, Eng=S • **Work Field:** 191 • **MPSMS:** 420, 434 • **Aptitudes:** G3, V4, N4, S3, P2, Q4, K3, F3, M3, E5, C2 • **Temperaments:** M, T • **Physical:** V=L, H=N, L=M, W, S, H • **Work Env:** I, N • **Salary:** 4 • **Outlook:** 2

CRYSTAL SLICER (electronics) • D.O.T. #677.382-018 • OES #92902 • CRYSTAL CUTTER; SAW OPERATOR; WAFER SLICER. Operates precision saws to slice wafers from semiconductor crystal ingots, such as silicon or gallium arsenide: Attaches mounted crystal to holding fixture of automatic feed on saw, using clamps. Adjusts saw controls to set speed and angle of saw blade, thickness of cut, and angle of holding fixture. Operates saw to cut sample wafer from crystal ingot. Measures crystal orientation of sample wafer, using x-ray machine, and measures thickness of sample wafer, using calipers or thickness gauge. Inspects sample wafer for flaws, such as saw marks, chips, bow, and taper. Readjusts saw controls based on measurements and inspection. Starts saw and observes operation of saw to ensure wafers are sliced according to specifications. Removes sliced wafers from saw and cleans wafers in sink or ultrasonic cleaner. May mount crystal ingot to mounting block [CRYSTAL MOUNTER (electronics) 677.687-014]. May be designated according to type of saw operated as V-BLOCK SAW OPERATOR (electronics); WIRE SAW OPERATOR (electronics). • **GED:** R3, M2, L2 • **SVP:** 3-6 mos • **Academic:** Ed=N, Eng=N • **Work Field:** 056 • **MPSMS:** 587 • **Aptitudes:** G3, V4, N4, S3, P3, Q4, K4, F3, M3, E5, C5 • **Temperaments:** J, T • **Physical:** V=L, H=N, L=M, W, H • **Work Env:** I • **Salary:** 4 • **Outlook:** 4

CUTTER OPERATOR (any ind.) • D.O.T. #699.682-018 • OES #92944 • SHEETER OPERATOR. Operates cutting machine equipped with rotary or reciprocating blades to cut rolls of material, such as cloth, paper, paperboard, cellophane, or plastic into sheets, according to specification: Inserts shaft into core of roll, and raises and positions roll on cutter rack, using hoist. Threads ends of material through feed rollers, under or across cutting blades, and alines material against machine guides. Turns rheostat or handwheel to adjust tension of material, and to synchronize timing of cutting blades with rate of material feed to regulate length and width of cut. Starts machine and verifies size of cut material, using rule, or notes accuracy of knife cut on spots of premarked paper. Readjusts machine toeinsure specified dimensions of sheet. Replaces worn cutting blades, using handtools. May operate machine equipped with electronic eye to control timing of cutting blades, and be designated SPOT CUTTER (any ind.). May be designated according to material cut as CELLOPHANE SHEETER (any ind.); FOIL CUTTER (electronics); PAPER SHEETER (any ind.); or according to purpose for which material is cut as LINER SHEETER (any ind.); WRAPPER SHEETER (any ind.). • **GED:** R3, M2, L2 • **SVP:** 3-6 mos • **Academic:** Ed=N, Eng=N • **Work Field:** 054 • **MPSMS:** 420, 470, 492 • **Aptitudes:** G3, V4, N4, S4, P4, Q4, K4, F4, M3, E5, C5 • **Temperaments:** R, T • **Stress:** T • **Physical:** V=L, H=N, L=M, W, H • **Work Env:** I, N • **Salary:** 3 • **Out look:** 2

DIE CUTTER (any ind.) • D.O.T. #699.682-022 • OES #92944 • BEAM-MACHINE OPERATOR; CLICKER; CLICKER OPERATOR; CLICKING-MACHINE OPERATOR; DIE-PRESS OPERATOR; DINKING-MACHINE OPERATOR; POWER-PRESS OPERATOR. Operates machine to cut out parts of specified size and shape from materials, such as cardboard, cloth, leather, mica, paper, plastic, or rubber: Places single or multiple layers of material on bed of machine. Turns handwheel to raise or lower head of machine (ram) according to thickness of material or depth of die. Positions one or more cutting dies on material or clamps dies to head of machine and positions material under dies to ensure maximum utilization of material. Depresses pedal or moves lever to activate ram that forces die through material. Removes cut parts from die or bed of machine. Measures parts with rule or compares parts with standard to verify conformance to specifications. Stacks parts in storage area according to size and shape. May sharpen cutting edges of dies, using file or hone. When operating machine to trim hat brims is designated as ROUNDING-MACHINE OPERATOR (hat & cap). May be designated according to type of die used as ADJUSTABLE-DIE CUTTER (paper goods); SOLID-DIE CUTTER (paper goods); or according to part cut as SOLE-LEATHER-CUTTING-MACHINE OPERATOR (boot & shoe); TOPPIECE CUTTER (boot & shoe); TRIMMING CUTTER (garment). Additional titles: BEAM-PRESS OPERATOR (rubber goods); BOX-TOE CUTTER (boot & shoe); BRIM CUTTER (hat & cap.); BUCKRAM CUTTER (boot & shoe; hat & cap; leather prod.); CAP-PARTS CUTTER (hat & cap); DOUBLE CUTTER (boot & shoe); GLOVE-PARTS CUTTER (glove & mit.); HANDBAG-PARTS CUTTER (leather prod.); HAT PARTS CUTTER (leather prod.); HEEL-LIFT-BEAM CUTTER (boot & shoe); HELMET-HAT-BRIM CUTTER (hat & cap); INSOLE CUTTER, MACHINE (boot & shoe); LABEL CUTTER (garment); LEATHER-NOVELTY-PARTS CUTTER (leather prod.); LINING CUTTER, MACHINE (boot & shoe); OUTSOLE CUTTER, MACHINE (boot & shoe); SHOE-PARTS CUTTER (boot & shoe); SILK-LINING CUTTER, MACHINE (boot & shoe; hat & cap; leather prod.); SINGLE-BEAM CLICKER (boot & shoe; hat & cap; leather prod.); SOLE-CUTTING-MACHINE OPERATOR (boot & shoe); TOP- LIFT CUTTER (boot & shoe); TRIMMING CUTTER, MACHINE (boot & shoe); TWIN-BEAM CLICKER (boot & shoe; hat & cap; leather prod.); UPPER CUTTER, MACHINE (boot & shoe). • **GED:** R3, M2, L3 • **SVP:** 3-6 mos • **Academic:** Ed=N, Eng=S • **Work Field:** 134 • **MPSMS:** 420, 470, 529 • **Aptitudes:** G3, V4, N4, S4, P4, Q4, K3, F4, M3, E4, C4 • **Temperaments:** R, T • **Stress:** T • **Physical:** V=G, H=N, L=L, W, H • **Work Env:** I • **Salary:** 3 • **Outlook:** 2

DYNAMITE-PACKING-MACHINE OPERATOR (explosives) • D.O.T. #692.662-010 • OES #92997 • Sets up and operates machine to pack dynamite into paper cartridge shells to form sticks: Installs and adjusts tamping sticks and nipple plates in packing machine according to diameter and length of cartridges to be packed, using nonsparking handtools. Starts machine, directs DYNAMITE-PACKING-MACHINE FEEDER (explosives) to fill powder hopper with dynamite, and fills shuttle board (cartridge forming block) with paper cartridge shells. Secures shuttle board in filling position on machine, and scoops dynamite from hopper into box above tamping sticks. Lifts shuttle board of filled cartridges from machine and tends crimping press to finish ends, or passes filled cartridges to DYNAMITE-CARTRIDGE CRIMPER (explosives). • **GED:** R3, M2, L3 • **SVP:** 6 mos-1 yr • **Academic:** Ed=N, Eng=S • **Work Field:** 041 • **MPSMS:** 499 • **Aptitudes:** G3, V4, N4, S3, P3, Q4, K3, F4, M3, E5, C4 • **Temperaments:** M, S, T • **Stress:** S • **Physical:** V=L, H=N, L=M, W, S, H • **Work Env:** I, N, R • **Salary:** 3 • **Outlook:** 2

HONEYCOMB-BLANKET MAKER (aircraft-aerospace mfg.) • D.O.T. #806.684-062 • OES #93999 • HONEYCOMB-PAPER FABRICATOR; METAL-HONEYCOMB PROCESSOR. Fabricates fiberglass, paper, or aluminum foil honeycomb-core blankets, used to insulate and strengthen aircraft wing, tail, and fuselage sections, using handtools and fabricating machines: Tends machines that automatically crimp, glue, and cut paper, foil, and fiberglass sheets to form honeycomb. Builds up honeycomb core sections in sequence to form blanket of specified thickness. Dips blankets formed from paper in chemical solution, and dries them in oven to increase strength of paper. Cuts and trims blanket to shape of part to be reinforced, using power shear, hand knife, router equipped with milling head, or bandsaw. Bonds metal or fiberglass skin to shaped blanket, using adhesive and press, or vacuum pressure and oven heat. May operate stretching machine to stretch and smooth out surface skin of honeycomb blanket. May be designated according to operation performed as ADHESIVE-SPREADER OPERATOR (aircraft- aerospace mfg.); BLANKET-MACHINE OPERATOR (aircraft-aero space mfg.); CORE-SAW OPERATOR (aircraft-aerospace mfg.); CORRUGATING- MACHINE OPERATOR (aircraft-aerospace mfg.); PANEL-LAY-UP WORKER (aircraft-aerospace mfg.); PRESS OPERATOR (aircraft-aero space mfg.). • **GED:** R3, M2, L1 • **SVP:** 6 mos-1 yr • **Academic:** Ed=N, Eng=N • **Work Field:** 102 • **MPSMS:** 592 • **Aptitudes:** G3, V4, N4, S3, P4, Q5, K3, F3, M3, E5, C5 • **Temperaments:** M, T • **Physical:** V=N, H=N, L=M, W, H • **Work Env:** I • **Salary:** 3 • **Outlook:** 3

NUMERICAL-CONTROL ROUTER OPERATOR, PRINTED CIRCUIT BOARDS (electronics) • D.O.T. #605.382-046 • OES #91502 • Sets up and operates computer-assisted, numerically-controlled routing machine to automatically rout (cut) individual printed circuit boards (PCBs) from printed circuit panels: Reviews setup instructions and specifications. Inserts or threads specified pre-programmed tape containing machine instructions into reader of machine. Selects specified cutting tools and installs routing bit in machine spindle or magazine. Positions and secures panels of PCBs to indexing table of machine. Pushes button or keys in commands on keyboard to activate machine that automatically aligns indexing table with printed circuit panels under tool spindle and routs or notches individual circuit boards that separate boards from circuit panels according to programmed instruction. Monitors machine operation and display readouts to detect malfunction. Measures dimensions of routed PCB samples to verify conformance to specification, using calipers. Notifies supervisor when boards do not meet specifications or machine malfunctions. May make machine adjustments, such as cleaning machine bed, inspecting router bits, and replacing worn or damaged bits. May maintain production records. • **GED:** R3, M3, L2 • **SVP:** 3-6 mos • **Academic:** Ed=N, Eng=S • **Work Field:** 055 • **MPSMS:** 587 • **Aptitudes:** G3, V3, N3, S3, P4, Q4, K4, F3, M4, E5, C5 • **Temperaments:** J, T • **Physical:** V=L, H=N, L=S, W, H • **Work Env:** I • **Salary:** 3 • **Outlook:** 4

WIRE-WRAPPING-MACHINE OPERATOR (electronics) • D.O.T. #726.682-014 • OES #93908 • Operates computer controlled semiautomatic machine that wraps wires around electronic-pin connectors: Mounts connector panel on machine pallet that moves panel along programmed path, using wrench and screw driver. Depresses specified button to start automatic programmed tape for pin sequence and observes panel lights that indicate size of wire prescribed in program. Selects and mounts specified wire on machine spindle. Threads wire through bit of wire-wrap gun, positions gun in support to align gun with pins on connector panel, and depresses trigger of wire-wrap gun to wrap wire on pins. Observes directional lights of machine to determine movement of pallet and gun support. Inspects wire-wrap of completed panels for tightness, neatness of fold, or broken wire. • **GED:** R4, M3, L4 •

SVP: 2-30 days • **Aca demic:** Ed=N, Eng=S • **Work Field:** 163 • **MPSMS:** 587 • **Aptitudes:** G4, V4, N5, S3, P4, Q4, K4, F2, M3, E5, C5 • **Temperaments:** R, T • **Stress:** T • **Physical:** V=L, H=N, L=L, H • **Work Env:** I • **Salary:** 3 • **Outlook:** 3

GOE: 06.02.10 Equipment Operator, Metal Processor, Skilled

CARBIDE-POWDER PROCESSOR (mach. shop) • **D.O.T.** #510.465-010 • **OES** #92965 • Tends machine and ovens to mix and dry ingredients used to fabricate carbide cutting-tool inserts, following work orders and charts: Reads work order to determine amount and grade of carbide specified. Computes amounts of ingredients required, using charts. Scoops ingredients from canisters, and weighs ingredients on scale to obtain specified amounts. Pours ingredients into cylindrical-tumbler mixing machine, starts tumbler, and stops it after specified time. Pours mixed ingredients into pans, and places them in decarbonizing oven to dry and burn off impurities. Removes pans from oven, adds other ingredients, and sifts mixture through screen to obtain powder of even consistency. Cleans equipment after each batch. • **GED:** R3, M2, L2 • **SVP:** 6 mos-1 yr • **Academic:** Ed=N, Eng=N • **Work Field:** 147 • **MPSMS:** 549 • **Aptitudes:** G3, V4, N4, S4, P4, Q4, K4, F4, M3, E5, C5 • **Temperaments:** M, T • **Physical:** V=L, H=N, L=H, W, H • **Work Env:** I, R • **Salary:** 3 • **Outlook:** 3

COLD-MILL OPERATOR (iron & steel) • **D.O.T.** #613.462-010 • **OES** #91314 • Sets up and operates rolling mill to flatten, temper, and reduce gage of steel strip, following rolling orders and using measuring instruments: Reads rolling order to determine setup and work sequence. Calculates draft (space between rolls) and roll speed for each mill stand to roll strip to specified dimensions and temper. Turns controls to adjust roll speed, draft, and tension of strip between reels of coiling mechanism. Installs guides, guards, and cooling equipment in stands, using handtools. Starts mill to roll test strip and adjusts roll screws, hydraulic sprays, and mill speeds. Moves controls to start production rolling of steel strip. Examines steel for surface defects, such as cracks and scratches. Verifies dimensions of steel for conformance to specifications, using micrometers, thickness gages, and measuring tape. Directs other workers in changing rolls, operating mill equipment, removing coils, and banding and loading strip steel. May be designated according to type of mill operated as REVERSING-MILL ROLLER (iron & steel); TANDEM-MILL ROLLER (iron & steel). May operate mill to temper steel strip and be designated TEMPER-MILL ROLLER (iron & steel). • **GED:** R4, M3, L3 • **SVP:** 2-4 yrs • **Academic:** Ed=N, Eng=S • **Work Field:** 135 • **MPSMS:** 541 • **Aptitudes:** G3, V3, N3, S3, P3, Q4, K3, F4, M3, E5, C5 • **Temperaments:** D, M, T • **Physical:** V=L, H=N, L=M, W, H • **Work Env:** I, W, N, R • **Salary:** 4 • **Outlook:** 2

HEAT TREATER 1 (heat treat.) • **D.O.T.** #504.382-014 • **OES** #91932 • Controls heat-treating furnaces, baths and quenching equipment to alter physical and chemical properties of metal objects, using specifications and methods of controlled heating and cooling, such as hardening, tempering, annealing, case-hardening, and normalizing: Determines temperature and time of heating cycle, and type and temperature of baths and quenching medium to attain specified hardness, toughness, and ductility of parts, using standard heat-treating charts, and utilizing knowledge of heat-treating methods, equipment, and properties of metals. Adjusts furnace controls and observes pyrometer to bring furnace to prescribed temperature. Loads parts into furnace. Removes parts after prescribed time and quenches parts in water, oil, brine, or other bath, or allows parts to cool in air. May test hardness of parts [HARDNESS INSPECTOR (heat treat.)]. May set up and operate die-quenching machine to prevent parts from warping. May set up and operate electronic induction equipment to heat objects [INDUCTION-MACHINE SETTER (heat treat.)]. May aline warped fuel elements, containing radioactive uranium, using hydraulic ram straightener. • **GED:** R4, M3, L3 • **SVP:** 2-4 yrs • **Academic:** Ed=N, Eng=S • **Work Field:** 133 • **MPSMS:** 540 • **Aptitudes:** G3, V3, N3, S4, P4, Q4, K3, F4, M3, E5, C3 • **Temperaments:** M, T, V • **Physical:** V=L, H=N, L=M, W, H • **Work Env:** I, H, R • **Salary:** 3 • **Outlook:** 3

PICKLER, CONTINUOUS PICKLING LINE (any ind.) •

D.O.T. #503.362-010 • **OES** #92997 • CLEANER OPERATOR; CONTINUOUS-DRYOUT OPERATOR; PICKLER OPERATOR; STRIP CLEANER. Sets up and controls continuous pickling or electrolytic-cleaning line to remove dirt, oil, and scale from coils of brass, copper, or steel strip and wire: Turns valve to add acid to processing tanks and shovels inhibitor into tanks to obtain baths of specified acid concentration. Installs and adjusts guides, pinch and leveler rolls, and side shears on processing line, according to specified dimensions of coils to be cleaned, using handtools. Moves controls to regulate speed of coil through line, to shear coil on each side of weld or stitch, and to remove coil from upcoiler machine. Verifies dimensions of pickled coils, using micrometer and measuring tapes. Examines surface of coils to verify removal of dirt, oil, and scale. Tests solution concentration in baths, using titration test equipment, and adjusts processing line controls to ensure conformance to specifications. May be designated according to type of line operated as ELECTROLYTIC DE-SCALER (any ind.). • **GED:** R3, M3, L3 • **SVP:** 1-2 yrs • **Academic:** Ed=N, Eng=S • **Work Field:** 031 • **MPSMS:** 540 • **Aptitudes:** G3, V4, N4, S3, P3, Q4, K3, F4, M3, E5, C5 • **Temperaments:** M, T • **Physical:** V=L, H=N, L=M, W, H • **Work Env:** I, R • **Salary:** 3 • **Outlook:** 3

SAND MIXER, MACHINE (foundry) • **D.O.T.** #570.682-018 • **OES** #92965 • SAND CONDITIONER, MACHINE; SAND MILL OPERATOR; SAND-SYSTEM OPERATOR. Operates machine to mix or recondition molding sand: Weighs out specified amounts of ingredients, such as sand, sea coal, and bonding agents, and shovels them into machine or automatic hopper. Sets dials for specified amounts of water, core oil, and other ingredients that are automatically measured and fed into machine. Turns dials to time mixing cycle of machine. Removes sample of sand and feels sand for consistency. Adjusts controls and adds ingredients to vary mixture according to sampling. May be designated according to purpose for which sand is to be used, such as SAND-MILL OPERATOR, CORE-SAND (found.); SAND-MILL OPERATOR, FACING-SAND (found.); SAND-MILL OPERATOR, MOLDING-SAND (found.). • **GED:** R3, M1, L1 • **SVP:** 3-6 mos • **Academic:** Ed=N, Eng=N • **Work Field:** 143 • **MPSMS:** 345 • **Aptitudes:** G3, V4, N4, S4, P3, Q4, K4, F4, M3, E5, C5 • **Temperaments:** J, T • **Physical:** V=L, H=N, L=M, W, H • **Work Env:** I, N • **Salary:** 4 • **Outlook:** 2

GOE: 06.02.11 Equipment Operator Chemical Processor, Skilled

WASTE-TREATMENT OPERATOR (chem.) • **D.O.T.** #955.382-014 • **OES** #95002 • Controls heat exchange unit, pumps, compressors, and related equipment to decontaminate, neutralize, and dispose of radioactive waste liquids collected from chemical processing operations: Removes sample of liquid from collection tank, using pipette. Pours sample into dish and bakes dish under heat lamp to evaporate water, leaving radioactive residue. Tests residue with Geiger counter and compares reading with chart to determine whether radioactivity level is within prescribed safety limits. Determines degree of acidity or alkalinity in liquid, using pH meter, and adds acid or alkali to neutralize liquid. Starts pump and admits waste liquid into sewer for disposal or into storage tanks for evaporation, according to degree of radioactivity. Transfers radioactive waste liquid from storage tanks to heat exchange unit. Operates heat evaporation system to reduce volume of liquid, and observes gages and adjusts controls during process to maintain steam pressure, temperature, and liquid at specified levels. Starts compressed-air pump to blow slurry on bottom of evaporator into lead container for permanent storage. Records data, such as number of gallons of waste pumped into sewer system or storage tanks, or reduced by heat exchange unit, and radioactivity levels. May monitor panel board to control operation of recovery systems that store or dispose of radioactive waste and be designated NUCLEAR-WASTE-PROCESS OPERATOR (any ind.). • **GED:** R4, M4, L4 • **SVP:** 1-2 yrs • **Academic:** Ed=H, Eng=S • **Work Field:** 014, 147 • **MPSMS:** 499, 870 • **Aptitudes:** G3, V3, N3, S4, P3, Q3, K3, F4, M3, E4, C4 • **Temperaments:** M, T • **Physical:** V=L, H=L, L=L, H • **Work Env:** I, R • **Salary:** 4 • **Out look:** 3

GOE: 06.02.12 Equipment Operator, Petroleum Processor, Skilled

CYLINDER FILLER (comp. & liq. gases) • D.O.T. #559.565-010 • OES #92974 • CHARGING OPERATOR; CYLINDER LOADER; DRUM FILLER; FILLER; GAS WORKER; MANIFOLD OPERATOR; PUMPER. Tends equipment to fill cylinders and other containers with liquefied or compressed gases: Changes cylinder valves with wrench, or adjusts them to prescribed tension, using torque wrench. Rolls cylinders onto platform scale, or positions cylinders in manifold racks manually or with chain hoist. Connects lines from manifold to cylinders, using wrench. Fills cylinders by any of following methods: (1) Sets pressure gage to specified reading and listens for buzzer indicating completion of filling. (2) Adjusts valves and observes gage to fill cylinders to specified pressure. (3) Observes scale indicator to fill cylinders to specified weight. (4) Fills cylinder to excess, rolls cylinder onto scale, and connects exhaust line to release excess gas and attain prescribed gross weight. Sprays or brushes chemical solution onto cylinder valve to test for leaks. Fills out and attaches warning and identification tags or decals, specifying tare and gross weight, cylinder number, type of gas, and date filled, and records data. May test gas for purity, using burette or other testing equipment. May inspect or test empty cylinder [CYLINDER INSPECTOR-AND-TESTER (comp. & liquefied gases)]. May evacuate residual gases from cylinders. May test filled cylinders for specified gas pressure by connecting gage and comparing reading with chart. May tend and maintain generator or compressor in filling process. May be designated according to type of container filled as TON-CONTAINER FILLER (comp. & liquefied gases); TUBE-TRAILER FILLER (comp. & liquefied gases). • **GED:** R3, M2, L2 • **SVP:** 30 days-3 mos • **Academic:** Ed=N, Eng=N • **Work Field:** 014 • **MPSMS:** 491, 496, 568 • **Aptitudes:** G4, V4, N4, S4, P3, Q4, K3, F4, M3, E5, C5 • **Temperaments:** T • **Physical:** V=L, H=N, L=H, W, S, H • **Work Env:** I, R • **Salary:** 2 • **Outlook:** 3

GOE: 06.02.13 Equipment Operator, Rubber & Plastics Processor, Skilled

BLANKMAKER (glass mfg.) • D.O.T. #579.382-022 • OES #92998 • Operates glass lathe to form glass tubes into glass blanks used in fabrication of laser light conductors: Reads work orders and technical manuals to determine lathe setup procedures, and pushes buttons and turns knobs to adjust lathe gas-injection and temperature controls. Locks glass tube into spindle chuck, using wrench. Trues and flares glass tube, using lathe carriage burner, ruler, and calipers. Attaches chemical spray nozzle to glass tube to coat interior of tube with gases, and inserts auger into tube to remove chemical residue. Lowers and locks spindle shield to form dust-free chamber. Presses keys on keyboard to transmit production specifications to computer and to transfer lathe operation from manual to automatic control for duration of blankmaking process. Observes lathe dials and gauges, computer display panel, and color of flame on lathe carriage burner to verify adherence to manufacturing specifications. Calculates data, such as blank weights, diameters, and densities, using calculator, and enters data on record sheet. Repairs lathe, using wrenches, pliers, and screwdrivers to correct malfunctions. • **GED:** R3, M3, L3 • **SVP:** 1-2 yrs • **Academic:** Ed=N, Eng=S • **Work Field:** 147 • **MPSMS:** 532 • **Aptitudes:** G3, V3, N3, S3, P2, Q2, K3, F4, M4, E5, C3 • **Temperaments:** T • **Physical:** V=L, H=N, L=L, H • **Work Env:** I • **Salary:** 4 • **Outlook:** 2

MIXING-MACHINE OPERATOR (any ind.) • D.O.T. #550.382-022 • OES #92965 • Operates mixing machine to blend ingredients into compounds for processing into plastic or rubber materials and products: Loads ingredients into mixing machine hopper from conveyor, scales, or handtrucks, or directs other workers in performing this task. Starts machine and adjusts valves to admit steam or cooling fluids to steam jacket or devices in mixing chamber to aid in blending and densifying mixture. Operates machine until mixture reaches desired consistency, and turns lever to unload mixture into container, conveyor, or mill for sheeting. May operate auxiliary equipment to break up, grind, dry mix, or otherwise prepare mixture for final processing. May tend automatic mixing machine. May be designated according to trade name of machine. • **GED:** R3, M2, L2 • **SVP:** 3-6 mos • **Academic:** Ed=N, Eng=N • **Work Field:** 143 • **MPSMS:** 492, 510 • **Aptitudes:** G3, V3, N4, S4, P3, Q4, K4, F4, M3, E5, C5 • **Temperaments:** M, T • **Physical:** V=L, H=N, L=H, W, H • **Work Env:** I, N • **Salary:** 3 • **Outlook:** 2

GOE: 06.02.15 Equipment Operator, Food Processor, Skilled

BAKER (bake. prod.) • D.O.T. #526.381-010 • OES #89805 • Mixes and bakes ingredients according to recipes to produce breads, pastries, and other baked goods: Measures flour, sugar, shortening, and other ingredients to prepare batters, doughs, fillings, and icings, using scale and graduated containers. Dumps ingredients into mixing-machine bowl or steam kettle to mix or cook ingredients according to specifications. Rolls, cuts, and shapes dough to form sweet rolls, piecrust, tarts, cookies, and related products preparatory to baking. Places dough in pans, molds, or on sheets and bakes in oven or on grill. Observes color of products being baked and turns thermostat or other controls to adjust oven temperature. Applies glaze, icing, or other topping to baked goods, using spatula or brush. May specialize in baking one type of product, such as breads, rolls, pies, or cakes. May decorate cakes [CAKE DECORATOR (bake. prod.)]. May develop new recipes for cakes and icings. • **GED:** R3, M2, L2 • **SVP:** 2-4 yrs • **Academic:** Ed=N, Eng=N • **Work Field:** 146 • **MPSMS:** 384 • **Aptitudes:** G3, V3, N3, S4, P3, Q4, K3, F3, M3, E5, C3 • **Temperaments:** J, T, V • **Physical:** V=L, H=N, L=H, W, S, H • **Work Env:** I • **Salary:** 3 • **Outlook:** 3

BUTTERMAKER (dairy prod.) • D.O.T. #529.362-010 • OES #92962 • Controls equipment to make grades of butter by either of following methods: (1) Butter churn method: Connects sanitary pipe between cream storage vat and churn. Starts pump to convey sterile solution through equipment and to admit measured amount of pasteurized cream into churn, and starts churn. Observes separation of buttermilk from butter and pumps buttermilk from churn. Opens churn and sprays butter with chlorinated water to remove residue buttermilk. Compares butter with color chart and adds coloring to meet specifications. Tests butter for moisture, salt content, and consistency, using testing apparatus, and achieves specified consistency by adding or removing water. Examines, smells, and tastes butter to grade it according to prescribed standard. (2) Butter chilling method: Pasteurizes and separates cream to obtain butter oil, and tests butter oil in standardizing vat for butter fat, moisture, salt content, and acidity, using testing apparatus. Adds water, alkali, and coloring to butter oil to achieve specified grade and starts agitator to mix ingredients. Turns valves and observes gages to regulate temperature and flow of water, refrigerant, and butter oil through chilling vat. Smells, tastes, and feels sample to grade butter emerging from chilling vat. May be designated according to equipment operated as BUTTER-CHILLING EQUIPMENT OPERATOR (dairy prod.); BUTTER CHURNER (dairy prod.). • **GED:** R3, M3, L2 • **SVP:** 1-2 yrs • **Academic:** Ed=N, Eng=N • **Work Field:** 146 • **MPSMS:** 383 • **Aptitudes:** G3, V3, N3, S4, P4, Q4, K3, F3, M3, E5, C3 • **Temperaments:** J, M, T • **Physical:** V=L, H=N, L=H, W, S, H • **Work Env:** I, C, W • **Salary:** 4 • **Outlook:** 2

CENTER-MACHINE OPERATOR (confection.) • D.O.T. #520.682-014 • OES #92968 • CASTING-MACHINE OPERATOR; EXTRUDING-MACHINE OPERATOR. Sets up and operates machine that extrudes soft candy, such as fondant, to form centers of specified size and shape for bonbons and chocolates: Inserts die plate in machine and tightens thumbscrews to secure plate. Examines and feels candy for specified consistency. Dumps candy into machine hopper. Starts machine that automatically feeds candy through openings in die plate and cuts off and deposits formed pieces on conveyor, or moves control to force candy through openings in die plate and moves wires that cut extruded candy to specified thickness. Weighs formed pieces at random to determine adherence to specifications. Adjusts wire or knife that cuts extruded candy to specified dimensions. When making cream centers to be coated with chocolate, may synchronize speed of center machine with enrobing machine. May be designated by product formed as FONDANT-PUFF MAKER (confection.); MARSHMALLOW RUNNER (confection.). • **GED:** R3, M2, L2 • **SVP:** 6 mos-1 yr • **Academic:** Ed=N, Eng=N • **Work Field:** 135 • **MPSMS:** 393 • **Aptitudes:** G3, V3, N3, S3, P3, Q4, K3, F4, M3, E5, C5 • **Temperaments:** M, T • **Physical:** V=L, H=N, L=M, W, H • **Work Env:** I • **Salary:** 3 • **Outlook:** 2

CHOCOLATE-PRODUCTION-MACHINE OPERATOR (choc. & cocoa) • D.O.T. #529.382-014 • OES #92998 • GENERAL UTILITY MACHINE OPERATOR. Operates any of following machines and equipment to relieve regular operators engaged in processing cocoa beans into chocolate liquor and in producing cocoa powder and sweet chocolate, according to formula: Controls roaster that roasts cocoa beans to develop specified color and flavor and reduces moisture content of beans [COCOA-BEAN ROASTER (choc. & cocoa) I; COCOA-BEAN ROASTER (choc. & cocoa) II]. Tends mill to grind nibs (cracked cocoa beans) into liquid chocolate of specified fineness [LIQUOR-GRINDING-MILL OPERATOR (choc. & cocoa)]. Tends hydraulic press to extract cocoa butter from chocolate liquor, and operates cocoa room machinery and equipment to grind and pulverize cocoa cakes into cocoa powder [COCOA-PRESS OPERATOR (choc. & cocoa); COCOA-ROOM OPERATOR (choc. & cocoa)]. Mixes ingredients, such as chocolate liquor, sugar, and powdered milk to make sweet chocolate [MIXER OPERATOR (choc. & cocoa)]. Operates refining machine to grind chocolate paste to specified consistency [REFINING-MACHINE OPERATOR (choc. & cocoa)]. Operates tempering equipment to control temperature of chocolate in cooling process before molding [CHOCOLATE TEMPERER (bake. prod.; cereal)]. May tend molding machines, pressure cookers, and dryers. May assist in supervising and training production line workers. • **GED:** R4, M3, L3 • **SVP:** 1-2 yrs • **Academic:** Ed=N, Eng=S • **Work Field:** 146 • **MPSMS:** 393 • **Aptitudes:** G3, V3, N3, S4, P4, Q4, K3, F4, M3, E5, C4 • **Temperaments:** T, V • **Physical:** V=L, H=N, L=H, W, S, H • **Work Env:** I, H, N • **Salary:** 4 • **Outlook:** 2

COFFEE ROASTER (food prep nec) • D.O.T. #523.682-014 • OES #92921 • Controls gas fired roasters to remove moisture from coffee beans: Weighs batch of coffee beans in scale-hopper, and opens chute to allow beans to flow into roasting oven. Observes thermometer and adjusts controls to maintain required temperature. Compares color of roasting beans in oven with standard to estimate roasting time. Opens discharge gate to dump roasted beans into cooling tray. Starts machine that blows air through beans to cool them. Records amounts, types, and blends of coffee beans roasted. • **GED:** R3, M2, L2 • **SVP:** 6 mos-1 yr • **Academic:** Ed=N, Eng=N • **Work Field:** 141, 212 • **MPSMS:** 391 • **Aptitudes:** G3, V3, N4, S4, P4, Q4, K3, F4, M4, E4, C3 • **Temperaments:** J, M, T • **Physical:** V=L, H=N, L=L, W, H • **Work Env:** I • **Salary:** 3 • **Outlook:** 3

DAIRY-PROCESSING-EQUIPMENT OPERATOR (dairy prod.) • D.O.T. #529.382-018 • OES #92932 • Operates continuous flow or vat-type equipment to process milk, cream, and other dairy products, following specified methods and formulas: Connects pipes between vats and processing equipment. Assembles fittings, valves, bowls, plates, disks, impeller shaft, and other parts to equipment with wrench to prepare for operation. Turns valves to pump sterilizing solution and rinse water through pipes and equipment and spray vats with atomizer. Starts pumps and equipment, observes temperature and pressure gages, and opens valves on continuous flow equipment to force milk through centrifuge to separate cream from milk, through homogenizer to produce specified emulsion, and through filter to remove sediment. Turns valves to admit steam and water into pipes to pasteurize milk and to circulate refrigerant through coils to cool milk. Starts pump and agitator, observes pressure and temperature gages, and opens valves on vat equipment to fill, stir, and steam-heat milk in vat. Pumps or pours specified amounts of liquid or powder ingredients, such as skim milk, lactic culture, stabilizer, neutralizer, and vitamins into vat to make dairy products, such as butter milk, chocolate milk, or ice cream mix. Tests product for acidity at various stages of processing. Records specified time, temperature, pressure, and volume readings. May be designated according to process performed as BYPRODUCTS MAKER (dairy prod.); CLARIFIER OPERATOR (dairy prod.); COOLER OPERATOR (dairy prod.); HOMOGENIZER OPERATOR (dairy prod.); MIX MAKER (dairy prod.); PASTEURIZER OPERATOR (dairy prod.); SEPARATOR OPERATOR (dairy prod.). May be required to hold license from state board of health or local government unit. • **GED:** R4, M2, L3 • **SVP:** 6 mos-1 yr • **Academic:** Ed=N, Eng=S • **Work Field:** 146 • **MPSMS:** 383 • **Aptitudes:** G3, V3, N4, S3, P3, Q4, K3, F3, M3, E5, C4 • **Temperaments:** M, T • **Physical:** V=L, H=N, L=H, W, C, S, H • **Work Env:** I, W, N, R • **Salary:** 3 • **Outlook:** 2

DOUGH MIXER (bake. prod.) • D.O.T. #520.582-010 • OES #92965 • MIXING-MACHINE ATTENDANT. Operates machines and equipment to mix ingredients to make straight and sponge (yeast) doughs according to formula: Moves controls and turns valves to adjust metering devices and to weigh, measure, sift, and convey water, flour, and shortening into mixer. Measures and dumps yeast, vitamins, yeast food, sugar, salt, and other ingredients into mixing machine. Turns knobs to set mixing cycle time and maintain temperature of dough. Starts machine. Feels dough for desired consistency. Dumps dough into trough. Pushes troughs of sponge dough into room to ferment for specified time. Dumps raised sponge dough into mixer, using hoist, and adds ingredients to complete mixture. Records number of batches mixed. May dump all ingredients into mixer by hand. May be designated according to type of dough mixed as BREAD-DOUGH MIXER (bake. prod.); COOKY MIXER (bake. prod.); DOG-FOOD DOUGH MIXER (bake. prod.); DOUGHNUT-DOUGH MIXER (bake. prod.); PASTRY MIXER (bake. prod.); PIE-CRUST MIXER (bake. prod.). Additional titles: CRACKER-DOUGH MIXER (bake. prod.); PRETZEL-DOUGH MIXER (bake. prod.); SWEET-DOUGH MIXER (bake. prod.). • **GED:** R3, M2, L3 • **SVP:** 6 mos-1 yr • **Academic:** Ed=N, Eng=S • **Work Field:** 143 • **MPSMS:** 384 • **Aptitudes:** G3, V4, N3, S4, P4, Q3, K3, F4, M3, E5, C4 • **Temperaments:** M, T • **Physical:** V=L, H=N, L=H, W, H • **Work Env:** I • **Salary:** 3 • **Outlook:** 2

DOUGHNUT-MACHINE OPERATOR (bake. prod.) • D.O.T. #526.682-022 • OES #92998 • CRULLER MAKER, MACHINE; DOUGHNUT-COOKING-MACHINE OPERATOR; FRIED-CAKE MAKER. Operates machine that shapes and fries doughnuts: Slides block of ejectors (cutters) into machine and tightens them, using wing nuts. Turns switch to heat frying tank to desired temperature. Mixes prepared ingredients with specified amount of water in mixing machine to form batter. Dumps batter into doughnut machine hopper, using chain hoist. Turns and adjusts valves to control air pressure for ejecting batter into frying tank and to regulate size of doughnuts, temperature and feed of grease, and speed of conveyor. Starts machine and observes color and verifies weight of doughnuts to ensure conformity to standards. Dismantles doughnut ejectors for cleaning. May melt and temper chocolate [CHOCOLATE TEMPERER (bake. prod.; cereal)]. • **GED:** R3, M2, L3 • **SVP:** 3-6 mos • **Academic:** Ed=N, Eng=S • **Work Field:** 146 • **MPSMS:** 384 • **Aptitudes:** G3, V4, N4, S4, P4, Q4, K4, F3, M3, E5, C4 • **Temperaments:** J, M, T • **Physical:** V=L, H=N, L=L, W, H • **Work Env:** I • **Salary:** 2 • **Outlook:** 3

DRIER OPERATOR (macaroni & related) • D.O.T. #523.362-014 • OES #92921 • Controls equipment that dries macaroni according to laboratory specifications: Turns dials and opens steam valves on panelboard to regulate temperature, humidity, and drying time in preliminary, secondary, and final drying chambers, according to outside atmospheric conditions, specific product requirements, and drying stage. Enters chambers and feels macaroni to determine if product is drying according to specifications, relying upon knowledge and experience. Opens chamber hatch to admit cold air and adjusts controls to change drying speed at particular drying stages to comply with laboratory recommendation or to meet changing atmospheric conditions. Regulates temperature and humidity in pressroom to maintain required atmospheric conditions. Evaluates quality of dried macaroni on basis of color. • **GED:** R4, M2, L3 • **SVP:** 2-4 yrs • **Academic:** Ed=N, Eng=S • **Work Field:** 141 • **MPSMS:** 397 • **Aptitudes:** G3, V3, N3, S4, P4, Q4, K3, F4, M3, E5, C2 • **Temperaments:** J, T • **Physical:** V=L, H=N, L=L, W, H • **Work Env:** I, H, W • **Salary:** 3 • **Outlook:** 1

FREEZER OPERATOR (dairy prod.) • D.O.T. #529.482-010 • OES #92928 • FREEZER; ICE-CREAM FREEZER. Operates one or more continuous freezers and other equipment to freeze ice cream mix into semisolid consistency: Weighs or measures powder and liquid ingredients, such as color, flavoring, or fruit puree, using graduate, and dumps ingredients into flavor vat. Starts agitator to blend contents. Starts pumps and turns valves to force mix into freezer barrels, admit refrigerant into freezer coils, and inject air into mix. Starts beater, scraper, and expeller blades to mix contents with air and prevent adherence of mixture to barrel walls. Observes ammeter and pressure gage and adjusts controls to obtain specified freezing temperature, air pressure, and machine speed. Fills hopper of fruit feeder with candy bits, fruit, and nuts, using scoop, or pours sirups into holder of rippling pump. Sets controls according to freezer speed to feed or ripple ingredients evenly into ice cream expelled from freezer. Opens valve to transfer contents to filling machine that pumps ice cream into cartons, cups, and cones, or molds for pies, rolls, and tarts. Places novelty dies in filler head that separates flavors and forms center designs or rosettes in packaged product. Weighs package and adjusts freezer air valve or switch on filler head to obtain specified amount of product in each container. Assembles pipes, fittings, and equipment for operation, using wrench. Sprays equipment with sterilizing solution. • **GED:** R3, M2, L2 • **SVP:** 6 mos-1 yr • **Academic:** Ed=N, Eng=N • **Work Field:** 146 • **MPSMS:** 383 • **Aptitudes:** G3, V4, N4, S4, P4, Q4, K4, F4, M3, E4, C5 • **Temperaments:** M, T • **Physical:** V=L, H=N, L=L, W, H • **Work Env:** I, W, R • **Salary:** 3 • **Outlook:** 2

GRINDER OPERATOR (grain & feed mill) • D.O.T. #521.682-026 • OES #92965 • FEED MILLER; GRISTMILLER; MILL OPERATOR; ROLLER-MILL OPERATOR. Operates bank of roll grinders to grind grain into meal or flour: Opens and closes slides in spouts to route grain to various grinders and sifters. Turns wheels to adjust pressure of grinding rollers for each break (passage of grain between rollers), according to grain size and hardness, and adjusts feed chutes to regulate flow of grain to rollers. Inspects product and sifts out chaff to determine percentage of yield. Adjusts rollers to maintain maximum yield. Replaces worn grinding rollers, using handtools. May sift and bolt meal or flour. May clean and temper grain prior to grinding. May direct workers who drain and temper grain and bolt meal or flour. May be designated according to grain milled as CORN MILLER (grain & feed mill.). May operate bur mills instead of roll grinders to grind grain and be designated BURR-MILL OPERATOR (grain & feed mill.). • **GED:** R3, M1, L2 • **SVP:** 2-4 yrs • **Academic:** Ed=N, Eng=N • **Work Field:** 142 • **MPSMS:** 381 • **Aptitudes:** G3, V3, N4, S4, P3, Q4, K4, F4, M3, E5, C4 • **Temperaments:** J, T • **Physical:** V=L, H=N, L=M, W, H • **Work Env:** I, N • **Salary:** 3 • **Outlook:** 2

OVEN OPERATOR, AUTOMATIC (bake. prod.) • D.O.T. #526.682-030 • OES #92921 • BAKER OPERATOR, AUTOMATIC. Controls reel or conveyor type oven to bake bread, pastries, and other bakery products: Observes steam pressure and temperature gages, and turns valves to regulate and maintain oven heat and humidity at prescribed levels. Turns rheostat to govern speed of conveyor or reel and to regulate baking time. Observes color of products during baking process to verify uniformity of finished products. May load and unload ovens. May be designated according to type of oven controlled as CONVEYORIZED OVEN TENDER (bake. prod.); REEL OVEN TENDER (bake. prod.). • **GED:** R3, M2, L2 • **SVP:** 3-6 mos • **Academic:** Ed=N, Eng=N • **Work Field:** 146 • **MPSMS:** 384 • **Aptitudes:** G3, V4, N4, S3, P3, Q4, K4, F4, M3, E5, C3 • **Temperaments:** J, M, T • **Physical:** V=L, H=N, L=L, W, H • **Work Env:** I, H • **Salary:** 2 • **Outlook:** 2

SIRUP MAKER (flav. ext. & sirup) • D.O.T. #520.485-026 • OES #92965 • COOKER, SIRUP; SAUCE MAKER. Tends equipment to mix ingredients that produce sirups used in canned fruits and preserves, flavorings, frozen novelty confections, or non-alcoholic beverages: Determines amounts of ingredients, such as sugar, water, and flavoring, required for specified quantity of sirup of designated specific gravity, using sugar-concentration and dilution charts. Opens valve to admit liquid sugar and water into mixer, or dumps crystalline sugar into mixer and admits water. Adds flavoring ingredients and starts mixer to make sirup. Opens valve to admit steam into jacket of mixer to invert sugar, eliminate air, and sterilize sirup. Tests sirup for sugar content, using hydrometer or refractometer. Pumps sirup to storage tank. May filter sirup to remove impurities and be designated as SIRUP FILTERER (flav.

ext. & sirup). May blend raw sirups and be designated as SIRUP BLENDER (flav. ext. & sirup). • **GED:** R3, M2, L3 • **SVP:** 3-6 mos • **Academic:** Ed=N, Eng=S • **Work Field:** 143 • **MPSMS:** 394 • **Aptitudes:** G3, V4, N3, S4, P3, Q4, K4, F4, M3, E5, C4 • **Temperaments:** M, T • **Physical:** V=L, H=N, L=M, W, S • **Work Env:** I, W • **Salary:** 3 • **Outlook:** 2

GOE: 06.02.17 Equipment Operator, Clay Processor, Skilled

BRIQUETTE-MACHINE OPERATOR (fuel briquettes) • D.O.T. #549.662-010 • OES #92998 • BRIQUETTE MOLDER; MOLDING-MACHINE OPERATOR. Operates machines and equipment to dehydrate, pulverize, mix, and mold ingredients to produce fuel briquettes: Shovels or empties sacks of materials into hoppers or bins, or starts elevator-conveyors. Turns valves, handwheels, or rheostats to move and control flow of fuels, water, and dry or liquid binders to machines. Starts conveyors, rotary drier, mixers, pulverizer, mixing augers, and compressing machines. Inspects briquettes and adjusts flow of materials to produce briquettes of specified dimensions. Removes and replaces broken bolts and worn shafts, using handtools. Lubricates machinery or directs oiling of equipment. May be designated according to type of briquette produced as BARBEQUE-BRIQUETTE-MACHINE OPERATOR (fuel briquettes); CHARCOAL-BRIQUETTE-MACHINE OPERATOR (fuel briquettes); COAL-BRIQUETTE-MACHINE OPERATOR (fuel briquettes). • **GED:** R3, M2, L2 • **SVP:** 3-6 mos • **Academic:** Ed=N, Eng=N • **Work Field:** 132, 147 • **MPSMS:** 504 • **Aptitudes:** G3, V4, N4, S4, P4, Q4, K4, F4, M3, E5, C5 • **Temperaments:** R, T • **Stress:** T • **Physical:** V=L, H=N, L=M, W, C, H • **Work Env:** I, N • **Salary:** 3 • **Outlook:** 3

GOE: 06.02.18 Equipment Operator, Assorted Materials Processor, Skilled

CRYSTAL GROWER (electronics) • D.O.T. #590.382-014 • OES #92902 • CRYSTAL GROWING FURNACE OPERATOR. Sets up and operates furnaces to grow semiconductor crystals from materials, such as silicon or gallium arsenide: Loads furnace with seed crystal, dopant, and crystal growing materials, such as polysilicon, gallium arsenide, or remelt. Reads work order and adjusts furnace controls to regulate operating conditions, such as power level, temperature, vacuum, and rotation speed, according to crystal growing specifications. Monitors meltdown of growing material and crystal growth, and adjusts furnace controls. Shuts down furnace and unloads crystal ingot after cooling. May clean inside furnace, using vacuum cleaner and cleaning supplies, and replace furnace liner and other parts. May weigh and crop crystal ingot, slice sample wafer, measure and test ingot for resistivity, and determine crystal orientation [INSPECTOR, CRYSTAL (electronics) 726.684-054]. May operate computer controls to regulate furnace conditions. May be designated according to type of crystal grown as GALLIUM ARSENIDE CRYSTAL GROWER (electronics) or SILICON CRYSTAL GROWER (electronics). • **GED:** R3, M2, L2 • **SVP:** 6 mos-1 yr • **Academic:** Ed=N, Eng=N • **Work Field:** 147 • **MPSMS:** 587 • **Aptitudes:** G3, V4, N3, S2, P2, Q3, K3, F3, M3, E5, C3 • **Temperaments:** J, T • **Physical:** V=L, H=N, L=M, W, H • **Work Env:** I • **Salary:** 3 • **Outlook:** 4

CRYSTAL GROWING TECHNICIAN (electronics) • D.O.T. #590.262-010 • OES #92902 • Analyzes processing procedures and equipment functions to identify and resolve problems in growing semiconductor crystals, utilizing knowledge of crystal growing and trains other workers to grow crystals: Observes furnace operation and crystal growth and reads logbook entries to identify deviations from specifications and procedures and advises CRYSTAL GROWER (electronics) 590.382-014 on techniques to adjust furnace controls to alter crystal growth to meet company specifications. Demonstrates and explains crystal growing procedures to train CRYSTAL GROWER (electronics) 590.382-014 and to improve worker's crystal growing techniques. Inspects furnaces for gas leaks, diagnoses equipment malfunctions, and requests equipment repairs. Sets up and operates furnaces in absence of CRYSTAL GROWER (electronics) 590.382-014. • **GED:** R4, M3, L3 • **SVP:** 1-2 yrs • **Academic:** Ed=H, Eng=S • **Work Field:** 147 •

MPSMS: 587 • **Aptitudes:** G2, V3, N2, S2, P2, Q3, K3, F3, M3, E5, C3 • **Temperaments:** J, T • **Physical:** V=L, H=N, L=M, W, H • **Work Env:** I • **Salary:** 4 • **Outlook:** 4

IMPREGNATOR (electronics) • D.O.T. #590.682-014 • OES #92953 • Controls equipment to impregnate electronic components, such as transformers, capacitors, coils, stators, rotors, and solenoids, with wax, varnish, oil, or plastic to seal or insulate them by any of following methods: (1) Places components on rack and ties lead wires to rack to avoid coating leads with liquid. Sets dial to regulate heater controls and maintain specified temperature of liquid in storage tank. Test viscosity, using viscometer, and adds thinner as required. Lowers rack into impregnation tank, using hoist, and locks lid in place. Turns valve to release specified amount of liquid from storage tank into impregnation tank and starts pump to create vacuum in impregnation tank. Stops pump, after specified time, and turns valve to drain tank. Removes impregnated components from tank and places them in curing oven. (2) Weighs out ingredients, such as plastic resins, mica, and silica and mixes them in bucket, following formula, to form sealant. Places components in bucket of sealant, or fills cases containing components with sealant, using cup or caulking gun. Places bucket or tray of components in vacuum tank, locks lid, and starts pump to create vacuum that impregnates components. Removes components from tank after specified time, and places them in oven. Removes components from oven after specified time, and examines them for sealing defects, such as pinholes or peeling. Trims excess material from components, using knife, and cleans terminals and cases, using solvent and cloth. Sprays plastic coating on components, using spray gun. May operate molding press to impregnate components with various protective compounds. May be designated according to impregnation material used as WAX IMPREGNATOR (electronics). May be designated IMPREGNATOR, ELECTRO-LYTIC CAPACITORS (electronics). • **GED:** R3, M2, L2 • **SVP:** 3-6 mos • **Academic:** Ed=N, Eng=N • **Work Field:** 141, 152 • **MPSMS:** 587 • **Aptitudes:** G4, V4, N4, S4, P3, Q5, K4, F4, M3, E5, C5 • **Temperaments:** R, T • **Stress:** T • **Physical:** V=L, H=N, L=M, W, H • **Work Env:** I • **Salary:** 3 • **Outlook:** 4

ION IMPLANT MACHINE OPERATOR (electronics) • D.O.T. #590.382-022 • OES #92902 • Operates ion implanting machine to implant semiconductor wafers with gases, such as arsenic, boron, or phosphorus, to implant electrical properties in wafers: Turns valves, flips switches, and presses buttons to start and regulate flow of gases into implant machine. Places semiconductor wafers in holders, such as carousel, wheels, or boats, using tweezers. Places loaded holder in machine and secures clamps. Presses buttons to start feeding and implanting process. Monitors gas gauges and meters and turns dials to adjust gases, following specifications, if required. Maintains processing reports. May test semiconductor wafers, using test equipment, to verify that voltage, current, and resistivity of implantation meet company specifications. • **GED:** R3, M3, L3 • **SVP:** 3-6 mos • **Academic:** Ed=N, Eng=S • **Work Field:** 147 • **MPSMS:** 587 • **Aptitudes:** G3, V3, N3, S4, P4, Q3, K4, F3, M4, E5, C5 • **Temperaments:** J, T • **Physical:** V=L, H=N, L=L, H • **Work Env:** I, R • **Salary:** 3 • **Outlook:** 4

ROOF-CEMENT-AND-PAINT MAKER (build. mat. nec) • D.O.T. #550.382-030 • OES #92965 • MIXER. Operates one or more mixing machines to combine tar, asbestos fiber, asphalt, or similar ingredients to make roof coating and cement: Starts mixing machine and pump and opens line valve to admit asphalt into mixing machine. Observes indicator or measuring stick and stops asphalt flow when specified amount has entered mixing machine. Dumps specified ingredients through well into mixing tank or starts conveyor and dumps ingredients onto convey or leading to mixing machine. Reads ammeter to determine consistency of mixture and adds materials as needed, or visually determines when mixture has attained consistency and stops mixing machine. Draws off sample of mixture for laboratory testing. Turns lock bolts to open lines between mixing tank and storage tank, using wrench. Keeps record of batch made, including deviations from written formula. • **GED:** R3, M2, L2 • **SVP:** 6 mos-1 yr • **Academic:** Ed=N, Eng=N • **Work Field:** 143 • **MPSMS:** 502, 503 • **Aptitudes:** G3, V4, N4, S3, P3, Q4, K3, F4, M3, E5, C4 • **Temperaments:** M, T • **Physical:** V=L, H=N, L=H, W, S, H • **Work Env:**

I • **Salary:** 3 • **Outlook:** 2

ROOFING-MACHINE OPERATOR (build. mat. nec) • D.O.T. #554.682-022 • OES #92953 • Operates machine to coat continuous rolls of roofing felt with asphalt, colored slate granules, powdered mica, or tar, to make roll roofing or shingles: Threads felt through or around series of coating rollers. Pulls felt through rollers and adjusts tension. Sets machine controls to gradually increase speed of rollers to specified operating speeds, or pulls levers and turns valves and wheels to synchronize machine speed and flow of coating material. Observes gage and adjusts rheostat to regulate temperature of coating material in reservoir. Examines felt as it emerges from rollers to ensure that coating material is applied according to specifications. May feel moving felt to determine whether granules are being deposited uniformly and are adhering as specified. May be designated according to type of coating applied as COATER, ASPHALT (build. mat., n.e.c.); COATER, SLATE (build. mat., n.e.c.). • **GED:** R3, M1, L2 • **SVP:** 3-6 mos • **Academic:** Ed=N, Eng=N • **Work Field:** 151 • **MPSMS:** 502, 503 • **Aptitudes:** G3, V4, N4, S3, P3, Q4, K3, F4, M3, E5, C5 • **Temperaments:** M, T • **Physical:** V=L, H=N, L=L, W, H • **Work Env:** I • **Salary:** 3 • **Outlook:** 2

SOAP MAKER (soap) • D.O.T. #559.382-054 • OES #92965 • SOAP BOILER. Controls equipment that produces soap according to formula: Opens valves to charge kettle with prescribed amounts of ingredients. Turns valve to admit steam through bottom of tank to boil and agitate mixture. Observes mixture through opening in top of tank to detect variations of color, consistency, and homogeneity of boiling ingredients. Adds soda or water to mixture as directed by laboratory; or determines degree of alkalinity of caustic soda in mixture, using meter, and adds soda or water as required. Observes color, consistency, and homogeneity of product to determine when boiling and agitating cycle are completed, and allows batch to cool and settle for specified period of time. Raises or lowers pumpline to locate separation level of neat (pure soap) and nigre (residue). Starts pump to transfer neat to designated department. Lowers pump line to bottom of tank to transfer residue to reclaiming tank. May calculate amount of ingredients needed to make various soaps, using formula. • **GED:** R3, M2, L3 • **SVP:** 2-4 yrs • **Academic:** Ed=N, Eng=S • **Work Field:** 147 • **MPSMS:** 494 • **Aptitudes:** G3, V3, N4, S4, P3, Q4, K4, F4, M3, E5, C3 • **Temperaments:** M, T • **Physical:** V=L, H=N, L=L, W, H • **Work Env:** I, N • **Salary:** 4 • **Outlook:** 2

STILL TENDER (any ind.) • D.O.T. #552.685-026 • OES #92962 • Tends flash-type still that reclaims or separates liquids, such as solvents, through volatilization and condensation: Starts pump to draw liquid into tank and allows impurities to settle. Turns valve to transfer liquids into still. Observes temperature gage and adjusts valve to heat liquid to specified temperature and vaporize liquid in tank. Turns valve to circulate water through tank jackets to condense vapors. Observes distillate for clarity, through pipeline viewer. May be designated according to liquid recovered as SOLVENT RECOVERER (plastics mat.). • **GED:** R3, M2, L2 • **SVP:** 30 days-3 mos • **Academic:** Ed=N, Eng=N • **Work Field:** 144 • **MPSMS:** 490 • **Aptitudes:** G4, V4, N4, S4, P4, Q4, K4, F4, M3, E5, C5 • **Temperaments:** M, T • **Physical:** V=L, H=N, L=L, H • **Work Env:** I • **Salary:** 3 • **Outlook:** 2

GOE: 06.02.19 Equipment Operator, Welding & Soldering, Skilled

LASER-BEAM-MACHINE OPERATOR (welding) • D.O.T. #815.682-010 • OES #91705 • Operates laser-beam machine, which produces heat from concentrated light beam, to weld metal components: Pushes button to open safety enclosure at rear of laser cavity. Positions metal components in fixture and places components on fixture-holding table inside cavity. Pushes button to close safety enclosure. Alines rear mirror of laser cavity, using micrometer screws, according to chart specifications. Types instructions, using teletype machine, to computer that automatically places fixture-holding table in operative position. Sights reference mark through microscope and turns controls to move fixture to welding position. Teletypes instructions to initiate weld cycle and to return fixture-holding table to unload position. Pushes button to open safety enclosure and removes fixtures containing welded components. Cleans optics, using brush, and replaces used flash tubes. May cut metal components, using laser-beam machine, and be designated LASER-BEAM CUTTER (welding). • **GED:** R3, M3, L3 • **SVP:** 3-6 mos • **Academic:** Ed=N, Eng=S • **Work Field:** 081 • **MPSMS:** 566 • **Aptitudes:** G3, V3, N3, S3, P3, Q3, K3, F3, M4, E5, C5 • **Temperaments:** T • **Physical:** V=L, H=N, L=L, H • **Work Env:** I • **Salary:** 3 • **Outlook:** 3

WELDING-MACHINE OPERATOR, ARC (welding) • D.O.T. #810.382-010 • OES #91702 • Sets up and operates arc welding machine that welds together parts of fabricated metal products, as specified by blueprints, layouts, welding procedures, and operating charts: Welds flat, cylindrical, or irregular parts that may be clamped, tack-welded, or otherwise positioned. May position weld line parallel to carriage. Turns cranks or pushes buttons to aline electrode on welding head over weld joint to weld linear joints, or adjust length of radial arm to position electrode over weld joint when welding radial joints. Clamps cylindrical workpieces onto turning rolls under stationary head to weld circular joints. Threads specified electrode wire from reel through feed rolls and welding head. Turns welding head to set specified angle of electrode. May fill hopper with specified flux and direct nozzle or gravity feed over weld line, or adjust shielding gas or gas mixture flow rate. Turns knobs to set current, voltage, and slope, and synchronize feed of wire and flux with speed of welding action. May set limit switch which automatically stops machine at end of weld. Starts machine and observes meters and gages, or observes welding action for compliance with procedures. Visually examines welds for adherence to specifications. May grind welded surfaces for penetrant test. Adjusts machine setup to vary size, location, and penetration of bead. May install track template to weld irregularly-shaped seams. May make trial run before welding and record setup and operating data. May layout, fit, and tack workpieces together. May preheat workpiece, using hand torch or heating furnace. May reweld defective joints, using hand welding equipment. May remove surplus slag, flux, and spatter, using brush, portable grinder, and hand scraper. May operate machine equipped with two or more heads. May be designated according to type of welding machine operated as WELDING-MACHINE OPERATOR, ELECTRO-GAS (welding); WELDING-MACHINE OPERATOR, GAS-METAL ARC (welding); WELDING-MACHINE OPERATOR, GAS-TUNGSTEN ARC (welding); WELDING-MACHINE OPERATOR, PLASMA ARC (welding); WELDING-MACHINE OPERATOR, SUBMERGED ARC (welding). • **GED:** R4, M4, L3 • **SVP:** 1-2 yrs • **Academic:** Ed=N, Eng=S • **Work Field:** 081 • **MPSMS:** 540, 554 • **Aptitudes:** G3, V4, N3, S4, P3, Q4, K3, F4, M4, E5, C4 • **Temperaments:** M, T • **Physical:** V=L, H=N, L=M, W, H • **Work Env:** I, N, R • **Salary:** 4 • **Outlook:** 3

WELDING-MACHINE OPERATOR, GAS (welding) • D.O.T. #811.482-010 • OES #91702 • WELDER, GAS, AUTOMATIC. Sets up and operates oxy-fuel-gas-welding machine to weld metal parts, according to work order, blueprints, layout, and operating charts: Clamps workpieces into holding fixture on machine bed, movable carriage, or turntable. Positions and clamps or bolts welding torch onto overhead carriage, radial arm, or into stationary fixture at specified angle and distance from workpiece. Turns cranks to aline torch with weld line. Selects torch tip, filler wire, and flux, according to charts or thickness and type of metal. Fills hoppers with flux and positions spout over weld line. Places reel of filler wire onto spindle and threads end through feed rolls to welding seam. Connects hoses from torch to regulator valves and cylinders of oxygen and fuel gas. Turns regulator valves to start flow of gases, lights torch, and adjusts gas mixture and pressure to obtain flame of desired size and color. Turns knobs to synchronize movement of torch or workpiece, feed of flux and filler with welding action, and sets switch to stop machine at end of weld. Starts machine, observes welding action, and examines weld for defects. Adjusts machine setup to vary bead size and other weld characteristics. May record setup and operating data. May reweld defective joints, using handtorch. May preheat workpiece in furnace. May lay out, fit, and tack-weld workpieces together. May operate machine equipped with two or more welding torches. May remove surplus flux, slag, and splatter, using wirebrush, portable grinder, and hand scraper. • **GED:** R3, M3, L2 • **SVP:** 1-2 yrs • **Academic:** Ed=N, Eng=N • **Work Field:** 081 • **MPSMS:** 540 • **Aptitudes:** G3, V4, N3, S3, P3, Q4, K3, F3, M3, E5, C4 • **Temperaments:** M,

T • **Physical:** V=L, H=N, L=M, W, S, H • **Work Env:** I, N, R • **Salary:** 4 • **Outlook:** 3

GOE: 06.02.20 Machine Assembling, Skilled

ARBOR-PRESS OPERATOR 1 (any ind.) • D.O.T. #616.682-010 • OES #92197 • FLOOR-PRESS OPERATOR. Sets up and operates arbor press to press-fit parts, such as bearings, linings, armatures, or wheels to housings or shafts: Installs specified holding fixtures and dies on press, using rule, gages, and handtools. Positions workpiece on press bed under ram, manually or using hoist. Moves controls to lower ram that presses part onto shaft or into housing. May mix white lead and apply it to parts as necessary, using brush, and remove scale, rust, burs, and excess white lead, using files, wire brush, and rags. May be designated according to parts assembled as BEARING-PRESS-MACHINE OPERATOR (loco. & car bldg. & rep.); CYLINDER-BLOCK-HOLE RELINER (auto. ser.); WHEEL-PRESS OPERATOR (loco. & car bldg. & rep.). • **GED:** R3, M1, L1 • **SVP:** 30 days-3 mos • **Academic:** Ed=N, Eng=N • **Work Field:** 061 • **MPSMS:** 610 • **Aptitudes:** G3, V4, N4, S3, P4, Q5, K3, F4, M3, E4, C5 • **Temperaments:** R, T • **Stress:** T • **Physical:** V=L, H=N, L=M, W, H • **Work Env:** I, N • **Salary:** 4 • **Outlook:** 3

COVERING-MACHINE OPERATOR (print. & pub.) • D.O.T. #653.682-014 • OES #92546 • Operates automatic book-covering machine to glue paper covers to wire-stitched books, pamphlets, and catalogs: Adjusts guide, spacing, and tension bars, and glue-distribution device according to size of book, by turning setscrews and handwheels. Fills glue reservoir, and loads feed hoppers of machine with covers and books. Pulls control lever to start machine. Removes finished books from discharge table. May direct other workers in keeping hoppers supplied with covers and books, and in removing and stacking finished books. May operate machine arranged in tandem with other bookbinding machines. • **GED:** R3, M2, L1 • **SVP:** 6 mos-1 yr • **Academic:** Ed=N, Eng=N • **Work Field:** 063 • **MPSMS:** 486 • **Aptitudes:** G3, V4, N4, S3, P4, Q4, K4, F4, M3, E5, C5 • **Temperaments:** M, R, T • **Stress:** T • **Physical:** V=L, H=N, L=L, H • **Work Env:** I, N • **Salary:** 3 • **Outlook:** 2

KICK-PRESS OPERATOR 1 (any ind.) • D.O.T. #616.682-026 • OES #92197 • ASSEMBLER, PRESS OPERATOR; BENCH-PRESS OPERATOR. Sets up and operates power press to assemble metal, plastic, rubber, or glass products by crimping, shaping, locking, staking, or press fitting: Installs specified dies on machine bed and ram, using measuring instruments and hand tools. Positions and clamps holding fixtures to machine bed, using sample workpiece, template, rule, and gage. Adjusts set screws to regulate stroke of ram. Alines parts between dies or positions them against fixtures on machine. Moves controls to lower ram that bends, clinches, or forces parts together. May operate machine to separate parts. May set up and operate machine to punch, cut, face, chamfer, or compress parts preparatory to assembly. May install gears and cams to synchronize action of multiple ram, feed, and positioning action of automatic presses. • **GED:** R3, M2, L2 • **SVP:** 3-6 mos • **Academic:** Ed=N, Eng=N • **Work Field:** 134 • **MPSMS:** 610 • **Aptitudes:** G3, V4, N4, S3, P3, Q4, K4, F3, M3, E4, C5 • **Temperaments:** M, T • **Physical:** V=L, H=N, L=L, W, S, H • **Work Env:** I, N, R • **Salary:** 4 • **Outlook:** 2

STACKING-MACHINE OPERATOR 1 (any ind.) • D.O.T. #692.682-054 • OES #97989 • LAMINATION STACKER, MACHINE; PLATE STACKER, MACHINE. Operates machine to stack plates or sheets of material, such as metal or plastic, to assemble laminated products, such as rotor cores and storage battery elements or to form bundles for shipment: Places specified material into one or more feed magazines or holding devices. Moves lever to set automatic feed for number of items specified for stack. Turns screws to adjust opening in feed mechanism to size of item, using measuring instruments or built-in scale and hand tools. Starts machine that automatically measures or counts and stacks specified number of pieces in desired arrangement. Clears jams and adjusts machine to correct malfunction, using handtools. Removes finished stack from machine and places stack into basket or into magazine of machine performing subsequent operation.

May insert spacers between bundles to form continuous stack. • **GED:** R3, M2, L3 • **SVP:** 3-6 mos • **Academic:** Ed=N, Eng=S • **Work Field:** 061 • **MPSMS:** 554 • **Aptitudes:** G3, V4, N4, S3, P4, Q4, K3, F4, M4, E5, C5 • **Temperaments:** M, R, T • **Stress:** T • **Physical:** V=L, H=N, L=L, S, H • **Work Env:** I, N • **Salary:** 2 • **Outlook:** 2

GOE: 06.02.21 Coating & Plating, Skilled

ANODIZER (any ind.) • D.O.T. #500.682-010 • OES #91921 • WHITE-METAL CORROSION PROOFER. Controls anodizing equipment to provide corrosion resistant surface to aluminum objects: Selects holding rack according to size, shape, and number of objects to be anodized. Wires or clips objects to anodizing rack and immerses rack in series of cleaning, etching, and rinsing baths. Positions objects in anodizing tank by suspending them from anode. Estimates amount of electric current and time required to anodize material. Turns rheostat to regulate flow of current. Removes objects from tank after specified time, rinses objects, and immerses them in bath of hot water or dichromate solution to seal oxide coating. Hangs objects on racks to air-dry. May immerse objects in dye bath to color them for decorative or identification purposes. May anodize workpiece with corrosion resistant material, using automated equipment that automatically cleans, rinses, and coats. • **GED:** R3, M2, L3 • **SVP:** 3-6 mos • **Academic:** Ed=N, Eng=S • **Work Field:** 154 • **MPSMS:** 550 • **Aptitudes:** G3, V4, N4, S3, P3, Q4, K4, F4, M3, E5, C4 • **Temperaments:** R, T • **Stress:** T • **Physical:** V=L, H=N, L=H, W, H • **Work Env:** B, H, W • **Salary:** 3 • **Outlook:** 3

COATER OPERATOR (any ind.) • D.O.T. #509.382-010 • OES #91926 • Operates roll-coating machine and auxiliary equipment to coat coils of sheet metal, flat metal blanks, or fabricated metal parts with paint, vinyl plastic, or adhesive film: Positions coiled metal strip on mandrel of feed reel or places metal blanks onto feed carriage of machine. Feeds coils of sheet metal into take-up rolls of stitching machine. Starts stitching machine that staples strips together to form endless metal strip. Turns control dials of machines to regulate speed of metal strip, temperature of drying ovens, and flow of chemicals that maintain specified viscosity of solutions in cleaning tanks. Mixes paint or coating solution to specified viscosity and starts equipment to pump mixture into machine reservoir. Turns setscrews to adjust distance between coating rollers that control thickness of coating. Measures thickness of coating to test viscosity, using wet film gage. Starts pump that fills printing machine reservoir. Adjusts printing cylinder that prints designs on painted metal strip and hydraulic pressure valve of laminating machine that applies plastic vinyl or adhesives to heated metal strip. Turns valve to control spray of water in quenching process that tempers paint, adhesives, or plastic vinyl. Presses pedal of shear machine to cut metal strips. Pushes reel lever to rewind coated metal strip into coil. Examines coated metal workpieces for defects, such as air bubbles or uncoated surfaces. • **GED:** R3, M3, L2 • **SVP:** 1-2 yrs • **Academic:** Ed=N, Eng=N • **Work Field:** 031, 153, 191 • **MPSMS:** 559 • **Aptitudes:** G3, V3, N4, S4, P3, Q4, K3, F4, M3, E4, C3 • **Temperaments:** M, T, V • **Physical:** V=L, H=N, L=M, W, H • **Work Env:** I, N, R • **Salary:** 3 • **Outlook:** 3

COATING-MACHINE OPERATOR (coated fabrics) • D.O.T. #584.382-010 • OES #92953 • SATURATOR. Operates machine to coat cloth, paper, or other sheet material used in production of artificial leather and other coated fabrics: Installs uncoated sheeting roll on machine brackets, using hoist, or threads sheeting from calender machine through coating machine rollers onto takeup roll. Operates sewing machine to join uncoated roll to end of processed roll, and cuts material at seam after seam passes through coating and drying units. Adjusts doctor blade or roller clearance to produce coating of specified thickness. Starts machine when dryer temperature reaches specified setting. Turns valves to control flow of coating solution onto sheeting, or applies solution to fabric surface, using dipper and bucket. Observes process to prevent slippage of sheeting from width guides and turns valves and moves machine controls to correct such defects as streaks, wrinkles, and turned edges in material being processed. Applies gummed tape to repair holes or tears in sheeting. May be designated according to type of coating applied as DULL-COAT-MILL

OPERATOR (coated fabrics); FINISH-COAT-MILL OPERATOR (coated fabrics); FIRST-COAT OPERATOR (coated fabrics). May remove coated rolls from machine, using hoist. • **GED:** R3, M2, L2 • **SVP:** 6 mos-1 yr • **Academic:** Ed=N, Eng=N • **Work Field:** 153 • **MPSMS:** 434 • **Aptitudes:** G3, V4, N3, S4, P3, Q4, K3, F4, M3, E4, C4 • **Temperaments:** M, T • **Physical:** V=L, H=N, L=M, W, H • **Work Env:** I • **Salary:** 3 • **Outlook:** 2

OPTICAL-ELEMENT COATER (optical goods) • D.O.T. #716.382-014 • OES #89917 • Controls vacuum coating equipment to coat optical elements with chemical or metal film to alter reflective properties of elements: Reads work order to ascertain thickness of optical element and type coating material specified. Installs heating filament in coating machine according to type coating applied, using screwdriver. Fills crucible with coating material and positions crucible under heating filament. Secures optical element in jig and centers jig in vacuum chamber of machine to ensure uniform coating of optical surface. Places dome-shaped lid (vacuum bell) over jig or lowers lid equipped with window depending upon machine used. Starts machine that creates vacuum and releases chemicals or metal to form coating on optical element by process of sublimation or atomization. Observes changing colors of element through vacuum bell or through window in lid to determine when element is coated to specifications, or reads exposure meter to determine coating thickness. Applies and removes strip of cellophane to test adherence of coating to optical element. May immerse elements in chemical solution to clean elements. May operate ultrasonic vibrator to clean element. May inspect optical elements prior to coating to detect defects, such as blemishes, abrasions, and rough edges, using microscope. May cement optical elements to gether to form multiple laminated elements [CEMENTER (optical goods)]. May spray emulsion on lens preparatory to coating. • **GED:** R3, M2, L2 • **SVP:** 6 mos-1 yr • **Academic:** Ed=N, Eng=N • **Work Field:** 151, 154 • **MPSMS:** 603 • **Aptitudes:** G3, V3, N4, S4, P3, Q4, K4, F3, M3, E5, C3 • **Temperaments:** M, T • **Physical:** V=L, H=N, L=L, H • **Work Env:** I • **Salary:** 3 • **Outlook:** 3

PAINT-SPRAYER OPERATOR, AUTOMATIC (any ind.) • D.O.T. #599.382-010 • OES #92951 • SPRAY-MACHINE OPERATOR. Sets up and operates painting and drying units along convey or line to coat metal, plastic, ceramic, and wood products with lacquer, paint, varnish, enamel, oil, or rustproofing material: Places or racks workpieces on conveyor. Turns valve to regulate water shield spray. Starts pumps to mix chemicals and paints, to fill tanks, and to control viscosity, adding prescribed amounts or proportions of paints, thinner, and chemicals to mixture. Screws specified nozzles into spray guns and positions nozzles to direct spray onto workpiece. Lights ovens, turns knobs, and observes gages on control panel to set specified temperature and air circulation in oven, to synchronize speed of conveyor with action of spray guns and ovens, and to regulate air pressure in spray guns that atomize spray. Determines flow and viscosity of paints and quality of coating visually or by use of viscometer. May spray coated product with salt solution for prescribed time to determine resistance to corrosion. May be designated according to coating applied as BONDERITE OPERATOR (any ind.); CONTROL OPERATOR, FLOW COAT (elec. equip.); or according to article coated as GUNSTOCK-SPRAY-UNIT ADJUSTER (firearms). • **GED:** R3, M2, L3 • **SVP:** 6 mos-1 yr • **Academic:** Ed=N, Eng=S • **Work Field:** 141, 153 • **MPSMS:** 495, 550 • **Aptitudes:** G3, V4, N3, S4, P3, Q4, K3, F4, M3, E5, C4 • **Temperaments:** M, T • **Physical:** V=L, H=N, L=M, W, H • **Work Env:** I, N • **Salary:** 3 • **Outlook:** 3

PAINTER, ELECTROSTATIC (any ind.) • D.O.T. #599.682-010 • OES #93947 • ELECTRONIC PAINT OPERATOR. Operates cone, disk, or nozzle-type electro-static painting equipment to spray negatively charged paint particles onto positively charged workpieces: Moves switches and dials to start flow current and to activate conveyor and paint spraying equipment. Turns valves and observes gages to set pressure and to control flow of paint to each spray station. Adjusts thermostat to maintain specified temperature in paint tanks. Inspects painted units for runs, sags, and unpainted areas. Readjusts pressure valves to control direction and pattern of spray and to correct flaws in coating. Cleans paint from ceiling and walls of booth, conveyor hooks or grid, and from disks, cones, spray heads, and hoses, using solvent and brush. May hand-spray parts to cover unpainted areas or apply rust preventative. May mix paint according to specifications, using viscometer to regulate consistency according to changes in atmospheric conditions. • **GED:** R3, M2, L3 • **SVP:** 3-6 mos • **Academic:** Ed=N, Eng=S • **Work Field:** 153 • **MPSMS:** 495, 550 • **Aptitudes:** G3, V3, N3, S4, P4, Q4, K3, F4, M3, E5, C3 • **Temperaments:** M, R, T • **Stress:** T • **Physical:** V=L, H=N, L=L, W, H • **Work Env:** I • **Salary:** 3 • **Outlook:** 3

PLATER (electroplating) • D.O.T. #500.380-010 • OES #91917 • ELECTROPLATER; PLATING-TANK OPERATOR. Sets up and controls plating equipment to coat metal objects electrolytically with chromium, copper, cadmium, or other metal to provide protective or decorative surfaces or to build up worn surfaces according to specifications: Reads work order to determine size and composition of object to be plated; type concentration and temperature of plating solution; type and thickness and location of specified plating metal; and amount of electrical current and time required to complete plating process. Immerses object in cleaning and rinsing baths [METAL-CLEANER, IMMERSION (any ind.)]. Suspends object, such as part or mold, from cathode rod (negative terminal) and immerses object in plating solution. Suspends stick or piece of plating metal from anode (positive terminal) and immerses metal in plating solution. Moves controls on rectifier to adjust flow of current through plating solution from anode to cathode and to permit electrodeposition of metal on object. Removes plated object from solution at periodic intervals and observes object to insure conformance to specifications. Adjusts voltage and amperage based on observation. Examines object visually at end of process to determine thickness of metal deposit or measures thickness, using instruments, such as micrometers or calipers. Grinds, polishes or rinses object in water and dries object to maintain clean even surface. May mix, and test strength of plating solution, using instruments and chemical tests. May measure, mark, and mask areas excluded from plating. May plate small objects, such as nuts or bolts, using motor-driven barrel. May direct other workers performing variety of duties, such as racking, cleaning, or plating objects. May operate electroplating equipment with reverse polarity and be known as PLATING STRIPPER (electroplating). May be designated according to plating materials used as BRASS PLATER (electroplating); BRONZE PLATER (electroplating); CADMIUM PLATER (electroplating); CHROMIUM PLATER (electroplating); COPPER PLATER (electroplating); GOLD PLATER (electroplating). Additional titles: NICKEL PLATER (electroplating); PLASTICS PLATER (fabric. plastics prod.); SILVER PLATER (electroplating); TIN PLATER (electroplating). • **GED:** R4, M3, L3 • **SVP:** 2-4 yrs • **Academic:** Ed=H, Eng=S • **Work Field:** 154 • **MPSMS:** 540 • **Aptitudes:** G3, V3, N3, S3, P3, Q4, K3, F3, M3, E5, C4 • **Temperaments:** M, T • **Physical:** V=L, H=L, L=M, W, H • **Work Env:** I, W • **Salary:** 4 • **Outlook:** 3

PLATER, PRINTED CIRCUIT BOARD PANELS (electronics) • D.O.T. #500.684-026 • OES #91921 • Electroplates printed circuit board (PCB) panels with metals, such as copper, tin, gold, nickel, or solder, to resist corrosion, improve electrical conductivity, and facilitate solder connections: Dip panels in cleaning solutions or wipes panels with cloth to clean panels. Clamps panels or rack of panels to overhead bar above tanks to complete electrolytic current. Immerses panels in plating solution. Sets timer for specified plating time and turns on electrical current. Observes meter and turns dial to maintain specified current in plating solution. Removes plated panels and immerses panels in rinsing tank. Examines plated panels for defects. May test thickness of plating, using gauge or test equipment. May tape areas to be excluded from plating, using tape machine. May trim excess material from PCB panels, using shearing machine. May calculate amperage setting, following specified formula. May be designated according to plating material used as GOLD PLATER (electronics) or NICKEL PLATER (electronics). • **GED:** R2, M1, L2 • **SVP:** 30 days-3 mos • **Academic:** Ed=N, Eng=N • **Work Field:** 154 • **MPSMS:** 587 • **Aptitudes:** G4, V4, N4, S4, P4, Q4, K4, F4, M3, E5, C5 • **Temperaments:** T • **Physical:** V=L, H=N, L=H, W, H • **Work Env:** I, R, F • **Salary:** 2 • **Outlook:** 3

ASSEMBLER, INTERNAL COMBUSTION ENGINE (engine & turbine) • D.O.T. #806.481-014 • OES #93105 • ENGINE ASSEMBLER. Assembles internal combustion engines according to standard procedures, using handtools, power wrenches, and gages, performing any of following operations on assembly line: Positions and bolts crankcase, block, and trunion support together to form basic unit of engine, using wrenches, hammer, and power hoist. Mounts crankshaft and camshaft to bearings and tightens bearing caps, using power wrench. Presses gears, sheave, fly wheel, or sprocket to shafts, using hand or hydraulic press, and locks them with keys and pins. Inserts cylinder sleeves into engine block or casing and fits piston and connecting rod assembly into cylinder and bolts it to crankshaft. Alines engine parts, such as camshaft and crankshaft gears, and sets timing and clearances between fixed or moving parts, using alining gages, dial indicator, feeler gages, and timing light. Examines parts or observes movement of completed assemblies to detect malfunction, and discards or replaces defective parts or assemblies. Bolts subassemblies, such as cylinder head, camshaft assembly, fuel pump, carburetor, governor, and water pump, to engine, using torque wrench and other handtools. Flares and connects copper or brass tubing for lubricating and cooling systems, using flaring tools and wrenches. May cut and bend tubing to conform to curvature of engine, using bending fixtures and tubing cutters. May lap cylinder counterbore and valve seats to seat cylinder sleeves and valves, using hand lapping tool and compound. May disassemble, polish, buff, and reassemble motors for demonstration purposes and be designated ASSEMBLER, SHOW MOTOR (engine & turbine). May be designated according to type of engine assembled as DIESEL-ENGINE ASSEMBLER (engine & turbine); GASOLINE-ENGINE ASSEMBLER (engine & turbine); MOTORCYCLE-ENGINE ASSEMBLER (engine & turbine); OUTBOARD-MOTOR ASSEMBLER (engine & turbine). • **GED:** R4, M3, L3 • **SVP:** 1-2 yrs • **Academic:** Ed=N, Eng=S • **Work Field:** 121 • **MPSMS:** 561 • **Aptitudes:** G3, V3, N3, S3, P4, Q4, K3, F3, M2, E5, C5 • **Temperaments:** M, T • **Physical:** V=L, H=N, L=M, W, S, H • **Work Env:** I, N • **Salary:** 4 • **Outlook:** 3

ASSEMBLER, SUBASSEMBLY (aircraft-aerospace mfg.) • D.O.T. #806.484-010 • OES #93102 • DETAIL ASSEMBLER; METAL FABRICATOR. Assembles parts, such as spars, ribs, and braces, to form structural subassemblies, such as air foils, rudders, flaps, stabilizers, elevators, ailerons, fins, fuselage tops and bulkheads, doorframes, doors, and windows, according to specifications, using handtools and portable power tools: Alines parts on jigs, using templates and fixtures, or by measuring from blueprint index points and station lines with rule, protractor, and divider. Files, saws, and deburrs parts, using handtools or portable power tools. Measures parts with micrometers and calipers to verify dimensions. Clamps parts together and drills, reams, and countersinks holes, using power hand drill. Assembles parts and fittings, such as braces, hinges, brackets, keyways, and nut plates, using wrenches. Deburrs keyways, holes, and cable grooves, using burring tool. Marks color symbols on work as guide for riveting. Cements rubber or felt weather stripping to metal doors, glass and plastic windows, and assemblies. May install electric and hydraulic components. May bend tubing. May rivet parts. May make temporary assembly fixtures and templates. • **GED:** R3, M2, L1 • **SVP:** 6 mos-1 yr • **Academic:** Ed=N, Eng=N • **Work Field:** 102 • **MPSMS:** 592 • **Aptitudes:** G3, V4, N4, S3, P5, Q4, K4, F3, M3, E5, C4 • **Temperaments:** M, T • **Physical:** V=L, H=N, L=M, W, S, H • **Work Env:** I • **Salary:** 3 • **Outlook:** 3

BRAZER, ASSEMBLER (welding) • D.O.T. #813.684-010 • OES #93914 • BRAZER; TORCH BRAZER. Brazes (bonds) together components to assemble metal parts as specified by layout, work order, or blueprints, using hand torch: Alines and clamps workpieces together, using rule, square, or template or sets up and places them in fixtures, jigs, or vise. Cleans joints of workpieces, using wire brush or by dipping them into cleaning solution. Selects torch tip, flux, and brazing alloy from data charts or work order. Connects hoses from torch to regulator valves and cylinders of oxygen and specified fuel gas, acetylene or natural. Turns valves to start flow of gases, lights flame, and adjusts pressure and mixture of gases to obtain desired color and size of flame. Brushes flux onto joint of workpiece or dips braze rod into flux to prevent oxidation of metal. Guides torch and rod along joint or seam of workpiece to heat to brazing temperature and melt braze alloy to bond workpieces together. Examines seam and rebrazes defective joints. May braze together broken parts and cover holes to repair leaks. May specialize in bonding parts with soft solder and be designated SOLDERER, TORCH (welding) II. May melt and separate brazed joints, using hand torch or furnace, remove and straighten components, and rebraze joints to repair misalined or damaged assemblies and be designated BRAZER, REPAIR AND SALVAGE (welding). May braze together seams of metal sheets, strips, screening, or wire cloth, using torch mounted on manually guided crawler, and be designated BRAZER, CRAWLER TORCH (welding). • **GED:** R4, M3, L3 • **SVP:** 6 mos-1 yr • **Academic:** Ed=N, Eng=S • **Work Field:** 083 • **MPSMS:** 540, 554 • **Aptitudes:** G3, V4, N4, S3, P4, Q4, K3, F3, M3, E5, C4 • **Temperaments:** M, T • **Physical:** V=L, H=N, L=M, W, S, H • **Work Env:** I, R • **Salary:** 3 • **Outlook:** 3

CABINET ASSEMBLER (furn.) • D.O.T. #763.684-014 • OES #93956 • Assembles radio, television, and phonograph cabinets, using handtools: Fits prefabricated wooden parts together. Trims and smooths parts to fit, using handtools and sandpaper. Inserts screws or dowels in predrilled holes, and fastens parts together with screwdriver, glue, and clamps. Installs hardware, such as hinges, catches, and knobs, on assembled cabinet. May cut baffle cloths and plastic screens to specified size and install them in cabinets, using hand or machine cutters, screwdriver, and stapling gun. • **GED:** R3, M2, L3 • **SVP:** 30 days-3 mos • **Academic:** Ed=N, Eng=S • **Work Field:** 102 • **MPSMS:** 461 • **Aptitudes:** G3, V4, N4, S3, P4, Q4, K3, F3, M3, E5, C5 • **Temperaments:** R, T • **Stress:** T • **Physical:** V=L, H=N, L=L, W, H • **Work Env:** I • **Salary:** 3 • **Outlook:** 3

CASKET ASSEMBLER (mort. goods) • D.O.T. #739.481-010 • OES #89399 • FITTER. Assembles wooden caskets from preformed panels and moldings and attaches supplemental hardware: Nails and glues side, end, and bottom sections together to form casket body. Assembles preformed sections of top frame, using hammer, glue, clamping nails, and bar clamps. Locates and marks midpoint of top frame, using ruler and pencil. Glues and nails panelboard and brace block between sides at midpoint for reinforcement. Positions template over top edge of body or measures body with ruler to locate position of hinges and catches, and recesses positions, using hammer and chisel or portable router. Drills holes at specified locations, using portable power drill. Installs hardware, such as corners, handles, hinges, and catches, using hand or power screwdriver. Sands and planes edges between body, top frame, and top panel to form tight joint, using planer or portable sander. Attaches top panel to top frame, using hand or powered screwdriver. Measures, cuts, and attaches ornamental molding or beading to casket body, using saw, hammer, miter box, and ruler. Sets nailheads, using hammer and nail set. Fills cracks and nail holes with wood filler or plaster of paris by hand or with putty knife. Smooths joints and edges, using sandpaper and handtools. May cut or trim wood to specified size for use in assembly of casket, using cutoff saw. May be designated according to part of casket assembled as BODY MAKER (mort. goods); CAP MAKER (mort. goods); MOLDING FITTER (mort. goods); PANEL FITTER (mort. goods); TOP-FRAME FITTER (mort. goods); TOP-FRAME MAKER (mort. goods). • **GED:** R3, M2, L2 • **SVP:** 1-2 yrs • **Academic:** Ed=N, Eng=N • **Work Field:** 102 • **MPSMS:** 619 • **Aptitudes:** G3, V4, N3, S3, P3, Q4, K3, F3, M3, E5, C5 • **Temperaments:** M, T • **Physical:** V=L, H=N, L=M, W, S, H • **Work Env:** I, N • **Salary:** 2 • **Outlook:** 3

ELECTRIC-SIGN ASSEMBLER (signs) • D.O.T. #729.684-022 • OES #93905 • Assembles electric signs, mounts tubing, and connects electrical equipment to sign box: Fastens back of sign to precut metal frame to form sign box, using screws and screwdriver. Fits precut glass, plexiglass, or plastic pane into bottom channel of metal frame. Crimps frame channel to secure pane, using pliers. Attaches tubing support brackets to sign box with self-tapping screws, using screwdriver. Screws or clamps glass elevation posts to brackets. Binds neon sign scroll to posts with wire. Connects wires between tubing electrodes and secondary-winding terminals of transformer. Attaches animation mechanism to back of sign, and connects part to be animated. May assemble fiberboard or cardboard cutout parts for animated window display signs. • **GED:** R3, M2, L2 • **SVP:** 30 days-3 mos • **Academic:** Ed=N, Eng=N • **Work Field:** 111 • **MPSMS:** 584 • **Aptitudes:** G3, V4, N4, S3, P3, Q4, K3, F3, M3, E5, C4 • **Temperaments:** R, T • **Stress:** T • **Physical:** V=L, H=N, L=M, W, H • **Work Env:** I • **Salary:** 2 • **Outlook:** 2

FURNITURE ASSEMBLER (furn.) • D.O.T. #763.684-038 • OES #93956 • PARTS ASSEMBLER. Assembles wooden parts or assemblies to form sections, frames, or complete articles of furniture: Trims joints to fit, using handtools. Blows dust from mortises and areas to be glued, using airhose. Spreads glue on surfaces to be joined by drawing wood across roller partially submerged in glue, by using brush dipped in glue, or by using glue-filled squeeze bottle. Knocks connecting parts together with mallet or compresses assembled parts in clamp until glue has dried. Wipes excess glue from joints with rag. Drills holes and drives screws into parts to join parts or to reinforce glued joints, using power drill and screwdriver. Attaches glue blocks, metal braces, corner blocks, drawer guides, tops, molding, shelves, dust bottoms, back panels, or skids with nails, screws, glue, or staples, using handtools and power tools. Inspects and verifies accuracy of assembled article for conformance to specified standards, using square and tape measure. Smooths irregular joints with rasp and sandpaper, and levels chair legs, using circular leveling saw. May drill holes and attach hardware, such as drawer guides, drawer locks, catches, and latches, using power drill and handtools. May slide drawers in and out to test ease of movement, and adjust ill-fitting drawers, using handtools. May be designated according to part or article assembled. • **GED:** R3, M2, L2 • **SVP:** 3-6 mos • **Academic:** Ed=N, Eng=N • **Work Field:** 102 • **MPSMS:** 460 • **Aptitudes:** G3, V4, N4, S4, P4, Q4, K3, F3, M3, E5, C5 • **Temperaments:** R, T • **Stress:** T • **Physical:** V=L, H=N, L=M, W, H • **Work Env:** I • **Salary:** 2 • **Outlook:** 2

MACHINE ASSEMBLER (mach. mfg.) • D.O.T. #638.361-010 • OES #93105 • Assembles machines, equipment, and their subassemblies, such as baling presses, stokers, blowers, compression pumps, and food wrapping machines according to customer's needs following blueprints and other written and verbal specifications: Plans assembly procedures, following specifications and using knowledge gained by experience. Removes small quantities of metal, using hand files or portable grinders to clean parts or to produce close fit between parts. Drills, taps, or reams holes, using drill press or portable drill. Alines components, and bolts, screws, or rivets them together, using handtools or portable powered tools. Installs moving parts, such as shafts, levers, or bearings and works them to test free movement. May bend and install pipe for hydraulic systems. May aline and mesh gears in gearbox to assemble system of gears. May test or assist in testing operation of completed product. • **GED:** R3, M3, L3 • **SVP:** 1-2 yrs • **Academic:** Ed=N, Eng=S • **Work Field:** 121 • **MPSMS:** 567 • **Aptitudes:** G3, V3, N3, S3, P3, Q4, K3, F3, M2, E5, C5 • **Temperaments:** M, T • **Physical:** V=G, H=N, L=M, W, C, S, H • **Work Env:** I, N • **Salary:** 4 • **Outlook:** 3

MOTORCYCLE ASSEMBLER (motor. & bicycles) • D.O.T. #806.684-090 • OES #93956 • Assembles complete motorcycles, performing any combination of following tasks: Positions and clamps frame in fixture on conveyor line. Bolts fork, motor, transmission, rear and front wheels, chain drives, handlebars, lights, seats, and other parts to frame, using hand tools or power tools. Turns gas or spark handle controls, and adjustment screws on distributor and carburetor to set spark and gas feed. Turns screws to adjust chain drive and clutch to specified tension. Focuses headlight on testing board and turns adjustment screws to aline beam of light. Lubricates motorcycle with grease gun. Records motor and sales numbers. May relieve assemblers and be known as UTILITY ASSEMBLER (motor. & bicycles). • **GED:** R3, M1, L1 • **SVP:** 6 mos-1 yr • **Academic:** Ed=N, Eng=N • **Work Field:** 102, 121 • **MPSMS:** 595 • **Aptitudes:** G3, V4, N4, S3, P3, Q4, K3, F3, M3, E4, C5 • **Temperaments:** T • **Physical:** V=L, H=N, L=H, W, S, H • **Work Env:** I • **Salary:** 4 • **Outlook:** 3

UTILITY WORKER (mfg. bldgs.) • D.O.T. #869.684-074 • OES

#93999 • Performs any combination of following tasks in manufacture of mobile homes and travel trailers: Tends woodworking and metalworking machines to cut and shape wood and metal parts. Cuts, shapes, and assembles parts, using handtools and power tools. Installs parts, household appliances, furnishings, and fixtures, using handtools and power tools. Trains inexperienced workers. Assists, relieves, or substitutes for INSTALLER (mfd. bldgs.; trans. equip.); ASSEMBLER (mfd. bldgs.; trans. equip.); and PLUMBER (mfd. bldgs.). • **GED:** R3, M2, L2 • **SVP:** 6 mos-1 yr • **Academic:** Ed=N, Eng=N • **Work Field:** 102 • **MPSMS:** 361, 597 • **Aptitudes:** G3, V4, N3, S3, P4, Q4, K3, F4, M3, E4, C4 • **Temperaments:** T, V • **Physical:** V=L, H=N, L=M, W, C, S, H • **Work Env:** I, N • **Salary:** 4 • **Outlook:** 3

GOE: 06.02.23 Manual Work, Assemble Small Parts, Skilled

ASSEMBLER, MUSICAL INSTRUMENTS (musical inst.) • D.O.T. #730.684-010 • OES #93956 • Performs any combination of the following tasks to assemble and fasten together parts to form subassemblies or complete musical instruments, such as drums, keyed brass, woodwind, or stringed instruments according to specified instructions or diagrams: Drills, taps, or reams holes to prepare parts for assembly, using drill press or bench-mounted drill. Bends tubing and laps parts by hand to form or join parts. Applies abrasive solvents to sliding joints to cause parts to move freely. Fits or faces parts, using hand file or bench grinder to trim parts to fit. Alines metal brass-wind parts, such as valves, knobs, keys, and bars by sight, by placing them in jigs and clamping them on instrument, or by positioning parts, using rulers or gages. Screws, clips, solders, and glues parts, such as drum hardware, corks, violin necks, wooden bridges, and metal snares, using handtools, portable powered tools, or hand torches. Removes excess solder, using scraping tool. Winds and bends spring wire around valve keys by hand to install valves on brass-wind instruments. Inserts steel bars and squeezes or separates bars to adjust tube spacing on brass-wind instruments. Cleans inside of tubes of brass-wind instruments with swab and cleaning solvent. Installs electric pick-ups in electrically amplified instruments, using screwdriver and soldering gun. May polish or buff exterior of instruments, using rotating buffing wheel. May cut tubing, using powersaw. May inspect instruments for defects and reject instruments not meeting specifications. May be designated according to instrument assembled as FINAL ASSEMBLER, BRASS-WIND INSTRUMENTS (musical inst.); MOUNTER, BRASS-WIND INSTRUMENTS (musical inst.); STRINGED-INSTRUMENT ASSEMBLER (musical inst.); or by part assembled as BRIDGE FITTER (musical inst.); KNOBBER (musical inst.); NECK FITTER (musical inst.). Additional titles: MOUNTER, CLARINETS (musical inst.); MOUNTER, FLUTES AND PICCOLOS (musical inst.); MOUNTER, KEYED INSTRUMENTS (musical inst.); MOUNTER, SAXOPHONES (musical inst.); MOUNTER, SOUSAPHONES (musical inst.); MOUNTER, TROMBONES (musical inst.); MOUNTER, TRUMPETS AND CORNETS (musical inst.). • **GED:** R3, M2, L2 • **SVP:** 30 days-3 mos • **Academic:** Ed=N, Eng=N • **Work Field:** 102 • **MPSMS:** 614 • **Aptitudes:** G3, V4, N4, S3, P3, Q4, K3, F3, M3, E5, C5 • **Temperaments:** R, T • **Stress:** T • **Physical:** V=L, H=L, L=L, W, H • **Work Env:** I • **Salary:** 2 • **Outlook:** 2

ASSEMBLER, PRODUCTION LINE (photo. apparatus) • D.O.T. #714.684-010 • OES #93956 • Assembles components of cameras, camera magazines, camera shutters, movie projectors, electronic photographic apparatus, such as exposure meters, using electric riveting press, punch press, soldering iron, and handtools: Screws, rivets, solders, and otherwise fastens and installs parts, following blueprints. Operates assemblies to test for specified functioning and adjusts mechanisms to attain specified functioning, using handtools, gages, and meters. May be designated according to type of apparatus assembled as CAMERA ASSEMBLER (photo. apparatus); METER ASSEMBLER (photo. apparatus); PROJECTOR ASSEMBLER (photo. apparatus) or according to part assembled as SYNCHRO ASSEMBLER (photo. apparatus). • **GED:** R3, M2, L2 • **SVP:** 3-6 mos • **Academic:** Ed=N, Eng=N • **Work Field:** 111, 121 • **MPSMS:** 606 • **Aptitudes:** G3, V4, N4, S3, P3, Q4, K3, F3, M3, E5, C4 • **Temperaments:** M, T •

Physical: V=G, H=N, L=S, H • **Work Env:** I • **Salary:** 2 • **Outlook:** 3

ASSEMBLER, SEMICONDUCTOR (electronics) • D.O.T. #726.684-034 • OES #93905 • MICROELECTRONICS PROCESSOR. Assembles microelectronic semiconductor devices, components, and subassemblies according to drawings and specifications, using microscope, bonding machines, and handtools, performing any combination of following duties: Reads work orders and studies assembly drawings to determine operation to be performed. Observes processed semiconductor wafer under scribing machine microscope and alines scribing tool with markings on wafer. Adjusts scribing machine controls, according to work order specifications, and presses switch to start scribing. Removes scribed wafer and breaks wafer into dice (chips), using probe. Places dice under microscope, visually examines dice for defects, according to learned procedures, and rejects defective dice. Positions mounting device on holder under bonding machine microscope, and adjusts bonding machine controls according to work order specifications. Positions die (chip) on mounting surface according to diagram. Presses switch on bonding machine to bond die to mounting surface. Places mounted die into holding fixture under microscope of lead bonding machine. Adjusts bonding machine controls according to work order specifications. Views die and moves controls to aline and position bonding head for lead bonding according to diagram. Presses switch to bond lead and moves bonding head to points indicated in bonding diagram to attach and route leads as illustrated. Inserts and seals unprotected assembly into designated assembly container device, using welding machine and epoxy syringe, to protect microelectronic assembly and complete device, component, or subassembly package. Examines and tests assembly at various stages of production, using microscope, go-not-go test equipment, measuring instruments, pressure-vacuum tanks, and related devices, according to standard procedures, to detect nonstandard or defective assemblies. Rejects or routes nonstandard components for rework. Cleans parts and assemblies at various stages of production, using cleaning devices and equipment. Maintains records of production and defects. Bonds multiple dice to headers or other mounting devices. Important variations are kinds of equipment used, such as thermal compression, wedge, wire ball, and wobble bonders, items assembled, or procedure performed. • **GED:** R3, M2, L2 • **SVP:** 30 days-3 mos • **Academic:** Ed=N, Eng=N • **Work Field:** 111 • **MPSMS:** 587 • **Aptitudes:** G3, V3, N4, S3, P2, Q3, K3, F2, M3, E4, C4 • **Temperaments:** J, R, T • **Stress:** T • **Physical:** V=G, H=N, L=S, H • **Work Env:** I • **Salary:** 3 • **Outlook:** 4

ASSEMBLER, SURGICAL GARMENT (per. protect. & med. device) • D.O.T. #712.684-010 • OES #93956 • Performs any combination of the following tasks to assemble surgical garments, such as trusses, knee, wrist, elbow, and ankle braces, belts, cervical collars, back braces, and hosiery: Reads work order to determine number and type of parts required to assemble garment. Measures and cuts required pieces, using ruler, templates, and electric or hand shears. Punches holes in material for attachment of fasteners, using punch press or hand punch. Attaches fasteners, such as eyelets or snaps, using rivet, snap-fastening, or eyelet machine. Grinds and polishes parts, using grinding wheel. Bends metal stays (springs) to specified curvature, using bending machine. Applies laytex coating to parts or specified areas of parts, using coating machine. Fits and fastens parts together, such as straps, buckles, pads, belts, and stays to assemble garment, using handtools, gluing equipment, and machines, such as punch press, riveting machine, and sewing machine. Weaves elastic thread into outer edges of garments, such as knee, wrist, and elbow braces to increase elasticity. Places completed garment in boxes or plastic bags for packaging. May be designated according to type garment assembled or material worked with as ELASTIC ASSEMBLER (per. protect. & med. dev.); LATEXER (per. protect. & med. dev.) II; LEATHER WORKER (per. protect. & med. dev.); SPRING BENDER (per. protect. & med. dev.); TRUSS ASSEMBLER (per. protect. & med. dev.). • **GED:** R2, M2, L2 • **SVP:** 30 days-3 mos • **Academic:** Ed=N, Eng=N • **Work Field:** 102 • **MPSMS:** 604 • **Aptitudes:** G3, V4, N4, S3, P3, Q4, K3, F3, M3, E4, C5 • **Temperaments:** M, T, V • **Physical:** V=L, H=N, L=L, W, H • **Work Env:** I • **Salary:** 2 • **Outlook:** 3

BITE-BLOCK MAKER (medical ser.) • D.O.T. #712.684-014 • OES #93956 • Forms wax bite blocks and impression trays used by DENTIST (medical ser.) to take impressions of patients' teeth and adjacent portions of jaw, using molding equipment and handtools: Softens shellac wafer, using gas burner. Spreads and shapes wafer over model of preliminary im pression to form tray, using flat-bladed molding tool. Imbeds metal strip in soft shellac for convenience in handling. Presses soft wax over plaster model of denture to form bite block. Trims excess wax from mold and smooths surface, using knife, spatula, and gas burner. Immerses mold in water to harden wax. Trims and smooths edges and surfaces of trays and bite blocks, using bench lathe equipped with grinding and buffing wheels. Rubs finished piece with cotton to obtain lustrous finish. • **GED:** R3, M1, L1 • **SVP:** 3-6 mos • **Academic:** Ed=N, Eng=N • **Work Field:** 136 • **MPSMS:** 604 • **Aptitudes:** G3, V4, N4, S3, P3, Q4, K3, F3, M4, E5, C4 • **Temperaments:** M, T • **Physical:** V=L, H=N, L=S, H • **Work Env:** I • **Salary:** 3 • **Outlook:** 2

CAPACITOR ASSEMBLER (elec. equip.) • D.O.T. #729.684-014 • OES #93905 • Assembles capacitors for electric transmission equipment, using handtools and soldering equipment: Solders banded porcelain bushing to cover, terminal and tube to top of bushing, and tins areas of bushing holes in top cover, using stationary or hand gas-heating equipment. Covers bushings with protective cap to prepare covers for sandblasting, buffing, and degreasing. Folds, creases, and pounds insulation to fit over top of wound foil and tissue, using rawhide hammer. Hammers drive screws to fasten nameplate to capacitor. Places cover on capacitor and tightens seal-off screw to hold cover during assembly, using screwdriver. Twists goose-neck filler pipe to capacitor tank and removes pipe after impregnation. Inserts brass plug and seals plug with solder, using gas torch. May bolt capacitors to frames and connect capacitors in banks, using bare copper or insulated conductor. May repair capacitors and be designated CAPACITOR REPAIRER (elec. equip.). • **GED:** R3, M2, L2 • **SVP:** 3-6 mos • **Academic:** Ed=N, Eng=N • **Work Field:** 111 • **MPSMS:** 581 • **Aptitudes:** G3, V4, N4, S4, P3, Q4, K3, F3, M3, E5, C5 • **Temperaments:** R, T • **Stress:** T • **Physical:** V=L, H=N, L=M, W, H • **Work Env:** I • **Salary:** 3 • **Outlook:** 2

CHAIN MAKER, MACHINE (jewelry) • D.O.T. #700.684-022 • OES #93999 • Forms chains for watches and other jewelry articles: Feeds wire into machine. Hooks together ends of chain formed by machine, using pliers, and solders on trimming. May be designated according to type of chain as NOVELTY-CHAIN MAKER (jewelry). • **GED:** R3, M2, L2 • **SVP:** 30 days-3 mos • **Academic:** Ed=N, Eng=N • **Work Field:** 102 • **MPSMS:** 611 • **Aptitudes:** G3, V4, N4, S4, P4, Q5, K4, F4, M3, E4, C5 • **Temperaments:** R, T • **Physical:** T • V=L, H=N, L=L, H • **Work Env:** I • **Salary:** 2 • **Outlook:** 2

ELECTRICAL-CONTROL ASSEMBLER (elec. equip.) • D.O.T. #729.684-026 • OES #93905 • Assembles protection, communication, and control devices, such as switches, relays, rheostats, transmitters, and switchboards, as laid out in drawings and wiring diagrams: Assembles in predetermined order, contact fingers, shafts, springs, gears, coils, terminals, and push buttons, using handtools, hand arbor press, and assembly fixtures. Fastens units in specified locations in switchbox or case. Cuts, strips, and mounts wires to connect electrical units, using soldering iron, staking machine, and plugging devices. Connects lead wires to buzzer, ohmmeter, or resistance tester to test connections for resistance, shorts, and grounds. May adjust contacts, springs, and shafts to meet specifications. May be designated according to unit assembled as RELAY ASSEMBLER (elec. equip.); RHEOSTAT ASSEMBLER (elec. equip.); SPEAKING-UNIT ASSEMBLER (elec. equip.); SWITCHBOX ASSEMBLER (elec. equip.) II; TELEPHONE-DIAPHRAGM ASSEMBLER (elec. equip.); or according to type of equipment assembled as ASSEMBLER, COMMUNICATIONS EQUIPMENT (elec. equip.). May assemble strip of switches, of telephone switchboard type, and be designated JACK-STRIP ASSEMBLER (elec. equip.). • **GED:** R3, M2, L2 • **SVP:** 3-6 mos • **Academic:** Ed=N, Eng=N • **Work Field:** 111 • **MPSMS:** 580 • **Aptitudes:** G3, V4, N3, S3, P2, Q4, K3, F3, M3, E4, C4 • **Temperaments:** R, T • **Stress:** T • **Physical:** V=L, H=N, L=L, H • **Work Env:** I • **Salary:** 3 • **Outlook:** 2

ELECTRONICS ASSEMBLER (electronics) • D.O.T. #726.684-018 • OES #93905 • Assembles electronic components, subassemblies, and systems by any one or combination of following methods: Reads work orders, follows production drawings and sample assemblies, and receives verbal instructions regarding duties to be performed. Positions and aligns parts in specified relationship to each other in jig, fixture, or other holding device, using tweezers, vacuum probe, or hand instruments. (1) Tends machines or uses handtools and power tools to crimp, stake, bolt, rivet, weld, solder, cement, press fit, or perform similar operation to secure parts in place. (2) Mounts assembled compo nents, such as transformers, resistors, capacitors, integrated circuits, and sockets on chassis panel. (3) Connects component lead wires to printed circuit or routes and connects wires between individual component leads and other components, connectors, terminals, and contact points, using soldering, welding, thermocompression, or related bonding procedures. (4) Installs finished assemblies or subassemblies in cases and cabinets. (5) Assembles and attaches functional and cosmetic hardware, such as caps, clamps, and knobs, to assemblies, using handtools and power tools. (6) Performs intermediate assembly tasks, such as potting, encapsulating, cleaning, coating, epoxy bonding, curing, stamping, etching, impregnating, and color coding parts and assemblies. (7) Tends machines which press or shape component parts, such as contacts, shells, and insulators. (8) Tends automatic assembly equipment which joins components and parts. (9) Winds capacitors on manual or automatic winding equipment. (10) Adjusts or trims material from components, such as capacitors and potentiometers, to change electronic characteristic to specification measured by electronic test instrument. (11) Performs on-line go-not-go testing and inspection, using magnifying devices, fixed and movable measuring instruments, and electronic test equipment, to ensure parts and assemblies meet production specifications and are free from defects. May perform assembly operations under microscope or other magnifying device. Occupations related to assembly of printed circuit boards and fabrication of integrated circuit chips are defined elsewhere under separate definitions. • **GED:** R3, M1, L2 • **SVP:** 30 days-3 mos • **Academic:** Ed=N, Eng=N • **Work Field:** 102, 111, 134 • **MPSMS:** 586, 587, 589 • **Aptitudes:** G4, V4, N4, S3, P3, Q3, K4, F2, M2, E5, C3 • **Temperaments:** R, T • **Stress:** T • **Physical:** V=L, H=N, L=L, H • **Work Env:** I • **Salary:** 3 • **Outlook:** 4

ELECTRONICS ASSEMBLER (inst. & app.) • D.O.T. #726.384-010 • OES #93905 • Installs and wires electronic subassemblies, such as integrators, channel controls, and power sources for spectroscopic equipment, working from wire-prints, schematics, and verbal instructions: Routes wiring through assembly to terminals according to color code, and loops wires to panel. Strips insulation from ends of wire and cable, using wire stripper, and solders or wraps wires around terminals to provide electrical connection. Drills holes into frame and bolts or screws parts and assembled units to frame, using handtools. • **GED:** R3, M2, L2 • **SVP:** 1-2 yrs • **Academic:** Ed=N, Eng=N • **Work Field:** 111 • **MPSMS:** 602, 603 • **Aptitudes:** G3, V4, N4, S3, P3, Q4, K3, F3, M3, E5, C4 • **Temperaments:** R, T • **Stress:** T • **Physical:** V=G, H=N, L=S, H • **Work Env:** I • **Salary:** 3 • **Outlook:** 4

LAMINATION ASSEMBLER (elec. equip.) • D.O.T. #729.484-010 • OES #93905 • STACKER; STACKING ASSEMBLER. Stacks, alines, and secures segment or ring type copper bars, or metal laminations and insulating separators, to assemble laminated cores for electrical parts, such as commutators, coils, armatures, and stators, by either of following methods: (1) Places core laminations and separators in holding device of machine. Starts machine that automatically measures and stacks specified quantity of laminations for each core and inserts separators between laminations. Offbears laminations from machine and secures laminations, using tape or other material. (2) Stacks specified quantity of laminations in holding fixture. Squeezes stack manually or presses laminations together in vise or press to reduce kinks or bulges. Measures stack, using rule, and adds or removes laminations and separators to obtain stack of specified dimensions. Alines edges of laminations, using hammer, and secures laminations with rubber wrapping material. May place stack of laminated cores into machine that automatically welds laminations into individual cores. May rivet laminations into cores, using peening hammer.

May be designated according to method used, as LAMINATION STACKER, HAND (elec. equip.); LAMINATION STACKER, MACHINE (elec. equip.), part assembled as COMMUTATOR STACKER (elec. equip.); POLE-SHOE ASSEMBLER (elec. equip.), or type core assembled as ROTOR-CORE ASSEMBLER (elec. equip.); STATOR-CORE ASSEMBLER (elec. equip.); TRANSFORMER-CORE ASSEMBLER (elec. equip.). • **GED:** R3, M2, L2 • **SVP:** 30 days-3 mos • **Academic:** Ed=N, Eng=N • **Work Field:** 111 • **MPSMS:** 582 • **Aptitudes:** G3, V4, N4, S4, P3, Q5, K3, F3, M3, E5, C5 • **Temperaments:** R, T • **Stress:** T • **Physical:** V=L, H=N, L=L, H • **Work Env:** I • **Salary:** 2 • **Outlook:** 3

LENS-MOLD SETTER (optical goods) • D.O.T. #713.381-010 • OES #89917 • MOLD SETTER. Assembles molds for casting contact lenses, using handtools, and inspects cast lenses for conformance to specifications, using precision measuring instruments: Selects mold and mold inserts. Positions inserts in mold and shims inserts as indicated by mold insert records. Sets holding pins, using wrench, and routes mold to CONTACT-LENS MOLDER (optical goods). Breaks seal on mold after casting and prys mold apart, using screwdriver and handpress. Peels lens and flashing from mold, using scalpel-like knife. Cuts lenses apart and places lenses in storage box. Inspects lenses, using power determining and optical centering instruments, thickness gage, shadowgraph, and loupe magnifier, to verify correctness of characteristics, such as inside curve dimension and power, and to detect defects, such as scratches. Alters position of mold in serts to correct lens thickness, using shims. Cleans mold with solvent or routes mold to grinding room for polishing to eliminate defects. • **GED:** R3, M3, L2 • **SVP:** 6 mos-1 yr • **Academic:** Ed=N, Eng=N • **Work Field:** 061, 211 • **MPSMS:** 605 • **Aptitudes:** G3, V3, N3, S3, P2, Q4, K3, F3, M3, E5, C4 • **Temperaments:** M, T • **Physical:** V=L, H=N, L=L, H • **Work Env:** I • **Salary:** 3 • **Outlook:** 3

PRINTED CIRCUIT BOARD ASSEMBLER, HAND (electronics) • D.O.T. #726.684-070 • OES #93905 • Performs combination of following tasks in assembly of electronic components onto printed circuit boards (PCBs) according to specifications, using handtools: Reads worksheets and wiring diagrams, receives verbal instructions, follows sample board to determine assembly duties, and selects components, such as transistors, resistors, relays, capacitors, and integrated circuits. Twists, bends, trims, strips, or files wire leads of components or reams holes in boards to insert wire leads, using handtools. Inserts color-coded wires in designated holes and clinches wire ends, using pliers. Press-fits (mounts) component leads onto board. Places plastic insulating sleeves around specified wire leads of components and shrinks sleeves into place, using heat gun. Crimps wire leads on underside of board, using handtools or press. Applies sealer or masking compound to selected parts of board to protect parts from effects of wave solder process. Solders wire leads and joints on underside of board, using soldering iron, to route and connect lead wires to board and between individual components. Installs heat sinks, sockets, face plates, and accessories on boards, using handtools. May be designated according to unit installed as SOCKET ASSEMBLER (electronics) or stage of production as POST-WAVE ASSEMBLER (electronics); PRE-WAVE ASSEMBLER (electronics). May assist other workers in duties concerned with wave-soldering PCBs. • **GED:** R3, M1, L2 • **SVP:** 3-6 mos • **Academic:** Ed=N, Eng=N • **Work Field:** 111 • **MPSMS:** 587 • **Aptitudes:** G4, V4, N4, S3, P3, Q4, K3, F2, M3, E5, C4 • **Temperaments:** R, T • **Stress:** T • **Physical:** V=L, H=N, L=L, H • **Work Env:** I • **Salary:** 3 • **Outlook:** 4

TUBE ASSEMBLER, CATHODE RAY (electronics) • D.O.T. #725.684-022 • OES #93956 • Performs any of the following tasks to assemble cathode-ray tubes for television receivers and display instruments: Removes funnel from rack and places on conveyor leading through washing, rinsing, and drying equipment. Positions funnel in holding chuck to secure for painting. Inserts brush into funnel and paints dag (conductive graphite) coating to delineate inspection window as indicated by chuck guide. Depresses pedal to rotate chuck and dag coats remainder of funnel and neck. Positions funnel in rotatable chuck equipped with automatic frit dispenser. Moves controls that index frit dispenser around edge of funnel mouth to apply sealant. Removes frit-coated funnel from jug and places on conveyor leading to drying chamber. Verifies that

aperture mask and display screen (top cap) mate according to matching numbers. Examines aperture mask and screen in light box to detect misaligned color dots, using microscope. Secures funnel in jig for joining display screen assembly onto funnel. Positions display screen assembly on funnel edge and aligns screen with reference points on funnel. Pushes jig into conveyor leading into lehr to fuse funnel and display screen assembly into bulb. Lifts bulb from lehr conveyor and places in holding fixture which conveys bulb through processing stations that preheat, insert and fuse gun into neck, anneal, and cool bulb assembly. Places bulb in holding fixture and connects wires and glass probe to vacuum evaporation equipment which rotates bulb through series of processes to apply aluminized coating, cool and create vacuum within tube. Disconnects wires and removes tube from equipment and places on conveyor for further processing. May be designated according to assembly station as BULB ASSEMBLER (electronics); DAG COATER (electronics); FUNNEL COATER (electronics); FRIT COATER (electronics); GUN-SEALING-MACHINE OPERATOR (electronics). • **GED:** R2, M1, L1 • **SVP:** 30 days-3 mos • **Academic:** Ed=N, Eng=N • **Work Field:** 111 • **MPSMS:** 587 • **Aptitudes:** G3, V4, N4, S3, P3, Q4, K3, F3, M3, E5, C5 • **Temperaments:** R • **Stress:** T • **Physical:** V=L, H=N, L=M, W, H • **Work Env:** I • **Salary:** 3 • **Outlook:** 3

WHEEL LACER AND TRUER (motor. & bicycles) • D.O.T. #706.684-106 • OES #93956 • WHEEL ASSEMBLER; WHEEL TRUER. Laces and trues-up (alines) motorcycle and bicycle wheels according to specifications, using gages and handtools or power tools: Hooks wire spokes onto perforated hubs and screws nipples of spokes onto rim to lace (assemble) wheel, using special hand wrench. Measures diameter of wheel, using fixed gage. Grinds protruding end of spokes from inside surface of rim, using portable hand grinder. Mounts tires on wheels [TIRE MOUNTER (fabric. prod., n.e.c.)] and clamps wheel in fixture. Positions dial indicator against tire and rim, turns wheel, and notes points at which wheel needs alinement as indicated by needle deflection on indicator. Turns spoke nipples with wrench to adjust tension of spokes at indicated points to aline wheel. • **GED:** R2, M1, L2 • **SVP:** 3-6 mos • **Academic:** Ed=N, Eng=N • **Work Field:** 061 • **MPSMS:** 595 • **Aptitudes:** G4, V4, N4, S4, P3, Q4, K4, F3, M3, E5, C5 • **Temperaments:** J, R, T • **Stress:** T • **Physical:** V=G, H=N, L=M, W, H • **Work Env:** I • **Salary:** 2 • **Outlook:** 3

WIRER, SUBASSEMBLIES (office mach.) • D.O.T. #729.684-062 • OES #93956 • Installs color-coded wires and cables in subassemblies, such as fuse panels, control key assemblies, and relay panels, for punched-card office machines according to wiring diagrams and blueprints by any combination of following tasks: Fastens eyelet or spade types of wire lugs to bolt or screw terminals, using wrenches and screwdrivers. Inserts plug ends of wires and cables into jacks, using pliers or special insertion tools. Attaches wire ends to terminal posts, using pneumatic wirewrapping gun. May test wiring continuity and connections, using ohmmeter, test lights, or other testing devices. • **GED:** R3, M2, L1 • **SVP:** 3-6 mos • **Academic:** Ed=N, Eng=N • **Work Field:** 111 • **MPSMS:** 571 • **Aptitudes:** G3, V4, N4, S3, P3, Q4, K3, F3, M3, E5, C4 • **Temperaments:** R, T • **Stress:** T • **Physical:** V=L, H=N, L=L, H • **Work Env:** I • **Salary:** 3 • **Outlook:** 3

GOE: 06.02.24 Manual Work, Metal & Plastics, Skilled

ARMATURE BANDER (any ind.) • D.O.T. #724.684-010 • OES #93999 • Winds steel wire around coil slots in armature core to hold coils in position when armature rotates, using banding machine: Lifts or hoists armature to horizontal spindle of banding machine. Shapes exposed parts of coils to specified size, using rawhide hammer. Mounts spool of specified wire and threads wire through guides of machine. Wraps sheet of insulation around core and attaches wire to pin wedged in core or twists first turn around armature, using pliers. Inserts metal clips under wire and turns crank to rotate armature or starts machine that winds wire around armature. Guides wire manually or mechanically to maintain tension. Turns ends of metal clips over wire and solders to hold wires into place. Solders armature leads to commutator and caps riser, using electric soldering iron. May shape coils [COIL SHAPER (any ind.)]. • **GED:** R3, M2, L2 • **SVP:** 6 mos-1 yr • **Academic:** Ed=N, Eng=N • **Work Field:** 163 • **MPSMS:** 582 • **Aptitudes:** G3, V4, N4, S3, P3, Q4, K3, F3, M3, E4, C5 • **Temperaments:** R, T • **Stress:** T • **Physical:** V=L, H=N, L=M, W, H • **Work Env:** I • **Salary:** 3 • **Outlook:** 2

ASSEMBLER, METAL BONDING (aircraft-aerospace mfg.) • D.O.T. #806.684-030 • OES #93956 • Bonds aircraft or space vehicle sheet metal skins (surface section) to metal honeycomb cores to assemble wing, tail, and fuselage sections, following blueprints, shop orders, and process chart specifications, using handtools and power tools: Examines parts and compares them with specifications to identify parts and to verify that prior processes have been completed. Measures mating surfaces to ensure required contact can be made. Cleans dust, dirt, oil, and other foreign matter from contact surfaces, using cleaning fluids and rags. Removes burs, waves, and other surface imperfections, using files and mallets. Places precut, compacted honeycomb section on assembly bench, hooks lines of drawbar to section and turns windlass crank to stretch honeycomb to specified size, following guide marks on edge of bench. Trims excess metal with hand shears and files mating surfaces to obtain close fit. Sprays metal bonding fluid on contact surfaces and daubs adhesive on edges of expanded honeycomb. Positions flat or contoured metal skin under and over honeycomb in jig conforming to shape of wing, tail, or fuselage section being formed. Turns clamps of jig or encases assembly in plastic or rubber vacuum bag to press skin evenly against honeycomb during subsequent curing process. Turns autoclave controls to specified temperature for bonding. Lifts or hoists assemblies onto dollies and pushes them into oven. Pulls assemblies from oven after curing cycle and removes vacuum bags or jigs. May bond paper honeycomb to metal surfaces of missile tank domes to insulate vehicle sections and strengthen dome, using bonding fluid and handtools. • **GED:** R3, M2, L1 • **SVP:** 6 mos-1 yr • **Academic:** Ed=N, Eng=N • **Work Field:** 102 • **MPSMS:** 592 • **Aptitudes:** G3, V4, N4, S3, P3, Q4, K3, F3, M3, E5, C5 • **Temperaments:** M, T • **Physical:** V=L, H=N, L=M, W, H • **Work Env:** I, N • **Salary:** 3 • **Outlook:** 3

BOAT PATCHER, PLASTIC (ship bldg. & rep.) • D.O.T. #807.684-014 • OES #85999 • ASSEMBLY DETAILER; PATCHER, PLASTIC BOAT. Repairs and repaints defects in fiberglass boat hulls, decks, and cabins, using handtools and power tools: Examines parts for defects, such as cracks and holes. Drills out defective areas or smooths rough edges, using portable electric drill and grinder. Cuts out patch of fiberglass material, using shears. Mixes resin and catalyst, dips patch in solution, and places patch over defect. Shapes and smooths edges to match contour of patched area. Fills holes with plastic filler material. Smooths repaired surfaces, using sandpaper or power disk sander. Mixes plastic paint with catalyst and sprays repaired surfaces, using spray gun. Cuts out damaged wood bracing strips, using portable electric saw. Replaces and bonds strips in place with saturated fiberglass mat. Touches up flaws, using paint brush. May polish repainted sections. • **GED:** R3, M1, L1 • **SVP:** 3-6 mos • **Academic:** Ed=N, Eng=N • **Work Field:** 102 • **MPSMS:** 593 • **Aptitudes:** G3, V4, N4, S4, P3, Q4, K3, F3, M3, E5, C3 • **Temperaments:** T • **Physical:** V=L, H=N, L=M, W, S, H • **Work Env:** B, N • **Salary:** 3 • **Outlook:** 3

BRIGHT CUTTER (jewelry) • D.O.T. #700.684-018 • OES #93926 • Cuts layer of metal from walls of settings and other surfaces of jewelry articles to reveal bright inner metals: Clamps article in chuck preparatory to cutting. Lubricates cutting tool and pushes tool over surface to remove specified layer of metal. • **GED:** R3, M2, L2 • **SVP:** 30 days-3 mos • **Academic:** Ed=N, Eng=N • **Work Field:** 054 • **MPSMS:** 611 • **Aptitudes:** G3, V4, N4, S4, P3, Q5, K3, F4, M3, E5, C4 • **Temperaments:** R, T • **Stress:** T • **Physical:** V=L, H=N, L=S, H • **Work Env:** I • **Salary:** 2 • **Outlook:** 2

CASTER (jewelry) • D.O.T. #502.381-010 • OES #89126 • MOLDER; SLUSH CASTER. Casts jewelry pieces and ornamental figures for trophies and placques from molten lead or zinc: Melts zinc or lead alloy bars in kettle. Assembles sections of mold and secures mold with C-clamp. Pours molten metal into mold, using hand ladle. Disassembles mold after specified time and knocks sand from casting, using mallet. Places jewelry piece or figure in tray to cool. • **GED:** R3, M2, L2 • **SVP:** 1-2 yrs • **Academic:** Ed=N,

Eng=N • **Work Field:** 132 • **MPSMS:** 611 • **Aptitudes:** G3, V4, N4, S3, P3, Q5, K3, F3, M3, E5, C5 • **Temperaments:** R, T • **Stress:** T • **Physical:** V=L, H=N, L=M, W, H • **Work Env:** I • **Salary:** 3 • **Outlook:** 3

FABRICATOR-ASSEMBLER, METAL PRODUCTS (any ind.) • D.O.T. #809.381-010 • OES #93197 • Fabricates and assembles metal products, such as window sashes, casements, doors, awning frames, shells, cases, and tubular products, such as golf carts or furniture, as specified by work orders, diagrams, and templates, using handtools, power tools, and metal working machinery: Lays out and marks reference points onto components, using template, rule, square, compass, and scale [LAY-OUT WORKER (any ind.) II]. Operates machines, such as shears, cutoff saws, brakes, punch press, form rolls, and drill press to cut and shape components to specified dimensions [MACHINE OPERATOR (any ind.) II]. Fits [FITTER (any ind.) II] and assembles components, using fixtures, handtools, and portable power tools, such as grinders, drills, power wrenches, and riveters. Operates machines, such as arbor presses, riveting press, brazing machine, and resistance-welding machines to complete assembly. May weld components together. May be designated by specialty as AWNING-FRAME MAKER (fabric. prod., n.e.c.); METAL SCREEN, STORM DOOR, AND WINDOW BUILDER (struct. & ornam. metal work); TUBULAR-PRODUCTS FABRICATOR (any ind.). • **GED:** R3, M2, L2 • **SVP:** 6 mos-1 yr • **Academic:** Ed=N, Eng=N • **Work Field:** 102 • **Aptitudes:** G3, V4, N3, S3, P3, Q5, K4, F3, M3, E4, C4 • **Temperaments:** M, T • **Physical:** V=L, H=N, L=M, W, S, H • **Work Env:** I, N, R • **Salary:** 3 • **Outlook:** 3

GREASE BUFFER (silverware) • D.O.T. #705.684-022 • OES #93953 • Holds and turns silverware, such as bowls, tea sets, trays, or flatware, against grease-coated cloth wheel or leather belt to impart specified finish. May remove scratches, spots, or blemishes with pumice stone. May bolt layers of precut cloth onto spindle and form into buff of desired shape by holding rakelike handtool against rotating cloth. May buff silverware to specified final finish, using soft cloth buffing wheel and fine grained rouge or buffing compound and be designated FINISHER (silverware). • **GED:** R3, M1, L2 • **SVP:** 3-6 mos • **Academic:** Ed=N, Eng=N • **Work Field:** 051 • **MPSMS:** 612 • **Aptitudes:** G3, V4, N4, S4, P3, Q4, K3, F3, M3, E5, C4 • **Temperaments:** J, R, T • **Stress:** T • **Physical:** V=L, H=N, L=L, H • **Work Env:** I, N, R • **Salary:** 2 • **Outlook:** 2

MESH CUTTER (jewelry) • D.O.T. #700.684-050 • OES #93926 • Cuts metal mesh to specified dimensions to make jewelry articles, such as women's handbags, belts, and watchbands: Detaches small metal squares from mesh by cutting corner rings until desired size and shape of mesh is attained. May complete shaping of mesh with scissors. • **GED:** R3, M1, L2 • **SVP:** 30 days-3 mos • **Academic:** Ed=N, Eng=N • **Work Field:** 054 • **MPSMS:** 611 • **Aptitudes:** G3, V4, N4, S3, P3, Q5, K3, F3, M3, E5, C5 • **Temperaments:** R, T • **Stress:** T • **Physical:** V=N, H=N, L=S, H • **Work Env:** I • **Salary:** 2 • **Outlook:** 2

PRESSURE SEALER-AND-TESTER (aircraft-aerospace mfg.) • D.O.T. #806.684-110 • OES #85323 • SEALER, AIRCRAFT. Cleans, seals, and tests aircraft pressurized sections and cavities, according to specifications, using cleaning solvent, calking gun, sealing compounds, and pressure testing equipment: Applies cleaning solvent to interior and exterior surfaces of compartments, such as fuel and water tanks, fuel vent systems, cabins, and cockpits, preparatory to sealing, using brush and rag waste. Applies sealing compounds to surfaces, using hand sealing tool or pressure gun. Dries sealant, using heat lamps and compressed hot air. Bolts access doors and hatches, disconnects plumbing lines, electrical cable and rigging, and caps connections with plugs and threaded fixtures to make section airtight. Connects airhoses of pressure-testing equipment to sealed section, using wrench. Turns valves to admit air pressure and observes air pressure gages to determine leakage. Brushes soapy solution on seams and rivets of section to locate leaks indicated by air bubbles. Applies sealing compound to leaks. Reinstalls plumbing and electrical and rigging connections. May repair leaks and defects by filing, reaming, and riveting. May assemble and air-test tank fittings and dump valves. May fabricate protective cages for high pressure tank testing. May be designated according to section tested as CABIN PRESSURIZER (aircraft-aerospace mfg.); FUEL-CELL SEALER (aircraft-aerospace mfg.); FUSELAGE-PRESSURIZATION ME-CHANIC (aircraft-aerospace mfg.); INTEGRAL TANK-SEALER-AND-REPAIRER (aircraft-aerospace mfg.). • **GED:** R3, M1, L1 • **SVP:** 3-6 mos • **Academic:** Ed=N, Eng=N • **Work Field:** 102 • **MPSMS:** 592 • **Aptitudes:** G3, V4, N4, S3, P3, Q4, K3, F3, M3, E4, C4 • **Temperaments:** M, T • **Physical:** V=L, H=N, L=L, W, S, H • **Work Env:** I • **Salary:** 3 • **Outlook:** 3

REPAIRER, FINISHED METAL (any ind.) • D.O.T. #809.684-034 • OES #85999 • Repairs surface defects, such as dings, dents, and buckles, in finished metal items, such as automobile bodies, refrigerators, or other appliances, using dolly blocks, ding and pick hammers, and other handtools: Visually examines and feels surface of workpiece to determine extent of defect. Holds dolly block against defect and hammers opposite side to smooth surface, being careful not to stretch surface or mar finish. Cleans and polishes repaired area, using buffer and cloth. May file dings to remove burs and rough spots. Polishes working surfaces of dolly blocks and hammers, using naphtha-soaked emery cloth to prevent scratching or gouging of workpiece. • **GED:** R3, M1, L1 • **SVP:** 6 mos-1 yr • **Academic:** Ed=N, Eng=N • **Work Field:** 102 • **MPSMS:** 583, 591 • **Aptitudes:** G3, V4, N4, S4, P3, Q4, K3, F4, M3, E4, C5 • **Temperaments:** J, T • **Physical:** V=L, H=N, L=H, W, H • **Work Env:** I • **Salary:** 3 • **Outlook:** 2

REPAIRER, TYPEWRITER (office mach.) • D.O.T. #706.381-030 • OES #85926 • Repairs and adjusts defective typewriters removed from production line, using handtools, power tools, and gages: Operates typewriter to test functioning of parts and mechanisms to determine repairs required. Disassembles machines to repair or replace defective components, using hand tools and holding devices. Bends, taps, turns parts such as screws, nuts, and type bar to eliminate binding, looseness, and misalinement, using special handtools. Verifies specified clearance between parts, using spacebars, tension scales, dial indicators and feeler gages. Measures rotation of motor drive-wheel to determine speed of wheel, using tachometer. May adjust interrelated typewriter parts to synchronize machine operation and be designated as ADJUSTER (office mach.). • **GED:** R3, M2, L3 • **SVP:** 1-2 yrs • **Academic:** Ed=N, Eng=S • **Work Field:** 121 • **MPSMS:** 571 • **Aptitudes:** G3, V3, N3, S3, P3, Q4, K3, F3, M3, E5, C5 • **Temperaments:** M, T • **Physical:** V=L, H=N, L=M, W, H • **Work Env:** I • **Salary:** 4 • **Outlook:** 2

RING STAMPER (jewelry) • D.O.T. #700.684-066 • OES #92198 • RING STRIKER. Stamps out, shapes, and trims ring and findings II blanks for jewelry, such as bracelets, pins, and earrings, performing any of following tasks: Stamps out ring and finding blanks from metal strips, using kick-press or power press. Forms contoured ring body from blank metal, using drop-press. Trims excess metal from edges of contoured ring body. Heats and softens metal blanks preparatory to stamping and shaping operations, using annealing furnace or gas torch. May operate rolling mill to decrease thickness of metal ingots. • **GED:** R2, M1, L1 • **SVP:** 6 mos-1 yr • **Academic:** Ed=N, Eng=N • **Work Field:** 134 • **MPSMS:** 611 • **Aptitudes:** G3, V4, N5, S3, P3, Q5, K3, F4, M3, E5, C4 • **Temperaments:** M, R, T • **Stress:** T • **Physical:** V=L, H=N, L=L, H • **Work Env:** I, N, R • **Salary:** 3 • **Outlook:** 2

SKI REPAIRER, PRODUCTION (sports equip.) • D.O.T. #732.684-118 • OES #93999 • Repairs defects in skis damaged in production or defective in material, using hand tools and power tools: Examines designated defects and markings on ski to determine type repair required. Selects specified fiberglass mat patch and positions patch over defect. Pours epoxy resin on patch to cause patch to adhere to ski. Places patched area into heated mold press to shape and dry patch. Removes ski from mold press and trims patched area with knife. Drills holes and trims damaged area to provide access to defect for skis having defects in plastic base layer, using portable drill and knife. Alines polyethylene-plastic sliver with defect in base layer and rubs soldering iron over sliver to melt plastic into defect. Smooths repaired ski to remove excess patching, using belt sander. May repair and refinish user-damaged skis in ski manufacturer's service shop. • **GED:** R2, M1, L1 • **SVP:** 6 mos-1 yr • **Academic:** Ed=N, Eng=N • **Work Field:** 102 • **MPSMS:** 616 • **Aptitudes:** G4, V4, N4, S4, P3, Q4, K3, F4, M3, E5, C4 • **Temperaments:** J, T • **Physical:** V=L, H=N, L=L, W, H • **Work Env:** I, N • **Salary:** 3 • **Outlook:** 3

SOLAR-FABRICATION TECHNICIAN (mach. shop) • D.O.T. #809.381-034 • OES #93197 • Fabricates and assembles metal solar collectors according to job order specifications, using machine shop tools and equipment: Lays out and marks reference points on metal tubing and sheets according to job order specifications, using rule and scriber. Aligns, cuts, and drills copper tubing to form pipe sections, using jig, bandsaw, and drill press. Smooths edges of pipe sections, using file and T-bar. Inserts other precut pipes into drilled holes of pipe sections according to job order specifications, and brazes joints to form manifold unit. Aligns and bends copper sheeting to form absorber plate, using power brake. Aligns manifold unit with grooves of absorber plate, squirts liquid solder into grooves, and bakes assembly to permanently bond joints, using oven. Sprays black paint on assembly to facilitate solar heat absorption, using paint sprayer. Aligns and bends galvanized sheeting to form enclosure frame parts of solar collector, using power brake. Drills holes into frame parts and screws or rivets parts together, using pneumatic drill and rivet gun. Inserts absorber plate and manifold assembly into enclosure frame, and rivets sections together. Calks assembly corners to prevent water leaks, using calk gun. Cuts and inserts insulation into enclosure frame to provide heat retention. Aligns and rivets frame end to assembly. Rivets covering to unit to complete solar collector assembly. Packs solar collectors into cardboard boxes for shipment, using tape, strapping, and crimper. Records product identification information on packed boxes. • **GED:** R3, M3, L2 • **SVP:** 3-6 mos • **Academic:** Ed=N, Eng=N • **Work Field:** 102 • **MPSMS:** 553 • **Aptitudes:** G3, V4, N3, S2, P2, Q3, K3, F3, M2, E4, C4 • **Temperaments:** T, V • **Physical:** V=L, H=N, L=H, W, S, H • **Work Env:** I, R • **Salary:** 3 • **Outlook:** 3

SPINNER (jewelry) • D.O.T. #700.684-074 • OES #93999 • Stretches and shapes metal into symmetrical forms, using handtools and bench lathe, for use in making jewelry: Mounts work in lathe chuck. Starts lathe and forces handtools against metal to bend and stretch it as specified. • **GED:** R3, M2, L2 • **SVP:** 6 mos-1 yr • **Academic:** Ed=N, Eng=N • **Work Field:** 134 • **MPSMS:** 611 • **Aptitudes:** G3, V4, N4, S3, P3, Q4, K3, F3, M3, E5, C5 • **Temperaments:** M, T • **Physical:** V=L, H=N, L=L, H • **Work Env:** I • **Salary:** 3 • **Outlook:** 2

STRAIGHTENER, HAND (any ind.) • D.O.T. #709.484-014 • OES #93999 • Straightens metal workpieces to blueprint specifications, using handtools and knowledge of metal properties: Rolls workpiece on flat surface or mounts and rotates it between centers to ascertain irregularities visually or with dial indicator. Positions workpiece on surface plate or anvil and hammers workpiece at points of irregularity to straighten it. Hammers mandrel through cylindrical objects, such as pipes or tubing to remove dents or kinks. Measures straightened workpiece for conformance with specifications, using straightedge, micrometers, and calipers. May straighten workpiece in straightening press. May heat workpiece in furnace or with heating torch to straighten it. May be designated according to parts straightened as TOOL STRAIGHTENER (any ind.); STRAIGHTENER, GUN PARTS (firearms). • **GED:** R3, M2, L2 • **SVP:** 6 mos-1 yr • **Academic:** Ed=N, Eng=N • **Work Field:** 134 • **MPSMS:** 540 • **Aptitudes:** G3, V3, N3, S3, P3, Q4, K3, F3, M3, E5, C4 • **Temperaments:** R, T • **Stress:** T • **Physical:** V=L, H=N, L=M, W, H • **Work Env:** I, N • **Salary:** 3 • **Outlook:** 3

SUBASSEMBLER (mach. mfg.) • D.O.T. #706.381-038 • OES #93105 • Assembles machinery components, such as operating cylinders, electric control cases, transmissions, clutches, and special tools according to specifications: Transports specified parts from storage to work area manually or by using overhead crane. Removes burs and rough surfaces from metal parts with hand file or portable pneumatic grinder. Brushes lubricant on moving parts and fits parts together on bench, following blueprints. Inserts shims between parts to realine or level parts and verifies alinement and clearance of parts, using micrometers, scale, and gages. Bolts, screws, and rivets parts together, using handtools. May operate hydraulic press to force bearings into sleeves and flatten rivets. May set up and operate drill press, bench lathe, and speed lathe. May connect electric wires to terminals of subassembly, using screwdriver. May move subassembly to storage area, using overhead crane. • **GED:** R3, M3, L2 • **SVP:** 1-2 yrs • **Academic:** Ed=N, Eng=N • **Work Field:** 121 • **MPSMS:** 567 • **Aptitudes:** G3, V4,

N3, S2, P2, Q4, K4, F4, M3, E5, C5 • **Temperaments:** M, T • **Physical:** V=L, H=N, L=M, W, H • **Work Env:** I, R • **Salary:** 3 • **Outlook:** 2

TROPHY ASSEMBLER (jewelry) • D.O.T. #735.684-018 • OES #93956 • Assembles trophies to customer's specifications, using drill press and handtools: Selects parts, such as base, tubing, metal plates, figures, and hardware from stock. Drills holes in base or plaque, using electric drill or drill press. Glues felt to bottom of base, or screws in metal feet. Staples or tapes metal plate to base. Bolts parts together, using screwdriver and socket wrench. Touches up scratch marks with scratch remover and polishes assembled trophy. May attach marble or onyx decoration to formed column with adhesive tape. May wrap trophy in tissue paper preparatory to shipping. • **GED:** R3, M2, L2 • **SVP:** 6 mos-1 yr • **Academic:** Ed=N, Eng=N • **Work Field:** 102 • **MPSMS:** 612 • **Aptitudes:** G3, V4, N4, S3, P3, Q4, K3, F3, M3, E5, C4 • **Temperaments:** R, T • **Stress:** T • **Physical:** V=L, H=N, L=L, H • **Work Env:** I • **Salary:** 3 • **Outlook:** 3

GOE: 06.02.25 Manual Work, Wood, Skilled

BOX MAKER, WOOD (wood. box) • D.O.T. #760.684-014 • OES #93956 • CARPENTER, BOX; CASE MAKER; CRATE BUILDER. Cuts lumber and assembles cut lumber into boxes and crates, using handtools or power tools: Measures, marks, and saws boards to specified size, using ruler, pencil, and powersaws. Assembles and nails boards together, using hammer, power stapler, or nailing machine. Repairs damaged containers by replacing damaged parts, using handtools. Salvages used crating by removing nails from board with hammer, nail puller, or crowbar and by sawing ends with portable electric handsaw. May sharpen saw, using file. May insert cardboard fillers, felt pads, and wooden separators in containers. May build crate around material, using ruler, handtools, and pneumatic nailer. When repairing wooden boxes, may be known as BOX REPAIRER (wood. box) I. • **GED:** R3, M2, L2 • **SVP:** 30 days-3 mos • **Academic:** Ed=N, Eng=N • **Work Field:** 102 • **MPSMS:** 454 • **Aptitudes:** G3, V4, N4, S3, P4, Q4, K3, F3, M3, E5, C5 • **Temperaments:** R, T • **Stress:** T • **Physical:** V=N, H=N, L=M, W, H • **Work Env:** I, N • **Salary:** 3 • **Outlook:** 2

GOE: 06.02.26 Manual Work, Paper, Skilled

PRESSER (print. & pub.) • D.O.T. #977.684-018 • OES #93956 • CASER-IN. Folds prefabricated bookcases (separately made bindings) over pasted book bodies and compresses assembly in press to secure cases to bodies: Folds upper half of case over top sheet of book body, stretching case tight over back of book and holding book in place on lower half of case. Presses case down on book body, centering book in case with fingers. Stacks enfolded books in press and places pressboards at intervals in stack. Turns handwheel to lower press head and clamp stack. Retains books in press until glue or paste has dried. Reverses handwheel, removes books, and stacks books for finishing. • **GED:** R3, M1, L1 • **SVP:** 3-6 mos • **Academic:** Ed=N, Eng=N • **Work Field:** 063 • **MPSMS:** 486 • **Aptitudes:** G3, V4, N4, S3, P4, Q4, K3, F3, M3, E5, C5 • **Temperaments:** R, T • **Stress:** T • **Physical:** V=N, H=N, L=L, H • **Work Env:** I • **Salary:** 3 • **Outlook:** 1

GOE: 06.02.27 Manual Work, Textile, Fabric & Leather, Skilled

BLOCKER, HAND 1 (hat & cap) • D.O.T. #580.684-010 • OES #93956 • BLOCKER, HEATED METAL-FORMS; FELT PULLER; HAT BLOCKER; ROPER. Shrinks felt cones to size and shapes cones to form unfinished hat bodies: Immerses cone in hot water, places cone in steam cabinet, or holds cone over steam jet, to shrink and soften cone. Positions softened cone over heated head-shaped block. Presses and rubs cone to smooth and shape cone by hand or using iron. Ties cord around base of crown and pulls edge of cone over base of block to form brim of hat. Removes cord and block from hat body after drying. May place cones in drying cabinet following blocking process. • **GED:** R2, M1, L2 • **SVP:** 30 days-3 mos •

Academic: Ed=N, Eng=N • **Work Field:** 032, 152 • **MPSMS:** 446, 449 • **Aptitudes:** G4, V4, N4, S3, P3, Q4, K4, F4, M3, E5, C5 • **Temperaments:** R, T • **Stress:** T • **Physical:** V=L, H=N, L=L, W, H • **Work Env:** I, H, W • **Salary:** 2 • **Outlook:** 2

COBBLER (boot & shoe) • D.O.T. #788.381-010 • OES #89511 • SHOE REPAIRER; SHOE STITCHER, ODD. Repairs shoes damaged in manufacturing process: Inspects shoe or reads ticket to determine defects. Removes damaged parts, using hand tools, such as knife, hammer, lasting tool, prying tool, and tack puller. Operates stitching machine or stitches by hand to repair broken or missed stitches and to replace parts. Relasts shoe to remove defects, such as wrinkles from outer parts, bunching of inner parts, and crooked seams. Alines and cements parts, such as edges, bindings, heels, soles, and uppers of shoe by hand. May fill holes and cracks in shoes, using colored wax filler. May be designated according to part of shoe repaired as COBBLER, SOLE (boot & shoe); COBBLER, UPPER (boot & shoe); LINING REPAIRER (boot & shoe); or according to method of shoe construction as COBBLER, MCKAY (boot & shoe). • **GED:** R3, M1, L2 • **SVP:** 6 mos-1 yr • **Academic:** Ed=N, Eng=N • **Work Field:** 102 • **MPSMS:** 522 • **Aptitudes:** G3, V4, N5, S3, P3, Q5, K3, F3, M3, E4, C4 • **Temperaments:** M, T, V • **Physical:** V=G, H=N, L=M, W, H • **Work Env:** I, N • **Salary:** 2 • **Outlook:** 3

CUTTER, HAND 1 (any ind.) • D.O.T. #781.584-014 • OES #93926 • Cuts out, shapes, or trims material or articles, such as canvas goods, garment parts, hats and caps, house furnishings, or knit goods, to facilitate subsequent operations, using scissors or knife: (1) Unrolls and lays out material along calibrated scale on cutting table or measures material with ruler and cuts material into lengths, using scissors or knife. (2) Positions pattern or template on material or marks around pattern or template, using chalk or pencil, and cuts out parts, using scissors or knife. Cuts notches in edges of parts to mark them for assembly. Shapes or trims excess material from parts. May match materials for color or shade. May cut or trim knit goods, using hot-wire device. May mark identification numbers on parts. May spread cloth on table in single or multiple lays prior to cutting. May assemble and fold articles after cutting. May be designated according to type of material or article cut as APPLIQUE CUTTER, HAND (trim. & embroid.); BED-SPREAD CUTTER, HAND (house furn.); BLANKET CUTTER, HAND (house furn.); CANVAS CUTTER, HAND (canvas goods); CURTAIN CUTTER, HAND (house furn.); DRAPERY CUTTER, HAND (house furn.); GARMENT-PARTS CUTTER, HAND (garment). Additional titles: HAT-AND-CAP-PARTS CUTTER, HAND (hat & cap); KNIT-GOODS CUTTER, HAND (knit goods); TERRY-CLOTH CUTTER, HAND (house furn.). • **GED:** R3, M1, L2 • **SVP:** 6 mos-1 yr • **Academic:** Ed=N, Eng=N • **Work Field:** 054, 241 • **MPSMS:** 420, 430, 440 • **Aptitudes:** G4, V4, N4, S3, P3, Q4, K3, F3, M3, E5, C4 • **Temperaments:** R, T • **Stress:** T • **Physical:** V=L, H=N, L=L, H • **Work Env:** I • **Salary:** 3 • **Outlook:** 2

CUTTER, MACHINE 1 (any ind.) • D.O.T. #781.684-014 • OES #93928 • CLOTH-CUTTING-MACHINE OPERATOR. Cuts multiple layers of fabric into parts for articles, such as canvas goods, house furnishings, garments, hats, stuffed toys, and upholstered furniture, using portable electric cutter: Inserts base of cutter under layers of fabric, starts cutter, and guides cutter around edges of pattern or template or along markings on fabric to cut out parts. Drills holes through layers of fabric, using electric drill, or cuts notches in edges of parts with scissors or electric cutter to mark parts for assembly. Sharpens blade with abrasive stone or belt attached to cutter as quality of cut indicates dull blade. Changes cutter blades, using screw driver or wrench. May guide lays of fabric around blade of stationary cutter (bandsaw), according to pattern markings. May spread fabric on table preparatory to cutting [SPREADER, MACHINE (any ind.)]. May arrange patterns on top ply of fabric and mark outline of pattern on fabric with chalk or crayon [MARKER (any ind.) I]. May separate cutting waste according to color of material. May be designated according to type of cutting machine used as CIRCULAR-KNIFE CUTTER, MACHINE (any ind.); STRAIGHT-KNIFE CUTTER, MACHINE (any ind.); or according to type of material, article, or part cut as CANVAS CUTTER, MACHINE (canvas goods); COVER CUTTER, MACHINE (house furn.; matt. & bedspring); DRAPERY CUTTER, MACHINE (house furn.); GARMENT-PARTS CUTTER, MA-

CHINE (garment); HAT-PARTS CUTTER, MACHINE (hat & cap). Additional titles: HOUSE-FURNISHINGS CUTTER, MACHINE (house furn.); TERRY CLOTH CUTTER, MACHINE (house furn.); UPHOLSTERY CUTTER, MACHINE (furn.). • **GED:** R3, M2, L2 • **SVP:** 6 mos-1 yr • **Academic:** Ed=N, Eng=N • **Work Field:** 054, 241 • **MPSMS:** 420, 430, 440 • **Aptitudes:** G3, V4, N4, S3, P3, Q4, K3, F4, M3, E5, C4 • **Temperaments:** M, T • **Physical:** V=L, H=N, L=M, W, S, H • **Work Env:** I • **Salary:** 3 • **Outlook:** 2

LEATHER CUTTER (leather prod.) • D.O.T. #783.684-022 • OES #93926 • Lays out, marks, and cuts leather or skins into parts for articles, such as holsters, belts, gun cases, garments and garment trim, surgical appliances, and paint roller covers, using leather knife or shears: Lays leather or skins on cutting table and positions pattern pieces on leather or skins to determine number of cuts. Marks outline of pattern on leather or skins, using pencil. Cuts around outline, using leather knife or shears. Turns screws on strap knife to adjust width of cut when cutting leather for rifle slings and gun case handles. Lays leather side on table, positions dies on leather to obtain maximum number of cuts from side, and strikes die with mallet to cut out part. May stack and tie cut pieces together. May cut parts with guillotine cutter. May punch holes in parts, using kick press. • **GED:** R3, M2, L2 • **SVP:** 3-6 mos • **Academic:** Ed=N, Eng=N • **Work Field:** 054, 241 • **MPSMS:** 529 • **Aptitudes:** G3, V4, N4, S3, P3, Q4, K3, F3, M3, E5, C5 • **Temperaments:** M, T • **Physical:** V=L, H=N, L=L, H • **Work Env:** I • **Salary:** 3 • **Outlook:** 3

LEATHER WORKER (leather prod.) • D.O.T. #783.684-026 • OES #93999 • Punches holes, installs rivets, and finishes edges of leather products, such as holsters, rifle cases, and belts, using handtools: Marks holes in article, using template and marking pencil. Punches holes for rivets, snaps, or buttons, using hand punch. Fastens parts together, using rivets, stitching machine, needle and thread, or adhesive. Attaches eyelets and metal decorations to article, using hammer and punch. Cuts around edge of article to smooth edge, using knife. Brushes stain on cut edge to match color of article. Rubs finished article with damp cloth to clean leather and rubs paste wax on surface, using cloth, to produce shine. May emboss designs on leather surface. May be designated according to article fabricated or repaired as HOLSTER MAKER (leather prod.); RIFLE-CASE REPAIRER (leather prod.). • **GED:** R3, M2, L2 • **SVP:** 6 mos-1 yr • **Academic:** Ed=N, Eng=N • **Work Field:** 102 • **MPSMS:** 529 • **Aptitudes:** G4, V4, N4, S3, P3, Q4, K3, F3, M3, E4, C4 • **Temperaments:** T, V • **Physical:** V=G, H=N, L=M, W, H • **Work Env:** I • **Salary:** 3 • **Outlook:** 3

MATTRESS MAKER (matt. & bedspring) • D.O.T. #780.684-074 • OES #93999 • Pads and covers innerspring assemblies to form mattresses: Cuts cover material, using electric cutting knife and scissors, and spreads and staples burlap, leno, or sisal cloth to both sides of innerspring assemblies. Spreads padding over sides of innerspring and tends tape-edge machine that sews cover over padding. Tufts mattresses by hand or by tending machine to hold padding in place. Sews roll edges on mattress by hand or by machine. • **GED:** R3, M1, L2 • **SVP:** 3-6 mos • **Academic:** Ed=N, Eng=N • **Work Field:** 102 • **MPSMS:** 464 • **Aptitudes:** G3, V4, N4, S3, P3, Q4, K3, F3, M3, E5, C5 • **Temperaments:** R, T • **Stress:** T • **Physical:** V=L, H=N, L=M, W, H • **Work Env:** I • **Salary:** 3 • **Outlook:** 2

MENDER (carpet & rug) • D.O.T. #782.684-042 • OES #93923 • Mends torn or defective portions of unfinished or finished cloth or carpets and rugs by handweaving: Examines cloth or rug for tears or defects, or marking that indicate imperfections. Reweaves thread or yarn to close holes or repair defects, using needle and thread or burling iron, and blends repair thread or yarn with existing pattern. Draws missing warp or filling threads through cloth and pulls out coarse and surplus threads, using burling iron, tweezers, and needle and thread. Pulls loosely woven threads through back of cloth to reduce slack, using tweezers. May trim yarn from defect, using scissors. May weave patch into hole, pounding repaired area smooth, and be designated RUG MENDER (carpet & rug). • **GED:** R3, M1, L2 • **SVP:** 3-6 mos • **Academic:** Ed=N, Eng=N • **Work Field:** 164, 171 • **MPSMS:** 420, 431 • **Aptitudes:** G3, V4, N4, S4, P3, Q4, K3, F3, M3, E5, C3 • **Temperaments:** M, T • **Physical:** V=G, H=N, L=S, H • **Work Env:** I • **Salary:** 2 • **Outlook:** 3

SPOTTER (laundry) • D.O.T. #361.684-018 • OES #93999 • Identifies stains in washable cotton and synthetic garments or household linens prior to laundering and applies chemicals until stain dissolves, using brush, sponge, or bone spatula: Sorts stained articles to segregate items stained with oil, grease or blood. Applies and rubs chemicals into garment, using bone spatula, sponge or brush, until stain dissolves. Places spotted articles in net bags for return to washroom. Bleaches and washes some articles in small washing machine. • **GED:** R3, M1, L1 • **SVP:** 30 days-3 mos • **Academic:** Ed=N, Eng=N • **Work Field:** 031 • **MPSMS:** 420, 440, 906 • **Aptitudes:** G4, V4, N5, S4, P3, Q5, K3, F4, M3, E5, C3 • **Temperaments:** M, R, T • **Stress:** T • **Physical:** V=L, H=N, L=L, H • **Work Env:** I • **Salary:** 2 • **Outlook:** 2

GOE: 06.02.28 Manual Work, Food Processing, Skilled

BENCH HAND (bake. prod.) • D.O.T. #520.384-010 • OES #93999 • BAKER, BENCH; DOUGH MOLDER, HAND. Forms dough for bread, buns, and other bakery products: Rolls dough to desired thickness with rolling pin or guides dough through rolling machine. Sprinkles flour on dough and workbench to prevent dough from sticking. Kneads dough to eliminate gases formed by yeast. Cuts dough into pieces with knife or handcutter. Adds spices, fruits, or seeds when making special rolls or breads. Weighs pieces on scales and keeps record of production. Places dough in baking pans. May cut dough into bun divisions by machine. May form dough into special shapes and add fillings or flavorings. • **GED:** R3, M2, L2 • **SVP:** 1-2 yrs • **Academic:** Ed=N, Eng=N • **Work Field:** 146 • **MPSMS:** 384 • **Aptitudes:** G3, V4, N3, S3, P3, Q4, K3, F3, M3, E5, C4 • **Temperaments:** J, T • **Physical:** V=L, H=N, L=M, W, H • **Work Env:** I • **Salary:** 3 • **Outlook:** 2

BUTCHER, ALL-ROUND (slaught. & meat pack.) • D.O.T. #525.381-014 • OES #89802 • Performs slaughtering and butchering tasks in small slaughtering and meat packing establishment, using cutting tools, such as cleaver, knife, and saw: Stuns animals prior to slaughtering [STUNNER, ANIMAL (slaught. & meat pack.)]. Shackles hind legs of animals, such as cattle, sheep, and hogs, to raise them for slaughtering or skinning [SHACKLER (slaught. & meat pack.)]. Severs jugular vein to drain blood and facilitate slaughtering [STICKER, ANIMAL (slaught. & meat pack.)]. Trims head meat and otherwise severs or removes parts of animal heads or skulls [HEAD TRIMMER (slaught. & meat pack.)]. Saws, splits, or scribes slaughtered animals to reduce carcass [CARCASS SPLITTER (slaught. & meat pack.)]. Slits open, eviscerates, and trims carcasses of slaughtered animals. Cuts, trims, skins, sorts, and washes viscera of slaughtered animals to separate edible portions from offal [OFFAL SEPARATOR (slaught. & meat pack.)]. Washes carcasses [WASHER, CARCASS (slaught. & meat pack.)]. Wraps muslin cloth about dressed animal carcasses or sides to enhance appearance and protect meat [SHROUDER (slaught. & meat pack.)]. Shaves hog carcasses [SHAVER (slaught. & meat pack.)]. Trims and cleans animal hides, using knife [HIDE TRIMMER (grease & tallow; slaught. & meat pack.)]. Cuts bones from standard cuts of meat, such as chucks, hams, loins, plates, rounds, and shanks, to prepare meat for marketing [BONER, MEAT (slaught. & meat pack.)]. Examines, weighs, and sorts fresh pork cuts [GRADER, GREEN MEAT (slaught. & meat pack.)]. Skins sections of animals or whole animals, such as cattle, sheep, and hogs [SKINNER (slaught. & meat pack.)]. Works in small slaughtering and meat packing establishment. May prepare meats for smoking [SMOKED MEAT PREPARER (slaught. & meat pack.)]. May cut and wrap meat. May salt (cure) and trim hides [HIDE HANDLER (grease & tallow; slaught. & meat pack.)]. • **GED:** R3, M2, L2 • **SVP:** 1-2 yrs • **Academic:** Ed=N, Eng=N • **Work Field:** 034 • **MPSMS:** 382 • **Aptitudes:** G3, V3, N4, S4, P3, Q4, K3, F3, M3, E5, C4 • **Temperaments:** T, V • **Physical:** V=L, H=N, L=H, W, S, H • **Work Env:** I, W • **Salary:** 4 • **Outlook:** 3

CANDY MAKER (confection.) • D.O.T. #529.361-014 • OES #89808 • BATCH MAKER; BOILER; CONFECTIONER; COOK, CANDY. Mixes and cooks candy ingredients by following, modifying, or formulating recipes to produce product of specified flavor, texture, and color: Cooks ingredients [CONFECTIONERY

COOKER (chew. gum; confection.)] at specified temperatures in open-fire or steam-jacketed kettles or in batch or continuous pressure cookers. Casts candy by hand, using molds and funnel, or tends machine that casts candy in starch or rubber molds [DEPOSITING-MACHINE OPERATOR (confection.)]. Spreads candy onto cooling and heating slabs. Kneads and machine-pulls candy [CANDY PULLER (confection.)]. Spins or rolls candy into strips ready for cutting [SPINNER (confection.)]. Examines, feels, and tastes product to evaluate color, texture, and flavor. Adds ingredients or modifies cooking and forming operations as needed. May direct CANDY-MAKER HELPERS (confection.). May be designated according to type of candy produced as CARAMEL-CANDY MAKER (confection.); COCONUT-CANDY MAKER (confection.); FUDGE-CANDY MAKER (confection.); HARD-CANDY MAKER (confection.); NOUGAT-CANDY MAKER (confection.); TAFFY-CANDY MAKER (confection.). • GED: R4, M3, L4 • SVP: 2-4 yrs • Academic: Ed=N, Eng=S • Work Field: 146 • MPSMS: 393 • Aptitudes: G3, V3, N3, S3, P3, Q4, K3, F3, M3, E5, C3 • Temperaments: J, M, T, V • Physical: V=L, H=N, L=M, W, S, H • Work Env: I • Salary: 4 • Outlook: 3

DOUGHNUT MAKER (bake. prod.) • D.O.T. #526.684-010 • OES #93999 • BAKER, DOUGHNUT; CRULLER MAKER. Mixes, forms, and fries dough to produce doughnuts: Dumps prepared doughnut mix into mixing-machine bowl, adds water and dehydrated eggs, and starts mixer. Turns switch on heating unit of frying tank and sets thermostat at specified temperature. Dumps dough from mixing bowl into hopper of doughnut cutter. Sets lever to control amount of dough that doughnut cutter will portion to frying tank. Moves cutter machine back and forth over frying tank and depresses trigger to eject individual doughnuts into hot grease. Turns doughnuts over in tank, using stick. Lifts wire tray of fried doughnuts from tank and places it in glazing tank. Slides trough containing glazing sirup over doughnuts. May glaze doughnuts, using hand dipper. May roll dough with rolling pin and form doughnuts with hand cutter. May lower wire tray of uncooked doughnuts into frier, using hooks. • GED: R3, M1, L1 • SVP: 6 mos-1 yr • Academic: Ed=N, Eng=N • Work Field: 146 • MPSMS: 384 • Aptitudes: G3, V4, N4, S4, P3, Q5, K4, F4, M3, E5, C4 • Temperaments: J, T • Physical: V=L, H=N, L=M, W, S, H • Work Env: I, H • Salary: 2 • Outlook: 4

GOE: 06.02.29 Manual Work, Rubber, Skilled

RUBBER-GOODS REPAIRER (any ind.) • D.O.T. #759.684-054 • OES #85999 • Repairs rubber products, such as life rafts and vests, gas-tank linings, inner tubes, and rubber vent systems, using oven or autoclave and steam curing iron: Cements rubber patch to torn or damaged areas and vulcanizes patch, using steam curing iron. Cuts rubber into pieces, covers metal and other surfaces with pieces, and places rubber article in oven or autoclave to bond surfaces. May make gaskets, washers, and hose, using molds and dies. • GED: R3, M1, L1 • SVP: 3-6 mos • Academic: Ed=N, Eng=N • Work Field: 063 • MPSMS: 519 • Aptitudes: G3, V4, N4, S4, P3, Q5, K4, F4, M3, E5, C5 • Temperaments: R, T • Stress: T • Physical: V=L, H=N, L=L, H • Work Env: I • Salary: 3 • Outlook: 2

GOE: 06.02.30 Manual Work, Stone, Glass & Clay, Skilled

GLASS CUTTER (any ind.) • D.O.T. #775.684-022 • OES #93926 • CUTTER; PATTERN CUTTER; STRAIGHT CUTTER. Cuts flat glass and mirrors to specified size and shape, using patterns, straightedge, tape measure, and glass cutting tools: Positions pattern on glass or measures dimensions and marks cutting lines, using glass cutting tool. Scribes around pattern or along straightedge, using cutting tool. Breaks away excess glass by hand or with notched tool or glass pinchers. May smooth rough edges, using belt sander. • GED: R3, M2, L1 • SVP: 3-6 mos • Academic: Ed=N, Eng=N • Work Field: 054 • MPSMS: 531 • Aptitudes: G3, V4, N4, S4, P3, Q4, K3, F3, M3, E5, C5 • Temperaments: R, T • Stress: T • Physical: V=L, H=N, L=H, W, H • Work Env: I • Salary: 3 • Outlook: 2

MOLDER (optical goods) • D.O.T. #575.381-010 • OES #89905 • Molds optical glass into various shaped blanks: Reads work order to determine type and quantity of optical glass to be molded. Changes dies and adjusts length of stroke and pressure of press, and regulates temperature of ovens and die heater according to type of glass to be processed. Places glass pieces in preheating oven to prepare glass for molding. Spreads refractory powder on oven floor to prevent glass from sticking and places preheated glass in oven. Presses glass pieces with paddles to determine readiness for molding and to shape glass to approximate shape of spoon die. Slides glass into spoon die, positions die in press, and depresses pedal to lower ram of press to mold glass blank. Removes spoon die from press and drops molded blank onto floor of cooling oven. • GED: R3, M2, L2 • SVP: 1-2 yrs • Academic: Ed=N, Eng=N • Work Field: 136 • MPSMS: 603 • Aptitudes: G3, V4, N4, S3, P3, Q5, K3, F4, M3, E4, C4 • Temperaments: J, T • Physical: V=L, H=N, L=M, W, H • Work Env: I, H, R • Salary: 4 • Outlook: 2

PLASTER MAKER (statue & art) • D.O.T. #779.684-046 • OES #93944 • CASTER. Casts plaster art objects, such as statuary and plaques, using flexible molds: Assembles mold that consists of inner shell and outer casing. Mixes specified proportions of water and plaster, by hand or using mechanical mixer, and pours mixture into rubber mold. Shakes and squeezes mold to eliminate air bubbles, and smooths plaster mixture at mouth of mold, using spatula. Flexes mold to remove casting, when plaster has set. Places casting in oven to dry. May be designated according to object cast as PLAQUE MAKER (stat. & art goods). • GED: R3, M1, L2 • SVP: 6 mos-1 yr • Academic: Ed=N, Eng=N • Work Field: 132 • MPSMS: 538 • Aptitudes: G3, V4, N4, S4, P3, Q5, K3, F4, M3, E5, C4 • Temperaments: J, R, T • Stress: T • Physical: V=L, H=N, L=M, W, H • Work Env: I, W, R • Salary: 3 • Outlook: 2

PLASTER-DIE MAKER (pottery & porc.) • D.O.T. #774.684-026 • OES #93944 • RAM-DIE MAKER. Casts plaster dies for hydraulic ram press that forms pottery ware: Places wire mesh over die face of master model and presses or taps mesh with wooden mallet to contour of model. Wires non-metallic conduit to wire mesh. Removes wire mesh assembly and sponges soap solution on model surface to separate die halves after casting. Lowers steel die rings over outside rim of each half of model and places wire mesh assembly over model face. Wires assembly to die rings. Mixes hydrostone (powdered plaster) with water and pours mixture into each half of model to top of die ring. Separates die from model and attaches airhose to die to remove water from dies. Sponges remaining moisture from dies. Places finished dies in storage rack. • GED: R3, M1, L1 • SVP: 6 mos-1 yr • Academic: Ed=N, Eng=N • Work Field: 132, 143 • MPSMS: 536 • Aptitudes: G3, V4, N4, S4, P3, Q4, K3, F3, M3, E5, C5 • Temperaments: R, T • Stress: T • Physical: V=N, H=N, L=H, W, H • Work Env: I, W • Salary: 3 • Outlook: 2

THROWER (pottery & porc.) • D.O.T. #774.381-010 • OES #89905 • CLAY THROWER; POT MAKER. Molds plastic clay into such ware as vases, urns, saggers, and pitchers, as clay revolves on potter's wheel: Positions ball of clay in center of potter's wheel and starts motor, or pumps treadle with foot to revolve wheel. Presses thumbs down into center of revolving clay to form hollow. Presses on inside and outside of emerging clay cylinder with hands and fingers, gradually raising and shaping clay to desired form and size. Constantly adjusts speed of wheel to conform with changing tenacity (firmness) of clay as piece enlarges and walls become thinner, judging degrees of change by feel. Smooths surfaces of finished piece, using rubber scrapers and wet sponge. Verifies size and form, using calipers and templates. Pulls wire held taut between both hands through base of article and wheel to separate finished piece, or removes piece from wheel to dry. May form saggers only and be known as SAGGER FORMER (pottery & porc.). • GED: R3, M2, L3 • SVP: 2-4 yrs • Academic: Ed=N, Eng=S • Work Field: 136 • MPSMS: 535 • Aptitudes: G3, V4, N4, S2, P2, Q5, K2, F2, M2, E2, C4 • Temperaments: M, R, T • Stress: T • Physical: V=L, H=N, L=M, W, H • Work Env: I, W • Salary: 4 • Outlook: 2

GOE: 06.02.31 Manual Work, Laying Out & Marking, Skilled

LAY-OUT WORKER 2 (any ind.) • D.O.T. #809.381-014 • OES #89117 • DUPLICATOR; LAY-OUT MAKER. Traces patterns and marks specifications for fabricating operations onto sheet metal, metal plates, and structural shapes, using templates, measuring instruments, and handtools: Measures stock, using rule to locate center line for positioning template. Tapes, clamps, bolts, or holds template on workpiece. Marks bending and cutting lines, using scribe; punches or spot drills location of holes, using center punch or hand drill. May lay out straight lines and location of holes detailed on blueprints. • **GED:** R3, M3, L2 • **SVP:** 6 mos-1 yr • **Academic:** Ed=N, Eng=N • **Work Field:** 241 • **MPSMS:** 554 • **Aptitudes:** G3, V4, N3, S3, P3, Q4, K3, F3, M3, E5, C5 • **Temperaments:** M, T • **Physical:** V=L, H=N, L=M, W, S, H • **Work Env:** I, N • **Salary:** 3 • **Outlook:** 3

GOE: 06.02.32 Manual Work, Assorted Materials, Skilled

BONDED STRUCTURES REPAIRER (aircraft-aerospace mfg.) • D.O.T. #807.381-014 • OES #85323 • Repairs aircraft and space vehicle bonded structures according to blueprints and written specifications, using handtools and power tools: Reads inspection reports, rework instructions, and blue prints to determine type of repair, tools required, and to plan sequence of operations. Positions and fastens bonded structure in assembly fixture or bonding form, using clamps, wrenches, and screwdriver. Examines structure to locate damaged area and identify type of imperfection. Spreads plastic film over area to be repaired to prevent damage to skin of structure. Drills holes in structure to gain access to internal damage, using portable drill. Scribes around damaged areas and cuts out damaged sections of structure, using knife and abrasive wheel. Laminates combination of materials such as honeycomb blanket, fiberglass cloth, and aluminum sheeting together to form bonded repair section. Trims and shapes repair sections to specified size, using knives, rotary files, and portable power tools. Sprays and injects adhesive in cut-out areas of bonded structure, using spray and pres sure-injection guns. Fits repair sections into cut-out areas and fastens sections in place, using adhesive tape and tack-iron. • **GED:** R3, M2, L2 • **SVP:** 1-2 yrs • **Academic:** Ed=N, Eng=N • **Work Field:** 102 • **MPSMS:** 592 • **Aptitudes:** G3, V3, N3, S3, P2, Q4, K4, F3, M3, E5, C5 • **Temperaments:** M, T • **Physical:** V=L, H=N, L=L, W, H • **Work Env:** I, R • **Salary:** 4 • **Outlook:** 3

BOW MAKER, PRODUCTION (sports equip.) • D.O.T. #732.684-038 • OES #93999 • Fabricates and shapes laminated archery bows: Selects dies according to type bow to be produced and bolts dies to bow press. Applies epoxy resin to precut wood and fiberglass parts for laminating. Alines parts following reference marks and clamps parts to press. Cures bows for specified time to form contour of bow, using bow press. Cuts string nocks in bow tips and bevels bow edge, using abrasive wheels and sanders. Shapes and finishes contour of bow, using belt sanders. Examines bow for twist and adjusts string position to compensate for deficiencies noted. Buffs bow to smooth finish, using power buffer. Measures force required to pull bow string to full draw, using scale and pulley device, to determine if bow meets specifications. May apply decorative or identifying decal to bow. May varnish and stain bow to protect surface. May assemble crossbows and be designated as CROSSBOW MAKER (sports equip.). May repair defects in bows damaged in production or returned to factory for repair. • **GED:** R3, M3, L2 • **SVP:** 6 mos-1 yr • **Academic:** Ed=N, Eng=N • **Work Field:** 102 • **MPSMS:** 616 • **Aptitudes:** G4, V4, N3, S4, P3, Q4, K3, F3, M3, E4, C4 • **Temperaments:** M, T • **Physical:** V=L, H=N, L=L, H • **Work Env:** I • **Salary:** 3 • **Outlook:** 3

BRUSH MATERIAL PREPARER (brush & broom) • D.O.T. #739.684-022 • OES #93999 • Prepares hog bristles and other brush-filling materials, such as horsehair, nylon, and vegetable fibers for use in brushes: Alines bristles, to ensure that flagged ends are together, and discards defective bristles. Ties bundle of bristles to prevent bending and places it in rack. Uses hoist to lower rack of bundles into vat of boiling water to remove natural curl of bristle. Removes rack after specified time and places it on dolly or in oven to dry. Places bundle of bristles in carton and labels carton according to length, origin, grade, and color of contents or spreads bristles in rows on tray for mixing and blending operations. Prepares other brush-filling materials by straightening, combing, cutting, and tying them according to type of material and intended use. Holds bundle of material against grinding wheel to flag ends, to trim butt ends, and to polish material. Selects filling material according to formula and lays it on workbench in prescribed manner prior to processing by mixing machine. May pack material in carton. May place bristles in sterilizer to kill germs. May dye bristles specified color, using dyeing vat. May shape, soften, and clean bristles, using machines that cut, split, and grind bristles. • **GED:** R2, M1, L1 • **SVP:** 6 mos-1 yr • **Academic:** Ed=N, Eng=N • **Work Field:** 062, 147 • **MPSMS:** 619 • **Aptitudes:** G4, V4, N4, S4, P4, Q4, K4, F3, M3, E5, C4 • **Temperaments:** R, T • **Stress:** T • **Physical:** V=N, H=N, L=M, W, H • **Work Env:** I, N, R • **Salary:** 2 • **Outlook:** 2

CABLE MAKER (elec. equip.) • D.O.T. #728.684-010 • OES #93999 • Lays wire around pegs on harness board and ties wires together to form harness (cable) used in electrical and electronic equipment, such as communication equipment, aircraft and ignition systems, electrical appliances, or other electrical or electronic systems: Selects wires of color, marking, or length specified by wire lists or diagrams, and loops them between guide pegs on board, following colored lines or numbers marked on board. Laces wires together at specified points by wrapping and tying with waxed twine, plastic or nylon strips. Applies sealing varnish to laces with brush to secure knots. May solder ends of cable wires to terminal strip or multiple-pin plug, using soldering iron. May insert cable in plastic tubing to protect cable from dust and moisture. May paint identifying colors on wire. • **GED:** R3, M2, L2 • **SVP:** 30 days-3 mos • **Academic:** Ed=N, Eng=N • **Work Field:** 111 • **MPSMS:** 584, 586, 587 • **Aptitudes:** G3, V4, N4, S3, P3, Q3, K3, F3, M3, E5, C3 • **Temperaments:** R, T • **Stress:** T • **Physical:** V=L, H=N, L=L, H • **Work Env:** I • **Salary:** 3 • **Outlook:** 4

CHARGE PREPARATION TECHNICIAN (electronics) • D.O.T. #590.384-010 • OES #92902 • Prepares ampoule containing charge (specified amounts of materials for crystal growing process) to grow gallium arsenide crystal ingot in crystal growing furnace: Cleans ampoules, plugs, and boats, using etch tanks and/or sandblasting equipment. Operates saw to cut remelt into sections of specified size. Immerses remelt into etch tank to remove contaminants, and dries remelt in oven. Measures and weighs specified amounts of crystal growing material, such as seed, seed powder, remelt, and dopant, and loads material into boat and ampoule, following prescribed procedure. Attaches ampoule to diffusion pump to remove air from ampoule, and seals ampoule, using blowtorch. Transports sealed ampoule to holding rack in furnace room for further processing by CRYSTAL GROWER (electronics) 590.382-014. Records production information. • **GED:** R2, M2, L2 • **SVP:** 3-6 mos • **Academic:** Ed=N, Eng=N • **Work Field:** 147 • **MPSMS:** 587 • **Aptitudes:** G3, V4, N4, S4, P3, Q3, K3, F3, M3, E5, C5 • **Temperaments:** R, T • **Stress:** T • **Physical:** V=L, H=N, L=L, H • **Work Env:** I, R • **Salary:** 3 • **Outlook:** 4

COIL WINDER, REPAIR (any ind.) • D.O.T. #724.381-014 • OES #89999 • Winds coils for repair of electric motor and generator parts, such as rotors, stators, and armatures, using original winding as guide to determine number of turns and size of wire: Winds coil on machine or directly into slots of rotors, stators, and armatures or pounds heavy copper over template to form coils. Operates coil spreading machine to shape rigid coils for placement into slots. Tends coil taping machine or winds tape around coils by hand to insulate coils. Cuts and forms sheet insulation to fit slots, using paper cutter and forming fixture. Inserts coils into slots and pounds, using mallet and block, to compress and shape windings. Twists coil leads together to form groups of coils according to original winding and solders connections, using soldering iron. May paint coils with insulating varnish or enamel. May be designated according to coil wound as FIELD-COIL WINDER (any ind.). • **GED:** R3, M2, L2 • **SVP:** 6 mos-1 yr • **Academic:** Ed=N, Eng=N • **Work Field:** 163 • **MPSMS:** 582 • **Aptitudes:** G3, V4, N3, S3, P3, Q4, K3, F3, M3, E4, C4 • **Temperaments:** R, T • **Stress:** T • **Physical:** V=L, H=N, L=L, H • **Work Env:** I • **Salary:** 3 • **Outlook:** 3

DENTURE WAXER (medical ser.) • D.O.T. #712.681-010 • OES #93956 • WAXER, METAL, PARTIAL DENTURE. Molds wax over denture setup to form contour molds of gums, palates, bridges, and other denture surfaces for use in casting plaster models or metal framework of dentures, using molding equipment and handtools: Applies softened wax to base of denture setup and fills space between adjacent teeth, using spatula and fingers. Carves and shapes wax, using scraper, knife, and heated spatula to form natural-appearing denture contours. Immerses denture in cold water to harden wax. Rubs surface with cotton to obtain lustrous finish. Attaches wax rod to pattern to form sprue for casting. May mix plaster or melt metals and pour plaster or molten metal in contour molds to form model for duplicate casting [DENTURE-MODEL MAKER (medical ser.)]. May verify occlusion of teeth, using articulator. May construct wax bite blocks and plastic trays [BITE-BLOCK MAKER (medical ser.)]. • **GED:** R3, M2, L3 • **SVP:** 1-2 yrs • **Academic:** Ed=N, Eng=S • **Work Field:** 136 • **MPSMS:** 604, 925 • **Aptitudes:** G3, V3, N4, S2, P2, Q4, K3, F3, M3, E5, C4 • **Temperaments:** M, T • **Physical:** V=L, H=N, L=L, H • **Work Env:** I • **Salary:** 4 • **Outlook:** 2

ETCHED-CIRCUIT PROCESSOR (electronics) • D.O.T. #590.684-018 • OES #93951 • Performs any combination of following duties to print and etch conductive patterns on copper-faced plastic, fiberglass, or epoxy board to fabricate printed circuit boards (PCBs): Cuts board to designated size, using sheet metal shears, following work order, shop sheet, or verbal instructions. Sands board, places it in vapor degreaser, or immerses it in chemical solution to clean and remove oxides or other contaminants. Sprays or brushes light-sensitive enamel on copper surface and places board in whirler machine to spread enamel evenly or tends machine that flows light-sensitive resist over board. Laminates light-sensitive dry film to board, using heat and pressure. Positions board and circuit negative in contact printer and exposes them to light for specified period of time to transfer image of circuit to board. Immerses exposed board in solution to develop acid-resistant circuit pattern on surface. Examines board to verify development of pattern by comparing it to sample. Touches up board, using brush to apply acid resist over sections of pattern not developed. Immerses board in acid or tends etching machine to etch conductive pattern on copper surface. Immerses board in solution to dissolve enamel. Drills holes in board, using drill press, following work sample, drawing, and diagrams. Installs hardware, such as brackets, eyelets, and terminals, using eyelet machine and hand arbors. May reduce circuit artwork prior to printing onto board, using reduction camera. May use silk-printing device to print conductive pattern onto board. May fabricate PCB used as prototype of production model. • **GED:** R3, M3, L3 • **SVP:** 3-6 mos • **Academic:** Ed=N, Eng=S • **Work Field:** 111, 182, 191 • **MPSMS:** 587 • **Aptitudes:** G3, V4, N4, S3, P2, Q5, K4, F3, M3, E5, C5 • **Temperaments:** R, T • **Stress:** T • **Physical:** V=L, H=N, L=L, H • **Work Env:** I • **Salary:** 3 • **Outlook:** 4

OPAQUER (medical ser.) • D.O.T. #712.684-030 • OES #93947 • PORCELAIN-BUILDUP ASSISTANT. Applies coating of opaque porcelain over cast metal tooth cap, using brush: Mixes porcelain of specified color and water to required consistency. Brushes porcelain mixture over surfaces of metal cap. Places cap in electric oven for specified time to dry and harden porcelain. Removes cap and examines cap to ensure even application and smoothness of coating. Routes workpiece to specified department for application of finish porcelain. May grind and shape dried porcelain to contours of metal cap, using abrasive wheels. May measure dimensions of tooth cap and verify occlusion, using gages and articulator. • **GED:** R3, M2, L2 • **SVP:** 3-6 mos • **Academic:** Ed=N, Eng=N • **Work Field:** 141, 153 • **MPSMS:** 925 • **Aptitudes:** G3, V4, N4, S4, P3, Q4, K3, F3, M3, E5, C3 • **Temperaments:** M, T • **Physical:** V=L, H=N, L=S, H • **Work Env:** I • **Salary:** 3

RACKET STRINGER (sports equip.) • D.O.T. #732.684-094 • OES #93999 • Strings tennis and badminton rackets with synthetic fiber or animal gut strings: Clamps racket in stand and threads warp (main strings) through holes in bow. Clamps ends of strings in jaws of tensioner arms, depresses pedal to tighten strings to prescribed tension, and locks strings in place by wedging awl in hole with string until next set of holes are strung, or string is tied. Threads weave (cross strings) through holes in bow, weaves them through main strings, applies tension, and secures them similarly to main strings. May wrap bow at intervals with bands of colored thread to strengthen and decorate it. May varnish wooden parts of racket. May replace leather or plastic grips on racket handle. • **GED:** R3, M2, L2 • **SVP:** 6 mos-1 yr • **Academic:** Ed=N, Eng=N • **Work Field:** 164 • **MPSMS:** 616 • **Aptitudes:** G3, V4, N4, S3, P3, Q4, K3, F3, M3, E3, C4 • **Temperaments:** R, T • **Stress:** T • **Physical:** V=L, H=N, L=L, H • **Work Env:** I • **Salary:** 3 • **Outlook:** 3

SKI MOLDER (sports equip.) • D.O.T. #732.684-114 • OES #93999 • Fabricates sock (inner-construction, ski-component) and alines sock with other ski parts in die press that molds components into partially fabricated ski: Places fiberglass lay-up (mat of specified size) on work table, pours epoxy resin over lay-up, and spreads resin with paddle to facilitate saturation. Positions ski core on lay-up, places foot-pad on top of core, and pours resin over core and foot-pad. Folds lay-up around core and foot-pad to form sock, cuts sock to contour of ski toe (front) with scissors and template, and alines sock assembly in specified manner within mold press. Places ski base layer in press with sock assembly in specified alinement and activates press to shape and mold layers. • **GED:** R3, M1, L2 • **SVP:** 30 days-3 mos • **Academic:** Ed=N, Eng=N • **Work Field:** 102 • **MPSMS:** 616 • **Aptitudes:** G4, V4, N4, S3, P3, Q5, K3, F4, M3, E4, C5 • **Temperaments:** J, T • **Physical:** V=L, H=N, L=L, H • **Work Env:** I • **Salary:** 3 • **Outlook:** 2

WIRER (office mach.) • D.O.T. #729.281-042 • OES #93114 • Installs, adjusts, and repairs wiring and cables in punched card office machines and adding machines according to wiring diagrams, blueprints, and engineering specifications, using handtools, soldering iron, and plugging gun: Reads wiring diagrams, blueprints, wire routing and standards sheets, and engineering specifications to determine lengths, types, routing, and colors of wiring and cables to be installed in machines, such as collators, adding machines, reproducing punches, card reader punches, and interpreters. Selects specified wires and cables, routes according to instructions, and fastens connections by bolting, screwing, soldering, or plugging, using wrenches, screwdrivers, soldering iron, and plugging gun (pneumatic gun that forces plug ends of wires into jacks). Inspects previously wired units, such as plugboards, fuse holders, key boards, and indicator lights, for conformance to specifications, using test devices, such as voltmeters and ohmmeters. • **GED:** R3, M3, L2 • **SVP:** 1-2 yrs • **Academic:** Ed=N, Eng=N • **Work Field:** 111 • **MPSMS:** 571 • **Aptitudes:** G3, V4, N4, S2, P3, Q4, K3, F2, M3, E5, C3 • **Temperaments:** M, T • **Physical:** V=L, H=N, L=L, H • **Work Env:** I • **Salary:** 4 • **Outlook:** 3

06.03 Quality Control

Workers in this group check the quality and quantity of products and materials being manufactured. They inspect, test, weigh, sort, and grade specific items to be sure that they meet certain standards. Some may also keep inspection records of the number or kind of defects and flaws they find. They work in factories and other large plants that process materials and manufacture products.

✔ **What kind of work would you do?**

Your work activities would depend upon your specific job. For example, you might:

- examine unground optical lenses for flaws and sort them according to defects.
- inspect watch dials and hands for flaws and proper alignment.
- inspect the dimensions of fountain pen nibs by using measuring instruments such as calipers.
- examine rejected rubber footwear and sort according to whether pairs should be salvaged or scrapped.

✔ **What skills and abilities do you need for this kind of work?**

To do this kind of work, you must be able to:

- do the same thing over and over according to a set procedure.
- use eyes, hands, and fingers to handle gauges and measuring tools.
- use math skills to count, measure, or keep inspection records.
- make decisions based on standards that can be measured or checked.

The above statements may not apply to every job in this group.

✔ **How do you know if you would like or could learn to do this kind of work?**

The following questions may give you clues about yourself as you consider this group of jobs.

- Have you had industrial arts or machine shop courses? Did you learn how to use measuring devices such as gages, calipers, and micrometers?
- Have you sorted paper, metal, or glass for recycling? Were you able to tell the difference between similar types of materials?
- Have you had general or applied mathematics courses? Do you like to keep tallies or other simple records?

✔ **How can you prepare for and enter this kind of work?**

Occupations in this group usually require education and/or training extending from thirty days to over one year, depending upon the specific kind of work. Most jobs in this group have no specific educational requirements. However vocational shop courses are helpful.

Employers usually train workers through on-the-job training programs.

✔ **What else should you consider about these jobs?**

Overtime or night and shift work may be required. Many of these jobs are available to persons without any training. After gaining skill and experience in these jobs, workers often move up to better paying jobs.

Workers are exposed to different types of factory conditions. However, these jobs usually do not require working near machinery.

If you think you would like to do this kind of work, look at the job titles listed below.

GOE: 06.03.01 Inspecting, Testing & Repairing

CABLE STRETCHER AND TESTER (aircraft-aerospace mfg.) • D.O.T. #806.685-010 • OES #92198 • Tends cable-stretching machine that stretches aircraft control cables to specified length and tests holding capacity of terminal fittings: Inserts pins through cable terminal fittings and attaches cable ends to stretching machine fixtures. Slides movable fixture along track on machine bed to take up slack in cable and bolts fixture in place. Sets regulator dial at specified tension reading according to length and thickness of cable. Starts machine that stretches cable to specified length and tests holding capacity of terminal fittings. Examines cables to detect loosened fittings or broken strands. May mix corrosion-proofing solution according to formula and immerse cables in solution. May tape identification tags to cables. May pack cables in bags and seal bag opening, using sealing machine. • **GED:** R3, M2, L1 • **SVP:** 3-6 mos • **Academic:** Ed=N, Eng=N • **Work Field:** 134, 211 • **MPSMS:** 557 • **Aptitudes:** G3, V4, N4, S4, P3, Q4, K3, F3, M3, E5, C5 • **Temperaments:** M, T • **Physical:** V=L, H=N, L=L, W, H • **Work Env:** I, N • **Salary:** 3 • **Outlook:** 3

COMPARATOR OPERATOR (any ind.) • D.O.T. #699.384-010 • OES #83005 • SHADOWGRAPH OPERATOR. Inspects parts for defects in finish and dimensions, using machine that projects magnified shadows of parts on screen: Reads specifications of part to ascertain form and degree to be magnified. Draws enlarged outline of part to scale on chart (celluloid disk), using scribers, dividers, and straightedge. Places chart over translucent glass disk of comparator (shadowgraph) machine. Inserts specified lens into machine and adjusts mirrors to magnify parts. Positions and secures parts on machine table. Turns light on and moves levers of machine to bring shadows of parts into focus with chart outline. Inspects shadows for imperfections of finish and incorrect dimensions. Prepares reports of findings. May rotate part in holding fixture to examine surfaces and to verify concentricity of parts. • **GED:** R3, M3, L3 • **SVP:** 3-6 mos • **Academic:** Ed=N, Eng=S • **Work Field:** 121, 211 • **MPSMS:** 587, 607 • **Aptitudes:** G3, V3, N4, S3, P2, Q3, K3, F3, M4, E5, C5 • **Temperaments:** M, T • **Physical:** V=G, H=N, L=L, H • **Work Env:** I • **Salary:** 3 • **Outlook:** 2

INSPECTOR (fabric. plastic prod.) • D.O.T. #559.381-010 • OES #83002 • CUSTOMER-RETURN INSPECTOR; PROCESS INSPECTOR. Inspects and tests plastic sheets, rods, tubes, powders, or fabricated articles for uniformity of color, surface defects, hardness, and dimensional accuracy, following plant specifications or blueprints and using measuring instruments and test equipment: Examines surface of product for defects, such as scratches, burns, and discolorations. Positions transparent sheet between light and calibrated screen and observes shadow pattern of sheet projected on screen to determine optical distortion. Verifies weight and dimensions of product, using scales, gages, calipers, micrometers, and templates. Compares color of product with color standard. Determines hardness and structural strength of product, using acid bath, burst tester, and hardness tester. Records test data, and grades and labels product according to type of defect. May investigate cause of recurring defects and recommend changes in production procedures. May file, buff, or sand product to remove defects. • **GED:** R3, M3, L3 • **SVP:** 6 mos-1 yr • **Academic:** Ed=N, Eng=S • **Work Field:** 211 • **MPSMS:** 510 • **Aptitudes:** G3, V3, N3, S3, P3, Q3, K4, F4, M3, E5, C3 • **Temperaments:** M, T • **Physical:** V=G, H=N, L=S, H • **Work Env:** I, N • **Salary:** 3 • **Outlook:** 2

MACHINE TESTER (office mach.) • D.O.T. #706.387-014 • OES #83005 • Tests machines, such as calculating or adding machines, manually or automatically to detect malfunctions, using handtools, alinement gage, and tester: Sets machine on ball swivel mount to facilitate turning in all directions when examining parts. Plugs cord of machine into electrical outlet. Presses keys on keyboard and moves levers in prescribed sequence to test alinement of printing, repeat latch, ribbon and paper feed, correction release, noise, and clearance of type bars, according to checklist. Test-runs battery of machines through fixed computation cycle automatically, using autotypist or tester. Reads arithmetic results recorded on paper tapes of machines and compares them with test chart to verify accuracy. Indicates defects on inspection worksheet and gives worksheet and machine to repairer. May disassemble machine to determine cause of defect. May be designated according to type of inspection done as CLEARING INSPECTOR (office mach.); FINAL INSPECTOR (office mach.); SAMPLING INSPECTOR (office mach.); UTILITY INSPECTOR (office mach.). • **GED:** R3, M2, L2 • **SVP:** 3-6 mos • **Academic:** Ed=N, Eng=N • **Work Field:** 211 • **MPSMS:** 571 • **Aptitudes:** G3, V3, N4, S4, P3, Q3, K3, F3, M3, E5, C5 • **Temperaments:** M, R, T • **Stress:** T • **Physical:** V=L, H=N, L=L, H • **Work Env:** I • **Salary:** 3 • **Outlook:** 2

MOTORCYCLE TESTER (motor. & bicycles) • D.O.T. #620.384-010 • OES #83005 • Inspects and tests motorcycles, performing any combination of following tasks according to standard procedures, using handtools and testing instruments: Mounts motorcycle on test stand. Attaches lead wires of test panel to ignition system of motor and runs motor at various speeds to measure generator output, oil pressure, revolution per minute, and other specified operating characteristics. Compares test instrument readings with operational charts to detect malfunctions. Engages clutch and transmission of motorcycle and listens for sounds denoting malfunction. Records findings on worksheet. Turns adjustment screw on carburetor to regulate idling speed of motor, using screwdriver. Inspects frame and fenders for dents and scratches. Tightens frame nuts and bolts, using handtools. Tests operation of horn and lights. Verifies identification number and optional equipment against data on work order. • **GED:** R3, M3, L3 • **SVP:** 6 mos-1 yr • **Academic:** Ed=N, Eng=S • **Work Field:** 121 • **MPSMS:** 595 • **Aptitudes:** G3, V3, N3, S3, P3, Q4, K3, F3, M3,

E4, C4 • **Temperaments:** R, T • **Stress:** T • **Physical:** V=L, L=M, W, S, H • **Work Env:** I • **Salary:** 4 • **Outlook:** 3

QUALITY-CONTROL INSPECTOR (phonograph) • D.O.T. #194.387-010 • OES #83005 • MATRIX INSPECTOR; MOTHER TESTER. Inspects metal phonograph record mothers for surface defects, using optical and sound-reproducing equipment: Places matrix on turntable and measures grooved surface and width of grooves in matrix, using ruler and calibrated microscope. Places tone arm on matrix and starts sound-reproducing machine. Listens for defects in matrix, such as pops and ticks, and observes meter that indicates surface noise and sound level. Stops machine and locates defects in matrix, using microscope and magnifying glass. Marks location of defects with bar soap and returns matrix for repair. Notes reasons for rejection on worksheet. Listens to repaired matrices to ensure that defects have been eliminated. • **GED:** R3, M2, L2 • **SVP:** 3-6 mos • **Academic:** Ed=H, Eng=S • **Work Field:** 211 • **MPSMS:** 585 • **Aptitudes:** G3, V4, N3, S4, P2, Q4, K4, F4, M4, E5, C5 • **Temperaments:** J, M, T • **Physical:** V=G, H=G, L=S, H • **Work Env:** I • **Salary:** 3 • **Outlook:** 3

SPECIAL TESTER (tobacco) • D.O.T. #529.487-010 • OES #83005 • Tests tobacco samples from various stages of processing to determine conformance to quality standards: Obtains tobacco samples from various processing areas to ensure representative sampling. Conducts tests to determine characteristics of tobacco batch, such as stem length, percentage of lamina, stem, and foreign matter content, using scales, laboratory equipment, and calculator. • **GED:** R3, M3, L3 • **SVP:** 30 days-3 mos • **Academic:** Ed=N, Eng=S • **Work Field:** 211 • **MPSMS:** 401, 403, 409 • **Aptitudes:** G3, V3, N3, S4, P4, Q3, K4, F4, M4, E5, C5 • **Temperaments:** M, T • **Physical:** V=L, H=N, L=L, W, H • **Work Env:** I • **Salary:** 2 • **Outlook:** 2

TEST DRIVER 1 (auto. mfg.) • D.O.T. #806.281-050 • OES #83002 • CAR TESTER; CHASSIS DRIVER; OVERLAND DRIVER; ROAD TESTER. Drives completed automobile, as vehicle comes from assembly line, on proving ground under simulated road conditions and observes performance to detect mechanical and structural defects: Examines car before road testing to ensure that equipment, such as electrical wiring, hydraulic lines, and fan belts are installed as specified and verifies that car has been serviced with oil, gas, and water. Drives car to simulate actual driving conditions. Listens for rattles and excessive mechanical noise, and moves controls to test functioning of equipment, such as horn, heater, wipers, and power windows. Drives car through water spray and visually inspects interior for leaks. Writes inspection report on standardized form indicating defects or malfunctions. • **GED:** R3, M2, L3 • **SVP:** 1-2 yrs • **Academic:** Ed=N, Eng=S • **Work Field:** 121 • **MPSMS:** 591 • **Aptitudes:** G3, V3, N4, S3, P3, Q4, K3, F4, M3, E3, C4 • **Temperaments:** M, T • **Physical:** V=G, H=L, L=L, W, H • **Work Env:** I • **Salary:** 4 • **Outlook:** 3

GOE: 06.03.02 Inspecting, Grading, Sorting, Weighing & Recording

CALIBRATION CHECKER 2 (inst. & app.) • D.O.T. #710.687-018 • OES #83005 • AIR CHECKER. Tests accuracy of pressure-activated controls: Seats control in holding fixture and couples air-pressure lines to capillary tube of control. Opens air valve and observes action of contact points within specified pressure range. Compares reading of scale pointer on control with reading on pressure gage to verify accuracy of control. • **GED:** R3, M2, L2 • **SVP:** 3-6 mos • **Academic:** Ed=N, Eng=N • **Work Field:** 211 • **MPSMS:** 602 • **Aptitudes:** G3, V4, N4, S4, P3, Q4, K3, F4, M4, E5, C5 • **Temperaments:** M, T • **Physical:** V=L, H=N, L=L, W, H • **Work Env:** I, R • **Salary:** 3 • **Outlook:** 3

ELECTRONICS INSPECTOR II (electronics) • D.O.T. #726.684-022 • OES #83005 • CHECKER; INSPECTOR, COMPONENT PARTS; INSPECTOR, VISUAL; LINE INSPECTOR. Inspects electronic assemblies, subassemblies, parts, and components by comparing them with samples or production illustrations: Examines unit visually for physical defects, such as broken wire, excess solder, holes in sealing material, unevenly wound coil, coating and plating blemishes, oil leaks, faulty resistance weld, scratches, and cracks. Compares hardware, such as eyelets, brackets, and lugs, on assemblies, subassemblies, and parts with parts list to verify installation. Examines hardware for specified contact with conductor area. Rejects faulty assembly, part, or component. Records type and quantity of defects to keep record control. May measure parts to verify accuracy of dimensions, using standard gauges. May sort defective components and parts for salvage or scrap. May be designated according to item inspected as CAPAC-ITOR INSPECTOR (electronics); CATHODE-COATING INSPEC-TOR (electronics); CONNECTOR INSPECTOR (electronics); FIL-TER INSPECTOR (electronics); GRID INSPECTOR (electronics). Additional titles: RESISTOR INSPECTOR (electronics); TELEVI-SION-CHASSIS INSPECTOR (electronics); TUBE INSPECTOR (electronics). • **GED:** R3, M2, L2 • **SVP:** 30 days-3 mos • **Academic:** Ed=N, Eng=N • **Work Field:** 212 • **MPSMS:** 587 • **Aptitudes:** G3, V4, N4, S4, P3, Q4, K4, F3, M3, E5, C4 • **Temperaments:** J, R, T • **Stress:** T • **Physical:** V=G, H=N, L=S, H • **Work Env:** I • **Salary:** 3 • **Outlook:** 4

ELECTRONICS TESTER II (electronics) • D.O.T. #726.684-026 • OES #83005 • COMPONENT TESTER; PRODUCTION TES-TER; QUALITY-CONTROL TESTER; TESTING-MACHINE OP-ERATOR. Tests electronic function of assemblies, components, and parts, using standard test equipment and procedures: Connects unit to test instrument, such as ohmmeter, voltmeter, ammeter, resistance bridge, or oscilloscope and turns switch. Reads instrument dial or scope that indicates resistance, capacitance, continuity, and wave pattern or defect, such as short or current leakage. Compares instrument reading with standard and rejects defective units. Records type and quantity of defect. May verify dimensions of parts, using standard gauges. May examine assembly, component, or part for defects, such as short leads, bent plate, or cracked seal. May tend equipment to subject unit to stress and strain prior to testing. May tend automatic test equipment. May operate x-ray photograph and closed circuit television viewing equipment to observe internal image of unit for assembly defect prior to testing. May adjust circuits in radio and television receivers for maximum signal response and be designated ALIGNER (electronics). May be designated according to unit tested as COIL TESTER (electronics); FILTER TESTER (electronics); TUBE TESTER (electronics). • **GED:** R3, M3, L3 • **SVP:** 30 days-3 mos • **Academic:** Ed=N, Eng=S • **Work Field:** 211 • **MPSMS:** 586, 587 • **Aptitudes:** G3, V4, N4, S4, P4, Q4, K4, F4, M4, E5, C4 • **Temperaments:** R • **Stress:** T • **Physical:** V=G, H=N, L=L, H • **Work Env:** I • **Salary:** 3 • **Outlook:** 4

GARMENT INSPECTOR (any ind.) • D.O.T. #789.687-070 • OES #83005 • TRIMMER. Inspects garments for defects in sewing, knitting, or finishing: Spreads garment on table or draws it over inspection form. Scans garment to detect defects, such as faulty seaming, incorrect sleeve or collar setting, misalined fasteners or trim, and variations in color of fabric. Examines fabric for mispicks, slubs, runs, dropped stitches, holes, or stains. Marks defects, using chalk, thread, tags, tape, or pins. Measures garment at designated places, using tape measure or following markings on table, to determine that garments conform to standard size. Trims excess material and thread ends from garment, using scissors, or tends trimming machine to remove excess material and loose threads [THREAD CUTTER (any ind.)]. Folds garment or hangs it on hanger or rack. May remove spots and stains from garments [SPOT CLEANER (garment; knit goods)]. May inspect surgical garments and appliances, such as belts, hosiery, or knee and ankle braces, and be designated INSPECTOR (surgical appl.). May examine cut garment parts to detect inaccuracies in cutting and be designated CUTTING INSPECTOR (garment). May be designated according to production stage as FINISHED-GARMENT INSPEC-TOR (garment; knit goods); GREY-GOODS INSPECTOR (knit goods); SECONDS INSPECTOR (garment; knit goods). • **GED:** R2, M1, L2 • **SVP:** 30 days-3 mos • **Academic:** Ed=N, Eng=N • **Work Field:** 165, 171 • **MPSMS:** 424, 440, 604 • **Aptitudes:** G4, V4, N4, S4, P3, Q4, K4, F3, M3, E5, C4 • **Temperaments:** M, R, T • **Stress:** T • **Physical:** V=L, H=N, L=L, H • **Work Env:** I • **Salary:** 2 • **Outlook:** 3

GLASS INSPECTOR (any ind.) • D.O.T. #579.687-022 • OES #83005 • Visually inspects plate glass or glass products for defects, such as scratches, cracks, chips, holes, or bubbles: Places workpiece on inspection stand or table. Visually examines workpiece and marks defects. Rejects or classifies pieces for potential use,

such as mirrors, glass pane, or furniture tops. Scrapes or washes foreign material from surface, using scraper, sponge, or brush. May clean or polish glass by washing with water or solvent and drying with cloth. May place straight edge over glass plates to determine if plates are warped. May attach identifying label to glassware. • **GED:** R2, M1, L2 • **SVP:** 30 days-3 mos • **Academic:** Ed=N, Eng=N • **Work Field:** 031, 211 • **MPSMS:** 530 • **Aptitudes:** G4, V4, N4, S4, P3, Q4, K4, F4, M3, E5, C4 • **Temperaments:** R, T • **Stress:** T • **Physical:** V=G, H=N, L=L, W, H • **Work Env:** I • **Salary:** 2 • **Outlook:** 2

GRADER (woodworking) • D.O.T. #669.587-010 • OES #83005 • LUMBER INSPECTOR; SIZER GRADER. Inspects and grades milled, rough-sawed, or dimensional stock lumber according to standards: Examines lumber on table, moving belt, chain conveyor, or in racks for defects, such as knots, stains, decay, splits, faulty edges, pitch pockets, wormholes, and defective milling. Grades and marks lumber, using caliper rule, to ensure specified dimensions. May determine cuts to be made to obtain highest marketable value from material. May remove unsatisfactory pieces from conveyor or table and place pieces on stacks, in bins, or on carts. May scale board footage, using calibrated scale on lumber ruler, and record results. May tally pieces of lumber according to grade and board footage. May be designated according to lumber graded as FLOOR-ING GRADER (plan. mill); GREEN-LUMBER GRADER (woodworking); or according to location of work as DOCK GRADER (woodworking); GREEN-CHAIN MARKER (sawmill); PLANER-MILL GRADER (plan. mill). May review work of other graders and be designated CHECK GRADER (woodworking). Additional titles: DRY-LUMBER GRADER (woodworking); MILLED-LUMBER GRADER (woodworking); PUNCHER (plan. mill); ROUGH-LUM-BER GRADER (woodworking). • **GED:** R3, M3, L2 • **SVP:** 3-6 mos • **Academic:** Ed=N, Eng=N • **Work Field:** 211 • **MPSMS:** 450 • **Aptitudes:** G3, V3, N3, S3, P3, Q4, K3, F4, M3, E4, C4 • **Temperaments:** D, J, M, T • **Physical:** V=L, H=N, L=L, H • **Work Env:** I, N • **Salary:** 3 • **Outlook:** 2

HYDRO-PNEUMATIC TESTER (any ind.) • D.O.T. #862.687-018 • OES #83005 • Tests boilers, tanks, fittings, pipes, and similar objects to detect and locate leaks, using compressed air or water pressure: Installs fittings on object to seal outlets and connects object to high-pressure air or water line, using handtools. Activates air compressor or water pump until gage registers specified internal pressure. Observes gage for loss of pressure indicative of leaks, and examines object for escaping air or water to detect leaks. Marks object at source of leaks for subsequent repair. May apply soap solution to surface of object or immerse object to facilitate location of air leaks. May test object under high pressure to ensure compliance with product safety ratings. May be designated according to type of test used as HYDROSTATIC TESTER (any ind.); PNEUMATIC TESTER (any ind.). • **GED:** R3, M2, L3 • **SVP:** 3-6 mos • **Academic:** Ed=N, Eng=N • **Work Field:** 211 • **MPSMS:** 550 • **Aptitudes:** G3, V4, N4, S4, P4, Q4, K4, F4, M3, E5, C5 • **Temperaments:** M, T • **Physical:** V=G, H=N, L=L, W, H • **Work Env:** B, N • **Salary:** 5 • **Outlook:** 3

INKER (print. & pub.) • D.O.T. #659.667-010 • OES #83005 • Compares color of printing ink with sample to ensure adherence to formula or customer specifications: Determines ink viscosity by timing flow from test cup and adds desired amount of solvent to meet viscosity requirements for kind of ink and application. Fills ink reservoirs in presses and adds more solvent to thin ink or uncovers reservoirs to allow evaporation of excess solvent during press run. May fill lubricating cups with oil and grease. May assist press operator to set up printing press. • **GED:** R3, M2, L2 • **SVP:** 3-6 mos • **Academic:** Ed=N, Eng=N • **Work Field:** 191 • **MPSMS:** 499 • **Aptitudes:** G3, V4, N3, S4, P3, Q3, K4, F4, M4, E5, C2 • **Temperaments:** M, R, T • **Stress:** T • **Physical:** V=L, H=N, L=L, W • **Work Env:** I, N • **Salary:** 3 • **Outlook:** 2

INSPECTOR (drug prep. & related) • D.O.T. #559.387-014 • OES #83005 • Inspects pharmaceutical ingredients and products to detect deviations from manufacturing standards: Selects samples of in-process pharmaceutical ingredients, capsules, tablets, and related products for testing, according to prescribed procedures. Weighs samples, using scales, and measures samples, using micrometer. Places specified samples in disintegration baths and observes and times rate of dissolution. Records inspection results on designated forms. Checks incoming purchased pharmaceutical ingredients against invoice to verify conformity of product name, count, and labeling. Carries samples of incoming products to analytical laboratory for quality assurance testing. • **GED:** R3, M2, L3 • **SVP:** 3-6 mos • **Academic:** Ed=N, Eng=S • **Work Field:** 211, 212 • **MPSMS:** 493 • **Aptitudes:** G3, V3, N4, S4, P3, Q3, K4, F4, M4, E5, C4 • **Temperaments:** T • **Physical:** V=G, H=N, L=L, H • **Work Env:** I • **Salary:** 3 • **Outlook:** 3

INSPECTOR (jewelry) • D.O.T. #700.687-034 • OES #83005 • Examines findings and finished pieces of jewelry for specified size and shape and for defects in enameling, painting, plating, and polishing. Straightens parts or inserts links, using pointed pliers. May measure and weigh completed articles of sterling silver or pieces of jewelry, using balance scale, micrometer, calipers, rulers, and height gage. May inspect filled books of gold leaf or rolls of metal foil for defects, such as dimensional accuracy, holes or torn corners. • **GED:** R3, M2, L2 • **SVP:** 3-6 mos • **Academic:** Ed=N, Eng=N • **Work Field:** 211 • **MPSMS:** 611 • **Aptitudes:** G3, V4, N4, S4, P3, Q4, K4, F3, M4, E5, C4 • **Temperaments:** R, T • **Stress:** T • **Physical:** V=G, H=N, L=S, H • **Work Env:** I • **Salary:** 2 • **Outlook:** 3

INSPECTOR, FABRIC (any ind.) • D.O.T. #789.587-014 • OES #83005 • FOLDER INSPECTOR; INSPECTOR AND CLIPPER. Examines articles made from fabric, such as bags, bed linens, canvas products, or house furnishings, to detect soil and assembly defects: Measures length or width of article to detect variation from customer or plant specifications, using tape or rule. Spreads article over table or rack and scans article to detect defective stitching, loose threads, color variations between thread and fabric, and uneven seams, corners, pleats, or hems. Cuts excess threads with scissors. Marks defects with gummed label or chalk. Stacks articles that fail to meet specifications on handtruck or table. Records number and type of defects. Folds articles according to customer or plant specifications. May examine paired articles, comparing designs to detect irregular alinement. May inspect tufted articles, scanning article to detect uneven or ragged tufts. May work as member of team to examine large articles, such as blankets, bedspreads, and draperies. May be designated according to article inspected as BAG INSPECTOR (tex. bag); BEDSPREAD INSPECTOR (house furn.); BLANKET INSPECTOR (house furn.); CURTAIN INSPECTOR (house furn.); DISH-CLOTH INSPECTOR (house furn.); DRAPERY INSPECTOR (house furn.). Additional titles: INSPECTOR, CANVAS PRODUCTS (canvas goods; tex. prod., n.e.c.); RETURNED-GOODS INSPECTOR (house furn.); SHEET INSPECTOR (house furn.); TOWEL INSPECTOR (house furn.). • **GED:** R3, M1, L2 • **SVP:** 30 days-3 mos • **Academic:** Ed=N, Eng=N • **Work Field:** 211 • **MPSMS:** 420, 430 • **Aptitudes:** G3, V4, N4, S4, P3, Q4, K4, F3, M4, E5, C3 • **Temperaments:** M, R, T • **Stress:** T • **Physical:** V=G, H=N, L=L, H • **Work Env:** I • **Salary:** 2 • **Outlook:** 3

INSPECTOR, INTEGRATED CIRCUITS (electronics) • D.O.T. #726.684-058 • OES #83005 • Inspects integrated circuit (IC) assemblies, semiconductor wafers, and IC dies for conformance to company standards, using microscope: Reads work order to determine inspection criteria. Places group of items in trays on microscope stage, or positions items individually on stage for inspection, using vacuum pencil or tweezers. Turns knobs on microscope to adjust focus and magnification as required to view items for inspection. Views and inspects items according to company standards to detect defects, such as broken circuit lines, bridged circuits, misalignments, symbol errors, and missing solder. Discards defective items. May remove contaminants from items, using brush or airhose. May use magnifying glass to inspect electronic items. • **GED:** R2, M2, L2 • **SVP:** 30 days-3 mos • **Academic:** Ed=N, Eng=S • **Work Field:** 212 • **MPSMS:** 587 • **Aptitudes:** G4, V4, N4, S3, P3, Q4, K4, F3, M4, E5, C5 • **Temperaments:** R, T • **Stress:** T • **Physical:** V=G, H=N, L=S, W, H • **Work Env:** I • **Salary:** 2 • **Outlook:** 4

INSPECTOR, PRINTED CIRCUIT BOARDS (electronics) • D.O.T. #726.684-062 • OES #83005 • BOARD INSPECTOR; CIRCUIT BOARD INSPECTOR; TOUCH-UP INSPECTOR, PRINTED CIRCUIT BOARDS; TOUCH-UP OPERATOR, PRINTED CIRCUIT BOARDS. Inspects printed circuit boards (PCBs) for conformance to specifications and touches up defects:

Inserts plug gauges into drilled holes in PCB panels to verify conformance to specified dimensions. Measures plated areas on PCB panels, using devices such as micrometers and dial indicators, to verify uniformity and thickness of plating. Brushes liquid photoresist on sections of circuitry pattern not completed and scrapes excess photoresist from panels, using artist's knife. Examines PCB circuitry, using light table, eye-loupe, magnifier or binocular microscope, and specifications or artwork, to detect defects, such as shorts, breaks, excess or missing solder, scratches, cracks and incorrect layout, and scrapes excess copper and solder from board, using artist's knife. Measures PCBs for conformance to specified dimensions, using calipers, micrometers, dial indicators, rulers, and eye-loupes. Rejects defective boards and records type and quantity of defects to keep record control. May inspect plating in holes and remove excess plating. May test adherence of photoresist to PCBs, using tape. May repair broken circuitry, using soldering iron or circuit bonding equipment. May test circuit continuity of boards, using bare board testers. May inspect inner layers of multilayer PCBs to verify that internal alignment and location of drilled component mounting holes meet specifications, using computer-controlled x-ray equipment, and be designated X RAY TECHNICIAN, PRINTED CIRCUIT BOARDS (electronics). • **GED:** R3, M2, L2 • **SVP:** 30 days-3 mos • **Academic:** Ed=N, Eng=S • **Work Field:** 212 • **MPSMS:** 587 • **Aptitudes:** G3, V3, N4, S4, P3, Q4, K3, F3, M3, E5, C5 • **Temperaments:** R, T • **Stress:** T • **Physical:** V=G, H=N, L=S, H • **Work Env:** I • **Salary:** 2 • **Outlook:** 5

INSPECTOR, SEMICONDUCTOR WAFER (electronics) • D.O.T. #726.684-066 • OES #83005 • Performs any of following duties to inspect, measure, and test semiconductor wafers for conformance to specifications: Inspects wafers under high intensity lamp to detect surface defects, such as scratches, chips, stains, burns, or haze. Measures thickness and resistivity of wafers, using electronic gauges or automated sorting machine. Measures diameter and flat of wafers, using calipers. Inspects bow or flatness of wafers, using electronic gauges, or examines surface of wafers under high intensity lamp. Tests for positive or negative conductivity of wafers, using electronic probe and gauge. Determines crystal orientation of wafers, using x-ray equipment. Encloses containers of inspected wafers in plastic bags for protection, using heat sealer. Records inspection data on production records or in computer, using computer terminal. May tend equipment that cleans surface of wafers [WAFER CLEANER (electronics) 590.685-102]. • **GED:** R3, M2, L2 • **SVP:** 30 days-3 mos • **Academic:** Ed=N, Eng=S • **Work Field:** 212 • **MPSMS:** 587 • **Aptitudes:** G3, V4, N4, S4, P3, Q4, K3, F3, M4, E5, C5 • **Temperaments:** T • **Physical:** V=G, H=N, L=S, W, H • **Work Env:** I • **Salary:** 2 • **Outlook:** 5

LENS EXAMINER (optical goods) • D.O.T. #716.687-022 • OES #83005 • INSPECTOR-IN-PROCESS; LENS ASSORTER; LENS INSPECTOR. Performs one or more of following tasks to inspect glass and plastic lens blanks for defects: Removes paint and wax from blank with solvent and razor blade. Rinses blank in water. Examines surface and edges to detect defects, such as pits, scratches, and chips. Inspects blanks with polariscope to detect annealing defects, such as bubbles, striae, fire cracks, or seal checks. Marks defective blanks for rework or salvage, using crayon or pencil. Sorts blanks by grade and type of defect. Weighs lens blanks and records weight for determining shipping costs. May pack blanks in cartons for shipping. May gage blanks [LENS-BLANK GAGER (optical goods)]. May assemble nonprecision optical element into mechanical housing. • **GED:** R2, M1, L2 • **SVP:** 3-6 mos • **Academic:** Ed=N, Eng=N • **Work Field:** 211 • **MPSMS:** 603 • **Aptitudes:** G3, V4, N5, S4, P3, Q5, K4, F4, M5, E5, C4 • **Temperaments:** M, T • **Physical:** V=G, H=N, L=L, H • **Work Env:** I • **Salary:** 3 • **Outlook:** 3

LUMBER SORTER (woodworking) • D.O.T. #922.687-074 • OES #83005 • LUMBER PULLER; RACKER; SEPARATOR. Sorts lumber or veneer according to grade markings and size: Removes boards from sorting table, handtruck, or conveyor and stacks in piles or places boards in rack or on conveyor, according to grade marking, length, or use of boards. Gages length of boards by sight, by marks on sorting table, or by measuring with rule. May remove defective lumber from conveyor and stack lumber according to grade, length, species, and color. May hand-stamp grade markings on boards or stack of lumber. May be designated according to sorting equipment used as RACKER (plan. mill; saw mill). • **GED:** R1, M1, L1 • **SVP:** 2-30 days • **Academic:** Ed=N, Eng=N • **Work Field:** 011, 211 • **MPSMS:** 450 • **Aptitudes:** G4, V4, N4, S3, P4, Q4, K4, F4, M3, E5, C4 • **Temperaments:** M, T • **Physical:** V=G, H=N, L=M, W, H • **Work Env:** I • **Salary:** 4 • **Outlook:** 3

METAL-FINISH INSPECTOR (any ind.) • D.O.T. #703.687-014 • OES #83005 • Inspects surfaces of sheet metal articles, such as refrigerator and freezer cabinets, or automobile bodies for burs, dings, scratches, laminated metal, or other surface defects prior to painting or porcelainizing: Rubs gloved hand over surfaces and examines workpiece. Marks defects for repair, using knowledge of acceptable metal finish standards and specifications. Records recurring defects on inspection report and submits report to quality control department for action. Records and submits daily inspection report. • **GED:** R3, M2, L2 • **SVP:** 6 mos-1 yr • **Academic:** Ed=N, Eng=N • **Work Field:** 211 • **MPSMS:** 556, 583 • **Aptitudes:** G3, V3, N4, S4, P3, Q4, K4, F4, M3, E5, C5 • **Temperaments:** R, T • **Stress:** T • **Physical:** V=G, H=N, L=L, H • **Work Env:** I • **Salary:** 3 • **Outlook:** 2

PAINT-SPRAY INSPECTOR (any ind.) • D.O.T. #741.687-010 • OES #83005 • FINISH INSPECTOR. Inspects finishes, such as paint, lacquer, or porcelain enamel on items, such as household appliances, automobiles, toys, or bicycles while items move along production line or in inspection bays to ascertain conformance to standards: Examines workpiece for scale, cracks, shade variances, or unpainted areas. Marks workpiece with symbol to indicate defective area and type of repair needed. Records number and type of units rejected and reasons for rejection. May mark other defects, such as loose welds and loose or missing parts. May inspect decals, identification markings or stenciling on workpiece to ensure specified location, clarity, and alinement. • **GED:** R2, M1, L2 • **SVP:** 2-30 days • **Academic:** Ed=N, Eng=N • **Work Field:** 211 • **MPSMS:** 550, 590 • **Aptitudes:** G4, V4, N4, S4, P3, Q4, K4, F4, M3, E5, C3 • **Temperaments:** R, T • **Stress:** T • **Physical:** V=G, H=N, L=L, H • **Work Env:** I • **Salary:** 2 • **Outlook:** 2

PHOTO CHECKER AND ASSEMBLER (photofinish.) • D.O.T. #976.687-014 • OES #83005 • CHECKER; INSPECTOR. Inspects, assembles, and packs mounted or unmounted negatives, color film transparencies, and photographic prints: Examines items for natural color shading, density, sharpness of image, or identifying numbers, using lighted viewing screen. Marks defective prints, using grease pencil and standardized symbols to indicate nature of defect and corrective action required in reprinting. Removes defects, such as dust and smudges from prints, using brush, cloth, and cleaning fluid. Packages and labels satisfactory prints and negatives. Maintains daily production records. May cut negatives and prints from roll, using cutting machine. May be designated according to type of print inspected as COLOR PRINT INSPECTOR (photofinish.); FULL-ROLL INSPECTOR (photofinish.); MOUNTING INSPECTOR (photofinish.); REVERSAL-PRINT INSPECTOR (photofinish.); May inspect prints for tears, dirt, scum, or other surface defects preparatory to mounting and be designated TAKE-DOWN INSPECTOR (photofinish.). • **GED:** R3, M1, L1 • **SVP:** 3-6 mos • **Academic:** Ed=N, Eng=N • **Work Field:** 041, 211, 221 • **MPSMS:** 867 • **Aptitudes:** G3, V4, N4, S3, P3, Q4, K4, F3, M3, E4, C2 • **Temperaments:** J, T • **Physical:** V=L, H=N, L=S, H • **Work Env:** I • **Salary:** 2 • **Outlook:** 2

PHOTOFINISHING LABORATORY WORKER (photofinish.) • D.O.T. #976.687-018 • OES #58028 • FILM NUMBERER; FILM SORTER; PRICER-BAGGER; PROOF SORTER; RACKER; REPRINT SORTER; SORTER-PACKER. Performs any combination of following tasks to prepare and disseminate negatives, positives, and prints in photofinishing laboratory: Reads instructions written on orders, and examines contents of orders to ascertain size, type and number of pieces. Sorts orders according to size and type processing required. Pastes identifying label on customer order envelopes and transfer bags to ensure matching of orders subsequent to processing. Removes finished work from transfer bags subsequent to processing and computes customer charges according to pricelist. Inserts order in bag or envelope, and staples bag together or seals envelope. Pastes address label on bag or envelope. May convey orders between departments. May distribute supplies to other photofinishing workers. May maintain records of order sorted and packaged. • **GED:** R2, M2, L2 • **SVP:** 30 days-3 mos • **Academic:** Ed=N, Eng=N • **Work Field:** 041, 221 • **MPSMS:** 568 • **Aptitudes:** G4, V4, N4, S4, P4, Q3, K4, F3, M3, E5, C4 • **Temperaments:** V • **Physical:** V=L, H=N, L=L, H • **Work Env:** I • **Salary:** 2 • **Outlook:** 4

PRINT INSPECTOR (pottery & porc.) • D.O.T. #774.687-018 • OES #83005 • DECORATOR INSPECTOR. Inspects printed decoration on pottery and porcelain ware: Compares printed decoration and quality of workmanship of ware with sample and discards misprinted ware. Returns salvageable pieces for rework. Rubs ware with abrasive stone or wet sponge to remove paint spots. • **GED:** R3, M1, L1 • **SVP:** 3-6 mos • **Academic:** Ed=N, Eng=N • **Work Field:** 211 • **MPSMS:** 535 • **Aptitudes:** G3, V4, N3, S3, P3, Q4, K3, F4, M3, E5, C3 • **Temperaments:** M, R, T • **Stress:** T • **Physical:** V=G, H=N, L=L, W, H • **Work Env:** I • **Salary:** 3 • **Outlook:** 2

WEIGHER, PRODUCTION (any ind.) • D.O.T. #929.587-014 • OES #83005 • Weighs out specified quantities of materials for use in production processes, using balance, platform, or floor scales: Places material on scales and adds or removes portions of material to obtain specified weight. May read work order or follow formula to determine types and quantities of materials to weigh. May record weight of materials used for production records, or maintain perpetual inventory of materials used and on hand. May dump materials in prescribed sequence into chute or hopper or onto conveyor belt. May transfer weighed materials to production or storage areas, using hand-or-power truck. May sort weighed materials into designated bins or containers, according to weight or type. May be designated according to type of scale used or material weighed as BATCH WEIGHER (chem.); COMPOUNDER (rubber reclaim.); FEATHER GRADER (house furn.); OPERATOR, SCALES (plastics mat.); RUBBER COMPOUNDER (insulated wire; plastics mat.; rubber goods; rubber tire & tube); SHADOW-GRAPH-WEIGHT OPERATOR (sports equip.); STOCK MIXER (felt goods; textile); WEIGHER-AND-CHARGER (floor covering, n.e.c.). May weigh plant products as part of packing process and be designated WEIGHER, PACKING (any ind.). • **GED:** R2, M1, L2 • **SVP:** 30 days-3 mos • **Academic:** Ed=N, Eng=N • **Work Field:** 212 • **MPSMS:** 490, 510, 610 • **Aptitudes:** G4, V4, N4, S4, P4, Q4, K4, F4, M3, E5, C5 • **Temperaments:** R, T • **Stress:** T • **Physical:** V=L, H=N, L=L, W, H • **Work Env:** I • **Salary:** 3 • **Outlook:** 3

06.04 Elemental Work: Industrial

Workers in this group feed, off bear, or tend machines and equipment, or do manual work. They perform routine, uncomplicated work that requires little training or experience. They also assist other, more skilled workers. They work in a factory setting.

✔ **What kind of work would you do?**

Your work activities would depend upon your specific job. For example, you might:

- use a handtruck to move supplies to workers on an assembly line.
- smooth wooden furniture posts using sandpaper and steel wool.
- tend a machine that seals paper cartons.
- carry containers and materials and wash mixing vats to assist syrup-mixer in making table syrup.

- tend machine that cuts continuous strips of zipper into certain lengths.
- clean and polish plated products with a cloth and liquid cleanser.
- tend a machine that rivets metal furniture parts together.
- sort and bag scrap leather to salvage usable pieces.

✔ What skills and abilities do you need for this kind of work?
To do this kind of work, you must be able to:

- follow instructions carefully.
- adjust to doing the same thing over and over.

- move or lift heavy objects.
- pay attention to safety rules when working around machinery.

✔ How do you know if you would like or could learn to do this kind of work?
The following questions may give you clues about yourself as you consider this group of jobs.

- Have you taken an industrial arts course? Would you like to work in an industrial setting?

- Have you helped a worker install, repair, or build something in your home? Can you follow directions?
- Have you helped a custodian at school or church?

✔ How can you prepare for and enter this kind of work?
Occupations in this group usually require education and/or training extending from a short demonstration to over three months, depending upon the specific kind of work. Most jobs in this group do not require specific training before employment. Brief on-the-job training is often provided at the time of employment or as work assignments are changed. Industrial arts or shop courses provide useful background for jobs in this group.

✔ What else should you consider about these jobs?
Many people accept jobs in this group as their first full-time employment. As they develop experience and skills, they may advance to other jobs in the work setting.

Work activities change very little from day to day because workers must follow set procedures. It is important that workers follow strict safety rules when working around machines.

If you think you would like to do this kind of work, look at the job titles listed on the following pages.

GOE: 06.04.02 Machine Work, Metal & Plastics, Elemental

BENDING-MACHINE OPERATOR 2 (any ind.) • D.O.T. #617.685-010 • OES #91321 • Tends machine that bends metal structural shapes, such as bars, strips, rods, angles, and tubes to specified angle or contour: Positions workpiece against end stops. Locks holding clamp and guide clamp onto workpiece. Lubricates workpiece with oil. Pulls lever or depresses pedal to activate turntable which draws workpiece through guide clamp and around die block until stopped by plug stops. May slide mandrel into tubing instead of using guide clamp. May perform such fabricating tasks as flaring tube ends, using tube flarer, or cutting metal stock to length, using power shears or saws. May attach specified die to machine, using wrench. May be designated according to type of stock bent as ROD-BEND-ING-MACHINE OPERATOR (any ind.) II; TUBE-BENDING-MA-CHINE OPERATOR (any ind.) II or type of machine tended as TWO-STAGE, STEEL-BENDER ANNEALER (sports equip.). • **GED:** R2, M1, L1 • **SVP:** 30 days-3 mos • **Academic:** Ed=N, Eng=N • **Work Field:** 134 • **MPSMS:** 554 • **Aptitudes:** G4, V4, N4, S4, P4, Q5, K4, F4, M3, E4, C5 • **Temperaments:** R, T • **Stress:** T • **Physical:** V=L, H=N, L=M, W, H • **Work Env:** I, N • **Salary:** 3 • **Outlook:** 2

BUFFING-MACHINE TENDER (any ind.) • D.O.T. #603.665-010 • OES #91117 • Tends automatic buffing machine that buffs parts, such as automobile hardware or trim: Loads parts on holding fixture of revolving table that is preset for regular indexing and starts machine. Removes buffed parts and examines them for surface defects. Places buffed parts into shallow tray and covers them with cardboard separators. Informs BUFFER (any ind.) I or BUFFING-LINE SET-UP WORKER (any ind.) of buffing defects. May maintain count of buffed parts and parts which do not meet specifications. • **GED:** R2, M1, L1 • **SVP:** 2-30 days • **Academic:** Ed=N, Eng=N • **Work Field:** 051 • **MPSMS:** 550 • **Aptitudes:**

G4, V4, N4, S4, P4, Q4, K4, F4, M3, E5, C5 • **Temperaments:** R, T • **Stress:** T • **Physical:** V=L, H=N, L=L, H • **Work Env:** I, N • **Salary:** 2 • **Outlook:** 2

DRILL-PRESS OPERATOR, PRODUCTION (mach. shop) • D.O.T. #606.685-026 • OES #91117 • Tends one or more previously setup single-spindle or multiple-spindle drill presses to perform machining operations, such as drilling, tapping, reaming, or countersinking holes in metal on production basis: Lifts workpiece manually or with hoist and clamps it in drilling jig or holding fixture on machine table. Starts machine, engages automatic feed or pulls lever or turns handwheel to lower cutting tool into workpiece. Turns valve to direct flow of coolant and cutting oils over cutting area. Observes operation and releases lever or turns handwheel to raise cutting tool from workpiece when operation is completed. Inspects or measures machined work piece for conformance to specifications and shop standards, using instruments, such as fixed gages, templates, or micrometers. Changes worn cutting tools, using wrenches. May machine plastics or other nonmetallic materials. • **GED:** R2, M1, L1 • **SVP:** 2-30 days • **Academic:** Ed=N, Eng=N • **Work Field:** 053 • **MPSMS:** 540 • **Aptitudes:** G4, V4, N4, S4, P4, Q4, K3, F4, M4, E5, C5 • **Temperaments:** R, T • **Stress:** T • **Physical:** V=G, H=N, L=M, W, H • **Work Env:** I, N • **Salary:** 4 • **Outlook:** 3

DRUM STRAIGHTENER 1 (any ind.) • D.O.T. #619.685-034 • OES #91321 • CONTAINER REPAIRER; DEDENTER. Tends machine equipped with rolls to remove dents and reform bodies and chimes (rims) of metal barrels or drums: Slides open end of barrel over cylinder in machine. Pulls lever to lower rolls against barrel. Starts machine that rotates barrel against rolls to reform or straighten side, bead, or chime. Raises rolls and slides barrel off cylinder. • **GED:** R2, M1, L1 • **SVP:** 2-30 days • **Academic:** Ed=N, Eng=N • **Work Field:** 559 • **MPSMS:** 559 • **Aptitudes:** G4, V4, N5, S4, P4, Q5, K4, F4, M3, E5, C5 • **Temperaments:** R, T • **Stress:** T • **Physical:** V=L, H=N, L=H, W, S, H • **Work Env:** I, N • **Salary:** 2 • **Outlook:** 3

EMBOSSER (any ind.) • D.O.T. #583.685-030 • OES #92998 • EMBOSSING-CALENDER OPERATOR; EMBOSSING-MACHINE OPERATOR; ROLLER EMBOSSER. Tends machine that imparts raised design or finish on cloth, coated fabrics, or plastic sheeting, by means of heat and pressure from engraved steel rollers: Adjusts automatic device that regulates heat or turns valve to admit steam to rollers. Slides bar through center of material roll and lifts it onto machine feed brackets. Threads material between rollers and laps end onto takeup tube. Starts machine and moves controls to adjust speed, pressure of rollers, and tension of material. Observes material as it passes through machine to prevent seams, rolled selvages, or trash from damaging rollers. May guide material by hand. May verify temperature of roller, using pyrometer. May sew cuts of cloth together, using portable sewing machine. May be designated according to material embossed as SILK-CREPE-MACHINE OPERATOR (textile). May tend machine that imparts artificial graining, size, trademark, or other designs to sweatbands and be designated SWEATBAND-DECORATING-MACHINE OPERATOR (hat & cap). Important variables may be indicated by trade names of machine used. • **GED:** R2, M1, L2 • **SVP:** 30 days-3 mos • **Academic:** Ed=N, Eng=N • **Work Field:** 032, 192 • **MPSMS:** 420 • **Aptitudes:** G3, V4, N4, S4, P3, Q4, K4, F4, M3, E4, C5 • **Temperaments:** R, T • **Stress:** T • **Physical:** V=L, H=N, L=M, W, H • **Work Env:** I, N • **Salary:** 2 • **Outlook:** 2

GRAINER, MACHINE (any ind.) • D.O.T. #652.686-014 • OES #98502 • Feeds metal or simulated wood panels, sheets, or strips into machine that prints lines resembling natural wood grain. Holds or moves irregularly shaped pieces against printing roller to impart grainlike appearance. Stacks grained pieces for further processing or assembly into articles, such as television cabinets, automobile dashboards, and office furniture. • **GED:** R2, M1, L1 • **SVP:** 2-30 days • **Academic:** Ed=N, Eng=N • **Work Field:** 191 • **MPSMS:** 459, 556 • **Aptitudes:** G3, V4, N4, S3, P3, Q5, K3, F3, M3, E5, C4 • **Temperaments:** R • **Stress:** T • **Physical:** V=L, H=N, L=M, W, H • **Work Env:** I • **Salary:** 2 • **Outlook:** 2

LATHE OPERATOR, PRODUCTION (mach. shop) • D.O.T. #604.685-026 • OES #91117 • AUTOMATIC-LATHE OPERATOR; ENGINE-LATHE OPERATOR, PRODUCTION; TURRET-LATHE OPERATOR, PRODUCTION. Tends one or more previously setup lathes, such as turret lathes, engine lathes, and chucking machines, to perform one or series of repetitive operations, such as turning, boring, threading, or facing, of metal workpieces according to specifica tions on production basis: Lifts workpiece manually or with hoist, and positions and secures it between lathe centers, in chuck or in holding fixture, using wrench, or places it in auto matic loading mechanism. Starts machine and turns handwheels to feed tools to workpiece, or engages automatic feed. Observes machining operation to detect malfunction or excessive tool wear. Verifies conformance of machined work to specifications, using fixed gages, calipers, and micrometers. Changes worn tools, using wrenches. May machine plastics or other non-metallic materials. May be designated by type of machine tended or operation per formed as KNURLING-MACHINE OPERATOR (pen & pencil); TAPPER (clock & watch) I. • **GED:** R2, M2, L2 • **SVP:** 30 days-3 mos • **Academic:** Ed=N, Eng=N • **Work Field:** 055 • **MPSMS:** 566 • **Aptitudes:** G4, V4, N4, S4, P3, Q4, K3, F3, M3, E5, C5 • **Temperaments:** M, R, T • **Stress:** T • **Physical:** V=G, H=N, L=M, W, H • **Work Env:** I, N • **Salary:** 4 • **Out look:** 4

MACHINE OPERATOR 2 (any ind.) • D.O.T. #619.685-062 • OES #91714 • Tends fabricating machines, such as cutoff saws, shears, brakes, ironworker, straightening press, and punch, to cut, shape, bend metal plates, sheets, and structural shapes: Sets stops or guides to specified length as indicated by scale, rule, or template. Positions workpiece, manually or using hoist, against stops or alines layout marks with die or blade. Pushes button or depresses treadle to activate machine. Measures work, using rule or template. Removes burs, sharp edges, rust, or scale, using file, hand grinder, or wire brush. Performs other shop tasks, such as oiling machines, dies, or workpieces, assisting machine operators to set up machine, and stacking, marking, packing, and transporting finished pieces. May tend other machines, such as drill press, spot welder, or rivet ing machines. May tend breaks, rolls, shears, riveting, and spot- welding machines to join together sheet metal and be designated SHEET-METAL PRODUCTION WORKER (any ind.). • **GED:** R2, M2, L2 • **SVP:** 30 days-3 mos • **Academic:** Ed=N, Eng=N • **Work Field:** 054, 134 • **MPSMS:** 554 • **Aptitudes:** G4, V4, N4, S3, P4, Q4, K4, F4, M3, E4, C5 • **Temperaments:** R, T • **Stress:** T • **Physical:** V=L, H=N, L=M, W, H • **Work Env:** I, N, R • **Salary:** 4 • **Outlook:** 3

MAGNETIC-TAPE WINDER (electronics) • D.O.T. #726.685-010 • OES #92998 • CARTRIDGE LOADER. Tends machines that wind magnetic tape into reels or cassette hubs for use in communication and control equipment, instruments, and computers: Positions tape supply reels or cassette hubs on letoff and windup spindles of tape winding machines. Loops tape from supply reels through machine guides and into blank reels or hubs. Turns knob of footage counter devices that automatically cut tape and stop machines when specified length of tape has been wound into blank reels or hubs. Pushes switches to start individual machines and removes wound reels or hubs when machines stop. Scrapes detected surface defects from tape with knife. Splices tape ends together to form continuous loops in cassettes, using bench splicer. Inserts filled and blank hubs into cassettes and attaches covers. Packs reels and cassettes into containers and labels containers for shipment. • **GED:** R2, M1, L1 • **SVP:** 2-30 days • **Academic:** Ed=N, Eng=N • **Work Field:** 163 • **MPSMS:** 589 • **Aptitudes:** G4, V4, N4, S4, P4, Q4, K3, F3, M3, E4, C5 • **Temperaments:** R, T • **Stress:** T • **Physical:** V=L, H=N, L=L, H • **Work Env:** I • **Salary:** 3 • **Outlook:** 3

NIBBLER OPERATOR (any ind.) • D.O.T. #615.685-026 • OES #91321 • Tends machine that cuts metal plates, sheets, or structural shapes into specified radial or irregular shapes by action of reciprocating cutting knives or punches: Positions and clamps specified cutter or punch into ram and bed of machine. Turns thumbscrews to adjust depth of stroke to thick ness of metal. Turns handwheel to set specified distance between cutter or punch and center point of turntable or fixtures, using built-in scale or rule. Clamps guide and drive rollers over workpiece. Depresses pedal which activates ram and feed rollers to cut or punch along radius. Guides workpiece manually along cutting lines or template to cut irregular shapes. May lay out guidelines onto workpiece by tracing from template. May drill center hole into workpiece, using portable drill. May bevel edges of steel plates, using portable pneumatic nibbler. • **GED:** R2, M2, L2 • **SVP:** 30 days-3 mos • **Academic:** Ed=N, Eng=N • **Work Field:** 054 • **MPSMS:** 554 • **Aptitudes:** G3, V4, N4, S3, P4, Q5, K4, F4, M3, E4, C5 • **Temperaments:** R, T • **Stress:** T • **Physical:** V=L, H=N, L=M, W, H • **Work Env:** I, N, R • **Salary:** 4 • **Outlook:** 2

POWER-PRESS TENDER (any ind.) • D.O.T. #617.685-026 • OES #91321 • Tends power press that cuts, punches, or stamps articles of various sizes and shapes from sheets or blocks of materials: Positions or clamps sheet or block on machine bed or in holding fixture to obtain maximum cuts from each sheet. Turns on power and depresses pedal or moves lever that rotates or forces cutting die through sheet or block to obtain article of specified size and shape. May bolt or clamp die to machine, using handtools. May tend machine that automatically feeds and positions material under die for cutting. May examine parts for defects and discard parts not meeting specifications. May be designated according to kind of article as CORK BLOCKER (cork prod.); GASKET CUT-TER (cork prod.), or according to type of machine tended as PUNCH-PRESS OPERATOR (any ind.) IV; STAMPING- PRESS OPERATOR (any ind.); TURNING-MACHINE OPERATOR (any ind.). • **GED:** R2, M1, L1 • **SVP:** 30 days-3 mos • **Academic:** Ed=N, Eng=N • **Work Field:** 055, 134 • **MPSMS:** 556 • **Aptitudes:** G4, V4, N4, S4, P4, Q4, K3, F4, M3, E4, C5 • **Temperaments:** R • **Stress:** T • **Physical:** V=L, H=N, L=L, H • **Work Env:** I, N • **Salary:** 3 • **Outlook:** 2

PRODUCTION-MACHINE TENDER (nut & bolt) • D.O.T. #619.365-010 • OES #92198 • Tends one or more automatic machines to head, trim, roll-thread, slot, or tap metal stock to produce nuts, bolts, or other fasteners: Feeds machine by filling hoppers or loading coiled steel on reel and threading end of coil through feed rolls. Starts machine and observes operation. Measures parts, using rule or fixed gage, to determine conformance to specifications. Frees stock jammed in feed mechanism, using rod. Stops machine and notifies supervisor when machine malfunctions or parts do not conform to specifications. Installs and adjusts cutting tools on machine, using wrench and rule. May be designated according to type of machine tended as TAPPING-MACHINE OPERA TOR, AUTOMATIC (nut & bolt). • **GED:** R2, M2, L2 • **SVP:** 2-30 days • **Academic:** Ed=N, Eng=N • **Work Field:** 057, 134 • **MPSMS:** 540, 555 • **Aptitudes:** G4, V4, N4, S4, P4, Q4, K4, F4, M3, E5, C5 • **Temperaments:** R, T • **Stress:** T • **Physical:** V=L, H=N, L=M, W, H • **Work Env:** I, N • **Salary:** 3 • **Outlook:** 2

PUNCH-PRESS OPERATOR II (any ind.) • D.O.T. #615.685-030 • OES #91321 • Tends one or more power presses that trim, punch, shape, notch, draw, or crimp metal or plastic stock between preset dies: Places workpiece against fixtures or stops on machine bed, positions it under die, or threads roll of metal into jig and starts press. May inspect parts visually or with fixed gauges. May tend press that imprints identifying information on product or product part. May be designated according to product worked on as FIN-MACHINE OPERATOR (auto. mfg.); SPRUE-CUTTING-PRESS OPERATOR (found.); or according to type of press as MULTIPLE-PUNCH-PRESS OPERATOR (any ind.) II; or function of machine as COLD-TRIMMING-PRESS OPERATOR (forging); DRAW-PRESS OPERATOR (any ind.) II; FORMING-PRESS OP-ERATOR (any ind.) II; HOT-TRIMMING-PRESS OPERATOR (forging). May tend press that pierces pivot holes and reduces watch hands to specified thickness and be designated SWAGER AND PIERCER (clock & watch). May tend press that cuts fiberglass panels or sheets to produce printed circuit boards and be designated PUNCH-PRESS OPERATOR, PRINTED CIRCUIT BOARDS (electronics). • **GED:** R2, M1, L1 • **SVP:** 30 days-3 mos • **Academic:** Ed=N, Eng=N • **Work Field:** 134 • **MPSMS:** 541, 554, 607 • **Aptitudes:** G4, V4, N4, S4, P4, Q4, K4, F4, M3, E4, C5 • **Temperaments:** R • **Stress:** T • **Physical:** V=L, H=N, L=M, W, H • **Work Env:** I • **Salary:** 4 • **Outlook:** 4

SCROLL-MACHINE OPERATOR (struct. & ornam. metal work) • D.O.T. #616.685-062 • OES #92198 • Tends machine that forms metal stock, such as bars, rods, squares, tubing, and wire, into coils or ornamental scrolls: Positions and clamps specified scroll (die) into bed of machine. Threads work piece through drag roll and clamps roll to center of die. Starts machine that turns die to draw workpiece along contour of die as vertical rod pushes workpiece into center of die, forming scroll or coil. May tend power shear or cutoff saw to cut stock to specified length. May insert leather strip along edge of die to protect finish of workpiece. May bend workpieces along edge of die manually. • **GED:** R2, M1, L1 • **SVP:** 2-30 days • **Academic:** Ed=N, Eng=N • **Work Field:** 135 • **MPSMS:** 554 • **Aptitudes:** G4, V4, N4, S4, P4, Q5, K4, F4, M4, E5, C5 • **Temperaments:** R, T • **Stress:** T • **Physical:** V=L, H=N, L=M, W, H • **Work Env:** I, N • **Salary:** 4 • **Outlook:** 3

TOOL DRESSER (any ind.) • D.O.T. #601.682-010 • OES #92198 • DRILL-SHARPENER OPERATOR. Operates compressed-air or steam-driven machine to sharpen large drills, such as rock drills, used in construction, mining, quarrying, and well-drilling: Places cutting end of drill in forge to heat cutting edge to increase malleability. Inserts heated drill into die space on machine. Starts hammering action of die to shape cutting edge of drill. Stops machine and removes edged drill. Tempers drill by heating it in forge and quenching it in water, brine, or oil. • **GED:** R3, M2, L2 • **SVP:** 6 mos-1 yr • **Academic:** Ed=N, Eng=N • **Work Field:** 134 • **MPSMS:** 552 • **Aptitudes:** G3, V4, N4, S4, P3, Q4, K3, F4, M3, E5, C4 • **Temperaments:** M, T • **Physical:** V=L, H=N, L=M, W, H • **Work Env:** I • **Salary:** 3 • **Outlook:** 2

TURRET-PUNCH-PRESS OPERATOR, TAPE-CONTROL (any ind.) • D.O.T. #615.685-042 • OES #91321 • Tends tape-controlled turret or hydraulic-powered punch press that automatically positions indexing table, selects punch, and punches holes, or layout marks in metal sheets, plates, strips, or bars: Positions and clamps workpiece against fixtures or to specified point on built-in scale. Threads tape through electronic reader to specified position. Starts machine and observes operation. May verify first piece, using rule and plug gages. May open chucks, using wrench to replace worn or broken punches and dies. • **GED:** R2, M2, L2 • **SVP:** 30 days-3 mos • **Academic:** Ed=N, Eng=N • **Work Field:** 134 • **MPSMS:** 554 • **Aptitudes:** G4, V4, N4, S4, P4, Q5, K4, F3, M4, E5, C5 • **Temperaments:** R, T • **Stress:** T • **Physical:** V=L, H=N, L=H, W, H • **Work Env:** I, N, R • **Salary:** 4 • **Outlook:** 4

WIRE-DRAWING-MACHINE TENDER (wire) • D.O.T. #614.685-026 • OES #91321 • Tends machines that weld ends of wire together to form continuous coil and draw wire through dies to reduce wire to specified diameter: Lifts reels of wire onto spindle of floor stand, manually, or using hoist. Welds ends of wire together, using welding machine. Smooths weld to diameter of wire, using abrasive cloth. Threads wire around tension rollers, and through reducing dies, and fastens end of wire to spindle. Starts machine that draws wire through dies and around takeup reel. May verify diameter of drawn wire, using micrometer. May record production. • **GED:** R2, M1, L2 • **SVP:** 30 days-3 mos • **Academic:** Ed=N, Eng=N • **Work Field:** 081, 135 • **MPSMS:** 557 • **Aptitudes:** G4, V4, N4, S4, P3, Q4, K4, F4, M3, E5, C5 • **Temperaments:** R, T • **Stress:** T • **Physical:** V=L, H=N, L=M, W, H • **Work Env:** I, W, N • **Salary:** 3 • **Outlook:** 3

GOE: 06.04.03 Machine Work, Wood, Elemental

ARTIFICIAL-LOG-MACHINE OPERATOR (fuel briquettes) • D.O.T. #569.685-010 • OES #92314 • Tends machines that automatically compress sawdust into artificial fuel logs and extrude them onto conveyors: Starts machines. Observes compression marks on finished logs to insure that logs are compressed according to specifications, and turns thumbscrews to adjust degree of compression. Weighs sample log periodically to verify conformance to standards. May replace sawdust-feeding screws, using screwdriver and wrenches. May add chemicals to sawdust to produce log that burns colored flame. • **GED:** R2, M2, L1 • **SVP:** 3-6 mos • **Academic:** Ed=N, Eng=N • **Work Field:** 135 • **MPSMS:** 459 • **Aptitudes:** G3, V4, N4, S4, P3, Q4, K4, F4, M3, E4, C4 • **Temperaments:** R, T • **Stress:** T • **Physical:** V=L, H=N, L=L, W, H • **Work Env:** I, N, R • **Salary:** 3 • **Outlook:** 2

BUZZSAW OPERATOR (any ind.) • D.O.T. #667.685-026 • OES #92308 • Tends circular cutoff saw that custom cuts fireplace and stove fuel wood from random lengths of wood: Places wood on carriage and adjusts guides to specified length. Starts saw and moves carriage past saw to cut wood to length. Advances wood to carriage guides and repeats moving carriage past saw. • **GED:** R2, M1, L1 • **SVP:** 30 days-3 mos • **Academic:** Ed=N, Eng=N • **Work**

Field: 056 • **MPSMS:** 452 • **Aptitudes:** G4, V4, N4, S4, P4, Q5, K3, F4, M3, E4, C5 • **Temperaments:** R, T • **Stress:** T • **Physical:** V=L, H=N, L=H, W, C, S, H • **Work Env:** O, N, R • **Salary:** 5 • **Outlook:** 2

CHAIN OFFBEARER (planing mill) • D.O.T. #669.686-018 • OES #98502 • Pulls lumber from moving conveyor coming from ripsaw, resaw, planer, trimmer, and grading tables, and slides and stacks lumber on piles, according to grade marked on each piece. May push buttons to start and stop conveyor and deposit waste material onto slasher conveyor for waste recovery. May be designated according to condition of lumber removed from conveyor as DRY-CHAIN OFFBEARER (sawmill); GREEN-CHAIN OFFBEARER (plan. mill; sawmill), or may be designated according to machine from which lumber is conveyed as PLANER-CHAIN OFFBEARER (plan. mill). • **GED:** R2, M1, L1 • **SVP:** 2-30 days • **Academic:** Ed=N, Eng=N • **Work Field:** 011 • **MPSMS:** 452 • **Aptitudes:** G4, V4, N5, S4, P4, Q5, K4, F4, M3, E4, C5 • **Temperaments:** R • **Stress:** T • **Physical:** V=L, H=N, L=H, W, H • **Work Env:** B, N, R • **Salary:** 4 • **Outlook:** 2

LATHE SPOTTER (veneer & plywood) • D.O.T. #663.686-022 • OES #98999 • Positions veneer blocks (logs cut to length) between spindles of veneer lathe, using electric hoist: Measures diameter of block to locate and mark center, using ruler. Examines end of log to detect rot, cracks, and splits. Selects chuck of minimum diameter according to size and condition of block, and places block on lathe spindle. Secures hooks to ends of block, activates hoist to suspend block between lathe chucks, and signals VENEER-LATHE OPERATOR (basketry; veneer & plywood) to press chucks into block. Removes knots, dirt, and other foreign matter, using ax, steam hose, and pick. May assist in chaining lathe knives. May operate lathe-charging-machine, from console, to position logs for automatic loading into rotary veneer lathe. May be designated according to type of log peeled as FLITCH HANGER (veneer & plywood). • **GED:** R2, M1, L1 • **SVP:** 30 days-3 mos • **Academic:** Ed=N, Eng=N • **Work Field:** 054 • **MPSMS:** 453 • **Aptitudes:** G4, V4, N3, S3, P4, Q4, K3, F4, M3, E5, C5 • **Temperaments:** R • **Stress:** T • **Physical:** V=L, H=N, L=H, W, S, H • **Work Env:** I, N • **Salary:** 5 • **Outlook:** 2

POWER-BARKER OPERATOR (paper & pulp) • D.O.T. #669.485-010 • OES #92998 • Tends machine that removes bark and dirt from logs by one of following methods: (1) Starts conveyor to move logs from pond to drum of barking machine. Moves lever to activate chains or start drum revolving to tumble logs and knock off bark. Turns valve to regulate water spray that removes chips and dirt from log. Breaks up log jams in drum, using peavey or pike pole and chain hoist. (2) Moves lever to activate kicker arms that kick log into machine cradle. Turns controls that start log rotating between toothed gears that remove bark from log, and regulates and directs pressurized water jet to remove loose bark and dirt. (3) Turns levers to control movement and centering of log in jet ring and to regulate pressure of water jets. Starts conveyors that carry logs from barking machine to saw deck. May be designated according to machine operated as DRUM-BARKER OPERATOR (paper & pulp); HYDRAULIC-BARKER OPERATOR (paper & pulp; sawmill); RING-BARKER OPERATOR (sawmill). • **GED:** R3, M2, L2 • **SVP:** 30 days-3 mos • **Academic:** Ed=N, Eng=N • **Work Field:** 031 • **MPSMS:** 452 • **Aptitudes:** G3, V4, N4, S3, P4, Q5, K3, F4, M3, E4, C5 • **Temperaments:** R, T • **Stress:** T • **Physical:** V=L, H=N, L=L, H • **Work Env:** B, N, R • **Salary:** 5 • **Outlook:** 2

GOE: 06.04.04 Machine Work, Paper, Elemental

BAG-MACHINE OPERATOR (paper goods) • D.O.T. #649.685-014 • OES #92998 • BAG-MAKING-MACHINE OPERATOR. Tends machine that automatically measures, prints, cuts, folds, and glues, or seals plain or wax papers, polyethylene film, or cellophane to form bags: Threads materials from parent roll through guides and rollers to cutters, gluer, printer, folding device, or electric sealer. Starts machine, observes operation, and adjusts machine to insure uniform shearing, printing, folding, gluing, or sealing of continuous roll of material into finished bags. May insert shaft into core of parent roll and secure with steel collars, using handtools, and mount roll onto machine, using hoist. May be designated according to material processed as CELLOPHANE-

BAG-MACHINE OPERATOR (paper goods); POLYETHYLENE-BAG-MACHINE OPERATOR (paper goods); WAXED-BAG-MACHINE OPERATOR (paper goods). • **GED:** R2, M1, L1 • **SVP:** 30 days-3 mos • **Academic:** Ed=N, Eng=N • **Work Field:** 102 • **MPSMS:** 474 • **Aptitudes:** G4, V4, N4, S3, P4, Q5, K4, F4, M3, E5, C4 • **Temperaments:** M, T • **Physical:** V=L, H=N, L=M, W, H • **Work Env:** I, N • **Salary:** 2 • **Outlook:** 3

BINDERY WORKER (print. & pub.) • D.O.T. #653.685-010 • OES #92546 • BINDERY OPERATOR; TABLE WORKER. Tends one or more machines and performs any combination of following duties involved in binding books, magazines, pamphlets, directories, and catalogs: Punches holes in paper sheets, using gang-punch press. Stamps numbers on sheets by hand or machine. Creases and compresses signatures prior to affixing covers, using handpress. Fastens sheets or signatures together, using hand or machine stapler, or tends machine that inserts wire or plastic binding strips into punched holes to fasten pages and covers together. Feeds covers, signatures, and sheets into various machines for stitching, folding, ruling, roughing, indexing, and gluing operations. Removes, stacks, and packs printed material in various stages of completion as it accumulates on delivery table of machines. Examines stitched or bound books and magazines to ascertain that pages or signatures are bound in numerical or folio order according to sample copy, and for such defects as imperfect bindings, ink spots, and torn, loose, and uneven pages. Inserts illustrated pages or extra sheets into catalogs or directories by machine. Places paper jackets on acceptable books. Applies goldleaf, silver leaf, or metallic foil on book covers. Stamps designs or lettering on covers, using stamping machine. • **GED:** R2, M2, L2 • **SVP:** 3-6 mos • **Academic:** Ed=N, Eng=N • **Work Field:** 062, 134 • **MPSMS:** 486 • **Aptitudes:** G4, V4, N4, S4, P3, Q4, K3, F3, M3, E5, C4 • **Temperaments:** R • **Stress:** T • **Physical:** V=L, H=N, L=L, H • **Work Env:** I, N • **Salary:** 3 • **Outlook:** 2

CARTON-FORMING-MACHINE OPERATOR (any ind.) • D.O.T. #641.685-022 • OES #92998 • Tends machine that forms and glues flat blanks or continuous roll of paperboard into finished cartons for packing merchandise: Adjusts forming bars to accommodate size of box to be shaped, using handtools. Fills glue pots with adhesive and positions rollers to dispense glue onto paperboard. Loads feeding magazine with blanks, or mounts roll of paper on machine standard and threads paper to feeding mechanism and starts machine. Observes machine operation to detect malfunction. May load machine with roll of waxed, parchment, or other paper used to line cartons. May mount roll of metal strip to form cutting edge on cartons. May stamp data with handstamp or attach automatic stamping device. • **GED:** R2, M1, L1 • **SVP:** 2-30 days • **Academic:** Ed=N, Eng=N • **Work Field:** 062, 063 • **MPSMS:** 475 • **Aptitudes:** G4, V4, N4, S4, P4, Q5, K4, F4, M4, E5, C5 • **Temperaments:** R, T • **Stress:** T • **Physical:** V=L, H=N, L=M, W, H • **Work Env:** I, N • **Salary:** 2 • **Outlook:** 3

CARTON-FORMING-MACHINE TENDER (paper goods) • D.O.T. #641.685-026 • OES #92998 • Tends one or more machines that automatically cut, glue, and form cartons or caddies from pasteboard rolls for kitchen, penny, and book matches: Rolls pasteboard to machine, positions on let-off rack, and threads end of pasteboard strip into machine. Starts and observes machine operation and corrects malfunctions, such as improper forming, glue flow, or pasteboard tension, using handtools. Observes finished cartons as they drop from forming machine into rotating hopper, then into gravity feed chute, to prevent jamming. May lift tote box of finished cartons and dump into feed hopper. • **GED:** R2, M1, L1 • **SVP:** 2-30 days • **Academic:** Ed=N, Eng=N • **Work Field:** 102 • **MPSMS:** 475 • **Aptitudes:** G4, V4, N4, S4, P4, Q4, K4, F4, M3, E5, C5 • **Temperaments:** R • **Stress:** T • **Physical:** V=L, H=N, L=H, W, H • **Work Env:** I, N • **Salary:** 2 • **Outlook:** 3

FOLDING-MACHINE FEEDER (print. & pub.) • D.O.T. #653.686-014 • OES #98502 • Feeds printed sheets into fold guide of machine that automatically folds and cuts them into signatures (pages) for binding. Notifies FOLDING-MACHINE SETTER (print. & pub.) of machine malfunction. • **GED:** R1, M1, L1 • **SVP:** 2-30 days • **Academic:** Ed=N, Eng=N • **Work Field:** 062 • **MPSMS:** 486 • **Aptitudes:** G4, V4, N5, S4, P4, Q5, K4, F4, M3, E5, C5 • **Temperaments:** R • **Stress:** T • **Physical:** V=L, H=N, L=L, H • **Work Env:** I, N • **Salary:** 2 • **Outlook:** 2

GOE: 06.04.05 Machine Work, Fabric & Leather, Elemental

ADHESIVE-BANDAGE-MACHINE OPERATOR (per. protect. & med. device) • D.O.T. #692.685-014 • OES #92998 • Tends machine that automatically makes adhesive bandages from cloth and plastic material: Positions specified rolls of materials on machine spindles and locks them in place with plates and set-screws to prevent unrolling. Threads materials through rollers in prescribed sequence. Starts machine that cuts materials to required length, affixes gauze to cloth or plastic tape, fastens crinoline strips to ends, seals completed bandage in paper wrapper, and deposits it on conveyor belt or in bin for subsequent packing. Observes machine during operations to detect jamming, twisted materials, or malfunctions and makes minor adjustments to correct faults. • **GED:** R2, M1, L2 • **SVP:** 30 days-3 mos • **Academic:** Ed=N, Eng=N • **Work Field:** 054, 062 • **MPSMS:** 604 • **Aptitudes:** G3, V4, N4, S3, P3, Q4, K3, F3, M3, E5, C3 • **Temperaments:** R, T • **Stress:** T • **Physical:** V=L, H=N, L=L, H • **Work Env:** I • **Salary:** 2 • **Outlook:** 2

BUTTONHOLE-AND-BUTTON-SEWING-MACHINE OPERATOR (garment) • D.O.T. #786.685-042 • OES #92717 • Tends semiautomatic sewing machines that cut and stitch buttonholes and sew buttons and other fasteners to garments: Pours buttons into hopper for automatic feeding into holding clamp of sewing machine or places buttons and fasteners in clamp. Turns knobs to adjust stitching and cutting mechanisms of machine to set size of buttonholes according to garment styles. Positions garment, garment parts, buttons, or fasteners under needle, and starts short-cycle sewing machine that cuts and stitches button holes in garment or parts or sews buttons and fasteners to garment. Cuts threads, using scissors. • **GED:** R2, M1, L2 • **SVP:** 2-30 days • **Academic:** Ed=N, Eng=N • **Work Field:** 171 • **MPSMS:** 440 • **Aptitudes:** G4, V4, N4, S4, P3, Q5, K4, F4, M3, E4, C4 • **Temperaments:** R, T • **Stress:** T • **Physical:** V=L, H=N, L=L, H • **Work Env:** I, N • **Salary:** 2 • **Outlook:** 2

CEMENTER, MACHINE APPLICATOR (boot & shoe) • D.O.T. #690.686-018 • OES #98502 • Applies cement onto separate shoe parts prior to joining, performing any of following operations: (1) Feeds parts between pressure and cementing rollers of machine and removes cemented parts. (2) Holds part against cement-covered roller or revolving brush that applies cement to part. (3) Feeds parts between rollers that move parts under spray nozzle. (4) Holds parts under machine applicator nozzle. May fill cement reservoir. May join parts together. May be designated according to parts coated as BINDING CEMENTER, FRENCH CORD (boot & shoe); BOTTOM CEMENTER (boot & shoe) I; CEMENTER FOR FOLDING, MACHINE (boot & shoe); CHANNEL CEMENTER, INSOLE, MACHINE (boot & shoe); CHANNEL CEMENTER, OUTSOLE, MACHINE (boot & shoe); HEEL CEMENTER, MACHINE (boot & shoe). Additional titles: HEEL-LINING PASTER (boot & shoe); PLATFORM CEMENTER (boot & shoe); POTDEVIN CEMENTER, MACHINE (boot & shoe); OUTSOLE CEMENTER, MACHINE (boot & shoe); RAND CEMENTER (boot & shoe); TUCK-AND-INSOLE CEMENTER (boot & shoe); UPPER-LINING CEMENTER (boot & shoe); WELT-STRIP CEMENTER, MACHINE (boot & shoe). • **GED:** R1, M1, L1 • **SVP:** 2-30 days • **Academic:** Ed=N, Eng=N • **Work Field:** 063 • **MPSMS:** 522 • **Aptitudes:** G4, V4, N5, S4, P4, Q5, K4, F4, M3, E4, C5 • **Temperaments:** R • **Stress:** T • **Physical:** V=L, H=N, L=L, H • **Work Env:** I • **Salary:** 3 • **Outlook:** 3

EYELET-MACHINE OPERATOR (any ind.) • D.O.T. #699.685-018 • OES #92998 • BUTTON BRADDER; BUTTON CLAMPER; BUTTON RIVETER; EYELET MAKER; EYELET RIVETER; EYELETTER; GROMMET-MACHINE OPERATOR; GROMMET MAKER. Tends machine that crimps eyelets, grommets, snaps, buttons, or similar fasteners to material, such as cloth, canvas, paper, plastic, leather, or rubber to reinforce holes, attach fasteners, or to attach parts, by any of following methods: (1) Pours metal fasteners into hopper of machine. Positions material under machine head according to marking on machine bed or material. Depresses pedal to start machine that feeds fastener from fastener holder, lowers ram to force fastener through material and to crimp fastener edges into material, and material into position for suc-

ceeding fasteners. (2) Lays fastener in holder of machine. Positions material over fastener according to marks on material or pre-punched holes in material. Depresses pedal to lower machine ram which forces edges of fastener into material. (3) Inserts bottom section of two piece fastener in slot in bed of machine and top section into hole in material. Depresses pedal to lower ram and rivet both sections together. May locate and mark positions of fastener on material. May tend machine that also punches holes for fasteners. May be designated according to type of fastener used as BLIND EYELETTER (boot & shoe); BLIND HOOKER (boot & shoe); according to part attached as BUCKLE-ATTACHING-MACHINE OPERATOR (hat & cap); HOOK-AND-EYE ATTACHER, MACHINE (garment); or according to part made, as CHIN-STRAP MAKER (hat & cap); SWEATBAND MAKER (hat & cap). Additional titles: BUTTON-ATTACHING-MACHINE OPERATOR (any ind.); CAP-AND-STUD-MACHINE OPERATOR (rubber goods); FASTENER ATTACHER (any ind.); GRIPPER ATTACHER (any ind.); SNAP ATTACHER (any ind.); SNAP-FASTENER-MACHINE OPERATOR (any ind.). • **GED:** R2, M1, L1 • **SVP:** 2-30 days • **Academic:** Ed=N, Eng=N • **Work Field:** 062 • **MPSMS:** 430, 446, 522 • **Aptitudes:** G4, V4, N4, S4, P4, Q4, K3, F3, M3, E4, C5 • **Temperaments:** R • **Stress:** T • **Physical:** V=L, H=N, L=L, W, H • **Work Env:** I • **Salary:** 3 • **Outlook:** 2

FASTENER-SEWING-MACHINE OPERATOR (any ind.) • D.O.T. #787.685-010 • OES #92721 • HOOK-AND-EYE-SEWING-MACHINE OPERATOR. Tends one or more machines that automatically sew fasteners, such as hooks and eyes, to continuous strips of binding tape. Fills hopper of machine with fasteners. May measure hook and eye spacing, using ruler, and examine tape for defects, such as misplaced stitching or discoloration. May tend machine equipped with button sewing adaptor to stitch metal tips to corners of umbrella covers and be designated TIPPING-MACHINE OPERATOR (umbrella). Performs duties as described under SEWING-MACHINE OPERATOR, AUTOMATIC (any ind.). • **GED:** R2, M1, L2 • **SVP:** 2-30 days • **Academic:** Ed=N, Eng=N • **Work Field:** 171 • **MPSMS:** 618 • **Aptitudes:** G4, V4, N4, S4, P3, Q4, K3, F3, M3, E4, C4 • **Temperaments:** R, T • **Stress:** T • **Physical:** V=L, H=N, L=L, H • **Work Env:** I, N • **Salary:** 2 • **Outlook:** 2

FOLDER-SEAMER, AUTOMATIC (any ind.) • D.O.T. #787.685-014 • OES #92721 • Tends machine that folds, stitches, and cuts cloth into lengths to form articles, such as bags, finger-buffs, pillowcases, straps, or tie-backs. May turn handwheel or thumb-screw to adjust tension on roll of cloth. May tend machine that sews string into hem of draw-string bag and be designated SHEET CUTTER (tex. bag). May be designated according to article fabricated as BAG-MAKING-MACHINE TENDER (tex. bag); BELT-LOOP MAKER (garment); PILLOWCASE SEWER, AUTOMATIC (house furn.); SEWER-AND-CUTTER, FINGER-BUFF MATERIAL (tex. prod., n.e.c.); STRAP-MACHINE OPERATOR, AUTOMATIC (garment); TIE-BACK SEWER, AUTOMATIC (house furn.). Performs duties as described under SEWING-MACHINE OPERATOR, AUTOMATIC (any ind.). • **GED:** R2, M1, L2 • **SVP:** 30 days-3 mos • **Academic:** Ed=N, Eng=N • **Work Field:** 054, 171 • **MPSMS:** 421, 439, 449 • **Aptitudes:** G4, V4, N4, S4, P4, Q4, K4, F3, M3, E5, C4 • **Temperaments:** R, T • **Stress:** T • **Physical:** V=L, H=N, L=L, H • **Work Env:** I, N • **Salary:** 2 • **Outlook:** 2

GLOVE TURNER AND FORMER, AUTOMATIC (glove & mitten) • D.O.T. #583.686-018 • OES #98502 • TURNER AND FORMER, AUTOMATIC. Feeds or offbears machine that turns, shapes, and presses gloves: Dumps box of gloves into bin over machine. Pulls each glove over turner tubes to feed machine. Removes turned, shaped (formed), and pressed glove from conveyor. Examines gloves for defective pressing or punched-out finger tips and pairs gloves without defects. • **GED:** R1, M1, L1 • **SVP:** 2-30 days • **Academic:** Ed=N, Eng=N • **Work Field:** 032, 062 • **MPSMS:** 449 • **Aptitudes:** G4, V4, N4, S4, P4, Q4, K2, F3, M2, E5, C5 • **Temperaments:** R • **Stress:** T • **Physical:** V=L, H=N, L=L, H • **Work Env:** I, N • **Salary:** 2 • **Outlook:** 2

HEMMER, AUTOMATIC (house. furn.) • D.O.T. #787.685-018 • OES #92721 • SIDE HEMMER. Tends one or more automatic sewing machines that hem continuous lengths of material: Threads material through feed rollers, machine guides, and hem-folding attachment. Starts machine that sews continuous hem and stops as material runs out or thread breaks. When tending machine that sews hemstitch, may be designated GANG-HEM-STITCHING-MACHINE OPERATOR (house furn.). May be designated according to product hemmed as CURTAIN HEMMER, AUTOMATIC (house furn.); DRAPERY HEMMER, AUTOMATIC (house furn.); RUFFLING HEMMER, AUTOMATIC (house furn.). Performs duties as described under SEWING-MACHINE OPERATOR, AUTOMATIC (any ind.). • **GED:** R3, M1, L1 • **SVP:** 30 days-3 mos • **Academic:** Ed=N, Eng=N • **Work Field:** 171 • **MPSMS:** 420 • **Aptitudes:** G4, V4, N4, S4, P4, Q5, K4, F3, M3, E5, C4 • **Temperaments:** R, T • **Stress:** T • **Physical:** V=L, H=N, L=L, H • **Work Env:** I • **Salary:** 2 • **Outlook:** 3

PLEATING-MACHINE OPERATOR (any ind.) • D.O.T. #583.685-082 • OES #92998 • Tends one or more machines that fold and press pleats into materials, such as cloth, paper, plastic, or parchment: Turns thumbscrews or levers to adjust pleating knife according to width specified for pleats and for distance specified between pleats, and to adjust temperature of pressing rollers. Places roll of material on rod at entry end of machine and draws end of fabric through guides, pleating knife, and between heated pressing rollers. Laps end of fabric around takeup roll or guides end into box. Starts machine and observes pleating for conformance to specifications. May thread material between layers of paper to prevent heated rollers from scorching material. May tend machine that attaches waxed thread to edges of material to hold pleats in fabric. • **GED:** R3, M2, L3 • **SVP:** 3-6 mos • **Academic:** Ed=N, Eng=S • **Work Field:** 032, 062 • **MPSMS:** 420, 439, 474 • **Aptitudes:** G4, V4, N4, S4, P4, Q4, K3, F4, M3, E5, C5 • **Temperaments:** R • **Stress:** T • **Physical:** V=G, H=N, L=L, W, H • **Work Env:** I • **Salary:** 3 • **Outlook:** 2

PRESSER, MACHINE (any ind.) • D.O.T. #363.682-018 • OES #92728 • BUCK PRESSER; FINISHER, MACHINE; FLATTENING-MACHINE OPERATOR; IRONER, MACHINE; PRESSING MACHINE OPERATOR; PRESS OPERATOR; STEAM FLATTENER; STEAM-HEATED-POWER-PRESS OPERATOR; STEAM PRESSER; STEAM-PRESS OPERATOR. Operates pressing machine to smooth surfaces, flatten seams, or shape articles, such as garments, drapes, slipcovers, and hose, in manufacturing or dry cleaning establishments: (1) Spreads articles to be pressed on buck (padded table) of machine. Pulls pressing head onto article and depresses pedals or presses buttons to lock head, admit steam into buck, and exhaust steam. Rearranges articles on buck and repeats process until pressing is completed. (2) Positions garment on buck and depresses pedal to lower jump iron onto garment and to apply pressure. Pushes lever to release steam from iron. Pushes iron, attached to movable arm, back and forth over garment and shifts garment under iron until pressed. May operate two presses simultaneously, positioning articles on one press while another article is steamed on other press. May finish pressed articles, using hand or puff-irons. May tend machine that presses and shapes articles, such as shirts, blouses, and sweaters [PRESSER, FORM (any ind.)]. May be designated according to article pressed as COAT PRESSER (any ind.); PANTS PRESSER (any ind.); or according to fabric pressed as SILK PRESSER (garment) II; or according to part of garment pressed as ARMHOLE-AND-SHOULDER OFF-PRESSER (garment); LINING PRESSER (clean., dye., & press.); or according to type of machine used as JUMP-IRON-MACHINE PRESSER (garment). Additional Titles: BAND PRESSER (garment); COLLAR FUSER (garment); FORM-PRESS OPERATOR (clean., dye., & press.; laund.); LEGGER-PRESS OPERATOR (clean., dye., & press.; laund.); MUSHROOM-PRESS OPERATOR (clean., dye., & press.; laund.); PUFF-IRON OPERATOR (clean., dye., & press.; laund.) II; SHIRT FINISHER (garment); TOPPER-PRESS OPERATOR (clean., dye., & press.; laund.); TOPPER-PRESS OPERATOR, AUTOMATIC (clean., dye., & press.; laund.); VEST-FRONT PRESSER (garment); WASH-CLOTHES PRESSER (clean., dye., & press.); WOOL PRESSER (clean., dye., & press.). • **GED:** R2, M1, L1 • **SVP:** 2-30 days • **Academic:** Ed=N, Eng=N • **Work Field:** 032 • **MPSMS:** 420, 440, 906 • **Aptitudes:** G4, V4, N5, S4, P4, Q5, K3, F3, M3, E4, C5 • **Temperaments:** R • **Stress:** T • **Physical:** V=L, H=N, L=L, W, S, H • **Work Env:** I, H, W, R • **Salary:** 2 • **Outlook:** 2

SEWING-MACHINE OPERATOR, SPECIAL EQUIPMENT

(matt. & bedspring) • D.O.T. #689.685-118 • OES #92721 • Tends machine that automatically stitches designs to decorate mattress covers and to hold padding in place: Places spools of thread on spindles and draws ends through guides, tensions, and needle eyes. Inserts bobbin in shuttle and draws thread through slot in shuttle wall. Clamps covering material and padding in frame and places frame in rack under sewing head of machine. Bolts pilot pattern plate on platform beneath frame, using wrench. Places pilot or guide bar extending from frame in guide channels of pilot pattern and starts machine. May move pilot or guide bar by hand. May attach framed cover to pulleys that draw it away from machine as cover is stitched, and guide cover under presser foot by hand to stitch design. • **GED:** R2, M1, L2 • **SVP:** 2-30 days • **Academic:** Ed=N, Eng=N • **Work Field:** 171 • **MPSMS:** 464 • **Aptitudes:** G4, V4, N4, S4, P3, Q5, K4, F4, M3, E5, C4 • **Temperaments:** R, T • **Stress:** T • **Physical:** V=G, H=N, L=L, H • **Work Env:** I • **Salary:** 2 • **Outlook:** 3

SPREADER, MACHINE (any ind.) • D.O.T. #781.685-010 • OES #92998 • LAYER UP. Tends machine that spreads cloth in successive layers on table to prepare cloth for cutting: Positions bolt of cloth on carriage of machine, turns handle to aline edge of cloth with marks on table, threads cloth end through feed rollers, and clamps cloth to end of table. Starts machine that automatically spreads cloth in even layers as it moves back and forth over table, or pushes machine along track over cutting table. Inspects cloth as it is spread to detect defects, such as dye shadings and holes. Cuts out defects with hand shears. Laps ends of cloth at points marked on table. Straightens edges and smooths layers of cloth with hands. Turns handwheel to adjust feeding mechanism of machine according to weight of cloth. Cuts cloth from roll, using hand shears. May mark pattern outlines on top ply of cloth [MARKER (any ind.) I]. May cut spread cloth [CUTTER, MACHINE (any ind.) I]. • **GED:** R2, M1, L1 • **SVP:** 30 days-3 mos • **Academic:** Ed=N, Eng=N • **Work Field:** 054, 062 • **MPSMS:** 420 • **Aptitudes:** G4, V4, N4, S4, P3, Q4, K3, F3, M3, E5, C3 • **Temperaments:** R, T • **Stress:** T • **Physical:** V=L, H=N, L=H, W, H • **Work Env:** I • **Salary:** 2 • **Outlook:** 2

STRIP-CUTTING-MACHINE OPERATOR (any ind.) • D.O.T. #686.685-066 • OES #92705 • SLICER; SLITTER. Tends machine that cuts rolls of textile material into narrow rolls of specified width: Lifts roll of material onto machine bar and hammers wedge into core of roll to secure roll to bar. Turns handwheel to move rotary blade into cutting position, following markings on calibrated scale to obtain specified cutting width. Starts machine that rotates blade and roll in opposite directions. Presses lever to move rotating blade forward and cut through roll of material. Releases lever and positions blade for subsequent cut. Removes narrow rolls of material from machine and stacks rolls on shelf according to width. When cutting rolls of bias material into narrow widths, is designated BIAS-BINDING CUTTER (trim. & embroid.). May be designated according to product cut as BAND-CUTTING-MACHINE OPERATOR (garment; knit goods); BINDING CUTTER (garment; textile); FACING-CUTTING-MACHINE OPERATOR (garment); HANDKERCHIEF CUTTER (textile); PIPING-CUTTING-MACHINE OPERATOR (garment); SUSPENDER CUTTER (garment); TAPE-CUTTING-MACHINE OPERATOR (garment; trim. & embroid.). • **GED:** R2, M1, L1 • **SVP:** 2-30 days • **Academic:** Ed=N, Eng=N • **Work Field:** 054 • **MPSMS:** 420 • **Aptitudes:** G4, V4, N4, S4, P4, Q4, K3, F4, M3, E5, C4 • **Temperaments:** R, T • **Stress:** T • **Physical:** V=L, H=N, L=H, W, H • **Work Env:** I • **Salary:** 3 • **Outlook:** 2

SURGICAL-DRESSING MAKER (per. protect. & med. device) • D.O.T. #689.685-130 • OES #92998 • PAD MAKER. Tends machine that automatically cuts and folds gauze backing around absorbent cotton to form surgical dressings: Starts machine that cuts gauze and absorbent cotton to size, folds gauze around cotton in prescribed manner to form surgical pad, and ejects pad. Examines ejected pads for size, folding of gauze and defects in absorbent cotton. May pack specified quantity of pads in bags or cartons. • **GED:** R2, M1, L1 • **SVP:** 2-30 days • **Academic:** Ed=N, Eng=N • **Work Field:** 054, 062 • **MPSMS:** 604 • **Aptitudes:** G4, V4, N4, S4, P4, Q4, K4, F4, M4, E4, C4 • **Temperaments:** R, T • **Stress:** T • **Physical:** V=L, H=N, L=L, H • **Work Env:** I • **Salary:** 2 • **Outlook:** 2

TACKING-MACHINE OPERATOR (any ind.) • D.O.T. #787.685-042 • OES #92721 • Tends machine that sews pattern of stitches, such as circles or rectangles, to attach parts, such as labels or straps, reinforce seam ends, or decorate articles. May be designated according to parts tacked as BAND TACKER (any ind.); BOW TACKER (hat & cap) II; LABEL TACKER (house furn.); or according to stitches sewn as BAR TACKER (any ind.). May attach reinforcing pieces to finger tips of gloves and be designated TIP SEWER (glove & mit.). May tend machine that tacks lead wire, thermostats, and line cord onto fabric body and be designated TACKER (elec. equip.). Performs duties as described under SEWING-MACHINE OPERATOR, AUTOMATIC (any ind.). • GED: R2, M1, L1 • SVP: 30 days-3 mos • Academic: Ed=N, Eng=N • Work Field: 171 • MPSMS: 420, 430, 440 • Aptitudes: G4, V4, N4, S4, P3, Q4, K3, F3, M3, E4, C4 • Temperaments: R, T • Stress: T • Physical: V=G, H=N, L=S, H • Work Env: I, N • Salary: 1 • Outlook: 3

GOE: 06.04.06 Machine Work, Textiles, Elemental

BEAM-WARPER TENDER, AUTOMATIC (asbestos prod.) • D.O.T. #681.685-018 • OES #92705 • BEAM WARPER; SECTION BEAMER; SECTION WARPER; TRICOT-WARPER TENDER; WARPER TENDER. Tends high-speed warpers that automatically wind yarn in parallel sheets onto beams I preparatory to dyeing, weaving, or knitting: Examines yarn in creel to ensure that it corresponds to warp pattern sheet specifications for number of yarn ends, arrangement of yarn in creel, yarn size, and color. Requests CREELER (any ind.) to alter creel setup to correspond with warp pattern sheet. Pulls yarn ends from packages mounted on creel, through drop wires, and tension, measuring, and spreading devices, and fastens ends to empty warp beam to thread machine. Sets yardage counter to record amount of yarn wound and starts machine. Observes operation to detect yarn breaks which cause machine to stop. Turns beam back to point of break, locates and ties broken ends, and cuts excess yarn, using scissors. Stops machine when specified yardage is wound on beam, cuts yarn, and places gummed tape over ends or loops ends together to secure ends. May wrap beam with paper. May doff full beams and set in empties [BEAM RACKER (textile)]. May replace empty yarn packages [CREELER (any ind.)]. • GED: R2, M1, L1 • SVP: 3-6 mos • Academic: Ed=N, Eng=N • Work Field: 163 • MPSMS: 411 • Aptitudes: G4, V4, N4, S4, P3, Q4, K3, F3, M3, E5, C4 • Temperaments: R, T • Stress: T • Physical: V=L, H=N, L=L, H • Work Env: I, N • Salary: 3 • Outlook: 2

CLOTH DOFFER (textile) • D.O.T. #689.586-010 • OES #98502 • CLOTH HANDLER; LOOM DOFFER; SHORT PIECE HANDLER. Removes rolls of cloth from looms or knitting machines and trucks cloth to storage: Stops machine when roll has sufficient yardage as indicated by yardage clock or mark on cloth. Cuts cloth, using scissors, and places cloth roll on handtruck. Places empty takeup beam I on bracket of machine, attaches cloth to beam, and restarts machine. Writes identifying information, such as lot and style number, on ticket and attaches ticket to cloth roll. Trucks cloth to storage or inspection department. May weigh and keep record of cloth beams doffed. • GED: R2, M1, L2 • SVP: 2-30 days • Academic: Ed=N, Eng=N • Work Field: 011, 164 • MPSMS: 420 • Aptitudes: G4, V4, N4, S4, P4, Q4, K4, F4, M3, E4, C4 • Temperaments: R • Stress: T • Physical: V=L, H=N, L=H, W, S, H • Work Env: I, N • Salary: 3 • Outlook: 2

KNITTING-MACHINE OPERATOR (knit goods) • D.O.T. #685.665-014 • OES #92705 • KNITTER; KNITTER, MACHINE. Tends one or more machines that knit fabrics, garment parts, or other articles from yarn: Creels machine and ties end of yarn to yarn in machine or threads yarn through guides, tension springs, stop-motion devices, and yarn carrier or needles, using hook. Starts machine and laps end of knitted goods around takeup roller. Observes knitting to detect yarn breaks, exhausted yarn packages, and knitting defects. Ties broken yarn ends, replaces exhausted yarn packages, and notifies KNITTING-MACHINE FIXER (hosiery; knit goods) of mechanical defects. Cuts knitted fabric, using scissors, and doffs roll of cloth from machine. May mark ticket to indicate number of holes in knitted goods. May replace defective needles, using needle pliers or wrench. May weigh roll of knitted goods and record weight. May oil machine. May be designated according to type of machine tended as CIRCULAR KNITTER (knit goods); FLAT KNITTER (knit goods). May be designated according to type of fabric knitted as JERSEY KNITTER (knit goods); PILE-FABRIC KNITTER (knit goods); RIB-CLOTH KNITTER (knit goods), or garment part as COLLAR KNITTER (knit goods); CUFF KNITTER (knit goods). • GED: R2, M1, L2 • SVP: 30 days-3 mos • Academic: Ed=N, Eng=N • Work Field: 165 • MPSMS: 424 • Aptitudes: G4, V4, N4, S4, P3, Q4, K4, F3, M3, E5, C4 • Temperaments: M, R, T • Stress: T • Physical: V=L, H=N, L=M, W, H • Work Env: I, N • Salary: 3 • Outlook: 2

PICKING-MACHINE OPERATOR (any ind.) • D.O.T. #680.685-082 • OES #92998 • BLENDER OPERATOR; SHREDDER; WILLOWER. Tends picking machine that opens or shreds and fluffs raw or used materials, such as wool, kapok, foam rubber, or hair to facilitate further processing: Cuts open bales of raw materials. Starts machine and deposits handfuls of raw material on feeding apron that conveys material into picking or shredding rollers. Observes machine to detect clogged rollers. Stops machine, and strips fiber from rollers, using knife, scissors, or hands. May spray raw material with oil emulsion. May be designated according to material processed as HAIR-PICKING-MACHINE OPERATOR (felt goods; furn.); TOW-PICKER OPERATOR (furn.); WOOL-PICKER OPERATOR (textile). • GED: R2, M1, L1 • SVP: 2-30 days • Academic: Ed=N, Eng=N • Work Field: 161 • MPSMS: 410 • Aptitudes: G4, V4, N5, S4, P4, Q5, K4, F4, M4, E5, C5 • Temperaments: R • Stress: T • Physical: V=L, H=N, L=M, W, S, H • Work Env: I, N • Salary: 2 • Outlook: 3

YARN WINDER (any ind.) • D.O.T. #681.685-154 • OES #92705 • BACK WINDER; PACKAGE WINDER; REWINDER; SPOOLER; WINDER; WINDING-MACHINE OPERATOR. Tends machine that winds strands of yarn from bobbins, cakes, pirns, and other yarn packages into packages specified for further processing, shipment, or storage: Places supply packages on spindles or holders. Threads ends of yarn from each package through guides and tension device and attaches them to takeup package. Observes winding units to detect breaks in yarn and ties broken ends by hand or with knotter. Stops machine or winding unit and doffs packages. Inspects yarn for defects. Reports malfunction of machine to MACHINE FIXER (textile). May weigh yarn package or keep production records. May tend machine that winds yarn through emulsion-filled trough or against paraffin disk to soften or strengthen yarn. May be designated according to package wound or supply package used as BOBBIN WINDER (textile); CAKE WINDER (textile); or according to material wound as WORSTED WINDER (textile). When winding continuous filament yarn to or from packages used in throwing processes, is known as REDRAW OPERATOR (textile). When rewinding tangled or short lengths of yarn, is known as SALVAGE WINDER (textile). Important variables may be indicated by trade names or machines used. Additional Titles: BRASS-BOBBIN WINDER (tex. prod., n.e.c.); CONE SPOOLER (any ind.); CONE WINDER (textile); COP WINDER (asbestos prod.; textile); MUFF WINDER (textile); PIECE HAND (textile); PIRN WINDER (textile); QUILL WINDER (narrow fabrics); SPOOL WINDER (textile); TAILING-MACHINE OPERATOR (textile); TUBE WINDER (any ind.); TWINE WINDER (cord. & twine). • GED: R2, M1, L1 • SVP: 30 days-3 mos • Academic: Ed=N, Eng=N • Work Field: 163 • MPSMS: 411 • Aptitudes: G4, V4, N4, S4, P4, Q4, K4, F3, M3, E4, C4 • Temperaments: R, T • Stress: T • Physical: V=L, H=N, L=M, W, S, H • Work Env: I, N • Salary: 3 • Outlook: 2

GOE: 06.04.07 Machine Work, Rubber, Elemental

DESIGN PRINTER, BALLOON (rubber goods) • D.O.T. #651.685-014 • OES #92543 • Tends cylinder press that prints designs and lettering on balloons: Rolls preinflated balloon against printing plate on revolving cylinder press that prints design. Pours ink and solvent in trough of cylinder press and adjusts ink flow. Cleans machine rollers, plates, and troughs with solvent and rag when color changes are specified. May inflate balloon on air nozzle, aline and press one or more inked block dies against balloon, deflate balloon, and place balloon in box. • **GED:** R2, M1, L1 • **SVP:** 2-30 days • **Academic:** Ed=N, Eng=N • **Work Field:** 191 • **MPSMS:** 519 • **Aptitudes:** G4, V4, N4, S4, P3, Q4, K3, F3, M3, E5, C4 • **Temperaments:** R • **Stress:** T • **Physical:** V=L, H=N, L=L, W, H • **Work Env:** I • **Salary:** 3 • **Outlook:** 2

RUBBER CUTTER (rubber goods) • D.O.T. #559.685-158 • OES #92944 • Tends machine that cuts bales of crude rubber into pieces: Removes wired wooden wrapping or metal straps, using cutters. Loads bale into machine bed, using electric hoist or pulls bale from chute, using hook. Moves lever to release hydraulic ram that pushes bale through stationary knives. May remove burlap covering from bales and truck them to machine. May push bales onto bed of cutting machine. May pull layers of smoked or crepe rubber apart, using hook. • **GED:** R1, M1, L1 • **SVP:** 2-30 days • **Academic:** Ed=N, Eng=N • **Work Field:** 054 • **MPSMS:** 519 • **Aptitudes:** G4, V4, N5, S4, P4, Q5, K4, F4, M3, E5, C5 • **Temperaments:** R • **Stress:** T • **Physical:** V=L, H=N, L=H, W, H • **Work Env:** I • **Salary:** 2 • **Outlook:** 2

GOE: 06.04.08 Machine Work, Stone, Clay & Glass, Elemental

CERAMIC CAPACITOR PROCESSOR (electronics) • D.O.T. #590.684-010 • OES #92998 • Processes substrate, electrode, and termination materials to form ceramic monolithic capacitors: Adds or evaporates ingredients from mixture to maintain specified viscosity. Grinds designated mixture to specified grain size, using mill and micron gage. Casts ceramic material into sheets, using automatic tape casting equipment. Cuts sheets into blanks. Inspects and sorts blanks according to thickness and quality, using thickness gage and magnifying device. Applies electrode material onto blanks, using silk screen printing equipment. Stacks printed blanks in sequence and presses, using laminating press to form laminate. Cuts laminate into chips, using automatic cutter. Loads chips onto boat and fires in kiln to fuse laminated material. Applies termination paste to designated ends of fused chip manually or using automatic dipping equipment. Fuses termination material to chip, using automatic oven. May polish finished monolithic capacitor chips, using tumbler. May attach lead wires and encase capacitors in epoxy material. • **GED:** R2, M2, L2 • **SVP:** 30 days-3 mos • **Academic:** Ed=N, Eng=N • **Work Field:** 147 • **MPSMS:** 587 • **Aptitudes:** G4, V4, N4, S4, P3, Q5, K3, F3, M3, E5, C4 • **Temperaments:** R, T • **Stress:** T • **Physical:** V=L, H=N, L=S, H • **Work Env:** I • **Salary:** 3 • **Outlook:** 4

COREMAKER, MACHINE 1 (foundry) • D.O.T. #518.685-014 • OES #91911 • CORE STRIPPER. Tends turnover draw-type coremaking machine that makes sand cores for use in casting metal: Clamps core box over die on front table of machine, and partly fills core box with sand from overhead chute, or by using hands or shovel. Depresses pedal to open compressed-air valve that causes table to rise and fall with series of jolts, to compress sand in box. Positions reinforcing wires in sand, fills box with sand, and repeats jolting. Tamps sand into core box with hand or pneumatic tool. Removes excess sand from top of core box with hands or straightedge and clamps metal plate to top of box. Pulls lever to roll front table over and deposit box top down on rear table. Pushes rear table down to withdraw core from core box and lifts core from machine. • **GED:** R2, M1, L2 • **SVP:** 30 days-3 mos • **Academic:** Ed=N, Eng=N • **Work Field:** 132 • **MPSMS:** 567 • **Aptitudes:** G4, V4, N5, S4, P3, Q5, K3, F4, M3, E4, C5 • **Temperaments:** R, T • **Stress:** T • **Physical:** V=L, H=N, L=M, W, H • **Work Env:** I, N • **Salary:** 4 • **Outlook:** 2

CRUSHER TENDER (any ind.) • D.O.T. #570.685-022 • OES #92965 • CRUSHER OPERATOR; ROLL ATTENDANT; PRIMARY-CRUSHER OPERATOR. Tends any of several types of crushers that size coal, rock, salt, or ore for industrial use or for further processing: Moves levers to regulate flow of materials to and from conveyors, chutes, pumps, or storage bins. Starts crusher and prods, breaks, or discards lumps to prevent plugging, using bar, sledge hammer, or jackhammer. Adjusts equipment, such as screens, conveyors, and fans, to control or vary size or grade of product, or to maintain uniform flow of materials. Cleans and lubricates equipment. May keep record of materials processed. • **GED:** R2, M2, L1 • **SVP:** 30 days-3 mos • **Academic:** Ed=N, Eng=N • **Work Field:** 142 • **MPSMS:** 340, 350 • **Aptitudes:** G4, V4, N4, S4, P3, Q4, K4, F4, M3, E5, C4 • **Temperaments:** R • **Stress:** T • **Physical:** V=L, H=N, L=M, W, H • **Work Env:** I, N • **Salary:** 2 • **Outlook:** 3

LENS-FABRICATING-MACHINE TENDER (optical goods) • D.O.T. #716.685-022 • OES #92965 • Tends one or more bench machines that generate, grind, edge, or polish ophthalmic lenses and precision optical elements: Mounts blocked element in machine holding device. Verifies machine settings or adjusts machines for variables, such as speed, machining time, and flow rate of abrasive or coolant. Starts machine that automatically generates, grinds, polishes, or edges optical element. Removes element after specified machining time, rinses element in water, and measures to verify specified dimensions of element, using micrometer, caliper, dial gage, and shadowgraph. May de-block and clean element in degreasing tank. May be designated according to fabricating process or type lens fabricated as CONTACT-LENS-CURVE GRINDER (optical goods); CONTACT-LENS-EDGE BUFFER (optical goods); FUSION-JUNCTURE GRINDER (optical goods); LENS-EDGE GRINDER, MACHINE (optical goods); LENS-GENERATING-MACHINE TENDER (optical goods); MULTIFOCAL-BUTTON COUNTERSINK GRINDER (optical goods). • **GED:** R2, M2, L2 • **SVP:** 3-6 mos • **Academic:** Ed=N, Eng=N • **Work Field:** 051 • **MPSMS:** 603, 605 • **Aptitudes:** G4, V4, N4, S4, P3, Q4, K4, F4, M3, E5, C5 • **Temperaments:** R, T • **Stress:** T • **Physical:** V=L, H=N, L=L, H • **Work Env:** I • **Salary:** 3 • **Outlook:** 3

MILLER (cement) • D.O.T. #570.685-046 • OES #92965 • GRINDER OPERATOR. Tends machines that crush, mix, or pulverize materials, such as limestone, shale, oyster shells, clay, iron ore, silica, gypsum, and cement clinkers, used in making cement: Starts mill and conveyors. Observes conveyor system to ensure continuous flow of material. Stops conveyor and removes clogged material, using bar. Opens chute over conveyor to add materials, such as iron, silica, or gypsum, according to specifications. Observes operation of auxiliary equipment, such as cement pumps, air or screen separators, air slides, cement coolers, and dust collectors. Turns valves to regulate water, air, and oil lines on machine, according to laboratory specifications. May regulate feeder mechanism on machines not equipped with automatic regulators. May add moisture to materials to facilitate flow into machine. May be designated according to type of mill tended as BALL-MILL OPERATOR (cement); FINISH-MILL OPERATOR (cement); HAMMER-MILL OPERATOR (cement); MILLER, ROD-MILL (cement); PUG-MILL OPERATOR (cement); RAW-FINISH-MILL OPERATOR (cement); TUBE-MILL OPERATOR (cement); VERTICAL-MILL OPERATOR (cement). • **GED:** R2, M2, L1 • **SVP:** 30 days-3 mos • **Academic:** Ed=N, Eng=N • **Work Field:** 142, 143 • **MPSMS:** 533 • **Aptitudes:** G4, V4, N4, S4, P4, Q4, K4, F4, M4, E5, C4 • **Temperaments:** M, T • **Physical:** V=L, H=N, L=M, W, H • **Work Env:** I, N • **Salary:** 2 • **Outlook:** 3

GOE: 06.04.09 Machine Work, Assorted Materials, Elemental

CROWN-ASSEMBLY-MACHINE OPERATOR (any ind.) • D.O.T. #692.685-062 • OES #92956 • CAP-LINING-MACHINE OPERATOR; INSERTING-PRESS OPERATOR; LINING-MACHINE TENDER; SPOT-MACHINE OPERATOR. Tends machine that inserts and glues cork, paper, plastic, or aluminum foil in bottlecap shells: Pours glue into pot. Turns valves to adjust gas flame for heating glue and to regulate flow of glue into machine. Mounts roll of lining material on machine spindle and starts machine. Observes discs and shells flowing from hopper into machine and pries jammed discs or shells loose, using poker. Examines glued shells on conveyor and rejects bent shells and offcenter or chipped discs. Pries glued disc from sample shell, using pick, observes quantity and texture of glue on sample, and adjusts valves to maintain specified temperature and rate of flow of glue. • **GED:** R2, M1, L1 • **SVP:** 2-30 days • **Academic:** Ed=N, Eng=N • **Work Field:** 063 • **MPSMS:** 556 • **Aptitudes:** G4, V4, N4, S4, P3, Q4, K3, F4, M3, E5, C5 • **Temperaments:** R • **Stress:** T • **Physical:** V=L, H=N, L=L, H • **Work Env:** I, N • **Salary:** 2 • **Outlook:** 2

CUTTER (photofinish.) • D.O.T. #976.685-010 • OES #92944 • FILM CUTTER; PRINT CUTTER. Tends automatic or semi-automatic machines that cut processed film or prints into single or multiple units: Examines film or print roll to determine size, number of cuts required, and type machine to use. Turns setscrews to adjust machine guides to roll width and sets density meter on automatic machine to coincide with sensitized marks on roll that control release of cutting blade. Threads roll through machine guides and starts machine that automatically cuts roll into individual or multiple units or depresses pedal of semi-automatic machine to cut roll. Cuts rolls of non-standard width, using scissors or hand-operated paper cutter. Inserts units in customer envelope. Keeps production records. • **GED:** R2, M1, L1 • **SVP:** 2-30 days • **Academic:** Ed=N, Eng=N • **Work Field:** 054 • **MPSMS:** 867 • **Aptitudes:** G4, V4, N4, S4, P4, Q4, K4, F3, M3, E5, C4 • **Temperaments:** R, T • **Stress:** T • **Physical:** V=L, H=N, L=L, H • **Work Env:** I • **Salary:** 1 • **Outlook:** 2

CUTTER, MACHINE 2 (any ind.) • D.O.T. #699.685-014 • OES #92944 • SHEARER; STRAIGHT CUTTER. Tends machine that cuts materials, such as braid, cardboard, cloth, felt, leather, ribbon, roofing paper, strands of wire, or tape to specified dimensions, by any of following methods: (1) Spaces guide or stop gage along calibrated scale of cutting table according to length of cut specified and tightens setscrew to secure guide or gage in position. Stacks single or multiple layers of material on cutting table with edges against stop gage or pulls material across cutting table to guide. Lowers lever-type blade by hand to cut material. (2) Spaces stop gage along calibrated scale, according to length of cut specified, and tightens setscrew to secure gage in position. Places single or multiple layers of material on bed of machine with edges against stop gage or moves lever to advance material on bed of machine against stop gage. Depresses pedal to activate lever-type blade that lowers and cuts material. May tend machine that trims excess material or irregular edges from variety of materials or garment and shoe parts. (3) Mounts roll of material on shaft or positions container of flat-folded material at feed end of machine. Threads end of material through guides and automatic feeding device. Turns setscrew to regulate feeding device according to length of cut specified. Starts machine that automatically feeds material under lever-type blade and cuts material into lengths. Stacks lengths of material on table or in handtruck. May change blade, using handtools. When cutting materials for use in making rubber stamp pads is designated as GUILLOTINE OPERATOR (pen & pencil). When trimming feathers for use in making shuttlecocks is designated as SHUTTLECOCK-FEATHER TRIMMER (sports equip.). May be designated according to material or article cut or trimmed as BELT-LOOP CUTTER (garment); COLLAR TRIMMER (garment); SAMPLE CUTTER (garment; textile). Additional titles: BAND CUTTER (garment); BELT CUTTER (garment); BRAID CUTTER (rubber goods); ELASTIC CUTTER (garment); FOIL CUTTER (any ind.); HOSE-SUSPENDER CUTTER (garment); LABEL CUTTER (garment; knit goods); PIPING BLOCKER (boot & shoe); RIBBON CUTTER (garment); SHEET CUTTER (house furn.); STRAP CUTTER (garment); TAPE CUTTER (garment); TOPPIECE CHOPPER (boot & shoe). • **GED:** R2, M1, L2 • **SVP:** 2-30 days • **Academic:** Ed=N, Eng=N • **Work Field:** 054 • **MPSMS:** 420, 520 • **Aptitudes:** G4, V4, N4, S4, P3, Q4, K4, F4, M3, E4, C4 • **Temperaments:** R, T • **Stress:** T • **Physical:** V=L, H=N, L=L, W, H • **Work Env:** I • **Salary:** 3 • **Outlook:** 2

CUTTING-MACHINE TENDER (any ind.) • D.O.T. #690.685-122 • OES #92944 • Tends power shear that cuts sheets of material, such as paper, pressboard, foil, cardboard, cork, or plastic material to specified dimension for items, such as cartons, wrappers, labels, business forms, or gaskets: Adjusts guides on machine to regulate width of cut, using ruler or by following calibrated scale on machine bed. Positions and alines sheets against guides and presses lever to clamp sheets to bed of machine. Moves controls to force shear blade through sheets. Adjusts guides and repositions material to trim or square edges to specifications. May change shear blade, using handtools. May be designated according to type of material cut as CARDBOARD CUTTER (any ind.); CUTTER, PLASTICS SHEETS (fabric. plastics prod.; plastics mat.); PAPER CUTTER (any ind.). May cut material manually, using hand-powered shear and be designated PAPER CUTTER, HAND (any ind.). • **GED:** R3, M2, L2 • **SVP:** 30 days-3 mos • **Academic:** Ed=N,

Eng=N • **Work Field:** 054 • **MPSMS:** 470, 492, 510 • **Aptitudes:** G4, V4, N4, S4, P4, Q4, K3, F3, M3, E4, C5 • **Temperaments:** R, T • **Stress:** T • **Physical:** V=L, H=N, L=L, S, H • **Work Env:** I, R • **Salary:** 2 • **Outlook:** 3

EMBOSSING-PRESS OPERATOR (any ind.) • D.O.T. #652.685-030 • OES #92543 • STAMPING-PRESS OPERATOR. Tends machine that embosses and imprints designs or lettering onto surfaces of materials, such as paper, cloth, rubber, leather, or plastic by pressing heated die through foil, gold-leaf, or coated ribbon onto workpiece: Positions specified type or stamping die in chase and locks chase in machine, using handtools. Places reel of specified foil, gold-leaf, or coated ribbon onto play-out spindle and threads end through rolls which feed and guide it under die mounted on ram of machine. Turns on heating element over die. Positions workpiece in bed of hand fed or feed hopper of automatically fed machine. Starts machine which lowers ram to lower heated die and ribbon to emboss and imprint work piece, and automatically moves coated ribbon with each stroke of machine. May tend machine that imprints trade names, brand, and grade onto leather sweatbands and be designated SWEATBAND PRINTER (hat & cap). • **GED:** R2, M1, L1 • **SVP:** 2-30 days • **Academic:** Ed=N, Eng=N • **Work Field:** 192 • **MPSMS:** 567 • **Aptitudes:** G4, V4, N4, S4, P3, Q4, K3, F3, M3, E4, C4 • **Temperaments:** R, T • **Stress:** T • **Physical:** V=L, H=N, L=L, H • **Work Env:** I, R • **Salary:** 2 • **Outlook:** 2

KEYMODULE-ASSEMBLY-MACHINE TENDER (office mach.) • D.O.T. #692.685-274 • OES #92998 • Tends machine that automatically assembles components to form modules used in keyboards of electronic computer equipment: Observes machine operations to detect defective parts and to ensure continuous movement of parts, subassemblies, and final assemblies along feed tracks. Removes defective parts from feed tracks and repositions disoriented parts, using pick. Pries jammed parts from track, using pick, or replenishes supply of parts in feeder bowl to remedy machine stoppage. Packs completed assemblies into containers. Notifies mechanic when machine malfunctions repeatedly occur. Periodically cleans feed tracks, machine surface, and work area, using handbrush, broom, airhose, or vacuum cleaner. • **GED:** R2, M2, L2 • **SVP:** 2-30 days • **Academic:** Ed=N, Eng=N • **Work Field:** 121 • **MPSMS:** 601 • **Aptitudes:** G4, V4, N4, S4, P3, Q4, K4, F4, M3, E5, C5 • **Temperaments:** R, T • **Stress:** T • **Physical:** V=L, H=N, L=L, H • **Work Env:** I, R • **Salary:** 3 • **Outlook:** 3

LEAF STAMPER (any ind.) • D.O.T. #979.682-018 • OES #92998 • GOLD-LEAF PRINTER; GOLD MARKER; GOLD STAMPER; HOT STAMPER; LETTERING-MACHINE OPERATOR; STAMPING-PRESS OPERATOR. Operates stamping press that imprints gold, silver, or carbon letters or designs on leather, fabric, or plastic articles or material: Positions and locks line of type or specified stamping die in heated chase. Sets heat, pressure, and time controls, according to material to be stamped. Places material in bed of stamping press. Pulls lever or presses switch to lower ram and imprint material. Examines imprint for alinement and clarity. Places spool of gold, silver, or carbon foil on spindle and threads foil through stamper or places sheet of foil over impression. Lowers stamping ram to force and fuse foil into impression. May use stamper that imprints and applies foil simultaneously. • **GED:** R2, M1, L1 • **SVP:** 30 days-3 mos • **Academic:** Ed=N, Eng=N • **Work Field:** 191, 192 • **MPSMS:** 610 • **Aptitudes:** G4, V4, N4, S3, P3, Q4, K3, F3, M3, E5, C4 • **Temperaments:** R, T • **Stress:** T • **Physical:** V=L, H=N, L=L, H • **Work Env:** I • **Salary:** 3 • **Outlook:** 2

MACHINE FEEDER (any ind.) • D.O.T. #699.686-010 • OES #98502 • Feeds or removes metal, plastic, or other stock and material from automatic fabricating machines: Places stock into hoppers, onto conveyors of self-centering machine bed, or lifts coils of sheet metal or wire onto feedrack. Removes stock from conveyor and piles it into boxes, truck, or on feed conveyor for next operation. May push dual control buttons to activate machine. May work in pairs to feed or remove pieces from machine. May thread sheet metal or wire through machine. May be designated by machine fed as SHEAR OPERATOR, AUTOMATIC (any ind.) II; or by task performed as PUNCH-PRESS FEEDER (any ind.); PUNCH-PRESS OFFBEARER (any ind.); STRAIGHTENING-MACHINE FEEDER (any ind.). • **GED:** R1, M1, L1 • **SVP:** 2-30 days •

Academic: Ed=N, Eng=N • **Work Field:** 054, 134 • **MPSMS:** 492, 540, 582 • **Aptitudes:** G4, V4, N5, S4, P4, Q5, K4, F4, M4, E5, C5 • **Temperaments:** R • **Stress:** T • **Physical:** V=L, H=N, L=M, H • **Work Env:** I, N, R • **Salary:** 2 • **Outlook:** 3

PHOTORESIST LAMINATOR, PRINTED CIRCUIT BOARD (electronics) • D.O.T. #699.685-042 • OES #92998 • HOT ROLL LAMINATOR. Tends machine that laminates dry photoresist film to surfaces of panels used in the manufacture of printed circuit boards (PCBs): Mounts rolls of photoresist film and plastic protective film on machine spindles. Threads film through machine rollers and secures film to takeup spindles. Presses button to activate machine. Adjusts controls to regulate speed, temperature, and pressure of laminating rollers. Moves levers and adjusts control to align panels with edge of film. Feeds panels into roller, or positions panels on conveyor that feeds laminating machine. Observes lamination process, monitors speed and temperature gauges, and adjusts controls to ensure compliance with standards. Removes laminated panels from machine. Cuts excess photoresist and protective plastic film from panel edges, using knife. May tend scrubber machine that cleans PCB panels prior to laminating process. May count and record number of panels completed. May examine laminated panels to detect defects. • **GED:** R2, M1, L1 • **SVP:** 2-30 days • **Academic:** Ed=N, Eng=N • **Work Field:** 063 • **MPSMS:** 587 • **Aptitudes:** G4, V4, N4, S4, P4, Q4, K4, F4, M4, E5, C5 • **Temperaments:** R • **Stress:** T • **Physical:** V=L, H=N, L=L, H • **Work Env:** I • **Salary:** 3 • **Outlook:** 2

SCRAP HANDLER (any ind.) • D.O.T. #509.685-050 • OES #92998 • Tends machines, such as baling machine, centrifugal separator, and oil purifier to salvage metal parts and cutting oil: Loads and moves barrels or crates of metal chips, shavings, or clippings from machining operations, using handtruck. Dumps metal scrap into baling machine and activates machine to compress scrap into bales. Binds bales of metal scrap with wire or metal strapping. Shovels scrap in spinner bucket. Clamps covers, sets timer, adjusts sump pump and oil line valves, and flips switches to start automatic cycle of centrifugal machine that spins metal scrap to separate cutting oil from scrap. Starts centrifugal oil purifier that filters foreign matter from used cutting oil to make oil reusable. Disassembles rejected devices and materials, such as thermostats, valves, conduit, and connectors, using handtools, arbor press, vises, and power hack saw. Sorts parts according to type of metal or part. Weighs bales and barrels of scrap metal and ties identification tags on scrap. May oversee and demonstrate salvaging procedures to other SCRAP HANDLERS (any ind.). • **GED:** R3, M2, L2 • **SVP:** 30 days-3 mos • **Academic:** Ed=N, Eng=N • **Work Field:** 011, 041, 145 • **MPSMS:** 549 • **Aptitudes:** G3, V4, N4, S4, P4, Q4, K3, F4, M3, E5, C5 • **Temperaments:** R • **Stress:** T • **Physical:** V=L, H=N, L=H, W, H • **Work Env:** I • **Salary:** 4 • **Outlook:** 3

SILK-SCREEN PRINTER, MACHINE (any ind.) • D.O.T. #979.665-010 • OES #92549 • Tends silk-screen machine that prints designs or lettering on glassware, pottery, metal, plastic, or electronic items: Bolts framed silk-screen onto machine, and installs and adjusts workpiece holding fixture, stops, and guides, using handtools, ruler, and workpiece pattern. Attaches squeegee to pneumatic drive mechanism, using wrench, and couples air line to mechanism. Regulates air pressure and manipulates squeegee to adjust squeegee pressure and angle of sweep. Applies printing compound to screen, using spatula or brush. Places workpiece in or on holding fixture, presses button to lower screen, and depresses pedal or pushes button to activate squeegee. Observes silk-screen and workpiece to detect printing defects caused by rip in screen and applies glue to rip to repair screen. Cleans silk-screen, using brush and solvent. May thin printing compound, using specified thinner. May tend firing oven to dry printed workpiece. May sharpen squeegee on sanding machine. May transfer image of original artwork to screen, using vacuum printer. May be known as DECORATING-MACHINE OPERATOR (glass mfg.); SQUEEGEE-MACHINE OPERATOR (glass mfg.); or STENCILING-MACHINE TENDER (glass mfg.; glass prod.). May tend machine that screen-prints circuit pattern and nomenclature on printed circuit board panels used in fabricating printed circuit boards and be known as SCREEN-PRINTING-MACHINE TENDER, PRINTED CIRCUIT BOARDS (electronics). • **GED:** R3, M1, L2 • **SVP:** 30

days-3 mos • **Academic:** Ed=N, Eng=N • **Work Field:** 191 • **MPSMS:** 530, 570, 580 • **Aptitudes:** G4, V4, N4, S4, P3, Q4, K3, F4, M3, E4, C4 • **Temperaments:** R, T • **Stress:** T • **Physical:** V=L, H=N, L=S, H • **Work Env:** I • **Salary:** 1 • **Outlook:** 3

SPRAY-PAINTING-MACHINE OPERATOR (any ind.) • D.O.T. #741.685-010 • OES #92953 • AUTOMATIC-SPRAY-MACHINE OPERATOR. Tends spray-painting machine that automatically applies lettering, diagrams, or designs on products, such as speedometer faces, automobile steering-wheel hubs, and radio or television control knobs: Places workpiece in masking jig and depresses pedal to clamp workpiece against stencil mask. Depresses pedal to spray exposed area of workpiece through mask. Removes product from jig and examines coating for smears, runs, incomplete painting, and similar flaws. Removes and places paint saturated masks in mask-washing machine for cleaning. May record production. • **GED:** R2, M1, L1 • **SVP:** 2-30 days • **Academic:** Ed=N, Eng=N • **Work Field:** 262 • **MPSMS:** 580, 615, 617 • **Aptitudes:** G4, V4, N4, S4, P4, Q5, K3, F3, M3, E4, C4 • **Temperaments:** R • **Stress:** T • **Physical:** V=L, H=N, L=M, W, H • **Work Env:** I • **Salary:** 2 • **Outlook:** 2

WAX MOLDER (foundry) • D.O.T. #549.685-038 • OES #92971 • Tends semiautomatic wax-molding machine that produces wax patterns used in lost-wax casting process: Sprays interior surface of die with parting agent. Places die against stops in bed of machine and starts machine that forces melted wax into die by injection or centrifugal process. Loosens pattern from die, using airhose. Removes pattern from die and inspects it for defects. Cleans excess wax from pattern, using knife. May pour melted wax into holding cup of machine. May be designated according to molding process used as CENTRIFUGAL-WAX MOLDER (found.; jewelry); INJECTION-WAX MOLDER (found.; jewelry). • **GED:** R2, M1, L2 • **SVP:** 2-30 days • **Academic:** Ed=N, Eng=N • **Work Field:** 132 • **MPSMS:** 567 • **Aptitudes:** G4, V4, N4, S4, P3, Q5, K4, F3, M3, E5, C5 • **Temperaments:** R, T • **Stress:** T • **Physical:** V=L, H=N, L=L, H • **Work Env:** I • **Salary:** 2 • **Outlook:** 2

GOE: 06.04.10 Equipment Operator, Metal, Elemental

DIE-CASTING-MACHINE OPERATOR 2 (foundry) • D.O.T. #514.685-018 • OES #91911 • Tends diecasting machine that casts parts, such as automobile trim, carburetor housings, and motor parts from nonferrous metals, such as zinc, aluminum, or magnesium: Turns valves to regulate flow of water circulating through dies. Blows metal fragments from die surfaces, using airhose, and brushes lubricant over die cavity and plunger. Ladles molten metal into chamber by hand when using cold chamber machine. Pushes button to close and lock dies and activate plunger that forces molten metal into die cavities. Removes casting after dies open automatically, using tongs or pliers. Inspects casting for defects, such as cracks or bubbles. May measure casting, using fixed gages. May dip castings in water to cool. May regulate speed of machine. • **GED:** R2, M1, L1 • **SVP:** 2-30 days • **Academic:** Ed=N, Eng=N • **Work Field:** 132 • **MPSMS:** 542 • **Aptitudes:** G4, V4, N4, S4, P3, Q4, K3, F4, M3, E5, C5 • **Temperaments:** R, T • **Stress:** T • **Physical:** V=L, H=N, L=M, W, H • **Work Env:** I, H, R • **Salary:** 4 • **Outlook:** 3

INJECTION-MOLDING-MACHINE TENDER (fabric. plastic prod.) • D.O.T. #556.685-038 • OES #91905 • Tends injection-molding machines that form plastic or rubber products, such as typewriter keys, phonograph records, and luggage handles: Dumps plastic powder, preformed plastic pellets, or preformed rubber slugs into hopper of molding machine. Starts machine that automatically liquefies pellets, slugs, or powder in heating chamber, injects liquefied material into mold, and ejects molded product. Observes gages to ensure specified molding temperature and pressure are maintained. Examines molded product for surface defects, such as dents and cracks. May heat plastic material over steamtable or in oven to prepare material for molding. May remove product from mold, using handtools. May trim flash from product, using shears or knife. May place product in cold water or position it on cooling fixture to prevent distortion. • **GED:** R2, M1, L1 • **SVP:** 2-30 days • **Academic:** Ed=N, Eng=N • **Work Field:** 132 • **MPSMS:** 519 • **Aptitudes:** G4, V4, N4, S4, P4, Q5, K4, F4, M4,

E5, C5 • **Temperaments:** M, T • **Physical:** V=L, H=N, L=L, H • **Work Env:** I • **Salary:** 3 • **Outlook:** 2

LABORER, GENERAL (nonfer. metal prod.) • D.O.T. #519.686-010 • OES #98502 • Performs any combination of tasks to aid other workers in production of nonferrous metal products: Transfers boxes of metal scrap from work areas to storage areas, using handtruck, and records quantity and type of scrap transferred. Dumps scrap metal into crusher that reduces bulk of metal. Shovels metal scrap onto furnace conveyor to dry scrap preparatory to melting. Dumps paste oil or fat into drum, adds water, and mixes solution, using steam hose, to prepare lubricant used in drawing tubes and rods. Examines metal products for defects, such as dents, cracks, and scratches. Taps dents from products, using mallet. Feeds metal castings into automatic finishing machine that performs operations, such as reaming, stamping, and cleaning. Scrapes carbon, dirt, and metal particles from interior surface of casting molds. May be known according to specific duties performed as CHIP-CRUSHER OPERATOR (nonfer. metal alloys); CHIP DRIER (nonfer. metal alloys); INSPECTOR (nonfer. metal alloys) II; GENERAL SCRAP WORKER (nonfer. metal alloys); SOAP WORKER (nonfer. metal alloys). • **GED:** R2, M1, L1 • **SVP:** 2-30 days • **Academic:** Ed=N, Eng=N • **Work Field:** 011, 142, 143 • **MPSMS:** 540 • **Aptitudes:** G4, V4, N4, S4, P4, Q4, K4, F4, M3, E5, C5 • **Temperaments:** R • **Stress:** T • **Physical:** V=L, H=N, L=H, W, H • **Work Env:** I • **Salary:** 3 • **Outlook:** 2

MILL OPERATOR (any ind.) • D.O.T. #599.685-058 • OES #92965 • Tends one or more mills that grind materials, such as rock, ore, ingredients for food, drugs, and chemicals with steel, stone, or ceramic balls or rods: Pushes lever or adds balls to mill as needed or specified. Dumps material or opens flow gate to load mill. Secures cover plate. Starts and runs mill for specified time depending on size of load, grind ability of material, and required fineness. Removes cover plate, attaches grid, and starts mill to discharge contents. When operating continuous ball mills, regulates inflow of materials and observes outflow to ensure attainment of specified product. May tend mill utilizing vacuum or other pressure. May tend steam-jacketed mill that heats materials during processing. May use mill to mix materials for wet or dry grinding. May keep production records. May be designated according to grinding agent as BALL-MILL OPERATOR (any ind.); PEBBLE-MILL OPERATOR (chem.; paint & varn.); ROD-MILL OPERATOR (any ind.); or according to powder ground as BARYTES GRINDER (paint & varn.). • **GED:** R2, M1, L2 • **SVP:** 30 days-3 mos • **Academic:** Ed=N, Eng=N • **Work Field:** 142 • **MPSMS:** 344, 347, 490 • **Aptitudes:** G4, V4, N4, S4, P4, Q4, K3, F4, M3, E5, C5 • **Temperaments:** R, T • **Stress:** T • **Physical:** V=L, H=N, L=M, W, S, H • **Work Env:** I, N • **Salary:** 2 • **Outlook:** 2

OXIDIZED-FINISH PLATER (any ind.) • D.O.T. #599.685-062 • OES #91926 • PLATER HELPER. Tends oxidizing tank that produces dark, lusterless, decorative finish on surface of metal articles, such as door lock parts, buttons, buckles, and small-arm parts: Places containers of workpieces in tank of oxidizing solution for specified time. Dips articles in successive baths to neutralize oxidization. May start tumbling barrel to dry oxidized pieces in sawdust [TUMBLER OPERATOR (any ind.)]. May mix chemical solutions according to formula. May tend degreasing tank to clean workpieces before oxidizing. • **GED:** R2, M1, L2 • **SVP:** 2-30 days • **Academic:** Ed=N, Eng=N • **Work Field:** 151 • **MPSMS:** 373, 550, 618 • **Aptitudes:** G4, V4, N4, S4, P4, Q4, K4, F4, M3, E5, C4 • **Temperaments:** R, T • **Stress:** T • **Physical:** V=L, H=N, L=M, W, H • **Work Env:** I, N, R • **Salary:** 2 • **Outlook:** 2

GOE: 06.04.11 Equip. Oper., Chemical Proc., Elemental

CENTRIFUGE OPERATOR, PLASMA PROCESSING (drug prep. & related) • D.O.T. #599.685-018 • OES #92962 • Tends centrifuges which separate plasma from whole blood for extraction of plasma: Packs plastic bags containing freshly drawn whole blood (whole blood units) into designated containers in centrifuge. Fastens centrifuge cover and depresses switch to activate centrifuge mechanism. Removes centrifuged whole blood units after designated time, examines each to confirm separation of plasma from whole blood, and places each whole blood unit in plasma extractor,

positioning holes at top of plastic bag on metal prongs. Inserts plastic tube of transfer unit into each whole blood unit and observes process as plasma is extracted from upper portion of plastic bag into bottle, to make certain that no red blood cells are drawn into plasma bottle. Seals off bottle and returns plasma bottle to rack. Removes blood unit from holder and gives to nursing personnel for return to donor. Marks each plasma bottle with blood group as indicated on plastic bag to assure separation of blood groups and prevent cross-contamination of blood groups during fractionation. Stores filled bottles of plasma in freezer. Cleans centrifuges and work area. • **GED:** R2, M2, L2 • **SVP:** 2-30 days • **Academic:** Ed=N, Eng=N • **Work Field:** 211 • **MPSMS:** 493 • **Aptitudes:** G3, V3, N3, S4, P4, Q3, K3, F3, M3, E5, C3 • **Temperaments:** J, R, T • **Stress:** T • **Physical:** V=L, H=N, L=L, W, H • **Work Env:** I • **Salary:** 2 • **Outlook:** 3

CHEMICAL OPERATOR 2 (chem.) • D.O.T. #558.585-014 • OES #92938 • REACTOR OPERATOR. Tends equipment units or semi-automatic system that processes chemical substances into industrial or consumer products, such as detergents, emulsifiers, salts, bleaching agents, acids, and synthetic resins: Dumps specified amounts of solid materials into heating vessels or blending tanks; and turns valves to feed liquid and gaseous materials through equipment units, or sets controls in specified sequence on control panel to start automatic feed. Turns valves or moves controls to maintain system at specified temperature, pressure, and vacuum levels. Observes chemical reactions; monitors gages, signals, and recorders; and receives notification from control laboratory, supervisor, or other workers to make specified operating adjustments. Draws samples of products for laboratory analysis. Maintains log of gage readings and shift production. May perform chemical tests on product to ensure conformance with specifications, using standard test equipment, materials, and procedure. May be designated according to substance processed as LOW-CHLORIDE SODA OPERATOR (chem.); SALT-PLANT OPERATOR (chem.); SODIUM-METHYLATE OPERATOR (chem.); equipment tended as STYRENE-DEHYDRATION-REACTOR OPERATOR (chem.); TOWER OPERATOR (chem.) II; or reaction produced as EMULSIFICATION OPERATOR (oils & fats); PRECIPITATION EQUIPMENT TENDER (chem.). • **GED:** R3, M2, L2 • **SVP:** 3-6 mos • **Academic:** Ed=N, Eng=N • **Work Field:** 147 • **MPSMS:** 490 • **Aptitudes:** G3, V4, N4, S4, P4, Q4, K3, F4, M3, E5, C5 • **Temperaments:** M, T • **Physical:** V=L, H=N, L=M, W, H • **Work Env:** I, R • **Salary:** 3 • **Outlook:** 2

CHEMICAL PREPARER 1 (chem.) • D.O.T. #550.685-030 • OES #92965 • Compounds liquid and powdered chemical ingredients and deionized water into chemical solutions, such as frit or conductive graphite, to produce adhesive or conductive coatings on cathode ray television or oscilloscope tubes. May perform standard chemical tests on product, using analytical balance, graduates, pH meter, resistivity meter, titration apparatus, colorimeter, and thermometer. Pours compounded product into containers for application to tube seams or funnel by other workers. • **GED:** R3, M3, L3 • **SVP:** 3-6 mos • **Academic:** Ed=N, Eng=S • **Work Field:** 143 • **MPSMS:** 490 • **Aptitudes:** G3, V3, N3, S4, P3, Q3, K3, F3, M3, E5, C4 • **Temperaments:** J, M • **Physical:** V=L, H=N, L=M, W, H • **Work Env:** I • **Salary:** 3 • **Outlook:** 2

DRIER OPERATOR (chem.) • D.O.T. #553.685-042 • OES #92923 • DRUM-DRIER OPERATOR; VACUUM-DRUM-DRIER OPERATOR. Tends vacuum drum driers that heat liquid compounds to form caked or powdered chemical products: Connects tube from feed inlet to drum containing liquid to be dried. Turns steam and coolant valves and observes thermometer to regulate temperature of steam-jacketed drum enclosed in vacuum chamber, according to specifications. Starts pump and observes vacuum gage to maintain prescribed vacuum in chamber. Starts revolving drum that dries liquid as it splashes against heated drum, forming caked or powdered product that is removed from surface of drum by scraper blade. Observes and feels dried product, periodically submits sample for laboratory moisture analysis, and adjusts drying temperature and vacuum if product does not meet plant standards. Records drying time of batch, gage readings, and amount or weight of materials dried. May set scraper blade at specified distance from drum, using handtools. May fill containers with dried materials, weigh containers, and tag containers for shipment or storage. •

GED: R3, M2, L2 • **SVP:** 30 days-3 mos • **Academic:** Ed=N, Eng=N • **Work Field:** 141 • **MPSMS:** 490 • **Aptitudes:** G3, V4, N4, S4, P4, Q4, K3, F4, M3, E5, C5 • **Temperaments:** M, T • **Physical:** V=L, H=N, L=M, W, H • **Work Env:** I, H • **Salary:** 3 • **Outlook:** 2

MIXER (paint & varn.) • D.O.T. #550.685-078 • OES #92965 • BATCH MIXER; BLENDER; DISPERSION MIXER. Tends mixing machines to blend solid and liquid ingredients to make products, such as paints, lacquers, putty, paint pigments, and binders, following formula: Turns valves or sets pump meters to admit specified amounts of liquids, such as oils, solvents, and water into mixer. Weighs and dumps specified amounts of dry ingredients, such as plastic flash, color concentrates, and resins into mixer, as indicated on batch ticket, or dumps preweighed ingredients into tank. Pushes or pulls tank to dispersion mixing machine. Depresses pedal to lower mixing blades into tank and presses button to start blades revolving to mix and disperse ingredients. Turns valves to drain batch through hoses into pebble or ball mill or into holding tank. May draw sample from batch for laboratory test and add ingredients to mixture as specified by laboratory. May clean equipment, using rags, solvent, and scraper. May be designated according to product mixed as GLASS ENAMEL MIXER (paint & varn.); LACQUER BLENDER (paint & varn.); PAINT MAKER (paint & varn.); PASTE MIXER (paint & varn.); PIGMENT MIXER (paint & varn.); PUTTY MAKER (paint & varn.). • **GED:** R3, M1, L2 • **SVP:** 30 days-3 mos • **Academic:** Ed=N, Eng=N • **Work Field:** 143 • **MPSMS:** 495 • **Aptitudes:** G4, V4, N4, S4, P4, Q4, K3, F4, M3, E5, C4 • **Temperaments:** M, R, T • **Stress:** T • **Physical:** V=L, H=N, L=H, W, H • **Work Env:** I, N • **Salary:** 3 • **Outlook:** 2

PAINT MIXER, MACHINE (any ind.) • D.O.T. #550.485-018 • OES #92965 • Tends paint-mixing machines that mix paint, lacquer, and stain: Attaches powered mixer to barrels of unmixed paint and starts mixer to stir paint for specified time to obtain specified consistency. Computes amounts and weights of paint, lacquer, solvent, or thinner required from standard formula, and pours specified amounts into mixing machine. Starts mixer and allows it to run for prescribed time to attain specified viscosity and color. Measures viscosity, using viscosimeter and stop watch. May pump paint from central pumping station to spray booths. May filter paint or pyroxylin to remove impurities. May maintain record of paint issued and inventory of supplies on hand. • **GED:** R2, M1, L1 • **SVP:** 30 days-3 mos • **Academic:** Ed=N, Eng=N • **Work Field:** 143 • **MPSMS:** 495 • **Aptitudes:** G3, V4, N4, S4, P4, Q4, K3, F4, M3, E5, C3 • **Temperaments:** R, T • **Stress:** T • **Physical:** V=L, H=N, L=H, W, H • **Work Env:** I, N • **Salary:** 3 • **Outlook:** 2

GOE: 06.04.13 Equip. Oper., Rubber, Plastics & Glass Proc., Elemental

BOWLING-BALL MOLDER (sports equip.) • D.O.T. #556.685-018 • OES #92971 • Tends presses that mold cover material on bowling-ball cores preparatory to steam curing, performing any combination of following duties: (1) Cuts rubber cover stock to approximate size, using knife, and lays specified number of rubber squares in mold half. (2) Positions mold half under press ram and presses button to lower ram into mold to shape rubber. Places bowling-ball core in every other mold with marked, weighted area away from seam. (3) Places cover, mold half on core, and pushes pins through mold flanges to hold halves in position. Places mold into press and presses button to lower ram and to mold cover to core. (4) Pulls flash from mold seam and places or pounds brackets onto mold flange to hold mold together during curing. Opens press, pounds pins out of flange, and stacks mold on pallet. May clean cores prior to molding operations, using cabinet sandblast equipment. • **GED:** R2, M1, L1 • **SVP:** 30 days-3 mos • **Academic:** Ed=N, Eng=N • **Work Field:** 132 • **MPSMS:** 616 • **Aptitudes:** G4, V4, N4, S4, P4, Q5, K3, F4, M3, E5, C5 • **Temperaments:** R • **Stress:** T • **Physical:** V=L, H=N, L=M, W, H • **Work Env:** I, N • **Salary:** 3 • **Outlook:** 2

COMPRESSION-MOLDING-MACHINE TENDER (fabric. plastic prod.) • D.O.T. #556.685-022 • OES #91905 • MOLDER; PLASTIC-PRESS MOLDER. Tends compression-molding machines that mold thermosetting plastics into products, such as automobile heater housings, ashtrays, buttons, electronic parts, plastic panels, and dishes: Dumps specified amount of plastic powders or pellets into hopper of machine, or positions pellets or sausage-shaped plastics in mold installed on machine. Starts machine that compresses plastic into mold under heat and pressure, and allows plastic to set for specified time. Removes product from mold and cleans mold, hopper, and bed of machine, using airhose and hand tools. May place plastics material on hot grid or in oven to soften it prior to molding. May weigh prescribed amount of material for molding. May place plastic sheet into machine fixture to fabricate buttons. • **GED:** R2, M1, L1 • **SVP:** 2-30 days • **Academic:** Ed=N, Eng=N • **Work Field:** 132 • **MPSMS:** 519 • **Aptitudes:** G4, V4, N5, S4, P4, Q5, K3, F4, M3, E5, C5 • **Temperaments:** R, T • **Stress:** T • **Physical:** V=L, H=N, L=L, H • **Work Env:** I • **Salary:** 3 • **Outlook:** 2

CONTACT-LENS MOLDER (optical goods) • D.O.T. #690.685-090 • OES #91905 • Tends heating equipment and hydraulic casting press that casts plastic contact lenses: Lays separate top and bottom sections of previously setup mold on heated metal block for specified time. Fills lens cavities in heated mold with plastic powder. Alines guide pins and holes to join top and bottom sections of mold. Places filled mold on bed of press, sets timer, and starts press to lower ram until dial indicates mold sections are under specified pressure. Removes mold from press. Inspects first run of lenses to verify accuracy of lens power, using power determining and optical centering instrument. Reports defects in new molds. • **GED:** R2, M2, L2 • **SVP:** 30 days-3 mos • **Academic:** Ed=N, Eng=N • **Work Field:** 132 • **MPSMS:** 605 • **Aptitudes:** G3, V4, N4, S3, P2, Q4, K3, F3, M3, E5, C4 • **Temperaments:** M, R, T • **Stress:** T • **Physical:** V=L, H=N, L=L, W, H • **Work Env:** I • **Salary:** 3 • **Outlook:** 2

FUSING-FURNACE LOADER (optical goods) • D.O.T. #573.686-014 • OES #98502 • FURNACE CLERK; PICKER. Loads and unloads conveyor of furnace that fuses multifocal lens parts: Positions multifocal lens blank and button assemblies, or assembled button parts, on emery disks, places disks on trays, and places filled trays on conveyor that passes through fusing furnace. Removes trays of fused items from end of conveyor and places them in rack to cool. Records production count. May mark identification number on lenses, using marking pen. May observe temperature indicators and inform supervisor of furnace malfunction. • **GED:** R2, M1, L1 • **SVP:** 2-30 days • **Academic:** Ed=N, Eng=N • **Work Field:** 131 • **MPSMS:** 605 • **Aptitudes:** G4, V4, N4, S4, P4, Q4, K3, F3, M3, E5, C5 • **Temperaments:** R • **Stress:** T • **Physical:** V=L, H=N, L=L, W, H • **Work Env:** I • **Salary:** 2 • **Outlook:** 2

LENS HARDENER (optical goods) • D.O.T. #573.685-030 • OES #92923 • Tends electric oven-type machine that hardens lenses used in safety eyeglasses, and tests hardness of lens, using steel-ball drop-test: Measures lens thickness with calipers to determine if lens meets thickness requirements for prescribed hardening. Positions lenses in holding fixture and pushes fixture into electric oven. Sets timer and temperature controls on oven according to chart specifications for prescribed hardness of lens. Removes lenses at end of cooling cycle, or places lenses in airflow to cool. Holds finished lens in polarized light fixture to detect defects produced by hardening. Places lens on bed of drop-test fixture and covers lens with cloth or plastic. Places steel ball of specified weight in release mechanism of fixture. Positions mechanism at specified distance from lens and releases ball. Discards broken lenses. • **GED:** R2, M2, L1 • **SVP:** 2-30 days • **Academic:** Ed=N, Eng=N • **Work Field:** 133 • **MPSMS:** 605 • **Aptitudes:** G4, V4, N4, S4, P3, Q4, K4, F4, M3, E5, C4 • **Temperaments:** R, T • **Stress:** T • **Physical:** V=L, H=N, L=L, W, H • **Work Env:** I • **Salary:** 2 • **Outlook:** 3

RECORD-PRESS TENDER (phonograph) • D.O.T. #556.685-070 • OES #92971 • Tends automatic steam-hydraulic press that molds plastic compound into phonograph records: Places record labels over top and bottom center pins of press, and places preweighed and heated biscuit (plastic compound) into press mold. Moves lever to close mold and start press on cycle that molds biscuit under pressure and heat to form phonograph record. Removes record at end of cycle, places record onto spindle of edge trimmer, and presses lever to start turntable that rotates record against circular blades to trim flash from record edge. Examines record for flaws, such as discoloration and scratches. Retains specified record samples for audio testing. May tend machine that automatically inserts labels and compound into mold, forms record, punches center hole, and trims flash from record edge. • **GED:** R2, M1, L1 • **SVP:** 30 days-3 mos • **Academic:** Ed=N, Eng=N • **Work Field:** 132 • **MPSMS:** 585 • **Aptitudes:** G4, V4, N4, S4, P3, Q4, K4, F4, M3, E5, C4 • **Temperaments:** R, T • **Stress:** T • **Physical:** V=L, H=N, L=L, H • **Work Env:** I, N • **Salary:** 2 • **Outlook:** 3

TIRE MOLDER (rubber tire & tube) • D.O.T. #553.685-102 • OES #92998 • CURING FINISHER; RETREAD-MOLD OPERATOR. Tends retreading mold that vulcanizes camelback (raw rubber tread) onto tire casing and molds tread design: Places air bag of specified size inside tire, using tire-spreading device, and clamps tire into mold. Inflates air bag to specified pressure and heats mold to specified temperature to cook and mold tread. Removes tire after predetermined time and trims loose ends from molded tread, using knife. • **GED:** R2, M1, L1 • **SVP:** 30 days-3 mos • **Academic:** Ed=N, Eng=N • **Work Field:** 132, 136 • **MPSMS:** 511 • **Aptitudes:** G4, V4, N5, S4, P4, Q5, K4, F4, M3, E5, C5 • **Temperaments:** R, T • **Stress:** T • **Physical:** V=L, H=N, L=H, W, H • **Work Env:** I, H • **Salary:** 4 • **Outlook:** 2

GOE: 06.04.15 Equip. Oper., Food Proc., Elemental

BAKER HELPER (bake. prod.) • D.O.T. #526.686-010 • OES #98999 • Performs any combination of the following tasks in production of baked goods: Moves and distributes bakery supplies and products in and around production area of bakery, using handtrucks, dollies, troughs, and rack trucks. Weighs and measures ingredients, such as sugar, flour, yeast, sirup, and dough. Lifts and dumps containers of materials to help load and unload machines, bins, hoppers, racks, and ovens. Feeds lumps or sheets of dough into hopper or between rolls of machine. Cleans equipment, using brushes, cleanser, and water. Greases, lines, or dusts pans or boards preparatory to receiving product for baking. May be designated according to worker assisted as BATTER-MIXER HELPER (bake. prod.); BENCH-HAND HELPER (bake. prod.) or according to machine operator assisted as CRACKER-AND-COOKY-MACHINE-OPERATOR HELPER (bake. prod.); DOUGHNUT-MACHINE-OPERATOR HELPER (bake. prod.). Additional titles: COOKY-MIXER HELPER (bake. prod.); DIVIDING-MACHINE-OPERATOR HELPER (bake. prod.); DOUGH-MIXER HELPER (bake. prod.); DOUGHNUT-MAKER HELPER, HAND (bake. prod.); ICER HELPER, HAND (bake. prod.); INGREDIENT- SCALER HELPER (bake. prod.); MOLDING-MACHINE-OPERATOR HELPER (bake. prod.). • **GED:** R2, M1, L1 • **SVP:** 2-30 days • **Academic:** Ed=N, Eng=N • **Work Field:** 146 • **MPSMS:** 384 • **Aptitudes:** G4, V4, N4, S4, P4, Q4, K4, F3, M3, E4, C4 • **Temperaments:** R, T • **Stress:** T • **Physical:** V=L, H=N, L=H, W, S, H • **Work Env:** I, W, N • **Salary:** 2 • **Outlook:** 4

BAND-SAW OPERATOR (slaught. & meat pack.) • D.O.T. #525.685-010 • OES #92944 • Tends electrically powered bandsaw that cuts portions from hams to prepare hams for smoking, curing, or packing processes: Lifts ham from meat tank onto saw table, using meat hook. Presses button to start saw and adjusts saw gages according to size of ham. Pushes and guides ham into saw blade by hand or with wooden device to cut shank from ham or to remove tip from shank. Pushes sawed meat onto conveyor for further processing. May tend bandsaw that cuts poultry into serving pieces for packaging. • **GED:** R2, M1, L1 • **SVP:** 2-30 days • **Academic:** Ed=N, Eng=N • **Work Field:** 034 • **MPSMS:** 382 • **Aptitudes:** G4, V4, N4, S4, P4, Q4, K4, F4, M3, E5, C5 • **Temperaments:** R • **Stress:** T • **Physical:** V=L, H=N, L=M, W, H • **Work Env:** I, W, N, R • **Salary:** 2 • **Outlook:** 2

BREWERY CELLAR WORKER (beer prod.) • D.O.T. #522.685-014 • OES #92998 • Tends equipment that cools and adds yeast to wort to produce beer: Starts pumps and turns valves to control flow of refrigerant through cooler coils, to regulate flow of hot wort from tank through cooler into starting tank, and to admit specified amounts of air into wort [COOLING-MACHINE OPERATOR (malt liquors)]. Turns valves to add yeast to wort and to transfer wort to fermenting tanks [RECEIVER, FERMENTING CELLARS (malt liquors)]. • **GED:** R2, M1, L1 • **SVP:** 2-30 days • **Academic:** Ed=N, Eng=N • **Work Field:** 146 • **MPSMS:** 395 • **Aptitudes:** G4, V4, N4, S4, P4, Q4, K4, F4, M3, E5, C5 • **Temperaments:** R, T • **Stress:** T • **Physical:** V=L, H=N, L=M, W, S, H • **Work Env:** I, C, W • **Salary:** 3 • **Outlook:** 2

CANNERY WORKER (can. & preserv.) • D.O.T. #529.686-014 • OES #93935 • Feeds products into processing equipment, such as washer, peeler, corer, pitter, and trimmer, and performs any combination of following tasks in canning, freezing, preserving, or packing food products: Dumps or places food products in hopper, on sorting table, or on conveyor. Sorts or grades products according to size, color, or quality. Feeds products into processing equipment, such as washing, refrigerating, peeling, coring, pitting, trimming, grinding, dicing, cooking, or slicing machines. Trims, peels, and slices products with knife or paring tool. Feeds empty containers onto conveyor or forming machines. Fills containers, using scoop or filling form, or packs by hand [PACKAGER, HAND (any ind.)]. Counts, weighs, or tallies processed items according to specifications. Inspects and weighs filled containers to ensure product conforms with quality and weight standards. Places filled containers on trays, racks, or into boxes. Loads, moves, or stacks containers by hand or handtruck and cleans glass jar containers, using airhose. May be designated according to work performed as DUMPER (can. & preserv.); PEELER (can. & preserv.); SORTER (can. & preserv.); TRIMMER (can. & preserv.). • **GED:** R2, M2, L2 • **SVP:** 2-30 days • **Academic:** Ed=N, Eng=N • **Work Field:** 041, 146, 212 • **MPSMS:** 380 • **Aptitudes:** G4, V4, N4, S4, P4, Q4, K3, F3, M3, E5, C4 • **Temperaments:** R, T • **Stress:** T • **Physical:** V=L, H=N, L=L, W, S, H • **Work Env:** I, W, N, R • **Salary:** 3 • **Outlook:** 2

CENTRIFUGE OPERATOR (dairy prod.) • D.O.T. #521.685-042 • OES #92962 • Tends centrifuge machines that refine liquid wort for use in making malted milk: Assembles and attaches bowl, rings, and cover onto centrifuge, using hoist and handtools. Starts machine, observes tachometer, and adjusts controls to regulate speed. Starts pumps, turns valves, and observes gages to convey wort through machine at specified pressure. Regulates clarity of wort by observing color and turning valves to alter pressure flow. Removes solids from machine with wooden paddle. Cleans machine with water. • **GED:** R2, M2, L2 • **SVP:** 2-30 days • **Academic:** Ed=N, Eng=N • **Work Field:** 145 • **MPSMS:** 383 • **Aptitudes:** G4, V4, N4, S4, P4, Q4, K4, F4, M3, E5, C3 • **Temperaments:** R, T • **Stress:** T • **Physical:** V=L, H=N, L=H, W, H • **Work Env:** I, W, N • **Salary:** 3 • **Outlook:** 3

CHEESE CUTTER (dairy prod.) • D.O.T. #529.585-010 • OES #92944 • Tends machine that cuts blocks of cheese into pieces of specified shape and size: Examines cheese for defects in color, texture, and body. Bolts specified cutting head to machine, using wrench, adjusts stops on cutting table, and turns wheels to position cutting wires. Places block on table, and moves lever to lower cutting head or raise table to cut cheese. Weighs cut cheese, places pieces on conveyor, and records amount cut. May measure cheese with ruler and cut with hand cutter. May trim rind, mold, or sediment from cheese, using knife. • **GED:** R2, M1, L1 • **SVP:** 2-30 days • **Academic:** Ed=N, Eng=N • **Work Field:** 054, 212 • **MPSMS:** 383 • **Aptitudes:** G4, V4, N4, S4, P3, Q4, K3, F4, M3, E5, C3 • **Temperaments:** M, R, T • **Stress:** T • **Physical:** V=L, H=N, L=M, W, H • **Work Env:** I • **Salary:** 2 • **Outlook:** 2

CHOCOLATE MOLDER, MACHINE (choc. & cocoa) • D.O.T. #529.685-054 • OES #92971 • Tends machine and equipment that deposit tempered chocolate into molds to form bars, blocks, and assorted figures: Opens valves to draw chocolate from tempering kettle or automatic tempering equipment into water-jacketed depositor of molding machine. Observes thermometer and turns valves to admit and circulate water in jacket to maintain specified temperature of chocolate in depositor. Adjusts piston stroke of depositor that forces measured amounts of chocolate into conveyorized molds, using handtools. Turns handwheel to adjust speed of conveyor. Starts machine. Weighs filled molds to ensure that weight of chocolate casts meet specifications. Observes thermometer and turns thermostat and valve to control temperature in cooling tunnel. Observes action of machine to insure that molds do not jam. May temper chocolate [CHOCOLATE TEMPERER (bake. prod.; cereal)]. • **GED:** R3, M2, L2 • **SVP:** 3-6 mos • **Academic:**

Ed=N, Eng=N • **Work Field:** 132 • **MPSMS:** 393 • **Aptitudes:** G3, V4, N4, S4, P4, Q4, K4, F4, M3, E5, C4 • **Temperaments:** M, T • **Physical:** V=L, H=N, L=L, W, H • **Work Env:** I, N • **Salary:** 3 • **Outlook:** 3

COFFEE GRINDER (food prep nec) • D.O.T. #521.685-078 • OES #92965 • GRANULIZING-MACHINE OPERATOR. Tends machines that grind coffee beans to specified fineness: Pulls lever or adjusts control to regulate flow of coffee beans into grinding machines. Starts machines and turns dials or moves levers to adjust grinding rollers. May control conveyors that carry ground coffee to storage bins. • **GED:** R1, M1, L1 • **SVP:** 2-30 days • **Academic:** Ed=N, Eng=N • **Work Field:** 142 • **MPSMS:** 391 • **Aptitudes:** G4, V4, N4, S4, P4, Q4, K4, F4, M4, E5, C5 • **Temperaments:** R, T • **Stress:** T • **Physical:** V=N, H=N, L=L, H • **Work Env:** I, N • **Salary:** 3 • **Outlook:** 3

COOK, FRY, DEEP FAT (can. & preserv.) • D.O.T. #526.685-014 • OES #92917 • Tends deep-fat cookers to fry meats, vegetables, or fish in cooking oil: Empties containers or opens valves to fill cookers with oil. Sets thermostat to heat oil to specified temperature. Empties containers of meat, vegetable, or fish into metal basket and immerses basket into vat manually or by hoist. Sets timer. Observes color at end of frying time to determine conformity to standards and extends frying time accordingly. Removes basket from cooker, drains it, and dumps contents onto tray. May dip foods into batter or dye before frying. May specialize in a particular food product for canning or freezing or may fry variety of foods for immediate consumption. • **GED:** R2, M1, L1 • **SVP:** 2-30 days • **Academic:** Ed=N, Eng=N • **Work Field:** 146 • **MPSMS:** 386, 387, 903 • **Aptitudes:** G4, V4, N4, S4, P4, Q5, K4, F4, M3, E5, C4 • **Temperaments:** R, T • **Stress:** T • **Physical:** V=L, H=N, L=M, W, H • **Work Env:** I • **Salary:** 2 • **Outlook:** 3

COOKER, PROCESS CHEESE (dairy prod.) • D.O.T. #526.665-010 • OES #92917 • COOK BLENDER. Tends vat to cook blended cheeses or cheese curd and other ingredients to make process cheese: Starts agitator and signals for cheese to be dropped into vat. Turns steam valve and observes thermometer to heat vat to specified temperature. Measures or weighs out prescribed ingredients, such as sodium citrate, disodium phosphate, and cream, using scale and measuring glass. Dumps ingredients into vat. Cooks mixture at specified temperature for specified time or observes consistency of mixture to determine when it is cooked to specifications. Pulls lever to drain cheese into hopper or bucket. May pump cheese through viscolizer to achieve finer texture. May mix unheated cheese or cheese curd and other ingredients to make cold pack cheese or creamed cheese and be designated CREAM-CHEESE MAKER (dairy prod.). • **GED:** R3, M2, L2 • **SVP:** 30 days-3 mos • **Academic:** Ed=N, Eng=N • **Work Field:** 146 • **MPSMS:** 383 • **Aptitudes:** G3, V4, N4, S4, P4, Q4, K4, F4, M3, E5, C5 • **Temperaments:** J, T • **Physical:** V=L, H=N, L=M, W, H • **Work Env:** I, W • **Salary:** 2 • **Outlook:** 2

FLOUR BLENDER (grain & feed mill) • D.O.T. #520.685-106 • OES #92965 • BLENDER. Tends machines that blend and sift flour, and conveyors that carry flour between machines: Starts screw conveyors or turns valves on feed chutes to transfer flour from storage bins to mixing machine, or dumps designated bags of flour into hopper of machine. Starts machine to mix flour and pulls lever to open gate and allow blended flour to flow from machine. Starts separator that sifts mixed flour to remove lumps. Starts conveyors that transfer blended and sifted flour to packing machine. • **GED:** R2, M1, L1 • **SVP:** 30 days-3 mos • **Academic:** Ed=N, Eng=N • **Work Field:** 143 • **MPSMS:** 381 • **Aptitudes:** G4, V4, N4, S4, P4, Q4, K4, F4, M3, E5, C5 • **Temperaments:** R • **Stress:** T • **Physical:** V=L, H=N, L=H, W, H • **Work Env:** I, N • **Salary:** 3 • **Outlook:** 2

HONEY PROCESSOR (food prep nec) • D.O.T. #522.685-070 • OES #92962 • PASTEURIZER. Tends equipment that pasteurizes and filters liquid honey, and seeds honey with crystals to make crystallized honey for use as food spread: Turns valve to admit honey from blending tanks to pasteurizer, and to adjust and control pasteurizing temperature. Installs pads in filter press and turns handcrank to tighten pads. Starts pumps and adjusts pressure to force honey through filter and transfer honey to bottling machine or cooling vats. Pours container of honey crystals into vat of liquid honey and mixes it with paddle or electric stirring rod to induce controlled crystallization. May bottle honey. • **GED:** R2, M1, L1 • **SVP:** 30 days-3 mos • **Academic:** Ed=N, Eng=N • **Work Field:** 146 • **MPSMS:** 399 • **Aptitudes:** G3, V4, N4, S4, P3, Q4, K3, F4, M3, E4, C4 • **Temperaments:** R, T • **Stress:** T • **Physical:** V=N, H=N, L=L, W, C, H • **Work Env:** I, W • **Salary:** 2 • **Outlook:** 2

MILL OPERATOR (corn prod.) • D.O.T. #521.685-226 • OES #92965 • Tends mills that grind stockfeed: Turns gate valves on feed chute to regulate flow of materials into mills. Starts mills and turns handwheel to adjust distance between rollers to attain desired fineness of grind. Feels sample of product to verify fineness of grind. • **GED:** R1, M1, L1 • **SVP:** 2-30 days • **Academic:** Ed=N, Eng=N • **Work Field:** 142 • **MPSMS:** 381 • **Aptitudes:** G4, V4, N4, S3, P4, Q4, K4, F3, M3, E5, C5 • **Temperaments:** J, T • **Physical:** V=N, H=N, L=L, W, C, H • **Work Env:** I • **Salary:** 4 • **Outlook:** 3

MIXING-MACHINE OPERATOR (food prep. n.e.c.) • D.O.T. #520.665-014 • OES #92965 • Tends machine that mixes compressed yeast with oils and whiteners preparatory to extrusion and packing: Signals worker to fill mixer with specified amount of compressed yeast. Pours specified quantity of cutting oils and whitening agents into yeast and starts agitators to mix ingredients for specified time. Observes and feels mixed yeast to determine its consistency and pours specified amount of water into yeast to achieve required consistency. Starts screw conveyor to transfer yeast to extruders. • **GED:** R2, M1, L1 • **SVP:** 2-30 days • **Academic:** Ed=N, Eng=N • **Work Field:** 143 • **MPSMS:** 399 • **Aptitudes:** G3, V4, N4, S3, P4, Q4, K4, F4, M4, E5, C5 • **Temperaments:** J, T • **Physical:** V=L, H=N, L=M, W, C, H • **Work Env:** I, N • **Salary:** 3 • **Outlook:** 2

OVEN TENDER (bake. prod.) • D.O.T. #526.685-030 • OES #92921 • Tends stationary or rotary hearth oven that bakes bread, pastries, and other bakery products: Places pans of unbaked goods on blade of long-handled paddle (peel). Opens oven door and slides loaded peel into oven. Jerks paddle from under pans to deposit them on hearth. Observes gages and turns valves to regulate heat and humidity of oven. Notes color of products during baking to ensure uniformity of finished products. Removes baked goods from oven with peel, and places them on tiered racks. Flips switch to position hearth for loading and unloading when tending rotary hearth oven. May be designated according to type of oven tended as PEEL OVEN TENDER (bake. prod.); ROTARY-PEEL OVEN TENDER (bake. prod.). • **GED:** R3, M1, L1 • **SVP:** 3-6 mos • **Academic:** Ed=N, Eng=N • **Work Field:** 141 • **MPSMS:** 384 • **Aptitudes:** G3, V4, N4, S4, P3, Q4, K3, F4, M3, E5, C4 • **Temperaments:** J, T • **Physical:** V=L, H=N, L=M, W, S, H • **Work Env:** I, H • **Salary:** 2 • **Outlook:** 2

PRESS OPERATOR, MEAT (slaught. & meat pack.) • D.O.T. #520.685-182 • OES #92971 • Tends machine that presses such meats as bacon slabs, beef cuts, hams, and hog butts, into shape to facilitate slicing or packing: Positions meat on table of pressing machine and depresses pedal or pulls lever to lower ram onto meat that compresses meat into shape. Removes meat from machine and places in container, or on conveyor for transfer to slicing machine. May tend slicing machine [SLICING-MACHINE OPERATOR (dairy prod.; slaught. & meat pack.)]. May be designated according to cut of meat pressed, as BUTT PRESSER (slaught. & meat pack.); HAM MOLDER (slaught. & meat pack.). • **GED:** R1, M1, L1 • **SVP:** 2-30 days • **Academic:** Ed=N, Eng=N • **Work Field:** 034, 134 • **MPSMS:** 382 • **Aptitudes:** G4, V4, N5, S4, P4, Q5, K4, F4, M3, E5, C5 • **Temperaments:** R • **Stress:** T • **Physical:** V=L, H=N, L=M, W, H • **Work Env:** I • **Salary:** 3 • **Outlook:** 2

YEAST-CUTTING-AND-WRAPPING-MACHINE OPERATOR (food prep nec) • D.O.T. #529.665-022 • OES #92974 • YEAST-CAKE CUTTER. Tends machines that compress and extrude bulk yeast into continuous bars, cut bars into cakes of specified size, and wrap and heat-seal cakes: Signals worker to fill hopper of extruder with yeast. Positions and threads roll of paper, plastic film, or foil through roller guide of wrapping mechanism, and starts machines. Removes yeast cakes from conveyor emerging from cutter and feeds cakes into wrapping machine, discarding cracked or malformed cakes. Observes cutting and wrapping operation to detect jamming or twisted wrapping. Packs wrapped yeast cakes in cartons. • **GED:** R2, M1, L1 • **SVP:** 2-30 days • **Academic:** Ed=N, Eng=N • **Work Field:** 146 • **MPSMS:** 399 •

Aptitudes: G4, V4, N4, S4, P4, Q5, K3, F4, M3, E5, C5 • **Temperaments:** R, T • **Stress:** T • **Physical:** V=L, H=N, L=L, W, H • **Work Env:** I • **Salary:** 2 • **Outlook:** 2

GOE: 06.04.16 Equip. Oper., Textile, Fabric & Leather Proc., Elemental

EXTRACTOR OPERATOR (any ind.) • D.O.T. #581.685-038 • OES #92998 • CENTRIFUGAL-EXTRACTOR OPERATOR; CLOTHES WRINGER; DRYING-MACHINE TENDER; EXTRACTOR; RAPID-EXTRACTOR OPERATOR; WRINGER. Tends centrifugal extractor that removes surplus moisture or dye from materials, such as wet cloth, garments, knit goods, linens, raw fibers, or yarn: Pushes loaded handtrucks or portable extractor baskets into position at machine or under hoist. Lifts material from handtruck, or raises baskets, using chain or electric hoist to load extractor. Distributes material uniformly in extractor baskets to balance load and reduce vibration. Observes tilt of portable baskets to verify balance when using hoist. Closes cover and starts machine. Unloads materials into handtruck for transfer to subsequent work station. May unload washing machines. May work with raw cotton and be designated as EXTRACTOR TENDER, RAW STOCK (textile). May tend drying machine [TUMBLER OPERATOR (clean., dye., & press.; laund.)]. May tend machine that extracts moisture from cakes of rayon or other synthetic yarn and be designated CAKE WRINGER (synthetic fibers). • **GED:** R1, M1, L1 • **SVP:** 2-30 days • **Academic:** Ed=N, Eng=N • **Work Field:** 145 • **MPSMS:** 410, 420, 440 • **Aptitudes:** G4, V4, N5, S4, P4, Q5, K4, F4, M3, E4, C5 • **Temperaments:** R • **Stress:** T • **Physical:** V=L, H=N, L=M, W, H • **Work Env:** I, W, N • **Salary:** 2 • **Outlook:** 2

HARDENING-MACHINE OPERATOR (hat & cap) • D.O.T. #586.685-026 • OES #92998 • HARDENER. Tends machine that agitates fur felt hat cones to mat together interlocking fibers and harden cones preparatory to forming into hats: Wraps wet cones in burlap and wrings or places cones in extractor and starts machine to remove excess water. Wraps cones in woolen cloth and places cloth containing cones on rollers of hardening machine. Pulls handle to lower upper rollers onto cones and simultaneously start timed rollers that agitate cones and tighten fibers in tip of cones. Removes cloth containing cones and repeats operation to tighten fibers in brim area of cones. May inspect cones and work fibers into holes and thin spots, using fingers, to repair damaged cones. • **GED:** R2, M1, L2 • **SVP:** 30 days-3 mos • **Academic:** Ed=N, Eng=N • **Work Field:** 062, 134 • **MPSMS:** 529 • **Aptitudes:** G4, V4, N4, S4, P3, Q4, K3, F3, M3, E5, C5 • **Temperaments:** R • **Stress:** T • **Physical:** V=L, H=N, L=L, W, H • **Work Env:** I, W, N • **Salary:** 2 • **Outlook:** 2

MACHINE FEEDER, RAW STOCK (felt goods) • D.O.T. #680.686-018 • OES #98502 • FEEDER TENDER; GUILLOTINE OPERATOR; HOPPER FEEDER; SHREDDER PICKER. Feeds raw fiber stock into machines that loosen, shred, separate, clean, form nubs, or straighten fibers: Places fibers on conveyor belt or into machine hopper for processing by machine. Opens and closes gates of belt and pneumatic conveyors on machines fed directly from preceding machines. Loosens material before dumping it into hoppers by pulling fibers apart. May truck stock from storage or other departments to machine. May be designated according to type of machine fed as CARDING-MACHINE FEEDER (textile); GARNETT FEEDER (house furn.; waste & batting); NUB-CARD TENDER (textile); PICKER FEEDER (house furn.; textile). • **GED:** R1, M1, L1 • **SVP:** 2-30 days • **Academic:** Ed=N, Eng=N • **Work Field:** 161 • **MPSMS:** 410 • **Aptitudes:** G4, V4, N5, S4, P4, Q5, K4, F4, M4, E5, C5 • **Temperaments:** R • **Stress:** T • **Physical:** V=L, H=N, L=H, W, S, H • **Work Env:** I, N • **Salary:** 3 • **Outlook:** 3

SLASHER TENDER (textile) • D.O.T. #582.562-010 • OES #92998 • SIZER. Operates machine to saturate warp yarn with size and wind sized yarn onto loom beam: Positions section beams onto creel with aid of another worker, using hoist. Gathers ends of warp together and ties warp to corresponding leaders left in machine from previous run, or when machine is empty, bunches ends together and threads yarn through size pot, around drying cylinders, and onto loom beams. Inserts lease rods between alternate strands of yarn to prevent yarn from sticking together. Lays individual warp ends between teeth of expansion comb for even distribution across loom beam. Turns valves to admit size into vat and steam into drying cylinders. Sets yardage clock to indicate yardage to be wound on loom beam. Starts machine and observes flow of warp through machine to detect breaks and tangles in yarn. Disentangles yarn and ties broken ends with fingers. Feels yarn to verify adherence of size to yarn and insure that yarn is dry but not burned. Inserts lease string in warp yarn and secures yarn ends with tape. Doffs loom beam onto handtruck and replaces with empty beam, using hoist. Records style number, yardage beamed, yarn breaks, and machine stops. May change temperature control chart on control panel. May clean machine. May process yarn for use on narrow fabric looms and be designated WARP-SPOOL SLASHER (narrow fabrics). • **GED:** R3, M2, L3 • **SVP:** 1-2 yrs • **Academic:** Ed=N, Eng=S • **Work Field:** 152 • **MPSMS:** 411 • **Aptitudes:** G3, V4, N4, S3, P3, Q4, K3, F3, M3, E5, C4 • **Temperaments:** R, T • **Stress:** T • **Physical:** V=L, H=N, L=H, W, S, H • **Work Env:** I, H, W, N • **Salary:** 4 • **Outlook:** 2

GOE: 06.04.17 Equip. Oper., Clay Proc., Elemental

AUXILIARY-EQUIPMENT TENDER (cement) • D.O.T. #570.685-010 • OES #92965 • CEMENT MIXER; SLIP MIXER; SLURRY BLENDER; SLURRY-TANK TENDER. Tends auxiliary equipment such as pumps, motors, and conveyors to supply materials and power to slurry tanks and other equipment to mix cement slurry for kilns: Receives signal from ROTARY-KILN OPERATOR (cement; chem.; minerals & earths). and starts pumps and conveyors to feed raw materials into kiln. Opens valves to fill slurry tanks with specified amounts of water and raw materials or to correct slurry mixture. Starts tank agitators that mix slurry. Greases and oils equipment. May be designated according to equipment tended as KILN FEEDER (cement) or MIXER TENDER (cement). • **GED:** R2, M2, L1 • **SVP:** 30 days-3 mos • **Academic:** Ed=N, Eng=N • **Work Field:** 143 • **MPSMS:** 533 • **Aptitudes:** G4, V4, N4, S4, P4, Q4, K4, F4, M3, E4, C5 • **Temperaments:** R, T • **Stress:** T • **Physical:** V=L, H=N, L=M, W, S, H • **Work Env:** B, N • **Salary:** 2 • **Outlook:** 3

KILN WORKER (pottery & porc.) • D.O.T. #573.687-022 • OES #98999 • KILN MAINTENANCE LABORER. Performs routine tasks concerned with maintenance and repair of kilns under direction of such workers as KILN PLACERS (pottery & porc.) or BRICKLAYERS (brick & tile). • **GED:** R1, M1, L1 • **SVP:** 2-30 days • **Academic:** Ed=N, Eng=N • **Work Field:** 102 • **MPSMS:** 568 • **Aptitudes:** G4, V4, N5, S4, P3, Q5, K4, F4, M3, E4, C5 • **Temperaments:** R • **Stress:** T • **Physical:** V=L, H=N, L=M, W, S, H • **Work Env:** I • **Salary:** 2 • **Outlook:** 2

SHELL MOLDER (foundry) • D.O.T. #518.685-026 • OES #91911 • Tends machine that makes shell molds used to produce metal castings: Starts machine that automatically forms and cures shell. Strips cured shell halves from machine and positions shell half on fixture of mold-closing machine. Brushes glue around edges of shell half. Positions remaining shell half on top of lower half and activates ram that exerts pressure on shell until glue has set. May glue and assemble shell halves by hand. May clamp, wire, or bolt shell halves together. May bolt pattern and core box to bed of machine. May produce cores on shell making machine and be designated SHELL COREMAKER (found.). • **GED:** R2, M1, L2 • **SVP:** 2-30 days • **Academic:** Ed=N, Eng=N • **Work Field:** 136, 141 • **MPSMS:** 567 • **Aptitudes:** G4, V4, N4, S4, P3, Q4, K3, F3, M3, E4, C5 • **Temperaments:** R, T • **Stress:** T • **Physical:** V=L, H=N, L=H, W, H • **Work Env:** I, R • **Salary:** 4 • **Outlook:** 2

GOE: 06.04.18 Equip. Oper., Wood Processing

DIGESTER-OPERATOR HELPER (build. board) • D.O.T. #532.686-010 • OES #98502 • COOK HELPER; DIGESTER-COOK HELPER; PULP-MAKING-PLANT OPERATOR. Feeds wood chips and soda ash or acid into digester that processes wood chips into pulp: Unbolts and removes digester cover, using wrench and chain hoist. Lowers feed pipe into digester, using hoist, and pushes button or turns handwheel to load digester with wood chips. Pushes control panel button or turns valve to admit specified quantities of soda ash or acid into digester. Replaces and bolts cover. May remove cover and blow steam from digester at completion of cooking cycle. May tend conveyors that convey chips to hopper or cooked pulp to storage bins. May open valves to blow cooked pulp into pit. May pull lever to dump cooked pulp from rotary digester. May draw and deliver pulp sample to laboratory for analysis. • **GED:** R2, M2, L1 • **SVP:** 2-30 days • **Academic:** Ed=N, Eng=N • **Work Field:** 147 • **MPSMS:** 471, 473 • **Aptitudes:** G4, V4, N4, S4, P4, Q5, K4, F4, M3, E5, C5 • **Temperaments:** R • **Stress:** T • **Physical:** V=L, H=N, L=L, W, H • **Work Env:** I • **Salary:** 4 • **Outlook:** 2

TANKER (wood preserving) • D.O.T. #561.665-010 • OES #92998 • DIP TANKER; PLATFORM WORKER; SCAFFOLD WORKER. Tends open tank to impregnate wood products with preservatives: Signals BRIDGE-OR-GANTRY-CRANE OPERATOR (any ind.) to lift load of material over tank and guides load into tank by hand or with rod, working from elevated platform. Chains tank loads of poles to high rack to prevent toppling. Observes gages and turns valves to regulate heat and flow of preserving solution in tank. Impregnates sashes, doors, and other millwork products, using hand or power hoist to load and unload tank. May tend vacuum-type dip tank that impregnates wood by pressure. • **GED:** R2, M1, L1 • **SVP:** 30 days-3 mos • **Academic:** Ed=N, Eng=N • **Work Field:** 152 • **MPSMS:** 452 • **Aptitudes:** G4, V4, N4, S3, P4, Q4, K4, F4, M3, E4, C5 • **Temperaments:** R, T • **Stress:** T • **Physical:** V=L, H=N, L=M, W, S, H • **Work Env:** B, R • **Salary:** 2 • **Outlook:** 2

GOE: 06.04.19 Equip. Oper., Assorted Materials Proc., Elemental

COATING EQUIPMENT OPERATOR, PRINTED CIRCUIT BOARDS (electronics) • D.O.T. #590.685-066 • OES #92953 • Tends automated equipment that applies photosensitive coating of masking ink to printed circuit board (PCB) panels to facilitate development of circuit design on boards in fabrication of PCBs: Pushes buttons and switches to start heater, conveyor, and coating equipment. Measures conveyor travel time of sample panel, using stopwatch, and weighs sample panel, using digital scale, to ensure that specifications are met. Turns dials to adjust conveyor speed and to add or delete masking ink in solution, as needed. Feeds panels onto conveyor of automated equipment that cleans, heats, and applies masking ink to panels. Removes panels from unloading rack upon completion of coating process and dries panels in oven. Records production data. • **GED:** R2, M2, L2 • **SVP:** 30 days-3 mos • **Academic:** Ed=N, Eng=S • **Work Field:** 151 • **MPSMS:** 587 • **Aptitudes:** G3, V4, N4, S4, P4, Q4, K3, F4, M3, E5, C5 • **Temperaments:** R • **Stress:** T • **Physical:** V=N, H=N, L=M, W, H • **Work Env:** I • **Salary:** 2 • **Outlook:** 4

CREMATOR (per. ser.) • D.O.T. #359.685-010 • OES #69999 • Tends retort furnace that cremates human bodies: Slides casket containing body into furnace. Starts furnace. Adjusts valves to attain extreme heat and to maintain temperature for specified time. Allows furnace to cool. Removes unburned metal casket parts from furnace. Scrapes ashes of casket and body from furnace, using handtools. Sifts ashes through fine screen and removes extraneous material. Places remains in canister and attaches metal identification tag to canister. Cleans furnace and sweeps and washes floors. May place rings and jewelry in temporary box for return to relatives. May clean building and fixtures. May care for lawns and shrubs. • **GED:** R3, M2, L2 • **SVP:** 30 days-3 mos • **Academic:** Ed=N, Eng=N • **Work Field:** 291 • **MPSMS:** 909 • **Aptitudes:** G3, V4, N4, S4, P4, Q4, K3, F4, M3, E5, C5 • **Temperaments:** R, T • **Stress:** T • **Physical:** V=N, H=N, L=H, W, H • **Work Env:** I, H • **Salary:** 2 • **Outlook:** 2

DEVELOPER, AUTOMATIC (photofinish.) • D.O.T. #976.685-014 • OES #92908 • CONTINUOUS PROCESS MACHINE OPERATOR; FILM MACHINE OPERATOR. Tends machine that develops sheets, strips, or continuous roll of film preparatory to printing: Pulls film through trapdoor into darkroom. Strips paper backing from film and attaches identifying label. Feels edges of film to detect tears and repairs film, using stapler. Reads work order or feels film for size or notches to determine type of process and developing time required. Positions racks of film on machine chain links according to developing time required or threads leader of continuous roll through machine preparatory to processing. Activates machine that automatically transports film through series of chemical baths to develop, fix, harden, bleach, and wash film. Listens for sounds that indicate machine malfunctioning and notifies supervisor or maintenance personnel when repairs are needed. May run test strip through machine for inspection by supervisor and add chemicals to or adjust machine as directed. May tend equipment that develops, fixes image, and dries X-ray plates and be designated X-RAY-DEVELOPING-MACHINE OPERATOR (medical ser.). • **GED:** R2, M1, L1 • **SVP:** 2-30 days • **Academic:** Ed=N, Eng=N • **Work Field:** 202 • **MPSMS:** 867 • **Aptitudes:** G3, V4, N4, S4, P3, Q4, K3, F3, M3, E5, C5 • **Temperaments:** R, T • **Stress:** T • **Physical:** V=N, H=N, L=L, H • **Work Env:** I, N • **Salary:** 3 • **Outlook:** 3

DISPLAY-SCREEN FABRICATOR (electronics) • D.O.T. #725.685-010 • OES #92198 • Tends a variety of machines that form and prepare aperture masks and display screens for color-television picture tubes: Feeds specified sections of sensitized steel between plates in photographic printing chase to flatten sheet to specification. Sets timer for specified exposure time and turns on heliarc lamp to imprint pattern of aperture mask from photographic plate onto steel. Verifies alinement of plates, using microscope. Tends furnace that blackens aperture masks and rings used in color television picture tubes. Feeds mask through series of rollers to flatten mask. Positions mask on bed of forming press and lowers die to form mask. Places display screen on conveyor leading through cleaning, drying, and phosphor coating operations. Positions aperture mask and screen on fixture over time-cycled light source to print color-emitting dots on phospher coating. Starts cycle to expose coating to light through mask aperture. Marks mating screen and aperture mask with matching numbers for future assembly. Fastens screen in holder on conveyor that carries screen through equipment to develop exposed phosphor, remove unexposed phosphor, and dry screen. May be designated according to process as APERTURE-MASK ETCHER (electronics); MASK FORMER (electronics); PHOSPHOR-APPLICATION MACHINE ATTENDANT (electronics). • **GED:** R2, M1, L1 • **SVP:** 2-30 days • **Academic:** Ed=N, Eng=N • **Work Field:** 134, 182 • **MPSMS:** 554 • **Aptitudes:** G4, V4, N5, S3, P4, Q5, K3, F3, M3, E4, C4 • **Temperaments:** R, T • **Stress:** T • **Physical:** V=L, H=N, L=L, H • **Work Env:** I, W • **Salary:** 3 • **Outlook:** 3

ELECTRONIC-COMPONENT PROCESSOR (electronics) • D.O.T. #590.684-014 • OES #92902 • Performs any combination of following duties to process materials into finished or semi-finished electronic components: Reads work orders, formulas, and processing charts and receives verbal instructions to determine specifications and sequence of operations to be followed. Weighs or measures specified ingredients and binding agents, using scales and graduates. Mixes and grinds material, using manual or automatic machines and equipment. Loads, unloads, monitors operation, and adjusts controls of various processing machines and equipment that bake, diffuse, cast, xray, cut, polish, coat, plate, silk-screen, and perform other similar operations to prepare, combine, or change structure of materials to produce compositions with specific electronics properties. Cleans materials as required prior to processing operations, using solvents. May inspect, measure, and test components according to specifications, using measuring instruments and test equipment. May enclose components in housings. May stamp or etch identifying information on finished component. May count, sort, and weigh processed items. May be designated according to duties performed as BAKER BEADS (electronics); FIRER (electronics); PELLET-PREPARATION OPERATOR (electronics); PREFORMING-MACHINE OPERATOR (electronics); VACUUM-EVAPORATION OPERATOR (electronics); WEIGHT-COUNT OPERATOR (electronics). Assembly of processed materials, parts, and components is covered under ELECTRONICS ASSEMBLER (electronics) 726.684-018 and ELECTRONICS ASSEMBLER, DEVELOPMENTAL (electronics) 726.261-010. • **GED:** R2, M2, L2 • **SVP:** 30 days-3 mos • **Academic:** Ed=N, Eng=N • **Work Field:** 147 • **MPSMS:** 587 • **Aptitudes:** G4, V4, N4, S4, P4, Q4, K3, F3, M3, E5, C4 • **Temperaments:** R, T • **Stress:** T • **Physical:** V=L, H=N, L=L, H • **Work**

Env: I • Salary: 3 • Outlook: 4

ETCHER-STRIPPER, PRINTED CIRCUIT BOARDS (electronics) • D.O.T. #590.685-082 • OES #92198 • Tends equipment that automatically acid-etches away unprotected copper and strips etch-resistant coating (photoresist) from substrate boards or panels, leaving conductive copper pattern to form printed circuit boards (PCBs): Reads process specifications and sets equipment controls to regulate conveyor speed, spray intensity, and solution temperatures and strengths. Places copper clad boards or panels with etch-resistant coating protecting circuitry pattern on motorized conveyor leading into series of processing units, such as sprayers, rinsers, scrubbers, and dryers, that acid-etch copper from unprotected areas and chemically strip off etch-resistant coating. Monitors equipment operation, gauges, and meters to detect malfunctions or variance from specifications. Visually examines sample boards during and after processing for completeness of etching and stripping. Notifies supervisor when equipment malfunctions or when boards fail to meet specifications. May adjust machine controls or alignment of boards on conveyor rollers to correct defects. May reroute boards through processing units to complete etching or stripping process. May periodically change or adjust chemicals and solutions. May test acid solution, using pH meter. May immerse boards in tanks of chemicals and solutions when equipment malfunctions. May use microscope to examine boards. May tend developing unit attached to etching-stripping equipment. May immerse boards in acid solution or tend machine that etches conductive pattern on copper surface and be designated ETCHER, PRINTED CIRCUITS (electronics). • **GED:** R2, M2, L2 • **SVP:** 30 days-3 mos • **Academic:** Ed=N, Eng=N • **Work Field:** 182 • **MPSMS:** 587 • **Aptitudes:** G4, V4, N4, S4, P3, Q4, K3, F4, M3, E5, C5 • **Temperaments:** R, T • **Stress:** T • **Physical:** V=G, H=N, L=M, W, H • **Work Env:** I, R, F • **Salary:** 2 • **Outlook:** 4

FILTER OPERATOR (any ind.) • D.O.T. #551.685-078 • OES #92962 • SLUDGE-FILTER OPERATOR; VACUUM-FILTER OPERATOR. Tends rotary drum-filters that separate slurries into liquid and filter cake (insoluble material): Couples flexible hose or pipe to vat, starts pump, and turns valves to regulate flow of slurry to filter tanks. Adjusts controls to regulate rotation speed of drums. Turns valve to regulate pressure that forces slurry through filter, separating filter cake from liquid. Observes discharge to ensure that scrapers are removing filter cake from drum. May tend thickeners, washing sprays, settlers, or related equipment. May draw sample for laboratory analysis. May be designated according to trade name of machine. • **GED:** R2, M1, L1 • **SVP:** 2-30 days • **Academic:** Ed=N, Eng=N • **Work Field:** 145 • **MPSMS:** 380, 490 • **Aptitudes:** G4, V4, N4, S4, P4, Q4, K4, F4, M3, E5, C4 • **Temperaments:** R, T • **Stress:** T • **Physical:** V=L, H=N, L=M, W, S, H • **Work Env:** I, N • **Salary:** 3 • **Out look:** 2

HEAT TREATER (electronics) • D.O.T. #504.686-022 • OES #91932 • Feeds and offbears furnace that heats semiconductor wafers to relieve stress caused by sawing and to stabilize resistivity: Transfers wafers from storage container to quartz boat. Places boat on conveyor belt that automatically moves wafers through furnace. Removes boat from conveyor belt at furnace exit. Transfers wafers from boat to storage container after cooling. Records production information on work order. • **GED:** R1, M1, L1 • **SVP:** 1 day • **Academic:** Ed=N, Eng=N • **Work Field:** 133 • **MPSMS:** 587 • **Aptitudes:** G4, V4, N5, S5, P5, Q5, K4, F5, M4, E5, C5 • **Temperaments:** R • **Stress:** T • **Physical:** V=L, H=N, L=L, H • **Work Env:** I, R • **Salary:** 2 • **Outlook:** 3

LABORER (drug prep. & related) • D.O.T. #559.686-022 • OES #98502 • BATCHER. Performs any combination of the following duties concerned with processing and packaging drug and toilet products: Transfers specified ingredients from storage to production area, using handtruck. Assembles specified ingredients for compounding. Feeds plants, roots, and herbs into machines, such as silage cutters, fanning mills, and washing machines. Loads botanicals into driers. Cuts animal tissue into strips, using saws. Feeds strips into meat grinders. Opens drums and scoops or dumps contents into kettles, tanks, or machine hopper. Removes filled cartons from packaging machine conveyor. • **GED:** R2, M1, L2 • **SVP:** 2-30 days • **Academic:** Ed=N, Eng=N • **Work Field:** 147 • **MPSMS:** 493 • **Aptitudes:** G4, V4, N4, S4, P4, Q5, K4, F4, M3, E5, C5 • **Temperaments:** R • **Stress:** T • **Physical:** V=L, H=N,

L=H, W, S, H • **Work Env:** I • **Salary:** 2 • **Outlook:** 2

METALLIZATION EQUIPMENT OPERATOR, SEMICONDUCTOR WAFERS (electronics) • D.O.T. #590.685-086 • OES #92902 • Tends machines that deposit layer of metal, such as aluminum, gold, or platinum, on semiconductor wafer surfaces to provide electrical contact between circuit components: Places semiconductor wafers in container, such as boat or cassette, using vacuum wand or tweezers. Cleans wafers, using chemical baths or automatic cleaning equipment, to remove contaminants prior to metal deposition. Loads wafers into metallization equipment holders, using vacuum wand or tweezers. Places loaded holders in equipment chamber. Pushes buttons, turns dials, and flips switches to start and adjust metallization process, following processing specifications. Tests and inspects processed wafers, using testing equipment, to measure electrical conductivity and thickness of metal layer. Maintains production records. Maintains chemicals and metals for equipment. Cleans work area. • **GED:** R3, M2, L2 • **SVP:** 30 days-3 mos • **Academic:** Ed=N, Eng=S • **Work Field:** 147 • **MPSMS:** 587 • **Aptitudes:** G3, V4, N4, S4, P4, Q4, K4, F3, M3, E5, C5 • **Temperaments:** R, T • **Stress:** T • **Physical:** V=L, H=N, L=L, W, H • **Work Env:** I • **Salary:** 2 • **Outlook:** 4

PLATER, SEMICONDUCTOR WAFERS AND COMPONENTS (electronics) • D.O.T. #500.684-030 • OES #91921 • Electroplates semiconductor wafers and electronic components, such as copper leads and rectifiers, with metals, such as gold, silver, and lead: Reads processing sheet to determine plating time and specifications. Places components or wafers in basket or fixture, using tweezers, and immerses components or wafers in chemical solution baths for specified time to clean and plate components or wafers. May measure thickness of photoresist and metal on wafer surface, using micrometer, and test electrical circuitry of individual die on wafer, using test probe equipment. May measure anode width on wafer surface, using microscope measuring equipment. • **GED:** R3, M2, L2 • **SVP:** 30 days-3 mos • **Academic:** Ed=N, Eng=N • **Work Field:** 154 • **MPSMS:** 587 • **Aptitudes:** G3, V4, N4, S3, P3, Q4, K4, F4, M4, E5, C3 • **Temperaments:** T • **Physical:** V=L, H=N, L=L, H • **Work Env:** I, R, F • **Salary:** 2 • **Outlook:** 3

POLYSILICON PREPARATION WORKER (electronics) • D.O.T. #590.684-038 • OES #92998 • Performs any combination of following tasks to prepare polysilicon for crystal growing process: Operates drilling machine to remove core sample from polysilicon rod for evaluation. Breaks polysilicon rod into chunks, using hammer. Removes tungsten filament from chunks, using circular saw or drill. Immerses polysilicon chunks into series of vats containing chemical solutions to remove contaminants, using steel basket and hoist. Breaks chunks of polysilicon into pieces, using hammer, to prepare polysilicon for meltdown in crystal growing process. Records production information. • **GED:** R2, M2, L2 • **SVP:** 2-30 days • **Academic:** Ed=N, Eng=N • **Work Field:** 031, 057 • **MPSMS:** 349 • **Aptitudes:** G4, V4, N4, S3, P3, Q4, K3, F4, M3, E4, C4 • **Temperaments:** R • **Stress:** T • **Physical:** V=L, H=N, L=V, W, H • **Work Env:** I, R • **Salary:** 2 • **Outlook:** 4

PRINT DEVELOPER, AUTOMATIC (photofinish.) • D.O.T. #976.685-026 • OES #92908 • Tends one or more machines that automatically develop, fix, wash, and dry photographic prints: Threads leaders (paper strips) around rollers, through processing tanks and dryer, around polished drum, and onto takeup reel. Turns valves to fill tanks with premixed solutions, such as developer, dyes, stop-baths, fixers, bleaches, and washes. Moves thermostatic control to keep steam-heated drum at specified temperature. Splices sensitized paper to leaders, using tape. Starts machine and throws switches to synchronize drive speeds of processing and drying units. Compares processed prints with color standard and reports variations to control department. Adds specified amounts of chemicals to renew solutions. Maintains production records. • **GED:** R2, M1, L1 • **SVP:** 3-6 mos • **Academic:** Ed=N, Eng=N • **Work Field:** 202 • **MPSMS:** 867 • **Aptitudes:** G4, V4, N4, S4, P4, Q4, K4, F3, M3, E5, C3 • **Temperaments:** R, T • **Stress:** T • **Physical:** V=G, H=N, L=S, H • **Work Env:** I, N, R • **Salary:** 3 • **Outlook:** 4

SEMICONDUCTOR PROCESSOR (electronics) • D.O.T. #590.684-022 • OES #92902 • WAFER FAB OPERATOR. Processes materials used in manufacture of electronic semiconductors: Loads semiconductor material into furnace to fuse and form ingot. Saws ingot into segments, using power saw. Loads individual segment into crystal growing chamber and monitors controls to produce specified crystalline structure in ingot. Locates crystal axis in ingot, using x-ray equipment and saws ingot into wafers, using power saw. Cleans, polishes, and loads wafer into series of special purpose furnaces, chemical baths, and equipment used to form circuitry and change conductive properties of individual segments of wafer. May scribe or separate wafer into dice (segments). • **GED:** R2, M2, L2 • **SVP:** 30 days-3 mos • **Academic:** Ed=N, Eng=N • **Work Field:** 147 • **MPSMS:** 587 • **Aptitudes:** G4, V4, N4, S4, P3, Q5, K3, F3, M3, E5, C5 • **Temperaments:** R, T • **Stress:** T • **Physical:** V=G, H=N, L=L, W, H • **Work Env:** I • **Salary:** 2 • **Outlook:** 4

STERILIZER (drug prep. & related) • D.O.T. #599.585-010 • OES #92998 • AUTOCLAVE OPERATOR. Tends autoclave that sterilizes drug products, containers, supplies, instruments, and equipment: Places articles in autoclave manually or by use of electric hoist. Secures door or lid, turns dials to adjust temperature and pressure, and opens steam valve. Shuts off steam and removes sterilized articles after specified time. Records time and temperature setting and gage readings. May wrap supplies and instruments in paper or cloth preparatory to sterilizing. • **GED:** R3, M2, L3 • **SVP:** 30 days-3 mos • **Academic:** Ed=N, Eng=S • **Work Field:** 141 • **MPSMS:** 493 • **Aptitudes:** G3, V3, N4, S4, P4, Q4, K4, F4, M3, E5, C5 • **Temperaments:** R, T • **Stress:** T • **Physical:** V=L, H=N, L=L, S, H • **Work Env:** I • **Salary:** 2 • **Outlook:** 3

UTILITY WORKER, FILM PROCESSING (photofinish.) • D.O.T. #976.685-030 • OES #92908 • Performs a variety of tasks to assist or substitute for other workers in a photofinishing laboratory: Sorts prints according to size and order number to facilitate handling. Tends automatic cutting machine that cuts roll into individual prints [CUTTER (photofinish.)]. Tends automatic film developing machine that develops and fixes image on film [DEVELOPER, AUTOMATIC (photofinish)]. Removes prints from print developer rinse tray and tends drum-type drier that dries prints. Prepares daily production sheet noting quantity and kind of work performed. • **GED:** R3, M1, L2 • **SVP:** 30 days-3 mos • **Academic:** Ed=N, Eng=N • **Work Field:** 054, 202, 221 • **MPSMS:** 867 • **Aptitudes:** G3, V3, N4, S4, P4, Q4, K3, F3, M3, E5, C4 • **Temperaments:** V • **Physical:** V=L, H=N, L=L, W, H • **Work Env:** I • **Salary:** 2 • **Outlook:** 2

GOE: 06.04.20 Machine Assembling, Elemental

ASSEMBLY-PRESS OPERATOR (any ind.) • D.O.T. #690.685-014 • OES #92998 • BENCH-PRESS OPERATOR. Tends hand or power press that shapes or assembles metal, plastic, rubber, or glass parts by crimping, shaping, locking, staking, or press fitting: Alines workpiece against fixtures under ram as specified. Moves controls to lower ram that shapes parts or presses parts together. May tend machine to separate parts or punch, face, cut, chamfer, or compress parts preparatory to assembly. May tend machine equipped with multiple rams or automatic positioning device. May be designated according to type of press tended as ARBOR-PRESS OPERATOR (any ind.) II; KICK-PRESS OPERATOR (any ind.) II; or according to parts assembled as HANDLE ATTACHER (any ind.); LENS MOUNTER (optical goods) I. • **GED:** R2, M1, L2 • **SVP:** 2-30 days • **Academic:** Ed=N, Eng=N • **Work Field:** 061, 134 • **MPSMS:** 550, 580, 610 • **Aptitudes:** G4, V4, N4, S4, P3, Q4, K3, F3, M3, E4, C4 • **Temperaments:** R, T • **Stress:** T • **Physical:** V=L, H=N, L=L, W, H • **Work Env:** I, N • **Salary:** 2 • **Outlook:** 2

CORRUGATED-FASTENER DRIVER (woodworking) • D.O.T. #669.685-042 • OES #92314 • CORRUGATOR OPERATOR; SHOOK SPLICER; SPLICER-MACHINE OPERATOR; STITCHER OPERATOR. Tends machine that cuts metal fasteners from corrugated metal stripping and drives fasteners into boards across joints to fasten boards together: Positions spool of corrugated metal stripping onto machine spindles and threads end of stripping between clamps of automatic feed driver-head. Positions and tightens machine driver-head above workpiece joint, using

wrench. Starts machine, positions workpiece against machine table stop, and depresses foot pedal to activate machine driver-head and force fastener into workpiece. May be designated according to parts fastened as BOX-TOP-STITCHING-MACHINE OPERATOR (wood. box); DOOR-FRAME ASSEMBLER, MACHINE (woodworking). • **GED:** R2, M1, L1 • **SVP:** 2-30 days • **Academic:** Ed=N, Eng=N • **Work Field:** 072 • **MPSMS:** 450 • **Aptitudes:** G4, V4, N5, S4, P4, Q5, K3, F4, M3, E4, C5 • **Temperaments:** R • **Stress:** T • **Physical:** V=L, H=N, L=M, W, S, H • **Work Env:** I, N • **Salary:** 3 • **Outlook:** 2

MOUNTER, AUTOMATIC (photofinish.) • D.O.T. #976.685-022 • OES #92908 • Tends automatic-mounting press that cuts film into individual transparencies, and inserts and seals transparencies in mounting frames: Loads mounting frames into machine and depresses lever to lock frames into feed position. Compares identifying labels to insure numbers on film reel and customer envelope match. Records customer charges on envelope according to standard price listing. Mounts film reel on machine spindle and trims rough edges of film, using scissors. Threads film through machine guides and activates machine that automatically cuts film and mounts transparencies. Observes movement of film through machine to detect jamming and adjusts machine guides, using screwdriver. Notifies supervisor of major machine malfunction. • **GED:** R2, M1, L1 • **SVP:** 2-30 days • **Academic:** Ed=N, Eng=N • **Work Field:** 054, 062 • **MPSMS:** 867 • **Aptitudes:** G4, V4, N4, S4, P3, Q4, K3, F3, M3, E5, C5 • **Temperaments:** R • **Stress:** T • **Physical:** V=L, H=N, L=L, H • **Work Env:** I • **Salary:** 1 • **Outlook:** 2

STAPLING-MACHINE OPERATOR (any ind.) • D.O.T. #692.685-202 • OES #92998 • WIRE-STITCHER OPERATOR. Tends machine that staples together parts of products made from materials, such as plastic, paper, leather, felt, and canvas: Loads machine with wire staples or spool of wire, and positions material under head of machine. Steps on pedal to lower ram that cuts off wire staple and forces it through material to clinch it together. May adjust machine table to accommodate different sizes of materials being stapled. • **GED:** R2, M1, L2 • **SVP:** 2-30 days • **Academic:** Ed=N, Eng=N • **Work Field:** 062 • **MPSMS:** 610 • **Aptitudes:** G4, V4, N4, S4, P4, Q4, K3, F3, M3, E5, C5 • **Temperaments:** R • **Stress:** T • **Physical:** V=L, H=N, L=M, W, H • **Work Env:** I, N • **Salary:** 2 • **Outlook:** 2

GOE: 06.04.21 Machine Work, Brushing & Coating, Elemental

CERAMIC COATER, MACHINE (any ind.) • D.O.T. #509.685-022 • OES #91926 • CERAMIC PLATER. Tends machine that coats metal objects with ceramic material: Places workpiece on rack, observing reflection in mirror below rack to determine when surface to be coated is exposed. Closes machine door and presses button to start rack revolving and initiate coating cycle. Observes gages and turns valves to maintain specified flow through coating nozzle. Fills reservoir with ceramic material and turns valves on hydrogen supply tanks to maintain flow of gas to machine. Removes coated parts, blows away excess material with airhose, and places parts in container. • **GED:** R2, M2, L1 • **SVP:** 2-30 days • **Academic:** Ed=N, Eng=N • **Work Field:** 153 • **MPSMS:** 559 • **Aptitudes:** G4, V4, N4, S3, P3, Q5, K3, F3, M3, E5, C4 • **Temperaments:** R, T • **Stress:** T • **Physical:** V=L, H=N, L=M, W, H • **Work Env:** I, H • **Salary:** 2 • **Outlook:** 3

DIPPER (any ind.) • D.O.T. #599.685-026 • OES #92953 • DIP PAINTER; IMPREGNATOR. Tends dipping tanks and auxiliary equipment that immerses and coats articles with liquids, such as paint, molten tin, latex, stain, or asphalt: Moves controls to maintain temperature, flow, and composition of liquid. Coats articles, using either of following methods: (1) Loads conveyor or transfer rack that automatically dips articles; (2) Loads wire basket and starts power hoist to lift and dip basket; (3) Dips articles in liquid. Removes excess coating, using rag or brush. May test quality of liquid, using chemically treated paper, color charts, or other devices. Adds coating solution according to test results or specifications. May tend centrifugal drier to dry coating and remove excess. May be designated according to coating applied as ASPHALT COATER (elec. equip.); ENAMEL DIPPER (any ind.); PORCE-

LAIN SLUSHER (any ind.); VARNISH DIPPER (furn.); or according to article dipped as BROOM-HANDLE DIPPER (brush & broom); PAINTER, SPRING (matt. & bed spring; wirework). Additional titles: BLUER (firearms); BONDERIZER (auto. mfg.); CLAY-PRODUCTS GLAZER (elec. equip.); PAINT DIPPER (any ind.); RUST PROOFER (auto. mfg.); SCREEN-FRAME ENAMELER (struct. & ornam. metalwork); STAIN DIPPER (furn.); TINNER OPERATOR, CONNECTING RODS (auto. mfg.); VINYL DIPPER (rubber goods). • **GED:** R2, M1, L1 • **SVP:** 2-30 days • **Academic:** Ed=N, Eng=N • **Work Field:** 151 • **MPSMS:** 460, 510, 610 • **Aptitudes:** G4, V4, N4, S4, P4, Q4, K4, F4, M4, E5, C4 • **Temperaments:** R • **Stress:** T • **Physical:** V=L, H=N, L=M, W, H • **Work Env:** I • **Salary:** 2 • **Outlook:** 2

DIPPER AND BAKER (any ind.) • D.O.T. #599.685-030 • OES #92953 • IMPREGNATING-TANK OPERATOR. Dips assembled electrical equipment components into materials, such as varnish, enamel, or asphalt to insulate wires and coils and tends oven that dries dipped components: Pours dipping solution into vat and measures consistency with hydrometer, adding thinner to control density. Sets vat thermostat at prescribed temperature. Hangs or bolts components to be dipped, such as armatures or transformers, on racks, lifts them manually or by use of hand-operated hoist, and immerses them in vat for prescribed time. Removes components and places them on racks to drain. Sets oven temperature controls and places dipped units in oven to bake and dry for specified time. May clean and coat electrical leads by dipping them in molten solder. May paint armatures and field coils, using brush, or pour insulating compound over coils. May be designated according to unit impregnated as ARMATURE VARNISHER (any ind.); FIELD-COIL ENAMELER (any ind.). • **GED:** R2, M1, L1 • **SVP:** 2-30 days • **Academic:** Ed=N, Eng=N • **Work Field:** 141, 151 • **MPSMS:** 582 • **Aptitudes:** G4, V4, N4, S4, P4, Q4, K4, F4, M3, E4, C4 • **Temperaments:** R, T • **Stress:** T • **Physical:** V=L, H=N, L=M, W, H • **Work Env:** I, H • **Salary:** 2 • **Outlook:** 3

ELECTROLESS PLATER, PRINTED CIRCUIT BOARD PANELS (electronics) • D.O.T. #501.685-022 • OES #91926 • DEPOSITION OPERATOR. Tends electroless plating equipment that immerses printed circuit board (PCB) panels into series of chemical tanks to clean, rinse, and deposit metal plating on panels to improve electrical conductivity and facilitate solder connections in production of PCBs: Turns valves to fill tanks with solutions to specified levels. Loads panels onto dipping racks and attaches racks to bar, hoist, overhead crane, or holding fixture. Sets timer for deposition cycle. Keys data into computer keyboard, presses buttons or pulls levers to activate equipment that moves racks of panels through tanks, or lowers racks into tanks manually. Observes gauges and adjusts valves on tanks to maintain required temperature. Removes PCB upon completion of deposition cycle. May compute length of deposition cycle, using calculator. May add chemicals to tanks. May be designated according to type of coating applied as COPPER DEPOSITION OPERATOR (electronics). • **GED:** R2, M2, L2 • **SVP:** 2-30 days • **Academic:** Ed=N, Eng=N • **Work Field:** 151 • **MPSMS:** 587 • **Aptitudes:** G4, V4, N4, S4, P4, Q4, K4, F4, M4, E5, C5 • **Temperaments:** R • **Stress:** T • **Physical:** V=L, H=N, L=H, W, H • **Work Env:** I • **Salary:** 2 • **Outlook:** 3

JEWELRY COATER (jewelry) • D.O.T. #590.685-046 • OES #91926 • Tends equipment that coats jewelry parts with powdered enamel: Places jewelry on racks, rods, or in wire trays, and sprays jewelry with agar solution for subsequent application of powdered enamel on metal, using spray gun. Fills hopper of machine with specified shade of powdered enamel. Places rods or racks on conveyor and starts vibrating machine that shakes powder onto parts passing under opening. Dries enamel-coated parts in oven preparatory to firing them at high temperature. • **GED:** R2, M1, L2 • **SVP:** 2-30 days • **Academic:** Ed=N, Eng=N • **Work Field:** 153 • **MPSMS:** 611 • **Aptitudes:** G4, V4, N4, S4, P4, Q4, K4, F4, M4, E5, C4 • **Temperaments:** R, T • **Stress:** T • **Physical:** V=L, H=N, L=L, W, H • **Work Env:** I • **Salary:** 2 • **Outlook:** 3

PAINTER, TUMBLING BARREL (any ind.) • D.O.T. #599.685-070 • OES #92953 • BARREL PAINTER. Tends tumbling barrel-painting machine that coats articles of porous materials, such as wooden shoe tree turnings or toy parts, with coating materials, such as paint, varnish, or lacquer: Places parts into tumbling barrel. Mixes coating material and thinner as specified and pours over parts in barrel. Starts barrel rotating to impart coating material on articles while heated air is blown through barrel to dry articles. Stops rotation of barrel, examines articles for uniformity of coating, adds more paint as required, and restarts rotation. Unloads barrel, breaking apart any articles that are stuck together. • **GED:** R3, M2, L2 • **SVP:** 30 days-3 mos • **Academic:** Ed=N, Eng=N • **Work Field:** 151 • **MPSMS:** 457, 495 • **Aptitudes:** G4, V4, N4, S4, P3, Q4, K3, F4, M3, E5, C4 • **Temperaments:** J • **Physical:** V=L, H=N, L=M, W, H • **Work Env:** I • **Salary:** 2 • **Outlook:** 2

PAINTING-MACHINE OPERATOR (any ind.) • D.O.T. #599.685-074 • OES #92953 • SPRAY-MACHINE OPERATOR. Tends machine equipped with compressed-air spray nozzles that coat products or materials with oil, paint, lacquer, varnish, shellac, or rustproofing agents: Pours premixed paint or lacquer into reservoir of machine and couples hose to spray nozzles. Moves sleeve on nozzles to attain specified spraying pressure and turns thumbscrew to direct nozzles toward articles or materials to be coated. Places articles or material onto conveyor or onto transfer table that carries them between spray nozzles. May mix paints with thinner solution according to formula. May regulate temperature of coating solution. May remove articles or materials from conveyor belt and place articles or materials in drying racks or container. May be designated according to coating applied as LACQUER COATER (fabric. plastics prod.); OILING-MACHINE OPERATOR (iron & steel); SPRAY-PAINTER, MACHINE (build. board). • **GED:** R2, M1, L2 • **SVP:** 30 days-3 mos • **Academic:** Ed=N, Eng=N • **Work Field:** 153 • **MPSMS:** 471, 534, 583 • **Aptitudes:** G4, V4, N4, S4, P4, Q4, K4, F4, M3, E5, C4 • **Temperaments:** R, T • **Stress:** T • **Physical:** V=L, H=N, L=M, W, H • **Work Env:** I • **Salary:** 2 • **Outlook:** 3

PLATER, HOT DIP (galvanizing) • D.O.T. #501.685-010 • OES #91926 • GALVANIZING DIPPER; POT RUNNER. Tends equipment to coat iron and steel products with corrosion-resistant molten nonferrous metal: Suspends metal objects, such as pails, shelving, nuts and bolts, and structural steel from conveyor hooks or places them in wire baskets. Immerses objects in chemical solution to clean surface of scale and foreign matter. Lowers objects into tank of ammonium chloride or other flux to protect surface from oxidation and facilitate coating. Dips objects into tank of molten metal to coat objects, using hoist or conveyor. Removes objects from tanks after specified time. Places objects, such as nuts and bolts, in centrifuge and starts machine to cool objects and remove excessive coating. Places objects, such as shelving and structural steel, into water tank or transfers them to storage area to cool. Smooths coating, using wire brush and file. Inspects objects for even and complete coating and returns defective objects for reprocessing. Scoops dross from tank, using long-handled scoop, pours dross into molds, and weighs molded dross. Turns valves to regulate temperature in dipping tank. Adds coating metal and chemicals to maintain specified levels and mixtures in cleaning, dipping, and fluxing tanks. May be designated according to type of coating applied as GALVANIZER, ZINC (galvanizing); TIN DIPPER (galvanizing). • **GED:** R2, M1, L1 • **SVP:** 3-6 mos • **Academic:** Ed=N, Eng=N • **Work Field:** 151 • **MPSMS:** 550 • **Aptitudes:** G4, V4, N4, S4, P3, Q5, K4, F4, M3, E5, C4 • **Temperaments:** R, T • **Stress:** T • **Physical:** V=L, H=N, L=H, W, H • **Work Env:** I, W, N, R • **Salary:** 3 • **Outlook:** 3

PLATER, PRODUCTION (electroplating) • D.O.T. #500.665-010 • OES #91921 • ELECTROPLATER, AUTOMATIC. Tends automatic equipment that conveys objects through series of cleaning, rinsing, and electrolytic plating solutions to plate objects with decorative or protective metallic coating: Starts equipment and regulates flow of electricity through plating solution, and immersion time of objects in solutions, following oral instructions or written specifications. Observes plating operation to ensure conformance with company standards. Adds water or other materials according to specifications to maintain mixture and level of cleaning, rinsing, and plating solutions. Observes temperature gauges and turns steam valves to maintain specified temperatures of cleaning and rinsing solutions. Lubricates moving parts of plating conveyor. Cleans plating and cleaning tanks. May test plating solution, using hydrometer and litmus paper, or gather random sample of solution for laboratory analy sis. May replace anodes and cathodes of plating equipment. May fasten objects to hooks, racks, or place them in containers of plating equipment. May start and monitor plating process, using computer equipment. • **GED:** R2, M2, L2 • **SVP:** 30 days-3 mos • **Academic:** Ed=N, Eng=N • **Work Field:** 154 • **MPSMS:** 540, 587 • **Aptitudes:** G4, V4, N4, S3, P4, Q4, K4, F4, M4, E5, C4 • **Temperaments:** R, T • **Stress:** T • **Physical:** V=L, H=N, L=M, W, H • **Work Env:** I • **Salary:** 3 • **Outlook:** 3

SEED PELLETER (agric.) • D.O.T. #599.685-126 • OES #92953 • Tends equipment that applies coating to agricultural seeds and separates coated seeds according to size specifications to allow for uniform planting: Dumps seeds into rotary drum and presses buttons to start drum rotation. Adds water, powder, and glue for specified period, using spray guns and scoop and following work order specifications. Stops drum and scoops coated seeds (pellets) from drum, dumps pellets into electric sizing mill or onto manual sizing screen to remove undersized pellets. Returns undersized pellets to drums for additional coating. Dumps and spreads pellets on trays in drying tunnel for drying. Repeats sizing procedure for dried pellets to ensure that pellets meet sizing specifications. Fills pails with pellets specified on shipping order, using scoop, covers pails with lids, and places pails on pallet for shipment. Cleans interior and exterior of drums and work area, using brushes, rags, mop, detergent, and water. • **GED:** R2, M1, L2 • **SVP:** 2-30 days • **Academic:** Ed=N, Eng=N • **Work Field:** 145, 151 • **MPSMS:** 311 • **Aptitudes:** G4, V4, N4, S4, P4, Q4, K4, F4, M3, E5, C5 • **Temperaments:** R • **Stress:** T • **Physical:** V=L, H=N, L=L, W, H • **Work Env:** I, W • **Salary:** 2 • **Outlook:** 3

SPRAY-UNIT FEEDER (any ind.) • D.O.T. #599.686-014 • OES #98502 • MACHINE SPRAYER. Feeds manufactured articles or parts onto conveyor or feed mechanism that carries them through paint dipping and spraying operations. May be designated according to coating applied as LACQUERER (needle, pin, & rel. prod.); or according to article sprayed as GUNSTOCK-SPRAY-UNIT FEEDER (firearms); SPRAYER, LIGHT BULBS (elec. equip.); or according to mechanism fed as HOOK LOADER (toys & games). • **GED:** R2, M1, L1 • **SVP:** 2-30 days • **Academic:** Ed=N, Eng=N • **Work Field:** 151, 153 • **MPSMS:** 495 • **Aptitudes:** G4, V4, N4, S4, P4, Q4, K4, F4, M3, E5, C5 • **Temperaments:** R • **Stress:** T • **Physical:** V=L, H=N, L=L, W, H • **Work Env:** I • **Salary:** 2 • **Outlook:** 2

GOE: 06.04.22 Manual Work, Ass. Large Parts, Elemental

ASSEMBLER, AUTOMOBILE (auto. mfg.) • D.O.T. #806.684-010 • OES #93956 • Assembles automobiles and trucks or automobile and truck components, such as axles, transmissions, bodies, and motors, performing any combination of following tasks: Fits and fastens parts, such as brackets and small body-hardware or subassemblies, such as manifolds, transmissions, engines, and axle units, using handtools or powered handtools. Adjusts brakes, inflates tires, lubricates chassis, and pours in oil or brake fluid. May be designated according to component assembled as ASSEMBLER, AXLE (auto. mfg.); ASSEMBLER, BODY (auto. mfg.); ASSEMBLER, MOTOR (auto. mfg.); ASSEMBLER, SOFT TRIM (auto. mfg.); ASSEMBLER, TRANSMISSION (auto. mfg.); or according to stage of assembly as ASSEMBLER, FINAL (auto. mfg.). Additional titles: ADJUSTER AND FITTER (auto. mfg.); ASSEMBLER, DOOR-PANEL (auto. mfg.); ASSEMBLER, FIRE-TRUCK BODY (auto. mfg.); DECK-LID FITTER (auto. mfg.); DOOR FITTER (auto. mfg.). • **GED:** R2, M1, L2 • **SVP:** 2-30 days • **Academic:** Ed=N, Eng=N • **Work Field:** 102, 121 • **MPSMS:** 591 • **Aptitudes:** G4, V4, N4, S4, P4, Q4, K4, F4, M3, E5, C5 • **Temperaments:** R • **Stress:** T • **Physical:** V=L, H=N, L=M, W, H • **Work Env:** I • **Salary:** 3 • **Outlook:** 2

ASSEMBLER, BICYCLE 2 (motor. & bicycles) • D.O.T. #806.687-010 • OES #93956 • Assembles bicycles on assembly line, performing one or a combination of tasks as described under ASSEMBLER, BICYCLE (motor. & bicycles) I, using handtools and portable power tools. May assemble and package bicycle subassemblies, such as shift levers, axles, and reflectors and be designated as BICYCLE SUBASSEMBLER (motor. & bicycles).

GED: R1, M1, L1 • **SVP:** 2-30 days • **Academic:** Ed=N, Eng=N • **Work Field:** 121 • **MPSMS:** 595 • **Aptitudes:** G4, V4, N4, S4, P4, Q5, K3, F4, M3, E5, C5 • **Temperaments:** R • **Stress:** T • **Physical:** V=N, H=N, L=L, W, H • **Work Env:** I • **Salary:** 2 • **Outlook:** 3

ASSEMBLER, PRODUCTION (any ind.) • D.O.T. #706.687-010 • OES #93956 • Performs one or more repetitive bench or line assembly operations to mass-produce products, such as automobile or tractor radiators, blower wheels, refrigerators, or gas stoves. Places parts in specified relationship to each other. Bolts, clips, screws, cements, or otherwise fastens parts together by hand, or using handtools or portable powered tools. May tend machines, such as arbor presses or riveting machine, to perform force fitting or fastening operations on assembly line. May be assigned to different work stations as production needs require. May work on line where tasks vary as different model of same article moves along line. May be specified according to part or product produced. • **GED:** R2, M1, L1 • **SVP:** 2-30 days • **Academic:** Ed=N, Eng=N • **Work Field:** 102, 121 • **MPSMS:** 550, 568 • **Aptitudes:** G4, V4, N4, S4, P4, Q4, K3, F4, M3, E5, C5 • **Temperaments:** R, T • **Stress:** T • **Physical:** V=L, H=N, L=M, W, H • **Work Env:** I • **Salary:** 2 • **Outlook:** 2

LAMINATOR, HAND (furn.) • D.O.T. #763.684-050 • OES #93999 • Cements precut laminated plastic covering materials to plywood panels to form furniture parts, such as cabinet tops, countertops, tabletops, and desktops: Applies cement to surface of plywood panels, using brush. Glues plastic laminated covering material to plywood panel to form furniture part and smooths surface with rollers. Wipes acetone on edges of covering and panel with rag and solvent to remove excess cement. Examines edges of laminated part to detect ridges, and removes excess material with file or electric hand trimmer. May attach metal molding trim to edges, using glue and handtools. May cut plastic laminated material and plywood to specified size and shape, using handtools and power tools. May clamp laminated plastic in place until glue sets, using clamps or vise. May install laminated plastic tops on furniture and be designated PLASTIC-TOP INSTALLER (furn.). May cover tops of kitchen and bathroom fixtures and be designated CABINET ASSEMBLER (mfd. bldgs.). • **GED:** R2, M1, L1 • **SVP:** 30 days-3 mos • **Academic:** Ed=N, Eng=N • **Work Field:** 063 • **MPSMS:** 460 • **Aptitudes:** G3, V4, N4, S3, P4, Q5, K4, F4, M3, E5, C5 • **Temperaments:** T • **Physical:** V=N, H=N, L=M, W, H • **Work Env:** I • **Salary:** 2 • **Outlook:** 2

NAILER, HAND (any ind.) • D.O.T. #762.684-050 • OES #93956 • Assembles wooden products, such as boxes, packing cases, kegs, pallets, furniture frames, door and window units, and hogshead subassemblies, using handtools: Positions workpiece on table, floor, easel, or jig, according to verbal instructions, and nails or staples materials together at designated points, using hammer, pneumatic gun, or staple gun. Drives nails in carvings, molding, and scroll work, using hammer, before attaching to furniture. Attaches metal cleats to bottoms of nail kegs to reinforce containers, using hammer and nails. Clinches exposed nail ends and places assembled unit aside for further processing or shipment. May insert bolts in predrilled holes and tighten bolts with wrench. May glue joints before nailing. May record production. May repair containers and be designated BOX REPAIRER (any ind.). May be designated according to product assembled as BOX MAKER, WOOD (any ind.); PANEL MAKER (woodworking). • **GED:** R2, M1, L1 • **SVP:** 30 days-3 mos • **Academic:** Ed=N, Eng=N • **Work Field:** 072 • **MPSMS:** 450, 460 • **Aptitudes:** G4, V4, N4, S4, P4, Q5, K3, F4, M3, E5, C5 • **Temperaments:** R, T • **Stress:** T • **Physical:** V=L, H=N, L=H, W, S, H • **Work Env:** I • **Salary:** 2 • **Outlook:** 2

PLASTIC-TOP ASSEMBLER (furn.) • D.O.T. #763.684-062 • OES #93956 • Stacks sheets of glue-coated plywood, fiberboard, and plastic, in specified sequence for pressing into laminated tops for furniture, such as dressers, tables, and desks. Builds tops for matched sets, by matching color, type of finish, and grain pattern of face sheets. May tend cold press to compress stack [HYDRAULIC-PRESS OPERATOR (veneer & plywood)]. • **GED:** R2, M1, L1 • **SVP:** 2-30 days • **Academic:** Ed=N, Eng=N • **Work Field:** 063 • **MPSMS:** 460 • **Aptitudes:** G4, V4, N4, S4, P3, Q4, K4, F4, M3, E5, C4 • **Temperaments:** R, T • **Stress:** T • **Physical:** V=L, H=N,

L=H, W, S, H • **Work Env:** I • **Salary:** 2 • **Outlook:** 2

RIVETER, HAND (any ind.) • D.O.T. #709.684-066 • OES #93956 • Rivets together light-gage metal parts to assemble articles, such as kitchenware, household appliances, and metal furniture, using portable riveting gun, or rivet set and hammer: Alines parts and inserts rivets in rivet holes. Positions parts with rivet head against anvil or die. Places die of rivet gun or rivet set over end of rivet shank. Presses trigger of gun, or strikes end of rivet set with hammer to spread rivet over rivet hole. May drill or ream rivet holes, using portable drill. May remove defective rivets, using hand punch. • **GED:** R2, M1, L1 • **SVP:** 2-30 days • **Academic:** Ed=N, Eng=N • **Work Field:** 073 • **MPSMS:** 463, 466 • **Aptitudes:** G4, V4, N4, S4, P4, Q5, K4, F3, M3, E5, C5 • **Temperaments:** R, T • **Stress:** T • **Physical:** V=L, H=N, L=M, W, H • **Work Env:** I, N • **Salary:** 3 • **Outlook:** 2

GOE: 06.04.23 Manual Work, Ass. Small Parts, Elemental

ASSEMBLER (elec. equip.) • D.O.T. #723.684-010 • OES #93905 • Assembles parts and subassemblies to form portable electrical appliances, power tools, and other products, using fixtures, handtools, and power tools: Inserts screws, bolts, or rivets through holes in parts or subassemblies and tightens fasteners to secure components, such as field windings, fan blades, pulleys, heating elements, thermostats, switches, and timers, using handtools and power tools. Reams bearing holes in housing assembly, using hand reamer, and places armature shaft in bearings of product. Turns setscrew to adjust end play of motor. Hooks lug ends of wires to terminals, tightens bolts, or solders connection to fasten instruments with burner, motor, or outlet cord. May be designated according to product assembled as DEEP-FRYER ASSEMBLER (elec. equip.); ELECTRIC-FAN ASSEMBLER (elec. equip.); ELECTRIC-HEATER ASSEMBLER (elec. equip.); FOOD-MIXER ASSEMBLER (elec. equip.); POWER-TOOL ASSEMBLER (elec. equip.); STEAM-IRON ASSEMBLER (elec. equip.) • **GED:** R2, M2, L2 • **SVP:** 30 days-3 mos • **Academic:** Ed=N, Eng=N • **Work Field:** 111 • **MPSMS:** 566, 583 • **Aptitudes:** G4, V4, N4, S4, P3, Q5, K3, F3, M3, E5, C4 • **Temperaments:** R, T • **Stress:** T • **Physical:** V=G, H=N, L=S, H • **Work Env:** I • **Salary:** 2 • **Outlook:** 3

ASSEMBLER (jewelry) • D.O.T. #700.684-014 • OES #93956 • Assembles jewelry, such as rings, lockets, bracelets, brooches, and watchcases, using pliers, screwdriver, and jeweler's hammer. May use foot press. May be designated according to type of product assembled as BRACELET MAKER, NOVELTY (jewelry); BROOCH MAKER, NOVELTY (jewelry). • **GED:** R2, M1, L1 • **SVP:** 30 days-3 mos • **Academic:** Ed=N, Eng=N • **Work Field:** 061 • **MPSMS:** 611 • **Aptitudes:** G3, V4, N4, S4, P3, Q5, K3, F3, M3, E5, C5 • **Temperaments:** R, T • **Stress:** T • **Physical:** V=L, H=N, L=S, H • **Work Env:** I • **Salary:** 2 • **Outlook:** 2

ASSEMBLER (sports equip.) • D.O.T. #732.684-014 • OES #93956 • Assembles water sports equipment, such as diving boards, under-water equipment, and water skis, using handtools and power tools: Positions parts in sequence of assembly following work orders, guides, holes, or edges. Screws precut parts together, using handtools, or glues parts together, using glue and clamps. Reams threads on tanks, using die cutting tool. May bore holes for attachment of accessories, using portable drill. May examine completed items for functioning and conformance to specifications. May be designated according to article assembled as AIR-TANK ASSEMBLER (sports equip.); DIVING-BOARD ASSEMBLER (sports equip.); WATER-SKI ASSEMBLER (sports equip.). • **GED:** R2, M2, L2 • **SVP:** 30 days-3 mos • **Academic:** Ed=N, Eng=N • **Work Field:** 102 • **MPSMS:** 616 • **Aptitudes:** G3, V4, N4, S3, P3, Q4, K3, F3, M3, E5, C5 • **Temperaments:** R, T • **Stress:** T • **Physical:** V=L, H=N, L=L, H • **Work Env:** I • **Salary:** 3 • **Outlook:** 3

ASSEMBLER, MOLDED FRAMES (optical goods) • D.O.T. #713.684-014 • OES #93956 • FRAME ASSEMBLER. Assembles plastic eyeglass frames, using drill press and rivet press: Positions frame parts in jig and drills holes in parts, using drill press. Inserts rivets through holes, positions clips and hinges on rivets, and depresses pedal of pneumatic press to set rivets. • **GED:** R2, M1,

L1 • **SVP:** 2-30 days • **Academic:** Ed=N, Eng=N • **Work Field:** 053, 073 • **MPSMS:** 605 • **Aptitudes:** G4, V4, N4, S4, P4, Q4, K4, F3, M4, E4, C5 • **Temperaments:** R • **Stress:** T • **Physical:** V=N, H=N, L=L, H • **Work Env:** I • **Salary:** 2 • **Outlook:** 3

ASSEMBLER, SMALL PARTS (any ind.) • D.O.T. #706.684-022 • OES #93956 • BENCH ASSEMBLER. Performs one or more repetitive operations on assembly line to mass-produce small products, such as ball bearings, automobile door locking units, speedometers, condensers, distributors, ignition coils, or carburetors: Positions parts in specified relationship to each other, using hands, tweezers, or tongs. Bolts, screws, clips, cements, or otherwise fastens parts together by hand or using handtools or portable powered tools. Frequently works at bench as member of assembly group assembling one or two specific parts and passing unit to another worker. May load and unload previously setup machines, such as arbor presses, drill presses, taps, spot-welding machines, riveting machines, milling machines, or broaches to perform fastening, force fitting, or light metal-cutting operation on assembly line. May be assigned to different work stations as production needs require, or shift from one station to another to reduce fatigue factor. May be specified according to product assembled. • **GED:** R2, M1, L2 • **SVP:** 2-30 days • **Academic:** Ed=N, Eng=N • **Work Field:** 102, 121 • **MPSMS:** 550, 568 • **Aptitudes:** G4, V4, N5, S4, P3, Q4, K3, F3, M3, E5, C5 • **Temperaments:** R, T • **Stress:** T • **Physical:** V=G, H=N, L=L, H • **Work Env:** I • **Salary:** 2 • **Outlook:** 3

ASSEMBLER, SMALL PRODUCTS (any ind.) • D.O.T. #739.687-030 • OES #93956 • Assembles parts of various materials, such as plastic, wood, metal, rubber, or paperboard, to mass produce small products, such as roller skates, toys, shoe lasts, musical instrument parts, or loudspeakers, performing any combination of following repetitive operations: Positions parts in specified relationship to each other, using hand, tweezers, or tongs. Bolts, screws, clips, cements, or otherwise fastens parts together by hand, using handtools, portable powered tools, or bench machines. May tend previously setup machines, such as arbor presses, punch presses, taps, spot-welding machines, or riveting machines to perform fastening, force fitting, or light cutting operation on assembly line. Frequently works at bench as member of assembly group assembling one or two specific parts and passing unit on to another worker. May be assigned to different work stations as production needs require or shift from one station to another to reduce fatigue factor. • **GED:** R2, M1, L1 • **SVP:** 2-30 days • **Academic:** Ed=N, Eng=N • **Work Field:** 102, 121 • **MPSMS:** 610 • **Aptitudes:** G4, V4, N5, S4, P4, Q5, K3, F3, M3, E5, C4 • **Temperaments:** R, T • **Stress:** T • **Physical:** V=G, H=N, L=S, H • **Work Env:** I • **Salary:** 2 • **Outlook:** 3

BENCH ASSEMBLER (agric. equip.) • D.O.T. #706.684-042 • OES #93956 • SUBASSEMBLER. Assembles parts to form yard and garden care equipment components, such as reels, steering handles, and gear boxes, following specifications and using handtools and power tools: Fits parts of components together and fastens them with bolts and cotter pins, using handtools and pneumatic impact wrench. Seats inserts, such as bearings and grease seals in hubs and sleeves, using power press. Rivets reel blades to hubs on reel shaft, using pneumatic clinching gun, and sets rivets, using rivet press [RIVETING-MACHINE OPERATOR (any ind.) I]. May be designated according to part assembled as REEL FABRICATOR (agric. equip.). • **GED:** R2, M1, L2 • **SVP:** 2-30 days • **Academic:** Ed=N, Eng=N • **Work Field:** 121 • **MPSMS:** 562 • **Aptitudes:** G3, V4, N4, S3, P4, Q4, K3, F3, M3, E5, C5 • **Temperaments:** R, T • **Stress:** T • **Physical:** V=L, H=N, L=L, H • **Work Env:** I • **Salary:** 3 • **Outlook:** 2

COIL WINDER (elec. equip.) • D.O.T. #724.684-026 • OES #93908 • Winds coils to be used in electrical equipment and instruments, or as electronic components, according to wiring diagrams, sample coil, or work order, using coil-winding machines and handtools: Reviews wiring diagrams and work order, or examines sample coil to ascertain type and size of wire specified and type, size, length, circumference, and primary and secondary windings of coil to be wound. Selects coil-forming device for specified coil to be wound and fastens it onto machine arbor, mandrel, or spindle or fastens it in between chuck and tail stock. Threads end of wire from reel through tension device, guides, and spreader, bends ends of wire to form lead, and attaches lead to coil core. Turns setscrews to adjust tension on wire and sets counter for number of turns specified for coil. Starts machine and manually feeds wire over coil core or using spreader to obtain even and uniform winding and shape of coil. Observes counter and stops machine, when specified number of turns have been made. Wraps insulation between layers and around wound coil and in larger coils inserts plastic blocks between turns to form cooling ducts. Ties coil with tape to hold wires and inside form in place. Cuts wire to form leads, using wire or bolt cutters. Pounds coil with hammer or mallet to shape end windings or remove coil from fixture. Winds asbestos, cotton, glass, mica, paper, or tape, and brushes varnish on coil or dips coil in varnish, epoxy, or wax to reinforce and seal coil. Strips insulation from end of lead wires, threads lead wires through insulating sleeves or slides sleeves over leads, and solders lead wires to terminals. May test coils for continuity of windings, using test lamp. May cut and form insulating materials and be known as INSULATOR CUTTER AND FORMER (elec. equip.) or insert insulation in core slots and be known as INSULATOR (elec. equip.). May wind heavy ribbon, strap, or round wire over fixture to form coil and be designated as COIL FORMER, TEMPLATE (elec. equip.); COIL WINDER, OPEN SLOT (elec. equip.); COIL WINDER, STRAP (elec. equip.). May be designated according to type of coil wound or work station as ARMATURE COIL WINDER (elec. equip.); AUDIO-COIL WINDER (electronics); BENDER, ARMATURE COIL (elec. equip.); BOBBIN-COIL WINDER (electronics); COIL FINISHER (elec. equip.; electronics); COIL TAPER, HAND (elec. equip.). Additional titles: COIL TAPER, MACHINE (elec. equip.); COIL-UNIT BUILDER, EXPERIMENTAL (electronics); COIL WINDER, HAND (electronics); COIL WRAPPER (electronics); FIELD-AND-YOKE ASSEMBLER (elec. equip.); FIELD-COIL ASSEMBLER (elec. equip.); FIELD-COIL WINDER (elec. equip.); FILAMENT-COIL WINDER (electronics); FORMER, ARMATURE COILS (elec. equip.); FORMER, ROTOR-COIL (elec. equip.); HELIX-COIL WINDER (elec. equip.); INTER-COIL WINDER (elec. equip.); INTER-POLE WINDER (elec. equip.); RESISTOR WINDER (elec. equip.; electronics); ROTOR-COIL WINDER (elec. equip.); SPIDER-COIL WINDER (elec. equip.); TOROIDAL-COIL WINDER (elec. equip.; electronics); TRANSFORMER-COIL ASSEMBLER (elec. equip.); TRANSFORMER-COIL WINDER (elec. equip.; electronics); UNIVERSAL-WINDING-MACHINE OPERATOR (elec. equip.; electronics). • **GED:** R2, M2, L2 • **SVP:** 3-6 mos • **Academic:** Ed=N, Eng=N • **Work Field:** 111, 163 • **MPSMS:** 582, 587 • **Aptitudes:** G4, V4, N4, S4, P3, Q4, K3, F3, M3, E5, C5 • **Temperaments:** M, R, T • **Stress:** T • **Physical:** V=L, H=N, L=L, H • **Work Env:** I • **Salary:** 3 • **Outlook:** 2

EARRING MAKER (jewelry) • D.O.T. #700.684-030 • OES #93999 • Assembles pearl earrings according to designs or instructions: Winds wire-threaded pearls, by hand, around metal-looped earring blanks. Cuts end of wire thread with cutter. Fastens pearls on loops by twisting wire with pliers. May paste loops of pearls and single pearls to facing of other loop blank. • **GED:** R3, M2, L2 • **SVP:** 30 days-3 mos • **Academic:** Ed=N, Eng=N • **Work Field:** 061 • **MPSMS:** 611 • **Aptitudes:** G3, V4, N4, S4, P3, Q5, K4, F3, M4, E5, C4 • **Temperaments:** R, T • **Stress:** T • **Physical:** V=L, H=N, L=S, H • **Work Env:** I • **Salary:** 2 • **Outlook:** 2

ELECTRIC-MOTOR ASSEMBLER (elec. equip.) • D.O.T. #721.684-022 • OES #93905 • Assembles subassemblies and parts of dynamotors, converters, and electric motors used in instruments, appliances, and power tools, performing any combination of following tasks, using power tools and handtools: Bolts field windings and brush holders into motor housings, using wrenches, screwdrivers, and holding fixtures. Presses bushings and bearings into motor head, using arbor press. Secures fans and gears to armature shaft, using nuts and lock washers, and places armature shaft in bearings. Solders or screws electrical leads to brushes, and switch base to housing and fastens with screws. Lubricates gears and other moving parts, using oil can, paddle, or grease gun. Turns shaft to insure free movement of parts. May screw covers on motor ends to keep out dirt and moisture during shipment. When replacing defective parts in motors is designated REPAIRER, ELECTRIC MOTORS (elec. equip.). May be designated according to type motor assembled as ASSEMBLER, INSTRUMENT MOTORS (elec. equip.) or part assembled as BRUSH-HOLDER ASSEM-

BLER (elec. equip.). • **GED:** R2, M1, L2 • **SVP:** 30 days-3 mos • **Academic:** Ed=N, Eng=N • **Work Field:** 111 • **MPSMS:** 582 • **Aptitudes:** G4, V4, N4, S4, P4, Q5, K3, F2, M3, E5, C4 • **Temperaments:** R, T • **Stress:** T • **Physical:** V=L, H=L, L=L, H • **Work Env:** I • **Salary:** 2 • **Outlook:** 3

FILLER (house. furn.) • D.O.T. #780.684-066 • OES #93956 • STUFFER. Fills pillows, cushions, and comforters with down, kapok, wool, or other filler, using filling machine: Ties or holds opening of cover around discharge tube of filling machine and presses button to start blower that sucks filling into cover. Estimates amount of filler blown into cover by either timing blower or weighing articles. Stuffs filling into open end of cover, using metal rod. May stuff covers by hand. May be designated according to article filled as CUSHION FILLER (house furn.); PILLOW FILLER (house furn.); SLEEPING-BAG FILLER (tex. prod., n.e.c.); or according to kind of filler used as DOWN FILLER (house furn.). • **GED:** R2, M1, L1 • **SVP:** 2-30 days • **Academic:** Ed=N, Eng=N • **Work Field:** 041 • **MPSMS:** 433, 439 • **Aptitudes:** G4, V4, N4, S4, P4, Q5, K3, F4, M4, E5, C5 • **Temperaments:** R • **Stress:** T • **Physical:** V=N, H=N, L=L, H • **Work Env:** I • **Salary:** 2 • **Outlook:** 2

LOCK ASSEMBLER (hardware) • D.O.T. #706.684-074 • OES #93956 • Fastens together parts of locks with screws, bolts, and rivets, using handtools and power tools: Files and fits parts to obtain smooth functioning of lock. Assembles inside lock parts in lock case and rivets side plate in place, using rivet tool. May pack locks in cartons and mark cartons to identify contents. • **GED:** R2, M1, L2 • **SVP:** 30 days-3 mos • **Academic:** Ed=N, Eng=N • **Work Field:** 071, 073 • **MPSMS:** 552 • **Aptitudes:** G4, V4, N5, S3, P4, Q5, K4, F3, M4, E4, C5 • **Temperaments:** R, T • **Stress:** T • **Physical:** V=L, H=N, L=S, H • **Work Env:** I, N • **Salary:** 3 • **Outlook:** 2

MULTIFOCAL-LENS ASSEMBLER (optical goods) • D.O.T. #713.684-034 • OES #93956 • MULTIFOCAL-BUTTON ASSEMBLER. Fits and secures multifocal lens parts together preparatory to fusing, utilizing adhesive compound or asbestos tape: Dips multifocal button in cleaning solution and wipes dry. Brushes button and countersink blank to remove dust and lint. Positions button on polished surface of countersink blank. Performs test to detect presence of foreign matter between button and countersink blank, using instrument that indicates foreign matter when pressure is applied to outside edge of button. Recleans surfaces and performs test until instrument indicates lens parts are free of foreign matter. Places spring clamp on blank to hold button in position. Inserts metal peg between button and blank to allow air to escape during fusing, using tweezers. Applies cement to surface contact points around edge of button, using needle applicator, or wraps asbestos tape around button and countersink blank assembly to hold button in place. Removes spring clip and metal peg after cement is set. Places assembled unit in tray for transfer to fusing room. • **GED:** R2, M1, L2 • **SVP:** 30 days-3 mos • **Academic:** Ed=N, Eng=N • **Work Field:** 061, 063 • **MPSMS:** 605 • **Aptitudes:** G4, V4, N4, S3, P3, Q5, K3, F3, M4, E5, C4 • **Temperaments:** R, T • **Stress:** T • **Physical:** V=L, H=N, L=S, H • **Work Env:** I • **Salary:** 2 • **Outlook:** 3

SILK-SCREEN-FRAME ASSEMBLER (any ind.) • D.O.T. #709.484-010 • OES #93956 • FRAME BUILDER, SILK-SCREEN; SETTER-UP, SILK-SCREEN FRAME. Builds frames for silk or metal screens used to stencil identifying or operational data on parts or products following blueprints: Bends bar stock to specified shape and dimensions to form frame, using vise and handtools. Solders joints, using soldering iron. Measures and marks location of holes on frame, using rule. Drills and threads holes, using drill press and handtap. Screws guides and stops in holes for use in positioning part in frame. • **GED:** R3, M2, L2 • **SVP:** 30 days-3 mos • **Academic:** Ed=N, Eng=N • **Work Field:** 102 • **MPSMS:** 567 • **Aptitudes:** G4, V4, N4, S4, P3, Q4, K3, F3, M3, E5, C5 • **Temperaments:** R, T • **Stress:** T • **Physical:** V=L, H=N, L=L, H • **Work Env:** I • **Salary:** 2 • **Outlook:** 3

TIRE MOUNTER (fabric. prod. nec) • D.O.T. #739.684-158 • OES #93956 • TIRE ASSEMBLER. Assembles hard rubber tires and wheel rims for articles, such as lawn mowers and baby carriages: Places rubber tire into jaws of spreading device and depresses pedal to close jaws and stretch tire. Positions wheel rim on spindle mandrel at center of tire. Pushes button to open jaws that release tire onto rim and removes wheel from spreading device. • **GED:** R2, M1, L1 • **SVP:** 2-30 days • **Academic:** Ed=N, Eng=N • **Work Field:** 061 • **MPSMS:** 559 • **Aptitudes:** G4, V4, N5, S4, P4, Q5, K3, F4, M3, E4, C5 • **Temperaments:** R • **Stress:** T • **Physical:** V=L, H=N, L=L, H • **Work Env:** I, N • **Salary:** 3 • **Outlook:** 3

TOY ASSEMBLER (toys & games) • D.O.T. #731.687-034 • OES #93956 • Assembles parts of various materials, such as plastic, wood, metal, or fabric to mass produce toys performing any combination of following tasks: Selects parts specified and positions parts in designated relationship to each other, using hands, tweezers, or pliers. Assembles and fastens parts of toys together, using clips, glue, jig, screws, dowels, nails, handtools, and portable powered tools. Inspects toys for specified color and operation of parts. May tend previously setup machines, such as drill press, reamer, welding machine, nailing machine, flanging press, and punch press to drill, cut, weld, trim, fit, or insert toy parts on assembly line. May be designated according to item assembled or material used as ASSEMBLER, TOY VOICES (toys & games); DOLL-EYE-SETTER (toys & games); STUFFED-TOY JOINER (toys & games); TOY ASSEMBLER, PLASTIC (toys & games); TOY ASSEMBLER, WOOD (toys & games); and WHEEL ASSEMBLER, BABY CARRIAGE (toys & games). • **GED:** R2, M1, L1 • **SVP:** 2-30 days • **Academic:** Ed=N, Eng=N • **Work Field:** 102, 121 • **MPSMS:** 615 • **Aptitudes:** G4, V4, N5, S4, P4, Q5, K3, F3, M3, E4, C4 • **Temperaments:** R, T • **Stress:** T • **Physical:** V=N, H=N, L=L, H • **Work Env:** I • **Salary:** 2 • **Outlook:** 3

GOE: 06.04.24 Manual Work, Metal & Plastics, Elemental

ARBORER (jewelry) • D.O.T. #700.684-010 • OES #93999 • BENDER; RING MAKER; SIZER. Forms ring blank into circular shape, using ring mandrel and rawhide mallet: Files ends of ring blank smooth and square and places blank in ring bending device. Pulls lever to bend blank into semicircle. Places blank on mandrel and hammers blank into circular shape, using rawhide mallet. Slides ring over sizing (measuring) mandrel to verify conformity to specifications. • **GED:** R2, M1, L1 • **SVP:** 2-30 days • **Academic:** Ed=N, Eng=N • **Work Field:** 134 • **MPSMS:** 611 • **Aptitudes:** G4, V4, N5, S4, P4, Q5, K4, F3, M3, E5, C5 • **Temperaments:** R, T • **Stress:** T • **Physical:** V=N, H=N, L=L, H • **Work Env:** I • **Salary:** 2 • **Outlook:** 2

BENCH GRINDER (any ind.) • D.O.T. #705.684-010 • OES #91117 • Moves metal objects, such as castings, billets, machine parts, sheet metal subassemblies, or arrowheads, against abrasive wheel of bench grinder to grind, smooth, or rough-finish objects to specifications: Clamps workpiece in workholder or jig, or holds it in hands, and feeds it against rotating grinding wheel to remove excess metal, scratches, or burs. Examines or measures workpiece for conformance to standards. Guides dressing tool across wheel to true surface. Replaces worn wheels, using wrench. May position workpiece in automatic feed mechanism. May select and mount abrasive wheels of different grit size to grinder to obtain specified finish on workpiece. May start pump and direct coolant flow against wheel. • **GED:** R2, M1, L1 • **SVP:** 30 days-3 mos • **Academic:** Ed=N, Eng=N • **Work Field:** 051 • **MPSMS:** 540, 566 • **Aptitudes:** G4, V4, N4, S4, P3, Q4, K3, F4, M3, E5, C5 • **Temperaments:** M, R, T • **Stress:** T • **Physical:** V=L, H=N, L=M, W, H • **Work Env:** I, W, N, R • **Salary:** 2 • **Outlook:** 2

BENCH WORKER (optical goods) • D.O.T. #713.684-018 • OES #93999 • Performs any combination of the following activities to prepare plastic eyeglass frames for assembly, using bench-mounted machines and handtools or power tools: Drills or punches holes in frame components, using drill or punch press. Inserts and tightens screws, nuts, and bolts to assemble parts, using handtools. Inserts and expands rivets to assemble parts, using rivet gun. Alines and miters frame part edges, using mitering machine. Cuts grooves in parts for insertion of lenses, using grooving machine. May be designated according to activity as GROOVER (optical goods). • **GED:** R2, M1, L1 • **SVP:** 30 days-3 mos • **Academic:** Ed=N, Eng=N • **Work Field:** 102 • **MPSMS:** 605 • **Aptitudes:** G4, V4, N4, S3, P4, Q5, K3, F3, M4, E4, C5 • **Temperaments:** R • **Stress:** T • **Physical:** V=L, H=N, L=L, H • **Work Env:** I •

Salary: 2 • **Outlook:** 3

BUFFER 1 (any ind.) • D.O.T. #705.684-014 • OES #91117 • COLOR BUFFER. Buffs items, such as automobile trim or accessories, hardware, or fabricated plastic parts with cloth buffing wheel: Holds and moves parts against wheel to smooth surfaces, produce specified finish, or cut down plating defects, such as burns or salt deposits, using knowledge of metals and buffing operations. Coats buffing wheel by holding buffing compound stick against revolving wheel. Pushes and manipulates workpiece against buffing wheel to remove scratches and defects and produce specified finish, using knowledge of buffing operations and finishes. Replaces worn buffs, using wrench. Uses care not to cut through plate when buffing plated surfaces. May be designated according to type of material buffed as BUFFER, CHROME (any ind.); BUFFER, COPPER (any ind.); BUFFER, NICKEL (any ind.). May polish articles [POLISHER (any ind.)] and buff articles and be designated POLISHER AND BUFFER (any ind.) I. May polish brass eye castings used in fitting wooden shuttles and clean castings in series of chemical solutions and be designated STRAPPER AND BUFFER (woodworking). • **GED:** R2, M1, L2 • **SVP:** 3-6 mos • **Academic:** Ed=N, Eng=N • **Work Field:** 051 • **MPSMS:** 542, 556 • **Aptitudes:** G3, V4, N4, S4, P3, Q4, K3, F3, M3, E5, C4 • **Temperaments:** J, R, T • **Stress:** T • **Physical:** V=L, H=N, L=M, W, H • **Work Env:** I, R • **Salary:** 2 • **Outlook:** 2

CONTACT-LENS-FLASHING PUNCHER (optical goods) • D.O.T. #713.687-014 • OES #93999 • PUNCHER. Punches flashing from molded plastic contact lenses, using handpress: Places compartmentalized box under openings in press-holding fixture to catch lens after punching. Positions lens in holding fixture and pulls lever to lower hollow punch which cuts flashing from lens. Repeats punching, allowing only lenses of same specifications to fall in same compartment. Labels and routes lenses in envelopes or boxes to stockroom or other work stations. • **GED:** R2, M1, L1 • **SVP:** 2-30 days • **Academic:** Ed=N, Eng=N • **Work Field:** 054 • **MPSMS:** 605 • **Aptitudes:** G4, V4, N4, S4, P4, Q4, K4, F4, M4, E5, C5 • **Temperaments:** R • **Stress:** T • **Physical:** V=L, H=N, L=L, H • **Work Env:** I • **Salary:** 2 • **Outlook:** 3

FILER (jewelry) • D.O.T. #700.684-034 • OES #93953 • FITTER; SHAPER. Trims and smooths edges, surfaces, and impressed or raised designs of jewelry articles and jewelry findings II, using files, chisels, and saws: Places article in holding device or against bench pin. Files or cuts excess metal from surfaces and ornamentations, such as filigree or relief designs. Miters joints and ends of formed ring blanks, using file. May smooth and polish edges and soldered areas of jewelry, using abrasive wheel. May operate motor-driven filing machine. • **GED:** R3, M1, L2 • **SVP:** 30 days-3 mos • **Academic:** Ed=N, Eng=N • **Work Field:** 051, 057 • **MPSMS:** 611 • **Aptitudes:** G4, V4, N5, S3, P3, Q5, K3, F3, M3, E5, C4 • **Temperaments:** R, T • **Stress:** T • **Physical:** V=L, H=N, L=L, H • **Work Env:** I • **Salary:** 2 • **Outlook:** 2

GRINDER 1 (any ind.) • D.O.T. #705.684-026 • OES #93953 • Grinds and smooths surfaces of items, such as automobile or appliance components, prior to finishing operations, using powered portable wheel, disk, or belt grinder: Examines and feels surface of workpiece for defects. Selects grade of abrasive belt, wheel, or disk according to specifications, knowledge of abrasives, and condition of metal, and attaches to grinder. Starts grinder and moves it over surface of workpiece to remove scratches, laminated metal, excess weld material, and burs. Polishes ground areas with finer abrasive to produce smooth, unmarred surface. Replaces worn abrasive disks, wheels, and belts, using wrench. May be designated according to type of grinder operated as GRINDER, BELT (any ind.); GRINDER, WHEEL OR DISK (any ind.). May grind leaded-in portions of automobile bodies and be designated GRINDER, LEAD (auto. mfg.). • **GED:** R2, M1, L2 • **SVP:** 30 days-3 mos • **Academic:** Ed=N, Eng=N • **Work Field:** 051 • **MPSMS:** 540 • **Aptitudes:** G4, V4, N4, S4, P3, Q4, K3, F4, M3, E5, C5 • **Temperaments:** J, R, T • **Stress:** T • **Physical:** V=L, H=N, L=M, W, H • **Work Env:** I, N, R • **Salary:** 2 • **Outlook:** 3

GRINDER-CHIPPER 2 (any ind.) • D.O.T. #809.684-026 • OES #93953 • GRINDER, ROUGH. Grinds and chips weld splatter, high spots, burs, slag, and rust from surface of fabricated metal structures and parts to improve appearance or prepare for painting, using portable or pedestal grinders, chipping hammers and wire brushes: Positions workpiece on worktable manually or using jib or crane. Inserts specified grinding wheel, wire brush, or cutting chisel into portable grinder or power hammer. Pulls trigger to activate power tool and positions and guides tool along high or defective spots on surface of work piece. May chip or grind out pits or cracks. Grinds portable pieces, using pedestal grinder. May sharpen chisels and dress grinding wheel, using pedestal grinder or wheel dresser. May paint fabricated parts, using spray gun [PAINTER, SPRAY (any ind.) I]. May be designated according to tool used as CHIPPER (any ind.) II; GRINDER (any ind.) IV. • **GED:** R2, M1, L1 • **SVP:** 30 days-3 mos • **Academic:** Ed=N, Eng=N • **Work Field:** 051, 052 • **MPSMS:** 554 • **Aptitudes:** G3, V4, N4, S4, P3, Q5, K3, F4, M3, E5, C5 • **Temperaments:** J, T • **Physical:** V=L, H=N, L=H, W, C, S, H • **Work Env:** I, N, R • **Salary:** 2 • **Outlook:** 2

JIGSAWYER (jewelry) • D.O.T. #700.684-046 • OES #91117 • JIGSAW OPERATOR. Cuts out metal jewelry findings II according to pattern, using jigsaw: Receives metal sheets with patterns cemented to tops, or prints patterns on printing press and cements onto metal sheets. Assembles several sheets into laminated block with oiled paper between layers to produce multiple findings in one cutting operation. Drills holes for saw blade, using drill press. Mounts blade on jigsaw, starts saw, and guides metal sheet against blade to cut along lines of pattern. • **GED:** R2, M1, L1 • **SVP:** 3-6 mos • **Academic:** Ed=N, Eng=N • **Work Field:** 056 • **MPSMS:** 611 • **Aptitudes:** G3, V4, N4, S4, P3, Q5, K3, F3, M3, E5, C5 • **Temperaments:** R, T • **Stress:** T • **Physical:** V=L, H=N, L=L, H • **Work Env:** I • **Salary:** 3 • **Outlook:** 2

LABORER, GOLD LEAF (gold leaf & foil) • D.O.T. #700.687-038 • OES #98902 • Places gold strips between sheets of plastic or skin to form packets (stacks) for beating by GOLDBEATER (gold leaf & foil). May be designated SHODER FILLER (gold leaf & foil) when forming packet for second beating, or MOLD FILLER (gold leaf & foil) when forming packet for third beating. • **GED:** R2, M1, L1 • **SVP:** 2-30 days • **Academic:** Ed=N, Eng=N • **Work Field:** 061 • **MPSMS:** 559 • **Aptitudes:** G4, V4, N5, S4, P4, Q5, K4, F4, M3, E5, C5 • **Temperaments:** R • **Stress:** T • **Physical:** V=L, H=N, L=L, H • **Work Env:** I, N • **Salary:** 2 • **Outlook:** 2

MELTER (jewelry) • D.O.T. #700.687-042 • OES #92198 • Melts gold, or gold and silver alloys, using furnace, electric heating unit, or torch, and pours molten metal into ingot molds to prepare metal for use in making jewelry: Places metal in clay crucible. Places crucible in preheated oven or heats crucible with torch to melt metal. Observes color changes in metals to ensure that specified temperature is attained. Pours molten metal into ingot mold. Opens mold, lifts out ingot with tongs, and quenches ingot in water. May operate roller machine to roll ingots into metal strips for use in stamping out jewelry blanks [ROLLER (jewelry)]. • **GED:** R2, M1, L2 • **SVP:** 2-30 days • **Academic:** Ed=N, Eng=N • **Work Field:** 131, 132 • **MPSMS:** 541 • **Aptitudes:** G4, V4, N4, S4, P4, Q5, K4, F4, M4, E5, C4 • **Temperaments:** M, R, T • **Stress:** T • **Physical:** V=N, H=N, L=M, W, H • **Work Env:** I, H, R • **Salary:** 2 • **Outlook:** 2

METAL FINISHER (any ind.) • D.O.T. #705.684-034 • OES #92198 • Grinds, files, or sands surfaces of metal items, such as automobile bodies and household appliances, using handtools, power tools, and knowledge of metal finishing techniques: Examines and feels surface of metal to detect defects, such as dents, scratches, or breaks in metal. Removes dents, using hammer and dolly block, and fills uneven surface with molten solder. Smooths surface of item to specified finish, using handtools and powered tools. May polish metal surface, using powered polishing wheel or belt [POLISHER (any ind.)]. • **GED:** R2, M1, L2 • **SVP:** 3-6 mos • **Academic:** Ed=N, Eng=N • **Work Field:** 051 • **MPSMS:** 556, 583 • **Aptitudes:** G4, V4, N4, S3, P3, Q4, K3, F4, M3, E5, C5 • **Temperaments:** R, T • **Stress:** T • **Physical:** V=L, H=N, L=L, H • **Work Env:** I, N • **Salary:** 2 • **Outlook:** 2

MOLD DRESSER (any ind.) • D.O.T. #519.684-018 • OES #93953 • MOLD REPAIRER. Removes residue, blemishes, corrosion, and similar defects from interior of molds, using handtools and power tools: Inspects interior surfaces of molds to locate pits and holes. Positions molds for work, using hoist. Repairs defects, using hammers, drills, chisels, routers, or grinding wheel. Smooths interior of mold, using file, buffing wheel, emery paper, or steelwool. May add metal to or remove metal from plates, rings, and molds, using welding equipment and files. May reassemble molds after repairing. May be designated according to type of mold repaired as GLASS-MOLD REPAIRER (glass mfg.). • **GED:** R2, M1, L1 • **SVP:** 3-6 mos • **Academic:** Ed=N, Eng=N • **Work Field:** 031, 102 • **MPSMS:** 567 • **Aptitudes:** G4, V4, N4, S4, P3, Q4, K3, F3, M3, E5, C5 • **Temperaments:** R, T • **Stress:** T • **Physical:** V=L, H=N, L=M, W, H • **Work Env:** I, N, R • **Salary:** 4 • **Outlook:** 2

OXIDIZER (silverware) • D.O.T. #700.684-054 • OES #93947 • Brushes oxide solution on ornamentation (patterned surfaces) of silverware and silver-plated ware to darken crevasses to make design stand out after buffing: Brushes oxide on ornamentation of holloware, such as bowls, trays, and coffee pots. Dips ornamented end of knives, forks, and spoons in solution, and wipes excess solution from silverware with cloth to prevent discoloration. Places silverware in mesh basket and immerses it in water to neutralize oxidization. May tend convey orized machine that automatically oxidizes stainless steel flatware items. • **GED:** R2, M1, L2 • **SVP:** 2-30 days • **Academic:** Ed=N, Eng=N • **Work Field:** 151 • **MPSMS:** 612 • **Aptitudes:** G4, V4, N4, S4, P3, Q5, K3, F4, M3, E5, C5 • **Temperaments:** R, T • **Stress:** T • **Physical:** V=L, H=N, L=L, S, H • **Work Env:** I • **Salary:** 2 • **Outlook:** 2

POLISHER (any ind.) • D.O.T. #705.684-058 • OES #91117 • Removes excess metal and surface defects from such items as hardware, small arms barrels, automobile trim, or accessory parts prior to buffing, bluing, or plating, using revolving abrasive wheel or belt: Selects abrasive belt or wheel according to grain size, type of finish specified, product being polished, or amount of metal to be removed, using knowledge of polishing operations and abrasives. Attaches wheel or belt to drive mechanism. Starts polisher and manipulates workpiece against abrasive wheel or portable wheel against workpiece to remove metal and surface defects. Examines part for acceptability of finish. May be designated according to type of material polished as POLISHER, ALUMINUM (any ind.); POLISHER, BRASS (any ind.); POLISHER, BRONZE (any ind.); POLISHER, ZINC (any ind.). • **GED:** R3, M2, L2 • **SVP:** 1-2 yrs • **Academic:** Ed=N, Eng=N • **Work Field:** 051 • **MPSMS:** 550 • **Aptitudes:** G3, V4, N4, S3, P3, Q4, K3, F3, M3, E5, C5 • **Temperaments:** R, T • **Stress:** T • **Physical:** V=L, H=N, L=M, W, H • **Work Env:** I, N • **Salary:** 3 • **Outlook:** 2

POLISHER, EYEGLASS FRAMES (optical goods) • D.O.T. #713.684-038 • OES #91117 • Polishes plastic eyeglass frames and temple pieces to remove scratches and pit marks, using polishing wheel: Applies abrasive compound to wheel surface, using brush. Starts machine and holds and turns frame parts against wheel to polish parts and remove defects. Inspects and feels polished parts to verify removal of flaws. Presses sandpaper against polishing wheel to remove abrasive residue in preparation for next sequence. • **GED:** R2, M1, L1 • **SVP:** 2-30 days • **Academic:** Ed=N, Eng=N • **Work Field:** 051 • **MPSMS:** 605 • **Aptitudes:** G4, V4, N5, S4, P3, Q5, K4, F3, M4, E5, C5 • **Temperaments:** R • **Stress:** T • **Physical:** V=L, H=N, L=S, H • **Work Env:** I • **Salary:** 2 • **Outlook:** 3

PREPARER (jewelry) • D.O.T. #700.687-062 • OES #93999 • BENCH HAND. Performs any combination of following tasks in preparing cast jewelry findings II for further processing: Cuts, saws, or breaks off gates from jewelry castings, using shears, jeweler's saw, pliers, or foot press equipped with cutting tool. Removes burs and smooths rough edges of casting, using file or grinding wheel. Straightens distorted castings, using foot press equipped with shaping dies. May remove plaster from castings by dipping castings in water and acid solution. May count and separate jewelry casting into containers, according to type, and marks containers with identifying information. May specialize in breaking off gates from jewelry castings and be designated BREAKER-OFF (jewelry). • **GED:** R2, M1, L1 • **SVP:** 2-30 days • **Academic:** Ed=N, Eng=N • **Work Field:** 054 • **MPSMS:** 611 • **Aptitudes:** G4, V4, N5, S4, P4, Q5, K4, F4, M4, E4, C5 • **Temperaments:** R • **Stress:** T • **Physical:** V=L, H=N, L=S, H • **Work Env:** I • **Salary:** 2 • **Outlook:** 2

REFINER (medical ser.) • D.O.T. #712.684-038 • OES #93999 • Recovers precious metals, such as gold, platinum, and palladium from scrap dentures and extracted teeth, using furnace, retort, and laboratory equipment: Breaks scrap dentures, using hammer, and removes precious metals. Weighs each type metal and records weights. Places metal in retort and positions retort in furnace to melt metal particles. Turns valves to adjust temperature of furnace. Removes retort and pours molten metal solution into beaker, using tongs. Adds specified amounts of chemicals to molten metal solution to separate metal from solution. Pours solution through filter to recover precious dental metals. • GED: R3, M2, L2 • SVP: 3-6 mos • Academic: Ed=N, Eng=N • Work Field: 145 • MPSMS: 549 • Aptitudes: G3, V4, N4, S4, P3, Q4, K4, F4, M3, E5, C5 • Temperaments: M, T • Physical: V=L, H=N, L=L, H • Work Env: I • Salary: 3 • Outlook: 2

SILK-SCREEN ETCHER (engraving) • D.O.T. #704.684-014 • OES #93951 • ETCHER, HAND. Etches lettering, trademarks, or designs through silk screen onto metal objects, such as plates, jewelry, trophies, cutlery, and tools: Positions object to be etched on setup board. Places silk screen of specified design or lettering over object. Brushes specified acid solution through silk screen to etch design on object. Rinses workpiece in neutralizing solution after specified time to remove acid, or places it on conveyor which carries workpiece into bath. May brush acid resistant solution through screen and place workpiece into acid bath to etch pattern on unprotected surface. • GED: R2, M1, L1 • SVP: 30 days-3 mos • Academic: Ed=N, Eng=N • Work Field: 182 • MPSMS: 550, 610 • Aptitudes: G4, V4, N4, S4, P3, Q5, K4, F4, M3, E5, C5 • Temperaments: R, T • Stress: T • Physical: V=L, H=N, L=L, H • Work Env: I • Salary: 2 • Outlook: 3

STONER (jewelry) • D.O.T. #735.684-014 • OES #93953 • Smooths enameled surface of jewelry articles, using abrasive stone: Fastens jewelry article in wooden chuck (jeweler's block). Rubs moist abrasive stone across article to remove excess enamel and produce smooth surface. Brushes or washes article to remove loose particles. May remove excess enamel, using buffing machine. • GED: R2, M1, L2 • SVP: 3-6 mos • Academic: Ed=N, Eng=N • Work Field: 051 • MPSMS: 611 • Aptitudes: G4, V4, N5, S4, P3, Q5, K3, F3, M3, E5, C5 • Temperaments: R, T • Stress: T • Physical: V=L, H=N, L=S, H • Work Env: I • Salary: 3 • Outlook: 3

STRETCHER (jewelry) • D.O.T. #700.684-078 • OES #93999 • Stretches rings to specified size and shape, using stretching device: Slides ring onto hollow arbor (female) having slits running down its length that permit it to contract or expand. Turns wheel to force tapered male arbor into hollow arbor to expand and stretch ring. Repeats operation until ring is stretched and formed as specified. • GED: R2, M1, L2 • SVP: 30 days-3 mos • Academic: Ed=N, Eng=N • Work Field: 134 • MPSMS: 611 • Aptitudes: G3, V4, N4, S4, P4, Q5, K3, F4, M3, E5, C5 • Temperaments: R, T • Stress: T • Physical: V=N, H=N, L=S, H • Work Env: I • Salary: 2 • Outlook: 2

GOE: 06.04.25 Manual Work, Wood, Elemental

CANER 2 (furn.) • D.O.T. #763.684-022 • OES #85999 • Installs or replaces prewoven panels of cane, willow, or rattan in furniture frames: Cuts damaged panel from furniture frame, using knife. Pries wooden splines from grooves in frame, using chisel. Places frame in water to soften dried glue and adhering panel, and scrapes surfaces clean. Brushes glue into grooves around frame opening and stretches water-soaked panel over opening. Forces edges of panel into grooves, using wedge and mallet or pneumatic press. Brushes glue over panel edges in grooves, and forces splines into grooves flush with surface. Trims excess material, using knife. May cut prewoven panels to size, using pattern and scissors or cutting machine. • GED: R2, M1, L1 • SVP: 30 days-3 mos • Academic: Ed=N, Eng=N • Work Field: 102 • MPSMS: 460 • Aptitudes: G4, V4, N4, S4, P4, Q4, K4, F4, M3, E5, C5 • Temperaments: R, T • Stress: T • Physical: V=L, H=N, L=L, H • Work Env: I • Salary: 2 • Outlook: 2

CROSSBAND LAYER (veneer & plywood) • D.O.T. #762.687-026 • OES #98999 • CORE LAYER, PLYWOOD; GLUE SPREADER HELPER. Stacks glued crossbands alternately with core stock to assemble plywood panels for bonding, working as member of team: Grasps glue-coated crossbands as they emerge from glue spreader and places them cross-grained between back sheet, core stock, and

face sheet placed by VENEER-STOCK LAYER (veneer & plywood) until specified ply is obtained. Discards broken cross bands. Pushes assembled panels down conveyor to hot-plate press for bonding into plywood. May assist GLUE SPREADER, VENEER (veneer & plywood) to clean rollers of glue spreader. May brush glue on irregularly shaped veneer sheets that will not fit in glue spreader. May assemble 3-ply panels alone, laying back sheet, glued core or inner sheet, and face sheet in sequence, and be designated PLY-WOOD BUILDER (veneer & plywood). • GED: R2, M1, L1 • SVP: 2-30 days • Academic: Ed=N, Eng=N • Work Field: 063 • MPSMS: 453 • Aptitudes: G4, V4, N4, S4, P4, Q5, K3, F4, M3, E5, C5 • Temperaments: R • Stress: T • Physical: V=L, H=N, L=M, W, S, H • Work Env: I, W, N • Salary: 2 • Outlook: 3

WOODWORKING-SHOP HAND (woodworking) • D.O.T. #769.687-054 • OES #98999 • MILL LABORER; WOODWORK-ING-SHOP LABORER. Performs any combination of following duties to facilitate cutting, finishing, storing, cleaning, and shipping wood products, and inspects products prior to shipment: Stacks lumber or wood products on floor or in bins to supply machine operators or assemblers, or in kiln cars, yard, or shed for storage or seasoning. Places sticks between lumber to permit air circulation, and binds stacks together during seasoning. Hammers shaped steel bands into timbers and railroad ties to prevent splitting during seasoning and inserts bolts or metal dowels through split timbers to hold parts together. Dismantles crates and removes nails and other metal from wooden parts to salvage material, using handtools. Applies filler, putty, or other material, using brush, putty knife, and fingers to fill wood pores, holes, cracks, or other indentations. Removes paint, lacquer, and other finishes from wood products, using solvent, steel wool, brush, and cloths, and sands rough spots, using sandpaper or sanding machine, to prepare surfaces for finishing. Traces patterns on lumber stock as guide for machine operator. Attaches articles to wires, cord, or hooks preparatory to dipping. Dips article into vats to coat them with paint, asphalt, or other ingredients. Marks furniture surfaces with crayon or rough-edged object to simulate antique finish. Brushes surfaces with glue preparatory to covering with leather, paper, or other materials. Nails together lumber for cutting, and places lumber on machine table. Examines materials and products for defects, finish, and grade, and accuracy of dimensions and matching panels, using measuring instruments. Stamps grade on product and weighs and records units processed and inspected. Changes cutterheads and blades, adjusts belts, and performs other duties as instructed to facilitate setting up woodworking machines. Loads and unloads materials from railroad cars, trucks, and barges by hand, using handtruck or industrial truck to move material to designated areas. Cleans cars and trucks and lines them with paper preparatory to loading. • GED: R2, M1, L1 • SVP: 2-30 days • Academic: Ed=N, Eng=N • Work Field: 102, 211 • MPSMS: 450, 460 • Aptitudes: G4, V4, N4, S4, P3, Q4, K4, F4, M3, E4, C4 • Temperaments: R, T • Stress: T • Physical: V=L, H=N, L=V, W, S, H • Work Env: B, N • Salary: 2 • Outlook: 3

GOE: 06.04.26 Manual Work, Paper, Elemental

LABEL CODER (any ind.) • D.O.T. #920.587-014 • OES #98999 • LABEL MARKER. Cuts notches in container or bottle labels to indicate data, such as type, batch, date, and destination of product, following predetermined code: Turns setscrews to space and lock blades of notching device according to coding guide, using ruler. Clamps stack of labels on bed of notching device and pushes bed forward to force labels against blades. Prepares label-coding report. May insert or remove symbols, using tweezers to set up carton-coding wheels. May wash defective labels from bottles. • GED: R2, M1, L1 • SVP: 2-30 days • Academic: Ed=N, Eng=N • Work Field: 054 • MPSMS: 470 • Aptitudes: G4, V4, N4, S4, P4, Q4, K4, F3, M4, E5, C5 • Temperaments: R, T • Stress: T • Physical: V=L, H=N, L=L, H • Work Env: I • Salary: 2 • Outlook: 3

TRIM-STENCIL MAKER (any ind.) • D.O.T. #781.684-058 • OES #93999 • PATTERN-PUNCHING-MACHINE OPERATOR. Lays out and traces patterns on paper to make stencils used for cutting cloth upholstery: Arranges master patterns on paper in such manner as to minimize waste when cloth is cut. Traces patterns on paper, using pencil. Perforates paper, using hand punch or by guiding automatic punch around traced lines so that pattern will be transferred to material when chalk powder is dusted over stencil. • **GED:** R2, M2, L2 • **SVP:** 30 days-3 mos • **Academic:** Ed=N, Eng=N • **Work Field:** 241 • **MPSMS:** 479 • **Aptitudes:** G3, V4, N4, S3, P3, Q4, K4, F3, M3, E5, C5 • **Temperaments:** M, T • **Physical:** V=L, H=N, L=L, H • **Work Env:** I • **Salary:** 2 • **Outlook:** 2

GOE: 06.04.27 Manual Work, Textile, Fabric & Leather, Elemental

BOW MAKER (any ind.) • D.O.T. #789.684-010 • OES #93999 • Forms ornamental bows for hair or dress wear, by hand: Winds length of ribbon on rack to form bows. Cuts ribbon into sections with scissors and ties folds together at middle with twine to form bow. Inserts bobby pin or safety pin through twine, and removes bows from rack. Arranges artificial flower or lace medallion on bow as specified, and ties them together with twine or ribbon. May sew comb attachment to middle section of underside of bow, using needle and thread. • **GED:** R2, M1, L2 • **SVP:** 30 days-3 mos • **Academic:** Ed=N, Eng=N • **Work Field:** 062 • **MPSMS:** 618 • **Aptitudes:** G4, V4, N4, S4, P4, Q5, K4, F3, M4, E5, C5 • **Temperaments:** R, T • **Stress:** T • **Physical:** V=N, H=N, L=L, H • **Work Env:** I • **Salary:** 2 • **Outlook:** 2

CANVAS REPAIRER (any ind.) • D.O.T. #782.684-010 • OES #85956 • Repairs damaged or worn tent, awning, or other canvas articles: Spreads canvas on worktable and examines it for holes, tears, and worn areas. Trims edges of damaged area, using scissors or knife. Patches holes, sews tears, or darns defective area, using needle and thread or sewing machine. Stamps grommets into edges of canvas, using mallet and punch or eyelet machine. May repair leatherette fabrics. May measure structures for canvas coverings, using tape measure. • **GED:** R2, M1, L1 • **SVP:** 3-6 mos • **Academic:** Ed=N, Eng=N • **Work Field:** 171 • **MPSMS:** 436 • **Aptitudes:** G4, V4, N4, S4, P3, Q5, K3, F3, M3, E4, C4 • **Temperaments:** R, T • **Stress:** T • **Physical:** V=L, H=N, L=H, W, H • **Work Env:** I • **Salary:** 3 • **Outlook:** 2

CARPET CUTTER 2 (carpet & rug) • D.O.T. #585.687-014 • OES #98999 • Cuts specified lengths from continuous roll of carpet, using power cut-off knife or long-handled cutting blade. May cut felt padding to specified lengths and be designated as FELT-PAD CUTTER (felt goods). • **GED:** R2, M1, L1 • **SVP:** 30 days-3 mos • **Academic:** Ed=N, Eng=N • **Work Field:** 054 • **MPSMS:** 430 • **Aptitudes:** G4, V4, N4, S4, P4, Q4, K4, F4, M3, E5, C5 • **Temperaments:** R • **Stress:** T • **Physical:** V=L, H=N, L=L, W, H • **Work Env:** I • **Salary:** 3 • **Outlook:** 2

LABORER, GENERAL (leather mfg.) • D.O.T. #589.686-026 • OES #98999 • BLUE-LINE HANGER; CELLAR HAND; DEPARTMENT HELPER; ROUSTABOUT; TOGGLER. Performs any combination of following duties in various sections of tannery, such as drying department, beam house, hide house, or tan house: Cuts cord from hide bundles and spreads hides on floor for processing. Dumps tannery refuse, such as skin and fat, in bin and covers refuse with lime to prevent putrefaction. Covers fleshy side of hides with lime solution to prevent putrefaction of hides. Applies solvent to wool of sheepskin to remove painted brands, using rag and brush. Hangs hides in steam room and turns valve to admit steam that loosens hair and wool on hides. Moves steamed hides to dehairing machine or manually pulls loosened wool from hides. Collects hair after dehairing operation and dumps hair into washing machine. Shovels washed hair into centrifugal drier or onto screen over steam coils to remove moisture. Punches holes in hides, using awl or punch press, to facilitate tying hides into bundles for tanning. Counts and ties specified number of hides into bundles. Dumps hides into drums or vats containing various chemical solutions that dehair, delime, or preserve hides. Dampens hides with water in preparation for oiling. Pastes or clips wet hides on frames to prevent wrinkling and slides frames into drying tunnel. Removes dry hides from frames and stacks hides on cart. Feeds and offbears machines that clean and smooth finished hides by pressing, brushing, or vacuuming. Cleans vats, tanks, and drums of lime, tanbark, and refuse and scrubs walls and floors of tannery,

using brushes, scrapers, and solvents. Sprays disinfectant in trucks or freight cars used to haul hides to tannery. May be assigned to specific section of tannery and be designated LABORER, BEAM HOUSE (leather mfg.); LABORER, DRYING DEPARTMENT (leather mfg.); LABORER, HIDE HOUSE (leather mfg.); LABORER, TAN HOUSE (leather mfg.). • **GED:** R2, M1, L1 • **SVP:** 2-30 days • **Academic:** Ed=N, Eng=N • **Work Field:** 011, 031, 032 • **MPSMS:** 521 • **Aptitudes:** G4, V4, N4, S4, P4, Q4, K4, F4, M3, E5, C5 • **Temperaments:** R • **Stress:** T • **Physical:** V=L, H=N, L=M, W, H • **Work Env:** B • **Salary:** 2 • **Outlook:** 2

SEWER, HAND (any ind.) • D.O.T. #782.684-058 • OES #93923 • ASSEMBLER; BANDER; BAND SEWER; GARMENT FINISHER; GARMENT SEWER, HAND; HAND STITCHER; HAND TACKER; NEEDLEWORKER; TABLE WORKER, SEWING; TRIMMER. Joins and reinforces parts of articles, such as garments, curtains, parachutes, stuffed toys, or sews buttonholes and attaches fasteners to articles, or sews decorative trimmings to articles, using needle and thread: Selects thread, according to specifications or color of parts. Alines parts, fasteners, or trimmings, following seams, edges, or markings on parts. Sews parts with various types of stitches, such as felling tacking, stitch and basting. Trims excess threads, using scissors or knife. May trim edges of parts, using scissors. When sewing fasteners or trimmings to articles, may be designated FINISHER, HAND (garment). May be designated according to stitch sewn as BASTER, HAND (garment); FELLER, HAND (garment). May be designated according to article or part sewn as ARMHOLE BASTER, HAND (garment); BOW ATTACHER (garment); BOW TACKER (hat & cap) I; BUTTONHOLE MAKER, HAND (garment); BUTTON HOLE TACKER (garment); BUTTON SEWER, HAND (garment); COLLAR FELLER (garment). Additional titles: COLLAR TACKER (garment); DRAPERY SEWER, HAND (house furn.); DRESSMAKER (garment); EDGE MAKER (garment); HOOK-AND-EYE ATTACHER (garment); LABEL SEWER, HAND (any ind.); LAPEL BASTER (garment); LAPEL PADDER (garment); LINING FINISHER (garment); NECK FELLER (garment); SLEEVE BASTER (garment); SLEEVE-BOTTOM FELLER (garment); TACKER (garment); TOP-COLLAR BASTER (garment); TRIMMING FINISHER (garment). • **GED:** R2, M1, L1 • **SVP:** 30 days-3 mos • **Academic:** Ed=N, Eng=N • **Work Field:** 171 • **MPSMS:** 439, 440 • **Aptitudes:** G4, V4, N4, S4, P3, Q5, K3, F2, M3, E5, C4 • **Temperaments:** R, T • **Stress:** T • **Physical:** V=G, H=N, L=S, H • **Work Env:** I • **Salary:** 2 • **Outlook:** 3

THREAD CUTTER (any ind.) • D.O.T. #789.684-050 • OES #93926 • TRIMMING-MACHINE OPERATOR. Trims loose threads from edges or seams of articles, such as garments, hats, linens, and surgical appliances: (1) Moves edges or seams of article over stationary cutting head equipped with vacuum attachment that draws threads between reciprocal blades to cut threads. (2) Spreads article on table or pulls article over form and guides electric hand clippers equipped with vacuum hose along edges or seams of article to cut threads. When trimming knitted garments, pulls loose threads through several stitches with latch needle or ties threads from converging seams to secure stitching. May cut short or thick threads unsuitable for machine cutting, using scissors. • **GED:** R2, M1, L1 • **SVP:** 2-30 days • **Academic:** Ed=N, Eng=N • **Work Field:** 054 • **MPSMS:** 420, 440, 604 • **Aptitudes:** G4, V4, N5, S4, P4, Q5, K4, F4, M3, E5, C5 • **Temperaments:** R • **Stress:** T • **Physical:** V=L, H=N, L=L, H • **Work Env:** I • **Salary:** 2 • **Outlook:** 2

GOE: 06.04.28 Manual Work, Food Processing, Elemental

BONER, MEAT (slaught. & meat pack.) • D.O.T. #525.684-010 • OES #93938 • RIBBER. Cuts bones from standard cuts of meat, such as chucks, hams, loins, plates, rounds, and shanks to prepare meat for packing and marketing, using knife and meat hook: Inserts knife in meat around bones to separate meat, fat, or tissue. Pulls and twists bones loose from meat. Cuts and trims such meat cuts as butts, hams, flanks, and shoulders to shape meat and remove fat and defects. Trims meat from bones and ribs. May pull bones and skin from cooked pigs feet, and cut out toe bones and nails. May be designated according to cut of meat boned as BLADE

BONER (slaught. & meat pack.); CHUCK BONER (slaught. & meat pack.); HAM BONER (slaught. & meat pack.); or type of animal boned as BEEF BONER (slaught. & meat pack.); HOG RIBBER (slaught. & meat pack.); SHEEP BONER (slaught. & meat pack.). Additional titles: LOIN BONER (slaught. & meat pack.); PLATE BONER (slaught. & meat pack.); RIB BONER (slaught. & meat pack.); ROUND BONER (slaught. & meat pack.); SHANK BONER (slaught. & meat pack.); SHOULDER BONER (slaught. & meat pack.). • **GED:** R2, M1, L2 • **SVP:** 3-6 mos • **Academic:** Ed=N, Eng=N • **Work Field:** 034 • **MPSMS:** 382 • **Aptitudes:** G4, V4, N5, S3, P3, Q5, K3, F3, M3, E5, C4 • **Temperaments:** R, T • **Stress:** T • **Physical:** V=L, H=N, L=M, W, H • **Work Env:** I, C, W, R • **Salary:** 3 • **Out look:** 2

CANDY DIPPER, HAND (confection.) • D.O.T. #524.684-010 • OES #93947 • Dips candy centers, fruit, or nuts into coatings to coat, decorate, and identify product: Scoops liquid coating material onto slab of heated dipping table and kneads material, such as chocolate, fondant, or icing to attain specified consistency. Drops candy into mass and swirls candy about until thoroughly coated, using fingers or fork. Removes candy and marks identifying design or symbol on top, using fingers or fork, to identify type of center or brand. May decorate top of candy with nuts, coconut, or other garnishment. May mix coating ingredients and dip candy into vat containing coating material, regulating vat temperature to maintain specified consistency. May pour liquid chocolate into molds to form figures [CANDY MOLDER, HAND (confection.)]. May be designated according to type of center dipped as BONBON DIPPER (confection.); CHERRY DIPPER (confection.); CREAM DIPPER (confection.); PECAN-MALLOW DIPPER (confection.); or according to type of coating as CHOCOLATE COATER (confection.); ICING COATER (confection.). • **GED:** R2, M1, L1 • **SVP:** 3-6 mos • **Academic:** Ed=N, Eng=N • **Work Field:** 151 • **MPSMS:** 393 • **Aptitudes:** G4, V4, N5, S4, P3, Q5, K3, F3, M3, E5, C4 • **Temperaments:** R, T • **Stress:** T • **Physical:** V=N, H=N, L=L, H • **Work Env:** I • **Salary:** 2 • **Outlook:** 2

CANDY MOLDER, HAND (confection.) • D.O.T. #520.687-018 • OES #93944 • MOLDER, HAND; NOVELTY-CANDY MAKER; PASTE WORKER. Pours liquid candy into chilled molds to form solid candy figures, such as animals or Christmas trees: Dumps or pours candy into warming pan and turns dial to heat product to pouring temperature. Stirs candy to facilitate melting and pours it into chilled mold. Taps or tilts mold to distribute candy uniformly throughout mold. Opens mold when candy has congealed and removes figure. May be designated by type of candy molded as CHOCOLATE MOLDER (choc. & cocoa; confection.). • **GED:** R2, M1, L1 • **SVP:** 30 days-3 mos • **Academic:** Ed=N, Eng=N • **Work Field:** 132 • **MPSMS:** 393 • **Aptitudes:** G4, V4, N5, S4, P3, Q5, K4, F4, M4, E5, C5 • **Temperaments:** R, T • **Stress:** T • **Physical:** V=N, H=N, L=L, H • **Work Env:** I • **Salary:** 2 • **Outlook:** 3

CIGAR MAKER (tobacco) • D.O.T. #790.684-014 • OES #93999 • FINISHED-CIGAR MAKER; OUT-AND-OUT CIGAR MAKER, HAND; STOGIE MAKER, HAND. Rolls cigars by hand: Rolls filler, wraps filler with binder [BUNCH MAKER, HAND (tobacco)], and wraps bunch with wrapper leaf [ROLLER, HAND (tobacco)]. Presses cigars in molds to obtain finished shape [MOLD PRESSER (tobacco)]. • **GED:** R2, M2, L2 • **SVP:** 6 mos-1 yr • **Academic:** Ed=N, Eng=N • **Work Field:** 041, 136 • **MPSMS:** 401, 403, 409 • **Aptitudes:** G4, V4, N4, S4, P3, Q5, K3, F3, M3, E5, C5 • **Temperaments:** R, T • **Stress:** T • **Physical:** V=N, H=N, L=S, H • **Work Env:** I • **Salary:** 3 • **Outlook:** 3

DECORATOR (bake. prod.) • D.O.T. #524.684-014 • OES #93947 • DECORATOR, HAND; ORNAMENTER. Decorates confectionery products with chocolate, colored icings, or pastry cream: Screws nozzle of specified size and shape into outlet of decorating bag. Fills bag with icing, chocolate, or pastry cream. Squeezes bag to force material through nozzle, forming decorations, such as lines, letters, figures, or flowers. May mix, cook, and color decorating material. May spread material with brush, fingers, pronged instrument, or spatula. May fill molds with icing to form decorations, such as bells, birds, and bootees. May be designated according to product decorated as CANDY DECORATOR (confection.). • **GED:** R2, M1, L1 • **SVP:** 30 days-3 mos • **Academic:** Ed=N, Eng=N • **Work Field:** 146 • **MPSMS:** 384, 393 • **Aptitudes:** G4, V4, N4, S3, P3, Q4, K3, F3, M2, E5, C3 • **Temperaments:** R, T • **Stress:**

T • **Physical:** V=L, H=N, L=L, H • **Work Env:** I • **Salary:** 2 • **Outlook:** 2

FISH CLEANER (can. & preserv.) • D.O.T. #525.684-030 • OES #93938 • DRESS-GANG WORKER; FISH CUTTER; FISH DRESSER. Cleans fish aboard ship or ashore, performing any combination of the following tasks, alone or as member of crew: (1) Scrapes scales from fish with knife. (2) Cuts or rips fish from vent to throat with knife, and tears out viscera and gills. (3) Cuts off head of fish with knife, drops head in tub, and slides fish along table to next worker. (4) Washes blood from abdominal cavity by dropping fish in tub of water or by use of hose, and removes discolored membrane from abdomen lining with knife, spoon, scraper, glove, or piece of burlap. (5) Cuts gashes along sides of fish to facilitate salt penetration during curing. (6) Cuts fish behind gill slits and draws knife along backbone and ribs to free fillet (boneless portion of flesh). Lays fillet skinside down on table and draws knife laterally between skin and flesh to remove skin. (7) Slices flesh from bones in fletches (longitudinal quarter sections) for further processing into boneless slices of fish. Unloads catch from fishing vessels [LABORER, WHARF (can. & preserv.)]. May pack fish in containers. May remove slime from fish preparatory to canning and be designated as SLIMER (can. & preserv.; fish.). May clean, dress, wrap, label, and store fish for guests at resort establishments and be designated FISH HOUSEKEEPER (hotel & rest.). • **GED:** R1, M1, L1 • **SVP:** 2-30 days • **Academic:** Ed=N, Eng=N • **Work Field:** 034 • **MPSMS:** 331 • **Aptitudes:** G4, V4, N4, S3, P4, Q5, K3, F3, M3, E5, C4 • **Temperaments:** R • **Stress:** T • **Physical:** V=L, H=N, L=M, W, H • **Work Env:** I, W, R • **Salary:** 2 • **Outlook:** 2

POULTRY DRESSER (agric.) • D.O.T. #525.687-070 • OES #93999 • TIPPER. Slaughters and dresses fowl in preparation for marketing, performing any combination of the following tasks: Chops off bird's head or slits bird's throat to slaughter bird, using knife. Hangs bird by feet to drain blood. Dips bird into scalding water to loosen feathers. Holds bird against projecting rubber fingers of rotating drum to remove feathers. Cuts bird open, removes viscera, and washes bird and giblets. May pluck chickens by hand. May be designated according to type of fowl dressed as CHICKEN DRESSER (slaught. & meat pack.); TURKEY DRESSER (slaught. & meat pack.). May be known according to specific duties performed as POULTRY PICKER (slaught. & meat pack.); POULTRY SCALDER (slaught. & meat pack.). • **GED:** R1, M1, L1 • **SVP:** 2-30 days • **Academic:** Ed=N, Eng=N • **Work Field:** 034 • **MPSMS:** 324 • **Aptitudes:** G4, V4, N5, S4, P4, Q5, K4, F4, M3, E5, C5 • **Temperaments:** R • **Stress:** T • **Physical:** V=L, H=N, L=L, W, H • **Work Env:** I, W • **Salary:** 2 • **Outlook:** 3

TRIMMER, MEAT (slaught. & meat pack.) • D.O.T. #525.684-054 • OES #93926 • Trims fat, skin, tendons, tissues, and ragged edges from meat cuts, such as loins, spare ribs, butts, hams, rounds, sirloins, fillets, and chops, using meat-hook and knife: Trims meat and fat from bones and places trimmings and bones in separate containers. Trims fatback from hog bellies and cuts bellies into specified shapes, using knife. Feeds bacon bellies through rolls to flatten bellies to prescribed thickness. May wash or scrape dirt and blood from meat. May be designated according to section of meat trimmed as BELLY TRIMMER (slaught. & meat pack.); BUTT TRIMMER (slaught. & meat pack.); FATBACK TRIMMER (slaught. & meat pack.); LOIN TRIMMER (slaught. & meat pack.); SPARERIBS TRIMMER (slaught. & meat pack.). • **GED:** R1, M1, L1 • **SVP:** 2-30 days • **Academic:** Ed=N, Eng=N • **Work Field:** 034 • **MPSMS:** 382 • **Aptitudes:** G4, V4, N5, S4, P4, Q5, K3, F3, M3, E5, C4 • **Temperaments:** R, T • **Stress:** T • **Physical:** V=L, H=N, L=M, W, H • **Work Env:** I, C, W, R • **Salary:** 2 • **Out look:** 2

GOE: 06.04.29 Manual Work, Rubber, Elemental

FABRICATOR, FOAM RUBBER (any ind.) • D.O.T. #780.684-062 • OES #93999 • ASSEMBLER; CEMENTER; FOAM FABRICATOR. Cuts and assembles padded articles, such as mattresses or cushions, from molded foam rubber sheets, pads, or scrap: Positions and measures or marks pattern outline on foam rubber piece, using tape measure and crayon or pencil. Cuts around measurement or pattern outline, using electric knife or bandsaw. May place two identical pieces together, brush cement along edge, and press edges of pieces together to form cushion or mattress. May cement strips around edges of assembled pieces and over seams to provide smooth finish and reinforce seams. May staple spring assembly to wood frame and leno or sisal cloth to top of springs to form box-spring unit. • **GED:** R2, M1, L1 • **SVP:** 2-30 days • **Academic:** Ed=N, Eng=N • **Work Field:** 054 • **MPSMS:** 519 • **Aptitudes:** G4, V4, N4, S4, P3, Q4, K3, F4, M3, E5, C5 • **Temperaments:** R, T • **Stress:** T • **Physical:** V=L, H=N, L=L, H • **Work Env:** I • **Salary:** 2 • **Outlook:** 2

GOE: 06.04.30 Manual Work, Stone, Glass & Clay, Elemental

GLASS FINISHER (glass prod.) • D.O.T. #775.684-026 • OES #93926 • Cuts and finishes plate glass to make variety of glass products: Lays out pattern on plate glass and cuts it, using glasscutter. Holds glass against series of rotating grinding and polishing wheels to bevel and polish edges. Sprays silver solution on glass to provide mirrored surface, using spray gun. Assembles glass pieces to make various novel ties. May lay out design or monogram on glass and sandblast surface within guidelines, using sandblasting tool. • **GED:** R3, M2, L2 • **SVP:** 6 mos-1 yr • **Academic:** Ed=N, Eng=N • **Work Field:** 051, 054 • **MPSMS:** 531 • **Aptitudes:** G3, V4, N4, S3, P3, Q5, K3, F4, M3, E5, C5 • **Temperaments:** R, T • **Stress:** T • **Physical:** V=L, H=N, L=L, H • **Work Env:** I • **Salary:** 3 • **Outlook:** 2

SAGGER MAKER (pottery & porc.) • D.O.T. #774.684-030 • OES #93999 • Pounds clay over mold or frame to shape sagger sides and bottom, using maul: Lays pliable clay in circular or rectangular frame and pounds to shape to form of frame, using maul. Hammers slabs of clay over iron frame and cuts into strips to form sides, using knife. Folds strips around drum or wooden mold placed on prepared bottom to form sagger sides. Wets ends of strip and applies hand pressure to join. Plucks spare clay off bottom to fasten to sides, using wooden plucking tool. Smooths surface, using knife and wooden paddle and removes mold. Places sagger in drying room. • **GED:** R2, M1, L1 • **SVP:** 30 days-3 mos • **Academic:** Ed=N, Eng=N • **Work Field:** 136 • **MPSMS:** 535 • **Aptitudes:** G4, V4, N4, S4, P3, Q5, K3, F4, M3, E5, C5 • **Temperaments:** R, T • **Stress:** T • **Physical:** V=N, H=N, L=M, W, S, H • **Work Env:** I • **Salary:** 2 • **Outlook:** 2

TABLE-TOP TILE SETTER (brick & tile) • D.O.T. #763.684-074 • OES #93999 • Covers tabletops with mosaic tile squares to form decorative design: Glues cardboard pattern to top of table. Places template over pattern and marks off design, using pencil. Cuts out marked-off portion, using hand knife. Applies glue to surface of mosaic tile and tabletop. Sets multicolored squares in position to form prescribed design and color pattern. • **GED:** R2, M2, L2 • **SVP:** 3- 6 mos • **Academic:** Ed=N, Eng=N • **Work Field:** 092 • **MPSMS:** 534 • **Aptitudes:** G4, V4, N4, S3, P3, Q4, K3, F4, M3, E5, C2 • **Temperaments:** T • **Physical:** V=G, H=N, L=S, W, H • **Work Env:** I • **Salary:** 2 • **Outlook:** 3

GOE: 06.04.31 Manual Work, Welding & Flame Cutting, Elemental

WELDER, GUN (welding) • D.O.T. #810.664-010 • OES #93914 • Welds or tack-welds overlapping edges of prepositioned components to fabricate sheet metal assemblies, such as panels, refrigerator shells, and automobile bodies, using portable spot-welding gun: Positions and clamps electrode under overlapping edges of workpiece. Presses electrode against work piece at specified weld points to complete circuit between electrodes and heat metal to joining temperature. Removes electrode after specified period of time. May adjust equipment for automatic timing of current. May position and clamp workpieces together. • **GED:** R2, M2, L2 • **SVP:** 2-30 days • **Academic:** Ed=N, Eng=N • **Work Field:** 081 • **MPSMS:** 540, 554, 591 • **Aptitudes:** G4, V4, N4, S4, P4, Q4, K3, F3, M3, E5, C4 • **Temperaments:** R, T • **Stress:** T • **Physical:** V=L, H=N, L=M, W, H • **Work Env:** I, N, R • **Salary:** 2 • **Outlook:** 3

WELDER, PRODUCTION LINE (welding) • D.O.T. #819.684-010 • OES #93914 • Welds metal parts on production line, using previously set up gas-or arc-welding equipment: Turns valves to release fuel gas and oxygen and ignites mixture, or inserts specified weld rod into portable holder, clamps cable onto workpiece or jig, and strikes arc. Guides electrodes, or torch and filler rod, along horizontal weld line at specified speed and angle to melt and deposit metal from filler rod or electrode onto workpiece. May skip (tack) weld designated spots to secure workpieces for other welders. May use different equipment and be designated as BRAZER, PRODUCTION LINE (welding); WELDER, PRODUCTION LINE, ARC (welding); WELDER, PRODUCTION LINE, COMBINATION (welding); WELDER, PRODUCTION LINE, GAS (welding). • **GED:** R2, M2, L2 • **SVP:** 2-30 days • **Academic:** Ed=N, Eng=N • **Work Field:** 081 • **MPSMS:** 540, 554, 591 • **Aptitudes:** G4, V4, N4, S4, P4, Q4, K3, F3, M3, E5, C4 • **Temperaments:** R, T • **Stress:** T • **Physical:** V=L, H=N, L=M, W, H • **Work Env:** I, N, R • **Salary:** 2 • **Outlook:** 3

GOE: 06.04.32 Manual Work, Casting & Molding, Elemental

CANDLEMAKER (candle) • D.O.T. #739.664-010 • OES #92998 • Forms candles according to one of following methods: (1) Strings wicks through notches or rings of dipping frame, according to length of candle to be formed. Dips wicks manually or with aid of motorized mechanism into vat of molten wax mixture to build up candles to specified circumference. Cuts or trims candles to specified sizes, using knife or hand die. Grades candles according to type, color, and size. (2) Inserts wick through center of molds and attaches ends to racks. Pours molten wax mixture into molds, using container or opens valves to admit wax into molds. Adjusts steam and coolant valves to maintain prescribed thermometer reading in mold. Turns hand crank of ejection mechanism to release candles from molds into rack after specified time. Scrapes remaining wax from molds, using handtools. May record production data, such as name, color, and quantity of candles. May add color ingredients to molten wax, according to specifications. • **GED:** R2, M1, L1 • **SVP:** 3-6 mos • **Academic:** Ed=N, Eng=N • **Work Field:** 054, 136 • **MPSMS:** 619 • **Aptitudes:** G3, V4, N4, S4, P4, Q4, K3, F3, M3, E5, C3 • **Temperaments:** R, T • **Stress:** T • **Physical:** V=L, H=N, L=M, W, H • **Work Env:** I • **Salary:** 3 • **Outlook:** 3

MACHINE MOLDER (foundry) • D.O.T. #518.682-010 • OES #91911 • MACHINE LINE MOLDER. Operates molding machine to form sand molds used in production of metal castings: Assembles flask, pattern, and follow board on molding table of machine. Sifts sand over pattern, using riddle, and fills flask with sand by opening hopper or using shovel. Packs sand around pattern contours, using ramming tool or pneumatic hammer. Starts machine that compacts sand in flask to form mold. Cuts pouring spout and vents in mold, using sprue cutter and wire. Lifts cope half of flask off drag half and removes pattern. Cleans cavity of mold, using airhose. Positions cores in drag, and assembles cope and drag. May set cores in mold cavity. May install pattern on bed of machine, and adjust pressure of ram. May be designated by machine operated as MACHINE MOLDER, SQUEEZE (found.) or MACHINE MOLDER, ROLL-OVER (found.), or product molded as MOLDER, FITTING (found.). • **GED:** R3, M2, L2 • **SVP:** 3-6 mos • **Academic:** Ed=N, Eng=N • **Work Field:** 136 • **MPSMS:** 567 • **Aptitudes:** G3, V4, N4, S3, P3, Q5, K3, F4, M3, E4, C5 • **Temperaments:** M, T • **Physical:** V=L, H=N, L=M, W, H • **Work Env:** I, N • **Salary:** 4 • **Outlook:** 2

GOE: 06.04.33 Manual Work, Brushing & Coating, Elemental

ENAMELER (plumb. supplies) • D.O.T. #509.684-010 • OES #91926 • ENAMEL DRIER. Sprays finish coat of enamel onto cast-iron sanitary units, such as bathtubs and sinks and bakes unit to provide permanent finish: Wheels units into furnace for preheating, using steel fork mounted on overhead conveyor. Observes color of unit through window in furnace to determine when desired temperature has been reached. Removes unit from furnace and sprays powdered enamel over it, using pneumatic gun. Returns unit to furnace to fuse and glaze enamel, repeating heating and enameling process until unit is coated without discolorations, blisters, or pinholes. • **GED:** R3, M2, L2 • **SVP:** 6 mos-1 yr • **Academic:** Ed=N, Eng=N • **Work Field:** 141, 153 • **MPSMS:** 553 • **Aptitudes:** G4, V4, N4, S3, P3, Q5, K3, F4, M2, E5, C3 • **Temperaments:** V • **Physical:** V=L, H=N, L=L, W, H • **Work Env:** I, H • **Salary:** 2 • **Out look:** 2

METAL SPRAYER, PRODUCTION (any ind.) • **D.O.T.** #505.684-014 • **OES** #91926 • Sprays variety of objects, such as valves, clutch plates, and cylinder linings, on production basis, to coat them with specified thickness of metal: Cleans and roughens surface of object in sand or shotblast cabinet [CABINET-ABRASIVE SANDBLASTER (any ind.)]. Fastens objects in fixture or between bench centers. Preheats object for spraying, using oxyacetylene torch or metalizing gun. Moves controls to set specified rate of wire feed and flow of oxygen and fuel gases through metalizing gun. Ignites gases to melt wire and presses button or trigger to release compressed air which atomizes and sprays molten metal onto workpiece. Manually directs spray over object to apply coating of specified thickness. May spray metal objects with soft solder preparatory to assembly and be designated SOLDER SPRAYER (any ind.). • **GED:** R2, M2, L2 • **SVP:** 30 days-3 mos • **Academic:** Ed=N, Eng=N • **Work Field:** 051, 153 • **MPSMS:** 541 • **Aptitudes:** G4, V4, N4, S4, P3, Q5, K3, F4, M3, E5, C4 • **Temperaments:** R, T • **Stress:** T • **Physical:** V=L, H=N, L=M, W, H • **Work Env:** I, N • **Salary:** 3 • **Outlook:** 3

PAINTER (jewelry) • **D.O.T.** #735.687-018 • **OES** #93947 • Brushes protective covering onto specified sections of jewelry articles to protect sections during electroplating, sandblasting, and polishing operations: Brushes or dabs lacquer or molten wax onto jewelry to prevent damage to coated areas during electroplating or sandblasting. Brushes shellac on sandblasted areas to protect areas during polishing. May correct plating defects, using paint and brush. • **GED:** R2, M1, L2 • **SVP:** 2-30 days • **Academic:** Ed=N, Eng=N • **Work Field:** 153 • **MPSMS:** 611 • **Aptitudes:** G4, V4, N4, S4, P3, Q4, K3, F3, M3, E5, C4 • **Temperaments:** R, T • **Stress:** T • **Physical:** V=G, H=N, L=S, H • **Work Env:** I • **Salary:** 2 • **Outlook:** 3

PAINTER, BRUSH (any ind.) • **D.O.T.** #740.684-022 • **OES** #93947 • PAINTER, HAND. Brushes paint, lacquer, rustproofing agent, or other coating onto metal, woodstock, or fabricated items, using brush: Places workpiece on bench, stanchion, or floor. Cleans surfaces, using hand scraper, wire brush, sandpaper, or turpentine. Pours desired amount of thinner into paint. Paints articles, using brush. Cleans brushes and floor, using solvent or soap and water. May transfer items to and from work area, using hoist or handtruck. May be designated according to article painted as LAST-CODE STRIPER (lasts & rel. forms); PAINTER, DRUM (any ind.); PAINTER, MANNEQUIN (model & pattern); PIPE COATER (iron & steel); or according to coating applied as JAPANNER (any ind.); LACQUERER (mach. shop); CAR VARNISHER (loco. & car bldg. & rep.). • **GED:** R2, M1, L1 • **SVP:** 2-30 days • **Academic:** Ed=N, Eng=N • **Work Field:** 153 • **MPSMS:** 495 • **Aptitudes:** G4, V4, N4, S4, P4, Q5, K4, F4, M3, E5, C4 • **Temperaments:** R, T • **Stress:** T • **Physical:** V=L, H=N, L=M, W, H • **Work Env:** I • **Salary:** 3 • **Outlook:** 3

PAINTER, SPRAY 2 (any ind.) • **D.O.T.** #741.687-018 • **OES** #93947 • PAINTER, ROUGH. Performs duties as described under PAINTER, SPRAY (any ind.) I where coating of surface or product is required without need for finished appearance. Workers spray manufactured articles on assembly line, or travel to work site to spray materials, such as waterproofing, adhesive, foam, or paint onto surfaces of articles. May be designated according to article sprayed as COIL SPRAYER (electronics); MICA-PARTS SPRAYER (electronics); PAINTER, BARREL (petrol. refin.); or according to coating applied as ENAMEL SPRAYER (any ind.) II; LACQUER SPRAYER (any ind.) II; SIZING SPRAYER (window shade & fix.). Additional titles: DAG SPRAYER (electronics); DOPER OPERATOR (tinware); LIPCOAT SPRAYER (any ind.); PAINTER, BLACKWALL TIRE (rubber tire & tube); PAINTER CHASSIS (auto. mfg.); PAINTER, ELECTRIC MOTOR (any ind.); SILICATOR (chem.); SPECIAL-LINING APPLIER (any ind.); SPRAY CEMENTER (leather prod.); SPRAYER (boot & shoe); TILE SPRAYER (brick & tile); TIMBER SPRINKLER (mining & quar-

rying); WATERPROOFER (boot & shoe). • **GED:** R2, M1, L1 • **SVP:** 2-30 days • **Academic:** Ed=N, Eng=N • **Work Field:** 153 • **MPSMS:** 495 • **Aptitudes:** G4, V4, N4, S4, P4, Q5, K4, F4, M3, E5, C4 • **Temperaments:** R • **Stress:** T • **Physical:** V=L, H=N, L=M, W, H • **Work Env:** B • **Salary:** 2 • **Outlook:** 2

PUTTY GLAZER (any ind.) • **D.O.T.** #749.684-042 • **OES** #93947 • Applies coating of putty, mastic, or similar material to imperfections in manufactured articles, preparatory to application of paint or other final coating: Inspects surface of article for defects, such as holes, cracks, and indentations. Spreads material over flaws, using dauber or knife, and brushes or spreads thinned putty or sealer over surface to conceal blemish. May spray article with prescribed coating, using spray gun. May prepare surface for finishing coat, using wire brushes, sandpaper, power grinder, or sandblasting equipment. May tend oven to bake article before or after application of final coating. May be designated according to article coated as WHEEL FILLER (auto. mfg.). • **GED:** R2, M1, L1 • **SVP:** 30 days-3 mos • **Academic:** Ed=N, Eng=N • **Work Field:** 094 • **MPSMS:** 495 • **Aptitudes:** G4, V4, N5, S4, P3, Q5, K3, F4, M3, E5, C5 • **Temperaments:** R, T • **Stress:** T • **Physical:** V=L, H=N, L=M, W, H • **Work Env:** I • **Salary:** 3 • **Outlook:** 2

TOUCH-UP PAINTER, HAND (any ind.) • **D.O.T.** #740.684-026 • **OES** #93947 • HAND PAINTER; RETOUCHER; SALVAGE PAINTER. Paints to cover or touch up articles, such as clock or instrument hands and dials, cases, engraved surfaces, glass tubes, and ceramics, using brush: Inspects workpiece for inspector's markings or defects. Wipes, scrapes, sands, or applies cleaning solution to surface to prepare for retouching. Dips brush into specified paint or protective coating solution and applies it to surface of article specified. Brushes paint over surface and wipes it from unengraved area to paint engraved etchings. May apply coating of material, such as plastic wax or removable paint to mask surfaces for plating, painting, or metalizing. May straighten parts, such as clock dials or hands, using jig or bench press preparatory to painting. May paint original items, such as dials for custom-built instruments, freehand, or using stencil or tracing device. May be designated according to article retouched as DIAL RETOUCHER (inst. & app.). • **GED:** R2, M1, L1 • **SVP:** 2-30 days • **Academic:** Ed=N, Eng=N • **Work Field:** 153, 262 • **MPSMS:** 495 • **Aptitudes:** G4, V4, N5, S4, P3, Q5, K3, F3, M4, E5, C4 • **Temperaments:** R, T • **Stress:** T • **Physical:** V=L, H=N, L=L, W, H • **Work Env:** I • **Salary:** 3 • **Outlook:** 3

GOE: 06.04.34 Manual Work, Assorted Materials, Elemental

ARTIFICIAL-FLOWER MAKER (artif. flower) • **D.O.T.** #739.684-014 • **OES** #93956 • FLOWER ARRANGER; FOLIAGE ARRANGER. Cuts out and assembles materials, such as fabric, wood, and paper, performing any combination of the following tasks to make artificial foliage, such as flowers, wreaths, and trees: Cuts out flower parts, such as leaves and petals from paper, fabric, or plastic, using handtools, such as scissors, knives, hammers, and dies. Stamps out flower parts with hand-operated or power-driven machine. Places roll of material on spindle of machine that automatically forms artificial-flower stems. Prints veining on artificial leaves, using stamps and handpress. Dips flowers into specified dye and squeezes out excess dye, using hands. Fastens twigs and buds to steel wire to form branches by hand or using twisting machine. Wires or glues flower parts to stem or branch. Fastens artificial flowers and foliage to wreath stand and inserts cones and grass decorations to form artificial wreath. May wrap stems with green and brown paper to effect natural appearance. May be designated according to product produced as WREATH AND GARLAND MAKER, HAND (artif. flower); or shape artificial flower petals from fabric, using tweezers, heated metal ball, and wooden form, and be designated PETAL SHAPER, HAND (artif. flower). • **GED:** R2, M1, L1 • **SVP:** 30 days-3 mos • **Academic:** Ed=N, Eng=N • **Work Field:** 102 • **MPSMS:** 618 • **Aptitudes:** G4, V4, N4, S3, P3, Q4, K3, F3, M3, E5, C3 • **Temperaments:** R, T • **Stress:** T • **Physical:** V=L, H=N, L=L, H • **Work Env:** I • **Salary:** 2 • **Outlook:** 3

BROOMMAKER (brush & broom) • **D.O.T.** #739.684-018 • **OES** #93999 • WINDER. Fabricates brooms from broom corn fibers, using one of following methods: (1) Inserts and clamps broom handle in winder (rotating vise). Threads end of wire from reel through hole in handle and nails, ties, or staples wire to handle. Places layers of fiber onto handle and depresses pedal to rotate handle to wrap wire around fiber. Spreads fibers around under wire as winder turns. Trims excess fiber around each layer, using knife. Hooks leather strap around body of broom to secure it while winding subsequent layers. Pounds fibers to pack and shape broom shoulders, using mallet. Wraps and fastens wire around neck of broom handle with stapler. Weighs brooms on scales to verify conformance to standard. (2) Gathers cut and graded broomcorn into bundle according to size required for broom. Inserts broom handle into plastic cone and staples cone to broom handle, using stapling machine. Dips base of broomcorn bundle in pot of hot tar, inserts base into cone, flattens cone and broom corn into fan-flare shape, using vise. Staples cone to broomcorn, using stapling machine, and stacks brooms for further processing. May pull broom through stemmer (comblike device) to remove coarse or short fibers. • **GED:** R2, M1, L1 • **SVP:** 3-6 mos • **Academic:** Ed=N, Eng=N • **Work Field:** 102 • **MPSMS:** 619 • **Aptitudes:** G4, V4, N4, S4, P3, Q4, K3, F4, M3, E4, C5 • **Temperaments:** R, T • **Stress:** T • **Physical:** V=N, H=N, L=L, H • **Work Env:** I • **Salary:** 1 • **Outlook:** 1

DECAL APPLIER (any ind.) • D.O.T. #749.684-010 • OES #93947 • DECAL TRANSFERRER; DESIGN TRANSFERRER; PRINT APPLIER. Applies decal designs to surfaces by moisture process: Cleans surface to be covered, using moist cloth. Submerges decal in water to moisten adhesive and backing paper. Positions decal on surface visually or using template and smooths out air bubbles with roller or edge board. Slides backing paper from decal and wipes off excess adhesive with damp cloth. May cut out decals from sheet with scissors. May varnish over design. When applying decals to chinaware may be designated as PRINT DECORATOR (pottery & porc.). • **GED:** R2, M1, L1 • **SVP:** 2-30 days • **Academic:** Ed=N, Eng=N • **Work Field:** 063 • **MPSMS:** 479 • **Aptitudes:** G4, V4, N5, S4, P3, Q4, K3, F3, M3, E5, C3 • **Temperaments:** R, T • **Stress:** T • **Physical:** V=L, H=N, L=L, H • **Work Env:** I, W • **Salary:** 2 • **Outlook:** 2

DRILLER, HAND (any ind.) • D.O.T. #809.684-018 • OES #92198 • DRILLER, PORTABLE. Drills rivet or bolt holes in material, such as metal, wood, or plastic, following layout marks and using portable power drill: Punches indentations along layout marks to guide drill bit, using center punch and hammer. Fastens specified drill bit in chuck of drill. Drills holes, replaces drill bit with specified reamer, tap, or counter sink, and enlarges, threads, or countersinks holes. Sharpens cutting tools, using power grinder. May aline offcenter holes in structural members, using drift pins, and bolt members together, using wrench. • **GED:** R2, M1, L1 • **SVP:** 2-30 days • **Academic:** Ed=N, Eng=N • **Work Field:** 053 • **MPSMS:** 573, 594, 610 • **Aptitudes:** G4, V4, N4, S4, P3, Q5, K4, F4, M3, E5, C5 • **Temperaments:** M, T • **Physical:** V=L, H=N, L=M, W, H • **Work Env:** I, N • **Salary:** 2 • **Outlook:** 2

ELECTRONICS UTILITY WORKER (electronics) • D.O.T. #726.367-014 • OES #58008 • Arranges layout of work station for other workers who fabricate, process, or assemble electronic equipment, and components, such as semiconductor devices, printed circuit boards (PCBs), chassis assemblies, and wire harnesses and cables: Reads specifications, such as process guide, bill of material, wiring diagram, mechanical print, and schematic diagram, to determine equipment needed, such as piece parts, chemicals and gases, tools, test instruments, and jigs and fixtures, for work stations. Prepares and submits requisition. Positions equipment in specified arrangement at work stations. Notifies stockroom when stations need resupply of materials, such as chemicals, resistors, transistors, and color-coded wire, during processing or assembly operations. May assist workers to follow new work procedures and relieve operators from work stations. May set and adjust controls for processing, fabricating, and assembly line equipment, such as furnaces, process chambers, power supplies, timers, and multimeters. May test and repair assembled items by removing or adding piece parts or resoldering or rebonding defective connections, using handtools, production equipment, test machines, and test instruments, such as meters, resistance bridges, and automatic component testers. • **GED:** R3, M1, L2 • **SVP:** 6

mos-1 yr • **Academic:** Ed=N, Eng=N • **Work Field:** 011 • **MPSMS:** 587 • **Aptitudes:** G3, V3, N3, S3, P3, Q3, K4, F4, M3, E5, C3 • **Temperaments:** R • **Stress:** T • **Physical:** V=L, H=N, L=L, W, H • **Work Env:** I • **Salary:** 3 • **Outlook:** 3

ELECTRONICS WORKER (electronics) • D.O.T. #726.687-010 • OES #93990 • Performs one or combination of duties to clean, trim, or prepare components or parts for assembly by other workers: Receives work directions from supervisor or reads work order for instructions regarding work to be performed. Cleans and deglosses parts, using various cleaning devices, solutions, and abrasives. Trims flashing from molded or cast parts, using cutting tool or file. Applies primers, plastics, adhesives, and other coatings to designated surfaces, using applicators, such as spray guns, brushes, or rollers. Fills shells, caps, cases, and other cavities with plastic encapsulating fluid or dips parts in fluid to protect, coat, and seal them [ENCAPSULATOR (elec. equip.; electronics) 726.687-022]. Prepares wires for assembly by measuring, cutting, stripping, twisting, tinning, and attaching contacts, lugs, and other terminal devices, using a variety of handtools and power tools and equipment [WIREWORKER (elec. equip.; electronics) 728.684-022]. Positions and fastens together parts, such as transformer laminates, glass tube laminates, electron tube mounts and cages, variable capacitor rotors and stators, paper loudspeaker cones, and shells and cases for various other components, using handtools and power tools. Charges rectifier plates, using current-generating device. Prints identifying information on component shells, using silk screen, transfer press, or electro-etch printing devices or equipment. Moves parts and finished components to designated areas of plant to supply assemblers or prepare for shipping or storage. Loads and unloads parts from ovens, baskets, pallets, and racks. Disassembles and reclaims parts, using heating equipment and handtools. Maintains records of production. May load mold with wound resistor forms and pour molten metal into mold to encase resistors. May be designated according to work performed as CAPACITOR ASSEMBLER, VARIABLE (electronics); CLEANER (electronics); CRIMPER (electronics); DIE CASTER (electronics); INSULATOR ASSEMBLER (electronics); METAL-BASE RECLAIMER (electronics). Additional titles: PAPER-CONE MAKER (electronics) I; RECTIFIER-PLATE CHARGER (electronics); TAPER (electronics); TINNER (electronics); WIRE STRIPPER (electronics). • **GED:** R2, M1, L2 • **SVP:** 2-30 days • **Academic:** Ed=N, Eng=N • **Work Field:** 111 • **MPSMS:** 585, 587 • **Aptitudes:** G4, V4, N4, S4, P4, Q4, K4, F3, M3, E5, C4 • **Temperaments:** R • **Stress:** T • **Physical:** V=L, H=N, L=L, H • **Work Env:** I • **Salary:** 3 • **Outlook:** 3

INSULATION-BLANKET MAKER (aircraft-aerospace mfg.) • D.O.T. #806.684-078 • OES #93999 • Fabricates and assembles heat-insulation blankets for aircraft jet engines, using handtools: Positions templates on insulation material, such as knitted wire cloth, glass cloth, sheet metal, foil, and felt, and cuts material to size, using tin shears. Cuts holes in metal strips, using hand punch. Welds metal strips to wire screens, using spot-welder. Assembles foil, screens, and felt in sequence and fastens edges to form insulation blanket, using hand crimper. • **GED:** R2, M1, L1 • **SVP:** 30 days-3 mos • **Academic:** Ed=N, Eng=N • **Work Field:** 102 • **MPSMS:** 592 • **Aptitudes:** G4, V4, N4, S3, P4, Q4, K4, F4, M3, E5, C5 • **Temperaments:** M, T • **Physical:** V=L, H=N, L=L, H • **Work Env:** I • **Salary:** 2 • **Outlook:** 3

LABORER, GRINDING AND POLISHING (any ind.) • D.O.T. #705.687-014 • OES #98999 • FINISHER. Cleans, deburrs, polishes, or grinds items of metal, plastic, or rubber, using handtools or powered equipment, performing any combination of following tasks: Scrapes or rubs parts with file, wire brush, or buffing cloth. Holds part against buffing or grinding wheel. Deburrs or polishes parts, using portable grinder, chipping hammer, buffer, deburring tool, or hand pick. Mounts part on revolving spindle or chuck and holds or moves tools, such as file, abrasive stone, or cloth against workpiece to file, grind, polish, or buff surface. Cleans interior surfaces of holes, using reamer. Changes tools on powered equipment. Applies abrasive compound, wax, or other dressing to facilitate cleaning or polishing operation. May be known according to process performed as BUFFER (any ind.) II; BURRER (mach. shop); BURRER-MARKER, AXLE (mach. shop.); TOP-EDGE BEVELER (any ind.); WIRE BRUSHER (any ind.). • **GED:** R2,

M2, L2 • **SVP:** 2-30 days • **Academic:** Ed=N, Eng=N • **Work Field:** 051, 052 • **MPSMS:** 540, 610 • **Aptitudes:** G4, V4, N4, S4, P3, Q4, K3, F3, M3, E5, C5 • **Temperaments:** R, T • **Stress:** T • **Physical:** V=G, H=N, L=M, W, H • **Work Env:** I, N • **Salary:** 2 • **Outlook:** 3

LEADER TIER (sports equip.) • D.O.T. #732.687-038 • OES #93956 • LEADER ASSEMBLER. Fabricates fishing leaders from cable wire and synthetic fiber line: Attaches snaps, swivels, and other accessories to precut lengths of plastic-or nylon-coated cable wire, and secures ends of cable with plastic or nylon sleeves and adhesives. Forms loop in ends of precut lengths of stainless steel wire and wraps ends back around wire to secure them. Ties loop knots in centers and ends of precut lengths of line to facilitate attachment of weights or hooks. May coil completed leaders and attach them to display cards or insert them in plastic envelopes. May test tensile strength of leader material, using tensiometer. May attach precut length of line to fishhook in manner to facilitate attachment to line or lure and be designated as SNELLER, HAND (sports equip.). • **GED:** R2, M1, L1 • **SVP:** 2-30 days • **Academic:** Ed=N, Eng=N • **Work Field:** 062 • **MPSMS:** 616 • **Aptitudes:** G4, V4, N4, S3, P4, Q5, K3, F2, M2, E5, C5 • **Temperaments:** R • **Stress:** T • **Physical:** V=L, H=N, L=L, H • **Work Env:** I • **Salary:** 2 • **Outlook:** 2

MACHINE SNELLER (sports equip.) • D.O.T. #732.685-026 • OES #92998 • Tends machine that attaches snells (leaders) to fishhooks: Threads snell from spool through guides to machine chuck. Starts machine and inserts hook between chuck jaws. Depresses pedal to actuate chuck that spins and wraps snell around hook shank, and cuts snell to predetermined length. Removes snelled hook from machine, threads snell through eye of hook, and ties overhand loop knot in end to facilitate attaching to fishing line. May attach snelled hooks to display cards. May tie a second hook above first to make special baiting hookup. • **GED:** R2, M1, L1 • **SVP:** 2-30 days • **Academic:** Ed=N, Eng=N • **Work Field:** 062 • **MPSMS:** 616 • **Aptitudes:** G4, V4, N4, S3, P3, Q5, K3, F2, M2, E4, C5 • **Temperaments:** R • **Stress:** T • **Physical:** V=L, H=N, L=L, H • **Work Env:** I • **Salary:** 2 • **Outlook:** 2

MASKER (any ind.) • D.O.T. #749.687-018 • OES #93999 • BODY MASKER; TAPER. Covers specified areas of metal or wooden parts to be spray-painted, using masking tape, cardboard, or paper: Marks area to be masked on parts or articles, such as aircraft and automobile assemblies, lamp bases, or motorcycle fenders, using rule or template. Cuts or tears paper or cardboard to specified size. Secures masking in place with gummed tape to protect parts while surrounding areas are spray-painted. May smooth unmasked surface, using sandpaper. May dip or coat article with liquid wax instead of applying masking. May tape precut masks or stencils to article. • **GED:** R2, M1, L1 • **SVP:** 30 days-3 mos • **Academic:** Ed=N, Eng=N • **Work Field:** 062, 153 • **MPSMS:** 495 • **Aptitudes:** G4, V4, N4, S4, P4, Q5, K4, F4, M3, E5, C5 • **Temperaments:** R • **Stress:** T • **Physical:** V=L, H=N, L=L, H • **Work Env:** I • **Salary:** 3 • **Outlook:** 2

MAT CUTTER (framing) • D.O.T. #739.684-126 • OES #93926 • Cuts materials to form bordering frames (mats) for pictures: Measures and marks materials, such as mat boards, fabrics, or paper according to size and width of picture. Inserts material in holding device and cuts with knife or razor blade to form bordering frame. May cut backing board to size, using knife or saw. • **GED:** R2, M1, L1 • **SVP:** 2-30 days • **Academic:** Ed=N, Eng=N • **Work Field:** 054 • **MPSMS:** 457 • **Aptitudes:** G4, V4, N4, S3, P3, Q5, K3, F4, M4, E4, C5 • **Temperaments:** R, T • **Stress:** T • **Physical:** V=L, H=N, L=L, H • **Work Env:** I • **Salary:** 2 • **Outlook:** 2

MOUNTER, HAND (photofinish.) • D.O.T. #976.684-018 • OES #93926 • Cuts and mounts photographic film transparencies, using film cutter and heatsealing press: Positions film roll on spindle of cutting machine and threads end of film into rack or along track in front of lighted screen, and under cutter knives. Inspects film for defects, such as blank or black film and double exposures. Alines exposure separation line with cutter knives and depresses pedal to cut film along line. Positions cut film in center of mount and folds edges of mount over film. Inserts mount in heating press that automatically numbers, seals, and ejects mount into tray. Packs mounts in boxes for shipment. • **GED:** R2, M1, L1 • **SVP:** 2-30 days • **Academic:** Ed=N, Eng=N • **Work Field:** 054,

062 • **MPSMS:** 867 • **Aptitudes:** G4, V4, N4, S4, P4, Q4, K3, F3, M3, E4, C4 • **Temperaments:** R, T • **Stress:** T • **Physical:** V=L, H=N, L=S, H • **Work Env:** I • **Salary:** 2 • **Outlook:** 1

PAINT MIXER, HAND (any ind.) • D.O.T. #550.684-018 • OES #93999 • MIXER. Mixes stains, paints, and other coatings for use in painting according to formulas: Pours pigments, paint paste, vehicle, and thinner into can. Stirs mixture with paddle. Compares mixed liquid with desired color sample to ensure that it matches. May blend colors to obtain desired shades. May test specific gravity of mixture, using hydrometer. When mixing colors for spray painting may be designated as SPRAY BLENDER (any ind.). • **GED:** R2, M1, L1 • **SVP:** 30 days-3 mos • **Academic:** Ed=N, Eng=N • **Work Field:** 143 • **MPSMS:** 495 • **Aptitudes:** G4, V4, N4, S4, P4, Q4, K4, F4, M3, E5, C3 • **Temperaments:** M, R • **Stress:** T • **Physical:** V=L, H=N, L=L, W, H • **Work Env:** I • **Salary:** 3 • **Outlook:** 2

PHOTO MASK CLEANER (electronics) • D.O.T. #590.684-034 • OES #98905 • Performs any combination of following tasks to clean production photo mask plates used in fabrication of semiconductor devices: Reads specifications sheet to verify type of photo mask plate and number of production runs for each plate. Marks number of production runs on border of each photo mask plate, using diamond scribe. Immerses photo mask plates into series of chemical baths to strip photoresist from photo mask. Places photo mask plates in chamber of specified cleaning machine and starts machine that automatically cleans and dries photo mask plates. Places photo mask plates in chamber of coating machine and starts machine that automatically deposits specified coating onto photo mask. Monitors operation of machines. Inspects photo mask plates for defects or insufficient cleaning, using microscope. Records process and inspection information in logbook. • **GED:** R2, M1, L2 • **SVP:** 2-30 days • **Academic:** Ed=N, Eng=N • **Work Field:** 031, 182 • **MPSMS:** 587 • **Aptitudes:** G4, V4, N5, S4, P4, Q4, K4, F4, M4, E5, C5 • **Temperaments:** T • **Physical:** V=G, H=N, L=L, H • **Work Env:** I • **Salary:** 2 • **Outlook:** 4

SCREEN PRINTER (any ind.) • D.O.T. #979.684-034 • OES #93951 • DECORATOR; LETTERER; SCREENER; SILK-SCREEN OPERATOR; SILK-SCREEN PAINTER. Prints lettering and designs on objects, such as posters, targets, instrument dials, furniture, glass, and toys, using screen printing device. Positions object against guides on setup board or holding fixture of screening device and lowers screen. Pours paint into screen frame or dips squeegee in paint and draws squeegee across screen to transfer design to object. Cleans screen with solvent at end of run and when using different colors. May mix paints according to standard formulas. May affix decals to parts and assemblies, using roller. May examine printed object for defects. May fabricate silk-screen stencil, using photographic equipment. May be designated according to object printed as TARGET-FACE MAKER (sports equip.). May tend semi-automatic machine that advances wallpaper under printing screen and be designated WALLPAPER PRINTER (wallpaper) II. May screen-print electrode material onto substrate used in electronic components, such as ceramic capacitors and film resistors and be known as SILK-SCREEN PRINTER (electronics). May screen-print solder mask or nomenclature on printed circuit boards and be designated as SCREEN PRINTER, PRINTED CIRCUIT BOARDS, (electronics). • **GED:** R2, M1, L1 • **SVP:** 30 days-3 mos • **Academic:** Ed=N, Eng=N • **Work Field:** 191 • **MPSMS:** 480, 580 • **Aptitudes:** G3, V4, N4, S3, P3, Q4, K3, F4, M3, E5, C3 • **Temperaments:** R, T • **Stress:** T • **Physical:** V=L, H=N, L=L, H • **Work Env:** I • **Salary:** 1 • **Outlook:** 3

STUFFER (toys & games) • D.O.T. #731.685-014 • OES #92974 • BLOWER; TOY STUFFER. Tends machine that blows filler into stuffed-toy shells: Inserts precut supporting wire into shell. Places shell opening over stuffing machine nozzle. Depresses pedal to blow cotton or chopped foam rubber filler into shell to impart shape to toy. Places stuffed toy in tote box. Records production. May stuff toys by hand. • **GED:** R2, M1, L1 • **SVP:** 2-30 days • **Academic:** Ed=N, Eng=N • **Work Field:** 102 • **MPSMS:** 615 • **Aptitudes:** G4, V4, N4, S4, P4, Q4, K4, F4, M3, E4, C5 • **Temperaments:** R • **Stress:** T • **Physical:** V=N, H=N, L=S, H • **Work Env:** I • **Salary:** 2 • **Outlook:** 2

WIREWORKER (elec. equip.) • D.O.T. #728.684-022 • OES #93999 • WIRE-PREPARATION WORKER. Performs any combination of tasks involved in cutting, stripping, taping, forming, and soldering wires or wire leads of components used in electrical and electronic units, such as communication equipment, aircraft, ignition systems, electrical appliances, or other electrical or electronic control systems: Cuts wires to specified lengths, using wire cutters and ruler or measuring jig. Strips insulation from wire ends, using stripping tool. Twists wire ends and dips them into pot of solder to prevent fraying. Solders wires to specified connectors and terminals, using soldering iron, or crimps connectors and terminals to wire ends, using handtools. Wraps numbered or colored identification tape around wires. Rolls wires of identical number or color together and attaches tag to roll. Inserts wires into plastic insulation tubing. Bends, cuts, and crimps component leads to prepare component for mounting on printed circuit board or other assembly, using handtools. May insert wires in automatic numbering or color-coding machine to imprint part numbers or color codes. May insulate wire or component leads by dipping them into paraffin solution. May paint various protective coatings on wires with brush. May test wire and cable assemblies and repair defective assemblies. May use automated equipment or bench-mounted devices to cut, strip, bend, or crimp wire. May be designated by type of wire worked as COMPONENT LEAD FORMER (electronics). • **GED:** R2, M1, L2 • **SVP:** 2-30 days • **Academic:** Ed=N, Eng=N • **Work Field:** 054, 061, 111 • **MPSMS:** 587 • **Aptitudes:** G4, V4, N4, S4, P3, Q4, K3, F3, M3, E5, C4 • **Temperaments:** R, T • **Stress:** T • **Physical:** V=G, H=N, L=L, H • **Work Env:** I • **Salary:** 3 • **Outlook:** 3

GOE: 06.04.35 Laundering, Dry Cleaning

LAUNDERER, HAND (laundry) • D.O.T. #361.684-010 • OES #92726 • Washes, dries, and irons articles in hand-laundries and laundromats, using equipment, such as hand iron, and small washing and drying machines: Sorts articles on worktable or in baskets on floor to separate special washes, such as fugitives and starch work. Loads and unloads washing and drying machines, and adds detergent powder and bleach as required. Folds fluff-dry articles preparatory to wrapping. Presses wearing apparel, using hand iron [PRESSER, HAND (any ind.)]. Assembles, wraps, or bags laundered articles for delivery to customer. Some hand laundries are machine-equipped and only touching-up is done by hand iron; in others, some articles, such as flatwork and shirts, are sent to larger machine-equipped plants. • **GED:** R2, M1, L2 • **SVP:** 2-30 days • **Academic:** Ed=N, Eng=N • **Work Field:** 031, 032 • **MPSMS:** 440, 906 • **Aptitudes:** G4, V4, N4, S4, P3, Q4, K3, F3, M3, E5, C4 • **Temperaments:** J, V • **Physical:** V=G, H=L, L=M, W, H • **Work Env:** I, W • **Salary:** 1 • **Outlook:** 3

LAUNDRY LABORER (laundry) • D.O.T. #361.687-018 • OES #98999 • BUNDLE CLERK. Prepares laundry for processing and distributes laundry, performing any combination of the following duties: Opens bundles of soiled laundry. Places bundles onto conveyor belt or drops down chute for distribution to marking and classification sections. Weighs laundry on scales and records weight on tickets. Removes bundles from conveyor and distributes to workers, using handtruck. Fastens identification pins or clips onto laundry to facilitate subsequent assembly of customers' orders. Sorts net bags containing clean wash according to customers' identification tags. Sorts empty net bags according to color and size. Collects identification tags from lots of laundered articles for reuse. Moistens clean wash preparatory to ironing. Operates power hoist to load and unload washing machines and extractors. Stacks linen supplies on storage room shelves. Unloads soiled linen from trucks. May be designated according to duty performed as BUNDLE WEIGHER (laund.); CHUTE WORKER (laund.); CLIPPER (laund.); LINEN-SUPPLY-ROOM WORKER (laund.); NET SORTER (laund.). Additional titles: PIN SORTER AND BAGGER (laund.); PIN WORKER (laund.); WASHING-MACHINE LOADER (laund.) II. • **GED:** R1, M1, L1 • **SVP:** 2-30 days • **Academic:** Ed=N, Eng=N • **Work Field:** 011 • **MPSMS:** 906 • **Aptitudes:** G4, V4, N4, S4, P4, Q4, K4, F4, M4, E5, C4 • **Temperaments:** R • **Stress:** T • **Physical:** V=L, H=N, L=M, W, S, H • **Work Env:** I, W • **Salary:** 2 • **Outlook:** 3

LAUNDRY OPERATOR (laundry) • D.O.T. #369.684-014 • OES #92726 • Receives, marks, washes, finishes, checks, and wraps articles in laundry performing any combination of following tasks:

Classifies and marks incoming laundry with identifying code number, by hand or using machine [MARKER (clean., dye., & press.; laund.)]. Tends washing machine, extractor, and tumbler to clean and dry laundry. Finishes laundered articles, using hand iron, pressing machine, or feeds and folds flatwork on flatwork ironing machine. Sorts laundry and verifies count on laundry ticket [ASSEMBLER (clean., dye., & press.; laund.); CHECKER (clean., dye., & press.; laund.)]. May perform related tasks, such as mending torn articles, using sewing machine or by affixing adhesive patches. May wrap articles. May specialize in receiving and washing, or in finishing and checking, and be designated according to unit in which work is performed as LAUNDRY OPERATOR, FINISHING (laund.); LAUNDRY OPERATOR, WASH ROOM (laund.). • **GED:** R2, M1, L2 • **SVP:** 30 days-3 mos • **Academic:** Ed=N, Eng=N • **Work Field:** 031, 032 • **MPSMS:** 906 • **Aptitudes:** G4, V4, N4, S4, P4, Q4, K4, F4, M3, E4, C4 • **Temperaments:** R • **Stress:** T • **Physical:** V=N, H=N, L=M, W, H • **Work Env:** I, H, W, N, R • **Salary:** 2 • **Outlook:** 2

LEATHER FINISHER (clean., dye., & press.) • D.O.T. #363.682-010 • OES #92728 • PRESSER, LEATHER GARMENTS. Operates hot-head pressing machine to press and shape drycleaned leather or suede garments: Positions garment on buck of machine and pushes buttons to lower pressing head of machine onto garment. Rearranges garment on buck, repeating process until pressing is completed. Brushes suede to raise nap. • **GED:** R3, M1, L2 • **SVP:** 3-6 mos • **Academic:** Ed=N, Eng=N • **Work Field:** 032 • **MPSMS:** 529, 906 • **Aptitudes:** G4, V4, N4, S4, P3, Q4, K3, F4, M3, E4, C5 • **Temperaments:** R, T • **Stress:** T • **Physical:** V=L, H=N, L=L, H • **Work Env:** I, N • **Salary:** 3 • **Outlook:** 2

PRESS OPERATOR (laundry) • D.O.T. #363.685-010 • OES #92728 • WEARING-APPAREL PRESSER. Tends pressing-machine (hot-head type) to press washed wearing apparel, such as uniforms, jackets, aprons, and shirts: Smooths section of garment on buck (table) of machine, and moistens dry portions of garment with wet cloth or water spray. Pushes buttons to lower pressing head of machine to press and dry garment. Rearranges garment on buck, repeating process until pressing is completed. May work as part of team and press only portion of garment. May tend two or three presses simultaneously, positioning garment on one press while other presses are closed. • **GED:** R2, M1, L1 • **SVP:** 2-30 days • **Academic:** Ed=N, Eng=N • **Work Field:** 032 • **MPSMS:** 906 • **Aptitudes:** G4, V4, N5, S4, P4, Q5, K4, F4, M3, E5, C5 • **Temperaments:** R • **Stress:** T • **Physical:** V=L, H=N, L=L, W, S, H • **Work Env:** I, H, W • **Salary:** 2 • **Outlook:** 3

PRESSER, ALL-AROUND (clean., dye., & press.) • D.O.T. #363.682-014 • OES #92728 • COMBINATION PRESSER. Operates steam pressing machine or uses hand iron to press garments, such as trousers, sweaters, and dresses, usually in small cleaning establishment. Presses silk garments [SILK FINISHER (clean., dye., & press.)] and wool garments. • **GED:** R2, M2, L1 • **SVP:** 30 days-3 mos • **Academic:** Ed=N, Eng=N • **Work Field:** 032 • **MPSMS:** 906 • **Aptitudes:** G4, V4, N4, S4, P3, Q5, K3, F3, M3, E4, C5 • **Temperaments:** R • **Stress:** T • **Physical:** V=L, H=N, L=M, W, S, H • **Work Env:** I, H, W, N, R • **Salary:** 2 • **Outlook:** 3

PRESSER, FORM (any ind.) • D.O.T. #363.685-018 • OES #92728 • BLOCKER; PRESSING-MACHINE OPERATOR. Tends machine that presses and blocks (shapes) garments, such as blouses, coats, dresses, shirts, and sweaters in manufacturing or drycleaning establishment: Selects pressing form (dummy) according to shape of garment. Positions form on holder over steaming device, expands or contracts form according to size of garment, and inserts pin into slot to lock form. Pulls garment over form. Turns dial to regulate steam pressure according to type of material pressed. Depresses pedals that activate steam and air to press, block, and dry garment. Removes garment from form and lays garment on table. • **GED:** R2, M2, L1 • **SVP:** 2-30 days • **Academic:** Ed=N, Eng=N • **Work Field:** 032 • **MPSMS:** 440, 906 • **Aptitudes:** G4, V4, N4, S4, P3, Q5, K3, F3, M3, E3, C5 • **Temperaments:** R, T • **Stress:** T • **Physical:** V=L, H=N, L=L, W, H • **Work Env:** I, H, W, N, R • **Salary:** 2 • **Outlook:** 3

PRESSER, HAND (any ind.) • D.O.T. #363.684-018 • OES #93921 • FINISHER, HAND; IRONER, HAND. Presses articles, such as drapes, knit goods, millinery parts, parachutes, garments, and slip covers, or delicate textiles, such as lace, synthetics, and silks to remove wrinkles, flatten seams, and give shape to article, using hand iron: Places article in position on ironing board or worktable. Smooths and shapes fabric prior to pressing. Sprays water over fabric to soften fibers when not using steam iron. Adjusts temperature of iron, according to type of fabric, and uses covering cloths to prevent scorching or to avoid sheen on delicate fabrics. Pushes and pulls iron over surface of article, according to type of fabric. Fits odd-shaped pieces which cannot be pressed flat over puff iron. May pin, fold, and hang article after pressing. May be designated according to article or part pressed as COAT IRONER, HAND (garment); LINING PRESSER (clean., dye., & press.; garment); SEAM PRESSER (garment); VEST PRESSER (garment); or according to type of cloth pressed as COTTON PRESSER (garment); SILK PRESSER (garment) I. Additional titles: FLATWORK FINISHER, HAND (laund.); PIECE PRESSER (garment); POCKET PRESSER (garment); UNDERPRESSER, HAND (garment); WAIST PRESSER (garment); WEARING-APPAREL FINISHER, HAND (laund.). • **GED:** R2, M1, L1 • **SVP:** 2-30 days • **Academic:** Ed=N, Eng=N • **Work Field:** 032 • **MPSMS:** 440, 906 • **Aptitudes:** G4, V4, N5, S4, P4, Q5, K3, F4, M3, E5, C5 • **Temperaments:** R • **Stress:** T • **Physical:** V=L, H=N, L=L, W, H • **Work Env:** I, H, W, N, R • **Salary:** 2 • **Outlook:** 3

SILK FINISHER (clean., dye., & press.) • D.O.T. #363.681-010 • OES #89517 • Presses drycleaned and wet-cleaned silk and synthetic fiber garments, using hot-head press or steamtable, puff irons, and hand iron: Operates machine presses to finish those parts that can be pressed flat and completes other parts of garments by pressing with hand iron. Finishes parts difficult to reach, such as flounces, by fitting parts over puff irons. Finishes velvet garments by steaming on buck of hot-head press or steamtable, and brushing pile (nap) with handbrush. Finishes fancy garments, such as evening gowns and costumes, with hand iron, applying knowledge of fabrics and heats to produce high quality finishes which cannot be obtained on machine presses. Presses ties on small pressing machine or by inserting heated metal form into tie and touching up rough places with hand iron. Finishes pleated garments, determining size of pleat from evidence of old pleat or from work order (for new garments) and presses with machine press or hand iron. May press wool fabrics requiring precision finishing. In establishments where many SILK FINISHERS (clean., dye., & press.) are employed may be designated according to specialty as FINISHER, HAND (clean., dye., & press.); FORM-FINISHING-MACHINE OPERATOR (clean., dye., & press.; laund.); HOT-HEAD-MACHINE OPERATOR (clean., dye., & press.; laund.); PLEAT PRESSER (clean., dye., & press.); PUFF-IRON OPERATOR (clean., dye., & press.; laund.) I; TIE PRESSER (clean., dye., & press.); VELVET STEAMER (clean., dye., & press.). • **GED:** R3, M1, L2 • **SVP:** 3-6 mos • **Academic:** Ed=N, Eng=N • **Work Field:** 032 • **MPSMS:** 906 • **Aptitudes:** G3, V4, N4, S4, P3, Q5, K3, F3, M3, E4, C4 • **Temperaments:** R, T • **Stress:** T • **Physical:** V=L, H=N, L=L, H • **Work Env:** I, H, W, N, R • **Salary:** 3 • **Outlook:** 2

WASHER, MACHINE (laundry) • D.O.T. #361.665-010 • OES #92726 • STEAM CLEANER, MACHINE; WET CLEANER, MACHINE; WET WASHER, MACHINE. Tends one or more machines that wash commercial, industrial, or household articles, such as garments, blankets, curtains, draperies, fine linens, and rags: Loads, or directs workers engaged in loading, machine with articles requiring identical treatment. Starts machine and turns valves to admit specified amounts of soap, detergent, water, bluing, and bleach. Adds starch to loads of such articles as curtains or linens, when bell signal indicates that washing cycle is completed. Removes, or directs workers in removing articles from washer and into handtrucks or extractors. May wash delicate fabrics by hand. May mix solutions, such as bleach, bluing, or starch, and apply them to articles before or after washing to remove color or improve appearance. May spot-clean articles, before washing, to remove heavy stains. May sterilize items. May hang curtains, draperies, or blankets on stretch-frames to dry. May brush blankets, or feed into carding machine, to raise and fluff nap. May pull trousers over heated metal forms to dry and stretch legs. May load and remove articles from extractor or drier by hand or hoist, using metal basket or cord mesh bag. When washing contaminated laundry from

hospital isolation wards, may be designated ISOLATION-WASHER (laund.). May be designated according to type of articles washed as FLATWORK WASHER (laund.); OVERALL WASHER (laund.); RAG WASHER (laund.); WASHER, BLANKET (laund.). • **GED:** R3, M2, L2 • **SVP:** 3-6 mos • **Academic:** Ed=N, Eng=N • **Work Field:** 031 • **MPSMS:** 440, 906 • **Aptitudes:** G3, V4, N4, S4, P4, Q5, K4, F4, M4, E5, C5 • **Temperaments:** R • **Stress:** T • **Physical:** V=N, H=N, L=M, W, S, H • **Work Env:** I, W, N • **Salary:** 3 • **Outlook:** 2

WASHING-MACHINE LOADER-AND-PULLER (laundry) • D.O.T. #361.686-010 • OES #98502 • Loads and unloads washing machines in laundry: Pushes handtruck containing soiled laundry from marking and classifying department to washing machine and loads articles into machine. Removes washed laundry from machine and places in extractor baskets. May lift loaded extractor baskets, using power hoist. May place baskets in extractor and start extractor. May be known according to task performed as PULLER (laund.); WASHER HELPER, MACHINE (laund.); WASHING-MACHINE LOADER (laund.) I. • **GED:** R2, M1, L1 • **SVP:** 2-30 days • **Academic:** Ed=N, Eng=N • **Work Field:** 011 • **MPSMS:** 906 • **Aptitudes:** G4, V4, N5, S4, P4, Q5, K4, F4, M4, E5, C5 • **Temperaments:** R • **Stress:** T • **Physical:** V=L, H=N, L=H, W, H • **Work Env:** I, W, N • **Salary:** 2 • **Outlook:** 3

GOE: 06.04.37 Manual Work, Stamping & Labeling, Elemental

MARKER 2 (any ind.) • D.O.T. #920.687-126 • OES #98999 • LABELER; STAMPER. Marks or affixes trademarks or other identifying information, such as size, color, grade, or process code, on merchandise, material, or product, using one or more methods, such as metal punch and hammer, crayon, rubber stamp and ink, electric pencil, branding iron, acid and stencil, sand-grit and stencil, or tags. May inspect items before marking. May clean items. May use printing mechanism or labeling press. When marking is performed as task of packaging duties, worker should be classified according to type of packaging performed as PACKAGER, HAND (any ind.); PACKAGER, MACHINE (any ind.); or BALING-MACHINE TENDER (any ind.). • **GED:** R2, M1, L1 • **SVP:** 2-30 days • **Academic:** Ed=N, Eng=N • **Work Field:** 191, 192 • **MPSMS:** 898 • **Aptitudes:** G4, V4, N4, S4, P4, Q4, K4, F4, M3, E5, C5 • **Temperaments:** R • **Stress:** T • **Physical:** V=L, H=N, L=S, H • **Work Env:** I • **Salary:** 1 • **Outlook:** 3

MARKER, SEMICONDUCTOR WAFERS (electronics) • D.O.T. #920.587-026 • OES #98999 • Scribes identifying information onto semiconductor wafer, using metal stylus (scribe): Obtains container loaded with semiconductor wafers and removes wafers from container, using tweezers. Marks lot number and description number in designated area of wafers, following specifications and using metal stylus. Records production data. Cleans containers, using soap and water. • **GED:** R2, M1, L2 • **SVP:** 2-30 days • **Academic:** Ed=N, Eng=N • **Work Field:** 183, 231 • **MPSMS:** 587 • **Aptitudes:** G4, V4, N5, S5, P4, Q3, K4, F3, M4, E5, C5 • **Temperaments:** R • **Stress:** T • **Physical:** V=L, H=N, L=L, H • **Work Env:** I • **Salary:** 3 • **Outlook:** 3

NAME-PLATE STAMPER (any ind.) • D.O.T. #652.685-054 • OES #92543 • Tends machine that stamps or embosses identifying data on nameplates for manufactured products, using one of following methods: (1) Assembles dies or alines type in die block, using setscrews. Positions die block on press bed, lowers ram with handwheel, and feeds blank plates into powered machine or pulls lever to imprint data on blank. (2) Turns wheel to specified character and pulls lever to stamp character on blank. Repeats operation for each character until specified information is embossed on plate. May place nameplate in hinged forming block and close block manually to shape plate to specified curvature. • **GED:** R2, M1, L1 • **SVP:** 2-30 days • **Academic:** Ed=N, Eng=N • **Work Field:** 192 • **MPSMS:** 567 • **Aptitudes:** G4, V4, N4, S4, P3, Q3, K3, F4, M4, E4, C5 • **Temperaments:** R • **Stress:** T • **Physical:** V=G, H=N, L=L, H • **Work Env:** I • **Salary:** 2 • **Outlook:** 2

STENCILER (any ind.) • D.O.T. #920.687-178 • OES #93947 • MARKER, SHIPMENTS. Marks size, lot number, contents, or other identifying information or symbols on containers or directly on article by placing stencil on container or article and rubbing ink or paint brush across open lettering, or by spraying paint on stencil. May mix paints or lacquers. May be designated according to type of container stenciled as CARTON STENCILER (any ind.); DRUM STENCILER (distilled liquors); SACK STENCILER (any ind.). • **GED:** R1, M1, L1 • **SVP:** 2-30 days • **Academic:** Ed=N, Eng=N • **Work Field:** 191, 262 • **MPSMS:** 898 • **Aptitudes:** G4, V4, N4, S4, P4, Q5, K4, F4, M3, E5, C4 • **Temperaments:** R • **Stress:** T • **Physical:** V=L, H=N, L=L, H • **Work Env:** I • **Salary:** 2 • **Outlook:** 2

TICKETER (any ind.) • D.O.T. #652.685-098 • OES #92543 • LABEL STAMPER; TICKET MAKER; TICKET PRINTER. Tends machine that prints information, such as price, size, style, or color, on identification tags or labeling material: Selects type, according to specifications, and inserts type into machine, using tweezers, or turns dial on machine to move type into printing position. Mounts roll of tags or labeling material on machine brackets and threads end of roll through feeding device. Turns crank to print information on tags or material, or starts machine that automatically prints information on material. Removes printed material from delivery end of machine. May cut individual labels or tags from rolls of material, using scissors. May apply ink to printing rollers or printing pad on machine, using liquid or paste ink. May tend machine equipped with automatic cutter and counting control that stops machine when specified number of tickets have been printed. May tend machine that threads string through holes in tags or labels [STRINGING-MACHINE OPERATOR (paper goods)]. May tend machine that prints identifying information on tags or tickets and sews tickets to garments or garment parts [TICKET PRINTER AND TAGGER (garment)]. May tend machine that automatically prints identifying information on ticket and pins ticket to articles and be designated PIN-TICKET-MACHINE OPERATOR (any ind.). • **GED:** R2, M1, L2 • **SVP:** 2-30 days • **Academic:** Ed=N, Eng=N • **Work Field:** 191 • **MPSMS:** 479 • **Aptitudes:** G4, V4, N4, S4, P4, Q4, K4, F3, M4, E5, C4 • **Temperaments:** R • **Stress:** T • **Physical:** V=G, H=N, L=L, H • **Work Env:** I • **Salary:** 1 • **Outlook:** 4

GOE: 06.04.38 Wrapping & Packing

ASSEMBLER, HOSPITAL SUPPLIES (inst. & app.) • D.O.T. #712.687-010 • OES #93956 • Performs any combination of the following duties to assemble, package, and sterilize disposable plastic hospital supplies, such as hypodermic syringes, catheters, and intravenous transfusion apparatus: Selects parts required for product to be assembled. Lines up edges of plastic bags, inserts hypodermic plunger in cylinder, slides needle over base of cylinder, and positions other parts together to prepare for bonding. Positions assembled parts in equipment that heats and bonds plastic parts together. Places assembled product in plastic bag or other container, seals container, and packs items in cartons. Stacks cartons in sterilization chamber, seals chamber, and turns valve to admit gas into chamber that sterilizes products. Inspects products for defects and discards defective products. • **GED:** R2, M1, L1 • **SVP:** 2-30 days • **Academic:** Ed=N, Eng=N • **Work Field:** 041, 102 • **MPSMS:** 604 • **Aptitudes:** G4, V4, N5, S4, P4, Q5, K3, F3, M4, E5, C5 • **Temperaments:** R, T • **Stress:** T • **Physical:** V=L, H=N, L=L, H • **Work Env:** I • **Salary:** 2 • **Outlook:** 2

BAKERY WORKER (bake. prod.) • D.O.T. #929.686-010 • OES #98502 • BELT CONVEYOR LOADER; BISCUIT PACKER; PACKER HELPER; WEIGHT CHECKER. Works at conveyor belt or bench performing any combination of the following tasks in finishing, packaging, wrapping, and packing bakery goods: Feeds or offbears such machines as filling, depositing, enrobing, slicing, bag-filling, bag-sealing, wrapping, and carton-folding machines. Guides, stacks, separates, counts, packs, wraps, and weighs cookies, crackers, doughnuts, cakes, sweet rolls, and specialty items, such as toast and peanut butter crackers, as products progress on conveyor belt. Peels paper pan liners from baked cakes. Forms cartons by hand. Places labels inside or around packages, bags, or cartons. • **GED:** R1, M1, L1 • **SVP:** 2-30 days • **Academic:** Ed=N, Eng=N • **Work Field:** 011, 041 • **MPSMS:** 384 • **Aptitudes:** G4, V4, N4, S4, P4, Q4, K3, F3, M3, E5, C5 • **Temperaments:** R • **Stress:** T • **Physical:** V=L, H=N, L=M, W, H • **Work Env:** I, N • **Salary:** 3 • **Outlook:** 3

CARDER (any ind.) • D.O.T. #920.685-034 • OES #92974 • CARD ASSEMBLER; CARDING-MACHINE OPERATOR. Tends machine that stitches articles, such as hairpins, hooks and eyes, knitting needles, and snap fasteners, onto cards for sales presentation: Mounts cones of threads onto spindles and threads ends through guides. Stacks cards in gravity feed hopper. Starts machine and observes machine for jams as articles drop down feeder tubes and are stitched onto moving card. Cuts stitching between cards to separate cards, using scissors, and stacks filled cards. May attach articles on cards, using staples, elastic, or metal fasteners. May be designated according to type of article mounted as METAL-HAIRPIN CARDER (any ind.); PIN INSERTER (any ind.). • **GED:** R2, M1, L1 • **SVP:** 2-30 days • **Academic:** Ed=N, Eng=N • **Work Field:** 171 • **MPSMS:** 618 • **Aptitudes:** G4, V4, N4, S4, P4, Q4, K4, F3, M3, E4, C5 • **Temperaments:** R • **Stress:** T • **Physical:** V=L, H=N, L=L, H • **Work Env:** I • **Salary:** 2 • **Outlook:** 3

CRATER (any ind.) • D.O.T. #920.484-010 • OES #98902 • BOXER; CARPENTER, PACKING; CASE MAKER. Fabricates wooden crates or boxes, using woodworking handtools and powered tools, and packs such items as machinery, vehicles, or other large or odd-shaped products: Reads blueprints, shipping notices, and other specifications, and inspects product to determine size and shape of container, materials to be used, and types of supports and braces to be used. Lays out dimensions on materials with ruler, measuring tape, and pencil. Saws materials to size, using handsaws and powered saws. Assembles materials, using nailing or stapling machine, screws, bolts, glue, and handtools. Places product in container, manually or using hoist. Bolts heavy pieces to bottom of container or skid. Wraps and pads product with excelsior, paper, or other packing material. Builds crate around large or odd-shaped articles. Nails cover on crate. Wraps and tightens metal bands around crate, using banding equipment. Attaches identification labels or stencils containing such information as shipping destination, weight, and type of product contained on crate. Repairs broken crates. May cover military tanks and other equipment with neoprene or other protective covering to protect them during shipment. May count items to be packed to ensure compliance with shipping orders. May weigh loaded crate. May move container to shipping area, and lumber, paper, and other wrapping supplies to crating area, using hand or industrial truck. May sharpen saw blades, using file. May be designated according to item crated as MACHINERY CRATER (mach. mfg.); REFRIGERATOR CRATER (refrigerat. equip.), or specific duty performed as CRATE REPAIRER (any ind.). • **GED:** R3, M1, L2 • **SVP:** 30 days-3 mos • **Academic:** Ed=N, Eng=N • **Work Field:** 041, 102 • **MPSMS:** 454 • **Aptitudes:** G3, V4, N3, S3, P4, Q4, K3, F3, M3, E5, C5 • **Temperaments:** R, T • **Stress:** T • **Physical:** V=L, H=N, L=M, W, H • **Work Env:** I • **Salary:** 2 • **Outlook:** 3

FLOOR WORKER (chew. gum) • D.O.T. #920.687-090 • OES #98902 • Performs any combination of following tasks to facilitate wrapping and packing of chewing gum: Copies from registers (counters) on machines number of cartons of chewing gum filled by each packing machine. Empties containers of scrap gum into barrel for reprocessing. Distributes packaging materials to workers. Replaces packages of gum that were previously removed from carton for inspection. Scans stacks of cellophane-wrapped cartons passing on conveyor belt to detect defective wrapping. Removes cellophane from defectively wrapped cartons and returns cartons for rewrapping. • **GED:** R2, M1, L1 • **SVP:** 2-30 days • **Academic:** Ed=N, Eng=N • **Work Field:** 041, 231 • **MPSMS:** 393 • **Aptitudes:** G4, V4, N4, S4, P4, Q4, K4, F3, M4, E5, C5 • **Temperaments:** R • **Stress:** T • **Physical:** V=L, H=N, L=L, W, H • **Work Env:** I • **Salary:** 2 • **Outlook:** 1

MAILING-MACHINE OPERATOR (print. & pub.) • D.O.T. #208.462-010 • OES #56008 • Operates machine that automatically addresses, weighs, and ties into bundles printed publications, such as magazines, catalogs, and pamphlets, for mailing according to zip code: Reads production order to determine type and size of publication scheduled for mailing. Adjusts guides, rollers, loose card inserter, weighing machine, and tying arm, using rule and handtools. Fills paste reservoir. Mounts roll of subscriber address labels onto machine spindle and threads twine through tying arm. Starts machine and observes operation to detect evidence of malfunctions throughout production run. Stops machine to make adjustments or clear jams. Records production according to customer name and zip code, and machine down time due to malfunctions or lack of work. • **GED:** R4, M2, L3 • **SVP:** 6 mos-1 yr • **Academic:** Ed=N, Eng=S • **Work Field:** 041, 063 • **MPSMS:** 899 • **Aptitudes:** G3, V4, N3, S3, P3, Q4, K3, F3, M3, E5, C5 • **Temperaments:** M, T • **Physical:** V=L, H=N, L=M, H • **Work Env:** I, N • **Salary:** 2 • **Outlook:** 2

PACKAGE SEALER, MACHINE (any ind.) • D.O.T. #920.685-074 • OES #92974 • Tends machines that seal filled cardboard boxes, cartons, paper, cellophane, or plastic bags: Fills glue and water reservoir. Inserts rolls of paper tape into holders. Starts sealing machine and observes operation to detect faulty sealing and prevent conveyor jamming. Feeds cartons into machine and removes cartons from discharge conveyor. Feeds filled cellophane or glassine bags into machine that heats and seals top of bag. May adjust holding guides and conveyor line tripping mechanism that regulates movement of carton through gluing and flap-turning mechanism. May pack containers. May stamp identifying data on carton. May inspect contents of package to verify size, color, or brand of article. May be designated according to product packaged as CIGARETTE-CARTON SEALER (tobacco); type of machine operated as BOX-SEALING-MACHINE CATCHER (any ind.); HOT-SEALING-MACHINE OPERATOR (any ind.); or task performed as BOX-SEALING-MACHINE FEEDER (any ind.). • **GED:** R2, M1, L1 • **SVP:** 2-30 days • **Academic:** Ed=N, Eng=N • **Work Field:** 041 • **MPSMS:** 470 • **Aptitudes:** G4, V4, N5, S4, P4, Q4, K3, F4, M3, E4, C5 • **Temperaments:** R • **Stress:** T • **Physical:** V=N, H=N, L=M, W, H • **Work Env:** I • **Salary:** 2 • **Outlook:** 3

PACKAGER, HAND (any ind.) • D.O.T. #920.587-018 • OES #98902 • HAND PACKAGER. Packages materials and products manually, performing any combination of following duties: Cleans packaging containers. Lines and pads crates and assembles cartons. Obtains and sorts product. Wraps protective material around product. Starts, stops, and regulates speed of conveyor. Inserts or pours product into containers or fills containers from spout or chute. Weighs containers and adjusts quantity. Nails, glues, or closes and seals containers. Labels containers, container tags, or products. Sorts bundles or filled containers. Packs special arrangements or selections of product. Inspects materials, products, and containers at each step of packaging process. Records information, such as weight, time, and date packaged. May be designated according to whether high-production or small-lot packaging as FANCY PACKER (ret. tr.; whole. tr.); PACKAGING-LINE ATTENDANT (any ind.); specific packaging duty performed, such as filling, wrapping, packing, labeling, and container cleaning as SACK SEWER, HAND (any ind.); kinds of equipment used or product packaged as CANDLE WRAPPER (candle); CARTON STAPLER (any ind.); or whether packager performs associated duties, such as final assembly, before packaging product as NOVELTY-BALLOON ASSEMBLER AND PACKER (rubber goods). May weigh and package meat in retail store and be designated MEAT WRAPPER (ret. tr.). Additional titles: BAGGER (any ind.); BOW MAKER, GIFT WRAPPING (any ind.); BOX MAKER, CARDBOARD (any ind.); BOX WRAPPER (any ind.); BUNDLER (any ind.); CANDY PACKER (confection.); CASER, ROLLED GLASS (glass mfg.); COIL STRAPPER (iron & steel); CONTAINER FILLER (any ind.); FILLER (any ind.); FURNITURE PACKER (ret. tr.); GRADER, SAUSAGE AND WEINER (slaught. & meat pack.); GUNCOTTON PACKER (explosives); INSERTER, PROMOTIONAL ITEM (any ind.); INSPECTOR-PACKAGER (any ind.); LIDDER (any ind.); MATTRESS PACKER (matt. & bedspring); PACKAGER, MEAT (slaught. & meat pack.); PACKER, DRIED BEEF (slaught. & meat pack.); PACKER, FOAMED-IN-PLACE (any ind.); PACKER, SAUSAGE AND WIENER (slaught. & meat pack.); PIECE-GOODS PACKER (textile); SCALER, SLICED BACON (slaught. & meat pack.); SPONGE PACKER (whole. tr.); STAMPER (any ind.); TABLE WORKER (any ind.); TUBE PACKER (rubber tire & tube); WRAPPER (any ind.); WRAPPER, HAND (can. & preserv.); WRAPPING REMOVER (any ind.). [Workers who tend packaging machines are classified under PACKAGER, MACHINE (any ind.)]. • **GED:** R2, M1, L1 • **SVP:** 2-30 days • **Academic:** Ed=N, Eng=N • **Work Field:** 041 • **MPSMS:** 898 • **Aptitudes:** G4, V4, N4, S4, P4, Q4, K3, F3, M3, E5, C4 • **Temperaments:** R • **Stress:** T • **Physical:** V=N, H=N, L=M, W, H • **Work Env:** I • **Salary:** 3 • **Outlook:** 3

PACKAGER, MACHINE (any ind.) • D.O.T. #920.685-078 • OES

#92974 • **MACHINE OPERATOR, PACKAGING.** Tends machine that performs one or more packaging functions, such as filling, marking, labeling, tying, packing, or wrapping containers: Starts machine and observes operation to detect malfunctions of machine. Stops machine and reports malfunction to supervisor. Makes minor adjustments or repairs, such as opening valves, changing forming and cutting dies, setting guides, or clearing away damaged products of containers. Inspects filled container to ensure that product is packaged according to specifications. May feed product to conveyors, hoppers, or other feeding devices, and unload packaged product. May replenish packaging supplies, such as wrapping paper, plastic sheet, boxes, cartons, glue, ink, or labels. May mount supplies on spindles or place supplies in hopper or other feeding devices. May position and hold container in machine and press pedal or button or move lever to clean, glue, label, sew, or staple container. May cut stencils and stencil information on container, such as lot number or shipping destination. May tally number of units of product packaged or record information, such as size, weight, and type of products packaged. May be designated according to specific function or functions performed by machine tended as BOTTLE WASHER, MACHINE (any ind.) II; CAPPING-MACHINE OPERATOR (any ind.); CONTAINER-MAKER-FILLER-PACKER OPERATOR (any ind.); FILLING-MACHINE OPERATOR (any ind.); LABELER, MACHINE (any ind.); WRAPPING-MACHINE OPERATOR (any ind.). Additional titles: AEROSOL-LINE OPERATOR (any ind.); BAG PRINTER (bone, carbon, & lampblack; chem.); BLISTER-PACKING-MACHINE TENDER (any ind.); BREAD-WRAPPING-MACHINE FEEDER (bake. prod.); CANDY-WRAPPING-MACHINE OPERATOR (confection.); CARTON-GLUING-MACHINE OPERATOR (any ind.); CELLOPHANE WRAPPER, MACHINE (any ind.); COVER MARKER (paint & varn.); GLASSINE-MACHINE TENDER (any ind.); PACKING-MACHINE TENDER (any ind.); PALLETIZER OPERATOR (any ind.) II; SACK SEWER, MACHINE (any ind.); SILK SCREENER (optical goods); SPRING CRATER (matt. & bedspring); STENCIL CUTTER, MACHINE (any ind.); TEA-BAG-MACHINE TENDER (food prep., n.e.c.); TIRE WRAPPER (auto. ser.; rubber tire & tube); TUBE-FILLING-MACHINE OPERATOR (can. & preserv.; chem.); TYING-MACHINE OPERATOR (any ind.); WRAPPING-AND-PACKING-MACHINE OPERATOR (any ind.). [Workers who package products by hand are classified under PACKAGER, HAND (any ind.)]. • **GED:** R2, M1, L1 • **SVP:** 2-30 days • **Academic:** Ed=N, Eng=N • **Work Field:** 041 • **MPSMS:** 567 • **Aptitudes:** G4, V4, N4, S4, P4, Q4, K3, F3, M3, E4, C4 • **Temperaments:** R • **Stress:** T • **Physical:** V=N, H=N, L=M, W, H • **Work Env:** I • **Salary:** 2 • **Outlook:** 3

PACKING-LINE WORKER (rubber goods) • D.O.T. #753.687-038 • OES #98902 • Performs any combination of the following tasks as member of conveyor line crew, to finish and pack plastic or rubber footwear: Sorts and mates pairs and places them on conveyor. Opens or closes buckles, snaps fasteners together, inserts laces in eyelets, and ties loops (frogs) around buttons. Counts and tallies production or records on counter. Wraps pair in tissue, places them in shoe box, and packs boxes in cartons. Places rejects in boxes or racks for repair or mating. • **GED:** R2, M2, L1 • **SVP:** 2-30 days • **Academic:** Ed=N, Eng=N • **Work Field:** 041 • **MPSMS:** 512 • **Aptitudes:** G4, V4, N4, S4, P4, Q4, K4, F3, M3, E5, C4 • **Temperaments:** R • **Stress:** T • **Physical:** V=L, H=N, L=L, H • **Work Env:** I • **Salary:** 3 • **Outlook:** 3

PARACHUTE RIGGER (air trans.) • D.O.T. #912.684-010 • OES #93999 • PARACHUTE PACKER. Folds parachutes according to specifications and packs chutes in bag: Draws canopy of parachute from pack cover to its full length on surface of long bench. Straightens shrouds to eliminate coils or tangles. Folds canopy lengthwise on its seams, one segment over the other. Loops each shroud and forces it into retaining clip of pack cover. Folds canopy in fanfold arrangement and places in pack cover. Places pilot chute over parachute canopy, forces spring flat with hands, and secures it in place with release devices, such as ripcord, barometric pressure release, electromechanical release, or explosive charge. Inspects canopy, shroud, buckles and harness straps for damage or wear. Must be licensed by Federal Aviation Administration. May be designated as MASTER RIGGER (air trans.) when additionally qualified through experience to meet Federal Aviation Administration requirements. • **GED:** R3, M2, L2 • **SVP:** 6 mos-1 yr •

Academic: Ed=N, Eng=N • **Work Field:** 041, 062 • **MPSMS:** 439 • **Aptitudes:** G3, V4, N4, S3, P2, Q4, K3, F3, M3, E5, C5 • **Temperaments:** M, R, T • **Stress:** T • **Physical:** V=L, H=N, L=M, W, H • **Work Env:** I • **Salary:** 3 • **Outlook:** 3

GOE: 06.04.39 Cleaning, Industrial

CLEANER AND POLISHER (any ind.) • D.O.T. #709.687-010 • OES #98999 • Cleans and polishes chromium or nickel plated articles with cloth and liquid cleanser. May remove paint or other foreign matter adhering to surface of article with solvent, knife, or steel wool. May be designated according to type of metal cleaned as CHROME CLEANER (any ind.); NICKEL CLEANER (any ind.). • **GED:** R1, M1, L1 • **SVP:** 2-30 days • **Academic:** Ed=N, Eng=N • **Work Field:** 031 • **MPSMS:** 550 • **Aptitudes:** G4, V4, N5, S4, P4, Q5, K4, F3, M3, E5, C4 • **Temperaments:** R • **Stress:** T • **Physical:** V=L, H=N, L=L, H • **Work Env:** I • **Salary:** 2 • **Outlook:** 2

DIPPER (jewelry) • D.O.T. #735.687-010 • OES #98999 • ETCHER, ENAMELING; WASHER-OFF. Immerses enameled jewelry, jewelry findings, and other articles in acid and water baths to clean them. Dries cleaned articles by placing them in sieve and exposing them to steam or hot air, placing them in oven, by rolling them in heated sawdust, or by placing them in centrifugal drier. • **GED:** R2, M1, L1 • **SVP:** 2-30 days • **Academic:** Ed=N, Eng=N • **Work Field:** 031 • **MPSMS:** 611 • **Aptitudes:** G4, V4, N5, S5, P5, Q5, K4, F4, M4, E5, C5 • **Temperaments:** R • **Stress:** T • **Physical:** V=N, H=N, L=L, H • **Work Env:** I • **Salary:** 2 • **Outlook:** 3

EQUIPMENT CLEANER (any ind.) • D.O.T. #599.684-010 • OES #98905 • NIGHT CLEANER. Cleans and sterilizes machinery, utensils, and equipment used to process or store products, such as chemicals, paint, food, or beverages: Turns valves to drain machines or tanks and disconnects pipes, using wrenches. Sprays machines, tanks, and conveyors with water to loosen and remove dirt or other foreign matter. Scrubs machines, tanks, tables, pans, bowls, compartments, and conveyors, using brushes, rags, cleaning preparations, and diluted acids. Rinses articles with water, and dries them with compressed air. Scrubs floors and walls, using brushes, rags, and diluted acids. Connects hoses and lines to pump and starts pump to circulate cleaning and sterilizing solution through hoses and lines. Scrubs interior of disconnected pipes, valves, spigots, gages, and meters, using spiral brushes. Mixes cleaning solutions and diluted acids, according to formula. Draws off samples of cleaning solutions from mixing tanks for laboratory analysis. May replace defective sections of metal coils and lines, using handtools, soldering iron, and pipe couplings. May lubricate machinery. May be designated according to equipment cleaned as BEER-COIL CLEANER (any ind.); LARD-TUB WASHER (slaught. & meat pack.); LINE CLEANER (dairy prod.; malt liquors); PIPE WASHER (dairy prod.). May sterilize equipment and be designated EQUIPMENT STERILIZER (dairy prod.). • **GED:** R2, M1, L2 • **SVP:** 2-30 days • **Academic:** Ed=N, Eng=N • **Work Field:** 031 • **MPSMS:** 567, 568 • **Aptitudes:** G4, V4, N4, S4, P3, Q4, K3, F4, M3, E4, C4 • **Temperaments:** R • **Stress:** T • **Physical:** V=L, H=N, L=H, W, C, S, H • **Work Env:** I, W, N • **Salary:** 2 • **Outlook:** 4

LABORER, GENERAL (mach. shop) • D.O.T. #609.684-014 • OES #92198 • Performs any combination of following tasks to assist in machine shop activities: Loads and unloads materials, parts, or products onto or from pallets, skids, conveyors, or trucks manually or using hoist. Delivers metal parts or stock to designated work areas for machining, using electric pallet mover, hoist, or overhead crane. Lifts metal part or stock onto machine, manually or using hoist, and secures it on machine table, in chuck, or holding fixture, using wrenches, to assist in setting up machine. Feeds metal parts or stock into automatic metal working machines and removes machined part from machine after prescribed period of time or at end of machining cycle. Adds coolant to reservoirs of machines and lubricates machine parts and ways, using grease gun and oilcan. Reclaims cutting and lubricating oils from machines by pumping oil from machine reservoir into barrel, dumping oil from barrel into centrifugal separator that removes metal chips and dirt from oil, and drains clean oil from separator into containers. Removes metal chips and shavings from surfaces of machines, using rag or airhose, and wipes surfaces of machines with rag to remove excess oil. Cleans around work areas, using broom and shovel. Separates metal shavings, chips, and scrap materials from trash and places them in bins for resale. May remove burs or excess metal from machined parts, using files, sandpaper, emory cloth, or grinding machine. May be designated by specific task performed as BRASS RECLAIMER (mach. shop); GEAR CLEANER (mach. shop); OIL EXTRACTOR (mach. shop); SORTER (mach. shop); THREADING-MACHINE FEEDER, AUTOMATIC (mach. shop) II; TOOL MARKER (mach. shop). • **GED:** R2, M1, L1 • **SVP:** 2-30 days • **Academic:** Ed=N, Eng=N • **Work Field:** 011, 031 • **MPSMS:** 540 • **Aptitudes:** G4, V4, N4, S4, P4, Q4, K3, F4, M3, E5, C5 • **Temperaments:** R • **Stress:** T • **Physical:** V=L, H=N, L=H, W, S, H • **Work Env:** I, N • **Salary:** 3 • **Outlook:** 3

WASHER (optical goods) • D.O.T. #713.684-042 • OES #93947 • Performs any combination of following duties to clean finished eyeglasses, dye plastic eyeglass lenses, and electroplate metal frames: Washes, rinses, dries, and buffs eyeglasses, using cleaning solution, cloth, and buffing wheel. Mixes trays of dye according to formula and places trays on heating plate to maintain specified temperature. Mounts plastic lenses in holder and immerses lenses in dye for specified period. Compares lens with sample to verify color and immerses lens in dye to correct color as necessary. Immerses metal frames in plating solution for specified period to electroplate frames. • **GED:** R2, M1, L1 • **SVP:** 30 days-3 mos • **Academic:** Ed=N, Eng=N • **Work Field:** 031, 151, 154 • **MPSMS:** 605 • **Aptitudes:** G4, V4, N4, S4, P3, Q4, K4, F3, M3, E5, C3 • **Temperaments:** R, T • **Stress:** T • **Physical:** V=L, H=N, L=L, H • **Work Env:** I • **Salary:** 2 • **Outlook:** 3

WASHER, MACHINE (any ind.) • D.O.T. #599.685-114 • OES #92958 • Tends machine that washes flat ob jects, such as plate glass, plastic sheets, or metal: Places workpiece into movable bed of machine or between pinch rolls. Turns valves and observes gages to set specified flow of water or steam from jets in machine. Starts machine that moves workpiece by action of conveyor or pinch rolls into bath tank through spray of washing water, or steam under rotating brush and through spray of rinse water. Examines workpiece and removes remaining foreign matter, using hand scraper, brush, or sponge. May measure or weigh out and pour specified quantity of soap or detergent into wash water. • **GED:** R2, M1, L2 • **SVP:** 2-30 days • **Academic:** Ed=N, Eng=N • **Work Field:** 031 • **MPSMS:** 492, 530 • **Aptitudes:** G4, V4, N4, S4, P4, Q4, K4, F4, M4, E5, C4 • **Temperaments:** R • **Stress:** T • **Physical:** V=L, H=N, L=M, W, S, H • **Work Env:** I, N • **Salary:** 2 • **Outlook:** 2

WASHING-MACHINE OPERATOR (any ind.) • D.O.T. #599.685-118 • OES #92958 • Tends machines that wash and dry manufactured articles or their components, such as rubber gloves, pen and mechanical pencil barrels and lens blanks: Dumps detergent into machine. Places objects or racks of objects in washing machine. Sets controls to regulate length of cycle and water temperature as specified. Starts washing machine. Removes objects and places them in drying machine. Starts drying machine. Removes objects from machine when dry. May tend machine that rinses articles. • **GED:** R2, M1, L2 • **SVP:** 2-30 days • **Academic:** Ed=N, Eng=N • **Work Field:** 031 • **MPSMS:** 519, 609, 610 • **Aptitudes:** G4, V4, N4, S4, P4, Q4, K4, F4, M3, E5, C5 • **Temperaments:** R • **Stress:** T • **Physical:** V=L, H=N, L=M, W, H • **Work Env:** I, W, N • **Salary:** 2 • **Outlook:** 3

GOE: 06.04.40 Loading, Moving, Hoisting & Conveying

CHAR-CONVEYOR TENDER (sugar) • D.O.T. #529.685-050 • OES #97951 • Tends conveyor-belt system to distribute wet char from filters to drying hoppers and dried char from driers or bins to filters: Starts conveyor system under filter being emptied, and positions gate on belt over designated hopper to divert char from belt into hopper. Rakes char from one hopper to another to keep hoppers full. Starts shaker machine that distributes dried char from hopper or bins onto conveyor for transmission to filters. Inspects and cleans drier screens and pots. Sweeps and weighs char dust from dust-cooler room. May be designated according to condition of char as WET-CHAR CONVEYOR TENDER (sugar), or location of job as CHAR CONVEYOR TENDER, CELLAR (sugar). • **GED:** R2, M1, L1 • **SVP:** 2-30 days • **Academic:** Ed=N, Eng=N • **Work Field:** 011 • **MPSMS:** 499 • **Aptitudes:** G4, V4, N4, S4, P4, Q5, K4, F4, M3, E5, C5 • **Temperaments:** R, T • **Stress:** T • **Physical:** V=L, H=N, L=M, W, H • **Work Env:** I, H, W, R • **Salary:** 2 • **Out look:** 2

CLAMP REMOVER (veneer & plywood) • D.O.T. #569.687-010 • OES #98999 • Detaches clamping devices and stacks glued veneer panels after removal from cold press, working as member of team: Loosens turn buckles with metal rod and removes retaining rod attached to rails at top and bottom of stack. Removes top rail from stack and stacks veneer panels and caul boards on separate handtrucks. Pushes handtruck with veneer panels to drying oven or storage area for drying. May separate layers of veneer panels with spacer sticks. May clean glue from caul boards, using scraper. May be known according to specific task performed as VENEER STACKER (veneer & plywood). • **GED:** R1, M1, L1 • **SVP:** 2-30 days • **Academic:** Ed=N, Eng=N • **Work Field:** 063 • **MPSMS:** 453 • **Aptitudes:** G4, V4, N5, S4, P4, Q5, K4, F4, M3, E5, C5 • **Temperaments:** R • **Stress:** T • **Physical:** V=L, H=N, L=M, W, S, H • **Work Env:** I • **Salary:** 2 • **Outlook:** 3

COMPRESSED-GAS-PLANT WORKER (comp. & liq. gases) • D.O.T. #549.587-010 • OES #98999 • Performs any combination of following tasks in establishment making compressed and liquefied gas: Loads cylinders or ton-containers on vehicles, using handtruck or chain hoist, and records type and quantity of cylinders. Examines returned cylinders for surface defects, such as dents, cracks, and burns, and rolls cylinders to designated work area. Removes valves and installs reconditioned valves on cylinders, using wrenches. Connects exhaust manifold to cylinders and turns valve to draw off residual gas. Bounces or hammers cylinders to loosen rust and scale, and inserts water, steam, and air nozzles and turns valves to clean and dry cylinders. Tests filled cylinders for leaks by brushing or spraying chemical solution around valve. Weighs filled cylinders on platform scale and records weight. Screws protection cap over valve and ties warning and identification tags on cylinder. Wraps cakes of dry ice in paper and stores them in icehouse. May clean cylinder exteriors with wire brush. May place cylinders on heating rack to expand gas to ensure complete removal. May be known according to work performed as BLOW-OFF WORKER (comp. & liquefied gases); CYLINDER HANDLER (comp. & liquefied gases); CYLINDER VALVER (comp. & liquefied gases); HOIST-CYLINDER LOADER (comp. & liquefied gases); ICE HANDLER (comp. & liquefied gases); VALVE STEAMER (comp. & liquefied gases). Additional titles: CYLINDER CHECKER (comp. & liquefied gases); CYLINDER DEVALVER (comp. & liquefied gases); CYLINDER STEAMER (comp. & liquefied gases); TON-CONTAINER SHIPPER (comp. & liquefied gases). • **GED:** R2, M2, L2 • **SVP:** 2-30 days • **Academic:** Ed=N, Eng=N • **Work Field:** 011, 031 • **MPSMS:** 559 • **Aptitudes:** G4, V4, N4, S4, P3, Q4, K3, F3, M3, E4, C5 • **Temperaments:** R • **Stress:** T • **Physical:** V=L, H=N, L=M, W, H • **Work Env:** I • **Salary:** 2 • **Outlook:** 2

CONVEYOR FEEDER-OFFBEARER (any ind.) • D.O.T. #921.686-014 • OES #98502 • CARTON CATCHER; DUMPER-BULK SYSTEM. Feeds and offbears conveyor or conveyor system that moves materials or products by belt, roller, chain, or overhead convey or to and from loading dock, storage areas, work areas, and between departments or processing operations: Picks up materials or products from pallet, handtruck, or dolly, and places materials or products onto conveyor, or opens bins or chutes to dump bulk materials onto conveyor, or hangs products on chain or overhead conveyor, or transfers materials or products from one conveyor to another conveyor, and alines materials or products on conveyor to prevent jams. Dislodges jams by hand or pole. Removes materials or products from discharge end of conveyor and stacks materials or products on trays, pallets, or handtrucks. May feed and offbear conveyor that conveys material or products through machines or equipment operated or tended by another worker. May inspect materials or products for damage or for conformity to specifications. May push material or products between machines or departments on roller conveyor. May move materials or products to or from conveyor, using handtruck, dolly, or electric handtruck. May start or stop conveyor. May open cartons or shipping containers and place contents on conveyor. May use hoist to load or unload

conveyor. May stencil, tag, stamp, or write identifying information on packaged products. May record production. May keep work area clean and orderly. • **GED:** R1, M1, L1 • **SVP:** 2-30 days • **Academic:** Ed=N, Eng=N • **Work Field:** 011 • **MPSMS:** 565 • **Aptitudes:** G4, V4, N4, S4, P4, Q4, K4, F4, M4, E5, C5 • **Temperaments:** R • **Stress:** T • **Physical:** V=L, H=N, L=M, W, S, H • **Work Env:** I • **Salary:** 2 • **Outlook:** 3

CONVEYOR TENDER (any ind.) • D.O.T. #921.685-026 • OES #97951 • BELT TENDER; CONVEYOR MONITOR; RECEIVER, BULK SYSTEM. Tends conveyor or conveyor system that moves materials or products by belt, auger, or bucket conveyors to and from stockpiles, bins, silos, processing operations, or departments, or to load and unload railroad cars and trucks: Moves levers or pushes buttons to start conveyor. Loads conveyor by hand, lift, hoist, or by opening gates, chutes, or hoppers. Observes movement of materials or products on conveyor and dislodges jams, using pole, bar, handtools, or by hand. Notifies supervisor of equipment malfunction. Lubricates moving parts, using grease gun and oilcan. May position deflector bars, gates, chutes, or spouts to divert flow of materials from one conveyor onto another conveyor. May move and assemble portable conveyor sections and plug in electric cords to start conveyors. May clean work area, using shovel and broom. May tend conveyor motors in grain elevator and be designated GRAIN-ELEVATOR-MOTOR STARTER (grain & feed mill.). • **GED:** R1, M1, L1 • **SVP:** 2-30 days • **Academic:** Ed=N, Eng=N • **Work Field:** 011 • **MPSMS:** 565 • **Aptitudes:** G4, V4, N4, S4, P4, Q5, K4, F4, M3, E5, C5 • **Temperaments:** R • **Stress:** T • **Physical:** V=L, H=N, L=M, W, H • **Work Env:** B, N • **Salary:** 2 • **Outlook:** 2

DISTILLERY WORKER, GENERAL (distilled liquor) • D.O.T. #529.687-066 • OES #98999 • Cleans, transports and applies identifying data on steel drums in liquor distilling plant, performing any combination of following duties: Cleans interior of metal drums, using steam-cleaning apparatus, or interiors of barrels by rinsing them with water and alcohol. Stencils identifying information on barrelheads, using paint brush or spray gun to paint over cut-out stencils, or cuts identifying information on barrelheads, using metal dies and mallet. Paints or scrapes heads of used barrels to remove identifying information. Removes bungs from drums, using wrench or chisel and hammer. Rolls barrels into position for filling. Empties barrels or drums filled with liquor into dumping trough. Stamps serial numbers on barrelheads, using hand-stamping machine. Empties cartons of empty whisky bottles on conveyor belt for filling. Stacks cartons filled with whisky bottles. Repairs damaged cartons, using adhesive tape to cover tears and rips in cartons. Removes metal sealing rings from improperly labeled whisky bottles preparatory to removal of labels. May be known according to specific work performed as BARREL CUTTER (distilled liquors); BARREL ROLLER (distilled liquors); BARREL SCRAPER (distilled liquors); BUNG REMOVER (distilled liquors); CARTON REPAIRER (distilled liquors); DRUM CLEANER (distilled liquors); DRUM SEALER (distilled liquors); DUMPER (distilled liquors). • **GED:** R2, M1, L1 • **SVP:** 2-30 days • **Academic:** Ed=N, Eng=N • **Work Field:** 011, 031 • **MPSMS:** 454, 559 • **Aptitudes:** G4, V4, N4, S4, P4, Q3, K3, F4, M4, E4, C5 • **Temperaments:** R • **Stress:** T • **Physical:** V=L, H=N, L=H, W, S, H • **Work Env:** I, N • **Salary:** 4 • **Out look:** 2

GENERAL HELPER (oils & fats) • D.O.T. #529.687-094 • OES #98999 • Performs any combination of duties, such as carrying supplies to work area, forming cartons for packing, feeding cans onto conveyor, removing scrap, cleaning work area, and reclaiming oil stock from damaged containers. Dumps containers into steam tub, covers tub with canvas, and opens valve to introduce heat to melt and reclaim contents. Cleans work area using brooms, mops, and detergents. • **GED:** R1, M1, L1 • **SVP:** 2-30 days • **Academic:** Ed=N, Eng=N • **Work Field:** 011, 031 • **MPSMS:** 475 • **Aptitudes:** G4, V4, N5, S4, P4, Q5, K4, F4, M3, E5, C5 • **Temperaments:** R • **Stress:** T • **Physical:** V=L, H=N, L=M, W, H • **Work Env:** I, W • **Salary:** 2 • **Outlook:** 2

INDUSTRIAL-TRUCK OPERATOR (any ind.) • D.O.T. #921.683-050 • OES #97947 • Drives gasoline-, liquified gas-, or electric-powered industrial truck equipped with lifting devices, such as forklift, boom, scoop, lift beam and swivel-hook, fork-grapple, clamps, elevating platform, or trailer hitch, to push, pull, lift, stack, tier, or move products, equipment, or materials in warehouse, storage yard, or factory: Moves levers and presses pedals to drive truck and control movement of lifting apparatus. Positions forks, lifting platform, or other lifting device under, over, or around loaded pallets, skids, boxes, products, or materials or hooks tow trucks to trailer hitch, and transports load to designated area. Unloads and stacks material by raising and lowering lifting device. May inventory materials on work floor, and supply workers with materials as needed. May weigh materials or products and record weight on tags, labels, or production schedules. May load or unload materials onto or off of pallets, skids, or lifting device. May lubricate truck, recharge batteries, fill fuel tank, or replace liquified-gas tank. May be designated according to article moved as LEAD LOADER (ore dress., smelt., & refin.); process in which involved as STRIPPER TRUCK OPERATOR (ore dress., smelt., & refin.); or type of truck operated as ELECTRIC-TRUCK-CRANE OPERATOR (any ind.); FORK-LIFT-TRUCK OPERATOR (any ind.); TIER-LIFT-TRUCK OPERATOR (any ind.). Additional titles: BURNT-LIME DRAWER (lime); CASTING TRUCKER (found.); ELECTRIC-FREIGHT-CAR OPERATOR (r.r. trans.); ELECTRIC-TRUCK OPERATOR (any ind.); GASOLINE-TRUCK OPERATOR (any ind.); METAL-STORAGE WORKER (nonfer. metal alloys); PACKAGE-LIFT OPERATOR (any ind.). • **GED:** R2, M1, L1 • **SVP:** 30 days-3 mos • **Academic:** Ed=N, Eng=N • **Work Field:** 011, 013 • **MPSMS:** 565 • **Aptitudes:** G4, V4, N4, S3, P4, Q4, K3, F4, M3, E3, C5 • **Temperaments:** R, T • **Stress:** T • **Physical:** V=G, H=N, L=M, W, H • **Work Env:** B • **Salary:** 4 • **Outlook:** 2

LABORER (slaught. & meat pack.) • D.O.T. #529.687-130 • OES #98999 • Performs any combination of the following tasks in a slaughtering and meat packing establishment: Holds meat while it is being cut. Straightens and washes carcasses or parts on conveyor lines. Distributes meat to various work areas for further processing, using cart. Scrapes excess meat from surfaces of filled casings, such as sausages and bologna, and hangs them on conveyor racks. Pushes conveyor racks, hanging attachments, and meat carts, to various departments. Unloads smoked meats from conveyor racks and weighs, stamps, and tags them. Removes empty trolleys from overhead rail and places them in chute or onto other rails. Trucks empty ham molds to washing machines for cleaning process. Loads meat onto conveyor racks, carts, worktables, or trucks, using hook. Transports offal (carcass waste) from killing floor to rendering room and dumps offal into tankage cookers. Weighs and sacks rendered inedible offal. Fills ice trucks, using shovel. Stacks cartons of meat products on pallets or trucks and moves load to shipping or storage areas, using hand or power operated truck. Pushes meat through spray cabinet to wash meat. Washes equipment and uten sils, using water hose and spray cabinet. Sweeps and washes railroad refrigeration cars. May cut specific parts such as hooves or tendons, using knife. • **GED:** R2, M1, L1 • **SVP:** 2-30 days • **Academic:** Ed=N, Eng=N • **Work Field:** 011, 031, 212 • **MPSMS:** 382 • **Aptitudes:** G4, V4, N4, S4, P4, Q4, K3, F4, M3, E5, C5 • **Temperaments:** R • **Stress:** T • **Physical:** V=L, H=N, L=H, W, S, H • **Work Env:** I, W • **Salary:** 4 • **Outlook:** 3

LABORER, CHEMICAL PROCESSING (chem.) • D.O.T. #559.687-050 • OES #98999 • DRUM CARRIER. Performs any combination of following tasks in chemical plants: Fills or empties equipment and containers by pumping, opening valves, scooping, dumping, scraping or shoveling liquid, gaseous, or solid materials. Weighs materials and writes or stencils identifying information on containers. Fastens caps or covers on container, or screws bungs in place. Transports materials, using handtruck. Cleans stills and other equipment, using detergents, brushes, or scrapers. Loads railroad cars or trucks. Delivers samples to laboratory. Cleans work areas. Prepares materials by pulverizing, milling, crushing, or liquefying. Paints containers, using spray gun. May be known according to task performed as CARBOY FILLER (chem.); DRUM FILLER (chem.); KETTLE-ROOM HELPER (chem.); SHIPPING HAND (chem.); WHEELER (chem.). • **GED:** R2, M1, L1 • **SVP:** 30 days-3 mos • **Academic:** Ed=N, Eng=N • **Work Field:** 031, 041, 212 • **MPSMS:** 490 • **Aptitudes:** G4, V4, N4, S4, P4, Q4, K3, F4, M3, E5, C5 • **Temperaments:** R • **Stress:** T • **Physical:** V=L, H=N, L=H, W, S, H • **Work Env:** I, W • **Salary:** 2 • **Out look:** 2

LABORER, CONCRETE PLANT (concrete prod.) • D.O.T.

#579.686-010 • OES #98999 • Performs variety of tasks in establishment manufacturing concrete products: Ties strip of cloth around bell of freshly cast concrete pipe to maintain circular shape of bell during curing. Arranges pipe in storage yard and stacks pipe for shipment. Places rubber gaskets on pipe. Stacks concrete blocks on pallets for removal by fork lift truck. Feeds concrete blocks into block-breaking machine or abrasive saw to shape blocks. Immerses chimney flue liner sections in sealing compound. Brushes stone facings to remove loose material, applies acid solution, using brush to remove concrete around stones, and washes acid from stone, using water hose. Repairs defects in concrete surfaces, using mortar or grout and trowel, and smooths rough spots, using chisel and abrasive stone. Opens gates of railroad cars to allow materials to flow into storage chutes. Loads, unloads, and moves cement, sand, and gravel to work areas, using wheelbarrow, handtruck, or industrial truck. Cleans yard and plant, using shovel, broom, and water hose, and performs other duties as assigned. May be designated according to specific duties performed as ACID CUTTER (conc. prod.); BELL TIER (conc. prod.); BLOCK BREAKER (conc. prod.); BLOCK CUBER (conc. prod.); FLUE-LINING DIPPER (conc. prod.); ROUGH PATCHER (conc. prod.); YARDER (conc. prod.). • **GED:** R2, M1, L1 • **SVP:** 2-30 days • **Academic:** Ed=N, Eng=N • **Work Field:** 011, 031 • **MPSMS:** 536 • **Aptitudes:** G4, V4, N4, S5, P4, Q5, K4, F4, M3, E5, C5 • **Temperaments:** R • **Stress:** T • **Physical:** V=L, H=N, L=H, W, H • **Work Env:** B, W, N • **Salary:** 2 • **Outlook:** 3

LABORER, GENERAL (iron & steel) • D.O.T. #509.686-010 • OES #98502 • Performs any combination of tasks to assist workers engaged in production of iron and steel: Feeds and offbears equipment, such as conveyors, pilers, and loaders, to charge furnaces, transport hot metal to rollers, and store finished products. Bundles and ties metal rods, sheets, and wire, using banding machine and handtools. Attaches crane hooks, slings, or cradles to material for moving by BRIDGE-OR-GANTRY-CRANE OPERATOR (any ind.). Transports material to and from pro duction stations, using handtruck. Feeds material, such as ganister, magnesite, and limestone into crushers to prepare additives for molten metal. Grinds defects, such as burs, seams, and scratches from rolled steel, using portable grinder. Sweeps scale from work area and empties dust bins, using wheelbarrow, broom, and shovel. Breaks up manganese and scrap metal to facilitate handling, using sledge and pneumatic hammer. Marks identification numbers on steel billets, using chalk. Verifies dimension of products, using fixed gage. Wipes grease and oil from machinery with rags and solvent. May be known according to specific task performed as CONVEYOR FEEDER (iron & steel); CRUSHER FEEDER (iron & steel); LOADING CHECKER (iron & steel); MARKER (iron & steel); RACKER (iron & steel); SCRAP BREAKER (iron & steel). • **GED:** R2, M1, L1 • **SVP:** 2-30 days • **Academic:** Ed=N, Eng=N • **Work Field:** 011, 031 • **MPSMS:** 540 • **Aptitudes:** G4, V4, N4, S4, P4, Q5, K4, F4, M3, E5, C5 • **Temperaments:** R • **Stress:** T • **Physical:** V=L, H=N, L=H, W, C, S, H • **Work Env:** B, H, W, N, R • **Salary:** 3 • **Outlook:** 3

LABORER, GENERAL (plastics mat.) • D.O.T. #559.567-010 • OES #98999 • Performs any combination of following tasks involved in manufacturing plastics materials, synthetic resins, and synthetic rubber: Transports materials to workers and machines, using hoist or handtruck. Inserts metal core in rolls of plastics film. Tightens clamps on supply racks, using wrenches. Cleans machinery and work area, using vacuum cleaner, brushes, and cleaning solvents. Measures out, weighs, and dumps ingredients into mills, kettles, or hoppers. Replaces spools or coils of materials on supply racks or reels. Delivers samples of materials to testing laboratory. Records weights, types, and amounts of materials used, stored, or shipped. • **GED:** R2, M1, L1 • **SVP:** 2-30 days • **Academic:** Ed=N, Eng=N • **Work Field:** 011, 031 • **MPSMS:** 492 • **Aptitudes:** G4, V4, N4, S4, P4, Q4, K4, F4, M3, E5, C5 • **Temperaments:** R • **Stress:** T • **Physical:** V=L, H=N, L=M, W, C, S, H • **Work Env:** I • **Salary:** 2 • **Outlook:** 3

LABORER, SALVAGE (any ind.) • D.O.T. #929.687-022 • OES #98999 • RECLAIMER; SALVAGER; TRASH COLLECTOR; WASTE COLLECTOR. Salvages materials in industrial or commercial establishment, performing any combination of duties: Collects reusable items or waste materials, such as lumber, paper, rags, fiber, yarn, rubber, beer and soft drink bottles, chemicals, and scrap metal, in scrap gondolas, barrels, or other containers, using handtruck, industrial truck, or wheelbarrow. Inspects materials and sorts items or materials into piles or places in bins or barrels according to type, size, condition, coloring, marking, or other characteristics. Salvages reusable materials and disposes of waste by pouring into sewer or waste containers, loading onto vehicle, or by burning or baling waste. Moves reusable materials to production department or storage. Separates metal particles from waste, using wire screen or magnet. Attaches labels to waste and salvage containers to identify contents. Weighs materials and containers and keeps records of total amount of waste collected. Dumps waste material, such as broke (waste paper and pulp), into machine tank for reprocessing. Makes minor repairs to scrap containers, such as bumping out dents, using handtools. May be designated according to kind of material salvaged as BROKE HANDLER (paper & pulp); LUMBER SALVAGER (any ind.); METAL SORTER (any ind.); RAG SORTER (any ind.); SACK SORTER (any ind.); SCRAP SORTER (any ind.); or specialized as signment as SCRAP BURNER (any ind.). • **GED:** R2, M1, L1 • **SVP:** 2-30 days • **Academic:** Ed=N, Eng=N • **Work Field:** 211, 212, 221 • **MPSMS:** 898 • **Aptitudes:** G4, V4, N4, S4, P4, Q4, K4, F4, M3, E5, C3 • **Temperaments:** R • **Stress:** T • **Physical:** V=L, H=N, L=M, W, S, H • **Work Env:** I • **Salary:** 2 • **Outlook:** 2

LOADER 1 (any ind.) • D.O.T. #914.667-010 • OES #97905 • CAR FILLER; LIQUID LOADER; TANK-CAR LOADER; TRUCK LOADER. Pumps liquid chemicals, liquid petroleum products, and other liquids into or from tank cars, trucks, or barges: Verifies tank car numbers with loading instructions to ensure accurate placement of cars by crew. Connects ground cable to carry off static electricity. Removes and replaces or gives directions to another worker to remove and replace dome caps, using wrenches. Inspects interior for cleanliness and exterior for leaks or damage. Swings loading spout over dome and turns valve to admit liquids to tank. Lowers gage rod into tank or reads meter to verify specified volume of liquids loaded. Lowers sample bottle into tank for laboratory testing. Copies load specification on placard and tacks placard to tank. Seals outlet valves on car. When unloading cars, connects hose to outlet plugs on cars and attaches special dome, using wrenches. Starts pumps or turns valves to admit compressed air into tank car and force liquids into storage tanks. May test sample for specific gravity, using hydrometer, and record reading on loading slip. May clean interior of tank cars or tank trucks, using mechanical spray nozzle. May inspect rupture disc, vacuum relief valve, rubber gaskets on valves and cover plates, and replace defective parts, using wrenches. May pump nitrogen or compressed air into car to test for leaks. May be designated according to material loaded and unloaded as ACID LOADER (chem.); CAUSTIC LOADER (chem.); FATS AND OILS LOADER (soap). • **GED:** R3, M2, L2 • **SVP:** 6 mos-1 yr • **Academic:** Ed=N, Eng=N • **Work Field:** 014 • **MPSMS:** 380, 490, 501 • **Aptitudes:** G3, V4, N4, S3, P3, Q3, K3, F4, M3, E4, C4 • **Temperaments:** R, T • **Stress:** T • **Physical:** V=L, H=N, L=M, W, C, S, H • **Work Env:** B, R • **Salary:** 3 • **Outlook:** 3

MUNITIONS HANDLER (ammunition) • D.O.T. #929.687-034 • OES #98799 • Loads, unloads, and stores ammunition and ammunition components in magazines (storage areas): Moves materials between magazines and carries materials by hand, handtrucks, and roller conveyors. Secures cargoes in carriers, using blocks and stays. Cleans magazines and adjacent area. Crates and cases materials for specific orders. Inspects packaging and materials. • **GED:** R2, M1, L1 • **SVP:** 2-30 days • **Academic:** Ed=N, Eng=N • **Work Field:** 011, 211 • **MPSMS:** 370 • **Aptitudes:** G4, V4, N4, S4, P4, Q4, K4, F4, M3, E5, C5 • **Temperaments:** R • **Stress:** T • **Physical:** V=L, H=N, L=H, W, S, H • **Work Env:** B, R • **Salary:** 5 • **Outlook:** 2

NITROGLYCERIN DISTRIBUTOR (explosives) • D.O.T. #559.664-010 • OES #92965 • Distributes nitroglycerin to processing departments of dynamite plant and prepares nitroglycerin for shipment: Signals NITROGLYCERIN NEUTRALIZER (explosives) to release specified amounts of nitroglycerin to storage tanks. Tests acidity of nitroglycerin, using litmus paper. Turns valve to release sodium carbonate solution into nitroglycerin to neutralize excess acid that could cause decomposition of material and explosion. Transfers nitroglycerin from storage tank to lead-lined or stainless steel tanks mounted on wheels. Pushes tanks to mix house or other processing department. Washes tanks between loads with sodium carbonate solution and water, using hose and brush. Fills glass or stainless steel vials with nitroglycerin, using filling spout, and packs vials in boxes. • **GED:** R2, M1, L1 • **SVP:** 2-30 days • **Academic:** Ed=N, Eng=N • **Work Field:** 011, 041 • **MPSMS:** 499 • **Aptitudes:** G4, V4, N4, S4, P3, Q4, K3, F4, M3, E5, C4 • **Temperaments:** S, T • **Stress:** S • **Physical:** V=L, H=N, L=H, W, H • **Work Env:** I, R • **Salary:** 2 • **Outlook:** 2

PALLETIZER OPERATOR 1 (any ind.) • D.O.T. #921.682-014 • OES #97951 • Operates console that controls automatic palletizing equipment to sort, transfer, and stack on pallets containers of finished products, such as sugar, canned vegetables, citrus juice, and cigarettes: Reads production and delivery schedules and stacking pattern to determine sorting and transfer procedures, arrangement of packages on pallet, and destination of loaded pallet. Observes packages moving along conveyor to identify packages and to detect defective packaging, and presses console buttons to deflect packages to predetermined accumulator or reject lines. Turns selector switch on palletizer to control stacking arrangement of packages on pallet and to transfer loaded pallet to storage or delivery platform. Supplies loading equipment with empty pallets. Stops equipment to clear jams. Informs supervisor of equipment malfunction. May keep record of production and equipment performance. May operate depalletizing equipment and be designated DEPALLETIZER OPERATOR (any ind.). • **GED:** R3, M1, L1 • **SVP:** 3-6 mos • **Academic:** Ed=N, Eng=N • **Work Field:** 011, 145, 211 • **MPSMS:** 565 • **Aptitudes:** G3, V3, N4, S3, P3, Q4, K4, F4, M3, E5, C5 • **Temperaments:** M, T • **Physical:** V=L, H=N, L=L, H • **Work Env:** I • **Salary:** 4 • **Outlook:** 4

PUMPER, BREWERY (beer prod.) • D.O.T. #914.665-014 • OES #97953 • CELLAR WORKER. Tends power-driven pumps that transfer wort, beer, or liquified yeast mixture to various sections of brewery: Receives signal from point of destination indicating time of fluid transfer. Connects flexible hose and stationary lines to pumps and vessels containing specified fluid and notifies worker at destination point of line prior to transfer of fluid. Turns valves and starts pump to admit and control flow of liquid through lines. Collects random samples of fluid from vessels for laboratory testing, using beaker. May tend automated equipment to transfer liquids through various processes. May observe thermometers and turn valves to regulate flow of beer through refrigeration unit to maintain specified temperature of product [COOLING-MACHINE OPERATOR (malt liquors)]. May pump two or more varieties of beer into one tank to blend mixture. May record types and amounts of beer pumped. May clean pumps and lines by flushing with cleansing solutions and water. May be designated according to plant location, or product transferred as BOTTLE-HOUSE PUMPER (malt liquors); CELLAR PUMPER (malt liquors); WORT PUMPER (malt liquors); YEAST PUMPER (malt liquors). • **GED:** R3, M2, L2 • **SVP:** 30 days-3 mos • **Academic:** Ed=N, Eng=N • **Work Field:** 014 • **MPSMS:** 395 • **Aptitudes:** G3, V4, N4, S3, P4, Q4, K3, F4, M3, E5, C5 • **Temperaments:** R • **Stress:** T • **Physical:** V=L, H=N, L=M, W, S, H • **Work Env:** I, W • **Salary:** 2 • **Out look:** 3

SAWMILL WORKER (sawmill) • D.O.T. #667.686-014 • OES #92308 • SWAMPER. Performs any combination of following duties in preparing logs for cutting into lumber and storing cut lumber in sawmill: Unloads logs from trucks or cars. Rolls logs onto sawmill deck. Examines logs for defects, such as imbedded pieces of iron or stone, decayed wood from splits, and marks defects for removal by other workers. Rolls logs from deck onto log or carriage. Rides log carriage of head saw and adjusts position of logs on carriage to cut planks of required thickness. Sorts and guides planks emerging from saw onto roller tables or conveyors for trimming edges. Straightens lumber on moving conveyors. May straighten edges of rough lumber, using saw. May operate and maintain donkey engines. May sharpen and adjust teeth of woodworking saws. May tend fires in donkey engine. May relieve designated workers engaged in preparing or cutting logs into lumber and be designated SAWMILL-RELIEF WORKER (sawmill). • **GED:** R3, M1, L1 • **SVP:** 30 days-3 mos • **Academic:** Ed=N, Eng=N • **Work Field:** 056 • **MPSMS:** 451 • **Aptitudes:** G3, V4, N4, S3, P4, Q5, K3, F4, M3, E4, C5 • **Temperaments:** R, T • **Stress:** T • **Physical:** V=L, H=N, L=M, W, C, S, H • **Work Env:** I, N, R • **Salary:** 3 • **Outlook:** 3

Business Detail 07

An interest in organized, clearly defined activities requiring accuracy and attention to details, primarily in an office setting. You can satisfy this interest in a variety of jobs in which you can attend to the details of a business operation. You may enjoy using your math skills. Perhaps a job in billing, computing, or financial recordkeeping would satisfy you. You may prefer to deal with people. You may want a job in which you meet the public, talk on the telephone, or supervise other workers. You may like to operate computer terminals, typewriters, or bookkeeping machines. Perhaps a job in recordkeeping, filing, or recording would satisfy you. You may wish to use your training and experience to manage offices and supervise other workers.

Workers in this group perform clerical work which requires special skills and knowledge. They perform management activities according to established regulations and procedures. Jobs in this group are found in the offices of businesses, industries, courts of law, and government agencies, as well as in offices of doctors, lawyers, and other professionals.

✔ **What kind of work would you do?**
Your work activities would depend upon your specific job. For example, you might:

- organize and oversee all clerical operations in a business office.
- prepare correspondence and keep records for a board of education.
- use knowledge of medical terms and procedures to prepare and maintain medical records and correspondence.
- search public records to identify title restrictions for a title insurance company.
- use knowledge of insurance underwriting to select and process routine policy applications.
- administer and score psychological, vocational, or educational tests.

✔ **What skills and abilities do you need for this kind of work?**
To do this kind of work, you must be able to:

- use logical thinking and personal judgment to perform a variety of office tasks that require special skills and knowledge.
- make decisions based on your own judgment and company policy.
- follow instructions without close supervision.
- speak and write clearly and accurately.
- plan your own work and sometimes the work of others.
- deal with people.
- change work activities frequently; for example, typing, interviewing, taking dictation, supervising others.

✔ **How do you know if you would like or could learn to do this kind of work?**
The following questions may give you clues about yourself as you consider this group of jobs.

- Have you taken courses in typing or shorthand? Can you type rapidly and accurately?
- Have you written a letter of inquiry to a business? Can you write concisely and to the point, using proper grammar and punctuation?

- Have you been a secretary of an organization or club? Did you keep minutes of the meetings? Do you enjoy this type of activity?

- Have you had clerical work experience in the armed services?

✔ **How can you prepare for and enter this kind of work?**

Occupations in this group usually require education and/or training extending from six months to over four years, depending upon the specific kind of work. People who have a good working knowledge of English, grammar, and basic math can qualify for beginning jobs in this group. These workers will receive training on the job. Some workers will need special vocational training in a specific technology such as shorthand, stenotype, legal stenography, and business management.

✔ **What else should you consider about these jobs?**

Some positions require workers who can be trusted to handle confidential information. Workers in small offices often do a variety of tasks. They may serve as bookkeeper, clerk, and receptionist. Working conditions usually are pleasant, in a modern well-lighted office building.

If you think you would like to do this kind of work, look at the job titles listed on the following pages.

GOE: 07.01.01 Interviewing, Admin. Detail

CONTACT REPRESENTATIVE (gov. ser.) • D.O.T. #169.167-018 • OES #21911 • Provides information and assistance to public on government agency programs and procedures: Advises individuals of procedures for obtaining benefits or fulfilling obligations by explaining regulations, policies, and determinations of agency. Advises in preparation of applications required to obtain benefits or documents required to fulfill obligations. Analyzes applications for benefits, privileges, or relief from obligations, using knowledge of rules, regulations, and precedent decisions to determine qualifications for benefits and privileges or liability for obligations. Investigates errors or delays in processing of applications for benefits and initiates corrective action. May be designated according to title of agency represented. • **GED:** R5, M3, L5 • **SVP:** 1-2 yrs • **Academic:** Ed=A, Eng=S • **Work Field:** 282 • **MPSMS:** 959 • **Aptitudes:** G2, V2, N3, S4, P4, Q2, K4, F4, M4, E5, C5 • **Temperaments:** J, P • **Physical:** V=L, H=L, L=S • **Work Env:** I • **Salary:** 4 • **Outlook:** 3

CREDIT COUNSELOR (profess. & kin.) • D.O.T. #160.207-010 • OES #21199 • Provides financial counseling to individuals in debt: Confers with client to ascertain available monthly income after living expenses to meet credit obligations. Calculates amount of debt and funds available to plan method of payoff and estimate time for debt liquidation. Contacts creditors to explain client's financial situation and to arrange for payment adjustments so that payments are feasible for client and agreeable to creditors. Establishes payment priorities to reduce client's overall costs by liquidating high-interest, short-term loans or contracts first. Opens account for client and disburses funds from account to creditors as agent for client. Keeps records of account activity. May counsel client on personal and family financial problems, such as excessive spending and borrowing of funds, and be designated BUDGET CONSULTANT (profess. & kin.). May be required to be licensed by state agency. • **GED:** R5, M5, L5 • **SVP:** 2-4 yrs • **Academic:** Ed=A, Eng=S • **Work Field:** 232, 271, 282 • **MPSMS:** 890 • **Aptitudes:** G2, V2, N1, S4, P4, Q2, K5, F5, M4, E5, C5 • **Temperaments:** D, I, M, P • **Stress:** A • **Physical:** V=N, H=G, L=S • **Work Env:** I • **Salary:** 4 • **Outlook:** 4

ELIGIBILITY WORKER (gov. ser.) • D.O.T. #195.267-010 • OES #53502 • Interviews applicants or recipients to determine eligibility for public assistance: Interprets and explains rules and regulations governing eligibility and grants, methods of payment, and legal rights to applicant or recipient. Records and evaluates personal and financial data obtained from applicant or recipient to determine initial or continuing eligibility, according to departmental directives. Initiates procedures to grant, modify, deny, or terminate eligibility and grants for various aid programs, such as public welfare, employment, and medical assistance. Authorizes amount of grants, based on determination of eligibility for amount of money payments, food stamps, medical care, or other general assistance. Identifies need for social services, and makes referrals to various agencies and community resources available. Prepares regular and special reports as required, and submits individual recommendations for consideration by supervisor. Prepares and keeps records of assigned cases. • **GED:** R4, M3, L4 • **SVP:** 1-2 yrs • **Academic:** Ed=H, Eng=G • **Work Field:** 271 • **MPSMS:** 941 • **Aptitudes:** G2, V2, N3, S4, P4, Q2, K4, F4, M4, E5, C5 • **Temperaments:** J, M, P • **Stress:** E • **Physical:** V=N, H=L, L=S • **Work Env:** I • **Salary:** 4 • **Outlook:** 3

ELIGIBILITY-AND-OCCUPANCY INTERVIEWER (gov. ser.) • D.O.T. #168.267-038 • OES #53502 • Interviews and investigates prospective tenants to determine eligibility for public low-rent housing: Receives and processes initial or reactivated applications for public housing. Interviews applicant to obtain additional information such as family composition, health and social problems, veteran status, rent paying ability, net assets, and need for housing assistance. Advises applicant on eligibility requirements, methods of selecting tenants, and housing opportunities. Contacts employers, and public and private health and welfare agencies to verify applicant information. Provides information to tenant or applicant on availability of community resources for financial or social welfare assistance. Determines applicant eligibility according to agency rules and policies. Selects and refers eligible applicant to MANAGER, HOUSING PROJECT (profess. & kin.). Notifies eligible applicant of vacancy and assignment procedures. Computes rent in proportion to applicant's income. Receives and records security deposit and advance rent from selected applicant. Conducts annual, interim, and special housing reviews with tenants. May assist in resolving tenant complaints on maintenance problems. May visit home to determine housekeeping habits, verify housing condition, and establish housing need. • **GED:** R4, M3, L4 • **SVP:** 6 mos-1 yr • **Academic:** Ed=H, Eng=S • **Work Field:** 271 • **MPSMS:** 941 • **Aptitudes:** G3, V3, N3, S5, P3, Q2, K4, F4, M4, E4, C4 • **Temperaments:** M, P, T, V • **Physical:** V=L, H=L, L=L • **Work Env:** I • **Salary:** 3 • **Outlook:** 3

FINANCIAL-AID COUNSELOR (educ.) • D.O.T. #169.267-018

• OES #21199 • Interviews students applying for financial aid, such as loans, grants-in-aid, or scholarships, to determine eligibility for assistance in college or university: Confers with individuals and groups to disseminate information and answer questions relating to financial assistance available to students enrolled in college or university. Interviews students to obtain information needed to determine eligibility for aid. Compares data on students' applications, such as proposed budget, family income, or transcript of grades, with eligibility requirements of assistance program. Determines amount of aid, considering such factors as funds available, extent of demand, and needs of students. Authorizes release of funds to students and prepares required records and reports. May assist in selection of candidates for financial awards or aid granted by specific department. May specialize in specific aid program and be designated as LOAN COUNSELOR (education); SCHOLARSHIP COUNSELOR (education). • **GED:** R4, M4, L4 • **SVP:** 6 mos-1 yr • **Academic:** Ed=B, Eng=G • **Work Field:** 271, 295 • **MPSMS:** 894 • **Aptitudes:** G3, V2, N3, S4, P3, Q2, K4, F4, M4, E5, C5 • **Temperaments:** J, M, P • **Stress:** E • **Physical:** V=N, H=L, L=S • **Work Env:** I • **Salary:** 4 • **Outlook:** 3

LOAN COUNSELOR (finan. inst.) • D.O.T. #186.267-014 • OES #21108 • COLLECTION ANALYST; LOAN-SERVICING OFFICER. Analyzes loan contracts and attempts to obtain payment of overdue installments: Studies record of delinquent account and contacts borrower to discuss payments due. Analyzes financial problems of borrower and adjusts loan agreement to restore loan to good standing. Receives and records payments. Prepares reports of delinquent accounts that cannot be collected. Answers loan inquiries concerning loan balance, taxes, and penalties. May be called upon to testify at legal proceedings. • **GED:** R5, M4, L5 • **SVP:** 2-4 yrs • **Academic:** Ed=A, Eng=S • **Work Field:** 271 • **MPSMS:** 894 • **Aptitudes:** G2, V2, N3, S4, P4, Q3, K4, F4, M4, E5, C5 • **Temperaments:** I, J, M, P • **Physical:** V=N, H=L, L=S • **Work Env:** I • **Salary:** 4 • **Outlook:** 4

MANAGEMENT AIDE (social ser.) • D.O.T. #195.367-014 • OES #27308 • Aids residents of public and private housing projects and apartments in relocation and provides information concerning regulations, facilities, and services: Explains rules established by owner or management, such as sanitation and maintenance requirements, and parking regulations. Demonstrates use and care of equipment for tenant use. Informs tenants of facilities, such as laundries and playgrounds. Advises homemakers needing assistance in child care, food, money management, and housekeeping problems. Provides information on location and nature of available community services, such as clinics and recreation centers. Keeps records and prepares reports for owner or management. • **GED:** R4, M3, L4 • **SVP:** 6 mos-1 yr • **Academic:** Ed=H, Eng=G • **Work Field:** 282, 291 • **MPSMS:** 941 • **Aptitudes:** G3, V3, N4, S5, P4, Q4, K4, F4, M4, E5, C5 • **Temperaments:** J, P • **Stress:** E • **Physical:** V=N, H=L, L=S, H • **Work Env:** I • **Salary:** 3 • **Outlook:** 3

PROBATION OFFICER (profess. & kin.) • D.O.T. #195.167-034 • OES #27305 • Engages in activities related to probation of juvenile or adult offenders: Determines which juvenile cases fall within jurisdiction of court and which should be adjusted informally or referred to other agencies. May release children to parents or authorize detention pending preliminary hearing. Conducts prehearing or presentence investigations of adults and juveniles by interviewing offender, family, and others concerned. Prepares social history for court. Interprets findings and suggests plan of treatment. Arranges for placement or clinical services if ordered by court and works with offender on probation according to treatment plan toward discharge from probation. Evaluates probationer's progress on follow-up basis. Secures remedial action if necessary, by court. May specialize in working with either juvenile or adult offenders, or both. May be administratively attached to court or to separate agency serving court. Usually required to have knowledge and skill in casework methods acquired through degree program at school of social work. • **GED:** R5, M3, L5 • **SVP:** 2-4 yrs • **Academic:** Ed=B, Eng=S • **Work Field:** 271, 294 • **MPSMS:** 941 • **Aptitudes:** G2, V2, N3, S4, P4, Q4, K4, F4, M4, E5, C5 • **Temperaments:** D, J, P, V • **Stress:** E, A • **Physical:** V=L, H=G, L=S • **Work Env:** I • **Salary:** 4 • **Outlook:** 4

RETIREMENT OFFICER (gov. ser.) • D.O.T. #166.267-030 • OES #21511 • Provides information and advice concerning provisions and regulations of state-administered retirement program for public employees: Explains retirement annuity system to personnel officers of state or local governmental entities covered by system, utilizing knowledge of rules and policies of retirement plan. Explains retirement policies and regulations of retirement board to covered employee groups, utilizing knowledge of annuity payments, procedure manuals, and official interpretations. Audits retirement accounts and examines records of employing entities to ensure compliance with prescribed standards and regulations. Attends and addresses conferences and other meetings of employees concerned, as representative of retirement board. • **GED:** R5, M5, L4 • **SVP:** 2-4 yrs • **Academic:** Ed=A, Eng=S • **Work Field:** 271, 282 • **MPSMS:** 894, 895 • **Aptitudes:** G3, V2, N2, S5, P5, Q3, K5, F5, M5, E5, C5 • **Temperaments:** M, P, T • **Physical:** V=N, H=G, L=L • **Work Env:** I • **Salary:** 4 • **Outlook:** 3

GOE: 07.01.02 Administrative Detail

ADMINISTRATIVE CLERK (clerical) • D.O.T. #219.362-010 • OES #55347 • CLERK, GENERAL OFFICE. Compiles and maintains records of business transactions and office activities of establishment, performing variety of following or similar clerical duties and utilizing knowledge of systems or procedures: Copies data and compiles records and reports. Tabulates and posts data in record books. Computes wages, taxes, premiums, commissions, and payments. Records orders for merchandise or service. Gives information to and interviews customers, claimants, employees, and sales personnel. Receives, counts, and pays out cash. Prepares, issues, and sends out receipts, bills, policies, invoices, statements, and checks. Prepares stock inventory. Adjusts complaints. Operates office machines, such as typewriter, adding, calculating, and duplicating machines. Opens and routes incoming mail, answers correspondence, and prepares outgoing mail. May take dictation. May prepare payroll. May keep books. May purchase supplies. May be designated according to field of activity or according to location of employment as ADJUSTMENT CLERK (ret. tr.; tel. & tel.); AIRPORT CLERK (air trans.); COLLIERY CLERK (mining & quarrying); DEATH-CLAIM CLERK (insurance); FIELD CLERK (clerical). Additional titles: AGENCY CLERK (insurance); AUCTION CLERK (clerical); BENEFITS CLERK (clerical); CONSTRUCTION-RECORDS CLERK (const.; light, heat, & power); SHOP CLERK (clerical). • **GED:** R4, M3, L3 • **SVP:** 3-6 mos • **Academic:** Ed=N, Eng=G • **Work Field:** 231, 232, 282 • **MPSMS:** 890 • **Aptitudes:** G3, V3, N3, S4, P4, Q2, K3, F3, M4, E5, C5 • **Temperaments:** P, T, V • **Physical:** V=L, H=N, L=S, H • **Work Env:** I • **Salary:** 3 • **Outlook:** 3

ADMINISTRATIVE SECRETARY (any ind.) • D.O.T. #169.167-014 • OES #39999 • EXECUTIVE SECRETARY. Keeps official corporation records and executes administrative policies determined by or in conjunction with other officials: Prepares memorandums outlining and explaining administrative procedures and policies to supervisory workers. Plans conferences. Directs preparation of records, such as notices, minutes, and resolutions for stockholders' and directors' meetings. Directs recording of company stock issues and transfers. Acts as custodian of corporate documents and records. Directs preparation and filing of corporate legal documents with government agencies to conform with statutes. In small organizations, such as trade, civic, or welfare associations, often performs publicity work. Depending on organization, works in line or staff capacity. • **GED:** R5, M4, L5 • **SVP:** 4-10 yrs • **Academic:** Ed=A, Eng=G • **Work Field:** 231, 295 • **MPSMS:** 891 • **Aptitudes:** G2, V2, N3, S4, P4, Q3, K4, F4, M4, E5, C5 • **Temperaments:** D, J, M, P, V • **Stress:** E, A • **Physical:** V=L, H=L, L=S • **Work Env:** I • **Salary:** 4 • **Outlook:** 4

COORDINATOR, SKILL-TRAINING PROGRAM (gov. ser.) • D.O.T. #169.167-062 • OES #21511 • Plans and arranges for cooperation with and participation in skill training program by private industry, agencies, and concerned individuals: Organizes and coordinates recruiting, training, and placement of participants. Contacts various service agencies on behalf of trainees with social problems and refers trainees to appropriate agencies to ensure trainees receive maximum available assistance. Prepares periodic reports to monitor and evaluate progress of program. •

GED: R5, M4, L4 • **SVP:** 1-2 yrs • **Academic:** Ed=H, Eng=G • **Work Field:** 295 • **MPSMS:** 931 • **Aptitudes:** G2, V2, N2, S3, P4, Q3, K4, F4, M3, E4, C4 • **Temperaments:** D, I, M, P • **Stress:** E • **Physical:** V=N, H=N, L=S, H • **Work Env:** I • **Salary:** 4 • **Outlook:** 2

COURT CLERK (gov. ser.) • D.O.T. #243.362-010 • OES #53702 • Performs clerical duties in court of law: Prepares docket or calendar of cases to be called, using typewriter. Examines legal documents submitted to court for adherence to law or court procedures, prepares case folders, and posts, files, or routes documents. Explains procedures or forms to parties in case. Secures information for judges, and contacts witnesses, attorneys, and litigants to obtain information for court, and instructs parties when to appear in court. Notifies district attorney's office of cases prosecuted by district attorney. Administers oath to witnesses. Records minutes of court proceedings, using stenotype machine or shorthand, and transcribes testimony, using typewriter. Records case disposition, court orders, and arrangement for payment of court fees. Collects court fees or fines and records amounts collected. • **GED:** R4, M2, L4 • **SVP:** 1-2 yrs • **Academic:** Ed=H, Eng=G • **Work Field:** 231, 282 • **MPSMS:** 950 • **Aptitudes:** G3, V3, N3, S4, P4, Q2, K3, F3, M3, E5, C5 • **Temperaments:** P, V • **Stress:** E • **Physical:** V=N, H=N, L=S • **Work Env:** I • **Salary:** 4 • **Outlook:** 3

LABOR EXPEDITER (const.) • D.O.T. #249.167-018 • OES #58008 • Expedites movement of labor to construction locations: Contacts representatives of transportation, feeding, and housing facilities to arrange for servicing workers at transient points. Issues permits, identification cards, and tickets to workers for travel to specified areas. May contact labor union with jurisdiction, where project is located, to inform labor official of recruited workers and to determine union regulations in area. May direct workers to report to local union after arrival in area. May meet recruited workers at designated depot, airport, or dock. • **GED:** R4, M3, L4 • **SVP:** 6 mos-1 yr • **Academic:** Ed=N, Eng=G • **Work Field:** 282, 291 • **MPSMS:** 850, 900 • **Aptitudes:** G3, V3, N3, S5, P4, Q3, K4, F4, M4, E5, C5 • **Temperaments:** D, P, V • **Stress:** E, A • **Physical:** V=N, H=L, L=L • **Work Env:** B • **Salary:** 3 • **Outlook:** 3

MANAGER, OFFICE (any ind.) • D.O.T. #169.167-034 • OES #13014 • CHIEF CLERK; MANAGER, ADMINISTRATIVE SERVICES. Coordinates activities of clerical personnel in establishment or organization: Analyzes and organizes office operations and procedures, such as typing, bookkeeping, preparation of payrolls, flow of correspondence, filing, requisition of supplies, and other clerical services. Evaluates office production, revises procedures, or devises new forms to improve efficiency of workflow. Establishes uniform correspondence procedures and style practices. Formulates procedures for systematic retention, protection, retrieval, transfer, and disposal of records. Plans office layouts and initiates cost reduction programs. Reviews clerical and personnel records to ensure completeness, accuracy, and timeliness. Prepares activities reports for guidance of management. Prepares employee ratings and conducts employee benefit and insurance programs. Coordinates activities of various clerical departments or workers within department. • **GED:** R4, M3, L4 • **SVP:** 2-4 yrs • **Academic:** Ed=H, Eng=S • **Work Field:** 231, 232 • **MPSMS:** 890 • **Aptitudes:** G2, V2, N3, S4, P4, Q3, K4, F4, M4, E5, C5 • **Temperaments:** D, J, M, P, V • **Stress:** A • **Physical:** V=L, H=L, L=S • **Work Env:** I • **Salary:** 4 • **Outlook:** 4

MANAGER, TRAFFIC 1 (motor trans.) • D.O.T. #184.167-102 • OES #15023 • Directs and coordinates activities concerned with documentation and routing of outgoing freight, and verification and reshipment of incoming freight, at motor-transportation company warehouse: Directs activities of workers engaged in assigning tariff classifications according to type and weight of freight or merchandise, routing and scheduling shipment by air, rail, or truck, and preparing billings from tariff and classification manuals. Reviews documents to ensure that assigned classifications and tariffs are in accordance with mode of transportation and destination of shipment. Investigates shipper or consignee complaints regarding lost or damaged merchandise or shortages in shipment to determine responsibility. Directs preparation of claims against carrier responsible and corresponds with shipper or consignee to effect settlement. Schedules shipments to ensure compliance with interstate traffic laws and regulations and company policies. • **GED:** R5, M4, L5 •

SVP: 4-10 yrs • **Academic:** Ed=A, Eng=G • **Work Field:** 221 • **MPSMS:** 853 • **Aptitudes:** G2, V2, N2, S4, P4, Q2, K4, F4, M4, E5, C5 • **Temperaments:** D, P • **Stress:** E, A • **Physical:** V=N, H=G, L=S • **Work Env:** I • **Salary:** 5 • **Outlook:** 2

MEMBERSHIP SECRETARY (nonprofit org.) • D.O.T. #201.362-018 • OES #55108 • Compiles and maintains membership lists, records receipts of dues and contributions, and gives information to members of nonprofit organization: Compiles and maintains membership lists and contribution records. Welcomes new members and issues membership cards. Explains privileges and obligations of membership, discusses organization problems, adjusts complaints, and gives information to members. Types and sends notices of dues. Collects and records receipts of dues and contributions. Sends newsletters, promotional materials, and other publications to persons on mailing list. May compile financial reports. • **GED:** R4, M3, L4 • **SVP:** 30 days-3 mos • **Academic:** Ed=H, Eng=G • **Work Field:** 231, 282 • **MPSMS:** 891 • **Aptitudes:** G3, V3, N4, S5, P3, Q2, K3, F3, M4, E5, C5 • **Temperaments:** P, T, V • **Stress:** E • **Physical:** V=L, H=L, L=S, H • **Work Env:** I • **Salary:** 2 • **Outlook:** 3

PROCUREMENT CLERK (clerical) • D.O.T. #249.367-066 • OES #55326 • AWARD CLERK; BID CLERK; BUYER, ASSISTANT; PURCHASE-REQUEST EDITOR; PURCHASING-AND-FISCAL CLERK; PURCHASING CLERK; PURCHASING-CONTRACTING CLERK. Compiles information and records to prepare purchase orders for procurement of material for industrial firm, governmental agency, or other establishment. Verifies nomenclature and specifications of purchase requests. Searches inventory records or warehouse to determine if material on hand is in sufficient quantity. Consults catalogs and interviews suppliers to obtain prices and specifications. Types or writes invitation-of-bid forms and mails forms to supplier firms or for public posting. Writes or types purchase order and sends copy to supplier and department originating request. Compiles records of items purchased or transferred between departments, prices, deliveries, and inventories. Confers with suppliers concerning late delivery. May compare prices, specifications, and delivery dates and award contract to bidders or place orders with suppliers or mail-order firms. May compute total cost of items purchased, using calculating machine. May classify priority regulations. May verify bills from suppliers with bids and purchase orders and approve for payment. • **GED:** R4, M3, L3 • **SVP:** 3-6 mos • **Academic:** Ed=N, Eng=S • **Work Field:** 221, 232 • **MPSMS:** 898 • **Aptitudes:** G3, V3, N3, S4, P3, Q2, K4, F4, M4, E5, C5 • **Temperaments:** M, P, T, V • **Stress:** E • **Physical:** V=N, H=L, L=S, H • **Work Env:** I • **Salary:** 2 • **Outlook:** 3

TEACHER AIDE II (educ.) • D.O.T. #249.367-074 • OES #31521 • Assists teaching staff of public or private elementary or secondary school by performing any combination of following duties in classroom: Calls roll and prepares attendance records. Grades homework and objective examinations, using answer sheets, and records results. Distributes teaching materials to students, such as textbooks, workbooks, or writing paper and pencils. Keeps order in classroom, library, halls, and on school grounds. Sets up and operates equipment, such as film and slide projectors and tape recorders. Prepares requisitions for library materials and stockroom supplies. May type and operate duplicating equipment to reproduce instructional materials. May be designated by school level as TEACHER AIDE, ELEMENTARY SCHOOL (education); TEACHER AIDE, SECONDARY SCHOOL (education) II. • **GED:** R3, M3, L3 • **SVP:** 30 days-3 mos • **Academic:** Ed=N, Eng=G • **Work Field:** 231, 296 • **MPSMS:** 931 • **Aptitudes:** G3, V3, N3, S5, P4, Q3, K4, F4, M4, E5, C4 • **Temperaments:** V • **Physical:** V=L, H=L, L=L, W, H • **Work Env:** I • **Salary:** 2 • **Outlook:** 3

TOWN CLERK (gov. ser.) • D.O.T. #243.367-018 • OES #53705 • Performs variety of clerical and administrative duties required by municipal government: Prepares agendas and bylaws for town council; records minutes of council meetings; answers official correspondence; keeps fiscal records and accounts; and prepares reports on civic needs. • **GED:** R4, M4, L3 • **SVP:** 6 mos-1 yr • **Academic:** Ed=N, Eng=G • **Work Field:** 231, 232 • **MPSMS:** 890 • **Aptitudes:** G2, V2, N2, S4, P2, Q2, K4, F4, M5, E5, C5 • **Temperaments:** M, P • **Physical:** V=L, H=L, L=S • **Work Env:** I • **Salary:** 3 • **Outlook:** 3

GOE: 07.01.03 Secretarial Work

LEGAL SECRETARY (clerical) • D.O.T. #201.362-010 • OES #55102 • Prepares legal papers and correspondence of legal nature, such as summonses, complaints, motions, and subpoenas. May review law journals and other legal publications to identify court decisions pertinent to pending cases and submit articles to company officials. • **GED:** R4, M2, L4 • **SVP:** 1-2 yrs • **Academic:** Ed=H, Eng=G • **Work Field:** 231 • **MPSMS:** 891 • **Aptitudes:** G2, V2, N3, S4, P2, Q2, K2, F2, M3, E5, C4 • **Temperaments:** J, P, T, V • **Stress:** E • **Physical:** V=L, H=N, L=S, H • **Work Env:** I • **Salary:** 4 • **Outlook:** 4

MEDICAL SECRETARY (medical ser.) • D.O.T. #201.362-014 • OES #55105 • Performs secretarial duties utilizing knowledge of medical terminology and hospital, clinic, or laboratory procedures: Takes dictation in shorthand or using transcribing machine. Compiles and records medical charts, reports, and correspondence, using typewriter. May prepare and send bills to patients and record appointments. • **GED:** R4, M3, L4 • **SVP:** 2-4 yrs • **Academic:** Ed=H, Eng=G • **Work Field:** 231 • **MPSMS:** 891 • **Aptitudes:** G2, V2, N3, S4, P2, Q2, K2, F2, M3, E5, C4 • **Temperaments:** J, P, T • **Stress:** E • **Physical:** V=L, H=G, L=S, H • **Work Env:** I • **Salary:** 3 • **Outlook:** 4

SECRETARY (clerical) • D.O.T. #201.362-030 • OES #55108 • SECRETARIAL STENOGRAPHER. Schedules appointments, gives information to callers, takes dictation, and otherwise relieves officials of clerical work and minor administrative and business detail: Reads and routes incoming mail. Locates and attaches appropriate file to correspondence to be answered by employer. Takes dictation in shorthand or by machine [STENOTYPE OPERATOR (clerical)] and transcribes notes on typewriter, or transcribes from voice recordings [TRANSCRIBING-MACHINE OPERATOR (clerical)]. Composes and types routine correspondence. Files correspondence and other records. Answers telephone and gives information to callers or routes call to appropriate official and places outgoing calls. Schedules appointments for employer. Greets visitors, ascertains nature of business, and conducts visitors to employer or appropriate person. May not take dictation. May arrange travel schedule and reservations. May compile and type statistical reports. May oversee clerical workers. May keep personnel records [PERSONNEL CLERK (clerical)]. May record minutes of staff meetings. May make copies of correspondence or other printed matter, using copying or duplicating machine. May prepare outgoing mail, using postage-metering machine. • **GED:** R4, M3, L4 • **SVP:** 1-2 yrs • **Academic:** Ed=H, Eng=G • **Work Field:** 231, 282 • **MPSMS:** 891 • **Aptitudes:** G2, V2, N3, S4, P2, Q2, K2, F2, M3, E5, C4 • **Temperaments:** J, P, T, V • **Stress:** E • **Physical:** V=L, H=L, L=S, H • **Work Env:** I • **Salary:** 4 • **Outlook:** 4

SOCIAL SECRETARY (clerical) • D.O.T. #201.162-010 • OES #55108 • Coordinates social, business, and personal affairs of employer. Confers with employer on contemplated social functions, sends invitations, and arranges for decorations and entertainment. Advises employer on etiquette, dress, and current events. Reads and answers routine correspondence, using typewriter or in own handwriting as situation demands. May manage financial affairs of entire house. • **GED:** R4, M2, L4 • **SVP:** 1-2 yrs • **Academic:** Ed=N, Eng=G • **Work Field:** 231, 291 • **MPSMS:** 891, 909 • **Aptitudes:** G2, V2, N3, S4, P3, Q3, K3, F3, M3, E5, C4 • **Temperaments:** J, P, V • **Stress:** E • **Physical:** V=N, H=L, L=S, H • **Work Env:** I • **Salary:** 2 • **Outlook:** 2

GOE: 07.01.04 Financial Work, Admin. Detail

ESCROW OFFICER (profess. & kin.) • D.O.T. #119.367-010 • OES #28399 • Holds in escrow, funds, legal papers, and other collateral posted by contracting parties to ensure fulfillment of contracts or trust agreements: Prepares escrow agreement. Executes terms of contract or trust agreement, such as holding money or legal papers, paying off mortgages, or paying sums to designated parties. Files and delivers deeds and other legal papers. May assist buyer to secure financing. • **GED:** R4, M3, L3 • **SVP:** 4-10 yrs • **Academic:** Ed=H, Eng=G • **Work Field:** 231, 272 • **MPSMS:** 895,

932 • **Aptitudes:** G2, V3, N2, S4, P4, Q2, K3, F3, M3, E4, C4 • **Temperaments:** M, T • **Physical:** V=L, H=N, L=S • **Work Env:** I • **Salary:** 4 • **Outlook:** 3

LOAN CLOSER (finan. inst.) • D.O.T. #249.367-050 • OES #53121 • Prepares papers and assembles documents to obtain loans for builders to finance new construction: Forwards applications for loans, construction plans, and credit ratings to loan company for approval. Receives approval of company and orders preliminary title reports and covenants. Draws up closing papers showing financial transactions, conditions, and restrictions upon which sale is based. Records deeds with title company and municipal authorities. May draw up notes, trust deeds and agreements, and obtain signatures. • **GED:** R4, M4, L4 • **SVP:** 1-2 yrs • **Academic:** Ed=N, Eng=G • **Work Field:** 231 • **MPSMS:** 894 • **Aptitudes:** G3, V3, N2, S4, P4, Q3, K4, F4, M4, E5, C5 • **Temperaments:** M, P • **Physical:** V=L, H=L, L=S • **Work Env:** I • **Salary:** 4 • **Outlook:** 4

MORTGAGE CLERK (finan. inst.) • D.O.T. #249.382-010 • OES #53121 • Performs any combination of following duties to process and maintain records of real estate loans: Prepares legal papers and other documents affecting title to real estate, using typewriter. Examines loan documents, such as deeds, assignments, and mortgages, to ensure conformance to escrow instructions, policy, and legal requirements. Obtains title and hazard insurance policies and computes fees, charges, and mortgage settlement figures; allocates charges; orders disbursement of funds; and records loan documents to complete real-estate loan transactions. Examines hazard insurance policies to insure adequate protection against loss on mortgaged property. Records loan data on file cards and keeps files to guard against tax delinquencies and expiration of insurance policies. Types and mails tax and insurance premium notices to remind customers of payment due. May interview applicants for loans to obtain information for bank official. May compute capital gains and keep expense and depreciation ledgers for tax purposes. May be designated according to type of work assigned as ESCROW CLERK (clerical); FORECLOSURE CLERK (clerical); HAZARD-INSURANCE CLERK (insurance); RELEASE CLERK (clerical); TAX CLERK (clerical) II. • **GED:** R3, M3, L3 • **SVP:** 6 mos-1 yr • **Academic:** Ed=N, Eng=G • **Work Field:** 232 • **MPSMS:** 891, 894 • **Aptitudes:** G3, V3, N2, S4, P4, Q2, K3, F3, M3, E5, C5 • **Temperaments:** M, T, V • **Physical:** V=N, H=N, L=S, H • **Work Env:** I • **Salary:** 2 • **Outlook:** 3

REAL-ESTATE CLERK (clerical) • D.O.T. #219.362-046 • OES #53914 • Maintains records concerned with rental, sale, and management of real estate, performing any combination of following duties: Types copies of listings of real estate rentals and sales for distribution to trade publications, and for use as reference data by other departments. Computes interest owed, penalty payment, amount of principal, and taxes due on mortgage loans, using calculating machine. Holds in escrow collateral posted to ensure fulfillment of contracts in transferring real estate and property titles. Checks due notices on taxes and renewal dates of insurance and mortgage loans to take follow-up action. Sends out rent-due notices to tenants. Writes checks in payment of bills due, keeps record of disbursements, and examines cancelled returned checks for endorsement. Secures estimates from contractors for building repairs. May compile list of prospects from leads in newspapers and trade periodicals to locate prospective purchasers of real estate. • **GED:** R4, M3, L3 • **SVP:** 6 mos-1 yr • **Academic:** Ed=N, Eng=G • **Work Field:** 232 • **MPSMS:** 895 • **Aptitudes:** G3, V3, N2, S4, P4, Q2, K3, F3, M3, E5, C5 • **Temperaments:** R, T • **Stress:** T • **Physical:** V=L, H=N, L=S, H • **Work Env:** I • **Salary:** 3 • **Outlook:** 3

UNDERWRITING CLERK (insurance) • D.O.T. #219.367-038 • OES #59999 • UNDERWRITING ANALYST. Compiles data and performs routine clerical tasks to relieve UNDERWRITER (insurance) of minor administrative detail, using knowledge of underwriting and policy issuing procedures: Reviews correspondence, records, and reports to select routine matters for processing. Routes risk-involved matters to UNDERWRITER (insurance) for evaluation. Prepares requisitions for and reviews credit and motor vehicle reports and results of investigations to compile and summarize pertinent data onto underwriting work sheets. Consults manuals to determine rate classifications and assigns rates to pending applications, using adding machine. Corresponds with or telephones field personnel to inform them of underwriting actions taken. Maintains related files. • **GED:** R3, M3, L3 • **SVP:** 3-6 mos • **Academic:** Ed=H, Eng=S • **Work Field:** 232 • **MPSMS:** 895 • **Aptitudes:** G3, V3, N3, S4, P4, Q3, K3, F3, M4, E5, C5 • **Temperaments:** R, T • **Stress:** T • **Physical:** V=L, H=N, L=L, H • **Work Env:** I • **Salary:** 3 • **Outlook:** 3

VAULT CASHIER (bus. ser.) • D.O.T. #222.137-050 • OES #51002 • VAULT SUPERVISOR. Supervises and coordinates activities of workers engaged in receiving, processing, routing, and shipping money and other valuables in armored car firm: Prepares route and work schedules. Oversees loading, unloading, and moving of money and other valuables to and from vault. Issues work and route sheets to workers and collects delivery and pickup receipts from guards. Supervises workers preparing payroll envelopes for customers. Observes workers to ensure that security regulations are followed. Performs other duties as described under SUPERVISOR (clerical). • **GED:** R4, M3, L3 • **SVP:** 6 mos-1 yr • **Academic:** Ed=N, Eng=G • **Work Field:** 013, 221, 293 • **MPSMS:** 899 • **Aptitudes:** G3, V3, N3, S4, P3, Q3, K3, F4, M4, E5, C4 • **Temperaments:** D, P, T • **Stress:** E • **Physical:** V=N, H=N, L=L • **Work Env:** I • **Salary:** 2 • **Outlook:** 3

GOE: 07.01.05 Certifying

ADMISSIONS EVALUATOR (educ.) • D.O.T. #205.367-010 • OES #59999 • ADMINISTRATIVE ASSISTANT; DEGREE CLERK. Examines academic records of students to determine eligibility for graduation or for admission to college, university, or graduate school: Compares transcripts of courses with school entrance or degree requirements and prepares evaluation form listing courses for graduation. Studies course prerequisites, degree equivalents, and accreditation of schools, and computes grade-point averages to establish students' qualifications for admission, transfer, or graduation. Explains evaluations to students. Refers students with academic discrepancies to proper department heads for further action. Types list of accepted applicants or of degree candidates and submits it for approval. Issues registration permits and records acceptances and fees paid. Performs related duties, such as preparing commencement programs and computing student averages for honors. May advise students concerning their eligibility for teacher certificates. May specialize in evaluation of transfer students' records and be designated EVALUATOR, TRANSFER STUDENTS (education). • **GED:** R4, M2, L4 • **SVP:** 1-2 yrs • **Academic:** Ed=H, Eng=G • **Work Field:** 271, 282 • **MPSMS:** 931 • **Aptitudes:** G2, V2, N2, S4, P4, Q3, K4, F4, M4, E5, C5 • **Temperaments:** M, P • **Stress:** E • **Physical:** V=N, H=L, L=S, H • **Work Env:** I • **Salary:** 3 • **Outlook:** 4

CONTRACT CLERK (profess. & kin.) • D.O.T. #119.267-018 • OES #28399 • CONTRACT CONSULTANT; CONTRACT TECHNICIAN. Reviews agreements or proposed agreements for conformity to company rates, rules, and regulations: Analyzes contracts and confers with various department heads to detect ambiguities, inaccurate statements, omissions of essential terms, and conflicts with possible legal prohibitions. Recommends modifications. Converts agreements into contract form or prepares amended agreement for approval by legal department. May initiate changes in standard form contracts. • **GED:** R5, M2, L5 • **SVP:** 2-4 yrs • **Academic:** Ed=H, Eng=G • **Work Field:** 261, 272 • **MPSMS:** 932 • **Aptitudes:** G2, V1, N3, S4, P4, Q3, K4, F4, M4, E5, C5 • **Temperaments:** J, M, T, V • **Physical:** V=L, H=N, L=S, H • **Work Env:** I • **Salary:** 4 • **Outlook:** 3

EXAMINER (gov. ser.) • D.O.T. #169.267-014 • OES #21911 • Examines and evaluates data to determine persons' or organizations' eligibility for, conformity with, or liability under, government regulated activity or program: Examines data contained in application forms, agency reports, business records, public documents or other records to gather facts, verify correctness, or establish authenticity. Interviews persons, visits establishments, or confers with technical or professional specialists, to obtain information or clarify facts. Analyzes data obtained, utilizing knowledge of administrative policies, regulatory codes, legislative directives, precedent, or other guidelines. Determines eligibility for participation in activity, conformity to program requirements, or liability for damages or financial losses incurred, based on findings.

Prepares correspondence to inform concerned parties of decision and rights to appeal. Prepares reports of examinations, evaluations, and decisions. May be classified according to job function, program involved, or agency concerned. • **GED:** R4, M4, L4 • **SVP:** 1-2 yrs • **Academic:** Ed=H, Eng=G • **Work Field:** 211, 271 • **MPSMS:** 959 • **Aptitudes:** G2, V2, N2, S3, P3, Q3, K4, F4, M5, E5, C5 • **Temperaments:** J, M, P • **Stress:** E • **Physical:** V=N, H=L, L=S • **Work Env:** I • **Salary:** 4 • **Outlook:** 3

HOSPITAL-INSURANCE REPRESENTATIVE (insurance) • D.O.T. #166.267-014 • OES #21511 • Interprets hospital and medical insurance services and benefits to contracting hospital personnel: Discusses contract provisions and hospital claims forms with medical and hospital personnel. Instructs hospital clerical staff in resolving problems concerning billing and admitting procedures. Writes reports outlining hospital and contract benefits for incorporation into brochures and pamphlets. May travel from city to city. • **GED:** R4, M3, L4 • **SVP:** 1-2 yrs • **Academic:** Ed=H, Eng=S • **Work Field:** 282 • **MPSMS:** 895 • **Aptitudes:** G2, V2, N3, S4, P3, Q2, K4, F4, M4, E5, C5 • **Temperaments:** M, P • **Physical:** V=N, H=L, L=S • **Work Env:** I • **Salary:** 4 • **Outlook:** 4

PASSPORT-APPLICATION EXAMINER (gov. ser.) • D.O.T. #169.267-030 • OES #21911 • Approves applications for United States passports and related privileges and services: Reviews information on applications, such as applicant's birthplace and birthplaces of applicant's parents, to determine eligibility according to nationality laws and governmental policies. Examines supporting documents, such as affidavits, records, newspaper files, and Bibles, to evaluate relevance and authenticity of documents. Queries applicants to obtain additional or clarifying data. Forwards approved applications to designated official, and prepares summaries for cases not approved indicating points of law. Answers questions of individuals concerning passport applications and related services. • **GED:** R4, M3, L4 • **SVP:** 6 mos-1 yr • **Academic:** Ed=H, Eng=S • **Work Field:** 271 • **MPSMS:** 959 • **Aptitudes:** G2, V3, N3, S4, P3, Q3, K4, F4, M4, E5, C5 • **Temperaments:** J, P • **Physical:** V=L, H=L, L=L • **Work Env:** I • **Salary:** 3 • **Outlook:** 3

TITLE CLERK (petrol. production) • D.O.T. #162.267-010 • OES #28399 • Procures testimonial documents required to remove restrictions affecting title of landowners to property, and requisitions purchase orders and bank checks to satisfy requirements of contracts and agreements covering lease or purchase of land and gas, oil, and mineral rights: Examines leases, contracts, and purchase agreements to assure conformity to specified requirements. Examines abstract to assure complete title-coverage of land described, completeness of land description, and to detect lapses of time in abstract coverage of landowner's title. Prepares correspondence and other records to transmit leases and abstracts. Reviews title opinion to determine nature of testimonial documents needed to meet legal objections and to assure accuracy in terms of trade. Confers with personnel of abstract company, landowners, and LEASE BUYERS (mining & quarrying; petrol. production) to explain reasons for and to obtain testimonial documents needed to clear title. Prepares or requests deeds, affidavits, and other documents and transmits them to appropriate persons for execution to meet title requirements. Investigates whether delinquent taxes are due on land involved in agreements and confers or corresponds with landowner to assure payment. Verifies computations of fees, rentals, bonuses, brokerage commissions and other expenses and prepares records to initiate requests for payment. Prepares purchase data sheet for records unit covering each trade or exchange. Answers queries regarding leases and contracts by mail, telephone, or personal discussion. • **GED:** R5, M4, L5 • **SVP:** 1-2 yrs • **Academic:** Ed=A, Eng=S • **Work Field:** 232, 271 • **MPSMS:** 891 • **Aptitudes:** G3, V3, N3, S4, P4, Q2, K4, F4, M4, E4, C4 • **Temperaments:** J, P, V • **Physical:** V=G, H=L, L=S • **Work Env:** I • **Salary:** 4 • **Outlook:** 4

TITLE EXAMINER (profess. & kin.) • D.O.T. #119.287-010 • OES #28311 • Searches public records and examines titles to determine legal condition of property title: Examines copies of records, such as mortgages, liens, judgments, easements, vital statistics, and plat and map books to determine ownership and legal restrictions and to verify legal description of property. Copies or summarizes (abstracts) recorded documents, such as mortgages, trust deeds, and contracts affecting condition of title to property. Analyzes restrictions and prepares report outlining restrictions and actions required to clear title. When working in title-insurance company, prepares and issues policy that guarantees legality of title. • **GED:** R5, M3, L5 • **SVP:** 2-4 yrs • **Academic:** Ed=A, Eng=S • **Work Field:** 231, 271 • **MPSMS:** 932 • **Aptitudes:** G2, V2, N3, S4, P4, Q2, K4, F4, M4, E5, C5 • **Temperaments:** J, M, T • **Physical:** V=G, H=N, L=S, H • **Work Env:** I • **Salary:** 4 • **Outlook:** 4

TITLE SUPERVISOR (profess. & kin.) • D.O.T. #119.167-018 • OES #28311 • Directs and coordinates activities of subordinates engaged in searching public records and examining titles to determine legal condition of property title. • **GED:** R5, M3, L5 • **SVP:** 4-10 yrs • **Academic:** Ed=A, Eng=S • **Work Field:** 271 • **MPSMS:** 932 • **Aptitudes:** G2, V1, N3, S3, P3, Q2, K4, F4, M4, E5, C5 • **Temperaments:** D, J, M, P, T • **Physical:** V=G, H=N, L=S, H • **Work Env:** I • **Salary:** 5 • **Outlook:** 3

GOE: 07.01.06 Investigating, Admin. Detail

ATTENDANCE OFFICER (educ.) • D.O.T. #168.367-010 • OES #21911 • TRUANT OFFICER. Investigates continued absences of pupils from public schools to determine if such absences are lawful and known to parents. • **GED:** R4, M2, L4 • **SVP:** 2-4 yrs • **Academic:** Ed=H, Eng=S • **Work Field:** 271 • **MPSMS:** 931, 932 • **Aptitudes:** G2, V2, N4, S4, P4, Q3, K4, F4, M4, E4, C5 • **Temperaments:** J, P • **Physical:** V=G, H=G, L=L, W, H • **Work Env:** B • **Salary:** 4 • **Outlook:** 3

CASEWORKER (gov. ser.) • D.O.T. #169.262-010 • OES #21999 • Performs research into laws of United States and procedures of Federal agencies and prepares correspondence in office of Member of Congress to resolve problems or complaints of constituents: Confers with individuals who have requested assistance to determine nature and extent of problems. Analyzes U.S. Code to become familiar with laws relating to specific complaints of constituents. Researches procedures and systems of governmental agencies and contacts representatives of Federal agencies to obtain information on policies. Contacts Congressional Research Service to collect information relating to agency policies and laws. Contacts colleges and universities to obtain information relating to constituent problems. Determines action to facilitate resolution of constituent problems. Composes and types letters to Federal agencies and Congressional committees concerning resolution of problems of constituents. Prepares memoranda to inform Member of Congress of problems which require legislative attention. Confers with personnel assisting Member of Congress to discuss introduction of legislation to solve constituent problems. Calculates social security benefits, veterans' benefits, tax assessments, and other data concerning constituent complaints, using desk calculator. • **GED:** R5, M3, L4 • **SVP:** 6 mos-1 yr • **Academic:** Ed=A, Eng=S • **Work Field:** 231, 271 • **MPSMS:** 891, 893 • **Aptitudes:** G2, V2, N3, S4, P4, Q2, K2, F3, M4, E5, C5 • **Temperaments:** J, P • **Physical:** V=L, H=L, L=S, H • **Work Env:** I • **Salary:** 3 • **Outlook:** 4

IDENTIFICATION OFFICER (gov. ser.) • D.O.T. #377.264-010 • OES #63028 • Collects, analyzes, classifies and photographs physical evidence and fingerprints to identify criminals: Searches for evidence and dusts surfaces to reveal latent fingerprints. Photographs crime site and fingerprints to obtain record of evidence. Lifts print on tape and transfers to permanent record cards.

Vacuums site to collect physical evidence and submits to SUPERVISOR, IDENTIFICATION AND COMMUNICATIONS (gov. ser.) for verifications. Photographs, fingerprints, and measures height and weight of arrested suspects, noting physical characteristics and posts data on record for filing. Prepares and photographs plastic moulage of footprints and tire tracks. Compares fingerprints obtained with suspect or unknown files to identify perpetrator [FINGERPRINT CLASSIFIER (gov. ser.)]. Manipulates mask mirror on specialized equipment to prepare montage of suspect according to description from witnesses. May fingerprint applicant for employment or federal clearance and forward prints to other law enforcement agencies. May testify in court as qualified fingerprint expert. • **GED:** R4, M3, L4 • **SVP:** 4-10 yrs • **Academic:** Ed=H, Eng=G • **Work Field:** 201, 231, 271 • **MPSMS:** 951 • **Aptitudes:** G2, V2, N3, S2, P2, Q3, K2, F3, M3, E4, C4 • **Temperaments:** J, M, T, V • **Physical:** V=G, H=N, L=L, W, H • **Work Env:** B • **Salary:** 4 • **Outlook:** 3

GOE: 07.01.07 Test Administration

DRIVER'S LICENSE EXAMINER (gov. ser.) • D.O.T. #168.267-034 • OES #21911 • Gives written and visual acuity tests and conducts road performance tests to determine applicant's eligibility for driver's license: Scores written and visual acuity tests and issues and collects fees for instruction permits. Conducts road tests and observes applicant's driving ability throughout specified maneuvers and compliance with traffic safety rules. Rates ability for each maneuver. Collects fees and issues licenses. Lectures to school and community groups concerning driver improvement program. May inspect brakes, stop and signal lights, and horn to determine if applicant's vehicle is safe to operate. • **GED:** R3, M2, L3 • **SVP:** 3-6 mos • **Academic:** Ed=H, Eng=S • **Work Field:** 211 • **MPSMS:** 950 • **Aptitudes:** G3, V3, N3, S3, P3, Q3, K3, F3, M3, E4, C4 • **Temperaments:** J, M, P • **Physical:** V=G, H=G, L=L, W, H • **Work Env:** I • **Salary:** 3 • **Outlook:** 3

EXAMINATION PROCTOR (gov. ser.) • D.O.T. #199.267-018 • OES #39999 • Administers civil service qualifying examinations: Verifies admissions credentials of examinees, maintains order, distributes and collects examination materials, keeps time, and answers questions relative to examination procedures. May participate in oral interviews of candidates. May score examinations, using scoring template or answer sheet. • **GED:** R4, M3, L4 • **SVP:** 6 mos- 1 yr • **Academic:** Ed=H, Eng=S • **Work Field:** 295 • **MPSMS:** 712 • **Aptitudes:** G3, V2, N3, S4, P3, Q3, K4, F4, M4, E5, C5 • **Temperaments:** M, P • **Physical:** V=G, H=G, L=L, H • **Work Env:** I • **Salary:** 3 • **Outlook:** 3

TEST TECHNICIAN (clerical) • D.O.T. #249.367-078 • OES #59999 • TEST EXAMINER. Administers and scores psychological, vocational, or educational tests: Distributes test blanks or apparatus to individuals being tested. Reads directions orally from testing manual, or gives other standardized directions. Demonstrates use of test apparatus or discusses practice exercises to familiarize individuals with testing material. Monitors test group to ensure compliance with directions. Times test with stop watch or electric timer. Scores test with test-scoring key and records results on test paper, work application, or test profile form. May operate test-scoring machine to score tests. • **GED:** R3, M2, L3 • **SVP:** 3-6 mos • **Academic:** Ed=H, Eng=G • **Work Field:** 296 • **MPSMS:** 940 • **Aptitudes:** G3, V3, N3, S4, P3, Q2, K3, F3, M3, E5, C4 • **Temperaments:** J, M, P, T • **Stress:** E • **Physical:** V=L, H=L, L=L, W • **Work Env:** I • **Salary:** 3 • **Outlook:** 3

07.02 Mathematical Detail

Workers in this group use clerical and math skills to gather, organize, compute, and record, with or without machines, the numerical information used in business or in financial transactions. Jobs in this group are found wherever numerical record-keeping is important. Banks, finance companies, accounting firms, or the payroll and inventory control departments in business and government are typical of places where this work is done.

✔ **What kind of work would you do?**

Your work activities would depend upon your specific job. For example, you might:

- use a calculator to compute wages for payroll records.
- compute the cost of labor and materials for production records of a factory.
- compute freight charges and prepare bills for a truck company.

- compute or verify credit card data to keep customer accounts.
- supervise statistical clerks or insurance underwriting clerks.

✔ **What skills and abilities do you need for this kind of work?**

To do this kind of work, you must be able to:

- compute and record numbers correctly.
- follow procedures for keeping records.
- use eyes, hands, and fingers at the same time to enter figures in books and forms, or to operate a calculating machine.

- perform work that is routine and detailed.
- read and copy large amounts of numbers without error.

The above statements may not apply to every job in this group.

✔ **How do you know if you would like or could learn to do this kind of work?**

The following questions may give you clues about yourself as you consider this group of jobs.

- Have you had courses in arithmetic or business math? Are you accurate?
- Have you taken bookkeeping or accounting? Do you like working with numbers?

- Have you balanced a checking account or figured interest rates? Do you spot errors quickly?
- Have you had experience working with numbers while in the armed forces? Do you like routine work of this kind?

✔ **How can you prepare for and enter this kind of work?**

Occupations in this group usually require education and/or training extending from thirty days to over two years, depending upon the specific kind of work. People with basic math skills can enter many of the jobs in this group. They receive on-the-job training for specific tasks. To enter some jobs, training in bookkeeping or other business subjects is required. Business training is offered by high schools and business schools.

✔ **What else should you consider about these jobs?**

Workers in small offices may do a variety of tasks. Some may keep all records for a business or agency. Usually, experience is needed for some positions.

In large offices, workers may have only certain tasks to do, and may repeat these tasks every day. Most jobs of this nature are entry jobs requiring little or no experience.

If you think you would like to do this kind of work, look at the job titles listed on the following pages.

GOE: 07.02.01 Bookkeeping & Auditing

BALANCE CLERK (clerical) • D.O.T. #216.382-018 • OES #55338 • BALANCING CLERK. Calculates, verifies, and compares balances of one record book with prior balances of same or other record books: Adds debit and credit items on ledger and journal sheets, using adding machine. Compares totals and subtracts to obtain balance. Examines individual items for errors in computation or transposition of numerals. Corrects errors or lists those to be corrected. May operate keypunch machine to post entries on tabulating cards. May be designated according to type of accounts balanced as ACCOUNTS-RECEIVABLE-BALANC-

ING CLERK (clerical). May reconcile company's bank ledger with bank statements and be designated BANK-RECONCILIATION CLERK (clerical). • **GED:** R3, M2, L2 • **SVP:** 3-6 mos • **Academic:** Ed=N, Eng=S • **Work Field:** 232 • **MPSMS:** 892 • **Aptitudes:** G3, V3, N3, S4, P4, Q2, K3, F3, M4, E5, C5 • **Temperaments:** R, T • **Stress:** T • **Physical:** V=L, H=N, L=S, H • **Work Env:** I • **Salary:** 3 • **Outlook:** 3

BOOKKEEPER 1 (clerical) • D.O.T. #210.382-014 • OES #55338 • FULL-CHARGE BOOKKEEPER; GENERAL BOOKKEEPER. Keeps complete set of records of financial transactions of establishment: Verifies and enters details of transactions as they occur or in chronological order in account and cash journals from items, such as sales slips, invoices, check stubs, inventory records, and requisitions. Summarizes details on separate ledgers, using adding or calculating machine, and transfers data to general ledger. Balances books and compiles reports to show statistics, such as cash receipts and expenditures, accounts payable and receivable, profit and loss, and other items pertinent to operation of business. Calculates employee wages from plant records or timecards and prepares checks or withdraws cash from bank for payment of wages. May prepare withholding, Social Security, and other tax reports. May compute, type, and mail monthly statements to customers. May complete books to or through trial balance. May operate bookkeeping machines [BOOKKEEPING-MACHINE OPERATOR (clerical) I]. • **GED:** R4, M4, L3 • **SVP:** 1-2 yrs • **Academic:** Ed=H, Eng=S • **Work Field:** 232 • **MPSMS:** 892 • **Aptitudes:** G2, V3, N2, S4, P3, Q2, K3, F3, M3, E5, C5 • **Temperaments:** T, V • **Physical:** V=G, H=N, L=S, H • **Work Env:** I • **Salary:** 4 • **Outlook:** 3

GENERAL-LEDGER BOOKKEEPER (clerical) • D.O.T. #210.382-046 • OES #55338 • Compiles and posts in general ledgers information or summaries concerning various business transactions that have been recorded in separate ledgers by other clerks, using calculating or adding machine. • **GED:** R4, M4, L3 • **SVP:** 6 mos-1 yr • **Academic:** Ed=H, Eng=S • **Work Field:** 232 • **MPSMS:** 892 • **Aptitudes:** G3, V3, N2, S4, P3, Q2, K3, F3, M3, E5, C5 • **Temperaments:** R, T • **Stress:** T • **Physical:** V=L, H=N, L=S, H • **Work Env:** I • **Salary:** 3 • **Outlook:** 2

RECONCILEMENT CLERK (finan. inst.) • D.O.T. #210.382-058 • OES #55338 • Reconciles bank statements received from other banks, such as branch banks and Federal Reserve banks. Compiles reports for bank examiners to expedite auditing of accounts. Compiles and mails monthly reconcilement report to Federal Reserve bank. May make copies of reconciled statements, using photocopying machine, and file copies. • **GED:** R3, M3, L2 • **SVP:** 6 mos-1 yr • **Academic:** Ed=N, Eng=S • **Work Field:** 232 • **MPSMS:** 892 • **Aptitudes:** G3, V3, N2, S4, P3, Q2, K4, F3, M4, E5, C5 • **Temperaments:** R, T • **Stress:** T • **Physical:** V=L, H=N, L=S, H • **Work Env:** I • **Salary:** 3 • **Outlook:** 3

RESERVES CLERK (finan. inst.) • D.O.T. #216.362-034 • OES #55338 • Compiles records of fund reserves of bank and branches to ensure conformance with Federal Reserve requirements: Reviews cash orders from branches to determine that order follows established procedure and amount meets with bank limitations and requirements. Posts order to department record sheet, telephones order to Federal Reserve bank, and prepares letter to Federal Reserve confirming each order, using typewriter. Charges or credits accounts following bank regulations. Keeps records of bank's balance with Federal Reserve bank. Photocopies records, using photographic machine [PHOTOGRAPHIC-MACHINE OPERATOR (clerical)]. • **GED:** R4, M3, L3 • **SVP:** 6 mos-1 yr • **Academic:** Ed=N, Eng=G • **Work Field:** 232 • **MPSMS:** 892 • **Aptitudes:** G3, V3, N2, S5, P4, Q2, K3, F3, M3, E5, C4 • **Temperaments:** R, T • **Stress:** T • **Physical:** V=L, H=N, L=S, H • **Work Env:** I • **Salary:** 3 • **Outlook:** 3

GOE: 07.02.02 Accounting Detail

ACCOUNTING CLERK (clerical) • D.O.T. #216.482-010 • OES #55338 • Performs any combination of routine calculating, posting, and verifying duties to obtain primary financial data for use in maintaining accounting records: Posts details of business transactions, such as allotments, disbursements, deductions from payrolls, pay and expense vouchers, remittances paid and due, checks, and claims. Totals accounts, using adding machine. Computes and records interest charges, refunds, cost of lost or damaged goods, freight or express charges, rentals, and similar items. May type vouchers, invoices, account statements, payrolls, periodic reports, and other records. May reconcile bank statements. May be designated according to type of accounting performed as ACCOUNTS-PAYABLE CLERK (clerical); ACCOUNTS-RECEIVABLE CLERK (clerical); ADVANCE-PAYMENT CLERK (clerical); BILL-RECAPITULATION CLERK (light, heat, & power); CASH-POSTING CLERK (clerical); RENT AND MISCELLANEOUS REMITTANCE CLERK (insurance); TAX-RECORD CLERK (light, heat, & power). • **GED:** R4, M3, L3 • **SVP:** 3-6 mos • **Academic:** Ed=H, Eng=S • **Work Field:** 232 • **MPSMS:** 892 • **Aptitudes:** G3, V4, N3, S4, P3, Q2, K3, F3, M4, E5, C5 • **Temperaments:** R, T • **Stress:** T • **Physical:** V=L, H=N, L=S, H • **Work Env:** I • **Salary:** 3 • **Outlook:** 1

ACCOUNTING CLERK, DATA PROCESSING (clerical) • D.O.T. #216.382-010 • OES #55338 • Compiles financial and business transaction data from vouchers, invoices, transmittal sheets, and other source documents to prepare computer-input forms, and verifies and reconciles errors on computer printouts to maintain accounting records: Reviews source documents, such as vouchers, invoices, cash receipts, and purchase orders, for completeness and accuracy. Posts items such as revenue, expense, and cash receipt amounts in journal, assigning as debits or credits to appropriate accounts. Prepares computer-input forms for processing of transaction data, using code book. Compares computer-printout data against source documents and journal entries to verify accuracy, and prepares input forms to reconcile errors. Batches documents after processing, totals amounts in batch, using adding machine, and files documents. Periodically reviews records and subsequent computer printouts to balance accounts and to identify suspense items or delinquent accounts for further action. • **GED:** R3, M3, L2 • **SVP:** 6 mos-1 yr • **Academic:** Ed=N, Eng=S • **Work Field:** 232 • **MPSMS:** 892 • **Aptitudes:** G3, V3, N3, S4, P3, Q2, K3, F3, M4, E5, C5 • **Temperaments:** R, T • **Stress:** T • **Physical:** V=L, H=N, L=S, H • **Work Env:** I • **Salary:** 3 • **Outlook:** 3

BROKERAGE CLERK 1 (finan. inst.) • D.O.T. #219.482-010 • OES #53128 • Records purchases and sales of securities, such as stocks and bonds, in investment firm: Computes Federal and state transfer taxes and commission rates, using calculating machine and rate tables. Verifies details on stock certificates, such as owners' names, transaction dates, and distribution instructions, to ensure accuracy and conformance with government regulations. Posts transaction data to ledgers and accounting and certificate records. Types data on customer's confirmation form to effect transfer of securities bought and sold. Accepts and routes for delivery customer's securities and cash for investment firm. • **GED:** R4, M3, L3 • **SVP:** 6 mos-1 yr • **Academic:** Ed=N, Eng=G • **Work Field:** 232 • **MPSMS:** 894 • **Aptitudes:** G3, V3, N3, S4, P4, Q3, K4, F4, M4, E5, C5 • **Temperaments:** R, T • **Stress:** T • **Physical:** V=N, H=N, L=S, H • **Work Env:** I • **Salary:** 2 • **Outlook:** 3

CALCULATING-MACHINE OPERATOR (clerical) • D.O.T. #216.482-022 • OES #56002 • CALCULATOR OPERATOR. Computes and records statistical, accounting and other numerical data, utilizing knowledge of mathematics and using machine that automatically performs mathematical processes, such as addition, subtraction, multiplication, division, and extraction of roots: Presses keys and moves levers to feed data into machine. Posts totals to records, such as inventories and summary sheets. May verify computations made by other workers. Important variables may be indicated by trade name of machines used. May be designated according to type of computations made as WEIGHT CALCULATOR (ship & boat bldg. & rep.). May be designated according to subject matter as FORMULA FIGURER (paint & varn.); PREMIUM-NOTE INTEREST-CALCULATOR CLERK (insurance). May compute and record inventory data from audio transcription, using transcribing machine and calculator, and be designated INVENTORY TRANSCRIBER (bus. ser.). • **GED:** R3, M2, L2 • **SVP:** 30 days-3 mos • **Academic:** Ed=N, Eng=S • **Work Field:** 232 • **MPSMS:** 892 • **Aptitudes:** G3, V4, N3, S5, P3, Q2, K3, F3, M4, E5, C5 • **Temperaments:** R, T • **Stress:** T • **Physical:** V=L, H=N, L=S, H • **Work Env:** I • **Salary:** 2 • **Outlook:** 2

CANCELLATION CLERK (insurance) • D.O.T. #203.382-014 • OES #53314 • MEMORANDUM-STATEMENT CLERK; POLICY-CANCELLATION CLERK; PREMIUM-CANCELLATION CLERK; PREMIUM-CARD-CANCELLATION CLERK; TERMINATION CLERK. Cancels insurance policies as requested by agents: Receives computer printout of cancellation data or retrieves expiration card from file. Checks number on card with number of policy. Computes refunds, using calculator, adding machine, and rate tables. Types cancellation correspondence and mails with canceled policy to policyholder. Types cancellation notice and routes to bookkeeping department for recording. Mails cancellation notice to agent. • **GED:** R3, M3, L3 • **SVP:** 6 mos-1 yr • **Academic:** Ed=N, Eng=G • **Work Field:** 231, 232 • **MPSMS:** 895 • **Aptitudes:** G3, V3, N3, S4, P3, Q2, K4, F3, M4, E5, C4 • **Temperaments:** R, T • **Stress:** T • **Physical:** V=L, H=N, L=S, H • **Work Env:** I • **Salary:** 2 • **Outlook:** 3

CHECK-PROCESSING CLERK 1 (finan. inst.) • D.O.T. #216.387-010 • OES #55338 • CUSTOMER-ACCOUNT CLERK; PAYMENT-PROCESSING CLERK. Examines and processes incoming checks and credit-card-payment coupons in bank: Scans incoming checks for irregularities, such as incorrect dates and missing, altered, and illegible entries. Date-stamps items to record receipt. Photographs checks and coupons for bank copies. Sorts checks by account number and date or type of payment. Compares signatures on checks with signature cards. Verifies that check and coupon amounts are identical. Computes, using adding machine, check totals for each account, compares total with account balance, and notifies supervisor of insufficient funds. Identifies, stamps, and forwards checks listed on stop-payment report and coupons to other bank personnel. May post figures to bank records. May submit checks above specified amount to supervisor for review. • **GED:** R3, M3, L3 • **SVP:** 30 days-3 mos • **Academic:** Ed=N, Eng=S • **Work Field:** 232 • **MPSMS:** 894 • **Aptitudes:** G3, V3, N3, S4, P3, Q2, K3, F3, M4, E5, C5 • **Temperaments:** R, T • **Stress:** T • **Physical:** V=L, H=N, L=S • **Work Env:** I • **Salary:** 2 • **Outlook:** 2

COLLECTION CLERK (finan. inst.) • D.O.T. #216.362- 014 • OES #55338 • Receives and processes collection items (negotiable instruments), such as checks, drafts, and coupons, presented to bank by customers or corresponding banks: Reads letter of instructions accompanying negotiable instruments to determine disposition of items. Debits bank's account and credits customer's account to liquidate outstanding collections. Computes interest on bills of exchange (drafts), using adding machine, and lists debits and credits on liability sheet to record customer's outstanding balance. Examines, calculates interest on, endorses, records, issues receipts, and mails outgoing collections for payment. Traces unpaid items to determine reasons for nonpayment and notifies customer of disposition. May prove and balance daily transactions. May act as agent for collections payable in United States and possessions and be designated COUNTRY-COLLECTION CLERK (finan. inst.). May process collection items drawn on local bonds and securities exchanges or transfers within a locality and be designated CITY-COLLECTION CLERK (finan. inst.). May collect foreign bills of exchange and be designated FOREIGN-COLLECTION CLERK (finan. inst.). May process matured bonds and coupons and be designated COUPON-AND-BOND-COLLECTION CLERK (finan. inst.); COUPON-COLLECTION CLERK (finan. inst.). • **GED:** R4, M4, L4 • **SVP:** 6 mos-1 yr • **Academic:** Ed=H, Eng=G • **Work Field:** 232 • **MPSMS:** 894 • **Aptitudes:** G3, V3, N3, S4, P3, Q2, K2, F3, M4, E5, C5 • **Temperaments:** R, T • **Stress:** T • **Physical:** V=L, H=N, L=S, H • **Work Env:** I • **Salary:** 3 • **Outlook:** 4

CONTRACT CLERK, AUTOMOBILE (ret. tr.) • D.O.T. #219.362-026 • OES #55347 • Verifies accuracy of automobile sales contracts: Calculates tax, transfer and license fees, insurance premiums, and interest rates, using tables, schedules, and calculating machine. Verifies amount and number of payments, trade-in allowance, and total price of automobile. Interviews customer to obtain additional information and explain terms of contract. Corresponds with motor vehicle agencies to clear automobile titles. Obtains license, signs registration documents on cars traded in, and transfers titles on cars sold. Keeps file of sales contracts. • **GED:** R4, M3, L3 • **SVP:** 6 mos-1 yr • **Academic:** Ed=N, Eng=G • **Work Field:** 231, 232 • **MPSMS:** 890 • **Aptitudes:** G3, V3, N3, S4, P4, Q2, K3, F3, M3, E5, C5 • **Temperaments:** T, V • **Physical:** V=L, H=N, L=S, H • **Work Env:** I • **Salary:** 3 • **Outlook:** 3

COST CLERK (clerical) • D.O.T. #216.382-034 • OES #55344 • COST-ACCOUNTING CLERK; EXPENSE CLERK. Compiles production or sales cost reports on unit or total basis for department or working unit: Calculates individual items, such as labor, material, and time costs, relationship of sales or revenues to costs, and overhead expenditures, using calculating machine. Examines records, such as time and production sheets, payrolls, operations charts and schedules, to obtain data for calculations. Prepares reports showing total cost, selling prices or rates profits. May be designated according to work performed as COST-ESTIMATING CLERK (light, heat, & power); OPERATING-COST CLERK (clerical). • **GED:** R4, M4, L3 • **SVP:** 6 mos-1 yr • **Academic:** Ed=H, Eng=S • **Work Field:** 232 • **MPSMS:** 892 • **Aptitudes:** G2, V4, N2, S4, P3, Q2, K3, F3, M4, E5, C5 • **Temperaments:** R, T • **Stress:** T • **Physical:** V=L, H=N, L=S, H • **Work Env:** I • **Salary:** 3 • **Outlook:** 2

COUPON CLERK (finan. inst.) • D.O.T. #219.462-010 • OES #53102 • Receives matured bond coupons from bank departments, local banks, and customers to effect collection on cash basis, or for payment when future collection is made: Examines coupons presented for payment to verify issue, payment date, and amount due. Enters credit in customer's passbook for coupons accepted for payment. Liquidates collection payments by debiting and crediting accounts. Issues checks to bond owners in settlement of transactions. Totals and proves daily transactions, using adding machine. Composes, types, and sends correspondence relating to discrepancies, errors, and outstanding unpaid items. Keeps record of outstanding unpaid cash coupons, using adding machine. • **GED:** R4, M3, L4 • **SVP:** 6 mos-1 yr • **Academic:** Ed=N, Eng=S • **Work Field:** 232 • **MPSMS:** 892, 894 • **Aptitudes:** G3, V3, N3, S4, P4, Q2, K3, F3, M3, E5, C5 • **Temperaments:** T, V • **Physical:** V=L, H=N, L=S, H • **Work Env:** I • **Salary:** 2 • **Outlook:** 2

FEE CLERK (finan. inst.) • D.O.T. #214.362-018 • OES #55338 • Compiles data from trust-account records and verifies charges for services performed by trust division of commercial bank: Reviews trust-account records, such as securities, purchases and sales, interest or dividend collections, and withdrawals of funds, to determine nature of trust services performed. Consults rate book to verify fees charged. Records charges and transactions on fee tickets and routes tickets for computer processing. Computes debits and credits, using adding machine, adds amounts on account records, and compares totals to verify computations and balance accounts. • **GED:** R3, M3, L3 • **SVP:** 30 days-3 mos • **Academic:** Ed=N, Eng=G • **Work Field:** 232 • **MPSMS:** 892 • **Aptitudes:** G3, V3, N3, S4, P4, Q2, K3, F3, M4, E5, C5 • **Temperaments:** R, T • **Stress:** T • **Physical:** V=L, H=N, L=S, H • **Work Env:** I • **Salary:** 2 • **Outlook:** 3

NIGHT AUDITOR (hotel & rest.) • D.O.T. #210.382-054 • OES #55338 • NIGHT-CLERK AUDITOR. Verifies and balances entries and records of financial transactions reported by various hotel departments during day, using adding, bookkeeping, and calculating machines. May perform duties of HOTEL CLERK (hotel & rest.) in smaller establishment. • **GED:** R4, M4, L3 • **SVP:** 6 mos-1 yr • **Academic:** Ed=N, Eng=S • **Work Field:** 232 • **MPSMS:** 892 • **Aptitudes:** G3, V3, N2, S4, P3, Q2, K3, F3, M3, E5, C5 • **Temperaments:** R, T • **Stress:** T • **Physical:** V=L, H=N, L=S, H • **Work Env:** I • **Salary:** 3 • **Outlook:** 3

POLICY-CHANGE CLERK (insurance) • D.O.T. #219.362-042 • OES #53314 • BENEFICIARY-CHANGE CLERK; CHANGE APPROVER; RECORDS-CHANGE CLERK; TITLE AND BENEFICIARY CLERK. Compiles data on changes in insurance policies and changes policy records to conform to insured's specifications: Examines letter from insured or agent, original application, and other company documents to determine how to effect proposed changes, such as change in beneficiary or method of payment, increase in principal sum or type of insurance. Corresponds with insured or agent to obtain supplemental information or to explain how change would not conform to company regulations or State laws, or routes file to POLICYHOLDER-INFORMATION CLERK (insurance). Calculates premium, commission adjustments, and new reserve requirements, using rate books, statistical tables, calculator, and knowledge of specific types of policies. Transcribes data to abstract (worksheet) and assigns computer codes for use in preparing documents and adjusting accounts. May prepare abstract for typing new policy or rider to existing policy. May underwrite changes when increase in amount of risk occurs. • **GED:** R4, M3, L3 • **SVP:** 6 mos-1 yr • **Academic:** Ed=N, Eng=G • **Work Field:** 232 • **MPSMS:** 895 • **Aptitudes:** G3, V3, N3, S5, P4, Q2, K3, F3, M4, E5, C5 • **Temperaments:** M, T • **Physical:** V=L, H=N, L=S, H • **Work Env:** I • **Salary:** 3 • **Outlook:** 3

POSTING CLERK (clerical) • D.O.T. #216.587-014 • OES #55338 • ENTRY CLERK; POSTER; TRANSCRIBING CLERK.

Records business transactions in journals, ledgers, and on special forms, and transfers entries from one accounting record to another: Records information, such as date, address, identification number, disposition of correspondence, purchase orders, invoices, or checks. May compute debits and credits, using calculating machine or adding machine. May be designated according to type of accounting book in which entries are made as CONSTRUCTION-LEDGER CLERK (light, heat, & power); JOURNAL CLERK (clerical); LEDGER CLERK (clerical) or according to type of transaction recorded as REMITTANCE CLERK (finan. inst.; insurance). May use bookkeeping machine and be designated POSTING-MACHINE OPERATOR (clerical). When keeping records of suspense accounts is designated SUSPENSE CLERK (light, heat, & power). May be known according to specialty, and designated as CARD-INDEX CLERK (clerical); DATA- CHANGE CLERK (clerical); or ERROR-LEDGER CLERK (clerical). • **GED:** R3, M2, L2 • **SVP:** 30 days-3 mos • **Academic:** Ed=N, Eng=S • **Work Field:** 232 • **MPSMS:** 892 • **Aptitudes:** G3, V4, N3, S5, P4, Q2, K3, F4, M4, E5, C5 • **Temperaments:** R • **Stress:** T • **Physical:** V=L, H=N, L=S, H • **Work Env:** I • **Salary:** 2 • **Outlook:** 3

PROBATE CLERK (finan. inst.) • D.O.T. #216.362-030 • OES #59999 • Compiles data to assist trust department in settling estates and accounts that are under probate: Verifies legal descriptions of real estate and clearance of titles to real estate and personal property. Confers with estate executors, creditors, legal personnel and co-workers to obtain data. Prepares certified claim forms for creditors of estate, using typewriter. Maintains probate files showing payment of bills and taxes. May compute taxes. May prepare reports for beneficiaries, banks, and courts. • **GED:** R4, M4, L4 • **SVP:** 6 mos-1 yr • **Academic:** Ed=N, Eng=G • **Work Field:** 232 • **MPSMS:** 891, 894 • **Aptitudes:** G3, V3, N2, S4, P4, Q2, K3, F3, M3, E5, C5 • **Temperaments:** R, T • **Stress:** T • **Physical:** V=L, H=N, L=S, H • **Work Env:** I • **Salary:** 3 • **Outlook:** 2

STATEMENT CLERK (finan. inst.) • D.O.T. #219.362-058 • OES #53126 • Records previously prepared bank statements, distributes statements to customers, and reconciles discrepancies in records and accounts: Records previously prepared statements, using typewriter. Inserts statements and cancelled checks in envelopes, affixes postage, and routes statements for mailing or delivers statements and cancelled checks to customers over counter and obtains signature as receipt. Keeps cancelled check and customers' signature files. May recover checks returned to customer in error and adjust customer complaints. May post stop payment notices to prevent payment of protested checks. May cancel checks, using perforating machine. May take orders for imprinted checks. May answer customers' inquiries. • **GED:** R3, M2, L3 • **SVP:** 3-6 mos • **Academic:** Ed=N, Eng=G • **Work Field:** 231, 232 • **MPSMS:** 894 • **Aptitudes:** G3, V3, N3, S4, P3, Q2, K3, F3, M4, E5, C5 • **Temperaments:** R, T • **Stress:** T • **Physical:** V=L, H=N, L=L, H • **Work Env:** I • **Salary:** 2 • **Outlook:** 3

TAX PREPARER (bus. ser.) • D.O.T. #219.362-070 • OES #21111 • INCOME-TAX-RETURN PREPARER; TAX FORM PREPARER. Prepares income tax return forms for individuals and small businesses: Reviews financial records, such as prior tax return forms, income statements, and documentation of expenditures to determine forms needed to prepare return. Interviews client to obtain additional information on taxable income and deductible expenses and allowances. Computes taxes owed, using adding machine, and completes entries on forms, following tax form instructions and tax tables. Consults tax law handbooks or bulletins to determine procedure for preparation of atypical returns. Occasionally verifies totals on forms prepared by others to detect errors of arithmetic or procedure. Calculates form preparation fee according to complexity of return and amount of time required to prepare forms. • **GED:** R4, M4, L3 • **SVP:** 3-6 mos • **Academic:** Ed=H, Eng=G • **Work Field:** 232 • **MPSMS:** 892 • **Aptitudes:** G3, V3, N3, S4, P4, Q2, K4, F3, M4, E5, C5 • **Temperaments:** J, P, T • **Stress:** E • **Physical:** V=G, H=L, L=S • **Work Env:** I • **Salary:** 3 • **Outlook:** 3

TELLER, COLLECTION AND EXCHANGE (finan. inst.) • D.O.T. #211.362-022 • OES #53102 • Accepts contracts, escrows, notes, bonds, mortgages, trade acceptances, checks, drafts, coupons, and other negotiable instruments for collection, exchange, and distribution of payment: Prepares or reviews collection forms, such as transmittal letters and advice records. Maintains file on items with due dates. Routes collection items for collection, records payments, manually or using teller machine, and issues receipts. Computes and deducts or adds new principal, interest, and collection or discount charges, using adding or calculating machine. Credits or remits proceeds, and releases documents and instruments upon full payment. May collect and remit Federal withholding tax payments. May prepare and service escrow and trust accounts. May purchase and sell domestic and foreign exchange. May handle foreign collections and bills of exchange. May initiate correspondence with submitting banks or individuals to ensure compliance with governmental regulations and procedures regarding redemption, exchange, or transfer of securities. May be designated according to type of transactions handled as TELLER, BOND (finan. inst.); TELLER, CONTRACT COLLECTIONS (finan. inst.); TELLER, DOMESTIC EXCHANGE (finan. inst.); TELLER, FOREIGN EXCHANGE (finan. inst.). • **GED:** R4, M3, L3 • **SVP:** 6 mos-1 yr • **Academic:** Ed=H, Eng=G • **Work Field:** 232 • **MPSMS:** 894 • **Aptitudes:** G2, V2, N2, S4, P3, Q2, K2, F2, M3, E5, C4 • **Temperaments:** P, T, V • **Stress:** E • **Physical:** V=L, H=L, L=S, H • **Work Env:** I • **Salary:** 3 • **Outlook:** 3

TRUST-SECURITIES CLERK (finan. inst.) • D.O.T. #219.362-062 • OES #55338 • EVALUATION ASSISTANT. Performs any combination of following duties to compile and record data concerning asset value and financial status of customer accounts in trust division of commercial bank: Searches files to ascertain quantity and type of assets owned by trust-account customers. Records securities transactions [SECURITIES CLERK (finan. inst.)]. Computes interest, income, profit or loss, and unit values of securities purchased and sold, using calculator. Consults financial newspapers and periodicals or reports from investment specialists to obtain price, dividend, yield, and other data pertinent to securities, mortgages, or other assets held in trust accounts. Reviews trust accounts affected by such market actions as stock splits, mergers, and rights offerings and compiles reports on affected accounts to guide TRUST OFFICER (finan. inst.) in determining needed action. May record and process proxy cards. May review investment fund transactions to compile annual report. • **GED:** R3, M3, L3 • **SVP:** 3-6 mos • **Academic:** Ed=N, Eng=G • **Work Field:** 232 • **MPSMS:** 892 • **Aptitudes:** G3, V3, N3, S4, P4, Q2, K3, F3, M3, E5, C5 • **Temperaments:** M, T • **Physical:** V=L, H=N, L=S, H • **Work Env:** I • **Salary:** 2 • **Outlook:** 3

GOE: 07.02.03 Statistical Reporting & Analysis

ACCOUNT-INFORMATION CLERK (light, heat, & power) • D.O.T. #210.367-010 • OES #55338 • Keeps accounting records and compiles information requested by customer and others pertaining to customer accounts: Keeps records and prepares report of meters registering use of gas- or electric-power, showing results of investigations and amounts recovered or lost. Prepares lists and enters charges and payments to customers' accounts for losses, additional deposits, special and irregular charges. Keeps records of overpayments on customer accounts. Applies overpayments to charges on customers' account or prepares voucher for refund. Investigates incorrect billings due to charges or credits on customers' accounts and prepares written instructions for correction. Reviews accounts not billed and prepares bill from available information. Enters information in meter books which was received too late for billing, such as meter test reports and missed meter readings. Prepares lists of special billing instructions, incorporating charges shown on customers' account. Processes final bills that exceed amount of deposit to enter amount of net bill. Prepares and mails duplicate bills as requested. Interviews customers and others in person or by telephone to answer inquiries and complaints pertaining to bills, customer deposits, and accounts. May specialize in handling inquiries received by mail, compiling information from customer accounting records for replies dictated by others. • **GED:** R4, M3, L3 • **SVP:** 1-2 yrs • **Academic:** Ed=H, Eng=G • **Work Field:** 232 • **MPSMS:** 892 • **Aptitudes:** G3, V3, N3, S4, P4, Q2, K4, F3, M3, E5, C5 • **Temperaments:** P, T, V • **Stress:** E • **Physical:** V=L, H=L, L=S, H • **Work Env:** I • **Salary:** 4 • **Outlook:** 3

CLAIM EXAMINER (insurance) • D.O.T. #168.267-014 • OES #21921 • Reviews settled insurance claims to determine that payments and settlements have been made in accordance with company practices and procedures: Analyzes data used in settling claim to determine its validity in payment of claims. Reports overpayments, underpayments, and other irregularities. Confers with legal counsel on claims requiring litigation. • **GED:** R5, M3, L4 • **SVP:** 2-4 yrs • **Academic:** Ed=A, Eng=S • **Work Field:** 271 • **MPSMS:** 895 • **Aptitudes:** G2, V2, N3, S4, P4, Q3, K4, F4, M4, E5, C5 • **Temperaments:** M, V • **Physical:** V=L, H=L, L=S, H • **Work Env:** I • **Salary:** 4 • **Outlook:** 3

GRADING CLERK (educ.) • D.O.T. #219.467-010 • OES #53905 • GRADE RECORDER; TEST CLERK. Scores objective-type examination papers and computes and records test grades and averages of students in school or college: Grades papers, using electric marking machine. Totals errors found and computes and records percentage grade on student's grade card. Averages test grades to compute student's grade for course. May use weight factors in computing test grades and arriving at final averages. • **GED:** R4, M3, L3 • **SVP:** 30 days-3 mos • **Academic:** Ed=H, Eng=S • **Work Field:** 232 • **MPSMS:** 899 • **Aptitudes:** G3, V3, N3, S4, P4, Q3, K4, F4, M4, E5, C5 • **Temperaments:** R, T • **Stress:** T • **Physical:** V=N, H=N, L=S, H • **Work Env:** I • **Salary:** 2 • **Outlook:** 3

STATISTICAL CLERK (clerical) • D.O.T. #216.382-062 • OES #55328 • RECORD CLERK; REPORT CLERK; TABULATING CLERK. Compiles data and computes statistics for use in statistical studies, using calculator and adding machine: Compiles statistics from source materials, such as production and sales records, quality-control and test records, personnel records, timesheets, survey sheets, and questionnaires. Assembles and classifies statistics, following prescribed procedures. Computes statistical data according to formulas, using calculator. May verify authenticity of source material. May be designated according to type of statistics compiled as CENSUS CLERK (gov. ser.); MILEAGE CLERK (r.r. trans.); PRODUCTION- STATISTICAL CLERK (clerical); SALES-RECORD CLERK (clerical); STEAM-PLANT RECORDS CLERK (light, heat, & power); TIME-ANALYSIS CLERK (clerical); TRAFFIC ENUMERATOR (clerical). May compile actuarial statistics, charts, and graphs and be designated ACTUARIAL CLERK (insurance). • **GED:** R3, M3, L3 • **SVP:** 3-6 mos • **Academic:** Ed=H, Eng=S • **Work Field:** 232 • **MPSMS:** 891 • **Aptitudes:** G3, V4, N3, S4, P3, Q2, K3, F3, M3, E5, C5 • **Temperaments:** R, T • **Stress:** T • **Physical:** V=G, H=N, L=S, H • **Work Env:** I • **Salary:** 3 • **Outlook:** 3

GOE: 07.02.04 Billing & Rate Computation

ADVERTISING CLERK (bus. ser.) • D.O.T. #247.387-010 • OES #53908 • Compiles advertising orders for submission to publishers and verifies conformance of published advertisements to specifications, for billing purposes: Reviews order received from advertising agency or client to determine specifications. Computes cost of advertisement, based on size, date, position, number of insertions, and other requirements, using rate charts. Posts cost data on order and worksheet. Types and mails order and specifications to designated publishers. Files order data pending receipt of publication. Scans publication to locate published advertisement. Measures advertisement, using ruler or transparent calibrated overlay, to verify conformance to size specifications [ADVERTISING-SPACE CLERK (print. & pub.)]. Compares advertisement with order to verify conformance to other specifications. Computes difference in cost when published advertisement varies from specifications and posts corrected costs on order controls. Separates tear sheet (page upon which advertisement appears) from publication, types and attaches identifying information to tear sheet; and routes with order and worksheet to billing department. • **GED:** R3, M2, L2 • **SVP:** 3-6 mos • **Academic:** Ed=N, Eng=G • **Work Field:** 231, 232 • **MPSMS:** 896 • **Aptitudes:** G3, V3, N3, S4, P3, Q2, K3, F3, M4, E5, C5 • **Temperaments:** T • **Physical:** V=L, H=N, L=S, H • **Work Env:** I • **Salary:** 2 • **Outlook:** 3

BILLING CLERK (clerical) • D.O.T. #214.362-042 • OES #55344 • Operates calculator and typewriter to compile and prepare customer charges, such as labor and material costs: Reads computer printout to ascertain monthly costs, schedule of work completed, and type of work performed for customer, such as plumbing, sheetmetal, and insulation. Computes costs and percentage of work completed, using calculator. Compiles data for billing personnel. Types invoices indicating total items for project and cost amounts. • **GED:** R4, M3, L3 • **SVP:** 3-6 mos • **Academic:** Ed=H, Eng=S • **Work Field:** 232 • **MPSMS:** 899 • **Aptitudes:** G3, V3, N3, S4, P4, Q2, K2, F3, M4, E5, C4 • **Temperaments:** R, T • **Stress:** T • **Physical:** V=L, H=N, L=S, H • **Work Env:** I • **Salary:** 3 • **Outlook:** 3

BILLING-CONTROL CLERK (light, heat, & power) • D.O.T. #214.387-010 • OES #55344 • Reviews and posts data from meter books, computes charges for utility services, and marks special accounts for billing purposes: Marks accounts with fixed demands, combined bills for more than one meter connection, and those requiring use of constant multipliers to extend meter reading to actual consumption. Posts late and special meter readings and estimated readings. Examines meter-reading entries for evidence of irregular conditions, such as defective meters or use of service without contract, and prepares forms for corrective actions by others. Marks accounts for no bill when irregular conditions cannot be resolved before billing date. • **GED:** R3, M3, L3 • **SVP:** 6 mos-1 yr • **Academic:** Ed=N, Eng=S • **Work Field:** 231, 232 • **MPSMS:** 892 • **Aptitudes:** G3, V3, N3, S4, P4, Q2, K3, F3, M3, E5, C5 • **Temperaments:** R, T • **Stress:** T • **Physical:** V=L, H=N, L=S, H • **Work Env:** I • **Salary:** 2 • **Outlook:** 3

DEMURRAGE CLERK (r.r. trans.) • D.O.T. #214.362-010 • OES #55344 • CAR-RECORD CLERK. Compiles demurrage charges, using basic rates from rate tables: Communicates with consignee by telephone or letter to notify consignee of date and time of arrival of freight shipment, location, and allowable time for moving or unloading freight before demurrage charges are levied. Reviews bills of lading and other shipping documents to ascertain number of carloads of shipment and computes demurrage charges, using basic rates from rate table and adding or calculating machine. Prepares demurrage bill and for wards it to consignee or shipper. May reconsign or reroute cars on order from shippers. May prepare new waybills and bills of lading on receipt of notice of sale of carload of freight from shipper. • **GED:** R3, M3, L3 • **SVP:** 6 mos-1 yr • **Academic:** Ed=N, Eng=G • **Work Field:** 232 • **MPSMS:** 892 • **Aptitudes:** G3, V3, N3, S4, P4, Q3, K3, F3, M4, E5, C5 • **Temperaments:** M, T • **Physical:** V=L, H=N, L=S, H • **Work Env:** I • **Salary:** 3 • **Outlook:** 3

INSURANCE CLERK (medical ser.) • D.O.T. #214.362-022 • OES #55344 • HOSPITAL-INSURANCE CLERK; PATIENT-INSURANCE CLERK. Verifies hospitalization insurance coverage, computes patients' benefits, and compiles itemized hospital bills: Types insurance assignment form with data, such as names of insurance company and policy holder, policy number, and PHYSICIAN'S (medical ser.) diagnosis. Telephones, writes, or wires insurance company to verify patient's coverage and to obtain information concerning extent of benefits. Computes total hospital bill showing amounts to be paid by insurance company and by patient, using adding and calculating machines. Answers patient's questions regarding statements and insurance coverage. Telephones or writes companies with unpaid insurance claims to obtain settlement of claim. Prepares forms outlining hospital expenses for governmental, welfare, and other agencies paying bill of specified patient. • **GED:** R4, M3, L4 • **SVP:** 6 mos-1 yr • **Academic:** Ed=N, Eng=G • **Work Field:** 232 • **MPSMS:** 895, 899 • **Aptitudes:** G3, V3, N3, S4, P4, Q3, K4, F4, M4, E5, C5 • **Temperaments:** P, R, T • **Stress:** E, T • **Physical:** V=L, H=N, L=S, H • **Work Env:** I • **Salary:** 3 • **Outlook:** 4

INVOICE-CONTROL CLERK (clerical) • D.O.T. #214.362-026 • OES #55344 • ACCOUNTS-PAYABLE CLERK; PURCHASE-ORDER CHECKER. Compiles data from vendors' invoices and supporting documents to verify accuracy of billing data and to ensure receipt of items ordered: Compares invoices against purchase orders and shipping and receiving documents to verify receipt of items ordered. Computes entries on invoices and credit memorandums to determine prices and discounts, using calculator. Posts data to control records. Contacts vendors or buyers regarding errors in partial or duplicate shipments, prices, substitutions, and extensions. Maintains file of returnable items received from or returned to vendors. Writes check or prepares voucher authorizing payment to vendors. • **GED:** R4, M3, L3 • **SVP:** 3-6 mos • **Academic:** Ed=N, Eng=S • **Work Field:** 232 • **MPSMS:** 892 • **Aptitudes:** G3, V3, N3, S4, P3, Q3, K4, F4, M4, E5, C5 • **Temperaments:** R, T • **Stress:** T • **Physical:** V=L, H=N, L=S, H • **Work Env:** I • **Salary:** 3 • **Outlook:** 3

RATER (insurance) • D.O.T. #214.482-022 • OES #55344 • POLICY RATER; RATE INSERTER; RATING CLERK. Calculates amount of premium to be charged for various types of insurance, using rate book, calculator, and adding machine: Selects premium rate based on information in case record folder relating to type and amount of policy based on standard risk factors, such as use and age of automobile, location and value of property, or age of applicant. Adds premium rates of basic policy and endorsements to compute total annual premium. Records rates on abstract sheet (worksheet), from which policies will be typed. May calculate commissions. • **GED:** R3, M3, L3 • **SVP:** 3-6 mos • **Academic:** Ed=N, Eng=S • **Work Field:** 232 • **MPSMS:** 895 • **Aptitudes:** G3, V3, N3, S4, P4, Q2, K3, F3, M4, E5, C5 • **Temperaments:** R, T • **Stress:** T • **Physical:** V=L, H=N, L=S, H • **Work Env:** I • **Salary:** 3 • **Outlook:** 3

REINSURANCE CLERK (insurance) • D.O.T. #219.482-018 • OES #59999 • Types reinsurance applications and contracts and calculates reinsurance liability, working for either prime insurer or reinsurer and by either of following methods: (1) Calculates reinsurance required on each risk, considering limit of liability. Selects reinsurers who may accept part of ceded liability. Types applications. Computes amount of each premium due, using calculating machine. Accepts reinsurers and their liability for cash values and dividends. Prepares abstract for typing of contracts. (2) Receives reinsurance application from prime insurer. Determines amount of insurance already held on risk from company records and calculates reinsurance that company can accept, based on limit of liability. Determines if reinsurance is automatic from treaty provisions and sends application to underwriting department when it is not automatic. Types notice of acceptance or rejection, based on limit of liability, and action of UNDERWRITER (insurance). Operates calculator to verify computations made by prime insurer. • **GED:** R4, M3, L3 • **SVP:** 6 mos-1 yr • **Academic:** Ed=N, Eng=G • **Work Field:** 231, 232 • **MPSMS:** 895 • **Aptitudes:** G3, V3, N3, S5, P4, Q2, K3, F3, M3, E5, C5 • **Temperaments:** M, T • **Physical:** V=L, H=N, L=S, H • **Work Env:** I • **Salary:** 2 • **Outlook:** 3

TAX CLERK 1 (clerical) • D.O.T. #219.487-010 • OES #55338 • REVENUE-STAMP CLERK. Computes state or federal taxes on sales transactions, production processes, or articles produced, and keeps record of amount due and paid. May affix revenue stamps to tax reports to cover amount of tax due. • **GED:** R3, M2, L2 • **SVP:** 30 days-3 mos • **Academic:** Ed=N, Eng=G • **Work Field:** 232 • **MPSMS:** 892 • **Aptitudes:** G3, V3, N3, S4, P4, Q3, K3, F3, M4,

E5, C5 • **Temperaments:** R, T • **Stress:** T • **Physical:** V=N, H=N, L=S, H • **Work Env:** I • **Salary:** 2 • **Outlook:** 3

TRAFFIC CLERK (clerical) • D.O.T. #214.587-014 • OES #58028 • Records incoming and outgoing freight data, such as destination, weight, route-initiating department, and charges: Ensures accuracy of rate charges by comparing classification of materials with rate chart. May keep file of claims for overcharges and for damages to goods in transit. • **GED:** R3, M3, L2 • **SVP:** 3-6 mos • **Academic:** Ed=N, Eng=S • **Work Field:** 232 • **MPSMS:** 892 • **Aptitudes:** G3, V3, N4, S4, P4, Q3, K4, F3, M4, E5, C5 • **Temperaments:** M, T • **Physical:** V=N, H=N, L=S, H • **Work Env:** I • **Salary:** 3 • **Outlook:** 3

GOE: 07.02.05 Payroll & Timekeeping

PAYROLL CLERK (clerical) • D.O.T. #215.482-010 • OES #55341 • Computes wages and posts wage data to payroll records, using calculator: Operates posting machine to compute and record earnings from timesheets and work tickets, subtracting deductions, such as income-tax withholdings, social security payments, union dues, insurance, credit union payments, and bond purchases. Enters net wages on earning record card, check, check stub, and payroll sheet. May prepare periodic reports of earnings and income tax deductions. May keep records of sick leave pay and nontaxable wages. May prepare and distribute pay envelopes. May keep records of goods produced by individual workers, units, or departments. May prepare time records. May compute wages for employees working on bonus, commission, or piecework systems, and be designated as BONUS CLERK (clerical); COMMISSION CLERK (clerical); PIECEWORK TIME CLERK (clerical). • **GED:** R3, M3, L2 • **SVP:** 3-6 mos • **Academic:** Ed=N, Eng=S • **Work Field:** 232 • **MPSMS:** 892 • **Aptitudes:** G3, V3, N3, S4, P4, Q2, K2, F2, M3, E5, C5 • **Temperaments:** R, T • **Stress:** T • **Physical:** V=L, H=N, L=S, H • **Work Env:** I • **Salary:** 3 • **Outlook:** 3

TIMEKEEPER (clerical) • D.O.T. #215.367-022 • OES #55341 • Compiles employees' time and production records: Reviews timesheets, workcharts, and timecards for completeness. Computes total time worked by employees, posts to master timesheet, and routes to payroll department. May pay employees. May calculate time worked and units produced by piece-work or bonus-work employees and be designated TIME CHECKER (clerical) or WORK CHECKER (clerical). May locate workers on jobs at various times to verify attendance of workers listed on daily spot sheet and be designated SPOTTER (any ind.). May interview employees to discuss hours worked and pay adjustments to be made and be designated PAY AGENT (clerical). • **GED:** R3, M2, L2 • **SVP:** 30 days-3 mos • **Academic:** Ed=N, Eng=S • **Work Field:** 232 • **MPSMS:** 898 • **Aptitudes:** G3, V3, N3, S4, P4, Q2, K3, F3, M3, E5, C5 • **Temperaments:** R, T • **Stress:** T • **Physical:** V=L, H=N, L=S, H • **Work Env:** I • **Salary:** 2 • **Outlook:** 3

07.03 Financial Detail

Workers in this group use basic math skills as they deal with the public. Keeping records, answering customers' questions, and supervising others is often part of the job. Jobs in this group are found where money is paid to or received from the public. Banks, grocery check-out counters, and ticket booths are typical places of employment.

✔ What kind of work would you do?

Your work activities would depend upon your specific job. For example, you might:

- receive money from customers and compute payments and interest for a loan company.
- operate a cash register, receive cash, and make change in a grocery store.
- cash winning tickets at a race track.
- record bids for items and collect deposits at an auction.
- keep records of the money you receive and pay out in a bank.

✔ **What skills and abilities do you need for this kind of work?**

To do this kind of work, you must be able to:

- use math to figure the cost of things and make change.
- use eyes, hands, and fingers at the same time to operate an adding machine, calculator, or cash register.
- deal with the public with tact and courtesy.
- perform work that is routine and organized.
- make decisions based on information that can be checked or verified.

✔ **How do you know if you would like or could learn to do this kind of work?**

The following questions may give you clues about yourself as you consider this group of jobs.

- Have you balanced a checking account? Did your balance agree with the bank statement?
- Have you used a calculator or adding machine? Do you like operating this type of equipment?
- Have you sold tickets, candy, or other items? Can you make change rapidly and accurately?
- Have you been the treasurer of a club or social group? Did your records balance at the end of your term in office?
- Have you worked as a cashier in a military PX? Do you like working with the public?

✔ **How can you prepare for and enter this kind of work?**

Occupations in this group usually require education and/or training extending from a short demonstration to over two years, depending upon the specific kind of work. Basic math skills are required for most of the jobs in this group. Workers usually receive on-the-job training for specific tasks. A few jobs may require experience or more formal business training. This training is offered by high schools, business schools, and government training programs. Jobs with the federal government usually require a civil service examination.

✔ **What else should you consider about these jobs?**

Workers who handle money may have to be bonded to protect the employer against dishonest activities. At the end of their shift, workers must make sure that their cash on hand balances with their records. Sometimes this may mean working after the firm or company closes to the public.

If you think you would like to do this kind of work, look at the job titles listed on the following pages.

GOE: 07.03.01 Paying & Receiving

AUCTION CLERK (ret. tr.) • D.O.T. #294.567-010 • OES #49023 • Records amounts of final bids for merchandise at auction sales, and receives money from final bidders at auction: Locates lot and item number of article up for bidding on record sheet. Listens to amount of bids called for by AUCTIONEER (ret. tr.; whole. tr.) and records final amount bid for article. Receives deposit money or full payment from final bidders. • **GED:** R2, M2, L2 • **SVP:** 30 days-3 mos • **Academic:** Ed=N, Eng=G • **Work Field:** 231 • **MPSMS:** 881, 882 • **Aptitudes:** G3, V4, N3, S5, P5, Q3, K4, F4, M5, E5, C5 • **Temperaments:** P, R • **Physical:** V=N, H=L, L=S, W, H • **Work Env:** I • **Salary:** 2 • **Outlook:** 3

CASHIER 1 (clerical) • D.O.T. #211.362-010 • OES #49023 • CASH-ACCOUNTING CLERK; CASH CLERK; CASHIER, GENERAL. Performs any combination of following duties to receive funds from customers and employees, to disburse funds, and to record monetary transactions in a business establishment or place of public accommodation: Receives cash or checks from customers and employees in person or by mail. Completes credit-card charge transactions for customers using charge plate. Counts money to verify amounts and issues receipts for funds received. Issues change and cashes checks. Compares totals on cash register with amount of currency in register to verify balances. Endorses checks and lists and totals cash and checks for bank deposit. Prepares bank deposit slips. Withdraws cash from bank accounts and keeps custody of cash fund. Disburses cash and writes vouchers and checks in payment of company expenditures. Posts data to accounts and balances receipts and disbursements. Compiles collection, disbursement, and bank-reconciliation reports. Operates office machines, such as typewriter, calculating, bookkeeping, and check-writing machines. May authorize various plant expenditures and purchases. May prepare payroll and paychecks. May be designated according to specialization as AGENCY CASHIER (insurance); CASHIER, FRONT OFFICE (hotel & rest.); CIRCULATION CASHIER (print. & pub.). When disbursing money in payment of wages, materials, taxes, plant maintenance, and other company expenses, is designated as DISBURSEMENT CLERK (clerical). When keeping records of cash receipts and maintaining operating reserves in bank for various hotel departments may be designated as HOTEL CASHIER, GENERAL (hotel & rest.). When clearing accounts and issuing financial statements and receipts to hospital or nursing-home patients, is designated as HOSPITAL CASHIER (medical ser.). • **GED:** R4, M3, L3 • **SVP:** 6 mos-1 yr • **Academic:** Ed=H, Eng=G • **Work Field:** 232 • **MPSMS:** 899 • **Aptitudes:** G2, V2, N2, S4, P3, Q2, K2, F2, M3, E5, C4 • **Temperaments:** P, T, V • **Stress:** E • **Physical:** V=G, H=N, L=S, H • **Work Env:** I • **Salary:** 3 • **Outlook:** 3

CASHIER 2 (clerical) • D.O.T. #211.462-010 • OES #49023 • CASH CLERK; CASHIER, GENERAL; CASHIER, OFFICE; TICKET CLERK. Receives cash from customers or employees in payment for goods or services and records amounts received: Recomputes or computes bill, itemized lists, and tickets showing amount due, using adding machine or cash register. Makes change, cashes checks, and issues receipts or tickets to customers. Records amounts received and prepares reports of transactions. Reads and records totals shown on cash register tape and verifies against cash on hand. May be required to know value and features of items for which money is received. May give cash refunds or issue credit memorandums to customers for returned merchandise. May operate ticket-dispensing machine. May sell candy, cigarettes, gum, and gift certificates, and issue trading stamps. Usually employed in restaurants, cafeterias, theaters, retail stores, and other establishments. May be designated according to nature of establishment as CAFETERIA CASHIER (hotel & rest.); CASHIER, PARKING LOT (auto. ser.); DINING-ROOM CASHIER (hotel & rest.); SERVICE-BAR CASHIER (hotel & rest.); STORE CASHIER (clerical); or according to type of account as CASHIER, CREDIT (clerical); CASHIER, PAYMENTS RECEIVED (clerical). When working on same floor, and receiving money, making change, and cashing checks for sales personnel is designated FLOOR CASHIER (clerical). When making change for patrons at places of amusement other than gambling establishments, is designated CHANGE-BOOTH CASHIER (amuse. & rec.). • **GED:** R3, M3, L2 • **SVP:** 2-30 days • **Academic:** Ed=N, Eng=S • **Work Field:** 232 • **MPSMS:** 899 • **Aptitudes:** G3, V3, N3, S4, P4, Q3, K3, F3, M3, E5, C5 • **Temperaments:** P, T • **Stress:** E • **Physical:** V=L, H=L, L=S, H • **Work Env:** I • **Salary:** 2 • **Outlook:** 3

CASHIER-CHECKER (ret. tr.) • D.O.T. #211.462-014 • OES #49023 • Operates cash register to itemize and total customer's purchases in self-service grocery or department store: Reviews price sheets to note price changes and sale items. Records prices and departments, subtotals taxable items, and totals purchases on cash register. Collects money from customer and makes change. Stocks shelves and marks prices on containers. May weigh items, bag merchandise, issue trading stamps, and redeem food stamps and promotional coupons. May cash checks. May be designated according to items checked as GROCERY CHECKER (ret. tr.). • **GED:** R3, M2, L2 • **SVP:** 30 days-3 mos • **Academic:** Ed=N, Eng=S • **Work Field:** 221, 232 • **MPSMS:** 899 • **Aptitudes:** G3, V3, N3, S4, P3, Q3, K2, F2, M3, E5, C4 • **Temperaments:** P, R, S, T • **Stress:** E, T, S • **Physical:** V=L, H=L, L=L, H • **Work Env:** I • **Salary:** 2 • **Outlook:** 4

CHECK CASHIER (bus. ser.) • D.O.T. #211.462-026 • OES #49023 • CASHIER, CHECK-CASHING AGENCY. Cashes checks, prepares money orders, receives payment for utilities bills, and collects and records fees charged for check-cashing service. May receive payment and issue receipts for such items as license plates. • **GED:** R3, M3, L2 • **SVP:** 30 days-3 mos • **Academic:** Ed=N, Eng=S • **Work Field:** 232 • **MPSMS:** 899 • **Aptitudes:** G3, V3, N3, S4, P4, Q3, K4, F4, M4, E5, C5 • **Temperaments:** P, R, T • **Stress:** E, T • **Physical:** V=L, H=L, L=S, H • **Work Env:** I • **Salary:** 2 • **Outlook:** 3

COUNTER CLERK (photofinish.) • D.O.T. #249.366-010 • OES #49017 • Receives film for processing, loads film into equipment that automatically processes film for subsequent photo printing, and collects payment from customers of photofinishing establishment: Answers customer's questions regarding prices and services. Receives film to be processed from customer and enters identification data and printing instructions on service log and customer order envelope. Loads film into equipment that automatically processes film, and routes processed film for subsequent photo printing. Files processed film and photographic prints according to customer's name. Locates processed film and prints for customer. Totals charges, using cash register, collects payment, and returns prints and processed film to customer. Sells photo supplies, such as film, batteries, and flashcubes. • **GED:** R2, M2, L2 • **SVP:** 2-30 days • **Academic:** Ed=N, Eng=S • **Work Field:** 202, 232 • **MPSMS:** 899 • **Aptitudes:** G4, V4, N4, S4, P4, Q3, K4, F4, M4, E5, C5 • **Temperaments:** P • **Stress:** E • **Physical:** V=L, H=N, L=S, H • **Work Env:** I • **Salary:** 1 • **Outlook:** 4

LAYAWAY CLERK (ret. tr.) • D.O.T. #299.467-010 • OES #49011 • WILL-CALL CLERK. Stores and releases merchandise and receives payments for merchandise held in layaway department: Places ordered merchandise on shelves in storeroom. Receives payments on account and final payments for merchandise and issues receipts, using cash register. Keeps records of packages held, amount of each payment, and balance due. Contacts customer when specified period of time has passed without payment to determine if customer still wants merchandise. Releases merchandise to customer upon receipt of final payment, or when customer opens charge account, or routes merchandise for delivery to shipping or delivery department. Packs merchandise when picked up by or being delivered to customer. • **GED:** R3, M3, L3 • **SVP:** 30 days-3 mos • **Academic:** Ed=N, Eng=G • **Work Field:** 221, 232 • **MPSMS:** 881 • **Aptitudes:** G3, V4, N3, S4, P4, Q3, K4, F4, M4, E5, C5 • **Temperaments:** P, T • **Stress:** E • **Physical:** V=N, H=L, L=L, H • **Work Env:** I • **Salary:** 2 • **Outlook:** 3

PARIMUTUEL-TICKET SELLER (amuse. & rec.) • D.O.T. #211.467-022 • OES #49023 • MUTUEL CLERK; PARIMUTUEL CLERK. Sells parimutuel tickets to patrons at racetrack: Reads entry sheets to ascertain entry number of specific horses in designated race and depresses corresponding numbered key of ticket-dispensing machine that automatically ejects ticket requested by patron. Accepts money and makes change. After start of race records totals of tickets sold and cash received and forwards to money room for counting and verification. • **GED:** R3, M2, L2 • **SVP:** 2-30 days • **Academic:** Ed=N, Eng=S • **Work Field:** 232 • **MPSMS:** 899 • **Aptitudes:** G3, V3, N3, S5, P4, Q3, K4, F3, M4, E5, C4 • **Temperaments:** P, R, T • **Stress:** E, T • **Physical:** V=L, H=L, L=S, H • **Work Env:** I • **Salary:** 2 • **Outlook:** 3

POST-OFFICE CLERK (gov. ser.) • D.O.T. #243.367-014 • OES #57308 • POSTAL CLERK. Performs any combination of following tasks in post office: Sells postage stamps, postal cards, and stamped envelopes. Issues money orders. Registers and insures mail and computes mailing costs of letters and parcels. Places mail into pigeonholes of mail rack, or into bags, according to state, address, name of person, organization, or other scheme. Examines mail for correct postage and cancels mail, using rubber stamp or canceling machine. Weighs parcels and letters on scale and computes mailing cost based on weight and destination. Records daily transactions. Receives complaints concerning mail delivery, mail theft, and lost mail, completes and routes appropriate forms for investigation. Answers questions pertaining to mail regulations or procedures. Posts circulars on bulletin board for public information; distributes public announcements; and assists public in complying with other federal agency requirements, such as registration of aliens. May drive motorcycle or light truck to deliver special delivery letters. May be employed in remote retail store contracted by post office to provide postal services and be designated as CONTRACT-POST-OFFICE CLERK (ret. tr.). • **GED:** R3, M3, L3 • **SVP:** 3-6 mos • **Academic:** Ed=H, Eng=G • **Work Field:** 221, 292 • **MPSMS:** 954 • **Aptitudes:** G3, V3, N3, S4, P3, Q2, K3, F3, M3, E5, C5 • **Temperaments:** P, V • **Stress:** E • **Physical:** V=G, H=L, L=L, H • **Work Env:** I • **Salary:** 4 • **Outlook:** 1

TELLER (finan. inst.) • D.O.T. #211.362-018 • OES #53102 • GENERAL TELLER. Receives and pays out money, and keeps records of money and negotiable instruments involved in various banking and other financial transactions, performing any combination of following tasks: Receives checks and cash for deposit, verifies amounts, and examines checks for endorsements. Enters deposits in depositors' passbooks or issues receipts. Cashes checks and pays out money upon verification of signatures and customer balances. Places holds on accounts for uncollected funds. Orders supply of cash to meet daily needs, counts incoming cash, and prepares cash for shipment. May compute service charges, file checks, and accept utility bill payments. May photograph records, using microfilming device. May operate various office machines. May sell domestic exchange, travelers' checks, and savings bonds. May open new accounts and compute interest and discounts. May be designated according to type of transactions handled as TELLER, MAIL CREDIT (finan. inst.); TELLER, PAYING AND RECEIVING (finan. inst.); TELLER, PAYROLL (finan. inst.); TELLER, RETURN ITEMS (finan. inst.); TELLER, SAVINGS (finan. inst.); TELLER, SPECIAL DEPOSITS (finan. inst.). • **GED:** R4, M3, L2 • **SVP:** 6 mos-1 yr • **Academic:** Ed=H, Eng=G • **Work Field:** 232 • **MPSMS:** 894 • **Aptitudes:** G2, V3, N2, S4, P3, Q2, K2, F2, M3, E5, C4 • **Temperaments:** P, R, T • **Stress:** E, T • **Physical:** V=G, H=G, L=S, H • **Work Env:** I • **Salary:** 2 • **Outlook:** 3

TELLER, HEAD (finan. inst.) • D.O.T. #211.132-010 • OES #51002 • Supervises and coordinates activities of workers engaged in receiving and paying out money and keeping records of transactions in banks and similar financial institutions: Assigns duties and work schedules to workers to ensure efficient functioning of department. Trains employees in customer service and banking procedures. Approves checks for payment. Adjusts customer complaints. Examines TELLERS (finan. inst.) reports of daily transactions for accuracy. Consolidates and balances reports, using adding machine. Insures supply of money for bank's needs based on legal requirements and business demand. May be designated according to transactions involved as TELLER, COLLECTION AND EXCHANGE, HEAD (finan. inst.); TELLER, FOREIGN EXCHANGE, HEAD (finan. inst.); TELLER, NOTE, HEAD (finan. inst.); TELLER, PAYING AND RECEIVING, HEAD (finan. inst.); TELLER, SAVINGS, HEAD (finan. inst.). Performs other duties as described under SUPERVISOR (clerical). • **GED:** R4, M3, L4 • **SVP:** 4- 10 yrs • **Academic:** Ed=N, Eng=G • **Work Field:** 232 • **MPSMS:** 894 • **Aptitudes:** G2, V2, N2, S4, P3, Q2, K4, F4, M4, E5, C4 • **Temperaments:** D, M, P, T • **Stress:** E • **Physical:** V=L, H=L, L=S, W, H • **Work Env:** I • **Salary:** 4 • **Outlook:** 3

TELLER, NOTE (finan. inst.) • D.O.T. #211.362-026 • OES #53102 • LOAN TELLER. Accepts payments on loans, and maintains custody of securities: Accepts cash or checks and issues receipts. Computes principal, interest, and discounts, using adding or calculating machine, and posts entries to ledgers and payment books. Types loan forms and documents, such as notes, contracts, and loan renewals. Examines collateral for negotiability. Examines documents on secured loans to ascertain that necessary pledges, powers, chattel mortgages, and assignments are present. Surrenders note and collateral to customer upon payment of loan. May secure or renew insurance policies containing loss-payable clauses. May record deeds, mortgages, and other legal conveyances and instruments. May review daily market quotations and compute current value of loan collateral held. May request borrowers to pledge additional collateral. May clip and collect coupons on securities held. May be designated according to type of transactions handled as TELLER, COLLATERAL (finan. inst.); TELLER, COMMERCIAL NOTE (finan. inst.); TELLER, DISCOUNT (finan. inst.); TELLER, REAL ESTATE LOAN (finan. inst.). • **GED:** R4, M3, L3 • **SVP:** 6 mos-1 yr • **Academic:** Ed=H, Eng=G • **Work Field:** 232 • **MPSMS:** 894 • **Aptitudes:** G2, V2, N2, S4, P3, Q2, K2, F2, M3, E5, C4 • **Temperaments:** P, T, V • **Stress:** E • **Physical:** V=L, H=L, L=S, H • **Work Env:** I • **Salary:** 3 • **Outlook:** 3

TOLL COLLECTOR (gov. ser.) • D.O.T. #211.462-038 • OES #49023 • Collects toll charged for use of bridges, highways, or tunnels by motor vehicles, or fare for vehicle and passengers on ferryboats: Collects money and gives customer change. Accepts toll and fare tickets previously purchased. At end of shift balances cash and records money and tickets received. May sell round-trip booklets. May be designated according to place of employment as TOLL-BRIDGE ATTENDANT (gov. ser.); or type of fare as VEHICLE-FARE COLLECTOR (motor trans.; water trans.). May admit passengers through turnstile and be designated as TURNSTILE COLLECTOR (water trans.). • **GED:** R3, M2, L2 • **SVP:** 2-30 days • **Academic:** Ed=N, Eng=S • **Work Field:** 232 • **MPSMS:** 899 • **Aptitudes:** G3, V3, N3, S4, P4, Q3, K3, F3, M4, E5, C4 • **Temperaments:** R, T • **Stress:** T • **Physical:** V=L, H=N, L=S, H • **Work Env:** B • **Salary:** 2 • **Outlook:** 3

07.04 Oral Communications

Workers in this group give and receive information verbally. Workers may deal with people in person, by telephone, telegraph, or radio. Recording of information in an organized way is frequently required. Private businesses, institutions such as schools and hospitals, and government agencies hire these workers in their offices, reception areas, registration desks, and other areas of information exchange.

✔ **What kind of work would you do?**
Your work activities would depend upon your specific job. For example, you might:

- interview people and compile information for a survey or census.
- give information to bus or train travelers.
- operate a telephone switchboard.
- register hotel guests and assign rooms.
- prepare reports and insurance-claim forms for customers.

- receive callers at an office and direct them to the proper area.
- use a radio to receive trouble calls and dispatch repairers.
- register park visitors and explain rules and hazards.

✔ **What skills and abilities do you need for this kind of work?**
To do this kind of work, you must be able to:

- speak clearly and listen carefully.
- use personal judgment and specialized knowledge to give information to people orally.

- communicate well with many different kinds of people.

- change easily and frequently from one activity to another, such as from typing, to interviewing, to searching in a directory, to using a telephone or radio transmitter.

- use eyes, hands, and fingers accurately while operating a switchboard or computer keyboard.

✔ **How do you know if you would like or could learn to do this kind of work?**

The following questions may give you clues about yourself as you consider this group of jobs.

- Have you participated in a school or community survey? Do you enjoy meeting and interviewing people?
- Have you given directions to others for finding your home? Were they able to follow your directions?
- Have you had speech courses? Do you have a clear speaking voice? Do you use good grammar?

- Have you operated a CB radio? Do you like to use the equipment?
- Have you been involved in a communications unit of the armed forces? Would you like to continue doing this type of work?

✔ **How can you prepare for and enter this kind of work?**

Occupations in this group usually require education and/or training extending from thirty days to over four years, depending upon the specific kind of work. People with a good speaking vocabulary and who like contact with the public usually enter these jobs. Some jobs require typing or general clerical skills. On-the-job training ranging from one month to two years is usually provided. Many employers prefer workers with a high school education or its equal. Chances for promotion are improved with additional education and training. Jobs in the federal government usually require a civil service examination.

✔ **What else should you consider about these jobs?**

Often the worker may have to ask for information that is considered personal or confidential. People may have an unfavorable attitude about giving this information.

Workers may be assigned a wide range of duties, depending on the size of their company.

If you think you would like to do this kind of work, look at the job titles listed on the following pages.

GOE: 07.04.01 Interviewing, Communications

ADMITTING OFFICER (medical ser.) • D.O.T. #205.137-010 • OES #51002 • Supervises, coordinates, and participates in activities of workers engaged in admitting hospital patients and preparing required records: Interviews patient or patient's representative to obtain necessary personal and financial data and to determine eligibility for admission. Assigns accommodations based on PHYSICIAN'S (medical ser.) admittance orders, patient's preference, nature of illness, and availability of space. Prepares records of admission, transfer, and other required data. Sends notices of patient's admission to pertinent departments. Directs and reviews work of clerical and other personnel in admitting patients with minimum delay and inconvenience. Keeps records of admissions and discharges, and compiles perpetual occupancy-census data. Performs duties described under SUPERVISOR (clerical). • **GED:** R4, M2, L3 • **SVP:** 2-4 yrs • **Academic:** Ed=H, Eng=G • **Work Field:** 231, 291 • **MPSMS:** 924 • **Aptitudes:** G3, V3, N3, S3, P4, Q3, K4, F4, M4, E5, C5 • **Temperaments:** M, P, V • **Stress:** E • **Physical:** V=N, H=L, L=S • **Work Env:** I • **Salary:** 3 • **Outlook:** 4

BLOOD-DONOR-UNIT ASSISTANT (medical ser.) • D.O.T. #245.367-014 • OES #55347 • Performs any combination of following supportive duties at blood-collection unit of blood bank: Schedules appointments over telephone for blood donors. Interviews blood donors and records identifying and blood-credit information on registration form. Notifies nurse if donor appears to be underweight or too old to give blood. Takes blood donor's temperature and pulse to assist during medical interview. Unpacks, labels, and stamps date on empty blood packs. Posts donor names, blood-control numbers, and donor-group numbers to unit log sheet. Seals filled blood packs and sample tubes, using handtools and heat-sealing machine. Serves refreshments, such as coffee, juice, cookies, and jelly beans, to donors to prevent or relieve adverse reactions and to begin replenishment of blood fluids. • **GED:** R2, M1, L2 • **SVP:** 2-30 days • **Academic:** Ed=N, Eng=S • **Work Field:** 041, 231, 291 • **MPSMS:** 903, 929 • **Aptitudes:** G4, V3, N4, S4, P3, Q3, K3, F4, M3, E5, C4 • **Temperaments:** P, T, V • **Stress:** E • **Physical:** V=N, H=L, L=L, W, H • **Work Env:** I • **Salary:** 2 • **Outlook:** 2

BONDING AGENT (bus. ser.) • D.O.T. #186.267-010 • OES #21199 • BAIL BONDING AGENT. Investigates arrested person to determine bondability: Interviews bond applicant to ascertain character and financial status. Furnishes bond for prescribed fee upon determining intention of accused to appear in court. Posts and signs bond with court clerk to obtain release of client. Forfeits amount of bond if client fails to appear for trial. • **GED:** R4, M3, L4 • **SVP:** 1-2 yrs • **Academic:** Ed=H, Eng=G • **Work Field:** 271 • **MPSMS:** 895, 949 • **Aptitudes:** G3, V3, N4, S5, P5, Q3, K4, F4, M4, E5, C5 • **Temperaments:** J, P, V • **Stress:** E, A • **Physical:**

V=N, H=G, L=S, W • **Work Env:** I • **Salary:** 4 • **Outlook:** 2

CREDIT CLERK (clerical) • D.O.T. #205.367-022 • OES #53121 • LOAN CLERK. Processes applications of individuals applying for loans and credit: Interviews applicant to obtain personal and financial data and fills out application. Calls or writes to credit bureaus, employers, and personal references to check credit and personal references. Verifies credit limit, considering such factors as applicant's assets, credit experience, and personal references, based on predetermined standards. Notifies customer by mail, telephone, or in person of acceptance or rejection of application. May keep record or file of credit transactions, deposits, and payments, and sends letters or confers with customers having delinquent accounts to make payment [COLLECTION CLERK (clerical)]. May solicit business by sending form letters and brochures to prospective customers. May adjust incorrect credit charges and grant extensions of credit on overdue accounts. May accept payment on accounts. May keep record of applications for loans and credit. May compute interest and payments, using adding and calculating machine. May provide credit information or rating on request to retail stores, credit agencies, or other banks about customer. May check value of customer's collateral, such as securities, held as security for loan. May advise customer by phone or in writing about loan or credit information. May assist customer to fill out loan or credit application. May take loan applications and be designated as LOAN-APPLICATION CLERK (finan. inst.); LOAN-APPROVAL AGENT (gov. ser.). • **GED:** R4, M3, L4 • **SVP:** 3-6 mos • **Academic:** Ed=H, Eng=G • **Work Field:** 231, 282 • **MPSMS:** 894 • **Aptitudes:** G3, V3, N3, S5, P4, Q2, K4, F4, M4, E5, C5 • **Temperaments:** P, T • **Stress:** E • **Physical:** V=N, H=L, L=S • **Work Env:** I • **Salary:** 3 • **Outlook:** 4

CUSTOMER-SERVICE REPRESENTATIVE (light, heat, & power) • D.O.T. #239.367-010 • OES #55335 • ADJUSTMENT CLERK; APPLICATION CLERK; ORDER CLERK; OUTSIDE CONTACT CLERK; SERVICE REPRESENTATIVE. Interviews applicants for water, gas, electric, or telephone service: Talks with customers by phone or in person and receives orders for installation, turn-on, discontinuance, or change in services. Fills out contract forms, determines charges for service requested, collects deposits, prepares change of address records, and issues discontinuance orders. May solicit sale of new or additional services. May adjust complaints concerning billing or service rendered, referring complaints of service failures, such as low voltage or low pressure to designated departments for investigation. May specialize in visiting customers at their place of residence to investigate conditions preventing completion of service-connection orders and to obtain contract and deposit when service is being used without contract. • **GED:** R3, M2, L3 • **SVP:** 6 mos-1 yr • **Academic:** Ed=H, Eng=G • **Work Field:** 231 • **MPSMS:** 891 • **Aptitudes:** G3, V3, N4, S4, P4, Q3, K4, F4, M4, E5, C5 • **Temperaments:** P, V • **Stress:** E • **Physical:** V=N, H=G, L=S • **Work Env:** I • **Salary:** 3 • **Outlook:** 4

EMPLOYMENT CLERK (clerical) • D.O.T. #205.362-014 • OES #55314 • INTERVIEWER; RECEPTION INTERVIEWER. Interviews applicants for employment and processes application forms: Interviews applicants to obtain information, such as age, marital status, work experience, education, training, and occupational interest. Informs applicants of company employment policies. Refers qualified applicants to employing official. Types letters to references indicated on application, or telephones agencies, such as credit bureaus and finance companies. Files applications forms. Compiles and types reports for supervisors on applicants and employees from personnel records. May review credentials to establish eligibility of applicant in regard to identification and naturalization. May telephone or write applicant to inform of acceptance or rejection for employment. May administer aptitude, personality, and interest tests. May compile personnel records [PERSONNEL CLERK (clerical)]. • **GED:** R4, M2, L4 • **SVP:** 6 mos-1 yr • **Academic:** Ed=H, Eng=G • **Work Field:** 231, 271 • **MPSMS:** 943 • **Aptitudes:** G2, V2, N3, S4, P4, Q2, K3, F3, M4, E5, C5 • **Temperaments:** M, P, V • **Stress:** E • **Physical:** V=N, H=L, L=S, H • **Work Env:** I • **Salary:** 3 • **Outlook:** 4

EMPLOYMENT-AND-CLAIMS AIDE (gov. ser.) • D.O.T. #169.367-010 • OES #21502 • Assists applicants completing application forms for job referrals or unemployment compensation claims: Answers questions concerning registration for jobs or application for unemployment insurance benefits. Reviews data on job application to claim forms to ensure completeness. Refers applicants to job opening or interview with EMPLOYMENT INTERVIEWER (profess. & kin.), in accordance with administrative guide lines or office procedures. Schedules unemployment insurance claimants for interview by CLAIMS ADJUDICATOR (gov. ser.), when question of eligibility arises. Interviews claimants returning at specified intervals to certify claimants for continuing benefits. May assist applicants in filling out forms using knowledge of information required or native language of applicant. • **GED:** R3, M3, L3 • **SVP:** 6 mos-1 yr • **Academic:** Ed=N, Eng=S • **Work Field:** 282 • **MPSMS:** 959 • **Aptitudes:** G3, V3, N3, S3, P3, Q3, K4, F4, M4, E5, C3 • **Temperaments:** P, R, V • **Physical:** V=L, H=L, L=S • **Work Env:** I • **Salary:** 3 • **Outlook:** 4

HOSPITAL-ADMITTING CLERK (medical ser.) • D.O.T. #205.362-018 • OES #55332 • ADMISSIONS CLERK; CLINIC CLERK; HOSPITAL-RECEIVING CLERK; MEDICAL CLERK. Interviews incoming patient or representative and records information required for admission and assigns patient to room: Interviews patient or representative to obtain and record name, address, age, religion, persons to notify in case of emergency, attending physician, and individual or insurance company responsible for payment of bill. Explains hospital regulations, such as visiting hours, payment of accounts, and schedule of charges. Assigns patient to room or ward and escorts patient or arranges for escort to assigned room. Types admitting records and routes to designated department. Obtains signed statement from patient to protect hospital's interests. May compile data for occupancy and census records. May store patient's valuables. May receive payments on account. May arrange for such services as kosher diet, telephone, or television in patient's room. May be assigned to clinic reception desk to record appointments and be designated APPOINTMENT CLERK (medical ser.). • **GED:** R3, M2, L3 • **SVP:** 1-2 yrs • **Academic:** Ed=H, Eng=G • **Work Field:** 231, 282 • **MPSMS:** 890 • **Aptitudes:** G3, V3, N3, S4, P4, Q3, K3, F3, M4, E5, C5 • **Temperaments:** P, V • **Stress:** E • **Physical:** V=N, H=L, L=S, H • **Work Env:** I • **Salary:** 3 • **Outlook:** 4

IDENTIFICATION CLERK (clerical) • D.O.T. #205.362-022 • OES #55314 • SECURITY CLERK. Compiles and records personal data about civilian workers, vendors, contractors, military personnel, and dependents of military personnel at defense installation and prepares badges, passes, and identification cards: Interviews applicants to obtain and verify information, such as name, date of birth, physical description, and type of security clearance held. Corresponds with law enforcement officials, previous employers, and other references to obtain applicant's social, moral, and political background for use by department in determining employment acceptability. Photographs new workers, using automatic identification camera. May finger print workers and keep other supplemental identification systems. May keep records of badges issued, lost, and reissued. May issue temporary identification badges to visitors. • **GED:** R3, M1, L3 • **SVP:** 30 days-3 mos • **Academic:** Ed=H, Eng=G • **Work Field:** 231 • **MPSMS:** 891 • **Aptitudes:** G3, V3, N4, S5, P4, Q3, K2, F3, M3, E5, C5 • **Temperaments:** P, T, V • **Stress:** E • **Physical:** V=L, H=L, L=S, H • **Work Env:** I • **Salary:** 2 • **Outlook:** 3

LOAN INTERVIEWER (finan. inst.) • D.O.T. #241.367-018 • OES #53111 • LOAN OFFICER. Interviews applicants applying for mortgage loans: Interviews loan applicants to elicit information, prepares loan request papers, and obtains related documents from applicants, such as blueprints and construction reports. Investigates applicant's background and verifies credit and bank references. Forwards findings reports and documents to appraisal department. Informs applicants whether loan requests have been approved or rejected. Prepares forms for forwarding to insuring agency. • **GED:** R4, M3, L3 • **SVP:** 1-2 yrs • **Academic:** Ed=H, Eng=G • **Work Field:** 271 • **MPSMS:** 894 • **Aptitudes:** G3, V3, N3, S5, P5, Q3, K4, F4, M4, E5, C5 • **Temperaments:** M, P • **Stress:** E • **Physical:** V=N, H=L, L=S • **Work Env:** I • **Salary:** 3 • **Outlook:** 4

NEW-ACCOUNTS CLERK (finan. inst.) • D.O.T. #205.362-026 • OES #53105 • NEW-ACCOUNTS TELLER. Interviews persons desiring to open checking or savings accounts, records data on application forms, and keeps related records: Interviews prospective customers, explains services available, and assists customers in completing application forms. Compiles, types, and files lists of new accounts. Prepares forms for items, such as signature cards, cashier checks, drafts, and money orders, using typewriter and adding machine. Answers telephone inquiries relating to opening or closing of accounts. May duplicate records for distribution to branch banks. • **GED:** R4, M4, L4 • **SVP:** 6 mos-1 yr • **Academic:** Ed=H, Eng=G • **Work Field:** 231, 282 • **MPSMS:** 891, 894 • **Aptitudes:** G3, V3, N4, S4, P4, Q2, K3, F3, M4, E5, C5 • **Temperaments:** P, T • **Stress:** E • **Physical:** V=N, H=L, L=S, H • **Work Env:** I • **Salary:** 3 • **Outlook:** 4

OUTPATIENT-ADMITTING CLERK (medical ser.) • D.O.T. #205.362-030 • OES #55332 • Interviews new outpatients at hospital or clinic and records data on medical charts: Obtains specified information from patient, such as age, insurance coverage, and symptoms, and types information onto prescribed forms. Places records and blank history sheets in order and files them in folder. Schedules appointments for examinations in hospital clinics, according to nature of illness. Gives general information about outpatient care and answers telephone. May tally number of outpatients entering each day or week. May give first aid. • **GED:** R3, M2, L3 • **SVP:** 3-6 mos • **Academic:** Ed=H, Eng=G • **Work Field:** 231 • **MPSMS:** 924 • **Aptitudes:** G3, V3, N4, S4, P4, Q3, K3, F3, M3, E5, C5 • **Temperaments:** P, V • **Stress:** E • **Physical:** V=L, H=L, L=S, H • **Work Env:** I • **Salary:** 3 • **Outlook:** 4

REGISTRATION CLERK (gov. ser.) • D.O.T. #205.367-042 • OES #55332 • Interviews persons to compile information for legal or other records: Records answers to personal history queries, such as date of birth, length of residence in United States, and change of address to enroll persons for voting, citizenship applications, or other purposes. May record number of applicants registered. May fingerprint registrants [FINGERPRINT CLERK (gov. ser.) I]. May take affidavits concerning registrants' statement. • **GED:** R3, M2, L3 • **SVP:** 30 days-3 mos • **Academic:** Ed=H, Eng=G • **Work Field:** 271 • **MPSMS:** 950 • **Aptitudes:** G3, V3, N4, S5, P3, Q3, K4, F3, M3, E5, C5 • **Temperaments:** P, R, T • **Stress:** E, T • **Physical:** V=N, H=L, L=S • **Work Env:** I • **Salary:** 3 • **Outlook:** 3

REHABILITATION CLERK (nonprofit org.) • D.O.T. #205.367-046 • OES #59999 • Compiles, verifies, and records client data in vocational rehabilitation facility: Interviews clients to obtain information, such as medical history and work limitations. Prepares and assists clients to complete routine intake and personnel forms. Gives and receives client information in person, by telephone, or mail to authorized persons. Prepares and types client attendance, training, and counseling reports from client records. Reviews training approval forms and payment vouchers for completeness and accuracy. • **GED:** R3, M2, L2 • **SVP:** 3-6 mos • **Academic:** Ed=H, Eng=G • **Work Field:** 231, 282 • **MPSMS:** 891, 931 • **Aptitudes:** G3, V3, N4, S4, P3, Q2, K3, F3, M3, E5, C5 • **Temperaments:** P, T • **Stress:** E • **Physical:** V=N, H=L, L=S, H • **Work Env:** I • **Salary:** 3 • **Outlook:** 3

SKIP TRACER (clerical) • D.O.T. #241.367-026 • OES #53117 • DEBTOR; TRACER. Traces skips (debtors who change residence without notifying creditors to evade payment of bills) for creditors or other concerned parties: Searches city and telephone directories, and street listings, and inquires at post office. Interviews, telephones, or writes former neighbors, stores, friends, relatives, and former employers to elicit information pertaining to whereabouts of skips. Follows up each lead and prepares report of investigation to creditor. May trace individuals for purposes of serving legal papers. May contact debtors by mail or phone to attempt collection of money owed [COLLECTION CLERK (clerical)]. • **GED:** R4, M2, L4 • **SVP:** 3-6 mos • **Academic:** Ed=N, Eng=G • **Work Field:** 231, 271 • **MPSMS:** 894 • **Aptitudes:** G3, V3, N4, S5, P4, Q3, K4, F4, M4, E5, C5 • **Temperaments:** P • **Stress:** E • **Physical:** V=N, H=L, L=S • **Work Env:** I • **Salary:** 3 • **Outlook:** 3

SURVEY WORKER (clerical) • D.O.T. #205.367-054 • OES #55332 • INTERVIEWER; MERCHANDISING REPRESENTATIVE; PUBLIC INTERVIEWER. Interviews people and compiles statistical information on topics, such as public issues or consumer buying habits: Contacts people at home or place of business, or approaches persons at random on street, or contacts them by telephone following specified sampling procedures. Asks questions following specified outline on questionnaire and records answers. Reviews, classifies, and sorts questionnaires following specified procedures and criteria. May participate in Federal, state, or local population survey and be known as CENSUS ENUMERATOR (gov. ser.). • **GED:** R3, M1, L2 • **SVP:** 30 days-3 mos • **Academic:** Ed=N, Eng=G • **Work Field:** 231 • **MPSMS:** 899 • **Aptitudes:** G3, V3, N4, S4, P4, Q3, K4, F3, M3, E5, C5 • **Temperaments:** P, T • **Stress:** E • **Physical:** V=L, H=L, L=S, W, H • **Work Env:** B • **Salary:** 2 • **Outlook:** 2

TRAFFIC CHECKER (gov. ser.) • D.O.T. #205.367-058 • OES #55332 • Interviews motor vehicle drivers at specified road intersection or highway to secure information for use in highway planning: Places equipment, such as barricades, signs, and automatic vehicle counting devices. Signals driver to stop, presents identification credentials, and explains reason for halting vehicle. Questions driver to obtain data, such as itinerary and purpose of trip. Records results of interview, and permits driver to continue journey. May secure information on load (either passenger or cargo) carried and type and weight of vehicle. • **GED:** R2, M2, L2 • **SVP:** 2-30 days • **Academic:** Ed=N, Eng=G • **Work Field:** 231 • **MPSMS:** 959 • **Aptitudes:** G3, V3, N3, S3, P3, Q3, K3, F4, M4, E5, C5 • **Temperaments:** P • **Stress:** E • **Physical:** V=N, H=L, L=S, W, H • **Work Env:** O • **Salary:** 2 • **Outlook:** 2

GOE: 07.04.02 Order, Complaint & Claims Handling

CLAIMS CLERK 2 (insurance) • D.O.T. #205.367-018 • OES #53311 • LOSS-CLAIM CLERK. Prepares reports and insurance-claim forms for damage or loss against insurance companies: Obtains information from insured to prepare claim form. Forwards report of claim or claim form to insurance company. Acts as intermediary between company and insured. May assist in settling claims. • **GED:** R3, M3, L3 • **SVP:** 3-6 mos • **Academic:** Ed=N, Eng=G • **Work Field:** 231 • **MPSMS:** 895 • **Aptitudes:** G3, V3, N3, S5, P4, Q3, K4, F4, M4, E5, C5 • **Temperaments:** M, P • **Stress:** E • **Physical:** V=N, H=L, L=S • **Work Env:** I • **Salary:** 3 • **Outlook:** 4

COLLECTION CLERK (clerical) • D.O.T. #241.357-010 • OES #53508 • COLLECTION CORRESPONDENT; DELINQUENT-ACCOUNT CLERK; DUNNING CLERK; PAST-DUE-ACCOUNTS CLERK. Notifies or locates customers of delinquent accounts and attempts to secure payment, using postal services, telephone, or personal visit: Mails form letters to customers to encourage payment of delinquent accounts. Confers with customer by telephone in attempt to determine reason for overdue payment, reviewing terms of sales, service, or credit contract with customer. Prepares statements for credit department if customer fails to respond. May order repossession or service disconnection, or turn over account to attorney. May sort, read, answer, and file correspondence. May receive payments and post amount paid to customer's account. May grant extensions of credit. May void sales tickets for unclaimed c.o.d. and lay-away merchandise. May be designated according to type of establishment as BANK-CREDIT-CARD-COLLECTION CLERK (finan. inst.); DEPARTMENT-STORE-COLLECTION CLERK (ret. tr.); HOSPITAL-COLLECTION CLERK (medical ser.); UTILITY-BILL-COLLECTION CLERK (clerical). May personally interview or respond to correspondence or telephone inquiry from customers regarding delinquent bills, and whether any action taken is correct and whether adjustment of action taken is recommnded. See COLLECTOR (clerical) when performing personal-visit collections. May trace customer to new address by inquiring at post office or by questioning neighbors [SKIP TRACER (clerical)]. May attempt to repossess merchandise, such as automobile, furniture, and appliances when customer fails to make payment [REPOSSESSOR (clerical)]. • **GED:** R4, M3, L4 • **SVP:** 3-6 mos • **Academic:** Ed=N, Eng=G • **Work Field:** 231, 282 • **MPSMS:** 894 • **Aptitudes:** G3, V3, N3, S5, P5, Q3, K4, F4, M4, E5, C5 • **Temperaments:** I, P • **Stress:** E • **Physical:** V=N, H=L, L=S • **Work Env:** B • **Salary:** 3 • **Outlook:** 4

CORRESPONDENCE CLERK (clerical) • D.O.T. #209.262-010 • OES #55317 • CORRESPONDENT. Composes letters in reply to correspondence concerning such items as requests for merchandise, damage claims, credit information, delinquent accounts, incorrect billing, unsatisfactory service, or to request information: Reads incoming correspondence and gathers data to formulate reply. Operates typewriter to prepare correspondence or to complete form letters, or dictates reply. May route correspondence to other departments for reply. May keep files of correspondence sent, received, or requiring further action. May be designated according to type of correspondence handled as CLAIM CLERK (clerical); CREDIT-CORRESPONDENCE CLERK (clerical); FAN-MAIL CLERK (amuse. & rec.); FOREIGN-TRADE- SERVICES CLERK (finan. inst.); SALES-CORRESPONDENCE CLERK (clerical) • **GED:** R4, M2, L4 • **SVP:** 1-2 yrs • **Academic:** Ed=H, Eng=G • **Work Field:** 231 • **MPSMS:** 891 • **Aptitudes:** G3, V2, N3, S4, P4, Q3, K3, F3, M3, E5, C5 • **Temperaments:** J, M • **Physical:** V=L, H=L, L=S, H • **Work Env:** I • **Salary:** 4 • **Outlook:** 2

REFERRAL-AND-INFORMATION AIDE (gov. ser.) • D.O.T. #237.367-042 • OES #55305 • Receives callers and responds to complaints in person or by telephone for government agency: Questions callers to ascertain nature of complaints against government agency; records complaint on standard form; and routes form to appropriate department or office for action. Contacts department or office to which complaint was referred to determine disposition. Contacts complainant to verify data and follow-up on results of referral. Compiles complaint records, by category, department office, and disposition. Notifies supervisor of patterns of poor provision of service. Maintains up-to-date reference materials and files. • **GED:** R3, M2, L3 • **SVP:** 30 days-3 mos • **Academic:** Ed=N, Eng=G • **Work Field:** 231, 282 • **MPSMS:** 959 • **Aptitudes:** G3, V2, N4, S4, P4, Q3, K4, F4, M4, E5, C5 • **Temperaments:** J, P • **Stress:** E • **Physical:** V=N, H=L, L=S, H • **Work Env:** I • **Salary:** 2 • **Outlook:** 3

GOE: 07.04.03 Registration

ANIMAL-HOSPITAL CLERK (medical ser.) • D.O.T. #245.367-010 • OES #55347 • Registers and admits animals brought to animal hospital; advises owners about condition of pets being treated; prepares case records of treated animals; and computes and records payment of fees: Questions animal owners to determine symptoms and to complete admission form. Answers questions by phone, letter, or in person about condition of animals treated, visiting hours, first aid, and discharge date. Prepares case record on each animal treated, including identifying information, diagnosis, and treatment. Computes treatment cost and records fees collected. • **GED:** R3, M2, L3 • **SVP:** 3-6 mos • **Academic:** Ed=N, Eng=G • **Work Field:** 232, 282 • **MPSMS:** 929 • **Aptitudes:** G3, V3, N3, S5, P4, Q3, K4, F4, M4, E5, C5 • **Temperaments:** P • **Stress:** E • **Physical:** V=N, H=L, L=S, W, H • **Work Env:** I • **Salary:** 3 • **Outlook:** 2

DOG LICENSER (nonprofit org.) • D.O.T. #249.367-030 • OES #53708 • Canvasses assigned area to locate and advise dog owners of licensing law; to assist with license applications; and to collect license fees: Visits homes and questions dog owners to determine compliance with licensing law. Explains requirements to dog owners, fills out applications, and collects license fees or gives application to owners for mailing. Counts collected fees and applications. Submits fees and reports to department for record. • **GED:** R3, M2, L3 • **SVP:** 3-6 mos • **Academic:** Ed=N, Eng=G • **Work Field:** 231, 271, 282 • **MPSMS:** 329 • **Aptitudes:** G3, V3, N3, S4, P4, Q4, K5, F4, M4, E5, C5 • **Temperaments:** P • **Stress:** E • **Physical:** V=N, H=N, L=S • **Work Env:** B • **Salary:** 3 • **Outlook:** 3

ELECTION CLERK (gov. ser.) • D.O.T. #205.367-030 • OES #59999 • POLL CLERK; RETURNING OFFICER. Performs any combination of the following duties during elections: Compiles and verifies voter lists from official registration records. Requests identification of voters at polling place. Obtains signatures and records names of voters to prevent voting of unauthorized persons. Distributes ballots to voters and answers questions concerning voting procedure. Counts valid ballots and prepares official reports of election results. • **GED:** R3, M2, L2 • **SVP:** 2-30 days • **Academic:** Ed=N, Eng=G • **Work Field:** 231 • **MPSMS:** 959 • **Aptitudes:** G3, V3, N4, S5, P4, Q3, K4, F4, M4, E5, C5 • **Temperaments:** M, P, T • **Stress:** E • **Physical:** V=L, H=L, L=S • **Work Env:** I • **Salary:** 1 • **Outlook:** 1

HOTEL CLERK (hotel & rest.) • D.O.T. #238.362-010 • OES #53808 • MOTEL CLERK; MOTOR-LODGE CLERK. Performs any combination of following duties for guests of hotel, motel, motor lodge, or condominium-hotel: Registers and assigns rooms to guests. Issues room key and escort instructions to BELLHOP (hotel & rest.). Date-stamps, sorts, and racks incoming mail and messages. Transmits and receives messages, using equipment, such as telegraph, telephone, Teletype, and switchboard. Answers inquiries pertaining to hotel services; registration of guests; and shopping, dining, entertainment, and travel directions. Keeps records of room availability and guests' accounts. Computes bill, collects payment, and makes change for guests [CASHIER (clerical) I]. Makes and confirms reservations. May sell tobacco, candy, and newspapers. May post charges, such as room, food, liquor, or telephone, to cashbooks, by hand [BOOKKEEPER (clerical) II] or by machine [BOOKKEEPING-MACHINE OPERATOR (clerical) II]. May make restaurant, transportation, or entertainment reservation, and arrange for tours. May deposit guest's valuables in hotel safe or safe-deposit box. May order complimentary flowers or champagne for honeymoon couples or special guests. May rent dock space at marina-hotel. May work on one floor and be designated FLOOR CLERK (hotel & rest.). May be known according to specific task performed as KEY CLERK (hotel & rest.); RESERVATION CLERK (hotel & rest.); ROOM CLERK (hotel & rest.) or area worked as DESK CLERK (per. ser.); FRONT CLERK (hotel & rest.). • **GED:** R3, M3, L3 • **SVP:** 3-6 mos • **Academic:** Ed=N, Eng=G • **Work Field:** 232, 291 • **MPSMS:** 902 • **Aptitudes:** G3, V3, N3, S4, P4, Q3, K4, F3, M4, E5, C4 • **Temperaments:** P, V • **Stress:** E • **Physical:** V=N, H=L, L=S • **Work Env:** I • **Salary:** 3 • **Outlook:** 3

LICENSE CLERK (gov. ser.) • D.O.T. #205.367-034 • OES #53708 • Issues licenses or permits to qualified applicants: Questions persons to obtain information, such as name, address, and age, and records data on prescribed forms. Collects prescribed fee. Issues drivers's automobile, liquor, marriage, or other licenses. May conduct oral, visual, written, or performance test to determine applicant's qualifications. • **GED:** R3, M2, L3 • **SVP:** 30 days-3 mos • **Academic:** Ed=H, Eng=G • **Work Field:** 231 • **MPSMS:** 950 • **Aptitudes:** G3, V3, N4, S5, P4, Q3, K4, F4, M4, E5, C5 • **Temperaments:** P, T • **Stress:** E • **Physical:** V=N, H=L, L=S, H • **Work Env:** I • **Salary:** 3 • **Outlook:** 3

PARK AIDE (gov. ser.) • D.O.T. #249.367-082 • OES #55305 • PARK TECHNICIAN; RANGER AIDE. Assists PARK RANGER (gov. ser.) 169.167-042 or PARK SUPERINTENDENT (gov. ser.) 188.167-062 in operation of State or national park, monument, historic site, or recreational area through performance of any combination of clerical and other duties: Greets visitors at facility entrance and explains regulations. Assigns campground or recreational vehicle sites and collects fees at park offering camping facilities. Monitors campgrounds, cautions visitors against infractions of rules, and notifies PARK RANGER (gov. ser.) 169.167-042 of problems. Replenishes firewood and assists GROUNDS-KEEPER, PARKS AND GROUNDS (gov. ser.) 406.687-010 to maintain camping and recreational areas in clean and orderly condition. Conducts tours of premises and answers visitors' questions when stationed at historic park, site, or monument. Operates projection and sound equipment and assists PARK RANGER (gov. ser.) 169.167-042 in presentation of interpretive programs. Provides simple first-aid treatment to visitors injured on premises and assists persons with more serious injuries to obtain appropriate medical care. Participates in carrying out fire-fighting or conservation activities. Assists other workers in activities concerned with restoration of buildings and other facilities, or excavation and preservation of artifacts when stationed at historic or archeological site. • **GED:** R4, M3, L4 • **SVP:** 30 days-3 mos • **Academic:** Ed=H, Eng=G • **Work Field:** 282, 293 • **MPSMS:** 919, 959 • **Aptitudes:** G3, V3, N4, S4, P3, Q3, K3, F4, M3, E5, C4 • **Temperaments:** P, V • **Stress:** E • **Physical:** V=L, H=L, L=L • **Work Env:** I • **Salary:** 2 • **Outlook:** 3

PUBLIC HEALTH REGISTRAR (gov. ser.) • D.O.T. #169.167-046 • OES #21999 • Records and maintains birth and death certificates and communicable disease reports, and prepares statistical data and medical reports for city or county public health department: Registers birth, death, and communicable disease statistics from information supplied by physicians, hospital personnel, funeral directors, and representatives from other agencies. Analyzes cause of death statements and communicable disease reports for compliance with laws and local regulations, consistency, and completeness. Contacts information sources concerning vital statistics and disease reports to resolve discrepancies and obtain additional information. Makes certified copies of documents and issues permits to remove and bury bodies. Prepares reports, such as epidemiological case history and morbidity report and keeps file of communicable disease cases. Refers tuberculosis cases and contacts to appropriate health agencies for consultation, treatment referral, and assistance in disease control. Obtains medical, statistical, and sociological data for use by workers in various public health departments. Assists in maintaining statistical data file and medical information reference library. • **GED:** R4, M3, L4 • **SVP:** 2-4 yrs • **Academic:** Ed=H, Eng=G • **Work Field:** 231 • **MPSMS:** 721, 729, 929 • **Aptitudes:** G3, V3, N3, S4, P4, Q3, K4, F4, M4, E4, C5 • **Temperaments:** M, P, V • **Stress:** E • **Physical:** V=L, H=L, L=S • **Work Env:** I • **Salary:** 4 • **Outlook:** 3

RECREATION-FACILITY ATTENDANT (amuse. & rec.) • D.O.T. #341.367-010 • OES #68014 • Schedules use of recreation facilities, such as golf courses, tennis courts, and softball and sandlot diamonds, in accordance with private club or public park rules: Makes reservations for use of facilities by players. Settles disputes between groups or individual players regarding use of facilities. Coordinates use of facilities to prevent players from interfering with one another. May collect fees from players. May inform players of rules concerning dress, conduct, or equipment and enforce rules or eject unruly player or unauthorized persons as necessary. May sell or rent golf and tennis balls, racquets, golf clubs, and other equipment. May render emergency first aid to injured or striken players. May patrol facilities to detect damage to facilities and report damages to appropriate authority. May be designated according to facility tended as GOLF-COURSE STARTER (amuse. & rec.); TENNIS-COURT ATTENDANT (amuse. & rec.). • **GED:** R3, M3, L3 • **SVP:** 30 days-3 mos • **Academic:** Ed=N, Eng=S • **Work Field:** 291 • **MPSMS:** 914 • **Aptitudes:** G3, V3, N3, S4, P4, Q3, K4, F4, M4, E5, C5 • **Temperaments:** D, P, V • **Stress:** E • **Physical:** V=N, H=N, L=L, W • **Work Env:** B • **Salary:** 2 • **Outlook:** 2

RESERVATIONS AGENT (air trans.) • D.O.T. #238.367-018 • OES #53805 • TELEPHONE-SALES AGENT. Makes and confirms reservations for passengers on scheduled airline flights: Arranges reservations and routing for passengers at request of TICKET AGENT (any ind.) or customer, using timetables, airline manuals, reference guides, and tariff book. Types requested flight number on keyboard of on-line computer reservation system and scans screen to determine space availability. Telephones customer or TICKET AGENT (any ind.) to advise of changes in flight plan or to cancel or confirm reservation. May maintain advance or current inventory of available passenger space on flights. May advise load control personnel and other stations of changes in passenger itinerary to control space and ensure utilization of seating capacity on flights. • **GED:** R4, M3, L3 • **SVP:** 3-6 mos • **Academic:** Ed=H, Eng=G • **Work Field:** 291 • **MPSMS:** 855 • **Aptitudes:** G3, V3, N3, S4, P4, Q3, K3, F3, M3, E5, C5 • **Temperaments:** I, P, R • **Stress:** E, T • **Physical:** V=N, H=L, L=S, H • **Work Env:** I • **Salary:** 2 • **Outlook:** 3

GOE: 07.04.04 Recepting & Information Giving

INFORMATION CLERK (clerical) • D.O.T. #237.367-022 • OES #55305 • Answers inquiries of persons coming into establishment: Provides information regarding activities conducted at establishment, and location of departments, offices, and employees within organization. In retail establishment informs customer of location of store merchandise. In hotel supplies information concerning services, such as laundry and valet services. Receives and answers requests for information from company officials and employees. May call employees or officials to information desk to answer inquiries. May keep record of questions asked. • **GED:** R4, M2, L3 • **SVP:** 3-6 mos • **Academic:** Ed=H, Eng=G • **Work Field:** 282 • **MPSMS:** 899 • **Aptitudes:** G3, V3, N3, S4, P3, Q3, K4, F4, M4,

E5, C5 • **Temperaments:** P, V • **Stress:** E • **Physical:** V=N, H=L, L=S, H • **Work Env:** I • **Salary:** 2 • **Outlook:** 3

LAND-LEASING EXAMINER (gov. ser.) • D.O.T. #237.367-026 • OES #55305 • LAND-LEASE-INFORMATION CLERK. Furnishes information to public concerning status of state-owned lands for lease, and assists applicants to file documents required to lease land: Answers public inquiries concerning types of land leases available. Furnishes current information concerning land classification, withdrawals from market, or mineral reservations. Assists applicant in completing required documents. Examines applications, transfers, and supporting documents for conformance with agency specifications. Processes documents, collects fees, and maintains history ledgers of state-owned land. • **GED:** R4, M3, L4 • **SVP:** 2-4 yrs • **Academic:** Ed=H, Eng=G • **Work Field:** 282 • **MPSMS:** 959 • **Aptitudes:** G3, V3, N3, S4, P3, Q2, K5, F5, M4, E5, C5 • **Temperaments:** M, P • **Stress:** E • **Physical:** V=N, H=L, L=S, H • **Work Env:** I • **Salary:** 2 • **Outlook:** 3

MUSEUM ATTENDANT (museum) • D.O.T. #109.367-010 • OES #31511 • Conducts operation of museum and provides information about regulations, facilities, and exhibits to visitors: Opens museum at designated hours, greets visitors, and invites visitors to sign guest register. Monitors visitors viewing exhibits, cautions persons not complying with museum regulations, distributes promotional materials, and answers questions concerning exhibits, regulations, and facilities. Arranges tours of facility for schools or other groups, and schedules volunteers or other staff members to conduct tours. Examines exhibit facilities and collection objects periodically and notifies museum professional personnel or governing body when need for repair or replacement is observed. • **GED:** R4, M3, L4 • **SVP:** 30 days-3 mos • **Academic:** Ed=H, Eng=S • **Work Field:** 231, 282, 293 • **MPSMS:** 933 • **Aptitudes:** G3, V3, N4, S4, P3, Q3, K3, F4, M4, E5, C5 • **Temperaments:** P, V • **Stress:** E • **Physical:** V=L, H=L, L=S, W • **Work Env:** I • **Salary:** 2 • **Outlook:** 2

POLICYHOLDER-INFORMATION CLERK (insurance) • D.O.T. #249.262-010 • OES #55305 • CORRESPONDENT; CUSTOMER-SERVICE CLERK. Analyzes and answers requests by mail, telephone, or in person from policyholders, beneficiaries, or others for information concerning insurance policies: Searches company records to obtain information requested by customer. Estimates loan or cash value of policy for policyholders, using rate books and calculating machine. Interprets policy provisions to determine methods of effecting desired changes, such as change of beneficiary or type of insurance, or change in method of payment. Mails or gives out specified forms and routes completed forms to various units for processing. Analyzes policy transactions and corrects company records to adjust errors. May compose formal synopses of company and competitor policies for use by sales force. May provide information for pensioners and be designated PENSIONHOLDER-INFORMATION CLERK (insurance). • **GED:** R4, M2, L4 • **SVP:** 1-2 yrs • **Academic:** Ed=N, Eng=G • **Work Field:** 282 • **MPSMS:** 895 • **Aptitudes:** G2, V2, N3, S5, P4, Q2, K4, F4, M4, E5, C5 • **Temperaments:** M, P, T • **Stress:** E • **Physical:** V=N, H=L, L=S, H • **Work Env:** I • **Salary:** 3 • **Outlook:** 3

RECEPTIONIST (clerical) • D.O.T. #237.367-038 • OES #55305 • RECEPTION CLERK. Receives callers at establishment, determines nature of business, and directs callers to destination: Obtains caller's name and arranges for appointment with person called upon. Directs caller to destination and records name, time of call, nature of business, and person called upon. May issue visitor's pass when required. May make future appointments and answer inquiries [INFORMATION CLERK (clerical)]. May perform variety of clerical duties [ADMINISTRATIVE CLERK (clerical)] and other duties pertinent to type of establishment. May collect and distribute mail and messages. May receive patients in office of DENTIST (medical ser.); PHYSICIAN (medical ser.), or other health service, and be designated as OUTPATIENT RECEPTIONIST (medical ser.) or RECEPTIONIST, DOCTOR'S OFFICE (medical ser.). • **GED:** R3, M2, L3 • **SVP:** 6 mos-1 yr • **Academic:** Ed=N, Eng=G • **Work Field:** 231, 282 • **MPSMS:** 899 • **Aptitudes:** G3, V3, N4, S4, P4, Q3, K4, F4, M4, E5, C5 • **Temperaments:** P, R • **Stress:** E, T • **Physical:** V=N, H=G, L=S, H • **Work Env:** I • **Salary:** 2 • **Outlook:** 3

GOE: 07.04.05 Information Transmitting & Receiving

AIRLINE-RADIO OPERATOR (air trans.) • D.O.T. #193.262-010 • OES #39008 • Transmits and receives messages between station and aircraft or other ground stations by radiotelephone: Sends meteorological data to aircraft by radio telephone. Relays by telegraphic typewriter to DISPATCHER (air trans.) transmissions from aircraft, such as number of passengers aboard, estimated time of arrival, mechanical condition of plane, and requests for repairs. Relays instructions of air traffic control centers to airplane when communication fails. Makes connections between telephone and radio equipment to permit direct communication between DISPATCHER (air trans.) and airplane. Must be licensed by Federal Communications Commission. • **GED:** R4, M4, L4 • **SVP:** 2-4 yrs • **Academic:** Ed=H, Eng=G • **Work Field:** 281 • **MPSMS:** 860 • **Aptitudes:** G2, V2, N3, S4, P3, Q2, K3, F2, M2, E5, C4 • **Temperaments:** M, P, V • **Physical:** V=N, H=G, L=S, H • **Work Env:** I • **Salary:** 4 • **Outlook:** 2

ALARM OPERATOR (gov. ser.) • D.O.T. #379.162-010 • OES #58002 • FIRE-ALARM DISPATCHER. Operates municipal fire alarm system, radio transmitter and receiver, and telephone switchboard: Receives incoming fire calls by telephone or through alarm system. Questions caller, observes alarm register that codes location of fire, and scans map of city to determine whether fire is located within area served by city fire department. Determines type and number of units to respond to emergency. Notifies fire station, using radio, and starts alarm system that automatically contacts all fire stations and indicates location of fire. Relays messages from scene of fire, such as requests for additional help and medical assistance. Records date, time, type of call and destination of messages received or transmitted. Maintains activity, code, and locator files. Tests various communications systems and reports malfunctions to maintenance units. May operate telegraph to relay code as back-up if transmitter fails. • **GED:** R4, M3, L4 • **SVP:** 1-2 yrs • **Academic:** Ed=H, Eng=S • **Work Field:** 281 • **MPSMS:** 860, 951 • **Aptitudes:** G3, V3, N3, S4, P4, Q3, K4, F3, M4, E5, C4 • **Temperaments:** D, P, S • **Stress:** E, S • **Physical:** V=N, H=L, L=S, H • **Work Env:** I • **Salary:** 3 • **Outlook:** 2

DISPATCHER, MAINTENANCE SERVICE (clerical) • D.O.T. #239.367-014 • OES #58005 • DISPATCHER; MAINTENANCE CLERK. Receives telephone and written orders from plant departments for maintenance service, such as repair work, machine adjustments, and renewals or installation of other plant property, and relays requests to appropriate maintenance division. Keeps record of requests and services rendered. Requisitions supplies for maintenance and clerical workers. • **GED:** R3, M2, L3 • **SVP:** 30 days-3 mos • **Academic:** Ed=N, Eng=G • **Work Field:** 231 • **MPSMS:** 891 • **Aptitudes:** G3, V3, N3, S4, P4, Q3, K4, F4, M4, E5, C5 • **Temperaments:** R • **Stress:** T • **Physical:** V=N, H=L, L=S, H • **Work Env:** I • **Salary:** 2 • **Outlook:** 2

FIRE LOOKOUT (forestry) • D.O.T. #452.367-010 • OES #63005 • WATCHER, LOOKOUT TOWER. Locates and reports forest fires and weather phenomena from remote fire-lookout station: Maintains surveillance from station to detect evidence of fires and observe weather conditions. Locates fires on area map, using azimuth sighter and known landmarks, estimates size and characteristics of fire, and reports findings to base camp by radio or telephone. Observes instruments and reports daily meteorological data, such as temperature, relative humidity, wind direction and velocity, and type of cloud formations. Relays messages from base camp, mobile units, and law enforcement and governmental agencies relating to weather forecasts, fire hazard conditions, emergencies, accidents, and location of crews and personnel. Explains state and Federal laws, timber company policies, fire hazard conditions, and fire prevention methods to visitors of forest. Maintains records and logbooks. • **GED:** R3, M2, L3 • **SVP:** 6 mos-1 yr • **Academic:** Ed=N, Eng=S • **Work Field:** 293 • **MPSMS:** 313 • **Aptitudes:** G3, V3, N4, S3, P3, Q3, K4, F4, M4, E4, C3 • **Temperaments:** M, S • **Stress:** S • **Physical:** V=L, H=L, L=L, W, C, H • **Work Env:** B • **Salary:** 1 • **Outlook:** 3

FLIGHT-INFORMATION EXPEDITER (air trans.) • D.O.T. #912.367-010 • OES #58008 • Determines flight times of airplanes and transmits information to flight operations and Air Traffic Command centers: Evaluates data, such as weather conditions, flight plans, ramp delays, and enroute stopovers, to determine arrival and departure times for each flight, using aids, such as weather charts, slide rule, and computer. Transmits identity and type of airplane, flight locations, time of arrival and departure, and names of crew members to Air Traffic Command to obtain clearance for flight over restricted areas. Notifies departments of airline of pending arrival of inbound flight to ensure that personnel are available to load or unload fuel, baggage, and cargo. • **GED:** R4, M4, L4 • **SVP:** 6 mos- 1 yr • **Academic:** Ed=N, Eng=G • **Work Field:** 211, 231 • **MPSMS:** 855 • **Aptitudes:** G3, V3, N3, S4, P3, Q3, K4, F4, M4, E5, C4 • **Temperaments:** M, P, V • **Stress:** E • **Physical:** V=L, H=G, L=L, H • **Work Env:** I • **Salary:** 3 • **Outlook:** 3

POLICE AIDE (gov. ser.) • D.O.T. #243.362-014 • OES #55347 • Performs any combination of following tasks in police department to relieve police officers of clerical duties: Types and files police forms. Posts information to police records, by hand, typewriter, or keypunch machine. Gives information to public, over phone or in person, concerning arrests, missing persons, or other police related business. Operates telephone switchboard to take or relay information. Operates computer terminal to input and retrieve information into and from computer. May be designated by work location as STATION-HOUSE CLERK (gov. ser.). • **GED:** R3, M2, L3 • **SVP:** 30 days-3 mos • **Academic:** Ed=H, Eng=G • **Work Field:** 231, 282 • **MPSMS:** 951 • **Aptitudes:** G3, V3, N4, S5, P4, Q3, K4, F4, M4, E5, C5 • **Temperaments:** P, V • **Stress:** E • **Physical:** V=N, H=L, L=S • **Work Env:** I • **Salary:** 2 • **Outlook:** 3

PROTECTIVE-SIGNAL OPERATOR (any ind.) • D.O.T. #379.362-014 • OES #57199 • ALARM-SIGNAL OPERATOR; DROP-BOARD OPERATOR; DX BOARD OPERATOR; OPERATOR, CIRCUIT; OPERATOR, DIRECT WIRE; SIGNAL TIMER. Reads and records coded signals received in central station of electrical protective signaling system: Interprets coded audible or visible signals received on alarm signal board by direct wire or register tape from subscribers' premises that indicate opening and closing of protected premises, progress of security guard, unlawful intrusions, or fire. Reports irregular signals for corrective action. Reports alarms to police or fire department. Posts changes of subscriber opening and closing schedules. Prepares daily alarm activity and subscriber service reports. May adjust central station equipment to ensure uninterrupted service. May dispatch security personnel to premises after receiving alarm. • **GED:** R3, M2, L3 • **SVP:** 6 mos-1 yr • **Academic:** Ed=N, Eng=S • **Work Field:** 231, 281, 293 • **MPSMS:** 899 • **Aptitudes:** G3, V3, N3, S3, P3, Q3, K3, F3, M4, E5, C3 • **Temperaments:** M, P, S, V • **Stress:** E, S • **Physical:** V=L, H=L, L=S, H • **Work Env:** I • **Salary:** 3 • **Outlook:** 2

SCOREBOARD OPERATOR (amuse. & rec.) • D.O.T. #349.665-010 • OES #69999 • Watches players and officials at athletic event and posts or moves indicators and buttons to record progress of game on scoreboard to inform spectators. Confers, by telephone, with ANNOUNCER (amuse. & rec.) or sideline officials to verify observation of plays. • **GED:** R3, M2, L3 • **SVP:** 2-30 days • **Academic:** Ed=N, Eng=S • **Work Field:** 281 • **MPSMS:** 914 • **Aptitudes:** G3, V3, N4, S4, P3, Q4, K3, F5, M4, E5, C5 • **Temperaments:** R, T • **Stress:** T • **Physical:** V=L, H=N, L=S, H • **Work Env:** B • **Salary:** 1 • **Outlook:** 2

SERVICE CLERK (clerical) • D.O.T. #221.367-070 • OES #58005 • REPAIR-SERVICE CLERK; SERVICE-ORDER DISPATCHER. Receives, records, and distributes work orders to service crews upon customers' requests for service on articles or utilities purchased from wholesale or retail establishment or utility company: Records information, such as name, address, article to be repaired, or service to be rendered. Prepares work order and distributes to service crew. Schedules service call and dispatches service crew. Calls or writes customer to ensure satisfactory performance of service. Keeps record of service calls and work orders. May dispatch orders and relay messages and special instructions to mobile crews and other departments, using radio-telephone equipment. • **GED:** R3, M2, L2 • **SVP:** 3-6 mos • **Academic:** Ed=N, Eng=G • **Work Field:** 231 • **MPSMS:** 898 • **Aptitudes:** G3, V3, N4, S4, P4, Q3, K4, F4, M4, E5, C5 • **Temperaments:** P, V • **Stress:** E •

Physical: V=N, H=L, L=S, H • **Work Env:** I • **Salary:** 2 • **Outlook:** 3

SWITCHBOARD OPERATOR, POLICE DISTRICT (gov. ser.) • D.O.T. #235.562-014 • OES #57102 • Operates switch board to receive and transmit police communications: Talks to police officers reporting from callboxes and records messages on special forms. Enters time of call and callbox number. Telephones for ambulances or fire-fighting equipment when requested. Routes messages for radio broadcast to DISPATCHER, RADIO (gov. ser.). • **GED:** R3, M1, L2 • **SVP:** 3-6 mos • **Academic:** Ed=N, Eng=G • **Work Field:** 281 • **MPSMS:** 861 • **Aptitudes:** G3, V3, N4, S4, P4, Q4, K3, F3, M3, E5, C5 • **Temperaments:** P, R • **Stress:** E, T • **Physical:** V=N, H=L, L=L, H • **Work Env:** I • **Salary:** 3 • **Outlook:** 3

TELECOMMUNICATOR (gov. ser.) • D.O.T. #379.362-018 • OES #58002 • DISPATCHER. Operates communication equipment to receive incoming calls for assistance and dispatches personnel and equipment to scene of emergency: Operates telephone console to receive incoming calls for assistance. Questions caller to determine nature of problem and type and number of personnel and equipment needed, following established guidelines. Scans status charts and computer screen to determine units available. Monitors alarm system signals that indicate location of fire or other emergency. Operates two-way radio to dispatch police, fire, medical, and other personnel and equipment and to relay instructions or information to remove units. Types commands on computer keyboard to update files and maintain logs. Tests communications and alarm equipment and backup systems to ensure serviceability. May provide pre-arrival instructions to caller, utilizing knowledge of emergency medical techniques. May activate alarm system to notify fire stations. • **GED:** R4, M2, L4 • **SVP:** 6 mos-1 yr • **Academic:** Ed=H, Eng=G • **Work Field:** 281 • **MPSMS:** 861 • **Aptitudes:** G2, V2, N4, S3, P3, Q2, K3, F3, M3, E5, C5 • **Temperaments:** J, P, S, V • **Stress:** E, S • **Physical:** V=L, H=L, L=S, H • **Work Env:** I • **Salary:** 3 • **Outlook:** 2

TRAIN DISPATCHER (r.r. trans.) • D.O.T. #184.167-262 • OES #81011 • CTC OPERATOR; DISPATCHER; TRAFFIC-CONTROL OPERATOR. Coordinates railroad traffic on specified section of line from CTC (centralized-traffic-control) unit that electrically activates track switches and signals: Reads train orders and schedules to familiarize self with scheduled runs, destination of trains, times of arrivals and departures, and priority of trains. Monitors CTC panelboard that indicates location of trains by lights that illuminate as train passes specified positions on run. Operates controls to activate track switches and traffic signals. Reroutes trains or signals LOCOMOTIVE ENGINEER (r.r. trans.) to stop train or change speed according to traffic conditions. Talks by telephone with crew members to relay changes in train orders and schedules, and to receive notification of emergency stops, delays, or accidents. Records time each train reaches specified point, time messages are given or received, and name of person giving or receiving message. May chart train movements on graph to estimate arrival times at specified points. May operate teletypewriter to transmit messages to freight offices or other points along line. • **GED:** R4, M3, L4 • **SVP:** 2-4 yrs • **Academic:** Ed=H, Eng=S • **Work Field:** 013, 281 • **MPSMS:** 851 • **Aptitudes:** G2, V3, N3, S4, P3, Q3, K4, F4, M4, E5, C4 • **Temperaments:** D, M, P, T • **Stress:** A • **Physical:** V=L, H=L, L=S • **Work Env:** I • **Salary:** 4 • **Outlook:** 1

UTILITY CLERK (light, heat, & power) • D.O.T. #239.367-034 • OES #55335 • Responds to telephone requests for information concerning location of underground utility distribution lines: Informs construction contractors and others excavating near company installations of buried line locations to prevent safety hazards and damage to company equipment, utilizing plat and distribution line maps. Updates maps to indicate extensions and revisions of utility distribution lines within specified jurisdiction. May relay telephone reports of gas emergencies to specified personnel [GAS-DISTRIBUTION-AND-EMERGENCY CLERK (light, heat, & power) 249.367-042] or radio customer service requests to mobile service crews, using two-way radio. May issue tools and parts used by company work crews [STOCK CLERK (clerical) 222.387-058]. • **GED:** R4, M3, L3 • **SVP:** 6 mos-1 yr • **Academic:** Ed=H, Eng=G

• **Work Field:** 282 • **MPSMS:** 870 • **Aptitudes:** G3, V3, N3, S4, P4, Q2, K3, F4, M3, E5, C4 • **Temperaments:** P, T • **Stress:** E • **Physical:** V=L, H=L, L=L, H • **Work Env:** I • **Salary:** 3 • **Outlook:** 3

GOE: 07.04.06 Switchboard Services

CENTRAL-OFFICE OPERATOR (tel. & tel.) • D.O.T. #235.462-010 • OES #57108 • SWITCHBOARD OPERATOR; TELEPHONE OPERATOR. Operates telephone switchboard to establish or assist customers in establishing local or long-distance telephone connections: Observes signal light on switchboard, plugs cords into trunk-jack, and dials or presses button to make connections. Inserts tickets in calculagraph (time-stamping device) to record time of toll calls. Consults charts to determine charges for pay-telephone calls, and requests coin deposits for calls. May give information regarding subscribers' telephone numbers [DIRECTORY-ASSISTANCE OPERATOR (tel. & tel.)]. Calculates and quotes charges on long-distance calls. May make long-distance connections and be designated LONG-DISTANCE OPERATOR (tel. & tel.). • **GED:** R3, M1, L3 • **SVP:** 30 days- 3 mos • **Academic:** Ed=N, Eng=G • **Work Field:** 281 • **MPSMS:** 861 • **Aptitudes:** G3, V3, N4, S4, P5, Q3, K3, F3, M3, E5, C5 • **Temperaments:** P, R • **Stress:** E, T • **Physical:** V=N, H=G, L=S, H • **Work Env:** I • **Salary:** 3 • **Outlook:** 3

DIRECTORY-ASSISTANCE OPERATOR (tel. & tel.) • D.O.T. #235.662-018 • OES #57105 • Provides telephone information from cord or cordless central office switchboard: Plugs in headphones when signal light flashes on cord switch board, or pushes switch keys on cordless switchboard to make connections. Refers to alphabetical or geographical reels or directories to answer questions and suggests alternate locations and spelling under which number could be listed. May type location and spelling of name on computer terminal keyboard, and scan directory or microfilm viewer to locate number. May keep record of calls received. May keep reels and directories up to date. • **GED:** R3, M2, L3 • **SVP:** 30 days-3 mos • **Academic:** Ed=N, Eng=G • **Work Field:** 282 • **MPSMS:** 861 • **Aptitudes:** G3, V3, N4, S4, P3, Q3, K3, F3, M3, E5, C5 • **Temperaments:** P, R • **Stress:** E, T • **Physical:** V=N, H=L, L=S, H • **Work Env:** I • **Salary:** 2 • **Outlook:** 3

TELEPHONE OPERATOR (clerical) • D.O.T. #235.662-022 • OES #57102 • CONTROL-BOARD OPERATOR; PBX OPERATOR; PRIVATE-BRANCH-EXCHANGE OPERATOR; SWITCHBOARD OPERATOR; TELEPHONE-SWITCHBOARD OPERATOR. Operates cord or cordless switch board to relay incoming, outgoing, and interoffice calls: On cordless switchboard, pushes switch keys to make connections and relay calls. On cord type equipment, plugs cord into switchboard jacks. May supply information to callers and record messages. May keep record of calls placed and toll charges. May perform clerical duties, such as typing, proofreading, and sorting mail. May operate system of bells or buzzers to call individuals in establishment to phone. May receive visitors, obtain name and nature of business, and schedule appointments [RECEPTIONIST (clerical)]. • **GED:** R3, M2, L3 • **SVP:** 30 days-3 mos • **Academic:** Ed=N, Eng=G • **Work Field:** 281 • **MPSMS:** 861 • **Aptitudes:** G3, V3, N4, S4, P3, Q4, K3, F3, M3, E5, C5 • **Temperaments:** P, R • **Stress:** E, T • **Physical:** V=N, H=L, L=S, H • **Work Env:** I • **Salary:** 2 • **Outlook:** 3

TELEPHONE-ANSWERING-SERVICE OPERATOR (bus. ser.) • D.O.T. #235.662-026 • OES #57102 • INTERCEPTOR OPERATOR; TELEPHONE-INTERCEPTOR OPERATOR. Operates cord or cord less switchboard to provide answering service for clients. Greets caller and announces name or phone number of client. Records and delivers messages, furnishes information, accepts orders, and relays calls. Places telephone calls at request of client and to locate client in emergencies. Date stamps and files messages. • **GED:** R3, M2, L3 • **SVP:** 30 days-3 mos • **Academic:** Ed=N, Eng=G • **Work Field:** 231, 281 • **MPSMS:** 861 • **Aptitudes:** G3, V3, N4, S4, P5, Q3, K3, F3, M3, E5, C5 • **Temperaments:** P, R • **Stress:** E, T • **Physical:** V=N, H=L, L=S, H • **Work Env:** I • **Salary:** 2 • **Outlook:** 3

07.05 Records Processing

Workers in this group prepare, review, maintain, route, distribute, and coordinate recorded information. They check records and schedules for accuracy. They may schedule the activities of people or the use of equipment. Jobs in this group are found in most businesses, institutions, and government agencies.

✔ **What kind of work would you do?**
Your work activities would depend upon your specific job. For example, you might:

- issue route slips to drivers to pick up items.
- file correspondence, cards, invoices, receipts, and other records.
- sort and deliver mail in a city or rural mail route.
- open and inspect incoming correspondence and packages and route them to proper person in an office.
- read typeset copy and mark errors in a publishing company.

- keep records of securities held as collateral by a bank.
- take dictation in shorthand and type letters or other documents from your notes.
- compile records showing cost and volume of advertising.
- compile, verify, and file medical records in a hospital.
- help to prepare duty rosters for crew members of scheduled airline flights.

✔ **What skills and abilities do you need for this kind of work?**
To do this kind of work, you must be able to:

- use specialized recordkeeping procedures.
- recognize errors in recorded information.

- plan the activities of others.
- perform work which may be routine or repetitive.

✔ **How do you know if you would like or could learn to do this kind of work?**
The following questions may give you clues about yourself as you consider this group of jobs.

- Have you taken business or office practice courses? Do you like to work with business forms and filing systems?
- Have you used the library card catalog to compile a report? Can you locate the information you need quickly and easily by using the library system?

- Have you collected stamps or coins? Do you have them classified and arranged according to a plan?
- Have you been in charge of records for a club or social group? Do you enjoy maintaining files?
- Have you have experience in the armed forces requiring processing or keeping information?

✔ **How can you prepare for and enter this kind of work?**
Occupations in this group usually require education and/or training extending from thirty days to over one year, depending upon the specific kind of work. A high school education or its equal is usually required. Special courses in language skills such as punctuation, grammar, and spelling, as well as basic math courses, are helpful. Some employers prefer workers who have completed general business or clerical courses. Training programs for many of these jobs are available through federal or state agencies.

On-the-job training, ranging from a short demonstration to a one-year program, may be provided. Through this training, workers become familiar with their duties.

Sometimes applicants are tested to determine their ability to do or to learn to do the tasks involved.

✔ What else should you consider about these jobs?

Many of these jobs offer advancement possibilities. Part-time or temporary work is usually available. Job duties are assigned to workers according to the size of the company.

If you think you would like to do this kind of work, look at the job titles listed on the following pages.

GOE: 07.05.01 Coordinating & Scheduling

ADVERTISING-DISPATCH CLERK (print. & pub.) • D.O.T. #247.387-014 • OES #58008 • SCHEDULE CLERK. Compiles and dispatches advertising schedule and material to composing room of daily or weekly publication: Reviews advertising order and prepares advertising schedule, listing size of ad, date(s) to appear, and page and position of ad. Searches advertising files and selects mat that corresponds to advertising layout. Dispatches mat, advertising layout and copy, and advertising schedule to composing department. Obtains advertising proofs from composing department and dispatches them to advertising department for proofreading. Maintains files of all advertising material. May proofread and correct advertising proofs. May read advertisement in first edition of publication for errors. • **GED:** R3, M2, L3 • **SVP:** 3-6 mos • **Academic:** Ed=N, Eng=G • **Work Field:** 231 • **MPSMS:** 480, 896 • **Aptitudes:** G3, V3, N4, S4, P3, Q2, K4, F4, M4, E5, C5 • **Temperaments:** R, T • **Stress:** T • **Physical:** V=N, H=N, L=S, H • **Work Env:** I • **Salary:** 2 • **Outlook:** 3

CREW SCHEDULER (air trans.) • D.O.T. #215.362-010 • OES #58008 • Compiles duty rosters of flight crews and maintains records of crew members' flying time for scheduled airline flights: Prepares flight register which crew members sign to indicate their preference and availability for flights and time they wish to be called prior to each flight. Types names of crew members onto flight schedule in order of seniority to indicate flights to which crew members are assigned. Posts names of extra crew members in order of seniority on reserve list. Selects replacements from reserve list and notifies replacement when needed. Computes and logs cumulative flight time for crew members and removes crew member's name from flight schedule when flying time limit, as prescribed by Federal Aviation Administration, has been reached. Schedules vacations as requested by crew members. May notify crew members of assignments, using telephone. • **GED:** R3, M3, L3 • **SVP:** 6 mos-1 yr • **Academic:** Ed=N, Eng=S • **Work Field:** 232 • **MPSMS:** 898 • **Aptitudes:** G3, V3, N3, S4, P3, Q3, K4, F3, M4, E5, C5 • **Temperaments:** R, T • **Stress:** T • **Physical:** V=L, H=N, L=S, H • **Work Env:** I • **Salary:** 3 • **Outlook:** 3

DISPATCHER, MOTOR VEHICLE (clerical) • D.O.T. #249.167-014 • OES #58005 • Assigns motor vehicles and drivers for conveyance of freight or passengers: Compiles list of available vehicles. Assigns vehicles according to factors, such as length and purpose of trip, freight or passenger requirements, and preference of user. Issues keys, record sheets, and credentials to drivers. Records time of departure, destination, cargo, and expected time of return. Investigates overdue vehicles. May confer with customers to expedite or locate missing, misrouted, delayed, or damaged merchandise. May maintain record of mileage, fuel used, repairs made, and other expenses. May establish service or delivery routes. May supervise loading and unloading. May issue equipment to drivers, such as handtrucks, dollies, and blankets. May direct activities of drivers, using two-way radio. May assign helpers to drivers. May be designated according to type of motor vehicle dispatched as DISPATCHER, AUTOMOBILE RENTAL (auto. ser.); DISPATCHER, TOW TRUCK (auto. ser.). • **GED:** R3, M2, L3 • **SVP:** 6 mos-1 yr • **Academic:** Ed=N, Eng=G • **Work Field:** 231, 232 • **MPSMS:** 850 • **Aptitudes:** G3, V3, N4, S4, P4, Q3, K4, F4, M4, E5, C5 • **Temperaments:** D, P, V • **Stress:** E, A • **Physical:** V=N, H=L, L=S • **Work Env:** I • **Salary:** 3 • **Outlook:** 3

EXPEDITER (clerical) • D.O.T. #222.367-018 • OES #58008 • Contacts or writes vendors and shippers to ensure that merchandise, supplies, and equipment are forwarded on specified shipping date: Contacts vendor by mail, phone, or visit to verify shipment of goods on promised date or to ensure that goods will be shipped when promised. Communicates with transportation company to preclude delays in transit. May arrange for distribution of materials upon arrival. May contact vendors to requisition materials. May inspect products for quality and quantity to ensure adherence to specifications. • **GED:** R4, M3, L3 • **SVP:** 3-6 mos • **Academic:** Ed=H, Eng=G • **Work Field:** 221 • **MPSMS:** 898 • **Aptitudes:** G3, V3, N4, S5, P4, Q3, K4, F4, M4, E5, C5 • **Temperaments:** P • **Stress:** E • **Physical:** V=N, H=L, L=S, H • **Work Env:** I • **Salary:** 5 • **Outlook:** 3

GUIDE, TRAVEL (per. ser.) • D.O.T. #353.167-010 • OES #68017 • GUIDE, EXCURSION; GUIDE, ITINERARY; GUIDE, TOUR. Arranges transportation and other accommodations for groups of tourists, following planned itinerary, and escorts groups during entire trip, within single area or at specified stopping points of tour: Makes reservations on ships, trains, and other modes of transportation, and arranges for other accommodations, such as baggage handling, dining and lodging facilities, and recreational activities, using communication media, such as cable, telegraph, or telephone. Accompanies tour group and describes points of interest. May assist tourists to plan itinerary, obtain travel certificates, such as visas, passports, and health certificates, and convert currency into travelers' checks or foreign moneys. May be designated according to method of transportation used as GUIDE, CRUISE (per. ser.); or locality of tour as GUIDE, DOMESTIC TOUR (per. ser.); GUIDE, FOREIGN TOUR (per. ser.). • **GED:** R4, M3, L4 • **SVP:** 1-2 yrs • **Academic:** Ed=N, Eng=G • **Work Field:** 282, 291 • **MPSMS:** 859 • **Aptitudes:** G2, V2, N3, S4, P4, Q3, K4, F4, M4, E5, C4 • **Temperaments:** D, P, V • **Stress:** E, A • **Physical:** V=L, H=L, L=L, W, H • **Work Env:** I • **Salary:** 3 • **Outlook:** 1

PERSONNEL SCHEDULER (clerical) • D.O.T. #215.367-014 • OES #58008 • SCHEDULER AND PLANNER. Compiles weekly personnel assignment schedules for production department in manufacturing plant: Studies production schedules and staffing tables to ascertain personnel requirements. Determines and records work assignments according to worker availability, seniority, job classification, and preferences. Compiles and oversees in-plant distribution of work schedule. Adjusts schedules to meet emergencies caused by extended leave or increased production demands. Compiles annual seniority lists on which employees indicate vacation preferences and approves leave requests to prevent production losses. • **GED:** R4, M3, L3 • **SVP:** 3-6 mos • **Academic:** Ed=N, Eng=S • **Work Field:** 232 • **MPSMS:** 898 • **Aptitudes:** G3, V3, N3, S4, P4, Q2, K3, F3, M4, E5, C5 • **Temperaments:** M, T • **Physical:** V=L, H=N, L=S, H • **Work Env:** I • **Salary:** 3 • **Outlook:** 3

POLICE CLERK (gov. ser.) • D.O.T. #375.362-010 • OES #55347 • Compiles daily duty roster and types and maintains various records and reports in municipal police department to document information, such as daily work assignments, equipment issued, vacation scheduled, training records, and personnel data: Prepares duty roster to indicate such personnel information as days on, days off, equipment assigned, and watch. Arranges schedule to most efficiently use personnel and equipment and ensure availability of personnel for court dates. Submits roster to superior for approval. Compiles and records data to maintain personnel folders. Reviews duty roster, personnel folders, and training schedules to schedule training for police personnel. Performs other duties as described under POLICE AIDE (gov. ser.) 243.362-014. • **GED:** R4, M3, L3 • **SVP:** 1-2 yrs • **Academic:** Ed=H, Eng=G • **Work Field:** 231, 293 • **MPSMS:** 951 • **Aptitudes:** G3, V3, N3, S4, P3, Q3, K2, F3, M4, E5, C5 • **Temperaments:** T • **Physical:** V=L, H=N, L=S, H • **Work Env:** I • **Salary:** 3 • **Outlook:** 2

RESERVATION CLERK (clerical) • D.O.T. #238.362-014 • OES #53802 • CLERK, TRAVEL RESERVATIONS; TRAVEL CLERK. Obtains travel and hotel accommodations for guests and employees of industrial concern, issues tickets, types itineraries, and compiles reports of transactions: Obtains confirmation of travel and lodging space and rate information. Issues and validates airline tickets from stock or teleticketer and obtains rail and bus tickets from carriers. Prepares passenger travel booklet containing tickets, copy of itinerary, written lodging confirmations, pertinent credit cards, and travel suggestions. Keeps current directory of hotels, motels, and timetables, and answers inquiries concerning routes, fares, and accommodations. Reviews routine invoices of transportation charges, and types and submits reports to company and to transportation agencies. Prepares and types claim forms for refunds and adjustments and reports of transactions processed. • GED: R3, M3, L3 • SVP: 6 mos-1 yr • Academic: Ed=H, Eng=G • Work Field: 282, 291 • MPSMS: 859 • Aptitudes: G3, V3, N3, S4, P4, Q2, K2, F3, M3, E5, C5 • Temperaments: P, T, V • Stress: E • Physical: V=N, H=G, L=S, H • Work Env: I • Salary: 4 • Outlook: 2

SCHEDULER (museum) • D.O.T. #238.367-034 • OES #55305 • EDUCATION DEPARTMENT REGISTRAR; MUSEUM SERVICE SCHEDULER. Makes reservations and accepts payment for group tours, classes, field trips, and other educational activities offered by museum, zoo, or similar establishment: Provides information regarding tours for school, civic, or other groups, suggests tours on institution calendar, and contacts group leaders prior to scheduled dates to confirm reservations. Provides information regarding classes, workshops, field trips, and other educational programs designed for such special groups as school or college students, teachers, or handicapped persons. Registers groups and individuals for participation in programs, enters registration information in department records, and contacts participants prior to program dates to confirm registration and provide preparatory information. Prepares lists of groups scheduled for tours and persons registered for other activities for use of DIRECTOR, EDUCATION (museum) 099.117-030 or other personnel. Collects and records receipts of fees for tours, classes, and other activities. Maintains records of participating groups, fees received, and other data related to educational programs for use in preparation of department reports. May take reservations and sell advance tickets to exhibits, concerts, and other events sponsored by institution, prepare periodic summaries of department activities for review by administrative personnel, or arrange for various support services to facilitate presentation of special activities. • GED: R3, M3, L3 • SVP: 30 days-3 mos • Academic: Ed=H, Eng=G • Work Field: 232, 282 • MPSMS: 939 • Aptitudes: G3, V3, N3, S4, P4, Q2, K3, F3, M3, E5, C5 • Temperaments: J, P, V • Stress: E • Physical: V=L, H=N, L=S, H • Work Env: I • Salary: 3 • Outlook: 3

SCHEDULER, MAINTENANCE (clerical) • D.O.T. #221.367-066 • OES #58008 • DISPATCHER, MAINTENANCE. Schedules repairs and lubrication of motor vehicles for vehicle-maintenance concern or company automotive-service shop: Schedules vehicles for lubrication or repairs based on date of last lubrication and mileage traveled or urgency of repairs. Contacts garage to verify availability of facilities. Notifies parking garage workers to deliver specified vehicles. Maintains file of requests for services. • GED: R3, M2, L3 • SVP: 3-6 mos • Academic: Ed=N, Eng=S • Work Field: 231 • MPSMS: 591 • Aptitudes: G3, V3, N3, S4, P4, Q3, K4, F4, M4, E5, C5 • Temperaments: P • Stress: E • Physical: V=N, H=L, L=S, H • Work Env: I • Salary: 2 • Outlook: 3

TELEVISION-SCHEDULE COORDINATOR (radio & tv broad.) • D.O.T. #199.387-010 • OES #59999 • LOG OPERATIONS COORDINATOR; PROGRAM SCHEDULE CLERK. Prepares daily operations schedules and advance program log for newspapers, magazines, and traffic department: Provides for clearance and rotation of spot-commercial films and slides for television programs, and performs related clerical duties for DIRECTOR, PROGRAM (radio & tv broad.). May compose courtesy, apology, and stay-tuned announcements. • GED: R4, M3, L4 • SVP: 3-6 mos • Academic: Ed=H, Eng=S • Work Field: 231 • MPSMS: 863 • Aptitudes: G3, V3, N3, S4, P4, Q2, K4, F4, M4, E5, C5 • Temperaments: M, T • Physical: V=L, H=L, L=S, H • Work Env: I • Salary: 3 • Outlook: 3

TRAFFIC CLERK (bus. ser.) • D.O.T. #221.367-078 • OES #58008 • Compiles schedules and control records on work in process in advertising agency to ensure completion of artwork, copy, and layouts prior to deadline and notifies staff and clients of schedule changes: Keeps schedules and records on work to ensure arrival of printing and artwork, as needed, and to ensure completion of copy. Contacts vendors and notifies agency personnel and clients of changes in schedules. • GED: R4, M2, L3 • SVP: 3-6 mos • Academic: Ed=N, Eng=S • Work Field: 231 • MPSMS: 896, 898 • Aptitudes: G3, V3, N4, S4, P4, Q3, K4, F4, M4, E5, C5 • Temperaments: P, T • Stress: E • Physical: V=N, H=L, L=S • Work Env: I • Salary: 2 • Outlook: 3

TRANSPORTATION AGENT (air trans.) • D.O.T. #912.367-014 • OES #58011 • DEPARTURE CLERK; OPERATIONS AGENT; SERVICE COORDINATOR. Expedites movement of freight, mail, baggage, and passengers through airline terminal by performing following tasks: Prepares airway bill of lading on freight from consignors and routes freight on first available flight. Telephones consignees to report arrival of air freight. Obtains flight number, airplane number, and names of crew members from teletyped message of DISPATCHER (air trans.), and records data on airplane's flight papers. Records baggage, mail, and freight weights, and number of passengers on airplane's papers and teletypes data to flight's destination. Positions ramp for loading of airplane. Verifies passengers' tickets as they board plane. Oversees or participates in loading cargo to ensure completeness of load and even distribution of weight. Removes ramp, and signals pilot that personnel and equipment are clear of plane. May load and unload freight and baggage by operating forklift truck. • GED: R3, M3, L3 • SVP: 6 mos-1 yr • Academic: Ed=N, Eng=G • Work Field: 221, 281 • MPSMS: 855 • Aptitudes: G3, V3, N3, S4, P4, Q3, K3, F3, M3, E4, C4 • Temperaments: P, V • Stress: E • Physical: V=L, H=G, L=L, W, H • Work Env: B, N • Salary: 3 • Outlook: 3

GOE: 07.05.02 Record Verification & Proofing

BRAILLE PROOFREADER (nonprofit org.) • D.O.T. #209.367-014 • OES #53911 • Verifies proof copy of braille transcription against original script, such as pamphlet, book, or newspaper, to detect grammatical, typographical, or compositional errors and marks proof for correction: Reads original script to compare it with proof copy (if sighted); or listens to reading or recording of original and slides fingers over braille characters to feel discrepancies in proof (if blind). Consults reference books or secures aid of reader to check references to rules of grammar and composition. Marks proof with braille stylus or pencil to correct errors, using standard printers' marks. May direct workers in use of braille slates (printing devices). May select material for transcription. • GED: R4, M1, L4 • SVP: 6 mos-1 yr • Academic: Ed=H, Eng=G • Work Field: 261 • MPSMS: 898 • Aptitudes: G2, V2, N4, S3, P3, Q2, K4, F4, M4, E5, C5 • Temperaments: M, T • Physical: V=N, H=L, L=S, H • Work Env: I • Salary: 3 • Outlook: 3

CLASSIFIED-AD CLERK 2 (print. & pub.) • D.O.T. #247.387-022 • OES #53908 • CLASSIFIED-COPY-CONTROL CLERK. Examines and marks classified advertisements of newspaper according to copy sheet specifications to guide composing room in assembling type: Marks advertisements that have expired and indicates number of days others are to continue, using classified file copy and copy sheet for current day. Computes and records total number of lines expired and number of lines for new advertisements. • GED: R3, M3, L2 • SVP: 6 mos-1 yr • Academic: Ed=N, Eng=G • Work Field: 231 • MPSMS: 898 • Aptitudes: G3, V3, N3, S5, P4, Q2, K4, F4, M4, E5, C5 • Temperaments: R, T • Stress: T • Physical: V=L, H=N, L=S, H • Work Env: I • Salary: 2 • Outlook: 3

CREDIT AUTHORIZER (clerical) • D.O.T. #249.367-022 • OES #53114 • AUTHORIZER; CHARGE-ACCOUNT AUTHORIZER. Authorizes credit charges against customer's account: Receives charge slip or credit application by mail, or receives information from salespeople or merchants over telephone. Verifies credit standing of customer from information in files, and approves or disapproves credit, based on predetermined standards. May file sales slips in customer's ledger for billing purposes. May prepare credit cards or charge account plates. May keep record of customer's charges and payments and mail charge statement to customer. • **GED:** R3, M2, L2 • **SVP:** 30 days-3 mos • **Academic:** Ed=N, Eng=G • **Work Field:** 231, 282 • **MPSMS:** 894 • **Aptitudes:** G3, V3, N4, S5, P4, Q3, K3, F4, M4, E5, C5 • **Temperaments:** M, P • **Stress:** E • **Physical:** V=L, H=N, L=S • **Work Env:** I • **Salary:** 2 • **Outlook:** 3

CREDIT-REFERENCE CLERK (ret. tr.) • D.O.T. #209.362-018 • OES #53117 • Telephones or writes to references listed on application form to investigate credit standing of applicant. Verifies information on previous employment with employers. Operates typewriter to record information received on credit application form. Reciprocates credit information with credit bureaus. • **GED:** R3, M2, L3 • **SVP:** 3-6 mos • **Academic:** Ed=H, Eng=S • **Work Field:** 271 • **MPSMS:** 891, 894 • **Aptitudes:** G3, V3, N4, S4, P4, Q3, K2, F2, M3, E5, C5 • **Temperaments:** M, P, T • **Physical:** V=L, H=L, L=S, H • **Work Env:** I • **Salary:** 3 • **Outlook:** 4

DATA-EXAMINATION CLERK (clerical) • D.O.T. #209.387-022 • OES #59999 • Reviews input-and-output data to verify adequacy and appropriateness of material required for data-processing operations: Reviews worksheet listing materials required for specific data-processing project and accompanying source documents and materials to determine completeness of documents and adequacy and appropriateness of materials required, such as punch cards and tape reels or decks. Examines notations, code indications, and instructions written on source documents for legibility and to detect errors and verify conformance with established policies and specifications. Notifies supervisor when input data errors or shortages of documents or materials are detected, and corrects errors. Reviews corrected input data and output data, such as punched cards or computer printouts with source documents and worksheets to verify completeness, accuracy, and conformance to specifications. May be designated according to type of data examined as INPUT EXAMINER (clerical); OUTPUT EXAMINER (clerical). • **GED:** R4, M2, L3 • **SVP:** 30 days-3 mos • **Academic:** Ed=H, Eng=G • **Work Field:** 231 • **MPSMS:** 891 • **Aptitudes:** G3, V3, N4, S4, P3, Q2, K4, F4, M4, E5, C5 • **Temperaments:** M, T • **Physical:** V=L, H=N, L=S • **Work Env:** I • **Salary:** 2 • **Outlook:** 3

DISBURSEMENT CLERK (finan. inst.) • D.O.T. #209.367-022 • OES #53121 • Verifies accuracy of loan applications and prepares file for each loan transaction: Compares original application against credit report. Approves loan and prepares check. Delivers or mails check to branch office. Prepares loan worksheet, insurance record, credit report, and application copy for each loan. Compiles daily report of loan transactions. Prepares payment book and mails to customer. • **GED:** R3, M3, L3 • **SVP:** 3-6 mos • **Academic:** Ed=N, Eng=G • **Work Field:** 231 • **MPSMS:** 894 • **Aptitudes:** G3, V3, N3, S4, P3, Q3, K4, F4, M4, E5, C5 • **Temperaments:** M, T • **Physical:** V=L, H=N, L=S • **Work Env:** I • **Salary:** 3 • **Outlook:** 3

INVESTIGATOR, UTILITY-BILL COMPLAINTS (light, heat, & power) • D.O.T. #241.267-034 • OES #53123 • CUSTOMER-SERVICE REPRESENTATIVE. Investigates customers' bill complaints for gas and electric-power service: Examines weather reports for weather conditions during billing period that might have contributed to increased use of service. Examines meter reading schedules to determine if early readings increased billing period. Reviews meter books, microfilm, computer printouts, and machine accounting records for errors causing high bill. Orders tests to detect meter malfunctions. Confers with customer in person, by telephone, or dictates correspondence to explain reasons for high bill. Prepares forms required for correction of meter reading or billing errors. • **GED:** R4, M4, L4 • **SVP:** 1-2 yrs • **Academic:** Ed=H, Eng=G • **Work Field:** 271 • **MPSMS:** 891 • **Aptitudes:** G3, V3, N2, S4, P4, Q2, K4, F4, M4, E5, C4 • **Temperaments:** M, P • **Stress:** E • **Physical:** V=L, H=L, L=S • **Work Env:** I • **Salary:** 3 • **Outlook:** 4

LETTER-OF-CREDIT CLERK (finan. inst.) • D.O.T. #219.387-018 • OES #55338 • Accepts import and export letters of credit and advances or accepts payments: Studies terms of credit, such as amount, insurance coverage, and shipping conditions to determine mode of processing. Notifies exporters or importers of issuance of letters of credit covering shipments of merchandise. Verifies

items, such as endorsements, amounts and charges, interest, foreign exchange conversion rates, and pay drafts. Maintains file of borrower's resolutions, authorized signatures, and insurance policies. May translate correspondence into English or foreign language. • **GED:** R4, M3, L3 • **SVP:** 6 mos-1 yr • **Academic:** Ed=H, Eng=G • **Work Field:** 232 • **MPSMS:** 894 • **Aptitudes:** G3, V3, N3, S4, P4, Q3, K3, F2, M4, E5, C5 • **Temperaments:** R, T • **Stress:** T • **Physical:** V=L, H=N, L=S, H • **Work Env:** I • **Salary:** 3 • **Outlook:** 3

PRODUCTION PROOFREADER (print. & pub.) • D.O.T. #247.667-010 • OES #53911 • Compares proofs of store advertisements with original copy to detect errors in printed material. Reads proofs and corrects errors in type, arrangement, grammar, punctuation, or spelling, using proofreader's marks. Routes proofs with corrections to be reprinted and reads corrected proofs. • **GED:** R3, M2, L3 • **SVP:** 3-6 mos • **Academic:** Ed=N, Eng=G • **Work Field:** 211, 261 • **MPSMS:** 896 • **Aptitudes:** G3, V3, N4, S5, P4, Q1, K4, F4, M4, E5, C5 • **Temperaments:** M, T • **Physical:** V=L, H=N, L=S • **Work Env:** I • **Salary:** 3 • **Outlook:** 2

PROOFREADER (print. & pub.) • D.O.T. #209.387-030 • OES #53911 • Reads typescript (original copy) or proof of type set-up to detect and mark for correction any grammatical, typographical, or compositional errors, by either of following methods: (1) Places proof and copy side by side on reading board. Reads proof against copy, marking by standardized code, errors that appear in proof. Returns marked proof for correction and later checks corrected proof against copy. (2) Reads and corrects proof while COPY HOLDER (print. & pub.) reads aloud from original copy or reads proof aloud to COPY HOLDER (print. & pub.) who calls out discrepancies between proof and copy. May measure dimensions, spacing, and positioning of page elements (copy and illustrations) to verify conformance to specifications, using printer's ruler. • **GED:** R4, M1, L4 • **SVP:** 6 mos-1 yr • **Academic:** Ed=H, Eng=G • **Work Field:** 261 • **MPSMS:** 480 • **Aptitudes:** G2, V2, N4, S3, P3, Q2, K4, F4, M4, E5, C4 • **Temperaments:** M, T • **Physical:** V=L, H=N, L=S, H • **Work Env:** I • **Salary:** 3 • **Outlook:** 3

READER (bus. ser.) • D.O.T. #249.387-022 • OES #59999 • CLIPPING MARKER; PRESS READER; PRESS-SERVICE READER. Reads newspapers, magazines, and other periodicals for articles of prescribed subject matter, and marks items to be clipped, using colored pencils and customer code system. • **GED:** R3, M1, L3 • **SVP:** 3-6 mos • **Academic:** Ed=N, Eng=G • **Work Field:** 231 • **MPSMS:** 899 • **Aptitudes:** G3, V3, N4, S4, P4, Q3, K4, F4, M4, E5, C4 • **Temperaments:** M, R • **Stress:** T • **Physical:** V=L, H=N, L=S • **Work Env:** I • **Salary:** 2 • **Outlook:** 2

REVIEWER (insurance) • D.O.T. #209.687-018 • OES #53314 • FINAL-APPLICATION REVIEWER; NEW-BUSINESS CLERK; SALES-REVIEW CLERK. Reviews insurance applications to ensure that all questions have been answered. Corresponds with sales personnel to inform them of status of application being processed, and to encourage prompt delivery of policies to policyholders. May collect initial premiums and issue receipts. May compile periodic reports on new business for management. • **GED:** R3, M1, L3 • **SVP:** 3-6 mos • **Academic:** Ed=H, Eng=G • **Work Field:** 211, 231 • **MPSMS:** 895 • **Aptitudes:** G3, V3, N4, S4, P4, Q3, K4, F4, M4, E5, C5 • **Temperaments:** R • **Stress:** T • **Physical:** V=L, H=N, L=S, H • **Work Env:** I • **Salary:** 3 • **Outlook:** 3

THROW-OUT CLERK (ret. tr.) • D.O.T. #241.367-030 • OES #53117 • CHARGE-ACCOUNT IDENTIFICATION CLERK. Processes records of department-store transactions which cannot be applied to customer's account by routine procedures in order that charges, cash payments, and refunds may be recorded, collected, or credited: Reviews and talks to sales-audit, charge-account-authorization, and collection personnel to identify missing information or compare signatures on sales or credit slips. Telephones or writes to customers for additional information. Corrects or adds information to customer accounts as necessary. Mails dunning correspondence to customers in arrears on their charge accounts [COLLECTION CLERK (clerical)]. • **GED:** R3, M3, L3 • **SVP:** 3-6 mos • **Academic:** Ed=N, Eng=G • **Work Field:** 232, 271 • **MPSMS:** 894 • **Aptitudes:** G3, V3, N3, S5, P3, Q2, K4, F4, M4, E5, C5 • **Temperaments:** P • **Stress:** E • **Physical:** V=L, H=L, L=S • **Work Env:** I • **Salary:** 2 • **Outlook:** 3

TITLE SEARCHER (real estate) • D.O.T. #209.367-046 • OES #28308 • Searches public and private records and indices to compile list of legal instruments pertaining to property titles, such as mortgages, deeds, and assessments, for insurance, real estate, or tax purposes: Reads search request to ascertain type of title evidence required, and to obtain legal description of property and names of involved parties. Compares legal description of property with legal description contained in records and indices, to verify such factors as deed of ownership, tax code and parcel number, and description of property's bound aries. Requisitions maps or drawings delineating property from company title plant, county surveyor, or assessor's office. Compiles list of transactions pertaining to property, using address or name of owner to search lot books, geographic and general indices, or assessor's rolls. Records date of transaction, name of involved parties, and source of documents in chronological order on work sheets, and indicates judgments, mechanics liens, or other factors which affect title to property. May specialize in searching tax records and be designated as TAX SEARCHER (real estate). • **GED:** R3, M1, L3 • **SVP:** 6 mos-1 yr • **Academic:** Ed=N, Eng=G • **Work Field:** 231, 271 • **MPSMS:** 895 • **Aptitudes:** G3, V3, N3, S4, P4, Q2, K4, F4, M4, E5, C5 • **Temperaments:** M, T • **Physical:** V=L, H=N, L=S, W, S, H • **Work Env:** I • **Salary:** 3 • **Outlook:** 3

GOE: 07.05.03 Record Preparation & Maintenance

ASSIGNMENT CLERK (clerical) • D.O.T. #249.367-090 • OES #55314 • Compiles data to notify establishment personnel of position vacancies and identifies and assigns qualified applicants, following specified guidelines and procedures: Scans reports to detect listings of vacancies or receives telephone notices of vacancies from establishment personnel. Types or writes information, such as position titles, shifts, days off, and application deadlines, on vacancy advertisement forms. Reviews bid slips or similar application forms submitted by employees in response to advertisement and verifies relevant data on application against data in personnel records. Selects applicants meeting specified criterion, such as seniority, and notifies concerned personnel of selection. Compiles and disperses position assignment notices to notify other establishment personnel of applicants selected to fill vacancies. Records data on specified forms to update personnel and employment records. • **GED:** R3, M2, L2 • **SVP:** 6 mos-1 yr • **Academic:** Ed=N, Eng=G • **Work Field:** 231, 282 • **MPSMS:** 891 • **Aptitudes:** G3, V3, N4, S4, P4, Q3, K3, F3, M4, E5, C5 • **Temperaments:** J, P, V • **Stress:** E • **Physical:** V=N, H=N, L=S, H • **Work Env:** I • **Salary:** 2 • **Outlook:** 2

ATTENDANCE CLERK (educ.) • D.O.T. #219.362-014 • OES #59999 • Compiles attendance records for school district, issues attendance permits, and answers inquiries: Obtains district attendance figures from each school daily, using telephone. Records figures by grade level and for special classes, such as mentally retarded or gifted, in workbook. Totals figures, using calculator. Collates data and prepares standard state reports, using typewriter. Computes average daily attendance figures and forwards to state for compensation and to school cafeteria for meal planning. Interviews applicants for interdistrict attendance permits to attend elementary and secondary schools in district and issues permits, if requirements are met. Sends copy of permit to applicable school and retains file copy. Maintains file of inter-district attendance agreements, bills outside districts for attendance within district, and notifies supervisor of agreement expirations. Answers inquiries from parents and school officials, using state education code as guide. Prepares special reports, such as ethnic or racial-distribution surveys, requested by state or district education officials. • **GED:** R4, M3, L4 • **SVP:** 1-2 yrs • **Academic:** Ed=N, Eng=G • **Work Field:** 232, 282 • **MPSMS:** 891, 931 • **Aptitudes:** G3, V3, N3, S4, P4, Q2, K4, F3, M4, E5, C5 • **Temperaments:** P, T, V • **Physical:** V=L, H=N, L=S, H • **Work Env:** I • **Salary:** 4 • **Outlook:** 3

AUTOMOBILE LOCATOR (ret. tr.) • D.O.T. #296.367-010 • OES #49999 • Phones other new or used automobile dealers to locate type of automobile desired by customer. Prepares papers for transfer of automobile. Keeps records of automobiles traded. • **GED:** R3, M2,

L3 • **SVP:** 30 days-3 mos • **Academic:** Ed=N, Eng=S • **Work Field:** 231 • **MPSMS:** 899 • **Aptitudes:** G3, V3, N4, S4, P4, Q3, K4, F4, M4, E5, C5 • **Temperaments:** P • **Physical:** V=L, H=L, L=S • **Work Env:** I • **Salary:** 2 • **Outlook:** 3

BORDEREAU CLERK (insurance) • D.O.T. #203.382-010 • OES #55308 • Compiles data and operates typewriter to prepare applications for insurance, such as fire or tornado, on property in which company has interest: Records amount loaned on property, and operates typewriter to post data to application form, such as description of property, name of mortgagor, and amount of insurance desired. Forwards completed application to insurance company. • **GED:** R3, M2, L3 • **SVP:** 3-6 mos • **Academic:** Ed=N, Eng=G • **Work Field:** 231 • **MPSMS:** 895 • **Aptitudes:** G3, V3, N4, S4, P3, Q2, K3, F3, M4, E5, C5 • **Temperaments:** R, T • **Stress:** T • **Physical:** V=L, H=N, L=S, H • **Work Env:** I • **Salary:** 2 • **Outlook:** 3

CALL-OUT OPERATOR (bus. ser.) • D.O.T. #237.367-014 • OES #53117 • Compiles credit information, such as status of credit accounts, personal references, and bank accounts to fulfill subscribers' requests, using telephone. Copies information onto form to update information for credit record on file, or for computer input. Telephones subscriber to relay requested information or submits data obtained for type written report to subscriber. • **GED:** R3, M2, L3 • **SVP:** 2-30 days • **Academic:** Ed=N, Eng=G • **Work Field:** 231, 282 • **MPSMS:** 894 • **Aptitudes:** G3, V3, N4, S4, P5, Q3, K3, F3, M4, E5, C5 • **Temperaments:** P, R, T • **Stress:** E, T • **Physical:** V=N, H=L, L=S • **Work Env:** I • **Salary:** 2 • **Outlook:** 3

CLASSIFICATION CLERK (clerical) • D.O.T. #206.387-010 • OES #55321 • CODING FILE CLERK. Classifies materials according to subject matter and assigns numbers or symbols from predetermined coding system to facilitate accurate filing and reference: Scans correspondence, reports, drawings, and other materials to be filed to determine subject matter. Ascertains specified number or symbol, using code book or chart, and marks or stamps code on material. Assigns cross-indexing numbers if subject matter should be classified and filed under more than one heading. May revise coding system to improve code usage. • **GED:** R3, M2, L3 • **SVP:** 6 mos-1 yr • **Academic:** Ed=H, Eng=G • **Work Field:** 231 • **MPSMS:** 891 • **Aptitudes:** G3, V3, N3, S4, P4, Q3, K4, F4, M4, E5, C4 • **Temperaments:** M, T • **Physical:** V=L, H=N, L=L • **Work Env:** I • **Salary:** 3 • **Outlook:** 2

CODING CLERK (clerical) • D.O.T. #209.387-010 • OES #59999 • Converts routine items of information, obtained from records and reports, into codes for processing by data typing or keypunch units, using predetermined coding systems: Manually records alphabetic, alphanumeric, or numeric codes in prescribed sequence on worksheet or margin of source document for transfer to punchcards or machine input tape. Important variations may be indicated by trade name of computer system for which coding is accomplished. • **GED:** R3, M1, L3 • **SVP:** 30 days-3 mos • **Academic:** Ed=N, Eng=G • **Work Field:** 231 • **MPSMS:** 890 • **Aptitudes:** G3, V3, N4, S5, P4, Q3, K4, F4, M4, E5, C5 • **Temperaments:** T • **Physical:** V=L, H=N, L=S, H • **Work Env:** I • **Salary:** 2 • **Outlook:** 3

COMPILER (clerical) • D.O.T. #209.387-014 • OES #55328 • Compiles directories, survey findings, opinion polls, and census reports from data obtained from surveys or census: Compiles names, addresses, vital statistics, and other facts or opinions from business subscribers or persons in communities or cities. Verifies information for completeness and accuracy. Records and arranges information in specified order or groupings, such as by name, location, sex, occupation, or affiliation. May use typewriter or other recording device to duplicate information for filing or distribution. May prepare graphs or charts to show survey results. May be designated according to type of information compiled as DIRECTORY COMPILER (clerical); SURVEY COMPILER (clerical). May compile lists of prospective customers and be designated MAILING-LIST COMPILER (clerical). • **GED:** R3, M2, L3 • **SVP:** 3-6 mos • **Academic:** Ed=N, Eng=G • **Work Field:** 231 • **MPSMS:** 890 • **Aptitudes:** G3, V3, N4, S5, P4, Q3, K4, F4, M4, E5, C5 • **Temperaments:** T • **Physical:** V=L, H=N, L=S, H • **Work Env:** I • **Salary:** 3 • **Outlook:** 3

CREDIT-CARD-CONTROL CLERK (finan. inst.) • D.O.T.

#249.367-026 • OES #59999 • Compiles, verifies, and files records and forms to control procedures for issuance, blocking (withholding), or renewal of bank credit cards, performing any combination of following duties: Receives shipments of plastic credit-card blanks and verifies totals received against invoices. Assigns consecutive batch numbers to blank cards, using ticket-counting machine, and stores cards in vault. Issues blank cards on requisition to embossing workers for printing of cards and keeps records of batch numbers issued. Receives new or reissued printed cards, verifies number sequence, and compares identifying data on cards with data on application files to detect errors. Compiles lists of cards containing errors and initiates correction forms. Places completed credit cards and bank literature into envelopes for mailing. Receives returned cards and reviews correspondence or searches bank records to determine customers' reasons for return. Receives blocking notices from bank officials and places designated cards in hold file. Releases blocked cards upon authorization from bank officials. Destroys inaccurate, mutilated, or expired cards, in presence of witnesses, using scissors. Compiles destroyed- plastics lists and records reasons for destruction, using typewriter. Occasionally verifies customers' account balances to expedite issuance or renewal of cards. Maintains related files and control records. • **GED:** R3, M2, L2 • **SVP:** 30 days-3 mos • **Academic:** Ed=N, Eng=G • **Work Field:** 231 • **MPSMS:** 891 • **Aptitudes:** G4, V3, N3, S4, P4, Q2, K3, F3, M3, E5, C5 • **Temperaments:** R, T • **Stress:** T • **Physical:** V=L, H=N, L=S, H • **Work Env:** I • **Salary:** 2 • **Outlook:** 3

DETAILER, SCHOOL PHOTOGRAPHS (photofinish.) • D.O.T. #976.564-010 • OES #58008 • Performs a variety of tasks to prepare and disseminate school photographs: Reads photographers' work orders and records information, such as number of prints and type finish specified as a guide for processing film. Assigns control number to each order. Records customer charges on worksheet and submits to accounting department for billing. Sorts and bags film according to processing required. Cuts prints to prepare composite for group photographs, using chopping block, die, and mallet. Assembles composite and mails to picture service for processing of negative. Routes composite negative to printing section and records cost of composite service. Feeds specified photographs in gluing machine that automatically applies adhesive backing to photographs. Confers with photographers to discuss school programs available, costs and shipping dates. Confers with customers to resolve complaints regarding missing or defective photographs. Cuts out, arranges, and pastes letters, numbers, and pictures to design advertising circulars. Maintains records indicating orders received, unit prices charged, and department earnings. • **GED:** R3, M2, L2 • **SVP:** 3-6 mos • **Academic:** Ed=N, Eng=N • **Work Field:** 264, 282 • **MPSMS:** 867 • **Aptitudes:** G3, V3, N3, S3, P3, Q3, K4, F3, M3, E5, C3 • **Temperaments:** J, M, T, V • **Physical:** V=L, H=N, L=L, H • **Work Env:** I • **Salary:** 1 • **Outlook:** 1

DIET CLERK (medical ser.) • D.O.T. #245.587-010 • OES #59999 • DIET AIDE; DIETARY CLERK. Compiles dietary information for use by kitchen personnel in preparation of foods for hospital patients: Examines diet order received from wards and tallies portions and foods of general and soft diets. Marks tally figures on master menu to inform kitchen personnel of food requirements. Processes new diets and changes as required. Tallies quantities of specific foods, such as vegetables and meats, to be prepared in kitchen. Types menus, discharge diets, and diet-tray cards. Maintains records of and prepares reports on perpetual inventory, food purchases, meals served, and food costs. • **GED:** R3, M3, L3 • **SVP:** 30 days-3 mos • **Academic:** Ed=N, Eng=G • **Work Field:** 232 • **MPSMS:** 903 • **Aptitudes:** G3, V3, N3, S4, P4, Q3, K4, F4, M4, E5, C5 • **Temperaments:** R • **Stress:** T • **Physical:** V=L, H=N, L=S, H • **Work Env:** I • **Salary:** 2 • **Outlook:** 2

DOCUMENT PREPARER, MICROFILMING (bus. ser.) • D.O.T. #249.587-018 • OES #58099 • Prepares documents, such as brochures, pamphlets, and catalogs, for microfilming, using paper cutter, photocopying machine, rubber stamps, and other work devices: Cuts documents into individual pages of standard microfilming size and format when allowed by margin space, using paper cutter or razor knife. Reproduces document pages as necessary to improve clarity or to reduce one or more pages into single page of standard microfilming size, using photocopying machine. Stamps standard symbols on pages or inserts instruction cards between pages of material to notify MICROFILM-CAMERA OPERATOR (bus. ser.) 976.682-022 of special handling, such as manual repositioning, during microfilming. Prepares cover sheet and document folder for material and index card for company files indicating information, such as firm name and address, product category, and index code, to identify material. Inserts material to be filmed in document folder and files folder for processing according to index code and filming priority schedule. • **GED:** R3, M1, L2 • **SVP:** 2-30 days • **Academic:** Ed=N, Eng=N • **Work Field:** 054, 201, 231 • **MPSMS:** 891 • **Aptitudes:** G3, V4, N4, S3, P4, Q3, K4, F4, M4, E5, C4 • **Temperaments:** T, V • **Physical:** V=G, H=N, L=S, H • **Work Env:** I • **Salary:** 2 • **Outlook:** 3

FILE CLERK 2 (clerical) • D.O.T. #206.367-014 • OES #55321 • Performs duties essentially same as those of FILE CLERK (clerical) I, except that in addition to putting material in and removing it from files, performs clerical work in searching and investigating information contained in files, inserting additional data on file records, making up reports, and keeping files current, which may require making calculations, and supplying written information from file data. Classifies material when classification is not readily discernible [CLASSIFICATION CLERK (clerical)]. Disposes of obsolete files in accordance with established retirement schedule or legal requirements. May operate keypunch to enter data on tabulating cards. May photograph records on microfilming devices. May type reports. May use calculating machine. May be designated according to material filed as FILE CLERK, FILM (clerical); FILE CLERK, GEOLOGICAL RECORDS (petrol. production); FILE CLERK, MAPS (clerical); FILE CLERK, MEDICAL RECORDS (clerical); FILE CLERK, X-RAYS (medical ser.); PAINT-SAMPLE CLERK (paint & varn.). • **GED:** R3, M2, L3 • **SVP:** 6 mos-1 yr • **Academic:** Ed=H, Eng=S • **Work Field:** 231, 271 • **MPSMS:** 891 • **Aptitudes:** G3, V3, N4, S4, P3, Q2, K4, F3, M3, E5, C5 • **Temperaments:** M, T • **Physical:** V=L, H=N, L=L, S, H • **Work Env:** I • **Salary:** 3 • **Outlook:** 2

FINGERPRINT CLERK 2 (gov. ser.) • D.O.T. #206.387-014 • OES #55321 • Examines fingerprint patterns and classifies prints according to standard system: Examines fingerprints, using magnifying glass, to determine pattern formations. Classifies fingerprints according to standard system and records classification on file cards. Files records, following prescribed sequence. Searches fingerprint identification files to provide information to authorized persons. • **GED:** R4, M2, L3 • **SVP:** 3-6 mos • **Academic:** Ed=H, Eng=S • **Work Field:** 231, 271 • **MPSMS:** 959 • **Aptitudes:** C3, V3, N4, S3, P2, Q3, K4, F4, M4, E5, C5 • **Temperaments:** M, T • **Physical:** V=L, H=N, L=S, H • **Work Env:** I • **Salary:** 3 • **Outlook:** 2

IDENTIFICATION TECHNICIAN (gov. ser.) • D.O.T. #209.362-022 • OES #59999 • Operates equipment to microfilm, store, retrieve, and reproduce police records; and takes, classifies, and matches fingerprints in identification-and-records section of police department: Operates equipment to microfilm and store crime-and-accident reports on cassettes. Operates equipment to retrieve microfilmed information upon request of police officials or public. Tends facsimile machine to transmit and receive photographs, fingerprints, and accompanying informational data. Fingerprints applicants for licenses and civil-service examinations and assists in preparation of applications. Classifies fingerprints and matches with prints filed as evidence in unsolved crimes. Compiles and submits periodic reports pertaining to police department activities. • **GED:** R3, M2, L3 • **SVP:** 3-6 mos • **Academic:** Ed=H, Eng=G • **Work Field:** 201, 211, 231 • **MPSMS:** 951 • **Aptitudes:** G3, V3, N4, S3, P3, Q3, K3, F4, M3, E5, C5 • **Temperaments:** M, P • **Physical:** V=L, H=N, L=S, H • **Work Env:** I • **Salary:** 3 • **Outlook:** 3

INSURANCE CLERK 2 (clerical) • D.O.T. #205.567-010 • OES #55314 • GROUP-INSURANCE-AUDITING CLERK; INSURED BENEFITS CLERK. Keeps records of group insurance policies, such as life, hospitalization, and workmen's compensation, covering company employees and dependents: Explains insurance plan to new employees. Writes data on application blanks or verifies data on blanks submitted by employees and forwards applications to insurance company. Files records of claims and fills out cancellation forms when employees leave company service. May correspond with or telephone physicians, hospitals, and employees regarding claims. • **GED:** R3, M2, L3 • **SVP:** 3-6 mos • **Academic:** Ed=H, Eng=G • **Work Field:** 231, 282 • **MPSMS:** 891 • **Aptitudes:** G3, V3, N3, S4, P4, Q3, K4, F4, M4, E5, C5 • **Temperaments:** P, T • **Stress:** E • **Physical:** V=N, H=N, L=S, H • **Work Env:** I • **Salary:** 3 • **Outlook:** 2

MEDICAL RECORD TECHNICIAN (medical ser.) • D.O.T. #079.367-014 • OES #32911 • HOSPITAL RECORD ADMINISTRATOR; MEDICAL RECORD ADMINISTRATOR. Compiles and maintains medical records of hospital and clinic patients: Reviews medical records for completeness and accuracy. Codes diseases, operations, diagnoses, and treatments. Compiles medical care and census data for statistical reports. Transcribes medical reports. Maintains indexes on patient, disease, operation, and other categories. Directs routine operation of medical record department. Files, or directs MEDICAL-RECORD CLERK (medical ser.) to file, patient records. Maintains flow of medical records and reports to departments. May assist medical staff in special studies or research. • **GED:** R5, M4, L5 • **SVP:** 1-2 yrs • **Academic:** Ed=A, Eng=G • **Work Field:** 231 • **MPSMS:** 920 • **Aptitudes:** G2, V2, N3, S4, P4, Q3, K4, F4, M4, E5, C5 • **Temperaments:** M, P, T, V • **Stress:** E • **Physical:** V=L, H=N, L=S, H • **Work Env:** I • **Salary:** 4 • **Outlook:** 4

MEDICAL-RECORD CLERK (medical ser.) • D.O.T. #245.362-010 • OES #55328 • Compiles, verifies, and files medical records of hospital or clinic patients and compiles statistics for use in reports and surveys: Prepares folders and maintains records of newly admitted patients. Reviews contents of patients' medical record folders, assembles into standard order, and files according to established procedure. Reviews inpatient and emergency room records to ensure presence of required reports and PHYSICIANS' (medical ser.) signatures, and routes incomplete records to appropriate personnel for completion or prepares reports of incomplete records to notify administration. Checks list of discharged patients to ensure receipt of all current records. Compiles daily and periodic statistical data, such as admissions, discharges, deaths, births, and types of treatment rendered. Records diagnoses and treatments, including operations performed, for use in completing hospital insurance billing forms. May maintain death log. May type and process birth certificates. May assist other workers with coding of records. May make copies of medical records, using duplicating equipment. May schedule and post results of laboratory tests to records and be designated CHARTING CLERK (medical ser.). • **GED:** R4, M3, L3 • **SVP:** 3-6 mos • **Academic:** Ed=N, Eng=G • **Work Field:** 231, 232 • **MPSMS:** 891 • **Aptitudes:** G3, V3, N3, S4, P4, Q3, K4, F4, M4, E5, C4 • **Temperaments:** M, T • **Physical:** V=L, H=N, L=L, H • **Work Env:** I • **Salary:** 3 • **Outlook:** 3

MEDICAL-SERVICE TECHNICIAN (military ser.) • D.O.T. #079.367-018 • OES #32999 • Administers medical aid to personnel aboard submarines, small ships, and isolated areas in absence of or under supervision of medical superior: Examines patients and diagnoses condition. Prescribes medication to treat condition of patient. Inoculates and vaccinates patients to immunize patients from communicable diseases. Treats cuts and burns, performs minor surgery and administers emergency medical care to patients during emergency situations in absence of superior. Inspects food and facilities to determine conformance to sanitary regulations. Recommends necessary measures to ensure sanitary conditions are maintained. Records, transcribes, and files medical case histories. Prepares requisitions for supplies, services, and equipment. • **GED:** R4, M3, L3 • **SVP:** 2-4 yrs • **Academic:** Ed=H, Eng=S • **Work Field:** 231, 294 • **MPSMS:** 924, 929 • **Aptitudes:** G2, V2, N3, S2, P3, Q3, K3, F3, M3, E4, C4 • **Temperaments:** J, P, S, T • **Stress:** S • **Physical:** V=G, H=L, L=L, W, H • **Work Env:** I, N • **Salary:** 4 • **Outlook:** 3

MORTGAGE-PROCESSING CLERK (finan. inst.) • D.O.T. #203.382-022 • OES #53121 • LOAN PROCESSOR; ESCROW SECRETARY. Compiles information and operates typewriter to process mortgage loans, performing various routine clerical duties: Reviews borrower's loan papers to ensure completeness of data. Operates typewriter to prepare correspondence, reports, and loan documents from rough draft. Compiles information from various

credit references to prepare credit reports. Completes bank papers and instruction forms for escrow agent. Types or makes hand entries on loan papers and keeps card file showing additions or withdrawals of papers from files. • **GED:** R3, M3, L3 • **SVP:** 6 mos-1 yr • **Academic:** Ed=N, Eng=G • **Work Field:** 231 • **MPSMS:** 894 • **Aptitudes:** G3, V3, N3, S4, P3, Q2, K4, F3, M3, E5, C5 • **Temperaments:** T • **Physical:** V=L, H=N, L=S, H • **Work Env:** I • **Salary:** 2 • **Outlook:** 3

NEWS ASSISTANT (radio & tv broad.) • D.O.T. #209.367-038 • OES #59999 • DESK ASSISTANT. Compiles, dispenses, and files news stories and related copy to assist editorial personnel in broadcasting newsroom: Telephones government agencies and sports facilities and monitors other stations to obtain weather, traffic, and sports information. Telephones people involved in news events to obtain further information or to arrange for on-air or background interviews by news broadcasting personnel. Files and retrieves news scripts, printouts, and recording tapes. May make written copies of news stories called in from remote locations. May record, edit, and play back tapes of news stories to assist COLUMNIST/COMMENTATOR (print. & pub.; radio & tv broad.), using recording and splicing machines and equipment. • **GED:** R4, M2, L4 • **SVP:** 30 days-3 mos • **Academic:** Ed=H, Eng=G • **Work Field:** 231 • **MPSMS:** 863 • **Aptitudes:** G3, V3, N4, S4, P4, Q3, K4, F4, M4, E5, C5 • **Temperaments:** M, T • **Physical:** V=N, H=L, L=S, W • **Work Env:** I • **Salary:** 2 • **Outlook:** 2

ORDER CLERK (clerical) • D.O.T. #249.367-054 • OES #55323 • CUSTOMER-ORDER CLERK; ORDER FILLER; ORDER TAKER. Processes orders for material or merchandise received by mail, telephone, or personally from customer or company employee: Edits orders received for price and nomenclature. Informs customer of unit prices, shipping date, anticipated delays, and any additional information needed by customer, using mail or telephone. Writes or types order form and computes total cost for customer. Records or files copy of orders received according to expected delivery date. May ascertain credit rating of customer [CREDIT CLERK (clerical)]. May check inventory control and notify stock control departments of orders that would deplete stock. May initiate purchase requisitions. May route orders to departments for filling and follow up on orders to ensure delivery by specified dates and be designated TELEPHONE-ORDER DISPATCHER (clerical). May compute price, discount, sales representative's commission, and shipping charges. May prepare invoices and shipping documents, such as bill of lading [BILLING TYPIST (clerical)]. May recommend type of packing or labeling needed on order. May receive and check customer complaints [CUSTOMER-COMPLAINT CLERK (clerical)]. May confer with production, sales, shipping, warehouse, or common carrier personnel to expedite or trace missing or delayed shipments [TRACER CLERK (clerical)]. May attempt to sell additional merchandise to customer [TELEPHONE SOLICITOR (any ind.)]. May compile statistics and prepare various reports for management. May be designated according to method of receiving orders as MAIL-ORDER CLERK (clerical); TELEPHONE-ORDER CLERK (clerical). • **GED:** R3, M3, L3 • **SVP:** 3-6 mos • **Academic:** Ed=N, Eng=S • **Work Field:** 231, 282 • **MPSMS:** 881, 882 • **Aptitudes:** G3, V3, N3, S4, P4, Q2, K4, F4, M4, E5, C5 • **Temperaments:** P • **Stress:** E • **Physical:** V=N, H=L, L=S • **Work Env:** I • **Salary:** 3 • **Outlook:** 3

ORDER-DEPARTMENT SUPERVISOR (any ind.) • D.O.T. #169.167-038 • OES #39999 • Coordinates activities of personnel of order-writing department: Plans and initiates order-writing procedures, using knowledge of company products, pricing methods, and discount classifications. Directs establishment and maintenance of customer order records, such as discount classifications, cost basis, special routing, and transportation information. Supervises workers writing master orders used by production, shipping, invoicing, advertising, cost, and estimating departments. • **GED:** R4, M3, L4 • **SVP:** 2-4 yrs • **Academic:** Ed=H, Eng=S • **Work Field:** 232 • **MPSMS:** 892 • **Aptitudes:** G2, V2, N3, S4, P4, Q3, K4, F4, M4, E5, C5 • **Temperaments:** D, M, P • **Stress:** A • **Physical:** V=N, H=L, L=S • **Work Env:** I • **Salary:** 4 • **Outlook:** 3

PERSONNEL CLERK (clerical) • D.O.T. #209.362-026 • OES #55314 • PERSONNEL-RECORDS CLERK. Compiles and keeps personnel records: Records data for each employee, such as address, weekly earnings, absences, amount of sales or production, supervisory reports on ability, and date of and reason for termination. Compiles and types reports from employment records. Files employment records. Searches employee files and furnishes information to authorized persons. May operate calculating machine. May administer and score aptitude, personality, and interest tests. May fill out and explain bonding application required by company. May prepare and file reports of accidents and injuries at industrial establishment and be designated as ACCIDENT-REPORT CLERK (clerical). • **GED:** R4, M2, L4 • **SVP:** 3-6 mos • **Academic:** Ed=H, Eng=G • **Work Field:** 231 • **MPSMS:** 891 • **Aptitudes:** G3, V3, N3, S3, P4, Q2, K3, F3, M3, E5, C5 • **Temperaments:** T • **Physical:** V=L, H=N, L=S, H • **Work Env:** I • **Salary:** 3 • **Outlook:** 3

PROPERTY CLERK (gov. ser.) • D.O.T. #222.367-054 • OES #59999 • PROPERTY CUSTODIAN. Receives, stores, records, and issues money, valuables, and other articles seized as evidence, removed from prisoner, or recovered, lost, or stolen property: Prepares record of articles and valuables received including description of article, name of owner (if known), name of police officer from whom received, and reason for retention. Issues property being retained as evidence to officer at time of trial upon receipt of authorization. Telephones owners or mails letters to notify owners to claim property, and releases lost or stolen property to owners upon proof of ownership. Returns property to released prisoners. Prepares list of articles required by law to be destroyed and destroys narcotics and drugs (upon authorization) in presence of official witnesses. Sends alcoholic beverages to state liquor commission. Lists and sends unclaimed or confiscated money to auditor's office. Sends unclaimed and illegal weapons for official destruction. Prepares inventory of unclaimed articles for possible sale at auction or donation to charitable organization. • **GED:** R3, M2, L3 • **SVP:** 6 mos-1 yr • **Academic:** Ed=N, Eng=G • **Work Field:** 221 • **MPSMS:** 959 • **Aptitudes:** G3, V3, N4, S4, P4, Q3, K4, F4, M4, E5, C5 • **Temperaments:** M, P, T • **Physical:** V=N, H=N, L=L, H • **Work Env:** I • **Salary:** 2 • **Outlook:** 3

RECORDS CUSTODIAN (finan. inst.) • D.O.T. #206.387-026 • OES #55321 • Stores bank records and oversees destruction of outdated records: Transfers records by truck or other means from banks to storage facility. Stacks or shelves boxed or packaged records according to designated plan. Searches records for data requested by bank officials. Receives and files microfilm records. Oversees destruction of records at expiration of legal retention dates by authorized method. Copies records or makes reproductions, as requested, by filming or other methods. • **GED:** R3, M2, L3 • **SVP:** 6 mos-1 yr • **Academic:** Ed=H, Eng=S • **Work Field:** 221 • **MPSMS:** 891 • **Aptitudes:** G3, V3, N3, S4, P3, Q3, K3, F3, M3, E5, C4 • **Temperaments:** M, T • **Physical:** V=L, H=N, L=L, S, H • **Work Env:** I • **Salary:** 3 • **Outlook:** 2

REFERRAL CLERK, TEMPORARY-HELP AGENCY (clerical) • D.O.T. #205.367-062 • OES #55314 • STAFFING CLERK. Compiles and records information about temporary job openings and refers qualified applicants from register of temporary help agency: Receives call from hospital, business, or other type of organization requesting temporary workers and obtains and records information regarding job requirements. Reviews records to locate registered workers who match organization requirements and are available for scheduled work shift. Notifies selected workers of job availability and records referral information on agency records. Sorts mail, files records, and performs related clerical duties. May give employment applications to applicants, schedule interviews with agency registration interviewers, or administer standard agency skill tests. May specialize in referring specific types of workers, such as nurses. • **GED:** R3, M3, L3 • **SVP:** 30 days-3 mos • **Academic:** Ed=H, Eng=G • **Work Field:** 231, 282 • **MPSMS:** 943 • **Aptitudes:** G3, V3, N4, S4, P4, Q3, K4, F3, M4, E5, C5 • **Temperaments:** P, V • **Stress:** E • **Physical:** V=L, H=N, L=S • **Work Env:** I • **Salary:** 2 • **Outlook:** 2

REPAIR-ORDER CLERK (clerical) • D.O.T. #221.382-022 • OES #58008 • WORK-ORDER CLERK. Receives interdepartmental work orders for construction or repairs, routes work orders to maintenance shop, and compiles cost reports: Files copy of each work order received, and routes original copy to maintenance shop.

Receives and files cost reports of work accomplished, and prepares bills to be charged against department requesting construction or repairs. Types cost reports of work completed or in progress. • **GED:** R3, M3, L3 • **SVP:** 30 days-3 mos • **Academic:** Ed=N, Eng=S • **Work Field:** 231, 232 • **MPSMS:** 898 • **Aptitudes:** G3, V3, N3, S4, P4, Q3, K3, F3, M3, E5, C5 • **Temperaments:** R, T • **Stress:** T • **Physical:** V=L, H=N, L=S, H • **Work Env:** I • **Salary:** 2 • **Outlook:** 3

REPRODUCTION ORDER PROCESSOR (clerical) • D.O.T. #221.367-058 • OES #58008 • Reviews request orders for duplication of printed, typed, and handwritten materials and determines appropriate reproduction method, based on knowledge of cost factors and duplicating machines and processes: Reads duplication requests to ascertain number of copies to be made and completion date requested. Confers with order requestor when additional information is necessary to facilitate completion of order. Designates method of duplication, such as photocopying or offset, and routes request orders for processing. Examines completed reproduced material for adherence to order specifications. Keeps files on status of request orders. Keeps supply of standard forms and issues forms as requested. • **GED:** R3, M2, L3 • **SVP:** 6 mos-1 yr • **Academic:** Ed=N, Eng=G • **Work Field:** 191, 201 • **MPSMS:** 898 • **Aptitudes:** G3, V3, N3, S4, P3, Q3, K4, F4, M4, E5, C5 • **Temperaments:** J, P • **Physical:** V=L, H=N, L=S, H • **Work Env:** I • **Salary:** 2 • **Outlook:** 3

SHORTHAND REPORTER (clerical) • D.O.T. #202.362-010 • OES #55302 • COURT REPORTER; LAW REPORTER. Records examination, testimony, judicial opinions, judge's charge to jury, judgment or sentence of court, or other proceedings in court of law by machine shorthand [STENOTYPE OPERATOR (clerical)], takes shorthand notes, or reports proceedings into steno-mask. Reads portions of transcript during trial on judge's request, and asks speakers to clarify inaudible statements. Operates typewriter to transcribe recorded material, or dictates material into recording machine. May record proceedings of quasi-judicial hearings, formal and informal meetings, and be designated HEARINGS REPORTER (clerical). May be self-employed, performing duties in court of law or at hearings and meetings, and be designated FREELANCE REPORTER (clerical). • **GED:** R3, M2, L3 • **SVP:** 1-2 yrs • **Academic:** Ed=H, Eng=G • **Work Field:** 231 • **MPSMS:** 891, 932 • **Aptitudes:** G2, V2, N4, S4, P2, Q2, K2, F2, M3, E5, C5 • **Temperaments:** P, S, T • **Stress:** E, S • **Physical:** V=L, H=L, L=S, H • **Work Env:** I • **Salary:** 4 • **Outlook:** 4

STENOGRAPHER (clerical) • D.O.T. #202.362-014 • OES #55302 • CLERK-STENOGRAPHER. Takes dictation in shorthand of correspondence, reports, and other matter, and operates typewriter to transcribe dictated material. Performs variety of clerical duties [ADMINISTRATIVE CLERK (clerical)], except when working in stenographic pool. May transcribe material from sound recordings [TRANSCRIBING-MACHINE OPERATOR (clerical)]. May perform stenographic duties in professional office and be designated as LEGAL STENOGRAPHER (clerical); MEDICAL STENOGRAPHER (clerical); TECHNICAL STENOGRAPHER (clerical). May take dictation in foreign language and be known as FOREIGN-LANGUAGE STENOGRAPHER (clerical). May be designated according to department in which employed as POLICE STENOGRAPHER (gov. ser.). May work for public stenographic service and be designated PUBLIC STENOGRAPHER (clerical). May transcribe dictation on electric typewriter that generates punched cards or tape for automatic reproduction and be designated STENOGRAPHER, AUTOMATIC REPRODUCTION (clerical). • **GED:** R3, M2, L3 • **SVP:** 6 mos-1 yr • **Academic:** Ed=H, Eng=G • **Work Field:** 231 • **MPSMS:** 891 • **Aptitudes:** G3, V2, N4, S4, P2, Q2, K2, F3, M3, E5, C5 • **Temperaments:** T • **Physical:** V=L, H=G, L=S, H • **Work Env:** I • **Salary:** 4 • **Outlook:** 3

STENOTYPE OPERATOR (clerical) • D.O.T. #202.362-022 • OES #55302 • STENOTYPE-MACHINE OPERATOR; STENOTYPIST. Takes dictation of correspondence, reports, and other matter on machine that writes contractions or symbols for full words on paper roll. Operates typewriter to transcribe notes. May dictate notes into recording machine for TRANSCRIBING-MACHINE OPERATOR (clerical) to transcribe. • **GED:** R4, M2, L4 • **SVP:** 6 mos-1 yr • **Academic:** Ed=N, Eng=G • **Work Field:** 231

• **MPSMS:** 891 • **Aptitudes:** G3, V3, N4, S4, P3, Q2, K2, F2, M3, E5, C5 • **Temperaments:** R, T • **Stress:** T • **Physical:** V=L, H=L, L=S, H • **Work Env:** I • **Salary:** 3 • **Outlook:** 4

STOCK-CONTROL CLERK (clerical) • D.O.T. #219.367-034 • OES #58023 • INVENTORY CONTROLLER; STOCK-ORDER LISTER. Performs any combination of following tasks to compile records concerned with ordering, receiving, storing, issuing, and shipping materials, supplies, and equipment: Compiles data from such records and documents as shipping and receiving papers, requisitions, contracts, and accounting reports and posts information to ledgers or other records. Keeps back-order file in established sequence and releases back orders for issuance or shipment as stock is available. Compiles stock-control records, consumption data, consumption rates, current market conditions, characteristics of items in storage, and related factors to establish or recommend stock levels or replenishment needs. Prepares requisitions, orders, or other papers for purchasing or requisitioning new or additional stock items. Compares nomenclature, stock numbers, authorized substitutes, and other listed information with catalogs, manuals, parts lists, and similar references to verify accuracy of requisitions and shipping orders. Reviews files to determine which items are not being used and recommends disposal of excess stock. • **GED:** R4, M3, L3 • **SVP:** 6 mos-1 yr • **Academic:** Ed=N, Eng=S • **Work Field:** 221 • **MPSMS:** 898 • **Aptitudes:** G3, V3, N3, S4, P4, Q3, K4, F4, M3, E5, C4 • **Temperaments:** M, T • **Physical:** V=L, H=N, L=L, H • **Work Env:** I • **Salary:** 3 • **Outlook:** 3

TAPE LIBRARIAN (clerical) • D.O.T. #206.387-030 • OES #55321 • Classifies, catalogs, and maintains library of reels of magnetic or punched paper tape or decks of magnetic cards or punchcards used for electronic data processing purposes: Classifies and catalogs material according to content, purpose of program, routine or subroutine, and date on which generated. Assigns code conforming with standardized system. Prepares index cards for file reference. Stores materials and records according to classification and catalog number. Issues materials and maintains charge-out records. Inspects returned tapes or cards and notifies supervisor if worn or damaged. May maintain files of program developmental records and run books (operating instructions). May operate keypunch to replace defective punchcards and produce data cards to identify punchcard decks [KEYPUNCH OPERATOR (clerical)]. May work in computer room operations, performing such tasks as loading and removing print-out forms, reels of tape, and decks of cards from machines. • **GED:** R4, M2, L4 • **SVP:** 3-6 mos • **Academic:** Ed=H, Eng=S • **Work Field:** 221, 231 • **MPSMS:** 890 • **Aptitudes:** G3, V3, N4, S4, P3, Q2, K3, F3, M4, E5, C5 • **Temperaments:** T • **Physical:** V=L, H=N, L=L, H • **Work Env:** I • **Salary:** 3 • **Outlook:** 2

WARD CLERK (medical ser.) • D.O.T. #245.362-014 • OES #55347 • FLOOR CLERK. Prepares and compiles records in hospital nursing unit, such as obstetrics, pediatrics, or surgery: Records name of patient, address, and name of attending physician to prepare medical records on new patients. Copies information, such as patient's temperature, pulse rate, and blood pressure from nurses' records onto patient's medical records. Records diet instructions. Keeps file of medical records on patients in unit. Prepares notice of patient's discharge to inform business office. Requisitions supplies designated by nursing staff. Answers telephone and relays messages to patients and medical staff. Directs visitors to patients' rooms. Distributes mail, newspapers, and flowers to patients. May compile census of patients. May assist in patient care and services, such as dressing and feeding patient. May keep record of absences and hours worked by unit personnel. • **GED:** R3, M3, L3 • **SVP:** 30 days-3 mos • **Academic:** Ed=N, Eng=G • **Work Field:** 231, 232 • **MPSMS:** 890 • **Aptitudes:** G3, V3, N3, S4, P3, Q3, K3, F3, M3, E5, C4 • **Temperaments:** T, V • **Physical:** V=L, H=L, L=S, H • **Work Env:** I • **Salary:** 3 • **Outlook:** 3

GOE: 07.05.04 Routing & Distribution

CORRESPONDENCE-REVIEW CLERK (clerical) • D.O.T. #209.367-018 • OES #55317 • Reads and routes incoming correspondence to individual or department concerned: Reviews correspondence, determines appropriate routing, and requisitions records needed to process correspondence. Types acknowledgement letter to person sending correspondence. Reviews requested records for completeness and accuracy and attaches records to correspondence for reply by other workers. May maintain files and control records to show status of action in processing correspondence. May compile data from records to prepare periodic reports. May investigate discrepancies in reports and records and confer with personnel in affected departments to ensure accuracy and compliance with procedures. • **GED:** R3, M1, L3 • **SVP:** 6 mos-1 yr • **Academic:** Ed=H, Eng=G • **Work Field:** 231 • **MPSMS:** 891 • **Aptitudes:** G3, V3, N4, S4, P4, Q3, K4, F3, M3, E5, C5 • **Temperaments:** T • **Physical:** V=L, H=N, L=S, H • **Work Env:** I • **Salary:** 3 • **Outlook:** 3

MAIL CARRIER (gov. ser.) • D.O.T. #230.367-010 • OES #57305 • CITY CARRIER; LETTER CARRIER. Sorts mail for delivery and delivers mail on established route: Inserts mail into slots of mail rack to sort for delivery. Delivers mail to residences and business establishments along route. Completes delivery forms, collects charges, and obtains signature on receipts for delivery of specified types of mail. Enters changes of address in route book and re-addresses mail to be forwarded. May drive vehicle over established route. May deliver specialized types of mail and be designated as PARCEL-POST CARRIER (gov. ser.) or SPECIAL-DELIVERY CARRIER (gov. ser.). • **GED:** R3, M2, L3 • **SVP:** 3-6 mos • **Academic:** Ed=N, Eng=G • **Work Field:** 221 • **MPSMS:** 954 • **Aptitudes:** G3, V3, N4, S4, P4, Q3, K3, F4, M3, E5, C4 • **Temperaments:** R • **Stress:** T • **Physical:** V=G, H=N, L=M, W, H • **Work Env:** I, R • **Salary:** 4 • **Outlook:** 2

MAIL CLERK (clerical) • D.O.T. #209.587-026 • OES #57302 • MAILROOM CLERK; MAIL SORTER; POSTAL CLERK. Sorts incoming mail for distribution and dispatches outgoing mail: Opens envelopes by hand or machine. Stamps date and time of receipt on incoming mail. Sorts mail according to destination and type, such as returned letters, adjustments, bills, orders, and payments. Readdresses undeliverable mail bearing incomplete or incorrect address. Examines outgoing mail for appearance and seals envelopes by hand or machine. Stamps outgoing mail by hand or with postage meter. May fold letters or circulars and insert into envelopes [FOLDING-MACHINE OPERATOR (clerical)]. May distribute and collect mail. May weigh mail to determine that postage is correct. May keep record of registered mail. May address mail, using addressing machine [ADDRESSING-MACHINE OPERATOR (clerical)]. May be designated according to type of mail handled as MAIL CLERK, BILLS (clerical). • **GED:** R3, M1, L2 • **SVP:** 2-30 days • **Academic:** Ed=N, Eng=N • **Work Field:** 212, 231 • **MPSMS:** 891 • **Aptitudes:** G3, V3, N4, S4, P3, Q3, K4, F4, M4, E5, C5 • **Temperaments:** R, T • **Stress:** T • **Physical:** V=L, H=N, L=L, W, H • **Work Env:** I • **Salary:** 2 • **Outlook:** 3

MAIL HANDLER (gov. ser.) • D.O.T. #209.687-014 • OES #57308 • DISTRIBUTION CLERK. Sorts and processes mail in post office: Sorts incoming or outgoing mail into mail rack pigeonholes or into mail sacks according to destination. May feed letters into electric canceling machine or hand-stamp mail with rubber stamp to cancel postage. May serve at public window or counter. May transport mail within post office [MATERIAL HANDLER (any ind.)]. May sort mail in mobile post office and be designated DISTRIBUTION CLERK, RAILWAY OR HIGHWAY POST OFFICE (gov. ser.). May sort mail which other workers have been unable to sort and be designated SPECIAL-DISTRIBUTION CLERK (gov. ser.). • **GED:** R3, M2, L2 • **SVP:** 3-6 mos • **Academic:** Ed=N, Eng=N • **Work Field:** 231 • **MPSMS:** 954 • **Aptitudes:** G3, V4, N4, S3, P4, Q2, K2, F4, M3, E5, C5 • **Temperaments:** R • **Stress:** T • **Physical:** V=G, H=N, L=L, W, H • **Work Env:** I • **Salary:** 2 • **Outlook:** 4

MERCHANDISE DISTRIBUTOR (ret. tr.) • D.O.T. #219.367-018 • OES #58023 • Compiles reports of stock on hand and kind and amount sold: Dispatches inventory data to units of retail chain. Routes merchandise from one branch store to another on the basis of sales. Usually specializes in one type of merchandise, such as dresses, sportswear, or lingerie. May give directions to one or more workers. • **GED:** R3, M2, L2 • **SVP:** 30 days-3 mos • **Academic:** Ed=N, Eng=N • **Work Field:** 232 • **MPSMS:** 891 • **Aptitudes:** G3, V3, N3, S4, P4, Q3, K4, F4, M4, E5, C5 • **Temperaments:** M, T • **Physical:** V=L, H=L, L=L, H • **Work Env:** I • **Salary:** 2 • **Outlook:** 4

MESSENGER, BANK (finan. inst.) • D.O.T. #230.367-014 • OES #57311 • COLLECTOR. Prepares lists of checks, drafts, notes, and other items drawn on other local banks and delivers to local clearing house or to drawee bank and business houses for payment or acceptance: Gathers items, such as checks, securities, and legal documents, from sections and departments. Sorts items and lists on collection form. Delivers items and obtains receipts. Posts data concerning collection items on settlement sheet. Delivers and picks up mail inside bank. May drive automobile to pick up and deliver items. • **GED:** R3, M2, L3 • **SVP:** 3-6 mos • **Academic:** Ed=N, Eng=S • **Work Field:** 231 • **MPSMS:** 894 • **Aptitudes:** G3, V3, N4, S4, P4, Q3, K3, F3, M4, E5, C5 • **Temperaments:** J, V • **Physical:** V=L, H=N, L=L, W, H • **Work Env:** B • **Salary:** 2 • **Outlook:** 3

PARCEL-POST CLERK (clerical) • D.O.T. #222.387-038 • OES #57302 • PARCEL-POST PACKER; PARCEL-POST WEIGHER. Wraps, inspects, weighs, and affixes postage to parcel-post packages and records c.o.d. and insurance information: Wraps packages or inspects wrapping for conformance to company standards and postal regulations. Weighs packages and determines postage, using scale and parcel-post zone book, and affixes postage stamps to packages. Records information, such as value, charges, and destination of insured and c.o.d. packages. Copies and attaches c.o.d. card to packages to indicate amount to be collected. Addresses packages or compares addresses with records to verify accuracy. May compute cost of merchandise, shipping fees, and other charges and bill customer. May sort parcels for shipment, according to destination or other classification, and place parcels in mail bags or bins and be designated as MAIL-ORDER SORTER (ret. tr.). May process incoming and outgoing mail [MAIL CLERK (clerical)]. May fill orders from stock and be designated as PARCEL-POST ORDER-CLERK (clerical). • **GED:** R3, M2, L3 • **SVP:** 3-6 mos • **Academic:** Ed=N, Eng=S • **Work Field:** 212, 232 • **MPSMS:** 898 • **Aptitudes:** G3, V3, N3, S4, P3, Q3, K4, F4, M4, E5, C5 • **Temperaments:** R, T • **Stress:** T • **Physical:** V=L, H=N, L=H, W, H • **Work Env:** I • **Salary:** 2 • **Outlook:** 3

ROUTE-DELIVERY CLERK (clerical) • D.O.T. #222.587-034 • OES #58028 • Prepares itemized delivery sheet for items of merchandise to be delivered by truck drivers, grouping and routing deliveries according to designated districts: Copies information, such as name, address of consignee, type of merchandise, number of pieces, and mailing designation, from records onto delivery sheet. Locates and selects merchandise and verifies against delivery sheet specifications. May arrange for unloading of merchandise from freight cars, transport trucks, or ships, into consignees' trucks. May keep records of and arrange for storage of undelivered merchandise. • **GED:** R2, M2, L2 • **SVP:** 30 days-3 mos • **Academic:** Ed=N, Eng=S • **Work Field:** 221 • **MPSMS:** 853 •

Aptitudes: G3, V3, N4, S4, P4, Q3, K4, F4, M4, E5, C4 • **Temperaments:** R, T • **Stress:** T • **Physical:** V=L, H=N, L=L, H • **Work Env:** B • **Salary:** 2 • **Outlook:** 3

ROUTING CLERK (nonprofit org.) • D.O.T. #249.367-070 • OES #58005 • Determines truck routes involved and issues route slips to drivers to pick up donated clothing, furniture, and general merchandise for vocational rehabilitation organization: Reviews presorted route slips and reviews street maps to determine appropriate route, based on type and quantity of merchandise pledged and location of donor. Issues route slips to drivers. Answers telephone and mail inquiries and complaints from donors concerning pickups; and advises drivers of problems or reschedules pickup. Occasionally takes pickup orders. Prepares daily truck-collection report based on information from drivers, and keeps attendance, safety, and maintenance records. • **GED:** R3, M2, L3 • **SVP:** 30 days-3 mos • **Academic:** Ed=N, Eng=G • **Work Field:** 231, 282 • **MPSMS:** 853 • **Aptitudes:** G3, V3, N4, S5, P3, Q3, K4, F4, M4, E5, C5 • **Temperaments:** M, P • **Stress:** E • **Physical:** V=L, H=L, L=S, H • **Work Env:** I • **Salary:** 2 • **Outlook:** 3

SHIPPING-ORDER CLERK (clerical) • D.O.T. #219.367-030 • OES #58028 • Requisitions transportation from freight carriers to ship plant products: Reads shipping orders to determine quantity and type of transportation needed. Contacts carrier representative to make arrangements and to issue instructions for loading products. Annotates shipping orders to inform shipping department of loading location and time of arrival of transportation. May perform other clerical tasks, such as typing and mailing bills, typing correspondence, and keeping files. • **GED:** R3, M2, L3 • **SVP:** 3-6 mos • **Academic:** Ed=N, Eng=S • **Work Field:** 232, 282 • **MPSMS:** 850, 898 • **Aptitudes:** G3, V3, N3, S4, P4, Q3, K4, F4, M4, E5, C5 • **Temperaments:** M, P, T • **Stress:** E • **Physical:** V=N, H=L, L=L, H • **Work Env:** I • **Salary:** 2 • **Outlook:** 3

VAULT WORKER (bus. ser.) • D.O.T. #222.587-058 • OES #58028 • Keeps records of, sorts, and routes sealed money bags received at and dispatched from vault of armored car firm: Receives bags and signs routing slip to acknowledge receipt. Sorts bags according to delivery routes. Records data, such as origin, routing, and destination of bags. Delivers bags to ARMORED-CAR GUARD (bus. ser.) for loading onto truck and verifies that guard has signed routing slip. Submits logs and routing slips to VAULT CASHIER (bus. ser.) for review. • **GED:** R3, M2, L2 • **SVP:** 30 days-3 mos • **Academic:** Ed=N, Eng=S • **Work Field:** 221 • **MPSMS:** 899 • **Aptitudes:** G3, V3, N4, S4, P4, Q3, K4, F4, M4, E5, C4 • **Temperaments:** M • **Physical:** V=N, H=N, L=M, W, S, H • **Work Env:** I • **Salary:** 2 • **Outlook:** 3

07.06 Clerical Machine Operation

Workers in this group use business machines to record or process data. They operate machines that type, print, sort, compute, send, or receive information. Their jobs are found in businesses, industries, government agencies, or wherever large amounts of data are processed, sent, or received.

✔ **What kind of work would you do?**
Your work activities would depend upon your specific job. For example, you might:

- type letters, forms, lists, and other materials.
- operate a special typewriter which automatically adjusts margins to prepare copy for reproduction.
- operate checkwriting machine to imprint checks.
- monitor and control a computer terminal to process data according to instructions.

- operate a telegraphic typewriter to send and receive messages.
- operate a keypunch machine to transcribe data onto punch cards or magnetic tape.
- operate billing machine to prepare bills, statements, and invoices.

✔ **What skills and abilities do you need for this kind of work?**

To do this kind of work, you must be able to:

- use eyes, hands, and fingers to operate keyboard of a clerical machine quickly and accurately.
- perform repetitive tasks.
- follow set or routine procedures.
- work with speed and accuracy.

The above statements may not apply to every job in this group.

✔ **How do you know if you would like or could learn to do this kind of work?**

The following questions may give you clues about yourself as you consider this group of jobs.

- Have you taken courses in typing? Were your speed test scores average or above? Do you enjoy typing?
- Have you had a part-time job in an office setting? Do you enjoy work that follows a set routine?
- Have you used a calculator or adding machine regularly? Can you use these machines rapidly and accurately?
- Have you had clerical work experience in the armed forces?

✔ **How can you prepare for and enter this kind of work?**

Occupations in this group usually require education and/or training extending from three months to over two years, depending upon the specific kind of work. Most employers require an applicant to have a high school education or its equal. Spelling and grammar are important to prepare for jobs in this group. Basic arithmetic skills are required for some jobs.

Some employers provide machine instruction and on- the-job training. However, graduation from a business school can be an advantage. The ability to operate several office machines improves chances for employment. Specialized training on a particular machine is required for certain jobs.

Supervisory positions are usually assigned to experienced workers who have leadership ability.

✔ **What else should you consider about these jobs?**

Some workers operate one machine all day. They may report malfunctions or make minor repairs. Large company offices usually have enough work to keep machines operating constantly. In small firms, however, machine operators may also do a variety of other clerical tasks.

Workers in supervisory jobs should enjoy dealing with people because they often train new workers, interview job applicants, and assign workers to jobs.

If you think you would like to do this kind of work, look at the job titles listed on the following pages.

GOE: 07.06.01 Computer Operation

COMPUTER OPERATOR (clerical) • D.O.T. #213.362-010 • OES #56011 • CONSOLE OPERATOR. Monitors and controls electronic computer to process business, scientific, engineering, or other data, according to operating instructions: Sets control switches on computer and peripheral equipment, such as external memory, data communicating, synchronizing, input, and output recording or display devices, to integrate and operate equipment according to program, routines, subroutines, and data requirements specified in written operating instructions. Selects and loads input and output units with materials, such as tapes or punchcards and printout forms, for operating runs or oversees operators of peripheral equipment who perform these functions. Moves switches to clear system and start operation of equipment. Observes machines and control panel on computer console for error lights, verification printouts and error messages, and machine stoppage or faulty output. Types alternate commands into computer console, according to predetermined instructions, to correct error or failure and resume operations. Notifies supervisor of errors or equipment stoppage. Clears unit at end of operating run and reviews schedule to determine next assignment. Records operating and down time. Wires control panels of peripheral equipment. May control computer to provide input or output service for another computer under instructions from operator of that unit. May operate small-scale computer (known variously as mini-limited-storage-, or desk-size computer) and related on-line or off-line equipment and be designated SMALL-SCALE-COMPUTER OPERATOR (clerical). • **GED:** R4, M2, L3 • **SVP:** 1-2 yrs • **Academic:** Ed=H, Eng=S • **Work Field:** 232 • **MPSMS:** 890 • **Aptitudes:** G3, V3, N3, S3, P3, Q2, K3, F3, M4, E4, C4 • **Temperaments:** S, T, V • **Stress:** S • **Physical:** V=L, H=N, L=S, W, H • **Work Env:** I • **Salary:** 4 • **Outlook:** 4

COMPUTER-PERIPHERAL-EQUIPMENT OPERATOR (clerical) • D.O.T. #213.382-010 • OES #56014 • ASSISTANT CONSOLE OPERATOR; TAPE HANDLER. Operates on-line or off-line peripheral machines, according to written or oral instructions, to transfer data from one form to another, print output, and read data into and out of digital computer: Mounts and positions materials, such as reels of magnetic tape or paper tape onto spindles, decks of cards in hoppers, bank checks in magnetic ink reader-sorter, notices in optical scanner, or output forms and carriage tape in printing devices. Sets guides, keys, and switches according to oral instructions or run book to prepare equipment for operation. Selects specified wired control panels or wires panels according to diagrams and inserts them into machines. Presses switches to start off-line machines, such as card tape converters, or to interconnect on-line equipment, such as tape or card computer input and output devices, and high speed printer or other output recorder. Observes materials for creases, tears, or printing defects and watches machine and error lights to detect machine malfunction. Removes faulty materials and notifies supervisor of machine stoppage or error. Unloads and labels card or tape input and output and places them in storage or routes them to library. Separates and sorts printed output forms, using decollator, to prepare them for distribution. May operate punchcard tabulating machines, such as sorters and collators. May be designated according to specialty of equipment operated as CARD-TAPE-CONVERTER OPERATOR (clerical); HIGH-SPEED-PRINTER OPERATOR (clerical). • GED: R4, M2, L3 • SVP: 3-6 mos • Academic: Ed=N, Eng=S • Work Field: 231 • MPSMS: 890 • Aptitudes: G3, V3, N4, S3, P4, Q3, K3, F3, M3, E5, C4 • Temperaments: T, V • Physical: V=L, H=N, L=L, H • Work Env: I • Salary: 3 • Outlook: 3

IN-FILE OPERATOR (bus. ser.) • D.O.T. #203.362-014 • OES #55305 • Operates CRT (Cathode-Ray Tube) to post or retrieve credit information and compiles and reports credit information to subscribers of credit-reporting agency: Receives telephone requests from subscribers for information about credit applicants and identifies caller by code. Types coded inquiry details on keyboard of CRT machine for computer input. Reads data from computer printout on display screen to subscriber over telephone, or activates machine to print out information for mailing to subscriber. Occasionally compiles and types additional credit data on machine for input into computer memory bank. • GED: R3, M2, L3 • SVP: 3-6 mos • Academic: Ed=N, Eng=G • Work Field: 281, 282 • MPSMS: 899 • Aptitudes: G3, V3, N4, S4, P4, Q3, K3, F3, M4, E5, C5 • Temperaments: P, R, T • Stress: T • Physical: V=L, H=L, L=S, H • Work Env: I • Salary: 2 • Outlook: 4

TERMINAL OPERATOR (clerical) • D.O.T. #203.582-054 • OES #56017 • COMPUTER-TERMINAL OPERATOR. Operates on-line computer typewriter terminal to transmit data to or to receive data from computer at remote location. Types alphabetic or numeric input data or request for data output on keyboard of computer terminal from source documents, using knowledge of coding system. Inserts specified paper into typewriter carriage and presses key to obtain printout or activates machine to display facsimile on viewing screen of information input or stored. Compares data on printout or screen with source documents to detect errors. Backspaces and strikes over original material, using terminal keyboard, to correct errors. Presses code key to transmit corrected data via telephone lines to computer. May operate terminal to record data on perforated tape. May place tape in transmitter to transmit data to remote computer. May maintain incoming and outgoing message logs. • GED: R4, M2, L3 • SVP: 3-6 mos • Academic: Ed=N, Eng=G • Work Field: 231, 281 • MPSMS: 891 • Aptitudes: G3, V3, N4, S4, P3, Q2, K3, F3, M4, E5, C5 • Temperaments: R, T • Stress: T • Physical: V=L, H=N, L=S, H • Work Env: I • Salary: 3 • Outlook: 4

TERMINAL-MAKEUP OPERATOR (print. & pub.) • D.O.T. #208.382-010 • OES #56021 • AD-TERMINAL-MAKEUP OPERATOR. Operates computer terminal and related equipment to transfer and typeset display advertising data from perforated tape onto computer tapes for subsequent reproduction as printed matter: Secures perforated tape roll on machine reel and presses button to feed perforated tape into terminal console. Presses button to activate video display screen. Reads work order to determine combination of type style, point size, line width, and spacing to be set. Pushes terminal controls and depresses keys to observe and arrange elements on screen according to specifications. Measures copy margins to verify margin specifications, using ruler. Presses buttons to transfer typeset copy onto computer tape and into computer for storage. • GED: R3, M2, L3 • SVP: 6 mos-1 yr • Academic: Ed=N, Eng=S • Work Field: 231, 264, 281 • MPSMS: 480, 752 • Aptitudes: G3, V3, N4, S4, P3, Q2, K2, F3, M4, E5, C5 • Temperaments: M, T • Physical: V=L, H=N, L=S, H • Work Env: I • Salary: 2 • Outlook: 2

TERMINAL-SYSTEM OPERATOR (clerical) • D.O.T. #203.362-018 • OES #56021 • Operates computer terminal and compiles data to produce business, scientific, or technical reports and publications in printlike format: Reviews source documents, such as correspondence, company records, statistical tables, and accompanying instructions to determine computer operations required to produce texts in format requested. Confers with source document originators to clarify instructions, such as paragraphing, indentation, line spacing, and other style requirements. Arranges data input sequence according to manuals. Types coded commands on computer terminal keyboard to enter, store, retrieve, or delete data, using knowledge of coding system. Proofreads printout of draft copy to correct errors and verify format specifications. Types coded command to computer to produce finished copy on paper, magnetic tape, or punched cards for subsequent reproduction as completed texts by peripheral equipment, such as high-speed printers. • GED: R4, M3, L4 • SVP: 6 mos-1 yr • Academic: Ed=N, Eng=G • Work Field: 231, 281 • MPSMS: 891 • Aptitudes: G2, V2, N3, S3, P4, Q2, K2, F3, M4, E5, C5 • Temperaments: M, T • Physical: V=N, H=N, L=S, H • Work Env: I • Salary: 2 • Outlook: 4

GOE: 07.06.02 Keyboard Machine Operation

ADDING-MACHINE OPERATOR (clerical) • D.O.T. #216.482-014 • OES #56002 • Computes details of business transactions, using knowledge of arithmetic and electrically powered or lever-operated adding machine that automatically performs addition and subtraction and records results on paper tape. Posts figures from tape onto records or reports. May verify and record totals of items on batch sheets and be designated BATCH CLERK (finan. inst.). May sort, list, total, and recapitulate batches of clearings for distribution to other banks and be designated OUT-CLEARING CLERK (finan. inst.). • GED: R2, M2, L2 • SVP: 30 days-3 mos • Academic: Ed=N, Eng=S • Work Field: 232 • MPSMS: 892 • Aptitudes: G3, V4, N3, S4, P4, Q3, K3, F3, M4, E5, C5 • Temperaments: R, T • Stress: T • Physical: V=L, H=N, L=S, H • Work Env: I • Salary: 2 • Outlook: 1

BRAILLE OPERATOR (print. & pub.) • D.O.T. #203.582-010 • OES #56017 • Operates machine, similar to typewriter, to impress dots in metal sheets for making braille books, transcribing from prepared copy or original script: Inserts metal sheet into machine carriage. Depresses one or combination of keys to form braille letter. Depresses pedal that forces punches to impress on metal sheet combinations of dots that distinguish braille letters. If worker is blind, transcribes from recorded rather than manuscript copy. • GED: R3, M1, L3 • SVP: 3-6 mos • Academic: Ed=N, Eng=G • Work Field: 192 • MPSMS: 567 • Aptitudes: G3, V3, N4, S4, P3, Q3, K3, F3, M3, E4, C5 • Temperaments: R, T • Stress: T • Physical: V=L, H=N, L=S, H • Work Env: I • Salary: 3 • Outlook: 3

BRAILLE TYPIST (educ.) • D.O.T. #203.582-014 • OES #56017 • BRAILLE CODER; BRAILLE TRANSCRIBER. Operates braille typewriter to transcribe reading matter for use by the blind: Reads copy and operates braille typewriter to emboss specially-treated paper with various combinations of dots that characterize braille alphabet, using braille code form. • GED: R4, M1, L3 • SVP: 6 mos-1 yr • Academic: Ed=H, Eng=G • Work Field: 192 • MPSMS: 567 • Aptitudes: G3, V3, N4, S3, P3, Q2, K3, F2, M3, E5, C5 • Temperaments: R, T • Stress: T • Physical: V=L, H=N, L=S, H • Work Env: I • Salary: 2 • Outlook: 3

CHECK WRITER (ret. tr.) • D.O.T. #219.382-010 • OES #59999 • Imprints payment data on checks, records payment details on check register, using checkwriting machine, and compiles summaries of daily disbursements: Receives checks and vouchers authorized for payment, selects specified check register form, and inserts form into checkwriting-machine slot. Depresses buttons to transcribe payment data from voucher into machine. Inserts blank check into additional slot and presses bar to imprint details on check register and check. Removes check and repeats procedure to process batch of checks. Turns key to release signature plate and removes plate when processing checks totalling more than designated amount and sets such checks aside for handwritten signature by authorized personnel. Pulls lever to clear machine and print total on individual register. Compares register total with total on adding-machine tape to verify accuracy of register totals. Corrects errors or returns vouchers to other personnel for correction. Compiles daily summary of payment amounts by bank, merchandise, and expense categories and totals amounts, using adding machine. • **GED:** R4, M4, L2 • **SVP:** 30 days-3 mos • **Academic:** Ed=N, Eng=S • **Work Field:** 232 • **MPSMS:** 892 • **Aptitudes:** G4, V4, N3, S4, P2, Q2, K3, F3, M4, E5, C5 • **Temperaments:** M, T • **Physical:** V=N, H=N, L=S, H • **Work Env:** I • **Salary:** 2 • **Outlook:** 4

CLERK-TYPIST (clerical) • D.O.T. #203.362-010 • OES #55308 • Compiles data and operates typewriter in performance of routine clerical duties to maintain business records and reports: Types reports, business correspondence, application forms, shipping tickets, and other matter. Files records and reports, posts information to records, sorts and distributes mail, answers telephone, and performs similar duties. May compute amounts, using adding or calculating machine. May be designated according to records typed as TRUST-REMITTANCE CLERK (finan. inst.). May type on or from specialized forms and be designated GUEST-HISTORY CLERK (hotel & rest.); SECURITY-INDEX CLERK (finan. inst.); STORAGE-RECEIPT POSTER (clerical). May compile reports and type prescription data on labels in hospital pharmacy and be designated DISPENSARY CLERK (medical ser.). Additional titles: COLLECTION-CARD CLERK (clerical); MOTOR-POOL CLERK (clerical); ORDER CLERK (light, heat, & power); POLICY-ISSUE CLERK (insurance); REMITTANCE-ACCOUNT CLERK (finan. inst.); VERIFICATION-AND-PROXY CLERK (finan. inst.). • **GED:** R3, M2, L3 • **SVP:** 3-6 mos • **Academic:** Ed=N, Eng=G • **Work Field:** 231, 232 • **MPSMS:** 891 • **Aptitudes:** G3, V3, N3, S4, P3, Q2, K3, F3, M3, E5, C5 • **Temperaments:** T • **Physical:** V=L, H=N, L=S, H • **Work Env:** I • **Salary:** 2 • **Outlook:** 4

CRYPTOGRAPHIC-MACHINE OPERATOR (clerical) • D.O.T. #203.582-018 • OES #56017 • CODE CLERK; CRYPTOGRAPHIC TECHNICIAN. Operates cryptographic equipment to code, transmit, and decode secret messages for units of armed forces, law enforcement agencies, or business organizations: Selects required code according to instructions, using code book. Inserts specified code card into machine station to program encoding machine. Types plain text data on keyboard of automatic machine which encrypts and transmits message, or on semiautomatic machine which converts plain text into taped code for transmission via teletype machine. Feeds incoming tape into decoder device on semiautomatic machine and distributes decoded messages. Resolves garbled or undecipherable messages, using cryptographic procedures and equipment or requests retransmission of message. May operate teletype or teleprinter equipment to transmit messages. May operate radio to send and receive data. • **GED:** R4, M2, L3 • **SVP:** 6 mos-1 yr • **Academic:** Ed=H, Eng=G • **Work Field:** 231 • **MPSMS:** 869 • **Aptitudes:** G3, V3, N3, S4, P3, Q2, K3, F3, M4, E5, C5 • **Temperaments:** M, T • **Physical:** V=L, H=N, L=S, H • **Work Env:** I • **Salary:** 2 • **Outlook:** 3

DATA TYPIST (clerical) • D.O.T. #203.582-022 • OES #56017 • Operates special-purpose electric typewriter to convert alphabetic, numeric, and symbolic data into coded form on punchcards or tapes: Loads decks of punchcards or reels of magnetic or paper tape into machine. Moves switches to adjust machine and auxiliary equipment to produce desired cards or tapes. Types computer program from worksheet, and input data, such as specified items from business forms, which machine converts to holes or magnetic impulses on cards or tapes. Proofreads typed copy to identify errors, and retypes copy or presses buttons to activate correctional devices built into machine. May insert tape or cards into reader

attachment for automatic duplication of business correspondence or records. Important variables may be trade name of machine operated. • **GED:** R4, M2, L3 • **SVP:** 3-6 mos • **Academic:** Ed=H, Eng=S • **Work Field:** 231 • **MPSMS:** 890 • **Aptitudes:** G3, V3, N4, S3, P3, Q2, K3, F3, M4, E5, C5 • **Temperaments:** T • **Physical:** V=G, H=N, L=S, H • **Work Env:** I • **Salary:** 3 • **Outlook:** 3

DATA-CODER OPERATOR (clerical) • D.O.T. #203.582-026 • OES #56017 • MAGNETIC-TAPE ENCODER. Operates machine with keyboard identical to keypunch machine to transcribe data onto magnetic tape for computer input: Examines codes on forms and source documents to determine work procedures. Positions reel of magnetic tape on spindle and clips source document to copy holder. Sets switches and presses keys which generate magnetic impulses onto tape to record data from forms and documents. Removes completed reel, marks and attaches identifying label, and sets reel and source documents aside for verification by co-workers. Positions tape completed by co-workers on spindle, sets switches, and depresses keys to recopy data from original source documents. Observes lights on machine console to note error indications and presses keys to make corrections. Removes verified reel and routes with source documents for computer processing. • **GED:** R4, M2, L4 • **SVP:** 3-6 mos • **Academic:** Ed=H, Eng=S • **Work Field:** 231 • **MPSMS:** 891 • **Aptitudes:** G3, V3, N4, S4, P3, Q2, K3, F3, M4, E5, C5 • **Temperaments:** R, T • **Stress:** T • **Physical:** V=L, H=N, L=S, H • **Work Env:** I • **Salary:** 2 • **Outlook:** 3

ELECTRONIC-TYPESETTING-MACHINE OPERATOR (print. & pub.) • D.O.T. #203.582-074 • OES #56021 • Operates terminal keyboard of electronic typesetting machine and auxiliary equipment, such as photocomposing and developing machines, to produce hard copy of text such as in-house publications: Measures lines of copy and size of type to be input to determine machine settings required, using printer's rule. Loads disk or tape into electronic typesetting machine and depresses keys to set length and thickness of printed lines. Depresses keys to input material and scans video screen to monitor input. Depresses keys to move cursor (indicator) to point where error occurs and to delete or correct error. Loads completed disk or tape and magazine of photosensitive paper into photocopying machine. Sets font selector controls to select type of specified face and size and starts machine that automatically prints text from disk or tape onto photosensitive paper. Removes magazine of photosensitive paper from photocopying machine at end of cycle, inserts magazine in developing machine, and starts machine. Proofreads developed copy to detect additional errors. Corrects errors on disk or tape, using typesetting machine and video screen, to prepare disk or tape to produce error-free copy. • **GED:** R4, M3, L4 • **SVP:** 1-2 yrs • **Academic:** Ed=H, Eng=G • **Work Field:** 201, 202, 231 • **MPSMS:** 891 • **Aptitudes:** G3, V3, N4, S4, P3, Q2, K3, F3, M3, E5, C5 • **Temperaments:** T • **Physical:** V=L, H=N, L=S, H • **Work Env:** I • **Salary:** 3 • **Outlook:** 4

FOOD TABULATOR, CAFETERIA (hotel & rest.) • D.O.T. #211.582-010 • OES #56002 • FOOD CHECKER, CAFETERIA; MULTI-COUNTER OPERATOR. Keeps record of all food items sold: Observes items on customer's tray. Presses key corresponding to food items listed on tabulating or multicounting machine which registers each item. May calculate cash receipts by multiplying total of each item by selling price and adding results, using adding machine. May act as CASHIER (clerical) II. May take customer order and simultaneously record order and tabulate bill in fast-food or other automated establishment and be designated FOOD TABULATOR, AUTOMATED SYSTEM (hotel & rest.). • **GED:** R3, M2, L1 • **SVP:** 30 days-3 mos • **Academic:** Ed=N, Eng=N • **Work Field:** 231 • **MPSMS:** 899 • **Aptitudes:** G3, V3, N3, S4, P4, Q3, K3, F3, M4, E5, C4 • **Temperaments:** R, T • **Stress:** T • **Physical:** V=N, H=N, L=S, H • **Work Env:** I • **Salary:** 2 • **Outlook:** 3

KEYPUNCH OPERATOR (clerical) • D.O.T. #203.582-030 • OES #56017 • CARD-PUNCH OPERATOR; PRINTING-CARD-PUNCH OPERATOR; PRINTING-PUNCH OPERATOR. Operates alphabetic and numeric keypunch machine, similar in operation to electric typewriter, to transcribe data from source material onto punchcards, paper or magnetic tape, or magnetic cards, and to record accounting or statistical data for subsequent processing by automatic or electronic data processing equipment: Attaches skip bar to machine and previously punched program card around machine drum to control duplication and spacing of constant data. Loads machine with decks of tabulating punchcards, paper or magnetic tape, or magnetic cards. Moves switches and depresses keys to select automatic or manual duplication and spacing, select alphabetic or numeric punching, and transfer cards or tape through machine stations. Depresses keys to transcribe new data in prescribed sequence from source material into perforations on card, or as magnetic impulses on specified locations on tape or card. Inserts previously processed card into card gage to verify registration of punches. Observes machine to detect faulty feeding, positioning, ejecting, duplicating, skipping, punching, or other mechanical malfunctions and notifies supervisor. Removes jammed cards, using prying knife. May tend machines that automatically sort, merge, or match punchcards into specified groups. May verify accuracy of data, using verifying machine [VERIFIER OPERATOR (clerical)]. May perform general typing tasks [TYPIST (clerical)]. May keypunch numerical data only and be designated KEYPUNCH OPERATOR, NUMERIC (clerical). • **GED:** R3, M2, L2 • **SVP:** 30 days-3 mos • **Academic:** Ed=H, Eng=N • **Work Field:** 231 • **MPSMS:** 890 • **Aptitudes:** G3, V3, N4, S3, P3, Q2, K2, F3, M4, E5, C5 • **Temperaments:** T • **Physical:** V=L, H=N, L=S, H • **Work Env:** I • **Salary:** 3 • **Outlook:** 3

MAGNETIC-TAPE-COMPOSER OPERATOR (print. & pub.) • D.O.T. #203.382-018 • OES #56021 • COMPOSING-MACHINE OPERATOR. Operates magnetic-tape recording and typographic composing machine to prepare copy used for offset printing of forms, documents, advertisements, and other matter, following copy and layout instructions and using knowledge of typesetting and typing techniques: Clips copy and instructions to copy holder. Inserts blank tape cartridges on tape-station hubs and starts recorder to thread tape. Selects and attaches specified type-font element to typewriter carrier. Adjusts margins and other spacing mechanisms to set line justification. Types from marked copy, using electric typewriter that simultaneously produces proof copy and master tape. Types in composer control codes according to program sequence to allow change of type font and format. Proofreads copy. Makes corrections by strikeover on proof copy, automatically correcting identical material on master tape, or retypes corrected portions only, generating correction tape. Reference codes correction tape to error location in original copy and tape. Removes tape cartridges from recorder and installs cartridges, with correction tape, if any, into composer-output printer. Installs specified type font and sets escapement and vertical spacing controls. Keys in layout and composing codes on control panel, following program sequence. Inserts coated paper and starts composer. Operates composer controls in response to function-light indicators and changes type font and format as work progresses. Removes copy from composer, examines copy for errors, and makes necessary corrections. May specialize in operation of recorder or composer units. May operate varitype machine to set headline copy [VARITYPE OPERATOR (clerical)]. May prepare final camera-ready copy and layout, using waxing machine and drafting tools and equipment. • **GED:** R4, M3, L3 • **SVP:** 6 mos-1 yr • **Academic:** Ed=N, Eng=G • **Work Field:** 191 • **MPSMS:** 480 • **Aptitudes:** G3, V3, N4, S3, P2, Q2, K2, F3, M3, E4, C4 • **Temperaments:** M, T • **Physical:** V=L, H=L, L=S, H • **Work Env:** I • **Salary:** 2 • **Outlook:** 3

MAGNETIC-TAPE-TYPEWRITER OPERATOR (clerical) • D.O.T. #203.582-034 • OES #55311 • Operates magnetic-tape typewriter and tape console to type positive proof copy and simultaneously to produce master tape for automatic reproduction of finished texts, such as letters, reports, and other data from manuscript or prepared material: Positions blank cartridge on tape spindle head and peg in tape station of console. Presses button to load tape into console. Inserts proof paper into typewriter carriage, sets controls for margins, spacing, and tabulation and turns dials for automatic preparation of magnetic tape. Types from draft and reads proof copy for errors. Backspaces and strikes over or presses line-return button and retypes entire line to correct individual character or line errors on both proof copy and tape. Presses button to stop tape or to mark end of tape section. Removes proof copy from carriage and completed tape cartridge from tape-station housing. Frequently combines or transfers data between two tapes, one with standard text and the other with personalized data, to prepare individualized correspondence. Keeps log of reference numbers and data recorded on each tape. Files tapes, correspondence, and reports. May transcribe data from recorded message, using earphones and recording unit. May use typewriter equipped with magnetic card rather than tape and be designated MAGNETIC-CARD-TYPEWRITER OPERATOR (clerical). • **GED:** R3, M2, L3 • **SVP:** 3-6 mos • **Academic:** Ed=N, Eng=S • **Work Field:** 231 • **MPSMS:** 891 • **Aptitudes:** G3, V3, N4, S3, P2, Q2, K2, F3, M3, E4, C5 • **Temperaments:** R, T • **Stress:** T • **Physical:** V=L, H=N, L=S, H • **Work Env:** I • **Salary:** 3 • **Outlook:** 3

PHOTOCOMPOSITION-KEYBOARD OPERATOR (print. & pub.) • D.O.T. #203.582-046 • OES #56021 • Operates keyboard of computer terminal equipped with video display screen to record data from manuscript for storage and retrieval into and from computer system for subsequent reproduction as printed matter: Reads instructions on worksheet to obtain codes which direct specific computer activity and depresses command keys on terminal keyboard to store or retrieve data. Reads manuscript and types on keyboard to record and store data into computer memory. Reads corrected proof sheet and depresses keys to retrieve specified portions of text for display on video screen. Observes screen to locate text to be corrected and types corrections. Maintains log of activities. If worker operates similar equipment to perforate paper tape used to activate photocomposing machine, see PHOTOCOMPOSING-PERFORATOR-MACHINE OPERATOR (print. & pub.). • **GED:** R3, M2, L3 • **SVP:** 3-6 mos • **Academic:** Ed=N, Eng=G • **Work Field:** 231, 281 • **MPSMS:** 480 • **Aptitudes:** G3, V3, N3, S3, P3, Q3, K3, F3, M3, E5, C5 • **Temperaments:** T • **Physical:** V=L, H=N, L=S, H • **Work Env:** I • **Salary:** 3 • **Outlook:** 3

PHOTOTYPESETTER OPERATOR (print. & pub.) • D.O.T. #650.582-022 • OES #92541 • PHOTOTYPESETTER. Operates keyboard of automatic phototypesetting machine to photographically print type matter onto film or strips of photosensitive paper to prepare positives or paper flats for making printing plates: Loads roll of photosensitive paper or film into camera magazine, positions magazine on machine, and pulls lever to open exposure slot. Starts typesetting mechanism. Turns dial to select lens and regulate gear that controls size (magnification or reproduction) of matrix letter, exposure, and light intensity, or moves selector levers, depresses keys or control buttons to select style and size of type. Depresses keys of keyboard to select fotomats for printing onto photopaper or film. Cuts photopaper with knife to separate exposed portion. Removes exposed photopaper or film from magazine for developing. May perform routine maintenance and adjustments on machine, using handtools. • **GED:** R4, M2, L3 • **SVP:** 6 mos-1 yr • **Academic:** Ed=N, Eng=G • **Work Field:** 191 • **MPSMS:** 567 • **Aptitudes:** G3, V3, N3, S3, P2, Q2, K3, F3, M3, E5, C4 • **Temperaments:** M, T • **Physical:** V=G, H=N, L=L, H • **Work Env:** I • **Salary:** 3 • **Outlook:** 3

PROOF-MACHINE OPERATOR (finan. inst.) • D.O.T. #217.382-010 • OES #56017 • PROOF CLERK; PROOF OPERATOR. Operates proof machine to sort, record, and prove records of bank transactions, such as checks, deposit slips, and withdrawal slips: Depresses keys to sort items into various categories and to list items simultaneously on master control tape and individual batch tapes. Positions items in machine to be endorsed and grouped automatically or manually sorts items. Totals tapes and locates, corrects, and records errors. Attaches tapes to sorted batches and prepares recapitulation sheet. Proves deposits, checks, debits, and credits listed on batch sheet. May photograph items, using microfilm or photocopying equipment, for bank records. May operate proof machine that magnetically encodes identification symbols on checks and deposit slips and be designated ENCODER (finan. inst.). Important variations may be indicated by trade names of machines operated. • **GED:** R3, M3, L2 • **SVP:** 3-6 mos • **Academic:** Ed=N, Eng=S • **Work Field:** 232 • **MPSMS:** 892, 894 • **Aptitudes:** G3, V3, N3, S4, P3, Q2, K3, F2, M3, E5, C5 • **Temperaments:** R, T • **Stress:** T • **Physical:** V=L, H=N, L=S, H • **Work Env:** I, N • **Salary:** 3 • **Outlook:** 3

TELEGRAPHIC-TYPEWRITER OPERATOR (clerical) • D.O.T. #203.582-050 • OES #57111 • TELEGRAPH OPERATOR, AUTOMATIC. Operates telegraphic typewriter to send and receive messages: Turns on machine and types identifying code for station called or acknowledges calls from other stations. Types outgoing messages when stations are connected. Reads incoming messages to detect errors and presses lever to stop transmission when messages are garbled or overlined. Types requests for clarification. Enters date, time, and serial number on messages sent and received. Pastes messages received on tape on paper forms. May type messages on tape attachment and transmit them by inserting tape into machine when stations are connected. May be designated according to system used as MULTIPLEX-MACHINE OPERATOR (tel. & tel.). Important variations are kinds (trade names) of telegraphic typewriters operated. • **GED:** R3, M2, L3 • **SVP:** 3-6 mos • **Academic:** Ed=N, Eng=G • **Work Field:** 281 • **MPSMS:** 862 • **Aptitudes:** G3, V3, N4, S4, P3, Q2, K2, F2, M3, E5, C5 • **Temperaments:** R, T • **Stress:** T • **Physical:** V=N, H=L, L=S, H • **Work Env:** I • **Salary:** 3 • **Outlook:** 1

TRANSCRIBING-MACHINE OPERATOR (clerical) • D.O.T. #203.582-058 • OES #55302 • DICTATING-MACHINE TRANSCRIBER; DICTATING-MACHINE TYPIST. Operates typewriter to transcribe letters, reports, or other recorded data heard through earphones of transcribing (voice reproducing) machine: Positions record or tape on machine spindle and sets needle on record, or threads tape through machine. Depresses pedal to rotate record or tape. Turns dials to control volume, tone, and speed of voice reproduction. Types message heard through earphones. Reads chart prepared by dictator to determine length of message and corrections to be made. May type unrecorded information, such as name, address, and date. May keep file of records. May condition records for reuse, using wax-shaving attachment. May receive and route callers [RECEPTIONIST (clerical)]. Important variations are kinds (trade names) of transcribing machines used. May be designated by subject matter transcribed as LEGAL TRANSCRIBER (clerical); MEDICAL TRANSCRIBER (clerical). • **GED:** R3, M1, L3 • **SVP:** 3-6 mos • **Academic:** Ed=N, Eng=G • **Work Field:** 231 • **MPSMS:** 891 • **Aptitudes:** G3, V3, N4, S4, P4, Q2, K2, F2, M3, E4, C5 • **Temperaments:** R, T • **Stress:** T • **Physical:** V=L, H=L, L=S, H • **Work Env:** I • **Salary:** 3 • **Outlook:** 4

TYPIST (clerical) • D.O.T. #203.582-066 • OES #55308 • Types letters, reports, stencils, forms, addresses, or other straight-copy material from rough draft or corrected copy. May verify totals on report forms, requisitions, or bills. May operate duplicating machines to reproduce copy. May be designated according to material typed as ADDRESS-CHANGE CLERK (insurance); ENDORSEMENT CLERK (insurance); POLICY WRITER (insurance); RECORD CLERK (hotel & rest.); STATISTICAL TYPIST (clerical); TICKETING CLERK (finan. inst.). Additional titles: APPLICATION-REGISTER CLERK (insurance); FILING WRITER (insurance); MASTER-SHEET CLERK (insurance); MORTGAGE-PAPERS-ASSIGNMENT-AND-ASSEMBLY CLERK (insurance); STENCIL CUTTER (clerical); TABULAR TYPIST (clerical); TITLE CLERK, AUTOMOBILE (clerical). • **GED:** R3, M2, L3 • **SVP:** 30 days-3 mos • **Academic:** Ed=N, Eng=G • **Work Field:** 231 • **MPSMS:** 891 • **Aptitudes:** G3, V3, N4, S4, P4, Q2, K2, F2, M3, E5, C5 • **Temperaments:** T • **Physical:** V=L, H=N, L=S, H • **Work Env:** I • **Salary:** 2 • **Outlook:** 4

VARITYPE OPERATOR (clerical) • D.O.T. #203.382-026 • OES #56021 • Operates one or a variety of electrically powered typewriting machines equipped with changeable type fonts to typeset master copies, such as stencils, direct plates, photo-offsets, and tracings, for reproduction of copies having a printed appearance: Plans layout of page elements (illustrations, headlines, and text) from rough draft or specifications, using knowledge of design. Pastes up preprinted type and reproduction proofs on master layout, using paste and brush. Determines size and style of type, horizontal and vertical spacing, and margins, using knowledge of typesetting. Calculates anticipated dimensions of photo-offset copy to be enlarged or reduced, using arithmetic percentages. Attaches

fonts to type holder. Attaches gear to platen to control spacing between lines. Moves lever to control spacing between characters. Sets stops to control right margin. Changes style and size of type by pressing type-change key and turning font from reserve to typing position. May draw decorative or illustrative designs on copy. May lay out and rule forms and charts, using drafting tools. • **GED:** R3, M2, L3 • **SVP:** 6 mos-1 yr • **Academic:** Ed=N, Eng=G • **Work Field:** 231, 264 • **MPSMS:** 752, 891 • **Aptitudes:** G3, V3, N4, S3, P2, Q2, K2, F2, M3, E5, C5 • **Temperaments:** J, M, T • **Physical:** V=L, H=N, L=S, H • **Work Env:** I • **Salary:** 2 • **Outlook:** 3

VERIFIER OPERATOR (clerical) • D.O.T. #203.582-070 • OES #56017 • KEYPUNCH VERIFIER. Operates keyboard type machine that verifies accuracy of data in punched tabulating cards and rejects incorrectly punched cards: Places punched cards in machine. Depresses keys in same sequence required to punch cards. Removes incorrectly punched cards as indicated by light or by key that will not depress. Stacks verified and corrected cards in rack for mailing. May punch corrected card, using keypunch machine. May tend machine that sorts perforated tabulating cards into specified groups [SORTING-MACHINE OPERATOR (clerical)]. • **GED:** R3, M2, L2 • **SVP:** 3-6 mos • **Academic:** Ed=N, Eng=N • **Work Field:** 231 • **MPSMS:** 891 • **Aptitudes:** G3, V3, N4, S3, P3, Q2, K2, F3, M4, E5, C5 • **Temperaments:** R, T • **Stress:** T • **Physical:** V=L, H=N, L=S, H • **Work Env:** I • **Salary:** 2 • **Outlook:** 4

WIRES-TRANSFER CLERK (finan. inst.) • D.O.T. #203.562-010 • OES #57111 • Operates telegraphic typewriter or facsimile machine to transfer funds or securities for bank or customers and maintains record of transactions: Types, codes, decodes, and stamps time on messages and keeps record of funds or securities transferred and their disposition. Keeps file of customers requiring daily transfer of funds or securities. Prepares entries to correspondent or branch accounts to record transactions. • **GED:** R3, M3, L3 • **SVP:** 3-6 mos • **Academic:** Ed=N, Eng=G • **Work Field:** 232, 281 • **MPSMS:** 894 • **Aptitudes:** G3, V3, N3, S4, P4, Q2, K3, F3, M4, E5, C5 • **Temperaments:** R, T • **Stress:** T • **Physical:** V=N, H=L, L=S, H • **Work Env:** I • **Salary:** 2 • **Outlook:** 3

WORD-PROCESSING-MACHINE OPERATOR (clerical) • D.O.T. #203.362-022 • OES #55311 • WORD PROCESSOR. Operates word processing equipment to record, edit, store, and revise correspondence, reports, statistical tables, forms, and other materials, utilizing clerical skills and knowledge of word processing functions: Reads instructions to determine procedures to be followed regarding material to be prepared or revised and required format for finished copy. Depresses keys on word processing equipment to adjust controls for spacing, margins, and tabulation, and places tape cassette, diskette, or other magnetic recording medium in holder. Keyboards (types) original material into machine memory, typing from printed copy, machine dictation, or related sources. Reads proof copy of material entered into machine memory, and depresses keys to correct typographical errors, print out final copy, and record material onto magnetic medium. Locates medium in file when revisions are required, places medium in holder and presses keys to insert (type), delete, correct, reposition, or reformat designated material. May operate equipment that extends word processing capabilities, such as cathode ray tube (CRT) displays, single or multiple printers, or optical character recognition (OCR). Important variations are kinds (trade names) of word processing equipment operated. May operate electronic typewriters with limited editing capabilities. • **GED:** R3, M1, L3 • **SVP:** 3-6 mos • **Academic:** Ed=N, Eng=G • **Work Field:** 231 • **MPSMS:** 891 • **Aptitudes:** G3, V3, N4, S4, P4, Q2, K2, F3, M3, E5, C5 • **Temperaments:** R, T • **Stress:** T • **Physical:** V=G, H=N, L=S, H • **Work Env:** I • **Salary:** 4 • **Outlook:** 4

07.07 Clerical Handling

Workers in this group perform clerical duties that require little special training or skill. Workers routinely file, sort, copy, route, or deliver things like letters, packages, or messages. Most large businesses, industries, and government agencies employ these workers.

✔ **What kind of work would you do?**

Your work activities would depend upon your specific job. For example, you might:

- wrap, inspect, weigh, and affix postage to packages and record COD and insurance information.
- pick up and deliver messages in an office or office building.
- put printed pages together in sequence.
- keep office workers supplied with pencils, paper, and other materials.

✔ **What skills and abilities do you need for this kind of work?**

To do this kind of work, you must be able to:

- perform clerical tasks that do not require special skills.
- follow directions.
- perform work that is routine.
- read or copy information correctly.
- work well with others.

The above statements may not apply to every job in this group.

✔ **How do you know if you would like or could learn to do this kind of work?**

The following questions may give you clues about yourself as you consider this group of jobs.

- Have you kept attendance records for a class or club? Do you enjoy this type of work?
- Have you helped to address and stamp newsletters?
- Have you maintained a checkbook for yourself or a club? Can you copy and compute numbers accurately?

✔ **How can you prepare for and enter this kind of work?**

Occupations in this group usually require education and/or training extending from a short demonstration to over three months, depending upon the specific kind of work. Basic arithmetic and English skills are required for many of these jobs. On-the-job training is provided by most employers. However, high school commercial or business courses are helpful in getting beginning jobs. Workers entering federal government jobs usually are required to take civil service examinations.

✔ **What else should you consider about these jobs?**

Both full- and part-time jobs are usually available for workers in this group. There are often opportunities for advancement or transfer, both within a company or to other employers.

If you think you would like to do this kind of work, look at the job titles listed on the following pages.

GOE: 07.07.02 Sorting & Distribution

ADDRESSER (clerical) • D.O.T. #209.587-010 • OES #59999 • ADDRESSING CLERK; ENVELOPE ADDRESSER. Addresses by hand or typewriter, envelopes, cards, advertising literature, packages, and similar items for mailing. May sort mail. • **GED:** R2, M1, L2 • **SVP:** 2-30 days • **Academic:** Ed=N, Eng=N • **Work Field:** 231 • **MPSMS:** 891 • **Aptitudes:** G4, V4, N4, S4, P4, Q3, K4, F4, M3, E5, C5 • **Temperaments:** R • **Stress:** T • **Physical:** V=L, H=N, L=S, H • **Work Env:** I • **Salary:** 2 • **Outlook:** 2

ADVERTISING-MATERIAL DISTRIBUTOR (any ind.) • D.O.T. #230.687-010 • OES #98999 • DISTRIBUTOR, ADVERTISING MATERIAL. Distributes advertising material, such as merchandise samples, handbills, and coupons, from house to house, to business establishments, or to persons on street, following oral instructions, street maps, or address lists. May be designated according to type of advertising material distributed as HANDBILL DISTRIBUTOR (any ind.); PAMPHLET DISTRIBUTOR (any ind.); SAMPLE DISTRIBUTOR (any ind.). • **GED:** R1, M1, L1 • **SVP:** 2-30 days • **Academic:** Ed=N, Eng=N • **Work Field:** 011 • **MPSMS:** 896 • **Aptitudes:** G4, V4, N5, S4, P4, Q4,

K4, F4, M3, E5, C5 • **Temperaments:** R • **Stress:** T • **Physical:** V=L, H=N, L=L, W, H • **Work Env:** O • **Salary:** 2 • **Outlook:** 3

AUCTION ASSISTANT (ret. tr.) • D.O.T. #294.667-010 • OES #59999 • LOT CALLER. Assists AUCTIONEER (ret. tr.; whole. tr.) at auction by tagging and arranging articles for sale, calling out lot and item numbers, and holding or displaying articles being auctioned: Receives and stores incoming merchandise to be auctioned. Writes assigned record numbers on tags and wires tags to articles. Arranges articles into group lots, according to similarity of type of merchandise, such as household goods, art objects, jewelry, and furniture. Assigns lot and item numbers to grouped articles and records numbers on tags and in record book. Calls out lot and item numbers of article being auctioned and holds or otherwise displays article during bidding. Assists final bidders in locating purchased items. • **GED:** R2, M1, L2 • **SVP:** 2-30 days • **Academic:** Ed=N, Eng=S • **Work Field:** 221 • **MPSMS:** 881, 882 • **Aptitudes:** G4, V4, N4, S4, P4, Q4, K4, F4, M4, E5, C4 • **Temperaments:** P, R • **Stress:** E • **Physical:** V=N, H=L, L=L, H • **Work Env:** I • **Salary:** 2 • **Outlook:** 3

CHECKER 1 (clerical) • D.O.T. #222.687-010 • OES #58017 • Verifies quantity, quality, condition, value, and type of articles purchased, sold, or produced against records or reports. May sort data or items into predetermined sequence or groups. May record items verified. May be designated according to type of establishment as WAREHOUSE CHECKER (cleri cal). • **GED:** R2, M2, L2 • **SVP:** 2-30 days • **Academic:** Ed=N, Eng=S • **Work Field:** 221 • **MPSMS:** 898 • **Aptitudes:** G3, V4, N3, S4, P4, Q3, K4, F4, M4, E5, C5 • **Temperaments:** M, R • **Stress:** T • **Physical:** V=L, H=N, L=L, H • **Work Env:** I • **Salary:** 2 • **Outlook:** 3

CONTROL CLERK, DATA PROCESSING 2 (clerical) • D.O.T. #221.687-010 • OES #58008 • Reads flow charts to ascertain sequence of materials required for machine operation. Provides workers with such materials as punched cards and reels of magnetic tape to expedite processing of data. May separate computer printouts for distribution to concerned departments, using detaching machine. • **GED:** R3, M2, L3 • **SVP:** 3-6 mos • **Academic:** Ed=N, Eng=S • **Work Field:** 221 • **MPSMS:** 898 • **Aptitudes:** G3, V3, N4, S4, P3, Q3, K4, F4, M3, E5, C4 • **Temperaments:** R • **Stress:** T • **Physical:** V=L, H=N, L=L, H • **Work Env:** I • **Salary:** 2 • **Outlook:** 3

DELIVERER, OUTSIDE (clerical) • D.O.T. #230.667-010 • OES #57311 • MESSENGER. Delivers messages, telegrams, documents, packages, and other items to business establishments and private homes, traveling on foot or by bicycle, motorcycle, automobile, or public conveyance. May keep log of items received and delivered. May obtain receipts or payment for articles delivered. May be designated according to item delivered as TELEGRAM MESSENGER (tel. & tel.). • **GED:** R2, M1, L2 • **SVP:** 2-30 days • **Academic:** Ed=N, Eng=S • **Work Field:** 011, 013 • **MPSMS:** 899 • **Aptitudes:** G4, V4, N4, S4, P4, Q4, K4, F4, M4, E5, C5 • **Temperaments:** P, R • **Stress:** T • **Physical:** V=L, H=N, L=L, W, H • **Work Env:** O • **Salary:** 2 • **Outlook:** 3

DIRECT-MAIL CLERK (clerical) • D.O.T. #209.587-018 • OES #57302 • Mails letters, merchandise samples, and promotional literature to prospective customers. Receives requests for samples and prepares required shipping slips. Maintains files and records of customer transactions. • **GED:** R3, M1, L2 • **SVP:** 3-6 mos • **Academic:** Ed=N, Eng=N • **Work Field:** 231 • **MPSMS:** 891 • **Aptitudes:** G3, V3, N3, S5, P4, Q3, K4, F4, M4, E5, C5 • **Temperaments:** R • **Stress:** T • **Physical:** V=L, H=N, L=L, W, H • **Work Env:** I • **Salary:** 3 • **Outlook:** 3

DISTRIBUTING CLERK (clerical) • D.O.T. #222.587-018 • OES #58028 • PACKING-AND-SHIPPING CLERK; PUBLICATIONS-DISTRIBUTION CLERK. Assembles and routes various types of printed material: Assembles specified number of forms, manuals, or circulars for each addressee as indicated by distribution tables or instructions. Wraps, ties, or places material in envelopes, boxes, or other containers. Stamps, types, or writes addresses on packaged materials. Forwards packages by mail, messenger, or through message center. Keeps records of materials sent. May requisition and store materials to maintain stock [STOCK CLERK (clerical)]. • **GED:** R3, M2, L3 • **SVP:** 30 days-3 mos • **Academic:** Ed=N, Eng=S • **Work Field:** 231 • **MPSMS:** 896 • **Aptitudes:** G3, V3,

N4, S4, P3, Q3, K4, F3, M3, E5, C4 • **Temperaments:** V • **Physical:** V=L, H=N, L=L, H • **Work Env:** I • **Salary:** 2 • **Outlook:** 3

MESSENGER, COPY (print. & pub.) • D.O.T. #239.677-010 • OES #57311 • PROOF RUNNER. Delivers and illustration material to and from advertisers and other outside agencies and within office. May read competitors' publications, clip items or stories not printed in own publication, and submit clippings to editor. • **GED:** R2, M1, L2 • **SVP:** 2-30 days • **Academic:** Ed=N, Eng=S • **Work Field:** 011 • **MPSMS:** 896, 899 • **Aptitudes:** G4, V4, N4, S4, P4, Q4, K4, F4, M4, E5, C5 • **Temperaments:** P, R • **Stress:** T • **Physical:** V=N, H=N, L=L, W, H • **Work Env:** B • **Salary:** 2 • **Outlook:** 3

PAGE (library) • D.O.T. #249.687-014 • OES #53902 • RUNNER; SHELVER; SHELVING CLERK; STACK CLERK. Locates library materials, such as books, periodicals, and pictures for loan, and replaces material in shelving area (stacks) or files, according to identification number and title. Trucks or carries material between shelving area and issue desk. May clip premarked articles from periodicals. • **GED:** R2, M1, L2 • **SVP:** 2-30 days • **Academic:** Ed=N, Eng=G • **Work Field:** 221 • **MPSMS:** 933 • **Aptitudes:** G3, V3, N4, S4, P4, Q3, K4, F4, M4, E5, C5 • **Temperaments:** R • **Physical:** V=N, H=N, L=S, W, S, H • **Work Env:** I • **Salary:** 2 • **Outlook:** 2

PROCESS SERVER (bus. ser.) • D.O.T. #249.367-062 • OES #59999 • Serves court orders and processes, such as summonses and subpoenas: Receives papers to be served from magistrate, court clerk, or attorney. Locates person to be served, using telephone directories, state, county, and city records, or public utility records, and delivers document. Records time and place of delivery. May deliver general messages and documents between courts and attorneys. • **GED:** R3, M2, L3 • **SVP:** 30 days-3 mos • **Academic:** Ed=N, Eng=G • **Work Field:** 282 • **MPSMS:** 959 • **Aptitudes:** G3, V3, N4, S5, P4, Q3, K4, F4, M4, E5, C5 • **Temperaments:** P • **Stress:** E • **Physical:** V=G, H=L, L=S, W • **Work Env:** B • **Salary:** 3 • **Outlook:** 3

ROUTER (clerical) • D.O.T. #222.587-038 • OES #58099 • DISPATCHER; MARKER, DELIVERY; ROUTING CLERK. Stamps, stencils, letters, or tags packages, boxes, or lots of merchandise to indicate delivery routes. Reads addresses on articles and determines route, using standard charts. • **GED:** R2, M1, L2 • **SVP:** 2-30 days • **Academic:** Ed=N, Eng=S • **Work Field:** 231 • **MPSMS:** 898 • **Aptitudes:** G4, V4, N4, S4, P3, Q3, K3, F3, M3, E5, C5 • **Temperaments:** R • **Stress:** T • **Physical:** V=N, H=N, L=L, H • **Work Env:** I • **Salary:** 2 • **Outlook:** 3

SORTER (clerical) • D.O.T. #209.687-022 • OES #59999 • Sorts data, such as forms, correspondence, checks, receipts, bills, and sales tickets, into specified sequence or grouping, such as by address, code, quantity, and class, for such purposes as filing, mailing, copying, or preparing records. May be designated according to work performed as BILL SORTER (clerical); SALES-SLIP SORTER (clerical). • **GED:** R2, M1, L2 • **SVP:** 30 days-3 mos • **Academic:** Ed=N, Eng=N • **Work Field:** 231 • **MPSMS:** 890 • **Aptitudes:** G4, V4, N4, S4, P3, Q3, K4, F3, M3, E5, C4 • **Temperaments:** R • **Stress:** T • **Physical:** V=L, H=N, L=S, H • **Work Env:** I • **Salary:** 2 • **Outlook:** 3

TELEPHONE-DIRECTORY DELIVERER (bus. ser.) • D.O.T. #230.667-014 • OES #98999 • PHONE-BOOK DELIVERER. Delivers telephone directories to residences and business establishments, on foot: Receives supply of directories from TELEPHONE-DIRECTORY-DISTRIBUTOR DRIVER (bus. ser.) or from other individual at central distribution point or from vehicle parked in distribution area, places books on handtruck or in sacks or other containers, and delivers books, following verbal instructions or address list. May pick up outdated directories for return for salvage purposes. • **GED:** R1, M1, L1 • **SVP:** 1 day • **Academic:** Ed=N, Eng=N • **Work Field:** 011 • **MPSMS:** 899 • **Aptitudes:** G4, V4, N5, S4, P5, Q4, K4, F4, M4, E5, C5 • **Temperaments:** R • **Stress:** T • **Physical:** V=L, H=N, L=H, W, S, H • **Work Env:** O • **Salary:** 1 • **Outlook:** 3

GOE: 07.07.03 General Clerical Work

CLERK, GENERAL (clerical) • D.O.T. #209.562-010 • OES

#55347 • OFFICE CLERK, ROUTINE. Performs any combination of following and similar clerical tasks requiring limited knowledge of systems or procedures: Writes or types bills, statements, receipts, checks, or other documents, copying information from one record to another. Proofreads records or forms. Counts, weighs, or measures material. Sorts and files records. Receives money from customers and deposits money in bank. Addresses envelopes or packages by hand or with typewriter or addressograph machine. Stuffs envelopes by hand or with envelope stuffing machine. Answers telephone, conveys messages, and runs errands. Stamps, sorts, and distributes mail. Stamps or numbers forms by hand or machine. Copies documents, using office duplicating equipment. • **GED:** R3, M2, L3 • **SVP:** 2-30 days • **Academic:** Ed=N, Eng=G • **Work Field:** 231 • **MPSMS:** 891 • **Aptitudes:** G3, V3, N3, S4, P3, Q3, K4, F3, M3, E5, C5 • **Temperaments:** T • **Physical:** V=L, H=N, L=L, W, H • **Work Env:** I • **Salary:** 2 • **Outlook:** 3

COIN-MACHINE COLLECTOR (bus. ser.) • D.O.T. #292.687-010 • OES #59999 • COIN-BOX COLLECTOR; PAY-STATION COLLECTOR. Collects coins or coin boxes from parking meters or telephone pay stations: Unlocks telephone faceplate and removes box containing money. Inserts empty box and locks face plate. Tags boxes to identify pay stations. Reports malfunctioning telephones or parking meters to repair department. Delivers boxes to central depot for machine counting, tabulating, and customer payment. May count coins and compute amount due subscriber, according to difference between minimum guaranteed rate and total cash in box. May pay subscriber percentage refund. May adjust or repair parking meters, using handtools. May keep records of collections, balances due, and refunds. May be designated according to type of equipment involved as PARKING-METER-COIN COLLECTOR (bus. ser.; gov. ser.); TELEPHONE COIN-BOX COLLECTOR (tel. & tel.). • **GED:** R2, M1, L2 • **SVP:** 2-30 days • **Academic:** Ed=N, Eng=N • **Work Field:** 221 • **MPSMS:** 899 • **Aptitudes:** G3, V4, N4, S4, P4, Q4, K4, F4, M3, E3, C5 • **Temperaments:** R • **Stress:** T • **Physical:** V=N, H=N, L=L, W, H • **Work Env:** O • **Salary:** 2 • **Outlook:** 3

OFFICE HELPER (clerical) • D.O.T. #239.567-010 • OES #57311 • Performs any combination of the following duties in business office of commercial or industrial establishment: Furnishes workers with clerical supplies. Opens, sorts, and distributes incoming mail, and collects, seals, and stamps outgoing mail. Delivers oral or written messages. Collects and distributes paperwork, such as records or timecards, from one department to another. Marks, tabulates, and files articles and records. May use office equipment, such as envelope-sealing machine, letter opener, record shaver, stamping machine, and transcribing machine. May deliver items to other business establishments [DELIVERER, OUTSIDE (clerical)]. May specialize in delivering mail, messages, documents, and packages between departments of establishment and be designated MESSENGER, OFFICE (clerical). May deliver stock certificates and bonds within and between stock brokerage offices and be designated RUNNER (finan. inst.). • **GED:** R2, M2, L2 • **SVP:** 2-30 days • **Academic:** Ed=N, Eng=G • **Work Field:** 221 • **MPSMS:** 890, 899 • **Aptitudes:** G3, V4, N4, S4, P4, Q3, K4, F3, M3, E5, C5 • **Temperaments:** V • **Physical:** V=N, H=L, L=L, W, H • **Work Env:** I • **Salary:** 2 • **Outlook:** 3

Selling 08

An interest in bringing others to a point of view by personal persuasion, using sales and promotional techniques. You can satisfy this interest in a variety of sales jobs. You may enjoy selling technical products or services. Perhaps you prefer a selling job requiring less background knowledge. You may work in stores, sales offices, or in customers' homes. You may wish to buy and sell products to make a profit. You can also satisfy this interest in legal work, business negotiations, advertising, and related fields found under other categories in the Guide.

08.01 Sales Technology

Workers in this group sell products such as industrial machinery, data processing equipment, and pharmaceuticals; services such as industrial shipping, insurance, and advertising. They advise customers of the capabilities, uses, and other important features of these products and services, and help them choose those best suited to their needs. They work for manufacturers, wholesalers, and insurance, financial, and business service institutions. Also included in this group are workers who buy products, materials, securities and properties for resale. Some work for themselves.

✔ **What kind of work would you do?**
Your work activities would depend upon your specific job. For example, you might:

- call on oil companies to sell them oilfield equipment.
- call on businesses to sell them radio and television time.
- call on businesses to sell them computers.
- advise people about the type and amount of insurance they should buy.
- buy clothing and accessories for stocking a department store.
- sell professional supplies and equipment to dentists, doctors, or engineers.
- buy the grain harvest from farmers for resale to processing plants.

✔ **What skills and abilities do you need for this kind of work?**
To do this kind of work, you must be able to:

- understand the principles of electronics, chemistry, economics, or communications, as they relate to the products you sell or buy.
- organize your own activities to make the best use of your time and effort.
- express yourself well when talking to potential buyers or sellers, to discuss features of the products or services involved and convince the other person of both your knowledge and integrity.
- use arithmetic in computing the mark-up on merchandise, cost of installing equipment or machinery in a plant, or quoting special rates for varying amounts of materials purchased.
- maintain enthusiasm and interest throughout all conferences with buyers or sellers.
- keep accurate records of contacts, sales, and purchases.

✔ **How do you know if you would like or could learn to do this kind of work?**
The following questions may give you clues about yourself as you consider this group of jobs.

- Have you taken business or sales related courses? Did you like the courses?
- Have you attended auctions? Can you estimate, in advance, the selling prices of the items?

- Have you bought items to sell? Did you make a profit on your sales? Do you enjoy doing this type of activity?
- Have you made speeches or been in debates? Do you enjoy presenting ideas to people?
- Have you worked as a salesperson in a store? Do you enjoy sales work?

✔ **How can you prepare for and enter this kind of work?**

Occupations in this group usually require education and/or training extending from six months to over ten years, depending upon the specific kind of work. A common way to prepare is to obtain a two- or four-year degree with a major in business administration, marketing, or a similar field. For jobs involving technical sales, a degree in a field such as engineering, chemistry, or physics is helpful. Sometimes workers in other sales groups advance after obtaining related work experience.

Most employers give new employees formal and informal training. This training may last up to one year. Workers learn the policies, procedures, and details involved.

Jobs in real estate or insurance may require a state or local license. Workers usually must take a written test to obtain these licenses.

✔ **What else should you consider about these jobs?**

Most of these jobs require meeting new people. Some jobs involve frequent travel. Many workers are under pressure as they make decisions which affect sales or investments involving large sums of money.

Some workers receive a salary, others work on a commission. A commission is usually a percent of the selling price of an item. Sometimes a worker may receive a combination of salary and commission. Some workers in this group own their own businesses.

If you think you would like to do this kind of work, look at the job titles listed below.

GOE: 08.01.01 Technical Sales

PHARMACEUTICAL DETAILER (whole. tr.) • D.O.T. #262.157-010 • OES #49005 • DETAILER, PHARMACEUTI-CALS. Promotes use of and sells ethical drugs and other pharmaceutical products to PHYSICIANS (medical ser.), DENTISTS (medical ser.), hospitals, and retail and wholesale drug establishments, utilizing knowledge of medical practices, drugs, and medicines: Calls on customers, informs customer of new drugs, and explains characteristics and clinical studies conducted with drug. Discusses dosage, use, and effect of new drugs and medicinal preparations. Gives samples of new drugs to customer. Promotes and sells other drugs and medicines manufactured by company. May sell and take orders for pharmaceutical supply items from persons contacted. • GED: R5, M3, L5 • SVP: 2-4 yrs • Academic: Ed=B, Eng=G • Work Field: 292 • MPSMS: 493 • Aptitudes: G2, V2, N3, S3, P3, Q3, K4, F4, M4, E5, C4 • Temperaments: I, J, P • Stress: E • Physical: V=N, H=L, L=L, W • Work Env: I • Salary: 5 • Outlook: 4

SALES REPRESENTATIVE, AIRCRAFT (ret. tr.) • D.O.T. #273.253-010 • OES #49005 • Sells aircraft to individuals and to business and industrial establishments: Discusses suitability of different types of aircraft to meet customer's requirements. Demonstrates aircraft in flight, stressing maneuverability, safety factors, and ease of handling. Verifies customer's credit rating. Prepares contracts for plane storage and maintenance service. Performs other duties as described under SALES REPRESENTATIVE (ret. tr.; whole. tr.). May appraise aircraft traded-in on new plane. May rent aircraft to customers [AIRPLANE-CHARTER CLERK (air trans.)]. May pilot aircraft during demonstrations and be required to have Private Pilot's License issued by Federal Aviation

Administration. • GED: R5, M3, L4 • SVP: 1-2 yrs • Academic: Ed=N, Eng=G • Work Field: 292 • MPSMS: 592 • Aptitudes: G2, V2, N3, S2, P3, Q3, K3, F4, M3, E3, C4 • Temperaments: I, J, M, P • Stress: E • Physical: V=N, H=L, L=S, W, H • Work Env: B, R • Salary: 4 • Outlook: 2

SALES REPRESENTATIVE, CHEMICALS AND DRUGS (whole. tr.) • D.O.T. #262.357-010 • OES #49005 • Sells chemical or pharmaceutical products, such as explosives, acids, industrial or agricultural chemicals, medicines, and drugs, performing duties as described under SALES REPRESENTATIVE (ret. tr.; whole. tr.). • GED: R4, M3, L4 • SVP: 6 mos-1 yr • Academic: Ed=A, Eng=G • Work Field: 292 • MPSMS: 490 • Aptitudes: G3, V3, N3, S4, P4, Q3, K4, F4, M4, E5, C5 • Temperaments: I, J, P • Stress: E • Physical: V=N, H=L, L=L, W • Work Env: I • Salary: 5 • Outlook: 4

SALES REPRESENTATIVE, COMMUNICATION EQUIPMENT (whole. tr.) • D.O.T. #271.257-010 • OES #49005 • Sells communication equipment, such as telephone and telegraph apparatus, intercommunication equipment, and radio broadcasting equipment, utilizing knowledge of electronics. Analyzes customer's communication needs and recommends equipment needed. Performs other duties as described under SALES REPRESENTATIVE (ret. tr.; whole. tr.). May train personnel of business establishments in use of equipment. • GED: R4, M4, L4 • SVP: 1-2 yrs • Academic: Ed=N, Eng=G • Work Field: 292 • MPSMS: 586 • Aptitudes: G2, V2, N2, S2, P3, Q3, K4, F4, M4, E5, C4 • Temperaments: I, J, P • Stress: E • Physical: V=N, H=L, L=L, W • Work Env: I • Salary: 4 • Outlook: 4

SALES REPRESENTATIVE, COMPUTERS AND EDP SYSTEMS (whole. tr.) • D.O.T. #275.257-010 • OES #49005 • Sells computers and electronic data-processing systems to business or industrial establishments, performing duties as described under SALES REPRESENTATIVE (ret. tr.; whole. tr.). Analyzes customer's needs and recommends computer system that best meets customer's requirements. Emphasizes salable features, such as flexibility, cost, capacity, and economy of operation. Consults with staff engineers on highly technical problems. • **GED:** R5, M4, L4 • **SVP:** 1-2 yrs • **Academic:** Ed=A, Eng=G • **Work Field:** 292 • **MPSMS:** 571 • **Aptitudes:** G2, V2, N3, S3, P4, Q3, K4, F4, M4, E5, C5 • **Temperaments:** I, J, P • **Stress:** E • **Physical:** V=N, H=L, L=S, W • **Work Env:** I • **Salary:** 5 • **Outlook:** 4

SALES REPRESENTATIVE, DENTAL AND MEDICAL EQUIPMENT AND SUPPLIES (whole. tr.) • D.O.T. #276.257-010 • OES #49005 • Sells medical and dental equipment and supplies, except drugs and medicines, to doctors, dentists, hospitals, medical schools, and retail establishments: Studies data describing new products to develop sales approach. Compiles data on equipment and supplies preferred by customers. Advises customers of equipment for given need based on technical knowledge of products. Provides customers with advice in such areas as office layout, legal and insurance regulations, cost analysis, and collection methods to develop goodwill and promote sales. Performs other duties as described under SALES REPRESENTATIVE (ret. tr.; whole. tr.). May be designated according to type of equipment and supplies sold as SALES REPRESENTATIVE, DENTAL EQUIPMENT AND SUPPLIES (whole. tr.). May sell orthopedic appliances, trusses, and artificial limbs and be designated SALES REPRESENTATIVE, PROSTHETIC AND ORTHOTIC APPLIANCES (whole. tr.). May sell services of dental laboratory and be designated as SALES REPRESENTATIVE, DENTAL PROSTHETICS (whole. tr.) • **GED:** R4, M3, L4 • **SVP:** 1-2 yrs • **Academic:** Ed=B, Eng=G • **Work Field:** 292 • **MPSMS:** 604 • **Aptitudes:** G2, V2, N3, S3, P3, Q3, K4, F4, M4, E5, C4 • **Temperaments:** I, J, P • **Stress:** E • **Physical:** V=N, H=L, L=L, W • **Work Env:** I • **Salary:** 5 • **Outlook:** 4

SALES REPRESENTATIVE, ELECTRONICS PARTS (whole. tr.) • D.O.T. #271.357-010 • OES #49005 • Sells radio, television, and other electronics parts to establishments, such as appliance stores, dealers, and repair shops or electronics and aircraft manufacturing firms, performing duties as described under SALES REPRESENTATIVE (ret. tr.; whole. tr.). • **GED:** R4, M3, L4 • **SVP:** 1-2 yrs • **Academic:** Ed=N, Eng=G • **Work Field:** 292 • **MPSMS:** 587 • **Aptitudes:** G2, V2, N3, S3, P3, Q3, K4, F4, M4, E5, C5 • **Temperaments:** I, J, P • **Stress:** E • **Physical:** V=N, H=L, L=L • **Work Env:** I • **Salary:** 4 • **Outlook:** 4

SALES REPRESENTATIVE, GRAPHIC ART (bus. ser.) • D.O.T. #254.251-010 • OES #43023 • Sells graphic art, such as layout, illustration, and photography, to advertising agencies and industrial organizations for use in advertising and illustration: Plans and sketches layouts to meet customer needs. Advises customer in methods of composing layouts, utilizing knowledge of photographic and illustrative art and printing terminology. Informs customer of types of artwork available by providing samples. Computes job costs. Delivers advertising or illustration proofs to customer for approval. May write copy as part of layout. • **GED:** R5, M3, L4 • **SVP:** 2-4 yrs • **Academic:** Ed=H, Eng=G • **Work Field:** 262, 292 • **MPSMS:** 752 • **Aptitudes:** G2, V2, N3, S2, P3, Q3, K3, F3, M4, E5, C2 • **Temperaments:** F, I, P, V • **Stress:** E • **Physical:** V=L, H=L, L=S, H • **Work Env:** I • **Salary:** 4 • **Outlook:** 3

SALES REPRESENTATIVE, SIGNS AND DISPLAYS (signs) • D.O.T. #254.257-010 • OES #43023 • Solicits and draws up contracts for signs and displays: Calls on advertisers and sales promotion people to obtain information concerning prospects for current advertising and sales promotion. Discusses advantages of and suggests ideas for signs and displays. Submits rendering or drawing of proposed sign or display to prospect. Draws up contract covering arrangements for designing, fabricating, erecting, and maintaining sign or display, depending on type of job and customer's wishes. May confer with architect in determining type of sign. May select and arrange for lease of site [SALES AGENT, REAL ESTATE (real estate)]. • **GED:** R4, M3, L4 • **SVP:** 1-2 yrs • **Academic:** Ed=H, Eng=G • **Work Field:** 292 • **MPSMS:** 896 • **Aptitudes:** G2, V2, N3, S2, P2, Q3, K4, F4, M4, E5, C3 • **Temper-**

aments: I, J, P • **Stress:** E • **Physical:** V=L, H=L, L=S, W • **Work Env:** I • **Salary:** 4 • **Outlook:** 3

GOE: 08.01.02 Intangible Sales

ESTATE PLANNER (insurance) • D.O.T. #186.167-010 • OES #21199 • Reviews assets and liabilities of estate to determine that insurance is adequate for financial protection of estate: Studies legal instruments, such as wills, trusts, business agreements, life insurance policies, and government benefits to estimate value and expenses of estate. Computes expenses, taxes, and debts to determine value of adjusted gross estate, using knowledge of accounting and tax laws. Prepares and discusses insurance program with client that will provide maximum financial security for family and protect investments. Suggests purchase of additional or new life insurance when analysis of estate indicates need for meeting cash demands at death. Discusses legal instruments with family attorney if study indicates need for change. May be required to hold State license. • **GED:** R5, M4, L5 • **SVP:** 2-4 yrs • **Academic:** Ed=H, Eng=G • **Work Field:** 211, 292 • **MPSMS:** 895 • **Aptitudes:** G1, V1, N2, S4, P4, Q3, K4, F4, M4, E5, C5 • **Temperaments:** J, M, P • **Stress:** E, A • **Physical:** V=N, H=G, L=S • **Work Env:** I • **Salary:** 4 • **Outlook:** 3

SALES AGENT, FINANCIAL SERVICES (finan. inst.) • D.O.T. #251.257-010 • OES #43014 • Calls on industrial, wholesale and retail establishments, real estate firms, contractors, and individuals to solicit applications for loans and new deposit accounts for bank or savings and loan association: Locates and contacts prospective customers to present bank's financing services and to ascertain banking needs, and consults with present customers concerning bank credit and financing. Develops financing plan based on type of loan service required by customer. Reviews business trends and advises customers regarding quality or quantity of fluctuations. Contacts customers to solicit increased deposit balances, transfer of accounts from other banks, and to offer bank's services. Attends sales and trade meetings as bank representative to develop new business and to gain information and leads on prospective accounts. • **GED:** R5, M4, L5 • **SVP:** 1-2 yrs • **Academic:** Ed=A, Eng=G • **Work Field:** 292 • **MPSMS:** 894 • **Aptitudes:** G2, V2, N2, S4, P4, Q3, K4, F4, M4, E5, C5 • **Temperaments:** I, J, P • **Stress:** E • **Physical:** V=N, H=L, L=L, H • **Work Env:** I • **Salary:** 4 • **Outlook:** 4

SALES AGENT, INSURANCE (insurance) • D.O.T. #250.257-010 • OES #43002 • INSURANCE AGENT. Sells insurance to new and present clients, recommending amount and type of coverage based on analysis of prospect's circumstances: Compiles lists of prospective clients to provide leads for additional business. Contacts prospects and explains features and merits of policies offered, utilizing persuasive sales techniques. Calculates and quotes premium rates for recommended policies, using adding machine and rate books. Calls on policyholders to deliver and explain policy, to suggest additions or changes in insurance program, or to make changes in beneficiaries. May collect weekly or monthly premiums from policyholders and keep record of payments. Must have license issued by State. May be designated according to type of insurance sold as SALES AGENT, CASUALTY INSURANCE (insurance); SALES AGENT, FIRE INSURANCE (insurance); SALES AGENT, LIFE INSURANCE (insurance); SALES AGENT, MARINE INSURANCE (insurance). May work independently, selling a variety of insurance, such as life, fire, casualty, and marine, for many companies and be designated as INSURANCE BROKER (insurance). May work independently, selling for one company, and be designated GENERAL AGENT (insurance). • **GED:** R4, M3, L4 • **SVP:** 1-2 yrs • **Academic:** Ed=H, Eng=G • **Work Field:** 292 • **MPSMS:** 895 • **Aptitudes:** G2, V2, N2, S4, P4, Q2, K3, F3, M4, E5, C5 • **Temperaments:** I, J, M, P • **Stress:** E • **Physical:** V=N, H=L, L=S • **Work Env:** I • **Salary:** 3 • **Outlook:** 4

SALES REPRESENTATIVE, ADVERTISING (print. & pub.) • D.O.T. #254.357-014 • OES #43023 • ADVERTISING-SALES REPRESENTATIVE; ADVERTISING SOLICITOR. Sells classified and display advertising space for publication: Prepares list of prospects from leads in other papers and from old accounts. Obtains pertinent information concerning prospect's past and current advertising for use in sales presentation. Visits advertisers to point out advantages of own publication and exhibits prepared layouts with mats and copy with headings. May collect payments due. Usually designated by type of advertising sold as SALES REPRESENTATIVE, CLASSIFIED ADVERTISING (print. & pub.); SALES REPRESENTATIVE, DISPLAY ADVERTISING (print. & pub.). • **GED:** R4, M3, L4 • **SVP:** 1-2 yrs • **Academic:** Ed=H, Eng=G • **Work Field:** 292 • **MPSMS:** 880, 896 • **Aptitudes:** G2, V2, N3, S2, P3, Q4, K4, F4, M4, E5, C4 • **Temperaments:** I, J, P • **Stress:** E • **Physical:** V=N, H=L, L=S • **Work Env:** I • **Salary:** 4 • **Outlook:** 3

SALES REPRESENTATIVE, DATA-PROCESSING SERVICES (bus. ser.) • D.O.T. #251.157-014 • OES #43017 • Contacts representatives of government, business, and industrial organizations to solicit business for data-processing establishment: Calls on prospective clients to explain types of services provided by establishment, such as inventory control, payroll processing, data conversion, sales analysis, and financial reporting. Analyzes data-processing requirements of prospective client and draws up prospectus of data-processing plan designed specifically to serve client's needs. Consults SYSTEMS ANALYST, ELECTRONIC DATA PROCESSING (profess. & kin.) 012.167-066 and SYSTEMS ENGINEER, ELECTRONIC DATA PROCESSING (profess. & kin.) 003.167-062 employed by data-processing establishment to secure information concerning methodology for solving unusual problems. Quotes prices for services outlined in prospectus. Revises or expands prospectus to meet client's needs. Writes order and schedules initiation of services. Periodically confers with clients and establishment personnel to verify satisfaction with service or to resolve complaints. • **GED:** R5, M5, L5 • **SVP:** 2-4 yrs • **Academic:** Ed=A, Eng=G • **Work Field:** 292 • **MPSMS:** 893 • **Aptitudes:** G2, V2, N2, S2, P3, Q2, K4, F4, M4, E5, C5 • **Temperaments:** I, J, P • **Stress:** E • **Physical:** V=L, H=L, L=L, W • **Work Env:** I • **Salary:** 4 • **Outlook:** 4

SALES REPRESENTATIVE, HOTEL SERVICES (hotel & rest.) • D.O.T. #259.157-014 • OES #43017 • Contacts representatives of government, business, and social groups to solicit business for hotel, motel, or resort: Selects prospective customers by reviewing information concerning functions, such as sales meetings, conventions, training classes, and routine travel by organization members. Calls on prospects, analyzes requirements of occasion, outlines types of service offered, and quotes prices. Verifies reservations by letter or draws up contract and obtains signatures. Confers with customer and hotel department heads to plan function details, such as space requirements, publicity, time schedule, food service, and decorations. May serve as convention advisor or hotel agent during function to minimize confusion and resolve problems, such as space adjustment and need for additional equipment. May select and release hotel's publicity. • **GED:** R4, M3, L4 • **SVP:** 1-2 yrs • **Academic:** Ed=H, Eng=G • **Work Field:** 292 • **MPSMS:** 900 • **Aptitudes:** G2, V2, N3, S3, P3, Q2, K4, F4, M4, E5, C4 • **Temperaments:** D, I, J, P, V • **Stress:** E • **Physical:** V=N, H=L, L=S, W • **Work Env:** I • **Salary:** 4 • **Outlook:** 3

SALES REPRESENTATIVE, PRINTING (whole. tr.) • D.O.T. #254.357-018 • OES #43017 • Visits business establishments to solicit business for printing firm: Interviews purchasing personnel and quotes prices on printed material from schedule or secures price from ESTIMATOR, PRINTING (print. & pub.). Explains technical phases, such as type size and style, paper stock, binding materials, and various methods of reproduction. Contacts prospects following leads submitted by management, established customers, or developed through other sources. May prepare sales promotional letters to be sent to prospective customers. May submit formal bids on large orders of printed matter. • **GED:** R4, M3, L4 • **SVP:** 6 mos-1 yr • **Academic:** Ed=H, Eng=G • **Work Field:** 292 • **MPSMS:** 480 • **Aptitudes:** G3, V3, N3, S4, P3, Q3, K4, F4, M4, E5, C4 • **Temperaments:** I, J, P • **Stress:** E • **Physical:** V=N, H=L, L=S • **Work Env:** I • **Salary:** 4 • **Outlook:** 3

SALES REPRESENTATIVE, PUBLIC UTILITIES (light, heat, & power) • D.O.T. #253.357-010 • OES #43017 • COMMERCIAL SERVICE REPRESENTATIVE. Solicits prospective and existing commercial and residential clients to promote increased or economical use of public utilities, such as gas, electric power, telephone, and telegraph service: Inspects installations in existing establishments or reviews plans for new construction to determine potential need or necessity for extension of utility service. Advises customers in most economical use of utility to promote energy conservation and reduce cost. Quotes approximate rates, installation charges, and operating costs and explains company services. Writes construction requisitions and service applications, conforming to needs and requests of consumer. May investigate customers' complaints concerning bills. May be designated by type of utility sold as SALES REPRESENTATIVE, ELECTRIC SERVICE (light, heat, & power); SALES REPRESENTATIVE, GAS SERVICE (light, heat, & power); SALES REPRESENTATIVE, TELEPHONE AND TELEGRAPH SERVICES (tel. & tel.) or by area in which utility is sold as SALES REPRESENTATIVE, RURAL POWER (light, heat, & power). • **GED:** R4, M3, L4 • **SVP:** 1-2 yrs • **Academic:** Ed=H, Eng=G • **Work Field:** 292 • **MPSMS:** 860, 870 • **Aptitudes:** G2, V2, N3, S3, P3, Q3, K4, F4, M4, E5, C5 • **Temperaments:** I, J, P • **Stress:** E • **Physical:** V=N, H=L, L=S • **Work Env:** I • **Salary:** 4 • **Outlook:** 3

SALES REPRESENTATIVE, RADIO AND TELEVISION TIME (radio & tv broad.) • D.O.T. #259.357-018 • OES #43023 • ACCOUNT EXECUTIVE. Contacts prospective customers to sell radio and television time for broadcasting station or network: Calls on prospects and presents outlines of various programs or commercial announcements. Discusses current popularity of various types of programs, such as news, dramatic, and variety. Arranges for and accompanies prospect to auditions. Prepares sales contracts. • **GED:** R4, M3, L4 • **SVP:** 1-2 yrs • **Academic:** Ed=H, Eng=G • **Work Field:** 292 • **MPSMS:** 863 • **Aptitudes:** G2, V2, N3, S3, P3, Q3, K4, F4, M4, E5, C5 • **Temperaments:** I, J, M, P • **Stress:** E • **Physical:** V=N, H=L, L=S • **Work Env:** I • **Salary:** 4 • **Outlook:** 3

SALES REPRESENTATIVE, SECURITY SYSTEMS (bus. ser.) • D.O.T. #259.257-022 • OES #43017 • Sells burglar, fire, and medical emergency alarm systems and security monitoring services to individuals and businesses: Contacts prospective customers to explain security monitoring services and to demonstrate alarm systems. Examines customer's home or business and analyzes customer's requirements to recommend security system to meet customer's needs. Explains operation of security system after installation. Performs other duties as described under SALES REPRESENTATIVE (ret. tr.; whole. tr.) Master Title. • **GED:** R4, M3, L4 • **SVP:** 6 mos-1 yr • **Academic:** Ed=H, Eng=G • **Work Field:** 211, 292 • **MPSMS:** 586, 951 • **Aptitudes:** G2, V2, N3, S3, P5, Q3, K4, F4, M4, E5, C5 • **Temperaments:** I, J, P • **Stress:** E • **Physical:** V=L, H=L, L=M, W, H • **Work Env:** I • **Salary:** 4 • **Outlook:** 3

SALES REPRESENTATIVE, TELEPHONE SERVICES (tel. & tel.) • D.O.T. #253.257-010 • OES #43017 • COMMERCIAL REPRESENTATIVE. Sells telephone services to business accounts: Contacts and visits commercial customers to review telephone service. Analyzes communication needs of business establishments, using knowledge of type of business, available telephone equipment, and traffic studies. Recommends services, such as additional telephone instruments and lines, switchboard systems, dial- and key-telephone systems, private-branch exchanges, and speaker telephones. Quotes rates for equipment and writes up orders. Explains equipment usage, using brochures and demonstration equipment. May specialize in selling services to a particular industry. • **GED:** R5, M3, L4 • **SVP:** 1-2 yrs • **Academic:** Ed=H, Eng=G • **Work Field:** 292 • **MPSMS:** 861 • **Aptitudes:** G2, V2, N3, S3, P3, Q3, K4, F4, M4, E5, C5 • **Temperaments:** I, J, P • **Stress:** E • **Physical:** V=N, H=L, L=S • **Work Env:** I • **Salary:** 4 • **Outlook:** 4

TRAFFIC AGENT (air trans.) • D.O.T. #252.257-010 • OES #43017 • SALES REPRESENTATIVE. Solicits freight business from industrial and commercial firms and passenger-travel business from travel agencies, schools, clubs, and other organizations: Calls on prospective shippers to explain advantages of using company facilities. Quotes tariffs, rates, and train schedules. Explains available routes, load limits, and special equipment available, and offers suggestions in method of loading, crating, and handling freight. Calls on travel agents, schools, clubs, and other organizations to explain available accommodations offered by company. Quotes fares, schedules, and available itineraries offered to groups by company. Speaks to members of groups and organizations and exhibits travel movies showing points of interest along routes to stimulate interest in travel. Distributes descriptive pamphlets.

Acts as liaison between shipper and carrier to obtain information for settling complaints. May specialize in soliciting freight or passenger contracts or may travel from community to community to solicit freight and passenger patronage and be designated as FREIGHT-TRAFFIC AGENT (air trans.; motor trans.; r.r. trans.; water trans.); PASSENGER TRAFFIC AGENT (air trans.; motor trans.; r.r. trans.; water trans.); TRAVELING-FREIGHT-AND-PASSENGER AGENT (air trans.; motor trans.; r.r. trans.; water trans.). • **GED:** R5, M3, L4 • **SVP:** 2-4 yrs • **Academic:** Ed=N, Eng=G • **Work Field:** 292 • **MPSMS:** 850 • **Aptitudes:** G2, V2, N3, S4, P3, Q2, K4, F4, M4, E5, C5 • **Temperaments:** I, J, M, P • **Stress:** E • **Physical:** V=N, H=L, L=L • **Work Env:** I • **Salary:** 3 • **Outlook:** 3

GOE: 08.01.03 Purchasing & Sales

BUSINESS OPPORTUNITY AND PROPERTY INVESTMENT BROKER (bus. ser.) • D.O.T. #189.157-010 • OES #15011 • BUSINESS INVESTOR; PROPERTY INVESTOR. Buys and sells business enterprises or investment property on speculative or commission basis: Reviews trade journals, business opportunity advertisements, or other publications to ascertain business enterprises or investment property up for sale. Investigates financial rating of business, customer appeal for type of merchandise, and desirability of location for type of business, or condition and location of investment property. Estimates cost of improving business or property and potential market value to determine resale value. Purchases business or property on speculative basis or on commission basis for client. Repairs, remodels, or redecorates building; purchases competitive merchandise; and installs sound management practices to improve value of property or business acquisition. Contacts prospective clients through newspaper advertisements or mailing lists. Describes to client selling points of property or business, emphasizing such factors as improvements made and profit potential. Sells business or property to buyer and makes arrangements for escrow and title change. Must be licensed by state. • **GED:** R5, M4, L4 • **SVP:** 2-4 yrs • **Academic:** Ed=N, Eng=G • **Work Field:** 292 • **MPSMS:** 890 • **Aptitudes:** G2, V2, N3, S3, P4, Q3, K4, F4, M4, E5, C5 • **Temperaments:** D, I, J, P • **Stress:** E • **Physical:** V=N, H=L, L=S, W • **Work Env:** B • **Salary:** 4 • **Outlook:** 3

BUYER (profess. & kin.) • D.O.T. #162.157-018 • OES #21302 • BROKER. Purchases merchandise or commodities for resale: Inspects and grades or appraises agricultural commodities, durable goods, apparel, furniture, livestock, or other merchandise offered for sale to determine value and yield. Selects and orders merchandise from showings by manufacturing representatives, growers, or other sellers, or purchases on open market for cash, basing selection on nature of clientele, or demand for specific commodity, merchandise, or other property, utilizing knowledge of various articles of commerce and experience as buyer. Transports purchases or contacts carriers to arrange transportation of purchases. Authorizes payment of invoices or return of merchandise. May negotiate contracts for severance of agricultural or forestry products from land. May conduct staff meetings with sales personnel to introduce new merchandise. May price items for resale. May be required to be licensed by state. May be identified according to type of commodities, merchandise, or goods purchased. • **GED:** R4, M3, L4 • **SVP:** 1-2 yrs • **Academic:** Ed=H, Eng=G • **Work Field:** 292 • **MPSMS:** 880 • **Aptitudes:** G2, V2, N2, S4, P3, Q3, K4, F4, M4, E5, C4 • **Temperaments:** D, I, J, P, V • **Stress:** E, A • **Physical:** V=L, H=L, L=S, H • **Work Env:** I • **Salary:** 4 • **Outlook:** 4

BUYER, ASSISTANT (ret. tr.) • D.O.T. #162.157-022 • OES #21302 • Performs following duties in connection with purchase and sale of merchandise to aid BUYER (profess. & kin.): Verifies quantity and quality of stock received from manufacturer. Authorizes payment of invoices or return of shipment. Approves advertising copy for newspaper. Gives MARKERS (ret. tr.; whole. tr.) information, such as price mark-ups or mark-downs, manufacturer number, season code, and style number to print on price tickets. Inspects exchanged or refunded merchandise. May sell merchandise to become familiar with customers' attitudes, preferences, and purchasing problems. • **GED:** R4, M3, L3 • **SVP:** 1-2 yrs • **Academic:** Ed=H, Eng=S • **Work Field:** 292 • **MPSMS:** 881 • **Aptitudes:** G2, V2, N3, S3, P3, Q3, K4, F4, M4, E5, C3 •

Temperaments: J, P • **Physical:** V=G, H=L, L=L • **Work Env:** I • **Salary:** 4 • **Outlook:** 3

COMMISSION AGENT, AGRICULTURAL PRODUCE (whole. tr.) • D.O.T. #260.357-010 • OES #49008 • BROKER, AGRICULTURAL PRODUCE. Sells bulk shipments of agricultural produce on commission basis to WHOLESALERS (whole. tr.) I or other buyers for growers or shippers. Deducts expenses and commission from payment received from sale of produce, and remits balance to shipper. May call on wholesalers' customers, such as restaurants and institutional food services, to promote sales and provide nutritional and other information about products. May be required to be licensed and bonded by State. • **GED:** R4, M3, L4 • **SVP:** 1-2 yrs • **Academic:** Ed=N, Eng=G • **Work Field:** 292 • **MPSMS:** 300, 882 • **Aptitudes:** G2, V2, N2, S4, P4, Q3, K4, F4, M4, E5, C5 • **Temperaments:** I, J, M, P • **Stress:** E • **Physical:** V=N, H=L, L=S • **Work Env:** I • **Salary:** 4 • **Outlook:** 3

COMPARISON SHOPPER (ret. tr.) • D.O.T. #296.367-014 • OES #49999 • Compares prices, packaging, physical characteristics, and styles of merchandise in competing stores: Visits stores to observe details of merchandise and gather information that will be valuable to employer in setting prices and determining buying policies. Verifies complaints of customers on price of merchandise by shopping at designated store to ascertain same quality and style for specified price. Prepares reports of findings. May check with BUYER (profess. & kin.) to verify that advertised merchandise will be available for customer purchase, and that merchandise, price, and sales dates are accurately described in advertising copy and illustration. May purchase merchandise in various locations for quality comparison tests. • **GED:** R4, M2, L3 • **SVP:** 30 days-3 mos • **Academic:** Ed=N, Eng=G • **Work Field:** 211, 292 • **MPSMS:** 889 • **Aptitudes:** G3, V3, N4, S5, P3, Q3, K5, F4, M4, E5, C3 • **Temperaments:** J, M • **Physical:** V=L, H=L, L=L, W • **Work Env:** I • **Salary:** 2 • **Outlook:** 3

FOREIGN BANKNOTE TELLER-TRADER (finan. inst.) • D.O.T. #211.362-014 • OES #53102 • Buys and sells foreign currencies and drafts and sells travelers' checks, according to daily international exchange rates, working at counter in foreign exchange office: Questions patrons to determine type of currency or draft desired or offered for sale. Quotes unit exchange rate, using daily international rate sheet. Computes exchange value including fee for transaction, using calculator, and counts out currency. Sells foreign and domestic denomination travelers' checks. Prepares sales slips and records transactions in daily log. Gives information to patrons about foreign currency regulations. Prepares daily inventory of currency, drafts, and travelers' checks. Computes amounts on logsheets and balances with inventory report. • **GED:** R4, M4, L4 • **SVP:** 6 mos-1 yr • **Academic:** Ed=H, Eng=G • **Work Field:** 232 • **MPSMS:** 894 • **Aptitudes:** G2, V3, N2, S4, P3, Q2, K2, F2, M3, E5, C1 • **Temperaments:** M, P, T • **Stress:** E • **Physical:** V=N, H=N, L=S, H • **Work Env:** I • **Salary:** 3 • **Outlook:** 3

PAWNBROKER (ret. tr.) • D.O.T. #191.157-010 • OES #49999 • Estimates pawn or pledge value of articles, such as jewelry, cameras, and musical instruments, and lends money to customer: Examines article to determine condition and worth. Weighs gold or silver articles on coin scales or employs acid tests to verify carat content and purity to verify value of articles. Inspects diamonds and other gems for flaws and color, using loupe (magnifying glass). Assigns pledge value to article based on knowledge of values or listing of wholesale prices. Rejects articles in unsatisfactory condition or having no pledge value. Issues pledge tickets and keeps record of loans. Computes interest when pledges are redeemed or extended. Sells unredeemed pledged items. May examine customer's identification and record thumbprints for police reports. May testify in court proceedings involving stolen merchandise. • **GED:** R4, M4, L4 • **SVP:** 1- 2 yrs • **Academic:** Ed=N, Eng=G • **Work Field:** 211 • **MPSMS:** 894 • **Aptitudes:** G3, V3, N3, S4, P3, Q3, K4, F4, M4, E5, C3 • **Temperaments:** J, M, P, V • **Physical:** V=L, H=N, L=S, H • **Work Env:** I • **Salary:** 3 • **Outlook:** 1

SALES REPRESENTATIVE, LIVESTOCK (whole. tr.) • D.O.T. #260.257-010 • OES #49008 • Sells cattle, horses, hogs, and other livestock on commission to packing houses, farmers, or other purchasers: Contacts prospective buyers to persuade them to purchase livestock. Reviews current market information and inspects livestock to determine their value. Informs buyers of market conditions, care, and breeding of livestock. Attends livestock meetings to keep informed of livestock trends and developments. • **GED:** R4, M3, L4 • **SVP:** 6 mos-1 yr • **Academic:** Ed=N, Eng=G

• **Work Field:** 282, 292 • **MPSMS:** 320 • **Aptitudes:** G2, V2, N3, S4, P4, Q3, K4, F4, M4, E5, C5 • **Temperaments:** I, J, P • **Stress:** E • **Physical:** V=N, H=L, L=S, W • **Work Env:** I • **Salary:** 3 • **Outlook:** 2

08.02 General Sales

Workers in this group sell, demonstrate, and solicit orders for products and services of many kinds. They are employed by retail and wholesale firms, manufacturers and distributors, business services, and non-profit organizations. Some spend all their time in a single location, such as a department store or automobile agency. Others call on businesses or individuals to sell products or services, or follow up on earlier sales.

✔ What kind of work would you do?
Your work activities would depend upon your specific job. For example, you might:

- demonstrate and sell radios and television sets in a department store.
- sell hardware supplies to stock stores.
- help customers find what they want in a jewelry store.
- sell pets and pet supplies in a pet store.
- call people on the telephone to sell them products.
- arrange and conduct demonstration parties in people's homes.
- drive a truck on a set route and sell products to people at their homes.
- call on people in their homes to sell pest control services.
- train or supervise workers in a sales department and keep records of merchandise on hand.

✔ What skills and abilities do you need for this kind of work?
To do this kind of work, you must be able to:

- understand and explain company policies about such things as deferred payment plans, financing charges, returned goods privileges, or service guarantees.
- use arithmetic to total costs of purchase, make change, compute percentages, fill out order and sales forms, and draw up time purchase contracts.
- treat customers with courtesy and respect, even in difficult situations.
- talk easily and persuasively to other people, using language that they'll understand.
- help customers to make up their minds about purchases by suggesting appropriate products.

✔ How do you know if you would like or could learn to do this kind of work?
The following questions may give you clues about yourself as you consider this group of jobs.

- Have you had courses in sales, bookkeeping, or business math? Did you like these courses? Do you have an ability to work with numbers?
- Have you sold items door-to-door? Have you collected money or items for a charity? Do you like to meet people this way?
- Have you given oral reports in front of a group? Do you express your ideas easily to strangers?
- Have you worked in a military PX or cafeteria? Do you enjoy selling items to people?

✔ How can you prepare for and enter this kind of work?

Occupations in this group usually require education and/or training extending from three months to over two years, depending upon the specific kind of work. Most employers require applicants to have a high school education or its equal. Courses in selling or retailing are helpful. Many high schools, junior colleges, and community colleges offer courses and programs in this field. Some schools provide work-study programs in which students work part-time as well as attend classes. Selling experience during vacations is also helpful in preparing for this kind of work.

Employers usually provide on-the-job training to teach new workers about the company policies and the products or services to be sold. These training programs may last from one week to three months. Some workers are required to have extra skills such as driving a truck or playing a musical instrument. Other workers are required to make minor repairs or adjustments on equipment they sell.

Some jobs in this group are supervisory or management positions to which workers with sales experience may be promoted.

✔ What else should you consider about these jobs?

Many retail sales jobs require workers to vary working hours. Some businesses are open to the public on Sundays, holidays, or evenings. Selling is usually done at the customer's convenience.

Some workers are paid by the hour. Others are paid according to how much they sell. However, some workers receive earnings from a combination of these ways.

If you think you would like to do this kind of work, look at the job titles listed on the following pages.

GOE: 08.02.01 Wholesale Sales

MANUFACTURERS' REPRESENTATIVE (whole. tr.) • D.O.T. #279.157-010 • OES #49008 • MANUFACTURERS' AGENT. Sells single, allied, diversified, or multi-line products to WHOLESALERS (whole. tr.) I or other customers for one or more manufacturers on commission basis: Contacts manufacturers and arranges to sell their products. Calls on regular or prospective customers to solicit orders. Demonstrates products and points out salable features. Answers questions concerning products, such as price, credit terms, and durability. May forward orders to manufacturer. • GED: R4, M3, L4 • SVP: 1-2 yrs • Academic: Ed=H, Eng=C • Work Field: 292 • MPSMS: 882 • Aptitudes: G2, V2, N3, S4, P3, Q3, K4, F4, M4, E5, C4 • Temperaments: I, J, P • Stress: E • Physical: V=L, H=L, L=S, W, H • Work Env: I • Salary: 4 • Outlook: 3

SALES REPRESENTATIVE, ANIMAL-FEED PRODUCTS (whole. tr.) • D.O.T. #272.357-010 • OES #49005 • Sells livestock- and poultry-feed products to farmers and retail establishments: Suggests feed changes to improve breeding of fowl and stock. Performs other duties as described under SALES REPRESENTATIVE (ret. tr.; whole. tr.). May specialize in selling feed supplements and be designated as SALES REPRESENTATIVE, CATTLE-AND-POULTRY FEED SUPPLEMENTS (whole. tr.). • GED: R4, M3, L4 • SVP: 1-2 yrs • Academic: Ed=N, Eng=G • Work Field: 292 • MPSMS: 381 • Aptitudes: G3, V3, N3, S4, P4, Q3, K4, F4, M4, E5, C5 • Temperaments: I, J, P • Stress: E • Physical: V=N, H=N, L=S, W • Work Env: I • Salary: 4 • Outlook: 2

SALES REPRESENTATIVE, CANVAS PRODUCTS (whole. tr.) • D.O.T. #261.357-014 • OES #49008 • Sells canvas goods, such as awnings, tents, tarpaulins, covers, and bags, to retail outlets and industrial and commercial establishments, performing duties as described under SALES REPRESENTATIVE (ret. tr.; whole. tr.). May rent tents for events, such as circuses, conventions, or revival meetings. May measure area to be covered by canvas product. May deliver and install awnings [AWNING HANGER (canvas goods; const.; ret. tr.)]. • GED: R4, M3, L4 • SVP: 1-2 yrs • Academic: Ed=N, Eng=G • Work Field: 292 • MPSMS: 436 • Aptitudes: G3, V3, N3, S3, P3, Q3, K4, F4, M4, E5, C4 • Temperaments: I, J, P • Stress: E • Physical: V=L, H=L, L=L, W • Work Env: B • Salary: 4 • Outlook: 3

SALES REPRESENTATIVE, FARM AND GARDEN EQUIPMENT AND SUPPLIES (whole. tr.) • D.O.T. #272.357-014 • OES #49005 • Sells farm and garden machinery, equipment, and supplies, such as tractors, feed, fertilizer, seed, insecticide, and farm and garden implements, performing duties as described under SALES REPRESENTATIVE (ret. tr.; whole. tr.). May sell spare parts and service contracts for machinery and equipment. • GED: R4, M3, L4 • SVP: 6 mos-1 yr • Academic: Ed=N, Eng=G • Work Field: 292 • MPSMS: 562 • Aptitudes: G3, V3, N3, S3, P4, Q3, K4, F4, M4, E5, C5 • Temperaments: I, J, P • Stress: E • Physical: V=N, H=N, L=S, W • Work Env: I • Salary: 4 • Outlook: 3

SALES REPRESENTATIVE, HOME FURNISHINGS (whole. tr.) • D.O.T. #270.357-010 • OES #49011 • Sells home furnishings, such as china, glassware, floor coverings, furniture, linens, brooms, and kitchen articles, performing duties as described under SALES REPRESENTATIVE (ret. tr.; whole. tr.). • GED: R4, M3, L4 • SVP: 6 mos-1 yr • Academic: Ed=N, Eng=G • Work Field: 292 • MPSMS: 882 • Aptitudes: G3, V3, N3, S3, P3, Q3, K4, F4, M4, E5, C4 • Temperaments: I, J, P • Stress: E • Physical: V=N, H=L, L=L, W • Work Env: I • Salary: 3 • Outlook: 4

SALES REPRESENTATIVE, HOUSEHOLD APPLIANCES (whole. tr.) • D.O.T. #270.357-014 • OES #49011 • Sells household appliances, such as refrigerators, ranges, laundry equipment, dishwashers, vacuum cleaners, and room air-conditioning units. Performs duties as described under SALES REPRESENTATIVE (ret. tr.; whole. tr.). May train dealers in operation and use of appliances. • GED: R4, M3, L4 • SVP: 6 mos-1 yr • Academic: Ed=N, Eng=G • Work Field: 292 • MPSMS: 583 • Aptitudes: G3, V3, N3, S4, P4, Q3, K4, F4, M4, E5, C5 • Temperaments: I, J, P • Stress: E • Physical: V=N, H=L, L=S, W • Work Env: I •

Salary: 4 • Outlook: 4

SALES REPRESENTATIVE, MALT LIQUORS (whole. tr.) • D.O.T. #260.357-018 • OES #49008 • Sells beer and other malt liquors to taverns, hotels, restaurants, cocktail lounges, bowling alleys, steamship companies, railroads, military establishments, delicatessens, and supermarkets for wholesale distributor. Performs other duties as described under SALES REPRESENTATIVE (ret. tr.; whole. tr.). Confers with SALES SUPERVISOR, MALT LIQUORS (whole. tr.) to resolve customer problems. • GED: R4, M3, L3 • SVP: 3-6 mos • Academic: Ed=N, Eng=G • Work Field: 292 • MPSMS: 882 • Aptitudes: G3, V3, N3, S4, P4, Q3, K4, F4, M4, E5, C4 • Temperaments: I, J, P • Stress: E • Physical: V=N, H=L, L=S, W • Work Env: I • Salary: 4 • Outlook: 3

SALES REPRESENTATIVE, MEN'S AND BOYS' APPAREL (whole. tr.) • D.O.T. #261.357-022 • OES #49008 • Sells men's and boys' clothing, such as suits, coats, sport jackets, and slacks, utilizing knowledge of garment construction, fabrics, and styles. Performs other duties as described under SALES REPRESENTATIVE (ret. tr.; whole. tr.). • GED: R4, M3, L4 • SVP: 1-2 yrs • Academic: Ed=N, Eng=G • Work Field: 292 • MPSMS: 441 • Aptitudes: G3, V3, N3, S3, P3, Q3, K4, F4, M4, E5, C4 • Temperaments: I, J, P • Stress: E • Physical: V=L, H=L, L=L, W • Work Env: I • Salary: 4 • Outlook: 3

SALES REPRESENTATIVE, NOVELTIES (whole. tr.) • D.O.T. #277.357-018 • OES #49008 • Sells novelties, such as souvenirs, toys, statuettes, glassware, and trinkets, to variety stores, toy stores, and carnivals, performing duties as described under SALES REPRESENTATIVE (ret. tr.; whole. tr.). • GED: R4, M3, L4 • SVP: 3-6 mos • Academic: Ed=A, Eng=G • Work Field: 292 • MPSMS: 610 • Aptitudes: G3, V3, N3, S4, P4, Q3, K4, F4, M4, E5, C5 • Temperaments: I, J, P • Stress: E • Physical: V=N, H=L, L=L, W • Work Env: I • Salary: 3 • Outlook: 3

SALES REPRESENTATIVE, PETROLEUM PRODUCTS (whole. tr.) • D.O.T. #269.357-014 • OES #49008 • Sells petroleum products, such as gasoline, oil, greases, and lubricants, performing duties as described under SALES REPRESENTATIVE (ret. tr.; whole. tr.). May be designated according to specific petroleum product sold as SALES REPRESENTATIVE, INDUSTRIAL LUBRICANTS (whole. tr.). • GED: R4, M3, L4 • SVP: 1-2 yrs • Academic: Ed=N, Eng=G • Work Field: 292 • MPSMS: 500 • Aptitudes: G3, V3, N3, S4, P4, Q3, K4, F4, M4, E5, C5 • Temperaments: I, J, P • Stress: E • Physical: V=N, H=L, L=S, W • Work Env: I • Salary: 4 • Outlook: 3

SALES REPRESENTATIVE, RECREATION AND SPORTING GOODS (whole. tr.) • D.O.T. #277.357-026 • OES #49008 • Sells amusement and sporting goods, such as hunting and fishing equipment, camping equipment, athletic equipment, playground equipment, toys, and games: Performs duties as described under SALES REPRESENTATIVE (ret. tr.; whole. tr.). May be designated according to product sold as SALES REPRESENTATIVE, PLAYGROUND EQUIPMENT (whole. tr.); SALES REPRESENTATIVE, SPORTING GOODS (whole. tr.); SALES REPRESENTATIVE, TOYS AND GAMES (ret. tr.; whole. tr.). • GED: R4, M3, L4 • SVP: 6 mos-1 yr • Academic: Ed=N, Eng=G • Work Field: 292 • MPSMS: 610 • Aptitudes: G3, V3, N3, S3, P3, Q3, K4, F4, M4, E5, C4 • Temperaments: I, J, P • Stress: E • Physical: V=N, H=N, L=L, W • Work Env: I • Salary: 2 • Outlook: 3

SALES REPRESENTATIVE, TEXTILES (whole. tr.) • D.O.T. #261.357-030 • OES #49008 • Sells textile fabrics, such as cottons, wools, synthetics, and combination blends, to garment manufacturers, retail stores, textile converters, and buying offices, utilizing knowledge of textile construction, fabrics, fashion, and textile products. Performs other duties as described under SALES REPRESENTATIVE (ret. tr.; whole. tr.). May sell raw fibers to spinning mills and be designated SALES REPRESENTATIVE, RAW FIBERS (whole. tr.). • GED: R4, M3, L4 • SVP: 1-2 yrs • Academic: Ed=N, Eng=G • Work Field: 292 • MPSMS: 410, 420, 430 • Aptitudes: G2, V2, N3, S4, P3, Q3, K4, F4, M4, E5, C3 • Temperaments: I, J, P • Stress: E • Physical: V=L, H=L, L=L, W • Work Env: I • Salary: 4 • Outlook: 3

SALES REPRESENTATIVE, VIDEOTAPE (whole. tr.) • D.O.T. #271.357-014 • OES #49011 • Sells television tape, used to record programs for delayed play-back, performing duties as described

under SALES REPRESENTATIVE (ret. tr.; whole. tr.). • GED: R4, M3, L4 • SVP: 30 days-3 mos • Academic: Ed=N, Eng=S • Work Field: 292 • MPSMS: 586 • Aptitudes: G3, V3, N3, S4, P4, Q3, K4, F4, M4, E5, C5 • Temperaments: I, J, P • Stress: E • Physical: V=N, H=N, L=S, W • Work Env: I • Salary: 2 • Outlook: 4

SALES REPRESENTATIVE, WOMEN'S AND GIRLS' APPAREL (whole. tr.) • D.O.T. #261.357-038 • OES #49008 • Sells women's and girls' apparel, such as coats, dresses, lingerie, and accessories, utilizing knowledge of fabrics, style, and prices. Performs other duties as described under SALES REPRESENTATIVE (ret. tr.; whole. tr.). May specialize according to price range of garment sold. May sell only girls' or women's apparel and be designated SALES REPRESENTATIVE, GIRLS' APPAREL (whole. tr.); SALES REPRESENTATIVE, WOMEN'S APPAREL (whole. tr.). • GED: R4, M3, L4 • SVP: 6 mos-1 yr • Academic: Ed=N, Eng=G • Work Field: 292 • MPSMS: 440 • Aptitudes: G3, V3, N3, S4, P3, Q3, K4, F4, M4, E5, C4 • Temperaments: I, J, P • Stress: E • Physical: V=L, H=L, L=L, W • Work Env: I • Salary: 4 • Outlook: 3

SALES-PROMOTION REPRESENTATIVE (whole. tr.) • D.O.T. #269.357-018 • OES #43023 • Persuades customers to use sales promotion display items of wholesale commodity distributor: Visits retail establishments, such as department stores, taverns, supermarkets, and clubs to persuade customers to use display items to promote sale of company products. Delivers promotion items, such as posters, glasses, napkins, and samples of product, and arranges display of items in customer's establishment. May take sales order from customer. • GED: R4, M2, L3 • SVP: 30 days-3 mos • Academic: Ed=N, Eng=G • Work Field: 292 • MPSMS: 882 • Aptitudes: G3, V3, N4, S4, P3, Q3, K3, F3, M3, E4, C4 • Temperaments: I, J, P • Stress: E • Physical: V=N, H=L, L=S, W, H • Work Env: I • Salary: 2 • Outlook: 3

GOE: 08.02.02 Retail

SALES EXHIBITOR (nonprofit org.) • D.O.T. #279.357-010 • OES #49032 • Sells variety of products made by the blind, such as wallets, mops, neckties, rugs, aprons, and babywear: Contacts businesses and civic establishments and arranges to exhibit and sell merchandise made by the blind on their premises. Sets up and displays merchandise to attract attention of prospective customers. Performs other duties as described under SALESPERSON (ret. tr.; whole. tr.). • GED: R3, M2, L3 • SVP: 30 days-3 mos • Academic: Ed=N, Eng=G • Work Field: 292 • MPSMS: 889 • Aptitudes: G3, V3, N3, S4, P4, Q4, K4, F4, M4, E5, C4 • Temperaments: I, J, P • Stress: E • Physical: V=L, H=L, L=L, W, H • Work Env: I • Salary: 2 • Outlook: 3

SALES-SERVICE REPRESENTATIVE, MILKING MACHINES (ret. tr.) • D.O.T. #299.251-010 • OES #49005 • Sells, installs, and repairs milking equipment: Calls on farmers to solicit repair business and to sell new milking equipment, such as vacuum pumps, buckets, pipelines, and replacement parts. Demonstrates milking machines. Cuts and threads pipe and attaches fittings, using plumber's tools, to install pipelines. Cleans and flushes pipelines, and repairs pulsators and vacuum pumps. • GED: R4, M3, L4 • SVP: 1-2 yrs • Academic: Ed=H, Eng=S • Work Field: 121, 292 • MPSMS: 562 • Aptitudes: G2, V3, N3, S2, P3, Q3, K3, F3, M3, E4, C5 • Temperaments: I, J, M, P • Physical: V=L, H=L, L=M, W, H • Work Env: B • Salary: 4 • Outlook: 3

SALESPERSON, ART OBJECTS (ret. tr.) • D.O.T. #277.457-010 • OES #49011 • Sells paintings, art materials, curios, and mirror and picture frames, performing duties as described under SALESPERSON (ret. tr.; whole. tr.). • GED: R3, M2, L3 • SVP: 3-6 mos • Academic: Ed=N, Eng=S • Work Field: 292 • MPSMS: 881 • Aptitudes: G3, V3, N3, S4, P4, Q3, K4, F4, M4, E5, C4 • Temperaments: I, J, P • Physical: V=G, H=G, L=L, H • Work Env: I • Salary: 3 • Outlook: 3

SALESPERSON, AUTOMOBILES (ret. tr.) • D.O.T. #273.353-010 • OES #49011 • SALESPERSON, CARS. Sells new or used automobiles on premises of automobile agency: Explains features and demonstrates operation of car in showroom or on road. Suggests optional equipment for customer to purchase. Computes and quotes sales price, including tax, trade-in allowance, license fee, and discount, and requirements for financing payment of car on credit. Performs other duties as described under SALESPERSON (ret. tr.; whole. tr.). May be designated as SALESPERSON, NEW CARS (ret. tr.); SALESPERSON, USED CARS (ret. tr.). • **GED:** R4, M3, L4 • **SVP:** 6 mos-1 yr • **Academic:** Ed=H, Eng=G • **Work Field:** 292 • **MPSMS:** 591 • **Aptitudes:** G3, V3, N3, S3, P3, Q3, K3, F4, M4, E3, C4 • **Temperaments:** I, P • **Stress:** E • **Physical:** V=L, H=L, L=S, W, H • **Work Env:** B • **Salary:** 4 • **Outlook:** 3

SALESPERSON, BOOKS (ret. tr.) • D.O.T. #277.357-034 • OES #49011 • Sells books in book or department store: Suggests selection of books, based on knowledge of current literature and familiarity with publishers' catalogs and book reviews. Arranges books on shelves and racks according to type, author, or subject matter. Performs other duties as described under SALESPERSON (ret. tr.; whole. tr.). May specialize in selling technical publications. • **GED:** R4, M3, L4 • **SVP:** 3-6 mos • **Academic:** Ed=N, Eng=G • **Work Field:** 292 • **MPSMS:** 480, 757 • **Aptitudes:** G3, V2, N3, S4, P4, Q3, K3, F3, M4, E5, C5 • **Temperaments:** I, J, P • **Stress:** E • **Physical:** V=L, H=N, L=L, H • **Work Env:** I • **Salary:** 2 • **Outlook:** 3

SALESPERSON, COSMETICS AND TOILETRIES (ret. tr.) • D.O.T. #262.357-018 • OES #49011 • Sells cosmetics and toiletries, such as skin creams, hair preparations, face powder, lipstick, and perfume, to customers in department store or specialty shop: Demonstrates methods of application of various preparations to customer. Explains beneficial properties of preparations and suggests shades or varieties of makeup to suit customer's complexion. May weigh and mix facial powders, according to established formula, to obtain desired shade, using spatula and scale. Performs other duties as described under SALESPERSON (ret. tr.; whole. tr.). • **GED:** R3, M3, L3 • **SVP:** 3-6 mos • **Academic:** Ed=N, Eng=G • **Work Field:** 292 • **MPSMS:** 494 • **Aptitudes:** G3, V3, N3, S4, P3, Q3, K3, F3, M3, E5, C3 • **Temperaments:** I, J, P • **Stress:** E • **Physical:** V=L, H=L, L=L, H • **Work Env:** I • **Salary:** 3 • **Outlook:** 3

SALESPERSON, CURTAINS AND DRAPERIES (ret. tr.) • D.O.T. #270.357-022 • OES #49011 • Sells curtains, draperies, slipcovers, bedspreads, and yard goods from which these may be made: Displays samples of fabric and advises customer regarding color and pattern of material or style that will complement furnishings in customer's home. Selects size or number of curtains or drapes required, based on customer's specifications or window measurements. May estimate cost of fabricating draperies, curtains, or slipcovers. May measure and cut fabric from bolt. May also sell curtain and drapery rods and window shades. Performs other duties as described under SALESPERSON (ret. tr.; whole. tr.). May sell custom-made draperies to customers in their homes and be designated SALESPERSON, CUSTOM DRAPERIES (ret. tr.). • **GED:** R4, M3, L4 • **SVP:** 3-6 mos • **Academic:** Ed=N, Eng=S • **Work Field:** 292 • **MPSMS:** 420, 439 • **Aptitudes:** G3, V3, N3, S3, P3, Q3, K4, F4, M4, E5, C3 • **Temperaments:** I, J, M, P • **Stress:** E • **Physical:** V=L, H=L, L=L, W, H • **Work Env:** I • **Salary:** 4 • **Outlook:** 4

SALESPERSON, FLOWERS (ret. tr.) • D.O.T. #260.357-026 • OES #49011 • Sells natural and artificial flowers, potted plants, floral pieces, and accessories: Advises customer regarding type of flowers, floral arrangements, and decorations desirable for specific occasions, utilizing knowledge of social and religious customs. Arranges display of flowers and decorative accessories, such as vases and ceramics. Performs other duties as described under SALESPERSON (ret. tr.; whole. tr.). May contact florists in other communities by telegraph or telephone to place orders for out-of-town delivery. May design and make up corsages, wreaths, sprays, and other floral decorations. • **GED:** R4, M3, L3 • **SVP:** 3-6 mos • **Academic:** Ed=N, Eng=S • **Work Field:** 292 • **MPSMS:** 311 • **Aptitudes:** G3, V3, N3, S3, P3, Q3, K3, F3, M3, E5, C3 • **Temperaments:** F, I, J, P • **Stress:** E • **Physical:** V=N, H=N, L=L, H • **Work Env:** I, W • **Salary:** 1 • **Outlook:** 4

SALESPERSON, FURNITURE (ret. tr.) • D.O.T. #270.357-030 • OES #49011 • Sells furniture, beds, and mattresses in department store or furniture store: Advises customer on type of furniture that will complement other furnishings in customer's home by suggesting period styles, colors, and woods. Discusses quality of fabric and trimmings, finish and grain of wood, and method of construction with customer. May resolve customer complaints regarding delivery of damaged or incorrect merchandise. Performs other duties as described under SALESPERSON (ret. tr.; whole. tr.). • **GED:** R4, M3, L4 • **SVP:** 3-6 mos • **Academic:** Ed=N, Eng=S • **Work Field:** 292 • **MPSMS:** 460 • **Aptitudes:** G3, V3, N3, S3, P3, Q3, K3, F3, M4, E5, C3 • **Temperaments:** I, J, P • **Stress:** E • **Physical:** V=L, H=L, L=S, W, H • **Work Env:** I • **Salary:** 4 • **Outlook:** 4

SALESPERSON, HEARING AIDS (ret. tr.) • D.O.T. #276.354-010 • OES #49011 • HEARING-AID TECHNICIAN. Sells hearing aids to customers in retail establishment: Tests customer's hearing, using audiometer, to determine need for hearing aid in cases where customer is not referred to store by PHYSICIAN (medical ser.). Confers with customer concerning particular hearing needs to select type and style of aid. Demonstrates use of aid to customer and fits aid. Performs other duties as described under SALESPERSON (ret. tr.; whole. tr.). May replace defective parts or make repairs to equipment returned by customer. • **GED:** R4, M3, L4 • **SVP:** 6 mos-1 yr • **Academic:** Ed=H, Eng=G • **Work Field:** 292 • **MPSMS:** 589 • **Aptitudes:** G3, V3, N3, S3, P3, Q3, K3, F3, M3, E5, C5 • **Temperaments:** I, J, M, P • **Stress:** E • **Physical:** V=N, H=L, L=L, H • **Work Env:** I • **Salary:** 3 • **Outlook:** 3

SALESPERSON, HOUSEHOLD APPLIANCES (ret. tr.) • D.O.T. #270.357-034 • OES #49011 • Sells radios, television sets, and other household appliances to customers: Explains features of appliances, such as stoves, refrigerators, vacuum cleaners, and washing machines. Demonstrates television, radio, and phonograph sets. Performs other duties as described under SALESPERSON (ret. tr.; whole. tr.). May sell service contracts for appliances sold. May demonstrate appliances on display floor of utility company and refer interested customers to appliance dealers for purchase. • **GED:** R4, M3, L4 • **SVP:** 3-6 mos • **Academic:** Ed=N, Eng=S • **Work Field:** 292 • **MPSMS:** 583, 585 • **Aptitudes:** G3, V3, N3, S4, P4, Q3, K4, F3, M3, E5, C4 • **Temperaments:** I, J, P • **Stress:** E • **Physical:** V=L, H=L, L=L, W, H • **Work Env:** I • **Salary:** 4 • **Outlook:** 4

SALESPERSON, INFANTS' AND CHILDREN'S WEAR (ret. tr.) • D.O.T. #261.357-046 • OES #49011 • Sells infants' and children's wearing apparel, nursery furniture, and bedding: Advises customer on durability of merchandise and quantity to purchase for infants. Suggests gift items or sizes of infants' clothes. May sell infants' and children's shoes. Performs other duties as described under SALESPERSON (ret. tr.; whole. tr.). • **GED:** R4, M3, L4 • **SVP:** 30 days-3 mos • **Academic:** Ed=N, Eng=S • **Work Field:** 292 • **MPSMS:** 881 • **Aptitudes:** G3, V3, N3, S4, P3, Q4, K3, F3, M3, E5, C4 • **Temperaments:** I, J, P • **Stress:** E • **Physical:** V=L, H=L, L=L, W, H • **Work Env:** I • **Salary:** 3 • **Outlook:** 3

SALESPERSON, JEWELRY (ret. tr.) • D.O.T. #279.357-058 • OES #49011 • Displays and sells jewelry and watches: Advises customer on quality, cuts, or value of jewelry and gems and in selecting mountings or settings for gems. Informs customer of various grades of watch movements and type of servicing offered by manufacturer. Performs other duties as described under SALESPERSON (ret. tr.; whole. tr.). May estimate cost of jewelry and watch repair. May suggest designs for custom jewelry. May sell flatware, hollowware, and tableware, and advise customer on quality, grades, and patterns. • **GED:** R4, M3, L4 • **SVP:** 6 mos-1 yr • **Academic:** Ed=H, Eng=S • **Work Field:** 292 • **MPSMS:** 607, 611 • **Aptitudes:** G3, V3, N3, S4, P3, Q3, K3, F3, M4, E5, C3 • **Temperaments:** I, J, P • **Physical:** V=G, H=G, L=L, H • **Work Env:** I • **Salary:** 3 • **Outlook:** 3

SALESPERSON, MEN'S AND BOYS' CLOTHING (ret. tr.) • D.O.T. #261.357-050 • OES #49011 • Sells men's and boys' outer garments, such as suits, trousers, and coats: Advises customer about prevailing styles and suitability of garments. Answers questions relative to fabric or design of garment. Selects standard-sized garments nearest to customer's measurements. May mark garment for alterations. Performs other duties as described under SALESPERSON (ret. tr.; whole. tr.). • **GED:** R4, M3, L4 • **SVP:** 6 mos-1 yr • **Academic:** Ed=N, Eng=S • **Work Field:** 292 • **MPSMS:** 441 • **Aptitudes:** G3, V3, N3, S3, P3, Q4, K3, F3, M3, E5, C3 • **Temperaments:** I, J, P • **Stress:** E • **Physical:** V=L,

H=L, L=L, W, H • **Work Env:** I • **Salary:** 4 • **Outlook:** 3

SALESPERSON, MUSICAL INSTRUMENTS AND ACCESSORIES (ret. tr.) • D.O.T. #277.357-038 • OES #49011 • Sells brass, percussion, stringed, and woodwind musical instruments, musical accessories, equipment, and supplies: Explains function, mechanisms, and care of musical instruments to customer. Demonstrates and discusses quality of tone and variations in instruments of different prices. Performs other duties as described under SALESPERSON (ret. tr.; whole. tr.). May make repairs. May solicit business of orchestras or other musical groups. May rent instruments to customers and prepare rental contracts. • **GED:** R4, M3, L4 • **SVP:** 1-2 yrs • **Academic:** Ed=N, Eng=G • **Work Field:** 292 • **MPSMS:** 614 • **Aptitudes:** G2, V3, N3, S3, P3, Q3, K3, F3, M3, E5, C4 • **Temperaments:** I, J, P • **Stress:** E • **Physical:** V=N, H=N, L=L, H • **Work Env:** I • **Salary:** 3 • **Outlook:** 2

SALESPERSON, PHONOGRAPH RECORDS AND TAPE RECORDINGS (ret. tr.) • D.O.T. #277.357-046 • OES #49011 • Sells phonograph records and tape recordings in music store, record shop, or department store, performing duties as described under SALESPERSON (ret. tr.; whole. tr.). Assists customers in selection of instrumental and vocal recordings in musical categories, such as popular, classical, folk, and religious, using knowledge of available releases, catalogs, and lists. May also sell recording maintenance equipment and supplies. • **GED:** R3, M3, L3 • **SVP:** 30 days- 3 mos • **Academic:** Ed=N, Eng=S • **Work Field:** 292 • **MPSMS:** 881 • **Aptitudes:** G3, V3, N3, S4, P4, Q3, K4, F4, M4, E5, C5 • **Temperaments:** I, M, P • **Physical:** V=L, H=G, L=L, H • **Work Env:** I • **Salary:** 2 • **Outlook:** 3

SALESPERSON, PIANOS AND ORGANS (ret. tr.) • D.O.T. #277.354-010 • OES #49011 • Sells pianos or organs: Plays instrument to demonstrate tonal qualities of piano or combinations of tones on organ. Discusses construction and operating techniques of organs, or construction of piano with effect on tone, quality, and limitations. Advises customer on style of organ or piano to harmonize with other furniture. May appraise used organs or pianos for trade-in allowance. May rent pianos or organs and prepare rental contracts. Performs duties as described under SALESPERSON (ret. tr.; whole. tr.). • **GED:** R4, M3, L4 • **SVP:** 1-2 yrs • **Academic:** Ed=H, Eng=S • **Work Field:** 292 • **MPSMS:** 614 • **Aptitudes:** G2, V3, N3, S4, P3, Q3, K3, F3, M3, E5, C4 • **Temperaments:** I, J, P • **Physical:** V=L, H=G, L=L, H • **Work Env:** I • **Salary:** 4 • **Outlook:** 2

SALESPERSON, SHOES (ret. tr.) • D.O.T. #261.357-062 • OES #49011 • Fits and sells shoes, boots, and other footwear: Ascertains customer's shoe size or measures customer's foot on measuring device. Obtains footwear of specified style, color, and size from stock. Stretches shoes, using hand stretchers, or inserts cotton or cork pads in heel seat or instep of shoe to tighten fit. May sell related products, such as handbags, hosiery, shoetrees, and shoe polish. Performs other duties as described under SALESPERSON (ret. tr.; whole. tr.). May be designated according to type of shoes sold as SALESPERSON, CHILDREN'S SHOES (ret. tr.); SALESPERSON, MEN'S SHOES (ret. tr.); SALESPERSON, WOMEN'S SHOES (ret. tr.). • **GED:** R4, M3, L4 • **SVP:** 30 days-3 mos • **Academic:** Ed=N, Eng=S • **Work Field:** 292 • **MPSMS:** 512, 522 • **Aptitudes:** G3, V3, N3, S4, P3, Q4, K3, F3, M3, E5, C3 • **Temperaments:** I, J, P • **Stress:** E • **Physical:** V=L, H=L, L=L, W, S, H • **Work Env:** I • **Salary:** 4 • **Outlook:** 3

SALESPERSON, SPORTING GOODS (ret. tr.) • D.O.T. #277.357-058 • OES #49011 • Sells sporting goods and athletic equipment: Advises customer on type of equipment for specific purposes, such as length of golf club, size of grip on tennis racket, weight of bowling ball, length of skis and poles, and caliber and make of gun or rifle. Explains care of equipment, regulations of games, and fish and game laws. Informs customer of areas for hunting, fishing, or skiing, and cost of such outings. Performs other duties as described under SALESPERSON (ret. tr.; whole. tr.). May repair sporting goods. • **GED:** R4, M3, L4 • **SVP:** 6 mos-1 yr • **Academic:** Ed=N, Eng=S • **Work Field:** 292 • **MPSMS:** 616 • **Aptitudes:** G3, V3, N3, S4, P3, Q3, K3, F3, M3, E5, C4 • **Temperaments:** I, J, P • **Stress:** E • **Physical:** V=N, H=L, L=L, H • **Work Env:** I • **Salary:** 2 • **Outlook:** 3

SALESPERSON, STEREO EQUIPMENT (ret. tr.) • D.O.T. #270.357-038 • OES #49011 • Sells home-entertainment electronic sound equipment and parts, such as stereophonic phonographs, recording equipment, radios, speakers, tuners, amplifiers, microphones, and record changers. Explains features of various brands, meaning of technical manufacturers' specifications, and method of installation, applying knowledge of electronics. Performs other duties as described under SALESPERSON (ret. tr.; whole. tr.). • **GED:** R4, M3, L4 • **SVP:** 3-6 mos • **Academic:** Ed=N, Eng=S • **Work Field:** 292 • **MPSMS:** 585 • **Aptitudes:** G3, V3, N3, S4, P3, Q3, K3, F3, M3, E5, C4 • **Temperaments:** I, J, P • **Stress:** E • **Physical:** V=L, H=L, L=M, W, H • **Work Env:** I • **Salary:** 4 • **Outlook:** 4

SALESPERSON, SURGICAL APPLIANCES (ret. tr.) • D.O.T. #276.257-022 • OES #49005 • FITTER; SURGICAL-APPLIANCE FITTER. Fits and sells surgical appliances, such as trusses, abdominal supports, braces, cervical collars, and artificial limbs, using knowledge of anatomy, orthopedics, orthotics, and prosthetics: Measures customer with tape measure or follows prescription from PHYSICIAN (medical ser.) to determine type and size of appliance required. Selects appliance from stock and fits appliance on customer. Writes specifications for and orders custom-made appliances. Performs other duties as described under SALESPERSON (ret. tr.; whole. tr.). May design and fabricate, or direct fabrication of custom-made appliances. • **GED:** R5, M3, L4 • **SVP:** 1-2 yrs • **Academic:** Ed=A, Eng=S • **Work Field:** 292 • **MPSMS:** 604 • **Aptitudes:** G2, V2, N3, S2, P3, Q3, K4, F4, M4, E5, C4 • **Temperaments:** I, J, M, P, T • **Physical:** V=L, H=L, L=L, W, S, H • **Work Env:** I • **Salary:** 4 • **Outlook:** 2

SALESPERSON, WOMEN'S APPAREL AND ACCESSORIES (ret. tr.) • D.O.T. #261.357-066 • OES #49011 • SALESPERSON, LADIES' WEAR. Sells women's clothing and fashion accessories, such as coats, sportswear, suits, dresses, formal gowns, lingerie, hosiery, belts, gloves, costume jewelry, handbags, and scarfs: Advises customer as to current fashion, style of garment to suit age and figure, and coordination of accessories with apparel. Answers questions regarding weave, washability, durability, or color fastness of various fabrics. May make repairs or alterations. Performs other duties as described under SALESPERSON (ret. tr.; whole. tr.). May be designated according to specific category or type of item sold as SALESPERSON, FASHION ACCESSORIES (ret. tr.); SALESPERSON, HANDBAGS (ret. tr.); SALESPERSON, HOSIERY (ret. tr.); SALESPERSON, LINGERIE (ret. tr.); SALESPERSON, WOMEN'S APPAREL (ret. tr.); SALESPERSON, WOMEN'S DRESSES (ret. tr.); SALESPERSON, WOMEN'S SPORTSWEAR (ret. tr.). • **GED:** R4, M3, L4 • **SVP:** 30 days-3 mos • **Academic:** Ed=N, Eng=S • **Work Field:** 292 • **MPSMS:** 880 • **Aptitudes:** G3, V3, N3, S3, P3, Q4, K3, F3, M3, E5, C3 • **Temperaments:** I, J, P • **Stress:** E • **Physical:** V=L, H=L, L=L, W, H • **Work Env:** I • **Salary:** 4 • **Outlook:** 3

SALESPERSON, YARD GOODS (ret. tr.) • D.O.T. #261.357-070 • OES #49011 • Sells yard goods made from cotton, linen, wool, silk, synthetic fibers, and other materials: Unrolls bolts of cloth to display assortment of fabrics to customer. Advises customer as to kind and quantity of material required to make garments, bed clothes, curtains, and other articles. Discusses features and qualities of fabric, such as weave, texture, color, and washability. Suggests harmonizing or matching colors of fabrics. Measures and cuts length of fabric from bolt, using scissors and measuring machine or yardstick. Performs other duties as described under SALESPERSON (ret. tr.; whole. tr.). May sell sewing accessories and notions, such as dress patterns, needlecraft books, needles, thread, buttons, and zippers. • **GED:** R4, M3, L4 • **SVP:** 30 days-3 mos • **Academic:** Ed=N, Eng=S • **Work Field:** 292 • **MPSMS:** 420 • **Aptitudes:** G3, V3, N3, S3, P3, Q4, K3, F3, M3, E5, C3 • **Temperaments:** I, J, P • **Stress:** E • **Physical:** V=L, H=L, L=L, H • **Work Env:** I • **Salary:** 2 • **Outlook:** 3

GOE: 08.02.03 Wholesale & Retail Sales

AUCTIONEER (ret. tr.) • D.O.T. #294.257-010 • OES #49999 • Sells articles at auction to highest bidder: Appraises merchandise before sale and assembles merchandise in lots according to estimated value of individual pieces or type of article. Selects article to be auctioned at suggestion of bidders or by own choice. Appraises article and determines or asks for starting bid. Describes merchandise and gives information about article, such as history and ownership, in order to encourage bidding. Continues to ask for bids, attempting to stimulate buying desire of bidders. Closes sale to highest bidder. May write auction catalog and advertising copy for local or trade newspapers and periodicals. May be designated according to property auctioned as AUCTIONEER, ART (ret. tr.; whole. tr.); AUCTIONEER, AUTOMOBILE (whole. tr.); AUCTIONEER, FURNITURE (ret. tr.; whole. tr.); AUCTIONEER, LIVESTOCK (ret. tr.; whole. tr.); AUCTIONEER, REAL ESTATE (ret. tr.; whole. tr.); AUCTIONEER, TOBACCO (whole. tr.). • **GED:** R3, M2, L3 • **SVP:** 1-2 yrs • **Academic:** Ed=N, Eng=G • **Work Field:** 211, 292 • **MPSMS:** 881, 882 • **Aptitudes:** G3, V2, N4, S5, P3, Q3, K4, F4, M4, E5, C4 • **Temperaments:** F, I, J, P • **Stress:** E • **Physical:** V=L, H=G, L=S, H • **Work Env:** I • **Salary:** 4 • **Outlook:** 1

SALES REPRESENTATIVE, BOATS AND MARINE SUPPLIES (ret. tr.) • D.O.T. #273.357-018 • OES #49011 • Sells boats and marine equipment and supplies, such as fixtures, pumps, instruments, cordage, paints, and motor parts: Shows boat on sales floor or shows catalog pictures and blueprints. Explains construction and performance of boat and differences between various types of marine equipment. Advises boat owners on selection of new equipment and problems pertaining to repairs. Performs other duties as described under SALES REPRESENTATIVE (ret. tr.; whole. tr.). May demonstrate boat in water. May arrange for delivery, registration, and inspection of boat. May sell water-sports equipment, such as water skis and scuba gear. May sell marine equipment and supplies, except boats, and be designated SALES REPRESENTATIVE, MARINE SUPPLIES (ret. tr.; whole. tr.). • **GED:** R4, M3, L4 • **SVP:** 6 mos-1 yr • **Academic:** Ed=N, Eng=G • **Work Field:** 292 • **MPSMS:** 593, 881, 882 • **Aptitudes:** G3, V3, N3, S3, P3, Q3, K4, F4, M3, E5, C4 • **Temperaments:** I, J, P • **Stress:** E • **Physical:** V=N, H=L, L=S, W, H • **Work Env:** I • **Salary:** 4 • **Outlook:** 3

SALES REPRESENTATIVE, OFFICE MACHINES (ret. tr.) • D.O.T. #275.357-034 • OES #49008 • Sells office machines, such as typewriters and adding, calculating, and duplicating machines, to business establishments: Performs duties as described under SALES REPRESENTATIVE (ret. tr.; whole. tr.). May instruct employees or purchasers in use of machine. May make machine adjustments. May sell office supplies, such as paper, ribbons, ink, and tapes. May rent or lease office machines. May be designated according to type of machine sold as SALES REPRESENTATIVE, ADDING MACHINES (whole. tr.); SALES REPRESENTATIVE, CALCULATING MACHINES (whole. tr.); SALES REPRESENTATIVE, CASH REGISTERS (whole. tr.); SALES REPRESENTATIVE, DICTATING MACHINES (whole. tr.); SALES REPRESENTATIVE, DUPLICATING MACHINES (whole. tr.); SALES REPRESENTATIVE, TYPEWRITERS (whole. tr.). Additional titles: SALES REPRESENTATIVE, ADDRESSING MACHINES (whole. tr.); SALES REPRESENTATIVE, BOOKKEEPING-AND-ACCOUNTING MACHINES (whole. tr.); SALES REPRESENTATIVE, CHECK-ENDORSING-AND-SIGNING MACHINES (whole. tr.); SALES REPRESENTATIVE, STENOGRAPHIC MACHINES (whole. tr.). • **GED:** R4, M3, L4 • **SVP:** 6 mos-1 yr • **Academic:** Ed=N, Eng=G • **Work Field:** 292 • **MPSMS:** 571 • **Aptitudes:** G3, V2, N3, S3, P3, Q3, K3, F3, M3, E5, C5 • **Temperaments:** I, J, P • **Stress:** E • **Physical:** V=N, H=L, L=M, W • **Work Env:** I • **Salary:** 4 • **Outlook:** 4

SALES REPRESENTATIVE, TOBACCO PRODUCTS AND SMOKING SUPPLIES (ret. tr.) • D.O.T. #260.357-022 • OES #49008 • Sells tobacco products, such as cigars, cigarettes, and pipe tobacco, and smoking supplies, such as pipes and tobacco pouches, performing duties as described under SALES REPRESENTATIVE (ret. tr.; whole. tr.). May also sell confectionery and chewing gum products. • **GED:** R4, M3, L3 • **SVP:** 6 mos-1 yr • **Academic:** Ed=N, Eng=G • **Work Field:** 292 • **MPSMS:** 403, 409, 619 • **Aptitudes:** G3, V3, N3, S4, P3, Q3, K4, F4, M4, E5, C4 • **Temperaments:** I, P • **Stress:** E • **Physical:** V=N, H=L, L=S, W • **Work Env:** I • **Salary:** 4 • **Outlook:** 3

SALESPERSON, AUTOMOBILE ACCESSORIES (ret. tr.) • D.O.T. #273.357-030 • OES #49011 • Sells automobile supplies and accessories, such as tires, batteries, seat covers, mufflers, and headlights: Ascertains make and year of automobile and reads catalog for stock number of item. Performs other duties as described under SALESPERSON (ret. tr.; whole. tr.). • **GED:** R4, M3, L4 • **SVP:** 3-6 mos • **Academic:** Ed=H, Eng=S • **Work Field:** 292 • **MPSMS:** 591 • **Aptitudes:** G3, V3, N3, S4, P4, Q3, K4, F4, M3, E5, C5 • **Temperaments:** I, J, P • **Physical:** V=G, H=G, L=L, W • **Work Env:** I • **Salary:** 3 • **Outlook:** 4

SALESPERSON, FLOOR COVERINGS (ret. tr.) • D.O.T. #270.357-026 • OES #49011 • Displays and sells floor coverings, such as carpets, rugs, and linoleum, in department store, specialty store, or showroom: Shows rugs or samples of carpets to customer. Explains qualities of various rugs and carpets, such as composition, method of fabrication, and wearing qualities. Estimates cost and amount of covering required, referring to customer's floor plans. Performs other duties as described under SALESPERSON (ret. tr.; whole. tr.). May measure floor and sell floor coverings in customer's home or place of business and be designated FLOOR-COVERINGS ESTIMATOR (ret. tr.; whole. tr.); SALESPERSON, TERRAZZO TILES (ret. tr.; whole. tr.). • **GED:** R4, M3, L4 • **SVP:** 3- 6 mos • **Academic:** Ed=N, Eng=S • **Work Field:** 292 • **MPSMS:** 431, 619 • **Aptitudes:** G3, V3, N3, S4, P4, Q3, K3, F4, M4, E5, C3 • **Temperaments:** I, J, M, P • **Stress:** E • **Physical:** V=L, H=L, L=S, W, S, H • **Work Env:** I • **Salary:** 4 • **Outlook:** 4

SALESPERSON, GENERAL HARDWARE (ret. tr.) • D.O.T. #279.357-050 • OES #49011 • FLOOR CLERK, HARDWARE. Sells hardware, such as builder's hardware, electrical equipment, gardening tools and equipment, household hardware, paints, plumbing supplies, and woodworking equipment: Advises customer concerning quality and demonstrates uses of hardware, tools, and equipment. Performs related duties, such as estimating amount of paint required to cover given area, advising customer on methods of mixing paint, and cutting screens, glass, wire, or window shades to specified sizes or lengths. Performs other duties as described under SALESPERSON (ret. tr.; whole. tr.). May specialize in selling paint and be designated as SALESPERSON, PAINT (ret. tr.; whole. tr.); SALESPERSON, WALL COVERINGS (ret. tr.; whole. tr.). • **GED:** R4, M3, L4 • **SVP:** 3-6 mos • **Academic:** Ed=N, Eng=S • **Work Field:** 292 • **MPSMS:** 881, 882 • **Aptitudes:** G3, V3, N3, S4, P3, Q3, K3, F3, M3, E5, C4 • **Temperaments:** I, J, P • **Stress:** E • **Physical:** V=N, H=N, L=L, W, H • **Work Env:** I • **Salary:** 3 • **Outlook:** 3

SALESPERSON, GENERAL MERCHANDISE (ret. tr.) • D.O.T. #279.357-054 • OES #49011 • Sells variety of commodities in sales establishment, performing duties as described under SALESPERSON (ret. tr.; whole. tr.). May demonstrate use of merchandise. May examine defective article returned by customer to determine if refund or replacement should be made. May estimate quantity of merchandise required to fill customer's need. • **GED:** R4, M3, L4 • **SVP:** 3-6 mos • **Academic:** Ed=N, Eng=S • **Work Field:** 292 • **MPSMS:** 880 • **Aptitudes:** G3, V3, N3, S4, P4, Q3, K3, F3, M3, E5, C4 • **Temperaments:** I, J, P • **Stress:** E • **Physical:** V=N, H=N, L=L, H • **Work Env:** I • **Salary:** 2 • **Outlook:** 3

SALESPERSON, HORTICULTURAL AND NURSERY PRODUCTS (ret. tr.) • D.O.T. #272.357-022 • OES #49011 • Sells container-grown plants and garden supplies in nursery, greenhouse, or department store: Advises customer on selection of plants and methods of planting and cultivation. Suggests trees and shrubbery suitable for specified growing conditions. Performs other duties as described under SALESPERSON (ret. tr.; whole. tr.). May water and trim growing plants on sales floor. • **GED:** R4, M3, L4 • **SVP:** 3-6 mos • **Academic:** Ed=N, Eng=G • **Work Field:** 292 • **MPSMS:** 310 • **Aptitudes:** G3, V3, N3, S4, P4, Q4, K3, F3, M3, E5, C4 • **Temperaments:** I, J, P • **Stress:** E • **Physical:** V=N, H=N, L=L, W, H • **Work Env:** I • **Salary:** 3 • **Outlook:** 3

SALESPERSON, PARTS (ret. tr.) • D.O.T. #279.357-062 • OES #49014 • COUNTER CLERK; PARTS CLERK. Sells spare and replaceable parts and equipment from behind counter in agency, repair shop, or parts store: Ascertains make, year, and type of part needed, inspects damaged part to determine part required, or advises customer of part needed according to description of malfunction. Discusses use and features of various parts, based on knowledge of engines, machinery, or equipment. Reads catalog for stock number, price, and replacement parts. Advises customer on substitution or modification of parts when replacement is not available. Examines returned part to determine if it is defective and exchanges part or refunds money. Fills customer orders from stock, finding parts by location and stock number from catalog. Marks and stores parts in stockroom according to prearranged plan. Receives and fills telephone orders for parts. Performs other duties as described under SALESPERSON (ret. tr.; whole. tr.). May measure engine parts to determine whether similar parts may be machined down or built up to required size, using micrometers and knowledge of part specifications, machining, metalizing, and rebuilding operations. Usually specializes in selling parts for one type of machinery or equipment and is designated according to part sold as COUNTER CLERK, APPLIANCE PARTS (ret. tr.; whole. tr.); COUNTER CLERK, AUTOMOTIVE PARTS (ret. tr.; whole. tr.); COUNTER CLERK, FARM EQUIPMENT PARTS (ret. tr.; whole. tr.); COUNTER CLERK, INDUSTRIAL MACHINERY AND EQUIPMENT PARTS (ret. tr.; whole. tr.); COUNTER CLERK, RADIO, TELEVISION, AND ELECTRONICS PARTS (ret. tr.; whole. tr.); COUNTER CLERK, TRACTOR PARTS (ret. tr.; whole. tr.); COUNTER CLERK, TRUCK PARTS (ret. tr.; whole. tr.). • **GED:** R4, M3, L4 • **SVP:** 1-2 yrs • **Academic:** Ed=N, Eng=S • **Work Field:** 292 • **MPSMS:** 880 • **Aptitudes:** G3, V3, N3, S3, P3, Q3, K4, F3, M3, E5, C4 • **Temperaments:** I, J, P, T • **Stress:** E • **Physical:** V=L, H=N, L=L, W, H • **Work Env:** I • **Salary:** 4 • **Outlook:** 3

SALESPERSON, PHOTOGRAPHIC SUPPLIES AND EQUIPMENT (ret. tr.) • D.O.T. #277.357-050 • OES #49014 • Sells photographic and optical equipment and supplies, such as cameras, projectors, film, and binoculars: Demonstrates equipment to customer and explains functioning of various cameras, filters, lenses, and other photographic accessories. Receives film for processing. Performs other duties as described under SALESPERSON (ret. tr.; whole. tr.). May repair photographic or optical equipment. • **GED:** R4, M3, L4 • **SVP:** 6 mos-1 yr • **Academic:** Ed=H, Eng=S • **Work Field:** 292 • **MPSMS:** 603, 606 • **Aptitudes:** G3, V3, N3, S3, P3, Q3, K3, F3, M3, E5, C4 • **Temperaments:** I, J, P • **Physical:** V=L, H=G, L=L, H • **Work Env:** I • **Salary:** 3 • **Outlook:** 3

GOE: 08.02.04 Real Estate

LEASING AGENT, RESIDENCE (real estate) • D.O.T. #250.357-014 • OES #43008 • RENTAL AGENT. Shows and rents apartments, condominiums, homes, or mobile home lots to prospective tenants: Interviews prospective tenants and records information to ascertain needs and qualifications. Accompanies prospects to model homes and apartments and discusses size and layout of rooms, available facilities, such as swimming pool and saunas, location of shopping centers, services available, and terms of lease. Completes lease form or agreement and collects rental deposit. May inspect condition of premises periodically and arrange for necessary maintenance. May compile listings of available rental property. May compose newspaper advertisements. May be required to have real estate agent's license. • **GED:** R4, M2, L4 • **SVP:** 6 mos-1 yr • **Academic:** Ed=N, Eng=G • **Work Field:** 292 • **MPSMS:** 895 • **Aptitudes:** G3, V3, N3, S4, P4, Q3, K4, F4, M4, E5, C5 • **Temperaments:** I, J, P • **Stress:** E • **Physical:** V=L, H=L, L=S, W • **Work Env:** I • **Salary:** 3 • **Outlook:** 3

SALES AGENT, REAL ESTATE (real estate) • D.O.T. #250.357-018 • OES #43005 • REAL-ESTATE AGENT. Rents, buys, and sells property for clients on commission basis: Studies property listings to become familiar with properties for sale. Reviews trade journals to keep informed of marketing conditions and property values. Interviews prospective clients to solicit listings. Accompanies prospects to property sites, quotes purchase price, describes features, and discusses conditions of sale or terms of lease. Draws up real estate contracts, such as deeds, leases, and mortgages and negotiates loans on property. Must have license issued by State. May hold brokerage license and be designated as REAL-ESTATE BROKER (real estate). • **GED:** R4, M3, L4 • **SVP:** 6 mos-1 yr • **Academic:** Ed=H, Eng=G • **Work Field:** 292 • **MPSMS:** 895 • **Aptitudes:** G2, V2, N3, S3, P3, Q3, K4, F4, M4, E5, C5 • **Temperaments:** I, J, P • **Stress:** E • **Physical:** V=L, H=L, L=S, W • **Work Env:** I • **Salary:** 3 • **Outlook:** 4

GOE: 08.02.05 Demonstration & Sales

DEMONSTRATOR (ret. tr.) • D.O.T. #297.354-010 • OES #49032 • Demonstrates merchandise and products to customers to promote sales: Displays product and explains features to customers. Answers customer's questions about product. Demonstrates use or production of product and simultaneously explains merits to persuade customers to buy product. May perform duties described under SALESPERSON (ret. tr.; whole. tr.). May suggest product improvements to employer. May use graphic aids, such as charts, slides, or films, to facilitate demonstration. May give product samples to customers. May conduct guided tours of plant where product is made. May train other demonstrators. May be designated according to type of merchandise demonstrated as BAKERY DEMONSTRATOR (ret. tr.); CERAMIC-MAKER DEMONSTRATOR (ret. tr.); COSMETICS DEMONSTRATOR (ret. tr.); FOOD DEMONSTRATOR (ret. tr.; whole. tr.); GLASSWARE-MAKER DEMONSTRATOR (ret. tr.); HOUSEWARES DEMONSTRATOR (ret. tr.; whole. tr.). • **GED:** R3, M3, L3 • **SVP:** 30 days-3 mos • **Academic:** Ed=N, Eng=G • **Work Field:** 292 • **MPSMS:** 880 • **Aptitudes:** G3, V3, N3, S4, P4, Q4, K3, F3, M3, E4, C4 • **Temperaments:** I, J, P • **Stress:** E • **Physical:** V=L, H=L, L=L, W, H • **Work Env:** I • **Salary:** 2 • **Outlook:** 3

DEMONSTRATOR, ELECTRIC-GAS APPLIANCES (light, heat, & power) • D.O.T. #297.357-010 • OES #49032 • Demonstrates and explains operation and care of electric or gas appliances to utility company customers to promote appliance sales, and advises customers on energy conservation methods: Visits community organizations and schools to demonstrate operating features and care of appliances, such as air conditioners, driers, ranges, and washers. Explains how electricity or gas is produced and transmitted, reasons for electricity and gas rate increases, and methods of efficiently using appliances to conserve energy and reduce utility bills. Lectures to dealers, sales personnel, and employees of utility company on efficient use and care of appliances, as part of training program. Answers telephone and written requests from customers for information about appliance use. May advise customers on related homemaking problems, such as kitchen planning, home lighting, heating-fuel conservation, food preparation, and laundering with new fabrics. May write articles and pamphlets on appliance use. May represent utility company as guest on radio or television programs to discuss conservation of electrical or gas energy. • **GED:** R5, M3, L5 • **SVP:** 1-2 yrs • **Academic:** Ed=N, Eng=G • **Work Field:** 282, 292 • **MPSMS:** 583, 931 • **Aptitudes:** G2, V2, N3, S3, P3, Q3, K4, F3, M3, E5, C3 • **Temperaments:** I, J, P, V • **Stress:** E • **Physical:** V=L, H=L, L=L, W • **Work Env:** I • **Salary:** 2 • **Outlook:** 3

DEMONSTRATOR, KNITTING (ret. tr.) • D.O.T. #297.354-014 • OES #49032 • Shows customers how to knit garments or accessories by hand: Demonstrates methods of holding needles and making various stitches. Interprets knitting terminology and how to read and follow knitting instructions for customer. Suggests yarn for use in particular style of garment and estimates amount to purchase. Takes customer's measurements for proposed garment and estimates number of stitches required for each part of garment. Sells customer yarn required for knitting specified garment or clothing accessory. • **GED:** R4, M4, L4 • **SVP:** 6 mos-1 yr • **Academic:** Ed=H, Eng=S • **Work Field:** 165, 292, 296 • **MPSMS:** 424 • **Aptitudes:** G3, V3, N3, S3, P4, Q5, K3, F3, M3, E5, C5 • **Temperaments:** J, M, P, T • **Physical:** V=L, H=L, L=S, H • **Work Env:** I • **Salary:** 3 • **Outlook:** 3

SALESPERSON-DEMONSTRATOR, PARTY PLAN (ret. tr.) • D.O.T. #279.357-038 • OES #49026 • Displays and sells merchandise, such as clothes, household items, jewelry, toiletries, or toys, to guests attending house party: Confers with party sponsor to arrange date, time, and number of guests. Sets up display of sample merchandise. Meets guests and converses with them to establish rapport. Discusses items on display or demonstrates uses of product, and explains program to guests. Hands out catalogs or brochures that picture merchandise available. Writes orders for merchandise and arranges for payment. Delivers orders to sponsor or individual and collects monies due. May give small sample items to guests. May discuss program with guests to persuade them to sponsor house party by describing benefits derived from sponsorship. May assist sponsor to serve refreshments. • **GED:** R4, M3, L4 • **SVP:** 3-6 mos • **Academic:** Ed=N, Eng=G • **Work Field:** 292 • **MPSMS:** 881 • **Aptitudes:** G3, V3, N3, S4, P4, Q3, K4, F4, M4, E4, C4 • **Temperaments:** I, J, P • **Stress:** E • **Physical:** V=L, H=L, L=L, W, H • **Work Env:** I • **Salary:** 2 • **Outlook:** 3

GOE: 08.02.06 Services, General Sales

SALES AGENT, BUSINESS SERVICES (bus. ser.) • D.O.T. #251.357-010 • OES #43017 • Sells business service, such as food-vending, trading stamps, detective, armored truck, telephone-answering, linen supply, and cleaning service: Develops list of prospective customers by studying business and telephone directories, consulting business associates, and observing business establishment while driving through sales territory. Reviews orders for ideas to expand services available to present customers. Calls on prospects to explain features of services, cost, and advantages. Writes orders and schedules initiation of services. Confers with customers and company officials to resolve complaints. May collect payments on accounts. May be designated according to service sold as SALES AGENT, FOOD-VENDING SERVICE (whole. tr.); SALES AGENT, PROTECTIVE SERVICE (bus. ser.); SALES AGENT, TRADING STAMPS (bus. ser.). • **GED:** R4, M3, L4 • **SVP:** 6 mos-1 yr • **Academic:** Ed=H, Eng=G • **Work Field:** 292 • **MPSMS:** 899 • **Aptitudes:** G3, V3, N3, S3, P4, Q3, K4, F4, M4, E5, C4 • **Temperaments:** I, J, P • **Stress:** E • **Physical:** V=L, H=L, L=S • **Work Env:** B • **Salary:** 3 • **Outlook:** 3

SALES REPRESENTATIVE, AUTOMOTIVE-LEASING (bus. ser.) • D.O.T. #273.357-014 • OES #43099 • Sells automotive-leasing services to businesses and individuals: Visits prospective customers to stimulate interest in establishing or expanding automotive-leasing programs. Explains advantages of leasing automotive equipment, such as tax savings and reduced capital expenditures. Recommends types and number of vehicles needed to satisfactorily perform job with minimal expense. Computes leasing charges, based on such factors as length of contract, anticipated mileage, and applicable taxes. Prepares and sends leasing contract to leasing agency. Performs other tasks to increase sales, such as evaluating advertising campaigns or revising administrative procedures. Performs other duties as described under SALES REPRESENTATIVE (ret. tr.; whole. tr.). • **GED:** R4, M3, L4 • **SVP:** 6 mos-1 yr • **Academic:** Ed=N, Eng=G • **Work Field:** 292 • **MPSMS:** 889 • **Aptitudes:** G3, V3, N3, S4, P4, Q3, K4, F4, M4, E5, C5 • **Temperaments:** I, J, P • **Stress:** E • **Physical:** V=N, H=L, L=S, W • **Work Env:** I • **Salary:** 4 • **Outlook:** 3

SALES REPRESENTATIVE, FRANCHISE (bus. ser.) • D.O.T. #251.357-022 • OES #43017 • Solicits purchase of franchise operation by contacting persons who meet organization's standards: Visits prospects to explain advantages of franchised business, services to be rendered, costs, location, and financial arrangements. Performs other duties as described under SALES REPRESENTATIVE (ret. tr.; whole. tr.). May assist franchise purchaser in early stages of operating business. May confer with purchaser and company officials to resolve complaints. • **GED:** R4, M3, L4 • **SVP:** 6 mos-1 yr • **Academic:** Ed=H, Eng=G • **Work Field:** 292 • **MPSMS:** 894 • **Aptitudes:** G3, V3, N3, S4, P4, Q3, K4, F4, M4, E5, C5 • **Temperaments:** I, J, P • **Stress:** E • **Physical:** V=N, H=L, L=L, W • **Work Env:** I • **Salary:** 3 • **Outlook:** 4

SALES REPRESENTATIVE, UPHOLSTERY AND FURNITURE REPAIR (ret. tr.) • D.O.T. #259.357-026 • OES #43099 • Calls on prospective customers to sell and estimate cost of furniture repair and upholstery service, utilizing knowledge of upholstery and repair procedures and material and labor costs: Examines worn or damaged furniture to determine extent of repairs required. Estimates amount of material required based on style and dimensions of furniture. Advises customer on color and type of fabric. Completes estimate form and gives form to customer. Prepares sales contract for upholstery work. • **GED:** R4, M3, L3 • **SVP:** 6 mos-1 yr • **Academic:** Ed=N, Eng=G • **Work Field:** 211, 292 • **MPSMS:** 420, 462 • **Aptitudes:** G3, V3, N3, S3, P3, Q3, K4, F4, M4, E5, C3 • **Temperaments:** I, J, M, P • **Stress:** E • **Physical:** V=L, H=L, L=S, W • **Work Env:** I • **Salary:** 3 • **Outlook:** 2

TRAVEL AGENT (bus. ser.) • D.O.T. #252.157-010 • OES #43021

• **TRAVEL COUNSELOR.** Plans itineraries, and arranges accommodations and other travel services for customers of travel agency: Converses with customer to determine destination, mode of transportation, travel dates, financial considerations, and accommodations required. Plans or describes and sells itinerary package tour. Gives customer brochures and publications concerning travel and containing information, such as local customs, points of interest, and special events occurring in various locations, or foreign country regulations, such as consular requirements, rates of monetary exchange, and currency limitations. Computes cost of travel and accommodations, using calculating machine, carrier tariff books, and hotel rate books, or quotes costs of package tours. Books customer on transportation carrier and makes hotel reservations, using telephone or teletypewriter. Writes or obtains travel tickets for transportation or tour and collects payment. May specialize in foreign or domestic service, individual or group travel, specific geographical area, airplane charters, or package tours by bus. May act as wholesaler and assemble tour packages. • **GED:** R3, M3, L3 • **SVP:** 3-6 mos • **Academic:** Ed=H, Eng=G • **Work Field:** 282, 292 • **MPSMS:** 850 • **Aptitudes:** G3, V2, N3, S4, P4, Q2, K4, F4, M4, E5, C4 • **Temperaments:** I, J, P • **Stress:** E • **Physical:** V=L, H=G, L=S • **Work Env:** I • **Salary:** 3 • **Outlook:** 3

WEDDING CONSULTANT (ret. tr.) • D.O.T. #299.357-018 • OES #49999 • Advises prospective brides in all phases of wedding planning, such as etiquette, attire of wedding party, and selection of trousseau: Compiles list of prospective brides from newspaper announcements of engagements. Mails promotional material to offer own and store's services as consultant. Recommends trousseau for bride, and costumes and accessories for attendants. Advises bride on selection of silverware style and pattern, china, glassware, stationery, invitations, flowers, and catering service. May display and sell wedding trousseau to bride, and attire for attendants, and silverware, china, and glassware to brides and wedding gift purchasers, performing duties as described under SALESPERSON (ret. tr.; whole. tr.). May compile and maintain gift register. May arrange for photographers to take pictures of wedding party. May attend rehearsals and wedding ceremony to give advice on etiquette. May accompany bride when shopping in store or shop for her. • **GED:** R4, M3, L4 • **SVP:** 1-2 yrs • **Academic:** Ed=H, Eng=S • **Work Field:** 292 • **MPSMS:** 881 • **Aptitudes:** G3, V2, N3, S4, P3, Q3, K4, F4, M4, E5, C3 • **Temperaments:** F, I, J, P, V • **Stress:** E • **Physical:** V=L, H=G, L=L, H • **Work Env:** I • **Salary:** 4 • **Outlook:** 2

GOE: 08.02.07 Driving-Selling

DRIVER, SALES ROUTE (ret. tr.) • D.O.T. #292.353-010 • OES #97117 • DELIVERY-ROUTE TRUCK DRIVER; ROUTE DRIVER; TRUCK DRIVER, SALES ROUTE. Drives truck or automobile over established route to deliver and sell products or render services, collects money from customers, and makes change: Drives truck to deliver such items as beer, beverages, bakery products, dry cleaning, ice, laundry, and milk to customer's home or place of business. Collects money from customers and makes change. Writes up customer order. Records sales or deliveries on daily sales or delivery record. Calls on prospective customers to solicit new business. Informs regular customers of new products or services. May place stock on shelves or racks. May set up merchandise and sales promotion displays or issue sales promotion materials to customers. May collect or pick up empty containers or rejected or unsold merchandise. May load truck. May issue or obtain customer signature on receipt for pickup or delivery. May clean inside of truck. May direct DRIVER HELPER, SALES ROUTE (ret. tr.; whole. tr.) to load and unload truck and carry merchandise. May be designated according to product delivered or service rendered as DRIVER, BAKERY-PRODUCTS ROUTE (ret. tr.; whole. tr.); DRIVER, BEER ROUTE (whole. tr.); DRIVER, BEVERAGE ROUTE (whole. tr.); DRIVER, DRY-CLEANING ROUTE (ret. tr.; whole. tr.); DRIVER, ICE-CREAM ROUTE (whole. tr.); DRIVER, ICE ROUTE (ret. tr.); DRIVER, LAUNDRY ROUTE (ret. tr.); DRIVER, MILK ROUTE (dairy prod.). • **GED:** R3, M2, L3 • **SVP:** 30 days-3 mos • **Academic:** Ed=N, Eng=S • **Work Field:** 013, 292 • **MPSMS:** 880 • **Aptitudes:** G3, V3, N3, S4, P4, Q3, K3, F4, M4, E3, C4 • **Temperaments:** I, P • **Stress:** E • **Physical:** V=L, H=L, L=M, W, H • **Work Env:** I • **Salary:** 2

• Outlook: 3

GOE: 08.02.08 Soliciting-Selling

FUND RAISER 2 (nonprofit org.) • D.O.T. #293.357-014 • OES #43099 • CONTRIBUTION SOLICITOR. Contacts individuals and firms by telephone, in person, or by mail to solicit funds for charities or other causes. Takes pledges for amounts to be contributed or accepts immediate cash payments. May sell emblems or other tokens of organization represented. • **GED:** R3, M2, L3 • **SVP:** 2-30 days • **Academic:** Ed=N, Eng=G • **Work Field:** 292 • **MPSMS:** 940 • **Aptitudes:** G3, V3, N3, S4, P4, Q4, K4, F4, M4, E5, C5 • **Temperaments:** I, P • **Stress:** E • **Physical:** V=N, H=L, L=S • **Work Env:** B • **Salary:** 2 • **Outlook:** 4

MEMBERSHIP SOLICITOR (any ind.) • D.O.T. #293.357-022 • OES #43099 • Solicits membership for club or trade association: Visits or contacts prospective members to explain benefits and costs of membership and to describe organization and objectives of club or association. May collect dues and payments for publications from members. May solicit funds for club or association [FUND RAISER (nonprofit organ.) II]. May speak to members at meetings about services available. • **GED:** R4, M3, L4 • **SVP:** 3-6 mos • **Academic:** Ed=N, Eng=G • **Work Field:** 292 • **MPSMS:** 896 • **Aptitudes:** G3, V3, N4, S5, P5, Q3, K5, F4, M5, E5, C5 • **Temperaments:** I, P • **Stress:** E • **Physical:** V=N, H=L, L=S • **Work Env:** I • **Salary:** 3 • **Outlook:** 4

SALES REPRESENTATIVE, DOOR-TO-DOOR (ret. tr.) • D.O.T. #291.357-010 • OES #49026 • CANVASSER; PEDDLER; SOLICITOR. Sells merchandise or service, such as books, magazines, notions, brushes, and cosmetics, going from door to door without making appointments or following leads from management, other workers, or from listings in city and telephone directories: Displays sample products, explains desirable qualities of products, and leaves samples, or distributes advertising literature explaining service or products. Writes orders. May deliver merchandise, collect money, and make change. May contact individuals previously solicited in person, by telephone, or by mail to close sale. May travel from one area to another, or be assigned to a territory. • **GED:** R3, M2, L3 • **SVP:** 2-30 days • **Academic:** Ed=N, Eng=G • **Work Field:** 292 • **MPSMS:** 881 • **Aptitudes:** G3, V3, N3, S4, P4, Q3, K4, F4, M4, E5, C4 • **Temperaments:** I, P • **Stress:** E • **Physical:** V=L, H=L, L=S, W • **Work Env:** B • **Salary:** 3 • **Outlook:** 4

TELEPHONE SOLICITOR (any ind.) • D.O.T. #299.357-014 • OES #49026 • TELEPHONE SALES REPRESENTATIVE. Solicits orders for merchandise or services over telephone: Calls prospective customers to explain type of service or merchandise offered. Quotes prices and tries to persuade customer to buy, using prepared sales talk. Records names, addresses, purchases, and reactions of prospects solicited. Refers orders to other workers for filling. May develop lists of prospects from city and telephone directories. May transcribe data from order card to keypunch card, using vari-punch machine. May type report periodically on sales activities, using typewriter. May contact DRIVER, SALES ROUTE (ret. tr.; whole. tr.) to arrange delivery of merchandise. • **GED:** R3, M3, L3 • **SVP:** 30 days-3 mos • **Academic:** Ed=N, Eng=G • **Work Field:** 292 • **MPSMS:** 889 • **Aptitudes:** G3, V3, N3, S4, P4, Q3, K4, F4, M4, E5, C5 • **Temperaments:** I, P • **Stress:** E • **Physical:** V=L, H=G, L=S, H • **Work Env:** I • **Salary:** 1 • **Outlook:** 4

08.03 Vending

Workers in this group sell novelties, snacks and other inexpensive items. They work at stadiums and street fairs, in night clubs or restaurants or wherever crowds gather for entertainment or recreation. Some of them sell products on the street, staying in one location, or moving through commercial and residential areas.

✔ What kind of work would you do?
Your work activities would depend upon your specific job. For example, you might:

- walk around a football stadium or baseball park calling out items to be sold.
- walk among guests in a nightclub, restaurant, or hotel selling cigars, cigarettes, or corsages.
- sell snacks to passengers on train.
- take pictures of people in restaurants and try to sell them the finished prints.
- sell merchandise such as flowers, fruit, or ice cream from a pushcart or truck.

✔ What skills and abilities do you need for this kind of work?
To do this kind of work, you must be able to:

- speak clearly, shout, sing, or call out to attract customers.
- accept payment and make change quickly and accurately.
- stand or walk for long periods of time, often climbing stairs or pushing through crowds while carrying heavy containers or pushing a cart.
- be very persuasive in getting people to buy your products.

The above statements may not apply to every job in this group.

✔ How do you know if you would like or could learn to do this kind of work?
The following questions may give you clues about yourself as you consider this group of jobs.

- Have you worked at a carnival or fair? Do you enjoy shouting or gesturing to get the attention of a crowd?
- Have you sold things to raise money for a school or civic project? Do you enjoy this type of activity?
- Have you sold magazines or candy door-to-door? Do you like work in which you persuade others to buy products?
- Have you worked as a cashier in a store? Can you figure the cost of several items and make change accurately?

✔ **How can you prepare for and enter this kind of work?**

Occupations in this group usually require education and/or training extending from a short demonstration to over three months, depending upon the specific kind of work. Most jobs in this group are open to almost anyone. Formal training, experience, or education is seldom required.

✔ **What else should you consider about these jobs?**

Jobs in this group are usually short-term and opportunities for advancement are few. In many cases, payment is based only on how many items are sold, so workers must use all possible means to convince customers to buy. However, some jobs provide permanent employment. These jobs provide experience that can be applied to other saleswork. Some jobs in this group require the worker to be outside in all kinds of weather. Some workers own their own carts and are in business for themselves.

If you think you would like to do this kind of work, look at the job titles listed below.

GOE: 08.03.01 Peddling & Hawking

PHOTOGRAPHER (amuse. & rec.) • D.O.T. #143.457-010 • OES #34023 • Persuades nightclub and restaurant patrons to pose for pictures and operates camera to photograph them: Carries camera and flashbulb equipment to tables and solicits customers' patronage. Adjusts camera and photographs customers. Takes exposed film to darkroom on premises for immediate processing by DEVELOPER (photofinish.). Returns to customers with finished photographs or proofs and writes orders for additional prints selected. Receives payment for photographs. May use camera which produces instant picture. • **GED:** R3, M1, L3 • **SVP:** 30 days-3 mos • **Academic:** Ed=N, Eng=S • **Work Field:** 292 • **MPSMS:** 753 • **Aptitudes:** G3, V2, N3, S5, P4, Q4, K4, F4, M4, E5, C5 • **Temper-**aments: I, P • **Physical:** V=G, H=G, L=L, W, H • **Work Env:** I • **Salary:** 2 • **Outlook:** 1

VENDOR (amuse. & rec.) • D.O.T. #291.457-022 • OES #49026 • PEDDLER. Sells refreshments, programs, novelties, or cushions at sports events, parades, or other entertainments: Circulates among patrons or spectators, calling out items for sale. Hands, passes, or throws item to purchaser, receives payment, and makes change as required. Checks out items to replenish stock and turns in monies from sales. • **GED:** R2, M2, L2 • **SVP:** 2-30 days • **Academic:** Ed=N, Eng=S • **Work Field:** 292 • **MPSMS:** 889 • **Aptitudes:** G4, V4, N4, S4, P4, Q4, K4, F4, M4, E5, C5 • **Temperaments:** P • **Stress:** E • **Physical:** V=N, H=N, L=M, W, H • **Work Env:** B • **Salary:** 2 • **Outlook:** 3

Accommodating 09

An interest in catering to the wishes and needs of others, usually on a one-to-one basis. You can satisfy this interest by providing services for the convenience of others, such as hospitality services in hotels, restaurants, airplanes, etc. You may enjoy improving the appearance of others. Perhaps working in the hair and beauty care field would satisfy you. You may wish to provide personal services, such as taking tickets, baggage, or ushering.

09.01 Hospitality Services

Workers in this group help persons, such as visitors, travelers, and customers, get acquainted with and feel at ease in an unfamiliar setting; provide escort and guide services; and plan and direct social activities. They may also be concerned with the safety and comfort of people when they are traveling or vacationing. These workers find employment with air-, rail-, and water transportation companies; radio and television broadcasting stations; hotels and restaurants; museums; retirement homes, and related establishments.

✔ **What kind of work would you do?**
Your work activities would depend upon your specific job. For example you might:

- greet guests and answer questions concerning social and recreational activities in a hotel.
- greet and seat customers in a restaurant.
- provide personal services to airplane passengers, such as answering questions and serving meals.
- escort a group of people through an industrial plant and explain what is taking place.
- take people on a tour of model homes and explain their features.
- conduct visitors on tour of television studios.

✔ **What skills and abilities do you need for this kind of work?**
To do this kind of work, you must be able to:

- speak clearly
- talk easily with all kinds of people to put them at ease.
- use judgment and reasoning to cope with emergencies, such as sudden illness, accident, or interrupted service.
- perform a variety of activities and change activities frequently and sometimes without notice.
- plan and carry out an activity, such as a card party or dance.

✔ **How do you know if you would like or could learn to do this kind of work?**
The following questions may give you clues about yourself as you consider this group of jobs.

- Have you been a member of a community or civil group? Do you like socializing with others?
- Have you had courses in speech? Do you like to speak to groups?
- Have you planned or organized a party? Can you lead others in games and group activities?
- Have you taught friends to dance? Did they enjoy the lessons?

- Have you been a treasurer or secretary for an organization? Can you keep accurate records?

✔ **How can you prepare for and enter this kind of work?**

Occupations in this group usually require education and/or training extending from thirty days to over two years, depending upon the specific kind of work. The methods of entry for these jobs vary. For example, guides in public buildings receive on-the-job training after they are hired. Airplane flight attendants are usually trained by employers. Dude wranglers and stewards enter through experience in lower level jobs. Hostesses, chaperones, and escorts are hired because of their manners and charming personalities.

✔ **What else should you consider about these jobs?**

Workers in this group may have to travel and live in hotels or resorts instead of at home. Night or holiday work may be required. Some workers must wear uniforms.

If you think you would like to do this kind of work, look at the job titles listed on the following pages.

GOE: 09.01.01 Social & Recreational Activities

AMUSEMENT PARK WORKER (amuse. & rec.) • D.O.T. #349.664-010 • OES #68014 • Performs any combination of following duties in amusement park: Escorts patrons on tours of park's points of interest. Takes pictures of patrons to impart pictures onto T-shirts, using camera, automatic printing equipment, and heating press. Maintains and distributes uniforms worn by park employees. Cleans park grounds, office facilities, and restroom areas, using broom, dust pan, or vacuum cleaner. Distributes literature, such as maps, show schedules, and pass information, to acquaint visitors with park facilities. Monitors activities of children using park playground area to ensure safe use of equipment. Directs patrons to seats for park attractions and opens doors to assist patrons' entry and exit from attractions. Receives cash for tickets or items sold to patrons and records sales, using cash register. • **GED:** R2, M2, L2 • **SVP:** 2-30 days • **Academic:** Ed=N, Eng=S • **Work Field:** 282, 291 • **MPSMS:** 919 • **Aptitudes:** G3, V3, N4, S4, P4, Q4, K3, F4, M3, E5, C4 • **Temperaments:** P • **Stress:** E • **Physical:** V=L, H=L, L=M, W, H • **Work Env:** I • **Salary:** 2 • **Outlook:** 4

COUNSELOR, CAMP (amuse. & rec.) • D.O.T. #159.124-010 • OES #27311 • Directs activities of children at vacation camp: Plans activities, such as hikes, cookouts, and campfires, to provide wide variety of camping experiences. Demonstrates use of camping equipment and explains principles and techniques of activities, such as backpacking, nature study, and outdoor cooking, to increase campers knowledge and competence. Plans and arranges competition in activities, such as team sports or housekeeping, to stimulate campers interest and participation. Demonstrates use of materials and tools to instruct children in arts and crafts. Instructs campers in skills, such as canoeing, sailing, swimming, archery, horseback riding, and animal care, explaining and demonstrating procedures and safety techniques. Organizes, leads, instructs, and referees games. Enforces camp rules and regulations to guide conduct, maintain discipline, and safeguard health of campers. May be identified according to type of camp activity. • **GED:** R4, M2, L4 • **SVP:** 1-2 yrs • **Academic:** Ed=N, Eng=G • **Work Field:** 296 • **MPSMS:** 919 • **Aptitudes:** G2, V2, N4, S3, P4, Q4, K3, F3, M3, E3, C4 • **Temperaments:** D, P, V • **Stress:** E • **Physical:** V=N, H=L, L=L, W, C, H • **Work Env:** B • **Salary:** 3 • **Outlook:** 3

DIRECTOR, SOCIAL (hotel & rest.) • D.O.T. #352.167-010 • OES #27311 • DIRECTOR, RECREATION. Plans and organizes recreational activities and creates friendly atmosphere for guests in hotels and resorts or for passengers on board ship: Greets new arrivals, introduces them to other guests, acquaints them with recreation facilities, and encourages them to participate in group activities. Ascertains interests of group and evaluates available equipment and facilities to plan activities, such as card parties, games, tournaments, dances, musicals, and field trips. Arranges for activity requirements, such as setting up equipment, transportation, decorations, refreshments, and entertainment. Associates with lonely guests and visits those who are ill. May greet and seat guests in dining room. May assist management in resolving guests' complaints. • **GED:** R4, M3, L4 • **SVP:** 1-2 yrs • **Academic:** Ed=N, Eng=G • **Work Field:** 291, 295 • **MPSMS:** 919 • **Aptitudes:** G3, V2, N3, S4, P4, Q3, K4, F4, M4, E4, C5 • **Temperaments:** D, J, P, V • **Stress:** E • **Physical:** V=L, H=L, L=S, W • **Work Env:** B • **Salary:** 4 • **Outlook:** 3

GROUP WORKER (social ser.) • D.O.T. #195.164-010 • OES #27305 • Organizes and leads groups, such as senior citizens, children, and street gangs, in activities that meet interests of individual members: Develops recreational, physical education, and cultural programs for various age groups. Demonstrates and instructs participants in activities, such as active sports, group dances and games, arts, crafts, and dramatics. Organizes current-events discussion groups, conducts consumer problem surveys, and performs similar activities to stimulate interest in civic responsibility. Promotes group work concept of enabling members to develop their own program activities through encouragement and leadership of membership discussions. Consults with other community resources regarding specific individuals, and makes referral when indicated. Keeps records. May recruit, train, and supervise paid staff and volunteers. Employed in settings, such as community center, neighborhood or settlement house, hospital, institution for children or aged, youth centers, and housing projects. • **GED:** R5, M4, L5 • **SVP:** 2-4 yrs • **Academic:** Ed=A, Eng=G • **Work Field:** 294 • **MPSMS:** 941 • **Aptitudes:** G2, V2, N3, S3, P3, Q4, K3, F3, M3, E3, C3 • **Temperaments:** D, I, J, P, V • **Stress:** E • **Physical:** V=N, H=L, L=S, H • **Work Env:** B • **Salary:** 4 • **Outlook:** 2

GUIDE, HUNTING AND FISHING (amuse. & rec.) • D.O.T. #353.161-010 • OES #68017 • Plans, organizes and conducts hunting and fishing trips for individuals and groups: Plans itinerary for hunting and fishing trips applying knowledge of countryside to determine best route and sites. Arranges for transporting sportsman, equipment and supplies to hunting or fishing area using horses, land vehicles, motorboat, or airplane. Explains hunting and fishing laws to ensure compliance. Instructs members of party in use of hunting or fishing gear. Prepares meals for members of party. Administers first aid to injured sportsmen. May care for animals. May sell or rent equipment, clothing and supplies. May pilot airplane or drive land and water vehicles. • **GED:** R4, M3, L3 • **SVP:** 2-4 yrs • **Academic:** Ed=N, Eng=G • **Work Field:** 146, 282, 291 • **MPSMS:** 914 • **Aptitudes:** G3, V3, N3, S3, P4, Q4, K3, F3, M2, E3, C4 • **Temperaments:** D, J, P, V • **Stress:** E, A •

Physical: V=L, H=L, L=H, W, S, H • **Work Env:** O • **Salary:** 3 • **Outlook:** 1

HOST/HOSTESS (any ind.) • D.O.T. #352.667-010 • OES #69999 • RECEPTIONIST. Greets guests arriving at country club, catered social function, or other gathering place. Introduces guests and suggests planned activities, such as dancing or games. Gives directions to personnel engaged in serving of refreshments. May plan menus and supervise activities of food-service workers. May plan and participate in social activities, games, and sports, depending on nature of establishment or function. May deposit or pick up guests at railway station, home, or other location as directed. • **GED:** R3, M2, L3 • **SVP:** 30 days-3 mos • **Academic:** Ed=N, Eng=G • **Work Field:** 291 • **MPSMS:** 909 • **Aptitudes:** G3, V3, N4, S4, P4, Q4, K4, F4, M4, E5, C5 • **Temperaments:** D, V • **Physical:** V=L, H=L, L=L, W • **Work Env:** I • **Salary:** 2 • **Outlook:** 3

RECREATION AIDE (social ser.) • D.O.T. #195.367-030 • OES #68014 • Assists RECREATION LEADER (social ser.) 195.227-014 in conducting recreation activities in community center or other voluntary recreation facility: Arranges chairs, tables, and sporting or exercise equipment in designated rooms or other areas for scheduled group activities, such as banquets, wedding receptions, parties, group meetings, or sports events. Welcomes visitors and answers incoming telephone calls. Notifies patrons of activity schedules and registration requirements. Monitors spectators and participants at sports events to ensure orderly conduct. Receives, stores, and issues sports equipment and supplies. May keep attendance records or scores at sporting events, operate audiovisual equipment, monitor activities of children during recreational trips or tours, or perform other duties as directed by RECREATION LEADER (social ser.) 195.227-014. • **GED:** R3, M2, L3 • **SVP:** 2-30 days • **Academic:** Ed=N, Eng=G • **Work Field:** 291 • **MPSMS:** 941 • **Aptitudes:** G3, V3, N3, S4, P4, Q4, K4, F4, M4, E5, C5 • **Temperaments:** P, V • **Stress:** E • **Physical:** V=N, H=N, L=S, W, H • **Work Env:** I • **Salary:** 2 • **Outlook:** 2

RECREATION LEADER (social ser.) • D.O.T. #195.227-014 • OES #27311 • Conducts recreation activities with assigned groups in public department of voluntary agency: Organizes, promotes, and develops interest in activities, such as arts and crafts, sports, games, music, dramatics, social recreation, camping, and hobbies. Cooperates with other staff members in conducting community wide events and works with neighborhood groups to determine recreation interests and needs of all ages. Works under close supervision of RECREATION SUPERVISOR (profess. & kin.). Cooperates with recreation and nonrecreation personnel when in agency setting, such as settlement house, institution for children or aged, hospital, armed services, or penal institution. • **GED:** R5, M3, L5 • **SVP:** 2-4 yrs • **Academic:** Ed=A, Eng=G • **Work Field:** 291 • **MPSMS:** 941 • **Aptitudes:** G2, V2, N4, S3, P3, Q1, K3, F3, M3, E3, C5 • **Temperaments:** D, P • **Stress:** E • **Physical:** V=N, H=L, L=L, W • **Work Env:** B • **Salary:** 4 • **Outlook:** 3

GOE: 09.01.02 Guide Services

CRAFT DEMONSTRATOR (museum) • D.O.T. #109.364-010 • OES #31511 • Demonstrates and explains techniques and purposes of handicraft or other activity, such as candle dipping, horseshoeing, or soap making, as part of display in history or folk museum, or restored or refurbished farm, village, or neighborhood: Studies historical and technical literature to acquire information about time period and lifestyle depicted in display and craft techniques associated with time and area, to devise plan for authentic presentation of craft. Drafts outline of talk, assisted by research personnel, to acquaint visitors with customs and crafts associated with folk life depicted. Practices techniques involved in handicraft to ensure accurate and skillful demonstrations. Molds candles, shoes horses, operates looms, or engages in other crafts or activities, working in appropriate period setting, to demonstrate craft to visitors. Explains techniques of craft, and points out relationship of craft to lifestyle depicted to assist visitors to comprehend traditional techniques of work and play peculiar to time and area. Answers visitor questions or refers visitor to other sources for information. • **GED:** R4, M2, L4 • **SVP:** 3-6 mos • **Academic:** Ed=H, Eng=S • **Work Field:** 282 • **MPSMS:** 919, 931, 939 • **Aptitudes:** G3, V3, N3, S3, P3, Q4, K3, F3, M3, E5, C3 • **Temper-**

aments: F, J, P, T • **Physical:** V=L, H=L, L=L, H • **Work Env:** I • **Salary:** 3 • **Outlook:** 3

EXHIBIT-DISPLAY REPRESENTATIVE (any ind.) • D.O.T. #297.367-010 • OES #49032 • Attends trade, traveling, promotional, educational, or amusement exhibit to answer visitors' questions, explain or describe exhibit, and to protect it against theft or damage. May set up or arrange display. May demonstrate use of displayed items. May lecture and show slides. May collect fees or accept donations. May solicit patronage. May distribute brochures. May obtain names and addresses of prospective customers. May drive truck and trailer to transport exhibit. May be designated TRADE-SHOW REPRESENTATIVE (any ind.). • **GED:** R4, M2, L4 • **SVP:** 6 mos-1 yr • **Academic:** Ed=N, Eng=G • **Work Field:** 282, 293 • **MPSMS:** 960 • **Aptitudes:** G3, V3, N4, S4, P3, Q4, K4, F4, M4, E5, C5 • **Temperaments:** P • **Stress:** E • **Physical:** V=L, H=L, L=L, W • **Work Env:** I • **Salary:** 2 • **Outlook:** 3

GUIDE (per. ser.) • D.O.T. #353.367-010 • OES #68017 • GUIDE, VISITOR. Escorts visitors around city or town: Advises visitors, such as convention delegates, foreign government personnel, or salesmen, as to location of buildings, points of interest, and other sites, or escorts visitors to designated locations, using private or public transportation. May carry equipment, luggage, or sample cases for visitors. May be required to speak foreign language when communicating with foreign visitors. May be designated according to type of visitor directed or escorted as GUIDE, DELEGATE (per. ser.). • **GED:** R3, M1, L2 • **SVP:** 30 days-3 mos • **Academic:** Ed=N, Eng=G • **Work Field:** 282, 291 • **MPSMS:** 909 • **Aptitudes:** G3, V3, N4, S4, P4, Q4, K4, F4, M4, E5, C5 • **Temperaments:** P, V • **Stress:** E • **Physical:** V=L, H=L, L=S, W • **Work Env:** B • **Salary:** 2 • **Outlook:** 2

GUIDE, PLANT (any ind.) • D.O.T. #353.367-018 • OES #68017 • PLANT TOUR GUIDE. Escorts group of people through industrial establishment, and describes features of interest: Leads way along specified route and explains various processes and operation of machines. Answers questions and supplies information on work of department or departments visited. • **GED:** R3, M2, L3 • **SVP:** 30 days-3 mos • **Academic:** Ed=N, Eng=G • **Work Field:** 282 • **MPSMS:** 931 • **Aptitudes:** G3, V3, N4, S4, P4, Q4, K4, F4, M4, E5, C4 • **Temperaments:** P, V • **Stress:** E • **Physical:** V=L, H=L, L=S, W • **Work Env:** B • **Salary:** 2 • **Outlook:** 2

GOE: 09.01.03 Food Services, Hospitality

HOST/HOSTESS, RESTAURANT (hotel & rest.) • D.O.T. #310.137-010 • OES #65002 • WAITER/WAITRESS, HEAD. Supervises and coordinates activities of dining room personnel to provide fast and courteous service to patrons: Schedules dining reservations and arranges parties or special services for diners. Greets guests, escorts them to tables, and provides menus. Adjusts complaints of patrons. Assigns work tasks and coordinates activities of dining room personnel to ensure prompt and courteous service to patrons. Inspects dining room serving stations for neatness and cleanliness, and requisitions table linens and other dining room supplies for tables and serving stations. May interview, hire and discharge dining room personnel. May train dining room employees. May schedule work hours and keep time records of dining room workers. May assist in planning menus. May act as [CASHIER (clerical) II]. • **GED:** R4, M3, L4 • **SVP:** 1-2 yrs • **Academic:** Ed=N, Eng=S • **Work Field:** 291 • **MPSMS:** 903 • **Aptitudes:** G3, V3, N3, S4, P4, Q3, K4, F4, M4, E5, C5 • **Temperaments:** D, P, V • **Stress:** E • **Physical:** V=L, H=L, L=L, W, H • **Work Env:** I • **Salary:** 2 • **Outlook:** 4

WAITER/WAITRESS, CAPTAIN (hotel & rest.) • D.O.T. #311.137-018 • OES #61099 • CAPTAIN. Supervises activities of workers in section of dining room: Receives guests and conducts them to tables. Describes or suggests food courses and appropriate wines. When serving banquets, may be designated as BANQUET CAPTAIN (hotel & rest.). • **GED:** R4, M2, L3 • **SVP:** 1-2 yrs • **Academic:** Ed=H, Eng=S • **Work Field:** 291 • **MPSMS:** 903 • **Aptitudes:** G3, V3, N4, S4, P4, Q3, K4, F4, M4, E5, C5 • **Temperaments:** D, P • **Stress:** E • **Physical:** V=L, H=G, L=L, W • **Work Env:** I • **Salary:** 2 • **Outlook:** 4

GOE: 09.01.04 Safety & Comfort Services

AIRPLANE-FLIGHT ATTENDANT (air trans.) • D.O.T. #352.367-010 • OES #68026 • AIRPLANE-CABIN ATTENDANT. Performs variety of personal services conducive to safety and comfort of airline passengers during flight: Greets passengers, verifies tickets, records destinations, and assigns seats. Explains use of safety equipment, such as seat belts, oxygen masks, and life jackets. Serves previously prepared meals and beverages. Observes passengers to detect signs of discomfort, and issues palliatives to relieve them of ailments, such as airsickness and insomnia. Answers questions regarding performance of aircraft, stopovers, and flight schedules. Performs other personal services, such as distributing reading material and pointing out places of interest. Prepares reports showing place of departure and destination, passenger ticket numbers, meal and beverage inventories, palliatives issued, and lost and found articles. May collect money for meals and beverages. • **GED:** R4, M3, L3 • **SVP:** 30 days-3 mos • **Academic:** Ed=H, Eng=G • **Work Field:** 282, 291 • **MPSMS:** 855 • **Aptitudes:** G3, V3, N3, S4, P4, Q3, K3, F4, M3, E3, C5 •

Temperaments: P, S, V • **Stress:** E, S • **Physical:** V=L, H=G, L=M, W, C, S, H • **Work Env:** I, N, R • **Salary:** 3 • **Outlook:** 1

FUNERAL ATTENDANT (per. ser.) • D.O.T. #359.677-014 • OES #68041 • UNDERTAKER ASSISTANT; USHER. Performs variety of tasks during funeral: Places casket in parlor or chapel prior to wake or funeral service and arranges floral offerings and lights around casket, following instructions of DIRECTOR, FUNERAL (per. ser.) or EMBALMER (per. ser.). Directs or escorts mourners to parlor or chapel in which wake or funeral is held. Assists DIRECTOR, FUNERAL (per. ser.) to close coffin. Carries flowers to hearse or limousine for transportation to place of interment. Assists mourners into and out of limousines. Issues and stores funeral equipment, such as casket lowering devices and grass mats used at place of interment. May carry casket [PALLBEARER (per. ser.)]. • **GED:** R2, M1, L2 • **SVP:** 30 days-3 mos • **Academic:** Ed=N, Eng=N • **Work Field:** 291 • **MPSMS:** 909 • **Aptitudes:** G4, V4, N4, S4, P4, Q4, K4, F4, M4, E5, C4 • **Temperaments:** P • **Stress:** E • **Physical:** V=L, H=N, L=M, W, H • **Work Env:** I • **Salary:** 2 • **Outlook:** 2

09.02 Barber and Beauty Services

Workers in this group provide people with a variety of barbering and beauty services. These services involve care of the hair, skin, and nails. These workers find employment in barber and beauty shops, department stores, hotel, and retirement homes. A few workers find jobs on passenger ships. Some are self-employed and work in their own homes or go to the customer.

✔ **What kind of work would you do?**
Your work activities would depend upon your specific job. For example, you might:

- cut, trim, shampoo, curl, or style hair.
- lather and shave facial hair.
- remove unwanted facial hair by using an electrically-charged needle.

- give hair and scalp-conditioning treatments.

✔ **What skills and abilities do you need for this kind of work?**
To do this kind of work, you must be able to:

- understand written and diagram instructions for applying hair coloring and permanent waving solutions.
- adapt a procedure to an individual customer's physical features.
- use a variety of tools, such as scissors, tweezers, combs, curlers, and hair blowers.

- add and subtract to mix solutions in proper proportions.
- see differences in shapes, widths, and lengths of lines when cutting hair and shaping eyebrows.
- deal pleasantly with all kinds of people.
- use hands and fingers skillfully to wrap hair around rollers.

✔ **How do you know if you would like or could learn to do this kind of work?**
The following questions may give you clues about yourself as you consider this group of jobs.

- Have you cut someone's hair? Do you style your own hair? Do you like to try new and different hairstyles?
- Have you read health and beauty magazines? Can you recognize various skin tones or hair textures?

- Have you applied theatrical make-up? Do you enjoy changing the appearance of others?
- Have you worked at a health spa or athletic club? Do you enjoy helping others?

✔ How can you prepare for and enter this kind of work?

Occupations in this group usually require education and/or training extending from six months to over two years, depending upon the specific kind of work. Both public and private vocational schools offer courses in cosmetology and barbering. In a few areas, apprenticeships in cosmetology are available. Manufacturers of barbering and cosmetology equipment and materials offer training courses about the use of their products.

Formal training requirements vary according to the occupation and state. Studies usually include anatomy, bacteriology, dermatology, and physiology. Techniques such as hair cutting, permanent waving, electrolysis, and hair and scalp analysis are also included.

Students of cosmetology or barbering schools get supervised practical experience. Trainees and workers develop further expertise by attending and participating in seminars and contests sponsored by schools, trade associations, and manufacturers.

✔ What else should you consider about these jobs?

Workers may be required to furnish and wear uniforms. Irregular hours may be required, including evening and weekends. Standing for varying lengths of time is typical of this work but it is not a requirement.

Many workers use stools with rolling casters to move around the customer's chair. Changing hair styles and the development of new products and techniques make it necessary for workers to attend training and demonstration classes frequently.

Workers usually are paid on the basis of how many customers they serve. They rarely receive a straight salary. Most employers set the prices for the services offered and the worker receives a part of these prices. The amount a worker is paid may vary and may depend on the supplies and tools provided by the employer. For example, some employers provide the needed towels, shampoo, or lotions and keep a larger share of the money collected. Workers may or may not be allowed to accept tips. They may be expected to join a union and pay membership dues.

If you think you would like to do this kind of work, look at the job titles listed below.

GOE: 09.02.01 Cosmetology

COSMETOLOGIST (per. ser.) • D.O.T. #332.271-010 • OES #68011 • BEAUTICIAN; BEAUTY CULTURIST; BEAUTY OPERATOR; COSMETICIAN. Provides beauty services for customers: Analyzes hair to ascertain condition of hair. Applies bleach, dye, or tint, using applicator or brush, to color customer's hair, first applying solution to portion of customer's skin to determine if customer is allergic to solution. Shampoos hair and scalp with water, liquid soap, dry powder, or egg, and rinses hair with vinegar, water, lemon, or prepared rinses. Massages scalp and gives other hair and scalp-conditioning treatments for hygienic or remedial purposes[SCALP-TREATMENT OPERATOR (per. ser.)]. Styles hair by blowing, cutting, trimming, and tapering, using clippers, scissors, razors, and blow-wave gun. Suggests coiffure according to physical features of patron and current styles, or determines coiffure from instructions of patron. Applies water or waving solutions to hair and winds hair around rollers, or pin curls and finger-waves hair. Sets hair by blow-dry or natural-set, or presses hair with straightening comb. Suggests cosmetics for conditions, such as dry or oily skin. Applies lotions and creams to customer's face and neck to soften skin and lubricate tissues. Performs other beauty services, such as massaging face or neck, shaping and coloring eyebrows or eyelashes, removing unwanted hair, applying solutions that straighten hair or retain curls or waves in hair, and waving or curling hair. Cleans, shapes, and polishes fingernails and toe nails [MANICURIST (per. ser.)]. May be designated according to beauty service provided as FACIAL OPERATOR (per. ser.); FINGER WAVER (per. ser.); HAIR COLORIST (per. ser.); HAIR TINTER (per. ser.); MARCELLER (per. ser.); PERMANENT WAVER (per. ser.); SHAMPOOER (per. ser.). • GED: R4, M3, L3

• SVP: 1-2 yrs • Academic: Ed=H, Eng=S • Work Field: 264, 291 • MPSMS: 904 • Aptitudes: G3, V3, N4, S3, P2, Q4, K2, F2, M3, E5, C2 • Temperaments: J, P, V • Stress: E • Physical: V=G, H=N, L=S, W, H • Work Env: I • Salary: 2 • Outlook: 3

HAIR STYLIST (per. ser.) • D.O.T. #332.271-018 • OES #68005 • HAIRDRESSER. Specializes in dressing hair according to latest style, period, or character portrayal, following instructions of patron, MAKE-UP ARTIST (amuse. & rec.; motion pic.; radio & tv broad.), or script: Questions patron or reads instructions of MAKE-UP ARTIST (amuse. & rec.; motion pic.; radio & tv broad.) or script to determine hairdressing requirements. Studies facial features of patron or performing artist and arranges, shapes, and trims hair to achieve desired effect, using fingers, combs, barber scissors, hair-waving solutions, hairpins, and other accessories. Dyes, tints, bleaches, or curls or waves hair as required. May create new style especially for patron. May clean and style wigs. May style hairpieces and be designated HAIRPIECE STYLIST (hairwork). • GED: R4, M3, L3 • SVP: 1-2 yrs • Academic: Ed=N, Eng=S • Work Field: 264, 291 • MPSMS: 904 • Aptitudes: G3, V3, N4, S3, P3, Q4, K2, F3, M3, E5, C3 • Temperaments: J, P, V • Stress: E • Physical: V=L, H=N, L=L, W, H • Work Env: I • Salary: 3 • Outlook: 3

SCALP-TREATMENT OPERATOR (per. ser.) • D.O.T. #339.371-014 • OES #68005 • HAIR-AND-SCALP SPECIALIST; SCALP SPECIALIST; TRICHOLOGIST. Gives hair and scalp conditioning treatments for hygienic or remedial purposes: Massages, shampoos, and steams hair and scalp of patron to clean and remove excess oil, using liquid soap, rinses, and hot towels. Applies medication to and massages scalp to increase blood circulation, stimulate glandular activity, and promote growth of hair, using hands and fingers or vibrating equipment. Administers other remedial treatments to relieve such conditions as dandruff or itching scalp, using such therapeutic equipment as infrared or ultraviolet lamps. Advises patrons with chronic or potentially contagious scalp conditions to seek medical treatment. May maintain treatment records. • **GED:** R3, M2, L3 • **SVP:** 6 mos-1 yr • **Academic:** Ed=N, Eng=S • **Work Field:** 294 • **MPSMS:** 904 • **Aptitudes:** G3, V3, N4, S3, P3, Q4, K3, F3, M3, E5, C4 • **Temperaments:** J, P, V • **Stress:** E • **Physical:** V=L, H=N, L=L, W, H • **Work Env:** I • **Salary:** 3 • **Outlook:** 3

GOE: 09.02.02 Barbering

BARBER (per. ser.) • D.O.T. #330.371-010 • OES #68002 •

HAIRCUTTER; TONSORIAL ARTIST. Provides customers with barbering services: Cuts, blows out, trims, and tapers hair, using clippers, comb, blow-out gun, and scissors. Applies lather and shaves beard or shapes hair contour (outline) on temple and neck, using razor. Performs other tonsorial services, such as applying hairdressings or lotions, dyeing, shampooing, singeing, or styling hair, and massaging face, neck, or scalp. Records service charge on ticket. May sell lotions, tonics, or other cosmetic supplies. • **GED:** R3, M2, L3 • **SVP:** 1-2 yrs • **Academic:** Ed=H, Eng=S • **Work Field:** 291 • **MPSMS:** 904 • **Aptitudes:** G3, V3, N4, S3, P2, Q4, K2, F3, M3, E5, C4 • **Temperaments:** J, P, T • **Stress:** E • **Physical:** V=G, H=N, L=S, W, H • **Work Env:** I • **Salary:** 3 • **Outlook:** 2

09.03 Passenger Services

Workers in this group drive buses, taxis, limousines, or other vehicles to transport people. Workers who teach driving are also included in this group. Taxi, bus, and street railway companies hire most of the workers in this group but they can also find employment with government agencies.

✔ **What kind of work would you do?**
Your work activities would depend upon your specific job. For example, you might:

- drive a taxi and pick up customers who signal and assist them with baggage.
- drive a bus on a regular route in a city.
- give directions and other information to passengers of your bus or taxi.
- record taxi fares and destinations in a log.

- drive a bus from city to city.
- enforce safety rules when loading or unloading your passengers.
- work as a chauffeur for an individual or company.

✔ **What skills and abilities do you need for this kind of work?**
To do this kind of work, you must be able to:

- follow written and oral instructions and use time schedules, meters, and traffic regulations.
- think, reason, and act quickly to cope with traffic situations.
- read maps to locate addresses and select the best routes.
- memorize routes and established passenger pick-up locations.
- speak clearly to give information to passengers.

- deal courteously with all kinds of people.
- judge distances and speeds to avoid accidents.
- move eyes, hands and feet easily and together to brake, steer, and use other vehicle controls, such as directional signals and windshield wipers.
- read street and traffic signs at a distance and identify colors of traffic lights.

✔ **How do you know if you would like or could learn to do this kind of work?**
The following questions may give you clues about yourself as you consider this group of jobs.

- Have you completed a driver's education course? Do you have a driver's or chauffeur's license?
- Have you driven a vehicle in heavy traffic? Did you stay calm?
- Have you driven in a bicycle rodeo, car rally, or other vehicle obstacle course? Did you receive a good score?

- Have you driven a church or school bus? Can you drive a vehicle loaded with passengers without being distracted?
- Have you had military experience driving a motor vehicle?

✔ How can our prepare for and enter this type of work?

Occupations in this group usually require education and/or training extending from thirty days to over six months, depending upon the specific kind of work. Many employers want workers with a high school education or its equal. The U.S. Department of Transportation requires intercity bus drivers to be able to communicate with passengers and prepare reports. These drivers must meet specific physical requirements. They must take a written test on motor vehicle regulations. They must pass a test in the type of bus they will drive. Many intercity bus lines want workers with driving experience. Most of these firms have their own training programs for new drivers.

Local bus drivers are usually required to have a chauffeur's license. Many employers require applicants to take a written test. Workers also need to be of normal adult height and weight and have good eyesight and health. They are usually required to have one or two years of experience driving a large vehicle. Most local transit companies hold training courses and behind-the-wheel sessions. Each state has special rules for drivers of school buses. These rules are set by the State Department of Education.

Taxi drivers also must have a chauffeur's license. they are required to have a special taxi operator's license issued by the local police department, state safety department, or the public utilities commission. Most large cities require an applicant for a taxi driver's license to pass a written test on traffic laws and street locations. Some cities also require workers to have a good driving record and no criminal history. Workers often need an eighth grade education or its equal to complete the required forms.

✔ What else should you consider about these jobs?

Workers in these jobs may have to work nights and weekends or report for work on short notice. Heavy traffic and long trips can cause nervous tension in drivers. Steering and controlling the larger vehicles will require free shoulder movements and more strength than is used in driving private passenger automobiles.

Chances for promotion in these jobs are limited. However, experienced drivers may be assigned preferred routes or may get more pay. A few drivers may become dispatchers or terminal managers. Some taxi drivers buy and drive their own cabs.

If you think you would like to do this kind of work, look at the job titles listed below.

GOE: 09.03.01 Group Transportation

BUS DRIVER (motor trans.) • D.O.T. #913.463-010 • OES #97108 • CHAUFFEUR, MOTORBUS; COACH OPERATOR. Drives bus to transport passengers over specified routes to local or distant points according to time schedule: Assists passengers with baggage and collects tickets or cash fares. Regulates heating, lighting, and ventilating systems for passenger comfort. Complies with local traffic regulations. Reports delays or accidents. Records cash receipts and ticket fares. May make repairs and change tires. May inspect bus and check gas, oil, and water before departure. May load or unload baggage or express checked by passengers in baggage compartment. May transport pupils between pickup points and school and be designated as BUS DRIVER, SCHOOL (motor trans.). May drive diesel or electric powered transit bus to transport passengers over established city route and be designated as MOTOR-COACH DRIVER (motor trans.); TROLLEY-COACH DRIVER (motor trans.). • GED: R3, M2, L2 • SVP: 6 mos-1 yr • Academic: Ed=N, Eng=S • Work Field: 013 • MPSMS: 852, 859 • Aptitudes: G3, V3, N4, S3, P4, Q4, K3, F4, M3, E3, C4 • Temperaments: J, M, P • Stress: E • Physical: V=G, H=G, L=M, W, H • Work Env: I, N • Salary: 3 • Outlook: 2

GOE: 09.03.02 Individual Transportation

CHAUFFEUR (any ind.) • D.O.T. #913.663-010 • OES #97114 • Drives automobile to transport office personnel and visitors of commercial or industrial establishment. Performs miscellaneous errands, such as carrying mail to and from post office. May make overnight drives and extended trips requiring irregular hours. May be required to have chauffeurs license. May clean vehicle and make minor repairs or adjustments. • GED: R3, M2, L2 • SVP: 30 days-3 mos • Academic: Ed=N, Eng=S • Work Field: 013 • MPSMS: 852 • Aptitudes: G3, V4, N4, S3, P4, Q4, K3, F4, M3, E3, C4 • Temperaments: J, M, P • Physical: V=G, H=N, L=L, W, H • Work Env: B • Salary: 2 • Outlook: 3

TAXI DRIVER (motor trans.) • D.O.T. #913.463-018 • OES #97114 • CAB DRIVER. Drives taxicab to transport passengers for fee: Picks up passengers in response to radio or telephone relayed request for service. Collects fee recorded on taximeter based on mileage or time factor and records transaction on log. Reports by radio or telephone to TAXICAB STARTER (motor trans.) on completion of trip. May drive limousine or custom-built sedan to pick up and discharge airport passengers arriving or leaving on scheduled flights and be designated CHAUFFEUR, AIRPORT LIMOUSINE (motor trans.). • GED: R3, M2, L2 • SVP: 30 days-3 mos • Academic: Ed=N, Eng=S • Work Field: 013 • MPSMS: 852 • Aptitudes: G3, V3, N3, S3, P4, Q4, K3, F4, M3, E3, C4 • Temperaments: J, M, P • Stress: E • Physical: V=G, H=G, L=M, W, H • Work Env: I • Salary: 3 • Outlook: 2

GOE: 09.03.03 Instruction & Supervision

INSTRUCTOR, DRIVING (educ.) • D.O.T. #099.223-010 • OES

#31317 • TEACHER, DRIVER EDUCATION. Instructs individuals and groups in theory and application of automobile driving skills: Demonstrates and explains handling of automobile in emergencies, driving techniques, and mechanical operation of automobile, using blackboard diagrams, audiovisual aids, and driving simulators. Observes individual's driving habits and reactions under various driving conditions to ensure conformance with vehicle operational standards and state vehicle code. May test hearing and vision of individuals, using lettered charts and colored lights. May teach motor vehicle regulations and insurance laws. May teach operation of vehicles other than automobile, and be identified according to type of vehicle. **• GED:** R4, M2, L3 **• SVP:** 3-6 mos **• Academic:** Ed=H, Eng=G **• Work Field:** 296 **• MPSMS:** 931 **• Aptitudes:** G3, V3, N4, S3, P3, Q3, K2, F3, M3, E2, C4 **• Temperaments:** I, J, S **• Stress:** S **• Physical:** V=G, H=L, L=S, W, H **• Work Env:** I, R **• Salary:** 3 **• Outlook:** 3

09.04 Customer Services

Workers in this group provide customers in commercial settings with various services ranging from delivering newspapers to serving food. Their duties usually include receiving payment and making change. Most of these workers find employment in hotels, restaurants, stores, and concessions. However, some do work on board trains and ships and at amusement parks and resorts.

✔ **What kind of work would you do?**
Your work activities would depend upon your specific job. For example, you might:

- sell sandwiches, drinks, and other food from a truck or cart.
- rent bicycles to patrons at recreational areas.
- collect fees and issue equipment in a bowling center.
- mix and sell drinks to patrons of a bar.
- rent canoes, rowboats, motorboats, or fishing equipment to people at a resort.
- total bills, receive money, and make change for drug store customers.
- write special orders for services and merchandise, and perform personal services for customers, such as gift wrapping or monogramming.
- fill out forms and receive payments for auto rental customers.
- serve meals in a diner or formal dining room.

✔ **What skills and abilities do you need for this kind of work?**
To do this kind of work, you must be able to:

- use arithmetic to total costs and make change
- talk with different kinds of people to find out what services they want and to give them information.
- stand or walk for varying lengths of time, sometimes for long periods.
- move fingers and hands easily and quickly to handle things like dishes, money, and merchandise.
- lift and carry things like heavy trays, sports equipment, and bundles of newspapers.

✔ **How do you know if you would like or could learn to do this kind of work?**
The following questions may give you clues about yourself as you consider this group of jobs.

- Have you sold things to raise money for clubs or local organizations? Did you collect money and keep records of sales?
- Have you given directions to anyone who was lost? Did you make the directions clear?
- Have you served food or beverage at a party or reception? Can you do so without dropping or spilling food or drink?

✔ **How can you prepare for and enter this kind of work?**

Occupations in this group usually require education and/or training extending from a short demonstration to over three months, depending upon the specific kind of work. People can learn most of the jobs in this group after being hired. However, some restaurants hire only persons with experience. Workers may get the training and experience they need by starting in a related job. For example, a person may start as a dining room attendant and become a waiter or waitress. Some schools offer classes in food service work.

✔ **What else should you consider about these jobs?**

Night and holiday work, changing work hours, and weekend work are often required. Uniforms may be required, especially for food service work.

Income for these workers is often a combination of wages and tips. Some jobs in this group require the worker to adapt to specific demands. For example, a newspaper carrier may have to be out very early in the morning regardless of weather. An attendant at a lodging facility may have to live on the premises.

If you think you would like to do this kind of work, look at the job titles listed on the following pages.

GOE: 09.04.01 Food Services, Customer Service

BARTENDER (hotel & rest.) • D.O.T. #312.474-010 • OES #65005 • BAR ATTENDANT; BARKEEPER. Mixes and serves alcoholic and nonalcoholic drinks to patrons of bar, following standard recipes: Mixes ingredients, such as liquor, soda, water, sugar, and bitters, to prepare cocktails and other drinks. Serves wine and draught or bottled beer. Collects money for drinks served. Orders or requisitions liquors and supplies. Places bottled goods and glasses to make attractive display. May slice and pit fruit for garnishing drinks. May prepare appetizers, such as pickles, cheese, and cold meats. When tending service bar, may be designated as SERVICE BARTENDER (hotel & rest.). • **GED:** R3, M2, L2 • **SVP:** 30 days-3 mos • **Academic:** Ed=N, Eng=S • **Work Field:** 143, 291 • **MPSMS:** 903 • **Aptitudes:** G3, V3, N4, S4, P4, Q4, K4, F4, M3, E5, C4 • **Temperaments:** M, P • **Stress:** E • **Physical:** V=L, H=G, L=S, W, H • **Work Env:** I • **Salary:** 2 • **Outlook:** 4

CANTEEN OPERATOR (any ind.) • D.O.T. #311.674-010 • OES #65017 • Serves sandwiches, salads, beverages, desserts, candies, and tobacco to employees in industrial establishment. May collect money for purchases. May order items to replace stocks. May serve hot dishes, such as soups. May serve employees from a mobile canteen. • **GED:** R2, M1, L2 • **SVP:** 30 days-3 mos • **Academic:** Ed=N, Eng=S • **Work Field:** 291 • **MPSMS:** 903 • **Aptitudes:** G4, V4, N4, S4, P4, Q4, K4, F4, M4, E5, C5 • **Temperaments:** P • **Stress:** E • **Physical:** V=N, H=N, L=S, H • **Work Env:** I • **Salary:** 2 • **Outlook:** 4

CAR HOP (hotel & rest.) • D.O.T. #311.477-010 • OES #65011 • DRIVE-IN WAITER/WAITRESS. Serves food and refreshments to patrons in cars: Takes order and relays it to kitchen or serving counter to be filled. Places filled order on tray and fastens tray to car door. Totals and presents check to customer and accepts payment for service. Removes tray and stacks dishes for return to kitchen. May prepare fountain drinks, such as sodas, milkshakes, and malted milks. • **GED:** R2, M2, L2 • **SVP:** 2-30 days • **Academic:** Ed=N, Eng=S • **Work Field:** 291 • **MPSMS:** 903 • **Aptitudes:** G4, V4, N4, S4, P4, Q4, K3, F4, M3, E3, C4 • **Temperaments:** P • **Stress:** E • **Physical:** V=L, H=L, L=L, W, H • **Work Env:** O • **Salary:** 2 • **Outlook:** 3

COUNTER ATTENDANT, LUNCHROOM OR COFFEE SHOP (hotel & rest.) • D.O.T. #311.477-014 • OES #65017 • WAITER/WAITRESS, COUNTER. Serves food to diners seated at counter: Calls order to kitchen and picks up and serves order when ready. Accepts payment or makes up itemized check for service. May prepare sandwiches, salads, and other short order items [COOK, SHORT ORDER (hotel & rest.) II]. May perform other duties, such as cleaning counters, washing dishes, and selling cigars and cigarettes. • **GED:** R2, M2, L2 • **SVP:** 2-30 days • **Academic:** Ed=N, Eng=S • **Work Field:** 291 • **MPSMS:** 903 • **Aptitudes:** G4, V4, N4, S4, P4, Q4, K4, F3, M3, E5, C5 • **Temperaments:** P, R • **Stress:** E, T • **Physical:** V=N, H=G, L=L, W, H • **Work Env:** I • **Salary:** 2 • **Outlook:** 4

FAST-FOODS WORKER (hotel & rest.) • D.O.T. #311.472-010 • OES #65041 • CASHIER, FAST FOODS RESTAURANT. Serves customer of fast food restaurant: Requests customer order and depresses keys of multi-counting machine to simultaneously record order and compute bill [FOOD TABULATOR, AUTOMATED SYSTEM (hotel & rest.) 211.582-010]. Selects requested food items from serving or storage areas and assembles items on serving tray or in takeout bag. Notifies kitchen personnel of shortages or special orders. Serves cold drinks, using drink-dispensing machine, or frozen milk drinks or desserts, using milkshake or frozen custard machine. Makes and serves hot beverages, using automatic water heater or coffeemaker. Presses lids onto beverages and places beverages on serving tray or in takeout container. Receives payment. May cook or apportion french-fries or perform other minor duties to prepare food, serve customers, or maintain orderly eating or serving areas. • **GED:** R2, M2, L2 • **SVP:** 2-30 days • **Academic:** Ed=N, Eng=S • **Work Field:** 291, 292 • **MPSMS:** 903 • **Aptitudes:** G4, V4, N4, S4, P4, Q3, K3, F3, M3, E5, C5 • **Temperaments:** P, T • **Stress:** E • **Physical:** V=L, H=L, L=L, W, H • **Work Env:** I • **Salary:** 1 • **Outlook:** 4

FOUNTAIN SERVER (hotel & rest.) • D.O.T. #319.474-010 • OES #65017 • FOUNTAIN DISPENSER; ICE-CREAM DISPENSER; SODA CLERK; SODA DISPENSER; SODA JERKER. Prepares and serves soft drinks and ice-cream dishes, such as ice-cream sundaes, malted milks, sodas, and fruitades, using memorized formulas and methods or following directions. Cleans glasses, dishes, and fountain equipment and polishes metalwork on fountain. May prepare and serve sandwiches [SANDWICH MAKER (hotel & rest.)] or other foods [COUNTER ATTENDANT, LUNCHROOM OR COFFEE SHOP (hotel & rest.)]. • **GED:** R2, M2, L2 • **SVP:** 2-30 days • **Academic:** Ed=N, Eng=S • **Work Field:** 146 • **MPSMS:** 903 • **Aptitudes:** G4, V4, N4, S4, P4, Q4, K4, F4, M3, E5, C4 • **Temperaments:** M, P, R • **Stress:** E, T • **Physical:** V=L, H=L, L=L, W, H • **Work Env:** I • **Salary:** 1 • **Outlook:** 4

LUNCH-TRUCK DRIVER (hotel & rest.) • D.O.T. #292.463-010 • OES #97117 • CATERING-TRUCK OPERATOR; LUNCH-

TRUCK OPERATOR. Drives lunch truck over regular scheduled route, and sells miscellaneous food specialties, such as sandwiches, box lunches, and beverages, to industrial and office workers, students, and to patrons of sports and public events. Loads and unloads truck. Maintains truck and food-dispensing equipment in sanitary condition and good working order. May prepare and wrap sandwiches for delivery. May push lunch-cart through departments of industrial establishment or office building to sell merchandise and be known as LUNCH-WAGON OPERATOR (hotel & rest.). • **GED:** R2, M2, L2 • **SVP:** 2-30 days • **Academic:** Ed=N, Eng=S • **Work Field:** 013, 292 • **MPSMS:** 903 • **Aptitudes:** G3, V3, N3, S3, P4, Q4, K3, F4, M3, E3, C4 • **Temperaments:** P • **Stress:** E • **Physical:** V=L, H=L, L=M, W, H • **Work Env:** B • **Salary:** 2 • **Outlook:** 3

MANAGER, FOOD CONCESSION (hotel & rest.) • D.O.T. #185.167-022 • OES #41002 • Manages refreshment stand or other food concession at public gatherings, sports events, amusement park, or similar facility: Purchases refreshments, according to anticipated demand and familiarity with public taste in food and beverages. Directs storage, preparation, and serving of refreshments by other workers at refreshment stand or circulating throughout audience. Assigns VENDORS (amuse. & rec.) to locations. Tabulates receipts and balances accounts. Inventories supplies on hand at end of each day or other designated period. • **GED:** R3, M3, L3 • **SVP:** 1-2 yrs • **Academic:** Ed=N, Eng=S • **Work Field:** 295 • **MPSMS:** 903 • **Aptitudes:** G3, V3, N3, S4, P4, Q2, K4, F4, M4, E5, C5 • **Temperaments:** D, M, P • **Stress:** A • **Physical:** V=L, H=L, L=L, W, H • **Work Env:** I • **Salary:** 4 • **Outlook:** 3

VENDING-MACHINE ATTENDANT (hotel & rest.) • D.O.T. #319.464-014 • OES #85947 • Stocks machines and assists customers in facility where food is dispensed from coin-operated machines: Places food or drink items on shelves of vending machines and changes shelf labels as required to indicate selections. Makes change for customers and answers questions regarding selections. Adjusts temperature gauges to maintain food items at specified temperatures. Performs minor repairs or adjustments on machines to correct jams or similar malfunctions, using handtools. Prepares requisitions for food and drink supplies. Cleans interior and exterior of machines, using damp cloth. Maintains eating area in orderly condition. May sell precooked foods from hot table. May remove money from vending machines and keep records of receipts. • **GED:** R2, M2, L2 • **SVP:** 2-30 days • **Academic:** Ed=N, Eng=N • **Work Field:** 221, 291 • **MPSMS:** 919 • **Aptitudes:** G3, V4, N4, S4, P4, Q4, K4, F4, M3, E5, C4 • **Temperaments:** P • **Stress:** E • **Physical:** V=L, H=N, L=L, W, H • **Work Env:** I • **Salary:** 2 • **Outlook:** 4

VENDING-STAND SUPERVISOR (gov. ser.) • D.O.T. #185.167-066 • OES #41002 • OPERATIONS SUPERVISOR; VENDING-ENTERPRISES SUPERVISOR. Coordinates activities of persons engaged in vending-stand operations of State program for rehabilitation of the blind: Observes stand operation and advises blind vendor on merchandise purchase and display, improved methods of operation, personal appearance, and sanitation. Inspects condition of stock and fixtures to ascertain adherence to regulations and to determine need for maintenance and repairs. Examines invoices and receipts to determine equity of charges and to prepare monthly profit and loss statement. Investigates and resolves problems varying from nuisance complaints to breach-of-contract. May address civic groups to promote public relations. May collect cash, invoices, receipts, and specified assessments as determined by State program requirements. May plan, locate, and arrange for installation of stands, train vendors, and negotiate contracts with building managers for stand operation [BUSINESS-ENTERPRISE OFFICER (gov. ser.)]. • **GED:** R5, M4, L4 • **SVP:** 2-4 yrs • **Academic:** Ed=A, Eng=S • **Work Field:** 292, 295 • **MPSMS:** 881, 940 • **Aptitudes:** G2, V2, N3, S3, P3, Q3, K4, F4, M4, E5, C4 • **Temperaments:** D, J, M, P, V • **Stress:** A • **Physical:** V=G, H=G, L=L, W • **Work Env:** I • **Salary:** 4 • **Outlook:** 2

WAITER/WAITRESS, FORMAL (hotel & rest.) • D.O.T. #311.477-026 • OES #65008 • Serves meals to patrons according to established rules of etiquette, working in formal setting: Presents menu to diner, suggesting dinner courses, appropriate wines, and answering questions regarding food preparation. Writes order

on check or memorizes it. Relays order to kitchen and serves courses from kitchen and service bars. Garnishes and decorates dishes preparatory to serving. Serves patrons from chafing dish at table. Observes diners to fulfill any additional request and to perceive when meal has been completed. Totals bill and accepts payment or refers patron to CASHIER (clerical) II. May carve meats, bone fish and fowl, and prepare flaming dishes and desserts at patron's table. When serving at banquets, may be designated WAITER/WAITRESS, BANQUET (hotel & rest.). • **GED:** R3, M2, L3 • **SVP:** 30 days-3 mos • **Academic:** Ed=N, Eng=S • **Work Field:** 291 • **MPSMS:** 903 • **Aptitudes:** G3, V3, N4, S4, P4, Q4, K3, F4, M3, E4, C5 • **Temperaments:** P, R • **Stress:** E • **Physical:** V=L, H=L, L=L, W, H • **Work Env:** I • **Salary:** 3 • **Outlook:** 4

WAITER/WAITRESS, INFORMAL (hotel & rest.) • D.O.T. #311.477-030 • OES #65008 • Serves food to patrons at counters and tables of coffeeshops, lunchrooms, and other dining establishments where food service is informal: Presents menu, answers questions, and makes suggestions regarding food and service. Writes order on check or memorizes it. Relays order to kitchen and serves courses from kitchen and service bars. Observes guests to fulfill any additional request and to perceive when meal has been completed. Totals bill and accepts payment or refers patron to CASHIER (clerical) II. May ladle soup, toss salads, portion pies and desserts, brew coffee, and perform other services as determined by establishment's size and practices. May clear and reset counters or tables at conclusion of each course [DINING ROOM ATTENDANT (hotel & rest.)]. • **GED:** R3, M2, L2 • **SVP:** 30 days-3 mos • **Academic:** Ed=N, Eng=S • **Work Field:** 291 • **MPSMS:** 903 • **Aptitudes:** G3, V3, N4, S4, P4, Q4, K4, F4, M3, E4, C5 • **Temperaments:** P • **Stress:** E • **Physical:** V=L, H=G, L=L, W, H • **Work Env:** I • **Salary:** 2 • **Outlook:** 4

WAITER/WAITRESS, TAKE OUT (hotel & rest.) • D.O.T. #311.477-038 • OES #65017 • Serves customers of a take out counter of a restaurant or lunchroom with food to be consumed elsewhere. Receives order from customer. Wraps sandwiches, hot entrees, desserts, and other menu items, and fills containers with coffee, tea, and other beverages. May accept payment for orders. May prepare fountain drinks, such as sodas and milk shakes. • **GED:** R3, M2, L2 • **SVP:** 30 days-3 mos • **Academic:** Ed=N, Eng=S • **Work Field:** 291 • **MPSMS:** 903 • **Aptitudes:** G3, V4, N4, S4, P4, Q4, K4, F4, M3, E5, C5 • **Temperaments:** P • **Stress:** E • **Physical:** V=L, H=L, L=L, W, H • **Work Env:** I • **Salary:** 2 • **Outlook:** 4

GOE: 09.04.02 Sales Services

AUTOMOBILE-RENTAL CLERK (auto. ser.) • D.O.T. #295.477-010 • OES #49017 • CAR-RENTAL CLERK. Rents automobiles to customers at airports, hotels, marinas, and other locations: Talks to customer to determine type of automobile desired and accessories, such as power steering or air-conditioning, location where car is to be picked up and returned, and number of days required. Examines customer's driver's license, and determines amount of deposit required. Quotes cost of rental, based on per-day and per-mile rates. Completes rental contract and obtains customer's signature and deposit, or checks charge-plate number against list of disapproved charge plates. Telephones storage and service area to determine if automobile desired is available and request delivery of automobile, and to check automobile upon return for damage and to record mileage reading. Computes rental charges based on rental time, miles traveled, type of car rented, taxes, and other incidental expenses incurred. May reconcile cash and rental agreements and charge slips and send them to management. May deliver automobile to customer. May keep log of location of rented automobiles. May be designated according to type of automobile rented as LIMOUSINE-RENTAL CLERK (auto. ser.). • **GED:** R3, M3, L3 • **SVP:** 3-6 mos • **Academic:** Ed=N, Eng=G • **Work Field:** 292 • **MPSMS:** 859 • **Aptitudes:** G3, V3, N3, S4, P4, Q3, K4, F4, M4, E5, C5 • **Temperaments:** M, P • **Stress:** E • **Physical:** V=L, H=L, L=S, H • **Work Env:** I • **Salary:** 2 • **Outlook:** 3

BICYCLE-RENTAL CLERK (ret. tr.) • D.O.T. #295.467-010 • OES #49017 • Rents bicycles to patrons at beach, resort, or retail bicycle-rental store: Explains bicycle-rental rates and conditions to customer. Issues bicycle to customer and records time of transaction. Receives returned bicycles and examines them for abuse or breakage. Computes rental charge according to elapsed time and accepts payment, imposing specified fee for damage to bicycle. Records time bicycle was returned. Prepares cash report at end of shift. Tags bicycles needing repair or service. May adjust bicycle seat to suit customer. May receive money deposit or identification, such as drivers license, as security toward return of bicycle. May explain operation of bicycle and features of certain bicycles, such as gear shifting and hand brakes to customers. • GED: R2, M2, L2 • SVP: 2- 30 days • Academic: Ed=N, Eng=S • Work Field: 292 • MPSMS: 881 • Aptitudes: G4, V4, N3, S4, P4, Q3, K4, F4, M4, E5, C5 • Temperaments: M, P • Stress: 2 • Physical: V=L, H=N, L=L, W • Work Env: B • Salary: 2 • Outlook: 3

CASHIER-WRAPPER (ret. tr.) • D.O.T. #211.462-018 • OES #49023 • Operates cash register to compute and record total sale and wraps merchandise for customers in department, variety, and specialty stores: Receives sales slip, money, and merchandise from salesperson or customer. Records amount of sale on cash register and makes change. Obtains credit authorization on charge purchases in excess of floor limit from designated official, using telephone or pneumatic tube carrier. Inspects merchandise prior to wrapping to see that it is in satisfactory condition and verifies sales slip with price tickets on merchandise. Places merchandise in bags or boxes and gives change and packages to selling personnel. Wraps packages for shipment and routes to delivery department. Balances cash received with cash sales daily. May gift wrap merchandise. • GED: R3, M2, L2 • SVP: 30 days-3 mos • Academic: Ed=N, Eng=S • Work Field: 041, 232 • MPSMS: 899 • Aptitudes: G3, V3, N3, S4, P4, Q3, K3, F3, M3, E5, C3 • Temperaments: P, R, T • Stress: E, T • Physical: V=L, H=N, L=L, H • Work Env: I • Salary: 2 • Outlook: 4

CUSTOMER-SERVICE CLERK (ret. tr.) • D.O.T. #299.367-010 • OES #49999 • CUSTOMER-SERVICE SPECIALIST, POST EXCHANGE. Performs any combination of following tasks in post exchange: Arranges for gift wrapping, monogramming, printing, and fabrication of such items as desk nameplates and rubber stamps, and repair or replacement of defective items covered by warranty. Takes orders for such items as decorated cakes, cut flowers, personalized greeting cards and stationery, and merchandise rentals and repairs. Prepares special-order worksheet. Keeps record of services in progress. Notifies customer when service is completed and accepts payment. Acts as WEDDING CONSULTANT (ret. tr.). Assists customers to select and purchase specified merchandise [PERSONAL SHOPPER (ret. tr.)]. Keeps records of items in layaway, receives and posts customer payments, and prepares and forwards delinquent notices [LAYAWAY CLERK (ret. tr.)]. Issues temporary identification cards from information on military records. Approves customer's checks and provides check-cashing service according to exchange policy. Answers customer's telephone, mail, and in-person inquiries and directs customers to appropriate sales area [INFORMATION CLERK (clerical)]. Resolves customer complaints and requests for refunds, exchanges, and adjustments. Provides customers with catalogs and information concerning prices, shipping time, and costs. • GED: R3, M3, L3 • SVP: 3-6 mos • Academic: Ed=N, Eng=G • Work Field: 231, 291, 292 • MPSMS: 881 • Aptitudes: G3, V3, N3, S4, P3, Q3, K4, F3, M4, E5, C3 • Temperaments: P, V • Stress: E • Physical: V=N, H=G, L=S, H • Work Env: I • Salary: 2 • Outlook: 3

DELIVERER, MERCHANDISE (ret. tr.) • D.O.T. #299.477-010 • OES #49999 • Delivers merchandise from retail store to customers on foot, bicycle, or public conveyance: Unpacks incoming merchandise, marks prices on articles, and stacks them on counters and shelves [STOCK CLERK, SELF-SERVICE STORE (ret. tr.)]. Walks, rides bicycle, or uses public convey ances to deliver merchandise to customer's home or place of business. Collects money from customers or signature from charge-account customers. Sweeps floors, runs errands, and waits on customers [SALES CLERK (ret. tr.)]. May drive light truck to deliver orders. May be designated according to merchandise delivered as DELIVERER, FOOD (ret. tr.); DELIVERER, PHARMACY (ret. tr.). • GED: R2, M2, L2 • SVP: 2-30 days • Academic: Ed=N, Eng=S • Work Field: 221, 291 • MPSMS: 881 • Aptitudes: G4, V4, N3, S4, P4, Q4, K4, F4, M4, E4, C5 • Temperaments: P • Stress: E • Physical: V=L, H=N, L=M, W, C, S, H • Work Env: B • Salary:

2 • Outlook: 3

FLOOR ATTENDANT (amuse. & rec.) • D.O.T. #343.467-014 • OES #68014 • Verifies winning bingo cards to award prize or pay prize money to players holding winning cards: Collects money (fee) for participation in game and issues game cards to players. Listens for shouts or looks for waving arms from players who have winning cards. Compares numbers on card with numbers called and displayed on board to verify winning cards. Gives prize or pays money to players holding winning cards. • GED: R2, M1, L1 • SVP: 2-30 days • Academic: Ed=N, Eng=S • Work Field: 232 • MPSMS: 919 • Aptitudes: G4, V4, N4, S4, P3, Q3, K4, F4, M4, E5, C5 • Temperaments: P, R • Stress: E • Physical: V=L, H=L, L=L, W, H • Work Env: I • Salary: 2 • Outlook: 3

FURNITURE-RENTAL CONSULTANT (ret. tr.) • D.O.T. #295.357-018 • OES #49017 • DECORATOR CONSULTANT; RENTAL CLERK, FURNITURE. Rents furniture and accessories to customers: Talks to customer to determine furniture preferences and requirements. Guides or accompanies customer through show room, answers questions, and advises customer on compatibility of various styles and colors of furniture items. Compiles list of customer-selected items. Computes rental fee, explains rental terms, and presents list to customer for approval. Prepares order form and lease agreement, explains terms of lease to customer, and obtains customer signature. Obtains credit information from customer. Forwards forms to credit office for verification of customer credit status and approval of order. Collects initial payment from customer. Contacts customers to encourage followup transactions. May visit commercial customer site to solicit rental contracts, or review floor plans of new construction and suggest suitable furnishings. May sell furniture or accessories [SALESPERSON, FURNITURE (ret. tr.) 270.357-030]. • GED: R3, M2, L2 • SVP: 2-30 days • Academic: Ed=N, Eng=G • Work Field: 292 • MPSMS: 460, 881 • Aptitudes: G3, V3, N3, S4, P4, Q4, K4, F4, M4, E5, C4 • Temperaments: I, P • Stress: E • Physical: V=L, H=L, L=L, H • Work Env: I • Salary: 2 • Outlook: 3

GAMBLING DEALER (amuse. & rec.) • D.O.T. #343.467-018 • OES #68014 • Conducts game at gambling table, such as dice, roulette, or cards, in gambling establishment: Exchanges paper currency for playing chips or coin money. Ensures that all wagers are placed before cards are dealt, roulette wheel is spun, or dice are tossed. Announces winning number or color to players. Computes payable odds to pay winning bets. Pays winning bets and collects losing bets. May be designated according to specialty as BACCARAT DEALER (amuse. & rec.); DICE DEALER (amuse. & rec.); ROULETTE DEALER (amuse. & rec.); TWENTY-ONE DEALER (amuse. & rec.). • GED: R3, M3, L3 • SVP: 30 days-3 mos • Academic: Ed=N, Eng=G • Work Field: 232, 282 • MPSMS: 919 • Aptitudes: G3, V3, N3, S4, P3, Q3, K3, F3, M3, E5, C4 • Temperaments: J, P, R, T • Stress: E • Physical: V=L, H=L, L=L, H • Work Env: I • Salary: 3 • Outlook: 3

GAME ATTENDANT (amuse. & rec.) • D.O.T. #342.457-010 • OES #68014 • GAME OPERATOR. Induces customers to participate in games at concession booths in parks, carnivals, stadiums, or similar amusement places: Attracts customers by describing to passing public, type of games available. Serves customers game equipment, such as toss rings or balls, distributes prizes to customers who win games, and collects fees for services. Cleans and repairs booth and keeps equipment in serviceable condition. May be designated according to type game operated as SHOOTING GALLERY OPERATOR (amuse. & rec.). • GED: R3, M3, L3 • SVP: 30 days-3 mos • Academic: Ed=N, Eng=S • Work Field: 292 • MPSMS: 919 • Aptitudes: G3, V3, N3, S4, P4, Q4, K3, F3, M3, E5, C5 • Temperaments: I, J, P • Stress: E • Physical: V=L, H=N, L=L, H • Work Env: B • Salary: 2 • Outlook: 3

NEWSPAPER CARRIER (ret. tr.) • D.O.T. #292.457-010 • OES #49026 • CARRIER; NEWSPAPER DELIVERER. Delivers and sells newspapers to subscribers along prescribed route and collects money periodically: Purchases newspapers at wholesale price for resale to subscriber at retail rate. Walks or rides bicycle to deliver newspapers to subscribers. Keeps records of accounts. Contacts prospective subscribers along route to solicit subscriptions. May attend training sessions to learn selling techniques. If worker delivers newspapers, using automobile or truck, see NEWSPAPER-DELIVERY DRIVER (whole. tr.). • GED: R2, M2, L2 • SVP:

2-30 days • **Academic:** Ed=N, Eng=S • **Work Field:** 292 • **MPSMS:** 889, 899 • **Aptitudes:** G4, V3, N4, S4, P4, Q4, K4, F4, M4, E3, C5 • **Temperaments:** I, P • **Stress:** E • **Physical:** V=L, H=N, L=L, W, H • **Work Env:** O • **Salary:** 1 • **Outlook:** 4

PARKING-LOT ATTENDANT (auto. ser.) • D.O.T. #915.473-010 • OES #97808 • AUTOMOBILE PARKER; PARKING ATTENDANT; PARKING-LOT CHAUFFEUR; PARKING-STATION ATTENDANT; SPOTTER. Parks automobiles for customers in parking lot or storage garage: Places numbered tag on windshield of automobile to be parked and hands customer similar tag to be used later in locating parked automobile. Records time and drives automobile to parking space, or points out parking space for customer's use. Patrols area to prevent thefts from parked automobiles. Collects parking fee from customer, based on charges for time automobile is parked. Takes numbered tag from customer, locates automobile, and surrenders it to customer, or directs customer to parked automobile. May service automobiles with gasoline, oil, and water. When parking automobiles in storage garage, may be designated as STORAGE- GARAGE ATTENDANT (auto. ser.). • **GED:** R2, M1, L1 • **SVP:** 2-30 days • **Academic:** Ed=N, Eng=S • **Work Field:** 291 • **MPSMS:** 961 • **Aptitudes:** G4, V4, N4, S4, P4, Q4, K4, F4, M3, E3, C5 • **Temperaments:** P, R • **Stress:** E, T • **Physical:** V=L, H=N, L=L, W, H • **Work Env:** B • **Salary:** 2 • **Outlook:** 3

PERSONAL SHOPPER (ret. tr.) • D.O.T. #296.357-010 • OES #49999 • PROFESSIONAL SHOPPER; SHOPPER'S AID; SPECIAL SHOPPER. Selects and purchases merchandise for department store customers, according to mail or telephone requests. Visits wholesale establishments or other department stores to purchase merchandise which is out-of-stock or which store does not carry. Records and processes mail orders and merchandise returned for exchange. May escort customer through store. • **GED:** R4, M3, L3 • **SVP:** 6 mos-1 yr • **Academic:** Ed=N, Eng=G • **Work Field:** 291, 292 • **MPSMS:** 880 • **Aptitudes:** G3, V3, N3, S4, P4, Q4, K4, F4, M4, E5, C5 • **Temperaments:** M, P • **Stress:** E • **Physical:** V=L, H=L, L=L, W • **Work Env:** I • **Salary:** 2 • **Outlook:** 3

SALES ATTENDANT, BUILDING MATERIALS (ret. tr.) • D.O.T. #299.677-014 • OES #49021 • YARD SALESPERSON. Assists customers and stocks merchandise in building materials and supplies department of self-service general store: Answers questions and advises customer in selection of building materials and supplies. Cuts lumber, screening, glass, and related materials to size requested by customer, using powersaws, holding fixtures, and various hand cutting tools. Assists customer in loading purchased materials into customer's vehicle. Moves materials and supplies from receiving area to display area, using forklift or handtruck. Marks prices on merchandise or price stickers, according to pricing guides, using marking devices. Straightens materials on display to maintain safe and orderly conditions in sales areas. Covers exposed materials when required to prevent weather damage. Counts materials and records totals on inventory sheets. • **GED:** R2, M2, L2 • **SVP:** 30 days-3 mos • **Academic:** Ed=N, Eng=S • **Work Field:** 011, 292 • **MPSMS:** 881 • **Aptitudes:** G4, V4, N4, S4, P4, Q4, K4, F4, M4, E4, C5 • **Temperaments:** P, V • **Stress:** E • **Physical:** V=L, H=L, L=H, W, S, H • **Work Env:** I • **Salary:** 2 • **Outlook:** 3

SALES CLERK (ret. tr.) • D.O.T. #290.477-014 • OES #49011 • Obtains or receives merchandise, totals bill, receives payment, and makes change for customers in such retail stores as tobacco shop, drug store, candy store, or liquor store: Stocks shelves, counters, or tables with merchandise. Sets up advertising displays or arranges merchandise on counters or tables to promote sales. Stamps, marks, or tags price on merchandise. Obtains merchandise requested by customer or receives merchandise selected by customer. Totals price and tax on merchandise selected by customer, using paper and pencil, cash register, or adding machine, to determine bill; receives payment, and makes change. Occasionally calculates sales discount in determining sales slip. Wraps or bags merchandise for customers. Cleans shelves, counters, or tables as necessary. May keep record of sales, prepare inventory of stock, or order merchandise. May be designated according to product sold or type of store. • **GED:** R3, M3, L2 • **SVP:** 30 days-3 mos • **Academic:** Ed=N, Eng=S • **Work Field:** 221, 292 • **MPSMS:** 881

• **Aptitudes:** G3, V3, N3, S4, P4, Q3, K3, F4, M4, E5, C4 • **Temperaments:** P • **Stress:** E • **Physical:** V=L, H=L, L=S, H • **Work Env:** I • **Salary:** 2 • **Outlook:** 3

SALES CLERK, FOOD (ret. tr.) • D.O.T. #290.477-018 • OES #49011 • Obtains or prepares food items requested by customers in retail food stores, such as groceries, produce, bakery goods, meat and fish, and totals customer bill, receives payment, and makes change: Sets up displays on counters, shelves, or in bins. Fills customer order, performing such duties as obtaining items from shelves, freezers, coolers, bins, tables, or containers, cleaning poultry, scaling and trimming fish, slicing meat or cheese, using slicing machine, or preparing take-out sandwiches and salads. Weighs items, such as produce, meat, and poultry to determine price. Lists and totals prices, using paper and pencil, adding machine, or cash register, and informs customer of total price of purchases. Receives money from customers for purchases, and makes change. Bags or wraps purchases for customers. Cleans shelves, bins, tables, and coolers as necessary. Stamps, marks, or tags price on merchandise. Stocks shelves, coolers, counter, bins, tables, freezers, containers, or trays with new merchandise. May make deliveries to customers' homes or places of business on foot or using vehicle [DELIVERER, MERCHANDISE (ret. tr.)]. May write up special orders, such as for birthday cakes in bakery store. May order merchandise from warehouse or supplier. May be designated according to type of food sold as GROCERY CLERK (ret. tr.); MEAT COUNTER CLERK (ret. tr.); PRODUCE CLERK (ret. tr.) I; SALES CLERK, FISH (ret. tr.). • **GED:** R3, M3, L2 • **SVP:** 30 days-3 mos • **Academic:** Ed=N, Eng=S • **Work Field:** 221, 292 • **MPSMS:** 881 • **Aptitudes:** G3, V3, N3, S4, P4, Q4, K3, F4, M4, E5, C5 • **Temperaments:** P • **Stress:** E • **Physical:** V=N, H=N, L=L, W, H • **Work Env:** I • **Salary:** 2 • **Outlook:** 3

SELF-SERVICE-LAUNDRY-AND-DRY-CLEANING ATTENDANT (clean., dye., & press.) • D.O.T. #369.677-010 • OES #49017 • ATTENDANT, COIN-OPERATED LAUNDRY; ATTENDANT, LAUNDRY-AND-DRY-CLEANING SERVICE; WASHATERIA ATTENDANT. Assists customer to launder or dryclean clothes, or launders or drycleans clothes for customer paying for complete service, using self-service equipment: Gives instructions to customer in clothes preparation, such as weighing, sorting, fog-spraying spots, and removing perishable buttons. Assigns machine and directs customer or points out posted instructions regarding equipment operation. Weighs soiled items and calculates amount charged customer requiring complete services. Dampens garments with cleaning solvent and rubs with sponge or brush to remove spots or stains. Places clothes, cleaning material, bleach, and coins in laundering or drycleaning equipment, and sets automatic controls to clean or dry clothes. Removes clothes from equipment. Hangs, bags, folds, and bundles clothes for delivery to customer. Receives payment for service. May sell cleansing agents. • **GED:** R3, M1, L3 • **SVP:** 2-30 days • **Academic:** Ed=N, Eng=S • **Work Field:** 291, 292 • **MPSMS:** 906 • **Aptitudes:** G4, V4, N4, S4, P4, Q4, K4, F4, M4, E5, C4 • **Temperaments:** P, V • **Stress:** E • **Physical:** V=N, H=N, L=M, W, H • **Work Env:** I • **Salary:** 2 • **Outlook:** 2

SERVICE-ESTABLISHMENT ATTENDANT (clean., dye., & press.) • D.O.T. #369.477-014 • OES #49017 • COUNTER ATTENDANT. Receives articles, such as shoes and clothing, to be repaired or cleaned, in personal-service establishment: Examines articles to determine nature of repair and advises customer of repairs needed. Quotes prices and prepares work ticket. Sends articles to work department. Returns finished articles to customer and collects amount due. May keep records of cash receipts and articles received and delivered. May sell articles, such as cleaner, polish, shoelaces, and accessories. • **GED:** R3, M2, L2 • **SVP:** 30 days-3 mos • **Academic:** Ed=N, Eng=S • **Work Field:** 291 • **MPSMS:** 906, 961 • **Aptitudes:** G3, V3, N3, S4, P4, Q3, K4, F4, M4, E5, C5 • **Temperaments:** J, P • **Stress:** E • **Physical:** V=N, H=N, L=S, H • **Work Env:** I • **Salary:** 2 • **Outlook:** 2

SKATE-SHOP ATTENDANT (amuse. & rec.) • D.O.T. #341.464-010 • OES #68014 • Repairs, rents, or sells ice skates and equipment at ice-skating rink: Removes skate blade from shoe, places it in guide frame, and sharpens blade on grinding wheel. Drills holes in shoe, using electric drill, and bolts blade to shoe, using wrench. Cleans skates with cloth or buffing tool and places them on shelf according to size. Issues skates to patrons and collects ticket or money for rental. Sells merchandise, such as skates, skate guards, and skating apparel. • **GED:** R3, M2, L2 • **SVP:** 30 days-3 mos • **Academic:** Ed=N, Eng=S • **Work Field:** 102, 292 • **MPSMS:** 616 • **Aptitudes:** G3, V4, N3, S4, P4, Q3, K3, F4, M3, E5, C5 • **Temperaments:** P, T • **Stress:** E • **Physical:** V=L, H=N, L=L, W, H • **Work Env:** I • **Salary:** 2 • **Outlook:** 2

STORAGE-FACILITY RENTAL CLERK (bus. ser.) • D.O.T. #295.367-026 • OES #49017 • Leases storage space to customers of rental storage facility: Informs customers of space availability, rental regulations, and rates. Assists customers in selection of storage unit size according to articles or material to be stored. Records terms of rental on rental agreement form and assists customer in completing form. Photographs completed form and customer to establish identification record, using security camera. Computes rental fee and collects payment. Maintains rental status record and waiting list for storage units. Notifies customers when rental term is about to expire or rent is overdue. Inspects storage area periodically to ensure storage units are locked. Observes individuals entering storage area to prevent access to or tampering with storage units by unauthorized persons. Loads film into security and surveillance cameras, records dates of film changes, and monitors camera operations to ensure performance as required. Cleans facility and maintains premises in orderly condition. • **GED:** R3, M3, L3 • **SVP:** 2-30 days • **Academic:** Ed=N, Eng=G • **Work Field:** 292 • **MPSMS:** 889 • **Aptitudes:** G3, V3, N3, S4, P4, Q3, K4, F4, M3, E5, C5 • **Temperaments:** P, V • **Stress:** E • **Physical:** V=L, H=N, L=S, W, H • **Work Env:** I • **Salary:** 2 • **Outlook:** 3

TOOL-AND-EQUIPMENT-RENTAL CLERK (bus. ser.) • D.O.T. #295.357-014 • OES #49017 • RENTAL CLERK, TOOL-AND-EQUIPMENT. Rents tools and equipment to customers: Suggests tools or equipment, based on work to be done. Prepares rental form and quotes rental rates to customer. Starts power equipment

to ensure performance prior to issuance to customer. Computes rental fee based on hourly or daily rate. Cleans, lubricates, and adjusts power tools and equipment. May drive truck or use hand-truck to deliver tools or equipment to customer. • **GED:** R3, M3, L3 • **SVP:** 3-6 mos • **Academic:** Ed=N, Eng=S • **Work Field:** 292 • **MPSMS:** 881 • **Aptitudes:** G3, V3, N3, S4, P3, Q3, K4, F4, M4, E4, C4 • **Temperaments:** I, J, P • **Stress:** E • **Physical:** V=L, H=L, L=M, H • **Work Env:** I • **Salary:** 2 • **Outlook:** 4

TRAILER-RENTAL CLERK (auto. ser.) • D.O.T. #295.467-022 • OES #49017 • Rents trailers, trucks, and power-driven mobile machinery and equipment: Talks with customer to determine type of equipment needed, such as vacation, boat, or open trailer, or moving truck or moving-van trailer, or cement mixer. Quotes rental rates and collects security deposit. Prepares rental-agreement form. Directs yard personnel to hitch trailer to customer's vehicle or bring truck or power-driven mobile equipment to customer. Computes rental charges, collects money, makes change, and returns deposit. May pull trailer into position and fasten appropriate hitch to customer's vehicle. May splice wires from trailer's taillights onto wires of customer's vehicle's taillights to provide brake and turn signals to trailer. May advise customer on type of equipment to rent, depending on work to be done. May rent power tools and equipment [TOOL-AND-EQUIPMENT-RENTAL CLERK (bus. ser.; ret. tr.)]. May be designated according to type of equipment rented as CONSTRUCTION-MACHINERY-AND-EQUIP-MENT-RENTAL CLERK (bus. ser.); FARM-MACHINERY-AND-EQUIPMENT-RENTAL CLERK (bus. ser.); TRUCK RENTAL CLERK (auto. ser.). • **GED:** R3, M3, L3 • **SVP:** 3-6 mos • **Academic:** Ed=N, Eng=G • **Work Field:** 292 • **MPSMS:** 881 • **Aptitudes:** G3, V3, N3, S4, P4, Q3, K4, F4, M4, E5, C5 • **Temperaments:** P • **Stress:** E • **Physical:** V=L, H=L, L=L, W, H • **Work Env:** I • **Salary:** 2 • **Outlook:** 3

09.05 Attendant Services

Workers in this group perform services that make life easier and more pleasant for people. They do things that people can't or don't want to do for themselves, like opening doors, delivering messages, carrying luggage and packages, and dishing up food. They find employment in a variety of settings, such as hotels, airports, golf courses, theaters, reducing salons, and gymnasiums.

✔ **What kind of work would you do?**

Your work activities would depend upon your specific job. For example, you might:

- serve or assist diners at a buffet table.
- carry food to a serving table in a cafeteria.
- carry and deliver messages.
- care for costumes of a theatrical or movie cast.
- carry pails of drinking water to farm or construction workers.
- serve food to cafeteria customers.
- check credentials of those entering a press box and run errands.

- retrieve bats and foul balls from baseball field and supply balls to the umpire.
- massage a customer's muscles to relieve tension.
- clean, shape, and polish fingernails.
- take tickets from persons attending a theater.
- carry baggage on and off trains.

✔ **What skills and abilities do you need for this kind of work?**

To do this kind of work, you must be able to:

- carry out specific oral or written instructions, frequently following a simple routine.

- do the same task over and over, frequently in the same way.
- get along with all kinds of people.
- stand and walk for long periods of time.

- use hands and fingers skillfully and easily when performing tasks, like giving rub-downs, manicuring fingernails, opening oysters, and bagging groceries.

- lift and carry things like luggage, trays of dishes, and bags of golf clubs.

✔ **How do you know if you would like or could learn to do this kind of work?**

The following questions may give you clues about yourself as you consider this group of jobs.

- Have you collected tickets or ushered at a play? Do you remain courteous when other people are rude to you?
- Have you served food or beverages in a cafeteria line? Can you walk or stand for long periods of time?
- Have you helped with the wardrobe for a school or community theatrical group? Do you enjoy assisting others?

- Have you been in charge of sports equipment for a team? Do you enjoy caring for other people's property?
- Have you served food in a mess hall as a member of a military force? Did you like doing this?

✔ **How can you prepare for and enter this kind of work?**

Occupations in this group usually require education and/or training extending from a short demonstration to over three months, depending upon the specific kind of work. Many jobs in this group require only on-the-job training. However, formal training is available. For example, massage techniques may be learned in a few class sessions through a public or private school. Manicurists usually learn their trade in a beauty school.

Some jobs require city or state licenses. Courses in food and beverage service are offered in many vocational schools. Employers usually train inexperienced people.

✔ **What else should you consider about these jobs?**

Income for these workers may be a combination of wages and tips. Their salary sometimes includes room and board. Weekend and evening work is required in some of these jobs. Some workers like Bellhops and Waiters/Waitresses are required to wear uniforms.

If you think you would like to do this kind of work, look at the job titles listed on the following pages.

GOE: 09.05.01 Physical Conditioning

COOLING-ROOM ATTENDANT (per. ser.) • D.O.T. #335.677-010 • OES #68032 • ALCOHOL RUBBER; SLUMBER-ROOM ATTENDANT. Attends to comfort and needs of thermal bath customers cooling off and resting after bath and massage: Assigns cot to customer. Rubs customer's body with alcohol and oil to soothe skin. Covers customer with sheet. Times length of rest period. Procures beverage, food, or other items on request. May arrange for valet services. May change bedding on cots. May shine shoes [SHOE SHINER (per. ser.)]. May sweep and mop floors and dust furniture [CLEANER, COMMERCIAL OR INSTITUTIONAL (any ind.)]. • **GED:** R2, M1, L2 • **SVP:** 2-30 days • **Academic:** Ed=N, Eng=S • **Work Field:** 291 • **MPSMS:** 909 • **Aptitudes:** G4, V4, N4, S4, P4, Q4, K4, F4, M3, E5, C5 • **Temperaments:** P, R • **Stress:** E, T • **Physical:** V=N, H=N, L=L, W, S, H • **Work Env:** I • **Salary:** 2 • **Outlook:** 2

ELECTROLOGIST (per. ser.) • D.O.T. #339.371-010 • OES #68005 • ELECTRIC-NEEDLE SPECIALIST; ELECTROLYSIS OPERATOR; HYPERTRICHOLOGIST. Removes hair from skin of patron by electrolysis: Positions sterile bulbous or round-tipped needles into holders (electrodes) of galvanic or short wave electrical equipment. Places secondary electrode in hand or immerses fingers or hand of patron in water-filled electrode cup to complete circuit and stabilize amount of electricity when equipment is operating.

Swabs skin area with antiseptic solution to sterilize it. Inserts needle or needles into hair follicle and into organ beneath hair root (papilla). Presses switch and adjusts timing and rheostat controls of equipment that regulate amount of electricity flowing through needle or needles to decompose cells of papilla. Removes needle or needles, and pulls hair from follicle, using tweezers. • **GED:** R3, M2, L3 • **SVP:** 6 mos- 1 yr • **Academic:** Ed=N, Eng=S • **Work Field:** 294 • **MPSMS:** 904 • **Aptitudes:** G3, V3, N4, S4, P2, Q4, K3, F2, M3, E4, C5 • **Temperaments:** M, P, T • **Stress:** E • **Physical:** V=L, H=N, L=L, W, H • **Work Env:** I • **Salary:** 3 • **Outlook:** 3

FINGERNAIL FORMER (per. ser.) • D.O.T. #331.674-014 • OES #68008 • Forms artificial fingernails on customer's fingers: Roughens surfaces of fingernails, using abrasive wheel. Attaches paper forms to tips of customer's fingers to support and shape artificial nails. Brushes coats of powder and solvent onto nails and paper forms with handbrush to extend nails to desired length. Removes paper forms and shapes and smooths edges of nails, using rotary abrasive wheel. Brushes additional powder and solvent onto new growth between cuticles and nails to maintain nail appearance. May soften, trim, or cut cuticles, using oil, water, knife, or scissors, to prepare customer's nails for application of artificial nails. • **GED:** R2, M1, L2 • **SVP:** 30 days-3 mos • **Academic:** Ed=N, Eng=S • **Work Field:** 291 • **MPSMS:** 904 • **Aptitudes:** G4, V4, N4, S4, P3, Q5, K3, F3, M3, E5, C4 • **Temperaments:** P, T •

Stress: E • Physical: V=L, H=N, L=S, H • **Work Env:** I • **Salary:** 1 • **Outlook:** 2

HOT-ROOM ATTENDANT (per. ser.) • D.O.T. #335.677-014 • OES #68032 • ELECTRIC-BATH ATTENDANT; PORTER, BATH; PUBLIC-BATH ATTENDANT; SWEAT-BOX ATTENDANT; TUB ATTENDANT. Serves patrons in dry-heat cabinet or room or steam room of athletic, bathing, or other establishment: Spreads sheet or towel over seating facility in cabinet or rooms and seats patrons. Supplies drinking water and renders other services requested, such as wrapping cool towels about patron's head, spraying body with water, or timing length of bath. Gives shower baths and furnishes towel or dries patron. Collects soiled linen and cleans bathing area and facilities, such as tubs and showers. May turn valves and switches to adjust heating equipment, regulating amount of steam or temperature. May pour water over heated rocks to prepare steamroom. May be designated according to bath facility served as DRY-HEAT-CABINET ATTENDANT (per. ser.); DRY-HEAT-ROOM ATTENDANT (per. ser.); SHOWER ATTENDANT (per. ser.); STEAM-ROOM ATTENDANT (per. ser.). • **GED:** R2, M1, L2 • **SVP:** 2-30 days • **Academic:** Ed=N, Eng=S • **Work Field:** 291 • **MPSMS:** 909, 919 • **Aptitudes:** G4, V4, N4, S4, P4, Q4, K4, F4, M3, E5, C5 • **Temperaments:** P, V • **Stress:** E • **Physical:** V=N, H=L, L=L, W, S, H • **Work Env:** I, H, W • **Salary:** 2 • **Outlook:** 2

MANICURIST (per. ser.) • D.O.T. #331.674-010 • OES #68008 • Cleans, shapes, and polishes customers' fingernails and toenails: Removes previously applied nail polish, using liquid remover and swabs. Shapes and smooths ends of nails, using scissors, files, and emery boards. Cleans customers' nails in soapy water, using swabs, files, and orange sticks. Softens nail cuticles with water and oil, pushes back cuticles, using cuticle knife, and trims cuticles, using scissors or nippers. Whitens underside of nails with white paste or pencil. Polishes nails, using powdered polish and buffer, or applies clear or colored liquid polish onto nails with brush. May perform other beauty services such as giving facials, and shampooing, tinting, and curling hair [COSMETOLOGIST (per. ser.)]. • **GED:** R2, M1, L2 • **SVP:** 30 days-3 mos • **Academic:** Ed=N, Eng=S • **Work Field:** 291 • **MPSMS:** 904 • **Aptitudes:** G4, V4, N4, S4, P3, Q5, K3, F3, M3, E5, C3 • **Temperaments:** J, P • **Stress:** E • **Physical:** V=L, H=N, L=S, H • **Work Env:** I • **Salary:** 2 • **Outlook:** 3

MASSEUR/MASSEUSE (per. ser.) • D.O.T. #334.374-010 • OES #69999 • BATH ATTENDANT; BATH-HOUSE ATTENDANT; RUBBER. Massages customers and administers other body conditioning treatments for hygienic or remedial purposes: Applies alcohol, lubricants, or other rubbing compounds. Massages body, using such techniques as kneading, rubbing, and stroking flesh, to stimulate blood circulation, relax contracted muscles, facilitate elimination of waste matter, or to relieve other conditions, using hands or vibrating equipment. Administers steam or dry heat, ultraviolet or infrared, or water treatments on request of customer or instructions of PHYSICIAN (medical ser.). May give directions to clients in activities, such as reducing or remedial exercises. May examine client and recommend body conditioning activities or treatments. May record treatments furnished to customers. • **GED:** R3, M2, L3 • **SVP:** 3-6 mos • **Academic:** Ed=N, Eng=S • **Work Field:** 291 • **MPSMS:** 909, 929 • **Aptitudes:** G3, V3, N4, S3, P3, Q4, K3, F3, M2, E5, C4 • **Temperaments:** J, P, V • **Stress:** E • **Physical:** V=N, H=N, L=M, W, H • **Work Env:** I • **Salary:** 3 • **Outlook:** 3

REDUCING-SALON ATTENDANT (per. ser.) • D.O.T. #359.567-010 • OES #69999 • Measures, weighs and records patron's body statistics, refers information to supervisor for evaluation and planning of exercise program, and demonstrates exercises and use of equipment. Monitors member's exercise activities to assure progress toward desired goals. Records patron's measurements periodically for re-evaluation. • **GED:** R2, M2, L2 • **SVP:** 2-30 days • **Academic:** Ed=N, Eng=S • **Work Field:** 291 • **MPSMS:** 909 • **Aptitudes:** G4, V4, N4, S4, P4, Q4, K3, F4, M3, E4, C5 • **Temperaments:** P • **Stress:** E • **Physical:** V=N, H=N, L=M, W, S, H • **Work Env:** I, H, W • **Salary:** 2 • **Outlook:** 2

WEIGHT-REDUCTION SPECIALIST (per. ser.) • D.O.T. #359.367-014 • OES #69999 • NUTRITION EDUCATOR. Assists clients in devising and carrying out weight-loss plan, using established dietary programs and positive reinforcement procedures: Interviews client to obtain information on weight development history, eating habits, medical restrictions, and nutritional objectives. Weighs and measures client, using measuring instruments, and enters data on client record. Discusses eating habits with client to identify dispensable food items and to encourage increased consumption of high nutrition, low calorie food items, or selects established diet program which matches client goals and restrictions. Explains program and procedures which should be followed to lose desired amount of weight, and answers client questions. Reviews client food diary at regular intervals to identify eating habits which do not coincide with established or agreed upon dietary program, and reviews weight loss statistics to determine progress. Counsels client to promote established goals and to reinforce positive results. May photograph client during therapy to provide visual record of progress. May conduct aversion therapy, utilizing electric shock, rancid odors, and other physical or visual stimuli to promote negative association with food designated for elimination from diet. May conduct positive conditioning therapy sessions, utilizing physical and visual stimuli to promote positive association with foods designated for increase in diet. May give client weight-loss aids, such as calorie counters, or sell nutritional products to be used in conjunction with diet program. • **GED:** R3, M2, L3 • **SVP:** 30 days-3 mos • **Academic:** Ed=N, Eng=G • **Work Field:** 291 • **MPSMS:** 909 • **Aptitudes:** G3, V3, N4, S5, P4, Q3, K4, F4, M4, E5, C5 • **Temperaments:** J, P • **Stress:** E • **Physical:** V=N, H=N, L=S, W, H • **Work Env:** I • **Salary:** 2 • **Outlook:** 2

GOE: 09.05.02 Food Services, Attendant Serv.

CAFETERIA ATTENDANT (hotel & rest.) • D.O.T. #311.677-010 • OES #65014 • DINING-ROOM ATTENDANT, CAFETERIA; SERVICE ATTENDANT, CAFETERIA; TABLE ATTENDANT, CAFETERIA; WAITER/WAITRESS, CAFETERIA. Carries trays from food counters to tables for cafeteria patrons. Carries dirty dishes to kitchen. Sets tables with clean linens, sugar bowls, and condiments. Washes tables. May wrap clean silver in napkins. May circulate among diners and serve coffee and be designated as COFFEE SERVER, CAFETERIA OR RESTAURANT (hotel & rest.). • **GED:** R2, M1, L1 • **SVP:** 2-30 days • **Academic:** Ed=N, Eng=S • **Work Field:** 291 • **MPSMS:** 903 • **Aptitudes:** G4, V4, N4, S4, P4, Q5, K4, F4, M3, E4, C5 • **Temperaments:** P, R • **Stress:** E, T • **Physical:** V=L, H=N, L=L, W, H • **Work Env:** I • **Salary:** 4 • **Outlook:** 4

COUNTER ATTENDANT, CAFETERIA (hotel & rest.) • D.O.T. #311.677-014 • OES #65017 • SERVER; STEAMTABLE ATTENDANT. Serves food from counters and steamtables to cafeteria patrons: Serves salads, vegetables, meat, breads, and cocktails, ladles soups and sauces, portions desserts, and fills beverage cups and glasses as indicated by customer. Adds relishes and garnishes according to instructions from COUNTER SUPERVISOR (hotel & rest.). Scrubs and polishes counters, steamtables, and other equipment. May replenish foods at serving stations. May brew coffee and tea. May carve meat. May accept payment for food, using cash register or adding machine to total check. May prepare and serve salads and be known as SALAD COUNTER ATTENDANT (hotel & rest.). May serve food to passenger from steamtable on railroad dining car and be known as STEAMTABLE ATTENDANT, RAILROAD (r.r. trans.). • **GED:** R2, M1, L2 • **SVP:** 30 days-3 mos • **Academic:** Ed=N, Eng=S • **Work Field:** 291 • **MPSMS:** 903 • **Aptitudes:** G4, V4, N4, S4, P3, Q4, K3, F3, M3, E5, C4 • **Temperaments:** P, R • **Stress:** E, T • **Physical:** V=L, H=N, L=L, W, H • **Work Env:** I • **Salary:** 1 • **Outlook:** 4

COUNTER-SUPPLY WORKER (hotel & rest.) • D.O.T. #319.687-010 • OES #65014 • Replenishes food and equipment at steamtables and serving counters of cafeteria to facilitate service to patrons: Carries food, dishes, trays, and silverware from kitchen and supply departments to serving counters. Garnishes foods and positions them on table to ensure their visibility to patrons and convenience in serving. Keeps assigned area and equipment free of spilled foods. Keeps shelves of vending machines stocked with food when working in automat. • **GED:** R2, M1, L1 • **SVP:** 2-30 days • **Academic:** Ed=N, Eng=N • **Work Field:** 221 • **MPSMS:**

903 • **Aptitudes:** G4, V4, N4, S4, P4, Q4, K4, F4, M3, E5, C4 • **Temperaments:** R • **Stress:** T • **Physical:** V=L, H=N, L=M, W, H • **Work Env:** I • **Salary:** 2 • **Outlook:** 3

DINING ROOM ATTENDANT (hotel & rest.) • D.O.T. #311.677-018 • OES #65014 • Performs any combination of the following duties to facilitate food service: Carries dirty dishes from dining room to kitchen. Replaces soiled table linens and sets tables with silverware and glassware. Replenishes supply of clean linens, silverware, glassware, and dishes in dining room. Supplies service bar with food, such as soups, salads, and desserts. Serves ice water and butter to patrons. Cleans and polishes glass shelves and doors of service bars and equipment, such as coffee urns and cream and milk dispensers. Makes coffee and fills fruit juice dispensers. Runs errands and delivers food orders to offices and is designated RUNNER (hotel & rest.). May transfer food and dishes between floors of establishment, using dumbwaiter. May be designated according to type of activity or area of work as CLEAN-UP HELPER, BANQUET (hotel & rest.); COUNTER DISH CARRIER (hotel & rest.); GLASS WASHER AND CARRIER (hotel & rest.); ROOM SERVICE ASSISTANT (hotel & rest.). Additional Titles: DISH CARRIER (hotel & rest.); STEAMTABLE WORKER (hotel & rest.); TABLE SETTER (hotel & rest.); WATER SERVER (hotel & rest.). • **GED:** R2, M1, L1 • **SVP:** 2-30 days • **Academic:** Ed=N, Eng=N • **Work Field:** 011, 031, 291 • **MPSMS:** 903 • **Aptitudes:** G4, V4, N4, S4, P4, Q4, K4, F4, M4, E4, C5 • **Temperaments:** P, R • **Stress:** T • **Physical:** V=L, H=N, L=M, W, S, H • **Work Env:** I • **Salary:** 1 • **Outlook:** 4

FOOD-SERVICE WORKER, HOSPITAL (medical ser.) • D.O.T. #355.677-010 • OES #65011 • DIETARY AIDE; DIET-KITCHEN AIDE; TRAY WORKER. Prepares and delivers food trays to hospital patients, performing any combination of following duties on tray line: Reads production orders on color-coded menu cards on trays to determine appropriate items to place on tray. Places items such as silver, fruit juice, sugar, cream, milk and butter on trays. Fills vacuum bottles with coffee and apportions food servings according to diet list on menu card. Places servings in blender to make foods for soft or liquid diets. Examines filled tray for completeness and places on cart or dumbwaiter. Pushes carts to halls or ward kitchens. Serves trays to patients. Collects and stacks dirty dishes on cart and returns cart to kitchen. Washes dishes and cleans work area, tables, cabinets, and ovens. Collects and places garbage and trash in designated containers. May record amounts and types of special food items served to patients. May be designated according to type of food trays prepared as NOURISHMENT WORKER (medical ser.); SPECIAL-DIET WORKER (medical ser.); or duty on tray line as TRAY-LINE WORKER (medical ser.). • **GED:** R3, M2, L2 • **SVP:** 2-30 days • **Academic:** Ed=N, Eng=S • **Work Field:** 031, 146, 291 • **MPSMS:** 903 • **Aptitudes:** G3, V4, N4, S4, P3, Q3, K4, F3, M3, E4, C4 • **Temperaments:** R, T • **Stress:** T • **Physical:** V=L, H=N, L=M, W, H • **Work Env:** I, W, N, R • **Salary:** 2 • **Outlook:** 2

MESS ATTENDANT (water trans.) • D.O.T. #350.677-010 • OES #65008 • Serves food to officers and crew aboard ship: Prepares hot and cold drinks, and fruits, for serving, and sets tables for meals. Serves food. Washes glassware and silverware after meals, cleans messroom, and disposes of trash and garbage. Makes beds and cleans bedrooms and bathrooms assigned to ship's officers. May be designated according to area in which work is performed or personnel served as MESS ATTENDANT, CREW (water trans.); MESS ATTENDANT, OFFICERS' ROOM (water trans.); MESS ATTENDANT, OFFICERS' SALON (water trans.). • **GED:** R2, M1, L2 • **SVP:** 30 days-3 mos • **Academic:** Ed=N, Eng=S • **Work Field:** 291 • **MPSMS:** 903 • **Aptitudes:** G4, V4, N4, S4, P4, Q4, K3, F4, M3, E4, C5 • **Temperaments:** P, R • **Stress:** E, T • **Physical:** V=L, H=L, L=M, W, S, H • **Work Env:** I • **Salary:** 2 • **Outlook:** 2

WAITER/WAITRESS, ROOM SERVICE (hotel & rest.) • D.O.T. #311.477-034 • OES #65011 • Serves meals to guests in their rooms. Carries silverware, linen, and food on tray or uses cart. Sets up table and serves food from cart. Removes equipment from rooms. • **GED:** R3, M2, L2 • **SVP:** 30 days-3 mos • **Academic:** Ed=N, Eng=S • **Work Field:** 291 • **MPSMS:** 903 • **Aptitudes:** G3, V4, N4, S4, P4, Q4, K3, F4, M3, E4, C5 • **Temperaments:** P • **Stress:** E • **Physical:** V=L, H=N, L=L, W, H • **Work Env:** I •

Salary: 2 • **Outlook:** 4

WINE STEWARD/STEWARDESS (hotel & rest.) • D.O.T. #310.357-010 • OES #65008 • SOMMELIER. Selects, requisitions, stores, sells, and serves wines in restaurant: Keeps inventory and orders wine to replenish stock. Stores wines on racks or shelves. Discusses wines with patrons and assists patrons to make wine selection, applying knowledge of wines. Tastes wines prior to serving and serves wines to patrons. • **GED:** R3, M3, L3 • **SVP:** 1-2 yrs • **Academic:** Ed=N, Eng=S • **Work Field:** 221, 291 • **MPSMS:** 903 • **Aptitudes:** G3, V3, N3, S4, P4, Q3, K4, F4, M4, E5, C3 • **Temperaments:** J, P • **Stress:** E • **Physical:** V=L, H=L, L=L, W, H • **Work Env:** I • **Salary:** 4 • **Outlook:** 3

GOE: 09.05.03 Portering & Baggage Services

BELLHOP (hotel & rest.) • D.O.T. #324.677-010 • OES #68023 • Serves hotel guests by performing the following tasks: Escorts incoming hotel guests to rooms, assists them with hand luggage, and offers information pertaining to available services and facilities of hotel, points of interest, and entertainment attractions. Inspects guest's room to ensure that it is in order and supplies are adequate. Explains features of room, such as operation of radio, television, and night-lock, and how to place telephone calls. Pages guests in lobby, dining room, or other parts of hotel. Delivers messages, and runs errands. May deliver room service orders. May pick up articles for laundry and valet service. May call taxi for guests. May transport guest about premises or local areas in car or motorized cart. May keep record of calls for service. May deliver packages, suitcases, and trunks, and set up sample rooms [PORTER, BAGGAGE (hotel & rest.)]. May tidy lobby [HOUSECLEANER (hotel & rest.)]. May operate elevator [ELEVATOR OPERATOR (any ind.)]. When paging guests, may be known as PAGE (hotel & rest.). • **GED:** R2, M2, L2 • **SVP:** 2-30 days • **Academic:** Ed=N, Eng=S • **Work Field:** 291 • **MPSMS:** 905 • **Aptitudes:** G4, V4, N4, S4, P4, Q4, K4, F4, M3, E4, C5 • **Temperaments:** P, V • **Stress:** E • **Physical:** V=L, H=N, L=M, W, H • **Work Env:** I • **Salary:** 2 • **Outlook:** 3

CHECKROOM ATTENDANT (any ind.) • D.O.T. #358.677-010 • OES #69999 • Stores wearing apparel, luggage, bundles, and other articles for patrons of an establishment or employees of business establishment, issuing claim check for articles checked and returning articles on receipt of check. May be designated according to article stored as BAGGAGE CHECKER (any ind.); COAT CHECKER (any ind.); HAT CHECKER (any ind.); STANDBY (motion pic.); WRAP CHECKER (any ind.). • **GED:** R2, M2, L2 • **SVP:** 2-30 days • **Academic:** Ed=N, Eng=S • **Work Field:** 221, 291 • **MPSMS:** 909 • **Aptitudes:** G4, V4, N4, S4, P4, Q3, K4, F4, M4, E5, C5 • **Temperaments:** P, R • **Stress:** E, T • **Physical:** V=L, H=N, L=L, W, H • **Work Env:** I • **Salary:** 2 • **Outlook:** 2

PORTER (air trans.) • D.O.T. #357.677-010 • OES #98999 • PORTER, BAGGAGE; REDCAP. Carries baggage for passengers of airline, railroad, or motorbus by hand or handtruck, to waiting or baggage room, onto train or bus, or to taxicab or private automobile. Performs related services, such as calling taxicabs, directing persons to ticket windows and rest rooms, and assisting handicapped passengers upon their arrival or departure. May clean terminal floors; wash walls, windows and counters; and dust furniture. When employed in airline terminal is designated as SKYCAP (air trans.). • **GED:** R2, M1, L2 • **SVP:** 2-30 days • **Academic:** Ed=N, Eng=S • **Work Field:** 011, 291 • **MPSMS:** 905 • **Aptitudes:** G4, V4, N4, S4, P4, Q4, K4, F4, M4, E4, C5 • **Temperaments:** P, R • **Stress:** E, T • **Physical:** V=L, H=N, L=M, W, S, H • **Work Env:** B, N • **Salary:** 2 • **Outlook:** 2

PORTER, BAGGAGE (hotel & rest.) • D.O.T. #324.477-010 • OES #68023 • PORTER, LUGGAGE. Delivers luggage to and from hotel rooms, sets up sample rooms for sales personnel and performs related services as requested by guest or BAGGAGE PORTER, HEAD (hotel & rest.). Transfers trunks, packages, and other baggage to room or loading area, using handtruck. Arranges for outgoing freight, express or mail shipments, computes charges, tags article, and records information, such as addressee, addressor, carrier, and charges, on specified forms. Sets up display tables, racks, or shelves and assists sales personnel in unpacking and arranging merchandise display. May supply guests with travel information, such as transportation rates, routes, and schedules. May escort incoming guest to room [BELLHOP (hotel & rest.)]. May arrange for cleaning, laundering, and repair of guests' clothing and other items. May compute charge slips for services rendered guests and forwards slips to bookkeeping department. • **GED:** R2, M2, L2 • **SVP:** 2-30 days • **Academic:** Ed=N, Eng=S • **Work Field:** 011, 291 • **MPSMS:** 905 • **Aptitudes:** G4, V4, N4, S4, P4, Q4, K4, F4, M3, E4, C5 • **Temperaments:** P • **Stress:** E • **Physical:** V=L, H=N, L=M, W, S, H • **Work Env:** I • **Salary:** 2 • **Outlook:** 3

ROOM-SERVICE CLERK (hotel & rest.) • D.O.T. #324.577-010 • OES #69999 • DELIVERY-ROOM CLERK; PACKAGE CLERK; RECEIVING-ROOM CLERK; RUNNER. Performs any combination of the following tasks related to serving guests in apartment hotels: Delivers and removes packages, laundry, clothes, groceries, and other articles to and from guests rooms or servidors (cabinets built into doors of hotel rooms). Collects supply orders from various departments and delivers to PURCHASING AGENT (profess. & kin.). Delivers mail to various departments and guests. Records information pertaining to services rendered. May arrange for pressing clothes and shining shoes, sending and receiving packages, and in maintaining valet service. May press clothes and shine shoes [SHOE SHINER (per. ser.)]. May supervise activities of workers engaged in delivering packages to hotel guests. • **GED:** R2, M2, L2 • **SVP:** 2-30 days • **Academic:** Ed=N, Eng=S • **Work Field:** 291 • **MPSMS:** 899 • **Aptitudes:** G4, V4, N4, S4, P4, Q3, K4, F3, M3, E5, C5 • **Temperaments:** P, V • **Stress:** E • **Physical:** V=L, H=N, L=L, W, H • **Work Env:** I • **Salary:** 2 • **Outlook:** 3

GOE: 09.05.04 Doorkeeping Services

DOORKEEPER (any ind.) • D.O.T. #324.677-014 • OES #69999 • Serves residents, guests, or patrons of hotel, store, apartment building, hospital, or similar establishment by opening doors, hailing taxicabs, answering inquiries, assisting the elderly or infirm into automobiles, and performing related services. Prevents entrance of unauthorized or undesirable persons. May forcibly eject inebriated or rowdy persons from premises. May notify guests by telephone of delivery of automobiles, packages, or arrival of visitors. May carry baggage. • **GED:** R2, M1, L2 • **SVP:** 2-30 days • **Academic:** Ed=N, Eng=N • **Work Field:** 291 • **MPSMS:** 909 • **Aptitudes:** G4, V4, N4, S4, P4, Q4, K4, F5, M4, E5, C5 • **Temperaments:** P, V • **Stress:** E • **Physical:** V=L, H=N, L=M, W, H • **Work Env:** B • **Salary:** 2 • **Outlook:** 3

DRIVE-IN THEATER ATTENDANT (amuse. & rec.) • D.O.T. #349.673-010 • OES #68021 • FIELD ATTENDANT. Performs any combination of following duties in rendering services to patrons of drive-in theaters: Greets patrons desiring to attend theater. Collects admission fee and purchases ticket for patron from TICKET SELLER (clerical). Parks car or directs patron to parking space, indicating available space with flashlight. Patrols theater on foot or bicycle to prevent disorderly conduct, rowdiness, or to detect other infractions of rules. Watches over children in playground during intermission. Serves patrons at refreshment stand during intermission. May attach loudspeaker to automobile door and turn controls to adjust volume. • **GED:** R2, M1, L2 • **SVP:** 2-30 days • **Academic:** Ed=N, Eng=S • **Work Field:** 291 • **MPSMS:** 912 • **Aptitudes:** G4, V3, N4, S4, P4, Q4, K4, F4, M4, E5, C5 • **Temperaments:** P, R • **Stress:** E • **Physical:** V=L, H=N, L=L, W, H • **Work Env:** O • **Salary:** 2 • **Outlook:** 2

HOSPITAL ENTRANCE ATTENDANT (medical ser.) • D.O.T. #355.677-014 • OES #66099 • HOSPITAL MESSENGER. Directs or escorts incoming patients or visitors from hospital admitting office or reception desk to designated area in hospital or clinic: Carries patient's luggage. Assists patient in walking to prevent accidents by falling, or transports nonambulatory patient, using wheelchair. Delivers messages and file papers for office staff. May be designated according to area assigned as ADMITTING-OFFICE GUIDE (medical ser.); OUT-PATIENT-CLINIC GUIDE (medical ser.). • **GED:** R2, M1, L2 • **SVP:** 2-30 days • **Academic:** Ed=N, Eng=S • **Work Field:** 291 • **MPSMS:** 924 • **Aptitudes:** G4, V4, N4, S4, P4, Q4, K4, F4, M4, E4, C5 • **Temperaments:** P, R • **Stress:** E, T • **Physical:** V=L, H=N, L=M, W, S, H • **Work Env:** I • **Salary:** 2 • **Outlook:** 3

GOE: 09.05.05 Card & Game Room Services

CARDROOM ATTENDANT 2 (amuse. & rec.) • D.O.T. #343.577-010 • OES #68014 • Seats cardroom patrons: Takes name of patron requesting seat at table and adds name, with chalk, to waiting list on board. Pages customer over loudspeaker when notified by SUPERVISOR, CARDROOM (amuse. & rec.) that seat is available. • **GED:** R2, M1, L2 • **SVP:** 2-30 days • **Academic:** Ed=N, Eng=S • **Work Field:** 291 • **MPSMS:** 919 • **Aptitudes:** G4, V4, N4, S4, P4, Q4, K4, F4, M4, E5, C5 • **Temperaments:** P, R • **Stress:** E, T • **Physical:** V=L, H=L, L=L • **Work Env:** I • **Salary:** 3 • **Outlook:** 3

GOE: 09.05.06 Individualized Services

CADDIE (amuse. & rec.) • D.O.T. #341.677-010 • OES #68014 • GOLF CADDIE. Carries golf bags or pushes or pulls cart that holds golf bags around golf course for players, handing clubs to players as requested: Advises players, as requested, on selection of proper club for stroke or concerning peculiarities of course. Locates driven balls and holds marker out of cup while players putt. • **GED:** R2, M2, L2 • **SVP:** 2-30 days • **Academic:** Ed=N, Eng=S • **Work Field:** 291 • **MPSMS:** 905 • **Aptitudes:** G4, V4, N4, S3, P3, Q4, K4, F4, M4, E5, C5 • **Temperaments:** P, R • **Stress:** E • **Physical:** V=L, H=N, L=M, W, S, H • **Work Env:** O • **Salary:** 2 • **Outlook:** 2

DRESSER (amuse. & rec.) • D.O.T. #346.674-010 • OES #68032 • Aids entertainer to dress and attends to clothing and costumes: Arranges costumes in order of use. Unpacks clothes and costumes and places them for convenient use. Cleans spots from apparel. Presses costumes. Mends ripped seams or makes other minor repairs. May arrange for cleaning, pressing or laundering of costumes. • **GED:** R2, M2, L2 • **SVP:** 30 days-3 mos • **Academic:** Ed=N, Eng=S • **Work Field:** 171, 291 • **MPSMS:** 449, 912 • **Aptitudes:** G4, V4, N4, S4, P4, Q4, K3, F3, M3, E4, C3 • **Temperaments:** P, V • **Stress:** E • **Physical:** V=L, H=N, L=L, W, H • **Work Env:** I • **Salary:** 2 • **Outlook:** 2

GOE: 09.05.07 General Wardrobe Services

CLOTHES-ROOM WORKER (medical ser.) • D.O.T. #355.687-010 • OES #58023 • Receives, stores, and issues clothing of patients in hospital: Hangs clothing on hangers or places on storage shelves or racks, according to admittance number on clothing record. Covers clothing with protective covering. Issues clothing to patients or other workers, according to signed receipt of patient's and clothing release slip. May arrange for clothing to be cleaned, pressed, or laundered. • **GED:** R2, M1, L2 • **SVP:** 2-30 days • **Academic:** Ed=N, Eng=N • **Work Field:** 221 • **MPSMS:** 924 • **Aptitudes:** G3, V4, N4, S4, P4, Q3, K4, F4, M4, E5, C4 • **Temperaments:** M, R • **Stress:** T • **Physical:** V=N, H=N, L=L, W, H • **Work Env:** I • **Salary:** 2 • **Outlook:** 2

LOCKER-ROOM ATTENDANT (per. ser.) • D.O.T. #358.677-014 • OES #69999 • CAGE CLERK; DRESSING-ROOM ATTENDANT; LOCKER ATTENDANT; LOCKER-ROOM CLERK; PERSONAL ATTENDANT; SUIT ATTENDANT. Assigns dressing room facilities, locker space or clothing containers, and supplies to patrons of athletic or bathing establishment: Issues dressing room or locker key. Receives patron's clothing-filled container, furnishes claim check, places container on storage shelf or rack, and returns container upon receipt of claim check. Issues athletic equipment, bathing suit, or supplies, such as soap and towels. May arrange for valet services, such as clothes pressing and shoeshining. May collect soiled linen and perform cleaning tasks, such as mopping dressing room floors and washing shower room walls. May collect fees for use of facilities, equipment, or supplies. May pack athletic uniforms and equipment for individual or team out-of-town sporting events. May attend to needs of athletic team in team clubhouse and be designated CLUBHOUSE ATTENDANT (amuse. & rec.). • **GED:** R2, M2, L2 • **SVP:** 2-30 days • **Academic:** Ed=N, Eng=S • **Work Field:** 291 • **MPSMS:** 909, 919 • **Aptitudes:** G4, V4, N4, S4, P4, Q4, K4, F4, M4, E5, C5 • **Temperaments:** P, V • **Stress:** E • **Physical:** V=L, H=N, L=L, W, S, H • **Work Env:** I, W • **Salary:** 2 • **Outlook:** 2

RESTROOM ATTENDANT (any ind.) • D.O.T. #358.677-018 • OES #68032 • LAVATORY ATTENDANT; TOILET ATTENDANT; WASHROOM ATTENDANT. Serves patrons of lavatories in store, public building, hotel, or similar establishment by providing soap and towels, brushing patrons' clothing, shining shoes, sewing on loose buttons, and performing related services. Replenishes restroom supplies. May scrub lavatory, floors, walls, mirrors, and fixtures, using brushes, detergent, and water. May administer first aid to ill or injured patrons. • **GED:** R2, M1, L1 • **SVP:** 2-30 days • **Academic:** Ed=N, Eng=S • **Work Field:** 291 • **MPSMS:** 909 • **Aptitudes:** G4, V4, N4, S5, P4, Q5, K4, F4, M4, E5, C5 • **Temperaments:** P, R • **Stress:** E, T • **Physical:** V=L, H=N, L=L, W, S, H • **Work Env:** I • **Salary:** 2 • **Outlook:** 2

GOE: 09.05.08 Ticket Taking, Ushering

CHILDREN'S ATTENDANT (amuse. & rec.) • D.O.T. #349.677-018 • OES #68021 • Monitors behavior of unaccompanied children in children's section of theater to maintain order: Escorts children who are unaccompanied by adult between theater entrance and children's section when children enter or leave theater. Maintains order among children and searches for lost articles. Notes when each child enters section and reminds child to go home after witnessing complete performance. • **GED:** R2, M1, L1 • **SVP:** 2-30 days • **Academic:** Ed=N, Eng=S • **Work Field:** 291 • **MPSMS:** 911 • **Aptitudes:** G4, V4, N4, S4, P4, Q4, K4, F4, M4, E5, C5 • **Temperaments:** P • **Stress:** E • **Physical:** V=L, H=N, L=L, W • **Work Env:** I • **Salary:** 2 • **Outlook:** 2

TICKET TAKER (amuse. & rec.) • D.O.T. #344.667-010 • OES #68021 • Collects admission tickets and passes from patrons at entertainment events: Examines ticket or pass to verify authenticity. Refuses admittance to patrons without ticket or pass, or who are undesirable for such reasons as intoxication or improper attire. May direct patrons to their seats. May distribute door checks to patrons temporarily leaving establishment. May count and record number of tickets collected. May be designated as GATE ATTEN-DANT (amuse. & rec.) or TURNSTILE ATTENDANT (amuse. & rec.) when collecting tickets at open-air event. • **GED:** R2, M1, L2 • **SVP:** 2-30 days • **Academic:** Ed=N, Eng=S • **Work Field:** 291 • **MPSMS:** 919 • **Aptitudes:** G4, V4, N4, S4, P4, Q4, K4, F4, M4, E5, C5 • **Temperaments:** P, R • **Stress:** E, T • **Physical:** V=L, H=N, L=S, W, H • **Work Env:** I • **Salary:** 2 • **Outlook:** 2

USHER (amuse. & rec.) • D.O.T. #344.677-014 • OES #68021 • Assists patrons at entertainment events to find seats, search for lost articles, and locate such facilities as restrooms and telephones. Distributes programs to patrons. Assists other workers to change advertising display. • **GED:** R2, M1, L1 • **SVP:** 2-30 days • **Academic:** Ed=N, Eng=S • **Work Field:** 291 • **MPSMS:** 910 • **Aptitudes:** G4, V4, N4, S5, P4, Q4, K4, F4, M4, E5, C5 • **Temperaments:** R • **Stress:** T • **Physical:** V=L, H=L, L=L, W • **Work Env:** B • **Salary:** 2 • **Outlook:** 2

GOE: 09.05.09 Elevator Services

ELEVATOR OPERATOR (any ind.) • D.O.T. #388.663-010 • OES #67011 • SERVICE-CAR OPERATOR. Operates elevator to transport passengers between floors of office building, apartment house, department store, hotel, or similar establishment: Pushes buttons or moves lever to control movement of elevator on signal or instructions from passengers or others. Opens and closes safety gate and door of elevator at each floor where stop is made. Supplies information to passengers, such as location of offices, merchandise, and individuals. May perform other duties, such as distributing mail to various floors, answering telephone, preventing unauthorized persons from entering building, and assisting other employees to load and unload freight. May sweep or vacuum elevator. May be designated according to location of elevator operated as FRONT-ELEVATOR OPERATOR (hotel & rest.). • **GED:** R2, M1, L2 • **SVP:** 2-30 days • **Academic:** Ed=N, Eng=S • **Work Field:** 011, 282 • **MPSMS:** 969 • **Aptitudes:** G4, V3, N4, S4, P4, Q4, K3, F4, M3, E5, C5 • **Temperaments:** P, R • **Stress:** E, T • **Physical:** V=N, H=N, L=S, H • **Work Env:** I • **Salary:** 1 • **Outlook:** 2

Humanitarian 10

An interest in helping individuals with their mental, spiritual, social, physical, or vocational concerns. You can satisfy this interest by work in which caring for the welfare of others is important. Perhaps the spiritual or mental well-being of others concerns you. You could prepare for a job in religion or counseling. You may wish to help others with physical problems. You could work in the nursing, therapy, or rehabilitation fields. You may like to provide needed but less difficult care by working as an aide, orderly, or technician.

10.01 Social Services

Workers in this group help people deal with their problems. They may work with one person at a time or with groups of people. Workers sometimes specialize in problems that are personal, social, vocational, physical, educational, or spiritual in nature. Schools, rehabilitation centers, mental health clinics, guidance centers, and churches employ these workers. Jobs are also found in public and private welfare and employment services, juvenile courts, and vocational rehabilitation programs.

✔ **What kind of work would you do?**
Your work activities would depend upon your specific job. For example, you might:

- observe and interview members of a family to determine their medical or psychological needs.
- help prison parolees find jobs and adjust to society.
- counsel persons about educational and vocational plans.

- promote physical healing or spiritual well-being through prayer or other religious activities.
- help individuals overcome emotional or social problems.
- assist parents with child-rearing problems.

✔ **What skills and abilities do you need for this kind of work?**
To do this kind of work, you must be able to:

- use logical thinking and special training to counsel others or to help a person define and solve personal problems.
- care about people, their needs, and their welfare enough to want to help in some way.

- understand the way government programs and social service organizations function.
- gain the trust and confidence of people.

✔ **How do you know if you would like or could learn to do this kind of work?**
The following questions may give you clues about yourself as you consider this group of jobs.

- Have you been active in church or civic groups? Do you like to work with other people toward a common goal?

- Have your friends come to you for advice or help with their personal problems? Did you help them find solutions?

- Have you had courses in psychology, sociology, or other social sciences? Do you like to study human behavior?

- Have you helped to teach someone who had a problem learning something? Are you patient and willing to stay with a task until it is finished?

✔ How can you prepare for and enter this kind of work?

Occupations in this group usually require education and/or training extending from two years to over ten years, depending upon the specific kind of work. More than four years of college study is required for most jobs in this group. Two or more years of graduate level study is often required for jobs in social work or psychology. Some jobs in religion, clinical psychology, or industrial psychology require additional education. School counselors are usually required to have one or more years of teaching experience.

Some workers begin as helpers in social, religious, or welfare organizations and receive on-the-job training. However, formal training is usually required for a worker to become a professional.

Private organizations dealing with problems such as drug addition and abortion sometimes hire people who can relate to these problems.

✔ What else should you consider about these jobs?

Workers in this group sometimes receive community recognition or personal satisfaction from helping others. These jobs may involve irregular working hours and often include weekends and evenings. The work may involve dealing with sensitive people and confidential information.

Knowledge and skills must be updated frequently through reading journals, or attending seminars, summer schools, and workshops.

If you think you would like to do this kind of work, look at the job titles listed on the following pages.

GOE: 10.01.01 Religious Services

CLERGY MEMBER (profess. & kin.) • D.O.T. #120.007-010 • OES #27502 • MINISTER; PREACHER; PRIEST; RABBI. Conducts religious worship and performs other spiritual functions associated with beliefs and practices of religious faith or denomination as authorized, and provides spiritual and moral guidance and assistance to members: Leads congregation in worship services. Prepares and delivers sermons and other talks. Interprets doctrine of religion. Instructs people who seek conversion to faith. Conducts wedding and funeral services. Administers rites or ordinances of church. Visits sick and shut-ins, and helps poor. Counsels those in spiritual need and comforts bereaved. Oversees religious education programs, such as Sunday school and youth groups. May write articles for publication and engage in interfaith, community, civic, educational, and recreational activities sponsored by or related to interest of denomination. May teach in seminaries and universities. May serve in armed forces, institutions, or industry and be designated CHAPLAIN (profess. & kin.). When in charge of Christian church, congregation, or parish may be designated PASTOR (profess. & kin.) or RECTOR (profess. & kin.). May carry religious message and medical or educational aid to nonchristian lands and people to obtain converts and establish native church and be designated MISSIONARY (profess. & kin.). • **GED:** R6, M4, L6 • **SVP:** 4-10 yrs • **Academic:** Ed=B, Eng=G • **Work Field:** 294, 296 • **MPSMS:** 944 • **Aptitudes:** G1, V1, N3, S4, P4, Q3, K4, F4, M4, E5, C5 • **Temperaments:** F, I, J, P, V • **Stress:** E • **Physical:** V=N, H=L, L=S • **Work Env:** I • **Salary:** 3 • **Outlook:** 1

GOE: 10.01.02 Counseling & Social Work

CASE AIDE (social ser.) • D.O.T. #195.367-010 • OES #27308 Works on simpler aspects of cases or provides service to less complex cases, under close and regular supervision and tutorage

of CASEWORKER (social ser.). • **GED:** R5, M3, L5 • **SVP:** 1-2 yrs • **Academic:** Ed=N, Eng=G • **Work Field:** 271, 294 • **MPSMS:** 941 • **Aptitudes:** G2, V2, N3, S5, P4, Q3, K4, F4, M4, E5, C5 • **Temperaments:** D, J, P, V • **Stress:** E • **Physical:** V=N, H=L, L=S, W • **Work Env:** I • **Salary:** 4 • **Outlook:** 3

CASEWORKER (social ser.) • D.O.T. #195.107-010 • OES #27305 • Counsels and aids individuals and families requiring assistance of social service agency: Interviews clients with problems, such as personal and family adjustments, finances, employment, and physical and mental impairments to determine nature and degree of problem. Secures information, such as physical, psychological, and social factors, contributing to client's situation and evaluates these and client's capacities. Counsels client individually, in family, or in other small groups regarding plans for meeting needs and aids client to mobilize inner capacities and environmental resources to improve social functioning. Helps client to modify attitudes and patterns of behavior by increasing understanding of self, personal problems, and client's part in creating them. Refers clients to community resources and other organizations. Compiles records. May secure supplementary information, such as employment, medical records, or school reports. May determine client's eligibility for financial assistance. May work in collaboration with other professional disciplines. Usually required to have knowledge and skill in casework method acquired through degree program at school of social work. When rendering advisory services to agencies, groups, or individuals, may be designated as SOCIAL-WORK CONSULTANT, CASEWORK (social ser.). • **GED:** R5, M4, L5 • **SVP:** 2-4 yrs • **Academic:** Ed=A, Eng=G • **Work Field:** 271, 294 • **MPSMS:** 941 • **Aptitudes:** G2, V2, N3, S4, P4, Q4, K4, F4, M4, E5, C5 • **Temperaments:** D, I, J, P, V • **Stress:** E, A • **Physical:** V=N, H=G, L=S • **Work Env:** I • **Salary:** 4 • **Outlook:** 2

COMMUNITY WORKER (gov. ser.) • D.O.T. #195.367-018 • OES #27305 • Investigates problems of residents of assigned neighborhood to determine needs of those disadvantaged because of income, age, or other economic or personal handicaps: Seeks out and assists persons in need of agency services, under direction of professional staff. Visits individuals and families, and addresses neighborhood groups to publicize supportive services available to the unemployed, parolees, or others needing special assistance. Follows-up all contacts and prepares and submits reports of activities. • **GED:** R5, M4, L4 • **SVP:** 1-2 yrs • **Academic:** Ed=N, Eng=G • **Work Field:** 291 • **MPSMS:** 941 • **Aptitudes:** G3, V3, N3, S4, P4, Q3, K4, F4, M4, E4, C4 • **Temperaments:** D, I, P, V • **Stress:** E • **Physical:** V=N, H=N, L=S • **Work Env:** I • **Salary:** 4 • **Outlook:** 2

COUNSELOR (profess. & kin.) • D.O.T. #045.107-010 • OES #31514 • GUIDANCE COUNSELOR; VOCATIONAL ADVISER; VOCATIONAL COUNSELOR. Counsels individuals and provides group educational and vocational guidance services: Collects, organizes, and analyzes information about individuals through records, tests, interviews, and professional sources, to appraise their interests, aptitudes, abilities, and personality characteristics, for vocational and educational planning. Compiles and studies occupational, educational, and economic information to aid counselees in making and carrying out vocational and educational objectives. Refers students to placement service. Assists individuals to understand and overcome social and emotional problems. May engage in research and follow-up activities to evaluate counseling techniques. May teach classes. May be designated according to area of activity as COUNSELOR, COLLEGE (education); COUNSELOR, EMPLOYMENT DEVELOPMENT DEPARTMENT (education); COUNSELOR, SCHOOL (education); COUNSELOR, VETERANS ADMINISTRATION (gov. ser.). • **GED:** R5, M5, L5 • **SVP:** 2-4 yrs • **Academic:** Ed=M, Eng=G • **Work Field:** 282, 291 • **MPSMS:** 931 • **Aptitudes:** G1, V1, N3, S4, P4, Q4, K4, F4, M4, E5, C5 • **Temperaments:** J, M, P, V • **Stress:** E • **Physical:** V=N, H=G, L=S, H • **Work Env:** I • **Salary:** 4 • **Outlook:** 2

FOOD-MANAGEMENT AIDE (gov. ser.) • D.O.T. #195.367-022 • OES #27308 • NUTRITION AIDE. Advises low income family members how to plan, budget, shop, prepare balanced meals, and handle and store food, following prescribed standards: Advises clients of advantages of food stamps, how to obtain stamps, and use of stamps during shopping trips. Transports clients to shopping area, using automobile. Observes clients' food selections. Recommends alternate economical and nutritional food choices. Observes and discusses meal preparation. Suggests alternate methods of food preparation. Assists in planning of food budget, utilizing charts and sample budgets. Advises clients on preferred methods of sanitation. Consults with supervisor concerning programs for individual families. Maintains records concerning results of family visits. • **GED:** R3, M2, L3 • **SVP:** 30 days-3 mos • **Academic:** Ed=N, Eng=G • **Work Field:** 282 • **MPSMS:** 941 • **Aptitudes:** G3, V3, N4, S4, P4, Q3, K4, F4, M4, E4, C5 • **Temperaments:** P • **Stress:** E • **Physical:** V=N, H=L, L=L • **Work Env:** I • **Salary:** 2 • **Outlook:** 3

PROBATION-AND-PAROLE OFFICER (profess. & kin.) • D.O.T. #195.107-046 • OES #27305 • Counsels juvenile or adult offenders in activities related to legal conditions of probation or parole: Reviews social history of institutionalized offenders due for parole, and talks with offenders regarding development of release plans by parole commission. Determines which juvenile cases fall within jurisdiction of courts and which should be adjusted informally or referred to other agencies. Confers with legal representatives, family, and other concerned persons to conduct prehearing or presentencing investigations. Compiles reports and testifies in courts when requested. Reviews file folders on assigned offenders to determine violation committed and legal stipulation of release. Explains legal requirements to offender, such as visits to office, payment of restitution, and employment requirements to inform offender of release conditions. Interviews offender to formulate release plan and to identify specific problems that hinder probation or parole, such as family indifference, need of employment, and health conditions in need of attention, utilizing interviewing and counseling techniques. Refers offender to other agencies to correct problems, such as drug addiction, educational deficiency, and personality adjustments. Visits and telephones business firms to develop jobs for unemployed offenders. Evaluates offender progress during release with visits to home and place of work. Secures remedial action, or requests leniency by courts, if necessary, when offender behavior justifies such action. • **GED:** R5, M3, L5 • **SVP:** 2-4 yrs • **Academic:** Ed=B, Eng=G • **Work Field:** 271 • **MPSMS:** 949 • **Aptitudes:** G2, V2, N3, S4, P4, Q4, K4, F4, M4, E4, C5 • **Temperaments:** D, J, P, V • **Stress:** E, A • **Physical:** V=L, H=G, L=S, W, H • **Work Env:** I • **Salary:** 4 • **Outlook:** 2

PSYCHOLOGIST, CLINICAL (profess. & kin.) • D.O.T. #045.107-022 • OES #27108 • Diagnoses or evaluates mental and emotional disorders of individuals, and administers programs of treatment: Interviews patients in clinics, hospitals, prisons, and other institutions, and studies medical and social case histories. Observes patients in play or other situations, and selects, administers, and interprets intelligence, achievement, interest, personality, and other psychological tests to diagnose disorders and formulate plans of treatment. Treats psychological disorders to effect improved adjustments utilizing various psychological techniques, such as milieu therapy, psychodrama, and play therapy. Selects approach to use in individual therapy, such as directive, nondirective, and supportive therapy, and plans frequency, intensity, and duration of therapy. May collaborate with PSYCHIATRISTS (medical ser.) and other specialists in developing treatment programs for patients. May instruct and direct students serving psychological internships in hospitals and clinics. May develop experimental designs and conduct research in fields of personality development and adjustment, diagnosis, treatment, and prevention of mental disorders. May serve as consultant to social, educational, welfare, and other agencies on individual cases or in evaluation, planning, and development of mental health programs. May specialize in behavior problems and therapy, crime and delinquency, group therapy, individual diagnosis and therapy, mental deficiency, objective tests, projective techniques, or speech pathology. • **GED:** R6, M5, L6 • **SVP:** 4-10 yrs • **Academic:** Ed=M, Eng=G • **Work Field:** 294 • **MPSMS:** 733 • **Aptitudes:** G1, V1, N3, S4, P3, Q4, K4, F3, M3, E5, C4 • **Temperaments:** J, M, P, V • **Stress:** E • **Physical:** V=N, H=L, L=S • **Work Env:** I • **Salary:** 5 • **Outlook:** 4

PSYCHOLOGIST, COUNSELING (profess. & kin.) • D.O.T. #045.107-026 • OES #27108 • Provides individual and group counseling services in universities and colleges, schools, clinics, rehabilitation centers, Veterans Administration hospitals, and industry, to assist individuals in achieving more effective personal, social, educational, and vocational development and adjustment: Collects data about individual through use of interview, case history, and observational techniques. Selects and interprets psychological tests designed to assess individual's intelligence, aptitudes, abilities, and interests, applying knowledge of statistical analysis. Evaluates data to identify causes of problem of individuals and to determine advisability of counseling or referral to other specialists or institutions. Conducts counseling or therapeutic interviews to assist individual to gain insight into personal problems, define goals, and plan action reflecting interests, abilities, and needs. Provides occupational, educational, and other information to enable individual to formulate realistic educational and vocational plans. Follows up results of counseling to determine reliability and validity of treatment used. May engage in research to develop and improve diagnostic and counseling techniques. May administer and score psychological tests. • **GED:** R6, M5, L5 • **SVP:** 4-10 yrs • **Academic:** Ed=M, Eng=G • **Work Field:** 294 • **MPSMS:** 733 • **Aptitudes:** G1, V1, N3, S4, P3, Q3, K4, F4, M4, E5, C5 • **Temperaments:** I, M, P, V • **Stress:** E • **Physical:** V=N, H=L, L=S • **Work Env:** I • **Salary:** 5 • **Outlook:** 4

RESIDENCE COUNSELOR (educ.) • D.O.T. #045.107-038 • OES #31514 • COUNSELOR, DORMITORY; DORMITORY SUPERVISOR; HEAD RESIDENT, DORMITORY. Provides individual and group guidance services relative to problems of scholastic, educational, and personal-social nature to dormitory students: Suggests remedial or corrective actions and assists students in making better adjustments and in planning intelligent life goals. Plans and directs program to orient new students and assists in their integration into campus life. Initiates and conducts group conferences to plan and discuss programs and policies related to assignment of quarters, social and recreational activities, and dormitory living. Supervises dormitory activities. Investigates reports of misconduct and attempts to resolve or eliminate causes of conflict. May interview all dormitory students to determine need for counseling. • **GED:** R5, M4, L5 • **SVP:** 2-4 yrs • **Academic:** Ed=A, Eng=S • **Work Field:** 282, 294 • **MPSMS:** 931 • **Aptitudes:** G1, V1, N4, S4, P4, Q4, K4, F4, M4, E5, C5 • **Temperaments:** I, J, P, V • **Physical:** V=N, H=L, L=S • **Work Env:** I • **Salary:** 4 • **Out look:** 5

SOCIAL-SERVICES AIDE (social ser.) • D.O.T. #195.367-034 • OES #27308 • Assists professional staff of public social service agency, performing any combination of following tasks: Interviews individuals and family members to compile information on social, educational, criminal, institutional, or drug history. Visits individuals in homes or attends group meetings to provide information on agency services, requirements, and procedures. Provides rudimentary counseling to agency clients. Oversees day-to-day group activities of residents in institution. Meets with youth groups to acquaint them with consequences of delinquent acts. Refers individuals to various public or private agencies for assistance. May care for children in client's home during client's appointments. May accompany handicapped individuals to appointments. • **GED:** R4, M3, L4 • **SVP:** 1-2 yrs • **Academic:** Ed=N, Eng=G • **Work Field:** 271, 294 • **MPSMS:** 941 • **Aptitudes:** G3, V3, N3, S4, P4, Q3, K4, F4, M4, E5, C5 • **Temperaments:** D, J, P, V • **Stress:** E • **Physical:** V=N, H=N, L=S • **Work Env:** I • **Salary:** 2 • **Outlook:** 2

VOCATIONAL-REHABILITATION COUNSELOR (gov. ser.) • D.O.T. #045.107-042 • OES #31514 • COUNSELOR, VOCATIONAL REHABILITATION. Counsels handicapped individuals to provide vocational rehabilitation services: Interviews and evaluates handicapped applicants to determine degree of handicap, eligibility for service, and feasibility of vocational rehabilitation. Accepts or recommends acceptance of suitable candidates. Determines suitable job or business consistent with applicant's desires, aptitude, and physical limitations. Plans and arranges for applicant to study or train for job opening. Assists applicant with personal adjustment throughout rehabilitation program. Aids applicant in obtaining medical service during training. Promotes and develops job openings and places qualified applicant in employment. May refer qualified applicant to BUSINESS-ENTERPRISE OFFICER (gov. ser.) for placement in business enterprise. • **GED:** R5, M3, L5 • **SVP:** 4-10 yrs • **Academic:** Ed=M, Eng=G • **Work Field:** 282, 294 • **MPSMS:** 931, 943 • **Aptitudes:** G2, V2, N3, S4, P4, Q3, K4, F4, M4, E4, C4 • **Temperaments:** D, J, M, V • **Stress:** A • **Physical:** V=N, H=G, L=S • **Work Env:** I • **Salary:** 4 • **Outlook:** 2

10.02 Nursing, Therapy, and Specialized Teaching Services

Workers in this group care for, treat, or train people to improve their physical and emotional well being. Most workers in this group deal with sick, injured, or handicapped people. Some workers are involved in health education and sickness prevention. Hospitals, nursing homes, and rehabilitation centers hire workers in this group, as do schools, industrial plants, doctors' offices, and private homes. Some sports also have a need for workers in this group.

✔ **What kind of work would you do?**
Your work activities would depend upon your specific job. For example, you might:

- provide general nursing care to patients in a hospital.
- give medications to patients as prescribed.
- care for and treat patients in a doctor's office.
- observe, record, and report information about the condition of patients in a hospital or clinic.
- plan and carry out a school health program.

- plan, organize, and direct music or art activities to help patients in a mental hospital.
- direct and aid patients in physical therapy exercises.
- provide physical therapy exercises and treatments as directed by a physician.
- train newly blinded people in daily routines, such as grooming, dressing, and using the telephone.

✔ **What skills and abilities do you need for this kind of work?**
To do this kind of work, you must be able to:

- use common sense and special medical skills to care for or treat sick or handicapped people.
- understand technical information you might get from supervisors, charts, reference books, manuals, or labels.
- use eyes, hands, and fingers with skill.

- work fast in an emergency.
- communicate with people when they are sick, handicapped, or nervous.
- change from one duty to another frequently.
- follow instructions exactly.
- record information accurately.

The above statements may not apply to every job in this group.

✔ **How do you know if you would like or could learn to do this kind of work?**
The following questions may give you clues about yourself as you consider this group of jobs.

- Have you worked as an aide in a hospital, day care center, nursing home, or other institution? Do you like helping people who are ill or injured?
- Have you had training or school courses in arts, crafts, speech, or music? Can you teach these skills to others?
- Have you assembled a plastic model of a human body? Are you interested in human anatomy?

- Have you taken a first aid course? Do you remember actions you should take in an emergency?
- Have you taken courses which require you to dissect an animal? Can you skillfully handle small instruments such as tweezers or probes?

✔ How can you prepare for and enter this kind of work?

Occupations in this group usually require education and/or training extending from one year to over ten years, depending upon the specific kind of work. People seeking entry into professional nursing and rehabilitation are required to have specialized training. Most schools of professional nursing require a high school education or its equal for admission. A few schools require some college credits for admission.

Most nursing schools offer one or more of the following programs: two-year associate degrees, three-year diploma programs, or four-year baccalaureate degrees. Studies in all programs include biological, physical, and social sciences as well as nursing theory and practice. Two and three year programs prepare graduates for general and private duty nursing. Graduates of four-year baccalaureate programs qualify for general duty nursing, positions in public health agencies, or advancement to supervisory and administrative work.

Jobs in therapy usually require a college degree in a specialized field such as speech, music, recreation, art, or physical education. On-the-job training is also required. People with degrees in other fields may become qualified by taking the necessary academic and clinical courses.

✔ What else should you consider about these jobs?

These jobs involve close physical contact with people. Workers may have to lift, bathe, groom, or massage patients. They may also take blood or apply dressings and medications. Conditions associated with mental, emotional, or physical problems must be tolerated.

Most professionals will work a 40-hour week. However they may be on call or required to work overtime. Workers with seniority usually can be selective about the days and shifts they work.

Jobs may involve direct patient care, research, teaching, or combinations of each. There are many areas of specialization in this field.

If you think you would like to do this kind of work, look at the job titles on the following pages.

GOE: 10.02.01 Nursing

NURSE ANESTHETIST (medical ser.) • D.O.T. #075.371-010 • OES #32502 • Administers intravenous, spinal, and other anesthetics to render persons insensible to pain during surgical operations, deliveries, or other medical and dental procedures: Positions patient and administers prescribed anesthetic in accordance with standardized procedures, regulating flow of gases or injecting fluids intravenously or rectally. Observes patient's reaction during anesthesia, periodically counting pulse and respiration, taking blood pressure, and noting skin color and dilatation of pupils. Administers oxygen or initiates other emergency measures to prevent surgical shock, asphyxiation, or other adverse conditions. Informs PHYSICIAN (medical ser.) of patient's condition during anesthesia. Records patient's preoperative, operative, and postoperative condition, anesthetic and medications administered, and related data. May give patient postoperative care as directed. • **GED:** R5, M4, L5 • **SVP:** 2-4 yrs • **Academic:** Ed=B, Eng=G • **Work Field:** 294 • **MPSMS:** 924 • **Aptitudes:** G2, V3, N2, S2, P2, Q3, K4, F2, M2, E5, C3 • **Temperaments:** M, P, S • **Stress:** E, A, S • **Physical:** V=L, H=L, L=M, W, H • **Work Env:** I • **Salary:** 4 • **Outlook:** 4

NURSE PRACTITIONER (medical ser.) • D.O.T. #075.264-010 • OES #32502 • PRIMARY CARE NURSE PRACTITIONER. Provides general medical care and treatment to assigned patients in facilities, such as clinics, health centers, or public health agency, working with PHYSICIAN (medical ser.): Performs physical examinations and preventive health measures within prescribed guidelines. Orders, interprets, and evaluates diagnostic tests to identify and assess patient's clinical problems and health care needs. Records physical findings, and formulates plan and prognosis, based on patient's condition. Discusses case with PHYSICIAN (medical ser.) and other health professionals to assure observation of specified practice. Submits health care plan and goals of individual patients for periodic review and evaluation by PHYSICIAN (medical ser.). Recommends drugs or other forms of treatment, such as physical therapy, inhalation therapy, or related therapeutic procedures. May refer patients to PHYSICIAN (medical ser.) for consultation or to specialized health resources for treatment. May determine when patient has recovered and release patient. Where state law permits, may engage in independent practice. • **GED:** R5, M5, L5 • **SVP:** 4-10 yrs • **Academic:** Ed=B, Eng=G • **Work Field:** 294 • **MPSMS:** 924 • **Aptitudes:** G2, V2, N3, S2, P2, Q4, K3, F3, M3, E5, C3 • **Temperaments:** D, J, M, P • **Stress:** E, A • **Physical:** V=L, H=L, L=L, W, H • **Work Env:** I • **Salary:** 5 • **Outlook:** 4

NURSE, GENERAL DUTY (medical ser.) • D.O.T. #075.374-010 • OES #32502 • NURSE, STAFF. Renders general nursing care to patients in hospital, infirmary, sanitarium, or similar institution: Administers prescribed medications and treatments in accordance with approved nursing techniques. Prepares equipment and aids PHYSICIAN (medical ser.) during treatments and examinations of patients. Observes patient, records significant conditions and reactions, and notifies supervisor or PHYSICIAN (medical ser.) of patient's condition and reaction to drugs, treatments, and significant incidents. Takes temperature, pulse, blood pressure, and other vital signs to detect deviations from normal and determine progress of patient. May rotate among various clinical services of institution, such as obstetrics, surgery, orthopedics, outpatient and admitting, pediatrics, psychiatry, and tuberculosis. May prepare rooms, sterile instruments, equipment, and supplies, and handing, in order of use, to assist SURGEON (medical ser.) I or OBSTETRICIAN (medical ser.) in operations and deliveries. May make beds, bathe and feed patients, and assist in their rehabilitation. May serve as leader for group of personnel rendering nursing care to number of patients. • **GED:** R5, M4, L5 • **SVP:** 2-4 yrs • **Academic:** Ed=B, Eng=G • **Work Field:** 294 • **MPSMS:** 924 • **Aptitudes:** G2, V2, N3, S3, P3, Q3, K3, F3, M3, E4, C4 • **Temperaments:** M, P, S, T • **Stress:** E, S • **Physical:** V=G, H=G, L=M, W, H • **Work Env:** I • **Salary:** 5 • **Outlook:** 5

NURSE, INSTRUCTOR (medical ser.) • D.O.T. #075.121-010 • OES #31114 • Demonstrates and teaches patient care in classroom and clinical units to nursing students and instructs students in principles and application of physical, biological, and psychological subjects related to nursing: Lectures to students, conducts and supervises laboratory work, issues assignments, and directs seminars and panels. Prepares and administers examinations, evaluates student progress, and maintains records of student classroom and clinical experience. Participates in planning curriculum, teaching schedule, and course outline. Cooperates with medical and nursing personnel in evaluating and improving teaching and nursing practices. May specialize in specific subject, such as anatomy, chemistry, psychology, or nutrition, or in type of nursing activity, such as nursing of medical or surgical patients. • **GED:** R5, M4, L5 • **SVP:** 2-4 yrs • **Academic:** Ed=A, Eng=S • **Work Field:** 296 • **MPSMS:** 924 • **Aptitudes:** G2, V1, N2, S3, P3, Q2, K4, F3, M4, E5, C4 • **Temperaments:** D, P, V • **Stress:** A • **Physical:** V=N, H=L, L=L, H • **Work Env:** I • **Salary:** 4 • **Outlook:** 5

NURSE, LICENSED PRACTICAL (medical ser.) • D.O.T. #079.374-014 • OES #32505 • Cares for ill, injured, convalescent, and handicapped persons in hospitals, clinics, private homes, sanitariums, and similar institutions: Takes and records temperature, blood pressure, and pulse and respiration rate. Dresses wounds, gives enemas, douches, alcohol rubs, and massages. Applies compresses, ice bags, and hot water bottles. Observes patient and reports adverse reactions to medical personnel in charge. Administers specified medication, and notes time and amount on patient's chart. Assembles and uses such equipment as catheters, tracheotomy tubes, and oxygen suppliers. Performs routine laboratory work, such as urinalysis. Sterilizes equipment and supplies, using germicides, sterilizer, or autoclave. Prepares food trays and feeds patient. Records food and fluid intake and output. Bathes, dresses, and assists patient in walking and turning. Cleans rooms, makes beds, and answers patient's calls. Washes and dresses bodies of deceased persons. Must pass state board examination and

be licensed. May assist in delivery, care, and feeding of infants. • **GED:** R4, M3, L4 • **SVP:** 1-2 yrs • **Academic:** Ed=A, Eng=G • **Work Field:** 294 • **MPSMS:** 924 • **Aptitudes:** G3, V3, N4, S3, P3, Q4, K3, F3, M3, E4, C4 • **Temperaments:** P, S, T, V • **Stress:** E, S • **Physical:** V=G, H=G, L=M, W, S, H • **Work Env:** I, R, F • **Salary:** 4 • **Outlook:** 3

NURSE, OFFICE (medical ser.) • D.O.T. #075.374-014 • OES #32502 • Cares for and treats patients in office, as directed by PHYSICIAN (medical ser.): Prepares patient for and assists with examinations. Administers injections and medications, dresses wounds and incisions, interprets PHYSICIAN'S (medical ser.) instructions to patients, assists with emergency and minor surgery, and performs related tasks as directed. Maintains records of vital statistics and other pertinent data of patient. Cleans and sterilizes instruments and equipment, and maintains stock of supplies. May conduct laboratory tests. May record and develop electrocardiographs and X-rays. May act as receptionist, perform secretarial duties, and prepare monthly statements. • **GED:** R5, M4, L5 • **SVP:** 2-4 yrs • **Academic:** Ed=B, Eng=G • **Work Field:** 294 • **MPSMS:** 924 • **Aptitudes:** G2, V2, N3, S2, P3, Q3, K3, F3, M3, E4, C4 • **Temperaments:** M, P, S, T • **Stress:** E, S • **Physical:** V=L, H=L, L=M, W, H • **Work Env:** I • **Salary:** 4 • **Outlook:** 4

NURSE, PRIVATE DUTY (medical ser.) • D.O.T. #075.374-018 • OES #32502 • NURSE, SPECIAL. Contracts independently to render nursing care, usually to one patient, in hospital or private home: Administers medications, treatments, dressings, and other nursing services, according to PHYSICIAN'S (medical ser.) instructions and condition of patient. Observes, evaluates, and records symptoms. Applies independent emergency measures to counteract adverse developments and notifies PHYSICIAN (medical ser.) of patient's condition. Directs patient in good health habits. Gives information to family in treatment of patient and maintenance of healthful environment. Maintains equipment and supplies. Cooperates with community agencies furnishing assistance to patient. May supervise diet when employed in private home. May specialize in one field of nursing, such as obstetrics, psychiatry, or tuberculosis. • **GED:** R5, M4, L5 • **SVP:** 2-4 yrs • **Academic:** Ed=B, Eng=G • **Work Field:** 294 • **MPSMS:** 924 • **Aptitudes:** G2, V2, N3, S2, P2, Q3, K3, F3, M3, E4, C4 • **Temperaments:** M, P, S, T • **Stress:** E, A, S • **Physical:** V=L, H=L, L=M, W, H • **Work Env:** I • **Salary:** 4 • **Outlook:** 4

NURSE, SCHOOL (medical ser.) • D.O.T. #075.124-010 • OES #32502 • DIRECTOR, STUDENT HEALTH SERVICES. Plans policies, standards, and objectives of school health program, in cooperation with medical authority and administrative school personnel: Participates in medical examinations and reviews findings to evaluate health status of pupils and progress of program. Instructs classes in subjects, such as child care, first aid, and home nursing, and establishes nursing policies to meet emergencies. Cooperates with school personnel in identifying and meeting social, emotional, and physical needs of school children. Administers immunizations and maintains health records of students. Works with community agencies in planning facilities to meet needs of children outside school situation. May assist in program for care of crippled children. May work in college and be designated NURSE, COLLEGE (medical ser.). • **GED:** R5, M4, L5 • **SVP:** 2-4 yrs • **Academic:** Ed=B, Eng=G • **Work Field:** 294, 296 • **MPSMS:** 924 • **Aptitudes:** G2, V2, N3, S3, P3, Q3, K4, F3, M3, E4, C3 • **Temperaments:** D, M, P, T, V • **Stress:** E, A • **Physical:** V=L, H=L, L=M, W, H • **Work Env:** I • **Salary:** 4 • **Outlook:** 3

NURSE, STAFF, COMMUNITY HEALTH (medical ser.) • D.O.T. #075.124-014 • OES #32502 • PUBLIC-HEALTH NURSE. Instructs individuals and families in health education and disease prevention in community health agency: Visits homes to determine patient and family needs, develops plan to meet needs, and provides nursing services. Instructs family in care and rehabilitation of patient, and in maintenance of health and prevention of disease for family members. Gives treatments to patient following PHYSICIAN'S (medical ser.) instructions. Assists community members and health field personnel to assess, plan for, and provide needed health and related services. Refers patients with sound and emotional problems to other community agencies for assistance. Teaches home nursing material and child care, and other subjects related to individual and community welfare. Participates in programs to safeguard health of children, including child health conferences, school health, group instruction for parents, and immunization programs. Assists in preparation of special studies and in research programs. Directs treatment of patient by NURSE, LICENSED PRACTICAL (medical ser.) and HOME ATTENDANT (per. ser.). Cooperates with families, community agencies, and medical personnel to arrange for convalescent and rehabilitative care of sick or injured persons. May specialize in one phase of community health nursing, such as clinical pediatrics or tuberculosis. • **GED:** R5, M4, L5 • **SVP:** 2-4 yrs • **Academic:** Ed=B, Eng=G • **Work Field:** 294 • **MPSMS:** 929 • **Aptitudes:** G2, V2, N2, S3, P3, Q3, K4, F3, M3, E4, C3 • **Temperaments:** I, M, P, T • **Stress:** E • **Physical:** V=L, H=L, L=M, W, H • **Work Env:** I • **Salary:** 4 • **Outlook:** 4

NURSE, STAFF, OCCUPATIONAL HEALTH NURSING (medical ser.) • D.O.T. #075.374-022 • OES #32502 • NURSE, STAFF, INDUSTRIAL. Provides nursing service to employees or persons who become ill or suffer an accident on premises of department store, factory, or other establishment: Administers first aid to injured persons. Attends to subsequent dressings of employees' injuries. Maintains record of persons treated, and prepares accident reports for compensation or other purposes. Gives information to employees in health education and illness prevention. Performs other duties, such as visiting employees' homes to provide nursing care and family health guidance. Cooperates with department heads and employees to promote accident prevention. Assists PHYSICIAN (medical ser.) in health examination programs. May take and develop X-rays. May oversee preparation and handling of food in company cafeteria. • **GED:** R5, M4, L5 • **SVP:** 2- 4 yrs • **Academic:** Ed=B, Eng=G • **Work Field:** 294 • **MPSMS:** 929 • **Aptitudes:** G2, V2, N3, S4, P3, Q3, K3, F3, M3, E4, C3 • **Temperaments:** M, P, V • **Stress:** E • **Physical:** V=L, H=L, L=L, W, H • **Work Env:** I • **Salary:** 4 • **Outlook:** 4

NURSE-MIDWIFE (medical ser.) • D.O.T. #075.264-014 • OES #32502 • Provides medical care and treatment to obstetrical patients under supervision of OBSTETRICIAN (medical ser.), delivers babies, and instructs patients in prenatal and postnatal health practices: Participates in initial examination of obstetrical patient, and is assigned responsibility for care, treatment, and delivery of patient. Examines patient during pregnancy, utilizing physical findings, laboratory test results, and patient's statements to evaluate condition and ensure that patient's progress is normal. Discusses case with OBSTETRICIAN (medical ser.) to assure observation of specified practices. Instructs patient in diet and prenatal health practices. Stays with patient during labor to reassure patient and to administer medication. Delivers infant and performs postpartum examinations and treatments to ensure that patient and infant are responding normally. When deviations from standard are encountered during pregnancy or delivery, administers stipulated emergency measures, and arranges for immediate contact of OBSTETRICIAN (medical ser.). Visits patient during postpartum period in hospital and at home to instruct patient in care of self and infant and examine patient. Maintains records of cases for inclusion in establishment file. Conducts classes for groups of patients and families to provide information concerning pregnancy, childbirth, and family orientation. May direct activities of other workers. May instruct in midwifery in establishment providing such training. • **GED:** R5, M5, L3 • **SVP:** 2-4 yrs • **Academic:** Ed=B, Eng=G • **Work Field:** 294 • **MPSMS:** 924 • **Aptitudes:** G2, V3, N3, S3, P3, Q3, K3, F3, M3, E4, C4 • **Temperaments:** M, P, V • **Stress:** E, A • **Physical:** V=L, H=L, L=M, W, H • **Work Env:** I • **Salary:** 4 • **Outlook:** 3

PHYSICIAN ASSISTANT (medical ser.) • D.O.T. #079.364-018 • OES #32511 • Provides patient services under direct supervision and responsibility of doctor of medicine or osteopathy: Elicits detailed patient histories and does complete physical examinations. Reaches tentative diagnosis and orders appropriate laboratory tests. Counsels patient and family on health and disease. Sutures minor wounds, assists in surgery, applies and removes cast and traction apparatus, and performs other therapeutic procedures under supervision of doctor of medicine or osteopathy. May have special training in particular medical specialty and be designated CHILD HEALTH ASSOCIATE (medical ser.); GYNECOLOGIST ASSISTANT (medical ser.); ORTHOPEDIC PHYSICIAN ASSISTANT (medical ser.); SURGEON'S ASSISTANT (medical ser.); UROLOGIC PHYSICIAN ASSISTANT (medical ser.). • **GED:** R5, M4, L5 • **SVP:** 2-4 yrs • **Academic:** Ed=A, Eng=G • **Work Field:** 294 • **MPSMS:** 929 • **Aptitudes:** G2, V2, N3, S2, P2, Q3, K2, F3, M3, E5, C3 • **Temperaments:** J, M • **Physical:** V=N, H=L, L=L, H • **Work Env:** I • **Salary:** 4 • **Outlook:** 4

GOE: 10.02.02 Therapy & Rehabilitation

ACUPRESSURIST (medical ser.) • D.O.T. #079.271-014 • OES #32199 • Examines patients and analyzes findings to diagnose and treat physical problems according to knowledge and techniques of acupressure: Directs patient to lie on treatment couch and positions patient's arms and legs in relaxed position to facilitate examination and treatment. Examines patient's muscular system visually and feels tissue around muscles, nerves, and blood vessels to locate knots and other blockages which indicate excessive accumulations of blood, water, and other substances in tissue. Determines cause of accumulations and treatment procedures, according to knowledge of acupressure and experience. Feels tissue around muscles, nerves, and blood vessels to locate pressure points and presses at pressure points, using thumbs, fingers, and elbows to redirect accumulated body fluids into normal channels according to acupressure knowledge, techniques, and experience. Discusses findings with patient and explains relationship to internal organs. Outlines course of treatment for patient and advises patient regarding methods and diet for prevention of problem recurrence. Uses specific method or combination of acupressure methods, such as Ghi Ahp, Jin Shin Do, or Shiatsu, and may be known accordingly. • **GED:** R5, M3, L4 • **SVP:** 2-4 yrs • **Academic:** Ed=A, Eng=G • **Work Field:** 294 • **MPSMS:** 924 • **Aptitudes:** G2, V2, N3, S2, P2, Q3, K2, F2, M3, E3, C5 • **Temperaments:** J, P • **Stress:** E • **Physical:** V=N, H=L, L=M, W, H • **Work Env:** I • **Salary:** 4 • **Outlook:** 3

ART THERAPIST (medical ser.) • D.O.T. #076.127-010 • OES #32317 • Plans and conducts art therapy programs in public and private institutions to rehabilitate mentally ill and physically disabled patients: Confers with members of medically oriented team to determine nature of patient illness. Recommends art therapy program for patients. Devises program and instructs patients in art techniques. Encourages and guides patient participation. Appraises patients' art projections and recovery progress. Reports findings to other members of treatment team and counsels on patient's response until art therapy is discontinued. Maintains and repairs art materials and equipment. • **GED:** R4, M4, L4 • **SVP:** 2-4 yrs • **Academic:** Ed=B, Eng=G • **Work Field:** 294 • **MPSMS:** 929 • **Aptitudes:** G2, V2, N3, S2, P2, Q3, K4, F3, M3, E4, C3 • **Temperaments:** D, M, V • **Physical:** V=L, H=L, L=L, H • **Work Env:** I • **Salary:** 4 • **Outlook:** 1

ATHLETIC TRAINER (amuse. & rec.) • D.O.T. #153.224-010 • OES #34058 • Evaluates physical condition and advises and treats professional and amateur athletes to maintain maximum physical fitness for participation in athletic competition: Prescribes routine and corrective exercises to strengthen muscles. Recommends special diets to build up health and reduce overweight athletes. Massages parts of players' bodies to relieve soreness, strains, and bruises. Renders first aid to injured players, such as giving artificial respiration, cleaning and bandaging wounds, and applying heat and cold to promote healing. Calls PHYSICIAN (medical ser.) for injured persons as required. Wraps ankles, fingers, or wrists of athletes in synthetic skin, protecting gauze, and adhesive tape to support muscles and ligaments. Treats chronic minor injuries and related disabilities to maintain athletes performance. May give heat and diathermy treatments as prescribed by health service. Workers are identified according to type of sport. • **GED:** R5, M4, L4 • **SVP:** 4-10 yrs • **Academic:** Ed=A, Eng=S • **Work Field:** 294 • **MPSMS:** 913, 914 • **Aptitudes:** G2, V2, N4, S3, P3, Q4, K3, F2, M3, E4, C5 • **Temperaments:** D, J, M, P, S • **Stress:** E, S • **Physical:** V=N, H=L, L=M, W, S, H • **Work Env:** B • **Salary:** 4 • **Outlook:** 2

CORRECTIVE THERAPIST (medical ser.) • D.O.T. #076.361-010 • OES #32311 • Provides medically prescribed program of physical exercises and activities designed to prevent muscular deterioration resulting from long convalescence or inactivity due to chronic illness: Collaborates with other members of rehabilitation team in organizing patients' course of treatment. Establishes rapport with patients to motivate them, choosing exercises and activities in accordance with prescription. Utilizes any or combination of resistive, assistive, or free movement exercises, utilizing bars, or hydrogymnastics. Instructs patients in use, function, and care of prostheses and devices, such as braces, crutches, or canes and in use of manually controlled vehicles. Directs blind persons in foot travel. Prepares progress reports of patient's emotional reactions to and progress in training by observing patient during exercises to provide clinical data for diagnosis and prognosis by rehabilitation team. Directs patients in techniques of personal hygiene to compensate for permanent disabilities. • **GED:** R4, M2, L4 • **SVP:** 2-4 yrs • **Academic:** Ed=H, Eng=G • **Work Field:** 294 • **MPSMS:** 929 • **Aptitudes:** G2, V2, N2, S4, P4, Q4, K2, F2, M2, E3, C5 • **Temperaments:** D, P, V • **Stress:** E • **Physical:** V=L, H=L, L=M, W, H • **Work Env:** I, W • **Salary:** 4 • **Outlook:** 2

DANCE THERAPIST (medical ser.) • D.O.T. #076.127-018 • OES #32317 • Plans, organizes, and leads dance and body movement activities to improve patients' mental outlooks and physical well-beings: Observes and evaluates patient's mental and physical disabilities to determine dance and body movement treatment. Confers with patient and medical personnel to develop dance therapy program. Conducts individual and group dance sessions to improve patient's mental and physical well-being. Makes changes in patient's program based on observation and evaluation of progress. Attends and participates in professional conferences and workshops to enhance efficiency and knowledge. • **GED:** R5, M3, L5 • **SVP:** 4-10 yrs • **Academic:** Ed=A, Eng=G • **Work Field:** 263, 294 • **MPSMS:** 924 • **Aptitudes:** G2, V2, N3, S2, P3, Q3, K4, F4, M4, E1, C5 • **Temperaments:** D, J, P, V • **Stress:** E • **Physical:** V=L, H=L, L=L, W, C, H • **Work Env:** I • **Salary:** 4 • **Outlook:** 1

DENTAL HYGIENIST (medical ser.) • D.O.T. #078.361-010 • OES #32908 • ORAL HYGIENIST. Performs dental prophylaxis: Removes calcareous deposits, accretions, and stains from teeth by scaling accumulation of tartar from teeth and beneath margins of gums, using rotating brush, rubber cup, and cleaning compound. Applies medicaments to aid in arresting dental decay. Charts conditions of decay and disease for diagnosis and treatment by DENTIST (medical ser.). May expose and develop X-ray film. May make impressions for study casts. May remove sutures and dressings. May administer local anesthetic agents. May place and remove rubber dams, matrices, and temporary restorations. May place, carve, and finish amalgam restorations. May remove excess cement from coronal surfaces of teeth. May specialize in providing clinical services and health education in program designed to improve and maintain oral health of school children, in compliance with school policies and under direction of DENTIST (medical ser.) and school administrator and be designated DENTAL HYGIENIST, PUBLIC SCHOOL (medical ser.). May specialize in lecturing community organizations and other interested groups on oral hygiene, using motion pictures, charts, and other visual aids, to augment service of PUBLIC-HEALTH DENTIST (medical ser.) and be designated DENTAL HYGIENIST, COMMUNITY HEALTH (medical ser.). • **GED:** R4, M3, L4 • **SVP:** 1-2 yrs • **Academic:** Ed=A, Eng=G • **Work Field:** 294 • **MPSMS:** 929 • **Aptitudes:** G2, V2, N2, S2, P3, Q4, K2, F2, M2, E5, C3 • **Temperaments:** P, T • **Stress:** E • **Physical:** V=G, H=N, L=S, W, H • **Work Env:** I • **Salary:** 4 • **Outlook:** 4

DIALYSIS TECHNICIAN (medical ser.) • D.O.T. #078.362-014 • OES #32999 • KIDNEY-MACHINE OPERATOR. Sets up and operates artificial kidney machine to provide dialyses treatment for patients with kidney disorders or failure: Attaches coil, tubing, and connectors to machine to assemble it for use. Mixes priming, heparin, dialysis, and other solutions, according to formula. Primes coil with saline solution, heparinized solution, and whole blood to prepare machine for osmotic action. Transports patient to dialysis room and positions patient on cart at kidney machine. Takes and records patient's predialysis weight, temperature, blood pressure, pulse rate, and respiration rate. Removes shunt dressing from patient's arm or leg and takes blood sample from artery shunt. Connects kidney machine coil tubes to artery shunt and vein shunt in patient's arm or leg to start blood circulating through coil. Takes osmolality reading of dialysis bath solution to ensure solution is at

specified strength, and fills circulating tank of kidney machine with solution. Starts electric pump that circulates solution through and around kidney coil to activate osmosis between blood in coil and dialysis solution in circulating tank to remove impurities from blood. Monitors patient for adverse reaction and kidney machine for malfunction. Adjusts machine to maintain temperature of solution in coil at compatible level with blood in patient's circulatory system. Takes periodic blood pressure readings and performs hematocrit and clotting time tests on patient's blood sample during dialysis. Administers oxygen or gives blood transfusion, as required. Takes blood samples and removes tubes from shunts at end of treatment. Takes reading of vital signs and records readings on chart. Inspects shunts for leakage and bandages shunts. Drains blood from coil and returns it to blood bank for reuse by patient, and delivers blood sample to laboratory for analysis. Cleans and sterilizes kidney machine and reusable connectors. Packs permanent tubing and connectors in sterile containers. Makes parts, such as connectors and shunts, from materials, such as plastic tubing and coated plastic, using handtools and prepare torch. May assist with surgical insertion of shunts into vein and artery of patient's arm or leg. May explain dialysis procedure and operation of kidney machine to patient before first treatment to alloy apprehension or fear of dialysis. May operate dialysis machine equipped with membrane instead of coil. • **GED:** R4, M3, L3 • **SVP:** 1-2 yrs • **Academic:** Ed=H, Eng=S • **Work Field:** 294 • **MPSMS:** 924 • **Aptitudes:** G3, V3, N3, S3, P3, Q3, K2, F2, M3, E4, C4 • **Temperaments:** P, T • **Stress:** E • **Physical:** V=L, H=N, L=L, W, H • **Work Env:** I • **Salary:** 4 • **Outlook:** 3

HORTICULTURAL THERAPIST (medical ser.) • D.O.T. #076.124-018 • OES #32399 • Plans, coordinates, and conducts therapeutic gardening program to facilitate rehabilitation of physically and mentally handicapped patients: Confers with medical staff and patients to determine patients' needs. Evaluates patients' disabilities to determine gardening programs. Conducts gardening sessions to rehabilitate, train, and provide recreation for patients. Revises gardening program, based on observations and evaluation of patients' progress. • **GED:** R5, M4, L5 • **SVP:** 2-4 yrs • **Academic:** Ed=A, Eng=G • **Work Field:** 003, 294, 296 • **MPSMS:** 731, 924 • **Aptitudes:** G2, V2, N3, S3, P4, Q3, K3, F3, M3, E5, C3 • **Temperaments:** D, J, P, V • **Stress:** E • **Physical:** V=L, H=L, L=L, S, H • **Work Env:** I • **Salary:** 4 • **Outlook:** 1

HYPNOTHERAPIST (profess. & kin.) • D.O.T. #079.157-010 • OES #32199 • HYPNOTIST; MASTER HYPNOTIST. Induces hypnotic state in client to increase motivation or alter behavior patterns: Consults with client to determine nature of problem. Prepares client to enter hypnotic state by explaining how hypnosis works and what client will experience. Tests subject to determine degree of physical and emotional suggestibility. Induces hypnotic state in client, using individualized methods and techniques of hypnosis based on interpretation of test results and analysis of client's problem. May train client in self-hypnosis conditioning. • **GED:** R4, M3, L4 • **SVP:** 2-4 yrs • **Academic:** Ed=H, Eng=G • **Work Field:** 294 • **MPSMS:** 931 • **Aptitudes:** G2, V2, N4, S4, P4, Q4, K4, F4, M4, E5, C5 • **Temperaments:** D, J, P • **Stress:** E • **Physical:** V=L, H=L, L=S, H • **Work Env:** I • **Salary:** 4 • **Outlook:** 2

INDUSTRIAL THERAPIST (medical ser.) • D.O.T. #076.167-010 • OES #32305 • Arranges salaried, productive employment in actual work environment for mentally ill patients, to enable patients to perform medically prescribed work activities, and to motivate and prepare patients to resume employment outside hospital environment: Determines work activities for greatest therapeutic value for particular patient within limits of patient's disability. Plans work activities in coordination with other members of rehabilitation team. Assigns patient to work activity and evaluates patient's progress. Processes payroll records and salary distribution. • **GED:** R5, M5, L5 • **SVP:** 2-4 yrs • **Academic:** Ed=A, Eng=G • **Work Field:** 294 • **MPSMS:** 920 • **Aptitudes:** G2, V2, N2, S3, P3, Q3, K3, F3, M3, E4, C5 • **Temperaments:** D, M, P • **Stress:** E • **Physical:** V=N, H=L, L=L, W, H • **Work Env:** I • **Salary:** 4 • **Outlook:** 2

MANUAL-ARTS THERAPIST (medical ser.) • D.O.T. #076.124-010 • OES #32311 • Instructs patients in prescribed manual arts activities to prevent anatomical and physiological deconditioning, and to assist in maintaining, improving, or developing work skills: Collaborates with other members of rehabilitation team in planning and organizing work activities consonant with patients' capabilities and disabilities. Teaches, by means of actual or simulated work situations, activities, such as woodworking, photography, metalworking, agriculture, electricity, and graphic arts. Prepares reports showing development of patient's work tolerance, and emotional and social adjustment to aid medical personnel in evaluating patient's progress and ability to meet physical and mental demands of employment. • **GED:** R4, M4, L4 • **SVP:** 2-4 yrs • **Academic:** Ed=H, Eng=G • **Work Field:** 296 • **MPSMS:** 929 • **Aptitudes:** G2, V2, N2, S4, P4, Q4, K2, F2, M2, E3, C5 • **Temperaments:** D, P, V • **Stress:** E • **Physical:** V=L, H=L, L=L, H • **Work Env:** I • **Salary:** 4 • **Outlook:** 3

MUSIC THERAPIST (medical ser.) • D.O.T. #076.127-014 • OES #32317 • Plans, organizes, and directs music activities and learning experiences as part of care and treatment of patients to influence behavioral changes leading to increased experience and comprehension of self and environment: Collaborates with other members of rehabilitation team in planning music activities in accordance with patients' needs, capabilities, and interests. Directs and participates in instrumental and vocal music activities designed to meet patients' needs, such as solo or group singing, rhythmic and other creative music activities, music listening, playing in bands or orchestras, or attending concerts. Instructs patients in prescribed instrumental or vocal music. Studies and analyzes patients' reactions to various experiences and prepares reports describing symptoms indicative of progress or regression. Submits periodic reports to treatment team or PHYSICIAN (medical ser.) to provide clinical data for evaluation. • **GED:** R6, M5, L6 • **SVP:** 2-4 yrs • **Academic:** Ed=B, Eng=G • **Work Field:** 294 • **MPSMS:** 929 • **Aptitudes:** G2, V2, N2, S4, P4, Q4, K4, F3, M3, E4, C5 • **Temperaments:** I, J, M, P • **Stress:** E • **Physical:** V=N, H=L, L=L • **Work Env:** I • **Salary:** 4 • **Outlook:** 1

NUCLEAR MEDICAL TECHNOLOGIST (medical ser.) • D.O.T. #078.361-018 • OES #32914 • RADIOISOTOPE TECHNOLOGIST. Prepares, administers, and measures radioactive isotopes in therapeutic, diagnostic, and tracer studies, utilizing variety of radioisotope equipment: Prepares stock solutions of radioactive materials, and calculates doses to be administered by RADIOLOGIST (medical ser.). Measures glandular activity, traces radioactive doses, and calculates amount of radiation, using equipment, such as Geiger counters, electroscopes, scalers, scintillation and positron scanners, and scintigrams. Calibrates equipment. Subjects patients to radiation as prescribed by RADIOLOGIST (medical ser.), using such equipment as radium emanation tubes and needles, X-ray machines, and similar instruments. Executes blood volume, red cell survival, and fat absorption studies, following standard laboratory techniques. • **GED:** R5, M4, L5 • **SVP:** 2-4 yrs • **Academic:** Ed=A, Eng=S • **Work Field:** 294 • **MPSMS:** 925 • **Aptitudes:** G2, V2, N1, S2, P2, Q3, K3, F2, M2, E4, C4 • **Temperaments:** M, T, V • **Physical:** V=L, H=L, L=L, W, H • **Work Env:** I, R • **Salary:** 4 • **Outlook:** 3

OCCUPATIONAL THERAPIST (medical ser.) • D.O.T. #076.121-010 • OES #32305 • Plans, organizes, and conducts occupational therapy program in hospital, institution, or community setting to facilitate rehabilitation of mentally, physically, or emotionally handicapped: Plans program involving activities, such as manual arts and crafts, practice in function, prevocational, vocational, and homemaking skills and activities of daily living, and participation in sensorimotor, educational, recreational, and social activities designed to help patients regain physical or mental functioning or adjust to handicaps. Consults with other members of rehabilitation team to select activity program consistent with needs and capabilities of each patient and to coordinate occupational therapy with other therapeutic activities. Selects constructive activities suited to individuals physical capacity, intelligence level, and interest to upgrade patient to maximum independence, prepare patient for return to employment, assist in restoration of functions, and aid in adjustment to disability. Teaches patients skills and techniques required for participation in activities and evaluates patients' progress. Designs and constructs special equipment for patient and suggests adaptations of patient's work-living environment. Requisitions supplies and equipment. Lays out ma-

terials for patients' use and cleans and repairs tools at end of sessions. May conduct training programs or participate in training medical and nursing students and other workers in occupations therapy techniques and objectives. May design, make, and fit adaptive devices, such as splints and braces, following medical prescription. May plan, direct, and coordinate occupational therapy program and be designated DIRECTOR, OCCUPATIONAL THERAPY (medical ser.). • **GED:** R5, M4, L5 • **SVP:** 2-4 yrs • **Academic:** Ed=B, Eng=G • **Work Field:** 294 • **MPSMS:** 929 • **Aptitudes:** G2, V2, N2, S3, P3, Q4, K4, F3, M3, E4, C5 • **Temperaments:** J, P, V • **Stress:** E • **Physical:** V=N, H=L, L=S, H • **Work Env:** I • **Salary:** 5 • **Outlook:** 4

OCCUPATIONAL THERAPY ASSISTANT (medical ser.) • D.O.T. #076.364-010 • OES #66021 • Assists OCCUPATIONAL THERAPIST (medical ser.) in administering occupational therapy program in hospital, related facility, or community setting for physically, developmentally, or emotionally handicapped clients: Assists in evaluation of clients daily living skills and capacities to determine extent of abilities and limitations. Assists in planning and implementing programs utilizing activities selected to restore, reinforce, and enhance task performances, diminish or correct pathology, and to promote and maintain health. Designs and adapts equipment and working-living environment. Fabricates splints. Reports information and observations to supervisor. Carries out general activity program for individuals or groups. Assists in instructing patient and family in home programs as well as care and use of adaptive equipment. Prepares work materials, assists in maintenance of equipment, and orders supplies. May be responsible for maintaining observed information in client records. • **GED:** R4, M3, L4 • **SVP:** 1-2 yrs • **Academic:** Ed=A, Eng=G • **Work Field:** 294 • **MPSMS:** 929 • **Aptitudes:** G2, V2, N3, S3, P3, Q3, K2, F2, M2, E3, C4 • **Temperaments:** J, P, T, V • **Stress:** E • **Physical:** V=L, H=L, L=M, W, S, H • **Work Env:** I, R • **Salary:** 4 • **Outlook:** 3

ORIENTATION THERAPIST FOR THE BLIND (educ.) • D.O.T. #076.221-010 • OES #32399 • INSTRUCTOR OF BLIND; ORIENTOR; THERAPIST FOR BLIND. Assists newly blinded patients to achieve personal adjustment and maximum independence through training in techniques of daily living: Trains patients to orient to physical surroundings and to travel alone, with or without cane, through use of variety of actual or simulated travel situations. Teaches patients to attend to such personal needs as eating, grooming, dressing, and using dial telephone. Instructs patients in handicrafts, such as leather working or weaving, to improve sense of touch. Teaches patients to read and write Braille. Instructs patient in use of reading machines, such as stereotoner and optacon, common electrical devices, and communications skills development, such as effective listening. Instructs patients in group activities, such as swimming, dancing, or playing modified baseball to increase capacity for social participation and to improve general health. Prepares progress report to allow members of rehabilitation team to evaluate patients' ability to perform varied activities essential to daily living. • **GED:** R5, M2, L5 • **SVP:** 2-4 yrs • **Academic:** Ed=A, Eng=S • **Work Field:** 296 • **MPSMS:** 931 • **Aptitudes:** G2, V2, N3, S3, P3, Q3, K3, F3, M3, E4, C4 • **Temperaments:** D, M, P, V • **Stress:** A • **Physical:** V=N, H=L, L=L, H • **Work Env:** I • **Salary:** 4 • **Outlook:** 4

ORTHOPTIST (medical ser.) • D.O.T. #079.371-014 • OES #32999 • Aids persons with correctable focusing defects to develop and use binocular vision (focusing of both eyes): Measures visual acuity, focusing ability, and eye-motor movement of eyes, separately and jointly. Aids patient to move, focus, and coordinate both eyes to aid in visual development. Develops visual skills, near-visual discrimination, and depth perception, using developmental glasses and prisms. Instructs adult patients or parents of young patients in utilization of corrective methods at home. • **GED:** R4, M4, L4 • **SVP:** 1-2 yrs • **Academic:** Ed=A, Eng=G • **Work Field:** 294 • **MPSMS:** 929 • **Aptitudes:** G2, V3, N3, S3, P3, Q4, K4, F3, M3, E5, C4 • **Temperaments:** I, J, M, P • **Stress:** E • **Physical:** V=L, H=L, L=S, H • **Work Env:** I, N, R • **Salary:** 4 • **Outlook:** 3

PHYSICAL THERAPIST (medical ser.) • D.O.T. #076.121-014 • OES #32308 • PHYSIOTHERAPIST. Plans and administers medically prescribed physical therapy treatment programs for patients to restore function, relieve pain, and prevent disability following disease, injury, or loss of body part, working at hospital, rehabilitation center, nursing home, home-health agency, or in private practice: Reviews and evaluates PHYSICIAN'S (medical ser.) referral (prescription) and patient's medical records to determine physical therapy treatment required. Performs patient tests, measurements, and evaluations, such as range-of-motion and manual-muscle tests, gait and functional analyses, and body-parts measurements, and records and evaluates findings to aid in establishing or revising specifics of treatment programs. Plans and prepares written treatment program based on evaluation of available patient data. Administers manual therapeutic exercises to improve or maintain muscle function, applying precise amounts of manual force and guiding patient's body parts through selective patterns and degrees of movement. Instructs, motivates, and assists patients in nonmanual exercises, such as active regimens, isometric, and progressive-resistive, and in functional activities, such as ambulation, transfer, and daily-living activities, using weights, pulleys, exercise machines, mats, steps, and inclined surfaces, and assistive and supportive devices, such as crutches, canes, parallel bars, orthoses, and prostheses. Administers treatments involving application of physical agents, such as light, heat, water, and electricity, using equipment such as hydrotherapy tanks and whirlpool baths, moist packs, ultraviolet and infrared lamps, low-voltage generators, and diathermy and ultrasound machines; evaluates effects of treatments at various intensities and durations and adjusts treatments to achieve maximum benefit. Administers massage, applying deep and superficial massage techniques. Administers traction to relieve neck and back pain, using intermittent and static traction equipment. Records patient treatment, response, and progress. Instructs patient and family in physical therapy procedures to be continued at home. Evaluates, fits, and adjusts prosthetic and orthotic devices and recommends modifications to ORTHOTIST (per. protect. & med. dev.). Confers with PHYSICIAN (medical ser.) and other health practitioners to obtain additional patient information, suggest revisions in treatment program, and integrate physical therapy treatment with other aspects of patient health care. Orients, instructs, and directs work activities of PHYSICAL THERAPIST ASSISTANTS (medical ser.) or PHYSICAL THERAPY AIDES (medical ser.). May plan and conduct lectures and training programs on physical therapy and related topics for medical staff, students, and community groups. May train and evaluate clinical students. May plan and develop physical therapy research programs and participate in conducting research. May write technical articles and reports for publications. May teach physical therapy techniques and procedures in educational institutions. May limit treatment to specific patient group or disability and be designated PHYSICAL THERAPIST, PEDIATRIC (medical ser.); PHYSICAL THERAPIST, PULMONARY (medical ser.); or specialize in conducting physical therapy research and be designated PHYSICAL THERAPIST, RESEARCH (medical ser.). In facilities where PHYSICAL THERAPIST ASSISTANTS (medical ser.) are also employed, PHYSICAL THERAPISTS (medical ser.) may primarily administer complex treatments, such as certain types of manual exercise and functional training, and monitor administration of other treatments. • **GED:** R5, M4, L5 • **SVP:** 2-4 yrs • **Academic:** Ed=A, Eng=G • **Work Field:** 294 • **MPSMS:** 929 • **Aptitudes:** G2, V2, N3, S2, P2, Q3, K2, F2, M2, E4, C4 • **Temperaments:** D, I, J, M, P • **Stress:** E • **Physical:** V=N, H=N, L=L, W, S, H • **Work Env:** I • **Salary:** 4 • **Outlook:** 4

PHYSICAL THERAPIST ASSISTANT (medical ser.) • D.O.T. #076.224-010 • OES #66017 • PHYSICAL THERAPY TECHNICIAN. Administers physical therapy treatments to patients, working under direction of and as assistant to PHYSICAL THERAPIST (medical ser.): Administers noncomplex active and passive manual therapeutic exercises, therapeutic massage, and heat, light, sound, water, and electrical modality treatments, such as ultra sound, electrical stimulation, ultraviolet, infrared, and hot and cold packs to treat patients with relatively stable conditions. Administers traction to relieve neck and back pain, using intermittent and static traction equipment. Instructs, motivates, and assists patients in learning and improving functional activities, such as preambulation, transfer, ambulation, and daily-living activities. Observes patients during treatments and compiles and evaluates

data on patients' responses to treatments and progress and reports orally or in writing to PHYSICAL THERAPIST (medical ser.). Fits patients for, adjusts, and trains in use and care of orthoses, prostheses, and supportive devices, such as crutches, canes, walkers, and wheelchairs. Confers with members of physical therapy staff and other health team members, individually and in conference, to exchange, discuss, and evaluate patient information for planning, modifying, and coordinating treatment programs. Gives orientation to new PHYSICAL THERAPIST ASSISTANTS (medical ser.) and directs and gives instructions to PHYSICAL THERAPY AIDES (medical ser.). Performs various clerical tasks, such as taking inventory, ordering supplies, answering telephone, taking messages, and filling out forms. May measure patient's range of joint motion, length and girth of body parts, and vital signs to determine effects of specific treatments or to assist PHYSICAL THERAPIST (medical ser.) to compile data for patient evaluations. May monitor treatments administered by PHYSICAL THERAPY AIDES (medical ser.). • **GED:** R4, M3, L4 • **SVP:** 1-2 yrs • **Academic:** Ed=H, Eng=G • **Work Field:** 294 • **MPSMS:** 929 • **Aptitudes:** G2, V2, N3, S3, P3, Q3, K2, F2, M2, E3, C4 • **Temperaments:** I, J, M, P, T • **Stress:** E • **Physical:** V=L, H=L, L=M, W, S, H • **Work Env:** I, R • **Salary:** 4 • **Outlook:** 3

PHYSICAL-INTEGRATION PRACTITIONER (per. ser.) • D.O.T. #076.264-010 • OES #32311 • Conducts physical integration program to improve client's muscular function and flexibility: Determines client's medical history regarding accidents, operations, or chronic health complaints to plan objectives of program, using questionnaire. Photographs client to obtain different views of client's posture to facilitate treatment, using camera. Instructs client to demonstrate arm and leg movement and flexion of spine to evaluate client against established program norms. Determines program treatment procedures and discusses goals of program with client. Applies skin lubricant to section of body specified for treatment and massages muscles to release subclinical adhesions either manually or using handheld tool, utilizing knowledge of anatomy. Demonstrates and directs client's participation in specific exercises designed to fatigue desired muscle groups and release tension. Observes client's progress during program through such factors as increased joint movement, improved posture, or coordination. Records client's treatment, response, and progress. • **GED:** R3, M1, L2 • **SVP:** 1-2 yrs • **Academic:** Ed=N, Eng=G • **Work Field:** 294 • **MPSMS:** 929 • **Aptitudes:** G3, V3, N4, S2, P2, Q4, K3, F3, M3, E4, C4 • **Temperaments:** J, P • **Stress:** E • **Physical:** V=L, H=L, L=L, W, H • **Work Env:** I • **Salary:** 4 • **Outlook:** 1

PROGRAM AIDE, GROUP WORK (social ser.) • D.O.T. #195.227-010 • OES #27311 • GROUP LEADER. Leads informal group work activities, as directed by agency program staff: Receives instructions from PROGRAM DIRECTOR, GROUP WORK (profess. & kin.) or GROUP WORKER (social ser.) prior to initiating therapeutic group activities. Plans program details to meet needs and interests of individual members. Interests participants in various activities, such as arts and crafts and dramatics. Demonstrates techniques for active sports, group dances, and games. Helps develop new skills and interests. May work with part-time or volunteer staff. Employed by social service agencies, such as community center, neighborhood house, settlement house, or hospital. • **GED:** R5, M3, L4 • **SVP:** 1-2 yrs • **Academic:** Ed=A, Eng=S • **Work Field:** 296 • **MPSMS:** 941 • **Aptitudes:** G2, V2, N3, S4, P4, Q4, K4, F4, M4, E5, C5 • **Temperaments:** D, P • **Stress:** A • **Physical:** V=L, H=L, L=L, W • **Work Env:** B • **Salary:** 4 • **Outlook:** 3

PSYCHIATRIC TECHNICIAN (medical ser.) • D.O.T. #079.374-026 • OES #32931 • Provides nursing care to mentally ill, emotionally disturbed, or mentally retarded patients in psychiatric hospital or mental health clinic and participates in rehabilitation and treatment programs: Helps patients with their personal hygiene, such as bathing and keeping beds, clothing, and living areas clean. Administers oral medications and hypodermic injections, following physician's prescriptions and hospital procedures. Takes and records measures of patient's general physical condition, such as pulse, temperature, and respiration, to provide daily information. Observes patients to detect behavior patterns and reports observations to medical staff. Intervenes to restrain violent or potentially violent or suicidal patients by verbal or physical means as required. Leads prescribed individual or group therapy sessions as part of specific therapeutic procedures. May complete initial admittance forms for new patients. May contact patient's relatives by telephone to arrange family conferences. May issue medications from dispensary and maintain records in accordance with specified procedures. May be required to hold State license. • **GED:** R4, M3, L4 • **SVP:** 1-2 yrs • **Academic:** Ed=A, Eng=G • **Work Field:** 294 • **MPSMS:** 924 • **Aptitudes:** G3, V3, N3, S4, P4, Q3, K3, F3, M3, E4, C5 • **Temperaments:** J, P, S, V • **Stress:** E, S • **Physical:** V=N, H=L, L=M, W, H • **Work Env:** I, R • **Salary:** 4 • **Out look:** 3

RADIOLOGIC TECHNOLOGIST (medical ser.) • D.O.T. #078.362-026 • OES #32917 • X-RAY TECHNOLOGIST. Applies roentgen rays and radioactive substances to patients for diagnostic and therapeutic purposes: Positions patient under X-ray machine, adjusts immobilization devices, and affixes lead plates to protect unaffected areas. Administers drugs or chemical mixtures orally or as enemas to render organs opaque. Adjusts switches regulating length and intensity of exposure. Assists in treating diseased or affected areas of body, under supervision of PHYSICIAN (medical ser.), by exposing area to specified concentrations of X-rays for prescribed periods of time. Prepares reports and maintains records of services rendered. Makes minor adjustments to equipment. May assist in therapy requiring application of radium or radioactive isotopes. May specialize in taking X-rays of specific areas of body. • **GED:** R5, M4, L5 • **SVP:** 1-2 yrs • **Academic:** Ed=A, Eng=S • **Work Field:** 294 • **MPSMS:** 925 • **Aptitudes:** G2, V3, N3, S3, P3, Q3, K3, F3, M3, E4, C4 • **Temperaments:** M, P, T • **Stress:** E • **Physical:** V=G, H=N, L=M, W, H • **Work Env:** I, R • **Salary:** 4 • **Outlook:** 4

RECREATIONAL THERAPIST (medical ser.) • D.O.T. #076.124-014 • OES #32317 • Plans, organizes, and directs medically approved recreation program for patients in hospitals and other institutions: Directs and organizes such activities as adapted sports, dramatics, social activities, and arts and crafts, regulating content of program in accordance with patients' capabilities, needs, and interest. Prepares reports for patient's physician or treatment team, describing patients' reactions, and symptoms indicative of progress or regression. • **GED:** R4, M2, L4 • **SVP:** 1-2 yrs • **Academic:** Ed=H, Eng=G • **Work Field:** 294 • **MPSMS:** 929 • **Aptitudes:** G2, V2, N3, S3, P3, Q2, K3, F3, M3, E4, C4 • **Temperaments:** D, P, V • **Stress:** E • **Physical:** V=N, H=N, L=S, W, H • **Work Env:** I • **Salary:** 4 • **Outlook:** 4

RESPIRATORY THERAPIST (medical ser.) • D.O.T. #079.361-010 • OES #32302 • INHALATION THERAPIST. Administers respiratory therapy care and life support to patients with deficiencies and abnormalities of cardiopulmonary system, under supervision of PHYSICIAN (medical ser.) and by prescription. Gets up and operates devices, such as respirators, mechanical ventilators, therapeutic gas administration apparatus, environmental control systems, and aerosol generators. Observes equipment gages to ensure specified volumes are maintained. Performs bronchopulmonary drainage and assists patient in performing breathing exercises. Monitors patient's physiological responses to therapy, as well as equipment function. Consults with PHYSICIAN (medical ser.) in event of adverse reactions. Maintains patient's chart that contains pertinent identification and therapy information. Inspects and tests respiratory therapy equipment to ensure proper operating condition. Orders major repairs when needed. May demonstrate respirator care procedures to trainees and other health care personnel. • **GED:** R4, M3, L3 • **SVP:** 1-2 yrs • **Academic:** Ed=H, Eng=G • **Work Field:** 294 • **MPSMS:** 929 • **Aptitudes:** G3, V3, N3, S3, P3, Q4, K3, F3, M2, E5, C5 • **Temperaments:** M, T, V • **Physical:** V=G, H=N, L=L, W, H • **Work Env:** I • **Salary:** 4 • **Outlook:** 5

GOE: 10.02.03 Specialized Teaching

EDUCATIONAL THERAPIST (educ.) • D.O.T. #094.227-010 • OES #31311 • TEACHER, EDUCATIONALLY HANDICAPPED. Teaches elementary and secondary school subjects to educationally-handicapped students with neurological or emotional disabilities in schools, institutions, or other specialized facilities: Plans curriculum and prepares lessons and other instructional materials to meet individual needs of students, considering factors, such as physical, emotional, and educational levels of development. Instructs students in specific subject areas, such as English, mathematics, and geography. Observes students for sign of disruptive behavior, such as violence, outbursts of temper, and episodes of destructiveness. Counsels students with regard to disruptive behavior, utilizing variety of therapeutic methods. Confers with other staff members to plan programs designed to promote educational, physical, and social development of students. • **GED:** R5, M4, L5 • **SVP:** 2-4 yrs • **Academic:** Ed=B, Eng=G • **Work Field:** 296 • **MPSMS:** 931 • **Aptitudes:** G2, V2, N3, S4, P3, Q2, K4, F4, M4, E5, C5 • **Temperaments:** D, I, P, V • **Stress:** E • **Physical:** V=L, H=L, L=S, S, H • **Work Env:** I • **Salary:** 4 • **Outlook:** 3

EVALUATOR (educ.) • D.O.T. #094.267-010 • OES #31311 • Assesses type and degree of disability of handicapped children to aid in determining special programs and services required to meet educational needs: Reviews referrals of children having or suspected of having learning disabilities, mental retardation, behavioral disorders, or physical handicaps to determine evaluation procedure. Confers with school or other personnel and scrutinizes records to obtain additional information on nature and severity of disability. Observes student behavior and rates strength and weakness of factors such as rapport, motivation, cooperativeness, aggression, attention span, and task completion. Selects, administers, and scores variety of preliminary tests to measure individual's aptitudes, educational achievements, perceptual motor skills, vision, and hearing. Reports findings for staff consideration in placement of children in educational programs. May test preschool children to detect learning handicaps and recommend followup activities, consultation, or services. May administer work related tests and review records and other data to assess student vocational interests and abilities. May specialize in evaluating student readiness to transfer from special classes to regular classroom, and in providing supportive services to regular classroom teacher and be designated MAINSTREAMING FACILITATOR (education). • **GED:** R5, M4, L5 • **SVP:** 2-4 yrs • **Academic:** Ed=B, Eng=G • **Work Field:** 271, 296 • **MPSMS:** 931 • **Aptitudes:** G2, V2, N3, S3, P3, Q2, K4, F4, M4, E5, C5 • **Temperaments:** I, J, P • **Stress:** E • **Physical:** V=L, H=L, L=S, H • **Work Env:** I • **Salary:** 4 • **Outlook:** 3

TEACHER, BLIND (educ.) • D.O.T. #094.227-014 • OES #31311 • INSTRUCTOR, BLIND; TEACHER, BRAILLE; TEACHER, VISUALLY HANDICAPPED. Teaches elementary and secondary school subjects to visually handicapped students, using braille system: Instructs students in reading and writing braille using slate and stylus or braille writer. Plans curriculum and prepares lessons and other instructional materials, according to grade level of students. Transcribes lessons and other materials into braille for blind students or bold faced type for partially sighted. Arranges for and conducts field trips designed to promote sensory learning experiences. Instructs students in specific subject areas, such as mathematics, English, and social studies. Encourages students to participate in verbal and sensory class room learning experiences to ensure their comprehension of subject matter, development of social skills, and ability to identify objects encountered in daily living. May counsel students. May teach braille to individuals with sight and be designated INSTRUCTOR, BRAILLE (education). • **GED:** R5, M4, L5 • **SVP:** 2-4 yrs • **Academic:** Ed=B, Eng=S • **Work Field:** 296 • **MPSMS:** 931 • **Aptitudes:** G2, V2, N3, S4, P3, Q2, K3, F3, M4, E5, C5 • **Temperaments:** D, I, J, P • **Stress:** A • **Physical:** V=N, H=L, L=L, H • **Work Env:** I • **Salary:** 4 • **Outlook:** 3

TEACHER, DEAF STUDENTS (educ.) • D.O.T. #094.224-010 • OES #31311 • INSTRUCTOR, DEAF-MUTE; TEACHER, AURALLY HANDICAPPED; TEACHER, ORAL-DEAF. Teaches elementary and secondary school subjects to aurally-handicapped students, using various methods, such as lip reading, finger spelling, cued speech, and sign language: Instructs deaf and hard-of-hearing students in communication skills, using hearing aid or other electronic or electrical amplifying equipment. Plans curriculum and prepares lessons and other instructional materials according to grade level of students, utilizing visual media, such as films, television, and charts. Instructs students in specific subject areas, such as geography, biology, and art. Encourages students to participate in verbal communication classroom learning experiences to ensure their comprehension of subject matter, development of social skills, and ability to communicate in situations encountered in daily living. May attend and interpret lectures and instructions for students enrolled in regular classes. May specialize in teaching lip reading and be designated as TEACHER, LIP READING (education). • **GED:** R5, M4, L5 • **SVP:** 2-4 yrs • **Academic:** Ed=B, Eng=S • **Work Field:** 296 • **MPSMS:** 931 • **Aptitudes:** G2, V2, N3, S3, P3, Q2, K3, F4, M4, E5, C5 • **Temperaments:** D, I, J, P • **Stress:** A • **Physical:** V=L, H=N, L=L, H • **Work Env:** I • **Salary:** 4 • **Outlook:** 3

TEACHER, HANDICAPPED STUDENTS (educ.) • D.O.T. #094.227-018 • OES #31311 • INSTRUCTOR, CRIPPLED STUDENTS; TEACHER, EXCEPTIONAL CHILDREN; TEACHER, ORTHOPEDICALLY HANDICAPPED. Teaches elementary and secondary school subjects to physically-handicapped students, adapting teaching techniques and methods of instruction to meet individual needs of students in schools, hospitals, and students' homes: Plans curriculum and prepares lessons and other materials, considering factors, such as individual needs, abilities, learning levels, and physical limitations of students. Arranges and adjusts tools, work aids, and equipment utilized by students in classroom, such as specially equipped worktables, typewriters, and mechanized page turners. Devises special teaching tools, techniques, and equipment. Instructs students in academic subjects and other activities designed to provide learning experience. Confers with other members of staff to develop programs to maximize students' potentials. May assist members of medical staff in rehabilitation programs for students. • **GED:** R5, M4, L5 • **SVP:** 2-4 yrs • **Academic:** Ed=M, Eng=G • **Work Field:** 296 • **MPSMS:** 931 • **Aptitudes:** G2, V2, N3, S4, P3, Q2, K3, F4, M4, E5, C5 • **Temperaments:** D, I, J, P • **Stress:** E • **Physical:** V=N, H=L, L=S, H • **Work Env:** I • **Salary:** 4 • **Outlook:** 1

TEACHER, HOME THERAPY (social ser.) • D.O.T. #195.227-018 • OES #31311 • CHILD DEVELOPMENT SPECIALIST; DEVELOPMENT DISABILITY SPECIALIST; INFANT EDUCATOR; PARENT TRAINER. Instructs parent of mentally- and physically-handicapped children in therapy techniques and behavior modification: Observes and plays with child and confers with child's parents and other professionals periodically to obtain information relating to child's mental and physical development. Evaluates child's responses to determine levels of child's physical and mental development. Determines parent's ability to comprehend and apply therapeutic and behavior modification techniques and parent's social and emotional needs to formulate teaching plan. Develops individual teaching plan covering self-help, motor, social, cognitive, and language skills development for parents to implement in home. Instructs parents individually or in groups in behavior modification, physical development, language development, and conceptual learning exercises and activities. Revises teaching plan to correspond with child's rate of development. Counsels parents and organizes groups of parents in similar situations to provide social and emotional support for parents. Refers parents and child to social service agencies and facilities for additional services and financial assistance. Consults and coordinates plans with other professionals. Teaches preschool subjects, such as limited vocabulary sign language and color recognition, to children capable of learning such subjects. • **GED:** R5, M3, L5 • **SVP:** 2-4 yrs • **Academic:** Ed=B, Eng=S • **Work Field:** 296 • **MPSMS:** 939, 941 • **Aptitudes:** G2, V2, N3, S4, P4, Q3, K3, F3, M3, E5, C5 • **Temperaments:** D, I, J, P, V • **Stress:** E, A • **Physical:** V=L, H=G, L=L, W, S, H • **Work Env:** I • **Salary:** 4 • **Outlook:** 3

TEACHER, MENTALLY-RETARDED STUDENTS (educ.) • D.O.T. #094.227-022 • OES #31311 • TEACHER, EDUCABLE MENTALLY RETARDED. Teaches basic academic and living skills to mentally-retarded students in schools, centers, and institutions, using various teaching techniques to reinforce learning: Plans curriculum and prepares lessons and other instructional materials according to achievement levels of students. Instructs students in subject areas, such as reading, writing, and basic arithmetic, utilizing various techniques, such as those of phonetics, multisensory learning, and repetition to reinforce learning. Instructs students in subjects and personal skills required to prepare them for independent maintenance and economic self-sufficiency. Administers ability and achievement tests and interprets results. Observes, evaluates, and prepares reports on progress of students. • **GED:** R5, M4, L5 • **SVP:** 2-4 yrs • **Academic:** Ed=B, Eng=S • **Work Field:** 296 • **MPSMS:** 931 • **Aptitudes:** G2, V2, N3, S4, P3, Q2, K4, F4, M4, E5, C5 • **Temperaments:** D, J, P • **Stress:** A • **Physical:** V=L, H=L, L=L • **Work Env:** I • **Salary:** 4 • **Outlook:** 3

TEACHER, PRESCHOOL (educ.) • D.O.T. #092.227-018 • OES #31302 • Instructs children in activities designed to promote social, physical, and intellectual growth in preparation for primary school in preschool, day care center, or other child development facility. Plans individual and group activities to stimulate learning, according to ages of children. May be designated as TEACHER, CHILD DEVELOPMENT CENTER (education); TEACHER, DAY CARE CENTER (education); TEACHER, EARLY CHILDHOOD EDUCATION (education); TEACHER, NURSERY SCHOOL (education). • **GED:** R4, M2, L3 • **SVP:** 2-4 yrs • **Academic:** Ed=A, Eng=S • **Work Field:** 296 • **MPSMS:** 931, 942 • **Aptitudes:** G3, V3, N3, S4, P4, Q3, K3, F3, M3, E3, C3 • **Temperaments:** D, J, P, V • **Stress:** A • **Physical:** V=L, H=G, L=L, W, S, H • **Work Env:** I • **Salary:** 4 • **Outlook:** 3

TEACHER, VOCATIONAL TRAINING (educ.) • D.O.T. #094.227-026 • OES #31311 • Teaches vocational skills to handicapped students: Confers with students, parents, school personnel, and other individuals to plan vocational training that meets needs, interests, and abilities of students. Instructs students in areas such as personal-social skills and work-related attitudes and behaviors. Develops work opportunities that allow students to experience success in performing tasks of increasing difficulty and that teach work values, such as self-improvement, independence, dependability, productivity, and pride of workmanship. Conducts field trips to enable students to learn about job activities and to explore work environments. May teach academic skills to students. May instruct students in one or more vocational skills, such as woodworking, building maintenance, cosmetology, food preparation, gardening, sewing, or nurse aiding. • **GED:** R5, M3, L5 • **SVP:** 2-4 yrs • **Academic:** Ed=A, Eng=S • **Work Field:** 296 • **MPSMS:** 931 • **Aptitudes:** G2, V2, N3, S4, P4, Q3, K4, F4, M4, E5, C5 • **Temperaments:** D, J, P • **Stress:** A • **Physical:** V=N, H=L, L=L, H • **Work Env:** I • **Salary:** 4 • **Outlook:** 4

WORK-STUDY COORDINATOR, SPECIAL EDUCATION (educ.) • D.O.T. #094.107-010 • OES #31311 • Plans and conducts special education work and study program for in-school youth: Establishes contacts with employers and employment agencies and surveys newspapers and other sources to locate work opportunities for students. Confers with potential employers to communicate objectives of work study program and to solicit cooperation in adapting work situations to special needs of students. Evaluates and selects program participants according to specified criteria and counsels and instructs selected students in matters such as vocational choices, job readiness, and job retention skills and behaviors. Assists students in applying for jobs and accompanies students to employment interviews. Confers with employer and visits worksite to monitor progress of student and to determine support needed to meet employer requirements and fulfill program goals. Counsels students to foster development of satisfactory job performance. Confers with school and community personnel to impart information about program and to coordinate program functions with related activities. • **GED:** R5, M3, L5 • **SVP:** 2-4 yrs • **Academic:** Ed=A, Eng=G • **Work Field:** 296, 298 • **MPSMS:** 931 • **Aptitudes:** G2, V2, N4, S4, P4, Q3, K4, F4, M4, E5, C5 • **Temperaments:** D, I, J, P • **Stress:** E • **Physical:** V=L, H=L, L=S • **Work Env:** I • **Salary:** 4 • **Outlook:** 3

10.03 Child and Adult Care

Workers in this group are concerned with the physical needs and the welfare of others. They assist professionals in treating the sick or injured. They care for the elderly, the very young, or the handicapped. Frequently these workers help people do the things they cannot do for themselves. Jobs are found in hospitals, clinics, day care centers, nurseries, schools, private homes, and centers for helping the handicapped.

✔ **What kind of work would you do?**

Your work activities would depend upon your specific job. For example, you might:

- help elderly persons bathe, feed, or dress themselves.
- collect medical data, using electronic equipment such as an electrocardiograph.
- assist physical therapists in providing treatment to patients.
- give emergency first aid in a commercial or industrial setting.
- ride in an ambulance and assist the driver in giving first aid and transporting patients.
- entertain and supervise children in a nursery.
- assist a dentist by recording information about patients and doing other simple office and clinical tasks.

✔ **What skills and abilities do you need for this kind of work?**

To do this kind of work, you must be able to:

- want to help people.
- deal with the young, elderly, sick, or handicapped.
- understand and follow instructions exactly in caring for those who depend on you.
- use arms, eyes, hands, and fingers with skill.
- talk and relate to sick or handicapped people.

The above statements may not apply to every job in this group.

✔ **How do you know if you would like or could learn to do this kind of work?**

The following questions may give you clues about yourself as you consider this group of jobs.

- Have you cared for children or sick people? Are you patient with and able to relate to those who cannot take care of themselves?
- Have you had courses in first aid? Can you react quickly and calmly in an emergency?
- Have you been a volunteer worker in a hospital? Do you like this kind of work?
- Have you participated in community services or charity work? Are you concerned for the welfare of others?
- Did you serve in the medical corps in the armed services?

✔ **How can you prepare for and enter this kind of work?**

Occupations in this group usually require education and/or training extending from thirty days to over two years, depending upon the specific kind of work. Employers usually require an applicant to have a high school education or its equal. Hospitals, community agencies, colleges, and public vocational schools offer training courses for many of these jobs. The average program requires about one year to complete. Some jobs in this group require state licenses.

Hospitals and clinics provide on-the-job training for many of these jobs. This training usually includes classroom instruction, demonstration of skills and techniques and practice. The length of training depends upon the job.

Interest and experience in homemaking, child care, or adult care provide good background for working with the aged, blind, or the very young.

✔ What else should you consider about these jobs?

Some of these jobs involve close physical contact with people. Workers may have to help lift, bathe, groom, or feed people. Working hours will vary, since health care is given 24 hours a day. The growing demand for health care gives workers in this group security.

The demand for both full- and part-time workers in this area is high. Qualified and experienced workers usually find the jobs that fit their needs.

Personal satisfaction is often received by helping others.

If you think you would like to do this kind of work, look at the job titles listed on the following pages.

GOE: 10.03.01 Data Collection, Child & Adult Care

AUDIOMETRIST (profess. & kin.) • D.O.T. #078.362-010 • OES #32999 • AUDIOMETRIC TECHNICIAN; HEARING-TEST TECHNICIAN. Administers audiometric screening and threshold tests, generally pure-tone air conduction, to individuals or groups, under supervision of AUDIOLOGIST (profess. & kin.), OTOLOGIST (medical ser.), or OTOLARYNGOLOGIST (medical ser.). Fits earphones on subject and provides instruction on procedures to be followed. Adjusts audiometer to control sound emitted and records subjects' responses. Refers individuals to AUDIOLOGIST (profess. & kin.) for interpretation of test results and need for more definitive hearing examination, or PHYSICIAN (medical ser.) for medical examination. • GED: R4, M3, L4 • SVP: 1-2 yrs • Academic: Ed=H, Eng=S • Work Field: 211 • MPSMS: 929 • Aptitudes: G2, V3, N3, S4, P3, Q2, K3, F3, M3, E4, C4 • Temperaments: M, P • Physical: V=N, H=N, L=L, H • Work Env: I • Salary: 4 • Outlook: 3

CARDIAC MONITOR TECHNICIAN (medical ser.) • D.O.T. #078.367-010 • OES #32999 • TELEMETRY TECHNICIAN. Monitors heart rhythm pattern of patients in special care unit of hospital to detect abnormal pattern variances, using telemetry equipment: Reviews patient information to determine normal heart rhythm pattern, current pattern, and prior variances. Observes screen of cardiac monitor and listens for alarm to identify abnormal variation in heart rhythm. Informs supervisor or NURSE, GENERAL DUTY (medical ser.) 075.374-010 of variances to initiate examination of patient. Measures length and height of patient's heart rhythm pattern on graphic tape readout, using calipers, and posts information on patient records. Answers calls for assistance from patients and inquiries concerning patients from medical staff, using intercom and call director. May perform duties as described under ELECTROCARDIOGRAPH TECHNICIAN (medical ser.) 078.362-018. • GED: R3, M2, L2 • SVP: 6 mos-1 yr • Academic: Ed=H, Eng=S • Work Field: 294 • MPSMS: 925 • Aptitudes: G3, V3, N4, S4, P4, Q3, K4, F4, M4, E5, C4 • Temperaments: J, S • Stress: S • Physical: V=L, H=N, L=S, H • Work Env: I • Salary: 3 • Outlook: 3

CARDIOPULMONARY TECHNOLOGIST (medical ser.) • D.O.T. #078.362-030 • OES #32925 • Performs diagnostic tests of cardiovascular and pulmonary systems of patients in hospital, using variety of laboratory machines and other work devices, to aid physicians in diagnosis and treatment: Conducts electrocardiogram, phonocardiography, vectorcardiography, ultra sound, stress, cardiac catherization, blood pressure, and other vascular tests to diagnose disorders of cardiovascular system, using variety of laboratory equipment, such as electrocardiograph and phonocardiograph machines, stethoscope, and catheter. Conducts tests of pulmonary system to diagnose pulmonary disorders, using respiratory equipment. Analyzes and interprets test findings and furnishes results to physician. • GED: R4, M4, L4 • SVP: 2-4 yrs • Academic: Ed=H, Eng=S • Work Field: 294 • MPSMS: 925 • Aptitudes: G2, V2, N2, S3, P2, Q2, K2, F3, M3, E5, C3 • Temperaments: J, P, T • Stress: E • Physical: V=L, H=L, L=L, W, H • Work Env: I • Salary: 4 • Outlook: 3

ELECTROCARDIOGRAPH TECHNICIAN (medical ser.) • D.O.T. #078.362-018 • OES #32926 • E.K.G. TECHNICIAN. Records electromotive variations in action of heart muscle, using electrocardiograph machine, to provide data for diagnosis of heart ailments: Attaches electrodes to specified areas of patient's body. Turns selector switch, and moves chest electrode to successive positions across chest to record electromotive variations occurring in various areas of heart muscle. Presses button to mark tracing paper to indicate positions of chest electrodes. Replenishes supply of paper and ink in machine and reports malfunctions. Edits and mounts final results and forwards results to CARDIOLOGIST (medical ser.) for analysis and interpretation. • GED: R4, M3, L4 • SVP: 1-2 yrs • Academic: Ed=H, Eng=S • Work Field: 294 • MPSMS: 925 • Aptitudes: G2, V3, N3, S3, P3, Q3, K3, F3, M3, E4, C5 • Temperaments: M, P, T • Stress: E • Physical: V=G, H=N, L=S, W, H • Work Env: I • Salary: 4 • Outlook: 4

ELECTROENCEPHALOGRAPHIC TECHNOLOGIST (medical ser.) • D.O.T. #078.362-022 • OES #32923 • E.E.G. TECHNICIAN. Measures impulse frequencies and differences in electrical potential from brain for use in diagnosis of brain disorders, using electroencephalograph: Fastens electrode to patient's head, using adhesive tape, adhesive paste, or pins inserted into skull epidermis according to specified pattern. Attaches electrode terminals to switchbox and turns selector switches to obtain combinations for complete set of graphic readings. Observes patient's behavior and makes notes on graph. Makes minor adjustments and repairs to equipment, such as replacing condensers and refilling tracing pins. Monitors other variables, such as electromyograms, electrocardiograms, electrooculograms, and respiration as directed. • GED: R4, M4, L4 • SVP: 1-2 yrs • Academic: Ed=H, Eng=S • Work Field: 294 • MPSMS: 925 • Aptitudes: G3, V3, N3, S3, P3, Q4, K4, F4, M4, E5, C5 • Temperaments: M, P, T • Stress: E • Physical: V=G, H=N, L=S, W, H • Work Env: I • Salary: 5 • Outlook: 3

HOLTER SCANNING TECHNICIAN (medical ser.) • D.O.T. #078.264-010 • OES #32999 • Analyzes tape from cardiac-function monitoring device (Holter monitor) worn by patient to provide data for diagnosis of cardiovascular disorders: Places magnetic tape from heart monitor worn by patient during specified test period onto spindle of tape scanner and pushes button to activate scanner. Turns knobs on scanner to adjust controls that regulate taped sounds associated with heart activity and focus video representation of sounds on screen of scanner. Observes scanner screen to identify irregularities in patient cardiac patterns, utilizing knowledge of regular and irregular cardiac-function patterns. Presses button on scanner to activate printer that prints sections of tape showing abnormal cardiac patterns. Tears strip of tape from printer and measures distances between peaks and valleys of heart activity patterns, using calipers, to obtain data for further analysis. Records findings on laboratory report forms and forwards tapes and forms to designated personnel. May fit patient with heart monitor, following instructions of supervisory personnel. May analyze patient diary to identify incidents that correspond to heart pattern irregularities detected on monitor tape. May perform other diagnostic procedures, such as electrocardiography and stress testing, to aid in medical evaluation of patient. • GED: R3, M3, L3 • SVP: 1-2 yrs • Academic: Ed=H, Eng=S • Work Field: 294 • MPSMS: 929 • Aptitudes: G3, V3, N3, S5, P3, Q3, K3, F3, M4, E4, C5 • Temperaments: J, T • Physical: V=L, H=N, L=M, W, H • Work Env: I • Salary: 4 • Outlook: 4

PULMONARY-FUNCTION TECHNICIAN (medical ser.) • D.O.T. #078.262-010 • OES #32999 • Performs pulmonary-function, lung-capacity, and blood-and-oxygen tests to gather data for medical evaluation, following instructions of supervisor: Confers with patient in treatment room to explain test procedures. Explains specified methods of breathing to patient and conducts pulmonary-function tests, such as helium dilution and gross spirometry tests, and lung-capacity tests, such as vital capacity and maximum breathing capacity tests, using spirometer. Activates co-oximeter and injects blood specimen into co-oximeter to perform blood analysis tests, such as oxygen saturation and red cell count. Collects and analyzes contents of expired air of patient, using oxygen analyzer. Observes and records readings on metering devices of analysis equipment, and conveys findings of tests and analyses to supervisor for evaluation. • **GED:** R4, M4, L4 • **SVP:** 1-2 yrs • **Academic:** Ed=H, Eng=S • **Work Field:** 294 • **MPSMS:** 925 • **Aptitudes:** G2, V2, N2, S3, P2, Q2, K4, F4, M4, E5, C4 • **Temperaments:** J, T • **Physical:** V=L, H=L, L=L, W, H • **Work Env:** I, R • **Salary:** 4 • **Outlook:** 4

GOE: 10.03.02 Patient Care

AMBULANCE ATTENDANT (medical ser.) • D.O.T. #355.374-010 • OES #66023 • Accompanies and assists AMBULANCE DRIVER (medical ser.) on calls: Assists in lifting patient onto wheeled cart or stretcher and into and out of ambulance. Renders first aid, such as bandaging, splinting, and administering oxygen. May be required to have Red Cross first-aid training certificate. • **GED:** R3, M2, L3 • **SVP:** 30 days-3 mos • **Academic:** Ed=N, Eng=G • **Work Field:** 294 • **MPSMS:** 929 • **Aptitudes:** G4, V4, N4, S4, P4, Q4, K3, F3, M3, E4, C4 • **Temperaments:** J, P, S, V • **Stress:** E, S • **Physical:** V=L, H=L, L=M, W, C, S, H • **Work Env:** I • **Salary:** 3 • **Outlook:** 3

BIRTH ATTENDANT (medical ser.) • D.O.T. #354.377-010 • OES #66008 • Provides assistance to women during childbirth, in absence of medical practitioner. May function under supervision of local or state health department. • **GED:** R3, M1, L2 • **SVP:** 3-6 mos • **Academic:** Ed=N, Eng=G • **Work Field:** 294 • **MPSMS:** 929 • **Aptitudes:** G4, V4, N4, S3, P3, Q4, K3, F3, M3, E5, C5 • **Temperaments:** J, P • **Stress:** E • **Physical:** V=L, H=L, L=M, W, H • **Work Env:** I • **Salary:** 3 • **Outlook:** 3

DENTAL ASSISTANT (medical ser.) • D.O.T. #079.371-010 • OES #66002 • Assists DENTIST (medical ser.) engaged in diagnostic, operative, surgical, periodontal, preventive, orthodontic, removable and fixed prosthdontic, endodontic, and pedodontic procedures during examination and treatment of patients: Provides diagnostic aids including exposing radiographs, taking and recording medical and dental histories, recording vital signs, making preliminary impressions for study casts, and making occlusal registrations for mounting study casts. Performs clinical supportive functions including preparing and dismissing patients; sterilizing and disinfecting instruments and equipment; providing postoperative instructions prescribed by DENTIST (medical ser.); and preparing tray setups for dental procedures. Assists DENTIST (medical ser.) in management of medical and dental emergencies. Assists in maintaining patient treatment records and maintaining operatory equipment and instruments. Performs such laboratory procedures as pouring, trimming, and polishing study casts; fabricating custom impression trays from preliminary impressions; cleaning and polishing removable appliances; and fabricating temporary restorations. Provides oral hygiene instruction, such as conducting plaque control program. Performs basic business office procedures, including maintaining appointment control, receiving payment for dental services, and maintaining supply order. • **GED:** R4, M3, L4 • **SVP:** 1-2 yrs • **Academic:** Ed=A, Eng=S • **Work Field:** 294 • **MPSMS:** 922 • **Aptitudes:** G3, V3, N3, S4, P3, Q3, K4, F3, M3, E5, C4 • **Temperaments:** P, T • **Stress:** E • **Physical:** V=L, H=N, L=S, H • **Work Env:** I • **Salary:** 4 • **Outlook:** 3

EMERGENCY MEDICAL TECHNICIAN (medical ser.) • D.O.T. #079.374-010 • OES #32508 • Administers first-aid treatment to and transports sick or injured persons to medical facility, working as member of emergency medical team: Responds to instructions from emergency medical dispatcher and drives specially equipped emergency vehicle to specified location. Monitors communication equipment to maintain contact with dispatcher. Removes or assists in removal of victims from scene of accident or catastrophe. Determines nature and extent of illness or injury, or magnitude of catastrophe, to establish first aid procedures to be followed or need for additional assistance, basing decisions on statements of persons involved, examination of victim or victims, and knowledge of emergency medical practice. Administers prescribed first-aid treatment at site of emergency, or in specially equipped vehicle, performing such activities as application of splints, administration of oxygen or intravenous injections, treatment of minor wounds or abrasions, or administration of artificial resuscitation. Communicates with professional medical personnel at emergency treatment facility to obtain instructions regarding further treatment and to arrange for reception of victims at treatment facility. Assists in removal of victims from vehicle and transfer of victims to treatment center. Assists treatment center admitting personnel to obtain and record information related to victims' vital statistics and circumstances of emergency. Maintains vehicles and medical and communication equipment and replenishes first-aid equipment and supplies. May assist in controlling crowds, protecting valuables, or performing other duties at scene of catastrophe. May assist professional medical personnel in emergency treatment administered at medical facility. • **GED:** R4, M3, L4 • **SVP:** 6 mos-1 yr • **Academic:** Ed=A, Eng=G • **Work Field:** 013, 294 • **MPSMS:** 929 • **Aptitudes:** G3, V3, N3, S3, P2, Q3, K2, F2, M2, E3, C3 • **Temperaments:** J, M, P, S • **Stress:** S • **Physical:** V=G, H=G, L=M, W, C, S, H • **Work Env:** B • **Salary:** 3 • **Outlook:** 3

FIRST-AID ATTENDANT (any ind.) • D.O.T. #354.677-010 • OES #66008 • NURSE, FIRST AID. Renders first aid and subsequent treatment to injured or ill employees at industrial plant, commercial establishment, mine, or construction site: Sterilizes, disinfects, anoints, and bandages minor cuts and burns. Applies artificial respiration or administers oxygen, in cases of suffocation and asphyxiation. Administers medications, such as aspirin or antiseptic solution, to relieve pain or prevent infection until patient can receive professional care, and gives prescribed medicines and treatments for illness. Changes beds, cleans equipment, and maintains infirmary for ward patients. Aids PHYSICIAN (medical ser.) during emergency situations. Keeps personal and medical records of employees. • **GED:** R3, M2, L3 • **SVP:** 30 days-3 mos • **Academic:** Ed=N, Eng=G • **Work Field:** 294 • **MPSMS:** 929 • **Aptitudes:** G3, V3, N4, S4, P3, Q3, K3, F3, M3, E5, C4 • **Temperaments:** J, P, S, V • **Stress:** E, S • **Physical:** V=L, H=L, L=L, W, H • **Work Env:** I • **Salary:** 2 • **Outlook:** 3

GERIATRIC NURSE ASSISTANT (medical ser.) • D.O.T. #355.674-026 • OES #66008 • Assists nursing staff in providing care to geriatric patients, applying knowledge of and techniques for dealing with problems associated with aging: Assists, instructs, or serves as role model for dysfunctional patients attempting to regain basic living skills, such as dressing, performing oral and personal hygiene, eating, grooming, communicating, ambulation, bladder and bowel control, and personal conduct. Gives direct patient care, such as bathing, dressing, and feeding patients, and assists in examinations and treatments [NURSE AIDE (medical ser.) 355.674-014]. May perform range of motion exercises with patients, such as flexing arms, legs, hands, feet, and neck, to prevent contraction of muscles and to maintain flexibility of joints. • **GED:** R3, M2, L3 • **SVP:** 30 days-3 mos • **Academic:** Ed=N, Eng=S • **Work Field:** 294 • **MPSMS:** 926 • **Aptitudes:** G4, V3, N4, S4, P4, Q3, K4, F4, M4, E5, C4 • **Temperaments:** P, S, V • **Stress:** E, S • **Physical:** V=L, H=L, L=M, W, H • **Work Env:** I • **Salary:** 2 • **Outlook:** 3

HOME HEALTH TECHNICIAN (medical ser.) • D.O.T. #079.224-010 • OES #66011 • Provides patient care, assistance, and instructions in household management and in-home medical care techniques to patients and families in home or homelike environment: Assists ambulatory and bedridden patient with dressing, bathing, grooming, and elimination. Transfers patient to and from wheelchair, and helps patient to walk to and from bed, shower, tub, and lavatory. Performs procedures and treatments as directed by professional staff, such as massages, hot and cold applications, dressing changes, wound irrigation, enemas, douches, catheterizations, and ostomy care, utilizing knowledge of body structures and function and aseptic techniques. Administers oral medications and injections under medical supervision. Measures and records patient temperature, pulse, and respiration rates, blood pressure, fluid intake and output, and performs throat inspection and urine tests to provide data for health-care team assessment. Teaches patients and family members approved medical techniques, such as mobility training in use of walkers, crutches, and other range-of-motion and supportive devices, to enable continuing home care, utilizing knowledge of physical rehabilitation techniques. Demonstrates basic home management techniques, such as housekeeping, nutrition, meal planning and preparation, and adapts techniques to patient's physical limitations. Guides and encourages patient and family to obtain optimal adjustment to illness or disability. • **GED:** R4, M3, L4 • **SVP:** 1-2 yrs • **Academic:** Ed=H, Eng=G • **Work Field:** 294, 296 • **MPSMS:** 926 • **Aptitudes:** G3, V3, N4, S3, P3, Q4, K3, F3, M3, E4, C4 • **Temperaments:** J, P, T, V • **Stress:** E • **Physical:** V=L, H=L, L=M, W, H • **Work Env:** I • **Salary:** 4 • **Outlook:** 4

MEDICAL ASSISTANT (medical ser.) • D.O.T. #079.367-010 • OES #66005 • Performs following duties under direction of PHYSICIAN (medical ser.) in examination and treatment of patients: Prepares treatment rooms for examination of patient. Drapes patients with covering and positions instruments and equipment. Hands instruments and materials to doctor as directed. Sterilizes and cleans instruments. Prepares inventory of supplies to determine items to be replenished. Interviews patients and checks pulse, temperature, blood pressure, weight, and height. May operate equipment, give injections or treatments, and assist in laboratory. May schedule appointments, receive money for bills, keep X-ray and other medical records, perform secretarial tasks, complete insurance forms, and maintain financial records. • **GED:** R4, M4, L4 • **SVP:** 1-2 yrs • **Academic:** Ed=H, Eng=G • **Work Field:** 294 • **MPSMS:** 929 • **Aptitudes:** G3, V3, N4, S4, P4, Q3, K3, F3, M3, E5, C5 • **Temperaments:** R • **Stress:** T • **Physical:** V=L, H=L, L=S, W, H • **Work Env:** I • **Salary:** 2 • **Outlook:** 4

MEDICATION AIDE (medical ser.) • D.O.T. #355.374-014 • OES #66026 • PHARMACY TECHNICIAN. Administers prescribed medications to patients and maintains related medical records under supervision of NURSE, GENERAL DUTY (medical ser.) 075.374-010, PHARMACIST, HOSPITAL (profess. & kin.) 074.161-010, or similar personnel: Receives supply of ordered medications and apportions, mixes, or assembles drugs for administration to patients. Verifies identity of patient receiving medication and records name of drug, dosage, and time of administration on specified forms or records. Presents medication to patient and observes ingestion or other application, or administers medication, using specified procedures. Takes vital signs or observes patient to detect response to specified types of medications and prepares report or notifies designated personnel of unexpected reactions. Documents reasons for which prescribed drugs are not administered, such as discharge of patient. May record and restock medication inventories. May give direct patient care such as bathing, dressing, and feeding patients, and assisting in examinations and treatments [NURSE AIDE (medical ser.) 355.674-014]. • **GED:** R3, M3, L3 • **SVP:** 3-6 mos • **Academic:** Ed=N, Eng=G • **Work Field:** 231, 294 • **MPSMS:** 926 • **Aptitudes:** G3, V3, N3, S3, P3, Q2, K2, F2, M3, E4, C4 • **Temperaments:** J, P, T • **Stress:** E • **Physical:** V=L, H=L, L=L, W, H • **Work Env:** I • **Salary:** 3 • **Outlook:** 3

MENTAL-RETARDATION AIDE (medical ser.) • D.O.T. #355.377-018 • OES #66014 • RESIDENT CARE AIDE. Assists in providing self-care training and therapeutic treatments to residents of mental retardation center: Demonstrates activities such as bathing and dressing to train residents in daily self-care practices. Converses with residents to reinforce positive behaviors and to promote social interaction. Serves meals and eats with residents to act as role model. Accompanies residents on shopping trips and instructs and counsels residents in purchase of personal items. Aids staff in administering therapeutic activities, such as physical exercises, occupational arts and crafts, and recreational games, to residents. Restrains disruptive residents to prevent injury to themselves and others. Observes and documents residents' behaviors, such as speech production, feeding patterns, and toilet training, to facilitate assessment and development of treatment goals. Attends to routine health-care needs of residents under supervision of medical personnel. May give medications as prescribed by PHYSICIAN

(medical ser.). May train parents or guardians in care of deinstitutionalized residents. • **GED:** R4, M3, L3 • **SVP:** 1-2 yrs • **Academic:** Ed=H, Eng=G • **Work Field:** 291, 294 • **MPSMS:** 926, 942 • **Aptitudes:** G3, V3, N4, S4, P4, Q4, K4, F4, M4, E5, C4 • **Temperaments:** J, P, V • **Stress:** E • **Physical:** V=L, H=L, L=M, W, H • **Work Env:** I, R • **Salary:** 3 • **Outlook:** 3

NURSE AIDE (medical ser.) • D.O.T. #355.674-014 • OES #66008 • HOSPITAL ATTENDANT; NURSING ASSISTANT. Assists in care of hospital patients, under direction of nursing and medical staff: Answers signal lights and bells to determine patients' needs. Bathes, dresses, and undresses patients. Serves and collects food trays and feeds patients requiring help. Transports patients to treatment units, using wheelchair or wheeled carriage, or assists them to walk. Drapes patients for examinations and treatments, and remains with patients, performing such duties as holding instruments and adjusting lights. Dusts and cleans patients' rooms. Changes bed linens, runs errands, directs visitors, and answers telephone. Takes and records temperature, pulse and respiration rates, and food and liquid intake and output, as directed. May apply compresses and hot water bottles. May clean, sterilize, store, prepare, and issue dressing packs, treatment trays, and other supplies and be designated as NURSE AIDE, CENTRAL SUPPLY (medical ser.). May prepare patients for delivery and clean delivery rooms, and be designated as NURSE AIDE, DELIVERY (medical ser.). May bathe, weigh, dress, and feed newborn babies and be designated as NURSE AIDE, NURSERY (medical ser.). May clean, sterilize, and assemble into packs, supplies and instruments used in surgery, and maintain cleanliness and order of operating rooms and be designated as NURSE AIDE, SURGERY (medical ser.). • **GED:** R3, M2, L2 • **SVP:** 3-6 mos • **Academic:** Ed=H, Eng=S • **Work Field:** 294 • **MPSMS:** 924 • **Aptitudes:** G4, V4, N4, S4, P4, Q4, K4, F3, M3, E4, C4 • **Temperaments:** P, S, V • **Stress:** E, S • **Physical:** V=G, H=L, L=M, W, S, H • **Work Env:** I, R • **Salary:** 3 • **Outlook:** 2

NURSE, PRACTICAL (medical ser.) • D.O.T. #354.374-010 • OES #66008 • Cares for patients and children in private homes, hospitals, sanitoriums, industrial plants, and similar institutions: Bathes and dresses bed patients, combs hair, and otherwise attends to their comfort and personal appearance. Cleans room, and changes bed linen. Takes and records temperature, pulse, and respiration rate. Gives medication as directed by PHYSICIAN (medical ser.) or NURSE, GENERAL DUTY (medical ser.), and makes notation of amount and time given. Gives enemas, douches, massages, and alcohol rubs. Applies hot and cold compresses and hot water bottles. Sterilizes equipment and supplies, using germicides, sterilizer, or autoclave. Prepares food trays, feeds patients, and records food and liquid intake and output. Cooks, washes, cleans, and does other housekeeping duties in private home. May give injections. May care for infants and small children in private home. For practical nurses meeting State licensing requirements see NURSE, LICENSED PRACTICAL (medical ser.). • **GED:** R3, M2, L3 • **SVP:** 3-6 mos • **Academic:** Ed=N, Eng=G • **Work Field:** 294 • **MPSMS:** 924 • **Aptitudes:** G3, V3, N4, S4, P4, Q4, K3, F4, M3, E4, C5 • **Temperaments:** P, S, V • **Stress:** E, S • **Physical:** V=L, H=L, L=M, W, S, H • **Work Env:** I • **Salary:** 3 • **Outlook:** 4

OCCUPATIONAL THERAPY AIDE (medical ser.) • D.O.T. #355.377-010 • OES #66021 • Assists OCCUPATIONAL THERAPIST (medical ser.) or OCCUPATIONAL THERAPY ASSISTANT (medical ser.) in occupational therapy program in hospital or similar institution: Performs program support services, such as transporting patient, assembling equipment, and preparing and maintaining work areas, as directed by OCCUPATIONAL THERAPIST (medical ser.) or OCCUPATIONAL THERAPY ASSISTANT (medical ser.). Assists in maintaining supplies and equipment. May assist in selected aspects or patient services as assigned. • **GED:** R4, M3, L4 • **SVP:** 6 mos-1 yr • **Academic:** Ed=H, Eng=G • **Work Field:** 294 • **MPSMS:** 924 • **Aptitudes:** G3, V3, N4, S3, P4, Q4, K4, F3, M3, E4, C4 • **Temperaments:** P, V • **Stress:** E • **Physical:** V=L, H=L, L=L, W, H • **Work Env:** I • **Salary:** 3 • **Outlook:** 3

ORDERLY (medical ser.) • D.O.T. #355.674-018 • OES #66008 • Performs any combination of following duties, as directed by nursing and medical staff, to care for hospitalized patients: Bathes patients and gives alcohol rubs. Cleans and shaves hair from skin area of operative cases. Measures and records intake and output of liquids, and takes and records temperature, and pulse and respiration rate. Gives enemas. Carries meal trays to patients. Lifts patients onto and from bed, and transports patients to hospital areas, such as operating and x-ray rooms, by rolling bed or using wheelchair or wheeled stretcher. Sets up equipment, such as oxygen tents, portable x-ray machines, and overhead irrigation bottles. Places anesthesia equipment near operating table, and assists in holding patient on table during administration of anesthetic. Sets up bone fracture equipment and assists PHYSICIAN (medical ser.) in putting on casts and braces. Maintains supply of hospital clothing for attending PHYSICIANS (medical ser.). Makes beds and collects soiled linen. Cleans rooms and corridors. Bathes deceased patients, accompanies body to morgue, and places personal belongings in mortuary box. May administer catheterizations and bladder irrigations. May accompany discharged mental patients home or those transferred to other institutions. • **GED:** R3, M2, L3 • **SVP:** 3-6 mos • **Academic:** Ed=H, Eng=S • **Work Field:** 294 • **MPSMS:** 926 • **Aptitudes:** G3, V3, N4, S4, P4, Q4, K3, F4, M3, E4, C4 • **Temperaments:** P, S, V • **Stress:** E, S • **Physical:** V=L, H=L, L=H, W, S, H • **Work Env:** I, W, R, F • **Salary:** 3 • **Outlook:** 2

ORTHOPEDIC ASSISTANT (medical ser.) • D.O.T. #712.661-010 • OES #32999 • ORTHOPEDIC CAST SPECIALIST. Applies, adjusts, and removes casts, assembles traction apparatus, and fits strappings and splints for orthopedic patients according to medical staff instructions, using handtools: Covers injured areas with specified protective materials, such as stockinette bandages, gauze, or rubber pads, preparatory to cast application. Wets, wraps, and molds plaster bandages around area of fracture. Trims plaster, using electric cutter. Removes whole and broken casts and alters position of cast to change setting of patient's limb or body part as directed. Assembles wooden, metal, plastic, or plaster material to make orthopedic splints, using handtools. Rigs pulleys, ropes, and frames to assemble fracture beds, using handtools. Attaches traction supports to patient's limb and adjusts support to specified tension. Assembles exercise frames, using handtools. Adjusts crutches and canes to fit patient. Instructs patients in care of and assists patients in walking with casts, braces, and crutches. • **GED:** R3, M2, L3 • **SVP:** 3-6 mos • **Academic:** Ed=N, Eng=S • **Work Field:** 294 • **MPSMS:** 604, 929 • **Aptitudes:** G3, V3, N4, S3, P3, Q4, K4, F3, M3, E5, C5 • **Temperaments:** M, P, T • **Physical:** V=L, H=N, L=M, W, S, H • **Work Env:** I • **Salary:** 3 • **Outlook:** 3

PERFUSIONIST (medical ser.) • D.O.T. #078.362-034 • OES #32999 • Sets up and operates heart-lung machine in hospital to take over functions of patient's heart and lungs during surgery or respiratory failure: Consults with surgeon or physician to obtain patient information needed to set up heart-lung machine. Assembles, sets up, and tests heart-lung machine to ensure that machine functions according to specifications. Operates heart-lung machine to regulate blood circulation and composition and oxygen and carbon dioxide levels, to administer drugs, and to control body temperature during surgery or respiratory failure of patient. Changes quantities administered at direction of physician, surgeon, or anesthesiologist. Cleans, repairs, and adjusts malfunctioning parts of heart-lung machine. • **GED:** R4, M3, L4 • **SVP:** 2-4 yrs • **Academic:** Ed=H, Eng=S • **Work Field:** 294 • **MPSMS:** 925 • **Aptitudes:** G2, V2, N3, S3, P3, Q3, K2, F3, M3, E5, C5 • **Temperaments:** P, S, T • **Stress:** E, S • **Physical:** V=L, H=L, L=L, H • **Work Env:** I • **Salary:** 4 • **Outlook:** 3

PHYSICAL THERAPY AIDE (medical ser.) • D.O.T. #355.354-010 • OES #68032 • PHYSICAL THERAPY ATTENDANT. Prepares patients for physical therapy treatments, assists PHYSICAL THERAPIST (medical ser.) or PHYSICAL THERAPIST ASSISTANT (medical ser.) during administration of treatments, and administers routine treatments: Assists patients to dress, undress, and put on and remove assistive and supportive devices, such as braces, splints, and slings, prior to and after treatments. Secures patients into or onto therapy equipment. Supports, turns, and stabilizes patients to assist PHYSICAL THERAPIST (medical ser.) or PHYSICAL THERAPIST ASSISTANT (medical ser.) to administer treatments, tests, and evaluations. Administers routine treatments, such as hydrotherapy, hot and cold packs, and paraffin bath. Safeguards, motivates, and assists patients practicing exercises and functional activities. Observes patients during treatments and reports signs of fatigue, distress, or other problems. Transports patients to and from treatment area and transfers patients between conveyances and treatment equipment, using transfer techniques appropriate to patients' conditions. Changes linens and arranges treatment supplies and equipment according to standard procedure or written or oral instructions. Cleans work area and equipment after treatment. Prepares hydrotherapy equipment at appropriate temperature and adds disinfectant solutions. Performs miscellaneous clerical and related duties, such as answering telephone, taking messages, running errands, delivering messages, and filing patient records. May record treatment given and equipment used. May inventory and requisition supplies and equipment. May adjust fit of supportive and assistive devices for patients, as instructed. May be assigned to specific type of treatment or patient service and be designated PHYSICAL THERAPY AIDE, HYDROTHERAPY (medical ser.); PHYSICAL THERAPY AIDE, TRANSPORT (medical ser.). • **GED:** R3, M2, L3 • **SVP:** 3-6 mos • **Academic:** Ed=N, Eng=G • **Work Field:** 294 • **MPSMS:** 924 • **Aptitudes:** G3, V3, N4, S4, P4, Q4, K3, F3, M3, E4, C4 • **Temperaments:** I, J, M, P, T • **Stress:** E • **Physical:** V=L, H=N, L=M, W, S, H • **Work Env:** I • **Salary:** 3 • **Outlook:** 3

PODIATRIC ASSISTANT (medical ser.) • D.O.T. #079.374-018 • OES #66005 • Assists PODIATRIST (medical ser.) in patient care. Prepares patients for treatment, sterilizes instruments, performs general office duties, and assists PODIATRIST (medical ser.) in preparing dressings, administering treatments, and developing X-rays. • **GED:** R4, M2, L4 • **SVP:** 1-2 yrs • **Academic:** Ed=H, Eng=S • **Work Field:** 231 • **MPSMS:** 929 • **Aptitudes:** G3, V4, N3, S4, P4, Q2, K3, F3, M3, E5, C5 • **Temperaments:** P, V • **Stress:** E • **Physical:** V=L, H=L, L=L • **Work Env:** I • **Salary:** 4 • **Outlook:** 3

PSYCHIATRIC AIDE (medical ser.) • D.O.T. #355.377-014 • OES #66014 • ASSISTANT THERAPY AIDE; ASYLUM ATTENDANT; CHARGE ATTENDANT; PSYCHIATRIC ATTENDANT; WARD ATTENDANT. Assists mentally ill patients, working under direction of nursing and medical staff: Accompanies patients to shower rooms, and assists them in bathing, dressing, and grooming. Accompanies patients to and from wards for examination and treatment, and administers prescribed medications. Assists patients in becoming accustomed to hospital routine and encourages them to participate in social and recreational activities, such as visiting, sports, and dramatics, to promote rehabilitation. Observes patients to ensure that none wanders from grounds. Feeds patients or attempts to persuade them to eat, and notes reasons for rejection of food. Observes patients to detect unusual behavior, and aids or restrains them to prevent injury to themselves or other patients. May escort patients off grounds for medical or dental treatment, to library for selection of reading materials, and to church services, motion pictures, or athletic contests. May clean rooms, ward furnishings, walls, and floors, using water, detergents, and disinfectants. May change bed linens. May be designated as WARD SUPERVISOR (medical ser.) when responsible for patient care and other services of a single ward. • **GED:** R3, M2, L3 • **SVP:** 3-6 mos • **Academic:** Ed=A, Eng=G • **Work Field:** 294 • **MPSMS:** 924 • **Aptitudes:** G3, V3, N4, S4, P4, Q4, K4, F4, M3, E5, C4 • **Temperaments:** J, P, V • **Stress:** E • **Physical:** V=L, H=L, L=M, W, H • **Work Env:** I • **Salary:** 3 • **Outlook:** 3

RESPIRATORY-THERAPY AIDE (medical ser.) • D.O.T. #355.674-022 • OES #66099 • Assists personnel in Respiratory Therapy Department of hospital, performing any or all of following tasks: Cleans, disinfects, and sterilizes equipment and supplies used in administration of respiratory therapy, using sponges, brushes, and cleaning solutions, and placing items in sterilization chamber for designated time period to ensure absence of contamination. Examines equipment to detect indications of disrepair, such as worn tubes or loose connections, and notifies supervisory staff when such indications are noted. Actuates equipment and observes gauges measuring pressure, rate of flow, and continuity to test equipment, and notifies supervisor when malfunctions are observed. Assists supervisory personnel in maintenance of inventory records. Delivers oxygen tanks and other equipment and supplies to specified hospital locations. Answers phone and takes and relays messages regarding department operations. Assists in administration of gas or aerosol therapy to patients. • **GED:** R3, M3, L3 • **SVP:** 3-6 mos • **Academic:** Ed=N, Eng=S • **Work Field:** 031, 212 • **MPSMS:** 926 • **Aptitudes:** G4, V4, N4, S3, P3, Q3, K3, F3, M4, E4, C5 • **Temperaments:** M, V • **Physical:** V=L, H=L, L=M, W, H • **Work Env:** I • **Salary:** 3 • **Outlook:** 3

SURGICAL TECHNICIAN (medical ser.) • D.O.T. #079.374-022 • OES #32928 • OPERATING-ROOM TECHNICIAN; SURGICAL ORDERLY. Performs any combination of following tasks before, during, and after operation: Washes, shaves, and sterilizes, operative area of patient. Scrubs hands and dons cap, mask, gown, and rubber gloves. Places equipment and supplies in operating room according to SURGEON'S (medical ser.) directions, and arranges instruments as specified by NURSE, GENERAL DUTY (medical ser.). Aids team to don gowns and gloves. Maintains specified supply of such fluids as plasma, saline, blood, and glucose for use during operation. Adjusts lights and other equipment as directed. Washes and sterilizes used equipment, using germicides, autoclave, and sterilizer. Cleans operating room. Counts sponges, needles, and instruments used during operation. May assist in administering blood, plasma, or other injections and transfusions. May hand SURGEON (medical ser.) I instruments and supplies, hold retractors, and cut sutures, as directed during operation. • **GED:** R4, M4, L3 • **SVP:** 1-2 yrs • **Academic:** Ed=A, Eng=S • **Work Field:** 294 • **MPSMS:** 929 • **Aptitudes:** G3, V3, N4, S4, P4, Q3, K4, F3, M3, E4, C4 • **Temperaments:** M, S, V • **Stress:** S • **Physical:** V=L, H=G, L=S, W, H • **Work Env:** I • **Salary:** 4 • **Outlook:** 4

GOE: 10.03.03 Care of Others

BLIND AIDE (per. ser.) • D.O.T. #359.573-010 • OES #68035 • CLERK GUIDE; ESCORT, BLIND. Performs any combination of the following duties to assist blind persons: Drives motor vehicle to transport blind persons to specified locations according to their personal and business activities. Carries brief or sample cases. Assists client with dressing, moving from one location to another, obtaining information or personal service. Prepares and maintains records of assistance rendered. May type correspondence and reports [CLERK-TYPIST (clerical)]. May assist teacher of blind in routine classroom activities such as toiletry or group school activities. • **GED:** R3, M2, L2 • **SVP:** 30 days-3 mos • **Academic:** Ed=N, Eng=G • **Work Field:** 291 • **MPSMS:** 909 • **Aptitudes:** G3, V3, N4, S3, P4, Q3, K3, F4, M3, E3, C4 • **Temperaments:** P, V • **Stress:** E • **Physical:** V=L, H=L, L=L, W, H • **Work Env:** B • **Salary:** 2 • **Outlook:** 2

CHILD-CARE ATTENDANT, SCHOOL (per. ser.) • D.O.T. #355.674-010 • OES #68038 • Attends to personal needs of handicapped children while in school to receive specialized academic and physical training: Wheels handicapped children to classes, lunchrooms, and treatment rooms. Secures children in equipment, such as slings or stretchers, and places into baths or pools for physical therapy treatment. Helps children to walk, board buses, put on prosthetic appliances, eat, dress, and perform other physical activities as their needs require. May use hoist to raise and lower children into pools or baths. • **GED:** R3, M1, L2 • **SVP:** 30 days-3 mos • **Academic:** Ed=N, Eng=S • **Work Field:** 294 • **MPSMS:** 929 • **Aptitudes:** G4, V4, N4, S4, P4, Q4, K4, F4, M4, E5, C5 • **Temperaments:** J, P, V • **Stress:** E • **Physical:** V=L, H=N, L=M, W, S, H • **Work Env:** I, W • **Salary:** 1 • **Outlook:** 4

CHILDREN'S TUTOR (dom. ser.) • D.O.T. #099.227-010 • OES #31399 • Cares for children in private home, overseeing their recreation, diet, health, and deportment: Teaches children foreign languages, and good health and personal habits. Arranges parties, outings, and picnics for children. Takes disciplinary measures to control children's behavior. Ascertains cause of behavior problems of children and devises means for solving them. When duties are confined to care of young children may be designated CHILDREN'S TUTOR, NURSERY (dom. ser.). • **GED:** R4, M2, L4 • **SVP:** 6 mos-1 yr • **Academic:** Ed=H, Eng=S • **Work Field:** 291,

296 • **MPSMS:** 942 • **Aptitudes:** G3, V3, N3, S4, P4, Q4, K4, F4, M4, E5, C5 • **Temperaments:** D, P, V • **Stress:** A • **Physical:** V=L, H=G, L=L, W, H • **Work Env:** I • **Salary:** 3 • **Outlook:** 4

GUARD, SCHOOL-CROSSING (gov. ser.) • D.O.T. #371.567-010 • OES #63044 • Guards street crossings during hours when children are going to or coming from school: Directs actions of children and traffic at street intersections to ensure safe crossing. Records license numbers of vehicles disregarding traffic signals and reports infractions to police. May escort children across street. May place caution signs at designated points before going on duty and remove signs at end of shift. May stop speeding vehicles and warn drivers. • **GED:** R2, M1, L2 • **SVP:** 2-30 days • **Academic:** Ed=N, Eng=S • **Work Field:** 293 • **MPSMS:** 959 • **Aptitudes:** G3, V3, N4, S4, P5, Q4, K4, F5, M4, E4, C4 • **Temperaments:** P • **Stress:** E • **Physical:** V=G, H=L, L=S, W, H • **Work Env:** O • **Salary:** 1 • **Outlook:** 2

HOME ATTENDANT (per. ser.) • D.O.T. #354.377-014 • OES #66011 • HOME HEALTH AIDE. Cares for elderly, convalescent, or handicapped persons in patient's home, performing any combination of the following tasks: Changes bed linens, washes and irons patient's laundry, and cleans patient's quarters. Purchases, prepares, and serves food for patient and other members of family, following special prescribed diets. Assists patients into and out of bed, automobile, or wheelchair, to lavatory, and up and downstairs. Assists patient to dress, bathe, and groom self. Massages patient and applies preparations and treatments, such as liniment or alcohol rubs and heat-lamp stimulation. Administers prescribed oral medications under written direction of physician or as directed by home care nurse. Accompanies ambulatory patients outside home, serving as guide, companion, and aide. Entertains patient, reads aloud, and plays cards or other games with patient. Performs variety of miscellaneous duties as requested, such as obtaining household supplies and running errands. May maintain records of services performed and of apparent condition of patient. May visit several households to provide daily health care to patients. • **GED:** R3, M2, L2 • **SVP:** 30 days-3 mos • **Academic:** Ed=N, Eng=G • **Work Field:** 291, 294 • **MPSMS:** 924, 941, 942 • **Aptitudes:** G3, V3, N4, S4, P4, Q4, K3, F4, M3, E4, C4 • **Temperaments:** J, P, V • **Stress:** E • **Physical:** V=L, H=L, L=M, W, H • **Work Env:** B • **Salary:** 2 • **Outlook:** 4

NURSERY SCHOOL ATTENDANT (any ind.) • D.O.T. #359.677-018 • OES #68038 • CHILD-CARE LEADER; CHILD-DAY-CARE CENTER WORKER; DAY CARE WORKER. Organizes and leads activities of prekindergarten children in nursery schools or in play rooms operated for patrons of theaters, department stores, hotels, and similar organizations: Helps children remove outer garments. Organizes and participates in games, reads to children, and teaches them simple painting, drawing, handwork, songs, and similar activities. Directs children in eating, resting, and toileting. Helps children develop habits of caring for own clothing and picking up and putting away toys and books. Maintains discipline. May serve meals and refreshments to children and regulate rest periods. May assist in such tasks as preparing food and cleaning quarters. • **GED:** R3, M2, L3 • **SVP:** 3-6 mos • **Academic:** Ed=N, Eng=S • **Work Field:** 291 • **MPSMS:** 942 • **Aptitudes:** G3, V3, N4, S4, P4, Q4, K4, F4, M4, E5, C4 • **Temperaments:** P, V • **Stress:** E • **Physical:** V=N, H=L, L=M, W, S, H • **Work Env:** B, N • **Salary:** 2 • **Outlook:** 2

PLAYROOM ATTENDANT (any ind.) • D.O.T. #359.677-026 • OES #68038 • KINDERGARTNER. Entertains children in nursery of department store, country club, or similar establishment as service to patrons. Reads aloud, organizes and participates in games, and gives elementary lessons in arts or crafts. • **GED:** R3, M2, L3 • **SVP:** 30 days-3 mos • **Academic:** Ed=N, Eng=S • **Work Field:** 291, 297 • **MPSMS:** 942 • **Aptitudes:** G3, V3, N3, S3, P3, Q4, K3, F3, M3, E4, C4 • **Temperaments:** F, P, V • **Stress:** E • **Physical:** V=N, H=L, L=L, W, S, H • **Work Env:** I • **Salary:** 2 • **Outlook:** 2

Leading-Influencing 11

An interest in leading and influencing others by using high-level verbal or numerical abilities. You can satisfy this interest through study and work in a variety of professional fields. You may enjoy the challenge and responsibility of leadership. You could seek work in administration or management. You may prefer working with technical details. You could find a job in finance, law, social research, or public relations. You may like to help others learn. Perhaps working in education would appeal to you.

11.01 Mathematics and Statistics

Workers in this group use advanced math and statistics to solve problems and conduct research. They analyze and interpret numerical data for planning and decision making. Some of these workers may first study and then determine how computers may best be used to solve problems or process information. Colleges, large businesses and industries, research organizations, and government agencies use these workers.

✔ **What kind of work would you do?**
Your work activities would depend upon your specific job. For example, you might:

- apply formulas and mathematical principles to solve technical problems in engineering or the physical sciences.
- develop systems for handling information for businesses and industries.

- design insurance and pension plans and set premiums and benefit rates.
- plan and write computer programs for control of automated operations.
- convert business problems into numbers and symbols for electronic data processing.

✔ **What skills and abilities do you need for this kind of work?**
To do this kind of work, you must be able to:

- use advanced logic and scientific thinking to solve a variety of complex problems.
- understand and use advanced math and statistics.
- use personal judgment, and known facts to make decisions and deal with problems.

- use computer technology to solve problems or process large amounts of information.
- speak and write clearly and accurately.
- use technical terms, math and computer symbols, and complex charts and graphs.

✔ **How do you know if you would like or could learn to do this kind of work?**
The following questions may give you clues about yourself as you consider this group of jobs.

- Have you had courses in advanced mathematics? Do you enjoy working with complex numerical ideas?

- Have you had experience using a pocket calculator? Can you enter long columns of numbers accurately? Can you use all of the mathematical functions on the machine?

- Do you like to solve written problems in mathematics? Can you easily identify the procedures for solving such problems?

✔ **How can you prepare for and enter this kind of work?**

Occupations in this group usually require education and/or training extending from two years to over ten years, depending upon the specific kind of work. Almost all jobs in this group require four or more years of study in mathematics and statistics at the college level. Experience in banking, accounting, or a related field is an additional requirement for some jobs. Other jobs require experience and training in a scientific or technical area.

Jobs with the federal government require a civil service examination.

✔ **What else should you consider about these jobs?**

Workers in this group are expected to keep up with developments and trends in their specific areas. They attend seminars and workshops, or study for advanced degrees.

If you think you would like to do this kind of work, look at the job titles listed on the following pages.

GOE: 11.01.01 Data Processing Design

CUSTOMER-SUPPORT SPECIALIST (whole. tr.) • D.O.T. #020.224-010 • OES #25102 • Converts client's manual accounting systems to computerized systems, trains client's employees to program systems, and diagnoses computer hardware malfunctions: Reviews and evaluates client's manual accounting and bookkeeping systems, using established accounting procedures to convert from manual system to computerized system. Contacts computer software vendor to order initial supply of forms. Teaches client's employees to program computer, using standardized programming methods and observing hands-on practices. Reviews client's operational procedures to implement improvements. Troubleshoots computer hardware malfunctions, using electronic test meter and tools, and repairs simple malfunctions or writes service order for use of repair personnel. • **GED:** R4, M4, L4 • **SVP:** 2-4 yrs • **Academic:** Ed=H, Eng=G • **Work Field:** 111, 232, 296 • **MPSMS:** 892 • **Aptitudes:** G2, V2, N2, S4, P3, Q1, K4, F4, M4, E5, C4 • **Temperaments:** P, T, V • **Stress:** E • **Physical:** V=L, H=L, L=S, W, H • **Work Env:** I • **Salary:** 4 • **Outlook:** 4

DIRECTOR, RECORDS MANAGEMENT (profess. & kin.) • D.O.T. #161.117-014 • OES #21905 • Plans, develops, and administers records management policies designed to facilitate effective and efficient handling of business records and other information: Plans development and implementation of records management policies intended to standardize filing, protecting, and retrieving records, reports, and other information contained on paper, microfilm, computer program, or other media. Coordinates and directs, through subordinate managers, activities of departments involved with records management analysis, reports analysis, and supporting technical, clerical micrographics, and printing services. Evaluates staff reports, utilizing knowledge of principles of records and information management, administrative processes and systems, cost control, governmental record keeping requirements, and organizational objectives. Confers with other administrators to assure compliance with policies, procedures, and practices of records management program. • **GED:** R5, M4, L5 • **SVP:** 4-10 yrs • **Academic:** Ed=B, Eng=G • **Work Field:** 211, 295 • **MPSMS:** 891 • **Aptitudes:** G2, V2, N3, S3, P3, Q2, K5, F5, M5, E5, C3 • **Temperaments:** D, M, P • **Stress:** E, A • **Physical:** V=N, H=N, L=S • **Work Env:** I • **Salary:** 5 • **Outlook:** 5

ENGINEERING ANALYST (profess. & kin.) • D.O.T. #020.067-010 • OES #22127 • APPLIED MATHEMATICIAN; COMPUTATIONAL ENGINEER; COMPUTING ANALYST; SYSTEMS ANALYST, ENGINEERING-SCIENTIFIC. Conducts logical analyses of scientific, engineering, and other technical problems and formulates mathematical models of problems for solution by digital computer: Analyzes assigned problem, such as optimal design configuration of ballistic missile or computer system for industrial process control. Consults with engineering or scientific personnel to refine definition of project and prepare mathematical simulation of physical system under study. Searches library for applicable mathematical formulations and data pertinent to problem. Prepares mathematical model of problem area, such as set of partial differential equations to relate constants, and variables, restrictions, alternatives, objectives, and their numerical parameters, and inserts relevant data. Reduces problem to computer-processable form, utilizing knowledge of numerical analysis. Confers with originator of problem, using knowledge of subject sciences and their language, to discuss adequacy and applicability of computer output or need for reformulation of model. Prepares reports. May use small scale analog or keyboard input digital computer to assist in or test parts of model formulation. May supervise other ENGINEERING ANALYSTS (profess. & kin.). • **GED:** R6, M6, L5 • **SVP:** 2-4 yrs • **Academic:** Ed=B, Eng=G • **Work Field:** 251 • **MPSMS:** 700, 710, 723 • **Aptitudes:** G1, V2, N1, S2, P2, Q2, K4, F4, M4, E5, C5 • **Temperaments:** J, M, V • **Physical:** V=L, H=N, L=S • **Work Env:** I • **Salary:** 4 • **Outlook:** 4

FORMS ANALYST (profess. & kin.) • D.O.T. #161.267-018 • OES #21905 • Examines and evaluates format and function of business forms to develop new, or improve existing forms format, usage, and control: Reviews forms to evaluate need for revision, consolidation, or discontinuation, using knowledge of form use, workflow, document flow, and compatibility with manual or machine processing. Confers with form users to gather recommendations for improvements, considering such characteristics as form necessity, completeness, design, text, and specifications as to size and color of paper, style of typeface, and number of copies. May design, draft or prepare finished master copy for new or modified form, or confer with printer's representative to specify changes in format and approve proof copies. Prepares and issues written instructions for use of forms in accordance with organizational policies, procedures, and practices. Keeps records to update information concerning form origin, function, necessity, usage, cost, and stock level. • **GED:** R4, M3, L4 • **SVP:** 2-4 yrs • **Academic:** Ed=B, Eng=S • **Work Field:** 211 • **MPSMS:** 891 • **Aptitudes:** G2, V2, N3, S3, P3, Q2, K5, F5, M5, E5, C3 • **Temperaments:** D, M, P, V • **Stress:** A • **Physical:** V=G, H=G, L=S • **Work Env:** I • **Salary:** 4 • **Outlook:** 3

INFORMATION SCIENTIST (profess. & kin.) • D.O.T. #109.067-010 • OES #25102 • Designs information system to provide management or clients with specific data from computer storage, utilizing knowledge of electronic data processing principles, mathematics, and computer capabilities: Develops and designs methods and procedures for collecting, organizing, interpreting, and classifying information for input into computer and retrieval of specific information from computer, utilizing knowledge of symbolic language and optical or pattern recognition principles. Develops alternate designs to resolve problems in input, storage, and retrieval of information. May specialize in specific field of information science, such as scientific or engineering research, or in specific discipline, such as business, medicine, education, aerospace, or library science. • GED: R5, M5, L5 • SVP: 2-4 yrs • **Academic:** Ed=B, Eng=G • **Work Field:** 244 • **MPSMS:** 933 • **Aptitudes:** G2, V2, N1, S2, P4, Q4, K4, F4, M4, E5, C5 • **Temperaments:** D, M, T • **Physical:** V=L, H=N, L=S • **Work Env:** I • **Salary:** 4 • **Outlook:** 4

MANAGER, ELECTRONIC DATA PROCESSING (profess. & kin.) • D.O.T. #169.167-030 • OES #13017 • DIRECTOR, DATA PROCESSING. Directs and coordinates planning and production activities of electronic data processing I division: Consults with management to define boundaries and priorities of tentative projects, discuss equipment acquisitions, determine specific information requirements of management, scientists, or engineers, and allocate operating time of computer systems. Confers with department heads involved with proposed projects to ensure cooperation and further define nature of project. Consults with SYSTEMS ENGINEER, ELECTRONIC DATA PROCESSING (profess. & kin.) to define equipment needs. Reviews project feasibility studies. Establishes work standards. Assigns, schedules, and reviews work. Interprets policies, purposes, and goals of organization to subordinates. Prepares progress reports to inform management of project development and deviation from predicted goals. Contracts with management specialists or technical personnel to solve problems. Revises computer operating schedule to introduce new program testing and operating runs. Reviews reports of computer and peripheral equipment production, malfunction, and maintenance to ascertain costs and plan operating changes within his department. Analyzes data requirements and flow to recommend reorganization or departmental realinement within company. Participates in decisions concerning personnel staffing and promotions within electronic data-processing department. Directs training of subordinates. Prepares proposals and solicits sales of systems analysis, programing, and computer services to outside firms. • GED: R6, M5, L5 • SVP: 4-10 yrs • **Academic:** Ed=B, Eng=G • **Work Field:** 295 • **MPSMS:** 890 • **Aptitudes:** G1, V1, N1, S2, P2, Q3, K4, F4, M4, E4, C5 • **Temperaments:** D, J, M, P, V • **Stress:** E, A • **Physical:** V=L, H=N, L=S, H • **Work Env:** I • **Salary:** 5 • **Outlook:** 4

OPERATIONS-RESEARCH ANALYST (profess. & kin.) • D.O.T. #020.067-018 • OES #25302 • Conducts analyses of management and operational problems and formulates mathematical or simulation models of problem for solution by computers or other methods: Analyzes problem in terms of management information and conceptualizes and defines problem. Studies information and selects plan from competitive proposals that affords maximum probability of profit or effectiveness in relation to cost or risk. Prepares model of problem in form of one or several equations that relates constants and variables, restrictions, alternatives, conflicting objectives and their numerical parameters. Defines data requirements and gathers and validates information applying judgment and statistical tests. Specifies manipulative or computational methods to be applied to model. Performs validation and testing of model to ensure adequacy, or determines need for reformulation. Prepares reports to management defining problem, evaluation, and possible solution. Evaluates implementation and effectiveness of research. May design, conduct, and evaluate experimental operational models where insufficient data exists to formulate model. May specialize in research and preparation of contract proposals specifying competence of organization to perform research, development, or production work. May develop and apply time and cost networks, such as Program Evaluation and Review Techniques (PERT), to plan and control large projects. May work in association with engineers, scientists, and management personnel in business, government, health, transportation, energy, manufacturing, environmental sciences or other technologies. • GED: R6, M6, L6 • SVP: 2-4 yrs • **Academic:** Ed=B, Eng=S • **Work Field:** 251 • **MPSMS:** 890 • **Aptitudes:** G1, V1, N1, S2, P3, Q3, K4, F4, M4, E4, C5 • **Temperaments:** J, M, V • **Physical:** V=N, H=N, L=S • **Work Env:** I • **Salary:** 4 • **Outlook:** 4

PROGRAMER, CHIEF, BUSINESS (profess. & kin.) • D.O.T. #020.167-018 • OES #25105 • COORDINATOR, COMPUTER PROGRAMING; LEAD PROGRAMER. Plans, schedules, and directs preparation of programs to process business data and solve business-oriented problems by the use of electronic data processing equipment: Consults with managerial and systems analysis personnel to clarify program intent, indicate problems, suggest changes, and determine extent of automatic programing and coding techniques to use. Assigns, coordinates, and reviews work of programing personnel. Develops own programs and routines from work flow charts or diagrams. Consolidates segments of program into complete sequence of terms and symbols. Breaks down program and input data for successive computer passes, depending on such factors as computer storage capacity and speed, extent of peripheral equipment, and intended use of output data. Analyzes test runs on computer to correct or direct correction of coded program and input data. Revises or directs revision of existing programs to increase operating efficiency or adapt to new requirements. Compiles documentation of program development and subsequent revisions. Trains subordinates in programing and program coding. Prescribes standards of terminology and symbology to simplify interpretation of programs. Collaborates with computer manufacturers and other users to develop new programing methods. Prepares records and reports. • GED: R5, M5, L5 • SVP: 2-4 yrs • **Academic:** Ed=B, Eng=G • **Work Field:** 232, 281 • **MPSMS:** 890 • **Aptitudes:** G2, V2, N2, S2, P3, Q2, K4, F4, M4, E4, C5 • **Temperaments:** D, J, M, P, V • **Stress:** E • **Physical:** V=L, H=L, L=S, H • **Work Env:** I • **Salary:** 4 • **Outlook:** 4

PROGRAMER, ENGINEERING AND SCIENTIFIC (profess. & kin.) • D.O.T. #020.167-022 • OES #25105 • Converts scientific, engineering, and other technical problem formulations to format processable by computer: Resolves symbolic formulations, prepares flow charts and block diagrams, and encodes resultant equations for processing by applying knowledge of advanced mathematics, such as differential equations and numerical analysis, and understanding of computer capabilities and limitations. Confers with engineering and technical personnel to resolve problems of intent, inaccuracy, or feasibility of computer processing. Reviews results of computer runs with interested personnel to determine necessity for modifications or reruns. Develops new subroutines or expands program to simplify statement, programming, or coding of future problems. For numerical control programming, see [TOOL PROGRAMER, NUMERICAL CONTROL (any ind.)]. • GED: R6, M6, L6 • SVP: 4-10 yrs • **Academic:** Ed=B, Eng=S • **Work Field:** 232, 244 • **MPSMS:** 700, 721, 723 • **Aptitudes:** G1, V1, N1, S2, P3, Q2, K4, F4, M4, E4, C5 • **Temperaments:** J, M • **Physical:** V=L, H=N, L=S • **Work Env:** I • **Salary:** 5 • **Outlook:** 3

PROGRAMER, INFORMATION SYSTEM (profess. & kin.) • D.O.T. #020.187-010 • OES #25105 • Develops and writes natural and artificial language computer programs to store, locate, and retrieve specific documents, data, and information: Develops computer programs for input and retrieval of physical science, engineering or medical information, text analysis, and language, law, military, or library science data. Writes programs for classification, indexing, input, storage, and retrieval of data and facts, display devices, and interfacing with other systems equipment. Devises sample input data to test adequacy of program and observes or runs test of program, using sample or actual data. Corrects program errors by altering program steps and sequence. Confers with INFORMATION SCIENTIST (profess. & kin.) to resolve questions of program intent, input data acquisition, time sharing, output requirements, coding use and modification, and inclusion of internal checks and controls for system integrity. • GED: R5, M5, L5 • SVP: 2-4 yrs • **Academic:** Ed=B, Eng=S • **Work Field:** 244 • **MPSMS:** 721, 933 • **Aptitudes:** G1, V1, N1, S2, P2, Q1, K4, F4, M4, E5, C5 • **Temperaments:** M, T • **Physical:** V=L, H=N, L=S, H • **Work Env:** I • **Salary:** 4 • **Outlook:** 4

PROGRAMER, PROCESS CONTROL (profess. & kin.) • D.O.T. #020.187-014 • OES #25111 • Plans and writes computer programs for control systems that automate operations: Writes complete sequence of machine instructions and routines necessary to complete processing cycle. Develops programs according to specification and standards of both process and computer system. Prepares flow charts, documents, and sequence logic; and methods of input, monitor, and display for open and closed loop, analog or digital systems. Writes programs for such systems as steel making and rolling mill operations, sanitation plants, combustion systems, chemical and fuel recovery systems, computerized production testing, automatic truck loading, steam boilers, and other commercial and industrial process control systems. For numerical control programming, see TOOL PROGRAMER, NUMERICAL CONTROL (any ind.). • **GED:** R5, M5, L5 • **SVP:** 2-4 yrs • **Academic:** Ed=A, Eng=S • **Work Field:** 244 • **MPSMS:** 567, 568 • **Aptitudes:** G1, V1, N1, S2, P3, Q2, K4, F4, M4, E5, C5 • **Temperaments:** M, R, T • **Physical:** V=N, H=N, L=S • **Work Env:** I • **Salary:** 4 • **Outlook:** 4

PROGRAMMER, BUSINESS (profess. & kin.) • D.O.T. #020.162-014 • OES #25105 • Converts symbolic statements of administrative data or business problems to detailed logical flow charts for coding into computer language: Analyzes all or part of workflow chart or diagram representing business problem by applying knowledge of computer capabilities, subject matter, algebra, and symbolic logic to develop sequence of program steps. Confers with supervisor and representatives of departments concerned with program to resolve questions of program intent, output requirements, input data acquisition, extent of automatic programming and coding use and modification, and inclusion of internal checks and controls. Writes detailed logical flow chart in symbolic form to represent work order of data to be processed by computer system, and to describe input, output, and arithmetic and logical operations involved. Converts detailed logical flow chart to language processable by computer [PROGRAMMER, DETAIL (clerical) 219.367- 026]. Devises sample input data to provide test of program adequacy. Prepares block diagrams to specify equipment configuration. Observes or operates computer to test coded program, using actual or sample input data. Corrects program errors by such methods as altering program steps and sequence. Prepares written instructions (run book) to guide operating personnel during production runs. Analyzes, reviews, and rewrites programs to increase operating efficiency or adapt to new requirements. Compiles documentation of program development and subsequent revisions. May specialize in writing programs for one make and type of computer. May operate computer to run daily programs. May direct and coordinate activities of other workers. • **GED:** R5, M5, L4 • **SVP:** 2-4 yrs • **Academic:** Ed=A, Eng=S • **Work Field:** 232, 244 • **MPSMS:** 890 • **Aptitudes:** G2, V2, N2, S2, P3, Q2, K4, F4, M4, E5, C4 • **Temperaments:** D, T • **Physical:** V=N, H=N, L=S, H • **Work Env:** I • **Salary:** 4 • **Outlook:** 4

PROGRAMMER, DETAIL (clerical) • D.O.T. #219.367-026 • OES #25108 • PROGRAM CODER; PROGRAMMER TRAINEE. Selects symbols from coding system peculiar to make or model of digital computer and codes II successive steps of completed program for conversion to machine instructions to process data or to control industrial processes: Reads and interprets sequence of alphabetic, numeric, or special characters from handbook or memory for each program step to translate into machine language or pseudo (symbolic) code that can be converted by computer processor into machine instructions. Records symbols on worksheet for transfer to punchcards or machine input tape. Marks code sheet to indicate relationship of code to program steps to simplify debugging of program. Confers with programming personnel to clarify intent of program steps. May work as understudy to PROGRAMMER, BUSINESS (profess. & kin.)020.162-014 or PROGRAMMER, ENGINEERING AND SCIENTIFIC (profess. & kin.)020.167-022 performing such additional tasks as converting flow charts and diagram of simple problem from rough to finished form or making minor changes in established programs to adapt programs to new requirements. May modify existing programs. May operate computer to run daily programs. • **GED:** R4, M3, L4 • **SVP:** 6 mos-1 yr • **Academic:** Ed=N, Eng=S • **Work Field:** 232 • **MPSMS:** 890 • **Aptitudes:** G3, V3, N4, S4, P3, Q3, K3, F4, M4, E5, C5 • **Temperaments:** J, T • **Physical:** V=L, H=N, L=S, H • **Work Env:** I • **Salary:** 2 • **Outlook:** 3

SOFTWARE TECHNICIAN (profess. & kin.) • D.O.T. #020.262-010 • OES #25105 • Analyzes problems, plans and develops software programs, transfers programs to memory chips, installs chips on printed circuit boards (PCB), and tests and corrects operation of chips and boards, using computer equipment: Assembles units into logical sequence and translates charts into programmed computer language to develop detailed flow charts. Enters coded commands into computer, tests printer for system errors, and corrects errors by altering commands until desired results are attained, using keyboard. Transfers program data onto disk, using terminal keyboard, mounts disk onto cathode-ray-tube (CRT) unit, checks screen for errors, and corrects errors as necessary. Mounts disk and blank chips in device which imprints program onto erasable memory chip. Writes specifications and instructs operator how to input data to obtain required results. Installs chips on printed circuit board and connects lead wires to board circuitry, utilizing diagrams and knowledge of electric circuitry and electronics. Observes operation of chip in terminal, changes sequence of program commands if necessary, and submits data specifications on tested chip to engineering department. • **GED:** R5, M4, L4 • **SVP:** 2-4 yrs • **Academic:** Ed=A, Eng=G • **Work Field:** 211, 233 • **MPSMS:** 571 • **Aptitudes:** G2, V2, N2, S4, P2, Q2, K4, F3, M3, E5, C5 • **Temperaments:** J, T • **Physical:** V=L, H=N, L=S, H • **Work Env:** I • **Salary:** 4 • **Outlook:** 4

STATISTICIAN, MATHEMATICAL (profess. & kin.) • D.O.T. #020.067-022 • OES #25312 • STATISTICIAN, THEORETICAL. Conducts research into mathematical theories and proofs that form basis of science of statistics and develops statistical methodology: Examines theories, such as those of probability and inference, to discover mathematical bases for new or improved methods of obtaining and evaluating numerical data. Develops and tests experimental designs, sampling techniques, and analytical methods, and prepares recommendations concerning their utilization in statistical surveys, experiments, and tests. Investigates, evaluates, and prepares reports on applicability, efficiency, and accuracy of statistical methods used by physical and social scientists, including STATISTICIANS, APPLIED (profess. & kin.), in obtaining and evaluating data. • **GED:** R6, M6, L6 • **SVP:** 4-10 yrs • **Academic:** Ed=B, Eng=G • **Work Field:** 251 • **MPSMS:** 721, 729 • **Aptitudes:** G1, V1, N1, S1, P2, Q3, K4, F4, M4, E5, C5 • **Temperaments:** D, J, M, T • **Physical:** V=N, H=N, L=S • **Work Env:** I • **Salary:** 5 • **Outlook:** 3

SYSTEMS ANALYST, ELECTRONIC DATA PROCESSING (profess. & kin.) • D.O.T. #012.167-066 • OES #25102 • Analyzes business procedures and problems to refine data and convert it to programmable form for electronic data processing: Confers with personnel of organizational units involved to ascertain specific output requirements, such as types of breakouts, degree of data summarization, and format for management reports. Studies existing data handling systems to evaluate effectiveness and develops new systems to improve production or workflow as required. Specifies in detail logical and/or mathematical operations to be performed by various equipment units and/or comprehensive computer programs, and operations to be performed by personnel in system. Conducts special studies and investigations pertaining to development of new information systems to meet current and projected needs. Plans and prepares technical reports, memoranda, and instructional manuals relative to the establishment and functioning of complete operational systems. May prepare programs for computer use, and be designated PROGRAMER-ANALYST (profess. & kin.). • **GED:** R5, M5, L5 • **SVP:** 2-4 yrs • **Academic:** Ed=B, Eng=G • **Work Field:** 232 • **MPSMS:** 890 • **Aptitudes:** G2, V2, N2, S3, P3, Q3, K4, F4, M4, E4, C5 • **Temperaments:** M, P • **Stress:** E • **Physical:** V=N, H=N, L=S • **Work Env:** I • **Salary:** 5 • **Outlook:** 5

GOE: 11.01.02 Data Analysis

ACTUARY (profess. & kin.) • D.O.T. #020.167-010 • OES #25313 • Applies knowledge of mathematics, probability, statistics, principles of finance and business to problems in life, health, social, and casualty insurance, annuities, and pensions: Determines mortality, accident, sickness, disability, and retirement rates; constructs probability tables regarding fire, natural disasters, and unemployment, based on analysis of statistical data and other pertinent information. Designs or reviews insurance and pension plans and calculates premiums. Ascertains premium rates required and cash reserves and liabilities necessary to ensure payment of future benefits. Determines equitable basis for distributing surplus earnings under participating insurance and annuity contracts in mutual companies. May specialize in one type of insurance and be designated as ACTUARY, CASUALTY (profess. & kin.); ACTUARY, LIFE (profess. & kin.). • **GED:** R5, M5, L5 • **SVP:** 4-10 yrs • **Academic:** Ed=B, Eng=G • **Work Field:** 232, 251 • **MPSMS:** 721 • **Aptitudes:** G2, V2, N1, S4, P3, Q1, K4, F4, M4, E5, C5 • **Temperaments:** D, M, T • **Physical:** V=L, H=N, L=S • **Work Env:** I • **Salary:** 5 • **Outlook:** 4

CONSULTANT (profess. & kin.) • D.O.T. #189.167-010 • OES #00000 • Consults with client to define need or problem, conducts studies and surveys to obtain data, and analyzes data to advise on or recommend solution, utilizing knowledge of theory, principles, or technology of specific discipline or field of specialization: Consults with client to ascertain and define need or problem area, and determine scope of investigation required to obtain solution. Conducts study or survey on need or problem to obtain data required for solution. Analyzes data to determine solution, such as installation of alternate methods and procedures, changes in processing methods and practices, modification of machines or equipment, or redesign of products or services. Advises client on alternate methods of solving need or problem, or recommends specific solution. May negotiate contract for consulting service. May specialize in providing consulting service to government in field of specialization. May be designated according to field of specialization such as engineering or science discipline, economics, education, labor, or in specialized field of work as health services, social services, or investment services. • **GED:** R5, M5, L5 • **SVP:** 4-10 yrs • **Academic:** Ed=B, Eng=G • **Work Field:** 244, 251, 271 • **MPSMS:** 700, 723, 950 • **Aptitudes:** G2, V2, N2, S2, P3, Q3, K4, F4, M4, E5, C5 • **Temperaments:** D, M, P • **Stress:** E • **Physical:** V=N, H=L, L=S • **Work Env:** I • **Salary:** 5 • **Outlook:** 3

FINANCIAL ANALYST (finan. inst.) • D.O.T. #020.167- 014 • OES #25315 • INVESTMENT ANALYST; SECURITIES ANALYST; SECURITIES-RESEARCH ANALYST. Conducts statistical analyses of information affecting investment program of public, industrial, and financial institutions, such as banks, insurance companies, and brokerage and investment houses: Interprets data concerning investments, their price, yield, stability, and future trends, using daily stock and bond reports, financial periodicals, securities manuals, and personal interviews. Constructs charts and graphs regarding investments. Summarizes data setting forth current and long term trends in investment risks and measurable economic influences pertinent to status of investments. May perform research and make analyses relative to losses and adverse financial trends and suggest remedial measures. May transmit buy-and-sell orders to broker based on securities analysis. May be designated according to type of securities handled as BOND ANALYST (finan. inst.); COMMODITY ANALYST (finan. inst.); or INSURANCE ANALYST (insurance). • **GED:** R5, M5, L4 • **SVP:** 2-4 yrs • **Academic:** Ed=B, Eng=G • **Work Field:** 211, 232 • **MPSMS:** 894 • **Aptitudes:** G2, V2, N2, S4, P4, Q2, K4, F4, M4, E5, C5 • **Temperaments:** J, M, T • **Physical:** V=L, H=N, L=S, H • **Work Env:** I • **Salary:** 4 • **Outlook:** 4

MATHEMATICAL TECHNICIAN (profess. & kin.) • D.O.T. #020.162-010 • OES #25323 • DATA-REDUCTION TECHNICIAN. Applies standardized mathematical formulas, principles, and methodology to technological problems in engineering and physical sciences in relation to specific industrial and research objectives, processes, equipment and products: Confers with professional, scientific, and engineering personnel to plan project. Analyzes raw data recorded on magnetic tape, punched cards, photographic film or other media. Selects most practical and accurate combination and sequence of computational methods, using algebra, trigonometry, geometry, vector analysis and calculus to reduce raw data to meaningful and manageable terms. Selects most economical and reliable combination of manual, mechanical, or electronic data processing methods and equipment consistent with data reduction requirements. Modifies standard formulas to conform to data processing method selected. Translates data into numerical values, equations, flow charts, graphs or other media. Analyzes processed data to detect errors. May operate card punching or sorting machines, calculators, or data processing equipment. • **GED:** R5, M5, L5 • **SVP:** 2-4 yrs • **Academic:** Ed=B, Eng=S • **Work Field:** 244, 251 • **MPSMS:** 721 • **Aptitudes:** G2, V2, N2, S3, P4, Q2, K3, F4, M4, E5, C4 • **Temperaments:** J, M, T, V • **Physical:** V=N, H=L, L=S • **Work Env:** I • **Salary:** 4 • **Outlook:** 4

STATISTICIAN, APPLIED (profess. & kin.) • D.O.T. #020.167-026 • OES #25312 • Plans data collection, and analyzes and interprets numerical data from experiments, studies, surveys, and other sources and applies statistical methodology to provide information for scientific research and statistical analysis: Plans methods to collect information and develops questionnaire techniques according to survey design. Conducts surveys utilizing sampling techniques or complete enumeration bases. Evaluates reliability of source information, adjusts and weighs raw data, and organizes results into form compatible with analysis by computers or other methods. Presents numerical information by computer readouts, graphs, charts, tables, written reports or other methods. Describes sources of information, and limitations on reliability and usability. May analyze and interpret statistics to point up significant differences in relationships among sources of information, and prepare conclusions and forecasts based on data summaries. May specialize in specific aspect of statistics or industrial activity reporting and be designated by specialty, such as DEMOGRAPHER (profess. & kin.) I; STATISTICIAN, ANALYTICAL (profess. & kin.); STATISTICIAN, ENGINEERING AND PHYSICAL SCIENCE (profess. & kin.). • **GED:** R5, M5, L4 • **SVP:** 2-4 yrs • **Academic:** Ed=B, Eng=S • **Work Field:** 251 • **MPSMS:** 721, 729 • **Aptitudes:** G1, V1, N1, S3, P2, Q2, K4, F4, M4, E5, C5 • **Temperaments:** J, M • **Physical:** V=N, H=N, L=S, H • **Work Env:** I • **Salary:** 4 • **Outlook:** 4

11.02 Educational and Library Services

Workers in this group do general and specialized teaching, vocational training, advising in agriculture and home economics, and library work of various kinds. Jobs are found in schools, colleges, libraries, and other educational facilities.

✔ **What kind of work would you do?**
Your work activities would depend upon your specific job. For example, you might:

- teach elementary or secondary school students.
- teach the skills for a specific trade to adults or youth.
- present ideas and information for effective home and farm management to adults.

- teach undergraduate or graduate college courses.
- check out, collect, and shelve books in a library.

✔ **What skills and abilities do you need for this kind of work?**
To do this kind of work, you must be able to:

- understand and use the basic principles of effective teaching.
- develop special skills and knowledge in one or more academic or vocational subjects.
- use an organized system for storing and using books and other library materials.
- develop a good teacher-student relationship.

✔ **How do you know if you would like or could learn to do this kind of work?**
The following questions may give you clues about yourself as you consider this group of jobs.

- Have you been a camp or playground instructor? Do you enjoy working with children?
- Have you helped friends or relatives with their homework? Can you explain things and communicate ideas?
- Have you been a member of FTA (Future Teachers of America) or a similar group? Do you have a desire to teach or train others?
- Have you been a school office worker or teacher's helper? Do you enjoy helping and assisting people?
- Have you assisted a librarian in cataloging or shelving books? Did you like this type of activity?

✔ **How can you prepare for and enter this kind of work?**
Occupations in this group usually require education and/or training extending from two years to over ten years, depending upon the specific kind of work. Four or more years of college is required for most jobs in this group. College and university teachers, supervisors, and librarians must have graduate degrees. Teachers in public schools must obtain state certificates. Requirements for certificates vary among the states, but specific amounts of education and experience are usually included. Vocational teachers are often required to have extensive work experience in their teaching field. Home economics and agricultural extension services workers need special coursework.

✔ **What else should you consider about these jobs?**
Openings for teachers vary according to the subject area or specialty, the enrollment, and the financial support of each institution. Most teachers are required to work only nine months each year. Therefore, some may have time to further their education or find summer employment.

Teachers and other education workers are frequently required to accept duties outside of the regular work day. These duties may include planning and grading activities; attending conferences, meetings, and workshops; advising students; or supervising student activities. Workers may receive additional pay for some of these duties.

If you think you would like to do this kind of work, look at the job titles listed on the following pages.

GOE: 11.02.01 Teaching & Instructing, General

FACULTY MEMBER, COLLEGE OR UNIVERSITY (educ.) • D.O.T. #090.227-010 • OES #31299 • Conducts college or university courses for undergraduate or graduate students: Teaches one or more subjects, such as economics, chemistry, law, or medicine, within a prescribed curriculum. Prepares and delivers lectures to students. Compiles bibliographies of specialized materials for outside reading assignments. Stimulates class discussions. Compiles, administers, and grades examinations, or assigns this work to others. Directs research of other teachers or graduate students working for advanced academic degrees. Conducts research in particular field of knowledge and publishes findings in professional journals. Performs related duties, such as advising students on academic and vocational curricula, and acting as adviser to student organizations. Serves on faculty committee providing professional consulting services to government and industry. May be designated according to faculty rank in traditional hierarchy as determined by institution's estimate of scholarly maturity as ASSOCIATE PROFESSOR (education); PROFESSOR (education); or according to rank distinguished by duties as signed or amount of time devoted to academic work as RESEARCH ASSISTANT (education); VISIT-

ING PROFESSOR (education). May teach in two-year college and be designated TEACHER, JUNIOR COLLEGE (education); or in technical institute and be designated FACULTY MEMBER, TECHNICAL INSTITUTE (education). Additional titles: ACTING PROFESSOR (education); ASSISTANT PROFESSOR (education); CLINICAL INSTRUCTOR (education); INSTRUCTOR (education); LECTURER (education); TEACHING ASSISTANT (education). • **GED:** R6, M5, L5 • **SVP:** 4-10 yrs • **Academic:** Ed=M, Eng=G • **Work Field:** 296 • **MPSMS:** 931 • **Aptitudes:** G1, V1, N2, S3, P3, Q2, K4, F4, M4, E5, C5 • **Temperaments:** D, I, J, P • **Stress:** E • **Physical:** V=N, H=N, L=S • **Work Env:** I • **Salary:** 5 • **Outlook:** 2

INSTRUCTOR, BUSINESS EDUCATION (educ.) • D.O.T. #090.222-010 • OES #31314 • Instructs students in commercial subjects, such as typing, filing, secretarial procedures, business mathematics, office equipment use, and personality development, in business schools, community colleges, or training programs: Instructs students in subject matter, utilizing various methods, such as lecture and demonstration, and uses audiovisual aids and other materials to supplement presentations. Prepares or follows teaching outline for course of study, assigns lessons, and corrects homework and classroom papers. Administers tests to evaluate students' progress, records results, and issues reports to inform students of their progress. Maintains discipline in classroom. • **GED:** R5, M4, L5 • **SVP:** 4-10 yrs • **Academic:** Ed=B, Eng=G • **Work Field:** 296 • **MPSMS:** 931 • **Aptitudes:** G2, V2, N3, S5, P4, Q1, K2, F3, M4, E5, C5 • **Temperaments:** D, I, J, P • **Stress:** E • **Physical:** V=L, H=L, L=S, H • **Work Env:** I • **Salary:** 5 • **Outlook:** 3

INSTRUCTOR, EXTENSION WORK (educ.) • D.O.T. #090.227-018 • OES #31399 • Conducts evening classes for extension service of college or university: Prepares course of study designed to meet community, organization, and student needs. Conducts and corrects examinations, and assigns course grades. • **GED:** R5, M3, L5 • **SVP:** 4-10 yrs • **Academic:** Ed=A, Eng=G • **Work Field:** 296 • **MPSMS:** 931 • **Aptitudes:** G2, V2, N3, S4, P3, Q2, K4, F4, M4, E5, C5 • **Temperaments:** D, I, P • **Stress:** E • **Physical:** V=N, H=L, L=S • **Work Env:** I • **Salary:** 3 • **Outlook:** 3

TEACHER (museum) • D.O.T. #099.227-038 • OES #31317 • Teaches classes, presents lectures, conducts workshops, and participates in other activities to further educational program of museum, zoo, or similar institution: Plans course content and method of presentation, and prepares outline of material to be covered and submits it for approval. Selects and assembles materials to be used in teaching assignment, such as pieces of pottery or samples of plant life, and arranges use of audiovisual equipment or other teaching aids. Conducts classes for children in various scientific, history, or art subjects, utilizing museum displays to augment standard teaching methods and adapting course content and complexity to ages and interests of students. Teaches adult classes in such subjects as art, history, astronomy, or horticulture, using audiovisual aids, demonstration, or laboratory techniques appropriate to subject matter. Presents series of lectures on subjects related to institution collections, often incorporating films or slides into presentation. Conducts seminars or workshops for school system teachers or lay persons to demonstrate methods of using institution facilities and collections to enhance school programs or to enrich other activities. Conducts workshops or field trips for students or community groups and plans and directs activities associated with projects. Plans and presents vacation or weekend programs for elementary or preschool children, combining recreational activities with teaching methods geared to age groups. Conducts classes for academic credit in cooperation with area schools or universities. Teaches courses in museum work to participants in work-study programs. Works with adult leaders of youth groups to assist youths to earn merit badges or fulfill other group requirements. Maintains records of attendance. Evaluates success of courses, basing evaluation on number and enthusiasm of persons participating and recommends retaining or dropping course in future plans. When course is offered for academic credit, evaluates class member performances, administers tests, and issues grades in accordance with methods used by cooperating educational institution. • **GED:** R5, M4, L5 • **SVP:** 2-4 yrs • **Academic:** Ed=B, Eng=S • **Work Field:** 296 • **MPSMS:** 931 •

Aptitudes: G2, V2, N3, S3, P3, Q3, K4, F4, M4, E5, C3 • **Temperaments:** D, P • **Stress:** A • **Physical:** V=L, H=L, L=L, H • **Work Env:** I • **Salary:** 4 • **Outlook:** 4

TEACHER AIDE I (educ.) • D.O.T. #099.327-010 • OES #31521 • ASSISTANT TEACHER. Assists teaching staff of public or private elementary or secondary school by performing any combination of following instructional tasks in classroom: Discusses assigned teaching area with classroom teacher to coordinate instructional efforts. Prepares lesson outline and plan in assigned area and submits it for review. Plans, prepares, and develops various teaching aids, such as bibliographies, charts, and graphs. Presents subject matter to students, utilizing variety of methods and techniques, such as lecture, discussion, and supervised role playing. Prepares, gives, and grades examinations. Assists students, individually or in groups, with lesson assignments to present or reinforce learning concepts. May confer with parents on progress of students. May specialize in specific subject area or total classroom experience. May be designated by school level as TEACHER AIDE, PRIMARY SCHOOL (education); TEACHER AIDE, SECONDARY SCHOOL (education) I. • **GED:** R4, M4, L4 • **SVP:** 1-2 yrs • **Academic:** Ed=H, Eng=G • **Work Field:** 296 • **MPSMS:** 931 • **Aptitudes:** G3, V2, N3, S3, P3, Q2, K3, F3, M3, E5, C3 • **Temperaments:** J, P, V • **Stress:** E • **Physical:** V=L, H=L, L=S, H • **Work Env:** I • **Salary:** 4 • **Outlook:** 1

TEACHER, ADULT EDUCATION (educ.) • D.O.T. #099.227-030 • OES #31317 • Instructs out-of-school youths and adults in academic and nonacademic courses in public or private schools or other organizations: Prepares outline of instructional program and studies and assembles material to be presented. Presents lectures and discussions to group to increase students' knowledge or vocational competence. Tests and grades students on achievement in class. Teaches courses, such as citizenship, fine arts, and homemaking, to enrich students' cultural and academic backgrounds. Conducts workshops and demonstrations to teach such skills as driving, sports, and dancing, or to provide training for parenthood. May teach basic courses in American history, principles, ideas, and customs and in English to foreign-born and be designated TEACHER, CITIZENSHIP (education). • **GED:** R4, M2, L4 • **SVP:** 2-4 yrs • **Academic:** Ed=B, Eng=S • **Work Field:** 296 • **MPSMS:** 931 • **Aptitudes:** G3, V2, N3, S3, P3, Q2, K4, F4, M4, E5, C5 • **Temperaments:** D, I, J • **Stress:** A • **Physical:** V=N, H=L, L=L, H • **Work Env:** I • **Salary:** 4 • **Outlook:** 4

TEACHER, ELEMENTARY SCHOOL (educ.) • D.O.T. #092.227-010 • OES #31305 • TEACHER, PRIMARY. Teaches elementary school pupils academic, social, and manipulative skills in public or private educational system: Prepares teaching outline for course of study. Lectures, demonstrates, and uses audiovisual teaching aids to present subject matter to class. Prepares, administers, and corrects tests, and records results. Assigns lessons, corrects papers, and hears oral presentations. Maintains order in classroom and on playground. Counsels pupils when adjustment and academic problems arise. Discusses pupils' academic and behavior problems with parents and suggests remedial action. Keeps attendance and grade records as required by school board. May teach combined grade classes in rural schools. • **GED:** R5, M3, L5 • **SVP:** 2-4 yrs • **Academic:** Ed=B, Eng=G • **Work Field:** 296 • **MPSMS:** 931 • **Aptitudes:** G2, V2, N3, S4, P3, Q2, K4, F4, M4, E4, C3 • **Temperaments:** J, P, V • **Stress:** E • **Physical:** V=N, H=L, L=S • **Work Env:** I • **Salary:** 4 • **Outlook:** 4

TEACHER, RESOURCE (educ.) • D.O.T. #099.227-042 • OES #31311 • MATHEMATICS IMPROVEMENT TEACHER; READING IMPROVEMENT TEACHER. Teaches basic academic subjects to students requiring remedial work, using special help programs to improve scholastic level: Teaches basic subjects, such as reading and math, applying lesson techniques designed for short attention spans. Administers achievement tests and evaluates test results to discover level of language and math skills. Selects and teaches reading material and math problems related to everyday life of individual student. Confers with school counselors and teaching staff to obtain additional testing information and to gain insight on student behavioral disorders affecting learning process. Designs special help programs for low achievers and encourages parent-teacher cooperation. Attends professional meetings, writes reports, and maintains records. • **GED:** R5, M5, L5 • **SVP:** 2-4 yrs

• **Academic:** Ed=B, Eng=S • **Work Field:** 296 • **MPSMS:** 931 • **Aptitudes:** G2, V2, N2, S4, P4, Q2, K4, F4, M4, E5, C5 • **Temperaments:** D, J, P • **Stress:** A • **Physical:** V=N, H=L, L=L • **Work Env:** I • **Salary:** 4 • **Outlook:** 3

TEACHER, SECONDARY SCHOOL (educ.) • D.O.T. #091.227-010 • OES #31308 • TEACHER, HIGH SCHOOL. Teaches one or more subjects, such as English, mathematics, or social studies, to students in public or private secondary schools: Instructs students in subject matter, utilizing various teaching methods, such as lecture and demonstration, and uses audiovisual aids and other materials to supplement presentations. Prepares teaching outline for course of study, assigns lessons, and corrects homework papers. Administers tests to evaluate pupils' progress, records results, and issues reports to inform parents of progress. Keeps attendance records. Maintains discipline in classroom and school yard. Participates in faculty and professional meetings, educational conferences, and teacher training workshops. Performs related duties, such as sponsoring one or more special activities or student organizations, assisting pupils in selecting course of study, and counseling them in adjustment and academic problems. May be identified according to subject matter taught. • **GED:** R5, M4, L5 • **SVP:** 2-4 yrs • **Academic:** Ed=B, Eng=G • **Work Field:** 296 • **MPSMS:** 931 • **Aptitudes:** G2, V2, N3, S4, P3, Q2, K4, F4, M4, E5, C5 • **Temperaments:** D, I, J, P • **Stress:** E • **Physical:** V=N, H=L, L=S • **Work Env:** I • **Salary:** 4 • **Outlook:** 4

TUTOR (educ.) • D.O.T. #099.227-034 • OES #31399 • INSTRUCTOR, PRIVATE; TEACHER, PRIVATE. Teaches academic subjects, such as English, mathematics, and foreign languages to pupils requiring private instruction, adapting curriculum to meet individual's needs. May teach in pupil's home. • **GED:** R5, M3, L5 • **SVP:** 2-4 yrs • **Academic:** Ed=A, Eng=S • **Work Field:** 296 • **MPSMS:** 931 • **Aptitudes:** G2, V2, N3, S4, P4, Q2, K4, F4, M4, E5, C5 • **Temperaments:** J, P • **Physical:** V=N, H=L, L=L • **Work Env:** I • **Salary:** 4 • **Outlook:** 4

GOE: 11.02.02 Vocational & Industrial Teaching

HUMAN RESOURCE ADVISOR (profess. & kin.) • D.O.T. #166.267-046 • OES #21511 • Provides establishment personnel assistance in identifying, evaluating, and resolving human relations and work performance problems within establishment to facilitate communication and improve employee human relations skills and work performance: Talks informally with establishment personnel and attends meetings of managers, supervisors, and work units to facilitate effective interpersonal communication among participants and to ascertain human relations and work related problems that adversely affect employee morale and establishment productivity. Evaluates human relations and work related problems and meets with supervisors and managers to determine effective remediation techniques, such as job skill training or personal intervention, to resolve human relations issues among personnel. Develops and conducts training to instruct establishment managers, supervisors, and workers in human relation skills, such as supervisory skills, conflict resolution skills, interpersonal communication skills, and effective group interaction skills. Schedules individuals for technical job-related skills training to improve individual work performance. May participate in resolving labor relations issues. May assist in screening applicants for establishment training programs. May write employee newsletter. • **GED:** R5, M3, L5 • **SVP:** 2-4 yrs • **Academic:** Ed=A, Eng=S • **Work Field:** 296, 298 • **MPSMS:** 893 • **Aptitudes:** G2, V2, N4, S5, P5, Q3, K5, F5, M5, E5, C5 • **Temperaments:** D, I, J, P • **Physical:** V=L, H=G, L=L • **Work Env:** I • **Salary:** 4 • **Outlook:** 3

INSTRUCTOR, TECHNICAL TRAINING (educ.) • D.O.T. #166.221-010 • OES #31314 • TRAINING SPECIALIST. Develops and conducts programs to train employees or customers of industrial or commercial establishment in installation, programming, safety, maintenance, and repair of machinery and equipment, such as robots, programmable controllers, and robot controllers, following manuals, specifications, blueprints, and schematics, and using handtools, measuring instruments, and testing equipment: Confers with management and staff or TECHNICAL TRAINING CO-

ORDINATOR (education) 166.167-054 to determine training objectives. Writes training program, including outline, text, handouts, and tests, and designs laboratory exercises, applying knowledge of electronics, mechanics, hydraulics, pneumatics, and programming, and following machine, equipment, and tooling manuals. Schedules classes based on classroom and equipment availability. Lectures class on safety, installation, programming, maintenance, and repair of machinery and equipment, following outline, handouts, and texts, and using visual aids, such as graphs, charts, videotape, and slides. Demonstrates procedures being taught, such as programming and repair, applying knowledge of electrical wire color coding, programming, electronics, mechanics, hydraulics, and pneumatics, using handtools, measuring instruments, and testing equipment, and following course outline. Observes trainees in laboratory and answers trainees' questions. Administers written and practical exams and writes performance reports to evaluate trainees' performance. Participates in meetings, seminars, and training sessions to obtain information useful to training facility and integrates information into training program. May repair electrical and electronic components of robots in industrial establishments. May install, program, maintain, and repair robots in customer's establishment [FIELD SERVICE TECHNICIAN (mach. mfg.) 638.261-026]. May be designated according to subject taught as INSTRUCTOR, PROGRAMMABLE CONTROLLERS (education); INSTRUCTOR, ROBOTICS (education). • **GED:** R5, M4, L5 • **SVP:** 4-10 yrs • **Academic:** Ed=A, Eng=G • **Work Field:** 111, 121, 296 • **MPSMS:** 560, 580, 931 • **Aptitudes:** G2, V2, N2, S2, P2, Q3, K3, F3, M2, E5, C4 • **Temperaments:** D, J, P, T, V • **Stress:** E • **Physical:** V=L, H=L, L=S, H • **Work Env:** I • **Salary:** 4 • **Outlook:** 4

INSTRUCTOR, VOCATIONAL TRAINING (educ.) • D.O.T. #097.227-014 • OES #31314 • TEACHER, VOCATIONAL TRAINING. Teaches vocational training subjects in specific trades to students in public or private schools or in industrial plants: Organizes program of practical and technical instruction, involving demonstrations of skills required in trade, and lectures on theory, practices, methods, processes, and terminology. Instructs students in subject areas, such as safety precautions, mathematics, science, drawing, use and maintenance of tools and equipment, and codes or regulations related to trade. Plans and supervises work of students in shop or laboratory. Tests and evaluates achievement of student in technical knowledge and trade skills. May be identified according to trade or theory taught or type of establishment in which training is conducted. • **GED:** R4, M4, L4 • **SVP:** 2-4 yrs • **Academic:** Ed=H, Eng=G • **Work Field:** 296 • **MPSMS:** 931 • **Aptitudes:** G2, V2, N2, S2, P2, Q3, K3, F3, M3, E3, C3 • **Temperaments:** J, P • **Stress:** E • **Physical:** V=N, H=L, L=S, H • **Work Env:** I • **Salary:** 4 • **Outlook:** 4

TECHNICAL SUPPORT SPECIALIST (profess. & kin.) • D.O.T. #199.224-010 • OES #39999 • Installs, modifies, and makes minor repairs to microcomputer hardware and software systems and provides technical assistance and training to system users: Installs or assists service personnel in installation of hardware and peripheral components, such as monitors, keyboards, printers, and disk drives on client's premises, following design or installation specifications. Loads specified software packages, such as operating systems, word processing, or spreadsheet programs into computer memory. Types commands on keyboard and observes system functions to verify correct system operation. Instructs clients in use of equipment, software, and manuals. Answers user's inquiries in person and via telephone concerning systems operation; diagnoses system hardware, software, and operator problems; and recommends or performs minor remedial actions to correct problems based on knowledge of system operation. Replaces defective or inadequate software packages. Refers major hardware problems to service personnel for correction. Attends technical conferences and seminars to keep abreast of new software and hardware product developments. • **GED:** R5, M4, L4 • **SVP:** 2-4 yrs • **Academic:** Ed=A, Eng=S • **Work Field:** 111, 233, 296 • **MPSMS:** 571, 893 • **Aptitudes:** G2, V2, N2, S3, P3, Q3, K4, F4, M4, E5, C4 • **Temperaments:** J, P, T, V • **Physical:** V=L, H=G, L=L, W, H • **Work Env:** I • **Salary:** 4 • **Outlook:** 3

TRAINING REPRESENTATIVE (educ.) • D.O.T. #166.227-010 • OES #31314 • TRAINING INSTRUCTOR. Prepares and conducts training programs for employees of industrial, commercial, service, or governmental establishment: Confers with management to gain knowledge of identified work situation requiring preventive or remedial training for employees. Formulates teaching outline in conformance with selected instructional methods, utilizing knowledge of specified training needs and effectiveness of such training methods as individual coaching, group instruction, lectures, demonstrations, conferences, meetings, and workshops. Selects or develops teaching aids, such as training handbooks, demonstration models, multimedia visual aids, and reference works. Conducts general or specialized training sessions covering specified areas, such as those concerned with new employees' orientation, specific on-the-job training, apprenticeship programs, sales techniques, health and safety practices, public relations, refresher training, promotional development, upgrading, retraining displaced workers, leadership development, and other such adaptations to changes in policies, procedures, regulations, and technologies. Tests trainees to measure their learning progress and to evaluate effectiveness of training presentations. • **GED:** R5, M4, L5 • **SVP:** 2-4 yrs • **Academic:** Ed=A, Eng=G • **Work Field:** 261, 296 • **MPSMS:** 712, 931 • **Aptitudes:** G2, V2, N2, S3, P3, Q3, K4, F4, M4, E5, C5 • **Temperaments:** D, J, P, T • **Stress:** E • **Physical:** V=N, H=L, L=S • **Work Env:** I • **Salary:** 4 • **Out look:** 3

GOE: 11.02.03 Teaching, Home Economics, Agriculture & Related

COMMUNITY DIETITIAN (profess. & kin.) • D.O.T. #077.127-010 • OES #32521 • Plans, organizes, coordinates, and evaluates nutritional component of health care services for organization: Develops and implements plan of care based on assessment of nutritional needs and available sources and correlates with other health care. Evaluates nutritional care and provides follow-up continuity of care. Instructs individuals and families in nutritional principles, diet, food selection, and economics and adapts teaching plans to individual lifestyle. Provides consultation to and works with community groups. Conducts or participates in in-service education and consultation with professional staff and supporting personnel of own and related organizations. Plans or participates in development of program proposals for funding. Plans, conducts, and evaluates dietary studies and participates in nutritional and epidemiologic studies with nutritional component. Evaluates food service systems and makes recommendation for conformance level that will provide optional nutrition and quality food if associated with group care institutions. May be employed by public health agency and be designated as NUTRITIONIST, PUBLIC HEALTH (gov. ser.). • **GED:** R5, M4, L5 • **SVP:** 4-10 yrs • **Academic:** Ed=A, Eng=G • **Work Field:** 282 • **MPSMS:** 924 • **Aptitudes:** G2, V2, N3, S3, P3, Q3, K4, F4, M4, E5, C5 • **Temperaments:** M, P, V • **Stress:** E • **Physical:** V=L, H=L, L=L • **Work Env:** I • **Salary:** 4 • **Outlook:** 3

COUNTY HOME-DEMONSTRATION AGENT (gov. ser.) • D.O.T. #096.121-010 • OES #31323 • HOME AGENT; HOME-DEMONSTRATION AGENT; HOME-EXTENSION AGENT. Develops, organizes, and conducts programs for individuals in rural communities to improve farm and family life: Lectures and demonstrates techniques in such subjects as nutrition, clothing, home management, home furnishing, and child care. Visits homes to advise families on problems, such as family budgeting and home remodeling. Organizes and advises clubs, and assists in selecting and training leaders to guide group discussions and demonstrations in subjects, such as sewing, food preparation, and home decoration. Writes leaflets and articles and talks over radio and television to disseminate information. Participates in community activities, such as judging at rural fairs and speaking before parent-teachers associations. May direct 4-H Club activities [FOUR-H CLUB AGENT (education)]. • **GED:** R5, M3, L5 • **SVP:** 2-4 yrs • **Academic:** Ed=A, Eng=S • **Work Field:** 295, 296 • **MPSMS:** 931, 959 • **Aptitudes:** G2, V2, N3, S3, P3, Q3, K4, F3, M3, E4, C3 • **Temperaments:** D, I, J, P, V • **Stress:** A • **Physical:** V=N, H=G, L=L, H • **Work Env:** I • **Salary:** 4 • **Outlook:** 2

COUNTY-AGRICULTURAL AGENT (gov. ser.) • D.O.T. #096.127-010 • OES #31323 • AGRICULTURAL AGENT; COUNTY ADVISER; COUNTY AGENT; EXTENSION AGENT; EXTENSION-SERVICE AGENT; EXTENSION WORKER; FARM ADVISER; FARM AGENT. Organizes and conducts cooperative extension program to advise and instruct farmers and individuals engaged in agri-business in applications of agricultural research findings: Collects, analyzes, and evaluates agricultural data; plans and develops techniques; and advises farmers to assist in solving problems, such as crop rotation and soil erosion. Delivers lectures and prepares articles concerning subjects, such as farm management and soil conservation. Demonstrates practical procedures used in solving agricultural problems. Discusses extension program with representatives of commercial organizations, county government, and other groups to inform them of program services and to obtain their cooperation in encouraging use of services. Prepares activity, planning, and other reports and maintains program records. Prepares budget requests, or assists in their preparation. May supervise and coordinate activities of other county extension workers. May direct 4-H Club activities. May be designated by specific program assignment as AGRI-BUSINESS AGENT (gov. ser.); FARM-MANAGEMENT AGENT (gov. ser.); HORTICULTURAL AGENT (gov. ser.); LIVESTOCK AGENT (gov. ser.); RESOURCE AGENT (gov. ser.). • **GED:** R5, M3, L5 • **SVP:** 2-4 yrs • **Academic:** Ed=A, Eng=S • **Work Field:** 282, 296 • **MPSMS:** 931, 959 • **Aptitudes:** G2, V2, N3, S4, P4, Q3, K4, F4, M4, E5, C3 • **Temperaments:** D, I, J, P, V • **Stress:** A • **Physical:** V=N, H=G, L=L • **Work Env:** B • **Salary:** 4 • **Outlook:** 3

EXTENSION SERVICE SPECIALIST (gov. ser.) • D.O.T. #096.127-014 • OES #31323 • COOPERATIVE EXTENSION ADVISER SPECIALIST. Instructs extension workers and develops specialized service activities in area of agriculture or home economics: Plans, develops, organizes, and evaluates training programs in subjects, such as home management, horticulture, and consumer information. Prepares leaflets, pamphlets, and other material for use as training aids. Conducts classes to train extension workers in specialized fields and in teaching techniques. Delivers lectures to commercial and community organizations and over radio and television to promote development of agricultural or domestic skills. Analyzes research data and plans activities to coordinate services with those offered by other departments, agencies, and organizations. May be designated according to field of specialization as AGRICULTURAL- EXTENSION SPECIALIST (gov. ser.); HOME ECONOMICS SPECIALIST (gov. ser.). • **GED:** R5, M3, L5 • **SVP:** 4-10 yrs • **Academic:** Ed=A, Eng=G • **Work Field:** 296 • **MPSMS:** 931, 959 • **Aptitudes:** G2, V2, N3, S4, P3, Q2, K4, F4, M4, E5, C3 • **Temperaments:** D, I, J, P, V • **Stress:** E • **Physical:** V=N, H=L, L=S • **Work Env:** I • **Salary:** 4 • **Outlook:** 3

HOME ECONOMIST (profess. & kin.) • D.O.T. #096.121-014 • OES #31323 • CONSUMER SERVICES CONSULTANT. Organizes and conducts consumer education service or research program for equipment, food, textile, or utility company, utilizing principles of home economics: Advises homemakers in selection and utilization of household equipment, food, and clothing, and interprets homemakers' needs to manufacturers of household products. Writes advertising copy and articles of interest to homemakers, tests recipes, equipment, and new household products, conducts radio and television homemakers' programs, and performs other public relations and promotion work for business firms, newspapers, magazines, and radio and television stations. Advises individuals and families on home management practices, such as budget planning, meal preparation, and energy conservation. Teaches improved homemaking practices to homemakers and youths through educational programs, demonstrations, discussions, and home visits. May engage in research in government, private industry, and colleges and universities to explore family relations or child development, develop new products for home, discover facts on food nutrition, and test serviceability of new materials. May specialize in specific area of home economics and be designated EQUIPMENT SPECIALIST (profess. & kin.); FASHION CONSULTANT (profess. & kin.); HOME ECONOMIST, CONSUMER SERVICE (profess. & kin.); NUTRITIONIST (profess. & kin.); PRODUCT REPRESENTATIVE (profess. & kin.); RESEARCH-HOME ECONOMIST (profess. & kin.); TEST-KITCHEN-HOME ECONOMIST (profess. & kin.). • **GED:** R5, M3, L5 • **SVP:** 2-4 yrs • **Academic:** Ed=A, Eng=G • **Work Field:** 282, 296 • **MPSMS:** 949 • **Aptitudes:** G2, V2, N3, S3, P3, Q2, K3, F3,

M3, E4, C3 • **Temperaments:** I, J, P, V • **Stress:** E • **Physical:** V=L, H=L, L=S, H • **Work Env:** I • **Salary:** 4 • **Outlook:** 3

HOMEMAKER (social ser.) • D.O.T. #309.354-010 • OES #68035 • Advises family in private home in dealing with problems, such as nutrition, cleanliness, and household utilities: Advises and assists family members in planning nutritious meals, purchasing and preparing foods, and utilizing commodities from surplus food programs. Assists head of household in training and disciplining children, assigns and schedules housekeeping duties to children according to their capabilities, and encourages parents to take interest in children's schoolwork and assist them in establishing good study habits. Explains fundamental hygiene principles and renders bedside care to individuals who are ill, and trains other family members to provide required care. Participates in evaluating needs of individuals served, and confers with CASEWORKER (social ser.) to plan for continuing additional services. • **GED:** R4, M2, L4 • **SVP:** 6 mos-1 yr • **Academic:** Ed=N, Eng=S • **Work Field:** 294 • **MPSMS:** 941 • **Aptitudes:** G3, V3, N4, S4, P4, Q3, K4, F4, M4, E5, C5 • **Temperaments:** I, J, P • **Stress:** E • **Physical:** V=N, H=L, L=L, W, H • **Work Env:** I • **Salary:** 3 • **Outlook:** 4

GOE: 11.02.04 Library Services

CAREER-GUIDANCE TECHNICIAN (educ.) • D.O.T. #249.367-014 • OES #55347 • CAREER-INFORMATION SPECIALIST; CAREER RESOURCE TECHNICIAN. Collects and organizes occupational data to provide source materials for school career information center, and assists students and teachers to locate and obtain materials: Orders, catalogues, and maintains files on materials relating to job opportunities, careers, technical schools, colleges, scholarships, armed forces, and other programs. Assists students and teachers to locate career information related to students' interests and aptitudes, or demonstrates use of files, shelf collections, and other information retrieval systems. Assists students to take and score self-administered vocational interest and aptitude tests. Keeps records of students enrolled in work experience program and other vocational programs to assist counseling and guidance staff. Schedules appointments with school guidance and counseling staff for students requiring professional assistance. May make presentations to parent and other groups to publicize activities of career center. May operate audio-visual equipment, such as tape recorders, record players, and film or slide projectors. • **GED:** R4, M3, L4 • **SVP:** 1-2 yrs • **Academic:** Ed=H, Eng=G • **Work Field:** 231, 282 • **MPSMS:** 931 • **Aptitudes:** G3, V3, N4, S4, P4, Q3, K4, F4, M4, E4, C5 • **Temperaments:** J, M, P • **Stress:** E • **Physical:** V=L, H=N, L=S, H • **Work Env:** I • **Salary:** 3 • **Outlook:** 3

CATALOG LIBRARIAN (library) • D.O.T. #100.387-010 • OES #31505 • CATALOGER; DESCRIPTIVE CATALOG LIBRARIAN. Compiles information on library materials, such as books and periodicals, and prepares catalog cards to identify materials and to integrate information into library catalog: Verifies author, title, and classification number on sample catalog card received from CLASSIFIER (library) against corresponding data on title page. Fills in additional information, such as publisher, date of publication, and edition. Examines material and notes additional information, such as bibliographies, illustrations, maps, and appendices. Copies classification number from sample card into library material for identification. Files cards into assigned sections of catalog. Tabulates number of sample cards according to quantity of material and catalog subject headings to determine amount of new cards to be ordered or reproduced. Prepares inventory card to record purchase information and location of library material. Requisitions additional cards. Records new information, such as death date of author and revised edition date, to amend cataloged cards. May supervise activities of other workers in unit. • **GED:** R4, M2, L4 • **SVP:** 6 mos-1 yr • **Academic:** Ed=B, Eng=G • **Work Field:** 221 • **MPSMS:** 933 • **Aptitudes:** G3, V3, N3, S4, P3, Q2, K4, F4, M4, E5, C5 • **Temperaments:** R, T • **Stress:** T • **Physical:** V=L, H=N, L=S, H • **Work Env:** I • **Salary:** 3 • **Outlook:** 3

CLASSIFIER (library) • D.O.T. #100.367-014 • OES #31505 • Classifies library materials, such as books, audiovisual materials, and periodicals, according to subject matter: Reviews materials to be classified and searches information sources, such as book re-

views, encyclopedias, and technical publications to determine subject matter of materials. Selects classification numbers and descriptive headings according to Dewey Decimal, Library of Congress, or other classification systems. Makes sample cards containing author, title, and classification number to guide CATALOG LIBRARIAN (library) in preparing catalog cards for books and periodicals. Assigns classification numbers, descriptive headings, and explanatory summaries to book and catalog cards to facilitate locating and obtaining materials. Composes annotations (explanatory summaries) of material content. • **GED:** R4, M3, L4 • **SVP:** 1-2 yrs • **Academic:** Ed=A, Eng=G • **Work Field:** 221 • **MPSMS:** 933 • **Aptitudes:** G2, V2, N4, S4, P3, Q2, K4, F4, M4, E5, C5 • **Temperaments:** J, R, T • **Stress:** T • **Physical:** V=L, H=N, L=S, H • **Work Env:** I • **Salary:** 4 • **Outlook:** 3

FILM-OR-TAPE LIBRARIAN (clerical) • D.O.T. #222.367-026 • OES #58023 • Classifies, catalogs, and maintains library of motion-picture films, photographic slides, video and audio tapes, or computer tapes and punchcards: Classifies and catalogs items according to contents and purpose and prepares index cards for file reference. Maintains records of items received, stored, issued, and returned. Stores items and records according to classification and catalog number. May store lecture notes or other documents related to documents stored. May be designated according to items stored as AUDIO-TAPE LIBRARIAN (clerical); COMPUTER-TAPE LIBRARIAN (clerical); FILM LIBRARIAN (motion pic.). • **GED:** R3, M2, L3 • **SVP:** 6 mos-1 yr • **Academic:** Ed=N, Eng=S • **Work Field:** 221 • **MPSMS:** 898 • **Aptitudes:** G3, V3, N3, S3, P3, Q2, K3, F4, M4, E5, C4 • **Temperaments:** R, T • **Stress:** T • **Physical:** V=L, H=N, L=L, H • **Work Env:** I • **Salary:** 2 • **Outlook:** 3

FILM-RENTAL CLERK (bus. ser.) • D.O.T. #295.367-018 • OES #55323 • AUDIO-VISUAL-EQUIPMENT-RENTAL CLERK; FILM BOOKER. Rents films and audio-visual equipment to individuals and organizations, such as schools, churches, clubs, and business firms: Views incoming films to familiarize self with content. Recommends films on specific subjects to show to designated group, utilizing knowledge of film content, availability of film, and rental charge. Determines and quotes rental charges for film, depending on purpose for showing film, number of times to be shown, and size of audience. Writes orders, listing shipping date, show date, and method of shipping film. Posts film rental dates on office records to complete reservation. May write or type correspondence, invoices, and shipping labels. May visit prospective or current customers to sell film-rental and audio-visual-equipment-renting service. • **GED:** R4, M3, L4 • **SVP:** 6 mos-1 yr • **Academic:** Ed=H, Eng=G • **Work Field:** 221, 292 • **MPSMS:** 889 • **Aptitudes:** G3, V3, N3, S4, P3, Q3, K4, F3, M4, E5, C5 • **Temperaments:** I, J, P • **Physical:** V=L, H=N, L=S, W, H • **Work Env:** I • **Salary:** 2 • **Outlook:** 3

LIBRARIAN (library) • D.O.T. #100.127-014 • OES #31502 • Maintains library collections of books, serial publications, documents, audiovisual, and other materials, and assists groups and individuals in locating and obtaining materials: Furnishes information on library activities, facilities, rules, and services. Explains and assists in use of reference sources, such as card or book catalog or book and periodical indexes to locate information. Describes or demonstrates procedures for searching catalog files. Searches catalog files and shelves to locate information. Issues and receives materials for circulation or for use in library. Assembles and arranges displays of books and other library materials. Maintains reference and circulation materials. Answers correspondence on special reference subjects. May compile list of library materials according to subject or interests. May select, order, catalog, and classify materials. May plan and direct or carry out special projects involving library promotion and outreach activity and be designated OUTREACH LIBRARIAN (library). May be designated according to specialized function as CIRCULATION LIBRARIAN (library); REFERENCE LIBRARIAN (library); or READERS'-ADVISORY-SERVICE LIBRARIAN (library). • **GED:** R5, M3, L5 • **SVP:** 2-4 yrs • **Academic:** Ed=B, Eng=G • **Work Field:** 221 • **MPSMS:** 933 • **Aptitudes:** G2, V2, N3, S4, P4, Q2, K4, F4, M4, E5, C5 • **Temperaments:** J, P, V • **Stress:** E • **Physical:** V=N, H=N, L=S, H • **Work Env:** I • **Salary:** 5 • **Outlook:** 3

LIBRARIAN, SPECIAL LIBRARY (library) • D.O.T. #100.167-

026 • OES #31502 • Manages library or section containing specialized materials for industrial, commercial, or governmental organizations, or for such institutions as schools and hospitals: Selects, orders, catalogs, and classifies special collections of technical books, periodicals, manufacturers' catalogs and specifications, slides, film strips, motion pictures, microforms, journal reprints, and other materials. Searches literature, compiles accession lists, and annotates or abstracts materials. Assists patrons in research problems. Translates or orders translation of materials from foreign languages into English. May be designated according to subject matter, specialty or library, or department as ART LIBRARIAN (library); BUSINESS LIBRARIAN (library); ENGINEERING LIBRARIAN (library); LAW LIBRARIAN (library); MAP LIBRARIAN (library); MEDICAL LIBRARIAN (library). • **GED:** R5, M3, L5 • **SVP:** 2-4 yrs • **Academic:** Ed=B, Eng=G • **Work Field:** 221 • **MPSMS:** 933 • **Aptitudes:** G2, V2, N3, S4, P3, Q2, K4, F4, M4, E5, C5 • **Temperaments:** D, J, P, V • **Physical:** V=L, H=N, L=S, H • **Work Env:** I • **Salary:** 4 • **Outlook:** 4

LIBRARY ASSISTANT (library) • D.O.T. #249.367-046 • OES #53902 • BOOK-LOAN CLERK; CIRCULATION CLERK; DESK ATTENDANT; LIBRARY ATTENDANT; LIBRARY CLERK; LIBRARY HELPER. Compiles records, sorts and shelves books, and issues and receives library materials, such as books, films, and phonograph records: Records identifying data and due date on cards by hand or using photographic equipment to issue books to patrons. Inspects returned books for damage, verifies due-date, and computes and receives overdue fines. Reviews records to compile list of overdue books and issues overdue notices to borrowers. Sorts books, publications, and other items according to classification code and returns them to shelves, files, or other designated storage area. Locates books and publications for patrons. Issues borrower's identification card according to established procedures. Files cards in catalog drawers according to system. Repairs books, using mending tape and paste and brush. Answers inquiries of nonprofessional nature on telephone and in person and refers persons requiring professional assistance to LIBRARIAN (library). May type material cards or issue cards and duty schedules. May be designated according to type of library as BOOKMOBILE CLERK (library); BRANCH-LIBRARY CLERK (library); or according to assigned department as LIBRARY CLERK, ART DE-PARTMENT (library). • **GED:** R3, M2, L3 • **SVP:** 3-6 mos • **Academic:** Ed=H, Eng=G • **Work Field:** 221, 282 • **MPSMS:** 933 • **Aptitudes:** G3, V3, N4, S4, P3, Q3, K3, F3, M4, E4, C4 • **Temperaments:** P, V • **Stress:** E • **Physical:** V=L, H=L, L=L, S, H • **Work Env:** I • **Salary:** 3 • **Outlook:** 3

LIBRARY TECHNICAL ASSISTANT (library) • D.O.T. #100.367-018 • OES #31505 • LIBRARY TECHNICIAN; LIBRARY ASSISTANT. Provides information service, such as answering questions regarding card catalogs, and assists public in use of bibliographic tools, such as Library of Congress catalog: Performs routine descriptive cataloging, such as fiction and children's literature. Files cards in catalog drawers according to system used. Answers routine inquiries, and refers persons requiring professional assistance to LIBRARIAN (library). Verifies bibliographic information on order requests. Directs activities of workers in maintenance of stacks or in section of department or division, such as ordering or receiving section of acquisitions department, card preparation activities in catalog department, or limited loan or reserve desk operation of circulation department. • **GED:** R4, M3, L3 • **SVP:** 6 mos-1 yr • **Academic:** Ed=H, Eng=G • **Work Field:** 221 • **MPSMS:** 933 • **Aptitudes:** G3, V3, N2, S4, P3, Q2, K4, F4, M4, E5, C5 • **Temperaments:** P, V • **Stress:** E • **Physical:** V=L, H=N, L=S, H • **Work Env:** I • **Salary:** 3 • **Outlook:** 2

MEDIA SPECIALIST, SCHOOL LIBRARY (library) • D.O.T. #100.167-030 • OES #31502 • LIBRARIAN, SCHOOL; MEDIA CENTER DIRECTOR, SCHOOL. Assesses and meets needs of students and faculty for information, and develops programs to stimulate students' interests in reading and use of types of resources: Selects and organizes books, films, tapes, records, and other materials and equipment. Plans and carries out program of instruction in use by school library media center. Prepares and administers budget for media center. Works with faculty to provide materials for classroom instruction. Confers with faculty, parents, public librarians, and community organizations to develop programs to enrich students' communication skills. • **GED:** R5, M3, L4 • **SVP:** 2-4 yrs • **Academic:** Ed=A, Eng=S • **Work Field:** 221 • **MPSMS:** 933 • **Aptitudes:** G2, V2, N3, S3, P2, Q3, K3, F3, M3, E5, C3 • **Temperaments:** D, I, J, P, V • **Stress:** A • **Physical:** V=L, H=L, L=L, H • **Work Env:** I • **Salary:** 4 • **Outlook:** 3

11.03 Social Research

Workers in this group gather, study, and analyze information about individuals, specific groups, or entire societies. They conduct research, both historical and current, into all aspects of human behavior, including abnormal behavior, language, work, politics, lifestyle, and cultural expression. They are employed by museums, schools and colleges, government agencies, and private research foundations.

✔ What kind of work would you do?

Your work activities would depend upon your specific job. For example, you might:

- collect and analyze data about jobs, including worker qualifications and characteristics.
- study articles from a historic site to learn about an ancient society.
- conduct research about the mental development of people.
- determine the origins, meanings, and pronunciations of words and define them for a dictionary.
- appraise, assemble, and direct the safekeeping of historic documents.
- conduct research in psychological problems related to engineering projects.
- study the structure of language to understand its social function.
- collect and interpret data on economic conditions.

✔ What skills and abilities do you need for this kind of work?

To do this kind of work, you must be able to:

- analyze and interpret both current and historical information that relates to the research subject.
- understand and use the theories and methods of research in your particular field.

- organize detailed research notes into a logical outline.
- write reports of findings.

✔ **How do you know if you would like or could learn to do this kind of work?**

The following questions may give you clues about yourself as you consider this group of jobs.

- Have you read magazines concerning world affairs and social problems? Do you keep informed of current events?
- Have you done research projects or surveys for social science classes? Do you enjoy this type of activity?

- Have you taken courses in sociology, psychology, or civics? Do you like to write reports or research papers?
- Have you visited museums or historical sites? Do you enjoy history?

✔ **How can you prepare for and enter this kind of work?**

Occupations in this group usually require education and/or training extending from two years to over ten years, depending upon the specific kind of work. Almost all jobs in this group require four or more years of college study in the social sciences. Some jobs require specialization in a particular field such as sociology, history, economics, or archeology. Courses in computer science and statistics are important because these technologies are used to handle research data.

✔ **What else should you consider about these jobs?**

Employers expect workers in this group to keep up with developments and trends in their specific area. This is done by attending seminars and workshops or studying for advanced degrees.

If you think you would like to do this kind of work, look at the job titles listed on the following pages.

GOE: 11.03.01 Psychological Research

PSYCHOLOGIST, EXPERIMENTAL (profess. & kin.) • D.O.T. #045.061-018 • OES #27108 • Plans, designs, conducts, and analyzes results of experiments to study problems in psychology: Formulates hypotheses and experimental designs to investigate problems of perception, memory, learning, personality, and cognitive processes. Designs and constructs equipment and apparatus for laboratory study. Selects, controls, and modifies variables in laboratory experiments with humans or animals, and observes and records behavior in relation to variables. Analyzes test results, using statistical techniques, and evaluates significance of data in relation to original hypothesis. Collaborates with other scientists in such fields as physiology, biology, and sociology in conducting interdisciplinary studies of behavior and formulating theories of behavior. Writes papers describing experiments and interpreting test results for publication or for presentation at scientific meetings. May specialize in aesthetics, memory, learning, autonomic functions, electro- encephalography, feeling and emotion, motivation, motor skills, perception, or higher-order cognitive processes. May conduct experiments to study relationship of behavior to various bodily mechanisms and be designated PSYCHOLOGIST, PHYSIOLOGICAL (profess. & kin.). May specialize in study of animal behavior to develop theories of animal and human behavior, and be designated PSYCHOLOGIST, COMPARATIVE (profess. & kin.). • GED: R6, M6, L5 • SVP: 4-10 yrs • Academic: Ed=M, Eng=G • Work Field: 251 • MPSMS: 733 • Aptitudes: G1, V1, N2, S3, P3, Q4, K3, F3, M3, E5, C4 • Temperaments: D, J, M, V • Physical: V=N, H=G, L=S, H • Work Env: I • Salary: 4 • Outlook: 3

PSYCHOLOGIST, INDUSTRIAL-ORGANIZATIONAL (profess. & kin.) • D.O.T. #045.107-030 • OES #27108 • Develops and applies psychological techniques to personnel administration, management, and marketing problems: Observes details of work and interviews workers and supervisors to establish physical, mental, educational, and other job requirements. Develops interview techniques, rating scales, and psychological tests to assess skills, abilities, aptitudes, and interests as aids in selection, placement, and promotion. Organizes training programs, applying principles of learning and individual differences, and evaluates and measures effectiveness of training methods by statistical analysis of production rate, reduction of accidents, absenteeism, and turnover. Counsels workers to improve job and personal adjustments. Conducts research studies of organizational structure, communication systems, group interactions, and motivational systems, and recommends changes to improve efficiency and effectiveness of individuals, organizational units, and organization. Investigates problems related to physical environment of work, such as illumination, noise, temperature, and ventilation, and recommends changes to increase efficiency and decrease accident rate. Conducts surveys and research studies to ascertain nature of effective supervision and leadership and to analyze factors affecting morale and motivation. Studies consumer reaction to new products and package designs, using surveys and tests, and measures effectiveness of advertising media to aid in sale of goods and services. May advise management on personnel policies and labor-management relations. May adapt machinery, equipment, workspace, and environment to human use. May specialize in development and application of such techniques as job analysis and classification, personnel interviewing, ratings, and vocational tests for use in selection, placement, promotion, and training of workers, and be designated PSYCHOLOGIST, PERSONNEL (profess. & kin.). May apply psychological principles and techniques to selection, training, classification, and assignment of military personnel, and be designated PSYCHOLOGIST, MILITARY PERSONNEL (profess. & kin.). May conduct surveys and tests to study consumer reaction to new products and package design, and to measure effectiveness of advertising media to aid manufacturers in sale of goods and services, and be designated MARKET-RESEARCH ANALYST (profess. & kin.) II. • **GED:** R6, M6, L5 • **SVP:** 4- 10 yrs • **Academic:** Ed=M, Eng=G • **Work Field:** 251, 271 • **MPSMS:** 733 • **Aptitudes:** G1, V1, N2, S3, P3, Q4, K4, F4, M4, E5, C5 • **Temperaments:** I, J, M, P, V • **Stress:** E • **Physical:** V=L, H=L, L=S • **Work Env:** I • **Salary:** 5 • **Outlook:** 4

GOE: 11.03.02 Sociological

CITY PLANNING AIDE (profess. & kin.) • D.O.T. #199.364-010 • OES #39999 • PLANNING ASSISTANT. Compiles data for use by URBAN PLANNER (profess. & kin.) in making planning studies: Summarizes information from maps, reports, field and file investigations, and books. Traces maps and prepares statistical tabulations, computations, charts, and graphs to illustrate planning studies in areas, such as population, transportation, traffic, land use, zoning, proposed subdivisions, and public utilities. Prepares and updates files and records. May answer public inquiries, conduct field interviews and make surveys of traffic flow, parking, housing, educational facilities, recreation, zoning, and other conditions which affect planning studies. • **GED:** R4, M4, L4 • **SVP:** 1-2 yrs • **Academic:** Ed=H, Eng=S • **Work Field:** 231, 271 • **MPSMS:** 719, 744 • **Aptitudes:** G3, V3, N3, S3, P2, Q2, K3, F3, M4, E5, C4 • **Temperaments:** T, V • **Physical:** V=G, H=L, L=L • **Work Env:** B • **Salary:** 4 • **Outlook:** 3

PLANNER, PROGRAM SERVICES (gov. ser.) • D.O.T. #188.167-110 • OES #27105 • Conducts studies, prepares reports, and advises public and private sector administrators on feasibility, cost-effectiveness, and regulatory conformance of proposals for special projects or ongoing programs in such fields as transportation, conservation, or health care: Consults with administrators or planning councils to discuss overall intent of programs or projects, and determines broad guidelines for studies, utilizing knowledge of subject area, research techniques, and regulatory limitations. Reviews and evaluates materials provided with proposals, such as environmental impact statements, construction specifications, or budget or staffing estimates, to determine additional data requirements. Conducts field investigations, economic or public opinion surveys, demographic studies, or other appropriate research to gather required information. Organizes and analyzes data from all sources, using statistical methods to ensure validity of results. Evaluates information to determine feasibility of proposals or to identify factors requiring amendment. Develops alternate plans for program or project, incorporating recommendations, for review of officials. Maintains collection of socioeconomic, environmental, and regulatory data related to agency functions, for use by planning and administrative personnel in government and private sectors. Reviews plans and proposals submitted by other governmental planning commissions or private organizations to assist in formulation of over all plans for region. • **GED:** R6, M5, L6 • **SVP:** 2-4 yrs • **Academic:** Ed=B, Eng=G • **Work Field:** 251 • **MPSMS:** 959 • **Aptitudes:** G1, V1, N1, S2, P2, Q2, K3, F4, M4, E5, C5 • **Temperaments:** D, J, P • **Stress:** E • **Physical:** V=N, H=N, L=S • **Work Env:** I • **Salary:** 4 • **Outlook:** 1

POLITICAL SCIENTIST (profess. & kin.) • D.O.T. #051.067-010 • OES #27199 • Studies phenomena of political behavior, such as origin, development, operation, and inter relationships of political institutions, to formulate and develop political theory: Conducts research into political philosophy and theories of political systems, utilizing information available on political phenomena, such as governmental institutions, public laws and administration, political party systems, and international law. Consults with government officials, civic bodies, research agencies, and political parties. Analyzes and interprets results of studies, and prepares reports detailing findings, recommendations or conclusions. May organize and conduct public opinion surveys and interpret results. May specialize in specific geographical, political, or philosophical aspect

of political behavior. • **GED:** R6, M5, L5 • **SVP:** 4-10 yrs • **Academic:** Ed=M, Eng=G • **Work Field:** 251 • **MPSMS:** 742, 743 • **Aptitudes:** G2, V2, N3, S4, P4, Q2, K4, F4, M4, E5, C5 • **Temperaments:** D, J • **Physical:** V=N, H=N, L=S • **Work Env:** I • **Salary:** 5 • **Outlook:** 2

RESEARCH WORKER, SOCIAL WELFARE (profess. & kin.) • D.O.T. #054.067-010 • OES #27199 • Plans, organizes, and conducts research for use in understanding social problems and for planning and carrying out social welfare programs: Develops research designs on basis of existing knowledge and evolving theory. Constructs and tests methods of data collection. Collects information and makes judgments through observation, interview, and review of documents. Analyzes and evaluates data. Writes reports containing descriptive, analytical, and evaluative content. Interprets methods employed and findings to individuals within agency and community. May direct work of statistical clerks, statisticians, and others. May collaborate with research workers in other disciplines. May be employed in voluntary or governmental social welfare agencies, community welfare councils, and schools of social work. • **GED:** R6, M5, L5 • **SVP:** 2-4 yrs • **Academic:** Ed=B, Eng=G • **Work Field:** 251 • **MPSMS:** 941 • **Aptitudes:** G1, V1, N2, S3, P4, Q4, K4, F4, M4, E5, C5 • **Temperaments:** J, M • **Physical:** V=N, H=L, L=S • **Work Env:** I • **Salary:** 4 • **Outlook:** 1

SCIENTIFIC LINGUIST (profess. & kin.) • D.O.T. #059.067-014 • OES #27199 • LINGUIST. Studies components, structure, and relationships within specified language to provide comprehension of its social functioning: Prepares description of sounds, forms, and vocabulary of language. Contributes to development of linguistic theory. Applies linguistic theory to any of following areas; development of improved methods in translation, including computerization; teaching of language to other than native speakers; preparation of language-teaching materials, dictionaries, and handbooks; reducing previously unwritten languages to standardized written form; preparation of literacy materials; preparation of tests for language-learning aptitudes and language proficiency; consultation with government agencies regarding language programs; or preparation of descriptions of comparative languages to facilitate improvement of teaching and translation. • **GED:** R6, M5, L6 • **SVP:** 4-10 yrs • **Academic:** Ed=B, Eng=S • **Work Field:** 251 • **MPSMS:** 745 • **Aptitudes:** G2, V2, N3, S2, P2, Q2, K4, F4, M4, E5, C5 • **Temperaments:** J, M, P • **Physical:** V=N, H=N, L=S, H • **Work Env:** I • **Salary:** 5 • **Outlook:** 2

SOCIOLOGIST (profess. & kin.) • D.O.T. #054.067-014 • OES #27199 • Conducts research into development, structure, and behavior of groups of human beings and patterns of culture and social organization which have arisen out of group life in society. Collects and analyzes scientific data concerning social phenomena, such as community, associations, social institutions, ethnic minorities, social classes, and social change. May teach sociology, direct research, prepare technical publications, or act as consultant to lawmakers, administrators, and other officials dealing with problems of social policy. May specialize in research on relationship between criminal law and social order in causes of crime and behavior of criminals and be designated CRIMINOLOGIST (profess. & kin.). May specialize in research on punishment for crime and control and prevention of crime, management of penal institutions, and rehabilitation of criminal offenders and be designated PENOLOGIST (profess. & kin.). May specialize in research on group relationships and processes in an industrial organization and be designated INDUSTRIAL SOCIOLOGIST (profess. & kin.). May specialize in research on rural communities in contrast with urban communities and special problems occasioned by impact of scientific and industrial revolutions on rural way of life and be designated RURAL SOCIOLOGIST (profess. & kin.). May specialize in research on interrelations between physical environment and technology in spatial distribution of people and their activities and be designated SOCIAL ECOLOGIST (profess. & kin.). May specialize in research on social problems arising from individual or group deviation from commonly accepted standards of conduct, such as crime and delinquency, or social problems and racial discrimination rooted in failure of society to achieve its collective purposes and be designated SOCIAL PROBLEMS SPECIALIST (profess. & kin.). May specialize in research on origin, growth, structure, and demographic characteristics of cities and social patterns and distinctive problems that result from urban environment and be designated URBAN SOCIOLOGIST (profess. & kin.). May specialize in research on social factors affecting health care, including definition of illness, patient and practitioner behavior, social epidemiology, and delivery of health care and be designated MEDICAL SOCIOLOGIST (profess. & kin.). May plan and conduct demographic research, surveys, and experiments to study human populations and affecting trends and be designated DEMOGRAPHER (profess. & kin.) II. • **GED:** R6, M5, L5 • **SVP:** 2-4 yrs • **Academic:** Ed=M, Eng=G • **Work Field:** 251 • **MPSMS:** 744 • **Aptitudes:** G1, V1, N3, S4, P4, Q3, K4, F4, M4, E5, C5 • **Temperaments:** D, J, M • **Physical:** V=N, H=N, L=S • **Work Env:** I • **Salary:** 4 • **Outlook:** 1

URBAN PLANNER (profess. & kin.) • D.O.T. #199.167-014 • OES #27105 • CITY PLANNER; CITY-PLANNING ENGINEER; LAND PLANNER; TOWN PLANNER. Develops comprehensive plans and programs for utilization of land and physical facilities of cities, counties, and metropolitan areas: Compiles and analyzes data on economic, social, and physical factors affecting land use, and prepares or requisitions graphic and narrative reports on data. Confers with local authorities, civic leaders, social scientists, and land planning and development specialists to devise and recommend arrangements of land and physical facilities for residential, commercial, industrial, and community uses. Recommends governmental measures affecting land use, public utilities, community facilities, and housing and transportation to control and guide community development and renewal. May review and evaluate environmental impact reports applying to specified private and public planning projects and programs. When directing activities of planning department, is known as CHIEF PLANNER (profess. & kin.) or DIRECTOR, PLANNING (profess. & kin.). Usually employed by local government jurisdictions, but may work for any level of government, or private consulting firms. • **GED:** R5, M4, L5 • **SVP:** 4-10 yrs • **Academic:** Ed=B, Eng=G • **Work Field:** 244, 295 • **MPSMS:** 704 • **Aptitudes:** G2, V1, N2, S2, P2, Q3, K4, F3, M4, E5, C4 • **Temperaments:** J, P, V • **Stress:** E • **Physical:** V=N, H=N, L=S • **Work Env:** I • **Salary:** 4 • **Outlook:** 2

GOE: 11.03.03 Historical

ANTHROPOLOGIST (profess. & kin.) • D.O.T. #055.067-010 • OES #27199 • Makes comparative studies in relations to distribution, origin, evolution, and races of humans, cultures they have created, and their distribution and physical characteristics: Gathers, analyzes, and reports data on human physique, social customs, and artifacts, such as weapons, tools, pottery, and clothing. May apply anthropological data and techniques to solution of problems in human relations in fields, such as industrial relations, race and ethnic relations, social work, political administration, education, public health, and programs involving transcultural or foreign relations. May specialize in application of anthropological concepts to current problems and be designated APPLIED ANTHROPOLOGIST (profess. & kin.). May specialize in study of relationships between language and culture and sociolinguistic studies and be designated ANTHROPOLOGICAL LINGUIST (profess. & kin.); or in study of relationship between individual personality and culture and be designated PSYCHOLOGICAL ANTHROPOLOGIST (profess. & kin.); or in study of complex, industrialized societies and be designated URBAN ANTHROPOLOGIST (profess. & kin.). • **GED:** R6, M5, L5 • **SVP:** 2-4 yrs • **Academic:** Ed=M, Eng=G • **Work Field:** 251 • **MPSMS:** 745 • **Aptitudes:** G1, V1, N3, S2, P2, Q4, K4, F4, M4, E4, C5 • **Temperaments:** J, M • **Physical:** V=N, H=L, L=S, W, H • **Work Env:** I • **Salary:** 4 • **Outlook:** 1

ARCHEOLOGIST (profess. & kin.) • D.O.T. #055.067-018 • OES #27199 • Reconstructs record of extinct cultures, especially preliterate cultures: Studies, classifies, and interprets artifacts, architectural features, and types of structures recovered by excavation in order to determine age and cultural identity. Establishes chronological sequence of development of each culture from simpler to more advanced levels. May specialize in study of literate periods of major civilizations in Near and Middle East and be designated ARCHEOLOGIST, CLASSICAL (profess. & kin.). May specialize in study of past Columbian history of the Americas and be designated HISTORICAL ARCHEOLOGIST (profess. & kin.). • **GED:**

R6, M5, L5 • **SVP:** 2-4 yrs • **Academic:** Ed=B, Eng=S • **Work Field:** 251 • **MPSMS:** 745 • **Aptitudes:** G1, V1, N3, S2, P2, Q4, K4, F4, M4, E4, C5 • **Temperaments:** J, M • **Physical:** V=N, H=N, L=L, H • **Work Env:** I • **Salary:** 4 • **Outlook:** 1

ARCHIVIST (profess. & kin.) • D.O.T. #101.167-010 • OES #31511 • Appraises and edits permanent records and historically valuable documents, participates in research activities based on archival materials, and directs safekeeping of archival documents and materials: Analyzes documents, such as government records, minutes of corporate board meetings, letters from famous persons, and charters of nonprofit foundations, by ascertaining date of writing, author, or original recipient of letter, to appraise value to posterity or to employing organization. Directs activities of workers engaged in cataloging and safekeeping of valuable materials and directs disposition of worthless materials. Prepares or directs preparation of document descriptions and reference aids for use of archives, such as accession lists, indexes, guides, bibliographies, abstracts, and microfilmed copies of documents. Directs filing and cross indexing of selected documents in alphabetical and chronological order. Advises government agencies, scholars, journalists, and others conducting research by supplying available materials and information according to familiarity with archives and with political, economic, military, and social history of period. Requests or recommends pertinent materials available in libraries, private collections, or other archives. Selects and edits documents for publication and display, according to knowledge of subject, literary or journalistic expression, and techniques for presentation and display. May be designated according to subject matter specialty as ARCHIVIST, ECONOMIC HISTORY (profess. & kin.); ARCHIVIST, MILITARY HISTORY (profess. & kin.); ARCHIVIST, POLITICAL HISTORY (profess. & kin.); or according to nature of employing institution as ARCHIVIST, NONPROFIT FOUNDATION (nonprofit organ.). In smaller organizations, may direct activities of libraries. • **GED:** R5, M3, L5 • **SVP:** 4-10 yrs • **Academic:** Ed=B, Eng=G • **Work Field:** 211, 251, 293 • **MPSMS:** 933 • **Aptitudes:** G2, V1, N2, S3, P2, Q3, K4, F4, M4, E5, C4 • **Temperaments:** D, F, J, P, V • **Physical:** V=L, H=N, L=S • **Work Env:** I • **Salary:** 4 • **Outlook:** 3

GENEALOGIST (profess. & kin.) • D.O.T. #052.067-018 • OES #27199 • Conducts research into genealogical background of individual or family in order to establish descent from specific ancestor or to discover and identify forebears of individual or family: Consults American and foreign genealogical tables and publications and documents, such as church and court records, for evidence of births, baptisms, marriages, deaths, and legacies in order to trace lines of descent or succession. Constructs chart showing lines of descent and family relationships. Prepares history of family in narrative form or writes brief sketches emphasizing points of interest in family background. • **GED:** R5, M2, L5 • **SVP:** 2-4 yrs • **Academic:** Ed=H, Eng=G • **Work Field:** 251 • **MPSMS:** 742, 743 • **Aptitudes:** G2, V2, N3, S4, P4, Q2, K4, F4, M4, E5, C5 • **Temperaments:** D, J, M • **Physical:** V=N, H=N, L=S, H • **Work Env:** I • **Salary:** 4 • **Outlook:** 1

HISTORIAN (profess. & kin.) • D.O.T. #052.067-022 • OES #27199 • Prepares in narrative, brief, or outline form chronological account or record of past or current events dealing with some phase of human activity, either in terms of individuals, or social, ethnic, political, or geographic groupings: Assembles historical data by consulting sources of information, such as historical indexes and catalogs, archives, court records, diaries, news files, and miscellaneous published and unpublished materials. Organizes and evaluates data on basis of authenticity and relative significance. Acts as adviser or consultant, and performs research for individuals, institutions, and commercial organizations on subjects, such as technological evolution within industry or manners and customs peculiar to certain historical period. May trace historical development within restricted field of research, such as economics, sociology, or philosophy. • **GED:** R5, M2, L5 • **SVP:** 2-4 yrs • **Academic:** Ed=B, Eng=G • **Work Field:** 251 • **MPSMS:** 742, 743 • **Aptitudes:** G2, V2, N3, S4, P4, Q2, K4, F4, M4, E5, C5 • **Temperaments:** D, J, M • **Physical:** V=L, H=N, L=S, H • **Work Env:** I • **Salary:** 4 • **Outlook:** 1

RESEARCH ASSISTANT (profess. & kin.) • D.O.T. #109.267-010 • OES #31511 • Conducts research on historic monuments, buildings, and scenes to reconstruct exhibits to scale in dioramas for use of fine-arts students or other purposes: Collects information from libraries, museums, and art institutes. Monitors construction of dioramas to ensure authenticity of proportions, color, and costumes in diorama. • **GED:** R5, M4, L4 • **SVP:** 2-4 yrs • **Academic:** Ed=A, Eng=S • **Work Field:** 251 • **MPSMS:** 750 • **Aptitudes:** G2, V2, N3, S2, P3, Q3, K4, F4, M4, E5, C3 • **Temperaments:** J, T, V • **Physical:** V=G, H=N, L=S • **Work Env:** I • **Salary:** 4 • **Outlook:** 3

RESEARCH ASSOCIATE (museum) • **D.O.T.** #109.067-014 • **OES** #31511 • Plans, organizes, and conducts research in scientific, cultural, historical, or artistic field for use in own work or in project of sponsoring institution: Develops plans for project or studies guidelines for project prepared by professional staff member to outline research procedures to be followed. Plans schedule according to variety of methods to be used, availability and quantity of resources, and number of subordinate personnel assigned to participate in project. Conducts research, utilizing institution library, archives, and collections, and other sources of information, to collect, record, analyze, and evaluate facts. Discusses findings with other personnel to evaluate validity of findings. Prepares reports of completed projects for publication in technical journals, for presentation to agency requesting project, or for use in further applied or theoretical research activities. • **GED:** R6, M6, L6 • **SVP:** 2-4 yrs • **Academic:** Ed=B, Eng=S • **Work Field:** 251 • **MPSMS:** 720, 730, 750 • **Aptitudes:** G1, V1, N1, S1, P2, Q2, K3, F4, M4, E5, C2 • **Temperaments:** J • **Physical:** V=G, H=L, L=S • **Work Env:** I • **Salary:** 4 • **Outlook:** 4

GOE: 11.03.04 Occupational Research

EMPLOYEE RELATIONS SPECIALIST (motor trans.) • **D.O.T.** #166.267-042 • **OES** #21511 • Interviews workers to gather information on worker attitudes toward work environment and supervision received to facilitate resolution of employee relations problems: Explains company and governmental rules, regulations, and procedures to inform workers of need for compliance. Gathers information on workers' feelings about factors that affect worker morale, motivation, and efficiency. Meets with management to discuss possible actions to be taken. Inspects work stations to ensure required changes or actions are implemented. Interviews workers to determine reactions to specific actions taken. Prepares reports on workers' comments and actions taken. Enrolls eligible workers in company programs, such as pension and savings plans. Maintains medical, insurance, and other personnel records and forms. • **GED:** R4, M2, L2 • **SVP:** 2-4 yrs • **Academic:** Ed=H, Eng=S • **Work Field:** 271 • **MPSMS:** 893 • **Aptitudes:** G2, V2, N3, S4, P4, Q3, K4, F4, M4, E5, C5 • **Temperaments:** J, P • **Physical:** V=L, H=G, L=S, H • **Work Env:** I • **Salary:** 4 • **Outlook:** 3

EMPLOYMENT INTERVIEWER (profess. & kin.) • **D.O.T.** #166.267-010 • **OES** #21508 • PLACEMENT INTERVIEWER. Interviews job applicants to select persons meeting employer qualifications: Reviews completed application and evaluates applicant's work history, education and training, job skills, salary desired, and physical and personal qualifications. Records additional skills, knowledges, abilities, interests, test results, and other data pertinent to classification, selection, and referral. Searches files of job orders from employers and matches applicant's qualifications with job requirements and employer specifications, utilizing manual file search, computer matching services, or employment service facilities. Informs applicant about job duties and responsibilities, pay and benefits, hours and working conditions, company and union policies, promotional opportunities, and other related information. Refers selected applicant to interview with person placing job order according to policy of school, agency, or company. Keeps for future reference records of applicants not immediately selected or hired. May perform reference and background checks. May refer applicant to vocational counseling services. May test or arrange for skills, intelligence, or psychological testing of applicant. May engage in research or follow-up activities to evaluate selection and placement techniques, by conferring with management and supervisory personnel. May specialize in interviewing and referring certain types of personnel, such as professional, technical, managerial, clerical, and other types of skilled or unskilled workers. May be known as PERSONNEL RECRUITER (profess. & kin.) and seek out potential applicants and try to interest them in applying for position openings. • **GED:** R5, M3, L5 • **SVP:** 6 mos-1 yr • **Academic:** Ed=B, Eng=G • **Work Field:** 271 • **MPSMS:** 943 • **Aptitudes:** G2, V2, N3, S4, P4, Q3, K4, F4, M4, E5, C5 • **Temperaments:** J, P • **Stress:** E • **Physical:** V=N, H=G, L=S • **Work Env:** I • **Salary:** 4 • **Outlook:** 4

JOB ANALYST (profess. & kin.) • **D.O.T.** #166.267-018 • **OES** #21511 • PERSONNEL ANALYST. Collects, analyzes, and prepares occupational information to facilitate personnel, administration, and management functions of organization: Consults with management to determine type, scope, and purpose of study. Studies current organizational occupational data and compiles distribution reports, organization and flow charts, and other background information required for study. Observes jobs and interviews workers and supervisory personnel to determine job and worker requirements. Analyzes occupational data, such as physical, mental, and training requirements of jobs and workers and develops written summaries, such as job descriptions, job specifications, and lines of career movement. Utilizes developed occupational data to evaluate or improve methods and techniques for recruiting, selecting, promoting, evaluating, and training workers, and administration of related personnel programs. May specialize in classifying positions according to regulated guidelines to meet job classification requirements of civil service system and be known as POSITION CLASSIFIER (gov. ser.). • **GED:** R5, M4, L5 • **SVP:** 1-2 yrs • **Academic:** Ed=B, Eng=G • **Work Field:** 295 • **MPSMS:** 712 • **Aptitudes:** G2, V2, N2, S3, P3, Q3, K4, F4, M4, E4, C4 • **Temperaments:** D, J, M, P • **Stress:** E • **Physical:** V=N, H=L, L=S • **Work Env:** I • **Salary:** 5 • **Outlook:** 4

JOB DEVELOPMENT SPECIALIST (profess. & kin.) • **D.O.T.** #166.267-034 • **OES** #21511 • Promotes and develops employment and on-the-job training opportunities for disadvantaged applicants: Assists employers in revising standards which exclude applicants from jobs. Demonstrates to employers effectiveness and profitability of employing chronically unemployed by identifying jobs that workers could perform. Establishes relationships with employers regarding problems, complaints, and progress of recently placed disadvantaged applicants and recommends corrective action. Assists employers in establishing wage scales commensurate with prevailing rates. Promotes, develops, and terminates on-the-job training program opportunities with employers and assists in writing contracts. Identifies need for and assists in development of auxiliary services to facilitate bringing disadvantaged applicants into job-ready status. Informs business, labor, and public about training programs through various media. • **GED:** R4, M3, L4 • **SVP:** 6 mos-1 yr • **Academic:** Ed=H, Eng=G • **Work Field:** 282 • **MPSMS:** 943 • **Aptitudes:** G3, V3, N4, S4, P4, Q4, K4, F4, M4, E5, C5 • **Temperaments:** I, J, P • **Stress:** E • **Physical:** V=N, H=L, L=S • **Work Env:** I • **Salary:** 3 • **Outlook:** 4

OCCUPATIONAL ANALYST (profess. & kin.) • **D.O.T.** #166.067-010 • **OES** #21511 • Researches occupations and analyzes and integrates data to develop and devise concepts of worker relationships, modify and maintain occupational classification system, and provide business, industry, and government with technical occupational information necessary for utilization of workforce: Confers with business, industry, government, and union officials to arrange for and develop plans for studies and surveys. Devises methods and establishes criteria for conducting studies and surveys. Researches jobs, industry and organizational concepts and techniques, and worker characteristics to determine job relationships, job functions and content, worker traits, and occupational trends. Prepares results of research for publication in form of books, brochures, charts, film, and manuals. Identifies need for and develops job analysis tools, such as manuals, reporting forms, training films, and slides. Prepares management tools, such as personnel distribution reports, organization and flow charts, job descriptions, tables of job relationships, and worker trait analysis. Conducts training and provides technical assistance to promote use of job analysis materials, tools, and concepts in areas of curriculum development, career planning, job restructuring, and government and employment training programs. May specialize in providing technical assistance to private, public, or governmental organizations and be designated INDUSTRIAL OCCUPA-

TIONAL ANALYST (profess. & kin.). • **GED:** R5, M4, L5 • **SVP:** 2-4 yrs • **Academic:** Ed=B, Eng=S • **Work Field:** 251 • **MPSMS:** 712 • **Aptitudes:** G1, V1, N2, S3, P3, Q3, K4, F4, M4, E4, C4 • **Temperaments:** D, J, M, P • **Stress:** A • **Physical:** V=G, H=G, L=L, W • **Work Env:** I • **Salary:** 4 • **Outlook:** 3

PERSONNEL RECRUITER (profess. & kin.) • D.O.T. #166.267-038 • OES #21511 • Seeks out, interviews, screens, and recruits job applicants to fill existing company job openings: Discusses personnel needs with department supervisors to prepare and implement recruitment program. Contacts colleges to set up on-campus interviews. Provides information on company facilities and job opportunities to potential applicants. Interviews college applicants to obtain work history, education, training, job skills, and salary requirements. Screens and refers qualified applicants to company hiring personnel for follow-up interview. Arranges travel and lodging for selected applicants at company expense. Performs reference and background checks on applicants. Corresponds with job applicants to notify them of employment consideration. Files and maintains employment records for future references. Projects yearly recruitment expenditures for budgetary control. • **GED:** R5, M3, L5 • **SVP:** 2-4 yrs • **Academic:** Ed=B, Eng=G • **Work Field:** 271 • **MPSMS:** 943 • **Aptitudes:** G2, V2, N3, S4, P4, Q3, K4, F4, M4, E5, C5 • **Temperaments:** I, J, P, V • **Stress:** E • **Physical:** V=N, H=L, L=S • **Work Env:** I • **Salary:** 5 • **Outlook:** 4

RECRUITER (military ser.) • D.O.T. #166.267-026 • OES #21511 • CAREER COUNSELOR. Interviews military and civilian personnel to recruit and inform individuals on matters concerning career opportunities, incentives, military rights and benefits, and advantages of military career: Assists and advises military commands in organizing, preparing, and implementing an enlisted recruiting and retention program. Interviews individuals to determine their suitability for placement into specific military occupation. Occasionally lectures to civic and social groups, military dependents, school officials, and religious leaders concerning military career opportunities. • **GED:** R4, M2, L3 • **SVP:** 6 mos-1 yr

• **Academic:** Ed=H, Eng=S • **Work Field:** 282, 295 • **MPSMS:** 943, 949 • **Aptitudes:** G3, V3, N4, S4, P4, Q2, K4, F4, M3, E5, C5 • **Temperaments:** J, P • **Physical:** V=N, H=G, L=L • **Work Env:** I • **Salary:** 3 • **Outlook:** 4

GOE: 11.03.05 Economic

ECONOMIST (profess. & kin.) • D.O.T. #050.067-010 • OES #27102 • ECONOMIC ANALYST. Plans, designs, and conducts research to aid in interpretation of economic relationships and in solution of problems arising from production and distribution of goods and services: Studies economic and statistical data in area of specialization, such as finance, labor, or agriculture. Devises methods and procedures for collecting and processing data, utilizing knowledge of available sources of data and various econometric and sampling techniques. Compiles data relating to research area, such as employment, productivity, and wages and hours. Reviews and analyzes economic data in order to prepare reports detailing results of investigation. Organizes data into report format and arranges for preparation of graphic illustrations of research findings. Formulates recommendations, policies, or plans to aid in market interpretation or solution of economic problems, such as recommending changes in methods of agricultural financing, domestic, and international monetary policies, or policies that regulate investment and transfer of capital. May specialize in specific economic area or commodity and be designated AGRICULTURAL ECONOMIST (profess. & kin.); COMMODITY-INDUSTRY ANALYST (profess. & kin.); FINANCIAL ECONOMIST (profess. & kin.); INDUSTRIAL ECONOMIST (profess. & kin.); INTERNATIONAL-TRADE ECONOMIST (profess. & kin.); LABOR ECONOMIST (profess. & kin.); PRICE ECONOMIST (profess. & kin.); TAX ECONOMIST (profess. & kin.). • **GED:** R5, M5, L5 • **SVP:** 2-4 yrs • **Academic:** Ed=B, Eng=G • **Work Field:** 251 • **MPSMS:** 741 • **Aptitudes:** G2, V2, N2, S4, P4, Q2, K4, F4, M4, E5, C5 • **Temperaments:** J, M, T • **Physical:** V=N, H=N, L=S • **Work Env:** I • **Salary:** 5 • **Outlook:** 2

11.04 Law

Workers in this group advise and represent others in legal matters. Those in small towns and cities conduct criminal or civil cases in court, draw up wills and other legal papers, abstract real estate, and perform related activities. Those in large cities usually specialize in one kind of law, such as criminal, civil, tax, labor, or patent. They work in law firms, unions, government agencies, and commercial and industrial establishments. Some are self-employed and have their own office. Lawyers are frequently elected to public office, particularly as legislators. Many State Governors and U.S. Presidents have been lawyers.

✔ What kind of work would you do?

Your work activities would depend upon your specific job. For example, you might:

- study court decisions and conduct investigations on claims filed against insurance companies.
- prepare wills, deeds, and other legal documents for people.
- preside in a court of law or at a formal hearing.
- conduct research in technical literature to recommend approval or rejection of patent applications.

- represent union or management in labor negotiations.
- defend people during prosecution under the law.
- represent clients who are suing or being sued for money or legal action.
- give advice concerning federal, state, local, and foreign taxes.

✔ What skills and abilities do you need for this kind of work?

To do this kind of work, you must be able to:

- understand, interpret, and apply legal procedures, principles, and laws.
- define problems, collect information, establish facts, and draw valid conclusions.
- deal with all kinds of clients, juries, judges, and other lawyers in a manner that will influence their opinions, attitudes, and judgments.

- read carefully and listen carefully to identify important details which could help a client win his case.
- use your judgment about how to conduct a case or deal with a problem.

✔ **How do you know if you would like or could learn to do this kind of work?**

The following questions may give you clues about yourself as you consider this group of jobs.

- Have you taken debate or speech courses? Do you feel at ease presenting a point of view in front of a group?
- Have you taken courses in journalism or composition? Can you communicate complex ideas effectively?

- Have you watched detective or lawyer television programs? Do you understand the legal terminology used?
- Have you attended a trial or court proceeding? Would you like to work in this type of atmosphere?

✔ **How can you prepare for and enter this kind of work?**

Occupations in this group usually require education and/or training extending from four years to over ten years, depending upon the specific kind of work. Lawyers are required to pass a bar examination and obtain a license for the particular state in which they want to practice. Educational requirements for taking the bar examination vary. Some states require proof of graduation from an approved law school. A four year college degree and completion of a program for law clerks may be accepted. Other states allow persons who study law with a licensed lawyer to take the bar examination. Correspondence courses in law are accepted as preparation for bar examinations in some states. Special requirements and licenses are necessary for those who wish to practice law in certain higher courts.

Entry requirements for law schools vary according to the institution. Some accept students directly from high school. Others require college graduation.

Some jobs in this group require legal education, but not a license. In these jobs, workers need legal knowledge, but do not practice law.

Licensed lawyers enter the field as junior partners in law firms, junior executives in business or industry, or workers in government agencies. A few establish their own law practices. However, self-employment is usually delayed because of the need for money, experience, and reputation. Some jobs in this group are elected or appointed positions.

Lawyers sometimes work long or irregular hours. They may be required to respond to emergency calls from clients. While the ability to see will make the study and practice of law easier, it is not required. There are many successful blind workers in this field.

The field of law is highly competitive, but salaried positions can be found in government agencies, private businesses, and in some law offices. Lawyers in private practice depend on collection of fees for their income. When they have several long-term retainers (fees paid in advance so that service is available when needed), they have a stable income.

If you think you would like to do this kind of work, look at the job titles listed below.

GOE: 11.04.01 Justice Administration

APPEALS REFEREE (gov. ser.) • D.O.T. #119.267-014 • OES #28105 • Adjudicates social welfare tax or benefit eligibility issues filed by disabled or unemployed claimants or employers: Arranges and conducts hearings to discover pertinent facts bearing on claim in accord with Federal and state laws and procedures. Renders decisions affirming or denying previous ruling, based on testimony, claim records, applicable provisions of law, and established precedents. Writes decision explaining ruling and informs interested parties of results. Confers with personnel of employer or agency involved to obtain additional information bearing on appeal, and to clarify future implications of decisions. May participate in court proceedings against claimants attempting to obtain benefits through fraud. May render informal opinions on points of law in questionable cases to facilitate initial determination of benefit eligibility or imposition of penalties. May be required to hold law degree or license to practice law. • **GED:** R6, M3, L6 • **SVP:** 4-10 yrs • **Academic:** Ed=B, Eng=G • **Work Field:** 271, 272 • **MPSMS:** 932, 959 • **Aptitudes:** G2, V2, N3, S4, P3, Q3, K4, F4, M4, E5, C5 • **Temperaments:** J, M, P, T • **Stress:** E, A • **Physical:** V=N, H=L, L=S • **Work Env:** I • **Salary:** 5 • **Outlook:** 4

HEARING OFFICER (gov. ser.) • D.O.T. #119.107-010 • OES #28105 • APPEALS BOARD REFEREE; REFEREE. Reviews previously adjudicated social welfare tax or eligibility issues, as member of appeals board, utilizing knowledge of regulations, policy, and precedent decisions: Researches laws, regulations, policies, and precedent decisions to prepare for appeal hearings. Schedules hearing, issues subpoenas, counsels parties, and administers oaths to prepare for formal hearing. Conducts hearing to obtain information and evidence relative to disposition of appeal. Questions witnesses and rules on exceptions, motions, and admissibility of evidence. Analyzes evidence and applicable law, regulations, policy, and precedent decisions to determine appropriate and permissible conclusions. Prepares written decision. May hear disability insurance appeals and be designated DISABILITY-INSURANCE-HEARING OFFICER (gov. ser.). May hear unemployment insurance appeals and be designated UNEMPLOYMENT- INSURANCE-HEARING OFFICER (gov. ser.). • **GED:** R6, M3, L6 • **SVP:** Over 10 yrs • **Academic:** Ed=B, Eng=G • **Work Field:** 272 • **MPSMS:** 959 • **Aptitudes:** G1, V2, N3, S4, P3, Q4, K4, F4, M4, E5, C5 • **Temperaments:** D, J, M, P • **Stress:** E, A • **Physical:** V=N, H=L, L=S • **Work Env:** I • **Salary:** 5 • **Outlook:** 3

GOE: 11.04.02 Legal Practice

LAWYER (profess. & kin.) • D.O.T. #110.107-010 • OES #28108 • ADVOCATE; ATTORNEY; BARRISTER; COUNSELOR; COUNSEL-AT LAW; JURIST; SOLICITOR. Conducts criminal and civil lawsuits, draws up legal documents, advises clients as to legal rights, and practices other phases of law: Gathers evidence in divorce, civil, criminal, and other cases to formulate defense or to initiate legal action. Represents client in court, and before quasi-judicial or administrative agencies of government. May act as trustee, guardian, or executor. May teach college courses in law. May specialize in particular phase of law. • **GED:** R6, M4, L6 • **SVP:** 4-10 yrs • **Academic:** Ed=M, Eng=G • **Work Field:** 272 • **MPSMS:** 932 • **Aptitudes:** G1, V1, N1, S4, P4, Q3, K4, F4, M4, E5, C5 • **Temperaments:** I, J, P, V • **Stress:** E, A • **Physical:** V=N, H=G, L=S • **Work Env:** I • **Salary:** 5 • **Outlook:** 3

LEGAL INVESTIGATOR (profess. & kin.) • D.O.T. #119.267-022 • OES #28302 • LEGAL ASSISTANT. Researches and prepares cases relating to administrative appeals of civil service members: Examines state government, personnel, college, or university rules and regulations. Answers members' questions regarding rights and benefits and advises on how rules apply to individual situations. Presents arguments and evidence to support appeal at appeal hearing. Calls upon witnesses to testify at hearing. • **GED:** R5, M2, L5 • **SVP:** 2-4 yrs • **Academic:** Ed=A, Eng=G • **Work Field:** 271, 272 • **MPSMS:** 949 • **Aptitudes:** G2, V1, N3, S4, P4, Q3, K4, F4, M4, E5, C5 • **Temperaments:** D, I, M, P • **Stress:** E • **Physical:** V=N, H=L, L=S • **Work Env:** I • **Salary:** 4 • **Outlook:** 4

PARALEGAL ASSISTANT (profess. & kin.) • D.O.T. #119.267-026 • OES #28302 • LAW CLERK; LEGAL AID. Researches law, investigates facts, and prepares documents to assist LAWYER (profess. & kin.): Researches and analyzes law sources such as statutes, recorded judicial decisions, legal articles, treaties, constitutions, and legal codes to prepare legal documents such as briefs, pleadings, appeals, wills, contracts, deeds, and trust instruments for review, approval, and use by attorney. Appraises and inventories real and personal property for estate planning. Investigates facts and law of case to determine causes of action and to prepare

case accordingly. Files pleadings with court clerk. Prepares affidavits of documents and maintains document file. Delivers or directs delivery of subpoenas to witnesses and parties to action. May direct and coordinate activities of law office employees. May prepare office accounts and tax returns. May specialize in litigation, probate, real estate, or corporation law. May search patent files to ascertain originality of patent application and be designated PATENT CLERK (gov. ser.). • **GED:** R5, M2, L5 • **SVP:** 2-4 yrs • **Academic:** Ed=A, Eng=G • **Work Field:** 271, 272 • **MPSMS:** 932 • **Aptitudes:** G2, V1, N3, S4, P4, Q3, K4, F4, M4, E5, C5 • **Temperaments:** M, P, T, V • **Stress:** E • **Physical:** V=G, H=N, L=S • **Work Env:** I • **Salary:** 4 • **Outlook:** 1

GOE: 11.04.03 Conciliation

ADJUDICATOR (gov. ser.) • D.O.T. #119.167-010 • OES #28105 • Adjudicates claims filed by government against individuals or organizations: Determines existence and amount of liability, according to law, administrative and judicial precedents and other evidence. Recommends acceptance or rejection of compromise settlement offers. • **GED:** R5, M4, L5 • **SVP:** 2-4 yrs • **Academic:** Ed=B, Eng=G • **Work Field:** 272 • **MPSMS:** 932 • **Aptitudes:** G2, V2, N2, S4, P4, Q4, K4, F4, M5, E5, C5 • **Temperaments:** J, P, V • **Stress:** E, A • **Physical:** V=N, H=L, L=S • **Work Env:** I • **Salary:** 4 • **Outlook:** 3

GOE: 11.04.04 Abstracting, Document Preparation

ABSTRACTOR (profess. & kin.) • D.O.T. #119.267-010 • OES #28311 • ABSTRACT CLERK; ABSTRACT MAKER; ABSTRACT SEARCHER; ABSTRACT WRITER; COURT ABSTRACTOR; TITLE ABSTRACTOR. Analyzes pertinent legal or insurance details or section of statute or case law to summarize for purposes of examination, proof, or ready reference. May search out titles to determine if title deed is correct [TITLE EXAMINER (profess. & kin.)]. • **GED:** R5, M3, L5 • **SVP:** 1-2 yrs • **Academic:** Ed=A, Eng=G • **Work Field:** 231, 271 • **MPSMS:** 895, 932 • **Aptitudes:** G2, V1, N4, S4, P4, Q2, K4, F4, M4, E5, C5 • **Temperaments:** M, T • **Physical:** V=L, H=N, L=S, H • **Work Env:** I • **Salary:** 3 • **Outlook:** 4

CUSTOMS-HOUSE BROKER (finan. inst.) • D.O.T. #186.117-018 • OES #19999 • Acts as intermediary between importers, steamship companies, or airlines and Bureau of Customs by preparing and compiling documents required by Federal Government for a ship or airplane of foreign origin to discharge its cargo at domestic port: Prepares entry papers from shippers' manifest in accordance with Bureau of Customs regulations. Files papers with Bureau of Customs and arranges for payment of duties. Quotes duty rates on commodities, based on knowledge of Federal tariffs and excise taxes. Prepares papers for shippers desiring to appeal excessive duty charges. Provides for storing of imported goods. Provides for bonds to cover dutiable goods being shipped into country via other ports. May register foreign ships with U.S. Coast Guard. Must be licensed by U.S. Government. • **GED:** R5, M4, L5 • **SVP:** 4-10 yrs • **Academic:** Ed=A, Eng=S • **Work Field:** 232 • **MPSMS:** 953 • **Aptitudes:** G2, V2, N2, S5, P4, Q3, K4, F5, M5, E5, C5 • **Temperaments:** D, M, P • **Stress:** A • **Physical:** V=L, H=L, L=S, H • **Work Env:** I • **Salary:** 5 • **Outlook:** 1

PATENT AGENT (profess. & kin.) • D.O.T. #119.167-014 • OES #28399 • Prepares and presents patent application to U. S. Patent Office and in patent courts, according to familiarity with patent law and filing procedures. Must be registered by U.S. Patent Office. Cannot practice law or appear in other courts. • **GED:** R6, M5, L6 • **SVP:** 2-4 yrs • **Academic:** Ed=B, Eng=S • **Work Field:** 272 • **MPSMS:** 932 • **Aptitudes:** G2, V1, N2, S2, P3, Q4, K4, F4, M5, E5, C4 • **Temperaments:** F, I, J • **Physical:** V=N, H=N, L=S • **Work Env:** I • **Salary:** 4 • **Outlook:** 1

11.05 Business Administration

Workers in this group are top level administrators and managers who work through lower level supervisors to direct all or a part of the activities in private establishments or Government agencies. They set policies, make important decisions, and set priorities. These jobs are found in large businesses, industry, and government. Labor unions and associations will also hire these workers.

✔ **What kind of work would you do?**

Your work activities would depend upon your specific job. For example, you might:

- serve as president of a company.
- plan and direct operations for an airport.
- administer city government according to policies set by city council or other elected officials.
- direct the business affairs of a university.
- approve the purchase of goods or services needed by a government agency.
- direct all sales activities of a company.
- plan and coordinate conventions, trade exhibits, and workshops for a professional association.

✔ **What skills and abilities do you need for this kind of work?**

To do this kind of work, you must be able to:

- think logically to make decisions.
- interpret information in mathematical, written, and diagram form, such as statistical reports, profit and loss statements, financial statements, and credit regulations.
- understand the effect politics and economic trends will have on company or agency plans.
- continually make decisions based on experience and personal feelings as well as on facts and figures.
- speak to large groups, such as the Chamber of Commerce and television audiences.
- deal with all kinds of people ranging from civic leaders to employees and from legislators to the general public.
- speak and write clearly and with authority.

✔ **How do you know if you would like or could learn to do this kind of work?**

The following questions may give you clues about yourself as you consider this group of jobs.

- Have you been president or treasurer of a club or social organization? Can you work with others to develop policies and plan programs of action?
- Have you taken business administration courses? Were you able to understand and contribute to class discussions about business practices?
- Have you read the business section of news magazines or newspapers? Do you understand the terms used?
- Have you supervised the activities of others? Were the activities carried out effectively?

✔ **How can you prepare for and enter this kind of work?**

Occupations in this group usually require education and/or training extending from two years to over ten years, depending upon the specific kind of work. Most jobs in this group require experience in related positions, usually within the same establishment, industry, or specialization. Degrees in business administration or law provide preparation for many jobs in this group. However, some administrative jobs require training and experience in such fields as engineering, chemistry, or sociology.

Some businesses offer management-trainee programs to advance employees to management positions. Some employers accept inexperienced college graduates with business degrees and place them in these training programs.

✔ **What else should you consider about these jobs?**

Workers in this group have heavy responsibilities. They may have to work long hours to meet specific situations or to solve problems. They may have to travel to different parts of the country or even to foreign countries to attend meetings and conduct businesses.

These workers sometimes change employers in order to move up the promotion ladder. These changes often require workers to relocate.

If you think you would like to do this kind of work, look at the job titles listed on the following pages.

GOE: 11.05.01 Management Services: Non-Government

ASSOCIATION EXECUTIVE (profess. & kin.) • D.O.T. #189.117-010 • OES #19999 • Directs and coordinates activities of professional or trade association in accordance with established policies to further achievement of goals, objectives, and standards of profession or association: Directs research surveys, compilation, and analysis of factors such as average income, benefits, standards, and common problems of profession, for presentation to association committees for action. Directs or participates in preparation of educational and informative materials for presentation to membership or public in newsletters, magazines, news releases, or on radio or television. Provides information and technical assistance to members, clients of members or public, relating to business operations, technology, or professional discipline represented by association. Represents association in negotiations with representatives of government, business, labor, and other organizations, and holds news conferences, delivers speeches, and appears before legislative bodies to present association's viewpoints and encourage acceptance of goals and objectives. Proposes, recommends, or assigns members to committees on association affairs. Recommends policy changes, actions on memberships, and levying of assessments to appropriate committees. Plans and coordinates association functions, such as conventions, exhibits or local or regional work shops, to present membership with committee proposals on goals or objectives, familiarize membership or public with new technology or products, and increase public acceptance of membership objectives. Directs and coordinates activities of workers performing office functions. May conduct investigations on members' professional ethics, competence, or conduct, or financial responsibility of members to enforce quasi-legal standards of membership. May be designated according to area of responsibility or activity directed, as DIRECTOR OF PUBLICATIONS (profess. & kin.); EXECUTIVE SECRETARY (profess. & kin.); MEMBERSHIP SECRETARY (profess. & kin.); REPRESENTATIVE, GOVERNMENT RELATIONS (profess. & kin.); RESEARCH DIRECTOR (profess. & kin.). • **GED:** R5, M4, L5 • **SVP:** 4-10 yrs • **Academic:** Ed=B, Eng=S • **Work Field:** 295 • **MPSMS:** 949 • **Aptitudes:** G2, V2, N2, S4, P4, Q3, K4, F4, M4, E5, C5 • **Temperaments:** D, I, P, S, V • **Stress:** A • **Physical:** V=L, H=L, L=S • **Work Env:** I • **Salary:** 5 • **Outlook:** 1

DIRECTOR, TRANSPORTATION (motor trans.) • D.O.T. #184.117-014 • OES #15023 • Formulates policies, programs, and procedures for transportation system, including schedules, rates, routes, assignment of drivers and vehicles and other terminal operations: Submits recommendations for development of, and compliance with transportation policies, procedures, and programs. Plans, directs, and implements vehicle scheduling, allocation, dispatching, licensing, and communication functions in accordance with established policies and objectives to effect economical utilization of vehicle facilities. Directs compilation and issuance of timetables. Conducts continuous analyses of vehicle and driver assignments and analyzes scheduling for possible consolidation. Reviews and revises driver schedules to ensure increased efficiency and to lower costs. Conducts field surveys to evaluate operations and recommends changes. Directs compilation and preparation of statistical surveys to determine traffic trends. Reviews and analyzes reports, such as revenue and performance records, and seat

occupancy patterns to secure information for recommended changes. Analyzes proposed schedules and rates, initiates preparation and distribution of proposed trip schedule changes, and submits analyses of data and rescheduling recommendations to administration. Directs operation and maintenance of communication systems, reviews procedures, provides guidance to resolve technical problems, analyzes costs and recommends cost control measures. Reviews cost statements to locate excessive expenses, and develops plans, policies, and budgets. Selects and recommends personnel for staff positions and trains and assigns personnel for supervisory positions. • **GED:** R5, M5, L5 • **SVP:** 4-10 yrs • **Academic:** Ed=A, Eng=S • **Work Field:** 013, 295 • **MPSMS:** 853, 859 • **Aptitudes:** G2, V2, N2, S4, P4, Q3, K4, F4, M4, E5, C4 • **Temperaments:** D, M, P • **Stress:** A • **Physical:** V=G, H=L, L=S • **Work Env:** I • **Salary:** 5 • **Outlook:** 1

MANAGER, AIRPORT (air trans.) • D.O.T. #184.117-026 • OES #15023 • DIRECTOR, AIRPORT; SUPERINTENDENT, AIRPORT. Plans, directs, and coordinates, through subordinate personnel, activities concerned with construction and maintenance of airport facilities and operation of airport in accordance with governmental agency or commission policies and regulations: Consults with commission members, governmental officials, or representatives of airlines to discuss and plan such matters as design and development of airport facilities, formulation of operating rules, regulations, and procedures, and aircraft landing, taxiing, and take-off patterns for various types of aircraft. Negotiates with representatives of airlines, utility companies, or individuals for acquisition of property for development of airport, lease of airport buildings and facilities, or use of rights-of-way over private property. Formulates procedures for use in event of aircraft accidents, fires, or other emergencies. Inspects airport facilities, such as runways, buildings, beacons and lighting, and automotive or construction equipment, or reviews inspection reports, to determine repairs, replacement, or improvements required. Coordinates activities of personnel involved in repair and maintenance of airport facilities, buildings, and equipment to minimize interruption of airport operations and improve efficiency. Directs personnel in investigating violations of aerial or ground traffic regulations, reviews investigation reports, and initiates actions to be taken against violators. Directs studies on noise abatement resulting from complaints of excessive noise from low flying aircraft or other operations. Reviews reports of expenditures for previous fiscal year, proposed improvements to facilities, and estimated increase in volume of traffic, in order to prepare budget estimates for upcoming fiscal year. Represents airport before civic or other organizational groups, courts, boards, and commissions. When management functions are divided at large or international airports workers may be designated according to activities directed as DIRECTOR, AIRPORT OPERATIONS (air trans.); MANAGER, AIRPORT-PROPERTY-AND-DEVELOPMENT (air trans.); SUPERINTENDENT, AIRPORT-BUILDINGS-MAINTENANCE (air trans.); SUPERINTENDENT, AIRPORT-FACILITIES-REPAIR-AND-MAINTENANCE (air trans.). • **GED:** R5, M5, L5 • **SVP:** 4-10 yrs • **Academic:** Ed=A, Eng=S • **Work Field:** 295 • **MPSMS:** 855 • **Aptitudes:** G2, V2, N2, S3, P3, Q3, K4, F4, M4, E5, C4 • **Temperaments:** D, J, P, V • **Stress:** A • **Physical:** V=G, H=L, L=L • **Work Env:** I • **Salary:** 5 • **Outlook:** 1

MANAGER, BAKERY (bake. prod.) • D.O.T. #189.117-046 • OES #19005 • Directs and coordinates activities involved with production, sale, and distribution of bakery products: Determines variety and quantity of bakery products to be produced, according to orders and sales projections. Develops budget for bakery operation, utilizing experience and knowledge of current market conditions. Directs sales activities following standard business practices. Plans product distribution to customers, and negotiates with suppliers to arrange purchase and delivery of bakery supplies. Implements, through subordinate managerial personnel, policies to make productive use of manpower, machines, and materials. Hires and discharges employees. May manage bakery that produces only speciality products, such as bagels or pastries. May manage bakery that sells products to general public. • **GED:** R5, M4, L4 • **SVP:** 4-10 yrs • **Academic:** Ed=A, Eng=G • **Work Field:** 295 • **MPSMS:** 384 • **Aptitudes:** G2, V2, N2, S4, P4, Q3, K4, F4, M4, E5, C5 • **Temperaments:** D, I, J, P, V • **Stress:** E, A • **Physical:** V=L, H=L, L=S, W • **Work Env:** I • **Salary:** 5 • **Outlook:** 3

MANAGER, INDUSTRIAL ORGANIZATION (any ind.) • D.O.T. #189.117-022 • OES #19005 • GENERAL MANAGER, INDUSTRIAL ORGANIZATION; MANAGER, GENERAL; PLANT SUPERINTENDENT, INDUSTRIAL ORGANIZATION. Directs and coordinates activities of industrial organization to obtain optimum efficiency and economy of operations and maximize profits: Plans, develops, and implements through subordinate administrative personnel, organizational policies and goals. Coordinates activities of divisions or departments, such as operating, manufacturing, engineering, planning, sales, maintenance, and research and development to effect operational efficiency and economy. Directs and coordinates preparation of sales promotion of products manufactured or services performed to develop new markets, increase share of market, and to obtain competitive position in industry. Analyses division or department budget requests to determine areas where reductions in expenditures can be made and allocates operating budgets. Confers with administrative personnel, reviews activity, operating, and sales reports to determine changes in programs or operations required. Directs preparation of administrative directives outlining changes in policy, programs, or operations for implementation by division or department administrative personnel concerned. Represents organization in industry manufacturing or trade associations to develop acceptance of organization. Workers are usually designated according to industry, such as petroleum production or refining, iron and steel, clock and watch; type of organization, such as air, rail, motor or water transportation; or type of product, such as paper, chemical, or plastics products. • **GED:** R5, M5, L5 • **SVP:** 4-10 yrs • **Academic:** Ed=A, Eng=S • **Work Field:** 295 • **MPSMS:** 712, 890 • **Aptitudes:** G2, V2, N3, S3, P3, Q4, K4, F4, M4, E5, C5 • **Temperaments:** D, P, V • **Stress:** A • **Physical:** V=N, H=L, L=S • **Work Env:** I • **Salary:** 5 • **Outlook:** 1

MANAGER, LAND DEVELOPMENT (real estate) • D.O.T. #186.117-042 • OES #15011 • Coordinates activities of land development company and negotiates with representatives of real estate, business, and industrial organizations, and community leaders to acquire and develop land: Supervises staff engaged in such activities as preparing appraisal reports on available land, showing availability and quality of water resources, mineral deposits, electric power, and labor supply. Prepares or directs preparation of statistical abstracts to reveal trends in tax rates in given communities, and proportion of total work force having specified skills. Plans and directs activities of field staff engaged in sampling mineral deposits, surveying land boundaries, and testing water supply to determine optimum usage of land. Negotiates with community, business, and public utility representatives to eliminate obstacles to land purchase, development, sale, or lease. Negotiates mortgage loans. Directs collection and auditing of funds from sale or lease of property. May perform duties of REAL-ESTATE AGENT (profess. & kin.). May cooperate with representatives of public utilities, universities, and other groups to coordinate research activities. May work for railroad, specialize in industrial development, and be designated MANAGER, INDUSTRIAL DEVELOPMENT (r.r. trans.). May work for government and be designated PROPERTY MANAGER (gov. ser.). • **GED:** R5, M5, L5 • **SVP:** 4-10 yrs • **Academic:** Ed=H, Eng=G • **Work Field:** 292, 295 • **MPSMS:** 851, 895 • **Aptitudes:** G2, V1, N1, S4, P3, Q2, K4, F4, M4, E5, C5 • **Temperaments:** D, I, J, M, P • **Stress:** A • **Physical:** V=N, H=G, L=S • **Work Env:** I • **Salary:** 4 • **Outlook:** 2

PRESIDENT (any ind.) • D.O.T. #189.117-026 • OES #19005 • Plans, develops, and establishes policies and objectives of business organization in accordance with board directives and corporation charter: Plans business objectives and develops organizational policies to coordinate functions and operations between divisions and departments and establish responsibilities and procedures for attaining objectives. Reviews activity reports and financial statements to determine progress and status in attaining objectives and revises objectives and plans in accordance with current conditions. Directs and coordinates formulation of financial programs to provide funding for new or continuing operations to maximize returns on investments, and to increase productivity. Plans and develops industrial, labor, and public relations policies designed to improve company's image and relations with customers, employees, stockholders, and public. Evaluates performance of executives for compliance with established policies and objectives of firm and contributions in attaining objectives. May preside over board of directors. May serve as chairman of committees, such as management, executive, engineering, and sales. • **GED:** R5, M5, L5 • **SVP:** Over 10 yrs • **Academic:** Ed=B, Eng=S • **Work Field:** 295 • **MPSMS:** 890 • **Aptitudes:** G2, V2, N3, S4, P4, Q3, K4, F4, M4, E5, C5 • **Temperaments:** D, J, P • **Stress:** A • **Physical:** V=L, H=L, L=S • **Work Env:** I • **Salary:** 5 • **Outlook:** 1

GOE: 11.05.02 Administrative Specialization

ADMINISTRATIVE ASSISTANT (any ind.) • D.O.T. #169.167-010 • OES #39999 • ADMINISTRATIVE ANALYST; ADMINISTRATIVE OFFICER. Aids executive in staff capacity by coordinating office services, such as personnel, budget preparation and control, housekeeping, records control, and special management studies: Studies management methods in order to improve workflow, simplify reporting procedures, or implement cost reductions. Analyzes unit operating practices, such as record keeping systems, forms control, office layout, suggestion systems, personnel and budgetary requirements, and performance standards to create new systems or revise established procedures. Analyzes jobs to delimit position responsibilities for use in wage-and-salary adjustments, promotions, and evaluation of work flow. Studies methods of improving work measurements or performance standards. Coordinates collection and preparation of operating reports, such as time-and-attendance records, terminations, new hires, transfers, budget expenditures, and statistical records of performance data. Prepares reports including conclusions and recommendations for solution of administrative problems. Issues and interprets operating policies. Reviews and answers correspondence. May assist in preparation of budget needs and annual reports of organization. May interview job applicants, conduct orientation of new employees, and plan training programs. May direct services, such as maintenance, repair, supplies, mail, and files. • **GED:** R5, M3, L5 • **SVP:** 2-4 yrs • **Academic:** Ed=A, Eng=G • **Work Field:** 251, 295 • **MPSMS:** 712 • **Aptitudes:** G2, V2, N3, S4, P4, Q3, K4, F4, M4, E5, C5 • **Temperaments:** D, J, M, P, V • **Stress:** E • **Physical:** V=L, H=L, L=S • **Work Env:** I • **Salary:** 4 • **Outlook:** 4

BUSINESS REPRESENTATIVE, LABOR UNION (profess. & kin.) • D.O.T. #187.167-018 • OES #19999 • Manages business affairs of labor union: Coordinates and directs such union functions as promoting local membership, placing union members on jobs, arranging local meetings, and maintaining relations between union and employers and press representatives. Visits worksites to ensure management and labor employees adhere to union contract specifications. May assist in developing plant production and safety and health measures. May negotiate with management on hours, wages, individual grievances, and other work-related matters affecting employees. • **GED:** R5, M3, L4 • **SVP:** 4-10 yrs • **Academic:** Ed=N, Eng=G • **Work Field:** 295 • **MPSMS:** 890 • **Aptitudes:** G2, V2, N3, S3, P4, Q4, K4, F4, M4, E4, C5 • **Temperaments:** P, V • **Stress:** E • **Physical:** V=N, H=L, L=S, W • **Work Env:** I • **Salary:** 5 • **Outlook:** 2

DIETITIAN, CHIEF (profess. & kin.) • D.O.T. #077.117-010 • OES #32521 • DIETITIAN, ADMINISTRATIVE; DIRECTOR, DIETETICS DEPARTMENT. Directs activities of institution department providing quantity food service and nutritional care: Administers, plans, and directs activities of department providing quantity food service. Establishes policies and procedures, and provides administrative direction for menu formulation, food preparation and service, purchasing, sanitation standards, safety practices, and personnel utilization. Selects professional dietetic staff, and directs departmental educational programs. Coordinates interdepartmental professional activities, and serves as consultant to management on matters pertaining to dietetics. • **GED:** R5, M4, L5 • **SVP:** 4-10 yrs • **Academic:** Ed=B, Eng=G • **Work Field:** 295 • **MPSMS:** 903 • **Aptitudes:** G2, V2, N2, S4, P4, Q3, K4, F4, M4, E4, C5 • **Temperaments:** D, J, M, P, V • **Stress:** E • **Physical:** V=N, H=N, L=S • **Work Env:** I • **Salary:** 4 • **Outlook:** 3

DIRECTOR, QUALITY ASSURANCE (profess. & kin.) • D.O.T. #189.117-042 • OES #15014 • DIRECTOR, PRODUCT ASSURANCE. Participates, as member of management team, in formulating and establishing organizational policies and operating procedures for company and develops, implements, and coordinates, through support staff and lower echelon managers, product assurance program to prevent or eliminate defects in new and/or existing products: Analyzes, evaluates, and presents information concerning factors, such as business situations, production capabilities, manufacturing problems, economic trends, and design and development of new products for consideration by other members of management team. Suggests and debates alternative methods and procedures in solving problems and meeting changing market opportunities. Cooperates with other top management personnel in formulating and establishing company policies, operating procedures, and goals. Develops initial and subsequent modifications of product assurance program to delineate areas of responsibility, personnel requirements, and operational procedures within program, according to and consistent with company goals and policies. Evaluates contents of reports from product assurance program department heads and confers with top management personnel preparatory to formulating fiscal budget for product assurance program. Conducts management meetings with product assurance program department heads to establish, delineate, and review program organizational policies, to coordinate functions and operations between departments, and to establish responsibilities and procedures for attaining objectives. Reviews technical problems and procedures of departments and recommends solutions to problems or changes in procedures. Visits and confers with representatives of material and component vendors to obtain information related to supply quality, capacity of vendor to meet orders, and vendor quality standards. Confers with engineers about quality assurance of new products designed and manufactured products on market to rectify problems. Reviews technical publications, articles, and abstracts to stay abreast of technical developments in industry. • **GED:** R5, M5, L5 • **SVP:** 4-10 yrs • **Academic:** Ed=N, Eng=G • **Work Field:** 295 • **MPSMS:** 893 • **Aptitudes:** G1, V1, N1, S4, P4, Q3, K4, F4, M4, E5, C5 • **Temperaments:** D, J, P, V • **Stress:** E, A • **Physical:** V=L, H=L, L=S, W, H • **Work Env:** I • **Salary:** 5 • **Outlook:** 1

DIRECTOR, SERVICE (ret. tr.) • D.O.T. #189.167-014 • OES #19999 • MANAGER, OPERATING AND OCCUPANCY; SUPERINTENDENT, NONSELLING; SUPERINTENDENT, OPERATING. Directs operating and nonselling services, such as building maintenance, warehousing, and payroll, in department store: Controls expenditures for items, such as remodeling and repairing of building, upkeep of elevators and air conditioning system, and repairing electrical system. Arranges for storage and display space for new merchandise. Acts as liaison for trucking company that delivers merchandise to customers. May hire and train new employees. • **GED:** R5, M4, L4 • **SVP:** 2-4 yrs • **Academic:** Ed=A, Eng=S • **Work Field:** 295 • **MPSMS:** 881 • **Aptitudes:** G2, V2, N3, S4, P3, Q3, K4, F4, M4, E5, C5 • **Temperaments:** D, J, P • **Stress:** A • **Physical:** V=L, H=L, L=S • **Work Env:** I • **Salary:** 4 • **Outlook:** 1

EXECUTIVE VICE PRESIDENT, CHAMBER OF COMMERCE (nonprofit org.) • D.O.T. #187.117-030 • OES #19999 • MANAGER, CHAMBER OF COMMERCE. Directs activities of chamber of commerce to promote business, industrial and job development, and civic improvements in community: Administers programs of departments and committees which perform such functions as providing members economic and marketing informa-

tion, promoting economic growth and stability in community, and counseling business organizations and industry on problems affecting local economy. Coordinates work with that of other community agencies to provide public services. Prepares and submits annual budget to elected officials for approval. Studies governmental legislation, taxation, and other fiscal matters to determine effect on community interests, and makes recommendations based on organizational policy. • **GED:** R5, M5, L5 • **SVP:** 4-10 yrs • **Academic:** Ed=A, Eng=S • **Work Field:** 295 • **MPSMS:** 949 • **Aptitudes:** G1, V1, N2, S4, P4, Q4, K4, F4, M4, E5, C5 • **Temperaments:** D, I, P • **Stress:** A • **Physical:** V=N, H=L, L=S • **Work Env:** I • **Salary:** 5 • **Outlook:** 1

GRANT COORDINATOR (profess. & kin.) • D.O.T. #169.117-014 • OES #21999 • Develops and coordinates grant-funded programs for agencies, institutions, local government, or units of local government, such as school systems or metropolitan police departments: Reviews literature dealing with funds available through grants from governmental agencies and private foundations to determine feasibility of developing programs to supplement local annual budget allocations. Discusses program requirements and sources of funds available with administrative personnel. Confers with personnel affected by proposed program to develop program goals and objectives, outline how funds are to be used, and explain procedures necessary to obtain funding. Works with fiscal officer in preparing narrative justification for purchase of new equipment and other budgetary expenditures. Submits proposal to officials for approval. Writes grant application, according to format required, and submits application to funding agency or foundation. Meets with representatives of funding sources to work out final details of proposal. Directs and coordinates evaluation and monitoring of grant-funded programs, or writes specifications for evaluation or monitoring of program by outside agency. Assists department personnel in writing periodic reports to comply with grant requirements. Maintains master files on all grants. Monitors all paper work connected with grant-funded programs. • **GED:** R6, M4, L6 • **SVP:** 2-4 yrs • **Academic:** Ed=B, Eng=S • **Work Field:** 295 • **MPSMS:** 893 • **Aptitudes:** G1, V1, N2, S4, P4, Q4, K4, F4, M4, E5, C5 • **Temperaments:** D, I, J, P • **Stress:** A • **Physical:** V=N, H=L, L=S, H • **Work Env:** I • **Salary:** 4 • **Outlook:** 1

IMPORT-EXPORT AGENT (any ind.) • D.O.T. #184.117-022 • OES #15023 • FOREIGN AGENT. Coordinates activities of international traffic division of import-export agency and negotiates settlements between foreign and domestic shippers: Plans and directs flow of air and surface traffic moving to overseas destinations. Supervises workers engaged in receiving and shipping freight, documentation, waybilling, assessing charges, and collecting fees for shipments. Negotiates with domestic customers, as intermediary for foreign customers, to resolve problems and arrive at mutual agreements. Negotiates with foreign shipping interests to contract for reciprocal freight-handling agreements. May examine invoices and shipping manifests for conformity to tariff and customs regulations. May contact customs officials to effect release of incoming freight and resolve customs delays. May prepare reports of transactions to facilitate billing of shippers and foreign carriers. • **GED:** R5, M4, L5 • **SVP:** 2-4 yrs • **Academic:** Ed=H, Eng=S • **Work Field:** 295 • **MPSMS:** 850 • **Aptitudes:** G2, V2, N3, S4, P4, Q3, K5, F5, M4, E5, C5 • **Temperaments:** D, I, J, P, V • **Stress:** E, A • **Physical:** V=N, H=G, L=S • **Work Env:** I • **Salary:** 4 • **Outlook:** 2

MANAGEMENT TRAINEE (any ind.) • D.O.T. #189.167-018 • OES #19999 • Performs assigned duties, under close direction of experienced personnel, to gain knowledge and experience required for promotion to management positions: Receives training and performs duties in departments, such as credit, customer relations, accounting, or sales to become familiar with line and staff functions and operations and management viewpoints and policies that affect each phase of business. Observes and studies techniques and traits of experienced workers in order to acquire knowledge of methods, procedures, and standards required for performance of departmental duties. Workers are usually trained in functions and operations of related or allied departments to facilitate transferability between departments and to provide greater promotional opportunities. • **GED:** R4, M4, L4 • **SVP:** 1-2 yrs • **Academic:** Ed=B, Eng=G • **Work Field:** 295 • **MPSMS:** 899 • **Aptitudes:**

G3, V2, N3, S4, P3, Q4, K4, F4, M4, E5, C5 • **Temperaments:** M, P, T, V • **Stress:** E • **Physical:** V=N, H=L, L=S • **Work Env:** I • **Salary:** 4 • **Outlook:** 1

MANAGER, BRANCH (any ind.) • D.O.T. #183.117-010 • OES #15014 • AGENT; MANAGER, AREA; MANAGER, DIVISION; MANAGER, PLANT. Directs production, distribution, and marketing operations for branch plant, or an assigned territory of industrial organization: Coordinates production, distribution, warehousing, and selling activities in accordance with policies, principles, and procedures established by MANAGER, INDUS-TRIAL ORGANIZATION (any ind.). Confers with customers and industrial representatives to evaluate and promote possibilities for improved and expanded services in area. Develops plans for efficient machine, manpower, and material utilization. Reviews and alters production costs, quality, and inventory control programs to maintain profitable operation of division. Plans and directs sales program by reviewing competitive position and developing new markets, using sales aids, advertising, promotional programs, and field services. Directs personnel program. Directs preparation of accounting records. Recommends budgets to management. May be designated according to title of area of jurisdiction as MANAGER, DISTRICT (any ind.); MANAGER, LOCAL (any ind.); MANAGER, REGIONAL (any ind.). • **GED:** R5, M4, L4 • **SVP:** 4-10 yrs • **Academic:** Ed=A, Eng=S • **Work Field:** 295 • **MPSMS:** 712 • **Aptitudes:** G2, V2, N3, S3, P4, Q3, K4, F4, M4, E5, C5 • **Temperaments:** D, I, M, P • **Stress:** A • **Physical:** V=N, H=L, L=S • **Work Env:** I • **Salary:** 5 • **Outlook:** 1

MANAGER, CONTRACTS (petrol. production) • D.O.T. #163.117-010 • OES #21308 • SUPPLY REPRESENTATIVE, PE-TROLEUM PRODUCTS. Negotiates contracts with representatives of oil producers, refiners, and pipeline carriers for purchase, sale, or delivery of crude oil, petroleum distillates, and natural gas and gasoline: Analyzes records of petroleum supply sources, movements of materials from plants to refineries, and current and prospective refinery demands. Coordinates work of sales, production, and shipping departments to implement procurance of products in accordance with refinery needs. Performs liaison work with engineering and production departments concerning contractual rights and obligations. May manage contracts for entire company, department, or for specified product, such as crude oil or natural gas. May be designated according to product contracted as SUP-PLY REPRESENTATIVE, DRY GAS (petrol. production; petrol. refin.; pipe lines); MANAGER, NATURAL-GAS UTILIZATION (petrol. production). • **GED:** R5, M5, L5 • **SVP:** 2-4 yrs • **Academic:** Ed=A, Eng=S • **Work Field:** 292 • **MPSMS:** 501, 856 • **Aptitudes:** G2, V1, N2, S4, P4, Q3, K4, F4, M4, E5, C5 • **Temperaments:** D, J, P, V • **Stress:** A • **Physical:** V=N, H=N, L=S • **Work Env:** I • **Salary:** 4 • **Outlook:** 4

MANAGER, CREDIT CARD OPERATIONS (profess. & kin.) • D.O.T. #186.167-022 • OES #13002 • Directs and coordinates credit card operations for bank, commercial concern, or credit card company: Develops and establishes procedures for verifying data on application form, such as applicant or company bank references, established credit rating, and personal data, to ascertain if applicant meets prescribed criteria for credit. Reviews documentation and recommendations on applications prepared by staff to determine credit validity and approves issuance to applicants meeting criteria. Establishes maximum credit ceiling from data for each account. Analyzes computer printouts, collection statistics, and reports to determine status of collection balances outstanding, and to evaluate effectiveness in current delinquency collection policies and procedures. Confers with administrative personnel relative to delinquency trends, and to recommend and assist in formulating changes in policy and procedures designed to provide for increased operational controls. Compiles and analyzes statistical data on fraudulent use of credit cards, such as number of cards lost or stolen, percentage of cards recovered, and losses incurred from use of cards, to develop procedures designed to deter or prevent use of cards. Conducts supervisory staff meetings to assign credit applications for verification, delinquent accounts for collection, fraud cases for investigation and possible legal action, and to obtain progress reports on activities. Audits delinquent accounts considered to be uncollectible to ensure maximum efforts and alternate recovery resources have been taken before assigning account bad

debt status. Ensures that prescribed actions on credit cards reported stolen are taken, such as alert coding of clients account and issuing of warning bulletins to establishments honoring use of card has been taken to minimize losses, prevent further use of card, and to assist in apprehension of user and in recovering card. Directs removal of charges in excess of client's liability from account. Coordinates credit card operations with activities of central collection department, company branches, and other credit card companies to exchange information and update credit card controls. May only manage one phase of credit card operations and be designated as COLLECTION MANAGER, DELINQUENT-CREDIT-CARD-ACCOUNTS (any ind.); CREDIT MANAGER, CREDIT CARD OPERATIONS (any ind.); FRAUD-AND-SECURITY MANAGER, CREDIT CARDS (any ind.). • **GED:** R5, M5, L5 • **SVP:** 4-10 yrs • **Academic:** Ed=A, Eng=G • **Work Field:** 271, 295 • **MPSMS:** 894 • **Aptitudes:** G2, V2, N2, S4, P4, Q3, K4, F4, M4, E5, C5 • **Temperaments:** D, F, J, V • **Stress:** A • **Physical:** V=N, H=G, L=S • **Work Env:** I • **Salary:** 4 • **Outlook:** 4

MANAGER, DEPARTMENT (any ind.) • D.O.T. #189.167-022 • OES #13014 • DEPARTMENT HEAD, SUPERINTENDENT. Directs and coordinates, through subordinate supervisory personnel, departmental activities and functions in commercial, industrial, or service establishment, utilizing knowledge of department functions and company policies, standards, and practices: Reviews and analyzes reports, records, and directives, and confers with supervisory personnel to obtain data required for planning department activities, such as new departmental commitments, status of work in progress, and problems encountered. Assigns, or delegates responsibility for specific work or functional activities and dissemination of policy to supervisory personnel. Gives work directions, resolves problems, prepares work schedules, and sets deadlines to ensure completion of operational functions. Coordinates activities of department with interrelated activities of other departments to ensure optimum efficiency and economy. Prepares reports and records on departmental activities for management. Evaluates current procedures and practices for accomplishing activities and functions of department to develop and implement alternate methods designed for improvement of work. Workers are designated according to department functions or activities or by type of department managed unless specifically described elsewhere. • **GED:** R4, M4, L4 • **SVP:** 2-4 yrs • **Academic:** Ed=H, Eng=G • **Work Field:** 295 • **MPSMS:** 890 • **Aptitudes:** G3, V3, N3, S3, P3, Q3, K4, F4, M4, E5, C5 • **Temperaments:** D, P • **Stress:** E, A • **Physical:** V=N, H=L, L=S • **Work Env:** I • **Salary:** 4 • **Outlook:** 3

MANAGER, DEPARTMENT STORE (ret. tr.) • D.O.T. #185.117-010 • OES #19005 • Directs and coordinates, through subordinate managerial personnel, activities of department store selling lines of merchandise in specialized departments: Formulates pricing policies for sale of merchandise, or implements policies set forth by merchandising board. Coordinates activities of non-merchandising departments, as purchasing, credit, accounting, and advertising with merchandising departments to obtain optimum efficiency of operations with minimum costs in order to maximize profits. Develops and implements, through subordinate managerial personnel, policies and procedures for store and departmental operations and customer personnel, and community relations. Negotiates or approves contracts negotiated with suppliers of merchandise, or with other establishments providing security, maintenance, or cleaning services. Reviews operating and financial statements and departmental sales records to determine merchandising activities that require additional sales promotion, clearance sales, or other sales procedures in order to turn over merchandise and achieve profitability of store operations and merchandising objectives. • **GED:** R5, M4, L5 • **SVP:** 4-10 yrs • **Academic:** Ed=A, Eng=S • **Work Field:** 292, 295 • **MPSMS:** 881 • **Aptitudes:** G2, V2, N2, S4, P4, Q3, K4, F4, M4, E5, C5 • **Temperaments:** D, J, P, V • **Stress:** A • **Physical:** V=L, H=L, L=S, H • **Work Env:** I • **Salary:** 5 • **Outlook:** 1

MANAGER, FINANCIAL INSTITUTION (finan. inst.) • D.O.T. #186.117-038 • OES #13002 • Manages branch or office of financial institutions, such as bank, finance company, mortgage banking company, savings and loan association or trust company: Directs and coordinates activities to implement institution's policies, procedures, and practices concerning granting or extending lines of credit, commercial loans, real estate loans, and consumer credit loans. Directs, through subordinate supervisory personnel, activities of workers engaged in performing such financial functions, as accounting and recording financial transactions, setting up trust or escrow accounts, probating estates, and administering trust or mortgage accounts. Establishes procedures for custody and control of assets, records, loan collateral, and securities to ensure safekeeping. Develops relationships with customers and business, community, and civic organizations to promote goodwill and generate new business. May be designated according to type of financial institution managed as MANAGER, BRANCH BANK (finan. inst.); MANAGER, FINANCE COMPANY (finan. inst.); MANAGER, MORTGAGE BANKING COMPANY (finan. inst.); MANAGER, SAVINGS-AND-LOAN ASSOCIATION (finan. inst.); MANAGER, TRUST COMPANY (finan. inst.) or according to type of loans made as MANAGER, CONSUMER CREDIT (finan. inst.). Managers that are also corporate officers of institution are designated according to title held, as [VICE-PRESIDENT, FINANCIAL INSTITUTION (finan. inst.)]. • **GED:** R5, M4, L4 • **SVP:** 4-10 yrs • **Academic:** Ed=H, Eng=G • **Work Field:** 295 • **MPSMS:** 894 • **Aptitudes:** G1, V1, N2, S3, P3, Q3, K4, F4, M4, E5, C5 • **Temperaments:** D, J, P • **Stress:** E, A • **Physical:** V=N, H=G, L=S • **Work Env:** I • **Salary:** 5 • **Outlook:** 2

MANAGER, OPERATIONS (air trans.) • D.O.T. #184.117-050 • OES #15023 • OPERATIONS MANAGER. Directs and coordinates activities of operations department of air, motor, railroad, or water transportation organization: Confers and cooperates with management personnel in formulating administrative and operational policies and procedures. Directs and coordinates, through subordinate managerial personnel, activities of operations department to obtain optimum use of equipment, facilities, and personnel. Reviews and analyzes expenditure, financial, and operations reports to determine requirements for increasing profits, such as need for increase in fares or tariffs, expansion of existing schedules, or extension of routes or new routes. Prepares recommendations on findings for management evaluation. Recommends capital expenditures for acquisition of new equipment which would increase efficiency and services of operations department. Approves requisitions for equipment, materials, and supplies within limits of operations department budget. Enforces compliance of operations personnel with administrative policies, procedures, safety rules, and governmental regulations. Directs investigations into causes of customer or shipper complaints relating to operations department. May negotiate contracts with equipment and materials suppliers. May act as representative of transportation organization before government commissions or regulatory bodies during hearings for increased fares or tariffs and on extension of or new rules. • **GED:** R5, M5, L5 • **SVP:** 4-10 yrs • **Academic:** Ed=A, Eng=S • **Work Field:** 295 • **MPSMS:** 850 • **Aptitudes:** G2, V2, N2, S3, P4, Q3, K4, F4, M4, E5, C5 • **Temperaments:** D, M, P • **Stress:** A • **Physical:** V=N, H=L, L=S • **Work Env:** I • **Salary:** 5 • **Outlook:** 1

MANAGER, PERSONNEL (profess. & kin.) • D.O.T. #166.117-018 • OES #13005 • Plans and carries out policies relating to all phases of personnel activity: Recruits, interviews, and selects employees to fill vacant positions. Plans and conducts new employee orientation to foster positive attitude toward company goals. Keeps record of insurance coverage, pension plan, and personnel transactions, such as hires, promotions, transfers, and terminations. Investigates accidents and prepares reports for insurance carrier. Conducts wage survey within labor market to determine competitive wage rate. Prepares budget of personnel operations. Meets with shop stewards and supervisors to resolve grievances. Writes separation notices for employees separating with cause and conducts exit interviews to determine reasons behind separations. Prepares reports and recommends procedures to reduce absenteeism and turnover. Contracts with outside suppliers to provide employee services, such as canteen, transportation, or relocation service. May keep records of hired employee characteristics for governmental reporting purposes. May negotiate collective bargaining agreement with BUSINESS REPRESENTATIVE, LABOR UNION (profess. & kin.). • **GED:** R5, M5, L5 • **SVP:** 4-10 yrs • **Academic:** Ed=B, Eng=G • **Work Field:** 295 • **MPSMS:** 712 • **Aptitudes:** G1, V1, N2, S3, P3, Q3, K4, F4, M4, E5, C5 • **Temper-**

aments: D, F, J, P, V • **Stress:** E, A • **Physical:** V=N, H=L, L=S • **Work Env:** I • **Salary:** 5 • **Outlook:** 4

MANAGER, PROCUREMENT SERVICES (profess. & kin.) • D.O.T. #162.167-022 • OES #13008 • DIRECTOR, PROCUREMENT SERVICES; MANAGER, MATERIAL CONTROL. Directs and coordinates activities of personnel engaged in purchasing and distributing raw materials, equipment, machinery, and supplies in industrial plant, public utility, or other organization: Prepares instructions regarding purchasing systems and procedures. Prepares and issues purchase orders and change notices to PURCHASING AGENTS (profess. & kin.). Analyzes market and delivery conditions to determine present and future material availability and prepares market analysis reports. Reviews purchase order claims and contracts for conformance to company policy. Develops and in stalls clerical and office procedures and practices, and studies work flow, sequence of operations, and office arrangement to determine expediency of installing new or improved office machines. Arranges for disposal of surplus materials. • **GED:** R4, M4, L4 • **SVP:** 2-4 yrs • **Academic:** Ed=H, Eng=G • **Work Field:** 292 • **MPSMS:** 898 • **Aptitudes:** G2, V2, N2, S4, P4, Q2, K4, F4, M4, E5, C5 • **Temperaments:** D, J, M, P, V • **Stress:** E, A • **Physical:** V=N, H=L, L=S • **Work Env:** I • **Salary:** 4 • **Outlook:** 3

MANAGER, PRODUCTION (radio & tv broad.) • D.O.T. #184.167-074 • OES #34056 • Coordinates work of various departments to produce radio or television programs: Trains, assigns duties, and supervises employees engaged in production and taping such programs as game shows, talk broadcasts, and special programs. Ensures that slanderous, libelous, and profane statements are avoided or deleted and that program is in conformance with station or network policy and regulations. May direct subordinates in auditioning talent and proposed programs. May be designated according to type of program produced or whether program is being broadcast to foreign countries as MANAGER, NEWS PRODUCTION (radio & tv broad.); MANAGER, PRODUCTION, INTERNATIONAL BROADCASTING (radio & tv broad.). • **GED:** R5, M4, L4 • **SVP:** 2-4 yrs • **Academic:** Ed=N, Eng=G • **Work Field:** 295, 297 • **MPSMS:** 863 • **Aptitudes:** G2, V2, N4, S4, P4, Q3, K4, F4, M4, E5, C5 • **Temperaments:** D, J, P, V • **Stress:** E, A • **Physical:** V=N, H=L, L=S • **Work Env:** I • **Salary:** 4 • **Outlook:** 1

MANAGER, REGIONAL (motor trans.) • D.O.T. #184.117-054 • OES #15023 • Directs and coordinates regional activities of motor transportation company: Examines and analyzes rates, tariffs, operating costs, and revenues to determine such needs or requirements as increase in rates and tariffs, reduction of operations and maintenance costs, and expansion of or changes in schedules or routes. Prepares, for management evaluation, recommendations designed to increase efficiency and revenues and lower costs. Directs, through subordinate management personnel, compliance of workers with established company policies, procedures, and standards, such as safekeeping of funds and tickets, personnel employment and grievance practices, and enforcement of union contracts and government regulations. Reviews operational records and reports and refers to manuals, company instructions, and government regulations to detect deviations from operational practices and prepares directives to eliminate such infractions. Investigates safeguards and inspects regional premises to ensure that adequate protection exists for company assets, property, and equipment. Participates in union contract negotiations and settling of grievances. Coordinates advertising and sales promotion programs for region. Reviews replies to passenger complaints and settlement of claims for conformance with company public relations policies and procedures. Inspects terminals for conformance with standards for cleanliness, appearance, and need of repair or maintenance, and directs corrective measures required to meet standards. • **GED:** R5, M5, L5 • **SVP:** 4-10 yrs • **Academic:** Ed=A, Eng=S • **Work Field:** 295 • **MPSMS:** 859 • **Aptitudes:** G2, V2, N2, S4, P4, Q3, K4, F4, M4, E5, C5 • **Temperaments:** D, P, V • **Stress:** A • **Physical:** V=L, H=L, L=S • **Work Env:** I • **Salary:** 5 • **Outlook:** 1

MANAGER, SCHEDULE PLANNING (air trans.) • D.O.T. #184.117-058 • OES #15023 • Negotiates with governmental regulatory body to change company's route application (fixed schedule for flights) over authorized routes as representative of certificated air carrier: Analyzes documentation on company operations and recommended changes in route application, prepared by subordinates, to determine if company position warrants requesting route application hearing, considering such factors as current and projected traffic load, route application of competitive carriers over same route, and profitability of route operations. Submits current and proposed schedules to Schedule Committee for consideration and approval to request hearing before regulatory body. Prepares company's position and arguments for presentation at route application hearing and negotiates with body for additional route applications or deletion of route applications on unprofitable routes in order to improve efficient utilization of flight personnel and equipment and to reduce losses or increase revenues. Directs and coordinates activities of workers compiling documentation on route application, analyzing data, and preparing recommendations for schedule changes. • **GED:** R5, M4, L5 • **SVP:** 4-10 yrs • **Academic:** Ed=A, Eng=S • **Work Field:** 295 • **MPSMS:** 855 • **Aptitudes:** G1, V1, N3, S4, P3, Q2, K4, F4, M4, E5, C5 • **Temperaments:** D, P • **Stress:** A • **Physical:** V=N, H=N, L=S, H • **Work Env:** I • **Salary:** 5 • **Outlook:** 1

MANAGER, STATION (radio & tv broad.) • D.O.T. #184.117-062 • OES #15023 • Directs and coordinates activities of radio or television station: Supervises directly, or through subordinates, personnel engaged in departments, such as sales, program, engineering, and personnel. Observes activities to ensure compliance with Federal regulations. Develops plans to promote sales of programs and time periods to advertisers and their agencies. Negotiates with motion picture companies for purchase of independent film programs. Confers with owners to discuss station policy and administrative procedures. May contact prospective buyers of station time to promote sale of station services. May manage station engaged in transmitting broadcasts to foreign countries and be known as DIRECTOR, INTERNATIONAL BROADCASTING (radio & tv broad.). Duties and responsibilities may vary in different stations, according to size and network affiliation. • **GED:** R5, M4, L5 • **SVP:** 4-10 yrs • **Academic:** Ed=A, Eng=S • **Work Field:** 295 • **MPSMS:** 863 • **Aptitudes:** G2, V2, N3, S4, P3, Q4, K4, F4, M4, E5, C5 • **Temperaments:** D, J, P, V • **Stress:** A • **Physical:** V=L, H=L, L=S • **Work Env:** I • **Salary:** 5 • **Outlook:** 1

MANAGER, TRAFFIC (any ind.) • D.O.T. #184.167-094 • OES #15023 • Directs and coordinates traffic activities of organization: Develops methods and procedures for transportation of raw materials to processing and production areas and commodities from departments to customers, warehouses, or other storage facilities. Determines most efficient and economical routing and mode of transportation, using rate and tariff manuals and motor freight and railroad guidebooks. Directs scheduling of shipments and notifies concerned departments or customers of arrival dates. Initiates investigations into causes of damages or shortages in consignments or overcharges for freight or insurance. Conducts studies in areas of packaging, warehousing, and loading of commodities and evaluates existing procedures and standards. Initiates changes designed to improve control and efficiency of traffic department. May negotiate contracts for leasing of transportation equipment or property. May assist in preparing department budget. • **GED:** R5, M4, L4 • **SVP:** 4-10 yrs • **Academic:** Ed=A, Eng=S • **Work Field:** 013, 221 • **MPSMS:** 851, 853 • **Aptitudes:** G2, V2, N3, S4, P3, Q3, K4, F4, M4, E5, C5 • **Temperaments:** D, M, P • **Stress:** A • **Physical:** V=L, H=L, L=S • **Work Env:** I • **Salary:** 5 • **Outlook:** 1

PROGRAM MANAGER (profess. & kin.) • D.O.T. #189.167-030 • OES #13014 • Manages program to ensure that implementation and prescribed activities are carried out in accordance with specified objectives: Plans and develops methods and procedures for implementing program, directs and coordinates program activities, and exercises control over personnel responsible for specific functions or phases of program. Selects personnel according to knowledge and experience in area with which program is concerned, such as social or public welfare, education, economics, or public relations. Confers with staff to explain program and individual responsibilities for functions and phases of program. Directs and coordinates personally, or through subordinate managerial personnel, activities concerned with implementation and carrying out objectives of program. Reviews reports and records of activities to ensure progress is being accomplished toward specified program objective and modifies or changes methodology as required to redirect activities and attain objectives. Prepares program reports for superiors. Controls expenditures in accordance with budget allocations. May specialize in managing governmental programs set up by legislative body or directive and be designated as MANAGER, GOVERNMENTAL PROGRAM (gov. ser.). • **GED:** R5, M5, L5 • **SVP:** 4-10 yrs • **Academic:** Ed=A, Eng=S • **Work Field:** 295 • **MPSMS:** 920, 930, 950 • **Aptitudes:** G2, V2, N2, S3, P3, Q2, K4, F4, M4, E5, C5 • **Temperaments:** D, M, P • **Stress:** A • **Physical:** V=L, H=L, L=S • **Work Env:** I • **Salary:** 5 • **Outlook:** 2

PROGRAM PROPOSALS COORDINATOR (radio & tv broad.) • D.O.T. #132.067-030 • OES #34002 • COORDINATOR, PROGRAM PLANNING. Develops, writes, and edits proposals for new radio or television programs: Reviews program proposals submitted by staff, station and independent producers, and other sources to determine proposal feasibility, based on knowledge of station's programming needs, policy and budgetary considerations, and potential underwriting (funding) sources. Edits proposals, or writes proposals for original program concepts, and submits proposals for review of programming, financial, and other departmental personnel. Participates in selection of researchers, consultants, producers, and on-air personalities to facilitate development of program ideas. Authorizes preparation of budget for final proposals. Maintains liaison between program production department and proposal originators to inform originators of status of accepted projects. • **GED:** R5, M3, L5 • **SVP:** 2-4 yrs • **Academic:** Ed=A, Eng=G • **Work Field:** 211, 261, 295 • **MPSMS:** 863, 864 • **Aptitudes:** G1, V1, N3, S4, P4, Q3, K4, F4, M4, E5, C5 • **Temperaments:** D, J, P, V • **Stress:** E, A • **Physical:** V=L, H=L, L=S, H • **Work Env:** I • **Salary:** 4 • **Outlook:** 3

PROGRAM SPECIALIST, EMPLOYEE-HEALTH MAINTENANCE (profess. & kin.) • D.O.T. #166.167-050 • OES #13005 • Coordinates activities of area employers in setting up local government funded program within establishments to help employees who are not functioning at satisfactory levels of job performance due to alcoholism or other behavioral medical problems: Writes and prepares newspaper advertisements, newsletters, and questionnaires and speaks before community groups to promote employee assistance program within business community. Analyzes character and type of business establishments in area, and compiles list of prospective employers appropriate for implementing assistance program. Contacts prospective employers, explains program and fees, points out advantages of program, and reaches agreement with interested employers on extent of proposed program. Develops program within establishment. Establishes committee composed of company officials and workers to develop statement of employee assistance program and policy and procedures. Plans and conducts training sessions for company officials to develop skills in identifying and handling employees troubled by alcoholism or other personal problems. Assists employer in setting up in-plant educational program to prevent alcoholism, using posters, pamphlets, and films, and establishes referral network providing for in-plant and out-of-plant group or individual counseling for troubled employees. Confers with team member of assistance program who provides counseling regarding planning and progress of counseling components. Confers with staff of employee assistance program regarding progress and evaluation of current programs and proposals for developing new programs. • **GED:** R5, M3, L5 • **SVP:** 1-2 yrs • **Academic:** Ed=A, Eng=S • **Work Field:** 282, 295 • **MPSMS:** 941 • **Aptitudes:** G2, V1, N3, S4, P4, Q3, K4, F4, M4, E5, C5 • **Temperaments:** D, I, J, P • **Physical:** V=L, H=L, L=S • **Work Env:** I • **Salary:** 4 • **Outlook:** 3

RESEARCH ANALYST (insurance) • D.O.T. #169.267-034 • OES #21999 • Evaluates insurance industry developments to update company products and procedures: Reviews industry publications and monitors pending legislation and regulations to determine impact of new developments on company insurance products. Consults with designated company personnel to disseminate information necessitating changes in language or provisions of insurance contracts and assists in preparation of documents or directives needed to implement changes. Corresponds or consults with agents, brokers, and other interested persons to determine feasibility and marketability of new products to meet competition and increase sales. Develops procedures and materials for introduction and administration of new products, and submits package for review by company personnel and regulatory bodies. May recommend lobbying activities to management. May direct or coordinate activities of other workers. May specialize in analyzing developments in group insurance operations and be designated GROUP-CONTRACT ANALYST (insurance). • **GED:** R5, M4, L5 • **SVP:** 4-10 yrs • **Academic:** Ed=B, Eng=G • **Work Field:** 251, 271 • **MPSMS:** 895, 939 • **Aptitudes:** G2, V2, N3, S4, P4, Q3, K4, F4, M4, E5, C5 • **Temperaments:** J, P • **Physical:** V=N, H=N, L=S, H • **Work Env:** I • **Salary:** 5 • **Outlook:** 3

SECURITY OFFICER (any ind.) • D.O.T. #189.167-034 • OES #39999 • Plans and establishes security procedures for company engaged in manufacturing products or processing data or material for Federal government: Studies Federal security regulations and restrictions relative to company operations. Directs activities of personnel in developing company security measures which comply with Federal regulations. Consults with local, district, or other Federal representatives for interpretation or application of particular regulations applying to company operations. Prepares security manual outlining and establishing measures and procedures for handling, storing, safekeeping, and destroying classified records and documents, and for granting company personnel or visitors access to classified material or entry into restricted areas. Directs and coordinates activities of personnel in revising or updating security measures due to new or revised regulations. May request deviations from restrictive regulations that interfere with normal operations. • **GED:** R4, M3, L4 • **SVP:** 2-4 yrs • **Academic:** Ed=H, Eng=G • **Work Field:** 293 • **MPSMS:** 959, 969 • **Aptitudes:** G2, V2, N3, S4, P4, Q4, K4, F4, M4, E5, C5 • **Temperaments:** D, J, P • **Stress:** E, A • **Physical:** V=L, H=L, L=S, W • **Work Env:** I • **Salary:** 4 • **Outlook:** 2

SPECIAL AGENT (insurance) • D.O.T. #166.167-046 • OES #21505 • SALES REPRESENTATIVE. Recruits independent SALES AGENTS, INSURANCE (insurance) in field and maintains contact between agent and home office: Selects SALES AGENT, INSURANCE (insurance), based on experience with other insurance companies. Drafts contract between agent and company. Advises agent on matters pertaining to conduct of business, such as cancellations, overdue accounts, and new business prospects. May gather information for UNDERWRITER (insurance). When working in life insurance, is designated as BROKERAGE MANAGER (insurance). • **GED:** R5, M3, L5 • **SVP:** 4-10 yrs • **Academic:** Ed=H, Eng=G • **Work Field:** 295 • **MPSMS:** 895 • **Aptitudes:** G2, V2, N3, S5, P3, Q2, K4, F4, M4, E5, C5 • **Temperaments:** D, I, P, T, V • **Stress:** E, A • **Physical:** V=N, H=L, L=S • **Work Env:** I • **Salary:** 5 • **Outlook:** 3

SUPERINTENDENT, PLANT PROTECTION (any ind.) • D.O.T. #189.167-050 • OES #19999 • PROTECTION CHIEF, INDUSTRIAL PLANT; SECURITY MANAGER. Directs personnel involved in establishing, promoting, and maintaining firm's security and property-protection programs: Establishes and supervises through subordinates, operational procedures for activities, such as fire prevention and firefighting, traffic control, guarding and patrolling physical property, orienting and monitoring of personnel involved with classified information, and investigation of accidents and criminal acts. Confers with representatives of management to formulate policies, determine need for programs, and coordinate programs with plant activities. Confers with representatives of local government to ensure cooperation and coordination of plant activities with law enforcement and firefighting agencies. May direct activities of workers involved in industrial safety programs. May direct activities of workers engaged in performing building maintenance and janitorial services. • **GED:** R5, M4, L4 • **SVP:** 4-10 yrs • **Academic:** Ed=H, Eng=G • **Work Field:** 293 • **MPSMS:** 951 • **Aptitudes:** G2, V2, N3, S4, P4, Q4, K4, F4, M4, E5, C5 • **Temperaments:** D, J, P, V • **Stress:** E, A • **Physical:** V=L, H=L, L=S, W • **Work Env:** I • **Salary:** 5 • **Outlook:** 1

UTILIZATION COORDINATOR (radio & tv broad.) • D.O.T. #169.167-078 • OES #21999 • Coordinates subscriber utilization of instructional television programming: Communicates with administrators, teaching staff, audiovisual specialists, and other personnel to assist subscribers in incorporating programs and

related materials into planned curricula. Conducts surveys to determine problems in use of programs and materials and develops workshops and other services to address identified needs. Confers with prospective users of programs to elicit interest in subscribing to services. Participates with other station personnel in developing advertising and promotional material. Oversees activities of workers engaged in processing subscriber accounts. • **GED:** R5, M3, L5 • **SVP:** 2-4 yrs • **Academic:** Ed=A, Eng=S • **Work Field:** 292, 295 • **MPSMS:** 860, 931 • **Aptitudes:** G2, V2, N4, S4, P4, Q3, K4, F4, M4, E5, C5 • **Temperaments:** J, P, V • **Physical:** V=L, H=L, L=S, H • **Work Env:** I • **Salary:** 4 • **Outlook:** 4

GOE: 11.05.03 Management Services: Government

DIRECTOR, REGULATORY AGENCY (gov. ser.) • D.O.T. #188.117-134 • OES #19005 • Directs agency, division, or major function of agency or division charged with investigating regulated activities to assure compliance with Federal, State, or municipal laws: Interprets and clarifies Federal, State, or municipal laws. Represents agency at meetings, conventions, and other forums to promote and explain agency objectives. Consults with other governmental agencies, business community, and private organizations to resolve problems. Plans and directs surveys and research studies to ensure effective program operation and to establish or modify standards. Recommends changes in legislation and administrative procedures to reflect technological and ecological changes and public sentiment. Confers with legislative liaison individuals or committees to develop legislative bills involving inspection procedures and to obtain wording for proposed inspection codes. Prepares or directs preparation and release of reports, studies, and other publications relating to program trends and accomplishments. Reviews and evaluates work of MANAGER, REGULATED PROGRAM (gov. ser.) 168.167-090 through conversations, meetings, and reports. Prepares or directs preparation of budget requests. May be required to testify in court or before control or review board. May be designated according to function or agency administered as ADMINISTRATOR, PESTICIDE (gov. ser.); ADMINISTRATOR, STRUCTURAL PEST CONTROL (gov. ser.); AGRICULTURAL COMMODITY GRADING SUPERVISOR (gov. ser.); DIRECTOR, REACTOR PROJECTS (gov. ser.); DIRECTOR, TRANSPORTATION UTILITIES REGULATION (gov. ser.); DIRECTOR, WEIGHTS AND MEASURES (gov. ser.); MANAGER FOR HEALTH, SAFETY, AND ENVIRONMENT (gov. ser.); PETROLEUM PRODUCTS INSPECTION SUPERVISOR (gov. ser.). • **GED:** R5, M4, L5 • **SVP:** 4-10 yrs • **Academic:** Ed=A, Eng=S • **Work Field:** 295 • **MPSMS:** 950 • **Aptitudes:** G2, V2, N3, S3, P3, Q2, K4, F4, M4, E5, C4 • **Temperaments:** D, J, P, V • **Stress:** A • **Physical:** V=L, H=L, L=S • **Work Env:** I • **Salary:** 5 • **Outlook:** 1

ENVIRONMENTAL ANALYST (gov. ser.) • D.O.T. #199.167-022 • OES #19005 • Directs, develops, and administers State governmental program for assessment of environmental impact of proposed recreational projects: Directs assessment of environmental impact and preparation of impact statements required for final evaluation of proposed actions. Directs identification and analysis of alternative proposals for handling projects in environmentally sensitive manner. Plans for enhancement of environmental setting for each proposed recreational project. Designs and directs special studies to obtain technical environmental information regarding planned projects, contacting and utilizing various sources, such as regional engineering offices, park region laboratories, and other governmental agencies. Prepares and controls budget for functions of impact-statement preparation program. Attends meetings and represents department on subjects related to program. • **GED:** R5, M3, L4 • **SVP:** 4-10 yrs • **Academic:** Ed=B, Eng=G • **Work Field:** 295 • **MPSMS:** 959 • **Aptitudes:** G2, V3, N3, S3, P4, Q2, K4, F4, M4, E5, C5 • **Temperaments:** D, J, P • **Stress:** E • **Physical:** V=N, H=N, L=S • **Work Env:** I • **Salary:** 5 • **Outlook:** 1

HOUSING-MANAGEMENT OFFICER (gov. ser.) • D.O.T. #188.117-110 • OES #19005 • Directs and coordinates activities concerned with providing advice and technical assistance to housing authorities and evaluating housing management programs: Develops policy and standards for guidance of local housing organizations in establishing and maintaining uniformity in operation of housing projects. Studies operation of housing projects, notes trends and needs, and evaluates efficiency of housing programs. Prepares regulations, procedures, and instructions for operation of housing projects based on analysis of operations. Approves or disapproves requests for waivers to policies, standards, and procedures. Consults with and advises housing personnel of public and private groups concerning needed improvements in housing operations. Advises and assists MANAGERS, HOUSING PROJECT (profess. & kin.) and staffs of local housing authorities concerning problems, such as eliminating excess costs, improving livability features and maintenance care of dwelling units, making more effective use of project facilities and community services, and promoting satisfactory relationships among tenants, housing project personnel, public officials, and private agencies. Leads public meetings and serves on committees to stimulate efforts of national, local, and private housing agencies and to emphasize housing needs of military personnel and low-income families. • **GED:** R5, M3, L4 • **SVP:** 4-10 yrs • **Academic:** Ed=A, Eng=S • **Work Field:** 295 • **MPSMS:** 959 • **Aptitudes:** G2, V2, N3, S4, P3, Q2, K4, F4, M4, E5, C5 • **Temperaments:** D, J, M, P, V • **Stress:** A • **Physical:** V=L, H=L, L=L • **Work Env:** I • **Salary:** 5 • **Outlook:** 1

LEGISLATIVE ASSISTANT (gov. ser.) • D.O.T. #169.167-066 • OES #21999 • Assists legislator in preparation of proposed legislation: Conducts research into subject of proposed legislation and develops preliminary draft of bill. Analyzes pending legislation and suggests to legislator action to be taken. Briefs legislator on policy issues. Attends committee meetings and prepares reports of proceedings. Speaks with lobbyists, constituents, and members of press to gather and provide information on behalf of legislator. Analyzes voting records of other legislators and political activity in legislator home district to derive data for legislator consideration. Maintains liaison with government agencies affected by proposed or pending legislation. Assists in campaign activities and drafts speeches for legislator. • **GED:** R5, M3, L5 • **SVP:** 2-4 yrs • **Academic:** Ed=H, Eng=G • **Work Field:** 251, 261 • **MPSMS:** 939 • **Aptitudes:** G2, V2, N3, S4, P4, Q3, K4, F4, M4, E5, C5 • **Temperaments:** I, J, P, V • **Stress:** E • **Physical:** V=N, H=N, L=S • **Work Env:** I • **Salary:** 4 • **Outlook:** 1

MANAGER, CITY (gov. ser.) • D.O.T. #188.117-114 • OES #19002 • MANAGER, COUNTY; MANAGER, TOWN. Directs and coordinates administration of city or county government in accordance with policies determined by city council or other authorized elected officials: Appoints department heads and staffs as provided by State laws or local ordinances. Supervises activities of departments performing functions such as collection and disbursement of taxes, law enforcement, maintenance of public health, construction of public works, and purchase of supplies and equipment. Prepares annual budget and submits estimates to authorized elected officials for approval. Plans for future development of urban and non-urban areas to provide for population growth and expansion of public services. May recommend zoning regulation controlling location and development of residential and commercial areas [URBAN PLANNER (profess. & kin.)]. May perform duties of one or more city or county officials as designated by local laws. • **GED:** R5, M4, L5 • **SVP:** 4-10 yrs • **Academic:** Ed=B, Eng=G • **Work Field:** 295 • **MPSMS:** 959 • **Aptitudes:** G2, V2, N3, S4, P4, Q4, K4, F4, M4, E5, C5 • **Temperaments:** D, J, P, V • **Stress:** E, A • **Physical:** V=N, H=G, L=S, W • **Work Env:** I • **Salary:** 5 • **Outlook:** 3

MANAGER, HOUSING PROJECT (profess. & kin.) • D.O.T. #186.167-030 • OES #15011 • Directs operations of housing project to provide low-income or military families, welfare recipients, or other eligible individuals with furnished or unfurnished housing in single or multi-unit dwellings or house trailers: Develops and implements plans for administration of housing project and procedures for making housing assignments. Reviews occupancy reports to ensure that applications, selection of tenants and assignment of dwelling units are in accordance with rules and regulations. Conducts surveys of local rental rates and participates in setting of rental rates according to occupants' income and accommodation requirements. Prepares operational budget requests and receives accounts for and disburses funds. Conducts analyses of management and maintenance costs to determine areas where cost reductions can be effected. Plans long range schedule of major repairs

on units, such as reroofing or painting exterior of dwellings. Studies housing demands occupancy and turnover rates and accommodation requirements of applicants to recommend policy and physical requirement changes. Promotes harmonious relations among tenants, housing project personnel, and persons of the community. Directs work activities of office and clerical staff in processing applications, collecting of rents and accounting for monies collected, and assigns building and grounds maintenance personnel to specific duties. Requisitions furnishings and furniture for housing units. May direct activities of other management personnel in housing project having commercial shops, concessions, theater, library, and recreational facilities. May refer applicants to private housing if all available units are occupied or if accommodation requirements are inadequate. • **GED:** R5, M4, L4 • **SVP:** 2-4 yrs • **Academic:** Ed=A, Eng=S • **Work Field:** 295 • **MPSMS:** 895 • **Aptitudes:** G2, V2, N3, S4, P4, Q3, K4, F4, M4, E5, C5 • **Temperaments:** D, I, P • **Stress:** A • **Physical:** V=N, H=L, L=S • **Work Env:** I • **Salary:** 4 • **Outlook:** 2

MANAGER, OFFICE (gov. ser.) • D.O.T. #188.167-058 • OES #19005 • Manages local, district, or regional office of governmental agency or department to provide public or other individuals with designated services, or implement laws, codes, programs, or policies prescribed by legislative bodies: Reviews official directives and correspondence to ascertain such data as changes prescribed in agency programs, policies, and procedures, and new assignments or responsibilities delegated to office. Confers with subordinate supervisory personnel and reads staff reports and records to obtain data, such as status of on-going work or projects, cases and investigations pending, indications of probable conclusions, and projected completion dates. Plans office activities and work projects and assigns unit supervisory personnel responsibility for carrying out and completing specific projects and duties. Coordinates activities of various office units in order to provide designated functions or services with minimum delay and optimum efficiency and accuracy. Informs supervisory personnel of changes or interpretations of laws, codes, programs, policies, or procedures. Conducts staff meetings for dissemination of pertinent information. Trains and evaluates performance of supervisory personnel and reviews performance reports prepared on staff. Prepares reports on office activities required by agency. Workers are usually designated according to type of office and agency or department managed, or by type of work performed by office staff. • **GED:** R4, M4, L4 • **SVP:** 4-10 yrs • **Academic:** Ed=H, Eng=S • **Work Field:** 295 • **MPSMS:** 950 • **Aptitudes:** G2, V2, N2, S3, P3, Q3, K4, F4, M4, E5, C5 • **Temperaments:** D, J, P, V • **Stress:** A • **Physical:** V=L, H=L, L=S, H • **Work Env:** I • **Salary:** 5 • **Outlook:** 4

MANAGER, REGULATED PROGRAM (gov. ser.) • D.O.T. #168.167-090 • OES #21911 • Directs and coordinates activities of departmental personnel engaged in investigating regulated activities to ensure compliance with Federal, State, or municipal laws, utilizing knowledge of agency's purposes, rules, regulations, procedures, and practices: Reviews agency's current workload status, schedules, and individual personnel assignments and expertise to establish priorities and to determine ability to accept and complete future commitments. Assigns specific duties to inspectors and/or INVESTIGATOR (gov. ser.) 168.267-062 either directly or through subordinate supervisors. Reviews work reports, papers, rulings, and other records prepared by subordinate personnel for clarity, completeness, accuracy, and conformance with agency policies. Routes approved reports and records to designated individuals, such as DIRECTOR, REGULATORY AGENCY (gov. ser.) 188.117-134 for action or for information. May participate in or make initial and/or advanced level investigations, tests, or rulings. May testify in court and/or before control or review board. May be required to be certified in designated speciality area. May be designated according to function or agency as BUSINESS REGULATION INVESTIGATOR (gov. ser.); CHILD DAY CARE PROGRAM SUPERVISOR (gov. ser.); FEED INSPECTION SUPERVISOR (gov. ser.); INSURANCE LICENSING SUPERVISOR (gov. ser.); MEAT AND POULTRY SPECIALIST SUPERVISOR (gov. ser.); PETROLEUM PRODUCTS DISTRICT SUPERVISOR (gov. ser.); POULTRY SPECIALIST SUPERVISOR (gov. ser.); PUBLIC UTILITIES COMPLAINT ANALYST SUPERVISOR (gov. ser.); or SUPERVISOR, WEIGHTS AND MEASURES, GAS AND OIL INSPECTION (gov. ser.). Workers involved in these activities may be identified by different titles, according to classification used by various agencies. • **GED:** R5, M5, L5 • **SVP:** 4-10 yrs • **Academic:** Ed=A, Eng=S • **Work Field:** 295 • **MPSMS:** 953 • **Aptitudes:** G1, V2, N2, S4, P2, Q2, K5, F5, M5, E5, C5 • **Temperaments:** D, J, P, T, V • **Stress:** A • **Physical:** V=L, H=L, L=L, H • **Work Env:** I • **Salary:** 5 • **Outlook:** 1

POSTMASTER (gov. ser.) • D.O.T. #188.167-066 • OES #15002 • Coordinates activities of workers engaged in postal and related work in assigned post office: Organizes and supervises directly, or through subordinates, such activities as processing incoming and outgoing mail; issuing and cashing money orders; selling stamps, bonds and certificates; and collecting box rents to ensure efficient service to patrons. Resolves customer complaints and informs public of postal laws and regulations. Confers with suppliers to obtain bids for proposed purchases, requisitions supplies, and disburses funds as specified by law. Prepares and submits detailed and summary reports of post office activities to designated superior. Selects, trains, and evaluates performance of employees and prepares work schedules. May perform or participate in post office activities depending on size of post office. May plan and implement labor relations program. May confer with employees to negotiate labor disputes. • **GED:** R4, M4, L4 • **SVP:** 2-4 yrs • **Academic:** Ed=H, Eng=S • **Work Field:** 295 • **MPSMS:** 954 • **Aptitudes:** G2, V2, N3, S4, P3, Q4, K4, F4, M4, E5, C5 • **Temperaments:** D, J, M, P, V • **Stress:** A • **Physical:** V=L, H=L, L=S • **Work Env:** I • **Salary:** 4 • **Outlook:** 1

SECRETARY OF STATE (gov. ser.) • D.O.T. #188.167-082 • OES #19005 • Directs and coordinates activities of secretary of state office to assist executive and legislative branches of state government under authority of state statutory and constitutional provisions: Directs activities of workers engaged in preserving records of official acts performed by governor and legislative bodies. Directs distribution of laws, resolutions, and other official state documents. Examines corporate articles or corporate statements of qualification to approve or disallow petitions for incorporation, amendments to corporate articles, dissolutions, and agreements of merger or consolidation. Administers Uniform Commercial Code to protect secured interest of retail merchants and lending institutions. Approves licensing of notaries public. Receives for processing, recording, and filing, documents such as deeds to state lands, claims to fraternal names and insignia, manuscripts, oaths of office, organization and boundaries of public districts, administrative rules and regulations adopted by state agencies, and statements of trust receipt financing. Directs activities involved in preserving historical documents and public records in state archives. May interpret and enforce election laws. May tabulate and certify accuracy of election returns. • **GED:** R5, M4, L5 • **SVP:** 4-10 yrs • **Academic:** Ed=M, Eng=G • **Work Field:** 295 • **MPSMS:** 959 • **Aptitudes:** G2, V2, N2, S4, P4, Q3, K4, F4, M4, E5, C5 • **Temperaments:** J, M, P, V • **Stress:** E • **Physical:** V=N, H=L, L=S • **Work Env:** I • **Salary:** 5 • **Outlook:** 1

GOE: 11.05.04 Sales & Purchasing Management

DIRECTOR, MEDIA MARKETING (radio & tv broad.) • D.O.T. #163.117-022 • OES #13011 • Plans and administers marketing and distribution of broadcasting television programs and negotiates agreements for ancillary properties, such as copyrights and distribution rights for films and audiovisual materials: Reviews inventory of television programs and films produced and distribution rights of broadcasting station to determine potential markets. Develops marketing strategy, based on knowledge of establishment policy, nature of market, copyright and royalty requirements, and cost and markup factors. Compiles catalog of audiovisual offerings and sets prices and rental fees. Negotiates with media agents to secure agreements for translation of materials into other media. Arranges for reproduction of materials for distribution and examines reproductions for conformity to standards. Edits materials according to specific market or customer requirements. Confers with legal staff to resolve problems, such as copyrights and royalty sharing with outside producers and distributors. • **GED:** R5, M4, L5 • **SVP:** 4-10 yrs • **Academic:** Ed=A, Eng=S • **Work Field:** 292, 295 • **MPSMS:** 864, 889 • **Aptitudes:** G2, V2, N3, S3, P3, Q2, K4, F4, M4, E5, C4 • **Temper-**

aments: D, I, J, P, V • **Stress:** A • **Physical:** V=L, H=L, L=S • **Work Env:** I • **Salary:** 5 • **Outlook:** 3

FIELD REPRESENTATIVE (bus. ser.) • D.O.T. #163.267-010 • OES #13011 • DISTRIBUTION MANAGER. Monitors dealers and distributors to ensure efficiency of franchise operation: Surveys proposed locations to determine feasibility of establishing dealerships or distributorships. Advises dealers and distributors of policies and operating procedures to ensure functional effectiveness of business, and also develops information concerning planning and developing of business modifications and expansions. Reviews operations records to evaluate effectiveness. • **GED:** R5, M4, L3 • **SVP:** 1-2 yrs • **Academic:** Ed=A, Eng=S • **Work Field:** 211, 292 • **MPSMS:** 899 • **Aptitudes:** G2, V2, N3, S3, P4, Q3, K4, F4, M4, E5, C5 • **Temperaments:** D, I, M, P • **Stress:** A • **Physical:** V=G, H=L, L=L • **Work Env:** I • **Salary:** 4 • **Outlook:** 4

MANAGER, CIRCULATION (print. & pub.) • D.O.T. #163.167-014 • OES #19999 • Directs sale and distribution of newspapers, books, and periodicals: Directs staffing, training, and performance evaluations to develop and control sales and distribution program. Establishes geographical areas of responsibility for subordinates to coordinate sales and distribution activities. May be designated according to type of circulation activity managed as MANAGER, NEWSPAPER CIRCULATION (print. & pub.); or area served as MANAGER, CITY CIRCULATION (print. & pub.). • **GED:** R5, M3, L4 • **SVP:** 4-10 yrs • **Academic:** Ed=A, Eng=S • **Work Field:** 292 • **MPSMS:** 480 • **Aptitudes:** G2, V2, N2, S3, P3, Q3, K4, F4, M4, E5, C5 • **Temperaments:** D, J, P, V • **Stress:** A • **Physical:** V=N, H=L, L=S • **Work Env:** I • **Salary:** 5 • **Outlook:** 3

MANAGER, PROFESSIONAL EQUIPMENT SALES-AND-SERVICE (bus. ser.) • D.O.T. #185.167-042 • OES #19999 • Directs and coordinates activities of establishment engaged in sale of professional equipment and supplies, and providing customer services, to organizations in such fields as medicine and medical services, engineering, and education: Plans and directs sales and service programs to promote new markets, improve competitive position in area, and provide fast and efficient customer service. Confers with potential customer to ascertain equipment, supplies, and service needs. Advises customer on types of equipment to purchase, considering such factors as costs, space availability, and intended use. Directs and coordinates activities of personnel engaged in sales and service accounting and record keeping, and receiving and shipping operations. Reviews articles in trade publications to keep abreast of technological developments in types of professional equipment merchandised. Resolves customer complaints regarding equipment, supplies, and services. Workers are usually classified according to type of firm managed or type of equipment and supplies sold such as dental, hospital, school, medical, or laboratory supply house. • **GED:** R5, M4, L4 • **SVP:** 2-4 yrs • **Academic:** Ed=A, Eng=S • **Work Field:** 292 • **MPSMS:** 589, 601, 604 • **Aptitudes:** G2, V2, N3, S4, P4, Q3, K4, F4, M4, E5, C5 • **Temperaments:** D, I, P, V • **Stress:** A • **Physical:** V=L, H=G, L=S, H • **Work Env:** I • **Salary:** 4 • **Outlook:** 1

MANAGER, SALES (any ind.) • D.O.T. #163.167-018 • OES #13011 • Manages sales activities of establishment: Directs staffing, training, and performance evaluations to develop and control sales program. Coordinates sales distribution by establishing sales territories, quotas, and goals, and advises dealers and distributors concerning sales and advertising techniques. Assigns sales territory to sales personnel. Analyzes sales statistics to formulate policy and to assist dealers in promoting sales. Reviews market analyses to determine customer needs, volume potential, price schedules, and discount rates, and develops sales campaigns to accommodate goals of company. Directs product simplification and standardization to eliminate unprofitable items from sales line. Represents company at trade association meetings to promote product. Coordinates liaison between sales department and other sales-related units. Analyzes and controls expenditures of division to conform to budgetary requirements. Assists engineering division to prepare manuals and technical publications. Prepares periodic sales report showing sales volume and potential sales. May direct sales for manufacturer, retail store, wholesale house, jobber, or other establishment. May direct product research and development. May recommend or approve budget, expenditures, and appropriations for research and development work. • **GED:** R5, M3, L5 • **SVP:**

4-10 yrs • **Academic:** Ed=H, Eng=G • **Work Field:** 292, 295 • **MPSMS:** 880, 896 • **Aptitudes:** G2, V2, N2, S3, P3, Q3, K4, F4, M4, E5, C5 • **Temperaments:** D, I, J, P, V • **Stress:** E, A • **Physical:** V=N, H=L, L=S • **Work Env:** I • **Salary:** 4 • **Outlook:** 3

PROPERTY-DISPOSAL OFFICER (any ind.) • D.O.T. #163.167-026 • OES #13014 • REDISTRIBUTION-AND-MAR-KETING OFFICER; SURPLUS-PROPERTY DISPOSALAGENT; SURPLUS SALES OFFICER. Disposes of surplus property, other than real property, using knowledge of merchandising practices: Inspects property to ascertain condition and estimate market value. Investigates market conditions and facilities to determine time, place, type of sale, and whether items shall be sold individually or in lots. Prepares advertising material and selects media for its release. Assigns and directs activities of sales personnel. Determines method of property display and sets prices of items to be sold in conformity with value and market. Advises interested parties of salvage possibilities. Recommends destruction or abandonment of property not deemed possible or practical to sell or salvage. • **GED:** R5, M5, L5 • **SVP:** 2-4 yrs • **Academic:** Ed=H, Eng=G • **Work Field:** 292, 295 • **MPSMS:** 592, 959 • **Aptitudes:** G2, V2, N3, S3, P4, Q2, K4, F4, M4, E5, C4 • **Temperaments:** D, J, M, P, V • **Stress:** E • **Physical:** V=N, H=L, L=S • **Work Env:** I • **Salary:** 4 • **Outlook:** 3

PURCHASING AGENT (profess. & kin.) • D.O.T. #162.157-038 • OES #21308 • BUYER; DIRECTOR, PURCHASING; MANAGER, PURCHASING; MANAGER, SUPPLY; PURCHASER.

Purchases raw materials or other unprocessed goods for processing, or machinery, equipment, tools, parts, produce, and other supplies or services necessary for operation of organization: Reviews requisitions. Interviews vendors to obtain information concerning product, price, ability of vendor to produce product or service, and delivery date. Selects purchase items by testing, observing, or otherwise examining. Estimates values according to knowledge of market price. Reviews bid proposals from vendors and enters into contracts within budgetary limitations. Keeps records pertaining to items purchased, costs, delivery, product performance, and inventories. Discusses defects of purchased goods with quality control or inspection personnel to determine source of trouble and takes corrective action. May approve bills for payment. May be designated according to type of goods purchased as BUYER, ELECTRONICS (elec. equip.); BUYER, FISH (can. & preserv.); BUYER, FOOD (hotel & rest.); BUYER, FURS (whole. tr.). May be designated according to position held as MANAGER, STOREROOM (hotel & rest.); SUPPLY REQUIREMENTS OFFICER (gov. ser.). Additional titles: BUYER, MAPLE SIRUP (food prep., n.e.c.); BUYER, TIME AND SPACE (bus. ser.); BUYER, TOBACCO (whole. tr.); LOGISTICS OFFICER (gov. ser.); PIECE-GOODS BUYER (garment); PURVEYOR (hotel & rest.); STOCK BUYER (any ind.). • **GED:** R4, M3, L4 • **SVP:** 2-4 yrs • **Academic:** Ed=H, Eng=G • **Work Field:** 292 • **MPSMS:** 880 • **Aptitudes:** G2, V2, N3, S4, P4, Q3, K4, F4, M4, E5, C4 • **Temperaments:** D, I, J, M, P • **Stress:** E, A • **Physical:** V=N, H=L, L=S • **Work Env:** I • **Salary:** 4 • **Outlook:** 4

11.06 Finance

Workers in this group use mathematical and analytical skills to design financial systems and examine and interpret financial records. They are concerned with accounting and auditing activities, records systems analysis, risk and profit analyses, brokering, and budget and financial control. They find employment in banks, loan companies, investment firms, colleges, government agencies, and miscellaneous business firms. Some workers, like accountants and appraisers are self-employed.

✔ **What kind of work would you do?**
Your work activities would depend upon your specific job. For example, you might:

- design an accounting system for a business to provide complete financial records.
- analyze financial records to prepare a financial status report.
- appraise materials and equipment to determine the total value of a business firm.
- analyze credit information to determine risk involved in lending money.

- study information to set schedules and rates for the transportation of merchandise and passengers.
- administer loan funds of a college or university and make arrangements for repayment.
- provide financial counseling to individuals in debt.
- regulate the cash flow in a bank by keeping loans, deposits, and Federal Reserve notes in balance.

✔ **What skills and abilities do you need for this kind of work?**
To do this kind of work, you must be able to:

- understand and use mathematical concepts in order to design a financial or economic system.

- interpret technical information presented in mathematical or diagram form in order to work with things like real estate property values, parimutuel betting systems and stock market reports.

- work math problems quickly and accurately.
- understand and use computers and related equipment.
- speak and write clearly to report financial information.

- make decisions about the value of real estate and personal property based on inspection of the property, how you think its location will be affected by future plans of the community, as well as established facts like past tax values.
- plan and direct the work of accounting clerks and other workers.

✔ **How do you know if you would like or could learn to do this kind of work?**
The following questions may give you clues about yourself as you consider this group of jobs.

- Have you had a checking or savings account? Did your balance always agree with the bank statement?
- Have you budgeted your own spending? Does your budget work?
- Have you had courses in accounting or bookkeeping? Do you enjoy this type of work?

- Have you been a treasurer of a school or community organization? Can you keep accurate financial records?
- Have you served in the accounting or payroll section of the armed forces?

✔ **How can you prepare for and enter this kind of work?**
Occupations in this group usually require education and/or training extending from two years to over ten years, depending upon the specific kind of work. Work experience is a major consideration in preparing for jobs in this group. Experience in related positions for the same employer is often required. However, courses in accounting, business law, economics, and investments are helpful. Some of these courses are available in high schools, but most are offered by business schools and colleges.

Some jobs in this group require licenses or certificates. Qualifications for credentials vary from state to state.

✔ **What else should you consider about these jobs?**
Jobs in this group are in offices which are usually well-lighted and ventilated. Some workers may be exposed to the noise of office machines. Other workers may have private offices.

Most of the work is detailed and workers may develop eyestrain if proper precautions are not taken.

The majority of these positions are salaried. Workers are seldom paid for overtime.

If you think you would like to do this kind of work, look at the job titles listed on the following pages.

GOE: 11.06.01 Accounting & Auditing

ACCOUNTANT (profess. & kin.) • D.O.T. #160.167-010 • OES #21114 • MANAGER, OFFICE. Directs and coordinates activities of workers engaged in general accounting, or applies principles of accounting to devise and implement system for general accounting: Directs and coordinates activities of workers engaged in keeping accounts and records, or performing such bookkeeping activities as recording disbursements, expenses, and tax payments. Prepares individual, division, or consolidated balance sheets to reflect company's assets, liabilities, and capital. Prepares profit and loss statements for specified accounting period. Audits contracts, orders, and vouchers, and prepares reports to substantiate individual transactions prior to settlement. May represent company before government agencies upon certification by agency involved. May work independently for fee or as member of accounting firm

and be designated as ACCOUNTANT, PUBLIC (profess. & kin.). • **GED:** R5, M5, L5 • **SVP:** 4-10 yrs • **Academic:** Ed=B, Eng=G • **Work Field:** 232 • **MPSMS:** 892 • **Aptitudes:** G2, V2, N2, S4, P4, Q2, K4, F4, M4, E5, C5 • **Temperaments:** D, J, P, T • **Stress:** E • **Physical:** V=G, H=N, L=S, H • **Work Env:** I • **Salary:** 5 • **Outlook:** 4

ACCOUNTANT, BUDGET (profess. & kin.) • D.O.T. #160.167-014 • OES #21114 • Applies principles of accounting to analyze past and present financial operations and estimates future revenues and expenditures to prepare budget: Estimates expenditures expected and submits to management. Analyzes records of present and past operations, trends and costs, estimated and realized revenues, administrative commitments, and obligations incurred. Develops, installs, and maintains budgeting systems which provide control of expenditures made to carry out activities, such as advertising and marketing, production and labor, maintenance, or project activities, such as construction of buildings. Advises management regarding matters, such as effective use of resources and methods for preventing capital being frozen. Interprets accounts and records to management. May supervise personnel performing routine phases of accounting operations. May assist in financial analysis of legislative projects to develop capital improvement budget and be designated PROGRAM ANALYST (gov. ser.). May assist communities to develop budget and efficient use of funds and be designated PUBLIC FINANCE SPECIALIST (gov. ser.). • **GED:** R5, M5, L5 • **SVP:** 4-10 yrs • **Academic:** Ed=A, Eng=G • **Work Field:** 232 • **MPSMS:** 892 • **Aptitudes:** G2, V2, N2, S4, P4, Q2, K4, F4, M4, E5, C5 • **Temperaments:** D, J, M, T • **Stress:** A • **Physical:** V=L, H=N, L=S • **Work Env:** I • **Salary:** 5 • **Outlook:** 4

ACCOUNTANT, COST (profess. & kin.) • D.O.T. #160.167-018 • OES #21114 • Applies principles of cost accounting and statistics to devise, implement, and administer systems to provide management with detailed cost data not ordinarily supplied by general accounting systems: Plans, implements, and directs cost finding and reporting systems to determine, record, and report unit costs of factors affecting production, such as raw material purchases, labor, inventory, and machine maintenance. Analyzes changes in product design, raw materials, overhead, manufacturing methods, or wages, for effects upon production costs. Analyzes actual manufacturing costs and prepares periodic report comparing standard costs to actual production costs. Provides management with cost and comparative reports to indicate needs for changes in pricing or production. May specialize in analyzing costs relating to public utility rate schedule and be designated RATE ENGINEER (profess. & kin.). May specialize in appraisal and evaluation of real property or equipment for sale, acquisition, or tax purposes for public utility and be designated VALUATION ENGINEER (profess. & kin.). • **GED:** R5, M5, L5 • **SVP:** 4-10 yrs • **Academic:** Ed=B, Eng=G • **Work Field:** 232 • **MPSMS:** 892 • **Aptitudes:** G2, V2, N1, S4, P4, Q2, K4, F4, M4, E5, C5 • **Temperaments:** D, J, P, T • **Stress:** E • **Physical:** V=N, H=N, L=S, H • **Work Env:** I • **Salary:** 5 • **Outlook:** 4

ACCOUNTANT, TAX (profess. & kin.) • D.O.T. #160.162-010 • OES #21114 • Prepares Federal, state, or local tax returns of individual, business establishment, or other organization: Examines accounts and records and computes tax returns according to prescribed rates, laws, and regulations. Advises management regarding effects of business, internal programs and activities, and other transactions upon taxes and represents principal before various governmental taxing bodies. May devise and install tax record systems. May specialize in particular phase of tax accounting, such as income, property, real estate, or Social Security taxes. • **GED:** R5, M5, L5 • **SVP:** 4-10 yrs • **Academic:** Ed=B, Eng=G • **Work Field:** 232 • **MPSMS:** 892 • **Aptitudes:** G2, V2, N2, S4, P3, Q2, K4, F4, M4, E5, C5 • **Temperaments:** D, I, M, P, T • **Stress:** E, A • **Physical:** V=L, H=N, L=S • **Work Env:** I • **Salary:** 5 • **Outlook:** 4

AUDITOR (profess. & kin.) • D.O.T. #160.162-014 • OES #21114 • Examines and analyzes accounting records of establishment and prepares reports concerning its financial status and operating procedures: Reviews data regarding material assets, net worth, liabilities, capital stock, surplus, income, and expenditures. Inspects items in books of original entry to determine if proper procedure in recording transactions was followed. Counts cash on hand, inspects notes receivable and payable, negotiable securities, and cancelled checks. Verifies journal and ledger entries of cash and check payments, purchases, expenses, and trial balances by examining and authenticating inventory items. Reports to management concerning scope of audit, financial conditions found, and source and application of funds. May make recommendations regarding improving operations and financial position of company. May audit banks and financial institutions and be designated BANK EXAMINER (gov. ser.). May examine company payroll and personnel records to determine worker's compensation coverage and be designated PAYROLL AUDITOR (insurance). • **GED:** R5, M5, L5 • **SVP:** 4-10 yrs • **Academic:** Ed=B, Eng=G • **Work Field:** 232 • **MPSMS:** 892 • **Aptitudes:** G2, V2, N1, S4, P4, Q2, K4, F4, M4, E5, C5 • **Temperaments:** D, M, T, V • **Physical:** V=G, H=N, L=S • **Work Env:** I • **Salary:** 5 • **Outlook:** 4

AUDITOR, INTERNAL (profess. & kin.) • D.O.T. #160.167-034

• OES #21114 • Conducts independent protective and constructive audits for managements to review effectiveness of controls, financial records, and operations: Examines records of departments to ensure proper recording of transactions and compliance with applicable laws. Inspects accounting systems to determine their efficiency and protective value. Reviews records pertaining to material assets, such as equipment, buildings, or manpower to determine degree to which they are utilized. Analyzes data obtained for evidence of deficiencies in controls, duplication of effort, extravagance, fraud, or lack of compliance with management's established policies or procedures. Prepares reports of findings and recommendations to management. May conduct special studies for management, such as those required to discover mechanics of detected frauds and to develop controls for their prevention. May audit business and governmental agency records to determine unemployment insurance premiums, liabilities, and employer compliance with state tax laws and be designated FINANCIAL-RECORDS EXAMINER (gov. ser.). • **GED:** R5, M5, L5 • **SVP:** 4-10 yrs • **Academic:** Ed=B, Eng=G • **Work Field:** 232, 271 • **MPSMS:** 892 • **Aptitudes:** G2, V2, N1, S4, P4, Q2, K4, F4, M4, E5, C5 • **Temperaments:** D, M, T, V • **Physical:** V=G, H=N, L=S • **Work Env:** I • **Salary:** 5 • **Outlook:** 4

AUDITOR, TAX (profess. & kin.) • D.O.T. #160.167-038 • OES #21114 • Audits financial records to determine tax liability: Reviews information gathered from tax payer, such as material assets, income, surpluses, liabilities, and expenditures to verify net worth or reported financial status and identify potential tax issues. Analyzes issues to determine nature, scope, and direction of investigation required. Develops and evaluates evidence of taxpayer finances to determine tax liability, using knowledge of interest and discount, annuities, valuation of stocks and bonds, sinking funds, and amortization valuation of depletable assets. Prepares written explanation of findings to notify taxpayer of tax liability. Advises taxpayer of appeal rights. May conduct onsite audits at taxpayer's place of business and be designated FIELD AUDITOR (gov. ser.). May audit individuals and small businesses through correspondence or by summoning taxpayer to branch office for interview and be designated OFFICE AUDITOR (gov. ser.). May perform legal and accounting work in examination of records, tax returns, and related documents pertaining to tax settlement of decedent's estates and be designated TAX ANALYST (gov. ser.). May review most complicated taxpayer accounts and be designated TAX EXAMINER (gov. ser.). • **GED:** R5, M5, L5 • **SVP:** 4-10 yrs • **Academic:** Ed=B, Eng=G • **Work Field:** 232, 271 • **MPSMS:** 953 • **Aptitudes:** G2, V2, N1, S4, P4, Q2, K4, F4, M4, E5, C5 • **Temperaments:** D, M, P, T, V • **Physical:** V=L, H=N, L=S • **Work Env:** I • **Salary:** 5 • **Outlook:** 4

OPERATIONS OFFICER (finan. inst.) • D.O.T. #186.167-050 • OES #21199 • Directs and coordinates activities of personnel involved in performing internal operations in department or branch office of financial institution, such as bank or savings and loan association: Audits accounts, records of proof, and certifications to ensure compliance of workers with established standard procedures and practices. Compiles required and special reports on operating functions of department or branch. Interviews, selects, and hires new employees. Directs employee training to improve efficiency and ensure conformance with standard procedures and practices. Verifies workers' count of incoming cash shipments. Controls supply of money on hand commensurate with branch's daily needs and legal requirements. Conducts staff meetings of operations personnel, or confers with subordinate supervisors to discuss operational problems or explain procedural changes or practices. May be designated according to financial institution as OPERATIONS OFFICER, BRANCH BANK (finan. inst.); OPERATIONS OFFICER, BRANCH OFFICE (finan. inst.) or department as OPERATIONS OFFICER, TRUST DEPARTMENT (finan. inst.). • **GED:** R5, M5, L4 • **SVP:** 2-4 yrs • **Academic:** Ed=H, Eng=G • **Work Field:** 232 • **MPSMS:** 894 • **Aptitudes:** G2, V2, N2, S4, P4, Q3, K4, F4, M4, E5, C5 • **Temperaments:** D, P, T • **Stress:** E, A • **Physical:** V=L, H=L, L=S, W, H • **Work Env:** I • **Salary:** 4 • **Outlook:** 2

REVENUE AGENT (gov. ser.) • D.O.T. #160.167-050 • OES #21914 • Conducts independent field audits and investigations of Federal income tax returns to verify or amend tax liabilities:

Examines selected tax returns to determine nature and extent of audits to be performed. Analyzes accounting books and records to determine appropriateness of accounting methods employed and compliance with statutory provisions. Investigates documents, financial transactions, operation methods, industry practices and such legal instruments as vouchers, leases, contracts, and wills, to develop information regarding inclusiveness of accounting records and tax returns. Confers with taxpayer or representative to explain issues involved and applicability of pertinent tax laws and regulations. (Workers who investigate and collect Federal tax delinquencies are defined under REVENUE OFFICER (gov. ser.). Secures taxpayer's agreement to discharge tax assessment or submits contested determination to other administrative or judicial conferees for appeals hearings. May participate in informal appeals hearings on contested cases from other agents. May serve as member of regional appeals board to reexamine unresolved issues in terms of relevant laws and regulations and be designated APPELLATE CONFEREE (gov. ser.). • **GED:** R5, M4, L4 • **SVP:** 2-4 yrs • **Academic:** Ed=B, Eng=G • **Work Field:** 232, 271 • **MPSMS:** 953 • **Aptitudes:** G2, V2, N2, S4, P3, Q3, K4, F4, M4, E5, C5 • **Temperaments:** I, J, M, P • **Stress:** E • **Physical:** V=L, H=L, L=S • **Work Env:** I • **Salary:** 4 • **Outlook:** 3

GOE: 11.06.02 Records Systems Analysis

REPORTS ANALYST (profess. & kin.) • D.O.T. #161.267- 026 • OES #21905 • Examines and evaluates purpose and content of business reports to develop new, or improve existing format, use, and control: Reviews reports to determine basic characteristics, such as origin and report flow, format, frequency, distribution and purpose or function of report. Confers with persons originating, handling, processing, or receiving reports to identify problems and to gather suggestions for improvements. Evaluates findings, using knowledge of workflow, operating practices, records retention schedules, and office equipment layout. Recommends establishment of new or modified reporting methods and procedures to improve report content and completeness of information. May prepare and issue instructions concerning generation, completion, and distribution of reports according to new or revised practices, procedures, or policies of reports management. • **GED:** R4, M3, L4 • **SVP:** 2-4 yrs • **Academic:** Ed=B, Eng=S • **Work Field:** 211 • **MPSMS:** 891 • **Aptitudes:** G2, V2, N3, S3, P3, Q2, K5, F5, M5, E5, C3 • **Temperaments:** D, M, P • **Physical:** V=L, H=G, L=S • **Work Env:** I • **Salary:** 4 • **Outlook:** 3

GOE: 11.06.03 Risk & Profit Analysis

APPRAISER (any ind.) • D.O.T. #191.287-010 • OES #49999 • Appraises merchandise, fixtures, machinery, and equipment of business firms to ascertain values for such purposes as approval of loans, issuance of insurance policies, disposition of estates, and liquidation of assets of bankrupt firms: Examines items and estimates their wholesale or auction-sale values, basing estimate on knowledge of equipment or goods, current market values, and industrial and economic trends. Prepares and submits reports of estimates to clients, such as insurance firms, lending agencies, government offices, creditors, courts, or attorneys. • **GED:** R5, M5, L5 • **SVP:** 2-4 yrs • **Academic:** Ed=A, Eng=S • **Work Field:** 211 • **MPSMS:** 899 • **Aptitudes:** G2, V3, N2, S3, P3, Q3, K4, F4, M4, E5, C5 • **Temperaments:** J, M • **Physical:** V=G, H=L, L=L, W, S, H • **Work Env:** I • **Salary:** 4 • **Outlook:** 1

APPRAISER (gov. ser.) • D.O.T. #188.167-010 • OES #21917 • DEPUTY ASSESSOR. Appraises real and personal property to determine fair value and assesses taxes in accordance with prescribed schedules: Inspects property and considers factors such as current market value, location of property, and building or replacement costs to make property appraisal. Computes amount of tax to be levied, using applicable tax tables, and writes reports of determinations for public record. May interpret laws, formulate policies, and direct activities of assessment office. May be designated according to type of property assessed as APPRAISER, AIRCRAFT (gov. ser.); APPRAISER, AUDITOR (gov. ser.); APPRAISER, BOATS AND MARINE (gov. ser.); APPRAISER, BUILDINGS (gov. ser.); APPRAISER, LAND (gov. ser.); APPRAISER, OIL AND WATER (gov. ser.); APPRAISER, PERSONAL PROPERTY (gov. ser.); APPRAISER, REAL ESTATE (gov. ser.); APPRAISER, TIMBER (gov. ser.). • **GED:** R5, M5, L5 • **SVP:** 2-4 yrs • **Academic:** Ed=A, Eng=G • **Work Field:** 211 • **MPSMS:** 895 • **Aptitudes:** G2, V2, N2, S3, P3, Q2, K4, F4, M4, E4, C4 • **Temperaments:** J, M, T • **Physical:** V=G, H=N, L=S, W, C, H • **Work Env:** B • **Salary:** 4 • **Outlook:** 1

APPRAISER, REAL ESTATE (real estate) • D.O.T. #191.267-010 • OES #43011 • Appraises improved or unimproved real property to determine value for purchase, sale, investment, mortgage, or loan purposes: Interviews persons familiar with property and takes measurements. Inspects property for construction, condition, and functional design. Computes depreciation and reproduction costs. Considers location and trends or impending changes that could influence future value of property. Searches public records of sales, leases, assessments, and other transactions. Compiles data and estimates value of property. Submits report to corroborate value established. • **GED:** R5, M4, L4 • **SVP:** 2-4 yrs • **Academic:** Ed=A, Eng=G • **Work Field:** 211 • **MPSMS:** 895 • **Aptitudes:** G2, V2, N2, S3, P4, Q2, K4, F4, M4, E5, C5 • **Temperaments:** J, P, V • **Physical:** V=G, H=N, L=S, W, C, S, H • **Work Env:** B • **Salary:** 4 • **Outlook:** 3

BOOKMAKER (amuse. & rec.) • D.O.T. #187.167-014 • OES #19999 • BOOKIE. Manages establishment to receive and pay off bets placed by horse racing patrons: Prepares and issues lists of approximate handicap odds on each horse prior to race, from knowledge of previous performance of horse under existing conditions of weather and track. Determines risks on each horse to refuse additional bets after maximum desired limit of liability has been reached. Records bets placed over counter, or by telephone or teletype. Issues betting receipts. Pays off bets on track parimutuel basis. May supervise and coordinate activities of CASHIERS, GAMBLING (amuse. & rec.). May balance betting accounts and keep records as required by State or municipal authorities. May place customers' bets with cooperating BOOKMAKERS (amuse. & rec.) to limit liability and apportion risk. May be designated as SPORTS-BOOKMAKER (amuse. & rec.) when taking bets on sports, such as football, boxing, baseball, and hockey. • **GED:** R4, M3, L3 • **SVP:** 1-2 yrs • **Academic:** Ed=H, Eng=G • **Work Field:** 295 • **MPSMS:** 914 • **Aptitudes:** G3, V3, N3, S4, P4, Q3, K4, F3, M3, E5, C5 • **Temperaments:** D, J, P, V • **Stress:** E, A • **Physical:** V=N, H=L, L=S, H • **Work Env:** I • **Salary:** 4 • **Outlook:** 1

CREDIT ANALYST (finan. inst.) • D.O.T. #191.267-014 • OES #21105 • Analyzes credit data to estimate degree of risk involved in extending credit or lending money to firms or individuals, and prepares reports of findings: Contacts banks, trade and credit associations, salesmen, and others to obtain credit information. Studies economic trends in firm's industry or branch of industry to predict probable success of new customer. Visits establishments to determine condition of plant and equipment and compare methods of operation with accepted practices in industry. Evaluates results of investigations, prepares reports of findings, and suggests credit limitations to management. Consults with management to assist in corporate planning. • **GED:** R5, M4, L5 • **SVP:** 4-10 yrs • **Academic:** Ed=A, Eng=G • **Work Field:** 271 • **MPSMS:** 894 • **Aptitudes:** G2, V2, N2, S4, P4, Q3, K4, F4, M5, E5, C5 • **Temperaments:** J, V • **Physical:** V=N, H=L, L=S • **Work Env:** I • **Salary:** 4 • **Outlook:** 2

DIRECTOR, UTILITY ACCOUNTS (gov. ser.) • D.O.T. #160.267-014 • OES #21114 • Evaluates financial condition of electric, telephone, gas, water, and public transit utility companies to facilitate work of regulatory commissions in setting rates: Analyzes annual reports, financial statements, and other records submitted by utility companies, applying accepted accounting and statistical analysis procedures to determine current financial condition of company. Evaluates reports from commission staff members and field investigators regarding condition of company property and other factors influencing solvency and profitability of company. Prepares and presents exhibits and testifies during commission hearings on regulatory or rate adjustments. Confers with company officials to discuss financial problems and regulatory matters. Directs workers engaged in filing company financial records. May conduct specialized studies, such as cost of service, revenue requirement, and cost allocation studies for commission, or design new rates in accordance with findings of commission and be designated RATE ANALYST (gov. ser.). • **GED:** R5, M5, L5 • **SVP:** 4-10 yrs • **Academic:** Ed=B, Eng=G • **Work Field:** 232 • **MPSMS:** 894 • **Aptitudes:** G2, V2, N1, S4, P3, Q3, K4, F4, M4, E5, C5 • **Temperaments:** M, P, T, V • **Physical:** V=L, H=N, L=S • **Work Env:** I • **Salary:** 5 • **Outlook:** 3

FACTORER (finan. inst.) • D.O.T. #186.117-026 • OES #21199 • Factors (purchases at discount) accounts receivable from business concerns requiring cash operating capital for continued operations: Directs collection of facts relative to prospective client's business activities, such as nature and salability of products or services, credit rating of client's customers, credit losses (bad debts) sustained over specified period, and sales data, such as terms of sales, due dates, average amount of invoices, and expected volume and turnover of receivable accounts to be assigned. Evaluates data to determine type of factoring plan to propose and percentage of net face value of accounts to advance which will yield favorable factoring profit margin and alleviate client's shortage of on-hand operating funds. Negotiates factoring agreement with client. Prepares and signs contract spelling out terms of agreement and rights and obligations of both parties. May furnish clients with other business services, such as management consulting services, credit and collection services, and accounts receivable bookkeeping services on contract or fee basis. May specialize in one or more aspects of factoring services, such as accounts receivables collection, credit monitoring, and bookkeeping control. • **GED:** R5, M5, L4 • **SVP:** 4-10 yrs • **Academic:** Ed=H, Eng=G • **Work Field:** 232, 295 • **MPSMS:** 894 • **Aptitudes:** G1, V1, N2, S4, P4, Q3, K4, F4, M4, E5, C5 • **Temperaments:** D, J, P • **Stress:** E, A • **Physical:** V=N, H=G, L=S • **Work Env:** I • **Salary:** 5 • **Outlook:** 2

FOREIGN-EXCHANGE TRADER (finan. inst.) • D.O.T. #186.167-014 • OES #21199 • INTERNATIONAL-BANKING OFFICER. Maintains bank's balances on deposit in foreign banks to ensure foreign exchange position, and determines prices at which such exchange shall be purchased and sold, based on demand, supply, and stability of currency: Refers to daily money market quotations to determine foreign exchange rates. Establishes local rates based upon money market quotations or customer's financial standing. Buys and sells foreign exchange drafts and computes proceeds. Adjusts deposit balances with foreign banks. Examines and approves bills of exchange. Issues letters of credit. Directs personnel engaged in foreign exchange. • **GED:** R5, M4, L4 • **SVP:** 4-10 yrs • **Academic:** Ed=A, Eng=S • **Work Field:** 232, 292 • **MPSMS:** 894 • **Aptitudes:** G2, V2, N2, S4, P4, Q3, K4, F4, M4, E5, C5 • **Temperaments:** D, J, M • **Stress:** A • **Physical:** V=N, H=N, L=S, H • **Work Env:** I • **Salary:** 5 • **Outlook:** 1

INVESTIGATOR (clerical) • D.O.T. #241.267-030 • OES #53117 • Investigates persons or business establishments applying for credit, employment, insurance, loans, or settlement of claims: Contacts former employers, neighbors, trade associations, and others by telephone, to verify employment record and to obtain health history and history of moral and social behavior. Examines city directories and public records to verify residence history, convictions and arrests, property ownership, bankruptcies, liens, and unpaid taxes of applicant. Obtains credit rating from banks and credit concerns. Analyzes information gathered by investigation and prepares reports of findings and recommendations. May interview applicant on telephone or in person to obtain other financial and personal data for completeness of report. When specializing in certain types of investigations, may be designated CREDIT REPORTER (bus. ser.); INSURANCE-APPLICATION INVESTIGATOR (insurance). • **GED:** R4, M2, L4 • **SVP:** 6 mos-1 yr • **Academic:** Ed=H, Eng=G • **Work Field:** 231, 271 • **MPSMS:** 890 • **Aptitudes:** G2, V2, N3, S5, P4, Q3, K4, F4, M4, E5, C5 • **Temperaments:** M, P • **Stress:** E • **Physical:** V=N, H=L, L=S, H • **Work Env:** B • **Salary:** 3 • **Outlook:** 3

LOAN OFFICER (finan. inst.) • D.O.T. #186.267-018 • OES #21108 • Examines, evaluates, authorizes or recommends approval of customer applications for lines or extension of lines of credit, commercial loans, real estate loans, consumer credit loans, or credit card accounts: Reviews loan application for completeness. Analyzes applicant's financial status, credit, and property evaluation to determine feasibility of granting loan request. Corresponds with or interviews applicant or creditors to resolve questions regarding application. Approves loan within specified limits or

refers loan to loan committee for approval. Completes loan agreement on accepted loans. May supervise loan personnel. May handle foreclosure proceedings. May analyze potential loan markets to develop prospects for loans. May buy and sell contracts, loans, or real estate by negotiating terms of transaction and drawing up requisite documents. May be designated according to type of loan concerned with as MORTGAGE-LOAN OFFICER (insurance). May solicit and negotiate conventional or government backed loans on commission basis and be known as MORTGAGE-LOAN AGENT (finan. inst.). • **GED:** R5, M4, L4 • **SVP:** 2-4 yrs • **Academic:** Ed=H, Eng=G • **Work Field:** 271 • **MPSMS:** 894 • **Aptitudes:** G2, V2, N3, S4, P4, Q3, K4, F4, M5, E5, C5 • **Temperaments:** J, M, P • **Stress:** A • **Physical:** V=N, H=G, L=S • **Work Env:** I • **Salary:** 4 • **Outlook:** 3

MANAGER, CREDIT AND COLLECTION (any ind.) • D.O.T. #168.167-054 • OES #21199 • Directs and coordinates activities of workers engaged in conducting credit investigations and collecting delinquent accounts of customers of commercial establishment, department store, bank, or similar establishment: Assigns subordinates to supervise workers investigating and verifying financial status and reputation of prospective customers applying for credit, preparing documents to substantiate findings, and recommending rejection or approval of applications. Reviews and evaluates applications, substantiated data, and recommendations, in order to determine credit validity. Establishes credit limitations on customer's account. Assigns responsibility for collecting on worthless checks and delinquent bills to specific supervisors. Reviews collection reports to ascertain status of collections and balances outstanding and to evaluate effectiveness of current collection policies and procedures. May also submit delinquent accounts to attorney or outside agency for collection. • **GED:** R5, M5, L5 • **SVP:** 4-10 yrs • **Academic:** Ed=A, Eng=S • **Work Field:** 271, 295 • **MPSMS:** 894 • **Aptitudes:** G2, V2, N2, S4, P4, Q2, K4, F4, M4, E5, C5 • **Temperaments:** D, J, M, P • **Stress:** A • **Physical:** V=L, H=N, L=S • **Work Env:** I • **Salary:** 5 • **Outlook:** 3

MARKET-RESEARCH ANALYST 1 (profess. & kin.) • D.O.T. #050.067-014 • OES #27102 • Researches market conditions in local, regional, or national area to determine potential sales of product or service: Establishes research methodology and designs format for data gathering, such as surveys, opinion polls, or questionnaires. Examines and analyzes statistical data to forecast future marketing trends. Gathers data on competitors and analyzes prices, sales, and methods of marketing and distribution. Collects data on customer preferences and buying habits. Prepares reports and graphic illustrations of findings. • **GED:** R5, M5, L5 • **SVP:** 2-4 yrs • **Academic:** Ed=A, Eng=G • **Work Field:** 251, 271 • **MPSMS:** 741 • **Aptitudes:** G2, V2, N2, S4, P4, Q2, K4, F4, M4, E5, C5 • **Temperaments:** J, M, P • **Physical:** V=N, H=N, L=S, H • **Work Env:** I • **Salary:** 4 • **Outlook:** 3

NEGOTIATOR, LETTER OF CREDIT (finan. inst.) • D.O.T. #186.117-050 • OES #21199 • Directs and coordinates activities concerned with processing of, and authorizing payment on letters of credit used in international banking: Examines documents, such as credit reports on client, bills of lading, or shipping manifests, for accuracy and completeness and to ensure that conditions of letter of credit are in accordance with policies and codes. Verifies document computations, using calculator or adding machine. Confers with lending official to verify credit rating of client. Contacts client relative to deficiencies in collateral that must be resolved prior to authorization. Negotiates with client to reach agreement on items, such as increase in collateral pledged or reduction in amount of purchases to ensure compliance with code and policies. Directs workers in preparing amendments to letter of credit contract resulting from negotiations. Contacts foreign banks, suppliers, or other sources to obtain documents required. Authorizes and specifies method of payments against letter of credit as per client instructions. Informs foreign banks when letter of credit loans remain unpaid for specified period of time. • **GED:** R5, M4, L4 • **SVP:** 2-4 yrs • **Academic:** Ed=H, Eng=G • **Work Field:** 232, 295 • **MPSMS:** 894 • **Aptitudes:** G2, V2, N2, S4, P4, Q2, K4, F4, M4, E5, C5 • **Temperaments:** D, M, P • **Stress:** E, A • **Physical:** V=N, H=G, L=S • **Work Env:** I • **Salary:** 3 • **Outlook:** 2

PERSONAL PROPERTY ASSESSOR (gov. ser.) • D.O.T. #191.367-010 • OES #21917 • DEPUTY ASSESSOR. Prepares lists of personal property owned by householders and merchants in assigned area to facilitate tax assessment, showing number and estimated value of taxable items designated in regulations. • **GED:** R3, M3, L3 • **SVP:** 3-6 mos • **Academic:** Ed=B, Eng=G • **Work Field:** 211, 231 • **MPSMS:** 953 • **Aptitudes:** G3, V3, N3, S4, P4, Q3, K4, F4, M4, E5, C5 • **Temperaments:** M, P • **Stress:** E • **Physical:** V=L, H=N, L=S, W • **Work Env:** I • **Salary:** 4 • **Outlook:** 2

SECURITIES TRADER 1 (finan. inst.) • D.O.T. #162.157-042 • OES #43014 • BROKER. Buys or sells securities in trading division of investment and brokerage firm for accounts of firm. Acts as agent for SALES AGENT, SECURITIES (finan. inst.). May be designated according to specialization as BROKER, BOND (finan. inst.); BROKER, COMMODITIES (finan. inst.); BROKER, STOCK (finan. inst.). • **GED:** R5, M5, L4 • **SVP:** 2- 4 yrs • **Academic:** Ed=A, Eng=G • **Work Field:** 292 • **MPSMS:** 894 • **Aptitudes:** G1, V2, N2, S4, P4, Q2, K4, F4, M4, E5, C5 • **Temperaments:** I, J, P • **Stress:** E, A • **Physical:** V=N, H=L, L=S • **Work Env:** I • **Salary:** 5 • **Outlook:** 3

SECURITIES TRADER 2 (finan. inst.) • D.O.T. #186.167-058 • OES #21199 • Trades securities and provides securities investment and counseling services for bank and its customers: Studies financial background and future trends of stocks and bonds, and advises bank officials and customers regarding investments. Transmits buy-and-sell orders to broker as directed, and recommends purchase, retention, or sale of issues. Notifies customer or bank of execution of trading orders. Negotiates stock and bond transactions. Computes extensions, commissions, and other charges for billing customers and for making payments for securities. Advises bank officials concerning sale of bond issues and trading of stock. May be designated according to type of securities handled as BOND TRADER (finan. inst.); STOCK TRADER (finan. inst.); or according to responsibilities assumed as BOND CASHIER (finan. inst.). • **GED:** R6, M5, L5 • **SVP:** 4-10 yrs • **Academic:** Ed=B, Eng=G • **Work Field:** 211, 232 • **MPSMS:** 894 • **Aptitudes:** G1, V1, N2, S4, P4, Q3, K4, F4, M4, E5, C5 • **Temperaments:** D, J, P, V • **Stress:** E, A • **Physical:** V=N, H=L, L=S • **Work Env:** I • **Salary:** 5 • **Outlook:** 3

UNDERWRITER (insurance) • D.O.T. #169.167-058 • OES #21102 • Reviews individual applications for insurance to evaluate degree of risk involved and accepts applications, following company's underwriting policies: Examines such documents as application form, inspection report, insurance maps, and medical reports to determine degree of risk from such factors as applicant's financial standing, age, occupation, accident experience, and value and condition of real property. Reviews company records to ascertain amount of insurance in force on single risk or group of closely related risks, and evaluates possibility of losses due to catastrophe or excessive insurance. Declines risks which are too excessive to obligate company. Dictates correspondence for field representatives, medical personnel, and other insurance or inspection companies to obtain further information, quote rates, or explain company's underwriting policies. When risk is excessive, authorizes reinsurance, or when risk is substandard, limits company's obligation by decreasing value of policy, specifying applicable endorsements, or applying rating to ensure safe and profitable distribution of risks, using rate books, tables, code books, and other reference material. Typically, workers who underwrite one type of insurance do not underwrite others, and are designated according to type of insurance underwritten as ACCIDENT-AND-SICKNESS UNDERWRITER (insurance); AUTOMOBILE UNDERWRITER (insurance); BOND UNDERWRITER (insurance); CASUALTY UNDERWRITER (insurance); COMPENSATION UNDERWRITER (insurance); CREDIT-LIFE UNDERWRITER (insurance); FIRE UNDERWRITER (insurance); GROUP UNDERWRITER (insurance); LIABILITY UNDERWRITER (insurance); LIFE UNDERWRITER (insurance); MARINE UNDERWRITER (insurance); MULTIPLE-LINE UNDERWRITER (insurance); PENSION-AND-ADVANCED UNDERWRITING SPECIALIST (insurance); REINSTATEMENT UNDERWRITER (insurance); SPECIAL-RISKS UNDERWRITER (insurance). When underwriting group policies solely on basis of medical examinations, may be designated as MEDICAL-STATEMENT APPROVER (insurance). • **GED:** R5, M4, L5 • **SVP:** 2-4 yrs • **Academic:** Ed=A, Eng=G •

Work Field: 211 • **MPSMS:** 895 • **Aptitudes:** G2, V2, N2, S4, P4, Q2, K4, F4, M4, E5, C5 • **Temperaments:** D, J, M, T • **Stress:** A • **Physical:** V=N, H=N, L=S, H • **Work Env:** I • **Salary:** 5 • **Outlook:** 3

GOE: 11.06.04 Brokering

SALES AGENT, SECURITIES (finan. inst.) • D.O.T. #251.157-010 • OES #43014 • BROKER, SECURITIES; REGISTERED REPRESENTATIVE; SECURITIES ADVISER; STOCKBROKER. Buys and sells stocks and bonds for individuals and organizations as representative of stock brokerage firm, applying knowledge of securities, market conditions, government regulations, and financial circumstances of customers: Gives information and advice regarding stocks, bonds, market conditions, and history and prospects of various corporations to prospective customers, based on interpretation of data from securities reports, financial periodicals, and stock-quotation-viewer screen, and persuades customers to buy or sell specific securities according to their financial needs. Records and transmits buy or sell orders to trading division in accordance with customer's wishes. Calculates and records cost of transaction for billing purposes, using quotations received during transmittal of order. Develops portfolio (list) of selected investments for customer. Compiles list of prospective customers and telephones prospects to obtain additional business. Must have broker's license issued by State. • **GED:** R5, M4, L5 • **SVP:** 2-4 yrs • **Academic:** Ed=B, Eng=G • **Work Field:** 292 • **MPSMS:** 894 • **Aptitudes:** G2, V2, N2, S4, P3, Q2, K4, F4, M4, E5, C5 • **Temperaments:** D, I, J, M, P • **Stress:** E, A • **Physical:** V=N, H=L, L=S, H • **Work Env:** I • **Salary:** 4 • **Outlook:** 3

GOE: 11.06.05 Budget & Financial Control

BUDGET ANALYST (gov. ser.) • D.O.T. #161.267-030 • OES #21117 • Analyzes current and past budgets, prepares and justifies budget requests, and allocates funds according to spending priorities in governmental service agency: Analyzes accounting records to determine financial resources required to implement program and submits recommendations for budget allocations. Recommends approval or disapproval of requests for funds. Advises staff on cost analysis and fiscal allocations. • **GED:** R5, M3, L4 • **SVP:** 2-4 yrs • **Academic:** Ed=B, Eng=G • **Work Field:** 232 • **MPSMS:** 892 • **Aptitudes:** G2, V2, N2, S4, P4, Q2, K4, F4, M4, E5, C5 • **Temperaments:** D, J, T • **Physical:** V=L, H=N, L=S, H • **Work Env:** I • **Salary:** 5 • **Outlook:** 3

BUDGET OFFICER (gov. ser.) • D.O.T. #161.117-010 • OES #21117 • Directs and coordinates activities of personnel responsible for formulation and presentation of budgets for controlling funds to implement program objectives of governmental organization: Directs compilation data based on statistical studies and analyses of past and current years to prepare budgets and to justify funds requested. Correlates appropriations for specific programs with appropriations for divisional programs and includes items for emergency funds. Reviews operating budgets periodically to analyze trends affecting budget needs. Consults with unit heads to ensure adjustments are made in accordance with program changes in order to facilitate long-term planning. Directs preparation of regular and special budget reports to interpret budget directives and to establish policies for carrying out directives. Prepares comparative analyses of operating programs by analyzing costs in relation to services performed during previous fiscal years and submits reports to director of organization with recommendations for budget revisions. Testifies regarding proposed budgets before examining and fund-granting authorities to clarify reports and gain support for estimated budget needs. Administers personnel functions of budget department, such as training, work scheduling, promotions, transfers, and performance ratings. • **GED:** R5, M5, L5 • **SVP:** 4-10 yrs • **Academic:** Ed=A, Eng=S • **Work Field:** 232, 295 • **MPSMS:** 892, 950 • **Aptitudes:** G2, V2, N1, S4, P3, Q2, K4, F4, M4, E5, C5 • **Temperaments:** D, J, M, P • **Stress:** A • **Physical:** V=N, H=G, L=S • **Work Env:** I • **Salary:** 5 • **Outlook:** 3

TRUST OFFICER (finan. inst.) • D.O.T. #186.117-074 • OES

#21199 • TRUST ADMINISTRATOR; TRUST INVESTMENT OFFICER. Directs and coordinates activities relative to creating and administering private, corporate, probate, and court-ordered guardianship trusts in accordance with terms creating trust, decedent's will, probate court, or court order: Directs drafting of, or drafts, agreement or legal documents specifying details, conditions, and duration of private or corporate trust, and placing of funds, securities, or other assets in trust account. Locates, inventories, and evaluates assets of probated trust. Directs realization of assets, liquidation of liabilities, payment of debts, and preparation of Federal and State returns on probated trusts. Interviews trust beneficiaries of court-ordered guardianship trusts in order to locate probable sources of assets. Negotiates with public agencies, such as Social Security, Railroad Retirement Board, Workman's Compensation Commission, in effort to accumulate all assets into trust. Directs collection of earnings, dividends, or sale of assets and placement of proceeds in trust account. Directs disbursement of funds according to conditions of trust or needs of court ward or beneficiary. Ensures that excess or surplus funds are invested in such manner as to obtain maximum earnings. May be designated according to type of trust as PROBATE TRUST OFFICER (finan. inst.); VETERAN'S GUARDIANSHIP OFFICER (gov. ser.). • **GED:** R5, M5, L5 • **SVP:** 4-10 yrs • **Academic:** Ed=A, Eng=S • **Work Field:** 272, 295 • **MPSMS:** 894 • **Aptitudes:** G1, V1, N2, S4, P4, Q3, K4, F4, M4, E5, C5 • **Temperaments:** D, J, P • **Stress:** A • **Physical:** V=L, H=G, L=S • **Work Env:** I • **Salary:** 5 • **Outlook:** 1

11.07 Services Administration

Workers in this group manage programs and projects in agencies that provide people with services in such areas as health, welfare, and recreation. They are in charge of program planning, policy making, and other managerial activities. The jobs are found in welfare and rehabilitation agencies and organizations, hospitals, schools, churches, libraries, and museums.

✔ What kind of work would you do?
Your work activities would depend upon your specific job. For example, you might:

- administer the affairs of a public or private school system under the direction of a board of education.
- plan and direct training and staff development programs for a business or government agency.
- serve as president of a college or university.
- direct a city or county welfare program.

- direct workers who classify prisoners and assign them to work and other activities within a prison.
- plan and coordinate community recreation programs.
- direct and coordinate the services and personnel of a hospital.
- coordinate emergency medical services for a city or county.

✔ What skills and abilities do you need for this kind of work?
To do this kind of work, you must be able to do:

- use language and mathematical skills to analyze and interpret financial reports, government funding requirements, and related materials.
- identify problems and make decisions based on your experience and judgment, as well as on established facts like budget allocations and legal requirements.

- deal with all kinds of people.
- speak and write clearly and effectively to influence people's actions and to be sure that your plans will be understood and followed.
- change your activities frequently.
- plan and direct programs and the activities of others.

✔ How do you know if you would like or could learn to do this kind of work?
The following questions may give you clues about yourself as you consider this group of jobs.

- Have you done volunteer work for a hospital or social agency? Do you enjoy helping people in such a setting?
- Have you taken courses in sociology or psychology? Do you enjoy these types of studies?

- Have you supervised the activities of others? Were the activities carried out effectively?

✔ **How can you prepare for and enter this kind of work?**

Occupations in this group usually require education and/or training extending from two years to over ten years, depending upon the specific kind of work. Most of these jobs require related work experience within the agency or institution involved. Some jobs require four to eight years of college study. In some cases, work experience within an institution or agency may be substituted for a portion of the educational requirements. College level courses in public administration or business administration are often a part of the formal preparation. Typing, while seldom required, will prove to be very useful.

✔ **What else should you consider about these jobs?**

Workers in this group have heavy responsibility from which they seldom escape, even at home or on vacation.

Some workers transfer to other agencies or institutions in order to move up the promotion ladder.

If you think you would like to do this kind of work, look at the job titles on the following pages.

GOE: 11.07.01 Social Services

COMMUNITY ORGANIZATION WORKER (social ser.) • D.O.T. #195.167-010 • OES #27305 • Plans, organizes, and works with community groups concerned with social problems of community: Stimulates, promotes, and coordinates agencies, groups, and individuals to meet identified needs. Studies and assesses strength and weakness of existing resources. Interprets needs, programs, and services to agencies, groups, and individuals involved and provides leadership and assistance. Prepares reports. May assist in budget preparation and presentation. May assist in raising funds. Works in specialized fields, such as aging, juvenile delinquency, urban renewal and redevelopment, and mental and physical health or in public or voluntary coordinating agency, such as community welfare or health council, or combined fund raising and welfare planning council. Usually required to have degree from school of social work. • **GED:** R5, M4, L5 • **SVP:** 2-4 yrs • **Academic:** Ed=N, Eng=G • **Work Field:** 295 • **MPSMS:** 941 • **Aptitudes:** G2, V2, N3, S4, P4, Q4, K4, F4, M4, E5, C5 • **Temperaments:** D, P • **Stress:** E • **Physical:** V=N, H=L, L=S, W • **Work Env:** I • **Salary:** 4 • **Outlook:** 2

COORDINATOR OF REHABILITATION SERVICES (medical ser.) • D.O.T. #076.117-010 • OES #32399 • Plans, administers, and directs operation of health therapy programs, such as physical, occupational, recreational, educational, music, and manual arts: Consults with medical and professional staff of other departments and personnel from associated health care fields to plan and coordinate joint patient and management objectives. Conducts staff conferences and plans training programs to maintain proficiency of staff in therapy techniques and use of new methods and equipment to meet patients' needs. Allocates personnel on basis of workload, space, and equipment available. Analyzes operating costs and prepares department budget. Coordinates research projects to develop new approaches to rehabilitative therapy. May recommend patient fees for therapy based on use of equipment and therapy staff. May serve as rehabilitative therapy consultant to employers, educational institutions, and community organizations. • **GED:** R5, M5, L5 • **SVP:** 4-10 yrs • **Academic:** Ed=A, Eng=S • **Work Field:** 295 • **MPSMS:** 929 • **Aptitudes:** G2, V2, N3, S4, P4, Q3, K4, F4, M4, E5, C5 • **Temperaments:** D, J, M, P • **Stress:** A • **Physical:** V=N, H=L, L=S • **Work Env:** I • **Salary:** 5 • **Outlook:** 4

DIRECTOR, COMMUNITY ORGANIZATION (nonprofit org.) • D.O.T. #187.117-014 • OES #19999 • COMMUNITY PLANNING DIRECTOR, COMMUNITY CHEST; DIRECTOR, COUNCIL OF SOCIAL AGENCIES; DIRECTOR; DIRECTOR, FEDERATED FUND; DIRECTOR, UNITED FUND; EXECUTIVE, COMMUNITY PLANNING. Directs activities of organization to coordinate functions of various community health and welfare programs: Organizes and develops planning program to ascertain community requirements and problems in specific fields of welfare work, and to determine agency responsibility for administering program. Surveys functions of member agencies to avoid duplication of efforts and recommends curtailment, extension, modification, or initiation of services. Advises health and welfare agencies in planning and providing services based on community surveys and analyses. Reviews estimated budgets of member agencies. Prepares and releases reports, studies, and publications to promote public understanding of and support for community programs. May recruit and train volunteer workers. May organize and direct campaign for solicitation of funds. • **GED:** R5, M5, L5 • **SVP:** 4-10 yrs • **Academic:** Ed=A, Eng=S • **Work Field:** 295 • **MPSMS:** 941 • **Aptitudes:** G2, V2, N3, S3, P4, Q3, K4, F4, M4, E5, C5 • **Temperaments:** D, P, V • **Stress:** A • **Physical:** V=N, H=L, L=S • **Work Env:** I • **Salary:** 5 • **Outlook:** 1

DIRECTOR, SERVICE (nonprofit org.) • D.O.T. #187.167-214 • OES #19999 • Directs and coordinates regional program activities of nonprofit agency to provide specialized human services, such as water safety programs, disaster relief, and emergency transportation: Consults with cooperating agencies, such as police, firefighters, and emergency ambulance services, to coordinate efforts and define areas of jurisdiction. Participates in program activities to serve clients of agency. Prepares budgets to control costs and to allocate funds in accordance with provisions and agency charter. May instruct agency staff and volunteers in skills required to provide services. May requisition and arrange for maintenance of equipment, such as two-way radios and agency vehicles. May coordinate services to disaster victims and be designated as DISASTER DIRECTOR (nonprofit organ.). May coordinate safety programs, such as water safety and emergency first aid, and be designated as SAFETY DIRECTOR (nonprofit organ.). May coordinate transportation of agency clients, blood, and medical supplies and equipment and be designated as TRANSPORTATION DIRECTOR (nonprofit organ.). • **GED:** R5, M3, L5 • **SVP:** 4-10 yrs • **Academic:** Ed=A, Eng=S • **Work Field:** 295 • **MPSMS:** 941 • **Aptitudes:** G1, V2, N3, S3, P4, Q3, K4, F4, M3, E5, C5 • **Temperaments:** D, J, P, V • **Stress:** A • **Physical:** V=G, H=G, L=M, W, H • **Work Env:** I • **Salary:** 5 • **Outlook:** 1

FIELD REPRESENTATIVE (profess. & kin.) • D.O.T. #189.267-010 • OES #27305 • Reviews and evaluates program operations of national or state affiliated or non-affiliated social service agency or organization, or community group to provide assistance and services in achieving goals: Interprets standards and program goals of national or state agency to assist local boards, committees, groups, or agencies in establishing program goals and standards. Confers with community councils to advise members on matters relating to program. Evaluates capabilities of local or community agencies or groups to achieve goals, considering such factors as administration and program finances, facilities and personnel staffing, and changing community needs. Prepares reports to inform national or state agency on conditions in local agencies or organizations and developing trends in local communities. May organize or conduct training or staff development programs. May organize regional meetings. May plan or conduct studies or surveys of local agency operation. May assist communities in establishing new local affiliates or programs. May confer with field representatives of other national agencies. • **GED:** R5, M4, L5 • **SVP:** 4-10 yrs • **Academic:** Ed=A, Eng=S • **Work Field:** 211 • **MPSMS:** 929, 940, 950 • **Aptitudes:** G2, V2, N3, S4, P4, Q4, K4, F4, M4, E5, C5 • **Temperaments:** I, J, P • **Physical:** V=G, H=G, L=S • **Work Env:** I • **Salary:** 5 • **Outlook:** 3

PROGRAM DIRECTOR, GROUP WORK (profess. & kin.) • D.O.T. #187.117-046 • OES #19999 • Plans, organizes, and directs activity program of group work agency or department, or scouting organization: Coordinates activities of program committees and other groups to plan procedures. Studies and analyzes member and community needs for basis of program development. Directs selection and training of staff and volunteer workers. Assigns work and evaluates performance of staff members and recommends indicated actions. Assists staff through individual and group conferences in analysis of specific programs, understanding of program development, and increasing use of individual skills. Interprets agency program and services to individuals or groups in community. May be designated according to agency or program directed as ACTIVITIES DIRECTOR, SCOUTING (nonprofit organ.); DIRECTOR, TEEN POST (profess. & kin.); PROGRAM DIRECTOR, SCOUTING (nonprofit organ.). • **GED:** R5, M5, L5 • **SVP:** 4-10 yrs • **Academic:** Ed=A, Eng=S • **Work Field:** 295 • **MPSMS:** 941 • **Aptitudes:** G1, V1, N3, S4, P4, Q4, K4, F4, M4, E5, C5 • **Temperaments:** D, P • **Stress:** A • **Physical:** V=N, H=G, L=L • **Work Env:** I • **Salary:** 5 • **Outlook:** 2

REHABILITATION CENTER MANAGER (gov. ser.) • D.O.T. #195.167-038 • OES #19999 • Coordinates activities and provides for physical and emotional needs of public-welfare recipients housed in indigent camp: Cooperates with welfare department investigators, psychologists, and physicians in assigning activities to indigents and in providing specialized attention to them in accordance with recommendations. Appoints leaders of activities, such as food preparation and maintenance of grounds, from camp inmates in accord with democratic leadership principles and welfare department policy. Coordinates sanitation, food management, health, education, spiritual counseling, and vocational activity programs in conformity with available facilities, needs of camp inmates, and policy of department. Interviews inmates and arranges with business and community leaders to place them in jobs. Maintains discipline and arbitrates disputes. Arranges for entertainment, such as movies, lectures, and musical programs. Maintains camp records, inventories supplies, and submits requisitions for camp needs. • **GED:** R5, M4, L5 • **SVP:** 2-4 yrs • **Academic:** Ed=B, Eng=S • **Work Field:** 294, 295 • **MPSMS:** 941 • **Aptitudes:** G2, V2, N3, S4, P3, Q3, K4, F4, M4, E5, C5 • **Temperaments:** D, F, I, J, V • **Stress:** E, A • **Physical:** V=L, H=G, L=L, W • **Work Env:** B • **Salary:** 4 • **Outlook:** 3

RESIDENCE SUPERVISOR (any ind.) • D.O.T. #187.167-186 • OES #27307 • ADVISER; CHAPERON; COTTAGE PARENT; HOUSE MANAGER. Coordinates variety of activities for residents of boarding school, college fraternity or sorority house, care and treatment institution, children's home, or similar establishment: Orders supplies and determines need for maintenance, repairs, and furnishings. Assigns rooms, assists in planning recreational activities, and supervises work and study programs. Counsels residents in identifying and resolving social or other problems. Compiles records of daily activities of residents. Chaperones group-sponsored trips and social functions. Ascertains need for and secures services of PHYSICIAN (medical ser.). Answers telephone and sorts and distributes mail. May escort individuals on trips outside establishment for shopping or to obtain medical or dental services. May hire and supervise activities of housekeeping personnel. May plan menus. • **GED:** R4, M3, L4 • **SVP:** 1-2 yrs • **Academic:** Ed=H, Eng=S • **Work Field:** 291, 295 • **MPSMS:** 942 • **Aptitudes:** G3, V3, N3, S4, P4, Q3, K4, F4, M4, E5, C5 •

Temperaments: D, P, V • **Stress:** A • **Physical:** V=L, H=G, L=S, H • **Work Env:** I • **Salary:** 4 • **Outlook:** 4

GOE: 11.07.02 Health & Safety Serv. Admin.

ADMINISTRATOR, HOSPITAL (medical ser.) • D.O.T. #187.117-010 • OES #15008 • SUPERINTENDENT, HOSPITAL. Directs administration of hospital within authority of governing board: Develops or expands programs or services for scientific research, preventive medicine, medical and vocational rehabilitation, and community health and welfare promotion. Administers fiscal operations such as budget planning, accounting, and establishing rates for hospital services. Directs hiring and training of personnel. Negotiates for improvement of and additions to hospital buildings and equipment. Directs and coordinates activities of medical, nursing, and administrative staffs and services. Develops policies and procedures for various hospital activities. May represent hospital at community meetings and promote programs through various news media. • **GED:** R5, M5, L5 • **SVP:** 4-10 yrs • **Academic:** Ed=M, Eng=G • **Work Field:** 295 • **MPSMS:** 924 • **Aptitudes:** G1, V2, N3, S4, P4, Q3, K4, F4, M4, E5, C5 • **Temperaments:** D, J, P, V • **Stress:** E, A • **Physical:** V=N, H=L, L=S, W • **Work Env:** I • **Salary:** 5 • **Outlook:** 3

CIVIL PREPAREDNESS TRAINING OFFICER (gov. ser.) • D.O.T. #169.127-010 • OES #21911 • Instructs paid and volunteer workers in techniques for meeting disaster situations: Conducts classes in emergency techniques, such as first aid, flood protection, firefighting, shelter management, disaster communications and organization, use of radiological monitoring equipment, and post-attack operations. Confers with local government and federal authorities, and with representatives of police, fire, sanitation, and public works departments, to coordinate training. May direct or participate in preparation of geographic surveys of local areas to aid in formulating emergency survival plans. May specialize in preparing and distributing emergency preparedness information and be designated CIVIL PREPAREDNESS PUBLIC INFORMATION OFFICER (gov. ser.). Workers involved in these and other civil preparedness activities may be identified according to classifications used by local, state, or federal authorities. • **GED:** R4, M3, L4 • **SVP:** 1-2 yrs • **Academic:** Ed=H, Eng=S • **Work Field:** 296 • **MPSMS:** 959 • **Aptitudes:** G2, V2, N3, S3, P3, Q4, K4, F4, M4, E5, C4 • **Temperaments:** I, S, V • **Stress:** S • **Physical:** V=L, H=L, L=L, W, H • **Work Env:** I • **Salary:** 4 • **Outlook:** 3

COMMUNITY-SERVICES-AND-HEALTH-EDUCATION OFFICER (gov. ser.) • D.O.T. #079.167-010 • OES #19005 • Plans and directs statewide program of public health education and promotes establishment of local health services: Directs workers engaged in preparation and distribution of health information materials, such as brochures, films, weight charts, and first-aid kits. Promotes establishment or expansion of local health services and provides technical assistance to individuals and groups conducting health conferences, workshops, and training courses. Answers health information requests received by department or reviews correspondence prepared by others. Coordinates special health education campaigns during epidemics, rabies outbreaks, instances of food poisoning, and similar emergencies. May direct health education activities in public schools. • **GED:** R6, M5, L6 • **SVP:** 4-10 yrs • **Academic:** Ed=B, Eng=S • **Work Field:** 295 • **MPSMS:** 929 • **Aptitudes:** G2, V2, N3, S3, P3, Q4, K4, F4, M5, E5, C5 • **Temperaments:** D, J, P • **Physical:** V=N, H=N, L=S • **Work Env:** I • **Salary:** 5 • **Outlook:** 3

MEDICAL-RECORD ADMINISTRATOR (medical ser.) • D.O.T. #079.167-014 • OES #15008 • HOSPITAL-RECORD ADMINISTRATOR. Plans, develops, and administers medical record systems for hospital, clinic, health center, or similar facility, to meet standards of accrediting and regulatory agencies: Collects and analyzes patient and institutional data. Assists medical staff in evaluating quality of patient care and in developing criteria and methods for such evaluation. Develops and implements policies and procedures for documenting, storing, and retrieving information, and for processing medical-legal documents, insurance and correspondence requests, in conformance with Federal, state, and local statutes. Develops in-service educational materials and conducts instructional programs for health care personnel. Supervises staff in preparing and analyzing medical documents. Provides consultant services to health care facilities, health data systems, related health organizations, and governmental agencies. Engages in basic and applied research in health care field. • **GED:** R6, M5, L6 • **SVP:** 4-10 yrs • **Academic:** Ed=B, Eng=G • **Work Field:** 221, 251 • **MPSMS:** 933 • **Aptitudes:** G1, V1, N3, S4, P4, Q3, K4, F4, M4, E5, C5 • **Temperaments:** M, P, T • **Stress:** E • **Physical:** V–N, H–L, L–S, H • **Work Env:** I • **Salary:** 5 • **Outlook:** 4

PUBLIC HEALTH EDUCATOR (profess. & kin.) • D.O.T. #079.117-014 • OES #31517 • COMMUNITY HEALTH EDUCATOR; TEACHER, PUBLIC HEALTH. Plans, organizes, and directs health education programs for group and community needs: Conducts community surveys and collaborates with other health specialists and civic groups to ascertain health needs, develop desirable health goals, and determine availability of professional health services. Develops and maintains cooperation between public, civic, professional, and voluntary agencies. Prepares and disseminates educational and informational materials. Promotes health discussions in schools, industry, and community agencies. May plan for and provide educational opportunities for health personnel. • **GED:** R5, M4, L5 • **SVP:** 4-10 yrs • **Academic:** Ed=M, Eng=G • **Work Field:** 271, 282 • **MPSMS:** 929 • **Aptitudes:** G1, V1, N3, S3, P4, Q3, K4, F4, M4, E4, C4 • **Temperaments:** D, I, J, P • **Stress:** E • **Physical:** V=N, H=L, L=S • **Work Env:** B • **Salary:** 5 • **Outlook:** 3

UTILIZATION-REVIEW COORDINATOR (medical ser.) • D.O.T. #079.137-010 • OES #15008 • Supervises and coordinates activities of utilization review staff and develops policies, standards, and procedures governing admissions and treatment of patients of health-care facility: Analyzes individual patient records to determine legitimacy of admission and continued stay in health-care facility, reviews patient treatment plans to ensure adherence to established criteria and standards, and supervises activities of utilization review staff. Reviews and analyzes governmental and accrediting agency standards governing admissions, treatment, and continued stay of patients to develop policies, procedures, and criteria for facility center. Reviews application for patient admission and determines necessity of each admission, applying established admission criteria. Approves admission or refers case to facility Utilization Review Committee for review and course of action when case fails to meet criteria. Reviews inpatient medical records to determine necessity of continued stay or discharge. Reviews physician treatment plans for inpatients to determine appropriateness of plan to patient manifested conditions and to ensure consistency with standard medical practice and facility policies. Makes clinical judgment regarding correctness of physician directed care. Determines next review date in accordance with established diagnostic criteria. Abstracts data from records. Assists review committee in planning and holding federally-mandated quality assurance reviews, periodic medical reviews, and professional reviews. Serves as review committee liaison with other committees within facility in development of policies and procedures. Participates in facility orientation and training programs. Supervises and coordinates activities of utilization review staff in maintenance of policy and procedure manuals, file, records, and correspondence. • **GED:** R5, M4, L5 • **SVP:** 2-4 yrs • **Academic:** Ed=B, Eng=G • **Work Field:** 294, 295 • **MPSMS:** 920 • **Aptitudes:** G2, V2, N2, S4, P4, Q2, K4, F4, M4, E5, C5 • **Temperaments:** D, J, P • **Stress:** E, A • **Physical:** V=L, H=N, L=S, H • **Work Env:** I • **Salary:** 4 • **Outlook:** 4

GOE: 11.07.03 Educational Services

CONSULTANT, EDUCATION (educ.) • D.O.T. #099.167-014 • OES #31517 • Plans and coordinates educational policies for specific subject area or grade level: Develops programs for in-service education of teaching personnel. Confers with Federal, state, and local school officials to develop curricula, and establish guidelines for educational programs. Confers with lay and professional groups to disseminate and receive input on teaching methods. Reviews and evaluates curricula for use in schools and assists in adaptation to local needs. Interprets and enforces provisions of state education codes and rules and regulations of state board of education. Conducts or participates in workshops, committees, and conferences designed to promote intellectual, social, and physical welfare of students. Studies and prepares recommendations on instructional materials, teaching aids, and related equipment. Prepares or approves manuals, guidelines, and reports on state educational policies and practices for distribution to school districts. Advises school officials on implementation of state and Federal programs and procedures. Conducts research into areas, such as teaching methods and techniques. May perform tasks at local school district level or as independent consultant in area of expertise. May be designated as consultant in specific area, such as reading, elementary education, or audio-visual education. • **GED:** R6, M6, L5 • **SVP:** 4-10 yrs • **Academic:** Ed=B, Eng=S • **Work Field:** 251, 296 • **MPSMS:** 931 • **Aptitudes:** G2, V1, N2, S4, P4, Q1, K4, F4, M4, E5, C5 • **Temperaments:** D, J, P • **Stress:** A • **Physical:** V=N, H=L, L=S • **Work Env:** I • **Salary:** 5 • **Outlook:** 4

DIRECTOR, EDUCATIONAL PROGRAM (educ.) • D.O.T. #099.117-010 • OES #15005 • Plans, develops, and administers programs to provide educational opportunities for students: Cooperates with business, civic, and other organizations to develop curriculums to meet needs and interests of students and community. Interviews and selects staff members and provides in-service training for teachers. Prepares budget and determines allocation of funds for staff, supplies and equipment, and facilities. Analyzes data from questionnaires, interviews, and group discussions to evaluate curriculums, teaching methods, and community participation in educational and other programs. May direct preparation of publicity to promote activities, such as personnel recruitment, educational programs or other services. May specialize in elementary, secondary, adult, or junior college education. • **GED:** R5, M3, L5 • **SVP:** 4-10 yrs • **Academic:** Ed=B, Eng=S • **Work Field:** 295 • **MPSMS:** 931 • **Aptitudes:** G2, V2, N2, S4, P3, Q2, K4, F4, M4, E5, C5 • **Temperaments:** D, J, P • **Stress:** A • **Physical:** V=N, H=L, L=S • **Work Env:** I • **Salary:** 5 • **Outlook:** 4

EDUCATIONAL RESOURCE COORDINATOR (museum) • D.O.T. #099.167-030 • OES #31511 • Directs operation of educational resource center of museum, zoo, or similar establishment: Maintains collections of slides, video tapes, programmed texts, and other educational materials related to institution specialty, storing or filing materials according to subject matter, geographic or ethnic association, or historical period. Composes or directs others in composition of descriptions of materials, and prepares catalog listing materials for use of museum staff members, area school teachers, and others. Compiles list of books, periodicals, and other materials designed to augment items available in resource center. Explains storage and cataloging systems to teachers and others who visit center and suggests materials for various projects, such as preparing school classes for tour of institution or presentation of lecture for community group. Issues loan materials to teachers or lecturer, or schedules and coordinates delivery of materials to designated locations. Maintains records of loans and prepares circulation reports for review by administrative personnel. Conducts work shops to acquaint educators with use of institution's facilities and materials. Attends teacher meetings and conventions to promote use of institution services. • **GED:** R5, M2, L5 • **SVP:** 2-4 yrs • **Academic:** Ed=A, Eng=S • **Work Field:** 295 • **MPSMS:** 931 • **Aptitudes:** G2, V2, N4, S4, P3, Q3, K4, F4, M4, E5, C3 • **Temperaments:** D, I, J, P • **Stress:** A • **Physical:** V=G, H=L, L=L • **Work Env:** I • **Salary:** 4 • **Outlook:** 4

EDUCATIONAL SPECIALIST (educ.) • D.O.T. #099.167-022 • OES #31517 • DIRECTOR, EVALUATION AND RESEARCH. Directs research activities concerned with educational programs in school system: Initiates procedures to determine if program objectives are being met. Devises tests to measure effectiveness of instructions and to interpret pupil intellectual and social development and group and school progress. Provides interpretation of research data gathered in other localities. Directs preparation and publication of guidance textbooks, documents, and materials used by guidance units. Develops procedures for current and proposed units of instruction. Directs report writing on effectiveness of educational program for release to public. May specialize in research activities concerned with elementary, secondary, college, or other specialized educational programs. • **GED:** R6, M5, L5 • **SVP:** 4-10 yrs • **Academic:** Ed=B, Eng=G • **Work Field:** 251 •

MPSMS: 931 • **Aptitudes:** G1, V1, N1, S4, P3, Q2, K4, F4, M4, E5, C5 • **Temperaments:** D, J, P • **Stress:** E • **Physical:** V=N, H=L, L=S • **Work Env:** I • **Salary:** 4 • **Outlook:** 3

FINANCIAL-AIDS OFFICER (educ.) • D.O.T. #090.117-030 • OES #15005 • DIRECTOR OF FINANCIAL AID AND PLACEMENTS; DIRECTOR OF STUDENT AID. Directs scholarship, grant-in-aid, and loan programs to provide financial assistance to students in college or university: Selects candidates and determines types and amounts of aid. Organizes and oversees student financial counseling activities. Coordinates activities with other departmental staff engaged in issuing or collecting student payments. May teach. May select financial aid candidates as members of committee and be designated CHAIRPERSON, SCHOLARSHIP AND LOAN COMMITTEE (education). • **GED:** R5, M3, L5 • **SVP:** 4-10 yrs • **Academic:** Ed=B, Eng=G • **Work Field:** 295 • **MPSMS:** 931 • **Aptitudes:** G2, V2, N2, S4, P4, Q2, K4, F4, M4, E5, C5 • **Temperaments:** D, P • **Stress:** E, A • **Physical:** V=N, H=L, L=S • **Work Env:** I • **Salary:** 5 • **Outlook:** 4

PARK NATURALIST (gov. ser.) • D.O.T. #049.127-010 • OES #24302 • Plans, develops, and conducts programs to inform public of historical, natural, and scientific features of national, state, or local park: Confers with park staff to determine subjects to be presented and program schedule. Surveys park to determine forest conditions and distribution and abundance of fauna and flora. Interviews specialists in desired fields to obtain and develop data for programs. Takes photographs and motion pictures to illustrate lectures and publications and to develop displays. Plans and develops audiovisual devices, prepares and presents illustrated lectures, constructs visitor-center displays, and conducts field trips to point out scientific, historic, and natural features of park. Performs emergency duties to protect human life, government property, and natural features of park. May plan, organize, and direct activities of seasonal staff members. May maintain official photographic and informational files for department. • **GED:** R5, M4, L5 • **SVP:** 2-4 yrs • **Academic:** Ed=A, Eng=G • **Work Field:** 251, 282 • **MPSMS:** 919, 959 • **Aptitudes:** G2, V2, N4, S2, P2, Q2, K3, F4, M3, E3, C3 • **Temperaments:** D, J, P, V • **Stress:** E • **Physical:** V=L, H=L, L=M, W, H • **Work Env:** B • **Salary:** 4 • **Outlook:** 3

SUPERVISOR, CONTRACT-SHELTERED WORKSHOP (nonprofit org.) • D.O.T. #187.134-010 • OES #31311 • Supervises and coordinates activities of handicapped individuals in sheltered workshop to train and improve vocational skills for gainful employment through productive work: Assigns individual to specific tasks, such as cleaning, sorting, assembling, repairing, or hand packing products or components. Demonstrates job duties to handicapped individual and observes worker performing tasks to ensure understanding of job duties. Monitors work performance at each individual's work station to ensure compliance with procedures and safety regulations and to note behavior deviations. Examines workpiece visually to verify adherence to specifications. Confers with individuals to explain or to demonstrate task again to resolve work related difficulties. Reassigns individual to simpler tasks when worker cannot perform assigned tasks, or to tasks containing higher degrees of complexity as level of competence is reached. Performs other duties described under SUPERVISOR (any ind.) Master Title. • **GED:** R3, M2, L2 • **SVP:** 2-4 yrs • **Academic:** Ed=N, Eng=G • **Work Field:** 295 • **MPSMS:** 949 • **Aptitudes:** G3, V3, N3, S3, P3, Q4, K3, F3, M3, E5, C5 • **Temperaments:** D, M, P, V • **Stress:** E, A • **Physical:** V=N, H=N, L=S, W, H • **Work Env:** I • **Salary:** 4 • **Outlook:** 1

TECHNICAL TRAINING COORDINATOR (educ.) • D.O.T. #166.167-054 • OES #21511 • Coordinates activities of instructors engaged in training employees or customers of industrial or commercial establishment: Confers with managers, instructors, or customer's representative to determine training needs. Assigns instructors to conduct training. Schedules classes, based on availability of classrooms, equipment, and instructors. Evaluates training packages, including outline, text, and handouts written by instructors. Assigns instructors to in-service or out-service training classes to learn new skills as needed. Monitors budget to ensure that training costs do not exceed allocated funds. Writes budget report listing training costs, such as instructors' wages and equipment costs, to justify expenditures. Attends meetings and seminars to obtain information useful to training staff and to inform management of training programs and goals. Monitors instructors during lectures and laboratory demonstrations to evaluate performance. Performs other duties as described under SUPERVISOR (any ind.) Master Title. May develop and conduct training programs for employees or customers of industrial or commercial establishment [INSTRUCTOR, TECHNICAL TRAINING (education) 166.221-010]. • **GED:** R5, M4, L5 • **SVP:** 4-10 yrs • **Academic:** Ed=A, Eng=S • **Work Field:** 295 • **MPSMS:** 893, 931 • **Aptitudes:** G2, V2, N2, S3, P3, Q3, K4, F4, M4, E5, C5 • **Temperaments:** D, J, P • **Physical:** V=L, H=L, L=L • **Work Env:** I • **Salary:** 5 • **Outlook:** 3

VOCATIONAL REHABILITATION CONSULTANT (gov. ser.) • D.O.T. #094.117-018 • OES #31517 • Develops and coordinates implementation of vocational rehabilitation programs: Consults with members of local communities and personnel of rehabilitation facilities, such as sheltered workshops and skills training centers, to identify need for new programs or modification of existing programs. Collects and analyzes data to define problems and develops proposals for programs to provide needed services, utilizing knowledge of vocational rehabilitation theory and practice, program funding sources, and government regulations. Provides staff training, negotiates contracts for equipment and supplies, and performs related functions to implement program changes. Monitors program operations and recommends additional measures to ensure programs meet defined needs. • **GED:** R5, M4, L5 • **SVP:** 4-10 yrs • **Academic:** Ed=M, Eng=G • **Work Field:** 251, 295 • **MPSMS:** 931, 940 • **Aptitudes:** G2, V2, N2, S3, P4, Q2, K4, F4, M4, E5, C5 • **Temperaments:** D, J, P • **Stress:** E, A • **Physical:** V=N, H=N, L=S • **Work Env:** I • **Salary:** 5 • **Outlook:** 4

GOE: 11.07.04 Recreational Services

CURATOR (museum) • D.O.T. #102.017-010 • OES #31511 • Directs and coordinates activities of workers engaged in operating exhibiting institution, such as museum, botanical garden, arboretum, art gallery, herbarium, or zoo: Directs activities concerned with instructional, acquisition, exhibitory, safekeeping, research, and public service objectives of institution. Assists in formulating and interpreting administrative policies of institution. Formulates plans for special research projects. Oversees curatorial, personnel, fiscal, technical, research, and clerical staff. Administers affairs of institution by corresponding and negotiating with administrators of other institutions to obtain exchange of loan collections or to exchange information or data, maintaining inventories, preparing budget, representing institution at scientific or association conferences, soliciting support for institution, and interviewing and hiring personnel. Obtains, develops, and organizes new collections to expand and improve educational and research facilities. Writes articles for publication in scientific journals. Consults with board of directors and professional personnel to plan and implement acquisitional, research, display and public service activities of institution. May participate in research activities. May be designated according to field of specialization as CURATOR, ART GALLERY (museum); CURATOR, HERBARIUM (muse um); CURATOR, HORTICULTURAL MUSEUM (museum); CURATOR, MEDICAL MUSEUM (museum); CURATOR, NATURAL HISTORY MUSEUM (museum); CURATOR, ZOOLOGICAL MUSEUM (museum); DIRECTOR, INDUSTRIAL MUSEUM (museum). • **GED:** R6, M5, L6 • **SVP:** Over 10 yrs • **Academic:** Ed=B, Eng=G • **Work Field:** 251, 295 • **MPSMS:** 949 • **Aptitudes:** G1, V1, N2, S3, P3, Q3, K4, F4, M4, E5, C3 • **Temperaments:** D, J, M, P, V • **Stress:** E • **Physical:** V=L, H=N, L=S, H • **Work Env:** B • **Salary:** 5 • **Outlook:** 3

LIBRARY CONSULTANT (library) • D.O.T. #100.117-014 • OES #21905 • Advises administrators of public libraries: Analyzes administrative policies, observes work procedures, and reviews data relative to book collections to determine effectiveness of library service to public. Compares allocations for building funds, salaries, and book collections with statewide and national standards, to determine effectiveness of fiscal operations. Gathers statistical data, such as population and community growth rates, and analyzes building plans to determine adequacy of programs for expansion. Prepares evaluation of library systems based on observations and surveys, and recommends measures to improve organization and administration of systems. • **GED:** R6, M4, L6 • **SVP:** 4-10 yrs • **Academic:** Ed=B, Eng=G • **Work Field:** 295 • **MPSMS:** 933 • **Aptitudes:** G1, V1, N3, S4, P3, Q2, K4, F4, M4, E5, C5 • **Temperaments:** I, P, V • **Stress:** E • **Physical:** V=L, H=L, L=S • **Work Env:** I • **Salary:** 4 • **Outlook:** 3

RECREATION SUPERVISOR (profess. & kin.) • **D.O.T. #187.137-010** • **OES #27311** • AREA SUPERVISOR; DISTRICT DIRECTOR; RECREATION SPECIALIST. Coordinates activities of paid and volunteer recreation service personnel in public department, voluntary agency, or similar type facility, such as community centers or swimming pools: Develops and promotes recreation program, including music, dance, arts and crafts, cultural arts, nature study, swimming, social recreation and games, or camping. Adapts recreation programs to meet needs of individual agency or institution, such as hospital, armed services, institution for chil-dren or aged, settlement house, or penal institution. Introduces new program activities, equipment, and materials to staff. Trains personnel and evaluates performance. Interprets recreation service to public and participates in community meetings and organizational planning. May work in team with administrative or other professional personnel, such as those engaged in medicine, social work, nursing, psychology, and therapy, to ensure that recreation is well balanced, coordinated, and integrated with special services. • **GED:** R5, M3, L4 • **SVP:** 4-10 yrs • **Academic:** Ed=A, Eng=G • **Work Field:** 295 • **MPSMS:** 941, 959 • **Aptitudes:** G1, V1, N3, S3, P3, Q4, K4, F4, M4, E4, C5 • **Temperaments:** D, P, V • **Stress:** E • **Physical:** V=L, H=L, L=S, W, H • **Work Env:** I • **Salary:** 4 • **Outlook:** 3

11.08 Communications

Workers in this group write, edit, report, and translate factual information. They find employment with radio and television broadcasting stations, newspapers, and publishing firms. Government agencies and professional groups provide some opportunities as do large firms which publish company newspapers and brochures.

✔ What kind of work would you do?

Your work activities would depend upon your specific job. For example, you might:

- rush to the scene of important happenings to gather information and write news stories.
- analyze news, attend public gatherings, interview public personalities and write a column for newspapers.
- examine materials received from foreign broadcasts and select and edit them for local use.

- supervise workers who gather information and write scripts for news, special events, and public affairs broadcasts.
- gather, analyze, select, arrange, and broadcast news for a television station.
- translate spoken or written information from one language into another.

✔ What skills and abilities do you need for this kind of work?

To do this kind of work, you must be able to:

- think logically to analyze written materials, organize facts, and interpret a wide variety of subject matter.
- understand and use a large vocabulary, sometimes in a technical or scientific language.
- speak clearly and easily when interviewing people and broadcasting news events.
- speak and write in a foreign language is an occasional requirement.
- see punctuation and spelling errors in written materials.

- identify the important and newsworthy aspects of a situation.
- change assignments and duties frequently.
- accept responsibility for the direction and planning of an activity.
- use accurate grammar, punctuation, spelling, and sentence structure.
- use words so that your readers and listeners have a clear mental picture of your ideas.

✔ How do you know if you would like or could learn to do this kind of work?

The following questions may give you clues about yourself as you consider this group of jobs.

- Have you worked on a school newspaper? Can you report events accurately?

- Have you had courses in journalism or broadcasting? Did these courses increase your interests in this type of writing?

- Have you proofread term papers or compositions? Can you spot errors in punctuation, spelling, or grammar?
- Have you spoken in front of an audience? Can you speak clearly when presenting a point of view?

✔ How can you prepare for and enter this kind of work?

Occupations in this group usually require education and/or training extending from four years to over ten years, depending upon the specific kind of work. College level courses such as journalism, English, and political science are usually required. In some cases, a four-year college degree is necessary for employment. However, writing or broadcasting experience is sometimes accepted. Some jobs in this group are open to people with experience gained in high school English or journalism courses, or by working on school newspapers. Some jobs require specific knowledge in areas such as current events, in addition to writing skills. Special courses, such as speech, may be required for some jobs.

✔ What else should you consider about these jobs?

Field work, such as that done by news reporters, will often require standing for long periods of time, walking considerable distance, and being exposed to all kinds of weather. Reporters are also exposed to hazards when reporting on fires, floods, and similar situations.

Workers in this group may be required to work nights or weekends. They are usually required to reflect the policies and points of view of their employers.

If you think you would like to do this kind of work, look at the job titles listed below.

GOE: 11.08.01 Editing, Communications

EDITOR, DEPARTMENT (print. & pub.) • D.O.T. #132.037-018 • OES #34002 • Supervises personnel engaged in selecting, gathering, and editing news and news photographs for one or more specialized news departments of newspaper: May select submitted material such as letters or articles for publication. May assign cartoons or editorials to staff members. May perform duties of REPORTER (print. & pub.; radio & tv broad.). May edit copy and perform related duties as required. Usually identified according to individual specialty or specialties. • **GED:** R5, M3, L5 • **SVP:** 4-10 yrs • **Academic:** Ed=A, Eng=G • **Work Field:** 261 • **MPSMS:** 480 • **Aptitudes:** G2, V1, N3, S4, P3, Q3, K4, F4, M4, E5, C5 • **Temperaments:** D, F, J, P, V • **Stress:** E • **Physical:** V=G, H=L, L=S • **Work Env:** I • **Salary:** 4 • **Outlook:** 2

EDITOR, NEWS (print. & pub.) • D.O.T. #132.067-026 • OES #34002 • MAKEUP EDITOR. Plans layout of newspaper edition: Receives news copy, photographs, and dummy page layouts marked to indicate columns occupied by advertising. Confers with management and editorial staff members regarding placement of developing news stories. Determines placement of stories based on relative significance, available space, and knowledge of layout principles. Marks layout sheets to indicate position of each story and accompanying photographs. Approves proofs submitted by composing room. May write or revise headlines. May edit copy. May perform related editorial duties as required. • **GED:** R5, M3, L5 • **SVP:** 4-10 yrs • **Academic:** Ed=A, Eng=G • **Work Field:** 261, 264 • **MPSMS:** 480 • **Aptitudes:** G2, V1, N3, S3, P3, Q3, K3, F4, M4, E5, C5 • **Temperaments:** D, F, J, M, T • **Stress:** A • **Physical:** V=L, H=N, L=S • **Work Env:** I • **Salary:** 5 • **Outlook:** 3

EDITOR, NEWSPAPER (print. & pub.) • D.O.T. #132.017-014 • OES #34002 • EDITOR-IN-CHIEF, NEWSPAPER. Formulates editorial policy and directs operation of newspaper: Confers with editorial policy committee and heads of production, advertising, and circulation departments to develop editorial and operating procedures and negotiate decisions affecting publication. Appoints editorial heads and supervises work of their departments in accordance with newspaper policy. Writes leading or policy editorials or notifies editorial department head of position to be taken on specific public issues. Reviews financial reports and takes appropriate action with respect to costs and revenues. Represents publication at professional and community functions. In smaller establishments may perform duties of one or more subordinate editors and direct activities of advertising, circulation, or production personnel. • **GED:** R6, M3, L6 • **SVP:** Over 10 yrs • **Academic:** Ed=B, Eng=G • **Work Field:** 261, 295 • **MPSMS:** 480 • **Aptitudes:** G1, V1, N3, S3, P3, Q3, K4, F4, M4, E5, C5 • **Temperaments:** D, F, I, J, P • **Stress:** E • **Physical:** V=N, H=N, L=S • **Work Env:** I • **Salary:** 4 • **Outlook:** 3

EDITORIAL ASSISTANT (print. & pub.) • D.O.T. #132.267-014 • OES #34002 • ASSISTANT EDITOR; ASSOCIATE EDITOR. Prepares written material for publication, performing any combination of following duties: Reads copy to detect errors in spelling, punctuation, and syntax. Verifies facts, dates, and statistics, using standard reference sources. Rewrites or modifies copy to conform to publication's style and editorial policy and marks copy for typesetter, using standard symbols to indicate how type should be set. Reads galley and page proofs to detect errors and indicates corrections, using standard proofreading symbols. May confer with authors regarding changes made to manuscript. May select and crop photographs and illustrative materials to conform to space and subject matter requirements. May prepare page layouts to position and space articles and illustrations. May write or rewrite headlines, captions, columns, articles, and stories according to publication requirements. May initiate or reply to correspondence regarding material published or being considered for publication. May read and evaluate submitted manuscripts and be designated MANUSCRIPT READER (print. & pub.). May be designated according to type of publication worked on as COPY READER (print. & pub.) when working on newspaper, and COPY READER, BOOK (print. & pub.) when working on books. • **GED:** R5, M3, L5 • **SVP:** 2-4 yrs • **Academic:** Ed=A, Eng=G • **Work Field:** 261 • **MPSMS:** 480, 757 • **Aptitudes:** G2, V2, N3, S3, P3, Q2, K4, F4, M4, E5, C5 • **Temperaments:** J, M, T • **Physical:** V=L, H=N, L=S, H • **Work**

©1991, JIST Works, Inc. • Indianapolis, IN

Env: I • Salary: 4 • Outlook: 3

GOE: 11.08.02 Writing

REPORTER (print. & pub.) • D.O.T. #131.267-018 • OES #34011 • Collects and analyzes information about newsworthy events to write news stories for publication or broadcast: Receives assignment or evaluates leads and news tips to develop story idea. Gathers and verifies factual information regarding story through interview, observation, and research. Organizes material, determines slant or emphasis, and writes story according to prescribed editorial style and format standards. May monitor police and fire department radio communications to obtain story leads. May take photographs to illustrate stories. May appear on television program when conducting taped or filmed interviews or narration. May give live reports from site of event or mobile broadcast unit. May transmit information to NEWSWRITER (print. & pub.; radio & tv broad.) for story writing. May specialize in one type of reporting, such as sports, fires, accidents, political affairs, court trials, or police activities. May be assigned to outlying areas or foreign countries and be designated CORRESPONDENT (print. & pub.; radio & tv broad.) or FOREIGN CORRESPONDENT (print. & pub.; radio & tv broad.). • **GED:** R5, M3, L5 • **SVP:** 2-4 yrs • **Academic:** Ed=A, Eng=G • **Work Field:** 261 • **MPSMS:** 480, 863, 864 • **Aptitudes:** G2, V1, N3, S4, P3, Q3, K3, F4, M4, E5, C5 • **Temperaments:** I, J, P • **Stress:** E • **Physical:** V=N, H=G, L=S, H • **Work Env:** B • **Salary:** 3 • **Outlook:** 1

RESEARCH ASSISTANT II (profess. & kin.) • D.O.T. #199.267-034 • OES #39999 • RESEARCHER. Compiles and analyzes verbal or statistical data to prepare reports and studies for use by professional workers in variety of areas, such as science, social science, law, medicine, or politics: Searches sources, such as reference works, literature, documents, newspapers, and statistical records, to obtain data on assigned subject. Analyzes and evaluates applicability of collected data. Prepares statistical tabulations, using calculator or adding machine. Writes reports or presents data in formats, such as abstracts, bibliographies, graphs, or maps. May interview individuals to obtain data or draft correspondence to answer inquiries. When conducting studies to assist lawmakers may be designated LEGISLATIVE AIDE (gov. ser.). • **GED:** R5, M3, L5 • **SVP:** 1-2 yrs • **Academic:** Ed=B, Eng=G • **Work Field:** 251, 261 • **MPSMS:** 939 • **Aptitudes:** G2, V2, N3, S4, P4, Q2, K4, F4, M4, E5, C4 • **Temperaments:** J, T • **Physical:** V=L, H=N, L=S • **Work Env:** I • **Salary:** 4 • **Outlook:** 4

WRITER, TECHNICAL PUBLICATIONS (profess. & kin.) • D.O.T. #131.267-026 • OES #34005 • TECHNICAL WRITER. Develops, writes, and edits material for reports, manuals, briefs, proposals, instruction books, catalogs, and related technical and administrative publications concerned with work methods and procedures, and installation, operation, and maintenance of machinery and other equipment: Receives assignment from supervisor. Observes production, developmental, and experimental activities to determine operating procedure and detail. Interviews production and engineering personnel and reads journals, reports, and other material to become familiar with product technologies and production methods. Reviews manufacturer's and trade catalogs, drawings and other data relative to operation, maintenance, and service of equipment. Studies blueprints, sketches, drawings, parts lists, specifications, mockups, and product samples to integrate and delineate technology, operating procedure, and production sequence and detail. Organizes material and completes writing assignment according to set standards regarding order, clarity, conciseness, style, and terminology. Reviews published materials and recommends revisions or changes in scope, format, content, and methods of reproduction and binding. May maintain records and files of work and revisions. May select photographs, drawings, sketches, diagrams, and charts to illustrate material. May assist in laying out material for publication. May arrange for typing, duplication, and distribution of material. May write speeches, articles, and public or employee relations releases. May edit, standardize, or make changes to material prepared by other writers or plant personnel and be designated STANDARD-PRACTICE ANALYST (profess. & kin.). May specialize in writing material regarding work methods and procedures and be designated PROCESS-DESCRIPTION WRITER (profess. & kin.). • **GED:** R5, M3,

L5 • **SVP:** 2-4 yrs • **Academic:** Ed=A, Eng=G • **Work Field:** 261 • **MPSMS:** 700, 710 • **Aptitudes:** G2, V1, N3, S2, P3, Q3, K4, F4, M4, E5, C5 • **Temperaments:** J, M, V • **Physical:** V=L, H=N, L=S, H • **Work Env:** I • **Salary:** 5 • **Outlook:** 4

GOE: 11.08.03 Writing & Broadcasting

COLUMNIST/COMMENTATOR (print. & pub.) • D.O.T. #131.067-010 • OES #34002 • Analyzes news and writes column or commentary, based on personal knowledge and experience with subject matter, for publication or broadcast: Gathers information and develops subject perspective through research, interview, experience, and attendance at functions, such as political conventions, news meetings, sports events, and social activities. Analyzes and interprets information to formulate and outline story idea. Selects material most pertinent to presentation, organizes into acceptable media form and format, and writes column or commentary. When working in broadcast medium usually records or presents commentary live. May be required to develop material to fit media time or space requirements. May analyze only current news items and be designated NEWS ANALYST (radio & tv broad.). May be designated according to medium worked in as COLUMNIST (print. & pub.); COMMENTATOR (radio & tv broad.). May specialize in particular field such as sports, fashion, society, or politics. • **GED:** R6, M3, L6 • **SVP:** 2-4 yrs • **Academic:** Ed=B, Eng=S • **Work Field:** 261 • **MPSMS:** 480, 863, 864 • **Aptitudes:** G1, V1, N3, S4, P3, Q3, K3, F4, M4, E5, C5 • **Temperaments:** I, J, M, P, V • **Physical:** V=N, H=N, L=S • **Work Env:** B • **Salary:** 4 • **Outlook:** 1

NEWSCASTER (radio & tv broad.) • D.O.T. #131.267-010 • OES #34014 • Analyzes and broadcasts news received from various sources: Examines news items of local, national, and international significance to determine selection or is assigned news items for broadcast by editorial staff. Prepares or assists in preparation of script. Presents news over radio or television. May specialize in particular field of news broadcasting, such as political, economic, or military. May gather information about newsworthy events. • **GED:** R5, M2, L5 • **SVP:** 2-4 yrs • **Academic:** Ed=A, Eng=G • **Work Field:** 261, 282 • **MPSMS:** 863 • **Aptitudes:** G2, V1, N3, S4, P4, Q3, K3, F4, M4, E5, C5 • **Temperaments:** I, J, M, P, V • **Stress:** E • **Physical:** V=N, H=G, L=S • **Work Env:** I • **Salary:** 5 • **Outlook:** 1

GOE: 11.08.04 Translating & Interpreting

INTERPRETER (profess. & kin.) • D.O.T. #137.267-010 • OES #39999 • Translates spoken passages from one language into another: Provides consecutive or simultaneous translation between languages. In consecutive interpreting listens to complete statements in one language, translates to second, and translates responses from second into first language. Expresses either approximate or exact translation, depending on nature of occasion. In simultaneous interpreting renders oral translation of material at time it is being spoken, usually hearing material over electronic audio system and broadcasting translation to listeners. Usually receives briefing on subject discussed prior to interpreting session. May be designated according to language or languages interpreted. May specialize in specific subject area. • **GED:** R5, M2, L5 • **SVP:** 1-2 yrs • **Academic:** Ed=A, Eng=G • **Work Field:** 281, 282 • **MPSMS:** 931 • **Aptitudes:** G2, V1, N4, S4, P4, Q3, K4, F4, M4, E5, C5 • **Temperaments:** M, P • **Stress:** E • **Physical:** V=N, H=L, L=S, H • **Work Env:** I • **Salary:** 4 • **Outlook:** 4

TRANSLATOR (profess. & kin.) • D.O.T. #137.267-018 • OES #39999 • Translates documents and other material from one language to another: Reads material and rewrites material in specified language or languages, following established rules pertaining to factors, such as word meanings, sentence structure, grammar, punctuation, and mechanics. May specialize in particular type of material, such as news, legal documents, or scientific reports and be designated accordingly. May be identified according to language translated. May represent or spell characters of another alphabet and be designated TRANSLITERATOR (profess. & kin.). • **GED:** R6, M3, L6 • **SVP:** 2-4 yrs • **Academic:** Ed=B,

Eng=G • Work Field: 261 • MPSMS: 931 • Aptitudes: G1, V1, N3, S3, P4, Q3, K4, F4, M4, E5, C5 • Temperaments: J, M, T • Physical: V=L, H=N, L=S, H • Work Env: I • Salary: 3 • Outlook: 2

11.09 Promotion

Workers in this group raise money, advertise products and services, and influence people in their actions or thoughts. They find employment in business and industry, with advertising agencies, professional groups, unions, colleges, and government agencies.

✔ **What kind of work would you do?**

Your work activities would depend upon your specific job. For example, you might:

- promote a business or industry by speaking to groups.
- plan and direct activities in an advertising agency.
- lobby for or against legislation for an industry, organization, or profession.
- develop plans for increasing the membership of an organization.
- write news releases, scripts, and other materials for an advertising campaign.
- develop materials to help dealers and distributors plan sales campaigns.

✔ **What skills and abilities do you need for this kind of work?**

To do this kind of work, you must be able to:

- originate and carry out sales campaigns.
- create new ways of presenting information that will attract peoples' attention.
- speak and write clearly and convincingly.
- frequently change from one activity to another, for example, writing a speech, giving a speech, and writing a report of campaign progress.
- understand how different kinds of people react to words, pictures, and color.
- work with all kinds of people.

✔ **How do you know if you would like or could learn to do this kind of work?**

The following questions may give you clues about yourself as you consider this group of jobs.

- Have you organized and directed ticket sales for a school or community event? Can you lead others in this type of activity?
- Have you made posters for a school or community activity? Did you use your own ideas in making them?
- Have you written advertising copy for a school yearbook or community newspaper?
- Have you worked for a political campaign? Can you understand and influence the public?
- Have you made ideas, products, or services better known and more acceptable to others?

✔ **How can you prepare for and enter this kind of work?**

Occupations in this group usually require education and/or training extending from four years to over ten years, depending upon the specific kind of work. Education at the college level would assist in entering this field. Another way to enter these jobs is to start at a related job in a public relations agency. Special courses in oral and visual communications may sometimes be required. The time needed to gain the necessary combination of education and experience may be as long as ten years. Typing is rarely a required skill, but being able to type will make many duties easier to perform, especially those concerned with public relations.

Employers often seek workers who have a favorable reputation in the field. Workers sometimes change employers in order to get better jobs.

✔ What else should you consider about these jobs?

Deadlines and performance standards often put pressure on these workers. Long hours and weekend work are not unusual in these situations.

If you think you would like to do this kind of work, look at the job titles below.

GOE: 11.09.01 Sales

ACCOUNT EXECUTIVE (bus. ser.) • D.O.T. #164.167-010 • OES #13011 • Plans, coordinates, and directs advertising campaign for clients of advertising agency: Confers with client to determine advertising requirements and budgetary limitations, utilizing knowledge of product or service to be advertised, media capabilities, and audience characteristics. Confers with agency artists, copywriters, photographers, and other media-production specialists to select media to be used and to estimate costs. Submits proposed program and estimated budget to client for approval. Coordinates activities of workers engaged in marketing research, writing copy, laying out artwork, purchasing media time and space, developing special displays and promotional items, and performing other media-production activities, in order to carry out approved campaign. • **GED:** R5, M3, L4 • **SVP:** 4-10 yrs • **Academic:** Ed=B, Eng=S • **Work Field:** 261 • **MPSMS:** 896 • **Aptitudes:** G2, V2, N3, S3, P3, Q3, K4, F4, M4, E5, C3 • **Temperaments:** D, F, I, J, P • **Stress:** E, A • **Physical:** V=G, H=L, L=S • **Work Env:** I • **Salary:** 5 • **Outlook:** 1

FASHION COORDINATOR (ret. tr.) • D.O.T. #185.157-010 • OES #13011 • FASHION STYLIST. Promotes new fashions and coordinates promotional activities, such as fashion shows, to induce consumer acceptance: Studies fashion and trade journals, travels to garment centers, attends fashion shows, and visits manufacturers and merchandise markets to obtain information on fashion trends. Consults with buying personnel to gain advice regarding type of fashions store will purchase and feature for season. Advises publicity and display departments of merchandise to be publicized. Selects garments and accessories to be shown at fashion shows. Provides information on current fashions, style trends, and use of accessories. May contract with models, musicians, caterers, and other personnel to manage staging of shows. May conduct teenage fashion shows and direct activities of store-sponsored club for teenage girls. • **GED:** R5, M4, L5 • **SVP:** 2-4 yrs • **Academic:** Ed=H, Eng=G • **Work Field:** 292 • **MPSMS:** 881 • **Aptitudes:** G2, V2, N3, S4, P3, Q4, K4, F4, M4, E5, C3 • **Temperaments:** I, J, P • **Stress:** E, A • **Physical:** V=L, H=G, L=S, W, H • **Work Env:** I • **Salary:** 4 • **Outlook:** 1

MANAGER, ADVERTISING (any ind.) • D.O.T. #164.117-010 • OES #13011 • DIRECTOR, ADVERTISING; SALES PROMOTION DIRECTOR. Plans and executes advertising policies of organization: Confers with department heads to discuss possible new accounts and to outline new policies or sales promotion campaigns. Confers with officials of newspapers, radio, and television stations, billboard advertisers, and advertising agencies to negotiate advertising contracts. Allocates advertising space to departments or products of establishment. Reviews and approves television and radio advertisements before release. Reviews rates and classifications applicable to various types of advertising and provides appropriate authorization. Directs workers in advertising department engaged in developing and producing advertisements. Directs research activities concerned with gathering information or with compilation of statistics pertinent to planning and execution of advertising sales promotion campaigns. May authorize information for publication, such as interviews with reporters or articles describing phases of establishment activity. May have responsibility for geographical district or department of establishment represented. May transact business as agent for advertising accounts. May direct preparation of special promotional features. • **GED:** R6, M5, L5 • **SVP:** 4-10 yrs • **Academic:** Ed=B, Eng=S • **Work Field:** 295 • **MPSMS:** 896 • **Aptitudes:** G2, V2, N2, S3, P4, Q4, K4, F4, M4, E5, C5 • **Temperaments:** D, J, P, V • **Stress:** A • **Physical:** V=G, H=G, L=S • **Work Env:** I • **Salary:** 5 • **Outlook:** 3

MANAGER, ADVERTISING (print. & pub.) • D.O.T. #163.167-010 • OES #13011 • Directs sale of display and classified advertising services for a publication: Plans sales campaigns. Consults with department heads and other officials to plan special campaigns and to promote sale of advertising services to various industry or trade groups. Corresponds with customers relative to advertising rates and policies, or to solicit new business. May select and train new sales personnel. May be designated according to type of advertising sold as MANAGER, CLASSIFIED ADVERTISING (print. & pub.); MANAGER, DISPLAY ADVERTISING (print. & pub.), or area or region served as MANAGER, LOCAL ADVERTISING (print. & pub.); MANAGER, NATIONAL ADVERTISING (print. & pub.). • **GED:** R5, M3, L5 • **SVP:** 4-10 yrs • **Academic:** Ed=A, Eng=S • **Work Field:** 292 • **MPSMS:** 896 • **Aptitudes:** G2, V2, N2, S3, P3, Q3, K4, F4, M4, E5, C5 • **Temperaments:** D, J, P • **Stress:** A • **Physical:** V=L, H=L, L=S • **Work Env:** I • **Salary:** 5 • **Outlook:** 3

MEDIA DIRECTOR (profess. & kin.) • D.O.T. #164.117-018 • OES #13011 • Plans and administers media programs in advertising department of food corporation: Confers with representatives of advertising agencies, product managers, and corporate advertising staff to establish media goals, objectives, and strategies within corporate advertising budget. Confers with advertising agents or media representatives to select specific programs and negotiate advertising to ensure optimum use of budgeted funds and long-term contracts. Adjusts broadcasting schedules due to program cancellations. Studies demographic data and consumer profiles to identify target audiences of media advertising. Reads trade journals and professional literature to stay informed of trends, innovations, and changes that affect media planning. • **GED:** R5, M4, L5 • **SVP:** 4-10 yrs • **Academic:** Ed=A, Eng=S • **Work Field:** 295 • **MPSMS:** 896 • **Aptitudes:** G2, V2, N2, S3, P3, Q2, K4, F4, M4, E5, C5 • **Temperaments:** D, J, P • **Stress:** A • **Physical:** V=L, H=L, L=S, H • **Work Env:** I • **Salary:** 5 • **Outlook:** 1

GOE: 11.09.02 Funds & Membership Solicitation

DIRECTOR, FUNDRAISING (nonprofit org.) • D.O.T. #165.117-010 • OES #19999 • Directs and coordinates solicitation and disbursement of funds for community social- welfare organization: Establishes fund-raising goals according to financial need of agency. Formulates policies for collecting and safeguarding contributions. Initiates public relations program to promote community understanding and support for organization's objectives. Develops schedule for disbursing solicited funds. Issues instructions to volunteer and paid workers regarding solicitations, public relations, and clerical duties. • **GED:** R5, M4, L5 • **SVP:** 4-10 yrs • **Academic:** Ed=B, Eng=S • **Work Field:** 295 • **MPSMS:** 941, 949 • **Aptitudes:** G2, V2, N2, S4, P4, Q3, K4, F4, M4, E5, C5 • **Temperaments:** D, I, J, P • **Stress:** A • **Physical:** V=N, H=N, L=S • **Work Env:** I • **Salary:** 5 • **Outlook:** 1

DIRECTOR, FUNDS DEVELOPMENT (profess. & kin.) • D.O.T. #165.117-014 • OES #19999 • Plans, organizes, directs, and coordinates ongoing and special project funding programs for museum, zoo, or similar institution: Prepares statement of planned activities and enlists support from members of institution staff and volunteer organizations. Develops public relations materials to enhance institution image and promote fundraising program. Identifies potential contributors to special project funds and supporters of institution's ongoing operations through examination of past records, individual and corporate contracts, and knowledge of community. Plans and coordinates fund drives for special projects. Assigns responsibilities for personal solicitation to members of staff, volunteer organizations, and governing body according to special interests or capabilities. Organizes direct mail campaign to reach other potential contributors. Plans and coordinates benefit events, such as banquets, balls, or auctions. Organizes solicitation drives for pledges of ongoing support from individuals, corporations, and foundations. Informs potential contributors of special needs of institution, and encourages individuals, corporations, and foundations to establish or contribute to special funds through endowments, trusts, donations of gifts-in-kind, or bequests, conferring with attorneys to establish methods of transferring funds to benefit both donors and institution. Researches public and private grant agencies and foundations to identify other sources of funding for research, community service, or other projects. Supervises and coordinates activities of workers engaged in maintaining records of contributors and grants and preparing letters of appreciation to be sent to contributors. • **GED:** R5, M4, L5 • **SVP:** 2-4 yrs • **Academic:** Ed=B, Eng=G • **Work Field:** 295 • **MPSMS:** 894, 896 • **Aptitudes:** G2, V2, N2, S4, P4, Q3, K4, F4, M4, E5, C5 • **Temperaments:** D, I, J, P • **Stress:** E, A • **Physical:** V=N, H=G, L=S • **Work Env:** I • **Salary:** 4 • **Outlook:** 3

FUND RAISER 1 (nonprofit org.) • D.O.T. #293.157-010 • OES #43099 • Plans fund-raising program for charities or other causes and writes to, telephones, or visits individuals or establishments to solicit funds: Compiles and analyzes information about potential contributors to develop mailing or contact list and to plan selling approach. Writes, telephones, or visits potential contributors and persuades them to contribute funds by explaining purpose and benefits of fund-raising program. Takes pledges or funds from contributors. Records expenses incurred and contributions received. May organize volunteers and plan social functions to raise funds. May prepare fund-raising brochures for mail-solicitation programs. • **GED:** R5, M3, L4 • **SVP:** 1-2 yrs • **Academic:** Ed=B, Eng=G • **Work Field:** 292, 295 • **MPSMS:** 920, 930, 940 • **Aptitudes:** G2, V2, N3, S5, P5, Q3, K5, F4, M4, E5, C5 • **Temperaments:** D, I, J, P • **Stress:** E • **Physical:** V=N, H=L, L=S • **Work Env:** I • **Salary:** 4 • **Outlook:** 4

MEMBERSHIP DIRECTOR (profess. & kin.) • D.O.T. #189.167-026 • OES #39999 • Organizes chapters of fraternal society, lodge, or similar organization and surveys conditions in branches already established: Contacts interested parties to present aims and ideals of organization. Coordinates group efforts in petitioning parent organization for charter and recognition. Advises societies or lodges having financial, organizational, and membership problems. • **GED:** R5, M4, L4 • **SVP:** 2-4 yrs • **Academic:** Ed=A, Eng=S • **Work Field:** 282, 292 • **MPSMS:** 949 • **Aptitudes:** G2, V2, N3, S4, P4, Q4, K4, F4, M4, E5, C5 • **Temperaments:** D, I, P, V • **Stress:** A • **Physical:** V=N, H=L, L=L, H • **Work Env:** I • **Salary:** 4 • **Outlook:** 1

GOE: 11.09.03 Public Relations

EMPLOYER RELATIONS REPRESENTATIVE (profess. & kin.) • D.O.T. #166.257-010 • OES #21511 • Establishes and maintains working relationships with local employers to promote use of public employment programs and services: Contacts employers new to area or company requiring revisit and arranges appointment to visit company representative or employer responsible for hiring workers. Establishes rapport between Employment Service and company to promote use of agency programs and services. Confers with employer to resolve problems, such as local employment office effectiveness, employer complaints, and alternative employer actions for recruiting qualified applicants. Answers employer questions concerning Employment Service programs or services available. Solicits employers to list job openings with Employment Service. Receives job orders from employers by phone or in person and records information to facilitate selection and referral process. • **GED:** R5, M2, L4 • **SVP:** 1-2 yrs • **Academic:** Ed=A, Eng=S • **Work Field:** 282 • **MPSMS:** 896, 943 • **Aptitudes:** G2, V2, N4, S4, P4, Q3, K4, F4, M4, E5, C5 • **Temperaments:** I, P • **Physical:** V=L, H=G, L=L, W, H • **Work Env:** I • **Salary:** 4 • **Outlook:** 3

FOREIGN-SERVICE OFFICER (gov. ser.) • D.O.T. #188.117-106 • OES #19005 • Represents interests of United States Government and Nationals by conducting relations with foreign nations and international organizations; protecting and advancing political, economic, and commercial interests overseas; and ren-dering personal services to Americans abroad and to foreign nationals traveling to the United States: Manages and administers diplomatic or consular post abroad. Conveys views of United States government to host government. Reports political and other developments in host country to superior or Secretary of State. Analyzes basic economic data, trends, and developments in host country or region. Advances trade by alerting United States businessmen to potential foreign trade and investment opportunities. Provides medical, legal, familial, and traveling advice and assistance to United States citizens. Issues passports to Americans and visas to foreigners wishing to enter the United States. Offers notarial services and assistance on benefit programs to Americans and eligible foreigners. Determines eligibility of persons to be documented as United States citizens. Takes testimony abroad for use in United States courts. May negotiate agreements between host and United States governments. May recommend how American policy can help improve foreign economic conditions. May coordinate American economic assistance programs. May serve in Washington, D. C. as counterpart to colleagues in the field, relating foreign service administrative needs to Department of State or United States Information Agency. May disseminate information overseas about the United States and its policies by engaging in cultural and educational interaction through United States Information Agency. May be designated according to basic field of specialization as ADMINISTRATIVE OFFICER (gov. ser.); COMMERCIAL OFFICER (gov. ser.); CONSULAR OFFICER (gov. ser.); CULTURAL AFFAIRS OFFICER (gov. ser.); DIPLOMATIC OFFICER (gov. ser.); ECONOMIC OFFICER (gov. ser.). Additional titles: INFORMATION OFFICER (gov. ser.); POLITICAL OFFICER (gov. ser.); PUBLIC AFFAIRS OFFICER (gov. ser.). • **GED:** R5, M4, L5 • **SVP:** 4-10 yrs • **Academic:** Ed=B, Eng=S • **Work Field:** 211, 271, 295 • **MPSMS:** 959 • **Aptitudes:** G2, V1, N3, S3, P3, Q3, K4, F4, M4, E5, C5 • **Temperaments:** F, I, J, P, V • **Stress:** E • **Physical:** V=L, H=L, L=S • **Work Env:** I • **Salary:** 5 • **Outlook:** 1

MANAGER, AREA DEVELOPMENT (light, heat, & power) • D.O.T. #184.117-030 • OES #15023 • AREA-DEVELOPMENT CONSULTANT. Negotiates with representatives of industrial, commercial, agricultural, or other interests utilizing electric power or fuel gas to encourage location of facilities in area served by utility: Directs and coordinates activities of workers engaged in preparation of surveys and studies of prospective development area to compile information of interest to companies desirous of relocation. Analyzes compiled data and formulates methods and procedures for developing industrial areas to determine industries that would enhance developmental plan. Plans promotional sales program and advertising to promote maximum utilization of land and consumption of electric power. Contacts companies to persuade them to locate in service area. • **GED:** R5, M3, L4 • **SVP:** 4-10 yrs • **Academic:** Ed=A, Eng=S • **Work Field:** 292, 295 • **MPSMS:** 871, 872 • **Aptitudes:** G2, V2, N2, S4, P4, Q3, K4, F4, M4, E5, C5 • **Temperaments:** D, I, J, P, V • **Stress:** A • **Physical:** V=N, H=L, L=S • **Work Env:** I • **Salary:** 5 • **Outlook:** 1

PUBLIC-RELATIONS REPRESENTATIVE (profess. & kin.) • D.O.T. #165.067-010 • OES #34008 • PUBLIC-RELATIONS PRACTITIONER. Plans and conducts public relations program designed to create and maintain favorable public image for employer or client: Plans and directs development and communication of information designed to keep public informed of employer's programs, accomplishments, or point of view. Arranges for public-relations efforts in order to meet needs, objectives, and policies of individual, special interest group, business concern, nonprofit organization, or governmental agency, serving as in-house staff member or as outside consultant. Prepares and distributes fact sheets, news releases, photographs, scripts, motion pictures, or tape recordings to media representatives and other persons who may be interested in learning about or publicizing employer's activities or message. Purchases advertising space and time as required. Arranges for and conducts public-contact programs designed to meet employer's objectives, utilizing knowledge of changing attitudes and opinions of consumers, clients, employees, or other interest groups. Promotes goodwill through such publicity efforts as speeches, exhibits, films, tours, and question/answer sessions. Represents employer during community projects and at public, social, and business gatherings. May specialize in researching data, creating ideas, writing copy, laying out artwork, contacting media representatives, or representing employer directly before general public. May specialize in one type of public-relations effort, such as fund-raising campaigns or political issues. May specialize in disseminating facts and information about organization's activities or governmental agency's programs to the general public and be known as PUBLIC INFORMATION OFFI-CER (profess. & kin.). • **GED:** R5, M4, L5 • **SVP:** 2-4 yrs • **Academic:** Ed=A, Eng=G • **Work Field:** 261 • **MPSMS:** 896 • **Aptitudes:** G1, V1, N3, S3, P3, Q3, K4, F4, M4, E5, C4 • **Temperaments:** D, I, J, P, V • **Stress:** E, A • **Physical:** V=N, H=G, L=S • **Work Env:** I • **Salary:** 4 • **Outlook:** 3

11.10 Regulations Enforcement

Workers in this group enforce government regulations and company policies that affect peoples' rights, health and safety, and finances. They examine records, inspect products, and investigate services, but do not engage in police work. Most workers find employment with government agencies, licensing departments, and health departments. Some are employed by retail establishments, mines, transportation companies, and non-profit organizations.

✔ What kind of work would you do?

Your work activities would depend upon your specific job. For example, you might:

- regulate the entry of people into the United States according to immigration laws.
- investigate employment practices to enforce equal employment opportunity laws.
- observe employees of a bus company to see that company rules are being followed.

- investigate shortages of cash, materials, tools, or equipment in a production or sales company.
- inspect buildings and equipment to detect fire hazards.
- direct the examination of insurance companies to see that state regulations are being followed.
- investigate animal cruelty and neglect complaints.

✔ What skills and abilities do you need for this kind of work?

To do this kind of work, you must be able to:

- think logically and apply technical knowledge when making investigations and inspections.
- establish facts and draw conclusions based on information collected.
- read and understand the laws and regulations to be enforced.
- write and speak clearly.
- make decisions based on laws and regulations.

- make decisions based on personal experience and your own opinions.
- cope with a variety of duties, such as questioning people, looking at the physical conditions in a manufacturing plant to identify hazards, and writing reports.
- deal with all kinds of people pleasantly but firmly.
- standing or walking for long periods of time.

✔ How do you know if you would like or could learn to do this kind of work?

The following questions may give you clues about yourself as you consider this group of jobs.

- Have you been in charge of a group or class? Can you enforce rules and regulations according to instructions?
- Have you been a member of an environmental or a consumer group? Would you like a job which promotes these interests?

- Have you taken courses in government, political science, or environmental health? Do you think rules and regulations are important?

✔ How can you prepare for and enter this kind of work?

Occupations in this group usually require education and/or training extending from one year to over ten years, depending upon the specific kind of work. The education and experience requirements vary greatly among the jobs in this group. Some jobs require prior knowledge of the regulations to be enforced and the procedures to be used. Others require special training such as insurance underwriting. Clerical and other workers within a company or government agency are sometimes promoted to positions in this group. Other jobs require skills and knowledges that are identified by special tests.

Many of the jobs in this group are in government agencies and are filled by those who qualify through civil service examinations. Some jobs are filled by appointment.

✔ What else should you consider about these jobs?

Some workers are required to wear uniforms. Some jobs involve shift work. Some workers sit at a desk in a comfortable office most of the day, while others must go from one place to another in order to inspect licenses and determine regulation compliance of people like beauty operators and food service workers. Other workers are stationed at inspection locations, such as port-of-entry and border crossings.

If you think you would like to do this kind of work, look at the job titles listed on the following pages.

GOE: 11.10.01 Finance, Regulations Enforcement

CHIEF BANK EXAMINER (gov. ser.) • D.O.T. #160.167-046 • OES #21911 • Directs investigation of banking practices throughout state to enforce laws governing banking procedures and solvency of financial institutions: Schedules bank examinations according to departmental policy, availability of personnel, and financial condition of each bank. Evaluates examination reports to determine action required to protect solvency of bank and interests of shareholders or depositors. Confers with financial advisors and banking commissioners to recommend or initiate action against banks failing to comply with standards and policies of commission. Confers with members of banking community to receive views and discuss common problems. Receives applications for establishment of banking institutions and evaluates results of investigations undertaken to determine whether such establishment is in public interest. Recommends acceptance or rejection of applications on basis of findings. • **GED:** R5, M5, L5 • **SVP:** 4-10 yrs • **Academic:** Ed=B, Eng=G • **Work Field:** 232, 271, 295 • **MPSMS:** 894 • **Aptitudes:** G2, V2, N1, S4, P4, Q2, K4, F4, M4, E5, C5 • **Temperaments:** D, J, M, P, V • **Stress:** E, A • **Physical:** V=L, H=N, L=S • **Work Env:** I • **Salary:** 5 • **Outlook:** 4

INSPECTOR, GOVERNMENT PROPERTY (gov. ser.) • D.O.T. #168.267-050 • OES #21911 • Inspects government-owned equipment and materials in hands of private contractors to prevent waste, damage, theft, and other irregularities. Reviews inventory reports and similar records to detect discrepancies in utilization of materials. Recommends legal or administrative action to protect government property. • **GED:** R4, M3, L4 • **SVP:** 1-2 yrs • **Academic:** Ed=H, Eng=S • **Work Field:** 271 • **MPSMS:** 892, 959 • **Aptitudes:** G2, V2, N2, S3, P3, Q3, K4, F4, M4, E5, C4 • **Temperaments:** J, M, T • **Physical:** V=G, H=N, L=L, W, H • **Work Env:** B • **Salary:** 4 • **Outlook:** 3

INVESTIGATOR (gov. ser.) • D.O.T. #168.267-062 • OES #21911 • Investigates regulated activities to assure compliance with federal, state, or municipal laws: Locates and interviews plaintiffs, witnesses, or representatives of business or government to gather facts relating to alleged violation. Observes conditions to verify facts indicating violation of law relating to such activities as revenue collection, employment practices, or fraudulent benefit claims. Examines business, personal, or public records and documents to establish facts and authenticity of data. Investigates character of applicant for special license or permit. Investigates suspected misuses of license or permit. Prepares correspondence and reports of investigations for use by administrative or legal authorities. Testifies in court or at administrative proceedings concerning findings of investigation. May serve legal papers. May be required to meet licensing or certification standards established by regulatory agency concerned. May be designated according to function or agency where employed as INSPECTOR, WEIGHTS AND MEASURES (gov. ser.); INVESTIGATOR, INTERNAL REVENUE (gov. ser.); INVESTIGATOR, WELFARE (gov. ser.); POSTAL INSPECTOR (gov. ser.); INVESTIGATOR, CLAIMS (gov. ser.). • **GED:** R5, M4, L4 • **SVP:** 1-2 yrs • **Academic:** Ed=A, Eng=G • **Work Field:** 271 • **MPSMS:** 950 • **Aptitudes:** G2, V2, N3, S3, P3, Q3, K5, F5, M5, E5, C5 • **Temperaments:** J, M, P • **Stress:** E • **Physical:** V=G, H=L, L=L, W • **Work Env:** B • **Salary:** 4 • **Outlook:** 2

INVESTIGATOR, FRAUD (ret. tr.) • D.O.T. #376.267-014 • OES #63035 • Investigates cases of fraud involving use of charge cards reported lost or stolen, cash refunds, and non-existent accounts in retail stores: Receives information from credit, sales, and collection departments regarding suspected fraud cases. Interviews store personnel, and observes and questions suspected customers to obtain evidence. Compiles detailed reports on fraud cases, and submits and discusses cases with police. Consults with postal officials when charge cards are reported stolen in mail. Testifies at court trials of offenders. Prepares reports of fraud cases and submits to security department and other store officials. • **GED:** R4, M4, L3 • **SVP:** 2-4 yrs • **Academic:** Ed=H, Eng=G • **Work Field:** 271 • **MPSMS:** 969 • **Aptitudes:** G3, V3, N3, S4, P4, Q3, K4, F4, M4, E5, C4 • **Temperaments:** J, P • **Stress:** E • **Physical:** V=G, H=L, L=S • **Work Env:** I • **Salary:** 4 • **Outlook:** 3

REVENUE OFFICER (gov. ser.) • D.O.T. #188.167-074 • OES #21911 • Investigates and collects delinquent Federal taxes and secures delinquent tax returns from individuals or business firms according to prescribed laws and regulations: Investigates delinquent tax cases referred by agency investigators, as well as leads found in newspapers, trade journals, and public stockbroker records. Confers with individuals or business representatives by telephone, correspondence, or in person to determine amount of delinquent taxes and enforce collection. Examines and analyzes tax assets and liabilities to determine solution for resolving tax problem. Selects appropriate remedy for delinquent taxes when necessary, such as part-payment agreements, offers of compromise, or seizure and sale of property. Directs service of legal documents, such as subpoenas, warrants, notices of assessment, and garnishments. Recommends criminal prosecutions and civil penalties when necessary. Writes reports of determinations and actions taken for departmental files. (Workers who examine and audit tax records to determine tax liabilities are defined under title REVENUE AGENT (gov. ser.). • **GED:** R5, M4, L4 • **SVP:** 2-4 yrs • **Academic:** Ed=A, Eng=S • **Work Field:** 232, 271 • **MPSMS:** 953 • **Aptitudes:** G2, V2, N2, S4, P3, Q3, K4, F4, M4, E4, C5 • **Temperaments:** D, I, M, P, S • **Stress:** A, S • **Physical:** V=G, H=G, L=L, W • **Work Env:** I • **Salary:** 4 • **Outlook:** 1

GOE: 11.10.02 Individual Rights

DIRECTOR, COMPLIANCE (gov. ser.) • **D.O.T.** #188.117-046 • OES #19005 • Directs human relations program: Plans, organizes, and executes compliance programs in areas of employment, housing, and education under authority of federal, state, or local discriminatory legislation. Establishes and coordinates activities of local community relations committees. Conducts investigations to resolve complaints and report violations for adjudication. Plans informational programs to stimulate and maintain community interest and support. Cooperates with local, state, and federal governmental units and other organizations in identifying needs and providing assistance in enforcement of statutes. • **GED:** R5, M4, L5 • **SVP:** 2-4 yrs • **Academic:** Ed=A, Eng=S • **Work Field:** 295 • **MPSMS:** 959 • **Aptitudes:** G2, V2, N2, S4, P4, Q3, K4, F4, M4, E5, C5 • **Temperaments:** D, P • **Stress:** A • **Physical:** V=N, H=L, L=L, H • **Work Env:** I • **Salary:** 4 • **Outlook:** 1

EQUAL OPPORTUNITY OFFICER (any ind.) • **D.O.T.** #168.267-114 • OES #21911 • Monitors company contracts to determine affirmative action requirements and facilitate compliance: Reviews contracts to determine company actions required to meet equal opportunity provisions of local, State, or Federal laws. Studies equal opportunity complaints to clarify issues, and meets with personnel involved to arbitrate and settle disputes. Confers with supervisory personnel to verify or document alleged violations of law, such as failure to post notices, process grievances, or correct ethnic or other imbalances. Prepares report of findings and makes recommendations for corrective action. Participates with MANAGER, PERSONNEL (profess. & kin.) 166.117-018 in addressing and resolving issues involving company hiring and related personnel policies. • **GED:** R5, M3, L5 • **SVP:** 2-4 yrs • **Academic:** Ed=H, Eng=G • **Work Field:** 271, 282 • **MPSMS:** 940 • **Aptitudes:** G2, V2, N2, S3, P4, Q3, K4, F4, M4, E5, C5 • **Temperaments:** J, P • **Stress:** E • **Physical:** V=N, H=L, L=S • **Work Env:** I • **Salary:** 4 • **Outlook:** 1

EQUAL-OPPORTUNITY REPRESENTATIVE (gov. ser.) • **D.O.T.** #168.167-014 • OES #21911 • Organizes and implements Federally funded programs related to equal employment opportunity by providing consultation, encouraging good will between employers and minority communities, and evaluating employment practices: Consults with community representatives to develop technical assistance agreements in accordance with statutory regulations. Informs minority community on Civil Rights laws. Assists employers to interpret State and Federal laws. Develops guidelines for nondiscriminatory employment practices for use by employers. Acts as liaison representative between minority placement agencies and large employers. Investigates existing employment practices to detect and correct discriminatory factors. Conducts surveys and evaluates findings to determine existence of systematic discrimination. • **GED:** R5, M3, L5 • **SVP:** 4-10 yrs • **Academic:** Ed=A, Eng=G • **Work Field:** 295 • **MPSMS:** 959 • **Aptitudes:** G2, V3, N3, S4, P4, Q3, K4, F4, M4, E4, C4 • **Temperaments:** D, I, J, M, P • **Stress:** E, A • **Physical:** V=N, H=L, L=S • **Work Env:** I • **Salary:** 4 • **Outlook:** 2

GOE: 11.10.03 Health & Safety Regulations Enf.

CHEMICAL-RADIATION TECHNICIAN (gov. ser.) • **D.O.T.** #015.261-010 • OES #24508 • Tests materials and monitors operations of nuclear-powered electric generating plant, using specialized laboratory equipment and chemical and radiation detection instruments: Collects samples of water, gases, and solids at specified intervals during production process, using automatic sampling equipment. Analyzes materials, according to specified procedures, to determine if chemical components and radiation levels are within established limits. Records test results and prepares reports for review by supervisor. Assists workers to set up equipment and monitors equipment that automatically detects deviations from standard operations. Notifies personnel to adjust processing equipment, quantity of additives, and rate of discharge of waste materials, when test results and monitoring of equipment indicate that radiation levels, chemical balance, and discharge of radionuclide materials are in excess of standards. Carries out decontamination procedures to ensure safety of workers and continued operation of processing equipment in plant. Calibrates and maintains chemical instrumentation sensing elements and sampling system equipment, using handtools. Assists workers in diagnosis and correction of problems in instruments and processing equipment. Advises plant personnel of methods of protection from excessive exposure to radiation. • **GED:** R4, M3, L3 • **SVP:** 1-2 yrs • **Academic:** Ed=H, Eng=S • **Work Field:** 211, 221 • **MPSMS:** 715 • **Aptitudes:** G3, V3, N3, S2, P2, Q4, K2, F3, M3, E5, C3 • **Temperaments:** J, T • **Physical:** V=L, H=N, L=L, W, H • **Work Env:** I • **Salary:** 4 • **Outlook:** 2

FOOD AND DRUG INSPECTOR (gov. ser.) • **D.O.T.** #168.267-042 • OES #21911 • Inspects establishment where foods, drugs, cosmetics, and similar consumer items are manufactured, handled, stored, or sold to enforce legal standards of sanitation, purity, and grading: Visits specified establishments to investigate sanitary conditions and health and hygiene habits of persons handling consumer products. Collects samples of products for bacteriological and chemical laboratory analysis. Informs individuals concerned of specific regulations affecting establishments. Destroys subgrades, or prohibits sale of impure, toxic, damaged, or misbranded items. Questions employees, vendors, consumers, and other principals to obtain evidence for prosecuting violators. Ascertains that required licenses and permits have been obtained and are displayed. Prepares reports on each establishment visited, including findings and recommendations for action. May negotiate with marketers and processors to effect changes in facilities and practices, where undesirable conditions are discovered that are not specifically prohibited by law. May grade products according to specified standards. May test products, using variety of specialized test equipment, such as ultraviolet lights and filter guns. May investigate compliance with or violation of public sanitation laws and regulations and be designated SANITARY INSPECTOR (gov. ser.). • **GED:** R5, M4, L5 • **SVP:** 1-2 yrs • **Academic:** Ed=A, Eng=G • **Work Field:** 271 • **MPSMS:** 929 • **Aptitudes:** G2, V2, N3, S3, P4, Q4, K4, F4, M4, E5, C3 • **Temperaments:** M, P, T • **Physical:** V=G, H=N, L=S, W, H • **Work Env:** I • **Salary:** 4 • **Outlook:** 3

HAZARDOUS-WASTE MANAGEMENT SPECIALIST (gov. ser.) • **D.O.T.** #168.267-086 • OES #21911 • Conducts studies on hazardous waste management projects and provides information on treatment and containment of hazardous waste: Participates in developing hazardous waste rules and regulations to protect people and environment. Surveys industries to determine type and magnitude of disposal problem. Assesses available hazardous waste treatment and disposal alternatives, and costs involved, to compare economic impact of alternative methods. Assists in developing comprehensive spill prevention programs and reviews facility plans for spill prevention. Participates in developing spill-reporting regulations and environmental damage assessment programs. Prepares reports of findings concerning spills and prepares material for use in legal actions. Answers inquiries and prepares informational literature to provide technical assistance to representatives of industry, government agencies, and to general public. Provides technical assistance in event of hazardous chemical spill and identifies pollutant, determines hazardous impact, and recommends corrective action. • **GED:** R5, M3, L5 • **SVP:** 2-4 yrs • **Academic:** Ed=A, Eng=G • **Work Field:** 271, 282 • **MPSMS:** 732, 953 • **Aptitudes:** G2, V2, N2, S4, P4, Q2, K4, F4, M4, E5, C5 • **Temperaments:** P, T • **Stress:** E, A • **Physical:** V=L, H=N, L=S, H • **Work Env:** I • **Salary:** 5 • **Outlook:** 2

HEALTH OFFICER, FIELD (gov. ser.) • **D.O.T.** #168.167-018 • OES #21911 • INVESTIGATOR, COMMUNICABLE DISEASE. Investigates reported cases of communicable diseases and advises exposed persons to obtain medical treatment and to prevent further spread of disease: Locates and interviews exposed person, using information obtained from records of state or local public health departments and from individual already under treatment for communicable disease. Advises person to obtain treatment from private physician or public health clinic. May take blood sample to assist in identifying presence of disease in suspected victim. Questions exposed person to obtain information concerning other persons who may have received exposure. Conducts follow-up interviews with patients and suspected carriers. Writes report of activities and findings. Visits physicians, laboratories, and community health facilities to stimulate reporting of cases and to provide information about government-sponsored health programs concerning immunization efforts, VD control, mosquito abatement, and rodent control. • **GED:** R5, M3, L5 • **SVP:** 1-2 yrs • **Academic:** Ed=B, Eng=S • **Work Field:** 271 • **MPSMS:** 929 • **Aptitudes:** G2, V2, N3, S4, P3, Q3, K4, F5, M4, E5, C4 • **Temperaments:** D, I, J, M, P • **Stress:** A • **Physical:** V=G, H=G, L=L, W • **Work Env:** I, R • **Salary:** 4 • **Outlook:** 3

INDUSTRIAL HYGIENIST (profess. & kin.) • D.O.T. #079.161-010 • OES #32999 • Conducts health program in industrial plant or governmental organization to recognize, eliminate, and control occupational health hazards and diseases: Collects samples of dust, gases, vapors, and other potentially toxic materials for analysis. Investigates adequacy of ventilation, exhaust equipment, lighting, and other conditions which may affect employee health, comfort, or efficiency. Conducts evaluations of exposure to ionizing and nonionizing radiation and to noise, and recommends measures to ensure maximum employee protection. Collaborates with INDUSTRIAL-HEALTH ENGINEER (profess. & kin.) and PHYSICIAN, OCCUPATIONAL (medical ser.) to institute control and remedial measures for hazardous and potentially hazardous conditions and equipment. Prepares reports including observations, analyses of contaminants, and recommendations for control and correction of hazards. Participates in educational meetings to instruct employees in matters pertaining to occupational health and prevention of accidents. May specialize in particular area, such as collection and analysis of samples. • **GED:** R5, M4, L5 • **SVP:** 4-10 yrs • **Academic:** Ed=A, Eng=G • **Work Field:** 244, 271 • **MPSMS:** 712, 929 • **Aptitudes:** G1, V2, N1, S1, P1, Q4, K3, F4, M3, E5, C4 • **Temperaments:** D, M • **Physical:** V=L, H=L, L=M, W, H • **Work Env:** I, N • **Salary:** 5 • **Outlook:** 3

INDUSTRIAL-SAFETY-AND-HEALTH TECHNICIAN (any ind.) • D.O.T. #168.161-014 • OES #21911 • Plans and directs safety and health activities in industrial plant to evaluate and control environmental hazards: Tests noise levels and measures air quality, using precision instruments. Maintains and calibrates instruments. Administers hearing tests to employees. Trains forklift operators to qualify for licensing. Enforces use of safety equipment. Lectures employees to obtain compliance with regulations. Develops and monitors emergency action plans. Investigates accidents and prepares accident reports. Assists management to prepare safety and health budget. Recommends changes in policies and procedures to prevent accidents and illness. • **GED:** R5, M4, L4 • **SVP:** 1-2 yrs • **Academic:** Ed=A, Eng=G • **Work Field:** 211 • **MPSMS:** 953 • **Aptitudes:** G3, V3, N3, S4, P4, Q3, K3, F3, M3, E4, C4 • **Temperaments:** D, T • **Physical:** V=L, H=L, L=L, H • **Work Env:** I • **Salary:** 4 • **Outlook:** 3

INSPECTOR, AGRICULTURAL COMMODITIES (gov. ser.) • D.O.T. #168.287-010 • OES #21911 • Inspects agricultural commodities, processing equipment, and facilities to enforce compliance with governmental regulations: Inspects horticultural products, such as fruits, vegetables, and ornamental plants to detect disease or infestations harmful to consumers or agricultural economy. Inspects live animals and processing establishments to detect disease or unsanitary conditions. Compares brand with registry to identify owner. Examines, weighs, and measures commodities such as poultry, eggs, mutton, beef, and seafood to certify wholesomeness, grade, and weight. Examines viscera to detect spots or abnormal growths. Collects sample of pests or suspected diseased material and routes to laboratory for identification and analysis. Writes report of findings and advises grower or processor of corrective action. May testify in legal proceedings. May be required to hold U. S. Department of Agriculture license for each

product inspected. May be designated according to type of commodity or animal inspected. • **GED:** R4, M3, L4 • **SVP:** 2-4 yrs • **Academic:** Ed=H, Eng=S • **Work Field:** 211 • **MPSMS:** 300, 310, 320 • **Aptitudes:** G2, V3, N3, S3, P2, Q4, K3, F3, M3, E5, C3 • **Temperaments:** J, M, V • **Physical:** V=G, H=L, L=L, W, S, H • **Work Env:** B • **Salary:** 4 • **Outlook:** 3

INSPECTOR, HEALTH CARE FACILITIES (gov. ser.) • D.O.T. #168.167-042 • OES #21911 • Inspects health care facilities, such as hospitals, nursing homes, sheltered care homes, maternity homes, and daycare centers, to enforce public health laws and to investigate complaints: Inspects physical facilities, equipment, accommodations, and operating procedures to ensure compliance with laws governing standards of sanitation, acceptability of facilities, record keeping, staff competence qualifications, and ethical practices. Reviews reports concerning staffing, personal references, floor plans, fire inspections, and sanitation. Recommends changes in facilities, standards, and administrative methods in order to improve services and efficiency, utilizing knowledge of good practices and legal requirements. Advises applicants for approval of health care facilities on license application and rules governing operation of such facilities. May testify at hearings or in court. May compile data on conditions of health care facilities, for use in determining construction needs in community or region. • **GED:** R4, M3, L4 • **SVP:** 1-2 yrs • **Academic:** Ed=H, Eng=S • **Work Field:** 271 • **MPSMS:** 929 • **Aptitudes:** G2, V2, N3, S3, P3, Q3, K4, F5, M5, E5, C4 • **Temperaments:** J, M, V • **Physical:** V=G, H=L, L=S • **Work Env:** I • **Salary:** 4 • **Outlook:** 3

INSPECTOR, MOTOR VEHICLES (gov. ser.) • D.O.T. #168.267-058 • OES #21911 • AUTOMOBILE INSPECTOR; MOTOR-TRANSPORT INSPECTOR; WEIGH-STATION INSPECTOR. Inspects motor vehicles and cargoes for compliance with statutory regulations: Reviews employer records to determine accidents, traffic violations, and medical information recorded according to Federal and State regulations. Advises shipper of methods to improve cargo security and record keeping to account for shortage or theft. Interprets applicable regulations and suggests method of self-inspection to accomplish voluntary compliance with code. Inspects vehicle systems, such as lights, brakes, tires, directional signals, exhaust systems, and warning devices, to detect excessive wear or malfunction. Measures interior and exterior noise levels, using decibel meter. Reviews shipping papers to identify hazardous cargo, such as explosives, poisons, or combustibles. Inspects manner in which hazardous cargo is secured to prevent accidental spillage. Computes and records weight of commercial trucks at highway weigh station or using portable scale to determine gross weight and distribution of load over axles. Reviews commercial vehicle log to verify driver has not exceeded allowable driving hours and required permits and licenses are displayed. Declares vehicle or driver out-of-service for violation of intra- or interstate commerce regulations. Inspects buses to determine compliance with public transport regulations. May accompany bus drivers to observe conduct and observance of safety precautions. May inspect establishments that rebuild containers used to hold hazardous materials. May testify in legal proceedings. Measures efficiency of emission-control devices, using electronic test apparatus. • **GED:** R5, M4, L5 • **SVP:** 2-4 yrs • **Academic:** Ed=A, Eng=S • **Work Field:** 271 • **MPSMS:** 590, 959 • **Aptitudes:** G2, V2, N3, S3, P3, Q3, K4, F4, M4, E5, C4 • **Temperaments:** J, M, P • **Physical:** V=G, H=L, L=L, W, C • **Work Env:** I • **Salary:** 4 • **Outlook:** 3

INSPECTOR, WATER-POLLUTION CONTROL (gov. ser.) • D.O.T. #168.267-090 • OES #21911 • Inspects sites where discharges enter State waters and investigates complaints concerning water pollution problems: Inspects wastewater treatment facilities at sites, such as mobile home parks, sewage treatment plants, and other sources of pollution. Inspects lagoons and area where effluent enters State waters for such features as obvious discoloration of water, sludge, algae, rodents, and other conditions. Informs owner when unacceptable or questionable conditions are present and recommends corrective action. Notifies mobile laboratory technicians when sampling is required. Advises property owners, facility managers, and equipment operators concerning pollution control regulations. Investigates complaints concerning water pollution problems. Compiles information for pollution control discharge permits. Prepares technical reports of investigations. • **GED:** R5,

M4, L5 • **SVP:** 2-4 yrs • **Academic:** Ed=A, Eng=S • **Work Field:** 211 • **MPSMS:** 874, 953 • **Aptitudes:** G2, V2, N3, S4, P3, Q3, K4, F4, M4, E5, C5 • **Temperaments:** J, P • **Physical:** V=G, H=L, L=L, W • **Work Env:** I • **Salary:** 4 • **Outlook:** 3

MARINE-CARGO SURVEYOR (bus. ser.) • D.O.T. #168.267-094 • OES #21911 • Inspects cargoes of seagoing vessels to certify compliance with national and international health and safety regulations in cargo handling and stowage: Reads vessel documents that set forth cargo loading and securing procedures, capacities, and stability factors to ascertain cargo capabilities according to design and cargo regulations. Advises crew in techniques of stowing dangerous and heavy cargo, such as use of extra support beams (deck bedding), shoring, and additional stronger lashings, according to knowledge of hazards present when shipping grain, explosives, logs, and heavy machinery. Inspects loaded, secured cargo in holds and lashed to decks to ascertain that pertinent cargo handling regulations have been observed. Issues certificate of compliance when violations are not detected. Recommends remedial procedures to correct deficiencies. Measures ship holds and depth of fuel and water in tanks, using sounding line and tape measure, and reads draft markings to ascertain depth of vessel in water. Times roll of ship, using stopwatch. Calculates hold capacities, volume of stored fuel and water, weight of cargo, and ship stability factors, using standard mathematical formulas and calculator. Analyzes data obtained from survey, formulates recommendations pertaining to vessel capacities, and writes report of findings. Inspects cargo handling devices, such as boom, hoists, and derricks, to identify need for maintenance. • **GED:** R4, M4, L4 • **SVP:** Over 10 yrs • **Academic:** Ed=H, Eng=S • **Work Field:** 211, 271 • **MPSMS:** 953 • **Aptitudes:** G2, V2, N2, S3, P3, Q2, K4, F4, M4, E5, C5 • **Temperaments:** J, P, T • **Physical:** V=G, H=L, L=L, W, C, H • **Work Env:** I, R • **Salary:** 5 • **Outlook:** 3

MINE INSPECTOR (mining) • D.O.T. #168.267-074 • OES #21911 • CHECK VIEWER; SAFETY INSPECTOR. Inspects underground or open-pit mines to ascertain compliance with contractual agreements and with health and safety laws: Inspects for rotted or incorrectly placed timbers, dangerously placed or defective electrical and mechanical equipment, improperly stored explosives, and other hazardous conditions. Tests air quality to detect toxic or explosive gas or dust, using portable gas-analysis equipment, in order to control health hazards and to reduce injuries and fatalities. Observes mine activities to detect violations of Federal and State health and safety standards. Inspects mine workings to verify compliance with contractual agreements concerning production rates or mining within specified limits. May instruct mine workers in safety and first aid procedures. May be designated according to type of mine inspected as COAL-MINE INSPECTOR (mining & quarrying); METAL-MINE INSPECTOR (mining & quarrying). May specialize in inspection of specific conditions and be designated GAS INSPECTOR (mining & quarrying). When employed by governmental agency (instead of mine operator), conducts periodic mine inspections specifically to enforce Federal or State mining laws and is known as MINE INSPECTOR, FEDERAL (gov. ser.) or MINE INSPECTOR, STATE (gov. ser.). • **GED:** R4, M3, L4 • **SVP:** 1-2 yrs • **Academic:** Ed=H, Eng=S • **Work Field:** 271 • **MPSMS:** 369 • **Aptitudes:** G3, V3, N3, S3, P3, Q4, K4, F4, M4, E3, C4 • **Temperaments:** M, T • **Physical:** V=G, H=L, L=L, C, S • **Work Env:** B, R • **Salary:** 4 • **Outlook:** 3

OCCUPATIONAL-SAFETY-AND-HEALTH INSPECTOR (gov. ser.) • D.O.T. #168.167-062 • OES #21911 • OCCUPATIONAL-SAFETY-AND-HEALTH-COMPLIANCE OFFICER. Inspects places of employment to detect unsafe or unhealthy working conditions: Inspects work environment, machinery, and equipment in establishments and other worksites for conformance with governmental standards according to procedure or in response to complaint or accident. Interviews supervisors and employees to obtain facts about work practice or accident. Rates unsafe condition according to factors, such as severity of potential injury, likelihood of recurrence, employers' accident record, and evidence of voluntary compliance. Observes employees at work to determine compliance with safety precautions and safety equipment used. Orders suspension of activity posing threat to workers. Writes new safety order proposal designed to protect workers from work methods, processes, or other hazard not previously covered, using knowledge of safety-engineering practices, available protective devices, safety testing, and occupational safety and health standards. Discusses reason for inspection and penalty rating system with employer. Reviews log of reportable accidents and preventive actions taken to determine employers' attitude toward compliance with regulations. Documents findings and code sections violated. Interprets applicable laws and regulations to advise employer on legal requirements. May specialize in inspection of specific machine, apparatus, or device. May specialize in inspection of specific industry, such as construction, manufacturing, mining, petroleum, or transportation. May testify in legal proceedings. May photograph work environment suspected of endangering workers to provide evidence in legal proceedings. May include INDUSTRIAL HYGIENIST (profess. & kin.) in inspection party. • **GED:** R5, M5, L5 • **SVP:** 1-2 yrs • **Academic:** Ed=A, Eng=S • **Work Field:** 244, 271 • **MPSMS:** 712 • **Aptitudes:** G2, V2, N3, S3, P3, Q3, K4, F4, M4, E5, C4 • **Temperaments:** J, M, T • **Physical:** V=G, H=L, L=L, W, C, S, H • **Work Env:** B • **Salary:** 4 • **Outlook:** 3

PESTICIDE-CONTROL INSPECTOR (gov. ser.) • D.O.T. #168.267-098 • OES #21911 • Inspects operations of distributors and commercial applicators of pesticides to determine compliance with government regulations on handling, sale, and use of pesticides: Inspects premises of wholesale and retail distributors to ensure that registered pesticides are handled in accordance with State and Federal regulations. Determines that handlers possess permits and sell restricted pesticides only to authorized users. Evaluates pesticides for correct labeling, misbranding, misrepresentation, or adulteration, and confiscates or quarantines unacceptable pesticides. Inspects operations of commercial applicators of pesticides and observes application methods to ensure correct use of equipment, application procedures, and that applicators possess valid permits. Determines that accurate records are kept to show pesticides used, dosage, times, places, and methods of applications. Inspects premises to ensure that storage and disposal of pesticides conform to regulations. Investigates complaints concerning pesticides and uses. Identifies insect or disease, recommends treatment, and authorizes emergency use of suitable restricted pesticides to respond to emergency situations, such as insect infestations or outbreaks of plant disease. • **GED:** R4, M2, L3 • **SVP:** 2-4 yrs • **Academic:** Ed=H, Eng=S • **Work Field:** 271 • **MPSMS:** 953 • **Aptitudes:** G2, V2, N3, S4, P4, Q2, K4, F4, M4, E4, C4 • **Temperaments:** J, P • **Physical:** V=G, H=L, L=L, W, H • **Work Env:** I • **Salary:** 4 • **Outlook:** 3

PUBLIC HEALTH SERVICE OFFICER (gov. ser.) • D.O.T. #187.117-050 • OES #21911 • Administers public-health program of county or city: Inspects public facilities for health hazards or directs inspection by others. Negotiates with school, State, Federal, or other authorities and with community groups to formulate health standards and legislation affecting jurisdiction. Participates in establishing free clinics, cancer detection centers, and other programs to improve public health. Develops and coordinates public relations campaigns to promote programs and services and participates in radio and television discussions, public meetings, and other activities. Conducts examinations of hospitals, indigent care centers, and other institutions under control of municipality to ensure conformance to accepted standards. Prohibits sale of unsafe milk and other food and dairy products. May impose quarantines on area, animals, or persons with contagious disease. May order closing of establishments not conforming to prescribed health standards. • **GED:** R5, M5, L5 • **SVP:** 4-10 yrs • **Academic:** Ed=B, Eng=G • **Work Field:** 295 • **MPSMS:** 929 • **Aptitudes:** G1, V1, N2, S2, P2, Q3, K3, F4, M4, E4, C4 • **Temperaments:** D, M, P, V • **Stress:** E, A • **Physical:** V=L, H=L, L=S, W • **Work Env:** I • **Salary:** 5 • **Outlook:** 2

RADIATION-PROTECTION SPECIALIST (gov. ser.) • D.O.T. #168.261-010 • OES #21911 • Tests x-ray equipment, inspects areas where equipment is used, and evaluates operating procedures to detect and control radiation hazards: Visits hospitals, medical offices, and other establishments to test x-ray machines and fluoroscopes and to inspect premises. Tests equipment to determine that kilovolt potential, alignment of components, and other elements of equipment meet standards for safe operation, using specialized instruments and procedures. Operates equipment to determine need for calibration, repair, or replacement of tubes or other parts. Measures density of lead shielding in walls, using radiometric equipment. Computes cumulative radiation levels and refers to regulations to determine if amount of shielding is sufficient to absorb radiation emissions. Examines license of equipment operator for authenticity and observes operating practices to determine competence of operator to use equipment. Confers with physicians, dentists, and x-ray personnel to explain procedures and legal requirements pertaining to use of equipment. Demonstrates exposure techniques to improve procedures and minimize amount of radiation delivered to patient and operator. Reviews plans and specifications for proposed x-ray installations for conformance to legal requirements and radiation safety practices. Contacts organizations submitting inadequate specifications to explain changes in shielding or layout needed to conform to regulations. • **GED:** R5, M4, L5 • **SVP:** 4-10 yrs • **Academic:** Ed=A, Eng=G • **Work Field:** 211 • **MPSMS:** 953 • **Aptitudes:** G2, V2, N3, S2, P3, Q3, K3, F3, M3, E5, C3 • **Temperaments:** P, T • **Stress:** E • **Physical:** V=L, H=L, L=L, W, H • **Work Env:** I • **Salary:** 4 • **Outlook:** 2

REVIEWING OFFICER, DRIVER'S LICENSE (gov. ser.) • D.O.T. #168.167-074 • OES #21911 • Evaluates traffic record, and other aspects of driver's attitude and behavior to recommend suspension, revocation, or reinstatement of State operator's license: Reviews written record of driver, considering applicable laws and factors, such as number and nature of accidents, interval between accidents or convictions, driver's occupation, and number and gravity of traffic convictions, to evaluate driver's attitude and determine probability of repeated offenses. Recommends probation, suspension, or revocation of license, following rules, regulations, and policies of agency. Conducts hearings at request of persons whose licenses have been suspended or revoked to receive testimony and facts bearing on action. Receives petitions for reinstatement of licenses and approves or disapproves petitions according to evaluation of all pertinent facts. Confers with police and court officials to compile information, facilitate location or punishment of violators, and promote traffic safety. May allocate points for accidents or convictions and mail warnings to violators facing automatic penalties. • **GED:** R4, M3, L4 • **SVP:** 2-4 yrs • **Academic:** Ed=H, Eng=S • **Work Field:** 211, 271 • **MPSMS:** 959 • **Aptitudes:** G2, V2, N4, S4, P4, Q3, K4, F4, M4, E5, C5 • **Temperaments:** J, M, P • **Physical:** V=L, H=L, L=S • **Work Env:** I • **Salary:** 4 • **Outlook:** 3

SAFETY INSPECTOR (any ind.) • D.O.T. #168.264-014 • OES #21911 • SAFETY TECHNICIAN. Inspects machinery, equipment, and working conditions in industrial or other setting to ensure compliance with occupational safety and health regulations: Inspects machines and equipment for accident prevention devices. Observes workers to determine use of prescribed safety equipment, such as glasses, helmets, goggles, respirators, and clothing. Inspects specified areas for fire- prevention equipment and other safety and first-aid supplies. Tests working areas for noise, toxic, and other hazards, using decibel meter, gas detector, and light meter. Prepares report of findings with recommendations for corrective action. Investigates accidents to ascertain causes for use in recommending preventive safety measures and developing safety program. May demonstrate use of safety equipment. • **GED:** R4, M3, L4 • **SVP:** 1-2 yrs • **Academic:** Ed=A, Eng=G • **Work Field:** 211, 271 • **MPSMS:** 712 • **Aptitudes:** G3, V3, N3, S3, P3, Q4, K4, F4, M4, E5, C4 • **Temperaments:** J, M, P, T • **Stress:** E • **Physical:** V=G, H=L, L=L, W • **Work Env:** B • **Salary:** 4 • **Outlook:** 2

SAFETY INSPECTOR (insurance) • D.O.T. #168.167-078 • OES #21911 • LOSS-CONTROL TECHNICIAN; SAFETY ENGINEER. Inspects insured properties to evaluate physical conditions and promote safety programs: Inspects properties such as buildings, industrial operations, vehicles, and recreational facilities to evaluate physical conditions, safety practices, and hazardous situations according to knowledge of safety and casualty underwriting standards and governmental regulations. Measures insured area, calculates frontage, and records description and amount of stock, and photographs or drafts scale drawings of properties, to identify factors affecting insurance premiums. Analyzes history of accidents and claims against insured and inspects scenes of accidents to determine causes and to develop accident-prevention programs.

Prepares written report of findings and recommendations for correction of unsafe or unsanitary conditions. Confers with employees of insured to induce compliance with safety standards, codes, and regulations. Conducts informational meetings among various educational, civic, and industrial groups, to promote general safety concepts, utilizing audiovisual aids and insurance statistics. May specialize in specific type of accident- prevention or safety program, such as fire safety or traffic safety. • **GED:** R5, M4, L5 • **SVP:** 4-10 yrs • **Academic:** Ed=A, Eng=S • **Work Field:** 211, 271 • **MPSMS:** 895 • **Aptitudes:** G2, V2, N3, S3, P3, Q3, K4, F4, M4, E5, C4 • **Temperaments:** D, I, J, M, P • **Stress:** A • **Physical:** V=G, H=L, L=L, W, C, S • **Work Env:** B, R • **Salary:** 5 • **Outlook:** 3

SAFETY MANAGER (medical ser.) • D.O.T. #168.167-086 • OES #21911 • Plans, implements, coordinates, and assesses hospital accident, fire prevention, and occupational safety and health programs under general direction of hospital officials, utilizing knowledge of industrial safety-related engineering discipline and operating regulations: Develops and recommends new procedures and approaches to safety and loss prevention based on reports of incidents, accidents, and other data gathered from hospital personnel. Disseminates information to department heads and others regarding toxic substances, hazards, carcinogens, and other safety information. Assists department heads and administrators in enforcing safety regulations and codes. Measures and evaluates effectiveness of safety program, using established goals. Conducts building and grounds surveys on periodic and regular basis to detect code violations, hazards, and incorrect work practices and procedures. Develops and reviews safety training for hospital staff. Maintains administrative control of records related to safety and health programs. Prepares and disseminates memos and reports. Maintains required records. Assists personnel department in administering worker compensation program. • **GED:** R5, M5, L5 • **SVP:** 2-4 yrs • **Academic:** Ed=A, Eng=G • **Work Field:** 211, 295 • **MPSMS:** 704, 712 • **Aptitudes:** G2, V2, N2, S2, P2, Q2, K4, F4, M3, E5, C5 • **Temperaments:** D, I, J, P, V • **Stress:** E, A • **Physical:** V=L, H=L, L=S, W, H • **Work Env:** I • **Salary:** 4 • **Outlook:** 3

SANITARIAN (any ind.) • D.O.T. #529.137-014 • OES #81008 • SANITATION SUPERVISOR. Supervises and coordinates activities of workers engaged in duties concerned with sanitation programs in food processing establishment: Inspects products and equipment for conformity to sanitation laws and plant standards. Directs food handlers and production personnel in sanitary and pest- control procedures. Directs cleaning of equipment and work areas. Inspects premises for unsanitary practices and conditions. Examines incoming shipments of food ingredients for foreign matter, such as insects, poisons, or dirt, and gathers samples of ingredients for laboratory analysis. Confers with management and production personnel on sanitation problems and recommends changes in equipment, plant layout, lighting, ventilation, or work practices to improve sanitation standards and purity of product. Performs other duties as described under SUPERVISOR (any ind.). May be designated according to type of establishment as SUPERVISOR, BAKERY SANITATION (bake. prod.); SUPERVISOR, DAIRY SANITATION (dairy prod.). • **GED:** R4, M2, L3 • **SVP:** 2-4 yrs • **Academic:** Ed=N, Eng=G • **Work Field:** 031 • **MPSMS:** 380 • **Aptitudes:** G3, V3, N3, S3, P3, Q3, K4, F4, M3, E5, C5 • **Temperaments:** D, P, T • **Stress:** E, A • **Physical:** V=L, H=N, L=L, W, C, S, H • **Work Env:** I, W • **Salary:** 4 • **Outlook:** 2

SANITARIAN (profess. & kin.) • D.O.T. #079.117-018 • OES #21911 • Plans, develops, and executes environmental health program: Organizes and conducts training program in environmental health practices for schools and other groups. Determines and sets health and sanitation standards and enforces regulations concerned with food processing and serving, collection and disposal of solid wastes, sewage treatment and disposal, plumbing, vector control, recreational areas, hospitals and other institutions, noise, ventilation, air pollution, radiation, and other areas. Confers with government, community, industrial, civil defense, and private organizations to interpret and promote environmental health programs. Collaborates with other health personnel in epidemiological investigations and control. Advises civic and other officials in development of environmental health laws and regulations. •

GED: R6, M5, L6 • SVP: 4-10 yrs • Academic: Ed=B, Eng=G • Work Field: 293, 296 • MPSMS: 874 • Aptitudes: G2, V2, N3, S3, P3, Q4, K4, F4, M4, E5, C3 • Temperaments: D, M, T • Physical: V=L, H=L, L=M, W • Work Env: B, R • Salary: 5 • Outlook: 3

SANITATION INSPECTOR (gov. ser.) • D.O.T. #168.267-110 • OES #21911 • Inspects community land areas and investigates complaints concerning neglect of property and illegal dumping of refuse to ensure compliance with municipal code: Inspects designated areas periodically for evidence of neglect, excessive litter, and presence of unsightly or hazardous refuse. Interviews residents and inspects area to investigate reports of illegal dumping and neglected land. Locates property owners to explain nature of inspection and investigation findings and to encourage voluntary action to resolve problems. Studies laws and statutes in municipal code to determine specific nature of code violation and type of action to be taken. Issues notices of violation to land owners not complying with request for voluntary correction of problems. Issues notices of abatement to known violators of dumping regulations and informs other municipal agencies of need to post signs forbidding illegal dumping at designated sites. Prepares case materials when legal action is required to solve problems. Conducts informational meetings for residents, organizes neighborhood cleanup projects, and participates in campaigns to beautify city to promote community interest in eliminating dangerous and unsightly land use practices. • GED: R3, M2, L3 • SVP: 6 mos-1 yr • Aca demic: Ed=N, Eng=G • Work Field: 271 • MPSMS: 953 • Aptitudes: G3, V3, N4, S3, P4, Q3, K4, F4, M4, E5, C4 • Temperaments: I, J, P • Stress: E • Physical: V=G, H=N, L=S, W • Work Env: I • Salary: 3 • Outlook: 2

GOE: 11.10.04 Immigration & Customs

CUSTOMS IMPORT SPECIALIST (gov. ser.) • D.O.T. #168.267-018 • OES #21911 • CUSTOMS EXAMINER. Examines, classifies, and appraises imported merchandise according to Federal revenue laws, in order to enforce regulations of U. S. Customs Service: Examines and appraises merchandise and accompanying documentation according to import requirements, considering legal restrictions, country of origin, import quotas, and current market values. Requests laboratory testing and analyses of merchandise as needed. Determines duty and taxes to be paid on imported merchandise, considering its classification and value. Interviews importers and examines their records to verify integrity of invoices. Determines and reports evidence of intent to defraud and violations of trademark, copyright, and marking laws. Notifies other governmental agencies responsible for particular import inspection, or when apparent import violations concerns other agency regulations. Issues or denies permits to release imported merchandise for delivery, depending on importer's meeting legal requirements. Appraises seized and unclaimed merchandise to be sold at public auction. Assists Federal attorneys in preparation and trial of cases in Customs Court by supplying technical information and advice, securing qualified witnesses and evidence, and appearing as a government witness. May plan, coordinate, and evaluate work of import inspection team. May defend appraisal of merchandise during court appeals by importers. • GED: R5, M3, L5 • SVP: 4-10 yrs • Academic: Ed=A, Eng=S • Work Field: 211, 271 • MPSMS: 953 • Aptitudes: G2, V2, N3, S4, P2, Q3, K3, F3, M3, E4, C3 • Temperaments: J, M, P, T • Physical: V=G, H=L, L=L, H • Work Env: I • Salary: 5 • Outlook: 3

CUSTOMS INSPECTOR (gov. ser.) • D.O.T. #168.267-022 • OES #21911 • Inspects cargo, baggage, articles worn or carried by persons, and vessels, vehicles, or aircraft entering or leaving United States to enforce customs and related laws: Boards carriers arriving from foreign ports, and inspects and searches carriers to determine nature of cargoes. Superintends loading and unloading of cargo to ensure compliance with customs, neutrality, and commerce laws. Weighs, measures, and gages imported goods, using calipers, measuring rods, scale, and hydrometer. Examines baggage of passengers arriving from foreign territory to discover contraband or undeclared merchandise. Conducts body search of passengers or crew members. Questions suspicious persons to clarify irregularities and explains laws and regulations to tourists or others unfamiliar with customs statutes and procedures. Seals

hold and compartments containing sea stores (supplies for ship's personnel) to prevent illegal sale or smuggling of dutiable merchandise. Examines crew and passenger lists, manifests, pratiques, store lists, declarations of merchandise, and ships' documents and issues required permits. Classifies articles and assesses and collects duty on merchandise. Writes reports of findings, transactions, violations, and discrepancies. Seizes contraband and undeclared merchandise and detains or arrests persons involved in violations. May perform preliminary immigration screening of persons entering United States. May take samples of merchandise for appraising. May be designated according to type of inspection performed as BAGGAGE INSPECTOR (gov. ser.); BORDER INSPECTOR (gov. ser.); CARGO INSPECTOR (gov. ser.). • GED: R4, M4, L4 • SVP: 1-2 yrs • Academic: Ed=A, Eng=G • Work Field: 271 • MPSMS: 953 • Aptitudes: G2, V2, N2, S3, P3, Q2, K3, F3, M3, E3, C3 • Temperaments: J, M, P • Stress: E • Physical: V=G, H=L, L=L, W, C, S, H • Work Env: I • Salary: 4 • Outlook: 2

IMMIGRATION INSPECTOR (gov. ser.) • D.O.T. #168.167-022 • OES #21911 • Regulates entry of persons into United States at designated port of entry in accordance with immigration laws: Examines applications, visas, and passports and interviews persons to determine eligibility for admission, residence, and travel privileges in United States. Interprets laws and explains decisions to persons seeking entry. Arrests, detains, paroles, or arranges for deportation of persons according to laws, regulations, and departmental orders. Writes reports of activities and decisions. May patrol border on foot or horseback, or by airplane, automobile, or boat to detect and apprehend persons entering United States illegally and be designated IMMIGRATION PATROL INSPECTOR (gov. ser.). • GED: R4, M3, L4 • SVP: 6 mos-1 yr • Academic: Ed=A, Eng=G • Work Field: 271 • MPSMS: 953 • Aptitudes: G3, V2, N4, S4, P3, Q3, K4, F4, M4, E5, C4 • Temperaments: J, M, P • Stress: E • Physical: V=G, H=L, L=S, W, H • Work Env: B, R • Salary: 4 • Outlook: 2

GOE: 11.10.05 Company Policy

DEALER-COMPLIANCE REPRESENTATIVE (ret. tr.) • D.O.T. #168.267-026 • OES #21911 • FIELD REPRESENTATIVE. Inspects franchise dealerships and distributorships to ascertain compliance with company operating policies and procedures and to require adherence in detected instances: Inspects inventory and operating records to ascertain that only approved products are sold and approved operating procedures followed by dealer. Inspects premises and observes working conditions to ensure compliance with company and governmental standards of safety and sanitation. May ascertain that dealers are paying bills due company and may collect monies due. May advise dealers on financial aspects of operating franchise. • GED: R4, M3, L3 • SVP: 1-2 yrs • Academic: Ed=H, Eng=S • Work Field: 211 • MPSMS: 899 • Aptitudes: G3, V3, N3, S4, P4, Q3, K4, F4, M4, E4, C4 • Temperaments: J, M, P • Physical: V=G, H=L, L=L, W • Work Env: B • Salary: 4 • Outlook: 3

RATER, TRAVEL ACCOMMODATIONS (profess. & kin.) • D.O.T. #168.367-014 • OES #21911 • Inspects and evaluates travel and tourist accommodations in order to rate facilities to be listed in guidebook produced by employing organization, such as automobile club, tourism promoters, or travel guide publishers: Travels to and inspects travel accommodations and tourist facilities, such as hotels, motels, restaurants, campgrounds, vacation resorts, and other similar year-round or seasonal recreational establishments in order to observe conditions and gather data to be used in determining ratings. Rates or re-rates establishment according to predetermined standards concerning quantity and quality of such factors as convenience of location, variety of facilities available, degree of cleanliness maintained, efficiency of services offered, range of rates charged, and other matters of concern to travelers. Reports findings to employer by filling out forms containing ratings and reasons for conclusions and judgments. May sell to establishments concerned advertising space in publication (such as dining guide, tourist magazine, or recreational-area catalogs) in which ratings are to appear. • GED: R3, M3, L3 • SVP: 1-2 yrs • Academic: Ed=H, Eng=S • Work Field: 211 • MPSMS: 896 • Aptitudes: G3, V3, N4, S4, P4, Q4, K4, F4, M4, E4, C4 • Temperaments: D, J, M, P • Stress: A • Physical: V=G, H=L, L=L, W •

Work Env: B • **Salary:** 4 • **Outlook:** 3

REGULATORY ADMINISTRATOR (tel. & tel.) • D.O.T. #168.167-070 • OES #15023 • Directs and coordinates activities of workers engaged in investigating and responding to complaints from telephone subscribers or regulatory agencies concerning rates and services: Directs investigations of telephone company rates and services to ensure that subscribers' complaints are answered and requirements of governmental utility- regulation agencies are met. Analyzes reports of resulting data and recommends response to complaint, considering nature of complaint and company interests and policies. Directs preparation of documents for use by company witnesses summoned to testify at governmental hearings. Reviews governmental rulings to determine changes in legal stipulations and probable effects on company activities. May provide advice and source data to management personnel concerned with preparing applications to regulatory bodies for changes in rates or service. • **GED:** R5, M5, L5 • **SVP:** 4-10 yrs • **Academic:** Ed=B, Eng=S • **Work Field:** 271 • **MPSMS:** 861 • **Aptitudes:** G2, V2, N2, S4, P4, Q3, K4, F4, M4, E5, C5 • **Temperaments:** D, M, P • **Stress:** A • **Physical:** V=L, H=N, L=S • **Work Env:** I • **Salary:** 5 • **Outlook:** 1

TRAFFIC INSPECTOR (motor trans.) • D.O.T. #184.163-010 • OES #21911 • DISPATCHER; TRANSPORTATION INSPECTOR. Coordinates scheduled service within assigned territory of streetcar, bus, or railway transportation system: Periodically observes vehicles along route to ensure that service is provided according to schedule. Investigates schedule delays, accidents, equipment failures, and complaints, and files written report. Reports disruptions to service, using radiotelephone. Determines need for changes in service, such as additional coaches, route changes, and revised schedules to increase operating efficiency and improve service. Drives automobile along route to detect conditions hazardous to equipment and passengers, and negotiates with local government personnel to eliminate hazards. Assists in dispatching equipment when necessary. Recommends promotions and disciplinary actions involving transportation personnel. Inspects mechanical malfunctions of vehicles along route and directs repair. • **GED:** R4, M2, L3 • **SVP:** 2-4 yrs • **Academic:** Ed=H, Eng=S • **Work Field:** 013 • **MPSMS:** 850 • **Aptitudes:** G2, V2, N3, S4, P4, Q3, K4, F4, M4, E4, C4 • **Temperaments:** D, M, P, V • **Stress:** A • **Physical:** V=G, H=L, L=L • **Work Env:** O • **Salary:** 4 • **Outlook:** 3

TRANSPORTATION INSPECTOR (motor trans.) • D.O.T. #168.167-082 • OES #21911 • SERVICE INSPECTOR; UNDERCOVER AGENT. Compiles information concerning activities and conduct of employees on railroads, streetcars, and buses and submits written reports of findings: Observes employees performing assigned duties, assuming role of passenger to note their deportment, treatment of passengers, and adherence to company regulations and schedules. Observes and records time required to load and unload passengers or freight, volume of traffic at different stops or stations, and on streetcars and buses, at different times of day. Inspects company vehicles and other property for damage and evidence of abuse. Submits written reports to management with recommendations for improving service. • **GED:** R4, M3, L4 • **SVP:** 2-4 yrs • **Academic:** Ed=H, Eng=S • **Work Field:** 271 • **MPSMS:** 852 • **Aptitudes:** G3, V3, N3, S4, P4, Q3, K5, F4, M4, E5, C5 • **Temperaments:** J, M, V • **Physical:** V=G, H=G, L=L, W, H • **Work Env:** B • **Salary:** 4 • **Outlook:** 3

11.11 Business Management

Workers in this group manage a business, such as a store or cemetery, a branch of a large company, such as a local office for a credit corporation, or a department within a company, such as a warehouse. They usually carry out operating policies and procedures determined by administrative workers, such as presidents, vice-presidents and directors. Some managers own their own businesses and are considered self-employed. Managers find employment in all kinds of businesses as well as government agencies.

✔ **What kind of work would you do?**
Your work activities would depend upon your specific job. For example, you might:

- coordinate the disposal of surplus government property.
- manage a cemetery.
- manage a beauty or barber shop.
- prepare an operating budget for a freight terminal where ships or trucks are unloaded.

- determine the need for hiring additional employees for a hotel or motel.
- operate a branch store according to the policies set by the home office.
- oversee the operation of a recreation establishment, like a skating rink or golf club.

✔ **What skills and abilities do you need for this kind of work?**
To do this kind of work, you must be able to:

- read and interpret business records and statistical reports.
- use mathematical skills to interpret financial information and prepare budgets.
- analyze and interpret policies established by administrators.
- understand the government regulations covering business operations.

- make business decisions based on production reports and similar facts.
- make business decisions based on your own experience and personal opinions.
- see differences in widths and lengths of lines such as those on graphs.
- deal with the general public, customers, employees, union and government officials with tact and courtesy.

- plan and organize the work of others.
- change activity frequently and cope with interruptions.
- speak and write clearly.
- accept the full responsibility for managing an activity.

✔ **How do you know if you would like or could learn to do this kind of work?**
The following questions may give you clues about yourself as you consider this group of jobs.

- Have you been in charge of a committee or group activity? Were you able to get others to work well together?
- Have you been class president or treasurer of a club or group? Are you able to use judgment to make decisions?
- Have you planned and organized a project? Do you enjoy this type of activity?

✔ **How can you prepare for and enter this kind of work?**
Occupations in this group usually require education and/or training extending from one to over ten years, depending upon the specific kind of work. Nearly all the jobs in this group are entered by promotion or by transfer from related jobs. A college education is not always essential, but may be helpful. Employers usually require applicants to have a high school education or its equal, combined with experience. Experience requirements vary from one to ten years. For some jobs, experience is accepted as a substitute for a high school or college education.

✔ **What else should you consider about these jobs?**
Workers in this group often work more than a standard 40 hour week. They must vary work hours because of emergencies, accidents, or staff shortages. Workers usually are not paid for overtime.

If you think you would like to do this kind of work, look at the job titles listed on the following pages.

GOE: 11.11.01 Lodging, Management

CONDOMINIUM MANAGER (real estate) • D.O.T. #186.167-062 • OES #15011 • Manages condominium complex in accordance with homeowners' property management contract: Confers with representatives of homeowners' association or board of directors to review financial status of association and to determine management priorities. Directs collection of monthly assessments from residents and payment of incurred operating expenses. Directs maintenance staff in routine repair and maintenance of buildings and grounds of complex. Arranges for outside contractors to perform specified repairs. Investigates tenant complaints, such as utility malfunctions. Resolves complaints concerning other tenants or visitors. Prepares annual budget and activity reports and submits reports to association members. May assist elderly residents with essential tasks, such as food shopping. • **GED:** R4, M3, L4 • **SVP:** 2-4 yrs • **Academic:** Ed=H, Eng=G • **Work Field:** 295 • **MPSMS:** 893, 895 • **Aptitudes:** G2, V2, N3, S4, P3, Q2, K3, F4, M4, E5, C5 • **Temperaments:** D, J, P • **Stress:** E, A • **Physical:** V=L, H=L, L=S, W • **Work Env:** I • **Salary:** 2 • **Outlook:** 2

EXECUTIVE HOUSEKEEPER (hotel & rest.) • D.O.T. #187.167-046 • OES #15026 • HOUSEKEEPER, ADMINISTRATIVE; HOUSEKEEPER, HEAD. Directs institutional housekeeping program to ensure clean, orderly, and attractive conditions of establishment: Establishes standards and procedures for work of housekeeping staff, and plans work schedules to ensure adequate service. Inspects and evaluates physical condition of establishment, and submits to management recommendations for painting, repairs, furnishings, relocation of equipment, and reallocation of space. Periodically inventories supplies and equipment, and investigates new and improved cleaning instruments. Organizes and directs departmental training programs, resolves personnel problems, and hires new employees. Writes activity and personnel reports for review by management. Coordinates activities with those of other departments. May select and purchase new furnishings. May evaluate records to forecast department personnel requirements, and to prepare budget. • **GED:** R5, M4, L4 • **SVP:** 1-2 yrs • **Academic:** Ed=H, Eng=G • **Work Field:** 295 • **MPSMS:** 900 • **Aptitudes:** G2, V2, N3, S3, P3, Q3, K4, F4, M4, E5, C4 • **Temperaments:** D, M, P, V • **Stress:** E • **Physical:** V=L, H=L, L=L, W • **Work Env:** I • **Salary:** 4 • **Outlook:** 1

MANAGER, APARTMENT HOUSE (real estate) • D.O.T. #186.167-018 • OES #15011 • Manages apartment house complex or development for owners or property management firm: Shows prospective tenants apartments and explains occupancy terms. Rents or leases apartments, collects impounds as required, and completes lease form outlining conditions and terms of occupancy if lease required. Collects rents due and issues receipts. Investigates tenant complaints about malfunctions of utilities or furnished household appliances or goods, and inspects vacated apartments to determine needed repairs or maintenance. Directs and coordinates activities of maintenance staff to repair plumbing or electrical malfunctions, paint apartments or buildings, and to perform landscaping or gardening work, or arranges for outside personnel to perform maintenance. Endeavors to resolve tenant complaints concerning other tenants or visitors. May arrange for other services, such as fuel delivery or trash collection. • **GED:** R3, M3, L3 • **SVP:** 1-2 yrs • **Academic:** Ed=N, Eng=S • **Work Field:** 295 • **MPSMS:** 895 • **Aptitudes:** G3, V3, N3, S4, P4, Q3, K4, F4, M4, E4, C3 • **Temperaments:** J, M, V • **Stress:** A • **Physical:** V=G, H=L, L=L • **Work Env:** I • **Salary:** 4 • **Outlook:** 4

MANAGER, FRONT OFFICE (hotel & rest.) • D.O.T. #187.167-110 • OES #15026 • Coordinates front-office activities of hotel or motel and resolves problems arising from guests' complaints, reservation and room assignment activities, and unusual requests and inquiries: Assigns duties and shifts to workers and observes performances to ensure adherence to hotel policies and established operating procedures. Confers and cooperates with other department heads to ensure coordination of hotel activities. Answers inquiries pertaining to hotel policies and services. Greets important guests. Arranges for private telephone line and other special services. May patrol public rooms, investigate disturbances, and warn troublemakers. May interview and hire applicants. • **GED:** R4, M4, L4 • **SVP:** 1-2 yrs • **Academic:** Ed=H, Eng=G • **Work Field:** 295 • **MPSMS:** 902 • **Aptitudes:** G2, V2, N3, S4, P4, Q3, K4, F4, M4, E5, C5 • **Temperaments:** D, P, V • **Stress:** E, A • **Physical:** V=N, H=L, L=S • **Work Env:** I • **Salary:** 3 • **Outlook:** 3

MANAGER, HOTEL OR MOTEL (hotel & rest.) • D.O.T. #187.117-038 • OES #15026 • MANAGER, GENERAL; MANAGER, MOTOR HOTEL; MANAGER, MOTOR INN; MANAGER, RESIDENT. Manages hotel or motel to ensure efficient and profitable operation: Establishes standards for personnel administration and performance, service to patrons, room rates, advertising, publicity, credit, food selection and service, and type of patronage to be solicited. Plans dining room, bar, and banquet operations. Allocates funds, authorizes expenditures, and assists in planning budgets for departments. Hires personnel. Delegates authority and assigns responsibilities to department heads. In small motels or hotels, processes reservations and adjusts guests' complaints. • **GED:** R5, M5, L5 • **SVP:** 4-10 yrs • **Academic:** Ed=A, Eng=S • **Work Field:** 295 • **MPSMS:** 902 • **Aptitudes:** G2, V2, N2, S3, P3, Q3, K4, F4, M4, E5, C5 • **Temperaments:** D, J, P, V • **Stress:** A • **Physical:** V=L, H=L, L=S • **Work Env:** I • **Salary:** 5 • **Outlook:** 3

MANAGER, LODGING FACILITIES (hotel & rest.) • D.O.T. #320.137-014 • OES #15026 • Manages and maintains temporary or permanent lodging facilities, such as small apartment houses, motels, small hotels, trailer parks, and boat marinas: Shows and rents or assigns accommodations. Registers guests. Collects rents and records data pertaining to rent funds and expenditures. Resolves occupants' complaints. Purchases supplies and arranges for outside services, such as fuel delivery, laundry, maintenance and repair, and trash collection. Provides telephone answering service for tenants, delivers mail and packages, and answers inquiries concerning travel routes, recreational facilities, scenic attractions, and eating establishments. Cleans public areas, such as entrances, halls, and laundry rooms, and fires boilers. Makes minor electrical, plumbing, and structural repairs. Mows and waters lawns, and cultivates flower beds and shrubbery. Cleans accommodations after guests' departure. Provides daily maid service in overnight accommodations. May rent equipment, such as rowboats, water skis, and fishing tackle. May coordinate intramural activities of patrons of park. May arrange for medical aid for park patron. May sell light lunches, candy, tobacco, and other sundry items. May be designated according to type of establishment managed as MANAGER, APARTMENT HOUSE (hotel & rest.); MANAGER, HOTEL (hotel & rest.); MANAGER, MARINA (hotel & rest.); MANAGER, MOTEL (hotel & rest.); MANAGER, TOURIST CAMP (hotel & rest.); MANAGER, TRAILER PARK (hotel & rest.). • **GED:** R4, M3, L4 • **SVP:** 2-4 yrs • **Academic:** Ed=N, Eng=G • **Work Field:** 295 • **MPSMS:** 902 • **Aptitudes:** G3, V3, N3, S4, P4, Q3, K4, F4, M4, E4, C5 • **Temperaments:** D, P, V • **Stress:** E, A • **Physical:** V=N, H=N, L=M, H • **Work Env:** I • **Salary:** 4 • **Outlook:** 3

GOE: 11.11.02 Recreating & Amusement

DIRECTOR, CAMP (social ser.) • D.O.T. #195.167-018 • OES #19999 • Directs activities of recreation or youth work camp: Plans programs of recreational and educational activities. Hires and supervises camp staff. Arranges for required licenses, certificates, and insurance coverage to meet health, safety, and welfare standards for campers and for camp operation. Keeps records regarding finances, personnel actions, enrollments, and program activities related to camp business operations and budget allotments. • **GED:** R5, M4, L5 • **SVP:** 2-4 yrs • **Academic:** Ed=A, Eng=S • **Work Field:** 295 • **MPSMS:** 941 • **Aptitudes:** G2, V2, N2, S4, P4, Q4, K4, F4, M4, E5, C5 • **Temperaments:** D, P • **Stress:** A • **Physical:** V=G, H=L, L=S • **Work Env:** B • **Salary:** 4 • **Outlook:** 3

DIRECTOR, RECREATION CENTER (social ser.) • D.O.T. #195.167-026 • OES #19999 • Plans, organizes, and directs comprehensive public and voluntary recreation programs at recreation building, indoor center, playground, playfield, or day camp: Studies and analyzes recreational needs and resources. Oversees and assigns duties to staff. Interprets recreation programs and their philosophy to individuals and groups through personal participation and staff assignments. Schedules maintenance and use of facilities. Coordinates recreation program of host agency, such as settlement house, institution for children or aged, hospital, armed services, or penal institution, with related activity programs of other services or allied agencies. Cooperates with recreation and nonrecreation personnel. Works under direction of RECREATION SUPERVISOR (profess. & kin.). • **GED:** R5, M3, L5 • **SVP:** 2-4 yrs • **Academic:** Ed=A, Eng=S • **Work Field:** 295 • **MPSMS:** 941 • **Aptitudes:** G2, V2, N3, S4, P4, Q4, K4, F4, M4, E5, C5 • **Temperaments:** D, P • **Stress:** A • **Physical:** V=L, H=L, L=L • **Work Env:** B • **Salary:** 4 • **Outlook:** 3

MANAGER, BOWLING ALLEY (amuse. & rec.) • D.O.T. #187.167-222 • OES #19999 • Manages bowling alley: Directs activities of workers engaged in providing services to patrons and in maintaining facilities and equipment. Assigns alleys for use, issues score sheets, and pushes controls to actuate automatic game-scoring equipment. Records number of games played and collects payment. Inspects alleys to ensure equipment is operative and observes patrons to detect disruptive behavior and misuse of alleys and equipment. Rents bowling shoes to patrons. Organizes bowling leagues and informs members of league requirements. Prepares and distributes announcements of league activities, collects member fees, and distributes tournament prizes. May sell bowling equipment. May hire and train workers. • **GED:** R4, M2, L3 • **SVP:** 6 mos-1 yr • **Academic:** Ed=H, Eng=G • **Work Field:** 211, 295 • **MPSMS:** 914 • **Aptitudes:** G3, V2, N3, S3, P4, Q3, K4, F4, M4, E5, C5 • **Temperaments:** D, P, V • **Stress:** E, A • **Physical:** V=L, H=L, L=L, W, H • **Work Env:** I • **Salary:** 3 • **Outlook:** 3

MANAGER, GOLF CLUB (amuse. & rec.) • D.O.T. #187.167-114 • OES #19999 • Manages golf club to provide entertainment for patrons: Directs activities of dining room and kitchen workers and crews that maintain club buildings, equipment, and golf course in good condition. Hires and discharges workers. Estimates quantities and costs of foodstuffs, beverages, and groundskeeping equipment to prepare operating budget. Explains necessity of items on budget to board of directors and requests approval. Inspects club buildings, equipment, and golf course. Requisitions materials, such as foodstuffs, beverages, seeds, fertilizers, and groundskeeping equipment. Keeps accounts of receipts and expenditures. May assist in planning tournaments. • **GED:** R4, M4, L4 • **SVP:** 1-2 yrs • **Academic:** Ed=H, Eng=S • **Work Field:** 295 • **MPSMS:** 914 • **Aptitudes:** G2, V2, N2, S4, P4, Q2, K4, F4, M4, E5, C5 • **Temperaments:** D, J, P, V • **Stress:** A • **Physical:** V=L, H=L, L=S • **Work Env:** I • **Salary:** 4 • **Outlook:** 2

MANAGER, RECREATION ESTABLISHMENT (amuse. & rec.) • D.O.T. #187.117-042 • OES #19999 • Manages recreation establishment, such as dancehall, sports arena, or auditorium, to provide entertainment to public: Negotiates with promoters to contract and schedule entertainment. Compiles record of future engagements. Supervises clerical, service, and other employees. Hires and discharges workers. Complies with State and local fire and liquor regulations governing operation of establishment. May order supplies. May oversee workers engaged in keeping premises of establishment clean and in good repair. May be designated according to type of recreational facility directed as MANAGER, DANCE FLOOR (amuse. & rec.). • **GED:** R5, M4, L4 • **SVP:** 2-4 yrs • **Academic:** Ed=A, Eng=S • **Work Field:** 295 • **MPSMS:** 919 • **Aptitudes:** G2, V2, N3, S4, P4, Q3, K4, F4, M4, E5, C5 • **Temperaments:** D, P, V • **Stress:** A • **Physical:** V=L, H=L, L=L • **Work Env:** I • **Salary:** 4 • **Outlook:** 3

MANAGER, RECREATION FACILITY I (amuse. & rec.) • D.O.T. #187.167-230 • OES #19999 • Manages recreation facilities, such as tennis courts, golf courses, or arcade, and coordinates activities of workers engaged in providing services of facility: Determines work activities necessary to operate facility, hires workers, and assigns specific tasks and work hours, accordingly.

Initiates projects, such as promotional mailing or telephone campaigns, to acquaint public with activities of facility. Discusses fees of facility with interested persons. Registers patrons and explains rules and regulations. Confers with patrons to resolve grievances. Hires craftsmen, such as carpenters, plumbers, and electricians to make needed facility repairs. Maintains financial records. Collects coins from arcade machines. Purchases items such as golf balls, tennis balls, and paper supplies. • **GED:** R4, M3, L4 • **SVP:** 1-2 yrs • **Academic:** Ed=H, Eng=S • **Work Field:** 295 • **MPSMS:** 910 • **Aptitudes:** G2, V2, N3, S4, P4, Q3, K4, F4, M4, E5, C5 • **Temperaments:** D, P, V • **Stress:** A • **Physical:** V=L, H=G, L=L, W, H • **Work Env:** I • **Salary:** 4 • **Outlook:** 1

MANAGER, THEATER (amuse. & rec.) • D.O.T. #187.167-154 • OES #19999 • MANAGER, HOUSE. Manages theater for stage productions or motion pictures: Coordinates activities of personnel to ensure efficient operation and to promote patronage of theater. Directs workers in making alterations to and repair of building. Manages financial business of theater. Requisitions or purchases supplies. May book pictures or stage attractions designed to meet tastes of patrons. • **GED:** R4, M4, L4 • **SVP:** 2-4 yrs • **Academic:** Ed=H, Eng=S • **Work Field:** 295 • **MPSMS:** 910 • **Aptitudes:** G2, V2, N3, S4, P4, Q3, K4, F4, M4, E5, C5 • **Temperaments:** D, J, P • **Stress:** A • **Physical:** V=L, H=L, L=L • **Work Env:** I • **Salary:** 4 • **Outlook:** 3

GOE: 11.11.03 Transportation

CONDUCTOR, PASSENGER CAR (r.r. trans.) • D.O.T. #198.167-010 • OES #97302 • Coordinates activities of train crew engaged in transporting passengers on passenger train: Reads train orders, timetable schedules, and other written instructions received from TRAIN DISPATCHER (r.r. trans.) and discusses contents with LOCOMOTIVE ENGINEER (r.r. trans.) and train crew. Compares watch with that of LOCOMOTIVE ENGINEER (r.r. trans.) to ensure that departure time from station or terminal is in accordance with timetable schedules. Assists passengers to board train. Signals LOCOMOTIVE ENGINEER (r.r. trans.) to begin train run, using radiotelephone, giving hand signals, or by waving lantern. Collects tickets, fares, or passes from passengers. Answers passengers' questions concerning train rules and regulations and timetable schedules. Announces names of train stations and terminals to passengers. Supervises workers who inspect air brakes, airhoses, couplings, and journal boxes, and who regulate air conditioning, lighting, and heating, to ensure safety and comfort to passengers. Assists passengers to get off train at stations or terminals. Prepares reports at end of run to explain accidents, unscheduled stops, or delays. • **GED:** R4, M3, L4 • **SVP:** 4-10 yrs • **Academic:** Ed=H, Eng=G • **Work Field:** 013 • **MPSMS:** 851 • **Aptitudes:** G2, V2, N3, S4, P4, Q2, K3, F4, M4, E3, C4 • **Temperaments:** D, M, P, V • **Stress:** E, A • **Physical:** V=L, H=L, L=L, W, C, H • **Work Env:** B, N • **Salary:** 5 • **Outlook:** 1

CONDUCTOR, ROAD FREIGHT (r.r. trans.) • D.O.T. #198.167-018 • OES #97302 • Coordinates activities of train crew engaged in transporting freight on freight train: Reads train orders, schedules, and other written instructions received from TRAIN DISPATCHER (r.r. trans.) and discusses their contents with LOCOMOTIVE ENGINEER (r.r. trans.) and train crew. Inspects couplings and airhoses to ensure that they are securely fastened. Inspects journal boxes to ensure that they are lubricated. Inspects handbrakes on cars to ensure that they are released before train begins to run. Inspects freight cars to ensure that they are securely sealed. Records number of car and corresponding seal number and compares listing with waybill to ensure accuracy of routes and destinations. Compares watch with watch of LOCOMOTIVE ENGINEER (r.r. trans.) to ensure that departure time from station or terminal is in accordance with timetable schedules. Signals LOCOMOTIVE ENGINEER (r.r. trans.) via radiotelephone or by waving lantern to begin train run. Talks to LOCOMOTIVE ENGINEER (r.r. trans.) and traffic control center personnel via telephone during run to give or receive instructions or information concerning stops, delays, or oncoming trains. Instructs workers to set warning signals in front of and at rear of train during emergency stops to warn oncoming trains. Supervises workers engaged in inspection and maintenance of cars and mechanical equipment during run to ensure that train is operating efficiently and safely.

Records time of departures and arrivals at all destinations. Prepares reports at end of run to explain accidents, unscheduled stops or delays. • **GED:** R4, M3, L3 • **SVP:** 4-10 yrs • **Academic:** Ed=H, Eng=G • **Work Field:** 013 • **MPSMS:** 851 • **Aptitudes:** G3, V3, N4, S3, P4, Q3, K4, F4, M4, E3, C4 • **Temperaments:** D, M, P, T, V • **Stress:** E, A • **Physical:** V=L, H=L, L=L, W, C, H • **Work Env:** B, N • **Salary:** 5 • **Outlook:** 2

MANAGER, BUS TRANSPORTATION (motor trans.) • D.O.T. #184.167-054 • OES #15023 • Directs and coordinates activities of motor bus company to provide passengers with fast, efficient, and safe transportation, either performing following duties personally or through subordinate supervisory personnel: Applies for or recommends fare revisions, extension of routes, or changes in schedules in order to improve passenger services and increase revenues. Coordinates terminal and dispatching activities, communication operations, and assignment of driving personnel to obtain optimum use of facilities, equipment, and manpower. Inspects physical facilities of terminal and buses for such factors as cleanliness, safety, and appearance, and takes required actions in order to meet prescribed standards. Processes passenger complaints and initiates corrective actions designed to improve customer relations and services. Initiates investigations into causes of accidents, interviews operators concerned to determine responsibility, and takes actions on findings or submits reports to management. Directs preparation and issuance of new schedules to terminal and operating personnel. Dispatches replacement buses for vehicles involved in accidents and buses and operators for special charter or tours. Directs and participates in training of personnel and issues manuals, bulletins, and technical guides to improve services and operational activities. Reviews operator bids for routes to determine assignments for driving personnel. Checks trip and dispatch logs for conformance with schedules. Verifies cash fares with operator reports and reviews errors with personnel concerned. Directs preparation of and keeping of dispatch and vehicle operations records and reports. • **GED:** R4, M4, L4 • **SVP:** 4-10 yrs • **Academic:** Ed=H, Eng=S • **Work Field:** 295 • **MPSMS:** 852, 859 • **Aptitudes:** G2, V3, N3, S4, P4, Q3, K4, F4, M4, E5, C4 • **Temperaments:** D, P, V • **Stress:** A • **Physical:** V=G, H=L, L=S • **Work Env:** I • **Salary:** 5 • **Outlook:** 1

MANAGER, DISTRIBUTION WAREHOUSE (whole. tr.) • D.O.T. #185.167-018 • OES #41002 • Directs and coordinates activities of wholesaler's distribution warehouse: Reviews bills of lading for incoming merchandise and customer orders in order to plan work activities. Assigns workers to specific duties, such as verifying amounts of and storing incoming merchandise and assembling customer orders for delivery. Establishes operational procedures for verification of incoming and outgoing shipments, handling and disposition of merchandise, and keeping of warehouse inventory. Coordinates activities of distribution warehouse with activities of sales, record control, and purchasing departments to ensure availability of merchandise. Directs reclamation of damaged merchandise. • **GED:** R5, M3, L4 • **SVP:** 1-2 yrs • **Academic:** Ed=A, Eng=S • **Work Field:** 221, 295 • **MPSMS:** 853 • **Aptitudes:** G2, V2, N3, S4, P4, Q3, K4, F4, M4, E5, C5 • **Temperaments:** D, M, P, V • **Stress:** A • **Physical:** V=L, H=L, L=S, H • **Work Env:** I • **Salary:** 4 • **Outlook:** 2

MANAGER, TRAFFIC (air trans.) • D.O.T. #184.117-066 • OES #15023 • MANAGER, RATES AND SCHEDULES. Conducts studies on company freight and passenger classifications, rates, and tariffs and formulates changes required to provide for increased revenues and profitability of operations: Analyzes financial reports on operations and evaluates existing classifications, rates, and tariffs to determine changes required and need for expansion or curtailment of schedules and routes. Documents data to support proposals for increased revenues, expansion of schedules or routes, and files application for new rates, schedules, or routes with regulatory agencies. Testifies before regulatory agencies to present company's position and need for increased revenues in order to operate profitably. Negotiates with personnel of other transportation companies on division of interline revenues and signs contract on terms of agreement. Consults with officials of other companies on traffic movement problems, such as freight handling, transfer, and in-transit storage. Directs and coordinates activities of workers in classification of shipments and in applying and enforcing rates and tariffs. • **GED:** R5, M5, L5 • **SVP:** 4-10 yrs • **Academic:** Ed=A, Eng=S • **Work Field:** 295 • **MPSMS:** 850 • **Aptitudes:** G2, V2, N2, S4, P4, Q3, K4, F4, M4, E5, C5 • **Temperaments:** D, I, J, P, V • **Stress:** A • **Physical:** V=N, H=L, L=S • **Work Env:** I • **Salary:** 5 • **Outlook:** 1

MANAGER, WAREHOUSE (any ind.) • D.O.T. #184.167-114 • OES #15023 • STOREKEEPER; SUPERINTENDENT, STORAGE AREA; SUPERINTENDENT, WAREHOUSE. Directs warehousing activities for commercial or industrial establishment: Establishes operational procedures for activities, such as verification of incoming and outgoing shipments, handling and disposition of materials, and keeping warehouse inventory current. Inspects physical condition of warehouse and equipment and prepares work order for repairs and requisitions for replacement of equipment. Confers with department heads to ensure coordination of warehouse activities with activities, such as production, sales, records control, and purchasing. Screens and hires warehouse personnel and issues work assignments. Directs salvage of damaged or used material. May participate in planning personnel-safety and plant-protection activities. • **GED:** R5, M5, L4 • **SVP:** 4-10 yrs • **Academic:** Ed=A, Eng=S • **Work Field:** 221, 295 • **MPSMS:** 898 • **Aptitudes:** G2, V2, N2, S3, P4, Q4, K4, F4, M4, E5, C5 • **Temperaments:** D, P, V • **Stress:** A • **Physical:** V=G, H=L, L=S • **Work Env:** I • **Salary:** 5 • **Outlook:** 2

OPERATIONS MANAGER (motor trans.) • D.O.T. #184.167-118 • OES #15023 • Directs and coordinates activities of workers engaged in crating, moving, and storing household goods and furniture: Inspects warehouse facilities and equipment and recommends changes in allocation of space, and crating procedures to WAREHOUSE SUPERVISOR (motor trans.). Purchases moving equipment such as dollies, pads, trucks, and trailers. Plans pickup and delivery schedules for TRUCK DRIVERS, HEAVY (any ind.). Answers such inquiries as type of service offered, rates, schedules, and areas serviced. Examines items to be moved, to ascertain approximate weights and type of crating required. Investigates customers' complaints involving such matters as damaged items, overcharges, and delay in shipment, and makes necessary adjustment. Interviews, selects, trains, and assigns new personnel. May call on customers to solicit new business. May prepare cost estimates for clients. • **GED:** R4, M3, L3 • **SVP:** 1-2 yrs • **Academic:** Ed=H, Eng=S • **Work Field:** 221, 295 • **MPSMS:** 853 • **Aptitudes:** G3, V3, N3, S3, P3, Q3, K3, F4, M3, E3, C5 • **Temperaments:** D, J, M, P • **Stress:** A • **Physical:** V=G, H=G, L=L, W • **Work Env:** I • **Salary:** 4 • **Outlook:** 1

PURSER (water trans.) • D.O.T. #197.167-014 • OES #39999 • SHIP PURSER. Coordinates activities of workers aboard ship concerned with shipboard business functions and social activities for passengers: Prepares shipping articles and signs on crew. Maintains payroll records and pays off crews at completion of voyage. Submits passenger and crew sailing lists to governmental agencies as required by regulations. Assists passengers in preparing declarations for customs, arranging for inspections of horticultural items being brought into country, and inspection of documents by immigration authorities. Prepares ship's entrance and clearance papers for foreign ports, and ship's cargo manifests when discharging cargo. Supervises stowage, care, and removal of hold baggage. Arranges for travel and scenic tours at ports of call. Provides banking services and safekeeping of valuables for passengers. Supervises preparing, editing, printing, and distribution of ship's daily newspaper. Plans and conducts games, tournaments, and parties for passengers' enjoyment. May conduct religious services. May provide first aid for passengers and crew. • **GED:** R4, M3, L3 • **SVP:** 2-4 yrs • **Academic:** Ed=H, Eng=G • **Work Field:** 013, 232 • **MPSMS:** 854 • **Aptitudes:** G2, V2, N2, S4, P3, Q3, K4, F4, M4, E5, C5 • **Temperaments:** P, V • **Stress:** E • **Physical:** V=N, H=L, L=S, W, H • **Work Env:** I • **Salary:** 4 • **Outlook:** 2

STATION MANAGER (r.r. trans.) • D.O.T. #184.167-130 • OES #15023 • Directs and coordinates activities of railroad station employees and authorizes departure of trains: Notifies employees of changes in arrival and departure times of trains, boarding track numbers, and other information affecting passengers for announcement over loudspeaker and for posting on callboard. Ensures that shift workers and train crews report as scheduled, or

that replacements are obtained. Authorizes departure of passenger trains after transfer of mail and baggage is completed, delaying departure for arrival of connecting train if necessary. Authorizes repairs to station facilities and directs activities of custodial and maintenance workers. Investigates passenger service complaints to ensure efficient and courteous service. May negotiate with concessionaires to lease station space or facilities for restaurants, newsstands, advertising displays, and parking. • **GED:** R4, M3, L3 • **SVP:** 2-4 yrs • **Academic:** Ed=H, Eng=S • **Work Field:** 295 • **MPSMS:** 851 • **Aptitudes:** G2, V2, N3, S4, P4, Q3, K4, F4, M4, E5, C5 • **Temperaments:** D, P, T, V • **Stress:** A • **Physical:** V=L, H=L, L=L • **Work Env:** I • **Salary:** 4 • **Outlook:** 1

GOE: 11.11.04 Services, Business Management

DIRECTOR, FUNERAL (per. ser.) • D.O.T. #187.167-030 • OES #39011 • MANAGER, FUNERAL HOME; MORTICIAN; UNDERTAKER. Arranges and directs funeral services: Coordinates activities of workers to remove body to mortuary for embalming. Interviews family or other authorized person to arrange details, such as preparation of obituary notice, selection of urn or casket, determination of location and time of cremation or burial, selection of PALLBEARERS (per. ser.), procurement of official for religious rites, and transportation of mourners. Plans placement of casket in parlor or chapel and adjusts lights, fixtures, and floral displays. Directs PALLBEARERS (per. ser.) in placement and removal of casket from hearse. Closes casket and leads funeral cortege to church or burial site. Directs preparations and shipment of body for out of State burial. May prepare body for interment [EMBALMER (per. ser.)]. • **GED:** R4, M4, L4 • **SVP:** 2-4 yrs • **Academic:** Ed=A, Eng=G • **Work Field:** 291 • **MPSMS:** 909 • **Aptitudes:** G2, V2, N3, S3, P3, Q3, K4, F4, M4, E5, C4 • **Temperaments:** D, J, M, P, V • **Stress:** E • **Physical:** V=N, H=L, L=S, H • **Work Env:** B • **Salary:** 3 • **Outlook:** 1

GENERAL MANAGER, ROAD PRODUCTION (amuse. & rec.) • D.O.T. #187.117-034 • OES #19999 • Directs and coordinates activities concerned with setting up facility for performances of circus, ice skating show, rodeo, or similar touring road show: Plans layout of performance and backstage areas to conform with specification considering such factors, as type and space of facility. Negotiates with local renting agent to arrange personal space for entertainers and animals at each facility used on tour. Coordinates activities of various departments to ensure arrangements are made for providing water and feed for animals and disposal of rubbish and garbage, and to ensure that work crew has equipment and other facilities prepared for each performance. May count daily receipts and verify amount against number of tickets sold. May be designated according to type of show as SUPERINTENDENT, CIRCUS (amuse. & rec.). • **GED:** R4, M3, L5 • **SVP:** 4-10 yrs • **Academic:** Ed=H, Eng=S • **Work Field:** 295 • **MPSMS:** 919 • **Aptitudes:** G2, V2, N3, S3, P2, Q3, K4, F4, M4, E5, C5 • **Temperaments:** D, J, P, V • **Stress:** A • **Physical:** V=L, H=L, L=L • **Work Env:** I • **Salary:** 5 • **Outlook:** 1

MANAGER, BARBER OR BEAUTY SHOP (per. ser.) • D.O.T. #187.167-058 • OES #61099 • Manages business operations and directs personal service functions of barber or beauty shop: Confers with employees to ensure quality services for patrons, such as haircuts, facials, hair styling, shaves, massages, shampoos, and manicures. Makes appointments and assigns patrons to BARBERS (per. ser.) or COSMETOLOGIST (per. ser.) to maintain uniform employee schedules. Adjusts customer complaints and promotes new business by expressing personal interest in efficient service for patrons. Directs sanitary maintenance of shop in compliance with health regulations and requires cleanliness, neatness, and courtesy of employees. Negotiates leases and orders equipment and supplies. Keeps accounts of receipts and expenditures and makes up payroll. Performs services of BARBER (per. ser.) or COSMETOLOGIST (per. ser.) in addition to management functions. May supervise on-the-job training and school attendance of apprentice. May train apprentice and master barbers. May supervise MANICURIST (per. ser.); SHOE SHINER (per. ser.) and other workers. • **GED:** R4, M4, L4 • **SVP:** 2-4 yrs • **Academic:** Ed=H, Eng=S • **Work Field:** 291, 295 • **MPSMS:** 904 • **Aptitudes:** G3,

V3, N3, S3, P3, Q3, K4, F3, M3, E5, C4 • **Temperaments:** D, J, P, V • **Stress:** A • **Physical:** V=G, H=G, L=L, H • **Work Env:** I • **Salary:** 4 • **Outlook:** 2

MANAGER, EMPLOYMENT AGENCY (profess. & kin.) • D.O.T. #187.167-098 • OES #41002 • Manages employment services and business operations of private employment agency: Directs hiring, training, and evaluation of employees. Analyzes placement reports to determine effectiveness of EMPLOYMENT INTERVIEWERS (profess. & kin.). Participates in development and utilization of job development methods to promote business for agency. Enforces, through subordinate staff, agency policies, procedures, safety rules, and regulations. Approves or disapproves requests for purchase of new equipment and supplies. Ensures maintenance and repair of facilities and equipment. Prepares budget requests. Investigates and resolves customer complaints. May negotiate leases and order equipment and supplies for agency. • **GED:** R4, M3, L4 • **SVP:** 2-4 yrs • **Academic:** Ed=H, Eng=S • **Work Field:** 295 • **MPSMS:** 943 • **Aptitudes:** G2, V2, N3, S4, P4, Q3, K4, F4, M4, E5, C5 • **Temperaments:** D, J, V • **Stress:** A • **Physical:** V=N, H=L, L=S • **Work Env:** I • **Salary:** 4 • **Outlook:** 2

MANAGER, FAST FOOD SERVICES (ret. tr.) • D.O.T. #185.137-010 • OES #15026 • Manages franchised or independent fast food or wholesale prepared food establishment: Directs, coordinates, and participates in preparation of, and cooking, wrapping or packing types of food served or prepared by establishment, collecting of monies from in-house or take-out customers, or assembling food orders for wholesale customers. Coordinates activities of workers engaged in keeping business records, collecting and paying accounts, ordering or purchasing supplies, and delivery of foodstuffs to wholesale or retail customers. Interviews, hires, and trains personnel. May contact prospective wholesale customers, such as mobile food vendors, vending machine operators, bar and tavern owners, and institutional personnel, to promote sale of prepared foods, such as doughnuts, sandwiches, and specialty food items. May establish delivery routes and schedules for supplying wholesale customers. Workers are usually classified according to type or name of franchised establishment or type of prepared foodstuff retailed or wholesaled. • **GED:** R4, M4, L4 • **SVP:** 2-4 yrs • **Academic:** Ed=H, Eng=G • **Work Field:** 292, 295 • **MPSMS:** 881, 882 • **Aptitudes:** G3, V3, N3, S4, P3, Q3, K4, F4, M4, E5, C5 • **Temperaments:** D, J, P, V • **Stress:** E, A • **Physical:** V=L, H=L, L=L, W, H • **Work Env:** I • **Salary:** 4 • **Outlook:** 3

MANAGER, FOOD SERVICE (hotel & rest.) • D.O.T. #187.167-106 • OES #15026 • Coordinates food service activities of hotel, restaurant, or other similar establishment or at social functions: Estimates food and beverage costs and requisitions or purchases supplies. Confers with food preparation and other personnel to plan menus and related activities, such as dining room, bar, and banquet operations. Directs hiring and assignment of personnel. Investigates and resolves food quality and service complaints. May be designated according to type of establishment or specialty as CATERER (per. ser.); MANAGER, BANQUET (hotel & rest.); MANAGER, CAFETERIA OR LUNCHROOM (hotel & rest.); MANAGER, CATERING (hotel & rest.); MANAGER, FOOD AND BEVERAGE (hotel & rest.); MANAGER, RESTAURANT OR COFFEE SHOP (hotel & rest.). • **GED:** R4, M4, L4 • **SVP:** 2-4 yrs • **Academic:** Ed=H, Eng=G • **Work Field:** 295 • **MPSMS:** 903 • **Aptitudes:** G2, V2, N3, S4, P4, Q3, K4, F4, M4, E5, C4 • **Temperaments:** D, M, P, V • **Stress:** E, A • **Physical:** V=G, H=G, L=S, W, H • **Work Env:** I • **Salary:** 4 • **Outlook:** 5

MANAGER, PROPERTY (real estate) • D.O.T. #186.167-046 • OES #15011 • Manages commercial, industrial, or residential real estate properties for clients: Negotiates with client terms and conditions for providing management services, and drafts agreement stipulating extent and scope of management responsibilities, services to be performed, and costs for services. Prepares lease or rental agreements for lessees and collects specified rents and impounds. Directs bookkeeping functions, or credits client account for receipts and debits account for disbursements, such as mortgage, taxes, and insurance premium payments, management services costs, and upkeep and maintenance costs. Arranges for alterations to, or maintenance, upkeep, or reconditioning of property as specified in management services or lessee's agreement. Employs, or contracts for services of, security, maintenance, and

groundskeeping personnel and onsite management personnel if required. Purchases supplies and equipment for use on leased properties. Directs preparation of financial statements and reports on status of properties, such as occupancy rates and dates of expiration of leases. Directs issuance of check for monies due client. May advise client relative to financing, purchasing, or selling of property. Usually required to have real estate broker's license and be certified in property management. • **GED:** R5, M4, L4 • **SVP:** 4-10 yrs • **Academic:** Ed=A, Eng=S • **Work Field:** 232, 295 • **MPSMS:** 895 • **Aptitudes:** G2, V2, N3, S4, P4, Q3, K4, F4, M4, E5, C5 • **Temperaments:** D, P • **Stress:** A • **Physical:** V=L, H=L, L=L • **Work Env:** B • **Salary:** 5 • **Outlook:** 2

MANAGER, REAL-ESTATE FIRM (real estate) • D.O.T. #186.167-066 • OES #15011 • Directs and coordinates activities of sales staff for real estate firm: Screens and hires sales agents. Conducts training sessions to present and discuss sales techniques, ethics, and methods of maintaining sales quotas. Accompanies sales agents and clients to observe sales methods utilized, and counsels agents regarding matters, such as professionalism, financing, and sales closings. Confers with agents and clients to resolve problems, such as adjusting sales price, repairing property, or accepting closing costs. Sells or rents property for clients [SALES AGENT, REAL ESTATE (real estate) 250.357-018]. Manages residential and commercial properties for clients [MANAGER, PROPERTY (real estate) 186.167- 046]. May own real estate firm or be employed by nationwide franchise. • **GED:** R4, M3, L4 • **SVP:** 2-4 yrs • **Academic:** Ed=H, Eng=S • **Work Field:** 295 • **MPSMS:** 895 • **Aptitudes:** G2, V2, N2, S3, P3, Q3, K4, F4, M4, E4, C5 • **Temperaments:** D, I, J, P • **Stress:** A • **Physical:** V=L, H=G, L=S • **Work Env:** I • **Salary:** 4 • **Outlook:** 1

MANAGER, SALES (clean., dye., & press.) • D.O.T. #187.167-138 • OES #41002 • Manages sales functions of drycleaning establishment: Coordinates activities of SERVICE-ESTABLISHMENT ATTENDANT (clean., dye., & press.; laund.; per. ser.) and DRIVERS, SALES ROUTE (ret. tr.; whole. tr.). Visits customers to make estimates on proposed work, such as cleaning draperies, rugs, and upholstered furniture. Adjusts customers' complaints. Directs advertising and promotion campaigns. • **GED:** R4, M4, L4 • **SVP:** 2-4 yrs • **Academic:** Ed=H, Eng=S • **Work Field:** 291, 292 • **MPSMS:** 906 • **Aptitudes:** G2, V2, N3, S4, P4, Q4, K4, F5, M5, E5, C4 • **Temperaments:** D, J, M, P • **Stress:** A • **Physical:** V=G, H=L, L=L • **Work Env:** I • **Salary:** 4 • **Outlook:** 2

MANAGER, TOURING PRODUCTION (amuse. & rec.) • D.O.T. #191.117-038 • OES #39999 • MANAGER, THEATRICAL PRODUCTION; MANAGER, TOURING. Travels with and manages business affairs of theatrical company on tour: Completes various arrangements, such as contracting union agreements, hiring stage hands, and procuring legal permits for performance. Approves budgetary items for advertising and promotional purposes. Audits box-office receipts and files accounting statements according to legal requirements. May compile payroll records and distribute paychecks. When coordinating business affairs of first touring company on road, may be designated as COMPANY MANAGER (amuse. & rec.). When managing second and third road show companies, may be designated as ROAD MANAGER (amuse. & rec.). • **GED:** R4, M3, L4 • **SVP:** 2-4 yrs • **Academic:** Ed=H, Eng=S • **Work Field:** 295 • **MPSMS:** 910 • **Aptitudes:** G3, V3, N3, S4, P4, Q3, K4, F4, M4, E5, C5 • **Temperaments:** D, J, P, V • **Stress:** A • **Physical:** V=G, H=G, L=S • **Work Env:** I • **Salary:** 4 • **Outlook:** 1

MANAGER, TRAVEL AGENCY (bus. ser.) • D.O.T. #187.167-158 • OES #19999 • Manages travel agency: Directs, coordinates, and participates in merchandising travel agency services, such as sale of transportation company carrier tickets, packaged or specialized tours, or vacation packages. Plans work schedules for employees. Trains employees in advising customers on current traveling conditions, planning customer travel and itineraries, ticketing and booking functions, and in calculating costs for transportation and accommodations from current transportation schedules and tariff books and accommodation rate books. Sells travel tickets, packaged and specialized tours, and advises customers on travel plans. Reviews employee ticketing and sales activities to ensure cost calculations, booking, and transportation scheduling are in accordance with current transportation carrier schedules, tariff rates, and regulations and that charges are made for accommodations. Reconciles sales slips and cash daily. Coordinates sales promotion activities, approves advertising copy, and travel display work. Keeps employee records and hires and discharges employees. • **GED:** R4, M4, L4 • **SVP:** 2-4 yrs • **Academic:** Ed=H, Eng=S • **Work Field:** 295 • **MPSMS:** 850 • **Aptitudes:** G3, V3, N3, S4, P4, Q3, K4, F4, M4, E5, C4 • **Temperaments:** D, J, P, V • **Stress:** A • **Physical:** V=L, H=L, L=L, H • **Work Env:** I • **Salary:** 4 • **Outlook:** 1

GOE: 11.11.05 Wholesale-Retail Management

COMMISSARY MANAGER (any ind.) • D.O.T. #185.167-010 • OES #41002 • Directs and coordinates activities of commissary store to sell to or provide company employees or other eligible customers with foodstuffs, clothing, or other merchandise: Determines quantities of foodstuffs or other merchandise required to stock commissary, from inventory records, and prepares requisitions or buys merchandise to replenish stock. Sells merchandise to company employees or other eligible customers or issues merchandise upon requisition by authorized personnel. Keeps records pertaining to purchases, sales, and requisitions. May issue foodstuffs and supplies to COOKS, CAMP (any ind.) for preparation of meals. • **GED:** R4, M4, L3 • **SVP:** 1-2 yrs • **Academic:** Ed=H, Eng=S • **Work Field:** 292 • **MPSMS:** 380, 390 • **Aptitudes:** G2, V3, N3, S4, P4, Q3, K4, F4, M4, E5, C5 • **Temperaments:** D, P, V • **Stress:** A • **Physical:** V=L, H=L, L=L, S • **Work Env:** I • **Salary:** 4 • **Outlook:** 2

MANAGER, AUTOMOBILE SERVICE STATION (ret. tr.) • D.O.T. #185.167-014 • OES #41002 • Manages automobile service station: Plans, develops, and implements policies for operating station, such as hours of operation, workers required and duties, scope of operations, and prices for products and services. Hires and trains workers, prepares work schedules, and assigns workers to specific duties, such as customer service, automobile maintenance, or repair work. Directs, coordinates, and participates in performing customer service activities, such as pumping gasoline, checking engine oil, tires, battery, and washing windows and windshield. Notifies customer when oil is dirty or low, tires are worn, hoses or fanbelts defective, or evidences indicates battery defects, to promote sale of products and services, such as oil change and lubrication, tires, battery, or other automotive accessories. Reconciles cash with gasoline pump meter readings, sales slips, and credit card charges. Orders, receives, and inventories gasoline, oil, automotive accessories and parts. May perform automotive maintenance and repair work, such as adjusting or relining brakes, motor tune- ups, valve grinding, and changing and repairing tires. May sell only gasoline and oil on self-service basis and be designated as MANAGER, SELF-SERVICE GASOLINE STATION (ret. tr.), if owner- manager of station or independent dealer is designated as PROPRIETOR-MANAGER, RETAIL AUTOMOTIVE SERVICE (ret. tr.). • **GED:** R4, M4, L4 • **SVP:** 2-4 yrs • **Academic:** Ed=H, Eng=S • **Work Field:** 292, 295 • **MPSMS:** 881 • **Aptitudes:** G3, V3, N3, S3, P3, Q3, K3, F3, M3, E4, C3 • **Temperaments:** D, M, P, V • **Stress:** A • **Physical:** V=G, H=G, L=L, W, H • **Work Env:** B • **Salary:** 4 • **Outlook:** 2

MANAGER, DEPARTMENT (ret. tr.) • D.O.T. #299.137-010 • OES #41002 • DEPARTMENT SUPERVISOR; MANAGER, FLOOR. Supervises and coordinates activities of workers in one department of retail store: Assigns duties to workers and schedules lunch and break periods, work hours, and vacations. Trains workers in store policies, department procedures, and job duties. Assists sales workers in completing difficult sales. Evaluates worker performance and recommends retention, transfer, or dismissal of worker. Listens to customer complaints, examines returned merchandise, and attempts to resolve problem and restore and promote good public relations. Orders merchandise, supplies, and equipment, as necessary. Ensures that merchandise is correctly priced and displayed. Prepares sales and inventory reports. May approve checks for payment of merchandise and issue credit or cash refund on returned merchandise. May suggest purchase of merchandise for department. May plan department layout or merchandise or advertising display [DISPLAYER, MERCHANDISE (ret. tr.)]. May

install and remove department cash-register-receipt tape and audit cash receipts. May be designated according to department managed or type of merchandise sold as CANDY-DEPARTMENT MANAGER (ret. tr.); TOY-DEPARTMENT MANAGER (ret. tr.); PRODUCE-DEPARTMENT MANAGER (ret. tr.). • **GED:** R4, M3, L4 • **SVP:** 1-2 yrs • **Academic:** Ed=H, Eng=S • **Work Field:** 292 • **MPSMS:** 881 • **Aptitudes:** G2, V2, N3, S4, P3, Q3, K4, F4, M4, E5, C4 • **Temperaments:** D, J, P, V • **Stress:** A • **Physical:** V=L, H=L, L=L • **Work Env:** I • **Salary:** 4 • **Outlook:** 1

MANAGER, MACHINERY-OR-EQUIPMENT, RENTAL AND LEASING (any ind.) • D.O.T. #185.167-026 • OES #41002 • Directs and coordinates activities of establishment engaged in renting or leasing machinery, tools and equipment to companies involved in business operations such as manufacturing, petroleum production, construction or materials handling, or to individuals for personal use: Confers with customer to ascertain article required, duration of rental time, and responsibility for maintenance and repair, in order to determine rental or leasing charges based on such factors as type and cost of article, type of usage, duration of rental or lease, and overhead costs. Prepares rental or lease agreement, specifying charges and payment procedures, for use of machinery, tools, or equipment. Directs activities of workers engaged in bookkeeping, record and inventory keeping, and in checking, handling, servicing or maintaining in-house, leased, or rented machines, tools and equipment. Managers of leasing or renting establishments may be designated according to type or use of machinery, tools or equipment. • **GED:** R4, M4, L4 • **SVP:** 1-2 yrs • **Academic:** Ed=H, Eng=S • **Work Field:** 292 • **MPSMS:** 567, 568, 571 • **Aptitudes:** G3, V3, N3, S4, P4, Q4, K4, F4, M4, E5, C5 • **Temperaments:** D, P • **Stress:** A • **Physical:** V=L, H=G, L=L • **Work Env:** I • **Salary:** 4 • **Outlook:** 1

MANAGER, MARKET (ret. tr.) • D.O.T. #186.167-042 • OES #15011 • Directs and coordinates activities of municipal, regional, or state fruit, vegetable, or meat market or exchange: Negotiates contracts between wholesalers and market authority or rents space to food buyers and sellers. Directs through subordinate supervisory personnel collection of fees or monies due market, maintenance and cleaning of buildings and grounds, and enforcement of market sanitation and security rules and regulations. Keeps records of current sales prices of food items and total sales volume. May endeavor to resolve differences arising between buyers and sellers. May prepare market activity reports for management or board. • **GED:** R4, M3, L3 • **SVP:** 2-4 yrs • **Academic:** Ed=H, Eng=S • **Work Field:** 292 • **MPSMS:** 880 • **Aptitudes:** G2, V2, N3, S3, P4, Q3, K4, F4, M4, E5, C5 • **Temperaments:** D, J, P • **Stress:** A • **Physical:** V=N, H=L, L=S • **Work Env:** I • **Salary:** 4 • **Outlook:** 2

MANAGER, MEAT SALES AND STORAGE (ret. tr.) • D.O.T. #185.167-030 • OES #41002 • Coordinates activities of workers engaged in buying, processing, and selling meats and poultry and renting frozen food lockers: Prepares daily schedule and directs activities of employees. Examines products bought for resale or received for storage. Cuts, trims, bones, and cleans meats and poultry. Displays and sells different cuts of meats and poultry to customers and advises customers on quality of food, method of handling, and other factors affecting preparing, freezing, and storing food. Conducts in-service training for employees. • **GED:** R4, M3, L3 • **SVP:** 1-2 yrs • **Academic:** Ed=H, Eng=S • **Work Field:** 292 • **MPSMS:** 382, 853 • **Aptitudes:** G3, V3, N3, S3, P3, Q3, K3, F4, M3, E5, C3 • **Temperaments:** D, J, P • **Stress:** A • **Physical:** V=L, H=L, L=M, H • **Work Env:** I, C • **Salary:** 4 • **Outlook:** 1

MANAGER, PARTS (ret. tr.) • D.O.T. #185.167-038 • OES #41002 • MANAGER, STOCKROOM. Manages retail or wholesale automotive parts establishment or department of repair shop or service station: Requisitions new stock. Verifies cash receipts and keeps sales records. Hires, trains, and discharges workers. Confirms credit references of customers by mail or telephone. May sell parts. • **GED:** R4, M3, L3 • **SVP:** 2-4 yrs • **Academic:** Ed=H, Eng=S • **Work Field:** 292 • **MPSMS:** 591 • **Aptitudes:** G2, V2, N3, S4, P3, Q4, K4, F4, M4, E5, C4 • **Temperaments:** D, P • **Stress:** A • **Physical:** V=L, H=G, L=L, W • **Work Env:** I • **Salary:** 4 • **Outlook:** 2

MANAGER, RETAIL STORE (ret. tr.) • D.O.T. #185.167-046 •

OES #41002 • Manages retail store engaged in selling specific line of merchandise, as groceries, meat, liquor, apparel, jewelry, or furniture; related lines of merchandise, as radios, televisions, and household appliances; or general line of merchandise, performing following duties personally or supervising employees performing duties: Plans and prepares work schedules and assigns employees to specific duties. Formulates pricing policies on merchandise according to requirements for profitability of store operations. Coordinates sales promotion activities and prepares, or directs workers preparing, merchandise displays and advertising copy. Supervises employees engaged in, or performs, sales work, taking of inventories, reconciling cash with sales receipts, keeping operating records, or preparing daily record of transactions for ACCOUNTANT (profess. & kin.). Orders merchandise or prepares requisitions to replenish merchandise on hand. Ensures compliance of employees with established security, sales, and record keeping procedures and practices. Workers managing retail stores are classified according to specific line of merchandise sold, as women's apparel or furniture; related lines of merchandise, as camera and photographic supplies, or gifts, novelties, and souvenirs; type of business, as mail order establishment or auto supply house; or general line of merchandise carried, as sporting goods, drugs and sundries, or variety store. • **GED:** R4, M4, L3 • **SVP:** 2-4 yrs • **Academic:** Ed=H, Eng=G • **Work Field:** 292 • **MPSMS:** 881 • **Aptitudes:** G2, V2, N3, S4, P3, Q3, K4, F4, M4, E5, C5 • **Temperaments:** D, P • **Stress:** E, A • **Physical:** V=N, H=L, L=S, W, H • **Work Env:** I • **Salary:** 4 • **Outlook:** 2

MANAGER, VEHICLE LEASING AND RENTAL (auto. ser.) • D.O.T. #187.167-162 • OES #13011 • Manages automobile and truck leasing business: Directs and evaluates leasing, sales, advertising, and administrative procedures, including collections, inventory financing, and used car sales. Directs and monitors audit of financial accounts to assure compliance with prescribed standards. May visit franchised dealers to stimulate interest in establishment or expansion of leasing programs. • **GED:** R5, M4, L4 • **SVP:** 4-10 yrs • **Academic:** Ed=A, Eng=S • **Work Field:** 295 • **MPSMS:** 859 • **Aptitudes:** G2, V3, N3, S4, P4, Q3, K4, F5, M4, E5, C5 • **Temperaments:** D, I, M, V • **Stress:** A • **Physical:** V=L, H=L, L=L • **Work Env:** I • **Salary:** 5 • **Outlook:** 2

SERVICE SUPERVISOR, LEASED MACHINERY AND EQUIPMENT (any ind.) • D.O.T. #183.167-030 • OES #19999 • Directs and coordinates activities of service department of establishment concerned with providing lessers of machinery and equipment with maintenance and repair services as stipulated in leasing contract: Organizes field service offices and facilities in locations that will provide greatest number of customers with services. Stocks offices with spare parts and supplies to enable offices to provide required services. May arrange for transportation of machinery to and from customer's establishment when repairs cannot be performed on site. May contact potential customers concerning leasing of machinery and equipment. May negotiate leasing and service contracts for machinery and equipment. • **GED:** R4, M4, L4 • **SVP:** 2-4 yrs • **Academic:** Ed=H, Eng=S • **Work Field:** 111, 121 • **MPSMS:** 568, 571, 580 • **Aptitudes:** G2, V2, N3, S3, P3, Q3, K4, F4, M4, E5, C5 • **Temperaments:** D, P, V • **Stress:** A • **Physical:** V=L, H=L, L=L • **Work Env:** I • **Salary:** 4 • **Outlook:** 1

11.12 Contracts and Claims

Workers in this group negotiate contracts and settle claims for companies and individuals. Some make arrangements for agreements between buyers and sellers. Others investigate claims involving damage, injury, and losses. Jobs are found in insurance and transportation companies; businesses; construction companies; and government agencies. Some are found in booking agencies. These agents are frequently self-employed.

✔ **What kind of work would you do?**
Your work activities would depend upon your specific job. For example, you might:

- interview property holders and settle damage claims resulting from prospecting or drilling for oil.
- negotiate with communities to rent a site for circus.
- negotiate leases for the use of a city arena or auditorium.

- arrange leases of sites for billboards.
- arrange contracts for the appearance of musicians for a concert or show.
- serve as agent for artists, musicians, or actors and negotiate bookings for them.

✔ **What skills and abilities do you need for this kind of work?**
To do this kind of work, you must be able to:

- understand laws used in writing contracts and settling claims.
- compute costs and prepare cost estimates.
- understand detailed legal information.
- persuade others to agree to terms.
- speak clearly to avoid misunderstandings.

- use your experience and judgment to make decisions.
- work with all kinds of people.
- make decisions based on repair estimates, doctors' statements, and other verifiable information.
- keep accurate records and write detailed reports.

✔ **How do you know if you would like or could learn to do this kind of work?**

The following questions may give you clues about yourself as you consider this group of jobs.

- Have you taken courses in business law? Did you understand the special concepts and terms used in the course?
- Have you argued a point of view in front of a group? Are you persuasive and able to gain the respect and confidence of others?

- Have you helped arrange for a group to entertain at a school or community function? Were the arrangements understood by all parties?

✔ **How can you prepare for and enter this kind of work?**

Occupations in this group usually require education and/or training extending from two to over ten years, depending upon the specific kind of work. Most jobs in this group require experience in insurance, real estate, and labor relations. Community colleges offer courses in some of these fields. The type and amount of education required varies among the jobs. Some require four or more years of college or university study.

✔ **What else should you consider about these jobs?**

Some jobs in this group require workers to travel frequently. Pay may be based on salary, commission, or a combination of the two. A civil service examination is usually required for jobs in government.

If you think you would like to do this kind of work, look at the job titles listed on the following pages.

GOE: 11.12.01 Claims Settlement

APPRAISER, AUTOMOBILE DAMAGE (bus. ser.) • D.O.T. #241.267-014 • OES #53305 • AUTOMOBILE-DAMAGE APPRAISER; ESTIMATOR, AUTOMOBILE DAMAGE. Appraises automobile or other vehicle damage to determine cost of repair for insurance claim settlement and attempts to secure agreement with automobile repair shop on cost of repair: Examines damaged vehicle to determine extent of structural, body, mechanical, electrical, or interior damage. Estimates cost of labor and parts to repair or replace each item of damage, using standard automotive labor and parts cost manuals and knowledge of automotive repair. Determines salvage value on total-loss vehicle. Evaluates practicality of repair as opposed to payment of market value of vehicle before accident. Prepares insurance forms to indicate repair-cost estimates and recommendations. Reviews repair-cost estimates with automobile-repair shop to secure agreement on cost of repairs. Occasionally arranges to have damage appraised by another appraiser to resolve disagreement with repair shop on repair cost. • **GED:** R4, M2, L4 • **SVP:** 2-4 yrs • **Academic:** Ed=H, Eng=G • **Work Field:** 121, 211 • **MPSMS:** 961 • **Aptitudes:** G3, V3, N3, S3, P2, Q3, K4, F4, M4, E5, C5 • **Temperaments:** J, M, P • **Stress:** E • **Physical:** V=L, H=L, L=S, W • **Work Env:** B • **Salary:** 4 • **Outlook:** 4

CLAIM ADJUSTER (bus. ser.) • D.O.T. #241.217-010 • OES #53302 • INSURANCE ADJUSTOR; INSURANCE-CLAIM REPRESENTATIVE; INSURANCE INVESTIGATOR. Investigates claims against insurance or other companies for personal, casualty, or property loss or damages and attempts to effect out-of-court settlement with claimant: Examines claim form and other records to determine insurance coverage. Interviews, telephones, or corresponds with claimant and witnesses; consults police and hospital records; and inspects property damage to determine extent of company's liability, varying method of investigation according to type of insurance. Prepares report of findings and negotiates settlement with claimant. Recommends litigation by legal department when settlement cannot be negotiated. May attend litigation hearings. May be designated according to type of claim adjusted

as AUTOMOBILE-INSURANCE-CLAIM ADJUSTER (bus. ser.; insurance); CASUALTY-INSURANCE-CLAIM ADJUSTER (clerical); FIDELITY-AND-SURETY-BONDS-CLAIM ADJUSTER (bus. ser.; insurance); FIRE-INSURANCE-CLAIM ADJUSTER (bus. ser.; insurance); MARINE-INSURANCE-CLAIM ADJUSTER (bus. ser.; insurance); PROPERTY-LOSS-INSURANCE-CLAIM ADJUSTER (clerical). • **GED:** R5, M3, L5 • **SVP:** 1-2 yrs • **Academic:** Ed=H, Eng=G • **Work Field:** 271 • **MPSMS:** 895 • **Aptitudes:** G2, V2, N3, S3, P3, Q2, K4, F4, M4, E5, C5 • **Temperaments:** I, J, M, P • **Stress:** E • **Physical:** V=N, H=L, L=S, W • **Work Env:** B • **Salary:** 4 • **Outlook:** 3

CLAIM EXAMINER (bus. ser.) • D.O.T. #241.267-018 • OES #53302 • INSURANCE-CLAIM AUDITOR; INSURANCE-CLAIM APPROVER. Analyzes insurance claims to determine extent of insurance carrier's liability and settles claims with claimants in accordance with policy provisions: Compares data on claim application, death certificate, or physician's statement with policy file and other company records to ascertain completeness and validity of claim. Corresponds with agents and claimants or interviews them in person to correct errors or omissions on claim forms, and to investigate questionable entries. Pays claimant amount due. Refers most questionable claims to INVESTIGATOR (clerical) or to CLAIM ADJUSTER (bus. ser.; insurance) for investigation and settlement. May investigate claims in field. May be designated according to type of claim handled as ACCIDENT-AND-HEALTH-INSURANCE-CLAIM EXAMINER (insurance); AUTOMOBILE-INSURANCE-CLAIM EXAMINER (bus. ser.; insurance); DEATH-CLAIM EXAMINER (insurance); DISABILITY- INSURANCE-CLAIM EXAMINER (insurance); FIRE-INSURANCE-CLAIM EXAMINER (bus. ser.; insurance); MARINE-INSURANCE-CLAIM EXAMINER (bus. ser.; insurance). • **GED:** R4, M3, L4 • **SVP:** 2-4 yrs • **Academic:** Ed=H, Eng=G • **Work Field:** 271 • **MPSMS:** 895 • **Aptitudes:** G2, V2, N3, S4, P4, Q2, K4, F4, M4, E5, C5 • **Temperaments:** M, P • **Stress:** E • **Physical:** V=G, H=L, L=S, H • **Work Env:** I • **Salary:** 3 • **Outlook:** 3

CLAIMS ADJUDICATOR (gov. ser.) • D.O.T. #169.267-010 • OES #28105 • Adjudicates claims for benefits offered under governmental social insurance program, such as those dealing with unemployed, retired, or disabled workers, veterans, dependents, or survivors: Reviews and evaluates data on documents and forms, such as claim applications, birth or death certificates, physician's statements, employer's records, vocational evaluation reports, and other similar records. Interviews or corresponds with claimants or agents to elicit information, correct errors or omissions on claim forms, and to investigate questionable data. Authorizes payment of valid claims, or notifies claimant of denied claim and appeal rights. Reevaluates evidence and procures additional information in connection with claims under appeal or in cases requiring investigation of claimant's continuing eligibility for benefits. Prepares written reports of findings. May specialize in one phase of claim program, such as assisting claimant to prepare forms, rating degree of disability, investigating appeals, or answering questions concerning filing requirements and benefits provided. May be designated according to type of benefit-claim adjudicated. May act as consultant to board rating disability. • **GED:** R5, M4, L4 • **SVP:** 2-4 yrs • **Academic:** Ed=A, Eng=S • **Work Field:** 271, 282 • **MPSMS:** 959 • **Aptitudes:** G2, V2, N3, S5, P5, Q3, K4, F4, M4, E5, C5 • **Temperaments:** J, M, P • **Physical:** V=L, H=N, L=S • **Work Env:** I • **Salary:** 4 • **Out look:** 3

GENERAL CLAIMS AGENT (air trans.) • D.O.T. #186.117-030 • OES #39999 • Directs and coordinates activities involving claims against transportation company for shortages in or damaged freight, accidental death or injury to persons or employees, and private property damages: Directs activities of workers investigating claims to ascertain validity of claims and extent of company liability. Processes freight and property claims for which company is liable and submits claims to head office for settlement, or negotiates settlement with claimant and authorizes payment. Reviews employee accident reports to determine compensation program under which accidents are covered, and doctor reports for type of injury and length of time disabled. Authorizes payment of disability compensation according to state or federal acts. Contacts medical personnel to ascertain need for extension of payments beyond specified recovery date. Negotiates with persons having valid claims against company or death or injury to effect out-of-court settlement and refers cases that cannot be settled to legal department. Represents company at industrial accident or compensation board hearings to present company position on accident liability. May testify at court hearings to present evidence on company liability from investigation documents. • **GED:** R4, M4, L4 • **SVP:** 4-10 yrs • **Academic:** Ed=H, Eng=S • **Work Field:** 295 • **MPSMS:** 895 • **Aptitudes:** G2, V2, N3, S4, P4, Q3, K4, F4, M4, E5, C5 • **Temperaments:** D, M, P • **Stress:** A • **Physical:** V=L, H=L, L=S, H • **Work Env:** I • **Salary:** 5 • **Outlook:** 3

MANAGER, CUSTOMER SERVICE (tel. & tel.) • D.O.T. #168.167-058 • OES #51002 • Plans, directs, and coordinates activities of workers engaged in receiving, investigating, evaluating, and settling complaints and claims of telegraph customers: Directs workers to investigate complaints, such as those concerning rates or service in connection with domestic, international, or special-gift telegrams. Analyzes reports of findings and recommends response to complaint, considering nature and complexity of complaint, requirements of governmental utility-regulation agencies, and policies of company. Reviews actions of subordinates to ensure settlements are made correctly. Authorizes retention of data and preparation of documents for use during governmental or customer inquiries. • **GED:** R5, M5, L5 • **SVP:** 4-10 yrs • **Academic:** Ed=A, Eng=S • **Work Field:** 271, 295 • **MPSMS:** 862 • **Aptitudes:** G2, V2, N3, S4, P3, Q3, K4, F4, M4, E5, C5 • **Temperaments:** D, I, M, P • **Stress:** A • **Physical:** V=N, H=L, L=S • **Work Env:** I • **Salary:** 5 • **Outlook:** 3

SERVICE REPRESENTATIVE (auto. mfg.) • D.O.T. #191.167-022 • OES #53123 • Investigates dealer's claims for reimbursement of defective automobile parts: Reviews claims for labor or material adjustments with automobile dealer, examines parts claimed to be defective, and approves or disapproves dealer's claim. Assists dealers in handling unsettled claims by consulting with service personnel or customers. Prepares reports showing volume, types, and disposition of claims handled, or settlement allowed. May train dealers or service personnel in service operations or construction of products. May study dealers' organizational needs and advise them on matters, such as parts, tools, equipment, and personnel needed to handle service volume. • **GED:** R5, M4, L4 • **SVP:** 2-4 yrs • **Academic:** Ed=A, Eng=S • **Work Field:** 271 • **MPSMS:** 591 • **Aptitudes:** G2, V2, N3, S4, P4, Q3, K4, F4, M4, E5, C5 • **Temperaments:** J, M, P • **Physical:** V=L, H=L, L=S • **Work Env:** I • **Salary:** 4 • **Outlook:** 3

GOE: 11.12.02 Rental & Leasing

LOCATION MANAGER (motion pic.) • D.O.T. #191.167-018 • OES #19999 • Arranges for leasing of suitable property for use as location for television or motion picture production: Confers with production or unit manager and DIRECTOR, TELEVISION (radio & tv broad.) or DIRECTOR, MOTION PICTURE (motion pic.) regarding scenic backgrounds, terrain, and other topographical details of locations required for photographing exterior scenes. Searches files for pictures or descriptions of suitable locations or seeks new locations. Contacts property owners and local officials to arrange leasing and use of public and private property, rental of housing facilities, hiring of extras, and to obtain sanction for production activities. Arranges for transportation of troupe to location. • **GED:** R4, M3, L4 • **SVP:** 1-2 yrs • **Academic:** Ed=H, Eng=S • **Work Field:** 292, 295 • **MPSMS:** 895 • **Aptitudes:** G2, V2, N3, S3, P4, Q3, K4, F4, M4, E5, C5 • **Temperaments:** F, J, V • **Physical:** V=G, H=L, L=L • **Work Env:** B • **Salary:** 4 • **Outlook:** 1

MANAGER, LEASING (petrol. production) • D.O.T. #186.117-046 • OES #15011 • GENERAL MANAGER, LAND DEPARTMENT; LAND-AND-LEASES SUPERVISOR; LAND DEPARTMENT HEAD; LEASE AGENT; LEASES-AND-LAND SUPERVISOR; MANAGER, LAND DEPARTMENT; SUPERINTENDENT, LAND DEPARTMENT. Directs land and leasing department of petroleum company to secure leases, options, rights-of-way, and special agreements covering land and mineral rights for drilling wells and producing gas and oil: Studies leases bought, prices paid, and other negotiations of competing companies in specified areas and determines expenditure necessary to obtain leases and other contracts in those areas. Determines and specifies date of termination of lease rentals. Negotiates with brokers or other individuals to sell interests in leases owned. Executes general policies established by company officials. May make final decisions on and sign agreements and contracts for purchase, sale and acquisition of land leases, mineral and royalty rights. May be designated according to area of operations as MANAGER, DIVISIONAL LEASING (petrol. production). • **GED:** R5, M5, L5 • **SVP:** 4-10 yrs • **Academic:** Ed=A, Eng=S • **Work Field:** 295 • **MPSMS:** 895 • **Aptitudes:** G1, V2, N2, S4, P4, Q3, K4, F4, M4, E5, C5 • **Temperaments:** D, J, P • **Stress:** A • **Physical:** V=N, H=L, L=S • **Work Env:** I • **Salary:** 5 • **Outlook:** 2

PROPERTY-UTILIZATION OFFICER (gov. ser.) • D.O.T. #188.117-122 • OES #13014 • BUSINESS-SERVICE OFFICER; MANAGER, SURPLUS PROPERTY. Coordinates property procurement and maintenance activities, and negotiates with representatives to effect property transfers and sales, rental, and leasing contracts for government agency: Reviews property-related data, such as inventories, budgets, planning reports, vendor brochures, and excess property and property request reports, to obtain information on property status, needs, and availability. Writes, fills out, and reviews bids, contract specifications, purchase orders and estimates, and transfer forms to effect property transactions. Contacts vendors and potential users, and inspects and inventories acquired and transferred property through visits to government installations and vendor sites. Negotiates and confers with administrators, vendors, or users to effect agreement on property transfer details, such as price, model, packaging, transportation, land boundaries, or building layout. Authorizes expenditures within specified limits for purchases of supplies and equipment, equipment repair and maintenance, and alterations to premises. Fills government agency or other qualifying organization requests from surplus inventories, considering factors, such as donation criteria, actual needs, and justification. Prepares plans, standards, and specifications for building and equipment maintenance, repair, and inspection. May be designated according to property involved as REAL-ESTATE-UTILIZATION OFFICER (gov. ser.); STATE-SURPLUS-COMMODITY-AND-PROPERTY REPRESENTATIVE (gov. ser.). • **GED:** R5, M4, L4 • **SVP:** 4-10 yrs • **Academic:**

Ed=A, Eng=S • **Work Field:** 295 • **MPSMS:** 890, 959 • **Aptitudes:** G2, V2, N3, S3, P3, Q3, K4, F4, M4, E5, C4 • **Temperaments:** D, I, J, P, V • **Stress:** A • **Physical:** V=L, H=L, L=L • **Work Env:** I • **Salary:** 5 • **Outlook:** 1

REAL-ESTATE AGENT (profess. & kin.) • D.O.T. #186.117-058 • OES #15011 • LAND AGENT. Coordinates activities of real-estate department of company and negotiates acquisition and disposition of properties in most beneficial manner: Supervises staff engaged in preparing lease agreements, recording rental receipts, and performing other activities necessary to efficient management of company properties, or in performing routine research on zoning ordinances and condemnation considerations. Directs appraiser to inspect properties and land under consideration for acquisition, and recommends acquisition, lease, disposition, improvement, or other action consistent with best interest of company. Authorizes or requests authorization for maintenance of company properties not under control of operating departments, such as dwellings, hotels, or commissaries. Evaluates and promotes industrial-development potential of company properties. Negotiates contracts with sellers of land and renters of properties. • **GED:** R5, M5, L5 • **SVP:** 4-10 yrs • **Academic:** Ed=A, Eng=S • **Work Field:** 292, 295 • **MPSMS:** 895 • **Aptitudes:** G2, V2, N2, S3, P3, Q3, K4, F4, M4, E5, C5 • **Temperaments:** D, I, J, M, P • **Stress:** A • **Physical:** V=L, H=L, L=L • **Work Env:** B • **Salary:** 5 • **Outlook:** 1

RIGHT-OF-WAY AGENT (any ind.) • D.O.T. #191.117-046 • OES #15011 • CLAIMS AGENT, RIGHT-OF-WAY; PERMIT AGENT. Negotiates with property owners and public officials to secure purchase or lease of land and right-of-way for utility lines, pipelines, and other construction projects: Determines roads, bridges, and utility systems that must be maintained during construction. Negotiates with landholders for access routes and restoration of roads and surfaces. May examine public records to determine ownership and property rights. May be required to know property law. • **GED:** R5, M4, L5 • **SVP:** 2-4 yrs • **Academic:** Ed=B, Eng=G • **Work Field:** 271, 272 • **MPSMS:** 870, 895 • **Aptitudes:** G2, V2, N3, S3, P3, Q3, K4, F4, M4, E5, C5 • **Temperaments:** I, P, V • **Stress:** E • **Physical:** V=N, H=L, L=S, W, H • **Work Env:** B • **Salary:** 4 • **Outlook:** 2

GOE: 11.12.03 Booking

ADVANCE AGENT (amuse. & rec.) • D.O.T. #191.167-010 • OES #39999 • Coordinates business and promotional activities concerned with production of entertainment in advance of touring theatrical company, circus, road show, motion picture, or other attraction: Inspects performance location and reports condition, and if stage presentation, inspects equipment and accommodations of theatre, such as size of stage, seating capacity, and number of dressing rooms. Completes business details, such as advance sale of tickets and lodging for members of touring group. Purchases advertising space or spot announcements in newspapers, radio and television, and other media. Distributes posters, signs, and other displays to stimulate interest in coming attraction and promote box-office sales [PUBLIC-RELATIONS REPRESENTATIVE (profess. & kin.)]. • **GED:** R4, M4, L4 • **SVP:** 2-4 yrs • **Academic:** Ed=N, Eng=G • **Work Field:** 291 • **MPSMS:** 910 • **Aptitudes:** G3, V3, N3, S3, P4, Q3, K4, F4, M4, E5, C5 • **Temperaments:** D, J, P • **Stress:** E, A • **Physical:** V=N, H=L, L=S, W • **Work Env:** I • **Salary:** 3 • **Outlook:** 2

ARTIST'S MANAGER (amuse. & rec.) • D.O.T. #191.117-010 • OES #39999 • ARTIST CONSULTANT; ARTIST's REPRESENTATIVE; PERSONAL AGENT; PERSONAL MANAGER; TALENT AGENT. Manages affairs of entertainers by participating in negotiations with agents and others concerning contracts and business matters affecting clients' interests, and advises clients on career development and advancement: Represents client in negotiations with officials of unions, motion picture or television studios, theatrical productions, or entertainment house, for favorable contracts and financial fees to be received for engagements. Advises client concerning contracts, wardrobe, and effective presentation of act, according to knowledge of show business. Procures services of professional personnel in particular phase of show business to create or design format of original act, or prepare special material for new act to advance client's career. Manages business details of tours and engagements, such as obtaining reservations for trans-

portation and hotel accommodations, and making disbursements for road expenses. Represents client in public contacts, such as handling fan mail, telephone inquiries, and requests for personal appearances. May audition new talent for representation purposes. May procure bookings for clients. • **GED:** R5, M4, L5 • **SVP:** 2-4 yrs • **Academic:** Ed=B, Eng=G • **Work Field:** 295 • **MPSMS:** 919 • **Aptitudes:** G2, V2, N3, S4, P4, Q3, K4, F4, M4, E5, C5 • **Temperaments:** D, I, J, P • **Stress:** E, A • **Physical:** V=N, H=L, L=S • **Work Env:** I • **Salary:** 4 • **Outlook:** 1

BOOKING MANAGER (amuse. & rec.) • D.O.T. #191.117-014 • OES #39999 • BOOKER; BOOKING AGENT. Books performers, theatrical or ballet productions, variety or night club acts, concert or lecture series, trade shows, or other popular or classical attractions for entertainment in various establishments, such as theaters, showplaces, clubs, or halls: Schedules attractions for season, considering such factors as entertainment policy, budget, and tastes of patrons of particular establishment represented. Negotiates with booking representatives or producers of attractions to arrange terms of contract, play dates, and fees to be paid for engagements. Auditions new talent. Arranges for billing in accordance with contract agreement. Books motion pictures for exhibit into theater chains or independent houses. Selects and rents pictures to be exhibited on basis of potential box-office sales, cast of players, advertising allotment allowed by distributor, and similar factors. May specialize in in-house bookings and be designated according to establishment as CONCERT OR LECTURE HALL MANAGER (amuse. & rec.); SHOWPLACE MANAGER (amuse. & rec.). May specialize in independent bookings and be designated according to type of talent or of entertainment package represented and placed as ARTISTS' BOOKING REPRESENTATIVE (amuse. & rec.); THEATRICAL VARIETY AGENT (amuse. & rec.). May specialize in rental and distribution of motion pictures and be designated as FILM BOOKER (amuse. & rec.). May represent popular or rock musical groups only and be designated as BAND BOOKER (amuse. & rec.). When sponsoring, managing, and producing an entertainment, may be designated as IMPRESARIO (amuse. & rec.). • **GED:** R4, M4, L4 • **SVP:** 1-2 yrs • **Academic:** Ed=B, Eng=G • **Work Field:** 292 • **MPSMS:** 910 • **Aptitudes:** G3, V3, N3, S4, P4, Q2, K4, F4, M4, E5, C5 • **Temperaments:** I, J, P • **Stress:** E • **Physical:** V=N, H=G, L=S • **Work Env:** I • **Salary:** 4 • **Outlook:** 1

BUSINESS MANAGER (amuse. & rec.) • D.O.T. #191.117-018 • OES #39999 • BUSINESS AGENT. Manages financial affairs of entertainers and negotiates with agents and representatives for contracts and appearances: Negotiates with officials of unions, motion picture or television studios, stage productions, or entertainment houses for contracts and financial return to be received for engagements. Promotes client's interests by advising on income, investments, taxes, legal, and other financial matters. Provides liaison between client and representatives concerning contractual rights and obligations to settle contracts. Summarizes statements on periodic basis concerning client's investments, property, and financial status. • **GED:** R5, M4, L5 • **SVP:** 2-4 yrs • **Academic:** Ed=A, Eng=S • **Work Field:** 295 • **MPSMS:** 910 • **Aptitudes:** G2, V2, N3, S4, P4, Q2, K4, F4, M4, E5, C4 • **Temperaments:** D, I, J, P, V • **Stress:** A • **Physical:** V=N, H=L, L=S • **Work Env:** I • **Salary:** 4 • **Outlook:** 3

LITERARY AGENT (bus. ser.) • D.O.T. #191.117-034 • OES #39999 • AUTHOR'S AGENT; WRITER's REPRESENTATIVE. Markets clients' manuscripts to editors, publishers, and other buyers: Reads and appraises manuscripts and suggests revisions. Contacts prospective purchaser of material, basing selection upon knowledge of market and specific content of manuscript. Negotiates contract between publisher and client. Usually works on commission basis. • **GED:** R5, M4, L5 • **SVP:** 2-4 yrs • **Academic:** Ed=B, Eng=G • **Work Field:** 292 • **MPSMS:** 757 • **Aptitudes:** G2, V2, N3, S3, P3, Q3, K4, F4, M4, E5, C5 • **Temperaments:** I, P • **Stress:** E, A • **Physical:** V=N, H=G, L=S • **Work Env:** I • **Salary:** 4 • **Outlook:** 1

MANAGER, ATHLETE (amuse. & rec.) • D.O.T. #153.117-014 • OES #34058 • Manages affairs of PROFESSIONAL ATHLETE (amuse. & rec.) by negotiating with promoters or others to settle contracts and business matters and directs training: Negotiates with team management and promoters to obtain favorable contracts for client [BUSINESS MANAGER (amuse. & rec.)]. May prescribe exercises, rest periods, and diet to be followed by PROFESSIONAL ATHLETE (amuse. & rec.). May direct ATHLETIC TRAINER (amuse. & rec.; education) in conditioning PROFESSIONAL ATHLETE (amuse. & rec.). May give directions to protege in athletic techniques. May determine strategy to be followed by PROFESSIONAL ATHLETE (amuse. & rec.) in competition with others. May be designated according to type of PROFESSIONAL ATHLETE (amuse. & rec.) managed as MANAGER, BOXER (amuse. & rec.); MANAGER, WRESTLER (amuse. & rec.). • **GED:** R5, M5, L5 • **SVP:** 2-4 yrs • **Academic:** Ed=H, Eng=G • **Work Field:** 292 • **MPSMS:** 914 • **Aptitudes:** G2, V2, N2, S4, P4, Q3, K5, F5, M5, E5, C5 • **Temperaments:** D, I, J, P, V • **Stress:** E, A • **Physical:** V=N, H=L, L=S, W • **Work Env:** B • **Salary:** 5 • **Outlook:** 1

GOE: 11.12.04 Procurement Negotiations

CONTRACT ADMINISTRATOR (any ind.) • D.O.T. #162.117-014 • OES #13014 • Directs activities concerned with contracts for purchase or sale of equipment, materials, products, or services: Examines estimates of material, equipment, and production costs, performance requirements, and delivery schedules to ensure completeness and accuracy. Prepares bids, process specifications, test and progress reports, and other exhibits that may be required. Reviews bids from other firms for conformity to contract requirements and determines acceptable bids. Negotiates contract with customer or bidder. Requests or approves amendments to or extensions of contracts. Advises planning and production departments of contractual rights and obligations. May compile data for preparing estimates. May coordinate work of sales department with production and shipping department to implement fulfillment of contracts. May act as liaison between company and subcontractors. May direct sales program [MANAGER, SALES (any ind.)]. • **GED:** R5, M3, L5 • **SVP:** 4-10 yrs • **Academic:** Ed=A, Eng=G • **Work Field:** 295 • **MPSMS:** 894 • **Aptitudes:** G2, V2, N3, S4, P4, Q2, K4, F4, M4, E5, C5 • **Temperaments:** D, I, M, P, V • **Stress:** E, A • **Physical:** V=L, H=L, L=S • **Work Env:** I • **Salary:** 4 • **Outlook:** 4

CONTRACT SPECIALIST (profess. & kin.) • D.O.T. #162.117-018 • OES #21308 • CONTRACT COORDINATOR. Negotiates with suppliers to draw up procurement contracts: Negotiates, administers, extends, terminates, and renegotiates contracts. Formulates and coordinates procurement policies and procedures. Directs and coordinates activities of workers engaged in formulating bid proposals. Evaluates contract performance to determine necessity for amendments or extensions of contracts. Approves or rejects requests for deviations from contract specifications and delivery schedules. Arbitrates claims or complaints occurring in performance of contracts. Analyzes price proposals, financial reports, and other data to determine reasonableness of prices. May serve as liaison officer to ensure fulfillment of obligations by contractors. • **GED:** R5, M3, L4 • **SVP:** 4-10 yrs • **Academic:** Ed=A, Eng=S • **Work Field:** 295 • **MPSMS:** 949 • **Aptitudes:** G2, V2, N3, S4, P4, Q2, K4, F4, M4, E5, C5 • **Temperaments:** D, I, M, P, V • **Stress:** A • **Physical:** V=N, H=L, L=S • **Work Env:** I • **Salary:** 5 • **Outlook:** 4

CONTRACTOR (const.) • D.O.T. #182.167-010 • OES #15017 • Contracts to perform specified construction work in accordance with architect's plans, blueprints, codes, and other specifications: Estimates costs of materials, labor, and use of equipment required to fulfill provisions of contract and prepares bids. Confers with clients to negotiate terms of contract. Subcontracts specialized craft work, such as electrical, structural steel, concrete, and plumbing. Purchases material for construction. Supervises workers directly or through subordinate supervisors. May be designated according to specialty license or scope of principal activities as CONTRACTOR, GENERAL ENGINEERING (const.); CONTRACTOR, GENERAL BUILDING (const.). • **GED:** R4, M4, L4 • **SVP:** 2-4 yrs • **Academic:** Ed=H, Eng=G • **Work Field:** 102, 295 • **MPSMS:** 360 • **Aptitudes:** G3, V3, N2, S2, P2, Q3, K3, F3, M3, E3, C3 • **Temperaments:** D, M, P, V • **Stress:** E, A • **Physical:** V=L, H=L, L=S, W • **Work Env:** B, N • **Salary:** 5 • **Outlook:** 1

Physical Performing 12

An interest in physical activities performed before an audience. You can satisfy this interest through jobs in athletics, sports, and the performance of physical feats. Perhaps a job as a professional player or official would appeal to you. You may wish to develop and perform special acts such as acrobat ics or wire walking.

12.01 Sports

Workers in this group compete in professional athletic or sporting events, coach players, and officiate at games. They also give individual and group instruction, recruit players, and regulate various aspects of sporting events. Jobs in this group are found in all types of professional sports, such as football, baseball, basketball, hockey, golf, tennis, and horse racing. Some jobs are also available with private recreational facilities, including ski resorts, skating rinks, athletic clubs, and gymnasiums.

✔ **What kind of work would you do?**
Your work activities would depend upon your specific job. For example, you might:

- coach a professional sports team.
- start, time, or certify winners in a major auto race.
- inspect equipment to see if rules are being followed before an event.
- practice and play on a professional sports team.
- stop a game and penalize players for breaking a rule.
- ride horses in several races each day.
- give karate lessons to an individual or group.
- teach people how to ski.

✔ **What skills and abilities do you need for this kind of work?**
To do this kind of work, you must be able to:

- master all the rules of a particular game or sport and interpret them accurately.
- make official decisions quickly and enforce them when necessary.
- coordinate eye, hand, body, and foot movements with skill.
- adjust to the physical and mental pressures of competition.
- follow training rules strictly.

✔ **How do you know if you would like or could learn to do this kind of work?**
The following questions may give you clues about yourself as you consider this group of jobs.

- Have you competed in sports? Do you know the rules of any sport well enough to be a referee, judge, or umpire?
- Have you been an official in intramural games, physical education classes, or sandlot sports? Can you make decisions quickly and firmly?
- Have you coached a team or individual in athletic events? Were your efforts effective?
- Have you competed against others in athletic events? Do you remain calm and alert during competition?
- Have you won any special sports events? Do you excel in any athletic skill? Have others asked you to teach them that skill?

✔ How can you prepare for and enter this kind of work?

Occupations in this group usually require education and/or training extending from six months to over ten years, depending upon the specific kind of work. Professional coaches and officials often obtain the necessary training and experience by working with high school and college athletic teams. Umpires in major league baseball usually receive training in special umpire schools and must have experience in the minor leagues. Officials in horse racing usually have some type of related work experience and receive on-the-job training.

Professional athletes often receive initial training while on high school or college teams. They are recruited by professional clubs or teams and work under a contract. Training continues as long as they remain in active competition.

✔ What else should you consider about these jobs?

Often sports officials make decisions that are unpopular with the players or fans. If a player or coach argues about a ruling too strongly, the official in charge must enforce discipline by sending that individual from the game.

Professional athletes must maintain or improve their physical skills to remain in competition. The risk of physical injury is great in all of the contact sports. Some injuries may shorten or end a player's worklife in sports. Also, after reaching a certain age, many competitive players must find work in areas other than team play.

Frequent travel is usually involved for officials and athletes.

If you think you would like to do this kind of work, look at the job titles listed below.

GOE: 12.01.01 Coaching & Instructing

COACH, PROFESSIONAL ATHLETES (amuse. & rec.) • D.O.T. #153.227-010 • OES #34058 • COACH. Analyzes performance and instructs PROFESSIONAL ATHLETES (amuse. & rec.) in game strategies and techniques to prepare them for athletic competition: Observes players while they perform to determine need for individual or team improvement. Coaches players individually or in groups, demonstrating techniques of sport coached. Oversees daily practice of players to instruct them in areas of deficiency. Determines strategy during game, independently or in conference with other COACH, PROFESSIONAL ATHLETES (amuse. & rec.) or HEAD COACH (amuse. & rec.) based on factors as weakness in opposing team. May be designated according to phase of game coached as DEFENSIVE-LINE COACH (amuse. & rec.) or PITCHING COACH (amuse. & rec.). May be designated according to game coached as BASKETBALL COACH (amuse. & rec.); FOOTBALL COACH (amuse. & rec.); SWIMMING COACH (amuse. & rec.); TENNIS COACH (amuse. & rec.). • **GED:** R5, M3, L4 • **SVP:** 4-10 yrs • **Academic:** Ed=A, Eng=G • **Work Field:** 296 • **MPSMS:** 913 • **Aptitudes:** G3, V2, N4, S3, P3, Q4, K3, F4, M3, E2, C5 • **Temperaments:** D, J, P • **Stress:** E • **Physical:** V=L, H=L, L=H, W, S, H • **Work Env:** B • **Salary:** 5 • **Outlook:** 2

INSTRUCTOR, SPORTS (amuse. & rec.) • D.O.T. #153.227-018 • OES #31321 • ATHLETIC COACH. Teaches sport activity to individual or groups at private or public recreational facility or school: Explains and demonstrates use of apparatus and equipment. Explains and demonstrates principles, techniques, and methods of regulating movement of body, hands, or feet to achieve proficiency in activity. Observes students during practice to detect and correct mistakes. Explains and enforces safety rules and regulations. Explains method of keeping score. Organizes and conducts competition and tournaments. May participate in competition to demonstrate skill. May purchase, display, sell, maintain, or repair equipment. May keep record of receipts and expenditures. May lecture on history and purpose of sport. Workers are identified according to sport instructed. • **GED:** R4, M3, L4 • **SVP:** 4-10 yrs • **Academic:** Ed=H, Eng=S • **Work Field:** 296 • **MPSMS:** 914, 931 • **Aptitudes:** G2, V2, N3, S4, P4, Q4, K2, F2, M2, E2, C4 • **Temperaments:** D, J, M, P • **Stress:** E • **Physical:** V=G, H=G,

L=M, W, C, S, H • **Work Env:** B • **Salary:** 5 • **Outlook:** 3

SCOUT, PROFESSIONAL SPORTS (amuse. & rec.) • D.O.T. #153.117-018 • OES #34058 • Evaluates athletic skills of PROFESSIONAL ATHLETES (amuse. & rec.) to determine fitness and potentiality for professional sports and negotiates with them to obtain services: Reviews prospects' exhibitions and past performance records. Negotiates with PROFESSIONAL ATHLETES (amuse. & rec.) to arrange contracts. Reports to team management results of scouting assignments, such as selection or rejection of PROFESSIONAL ATHLETES (amuse. & rec.) scouted and persons and areas sighted for future recruitment. May be designated according to type of sport in which engaged as BASEBALL SCOUT (amuse. & rec.); BASKETBALL SCOUT (amuse. & rec.); FOOTBALL SCOUT (amuse. & rec.). • **GED:** R4, M3, L4 • **SVP:** 4-10 yrs • **Academic:** Ed=H, Eng=G • **Work Field:** 211 • **MPSMS:** 914 • **Aptitudes:** G2, V2, N4, S3, P3, Q3, K5, F4, M5, E5, C5 • **Temperaments:** D, I, J, P, V • **Stress:** E • **Physical:** V=L, H=L, L=S, W • **Work Env:** B • **Salary:** 5 • **Outlook:** 1

GOE: 12.01.02 Officiating

CHARTER (amuse. & rec.) • D.O.T. #249.367-018 • OES #59999 • Observes horserace, calls out description of race to other worker, and records statistical and related data on race for use in racing publication: Focuses binoculars on distance markers along track during race and calls out horses' numbers, positions, estimate of distances of horses from inside rail and between horses, and related observable data for other worker to record. Revises record of order and distance between horses at finish line if different from intercom announcement of official results. Copies identifying information, such as horses' names and drivers, from racing form onto record. Transcribes race results, such as winning and intermediate times, purse, and prices paid to bettors from tote board onto record. Contacts judges, using intercom, for decisions on foul claims and notes record accordingly. Computes race completion times for all but winning horses, using formula. Mails completed record to printer for use in printing race results in racing publications. • **GED:** R3, M2, L3 • **SVP:** 30 days-3 mos • **Academic:** Ed=N, Eng=G • **Work Field:** 231, 282 • **MPSMS:** 891 • **Aptitudes:** G3, V3, N3, S2, P3, Q4, K4, F4, M4, E5, C5 • **Temperaments: J, M, T • **Physical:** V=L, H=N, L=S • **Work Env:** I • **Salary:** 2 • **Outlook:** 3

CLOCKER (amuse. & rec.) • D.O.T. #153.367-010 • OES #34058 • Clocks (times) racehorses at racetrack during morning workouts to obtain speed information: Identifies each horse on track by its particular identifying marks and color, and records name. Observes horse during workout and assigns speed rating according to effort extended by horse and rider, distance run, and time required as measured by stopwatch. Records information and submits it to track management. • **GED:** R3, M2, L2 • **SVP:** 2-30 days • **Academic:** Ed=N, Eng=N • **Work Field:** 211 • **MPSMS:** 914 • **Aptitudes:** G3, V4, N3, S3, P3, Q3, K4, F4, M5, E5, C4 • **Temperaments:** M, T • **Physical:** V=L, H=N, L=S, H • **Work Env:** O • **Salary:** 2 • **Outlook:** 1

FLAGGER (amuse. & rec.) • D.O.T. #372.667-026 • OES #63044 • Signals with checkered flag when first race horse crosses starting line after release from starting gate to notify racing timer when to start timing race. • **GED:** R2, M1, L1 • **SVP:** 2-30 days • **Academic:** Ed=N, Eng=N • **Work Field:** 282 • **MPSMS:** 914 • **Aptitudes:** G4, V4, N4, S3, P4, Q5, K4, F5, M4, E5, C5 • **Temperaments:** T • **Physical:** V=L, H=N, L=L, W, H • **Work Env:** O • **Salary:** 2 • **Outlook:** 2

GOLF-COURSE RANGER (amuse. & rec.) • D.O.T. #379.667-010 • OES #63047 • GOLF-COURSE PATROLLER. Patrols golf course to prevent unauthorized persons from using facilities, keep play running smoothly, and assist injured or ill players: Inspects player and CADDIE (amuse. & rec.) registration and green fee tickets for validity. Prevents players from entering course beyond starting tee. Advises players to speed up or slow down in order to alleviate bottlenecks. Explains rules of game to players to settle disputes. Locates damaged or hazardous areas and marks areas for repair, using lime marker or stake. Cautions players against tearing up turf or otherwise abusing course. Renders first aid to injured or ill players and carries their equipment to clubhouse. Returns lost equipment to owners or to clubhouse. Keeps log of daily activities. May deliver urgent messages to players on course. • **GED:** R3, M2, L3 • **SVP:** 3-6 mos • **Academic:** Ed=N, Eng=S • **Work Field:** 293 • **MPSMS:** 914 • **Aptitudes:** G3, V3, N4, S4, P4, Q4, K4, F4, M4, E5, C5 • **Temperaments:** P, V • **Stress:** E • **Physical:** V=L, H=L, L=L, W, H • **Work Env:** O • **Salary:** 3 • **Outlook:** 2

HORSE-RACE STARTER (amuse. & rec.) • D.O.T. #153.267-010 • OES #34058 • STARTER. Determines entry sequence into starting gate and gives directions to riders and other track personnel to get horses into position for horse race: Evaluates performance and training record and observes horse's behavior to determine entry sequence. Directs entry of horse and rider into starting gate according to planned sequence and stall number. Gives directions to track personnel to assist rider when horse refuses to enter starting gate. Reports undue starting delay to racing officials.

Presses button to open gate automatically when horses are correctly alined. May recommend removal of horse unfit to start race. May schedule morning workouts for horses requiring familiarization with starting gate procedures. • **GED:** R3, M3, L3 • **SVP:** 3-6 mos • **Academic:** Ed=N, Eng=G • **Work Field:** 282 • **MPSMS:** 914 • **Aptitudes:** G3, V3, N4, S3, P5, Q5, K4, F4, M5, E5, C5 • **Temperaments:** J, M, P, V • **Stress:** E • **Physical:** V=L, H=L, L=L • **Work Env:** O • **Salary:** 3 • **Outlook:** 2

HORSE-RACE TIMER (amuse. & rec.) • D.O.T. #153.367-014 • OES #34058 • Clocks and records time required for horse leading in race to run specified distance: Observes signal for official start and activates stopwatch to time race. Observes leading horse crossing markers denoting fractional parts and finish line of race to note and record time elapsed. Compares recorded results with those obtained by automatic electronic timer and reports difference to racing officials. Writes daily report of name, number of leading horse, fractional and total time required for each race to submit to track officials. • **GED:** R3, M3, L3 • **SVP:** 30 days-3 mos • **Academic:** Ed=N, Eng=S • **Work Field:** 211, 231 • **MPSMS:** 914 • **Aptitudes:** G4, V4, N3, S3, P4, Q3, K4, F4, M4, E5, C4 • **Temperaments:** M, T • **Physical:** V=L, H=N, L=S • **Work Env:** I • **Salary:** 2 • **Outlook:** 1

LEAD PONY RIDER (amuse. & rec.) • D.O.T. #153.674-014 • OES #34058 • Rides lead pony to lead JOCKEY (amuse. & rec.) and mount from paddock to starting gate at racetrack: Leads horse scheduled to race from receiving barn to paddock to be saddled. Leads procession of riders in post position order to starting gate. Rides after runaway horse to aid rider regain control. Diverts riders from competitor involved in accident on racetrack. Leads race horse to paddock or receiving barn after race. Assists horse ambulance workers to remove injured horse from track, using block and tackle. Grooms and feeds lead pony. • **GED:** R2, M1, L1 • **SVP:** 2-30 days • **Academic:** Ed=N, Eng=N • **Work Field:** 291 • **MPSMS:** 329 • **Aptitudes:** G4, V4, N5, S4, P5, Q5, K3, F3, M3, E3, C5 • **Temperaments:** R • **Physical:** V=L, H=L, L=M, W, C, H • **Work Env:** O, R • **Salary:** 2 • **Outlook:** 2

UMPIRE (amuse. & rec.) • D.O.T. #153.267-018 • OES #34058 • FIELD CAPTAIN; JUDGE; REFEREE. Officiates at sporting events: Observes actions of participants to detect infractions of rules. Decides disputable matters according to established regulations. When concerned only with determining validity of goals, finish line order, or out-of-bound plays, may be designated FINISH JUDGE (amuse. & rec.); GOAL UMPIRE (amuse. & rec.); LINE UMPIRE (amuse. & rec.). • **GED:** R4, M3, L4 • **SVP:** 4-10 yrs • **Academic:** Ed=N, Eng=G • **Work Field:** 211, 295 • **MPSMS:** 914 • **Aptitudes:** G2, V2, N3, S2, P3, Q4, K4, F5, M4, E4, C5 • **Temperaments:** D, J, M, P, S • **Stress:** E, S • **Physical:** V=L, H=L, L=L, W • **Work Env:** B • **Salary:** 5 • **Outlook:** 1

12.02 Physical Feats

Workers in this group perform unusual or daring acts of physical strength or skill to entertain people. They may perform alone or with others. Circuses, carnivals, theaters, and amusement parks hire these workers.

✔ **What kind of work would you do?**
Your work activities would depend upon your specific job. For example, you might:

- demonstrate gymnastic skill on a high wire or trapeze to entertain audiences.
- ski jump in a water show.
- dive from a high platform into a tank of water.

- juggle and balance things such as balls, knives, or plates.
- perform acrobatic stunts on a horse in a circus.
- swim in a water ballet.

✔ **What skills and abilities do you need for this kind of work?**
To do this kind of work, you must be able to:

- coordinate eye, hand, body, and foot movement with skill.
- demonstrate poise and confidence while performing before an audience.

- judge distance, speed, and movement of objects or people.
- follow strict training rules.
- take the risk of physical injury.
- excel in a particular athletic skill.

The above statements may not apply to every job in this group.

✔ **How do you know if you would like or could learn to do this kind of work?**
The following questions may give you clues about yourself as you consider this group of jobs.

- Have you performed stunts that required daring and skill? Did you perform them without great fear?

- Have you had a hobby or specialty act such as juggling, acrobatics, or wire walking? Do you perform well before an audience?

✔ **How can you prepare for and enter this kind of work?**
Occupations in this group usually require education and/or training extending from six months to over ten years, depending upon the specific kind of work. The usual method of training is by observation and practice. Another method is working with and learning from a skilled performer.

Performers of some specialty act such as wire walking, are hired by circuses and other amusement companies. Some workers own their own equipment and contract for individual appearances.

✔ **What else should you consider about these jobs?**
For their own safety, workers must maintain or improve their physical skills. The physical requirements of some jobs may limit the number of years a worker can perform. Frequent travel is usually required.

If you think you would like to do this kind of work, look at the job titles listed below.

GOE: 12.02.01 Performing, Physical Feats

AQUATIC PERFORMER (amuse. & rec.) • D.O.T. #159.347-014 • OES #34056 • Performs water-ballet routines to entertain audience, utilizing synchronized techniques of swimming: May swim underwater, using air lines. May serve as LIFEGUARD (amuse. & rec.), sell tickets, or perform other duties when not participating in show. • **GED:** R3, M3, L3 • **SVP:** 6 mos-1 yr • **Academic:** Ed=N, Eng=S • **Work Field:** 297 • **MPSMS:** 919 • **Aptitudes:** G3, V3, N4, S2, P2, Q4, K2, F3, M3, E2, C4 • **Temperaments:** J, P, V • **Stress:** E • **Physi cal:** V=L, H=N, L=M, W, C, H • **Work Env:** I, W • **Salary:** 3 • **Outlook:** 1

JUGGLER (amuse. & rec.) • D.O.T. #159.341-010 • OES #34056 • Juggles and balances objects, such as balls, knives, plates, tenpins, and hats, to entertain audience. • **GED:** R3, M2, L2 • **SVP:** 1-2 yrs • **Academic:** Ed=N, Eng=N • **Work Field:** 297 • **MPSMS:** 919 • **Aptitudes:** G3, V3, N4, S2, P3, Q4, K2, F2, M2, E1, C5 • **Temperaments:** J, S, T • **Stress:** S • **Physical:** V=L, H=N, L=L, W, H • **Work Env:** I • **Salary:** 3 • **Outlook:** 1

STUNT PERFORMER (amuse. & rec.) • D.O.T. #159.341-014 • OES #34056 • Performs stunts, such as overturning speeding automobile or falling from runaway horse, and participates in fight-action scenes for motion picture, television, or stage production: Reads script and confers with DIRECTOR, MOTION PICTURE (motion pic.) and DIRECTOR OF PHOTOGRAPHY (motion pic.; radio & tv broad.) to ascertain positions of cameras and other performers. Examines terrain and inspects equipment, such as harness, rigging bars, or nets to avoid in jury. Coordinates body movement and facial expression to simulate giving and receiving violent blows. Rehearses stunt routines alone or with other STUNT PERFORMER (amuse. & rec.; motion pic.; radio & tv broad.). May design, build, or repair own safety equipment. • **GED:** R3, M3, L3 • **SVP:** 1-2 yrs • **Academic:** Ed=N, Eng=S • **Work Field:** 297 • **MPSMS:** 911 • **Aptitudes:** G3, V3, N4, S2, P4, Q4, K2, F3, M1, E1, C5 • **Temperaments:** J, P, S, T • **Stress:** S • **Physical:** V=G, H=G, L=M, W, C, S, H • **Work Env:** B, R • **Salary:** 4 • **Outlook:** 1

Appendix A
Alphabetical Index of Occupations

Each of the occupations in *The Enhanced Guide for Occupational Exploration* is listed in alphabetical order below. The name is followed by the industry that the occupation is related to, its D.O.T number, and its G.O.E number. Since occupations are arranged in this book by their G.O.E number, you can use this number to find the occupation's description and obtain additional information.

ABLE SEAMAN (water trans.), 911.364-010, 05.12.03
ABSTRACTOR (profess. & kin.), 119.267-010, 11.04.04
ACCORDION REPAIRER (any ind.), 730.281-014, 05.05.12
ACCOUNT EXECUTIVE (bus. ser.), 164.167-010, 11.09.01
ACCOUNT-INFORMATION CLERK (light, heat, & power), 210.367-010, 07.02.03
ACCOUNTANT (profess. & kin.), 160.167-010, 11.06.01
ACCOUNTANT, BUDGET (profess. & kin.), 160.167-014, 11.06.01
ACCOUNTANT, COST (profess. & kin.), 160.167-018, 11.06.01
ACCOUNTANT, TAX (profess. & kin.), 160.162-010, 11.06.01
ACCOUNTING CLERK (clerical), 216.482-010, 07.02.02
ACCOUNTING CLERK, DATA PROCESSING (clerical), 216.382-010, 07.02.02
ACTUARY (profess. & kin.), 020.167-010, 11.01.02
ACUPRESSURIST (medical ser.), 079.271-014, 10.02.02
ACUPUNCTURIST (medical ser.), 079.271-010, 02.03.04
ADDING-MACHINE OPERATOR (clerical), 216.482-014, 07.06.02
ADDRESSER (clerical), 209.587-010, 07.07.02
ADDRESSING-MACHINE OPERATOR (clerical), 208.582-010, 05.12.19
ADHESIVE-BANDAGE-MACHINE OPERATOR (per. protect. & med. device), 692.685-014, 06.04.05
ADJUDICATOR (gov. ser.), 119.167-010, 11.04.03
ADMINISTRATIVE ASSISTANT (any ind.), 169.167-010, 11.05.02
ADMINISTRATIVE CLERK (clerical), 219.362-010, 07.01.02
ADMINISTRATIVE SECRETARY (any ind.), 169.167-014, 07.01.02

ADMINISTRATOR, HOSPITAL (medical ser.), 187.117-010, 11.07.02
ADMISSIONS EVALUATOR (educ.), 205.367-010, 07.01.05
ADMITTING OFFICER (medical ser.), 205.137-010, 07.04.01
ADVANCE AGENT (amuse. & rec.), 191.167-010, 11.12.03
ADVERTISING CLERK (bus. ser.), 247.387-010, 07.02.04
ADVERTISING-DISPATCH CLERK (print. & pub.), 247.387-014, 07.05.01
ADVERTISING-MATERIAL DISTRIBUTOR (any ind.), 230.687-010, 07.07.02
ADVERTISING-SPACE CLERK (print. & pub.), 247.387-018, 01.06.01
AERODYNAMIST (aircraft-aerospace mfg.), 002.061-010, 05.01.01
AERONAUTICAL ENGINEER (profess. & kin.), 002.061-014, 05.01.07
AERONAUTICAL TEST ENGINEER (aircraft-aerospace mfg.), 002.061-018, 05.01.04
AERONAUTICAL-DESIGN ENGINEER (aircraft-aerospace mfg.), 002.061-022, 05.01.07
AERONAUTICAL-RESEARCH ENGINEER (aircraft-aerospace mfg.), 002.061-026, 05.01.01
AGRICULTURAL ENGINEER (profess. & kin.), 013.061-010, 05.01.08
AGRICULTURAL-ENGINEERING TECHNICIAN (profess. & kin.), 013.161-010, 05.01.07
AGRONOMIST (profess. & kin.), 040.061-010, 02.02.02
AIR ANALYST (profess. & kin.), 012.261-010, 05.01.04
AIR-COMPRESSOR OPERATOR (any ind.), 950.685-010, 05.06.02
AIR-CONDITIONING INSTALLER, DOMESTIC (any ind.), 827.464-010, 05.10.04
AIR-CONDITIONING INSTALLER-SERVICER, WINDOW UNIT (any ind.), 637.261-010, 05.05.09

AIR-CONDITIONING MECHANIC (auto. ser.), 620.281-010, 05.05.09
AIR-TRAFFIC-CONTROL SPECIALIST, STATION (gov. ser.), 193.162-014, 05.03.03
AIR-TRAFFIC-CONTROL SPECIALIST, TOWER (gov. ser.), 193.162-018, 05.03.03
AIRCRAFT BODY REPAIRER (aircraft-aerospace mfg.), 807.261-010, 05.05.06
AIRFRAME-AND-POWER-PLANT MECHANIC (aircraft-aerospace mfg.), 621.281-014, 05.05.09
AIRLINE SECURITY REPRESENTATIVE (air trans.), 372.667-010, 04.02.02
AIRLINE-RADIO OPERATOR (air trans.), 193.262-010, 07.04.05
AIRPLANE INSPECTOR (air trans.), 621.261-010, 05.07.02
AIRPLANE PILOT (agric.), 196.263-010, 05.04.01
AIRPLANE PILOT, COMMERCIAL (air trans.), 196.263-014, 05.04.01
AIRPLANE-FLIGHT ATTENDANT (air trans.), 352.367-010, 09.01.04
AIRPORT ATTENDANT (air trans.), 912.364-010, 05.10.04
AIRPORT ENGINEER (profess. & kin.), 005.061-010, 05.01.07
AIRPORT UTILITY WORKER (air trans.), 912.663-010, 05.12.06
ALARM INVESTIGATOR (bus. ser.), 376.367-010, 04.02.04
ALARM OPERATOR (gov. ser.), 379.162-010, 07.04.05
ALTERATION TAILOR (garment), 785.261-010, 05.05.15
AMBULANCE ATTENDANT (medical ser.), 355.374-010, 10.03.02
AMBULANCE DRIVER (medical ser.), 913.683-010, 05.08.03
AMUSEMENT PARK ENTERTAINER (amuse. & rec.), 159.647-010, 01.07.03
AMUSEMENT PARK WORKER (amuse. & rec.), 349.664-010, 09.01.01

ANALYST, FOOD AND BEVERAGE
(hotel & rest.), 310.267-010, 05.05.17
ANIMAL BREEDER (profess. & kin.),
041.061-014, 02.02.01
ANIMAL CARETAKER (any ind.),
410.674-010, 03.03.02
ANIMAL HEALTH TECHNICIAN
(medical ser.), 079.361-014, 02.03.03
ANIMAL KEEPER (amuse. & rec.),
412.674-010, 03.03.02
ANIMAL SCIENTIST (profess. & kin.),
040.061-014, 02.02.01
ANIMAL TRAINER (amuse. & rec.),
159.224-010, 03.03.01
ANIMAL-HOSPITAL CLERK (medical
ser.), 245.367-010, 07.04.03
ANIMAL-RIDE ATTENDANT (amuse. &
rec.), 349.674-010, 03.03.02
ANNOUNCER (radio & tv broad.),
159.147-010, 01.03.03
ANNOUNCER (amuse. & rec.),
159.347-010, 01.07.02
ANODIZER (any ind.), 500.682-010,
06.02.21
ANTENNA INSTALLER (any ind.),
823.684-010, 05.12.16
ANTENNA INSTALLER, SATELLITE
COMMUNICATIONS (any ind.),
823.261-022, 05.05.05
ANTHROPOLOGIST (profess. & kin.),
055.067-010, 11.03.03
APPEALS REFEREE (gov. ser.),
119.267-014, 11.04.01
APPLIANCE REPAIRER (elec. equip.),
723.584-010, 05.10.03
APPLIANCE-SERVICE SUPERVISOR
(light, heat, & power), 187.167-010,
05.02.06
APPRAISER (gov. ser.), 188.167-010,
11.06.03
APPRAISER (any ind.), 191.287-010,
11.06.03
APPRAISER, ART (profess. & kin.),
191.287-014, 01.02.01
APPRAISER, AUTOMOBILE DAMAGE
(bus. ser.), 241.267-014, 11.12.01
APPRAISER, REAL ESTATE (real
estate), 191.267-010, 11.06.03
AQUARIST (amuse. & rec.), 449.674-010,
03.03.02
AQUATIC PERFORMER (amuse. & rec.),
159.347-014, 12.02.01
ARBOR-PRESS OPERATOR 1 (any ind.),
616.682-010, 06.02.20
ARBORER (jewelry), 700.684-010,
06.04.24
ARC CUTTER (welding), 816.364-010,
05.05.06
ARCH-SUPPORT TECHNICIAN (per.
protect. & med. device), 712.381-010,
05.10.01
ARCHEOLOGIST (profess. & kin.),
055.067-018, 11.03.03
ARCHITECT (profess. & kin.),
001.061-010, 05.01.07
ARCHITECT, MARINE (profess. & kin.),
001.061-014, 05.01.07
ARCHIVIST (profess. & kin.),
101.167-010, 11.03.03
ARMATURE BANDER (any ind.),
724.684-010, 06.02.24
ARMORED-CAR GUARD (bus. ser.),
372.567-010, 04.02.02
ARMORED-CAR GUARD AND DRIVER
(bus. ser.), 372.563-010, 04.02.02

ART DIRECTOR (profess. & kin.),
141.031-010, 01.02.03
ART DIRECTOR (motion pic.),
142.031-010, 01.02.03
ART THERAPIST (medical ser.),
076.127-010, 10.02.02
ARTIFICIAL-FLOWER MAKER (artif.
flower), 739.684-014, 06.04.34
ARTIFICIAL-LOG-MACHINE
OPERATOR (fuel briquettes),
569.685-010, 06.04.03
ARTIFICIAL-PLASTIC-EYE MAKER
(optical goods), 713.261-014, 05.05.11
ARTIST'S MANAGER (amuse. & rec.),
191.117-010, 11.12.03
ASPHALT-DISTRIBUTOR TENDER
(const.), 853.665-010, 05.12.14
ASPHALT-PAVING-MACHINE
OPERATOR (const.), 853.663-010,
05.11.01
ASSAYER (profess. & kin.), 022.281-010,
02.04.01
ASSEMBLER (jewelry), 700.684-014,
06.04.23
ASSEMBLER (inst. & app.), 710.681-010,
06.01.04
ASSEMBLER (elec. equip.), 723.684-010,
06.04.23
ASSEMBLER (sports equip.),
732.684-014, 06.04.23
ASSEMBLER, AUTOMOBILE (auto.
mfg.), 806.684-010, 06.04.22
ASSEMBLER, BICYCLE 2 (motor. &
bicycles), 806.687-010, 06.04.22
ASSEMBLER, HOSPITAL SUPPLIES
(inst. & app.), 712.687-010, 06.04.38
ASSEMBLER, INTERNAL
COMBUSTION ENGINE (engine &
turbine), 806.481-014, 06.02.22
ASSEMBLER, METAL BONDING
(aircraft-aerospace mfg.), 806.684-030,
06.02.24
ASSEMBLER, MOLDED FRAMES
(optical goods), 713.684-014, 06.04.23
ASSEMBLER, MUSICAL
INSTRUMENTS (musical inst.),
730.684-010, 06.02.23
ASSEMBLER, PRODUCTION (any ind.),
706.687-010, 06.04.22
ASSEMBLER, PRODUCTION LINE
(photo. apparatus), 714.684-010,
06.02.23
ASSEMBLER, SEMICONDUCTOR
(electronics), 726.684-034, 06.02.23
ASSEMBLER, SMALL PARTS (any ind.),
706.684-022, 06.04.23
ASSEMBLER, SMALL PRODUCTS (any
ind.), 739.687-030, 06.04.23
ASSEMBLER, SUBASSEMBLY
(aircraft-aerospace mfg.), 806.484-010,
06.02.22
ASSEMBLER, SURGICAL GARMENT
(per. protect. & med. device),
712.684-010, 06.02.23
ASSEMBLY-PRESS OPERATOR (any
ind.), 690.685-014, 06.04.20
ASSIGNMENT CLERK (clerical),
249.367-090, 07.05.03
ASSISTANT-PRESS OPERATOR (print.
& pub.), 651.585-010, 05.05.13
ASSOCIATION EXECUTIVE (profess. &
kin.), 189.117-010, 11.05.01
ATHLETIC TRAINER (amuse. & rec.),
153.224-010, 10.02.02

ATTENDANCE CLERK (educ.),
219.362-014, 07.05.03
ATTENDANCE OFFICER (educ.),
168.367-010, 07.01.06
ATTENDANT, CAMPGROUND (amuse.
& rec.), 329.683-010, 05.12.18
AUCTION ASSISTANT (ret. tr.),
294.667-010, 07.07.02
AUCTION CLERK (ret. tr.), 294.567-010,
07.03.01
AUCTIONEER (ret. tr.), 294.257-010,
08.02.03
AUDIO OPERATOR (radio & tv broad.),
194.262-010, 05.10.05
AUDIO-VIDEO REPAIRER (any ind.),
729.281-010, 05.05.10
AUDIOLOGIST (profess. & kin.),
076.101-010, 02.03.04
AUDIOMETRIST (profess. & kin.),
078.362-010, 10.03.01
AUDIOVISUAL PRODUCTION
SPECIALIST (profess. & kin.),
149.061-010, 01.02.03
AUDIOVISUAL TECHNICIAN (any ind.),
960.382-010, 05.10.05
AUDITOR (profess. & kin.), 160.162-014,
11.06.01
AUDITOR, INTERNAL (profess. & kin.),
160.167-034, 11.06.01
AUDITOR, TAX (profess. & kin.),
160.167-038, 11.06.01
AUTO-DESIGN CHECKER (auto. mfg.),
017.261-010, 05.03.02
AUTOMATED EQUIPMENT
ENGINEER-TECHNICIAN (mach.
mfg.), 638.261-010, 05.05.05
AUTOMATIC-DOOR MECHANIC
(const.), 829.281-010, 05.10.03
AUTOMATIC-EQUIPMENT
TECHNICIAN (tel. & tel.),
822.281-010, 05.05.05
AUTOMOBILE DETAILER (auto. ser.),
915.687-034, 05.12.18
AUTOMOBILE LOCATOR (ret. tr.),
296.367-010, 07.05.03
AUTOMOBILE MECHANIC (auto. ser.),
620.261-010, 05.05.09
AUTOMOBILE UPHOLSTERER (auto.
ser.), 780.381-010, 05.05.15
AUTOMOBILE WRECKER (whole. tr.),
620.684-010, 05.12.15
AUTOMOBILE-ACCESSORIES
INSTALLER (auto. ser.), 806.684-038,
05.10.02
AUTOMOBILE-BODY REPAIRER (auto.
ser.), 807.381-010, 05.05.06
AUTOMOBILE-BODY-REPAIRER
HELPER (auto. ser.), 807.687-010,
05.12.12
AUTOMOBILE-RADIATOR MECHANIC
(auto. ser.), 620.381-010, 05.10.02
AUTOMOBILE-RENTAL CLERK (auto.
ser.), 295.477-010, 09.04.02
AUTOMOBILE-SERVICE-STATION
ATTENDANT (auto. ser.), 915.467-010,
05.10.02
AUTOMOBILE-SERVICE-STATION
MECHANIC (auto. ser.), 620.261-030,
05.05.09
AUTOMOTIVE ENGINEER (auto. mfg.),
007.061-010, 05.01.08
AUTOMOTIVE-COOLING-SYSTEM
DIAGNOSTIC TECHNICIAN (auto.
ser.), 620.261-034, 05.05.09

AUTOMOTIVE-MAINTENANCE-EQUIP-
MENT SERVICER (any ind.),
620.281-018, 05.05.09
AUXILIARY-EQUIPMENT OPERATOR,
DATA PROCESSING (clerical),
213.685-010, 05.12.19
AUXILIARY-EQUIPMENT TENDER
(cement), 570.685-010, 06.04.17
AVIONICS TECHNICIAN
(aircraft-aerospace mfg.), 823.281-010,
05.05.10
BAG-MACHINE OPERATOR (paper
goods), 649.685-014, 06.04.04
BAGGAGE HANDLER (r.r. trans.),
910.687-010, 05.12.03
BAILIFF (gov. ser.), 377.667-010, 04.02.03
BAKER (hotel & rest.), 313.381-010,
05.10.08
BAKER (bake. prod.), 526.381-010,
06.02.15
BAKER HELPER (bake. prod.),
526.686-010, 06.04.15
BAKER, HEAD (hotel & rest.),
313.131-010, 05.10.08
BAKER, PIZZA (hotel & rest.),
313.381-014, 05.10.08
BAKERY WORKER (bake. prod.),
929.686-010, 06.04.38
BALANCE CLERK (clerical),
216.382-018, 07.02.01
BALLISTICS EXPERT, FORENSIC (gov.
ser.), 199.267-010, 02.04.01
BAND-SAW OPERATOR (slaught. &
meat pack.), 525.685-010, 06.04.15
BARBER (per. ser.), 330.371-010, 09.02.02
BARGE CAPTAIN (water trans.),
911.137-010, 05.12.03
BARTENDER (hotel & rest.),
312.474-010, 09.04.01
BARTENDER HELPER (hotel & rest.),
312.687-010, 05.12.18
BATTERY REPAIRER (any ind.),
727.381-014, 05.10.03
BEACH LIFEGUARD (amuse. & rec.),
379.364-014, 04.02.03
BEAM-WARPER TENDER, AUTOMATIC
(asbestos prod.), 681.685-018, 06.04.06
BEEKEEPER (agric.), 413.161-010,
03.01.02
BELLHOP (hotel & rest.), 324.677-010,
09.05.03
BELT REPAIRER (any ind.), 630.684-014,
05.12.15
BENCH ASSEMBLER (agric. equip.),
706.684-042, 06.04.23
BENCH GRINDER (any ind.),
705.684-010, 06.04.24
BENCH HAND (bake. prod.),
520.384-010, 06.02.28
BENCH HAND (jewelry), 735.381-010,
06.01.04
BENCH WORKER (optical goods),
713.684-018, 06.04.24
BENDING-MACHINE OPERATOR 2
(any ind.), 617.685-010, 06.04.02
BICYCLE REPAIRER (any ind.),
639.681-010, 05.10.02
BICYCLE-RENTAL CLERK (ret. tr.),
295.467-010, 09.04.02
BILLING CLERK (clerical), 214.362-042,
07.02.04
BILLING-CONTROL CLERK (light, heat,
& power), 214.387-010, 07.02.04
BILLPOSTER (any ind.), 299.667-010,
05.12.12

BILLPOSTER (bus. ser.), 841.684-010,
05.12.14
BINDER (any ind.), 787.682-010, 06.02.05
BINDERY WORKER (print. & pub.),
653.685-010, 06.04.04
BIOCHEMIST (profess. & kin.),
041.061-026, 02.02.03
BIOLOGICAL AIDE (agric.), 049.384-010,
02.04.02
BIOLOGIST (profess. & kin.),
041.061-030, 02.02.03
BIOLOGY SPECIMEN TECHNICIAN
(profess. & kin.), 041.381-010, 02.04.02
BIOMEDICAL ENGINEER (profess. &
kin.), 019.061-010, 02.02.01
BIOMEDICAL EQUIPMENT
TECHNICIAN (profess. & kin.),
019.261-010, 02.04.02
BIOMEDICAL EQUIPMENT
TECHNICIAN (inst. & app.),
719.261-010, 05.05.11
BIOPHYSICIST (profess. & kin.),
041.061-034, 02.02.03
BIRTH ATTENDANT (medical ser.),
354.377-010, 10.03.02
BITE-BLOCK MAKER (medical ser.),
712.684-014, 06.02.23
BLACKSMITH (forging), 610.381-010,
05.05.06
BLANKMAKER (glass mfg.),
579.382-022, 06.02.13
BLASTER (any ind.), 859.261-010,
05.10.06
BLIND AIDE (per. ser.), 359.573-010,
10.03.03
BLOCKER, HAND 1 (hat & cap),
580.684-010, 06.02.27
BLOOD-DONOR-UNIT ASSISTANT
(medical ser.), 245.367-014, 07.04.01
BLUEPRINTING-MACHINE
OPERATOR (any ind.), 979.682-014,
05.10.05
BOAT LOADER 1 (water trans.),
911.364-014, 05.12.06
BOAT PATCHER, PLASTIC (ship bldg. &
rep.), 807.684-014, 06.02.24
BOAT REPAIRER (ship bldg. & rep.),
807.361-014, 05.05.02
BOAT RIGGER (ret. tr.), 806.464-010,
05.10.01
BOATBUILDER, WOOD (ship bldg. &
rep.), 860.381-018, 05.05.02
BODYGUARD (per. ser.), 372.667-014,
04.02.02
BOILER OPERATOR (any ind.),
950.382-010, 05.06.02
BOILERHOUSE MECHANIC (any ind.),
805.361-010, 05.05.06
BOILERMAKER 1 (boilermaking),
805.261-014, 05.05.06
BONDED STRUCTURES REPAIRER
(aircraft-aerospace mfg.), 807.381-014,
06.02.32
BONDING AGENT (bus. ser.),
186.267-010, 07.04.01
BONER, MEAT (slaught. & meat pack.),
525.684-010, 06.04.28
BOOK REPAIRER (any ind.),
977.684-010, 05.12.19
BOOKBINDER (print. & pub.),
977.381-010, 05.05.15
BOOKING MANAGER (amuse. & rec.),
191.117-014, 11.12.03
BOOKKEEPER 1 (clerical), 210.382-014,
07.02.01

BOOKMAKER (amuse. & rec.),
187.167-014, 11.06.03
BOOM-CONVEYOR OPERATOR (any
ind.), 921.683-014, 05.12.04
BORDER GUARD (gov. ser.),
375.363-010, 04.02.03
BORDEREAU CLERK (insurance),
203.382-010, 07.05.03
BOTANIST (profess. & kin.), 041.061-038,
02.02.02
BOUNCER (amuse. & rec.), 376.667-010,
04.02.03
BOW MAKER (any ind.), 789.684-010,
06.04.27
BOW MAKER, CUSTOM (sports equip.),
732.381-010, 01.06.02
BOW MAKER, PRODUCTION (sports
equip.), 732.684-038, 06.02.32
BOWLING-BALL MOLDER (sports
equip.), 556.685-018, 06.04.13
BOX MAKER, WOOD (wood. box),
760.684-014, 06.02.25
BOX-FOLDING-MACHINE OPERATOR
(paper goods), 649.682-010, 06.02.04
BRAILLE OPERATOR (print. & pub.),
203.582-010, 07.06.02
BRAILLE PROOFREADER (nonprofit
org.), 209.367-014, 07.05.02
BRAILLE TYPIST (educ.), 203.582-014,
07.06.02
BRAILLE-DUPLICATING-MACHINE
OPERATOR (print. & pub.),
207.685-010, 05.12.19
BRAKE COUPLER, ROAD FREIGHT
(r.r. trans.), 910.367-010, 05.12.05
BRAKE HOLDER (any ind.),
932.664-010, 05.12.03
BRAKE OPERATOR 2 (any ind.),
619.685-026, 06.02.02
BRAKE REPAIRER (auto. ser.),
620.281-026, 05.10.02
BRAZER, ASSEMBLER (welding),
813.684-010, 06.02.22
BREWERY CELLAR WORKER (beer
prod.), 522.685-014, 06.04.15
BREWING DIRECTOR (beer prod.),
183.167-010, 05.02.03
BRICKLAYER (const.), 861.381-018,
05.05.01
BRIDGE-OR-GANTRY CRANE
OPERATOR (any ind.), 921.663-010,
05.11.04
BRIGHT CUTTER (jewelry), 700.684-018,
06.02.24
BRIQUETTE-MACHINE OPERATOR
(fuel briquettes), 549.662-010, 06.02.17
BROKERAGE CLERK 1 (finan. inst.),
219.482-010, 07.02.02
BROOM STITCHER (brush & broom),
692.682-022, 06.02.09
BROOMMAKER (brush & broom),
739.684-018, 06.04.34
BRUSH MATERIAL PREPARER (brush
& broom), 739.684-022, 06.02.32
BUCKER (logging), 454.684-010, 03.04.02
BUDGET ANALYST (gov. ser.),
161.267-030, 11.06.05
BUDGET OFFICER (gov. ser.),
161.117-010, 11.06.05
BUFFER 1 (any ind.), 705.684-014,
06.04.24
BUFFING-MACHINE TENDER (any
ind.), 603.665-010, 06.04.02
BUILDING CLEANER (any ind.),
891.684-022, 05.10.01

BUILDING INSPECTOR (insurance), 168.267-010, 05.03.06

BULLDOZER OPERATOR 1 (any ind.), 850.683-010, 05.11.01

BURSTING-MACHINE TENDER (clerical), 217.685-010, 05.12.19

BUS DRIVER (motor trans.), 913.463-010, 09.03.01

BUSINESS MANAGER (amuse. & rec.), 191.117-018, 11.12.03

BUSINESS REPRESENTATIVE, LABOR UNION (profess. & kin.), 187.167-018, 11.05.02

BUSINESS-OPPORTUNITY-AND-PRO- PERTY-INVESTMENT BROKER (bus. ser.), 189.157-010, 08.01.03

BUTCHER, ALL-ROUND (slaught. & meat pack.), 525.381-014, 06.02.28

BUTCHER, MEAT (hotel & rest.), 316.681-010, 05.10.08

BUTTERMAKER (dairy prod.), 529.362-010, 06.02.15

BUTTONHOLE-AND-BUTTON-SEWING- MACHINE OPERATOR (garment), 786.685-042, 06.04.05

BUYER (profess. & kin.), 162.157-018, 08.01.03

BUYER, ASSISTANT (ret. tr.), 162.157-022, 08.01.03

BUZZSAW OPERATOR (any ind.), 667.685-026, 06.04.03

CABINET ASSEMBLER (furn.), 763.684-014, 06.02.22

CABINETMAKER (woodworking), 660.280-010, 05.05.08

CABLE ENGINEER, OUTSIDE PLANT (tel. & tel.), 003.167-010, 05.01.03

CABLE INSTALLER-REPAIRER (light, heat, & power), 821.361-010, 05.05.05

CABLE MAINTAINER (light, heat, & power), 952.464-010, 05.06.01

CABLE MAKER (elec. equip.), 728.684-010, 06.02.32

CABLE PULLER (const.), 829.684-018, 05.12.16

CABLE SPLICER (const.), 829.361-010, 05.05.05

CABLE STRETCHER AND TESTER (aircraft-aerospace mfg.), 806.685-010, 06.03.01

CABLE SUPERVISOR (tel. & tel.), 184.161-010, 05.05.05

CABLE TESTER (tel. & tel.), 822.361-010, 05.05.05

CADDIE (amuse. & rec.), 341.677-010, 09.05.06

CAFETERIA ATTENDANT (hotel & rest.), 311.677-010, 09.05.02

CAKE DECORATOR (bake. prod.), 524.381-010, 05.05.17

CALCULATING-MACHINE OPERATOR (clerical), 216.482-022, 07.02.02

CALIBRATION CHECKER 2 (inst. & app.), 710.687-018, 06.03.02

CALIBRATION LABORATORY TECHNICIAN (aircraft-aerospace mfg.), 019.281-010, 02.04.01

CALL-OUT OPERATOR (bus. ser.), 237.367-014, 07.05.03

CAMERA REPAIRER (photo. apparatus), 714.281-014, 05.05.11

CANCELLATION CLERK (insurance), 203.382-014, 07.02.02

CANDLEMAKER (candle), 739.664-010, 06.04.32

CANDY DIPPER, HAND (confection.), 524.684-010, 06.04.28

CANDY MAKER (confection.), 529.361-014, 06.02.28

CANDY MOLDER, HAND (confection.), 520.687-018, 06.04.28

CANER 2 (furn.), 763.684-022, 06.04.25

CANNERY WORKER (can. & preserv.), 529.686-014, 06.04.15

CANTEEN OPERATOR (any ind.), 311.674-010, 09.04.01

CANVAS REPAIRER (any ind.), 782.684-010, 06.04.27

CANVAS WORKER (canvas goods), 739.381-010, 06.01.04

CAPACITOR ASSEMBLER (elec. equip.), 729.684-014, 06.02.23

CAR HOP (hotel & rest.), 311.477-010, 09.04.01

CAR INSPECTOR (r.r. car blgd. & rep.), 910.667-010, 05.07.01

CARBIDE-POWDER PROCESSOR (mach. shop), 510.465-010, 06.02.10

CARBURETOR MECHANIC (auto. ser.), 620.281-034, 05.10.02

CARDER (any ind.), 920.685-034, 06.04.38

CARDIAC MONITOR TECHNICIAN (medical ser.), 078.367-010, 10.03.01

CARDIOPULMONARY TECHNOLOGIST (medical ser.), 078.362-030, 10.03.01

CARDROOM ATTENDANT 2 (amuse. & rec.), 343.577-010, 09.05.05

CAREER-GUIDANCE TECHNICIAN (educ.), 249.367-014, 11.02.04

CARETAKER (dom. ser.), 301.687-010, 05.12.18

CARGO AGENT (air trans.), 248.367-018, 05.09.01

CARPENTER (const.), 860.381-022, 05.05.02

CARPENTER, MAINTENANCE (any ind.), 860.281-010, 05.05.02

CARPENTER, ROUGH (const.), 860.381-042, 05.05.02

CARPET CUTTER (ret. tr.), 929.381-010, 05.10.01

CARPET CUTTER 2 (carpet & rug), 585.687-014, 06.04.27

CARPET LAYER (ret. tr.), 864.381-010, 05.10.01

CARPET SEWER (carpet & rug), 787.682-014, 06.02.05

CARPET WEAVER (carpet & rug), 683.682-010, 06.02.06

CARPET-LAYER HELPER (ret. tr.), 864.687-010, 05.10.01

CARTON-FORMING-MACHINE OPERATOR (any ind.), 641.685-022, 06.04.04

CARTON-FORMING-MACHINE TENDER (paper goods), 641.685-026, 06.04.04

CARVER (hotel & rest.), 316.661-010, 05.10.08

CASE AIDE (social ser.), 195.367-010, 10.01.02

CASEWORKER (gov. ser.), 169.262-010, 07.01.06

CASEWORKER (social ser.), 195.107-010, 10.01.02

CASH-REGISTER SERVICER (any ind.), 633.281-010, 05.05.09

CASHIER 1 (clerical), 211.362-010, 07.03.01

CASHIER 2 (clerical), 211.462-010, 07.03.01

CASHIER-CHECKER (ret. tr.), 211.462-014, 07.03.01

CASHIER-WRAPPER (ret. tr.), 211.462-018, 09.04.02

CASKET ASSEMBLER (mort. goods), 739.481-010, 06.02.22

CASTER (jewelry), 502.381-010, 06.02.24

CASTING REPAIRER (any ind.), 619.281-010, 05.10.01

CATALOG LIBRARIAN (library), 100.387-010, 11.02.04

CEMENT MASON (const.), 844.364-010, 05.05.01

CEMENTER, MACHINE APPLICATOR (boot & shoe), 690.686-018, 06.04.05

CEMETERY WORKER (real estate), 406.684-010, 03.04.04

CENTER-MACHINE OPERATOR (confection.), 520.682-014, 06.02.15

CENTRAL-OFFICE EQUIPMENT ENGINEER (tel. & tel.), 003.187-010, 05.01.03

CENTRAL-OFFICE OPERATOR (tel. & tel.), 235.462-010, 07.04.06

CENTRAL-OFFICE REPAIRER (tel. & tel.), 822.281-014, 05.05.05

CENTRAL-SUPPLY WORKER (medical ser.), 381.687-010, 05.12.18

CENTRIFUGE OPERATOR (dairy prod.), 521.685-042, 06.04.15

CENTRIFUGE OPERATOR, PLASMA PROCESSING (drug prep. & related), 599.685-018, 06.04.11

CEPHALOMETRIC ANALYST (medical ser.), 078.384-010, 02.04.02

CERAMIC CAPACITOR PROCESSOR (electronics), 590.684-010, 06.04.08

CERAMIC COATER, MACHINE (any ind.), 509.685-022, 06.04.21

CERAMIC DESIGN ENGINEER (profess. & kin.), 006.061-010, 05.01.07

CERAMIC ENGINEER (profess. & kin.), 006.061-014, 05.01.07

CHAIN MAKER, MACHINE (jewelry), 700.684-022, 06.02.23

CHAIN OFFBEARER (planing mill), 669.686-018, 06.04.03

CHAINSAW OPERATOR (logging), 454.687-010, 03.04.02

CHANGE-HOUSE ATTENDANT (any ind.), 358.687-010, 05.12.18

CHAPERON (per. ser.), 359.667-010, 04.02.03

CHAR-CONVEYOR TENDER (sugar), 529.685-050, 06.04.40

CHARGE PREPARATION TECHNICIAN (electronics), 590.384-010, 06.02.32

CHARTER (amuse. & rec.), 249.367-018, 12.01.02

CHAUFFEUR (any ind.), 913.663-010, 09.03.02

CHAUFFEUR, FUNERAL CAR (per. ser.), 359.673-014, 05.08.03

CHECK CASHIER (bus. ser.), 211.462-026, 07.03.01

CHECK WRITER (ret. tr.), 219.382-010, 07.06.02

CHECK-PROCESSING CLERK 1 (finan. inst.), 216.387-010, 07.02.02

CHECKER 1 (clerical), 222.687-010, 07.07.02

CHECKER, DUMP GROUNDS (bus. ser.), 219.367-010, 05.09.03

CHECKROOM ATTENDANT (any ind.), 358.677-010, 09.05.03

CHEESE CUTTER (dairy prod.), 529.585-010, 06.04.15

CHEESEMAKER (dairy prod.), 529.361-018, 06.01.04

CHEF (hotel & rest.), 313.131-014, 05.05.17

CHEF DE FROID (hotel & rest.), 313.281-010, 05.05.17

CHEMICAL DESIGN ENGINEER, PROCESSES (profess. & kin.), 008.061-014, 05.01.07

CHEMICAL ENGINEER (profess. & kin.), 008.061-018, 05.01.07

CHEMICAL OPERATOR 2 (chem.), 558.585-014, 06.04.11

CHEMICAL PREPARER 1 (chem.), 550.685-030, 06.04.11

CHEMICAL RESEARCH ENGINEER (profess. & kin.), 008.061-022, 05.01.01

CHEMICAL-ENGINEERING TECHNICIAN (profess. & kin.), 008.261-010, 05.01.08

CHEMICAL-LABORATORY TECHNICIAN (profess. & kin.), 022.261-010, 02.04.01

CHEMICAL-RADIATION TECHNICIAN (gov. ser.), 015.261-010, 11.10.03

CHEMICAL-TEST ENGINEER (profess. & kin.), 008.061-026, 05.01.04

CHEMIST (profess. & kin.), 022.061-010, 02.01.01

CHEMIST, FOOD (profess. & kin.), 022.061-014, 02.02.04

CHEMISTRY TECHNOLOGIST (medical ser.), 078.261-010, 02.04.02

CHIEF BANK EXAMINER (gov. ser.), 160.167-046, 11.10.01

CHILD-CARE ATTENDANT, SCHOOL (per. ser.), 355.674-010, 10.03.03

CHILDREN'S ATTENDANT (amuse. & rec.), 349.677-018, 09.05.08

CHILDREN'S TUTOR (dom. ser.), 099.227-010, 10.03.03

CHIMNEY SWEEP (any ind.), 891.687-010, 05.12.18

CHIROPRACTOR (medical ser.), 079.101-010, 02.03.04

CHOCOLATE MOLDER, MACHINE (choc. & cocoa), 529.685-054, 06.04.15

CHOCOLATE-PRODUCTION-MACHINE OPERATOR (choc. & cocoa), 529.382-014, 06.02.15

CHOKE SETTER (logging), 921.687-014, 05.12.04

CHOREOGRAPHER (amuse. & rec.), 151.027-010, 01.05.01

CHRISTMAS-TREE FARM WORKER (forestry), 451.687-010, 03.04.01

CIGAR MAKER (tobacco), 790.684-014, 06.04.28

CITY PLANNING AIDE (profess. & kin.), 199.364-010, 11.03.02

CIVIL ENGINEER (profess. & kin.), 005.061-014, 05.01.07

CIVIL ENGINEERING TECHNICIAN (profess. & kin.), 005.261-014, 05.03.02

CIVIL PREPAREDNESS TRAINING OFFICER (gov. ser.), 169.127-010, 11.07.02

CLAIM ADJUSTER (bus. ser.), 241.217-010, 11.12.01

CLAIM EXAMINER (insurance), 168.267-014, 07.02.03

CLAIM EXAMINER (bus. ser.), 241.267-018, 11.12.01

CLAIMS ADJUDICATOR (gov. ser.), 169.267-010, 11.12.01

CLAIMS CLERK 2 (insurance), 205.367-018, 07.04.02

CLAMP REMOVER (veneer & plywood), 569.687-010, 06.04.40

CLASSIFICATION CLERK (clerical), 206.387-010, 07.05.03

CLASSIFIED-AD CLERK 2 (print. & pub.), 247.387-022, 07.05.02

CLASSIFIER (library), 100.367-014, 11.02.04

CLAY MODELER (any ind.), 779.281-010, 01.06.02

CLEANER 2 (any ind.), 919.687-014, 05.12.18

CLEANER AND POLISHER (any ind.), 709.687-010, 06.04.39

CLEANER, COMMERCIAL OR INSTITUTIONAL (any ind.), 381.687-014, 05.12.18

CLEANER, HOSPITAL (medical ser.), 323.687-010, 05.12.18

CLEANER, HOUSEKEEPING (any ind.), 323.687-014, 05.12.18

CLEANER, INDUSTRIAL (any ind.), 381.687-018, 05.12.18

CLEANER, LABORATORY EQUIPMENT (any ind.), 381.687-022, 05.12.18

CLEANER, SIGNS (signs), 739.687-062, 05.12.18

CLEANER, WINDOW (any ind.), 389.687-014, 05.12.18

CLERGY MEMBER (profess. & kin.), 120.007-010, 10.01.01

CLERK, GENERAL (clerical), 209.562-010, 07.07.03

CLERK-TYPIST (clerical), 203.362-010, 07.06.02

CLOCKER (amuse. & rec.), 153.367-010, 12.01.02

CLOTH DOFFER (textile), 689.586-010, 06.04.06

CLOTH PRINTER (any ind.), 652.382-010, 06.02.09

CLOTHES DESIGNER (profess. & kin.), 142.061-018, 01.02.03

CLOTHES-ROOM WORKER (medical ser.), 355.687-010, 09.05.07

CLOWN (amuse. & rec.), 159.047-010, 01.03.02

COACH, PROFESSIONAL ATHLETES (amuse. & rec.), 153.227-010, 12.01.01

COATER OPERATOR (any ind.), 509.382-010, 06.02.21

COATING EQUIPMENT OPERATOR, PRINTED CIRCUIT BOARDS (electronics), 590.685-066, 06.04.19

COATING-MACHINE OPERATOR (coated fabrics), 584.382-010, 06.02.21

COBBLER (boot & shoe), 788.381-010, 06.02.27

CODE INSPECTOR (gov. ser.), 168.367-018, 05.03.06

CODING CLERK (clerical), 209.387-010, 07.05.03

COFFEE GRINDER (food prep nec), 521.685-078, 06.04.15

COFFEE MAKER (hotel & rest.), 317.684-010, 05.12.17

COFFEE ROASTER (food prep nec), 523.682-014, 06.02.15

COIL WINDER (elec. equip.), 724.684-026, 06.04.23

COIL WINDER, REPAIR (any ind.), 724.381-014, 06.02.32

COIN WRAPPER (clerical), 217.686-010, 05.12.19

COIN-MACHINE COLLECTOR (bus. ser.), 292.687-010, 07.07.03

COIN-MACHINE OPERATOR (finan. inst.), 217.585-010, 05.12.19

COIN-MACHINE-SERVICE REPAIRER (coin mach.), 639.281-014, 05.10.02

COLD-MILL OPERATOR (iron & steel), 613.462-010, 06.02.10

COLLATOR OPERATOR (clerical), 208.685-010, 05.12.19

COLLECTION CLERK (finan. inst.), 216.362-014, 07.02.02

COLLECTION CLERK (clerical), 241.357-010, 07.04.02

COLOR-PRINTER OPERATOR (photofinish.), 976.382-014, 05.10.05

COLUMNIST/COMMENTATOR (print. & pub.), 131.067-010, 11.08.03

COMEDIAN (amuse. & rec.), 159.047-014, 01.03.02

COMMERCIAL DESIGNER (profess. & kin.), 141.081-014, 01.02.03

COMMERCIAL ENGINEER (radio & tv broad.), 003.187-014, 05.01.03

COMMISSARY MANAGER (any ind.), 185.167-010, 11.11.05

COMMISSION AGENT, AGRICULTURAL PRODUCE (whole. tr.), 260.357-010, 08.01.03

COMMUNITY DIETITIAN (profess. & kin.), 077.127-010, 11.02.03

COMMUNITY ORGANIZATION WORKER (social ser.), 195.167-010, 11.07.01

COMMUNITY WORKER (gov. ser.), 195.367-018, 10.01.02

COMMUNITY-SERVICES-AND-HEALTH-EDUCATION OFFICER (gov. ser.), 079.167-010, 11.07.02

COMPARATOR OPERATOR (any ind.), 699.384-010, 06.03.01

COMPARISON SHOPPER (ret. tr.), 296.367-014, 08.01.03

COMPILER (clerical), 209.387-014, 07.05.03

COMPOSITOR (print. & pub.), 973.381-010, 05.05.13

COMPRESSED-GAS-PLANT WORKER (comp. & liq. gases), 549.587-010, 06.04.40

COMPRESSION-MOLDING-MACHINE TENDER (fabric. plastic prod.), 556.685-022, 06.04.13

COMPUTER OPERATOR (clerical), 213.362-010, 07.06.01

COMPUTER-APPLICATIONS ENGINEER (profess. & kin.), 020.062-010, 02.01.01

COMPUTER-PERIPHERAL-EQUIPMENT OPERATOR (clerical), 213.382-010, 07.06.01

CONCRETE-MIXING-TRUCK DRIVER (const.), 900.683-010, 05.08.03

CONDOMINIUM MANAGER (real estate), 186.167-062, 11.11.01

CONDUCTOR, PASSENGER CAR (r.r. trans.), 198.167-010, 11.11.03

CONDUCTOR, ROAD FREIGHT (r.r. trans.), 198.167-018, 11.11.03

CONDUIT MECHANIC (const.),
869.361-010, 05.05.06
CONFIGURATION MANAGEMENT
ANALYST (profess. & kin.),
012.167-010, 05.01.06
CONSERVATION TECHNICIAN
(museum), 102.261-010, 01.06.02
CONSERVATOR, ARTIFACTS (profess. &
kin.), 055.381-010, 01.06.02
CONSTRUCTION INSPECTOR (const.),
182.267-010, 05.03.06
CONSTRUCTION WORKER 2 (const.),
869.687-026, 05.12.03
CONSTRUCTION-EQUIPMENT
MECHANIC (const.), 620.261-022,
05.05.09
CONSULTANT (profess. & kin.),
189.167-010, 11.01.02
CONSULTANT, EDUCATION (educ.),
099.167-014, 11.07.03
CONTACT REPRESENTATIVE (gov.
ser.), 169.167-018, 07.01.01
CONTACT-LENS MOLDER (optical
goods), 690.685-090, 06.04.13
CONTACT-LENS-FLASHING PUNCHER
(optical goods), 713.687-014, 06.04.24
CONTINUITY DIRECTOR (radio & tv
broad.), 132.037-010, 01.01.01
CONTRACT ADMINISTRATOR (any
ind.), 162.117-014, 11.12.04
CONTRACT CLERK (profess. & kin.),
119.267-018, 07.01.05
CONTRACT CLERK, AUTOMOBILE
(ret. tr.), 219.362-026, 07.02.02
CONTRACT SPECIALIST (profess. &
kin.), 162.117-018, 11.12.04
CONTRACTOR (const.), 182.167-010,
11.12.04
CONTROL CLERK, DATA PROCESSING
2 (clerical), 221.687-010, 07.07.02
CONTROLS DESIGNER (profess. & kin.),
003.261-014, 05.03.02
CONVEYOR FEEDER-OFFBEARER
(any ind.), 921.686-014, 06.04.40
CONVEYOR OPERATOR (any ind.),
921.683-026, 05.11.04
CONVEYOR TENDER (any ind.),
921.685-026, 06.04.40
CONVEYOR-MAINTENANCE
MECHANIC (any ind.), 630.381-010,
05.10.02
CONVEYOR-SYSTEM DISPATCHER
(any ind.), 921.662-018, 05.12.04
COOK (dom. ser.), 305.281-010, 05.10.08
COOK (hotel & rest.), 313.361-014,
05.05.17
COOK (any ind.), 315.361-010, 05.10.08
COOK HELPER (hotel & rest.),
317.687-010, 05.12.17
COOK, BARBECUE (hotel & rest.),
313.381-022, 05.10.08
COOK, FRY, DEEP FAT (can. & preserv.),
526.685-014, 06.04.15
COOK, MEXICAN FOOD (food prep nec),
526.134-010, 06.01.01
COOK, PASTRY (hotel & rest.),
313.381-026, 05.10.08
COOK, SHORT ORDER 1 (hotel & rest.),
313.361-022, 05.10.08
COOK, SHORT ORDER 2 (hotel & rest.),
313.671-010, 05.10.08
COOK, SPECIALTY (hotel & rest.),
313.361-026, 05.10.08
COOKER, PROCESS CHEESE (dairy
prod.), 526.665-010, 06.04.15

COOLING-ROOM ATTENDANT (per.
ser.), 335.677-010, 09.05.01
COORDINATOR OF REHABILITATION
SERVICES (medical ser.), 076.117-010,
11.07.01
COORDINATOR, SKILL-TRAINING
PROGRAM (gov. ser.), 169.167-062,
07.01.02
COPY WRITER (profess. & kin.),
131.067-014, 01.01.02
COPYIST (any ind.), 152.267-010,
01.04.02
CORE-DRILL OPERATOR (any ind.),
930.682-010, 05.11.02
COREMAKER (foundry), 518.381-014,
06.01.04
COREMAKER, MACHINE 1 (foundry),
518.685-014, 06.04.08
CORRECTION OFFICER (gov. ser.),
372.667-018, 04.02.01
CORRECTIVE THERAPIST (medical
ser.), 076.361-010, 10.02.02
CORRESPONDENCE CLERK (clerical),
209.262-010, 07.04.02
CORRESPONDENCE-REVIEW CLERK
(clerical), 209.367-018, 07.05.04
CORRUGATED-FASTENER DRIVER
(woodworking), 669.685-042, 06.04.20
COSMETOLOGIST (per. ser.),
332.271-010, 09.02.01
COST CLERK (clerical), 216.382-034,
07.02.02
COST-ANALYSIS ENGINEER
(aircraft-aerospace mfg.), 002.167-010,
05.01.06
COUNSELOR (profess. & kin.),
045.107-010, 10.01.02
COUNSELOR, CAMP (amuse. & rec.),
159.124-010, 09.01.01
COUNTER ATTENDANT, CAFETERIA
(hotel & rest.), 311.677-014, 09.05.02
COUNTER ATTENDANT, LUNCHROOM
OR COFFEE SHOP (hotel & rest.),
311.477-014, 09.04.01
COUNTER CLERK (photofinish.),
249.366-010, 07.03.01
COUNTER-SUPPLY WORKER (hotel &
rest.), 319.687-010, 09.05.02
COUNTY HOME-DEMONSTRATION
AGENT (gov. ser.), 096.121-010,
11.02.03
COUNTY-AGRICULTURAL AGENT (gov.
ser.), 096.127-010, 11.02.03
COUPON CLERK (finan. inst.),
219.462-010, 07.02.02
COURT CLERK (gov. ser.), 243.362-010,
07.01.02
COVERING-MACHINE OPERATOR
(print. & pub.), 653.682-014, 06.02.20
CRAFT DEMONSTRATOR (museum),
109.364-010, 09.01.02
CRATER (any ind.), 920.484-010, 06.04.38
CREDIT ANALYST (finan. inst.),
191.267-014, 11.06.03
CREDIT AUTHORIZER (clerical),
249.367-022, 07.05.02
CREDIT CLERK (clerical), 205.367-022,
07.04.01
CREDIT COUNSELOR (profess. & kin.),
160.207-010, 07.01.01
CREDIT-CARD-CONTROL CLERK
(finan. inst.), 249.367-026, 07.05.03
CREDIT-REFERENCE CLERK (ret. tr.),
209.362-018, 07.05.02

CREMATOR (per. ser.), 359.685-010,
06.04.19
CREW SCHEDULER (air trans.),
215.362-010, 07.05.01
CRIMINALIST (profess. & kin.),
029.281-010, 02.04.01
CRIMPING-MACHINE OPERATOR (any
ind.), 616.682-022, 06.02.02
CROSSBAND LAYER (veneer &
plywood), 762.687-026, 06.04.25
CROSSING TENDER (any ind.),
371.667-010, 05.12.20
CROWN-ASSEMBLY-MACHINE
OPERATOR (any ind.), 692.685-062,
06.04.09
CRUSHER TENDER (any ind.),
570.685-022, 06.04.08
CRYPTOGRAPHIC-MACHINE
OPERATOR (clerical), 203.582-018,
07.06.02
CRYSTAL GROWER (electronics),
590.382-014, 06.02.18
CRYSTAL GROWING TECHNICIAN
(electronics), 590.262-010, 06.02.18
CRYSTAL SLICER (electronics),
677.382-018, 06.02.09
CURATOR (museum), 102.017-010,
11.07.04
CURRENCY SORTER (finan. inst.),
217.485-010, 05.12.19
CUSTODIAN, ATHLETIC EQUIPMENT
(amuse. & rec.), 969.367-010, 05.09.01
CUSTOM TAILOR (garment),
785.261-014, 05.05.15
CUSTOM VAN INSTALLER (auto. mfg.),
860.581-074, 05.05.02
CUSTOMER-EQUIPMENT ENGINEER
(tel. & tel.), 003.187-018, 05.01.08
CUSTOMER-SERVICE CLERK (ret. tr.),
299.367-010, 09.04.02
CUSTOMER-SERVICE
REPRESENTATIVE (light, heat, &
power), 239.367-010, 07.04.01
CUSTOMER-SUPPORT SPECIALIST
(whole. tr.), 020.224-010, 11.01.01
CUSTOMS IMPORT SPECIALIST (gov.
ser.), 168.267-018, 11.10.04
CUSTOMS INSPECTOR (gov. ser.),
168.267-022, 11.10.04
CUSTOMS PATROL OFFICER (gov. ser.),
168.167-010, 04.01.02
CUSTOMS-HOUSE BROKER (finan.
inst.), 186.117-018, 11.04.04
CUT-OFF-SAW OPERATOR
(woodworking), 667.682-022, 06.02.03
CUTTER (photofinish.), 976.685-010,
06.04.09
CUTTER OPERATOR (any ind.),
699.682-018, 06.02.09
CUTTER, HAND 1 (any ind.),
781.584-014, 06.02.27
CUTTER, MACHINE 1 (any ind.),
781.684-014, 06.02.27
CUTTER, MACHINE 2 (any ind.),
699.685-014, 06.04.09
CUTTING-MACHINE TENDER (any
ind.), 690.685-122, 06.04.09
CYLINDER FILLER (comp. & liq. gases),
559.565-010, 06.02.12
CYLINDER-PRESS OPERATOR (print. &
pub.), 651.362-010, 05.05.13
CYTOTECHNOLOGIST (medical ser.),
078.281-010, 02.04.02
DAIRY SCIENTIST (profess. & kin.),
040.061-018, 02.02.01

DAIRY TECHNOLOGIST (profess. & kin.), 040.061-022, 02.02.04

DAIRY-PROCESSING-EQUIPMENT OPERATOR (dairy prod.), 529.382-018, 06.02.15

DANCE THERAPIST (medical ser.), 076.127-018, 10.02.02

DANCER (amuse. & rec.), 151.047-010, 01.05.02

DATA TYPIST (clerical), 203.582-022, 07.06.02

DATA-CODER OPERATOR (clerical), 203.582-026, 07.06.02

DATA-EXAMINATION CLERK (clerical), 209.387-022, 07.05.02

DEALER-COMPLIANCE REPRESENTATIVE (ret. tr.), 168.267-026, 11.10.05

DECAL APPLIER (any ind.), 749.684-010, 06.04.34

DECKHAND (water trans.), 911.687-022, 05.08.04

DECKHAND, FISHING VESSEL (fish.), 449.667-010, 03.04.03

DECONTAMINATOR (any ind.), 199.384-010, 02.04.01

DECORATOR (any ind.), 298.381-010, 01.06.02

DECORATOR (bake. prod.), 524.684-014, 06.04.28

DECORATOR, STREET AND BUILDING (any ind.), 899.687-010, 05.12.12

DELI CUTTER-SLICER (ret. tr.), 316.684-014, 05.12.17

DELIVERER, CAR RENTAL (auto. ser.), 919.663-010, 05.08.03

DELIVERER, MERCHANDISE (ret. tr.), 299.477-010, 09.04.02

DELIVERER, OUTSIDE (clerical), 230.667-010, 07.07.02

DEMONSTRATOR (ret. tr.), 297.354-010, 08.02.05

DEMONSTRATOR, ELECTRIC-GAS APPLIANCES (light, heat, & power), 297.357-010, 08.02.05

DEMONSTRATOR, KNITTING (ret. tr.), 297.354-014, 08.02.05

DEMURRAGE CLERK (r.r. trans.), 214.362-010, 07.02.04

DENTAL ASSISTANT (medical ser.), 079.371-010, 10.03.02

DENTAL CERAMIST (medical ser.), 712.281-010, 05.05.11

DENTAL CERAMIST ASSISTANT (medical ser.), 712.664-010, 05.05.11

DENTAL HYGIENIST (medical ser.), 078.361-010, 10.02.02

DENTAL-LABORATORY TECHNICIAN (medical ser.), 712.381-018, 05.05.11

DENTAL-LABORATORY-TECHNICIAN APPRENTICE (medical ser.), 712.381-022, 05.05.11

DENTIST (medical ser.), 072.101-010, 02.03.02

DENTURE WAXER (medical ser.), 712.681-010, 06.02.32

DENTURE-MODEL MAKER (medical ser.), 712.681-014, 05.05.11

DEPUTY, COURT (gov. ser.), 377.137-018, 04.01.01

DERRICK OPERATOR (any ind.), 921.663-022, 05.11.04

DESIGN DRAFTER, ELECTROMECHANISMS (profess. & kin.), 017.261-014, 05.03.02

DESIGN PRINTER, BALLOON (rubber goods), 651.685-014, 06.04.07

DESIGN TECHNICIAN, COMPUTER-AIDED (electronics), 003.362-010, 05.03.02

DETAILER (profess. & kin.), 017.261-018, 05.03.02

DETAILER, SCHOOL PHOTOGRAPHS (photofinish.), 976.564-010, 07.05.03

DETECTIVE 1 (any ind.), 376.367-014, 04.02.02

DEVELOPER (photofinish.), 976.681-010, 05.10.05

DEVELOPER, AUTOMATIC (photofinish.), 976.685-014, 06.04.19

DIALYSIS TECHNICIAN (medical ser.), 078.362-014, 10.02.02

DIE CUTTER (any ind.), 699.682-022, 06.02.09

DIE SINKER (mach. shop), 601.280-022, 05.05.07

DIE-CASTING-MACHINE OPERATOR 2 (foundry), 514.685-018, 06.04.10

DIESEL MECHANIC (any ind.), 625.281-010, 05.05.09

DIET CLERK (medical ser.), 245.587-010, 07.05.03

DIETETIC TECHNICIAN (profess. & kin.), 077.121-010, 05.05.17

DIETITIAN, CHIEF (profess. & kin.), 077.117-010, 11.05.02

DIETITIAN, CLINICAL (profess. & kin.), 077.127-014, 05.05.17

DIGESTER-OPERATOR HELPER (build. board), 532.686-010, 06.04.18

DINING ROOM ATTENDANT (hotel & rest.), 311.677-018, 09.05.02

DINKEY OPERATOR (any ind.), 919.663-014, 05.11.04

DIPPER (any ind.), 599.685-026, 06.04.21

DIPPER (jewelry), 735.687-010, 06.04.39

DIPPER AND BAKER (any ind.), 599.685-030, 06.04.21

DIRECT-MAIL CLERK (clerical), 209.587-018, 07.07.02

DIRECTOR OF PHOTOGRAPHY (motion pic.), 143.062-010, 01.02.03

DIRECTOR, CAMP (social ser.), 195.167-018, 11.11.02

DIRECTOR, COMMUNITY ORGANIZATION (nonprofit org.), 187.117-014, 11.07.01

DIRECTOR, COMPLIANCE (gov. ser.), 188.117-046, 11.10.02

DIRECTOR, EDUCATIONAL PROGRAM (educ.), 099.117-010, 11.07.03

DIRECTOR, FUNDRAISING (nonprofit org.), 165.117-010, 11.09.02

DIRECTOR, FUNDS DEVELOPMENT (profess. & kin.), 165.117-014, 11.09.02

DIRECTOR, FUNERAL (per. ser.), 187.167-030, 11.11.04

DIRECTOR, MEDIA MARKETING (radio & tv broad.), 163.117-022, 11.05.04

DIRECTOR, MOTION PICTURE (motion pic.), 159.067-010, 01.03.01

DIRECTOR, QUALITY ASSURANCE (profess. & kin.), 189.117-042, 11.05.02

DIRECTOR, QUALITY CONTROL (profess. & kin.), 012.167-014, 05.02.03

DIRECTOR, RECORDS MANAGEMENT (profess. & kin.), 161.117-014, 11.01.01

DIRECTOR, RECREATION CENTER (social ser.), 195.167-026, 11.11.02

DIRECTOR, REGULATORY AGENCY (gov. ser.), 188.117-134, 11.05.03

DIRECTOR, SERVICE (nonprofit org.), 187.167-214, 11.07.01

DIRECTOR, SERVICE (ret. tr.), 189.167-014, 11.05.02

DIRECTOR, SOCIAL (hotel & rest.), 352.167-010, 09.01.01

DIRECTOR, TRANSPORTATION (motor trans.), 184.117-014, 11.05.01

DIRECTOR, UTILITY ACCOUNTS (gov. ser.), 160.267-014, 11.06.03

DIRECTORY-ASSISTANCE OPERATOR (tel. & tel.), 235.662-018, 07.04.06

DISBURSEMENT CLERK (finan. inst.), 209.367-022, 07.05.02

DISK JOCKEY (radio & tv broad.), 159.147-014, 01.03.03

DISPATCHER (air trans.), 912.167-010, 05.03.03

DISPATCHER, MAINTENANCE SERVICE (clerical), 239.367-014, 07.04.05

DISPATCHER, MOTOR VEHICLE (clerical), 249.167-014, 07.05.01

DISPLAY DESIGNER (profess. & kin.), 142.051-010, 01.02.03

DISPLAY MAKER (signs), 739.361-010, 01.06.02

DISPLAY-SCREEN FABRICATOR (electronics), 725.685-010, 06.04.19

DISPLAYER, MERCHANDISE (ret. tr.), 298.081-010, 01.02.03

DISTILLERY WORKER, GENERAL (distilled liquor), 529.687-066, 06.04.40

DISTRESSER (furn.), 763.687-018, 01.06.02

DISTRIBUTING CLERK (clerical), 222.587-018, 07.07.02

DIVER (any ind.), 899.261-010, 05.10.01

DOCUMENT PREPARER, MICROFILMING (bus. ser.), 249.587-018, 07.05.03

DOCUMENTATION ENGINEER (profess. & kin.), 012.167-078, 05.01.06

DOG BATHER (per. ser.), 418.677-010, 03.03.02

DOG CATCHER (gov. ser.), 379.673-010, 03.04.05

DOG GROOMER (per. ser.), 418.674-010, 03.03.02

DOG LICENSER (nonprofit org.), 249.367-030, 07.04.03

DOLL REPAIRER (any ind.), 731.684-014, 05.10.04

DOLLY PUSHER (radio & tv broad.), 962.687-010, 05.12.03

DOOR-CLOSER MECHANIC (any ind.), 630.381-014, 05.10.02

DOORKEEPER (any ind.), 324.677-014, 09.05.04

DOUGH MIXER (bake. prod.), 520.582-010, 06.02.15

DOUGHNUT MAKER (bake. prod.), 526.684-010, 06.02.28

DOUGHNUT-MACHINE OPERATOR (bake. prod.), 526.682-022, 06.02.15

DRAFTER, AERONAUTICAL (profess. & kin.), 002.261-010, 05.03.02

DRAFTER, ARCHITECTURAL (profess. & kin.), 001.261-010, 05.03.02

DRAFTER, ASSISTANT (profess. & kin.), 017.281-018, 05.03.02

DRAFTER, AUTOMOTIVE DESIGN (auto. mfg.), 017.281-022, 05.03.02

DRAFTER, CARTOGRAPHIC (profess. & kin.), 018.261-010, 05.03.02

DRAFTER, CIVIL (profess. & kin.), 005.281-010, 05.03.02

DRAFTER, COMMERCIAL (profess. & kin.), 017.261-026, 05.03.02

DRAFTER, ELECTRICAL (profess. & kin.), 003.281-010, 05.03.02

DRAFTER, ELECTRONIC (profess. & kin.), 003.281-014, 05.03.02

DRAFTER, GEOLOGICAL (petrol. production), 010.281-014, 05.03.02

DRAFTER, GEOPHYSICAL (petrol. production), 010.281-018, 05.03.02

DRAFTER, LANDSCAPE (profess. & kin.), 001.261-014, 05.03.02

DRAFTER, MARINE (profess. & kin.), 014.281-010, 05.03.02

DRAFTER, MECHANICAL (profess. & kin.), 007.281-010, 05.03.02

DRAFTER, STRUCTURAL (profess. & kin.), 005.281-014, 05.03.02

DRAFTER, TOPOGRAPHICAL (profess. & kin.), 018.261-014, 05.03.02

DRAGLINE OPERATOR (any ind.), 850.683-018, 05.11.04

DRAPERY AND UPHOLSTERY ESTIMATOR (ret. tr.), 299.387-010, 05.09.02

DRAPERY HANGER (ret. tr.), 869.484-014, 05.10.01

DRAWINGS CHECKER, ENGINEERING (profess. & kin.), 007.267-010, 05.03.02

DRESSER (amuse. & rec.), 346.674-010, 09.05.06

DRESSMAKER (any ind.), 785.361-010, 05.05.15

DRIER OPERATOR (macaroni & related), 523.362-014, 06.02.15

DRIER OPERATOR (chem.), 553.685-042, 06.04.11

DRILL-PRESS OPERATOR, PRODUCTION (mach. shop), 606.685-026, 06.04.02

DRILLER, HAND (any ind.), 809.684-018, 06.04.34

DRIVE-IN THEATER ATTENDANT (amuse. & rec.), 349.673-010, 09.05.04

DRIVER'S LICENSE EXAMINER (gov. ser.), 168.267-034, 07.01.07

DRIVER, SALES ROUTE (ret. tr.), 292.353-010, 08.02.07

DROP-HAMMER OPERATOR (forging), 610.462-010, 06.02.02

DRUM STRAIGHTENER 1 (any ind.), 619.685-034, 06.04.02

DRY-WALL APPLICATOR (const.), 842.381-010, 05.05.04

DRY-WALL APPLICATOR (const.), 842.681-010, 05.10.01

DUMP OPERATOR (any ind.), 921.685-038, 05.11.04

DUMP-TRUCK DRIVER (any ind.), 902.683-010, 05.08.01

DUMPER (any ind.), 921.667-018, 05.12.03

DUPLICATING-MACHINE OPERATOR 1 (clerical), 207.682-010, 05.10.05

DYNAMITE-PACKING-MACHINE OPERATOR (explosives), 692.662-010, 06.02.09

EARRING MAKER (jewelry), 700.684-030, 06.04.23

ECONOMIST (profess. & kin.), 050.067-010, 11.03.05

EDITOR, DEPARTMENT (print. & pub.), 132.037-018, 11.08.01

EDITOR, FILM (motion pic.), 962.264-010, 01.01.01

EDITOR, MAP (profess. & kin.), 018.261-018, 05.03.02

EDITOR, NEWS (print. & pub.), 132.067-026, 11.08.01

EDITOR, NEWSPAPER (print. & pub.), 132.017-014, 11.08.01

EDITOR, PUBLICATIONS (print. & pub.), 132.037-022, 01.01.01

EDITORIAL ASSISTANT (print. & pub.), 132.267-014, 11.08.01

EDITORIAL WRITER (print. & pub.), 131.067-022, 01.01.02

EDUCATIONAL RESOURCE COORDINATOR (museum), 099.167-030, 11.07.03

EDUCATIONAL SPECIALIST (educ.), 099.167-022, 11.07.03

EDUCATIONAL THERAPIST (educ.), 094.227-010, 10.02.03

ELECTION CLERK (gov. ser.), 205.367-030, 07.04.03

ELECTRIC-GOLF-CART REPAIRER (amuse. & rec.), 620.261-026, 05.10.03

ELECTRIC-METER INSTALLER 1 (light, heat, & power), 821.361-014, 05.05.05

ELECTRIC-METER REPAIRER (light, heat, & power), 729.281-014, 05.05.10

ELECTRIC-METER TESTER (light, heat, & power), 821.381-010, 05.05.10

ELECTRIC-MOTOR ASSEMBLER (elec. equip.), 721.684-022, 06.04.23

ELECTRIC-MOTOR REPAIRER (any ind.), 721.281-018, 05.05.10

ELECTRIC-MOTOR-CONTROL ASSEMBLER (elec. equip.), 721.381-014, 06.01.04

ELECTRIC-ORGAN INSPECTOR AND REPAIRER (musical inst.), 730.281-018, 05.05.12

ELECTRIC-SIGN ASSEMBLER (signs), 729.684-022, 06.02.22

ELECTRIC-TOOL REPAIRER (any ind.), 729.281-022, 05.10.03

ELECTRICAL ENGINEER (profess. & kin.), 003.061-010, 05.01.08

ELECTRICAL ENGINEER, POWER SYSTEM (light, heat, & power), 003.167-018, 05.01.03

ELECTRICAL TECHNICIAN (profess. & kin.), 003.161-010, 05.01.01

ELECTRICAL TEST ENGINEER (profess. & kin.), 003.061-014, 05.01.04

ELECTRICAL-APPLIANCE PREPARER (any ind.), 827.584-010, 05.12.16

ELECTRICAL-APPLIANCE REPAIRER (any ind.), 723.381-010, 05.10.03

ELECTRICAL-APPLIANCE SERVICER (any ind.), 827.261-010, 05.05.10

ELECTRICAL-CONTROL ASSEMBLER (elec. equip.), 729.684-026, 06.02.23

ELECTRICAL-DESIGN ENGINEER (profess. & kin.), 003.061-018, 05.01.07

ELECTRICAL-INSTRUMENT REPAIRER (any ind.), 729.281-026, 05.05.10

ELECTRICIAN (any ind.), 824.261-010, 05.05.05

ELECTRICIAN, AUTOMOTIVE (auto. ser.), 825.281-022, 05.05.10

ELECTRICIAN, MAINTENANCE (any ind.), 829.261-018, 05.05.05

ELECTRICIAN, POWERHOUSE (light, heat, & power), 820.261-014, 05.05.05

ELECTRO-OPTICAL ENGINEER (profess. & kin.), 023.061-010, 05.01.07

ELECTROCARDIOGRAPH TECHNICIAN (medical ser.), 078.362-018, 10.03.01

ELECTROENCEPHALOGRAPHIC TECHNOLOGIST (medical ser.), 078.362-022, 10.03.01

ELECTROLESS PLATER, PRINTED CIRCUIT BOARD PANELS (electronics), 501.685-022, 06.04.21

ELECTROLOGIST (per. ser.), 339.371-010, 09.05.01

ELECTROMECHANICAL TECHNICIAN (inst. & app.), 710.281-018, 05.05.11

ELECTROMEDICAL-EQUIPMENT REPAIRER (any ind.), 729.281-030, 05.05.11

ELECTRONIC-COMPONENT PROCESSOR (electronics), 590.684-014, 06.04.19

ELECTRONIC-ORGAN TECHNICIAN (any ind.), 828.261-010, 05.05.12

ELECTRONIC-TYPESETTING-MACHINE OPERATOR (print. & pub.), 203.582-074, 07.06.02

ELECTRONICS ASSEMBLER (inst. & app.), 726.384-010, 06.02.23

ELECTRONICS ASSEMBLER (electronics), 726.684-018, 06.02.23

ELECTRONICS ASSEMBLER, DEVELOPMENTAL (electronics), 726.261-010, 05.05.05

ELECTRONICS ENGINEER (profess. & kin.), 003.061-030, 05.01.08

ELECTRONICS INSPECTOR I (electronics), 726.381-010, 06.01.05

ELECTRONICS INSPECTOR II (electronics), 726.684-022, 06.03.02

ELECTRONICS MECHANIC (any ind.), 828.281-010, 05.05.10

ELECTRONICS TECHNICIAN (profess. & kin.), 003.161-014, 05.01.01

ELECTRONICS TESTER I (electronics), 726.281-014, 06.01.05

ELECTRONICS TESTER II (electronics), 726.684-026, 06.03.02

ELECTRONICS UTILITY WORKER (electronics), 726.367-014, 06.04.34

ELECTRONICS WORKER (electronics), 726.687-010, 06.04.34

ELECTRONICS-DESIGN ENGINEER (profess. & kin.), 003.061-034, 05.01.07

ELECTROTYPER (print. & pub.), 974.381-010, 05.05.13

ELEVATOR CONSTRUCTOR (const.), 825.361-010, 05.05.06

ELEVATOR EXAMINER-AND-ADJUSTER (any ind.), 825.261-014, 05.07.03

ELEVATOR OPERATOR (any ind.), 388.663-010, 09.05.09

ELEVATOR OPERATOR, FREIGHT (any ind.), 921.683-038, 05.12.04

ELEVATOR REPAIRER (any ind.), 825.281-030, 05.05.05

ELIGIBILITY WORKER (gov. ser.), 195.267-010, 07.01.01

ELIGIBILITY-AND-OCCUPANCY INTERVIEWER (gov. ser.), 168.267-038, 07.01.01

EMBALMER (per. ser.), 338.371-014, 02.04.02

EMBOSSER (any ind.), 583.685-030, 06.04.02

EMBOSSING-PRESS OPERATOR (any ind.), 652.685-030, 06.04.09

EMERGENCY MEDICAL TECHNICIAN (medical ser.), 079.374-010, 10.03.02

EMPLOYEE RELATIONS SPECIALIST (motor trans.), 166.267-042, 11.03.04

EMPLOYER RELATIONS REPRESENTATIVE (profess. & kin.), 166.257-010, 11.09.03

EMPLOYMENT CLERK (clerical), 205.362-014, 07.04.01

EMPLOYMENT INTERVIEWER (profess. & kin.), 166.267-010, 11.03.04

EMPLOYMENT-AND-CLAIMS AIDE (gov. ser.), 169.367-010, 07.04.01

ENAMELER (plumb. supplies), 509.684-010, 06.04.33

ENGINEER (water trans.), 197.130-010, 05.06.02

ENGINEER, SOILS (profess. & kin.), 024.161-010, 05.01.08

ENGINEERING ANALYST (profess. & kin.), 020.067-010, 11.01.01

ENGINEERING ASSISTANT, MECHANICAL EQUIPMENT (profess. & kin.), 007.161-018, 05.03.02

ENGINEERING TECHNICIAN (profess. & kin.), 005.261-010, 05.03.08

ENGRAVER, HAND, HARD METALS (engraving), 704.381-026, 01.06.01

ENGRAVER, HAND, SOFT METALS (engraving), 704.381-030, 01.06.01

ENGRAVER, MACHINE 1 (engraving), 704.682-010, 05.10.05

ENGRAVER, PICTURE (print. & pub.), 979.281-018, 01.06.01

ENGRAVING-PRESS OPERATOR (print. & pub.), 651.382-010, 05.10.05

ENVIRONMENTAL ANALYST (profess. & kin.), 029.081-010, 02.01.02

ENVIRONMENTAL ANALYST (gov. ser.), 199.167-022, 11.05.03

ENVIRONMENTAL EPIDEMIOLOGIST (gov. ser.), 041.167-010, 02.02.01

ENVIRONMENTAL-CONTROL-SYSTEM INSTALLER-SERVICER (any ind.), 637.261-014, 05.05.09

EQUAL OPPORTUNITY OFFICER (any ind.), 168.267-114, 11.10.02

EQUAL-OPPORTUNITY REPRESENTATIVE (gov. ser.), 168.167-014, 11.10.02

EQUIPMENT CLEANER (any ind.), 599.684-010, 06.04.39

EQUIPMENT INSTALLER (any ind.), 828.381-010, 05.10.04

EQUIPMENT MONITOR, PHOTOTYPESETTING (print. & pub.), 650.682-010, 05.10.05

ESCROW OFFICER (profess. & kin.), 119.367-010, 07.01.04

ESTATE PLANNER (insurance), 186.167-010, 08.01.02

ESTIMATOR (profess. & kin.), 160.267-018, 05.03.02

ESTIMATOR AND DRAFTER (light, heat, & power), 019.261-014, 05.03.02

ESTIMATOR, PRINTING (print. & pub.), 221.367-014, 05.09.02

ETCHED-CIRCUIT PROCESSOR (electronics), 590.684-018, 06.02.32

ETCHER (engraving), 704.684-010, 01.06.01

ETCHER HELPER, HAND (print. & pub.), 971.687-010, 05.12.03

ETCHER-STRIPPER, PRINTED CIRCUIT BOARDS (electronics), 590.685-082, 06.04.19

EVALUATOR (educ.), 094.267-010, 10.02.03

EVALUATOR (nonprofit org.), 249.367-034, 05.09.02

EVAPORATIVE-COOLER INSTALLER (any ind.), 637.381-010, 05.10.04

EXAMINATION PROCTOR (gov. ser.), 199.267-018, 07.01.07

EXAMINER (gov. ser.), 169.267-014, 07.01.05

EXECUTIVE HOUSEKEEPER (hotel & rest.), 187.167-046, 11.11.01

EXECUTIVE VICE PRESIDENT, CHAMBER OF COMMERCE (nonprofit org.), 187.117-030, 11.05.02

EXERCISER, HORSE (amuse. & rec.), 153.674-010, 03.03.01

EXHIBIT BUILDER (museum), 739.261-010, 01.06.02

EXHIBIT DESIGNER (museum), 142.061-058, 01.02.03

EXHIBIT-DISPLAY REPRESENTATIVE (any ind.), 297.367-010, 09.01.02

EXPEDITER (clerical), 222.367-018, 07.05.01

EXPERIMENTAL ASSEMBLER (any ind.), 739.381-026, 05.05.11

EXPERIMENTAL MECHANIC 2 (aircraft-aerospace mfg.), 621.281-022, 05.05.09

EXTENSION SERVICE SPECIALIST (gov. ser.), 096.127-014, 11.02.03

EXTERMINATOR (any ind.), 389.684-010, 05.10.09

EXTERMINATOR, TERMITE (bus. ser.), 383.364-010, 05.10.09

EXTRACTOR OPERATOR (any ind.), 581.685-038, 06.04.16

EYEGLASS-LENS CUTTER (optical goods), 716.682-010, 06.02.08

EYELET-MACHINE OPERATOR (any ind.), 699.685-018, 06.04.05

FABRICATOR, FOAM RUBBER (any ind.), 780.684-062, 06.04.29

FABRICATOR-ASSEMBLER, METAL PRODUCTS (any ind.), 809.381-010, 06.02.24

FACILITIES PLANNER (any ind.), 019.261-018, 05.01.06

FACTORER (finan. inst.), 186.117-026, 11.06.03

FACTORY LAY-OUT ENGINEER (profess. & kin.), 012.167-018, 05.01.06

FACULTY MEMBER, COLLEGE OR UNIVERSITY (educ.), 090.227-010, 11.02.01

FALLER 2 (logging), 454.684-014, 03.04.02

FARM-EQUIPMENT MECHANIC 1 (agric. equip.), 624.281-010, 05.05.09

FARMER, FIELD CROP (agric.), 404.161-010, 03.01.01

FARMER, GENERAL (agric.), 421.161-010, 03.01.01

FARMER, VINE-FRUIT CROPS (agric.), 403.161-014, 03.01.01

FARMWORKER, FRUIT 1 (agric.), 403.683-010, 03.04.01

FARMWORKER, GENERAL 1 (agric.), 421.683-010, 03.04.01

FARMWORKER, GENERAL 2 (agric.), 421.687-010, 03.04.01

FARMWORKER, LIVESTOCK (agric.), 410.664-010, 03.04.01

FARMWORKER, VEGETABLE 2 (agric.), 402.687-010, 03.04.01

FASHION ARTIST (ret. tr.), 141.061-014, 01.02.03

FASHION COORDINATOR (ret. tr.), 185.157-010, 11.09.01

FAST-FOODS WORKER (hotel & rest.), 311.472-010, 09.04.01

FASTENER-SEWING-MACHINE OPERATOR (any ind.), 787.685-010, 06.04.05

FEE CLERK (finan. inst.), 214.362-018, 07.02.02

FELTING-MACHINE OPERATOR (felt goods), 586.662-010, 06.02.05

FENCE ERECTOR (const.), 869.684-022, 05.10.01

FIELD ENGINEER (radio & tv broad.), 193.262-018, 05.03.05

FIELD ENGINEER (electronics), 828.261-014, 05.05.05

FIELD ENGINEER, SPECIALIST (petrol. production), 010.261-010, 05.03.04

FIELD REPRESENTATIVE (bus. ser.), 163.267-010, 11.05.04

FIELD REPRESENTATIVE (profess. & kin.), 189.267-010, 11.07.01

FIELD SERVICE TECHNICIAN (mach. mfg.), 638.261-026, 05.05.09

FIELD-SERVICE ENGINEER (aircraft-aerospace mfg.), 002.167-014, 05.01.04

FILE CLERK 2 (clerical), 206.367-014, 07.05.03

FILER (jewelry), 700.684-034, 06.04.24

FILLER (house. furn.), 780.684-066, 06.04.23

FILM DEVELOPER (motion pic.), 976.382-018, 05.10.05

FILM LABORATORY TECHNICIAN (motion pic.), 976.684-014, 05.10.05

FILM LABORATORY TECHNICIAN 1 (motion pic.), 076.381-010, 02.04.01

FILM-OR-TAPE LIBRARIAN (clerical), 222.367-026, 11.02.04

FILM-RENTAL CLERK (bus. ser.), 295.367-018, 11.02.04

FILTER OPERATOR (any ind.), 551.685-078, 06.04.19

FINAL ASSEMBLER (office mach.), 706.381-018, 06.01.04

FINANCIAL ANALYST (finan. inst.), 020.167-014, 11.01.02

FINANCIAL-AID COUNSELOR (educ.), 169.267-018, 07.01.01

FINANCIAL-AIDS OFFICER (educ.), 090.117-030, 11.07.03

FINE ARTS PACKER (museum), 102.367-010, 05.03.09

FINGERNAIL FORMER (per. ser.), 331.674-014, 09.05.01

FINGERPRINT CLASSIFIER (gov. ser.), 375.387-010, 02.04.01

FINGERPRINT CLERK 2 (gov. ser.), 206.387-014, 07.05.03

FINISHER, DENTURE (medical ser.), 712.681-018, 05.05.11

FIRE FIGHTER (any ind.), 373.364-010, 04.02.04

FIRE LOOKOUT (forestry), 452.367-010, 07.04.05

FIRE RANGER (forestry), 452.367-014, 04.02.02

FIRE WARDEN (forestry), 452.167-010, 04.01.02

FIRE-CONTROL MECHANIC (gov. ser.), 632.261-014, 05.05.11

FIRE-EXTINGUISHER REPAIRER (any ind.), 709.384-010, 05.10.04

FIRE-PROTECTION ENGINEERING TECHNICIAN (profess. & kin.), 019.261-026, 05.03.02

FIRER, LOCOMOTIVE (r.r. trans.), 910.363-010, 05.08.02

FIRESETTER (elec. equip.), 692.360-018, 06.01.02

FIRST-AID ATTENDANT (any ind.), 354.677-010, 10.03.02

FISH AND GAME WARDEN (gov. ser.), 379.167-010, 04.01.02

FISH CLEANER (can. & preserv.), 525.684-030, 06.04.28

FISH FARMER (fish.), 446.161-010, 03.01.02

FISH HATCHERY WORKER (fish.), 446.684-010, 03.04.03

FISHER, DIVING (fish.), 443.664-010, 03.04.03

FISHER, LINE (fish.), 442.684-010, 03.04.03

FISHER, NET (fish.), 441.684-010, 03.04.03

FITTER 1 (any ind.), 801.261-014, 05.05.06

FIXTURE REPAIRER-FABRICATOR (any ind.), 630.384-010, 05.10.01

FLAGGER (amuse. & rec.), 372.667-026, 12.01.02

FLIGHT ENGINEER (air trans.), 621.261-018, 05.03.06

FLIGHT-INFORMATION EXPEDITER (air trans.), 912.367-010, 07.04.05

FLIGHT-TEST SHOP MECHANIC (aircraft-aerospace mfg.), 621.381-010, 05.05.09

FLOOR ATTENDANT (amuse. & rec.), 343.467-014, 09.04.02

FLOOR LAYER (const.), 864.481-010, 05.10.01

FLOOR WORKER (chew. gum), 920.687-090, 06.04.38

FLORAL DESIGNER (ret. tr.), 142.081-010, 01.02.03

FLOUR BLENDER (grain & feed mill), 520.685-106, 06.04.15

FOLDER-SEAMER, AUTOMATIC (any ind.), 787.685-014, 06.04.05

FOLDING-MACHINE FEEDER (print. & pub.), 653.686-014, 06.04.04

FOLDING-MACHINE OPERATOR (clerical), 208.685-014, 05.12.19

FOOD AND DRUG INSPECTOR (gov. ser.), 168.267-042, 11.10.03

FOOD ASSEMBLER, KITCHEN (hotel & rest.), 319.484-010, 05.12.17

FOOD TABULATOR, CAFETERIA (hotel & rest.), 211.582-010, 07.06.02

FOOD TECHNOLOGIST (profess. & kin.), 041.081-010, 02.02.04

FOOD TESTER (any ind.), 029.361-014, 02.04.02

FOOD-MANAGEMENT AIDE (gov. ser.), 195.367-022, 10.01.02

FOOD-SERVICE WORKER, HOSPITAL (medical ser.), 355.677-010, 09.05.02

FOREIGN BANKNOTE TELLER-TRADER (finan. inst.), 211.362-014, 08.01.03

FOREIGN-EXCHANGE TRADER (finan. inst.), 186.167-014, 11.06.03

FOREIGN-SERVICE OFFICER (gov. ser.), 188.117-106, 11.09.03

FOREST ECOLOGIST (profess. & kin.), 040.061-030, 02.02.02

FOREST WORKER (forestry), 452.687-010, 03.04.02

FOREST-FIRE FIGHTER (forestry), 452.687-014, 03.04.02

FORESTER (profess. & kin.), 040.061-034, 03.01.04

FORESTER AIDE (forestry), 452.364-010, 03.02.02

FORMER, HAND (any ind.), 619.361-010, 05.05.06

FORMS ANALYST (profess. & kin.), 161.267-018, 11.01.01

FORMULA-ROOM WORKER (dairy prod.), 520.487-014, 05.10.08

FOUNDRY METALLURGIST (foundry), 011.061-010, 05.01.01

FOUNTAIN SERVER (hotel & rest.), 319.474-010, 09.04.01

FRAME REPAIRER (furn.), 763.681-010, 05.10.01

FREEZER OPERATOR (dairy prod.), 529.482-010, 06.02.15

FRETTED-INSTRUMENT MAKER, HAND (musical inst.), 730.281-022, 05.05.12

FRETTED-INSTRUMENT REPAIRER (any ind.), 730.281-026, 05.05.12

FRONT-END LOADER OPERATOR (any ind.), 921.683-042, 05.11.04

FRONT-END MECHANIC (auto. ser.), 620.281-038, 05.10.01

FUEL ATTENDANT (any ind.), 953.362-010, 05.06.02

FUEL-INJECTION SERVICER (any ind.), 625.281-022, 05.05.09

FUEL-SYSTEM-MAINTENANCE WORKER (any ind.), 638.381-010, 05.05.09

FUMIGATOR (bus. ser.), 383.361-010, 05.10.09

FUND RAISER 1 (nonprofit org.), 293.157-010, 11.09.02

FUND RAISER 2 (nonprofit org.), 293.357-014, 08.02.08

FUNERAL ATTENDANT (per. ser.), 359.677-014, 09.01.04

FURNACE CLEANER (any ind.), 891.687-014, 05.12.18

FURNACE INSTALLER (light, heat, & power), 862.361-010, 05.05.05

FURNACE INSTALLER-AND-REPAIRER, HOT AIR (any ind.), 869.281-010, 05.05.09

FURNITURE ASSEMBLER (furn.), 763.684-038, 06.02.22

FURNITURE ASSEMBLER-AND-INSTALLER (ret. tr.), 739.684-082, 05.10.01

FURNITURE DESIGNER (furn.), 142.061-022, 01.02.03

FURNITURE FINISHER (woodworking), 763.381-010, 05.05.08

FURNITURE RESTORER (museum), 763.380-010, 05.05.08

FURNITURE UPHOLSTERER (any ind.), 780.381-018, 05.05.15

FURNITURE-RENTAL CONSULTANT (ret. tr.), 295.357-018, 09.04.02

FURRIER (fur goods), 783.261-010, 05.05.15

FUSING-FURNACE LOADER (optical goods), 573.686-014, 06.04.13

GAMBLING DEALER (amuse. & rec.), 343.467-018, 09.04.02

GAME ATTENDANT (amuse. & rec.), 342.457-010, 09.04.02

GARAGE SERVICER, INDUSTRIAL (any ind.), 915.687-014, 05.12.08

GARBAGE COLLECTOR (motor trans.), 909.687-010, 05.12.03

GARDE MANGER (hotel & rest.), 313.361-034, 05.10.08

GARMENT INSPECTOR (any ind.), 789.687-070, 06.03.02

GAS-APPLIANCE SERVICER (any ind.), 637.261-018, 05.10.02

GAS-COMPRESSOR OPERATOR (any ind.), 950.382-014, 05.06.02

GAS-ENGINE OPERATOR (any ind.), 950.382-018, 05.06.01

GAS-ENGINE REPAIRER (any ind.), 625.281-026, 05.05.09

GAS-WELDING-EQUIPMENT MECHANIC (any ind.), 626.381-014, 05.05.09

GATE TENDER (any ind.), 372.667-030, 04.02.02

GENEALOGIST (profess. & kin.), 052.067-018, 11.03.03

GENERAL CLAIMS AGENT (air trans.), 186.117-030, 11.12.01

GENERAL HELPER (oils & fats), 529.687-094, 06.04.40

GENERAL MANAGER, FARM (agric.), 180.167-018, 03.01.01

GENERAL MANAGER, ROAD PRODUCTION (amuse. & rec.), 187.117-034, 11.11.04

GENERAL PRACTITIONER (medical ser.), 070.101-022, 02.03.01

GENERAL-LEDGER BOOKKEEPER (clerical), 210.382-046, 07.02.01

GEOGRAPHER (profess. & kin.), 029.067-010, 02.01.01

GEOLOGICAL AIDE (petrol. production), 024.267-010, 02.04.01

GEOLOGIST (profess. & kin.), 024.061-018, 02.01.01

GEOLOGIST, PETROLEUM (petrol. production), 024.061-022, 02.01.02

GEOPHYSICIST (profess. & kin.), 024.061-030, 02.01.01

GERIATRIC NURSE ASSISTANT (medical ser.), 355.674-026, 10.03.02

GIFT WRAPPER (ret. tr.), 299.364-014, 01.06.03

GILDER (any ind.), 749.381-010, 01.06.03

GLASS BLOWER (glass mfg.), 772.681-010, 06.01.04

GLASS CUTTER (any ind.), 775.684-022, 06.02.30

GLASS FINISHER (glass prod.), 775.684-026, 06.04.30

GLASS INSPECTOR (any ind.), 579.687-022, 06.03.02

GLASS INSTALLER (auto. ser.), 865.684-010, 05.10.01

©1991, JIST Works, Inc. • Indianapolis, IN

GLAZIER (const.), 865.381-010, 05.10.01

GLOVE TURNER AND FORMER, AUTOMATIC (glove & mitten), 583.686-018, 06.04.05

GOLDBEATER (gold leaf & foil), 700.381-018, 06.01.04

GOLF-COURSE RANGER (amuse. & rec.), 379.667-010, 12.01.02

GOLF-RANGE ATTENDANT (amuse. & rec.), 341.683-010, 05.12.18

GRADER (woodworking), 669.587-010, 06.03.02

GRADING CLERK (educ.), 219.467-010, 07.02.03

GRAINER, MACHINE (any ind.), 652.686-014, 06.04.02

GRANT COORDINATOR (profess. & kin.), 169.117-014, 11.05.02

GRAPHIC DESIGNER (profess. & kin.), 141.061-018, 01.02.03

GRAPHOLOGIST (amuse. & rec.), 159.247-018, 01.07.01

GREASE BUFFER (silverware), 705.684-022, 06.02.24

GREENSKEEPER 1 (any ind.), 406.137-010, 03.04.04

GREENSKEEPER 2 (any ind.), 406.683-010, 03.04.04

GRINDER 1 (any ind.), 705.684-026, 06.04.24

GRINDER OPERATOR (grain & feed mill), 521.682-026, 06.02.15

GRINDER-CHIPPER 2 (any ind.), 809.684-026, 06.04.24

GRIP (amuse. & rec.), 962.684-014, 05.10.01

GRIP (motion pic.), 962.687-022, 05.12.04

GROUNDSKEEPER, INDUSTRIAL COMMERCIAL (any ind.), 406.684-014, 03.04.04

GROUNDSKEEPER, PARKS AND GROUNDS (gov. ser.), 406.687-010, 03.04.04

GROUP LEADER (agric.), 180.167-022, 03.01.01

GROUP WORKER (social ser.), 195.164-010, 09.01.01

GUARD, IMMIGRATION (gov. ser.), 372.567-014, 04.02.01

GUARD, SCHOOL-CROSSING (gov. ser.), 371.567-010, 10.03.03

GUARD, SECURITY (any ind.), 372.667-034, 04.02.02

GUIDE (per. ser.), 353.367-010, 09.01.02

GUIDE, HUNTING AND FISHING (amuse. & rec.), 353.161-010, 09.01.01

GUIDE, PLANT (any ind.), 353.367-018, 09.01.02

GUIDE, TRAVEL (per. ser.), 353.167-010, 07.05.01

GUNSMITH (any ind.), 632.281-010, 05.05.07

HAIR STYLIST (per. ser.), 332.271-018, 09.02.01

HARBOR MASTER (gov. ser.), 375.167-026, 04.01.01

HARDENING-MACHINE OPERATOR (hat & cap), 586.685-026, 06.04.16

HAT-AND-CAP SEWER (hat & cap), 784.682-014, 06.02.05

HAZARDOUS-WASTE MANAGEMENT SPECIALIST (gov. ser.), 168.267-086, 11.10.03

HEAD SAWYER (sawmill), 667.662-010, 06.02.03

HEALTH OFFICER, FIELD (gov. ser.), 168.167-018, 11.10.03

HEALTH PHYSICIST (profess. & kin.), 079.021-010, 05.01.02

HEALTH-EQUIPMENT SERVICER (medical ser.), 359.363-010, 05.08.03

HEARING OFFICER (gov. ser.), 119.107-010, 11.04.01

HEAT TREATER (electronics), 504.686-022, 06.04.19

HEAT TREATER 1 (heat treat.), 504.382-014, 06.02.10

HEAT-TRANSFER TECHNICIAN (profess. & kin.), 007.181-010, 05.03.07

HEATER (forging), 619.682-022, 06.02.02

HEMMER (any ind.), 787.682-026, 06.02.05

HEMMER, AUTOMATIC (house. furn.), 787.685-018, 06.04.05

HERBARIUM WORKER (profess. & kin.), 041.384-010, 02.04.02

HIGHWAY-MAINTENANCE WORKER (gov. ser.), 899.684-014, 05.12.12

HISTOPATHOLOGIST (medical ser.), 041.061-054, 02.02.01

HISTORIAN (profess. & kin.), 052.067-022, 11.03.03

HOISTING ENGINEER (any ind.), 921.663-030, 05.11.04

HOLTER SCANNING TECHNICIAN (medical ser.), 078.264-010, 10.03.01

HOME ATTENDANT (per. ser.), 354.377-014, 10.03.03

HOME ECONOMIST (profess. & kin.), 096.121-014, 11.02.03

HOME HEALTH TECHNICIAN (medical ser.), 079.224-010, 10.03.02

HOMEMAKER (social ser.), 309.354-010, 11.02.03

HONEY PROCESSOR (food prep nec), 522.685-070, 06.04.15

HONEYCOMB-BLANKET MAKER (aircraft-aerospace mfg.), 806.684-062, 06.02.09

HORSE-RACE STARTER (amuse. & rec.), 153.267-010, 12.01.02

HORSE-RACE TIMER (amuse. & rec.), 153.367-014, 12.01.02

HORSESHOER (agric.), 418.381-010, 03.03.02

HORTICULTURAL THERAPIST (medical ser.), 076.124-018, 10.02.02

HORTICULTURAL WORKER 2 (agric.), 405.687-014, 03.04.04

HORTICULTURIST (profess. & kin.), 040.061-038, 02.02.02

HOSPITAL ENTRANCE ATTENDANT (medical ser.), 355.677-014, 09.05.04

HOSPITAL-ADMITTING CLERK (medical ser.), 205.362-018, 07.04.01

HOSPITAL-INSURANCE REPRESENTATIVE (insurance), 166.267-014, 07.01.05

HOST/HOSTESS (any ind.), 352.667-010, 09.01.01

HOST/HOSTESS, RESTAURANT (hotel & rest.), 310.137-010, 09.01.03

HOT-CELL TECHNICIAN (profess. & kin.), 015.362-018, 02.04.01

HOT-ROOM ATTENDANT (per. ser.), 335.677-014, 09.05.01

HOTEL CLERK (hotel & rest.), 238.362-010, 07.04.03

HOUSEHOLD-APPLIANCE INSTALLER (any ind.), 827.661-010, 05.10.04

HOUSEKEEPER (hotel & rest.), 321.137-010, 05.12.18

HOUSING-MANAGEMENT OFFICER (gov. ser.), 188.117-110, 11.05.03

HUMAN RESOURCE ADVISOR (profess. & kin.), 166.267-046, 11.02.02

HYDRAULIC ENGINEER (profess. & kin.), 005.061-018, 05.01.03

HYDRO-PNEUMATIC TESTER (any ind.), 862.687-018, 06.03.02

HYDROELECTRIC-STATION OPERATOR (light, heat, & power), 952.362-018, 05.06.01

HYDROGRAPHER (waterworks), 025.264-010, 02.04.01

HYDROLOGIST (profess. & kin.), 024.061-034, 02.01.01

HYPNOTHERAPIST (profess. & kin.), 079.157-010, 10.02.02

IDENTIFICATION CLERK (clerical), 205.362-022, 07.04.01

IDENTIFICATION OFFICER (gov. ser.), 377.264-010, 07.01.06

IDENTIFICATION TECHNICIAN (gov. ser.), 209.362-022, 07.05.03

ILLUMINATING ENGINEER (profess. & kin.), 003.061-046, 05.01.03

ILLUSTRATOR (profess. & kin.), 141.061-022, 01.02.03

IMMIGRATION INSPECTOR (gov. ser.), 168.167-022, 11.10.04

IMMUNOHEMATOLOGIST (medical ser.), 078.221-010, 02.04.02

IMPORT-EXPORT AGENT (any ind.), 184.117-022, 11.05.02

IMPREGNATOR (electronics), 590.682-014, 06.02.18

IN-FILE OPERATOR (bus. ser.), 203.362-014, 07.06.01

INDUSTRIAL DESIGNER (profess. & kin.), 142.061-026, 01.02.03

INDUSTRIAL ENGINEER (profess. & kin.), 012.167-030, 05.01.06

INDUSTRIAL ENGINEERING TECHNICIAN (profess. & kin.), 012.267-010, 05.03.06

INDUSTRIAL HYGIENIST (profess. & kin.), 079.161-010, 11.10.03

INDUSTRIAL THERAPIST (medical ser.), 076.167-010, 10.02.02

INDUSTRIAL-HEALTH ENGINEER (profess. & kin.), 012.167-034, 05.01.02

INDUSTRIAL-ORDER CLERK (clerical), 221.367-022, 05.09.03

INDUSTRIAL-SAFETY-AND-HEALTH TECHNICIAN (any ind.), 168.161-014, 11.10.03

INDUSTRIAL-TRUCK OPERATOR (any ind.), 921.683-050, 06.04.40

INFORMATION CLERK (clerical), 237.367-022, 07.04.04

INFORMATION SCIENTIST (profess. & kin.), 109.067-010, 11.01.01

INJECTION-MOLDING-MACHINE TENDER (fabric. plastic prod.), 556.685-038, 06.04.10

INKER (print. & pub.), 659.667-010, 06.03.02

INSERTING-MACHINE OPERATOR (clerical), 208.685-018, 05.12.19

INSPECTOR (fabric. plastic prod.), 559.381-010, 06.03.01

INSPECTOR (drug prep. & related), 559.387-014, 06.03.02

INSPECTOR (jewelry), 700.687-034, 06.03.02

INSPECTOR, AGRICULTURAL COMMODITIES (gov. ser.), 168.287-010, 11.10.03

INSPECTOR, AIR-CARRIER (gov. ser.), 168.264-010, 05.03.06

INSPECTOR, ASSEMBLIES AND INSTALLATIONS (aircraft-aerospace mfg.), 806.281-022, 06.01.05

INSPECTOR, BUILDING (gov. ser.), 168.167-030, 05.03.06

INSPECTOR, FABRIC (any ind.), 789.587-014, 06.03.02

INSPECTOR, GOVERNMENT PROPERTY (gov. ser.), 168.267-050, 11.10.01

INSPECTOR, HEALTH CARE FACILITIES (gov. ser.), 168.167-042, 11.10.03

INSPECTOR, INDUSTRIAL WASTE (gov. ser.), 168.267-054, 05.03.06

INSPECTOR, INTEGRATED CIRCUITS (electronics), 726.684-058, 06.03.02

INSPECTOR, METAL FABRICATING (any ind.), 619.261-010, 06.01.05

INSPECTOR, MOTOR VEHICLES (gov. ser.), 168.267-058, 11.10.03

INSPECTOR, PRINTED CIRCUIT BOARDS (electronics), 726.684-062, 06.03.02

INSPECTOR, QUALITY ASSURANCE (gov. ser.), 168.287-014, 05.03.06

INSPECTOR, RAILROAD (gov. ser.), 168.287-018, 05.03.06

INSPECTOR, SEMICONDUCTOR WAFER (electronics), 726.684-066, 06.03.02

INSPECTOR, WATER-POLLUTION CONTROL (gov. ser.), 168.267-090, 11.10.03

INSTALLER (museum), 922.687-050, 05.12.03

INSTRUCTOR, BUSINESS EDUCATION (educ.), 090.222-010, 11.02.01

INSTRUCTOR, DANCING (educ.), 151.027-014, 01.05.01

INSTRUCTOR, DRIVING (educ.), 099.223-010, 09.03.03

INSTRUCTOR, EXTENSION WORK (educ.), 090.227-018, 11.02.01

INSTRUCTOR, FLYING 2 (educ.), 097.227-010, 05.04.01

INSTRUCTOR, SPORTS (amuse. & rec.), 153.227-018, 12.01.01

INSTRUCTOR, TECHNICAL TRAINING (educ.), 166.221-010, 11.02.02

INSTRUCTOR, VOCATIONAL TRAINING (educ.), 097.227-014, 11.02.02

INSTRUMENT MAKER (any ind.), 600.280-010, 05.05.11

INSTRUMENT MECHANIC (any ind.), 710.281-026, 05.05.10

INSTRUMENT REPAIRER (any ind.), 710.261-010, 05.05.11

INSTRUMENT-MAKER AND REPAIRER (petrol. production), 600.280-014, 05.05.10

INSTRUMENTATION TECHNICIAN (profess. & kin.), 003.261-010, 05.01.01

INSULATION WORKER (const.), 863.364-014, 05.10.01

INSULATION-BLANKET MAKER (aircraft-aerospace mfg.), 806.684-078, 06.04.34

INSURANCE CLERK (medical ser.), 214.362-022, 07.02.04

INSURANCE CLERK 2 (clerical), 205.567-010, 07.05.03

INTEGRATED CIRCUIT LAYOUT DESIGNER (profess. & kin.), 003.261-018, 05.03.02

INTERIOR DESIGNER (profess. & kin.), 142.051-014, 01.02.03

INTERPRETER (profess. & kin.), 137.267-010, 11.08.04

INTERPRETER, DEAF (profess. & kin.), 137.267-014, 01.03.02

INVENTORY CLERK (clerical), 222.387-026, 05.09.01

INVESTIGATOR (gov. ser.), 168.267-062, 11.10.01

INVESTIGATOR (clerical), 241.267-030, 11.06.03

INVESTIGATOR (light, heat, & power), 376.367-022, 04.01.02

INVESTIGATOR, FRAUD (ret. tr.), 376.267-014, 11.10.01

INVESTIGATOR, UTILITY-BILL COMPLAINTS (light, heat, & power), 241.267-034, 07.05.02

INVOICE-CONTROL CLERK (clerical), 214.362-026, 07.02.04

ION IMPLANT MACHINE OPERATOR (electronics), 590.382-022, 06.02.18

JAILER (gov. ser.), 372.367-014, 04.02.01

JANITOR (any ind.), 382.664-010, 05.12.18

JEWELER (jewelry), 700.281-010, 01.06.02

JEWELRY COATER (jewelry), 590.685-046, 06.04.21

JIGSAWYER (jewelry), 700.684-046, 06.04.24

JOB ANALYST (profess. & kin.), 166.267-018, 11.03.04

JOB DEVELOPMENT SPECIALIST (profess. & kin.), 166.267-034, 11.03.04

JOB PRINTER (print. & pub.), 973.381-018, 05.05.13

JOB TRACER (clerical), 221.387-034, 05.09.02

JUGGLER (amuse. & rec.), 159.341-010, 12.02.01

KEY CUTTER (any ind.), 709.684-050, 05.12.13

KEYMODULE-ASSEMBLY-MACHINE TENDER (office mach.), 692.685-274, 06.04.09

KEYPUNCH OPERATOR (clerical), 203.582-030, 07.06.02

KICK-PRESS OPERATOR 1 (any ind.), 616.682-026, 06.02.20

KILN WORKER (pottery & porc.), 573.687-022, 06.04.17

KITCHEN HELPER (hotel & rest.), 318.687-010, 05.12.18

KNITTER MECHANIC (knit goods), 685.360-010, 06.01.02

KNITTING-MACHINE FIXER (hosiery), 689.280-014, 06.01.02

KNITTING-MACHINE OPERATOR (knit goods), 685.665-014, 06.04.06

LABEL CODER (any ind.), 920.587-014, 06.04.26

LABOR EXPEDITER (const.), 249.167-018, 07.01.02

LABORATORY ASSISTANT (petrol. production), 024.381-010, 02.04.01

LABORATORY ASSISTANT (light, heat, & power), 029.361-018, 02.04.01

LABORATORY ASSISTANT (textile), 029.381-014, 02.04.01

LABORATORY ASSISTANT, BLOOD AND PLASMA (drug prep. & related), 078.687-010, 02.04.02

LABORATORY ASSISTANT, CULTURE MEDIA (drug prep. & related), 559.384-010, 02.04.02

LABORATORY ASSISTANT, METALLURGICAL (iron & steel), 011.281-010, 02.04.01

LABORATORY CLERK (clerical), 222.587-026, 05.09.01

LABORATORY SUPERVISOR (profess. & kin.), 022.137-010, 02.04.01

LABORATORY TECHNICIAN (auto. mfg.), 019.381-010, 02.04.01

LABORATORY TECHNICIAN, VETERINARY (medical ser.), 073.361-010, 02.04.02

LABORATORY TESTER (synthetic fibers), 022.281-018, 02.04.01

LABORATORY TESTER (any ind.), 029.261-010, 02.04.01

LABORER (slaught. & meat pack.), 529.687-130, 06.04.40

LABORER (drug prep. & related), 559.686-022, 06.04.19

LABORER (petrol. production), 939.687-018, 05.12.03

LABORER, CHEMICAL PROCESSING (chem.), 559.687-050, 06.04.40

LABORER, CONCRETE PLANT (concrete prod.), 579.686-010, 06.04.40

LABORER, CONCRETE-MIXING PLANT (const.), 579.665-014, 05.12.04

LABORER, GENERAL (iron & steel), 509.686-010, 06.04.40

LABORER, GENERAL (nonfer. metal prod.), 519.686-010, 06.04.10

LABORER, GENERAL (plastics mat.), 559.567-010, 06.04.40

LABORER, GENERAL (leather mfg.), 589.686-026, 06.04.27

LABORER, GENERAL (mach. shop), 609.684-014, 06.04.39

LABORER, GOLD LEAF (gold leaf & foil), 700.687-038, 06.04.24

LABORER, GRINDING AND POLISHING (any ind.), 705.687-014, 06.04.34

LABORER, HOISTING (any ind.), 921.667-022, 05.12.04

LABORER, LANDSCAPE (agric.), 408.687-014, 03.04.04

LABORER, PETROLEUM REFINERY (petrol. refin.), 549.687-018, 05.12.03

LABORER, POWERHOUSE (light, heat, & power), 952.665-010, 05.12.04

LABORER, SALVAGE (any ind.), 929.687-022, 06.04.40

LABORER, SHIPYARD (ship bldg. & rep.), 809.687-022, 05.12.03

LABORER, STORES (any ind.), 922.687-058, 05.09.01

LAMINATION ASSEMBLER (elec. equip.), 729.484-010, 06.02.23

LAMINATOR, HAND (furn.), 763.684-050, 06.04.22

LAND SURVEYOR (profess. & kin.), 018.167-018, 05.01.06

LAND-LEASING EXAMINER (gov. ser.), 237.367-026, 07.04.04

LANDSCAPE ARCHITECT (profess. & kin.), 001.061-018, 05.01.07

LANDSCAPE CONTRACTOR (const.), 182.167-014, 03.01.03

LASER TECHNICIAN (electronics), 019.181-010, 05.01.01

LASER-BEAM-MACHINE OPERATOR (welding), 815.682-010, 06.02.19

LASER-BEAM-TRIM OPERATOR (electronics), 726.682-010, 06.02.02

LATHE HAND (jewelry), 700.682-014, 06.02.02

LATHE OPERATOR, NUMERICAL CONTROL (mach. shop), 604.362-010, 06.01.03

LATHE OPERATOR, PRODUCTION (mach. shop), 604.685-026, 06.04.02

LATHE SPOTTER (veneer & plywood), 663.686-022, 06.04.03

LATHER (const.), 842.361-010, 05.10.01

LAUNDERER, HAND (laundry), 361.684-010, 06.04.35

LAUNDRY CLERK (clerical), 221.387-038, 05.09.02

LAUNDRY LABORER (laundry), 361.687-018, 06.04.35

LAUNDRY OPERATOR (laundry), 369.684-014, 06.04.35

LAUNDRY WORKER 1 (any ind.), 361.684-014, 05.12.18

LAWN-SERVICE WORKER (agric.), 408.684-010, 03.04.04

LAWYER (profess. & kin.), 110.107-010, 11.04.02

LAY-OUT WORKER 2 (any ind.), 809.381-014, 06.02.31

LAYAWAY CLERK (ret. tr.), 299.467-010, 07.03.01

LEAD PONY RIDER (amuse. & rec.), 153.674-014, 12.01.02

LEADER TIER (sports equip.), 732.687-038, 06.04.34

LEAF STAMPER (any ind.), 979.682-018, 06.04.09

LEASING AGENT, RESIDENCE (real estate), 250.357-014, 08.02.04

LEATHER CUTTER (leather prod.), 783.684-022, 06.02.27

LEATHER FINISHER (clean., dye., & press.), 363.682-010, 06.04.35

LEATHER WORKER (leather prod.), 783.684-026, 06.02.27

LEGAL INVESTIGATOR (profess. & kin.), 119.267-022, 11.04.02

LEGAL SECRETARY (clerical), 201.362-010, 07.01.03

LEGISLATIVE ASSISTANT (gov. ser.), 169.167-066, 11.05.03

LENS EXAMINER (optical goods), 716.687-022, 06.03.02

LENS HARDENER (optical goods), 573.685-030, 06.04.13

LENS MOUNTER 2 (optical goods), 713.681-010, 05.05.11

LENS POLISHER, HAND (optical goods), 716.681-018, 06.01.04

LENS-FABRICATING-MACHINE TENDER (optical goods), 716.685-022, 06.04.08

LENS-MOLD SETTER (optical goods), 713.381-010, 06.02.23

LETTER-OF-CREDIT CLERK (finan. inst.), 219.387-018, 07.05.02

LIBRARIAN (library), 100.127-014, 11.02.04

LIBRARIAN, SPECIAL LIBRARY (library), 100.167-026, 11.02.04

LIBRARY ASSISTANT (library), 249.367-046, 11.02.04

LIBRARY CONSULTANT (library), 100.117-014, 11.07.04

LIBRARY TECHNICAL ASSISTANT (library), 100.367-018, 11.02.04

LICENSE CLERK (gov. ser.), 205.367-034, 07.04.03

LIGHT TECHNICIAN (motion pic.), 962.362-014, 05.10.03

LIGHT-FIXTURE SERVICER (any ind.), 389.687-018, 05.12.18

LIGHTING-EQUIPMENT OPERATOR (amuse. & rec.), 962.381-014, 05.12.16

LINE ERECTOR (const.), 821.361-018, 05.05.05

LINE MAINTAINER (any ind.), 821.261-014, 05.05.05

LINE REPAIRER (light, heat, & power), 821.361-026, 05.05.05

LINE WALKER (petrol. production), 869.564-010, 05.07.01

LINE-SERVICE ATTENDANT (air trans.), 912.687-010, 05.12.06

LINEN-ROOM ATTENDANT (hotel & rest.), 222.387-030, 05.09.01

LITERARY AGENT (bus. ser.), 191.117-034, 11.12.03

LIVESTOCK-YARD ATTENDANT (any ind.), 410.674-018, 03.04.01

LOAD DISPATCHER (light, heat, & power), 952.167-014, 05.06.01

LOADER 1 (any ind.), 914.667-010, 06.04.40

LOAN CLOSER (finan. inst.), 249.367-050, 07.01.04

LOAN COUNSELOR (finan. inst.), 186.267-014, 07.01.01

LOAN INTERVIEWER (finan. inst.), 241.367-018, 07.04.01

LOAN OFFICER (finan. inst.), 186.267-018, 11.06.03

LOCATION MANAGER (motion pic.), 191.167-018, 11.12.02

LOCK ASSEMBLER (hardware), 706.684-074, 06.04.23

LOCKER-ROOM ATTENDANT (per. ser.), 358.677-014, 09.05.07

LOCKSMITH (any ind.), 709.281-010, 05.05.09

LOCOMOTIVE ENGINEER (r.r. trans.), 910.363-014, 05.08.02

LOFT WORKER (ship bldg. & rep.), 661.281-010, 05.05.08

LOGGER, ALL-ROUND (logging), 454.684-018, 03.04.02

LOGGING-OPERATIONS INSPECTOR (forestry), 168.267-070, 03.01.04

LOOM FIXER (asbestos prod.), 683.260-018, 06.01.02

LOT ATTENDANT (ret. tr.), 915.583-010, 05.08.03

LUBRICATION SERVICER (auto. ser.), 915.687-018, 05.12.08

LUBRICATION-EQUIPMENT SERVICER (any ind.), 630.381-022, 05.10.02

LUGGAGE REPAIRER (any ind.), 365.361-010, 05.10.01

LUMBER SORTER (woodworking), 922.687-074, 06.03.02

LUNCH-TRUCK DRIVER (hotel & rest.), 292.463-010, 09.04.01

MACHINE ASSEMBLER (mach. mfg.), 638.361-010, 06.02.22

MACHINE BUILDER (mach. mfg.), 600.281-022, 05.05.09

MACHINE FEEDER (any ind.), 699.686-010, 06.04.09

MACHINE FEEDER, RAW STOCK (felt goods), 680.686-018, 06.04.16

MACHINE MOLDER (foundry), 518.682-010, 06.04.32

MACHINE OPERATOR 1 (any ind.), 616.360-018, 06.01.03

MACHINE OPERATOR 2 (any ind.), 619.685-062, 06.04.02

MACHINE SET-UP OPERATOR (elec. equip.), 600.380-018, 06.01.03

MACHINE SETTER (any ind.), 616.360-022, 06.01.02

MACHINE SNELLER (sports equip.), 732.685-026, 06.04.34

MACHINE TESTER (office mach.), 706.387-014, 06.03.01

MACHINERY ERECTOR (engine & turbine), 638.261-014, 05.05.09

MACHINIST (mach. shop), 600.280-022, 05.05.07

MAGICIAN (amuse. & rec.), 159.041-010, 01.03.02

MAGNETIC-TAPE WINDER (electronics), 726.685-010, 06.04.02

MAGNETIC-TAPE-COMPOSER OPERATOR (print. & pub.), 203.382-018, 07.06.02

MAGNETIC-TAPE-TYPEWRITER OPERATOR (clerical), 203.582-034, 07.06.02

MAIL CARRIER (gov. ser.), 230.367-010, 07.05.04

MAIL CLERK (clerical), 209.587-026, 07.05.04

MAIL HANDLER (gov. ser.), 209.687-014, 07.05.04

MAIL-PROCESSING-EQUIPMENT MECHANIC (gov. ser.), 633.261-014, 05.05.09

MAILER (print. & pub.), 222.587-030, 05.09.01

MAILING-MACHINE OPERATOR (print. & pub.), 208.462-010, 06.04.38

MAINTENANCE MACHINIST (any ind.), 600.280-042, 05.05.07

MAINTENANCE MECHANIC (any ind.), 638.281-014, 05.05.09

MAINTENANCE MECHANIC, TELEPHONE (any ind.), 822.281-018, 05.05.05

MAINTENANCE REPAIRER, BUILDING (any ind.), 899.381-010, 05.10.01

MAINTENANCE REPAIRER, INDUSTRIAL (any ind.), 899.261-014, 05.05.09

MAKE-UP ARTIST (amuse. & rec.), 333.071-010, 01.06.02

MANAGEMENT AIDE (social ser.), 195.367-014, 07.01.01

MANAGEMENT ANALYST (profess. & kin.), 161.167-010, 05.01.06

MANAGEMENT TRAINEE (any ind.), 189.167-018, 11.05.02

MANAGER, ADVERTISING (print. & pub.), 163.167-010, 11.09.01

MANAGER, ADVERTISING (any ind.), 164.117-010, 11.09.01

MANAGER, AIRPORT (air trans.), 184.117-026, 11.05.01

MANAGER, APARTMENT HOUSE (real estate), 186.167-018, 11.11.01

MANAGER, AREA DEVELOPMENT (light, heat, & power), 184.117-030, 11.09.03

MANAGER, ATHLETE (amuse. & rec.), 153.117-014, 11.12.03

MANAGER, AUTOMOBILE SERVICE STATION (ret. tr.), 185.167-014, 11.11.05

MANAGER, BAKERY (bake. prod.), 189.117-046, 11.05.01

MANAGER, BARBER OR BEAUTY SHOP (per. ser.), 187.167-058, 11.11.04

MANAGER, BOWLING ALLEY (amuse. & rec.), 187.167-222, 11.11.02

MANAGER, BRANCH (any ind.), 183.117-010, 11.05.02

MANAGER, BUS TRANSPORTATION (motor trans.), 184.167-054, 11.11.03

MANAGER, CAMP (const.), 187.167-066, 05.10.04

MANAGER, CIRCULATION (print. & pub.), 163.167-014, 11.05.04

MANAGER, CITY (gov. ser.), 188.117-114, 11.05.03

MANAGER, CONTRACTS (petrol. production), 163.117-010, 11.05.02

MANAGER, CREDIT AND COLLECTION (any ind.), 168.167-054, 11.06.03

MANAGER, CREDIT CARD OPERATIONS (profess. & kin.), 186.167-022, 11.05.02

MANAGER, CUSTOMER SERVICE (tel. & tel.), 168.167-058, 11.12.01

MANAGER, CUSTOMER SERVICES (bus. ser.), 187.167-082, 05.10.02

MANAGER, DAIRY FARM (agric.), 180.167-026, 03.01.01

MANAGER, DEPARTMENT (any ind.), 189.167-022, 11.05.02

MANAGER, DEPARTMENT (ret. tr.), 299.137-010, 11.11.05

MANAGER, DEPARTMENT STORE (ret. tr.), 185.117-010, 11.05.02

MANAGER, DISPLAY (ret. tr.), 142.031-014, 01.02.03

MANAGER, DISTRIBUTION WAREHOUSE (whole. tr.), 185.167-018, 11.11.03

MANAGER, ELECTRONIC DATA PROCESSING (profess. & kin.), 169.167-030, 11.01.01

MANAGER, EMPLOYMENT AGENCY (profess. & kin.), 187.167-098, 11.11.04

MANAGER, FAST FOOD SERVICES (ret. tr.), 185.137-010, 11.11.04

MANAGER, FINANCIAL INSTITUTION (finan. inst.), 186.117-038, 11.05.02

MANAGER, FOOD CONCESSION (hotel & rest.), 185.167-022, 09.04.01

MANAGER, FOOD PROCESSING PLANT (can. & preserv.), 183.167-026, 05.02.03

MANAGER, FOOD SERVICE (hotel & rest.), 187.167-106, 11.11.04

MANAGER, FRONT OFFICE (hotel & rest.), 187.167-110, 11.11.01

MANAGER, GOLF CLUB (amuse. & rec.), 187.167-114, 11.11.02

MANAGER, HOTEL OR MOTEL (hotel & rest.), 187.117-038, 11.11.01

MANAGER, HOUSING PROJECT (profess. & kin.), 186.167-030, 11.05.03

MANAGER, INDUSTRIAL ORGANIZATION (any ind.), 189.117-022, 11.05.01

MANAGER, LAND DEVELOPMENT (real estate), 186.117-042, 11.05.01

MANAGER, LEASING (petrol. production), 186.117-046, 11.12.02

MANAGER, LODGING FACILITIES (hotel & rest.), 320.137-014, 11.11.01

MANAGER, MACHINERY-OR-EQUIPMENT, RENTAL AND LEASING (any ind.), 185.167-026, 11.11.05

MANAGER, MARINA DRY DOCK (amuse. & rec.), 187.167-226, 05.02.07

MANAGER, MARINE SERVICE (ship bldg. & rep.), 187.167-130, 05.05.09

MANAGER, MARKET (ret. tr.), 186.167-042, 11.11.05

MANAGER, MEAT SALES AND STORAGE (ret. tr.), 185.167-030, 11.11.05

MANAGER, NURSERY (agric.), 180.167-042, 03.01.03

MANAGER, OFFICE (any ind.), 169.167-034, 07.01.02

MANAGER, OFFICE (gov. ser.), 188.167-058, 11.05.03

MANAGER, OPERATIONS (air trans.), 184.117-050, 11.05.02

MANAGER, PARTS (ret. tr.), 185.167-038, 11.11.05

MANAGER, PERSONNEL (profess. & kin.), 166.117-018, 11.05.02

MANAGER, PROCUREMENT SERVICES (profess. & kin.), 162.167-022, 11.05.02

MANAGER, PRODUCTION (radio & tv broad.), 184.167-074, 11.05.02

MANAGER, PROFESSIONAL EQUIPMENT SALES-AND-SERVICE (bus. ser.), 185.167-042, 11.05.04

MANAGER, PROPERTY (real estate), 186.167-046, 11.11.04

MANAGER, REAL-ESTATE FIRM (real estate), 186.167-066, 11.11.04

MANAGER, RECREATION ESTABLISHMENT (amuse. & rec.), 187.117-042, 11.11.02

MANAGER, RECREATION FACILITY I (amuse. & rec.), 187.167-230, 11.11.02

MANAGER, REGIONAL (motor trans.), 184.117-054, 11.05.02

MANAGER, REGULATED PROGRAM (gov. ser.), 168.167-090, 11.05.03

MANAGER, RETAIL STORE (ret. tr.), 185.167-046, 11.11.05

MANAGER, SALES (any ind.), 163.167-018, 11.05.04

MANAGER, SALES (clean., dye., & press.), 187.167-138, 11.11.04

MANAGER, SCHEDULE PLANNING (air trans.), 184.117-058, 11.05.02

MANAGER, STATION (radio & tv broad.), 184.117-062, 11.05.02

MANAGER, THEATER (amuse. & rec.), 187.167-154, 11.11.02

MANAGER, TOURING PRODUCTION (amuse. & rec.), 191.117-038, 11.11.04

MANAGER, TRAFFIC (air trans.), 184.117-066, 11.11.03

MANAGER, TRAFFIC (any ind.), 184.167-094, 11.05.02

MANAGER, TRAFFIC 1 (motor trans.), 184.167-102, 07.01.02

MANAGER, TRAVEL AGENCY (bus. ser.), 187.167-158, 11.11.04

MANAGER, VEHICLE LEASING AND RENTAL (auto. ser.), 187.167-162, 11.11.05

MANAGER, WAREHOUSE (any ind.), 184.167-114, 11.11.03

MANICURIST (per. ser.), 331.674-010, 09.05.01

MANUAL-ARTS THERAPIST (medical ser.), 076.124-010, 10.02.02

MANUFACTURERS' REPRESENTATIVE (whole. tr.), 279.157-010, 08.02.01

MANUFACTURING ENGINEER (profess. & kin.), 012.167-042, 05.01.06

MARBLE FINISHER (const.), 861.664-010, 05.05.01

MARINE ENGINEER (profess. & kin.), 014.061-014, 05.01.03

MARINE OILER (water trans.), 911.584-010, 05.12.08

MARINE SURVEYOR (profess. & kin.), 014.167-010, 05.03.06

MARINE-CARGO SURVEYOR (bus. ser.), 168.267-094, 11.10.03

MARINE-SERVICES TECHNICIAN (ship bldg. & rep.), 806.261-026, 05.05.02

MARKER (ret. tr.), 209.587-034, 05.09.03

MARKER 2 (any ind.), 920.687-126, 06.04.37

MARKER, SEMICONDUCTOR WAFERS (electronics), 920.587-026, 06.04.37

MARKET-RESEARCH ANALYST 1 (profess. & kin.), 050.067-014, 11.06.03

MASKER (any ind.), 749.687-018, 06.04.34

MASSEUR/MASSEUSE (per. ser.), 334.374-010, 09.05.01

MAT CUTTER (framing), 739.684-126, 06.04.34

MATE, SHIP (water trans.), 197.133-022, 05.04.02

MATERIAL CLERK (clerical), 222.387-034, 05.09.03

MATERIAL COORDINATOR (clerical), 221.167-014, 05.09.02

MATERIAL EXPEDITER (clerical), 221.367-042, 05.09.02

MATERIAL HANDLER (any ind.), 929.687-030, 05.12.03

MATERIAL SCHEDULER (aircraft-aerospace mfg.), 012.187-010, 05.03.03

MATERIALS ENGINEER (profess. & kin.), 019.061-014, 05.01.06

MATERIALS SCIENTIST (profess. & kin.), 029.081-014, 02.01.02

MATHEMATICAL TECHNICIAN (profess. & kin.), 020.162-010, 11.01.02

MATHEMATICIAN (profess. & kin.), 020.067-014, 02.01.01

MATTRESS MAKER (matt. & bedspring), 780.684-074, 06.02.27

MEAT CLERK (ret. tr.), 222.684-010, 05.09.01

MEAT CUTTER (ret. tr.), 316.684-018, 05.10.08

MECHANIC, AIRCRAFT ACCESSORIES (aircraft-aerospace mfg.), 621.381-014, 05.10.02

MECHANIC, INDUSTRIAL TRUCK (any ind.), 620.281-050, 05.05.09

MECHANICAL ENGINEER (profess. & kin.), 007.061-014, 05.01.08

MECHANICAL-ENGINEERING TECHNICIAN (profess. & kin.), 007.161-026, 05.01.01

MEDIA DIRECTOR (profess. & kin.), 164.117-018, 11.09.01

MEDIA SPECIALIST, SCHOOL LIBRARY (library), 100.167-030, 11.02.04

MEDICAL ASSISTANT (medical ser.), 079.367-010, 10.03.02

MEDICAL PHYSICIST (profess. & kin.), 079.021-014, 02.02.01

MEDICAL RECORD TECHNICIAN (medical ser.), 079.367-014, 07.05.03

MEDICAL SECRETARY (medical ser.), 201.362-014, 07.01.03

MEDICAL TECHNOLOGIST (medical ser.), 078.361-014, 02.04.02

MEDICAL-EQUIPMENT REPAIRER (per. protect. & med. device), 639.281-022, 05.10.02

MEDICAL-LABORATORY ASSISTANT (medical ser.), 078.381-010, 02.04.02

MEDICAL-LABORATORY TECHNICIAN (medical ser.), 078.381-014, 02.04.02

MEDICAL-RECORD ADMINISTRATOR (medical ser.), 079.167-014, 11.07.02

MEDICAL-RECORD CLERK (medical ser.), 245.362-010, 07.05.03

MEDICAL-SERVICE TECHNICIAN (military ser.), 079.367-018, 07.05.03

MEDICATION AIDE (medical ser.), 355.374-014, 10.03.02

MELTER (jewelry), 700.687-042, 06.04.24

MEMBERSHIP DIRECTOR (profess. & kin.), 189.167-026, 11.09.02

MEMBERSHIP SECRETARY (nonprofit org.), 201.362-018, 07.01.02

MEMBERSHIP SOLICITOR (any ind.), 293.357-022, 08.02.08

MENDER (carpet & rug), 782.684-042, 06.02.27

MENDER (any ind.), 787.682-030, 06.02.05

MENTAL-RETARDATION AIDE (medical ser.), 355.377-018, 10.03.02

MERCHANDISE DISTRIBUTOR (ret. tr.), 219.367-018, 07.05.04

MESH CUTTER (jewelry), 700.684-050, 06.02.24

MESS ATTENDANT (water trans.), 350.677-010, 09.05.02

MESSENGER, BANK (finan. inst.), 230.367-014, 07.05.04

MESSENGER, COPY (print. & pub.), 239.677-010, 07.07.02

METAL FABRICATOR (any ind.), 619.360-014, 05.05.06

METAL FINISHER (any ind.), 705.684-034, 06.04.24

METAL SPRAYER, PRODUCTION (any ind.), 505.684-014, 06.04.33

METAL-FINISH INSPECTOR (any ind.), 703.687-014, 06.03.02

METALLIZATION EQUIPMENT OPERATOR, SEMICONDUCTOR WAFERS (electronics), 590.685-086, 06.04.19

METALLOGRAPHER (profess. & kin.), 011.061-014, 05.01.04

METALLURGICAL TECHNICIAN (profess. & kin.), 011.261-010, 02.04.01

METALLURGIST, EXTRACTIVE (profess. & kin.), 011.061-018, 05.01.06

METALLURGIST, PHYSICAL (profess. & kin.), 011.061-022, 02.01.02

METEOROLOGICAL-EQUIPMENT REPAIRER (any ind.), 823.281-018, 05.05.10

METEOROLOGIST (profess. & kin.), 025.062-010, 02.01.01

METER READER (light, heat, & power), 209.567-010, 05.09.03

METER REPAIRER (any ind.), 710.281-034, 05.10.02

METROLOGIST (profess. & kin.), 012.067-010, 05.01.04

MICROBIOLOGIST (profess. & kin.), 041.061-058, 02.02.03

MICROBIOLOGY TECHNOLOGIST (drug prep. & related), 078.261-014, 02.04.02

MICROELECTRONICS TECHNICIAN (electronics), 590.362-022, 06.01.03

MICROFICHE DUPLICATOR (bus. ser.), 976.381-014, 05.10.05

MICROFILM MOUNTER (clerical), 208.685-022, 05.12.19

MICROFILM PROCESSOR (bus. ser.), 976.385-010, 05.10.05

MIGRANT LEADER (agric.), 180.167-050, 03.01.01

MILK DRIVER (dairy prod.), 905.483-010, 05.08.01

MILL OPERATOR (corn prod.), 521.685-226, 06.04.15

MILL OPERATOR (any ind.), 599.685-058, 06.04.10

MILLER (cement), 570.685-046, 06.04.08

MILLWRIGHT (any ind.), 638.281-018, 05.05.06

MIME (amuse. & rec.), 159.047-022, 01.03.02

MINE INSPECTOR (mining), 168.267-074, 11.10.03

MINERALOGIST (profess. & kin.), 024.061-038, 02.01.01

MINING ENGINEER (mining), 010.061-014, 05.01.06

MIXER (paint & varn.), 550.685-078, 06.04.11

MIXING-MACHINE OPERATOR (food prep nec), 520.665-014, 06.04.15

MIXING-MACHINE OPERATOR (any ind.), 550.382-022, 06.02.13

MODEL MAKER 1 (any ind.), 777.261-010, 01.06.02

MODEL, ARTISTS' (any ind.), 961.667-010, 01.08.01

MOLD DRESSER (any ind.), 519.684-018, 06.04.24

MOLD MAKER 1 (jewelry), 700.381-034, 01.06.02

MOLDER (foundry), 518.361-010, 06.01.04

MOLDER (optical goods), 575.381-010, 06.02.30

MORGUE ATTENDANT (medical ser.), 355.667-010, 02.04.02

MORTGAGE CLERK (finan. inst.), 249.382-010, 07.01.04

MORTGAGE-PROCESSING CLERK (finan. inst.), 203.382-022, 07.05.03

MORTUARY BEAUTICIAN (per. ser.), 339.361-010, 01.06.02

MOTION-PICTURE PROJECTIONIST (amuse. & rec.), 960.362-010, 05.10.05

MOTORBOAT OPERATOR (any ind.), 911.663-010, 05.08.04

MOTORCYCLE ASSEMBLER (motor. & bicycles), 806.684-090, 06.02.22

MOTORCYCLE TESTER (motor. & bicycles), 620.384-010, 06.03.01

MOUNTER, AUTOMATIC (photofinish.), 976.685-022, 06.04.20

MOUNTER, HAND (photofinish.), 976.684-018, 06.04.34

MUFFLER INSTALLER (auto. ser.), 807.664-010, 05.10.01

MULTIFOCAL-LENS ASSEMBLER (optical goods), 713.684-034, 06.04.23

MUNITIONS HANDLER (ammunition), 929.687-034, 06.04.40

MUSEUM ATTENDANT (museum), 109.367-010, 07.04.04

MUSEUM TECHNICIAN (museum), 102.381-010, 01.06.02

MUSIC THERAPIST (medical ser.), 076.127-014, 10.02.02

MUSICIAN, INSTRUMENTAL (amuse. & rec.), 152.041-010, 01.04.04

NAILER, HAND (any ind.), 762.684-050, 06.04.22

NAILING-MACHINE OPERATOR (any ind.), 669.682-058, 06.02.03

NAME-PLATE STAMPER (any ind.), 652.685-054, 06.04.37

NARRATOR (motion pic.), 150.147-010, 01.03.03

NAVIGATOR (air trans.), 196.167-014, 05.03.01

NEGOTIATOR, LETTER OF CREDIT (finan. inst.), 186.117-050, 11.06.03

NEW-ACCOUNTS CLERK (finan. inst.), 205.362-026, 07.04.01

NEW-CAR GET-READY MECHANIC (auto. ser.), 806.361-026, 05.10.02

NEWS ASSISTANT (radio & tv broad.), 209.367-038, 07.05.03

NEWSCASTER (radio & tv broad.), 131.267-010, 11.08.03

NEWSPAPER CARRIER (ret. tr.), 292.457-010, 09.04.02

NEWSPAPER-DELIVERY DRIVER (whole. tr.), 292.363-010, 05.08.03

NIBBLER OPERATOR (any ind.), 615.685-026, 06.04.02

NIGHT AUDITOR (hotel & rest.), 210.382-054, 07.02.02

NITROGLYCERIN DISTRIBUTOR (explosives), 559.664-010, 06.04.40

NONDESTRUCTIVE TESTER (bus. ser.), 011.261-018, 05.07.01

NUCLEAR ENGINEER (profess. & kin.), 015.061-014, 05.01.03

NUCLEAR MEDICAL TECHNOLOGIST (medical ser.), 078.361-018, 10.02.02

NUCLEAR-CRITICALITY SAFETY ENGINEER (profess. & kin.), 015.067-010, 05.01.02

NUCLEAR-DECONTAMINATION RESEARCH SPECIALIST (profess. & kin.), 008.061-030, 05.01.01

NUMERICAL-CONTROL ROUTER OPERATOR, PRINTED CIRCUIT BOARDS (electronics), 605.382-046, 06.02.09

NUMERICAL-CONTROL-MACHINE
OPERATOR (mach. shop), 609.662-010,
06.02.02

NURSE AIDE (medical ser.), 355.674-014,
10.03.02

NURSE ANESTHETIST (medical ser.),
075.371-010, 10.02.01

NURSE PRACTITIONER (medical ser.),
075.264-010, 10.02.01

NURSE, GENERAL DUTY (medical ser.),
075.374-010, 10.02.01

NURSE, INSTRUCTOR (medical ser.),
075.121-010, 10.02.01

NURSE, LICENSED PRACTICAL
(medical ser.), 079.374-014, 10.02.01

NURSE, OFFICE (medical ser.),
075.374-014, 10.02.01

NURSE, PRACTICAL (medical ser.),
354.374-010, 10.03.02

NURSE, PRIVATE DUTY (medical ser.),
075.374-018, 10.02.01

NURSE, SCHOOL (medical ser.),
075.124-010, 10.02.01

NURSE, STAFF, COMMUNITY HEALTH
(medical ser.), 075.124-014, 10.02.01

NURSE, STAFF, OCCUPATIONAL
HEALTH NURSING (medical ser.),
075.374-022, 10.02.01

NURSE-MIDWIFE (medical ser.),
075.264-014, 10.02.01

NURSERY SCHOOL ATTENDANT (any
ind.), 359.677-018, 10.03.03

OCCUPATIONAL ANALYST (profess. &
kin.), 166.067-010, 11.03.04

OCCUPATIONAL THERAPIST (medical
ser.), 076.121-010, 10.02.02

OCCUPATIONAL THERAPY AIDE
(medical ser.), 355.377-010, 10.03.02

OCCUPATIONAL THERAPY
ASSISTANT (medical ser.),
076.364-010, 10.02.02

OCCUPATIONAL-SAFETY-AND-HEALTH
INSPECTOR (gov. ser.), 168.167-062,
11.10.03

OFFICE HELPER (clerical), 239.567-010,
07.07.03

OFFICE-MACHINE SERVICER (any
ind.), 633.281-018, 05.05.09

OFFSET-DUPLICATING-MACHINE
OPERATOR (clerical), 207.682-018,
05.10.05

OFFSET-PRESS OPERATOR 1 (print. &
pub.), 651.482-010, 05.05.13

OIL-BURNER-SERVICER-AND-INSTALL
ER (any ind.), 862.281-018, 05.05.03

OILER (any ind.), 699.687-018, 05.12.08

OPAQUER (medical ser.), 712.684-030,
06.02.32

OPERATIONS MANAGER (tel. & tel.),
184.117-070, 11.05.02

OPERATIONS MANAGER (motor trans.),
184.167-118, 11.11.03

OPERATIONS OFFICER (finan. inst.),
186.167-050, 11.06.01

OPERATIONS-RESEARCH ANALYST
(profess. & kin.), 020.067-018, 11.01.01

OPTICAL ENGINEER (profess. & kin.),
019.061-018, 05.01.07

OPTICAL-EFFECTS-CAMERA
OPERATOR (motion pic.), 143.260-010,
01.02.03

OPTICAL-ELEMENT COATER (optical
goods), 716.382-014, 06.02.21

OPTICIAN (optical goods), 716.280-008,
05.05.11

OPTICIAN (optical goods), 716.280-014,
05.05.11

OPTICIAN, DISPENSING 1 (ret. tr.),
713.361-014, 05.05.11

OPTOMECHANICAL TECHNICIAN
(optical goods), 007.161-030, 05.01.01

OPTOMETRIST (profess. & kin.),
079.101-018, 02.03.04

ORDER CALLER (clerical), 209.667-014,
05.09.03

ORDER CLERK (clerical), 249.367-054,
07.05.03

ORDER DETAILER (clerical),
221.387-046, 05.09.02

ORDER FILLER (ret. tr.), 222.487-014,
05.09.01

ORDER-DEPARTMENT SUPERVISOR
(any ind.), 169.167-038, 07.05.03

ORDERLY (medical ser.), 355.674-018,
10.03.02

ORDINARY SEAMAN (water trans.),
911.687-030, 05.12.18

ORIENTATION THERAPIST FOR THE
BLIND (educ.), 076.221-010, 10.02.02

ORNAMENTAL-METAL WORKER
(fabric. metal prod. nec), 619.260-008,
05.05.06

ORTHODONTIC TECHNICIAN (medical
ser.), 712.381-030, 05.05.11

ORTHOPEDIC ASSISTANT (medical
ser.), 712.661-010, 10.03.02

ORTHOPTIST (medical ser.),
079.371-014, 10.02.02

ORTHOTICS ASSISTANT (per. protect. &
med. device), 078.361-022, 05.05.11

ORTHOTICS TECHNICIAN (per. protect.
& med. device), 712.381-034, 05.05.11

ORTHOTIST (per. protect. & med.
device), 078.261-018, 05.05.11

OUTPATIENT-ADMITTING CLERK
(medical ser.), 205.362-030, 07.04.01

OVEN OPERATOR, AUTOMATIC (bake.
prod.), 526.682-030, 06.02.15

OVEN TENDER (bake. prod.),
526.685-030, 06.04.15

OXIDIZED-FINISH PLATER (any ind.),
599.685-062, 06.04.10

OXIDIZER (silverware), 700.684-054,
06.04.24

PACKAGE DESIGNER (profess. & kin.),
142.081-018, 01.02.03

PACKAGE SEALER, MACHINE (any
ind.), 920.685-074, 06.04.38

PACKAGER, HAND (any ind.),
920.587-018, 06.04.38

PACKAGER, MACHINE (any ind.),
920.685-078, 06.04.38

PACKAGING ENGINEER (profess. &
kin.), 019.187-010, 05.03.09

PACKER, DENTURE (medical ser.),
712.684-034, 05.05.11

PACKING-LINE WORKER (rubber
goods), 753.687-038, 06.04.38

PAGE (library), 249.687-014, 07.07.02

PAINT MIXER, HAND (any ind.),
550.684-018, 06.04.34

PAINT MIXER, MACHINE (any ind.),
550.485-018, 06.04.11

PAINT-SPRAY INSPECTOR (any ind.),
741.687-010, 06.03.02

PAINT-SPRAYER OPERATOR,
AUTOMATIC (any ind.), 599.382-010,
06.02.21

PAINTER (jewelry), 735.687-018, 06.04.33

PAINTER (const.), 840.381-010, 05.10.07

PAINTER, AIRBRUSH (any ind.),
741.684-018, 01.06.03

PAINTER, BRUSH (any ind.),
740.684-022, 06.04.33

PAINTER, ELECTROSTATIC (any ind.),
599.682-010, 06.02.21

PAINTER, HAND (any ind.), 970.381-022,
01.06.03

PAINTER, SIGN (any ind.), 970.381-026,
01.06.03

PAINTER, SPRAY 1 (any ind.),
741.684-026, 05.10.07

PAINTER, SPRAY 2 (any ind.),
741.687-018, 06.04.33

PAINTER, TOUCH-UP (any ind.),
749.684-038, 05.10.07

PAINTER, TUMBLING BARREL (any
ind.), 599.685-070, 06.04.21

PAINTING-MACHINE OPERATOR (any
ind.), 599.685-074, 06.04.21

PALLETIZER OPERATOR 1 (any ind.),
921.682-014, 06.04.40

PANTRY GOODS MAKER (hotel & rest.),
317.684-014, 05.10.08

PAPERHANGER (const.), 841.381-010,
05.05.04

PARACHUTE RIGGER (air trans.),
912.684-010, 06.04.38

PARALEGAL ASSISTANT (profess. &
kin.), 119.267-026, 11.04.02

PARASITOLOGIST (profess. & kin.),
041.061-070, 02.02.01

PARCEL-POST CLERK (clerical),
222.387-038, 07.05.04

PARIMUTUEL-TICKET SELLER
(amuse. & rec.), 211.467-022, 07.03.01

PARK AIDE (gov. ser.), 249.367-082,
07.04.03

PARK NATURALIST (gov. ser.),
049.127-010, 11.07.03

PARK RANGER (gov. ser.), 169.167-042,
04.02.03

PARKING ENFORCEMENT OFFICER
(gov. ser.), 375.587-010, 04.02.02

PARKING-LOT ATTENDANT (auto. ser.),
915.473-010, 09.04.02

PARTS CLERK (clerical), 222.367-042,
05.09.01

PARTS SALVAGER (any ind.),
638.281-026, 05.05.09

PARTS-ORDER-AND-STOCK CLERK
(clerical), 249.367-058, 05.09.01

PASSPORT-APPLICATION EXAMINER
(gov. ser.), 169.267-030, 07.01.05

PASTRY CHEF (hotel & rest.),
313.131-022, 05.10.08

PATENT AGENT (profess. & kin.),
119.167-014, 11.04.04

PATTERNMAKER, METAL (foundry),
600.280-050, 05.05.07

PAWNBROKER (ret. tr.), 191.157-010,
08.01.03

PAYROLL CLERK (clerical), 215.482-010,
07.02.05

PERCUSSION-INSTRUMENT
REPAIRER (any ind.), 730.381-042,
05.05.12

PERFUSIONIST (medical ser.),
078.362-034, 10.03.02

PERSONAL PROPERTY ASSESSOR
(gov. ser.), 191.367-010, 11.06.03

PERSONAL SHOPPER (ret. tr.),
296.357-010, 09.04.02

PERSONNEL CLERK (clerical),
209.362-026, 07.05.03

PERSONNEL RECRUITER (profess. & kin.), 166.267-038, 11.03.04
PERSONNEL SCHEDULER (clerical), 215.367-014, 07.05.01
PESTICIDE-CONTROL INSPECTOR (gov. ser.), 168.267-098, 11.10.03
PETROLEUM ENGINEER (petrol. production), 010.061-018, 05.01.08
PETROLOGIST (profess. & kin.), 024.061-046, 02.01.01
PHARMACEUTICAL DETAILER (whole. tr.), 262.157-010, 08.01.01
PHARMACIST (profess. & kin.), 074.161-010, 02.04.01
PHARMACIST ASSISTANT (military ser.), 074.381-010, 02.04.01
PHARMACOLOGIST (profess. & kin.), 041.061-074, 02.02.01
PHARMACY HELPER (medical ser.), 074.387-010, 05.09.01
PHLEBOTOMIST (medical ser.), 079.364-022, 02.04.02
PHOTO CHECKER AND ASSEMBLER (photofinish.), 976.687-014, 06.03.02
PHOTO MASK CLEANER (electronics), 590.684-034, 06.04.34
PHOTO-OPTICS TECHNICIAN (profess. & kin.), 029.280-010, 02.04.01
PHOTOCOMPOSING-MACHINE OPERATOR (print. & pub.), 650.582-018, 05.10.05
PHOTOCOMPOSITION-KEYBOARD OPERATOR (print. & pub.), 203.582-046, 07.06.02
PHOTOCOPYING-MACHINE OPERATOR (clerical), 207.685-014, 05.12.19
PHOTOENGRAVER (print. & pub.), 971.381-022, 01.06.01
PHOTOFINISHING LABORATORY WORKER (photofinish.), 976.687-018, 06.03.02
PHOTOGRAMMETRIC ENGINEER (profess. & kin.), 018.167-026, 05.03.01
PHOTOGRAMMETRIST (profess. & kin.), 018.261-026, 05.03.02
PHOTOGRAPH FINISHER (photofinish.), 976.487-010, 05.10.05
PHOTOGRAPHER (amuse. & rec.), 143.457-010, 08.03.01
PHOTOGRAPHER, MOTION PICTURE (profess. & kin.), 143.062-022, 01.02.03
PHOTOGRAPHER, SCIENTIFIC (profess. & kin.), 143.062-026, 02.04.01
PHOTOGRAPHER, STILL (profess. & kin.), 143.062-030, 01.02.03
PHOTOGRAPHIC-MACHINE OPERATOR (clerical), 207.685-018, 05.12.19
PHOTOGRAPHIC-PLATE MAKER (electronics), 714.381-018, 05.10.05
PHOTOJOURNALIST (print. & pub.), 143.062-034, 01.02.03
PHOTORESIST LAMINATOR, PRINTED CIRCUIT BOARD (electronics), 699.685-042, 06.04.09
PHOTOTYPESETTER OPERATOR (print. & pub.), 650.582-022, 07.06.02
PHYSICAL THERAPIST (medical ser.), 076.121-014, 10.02.02
PHYSICAL THERAPIST ASSISTANT (medical ser.), 076.224-010, 10.02.02
PHYSICAL THERAPY AIDE (medical ser.), 355.354-010, 10.03.02

PHYSICAL-INTEGRATION PRACTITIONER (per. ser.), 076.264-010, 10.02.02
PHYSICIAN ASSISTANT (medical ser.), 079.364-018, 10.02.01
PHYSICIST (profess. & kin.), 023.061-014, 02.01.01
PHYSIOLOGIST (profess. & kin.), 041.061-078, 02.02.03
PIANO TECHNICIAN (any ind.), 730.281-038, 05.05.12
PIANO TUNER (any ind.), 730.361-010, 05.05.12
PICKING-MACHINE OPERATOR (any ind.), 680.685-082, 06.04.06
PICKLER, CONTINUOUS PICKLING LINE (any ind.), 503.362-010, 06.02.10
PICTURE FRAMER (framing), 739.684-146, 01.06.02
PIE MAKER (hotel & rest.), 313.361-038, 05.10.08
PILOT, SHIP (water trans.), 197.133-026, 05.04.02
PINSETTER ADJUSTER, AUTOMATIC (sports equip.), 829.381-010, 05.05.10
PINSETTER MECHANIC, AUTOMATIC (any ind.), 638.261-022, 05.10.04
PIPE FITTER (any ind.), 862.281-022, 05.05.03
PIPE-FITTER HELPER (const.), 862.684-022, 05.12.12
PIPE-ORGAN INSTALLER (musical inst.), 730.381-046, 05.05.12
PIPE-ORGAN TUNER AND REPAIRER (any ind.), 730.361-014, 05.05.12
PLAN CHECKER (gov. ser.), 168.267-102, 05.03.06
PLANNER, PROGRAM SERVICES (gov. ser.), 188.167-110, 11.03.02
PLANT BREEDER (profess. & kin.), 041.061-082, 02.02.02
PLANT ENGINEER (profess. & kin.), 007.167-014, 05.01.08
PLANT OPERATOR (concrete prod.), 570.682-014, 05.11.02
PLANT PATHOLOGIST (profess. & kin.), 041.061-086, 02.02.02
PLANT-CARE WORKER (agric.), 408.364-010, 03.04.05
PLASTER MAKER (statue & art), 779.684-046, 06.02.30
PLASTER-DIE MAKER (pottery & porc.), 774.684-026, 06.02.30
PLASTERER (const.), 842.361-018, 05.05.04
PLASTIC-TOP ASSEMBLER (furn.), 763.684-062, 06.04.22
PLATER (electroplating), 500.380-010, 06.02.21
PLATER, HOT DIP (galvanizing), 501.685-010, 06.04.21
PLATER, PRINTED CIRCUIT BOARD PANELS (electronics), 500.684-026, 06.02.21
PLATER, PRODUCTION (electroplating), 500.665-010, 06.04.21
PLATER, SEMICONDUCTOR WAFERS AND COMPONENTS (electronics), 500.684-030, 06.04.19
PLAYROOM ATTENDANT (any ind.), 359.677-026, 10.03.03
PLEATING-MACHINE OPERATOR (any ind.), 583.685-082, 06.04.05
PLUMBER (const.), 862.381-030, 05.05.03

PNEUMATIC-TOOL REPAIRER (any ind.), 630.281-010, 05.05.09
PNEUMATIC-TUBE REPAIRER (any ind.), 630.281-014, 05.10.02
PODIATRIC ASSISTANT (medical ser.), 079.374-018, 10.03.02
PODIATRIST (medical ser.), 079.101-022, 02.03.01
POLICE AIDE (gov. ser.), 243.362-014, 07.04.05
POLICE ARTIST (gov. ser.), 141.061-034, 01.02.03
POLICE CLERK (gov. ser.), 375.362-010, 07.05.01
POLICE OFFICER 1 (gov. ser.), 375.263-014, 04.01.02
POLICE OFFICER III (gov. ser.), 375.267-038, 04.01.02
POLICY-CHANGE CLERK (insurance), 219.362-042, 07.02.02
POLICYHOLDER-INFORMATION CLERK (insurance), 249.262-010, 07.04.04
POLISHER (any ind.), 705.684-058, 06.04.24
POLISHER, EYEGLASS FRAMES (optical goods), 713.684-038, 06.04.24
POLISHING-MACHINE OPERATOR (any ind.), 603.682-026, 06.02.02
POLISHING-WHEEL SETTER (any ind.), 776.684-014, 05.10.04
POLITICAL SCIENTIST (profess. & kin.), 051.067-010, 11.03.02
POLLUTION-CONTROL ENGINEER (profess. & kin.), 019.081-018, 05.01.02
POLLUTION-CONTROL TECHNICIAN (profess. & kin.), 029.261-014, 05.03.08
POLYGRAPH EXAMINER (profess. & kin.), 199.267-026, 02.04.02
POLYSILICON PREPARATION WORKER (electronics), 590.684-038, 06.04.19
PORTER (air trans.), 357.677-010, 09.05.03
PORTER, BAGGAGE (hotel & rest.), 324.477-010, 09.05.03
POST-OFFICE CLERK (gov. ser.), 243.367-014, 07.03.01
POSTING CLERK (clerical), 216.587-014, 07.02.02
POSTMASTER (gov. ser.), 188.167-066, 11.05.03
POTTERY-MACHINE OPERATOR (pottery & porc.), 774.382-010, 06.02.08
POULTRY DRESSER (agric.), 525.687-070, 06.04.28
POWER-BARKER OPERATOR (paper & pulp), 669.485-010, 06.04.03
POWER-DISTRIBUTION ENGINEER (light, heat, & power), 003.167-046, 05.01.03
POWER-PRESS TENDER (any ind.), 617.685-026, 06.04.02
POWER-REACTOR OPERATOR (light, heat, & power), 952.362-022, 05.06.01
POWER-SAW MECHANIC (any ind.), 625.281-030, 05.05.09
POWER-SHOVEL OPERATOR (any ind.), 850.683-030, 05.11.01
POWER-TRANSMISSION ENGINEER (light, heat, & power), 003.167-050, 05.01.03
POWERHOUSE MECHANIC (light, heat, & power), 631.261-014, 05.05.09

PRECISION-LENS GRINDER (optical goods), 716.382-018, 06.02.08

PRECISION-LENS POLISHER (optical goods), 716.682-018, 06.02.08

PREPARER (jewelry), 700.687-062, 06.04.24

PRESCRIPTION CLERK, LENS-AND-FRAMES (optical goods), 222.367-050, 05.09.02

PRESIDENT (any ind.), 189.117-026, 11.05.01

PRESS BUCKER (any ind.), 920.686-042, 05.12.03

PRESS OPERATOR (laundry), 363.685-010, 06.04.35

PRESS OPERATOR (fabric. plastic prod.), 690.682-062, 06.02.02

PRESS OPERATOR, HEAVY DUTY (any ind.), 617.260-010, 06.02.02

PRESS OPERATOR, MEAT (slaught. & meat pack.), 520.685-182, 06.04.15

PRESSER (print. & pub.), 977.684-018, 06.02.26

PRESSER, ALL-AROUND (clean., dye., & press.), 363.682-014, 06.04.35

PRESSER, FORM (any ind.), 363.685-018, 06.04.35

PRESSER, HAND (any ind.), 363.684-018, 06.04.35

PRESSER, MACHINE (any ind.), 363.682-018, 06.04.05

PRESSURE SEALER-AND-TESTER (aircraft-aerospace mfg.), 806.684-110, 06.02.24

PREVENTIVE MAINTENANCE COORDINATOR (any ind.), 169.167-074, 05.01.06

PRINT CONTROLLER (photofinish.), 976.360-010, 06.01.02

PRINT DEVELOPER, AUTOMATIC (photofinish.), 976.685-026, 06.04.19

PRINT INSPECTOR (pottery & porc.), 774.687-018, 06.03.02

PRINT-SHOP HELPER (print. & pub.), 979.684-026, 05.12.18

PRINTED CIRCUIT BOARD ASSEMBLER, HAND (electronics), 726.684-070, 06.02.23

PRINTED CIRCUIT DESIGNER (profess. & kin.), 003.261-022, 05.03.02

PRINTER 2 (print. & pub.), 651.380-010, 06.01.03

PRIVATE-BRANCH-EXCHANGE REPAIRER (tel. & tel.), 822.281-022, 05.05.05

PROBATE CLERK (finan. inst.), 216.362-030, 07.02.02

PROBATION OFFICER (profess. & kin.), 195.167-034, 07.01.01

PROBATION-AND-PAROLE OFFICER (profess. & kin.), 195.107-046, 10.01.02

PROCESS SERVER (bus. ser.), 249.367-062, 07.07.02

PROCUREMENT CLERK (clerical), 249.367-066, 07.01.02

PRODUCER (radio & tv broad.), 159.117-010, 01.03.01

PRODUCER (motion pic.), 187.167-174, 01.01.01

PRODUCER (amuse. & rec.), 187.167-178, 01.03.01

PRODUCT-SAFETY ENGINEER (profess. & kin.), 012.061-010, 05.01.02

PRODUCTION COORDINATOR (clerical), 221.167-018, 05.09.02

PRODUCTION ENGINEER (profess. & kin.), 012.167-046, 05.01.06

PRODUCTION PLANNER (profess. & kin.), 012.167-050, 05.01.06

PRODUCTION PROOFREADER (print. & pub.), 247.667-010, 07.05.02

PRODUCTION REPAIRER (electronics), 726.381-014, 05.10.03

PRODUCTION SUPERINTENDENT (any ind.), 183.117-014, 05.02.03

PRODUCTION TECHNICIAN, SEMICONDUCTOR PROCESSING EQUIPMENT (electronics), 590.384-014, 05.09.01

PRODUCTION-MACHINE TENDER (nut & bolt), 619.365-010, 06.04.02

PROGRAM AIDE, GROUP WORK (social ser.), 195.227-010, 10.02.02

PROGRAM COORDINATOR (amuse. & rec.), 139.167-010, 01.03.02

PROGRAM DIRECTOR, GROUP WORK (profess. & kin.), 187.117-046, 11.07.01

PROGRAM MANAGER (profess. & kin.), 189.167-030, 11.05.02

PROGRAM PROPOSALS COORDINATOR (radio & tv broad.), 132.067-030, 11.05.02

PROGRAM SPECIALIST, EMPLOYEE-HEALTH MAINTENANCE (profess. & kin.), 166.167-050, 11.05.02

PROGRAMER, CHIEF, BUSINESS (profess. & kin.), 020.167-018, 11.01.01

PROGRAMER, ENGINEERING AND SCIENTIFIC (profess. & kin.), 020.167-022, 11.01.01

PROGRAMER, INFORMATION SYSTEM (profess. & kin.), 020.187-010, 11.01.01

PROGRAMER, PROCESS CONTROL (profess. & kin.), 020.187-014, 11.01.01

PROGRAMMER, BUSINESS (profess. & kin.), 020.162-014, 11.01.01

PROGRAMMER, DETAIL (clerical), 219.367-026, 11.01.01

PROJECT ENGINEER (profess. & kin.), 019.167-014, 05.01.08

PROJECT MANAGER, ENVIRONMENTAL RESEARCH (profess. & kin.), 029.167-014, 02.01.02

PROJECTION PRINTER (photofinish.), 976.381-018, 05.10.05

PROMPTER (amuse. & rec.), 152.367-010, 01.04.02

PROOF-MACHINE OPERATOR (finan. inst.), 217.382-010, 07.06.02

PROOFREADER (print. & pub.), 209.387-030, 07.05.02

PROP MAKER (amuse. & rec.), 962.281-010, 01.06.02

PROPERTY CLERK (gov. ser.), 222.367-054, 07.05.03

PROPERTY-DISPOSAL OFFICER (any ind.), 163.167-026, 11.05.04

PROPERTY-UTILIZATION OFFICER (gov. ser.), 188.117-122, 11.12.02

PROSTHETICS ASSISTANT (per. protect. & med. device), 078.361-026, 05.05.11

PROSTHETICS TECHNICIAN (per. protect. & med. device), 712.381-038, 05.05.11

PROSTHETIST (per. protect. & med. device), 078.261-022, 05.05.11

PROTECTIVE-SIGNAL INSTALLER (bus. ser.), 822.361-018, 05.05.05

PROTECTIVE-SIGNAL OPERATOR (any ind.), 379.362-014, 07.04.05

PROTECTIVE-SIGNAL REPAIRER (bus. ser.), 822.361-022, 05.05.05

PSYCHIATRIC AIDE (medical ser.), 355.377-014, 10.03.02

PSYCHIATRIC TECHNICIAN (medical ser.), 079.374-026, 10.02.02

PSYCHOLOGIST, CLINICAL (profess. & kin.), 045.107-022, 10.01.02

PSYCHOLOGIST, COUNSELING (profess. & kin.), 045.107-026, 10.01.02

PSYCHOLOGIST, EXPERIMENTAL (profess. & kin.), 045.061-018, 11.03.01

PSYCHOLOGIST, INDUSTRIAL-ORGANIZATIONAL (profess. & kin.), 045.107-030, 11.03.01

PUBLIC HEALTH EDUCATOR (profess. & kin.), 079.117-014, 11.07.02

PUBLIC HEALTH REGISTRAR (gov. ser.), 169.167-046, 07.04.03

PUBLIC HEALTH SERVICE OFFICER (gov. ser.), 187.117-050, 11.10.03

PUBLIC-ADDRESS SERVICER (any ind.), 823.261-010, 05.05.10

PUBLIC-HEALTH MICROBIOLOGIST (gov. ser.), 041.261-010, 02.04.02

PUBLIC-RELATIONS REPRESENTATIVE (profess. & kin.), 165.067-010, 11.09.03

PULMONARY-FUNCTION TECHNICIAN (medical ser.), 078.262-010, 10.03.01

PUMP INSTALLER (any ind.), 630.684-018, 05.10.01

PUMP SERVICER (any ind.), 630.281-018, 05.05.09

PUMP-STATION OPERATOR, WATERWORKS (waterworks), 954.382-010, 05.06.03

PUMPER (any ind.), 914.682-010, 05.06.03

PUMPER, BREWERY (beer prod.), 914.665-014, 06.04.40

PUNCH-PRESS OPERATOR 3 (any ind.), 615.682-014, 06.02.02

PUNCH-PRESS OPERATOR II (any ind.), 615.685-030, 06.04.02

PUPPETEER (amuse. & rec.), 159.041-014, 01.03.02

PURCHASING AGENT (profess. & kin.), 162.157-038, 11.05.04

PURSER (water trans.), 197.167-014, 11.11.03

PUTTY GLAZER (any ind.), 749.684-042, 06.04.33

QUALITY-CONTROL COORDINATOR (drug prep. & related), 168.167-066, 05.02.03

QUALITY-CONTROL ENGINEER (profess. & kin.), 012.167-054, 05.01.04

QUALITY-CONTROL INSPECTOR (phonograph), 194.387-010, 06.03.01

QUALITY-CONTROL TECHNICIAN (profess. & kin.), 012.261-014, 02.04.01

QUICK SKETCH ARTIST (amuse. & rec.), 149.041-010, 01.02.02

RACKET STRINGER (sports equip.), 732.684-094, 06.02.32

RADIATION-PROTECTION ENGINEER (gov. ser.), 015.137-010, 05.01.02

RADIATION-PROTECTION SPECIALIST (gov. ser.), 168.261-010, 11.10.03

RADIATION-THERAPY TECHNOLOGIST (medical ser.), 078.361-034, 02.03.04

RADIO MECHANIC (any ind.), 823.261-018, 05.05.10

RADIOGRAPHER (any ind.), 199.361-010, 05.03.05

RADIOISOTOPE-PRODUCTION OPERATOR (profess. & kin.), 015.362-022, 02.04.01

RADIOLOGIC TECHNOLOGIST (medical ser.), 078.362-026, 10.02.02

RADIOLOGICAL-EQUIPMENT SPECIALIST (medical ser.), 719.261-014, 05.05.11

RADIOPHARMACIST (medical ser.), 074.161-014, 02.04.01

RADIOTELEPHONE OPERATOR (any ind.), 193.262-034, 05.03.05

RANGE MANAGER (profess. & kin.), 040.061-046, 02.02.02

RATER (insurance), 214.482-022, 07.02.04

RATER, TRAVEL ACCOMMODATIONS (profess. & kin.), 168.367-014, 11.10.05

REACTOR OPERATOR, TEST-AND-RESEARCH (profess. & kin.), 015.362-026, 02.04.01

READER (bus. ser.), 249.387-022, 07.05.02

REAL-ESTATE AGENT (profess. & kin.), 186.117-058, 11.12.02

REAL-ESTATE CLERK (clerical), 219.362-046, 07.01.04

RECEIVING CHECKER (clerical), 222.687-018, 05.09.03

RECEPTIONIST (clerical), 237.367-038, 07.04.04

RECONCILEMENT CLERK (finan. inst.), 210.382-058, 07.02.01

RECORD-PRESS TENDER (phonograph), 556.685-070, 06.04.13

RECORDING ENGINEER (phonograph), 194.362-010, 05.10.05

RECORDING STUDIO SET-UP WORKER (phonograph), 962.664-014, 05.12.03

RECORDIST (motion pic.), 962.382-010, 05.10.05

RECORDS CUSTODIAN (finan. inst.), 206.387-026, 07.05.03

RECREATION AIDE (social ser.), 195.367-030, 09.01.01

RECREATION LEADER (social ser.), 195.227-014, 09.01.01

RECREATION SUPERVISOR (profess. & kin.), 187.137-010, 11.07.04

RECREATION-FACILITY ATTENDANT (amuse. & rec.), 341.367-010, 07.04.03

RECREATIONAL THERAPIST (medical ser.), 076.124-014, 10.02.02

RECRUITER (military ser.), 166.267-026, 11.03.04

REDUCING-SALON ATTENDANT (per. ser.), 359.567-010, 09.05.01

REFERRAL CLERK, TEMPORARY-HELP AGENCY (clerical), 205.367-062, 07.05.03

REFERRAL-AND-INFORMATION AIDE (gov. ser.), 237.367-042, 07.04.02

REFINER (medical ser.), 712.684-038, 06.04.24

REFINERY OPERATOR (petrol. refin.), 549.260-010, 06.01.03

REFRIGERATING ENGINEER (any ind.), 950.362-014, 05.06.02

REFRIGERATION MECHANIC (any ind.), 637.261-026, 05.05.09

REFRIGERATION MECHANIC (refrig. equip.), 827.361-014, 05.05.09

REGISTRATION CLERK (gov. ser.), 205.367-042, 07.04.01

REGULATORY ADMINISTRATOR (tel. & tel.), 168.167-070, 11.10.05

REHABILITATION CENTER MANAGER (gov. ser.), 195.167-038, 11.07.01

REHABILITATION CLERK (nonprofit org.), 205.367-046, 07.04.01

REINSURANCE CLERK (insurance), 219.482-018, 07.02.04

RELIABILITY ENGINEER (profess. & kin.), 019.061-026, 05.01.04

REPAIR-ORDER CLERK (clerical), 221.382-022, 07.05.03

REPAIRER (furn.), 709.684-062, 05.10.01

REPAIRER, ART OBJECTS (any ind.), 779.381-018, 01.06.02

REPAIRER, FINISHED METAL (any ind.), 809.684-034, 06.02.24

REPAIRER, TYPEWRITER (office mach.), 706.381-030, 06.02.24

REPORTER (print. & pub.), 131.267-018, 11.08.02

REPORTS ANALYST (profess. & kin.), 161.267-026, 11.06.02

REPOSSESSOR (clerical), 241.367-022, 04.02.03

REPRODUCTION ORDER PROCESSOR (clerical), 221.367-058, 07.05.03

REPRODUCTION TECHNICIAN (any ind.), 976.361-010, 05.10.05

RERECORDING MIXER (motion pic.), 194.362-014, 05.10.05

RESEARCH ANALYST (insurance), 169.267-034, 11.05.02

RESEARCH ASSISTANT (profess. & kin.), 109.267-010, 11.03.03

RESEARCH ASSISTANT II (profess. & kin.), 199.267-034, 11.08.02

RESEARCH ASSOCIATE (museum), 109.067-014, 11.03.03

RESEARCH MECHANIC (aircraft-aerospace mfg.), 002.280-010, 05.01.04

RESEARCH WORKER, SOCIAL WELFARE (profess. & kin.), 054.067-010, 11.03.02

RESERVATION CLERK (clerical), 238.362-014, 07.05.01

RESERVATIONS AGENT (air trans.), 238.367-018, 07.04.03

RESERVES CLERK (finan. inst.), 216.362-034, 07.02.01

RESIDENCE COUNSELOR (educ.), 045.107-038, 10.01.02

RESIDENCE SUPERVISOR (any ind.), 187.167-186, 11.07.01

RESOURCE-RECOVERY ENGINEER (gov. ser.), 019.167-018, 05.01.02

RESPIRATORY THERAPIST (medical ser.), 079.361-010, 10.02.02

RESPIRATORY-THERAPY AIDE (medical ser.), 355.674-022, 10.03.02

RESTORER, CERAMIC (museum), 102.361-014, 01.06.02

RESTROOM ATTENDANT (any ind.), 358.677-018, 09.05.07

RETICLE INSPECTOR (electronics), 719.361-010, 06.01.05

RETIREMENT OFFICER (gov. ser.), 166.267-030, 07.01.01

REVENUE AGENT (gov. ser.), 160.167-050, 11.06.01

REVENUE OFFICER (gov. ser.), 188.167-074, 11.10.01

REVIEWER (insurance), 209.687-018, 07.05.02

REVIEWING OFFICER, DRIVER'S LICENSE (gov. ser.), 168.167-074, 11.10.03

RIDE OPERATOR (amuse. & rec.), 342.663-010, 05.10.02

RIGGER (ship bldg. & rep.), 806.261-014, 05.05.06

RIGGER (any ind.), 921.260-010, 05.11.04

RIGHT-OF-WAY AGENT (any ind.), 191.117-046, 11.12.02

RING MAKER (jewelry), 700.381-042, 06.01.04

RING STAMPER (jewelry), 700.684-066, 06.02.24

RIVETER, HAND (any ind.), 709.684-066, 06.04.22

RIVETER, HYDRAULIC (any ind.), 800.662-010, 06.02.02

RIVETING-MACHINE OPERATOR 1 (any ind.), 699.482-010, 06.02.02

ROAD-ROLLER OPERATOR (const.), 859.683-030, 05.11.01

ROCK-DRILL OPERATOR 1 (const.), 850.683-034, 05.11.01

ROCKET-ENGINE-COMPONENT MECHANIC (aircraft-aerospace mfg.), 621.281-030, 05.05.09

ROLLER-SKATE REPAIRER (any ind.), 732.684-102, 05.12.15

ROLLING ATTENDANT (iron & steel), 613.662-010, 06.01.03

ROOF-CEMENT-AND-PAINT MAKER (build. mat. nec), 550.382-030, 06.02.18

ROOFER (const.), 866.381-010, 05.10.01

ROOFING-MACHINE OPERATOR (build. mat. nec), 554.682-022, 06.02.18

ROOM-SERVICE CLERK (hotel & rest.), 324.577-010, 09.05.03

ROTARY DRILLER (petrol. production), 930.382-026, 05.11.03

ROTOGRAVURE-PRESS OPERATOR (print. & pub.), 651.362-026, 05.05.13

ROUSTABOUT (petrol. production), 860.684-046, 05.10.01

ROUTE-DELIVERY CLERK (clerical), 222.587-034, 07.05.04

ROUTER (clerical), 222.587-038, 07.07.02

ROUTING CLERK (nonprofit org.), 249.367-070, 07.05.04

RUBBER CUTTER (rubber goods), 559.685-158, 06.04.07

RUBBER-GOODS REPAIRER (any ind.), 759.684-054, 06.02.29

RUG REPAIRER (clean., dye., & press.), 782.381-018, 05.05.15

SAFE-AND-VAULT SERVICE MECHANIC (bus. ser.), 869.381-022, 05.05.06

SAFETY ENGINEER (profess. & kin.), 012.061-014, 05.01.02

SAFETY ENGINEER, MINES (mining), 010.061-026, 05.01.02

SAFETY INSPECTOR (insurance), 168.167-078, 11.10.03

SAFETY INSPECTOR (any ind.), 168.264-014, 11.10.03

SAFETY MANAGER (profess. & kin.), 012.167-058, 05.01.02

SAFETY MANAGER (medical ser.), 168.167-086, 11.10.03

SAGGER MAKER (pottery & porc.), 774.684-030, 06.04.30

SALAD MAKER (water trans.), 317.384-010, 05.10.08

SALES AGENT, BUSINESS SERVICES (bus. ser.), 251.357-010, 08.02.06

SALES AGENT, FINANCIAL SERVICES (finan. inst.), 251.257-010, 08.01.02

SALES AGENT, INSURANCE (insurance), 250.257-010, 08.01.02

SALES AGENT, REAL ESTATE (real estate), 250.357-018, 08.02.04

SALES AGENT, SECURITIES (finan. inst.), 251.157-010, 11.06.04

SALES ATTENDANT, BUILDING MATERIALS (ret. tr.), 299.677-014, 09.04.02

SALES CLERK (ret. tr.), 290.477-014, 09.04.02

SALES CLERK, FOOD (ret. tr.), 290.477-018, 09.04.02

SALES CORRESPONDENT (clerical), 221.367-062, 05.09.02

SALES ENGINEER, AERONAUTICAL PRODUCTS (aircraft-aerospace mfg.), 002.151-010, 05.01.05

SALES EXHIBITOR (nonprofit org.), 279.357-010, 08.02.02

SALES REPRESENTATIVE, ADVERTISING (print. & pub.), 254.357-014, 08.01.02

SALES REPRESENTATIVE, AIRCRAFT (ret. tr.), 273.253-010, 08.01.01

SALES REPRESENTATIVE, ANIMAL-FEED PRODUCTS (whole. tr.), 272.357-010, 08.02.01

SALES REPRESENTATIVE, AUTOMOTIVE-LEASING (bus. ser.), 273.357-014, 08.02.06

SALES REPRESENTATIVE, BOATS AND MARINE SUPPLIES (ret. tr.), 273.357-018, 08.02.03

SALES REPRESENTATIVE, CANVAS PRODUCTS (whole. tr.), 261.357-014, 08.02.01

SALES REPRESENTATIVE, CHEMICALS AND DRUGS (whole. tr.), 262.357-010, 08.01.01

SALES REPRESENTATIVE, COMMUNICATION EQUIPMENT (whole. tr.), 271.257-010, 08.01.01

SALES REPRESENTATIVE, COMPUTERS AND EDP SYSTEMS (whole. tr.), 275.257-010, 08.01.01

SALES REPRESENTATIVE, DATA-PROCESSING SERVICES (bus. ser.), 251.157-014, 08.01.02

SALES REPRESENTATIVE, DENTAL AND MEDICAL EQUIPMENT AND SUPPLIES (whole. tr.), 276.257-010, 08.01.01

SALES REPRESENTATIVE, DOOR-TO-DOOR (ret. tr.), 291.357-010, 08.02.08

SALES REPRESENTATIVE, ELECTRONICS PARTS (whole. tr.), 271.357-010, 08.01.01

SALES REPRESENTATIVE, FARM AND GARDEN EQUIPMENT AND SUPPLIES (whole. tr.), 272.357-014, 08.02.01

SALES REPRESENTATIVE, FRANCHISE (bus. ser.), 251.357-022, 08.02.06

SALES REPRESENTATIVE, GRAPHIC ART (bus. ser.), 254.251-010, 08.01.01

SALES REPRESENTATIVE, HOME FURNISHINGS (whole. tr.), 270.357-010, 08.02.01

SALES REPRESENTATIVE, HOTEL SERVICES (hotel & rest.), 259.157-014, 08.01.02

SALES REPRESENTATIVE, HOUSEHOLD APPLIANCES (whole. tr.), 270.357-014, 08.02.01

SALES REPRESENTATIVE, LIVESTOCK (whole. tr.), 260.257-010, 08.01.03

SALES REPRESENTATIVE, MALT LIQUORS (whole. tr.), 260.357-018, 08.02.01

SALES REPRESENTATIVE, MEN'S AND BOYS' APPAREL (whole. tr.), 261.357-022, 08.02.01

SALES REPRESENTATIVE, NOVELTIES (whole. tr.), 277.357-018, 08.02.01

SALES REPRESENTATIVE, OFFICE MACHINES (ret. tr.), 275.357-034, 08.02.03

SALES REPRESENTATIVE, PETROLEUM PRODUCTS (whole. tr.), 269.357-014, 08.02.01

SALES REPRESENTATIVE, PRINTING (whole. tr.), 254.357-018, 08.01.02

SALES REPRESENTATIVE, PUBLIC UTILITIES (light, heat, & power), 253.357-010, 08.01.02

SALES REPRESENTATIVE, RADIO AND TELEVISION TIME (radio & tv broad.), 259.357-018, 08.01.02

SALES REPRESENTATIVE, RECREATION AND SPORTING GOODS (whole. tr.), 277.357-026, 08.02.01

SALES REPRESENTATIVE, SECURITY SYSTEMS (bus. ser.), 259.257-022, 08.01.02

SALES REPRESENTATIVE, SIGNS AND DISPLAYS (signs), 254.257-010, 08.01.01

SALES REPRESENTATIVE, TELEPHONE SERVICES (tel. & tel.), 253.257-010, 08.01.02

SALES REPRESENTATIVE, TEXTILES (whole. tr.), 261.357-030, 08.02.01

SALES REPRESENTATIVE, TOBACCO PRODUCTS AND SMOKING SUPPLIES (ret. tr.), 260.357-022, 08.02.03

SALES REPRESENTATIVE, UPHOLSTERY AND FURNITURE REPAIR (ret. tr.), 259.357-026, 08.02.06

SALES REPRESENTATIVE, VIDEOTAPE (whole. tr.), 271.357-014, 08.02.01

SALES REPRESENTATIVE, WOMEN'S AND GIRLS' APPAREL (whole. tr.), 261.357-038, 08.02.01

SALES-ENGINEER, ELECTRONICS PRODUCTS AND SYSTEMS (profess. & kin.), 003.151-014, 05.01.05

SALES-PROMOTION REPRESENTATIVE (whole. tr.), 269.357-018, 08.02.01

SALES-SERVICE REPRESENTATIVE, MILKING MACHINES (ret. tr.), 299.251-010, 08.02.02

SALESPERSON, ART OBJECTS (ret. tr.), 277.457-010, 08.02.02

SALESPERSON, AUTOMOBILE ACCESSORIES (ret. tr.), 273.357-030, 08.02.03

SALESPERSON, AUTOMOBILES (ret. tr.), 273.353-010, 08.02.02

SALESPERSON, BOOKS (ret. tr.), 277.357-034, 08.02.02

SALESPERSON, COSMETICS AND TOILETRIES (ret. tr.), 262.357-018, 08.02.02

SALESPERSON, CURTAINS AND DRAPERIES (ret. tr.), 270.357-022, 08.02.02

SALESPERSON, FLOOR COVERINGS (ret. tr.), 270.357-026, 08.02.03

SALESPERSON, FLOWERS (ret. tr.), 260.357-026, 08.02.02

SALESPERSON, FURNITURE (ret. tr.), 270.357-030, 08.02.02

SALESPERSON, GENERAL HARDWARE (ret. tr.), 279.357-050, 08.02.03

SALESPERSON, GENERAL MERCHANDISE (ret. tr.), 279.357-054, 08.02.03

SALESPERSON, HEARING AIDS (ret. tr.), 276.354-010, 08.02.02

SALESPERSON, HORTICULTURAL AND NURSERY PRODUCTS (ret. tr.), 272.357-022, 08.02.03

SALESPERSON, HOUSEHOLD APPLIANCES (ret. tr.), 270.357-034, 08.02.02

SALESPERSON, INFANTS' AND CHILDREN'S WEAR (ret. tr.), 261.357-046, 08.02.02

SALESPERSON, JEWELRY (ret. tr.), 279.357-058, 08.02.02

SALESPERSON, MEN'S AND BOYS' CLOTHING (ret. tr.), 261.357-050, 08.02.02

SALESPERSON, MUSICAL INSTRUMENTS AND ACCESSORIES (ret. tr.), 277.357-038, 08.02.02

SALESPERSON, PARTS (ret. tr.), 279.357-062, 08.02.03

SALESPERSON, PHONOGRAPH RECORDS AND TAPE RECORDINGS (ret. tr.), 277.357-046, 08.02.02

SALESPERSON, PHOTOGRAPHIC SUPPLIES AND EQUIPMENT (ret. tr.), 277.357-050, 08.02.03

SALESPERSON, PIANOS AND ORGANS (ret. tr.), 277.354-010, 08.02.02

SALESPERSON, SHOES (ret. tr.), 261.357-062, 08.02.02

SALESPERSON, SPORTING GOODS (ret. tr.), 277.357-058, 08.02.02

SALESPERSON, STEREO EQUIPMENT (ret. tr.), 270.357-038, 08.02.02

SALESPERSON, SURGICAL APPLIANCES (ret. tr.), 276.257-022, 08.02.02

SALESPERSON, WOMEN'S APPAREL AND ACCESSORIES (ret. tr.), 261.357-066, 08.02.02

SALESPERSON, YARD GOODS (ret. tr.), 261.357-070, 08.02.02

SALESPERSON-DEMONSTRATOR, PARTY PLAN (ret. tr.), 279.357-038, 08.02.05

SAMPLE MAKER 1 (jewelry), 700.381-046, 01.06.02

SAND MIXER, MACHINE (foundry), 570.682-018, 06.02.10

SANDBLASTER (any ind.), 503.687-010, 05.12.18

SANDWICH MAKER (hotel & rest.), 317.684-018, 05.12.17

SANITARIAN (profess. & kin.), 079.117-018, 11.10.03

SANITARIAN (any ind.), 529.137-014, 11.10.03

SANITARY ENGINEER (profess. & kin.), 005.061-030, 05.01.03

SANITATION INSPECTOR (gov. ser.), 168.267-110, 11.10.03

SAW FILER (any ind.), 701.381-014, 05.05.07

SAWMILL WORKER (sawmill), 667.686-014, 06.04.40

SCALP-TREATMENT OPERATOR (per. ser.), 339.371-014, 09.02.01

SCANNER (profess. & kin.), 015.384-010, 02.04.01

SCHEDULER (museum), 238.367-034, 07.05.01

SCHEDULER, MAINTENANCE (clerical), 221.367-066, 07.05.01

SCIENTIFIC GLASS BLOWER (glass prod.), 006.261-010, 05.05.11

SCIENTIFIC LINGUIST (profess. & kin.), 059.067-014, 11.03.02

SCOREBOARD OPERATOR (amuse. & rec.), 349.665-010, 07.04.05

SCOUT, PROFESSIONAL SPORTS (amuse. & rec.), 153.117-018, 12.01.01

SCRAP HANDLER (any ind.), 509.685-050, 06.04.09

SCREEN MAKER, PHOTOGRAPHIC PROCESS (any ind.), 979.384-010, 05.10.05

SCREEN PRINTER (any ind.), 979.684-034, 06.04.34

SCREEN WRITER (motion pic.), 131.087-018, 01.01.02

SCROLL-MACHINE OPERATOR (struct. & ornam. metalwork), 616.685-062, 06.04.02

SEAMLESS-HOSIERY KNITTER (hosiery), 684.685-010, 06.02.06

SECRETARY (clerical), 201.362-030, 07.01.03

SECRETARY OF STATE (gov. ser.), 188.167-082, 11.05.03

SECURITIES TRADER 1 (finan. inst.), 162.157-042, 11.06.03

SECURITIES TRADER 2 (finan. inst.), 186.167-058, 11.06.03

SECURITY CONSULTANT (bus. ser.), 189.167-054, 04.02.02

SECURITY OFFICER (any ind.), 189.167-034, 11.05.02

SEED PELLETER (agric.), 599.685-126, 06.04.21

SEISMOLOGIST (profess. & kin.), 024.061-050, 02.01.01

SELF-SERVICE-LAUNDRY-AND-DRY-CLEANING ATTENDANT (clean., dye., & press.), 369.677-010, 09.04.02

SEMICONDUCTOR PROCESSOR (electronics), 590.684-022, 06.04.19

SEPTIC-TANK INSTALLER (const.), 851.663-010, 05.11.01

SERVICE CLERK (clerical), 221.367-070, 07.04.05

SERVICE MANAGER (ret. tr.), 185.164-010, 05.10.02

SERVICE MANAGER (auto. ser.), 185.167-058, 05.10.02

SERVICE REPRESENTATIVE (auto. mfg.), 191.167-022, 11.12.01

SERVICE REPRESENTATIVE (light, heat, & power), 959.574-010, 05.10.01

SERVICE SUPERVISOR, LEASED MACHINERY AND EQUIPMENT (any ind.), 183.167-030, 11.11.05

SERVICE-ESTABLISHMENT ATTENDANT (clean., dye., & press.), 369.477-014, 09.04.02

SET DECORATOR (motion pic.), 142.061-042, 01.02.03

SET DESIGNER (motion pic.), 142.061-046, 01.02.03

SET DESIGNER (amuse. & rec.), 142.061-050, 01.02.03

SETTER, AUTOMATIC-SPINNING LATHE (any ind.), 604.360-010, 06.01.02

SEWAGE-DISPOSAL WORKER (sanitary ser.), 955.687-010, 05.12.18

SEWER, HAND (any ind.), 782.684-058, 06.04.27

SEWER-LINE PHOTO-INSPECTOR (sanitary ser.), 851.362-010, 05.07.01

SEWER-LINE REPAIRER (sanitary ser.), 869.664-018, 05.12.12

SEWER-LINE REPAIRER, TELE-GROUT (sanitary ser.), 851.262-010, 05.10.01

SEWER-PIPE CLEANER (bus. ser.), 899.664-014, 05.12.12

SEWING-MACHINE OPERATOR (leather prod.), 783.682-014, 06.02.05

SEWING-MACHINE OPERATOR (any ind.), 787.682-046, 06.02.05

SEWING-MACHINE OPERATOR, SPECIAL EQUIPMENT (matt. & bedspring), 689.685-118, 06.04.05

SEWING-MACHINE REPAIRER (any ind.), 639.281-018, 05.10.02

SHEAR OPERATOR 1 (any ind.), 615.482-034, 06.02.02

SHEET-METAL WORKER (any ind.), 804.281-010, 05.05.06

SHELL MOLDER (foundry), 518.685-026, 06.04.17

SHELLFISH DREDGE OPERATOR (fish.), 446.663-010, 03.04.03

SHELLFISH GROWER (fish.), 446.161-014, 03.01.02

SHERIFF, DEPUTY (gov. ser.), 377.263-010, 04.01.02

SHIPFITTER (ship bldg. & rep.), 806.381-046, 05.05.06

SHIPPING AND RECEIVING CLERK (clerical), 222.387-050, 05.09.01

SHIPPING CHECKER (clerical), 222.687-030, 05.09.01

SHIPPING-AND-RECEIVING WEIGHER (clerical), 222.367-058, 05.09.01

SHIPPING-ORDER CLERK (clerical), 219.367-030, 07.05.04

SHIPWRIGHT (ship bldg. & rep.), 860.381-058, 05.05.02

SHOE DYER (per. ser.), 364.684-014, 05.12.14

SHOE REPAIRER (per. ser.), 365.361-014, 05.05.15

SHOP ESTIMATOR (auto. ser.), 807.267-010, 05.07.01

SHOP TAILOR (garment), 785.361-022, 05.05.15

SHORTHAND REPORTER (clerical), 202.362-010, 07.05.03

SIDER (const.), 863.684-014, 05.10.01

SIGN ERECTOR 1 (signs), 869.381-026, 05.05.06

SIGN ERECTOR 2 (signs), 869.684-054, 05.10.01

SIGN WRITER, HAND (any ind.), 970.281-022, 01.06.03

SILK FINISHER (clean., dye., & press.), 363.681-010, 06.04.35

SILK-SCREEN CUTTER (any ind.), 979.681-022, 01.06.01

SILK-SCREEN ETCHER (engraving), 704.684-014, 06.04.24

SILK-SCREEN PRINTER, MACHINE (any ind.), 979.665-010, 06.04.09

SILK-SCREEN-FRAME ASSEMBLER (any ind.), 709.484-010, 06.04.23

SILVERSMITH (silverware), 700.281-022, 01.06.02

SILVICULTURIST (profess. & kin.), 040.061-050, 02.02.02

SINGER (amuse. & rec.), 152.047-022, 01.04.03

SIRUP MAKER (flav. ext. & sirup), 520.485-026, 06.02.15

SKATE-SHOP ATTENDANT (amuse. & rec.), 341.464-010, 09.04.02

SKI MOLDER (sports equip.), 732.684-114, 06.02.32

SKI REPAIRER, PRODUCTION (sports equip.), 732.684-118, 06.02.24

SKIFF OPERATOR (fish.), 441.683-010, 03.04.03

SKIN FITTER (aircraft-aerospace mfg.), 806.381-054, 06.01.04

SKIP TRACER (clerical), 241.367-026, 07.04.01

SLASHER TENDER (textile), 582.562-010, 06.04.16

SMALL ENGINE MECHANIC (any ind.), 625.281-034, 05.05.09

SMOKE JUMPER (forestry), 452.364-014, 04.02.04

SOAP MAKER (soap), 559.382-054, 06.02.18

SOCIAL SECRETARY (clerical), 201.162-010, 07.01.03

SOCIAL-SERVICES AIDE (social ser.), 195.367-034, 10.01.02

SOCIOLOGIST (profess. & kin.), 054.067-014, 11.03.02

SOFTWARE TECHNICIAN (profess. & kin.), 020.262-010, 11.01.01

SOIL CONSERVATIONIST (profess. & kin.), 040.061-054, 02.02.02

SOIL SCIENTIST (profess. & kin.), 040.061-058, 02.02.02

SOIL-CONSERVATION TECHNICIAN (profess. & kin.), 040.261-010, 02.02.02

SOLAR-ENERGY-SYSTEM INSTALLER (any ind.), 637.261-030, 05.05.09

SOLAR-ENERGY-SYSTEMS DESIGNER (profess. & kin.), 007.161-038, 05.03.07

SOLAR-FABRICATION TECHNICIAN (mach. shop), 809.381-034, 06.02.24

SOLDERER (jewelry), 700.381-050, 06.01.04

SORTER (clerical), 209.687-022, 07.07.02

SORTER, AGRICULTURAL PRODUCE (agric.), 529.687-186, 03.04.01

SORTER-PRICER (nonprofit org.), 222.387-054, 05.09.03

SOUND CONTROLLER (amuse. & rec.), 194.262-014, 05.10.03

SOUND MIXER (motion pic.), 194.262-018, 05.10.05

SOUS CHEF (hotel & rest.), 313.131-026, 05.05.17

SPECIAL AGENT (insurance), 166.167-046, 11.05.02

SPECIAL AGENT (gov. ser.), 375.167-042, 04.01.02

SPECIAL TESTER (tobacco), 529.487-010, 06.03.01

SPECIFICATION WRITER (profess. & kin.), 019.267-010, 05.03.02

SPECTROSCOPIST (profess. & kin.), 011.281-014, 02.04.01

SPEECH PATHOLOGIST (profess. & kin.), 076.107-010, 02.03.04

SPINNER (jewelry), 700.684-074, 06.02.24

SPINNER, HAND (any ind.), 619.362-018, 06.02.02

SPINNER, HYDRAULIC (any ind.), 619.362-022, 06.02.02

SPORTS-EQUIPMENT REPAIRER (any ind.), 732.684-122, 05.10.04

SPOTTER (laundry), 361.684-018, 06.02.27

SPOTTER, PHOTOGRAPHIC (photofinish.), 970.381-034, 01.06.03

SPRAY-PAINTING-MACHINE OPERATOR (any ind.), 741.685-010, 06.04.09

SPRAY-UNIT FEEDER (any ind.), 599.686-014, 06.04.21

SPREADER, MACHINE (any ind.), 781.685-010, 06.04.05

STABLE ATTENDANT (any ind.), 410.674-022, 03.03.02

STACKING-MACHINE OPERATOR 1 (any ind.), 692.682-054, 06.02.20

STANDARDS ENGINEER (profess. & kin.), 012.061-018, 05.01.06

STAPLING-MACHINE OPERATOR (any ind.), 692.685-202, 06.04.20

STATEMENT CLERK (finan. inst.), 219.362-058, 07.02.02

STATION INSTALLER-AND-REPAIRER (tel. & tel.), 822.261-022, 05.05.05

STATION MANAGER (r.r. trans.), 184.167-130, 11.11.03

STATIONARY ENGINEER (any ind.), 950.382-026, 05.06.02

STATISTICAL CLERK (clerical), 216.382-062, 07.02.03

STATISTICIAN, APPLIED (profess. & kin.), 020.167-026, 11.01.02

STATISTICIAN, MATHEMATICAL (profess. & kin.), 020.067-022, 11.01.01

STEAM CLEANER (auto. ser.), 915.687-026, 05.12.18

STEEL-PLATE CALKER (any ind.), 843.684-010, 05.12.14

STENCILER (any ind.), 920.687-178, 06.04.37

STENOGRAPHER (clerical), 202.362-014, 07.05.03

STENOTYPE OPERATOR (clerical), 202.362-022, 07.05.03

STEREOTYPER (print. & pub.), 974.382-014, 05.05.13

STERILIZER (drug prep. & related), 599.585-010, 06.04.19

STEVEDORE 1 (water trans.), 911.663-014, 05.11.04

STILL TENDER (any ind.), 552.685-026, 06.02.18

STITCHER, STANDARD MACHINE (boot & shoe), 690.682-082, 06.02.05

STOCK CLERK (clerical), 222.387-058, 05.09.02

STOCK CLERK, SELF-SERVICE STORE (ret. tr.), 299.367-014, 05.09.01

STOCK-CONTROL CLERK (clerical), 219.367-034, 07.05.03

STONE CARVER (stonework), 771.281-014, 01.06.02

STONE SETTER (jewelry), 700.381-054, 05.05.14

STONECUTTER, HAND (stonework), 771.381-014, 05.05.01

STONER (jewelry), 735.684-014, 06.04.24

STORAGE-FACILITY RENTAL CLERK (bus. ser.), 295.367-026, 09.04.02

STOVE REFINISHER (any ind.), 749.684-046, 05.12.14

STRAIGHTENER, HAND (any ind.), 709.484-014, 06.02.24

STRAIGHTENING-PRESS OPERATOR (any ind.), 617.482-026, 06.02.02

STRAIGHTENING-ROLL OPERATOR (any ind.), 613.462-022, 06.02.02

STREET CLEANER (gov. ser.), 955.687-018, 05.12.18

STREET-LIGHT SERVICER (light, heat, & power), 824.381-010, 05.05.05

STREET-SWEEPER OPERATOR (gov. ser.), 919.683-022, 05.11.01

STRESS ANALYST (aircraft-aerospace mfg.), 002.061-030, 05.01.04

STRESS ANALYST (profess. & kin.), 007.061-042, 05.01.04

STRETCHER (jewelry), 700.684-078, 06.04.24

STRIP-CUTTING-MACHINE OPERATOR (any ind.), 686.685-066, 06.04.05

STRIPER, HAND (any ind.), 740.484-010, 01.06.03

STRUCTURAL ENGINEER (const.), 005.061-034, 05.01.08

STRUCTURAL-STEEL WORKER (const.), 801.361-014, 05.05.06

STUFFER (toys & games), 731.685-014, 06.04.34

STUNT PERFORMER (amuse. & rec.), 159.341-014, 12.02.01

SUBASSEMBLER (mach. mfg.), 706.381-038, 06.02.24

SUBSTATION OPERATOR (light, heat, & power), 952.362-026, 05.06.01

SUPERINTENDENT, BUILDING (any ind.), 187.167-190, 05.02.02

SUPERINTENDENT, CONSTRUCTION (const.), 182.167-026, 05.02.02

SUPERINTENDENT, MAINTENANCE (any ind.), 189.167-046, 05.05.02

SUPERINTENDENT, PLANT PROTECTION (any ind.), 189.167-050, 11.05.02

SUPERVISOR, CENTRAL SUPPLY (medical ser.), 079.164-010, 05.12.18

SUPERVISOR, CONTRACT-SHELTERED WORKSHOP (nonprofit org.), 187.134-010, 11.07.03

SUPERVISOR, VENDOR QUALITY (any ind.), 012.167-062, 05.03.06

SUPPLY CLERK (per. ser.), 339.687-010, 05.09.01

SURGICAL TECHNICIAN (medical ser.), 079.374-022, 10.03.02

SURGICAL-DRESSING MAKER (per. protect. & med. device), 689.685-130, 06.04.05

SURVEILLANCE-SYSTEM MONITOR (gov. ser.), 379.367-010, 04.02.03

SURVEY WORKER (clerical), 205.367-054, 07.04.01

SURVEYOR ASSISTANT, INSTRUMENTS (profess. & kin.), 018.167-034, 05.03.01

SURVEYOR HELPER (any ind.), 869.567-010, 05.12.02

SWEEPER-CLEANER, INDUSTRIAL (any ind.), 389.683-010, 05.12.18

SWIMMING POOL INSTALLER-AND-SERVICER (const.), 869.463-010, 05.10.01

SWIMMING-POOL SERVICER (any ind.), 891.684-018, 05.10.04

SWITCH TENDER (r.r. trans.), 910.667-026, 05.12.05

SWITCHBOARD OPERATOR, POLICE DISTRICT (gov. ser.), 235.562-014, 07.04.05

SYSTEMS ANALYST, ELECTRONIC DATA PROCESSING (profess. & kin.), 012.167-066, 11.01.01

SYSTEMS ENGINEER, ELECTRONIC DATA PROCESSING (profess. & kin.), 003.167-062, 05.01.03

TABLE-TOP TILE SETTER (brick & tile), 763.684-074, 06.04.30

TACKING-MACHINE OPERATOR (any ind.), 787.685-042, 06.04.05

TAKE-DOWN SORTER (photofinish.), 976.665-010, 05.10.05

TANK CLEANER (any ind.), 891.687-022, 05.12.18

TANKER (wood preserving), 561.665-010, 06.04.18

TAPE LIBRARIAN (clerical), 206.387-030, 07.05.03

TAPE TRANSFERRER (phonograph), 194.382-014, 05.10.05

TAPE-RECORDER REPAIRER (any ind.), 720.281-014, 05.10.03

TAPER (const.), 842.664-010, 05.10.01

TAPER, PRINTED CIRCUIT LAYOUT (electronics), 017.684-010, 05.03.02

TAX CLERK 1 (clerical), 219.487-010, 07.02.04

TAX PREPARER (bus. ser.), 219.362-070, 07.02.02

TAXI DRIVER (motor trans.), 913.463-018, 09.03.02

TEACHER (museum), 099.227-038, 11.02.01

TEACHER AIDE I (educ.), 099.327-010, 11.02.01

TEACHER AIDE II (educ.), 249.367-074, 07.01.02

TEACHER, ADULT EDUCATION (educ.), 099.227-030, 11.02.01

TEACHER, BLIND (educ.), 094.227-014, 10.02.03

TEACHER, DEAF STUDENTS (educ.), 094.224-010, 10.02.03

TEACHER, ELEMENTARY SCHOOL (educ.), 092.227-010, 11.02.01

TEACHER, HANDICAPPED STUDENTS (educ.), 094.227-018, 10.02.03

TEACHER, HOME THERAPY (social ser.), 195.227-018, 10.02.03

TEACHER, MENTALLY-RETARDED STUDENTS (educ.), 094.227-022, 10.02.03

TEACHER, MUSIC (educ.), 152.021-010, 01.04.01

TEACHER, PRESCHOOL (educ.), 092.227-018, 10.02.03

TEACHER, RESOURCE (educ.), 099.227-042, 11.02.01

TEACHER, SECONDARY SCHOOL (educ.), 091.227-010, 11.02.01

TEACHER, VOCATIONAL TRAINING (educ.), 094.227-026, 10.02.03

TECHNICAL ILLUSTRATOR (profess. & kin.), 017.281-034, 05.03.02

TECHNICAL SUPPORT SPECIALIST (profess. & kin.), 199.224-010, 11.02.02

TECHNICAL TRAINING COORDINATOR (educ.), 166.167-054, 11.07.03

TECHNICIAN, SEMICONDUCTOR DEVELOPMENT (profess. & kin.), 003.161-018, 05.01.01

TELECOMMUNICATOR (gov. ser.), 379.362-018, 07.04.05

TELEGRAPHIC-TYPEWRITER OPERATOR (clerical), 203.582-050, 07.06.02

TELEPHONE OPERATOR (clerical), 235.662-022, 07.04.06

TELEPHONE SOLICITOR (any ind.), 299.357-014, 08.02.08

TELEPHONE-ANSWERING-SERVICE OPERATOR (bus. ser.), 235.662-026, 07.04.06

TELEPHONE-DIRECTORY DELIVERER (bus. ser.), 230.667-014, 07.07.02

TELEPHONE-DIRECTORY-DISTRIBUTOR DRIVER (bus. ser.), 906.683-018, 05.08.03

TELEVISION INSTALLER (any ind.), 823.361-010, 05.10.03

TELEVISION TECHNICIAN (radio & tv broad.), 194.062-010, 01.02.03

TELEVISION-AND-RADIO REPAIRER (any ind.), 720.281-018, 05.10.03

TELEVISION-CABLE INSTALLER (any ind.), 821.281-010, 05.10.03

TELEVISION-SCHEDULE COORDINATOR (radio & tv broad.), 199.387-010, 07.05.01

TELLER (finan. inst.), 211.362-018, 07.03.01

TELLER, COLLECTION AND EXCHANGE (finan. inst.), 211.362-022, 07.02.02

TELLER, HEAD (finan. inst.), 211.132-010, 07.03.01

TELLER, NOTE (finan. inst.), 211.362-026, 07.03.01

TEMPLATE MAKER (any ind.), 601.381-038, 05.05.07

TEMPLATE MAKER, TRACK (any ind.), 809.484-014, 05.10.01

TERMINAL OPERATOR (clerical), 203.582-054, 07.06.01

TERMINAL-MAKEUP OPERATOR (print. & pub.), 208.382-010, 07.06.01

TERMINAL-SYSTEM OPERATOR (clerical), 203.362-018, 07.06.01

TERRAZZO FINISHER (const.), 861.664-014, 05.05.01

TERRAZZO WORKER (const.), 861.381-046, 05.05.01

TEST DRIVER 1 (auto. mfg.), 806.281-050, 06.03.01

TEST ENGINEER, NUCLEAR EQUIPMENT (profess. & kin.), 015.061-022, 05.01.04

TEST TECHNICIAN (profess. & kin.), 019.161-014, 05.01.04

TEST TECHNICIAN (agric. equip.), 019.261-022, 05.03.07

TEST TECHNICIAN (clerical), 249.367-078, 07.01.07

TEST TECHNICIAN, SEMICONDUCTOR PROCESSING EQUIPMENT (electronics), 590.262-014, 06.01.05

TEST-ENGINE EVALUATOR (petrol. refin.), 010.261-026, 05.01.04

TESTER (profess. & kin.), 011.361-010, 02.04.01

TESTER (petrol. refin.), 029.261-022, 02.04.01

TESTER, FOOD PRODUCTS (any ind.), 199.251-010, 05.05.17

THERMAL CUTTER, HAND 2 (welding), 816.684-010, 05.12.11

THERMOSTAT REPAIRER (inst. & app.), 710.381-050, 05.10.02

THREAD CUTTER (any ind.), 789.684-050, 06.04.27

THROW-OUT CLERK (ret. tr.), 241.367-030, 07.05.02

THROWER (pottery & porc.), 774.381-010, 06.02.30

TICKET TAKER (amuse. & rec.), 344.667-010, 09.05.08

TICKETER (any ind.), 652.685-098, 06.04.37

TILE FINISHER (const.), 861.664-018, 05.05.01

TILE SETTER (const.), 861.381-054, 05.05.01

TILE SETTER HELPER (const.), 869.664-014, 05.10.01

TIMBER-SIZER OPERATOR (planing mill), 665.482-018, 06.02.03

TIME-STUDY ENGINEER (profess. & kin.), 012.167-070, 05.01.06

TIMEKEEPER (clerical), 215.367-022, 07.02.05

TIRE ADJUSTER (ret. tr.), 241.367-034, 05.09.01

TIRE MOLDER (rubber tire & tube), 553.685-102, 06.04.13

TIRE MOUNTER (fabric. prod. nec), 739.684-158, 06.04.23

TIRE REPAIRER (auto. ser.), 915.684-010, 05.12.15

TISSUE TECHNOLOGIST (medical ser.), 078.361-030, 02.04.02

TITLE CLERK (petrol. production), 162.267-010, 07.01.05

TITLE EXAMINER (profess. & kin.), 119.287-010, 07.01.05

TITLE SEARCHER (real estate), 209.367-046, 07.05.02

TITLE SUPERVISOR (profess. & kin.), 119.167-018, 07.01.05

TOLL COLLECTOR (gov. ser.), 211.462-038, 07.03.01

TOOL DESIGNER (profess. & kin.), 007.061-026, 05.01.07

TOOL DRESSER (any ind.), 601.682-010, 06.04.02

TOOL GRINDER 1 (any ind.), 701.381-018, 05.05.07

TOOL GRINDER 2 (any ind.), 603.664-010, 06.02.01

TOOL PLANNER (any ind.), 012.167-074, 05.01.06

TOOL PROGRAMER, NUMERICAL CONTROL (any ind.), 007.167-018, 05.01.06

TOOL PROGRAMMER, NUMERICAL CONTROL (electronics), 609.262-010, 05.01.06

TOOL-AND-DIE MAKER (mach. shop), 601.280-046, 05.05.07

TOOL-AND-EQUIPMENT-RENTAL CLERK (bus. ser.), 295.357-014, 09.04.02

TOOL-CRIB ATTENDANT (clerical), 222.367-062, 05.09.01

TOOL-MACHINE SET-UP OPERATOR (mach. shop), 601.280-054, 05.05.07

TORCH-STRAIGHTENER-AND HEATER (any ind.), 709.684-086, 05.10.01

TOUCH-UP PAINTER, HAND (any ind.), 740.684-026, 06.04.33

TOW-TRUCK OPERATOR (auto. ser.), 919.663-026, 05.08.03

TOWER ERECTOR (const.), 821.361-038, 05.05.05

TOWN CLERK (gov. ser.), 243.367-018, 07.01.02

TOXICOLOGIST (drug prep. & related), 022.081-010, 02.04.02

TOY ASSEMBLER (toys & games), 731.687-034, 06.04.23

TRACK REPAIRER (r.r. trans.), 910.682-010, 05.12.12

TRACKMOBILE OPERATOR (any ind.), 919.683-026, 05.08.02

TRACTOR MECHANIC (auto. ser.), 620.281-058, 05.05.09

TRACTOR OPERATOR (any ind.), 929.683-014, 05.11.04

TRACTOR-CRANE OPERATOR (any ind.), 921.663-058, 05.11.04

TRACTOR-TRAILER-TRUCK DRIVER (any ind.), 904.383-010, 05.08.01

TRAFFIC AGENT (air trans.), 252.257-010, 08.01.02

TRAFFIC CHECKER (gov. ser.), 205.367-058, 07.04.01

TRAFFIC CLERK (clerical), 214.587-014, 07.02.04

TRAFFIC CLERK (bus. ser.), 221.367-078, 07.05.01

TRAFFIC INSPECTOR (motor trans.), 184.163-010, 11.10.05

TRAILER-RENTAL CLERK (auto. ser.), 295.467-022, 09.04.02

TRAIN DISPATCHER (r.r. trans.), 184.167-262, 07.04.05

TRAINING REPRESENTATIVE (educ.), 166.227-010, 11.02.02

TRANSCRIBING-MACHINE OPERATOR (clerical), 203.582-058, 07.06.02

TRANSFORMER ASSEMBLER (elec. equip.), 820.381-014, 06.01.04

TRANSFORMER REPAIRER (any ind.), 724.381-018, 05.10.03

TRANSLATOR (profess. & kin.), 137.267-018, 11.08.04

TRANSMITTER OPERATOR (radio & tv broad.), 193.262-038, 05.03.05

TRANSPORTATION AGENT (air trans.), 912.367-014, 07.05.01

TRANSPORTATION ENGINEER (profess. & kin.), 005.061-038, 05.01.08

TRANSPORTATION INSPECTOR (motor trans.), 168.167-082, 11.10.05

TRAVEL AGENT (bus. ser.), 252.157-010, 08.02.06

TREE TRIMMER (light, heat, & power), 408.664-010, 03.04.05

TRIM-STENCIL MAKER (any ind.), 781.684-058, 06.04.26

TRIMMER, MACHINE (garment), 781.682-010, 06.02.05

TRIMMER, MEAT (slaught. & meat pack.), 525.684-054, 06.04.28

TROPHY ASSEMBLER (jewelry), 735.684-018, 06.02.24

TRUCK DRIVER, HEAVY (any ind.), 905.663-014, 05.08.01

TRUCK DRIVER, LIGHT (any ind.), 906.683-022, 05.08.01

TRUCK-CRANE OPERATOR (any ind.), 921.663-062, 05.11.04

TRUST OFFICER (finan. inst.), 186.117-074, 11.06.05

TRUST-SECURITIES CLERK (finan. inst.), 219.362-062, 07.02.02

TUBE ASSEMBLER, CATHODE RAY (electronics), 725.684-022, 06.02.23

TUBE ASSEMBLER, ELECTRON (electronics), 725.384-010, 06.01.04

TUBE CLEANER (any ind.), 891.687-030, 05.12.18

TUNE-UP MECHANIC (auto. ser.), 620.281-066, 05.05.09

TURBINE ATTENDANT (light, heat, & power), 952.567-010, 05.09.03

TURBINE OPERATOR (light, heat, & power), 952.362-042, 05.06.01

TURRET-PUNCH-PRESS OPERATOR, TAPE-CONTROL (any ind.), 615.685-042, 06.04.02

TUTOR (educ.), 099.227-034, 11.02.01

TYPE COPYIST (mach. mfg.), 970.381-042, 01.06.03

TYPESETTING-MACHINE TENDER (print. & pub.), 650.685-010, 05.10.05

TYPIST (clerical), 203.582-066, 07.06.02

ULTRASONIC TESTER (bus. ser.), 709.281-018, 05.07.01

ULTRASOUND TECHNOLOGIST (medical ser.), 078.364-010, 02.04.01

UMBRELLA REPAIRER (any ind.), 369.684-018, 05.10.01

UMPIRE (amuse. & rec.), 153.267-018, 12.01.02

UNDERCOATER (auto. ser.), 843.684-014, 05.12.14

UNDERWRITER (insurance), 169.167-058, 11.06.03

UNDERWRITING CLERK (insurance), 219.367-038, 07.01.04

URBAN PLANNER (profess. & kin.), 199.167-014, 11.03.02

USED-CAR RENOVATOR (ret. tr.), 620.684-034, 05.10.04

USHER (amuse. & rec.), 344.677-014, 09.05.08

UTILITY CLERK (light, heat, & power), 239.367-034, 07.04.05

UTILITY WORKER (mfg. bldgs.), 869.684-074, 06.02.22

UTILITY WORKER, FILM PROCESSING (photofinish.), 976.685-030, 06.04.19

UTILIZATION COORDINATOR (radio & tv broad.), 169.167-078, 11.05.02

UTILIZATION ENGINEER (light, heat, & power), 007.061-034, 05.01.06

UTILIZATION-REVIEW COORDINATOR (medical ser.), 079.137-010, 11.07.02

VACUUM CLEANER REPAIRER (any ind.), 723.381-014, 05.10.03

VARITYPE OPERATOR (clerical), 203.382-026, 07.06.02

VAULT CASHIER (bus. ser.), 222.137-050, 07.01.04

VAULT WORKER (bus. ser.), 222.587-058, 07.05.04

VECTOR CONTROL ASSISTANT (gov. ser.), 049.364-014, 02.04.02

VENDING-MACHINE ATTENDANT (hotel & rest.), 319.464-014, 09.04.01

VENDING-STAND SUPERVISOR (gov. ser.), 185.167-066, 09.04.01

VENDOR (amuse. & rec.), 291.457-022, 08.03.01

VENETIAN-BLIND CLEANER AND REPAIRER (any ind.), 739.687-198, 05.12.18

VERIFIER OPERATOR (clerical), 203.582-070, 07.06.02

VETERINARIAN (medical ser.), 073.101-010, 02.03.03

VIDEO OPERATOR (radio & tv broad.), 194.282-010, 05.03.05

VIOLIN MAKER, HAND (musical inst.), 730.281-046, 05.05.12

VOCATIONAL REHABILITATION CONSULTANT (gov. ser.), 094.117-018, 11.07.03

VOCATIONAL-REHABILITATION COUNSELOR (gov. ser.), 045.107-042, 10.01.02

WAITER/WAITRESS, CAPTAIN (hotel & rest.), 311.137-018, 09.01.03

WAITER/WAITRESS, FORMAL (hotel & rest.), 311.477-026, 09.04.01

WAITER/WAITRESS, INFORMAL (hotel & rest.), 311.477-030, 09.04.01

WAITER/WAITRESS, ROOM SERVICE (hotel & rest.), 311.477-034, 09.05.02

WAITER/WAITRESS, TAKE OUT (hotel & rest.), 311.477-038, 09.04.01

WARD CLERK (medical ser.), 245.362-014, 07.05.03

WASHER (optical goods), 713.684-042, 06.04.39

WASHER, MACHINE (laundry), 361.665-010, 06.04.35

WASHER, MACHINE (any ind.), 599.685-114, 06.04.39

WASHING-MACHINE LOADER-AND-PULLER (laundry), 361.686-010, 06.04.35

WASHING-MACHINE OPERATOR (any ind.), 599.685-118, 06.04.39

WASTE-DISPOSAL ATTENDANT (any ind.), 955.383-010, 05.12.03

WASTE-MANAGEMENT ENGINEER, RADIOACTIVE MATERIALS (profess. & kin.), 005.061-042, 05.01.03

WASTE-TREATMENT OPERATOR (chem.), 955.382-014, 06.02.11

WATER TENDER (any ind.), 599.685-122, 05.12.06

WATER-SOFTENER SERVICER-AND-INSTALLER (bus. ser.), 862.684-034, 05.10.01

WATER-TREATMENT-PLANT OPERATOR (waterworks), 954.382-014, 05.06.04

WAX MOLDER (foundry), 549.685-038, 06.04.09

WEATHER OBSERVER (profess. & kin.), 025.267-014, 02.04.01

WEAVER (asbestos prod.), 683.682-038, 06.02.06

WEB-PRESS OPERATOR (print. & pub.), 651.362-030, 05.05.13

WEDDING CONSULTANT (ret. tr.), 299.357-018, 08.02.06

WEIGHER, PRODUCTION (any ind.), 929.587-014, 06.03.02

WEIGHT-REDUCTION SPECIALIST (per. ser.), 359.367-014, 09.05.01

WELDER, ARC (welding), 810.384-014, 05.05.06

WELDER, COMBINATION (welding), 819.384-010, 05.05.06

WELDER, EXPERIMENTAL (welding), 819.281-022, 05.05.06

WELDER, GAS (welding), 811.684-014, 05.05.06

WELDER, GUN (welding), 810.664-010, 06.04.31

WELDER, PRODUCTION LINE (welding), 819.684-010, 06.04.31

WELDER, TACK (welding), 810.684-010, 05.10.01

WELDER-ASSEMBLER (mach. mfg.), 819.381-010, 05.05.06

WELDER-FITTER (welding), 819.361-010, 05.05.06

WELDING ENGINEER (profess. & kin.), 011.061-026, 05.01.08

WELDING TECHNICIAN (profess. & kin.), 011.261-014, 05.01.01

WELDING-MACHINE OPERATOR, ARC (welding), 810.382-010, 06.02.19

WELDING-MACHINE OPERATOR, GAS (welding), 811.482-010, 06.02.19

WHEEL LACER AND TRUER (motor. & bicycles), 706.684-106, 06.02.23

WIG DRESSER (hairwork), 332.361-010, 01.06.02

WIND-GENERATING-ELECTRIC-POWER INSTALLER (const.), 821.381-018, 05.05.05

WIND-INSTRUMENT REPAIRER (any ind.), 730.281-054, 05.05.12

WINDOW REPAIRER (any ind.), 899.684-042, 05.12.12

WINE MAKER (wine prod.), 183.161-014, 05.02.03

WINE STEWARD/STEWARDESS (hotel & rest.), 310.357-010, 09.05.02

WIRE-DRAWING-MACHINE TENDER (wire), 614.685-026, 06.04.02

WIRE-WRAPPING-MACHINE OPERATOR (electronics), 726.682-014, 06.02.09

WIRER (office mach.), 729.281-042, 06.02.32

WIRER, SUBASSEMBLIES (office mach.), 729.684-062, 06.02.23

WIRES-TRANSFER CLERK (finan. inst.), 203.562-010, 07.06.02

WIREWORKER (elec. equip.), 728.684-022, 06.04.34

WOOD TECHNOLOGIST (profess. & kin.), 040.061-062, 02.02.02

WOODWORKING-SHOP HAND (woodworking), 769.687-054, 06.04.25

WORD-PROCESSING-MACHINE OPERATOR (clerical), 203.362-022, 07.06.02

WORK-STUDY COORDINATOR, SPECIAL EDUCATION (educ.), 094.107-010, 10.02.03

WRITER, PROSE, FICTION AND NONFICTION (profess. & kin.), 131.067-046, 01.01.02

WRITER, TECHNICAL PUBLICATIONS (profess. & kin.), 131.267-026, 11.08.02

X-RAY-EQUIPMENT TESTER (any ind.), 729.281-046, 06.01.05

YARD LABORER (paper & pulp), 922.687-102, 05.12.03

YARN WINDER (any ind.), 681.685-154, 06.04.06

YEAST-CUTTING-AND-WRAPPING-MACHINE OPERATOR (food prep nec), 529.665-022, 06.04.15

ZIPPER SETTER (any ind.), 787.682-086, 06.02.05

ZOOLOGIST (profess. & kin.), 041.061-090, 02.02.01

Appendix B
Industry Groupings, Codes and Abbreviations

There are two separate listings in this appendix. The first provides an alphabetical listing of the industry abbreviations used in the occupational descriptions in *The Enhanced Guide for Occupational Exploration* and their related full titles. The second list provides the industries in clusters of related industries as well as the SIC code number assigned to that industry by the U.S. Department of Labor. This code number allows you to cross-reference other occupational information systems.

Table of Abbreviations for Industry Designation

abrasive & polish. prod. = Abrasive and Polishing Products
agric. = Agriculture
agric. equip. = Agricultural Equipment
air trans. = Air Transportation
aircraft-aerospace mfg. = Aircraft-Aerospace Manufacturing
ammunition = Ammunition
amuse. & rec. = Amusement and Recreation
any ind. = Any Industry
artif. flower = Artificial Flowers
asbestos prod. = Asbestos Products
auto. mfg. = Automobile Manufacturing
auto. ser. = Automobile Services
bake. prod. = Bakery Products
bal. & scales = Balances and Scales
basketry = Basketry
beer prod. = Malt Liquors
boilermaking = Boilermaking
bone, carbon, & lampblack = Bone, Carbon, and Lampblack
boot & shoe = Boot and Shoe
brick & tile = Brick and Tile
brush & broom = Brush and Broom
build. board = Building Board
build. mat. nec = Building Materials, n.e.c.
bus. ser. = Business Services
button = Buttons
can. & preserv. = Canning and Preserving
candle = Candles
canvas goods = Canvas Goods
carpet & rug = Carpet and Rug
cement = Cement
cereal = Cereal Preparations
chem. = Chemical
chew. gum = Chewing Gum
choc. & cocoa = Chocolate and Cocoa Products
clean., dye., & press. = Cleaning, Dyeing, and Pressing
clerical = Clerical and Kindred Occupations

clock & watch = Clocks, Watches, and Allied Products
coal tar prod. = Primary Coal Tar Products
coated fabrics = Coated Fabrics
coin mach. = Coin-Operated Machines
coke prod. = Coke Products
comp. & liq. gases = Compressed and Liqified Gases
concrete prod. = Concrete Products
confection. = Confectionary
const. = Construction
cooperage = Cooperage
cord & twine = Cords and Twine
cork prod. = Cork Products
corn prod. = Corn Products
cut & tools = Cutlery and Tools
dairy prod. = Dairy Products
distilled liquor = Distilled Liquors
dom. ser. = Domestic Service
drug prep. & related = Drug Preparations and Related Products
educ. = Education and Instruction
elec. equip. = Electrical Equipment
electronics = Electronics
electroplating = Electroplating
engine & turbine = Engine and Turbine
engraving = Engraving, Chasing, & Etching excelsior = Excelsior
explosives = Explosives
fabric. metal prod. nec = Fabricated Metal Products, n.e.c.
fabric. plastic prod. = Fabricated Plastics Products
fabric. prod. nec = Fabricated Products, n.e.c.
felt goods = Felt Goods
finan. inst. = Financial Institutions
firearms = Firearms
fireworks = Fireworks
fish. = Fisheries
flav. ext. & sirup = Flavoring Extract and Syrup
floor covering nec = Hard-Surface Floor Covering

food prep nec = Food Preparation, n.e.c.
forestry = Forestry
forging = Forging
foundry = Foundries
framing = Mirror and Picture Frames
fuel briquettes = Fuel Briquettes
fur dressing = Fur Dressing
fur goods = Fur Goods
furn. = Furniture
galvanizing = Galvanizing and Other Coating
garment = Garment
glass mfg. = Glass Manufacturing
glass prod. = Glass Products
glove & mitten = Gloves and Mittens
glue = Glue and Gelatin
gold leaf & foil = Gold Leaf and Foil
gov. ser. = Government Services
grain & feed mill = Grain and Feed Milling
graphite = Graphite
grease & tallow = Grease and Tallow
hairwork = Hairwork
hardware = Hardware
hat & cap = Hat and Cap
heat treat. = Heat Treating
hosiery = Hosiery
hotel & rest. = Hotel and Restaurant
house. furn. = Household Furniture
hunt. & trap. = Hunting and Trapping
ice = Ice
inst. & app. = Instruments and Appliances
insulated wire = Insulated Wire and Cable
insurance = Insurance
iron & steel = Iron and Steel
jewelry = Jewelry
jewelry cases = Jewelry Cases
knit goods = Knit Goods
lasts & related = Lasts and Related Forms
laundry = Laundry
leather mfg. = Leather Manufacturing
leather prod. = Leather Products
library = Library
light, heat, & power = Light, Heat and Power

light. fix. = Lighting Fixtures
lime = Lime
logging = Logging
macaroni & related = Macaroni and
    Related Products
mach. mfg. = Machinery Manufacturing
mach. shop = Machine Shop
mach. tool = Machine Tool and Accessories
match = Match
matt. & bedspring = Mattress and
    Bedspring
medical ser. = Medical Services
mfg. bldgs. = Manufactured Buildings
military ser. = Military Services
minerals & earths = Minerals and Earths
mining = Mining and Quarrying
mirror = Mirror
model & pattern = Model and Pattern
mort. goods = Mortuary Goods
motion pic. = Motion Pictures
motor trans. = Motor Vehicle
    Transportation
motor. & bicycles = Motorcycles, Bicycles
    and Parts
museum = Museums, Art Galleries, and
    Gardens
musical inst. = Musical Instruments and
    Parts
nail = Nail Production
narrow fabrics = Narrow Fabrics
needle & related = Needles, Pins,
    Fasteners, and Related Products
nonfer. metal prod. = Nonferrous Metal
    Alloys
nonprofit org. = Nonprofit Organizations
nut & bolt = Nut, Bolt, Washer, and Rivet
    nut process. = Nut Processing and
    Shelling
office mach. = Office, Computing, and
    Accounting Machines
oils & fats = Oils and Fats, n.e.c.
optical goods = Optical Goods
ordanance = Ordnance and Accessories,
    n.e.c.
ore smelt. & refin. = Nonferrous Metal
    Smelting and Refining

paint & varn. = Paint and Varnish
paper & pulp = Paper and Pulp
paper goods = Paper Goods
pen & pencil = Pens, Pencils, and Artists'
    Materials
per. protect. & med. device = Personal
    Protection and Medical Devices
per. ser. = Personal Service
petrol. production = Petroleum and
    Natural Gas Production
petrol. refin. = Petroleum Refineries
phonograph = Phonographs
photo. apparatus = Photographic
    Apparatus and Materials
photofinish. = Photofinishing
pipe & boiler cov. = Pipe and Boiler
    Coverings
pipe lines = Pipe-Line Operation
planing mill = Planing Mill
plastics mat. = Plastics Materials
plumb. supplies = Plumbers' Supplies
pottery & porc. = Pottery and Porcelain
print. & pub. = Printing and Publishing
profess. & kin. = Professional and Kindred
r.r. car blgd. & rep. = Locomotive and Car
    Building and Repair r.r. trans. =
    Railroad Transportation
radio & tv broad. = Radio and TV
    Broadcasting
real estate = Real Estate
refrig. equip. = Refrigeration Equipment
ret. tr. = Retail Trade
rubber goods = Rubber Goods
rubber reclaim. = Rubber Reclamation
rubber tire & tube = Rubber Tires and
    Tubes
salt production = Salt Production
sanitary ser. = Sanitary Services
sawmill = Sawmill
ship bldg. & rep. = Ship and Boat
    Building and Repairing
signs = Signs and Advertising Novelities
silverware = Silverware
slaught. & meat pack. = Slaughtering and
    Meat Packing
smoking pipe = Smoking Pipe

soap = Soap and Glycerin
social ser. = Social Services
sports equip. = Sporting and Athletic
    Goods
spring = Metal Spring
statue & art = Statue and Art Goods
stonework = Stoneworking
struct. & ornam. metalwork = Structural
    and Ornamental Metalwork
sugar = Sugar
synthetic fibers = Synthetic Fibers
tel. & tel. = Telegraph and Telephone
tex. bag = Textile Bag
tex. prod. nec = Textile Products, n.e.c.
textile = Textile
tin cans = Tin and Metal Cans and
    Containers
tobacco = Tobacco
toys & games = Toys and Games
trans. equip. = Transportation
    Equipment, n.e.c.
trim. & embroid. = Trimming and
    Embroidery
turp. & rosin = Turpentine and Rosin
type founding = Type Founding
umbrella = Umbrella, Parasol, and Cane
veneer & plywood = Veneer and Plywood
wallpaper = Wallpaper
waste & batting = Waste and Batting
water trans. = Water Transportation
waterworks = Waterworks
welding = Welding and Related Processes
whole. tr. = Wholesale Trade
window shade & fix. = Window Shades
    and Fixtures
wine prod. = Vinous Liquors
wire = Wire Drawing
wirework = Wirework
wood dist. & charcoal = Wood Distilling
    and Charcoal
wood preserving = Wood Preserving
wood. box = Wooden Boxes
woodworking = Woodworking

List of Industries Within Related Clusters

Agriculture, Forestry, and Fishing

116 Agriculture
381 Fisheries
387 Forestry
457 Hunting and Trapping

Mining and Construction

271 Construction
568 Manufactured Buildings
575 Minerals and Earths
578 Mining and Quarrying
677 Petroleum Production

Tobacco, Food, & Related Products

164 Bakery Products
214 Canning and Preserving
234 Cereals
239 Chewing Gum
241 Chocolate and Cocoa
268 Confectionaries

283 Corn Products
313 Dairy Products
317 Distilled Liquors
383 Flavoring Extract and Syrup
385 Food Preparation, n.e.c.
427 Grain and Feed Mills
431 Grease and Tallow
459 Ice
554 Macaroni and Related Products
567 Malt Liquors
639 Nut Processing
646 Oils and Fats
812 Salt Production
831 Slaughtering and Meat Packing
851 Sugar
881 Tobacco
931 Vinous Liquors

Textiles, Leather, Clothing, & Related

176 Boot and Shoe
222 Canvas Goods
226 Carpet and Rug
254 Coated Fabrics
279 Cords and Twine

366 Fabricated Products, n.e.c.
369 Felt Goods
399 Fur Goods
409 Garments
419 Gloves and Mittens
441 Hat and Cap
449 Hosiery
455 Household Furniture
494 Knit Goods
518 Leather Manufacturing
522 Leather Products
615 Narrow Fabrics
871 Textile Bags
873 Textile Products, n.e.c.
875 Textiles
887 Trimming and Embroidery
939 Waste and Batting

Lumber and Wood Products

169 Basketry
185 Building Board
275 Cooperage
281 Cork Products
354 Excelsior

384 Floor Coverings, n.e.c.
514 Lasts and Related Forms
544 Logging
568 Manufactured Buildings
583 Mirror and Picture Frames
689 Planing Mills
817 Sawmills
927 Veneer and Plywood
957 Wooden Boxes
962 Wood Preserving
964 Woodworking

Furniture and Fixtures

401 Furniture
437 Hardware
571 Mattresses and Bedsprings
951 Window Shades and Fixtures
964 Woodworking

Paper, Printing, & Related Products

369 Felt Goods
661 Paper and Pulp
664 Paper Goods
699 Printing and Publishing
937 Wallpaper

Chemicals and Allied Products

174 Bone, Carbon, and Lampblack
237 Chemicals
253 Coal Tar Products
261 Compressed and Liqified Gases
323 Drug Preparations and Related Products
357 Explosives
379 Fireworks
421 Glue
657 Paint and Varnish
835 Soap
858 Synthetic Fibers
891 Turpentine and Rosin
959 Wood Distilling and Charcoal

Petroleum Refining and Related Industries

261 Compressed and Liqified Gases
395 Fuel Briquettes
431 Grease and Tallow
646 Oils and Fats
679 Petroleum Refineries

Rubber and Plastic Products

364 Fabricated Plastics Products
384 Floor Coverings, n.e.c.
691 Plastics Material
754 Rubber Goods
756 Rubber Reclaimation
761 Rubber Tires and Tubes

Stone, Clay, Glass, and Concrete Products

114 Abrasive and Polishing Products
145 Asbestos Products
178 Brick and Tile
186 Building Materials, n.e.c.

231 Cement
264 Concrete Products
384 Floor Coverings, n.e.c.
411 Glass Manufacturing
415 Glass Products
429 Graphite
484 Jewelry
537 Lime
575 Minerals and Earths
581 Mirrors
685 Pipe and Boiler Coverings
696 Pottery and Porcelain
843 Statue and Art Goods
845 Stonework

Metal Refining & Working

131 Ammunition
172 Boilermaking
258 Coke Products
294 Cutlery and Tools
345 Electroplating
352 Engraving
362 Fabricated Metal Products, n.e.c.
377 Firearms
391 Forging
393 Foundries
405 Galvanizing
423 Gold Leaf and Foil
437 Hardware
444 Heat Treating
469 Insulated Wire
475 Iron and Steel
484 Jewelry
561 Machine Shop
609 Nails
632 Nonferrous Metal Alloys
636 Nuts and Bolts
651 Ordnance
654 Ore Dressing, Smelting, and Refining
693 Plumbers' Supplies
839 Springs
847 Structural and Ornamental Metalwork
877 Tinware
945 Welding
953 Wire
955 Wirework

Business and Industrial Machinery

121 Agricultural Equipment
166 Balances and Scales
255 Coin Machines
351 Engine and Turbine
557 Machinery Manufacturing
563 Machine Tool and Accessories
644 Office Machines
735 Refrigeration Equipment
894 Type Founding

Electronic/Electrical Equipment

341 Electrical Equipment
343 Electronics
529 Lighting Fixtures
681 Phonographs

Transportation Equipment

123 Aircraft-Aerospace Manufacturing
151 Automobile Manufacturing
542 Locomotive and Car Building and Repair
592 Motorcycles and Bicycles
824 Ship and Boat Building and Repairs
885 Transportation Equipment

Measuring, Analyzing and ControllingInstruments

166 Balances and Scales
251 Clock and Watch
466 Instruments and Appliances
648 Optical Goods
673 Personal Protection and Medical Devices
683 Photographic Apparatus
829 Silverware

Miscellaneous Manufacturing Industries

141 Artificial Flowers
184 Brush and Broom
191 Buttons
218 Candles
366 Fabricated Products, n.e.c.
397 Fur Dressing
434 Hairwork
466 Instruments and Appliances
486 Jewelry Cases
569 Matches
583 Mirror and Picture Frames
585 Models and Patterns
587 Mortuary Goods
595 Musical Instruments
617 Needles, Pins, and Related Products
671 Pens and Pencils
827 Signs
833 Smoking Pipes
837 Sports Equipment
883 Toys and Games
924 Umbrellas

Transportation Services

125 Air Transportation
154 Automobile Services
542 Locomotive and Car Building and Repair
593 Motor Transportation
687 Pipe Lines
751 Railroad Transportation
941 Water Transportation

Communications

699 Printing and Publishing
724 Radio and TV Broadcasting
869 Telegraph and Telephone

Electric, Gas, and Sanitary Services

532 Light, Heat and Power
815 Sanitary Services
943 Waterworks

Trade

741 Retail Trade
948 Wholesale Trade

Finance, Insurance, and Real Estate

375 Financial Institutions
473 Insurance
731 Real Estate

Services

133 Amusement and Recreation
187 Business Services
247 Cleaning, Dyeing, and Pressing
249 Clerical
319 Domestic Service
335 Education
453 Hotel and Restaurant
516 Laundry
524 Library
573 Medical Services
589 Motion Pictures
597 Museums

634 Nonprofit Organizations
674 Personal Service
684 Photofinishing
836 Social Services

Government and Military Services

138 Any Industry
249 Clerical
335 Education
425 Government Services
574 Military Services
705 Professional and Kindred

APPENDIX C
2,500 Occupations Within Major Industries

This index organizes all the occupations listed in *The Enhanced Guide for Occupational Exploration* within major industry groupings where that job is most often found. You can use this list to help you find other occupations within an industry with which you are already familiar. This allows you to use special knowledge you have already acquired in a new but related occupation within the same industry. It will also help you identify occupations within an industry that interests you. Use the GOE number preceding each occupation to look up the description in this book. The number following it is its DOT number for use in cross-referencing the occupation to other systems. An explanation of DOT numbers is provided in chapter 1.

Agriculture

02.04.02 BIOLOGICAL AIDE (049.384-010)
03.01.01 FARMER, FIELD CROP (404.161-010)
03.01.01 FARMER, GENERAL (421.161-010)
03.01.01 FARMER, VINE-FRUIT CROPS (403.161-014)
03.01.01 GENERAL MANAGER, FARM (180.167-018)
03.01.01 GROUP LEADER (180.167-022)
03.01.01 MANAGER, DAIRY FARM (180.167-026)
03.01.01 MIGRANT LEADER (180.167-050)
03.01.02 BEEKEEPER (413.161-010)
03.01.03 MANAGER, NURSERY (180.167-042)
03.03.02 HORSESHOER (418.381-010)
03.04.01 FARMWORKER, FRUIT 1 (403.683-010)
03.04.01 FARMWORKER, GENERAL 1 (421.683-010)
03.04.01 FARMWORKER, GENERAL 2 (421.687-010)
03.04.01 FARMWORKER, LIVESTOCK (410.664-010)
03.04.01 FARMWORKER, VEGETABLE 2 (402.687-010)
03.04.01 SORTER, AGRICULTURAL PRODUCE (529.687-186)
03.04.04 HORTICULTURAL WORKER 2 (405.687-014)
03.04.04 LABORER, LANDSCAPE (408.687-014)
03.04.04 LAWN-SERVICE WORKER (408.684-010)
03.04.05 PLANT-CARE WORKER (408.364-010)
05.04.01 AIRPLANE PILOT (196.263-010)
06.04.21 SEED PELLETER (599.685-126)
06.04.28 POULTRY DRESSER (525.687-070)

Agricultural Equipment

05.03.07 TEST TECHNICIAN (019.261-022)
05.05.09 FARM-EQUIPMENT MECHANIC 1 (624.281-010)
06.04.23 BENCH ASSEMBLER (706.684-042)

Aircraft-Aerospace Manufacturing

02.04.01 CALIBRATION LABORATORY TECHNICIAN (019.281-010)
05.01.01 AERODYNAMIST (002.061-010)
05.01.01 AERONAUTICAL-RESEARCH ENGINEER (002.061-026)
05.01.04 AERONAUTICAL TEST ENGINEER (002.061-018)
05.01.04 FIELD-SERVICE ENGINEER (002.167-014)
05.01.04 RESEARCH MECHANIC (002.280-010)
05.01.04 STRESS ANALYST (002.061-030)
05.01.05 SALES ENGINEER, AERONAUTICAL PRODUCTS (002.151-010)
05.01.06 COST-ANALYSIS ENGINEER (002.167-010)
05.01.07 AERONAUTICAL-DESIGN ENGINEER (002.061-022)
05.03.03 MATERIAL SCHEDULER (012.187-010)
05.05.06 AIRCRAFT BODY REPAIRER (807.261-010)
05.05.09 AIRFRAME-AND-POWER-PLANT MECHANIC (621.281-014)
05.05.09 EXPERIMENTAL MECHANIC 2 (621.281-022)
05.05.09 FLIGHT-TEST SHOP MECHANIC (621.381-010)
05.05.09 ROCKET-ENGINE-COMPONENT MECHANIC (621.281-030)
05.05.10 AVIONICS TECHNICIAN (823.281-010)
05.10.02 MECHANIC, AIRCRAFT ACCESSORIES (621.381-014)
06.01.04 SKIN FITTER (806.381-054)
06.01.05 INSPECTOR, ASSEMBLIES AND INSTALLATIONS (806.281-022)
06.02.09 HONEYCOMB-BLANKET MAKER (806.684-062)
06.02.22 ASSEMBLER, SUBASSEMBLY (806.484-010)
06.02.24 ASSEMBLER, METAL BONDING (806.684-030)
06.02.24 PRESSURE SEALER-AND-TESTER (806.684-110)
06.02.32 BONDED STRUCTURES REPAIRER (807.381-014)
06.03.01 CABLE STRETCHER AND TESTER (806.685-010)
06.04.34 INSULATION-BLANKET MAKER (806.684-078)

Air Transportation

04.02.02 AIRLINE SECURITY REPRESENTATIVE (372.667-010)
05.03.01 NAVIGATOR (196.167-014)
05.03.03 DISPATCHER (912.167-010)
05.03.06 FLIGHT ENGINEER (621.261-018)
05.04.01 AIRPLANE PILOT, COMMERCIAL (196.263-014)
05.05.06 AIRCRAFT BODY REPAIRER (807.261-010)
05.05.09 AIRFRAME-AND-POWER-PLANT MECHANIC (621.281-014)
05.05.10 AVIONICS TECHNICIAN (823.281-010)
05.07.02 AIRPLANE INSPECTOR (621.261-010)
05.09.01 CARGO AGENT (248.367-018)
05.10.04 AIRPORT ATTENDANT (912.364-010)
05.12.06 AIRPORT UTILITY WORKER (912.663-010)
05.12.06 LINE-SERVICE ATTENDANT (912.687-010)

06.01.04 SKIN FITTER (806.381-054)
06.04.38 PARACHUTE RIGGER (912.684-010)
07.04.03 RESERVATIONS AGENT (238.367-018)
07.04.05 AIRLINE-RADIO OPERATOR (193.262-010)
07.04.05 FLIGHT-INFORMATION EXPEDITER (912.367-010)
07.05.01 CREW SCHEDULER (215.362-010)
07.05.01 TRANSPORTATION AGENT (912.367-014)
08.01.02 TRAFFIC AGENT (252.257-010)
09.01.04 AIRPLANE-FLIGHT ATTENDANT (352.367-010)
09.05.03 PORTER (357.677-010)
11.05.01 MANAGER, AIRPORT (184.117-026)
11.05.02 MANAGER, OPERATIONS (184.117-050)
11.05.02 MANAGER, SCHEDULE PLANNING (184.117-058)
11.11.03 MANAGER, TRAFFIC (184.117-066)
11.12.01 GENERAL CLAIMS AGENT (186.117-030)

Ammunition

06.04.40 MUNITIONS HANDLER (929.687-034)

Amusement and Recreation

01.02.02 QUICK SKETCH ARTIST (149.041-010)
01.02.03 SET DESIGNER (142.061-050)
01.03.01 PRODUCER (187.167-178)
01.03.02 CLOWN (159.047-010)
01.03.02 COMEDIAN (159.047-014)
01.03.02 MAGICIAN (159.041-010)
01.03.02 MIME (159.047-022)
01.03.02 PUPPETEER (159.041-014)
01.03.03 PROGRAM COORDINATOR (139.167-010)
01.04.02 PROMPTER (152.367-010)
01.04.03 SINGER (152.047-022)
01.04.04 MUSICIAN, INSTRUMENTAL (152.041-010)
01.05.01 CHOREOGRAPHER (151.027-010)
01.05.02 DANCER (151.047-010)
01.06.02 MAKE-UP ARTIST (333.071-010)
01.06.02 PROP MAKER (962.281-010)
01.07.01 GRAPHOLOGIST (159.247-018)
01.07.02 ANNOUNCER (159.347-010)
01.07.03 AMUSEMENT PARK ENTERTAINER (159.647-010)
03.03.01 ANIMAL TRAINER (159.224-010)
03.03.01 EXERCISER, HORSE (153.674-010)
03.03.02 ANIMAL KEEPER (412.674-010)
03.03.02 ANIMAL-RIDE ATTENDANT (349.674-010)
03.03.02 AQUARIST (449.674-010)
04.02.03 BEACH LIFEGUARD (379.364-014)
04.02.03 BOUNCER (376.667-010)
05.02.07 MANAGER, MARINA DRY DOCK (187.167-226)
05.09.01 CUSTODIAN, ATHLETIC EQUIPMENT (969.367-010)
05.10.01 GRIP (962.684-014)
05.10.02 RIDE OPERATOR (342.663-010)
05.10.03 ELECTRIC-GOLF-CART REPAIRER (620.261-026)
05.10.03 SOUND CONTROLLER (194.262-014)
05.10.05 MOTION-PICTURE PROJECTIONIST (960.362-010)
05.12.16 LIGHTING-EQUIPMENT OPERATOR (962.381-014)
05.12.18 ATTENDANT, CAMPGROUND (329.683-010)
05.12.18 GOLF-RANGE ATTENDANT (341.683-010)
07.03.01 PARIMUTUEL-TICKET SELLER (211.467-022)
07.04.03 RECREATION-FACILITY ATTENDANT (341.367-010)
07.04.05 SCOREBOARD OPERATOR (349.665-010)
08.03.01 PHOTOGRAPHER (143.457-010)
08.03.01 VENDOR (291.457-022)
09.01.01 AMUSEMENT PARK WORKER (349.664-010)
09.01.01 COUNSELOR, CAMP (159.124-010)
09.01.01 GUIDE, HUNTING AND FISHING (353.161-010)
09.04.02 FLOOR ATTENDANT (343.467-014)
09.04.02 GAMBLING DEALER (343.467-018)
09.04.02 GAME ATTENDANT (342.457-010)
09.04.02 SKATE-SHOP ATTENDANT (341.464-010)
09.05.04 DRIVE-IN THEATER ATTENDANT (349.673-010)
09.05.05 CARDROOM ATTENDANT 2 (343.577-010)
09.05.06 CADDIE (341.677-010)
09.05.06 DRESSER (346.674-010)
09.05.08 CHILDREN'S ATTENDANT (349.677-018)
09.05.08 TICKET TAKER (344.667-010)
09.05.08 USHER (344.677-014)

10.02.02 ATHLETIC TRAINER (153.224-010)
11.06.03 BOOKMAKER (187.167-014)
11.11.02 MANAGER, BOWLING ALLEY (187.167-222)
11.11.02 MANAGER, GOLF CLUB (187.167-114)
11.11.02 MANAGER, RECREATION ESTABLISHMENT
   (187.117-042)
11.11.02 MANAGER, RECREATION FACILITY I (187.167-230)
11.11.02 MANAGER, THEATER (187.167-154)
11.11.04 GENERAL MANAGER, ROAD PRODUCTION
   (187.117-034)
11.11.04 MANAGER, TOURING PRODUCTION (191.117-038)
11.12.03 ADVANCE AGENT (191.167-010)
11.12.03 ARTIST'S MANAGER (191.117-010)
11.12.03 BOOKING MANAGER (191.117-014)
11.12.03 BUSINESS MANAGER (191.117-018)
11.12.03 MANAGER, ATHLETE (153.117-014)
12.01.01 COACH, PROFESSIONAL ATHLETES (153.227-010)
12.01.01 INSTRUCTOR, SPORTS (153.227-018)
12.01.01 SCOUT, PROFESSIONAL SPORTS (153.117-018)
12.01.02 CHARTER (249.367-018)
12.01.02 CLOCKER (153.367-010)
12.01.02 FLAGGER (372.667-026)
12.01.02 GOLF-COURSE RANGER (379.667-010)
12.01.02 HORSE-RACE STARTER (153.267-010)
12.01.02 HORSE-RACE TIMER (153.367-014)
12.01.02 LEAD PONY RIDER (153.674-014)
12.01.02 UMPIRE (153.267-018)
12.02.01 AQUATIC PERFORMER (159.347-014)
12.02.01 JUGGLER (159.341-010)
12.02.01 STUNT PERFORMER (159.341-014)

Any Industry

01.04.02 COPYIST (152.267-010)
01.06.01 SILK-SCREEN CUTTER (979.681-022)
01.06.02 CLAY MODELER (779.281-010)
01.06.02 DECORATOR (298.381-010)
01.06.02 MODEL MAKER 1 (777.261-010)
01.06.02 REPAIRER, ART OBJECTS (779.381-018)
01.06.03 GILDER (749.381-010)
01.06.03 PAINTER, AIRBRUSH (741.684-018)
01.06.03 PAINTER, HAND (970.381-022)
01.06.03 PAINTER, SIGN (970.381-026)
01.06.03 SIGN WRITER, HAND (970.281-022)
01.06.03 STRIPER, HAND (740.484-010)
01.08.01 MODEL, ARTISTS' (961.667-010)
02.04.01 DECONTAMINATOR (199.384-010)
02.04.01 LABORATORY TESTER (029.261-010)
02.04.02 FOOD TESTER (029.361-014)
03.03.02 ANIMAL CARETAKER (410.674-010)
03.03.02 STABLE ATTENDANT (410.674-022)
03.04.01 LIVESTOCK-YARD ATTENDANT (410.674-018)
03.04.04 GREENSKEEPER 1 (406.137-010)
03.04.04 GREENSKEEPER 2 (406.683-010)
03.04.04 GROUNDSKEEPER, INDUSTRIAL-COMMERCIAL
   (406.684-014)
04.02.02 DETECTIVE 1 (376.367-014)
04.02.02 GATE TENDER (372.667-030)
04.02.02 GUARD, SECURITY (372.667-034)
04.02.04 FIRE FIGHTER (373.364-010)
05.01.06 FACILITIES PLANNER (019.261-018)
05.01.06 PREVENTIVE MAINTENANCE COORDINATOR
   (169.167-074)
05.01.06 TOOL PLANNER (012.167-074)
05.01.06 TOOL PROGRAMER, NUMERICAL CONTROL
   (007.167-018)
05.02.02 SUPERINTENDENT, BUILDING (187.167-190)
05.02.03 PRODUCTION SUPERINTENDENT (183.117-014)
05.03.05 RADIOGRAPHER (199.361-010)
05.03.05 RADIOTELEPHONE OPERATOR (193.262-034)
05.03.06 SUPERVISOR, VENDOR QUALITY (012.167-062)
05.05.02 CARPENTER, MAINTENANCE (860.281-010)
05.05.02 SUPERINTENDENT, MAINTENANCE (189.167-046)
05.05.03 OIL-BURNER-SERVICER-AND-INSTALLER
   (862.281-018)
05.05.03 PIPE FITTER (862.281-022)

05.05.05 ANTENNA INSTALLER, SATELLITE COMMUNICATIONS (823.261-022)
05.05.05 ELECTRICIAN (824.261-010)
05.05.05 ELECTRICIAN, MAINTENANCE (829.261-018)
05.05.05 ELEVATOR REPAIRER (825.281-030)
05.05.05 LINE MAINTAINER (821.261-014)
05.05.05 MAINTENANCE MECHANIC, TELEPHONE (822.281-018)
05.05.06 BOILERHOUSE MECHANIC (805.361-010)
05.05.06 FITTER 1 (801.261-014)
05.05.06 FORMER, HAND (619.361-010)
05.05.06 METAL FABRICATOR (619.360-014)
05.05.06 MILLWRIGHT (638.281-018)
05.05.06 SHEET-METAL WORKER (804.281-010)
05.05.07 GUNSMITH (632.281-010)
05.05.07 MAINTENANCE MACHINIST (600.280-042)
05.05.07 SAW FILER (701.381-014)
05.05.07 TEMPLATE MAKER (601.381-038)
05.05.07 TOOL GRINDER 1 (701.381-018)
05.05.09 AIR-CONDITIONING INSTALLER-SERVICER, WINDOW UNIT (637.261-010)
05.05.09 AUTOMOTIVE-MAINTENANCE-EQUIPMENT SERVICER (620.281-018)
05.05.09 CASH-REGISTER SERVICER (633.281-010)
05.05.09 DIESEL MECHANIC (625.281-010)
05.05.09 ENVIRONMENTAL-CONTROL-SYSTEM INSTALLER-SERVICER (637.261-014)
05.05.09 FUEL-INJECTION SERVICER (625.281-022)
05.05.09 FUEL-SYSTEM-MAINTENANCE WORKER (638.381-010)
05.05.09 FURNACE INSTALLER-AND-REPAIRER, HOT AIR (869.281-010)
05.05.09 GAS-ENGINE REPAIRER (625.281-026)
05.05.09 GAS-WELDING-EQUIPMENT MECHANIC (626.381-014)
05.05.09 LOCKSMITH (709.281-010)
05.05.09 MAINTENANCE MECHANIC (638.281-014)
05.05.09 MAINTENANCE REPAIRER, INDUSTRIAL (899.261-014)
05.05.09 MECHANIC, INDUSTRIAL TRUCK (620.281-050)
05.05.09 OFFICE-MACHINE SERVICER (633.281-018)
05.05.09 PARTS SALVAGER (638.281-026)
05.05.09 PNEUMATIC-TOOL REPAIRER (630.281-010)
05.05.09 POWER-SAW MECHANIC (625.281-030)
05.05.09 PUMP SERVICER (630.281-018)
05.05.09 REFRIGERATION MECHANIC (637.261-026)
05.05.09 SMALL-ENGINE MECHANIC (625.281-034)
05.05.09 SOLAR-ENERGY-SYSTEM INSTALLER (637.261-030)
05.05.10 AUDIO-VIDEO REPAIRER (729.281-010)
05.05.10 ELECTRIC-MOTOR REPAIRER (721.281-018)
05.05.10 ELECTRICAL-APPLIANCE SERVICER (827.261-010)
05.05.10 ELECTRICAL-INSTRUMENT REPAIRER (729.281-026)
05.05.10 ELECTRONICS MECHANIC (828.281-010)
05.05.10 INSTRUMENT MECHANIC (710.281-026)
05.05.10 METEOROLOGICAL-EQUIPMENT REPAIRER (823.281-018)
05.05.10 PUBLIC-ADDRESS SERVICER (823.261-010)
05.05.10 RADIO MECHANIC (823.261-018)
05.05.11 ELECTROMEDICAL-EQUIPMENT REPAIRER (729.281-030)
05.05.11 EXPERIMENTAL ASSEMBLER (739.381-026)
05.05.11 INSTRUMENT MAKER (600.280-010)
05.05.11 INSTRUMENT REPAIRER (710.261-010)
05.05.12 ACCORDION REPAIRER (730.281-014)
05.05.12 ELECTRONIC-ORGAN TECHNICIAN (828.261-010)
05.05.12 FRETTED-INSTRUMENT REPAIRER (730.281-026)
05.05.12 PERCUSSION-INSTRUMENT REPAIRER (730.381-042)
05.05.12 PIANO TECHNICIAN (730.281-038)
05.05.12 PIANO TUNER (730.361-010)
05.05.12 PIPE-ORGAN TUNER AND REPAIRER (730.361-014)
05.05.12 WIND-INSTRUMENT REPAIRER (730.281-054)
05.05.15 DRESSMAKER (785.361-010)
05.05.15 FURNITURE UPHOLSTERER (780.381-018)

05.05.17 TESTER, FOOD PRODUCTS (199.251-010)
05.06.01 GAS-ENGINE OPERATOR (950.382-018)
05.06.02 AIR-COMPRESSOR OPERATOR (950.685-010)
05.06.02 BOILER OPERATOR (950.382-010)
05.06.02 FUEL ATTENDANT (953.362-010)
05.06.02 GAS-COMPRESSOR OPERATOR (950.382-014)
05.06.02 REFRIGERATING ENGINEER (950.362-014)
05.06.02 STATIONARY ENGINEER (950.382-026)
05.06.03 PUMPER (914.682-010)
05.07.03 ELEVATOR EXAMINER-AND-ADJUSTER (825.261-014)
05.08.01 DUMP-TRUCK DRIVER (902.683-010)
05.08.01 TRACTOR-TRAILER-TRUCK DRIVER (904.383-010)
05.08.01 TRUCK DRIVER, HEAVY (905.663-014)
05.08.01 TRUCK DRIVER, LIGHT (906.683-022)
05.08.02 TRACKMOBILE OPERATOR (919.683-026)
05.08.04 MOTORBOAT OPERATOR (911.663-010)
05.09.01 LABORER, STORES (922.687-058)
05.10.01 BUILDING CLEANER (891.684-022)
05.10.01 CASTING REPAIRER (619.281-010)
05.10.01 DIVER (899.261-010)
05.10.01 FIXTURE REPAIRER-FABRICATOR (630.384-010)
05.10.01 LUGGAGE REPAIRER (365.361-010)
05.10.01 MAINTENANCE REPAIRER, BUILDING (899.381-010)
05.10.01 PUMP INSTALLER (630.684-018)
05.10.01 TEMPLATE MAKER, TRACK (809.484-014)
05.10.01 TORCH-STRAIGHTENER-AND-HEATER (709.684-086)
05.10.01 UMBRELLA REPAIRER (369.684-018)
05.10.02 BICYCLE REPAIRER (639.681-010)
05.10.02 CONVEYOR-MAINTENANCE MECHANIC (630.381-010)
05.10.02 DOOR-CLOSER MECHANIC (630.381-014)
05.10.02 GAS-APPLIANCE SERVICER (637.261-018)
05.10.02 LUBRICATION-EQUIPMENT SERVICER (630.381-022)
05.10.02 METER REPAIRER (710.281-034)
05.10.02 PNEUMATIC-TUBE REPAIRER (630.281-014)
05.10.02 SEWING-MACHINE REPAIRER (639.281-018)
05.10.03 BATTERY REPAIRER (727.381-014)
05.10.03 ELECTRIC-TOOL REPAIRER (729.281-022)
05.10.03 ELECTRICAL-APPLIANCE REPAIRER (723.381-010)
05.10.03 TAPE-RECORDER REPAIRER (720.281-014)
05.10.03 TELEVISION INSTALLER (823.361-010)
05.10.03 TELEVISION-AND-RADIO REPAIRER (720.281-018)
05.10.03 TELEVISION-CABLE INSTALLER (821.281-010)
05.10.03 TRANSFORMER REPAIRER (724.381-018)
05.10.03 VACUUM CLEANER REPAIRER (723.381-014)
05.10.04 AIR-CONDITIONING INSTALLER, DOMESTIC (827.464-010)
05.10.04 DOLL REPAIRER (731.684-014)
05.10.04 EQUIPMENT INSTALLER (828.381-010)
05.10.04 EVAPORATIVE-COOLER INSTALLER (637.381-010)
05.10.04 FIRE-EXTINGUISHER REPAIRER (709.384-010)
05.10.04 HOUSEHOLD-APPLIANCE INSTALLER (827.661-010)
05.10.04 PINSETTER MECHANIC, AUTOMATIC (638.261-022)
05.10.04 POLISHING-WHEEL SETTER (776.684-014)
05.10.04 SPORTS-EQUIPMENT REPAIRER (732.684-122)
05.10.04 SWIMMING-POOL SERVICER (891.684-018)
05.10.05 AUDIOVISUAL TECHNICIAN (960.382-010)
05.10.05 BLUEPRINTING-MACHINE OPERATOR (979.682-014)
05.10.05 REPRODUCTION TECHNICIAN (976.361-010)
05.10.05 SCREEN MAKER, PHOTOGRAPHIC PROCESS (979.384-010)
05.10.06 BLASTER (859.261-010)
05.10.07 PAINTER, SPRAY 1 (741.684-026)
05.10.07 PAINTER, TOUCH-UP (749.684-038)
05.10.08 COOK (315.361-010)
05.10.09 EXTERMINATOR (389.684-010)
05.11.01 BULLDOZER OPERATOR 1 (850.683-010)
05.11.01 POWER-SHOVEL OPERATOR (850.683-030)
05.11.02 CORE-DRILL OPERATOR (930.682-010)

05.11.04 BRIDGE-OR-GANTRY-CRANE OPERATOR
(921.663-010)
05.11.04 CONVEYOR OPERATOR (921.683-026)
05.11.04 DERRICK OPERATOR (921.663-022)
05.11.04 DINKEY OPERATOR (919.663-014)
05.11.04 DRAGLINE OPERATOR (850.683-018)
05.11.04 DUMP OPERATOR (921.685-038)
05.11.04 FRONT-END LOADER OPERATOR (921.683-042)
05.11.04 HOISTING ENGINEER (921.663-030)
05.11.04 RIGGER (921.260-010)
05.11.04 TRACTOR OPERATOR (929.683-014)
05.11.04 TRACTOR-CRANE OPERATOR (921.663-058)
05.11.04 TRUCK-CRANE OPERATOR (921.663-062)
05.12.02 SURVEYOR HELPER (869.567-010)
05.12.03 BRAKE HOLDER (932.664-010)
05.12.03 DUMPER (921.667-018)
05.12.03 MATERIAL HANDLER (929.687-030)
05.12.03 PRESS BUCKER (920.686-042)
05.12.03 WASTE-DISPOSAL ATTENDANT (955.383-010)
05.12.04 BOOM-CONVEYOR OPERATOR (921.683-014)
05.12.04 CONVEYOR-SYSTEM DISPATCHER (921.662-018)
05.12.04 ELEVATOR OPERATOR, FREIGHT (921.683-038)
05.12.04 LABORER, HOISTING (921.667-022)
05.12.06 WATER TENDER (599.685-122)
05.12.08 GARAGE SERVICER, INDUSTRIAL (915.687-014)
05.12.08 OILER (699.687-018)
05.12.12 BILLPOSTER (299.667-010)
05.12.12 DECORATOR, STREET AND BUILDING (899.687-010)
05.12.12 WINDOW REPAIRER (899.684-042)
05.12.13 KEY CUTTER (709.684-050)
05.12.14 STEEL-PLATE CALKER (843.684-010)
05.12.14 STOVE REFINISHER (749.684-046)
05.12.15 BELT REPAIRER (630.684-014)
05.12.15 ROLLER-SKATE REPAIRER (732.684-102)
05.12.16 ANTENNA INSTALLER (823.684-010)
05.12.16 ELECTRICAL-APPLIANCE PREPARER (827.584-010)
05.12.18 CHANGE-HOUSE ATTENDANT (358.687-010)
05.12.18 CHIMNEY SWEEP (891.687-010)
05.12.18 CLEANER 2 (919.687-014)
05.12.18 CLEANER, COMMERCIAL OR INSTITUTIONAL
(381.687-014)
05.12.18 CLEANER, HOUSEKEEPING (323.687-014)
05.12.18 CLEANER, INDUSTRIAL (381.687-018)
05.12.18 CLEANER, LABORATORY EQUIPMENT
(381.687-022)
05.12.18 CLEANER, WINDOW (389.687-014)
05.12.18 FURNACE CLEANER (891.687-014)
05.12.18 JANITOR (382.664-010)
05.12.18 LAUNDRY WORKER 1 (361.684-014)
05.12.18 LIGHT-FIXTURE SERVICER (389.687-018)
05.12.18 SANDBLASTER (503.687-010)
05.12.18 SWEEPER-CLEANER, INDUSTRIAL (389.683-010)
05.12.18 TANK CLEANER (891.687-022)
05.12.18 TUBE CLEANER (891.687-030)
05.12.18 VENETIAN-BLIND CLEANER AND REPAIRER
(739.687-198)
05.12.19 BOOK REPAIRER (977.684-010)
05.12.20 CROSSING TENDER (371.667-010)
06.01.02 MACHINE SETTER (616.360-022)
06.01.02 SETTER, AUTOMATIC-SPINNING LATHE
(604.360-010)
06.01.03 MACHINE OPERATOR 1 (616.360-018)
06.01.05 INSPECTOR, METAL FABRICATING (619.261-010)
06.01.05 X-RAY-EQUIPMENT TESTER (729.281-046)
06.02.01 TOOL GRINDER 2 (603.664-010)
06.02.02 BRAKE OPERATOR 2 (619.685-026)
06.02.02 CRIMPING-MACHINE OPERATOR (616.682-022)
06.02.02 POLISHING-MACHINE OPERATOR (603.682-026)
06.02.02 PRESS OPERATOR, HEAVY DUTY (617.260-010)
06.02.02 PUNCH-PRESS OPERATOR 3 (615.682-014)
06.02.02 RIVETER, HYDRAULIC (800.662-010)
06.02.02 RIVETING-MACHINE OPERATOR 1 (699.482-010)
06.02.02 SHEAR OPERATOR 1 (615.482-034)
06.02.02 SPINNER, HAND (619.362-018)
06.02.02 SPINNER, HYDRAULIC (619.362-022)

06.02.02 STRAIGHTENING-PRESS OPERATOR (617.482-026)
06.02.02 STRAIGHTENING-ROLL OPERATOR (613.462-022)
06.02.03 NAILING-MACHINE OPERATOR (669.682-058)
06.02.05 BINDER (787.682-010)
06.02.05 HEMMER (787.682-026)
06.02.05 MENDER (787.682-030)
06.02.05 SEWING-MACHINE OPERATOR (787.682-046)
06.02.05 ZIPPER SETTER (787.682-086)
06.02.09 CLOTH PRINTER (652.382-010)
06.02.09 CUTTER OPERATOR (699.682-018)
06.02.09 DIE CUTTER (699.682-022)
06.02.10 PICKLER, CONTINUOUS PICKLING LINE
(503.362-010)
06.02.13 MIXING-MACHINE OPERATOR (550.382-022)
06.02.18 STILL TENDER (552.685-026)
06.02.20 ARBOR-PRESS OPERATOR 1 (616.682-010)
06.02.20 KICK-PRESS OPERATOR 1 (616.682-026)
06.02.20 STACKING-MACHINE OPERATOR 1 (692.682-054)
06.02.21 ANODIZER (500.682-010)
06.02.21 COATER OPERATOR (509.382-010)
06.02.21 PAINT-SPRAYER OPERATOR, AUTOMATIC
(599.382-010)
06.02.21 PAINTER, ELECTROSTATIC (599.682-010)
06.02.24 ARMATURE BANDER (724.684-010)
06.02.24 FABRICATOR-ASSEMBLER, METAL PRODUCTS
(809.381-010)
06.02.24 REPAIRER, FINISHED METAL (809.684-034)
06.02.24 STRAIGHTENER, HAND (709.484-014)
06.02.27 CUTTER, HAND 1 (781.584-014)
06.02.27 CUTTER, MACHINE 1 (781.684-014)
06.02.29 RUBBER-GOODS REPAIRER (759.684-054)
06.02.30 GLASS CUTTER (775.684-022)
06.02.31 LAY-OUT WORKER 2 (809.381-014)
06.02.32 COIL WINDER, REPAIR (724.381-014)
06.03.01 COMPARATOR OPERATOR (699.384-010)
06.03.02 GARMENT INSPECTOR (789.687-070)
06.03.02 GLASS INSPECTOR (579.687-022)
06.03.02 HYDRO-PNEUMATIC TESTER (862.687-018)
06.03.02 INSPECTOR, FABRIC (789.587-014)
06.03.02 METAL-FINISH INSPECTOR (703.687-014)
06.03.02 PAINT-SPRAY INSPECTOR (741.687-010)
06.03.02 WEIGHER, PRODUCTION (929.587-014)
06.04.02 BENDING-MACHINE OPERATOR 2 (617.685-010)
06.04.02 BUFFING-MACHINE TENDER (603.665-010)
06.04.02 DRUM STRAIGHTENER 1 (619.685-034)
06.04.02 EMBOSSER (583.685-030)
06.04.02 GRAINER, MACHINE (652.686-014)
06.04.02 MACHINE OPERATOR 2 (619.685-062)
06.04.02 NIBBLER OPERATOR (615.685-026)
06.04.02 POWER-PRESS TENDER (617.685-026)
06.04.02 PUNCH-PRESS OPERATOR II (615.685-030)
06.04.02 TOOL DRESSER (601.682-010)
06.04.02 TURRET-PUNCH-PRESS OPERATOR,
TAPE-CONTROL (615.685-042)
06.04.03 BUZZSAW OPERATOR (667.685-026)
06.04.04 CARTON-FORMING-MACHINE OPERATOR
(641.685-022)
06.04.05 EYELET-MACHINE OPERATOR (699.685-018)
06.04.05 FASTENER-SEWING-MACHINE OPERATOR
(787.685-010)
06.04.05 FOLDER-SEAMER, AUTOMATIC (787.685-014)
06.04.05 PLEATING-MACHINE OPERATOR (583.685-082)
06.04.05 PRESSER, MACHINE (363.682-018)
06.04.05 SPREADER, MACHINE (781.685-010)
06.04.05 STRIP-CUTTING-MACHINE OPERATOR
(686.685-066)
06.04.05 TACKING-MACHINE OPERATOR (787.685-042)
06.04.06 PICKING-MACHINE OPERATOR (680.685-082)
06.04.06 YARN WINDER (681.685-154)
06.04.08 CRUSHER TENDER (570.685-022)
06.04.09 CROWN-ASSEMBLY-MACHINE OPERATOR
(692.685-062)
06.04.09 CUTTER, MACHINE 2 (699.685-014)
06.04.09 CUTTING-MACHINE TENDER (690.685-122)
06.04.09 EMBOSSING-PRESS OPERATOR (652.685-030)

06.04.09 LEAF STAMPER (979.682-018)
06.04.09 MACHINE FEEDER (699.686-010)
06.04.09 SCRAP HANDLER (509.685-050)
06.04.09 SILK-SCREEN PRINTER, MACHINE (979.665-010)
06.04.09 SPRAY-PAINTING-MACHINE OPERATOR
  (741.685-010)
06.04.10 MILL OPERATOR (599.685-058)
06.04.10 OXIDIZED-FINISH PLATER (599.685-062)
06.04.11 PAINT MIXER, MACHINE (550.485-018)
06.04.16 EXTRACTOR OPERATOR (581.685-038)
06.04.19 FILTER OPERATOR (551.685-078)
06.04.20 ASSEMBLY-PRESS OPERATOR (690.685-014)
06.04.20 STAPLING-MACHINE OPERATOR (692.685-202)
06.04.21 CERAMIC COATER, MACHINE (509.685-022)
06.04.21 DIPPER (599.685-026)
06.04.21 DIPPER AND BAKER (599.685-030)
06.04.21 PAINTER, TUMBLING BARREL (599.685-070)
06.04.21 PAINTING-MACHINE OPERATOR (599.685-074)
06.04.21 SPRAY-UNIT FEEDER (599.686-014)
06.04.22 ASSEMBLER, PRODUCTION (706.687-010)
06.04.22 NAILER, HAND (762.684-050)
06.04.22 RIVETER, HAND (709.684-066)
06.04.23 ASSEMBLER, SMALL PARTS (706.684-022)
06.04.23 ASSEMBLER, SMALL PRODUCTS (739.687-030)
06.04.23 SILK-SCREEN-FRAME ASSEMBLER (709.484-010)
06.04.24 BENCH GRINDER (705.684-010)
06.04.24 BUFFER 1 (705.684-014)
06.04.24 GRINDER 1 (705.684-026)
06.04.24 GRINDER-CHIPPER 2 (809.684-026)
06.04.24 METAL FINISHER (705.684-034)
06.04.24 MOLD DRESSER (519.684-018)
06.04.24 POLISHER (705.684-058)
06.04.26 LABEL CODER (920.587-014)
06.04.26 TRIM-STENCIL MAKER (781.684-058)
06.04.27 BOW MAKER (789.684-010)
06.04.27 CANVAS REPAIRER (782.684-010)
06.04.27 SEWER, HAND (782.684-058)
06.04.27 THREAD CUTTER (789.684-050)
06.04.29 FABRICATOR, FOAM RUBBER (780.684-062)
06.04.33 METAL SPRAYER, PRODUCTION (505.684-014)
06.04.33 PAINTER, BRUSH (740.684-022)
06.04.33 PAINTER, SPRAY 2 (741.687-018)
06.04.33 PUTTY GLAZER (749.684-042)
06.04.33 TOUCH-UP PAINTER, HAND (740.684-026)
06.04.34 DECAL APPLIER (749.684-010)
06.04.34 DRILLER, HAND (809.684-018)
06.04.34 LABORER, GRINDING AND POLISHING
  (705.687-014)
06.04.34 MASKER (749.687-018)
06.04.34 PAINT MIXER, HAND (550.684-018)
06.04.34 SCREEN PRINTER (979.684-034)
06.04.35 PRESSER, FORM (363.685-018)
06.04.35 PRESSER, HAND (363.684-018)
06.04.37 MARKER 2 (920.687-126)
06.04.37 NAME-PLATE STAMPER (652.685-054)
06.04.37 STENCILER (920.687-178)
06.04.37 TICKETER (652.685-098)
06.04.38 CARDER (920.685-034)
06.04.38 CRATER (920.484-010)
06.04.38 PACKAGE SEALER, MACHINE (920.685-074)
06.04.38 PACKAGER, HAND (920.587-018)
06.04.38 PACKAGER, MACHINE (920.685-078)
06.04.39 CLEANER AND POLISHER (709.687-010)
06.04.39 EQUIPMENT CLEANER (599.684-010)
06.04.39 WASHER, MACHINE (599.685-114)
06.04.39 WASHING-MACHINE OPERATOR (599.685-118)
06.04.40 CONVEYOR FEEDER-OFFBEARER (921.686-014)
06.04.40 CONVEYOR TENDER (921.685-026)
06.04.40 INDUSTRIAL-TRUCK OPERATOR (921.683-050)
06.04.40 LABORER, SALVAGE (929.687-022)
06.04.40 LOADER 1 (914.667-010)
06.04.40 PALLETIZER OPERATOR 1 (921.682-014)
07.01.02 ADMINISTRATIVE SECRETARY (169.167-014)
07.01.02 MANAGER, OFFICE (169.167-034)
07.04.05 PROTECTIVE-SIGNAL OPERATOR (379.362-014)

07.05.03 ORDER-DEPARTMENT SUPERVISOR (169.167-038)
07.07.02 ADVERTISING-MATERIAL DISTRIBUTOR
  (230.687-010)
08.02.08 MEMBERSHIP SOLICITOR (293.357-022)
08.02.08 TELEPHONE SOLICITOR (299.357-014)
09.01.01 HOST/HOSTESS (352.667-010)
09.01.02 EXHIBIT-DISPLAY REPRESENTATIVE (297.367-010)
09.01.02 GUIDE, PLANT (353.367-018)
09.03.02 CHAUFFEUR (913.663-010)
09.04.01 CANTEEN OPERATOR (311.674-010)
09.05.03 CHECKROOM ATTENDANT (358.677-010)
09.05.04 DOORKEEPER (324.677-014)
09.05.07 RESTROOM ATTENDANT (358.677-018)
09.05.09 ELEVATOR OPERATOR (388.663-010)
10.03.02 FIRST-AID ATTENDANT (354.677-010)
10.03.03 NURSERY SCHOOL ATTENDANT (359.677-018)
10.03.03 PLAYROOM ATTENDANT (359.677-026)
11.05.01 MANAGER, INDUSTRIAL ORGANIZATION
  (189.117-022)
11.05.01 PRESIDENT (189.117-026)
11.05.02 ADMINISTRATIVE ASSISTANT (169.167-010)
11.05.02 IMPORT-EXPORT AGENT (184.117-022)
11.05.02 MANAGEMENT TRAINEE (189.167-018)
11.05.02 MANAGER, BRANCH (183.117-010)
11.05.02 MANAGER, DEPARTMENT (189.167-022)
11.05.02 MANAGER, TRAFFIC (184.167-094)
11.05.02 SECURITY OFFICER (189.167-034)
11.05.02 SUPERINTENDENT, PLANT PROTECTION
  (189.167-050)
11.05.04 MANAGER, SALES (163.167-018)
11.05.04 PROPERTY-DISPOSAL OFFICER (163.167-026)
11.06.03 APPRAISER (191.287-010)
11.06.03 MANAGER, CREDIT AND COLLECTION
  (168.167-054)
11.07.01 RESIDENCE SUPERVISOR (187.167-186)
11.09.01 MANAGER, ADVERTISING (164.117-010)
11.10.02 EQUAL OPPORTUNITY OFFICER (168.267-114)
11.10.03 INDUSTRIAL-SAFETY-AND-HEALTH TECHNICIAN
  (168.161-014)
11.10.03 SAFETY INSPECTOR (168.264-014)
11.10.03 SANITARIAN (529.137-014)
11.11.03 MANAGER, WAREHOUSE (184.167-114)
11.11.05 COMMISSARY MANAGER (185.167-010)
11.11.05 MANAGER, MACHINERY-OR-EQUIPMENT, RENTAL
  AND LEASING (185.167-026)
11.11.05 SERVICE SUPERVISOR, LEASED MACHINERY AND
  EQUIPMENT (183.167-030)
11.12.02 RIGHT-OF-WAY AGENT (191.117-046)
11.12.04 CONTRACT ADMINISTRATOR (162.117-014)

Artificial Flowers

06.04.34 ARTIFICIAL-FLOWER MAKER (739.684-014)

Asbestos Products

06.01.02 LOOM FIXER (683.260-018)
06.02.06 WEAVER (683.682-038)
06.04.06 BEAM-WARPER TENDER, AUTOMATIC (681.685-018)

Automobile Manufacturing

02.04.01 LABORATORY TECHNICIAN (019.381-010)
05.01.08 AUTOMOTIVE ENGINEER (007.061-010)
05.03.02 AUTO-DESIGN CHECKER (017.261-010)
05.03.02 DRAFTER, AUTOMOTIVE DESIGN (017.281-022)
05.05.02 CUSTOM VAN INSTALLER (860.381-074)
06.03.01 TEST DRIVER 1 (806.281-050)
06.04.22 ASSEMBLER, AUTOMOBILE (806.684-010)
11.12.01 SERVICE REPRESENTATIVE (191.167-022)

Automobile Services

05.05.02 CUSTOM VAN INSTALLER (860.381-074)
05.05.06 AUTOMOBILE-BODY REPAIRER (807.381-010)
05.05.09 AIR-CONDITIONING MECHANIC (620.281-010)
05.05.09 AUTOMOBILE MECHANIC (620.261-010)

05.05.09 AUTOMOBILE-SERVICE-STATION MECHANIC (620.261-030)
05.05.09 AUTOMOTIVE-COOLING-SYSTEM DIAGNOSTIC TECHNICIAN (620.261-034)
05.05.09 TRACTOR MECHANIC (620.281-058)
05.05.09 TUNE-UP MECHANIC (620.281-066)
05.05.10 ELECTRICIAN, AUTOMOTIVE (825.281-022)
05.05.15 AUTOMOBILE UPHOLSTERER (780.381-010)
05.07.01 SHOP ESTIMATOR (807.267-010)
05.08.03 DELIVERER, CAR RENTAL (919.663-010)
05.08.03 TOW-TRUCK OPERATOR (919.663-026)
05.10.01 FRONT-END MECHANIC (620.281-038)
05.10.01 GLASS INSTALLER (865.684-010)
05.10.01 MUFFLER INSTALLER (807.664-010)
05.10.02 AUTOMOBILE-ACCESSORIES INSTALLER (806.684-038)
05.10.02 AUTOMOBILE-RADIATOR MECHANIC (620.381-010)
05.10.02 AUTOMOBILE-SERVICE-STATION ATTENDANT (915.467-010)
05.10.02 BRAKE REPAIRER (620.281-026)
05.10.02 CARBURETOR MECHANIC (620.281-034)
05.10.02 NEW-CAR GET-READY MECHANIC (806.361-026)
05.10.02 SERVICE MANAGER (185.167-058)
05.10.03 ELECTRIC-GOLF-CART REPAIRER (620.261-026)
05.12.08 LUBRICATION SERVICER (915.687-018)
05.12.12 AUTOMOBILE-BODY-REPAIRER HELPER (807.687-010)
05.12.14 UNDERCOATER (843.684-014)
05.12.15 TIRE REPAIRER (915.684-010)
05.12.18 AUTOMOBILE DETAILER (915.687-034)
05.12.18 STEAM CLEANER (915.687-026)
09.04.02 AUTOMOBILE-RENTAL CLERK (295.477-010)
09.04.02 PARKING-LOT ATTENDANT (915.473-010)
09.04.02 TRAILER-RENTAL CLERK (295.467-022)
11.11.05 MANAGER, VEHICLE LEASING AND RENTAL (187.167-162)

Bakery Products

05.05.17 CAKE DECORATOR (524.381-010)
06.02.15 BAKER (526.381-010)
06.02.15 DOUGH MIXER (520.582-010)
06.02.15 DOUGHNUT-MACHINE OPERATOR (526.682-022)
06.02.15 OVEN OPERATOR, AUTOMATIC (526.682-030)
06.02.28 BENCH HAND (520.384-010)
06.02.28 DOUGHNUT MAKER (526.684-010)
06.04.15 BAKER HELPER (526.686-010)
06.04.15 OVEN TENDER (526.685-030)
06.04.28 DECORATOR (524.684-014)
06.04.38 BAKERY WORKER (929.686-010)
11.05.01 MANAGER, BAKERY (189.117-046)

Boilermaking

05.05.06 BOILERMAKER 1 (805.261-014)

Boot and Shoe

06.02.05 STITCHER, STANDARD MACHINE (690.682-082)
06.02.27 COBBLER (788.381-010)
06.04.05 CEMENTER, MACHINE APPLICATOR (690.686-018)

Brick and Tile

06.04.30 TABLE-TOP TILE SETTER (763.684-074)

Brush and Broom

06.02.09 BROOM STITCHER (692.682-022)
06.02.32 BRUSH MATERIAL PREPARER (739.684-022)
06.04.34 BROOMMAKER (739.684-018)

Building Board

06.04.18 DIGESTER-OPERATOR HELPER (532.686-010)

Building Materials, n.e.c.

06.02.18 ROOF-CEMENT-AND-PAINT MAKER (550.382-030)
06.02.18 ROOFING-MACHINE OPERATOR (554.682-022)

Business Services

04.02.02 ARMORED-CAR GUARD (372.567-010)
04.02.02 ARMORED-CAR GUARD AND DRIVER (372.563-010)
04.02.02 SECURITY CONSULTANT (189.167-054)
04.02.04 ALARM INVESTIGATOR (376.367-010)
05.05.05 PROTECTIVE-SIGNAL INSTALLER (822.361-018)
05.05.05 PROTECTIVE-SIGNAL REPAIRER (822.361-022)
05.05.06 SAFE-AND-VAULT SERVICE MECHANIC (869.381-022)
05.07.01 NONDESTRUCTIVE TESTER (011.261-018)
05.07.01 ULTRASONIC TESTER (709.281-018)
05.08.03 TELEPHONE-DIRECTORY-DISTRIBUTOR DRIVER (906.683-018)
05.09.03 CHECKER, DUMP GROUNDS (219.367-010)
05.10.01 WATER-SOFTENER SERVICER-AND-INSTALLER (862.684-034)
05.10.02 MANAGER, CUSTOMER SERVICES (187.167-082)
05.10.05 MICROFICHE DUPLICATOR (976.381-014)
05.10.05 MICROFILM PROCESSOR (976.385-010)
05.10.09 EXTERMINATOR, TERMITE (383.364-010)
05.10.09 FUMIGATOR (383.361-010)
05.12.12 SEWER-PIPE CLEANER (899.664-014)
05.12.14 BILLPOSTER (841.684-010)
07.01.04 VAULT CASHIER (222.137-050)
07.02.02 TAX PREPARER (219.362-070)
07.02.04 ADVERTISING CLERK (247.387-010)
07.03.01 CHECK CASHIER (211.462-026)
07.04.01 BONDING AGENT (186.267-010)
07.04.05 AIRLINE-RADIO OPERATOR (193.262-010)
07.04.06 TELEPHONE-ANSWERING-SERVICE OPERATOR (235.662-026)
07.05.01 TRAFFIC CLERK (221.367-078)
07.05.02 READER (249.387-022)
07.05.03 CALL-OUT OPERATOR (237.367-014)
07.05.03 DOCUMENT PREPARER, MICROFILMING (249.587-018)
07.05.04 VAULT WORKER (222.587-058)
07.06.01 IN-FILE OPERATOR (203.362-014)
07.07.02 PROCESS SERVER (249.367-062)
07.07.02 TELEPHONE-DIRECTORY DELIVERER (230.667-014)
07.07.03 COIN-MACHINE COLLECTOR (292.687-010)
08.01.01 SALES REPRESENTATIVE, GRAPHIC ART (254.251-010)
08.01.02 SALES REPRESENTATIVE, DATA-PROCESSING SERVICES (251.157-014)
08.01.02 SALES REPRESENTATIVE, SECURITY SYSTEMS (259.257-022)
08.01.03 BUSINESS-OPPORTUNITY-AND-PROPERTY-INVESTMENT BROKER (189.157-010)
08.02.06 SALES AGENT, BUSINESS SERVICES (251.357-010)
08.02.06 SALES REPRESENTATIVE, AUTOMOTIVE-LEASING (273.357-014)
08.02.06 SALES REPRESENTATIVE, FRANCHISE (251.357-022)
08.02.06 TRAVEL AGENT (252.157-010)
09.04.02 STORAGE-FACILITY RENTAL CLERK (295.367-026)
09.04.02 TOOL-AND-EQUIPMENT-RENTAL CLERK (295.357-014)
11.02.04 FILM-RENTAL CLERK (295.367-018)
11.05.04 FIELD REPRESENTATIVE (163.267-010)
11.05.04 MANAGER, PROFESSIONAL EQUIPMENT SALES-AND-SERVICE (185.167-042)
11.09.01 ACCOUNT EXECUTIVE (164.167-010)
11.10.03 MARINE-CARGO SURVEYOR (168.267-094)
11.11.04 MANAGER, TRAVEL AGENCY (187.167-158)
11.12.01 APPRAISER, AUTOMOBILE DAMAGE (241.267-014)
11.12.01 CLAIM ADJUSTER (241.217-010)
11.12.01 CLAIM EXAMINER (241.267-018)
11.12.03 LITERARY AGENT (191.117-034)

Canning and Preserving

03.04.01 SORTER, AGRICULTURAL PRODUCE (529.687-186)

05.02.03 MANAGER, FOOD PROCESSING PLANT
(183.167-026)
06.04.15 CANNERY WORKER (529.686-014)
06.04.15 COOK, FRY, DEEP FAT (526.685-014)
06.04.28 FISH CLEANER (525.684-030)

Candles

06.04.32 CANDLEMAKER (739.664-010)

Canvas Goods

06.01.04 CANVAS WORKER (739.381-010)

Carpet and Rug

06.02.05 CARPET SEWER (787.682-014)
06.02.06 CARPET WEAVER (683.682-010)
06.02.27 MENDER (782.684-042)
06.04.27 CARPET CUTTER 2 (585.687-014)

Cement

06.04.08 MILLER (570.685-046)
06.04.17 AUXILIARY-EQUIPMENT TENDER (570.685-010)

Cereal Preparations

06.02.15 OVEN OPERATOR, AUTOMATIC (526.682-030)

Chemical

06.02.11 WASTE-TREATMENT OPERATOR (955.382-014)
06.04.11 CHEMICAL OPERATOR 2 (558.585-014)
06.04.11 CHEMICAL PREPARER 1 (550.685-030)
06.04.11 DRIER OPERATOR (553.685-042)
06.04.40 LABORER, CHEMICAL PROCESSING (559.687-050)

Chewing Gum

06.04.38 FLOOR WORKER (920.687-090)

Chocolate and Cocoa Products

06.02.15 CHOCOLATE-PRODUCTION-MACHINE OPERATOR
(529.382-014)
06.04.15 CHOCOLATE MOLDER, MACHINE (529.685-054)

Cleaning, Dyeing, and Pressing

05.05.15 RUG REPAIRER (782.381-018)
06.04.35 LEATHER FINISHER (363.682-010)
06.04.35 PRESSER, ALL-AROUND (363.682-014)
06.04.35 SILK FINISHER (363.681-010)
09.04.02 SELF-SERVICE-LAUNDRY-AND-DRY-CLEANING
ATTENDANT (369.677-010)
09.04.02 SERVICE-ESTABLISHMENT ATTENDANT
(369.477-014)
11.11.04 MANAGER, SALES (187.167-138)

Clerical and Kindred Occupations

04.02.03 REPOSSESSOR (241.367-022)
05.09.01 INVENTORY CLERK (222.387-026)
05.09.01 LABORATORY CLERK (222.587-026)
05.09.01 PARTS CLERK (222.367-042)
05.09.01 PARTS-ORDER-AND-STOCK CLERK (249.367-058)
05.09.01 SHIPPING AND RECEIVING CLERK (222.387-050)
05.09.01 SHIPPING CHECKER (222.687-030)
05.09.01 SHIPPING-AND-RECEIVING WEIGHER
(222.367-058)
05.09.01 TOOL-CRIB ATTENDANT (222.367-062)
05.09.02 JOB TRACER (221.387-034)
05.09.02 LAUNDRY CLERK (221.387-038)
05.09.02 MATERIAL COORDINATOR (221.167-014)
05.09.02 MATERIAL EXPEDITER (221.367-042)
05.09.02 ORDER DETAILER (221.387-046)
05.09.02 PRODUCTION COORDINATOR (221.167-018)
05.09.02 SALES CORRESPONDENT (221.367-062)
05.09.02 STOCK CLERK (222.387-058)
05.09.03 INDUSTRIAL-ORDER CLERK (221.367-022)
05.09.03 MATERIAL CLERK (222.387-034)

05.09.03 ORDER CALLER (209.667-014)
05.09.03 RECEIVING CHECKER (222.687-018)
05.10.05 DUPLICATING-MACHINE OPERATOR 1
(207.682-010)
05.10.05 OFFSET-DUPLICATING-MACHINE OPERATOR
(207.682-018)
05.12.19 ADDRESSING-MACHINE OPERATOR (208.582-010)
05.12.19 AUXILIARY-EQUIPMENT OPERATOR, DATA
PROCESSING (213.685-010)
05.12.19 BURSTING-MACHINE TENDER (217.685-010)
05.12.19 COIN WRAPPER (217.686-010)
05.12.19 COLLATOR OPERATOR (208.685-010)
05.12.19 FOLDING-MACHINE OPERATOR (208.685-014)
05.12.19 INSERTING-MACHINE OPERATOR (208.685-018)
05.12.19 MICROFILM MOUNTER (208.685-022)
05.12.19 PHOTOCOPYING-MACHINE OPERATOR
(207.685-014)
05.12.19 PHOTOGRAPHIC-MACHINE OPERATOR
(207.685-018)
07.01.02 ADMINISTRATIVE CLERK (219.362-010)
07.01.02 PROCUREMENT CLERK (249.367-066)
07.01.03 LEGAL SECRETARY (201.362-010)
07.01.03 SECRETARY (201.362-030)
07.01.03 SOCIAL SECRETARY (201.162-010)
07.01.04 REAL-ESTATE CLERK (219.362-046)
07.01.07 TEST TECHNICIAN (249.367-078)
07.02.01 BALANCE CLERK (216.382-018)
07.02.01 BOOKKEEPER 1 (210.382-014)
07.02.01 GENERAL-LEDGER BOOKKEEPER (210.382-046)
07.02.02 ACCOUNTING CLERK (216.482-010)
07.02.02 ACCOUNTING CLERK, DATA PROCESSING
(216.382-010)
07.02.02 CALCULATING-MACHINE OPERATOR (216.482-022)
07.02.02 COST CLERK (216.382-034)
07.02.02 POSTING CLERK (216.587-014)
07.02.03 STATISTICAL CLERK (216.382-062)
07.02.04 BILLING CLERK (214.362-042)
07.02.04 INVOICE-CONTROL CLERK (214.362-026)
07.02.04 TAX CLERK 1 (219.487-010)
07.02.04 TRAFFIC CLERK (214.587-014)
07.02.05 PAYROLL CLERK (215.482-010)
07.02.05 TIMEKEEPER (215.367-022)
07.03.01 CASHIER 1 (211.362-010)
07.03.01 CASHIER 2 (211.462-010)
07.04.01 CREDIT CLERK (205.367-022)
07.04.01 EMPLOYMENT CLERK (205.362-014)
07.04.01 IDENTIFICATION CLERK (205.362-022)
07.04.01 SKIP TRACER (241.367-026)
07.04.01 SURVEY WORKER (205.367-054)
07.04.02 COLLECTION CLERK (241.357-010)
07.04.02 CORRESPONDENCE CLERK (209.262-010)
07.04.04 INFORMATION CLERK (237.367-022)
07.04.04 RECEPTIONIST (237.367-038)
07.04.05 DISPATCHER, MAINTENANCE SERVICE
(239.367-014)
07.04.05 SERVICE CLERK (221.367-070)
07.04.06 TELEPHONE OPERATOR (235.662-022)
07.05.01 DISPATCHER, MOTOR VEHICLE (249.167-014)
07.05.01 EXPEDITER (222.367-018)
07.05.01 PERSONNEL SCHEDULER (215.367-014)
07.05.01 RESERVATION CLERK (238.362-014)
07.05.01 SCHEDULER, MAINTENANCE (221.367-066)
07.05.02 CREDIT AUTHORIZER (249.367-022)
07.05.02 DATA-EXAMINATION CLERK (209.387-022)
07.05.03 ASSIGNMENT CLERK (249.367-090)
07.05.03 CLASSIFICATION CLERK (206.387-010)
07.05.03 CODING CLERK (209.387-010)
07.05.03 COMPILER (209.387-014)
07.05.03 FILE CLERK 2 (206.367-014)
07.05.03 INSURANCE CLERK 2 (205.567-010)
07.05.03 ORDER CLERK (249.367-054)
07.05.03 PERSONNEL CLERK (209.362-026)
07.05.03 REFERRAL CLERK, TEMPORARY-HELP AGENCY
(205.367-062)
07.05.03 REPAIR-ORDER CLERK (221.382-022)

07.05.03 REPRODUCTION ORDER PROCESSOR (221.367-058)
07.05.03 SHORTHAND REPORTER (202.362-010)
07.05.03 STENOGRAPHER (202.362-014)
07.05.03 STENOTYPE OPERATOR (202.362-022)
07.05.03 STOCK-CONTROL CLERK (219.367-034)
07.05.03 TAPE LIBRARIAN (206.387-030)
07.05.04 CORRESPONDENCE-REVIEW CLERK (209.367-018)
07.05.04 MAIL CLERK (209.587-026)
07.05.04 PARCEL-POST CLERK (222.387-038)
07.05.04 ROUTE-DELIVERY CLERK (222.587-034)
07.05.04 SHIPPING-ORDER CLERK (219.367-030)
07.06.01 COMPUTER OPERATOR (213.362-010)
07.06.01 COMPUTER-PERIPHERAL-EQUIPMENT
    OPERATOR (213.382-010)
07.06.01 TERMINAL OPERATOR (203.582-054)
07.06.01 TERMINAL-SYSTEM OPERATOR (203.362-018)
07.06.02 ADDING-MACHINE OPERATOR (216.482-014)
07.06.02 CLERK-TYPIST (203.362-010)
07.06.02 CRYPTOGRAPHIC-MACHINE OPERATOR
    (203.582-018)
07.06.02 DATA TYPIST (203.582-022)
07.06.02 DATA-CODER OPERATOR (203.582-026)
07.06.02 KEYPUNCH OPERATOR (203.582-030)
07.06.02 MAGNETIC-TAPE-TYPEWRITER OPERATOR
    (203.582-034)
07.06.02 TELEGRAPHIC-TYPEWRITER OPERATOR
    (203.582-050)
07.06.02 TRANSCRIBING-MACHINE OPERATOR
    (203.582-058)
07.06.02 TYPIST (203.582-066)
07.06.02 VARITYPE OPERATOR (203.382-026)
07.06.02 VERIFIER OPERATOR (203.582-070)
07.06.02 WORD-PROCESSING-MACHINE OPERATOR
    (203.362-022)
07.07.02 ADDRESSER (209.587-010)
07.07.02 CHECKER 1 (222.687-010)
07.07.02 CONTROL CLERK, DATA PROCESSING 2
    (221.687-010)
07.07.02 DELIVERER, OUTSIDE (230.667-010)
07.07.02 DIRECT-MAIL CLERK (209.587-018)
07.07.02 DISTRIBUTING CLERK (222.587-018)
07.07.02 ROUTER (222.587-038)
07.07.02 SORTER (209.687-022)
07.07.03 CLERK, GENERAL (209.562-010)
07.07.03 OFFICE HELPER (239.567-010)
11.01.01 PROGRAMMER, DETAIL (219.367-026)
11.02.04 FILM-OR-TAPE LIBRARIAN (222.367-026)
11.06.03 INVESTIGATOR (241.267-030)

Coated Fabrics

06.02.21 COATING-MACHINE OPERATOR (584.382-010)

Coin-Operated Machines

05.10.02 COIN-MACHINE-SERVICE REPAIRER (639.281-014)

Compressed and Liquified Gases

06.02.12 CYLINDER FILLER (559.565-010)
06.04.40 COMPRESSED-GAS-PLANT WORKER (549.587-010)

Concrete Products

05.11.02 PLANT OPERATOR (570.682-014)
06.04.40 LABORER, CONCRETE PLANT (579.686-010)

Confectionary

06.02.15 CENTER-MACHINE OPERATOR (520.682-014)
06.02.28 CANDY MAKER (529.361-014)
06.04.28 CANDY DIPPER, HAND (524.684-010)
06.04.28 CANDY MOLDER, HAND (520.687-018)
06.04.28 DECORATOR (524.684-014)

Construction

03.01.03 LANDSCAPE CONTRACTOR (182.167-014)
05.01.08 STRUCTURAL ENGINEER (005.061-034)

05.02.02 SUPERINTENDENT, CONSTRUCTION (182.167-026)
05.03.06 CONSTRUCTION INSPECTOR (182.267-010)
05.05.01 BRICKLAYER (861.381-018)
05.05.01 CEMENT MASON (844.364-010)
05.05.01 MARBLE FINISHER (861.664-010)
05.05.01 TERRAZZO FINISHER (861.664-014)
05.05.01 TERRAZZO WORKER (861.381-046)
05.05.01 TILE FINISHER (861.664-018)
05.05.01 TILE SETTER (861.381-054)
05.05.02 CARPENTER (860.381-022)
05.05.02 CARPENTER, ROUGH (860.381-042)
05.05.03 PLUMBER (862.381-030)
05.05.04 DRY-WALL APPLICATOR (842.381-010)
05.05.04 PAPERHANGER (841.381-010)
05.05.04 PLASTERER (842.361-010)
05.05.05 CABLE SPLICER (829.361-010)
05.05.05 LINE ERECTOR (821.361-018)
05.05.05 TOWER ERECTOR (821.361-038)
05.05.05 WIND-GENERATING-ELECTRIC-POWER
    INSTALLER (821.381-018)
05.05.06 CONDUIT MECHANIC (869.361-010)
05.05.06 ELEVATOR CONSTRUCTOR (825.361-010)
05.05.06 STRUCTURAL-STEEL WORKER (801.361-014)
05.05.09 CONSTRUCTION-EQUIPMENT MECHANIC
    (620.261-022)
05.08.03 CONCRETE-MIXING-TRUCK DRIVER (900.683-010)
05.10.01 DRY-WALL APPLICATOR (842.681-010)
05.10.01 FENCE ERECTOR (869.684-022)
05.10.01 FLOOR LAYER (864.481-010)
05.10.01 GLAZIER (865.381-010)
05.10.01 INSULATION WORKER (863.364-014)
05.10.01 LATHER (842.361-010)
05.10.01 ROOFER (866.381-010)
05.10.01 SIDER (863.684-014)
05.10.01 SWIMMING POOL INSTALLER-AND-SERVICER
    (869.463-010)
05.10.01 TAPER (842.664-010)
05.10.01 TILE SETTER HELPER (869.664-014)
05.10.03 AUTOMATIC-DOOR MECHANIC (829.281-010)
05.10.04 MANAGER, CAMP (187.167-066)
05.10.07 PAINTER (840.381-010)
05.11.01 ASPHALT-PAVING-MACHINE OPERATOR
    (853.663-010)
05.11.01 ROAD-ROLLER OPERATOR (859.683-030)
05.11.01 ROCK-DRILL OPERATOR 1 (850.683-034)
05.11.01 SEPTIC-TANK INSTALLER (851.663-010)
05.11.02 PLANT OPERATOR (570.682-014)
05.12.03 CONSTRUCTION WORKER 2 (869.687-026)
05.12.04 LABORER, CONCRETE-MIXING PLANT
    (579.665-014)
05.12.12 PIPE-FITTER HELPER (862.684-022)
05.12.14 ASPHALT-DISTRIBUTOR TENDER (853.665-010)
05.12.16 CABLE PULLER (829.684-018)
07.01.02 LABOR EXPEDITER (249.167-018)
11.12.04 CONTRACTOR (182.167-010)

Corn Products

06.04.15 MILL OPERATOR (521.685-226)

Dairy Products

05.08.01 MILK DRIVER (905.483-010)
05.10.08 FORMULA-ROOM WORKER (520.487-014)
06.01.04 CHEESEMAKER (529.361-018)
06.02.15 BUTTERMAKER (529.362-010)
06.02.15 DAIRY-PROCESSING-EQUIPMENT OPERATOR
    (529.382-018)
06.02.15 FREEZER OPERATOR (529.482-010)
06.04.15 CENTRIFUGE OPERATOR (521.685-042)
06.04.15 CHEESE CUTTER (529.585-010)
06.04.15 COOKER, PROCESS CHEESE (526.665-010)

Distilled Liquors

06.04.40 DISTILLERY WORKER, GENERAL (529.687-066)

Domestic Service

05.10.08 COOK (305.281-010)
05.12.18 CARETAKER (301.687-010)
10.03.03 CHILDREN'S TUTOR (099.227-010)

Drug Preparations and Related Products

02.04.02 LABORATORY ASSISTANT, BLOOD AND PLASMA
(078.687-010)
02.04.02 LABORATORY ASSISTANT, CULTURE MEDIA
(559.384-010)
02.04.02 MICROBIOLOGY TECHNOLOGIST (078.261-014)
02.04.02 TOXICOLOGIST (022.081-010)
05.02.03 QUALITY-CONTROL COORDINATOR (168.167-066)
06.03.02 INSPECTOR (559.387-014)
06.04.11 CENTRIFUGE OPERATOR, PLASMA PROCESSING
(599.685-018)
06.04.11 DRIER OPERATOR (553.685-042)
06.04.19 LABORER (559.686-022)
06.04.19 STERILIZER (599.585-010)

Education and Instruction

01.04.01 TEACHER, MUSIC (152.021-010)
01.05.01 INSTRUCTOR, DANCING (151.027-014)
05.04.01 INSTRUCTOR, FLYING 2 (097.227-010)
07.01.01 FINANCIAL-AID COUNSELOR (169.267-018)
07.01.02 TEACHER AIDE II (249.367-074)
07.01.05 ADMISSIONS EVALUATOR (205.367-010)
07.01.06 ATTENDANCE OFFICER (168.367-010)
07.02.03 GRADING CLERK (219.467-010)
07.05.03 ATTENDANCE CLERK (219.362-014)
07.06.02 BRAILLE TYPIST (203.582-014)
09.03.03 INSTRUCTOR, DRIVING (099.223-010)
10.01.02 RESIDENCE COUNSELOR (045.107-038)
10.02.02 ATHLETIC TRAINER (153.224-010)
10.02.02 ORIENTATION THERAPIST FOR THE BLIND
(076.221-010)
10.02.03 EDUCATIONAL THERAPIST (094.227-010)
10.02.03 EVALUATOR (094.267-010)
10.02.03 TEACHER, BLIND (094.227-014)
10.02.03 TEACHER, DEAF STUDENTS (094.224-010)
10.02.03 TEACHER, HANDICAPPED STUDENTS (094.227-018)
10.02.03 TEACHER, MENTALLY-RETARDED STUDENTS
(094.227-022)
10.02.03 TEACHER, PRESCHOOL (092.227-018)
10.02.03 TEACHER, VOCATIONAL TRAINING (094.227-026)
10.02.03 WORK-STUDY COORDINATOR, SPECIAL
EDUCATION (094.107-010)
11.02.01 FACULTY MEMBER, COLLEGE OR UNIVERSITY
(090.227-010)
11.02.01 INSTRUCTOR, BUSINESS EDUCATION (090.222-010)
11.02.01 INSTRUCTOR, EXTENSION WORK (090.227-018)
11.02.01 TEACHER AIDE I (099.327-010)
11.02.01 TEACHER, ADULT EDUCATION (099.227-030)
11.02.01 TEACHER, ELEMENTARY SCHOOL (092.227-010)
11.02.01 TEACHER, RESOURCE (099.227-042)
11.02.01 TEACHER, SECONDARY SCHOOL (091.227-010)
11.02.01 TUTOR (099.227-034)
11.02.02 INSTRUCTOR, TECHNICAL TRAINING (166.221-010)
11.02.02 INSTRUCTOR, VOCATIONAL TRAINING
(097.227-014)
11.02.02 TRAINING REPRESENTATIVE (166.227-010)
11.02.04 CAREER-GUIDANCE TECHNICIAN (249.367-014)
11.07.03 CONSULTANT, EDUCATION (099.167-014)
11.07.03 DIRECTOR, EDUCATIONAL PROGRAM (099.117-010)
11.07.03 EDUCATIONAL SPECIALIST (099.167-022)
11.07.03 FINANCIAL-AIDS OFFICER (090.117-030)
11.07.03 TECHNICAL TRAINING COORDINATOR
(166.167-054)
12.01.01 INSTRUCTOR, SPORTS (153.227-018)

Electrical Equipment

05.10.03 APPLIANCE REPAIRER (723.584-010)
06.01.02 FIRESETTER (692.360-018)
06.01.03 MACHINE SET-UP OPERATOR (600.380-018)

06.01.04 ELECTRIC-MOTOR-CONTROL ASSEMBLER
(721.381-014)
06.01.04 TRANSFORMER ASSEMBLER (820.381-014)
06.02.23 CAPACITOR ASSEMBLER (729.684-014)
06.02.23 ELECTRICAL-CONTROL ASSEMBLER (729.684-026)
06.02.23 LAMINATION ASSEMBLER (729.484-010)
06.02.32 CABLE MAKER (728.684-010)
06.04.23 ASSEMBLER (723.684-010)
06.04.23 COIL WINDER (724.684-026)
06.04.23 ELECTRIC-MOTOR ASSEMBLER (721.684-022)
06.04.34 WIREWORKER (728.684-022)

Electronics

02.04.01 CALIBRATION LABORATORY TECHNICIAN
(019.281-010)
05.01.01 LASER TECHNICIAN (019.181-010)
05.01.06 TOOL PROGRAMMER, NUMERICAL CONTROL
(609.262-010)
05.03.02 DESIGN TECHNICIAN, COMPUTER-AIDED
(003.362-010)
05.03.02 TAPER, PRINTED CIRCUIT LAYOUT (017.684-010)
05.05.05 ELECTRONICS ASSEMBLER, DEVELOPMENTAL
(726.261-010)
05.05.05 FIELD ENGINEER (828.261-014)
05.09.01 PRODUCTION TECHNICIAN, SEMICONDUCTOR
PROCESSING EQUIPMENT (590.384-014)
05.10.03 PRODUCTION REPAIRER (726.381-014)
05.10.05 PHOTOGRAPHIC-PLATE MAKER (714.381-018)
06.01.02 FIRESETTER (692.360-018)
06.01.03 MICROELECTRONICS TECHNICIAN (590.362-022)
06.01.04 TUBE ASSEMBLER, ELECTRON (725.384-010)
06.01.05 ELECTRONICS INSPECTOR I (726.381-014)
06.01.05 ELECTRONICS TESTER I (726.281-014)
06.01.05 RETICLE INSPECTOR (719.361-010)
06.01.05 TEST TECHNICIAN, SEMICONDUCTOR
PROCESSING EQUIPMENT (590.262-014)
06.02.02 LASER-BEAM-TRIM OPERATOR (726.682-010)
06.02.09 CRYSTAL SLICER (677.382-018)
06.02.09 NUMERICAL CONTROL ROUTER OPERATOR,
PRINTED CIRCUIT BOARDS (605.382-046)
06.02.09 WIRE-WRAPPING-MACHINE OPERATOR
(726.682-014)
06.02.18 CRYSTAL GROWER (590.382-014)
06.02.18 CRYSTAL GROWING TECHNICIAN (590.262-010)
06.02.18 IMPREGNATOR (590.682-014)
06.02.18 ION IMPLANT MACHINE OPERATOR (590.382-022)
06.02.21 PLATER, PRINTED CIRCUIT BOARD PANELS
(500.684-026)
06.02.23 ASSEMBLER, SEMICONDUCTOR (726.684-034)
06.02.23 ELECTRONICS ASSEMBLER (726.684-018)
06.02.23 PRINTED CIRCUIT BOARD ASSEMBLER, HAND
(726.684-070)
06.02.23 TUBE ASSEMBLER, CATHODE RAY (725.684-022)
06.02.32 CABLE MAKER (728.684-010)
06.02.32 CHARGE PREPARATION TECHNICIAN (590.384-010)
06.02.32 ETCHED-CIRCUIT PROCESSOR (590.684-018)
06.03.02 ELECTRONICS INSPECTOR II (726.684-022)
06.03.02 ELECTRONICS TESTER II (726.684-026)
06.03.02 INSPECTOR, INTEGRATED CIRCUITS (726.684-058)
06.03.02 INSPECTOR, PRINTED CIRCUIT BOARDS
(726.684-062)
06.03.02 INSPECTOR, SEMICONDUCTOR WAFER
(726.684-066)
06.04.02 MAGNETIC-TAPE WINDER (726.685-010)
06.04.08 CERAMIC CAPACITOR PROCESSOR (590.684-010)
06.04.09 PHOTORESIST LAMINATOR, PRINTED CIRCUIT
BOARD (699.685-042)
06.04.11 CHEMICAL PREPARER 1 (550.685-030)
06.04.19 COATING EQUIPMENT OPERATOR, PRINTED
CIRCUIT BOARDS (590.685-066)
06.04.19 DISPLAY-SCREEN FABRICATOR (725.685-010)
06.04.19 ELECTRONIC-COMPONENT PROCESSOR
(590.684-014)
06.04.19 ETCHER-STRIPPER, PRINTED CIRCUIT BOARDS
(590.685-082)

06.04.19 HEAT TREATER (504.686-022)
06.04.19 METALLIZATION EQUIPMENT OPERATOR, SEMICONDUCTOR WAFERS (590.685-086)
06.04.19 PLATER, SEMICONDUCTOR WAFERS AND COMPONENTS (500.684-030)
06.04.19 POLYSILICON PREPARATION WORKER (590.684-038)
06.04.19 SEMICONDUCTOR PROCESSOR (590.684-022)
06.04.21 ELECTROLESS PLATER, PRINTED CIRCUIT BOARD PANELS (501.685-022)
06.04.23 COIL WINDER (724.684-026)
06.04.34 ELECTRONICS UTILITY WORKER (726.367-014)
06.04.34 ELECTRONICS WORKER (726.687-010)
06.04.34 PHOTO MASK CLEANER (590.684-034)
06.04.34 WIREWORKER (728.684-022)
06.04.37 MARKER, SEMICONDUCTOR WAFERS (920.587-026)

Electroplating

06.02.21 PLATER (500.380-010)
06.04.21 PLATER, PRODUCTION (500.665-010)

Engine and Turbine

05.05.09 MACHINERY ERECTOR (638.261-014)
06.02.22 ASSEMBLER, INTERNAL COMBUSTION ENGINE (806.481-014)

Engraving, Chasing, & Etching

01.06.01 ENGRAVER, HAND, HARD METALS (704.381-026)
01.06.01 ENGRAVER, HAND, SOFT METALS (704.381-030)
01.06.01 ETCHER (704.684-010)
05.10.05 ENGRAVER, MACHINE 1 (704.682-010)
06.04.24 SILK-SCREEN ETCHER (704.684-014)

Explosives

06.02.09 DYNAMITE-PACKING-MACHINE OPERATOR (692.662-010)
06.04.40 NITROGLYCERIN DISTRIBUTOR (559.664-010)

Fabricated Metal Products, n.e.c.

05.05.06 ORNAMENTAL-METAL WORKER (619.260-008)

Fabricated Plastics Products

06.02.02 PRESS OPERATOR (690.682-062)
06.03.01 INSPECTOR (559.381-010)
06.04.10 INJECTION-MOLDING-MACHINE TENDER (556.685-038)
06.04.13 COMPRESSION-MOLDING-MACHINE TENDER (556.685-022)

Fabricated Products, n.e.c.

06.04.23 TIRE MOUNTER (739.684-158)

Felt Goods

06.02.05 FELTING-MACHINE OPERATOR (586.662-010)
06.04.16 MACHINE FEEDER, RAW STOCK (680.686-018)

Financial Institutions

05.12.19 COIN-MACHINE OPERATOR (217.585-010)
05.12.19 CURRENCY SORTER (217.485-010)
07.01.01 LOAN COUNSELOR (186.267-014)
07.01.04 LOAN CLOSER (249.367-050)
07.01.04 MORTGAGE CLERK (249.382-010)
07.02.01 RECONCILEMENT CLERK (210.382-058)
07.02.01 RESERVES CLERK (216.362-034)
07.02.02 BROKERAGE CLERK 1 (219.482-010)
07.02.02 CHECK-PROCESSING CLERK 1 (216.387-010)
07.02.02 COLLECTION CLERK (216.362-014)
07.02.02 COUPON CLERK (219.462-010)
07.02.02 FEE CLERK (214.362-018)
07.02.02 PROBATE CLERK (216.362-030)
07.02.02 STATEMENT CLERK (219.362-058)

07.02.02 TELLER, COLLECTION AND EXCHANGE (211.362-022)
07.02.02 TRUST-SECURITIES CLERK (219.362-062)
07.03.01 TELLER (211.362-018)
07.03.01 TELLER, HEAD (211.132-010)
07.03.01 TELLER, NOTE (211.362-026)
07.04.01 LOAN INTERVIEWER (241.367-018)
07.04.01 NEW-ACCOUNTS CLERK (205.362-026)
07.05.02 DISBURSEMENT CLERK (209.367-022)
07.05.02 LETTER-OF-CREDIT CLERK (219.387-018)
07.05.03 CREDIT-CARD-CONTROL CLERK (249.367-026)
07.05.03 MORTGAGE-PROCESSING CLERK (203.382-022)
07.05.03 RECORDS CUSTODIAN (206.387-026)
07.05.04 MESSENGER, BANK (230.367-014)
07.06.02 PROOF-MACHINE OPERATOR (217.382-010)
07.06.02 WIRES-TRANSFER CLERK (203.562-010)
08.01.02 SALES AGENT, FINANCIAL SERVICES (251.257-010)
08.01.03 FOREIGN BANKNOTE TELLER-TRADER (211.362-014)
11.01.02 FINANCIAL ANALYST (020.167-014)
11.04.04 CUSTOMS-HOUSE BROKER (186.117-018)
11.05.02 MANAGER, FINANCIAL INSTITUTION (186.117-038)
11.06.01 OPERATIONS OFFICER (186.167-050)
11.06.03 CREDIT ANALYST (191.267-014)
11.06.03 FACTORER (186.117-026)
11.06.03 FOREIGN-EXCHANGE TRADER (186.167-014)
11.06.03 LOAN OFFICER (186.267-018)
11.06.03 NEGOTIATOR, LETTER OF CREDIT (186.117-050)
11.06.03 SECURITIES TRADER 1 (162.157-042)
11.06.03 SECURITIES TRADER 2 (186.167-058)
11.06.04 SALES AGENT, SECURITIES (251.157-010)
11.06.05 TRUST OFFICER (186.117-074)

Firearms

06.01.03 MACHINE SET-UP OPERATOR (600.380-018)

Fisheries

03.01.02 FISH FARMER (446.161-010)
03.01.02 SHELLFISH GROWER (446.161-014)
03.04.03 DECKHAND, FISHING VESSEL (449.667-010)
03.04.03 FISH HATCHERY WORKER (446.684-010)
03.04.03 FISHER, DIVING (443.664-010)
03.04.03 FISHER, LINE (442.684-010)
03.04.03 FISHER, NET (441.684-010)
03.04.03 SHELLFISH DREDGE OPERATOR (446.663-010)
03.04.03 SKIFF OPERATOR (441.683-010)
06.04.28 FISH CLEANER (525.684-030)

Flavoring Extract and Syrup

06.02.15 SIRUP MAKER (520.485-026)

Food Preparation, n.e.c.

06.01.01 COOK, MEXICAN FOOD (526.134-010)
06.02.15 COFFEE ROASTER (523.682-014)
06.04.15 COFFEE GRINDER (521.685-078)
06.04.15 HONEY PROCESSOR (522.685-070)
06.04.15 MIXING-MACHINE OPERATOR (520.665-014)
06.04.15 YEAST-CUTTING-AND-WRAPPING-MACHINE OPERATOR (529.665-022)

Forestry

03.01.04 LOGGING-OPERATIONS INSPECTOR (168.267-070)
03.02.02 FORESTER AIDE (452.364-010)
03.04.01 CHRISTMAS-TREE FARM WORKER (451.687-010)
03.04.02 FOREST WORKER (452.687-010)
03.04.02 FOREST-FIRE FIGHTER (452.687-014)
04.01.02 FIRE WARDEN (452.167-010)
04.02.02 FIRE RANGER (452.367-014)
04.02.04 SMOKE JUMPER (452.364-014)
07.04.05 FIRE LOOKOUT (452.367-010)

Forging

05.05.06 BLACKSMITH (610.381-010)

06.02.02 DROP-HAMMER OPERATOR (610.462-010)
06.02.02 HEATER (619.682-022)

Foundries

05.01.01 FOUNDRY METALLURGIST (011.061-010)
05.05.07 PATTERNMAKER, METAL (600.280-050)
06.01.04 COREMAKER (518.381-014)
06.01.04 MOLDER (518.361-010)
06.02.10 SAND MIXER, MACHINE (570.682-018)
06.04.08 COREMAKER, MACHINE 1 (518.685-014)
06.04.09 WAX MOLDER (549.685-038)
06.04.10 DIE-CASTING-MACHINE OPERATOR 2 (514.685-018)
06.04.17 SHELL MOLDER (518.685-026)
06.04.32 MACHINE MOLDER (518.682-010)

Fuel Briquettes

06.02.17 BRIQUETTE-MACHINE OPERATOR (549.662-010)
06.04.03 ARTIFICIAL-LOG-MACHINE OPERATOR
(569.685-010)

Fur Goods

05.05.15 FURRIER (783.261-010)

Furniture

01.02.03 FURNITURE DESIGNER (142.061-022)
01.06.02 DISTRESSER (763.687-018)
05.10.01 FRAME REPAIRER (763.681-010)
05.10.01 REPAIRER (709.684-062)
06.02.22 CABINET ASSEMBLER (763.684-014)
06.02.22 FURNITURE ASSEMBLER (763.684-038)
06.04.22 LAMINATOR, HAND (763.684-050)
06.04.22 PLASTIC-TOP ASSEMBLER (763.684-062)
06.04.25 CANER 2 (763.684-022)

Galvanizing and Other Coating

06.04.21 PLATER, HOT DIP (501.685-010)

Garment

05.05.15 ALTERATION TAILOR (785.261-010)
05.05.15 CUSTOM TAILOR (785.261-014)
05.05.15 SHOP TAILOR (785.361-022)
06.02.05 TRIMMER, MACHINE (781.682-010)
06.04.05 BUTTONHOLE-AND-BUTTON-SEWING-MACHINE
OPERATOR (786.685-042)

Glass Manufacturing

06.01.04 GLASS BLOWER (772.681-010)
06.02.13 BLANKMAKER (579.382-022)

Glass Products

05.05.11 SCIENTIFIC GLASS BLOWER (006.261-010)
06.04.30 GLASS FINISHER (775.684-026)

Gloves and Mittens

06.04.05 GLOVE TURNER AND FORMER, AUTOMATIC
(583.686-018)

Gold Leaf and Foil

06.01.04 GOLDBEATER (700.381-018)
06.04.24 LABORER, GOLD LEAF (700.687-038)

Government Services

01.02.03 POLICE ARTIST (141.061-034)
02.02.01 ENVIRONMENTAL EPIDEMIOLOGIST (041.167-010)
02.04.01 BALLISTICS EXPERT, FORENSIC (199.267-010)
02.04.01 FINGERPRINT CLASSIFIER (375.387-010)
02.04.02 PUBLIC-HEALTH MICROBIOLOGIST (041.261-010)
02.04.02 VECTOR CONTROL ASSISTANT (049.364-014)
03.04.04 GROUNDSKEEPER, PARKS AND GROUNDS
(406.687-010)
03.04.05 DOG CATCHER (379.673-010)

04.01.01 DEPUTY, COURT (377.137-018)
04.01.01 HARBOR MASTER (375.167-026)
04.01.02 CUSTOMS PATROL OFFICER (168.167-010)
04.01.02 FISH AND GAME WARDEN (379.167-010)
04.01.02 POLICE OFFICER 1 (375.263-014)
04.01.02 POLICE OFFICER III (375.267-038)
04.01.02 SHERIFF, DEPUTY (377.263-010)
04.01.02 SPECIAL AGENT (375.167-042)
04.02.01 CORRECTION OFFICER (372.667-018)
04.02.01 GUARD, IMMIGRATION (372.567-014)
04.02.01 JAILER (372.367-014)
04.02.02 PARKING ENFORCEMENT OFFICER (375.587-010)
04.02.03 BAILIFF (377.667-010)
04.02.03 BORDER GUARD (375.363-010)
04.02.03 PARK RANGER (169.167-042)
04.02.03 SURVEILLANCE-SYSTEM MONITOR (379.367-010)
05.01.02 RADIATION-PROTECTION ENGINEER (015.137-010)
05.01.02 RESOURCE-RECOVERY ENGINEER (019.167-018)
05.03.03 AIR-TRAFFIC-CONTROL SPECIALIST, STATION
(193.162-014)
05.03.03 AIR-TRAFFIC-CONTROL SPECIALIST, TOWER
(193.162-018)
05.03.06 CODE INSPECTOR (168.367-018)
05.03.06 INSPECTOR, AIR-CARRIER (168.264-010)
05.03.06 INSPECTOR, BUILDING (168.167-030)
05.03.06 INSPECTOR, INDUSTRIAL WASTE (168.267-054)
05.03.06 INSPECTOR, QUALITY ASSURANCE (168.287-014)
05.03.06 INSPECTOR, RAILROAD (168.287-018)
05.03.06 PLAN CHECKER (168.267-102)
05.05.09 MAIL-PROCESSING-EQUIPMENT MECHANIC
(633.261-014)
05.05.11 FIRE-CONTROL MECHANIC (632.261-014)
05.11.01 STREET-SWEEPER OPERATOR (919.683-022)
05.12.12 HIGHWAY-MAINTENANCE WORKER (899.684-014)
05.12.18 STREET CLEANER (955.687-018)
07.01.01 CONTACT REPRESENTATIVE (169.167-018)
07.01.01 ELIGIBILITY WORKER (195.267-010)
07.01.01 ELIGIBILITY-AND-OCCUPANCY INTERVIEWER
(168.267-038)
07.01.01 RETIREMENT OFFICER (166.267-030)
07.01.02 COORDINATOR, SKILL-TRAINING PROGRAM
(169.167-062)
07.01.02 COURT CLERK (243.362-010)
07.01.02 TOWN CLERK (243.367-018)
07.01.05 EXAMINER (169.267-014)
07.01.05 PASSPORT-APPLICATION EXAMINER (169.267-030)
07.01.06 CASEWORKER (169.262-010)
07.01.06 IDENTIFICATION OFFICER (377.264-010)
07.01.07 DRIVER'S LICENSE EXAMINER (168.267-034)
07.01.07 EXAMINATION PROCTOR (199.267-018)
07.03.01 POST-OFFICE CLERK (243.367-014)
07.03.01 TOLL COLLECTOR (211.462-038)
07.04.01 EMPLOYMENT-AND-CLAIMS AIDE (169.367-010)
07.04.01 REGISTRATION CLERK (205.367-042)
07.04.01 TRAFFIC CHECKER (205.367-058)
07.04.02 REFERRAL-AND-INFORMATION AIDE (237.367-042)
07.04.03 ELECTION CLERK (205.367-030)
07.04.03 LICENSE CLERK (205.367-034)
07.04.03 PARK AIDE (249.367-082)
07.04.03 PUBLIC HEALTH REGISTRAR (169.167-046)
07.04.04 LAND-LEASING EXAMINER (237.367-026)
07.04.05 ALARM OPERATOR (379.162-010)
07.04.05 POLICE AIDE (243.362-014)
07.04.05 SWITCHBOARD OPERATOR, POLICE DISTRICT
(235.562-014)
07.04.05 TELECOMMUNICATOR (379.362-018)
07.05.01 POLICE CLERK (375.362-010)
07.05.03 FINGERPRINT CLERK 2 (206.387-014)
07.05.03 IDENTIFICATION TECHNICIAN (209.362-022)
07.05.03 PROPERTY CLERK (222.367-054)
07.05.04 MAIL CARRIER (230.367-010)
07.05.04 MAIL HANDLER (209.687-014)
07.07.03 COIN-MACHINE COLLECTOR (292.687-010)
09.04.01 VENDING-STAND SUPERVISOR (185.167-066)
10.01.02 COMMUNITY WORKER (195.367-018)

10.01.02 FOOD-MANAGEMENT AIDE (195.367-022)
10.01.02 VOCATIONAL-REHABILITATION COUNSELOR (045.107-042)
10.03.03 GUARD, SCHOOL-CROSSING (371.567-010)
11.02.03 COUNTY HOME-DEMONSTRATION AGENT (096.121-010)
11.02.03 COUNTY-AGRICULTURAL AGENT (096.127-010)
11.02.03 EXTENSION SERVICE SPECIALIST (096.127-014)
11.03.02 PLANNER, PROGRAM SERVICES (188.167-110)
11.04.01 APPEALS REFEREE (119.267-014)
11.04.01 HEARING OFFICER (119.107-010)
11.04.03 ADJUDICATOR (119.167-010)
11.05.03 DIRECTOR, REGULATORY AGENCY (188.117-134)
11.05.03 ENVIRONMENTAL ANALYST (199.167-022)
11.05.03 HOUSING-MANAGEMENT OFFICER (188.117-110)
11.05.03 LEGISLATIVE ASSISTANT (169.167-066)
11.05.03 MANAGER, CITY (188.117-114)
11.05.03 MANAGER, OFFICE (188.167-058)
11.05.03 MANAGER, REGULATED PROGRAM (168.167-090)
11.05.03 POSTMASTER (188.167-066)
11.05.03 SECRETARY OF STATE (188.167-082)
11.06.01 REVENUE AGENT (160.167-050)
11.06.03 APPRAISER (188.167-010)
11.06.03 DIRECTOR, UTILITY ACCOUNTS (160.267-014)
11.06.03 PERSONAL PROPERTY ASSESSOR (191.367-010)
11.06.05 BUDGET ANALYST (161.267-030)
11.06.05 BUDGET OFFICER (161.117-010)
11.07.01 REHABILITATION CENTER MANAGER (195.167-038)
11.07.02 CIVIL PREPAREDNESS TRAINING OFFICER (169.127-010)
11.07.02
    COMMUNITY-SERVICES-AND-HEALTH-EDUCATION OFFICER (079.167-010)
11.07.03 PARK NATURALIST (049.127-010)
11.07.03 VOCATIONAL REHABILITATION CONSULTANT (094.117-018)
11.09.03 FOREIGN-SERVICE OFFICER (188.117-106)
11.10.01 CHIEF BANK EXAMINER (160.167-046)
11.10.01 INSPECTOR, GOVERNMENT PROPERTY (168.267-050)
11.10.01 INVESTIGATOR (168.267-062)
11.10.01 REVENUE OFFICER (188.167-074)
11.10.02 DIRECTOR, COMPLIANCE (188.117-046)
11.10.02 EQUAL-OPPORTUNITY REPRESENTATIVE (168.167-014)
11.10.03 CHEMICAL-RADIATION TECHNICIAN (015.261-010)
11.10.03 FOOD AND DRUG INSPECTOR (168.267-042)
11.10.03 HAZARDOUS-WASTE MANAGEMENT SPECIALIST (168.267-086)
11.10.03 HEALTH OFFICER, FIELD (168.167-018)
11.10.03 INSPECTOR, AGRICULTURAL COMMODITIES (168.287-010)
11.10.03 INSPECTOR, HEALTH CARE FACILITIES (168.167-042)
11.10.03 INSPECTOR, MOTOR VEHICLES (168.267-058)
11.10.03 INSPECTOR, WATER-POLLUTION CONTROL (168.267-090)
11.10.03 OCCUPATIONAL-SAFETY-AND-HEALTH INSPECTOR (168.167-062)
11.10.03 PESTICIDE-CONTROL INSPECTOR (168.267-098)
11.10.03 PUBLIC HEALTH SERVICE OFFICER (187.117-050)
11.10.03 RADIATION-PROTECTION SPECIALIST (168.261-010)
11.10.03 REVIEWING OFFICER, DRIVER'S LICENSE (168.167-074)
11.10.03 SANITATION INSPECTOR (168.267-110)
11.10.04 CUSTOMS IMPORT SPECIALIST (168.267-018)
11.10.04 CUSTOMS INSPECTOR (168.267-022)
11.10.04 IMMIGRATION INSPECTOR (168.167-022)
11.12.01 CLAIMS ADJUDICATOR (169.267-010)
11.12.02 PROPERTY-UTILIZATION OFFICER (188.117-122)

Grain and Feed Milling

06.02.15 GRINDER OPERATOR (521.682-026)
06.04.15 FLOUR BLENDER (520.685-106)

Hairwork

01.06.02 WIG DRESSER (332.361-010)

Hardware

06.04.23 LOCK ASSEMBLER (706.684-074)

Hat and Cap

06.02.05 HAT-AND-CAP SEWER (784.682-014)
06.02.27 BLOCKER, HAND 1 (580.684-010)
06.04.16 HARDENING-MACHINE OPERATOR (586.685-026)

Heat Treating

06.02.10 HEAT TREATER 1 (504.382-014)

Hosiery

06.01.02 KNITTING-MACHINE FIXER (689.280-014)
06.02.06 SEAMLESS-HOSIERY KNITTER (684.685-010)

Hotel and Restaurant

05.05.17 ANALYST, FOOD AND BEVERAGE (310.267-010)
05.05.17 CHEF (313.131-014)
05.05.17 CHEF DE FROID (313.281-010)
05.05.17 COOK (313.361-014)
05.05.17 SOUS CHEF (313.131-026)
05.09.01 LINEN-ROOM ATTENDANT (222.387-030)
05.10.08 BAKER (313.381-010)
05.10.08 BAKER, HEAD (313.131-010)
05.10.08 BAKER, PIZZA (313.381-014)
05.10.08 BUTCHER, MEAT (316.681-010)
05.10.08 CARVER (316.661-010)
05.10.08 COOK, BARBECUE (313.381-022)
05.10.08 COOK, PASTRY (313.381-026)
05.10.08 COOK, SHORT ORDER 1 (313.361-022)
05.10.08 COOK, SHORT ORDER 2 (313.671-010)
05.10.08 COOK, SPECIALTY (313.361-026)
05.10.08 GARDE MANGER (313.361-034)
05.10.08 PANTRY GOODS MAKER (317.684-014)
05.10.08 PASTRY CHEF (313.131-022)
05.10.08 PIE MAKER (313.361-038)
05.12.17 COFFEE MAKER (317.684-010)
05.12.17 COOK HELPER (317.687-010)
05.12.17 FOOD ASSEMBLER, KITCHEN (319.484-010)
05.12.17 SANDWICH MAKER (317.684-018)
05.12.18 BARTENDER HELPER (312.687-010)
05.12.18 HOUSEKEEPER (321.137-010)
05.12.18 KITCHEN HELPER (318.687-010)
06.04.15 COOK, FRY, DEEP FAT (526.685-014)
07.02.02 NIGHT AUDITOR (210.382-054)
07.04.03 HOTEL CLERK (238.362-010)
07.06.02 FOOD TABULATOR, CAFETERIA (211.582-010)
08.01.02 SALES REPRESENTATIVE, HOTEL SERVICES (259.157-014)
09.01.01 DIRECTOR, SOCIAL (352.167-010)
09.01.03 HOST/HOSTESS, RESTAURANT (310.137-010)
09.01.03 WAITER/WAITRESS, CAPTAIN (311.137-018)
09.04.01 BARTENDER (312.474-010)
09.04.01 CAR HOP (311.477-010)
09.04.01 COUNTER ATTENDANT, LUNCHROOM OR COFFEE SHOP (311.477-014)
09.04.01 FAST-FOODS WORKER (311.472-010)
09.04.01 FOUNTAIN SERVER (319.474-010)
09.04.01 LUNCH-TRUCK DRIVER (292.463-010)
09.04.01 MANAGER, FOOD CONCESSION (185.167-022)
09.04.01 VENDING-MACHINE ATTENDANT (319.464-014)
09.04.01 WAITER/WAITRESS, FORMAL (311.477-026)
09.04.01 WAITER/WAITRESS, INFORMAL (311.477-030)
09.04.01 WAITER/WAITRESS, TAKE OUT (311.477-038)
09.05.02 CAFETERIA ATTENDANT (311.677-010)
09.05.02 COUNTER ATTENDANT, CAFETERIA (311.677-014)
09.05.02 COUNTER-SUPPLY WORKER (319.687-010)
09.05.02 DINING ROOM ATTENDANT (311.677-018)
09.05.02 WAITER/WAITRESS, ROOM SERVICE (311.477-034)
09.05.02 WINE STEWARD/STEWARDESS (310.357-010)

09.05.03 BELLHOP (324.677-010)
09.05.03 PORTER, BAGGAGE (324.477-010)
09.05.03 ROOM-SERVICE CLERK (324.577-010)
11.11.01 EXECUTIVE HOUSEKEEPER (187.167-046)
11.11.01 MANAGER, FRONT OFFICE (187.167-110)
11.11.01 MANAGER, HOTEL OR MOTEL (187.117-038)
11.11.01 MANAGER, LODGING FACILITIES (320.137-014)
11.11.04 MANAGER, FOOD SERVICE (187.167-106)

Household Furniture

06.04.05 HEMMER, AUTOMATIC (787.685-018)
06.04.16 MACHINE FEEDER, RAW STOCK (680.686-018)
06.04.23 FILLER (780.684-066)

Instruments and Appliances

05.01.01 LASER TECHNICIAN (019.181-010)
05.05.11 BIOMEDICAL EQUIPMENT TECHNICIAN (719.261-010)
05.05.11 ELECTROMECHANICAL TECHNICIAN (710.281-018)
05.10.02 THERMOSTAT REPAIRER (710.381-050)
06.01.04 ASSEMBLER (710.681-010)
06.01.05 RETICLE INSPECTOR (719.361-010)
06.02.23 ELECTRONICS ASSEMBLER (726.384-010)
06.03.02 CALIBRATION CHECKER 2 (710.687-018)
06.04.38 ASSEMBLER, HOSPITAL SUPPLIES (712.687-010)

Insurance

05.03.06 BUILDING INSPECTOR (168.267-010)
07.01.04 UNDERWRITING CLERK (219.367-038)
07.01.05 HOSPITAL-INSURANCE REPRESENTATIVE (166.267-014)
07.02.02 CANCELLATION CLERK (203.382-014)
07.02.02 POLICY-CHANGE CLERK (219.362-042)
07.02.03 CLAIM EXAMINER (168.267-014)
07.02.04 RATER (214.482-022)
07.02.04 REINSURANCE CLERK (219.482-018)
07.04.02 CLAIMS CLERK 2 (205.367-018)
07.04.04 POLICYHOLDER-INFORMATION CLERK (249.262-010)
07.05.02 REVIEWER (209.687-018)
07.05.03 BORDEREAU CLERK (203.382-010)
08.01.02 ESTATE PLANNER (186.167-010)
08.01.02 SALES AGENT, INSURANCE (250.257-010)
11.01.02 FINANCIAL ANALYST (020.167-014)
11.05.02 RESEARCH ANALYST (169.267-034)
11.05.02 SPECIAL AGENT (166.167-046)
11.06.03 LOAN OFFICER (186.267-018)
11.06.03 UNDERWRITER (169.167-058)
11.10.03 SAFETY INSPECTOR (168.167-078)
11.12.01 APPRAISER, AUTOMOBILE DAMAGE (241.267-014)
11.12.01 CLAIM ADJUSTER (241.217-010)
11.12.01 CLAIM EXAMINER (241.267-018)

Iron and Steel

02.04.01 LABORATORY ASSISTANT, METALLURGICAL (011.281-010)
06.01.03 ROLLING ATTENDANT (613.662-010)
06.02.10 COLD-MILL OPERATOR (613.462-010)
06.04.40 LABORER, GENERAL (509.686-010)

Jewelry

01.06.02 JEWELER (700.281-010)
01.06.02 MOLD MAKER 1 (700.381-034)
01.06.02 SAMPLE MAKER 1 (700.381-046)
05.05.14 STONE SETTER (700.381-054)
06.01.04 BENCH HAND (735.381-010)
06.01.04 RING MAKER (700.381-042)
06.01.04 SOLDERER (700.381-050)
06.02.02 LATHE HAND (700.682-014)
06.02.23 CHAIN MAKER, MACHINE (700.684-022)
06.02.24 BRIGHT CUTTER (700.684-018)
06.02.24 CASTER (502.381-010)
06.02.24 MESH CUTTER (700.684-050)
06.02.24 RING STAMPER (700.684-066)

06.02.24 SPINNER (700.684-074)
06.02.24 TROPHY ASSEMBLER (735.684-018)
06.03.02 INSPECTOR (700.687-034)
06.04.09 WAX MOLDER (549.685-038)
06.04.21 JEWELRY COATER (590.685-046)
06.04.23 ASSEMBLER (700.684-014)
06.04.23 EARRING MAKER (700.684-030)
06.04.24 ARBORER (700.684-010)
06.04.24 FILER (700.684-034)
06.04.24 JIGSAWYER (700.684-046)
06.04.24 MELTER (700.687-042)
06.04.24 PREPARER (700.687-062)
06.04.24 STONER (735.684-014)
06.04.24 STRETCHER (700.684-078)
06.04.33 PAINTER (735.687-018)
06.04.39 DIPPER (735.687-010)

Knit Goods

06.01.02 KNITTER MECHANIC (685.360-010)
06.01.02 KNITTING-MACHINE FIXER (689.280-014)
06.02.05 TRIMMER, MACHINE (781.682-010)
06.04.06 BEAM-WARPER TENDER, AUTOMATIC (681.685-018)
06.04.06 KNITTING-MACHINE OPERATOR (685.665-014)

Laundry

06.02.27 SPOTTER (361.684-018)
06.04.35 LAUNDERER, HAND (361.684-010)
06.04.35 LAUNDRY LABORER (361.687-018)
06.04.35 LAUNDRY OPERATOR (369.684-014)
06.04.35 PRESS OPERATOR (363.685-010)
06.04.35 WASHER, MACHINE (361.665-010)
06.04.35 WASHING-MACHINE LOADER-AND-PULLER (361.686-010)
09.04.02 SELF-SERVICE-LAUNDRY-AND-DRY-CLEANING ATTENDANT (369.677-010)
09.04.02 SERVICE-ESTABLISHMENT ATTENDANT (369.477-014)

Leather Manufacturing

06.04.27 LABORER, GENERAL (589.686-026)

Leather Products

06.02.05 SEWING-MACHINE OPERATOR (783.682-014)
06.02.27 LEATHER CUTTER (783.684-022)
06.02.27 LEATHER WORKER (783.684-026)

Library

07.07.02 PAGE (249.687-014)
11.02.04 CATALOG LIBRARIAN (100.387-010)
11.02.04 CLASSIFIER (100.367-014)
11.02.04 LIBRARIAN (100.127-014)
11.02.04 LIBRARIAN, SPECIAL LIBRARY (100.167-026)
11.02.04 LIBRARY ASSISTANT (249.367-046)
11.02.04 LIBRARY TECHNICAL ASSISTANT (100.367-018)
11.02.04 MEDIA SPECIALIST, SCHOOL LIBRARY (100.167-030)
11.07.04 LIBRARY CONSULTANT (100.117-014)

Light, Heat and Power

02.04.01 LABORATORY ASSISTANT (029.361-018)
03.04.05 TREE TRIMMER (408.664-010)
04.01.02 INVESTIGATOR (376.367-022)
05.01.03 ELECTRICAL ENGINEER, POWER SYSTEM (003.167-018)
05.01.03 POWER-DISTRIBUTION ENGINEER (003.167-046)
05.01.03 POWER-TRANSMISSION ENGINEER (003.167-050)
05.01.06 UTILIZATION ENGINEER (007.061-034)
05.02.06 APPLIANCE-SERVICE SUPERVISOR (187.167-010)
05.03.02 ESTIMATOR AND DRAFTER (019.261-014)
05.05.05 CABLE INSTALLER-REPAIRER (821.361-010)
05.05.05 CABLE SPLICER (829.361-010)
05.05.05 ELECTRIC-METER INSTALLER 1 (821.361-014)
05.05.05 ELECTRICIAN, POWERHOUSE (820.261-014)

05.05.05 FURNACE INSTALLER (862.361-010)
05.05.05 LINE ERECTOR (821.361-018)
05.05.05 LINE REPAIRER (821.361-026)
05.05.05 STREET-LIGHT SERVICER (824.381-010)
05.05.05 TOWER ERECTOR (821.361-038)
05.05.05 WIND-GENERATING-ELECTRIC-POWER
        INSTALLER (821.381-018)
05.05.06 CONDUIT MECHANIC (869.361-010)
05.05.09 POWERHOUSE MECHANIC (631.261-014)
05.05.10 ELECTRIC-METER REPAIRER (729.281-014)
05.05.10 ELECTRIC-METER TESTER (821.381-010)
05.06.01 CABLE MAINTAINER (952.464-010)
05.06.01 HYDROELECTRIC-STATION OPERATOR
        (952.362-018)
05.06.01 LOAD DISPATCHER (952.167-014)
05.06.01 POWER-REACTOR OPERATOR (952.362-022)
05.06.01 SUBSTATION OPERATOR (952.362-026)
05.06.01 TURBINE OPERATOR (952.362-042)
05.09.03 METER READER (209.567-010)
05.09.03 TURBINE ATTENDANT (952.567-010)
05.10.01 SERVICE REPRESENTATIVE (959.574-010)
05.12.04 LABORER, POWERHOUSE (952.665-010)
05.12.16 CABLE PULLER (829.684-018)
07.02.03 ACCOUNT-INFORMATION CLERK (210.367-010)
07.02.04 BILLING-CONTROL CLERK (214.387-010)
07.04.01 CUSTOMER-SERVICE REPRESENTATIVE
        (239.367-010)
07.04.05 UTILITY CLERK (239.367-034)
07.05.02 INVESTIGATOR, UTILITY-BILL COMPLAINTS
        (241.267-034)
08.01.02 SALES REPRESENTATIVE, PUBLIC UTILITIES
        (253.357-010)
08.02.05 DEMONSTRATOR, ELECTRIC-GAS APPLIANCES
        (297.357-010)
11.09.03 MANAGER, AREA DEVELOPMENT (184.117-030)

Locomotive and Car Building and Repair

05.07.01 CAR INSPECTOR (910.667-010)

Logging

03.01.04 LOGGING-OPERATIONS INSPECTOR (168.267-070)
03.04.02 BUCKER (454.684-010)
03.04.02 CHAINSAW OPERATOR (454.687-010)
03.04.02 FALLER 2 (454.684-014)
03.04.02 LOGGER, ALL-ROUND (454.684-018)
05.10.04 MANAGER, CAMP (187.167-066)
05.12.04 CHOKE SETTER (921.687-014)

Macaroni and Related Products

06.02.15 DRIER OPERATOR (523.362-014)

Machinery Manufacturing

01.06.03 TYPE COPYIST (970.381-042)
05.05.05 AUTOMATED EQUIPMENT
        ENGINEER-TECHNICIAN (638.261-010)
05.05.06 WELDER-ASSEMBLER (819.381-010)
05.05.09 FIELD SERVICE TECHNICIAN (638.261-026)
05.05.09 MACHINE BUILDER (600.281-022)
05.05.09 MACHINERY ERECTOR (638.261-014)
06.02.22 MACHINE ASSEMBLER (638.361-010)
06.02.24 SUBASSEMBLER (706.381-038)

Machine Shop

05.05.07 DIE SINKER (601.280-022)
05.05.07 MACHINIST (600.280-022)
05.05.07 TOOL-AND-DIE MAKER (601.280-046)
05.05.07 TOOL-MACHINE SET-UP OPERATOR (601.280-054)
06.01.03 LATHE OPERATOR, NUMERICAL CONTROL
        (604.362-010)
06.01.03 MACHINE SET-UP OPERATOR (600.380-018)
06.02.02 NUMERICAL-CONTROL-MACHINE OPERATOR
        (609.662-010)
06.02.10 CARBIDE-POWDER PROCESSOR (510.465-010)
06.02.24 SOLAR-FABRICATION TECHNICIAN (809.381-034)

06.04.02 DRILL-PRESS OPERATOR, PRODUCTION
        (606.685-026)
06.04.02 LATHE OPERATOR, PRODUCTION (604.685-026)
06.04.39 LABORER, GENERAL (609.684-014)

Machine Tool and Accessories

05.05.09 MACHINE BUILDER (600.281-022)

Malt Liquors

05.02.03 BREWING DIRECTOR (183.167-010)
06.04.15 BREWERY CELLAR WORKER (522.685-014)
06.04.40 PUMPER, BREWERY (914.665-014)

Manufactured Buildings

05.10.01 DRY-WALL APPLICATOR (842.681-010)
05.10.01 SIDER (863.684-014)
05.10.01 TAPER (842.664-010)
06.02.22 UTILITY WORKER (869.684-074)

Mattress and Bedspring

06.02.27 MATTRESS MAKER (780.684-074)
06.04.05 SEWING-MACHINE OPERATOR, SPECIAL
        EQUIPMENT (689.685-118)

Medical Services

02.02.01 HISTOPATHOLOGIST (041.061-054)
02.03.01 GENERAL PRACTITIONER (070.101-022)
02.03.01 PODIATRIST (079.101-022)
02.03.02 DENTIST (072.101-010)
02.03.03 ANIMAL HEALTH TECHNICIAN (079.361-014)
02.03.03 VETERINARIAN (073.101-010)
02.03.04 ACUPUNCTURIST (079.271-010)
02.03.04 CHIROPRACTOR (079.101-010)
02.03.04 RADIATION-THERAPY TECHNOLOGIST
        (078.361-034)
02.04.01 RADIOPHARMACIST (074.161-014)
02.04.01 ULTRASOUND TECHNOLOGIST (078.364-010)
02.04.02 CEPHALOMETRIC ANALYST (078.384-010)
02.04.02 CHEMISTRY TECHNOLOGIST (078.261-010)
02.04.02 CYTOTECHNOLOGIST (078.281-010)
02.04.02 IMMUNOHEMATOLOGIST (078.221-010)
02.04.02 LABORATORY ASSISTANT, BLOOD AND PLASMA
        (078.687-010)
02.04.02 LABORATORY TECHNICIAN, VETERINARY
        (073.361-010)
02.04.02 MEDICAL TECHNOLOGIST (078.361-014)
02.04.02 MEDICAL-LABORATORY ASSISTANT (078.381-010)
02.04.02 MEDICAL-LABORATORY TECHNICIAN (078.381-014)
02.04.02 MICROBIOLOGY TECHNOLOGIST (078.261-014)
02.04.02 MORGUE ATTENDANT (355.667-010)
02.04.02 PHLEBOTOMIST (079.364-022)
02.04.02 TISSUE TECHNOLOGIST (078.361-030)
05.05.11 BIOMEDICAL EQUIPMENT TECHNICIAN
        (719.261-010)
05.05.11 DENTAL CERAMIST (712.281-010)
05.05.11 DENTAL CERAMIST ASSISTANT (712.664-010)
05.05.11 DENTAL-LABORATORY TECHNICIAN (712.381-018)
05.05.11 DENTAL-LABORATORY-TECHNICIAN
        APPRENTICE (712.381-022)
05.05.11 DENTURE-MODEL MAKER (712.681-014)
05.05.11 FINISHER, DENTURE (712.681-018)
05.05.11 ORTHODONTIC TECHNICIAN (712.381-030)
05.05.11 PACKER, DENTURE (712.684-034)
05.05.11 RADIOLOGICAL-EQUIPMENT SPECIALIST
        (719.261-014)
05.08.03 AMBULANCE DRIVER (913.683-010)
05.08.03 HEALTH-EQUIPMENT SERVICER (359.363-010)
05.09.01 LINEN-ROOM ATTENDANT (222.387-030)
05.09.01 PHARMACY HELPER (074.387-010)
05.10.08 FORMULA-ROOM WORKER (520.487-014)
05.12.17 FOOD ASSEMBLER, KITCHEN (319.484-010)
05.12.18 CENTRAL-SUPPLY WORKER (381.687-010)
05.12.18 CLEANER, HOSPITAL (323.687-010)
05.12.18 HOUSEKEEPER (321.137-010)

05.12.18 SUPERVISOR, CENTRAL SUPPLY (079.164-010)
06.02.23 BITE-BLOCK MAKER (712.684-014)
06.02.32 DENTURE WAXER (712.681-010)
06.02.32 OPAQUER (712.684-030)
06.04.11 CENTRIFUGE OPERATOR, PLASMA PROCESSING (599.685-018)
06.04.19 STERILIZER (599.585-010)
06.04.24 REFINER (712.684-038)
07.01.03 MEDICAL SECRETARY (201.362-014)
07.02.04 INSURANCE CLERK (214.362-022)
07.04.01 ADMITTING OFFICER (205.137-010)
07.04.01 BLOOD-DONOR-UNIT ASSISTANT (245.367-014)
07.04.01 HOSPITAL-ADMITTING CLERK (205.362-018)
07.04.01 OUTPATIENT-ADMITTING CLERK (205.362-030)
07.04.03 ANIMAL-HOSPITAL CLERK (245.367-010)
07.05.03 DIET CLERK (245.587-010)
07.05.03 MEDICAL RECORD TECHNICIAN (079.367-014)
07.05.03 MEDICAL-RECORD CLERK (245.362-010)
07.05.03 WARD CLERK (245.362-014)
09.05.02 FOOD-SERVICE WORKER, HOSPITAL (355.677-010)
09.05.04 HOSPITAL ENTRANCE ATTENDANT (355.677-014)
09.05.07 CLOTHES-ROOM WORKER (355.687-010)
10.02.01 NURSE ANESTHETIST (075.371-010)
10.02.01 NURSE PRACTITIONER (075.264-010)
10.02.01 NURSE, GENERAL DUTY (075.374-010)
10.02.01 NURSE, INSTRUCTOR (075.121-010)
10.02.01 NURSE, LICENSED PRACTICAL (079.374-014)
10.02.01 NURSE, OFFICE (075.374-014)
10.02.01 NURSE, PRIVATE DUTY (075.374-018)
10.02.01 NURSE, SCHOOL (075.124-010)
10.02.01 NURSE, STAFF, COMMUNITY HEALTH (075.124-014)
10.02.01 NURSE, STAFF, OCCUPATIONAL HEALTH NURSING (075.374-022)
10.02.01 NURSE-MIDWIFE (075.264-014)
10.02.01 PHYSICIAN ASSISTANT (079.364-018)
10.02.02 ACUPRESSURIST (079.271-014)
10.02.02 ART THERAPIST (076.127-010)
10.02.02 CORRECTIVE THERAPIST (076.361-010)
10.02.02 DANCE THERAPIST (076.127-018)
10.02.02 DENTAL HYGIENIST (078.361-010)
10.02.02 DIALYSIS TECHNICIAN (078.362-014)
10.02.02 HORTICULTURAL THERAPIST (076.124-018)
10.02.02 INDUSTRIAL THERAPIST (076.167-010)
10.02.02 MANUAL-ARTS THERAPIST (076.124-010)
10.02.02 MUSIC THERAPIST (076.127-014)
10.02.02 NUCLEAR MEDICAL TECHNOLOGIST (078.361-018)
10.02.02 OCCUPATIONAL THERAPIST (076.121-010)
10.02.02 OCCUPATIONAL THERAPY ASSISTANT (076.364-010)
10.02.02 ORTHOPTIST (079.371-014)
10.02.02 PHYSICAL THERAPIST (076.121-014)
10.02.02 PHYSICAL THERAPIST ASSISTANT (076.224-010)
10.02.02 PSYCHIATRIC TECHNICIAN (079.374-026)
10.02.02 RADIOLOGIC TECHNOLOGIST (078.362-026)
10.02.02 RECREATIONAL THERAPIST (076.124-014)
10.02.02 RESPIRATORY THERAPIST (079.361-010)
10.03.01 CARDIAC MONITOR TECHNICIAN (078.367-010)
10.03.01 CARDIOPULMONARY TECHNOLOGIST (078.362-030)
10.03.01 ELECTROCARDIOGRAPH TECHNICIAN (078.362-018)
10.03.01 ELECTROENCEPHALOGRAPHIC TECHNOLOGIST (078.362-022)
10.03.01 HOLTER SCANNING TECHNICIAN (078.264-010)
10.03.01 PULMONARY-FUNCTION TECHNICIAN (078.262-010)
10.03.02 AMBULANCE ATTENDANT (355.374-010)
10.03.02 BIRTH ATTENDANT (354.377-010)
10.03.02 DENTAL ASSISTANT (079.371-010)
10.03.02 EMERGENCY MEDICAL TECHNICIAN (079.374-010)
10.03.02 GERIATRIC NURSE ASSISTANT (355.674-026)
10.03.02 HOME HEALTH TECHNICIAN (079.224-010)
10.03.02 MEDICAL ASSISTANT (079.367-010)
10.03.02 MEDICATION AIDE (355.374-014)
10.03.02 MENTAL-RETARDATION AIDE (355.377-018)

10.03.02 NURSE AIDE (355.674-014)
10.03.02 NURSE, PRACTICAL (354.374-010)
10.03.02 OCCUPATIONAL THERAPY AIDE (355.377-010)
10.03.02 ORDERLY (355.674-018)
10.03.02 ORTHOPEDIC ASSISTANT (712.661-010)
10.03.02 PERFUSIONIST (078.362-034)
10.03.02 PHYSICAL THERAPY AIDE (355.354-010)
10.03.02 PODIATRIC ASSISTANT (079.374-018)
10.03.02 PSYCHIATRIC AIDE (355.377-014)
10.03.02 RESPIRATORY-THERAPY AIDE (355.674-022)
10.03.02 SURGICAL TECHNICIAN (079.374-022)
11.07.01 COORDINATOR OF REHABILITATION SERVICES (076.117-010)
11.07.02 ADMINISTRATOR, HOSPITAL (187.117-010)
11.07.02 MEDICAL-RECORD ADMINISTRATOR (079.167-014)
11.07.02 UTILIZATION-REVIEW COORDINATOR (079.137-010)
11.10.03 SAFETY MANAGER (168.167-086)
11.11.01 EXECUTIVE HOUSEKEEPER (187.167-046)

Military Services

02.04.01 PHARMACIST ASSISTANT (074.381-010)
07.05.03 MEDICAL-SERVICE TECHNICIAN (079.367-018)
11.03.04 RECRUITER (166.267-026)

Mining and Quarrying

05.01.02 SAFETY ENGINEER, MINES (010.061-026)
05.01.06 MINING ENGINEER (010.061-014)
11.10.03 MINE INSPECTOR (168.267-074)

Mirror and Picture Frames

01.06.02 PICTURE FRAMER (739.684-146)
06.04.34 MAT CUTTER (739.684-126)

Mortuary Goods

06.02.22 CASKET ASSEMBLER (739.481-010)

Motion Pictures

01.01.01 EDITOR, FILM (962.264-010)
01.01.01 PRODUCER (187.167-174)
01.01.02 SCREEN WRITER (131.087-018)
01.02.03 ART DIRECTOR (142.031-010)
01.02.03 DIRECTOR OF PHOTOGRAPHY (143.062-010)
01.02.03 OPTICAL-EFFECTS-CAMERA OPERATOR (143.260-010)
01.02.03 SET DECORATOR (142.061-042)
01.02.03 SET DESIGNER (142.061-046)
01.03.01 DIRECTOR, MOTION PICTURE (159.067-010)
01.03.03 NARRATOR (150.147-010)
01.04.03 SINGER (152.047-022)
01.06.02 MAKE-UP ARTIST (333.071-010)
01.06.02 PROP MAKER (962.281-010)
02.04.01 FILM LABORATORY TECHNICIAN 1 (976.381-010)
05.10.03 LIGHT TECHNICIAN (962.362-014)
05.10.05 FILM DEVELOPER (976.382-018)
05.10.05 FILM LABORATORY TECHNICIAN (976.684-014)
05.10.05 MOTION-PICTURE PROJECTIONIST (960.362-010)
05.10.05 RECORDIST (962.382-010)
05.10.05 RERECORDING MIXER (194.362-014)
05.10.05 SOUND MIXER (194.262-018)
05.12.04 GRIP (962.687-022)
11.12.02 LOCATION MANAGER (191.167-018)
12.02.01 STUNT PERFORMER (159.341-014)

Motorcycles, Bicycles and Parts

06.02.22 MOTORCYCLE ASSEMBLER (806.684-090)
06.02.23 WHEEL LACER AND TRUER (706.684-106)
06.03.01 MOTORCYCLE TESTER (620.384-010)
06.04.22 ASSEMBLER, BICYCLE 2 (806.687-010)

Motor Vehicle Transportation

05.12.03 GARBAGE COLLECTOR (909.687-010)
07.01.02 MANAGER, TRAFFIC 1 (184.167-102)

08.01.02 TRAFFIC AGENT (252.257-010)
09.03.01 BUS DRIVER (913.463-010)
09.03.02 TAXI DRIVER (913.463-018)
09.05.03 PORTER (357.677-010)
11.03.04 EMPLOYEE RELATIONS SPECIALIST (166.267-042)
11.05.01 DIRECTOR, TRANSPORTATION (184.117-014)
11.05.02 MANAGER, OPERATIONS (184.117-050)
11.05.02 MANAGER, REGIONAL (184.117-054)
11.10.05 TRAFFIC INSPECTOR (184.163-010)
11.10.05 TRANSPORTATION INSPECTOR (168.167-082)
11.11.03 MANAGER, BUS TRANSPORTATION (184.167-054)
11.11.03 MANAGER, TRAFFIC (184.117-066)
11.11.03 OPERATIONS MANAGER (184.167-118)
11.12.01 GENERAL CLAIMS AGENT (186.117-030)

Musical Instruments and Parts

05.05.12 ELECTRIC-ORGAN INSPECTOR AND REPAIRER
      (730.281-018)
05.05.12 FRETTED-INSTRUMENT MAKER, HAND
      (730.281-022)
05.05.12 PIPE-ORGAN INSTALLER (730.381-046)
05.05.12 VIOLIN MAKER, HAND (730.281-046)
06.02.23 ASSEMBLER, MUSICAL INSTRUMENTS
      (730.684-010)

Museums, Art Galleries, and Gardens

01.02.03 EXHIBIT DESIGNER (142.061-058)
01.06.02 CONSERVATION TECHNICIAN (102.261-010)
01.06.02 EXHIBIT BUILDER (739.261-010)
01.06.02 MUSEUM TECHNICIAN (102.381-010)
01.06.02 RESTORER, CERAMIC (102.361-014)
05.03.09 FINE ARTS PACKER (102.367-010)
05.05.08 FURNITURE RESTORER (763.380-010)
05.12.03 INSTALLER (922.687-050)
07.04.04 MUSEUM ATTENDANT (109.367-010)
07.05.01 SCHEDULER (238.367-034)
09.01.02 CRAFT DEMONSTRATOR (109.364-010)
11.02.01 TEACHER (099.227-038)
11.03.03 RESEARCH ASSOCIATE (109.067-014)
11.07.03 EDUCATIONAL RESOURCE COORDINATOR
      (099.167-030)
11.07.04 CURATOR (102.017-010)

Narrow Fabrics

06.01.02 LOOM FIXER (683.260-018)
06.04.06 BEAM-WARPER TENDER, AUTOMATIC (681.685-018)

Nonferrous Metal Alloys

06.04.10 LABORER, GENERAL (519.686-010)

Nonprofit Organizations

05.09.02 EVALUATOR (249.367-034)
05.09.03 SORTER-PRICER (222.387-054)
07.01.02 MEMBERSHIP SECRETARY (201.362-018)
07.04.01 REHABILITATION CLERK (205.367-046)
07.04.03 DOG LICENSER (249.367-030)
07.05.02 BRAILLE PROOFREADER (209.367-014)
07.05.04 ROUTING CLERK (249.367-070)
07.06.02 BRAILLE TYPIST (203.582-014)
08.02.02 SALES EXHIBITOR (279.357-010)
08.02.08 FUND RAISER 2 (293.357-014)
11.05.02 EXECUTIVE VICE PRESIDENT, CHAMBER OF
      COMMERCE (187.117-030)
11.07.01 DIRECTOR, COMMUNITY ORGANIZATION
      (187.117-014)
11.07.01 DIRECTOR, SERVICE (187.167-214)
11.07.03 SUPERVISOR, CONTRACT-SHELTERED
      WORKSHOP (187.134-010)
11.09.02 DIRECTOR, FUNDRAISING (165.117-010)
11.09.02 FUND RAISER 1 (293.157-010)

Nut, Bolt, Washer, and Rivet

06.04.02 PRODUCTION-MACHINE TENDER (619.365-010)

Office, Computing, and Accounting Machines

06.01.04 FINAL ASSEMBLER (706.381-018)
06.02.23 WIRER, SUBASSEMBLIES (729.684-062)
06.02.24 REPAIRER, TYPEWRITER (706.381-030)
06.02.32 WIRER (729.281-042)
06.03.01 MACHINE TESTER (706.387-014)
06.04.09 KEYMODULE-ASSEMBLY-MACHINE TENDER
      (692.685-274)

Oils and Fats, n.e.c.

06.04.40 GENERAL HELPER (529.687-094)

Optical Goods

05.01.01 OPTOMECHANICAL TECHNICIAN (007.161-030)
05.05.11 ARTIFICIAL-PLASTIC-EYE MAKER (713.261-014)
05.05.11 LENS MOUNTER 2 (713.681-010)
05.05.11 OPTICIAN (716.280-008)
05.05.11 OPTICIAN (716.280-014)
05.05.14 STONE SETTER (700.381-054)
05.09.02 PRESCRIPTION CLERK, LENS-AND-FRAMES
      (222.367-050)
06.01.04 LENS POLISHER, HAND (716.681-018)
06.01.05 RETICLE INSPECTOR (719.361-010)
06.02.08 EYEGLASS-LENS CUTTER (716.682-010)
06.02.08 PRECISION-LENS GRINDER (716.382-018)
06.02.08 PRECISION-LENS POLISHER (716.682-018)
06.02.21 OPTICAL-ELEMENT COATER (716.382-014)
06.02.23 LENS-MOLD SETTER (713.381-010)
06.02.30 MOLDER (575.381-010)
06.03.02 LENS EXAMINER (716.687-022)
06.04.08 LENS-FABRICATING-MACHINE TENDER
      (716.685-022)
06.04.13 CONTACT-LENS MOLDER (690.685-090)
06.04.13 FUSING-FURNACE LOADER (573.686-014)
06.04.13 LENS HARDENER (573.685-030)
06.04.23 ASSEMBLER, MOLDED FRAMES (713.684-014)
06.04.23 MULTIFOCAL-LENS ASSEMBLER (713.684-034)
06.04.24 BENCH WORKER (713.684-018)
06.04.24 CONTACT-LENS-FLASHING PUNCHER
      (713.687-014)
06.04.24 POLISHER, EYEGLASS FRAMES (713.684-038)
06.04.39 WASHER (713.684-042)

Paint and Varnish

06.04.11 MIXER (550.685-078)

Paper and Pulp

05.12.03 YARD LABORER (922.687-102)
06.04.03 POWER-BARKER OPERATOR (669.485-010)
06.04.18 DIGESTER-OPERATOR HELPER (532.686-010)

Paper Goods

06.02.04 BOX-FOLDING-MACHINE OPERATOR (649.682-010)
06.04.04 BAG-MACHINE OPERATOR (649.685-014)
06.04.04 CARTON-FORMING-MACHINE TENDER
      (641.685-026)

Personal Protection and Medical Devices

05.05.11 ORTHOTICS ASSISTANT (078.361-022)
05.05.11 ORTHOTICS TECHNICIAN (712.381-034)
05.05.11 ORTHOTIST (078.261-018)
05.05.11 PROSTHETICS ASSISTANT (078.361-026)
05.05.11 PROSTHETICS TECHNICIAN (712.381-038)
05.05.11 PROSTHETIST (078.261-022)
05.10.01 ARCH-SUPPORT TECHNICIAN (712.381-010)
05.10.02 MEDICAL-EQUIPMENT REPAIRER (639.281-022)
06.02.23 ASSEMBLER, SURGICAL GARMENT (712.684-010)
06.04.05 ADHESIVE-BANDAGE-MACHINE OPERATOR
      (692.685-014)
06.04.05 SURGICAL-DRESSING MAKER (689.685-130)
06.04.19 STERILIZER (599.585-010)

Personal Service

01.06.02 MORTUARY BEAUTICIAN (339.361-010)
01.06.02 WIG DRESSER (332.361-010)
02.04.02 EMBALMER (338.371-014)
03.03.02 DOG BATHER (418.677-010)
03.03.02 DOG GROOMER (418.674-010)
04.02.02 BODYGUARD (372.667-014)
04.02.02 SECURITY CONSULTANT (189.167-054)
04.02.03 CHAPERON (359.667-010)
05.05.15 ALTERATION TAILOR (785.261-010)
05.05.15 CUSTOM TAILOR (785.261-014)
05.05.15 SHOE REPAIRER (365.361-014)
05.08.03 CHAUFFEUR, FUNERAL CAR (359.673-014)
05.09.01 SUPPLY CLERK (339.687-010)
05.12.14 SHOE DYER (364.684-014)
06.04.19 CREMATOR (359.685-010)
07.05.01 GUIDE, TRAVEL (353.167-010)
09.01.02 GUIDE (353.367-010)
09.01.04 FUNERAL ATTENDANT (359.677-014)
09.02.01 COSMETOLOGIST (332.271-010)
09.02.01 HAIR STYLIST (332.271-018)
09.02.01 SCALP-TREATMENT OPERATOR (339.371-014)
09.02.02 BARBER (330.371-010)
09.04.02 SERVICE-ESTABLISHMENT ATTENDANT
    (369.477-014)
09.05.01 COOLING-ROOM ATTENDANT (335.677-010)
09.05.01 ELECTROLOGIST (339.371-010)
09.05.01 FINGERNAIL FORMER (331.674-014)
09.05.01 HOT-ROOM ATTENDANT (335.677-014)
09.05.01 MANICURIST (331.674-010)
09.05.01 MASSEUR/MASSEUSE (334.374-010)
09.05.01 REDUCING-SALON ATTENDANT (359.567-010)
09.05.01 WEIGHT-REDUCTION SPECIALIST (359.367-014)
09.05.07 LOCKER-ROOM ATTENDANT (358.677-014)
10.02.02 PHYSICAL-INTEGRATION PRACTITIONER
    (076.264-010)
10.03.03 BLIND AIDE (359.573-010)
10.03.03 CHILD-CARE ATTENDANT, SCHOOL (355.674-010)
10.03.03 HOME ATTENDANT (354.377-014)
11.11.04 DIRECTOR, FUNERAL (187.167-030)
11.11.04 MANAGER, BARBER OR BEAUTY SHOP
    (187.167-058)
11.11.04 MANAGER, FOOD SERVICE (187.167-106)

Petroleum and Natural Gas Production

02.01.02 GEOLOGIST, PETROLEUM (024.061-022)
02.04.01 GEOLOGICAL AIDE (024.267-010)
02.04.01 LABORATORY ASSISTANT (024.381-010)
05.01.08 PETROLEUM ENGINEER (010.061-018)
05.03.02 DRAFTER, GEOLOGICAL (010.281-014)
05.03.02 DRAFTER, GEOPHYSICAL (010.281-018)
05.03.04 FIELD ENGINEER, SPECIALIST (010.261-010)
05.05.10 INSTRUMENT-MAKER AND REPAIRER (600.280-014)
05.07.01 LINE WALKER (869.564-010)
05.10.01 ROUSTABOUT (869.684-046)
05.11.03 ROTARY DRILLER (930.382-026)
05.12.03 LABORER (939.687-018)
07.01.05 TITLE CLERK (162.267-010)
11.05.02 MANAGER, CONTRACTS (163.117-010)
11.12.02 MANAGER, LEASING (186.117-046)

Petroleum Refineries

02.04.01 TESTER (029.261-022)
05.01.04 TEST-ENGINE EVALUATOR (010.261-026)
05.07.01 LINE WALKER (869.564-010)
05.12.03 LABORER, PETROLEUM REFINERY (549.687-018)
06.01.03 REFINERY OPERATOR (549.260-010)
07.01.05 TITLE CLERK (162.267-010)
11.05.02 MANAGER, CONTRACTS (163.117-010)

Phonographs

05.10.05 RECORDING ENGINEER (194.362-010)
05.10.05 SOUND MIXER (194.262-018)
05.10.05 TAPE TRANSFERRER (194.382-014)

05.12.03 RECORDING STUDIO SET-UP WORKER
    (962.664-014)
06.03.01 QUALITY-CONTROL INSPECTOR (194.387-010)
06.04.10 INJECTION-MOLDING-MACHINE TENDER
    (556.685-038)
06.04.13 RECORD-PRESS TENDER (556.685-070)

Photographic Apparatus and Materials

05.01.01 OPTOMECHANICAL TECHNICIAN (007.161-030)
05.05.11 CAMERA REPAIRER (714.281-014)
06.02.23 ASSEMBLER, PRODUCTION LINE (714.684-010)

Photofinishing

01.06.03 SPOTTER, PHOTOGRAPHIC (970.381-034)
05.10.05 COLOR-PRINTER OPERATOR (976.382-014)
05.10.05 DEVELOPER (976.681-010)
05.10.05 FILM DEVELOPER (976.382-018)
05.10.05 FILM LABORATORY TECHNICIAN (976.684-014)
05.10.05 PHOTOGRAPH FINISHER (976.487-010)
05.10.05 PROJECTION PRINTER (976.381-018)
05.10.05 TAKE-DOWN SORTER (976.665-010)
06.01.02 PRINT CONTROLLER (976.360-010)
06.03.02 PHOTO CHECKER AND ASSEMBLER (976.687-014)
06.03.02 PHOTOFINISHING LABORATORY WORKER
    (976.687-010)
06.04.09 CUTTER (976.685-010)
06.04.19 DEVELOPER, AUTOMATIC (976.685-014)
06.04.19 PRINT DEVELOPER, AUTOMATIC (976.685-026)
06.04.19 UTILITY WORKER, FILM PROCESSING
    (976.685-030)
06.04.20 MOUNTER, AUTOMATIC (976.685-022)
06.04.34 MOUNTER, HAND (976.684-018)
07.03.01 COUNTER CLERK (249.366-010)
07.05.03 DETAILER, SCHOOL PHOTOGRAPHS (976.564-010)

Pipe-Line Operation

05.07.01 LINE WALKER (869.564-010)
07.01.05 TITLE CLERK (162.267-010)
11.05.02 MANAGER, CONTRACTS (163.117-010)

Planing Mill

06.02.03 TIMBER-SIZER OPERATOR (665.482-018)
06.04.03 CHAIN OFFBEARER (669.686-018)

Plastics Materials

06.03.01 INSPECTOR (559.381-010)
06.04.40 LABORER, GENERAL (559.567-010)

Plumbers' Supplies

06.04.33 ENAMELER (509.684-010)

Pottery and Porcelain

06.02.08 POTTERY-MACHINE OPERATOR (774.382-010)
06.02.30 PLASTER-DIE MAKER (774.684-026)
06.02.30 THROWER (774.381-010)
06.03.02 PRINT INSPECTOR (774.687-018)
06.04.17 KILN WORKER (573.687-022)
06.04.30 SAGGER MAKER (774.684-030)

Printing and Publishing

01.01.01 EDITOR, PUBLICATIONS (132.037-022)
01.01.02 EDITORIAL WRITER (131.067-022)
01.02.03 PHOTOJOURNALIST (143.062-034)
01.06.01 ADVERTISING-SPACE CLERK (247.387-018)
01.06.01 ENGRAVER, PICTURE (979.281-018)
01.06.01 PHOTOENGRAVER (971.381-022)
05.05.13 ASSISTANT-PRESS OPERATOR (651.585-010)
05.05.13 COMPOSITOR (973.381-010)
05.05.13 CYLINDER-PRESS OPERATOR (651.362-010)
05.05.13 ELECTROTYPER (974.381-010)
05.05.13 JOB PRINTER (973.381-018)
05.05.13 OFFSET-PRESS OPERATOR 1 (651.482-010)

05.05.13 ROTOGRAVURE-PRESS OPERATOR (651.362-026)
05.05.13 STEREOTYPER (974.382-014)
05.05.13 WEB-PRESS OPERATOR (651.362-030)
05.05.15 BOOKBINDER (977.381-010)
05.09.01 MAILER (222.587-030)
05.09.02 ESTIMATOR, PRINTING (221.367-014)
05.10.05 ENGRAVING-PRESS OPERATOR (651.382-010)
05.10.05 EQUIPMENT MONITOR, PHOTOTYPESETTING
    (650.682-010)
05.10.05 PHOTOCOMPOSING-MACHINE OPERATOR
    (650.582-018)
05.10.05 TYPESETTING-MACHINE TENDER (650.685-010)
05.12.03 ETCHER HELPER, HAND (971.687-010)
05.12.18 PRINT-SHOP HELPER (979.684-026)
05.12.19 BRAILLE-DUPLICATING-MACHINE OPERATOR
    (207.685-010)
06.01.03 PRINTER 2 (651.380-010)
06.02.20 COVERING-MACHINE OPERATOR (653.682-014)
06.02.26 PRESSER (977.684-018)
06.03.02 INKER (659.667-010)
06.04.04 BINDERY WORKER (653.685-010)
06.04.04 FOLDING-MACHINE FEEDER (653.686-014)
06.04.38 MAILING-MACHINE OPERATOR (208.462-010)
07.05.01 ADVERTISING-DISPATCH CLERK (247.387-014)
07.05.02 BRAILLE PROOFREADER (209.367-014)
07.05.02 CLASSIFIED-AD CLERK 2 (247.387-022)
07.05.02 PRODUCTION PROOFREADER (247.667-010)
07.05.02 PROOFREADER (209.387-030)
07.06.01 TERMINAL-MAKEUP OPERATOR (208.382-010)
07.06.02 BRAILLE OPERATOR (203.582-010)
07.06.02 BRAILLE TYPIST (203.582-014)
07.06.02 ELECTRONIC-TYPESETTING-MACHINE
    OPERATOR (203.582-074)
07.06.02 MAGNETIC-TAPE-COMPOSER OPERATOR
    (203.382-018)
07.06.02 PHOTOCOMPOSITION-KEYBOARD OPERATOR
    (203.582-046)
07.06.02 PHOTOTYPESETTER OPERATOR (650.582-022)
07.07.02 MESSENGER, COPY (239.677-010)
08.01.02 SALES REPRESENTATIVE, ADVERTISING
    (254.357-014)
11.05.04 MANAGER, CIRCULATION (163.167-014)
11.08.01 EDITOR, DEPARTMENT (132.037-018)
11.08.01 EDITOR, NEWS (132.067-026)
11.08.01 EDITOR, NEWSPAPER (132.017-014)
11.08.01 EDITORIAL ASSISTANT (132.267-014)
11.08.02 REPORTER (131.267-018)
11.08.03 COLUMNIST/COMMENTATOR (131.067-010)
11.09.01 MANAGER, ADVERTISING (163.167-010)

Professional and Kindred

01.01.02 COPY WRITER (131.067-014)
01.01.02 WRITER, PROSE, FICTION AND NONFICTION
    (131.067-046)
01.02.01 APPRAISER, ART (191.287-014)
01.02.03 ART DIRECTOR (141.031-010)
01.02.03 AUDIOVISUAL PRODUCTION SPECIALIST
    (149.061-010)
01.02.03 CLOTHES DESIGNER (142.061-018)
01.02.03 COMMERCIAL DESIGNER (141.081-014)
01.02.03 DISPLAY DESIGNER (142.051-010)
01.02.03 GRAPHIC DESIGNER (141.061-018)
01.02.03 ILLUSTRATOR (141.061-022)
01.02.03 INDUSTRIAL DESIGNER (142.061-026)
01.02.03 INTERIOR DESIGNER (142.051-014)
01.02.03 PACKAGE DESIGNER (142.081-018)
01.02.03 PHOTOGRAPHER, MOTION PICTURE (143.062-022)
01.02.03 PHOTOGRAPHER, STILL (143.062-030)
01.03.02 INTERPRETER, DEAF (137.267-014)
01.06.02 CONSERVATOR, ARTIFACTS (055.381-010)
02.01.01 CHEMIST (022.061-010)
02.01.01 COMPUTER-APPLICATIONS ENGINEER
    (020.062-010)
02.01.01 GEOGRAPHER (029.067-010)
02.01.01 GEOLOGIST (024.061-018)

02.01.01 GEOPHYSICIST (024.061-030)
02.01.01 HYDROLOGIST (024.061-034)
02.01.01 MATHEMATICIAN (020.067-014)
02.01.01 METEOROLOGIST (025.062-010)
02.01.01 MINERALOGIST (024.061-038)
02.01.01 PETROLOGIST (024.061-046)
02.01.01 PHYSICIST (023.061-014)
02.01.01 SEISMOLOGIST (024.061-050)
02.01.02 ENVIRONMENTAL ANALYST (029.081-010)
02.01.02 MATERIALS SCIENTIST (029.081-014)
02.01.02 METALLURGIST, PHYSICAL (011.061-022)
02.01.02 PROJECT MANAGER, ENVIRONMENTAL
    RESEARCH (029.167-014)
02.02.01 ANIMAL BREEDER (041.061-014)
02.02.01 ANIMAL SCIENTIST (040.061-014)
02.02.01 BIOMEDICAL ENGINEER (019.061-010)
02.02.01 DAIRY SCIENTIST (040.061-018)
02.02.01 MEDICAL PHYSICIST (079.021-014)
02.02.01 PARASITOLOGIST (041.061-070)
02.02.01 PHARMACOLOGIST (041.061-074)
02.02.01 ZOOLOGIST (041.061-090)
02.02.02 AGRONOMIST (040.061-010)
02.02.02 BOTANIST (041.061-038)
02.02.02 FOREST ECOLOGIST (040.061-030)
02.02.02 HORTICULTURIST (040.061-038)
02.02.02 PLANT BREEDER (041.061-082)
02.02.02 PLANT PATHOLOGIST (041.061-086)
02.02.02 RANGE MANAGER (040.061-046)
02.02.02 SILVICULTURIST (040.061-050)
02.02.02 SOIL CONSERVATIONIST (040.061-054)
02.02.02 SOIL SCIENTIST (040.061-058)
02.02.02 SOIL-CONSERVATION TECHNICIAN (040.261-010)
02.02.02 WOOD TECHNOLOGIST (040.061-062)
02.02.03 BIOCHEMIST (041.061-026)
02.02.03 BIOLOGIST (041.061-030)
02.02.03 BIOPHYSICIST (041.061-034)
02.02.03 MICROBIOLOGIST (041.061-058)
02.02.03 PHYSIOLOGIST (041.061-078)
02.02.04 CHEMIST, FOOD (022.061-014)
02.02.04 DAIRY TECHNOLOGIST (040.061-022)
02.02.04 FOOD TECHNOLOGIST (041.081-010)
02.03.04 AUDIOLOGIST (076.101-010)
02.03.04 OPTOMETRIST (079.101-018)
02.03.04 SPEECH PATHOLOGIST (076.107-010)
02.04.01 ASSAYER (022.281-010)
02.04.01 CHEMICAL-LABORATORY TECHNICIAN
    (022.261-010)
02.04.01 CRIMINALIST (029.281-010)
02.04.01 HOT-CELL TECHNICIAN (015.362-018)
02.04.01 LABORATORY SUPERVISOR (022.137-010)
02.04.01 METALLURGICAL TECHNICIAN (011.261-010)
02.04.01 PHARMACIST (074.161-010)
02.04.01 PHOTO-OPTICS TECHNICIAN (029.280-010)
02.04.01 PHOTOGRAPHER, SCIENTIFIC (143.062-026)
02.04.01 QUALITY-CONTROL TECHNICIAN (012.261-014)
02.04.01 RADIOISOTOPE-PRODUCTION OPERATOR
    (015.362-022)
02.04.01 REACTOR OPERATOR, TEST-AND-RESEARCH
    (015.362-026)
02.04.01 SCANNER (015.384-010)
02.04.01 SPECTROSCOPIST (011.281-014)
02.04.01 TESTER (011.361-010)
02.04.01 WEATHER OBSERVER (025.267-014)
02.04.02 BIOLOGY SPECIMEN TECHNICIAN (041.381-010)
02.04.02 BIOMEDICAL EQUIPMENT TECHNICIAN
    (019.261-010)
02.04.02 HERBARIUM WORKER (041.384-010)
02.04.02 POLYGRAPH EXAMINER (199.267-026)
03.01.04 FORESTER (040.061-034)
05.01.01 CHEMICAL RESEARCH ENGINEER (008.061-022)
05.01.01 ELECTRICAL TECHNICIAN (003.161-010)
05.01.01 ELECTRONICS TECHNICIAN (003.161-014)
05.01.01 INSTRUMENTATION TECHNICIAN (003.261-010)
05.01.01 MECHANICAL-ENGINEERING TECHNICIAN
    (007.161-026)

05.01.01 NUCLEAR-DECONTAMINATION RESEARCH
SPECIALIST (008.061-030)
05.01.01 TECHNICIAN, SEMICONDUCTOR DEVELOPMENT
(003.161-018)
05.01.01 WELDING TECHNICIAN (011.261-014)
05.01.02 HEALTH PHYSICIST (079.021-010)
05.01.02 INDUSTRIAL-HEALTH ENGINEER (012.167-034)
05.01.02 NUCLEAR-CRITICALITY SAFETY ENGINEER
(015.067-010)
05.01.02 POLLUTION-CONTROL ENGINEER (019.081-018)
05.01.02 PRODUCT-SAFETY ENGINEER (012.061-010)
05.01.02 SAFETY ENGINEER (012.061-014)
05.01.02 SAFETY MANAGER (012.167-058)
05.01.03 HYDRAULIC ENGINEER (005.061-018)
05.01.03 ILLUMINATING ENGINEER (003.061-046)
05.01.03 MARINE ENGINEER (014.061-014)
05.01.03 NUCLEAR ENGINEER (015.061-014)
05.01.03 SANITARY ENGINEER (005.061-030)
05.01.03 SYSTEMS ENGINEER, ELECTRONIC DATA
PROCESSING (003.167-062)
05.01.03 WASTE-MANAGEMENT ENGINEER, RADIOACTIVE
MATERIALS (005.061-042)
05.01.04 AIR ANALYST (012.261-010)
05.01.04 CHEMICAL-TEST ENGINEER (008.061-026)
05.01.04 ELECTRICAL TEST ENGINEER (003.061-014)
05.01.04 METALLOGRAPHER (011.061-014)
05.01.04 METROLOGIST (012.067-010)
05.01.04 QUALITY-CONTROL ENGINEER (012.167-054)
05.01.04 RELIABILITY ENGINEER (019.061-026)
05.01.04 STRESS ANALYST (007.061-042)
05.01.04 TEST ENGINEER, NUCLEAR EQUIPMENT
(015.061-022)
05.01.04 TEST TECHNICIAN (019.161-014)
05.01.05 SALES-ENGINEER, ELECTRONICS PRODUCTS
AND SYSTEMS (003.151-014)
05.01.06 CONFIGURATION MANAGEMENT ANALYST
(012.167-010)
05.01.06 DOCUMENTATION ENGINEER (012.167-078)
05.01.06 FACTORY LAY-OUT ENGINEER (012.167-018)
05.01.06 INDUSTRIAL ENGINEER (012.167-030)
05.01.06 LAND SURVEYOR (018.167-018)
05.01.06 MANAGEMENT ANALYST (161.167-010)
05.01.06 MANUFACTURING ENGINEER (012.167-042)
05.01.06 MATERIALS ENGINEER (019.061-014)
05.01.06 METALLURGIST, EXTRACTIVE (011.061-018)
05.01.06 PRODUCTION ENGINEER (012.167-046)
05.01.06 PRODUCTION PLANNER (012.167-050)
05.01.06 STANDARDS ENGINEER (012.061-018)
05.01.06 TIME-STUDY ENGINEER (012.167-070)
05.01.07 AERONAUTICAL ENGINEER (002.061-014)
05.01.07 AGRICULTURAL-ENGINEERING TECHNICIAN
(013.161-010)
05.01.07 AIRPORT ENGINEER (005.061-010)
05.01.07 ARCHITECT (001.061-010)
05.01.07 ARCHITECT, MARINE (001.061-014)
05.01.07 CERAMIC DESIGN ENGINEER (006.061-010)
05.01.07 CERAMIC ENGINEER (006.061-014)
05.01.07 CHEMICAL DESIGN ENGINEER, PROCESSES
(008.061-014)
05.01.07 CHEMICAL ENGINEER (008.061-018)
05.01.07 CIVIL ENGINEER (005.061-014)
05.01.07 ELECTRICAL-DESIGN ENGINEER (003.061-018)
05.01.07 ELECTRO-OPTICAL ENGINEER (023.061-010)
05.01.07 ELECTRONICS-DESIGN ENGINEER (003.061-034)
05.01.07 LANDSCAPE ARCHITECT (001.061-018)
05.01.07 OPTICAL ENGINEER (019.061-018)
05.01.07 TOOL DESIGNER (007.061-026)
05.01.08 AGRICULTURAL ENGINEER (013.061-010)
05.01.08 CHEMICAL-ENGINEERING TECHNICIAN
(008.261-010)
05.01.08 ELECTRICAL ENGINEER (003.061-010)
05.01.08 ELECTRONICS ENGINEER (003.061-030)
05.01.08 ENGINEER, SOILS (024.161-010)
05.01.08 MECHANICAL ENGINEER (007.061-014)
05.01.08 PLANT ENGINEER (007.167-014)

05.01.08 PROJECT ENGINEER (019.167-014)
05.01.08 TRANSPORTATION ENGINEER (005.061-038)
05.01.08 WELDING ENGINEER (011.061-026)
05.02.03 DIRECTOR, QUALITY CONTROL (012.167-014)
05.03.01 PHOTOGRAMMETRIC ENGINEER (018.167-026)
05.03.01 SURVEYOR ASSISTANT, INSTRUMENTS
(018.167-034)
05.03.02 CIVIL ENGINEERING TECHNICIAN (005.261-014)
05.03.02 CONTROLS DESIGNER (003.261-014)
05.03.02 DESIGN DRAFTER, ELECTROMECHANISMS
(017.261-014)
05.03.02 DETAILER (017.261-018)
05.03.02 DRAFTER, AERONAUTICAL (002.261-010)
05.03.02 DRAFTER, ARCHITECTURAL (001.261-010)
05.03.02 DRAFTER, ASSISTANT (017.281-018)
05.03.02 DRAFTER, CARTOGRAPHIC (018.261-010)
05.03.02 DRAFTER, CIVIL (005.281-010)
05.03.02 DRAFTER, COMMERCIAL (017.261-026)   ·
05.03.02 DRAFTER, ELECTRICAL (003.281-010)
05.03.02 DRAFTER, ELECTRONIC (003.281-014)
05.03.02 DRAFTER, LANDSCAPE (001.261-014)
05.03.02 DRAFTER, MARINE (014.281-010)
05.03.02 DRAFTER, MECHANICAL (007.281-010)
05.03.02 DRAFTER, STRUCTURAL (005.281-014)
05.03.02 DRAFTER, TOPOGRAPHICAL (018.261-014)
05.03.02 DRAWINGS CHECKER, ENGINEERING (007.267-010)
05.03.02 EDITOR, MAP (018.261-018)
05.03.02 ENGINEERING ASSISTANT, MECHANICAL
EQUIPMENT (007.161-018)
05.03.02 ESTIMATOR (160.267-018)
05.03.02 FIRE-PROTECTION ENGINEERING TECHNICIAN
(019.261-026)
05.03.02 INTEGRATED CIRCUIT LAYOUT DESIGNER
(003.261-018)
05.03.02 PHOTOGRAMMETRIST (018.261-026)
05.03.02 PRINTED CIRCUIT DESIGNER (003.261-022)
05.03.02 SPECIFICATION WRITER (019.267-010)
05.03.02 TECHNICAL ILLUSTRATOR (017.281-034)
05.03.06 INDUSTRIAL ENGINEERING TECHNICIAN
(012.267-010)
05.03.06 MARINE SURVEYOR (014.167-010)
05.03.07 HEAT-TRANSFER TECHNICIAN (007.181-010)
05.03.07 SOLAR-ENERGY-SYSTEMS DESIGNER (007.161-038)
05.03.08 ENGINEERING TECHNICIAN (005.261-010)
05.03.08 POLLUTION-CONTROL TECHNICIAN (029.261-014)
05.03.09 PACKAGING ENGINEER (019.187-010)
05.05.17 DIETETIC TECHNICIAN (077.121-010)
05.05.17 DIETITIAN, CLINICAL (077.127-014)
07.01.01 CREDIT COUNSELOR (160.207-010)
07.01.01 PROBATION OFFICER (195.167-034)
07.01.04 ESCROW OFFICER (119.367-010)
07.01.05 CONTRACT CLERK (119.267-018)
07.01.05 TITLE EXAMINER (119.287-010)
07.01.05 TITLE SUPERVISOR (119.167-018)
08.01.03 BUYER (162.157-018)
10.01.01 CLERGY MEMBER (120.007-010)
10.01.02 COUNSELOR (045.107-010)
10.01.02 PROBATION-AND-PAROLE OFFICER (195.107-046)
10.01.02 PSYCHOLOGIST, CLINICAL (045.107-022)
10.01.02 PSYCHOLOGIST, COUNSELING (045.107-026)
10.02.02 HYPNOTHERAPIST (079.157-010)
10.03.01 AUDIOMETRIST (078.362-010)
11.01.01 DIRECTOR, RECORDS MANAGEMENT (161.117-014)
11.01.01 ENGINEERING ANALYST (020.067-010)
11.01.01 FORMS ANALYST (161.267-018)
11.01.01 INFORMATION SCIENTIST (109.067-010)
11.01.01 MANAGER, ELECTRONIC DATA PROCESSING
(169.167-030)
11.01.01 OPERATIONS-RESEARCH ANALYST (020.067-018)
11.01.01 PROGRAMER, CHIEF, BUSINESS (020.167-018)
11.01.01 PROGRAMER, ENGINEERING AND SCIENTIFIC
(020.167-022)
11.01.01 PROGRAMER, INFORMATION SYSTEM (020.187-010)
11.01.01 PROGRAMER, PROCESS CONTROL (020.187-014)
11.01.01 PROGRAMMER, BUSINESS (020.162-014)

11.01.01 SOFTWARE TECHNICIAN (020.262-010)
11.01.01 STATISTICIAN, MATHEMATICAL (020.067-022)
11.01.01 SYSTEMS ANALYST, ELECTRONIC DATA
PROCESSING (012.167-066)
11.01.02 ACTUARY (020.167-010)
11.01.02 CONSULTANT (189.167-010)
11.01.02 MATHEMATICAL TECHNICIAN (020.162-010)
11.01.02 STATISTICIAN, APPLIED (020.167-026)
11.02.02 HUMAN RESOURCE ADVISOR (166.267-046)
11.02.02 TECHNICAL SUPPORT SPECIALIST (199.224-010)
11.02.03 COMMUNITY DIETITIAN (077.127-010)
11.02.03 HOME ECONOMIST (096.121-014)
11.03.01 PSYCHOLOGIST, EXPERIMENTAL (045.061-018)
11.03.01 PSYCHOLOGIST, INDUSTRIAL-ORGANIZATIONAL
(045.107-030)
11.03.02 CITY PLANNING AIDE (199.364-010)
11.03.02 POLITICAL SCIENTIST (051.067-010)
11.03.02 RESEARCH WORKER, SOCIAL WELFARE
(054.067-010)
11.03.02 SCIENTIFIC LINGUIST (059.067-014)
11.03.02 SOCIOLOGIST (054.067-014)
11.03.02 URBAN PLANNER (199.167-014)
11.03.03 ANTHROPOLOGIST (055.067-010)
11.03.03 ARCHEOLOGIST (055.067-018)
11.03.03 ARCHIVIST (101.167-010)
11.03.03 GENEALOGIST (052.067-018)
11.03.03 HISTORIAN (052.067-022)
11.03.03 RESEARCH ASSISTANT (109.267-010)
11.03.04 EMPLOYMENT INTERVIEWER (166.267-010)
11.03.04 JOB ANALYST (166.267-018)
11.03.04 JOB DEVELOPMENT SPECIALIST (166.267-034)
11.03.04 OCCUPATIONAL ANALYST (166.067-010)
11.03.04 PERSONNEL RECRUITER (166.267-038)
11.03.05 ECONOMIST (050.067-010)
11.04.02 LAWYER (110.107-010)
11.04.02 LEGAL INVESTIGATOR (119.267-022)
11.04.02 PARALEGAL ASSISTANT (119.267-026)
11.04.04 ABSTRACTOR (119.267-010)
11.04.04 PATENT AGENT (119.167-014)
11.05.01 ASSOCIATION EXECUTIVE (189.117-010)
11.05.02 BUSINESS REPRESENTATIVE, LABOR UNION
(187.167-018)
11.05.02 DIETITIAN, CHIEF (077.117-010)
11.05.02 DIRECTOR, QUALITY ASSURANCE (189.117-042)
11.05.02 GRANT COORDINATOR (169.117-014)
11.05.02 MANAGER, CREDIT CARD OPERATIONS
(186.167-022)
11.05.02 MANAGER, PERSONNEL (166.117-018)
11.05.02 MANAGER, PROCUREMENT SERVICES
(162.167-022)
11.05.02 PROGRAM MANAGER (189.167-030)
11.05.02 PROGRAM SPECIALIST, EMPLOYEE-HEALTH
MAINTENANCE (166.167-050)
11.05.03 MANAGER, HOUSING PROJECT (186.167-030)
11.05.04 PURCHASING AGENT (162.157-038)
11.06.01 ACCOUNTANT (160.167-010)
11.06.01 ACCOUNTANT, BUDGET (160.167-014)
11.06.01 ACCOUNTANT, COST (160.167-018)
11.06.01 ACCOUNTANT, TAX (160.162-010)
11.06.01 AUDITOR (160.162-014)
11.06.01 AUDITOR, INTERNAL (160.167-034)
11.06.01 AUDITOR, TAX (160.167-038)
11.06.02 REPORTS ANALYST (161.267-026)
11.06.03 MARKET-RESEARCH ANALYST 1 (050.067-014)
11.07.01 FIELD REPRESENTATIVE (189.267-010)
11.07.01 PROGRAM DIRECTOR, GROUP WORK (187.117-046)
11.07.02 PUBLIC HEALTH EDUCATOR (079.117-014)
11.07.04 RECREATION SUPERVISOR (187.137-010)
11.08.02 RESEARCH ASSISTANT II (199.267-034)
11.08.02 WRITER, TECHNICAL PUBLICATIONS (131.267-026)
11.08.04 INTERPRETER (137.267-010)
11.08.04 TRANSLATOR (137.267-018)
11.09.01 MEDIA DIRECTOR (164.117-018)
11.09.02 DIRECTOR, FUNDS DEVELOPMENT (165.117-014)
11.09.02 MEMBERSHIP DIRECTOR (189.167-026)

11.09.03 EMPLOYER RELATIONS REPRESENTATIVE
(166.257-010)
11.09.03 PUBLIC-RELATIONS REPRESENTATIVE
(165.067-010)
11.10.03 INDUSTRIAL HYGIENIST (079.161-010)
11.10.03 SANITARIAN (079.117-018)
11.10.05 RATER, TRAVEL ACCOMMODATIONS (168.367-014)
11.11.04 MANAGER, EMPLOYMENT AGENCY (187.167-098)
11.12.02 REAL-ESTATE AGENT (186.117-058)
11.12.04 CONTRACT SPECIALIST (162.117-018)

Radio and TV Broadcasting

01.01.01 CONTINUITY DIRECTOR (132.037-010)
01.01.01 EDITOR, FILM (962.264-010)
01.01.02 SCREEN WRITER (131.087-018)
01.02.03 ART DIRECTOR (142.031-010)
01.02.03 DIRECTOR OF PHOTOGRAPHY (143.062-010)
01.02.03 PHOTOJOURNALIST (143.062-034)
01.02.03 SET DECORATOR (142.061-042)
01.02.03 SET DESIGNER (142.061-046)
01.02.03 TELEVISION TECHNICIAN (194.062-010)
01.03.01 PRODUCER (159.117-010)
01.03.03 ANNOUNCER (159.147-010)
01.03.03 DISK JOCKEY (159.147-014)
01.04.03 SINGER (152.047-010)
01.06.02 MAKE-UP ARTIST (333.071-010)
05.01.03 COMMERCIAL ENGINEER (003.187-014)
05.03.05 FIELD ENGINEER (193.262-018)
05.03.05 TRANSMITTER OPERATOR (193.262-038)
05.03.05 VIDEO OPERATOR (194.282-010)
05.10.01 GRIP (962.684-014)
05.10.03 LIGHT TECHNICIAN (962.362-014)
05.10.05 AUDIO OPERATOR (194.262-010)
05.10.05 RECORDING ENGINEER (194.362-010)
05.10.05 RERECORDING MIXER (194.362-014)
05.10.05 SOUND MIXER (194.262-018)
05.10.05 TAPE TRANSFERRER (194.382-014)
05.12.03 DOLLY PUSHER (962.687-010)
05.12.04 GRIP (962.687-022)
07.05.01 TELEVISION-SCHEDULE COORDINATOR
(199.387-010)
07.05.03 NEWS ASSISTANT (209.367-038)
08.01.02 SALES REPRESENTATIVE, RADIO AND
TELEVISION TIME (259.357-018)
11.05.02 MANAGER, PRODUCTION (184.167-074)
11.05.02 MANAGER, STATION (184.117-062)
11.05.02 PROGRAM PROPOSALS COORDINATOR
(132.067-030)
11.05.02 UTILIZATION COORDINATOR (169.167-078)
11.05.04 DIRECTOR, MEDIA MARKETING (163.117-022)
11.08.02 REPORTER (131.267-018)
11.08.03 COLUMNIST/COMMENTATOR (131.067-010)
11.08.03 NEWSCASTER (131.267-010)
11.12.02 LOCATION MANAGER (191.167-018)
12.02.01 STUNT PERFORMER (159.341-014)

Real Estate

03.04.04 CEMETERY WORKER (406.684-010)
05.12.18 HOUSEKEEPER (321.137-010)
07.05.02 TITLE SEARCHER (209.367-046)
08.01.03
BUSINESS-OPPORTUNITY-AND-PROPERTY-INVEST
MENT BROKER (189.157-010)
08.02.04 LEASING AGENT, RESIDENCE (250.357-014)
08.02.04 SALES AGENT, REAL ESTATE (250.357-018)
11.05.01 MANAGER, LAND DEVELOPMENT (186.117-042)
11.06.03 APPRAISER, REAL ESTATE (191.267-010)
11.11.01 CONDOMINIUM MANAGER (186.167-062)
11.11.01 MANAGER, APARTMENT HOUSE (186.167-018)
11.11.04 MANAGER, PROPERTY (186.167-046)
11.11.04 MANAGER, REAL-ESTATE FIRM (186.167-066)

Refrigeration Equipment

05.05.09 REFRIGERATION MECHANIC (827.361-014)

Retail Trade

01.02.03 DISPLAYER, MERCHANDISE (298.081-010)
01.02.03 FASHION ARTIST (141.061-014)
01.02.03 FLORAL DESIGNER (142.081-010)
01.02.03 MANAGER, DISPLAY (142.031-014)
01.06.02 PICTURE FRAMER (739.684-146)
01.06.03 GIFT WRAPPER (299.364-014)
03.01.03 MANAGER, NURSERY (180.167-042)
05.05.11 OPTICIAN (716.280-014)
05.05.11 OPTICIAN, DISPENSING 1 (713.361-014)
05.05.15 ALTERATION TAILOR (785.261-010)
05.05.15 CUSTOM TAILOR (785.261-014)
05.05.15 SHOP TAILOR (785.361-022)
05.08.03 DELIVERER, CAR RENTAL (919.663-010)
05.08.03 LOT ATTENDANT (915.583-010)
05.09.01 MEAT CLERK (222.684-010)
05.09.01 ORDER FILLER (222.487-014)
05.09.01 STOCK CLERK, SELF-SERVICE STORE (299.367-014)
05.09.01 TIRE ADJUSTER (241.367-034)
05.09.02 DRAPERY AND UPHOLSTERY ESTIMATOR (299.387-010)
05.09.03 MARKER (209.587-034)
05.10.01 BOAT RIGGER (806.464-010)
05.10.01 CARPET CUTTER (929.381-010)
05.10.01 CARPET LAYER (864.381-010)
05.10.01 CARPET-LAYER HELPER (864.687-010)
05.10.01 DRAPERY HANGER (869.484-014)
05.10.01 FLOOR LAYER (864.481-010)
05.10.01 FURNITURE ASSEMBLER-AND-INSTALLER (739.684-082)
05.10.01 SIDER (863.684-014)
05.10.02 MANAGER, CUSTOMER SERVICES (187.167-082)
05.10.02 MEDICAL-EQUIPMENT REPAIRER (639.281-022)
05.10.02 NEW-CAR GET-READY MECHANIC (806.361-026)
05.10.02 SERVICE MANAGER (185.164-010)
05.10.04 USED-CAR RENOVATOR (620.684-034)
05.10.08 MEAT CUTTER (316.684-018)
05.12.17 DELI CUTTER-SLICER (316.684-014)
06.02.05 CARPET SEWER (787.682-014)
07.02.02 CONTRACT CLERK, AUTOMOBILE (219.362-026)
07.03.01 AUCTION CLERK (294.567-010)
07.03.01 CASHIER-CHECKER (211.462-014)
07.03.01 LAYAWAY CLERK (299.467-010)
07.05.02 CREDIT-REFERENCE CLERK (209.362-018)
07.05.02 PRODUCTION PROOFREADER (247.667-010)
07.05.02 THROW-OUT CLERK (241.367-030)
07.05.03 AUTOMOBILE LOCATOR (296.367-010)
07.05.03 CALL-OUT OPERATOR (237.367-014)
07.05.04 MERCHANDISE DISTRIBUTOR (219.367-018)
07.06.02 CHECK WRITER (219.382-010)
07.07.02 AUCTION ASSISTANT (294.667-010)
08.01.01 SALES REPRESENTATIVE, AIRCRAFT (273.253-010)
08.01.03 BUYER, ASSISTANT (162.157-022)
08.01.03 COMPARISON SHOPPER (296.367-014)
08.01.03 PAWNBROKER (191.157-010)
08.02.02 SALES-SERVICE REPRESENTATIVE, MILKING MACHINES (299.251-010)
08.02.02 SALESPERSON, ART OBJECTS (277.457-010)
08.02.02 SALESPERSON, AUTOMOBILES (273.353-010)
08.02.02 SALESPERSON, BOOKS (277.357-034)
08.02.02 SALESPERSON, COSMETICS AND TOILETRIES (262.357-018)
08.02.02 SALESPERSON, CURTAINS AND DRAPERIES (270.357-022)
08.02.02 SALESPERSON, FLOWERS (260.357-026)
08.02.02 SALESPERSON, FURNITURE (270.357-030)
08.02.02 SALESPERSON, HEARING AIDS (276.354-010)
08.02.02 SALESPERSON, HOUSEHOLD APPLIANCES (270.357-034)
08.02.02 SALESPERSON, INFANTS' AND CHILDREN'S WEAR (261.357-046)
08.02.02 SALESPERSON, JEWELRY (279.357-058)
08.02.02 SALESPERSON, MEN'S AND BOYS' CLOTHING (261.357-050)
08.02.02 SALESPERSON, MUSICAL INSTRUMENTS AND ACCESSORIES (277.357-038)
08.02.02 SALESPERSON, PHONOGRAPH RECORDS AND TAPE RECORDINGS (277.357-046)
08.02.02 SALESPERSON, PIANOS AND ORGANS (277.354-010)
08.02.02 SALESPERSON, SHOES (261.357-062)
08.02.02 SALESPERSON, SPORTING GOODS (277.357-058)
08.02.02 SALESPERSON, STEREO EQUIPMENT (270.357-038)
08.02.02 SALESPERSON, SURGICAL APPLIANCES (276.257-022)
08.02.02 SALESPERSON, WOMEN'S APPAREL AND ACCESSORIES (261.357-066)
08.02.02 SALESPERSON, YARD GOODS (261.357-070)
08.02.03 AUCTIONEER (294.257-010)
08.02.03 SALES REPRESENTATIVE, BOATS AND MARINE SUPPLIES (273.357-018)
08.02.03 SALES REPRESENTATIVE, OFFICE MACHINES (275.357-034)
08.02.03 SALES REPRESENTATIVE, TOBACCO PRODUCTS AND SMOKING SUPPLIES (260.357-022)
08.02.03 SALESPERSON, AUTOMOBILE ACCESSORIES (273.357-030)
08.02.03 SALESPERSON, FLOOR COVERINGS (270.357-026)
08.02.03 SALESPERSON, GENERAL HARDWARE (279.357-050)
08.02.03 SALESPERSON, GENERAL MERCHANDISE (279.357-054)
08.02.03 SALESPERSON, HORTICULTURAL AND NURSERY PRODUCTS (272.357-022)
08.02.03 SALESPERSON, PARTS (279.357-062)
08.02.03 SALESPERSON, PHOTOGRAPHIC SUPPLIES AND EQUIPMENT (277.357-050)
08.02.05 DEMONSTRATOR (297.354-010)
08.02.05 DEMONSTRATOR, KNITTING (297.354-014)
08.02.05 SALESPERSON-DEMONSTRATOR, PARTY PLAN (279.357-038)
08.02.06 SALES REPRESENTATIVE, UPHOLSTERY AND FURNITURE REPAIR (259.357-026)
08.02.06 TRAVEL AGENT (252.157-010)
08.02.06 WEDDING CONSULTANT (299.357-018)
08.02.07 DRIVER, SALES ROUTE (292.353-010)
08.02.08 SALES REPRESENTATIVE, DOOR-TO-DOOR (291.357-010)
09.04.02 BICYCLE-RENTAL CLERK (295.467-010)
09.04.02 CASHIER-WRAPPER (211.462-018)
09.04.02 CUSTOMER-SERVICE CLERK (299.367-010)
09.04.02 DELIVERER, MERCHANDISE (299.477-010)
09.04.02 FURNITURE-RENTAL CONSULTANT (295.357-018)
09.04.02 NEWSPAPER CARRIER (292.457-010)
09.04.02 PERSONAL SHOPPER (296.357-010)
09.04.02 SALES ATTENDANT, BUILDING MATERIALS (299.677-014)
09.04.02 SALES CLERK (290.477-014)
09.04.02 SALES CLERK, FOOD (290.477-018)
09.04.02 STORAGE-FACILITY RENTAL CLERK (295.367-026)
09.04.02 TOOL-AND-EQUIPMENT-RENTAL CLERK (295.357-014)
11.02.04 FILM-RENTAL CLERK (295.367-018)
11.05.02 DIRECTOR, SERVICE (189.167-014)
11.05.02 MANAGER, DEPARTMENT STORE (185.117-010)
11.09.01 FASHION COORDINATOR (185.157-010)
11.10.01 INVESTIGATOR, FRAUD (376.267-014)
11.10.05 DEALER-COMPLIANCE REPRESENTATIVE (168.267-026)
11.11.04 MANAGER, FAST FOOD SERVICES (185.137-010)
11.11.04 MANAGER, TRAVEL AGENCY (187.167-158)
11.11.05 MANAGER, AUTOMOBILE SERVICE STATION (185.167-014)
11.11.05 MANAGER, DEPARTMENT (299.137-010)
11.11.05 MANAGER, MARKET (186.167-042)
11.11.05 MANAGER, MEAT SALES AND STORAGE (185.167-030)
11.11.05 MANAGER, PARTS (185.167-038)
11.11.05 MANAGER, RETAIL STORE (185.167-046)

Railroad Transportation

05.08.02 FIRER, LOCOMOTIVE (910.363-010)
05.08.02 LOCOMOTIVE ENGINEER (910.363-014)
05.12.03 BAGGAGE HANDLER (910.687-010)
05.12.05 BRAKE COUPLER, ROAD FREIGHT (910.367-010)
05.12.05 SWITCH TENDER (910.667-026)
05.12.12 TRACK REPAIRER (910.682-010)
07.02.04 DEMURRAGE CLERK (214.362-010)
07.04.05 TRAIN DISPATCHER (184.167-262)
08.01.02 TRAFFIC AGENT (252.257-010)
09.05.03 PORTER (357.677-010)
11.05.02 MANAGER, OPERATIONS (184.117-050)
11.10.05 TRAFFIC INSPECTOR (184.163-010)
11.10.05 TRANSPORTATION INSPECTOR (168.167-082)
11.11.03 CONDUCTOR, PASSENGER CAR (198.167-010)
11.11.03 CONDUCTOR, ROAD FREIGHT (198.167-018)
11.11.03 STATION MANAGER (184.167-130)
11.12.01 GENERAL CLAIMS AGENT (186.117-030)

Rubber Goods

06.04.07 DESIGN PRINTER, BALLOON (651.685-014)
06.04.07 RUBBER CUTTER (559.685-158)
06.04.10 INJECTION-MOLDING-MACHINE TENDER
 (556.685-038)
06.04.38 PACKING-LINE WORKER (753.687-038)

Rubber Tires and Tubes

06.04.07 RUBBER CUTTER (559.685-158)
06.04.13 TIRE MOLDER (553.685-102)

Sanitary Services

05.07.01 SEWER-LINE PHOTO-INSPECTOR (851.362-010)
05.10.01 SEWER-LINE REPAIRER, TELE-GROUT
 (851.262-010)
05.12.12 SEWER-LINE REPAIRER (869.664-018)
05.12.18 SEWAGE-DISPOSAL WORKER (955.687-010)

Sawmill

06.02.03 HEAD SAWYER (667.662-010)
06.04.03 ARTIFICIAL-LOG-MACHINE OPERATOR
 (569.685-010)
06.04.03 CHAIN OFFBEARER (669.686-018)
06.04.03 POWER-BARKER OPERATOR (669.485-010)
06.04.40 SAWMILL WORKER (667.686-014)

Ship and Boat Building and Repairing

05.05.02 BOAT REPAIRER (807.361-014)
05.05.02 BOATBUILDER, WOOD (860.381-018)
05.05.02 MARINE-SERVICES TECHNICIAN (806.261-026)
05.05.02 SHIPWRIGHT (860.381-058)
05.05.06 RIGGER (806.261-014)
05.05.06 SHIPFITTER (806.381-046)
05.05.08 LOFT WORKER (661.281-010)
05.05.09 MANAGER, MARINE SERVICE (187.167-130)
05.10.01 BOAT RIGGER (806.464-010)
05.12.03 LABORER, SHIPYARD (809.687-022)
06.01.04 CANVAS WORKER (739.381-010)
06.02.24 BOAT PATCHER, PLASTIC (807.684-014)

Signs and Advertising Novelities

01.06.02 DISPLAY MAKER (739.361-010)
05.05.06 SIGN ERECTOR 1 (869.381-026)
05.10.01 SIGN ERECTOR 2 (869.684-054)
05.12.18 CLEANER, SIGNS (739.687-062)
06.02.22 ELECTRIC-SIGN ASSEMBLER (729.684-022)
08.01.01 SALES REPRESENTATIVE, SIGNS AND DISPLAYS
 (254.257-010)

Silverware

01.06.02 SILVERSMITH (700.281-022)
06.02.24 GREASE BUFFER (705.684-022)
06.04.24 OXIDIZER (700.684-054)

Slaughtering and Meat Packing

06.02.28 BUTCHER, ALL-ROUND (525.381-014)
06.04.15 BAND-SAW OPERATOR (525.685-010)
06.04.15 PRESS OPERATOR, MEAT (520.685-182)
06.04.28 BONER, MEAT (525.684-010)
06.04.28 POULTRY DRESSER (525.687-070)
06.04.28 TRIMMER, MEAT (525.684-054)
06.04.40 LABORER (529.687-130)

Soap and Glycerin

06.02.18 SOAP MAKER (559.382-054)

Social Services

07.01.01 MANAGEMENT AIDE (195.367-014)
09.01.01 GROUP WORKER (195.164-010)
09.01.01 RECREATION AIDE (195.367-030)
09.01.01 RECREATION LEADER (195.227-014)
10.01.02 CASE AIDE (195.367-010)
10.01.02 CASEWORKER (195.107-010)
10.01.02 SOCIAL-SERVICES AIDE (195.367-034)
10.02.02 PROGRAM AIDE, GROUP WORK (195.227-010)
10.02.03 TEACHER, HOME THERAPY (195.227-018)
11.02.03 HOMEMAKER (309.354-010)
11.07.01 COMMUNITY ORGANIZATION WORKER
 (195.167-010)
11.11.02 DIRECTOR, CAMP (195.167-018)
11.11.02 DIRECTOR, RECREATION CENTER (195.167-026)

Sporting and Athletic Goods

01.06.02 BOW MAKER, CUSTOM (732.381-010)
05.05.10 PINSETTER ADJUSTER, AUTOMATIC (829.381-010)
06.02.24 SKI REPAIRER, PRODUCTION (732.684-118)
06.02.32 BOW MAKER, PRODUCTION (732.684-038)
06.02.32 RACKET STRINGER (732.684-094)
06.02.32 SKI MOLDER (732.684-114)
06.04.13 BOWLING-BALL MOLDER (556.685-018)
06.04.23 ASSEMBLER (732.684-014)
06.04.34 LEADER TIER (732.687-038)
06.04.34 MACHINE SNELLER (732.685-026)

Statue and Art Goods

06.02.30 PLASTER MAKER (779.684-046)

Stoneworking

01.06.02 STONE CARVER (771.281-014)
05.05.01 STONECUTTER, HAND (771.381-014)

Structural and Ornamental Metalwork

06.04.02 SCROLL-MACHINE OPERATOR (616.685-062)

Sugar

06.04.40 CHAR-CONVEYOR TENDER (529.685-050)

Synthetic Fibers

02.04.01 LABORATORY TESTER (022.281-018)

Telegraph and Telephone

03.04.05 TREE TRIMMER (408.664-010)
05.01.03 CABLE ENGINEER, OUTSIDE PLANT (003.167-010)
05.01.03 CENTRAL-OFFICE EQUIPMENT ENGINEER
 (003.187-010)
05.01.08 CUSTOMER-EQUIPMENT ENGINEER (003.187-018)
05.05.05 AUTOMATIC-EQUIPMENT TECHNICIAN
 (822.281-010)
05.05.05 CABLE SPLICER (829.361-010)
05.05.05 CABLE SUPERVISOR (184.161-010)
05.05.05 CABLE TESTER (822.361-010)
05.05.05 CENTRAL-OFFICE REPAIRER (822.281-014)
05.05.05 PRIVATE-BRANCH-EXCHANGE REPAIRER
 (822.281-022)
05.05.05 STATION INSTALLER-AND-REPAIRER (822.261-022)

07.04.01 CUSTOMER-SERVICE REPRESENTATIVE
(239.367-010)
07.04.06 CENTRAL-OFFICE OPERATOR (235.462-010)
07.04.06 DIRECTORY-ASSISTANCE OPERATOR (235.662-018)
07.07.03 COIN-MACHINE COLLECTOR (292.687-010)
08.01.02 SALES REPRESENTATIVE, PUBLIC UTILITIES
(253.357-010)
08.01.02 SALES REPRESENTATIVE, TELEPHONE
SERVICES (253.257-010)
11.05.02 OPERATIONS MANAGER (184.117-070)
11.10.05 REGULATORY ADMINISTRATOR (168.167-070)
11.12.01 MANAGER, CUSTOMER SERVICE (168.167-058)

Textile Products, n.e.c.

06.04.23 FILLER (780.684-066)

Textile

02.04.01 LABORATORY ASSISTANT (029.381-014)
06.01.02 LOOM FIXER (683.260-018)
06.02.06 WEAVER (683.682-038)
06.02.27 MENDER (782.684-042)
06.04.06 BEAM-WARPER TENDER, AUTOMATIC (681.685-018)
06.04.06 CLOTH DOFFER (689.586-010)
06.04.16 MACHINE FEEDER, RAW STOCK (680.686-018)
06.04.16 SLASHER TENDER (582.562-010)

Tobacco

06.03.01 SPECIAL TESTER (529.487-010)
06.04.28 CIGAR MAKER (790.684-014)

Toys and Games

06.04.23 TOY ASSEMBLER (731.687-034)
06.04.34 STUFFER (731.685-014)

Transportation Equipment, n.e.c.

06.02.22 UTILITY WORKER (869.684-074)

Veneer and Plywood

03.04.02 CHAINSAW OPERATOR (454.687-010)
06.04.03 LATHE SPOTTER (663.686-022)
06.04.25 CROSSBAND LAYER (762.687-026)
06.04.40 CLAMP REMOVER (569.687-010)

Vinous Liquors

05.02.03 WINE MAKER (183.161-014)

Waste and Batting

06.04.16 MACHINE FEEDER, RAW STOCK (680.686-018)

Water Transportation

05.02.07 MANAGER, MARINA DRY DOCK (187.167-226)
05.04.02 MATE, SHIP (197.133-022)
05.04.02 PILOT, SHIP (197.133-026)
05.06.02 ENGINEER (197.130-010)
05.08.04 DECKHAND (911.687-022)
05.10.08 SALAD MAKER (317.384-010)
05.11.04 STEVEDORE 1 (911.663-014)
05.12.03 ABLE SEAMAN (911.364-010)
05.12.03 BARGE CAPTAIN (911.137-010)
05.12.06 BOAT LOADER 1 (911.364-014)
05.12.08 MARINE OILER (911.584-010)
05.12.18 ORDINARY SEAMAN (911.687-030)
08.01.02 TRAFFIC AGENT (252.257-010)
09.01.01 DIRECTOR, SOCIAL (352.167-010)
09.05.02 MESS ATTENDANT (350.677-010)
11.05.02 MANAGER, OPERATIONS (184.117-050)
11.11.03 MANAGER, TRAFFIC (184.117-066)
11.11.03 PURSER (197.167-014)
11.12.01 GENERAL CLAIMS AGENT (186.117-030)

Waterworks

02.04.01 HYDROGRAPHER (025.264-010)

05.06.03 PUMP-STATION OPERATOR, WATERWORKS
(954.382-010)
05.06.04 WATER-TREATMENT-PLANT OPERATOR
(954.382-014)
05.09.03 METER READER (209.567-010)
05.10.01 SERVICE REPRESENTATIVE (959.574-010)
07.04.01 CUSTOMER-SERVICE REPRESENTATIVE
(239.367-010)

Welding and Related Processes

05.05.06 ARC CUTTER (816.364-010)
05.05.06 WELDER, ARC (810.384-014)
05.05.06 WELDER, COMBINATION (819.384-010)
05.05.06 WELDER, EXPERIMENTAL (819.281-022)
05.05.06 WELDER, GAS (811.684-014)
05.05.06 WELDER-FITTER (819.361-010)
05.10.01 WELDER, TACK (810.684-010)
05.12.11 THERMAL CUTTER, HAND 2 (816.684-010)
06.02.19 LASER-BEAM-MACHINE OPERATOR (815.682-010)
06.02.19 WELDING-MACHINE OPERATOR, ARC (810.382-010)
06.02.19 WELDING-MACHINE OPERATOR, GAS (811.482-010)
06.02.22 BRAZER, ASSEMBLER (813.684-010)
06.04.31 WELDER, GUN (810.664-010)
06.04.31 WELDER, PRODUCTION LINE (819.684-010)

Wholesale Trade

03.01.01 GENERAL MANAGER, FARM (180.167-018)
03.01.03 MANAGER, NURSERY (180.167-042)
03.04.01 SORTER, AGRICULTURAL PRODUCE (529.687-186)
05.05.06 SAFE-AND-VAULT SERVICE MECHANIC
(869.381-022)
05.08.03 NEWSPAPER-DELIVERY DRIVER (292.363-010)
05.09.01 ORDER FILLER (222.487-014)
05.09.03 MARKER (209.587-034)
05.10.08 MEAT CUTTER (316.684-018)
05.12.15 AUTOMOBILE WRECKER (620.684-010)
07.03.01 AUCTION CLERK (294.567-010)
07.07.02 AUCTION ASSISTANT (294.667-010)
08.01.01 PHARMACEUTICAL DETAILER (262.157-010)
08.01.01 SALES REPRESENTATIVE, AIRCRAFT (273.253-010)
08.01.01 SALES REPRESENTATIVE, CHEMICALS AND
DRUGS (262.357-010)
08.01.01 SALES REPRESENTATIVE, COMMUNICATION
EQUIPMENT (271.257-010)
08.01.01 SALES REPRESENTATIVE, COMPUTERS AND EDP
SYSTEMS (275.257-010)
08.01.01 SALES REPRESENTATIVE, DENTAL AND MEDICAL
EQUIPMENT AND SUPPLIES (276.257-010)
08.01.01 SALES REPRESENTATIVE, ELECTRONICS PARTS
(271.357-010)
08.01.02 SALES REPRESENTATIVE, PRINTING (254.357-018)
08.01.03 COMMISSION AGENT, AGRICULTURAL PRODUCE
(260.357-010)
08.01.03 COMPARISON SHOPPER (296.367-014)
08.01.03 SALES REPRESENTATIVE, LIVESTOCK
(260.257-010)
08.02.01 MANUFACTURERS' REPRESENTATIVE
(279.157-010)
08.02.01 SALES REPRESENTATIVE, ANIMAL-FEED
PRODUCTS (272.357-010)
08.02.01 SALES REPRESENTATIVE, CANVAS PRODUCTS
(261.357-014)
08.02.01 SALES REPRESENTATIVE, FARM AND GARDEN
EQUIPMENT AND SUPPLIES (272.357-014)
08.02.01 SALES REPRESENTATIVE, HOME FURNISHINGS
(270.357-010)
08.02.01 SALES REPRESENTATIVE, HOUSEHOLD
APPLIANCES (270.357-014)
08.02.01 SALES REPRESENTATIVE, MALT LIQUORS
(260.357-018)
08.02.01 SALES REPRESENTATIVE, MEN'S AND BOYS'
APPAREL (261.357-022)
08.02.01 SALES REPRESENTATIVE, NOVELTIES
(277.357-018)

08.02.01 SALES REPRESENTATIVE, PETROLEUM PRODUCTS (269.357-014)
08.02.01 SALES REPRESENTATIVE, RECREATION AND SPORTING GOODS (277.357-026)
08.02.01 SALES REPRESENTATIVE, TEXTILES (261.357-030)
08.02.01 SALES REPRESENTATIVE, VIDEOTAPE (271.357-014)
08.02.01 SALES REPRESENTATIVE, WOMEN'S AND GIRLS' APPAREL (261.357-038)
08.02.01 SALES-PROMOTION REPRESENTATIVE (269.357-018)
08.02.03 AUCTIONEER (294.257-010)
08.02.03 SALES REPRESENTATIVE, BOATS AND MARINE SUPPLIES (273.357-018)
08.02.03 SALES REPRESENTATIVE, OFFICE MACHINES (275.357-034)
08.02.03 SALES REPRESENTATIVE, TOBACCO PRODUCTS AND SMOKING SUPPLIES (260.357-022)
08.02.03 SALESPERSON, AUTOMOBILE ACCESSORIES (273.357-030)
08.02.03 SALESPERSON, FLOOR COVERINGS (270.357-026)
08.02.03 SALESPERSON, GENERAL HARDWARE (279.357-050)
08.02.03 SALESPERSON, GENERAL MERCHANDISE (279.357-054)
08.02.03 SALESPERSON, HORTICULTURAL AND NURSERY PRODUCTS (272.357-022)
08.02.03 SALESPERSON, PARTS (279.357-062)
08.02.03 SALESPERSON, PHOTOGRAPHIC SUPPLIES AND EQUIPMENT (277.357-050)
08.02.05 DEMONSTRATOR (297.354-010)
08.02.07 DRIVER, SALES ROUTE (292.353-010)
11.01.01 CUSTOMER-SUPPORT SPECIALIST (020.224-010)

11.05.04 FIELD REPRESENTATIVE (163.267-010)
11.10.05 DEALER-COMPLIANCE REPRESENTATIVE (168.267-026)
11.11.03 MANAGER, DISTRIBUTION WAREHOUSE (185.167-018)
11.11.04 MANAGER, FAST FOOD SERVICES (185.137-010)
11.11.05 MANAGER, MARKET (186.167-042)
11.11.05 MANAGER, MEAT SALES AND STORAGE (185.167-030)
11.11.05 MANAGER, PARTS (185.167-038)

Wire Drawing

06.04.02 WIRE-DRAWING-MACHINE TENDER (614.685-026)

Wooden Boxes

06.02.25 BOX MAKER, WOOD (760.684-014)

Wood Distilling and Charcoal

03.04.02 CHAINSAW OPERATOR (454.687-010)

Wood Preserving

06.04.18 TANKER (561.665-010)

Woodworking

05.05.08 CABINETMAKER (660.280-010)
05.05.08 FURNITURE FINISHER (763.381-010)
06.02.03 CUT-OFF-SAW OPERATOR (667.682-022)
06.03.02 GRADER (669.587-010)
06.03.02 LUMBER SORTER (922.687-074)
06.04.20 CORRUGATED-FASTENER DRIVER (669.685-042)
06.04.25 WOODWORKING-SHOP HAND (769.687-054)

Appendix D
Listing of Occupations by Educational Level

This index organizes all occupations listed in *The Enhanced Guide for Occupational Exploration* under the minimum amount or type of education normally required. It provides a useful way to find occupations with entry requirements which are acceptable to you. It is important to note that this list does have limitations as it lists the MINIMUM requirements for those who hold the jobs. In many cases, you will need to obtain additional training to be competitive for entry into these jobs since many of those who hold the jobs have higher levels of preparation. For example, most people who work as pharmacologists, chemists, and geologists have master's degrees or above, even though these jobs are listed as requiring a four-year college bachelor's degree. Some people with a bachelor's degree do hold these jobs, but few new college graduates will obtain these jobs without additional education. This is why it is most important for you to more thoroughly research a career decision and its requirements before making a major time commitment to it. In spite of its limitations, we hope you find this appendix helpful. This appendix is arranged by the GOE number followed by the job title, its major occupational cluster and the DOT code.

Master's Degree or Above

02.01.01 GEOGRAPHER (profess. & kin.), 029.067-010
02.01.01 MATHEMATICIAN (profess. & kin.), 020.067-014
02.01.01 PHYSICIST (profess. & kin.), 023.061-014
02.02.01 HISTOPATHOLOGIST (medical ser.), 041.061-054
02.02.01 MEDICAL PHYSICIST (profess. & kin.), 079.021-014
02.03.01 GENERAL PRACTITIONER (medical ser.), 070.101-022
02.03.02 DENTIST (medical ser.), 072.101-010
02.03.03 VETERINARIAN (medical ser.), 073.101-010
02.03.04 AUDIOLOGIST (profess. & kin.), 076.101-010
02.03.04 SPEECH PATHOLOGIST (profess. & kin.), 076.107-010
02.04.01 PHARMACIST (profess. & kin.), 074.161-010
02.04.02 TOXICOLOGIST (drug prep. & related), 022.081-010
05.01.02 HEALTH PHYSICIST (profess. & kin.), 079.021-010
05.01.07 ARCHITECT (profess. & kin.), 001.061-010
10.01.02 COUNSELOR (profess. & kin.), 045.107-010
10.01.02 PSYCHOLOGIST, CLINICAL (profess. & kin.), 045.107-022
10.01.02 PSYCHOLOGIST, COUNSELING (profess. & kin.), 045.107-026
10.01.02 VOCATIONAL-REHABILITATION COUNSELOR (gov. ser.), 045.107-042
10.02.03 TEACHER, HANDICAPPED STUDENTS (educ.), 094.227-018
11.02.01 FACULTY MEMBER, COLLEGE OR UNIVERSITY (educ.), 090.227-010
11.03.01 PSYCHOLOGIST, EXPERIMENTAL (profess. & kin.), 045.061-018
11.03.01 PSYCHOLOGIST, INDUSTRIAL-ORGANIZATIONAL (profess. & kin.), 045.107-030
11.03.02 POLITICAL SCIENTIST (profess. & kin.), 051.067-010
11.03.02 SOCIOLOGIST (profess. & kin.), 054.067-014
11.03.03 ANTHROPOLOGIST (profess. & kin.), 055.067-010
11.04.02 LAWYER (profess. & kin.), 110.107-010
11.05.03 SECRETARY OF STATE (gov. ser.), 188.167-082
11.07.02 ADMINISTRATOR, HOSPITAL (medical ser.), 187.117-010
11.07.02 PUBLIC HEALTH EDUCATOR (profess. & kin.), 079.117-014
11.07.03 VOCATIONAL REHABILITATION CONSULTANT (gov. ser.), 094.117-018

Bachelor's Degree

01.01.01 EDITOR, PUBLICATIONS (print. & pub.), 132.037-022
01.01.01 PRODUCER (motion pic.), 187.167-174
01.02.03 ART DIRECTOR (motion pic.), 142.031-010
01.02.03 AUDIOVISUAL PRODUCTION SPECIALIST (profess. & kin.), 149.061-010
01.02.03 DIRECTOR OF PHOTOGRAPHY (motion pic.), 143.062-010
01.02.03 INDUSTRIAL DESIGNER (profess. & kin.), 142.061-026
01.03.01 PRODUCER (radio & tv broad.), 159.117-010
01.03.01 PRODUCER (amuse. & rec.), 187.167-178
02.01.01 CHEMIST (profess. & kin.), 022.061-010
02.01.01 COMPUTER-APPLICATIONS ENGINEER (profess. & kin.), 020.062-010
02.01.01 GEOLOGIST (profess. & kin.), 024.061-018
02.01.01 GEOPHYSICIST (profess. & kin.), 024.061-030
02.01.01 HYDROLOGIST (profess. & kin.), 024.061-034
02.01.01 MINERALOGIST (profess. & kin.), 024.061-038
02.01.01 PETROLOGIST (profess. & kin.), 024.061-046
02.01.01 SEISMOLOGIST (profess. & kin.), 024.061-050
02.01.02 ENVIRONMENTAL ANALYST (profess. & kin.), 029.081-010

02.01.02 GEOLOGIST, PETROLEUM (petrol. production), 024.061-022

02.01.02 MATERIALS SCIENTIST (profess. & kin.), 029.081-014

02.01.02 METALLURGIST, PHYSICAL (profess. & kin.), 011.061-022

02.02.01 ANIMAL SCIENTIST (profess. & kin.), 040.061-014

02.02.01 BIOMEDICAL ENGINEER (profess. & kin.), 019.061-010

02.02.01 DAIRY SCIENTIST (profess. & kin.), 040.061-018

02.02.01 ENVIRONMENTAL EPIDEMIOLOGIST (gov. ser.), 041.167-010

02.02.01 PARASITOLOGIST (profess. & kin.), 041.061-070

02.02.01 PHARMACOLOGIST (profess. & kin.), 041.061-074

02.02.01 ZOOLOGIST (profess. & kin.), 041.061-090

02.02.02 AGRONOMIST (profess. & kin.), 040.061-010

02.02.02 BOTANIST (profess. & kin.), 041.061-038

02.02.02 FOREST ECOLOGIST (profess. & kin.), 040.061-030

02.02.02 HORTICULTURIST (profess. & kin.), 040.061-038

02.02.02 PLANT BREEDER (profess. & kin.), 041.061-082

02.02.02 PLANT PATHOLOGIST (profess. & kin.), 041.061-086

02.02.02 RANGE MANAGER (profess. & kin.), 040.061-046

02.02.02 SOIL CONSERVATIONIST (profess. & kin.), 040.061-054

02.02.02 SOIL SCIENTIST (profess. & kin.), 040.061-058

02.02.02 WOOD TECHNOLOGIST (profess. & kin.), 040.061-062

02.02.03 BIOCHEMIST (profess. & kin.), 041.061-026

02.02.03 BIOLOGIST (profess. & kin.), 041.061-030

02.02.03 BIOPHYSICIST (profess. & kin.), 041.061-034

02.02.03 MICROBIOLOGIST (profess. & kin.), 041.061-058

02.02.03 PHYSIOLOGIST (profess. & kin.), 041.061-078

02.02.04 CHEMIST, FOOD (profess. & kin.), 022.061-014

02.02.04 DAIRY TECHNOLOGIST (profess. & kin.), 040.061-022

02.02.04 FOOD TECHNOLOGIST (profess. & kin.), 041.081-010

02.03.01 PODIATRIST (medical ser.), 079.101-022

02.03.04 CHIROPRACTOR (medical ser.), 079.101-010

02.03.04 OPTOMETRIST (profess. & kin.), 079.101-018

02.04.01 RADIOPHARMACIST (medical ser.), 074.161-014

02.04.02 CHEMISTRY TECHNOLOGIST (medical ser.), 078.261-010

02.04.02 IMMUNOHEMATOLOGIST (medical ser.), 078.221-010

02.04.02 MEDICAL TECHNOLOGIST (medical ser.), 078.361-014

02.04.02 MICROBIOLOGY TECHNOLOGIST (drug prep. & related), 078.261-014

02.04.02 PUBLIC-HEALTH MICROBIOLOGIST (gov. ser.), 041.261-010

03.01.04 FORESTER (profess. & kin.), 040.061-034

04.02.03 PARK RANGER (gov. ser.), 169.167-042

05.01.01 AERODYNAMIST (aircraft-aerospace mfg.), 002.061-010

05.01.01 AERONAUTICAL-RESEARCH ENGINEER (aircraft-aerospace mfg.), 002.061-026

05.01.01 CHEMICAL RESEARCH ENGINEER (profess. & kin.), 008.061-022

05.01.01 INSTRUMENTATION TECHNICIAN (profess. & kin.), 003.261-010

05.01.01 TECHNICIAN, SEMICONDUCTOR DEVELOPMENT (profess. & kin.), 003.161-018

05.01.02 INDUSTRIAL-HEALTH ENGINEER (profess. & kin.), 012.167-034

05.01.02 NUCLEAR-CRITICALITY SAFETY ENGINEER (profess. & kin.), 015.067-010

05.01.02 POLLUTION-CONTROL ENGINEER (profess. & kin.), 019.081-018

05.01.02 PRODUCT-SAFETY ENGINEER (profess. & kin.), 012.061-010

05.01.02 RADIATION-PROTECTION ENGINEER (gov. ser.), 015.137-010

05.01.02 RESOURCE-RECOVERY ENGINEER (gov. ser.), 019.167-018

05.01.02 SAFETY ENGINEER (profess. & kin.), 012.061-014

05.01.02 SAFETY MANAGER (profess. & kin.), 012.167-058

05.01.03 CENTRAL-OFFICE EQUIPMENT ENGINEER (tel. & tel.), 003.187-010

05.01.03 COMMERCIAL ENGINEER (radio & tv broad.), 003.187-014

05.01.03 ELECTRICAL ENGINEER, POWER SYSTEM (light, heat, & power), 003.167-018

05.01.03 HYDRAULIC ENGINEER (profess. & kin.), 005.061-018

05.01.03 ILLUMINATING ENGINEER (profess. & kin.), 003.061-046

05.01.03 MARINE ENGINEER (profess. & kin.), 014.061-014

05.01.03 NUCLEAR ENGINEER (profess. & kin.), 015.061-014

05.01.03 POWER-DISTRIBUTION ENGINEER (light, heat, & power), 003.167-046

05.01.03 POWER-TRANSMISSION ENGINEER (light, heat, & power), 003.167-050

05.01.03 SANITARY ENGINEER (profess. & kin.), 005.061-030

05.01.03 SYSTEMS ENGINEER, ELECTRONIC DATA PROCESSING (profess. & kin.), 003.167-062

05.01.03 WASTE-MANAGEMENT ENGINEER, RADIOACTIVE MATERIALS (profess. & kin.), 005.061-042

05.01.04 AERONAUTICAL TEST ENGINEER (aircraft-aerospace mfg.), 002.061-018

05.01.04 ELECTRICAL TEST ENGINEER (profess. & kin.), 003.061-014

05.01.04 FIELD-SERVICE ENGINEER (aircraft-aerospace mfg.), 002.167-014

05.01.04 METROLOGIST (profess. & kin.), 012.067-010

05.01.04 QUALITY-CONTROL ENGINEER (profess. & kin.), 012.167-054

05.01.04 RELIABILITY ENGINEER (profess. & kin.), 019.061-026

05.01.04 STRESS ANALYST (aircraft-aerospace mfg.), 002.061-030

05.01.04 STRESS ANALYST (profess. & kin.), 007.061-042

05.01.04 TEST ENGINEER, NUCLEAR EQUIPMENT (profess. & kin.), 015.061-022

05.01.05 SALES ENGINEER, AERONAUTICAL PRODUCTS (aircraft-aerospace mfg.), 002.151-010

05.01.06 CONFIGURATION MANAGEMENT ANALYST (profess. & kin.), 012.167-010

05.01.06 COST-ANALYSIS ENGINEER (aircraft-aerospace mfg.), 002.167-010

05.01.06 FACTORY LAY-OUT ENGINEER (profess. & kin.), 012.167-018

05.01.06 INDUSTRIAL ENGINEER (profess. & kin.), 012.167-030

05.01.06 MANAGEMENT ANALYST (profess. & kin.), 161.167-010

05.01.06 MANUFACTURING ENGINEER (profess. & kin.), 012.167-042

05.01.06 MATERIALS ENGINEER (profess. & kin.), 019.061-014

05.01.06 METALLURGIST, EXTRACTIVE (profess. & kin.), 011.061-018

05.01.06 MINING ENGINEER (mining), 010.061-014

05.01.06 PRODUCTION PLANNER (profess. & kin.), 012.167-050

05.01.06 STANDARDS ENGINEER (profess. & kin.), 012.061-018

05.01.06 TIME-STUDY ENGINEER (profess. & kin.), 012.167-070

05.01.06 UTILIZATION ENGINEER (light, heat, & power), 007.061-034

05.01.07 AERONAUTICAL ENGINEER (profess. & kin.), 002.061-014

05.01.07 AERONAUTICAL-DESIGN ENGINEER (aircraft-aerospace mfg.), 002.061-022

05.01.07 AIRPORT ENGINEER (profess. & kin.), 005.061-010

05.01.07 ARCHITECT, MARINE (profess. & kin.), 001.061-014

05.01.07 CERAMIC ENGINEER (profess. & kin.), 006.061-014

05.01.07 CHEMICAL DESIGN ENGINEER, PROCESSES (profess. & kin.), 008.061-014

05.01.07 CHEMICAL ENGINEER (profess. & kin.), 008.061-018

05.01.07 CIVIL ENGINEER (profess. & kin.), 005.061-014

05.01.07 ELECTRICAL-DESIGN ENGINEER (profess. & kin.), 003.061-018

05.01.07 ELECTRO-OPTICAL ENGINEER (profess. & kin.), 023.061-010

05.01.07 ELECTRONICS-DESIGN ENGINEER (profess. & kin.), 003.061-034

05.01.07 LANDSCAPE ARCHITECT (profess. & kin.), 001.061-018

05.01.07 OPTICAL ENGINEER (profess. & kin.), 019.061-018

05.01.08 AGRICULTURAL ENGINEER (profess. & kin.), 013.061-010

05.01.08 AUTOMOTIVE ENGINEER (auto. mfg.), 007.061-010

05.01.08 ELECTRICAL ENGINEER (profess. & kin.), 003.061-010

05.01.08 ELECTRONICS ENGINEER (profess. & kin.), 003.061-030

05.01.08 ENGINEER, SOILS (profess. & kin.), 024.161-010

05.01.08 MECHANICAL ENGINEER (profess. & kin.), 007.061-014

05.01.08 PETROLEUM ENGINEER (petrol. production), 010.061-018

05.01.08 STRUCTURAL ENGINEER (const.), 005.061-034

05.01.08 TRANSPORTATION ENGINEER (profess. & kin.), 005.061-038

05.02.03 DIRECTOR, QUALITY CONTROL (profess. & kin.), 012.167-014

05.03.01 PHOTOGRAMMETRIC ENGINEER (profess. & kin.), 018.167-026

05.03.02 CONTROLS DESIGNER (profess. & kin.), 003.261-014

05.03.09 PACKAGING ENGINEER (profess. & kin.), 019.187-010

05.05.11 ORTHOTIST (per. protect. & med. device), 078.261-018

05.05.11 PROSTHETIST (per. protect. & med. device), 078.261-022

05.05.17 DIETITIAN, CLINICAL (profess. & kin.), 077.127-014

07.01.01 FINANCIAL-AID COUNSELOR (educ.), 169.267-018

07.01.01 PROBATION OFFICER (profess. & kin.), 195.167-034

08.01.01 PHARMACEUTICAL DETAILER (whole. tr.), 262.157-010

08.01.01 SALES REPRESENTATIVE, DENTAL AND MEDICAL EQUIPMENT AND SUPPLIES (whole. tr.), 276.257-010

10.01.01 CLERGY MEMBER (profess. & kin.), 120.007-010

10.01.02 PROBATION-AND-PAROLE OFFICER (profess. & kin.), 195.107-046

10.02.01 NURSE ANESTHETIST (medical ser.), 075.371-010

10.02.01 NURSE PRACTITIONER (medical ser.), 075.264-010

10.02.01 NURSE, GENERAL DUTY (medical ser.), 075.374-010

10.02.01 NURSE, OFFICE (medical ser.), 075.374-014

10.02.01 NURSE, PRIVATE DUTY (medical ser.), 075.374-018

10.02.01 NURSE, SCHOOL (medical ser.), 075.124-010

10.02.01 NURSE, STAFF, COMMUNITY HEALTH (medical ser.), 075.124-014

10.02.01 NURSE, STAFF, OCCUPATIONAL HEALTH NURSING (medical ser.), 075.374-022

10.02.01 NURSE-MIDWIFE (medical ser.), 075.264-014

10.02.02 ART THERAPIST (medical ser.), 076.127-010

10.02.02 MUSIC THERAPIST (medical ser.), 076.127-014

10.02.02 OCCUPATIONAL THERAPIST (medical ser.), 076.121-010

10.02.03 EDUCATIONAL THERAPIST (educ.), 094.227-010

10.02.03 EVALUATOR (educ.), 094.267-010

10.02.03 TEACHER, BLIND (educ.), 094.227-014

10.02.03 TEACHER, DEAF STUDENTS (educ.), 094.224-010

10.02.03 TEACHER, HOME THERAPY (social ser.), 195.227-018

10.02.03 TEACHER, MENTALLY-RETARDED STUDENTS (educ.), 094.227-022

11.01.01 DIRECTOR, RECORDS MANAGEMENT (profess. & kin.), 161.117-014

11.01.01 ENGINEERING ANALYST (profess. & kin.), 020.067-010

11.01.01 FORMS ANALYST (profess. & kin.), 161.267-018

11.01.01 INFORMATION SCIENTIST (profess. & kin.), 109.067-010

11.01.01 MANAGER, ELECTRONIC DATA PROCESSING (profess. & kin.), 169.167-030

11.01.01 OPERATIONS-RESEARCH ANALYST (profess. & kin.), 020.067-018

11.01.01 PROGRAMER, CHIEF, BUSINESS (profess. & kin.), 020.167-018

11.01.01 PROGRAMER, ENGINEERING AND SCIENTIFIC (profess. & kin.), 020.167-022

11.01.01 PROGRAMER, INFORMATION SYSTEM (profess. & kin.), 020.187-010

11.01.01 STATISTICIAN, MATHEMATICAL (profess. & kin.), 020.067-022

11.01.01 SYSTEMS ANALYST, ELECTRONIC DATA PROCESSING (profess. & kin.), 012.167-066

11.01.02 ACTUARY (profess. & kin.), 020.167-010

11.01.02 CONSULTANT (profess. & kin.), 189.167-010

11.01.02 FINANCIAL ANALYST (finan. inst.), 020.167-014

11.01.02 MATHEMATICAL TECHNICIAN (profess. & kin.), 020.162-010

11.01.02 STATISTICIAN, APPLIED (profess. & kin.), 020.167-026

11.02.01 INSTRUCTOR, BUSINESS EDUCATION (educ.), 090.222-010

11.02.01 TEACHER (museum), 099.227-038

11.02.01 TEACHER, ADULT EDUCATION (educ.), 099.227-030

11.02.01 TEACHER, ELEMENTARY SCHOOL (educ.), 092.227-010

11.02.01 TEACHER, RESOURCE (educ.), 099.227-042

11.02.01 TEACHER, SECONDARY SCHOOL (educ.), 091.227-010

11.02.04 CATALOG LIBRARIAN (library), 100.387-010

11.02.04 LIBRARIAN (library), 100.127-014

11.02.04 LIBRARIAN, SPECIAL LIBRARY (library), 100.167-026

11.03.02 PLANNER, PROGRAM SERVICES (gov. ser.), 188.167-110

11.03.02 RESEARCH WORKER, SOCIAL WELFARE (profess. & kin.), 054.067-010

11.03.02 SCIENTIFIC LINGUIST (profess. & kin.), 059.067-014

11.03.02 URBAN PLANNER (profess. & kin.), 199.167-014

11.03.03 ARCHEOLOGIST (profess. & kin.), 055.067-018

11.03.03 ARCHIVIST (profess. & kin.), 101.167-010

11.03.03 HISTORIAN (profess. & kin.), 052.067-022

11.03.03 RESEARCH ASSOCIATE (museum), 109.067-014

11.03.04 EMPLOYMENT INTERVIEWER (profess. & kin.), 166.267-010

11.03.04 JOB ANALYST (profess. & kin.), 166.267-018

11.03.04 OCCUPATIONAL ANALYST (profess. & kin.), 166.067-010

11.03.04 PERSONNEL RECRUITER (profess. & kin.), 166.267-038

11.03.05 ECONOMIST (profess. & kin.), 050.067-010

11.04.01 APPEALS REFEREE (gov. ser.), 119.267-014

11.04.01 HEARING OFFICER (gov. ser.), 119.107-010

11.04.03 ADJUDICATOR (gov. ser.), 119.167-010

11.04.04 PATENT AGENT (profess. & kin.), 119.167-014

11.05.01 ASSOCIATION EXECUTIVE (profess. & kin.), 189.117-010

11.05.01 PRESIDENT (any ind.), 189.117-026

11.05.02 DIETITIAN, CHIEF (profess. & kin.), 077.117-010

11.05.02 GRANT COORDINATOR (profess. & kin.), 169.117-014

11.05.02 MANAGEMENT TRAINEE (any ind.), 189.167-018

11.05.02 MANAGER, PERSONNEL (profess. & kin.), 166.117-018

11.05.02 RESEARCH ANALYST (insurance), 169.267-034

11.05.03 ENVIRONMENTAL ANALYST (gov. ser.), 199.167-022

11.05.03 MANAGER, CITY (gov. ser.), 188.117-114

11.06.01 ACCOUNTANT (profess. & kin.), 160.167-010

11.06.01 ACCOUNTANT, COST (profess. & kin.), 160.167-018

11.06.01 ACCOUNTANT, TAX (profess. & kin.), 160.162-010

11.06.01 AUDITOR (profess. & kin.), 160.162-014

11.06.01 AUDITOR, INTERNAL (profess. & kin.), 160.167-034

11.06.01 AUDITOR, TAX (profess. & kin.), 160.167-038

11.06.01 REVENUE AGENT (gov. ser.), 160.167-050

11.06.02 REPORTS ANALYST (profess. & kin.), 161.267-026

11.06.03 DIRECTOR, UTILITY ACCOUNTS (gov. ser.), 160.267-014

11.06.03 PERSONAL PROPERTY ASSESSOR (gov. ser.),
191.367-010
11.06.03 SECURITIES TRADER 2 (finan. inst.), 186.167-058
11.06.04 SALES AGENT, SECURITIES (finan. inst.),
251.157-010
11.06.05 BUDGET ANALYST (gov. ser.), 161.267-030
11.07.01 REHABILITATION CENTER MANAGER (gov. ser.),
195.167-038
11.07.02
COMMUNITY-SERVICES-AND-HEALTH-EDUCATION
OFFICER (gov. ser.), 079.167-010
11.07.02 MEDICAL-RECORD ADMINISTRATOR (medical ser.),
079.167-014
11.07.02 UTILIZATION-REVIEW COORDINATOR (medical
ser.), 079.137-010
11.07.03 CONSULTANT, EDUCATION (educ.), 099.167-014
11.07.03 DIRECTOR, EDUCATIONAL PROGRAM (educ.),
099.117-010
11.07.03 EDUCATIONAL SPECIALIST (educ.), 099.167-022
11.07.03 FINANCIAL-AIDS OFFICER (educ.), 090.117-030
11.07.04 CURATOR (museum), 102.017-010
11.07.04 LIBRARY CONSULTANT (library), 100.117-014
11.08.01 EDITOR, NEWSPAPER (print. & pub.), 132.017-014
11.08.02 RESEARCH ASSISTANT II (profess. & kin.),
199.267-034
11.08.03 COLUMNIST/COMMENTATOR (print. & pub.),
131.067-010
11.08.04 TRANSLATOR (profess. & kin.), 137.267-018
11.09.01 ACCOUNT EXECUTIVE (bus. ser.), 164.167-010
11.09.01 MANAGER, ADVERTISING (any ind.), 164.117-010
11.09.02 DIRECTOR, FUNDRAISING (nonprofit org.),
165.117-010
11.09.02 DIRECTOR, FUNDS DEVELOPMENT (profess. &
kin.), 165.117-014
11.09.02 FUND RAISER 1 (nonprofit org.), 293.157-010
11.09.02 FOREIGN-SERVICE OFFICER (gov. ser.), 188.117-106
11.10.01 CHIEF BANK EXAMINER (gov. ser.), 160.167-046
11.10.03 HEALTH OFFICER, FIELD (gov. ser.), 168.167-018
11.10.03 PUBLIC HEALTH SERVICE OFFICER (gov. ser.),
187.117-050
11.10.03 SANITARIAN (profess. & kin.), 079.117-018
11.10.05 REGULATORY ADMINISTRATOR (tel. & tel.),
168.167-070
11.12.02 RIGHT-OF-WAY AGENT (any ind.), 191.117-046
11.12.03 ARTIST'S MANAGER (amuse. & rec.), 191.117-010
11.12.03 BOOKING MANAGER (amuse. & rec.), 191.117-014
11.12.03 LITERARY AGENT (bus. ser.), 191.117-034

Associate Degree or Apprenticeship

01.01.01 CONTINUITY DIRECTOR (radio & tv broad.),
132.037-010
01.01.01 EDITOR, FILM (motion pic.), 962.264-010
01.01.02 COPY WRITER (profess. & kin.), 131.067-014
01.01.02 EDITORIAL WRITER (print. & pub.), 131.067-022
01.02.01 APPRAISER, ART (profess. & kin.), 191.287-014
01.02.02 QUICK SKETCH ARTIST (amuse. & rec.), 149.041-010
01.02.03 ART DIRECTOR (profess. & kin.), 141.031-010
01.02.03 CLOTHES DESIGNER (profess. & kin.), 142.061-018
01.02.03 COMMERCIAL DESIGNER (profess. & kin.),
141.081-014
01.02.03 DISPLAY DESIGNER (profess. & kin.), 142.051-010
01.02.03 EXHIBIT DESIGNER (museum), 142.061-058
01.02.03 FASHION ARTIST (ret. tr.), 141.061-014
01.02.03 FURNITURE DESIGNER (furn.), 142.061-022
01.02.03 GRAPHIC DESIGNER (profess. & kin.), 141.061-018
01.02.03 ILLUSTRATOR (profess. & kin.), 141.061-022
01.02.03 INTERIOR DESIGNER (profess. & kin.), 142.051-014
01.02.03 MANAGER, DISPLAY (ret. tr.), 142.031-014
01.02.03 PACKAGE DESIGNER (profess. & kin.), 142.081-018
01.02.03 POLICE ARTIST (gov. ser.), 141.061-034
01.02.03 SET DECORATOR (motion pic.), 142.061-042
01.02.03 SET DESIGNER (motion pic.), 142.061-046
01.02.03 SET DESIGNER (amuse. & rec.), 142.061-050
01.02.03 TELEVISION TECHNICIAN (radio & tv broad.),
194.062-010

01.03.01 DIRECTOR, MOTION PICTURE (motion pic.),
159.067-010
01.03.03 ANNOUNCER (radio & tv broad.), 159.147-010
01.03.03 DISK JOCKEY (radio & tv broad.), 159.147-014
01.03.03 NARRATOR (motion pic.), 150.147-010
01.04.01 TEACHER, MUSIC (educ.), 152.021-010
01.05.01 CHOREOGRAPHER (amuse. & rec.), 151.027-010
01.05.01 INSTRUCTOR, DANCING (educ.), 151.027-014
01.06.01 ENGRAVER, PICTURE (print. & pub.), 979.281-018
01.06.01 PHOTOENGRAVER (print. & pub.), 971.381-022
01.06.02 RESTORER, CERAMIC (museum), 102.361-014
02.01.01 METEOROLOGIST (profess. & kin.), 025.062-010
02.01.02 PROJECT MANAGER, ENVIRONMENTAL
RESEARCH (profess. & kin.), 029.167-014
02.02.01 ANIMAL BREEDER (profess. & kin.), 041.061-014
02.02.02 SILVICULTURIST (profess. & kin.), 040.061-050
02.02.02 SOIL-CONSERVATION TECHNICIAN (profess. &
kin.), 040.261-010
02.03.04 ACUPUNCTURIST (medical ser.), 079.271-010
02.03.04 RADIATION-THERAPY TECHNOLOGIST (medical
ser.), 078.361-034
02.04.01 ASSAYER (profess. & kin.), 022.281-010
02.04.01 BALLISTICS EXPERT, FORENSIC (gov. ser.),
199.267-010
02.04.01 CALIBRATION LABORATORY TECHNICIAN
(aircraft-aerospace mfg.), 019.281-010
02.04.01 CHEMICAL-LABORATORY TECHNICIAN (profess. &
kin.), 022.261-010
02.04.01 CRIMINALIST (profess. & kin.), 029.281-010
02.04.01 GEOLOGICAL AIDE (petrol. production), 024.267-010
02.04.01 LABORATORY ASSISTANT (light, heat, & power),
029.361-018
02.04.01 LABORATORY ASSISTANT, METALLURGICAL (iron
& steel), 011.281-010
02.04.01 LABORATORY SUPERVISOR (profess. & kin.),
022.137-010
02.04.01 METALLURGICAL TECHNICIAN (profess. & kin.),
011.261-010
02.04.01 PHOTO-OPTICS TECHNICIAN (profess. & kin.),
029.280-010
02.04.01 QUALITY-CONTROL TECHNICIAN (profess. & kin.),
012.261-014
02.04.01 SPECTROSCOPIST (profess. & kin.), 011.281-014
02.04.01 TESTER (profess. & kin.), 011.361-010
02.04.01 ULTRASOUND TECHNOLOGIST (medical ser.),
078.364-010
02.04.02 CYTOTECHNOLOGIST (medical ser.), 078.281-010
02.04.02 FOOD TESTER (any ind.), 029.361-014
02.04.02 LABORATORY TECHNICIAN, VETERINARY
(medical ser.), 073.361-010
02.04.02 MEDICAL-LABORATORY TECHNICIAN (medical
ser.), 078.381-014
02.04.02 TISSUE TECHNOLOGIST (medical ser.), 078.361-030
03.01.01 GENERAL MANAGER, FARM (agric.), 180.167-018
03.01.04 LOGGING-OPERATIONS INSPECTOR (forestry),
168.267-070
04.01.02 CUSTOMS PATROL OFFICER (gov. ser.), 168.167-010
04.01.02 FIRE WARDEN (forestry), 452.167-010
04.01.02 SPECIAL AGENT (gov. ser.), 375.167-042
04.02.02 SECURITY CONSULTANT (bus. ser.), 189.167-054
05.01.01 ELECTRONICS TECHNICIAN (profess. & kin.),
003.161-014
05.01.01 FOUNDRY METALLURGIST (foundry), 011.061-010
05.01.01 LASER TECHNICIAN (electronics), 019.181-010
05.01.01 MECHANICAL-ENGINEERING TECHNICIAN
(profess. & kin.), 007.161-026
05.01.01 NUCLEAR-DECONTAMINATION RESEARCH
SPECIALIST (profess. & kin.), 008.061-030
05.01.01 OPTOMECHANICAL TECHNICIAN (optical goods),
007.161-030
05.01.02 SAFETY ENGINEER, MINES (mining), 010.061-026
05.01.03 CABLE ENGINEER, OUTSIDE PLANT (tel. & tel.),
003.167-010
05.01.04 AIR ANALYST (profess. & kin.), 012.261-010

05.01.04 CHEMICAL-TEST ENGINEER (profess. & kin.), 008.061-026

05.01.04 METALLOGRAPHER (profess. & kin.), 011.061-014

05.01.04 TEST TECHNICIAN (profess. & kin.), 019.161-014

05.01.05 SALES-ENGINEER, ELECTRONICS PRODUCTS AND SYSTEMS (profess. & kin.), 003.151-014

05.01.06 DOCUMENTATION ENGINEER (profess. & kin.), 012.167-078

05.01.06 FACILITIES PLANNER (any ind.), 019.261-018

05.01.06 LAND SURVEYOR (profess. & kin.), 018.167-018

05.01.06 PRODUCTION ENGINEER (profess. & kin.), 012.167-046

05.01.06 TOOL PLANNER (any ind.), 012.167-074

05.01.06 TOOL PROGRAMER, NUMERICAL CONTROL (any ind.), 007.167-018

05.01.06 TOOL PROGRAMMER, NUMERICAL CONTROL (electronics), 609.262-010

05.01.07 AGRICULTURAL-ENGINEERING TECHNICIAN (profess. & kin.), 013.161-010

05.01.07 CERAMIC DESIGN ENGINEER (profess. & kin.), 006.061-010

05.01.07 TOOL DESIGNER (profess. & kin.), 007.061-026

05.01.08 CHEMICAL-ENGINEERING TECHNICIAN (profess. & kin.), 008.261-010

05.01.08 CUSTOMER-EQUIPMENT ENGINEER (tel. & tel.), 003.187-018

05.01.08 PLANT ENGINEER (profess. & kin.), 007.167-014

05.01.08 PROJECT ENGINEER (profess. & kin.), 019.167-014

05.01.08 WELDING ENGINEER (profess. & kin.), 011.061-026

05.02.03 BREWING DIRECTOR (beer prod.), 183.167-010

05.02.03 MANAGER, FOOD PROCESSING PLANT (can. & preserv.), 183.167-026

05.02.03 QUALITY-CONTROL COORDINATOR (drug prep. & related), 168.167-066

05.02.03 WINE MAKER (wine prod.), 183.161-014

05.03.01 NAVIGATOR (air trans.), 196.167-014

05.03.01 SURVEYOR ASSISTANT, INSTRUMENTS (profess. & kin.), 018.167-034

05.03.02 AUTO-DESIGN CHECKER (auto. mfg.), 017.261-010

05.03.02 DESIGN DRAFTER, ELECTROMECHANISMS (profess. & kin.), 017.261-014

05.03.02 DRAFTER, AERONAUTICAL (profess. & kin.), 002.261-010

05.03.02 DRAFTER, AUTOMOTIVE DESIGN (auto. mfg.), 017.281-022

05.03.02 DRAFTER, CIVIL (profess. & kin.), 005.281-010

05.03.02 DRAFTER, COMMERCIAL (profess. & kin.), 017.261-026

05.03.02 DRAFTER, ELECTRICAL (profess. & kin.), 003.281-010

05.03.02 DRAFTER, ELECTRONIC (profess. & kin.), 003.281-014

05.03.02 DRAFTER, GEOLOGICAL (petrol. production), 010.281-014

05.03.02 DRAFTER, GEOPHYSICAL (petrol. production), 010.281-018

05.03.02 DRAFTER, MARINE (profess. & kin.), 014.281-010

05.03.02 DRAFTER, MECHANICAL (profess. & kin.), 007.281-010

05.03.02 DRAFTER, STRUCTURAL (profess. & kin.), 005.281-014

05.03.02 DRAFTER, TOPOGRAPHICAL (profess. & kin.), 018.261-014

05.03.02 EDITOR, MAP (profess. & kin.), 018.261-018

05.03.02 ENGINEERING ASSISTANT, MECHANICAL EQUIPMENT (profess. & kin.), 007.161-018

05.03.02 ESTIMATOR (profess. & kin.), 160.267-018

05.03.02 ESTIMATOR AND DRAFTER (light, heat, & power), 019.261-014

05.03.02 INTEGRATED CIRCUIT LAYOUT DESIGNER (profess. & kin.), 003.261-018

05.03.02 PRINTED CIRCUIT DESIGNER (profess. & kin.), 003.261-022

05.03.02 SPECIFICATION WRITER (profess. & kin.), 019.267-010

05.03.02 TECHNICAL ILLUSTRATOR (profess. & kin.), 017.281-034

05.03.03 MATERIAL SCHEDULER (aircraft-aerospace mfg.), 012.187-010

05.03.05 FIELD ENGINEER (radio & tv broad.), 193.262-018

05.03.05 RADIOGRAPHER (any ind.), 199.361-010

05.03.05 TRANSMITTER OPERATOR (radio & tv broad.), 193.262-038

05.03.06 BUILDING INSPECTOR (insurance), 168.267-010

05.03.06 INDUSTRIAL ENGINEERING TECHNICIAN (profess. & kin.), 012.267-010

05.03.06 INSPECTOR, AIR-CARRIER (gov. ser.), 168.264-010

05.03.06 INSPECTOR, INDUSTRIAL WASTE (gov. ser.), 168.267-054

05.03.06 INSPECTOR, QUALITY ASSURANCE (gov. ser.), 168.287-014

05.03.06 MARINE SURVEYOR (profess. & kin.), 014.167-010

05.03.06 SUPERVISOR, VENDOR QUALITY (any ind.), 012.167-062

05.03.07 HEAT-TRANSFER TECHNICIAN (profess. & kin.), 007.181-010

05.03.07 SOLAR-ENERGY-SYSTEMS DESIGNER (profess. & kin.), 007.161-038

05.03.07 TEST TECHNICIAN (agric. equip.), 019.261-022

05.03.08 POLLUTION-CONTROL TECHNICIAN (profess. & kin.), 029.261-014

05.04.01 AIRPLANE PILOT (agric.), 196.263-010

05.04.01 AIRPLANE PILOT, COMMERCIAL (air trans.), 196.263-014

05.04.01 INSTRUCTOR, FLYING 2 (educ.), 097.227-010

05.04.02 MATE, SHIP (water trans.), 197.133-022

05.05.02 SHIPWRIGHT (ship bldg. & rep.), 860.381-058

05.05.03 PIPE FITTER (any ind.), 862.281-022

05.05.05 AUTOMATIC-EQUIPMENT TECHNICIAN (tel. & tel.), 822.281-010

05.05.05 ELEVATOR REPAIRER (any ind.), 825.281-030

05.05.05 FURNACE INSTALLER (light, heat, & power), 862.361-010

05.05.06 MILLWRIGHT (any ind.), 638.281-018

05.05.07 MACHINIST (mach. shop), 600.280-022

05.05.07 PATTERNMAKER, METAL (foundry), 600.280-050

05.05.07 TOOL-AND-DIE MAKER (mach. shop), 601.280-046

05.05.09 AIRFRAME-AND-POWER-PLANT MECHANIC (aircraft-aerospace mfg.), 621.281-014

05.05.09 EXPERIMENTAL MECHANIC 2 (aircraft-aerospace mfg.), 621.281-022

05.05.09 FIELD SERVICE TECHNICIAN (mach. mfg.), 638.261-026

05.05.09 FLIGHT-TEST SHOP MECHANIC (aircraft-aerospace mfg.), 621.381-010

05.05.09 ROCKET-ENGINE-COMPONENT MECHANIC (aircraft-aerospace mfg.), 621.281-030

05.05.10 AVIONICS TECHNICIAN (aircraft-aerospace mfg.), 823.281-010

05.05.11 BIOMEDICAL EQUIPMENT TECHNICIAN (inst. & app.), 719.261-010

05.05.11 OPTICIAN (optical goods), 716.280-014

05.05.11 OPTICIAN, DISPENSING 1 (ret. tr.), 713.361-014

05.05.11 RADIOLOGICAL-EQUIPMENT SPECIALIST (medical ser.), 719.261-014

05.05.13 COMPOSITOR (print. & pub.), 973.381-010

05.05.13 ELECTROTYPER (print. & pub.), 974.381-010

05.05.13 JOB PRINTER (print. & pub.), 973.381-018

05.05.13 STEREOTYPER (print. & pub.), 974.382-014

05.05.17 ANALYST, FOOD AND BEVERAGE (hotel & rest.), 310.267-010

05.05.17 DIETETIC TECHNICIAN (profess. & kin.), 077.121-010

05.07.01 NONDESTRUCTIVE TESTER (bus. ser.), 011.261-018

05.10.05 RECORDING ENGINEER (phonograph), 194.362-010

06.01.02 PRINT CONTROLLER (photofinish.), 976.360-010

06.02.02 NUMERICAL-CONTROL-MACHINE OPERATOR (mach. shop), 609.662-010

07.01.01 CONTACT REPRESENTATIVE (gov. ser.), 169.167-018

07.01.01 CREDIT COUNSELOR (profess. & kin.), 160.207-010

07.01.01 LOAN COUNSELOR (finan. inst.), 186.267-014

07.01.01 RETIREMENT OFFICER (gov. ser.), 166.267-030
07.01.02 ADMINISTRATIVE SECRETARY (any ind.), 169.167-014
07.01.02 MANAGER, TRAFFIC 1 (motor trans.), 184.167-102
07.01.05 TITLE CLERK (petrol. production), 162.267-010
07.01.05 TITLE EXAMINER (profess. & kin.), 119.287-010
07.01.05 TITLE SUPERVISOR (profess. & kin.), 119.167-018
07.01.06 CASEWORKER (gov. ser.), 169.262-010
07.02.03 CLAIM EXAMINER (insurance), 168.267-014
07.05.03 MEDICAL RECORD TECHNICIAN (medical ser.), 079.367-014
08.01.01 SALES REPRESENTATIVE, CHEMICALS AND DRUGS (whole. tr.), 262.357-010
08.01.01 SALES REPRESENTATIVE, COMPUTERS AND EDP SYSTEMS (whole. tr.), 275.257-010
08.01.02 SALES AGENT, FINANCIAL SERVICES (finan. inst.), 251.257-010
08.01.02 SALES REPRESENTATIVE, DATA-PROCESSING SERVICES (bus. ser.), 251.157-014
08.02.01 SALES REPRESENTATIVE, NOVELTIES (whole. tr.), 277.357-018
08.02.02 SALESPERSON, SURGICAL APPLIANCES (ret. tr.), 276.257-022
09.01.01 GROUP WORKER (social ser.), 195.164-010
09.01.01 RECREATION LEADER (social ser.), 195.227-014
09.04.01 VENDING-STAND SUPERVISOR (gov. ser.), 185.167-066
10.01.02 CASEWORKER (social ser.), 195.107-010
10.01.02 RESIDENCE COUNSELOR (educ.), 045.107-038
10.02.01 NURSE, INSTRUCTOR (medical ser.), 075.121-010
10.02.01 NURSE, LICENSED PRACTICAL (medical ser.), 079.374-014
10.02.01 PHYSICIAN ASSISTANT (medical ser.), 079.364-018
10.02.02 ACUPRESSURIST (medical ser.), 079.271-014
10.02.02 ATHLETIC TRAINER (amuse. & rec.), 153.224-010
10.02.02 DANCE THERAPIST (medical ser.), 076.127-018
10.02.02 DENTAL HYGIENIST (medical ser.), 078.361-010
10.02.02 HORTICULTURAL THERAPIST (medical ser.), 076.124-018
10.02.02 INDUSTRIAL THERAPIST (medical ser.), 076.167-010
10.02.02 NUCLEAR MEDICAL TECHNOLOGIST (medical ser.), 078.361-018
10.02.02 OCCUPATIONAL THERAPY ASSISTANT (medical ser.), 076.364-010
10.02.02 ORIENTATION THERAPIST FOR THE BLIND (educ.), 076.221-010
10.02.02 ORTHOPTIST (medical ser.), 079.371-014
10.02.02 PHYSICAL THERAPIST (medical ser.), 076.121-014
10.02.02 PROGRAM AIDE, GROUP WORK (social ser.), 195.227-010
10.02.02 PSYCHIATRIC TECHNICIAN (medical ser.), 079.374-026
10.02.02 RADIOLOGIC TECHNOLOGIST (medical ser.), 078.362-026
10.02.03 TEACHER, PRESCHOOL (educ.), 092.227-018
10.02.03 TEACHER, VOCATIONAL TRAINING (educ.), 094.227-026
10.02.03 WORK-STUDY COORDINATOR, SPECIAL EDUCATION (educ.), 094.107-010
10.03.02 DENTAL ASSISTANT (medical ser.), 079.371-010
10.03.02 EMERGENCY MEDICAL TECHNICIAN (medical ser.), 079.374-010
10.03.02 PSYCHIATRIC AIDE (medical ser.), 355.377-014
10.03.02 SURGICAL TECHNICIAN (medical ser.), 079.374-022
11.01.01 PROGRAMER, PROCESS CONTROL (profess. & kin.), 020.187-014
11.01.01 PROGRAMMER, BUSINESS (profess. & kin.), 020.162-014
11.01.01 SOFTWARE TECHNICIAN (profess. & kin.), 020.262-010
11.02.01 INSTRUCTOR, EXTENSION WORK (educ.), 090.227-018
11.02.01 TUTOR (educ.), 099.227-034
11.02.02 HUMAN RESOURCE ADVISOR (profess. & kin.), 166.267-046

11.02.02 INSTRUCTOR, TECHNICAL TRAINING (educ.), 166.221-010
11.02.02 TECHNICAL SUPPORT SPECIALIST (profess. & kin.), 199.224-010
11.02.02 TRAINING REPRESENTATIVE (educ.), 166.227-010
11.02.03 COMMUNITY DIETITIAN (profess. & kin.), 077.127-010
11.02.03 COUNTY HOME-DEMONSTRATION AGENT (gov. ser.), 096.121-010
11.02.03 COUNTY-AGRICULTURAL AGENT (gov. ser.), 096.127-010
11.02.03 EXTENSION SERVICE SPECIALIST (gov. ser.), 096.127-014
11.02.03 HOME ECONOMIST (profess. & kin.), 096.121-014
11.02.04 CLASSIFIER (library), 100.367-014
11.02.04 MEDIA SPECIALIST, SCHOOL LIBRARY (library), 100.167-030
11.03.03 RESEARCH ASSISTANT (profess. & kin.), 109.267-010
11.04.02 LEGAL INVESTIGATOR (profess. & kin.), 119.267-022
11.04.02 PARALEGAL ASSISTANT (profess. & kin.), 119.267-026
11.04.04 ABSTRACTOR (profess. & kin.), 119.267-010
11.04.04 CUSTOMS-HOUSE BROKER (finan. inst.), 186.117-018
11.05.01 DIRECTOR, TRANSPORTATION (motor trans.), 184.117-014
11.05.01 MANAGER, AIRPORT (air trans.), 184.117-026
11.05.01 MANAGER, BAKERY (bake. prod.), 189.117-046
11.05.01 MANAGER, INDUSTRIAL ORGANIZATION (any ind.), 189.117-022
11.05.02 ADMINISTRATIVE ASSISTANT (any ind.), 169.167-010
11.05.02 DIRECTOR, SERVICE (ret. tr.), 189.167-014
11.05.02 EXECUTIVE VICE PRESIDENT, CHAMBER OF COMMERCE (nonprofit org.), 187.117-030
11.05.02 MANAGER, BRANCH (any ind.), 183.117-010
11.05.02 MANAGER, CONTRACTS (petrol. production), 163.117-010
11.05.02 MANAGER, CREDIT CARD OPERATIONS (profess. & kin.), 186.167-022
11.05.02 MANAGER, DEPARTMENT STORE (ret. tr.), 185.117-010
11.05.02 MANAGER, OPERATIONS (air trans.), 184.117-050
11.05.02 MANAGER, REGIONAL (motor trans.), 184.117-054
11.05.02 MANAGER, SCHEDULE PLANNING (air trans.), 184.117-058
11.05.02 MANAGER, STATION (radio & tv broad.), 184.117-062
11.05.02 MANAGER, TRAFFIC (any ind.), 184.167-094
11.05.02 OPERATIONS MANAGER (tel. & tel.), 184.117-070
11.05.02 PROGRAM MANAGER (profess. & kin.), 189.167-030
11.05.02 PROGRAM PROPOSALS COORDINATOR (radio & tv broad.), 132.067-030
11.05.02 PROGRAM SPECIALIST, EMPLOYEE-HEALTH MAINTENANCE (profess. & kin.), 166.167-050
11.05.02 UTILIZATION COORDINATOR (radio & tv broad.), 169.167-078
11.05.03 DIRECTOR, REGULATORY AGENCY (gov. ser.), 188.117-134
11.05.03 HOUSING-MANAGEMENT OFFICER (gov. ser.), 188.117-110
11.05.03 MANAGER, HOUSING PROJECT (profess. & kin.), 186.167-030
11.05.03 MANAGER, REGULATED PROGRAM (gov. ser.), 168.167-090
11.05.04 DIRECTOR, MEDIA MARKETING (radio & tv broad.), 163.117-022
11.05.04 FIELD REPRESENTATIVE (bus. ser.), 163.267-010
11.05.04 MANAGER, CIRCULATION (print. & pub.), 163.167-014
11.05.04 MANAGER, PROFESSIONAL EQUIPMENT SALES-AND-SERVICE (bus. ser.), 185.167-042
11.06.01 ACCOUNTANT, BUDGET (profess. & kin.), 160.167-014
11.06.03 APPRAISER (gov. ser.), 188.167-010
11.06.03 APPRAISER (any ind.), 191.287-010
11.06.03 APPRAISER, REAL ESTATE (real estate), 191.267-010
11.06.03 CREDIT ANALYST (finan. inst.), 191.267-014

11.06.03 FOREIGN-EXCHANGE TRADER (finan. inst.), 186.167-014

11.06.03 MANAGER, CREDIT AND COLLECTION (any ind.), 168.167-054

11.06.03 MARKET-RESEARCH ANALYST 1 (profess. & kin.), 050.067-014

11.06.03 SECURITIES TRADER 1 (finan. inst.), 162.157-042

11.06.03 UNDERWRITER (insurance), 169.167-058

11.06.05 BUDGET OFFICER (gov. ser.), 161.117-010

11.06.05 TRUST OFFICER (finan. inst.), 186.117-074

11.07.01 COORDINATOR OF REHABILITATION SERVICES (medical ser.), 076.117-010

11.07.01 DIRECTOR, COMMUNITY ORGANIZATION (nonprofit org.), 187.117-014

11.07.01 DIRECTOR, SERVICE (nonprofit org.), 187.167-214

11.07.01 FIELD REPRESENTATIVE (profess. & kin.), 189.267-010

11.07.01 PROGRAM DIRECTOR, GROUP WORK (profess. & kin.), 187.117-046

11.07.03 EDUCATIONAL RESOURCE COORDINATOR (museum), 099.167-030

11.07.03 PARK NATURALIST (gov. ser.), 049.127-010

11.07.03 TECHNICAL TRAINING COORDINATOR (educ.), 166.167-054

11.07.04 RECREATION SUPERVISOR (profess. & kin.), 187.137-010

11.08.01 EDITOR, DEPARTMENT (print. & pub.), 132.037-018

11.08.01 EDITOR, NEWS (print. & pub.), 132.067-026

11.08.01 EDITORIAL ASSISTANT (print. & pub.), 132.267-014

11.08.02 REPORTER (print. & pub.), 131.267-018

11.08.02 WRITER, TECHNICAL PUBLICATIONS (profess. & kin.), 131.267-026

11.08.03 NEWSCASTER (radio & tv broad.), 131.267-010

11.08.04 INTERPRETER (profess. & kin.), 137.267-010

11.09.01 MANAGER, ADVERTISING (print. & pub.), 163.167-010

11.09.01 MEDIA DIRECTOR (profess. & kin.), 164.117-018

11.09.02 MEMBERSHIP DIRECTOR (profess. & kin.), 189.167-026

11.09.03 EMPLOYER RELATIONS REPRESENTATIVE (profess. & kin.), 166.257-010

11.09.03 MANAGER, AREA DEVELOPMENT (light, heat, & power), 184.117-030

11.09.03 PUBLIC-RELATIONS REPRESENTATIVE (profess. & kin.), 165.067-010

11.10.01 INVESTIGATOR (gov. ser.), 168.267-062

11.10.01 REVENUE OFFICER (gov. ser.), 188.167-074

11.10.02 DIRECTOR, COMPLIANCE (gov. ser.), 188.117-046

11.10.02 EQUAL-OPPORTUNITY REPRESENTATIVE (gov. ser.), 168.167-014

11.10.03 FOOD AND DRUG INSPECTOR (gov. ser.), 168.267-042

11.10.03 HAZARDOUS-WASTE MANAGEMENT SPECIALIST (gov. ser.), 168.267-086

11.10.03 INDUSTRIAL HYGIENIST (profess. & kin.), 079.161-010

11.10.03 INDUSTRIAL-SAFETY-AND-HEALTH TECHNICIAN (any ind.), 168.161-014

11.10.03 INSPECTOR, MOTOR VEHICLES (gov. ser.), 168.267-058

11.10.03 INSPECTOR, WATER-POLLUTION CONTROL (gov. ser.), 168.267-090

11.10.03 OCCUPATIONAL-SAFETY-AND-HEALTH INSPECTOR (gov. ser.), 168.167-062

11.10.03 RADIATION-PROTECTION SPECIALIST (gov. ser.), 168.261-010

11.10.03 SAFETY INSPECTOR (insurance), 168.167-078

11.10.03 SAFETY INSPECTOR (any ind.), 168.264-014

11.10.03 SAFETY MANAGER (medical ser.), 168.167-086

11.10.04 CUSTOMS IMPORT SPECIALIST (gov. ser.), 168.267-018

11.10.04 CUSTOMS INSPECTOR (gov. ser.), 168.267-022

11.10.04 IMMIGRATION INSPECTOR (gov. ser.), 168.167-022

11.11.01 MANAGER, HOTEL OR MOTEL (hotel & rest.), 187.117-038

11.11.02 DIRECTOR, CAMP (social ser.), 195.167-018

11.11.02 DIRECTOR, RECREATION CENTER (social ser.), 195.167-026

11.11.02 MANAGER, RECREATION ESTABLISHMENT (amuse. & rec.), 187.117-042

11.11.03 MANAGER, DISTRIBUTION WAREHOUSE (whole. tr.), 185.167-018

11.11.03 MANAGER, TRAFFIC (air trans.), 184.117-066

11.11.03 MANAGER, WAREHOUSE (any ind.), 184.167-114

11.11.04 DIRECTOR, FUNERAL (per. ser.), 187.167-030

11.11.04 MANAGER, PROPERTY (real estate), 186.167-046

11.11.05 MANAGER, VEHICLE LEASING AND RENTAL (auto. ser.), 187.167-162

11.12.01 CLAIMS ADJUDICATOR (gov. ser.), 169.267-010

11.12.01 MANAGER, CUSTOMER SERVICE (tel. & tel.), 168.167-058

11.12.01 SERVICE REPRESENTATIVE (auto. mfg.), 191.167-022

11.12.02 MANAGER, LEASING (petrol. production), 186.117-046

11.12.02 PROPERTY-UTILIZATION OFFICER (gov. ser.), 188.117-122

11.12.02 REAL-ESTATE AGENT (profess. & kin.), 186.117-058

11.12.03 BUSINESS MANAGER (amuse. & rec.), 191.117-018

11.12.04 CONTRACT ADMINISTRATOR (any ind.), 162.117-014

11.12.04 CONTRACT SPECIALIST (profess. & kin.), 162.117-018

12.01.01 COACH, PROFESSIONAL ATHLETES (amuse. & rec.), 153.227-010

High School Diploma or GED

01.01.02 SCREEN WRITER (motion pic.), 131.087-018

01.01.02 WRITER, PROSE, FICTION AND NONFICTION (profess. & kin.), 131.067-046

01.02.03 DISPLAYER, MERCHANDISE (ret. tr.), 298.081-010

01.02.03 FLORAL DESIGNER (ret. tr.), 142.081-010

01.02.03 OPTICAL-EFFECTS-CAMERA OPERATOR (motion pic.), 143.260-010

01.02.03 PHOTOGRAPHER, MOTION PICTURE (profess. & kin.), 143.062-022

01.02.03 PHOTOGRAPHER, STILL (profess. & kin.), 143.062-030

01.02.03 PHOTOJOURNALIST (print. & pub.), 143.062-034

01.03.02 INTERPRETER, DEAF (profess. & kin.), 137.267-014

01.03.03 PROGRAM COORDINATOR (amuse. & rec.), 139.167-010

01.04.02 COPYIST (any ind.), 152.267-010

01.04.02 PROMPTER (amuse. & rec.), 152.367-010

01.04.03 SINGER (amuse. & rec.), 152.047-022

01.05.02 DANCER (amuse. & rec.), 151.047-010

01.06.02 CONSERVATION TECHNICIAN (museum), 102.261-010

01.06.02 CONSERVATOR, ARTIFACTS (profess. & kin.), 055.381-010

01.06.02 JEWELER (jewelry), 700.281-010

01.06.02 MUSEUM TECHNICIAN (museum), 102.381-010

01.06.03 PAINTER, SIGN (any ind.), 970.381-026

01.06.03 TYPE COPYIST (mach. mfg.), 970.381-042

01.07.02 ANNOUNCER (amuse. & rec.), 159.347-010

02.03.03 ANIMAL HEALTH TECHNICIAN (medical ser.), 079.361-014

02.04.01 FINGERPRINT CLASSIFIER (gov. ser.), 375.387-010

02.04.01 HOT-CELL TECHNICIAN (profess. & kin.), 015.362-018

02.04.01 HYDROGRAPHER (waterworks), 025.264-010

02.04.01 LABORATORY ASSISTANT (petrol. production), 024.381-010

02.04.01 LABORATORY ASSISTANT (textile), 029.381-014

02.04.01 LABORATORY TECHNICIAN (auto. mfg.), 019.381-010

02.04.01 LABORATORY TESTER (synthetic fibers), 022.281-018

02.04.01 LABORATORY TESTER (any ind.), 029.261-010

02.04.01 PHARMACIST ASSISTANT (military ser.), 074.381-010

02.04.01 PHOTOGRAPHER, SCIENTIFIC (profess. & kin.), 143.062-026

02.04.01 RADIOISOTOPE-PRODUCTION OPERATOR (profess. & kin.), 015.362-022

02.04.01 REACTOR OPERATOR, TEST-AND-RESEARCH (profess. & kin.), 015.362-026

02.04.01 SCANNER (profess. & kin.), 015.384-010
02.04.01 TESTER (petrol. refin.), 029.261-022
02.04.01 WEATHER OBSERVER (profess. & kin.), 025.267-014
02.04.02 BIOLOGICAL AIDE (agric.), 049.384-010
02.04.02 BIOLOGY SPECIMEN TECHNICIAN (profess. & kin.), 041.381-010
02.04.02 BIOMEDICAL EQUIPMENT TECHNICIAN (profess. & kin.), 019.261-010
02.04.02 CEPHALOMETRIC ANALYST (medical ser.), 078.384-010
02.04.02 EMBALMER (per. ser.), 338.371-014
02.04.02 HERBARIUM WORKER (profess. & kin.), 041.384-010
02.04.02 LABORATORY ASSISTANT, BLOOD AND PLASMA (drug prep. & related), 078.687-010
02.04.02 MEDICAL-LABORATORY ASSISTANT (medical ser.), 078.381-010
02.04.02 PHLEBOTOMIST (medical ser.), 079.364-022
02.04.02 POLYGRAPH EXAMINER (profess. & kin.), 199.267-026
02.04.02 VECTOR CONTROL ASSISTANT (gov. ser.), 049.364-014
03.01.01 FARMER, FIELD CROP (agric.), 404.161-010
03.01.01 FARMER, GENERAL (agric.), 421.161-010
03.01.01 FARMER, VINE-FRUIT CROPS (agric.), 403.161-014
03.01.01 MANAGER, DAIRY FARM (agric.), 180.167-026
03.01.02 FISH FARMER (fish.), 446.161-010
03.01.02 SHELLFISH GROWER (fish.), 446.161-014
03.01.03 LANDSCAPE CONTRACTOR (const.), 182.167-014
03.01.03 MANAGER, NURSERY (agric.), 180.167-042
03.02.02 FORESTER AIDE (forestry), 452.364-010
03.04.04 GREENSKEEPER 1 (any ind.), 406.137-010
04.01.01 DEPUTY, COURT (gov. ser.), 377.137-018
04.01.01 HARBOR MASTER (gov. ser.), 375.167-026
04.01.02 FISH AND GAME WARDEN (gov. ser.), 379.167-010
04.01.02 POLICE OFFICER 1 (gov. ser.), 375.263-014
04.01.02 POLICE OFFICER III (gov. ser.), 375.267-038
04.01.02 SHERIFF, DEPUTY (gov. ser.), 377.263-010
04.02.01 CORRECTION OFFICER (gov. ser.), 372.667-018
04.02.03 BAILIFF (gov. ser.), 377.667-010
04.02.04 FIRE FIGHTER (any ind.), 373.364-010
05.01.01 ELECTRICAL TECHNICIAN (profess. & kin.), 003.161-010
05.01.01 WELDING TECHNICIAN (profess. & kin.), 011.261-014
05.01.04 RESEARCH MECHANIC (aircraft-aerospace mfg.), 002.280-010
05.01.04 TEST-ENGINE EVALUATOR (petrol. refin.), 010.261-026
05.01.06 PREVENTIVE MAINTENANCE COORDINATOR (any ind.), 169.167-074
05.02.03 PRODUCTION SUPERINTENDENT (any ind.), 183.117-014
05.02.06 APPLIANCE-SERVICE SUPERVISOR (light, heat, & power), 187.167-010
05.02.07 MANAGER, MARINA DRY DOCK (amuse. & rec.), 187.167-226
05.03.02 CIVIL ENGINEERING TECHNICIAN (profess. & kin.), 005.261-014
05.03.02 DESIGN TECHNICIAN, COMPUTER-AIDED (electronics), 003.362-010
05.03.02 DETAILER (profess. & kin.), 017.261-018
05.03.02 DRAFTER, ARCHITECTURAL (profess. & kin.), 001.261-010
05.03.02 DRAFTER, ASSISTANT (profess. & kin.), 017.281-018
05.03.02 DRAFTER, CARTOGRAPHIC (profess. & kin.), 018.261-010
05.03.02 DRAFTER, LANDSCAPE (profess. & kin.), 001.261-014
05.03.02 DRAWINGS CHECKER, ENGINEERING (profess. & kin.), 007.267-010
05.03.02 FIRE-PROTECTION ENGINEERING TECHNICIAN (profess. & kin.), 019.261-026
05.03.02 PHOTOGRAMMETRIST (profess. & kin.), 018.261-026
05.03.03 AIR-TRAFFIC-CONTROL SPECIALIST, STATION (gov. ser.), 193.162-014
05.03.03 AIR-TRAFFIC-CONTROL SPECIALIST, TOWER (gov. ser.), 193.162-018

05.03.04 FIELD ENGINEER, SPECIALIST (petrol. production), 010.261-010
05.03.05 RADIOTELEPHONE OPERATOR (any ind.), 193.262-034
05.03.05 VIDEO OPERATOR (radio & tv broad.), 194.282-010
05.03.06 CONSTRUCTION INSPECTOR (const.), 182.267-010
05.03.06 FLIGHT ENGINEER (air trans.), 621.261-018
05.03.06 INSPECTOR, RAILROAD (gov. ser.), 168.287-018
05.03.06 PLAN CHECKER (gov. ser.), 168.267-102
05.03.08 ENGINEERING TECHNICIAN (profess. & kin.), 005.261-010
05.03.09 FINE ARTS PACKER (museum), 102.367-010
05.04.02 PILOT, SHIP (water trans.), 197.133-026
05.05.01 BRICKLAYER (const.), 861.381-018
05.05.01 CEMENT MASON (const.), 844.364-010
05.05.01 TERRAZZO WORKER (const.), 861.381-046
05.05.01 TILE SETTER (const.), 861.381-054
05.05.02 CARPENTER (const.), 860.381-022
05.05.02 CARPENTER, MAINTENANCE (any ind.), 860.281-010
05.05.02 CARPENTER, ROUGH (const.), 860.381-042
05.05.02 CUSTOM VAN INSTALLER (auto. mfg.), 860.381-074
05.05.02 MARINE-SERVICES TECHNICIAN (ship bldg. & rep.), 806.261-026
05.05.02 SUPERINTENDENT, MAINTENANCE (any ind.), 189.167-046
05.05.03 PLUMBER (const.), 862.381-030
05.05.04 DRY-WALL APPLICATOR (const.), 842.381-010
05.05.04 PAPERHANGER (const.), 841.381-010
05.05.04 PLASTERER (const.), 842.361-018
05.05.05 AUTOMATED EQUIPMENT ENGINEER-TECHNICIAN (mach. mfg.), 638.261-010
05.05.05 CABLE INSTALLER-REPAIRER (light, heat, & power), 821.361-010
05.05.05 CABLE SUPERVISOR (tel. & tel.), 184.161-010
05.05.05 CABLE TESTER (tel. & tel.), 822.361-010
05.05.05 CENTRAL-OFFICE REPAIRER (tel. & tel.), 822.281-014
05.05.05 ELECTRICIAN (any ind.), 824.261-010
05.05.05 ELECTRICIAN, MAINTENANCE (any ind.), 829.261-018
05.05.05 FIELD ENGINEER (electronics), 828.261-014
05.05.05 LINE REPAIRER (light, heat, & power), 821.361-026
05.05.05 MAINTENANCE MECHANIC, TELEPHONE (any ind.), 822.281-018
05.05.05 PRIVATE-BRANCH-EXCHANGE REPAIRER (tel. & tel.), 822.281-022
05.05.05 PROTECTIVE-SIGNAL INSTALLER (bus. ser.), 822.361-018
05.05.05 PROTECTIVE-SIGNAL REPAIRER (bus. ser.), 822.361-022
05.05.05 STATION INSTALLER-AND-REPAIRER (tel. & tel.), 822.261-022
05.05.06 AUTOMOBILE-BODY REPAIRER (auto. ser.), 807.381-010
05.05.06 BOILERMAKER 1 (boilermaking), 805.261-014
05.05.06 ELEVATOR CONSTRUCTOR (const.), 825.361-010
05.05.06 METAL FABRICATOR (any ind.), 619.360-014
05.05.06 SHEET-METAL WORKER (any ind.), 804.281-010
05.05.06 WELDER, ARC (welding), 810.384-014
05.05.06 WELDER, COMBINATION (welding), 819.384-010
05.05.06 WELDER-FITTER (welding), 819.361-010
05.05.07 DIE SINKER (mach. shop), 601.280-022
05.05.07 MAINTENANCE MACHINIST (any ind.), 600.280-042
05.05.07 TEMPLATE MAKER (any ind.), 601.381-038
05.05.07 TOOL-MACHINE SET-UP OPERATOR (mach. shop), 601.280-054
05.05.08 CABINETMAKER (woodworking), 660.280-010
05.05.08 FURNITURE FINISHER (woodworking), 763.381-010
05.05.09 AIR-CONDITIONING INSTALLER-SERVICER, WINDOW UNIT (any ind.), 637.261-010
05.05.09 AUTOMOBILE MECHANIC (auto. ser.), 620.261-010
05.05.09 AUTOMOTIVE-MAINTENANCE-EQUIPMENT SERVICER (any ind.), 620.281-018
05.05.09 DIESEL MECHANIC (any ind.), 625.281-010

05.05.09 ENVIRONMENTAL-CONTROL-SYSTEM INSTALLER-SERVICER (any ind.), 637.261-014

05.05.09 FARM-EQUIPMENT MECHANIC 1 (agric. equip.), 624.281-010

05.05.09 FURNACE INSTALLER-AND-REPAIRER, HOT AIR (any ind.), 869.281-010

05.05.09 MACHINE BUILDER (mach. mfg.), 600.281-022

05.05.09 MAINTENANCE MECHANIC (any ind.), 638.281-014

05.05.09 MANAGER, MARINE SERVICE (ship bldg. & rep.), 187.167-130

05.05.09 OFFICE-MACHINE SERVICER (any ind.), 633.281-018

05.05.09 POWERHOUSE MECHANIC (light, heat, & power), 631.261-014

05.05.09 REFRIGERATION MECHANIC (any ind.), 637.261-026

05.05.09 TRACTOR MECHANIC (auto. ser.), 620.281-058

05.05.09 TUNE-UP MECHANIC (auto. ser.), 620.281-066

05.05.10 AUDIO-VIDEO REPAIRER (any ind.), 729.281-010

05.05.10 ELECTRIC-MOTOR REPAIRER (any ind.), 721.281-018

05.05.10 ELECTRICIAN, AUTOMOTIVE (auto. ser.), 825.281-022

05.05.10 ELECTRONICS MECHANIC (any ind.), 828.281-010

05.05.10 INSTRUMENT-MAKER AND REPAIRER (petrol. production), 600.280-014

05.05.10 METEOROLOGICAL-EQUIPMENT REPAIRER (any ind.), 823.281-018

05.05.10 RADIO MECHANIC (any ind.), 823.261-018

05.05.11 ARTIFICIAL-PLASTIC-EYE MAKER (optical goods), 713.261-014

05.05.11 DENTAL-LABORATORY TECHNICIAN (medical ser.), 712.381-018

05.05.11 DENTAL-LABORATORY-TECHNICIAN APPRENTICE (medical ser.), 712.381-022

05.05.11 ELECTROMECHANICAL TECHNICIAN (inst. & app.), 710.281-018

05.05.11 FIRE-CONTROL MECHANIC (gov. ser.), 632.261-014

05.05.11 INSTRUMENT MAKER (any ind.), 600.280-010

05.05.11 OPTICIAN (optical goods), 716.280-008

05.05.11 ORTHODONTIC TECHNICIAN (medical ser.), 712.381-030

05.05.11 ORTHOTICS ASSISTANT (per. protect. & med. device), 078.361-022

05.05.11 ORTHOTICS TECHNICIAN (per. protect. & med. device), 712.381-034

05.05.11 PROSTHETICS ASSISTANT (per. protect. & med. device), 078.361-026

05.05.11 PROSTHETICS TECHNICIAN (per. protect. & med. device), 712.381-038

05.05.11 SCIENTIFIC GLASS BLOWER (glass prod.), 006.261-010

05.05.12 FRETTED-INSTRUMENT REPAIRER (any ind.), 730.281-026

05.05.17 CHEF (hotel & rest.), 313.131-014

05.05.17 COOK (hotel & rest.), 313.361-014

05.05.17 TESTER, FOOD PRODUCTS (any ind.), 199.251-010

05.06.01 HYDROELECTRIC-STATION OPERATOR (light, heat, & power), 952.362-018

05.06.01 POWER-REACTOR OPERATOR (light, heat, & power), 952.362-022

05.06.01 SUBSTATION OPERATOR (light, heat, & power), 952.362-026

05.06.01 TURBINE OPERATOR (light, heat, & power), 952.362-042

05.06.02 ENGINEER (water trans.), 197.130-010

05.06.02 STATIONARY ENGINEER (any ind.), 950.382-026

05.06.04 WATER-TREATMENT-PLANT OPERATOR (waterworks), 954.382-014

05.07.01 SHOP ESTIMATOR (auto. ser.), 807.267-010

05.07.02 AIRPLANE INSPECTOR (air trans.), 621.261-010

05.08.02 LOCOMOTIVE ENGINEER (r.r. trans.), 910.363-014

05.09.02 ESTIMATOR, PRINTING (print. & pub.), 221.367-014

05.09.02 EVALUATOR (nonprofit org.), 249.367-034

05.09.02 MATERIAL COORDINATOR (clerical), 221.167-014

05.09.02 PRODUCTION COORDINATOR (clerical), 221.167-018

05.09.02 SALES CORRESPONDENT (clerical), 221.367-062

05.10.01 MAINTENANCE REPAIRER, BUILDING (any ind.), 899.381-010

05.10.02 MANAGER, CUSTOMER SERVICES (bus. ser.), 187.167-082

05.10.02 SERVICE MANAGER (ret. tr.), 185.164-010

05.10.03 SOUND CONTROLLER (amuse. & rec.), 194.262-014

05.10.03 TELEVISION-AND-RADIO REPAIRER (any ind.), 720.281-018

05.10.04 MANAGER, CAMP (const.), 187.167-066

05.10.05 AUDIO OPERATOR (radio & tv broad.), 194.262-010

05.10.05 PHOTOGRAPHIC-PLATE MAKER (electronics), 714.381-018

05.10.05 RERECORDING MIXER (motion pic.), 194.362-014

05.10.05 SCREEN MAKER, PHOTOGRAPHIC PROCESS (any ind.), 979.384-010

05.10.05 SOUND MIXER (motion pic.), 194.262-018

05.10.06 BLASTER (any ind.), 859.261-010

05.12.18 CENTRAL-SUPPLY WORKER (medical ser.), 381.687-010

05.12.18 SEWAGE-DISPOSAL WORKER (sanitary ser.), 955.687-010

05.12.18 SUPERVISOR, CENTRAL SUPPLY (medical ser.), 079.164-010

06.01.03 LATHE OPERATOR, NUMERICAL CONTROL (mach. shop), 604.362-010

06.01.03 MACHINE OPERATOR 1 (any ind.), 616.360-018

06.01.03 MACHINE SET-UP OPERATOR (elec. equip.), 600.380-018

06.01.03 MICROELECTRONICS TECHNICIAN (electronics), 590.362-022

06.01.03 REFINERY OPERATOR (petrol. refin.), 549.260-010

06.01.04 CHEESEMAKER (dairy prod.), 529.361-018

06.01.04 ELECTRIC-MOTOR-CONTROL ASSEMBLER (elec. equip.), 721.381-014

06.01.05 ELECTRONICS INSPECTOR I (electronics), 726.381-010

06.01.05 ELECTRONICS TESTER I (electronics), 726.281-014

06.01.05 INSPECTOR, ASSEMBLIES AND INSTALLATIONS (aircraft-aerospace mfg.), 806.281-022

06.01.05 TEST TECHNICIAN, SEMICONDUCTOR PROCESSING EQUIPMENT (electronics), 590.262-014

06.02.11 WASTE-TREATMENT OPERATOR (chem.), 955.382-014

06.02.18 CRYSTAL GROWING TECHNICIAN (electronics), 590.262-010

06.02.21 PLATER (electroplating), 500.380-010

06.03.01 QUALITY-CONTROL INSPECTOR (phonograph), 194.387-010

07.01.01 ELIGIBILITY WORKER (gov. ser.), 195.267-010

07.01.01 ELIGIBILITY-AND-OCCUPANCY INTERVIEWER (gov. ser.), 168.267-038

07.01.01 MANAGEMENT AIDE (social ser.), 195.367-014

07.01.02 COORDINATOR, SKILL-TRAINING PROGRAM (gov. ser.), 169.167-062

07.01.02 COURT CLERK (gov. ser.), 243.362-010

07.01.02 MANAGER, OFFICE (any ind.), 169.167-034

07.01.02 MEMBERSHIP SECRETARY (nonprofit org.), 201.362-018

07.01.03 LEGAL SECRETARY (clerical), 201.362-010

07.01.03 MEDICAL SECRETARY (medical ser.), 201.362-014

07.01.03 SECRETARY (clerical), 201.362-030

07.01.04 ESCROW OFFICER (profess. & kin.), 119.367-010

07.01.04 UNDERWRITING CLERK (insurance), 219.367-038

07.01.05 ADMISSIONS EVALUATOR (educ.), 205.367-010

07.01.05 CONTRACT CLERK (profess. & kin.), 119.267-018

07.01.05 EXAMINER (gov. ser.), 169.267-014

07.01.05 HOSPITAL-INSURANCE REPRESENTATIVE (insurance), 166.267-014

07.01.05 PASSPORT-APPLICATION EXAMINER (gov. ser.), 169.267-030

07.01.06 ATTENDANCE OFFICER (educ.), 168.367-010

07.01.06 IDENTIFICATION OFFICER (gov. ser.), 377.264-010

07.01.07 DRIVER'S LICENSE EXAMINER (gov. ser.), 168.267-034

07.01.07 EXAMINATION PROCTOR (gov. ser.), 199.267-018

07.01.07 TEST TECHNICIAN (clerical), 249.367-078
07.02.01 BOOKKEEPER 1 (clerical), 210.382-014
07.02.01 GENERAL-LEDGER BOOKKEEPER (clerical), 210.382-046
07.02.02 ACCOUNTING CLERK (clerical), 216.482-010
07.02.02 COLLECTION CLERK (finan. inst.), 216.362-014
07.02.02 COST CLERK (clerical), 216.382-034
07.02.02 TAX PREPARER (bus. ser.), 219.362-070
07.02.02 TELLER, COLLECTION AND EXCHANGE (finan. inst.), 211.362-022
07.02.03 ACCOUNT-INFORMATION CLERK (light, heat, & power), 210.367-010
07.02.03 GRADING CLERK (educ.), 219.467-010
07.02.03 STATISTICAL CLERK (clerical), 216.382-062
07.02.04 BILLING CLERK (clerical), 214.362-042
07.03.01 CASHIER 1 (clerical), 211.362-010
07.03.01 POST-OFFICE CLERK (gov. ser.), 243.367-014
07.03.01 TELLER (finan. inst.), 211.362-018
07.03.01 TELLER, NOTE (finan. inst.), 211.362-026
07.04.01 ADMITTING OFFICER (medical ser.), 205.137-010
07.04.01 BONDING AGENT (bus. ser.), 186.267-010
07.04.01 CREDIT CLERK (clerical), 205.367-022
07.04.01 CUSTOMER-SERVICE REPRESENTATIVE (light, heat, & power), 239.367-010
07.04.01 EMPLOYMENT CLERK (clerical), 205.362-014
07.04.01 HOSPITAL-ADMITTING CLERK (medical ser.), 205.362-018
07.04.01 IDENTIFICATION CLERK (clerical), 205.362-022
07.04.01 LOAN INTERVIEWER (finan. inst.), 241.367-018
07.04.01 NEW-ACCOUNTS CLERK (finan. inst.), 205.362-026
07.04.01 OUTPATIENT-ADMITTING CLERK (medical ser.), 205.362-030
07.04.01 REGISTRATION CLERK (gov. ser.), 205.367-042
07.04.01 REHABILITATION CLERK (nonprofit org.), 205.367-046
07.04.02 CORRESPONDENCE CLERK (clerical), 209.262-010
07.04.03 LICENSE CLERK (gov. ser.), 205.367-034
07.04.03 PARK AIDE (gov. ser.), 249.367-082
07.04.03 PUBLIC HEALTH REGISTRAR (gov. ser.), 169.167-046
07.04.03 RESERVATIONS AGENT (air trans.), 238.367-018
07.04.04 INFORMATION CLERK (clerical), 237.367-022
07.04.04 LAND-LEASING EXAMINER (gov. ser.), 237.367-026
07.04.04 MUSEUM ATTENDANT (museum), 109.367-010
07.04.05 AIRLINE-RADIO OPERATOR (air trans.), 193.262-010
07.04.05 ALARM OPERATOR (gov. ser.), 379.162-010
07.04.05 POLICE AIDE (gov. ser.), 243.362-014
07.04.05 TELECOMMUNICATOR (gov. ser.), 379.362-018
07.04.05 TRAIN DISPATCHER (r.r. trans.), 184.167-262
07.04.05 UTILITY CLERK (light, heat, & power), 239.367-034
07.05.01 EXPEDITER (clerical), 222.367-018
07.05.01 POLICE CLERK (gov. ser.), 375.362-010
07.05.01 RESERVATION CLERK (clerical), 238.362-014
07.05.01 SCHEDULER (museum), 238.367-034
07.05.01 TELEVISION-SCHEDULE COORDINATOR (radio & tv broad.), 199.387-010
07.05.02 BRAILLE PROOFREADER (nonprofit org.), 209.367-014
07.05.02 CREDIT-REFERENCE CLERK (ret. tr.), 209.362-018
07.05.02 DATA-EXAMINATION CLERK (clerical), 209.387-022
07.05.02 INVESTIGATOR, UTILITY-BILL COMPLAINTS (light, heat, & power), 241.267-034
07.05.02 LETTER-OF-CREDIT CLERK (finan. inst.), 219.387-018
07.05.02 PROOFREADER (print. & pub.), 209.387-030
07.05.02 REVIEWER (insurance), 209.687-018
07.05.03 CLASSIFICATION CLERK (clerical), 206.387-010
07.05.03 FILE CLERK 2 (clerical), 206.367-014
07.05.03 FINGERPRINT CLERK 2 (gov. ser.), 206.387-014
07.05.03 IDENTIFICATION TECHNICIAN (gov. ser.), 209.362-022
07.05.03 INSURANCE CLERK 2 (clerical), 205.567-010
07.05.03 MEDICAL-SERVICE TECHNICIAN (military ser.), 079.367-018
07.05.03 NEWS ASSISTANT (radio & tv broad.), 209.367-038

07.05.03 ORDER-DEPARTMENT SUPERVISOR (any ind.), 169.167-038
07.05.03 PERSONNEL CLERK (clerical), 209.362-026
07.05.03 RECORDS CUSTODIAN (finan. inst.), 206.387-026
07.05.03 REFERRAL CLERK, TEMPORARY-HELP AGENCY (clerical), 205.367-062
07.05.03 SHORTHAND REPORTER (clerical), 202.362-010
07.05.03 STENOGRAPHER (clerical), 202.362-014
07.05.03 TAPE LIBRARIAN (clerical), 206.387-030
07.05.04 CORRESPONDENCE-REVIEW CLERK (clerical), 209.367-018
07.06.01 COMPUTER OPERATOR (clerical), 213.362-010
07.06.02 BRAILLE TYPIST (educ.), 203.582-014
07.06.02 CRYPTOGRAPHIC-MACHINE OPERATOR (clerical), 203.582-018
07.06.02 DATA TYPIST (clerical), 203.582-022
07.06.02 DATA-CODER OPERATOR (clerical), 203.582-026
07.06.02 ELECTRONIC-TYPESETTING-MACHINE OPERATOR (print. & pub.), 203.582-074
07.06.02 KEYPUNCH OPERATOR (clerical), 203.582-030
08.01.01 SALES REPRESENTATIVE, GRAPHIC ART (bus. ser.), 254.251-010
08.01.01 SALES REPRESENTATIVE, SIGNS AND DISPLAYS (signs), 254.257-010
08.01.02 ESTATE PLANNER (insurance), 186.167-010
08.01.02 SALES AGENT, INSURANCE (insurance), 250.257-010
08.01.02 SALES REPRESENTATIVE, ADVERTISING (print. & pub.), 254.357-014
08.01.02 SALES REPRESENTATIVE, HOTEL SERVICES (hotel & rest.), 259.157-014
08.01.02 SALES REPRESENTATIVE, PRINTING (whole. tr.), 254.357-018
08.01.02 SALES REPRESENTATIVE, PUBLIC UTILITIES (light, heat, & power), 253.357-010
08.01.02 SALES REPRESENTATIVE, RADIO AND TELEVISION TIME (radio & tv broad.), 259.357-018
08.01.02 SALES REPRESENTATIVE, SECURITY SYSTEMS (bus. ser.), 259.257-022
08.01.02 SALES REPRESENTATIVE, TELEPHONE SERVICES (tel. & tel.), 253.257-010
08.01.03 BUYER (profess. & kin.), 162.157-018
08.01.03 BUYER, ASSISTANT (ret. tr.), 162.157-022
08.01.03 FOREIGN BANKNOTE TELLER-TRADER (finan. inst.), 211.362-014
08.02.01 MANUFACTURERS' REPRESENTATIVE (whole. tr.), 279.157-010
08.02.02 SALES-SERVICE REPRESENTATIVE, MILKING MACHINES (ret. tr.), 299.251-010
08.02.02 SALESPERSON, AUTOMOBILES (ret. tr.), 273.353-010
08.02.02 SALESPERSON, HEARING AIDS (ret. tr.), 276.354-010
08.02.02 SALESPERSON, JEWELRY (ret. tr.), 279.357-058
08.02.02 SALESPERSON, PIANOS AND ORGANS (ret. tr.), 277.354-010
08.02.03 SALESPERSON, AUTOMOBILE ACCESSORIES (ret. tr.), 273.357-030
08.02.03 SALESPERSON, PHOTOGRAPHIC SUPPLIES AND EQUIPMENT (ret. tr.), 277.357-050
08.02.04 SALES AGENT, REAL ESTATE (real estate), 250.357-018
08.02.05 DEMONSTRATOR, KNITTING (ret. tr.), 297.354-014
08.02.06 SALES AGENT, BUSINESS SERVICES (bus. ser.), 251.357-010
08.02.06 SALES REPRESENTATIVE, FRANCHISE (bus. ser.), 251.357-022
08.02.06 TRAVEL AGENT (bus. ser.), 252.157-010
08.02.06 WEDDING CONSULTANT (ret. tr.), 299.357-018
09.01.02 CRAFT DEMONSTRATOR (museum), 109.364-010
09.01.03 WAITER/WAITRESS, CAPTAIN (hotel & rest.), 311.137-018
09.01.04 AIRPLANE-FLIGHT ATTENDANT (air trans.), 352.367-010
09.02.01 COSMETOLOGIST (per. ser.), 332.271-010
09.02.02 BARBER (per. ser.), 330.371-010
09.03.03 INSTRUCTOR, DRIVING (educ.), 099.223-010

10.02.02 CORRECTIVE THERAPIST (medical ser.), 076.361-010
10.02.02 DIALYSIS TECHNICIAN (medical ser.), 078.362-014
10.02.02 HYPNOTHERAPIST (profess. & kin.), 079.157-010
10.02.02 MANUAL-ARTS THERAPIST (medical ser.), 076.124-010
10.02.02 PHYSICAL THERAPIST ASSISTANT (medical ser.), 076.224-010
10.02.02 RECREATIONAL THERAPIST (medical ser.), 076.124-014
10.02.02 RESPIRATORY THERAPIST (medical ser.), 079.361-010
10.03.01 AUDIOMETRIST (profess. & kin.), 078.362-010
10.03.01 CARDIAC MONITOR TECHNICIAN (medical ser.), 078.367-010
10.03.01 CARDIOPULMONARY TECHNOLOGIST (medical ser.), 078.362-030
10.03.01 ELECTROCARDIOGRAPH TECHNICIAN (medical ser.), 078.362-018
10.03.01 ELECTROENCEPHALOGRAPHIC TECHNOLOGIST (medical ser.), 078.362-022
10.03.01 HOLTER SCANNING TECHNICIAN (medical ser.), 078.264-010
10.03.01 PULMONARY-FUNCTION TECHNICIAN (medical ser.), 078.262-010
10.03.02 HOME HEALTH TECHNICIAN (medical ser.), 079.224-010
10.03.02 MEDICAL ASSISTANT (medical ser.), 079.367-010
10.03.02 MENTAL-RETARDATION AIDE (medical ser.), 355.377-018
10.03.02 NURSE AIDE (medical ser.), 355.674-014
10.03.02 OCCUPATIONAL THERAPY AIDE (medical ser.), 355.377-010
10.03.02 ORDERLY (medical ser.), 355.674-018
10.03.02 PERFUSIONIST (medical ser.), 078.362-034
10.03.02 PODIATRIC ASSISTANT (medical ser.), 079.374-018
10.03.03 CHILDREN'S TUTOR (dom. ser.), 099.227-010
11.01.01 CUSTOMER-SUPPORT SPECIALIST (whole. tr.), 020.224-010
11.02.01 TEACHER AIDE I (educ.), 099.327-010
11.02.02 INSTRUCTOR, VOCATIONAL TRAINING (educ.), 097.227-014
11.02.04 CAREER-GUIDANCE TECHNICIAN (educ.), 249.367-014
11.02.04 FILM-RENTAL CLERK (bus. ser.), 295.367-018
11.02.04 LIBRARY ASSISTANT (library), 249.367-046
11.02.04 LIBRARY TECHNICAL ASSISTANT (library), 100.367-018
11.03.02 CITY PLANNING AIDE (profess. & kin.), 199.364-010
11.03.03 GENEALOGIST (profess. & kin.), 052.067-018
11.03.04 EMPLOYEE RELATIONS SPECIALIST (motor trans.), 166.267-042
11.03.04 JOB DEVELOPMENT SPECIALIST (profess. & kin.), 166.267-034
11.03.04 RECRUITER (military ser.), 166.267-026
11.05.01 MANAGER, LAND DEVELOPMENT (real estate), 186.117-042
11.05.02 IMPORT-EXPORT AGENT (any ind.), 184.117-022
11.05.02 MANAGER, DEPARTMENT (any ind.), 189.167-022
11.05.02 MANAGER, FINANCIAL INSTITUTION (finan. inst.), 186.117-038
11.05.02 MANAGER, PROCUREMENT SERVICES (profess. & kin.), 162.167-022
11.05.02 SECURITY OFFICER (any ind.), 189.167-034
11.05.02 SPECIAL AGENT (insurance), 166.167-046
11.05.02 SUPERINTENDENT, PLANT PROTECTION (any ind.), 189.167-050
11.05.03 LEGISLATIVE ASSISTANT (gov. ser.), 169.167-066
11.05.03 MANAGER, OFFICE (gov. ser.), 188.167-058
11.05.03 POSTMASTER (gov. ser.), 188.167-066
11.05.04 MANAGER, SALES (any ind.), 163.167-018
11.05.04 PROPERTY-DISPOSAL OFFICER (any ind.), 163.167-026
11.05.04 PURCHASING AGENT (profess. & kin.), 162.157-038
11.06.01 OPERATIONS OFFICER (finan. inst.), 186.167-050
11.06.03 BOOKMAKER (amuse. & rec.), 187.167-014

11.06.03 FACTORER (finan. inst.), 186.117-026
11.06.03 INVESTIGATOR (clerical), 241.267-030
11.06.03 LOAN OFFICER (finan. inst.), 186.267-018
11.06.03 NEGOTIATOR, LETTER OF CREDIT (finan. inst.), 186.117-050
11.07.01 RESIDENCE SUPERVISOR (any ind.), 187.167-186
11.07.02 CIVIL PREPAREDNESS TRAINING OFFICER (gov. ser.), 169.127-010
11.09.01 FASHION COORDINATOR (ret. tr.), 185.157-010
11.10.01 INSPECTOR, GOVERNMENT PROPERTY (gov. ser.), 168.267-050
11.10.01 INVESTIGATOR, FRAUD (ret. tr.), 376.267-014
11.10.02 EQUAL OPPORTUNITY OFFICER (any ind.), 168.267-114
11.10.03 CHEMICAL-RADIATION TECHNICIAN (gov. ser.), 015.261-010
11.10.03 INSPECTOR, AGRICULTURAL COMMODITIES (gov. ser.), 168.287-010
11.10.03 INSPECTOR, HEALTH CARE FACILITIES (gov. ser.), 168.167-042
11.10.03 MARINE-CARGO SURVEYOR (bus. ser.), 168.267-094
11.10.03 MINE INSPECTOR (mining), 168.267-074
11.10.03 PESTICIDE-CONTROL INSPECTOR (gov. ser.), 168.267-098
11.10.03 REVIEWING OFFICER, DRIVER'S LICENSE (gov. ser.), 168.167-074
11.10.05 DEALER-COMPLIANCE REPRESENTATIVE (ret. tr.), 168.267-026
11.10.05 RATER, TRAVEL ACCOMMODATIONS (profess. & kin.), 168.367-014
11.10.05 TRAFFIC INSPECTOR (motor trans.), 184.163-010
11.10.05 TRANSPORTATION INSPECTOR (motor trans.), 168.167-082
11.11.01 CONDOMINIUM MANAGER (real estate), 186.167-062
11.11.01 EXECUTIVE HOUSEKEEPER (hotel & rest.), 187.167-046
11.11.01 MANAGER, FRONT OFFICE (hotel & rest.), 187.167-110
11.11.02 MANAGER, BOWLING ALLEY (amuse. & rec.), 187.167-222
11.11.02 MANAGER, GOLF CLUB (amuse. & rec.), 187.167-114
11.11.02 MANAGER, RECREATION FACILITY I (amuse. & rec.), 187.167-230
11.11.02 MANAGER, THEATER (amuse. & rec.), 187.167-154
11.11.03 CONDUCTOR, PASSENGER CAR (r.r. trans.), 198.167-010
11.11.03 CONDUCTOR, ROAD FREIGHT (r.r. trans.), 198.167-018
11.11.03 MANAGER, BUS TRANSPORTATION (motor trans.), 184.167-054
11.11.03 OPERATIONS MANAGER (motor trans.), 184.167-118
11.11.03 PURSER (water trans.), 197.167-014
11.11.03 STATION MANAGER (r.r. trans.), 184.167-130
11.11.04 GENERAL MANAGER, ROAD PRODUCTION (amuse. & rec.), 187.117-034
11.11.04 MANAGER, BARBER OR BEAUTY SHOP (per. ser.), 187.167-058
11.11.04 MANAGER, EMPLOYMENT AGENCY (profess. & kin.), 187.167-098
11.11.04 MANAGER, FAST FOOD SERVICES (ret. tr.), 185.137-010
11.11.04 MANAGER, FOOD SERVICE (hotel & rest.), 187.167-106
11.11.04 MANAGER, REAL-ESTATE FIRM (real estate), 186.167-066
11.11.04 MANAGER, SALES (clean., dye., & press.), 187.167-138
11.11.04 MANAGER, TOURING PRODUCTION (amuse. & rec.), 191.117-038
11.11.04 MANAGER, TRAVEL AGENCY (bus. ser.), 187.167-158
11.11.05 COMMISSARY MANAGER (any ind.), 185.167-010
11.11.05 MANAGER, AUTOMOBILE SERVICE STATION (ret. tr.), 185.167-014
11.11.05 MANAGER, DEPARTMENT (ret. tr.), 299.137-010
11.11.05 MANAGER, MACHINERY-OR-EQUIPMENT, RENTAL AND LEASING (any ind.), 185.167-026

11.11.05 MANAGER, MARKET (ret. tr.), 186.167-042
11.11.05 MANAGER, MEAT SALES AND STORAGE (ret. tr.), 185.167-030
11.11.05 MANAGER, PARTS (ret. tr.), 185.167-038
11.11.05 MANAGER, RETAIL STORE (ret. tr.), 185.167-046
11.11.05 SERVICE SUPERVISOR, LEASED MACHINERY AND EQUIPMENT (any ind.), 183.167-030
11.12.01 APPRAISER, AUTOMOBILE DAMAGE (bus. ser.), 241.267-014
11.12.01 CLAIM ADJUSTER (bus. ser.), 241.217-010
11.12.01 CLAIM EXAMINER (bus. ser.), 241.267-018
11.12.01 GENERAL CLAIMS AGENT (air trans.), 186.117-030
11.12.02 LOCATION MANAGER (motion pic.), 191.167-018
11.12.03 MANAGER, ATHLETE (amuse. & rec.), 153.117-014
11.12.04 CONTRACTOR (const.), 182.167-010
12.01.01 INSTRUCTOR, SPORTS (amuse. & rec.), 153.227-018
12.01.01 SCOUT, PROFESSIONAL SPORTS (amuse. & rec.), 153.117-018

No Diploma

01.03.02 CLOWN (amuse. & rec.), 159.047-010
01.03.02 COMEDIAN (amuse. & rec.), 159.047-014
01.03.02 MAGICIAN (amuse. & rec.), 159.041-010
01.03.02 MIME (amuse. & rec.), 159.047-022
01.03.02 PUPPETEER (amuse. & rec.), 159.041-014
01.04.04 MUSICIAN, INSTRUMENTAL (amuse. & rec.), 152.041-010
01.06.01 ADVERTISING-SPACE CLERK (print. & pub.), 247.387-018
01.06.01 ENGRAVER, HAND, HARD METALS (engraving), 704.381-026
01.06.01 ENGRAVER, HAND, SOFT METALS (engraving), 704.381-030
01.06.01 ETCHER (engraving), 704.684-010
01.06.01 SILK-SCREEN CUTTER (any ind.), 979.681-022
01.06.02 BOW MAKER, CUSTOM (sports equip.), 732.381-010
01.06.02 CLAY MODELER (any ind.), 779.281-010
01.06.02 DECORATOR (any ind.), 298.381-010
01.06.02 DISPLAY MAKER (signs), 739.361-010
01.06.02 DISTRESSER (furn.), 763.687-018
01.06.02 EXHIBIT BUILDER (museum), 739.261-010
01.06.02 MAKE-UP ARTIST (amuse. & rec.), 333.071-010
01.06.02 MODEL MAKER 1 (any ind.), 777.261-010
01.06.02 MOLD MAKER 1 (jewelry), 700.381-034
01.06.02 MORTUARY BEAUTICIAN (per. ser.), 339.361-010
01.06.02 PICTURE FRAMER (framing), 739.684-146
01.06.02 PROP MAKER (amuse. & rec.), 962.281-010
01.06.02 REPAIRER, ART OBJECTS (any ind.), 779.381-018
01.06.02 SAMPLE MAKER 1 (jewelry), 700.381-046
01.06.02 SILVERSMITH (silverware), 700.281-022
01.06.02 STONE CARVER (stonework), 771.281-014
01.06.02 WIG DRESSER (hairwork), 332.361-010
01.06.03 GIFT WRAPPER (ret. tr.), 299.364-014
01.06.03 GILDER (any ind.), 749.381-010
01.06.03 PAINTER, AIRBRUSH (any ind.), 741.684-018
01.06.03 PAINTER, HAND (any ind.), 970.381-022
01.06.03 SIGN WRITER, HAND (any ind.), 970.281-022
01.06.03 SPOTTER, PHOTOGRAPHIC (photofinish.), 970.381-034
01.06.03 STRIPER, HAND (any ind.), 740.484-010
01.07.01 GRAPHOLOGIST (amuse. & rec.), 159.247-018
01.07.03 AMUSEMENT PARK ENTERTAINER (amuse. & rec.), 159.647-010
01.08.01 MODEL, ARTISTS' (any ind.), 961.667-010
02.04.01 DECONTAMINATOR (any ind.), 199.384-010
02.04.01 FILM LABORATORY TECHNICIAN 1 (motion pic.), 976.381-010
02.04.02 LABORATORY ASSISTANT, CULTURE MEDIA (drug prep. & related), 559.384-010
02.04.02 MORGUE ATTENDANT (medical ser.), 355.667-010
03.01.01 GROUP LEADER (agric.), 180.167-022
03.01.01 MIGRANT LEADER (agric.), 180.167-050
03.01.02 BEEKEEPER (agric.), 413.161-010
03.03.01 ANIMAL TRAINER (amuse. & rec.), 159.224-010
03.03.01 EXERCISER, HORSE (amuse. & rec.), 153.674-010

03.03.02 ANIMAL CARETAKER (any ind.), 410.674-010
03.03.02 ANIMAL KEEPER (amuse. & rec.), 412.674-010
03.03.02 ANIMAL-RIDE ATTENDANT (amuse. & rec.), 349.674-010
03.03.02 AQUARIST (amuse. & rec.), 449.674-010
03.03.02 DOG BATHER (per. ser.), 418.677-010
03.03.02 DOG GROOMER (per. ser.), 418.674-010
03.03.02 HORSESHOER (agric.), 418.381-010
03.03.02 STABLE ATTENDANT (any ind.), 410.674-022
03.04.01 CHRISTMAS-TREE FARM WORKER (forestry), 451.687-010
03.04.01 FARMWORKER, FRUIT 1 (agric.), 403.683-010
03.04.01 FARMWORKER, GENERAL 1 (agric.), 421.683-010
03.04.01 FARMWORKER, GENERAL 2 (agric.), 421.687-010
03.04.01 FARMWORKER, LIVESTOCK (agric.), 410.664-010
03.04.01 FARMWORKER, VEGETABLE 2 (agric.), 402.687-010
03.04.01 LIVESTOCK-YARD ATTENDANT (any ind.), 410.674-018
03.04.01 SORTER, AGRICULTURAL PRODUCE (agric.), 529.687-186
03.04.02 BUCKER (logging), 454.684-010
03.04.02 CHAINSAW OPERATOR (logging), 454.687-010
03.04.02 FALLER 2 (logging), 454.684-014
03.04.02 FOREST WORKER (forestry), 452.687-010
03.04.02 FOREST-FIRE FIGHTER (forestry), 452.687-014
03.04.02 LOGGER, ALL-ROUND (logging), 454.684-018
03.04.03 DECKHAND, FISHING VESSEL (fish.), 449.667-010
03.04.03 FISH HATCHERY WORKER (fish.), 446.684-010
03.04.03 FISHER, DIVING (fish.), 443.664-010
03.04.03 FISHER, LINE (fish.), 442.684-010
03.04.03 FISHER, NET (fish.), 441.684-010
03.04.03 SHELLFISH DREDGE OPERATOR (fish.), 446.663-010
03.04.03 SKIFF OPERATOR (fish.), 441.683-010
03.04.04 CEMETERY WORKER (real estate), 406.684-010
03.04.04 GREENSKEEPER 2 (any ind.), 406.683-010
03.04.04 GROUNDSKEEPER, INDUSTRIAL-COMMERCIAL (any ind.), 406.684-014
03.04.04 GROUNDSKEEPER, PARKS AND GROUNDS (gov. ser.), 406.687-010
03.04.04 HORTICULTURAL WORKER 2 (agric.), 405.687-014
03.04.04 LABORER, LANDSCAPE (agric.), 408.687-014
03.04.04 LAWN-SERVICE WORKER (agric.), 408.684-010
03.04.05 DOG CATCHER (gov. ser.), 379.673-010
03.04.05 PLANT-CARE WORKER (agric.), 408.364-010
03.04.05 TREE TRIMMER (light, heat, & power), 408.664-010
04.01.02 INVESTIGATOR (light, heat, & power), 376.367-022
04.02.01 GUARD, IMMIGRATION (gov. ser.), 372.567-014
04.02.01 JAILER (gov. ser.), 372.367-014
04.02.02 AIRLINE SECURITY REPRESENTATIVE (air trans.), 372.667-010
04.02.02 ARMORED-CAR GUARD (bus. ser.), 372.567-010
04.02.02 ARMORED-CAR GUARD AND DRIVER (bus. ser.), 372.563-010
04.02.02 BODYGUARD (per. ser.), 372.667-014
04.02.02 DETECTIVE 1 (any ind.), 376.367-014
04.02.02 FIRE RANGER (forestry), 452.367-014
04.02.02 GATE TENDER (any ind.), 372.667-030
04.02.02 GUARD, SECURITY (any ind.), 372.667-034
04.02.02 PARKING ENFORCEMENT OFFICER (gov. ser.), 375.587-010
04.02.03 BEACH LIFEGUARD (amuse. & rec.), 379.364-014
04.02.03 BORDER GUARD (gov. ser.), 375.363-010
04.02.03 BOUNCER (amuse. & rec.), 376.667-010
04.02.03 CHAPERON (per. ser.), 359.667-010
04.02.03 REPOSSESSOR (clerical), 241.367-022
04.02.03 SURVEILLANCE-SYSTEM MONITOR (gov. ser.), 379.367-010
04.02.04 ALARM INVESTIGATOR (bus. ser.), 376.367-010
04.02.04 SMOKE JUMPER (forestry), 452.364-014
05.02.02 SUPERINTENDENT, BUILDING (any ind.), 187.167-190
05.02.02 SUPERINTENDENT, CONSTRUCTION (const.), 182.167-026
05.03.02 TAPER, PRINTED CIRCUIT LAYOUT (electronics), 017.684-010

05.03.03 DISPATCHER (air trans.), 912.167-010

05.03.06 CODE INSPECTOR (gov. ser.), 168.367-018

05.03.06 INSPECTOR, BUILDING (gov. ser.), 168.167-030

05.05.01 MARBLE FINISHER (const.), 861.664-010

05.05.01 STONECUTTER, HAND (stonework), 771.381-014

05.05.01 TERRAZZO FINISHER (const.), 861.664-014

05.05.01 TILE FINISHER (const.), 861.664-018

05.05.02 BOAT REPAIRER (ship bldg. & rep.), 807.361-014

05.05.02 BOATBUILDER, WOOD (ship bldg. & rep.), 860.381-018

05.05.03 OIL-BURNER-SERVICER-AND-INSTALLER (any ind.), 862.281-018

05.05.05 ANTENNA INSTALLER, SATELLITE COMMUNICATIONS (any ind.), 823.261-022

05.05.05 CABLE SPLICER (const.), 829.361-010

05.05.05 ELECTRIC-METER INSTALLER 1 (light, heat, & power), 821.361-014

05.05.05 ELECTRICIAN, POWERHOUSE (light, heat, & power), 820.261-014

05.05.05 ELECTRONICS ASSEMBLER, DEVELOPMENTAL (electronics), 726.261-010

05.05.05 LINE ERECTOR (const.), 821.361-018

05.05.05 LINE MAINTAINER (any ind.), 821.261-014

05.05.05 STREET-LIGHT SERVICER (light, heat, & power), 824.381-010

05.05.05 TOWER ERECTOR (const.), 821.361-038

05.05.05 WIND-GENERATING-ELECTRIC-POWER INSTALLER (const.), 821.381-018

05.05.06 AIRCRAFT BODY REPAIRER (aircraft-aerospace mfg.), 807.261-010

05.05.06 ARC CUTTER (welding), 816.364-010

05.05.06 BLACKSMITH (forging), 610.381-010

05.05.06 BOILERHOUSE MECHANIC (any ind.), 805.361-010

05.05.06 CONDUIT MECHANIC (const.), 869.361-010

05.05.06 FITTER 1 (any ind.), 801.261-014

05.05.06 FORMER, HAND (any ind.), 619.361-010

05.05.06 ORNAMENTAL-METAL WORKER (fabric. metal prod. nec), 619.260-008

05.05.06 RIGGER (ship bldg. & rep.), 806.261-014

05.05.06 SAFE-AND-VAULT SERVICE MECHANIC (bus. ser.), 869.381-022

05.05.06 SHIPFITTER (ship bldg. & rep.), 806.381-046

05.05.06 SIGN ERECTOR 1 (signs), 869.381-026

05.05.06 STRUCTURAL-STEEL WORKER (const.), 801.361-014

05.05.06 WELDER, EXPERIMENTAL (welding), 819.281-022

05.05.06 WELDER, GAS (welding), 811.684-014

05.05.06 WELDER-ASSEMBLER (mach. mfg.), 819.381-010

05.05.07 GUNSMITH (any ind.), 632.281-010

05.05.07 SAW FILER (any ind.), 701.381-014

05.05.07 TOOL GRINDER (any ind.), 701.381-018

05.05.08 FURNITURE RESTORER (museum), 763.380-010

05.05.08 LOFT WORKER (ship bldg. & rep.), 661.281-010

05.05.09 AIR-CONDITIONING MECHANIC (auto. ser.), 620.281-010

05.05.09 AUTOMOBILE-SERVICE-STATION MECHANIC (auto. ser.), 620.261-030

05.05.09 AUTOMOTIVE-COOLING-SYSTEM DIAGNOSTIC TECHNICIAN (auto. ser.), 620.261-034

05.05.09 CASH-REGISTER SERVICER (any ind.), 633.281-010

05.05.09 CONSTRUCTION-EQUIPMENT MECHANIC (const.), 620.261-022

05.05.09 FUEL-INJECTION SERVICER (any ind.), 625.281-022

05.05.09 FUEL-SYSTEM-MAINTENANCE WORKER (any ind.), 638.381-010

05.05.09 GAS-ENGINE REPAIRER (any ind.), 625.281-026

05.05.09 GAS-WELDING-EQUIPMENT MECHANIC (any ind.), 626.381-014

05.05.09 LOCKSMITH (any ind.), 709.281-010

05.05.09 MACHINERY ERECTOR (engine & turbine), 638.261-014

05.05.09 MAIL-PROCESSING-EQUIPMENT MECHANIC (gov. ser.), 633.261-014

05.05.09 MAINTENANCE REPAIRER, INDUSTRIAL (any ind.), 899.261-014

05.05.09 MECHANIC, INDUSTRIAL TRUCK (any ind.), 620.281-050

05.05.09 PARTS SALVAGER (any ind.), 638.281-026

05.05.09 PNEUMATIC-TOOL REPAIRER (any ind.), 630.281-010

05.05.09 POWER-SAW MECHANIC (any ind.), 625.281-030

05.05.09 PUMP SERVICER (any ind.), 630.281-018

05.05.09 REFRIGERATION MECHANIC (refrig. equip.), 827.361-014

05.05.09 SMALL-ENGINE MECHANIC (any ind.), 625.281-034

05.05.09 SOLAR-ENERGY-SYSTEM INSTALLER (any ind.), 637.261-030

05.05.10 ELECTRIC-METER REPAIRER (light, heat, & power), 729.281-014

05.05.10 ELECTRIC-METER TESTER (light, heat, & power), 821.381-010

05.05.10 ELECTRICAL-APPLIANCE SERVICER (any ind.), 827.261-010

05.05.10 ELECTRICAL-INSTRUMENT REPAIRER (any ind.), 729.281-026

05.05.10 INSTRUMENT MECHANIC (any ind.), 710.281-026

05.05.10 PINSETTER ADJUSTER, AUTOMATIC (sports equip.), 829.381-010

05.05.10 PUBLIC-ADDRESS SERVICER (any ind.), 823.261-010

05.05.11 CAMERA REPAIRER (photo. apparatus), 714.281-014

05.05.11 DENTAL CERAMIST (medical ser.), 712.281-010

05.05.11 DENTAL CERAMIST ASSISTANT (medical ser.), 712.664-010

05.05.11 DENTURE-MODEL MAKER (medical ser.), 712.681-014

05.05.11 ELECTROMEDICAL-EQUIPMENT REPAIRER (any ind.), 729.281-030

05.05.11 EXPERIMENTAL ASSEMBLER (any ind.), 739.381-026

05.05.11 FINISHER, DENTURE (medical ser.), 712.681-018

05.05.11 INSTRUMENT REPAIRER (any ind.), 710.261-010

05.05.11 LENS MOUNTER 2 (optical goods), 713.681-010

05.05.11 PACKER, DENTURE (medical ser.), 712.684-034

05.05.12 ACCORDION REPAIRER (any ind.), 730.281-014

05.05.12 ELECTRIC-ORGAN INSPECTOR AND REPAIRER (musical inst.), 730.281-018

05.05.12 ELECTRONIC-ORGAN TECHNICIAN (any ind.), 828.261-010

05.05.12 FRETTED-INSTRUMENT MAKER, HAND (musical inst.), 730.281-022

05.05.12 PERCUSSION-INSTRUMENT REPAIRER (any ind.), 730.381-042

05.05.12 PIANO TECHNICIAN (any ind.), 730.281-038

05.05.12 PIANO TUNER (any ind.), 730.361-010

05.05.12 PIPE-ORGAN INSTALLER (musical inst.), 730.381-046

05.05.12 PIPE-ORGAN TUNER AND REPAIRER (any ind.), 730.361-014

05.05.12 VIOLIN MAKER, HAND (musical inst.), 730.281-046

05.05.12 WIND-INSTRUMENT REPAIRER (any ind.), 730.281-054

05.05.13 ASSISTANT-PRESS OPERATOR (print. & pub.), 651.585-010

05.05.13 CYLINDER-PRESS OPERATOR (print. & pub.), 651.362-010

05.05.13 OFFSET-PRESS OPERATOR 1 (print. & pub.), 651.482-010

05.05.13 ROTOGRAVURE-PRESS OPERATOR (print. & pub.), 651.362-026

05.05.13 WEB-PRESS OPERATOR (print. & pub.), 651.362-030

05.05.14 STONE SETTER (jewelry), 700.381-054

05.05.15 ALTERATION TAILOR (garment), 785.261-010

05.05.15 AUTOMOBILE UPHOLSTERER (auto. ser.), 780.381-010

05.05.15 BOOKBINDER (print. & pub.), 977.381-010

05.05.15 CUSTOM TAILOR (garment), 785.261-014

05.05.15 DRESSMAKER (any ind.), 785.361-010

05.05.15 FURNITURE UPHOLSTERER (any ind.), 780.381-018

05.05.15 FURRIER (fur goods), 783.261-010

05.05.15 RUG REPAIRER (clean., dye., & press.), 782.381-018

05.05.15 SHOE REPAIRER (per. ser.), 365.361-014

05.05.15 SHOP TAILOR (garment), 785.361-022

05.05.17 CAKE DECORATOR (bake. prod.), 524.381-010
05.05.17 CHEF DE FROID (hotel & rest.), 313.281-010
05.05.17 SOUS CHEF (hotel & rest.), 313.131-026
05.06.01 CABLE MAINTAINER (light, heat, & power), 952.464-010
05.06.01 GAS-ENGINE OPERATOR (any ind.), 950.382-018
05.06.01 LOAD DISPATCHER (light, heat, & power), 952.167-014
05.06.02 AIR-COMPRESSOR OPERATOR (any ind.), 950.685-010
05.06.02 BOILER OPERATOR (any ind.), 950.382-010
05.06.02 FUEL ATTENDANT (any ind.), 953.362-010
05.06.02 GAS-COMPRESSOR OPERATOR (any ind.), 950.382-014
05.06.02 REFRIGERATING ENGINEER (any ind.), 950.362-014
05.06.03 PUMP-STATION OPERATOR, WATERWORKS (waterworks), 954.382-010
05.06.03 PUMPER (any ind.), 914.682-010
05.07.01 CAR INSPECTOR (r.r. car blgd. & rep.), 910.667-010
05.07.01 LINE WALKER (petrol. production), 869.564-010
05.07.01 SEWER-LINE PHOTO-INSPECTOR (sanitary ser.), 851.362-010
05.07.01 ULTRASONIC TESTER (bus. ser.), 709.281-018
05.07.03 ELEVATOR EXAMINER-AND-ADJUSTER (any ind.), 825.261-014
05.08.01 DUMP-TRUCK DRIVER (any ind.), 902.683-010
05.08.01 MILK DRIVER (dairy prod.), 905.483-010
05.08.01 TRACTOR-TRAILER-TRUCK DRIVER (any ind.), 904.383-010
05.08.01 TRUCK DRIVER, HEAVY (any ind.), 905.663-014
05.08.01 TRUCK DRIVER, LIGHT (any ind.), 906.683-022
05.08.02 FIRER, LOCOMOTIVE (r.r. trans.), 910.363-010
05.08.02 TRACKMOBILE OPERATOR (any ind.), 919.683-026
05.08.03 AMBULANCE DRIVER (medical ser.), 913.683-010
05.08.03 CHAUFFEUR, FUNERAL CAR (per. ser.), 359.673-014
05.08.03 CONCRETE-MIXING-TRUCK DRIVER (const.), 900.683-010
05.08.03 DELIVERER, CAR RENTAL (auto. ser.), 919.663-010
05.08.03 HEALTH-EQUIPMENT SERVICER (medical ser.), 359.363-010
05.08.03 LOT ATTENDANT (ret. tr.), 915.583-010
05.08.03 NEWSPAPER-DELIVERY DRIVER (whole. tr.), 292.363-010
05.08.03 TELEPHONE-DIRECTORY-DISTRIBUTOR DRIVER (bus. ser.), 906.683-018
05.08.03 TOW-TRUCK OPERATOR (auto. ser.), 919.663-026
05.08.04 DECKHAND (water trans.), 911.687-022
05.08.04 MOTORBOAT OPERATOR (any ind.), 911.663-010
05.09.01 CARGO AGENT (air trans.), 248.367-018
05.09.01 CUSTODIAN, ATHLETIC EQUIPMENT (amuse. & rec.), 969.367-010
05.09.01 INVENTORY CLERK (clerical), 222.387-026
05.09.01 LABORATORY CLERK (clerical), 222.587-026
05.09.01 LABORER, STORES (any ind.), 922.687-058
05.09.01 LINEN-ROOM ATTENDANT (hotel & rest.), 222.387-030
05.09.01 MAILER (print. & pub.), 222.587-030
05.09.01 MEAT CLERK (ret. tr.), 222.684-010
05.09.01 ORDER FILLER (ret. tr.), 222.487-014
05.09.01 PARTS CLERK (clerical), 222.367-042
05.09.01 PARTS-ORDER-AND-STOCK CLERK (clerical), 249.367-058
05.09.01 PHARMACY HELPER (medical ser.), 074.387-010
05.09.01 PRODUCTION TECHNICIAN, SEMICONDUCTOR PROCESSING EQUIPMENT (electronics), 590.384-014
05.09.01 SHIPPING AND RECEIVING CLERK (clerical), 222.387-050
05.09.01 SHIPPING CHECKER (clerical), 222.687-030
05.09.01 SHIPPING-AND-RECEIVING WEIGHER (clerical), 222.367-058
05.09.01 STOCK CLERK, SELF-SERVICE STORE (ret. tr.), 299.367-014
05.09.01 SUPPLY CLERK (per. ser.), 339.687-010
05.09.01 TIRE ADJUSTER (ret. tr.), 241.367-034
05.09.01 TOOL-CRIB ATTENDANT (clerical), 222.367-062

05.09.02 DRAPERY AND UPHOLSTERY ESTIMATOR (ret. tr.), 299.387-010
05.09.02 JOB TRACER (clerical), 221.387-034
05.09.02 LAUNDRY CLERK (clerical), 221.387-038
05.09.02 MATERIAL EXPEDITER (clerical), 221.367-042
05.09.02 ORDER DETAILER (clerical), 221.387-046
05.09.02 PRESCRIPTION CLERK, LENS-AND-FRAMES (optical goods), 222.367-050
05.09.02 STOCK CLERK (clerical), 222.387-058
05.09.03 CHECKER, DUMP GROUNDS (bus. ser.), 219.367-010
05.09.03 INDUSTRIAL-ORDER CLERK (clerical), 221.367-022
05.09.03 MARKER (ret. tr.), 209.587-034
05.09.03 MATERIAL CLERK (clerical), 222.387-034
05.09.03 METER READER (light, heat, & power), 209.567-010
05.09.03 ORDER CALLER (clerical), 209.667-014
05.09.03 RECEIVING CHECKER (clerical), 222.687-018
05.09.03 SORTER-PRICER (nonprofit org.), 222.387-054
05.09.03 TURBINE ATTENDANT (light, heat, & power), 952.567-010
05.10.01 ARCH-SUPPORT TECHNICIAN (per. protect. & med. device), 712.381-010
05.10.01 BOAT RIGGER (ret. tr.), 806.464-010
05.10.01 BUILDING CLEANER (any ind.), 891.684-022
05.10.01 CARPET CUTTER (ret. tr.), 929.381-010
05.10.01 CARPET LAYER (ret. tr.), 864.381-010
05.10.01 CARPET-LAYER HELPER (ret. tr.), 864.687-010
05.10.01 CASTING REPAIRER (any ind.), 619.281-010
05.10.01 DIVER (any ind.), 899.261-010
05.10.01 DRAPERY HANGER (ret. tr.), 869.484-014
05.10.01 DRY-WALL APPLICATOR (const.), 842.681-010
05.10.01 FENCE ERECTOR (const.), 869.684-022
05.10.01 FIXTURE REPAIRER-FABRICATOR (any ind.), 630.384-010
05.10.01 FLOOR LAYER (const.), 864.481-010
05.10.01 FRAME REPAIRER (furn.), 763.681-010
05.10.01 FRONT-END MECHANIC (auto. ser.), 620.281-038
05.10.01 FURNITURE ASSEMBLER-AND-INSTALLER (ret. tr.), 739.684-082
05.10.01 GLASS INSTALLER (auto. ser.), 865.684-010
05.10.01 GLAZIER (const.), 865.381-010
05.10.01 GRIP (amuse. & rec.), 962.684-014
05.10.01 INSULATION WORKER (const.), 863.364-014
05.10.01 LATHER (const.), 842.361-010
05.10.01 LUGGAGE REPAIRER (any ind.), 365.361-010
05.10.01 MUFFLER INSTALLER (auto. ser.), 807.664-010
05.10.01 PUMP INSTALLER (any ind.), 630.684-018
05.10.01 REPAIRER (furn.), 709.684-062
05.10.01 ROOFER (const.), 866.381-010
05.10.01 ROUSTABOUT (petrol. production), 869.684-046
05.10.01 SERVICE REPRESENTATIVE (light, heat, & power), 959.574-010
05.10.01 SEWER-LINE REPAIRER, TELE-GROUT (sanitary ser.), 851.262-010
05.10.01 SIDER (const.), 863.684-014
05.10.01 SIGN ERECTOR 2 (signs), 869.684-054
05.10.01 SWIMMING POOL INSTALLER-AND-SERVICER (const.), 869.463-010
05.10.01 TAPER (const.), 842.664-010
05.10.01 TEMPLATE MAKER, TRACK (any ind.), 809.484-014
05.10.01 TILE SETTER HELPER (const.), 869.664-014
05.10.01 TORCH-STRAIGHTENER-AND-HEATER (any ind.), 709.684-086
05.10.01 UMBRELLA REPAIRER (any ind.), 369.684-018
05.10.01 WATER-SOFTENER SERVICER-AND-INSTALLER (bus. ser.), 862.684-034
05.10.01 WELDER, TACK (welding), 810.684-010
05.10.02 AUTOMOBILE-ACCESSORIES INSTALLER (auto. ser.), 806.684-038
05.10.02 AUTOMOBILE-RADIATOR MECHANIC (auto. ser.), 620.381-010
05.10.02 AUTOMOBILE-SERVICE-STATION ATTENDANT (auto. ser.), 915.467-010
05.10.02 BICYCLE REPAIRER (any ind.), 639.681-010
05.10.02 BRAKE REPAIRER (auto. ser.), 620.281-026
05.10.02 CARBURETOR MECHANIC (auto. ser.), 620.281-034

05.10.02 COIN-MACHINE-SERVICE REPAIRER (coin mach.), 639.281-014

05.10.02 CONVEYOR-MAINTENANCE MECHANIC (any ind.), 630.381-010

05.10.02 DOOR-CLOSER MECHANIC (any ind.), 630.381-014

05.10.02 GAS-APPLIANCE SERVICER (any ind.), 637.261-018

05.10.02 LUBRICATION-EQUIPMENT SERVICER (any ind.), 630.381-022

05.10.02 MECHANIC, AIRCRAFT ACCESSORIES (aircraft-aerospace mfg.), 621.381-014

05.10.02 MEDICAL-EQUIPMENT REPAIRER (per. protect. & med. device), 639.281-022

05.10.02 METER REPAIRER (any ind.), 710.281-034

05.10.02 NEW-CAR GET-READY MECHANIC (auto. ser.), 806.361-026

05.10.02 PNEUMATIC-TUBE REPAIRER (any ind.), 630.281-014

05.10.02 RIDE OPERATOR (amuse. & rec.), 342.663-010

05.10.02 SERVICE MANAGER (auto. ser.), 185.167-058

05.10.02 SEWING-MACHINE REPAIRER (any ind.), 639.281-018

05.10.02 THERMOSTAT REPAIRER (inst. & app.), 710.381-050

05.10.03 APPLIANCE REPAIRER (elec. equip.), 723.584-010

05.10.03 AUTOMATIC-DOOR MECHANIC (const.), 829.281-010

05.10.03 BATTERY REPAIRER (any ind.), 727.381-014

05.10.03 ELECTRIC-GOLF-CART REPAIRER (amuse. & rec.), 620.261-026

05.10.03 ELECTRIC-TOOL REPAIRER (any ind.), 729.281-022

05.10.03 ELECTRICAL-APPLIANCE REPAIRER (any ind.), 723.381-010

05.10.03 LIGHT TECHNICIAN (motion pic.), 962.362-014

05.10.03 PRODUCTION REPAIRER (electronics), 726.381-014

05.10.03 TAPE-RECORDER REPAIRER (any ind.), 720.281-014

05.10.03 TELEVISION INSTALLER (any ind.), 823.361-010

05.10.03 TELEVISION-CABLE INSTALLER (any ind.), 821.281-010

05.10.03 TRANSFORMER REPAIRER (any ind.), 724.381-018

05.10.03 VACUUM CLEANER REPAIRER (any ind.), 723.381-014

05.10.04 AIR-CONDITIONING INSTALLER, DOMESTIC (any ind.), 827.464-010

05.10.04 AIRPORT ATTENDANT (air trans.), 912.364-010

05.10.04 DOLL REPAIRER (any ind.), 731.684-014

05.10.04 EQUIPMENT INSTALLER (any ind.), 828.381-010

05.10.04 EVAPORATIVE-COOLER INSTALLER (any ind.), 637.381-010

05.10.04 FIRE-EXTINGUISHER REPAIRER (any ind.), 709.384-010

05.10.04 HOUSEHOLD-APPLIANCE INSTALLER (any ind.), 827.661-010

05.10.04 PINSETTER MECHANIC, AUTOMATIC (any ind.), 638.261-022

05.10.04 POLISHING-WHEEL SETTER (any ind.), 776.684-014

05.10.04 SPORTS-EQUIPMENT REPAIRER (any ind.), 732.684-122

05.10.04 SWIMMING-POOL SERVICER (any ind.), 891.684-018

05.10.04 USED-CAR RENOVATOR (ret. tr.), 620.684-034

05.10.05 AUDIOVISUAL TECHNICIAN (any ind.), 960.382-010

05.10.05 BLUEPRINTING-MACHINE OPERATOR (any ind.), 979.682-014

05.10.05 COLOR-PRINTER OPERATOR (photofinish.), 976.382-014

05.10.05 DEVELOPER (photofinish.), 976.681-010

05.10.05 DUPLICATING-MACHINE OPERATOR 1 (clerical), 207.682-010

05.10.05 ENGRAVER, MACHINE 1 (engraving), 704.682-010

05.10.05 ENGRAVING-PRESS OPERATOR (print. & pub.), 651.382-010

05.10.05 EQUIPMENT MONITOR, PHOTOTYPESETTING (print. & pub.), 650.682-010

05.10.05 FILM DEVELOPER (motion pic.), 976.382-018

05.10.05 FILM LABORATORY TECHNICIAN (motion pic.), 976.684-014

05.10.05 MICROFICHE DUPLICATOR (bus. ser.), 976.381-014

05.10.05 MICROFILM PROCESSOR (bus. ser.), 976.385-010

05.10.05 MOTION-PICTURE PROJECTIONIST (amuse. & rec.), 960.362-010

05.10.05 OFFSET-DUPLICATING-MACHINE OPERATOR (clerical), 207.682-018

05.10.05 PHOTOCOMPOSING-MACHINE OPERATOR (print. & pub.), 650.582-018

05.10.05 PHOTOGRAPH FINISHER (photofinish.), 976.487-010

05.10.05 PROJECTION PRINTER (photofinish.), 976.381-018

05.10.05 RECORDIST (motion pic.), 962.382-010

05.10.05 REPRODUCTION TECHNICIAN (any ind.), 976.361-010

05.10.05 TAKE-DOWN SORTER (photofinish.), 976.665-010

05.10.05 TAPE TRANSFERRER (phonograph), 194.382-014

05.10.05 TYPESETTING-MACHINE TENDER (print. & pub.), 650.685-010

05.10.07 PAINTER (const.), 840.381-010

05.10.07 PAINTER, SPRAY 1 (any ind.), 741.684-026

05.10.07 PAINTER, TOUCH-UP (any ind.), 749.684-038

05.10.08 BAKER (hotel & rest.), 313.381-010

05.10.08 BAKER, HEAD (hotel & rest.), 313.131-010

05.10.08 BAKER, PIZZA (hotel & rest.), 313.381-014

05.10.08 BUTCHER, MEAT (hotel & rest.), 316.681-010

05.10.08 CARVER (hotel & rest.), 316.661-010

05.10.08 COOK (dom. ser.), 305.281-010

05.10.08 COOK (any ind.), 315.361-010

05.10.08 COOK, BARBECUE (hotel & rest.), 313.381-022

05.10.08 COOK, PASTRY (hotel & rest.), 313.381-026

05.10.08 COOK, SHORT ORDER 1 (hotel & rest.), 313.361-022

05.10.08 COOK, SHORT ORDER 2 (hotel & rest.), 313.671-010

05.10.08 COOK, SPECIALTY (hotel & rest.), 313.361-026

05.10.08 FORMULA-ROOM WORKER (dairy prod.), 520.487-014

05.10.08 GARDE MANGER (hotel & rest.), 313.361-034

05.10.08 MEAT CUTTER (ret. tr.), 316.684-018

05.10.08 PANTRY GOODS MAKER (hotel & rest.), 317.684-014

05.10.08 PASTRY CHEF (hotel & rest.), 313.131-022

05.10.08 PIE MAKER (hotel & rest.), 313.361-038

05.10.08 SALAD MAKER (water trans.), 317.384-010

05.10.09 EXTERMINATOR (any ind.), 389.684-010

05.10.09 EXTERMINATOR, TERMITE (bus. ser.), 383.364-010

05.10.09 FUMIGATOR (bus. ser.), 383.361-010

05.11.01 ASPHALT-PAVING-MACHINE OPERATOR (const.), 853.663-010

05.11.01 BULLDOZER OPERATOR 1 (any ind.), 850.683-010

05.11.01 POWER-SHOVEL OPERATOR (any ind.), 850.683-030

05.11.01 ROAD-ROLLER OPERATOR (const.), 859.683-030

05.11.01 ROCK-DRILL OPERATOR 1 (const.), 850.683-034

05.11.01 SEPTIC-TANK INSTALLER (const.), 851.663-010

05.11.01 STREET-SWEEPER OPERATOR (gov. ser.), 919.683-022

05.11.02 CORE DRILL OPERATOR (any ind.), 930.682-010

05.11.02 PLANT OPERATOR (concrete prod.), 570.682-014

05.11.03 ROTARY DRILLER (petrol. production), 930.382-026

05.11.04 BRIDGE-OR-GANTRY-CRANE OPERATOR (any ind.), 921.663-010

05.11.04 CONVEYOR OPERATOR (any ind.), 921.683-026

05.11.04 DERRICK OPERATOR (any ind.), 921.663-022

05.11.04 DINKEY OPERATOR (any ind.), 919.663-014

05.11.04 DRAGLINE OPERATOR (any ind.), 850.683-018

05.11.04 DUMP OPERATOR (any ind.), 921.685-038

05.11.04 FRONT-END LOADER OPERATOR (any ind.), 921.683-042

05.11.04 HOISTING ENGINEER (any ind.), 921.663-030

05.11.04 RIGGER (any ind.), 921.260-010

05.11.04 STEVEDORE 1 (water trans.), 911.663-014

05.11.04 TRACTOR OPERATOR (any ind.), 929.683-014

05.11.04 TRACTOR-CRANE OPERATOR (any ind.), 921.663-058

05.11.04 TRUCK-CRANE OPERATOR (any ind.), 921.663-062

05.12.02 SURVEYOR HELPER (any ind.), 869.567-010

05.12.03 ABLE SEAMAN (water trans.), 911.364-010

05.12.03 BAGGAGE HANDLER (r.r. trans.), 910.687-010

05.12.03 BARGE CAPTAIN (water trans.), 911.137-010

05.12.03 BRAKE HOLDER (any ind.), 932.664-010

05.12.03 CONSTRUCTION WORKER 2 (const.), 869.687-026

05.12.03 DOLLY PUSHER (radio & tv broad.), 962.687-010

05.12.03 DUMPER (any ind.), 921.667-018

05.12.03 ETCHER HELPER, HAND (print. & pub.), 971.687-010
05.12.03 GARBAGE COLLECTOR (motor trans.), 909.687-010
05.12.03 INSTALLER (museum), 922.687-050
05.12.03 LABORER (petrol. production), 939.687-018
05.12.03 LABORER, PETROLEUM REFINERY (petrol. refin.), 549.687-018
05.12.03 LABORER, SHIPYARD (ship bldg. & rep.), 809.687-022
05.12.03 MATERIAL HANDLER (any ind.), 929.687-030
05.12.03 PRESS BUCKER (any ind.), 920.686-042
05.12.03 RECORDING STUDIO SET-UP WORKER (phonograph), 962.664-014
05.12.03 WASTE-DISPOSAL ATTENDANT (any ind.), 955.383-010
05.12.03 YARD LABORER (paper & pulp), 922.687-102
05.12.04 BOOM-CONVEYOR OPERATOR (any ind.), 921.683-014
05.12.04 CHOKE SETTER (logging), 921.687-014
05.12.04 CONVEYOR-SYSTEM DISPATCHER (any ind.), 921.662-018
05.12.04 ELEVATOR OPERATOR, FREIGHT (any ind.), 921.683-038
05.12.04 GRIP (motion pic.), 962.687-022
05.12.04 LABORER, CONCRETE-MIXING PLANT (const.), 579.665-014
05.12.04 LABORER, HOISTING (any ind.), 921.667-022
05.12.04 LABORER, POWERHOUSE (light, heat, & power), 952.665-010
05.12.05 BRAKE COUPLER, ROAD FREIGHT (r.r. trans.), 910.367-010
05.12.05 SWITCH TENDER (r.r. trans.), 910.667-026
05.12.06 AIRPORT UTILITY WORKER (air trans.), 912.663-010
05.12.06 BOAT LOADER 1 (water trans.), 911.364-014
05.12.06 LINE-SERVICE ATTENDANT (air trans.), 912.687-010
05.12.06 WATER TENDER (any ind.), 599.685-122
05.12.08 GARAGE SERVICER, INDUSTRIAL (any ind.), 915.687-014
05.12.08 LUBRICATION SERVICER (auto. ser.), 915.687-018
05.12.08 MARINE OILER (water trans.), 911.584-010
05.12.08 OILER (any ind.), 699.687-018
05.12.11 THERMAL CUTTER, HAND 2 (welding), 816.684-010
05.12.12 AUTOMOBILE-BODY-REPAIRER HELPER (auto. ser.), 807.687-010
05.12.12 BILLPOSTER (any ind.), 299.667-010
05.12.12 DECORATOR, STREET AND BUILDING (any ind.), 899.687-010
05.12.12 HIGHWAY-MAINTENANCE WORKER (gov. ser.), 899.684-014
05.12.12 PIPE-FITTER HELPER (const.), 862.684-022
05.12.12 SEWER-LINE REPAIRER (sanitary ser.), 869.664-018
05.12.12 SEWER-PIPE CLEANER (bus. ser.), 899.664-014
05.12.12 TRACK REPAIRER (r.r. trans.), 910.682-010
05.12.12 WINDOW REPAIRER (any ind.), 899.684-042
05.12.13 KEY CUTTER (any ind.), 709.684-050
05.12.14 ASPHALT-DISTRIBUTOR TENDER (const.), 853.665-010
05.12.14 BILLPOSTER (bus. ser.), 841.684-010
05.12.14 SHOE DYER (per. ser.), 364.684-014
05.12.14 STEEL-PLATE CALKER (any ind.), 843.684-010
05.12.14 STOVE REFINISHER (any ind.), 749.684-046
05.12.14 UNDERCOATER (auto. ser.), 843.684-014
05.12.15 AUTOMOBILE WRECKER (whole. tr.), 620.684-010
05.12.15 BELT REPAIRER (any ind.), 630.684-014
05.12.15 ROLLER-SKATE REPAIRER (any ind.), 732.684-102
05.12.15 TIRE REPAIRER (auto. ser.), 915.684-010
05.12.16 ANTENNA INSTALLER (any ind.), 823.684-010
05.12.16 CABLE PULLER (const.), 829.684-018
05.12.16 ELECTRICAL-APPLIANCE PREPARER (any ind.), 827.584-010
05.12.16 LIGHTING-EQUIPMENT OPERATOR (amuse. & rec.), 962.381-014
05.12.17 COFFEE MAKER (hotel & rest.), 317.684-010
05.12.17 COOK HELPER (hotel & rest.), 317.687-010
05.12.17 DELI CUTTER-SLICER (ret. tr.), 316.684-014
05.12.17 FOOD ASSEMBLER, KITCHEN (hotel & rest.), 319.484-010

05.12.17 SANDWICH MAKER (hotel & rest.), 317.684-018
05.12.18 ATTENDANT, CAMPGROUND (amuse. & rec.), 329.683-010
05.12.18 AUTOMOBILE DETAILER (auto. ser.), 915.687-034
05.12.18 BARTENDER HELPER (hotel & rest.), 312.687-010
05.12.18 CARETAKER (dom. ser.), 301.687-010
05.12.18 CHANGE-HOUSE ATTENDANT (any ind.), 358.687-010
05.12.18 CHIMNEY SWEEP (any ind.), 891.687-010
05.12.18 CLEANER 2 (any ind.), 919.687-014
05.12.18 CLEANER, COMMERCIAL OR INSTITUTIONAL (any ind.), 381.687-014
05.12.18 CLEANER, HOSPITAL (medical ser.), 323.687-010
05.12.18 CLEANER, HOUSEKEEPING (any ind.), 323.687-014
05.12.18 CLEANER, INDUSTRIAL (any ind.), 381.687-018
05.12.18 CLEANER, LABORATORY EQUIPMENT (any ind.), 381.687-022
05.12.18 CLEANER, SIGNS (signs), 739.687-062
05.12.18 CLEANER, WINDOW (any ind.), 389.687-014
05.12.18 FURNACE CLEANER (any ind.), 891.687-014
05.12.18 GOLF-RANGE ATTENDANT (amuse. & rec.), 341.683-010
05.12.18 HOUSEKEEPER (hotel & rest.), 321.137-010
05.12.18 JANITOR (any ind.), 382.664-010
05.12.18 KITCHEN HELPER (hotel & rest.), 318.687-010
05.12.18 LAUNDRY WORKER 1 (any ind.), 361.684-014
05.12.18 LIGHT-FIXTURE SERVICER (any ind.), 389.687-018
05.12.18 ORDINARY SEAMAN (water trans.), 911.687-030
05.12.18 PRINT-SHOP HELPER (print. & pub.), 979.684-026
05.12.18 SANDBLASTER (any ind.), 503.687-010
05.12.18 STEAM CLEANER (auto. ser.), 915.687-026
05.12.18 STREET CLEANER (gov. ser.), 955.687-018
05.12.18 SWEEPER-CLEANER, INDUSTRIAL (any ind.), 389.683-010
05.12.18 TANK CLEANER (any ind.), 891.687-022
05.12.18 TUBE CLEANER (any ind.), 891.687-030
05.12.18 VENETIAN-BLIND CLEANER AND REPAIRER (any ind.), 739.687-198
05.12.19 ADDRESSING-MACHINE OPERATOR (clerical), 208.582-010
05.12.19 AUXILIARY-EQUIPMENT OPERATOR, DATA PROCESSING (clerical), 213.685-010
05.12.19 BOOK REPAIRER (any ind.), 977.684-010
05.12.19 BRAILLE-DUPLICATING-MACHINE OPERATOR (print. & pub.), 207.685-010
05.12.19 BURSTING-MACHINE TENDER (clerical), 217.685-010
05.12.19 COIN WRAPPER (clerical), 217.686-010
05.12.19 COIN-MACHINE OPERATOR (finan. inst.), 217.585-010
05.12.19 COLLATOR OPERATOR (clerical), 208.685-010
05.12.19 CURRENCY SORTER (finan. inst.), 217.485-010
05.12.19 FOLDING-MACHINE OPERATOR (clerical), 208.685-014
05.12.19 INSERTING-MACHINE OPERATOR (clerical), 208.685-018
05.12.19 MICROFILM MOUNTER (clerical), 208.685-022
05.12.19 PHOTOCOPYING-MACHINE OPERATOR (clerical), 207.685-014
05.12.19 PHOTOGRAPHIC-MACHINE OPERATOR (clerical), 207.685-018
05.12.20 CROSSING TENDER (any ind.), 371.667-010
06.01.01 COOK, MEXICAN FOOD (food prep nec), 526.134-010
06.01.02 FIRESETTER (elec. equip.), 692.360-018
06.01.02 KNITTER MECHANIC (knit goods), 685.360-010
06.01.02 KNITTING-MACHINE FIXER (hosiery), 689.280-014
06.01.02 LOOM FIXER (asbestos prod.), 683.260-018
06.01.02 MACHINE SETTER (any ind.), 616.360-022
06.01.02 SETTER, AUTOMATIC-SPINNING LATHE (any ind.), 604.360-010
06.01.03 PRINTER 2 (print. & pub.), 651.380-010
06.01.03 ROLLING ATTENDANT (iron & steel), 613.662-010
06.01.04 ASSEMBLER (inst. & app.), 710.681-010
06.01.04 BENCH HAND (jewelry), 735.381-010
06.01.04 CANVAS WORKER (canvas goods), 739.381-010

06.01.04 COREMAKER (foundry), 518.381-014
06.01.04 FINAL ASSEMBLER (office mach.), 706.381-018
06.01.04 GLASS BLOWER (glass mfg.), 772.681-010
06.01.04 GOLDBEATER (gold leaf & foil), 700.381-018
06.01.04 LENS POLISHER, HAND (optical goods), 716.681-018
06.01.04 MOLDER (foundry), 518.361-010
06.01.04 RING MAKER (jewelry), 700.381-042
06.01.04 SKIN FITTER (aircraft-aerospace mfg.), 806.381-054
06.01.04 SOLDERER (jewelry), 700.381-050
06.01.04 TRANSFORMER ASSEMBLER (elec. equip.), 820.381-014
06.01.04 TUBE ASSEMBLER, ELECTRON (electronics), 725.384-010
06.01.05 INSPECTOR, METAL FABRICATING (any ind.), 619.261-010
06.01.05 RETICLE INSPECTOR (electronics), 719.361-010
06.01.05 X-RAY-EQUIPMENT TESTER (any ind.), 729.281-046
06.02.01 TOOL GRINDER 2 (any ind.), 603.664-010
06.02.02 BRAKE OPERATOR 2 (any ind.), 619.685-026
06.02.02 CRIMPING-MACHINE OPERATOR (any ind.), 616.682-022
06.02.02 DROP-HAMMER OPERATOR (forging), 610.462-010
06.02.02 HEATER (forging), 619.682-022
06.02.02 LASER-BEAM-TRIM OPERATOR (electronics), 726.682-010
06.02.02 LATHE HAND (jewelry), 700.682-014
06.02.02 POLISHING-MACHINE OPERATOR (any ind.), 603.682-026
06.02.02 PRESS OPERATOR (fabric. plastic prod.), 690.682-062
06.02.02 PRESS OPERATOR, HEAVY DUTY (any ind.), 617.260-010
06.02.02 PUNCH-PRESS OPERATOR 3 (any ind.), 615.682-014
06.02.02 RIVETER, HYDRAULIC (any ind.), 800.662-010
06.02.02 RIVETING-MACHINE OPERATOR 1 (any ind.), 699.482-010
06.02.02 SHEAR OPERATOR 1 (any ind.), 615.482-034
06.02.02 SPINNER, HAND (any ind.), 619.362-018
06.02.02 SPINNER, HYDRAULIC (any ind.), 619.362-022
06.02.02 STRAIGHTENING-PRESS OPERATOR (any ind.), 617.482-026
06.02.02 STRAIGHTENING-ROLL OPERATOR (any ind.), 613.462-022
06.02.03 CUT-OFF-SAW OPERATOR (woodworking), 667.682-022
06.02.03 HEAD SAWYER (sawmill), 667.662-010
06.02.03 NAILING-MACHINE OPERATOR (any ind.), 669.682-058
06.02.03 TIMBER-SIZER OPERATOR (planing mill), 665.482-018
06.02.04 BOX-FOLDING-MACHINE OPERATOR (paper goods), 649.682-010
06.02.05 BINDER (any ind.), 787.682-010
06.02.05 CARPET SEWER (carpet & rug), 787.682-014
06.02.05 FELTING-MACHINE OPERATOR (felt goods), 586.662-010
06.02.05 HAT-AND-CAP SEWER (hat & cap), 784.682-014
06.02.05 HEMMER (any ind.), 787.682-026
06.02.05 MENDER (any ind.), 787.682-030
06.02.05 SEWING-MACHINE OPERATOR (leather prod.), 783.682-014
06.02.05 SEWING-MACHINE OPERATOR (any ind.), 787.682-046
06.02.05 STITCHER, STANDARD MACHINE (boot & shoe), 690.682-082
06.02.05 TRIMMER, MACHINE (garment), 781.682-010
06.02.05 ZIPPER SETTER (any ind.), 787.682-086
06.02.06 CARPET WEAVER (carpet & rug), 683.682-010
06.02.06 SEAMLESS-HOSIERY KNITTER (hosiery), 684.685-010
06.02.06 WEAVER (asbestos prod.), 683.682-038
06.02.08 EYEGLASS-LENS CUTTER (optical goods), 716.682-010
06.02.08 POTTERY-MACHINE OPERATOR (pottery & porc.), 774.382-010

06.02.08 PRECISION-LENS GRINDER (optical goods), 716.382-018
06.02.08 PRECISION-LENS POLISHER (optical goods), 716.682-018
06.02.09 BROOM STITCHER (brush & broom), 692.682-022
06.02.09 CLOTH PRINTER (any ind.), 652.382-010
06.02.09 CRYSTAL SLICER (electronics), 677.382-018
06.02.09 CUTTER OPERATOR (any ind.), 699.682-018
06.02.09 DIE CUTTER (any ind.), 699.682-022
06.02.09 DYNAMITE-PACKING-MACHINE OPERATOR (explosives), 692.662-010
06.02.09 HONEYCOMB-BLANKET MAKER (aircraft-aerospace mfg.), 806.684-062
06.02.09 NUMERICAL-CONTROL ROUTER OPERATOR, PRINTED CIRCUIT BOARDS (electronics), 605.382-046
06.02.09 WIRE-WRAPPING-MACHINE OPERATOR (electronics), 726.682-014
06.02.10 CARBIDE-POWDER PROCESSOR (mach. shop), 510.465-010
06.02.10 COLD-MILL OPERATOR (iron & steel), 613.462-010
06.02.10 HEAT TREATER 1 (heat treat.), 504.382-014
06.02.10 PICKLER, CONTINUOUS PICKLING LINE (any ind.), 503.362-010
06.02.10 SAND MIXER, MACHINE (foundry), 570.682-018
06.02.12 CYLINDER FILLER (comp. & liq. gases), 559.565-010
06.02.13 BLANKMAKER (glass mfg.), 579.382-022
06.02.13 MIXING-MACHINE OPERATOR (any ind.), 550.382-022
06.02.15 BAKER (bake. prod.), 526.381-010
06.02.15 BUTTERMAKER (dairy prod.), 529.362-010
06.02.15 CENTER-MACHINE OPERATOR (confection.), 520.682-014
06.02.15 CHOCOLATE-PRODUCTION-MACHINE OPERATOR (choc. & cocoa), 529.382-014
06.02.15 COFFEE ROASTER (food prep nec), 523.682-014
06.02.15 DAIRY-PROCESSING-EQUIPMENT OPERATOR (dairy prod.), 529.382-018
06.02.15 DOUGH MIXER (bake. prod.), 520.582-010
06.02.15 DOUGHNUT-MACHINE OPERATOR (bake. prod.), 526.682-022
06.02.15 DRIER OPERATOR (macaroni & related), 523.362-014
06.02.15 FREEZER OPERATOR (dairy prod.), 529.482-010
06.02.15 GRINDER OPERATOR (grain & feed mill), 521.682-026
06.02.15 OVEN OPERATOR, AUTOMATIC (bake. prod.), 526.682-030
06.02.15 SIRUP MAKER (flav. ext. & sirup), 520.485-026
06.02.17 BRIQUETTE-MACHINE OPERATOR (fuel briquettes), 549.662-010
06.02.18 CRYSTAL GROWER (electronics), 590.382-014
06.02.18 IMPREGNATOR (electronics), 590.682-014
06.02.18 ION IMPLANT MACHINE OPERATOR (electronics), 590.382-022
06.02.18 ROOF-CEMENT-AND-PAINT MAKER (build. mat. nec), 550.382-030
06.02.18 ROOFING-MACHINE OPERATOR (build. mat. nec), 554.682-022
06.02.18 SOAP MAKER (soap), 559.382-054
06.02.18 STILL TENDER (any ind.), 552.685-026
06.02.19 LASER-BEAM-MACHINE OPERATOR (welding), 815.682-010
06.02.19 WELDING-MACHINE OPERATOR, ARC (welding), 810.382-010
06.02.19 WELDING-MACHINE OPERATOR, GAS (welding), 811.482-010
06.02.20 ARBOR-PRESS OPERATOR 1 (any ind.), 616.682-010
06.02.20 COVERING-MACHINE OPERATOR (print. & pub.), 653.682-014
06.02.20 KICK-PRESS OPERATOR 1 (any ind.), 616.682-026
06.02.20 STACKING-MACHINE OPERATOR 1 (any ind.), 692.682-054
06.02.21 ANODIZER (any ind.), 500.682-010
06.02.21 COATER OPERATOR (any ind.), 509.382-010
06.02.21 COATING-MACHINE OPERATOR (coated fabrics), 584.382-010

06.02.21 OPTICAL-ELEMENT COATER (optical goods), 716.382-014

06.02.21 PAINT-SPRAYER OPERATOR, AUTOMATIC (any ind.), 599.382-010

06.02.21 PAINTER, ELECTROSTATIC (any ind.), 599.682-010

06.02.21 PLATER, PRINTED CIRCUIT BOARD PANELS (electronics), 500.684-026

06.02.22 ASSEMBLER, INTERNAL COMBUSTION ENGINE (engine & turbine), 806.481-014

06.02.22 ASSEMBLER, SUBASSEMBLY (aircraft-aerospace mfg.), 806.484-010

06.02.22 BRAZER, ASSEMBLER (welding), 813.684-010

06.02.22 CABINET ASSEMBLER (furn.), 763.684-014

06.02.22 CASKET ASSEMBLER (mort. goods), 739.481-010

06.02.22 ELECTRIC-SIGN ASSEMBLER (signs), 729.684-022

06.02.22 FURNITURE ASSEMBLER (furn.), 763.684-038

06.02.22 MACHINE ASSEMBLER (mach. mfg.), 638.361-010

06.02.22 MOTORCYCLE ASSEMBLER (motor. & bicycles), 806.684-090

06.02.22 UTILITY WORKER (mfg. bldgs.), 869.684-074

06.02.23 ASSEMBLER, MUSICAL INSTRUMENTS (musical inst.), 730.684-010

06.02.23 ASSEMBLER, PRODUCTION LINE (photo. apparatus), 714.684-010

06.02.23 ASSEMBLER, SEMICONDUCTOR (electronics), 726.684-034

06.02.23 ASSEMBLER, SURGICAL GARMENT (per. protect. & med. device), 712.684-010

06.02.23 BITE-BLOCK MAKER (medical ser.), 712.684-014

06.02.23 CAPACITOR ASSEMBLER (elec. equip.), 729.684-014

06.02.23 CHAIN MAKER, MACHINE (jewelry), 700.684-022

06.02.23 ELECTRICAL-CONTROL ASSEMBLER (elec. equip.), 729.684-026

06.02.23 ELECTRONICS ASSEMBLER (inst. & app.), 726.384-010

06.02.23 ELECTRONICS ASSEMBLER (electronics), 726.684-018

06.02.23 LAMINATION ASSEMBLER (elec. equip.), 729.484-010

06.02.23 LENS-MOLD SETTER (optical goods), 713.381-010

06.02.23 PRINTED CIRCUIT BOARD ASSEMBLER, HAND (electronics), 726.684-070

06.02.23 TUBE ASSEMBLER, CATHODE RAY (electronics), 725.684-022

06.02.23 WHEEL LACER AND TRUER (motor. & bicycles), 706.684-106

06.02.23 WIRER, SUBASSEMBLIES (office mach.), 729.684-062

06.02.24 ARMATURE BANDER (any ind.), 724.684-010

06.02.24 ASSEMBLER, METAL BONDING (aircraft-aerospace mfg.), 806.684-030

06.02.24 BOAT PATCHER, PLASTIC (ship bldg. & rep.), 807.684-014

06.02.24 BRIGHT CUTTER (jewelry), 700.684-018

06.02.24 CASTER (jewelry), 502.381-010

06.02.24 FABRICATOR-ASSEMBLER, METAL PRODUCTS (any ind.), 809.381-010

06.02.24 GREASE BUFFER (silverware), 705.684-022

06.02.24 MESH CUTTER (jewelry), 700.684-050

06.02.24 PRESSURE SEALER-AND-TESTER (aircraft-aerospace mfg.), 806.684-110

06.02.24 REPAIRER, FINISHED METAL (any ind.), 809.684-034

06.02.24 REPAIRER, TYPEWRITER (office mach.), 706.381-030

06.02.24 RING STAMPER (jewelry), 700.684-066

06.02.24 SKI REPAIRER, PRODUCTION (sports equip.), 732.684-118

06.02.24 SOLAR-FABRICATION TECHNICIAN (mach. shop), 809.381-034

06.02.24 SPINNER (jewelry), 700.684-074

06.02.24 STRAIGHTENER, HAND (any ind.), 709.484-014

06.02.24 SUBASSEMBLER (mach. mfg.), 706.381-038

06.02.24 TROPHY ASSEMBLER (jewelry), 735.684-018

06.02.25 BOX MAKER, WOOD (wood. box), 760.684-014

06.02.26 PRESSER (print. & pub.), 977.684-018

06.02.27 BLOCKER, HAND 1 (hat & cap), 580.684-010

06.02.27 COBBLER (boot & shoe), 788.381-010

06.02.27 CUTTER, HAND 1 (any ind.), 781.584-014

06.02.27 CUTTER, MACHINE 1 (any ind.), 781.684-014

06.02.27 LEATHER CUTTER (leather prod.), 783.684-022

06.02.27 LEATHER WORKER (leather prod.), 783.684-026

06.02.27 MATTRESS MAKER (matt. & bedspring), 780.684-074

06.02.27 MENDER (carpet & rug), 782.684-042

06.02.27 SPOTTER (laundry), 361.684-018

06.02.28 BENCH HAND (bake. prod.), 520.384-010

06.02.28 BUTCHER, ALL-ROUND (slaught. & meat pack.), 525.381-014

06.02.28 CANDY MAKER (confection.), 529.361-014

06.02.28 DOUGHNUT MAKER (bake. prod.), 526.684-010

06.02.29 RUBBER-GOODS REPAIRER (any ind.), 759.684-054

06.02.30 GLASS CUTTER (any ind.), 775.684-022

06.02.30 MOLDER (optical goods), 575.381-010

06.02.30 PLASTER MAKER (statue & art), 779.684-046

06.02.30 PLASTER-DIE MAKER (pottery & porc.), 774.684-026

06.02.30 THROWER (pottery & porc.), 774.381-010

06.02.31 LAY-OUT WORKER 2 (any ind.), 809.381-014

06.02.32 BONDED STRUCTURES REPAIRER (aircraft-aerospace mfg.), 807.381-014

06.02.32 BOW MAKER, PRODUCTION (sports equip.), 732.684-038

06.02.32 BRUSH MATERIAL PREPARER (brush & broom), 739.684-022

06.02.32 CABLE MAKER (elec. equip.), 728.684-010

06.02.32 CHARGE PREPARATION TECHNICIAN (electronics), 590.384-010

06.02.32 COIL WINDER, REPAIR (any ind.), 724.381-014

06.02.32 DENTURE WAXER (medical ser.), 712.681-010

06.02.32 ETCHED-CIRCUIT PROCESSOR (electronics), 590.684-018

06.02.32 OPAQUER (medical ser.), 712.684-030

06.02.32 RACKET STRINGER (sports equip.), 732.684-094

06.02.32 SKI MOLDER (sports equip.), 732.684-114

06.02.32 WIRER (office mach.), 729.281-042

06.03.01 CABLE STRETCHER AND TESTER (aircraft-aerospace mfg.), 806.685-010

06.03.01 COMPARATOR OPERATOR (any ind.), 699.384-010

06.03.01 INSPECTOR (fabric. plastic prod.), 559.381-010

06.03.01 MACHINE TESTER (office mach.), 706.387-014

06.03.01 MOTORCYCLE TESTER (motor. & bicycles), 620.384-014

06.03.01 SPECIAL TESTER (tobacco), 529.487-010

06.03.01 TEST DRIVER 1 (auto. mfg.), 806.281-050

06.03.02 CALIBRATION CHECKER 2 (inst. & app.), 710.687-018

06.03.02 ELECTRONICS INSPECTOR II (electronics), 726.684-022

06.03.02 ELECTRONICS TESTER II (electronics), 726.684-026

06.03.02 GARMENT INSPECTOR (any ind.), 789.687-070

06.03.02 GLASS INSPECTOR (any ind.), 579.687-022

06.03.02 GRADER (woodworking), 669.587-010

06.03.02 HYDRO-PNEUMATIC TESTER (any ind.), 862.687-018

06.03.02 INKER (print. & pub.), 659.667-010

06.03.02 INSPECTOR (drug prep. & related), 559.387-014

06.03.02 INSPECTOR (jewelry), 700.687-034

06.03.02 INSPECTOR, FABRIC (any ind.), 789.587-014

06.03.02 INSPECTOR, INTEGRATED CIRCUITS (electronics), 726.684-058

06.03.02 INSPECTOR, PRINTED CIRCUIT BOARDS (electronics), 726.684-062

06.03.02 INSPECTOR, SEMICONDUCTOR WAFER (electronics), 726.684-066

06.03.02 LENS EXAMINER (optical goods), 716.687-022

06.03.02 LUMBER SORTER (woodworking), 922.687-074

06.03.02 METAL-FINISH INSPECTOR (any ind.), 703.687-014

06.03.02 PAINT-SPRAY INSPECTOR (any ind.), 741.687-010

06.03.02 PHOTO CHECKER AND ASSEMBLER (photofinish.), 976.687-014

06.03.02 PHOTOFINISHING LABORATORY WORKER (photofinish.), 976.687-018

06.03.02 PRINT INSPECTOR (pottery & porc.), 774.687-018

06.03.02 WEIGHER, PRODUCTION (any ind.), 929.587-014

06.04.02 BENDING-MACHINE OPERATOR 2 (any ind.), 617.685-010

06.04.02 BUFFING-MACHINE TENDER (any ind.), 603.665-010

06.04.02 DRILL-PRESS OPERATOR, PRODUCTION (mach. shop), 606.685-026

06.04.02 DRUM STRAIGHTENER 1 (any ind.), 619.685-034

06.04.02 EMBOSSER (any ind.), 583.685-030

06.04.02 GRAINER, MACHINE (any ind.), 652.686-014

06.04.02 LATHE OPERATOR, PRODUCTION (mach. shop), 604.685-026

06.04.02 MACHINE OPERATOR 2 (any ind.), 619.685-062

06.04.02 MAGNETIC-TAPE WINDER (electronics), 726.685-010

06.04.02 NIBBLER OPERATOR (any ind.), 615.685-026

06.04.02 POWER-PRESS TENDER (any ind.), 617.685-026

06.04.02 PRODUCTION-MACHINE TENDER (nut & bolt), 619.365-010

06.04.02 PUNCH-PRESS OPERATOR II (any ind.), 615.685-030

06.04.02 SCROLL-MACHINE OPERATOR (struct. & ornam. metalwork), 616.685-062

06.04.02 TOOL DRESSER (any ind.), 601.682-010

06.04.02 TURRET-PUNCH-PRESS OPERATOR, TAPE-CONTROL (any ind.), 615.685-042

06.04.02 WIRE-DRAWING-MACHINE TENDER (wire), 614.685-026

06.04.03 ARTIFICIAL-LOG-MACHINE OPERATOR (fuel briquettes), 569.685-010

06.04.03 BUZZSAW OPERATOR (any ind.), 667.685-026

06.04.03 CHAIN OFFBEARER (planing mill), 669.686-018

06.04.03 LATHE SPOTTER (veneer & plywood), 663.686-022

06.04.03 POWER-BARKER OPERATOR (paper & pulp), 669.485-010

06.04.04 BAG-MACHINE OPERATOR (paper goods), 649.685-014

06.04.04 BINDERY WORKER (print. & pub.), 653.685-010

06.04.04 CARTON-FORMING-MACHINE OPERATOR (any ind.), 641.685-022

06.04.04 CARTON-FORMING-MACHINE TENDER (paper goods), 641.685-026

06.04.04 FOLDING-MACHINE FEEDER (print. & pub.), 653.686-014

06.04.05 ADHESIVE-BANDAGE-MACHINE OPERATOR (per. protect. & med. device), 692.685-014

06.04.05 BUTTONHOLE-AND-BUTTON-SEWING-MACHINE OPERATOR (garment), 786.685-042

06.04.05 CEMENTER, MACHINE APPLICATOR (boot & shoe), 690.686-018

06.04.05 EYELET-MACHINE OPERATOR (any ind.), 699.685-018

06.04.05 FASTENER-SEWING-MACHINE OPERATOR (any ind.), 787.685-010

06.04.05 FOLDER-SEAMER, AUTOMATIC (any ind.), 787.685-014

06.04.05 GLOVE TURNER AND FORMER, AUTOMATIC (glove & mitten), 583.686-018

06.04.05 HEMMER, AUTOMATIC (house. furn.), 787.685-018

06.04.05 PLEATING-MACHINE OPERATOR (any ind.), 583.685-082

06.04.05 PRESSER, MACHINE (any ind.), 363.682-018

06.04.05 SEWING-MACHINE OPERATOR, SPECIAL EQUIPMENT (matt. & bedspring), 689.685-118

06.04.05 SPREADER, MACHINE (any ind.), 781.685-010

06.04.05 STRIP-CUTTING-MACHINE OPERATOR (any ind.), 686.685-066

06.04.05 SURGICAL-DRESSING MAKER (per. protect. & med. device), 689.685-130

06.04.05 TACKING-MACHINE OPERATOR (any ind.), 787.685-042

06.04.06 BEAM-WARPER TENDER, AUTOMATIC (asbestos prod.), 681.685-018

06.04.06 CLOTH DOFFER (textile), 689.586-010

06.04.06 KNITTING-MACHINE OPERATOR (knit goods), 685.665-014

06.04.06 PICKING-MACHINE OPERATOR (any ind.), 680.685-082

06.04.06 YARN WINDER (any ind.), 681.685-154

06.04.07 DESIGN PRINTER, BALLOON (rubber goods), 651.685-014

06.04.07 RUBBER CUTTER (rubber goods), 559.685-158

06.04.08 CERAMIC CAPACITOR PROCESSOR (electronics), 590.684-010

06.04.08 COREMAKER, MACHINE 1 (foundry), 518.685-014

06.04.08 CRUSHER TENDER (any ind.), 570.685-022

06.04.08 LENS-FABRICATING-MACHINE TENDER (optical goods), 716.685-022

06.04.08 MILLER (cement), 570.685-046

06.04.09 CROWN-ASSEMBLY-MACHINE OPERATOR (any ind.), 692.685-062

06.04.09 CUTTER (photofinish.), 976.685-010

06.04.09 CUTTER, MACHINE 2 (any ind.), 699.685-014

06.04.09 CUTTING-MACHINE TENDER (any ind.), 690.685-122

06.04.09 EMBOSSING-PRESS OPERATOR (any ind.), 652.685-030

06.04.09 KEYMODULE-ASSEMBLY-MACHINE TENDER (office mach.), 692.685-274

06.04.09 LEAF STAMPER (any ind.), 979.682-018

06.04.09 MACHINE FEEDER (any ind.), 699.686-010

06.04.09 PHOTORESIST LAMINATOR, PRINTED CIRCUIT BOARD (electronics), 699.685-042

06.04.09 SCRAP HANDLER (any ind.), 509.685-050

06.04.09 SILK-SCREEN PRINTER, MACHINE (any ind.), 979.665-010

06.04.09 SPRAY-PAINTING-MACHINE OPERATOR (any ind.), 741.685-010

06.04.09 WAX MOLDER (foundry), 549.685-038

06.04.10 DIE-CASTING-MACHINE OPERATOR 2 (foundry), 514.685-018

06.04.10 INJECTION-MOLDING-MACHINE TENDER (fabric. plastic prod.), 556.685-038

06.04.10 LABORER, GENERAL (nonfer. metal prod.), 519.686-010

06.04.10 MILL OPERATOR (any ind.), 599.685-058

06.04.10 OXIDIZED-FINISH PLATER (any ind.), 599.685-062

06.04.11 CENTRIFUGE OPERATOR, PLASMA PROCESSING (drug prep. & related), 599.685-018

06.04.11 CHEMICAL OPERATOR 2 (chem.), 558.585-014

06.04.11 CHEMICAL PREPARER 1 (chem.), 550.685-030

06.04.11 DRIER OPERATOR (chem.), 553.685-042

06.04.11 MIXER (paint & varn.), 550.685-078

06.04.11 PAINT MIXER, MACHINE (any ind.), 550.485-018

06.04.13 BOWLING-BALL MOLDER (sports equip.), 556.685-018

06.04.13 COMPRESSION-MOLDING-MACHINE TENDER (fabric. plastic prod.), 556.685-022

06.04.13 CONTACT-LENS MOLDER (optical goods), 690.685-090

06.04.13 FUSING-FURNACE LOADER (optical goods), 573.686-014

06.04.13 LENS HARDENER (optical goods), 573.685-030

06.04.13 RECORD-PRESS TENDER (phonograph), 556.685-070

06.04.13 TIRE MOLDER (rubber tire & tube), 553.685-102

06.04.15 BAKER HELPER (bake. prod.), 526.686-010

06.04.15 BAND-SAW OPERATOR (slaught. & meat pack.), 525.685-010

06.04.15 BREWERY CELLAR WORKER (beer prod.), 522.685-014

06.04.15 CANNERY WORKER (can. & preserv.), 529.686-014

06.04.15 CENTRIFUGE OPERATOR (dairy prod.), 521.685-042

06.04.15 CHEESE CUTTER (dairy prod.), 529.585-010

06.04.15 CHOCOLATE MOLDER, MACHINE (choc. & cocoa), 529.685-054

06.04.15 COFFEE GRINDER (food prep nec), 521.685-078

06.04.15 COOK, FRY, DEEP FAT (can. & preserv.), 526.685-014

06.04.15 COOKER, PROCESS CHEESE (dairy prod.), 526.665-010

06.04.15 FLOUR BLENDER (grain & feed mill), 520.685-106

06.04.15 HONEY PROCESSOR (food prep nec), 522.685-070

06.04.15 MILL OPERATOR (corn prod.), 521.685-226

06.04.15 MIXING-MACHINE OPERATOR (food prep nec), 520.665-014

06.04.15 OVEN TENDER (bake. prod.), 526.685-030

06.04.15 PRESS OPERATOR, MEAT (slaught. & meat pack.), 520.685-182

06.04.15 YEAST-CUTTING-AND-WRAPPING-MACHINE OPERATOR (food prep nec), 529.665-022

06.04.16 EXTRACTOR OPERATOR (any ind.), 581.685-038

06.04.16 HARDENING-MACHINE OPERATOR (hat & cap), 586.685-026

06.04.16 MACHINE FEEDER, RAW STOCK (felt goods), 680.686-018

06.04.16 SLASHER TENDER (textile), 582.562-010

06.04.17 AUXILIARY EQUIPMENT TENDER (ccmcnt), 570.685-010

06.04.17 KILN WORKER (pottery & porc.), 573.687-022

06.04.17 SHELL MOLDER (foundry), 518.685-026

06.04.18 DIGESTER-OPERATOR HELPER (build. board), 532.686-010

06.04.18 TANKER (wood preserving), 561.665-010

06.04.19 COATING EQUIPMENT OPERATOR, PRINTED CIRCUIT BOARDS (electronics), 590.685-066

06.04.19 CREMATOR (per. ser.), 359.685-010

06.04.19 DEVELOPER, AUTOMATIC (photofinish.), 976.685-014

06.04.19 DISPLAY-SCREEN FABRICATOR (electronics), 725.685-010

06.04.19 ELECTRONIC-COMPONENT PROCESSOR (electronics), 590.684-014

06.04.19 ETCHER-STRIPPER, PRINTED CIRCUIT BOARDS (electronics), 590.685-082

06.04.19 FILTER OPERATOR (any ind.), 551.685-078

06.04.19 HEAT TREATER (electronics), 504.686-022

06.04.19 LABORER (drug prep. & related), 559.686-022

06.04.19 METALLIZATION EQUIPMENT OPERATOR, SEMICONDUCTOR WAFERS (electronics), 590.685-086

06.04.19 PLATER, SEMICONDUCTOR WAFERS AND COMPONENTS (electronics), 500.684-030

06.04.19 POLYSILICON PREPARATION WORKER (electronics), 590.684-038

06.04.19 PRINT DEVELOPER, AUTOMATIC (photofinish.), 976.685-026

06.04.19 SEMICONDUCTOR PROCESSOR (electronics), 590.684-022

06.04.19 STERILIZER (drug prep. & related), 599.585-010

06.04.19 UTILITY WORKER, FILM PROCESSING (photofinish.), 976.685-030

06.04.20 ASSEMBLY-PRESS OPERATOR (any ind.), 690.685-014

06.04.20 CORRUGATED-FASTENER DRIVER (woodworking), 669.685-042

06.04.20 MOUNTER, AUTOMATIC (photofinish.), 976.685-022

06.04.20 STAPLING-MACHINE OPERATOR (any ind.), 692.685-202

06.04.21 CERAMIC COATER, MACHINE (any ind.), 509.685-022

06.04.21 DIPPER (any ind.), 599.685-026

06.04.21 DIPPER AND BAKER (any ind.), 599.685-030

06.04.21 ELECTROLESS PLATER, PRINTED CIRCUIT BOARD PANELS (electronics), 501.685-022

06.04.21 JEWELRY COATER (jewelry), 590.685-046

06.04.21 PAINTER, TUMBLING BARREL (any ind.), 599.685-070

06.04.21 PAINTING-MACHINE OPERATOR (any ind.), 599.685-074

06.04.21 PLATER, HOT DIP (galvanizing), 501.685-010

06.04.21 PLATER, PRODUCTION (electroplating), 500.665-010

06.04.21 SEED PELLETER (agric.), 599.685-126

06.04.21 SPRAY-UNIT FEEDER (any ind.), 599.686-014

06.04.22 ASSEMBLER, AUTOMOBILE (auto. mfg.), 806.684-010

06.04.22 ASSEMBLER, BICYCLE 2 (motor. & bicycles), 806.687-010

06.04.22 ASSEMBLER, PRODUCTION (any ind.), 706.687-010

06.04.22 LAMINATOR, HAND (furn.), 763.684-050

06.04.22 NAILER, HAND (any ind.), 762.684-050

06.04.22 PLASTIC-TOP ASSEMBLER (furn.), 763.684-062

06.04.22 RIVETER, HAND (any ind.), 709.684-066

06.04.23 ASSEMBLER (jewelry), 700.684-014

06.04.23 ASSEMBLER (elec. equip.), 723.684-010

06.04.23 ASSEMBLER (sports equip.), 732.684-014

06.04.23 ASSEMBLER, MOLDED FRAMES (optical goods), 713.684-014

06.04.23 ASSEMBLER, SMALL PARTS (any ind.), 706.684-022

06.04.23 ASSEMBLER, SMALL PRODUCTS (any ind.), 739.687-030

06.04.23 BENCH ASSEMBLER (agric. equip.), 706.684-042

06.04.23 COIL WINDER (elec. equip.), 724.684-026

06.04.23 EARRING MAKER (jewelry), 700.684-030

06.04.23 ELECTRIC-MOTOR ASSEMBLER (clcc. cquip.), 721.684-022

06.04.23 FILLER (house. furn.), 780.684-066

06.04.23 LOCK ASSEMBLER (hardware), 706.684-074

06.04.23 MULTIFOCAL-LENS ASSEMBLER (optical goods), 713.684-034

06.04.23 SILK-SCREEN-FRAME ASSEMBLER (any ind.), 709.484-010

06.04.23 TIRE MOUNTER (fabric. prod. nec), 739.684-158

06.04.23 TOY ASSEMBLER (toys & games), 731.687-034

06.04.24 ARBORER (jewelry), 700.684-010

06.04.24 BENCH GRINDER (any ind.), 705.684-010

06.04.24 BENCH WORKER (optical goods), 713.684-018

06.04.24 BUFFER 1 (any ind.), 705.684-014

06.04.24 CONTACT-LENS-FLASHING PUNCHER (optical goods), 713.687-014

06.04.24 FILER (jewelry), 700.684-034

06.04.24 GRINDER 1 (any ind.), 705.684-026

06.04.24 GRINDER-CHIPPER 2 (any ind.), 809.684-026

06.04.24 JIGSAWYER (jewelry), 700.684-046

06.04.24 LABORER, GOLD LEAF (gold leaf & foil), 700.687-038

06.04.24 MELTER (jewelry), 700.687-042

06.04.24 METAL FINISHER (any ind.), 705.684-034

06.04.24 MOLD DRESSER (any ind.), 519.684-018

06.04.24 OXIDIZER (silverware), 700.684-054

06.04.24 POLISHER (any ind.), 705.684-058

06.04.24 POLISHER, EYEGLASS FRAMES (optical goods), 713.684-038

06.04.24 PREPARER (jewelry), 700.687-062

06.04.24 REFINER (medical ser.), 712.684-038

06.04.24 SILK-SCREEN ETCHER (engraving), 704.684-014

06.04.24 STONER (jewelry), 735.684-014

06.04.24 STRETCHER (jewelry), 700.684-078

06.04.25 CANER 2 (furn.), 763.684-022

06.04.25 CROSSBAND LAYER (veneer & plywood), 762.687-026

06.04.25 WOODWORKING-SHOP HAND (woodworking), 769.687-054

06.04.26 LABEL CODER (any ind.), 920.587-014

06.04.26 TRIM-STENCIL MAKER (any ind.), 781.684-058

06.04.27 BOW MAKER (any ind.), 789.684-010

06.04.27 CANVAS REPAIRER (any ind.), 782.684-010

06.04.27 CARPET CUTTER 2 (carpet & rug), 585.687-014

06.04.27 LABORER, GENERAL (leather mfg.), 589.686-026

06.04.27 SEWER, HAND (any ind.), 782.684-058

06.04.27 THREAD CUTTER (any ind.), 789.684-050

06.04.28 BONER, MEAT (slaught. & meat pack.), 525.684-010

06.04.28 CANDY DIPPER, HAND (confection.), 524.684-010

06.04.28 CANDY MOLDER, HAND (confection.), 520.687-018

06.04.28 CIGAR MAKER (tobacco), 790.684-014

06.04.28 DECORATOR (bake. prod.), 524.684-014

06.04.28 FISH CLEANER (can. & preserv.), 525.684-030

06.04.28 POULTRY DRESSER (agric.), 525.687-070

06.04.28 TRIMMER, MEAT (slaught. & meat pack.), 525.684-054

06.04.29 FABRICATOR, FOAM RUBBER (any ind.), 780.684-062

06.04.30 GLASS FINISHER (glass prod.), 775.684-026

06.04.30 SAGGER MAKER (pottery & porc.), 774.684-030

06.04.30 TABLE-TOP TILE SETTER (brick & tile), 763.684-074

06.04.31 WELDER, GUN (welding), 810.664-010

06.04.31 WELDER, PRODUCTION LINE (welding), 819.684-010

06.04.32 CANDLEMAKER (candle), 739.664-010

06.04.32 MACHINE MOLDER (foundry), 518.682-010

06.04.33 ENAMELER (plumb. supplies), 509.684-010

06.04.33 METAL SPRAYER, PRODUCTION (any ind.), 505.684-014

06.04.33 PAINTER (jewelry), 735.687-018

06.04.33 PAINTER, BRUSH (any ind.), 740.684-022

06.04.33 PAINTER, SPRAY 2 (any ind.), 741.687-018

06.04.33 PUTTY GLAZER (any ind.), 749.684-042
06.04.33 TOUCH-UP PAINTER, HAND (any ind.), 740.684-026
06.04.34 ARTIFICIAL-FLOWER MAKER (artif. flower), 739.684-014
06.04.34 BROOMMAKER (brush & broom), 739.684-018
06.04.34 DECAL APPLIER (any ind.), 749.684-010
06.04.34 DRILLER, HAND (any ind.), 809.684-018
06.04.34 ELECTRONICS UTILITY WORKER (electronics), 726.367-014
06.04.34 ELECTRONICS WORKER (electronics), 726.687-010
06.04.34 INSULATION-BLANKET MAKER (aircraft-aerospace mfg.), 806.684-078
06.04.34 LABORER, GRINDING AND POLISHING (any ind.), 705.687-014
06.04.34 LEADER TIER (sports equip.), 732.687-038
06.04.34 MACHINE SNELLER (sports equip.), 732.685-026
06.04.34 MASKER (any ind.), 749.687-018
06.04.34 MAT CUTTER (framing), 739.684-126
06.04.34 MOUNTER, HAND (photofinish.), 976.684-018
06.04.34 PAINT MIXER, HAND (any ind.), 550.684-018
06.04.34 PHOTO MASK CLEANER (electronics), 590.684-034
06.04.34 SCREEN PRINTER (any ind.), 979.684-034
06.04.34 STUFFER (toys & games), 731.685-014
06.04.34 WIREWORKER (elec. equip.), 728.684-022
06.04.35 LAUNDERER, HAND (laundry), 361.684-010
06.04.35 LAUNDRY LABORER (laundry), 361.687-018
06.04.35 LAUNDRY OPERATOR (laundry), 369.684-014
06.04.35 LEATHER FINISHER (clean., dye., & press.), 363.682-010
06.04.35 PRESS OPERATOR (laundry), 363.685-010
06.04.35 PRESSER, ALL-AROUND (clean., dye., & press.), 363.682-014
06.04.35 PRESSER, FORM (any ind.), 363.685-018
06.04.35 PRESSER, HAND (any ind.), 363.684-018
06.04.35 SILK FINISHER (clean., dye., & press.), 363.681-010
06.04.35 WASHER, MACHINE (laundry), 361.665-010
06.04.35 WASHING-MACHINE LOADER-AND-PULLER (laundry), 361.686-010
06.04.37 MARKER 2 (any ind.), 920.687-126
06.04.37 MARKER, SEMICONDUCTOR WAFERS (electronics), 920.587-026
06.04.37 NAME-PLATE STAMPER (any ind.), 652.685-054
06.04.37 STENCILER (any ind.), 920.687-178
06.04.37 TICKETER (any ind.), 652.685-098
06.04.38 ASSEMBLER, HOSPITAL SUPPLIES (inst. & app.), 712.687-010
06.04.38 BAKERY WORKER (bake. prod.), 929.686-010
06.04.38 CARDER (any ind.), 920.685-034
06.04.38 CRATER (any ind.), 920.484-010
06.04.38 FLOOR WORKER (chew. gum), 920.687-090
06.04.38 MAILING-MACHINE OPERATOR (print. & pub.), 208.462-010
06.04.38 PACKAGE SEALER, MACHINE (any ind.), 920.685-074
06.04.38 PACKAGER, HAND (any ind.), 920.587-018
06.04.38 PACKAGER, MACHINE (any ind.), 920.685-078
06.04.38 PACKING-LINE WORKER (rubber goods), 753.687-038
06.04.38 PARACHUTE RIGGER (air trans.), 912.684-010
06.04.39 CLEANER AND POLISHER (any ind.), 709.687-010
06.04.39 DIPPER (jewelry), 735.687-010
06.04.39 EQUIPMENT CLEANER (any ind.), 599.684-010
06.04.39 LABORER, GENERAL (mach. shop), 609.684-014
06.04.39 WASHER (optical goods), 713.684-042
06.04.39 WASHER, MACHINE (any ind.), 599.685-114
06.04.39 WASHING-MACHINE OPERATOR (any ind.), 599.685-118
06.04.40 CHAR-CONVEYOR TENDER (sugar), 529.685-050
06.04.40 CLAMP REMOVER (veneer & plywood), 569.687-010
06.04.40 COMPRESSED-GAS-PLANT WORKER (comp. & liq. gases), 549.587-010
06.04.40 CONVEYOR FEEDER-OFFBEARER (any ind.), 921.686-014
06.04.40 CONVEYOR TENDER (any ind.), 921.685-026
06.04.40 DISTILLERY WORKER, GENERAL (distilled liquor), 529.687-066

06.04.40 GENERAL HELPER (oils & fats), 529.687-094
06.04.40 INDUSTRIAL-TRUCK OPERATOR (any ind.), 921.683-050
06.04.40 LABORER (slaught. & meat pack.), 529.687-130
06.04.40 LABORER, CHEMICAL PROCESSING (chem.), 559.687-050
06.04.40 LABORER, CONCRETE PLANT (concrete prod.), 579.686-010
06.04.40 LABORER, GENERAL (iron & steel), 509.686-010
06.04.40 LABORER, GENERAL (plastics mat.), 559.567-010
06.04.40 LABORER, SALVAGE (any ind.), 929.687-022
06.04.40 LOADER 1 (any ind.), 914.667-010
06.04.40 MUNITIONS HANDLER (ammunition), 929.687-034
06.04.40 NITROGLYCERIN DISTRIBUTOR (explosives), 559.664-010
06.04.40 PALLETIZER OPERATOR 1 (any ind.), 921.682-014
06.04.40 PUMPER, BREWERY (beer prod.), 914.665-014
06.04.40 SAWMILL WORKER (sawmill), 667.686-014
07.01.02 ADMINISTRATIVE CLERK (clerical), 219.362-010
07.01.02 LABOR EXPEDITER (const.), 249.167-018
07.01.02 PROCUREMENT CLERK (clerical), 249.367-066
07.01.02 TEACHER AIDE II (educ.), 249.367-074
07.01.02 TOWN CLERK (gov. ser.), 243.367-018
07.01.03 SOCIAL SECRETARY (clerical), 201.162-010
07.01.04 LOAN CLOSER (finan. inst.), 249.367-050
07.01.04 MORTGAGE CLERK (finan. inst.), 249.382-010
07.01.04 REAL-ESTATE CLERK (clerical), 219.362-046
07.01.04 VAULT CASHIER (bus. ser.), 222.137-050
07.02.01 BALANCE CLERK (clerical), 216.382-018
07.02.01 RECONCILEMENT CLERK (finan. inst.), 210.382-058
07.02.01 RESERVES CLERK (finan. inst.), 216.362-034
07.02.02 ACCOUNTING CLERK, DATA PROCESSING (clerical), 216.382-010
07.02.02 BROKERAGE CLERK 1 (finan. inst.), 219.482-010
07.02.02 CALCULATING-MACHINE OPERATOR (clerical), 216.482-022
07.02.02 CANCELLATION CLERK (insurance), 203.382-014
07.02.02 CHECK-PROCESSING CLERK 1 (finan. inst.), 216.387-010
07.02.02 CONTRACT CLERK, AUTOMOBILE (ret. tr.), 219.362-026
07.02.02 COUPON CLERK (finan. inst.), 219.462-010
07.02.02 FEE CLERK (finan. inst.), 214.362-018
07.02.02 NIGHT AUDITOR (hotel & rest.), 210.382-054
07.02.02 POLICY-CHANGE CLERK (insurance), 219.362-042
07.02.02 POSTING CLERK (clerical), 216.587-014
07.02.02 PROBATE CLERK (finan. inst.), 216.362-030
07.02.02 STATEMENT CLERK (finan. inst.), 219.362-058
07.02.02 TRUST-SECURITIES CLERK (finan. inst.), 219.362-062
07.02.04 ADVERTISING CLERK (bus. ser.), 247.387-010
07.02.04 BILLING-CONTROL CLERK (light, heat, & power), 214.387-010
07.02.04 DEMURRAGE CLERK (r.r. trans.), 214.362-010
07.02.04 INSURANCE CLERK (medical ser.), 214.362-022
07.02.04 INVOICE-CONTROL CLERK (clerical), 214.362-026
07.02.04 RATER (insurance), 214.482-022
07.02.04 REINSURANCE CLERK (insurance), 219.482-018
07.02.04 TAX CLERK 1 (clerical), 219.487-010
07.02.04 TRAFFIC CLERK (clerical), 214.587-014
07.02.05 PAYROLL CLERK (clerical), 215.482-010
07.02.05 TIMEKEEPER (clerical), 215.367-022
07.03.01 AUCTION CLERK (ret. tr.), 294.567-010
07.03.01 CASHIER 2 (clerical), 211.462-010
07.03.01 CASHIER-CHECKER (ret. tr.), 211.462-014
07.03.01 CHECK CASHIER (bus. ser.), 211.462-026
07.03.01 COUNTER CLERK (photofinish.), 249.366-010
07.03.01 LAYAWAY CLERK (ret. tr.), 299.467-010
07.03.01 PARIMUTUEL-TICKET SELLER (amuse. & rec.), 211.467-022
07.03.01 TELLER, HEAD (finan. inst.), 211.132-010
07.03.01 TOLL COLLECTOR (gov. ser.), 211.462-038
07.04.01 BLOOD-DONOR-UNIT ASSISTANT (medical ser.), 245.367-014

07.04.01 EMPLOYMENT-AND-CLAIMS AIDE (gov. ser.), 169.367-010
07.04.01 SKIP TRACER (clerical), 241.367-026
07.04.01 SURVEY WORKER (clerical), 205.367-054
07.04.01 TRAFFIC CHECKER (gov. ser.), 205.367-058
07.04.02 CLAIMS CLERK 2 (insurance), 205.367-018
07.04.02 COLLECTION CLERK (clerical), 241.357-010
07.04.02 REFERRAL-AND-INFORMATION AIDE (gov. ser.), 237.367-042
07.04.03 ANIMAL-HOSPITAL CLERK (medical ser.), 245.367-010
07.04.03 DOG LICENSER (nonprofit org.), 249.367-030
07.04.03 ELECTION CLERK (gov. ser.), 205.367-030
07.04.03 HOTEL CLERK (hotel & rest.), 238.362-010
07.04.03 RECREATION-FACILITY ATTENDANT (amuse. & rec.), 341.367-010
07.04.04 POLICYHOLDER-INFORMATION CLERK (insurance), 249.262-010
07.04.04 RECEPTIONIST (clerical), 237.367-038
07.04.05 DISPATCHER, MAINTENANCE SERVICE (clerical), 239.367-014
07.04.05 FIRE LOOKOUT (forestry), 452.367-010
07.04.05 FLIGHT-INFORMATION EXPEDITER (air trans.), 912.367-010
07.04.05 PROTECTIVE-SIGNAL OPERATOR (any ind.), 379.362-014
07.04.05 SCOREBOARD OPERATOR (amuse. & rec.), 349.665-010
07.04.05 SERVICE CLERK (clerical), 221.367-070
07.04.05 SWITCHBOARD OPERATOR, POLICE DISTRICT (gov. ser.), 235.562-014
07.04.06 CENTRAL-OFFICE OPERATOR (tel. & tel.), 235.462-010
07.04.06 DIRECTORY-ASSISTANCE OPERATOR (tel. & tel.), 235.662-018
07.04.06 TELEPHONE OPERATOR (clerical), 235.662-022
07.04.06 TELEPHONE-ANSWERING-SERVICE OPERATOR (bus. ser.), 235.662-026
07.05.01 ADVERTISING-DISPATCH CLERK (print. & pub.), 247.387-014
07.05.01 CREW SCHEDULER (air trans.), 215.362-010
07.05.01 DISPATCHER, MOTOR VEHICLE (clerical), 249.167-014
07.05.01 GUIDE, TRAVEL (per. ser.), 353.167-010
07.05.01 PERSONNEL SCHEDULER (clerical), 215.367-014
07.05.01 SCHEDULER, MAINTENANCE (clerical), 221.367-066
07.05.01 TRAFFIC CLERK (bus. ser.), 221.367-078
07.05.01 TRANSPORTATION AGENT (air trans.), 912.367-014
07.05.02 CLASSIFIED-AD CLERK 2 (print. & pub.), 247.387-022
07.05.02 CREDIT AUTHORIZER (clerical), 249.367-022
07.05.02 DISBURSEMENT CLERK (finan. inst.), 209.367-022
07.05.02 PRODUCTION PROOFREADER (print. & pub.), 247.667-010
07.05.02 READER (bus. ser.), 249.387-022
07.05.02 THROW-OUT CLERK (ret. tr.), 241.367-030
07.05.02 TITLE SEARCHER (real estate), 209.367-046
07.05.03 ASSIGNMENT CLERK (clerical), 249.367-090
07.05.03 ATTENDANCE CLERK (educ.), 219.362-014
07.05.03 AUTOMOBILE LOCATOR (ret. tr.), 296.367-010
07.05.03 BORDEREAU CLERK (insurance), 203.382-010
07.05.03 CALL-OUT OPERATOR (bus. ser.), 237.367-014
07.05.03 CODING CLERK (clerical), 209.387-010
07.05.03 COMPILER (clerical), 209.387-014
07.05.03 CREDIT-CARD-CONTROL CLERK (finan. inst.), 249.367-026
07.05.03 DETAILER, SCHOOL PHOTOGRAPHS (photofinish.), 976.564-010
07.05.03 DIET CLERK (medical ser.), 245.587-010
07.05.03 DOCUMENT PREPARER, MICROFILMING (bus. ser.), 249.587-018
07.05.03 MEDICAL-RECORD CLERK (medical ser.), 245.362-010
07.05.03 MORTGAGE-PROCESSING CLERK (finan. inst.), 203.382-022
07.05.03 ORDER CLERK (clerical), 249.367-054

07.05.03 PROPERTY CLERK (gov. ser.), 222.367-054
07.05.03 REPAIR-ORDER CLERK (clerical), 221.382-022
07.05.03 REPRODUCTION ORDER PROCESSOR (clerical), 221.367-058
07.05.03 STENOTYPE OPERATOR (clerical), 202.362-022
07.05.03 STOCK-CONTROL CLERK (clerical), 219.367-034
07.05.03 WARD CLERK (medical ser.), 245.362-014
07.05.04 MAIL CARRIER (gov. ser.), 230.367-010
07.05.04 MAIL CLERK (clerical), 209.587-026
07.05.04 MAIL HANDLER (gov. ser.), 209.687-014
07.05.04 MERCHANDISE DISTRIBUTOR (ret. tr.), 219.367-018
07.05.04 MESSENGER, BANK (finan. inst.), 230.367-014
07.05.04 PARCEL-POST CLERK (clerical), 222.387-038
07.05.04 ROUTE-DELIVERY CLERK (clerical), 222.587-034
07.05.04 ROUTING CLERK (nonprofit org.), 249.367-070
07.05.04 SHIPPING-ORDER CLERK (clerical), 219.367-030
07.05.04 VAULT WORKER (bus. ser.), 222.587-058
07.06.01 COMPUTER-PERIPHERAL-EQUIPMENT OPERATOR (clerical), 213.382-010
07.06.01 IN-FILE OPERATOR (bus. ser.), 203.362-014
07.06.01 TERMINAL OPERATOR (clerical), 203.582-054
07.06.01 TERMINAL-MAKEUP OPERATOR (print. & pub.), 208.382-010
07.06.01 TERMINAL-SYSTEM OPERATOR (clerical), 203.362-018
07.06.02 ADDING-MACHINE OPERATOR (clerical), 216.482-014
07.06.02 BRAILLE OPERATOR (print. & pub.), 203.582-010
07.06.02 CHECK WRITER (ret. tr.), 219.382-010
07.06.02 CLERK-TYPIST (clerical), 203.362-010
07.06.02 FOOD TABULATOR, CAFETERIA (hotel & rest.), 211.582-010
07.06.02 MAGNETIC-TAPE-COMPOSER OPERATOR (print. & pub.), 203.382-018
07.06.02 MAGNETIC-TAPE-TYPEWRITER OPERATOR (clerical), 203.582-034
07.06.02 PHOTOCOMPOSITION-KEYBOARD OPERATOR (print. & pub.), 203.582-046
07.06.02 PHOTOTYPESETTER OPERATOR (print. & pub.), 650.582-022
07.06.02 PROOF-MACHINE OPERATOR (finan. inst.), 217.382-010
07.06.02 TELEGRAPHIC-TYPEWRITER OPERATOR (clerical), 203.582-050
07.06.02 TRANSCRIBING-MACHINE OPERATOR (clerical), 203.582-058
07.06.02 TYPIST (clerical), 203.582-066
07.06.02 VARITYPE OPERATOR (clerical), 203.382-026
07.06.02 VERIFIER OPERATOR (clerical), 203.582-070
07.06.02 WIRES-TRANSFER CLERK (finan. inst.), 203.562-010
07.06.02 WORD-PROCESSING-MACHINE OPERATOR (clerical), 203.362-022
07.07.02 ADDRESSER (clerical), 209.587-010
07.07.02 ADVERTISING-MATERIAL DISTRIBUTOR (any ind.), 230.687-010
07.07.02 AUCTION ASSISTANT (ret. tr.), 294.667-010
07.07.02 CHECKER 1 (clerical), 222.687-010
07.07.02 CONTROL CLERK, DATA PROCESSING 2 (clerical), 221.687-010
07.07.02 DELIVERER, OUTSIDE (clerical), 230.667-010
07.07.02 DIRECT-MAIL CLERK (clerical), 209.587-018
07.07.02 DISTRIBUTING CLERK (clerical), 222.587-018
07.07.02 MESSENGER, COPY (print. & pub.), 239.677-010
07.07.02 PAGE (library), 249.687-014
07.07.02 PROCESS SERVER (bus. ser.), 249.367-062
07.07.02 ROUTER (clerical), 222.587-038
07.07.02 SORTER (clerical), 209.687-022
07.07.02 TELEPHONE-DIRECTORY DELIVERER (bus. ser.), 230.667-014
07.07.03 CLERK, GENERAL (clerical), 209.562-010
07.07.03 COIN-MACHINE COLLECTOR (bus. ser.), 292.687-010
07.07.03 OFFICE HELPER (clerical), 239.567-010
08.01.01 SALES REPRESENTATIVE, AIRCRAFT (ret. tr.), 273.253-010

08.01.01 SALES REPRESENTATIVE, COMMUNICATION EQUIPMENT (whole. tr.), 271.257-010

08.01.01 SALES REPRESENTATIVE, ELECTRONICS PARTS (whole. tr.), 271.357-010

08.01.02 TRAFFIC AGENT (air trans.), 252.257-010

08.01.03 BUSINESS-OPPORTUNITY-AND-PROPERTY-INVESTMENT BROKER (bus. ser.), 189.157-010

08.01.03 COMMISSION AGENT, AGRICULTURAL PRODUCE (whole. tr.), 260.357-010

08.01.03 COMPARISON SHOPPER (ret. tr.), 296.367-014

08.01.03 PAWNBROKER (ret. tr.), 191.157-010

08.01.03 SALES REPRESENTATIVE, LIVESTOCK (whole. tr.), 260.257-010

08.02.01 SALES REPRESENTATIVE, ANIMAL-FEED PRODUCTS (whole. tr.), 272.357-010

08.02.01 SALES REPRESENTATIVE, CANVAS PRODUCTS (whole. tr.), 261.357-014

08.02.01 SALES REPRESENTATIVE, FARM AND GARDEN EQUIPMENT AND SUPPLIES (whole. tr.), 272.357-014

08.02.01 SALES REPRESENTATIVE, HOME FURNISHINGS (whole. tr.), 270.357-010

08.02.01 SALES REPRESENTATIVE, HOUSEHOLD APPLIANCES (whole. tr.), 270.357-014

08.02.01 SALES REPRESENTATIVE, MALT LIQUORS (whole. tr.), 260.357-018

08.02.01 SALES REPRESENTATIVE, MEN'S AND BOYS' APPAREL (whole. tr.), 261.357-022

08.02.01 SALES REPRESENTATIVE, PETROLEUM PRODUCTS (whole. tr.), 269.357-014

08.02.01 SALES REPRESENTATIVE, RECREATION AND SPORTING GOODS (whole. tr.), 277.357-026

08.02.01 SALES REPRESENTATIVE, TEXTILES (whole. tr.), 261.357-030

08.02.01 SALES REPRESENTATIVE, VIDEOTAPE (whole. tr.), 271.357-014

08.02.01 SALES REPRESENTATIVE, WOMEN'S AND GIRLS' APPAREL (whole. tr.), 261.357-038

08.02.01 SALES-PROMOTION REPRESENTATIVE (whole. tr.), 269.357-018

08.02.02 SALES EXHIBITOR (nonprofit org.), 279.357-010

08.02.02 SALESPERSON, ART OBJECTS (ret. tr.), 277.457-010

08.02.02 SALESPERSON, BOOKS (ret. tr.), 277.357-034

08.02.02 SALESPERSON, COSMETICS AND TOILETRIES (ret. tr.), 262.357-018

08.02.02 SALESPERSON, CURTAINS AND DRAPERIES (ret. tr.), 270.357-022

08.02.02 SALESPERSON, FLOWERS (ret. tr.), 260.357-026

08.02.02 SALESPERSON, FURNITURE (ret. tr.), 270.357-030

08.02.02 SALESPERSON, HOUSEHOLD APPLIANCES (ret. tr.), 270.357-034

08.02.02 SALESPERSON, INFANTS' AND CHILDREN'S WEAR (ret. tr.), 261.357-046

08.02.02 SALESPERSON, MEN'S AND BOYS' CLOTHING (ret. tr.), 261.357-050

08.02.02 SALESPERSON, MUSICAL INSTRUMENTS AND ACCESSORIES (ret. tr.), 277.357-038

08.02.02 SALESPERSON, PHONOGRAPH RECORDS AND TAPE RECORDINGS (ret. tr.), 277.357-046

08.02.02 SALESPERSON, SHOES (ret. tr.), 261.357-062

08.02.02 SALESPERSON, SPORTING GOODS (ret. tr.), 277.357-058

08.02.02 SALESPERSON, STEREO EQUIPMENT (ret. tr.), 270.357-038

08.02.02 SALESPERSON, WOMEN'S APPAREL AND ACCESSORIES (ret. tr.), 261.357-066

08.02.02 SALESPERSON, YARD GOODS (ret. tr.), 261.357-070

08.02.03 AUCTIONEER (ret. tr.), 294.257-010

08.02.03 SALES REPRESENTATIVE, BOATS AND MARINE SUPPLIES (ret. tr.), 273.357-018

08.02.03 SALES REPRESENTATIVE, OFFICE MACHINES (ret. tr.), 275.357-034

08.02.03 SALES REPRESENTATIVE, TOBACCO PRODUCTS AND SMOKING SUPPLIES (ret. tr.), 260.357-022

08.02.03 SALESPERSON, FLOOR COVERINGS (ret. tr.), 270.357-026

08.02.03 SALESPERSON, GENERAL HARDWARE (ret. tr.), 279.357-050

08.02.03 SALESPERSON, GENERAL MERCHANDISE (ret. tr.), 279.357-054

08.02.03 SALESPERSON, HORTICULTURAL AND NURSERY PRODUCTS (ret. tr.), 272.357-022

08.02.03 SALESPERSON, PARTS (ret. tr.), 279.357-062

08.02.04 LEASING AGENT, RESIDENCE (real estate), 250.357-014

08.02.05 DEMONSTRATOR (ret. tr.), 297.354-010

08.02.05 DEMONSTRATOR, ELECTRIC-GAS APPLIANCES (light, heat, & power), 297.357-010

08.02.05 SALESPERSON-DEMONSTRATOR, PARTY PLAN (ret. tr.), 279.357-038

08.02.06 SALES REPRESENTATIVE, AUTOMOTIVE-LEASING (bus. ser.), 273.357-014

08.02.06 SALES REPRESENTATIVE, UPHOLSTERY AND FURNITURE REPAIR (ret. tr.), 259.357-026

08.02.07 DRIVER, SALES ROUTE (ret. tr.), 292.353-010

08.02.08 FUND RAISER 2 (nonprofit org.), 293.357-014

08.02.08 MEMBERSHIP SOLICITOR (any ind.), 293.357-022

08.02.08 SALES REPRESENTATIVE, DOOR-TO-DOOR (ret. tr.), 291.357-010

08.02.08 TELEPHONE SOLICITOR (any ind.), 299.357-014

08.03.01 PHOTOGRAPHER (amuse. & rec.), 143.457-010

08.03.01 VENDOR (amuse. & rec.), 291.457-022

09.01.01 AMUSEMENT PARK WORKER (amuse. & rec.), 349.664-010

09.01.01 COUNSELOR, CAMP (amuse. & rec.), 159.124-010

09.01.01 DIRECTOR, SOCIAL (hotel & rest.), 352.167-010

09.01.01 GUIDE, HUNTING AND FISHING (amuse. & rec.), 353.161-010

09.01.01 HOST/HOSTESS (any ind.), 352.667-010

09.01.01 RECREATION AIDE (social ser.), 195.367-030

09.01.02 EXHIBIT-DISPLAY REPRESENTATIVE (any ind.), 297.367-010

09.01.02 GUIDE (per. ser.), 353.367-010

09.01.02 GUIDE, PLANT (any ind.), 353.367-018

09.01.03 HOST/HOSTESS, RESTAURANT (hotel & rest.), 310.137-010

09.01.04 FUNERAL ATTENDANT (per. ser.), 359.677-014

09.02.01 HAIR STYLIST (per. ser.), 332.271-018

09.02.01 SCALP-TREATMENT OPERATOR (per. ser.), 339.371-014

09.03.01 BUS DRIVER (motor trans.), 913.463-010

09.03.02 CHAUFFEUR (any ind.), 913.663-010

09.03.02 TAXI DRIVER (motor trans.), 913.463-018

00.04.01 BARTENDER (hotel & rest.), 312.474-010

09.04.01 CANTEEN OPERATOR (any ind.), 311.674-010

09.04.01 CAR HOP (hotel & rest.), 311.477-010

09.04.01 COUNTER ATTENDANT, LUNCHROOM OR COFFEE SHOP (hotel & rest.), 311.477-014

09.04.01 FAST-FOODS WORKER (hotel & rest.), 311.472-010

09.04.01 FOUNTAIN SERVER (hotel & rest.), 319.474-010

09.04.01 LUNCH-TRUCK DRIVER (hotel & rest.), 292.463-010

09.04.01 MANAGER, FOOD CONCESSION (hotel & rest.), 185.167-022

09.04.01 VENDING-MACHINE ATTENDANT (hotel & rest.), 319.464-014

09.04.01 WAITER/WAITRESS, FORMAL (hotel & rest.), 311.477-026

09.04.01 WAITER/WAITRESS, INFORMAL (hotel & rest.), 311.477-030

09.04.01 WAITER/WAITRESS, TAKE OUT (hotel & rest.), 311.477-038

09.04.02 AUTOMOBILE-RENTAL CLERK (auto. ser.), 295.477-010

09.04.02 BICYCLE-RENTAL CLERK (ret. tr.), 295.467-010

09.04.02 CASHIER-WRAPPER (ret. tr.), 211.462-018

09.04.02 CUSTOMER-SERVICE CLERK (ret. tr.), 299.367-010

09.04.02 DELIVERER, MERCHANDISE (ret. tr.), 299.477-010

09.04.02 FLOOR ATTENDANT (amuse. & rec.), 343.467-014

09.04.02 FURNITURE-RENTAL CONSULTANT (ret. tr.), 295.357-018

09.04.02 GAMBLING DEALER (amuse. & rec.), 343.467-018

09.04.02 GAME ATTENDANT (amuse. & rec.), 342.457-010

09.04.02 NEWSPAPER CARRIER (ret. tr.), 292.457-010

09.04.02 PARKING-LOT ATTENDANT (auto. ser.), 915.473-010

09.04.02 PERSONAL SHOPPER (ret. tr.), 296.357-010

09.04.02 SALES ATTENDANT, BUILDING MATERIALS (ret. tr.), 299.677-014

09.04.02 SALES CLERK (ret. tr.), 290.477-014

09.04.02 SALES CLERK, FOOD (ret. tr.), 290.477-018

09.04.02 SELF-SERVICE-LAUNDRY-AND-DRY-CLEANING ATTENDANT (clean., dye., & press.), 369.677-010

09.04.02 SERVICE-ESTABLISHMENT ATTENDANT (clean., dye., & press.), 369.477-014

09.04.02 SKATE-SHOP ATTENDANT (amuse. & rec.), 341.464-010

09.04.02 STORAGE-FACILITY RENTAL CLERK (bus. ser.), 295.367-026

09.04.02 TOOL-AND-EQUIPMENT-RENTAL CLERK (bus. ser.), 295.357-014

09.04.02 TRAILER-RENTAL CLERK (auto. ser.), 295.467-022

09.05.01 COOLING-ROOM ATTENDANT (per. ser.), 335.677-010

09.05.01 ELECTROLOGIST (per. ser.), 339.371-010

09.05.01 FINGERNAIL FORMER (per. ser.), 331.674-014

09.05.01 HOT-ROOM ATTENDANT (per. ser.), 335.677-014

09.05.01 MANICURIST (per. ser.), 331.674-010

09.05.01 MASSEUR/MASSEUSE (per. ser.), 334.374-010

09.05.01 REDUCING-SALON ATTENDANT (per. ser.), 359.567-010

09.05.01 WEIGHT-REDUCTION SPECIALIST (per. ser.), 359.367-014

09.05.02 CAFETERIA ATTENDANT (hotel & rest.), 311.677-010

09.05.02 COUNTER ATTENDANT, CAFETERIA (hotel & rest.), 311.677-014

09.05.02 COUNTER-SUPPLY WORKER (hotel & rest.), 319.687-010

09.05.02 DINING ROOM ATTENDANT (hotel & rest.), 311.677-018

09.05.02 FOOD-SERVICE WORKER, HOSPITAL (medical ser.), 355.677-010

09.05.02 MESS ATTENDANT (water trans.), 350.677-010

09.05.02 WAITER/WAITRESS, ROOM SERVICE (hotel & rest.), 311.477-034

09.05.02 WINE STEWARD/STEWARDESS (hotel & rest.), 310.357-010

09.05.03 BELLHOP (hotel & rest.), 324.677-010

09.05.03 CHECKROOM ATTENDANT (any ind.), 358.677-010

09.05.03 PORTER (air trans.), 357.677-010

09.05.03 PORTER, BAGGAGE (hotel & rest.), 324.477-010

09.05.03 ROOM-SERVICE CLERK (hotel & rest.), 324.577-010

09.05.04 DOORKEEPER (any ind.), 324.677-014

09.05.04 DRIVE-IN THEATER ATTENDANT (amuse. & rec.), 349.673-010

09.05.04 HOSPITAL ENTRANCE ATTENDANT (medical ser.), 355.677-014

09.05.05 CARDROOM ATTENDANT 2 (amuse. & rec.), 343.577-010

09.05.06 CADDIE (amuse. & rec.), 341.677-010

09.05.06 DRESSER (amuse. & rec.), 346.674-010

09.05.07 CLOTHES-ROOM WORKER (medical ser.), 355.687-010

09.05.07 LOCKER-ROOM ATTENDANT (per. ser.), 358.677-014

09.05.07 RESTROOM ATTENDANT (any ind.), 358.677-018

09.05.08 CHILDREN'S ATTENDANT (amuse. & rec.), 349.677-018

09.05.08 TICKET TAKER (amuse. & rec.), 344.667-010

09.05.08 USHER (amuse. & rec.), 344.677-014

09.05.09 ELEVATOR OPERATOR (any ind.), 388.663-010

10.01.02 CASE AIDE (social ser.), 195.367-010

10.01.02 COMMUNITY WORKER (gov. ser.), 195.367-018

10.01.02 FOOD-MANAGEMENT AIDE (gov. ser.), 195.367-022

10.01.02 SOCIAL-SERVICES AIDE (social ser.), 195.367-034

10.02.02 PHYSICAL-INTEGRATION PRACTITIONER (per. ser.), 076.264-010

10.03.02 AMBULANCE ATTENDANT (medical ser.), 355.374-010

10.03.02 BIRTH ATTENDANT (medical ser.), 354.377-010

10.03.02 FIRST-AID ATTENDANT (any ind.), 354.677-010

10.03.02 GERIATRIC NURSE ASSISTANT (medical ser.), 355.674-026

10.03.02 MEDICATION AIDE (medical ser.), 355.374-014

10.03.02 NURSE, PRACTICAL (medical ser.), 354.374-010

10.03.02 ORTHOPEDIC ASSISTANT (medical ser.), 712.661-010

10.03.02 PHYSICAL THERAPY AIDE (medical ser.), 355.354-010

10.03.02 RESPIRATORY-THERAPY AIDE (medical ser.), 355.674-022

10.03.03 BLIND AIDE (per. ser.), 359.573-010

10.03.03 CHILD-CARE ATTENDANT, SCHOOL (per. ser.), 355.674-010

10.03.03 GUARD, SCHOOL-CROSSING (gov. ser.), 371.567-010

10.03.03 HOME ATTENDANT (per. ser.), 354.377-014

10.03.03 NURSERY SCHOOL ATTENDANT (any ind.), 359.677-018

10.03.03 PLAYROOM ATTENDANT (any ind.), 359.677-026

11.01.01 PROGRAMMER, DETAIL (clerical), 219.367-026

11.02.03 HOMEMAKER (social ser.), 309.354-010

11.02.04 FILM-OR-TAPE LIBRARIAN (clerical), 222.367-026

11.05.02 BUSINESS REPRESENTATIVE, LABOR UNION (profess. & kin.), 187.167-018

11.05.02 DIRECTOR, QUALITY ASSURANCE (profess. & kin.), 189.117-042

11.05.02 MANAGER, PRODUCTION (radio & tv broad.), 184.167-074

11.07.01 COMMUNITY ORGANIZATION WORKER (social ser.), 195.167-010

11.07.03 SUPERVISOR, CONTRACT-SHELTERED WORKSHOP (nonprofit org.), 187.134-010

11.10.03 SANITARIAN (any ind.), 529.137-014

11.10.03 SANITATION INSPECTOR (gov. ser.), 168.267-110

11.11.01 MANAGER, APARTMENT HOUSE (real estate), 186.167-018

11.11.01 MANAGER, LODGING FACILITIES (hotel & rest.), 320.137-014

11.12.03 ADVANCE AGENT (amuse. & rec.), 191.167-010

12.01.02 CHARTER (amuse. & rec.), 249.367-018

12.01.02 CLOCKER (amuse. & rec.), 153.367-010

12.01.02 FLAGGER (amuse. & rec.), 372.667-026

12.01.02 GOLF-COURSE RANGER (amuse. & rec.), 379.667-010

12.01.02 HORSE-RACE STARTER (amuse. & rec.), 153.267-010

12.01.02 HORSE-RACE TIMER (amuse. & rec.), 153.367-014

12.01.02 LEAD PONY RIDER (amuse. & rec.), 153.674-014

12.01.02 UMPIRE (amuse. & rec.), 153.267-018

12.02.01 AQUATIC PERFORMER (amuse. & rec.), 159.347-014

12.02.01 JUGGLER (amuse. & rec.), 159.341-010

12.02.01 STUNT PERFORMER (amuse. & rec.), 159.341-014

Appendix E
Listing of Occupations by Skills Required with Data, People, and Things

This index arranges all occupations listed in *The Enhanced Guide for Occupational Exploration* in numerical order of the third through sixth digits of their *Dictionary of Occupational Titles* (DOT) code number. These digits correspond to the levels of skill required for each occupation in terms of data, people, and things. This list provides a useful way to look for occupations that require skills which are similar to yours.

The first number listed to the left of each job title is its GOE number. Use this number to find that job's description in this book. The number that follows each job title is its DOT number. The jobs are listed in numerical order of the fourth through sixth DOT digits, beginning with the fourth digit, having to do with data. This system avoids duplicate listings of the same job in multiple locations but does make it somewhat more difficult to find all jobs listed with similar fifth digits (people) and sixth digits (things). For example, if you wanted to find jobs that require high level skills with people but relatively lower skills with data and things, you would have to begin by finding occupations listed by the fourth DOT digit (data) within the range you find acceptable, then for occupations within each of these data codes that require higher levels of skills with people (fifth digit) and then those with lower skill requirements with things (sixth digit).

Chapter 2 provides additional details on the meaning of the DOT code number but here is a summary that may help you use this index:

DATA (high = 0, low = 6): This refers to the fourth digit in the DOT code number.
0 = Synthesizing, 1 = Coordinating, 2 = Analyzing, 3 = Compiling, 4 = Computing, 5 = Copying, 6 = Comparing

PEOPLE (high = 0, low = 8): This refers the fifth digit in the DOT code number.
0 = Mentoring, 1 = Negotiating, 2 = Instructing, 3 = Supervising, 4 = Diverting, 5 = Persuading, 6 = Speaking-Signaling, 7 = Serving, 8 = Taking Instructions-Helping

THINGS (high = 0, low = 7): This refers to the sixth digit in the DOT code number.
0 = Setting up, 1 = Precision Working, 2 = Operating-Controlling, 3 = Driving-Operating, 4 = Manipulating, 5 = Tending, 6 = Feeding-Offbearing, 7 = Handling

Data = Synthesizing

007 Synthesizing, Mentoring, Handling

10.01.01 CLERGY MEMBER (profess. & kin.), 120.007-010

017 Synthesizing, Negotiating, Handling

11.07.04 CURATOR (museum), 102.017-010
11.08.01 EDITOR, NEWSPAPER (print. & pub.), 132.017-014

021 Synthesizing, Instructing, Precision

01.04.01 TEACHER, MUSIC (educ.), 152.021-010
02.02.01 MEDICAL PHYSICIST (profess. & kin.), 079.021-014
05.01.02 HEALTH PHYSICIST (profess. & kin.), 079.021-010

027 Synthesizing, Instructing, Handling

01.05.01 CHOREOGRAPHER (amuse. & rec.), 151.027-010
01.05.01 INSTRUCTOR, DANCING (educ.), 151.027-014

031 Synthesizing, Supervising, Precision

01.02.03 ART DIRECTOR (profess. & kin.), 141.031-010
01.02.03 ART DIRECTOR (motion pic.), 142.031-010
01.02.03 MANAGER, DISPLAY (ret. tr.), 142.031-014

037 Synthesizing, Supervising, Handling

01.01.01 CONTINUITY DIRECTOR (radio & tv broad.), 132.037-010
01.01.01 EDITOR, PUBLICATIONS (print. & pub.), 132.037-022
11.08.01 EDITOR, DEPARTMENT (print. & pub.), 132.037-018

041 Synthesizing, Diverting, Precision

01.02.02 QUICK SKETCH ARTIST (amuse. & rec.), 149.041-010
01.03.02 MAGICIAN (amuse. & rec.), 159.041-010
01.03.02 PUPPETEER (amuse. & rec.), 159.041-014
01.04.04 MUSICIAN, INSTRUMENTAL (amuse. & rec.), 152.041-010

047 Synthesizing, Diverting, Handling

01.03.02 CLOWN (amuse. & rec.), 159.047-010
01.03.02 COMEDIAN (amuse. & rec.), 159.047-014
01.03.02 MIME (amuse. & rec.), 159.047-022
01.04.03 SINGER (amuse. & rec.), 152.047-022
01.05.02 DANCER (amuse. & rec.), 151.047-010

051 Synthesizing, Persuading, Precision

01.02.03 DISPLAY DESIGNER (profess. & kin.), 142.051-010
01.02.03 INTERIOR DESIGNER (profess. & kin.), 142.051-014

061 Synthesizing, Speaking-Signaling, Precision

01.02.03 AUDIOVISUAL PRODUCTION SPECIALIST (profess. & kin.), 149.061-010
01.02.03 CLOTHES DESIGNER (profess. & kin.), 142.061-018
01.02.03 EXHIBIT DESIGNER (museum), 142.061-058
01.02.03 FASHION ARTIST (ret. tr.), 141.061-014
01.02.03 FURNITURE DESIGNER (furn.), 142.061-022
01.02.03 GRAPHIC DESIGNER (profess. & kin.), 141.061-018
01.02.03 ILLUSTRATOR (profess. & kin.), 141.061-022
01.02.03 INDUSTRIAL DESIGNER (profess. & kin.), 142.061-026
01.02.03 POLICE ARTIST (gov. ser.), 141.061-034
01.02.03 SET DECORATOR (motion pic.), 142.061-042
01.02.03 SET DESIGNER (motion pic.), 142.061-046
01.02.03 SET DESIGNER (amuse. & rec.), 142.061-050
02.01.01 CHEMIST (profess. & kin.), 022.061-010
02.01.01 GEOLOGIST (profess. & kin.), 024.061-018
02.01.01 GEOPHYSICIST (profess. & kin.), 024.061-030
02.01.01 HYDROLOGIST (profess. & kin.), 024.061-034
02.01.01 MINERALOGIST (profess. & kin.), 024.061-038
02.01.01 PETROLOGIST (profess. & kin.), 024.061-046
02.01.01 PHYSICIST (profess. & kin.), 023.061-014
02.01.01 SEISMOLOGIST (profess. & kin.), 024.061-050

02.01.02 GEOLOGIST, PETROLEUM (petrol. production), 024.061-022
02.01.02 METALLURGIST, PHYSICAL (profess. & kin.), 011.061-022
02.02.01 ANIMAL BREEDER (profess. & kin.), 041.061-014
02.02.01 ANIMAL SCIENTIST (profess. & kin.), 040.061-014
02.02.01 BIOMEDICAL ENGINEER (profess. & kin.), 019.061-010
02.02.01 DAIRY SCIENTIST (profess. & kin.), 040.061-018
02.02.01 HISTOPATHOLOGIST (medical ser.), 041.061-054
02.02.01 PARASITOLOGIST (profess. & kin.), 041.061-070
02.02.01 PHARMACOLOGIST (profess. & kin.), 041.061-074
02.02.01 ZOOLOGIST (profess. & kin.), 041.061-090
02.02.02 AGRONOMIST (profess. & kin.), 040.061-010
02.02.02 BOTANIST (profess. & kin.), 041.061-038
02.02.02 FOREST ECOLOGIST (profess. & kin.), 040.061-030
02.02.02 HORTICULTURIST (profess. & kin.), 040.061-038
02.02.02 PLANT BREEDER (profess. & kin.), 041.061-082
02.02.02 PLANT PATHOLOGIST (profess. & kin.), 041.061-086
02.02.02 RANGE MANAGER (profess. & kin.), 040.061-046
02.02.02 SILVICULTURIST (profess. & kin.), 040.061-050
02.02.02 SOIL CONSERVATIONIST (profess. & kin.), 040.061-054
02.02.02 SOIL SCIENTIST (profess. & kin.), 040.061-058
02.02.02 WOOD TECHNOLOGIST (profess. & kin.), 040.061-062
02.02.03 BIOCHEMIST (profess. & kin.), 041.061-026
02.02.03 BIOLOGIST (profess. & kin.), 041.061-030
02.02.03 BIOPHYSICIST (profess. & kin.), 041.061-034
02.02.03 MICROBIOLOGIST (profess. & kin.), 041.061-058
02.02.03 PHYSIOLOGIST (profess. & kin.), 041.061-078
02.02.04 CHEMIST, FOOD (profess. & kin.), 022.061-014
02.02.04 DAIRY TECHNOLOGIST (profess. & kin.), 040.061-022
03.01.04 FORESTER (profess. & kin.), 040.061-034
05.01.01 AERODYNAMIST (aircraft-aerospace mfg.), 002.061-010
05.01.01 AERONAUTICAL-RESEARCH ENGINEER (aircraft-aerospace mfg.), 002.061-026
05.01.01 CHEMICAL RESEARCH ENGINEER (profess. & kin.), 008.061-022
05.01.01 FOUNDRY METALLURGIST (foundry), 011.061-010
05.01.01 NUCLEAR-DECONTAMINATION RESEARCH SPECIALIST (profess. & kin.), 008.061-030
05.01.02 PRODUCT-SAFETY ENGINEER (profess. & kin.), 012.061-010
05.01.02 SAFETY ENGINEER (profess. & kin.), 012.061-014
05.01.02 SAFETY ENGINEER, MINES (mining), 010.061-026
05.01.03 HYDRAULIC ENGINEER (profess. & kin.), 005.061-018
05.01.03 ILLUMINATING ENGINEER (profess. & kin.), 003.061-046
05.01.03 MARINE ENGINEER (profess. & kin.), 014.061-014
05.01.03 NUCLEAR ENGINEER (profess. & kin.), 015.061-014
05.01.03 SANITARY ENGINEER (profess. & kin.), 005.061-030
05.01.03 WASTE-MANAGEMENT ENGINEER, RADIOACTIVE MATERIALS (profess. & kin.), 005.061-042
05.01.04 AERONAUTICAL TEST ENGINEER (aircraft-aerospace mfg.), 002.061-018
05.01.04 CHEMICAL-TEST ENGINEER (profess. & kin.), 008.061-026
05.01.04 ELECTRICAL TEST ENGINEER (profess. & kin.), 003.061-014
05.01.04 METALLOGRAPHER (profess. & kin.), 011.061-014
05.01.04 RELIABILITY ENGINEER (profess. & kin.), 019.061-026
05.01.04 STRESS ANALYST (aircraft-aerospace mfg.), 002.061-030
05.01.04 STRESS ANALYST (profess. & kin.), 007.061-042
05.01.04 TEST ENGINEER, NUCLEAR EQUIPMENT (profess. & kin.), 015.061-022
05.01.06 MATERIALS ENGINEER (profess. & kin.), 019.061-014
05.01.06 METALLURGIST, EXTRACTIVE (profess. & kin.), 011.061-018
05.01.06 MINING ENGINEER (mining), 010.061-014

05.01.06 STANDARDS ENGINEER (profess. & kin.), 012.061-018

05.01.06 UTILIZATION ENGINEER (light, heat, & power), 007.061-034

05.01.07 AERONAUTICAL ENGINEER (profess. & kin.), 002.061-014

05.01.07 AERONAUTICAL-DESIGN ENGINEER (aircraft-aerospace mfg.), 002.061-022

05.01.07 AIRPORT ENGINEER (profess. & kin.), 005.061-010

05.01.07 ARCHITECT (profess. & kin.), 001.061-010

05.01.07 ARCHITECT, MARINE (profess. & kin.), 001.061-014

05.01.07 CERAMIC DESIGN ENGINEER (profess. & kin.), 006.061-010

05.01.07 CERAMIC ENGINEER (profess. & kin.), 006.061-014

05.01.07 CHEMICAL DESIGN ENGINEER, PROCESSES (profess. & kin.), 008.061-014

05.01.07 CHEMICAL ENGINEER (profess. & kin.), 008.061-018

05.01.07 CIVIL ENGINEER (profess. & kin.), 005.061-014

05.01.07 ELECTRICAL-DESIGN ENGINEER (profess. & kin.), 003.061-018

05.01.07 ELECTRO-OPTICAL ENGINEER (profess. & kin.), 023.061-010

05.01.07 ELECTRONICS-DESIGN ENGINEER (profess. & kin.), 003.061-034

05.01.07 LANDSCAPE ARCHITECT (profess. & kin.), 001.061-018

05.01.07 OPTICAL ENGINEER (profess. & kin.), 019.061-018

05.01.07 TOOL DESIGNER (profess. & kin.), 007.061-026

05.01.08 AGRICULTURAL ENGINEER (profess. & kin.), 013.061-010

05.01.08 AUTOMOTIVE ENGINEER (auto. mfg.), 007.061-010

05.01.08 ELECTRICAL ENGINEER (profess. & kin.), 003.061-010

05.01.08 ELECTRONICS ENGINEER (profess. & kin.), 003.061-030

05.01.08 MECHANICAL ENGINEER (profess. & kin.), 007.061-014

05.01.08 PETROLEUM ENGINEER (petrol. production), 010.061-018

05.01.08 STRUCTURAL ENGINEER (const.), 005.061-034

05.01.08 TRANSPORTATION ENGINEER (profess. & kin.), 005.061-038

05.01.08 WELDING ENGINEER (profess. & kin.), 011.061-026

11.03.01 PSYCHOLOGIST, EXPERIMENTAL (profess. & kin.), 045.061-018

062 Synthesizing, Speaking-Signaling, Operating — Controlling

01.02.03 DIRECTOR OF PHOTOGRAPHY (motion pic.), 143.062-010

01.02.03 PHOTOGRAPHER, MOTION PICTURE (profess. & kin.), 143.062-022

01.02.03 PHOTOGRAPHER, STILL (profess. & kin.), 143.062-030

01.02.03 PHOTOJOURNALIST (print. & pub.), 143.062-034

01.02.03 TELEVISION TECHNICIAN (radio & tv broad.), 194.062-010

02.01.01 COMPUTER-APPLICATIONS ENGINEER (profess. & kin.), 020.062-010

02.01.01 METEOROLOGIST (profess. & kin.), 025.062-010

02.04.01 PHOTOGRAPHER, SCIENTIFIC (profess. & kin.), 143.062-026

067 Synthesizing, Speaking-Signaling, Handling

01.01.02 COPY WRITER (profess. & kin.), 131.067-014

Data = Coordinating

101 Coordinating, Mentoring, Precision

02.03.01 GENERAL PRACTITIONER (medical ser.), 070.101-022

02.03.01 PODIATRIST (medical ser.), 079.101-022

02.03.02 DENTIST (medical ser.), 072.101-010

01.01.02 EDITORIAL WRITER (print. & pub.), 131.067-022

01.01.02 WRITER, PROSE, FICTION AND NONFICTION (profess. & kin.), 131.067-046

01.03.01 DIRECTOR, MOTION PICTURE (motion pic.), 159.067-010

02.01.01 GEOGRAPHER (profess. & kin.), 029.067-010

02.01.01 MATHEMATICIAN (profess. & kin.), 020.067-014

05.01.02 NUCLEAR-CRITICALITY SAFETY ENGINEER (profess. & kin.), 015.067-010

05.01.04 METROLOGIST (profess. & kin.), 012.067-010

11.01.01 ENGINEERING ANALYST (profess. & kin.), 020.067-010

11.01.01 INFORMATION SCIENTIST (profess. & kin.), 109.067-010

11.01.01 OPERATIONS-RESEARCH ANALYST (profess. & kin.), 020.067-018

11.01.01 STATISTICIAN, MATHEMATICAL (profess. & kin.), 020.067-022

11.03.02 POLITICAL SCIENTIST (profess. & kin.), 051.067-010

11.03.02 RESEARCH WORKER, SOCIAL WELFARE (profess. & kin.), 054.067-010

11.03.02 SCIENTIFIC LINGUIST (profess. & kin.), 059.067-014

11.03.02 SOCIOLOGIST (profess. & kin.), 054.067-014

11.03.03 ANTHROPOLOGIST (profess. & kin.), 055.067-010

11.03.03 ARCHEOLOGIST (profess. & kin.), 055.067-018

11.03.03 GENEALOGIST (profess. & kin.), 052.067-018

11.03.03 HISTORIAN (profess. & kin.), 052.067-022

11.03.03 RESEARCH ASSOCIATE (museum), 109.067-014

11.03.04 OCCUPATIONAL ANALYST (profess. & kin.), 166.067-010

11.03.05 ECONOMIST (profess. & kin.), 050.067-010

11.05.02 PROGRAM PROPOSALS COORDINATOR (radio & tv broad.), 132.067-030

11.06.03 MARKET-RESEARCH ANALYST 1 (profess. & kin.), 050.067-014

11.08.01 EDITOR, NEWS (print. & pub.), 132.067-026

11.08.03 COLUMNIST/COMMENTATOR (print. & pub.), 131.067-010

11.09.03 PUBLIC-RELATIONS REPRESENTATIVE (profess. & kin.), 165.067-010

071 Synthesizing, Serving, Precision

01.06.02 MAKE-UP ARTIST (amuse. & rec.), 333.071-010

081 Synthesizing, Taking Instructions — Helping, Precision

01.02.03 COMMERCIAL DESIGNER (profess. & kin.), 141.081-014

01.02.03 DISPLAYER, MERCHANDISE (ret. tr.), 298.081-010

01.02.03 FLORAL DESIGNER (ret. tr.), 142.081-010

01.02.03 PACKAGE DESIGNER (profess. & kin.), 142.081-018

02.01.02 ENVIRONMENTAL ANALYST (profess. & kin.), 029.081-010

02.01.02 MATERIALS SCIENTIST (profess. & kin.), 029.081-014

02.02.04 FOOD TECHNOLOGIST (profess. & kin.), 041.081-010

02.04.02 TOXICOLOGIST (drug prep. & related), 022.081-010

05.01.02 POLLUTION-CONTROL ENGINEER (profess. & kin.), 019.081-018

087 Synthesizing, Taking Instructions — Helping, Handling

01.01.02 SCREEN WRITER (motion pic.), 131.087-018

02.03.03 VETERINARIAN (medical ser.), 073.101-010

02.03.04 AUDIOLOGIST (profess. & kin.), 076.101-010

02.03.04 CHIROPRACTOR (medical ser.), 079.101-010

02.03.04 OPTOMETRIST (profess. & kin.), 079.101-018

107   Coordinating, Mentoring, Handling

02.03.04 SPEECH PATHOLOGIST (profess. & kin.), 076.107-010
10.01.02 CASEWORKER (social ser.), 195.107-010
10.01.02 COUNSELOR (profess. & kin.), 045.107-010
10.01.02 PROBATION-AND-PAROLE OFFICER (profess. & kin.), 195.107-046
10.01.02 PSYCHOLOGIST, CLINICAL (profess. & kin.), 045.107-022
10.01.02 PSYCHOLOGIST, COUNSELING (profess. & kin.), 045.107-026
10.01.02 RESIDENCE COUNSELOR (educ.), 045.107-038
10.01.02 VOCATIONAL-REHABILITATION COUNSELOR (gov. ser.), 045.107-042
10.02.03 WORK-STUDY COORDINATOR, SPECIAL EDUCATION (educ.), 094.107-010
11.03.01 PSYCHOLOGIST, INDUSTRIAL-ORGANIZATIONAL (profess. & kin.), 045.107-030
11.04.01 HEARING OFFICER (gov. ser.), 119.107-010
11.04.02 LAWYER (profess. & kin.), 110.107-010

117   Coordinating, Negotiating, Handling

01.03.01 PRODUCER (radio & tv broad.), 159.117-010
05.02.03 PRODUCTION SUPERINTENDENT (any ind.), 183.117-014
11.01.01 DIRECTOR, RECORDS MANAGEMENT (profess. & kin.), 161.117-014
11.04.04 CUSTOMS-HOUSE BROKER (finan. inst.), 186.117-018
11.05.01 ASSOCIATION EXECUTIVE (profess. & kin.), 189.117-010
11.05.01 DIRECTOR, TRANSPORTATION (motor trans.), 184.117-014
11.05.01 MANAGER, AIRPORT (air trans.), 184.117-026
11.05.01 MANAGER, BAKERY (bake. prod.), 189.117-046
11.05.01 MANAGER, INDUSTRIAL ORGANIZATION (any ind.), 189.117-022
11.05.01 MANAGER, LAND DEVELOPMENT (real estate), 186.117-042
11.05.01 PRESIDENT (any ind.), 189.117-026
11.05.02 DIETITIAN, CHIEF (profess. & kin.), 077.117-010
11.05.02 DIRECTOR, QUALITY ASSURANCE (profess. & kin.), 189.117-042
11.05.02 EXECUTIVE VICE PRESIDENT, CHAMBER OF COMMERCE (nonprofit org.), 187.117-030
11.05.02 GRANT COORDINATOR (profess. & kin.), 169.117-014
11.05.02 IMPORT-EXPORT AGENT (any ind.), 184.117-022
11.05.02 MANAGER, BRANCH (any ind.), 183.117-010
11.05.02 MANAGER, CONTRACTS (petrol. production), 163.117-010
11.05.02 MANAGER, DEPARTMENT STORE (ret. tr.), 185.117-010
11.05.02 MANAGER, FINANCIAL INSTITUTION (finan. inst.), 186.117-038
11.05.02 MANAGER, OPERATIONS (air trans.), 184.117-050
11.05.02 MANAGER, PERSONNEL (profess. & kin.), 166.117-018
11.05.02 MANAGER, REGIONAL (motor trans.), 184.117-054
11.05.02 MANAGER, SCHEDULE PLANNING (air trans.), 184.117-058
11.05.02 MANAGER, STATION (radio & tv broad.), 184.117-062
11.05.02 OPERATIONS MANAGER (tel. & tel.), 184.117-070
11.05.03 DIRECTOR, REGULATORY AGENCY (gov. ser.), 188.117-134
11.05.03 HOUSING-MANAGEMENT OFFICER (gov. ser.), 188.117-110
11.05.03 MANAGER, CITY (gov. ser.), 188.117-114
11.05.04 DIRECTOR, MEDIA MARKETING (radio & tv broad.), 163.117-022
11.06.03 FACTORER (finan. inst.), 186.117-026
11.06.03 NEGOTIATOR, LETTER OF CREDIT (finan. inst.), 186.117-050
11.06.05 BUDGET OFFICER (gov. ser.), 161.117-010
11.06.05 TRUST OFFICER (finan. inst.), 186.117-074
11.07.01 COORDINATOR OF REHABILITATION SERVICES (medical ser.), 076.117-010

11.07.01 DIRECTOR, COMMUNITY ORGANIZATION (nonprofit org.), 187.117-014
11.07.01 PROGRAM DIRECTOR, GROUP WORK (profess. & kin.), 187.117-046
11.07.02 ADMINISTRATOR, HOSPITAL (medical ser.), 187.117-010
11.07.02 PUBLIC HEALTH EDUCATOR (profess. & kin.), 079.117-014
11.07.03 DIRECTOR, EDUCATIONAL PROGRAM (educ.), 099.117-010
11.07.03 FINANCIAL-AIDS OFFICER (educ.), 090.117-030
11.07.03 VOCATIONAL REHABILITATION CONSULTANT (gov. ser.), 094.117-018
11.07.04 LIBRARY CONSULTANT (library), 100.117-014
11.09.01 MANAGER, ADVERTISING (any ind.), 164.117-010
11.09.01 MEDIA DIRECTOR (profess. & kin.), 164.117-018
11.09.02 DIRECTOR, FUNDRAISING (nonprofit org.), 165.117-010
11.09.02 DIRECTOR, FUNDS DEVELOPMENT (profess. & kin.), 165.117-014
11.09.02 FOREIGN-SERVICE OFFICER (gov. ser.), 188.117-106
11.09.03 MANAGER, AREA DEVELOPMENT (light, heat, & power), 184.117-030
11.10.02 DIRECTOR, COMPLIANCE (gov. ser.), 188.117-046
11.10.03 PUBLIC HEALTH SERVICE OFFICER (gov. ser.), 187.117-050
11.10.03 SANITARIAN (profess. & kin.), 079.117-018
11.11.01 MANAGER, HOTEL OR MOTEL (hotel & rest.), 187.117-038
11.11.02 MANAGER, RECREATION ESTABLISHMENT (amuse. & rec.), 187.117-042
11.11.03 MANAGER, TRAFFIC (air trans.), 184.117-066
11.11.04 GENERAL MANAGER, ROAD PRODUCTION (amuse. & rec.), 187.117-034
11.11.04 MANAGER, TOURING PRODUCTION (amuse. & rec.), 191.117-038
11.12.01 GENERAL CLAIMS AGENT (air trans.), 186.117-030
11.12.02 MANAGER, LEASING (petrol. production), 186.117-046
11.12.02 PROPERTY-UTILIZATION OFFICER (gov. ser.), 188.117-122
11.12.02 REAL-ESTATE AGENT (profess. & kin.), 186.117-058
11.12.02 RIGHT-OF-WAY AGENT (any ind.), 191.117-046
11.12.03 ARTIST'S MANAGER (amuse. & rec.), 191.117-010
11.12.03 BOOKING MANAGER (amuse. & rec.), 191.117-014
11.12.03 BUSINESS MANAGER (amuse. & rec.), 191.117-018
11.12.03 LITERARY AGENT (bus. ser.), 191.117-034
11.12.03 MANAGER, ATHLETE (amuse. & rec.), 153.117-014
11.12.04 CONTRACT ADMINISTRATOR (any ind.), 162.117-014
11.12.04 CONTRACT SPECIALIST (profess. & kin.), 162.117-018
12.01.01 SCOUT, PROFESSIONAL SPORTS (amuse. & rec.), 153.117-018

121   Coordinating, Instructing, Precision

05.05.17 DIETETIC TECHNICIAN (profess. & kin.), 077.121-010
10.02.01 NURSE, INSTRUCTOR (medical ser.), 075.121-010
10.02.02 OCCUPATIONAL THERAPIST (medical ser.), 076.121-010
10.02.02 PHYSICAL THERAPIST (medical ser.), 076.121-014
11.02.03 COUNTY HOME-DEMONSTRATION AGENT (gov. ser.), 096.121-010
11.02.03 HOME ECONOMIST (profess. & kin.), 096.121-014

124   Coordinating, Instructing, Manipulating

09.01.01 COUNSELOR, CAMP (amuse. & rec.), 159.124-010
10.02.01 NURSE, SCHOOL (medical ser.), 075.124-010
10.02.01 NURSE, STAFF, COMMUNITY HEALTH (medical ser.), 075.124-014
10.02.02 HORTICULTURAL THERAPIST (medical ser.), 076.124-018
10.02.02 MANUAL-ARTS THERAPIST (medical ser.), 076.124-010
10.02.02 RECREATIONAL THERAPIST (medical ser.), 076.124-014

127 Coordinating, Instructing, Handling

05.05.17 DIETITIAN, CLINICAL (profess. & kin.), 077.127-014
10.02.02 ART THERAPIST (medical ser.), 076.127-010
10.02.02 DANCE THERAPIST (medical ser.), 076.127-018
10.02.02 MUSIC THERAPIST (medical ser.), 076.127-014
11.02.03 COMMUNITY DIETITIAN (profess. & kin.), 077.127-010
11.02.03 COUNTY-AGRICULTURAL AGENT (gov. ser.), 096.127-010
11.02.03 EXTENSION SERVICE SPECIALIST (gov. ser.), 096.127-014
11.02.04 LIBRARIAN (library), 100.127-014
11.07.02 CIVIL PREPAREDNESS TRAINING OFFICER (gov. ser.), 169.127-010
11.07.03 PARK NATURALIST (gov. ser.), 049.127-010

130 Coordinating, Supervising, Setting Up

05.06.02 ENGINEER (water trans.), 197.130-010

131 Coordinating, Supervising, Precision

05.05.17 CHEF (hotel & rest.), 313.131-014
05.05.17 SOUS CHEF (hotel & rest.), 313.131-026
05.10.08 BAKER, HEAD (hotel & rest.), 313.131-010
05.10.08 PASTRY CHEF (hotel & rest.), 313.131-022

132 Coordinating, Supervising, Operating — Controlling

07.03.01 TELLER, HEAD (finan. inst.), 211.132-010

133 Coordinating, Supervising, Driving — Operating

05.04.02 MATE, SHIP (water trans.), 197.133-022
05.04.02 PILOT, SHIP (water trans.), 197.133-026

134 Coordinating, Supervising, Manipulating

06.01.01 COOK, MEXICAN FOOD (food prep nec), 526.134-010
11.07.03 SUPERVISOR, CONTRACT-SHELTERED WORKSHOP (nonprofit org.), 187.134-010

137 Coordinating, Supervising, Handling

02.04.01 LABORATORY SUPERVISOR (profess. & kin.), 022.137-010
03.04.04 GREENSKEEPER 1 (any ind.), 406.137-010
04.01.01 DEPUTY, COURT (gov. ser.), 377.137-018
05.01.02 RADIATION-PROTECTION ENGINEER (gov. ser.), 015.137-010
05.12.03 BARGE CAPTAIN (water trans.), 911.137-010
05.12.18 HOUSEKEEPER (hotel & rest.), 321.137-010
07.01.04 VAULT CASHIER (bus. ser.), 222.137-050
07.04.01 ADMITTING OFFICER (medical ser.), 205.137-010
09.01.03 HOST/HOSTESS, RESTAURANT (hotel & rest.), 310.137-010
09.01.03 WAITER/WAITRESS, CAPTAIN (hotel & rest.), 311.137-018
11.07.02 UTILIZATION-REVIEW COORDINATOR (medical ser.), 079.137-010
11.07.04 RECREATION SUPERVISOR (profess. & kin.), 187.137-010
11.10.03 SANITARIAN (any ind.), 529.137-014
11.11.01 MANAGER, LODGING FACILITIES (hotel & rest.), 320.137-014
11.11.04 MANAGER, FAST FOOD SERVICES (ret. tr.), 185.137-010
11.11.05 MANAGER, DEPARTMENT (ret. tr.), 299.137-010

147 Coordinating, Diverting, Handling

01.03.03 ANNOUNCER (radio & tv broad.), 159.147-010
01.03.03 DISK JOCKEY (radio & tv broad.), 159.147-014
01.03.03 NARRATOR (motion pic.), 150.147-010

151 Coordinating, Persuading, Precision

05.01.05 SALES ENGINEER, AERONAUTICAL PRODUCTS (aircraft-aerospace mfg.), 002.151-010
05.01.05 SALES-ENGINEER, ELECTRONICS PRODUCTS AND SYSTEMS (profess. & kin.), 003.151-014

157 Coordinating, Persuading, Handling

08.01.01 PHARMACEUTICAL DETAILER (whole. tr.), 262.157-010
08.01.02 SALES REPRESENTATIVE, DATA-PROCESSING SERVICES (bus. ser.), 251.157-014
08.01.02 SALES REPRESENTATIVE, HOTEL SERVICES (hotel & rest.), 259.157-014
08.01.03 BUSINESS-OPPORTUNITY-AND-PROPERTY-INVESTMENT BROKER (bus. ser.), 189.157-010
08.01.03 BUYER (profess. & kin.), 162.157-018
08.01.03 BUYER, ASSISTANT (ret. tr.), 162.157-022
08.01.03 PAWNBROKER (ret. tr.), 191.157-010
08.02.01 MANUFACTURERS' REPRESENTATIVE (whole. tr.), 279.157-010
08.02.06 TRAVEL AGENT (bus. ser.), 252.157-010
10.02.02 HYPNOTHERAPIST (profess. & kin.), 079.157-010
11.05.04 PURCHASING AGENT (profess. & kin.), 162.157-038
11.06.03 SECURITIES TRADER 1 (finan. inst.), 162.157-042
11.06.04 SALES AGENT, SECURITIES (finan. inst.), 251.157-010
11.09.01 FASHION COORDINATOR (ret. tr.), 185.157-010
11.09.02 FUND RAISER 1 (nonprofit org.), 293.157-010

161 Coordinating, Speaking-Signaling, Precision

02.04.01 PHARMACIST (profess. & kin.), 074.161-010
02.04.01 RADIOPHARMACIST (medical ser.), 074.161-014
03.01.01 FARMER, FIELD CROP (agric.), 404.161-010
03.01.01 FARMER, GENERAL (agric.), 421.161-010
03.01.01 FARMER, VINE-FRUIT CROPS (agric.), 403.161-014
03.01.02 BEEKEEPER (agric.), 413.161-010
03.01.02 FISH FARMER (fish.), 446.161-010
03.01.02 SHELLFISH GROWER (fish.), 446.161-014
05.01.01 ELECTRICAL TECHNICIAN (profess. & kin.), 003.161-010
05.01.01 ELECTRONICS TECHNICIAN (profess. & kin.), 003.161-014
05.01.01 MECHANICAL-ENGINEERING TECHNICIAN (profess. & kin.), 007.161-026
05.01.01 OPTOMECHANICAL TECHNICIAN (optical goods), 007.161-030
05.01.01 TECHNICIAN, SEMICONDUCTOR DEVELOPMENT (profess. & kin.), 003.161-018
05.01.04 TEST TECHNICIAN (profess. & kin.), 019.161-014
05.01.07 AGRICULTURAL-ENGINEERING TECHNICIAN (profess. & kin.), 013.161-010
05.01.08 ENGINEER, SOILS (profess. & kin.), 024.161-010
05.02.03 WINE MAKER (wine prod.), 183.161-014
05.03.02 ENGINEERING ASSISTANT, MECHANICAL EQUIPMENT (profess. & kin.), 007.161-018
05.03.07 SOLAR-ENERGY-SYSTEMS DESIGNER (profess. & kin.), 007.161-038
05.05.05 CABLE SUPERVISOR (tel. & tel.), 184.161-010
09.01.01 GUIDE, HUNTING AND FISHING (amuse. & rec.), 353.161-010
11.10.03 INDUSTRIAL HYGIENIST (profess. & kin.), 079.161-010
11.10.03 INDUSTRIAL-SAFETY-AND-HEALTH TECHNICIAN (any ind.), 168.161-014

162 Coordinating, Speaking-Signaling, Operating — Controlling

05.03.03 AIR-TRAFFIC-CONTROL SPECIALIST, STATION (gov. ser.), 193.162-014
05.03.03 AIR-TRAFFIC-CONTROL SPECIALIST, TOWER (gov. ser.), 193.162-018
07.01.03 SOCIAL SECRETARY (clerical), 201.162-010

07.04.05 ALARM OPERATOR (gov. ser.), 379.162-010
11.01.01 PROGRAMMER, BUSINESS (profess. & kin.), 020.162-014
11.01.02 MATHEMATICAL TECHNICIAN (profess. & kin.), 020.162-010
11.06.01 ACCOUNTANT, TAX (profess. & kin.), 160.162-010
11.06.01 AUDITOR (profess. & kin.), 160.162-014

163 Coordinating, Speaking-Signaling, Driving — Operating

11.10.05 TRAFFIC INSPECTOR (motor trans.), 184.163-010

164 Coordinating, Speaking-Signaling, Manipulating

05.10.02 SERVICE MANAGER (ret. tr.), 185.164-010
05.12.18 SUPERVISOR, CENTRAL SUPPLY (medical ser.), 079.164-010
09.01.01 GROUP WORKER (social ser.), 195.164-010

167 Coordinating, Speaking-Signaling, Handling

01.01.01 PRODUCER (motion pic.), 187.167-174
01.03.01 PRODUCER (amuse. & rec.), 187.167-178
01.03.03 PROGRAM COORDINATOR (amuse. & rec.), 139.167-010
02.01.02 PROJECT MANAGER, ENVIRONMENTAL RESEARCH (profess. & kin.), 029.167-014
02.02.01 ENVIRONMENTAL EPIDEMIOLOGIST (gov. ser.), 041.167-010
03.01.01 GENERAL MANAGER, FARM (agric.), 180.167-018
03.01.01 GROUP LEADER (agric.), 180.167-022
03.01.01 MANAGER, DAIRY FARM (agric.), 180.167-026
03.01.01 MIGRANT LEADER (agric.), 180.167-050
03.01.03 LANDSCAPE CONTRACTOR (const.), 182.167-014
03.01.03 MANAGER, NURSERY (agric.), 180.167-042
04.01.01 HARBOR MASTER (gov. ser.), 375.167-026
04.01.02 CUSTOMS PATROL OFFICER (gov. ser.), 168.167-010
04.01.02 FIRE WARDEN (forestry), 452.167-010
04.01.02 FISH AND GAME WARDEN (gov. ser.), 379.167-010
04.01.02 SPECIAL AGENT (gov. ser.), 375.167-042
04.02.02 SECURITY CONSULTANT (bus. ser.), 189.167-054
04.02.03 PARK RANGER (gov. ser.), 169.167-042
05.01.02 INDUSTRIAL-HEALTH ENGINEER (profess. & kin.), 012.167-034
05.01.02 RESOURCE-RECOVERY ENGINEER (gov. ser.), 019.167-018
05.01.02 SAFETY MANAGER (profess. & kin.), 012.167-058
05.01.03 CABLE ENGINEER, OUTSIDE PLANT (tel. & tel.), 003.167-010
05.01.03 ELECTRICAL ENGINEER, POWER SYSTEM (light, heat, & power), 003.167-018
05.01.03 POWER-DISTRIBUTION ENGINEER (light, heat, & power), 003.167-046
05.01.03 POWER-TRANSMISSION ENGINEER (light, heat, & power), 003.167-050
05.01.03 SYSTEMS ENGINEER, ELECTRONIC DATA PROCESSING (profess. & kin.), 003.167-062
05.01.04 FIELD-SERVICE ENGINEER (aircraft-aerospace mfg.), 002.167-014
05.01.04 QUALITY-CONTROL ENGINEER (profess. & kin.), 012.167-054
05.01.06 CONFIGURATION MANAGEMENT ANALYST (profess. & kin.), 012.167-010
05.01.06 COST-ANALYSIS ENGINEER (aircraft-aerospace mfg.), 002.167-010
05.01.06 DOCUMENTATION ENGINEER (profess. & kin.), 012.167-078
05.01.06 FACTORY LAY-OUT ENGINEER (profess. & kin.), 012.167-018
05.01.06 INDUSTRIAL ENGINEER (profess. & kin.), 012.167-030
05.01.06 LAND SURVEYOR (profess. & kin.), 018.167-018

05.01.06 MANAGEMENT ANALYST (profess. & kin.), 161.167-010
05.01.06 MANUFACTURING ENGINEER (profess. & kin.), 012.167-042
05.01.06 PREVENTIVE MAINTENANCE COORDINATOR (any ind.), 169.167-074
05.01.06 PRODUCTION ENGINEER (profess. & kin.), 012.167-046
05.01.06 PRODUCTION PLANNER (profess. & kin.), 012.167-050
05.01.06 TIME-STUDY ENGINEER (profess. & kin.), 012.167-070
05.01.06 TOOL PLANNER (any ind.), 012.167-074
05.01.06 TOOL PROGRAMER, NUMERICAL CONTROL (any ind.), 007.167-018
05.01.08 PLANT ENGINEER (profess. & kin.), 007.167-014
05.01.08 PROJECT ENGINEER (profess. & kin.), 019.167-014
05.02.02 SUPERINTENDENT, BUILDING (any ind.), 187.167-190
05.02.02 SUPERINTENDENT, CONSTRUCTION (const.), 182.167-026
05.02.03 BREWING DIRECTOR (beer prod.), 183.167-010
05.02.03 DIRECTOR, QUALITY CONTROL (profess. & kin.), 012.167-014
05.02.03 MANAGER, FOOD PROCESSING PLANT (can. & preserv.), 183.167-026
05.02.03 QUALITY-CONTROL COORDINATOR (drug prep. & related), 168.167-066
05.02.06 APPLIANCE-SERVICE SUPERVISOR (light, heat, & power), 187.167-010
05.02.07 MANAGER, MARINA DRY DOCK (amuse. & rec.), 187.167-226
05.03.01 NAVIGATOR (air trans.), 196.167-014
05.03.01 PHOTOGRAMMETRIC ENGINEER (profess. & kin.), 018.167-026
05.03.01 SURVEYOR ASSISTANT, INSTRUMENTS (profess. & kin.), 018.167-034
05.03.03 DISPATCHER (air trans.), 912.167-010
05.03.06 INSPECTOR, BUILDING (gov. ser.), 168.167-030
05.03.06 MARINE SURVEYOR (profess. & kin.), 014.167-010
05.03.06 SUPERVISOR, VENDOR QUALITY (any ind.), 012.167-062
05.05.02 SUPERINTENDENT, MAINTENANCE (any ind.), 189.167-046
05.05.09 MANAGER, MARINE SERVICE (ship bldg. & rep.), 187.167-130
05.06.01 LOAD DISPATCHER (light, heat, & power), 952.167-014
05.09.02 MATERIAL COORDINATOR (clerical), 221.167-014
05.09.02 PRODUCTION COORDINATOR (clerical), 221.167-018
05.10.02 MANAGER, CUSTOMER SERVICES (bus. ser.), 187.167-082
05.10.02 SERVICE MANAGER (auto. ser.), 185.167-058
05.10.04 MANAGER, CAMP (const.), 187.167-066
07.01.01 CONTACT REPRESENTATIVE (gov. ser.), 169.167-018
07.01.01 PROBATION OFFICER (profess. & kin.), 195.167-034
07.01.02 ADMINISTRATIVE SECRETARY (any ind.), 169.167-014
07.01.02 COORDINATOR, SKILL-TRAINING PROGRAM (gov. ser.), 169.167-062
07.01.02 LABOR EXPEDITER (const.), 249.167-018
07.01.02 MANAGER, OFFICE (any ind.), 169.167-034
07.01.02 MANAGER, TRAFFIC 1 (motor trans.), 184.167-102
07.01.05 TITLE SUPERVISOR (profess. & kin.), 119.167-018
07.04.03 PUBLIC HEALTH REGISTRAR (gov. ser.), 169.167-046
07.04.05 TRAIN DISPATCHER (r.r. trans.), 184.167-262
07.05.01 DISPATCHER, MOTOR VEHICLE (clerical), 249.167-014
07.05.01 GUIDE, TRAVEL (per. ser.), 353.167-010
07.05.03 ORDER-DEPARTMENT SUPERVISOR (any ind.), 169.167-038
08.01.02 ESTATE PLANNER (insurance), 186.167-010
09.01.01 DIRECTOR, SOCIAL (hotel & rest.), 352.167-010
09.04.01 MANAGER, FOOD CONCESSION (hotel & rest.), 185.167-022

09.04.01 VENDING-STAND SUPERVISOR (gov. ser.), 185.167-066

10.02.02 INDUSTRIAL THERAPIST (medical ser.), 076.167-010

11.01.01 MANAGER, ELECTRONIC DATA PROCESSING (profess. & kin.), 169.167-030

11.01.01 PROGRAMER, CHIEF, BUSINESS (profess. & kin.), 020.167-018

11.01.01 PROGRAMER, ENGINEERING AND SCIENTIFIC (profess. & kin.), 020.167-022

11.01.01 SYSTEMS ANALYST, ELECTRONIC DATA PROCESSING (profess. & kin.), 012.167-066

11.01.02 ACTUARY (profess. & kin.), 020.167-010

11.01.02 CONSULTANT (profess. & kin.), 189.167-010

11.01.02 FINANCIAL ANALYST (finan. inst.), 020.167-014

11.01.02 STATISTICIAN, APPLIED (profess. & kin.), 020.167-026

11.02.04 LIBRARIAN, SPECIAL LIBRARY (library), 100.167-026

11.02.04 MEDIA SPECIALIST, SCHOOL LIBRARY (library), 100.167-030

11.03.02 PLANNER, PROGRAM SERVICES (gov. ser.), 188.167-110

11.03.02 URBAN PLANNER (profess. & kin.), 199.167-014

11.03.03 ARCHIVIST (profess. & kin.), 101.167-010

11.04.03 ADJUDICATOR (gov. ser.), 119.167-010

11.04.04 PATENT AGENT (profess. & kin.), 119.167-014

11.05.02 ADMINISTRATIVE ASSISTANT (any ind.), 169.167-010

11.05.02 BUSINESS REPRESENTATIVE, LABOR UNION (profess. & kin.), 187.167-018

11.05.02 DIRECTOR, SERVICE (ret. tr.), 189.167-014

11.05.02 MANAGEMENT TRAINEE (any ind.), 189.167-018

11.05.02 MANAGER, CREDIT CARD OPERATIONS (profess. & kin.), 186.167-022

11.05.02 MANAGER, DEPARTMENT (any ind.), 189.167-022

11.05.02 MANAGER, PROCUREMENT SERVICES (profess. & kin.), 162.167-022

11.05.02 MANAGER, PRODUCTION (radio & tv broad.), 184.167-074

11.05.02 MANAGER, TRAFFIC (any ind.), 184.167-094

11.05.02 PROGRAM MANAGER (profess. & kin.), 189.167-030

11.05.02 PROGRAM SPECIALIST, EMPLOYEE-HEALTH MAINTENANCE (profess. & kin.), 166.167-050

11.05.02 SECURITY OFFICER (any ind.), 189.167-034

11.05.02 SPECIAL AGENT (insurance), 166.167-046

11.05.02 SUPERINTENDENT, PLANT PROTECTION (any ind.), 189.167-050

11.05.02 UTILIZATION COORDINATOR (radio & tv broad.), 169.167-078

11.05.03 ENVIRONMENTAL ANALYST (gov. ser.), 199.167-022

11.05.03 LEGISLATIVE ASSISTANT (gov. ser.), 169.167-066

11.05.03 MANAGER, HOUSING PROJECT (profess. & kin.), 186.167-030

11.05.03 MANAGER, OFFICE (gov. ser.), 188.167-058

11.05.03 MANAGER, REGULATED PROGRAM (gov. ser.), 168.167-090

11.05.03 POSTMASTER (gov. ser.), 188.167-066

11.05.03 SECRETARY OF STATE (gov. ser.), 188.167-082

11.05.04 MANAGER, CIRCULATION (print. & pub.), 163.167-014

11.05.04 MANAGER, PROFESSIONAL EQUIPMENT SALES-AND-SERVICE (bus. ser.), 185.167-042

11.05.04 MANAGER, SALES (any ind.), 163.167-018

11.05.04 PROPERTY-DISPOSAL OFFICER (any ind.), 163.167-026

11.06.01 ACCOUNTANT (profess. & kin.), 160.167-010

11.06.01 ACCOUNTANT, BUDGET (profess. & kin.), 160.167-014

11.06.01 ACCOUNTANT, COST (profess. & kin.), 160.167-018

11.06.01 AUDITOR, INTERNAL (profess. & kin.), 160.167-034

11.06.01 AUDITOR, TAX (profess. & kin.), 160.167-038

11.06.01 OPERATIONS OFFICER (finan. inst.), 186.167-050

11.06.01 REVENUE AGENT (gov. ser.), 160.167-050

11.06.03 APPRAISER (gov. ser.), 188.167-010

11.06.03 BOOKMAKER (amuse. & rec.), 187.167-014

11.06.03 FOREIGN-EXCHANGE TRADER (finan. inst.), 186.167-014

11.06.03 MANAGER, CREDIT AND COLLECTION (any ind.), 168.167-054

11.06.03 SECURITIES TRADER 2 (finan. inst.), 186.167-058

11.06.03 UNDERWRITER (insurance), 169.167-058

11.07.01 COMMUNITY ORGANIZATION WORKER (social ser.), 195.167-010

11.07.01 DIRECTOR, SERVICE (nonprofit org.), 187.167-214

11.07.01 REHABILITATION CENTER MANAGER (gov. ser.), 195.167-038

11.07.01 RESIDENCE SUPERVISOR (any ind.), 187.167-186

11.07.02 COMMUNITY-SERVICES-AND-HEALTH-EDUCATION OFFICER (gov. ser.), 079.167-010

11.07.02 MEDICAL-RECORD ADMINISTRATOR (medical ser.), 079.167-014

11.07.03 CONSULTANT, EDUCATION (educ.), 099.167-014

11.07.03 EDUCATIONAL RESOURCE COORDINATOR (museum), 099.167-030

11.07.03 EDUCATIONAL SPECIALIST (educ.), 099.167-022

11.07.03 TECHNICAL TRAINING COORDINATOR (educ.), 166.167-054

11.09.01 ACCOUNT EXECUTIVE (bus. ser.), 164.167-010

11.09.01 MANAGER, ADVERTISING (print. & pub.), 163.167-010

11.09.02 MEMBERSHIP DIRECTOR (profess. & kin.), 189.167-026

11.10.01 CHIEF BANK EXAMINER (gov. ser.), 160.167-046

11.10.01 REVENUE OFFICER (gov. ser.), 188.167-074

11.10.02 EQUAL-OPPORTUNITY REPRESENTATIVE (gov. ser.), 168.167-014

11.10.03 HEALTH OFFICER, FIELD (gov. ser.), 168.167-018

11.10.03 INSPECTOR, HEALTH CARE FACILITIES (gov. ser.), 168.167-042

11.10.03 OCCUPATIONAL-SAFETY-AND-HEALTH INSPECTOR (gov. ser.), 168.167-062

11.10.03 REVIEWING OFFICER, DRIVER'S LICENSE (gov. ser.), 168.167-074

11.10.03 SAFETY INSPECTOR (insurance), 168.167-078

11.10.03 SAFETY MANAGER (medical ser.), 168.167-086

11.10.04 IMMIGRATION INSPECTOR (gov. ser.), 168.167-022

11.10.05 REGULATORY ADMINISTRATOR (tel. & tel.), 168.167-070

11.10.05 TRANSPORTATION INSPECTOR (motor trans.), 168.167-082

11.11.01 CONDOMINIUM MANAGER (real estate), 186.167-062

11.11.01 EXECUTIVE HOUSEKEEPER (hotel & rest.), 187.167-046

11.11.01 MANAGER, APARTMENT HOUSE (real estate), 186.167-018

11.11.01 MANAGER, FRONT OFFICE (hotel & rest.), 187.167-110

11.11.02 DIRECTOR, CAMP (social ser.), 195.167-018

11.11.02 DIRECTOR, RECREATION CENTER (social ser.), 195.167-026

11.11.02 MANAGER, BOWLING ALLEY (amuse. & rec.), 187.167-222

11.11.02 MANAGER, GOLF CLUB (amuse. & rec.), 187.167-114

11.11.02 MANAGER, RECREATION FACILITY I (amuse. & rec.), 187.167-230

11.11.02 MANAGER, THEATER (amuse. & rec.), 187.167-154

11.11.03 CONDUCTOR, PASSENGER CAR (r.r. trans.), 198.167-010

11.11.03 CONDUCTOR, ROAD FREIGHT (r.r. trans.), 198.167-018

11.11.03 MANAGER, BUS TRANSPORTATION (motor trans.), 184.167-054

11.11.03 MANAGER, DISTRIBUTION WAREHOUSE (whole. tr.), 185.167-018

11.11.03 MANAGER, WAREHOUSE (any ind.), 184.167-114

11.11.03 OPERATIONS MANAGER (motor trans.), 184.167-118

11.11.03 PURSER (water trans.), 197.167-014

11.11.03 STATION MANAGER (r.r. trans.), 184.167-130

11.11.04 DIRECTOR, FUNERAL (per. ser.), 187.167-030

11.11.04 MANAGER, BARBER OR BEAUTY SHOP (per. ser.), 187.167-058

11.11.04 MANAGER, EMPLOYMENT AGENCY (profess. & kin.), 187.167-098

11.11.04 MANAGER, FOOD SERVICE (hotel & rest.), 187.167-106

11.11.04 MANAGER, PROPERTY (real estate), 186.167-046

11.11.04 MANAGER, REAL-ESTATE FIRM (real estate), 186.167-066

11.11.04 MANAGER, SALES (clean., dye., & press.), 187.167-138

11.11.04 MANAGER, TRAVEL AGENCY (bus. ser.), 187.167-158

11.11.05 COMMISSARY MANAGER (any ind.), 185.167-010

11.11.05 MANAGER, AUTOMOBILE SERVICE STATION (ret. tr.), 185.167-014

11.11.05 MANAGER, MACHINERY-OR-EQUIPMENT, RENTAL AND LEASING (any ind.), 185.167-026

11.11.05 MANAGER, MARKET (ret. tr.), 186.167-042

11.11.05 MANAGER, MEAT SALES AND STORAGE (ret. tr.), 185.167-030

11.11.05 MANAGER, PARTS (ret. tr.), 185.167-038

11.11.05 MANAGER, RETAIL STORE (ret. tr.), 185.167-046

11.11.05 MANAGER, VEHICLE LEASING AND RENTAL (auto. ser.), 187.167-162

11.11.05 SERVICE SUPERVISOR, LEASED MACHINERY AND EQUIPMENT (any ind.), 183.167-030

11.12.01 MANAGER, CUSTOMER SERVICE (tel. & tel.), 168.167-058

11.12.01 SERVICE REPRESENTATIVE (auto. mfg.), 191.167-022

11.12.02 LOCATION MANAGER (motion pic.), 191.167-018

11.12.03 ADVANCE AGENT (amuse. & rec.), 191.167-010

11.12.04 CONTRACTOR (const.), 182.167-010

181 Coordinating, Taking Instructions — Helping, Precision

05.01.01 LASER TECHNICIAN (electronics), 019.181-010

05.03.07 HEAT-TRANSFER TECHNICIAN (profess. & kin.), 007.181-010

187 Coordinating, Taking Instructions — Helping, Handling

05.01.03 CENTRAL-OFFICE EQUIPMENT ENGINEER (tel. & tel.), 003.187-010

05.01.03 COMMERCIAL ENGINEER (radio & tv broad.), 003.187-014

05.01.08 CUSTOMER-EQUIPMENT ENGINEER (tel. & tel.), 003.187-018

05.03.03 MATERIAL SCHEDULER (aircraft-aerospace mfg.), 012.187-010

05.03.09 PACKAGING ENGINEER (profess. & kin.), 019.187-010

11.01.01 PROGRAMER, INFORMATION SYSTEM (profess. & kin.), 020.187-010

11.01.01 PROGRAMER, PROCESS CONTROL (profess. & kin.), 020.187-014

Data = Analyzing

207 Analyzing, Mentoring, Handling

07.01.01 CREDIT COUNSELOR (profess. & kin.), 160.207-010

217 Analyzing, Negotiating, Handling

11.12.01 CLAIM ADJUSTER (bus. ser.), 241.217-010

221 Analyzing, Instructing, Precision

02.04.02 IMMUNOHEMATOLOGIST (medical ser.), 078.221-010

10.02.02 ORIENTATION THERAPIST FOR THE BLIND (educ.), 076.221-010

11.02.02 INSTRUCTOR, TECHNICAL TRAINING (educ.), 166.221-010

222 Analyzing, Instructing, Operating — Controlling

11.02.01 INSTRUCTOR, BUSINESS EDUCATION (educ.), 090.222-010

223 Analyzing, Instructing, Driving - Operating

09.03.03 INSTRUCTOR, DRIVING (educ.), 099.223-010

224 Analyzing, Instructing, Manipulating

03.03.01 ANIMAL TRAINER (amuse. & rec.), 159.224-010

10.02.02 ATHLETIC TRAINER (amuse. & rec.), 153.224-010

10.02.02 PHYSICAL THERAPIST ASSISTANT (medical ser.), 076.224-010

10.02.03 TEACHER, DEAF STUDENTS (educ.), 094.224-010

10.03.02 HOME HEALTH TECHNICIAN (medical ser.), 079.224-010

11.01.01 CUSTOMER-SUPPORT SPECIALIST (whole. tr.), 020.224-010

11.02.02 TECHNICAL SUPPORT SPECIALIST (profess. & kin.), 199.224-010

227 Analyzing, Instructiing, Handling

05.04.01 INSTRUCTOR, FLYING 2 (educ.), 097.227-010

09.01.01 RECREATION LEADER (social ser.), 195.227-014

10.02.02 PROGRAM AIDE, GROUP WORK (social ser.), 195.227-010

10.02.03 EDUCATIONAL THERAPIST (educ.), 094.227-010

10.02.03 TEACHER, BLIND (educ.), 094.227-014

10.02.03 TEACHER, HANDICAPPED STUDENTS (educ.), 094.227-018

10.02.03 TEACHER, HOME THERAPY (social ser.), 195.227-018

10.02.03 TEACHER, MENTALLY-RETARDED STUDENTS (educ.), 094.227-022

10.02.03 TEACHER, PRESCHOOL (educ.), 092.227-018

10.02.03 TEACHER, VOCATIONAL TRAINING (educ.), 094.227-026

10.03.03 CHILDREN'S TUTOR (dom. ser.), 099.227-010

11.02.01 FACULTY MEMBER, COLLEGE OR UNIVERSITY (educ.), 090.227-010

11.02.01 INSTRUCTOR, EXTENSION WORK (educ.), 090.227-018

11.02.01 TEACHER (museum), 099.227-038

11.02.01 TEACHER, ADULT EDUCATION (educ.), 099.227-030

11.02.01 TEACHER, ELEMENTARY SCHOOL (educ.), 092.227-010

11.02.01 TEACHER, RESOURCE (educ.), 099.227-042

11.02.01 TEACHER, SECONDARY SCHOOL (educ.), 091.227-010

11.02.01 TUTOR (educ.), 099.227-034

11.02.02 INSTRUCTOR, VOCATIONAL TRAINING (educ.), 097.227-014

11.02.02 TRAINING REPRESENTATIVE (educ.), 166.227-010

12.01.01 COACH, PROFESSIONAL ATHLETES (amuse. & rec.), 153.227-010

12.01.01 INSTRUCTOR, SPORTS (amuse. & rec.), 153.227-018

247 Analyzing, Diverting, Handling

01.07.01 GRAPHOLOGIST (amuse. & rec.), 159.247-018

251 Analyzing, Persuading, Precision

05.05.17 TESTER, FOOD PRODUCTS (any ind.), 199.251-010

08.01.01 SALES REPRESENTATIVE, GRAPHIC ART (bus. ser.), 254.251-010

08.02.02 SALES-SERVICE REPRESENTATIVE, MILKING MACHINES (ret. tr.), 299.251-010

253 Analyzing, Persuading, Driving — Operating

08.01.01 SALES REPRESENTATIVE, AIRCRAFT (ret. tr.), 273.253-010

257 Analyzing, Persuading, Handling

08.01.01 SALES REPRESENTATIVE, COMMUNICATION EQUIPMENT (whole. tr.), 271.257-010

08.01.01 SALES REPRESENTATIVE, COMPUTERS AND EDP SYSTEMS (whole. tr.), 275.257-010

08.01.01 SALES REPRESENTATIVE, DENTAL AND MEDICAL EQUIPMENT AND SUPPLIES (whole. tr.), 276.257-010

08.01.01 SALES REPRESENTATIVE, SIGNS AND DISPLAYS (signs), 254.257-010

08.01.02 SALES AGENT, FINANCIAL SERVICES (finan. inst.), 251.257-010

08.01.02 SALES AGENT, INSURANCE (insurance), 250.257-010

08.01.02 SALES REPRESENTATIVE, SECURITY SYSTEMS (bus. ser.), 259.257-022

08.01.02 SALES REPRESENTATIVE, TELEPHONE SERVICES (tel. & tel.), 253.257-010

08.01.02 TRAFFIC AGENT (air trans.), 252.257-010

08.01.03 SALES REPRESENTATIVE, LIVESTOCK (whole. tr.), 260.257-010

08.02.02 SALESPERSON, SURGICAL APPLIANCES (ret. tr.), 276.257-022

08.02.03 AUCTIONEER (ret. tr.), 294.257-010

11.09.03 EMPLOYER RELATIONS REPRESENTATIVE (profess. & kin.), 166.257-010

260 Analyzing, Speaking-Signaling, Setting Up

01.02.03 OPTICAL-EFFECTS-CAMERA OPERATOR (motion pic.), 143.260-010

05.05.06 ORNAMENTAL-METAL WORKER (fabric. metal prod. nec), 619.260-008

05.11.04 RIGGER (any ind.), 921.260-010

06.01.02 LOOM FIXER (asbestos prod.), 683.260-018

06.01.03 REFINERY OPERATOR (petrol. refin.), 549.260-010

06.02.02 PRESS OPERATOR, HEAVY DUTY (any ind.), 617.260-010

261 Analyzing, Speaking-Signaling, Precision

01.06.02 CONSERVATION TECHNICIAN (museum), 102.261-010

01.06.02 EXHIBIT BUILDER (museum), 739.261-010

01.06.02 MODEL MAKER 1 (any ind.), 777.261-010

02.02.02 SOIL-CONSERVATION TECHNICIAN (profess. & kin.), 040.261-010

02.04.01 CHEMICAL-LABORATORY TECHNICIAN (profess. & kin.), 022.261-010

02.04.01 LABORATORY TESTER (any ind.), 029.261-010

02.04.01 METALLURGICAL TECHNICIAN (profess. & kin.), 011.261-010

02.04.01 QUALITY-CONTROL TECHNICIAN (profess. & kin.), 012.261-014

02.04.01 TESTER (petrol. refin.), 029.261-022

02.04.02 BIOMEDICAL EQUIPMENT TECHNICIAN (profess. & kin.), 019.261-010

02.04.02 CHEMISTRY TECHNOLOGIST (medical ser.), 078.261-010

02.04.02 MICROBIOLOGY TECHNOLOGIST (drug prep. & related), 078.261-014

02.04.02 PUBLIC-HEALTH MICROBIOLOGIST (gov. ser.), 041.261-010

05.01.01 INSTRUMENTATION TECHNICIAN (profess. & kin.), 003.261-010

05.01.01 WELDING TECHNICIAN (profess. & kin.), 011.261-014

05.01.04 AIR ANALYST (profess. & kin.), 012.261-010

05.01.04 TEST-ENGINE EVALUATOR (petrol. refin.), 010.261-026

05.01.06 FACILITIES PLANNER (any ind.), 019.261-018

05.01.08 CHEMICAL-ENGINEERING TECHNICIAN (profess. & kin.), 008.261-010

05.03.02 AUTO-DESIGN CHECKER (auto. mfg.), 017.261-010

05.03.02 CIVIL ENGINEERING TECHNICIAN (profess. & kin.), 005.261-014

05.03.02 CONTROLS DESIGNER (profess. & kin.), 003.261-014

05.03.02 DESIGN DRAFTER, ELECTROMECHANISMS (profess. & kin.), 017.261-014

05.03.02 DETAILER (profess. & kin.), 017.261-018

05.03.02 DRAFTER, AERONAUTICAL (profess. & kin.), 002.261-010

05.03.02 DRAFTER, ARCHITECTURAL (profess. & kin.), 001.261-010

05.03.02 DRAFTER, CARTOGRAPHIC (profess. & kin.), 018.261-010

05.03.02 DRAFTER, COMMERCIAL (profess. & kin.), 017.261-026

05.03.02 DRAFTER, LANDSCAPE (profess. & kin.), 001.261-014

05.03.02 DRAFTER, TOPOGRAPHICAL (profess. & kin.), 018.261-014

05.03.02 EDITOR, MAP (profess. & kin.), 018.261-018

05.03.02 ESTIMATOR AND DRAFTER (light, heat, & power), 019.261-014

05.03.02 FIRE-PROTECTION ENGINEERING TECHNICIAN (profess. & kin.), 019.261-026

05.03.02 INTEGRATED CIRCUIT LAYOUT DESIGNER (profess. & kin.), 003.261-018

05.03.02 PHOTOGRAMMETRIST (profess. & kin.), 018.261-026

05.03.02 PRINTED CIRCUIT DESIGNER (profess. & kin.), 003.261-022

05.03.04 FIELD ENGINEER, SPECIALIST (petrol. production), 010.261-010

05.03.06 FLIGHT ENGINEER (air trans.), 621.261-018

05.03.07 TEST TECHNICIAN (agric. equip.), 019.261-022

05.03.08 ENGINEERING TECHNICIAN (profess. & kin.), 005.261-010

05.03.08 POLLUTION-CONTROL TECHNICIAN (profess. & kin.), 029.261-014

05.05.02 MARINE-SERVICES TECHNICIAN (ship bldg. & rep.), 806.261-026

05.05.05 ANTENNA INSTALLER, SATELLITE COMMUNICATIONS (any ind.), 823.261-022

05.05.05 AUTOMATED EQUIPMENT ENGINEER-TECHNICIAN (mach. mfg.), 638.261-010

05.05.05 ELECTRICIAN (any ind.), 824.261-010

05.05.05 ELECTRICIAN, MAINTENANCE (any ind.), 829.261-018

05.05.05 ELECTRICIAN, POWERHOUSE (light, heat, & power), 820.261-014

05.05.05 ELECTRONICS ASSEMBLER, DEVELOPMENTAL (electronics), 726.261-010

05.05.05 FIELD ENGINEER (electronics), 828.261-014

05.05.05 LINE MAINTAINER (any ind.), 821.261-014

05.05.05 STATION INSTALLER-AND-REPAIRER (tel. & tel.), 822.261-022

05.05.06 AIRCRAFT BODY REPAIRER (aircraft-aerospace mfg.), 807.261-010

05.05.06 BOILERMAKER 1 (boilermaking), 805.261-014

05.05.06 FITTER 1 (any ind.), 801.261-014

05.05.06 RIGGER (ship bldg. & rep.), 806.261-014

05.05.09 AIR-CONDITIONING INSTALLER-SERVICER, WINDOW UNIT (any ind.), 637.261-010

05.05.09 AUTOMOBILE MECHANIC (auto. ser.), 620.261-010

05.05.09 AUTOMOBILE-SERVICE-STATION MECHANIC (auto. ser.), 620.261-030

05.05.09 AUTOMOTIVE-COOLING-SYSTEM DIAGNOSTIC TECHNICIAN (auto. ser.), 620.261-034

05.05.09 CONSTRUCTION-EQUIPMENT MECHANIC (const.), 620.261-022

05.05.09 ENVIRONMENTAL-CONTROL-SYSTEM INSTALLER-SERVICER (any ind.), 637.261-014

05.05.09 FIELD SERVICE TECHNICIAN (mach. mfg.), 638.261-026

05.05.09 MACHINERY ERECTOR (engine & turbine), 638.261-014

05.05.09 MAIL-PROCESSING-EQUIPMENT MECHANIC (gov. ser.), 633.261-014

05.05.09 MAINTENANCE REPAIRER, INDUSTRIAL (any ind.), 899.261-014

05.05.09 POWERHOUSE MECHANIC (light, heat, & power), 631.261-014

05.05.09 REFRIGERATION MECHANIC (any ind.), 637.261-026

05.05.09 SOLAR-ENERGY-SYSTEM INSTALLER (any ind.), 637.261-030

05.05.10 ELECTRICAL-APPLIANCE SERVICER (any ind.), 827.261-010

05.05.10 PUBLIC-ADDRESS SERVICER (any ind.), 823.261-010

05.05.10 RADIO MECHANIC (any ind.), 823.261-018

05.05.11 ARTIFICIAL-PLASTIC-EYE MAKER (optical goods), 713.261-014

05.05.11 BIOMEDICAL EQUIPMENT TECHNICIAN (inst. & app.), 719.261-010

05.05.11 FIRE-CONTROL MECHANIC (gov. ser.), 632.261-014

05.05.11 INSTRUMENT REPAIRER (any ind.), 710.261-010

05.05.11 ORTHOTIST (per. protect. & med. device), 078.261-018

05.05.11 PROSTHETIST (per. protect. & med. device), 078.261-022

05.05.11 RADIOLOGICAL-EQUIPMENT SPECIALIST (medical ser.), 719.261-014

05.05.11 SCIENTIFIC GLASS BLOWER (glass prod.), 006.261-010

05.05.12 ELECTRONIC-ORGAN TECHNICIAN (any ind.), 828.261-010

05.05.15 ALTERATION TAILOR (garment), 785.261-010

05.05.15 CUSTOM TAILOR (garment), 785.261-014

05.05.15 FURRIER (fur goods), 783.261-010

05.07.01 NONDESTRUCTIVE TESTER (bus. ser.), 011.261-018

05.07.02 AIRPLANE INSPECTOR (air trans.), 621.261-010

05.07.03 ELEVATOR EXAMINER-AND-ADJUSTER (any ind.), 825.261-014

05.10.01 DIVER (any ind.), 899.261-010

05.10.02 GAS-APPLIANCE SERVICER (any ind.), 637.261-018

05.10.03 ELECTRIC-GOLF-CART REPAIRER (amuse. & rec.), 620.261-026

05.10.04 PINSETTER MECHANIC, AUTOMATIC (any ind.), 638.261-022

05.10.06 BLASTER (any ind.), 859.261-010

06.01.05 INSPECTOR, METAL FABRICATING (any ind.), 619.261-010

11.10.03 CHEMICAL-RADIATION TECHNICIAN (gov. ser.), 015.261-010

11.10.03 RADIATION-PROTECTION SPECIALIST (gov. ser.), 168.261-010

262 Analyzing, Speaking-Signaling, Operating — Controlling

05.01.06 TOOL PROGRAMMER, NUMERICAL CONTROL (electronics), 609.262-010

05.03.05 FIELD ENGINEER (radio & tv broad.), 193.262-018

05.03.05 RADIOTELEPHONE OPERATOR (any ind.), 193.262-034

05.03.05 TRANSMITTER OPERATOR (radio & tv broad.), 193.262-038

05.10.01 SEWER-LINE REPAIRER, TELE-GROUT (sanitary ser.), 851.262-010

05.10.03 SOUND CONTROLLER (amuse. & rec.), 194.262-014

05.10.05 AUDIO OPERATOR (radio & tv broad.), 194.262-010

05.10.05 SOUND MIXER (motion pic.), 194.262-018

06.01.05 TEST TECHNICIAN, SEMICONDUCTOR PROCESSING EQUIPMENT (electronics), 590.262-014

06.02.18 CRYSTAL GROWING TECHNICIAN (electronics), 590.262-010

07.01.06 CASEWORKER (gov. ser.), 169.262-010

07.04.02 CORRESPONDENCE CLERK (clerical), 209.262-010

07.04.04 POLICYHOLDER-INFORMATION CLERK (insurance), 249.262-010

07.04.05 AIRLINE-RADIO OPERATOR (air trans.), 193.262-010

10.03.01 PULMONARY-FUNCTION TECHNICIAN (medical ser.), 078.262-010

11.01.01 SOFTWARE TECHNICIAN (profess. & kin.), 020.262-010

263 Analyzing, Speaking-Signaling, Driving — Operating

04.01.02 POLICE OFFICER 1 (gov. ser.), 375.263-014

04.01.02 SHERIFF, DEPUTY (gov. ser.), 377.263-010

05.04.01 AIRPLANE PILOT (agric.), 196.263-010

05.04.01 AIRPLANE PILOT, COMMERCIAL (air trans.), 196.263-014

264 Analyzing, Speaking-Signaling, Manipulating

01.01.01 EDITOR, FILM (motion pic.), 962.264-010

02.04.01 HYDROGRAPHER (waterworks), 025.264-010

05.03.06 INSPECTOR, AIR-CARRIER (gov. ser.), 168.264-010

07.01.06 IDENTIFICATION OFFICER (gov. ser.), 377.264-010

10.02.01 NURSE PRACTITIONER (medical ser.), 075.264-010

10.02.01 NURSE-MIDWIFE (medical ser.), 075.264-014

10.02.02 PHYSICAL-INTEGRATION PRACTITIONER (per. ser.), 076.264-010

10.03.01 HOLTER SCANNING TECHNICIAN (medical ser.), 078.264-010

11.10.03 SAFETY INSPECTOR (any ind.), 168.264-014

267 Analyzing, Speaking-Signaling, Handling

01.03.02 INTERPRETER, DEAF (profess. & kin.), 137.267-014

01.04.02 COPYIST (any ind.), 152.267-010

02.04.01 BALLISTICS EXPERT, FORENSIC (gov. ser.), 199.267-010

02.04.01 GEOLOGICAL AIDE (petrol. production), 024.267-010

02.04.01 WEATHER OBSERVER (profess. & kin.), 025.267-014

02.04.02 POLYGRAPH EXAMINER (profess. & kin.), 199.267-026

03.01.04 LOGGING-OPERATIONS INSPECTOR (forestry), 168.267-070

04.01.02 POLICE OFFICER III (gov. ser.), 375.267-038

05.03.02 DRAWINGS CHECKER, ENGINEERING (profess. & kin.), 007.267-010

05.03.02 ESTIMATOR (profess. & kin.), 160.267-018

05.03.02 SPECIFICATION WRITER (profess. & kin.), 019.267-010

05.03.06 BUILDING INSPECTOR (insurance), 168.267-010

05.03.06 CONSTRUCTION INSPECTOR (const.), 182.267-010

05.03.06 INDUSTRIAL ENGINEERING TECHNICIAN (profess. & kin.), 012.267-010

05.03.06 INSPECTOR, INDUSTRIAL WASTE (gov. ser.), 168.267-054

05.03.06 PLAN CHECKER (gov. ser.), 168.267-102

05.05.17 ANALYST, FOOD AND BEVERAGE (hotel & rest.), 310.267-010

05.07.01 SHOP ESTIMATOR (auto. ser.), 807.267-010

07.01.01 ELIGIBILITY WORKER (gov. ser.), 195.267-010

07.01.01 ELIGIBILITY-AND-OCCUPANCY INTERVIEWER (gov. ser.), 168.267-038

07.01.01 FINANCIAL-AID COUNSELOR (educ.), 169.267-018

07.01.01 LOAN COUNSELOR (finan. inst.), 186.267-014

07.01.01 RETIREMENT OFFICER (gov. ser.), 166.267-030

07.01.05 CONTRACT CLERK (profess. & kin.), 119.267-018

07.01.05 EXAMINER (gov. ser.), 169.267-014

07.01.05 HOSPITAL-INSURANCE REPRESENTATIVE (insurance), 166.267-014

07.01.05 PASSPORT-APPLICATION EXAMINER (gov. ser.), 169.267-030

07.01.05 TITLE CLERK (petrol. production), 162.267-010

07.01.07 DRIVER'S LICENSE EXAMINER (gov. ser.), 168.267-034

07.01.07 EXAMINATION PROCTOR (gov. ser.), 199.267-018

07.02.03 CLAIM EXAMINER (insurance), 168.267-014

07.04.01 BONDING AGENT (bus. ser.), 186.267-010
07.05.02 INVESTIGATOR, UTILITY-BILL COMPLAINTS
(light, heat, & power), 241.267-034
10.02.03 EVALUATOR (educ.), 094.267-010
11.01.01 FORMS ANALYST (profess. & kin.), 161.267-018
11.02.02 HUMAN RESOURCE ADVISOR (profess. & kin.),
166.267-046
11.03.03 RESEARCH ASSISTANT (profess. & kin.), 109.267-010
11.03.04 EMPLOYEE RELATIONS SPECIALIST (motor trans.),
166.267-042
11.03.04 EMPLOYMENT INTERVIEWER (profess. & kin.),
166.267-010
11.03.04 JOB ANALYST (profess. & kin.), 166.267-018
11.03.04 JOB DEVELOPMENT SPECIALIST (profess. & kin.),
166.267-034
11.03.04 PERSONNEL RECRUITER (profess. & kin.),
166.267-038
11.03.04 RECRUITER (military ser.), 166.267-026
11.04.01 APPEALS REFEREE (gov. ser.), 119.267-014
11.04.02 LEGAL INVESTIGATOR (profess. & kin.), 119.267-022
11.04.02 PARALEGAL ASSISTANT (profess. & kin.), 119.267-026
11.04.04 ABSTRACTOR (profess. & kin.), 119.267-010
11.05.02 RESEARCH ANALYST (insurance), 169.267-034
11.05.04 FIELD REPRESENTATIVE (bus. ser.), 163.267-010
11.06.02 REPORTS ANALYST (profess. & kin.), 161.267-026
11.06.03 APPRAISER, REAL ESTATE (real estate), 191.267-010
11.06.03 CREDIT ANALYST (finan. inst.), 191.267-014
11.06.03 DIRECTOR, UTILITY ACCOUNTS (gov. ser.),
160.267-014
11.06.03 INVESTIGATOR (clerical), 241.267-030
11.06.03 LOAN OFFICER (finan. inst.), 186.267-018
11.06.05 BUDGET ANALYST (gov. ser.), 161.267-030
11.07.01 FIELD REPRESENTATIVE (profess. & kin.),
189.267-010
11.08.01 EDITORIAL ASSISTANT (print. & pub.), 132.267-014
11.08.02 REPORTER (print. & pub.), 131.267-018
11.08.02 RESEARCH ASSISTANT II (profess. & kin.),
199.267-034
11.08.02 WRITER, TECHNICAL PUBLICATIONS (profess. &
kin.), 131.267-026
11.08.03 NEWSCASTER (radio & tv broad.), 131.267-010
11.08.04 INTERPRETER (profess. & kin.), 137.267-010
11.08.04 TRANSLATOR (profess. & kin.), 137.267-018
11.10.01 INSPECTOR, GOVERNMENT PROPERTY (gov. ser.),
168.267-050
11.10.01 INVESTIGATOR (gov. ser.), 168.267-062
11.10.01 INVESTIGATOR, FRAUD (ret. tr.), 376.267-014
11.10.02 EQUAL OPPORTUNITY OFFICER (any ind.),
168.267-114
11.10.03 FOOD AND DRUG INSPECTOR (gov. ser.), 168.267-042
11.10.03 HAZARDOUS-WASTE MANAGEMENT SPECIALIST
(gov. ser.), 168.267-086
11.10.03 INSPECTOR, MOTOR VEHICLES (gov. ser.),
168.267-058
11.10.03 INSPECTOR, WATER-POLLUTION CONTROL (gov.
ser.), 168.267-090
11.10.03 MARINE-CARGO SURVEYOR (bus. ser.), 168.267-094
11.10.03 MINE INSPECTOR (mining), 168.267-074
11.10.03 PESTICIDE-CONTROL INSPECTOR (gov. ser.),
168.267-098
11.10.03 SANITATION INSPECTOR (gov. ser.), 168.267-110
11.10.04 CUSTOMS IMPORT SPECIALIST (gov. ser.),
168.267-018
11.10.04 CUSTOMS INSPECTOR (gov. ser.), 168.267-022
11.10.05 DEALER-COMPLIANCE REPRESENTATIVE (ret. tr.),
168.267-026
11.12.01 APPRAISER, AUTOMOBILE DAMAGE (bus. ser.),
241.267-014
11.12.01 CLAIM EXAMINER (bus. ser.), 241.267-018
11.12.01 CLAIMS ADJUDICATOR (gov. ser.), 169.267-010
12.01.02 HORSE-RACE STARTER (amuse. & rec.), 153.267-010
12.01.02 UMPIRE (amuse. & rec.), 153.267-018

271 Analyzing, Serving, Precision

02.03.04 ACUPUNCTURIST (medical ser.), 079.271-010

09.02.01 COSMETOLOGIST (per. ser.), 332.271-010
09.02.01 HAIR STYLIST (per. ser.), 332.271-018
10.02.02 ACUPRESSURIST (medical ser.), 079.271-014

280 Analyzing, Taking Instructions — Helping, Setting Up

02.04.01 PHOTO-OPTICS TECHNICIAN (profess. & kin.),
029.280-010
05.01.04 RESEARCH MECHANIC (aircraft-aerospace mfg.),
002.280-010
05.05.07 DIE SINKER (mach. shop), 601.280-022
05.05.07 MACHINIST (mach. shop), 600.280-022
05.05.07 MAINTENANCE MACHINIST (any ind.), 600.280-042
05.05.07 PATTERNMAKER, METAL (foundry), 600.280-050
05.05.07 TOOL-AND-DIE MAKER (mach. shop), 601.280-046
05.05.07 TOOL-MACHINE SET-UP OPERATOR (mach. shop),
601.280-054
05.05.08 CABINETMAKER (woodworking), 660.280-010
05.05.10 INSTRUMENT-MAKER AND REPAIRER (petrol.
production), 600.280-014
05.05.11 INSTRUMENT MAKER (any ind.), 600.280-010
05.05.11 OPTICIAN (optical goods), 716.280-008
05.05.11 OPTICIAN (optical goods), 716.280-014
06.01.02 KNITTING-MACHINE FIXER (hosiery), 689.280-014

281 Analyzing, Taking Instructions — Helping, Precision

01.06.01 ENGRAVER, PICTURE (print. & pub.), 979.281-018
01.06.02 CLAY MODELER (any ind.), 779.281-010
01.06.02 JEWELER (jewelry), 700.281-010
01.06.02 PROP MAKER (amuse. & rec.), 962.281-010
01.06.02 SILVERSMITH (silverware), 700.281-022
01.06.02 STONE CARVER (stonework), 771.281-014
01.06.03 SIGN WRITER, HAND (any ind.), 970.281-022
02.04.01 ASSAYER (profess. & kin.), 022.281-010
02.04.01 CALIBRATION LABORATORY TECHNICIAN
(aircraft-aerospace mfg.), 019.281-010
02.04.01 CRIMINALIST (profess. & kin.), 029.281 010
02.04.01 LABORATORY ASSISTANT, METALLURGICAL (iron
& steel), 011.281-010
02.04.01 LABORATORY TESTER (synthetic fibers), 022.281-018
02.04.01 SPECTROSCOPIST (profess. & kin.), 011.281-014
02.04.02 CYTOTECHNOLOGIST (medical ser.), 078.281-010
05.03.02 DRAFTER, ASSISTANT (profess. & kin.), 017.281-018
05.03.02 DRAFTER, AUTOMOTIVE DESIGN (auto. mfg.),
017.281-022
05.03.02 DRAFTER, CIVIL (profess. & kin.), 005.281-010
05.03.02 DRAFTER, ELECTRICAL (profess. & kin.),
003.281-010
05.03.02 DRAFTER, ELECTRONIC (profess. & kin.),
003.281-014
05.03.02 DRAFTER, GEOLOGICAL (petrol. production),
010.281-014
05.03.02 DRAFTER, GEOPHYSICAL (petrol. production),
010.281-018
05.03.02 DRAFTER, MARINE (profess. & kin.), 014.281-010
05.03.02 DRAFTER, MECHANICAL (profess. & kin.),
007.281-010
05.03.02 DRAFTER, STRUCTURAL (profess. & kin.),
005.281-014
05.03.02 TECHNICAL ILLUSTRATOR (profess. & kin.),
017.281-034
05.05.02 CARPENTER, MAINTENANCE (any ind.), 860.281-010
05.05.03 OIL-BURNER-SERVICER-AND-INSTALLER (any
ind.), 862.281-018
05.05.03 PIPE FITTER (any ind.), 862.281-022
05.05.05 AUTOMATIC-EQUIPMENT TECHNICIAN (tel. &
tel.), 822.281-010
05.05.05 CENTRAL-OFFICE REPAIRER (tel. & tel.),
822.281-014
05.05.05 ELEVATOR REPAIRER (any ind.), 825.281-030
05.05.05 MAINTENANCE MECHANIC, TELEPHONE (any
ind.), 822.281-018

05.05.05 PRIVATE-BRANCH-EXCHANGE REPAIRER (tel. & tel.), 822.281-022
05.05.06 MILLWRIGHT (any ind.), 638.281-018
05.05.06 SHEET-METAL WORKER (any ind.), 804.281-010
05.05.06 WELDER, EXPERIMENTAL (welding), 819.281-022
05.05.07 GUNSMITH (any ind.), 632.281-010
05.05.08 LOFT WORKER (ship bldg. & rep.), 661.281-010
05.05.09 AIR-CONDITIONING MECHANIC (auto. ser.), 620.281-010
05.05.09 AIRFRAME-AND-POWER-PLANT MECHANIC (aircraft-aerospace mfg.), 621.281-014
05.05.09 AUTOMOTIVE-MAINTENANCE-EQUIPMENT SERVICER (any ind.), 620.281-018
05.05.09 CASH-REGISTER SERVICER (any ind.), 633.281-010
05.05.09 DIESEL MECHANIC (any ind.), 625.281-010
05.05.09 EXPERIMENTAL MECHANIC 2 (aircraft-aerospace mfg.), 621.281-022
05.05.09 FARM-EQUIPMENT MECHANIC 1 (agric. equip.), 624.281-010
05.05.09 FUEL-INJECTION SERVICER (any ind.), 625.281-022
05.05.09 FURNACE INSTALLER-AND-REPAIRER, HOT AIR (any ind.), 869.281-010
05.05.09 GAS-ENGINE REPAIRER (any ind.), 625.281-026
05.05.09 LOCKSMITH (any ind.), 709.281-010
05.05.09 MACHINE BUILDER (mach. mfg.), 600.281-022
05.05.09 MAINTENANCE MECHANIC (any ind.), 638.281-014
05.05.09 MECHANIC, INDUSTRIAL TRUCK (any ind.), 620.281-050
05.05.09 OFFICE-MACHINE SERVICER (any ind.), 633.281-018
05.05.09 PARTS SALVAGER (any ind.), 638.281-026
05.05.09 PNEUMATIC-TOOL REPAIRER (any ind.), 630.281-010
05.05.09 POWER-SAW MECHANIC (any ind.), 625.281-030
05.05.09 PUMP SERVICER (any ind.), 630.281-018
05.05.09 ROCKET-ENGINE-COMPONENT MECHANIC (aircraft-aerospace mfg.), 621.281-030
05.05.09 SMALL-ENGINE MECHANIC (any ind.), 625.281-034
05.05.09 TRACTOR MECHANIC (auto. ser.), 620.281-058
05.05.09 TUNE-UP MECHANIC (auto. ser.), 620.281-066
05.05.10 AUDIO-VIDEO REPAIRER (any ind.), 729.281-010
05.05.10 AVIONICS TECHNICIAN (aircraft-aerospace mfg.), 823.281-010
05.05.10 ELECTRIC-METER REPAIRER (light, heat, & power), 729.281-014
05.05.10 ELECTRIC-MOTOR REPAIRER (any ind.), 721.281-018
05.05.10 ELECTRICAL-INSTRUMENT REPAIRER (any ind.), 729.281-026
05.05.10 ELECTRICIAN, AUTOMOTIVE (auto. ser.), 825.281-022
05.05.10 ELECTRONICS MECHANIC (any ind.), 828.281-010
05.05.10 INSTRUMENT MECHANIC (any ind.), 710.281-026
05.05.10 METEOROLOGICAL-EQUIPMENT REPAIRER (any ind.), 823.281-018
05.05.11 CAMERA REPAIRER (photo. apparatus), 714.281-014
05.05.11 DENTAL CERAMIST (medical ser.), 712.281-010
05.05.11 ELECTROMECHANICAL TECHNICIAN (inst. & app.), 710.281-018

05.05.11 ELECTROMEDICAL-EQUIPMENT REPAIRER (any ind.), 729.281-030
05.05.12 ACCORDION REPAIRER (any ind.), 730.281-014
05.05.12 ELECTRIC-ORGAN INSPECTOR AND REPAIRER (musical inst.), 730.281-018
05.05.12 FRETTED-INSTRUMENT MAKER, HAND (musical inst.), 730.281-022
05.05.12 FRETTED-INSTRUMENT REPAIRER (any ind.), 730.281-026
05.05.12 PIANO TECHNICIAN (any ind.), 730.281-038
05.05.12 VIOLIN MAKER, HAND (musical inst.), 730.281-046
05.05.12 WIND-INSTRUMENT REPAIRER (any ind.), 730.281-054
05.05.17 CHEF DE FROID (hotel & rest.), 313.281-010
05.07.01 ULTRASONIC TESTER (bus. ser.), 709.281-018
05.10.01 CASTING REPAIRER (any ind.), 619.281-010
05.10.01 FRONT-END MECHANIC (auto. ser.), 620.281-038
05.10.02 BRAKE REPAIRER (auto. ser.), 620.281-026
05.10.02 CARBURETOR MECHANIC (auto. ser.), 620.281-034
05.10.02 COIN-MACHINE-SERVICE REPAIRER (coin mach.), 639.281-014
05.10.02 MEDICAL-EQUIPMENT REPAIRER (per. protect. & med. device), 639.281-022
05.10.02 METER REPAIRER (any ind.), 710.281-034
05.10.02 PNEUMATIC-TUBE REPAIRER (any ind.), 630.281-014
05.10.02 SEWING-MACHINE REPAIRER (any ind.), 639.281-018
05.10.03 AUTOMATIC-DOOR MECHANIC (const.), 829.281-010
05.10.03 ELECTRIC-TOOL REPAIRER (any ind.), 729.281-022
05.10.03 TAPE-RECORDER REPAIRER (any ind.), 720.281-014
05.10.03 TELEVISION-AND-RADIO REPAIRER (any ind.), 720.281-018
05.10.03 TELEVISION-CABLE INSTALLER (any ind.), 821.281-010
05.10.08 COOK (dom. ser.), 305.281-010
06.01.05 ELECTRONICS TESTER I (electronics), 726.281-014
06.01.05 INSPECTOR, ASSEMBLIES AND INSTALLATIONS (aircraft-aerospace mfg.), 806.281-022
06.01.05 X-RAY-EQUIPMENT TESTER (any ind.), 729.281-046
06.02.32 WIRER (office mach.), 729.281-042
06.03.01 TEST DRIVER 1 (auto. mfg.), 806.281-050

282 Analyzing, Taking Instructions — Helping, Operating — Controlling

05.03.05 VIDEO OPERATOR (radio & tv broad.), 194.282-010

287 Analyzing, Taking Instructions — Helping, Handling

01.02.01 APPRAISER, ART (profess. & kin.), 191.287-014
05.03.06 INSPECTOR, QUALITY ASSURANCE (gov. ser.), 168.287-014
05.03.06 INSPECTOR, RAILROAD (gov. ser.), 168.287-018
07.01.05 TITLE EXAMINER (profess. & kin.), 119.287-010
11.06.03 APPRAISER (any ind.), 191.287-010
11.10.03 INSPECTOR, AGRICULTURAL COMMODITIES (gov. ser.), 168.287-010

Data = Compiling

327 Compiling, Instructing, Handling
11.02.01 TEACHER AIDE I (educ.), 099.327-010

341 Compiling, Diverting, Precision
12.02.01 JUGGLER (amuse. & rec.), 159.341-010
12.02.01 STUNT PERFORMER (amuse. & rec.), 159.341-014

347 Compiling, Diverting, Handling
01.07.02 ANNOUNCER (amuse. & rec.), 159.347-010
12.02.01 AQUATIC PERFORMER (amuse. & rec.), 159.347-014

353 Compiling, Persuading, Driving — Operating
08.02.02 SALESPERSON, AUTOMOBILES (ret. tr.), 273.353-010
08.02.07 DRIVER, SALES ROUTE (ret. tr.), 292.353-010

354 Compiling, Persuading, Manipulating
08.02.02 SALESPERSON, HEARING AIDS (ret. tr.), 276.354-010
08.02.02 SALESPERSON, PIANOS AND ORGANS (ret. tr.), 277.354-010
08.02.05 DEMONSTRATOR (ret. tr.), 297.354-010
08.02.05 DEMONSTRATOR, KNITTING (ret. tr.), 297.354-014

10.03.02 PHYSICAL THERAPY AIDE (medical ser.), 355.354-010

11.02.03 HOMEMAKER (social ser.), 309.354-010

357   Compiling, Persuading, Handling

07.04.02 COLLECTION CLERK (clerical), 241.357-010

08.01.01 SALES REPRESENTATIVE, CHEMICALS AND DRUGS (whole. tr.), 262.357-010

08.01.01 SALES REPRESENTATIVE, ELECTRONICS PARTS (whole. tr.), 271.357-010

08.01.02 SALES REPRESENTATIVE, ADVERTISING (print. & pub.), 254.357-014

08.01.02 SALES REPRESENTATIVE, PRINTING (whole. tr.), 254.357-018

08.01.02 SALES REPRESENTATIVE, PUBLIC UTILITIES (light, heat, & power), 253.357-010

08.01.02 SALES REPRESENTATIVE, RADIO AND TELEVISION TIME (radio & tv broad.), 259.357-018

08.01.03 COMMISSION AGENT, AGRICULTURAL PRODUCE (whole. tr.), 260.357-010

08.02.01 SALES REPRESENTATIVE, ANIMAL-FEED PRODUCTS (whole. tr.), 272.357-010

08.02.01 SALES REPRESENTATIVE, CANVAS PRODUCTS (whole. tr.), 261.357-014

08.02.01 SALES REPRESENTATIVE, FARM AND GARDEN EQUIPMENT AND SUPPLIES (whole. tr.), 272.357-014

08.02.01 SALES REPRESENTATIVE, HOME FURNISHINGS (whole. tr.), 270.357-010

08.02.01 SALES REPRESENTATIVE, HOUSEHOLD APPLIANCES (whole. tr.), 270.357-014

08.02.01 SALES REPRESENTATIVE, MALT LIQUORS (whole. tr.), 260.357-018

08.02.01 SALES REPRESENTATIVE, MEN'S AND BOYS' APPAREL (whole. tr.), 261.357-022

08.02.01 SALES REPRESENTATIVE, NOVELTIES (whole. tr.), 277.357-018

08.02.01 SALES REPRESENTATIVE, PETROLEUM PRODUCTS (whole. tr.), 269.357-014

08.02.01 SALES REPRESENTATIVE, RECREATION AND SPORTING GOODS (whole. tr.), 277.357-026

08.02.01 SALES REPRESENTATIVE, TEXTILES (whole. tr.), 261.357-030

08.02.01 SALES REPRESENTATIVE, VIDEOTAPE (whole. tr.), 271.357-014

08.02.01 SALES REPRESENTATIVE, WOMEN'S AND GIRLS' APPAREL (whole. tr.), 261.357-038

08.02.01 SALES-PROMOTION REPRESENTATIVE (whole. tr.), 269.357-018

08.02.02 SALES EXHIBITOR (nonprofit org.), 279.357-010

08.02.02 SALESPERSON, BOOKS (ret. tr.), 277.357-034

08.02.02 SALESPERSON, COSMETICS AND TOILETRIES (ret. tr.), 262.357-018

08.02.02 SALESPERSON, CURTAINS AND DRAPERIES (ret. tr.), 270.357-022

08.02.02 SALESPERSON, FLOWERS (ret. tr.), 260.357-026

08.02.02 SALESPERSON, FURNITURE (ret. tr.), 270.357-030

08.02.02 SALESPERSON, HOUSEHOLD APPLIANCES (ret. tr.), 270.357-034

08.02.02 SALESPERSON, INFANTS' AND CHILDREN'S WEAR (ret. tr.), 261.357-046

08.02.02 SALESPERSON, JEWELRY (ret. tr.), 279.357-058

08.02.02 SALESPERSON, MEN'S AND BOYS' CLOTHING (ret. tr.), 261.357-050

08.02.02 SALESPERSON, MUSICAL INSTRUMENTS AND ACCESSORIES (ret. tr.), 277.357-038

08.02.02 SALESPERSON, PHONOGRAPH RECORDS AND TAPE RECORDINGS (ret. tr.), 277.357-046

08.02.02 SALESPERSON, SHOES (ret. tr.), 261.357-062

08.02.02 SALESPERSON, SPORTING GOODS (ret. tr.), 277.357-058

08.02.02 SALESPERSON, STEREO EQUIPMENT (ret. tr.), 270.357-038

08.02.02 SALESPERSON, WOMEN'S APPAREL AND ACCESSORIES (ret. tr.), 261.357-066

08.02.02 SALESPERSON, YARD GOODS (ret. tr.), 261.357-070

08.02.03 SALES REPRESENTATIVE, BOATS AND MARINE SUPPLIES (ret. tr.), 273.357-018

08.02.03 SALES REPRESENTATIVE, OFFICE MACHINES (ret. tr.), 275.357-034

08.02.03 SALES REPRESENTATIVE, TOBACCO PRODUCTS AND SMOKING SUPPLIES (ret. tr.), 260.357-022

08.02.03 SALESPERSON, AUTOMOBILE ACCESSORIES (ret. tr.), 273.357-030

08.02.03 SALESPERSON, FLOOR COVERINGS (ret. tr.), 270.357-026

08.02.03 SALESPERSON, GENERAL HARDWARE (ret. tr.), 279.357-050

08.02.03 SALESPERSON, GENERAL MERCHANDISE (ret. tr.), 279.357-054

08.02.03 SALESPERSON, HORTICULTURAL AND NURSERY PRODUCTS (ret. tr.), 272.357-022

08.02.03 SALESPERSON, PARTS (ret. tr.), 279.357-062

08.02.03 SALESPERSON, PHOTOGRAPHIC SUPPLIES AND EQUIPMENT (ret. tr.), 277.357-050

08.02.04 LEASING AGENT, RESIDENCE (real estate), 250.357-014

08.02.04 SALES AGENT, REAL ESTATE (real estate), 250.357-018

08.02.05 DEMONSTRATOR, ELECTRIC-GAS APPLIANCES (light, heat, & power), 297.357-010

08.02.05 SALESPERSON-DEMONSTRATOR, PARTY PLAN (ret. tr.), 279.357-038

08.02.06 SALES AGENT, BUSINESS SERVICES (bus. ser.), 251.357-010

08.02.06 SALES REPRESENTATIVE, AUTOMOTIVE-LEASING (bus. ser.), 273.357-014

08.02.06 SALES REPRESENTATIVE, FRANCHISE (bus. ser.), 251.357-022

08.02.06 SALES REPRESENTATIVE, UPHOLSTERY AND FURNITURE REPAIR (ret. tr.), 259.357-026

08.02.06 WEDDING CONSULTANT (ret. tr.), 299.357-018

08.02.08 FUND RAISER 2 (nonprofit org.), 293.357-014

08.02.08 MEMBERSHIP SOLICITOR (any ind.), 293.357-022

08.02.08 SALES REPRESENTATIVE, DOOR-TO-DOOR (ret. tr.), 291.357-010

08.02.08 TELEPHONE SOLICITOR (any ind.), 299.357-014

09.04.02 FURNITURE-RENTAL CONSULTANT (ret. tr.), 295.357-018

09.04.02 PERSONAL SHOPPER (ret. tr.), 296.357-010

09.04.02 TOOL-AND-EQUIPMENT-RENTAL CLERK (bus. ser.), 295.357-014

09.05.02 WINE STEWARD/STEWARDESS (hotel & rest.), 310.357-010

360   Compiling, Speaking-Signaling, Setting Up

05.05.06 METAL FABRICATOR (any ind.), 619.360-014

06.01.02 FIRESETTER (elec. equip.), 692.360-018

06.01.02 KNITTER MECHANIC (knit goods), 685.360-010

06.01.02 MACHINE SETTER (any ind.), 616.360-022

06.01.02 PRINT CONTROLLER (photofinish.), 976.360-010

06.01.02 SETTER, AUTOMATIC-SPINNING LATHE (any ind.), 604.360-010

06.01.03 MACHINE OPERATOR 1 (any ind.), 616.360-018

361   Compiling, Speaking-Signaling, Precision

01.06.02 DISPLAY MAKER (signs), 739.361-010

01.06.02 MORTUARY BEAUTICIAN (per. ser.), 339.361-010

01.06.02 RESTORER, CERAMIC (museum), 102.361-014

01.06.02 WIG DRESSER (hairwork), 332.361-010

02.03.03 ANIMAL HEALTH TECHNICIAN (medical ser.), 079.361-014

02.03.04 RADIATION-THERAPY TECHNOLOGIST (medical ser.), 078.361-034

02.04.01 LABORATORY ASSISTANT (light, heat, & power), 029.361-018

02.04.01 TESTER (profess. & kin.), 011.361-010

02.04.02 FOOD TESTER (any ind.), 029.361-014
02.04.02 LABORATORY TECHNICIAN, VETERINARY
(medical ser.), 073.361-010
02.04.02 MEDICAL TECHNOLOGIST (medical ser.),
078.361-014
02.04.02 TISSUE TECHNOLOGIST (medical ser.), 078.361-030
05.03.05 RADIOGRAPHER (any ind.), 199.361-010
05.05.02 BOAT REPAIRER (ship bldg. & rep.), 807.361-014
05.05.04 PLASTERER (const.), 842.361-018
05.05.05 CABLE INSTALLER-REPAIRER (light, heat, &
power), 821.361-010
05.05.05 CABLE SPLICER (const.), 829.361-010
05.05.05 CABLE TESTER (tel. & tel.), 822.361-010
05.05.05 ELECTRIC-METER INSTALLER 1 (light, heat, &
power), 821.361-014
05.05.05 FURNACE INSTALLER (light, heat, & power),
862.361-010
05.05.05 LINE ERECTOR (const.), 821.361-018
05.05.05 LINE REPAIRER (light, heat, & power), 821.361-026
05.05.05 PROTECTIVE-SIGNAL INSTALLER (bus. ser.),
822.361-018
05.05.05 PROTECTIVE-SIGNAL REPAIRER (bus. ser.),
822.361-022
05.05.05 TOWER ERECTOR (const.), 821.361-038
05.05.06 BOILERHOUSE MECHANIC (any ind.), 805.361-010
05.05.06 CONDUIT MECHANIC (const.), 869.361-010
05.05.06 ELEVATOR CONSTRUCTOR (const.), 825.361-010
05.05.06 FORMER, HAND (any ind.), 619.361-010
05.05.06 STRUCTURAL-STEEL WORKER (const.), 801.361-014
05.05.06 WELDER-FITTER (welding), 819.361-010
05.05.09 REFRIGERATION MECHANIC (refrig. equip.),
827.361-014
05.05.11 OPTICIAN, DISPENSING 1 (ret. tr.), 713.361-014
05.05.11 ORTHOTICS ASSISTANT (per. protect. & med. device),
078.361-022
05.05.11 PROSTHETICS ASSISTANT (per. protect. & med.
device), 078.361-026
05.05.12 PIANO TUNER (any ind.), 730.361-010
05.05.12 PIPE-ORGAN TUNER AND REPAIRER (any ind.),
730.361-014
05.05.15 DRESSMAKER (any ind.), 785.361-010
05.05.15 SHOE REPAIRER (per. ser.), 365.361-014
05.05.15 SHOP TAILOR (garment), 785.361-022
05.05.17 COOK (hotel & rest.), 313.361-014
05.10.01 LATHER (const.), 842.361-010
05.10.01 LUGGAGE REPAIRER (any ind.), 365.361-010
05.10.02 NEW-CAR GET-READY MECHANIC (auto. ser.),
806.361-026
05.10.03 TELEVISION INSTALLER (any ind.), 823.361-010
05.10.05 REPRODUCTION TECHNICIAN (any ind.),
976.361-010
05.10.08 COOK (any ind.), 315.361-010
05.10.08 COOK, SHORT ORDER 1 (hotel & rest.), 313.361-022
05.10.08 COOK, SPECIALTY (hotel & rest.), 313.361-026
05.10.08 GARDE MANGER (hotel & rest.), 313.361-034
05.10.08 PIE MAKER (hotel & rest.), 313.361-038
05.10.09 FUMIGATOR (bus. ser.), 383.361-010
06.01.04 CHEESEMAKER (dairy prod.), 529.361-018
06.01.04 MOLDER (foundry), 518.361-010
06.01.05 RETICLE INSPECTOR (electronics), 719.361-010
06.02.22 MACHINE ASSEMBLER (mach. mfg.), 638.361-010
06.02.28 CANDY MAKER (confection.), 529.361-014
10.02.02 CORRECTIVE THERAPIST (medical ser.), 076.361-010
10.02.02 DENTAL HYGIENIST (medical ser.), 078.361-010
10.02.02 NUCLEAR MEDICAL TECHNOLOGIST (medical
ser.), 078.361-018
10.02.02 RESPIRATORY THERAPIST (medical ser.),
079.361-010

362 Compiling, Speaking-Signaling, Operating — Controlling

02.04.01 HOT-CELL TECHNICIAN (profess. & kin.),
015.362-018
02.04.01 RADIOISOTOPE-PRODUCTION OPERATOR (profess.
& kin.), 015.362-022

02.04.01 REACTOR OPERATOR, TEST-AND-RESEARCH
(profess. & kin.), 015.362-026
05.03.02 DESIGN TECHNICIAN, COMPUTER-AIDED
(electronics), 003.362-010
05.05.13 CYLINDER-PRESS OPERATOR (print. & pub.),
651.362-010
05.05.13 ROTOGRAVURE-PRESS OPERATOR (print. & pub.),
651.362-026
05.05.13 WEB-PRESS OPERATOR (print. & pub.), 651.362-030
05.06.01 HYDROELECTRIC-STATION OPERATOR (light, heat,
& power), 952.362-018
05.06.01 POWER-REACTOR OPERATOR (light, heat, & power),
952.362-022
05.06.01 SUBSTATION OPERATOR (light, heat, & power),
952.362-026
05.06.01 TURBINE OPERATOR (light, heat, & power),
952.362-042
05.06.02 FUEL ATTENDANT (any ind.), 953.362-010
05.06.02 REFRIGERATING ENGINEER (any ind.), 950.362-014
05.07.01 SEWER-LINE PHOTO-INSPECTOR (sanitary ser.),
851.362-010
05.10.03 LIGHT TECHNICIAN (motion pic.), 962.362-014
05.10.05 MOTION-PICTURE PROJECTIONIST (amuse. & rec.),
960.362-010
05.10.05 RECORDING ENGINEER (phonograph), 194.362-010
05.10.05 RERECORDING MIXER (motion pic.), 194.362-014
06.01.03 LATHE OPERATOR, NUMERICAL CONTROL (mach.
shop), 604.362-010
06.01.03 MICROELECTRONICS TECHNICIAN (electronics),
590.362-022
06.02.02 SPINNER, HAND (any ind.), 619.362-018
06.02.02 SPINNER, HYDRAULIC (any ind.), 619.362-022
06.02.10 PICKLER, CONTINUOUS PICKLING LINE (any
ind.), 503.362-010
06.02.15 BUTTERMAKER (dairy prod.), 529.362-010
06.02.15 DRIER OPERATOR (macaroni & related), 523.362-014
07.01.02 ADMINISTRATIVE CLERK (clerical), 219.362-010
07.01.02 COURT CLERK (gov. ser.), 243.362-010
07.01.02 MEMBERSHIP SECRETARY (nonprofit org.),
201.362-018
07.01.03 LEGAL SECRETARY (clerical), 201.362-010
07.01.03 MEDICAL SECRETARY (medical ser.), 201.362-014
07.01.03 SECRETARY (clerical), 201.362-030
07.01.04 REAL-ESTATE CLERK (clerical), 219.362-046
07.02.01 RESERVES CLERK (finan. inst.), 216.362-034
07.02.02 COLLECTION CLERK (finan. inst.), 216.362-014
07.02.02 CONTRACT CLERK, AUTOMOBILE (ret. tr.),
219.362-026
07.02.02 FEE CLERK (finan. inst.), 214.362-018
07.02.02 POLICY-CHANGE CLERK (insurance), 219.362-042
07.02.02 PROBATE CLERK (finan. inst.), 216.362-030
07.02.02 STATEMENT CLERK (finan. inst.), 219.362-058
07.02.02 TAX PREPARER (bus. ser.), 219.362-070
07.02.02 TELLER, COLLECTION AND EXCHANGE (finan.
inst.), 211.362-022
07.02.02 TRUST-SECURITIES CLERK (finan. inst.),
219.362-062
07.02.04 BILLING CLERK (clerical), 214.362-042
07.02.04 DEMURRAGE CLERK (r.r. trans.), 214.362-010
07.02.04 INSURANCE CLERK (medical ser.), 214.362-022
07.02.04 INVOICE-CONTROL CLERK (clerical), 214.362-026
07.03.01 CASHIER 1 (clerical), 211.362-010
07.03.01 TELLER (finan. inst.), 211.362-018
07.03.01 TELLER, NOTE (finan. inst.), 211.362-026
07.04.01 EMPLOYMENT CLERK (clerical), 205.362-014
07.04.01 HOSPITAL-ADMITTING CLERK (medical ser.),
205.362-018
07.04.01 IDENTIFICATION CLERK (clerical), 205.362-022
07.04.01 NEW-ACCOUNTS CLERK (finan. inst.), 205.362-026
07.04.01 OUTPATIENT-ADMITTING CLERK (medical ser.),
205.362-030
07.04.03 HOTEL CLERK (hotel & rest.), 238.362-010
07.04.05 POLICE AIDE (gov. ser.), 243.362-014
07.04.05 PROTECTIVE-SIGNAL OPERATOR (any ind.),
379.362-014

07.04.05 TELECOMMUNICATOR (gov. ser.), 379.362-018
07.05.01 CREW SCHEDULER (air trans.), 215.362-010
07.05.01 POLICE CLERK (gov. ser.), 375.362-010
07.05.01 RESERVATION CLERK (clerical), 238.362-014
07.05.02 CREDIT-REFERENCE CLERK (ret. tr.), 209.362-018
07.05.03 ATTENDANCE CLERK (educ.), 219.362-014
07.05.03 IDENTIFICATION TECHNICIAN (gov. ser.),
          209.362-022
07.05.03 MEDICAL-RECORD CLERK (medical ser.),
          245.362-010
07.05.03 PERSONNEL CLERK (clerical), 209.362-026
07.05.03 SHORTHAND REPORTER (clerical), 202.362-010
07.05.03 STENOGRAPHER (clerical), 202.362-014
07.05.03 STENOTYPE OPERATOR (clerical), 202.362-022
07.05.03 WARD CLERK (medical ser.), 245.362-014
07.06.01 COMPUTER OPERATOR (clerical), 213.362-010
07.06.01 IN-FILE OPERATOR (bus. ser.), 203.362-014
07.06.01 TERMINAL-SYSTEM OPERATOR (clerical),
          203.362-018
07.06.02 CLERK-TYPIST (clerical), 203.362-010
07.06.02 WORD-PROCESSING-MACHINE OPERATOR
          (clerical), 203.362-022
08.01.03 FOREIGN BANKNOTE TELLER-TRADER (finan.
          inst.), 211.362-014
10.02.02 DIALYSIS TECHNICIAN (medical ser.), 078.362-014
10.02.02 RADIOLOGIC TECHNOLOGIST (medical ser.),
          078.362-026
10.03.01 AUDIOMETRIST (profess. & kin.), 078.362-010
10.03.01 CARDIOPULMONARY TECHNOLOGIST (medical
          ser.), 078.362-030
10.03.01 ELECTROCARDIOGRAPH TECHNICIAN (medical
          ser.), 078.362-018
10.03.01 ELECTROENCEPHALOGRAPHIC TECHNOLOGIST
          (medical ser.), 078.362-022
10.03.02 PERFUSIONIST (medical ser.), 078.362-034

363 Compiling, Speaking-Signaling, Driving — Operating

04.02.03 BORDER GUARD (gov. ser.), 375.363-010
05.08.02 FIRER, LOCOMOTIVE (r.r. trans.), 910.363-010
05.08.02 LOCOMOTIVE ENGINEER (r.r. trans.), 910.363-014
05.08.03 HEALTH-EQUIPMENT SERVICER (medical ser.),
          359.363-010
05.08.03 NEWSPAPER-DELIVERY DRIVER (whole. tr.),
          292.363-010

364 Compiling, Speaking-Signaling, Manipulating

01.06.03 GIFT WRAPPER (ret. tr.), 299.364-014
02.04.01 ULTRASOUND TECHNOLOGIST (medical ser.),
          078.364-010
02.04.02 PHLEBOTOMIST (medical ser.), 079.364-022
02.04.02 VECTOR CONTROL ASSISTANT (gov. ser.),
          049.364-014
03.02.02 FORESTER AIDE (forestry), 452.364-010
03.04.05 PLANT-CARE WORKER (agric.), 408.364-010
04.02.03 BEACH LIFEGUARD (amuse. & rec.), 379.364-014
04.02.04 FIRE FIGHTER (any ind.), 373.364-010
04.02.04 SMOKE JUMPER (forestry), 452.364-014
05.05.01 CEMENT MASON (const.), 844.364-010
05.05.06 ARC CUTTER (welding), 816.364-010
05.10.01 INSULATION WORKER (const.), 863.364-014
05.10.04 AIRPORT ATTENDANT (air trans.), 912.364-010
05.10.09 EXTERMINATOR, TERMITE (bus. ser.), 383.364-010
05.12.03 ABLE SEAMAN (water trans.), 911.364-010
05.12.06 BOAT LOADER 1 (water trans.), 911.364-014
09.01.02 CRAFT DEMONSTRATOR (museum), 109.364-010
10.02.01 PHYSICIAN ASSISTANT (medical ser.), 079.364-018
10.02.02 OCCUPATIONAL THERAPY ASSISTANT (medical
          ser.), 076.364-010
11.03.02 CITY PLANNING AIDE (profess. & kin.), 199.364-010

365 Compiling, Speaking-Signaling, Tending

06.04.02 PRODUCTION-MACHINE TENDER (nut & bolt),
          619.365-010

366 Compiling, Speaking-Signaling, Feeding — Offbearing

07.03.01 COUNTER CLERK (photofinish.), 249.366-010

367 Compiling, Speaking-Signaling, Handling

01.04.02 PROMPTER (amuse. & rec.), 152.367-010
04.01.02 INVESTIGATOR (light, heat, & power), 376.367-022
04.02.01 JAILER (gov. ser.), 372.367-014
04.02.02 DETECTIVE 1 (any ind.), 376.367-014
04.02.02 FIRE RANGER (forestry), 452.367-014
04.02.03 REPOSSESSOR (clerical), 241.367-022
04.02.03 SURVEILLANCE-SYSTEM MONITOR (gov. ser.),
          379.367-010
04.02.04 ALARM INVESTIGATOR (bus. ser.), 376.367-010
05.03.06 CODE INSPECTOR (gov. ser.), 168.367-018
05.03.09 FINE ARTS PACKER (museum), 102.367-010
05.09.01 CARGO AGENT (air trans.), 248.367-018
05.09.01 CUSTODIAN, ATHLETIC EQUIPMENT (amuse. &
          rec.), 969.367-010
05.09.01 PARTS CLERK (clerical), 222.367-042
05.09.01 PARTS-ORDER-AND-STOCK CLERK (clerical),
          249.367-058
05.09.01 SHIPPING-AND-RECEIVING WEIGHER (clerical),
          222.367-058
05.09.01 STOCK CLERK, SELF-SERVICE STORE (ret. tr.),
          299.367-014
05.09.01 TIRE ADJUSTER (ret. tr.), 241.367-034
05.09.01 TOOL-CRIB ATTENDANT (clerical), 222.367-062
05.09.02 ESTIMATOR, PRINTING (print. & pub.), 221.367-014
05.09.02 EVALUATOR (nonprofit org.), 249.367-034
05.09.02 MATERIAL EXPEDITER (clerical), 221.367-042
05.09.02 PRESCRIPTION CLERK, LENS-AND-FRAMES
          (optical goods), 222.367-050
05.09.02 SALES CORRESPONDENT (clerical), 221.367-062
05.09.03 CHECKER, DUMP GROUNDS (bus. ser.), 219.367-010
05.09.03 INDUSTRIAL-ORDER CLERK (clerical), 221.367-022
05.12.05 BRAKE COUPLER, ROAD FREIGHT (r.r. trans.),
          910.367-010
06.04.34 ELECTRONICS UTILITY WORKER (electronics),
          726.367-014
07.01.01 MANAGEMENT AIDE (social ser.), 195.367-014
07.01.02 PROCUREMENT CLERK (clerical), 249.367-066
07.01.02 TEACHER AIDE II (educ.), 249.367-074
07.01.02 TOWN CLERK (gov. ser.), 243.367-018
07.01.04 ESCROW OFFICER (profess. & kin.), 119.367-010
07.01.04 LOAN CLOSER (finan. inst.), 249.367-050
07.01.04 UNDERWRITING CLERK (insurance), 219.367-038
07.01.05 ADMISSIONS EVALUATOR (educ.), 205.367-010
07.01.06 ATTENDANCE OFFICER (educ.), 168.367-010
07.01.07 TEST TECHNICIAN (clerical), 249.367-078
07.02.03 ACCOUNT-INFORMATION CLERK (light, heat, &
          power), 210.367-010
07.02.05 TIMEKEEPER (clerical), 215.367-022
07.03.01 POST-OFFICE CLERK (gov. ser.), 243.367-014
07.04.01 BLOOD-DONOR-UNIT ASSISTANT (medical ser.),
          245.367-014
07.04.01 CREDIT CLERK (clerical), 205.367-022
07.04.01 CUSTOMER-SERVICE REPRESENTATIVE (light,
          heat, & power), 239.367-010
07.04.01 EMPLOYMENT-AND-CLAIMS AIDE (gov. ser.),
          169.367-010
07.04.01 LOAN INTERVIEWER (finan. inst.), 241.367-018
07.04.01 REGISTRATION CLERK (gov. ser.), 205.367-042
07.04.01 REHABILITATION CLERK (nonprofit org.),
          205.367-046
07.04.01 SKIP TRACER (clerical), 241.367-026
07.04.01 SURVEY WORKER (clerical), 205.367-054
07.04.01 TRAFFIC CHECKER (gov. ser.), 205.367-058

07.04.02 CLAIMS CLERK 2 (insurance), 205.367-018
07.04.02 REFERRAL-AND-INFORMATION AIDE (gov. ser.),
237.367-042
07.04.03 ANIMAL-HOSPITAL CLERK (medical ser.),
245.367-010
07.04.03 DOG LICENSER (nonprofit org.), 249.367-030
07.04.03 ELECTION CLERK (gov. ser.), 205.367-030
07.04.03 LICENSE CLERK (gov. ser.), 205.367-034
07.04.03 PARK AIDE (gov. ser.), 249.367-082
07.04.03 RECREATION-FACILITY ATTENDANT (amuse. &
rec.), 341.367-010
07.04.03 RESERVATIONS AGENT (air trans.), 238.367-018
07.04.04 INFORMATION CLERK (clerical), 237.367-022
07.04.04 LAND-LEASING EXAMINER (gov. ser.), 237.367-026
07.04.04 MUSEUM ATTENDANT (museum), 109.367-010
07.04.04 RECEPTIONIST (clerical), 237.367-038
07.04.05 DISPATCHER, MAINTENANCE SERVICE (clerical),
239.367-014
07.04.05 FIRE LOOKOUT (forestry), 452.367-010
07.04.05 FLIGHT-INFORMATION EXPEDITER (air trans.),
912.367-010
07.04.05 SERVICE CLERK (clerical), 221.367-070
07.04.05 UTILITY CLERK (light, heat, & power), 239.367-034
07.05.01 EXPEDITER (clerical), 222.367-018
07.05.01 PERSONNEL SCHEDULER (clerical), 215.367-014
07.05.01 SCHEDULER (museum), 238.367-034
07.05.01 SCHEDULER, MAINTENANCE (clerical), 221.367-066
07.05.01 TRAFFIC CLERK (bus. ser.), 221.367-078
07.05.01 TRANSPORTATION AGENT (air trans.), 912.367-014
07.05.02 BRAILLE PROOFREADER (nonprofit org.),
209.367-014
07.05.02 CREDIT AUTHORIZER (clerical), 249.367-022
07.05.02 DISBURSEMENT CLERK (finan. inst.), 209.367-022
07.05.02 THROW-OUT CLERK (ret. tr.), 241.367-030
07.05.02 TITLE SEARCHER (real estate), 209.367-046
07.05.03 ASSIGNMENT CLERK (clerical), 249.367-090
07.05.03 AUTOMOBILE LOCATOR (ret. tr.), 296.367-010
07.05.03 CALL-OUT OPERATOR (bus. ser.), 237.367-014
07.05.03 CREDIT-CARD-CONTROL CLERK (finan. inst.),
249.367-026
07.05.03 FILE CLERK 2 (clerical), 206.367-014
07.05.03 MEDICAL RECORD TECHNICIAN (medical ser.),
079.367-014
07.05.03 MEDICAL-SERVICE TECHNICIAN (military ser.),
079.367-018
07.05.03 NEWS ASSISTANT (radio & tv broad.), 209.367-038
07.05.03 ORDER CLERK (clerical), 249.367-054
07.05.03 PROPERTY CLERK (gov. ser.), 222.367-054
07.05.03 REFERRAL CLERK, TEMPORARY-HELP AGENCY
(clerical), 205.367-062
07.05.03 REPRODUCTION ORDER PROCESSOR (clerical),
221.367-058
07.05.03 STOCK-CONTROL CLERK (clerical), 219.367-034
07.05.04 CORRESPONDENCE-REVIEW CLERK (clerical),
209.367-018
07.05.04 MAIL CARRIER (gov. ser.), 230.367-010
07.05.04 MERCHANDISE DISTRIBUTOR (ret. tr.), 219.367-018
07.05.04 MESSENGER, BANK (finan. inst.), 230.367-014
07.05.04 ROUTING CLERK (nonprofit org.), 249.367-070
07.05.04 SHIPPING-ORDER CLERK (clerical), 219.367-030
07.07.02 PROCESS SERVER (bus. ser.), 249.367-062
08.01.03 COMPARISON SHOPPER (ret. tr.), 296.367-014
09.01.01 RECREATION AIDE (social ser.), 195.367-030
09.01.02 EXHIBIT-DISPLAY REPRESENTATIVE (any ind.),
297.367-010
09.01.02 GUIDE (per. ser.), 353.367-010
09.01.02 GUIDE, PLANT (any ind.), 353.367-018
09.01.04 AIRPLANE-FLIGHT ATTENDANT (air trans.),
352.367-010
09.04.02 CUSTOMER-SERVICE CLERK (ret. tr.), 299.367-010
09.04.02 STORAGE-FACILITY RENTAL CLERK (bus. ser.),
295.367-026
09.05.01 WEIGHT-REDUCTION SPECIALIST (per. ser.),
359.367-014
10.01.02 CASE AIDE (social ser.), 195.367-010

10.01.02 COMMUNITY WORKER (gov. ser.), 195.367-018
10.01.02 FOOD-MANAGEMENT AIDE (gov. ser.), 195.367-022
10.01.02 SOCIAL-SERVICES AIDE (social ser.), 195.367-034
10.03.01 CARDIAC MONITOR TECHNICIAN (medical ser.),
078.367-010
10.03.02 MEDICAL ASSISTANT (medical ser.), 079.367-010
11.01.01 PROGRAMMER, DETAIL (clerical), 219.367-026
11.02.04 CAREER-GUIDANCE TECHNICIAN (educ.),
249.367-014
11.02.04 CLASSIFIER (library), 100.367-014
11.02.04 FILM-OR-TAPE LIBRARIAN (clerical), 222.367-026
11.02.04 FILM-RENTAL CLERK (bus. ser.), 295.367-018
11.02.04 LIBRARY ASSISTANT (library), 249.367-046
11.02.04 LIBRARY TECHNICAL ASSISTANT (library),
100.367-018
11.06.03 PERSONAL PROPERTY ASSESSOR (gov. ser.),
191.367-010
11.10.05 RATER, TRAVEL ACCOMMODATIONS (profess. &
kin.), 168.367-014
12.01.02 CHARTER (amuse. & rec.), 249.367-018
12.01.02 CLOCKER (amuse. & rec.), 153.367-010
12.01.02 HORSE-RACE TIMER (amuse. & rec.), 153.367-014

371 Compiling, Serving, Precision

02.04.02 EMBALMER (per. ser.), 338.371-014
09.02.01 SCALP-TREATMENT OPERATOR (per. ser.),
339.371-014
09.02.02 BARBER (per. ser.), 330.371-010
09.05.01 ELECTROLOGIST (per. ser.), 339.371-010
10.02.01 NURSE ANESTHETIST (medical ser.), 075.371-010
10.02.02 ORTHOPTIST (medical ser.), 079.371-014
10.03.02 DENTAL ASSISTANT (medical ser.), 079.371-010

374 Compiling, Serving, Manipulating

09.05.01 MASSEUR/MASSEUSE (per. ser.), 334.374-010
10.02.01 NURSE, GENERAL DUTY (medical ser.), 075.374-010
10.02.01 NURSE, LICENSED PRACTICAL (medical ser.),
079.374-014
10.02.01 NURSE, OFFICE (medical ser.), 075.374-014
10.02.01 NURSE, PRIVATE DUTY (medical ser.), 075.374-018
10.02.01 NURSE, STAFF, OCCUPATIONAL HEALTH
NURSING (medical ser.), 075.374-022
10.02.02 PSYCHIATRIC TECHNICIAN (medical ser.),
079.374-026
10.03.02 AMBULANCE ATTENDANT (medical ser.),
355.374-010
10.03.02 EMERGENCY MEDICAL TECHNICIAN (medical
ser.), 079.374-010
10.03.02 MEDICATION AIDE (medical ser.), 355.374-014
10.03.02 NURSE, PRACTICAL (medical ser.), 354.374-010
10.03.02 PODIATRIC ASSISTANT (medical ser.), 079.374-018
10.03.02 SURGICAL TECHNICIAN (medical ser.), 079.374-022

377 Compiling, Serving, Handling

10.03.02 BIRTH ATTENDANT (medical ser.), 354.377-010
10.03.02 MENTAL-RETARDATION AIDE (medical ser.),
355.377-018
10.03.02 OCCUPATIONAL THERAPY AIDE (medical ser.),
355.377-010
10.03.02 PSYCHIATRIC AIDE (medical ser.), 355.377-014
10.03.03 HOME ATTENDANT (per. ser.), 354.377-014

380 Compiling, Taking Instructions — Helping, Setting Up

05.05.08 FURNITURE RESTORER (museum), 763.380-010
06.01.03 MACHINE SET-UP OPERATOR (elec. equip.),
600.380-018
06.01.03 PRINTER 2 (print. & pub.), 651.380-010
06.02.21 PLATER (electroplating), 500.380-010

381 Compiling, Taking Instructions — Helping, Precision

01.06.01 ENGRAVER, HAND, HARD METALS (engraving), 704.381-026

01.06.01 ENGRAVER, HAND, SOFT METALS (engraving), 704.381-030

01.06.01 PHOTOENGRAVER (print. & pub.), 971.381-022

01.06.02 BOW MAKER, CUSTOM (sports equip.), 732.381-010

01.06.02 CONSERVATOR, ARTIFACTS (profess. & kin.), 055.381-010

01.06.02 DECORATOR (any ind.), 298.381-010

01.06.02 MOLD MAKER 1 (jewelry), 700.381-034

01.06.02 MUSEUM TECHNICIAN (museum), 102.381-010

01.06.02 REPAIRER, ART OBJECTS (any ind.), 779.381-018

01.06.02 SAMPLE MAKER 1 (jewelry), 700.381-046

01.06.03 GILDER (any ind.), 749.381-010

01.06.03 PAINTER, HAND (any ind.), 970.381-022

01.06.03 PAINTER, SIGN (any ind.), 970.381-026

01.06.03 SPOTTER, PHOTOGRAPHIC (photofinish.), 970.381-034

01.06.03 TYPE COPYIST (mach. mfg.), 970.381-042

02.04.01 FILM LABORATORY TECHNICIAN 1 (motion pic.), 976.381-010

02.04.01 LABORATORY ASSISTANT (petrol. production), 024.381-010

02.04.01 LABORATORY ASSISTANT (textile), 029.381-014

02.04.01 LABORATORY TECHNICIAN (auto. mfg.), 019.381-010

02.04.01 PHARMACIST ASSISTANT (military ser.), 074.381-010

02.04.02 BIOLOGY SPECIMEN TECHNICIAN (profess. & kin.), 041.381-010

02.04.02 MEDICAL-LABORATORY ASSISTANT (medical ser.), 078.381-010

02.04.02 MEDICAL-LABORATORY TECHNICIAN (medical ser.), 078.381-014

03.03.02 HORSESHOER (agric.), 418.381-010

05.05.01 BRICKLAYER (const.), 861.381-018

05.05.01 STONECUTTER, HAND (stonework), 771.381-014

05.05.01 TERRAZZO WORKER (const.), 861.381-046

05.05.01 TILE SETTER (const.), 861.381-054

05.05.02 BOATBUILDER, WOOD (ship bldg. & rep.), 860.381-018

05.05.02 CARPENTER (const.), 860.381-022

05.05.02 CARPENTER, ROUGH (const.), 860.381-042

05.05.02 CUSTOM VAN INSTALLER (auto. mfg.), 860.381-074

05.05.02 SHIPWRIGHT (ship bldg. & rep.), 860.381-058

05.05.03 PLUMBER (const.), 862.381-030

05.05.04 DRY-WALL APPLICATOR (const.), 842.381-010

05.05.04 PAPERHANGER (const.), 841.381-010

05.05.05 STREET LIGHT SERVICER (light, heat, & power), 824.381-010

05.05.05 WIND-GENERATING-ELECTRIC-POWER INSTALLER (const.), 821.381-018

05.05.06 AUTOMOBILE-BODY REPAIRER (auto. ser.), 807.381-010

05.05.06 BLACKSMITH (forging), 610.381-010

05.05.06 SAFE-AND-VAULT SERVICE MECHANIC (bus. ser.), 869.381-022

05.05.06 SHIPFITTER (ship bldg. & rep.), 806.381-046

05.05.06 SIGN ERECTOR 1 (signs), 869.381-026

05.05.06 WELDER-ASSEMBLER (mach. mfg.), 819.381-010

05.05.07 SAW FILER (any ind.), 701.381-014

05.05.07 TEMPLATE MAKER (any ind.), 601.381-038

05.05.07 TOOL GRINDER 1 (any ind.), 701.381-018

05.05.08 FURNITURE FINISHER (woodworking), 763.381-010

05.05.09 FLIGHT-TEST SHOP MECHANIC (aircraft-aerospace mfg.), 621.381-010

05.05.09 FUEL-SYSTEM-MAINTENANCE WORKER (any ind.), 638.381-010

05.05.09 GAS-WELDING-EQUIPMENT MECHANIC (any ind.), 626.381-014

05.05.10 ELECTRIC-METER TESTER (light, heat, & power), 821.381-010

05.05.10 PINSETTER ADJUSTER, AUTOMATIC (sports equip.), 829.381-010

05.05.11 DENTAL-LABORATORY TECHNICIAN (medical ser.), 712.381-018

05.05.11 DENTAL-LABORATORY-TECHNICIAN APPRENTICE (medical ser.), 712.381-022

05.05.11 EXPERIMENTAL ASSEMBLER (any ind.), 739.381-026

05.05.11 ORTHODONTIC TECHNICIAN (medical ser.), 712.381-030

05.05.11 ORTHOTICS TECHNICIAN (per. protect. & med. device), 712.381-034

05.05.11 PROSTHETICS TECHNICIAN (per. protect. & med. device), 712.381-038

05.05.12 PERCUSSION-INSTRUMENT REPAIRER (any ind.), 730.381-042

05.05.12 PIPE-ORGAN INSTALLER (musical inst.), 730.381-046

05.05.13 COMPOSITOR (print. & pub.), 973.381-010

05.05.13 ELECTROTYPER (print. & pub.), 974.381-010

05.05.13 JOB PRINTER (print. & pub.), 973.381-018

05.05.14 STONE SETTER (jewelry), 700.381-054

05.05.15 AUTOMOBILE UPHOLSTERER (auto. ser.), 780.381-010

05.05.15 BOOKBINDER (print. & pub.), 977.381-010

05.05.15 FURNITURE UPHOLSTERER (any ind.), 780.381-018

05.05.15 RUG REPAIRER (clean., dye., & press.), 782.381-018

05.05.17 CAKE DECORATOR (bake. prod.), 524.381-010

05.10.01 ARCH-SUPPORT TECHNICIAN (per. protect. & med. device), 712.381-010

05.10.01 CARPET CUTTER (ret. tr.), 929.381-010

05.10.01 CARPET LAYER (ret. tr.), 864.381-010

05.10.01 GLAZIER (const.), 865.381-010

05.10.01 MAINTENANCE REPAIRER, BUILDING (any ind.), 899.381-010

05.10.01 ROOFER (const.), 866.381-010

05.10.02 AUTOMOBILE-RADIATOR MECHANIC (auto. ser.), 620.381-010

05.10.02 CONVEYOR-MAINTENANCE MECHANIC (any ind.), 630.381-010

05.10.02 DOOR-CLOSER MECHANIC (any ind.), 630.381-014

05.10.02 LUBRICATION-EQUIPMENT SERVICER (any ind.), 630.381-022

05.10.02 MECHANIC, AIRCRAFT ACCESSORIES (aircraft-aerospace mfg.), 621.381-014

05.10.02 THERMOSTAT REPAIRER (inst. & app.), 710.381-050

05.10.03 BATTERY REPAIRER (any ind.), 727.381-014

05.10.03 ELECTRICAL-APPLIANCE REPAIRER (any ind.), 723.381-010

05.10.03 PRODUCTION REPAIRER (electronics), 726.381-014

05.10.03 TRANSFORMER REPAIRER (any ind.), 724.381-018

05.10.03 VACUUM CLEANER REPAIRER (any ind.), 723.381-014

05.10.04 EQUIPMENT INSTALLER (any ind.), 828.381-010

05.10.04 EVAPORATIVE-COOLER INSTALLER (any ind.), 637.381-010

05.10.05 MICROFICHE DUPLICATOR (bus. ser.), 976.381-014

05.10.05 PHOTOGRAPHIC-PLATE MAKER (electronics), 714.381-018

05.10.05 PROJECTION PRINTER (photofinish.), 976.381-018

05.10.07 PAINTER (const.), 840.381-010

05.10.08 BAKER (hotel & rest.), 313.381-010

05.10.08 BAKER, PIZZA (hotel & rest.), 313.381-014

05.10.08 COOK, BARBECUE (hotel & rest.), 313.381-022

05.10.08 COOK, PASTRY (hotel & rest.), 313.381-026

05.12.16 LIGHTING-EQUIPMENT OPERATOR (amuse. & rec.), 962.381-014

06.01.04 BENCH HAND (jewelry), 735.381-010

06.01.04 CANVAS WORKER (canvas goods), 739.381-010

06.01.04 COREMAKER (foundry), 518.381-014

06.01.04 ELECTRIC-MOTOR-CONTROL ASSEMBLER (elec. equip.), 721.381-014

06.01.04 FINAL ASSEMBLER (office mach.), 706.381-018

06.01.04 GOLDBEATER (gold leaf & foil), 700.381-018

06.01.04 RING MAKER (jewelry), 700.381-042

06.01.04 SKIN FITTER (aircraft-aerospace mfg.), 806.381-054

06.01.04 SOLDERER (jewelry), 700.381-050

06.01.04 TRANSFORMER ASSEMBLER (elec. equip.), 820.381-014

06.01.05 ELECTRONICS INSPECTOR I (electronics), 726.381-010

06.02.15 BAKER (bake. prod.), 526.381-010

06.02.23 LENS-MOLD SETTER (optical goods), 713.381-010

06.02.24 CASTER (jewelry), 502.381-010

06.02.24 FABRICATOR-ASSEMBLER, METAL PRODUCTS (any ind.), 809.381-010

06.02.24 REPAIRER, TYPEWRITER (office mach.), 706.381-030

06.02.24 SOLAR-FABRICATION TECHNICIAN (mach. shop), 809.381-034

06.02.24 SUBASSEMBLER (mach. mfg.), 706.381-038

06.02.27 COBBLER (boot & shoe), 788.381-010

06.02.28 BUTCHER, ALL-ROUND (slaught. & meat pack.), 525.381-014

06.02.30 MOLDER (optical goods), 575.381-010

06.02.30 THROWER (pottery & porc.), 774.381-010

06.02.31 LAY-OUT WORKER 2 (any ind.), 809.381-014

06.02.32 BONDED STRUCTURES REPAIRER (aircraft-aerospace mfg.), 807.381-014

06.02.32 COIL WINDER, REPAIR (any ind.), 724.381-014

06.03.01 INSPECTOR (fabric. plastic prod.), 559.381-010

382 Compiling, Taking Instructions - Helping, Operating — Controlling

05.05.13 STEREOTYPER (print. & pub.), 974.382-014

05.06.01 GAS-ENGINE OPERATOR (any ind.), 950.382-018

05.06.02 BOILER OPERATOR (any ind.), 950.382-010

05.06.02 GAS-COMPRESSOR OPERATOR (any ind.), 950.382-014

05.06.02 STATIONARY ENGINEER (any ind.), 950.382-026

05.06.03 PUMP-STATION OPERATOR, WATERWORKS (waterworks), 954.382-010

05.06.04 WATER-TREATMENT-PLANT OPERATOR (waterworks), 954.382-014

05.10.05 AUDIOVISUAL TECHNICIAN (any ind.), 960.382-010

05.10.05 COLOR-PRINTER OPERATOR (photofinish.), 976.382-014

05.10.05 ENGRAVING-PRESS OPERATOR (print. & pub.), 651.382-010

05.10.05 FILM DEVELOPER (motion pic.), 976.382-018

05.10.05 RECORDIST (motion pic.), 962.382-010

05.10.05 TAPE TRANSFERRER (phonograph), 194.382-014

05.11.03 ROTARY DRILLER (petrol. production), 930.382-026

06.02.08 POTTERY-MACHINE OPERATOR (pottery & porc.), 774.382-010

06.02.08 PRECISION-LENS GRINDER (optical goods), 716.382-018

06.02.09 CLOTH PRINTER (any ind.), 652.382-010

06.02.09 CRYSTAL SLICER (electronics), 677.382-018

06.02.09 NUMERICAL-CONTROL ROUTER OPERATOR, PRINTED CIRCUIT BOARDS (electronics), 605.382-046

06.02.10 HEAT TREATER 1 (heat treat.), 504.382-014

06.02.11 WASTE-TREATMENT OPERATOR (chem.), 955.382-014

06.02.13 BLANKMAKER (glass mfg.), 579.382-022

06.02.13 MIXING-MACHINE OPERATOR (any ind.), 550.382-022

06.02.15 CHOCOLATE-PRODUCTION-MACHINE OPERATOR (choc. & cocoa), 529.382-014

06.02.15 DAIRY-PROCESSING-EQUIPMENT OPERATOR (dairy prod.), 529.382-018

06.02.18 CRYSTAL GROWER (electronics), 590.382-014

06.02.18 ION IMPLANT MACHINE OPERATOR (electronics), 590.382-022

06.02.18 ROOF-CEMENT-AND-PAINT MAKER (build. mat. nec), 550.382-030

06.02.18 SOAP MAKER (soap), 559.382-054

06.02.19 WELDING-MACHINE OPERATOR, ARC (welding), 810.382-010

06.02.21 COATER OPERATOR (any ind.), 509.382-010

06.02.21 COATING-MACHINE OPERATOR (coated fabrics), 584.382-010

06.02.21 OPTICAL-ELEMENT COATER (optical goods), 716.382-014

06.02.21 PAINT-SPRAYER OPERATOR, AUTOMATIC (any ind.), 599.382-010

07.01.04 MORTGAGE CLERK (finan. inst.), 249.382-010

07.02.01 BALANCE CLERK (clerical), 216.382-018

07.02.01 BOOKKEEPER 1 (clerical), 210.382-014

07.02.01 GENERAL-LEDGER BOOKKEEPER (clerical), 210.382-046

07.02.01 RECONCILEMENT CLERK (finan. inst.), 210.382-058

07.02.02 ACCOUNTING CLERK, DATA PROCESSING (clerical), 216.382-010

07.02.02 CANCELLATION CLERK (insurance), 203.382-014

07.02.02 COST CLERK (clerical), 216.382-034

07.02.02 NIGHT AUDITOR (hotel & rest.), 210.382-054

07.02.03 STATISTICAL CLERK (clerical), 216.382-062

07.05.03 BORDEREAU CLERK (insurance), 203.382-010

07.05.03 MORTGAGE-PROCESSING CLERK (finan. inst.), 203.382-022

07.05.03 REPAIR-ORDER CLERK (clerical), 221.382-022

07.06.01 COMPUTER-PERIPHERAL-EQUIPMENT OPERATOR (clerical), 213.382-010

07.06.01 TERMINAL-MAKEUP OPERATOR (print. & pub.), 208.382-010

07.06.02 CHECK WRITER (ret. tr.), 219.382-010

07.06.02 MAGNETIC-TAPE-COMPOSER OPERATOR (print. & pub.), 203.382-018

07.06.02 PROOF-MACHINE OPERATOR (finan. inst.), 217.382-010

07.06.02 VARITYPE OPERATOR (clerical), 203.382-026

383 Compiling, Taking Instructions — Helping, Driving — Operating

05.08.01 TRACTOR-TRAILER-TRUCK DRIVER (any ind.), 904.383-010

05.12.03 WASTE-DISPOSAL ATTENDANT (any ind.), 955.383-010

384 Compiling, Taking Instructions — Helping, Manipulating

02.04.01 DECONTAMINATOR (any ind.), 199.384-010

02.04.01 SCANNER (profess. & kin.), 015.384-010

02.04.02 BIOLOGICAL AIDE (agric.), 049.384-010

02.04.02 CEPHALOMETRIC ANALYST (medical ser.), 078.384-010

02.04.02 HERBARIUM WORKER (profess. & kin.), 041.384-010

02.04.02 LABORATORY ASSISTANT, CULTURE MEDIA (drug prep. & related), 559.384-010

05.05.06 WELDER, ARC (welding), 810.384-014

05.05.06 WELDER, COMBINATION (welding), 819.384-010

05.09.01 PRODUCTION TECHNICIAN, SEMICONDUCTOR PROCESSING EQUIPMENT (electronics), 590.384-014

05.10.01 FIXTURE REPAIRER-FABRICATOR (any ind.), 630.384-010

05.10.04 FIRE-EXTINGUISHER REPAIRER (any ind.), 709.384-010

05.10.05 SCREEN MAKER, PHOTOGRAPHIC PROCESS (any ind.), 979.384-010

05.10.08 SALAD MAKER (water trans.), 317.384-010

06.01.04 TUBE ASSEMBLER, ELECTRON (electronics), 725.384-010

06.02.23 ELECTRONICS ASSEMBLER (inst. & app.), 726.384-010

06.02.28 BENCH HAND (bake. prod.), 520.384-010

06.02.32 CHARGE PREPARATION TECHNICIAN (electronics), 590.384-010

06.03.01 COMPARATOR OPERATOR (any ind.), 699.384-010

06.03.01 MOTORCYCLE TESTER (motor. & bicycles), 620.384-010

385 Compiling, Taking Instructions — Helping, Tending

05.10.05 MICROFILM PROCESSOR (bus. ser.), 976.385-010

387 Compiling, Taking Instructions — Helping, Handling

01.06.01 ADVERTISING-SPACE CLERK (print. & pub.), 247.387-018
02.04.01 FINGERPRINT CLASSIFIER (gov. ser.), 375.387-010
05.09.01 INVENTORY CLERK (clerical), 222.387-026
05.09.01 LINEN-ROOM ATTENDANT (hotel & rest.), 222.387-030
05.09.01 PHARMACY HELPER (medical ser.), 074.387-010
05.09.01 SHIPPING AND RECEIVING CLERK (clerical), 222.387-050
05.09.02 DRAPERY AND UPHOLSTERY ESTIMATOR (ret. tr.), 299.387-010
05.09.02 JOB TRACER (clerical), 221.387-034
05.09.02 LAUNDRY CLERK (clerical), 221.387-038
05.09.02 ORDER DETAILER (clerical), 221.387-046
05.09.02 STOCK CLERK (clerical), 222.387-058
05.09.03 MATERIAL CLERK (clerical), 222.387-034
05.09.03 SORTER-PRICER (nonprofit org.), 222.387-054
06.03.01 MACHINE TESTER (office mach.), 706.387-014
06.03.01 QUALITY-CONTROL INSPECTOR (phonograph), 194.387-010
06.03.02 INSPECTOR (drug prep. & related), 559.387-014

07.02.02 CHECK-PROCESSING CLERK 1 (finan. inst.), 216.387-010
07.02.04 ADVERTISING CLERK (bus. ser.), 247.387-010
07.02.04 BILLING-CONTROL CLERK (light, heat, & power), 214.387-010
07.05.01 ADVERTISING-DISPATCH CLERK (print. & pub.), 247.387-014
07.05.01 TELEVISION-SCHEDULE COORDINATOR (radio & tv broad.), 199.387-010
07.05.02 CLASSIFIED-AD CLERK 2 (print. & pub.), 247.387-022
07.05.02 DATA-EXAMINATION CLERK (clerical), 209.387-022
07.05.02 LETTER-OF-CREDIT CLERK (finan. inst.), 219.387-018
07.05.02 PROOFREADER (print. & pub.), 209.387-030
07.05.02 READER (bus. ser.), 249.387-022
07.05.03 CLASSIFICATION CLERK (clerical), 206.387-010
07.05.03 CODING CLERK (clerical), 209.387-010
07.05.03 COMPILER (clerical), 209.387-014
07.05.03 FINGERPRINT CLERK 2 (gov. ser.), 206.387-014
07.05.03 RECORDS CUSTODIAN (finan. inst.), 206.387-026
07.05.03 TAPE LIBRARIAN (clerical), 206.387-030
07.05.04 PARCEL-POST CLERK (clerical), 222.387-038
11.02.04 CATALOG LIBRARIAN (library), 100.387-010

Data = Computing

457 Computing, Persuading, Handling

08.02.02 SALESPERSON, ART OBJECTS (ret. tr.), 277.457-010
08.03.01 PHOTOGRAPHER (amuse. & rec.), 143.457-010
08.03.01 VENDOR (amuse. & rec.), 291.457-022
09.04.02 GAME ATTENDANT (amuse. & rec.), 342.457-010
09.04.02 NEWSPAPER CARRIER (ret. tr.), 292.457-010

462 Computing, Speaking-Signaling, Operating — Controlling

06.02.02 DROP-HAMMER OPERATOR (forging), 610.462-010
06.02.02 STRAIGHTENING-ROLL OPERATOR (any ind.), 613.462-022
06.02.10 COLD-MILL OPERATOR (iron & steel), 613.462-010
06.04.38 MAILING-MACHINE OPERATOR (print. & pub.), 208.462-010
07.02.02 COUPON CLERK (finan. inst.), 219.462-010
07.03.01 CASHIER 2 (clerical), 211.462-010
07.03.01 CASHIER-CHECKER (ret. tr.), 211.462-014
07.03.01 CHECK CASHIER (bus. ser.), 211.462-026
07.03.01 TOLL COLLECTOR (gov. ser.), 211.462-038
07.04.06 CENTRAL-OFFICE OPERATOR (tel. & tel.), 235.462-010
09.04.02 CASHIER-WRAPPER (ret. tr.), 211.462-018

463 Computing, Speaking-Signaling, Driving — Operating

05.10.01 SWIMMING POOL INSTALLER-AND-SERVICER (const.), 869.463-010
09.03.01 BUS DRIVER (motor trans.), 913.463-010
09.03.02 TAXI DRIVER (motor trans.), 913.463-018
09.04.01 LUNCH-TRUCK DRIVER (hotel & rest.), 292.463-010

464 Computing, Speaking-Signaling, Manipulating

05.06.01 CABLE MAINTAINER (light, heat, & power), 952.464-010
05.10.01 BOAT RIGGER (ret. tr.), 806.464-010
05.10.04 AIR-CONDITIONING INSTALLER, DOMESTIC (any ind.), 827.464-010
09.04.01 VENDING-MACHINE ATTENDANT (hotel & rest.), 319.464-014
09.04.02 SKATE-SHOP ATTENDANT (amuse. & rec.), 341.464-010

465 Computing, Speaking-Signaling, Tending

06.02.10 CARBIDE-POWDER PROCESSOR (mach. shop), 510.465-010

467 Computing, Speaking-Signaling, Handling

05.10.02 AUTOMOBILE-SERVICE-STATION ATTENDANT (auto. ser.), 915.467-010
07.02.03 GRADING CLERK (educ.), 219.467-010
07.03.01 LAYAWAY CLERK (ret. tr.), 299.467-010
07.03.01 PARIMUTUEL-TICKET SELLER (amuse. & rec.), 211.467-022
09.04.02 BICYCLE-RENTAL CLERK (ret. tr.), 295.467-010
09.04.02 FLOOR ATTENDANT (amuse. & rec.), 343.467-014
09.04.02 GAMBLING DEALER (amuse. & rec.), 343.467-018
09.04.02 TRAILER-RENTAL CLERK (auto. ser.), 295.467-022

472 Computing, Serving, Operating — Controlling

09.04.01 FAST-FOODS WORKER (hotel & rest.), 311.472-010

473 Computing, Serving, Driving — Operating

09.04.02 PARKING-LOT ATTENDANT (auto. ser.), 915.473-010

474 Computing, Serving, Manipulating

09.04.01 BARTENDER (hotel & rest.), 312.474-010
09.04.01 FOUNTAIN SERVER (hotel & rest.), 319.474-010

477 Computing, Serving, Handling

09.04.01 CAR HOP (hotel & rest.), 311.477-010
09.04.01 COUNTER ATTENDANT, LUNCHROOM OR COFFEE SHOP (hotel & rest.), 311.477-014
09.04.01 WAITER/WAITRESS, FORMAL (hotel & rest.), 311.477-026
09.04.01 WAITER/WAITRESS, INFORMAL (hotel & rest.), 311.477-030
09.04.01 WAITER/WAITRESS, TAKE OUT (hotel & rest.), 311.477-038
09.04.02 AUTOMOBILE-RENTAL CLERK (auto. ser.), 295.477-010
09.04.02 DELIVERER, MERCHANDISE (ret. tr.), 299.477-010
09.04.02 SALES CLERK (ret. tr.), 290.477-014

09.04.02 SALES CLERK, FOOD (ret. tr.), 290.477-018
09.04.02 SERVICE-ESTABLISHMENT ATTENDANT (clean.,
dye., & press.), 369.477-014
09.05.02 WAITER/WAITRESS, ROOM SERVICE (hotel & rest.),
311.477-034
09.05.03 PORTER, BAGGAGE (hotel & rest.), 324.477-010

481 Computing, Taking Instructions — Helping, Precision

05.10.01 FLOOR LAYER (const.), 864.481-010
06.02.22 ASSEMBLER, INTERNAL COMBUSTION ENGINE
(engine & turbine), 806.481-014
06.02.22 CASKET ASSEMBLER (mort. goods), 739.481-010

482 Computing, Taking Instructions — Helping, Operating — Controlling

05.05.13 OFFSET-PRESS OPERATOR 1 (print. & pub.),
651.482-010
06.02.02 RIVETING-MACHINE OPERATOR 1 (any ind.),
699.482-010
06.02.02 SHEAR OPERATOR 1 (any ind.), 615.482-034
06.02.02 STRAIGHTENING-PRESS OPERATOR (any ind.),
617.482-026
06.02.03 TIMBER-SIZER OPERATOR (planing mill),
665.482-018
06.02.15 FREEZER OPERATOR (dairy prod.), 529.482-010
06.02.19 WELDING-MACHINE OPERATOR, GAS (welding),
811.482-010
07.02.02 ACCOUNTING CLERK (clerical), 216.482-010
07.02.02 BROKERAGE CLERK 1 (finan. inst.), 219.482-010
07.02.02 CALCULATING-MACHINE OPERATOR (clerical),
216.482-022
07.02.04 RATER (insurance), 214.482-022
07.02.04 REINSURANCE CLERK (insurance), 219.482-018
07.02.05 PAYROLL CLERK (clerical), 215.482-010
07.06.02 ADDING-MACHINE OPERATOR (clerical),
216.482-014

Data = Copying

562 Copying, Speaking-Signaling, Operating — Controlling

06.04.16 SLASHER TENDER (textile), 582.562-010
07.04.05 SWITCHBOARD OPERATOR, POLICE DISTRICT
(gov. ser.), 235.562-014
07.06.02 WIRES-TRANSFER CLERK (finan. inst.), 203.562-010
07.07.03 CLERK, GENERAL (clerical), 209.562-010

563 Copying, Speaking-Signaling, Driving — Operating

04.02.02 ARMORED-CAR GUARD AND DRIVER (bus. ser.),
372.563-010

564 Copying, Speaking-Signaling, Manipulating

05.07.01 LINE WALKER (petrol. production), 869.564-010
07.05.03 DETAILER, SCHOOL PHOTOGRAPHS (photofinish.),
976.564-010

565 Copying, Speaking-Signaling, Tending

06.02.12 CYLINDER FILLER (comp. & liq. gases), 559.565-010

567 Copying, Speaking-Signaling, Handling

04.02.01 GUARD, IMMIGRATION (gov. ser.), 372.567-014
04.02.02 ARMORED-CAR GUARD (bus. ser.), 372.567-010
05.09.03 METER READER (light, heat, & power), 209.567-010
05.09.03 TURBINE ATTENDANT (light, heat, & power),
952.567-010
05.12.02 SURVEYOR HELPER (any ind.), 869.567-010
06.04.40 LABORER, GENERAL (plastics mat.), 559.567-010
07.03.01 AUCTION CLERK (ret. tr.), 294.567-010

483 Computing, Taking Instructions — Helping, Driving — Operating

05.08.01 MILK DRIVER (dairy prod.), 905.483-010

484 Computing, Taking Instructions — Helping, Manipu lating

01.06.03 STRIPER, HAND (any ind.), 740.484-010
05.10.01 DRAPERY HANGER (ret. tr.), 869.484-014
05.10.01 TEMPLATE MAKER, TRACK (any ind.), 809.484-014
05.12.17 FOOD ASSEMBLER, KITCHEN (hotel & rest.),
319.484-010
06.02.22 ASSEMBLER, SUBASSEMBLY (aircraft-aerospace
mfg.), 806.484-010
06.02.23 LAMINATION ASSEMBLER (elec. equip.), 729.484-010
06.02.24 STRAIGHTENER, HAND (any ind.), 709.484-014
06.04.23 SILK-SCREEN-FRAME ASSEMBLER (any ind.),
709.484-010
06.04.38 CRATER (any ind.), 920.484-010

485 Computing, Taking Instructions — Helping, Tending

05.12.19 CURRENCY SORTER (finan. inst.), 217.485-010
06.02.15 SIRUP MAKER (flav. ext. & sirup), 520.485-026
06.04.03 POWER-BARKER OPERATOR (paper & pulp),
669.485-010
06.04.11 PAINT MIXER, MACHINE (any ind.), 550.485-018

487 Computing, Taking Instructions — Helping, Handling

05.09.01 ORDER FILLER (ret. tr.), 222.487-014
05.10.05 PHOTOGRAPH FINISHER (photofinish.), 976.487-010
05.10.08 FORMULA-ROOM WORKER (dairy prod.), 520.487-014
06.03.01 SPECIAL TESTER (tobacco), 529.487-010
07.02.04 TAX CLERK 1 (clerical), 219.487-010

07.05.03 INSURANCE CLERK 2 (clerical), 205.567-010
07.07.03 OFFICE HELPER (clerical), 239.567-010
09.05.01 REDUCING-SALON ATTENDANT (per. ser.),
359.567-010
10.03.03 GUARD, SCHOOL-CROSSING (gov. ser.), 371.567-010

573 Copying, Serving, Driving — Operating

10.03.03 BLIND AIDE (per. ser.), 359.573-010

574 Copying, Serving, Manipulating

05.10.01 SERVICE REPRESENTATIVE (light, heat, & power),
959.574-010

577 Copying, Serving, Handling

09.05.03 ROOM-SERVICE CLERK (hotel & rest.), 324.577-010
09.05.05 CARDROOM ATTENDANT 2 (amuse. & rec.),
343.577-010

582 Copying, Taking Instructions — Helping, Operating — Controlling

05.10.05 PHOTOCOMPOSING-MACHINE OPERATOR (print.
& pub.), 650.582-018
05.12.19 ADDRESSING-MACHINE OPERATOR (clerical),
208.582-010
06.02.15 DOUGH MIXER (bake. prod.), 520.582-010
07.06.01 TERMINAL OPERATOR (clerical), 203.582-054
07.06.02 BRAILLE OPERATOR (print. & pub.), 203.582-010
07.06.02 BRAILLE TYPIST (educ.), 203.582-014
07.06.02 CRYPTOGRAPHIC-MACHINE OPERATOR (clerical),
203.582-018
07.06.02 DATA TYPIST (clerical), 203.582-022
07.06.02 DATA-CODER OPERATOR (clerical), 203.582-026

07.06.02 ELECTRONIC-TYPESETTING-MACHINE
OPERATOR (print. & pub.), 203.582-074
07.06.02 FOOD TABULATOR, CAFETERIA (hotel & rest.),
211.582-010
07.06.02 KEYPUNCH OPERATOR (clerical), 203.582-030
07.06.02 MAGNETIC-TAPE-TYPEWRITER OPERATOR
(clerical), 203.582-034
07.06.02 PHOTOCOMPOSITION-KEYBOARD OPERATOR
(print. & pub.), 203.582-046
07.06.02 PHOTOTYPESETTER OPERATOR (print. & pub.),
650.582-022
07.06.02 TELEGRAPHIC-TYPEWRITER OPERATOR (clerical),
203.582-050
07.06.02 TRANSCRIBING-MACHINE OPERATOR (clerical),
203.582-058
07.06.02 TYPIST (clerical), 203.582-066
07.06.02 VERIFIER OPERATOR (clerical), 203.582-070

583 Copying, Taking Instructions — Helping, Driving — Operating

05.08.03 LOT ATTENDANT (ret. tr.), 915.583-010

584 Copying, Taking Instructions — Helping, Manipulating

05.10.03 APPLIANCE REPAIRER (elec. equip.), 723.584-010
05.12.08 MARINE OILER (water trans.), 911.584-010
05.12.16 ELECTRICAL-APPLIANCE PREPARER (any ind.),
827.584-010
06.02.27 CUTTER, HAND 1 (any ind.), 781.584-014

585 Copying, Taking Instructions — Helping, Tending

05.05.13 ASSISTANT-PRESS OPERATOR (print. & pub.),
651.585-010
05.12.19 COIN-MACHINE OPERATOR (finan. inst.),
217.585-010

06.04.11 CHEMICAL OPERATOR 2 (chem.), 558.585-014
06.04.15 CHEESE CUTTER (dairy prod.), 529.585-010
06.04.19 STERILIZER (drug prep. & related), 599.585-010

586 Copying, Taking Instructions — Helping, Feeding — Offbearing

06.04.06 CLOTH DOFFER (textile), 689.586-010

587 Copying, Taking Instructions — Helping, Handling

04.02.02 PARKING ENFORCEMENT OFFICER (gov. ser.),
375.587-010
05.09.01 LABORATORY CLERK (clerical), 222.587-026
05.09.01 MAILER (print. & pub.), 222.587-030
05.09.03 MARKER (ret. tr.), 209.587-034
06.03.02 GRADER (woodworking), 669.587-010
06.03.02 INSPECTOR, FABRIC (any ind.), 789.587-014
06.03.02 WEIGHER, PRODUCTION (any ind.), 929.587-014
06.04.26 LABEL CODER (any ind.), 920.587-014
06.04.37 MARKER, SEMICONDUCTOR WAFERS (electronics),
920.587-026
06.04.38 PACKAGER, HAND (any ind.), 920.587-018
06.04.40 COMPRESSED-GAS-PLANT WORKER (comp. & liq.
gases), 549.587-010
07.02.02 POSTING CLERK (clerical), 216.587-014
07.02.04 TRAFFIC CLERK (clerical), 214.587-014
07.05.03 DIET CLERK (medical ser.), 245.587-010
07.05.03 DOCUMENT PREPARER, MICROFILMING (bus.
ser.), 249.587-018
07.05.04 MAIL CLERK (clerical), 209.587-026
07.05.04 ROUTE-DELIVERY CLERK (clerical), 222.587-034
07.05.04 VAULT WORKER (bus. ser.), 222.587-058
07.07.02 ADDRESSER (clerical), 209.587-010
07.07.02 DIRECT-MAIL CLERK (clerical), 209.587-018
07.07.02 DISTRIBUTING CLERK (clerical), 222.587-018
07.07.02 ROUTER (clerical), 222.587-038

Data = Comparing

647 Comparing, Diverting, Handling

01.07.03 AMUSEMENT PARK ENTERTAINER (amuse. & rec.),
159.647-010

661 Comparing, Speaking-Signaling, Precision

05.10.04 HOUSEHOLD-APPLIANCE INSTALLER (any ind.),
827.661-010
05.10.08 CARVER (hotel & rest.), 316.661-010
10.03.02 ORTHOPEDIC ASSISTANT (medical ser.), 712.661-010

662 Comparing, Speaking-Signaling, Operating — Controlling

05.12.04 CONVEYOR-SYSTEM DISPATCHER (any ind.),
921.662-018
06.01.03 ROLLING ATTENDANT (iron & steel), 613.662-010
06.02.02 NUMERICAL-CONTROL-MACHINE OPERATOR
(mach. shop), 609.662-010
06.02.02 RIVETER, HYDRAULIC (any ind.), 800.662-010
06.02.03 HEAD SAWYER (sawmill), 667.662-010
06.02.05 FELTING-MACHINE OPERATOR (felt goods),
586.662-010
06.02.09 DYNAMITE-PACKING-MACHINE OPERATOR
(explosives), 692.662-010
06.02.17 BRIQUETTE-MACHINE OPERATOR (fuel briquettes),
549.662-010
07.04.06 DIRECTORY-ASSISTANCE OPERATOR (tel. & tel.),
235.662-018
07.04.06 TELEPHONE OPERATOR (clerical), 235.662-022
07.04.06 TELEPHONE-ANSWERING-SERVICE OPERATOR
(bus. ser.), 235.662-026

663 Comparing, Speaking-Signaling, Driving — Operating

03.04.03 SHELLFISH DREDGE OPERATOR (fish.), 446.663-010
05.08.01 TRUCK DRIVER, HEAVY (any ind.), 905.663-014
05.08.03 DELIVERER, CAR RENTAL (auto. ser.), 919.663-010
05.08.03 TOW-TRUCK OPERATOR (auto. ser.), 919.663-026
05.08.04 MOTORBOAT OPERATOR (any ind.), 911.663-010
05.10.02 RIDE OPERATOR (amuse. & rec.), 342.663-010
05.11.01 ASPHALT-PAVING-MACHINE OPERATOR (const.),
853.663-010
05.11.01 SEPTIC-TANK INSTALLER (const.), 851.663-010
05.11.04 BRIDGE-OR-GANTRY-CRANE OPERATOR (any ind.),
921.663-010
05.11.04 DERRICK OPERATOR (any ind.), 921.663-022
05.11.04 DINKEY OPERATOR (any ind.), 919.663-014
05.11.04 HOISTING ENGINEER (any ind.), 921.663-030
05.11.04 STEVEDORE 1 (water trans.), 911.663-014
05.11.04 TRACTOR-CRANE OPERATOR (any ind.), 921.663-058
05.11.04 TRUCK-CRANE OPERATOR (any ind.), 921.663-062
05.12.06 AIRPORT UTILITY WORKER (air trans.), 912.663-010
09.03.02 CHAUFFEUR (any ind.), 913.663-010
09.05.09 ELEVATOR OPERATOR (any ind.), 388.663-010

664 Comparing, Speaking-Signaling, Manipulating

03.04.01 FARMWORKER, LIVESTOCK (agric.), 410.664-010
03.04.03 FISHER, DIVING (fish.), 443.664-010
03.04.05 TREE TRIMMER (light, heat, & power), 408.664-010
05.05.01 MARBLE FINISHER (const.), 861.664-010
05.05.01 TERRAZZO FINISHER (const.), 861.664-014
05.05.01 TILE FINISHER (const.), 861.664-018

05.05.11 DENTAL CERAMIST ASSISTANT (medical ser.), 712.664-010
05.10.01 MUFFLER INSTALLER (auto. ser.), 807.664-010
05.10.01 TAPER (const.), 842.664-010
05.10.01 TILE SETTER HELPER (const.), 869.664-014
05.12.03 BRAKE HOLDER (any ind.), 932.664-010
05.12.03 RECORDING STUDIO SET-UP WORKER (phonograph), 962.664-014
05.12.12 SEWER-LINE REPAIRER (sanitary ser.), 869.664-018
05.12.12 SEWER-PIPE CLEANER (bus. ser.), 899.664-014
05.12.18 JANITOR (any ind.), 382.664-010
06.02.01 TOOL GRINDER 2 (any ind.), 603.664-010
06.04.31 WELDER, GUN (welding), 810.664-010
06.04.32 CANDLEMAKER (candle), 739.664-010
06.04.40 NITROGLYCERIN DISTRIBUTOR (explosives), 559.664-010
09.01.01 AMUSEMENT PARK WORKER (amuse. & rec.), 349.664-010

665 Comparing, Speaking-Signaling, Tending

05.10.05 TAKE-DOWN SORTER (photofinish.), 976.665-010
05.12.04 LABORER, CONCRETE-MIXING PLANT (const.), 579.665-014
05.12.04 LABORER, POWERHOUSE (light, heat, & power), 952.665-010
05.12.14 ASPHALT-DISTRIBUTOR TENDER (const.), 853.665-010
06.04.02 BUFFING-MACHINE TENDER (any ind.), 603.665-010
06.04.06 KNITTING-MACHINE OPERATOR (knit goods), 685.665-014
06.04.09 SILK-SCREEN PRINTER, MACHINE (any ind.), 979.665-010
06.04.15 COOKER, PROCESS CHEESE (dairy prod.), 526.665-010
06.04.15 MIXING-MACHINE OPERATOR (food prep nec), 520.665-014
06.04.15 YEAST-CUTTING-AND-WRAPPING-MACHINE OPERATOR (food prep nec), 529.665-022
06.04.18 TANKER (wood preserving), 561.665-010
06.04.21 PLATER, PRODUCTION (electroplating), 500.665-010
06.04.35 WASHER, MACHINE (laundry), 361.665-010
06.04.40 PUMPER, BREWERY (beer prod.), 914.665-014
07.04.05 SCOREBOARD OPERATOR (amuse. & rec.), 349.665-010

667 Comparing, Speaking-Signaling, Handling

01.08.01 MODEL, ARTISTS' (any ind.), 961.667-010
02.04.02 MORGUE ATTENDANT (medical ser.), 355.667-010
03.04.03 DECKHAND, FISHING VESSEL (fish.), 449.667-010
04.02.01 CORRECTION OFFICER (gov. ser.), 372.667-018
04.02.02 AIRLINE SECURITY REPRESENTATIVE (air trans.), 372.667-010
04.02.02 BODYGUARD (per. ser.), 372.667-014
04.02.02 GATE TENDER (any ind.), 372.667-030
04.02.02 GUARD, SECURITY (any ind.), 372.667-034
04.02.03 BAILIFF (gov. ser.), 377.667-010
04.02.03 BOUNCER (amuse. & rec.), 376.667-010
04.02.03 CHAPERON (per. ser.), 359.667-010
05.07.01 CAR INSPECTOR (r.r. car bldg. & rep.), 910.667-010
05.09.03 ORDER CALLER (clerical), 209.667-014
05.12.03 DUMPER (any ind.), 921.667-010
05.12.04 LABORER, HOISTING (any ind.), 921.667-022
05.12.05 SWITCH TENDER (r.r. trans.), 910.667-026
05.12.12 BILLPOSTER (any ind.), 299.667-010
05.12.20 CROSSING TENDER (any ind.), 371.667-010
06.03.02 INKER (print. & pub.), 659.667-010
06.04.40 LOADER 1 (any ind.), 914.667-010
07.05.02 PRODUCTION PROOFREADER (print. & pub.), 247.667-010
07.07.02 AUCTION ASSISTANT (ret. tr.), 294.667-010
07.07.02 DELIVERER, OUTSIDE (clerical), 230.667-010

07.07.02 TELEPHONE-DIRECTORY DELIVERER (bus. ser.), 230.667-014
09.01.01 HOST/HOSTESS (any ind.), 352.667-010
09.05.08 TICKET TAKER (amuse. & rec.), 344.667-010
12.01.02 FLAGGER (amuse. & rec.), 372.667-026
12.01.02 GOLF-COURSE RANGER (amuse. & rec.), 379.667-010

671 Comparing, Serving, Precision

05.10.08 COOK, SHORT ORDER 2 (hotel & rest.), 313.671-010

673 Comparing, Serving, Driving — Operating

03.04.05 DOG CATCHER (gov. ser.), 379.673-010
05.08.03 CHAUFFEUR, FUNERAL CAR (per. ser.), 359.673-014
09.05.04 DRIVE-IN THEATER ATTENDANT (amuse. & rec.), 349.673-010

674 Comparing, Serving, Manipulating

03.03.01 EXERCISER, HORSE (amuse. & rec.), 153.674-010
03.03.02 ANIMAL CARETAKER (any ind.), 410.674-010
03.03.02 ANIMAL KEEPER (amuse. & rec.), 412.674-010
03.03.02 ANIMAL-RIDE ATTENDANT (amuse. & rec.), 349.674-010
03.03.02 AQUARIST (amuse. & rec.), 449.674-010
03.03.02 DOG GROOMER (per. ser.), 418.674-010
03.03.02 STABLE ATTENDANT (any ind.), 410.674-022
03.04.01 LIVESTOCK-YARD ATTENDANT (any ind.), 410.674-018
09.04.01 CANTEEN OPERATOR (any ind.), 311.674-010
09.05.01 FINGERNAIL FORMER (per. ser.), 331.674-014
09.05.01 MANICURIST (per. ser.), 331.674-010
09.05.06 DRESSER (amuse. & rec.), 346.674-010
10.03.02 GERIATRIC NURSE ASSISTANT (medical ser.), 355.674-026
10.03.02 NURSE AIDE (medical ser.), 355.674-014
10.03.02 ORDERLY (medical ser.), 355.674-018
10.03.02 RESPIRATORY-THERAPY AIDE (medical ser.), 355.674-022
10.03.03 CHILD-CARE ATTENDANT, SCHOOL (per. ser.), 355.674-010
12.01.02 LEAD PONY RIDER (amuse. & rec.), 153.674-014

677 Comparing, Serving, Handling

03.03.02 DOG BATHER (per. ser.), 418.677-010
07.07.02 MESSENGER, COPY (print. & pub.), 239.677-010
09.01.04 FUNERAL ATTENDANT (per. ser.), 359.677-014
09.04.02 SALES ATTENDANT, BUILDING MATERIALS (ret. tr.), 299.677-014
09.04.02 SELF-SERVICE-LAUNDRY-AND-DRY-CLEANING ATTENDANT (clean., dye., & press.), 369.677-010
09.05.01 COOLING-ROOM ATTENDANT (per. ser.), 335.677-010
09.05.01 HOT-ROOM ATTENDANT (per. ser.), 335.677-014
09.05.02 CAFETERIA ATTENDANT (hotel & rest.), 311.677-010
09.05.02 COUNTER ATTENDANT, CAFETERIA (hotel & rest.), 311.677-014
09.05.02 DINING ROOM ATTENDANT (hotel & rest.), 311.677-018
09.05.02 FOOD-SERVICE WORKER, HOSPITAL (medical ser.), 355.677-010
09.05.02 MESS ATTENDANT (water trans.), 350.677-010
09.05.03 BELLHOP (hotel & rest.), 324.677-010
09.05.03 CHECKROOM ATTENDANT (any ind.), 358.677-010
09.05.03 PORTER (air trans.), 357.677-010
09.05.04 DOORKEEPER (any ind.), 324.677-014
09.05.04 HOSPITAL ENTRANCE ATTENDANT (medical ser.), 355.677-014
09.05.06 CADDIE (amuse. & rec.), 341.677-010
09.05.07 LOCKER-ROOM ATTENDANT (per. ser.), 358.677-014
09.05.07 RESTROOM ATTENDANT (any ind.), 358.677-018
09.05.08 CHILDREN'S ATTENDANT (amuse. & rec.), 349.677-018
09.05.08 USHER (amuse. & rec.), 344.677-014
10.03.02 FIRST-AID ATTENDANT (any ind.), 354.677-010

10.03.03 NURSERY SCHOOL ATTENDANT (any ind.), 359.677-018
10.03.03 PLAYROOM ATTENDANT (any ind.), 359.677-026

681 Comparing, Taking Instructions — Helping, Precision

01.06.01 SILK-SCREEN CUTTER (any ind.), 979.681-022
05.05.11 DENTURE-MODEL MAKER (medical ser.), 712.681-014
05.05.11 FINISHER, DENTURE (medical ser.), 712.681-018
05.05.11 LENS MOUNTER 2 (optical goods), 713.681-010
05.10.01 DRY-WALL APPLICATOR (const.), 842.681-010
05.10.01 FRAME REPAIRER (furn.), 763.681-010
05.10.02 BICYCLE REPAIRER (any ind.), 639.681-010
05.10.05 DEVELOPER (photofinish.), 976.681-010
05.10.08 BUTCHER, MEAT (hotel & rest.), 316.681-010
06.01.04 ASSEMBLER (inst. & app.), 710.681-010
06.01.04 GLASS BLOWER (glass mfg.), 772.681-010
06.01.04 LENS POLISHER, HAND (optical goods), 716.681-018
06.02.32 DENTURE WAXER (medical ser.), 712.681-010
06.04.35 SILK FINISHER (clean., dye., & press.), 363.681-010

682 Comparing, Taking Instructions — Helping, Operating — Controlling

05.06.03 PUMPER (any ind.), 914.682-010
05.10.05 BLUEPRINTING-MACHINE OPERATOR (any ind.), 979.682-014
05.10.05 DUPLICATING-MACHINE OPERATOR 1 (clerical), 207.682-010
05.10.05 ENGRAVER, MACHINE 1 (engraving), 704.682-010
05.10.05 EQUIPMENT MONITOR, PHOTOTYPESETTING (print. & pub.), 650.682-010
05.10.05 OFFSET-DUPLICATING-MACHINE OPERATOR (clerical), 207.682-018
05.11.02 CORE-DRILL OPERATOR (any ind.), 930.682-010
05.11.02 PLANT OPERATOR (concrete prod.), 570.682-014
05.12.12 TRACK REPAIRER (r.r. trans.), 910.682-010
06.02.02 CRIMPING-MACHINE OPERATOR (any ind.), 616.682-022
06.02.02 HEATER (forging), 619.682-022
06.02.02 LASER-BEAM-TRIM OPERATOR (electronics), 726.682-010
06.02.02 LATHE HAND (jewelry), 700.682-014
06.02.02 POLISHING-MACHINE OPERATOR (any ind.), 603.682-026
06.02.02 PRESS OPERATOR (fabric. plastic prod.), 690.682-062
06.02.02 PUNCH-PRESS OPERATOR 3 (any ind.), 615.682-014
06.02.03 CUT-OFF-SAW OPERATOR (woodworking), 667.682-022
06.02.03 NAILING-MACHINE OPERATOR (any ind.), 669.682-058
06.02.04 BOX-FOLDING-MACHINE OPERATOR (paper goods), 649.682-010
06.02.05 BINDER (any ind.), 787.682-010
06.02.05 CARPET SEWER (carpet & rug), 787.682-014
06.02.05 HAT-AND-CAP SEWER (hat & cap), 784.682-014
06.02.05 HEMMER (any ind.), 787.682-026
06.02.05 MENDER (any ind.), 787.682-030
06.02.05 SEWING-MACHINE OPERATOR (leather prod.), 783.682-014
06.02.05 SEWING-MACHINE OPERATOR (any ind.), 787.682-046
06.02.05 STITCHER, STANDARD MACHINE (boot & shoe), 690.682-082
06.02.05 TRIMMER, MACHINE (garment), 781.682-010
06.02.05 ZIPPER SETTER (any ind.), 787.682-086
06.02.06 CARPET WEAVER (carpet & rug), 683.682-010
06.02.06 WEAVER (asbestos prod.), 683.682-038
06.02.08 EYEGLASS-LENS CUTTER (optical goods), 716.682-010
06.02.08 PRECISION-LENS POLISHER (optical goods), 716.682-018
06.02.09 BROOM STITCHER (brush & broom), 692.682-022
06.02.09 CUTTER OPERATOR (any ind.), 699.682-018

06.02.09 DIE CUTTER (any ind.), 699.682-022
06.02.09 WIRE-WRAPPING-MACHINE OPERATOR (electronics), 726.682-014
06.02.10 SAND MIXER, MACHINE (foundry), 570.682-018
06.02.15 CENTER-MACHINE OPERATOR (confection.), 520.682-014
06.02.15 COFFEE ROASTER (food prep nec), 523.682-014
06.02.15 DOUGHNUT-MACHINE OPERATOR (bake. prod.), 526.682-022
06.02.15 GRINDER OPERATOR (grain & feed mill), 521.682-026
06.02.15 OVEN OPERATOR, AUTOMATIC (bake. prod.), 526.682-030
06.02.18 IMPREGNATOR (electronics), 590.682-014
06.02.18 ROOFING-MACHINE OPERATOR (build. mat. nec), 554.682-022
06.02.19 LASER-BEAM-MACHINE OPERATOR (welding), 815.682-010
06.02.20 ARBOR-PRESS OPERATOR 1 (any ind.), 616.682-010
06.02.20 COVERING-MACHINE OPERATOR (print. & pub.), 653.682-014
06.02.20 KICK-PRESS OPERATOR 1 (any ind.), 616.682-026
06.02.20 STACKING-MACHINE OPERATOR 1 (any ind.), 692.682-054
06.02.21 ANODIZER (any ind.), 500.682-010
06.02.21 PAINTER, ELECTROSTATIC (any ind.), 599.682-010
06.04.02 TOOL DRESSER (any ind.), 601.682-010
06.04.05 PRESSER, MACHINE (any ind.), 363.682-018
06.04.09 LEAF STAMPER (any ind.), 979.682-018
06.04.32 MACHINE MOLDER (foundry), 518.682-010
06.04.35 LEATHER FINISHER (clean., dye., & press.), 363.682-010
06.04.35 PRESSER, ALL-AROUND (clean., dye., & press.), 363.682-014
06.04.40 PALLETIZER OPERATOR 1 (any ind.), 921.682-014

683 Comparing, Taking Instructions — Helping, Driving — Operating

03.04.01 FARMWORKER, FRUIT 1 (agric.), 403.683-010
03.04.01 FARMWORKER, GENERAL 1 (agric.), 421.683-010
03.04.03 SKIFF OPERATOR (fish.), 441.683-010
03.04.04 GREENSKEEPER 2 (any ind.), 406.683-010
05.08.01 DUMP-TRUCK DRIVER (any ind.), 902.683-010
05.08.01 TRUCK DRIVER, LIGHT (any ind.), 906.683-022
05.08.02 TRACKMOBILE OPERATOR (any ind.), 919.683-026
05.08.03 AMBULANCE DRIVER (medical ser.), 913.683-010
05.08.03 CONCRETE-MIXING-TRUCK DRIVER (const.), 900.683-010
05.08.03 TELEPHONE-DIRECTORY-DISTRIBUTOR DRIVER (bus. ser.), 906.683-018
05.11.01 BULLDOZER OPERATOR 1 (any ind.), 850.683-010
05.11.01 POWER-SHOVEL OPERATOR (any ind.), 850.683-030
05.11.01 ROAD-ROLLER OPERATOR (const.), 859.683-030
05.11.01 ROCK-DRILL OPERATOR 1 (const.), 850.683-034
05.11.01 STREET-SWEEPER OPERATOR (gov. ser.), 919.683-022
05.11.04 CONVEYOR OPERATOR (any ind.), 921.683-026
05.11.04 DRAGLINE OPERATOR (any ind.), 850.683-018
05.11.04 FRONT-END LOADER OPERATOR (any ind.), 921.683-042
05.11.04 TRACTOR OPERATOR (any ind.), 929.683-014
05.12.04 BOOM-CONVEYOR OPERATOR (any ind.), 921.683-014
05.12.04 ELEVATOR OPERATOR, FREIGHT (any ind.), 921.683-038
05.12.18 ATTENDANT, CAMPGROUND (amuse. & rec.), 329.683-010
05.12.18 GOLF-RANGE ATTENDANT (amuse. & rec.), 341.683-010
05.12.18 SWEEPER-CLEANER, INDUSTRIAL (any ind.), 389.683-010
06.04.40 INDUSTRIAL-TRUCK OPERATOR (any ind.), 921.683-050

684   Comparing, Taking Instructions — Helping, Manipulating

01.06.01 ETCHER (engraving), 704.684-010
01.06.02 PICTURE FRAMER (framing), 739.684-146
01.06.03 PAINTER, AIRBRUSH (any ind.), 741.684-018
03.04.02 BUCKER (logging), 454.684-010
03.04.02 FALLER 2 (logging), 454.684-014
03.04.02 LOGGER, ALL-ROUND (logging), 454.684-018
03.04.03 FISH HATCHERY WORKER (fish.), 446.684-010
03.04.03 FISHER, LINE (fish.), 442.684-010
03.04.03 FISHER, NET (fish.), 441.684-010
03.04.04 CEMETERY WORKER (real estate), 406.684-010
03.04.04 GROUNDSKEEPER, INDUSTRIAL-COMMERCIAL (any ind.), 406.684-014
03.04.04 LAWN-SERVICE WORKER (agric.), 408.684-010
05.03.02 TAPER, PRINTED CIRCUIT LAYOUT (electronics), 017.684-010
05.05.06 WELDER, GAS (welding), 811.684-014
05.05.11 PACKER, DENTURE (medical ser.), 712.684-034
05.09.01 MEAT CLERK (ret. tr.), 222.684-010
05.10.01 BUILDING CLEANER (any ind.), 891.684-022
05.10.01 FENCE ERECTOR (const.), 869.684-022
05.10.01 FURNITURE ASSEMBLER-AND-INSTALLER (ret. tr.), 739.684-082
05.10.01 GLASS INSTALLER (auto. ser.), 865.684-010
05.10.01 GRIP (amuse. & rec.), 962.684-014
05.10.01 PUMP INSTALLER (any ind.), 630.684-018
05.10.01 REPAIRER (furn.), 709.684-062
05.10.01 ROUSTABOUT (petrol. production), 869.684-046
05.10.01 SIDER (const.), 863.684-014
05.10.01 SIGN ERECTOR 2 (signs), 869.684-054
05.10.01 TORCH-STRAIGHTENER-AND-HEATER (any ind.), 709.684-086
05.10.01 UMBRELLA REPAIRER (any ind.), 369.684-018
05.10.01 WATER-SOFTENER SERVICER-AND-INSTALLER (bus. ser.), 862.684-034
05.10.01 WELDER, TACK (welding), 810.684-010
05.10.02 AUTOMOBILE-ACCESSORIES INSTALLER (auto. ser.), 806.684-038
05.10.04 DOLL REPAIRER (any ind.), 731.684-014
05.10.04 POLISHING-WHEEL SETTER (any ind.), 776.684-014
05.10.04 SPORTS-EQUIPMENT REPAIRER (any ind.), 732.684-122
05.10.04 SWIMMING-POOL SERVICER (any ind.), 891.684-018
05.10.04 USED-CAR RENOVATOR (ret. tr.), 620.684-034
05.10.05 FILM LABORATORY TECHNICIAN (motion pic.), 976.684-014
05.10.07 PAINTER, SPRAY 1 (any ind.), 741.684-026
05.10.07 PAINTER, TOUCH-UP (any ind.), 749.684-038
05.10.08 MEAT CUTTER (ret. tr.), 316.684-018
05.10.08 PANTRY GOODS MAKER (hotel & rest.), 317.684-014
05.10.09 EXTERMINATOR (any ind.), 389.684-010
05.12.11 THERMAL CUTTER, HAND 2 (welding), 816.684-010
05.12.12 HIGHWAY-MAINTENANCE WORKER (gov. ser.), 899.684-014
05.12.12 PIPE-FITTER HELPER (const.), 862.684-022
05.12.12 WINDOW REPAIRER (any ind.), 899.684-042
05.12.13 KEY CUTTER (any ind.), 709.684-050
05.12.14 BILLPOSTER (bus. ser.), 841.684-010
05.12.14 SHOE DYER (per. ser.), 364.684-014
05.12.14 STEEL-PLATE CALKER (any ind.), 843.684-010
05.12.14 STOVE REFINISHER (any ind.), 749.684-046
05.12.14 UNDERCOATER (auto. ser.), 843.684-014
05.12.15 AUTOMOBILE WRECKER (whole. tr.), 620.684-010
05.12.15 BELT REPAIRER (any ind.), 630.684-014
05.12.15 ROLLER-SKATE REPAIRER (any ind.), 732.684-102
05.12.15 TIRE REPAIRER (auto. ser.), 915.684-010
05.12.16 ANTENNA INSTALLER (any ind.), 823.684-010
05.12.16 CABLE PULLER (const.), 829.684-018
05.12.17 COFFEE MAKER (hotel & rest.), 317.684-010
05.12.17 DELI CUTTER-SLICER (ret. tr.), 316.684-014
05.12.17 SANDWICH MAKER (hotel & rest.), 317.684-018
05.12.18 LAUNDRY WORKER 1 (any ind.), 361.684-014
05.12.18 PRINT-SHOP HELPER (print. & pub.), 979.684-026

05.12.19 BOOK REPAIRER (any ind.), 977.684-010
06.02.09 HONEYCOMB-BLANKET MAKER (aircraft-aerospace mfg.), 806.684-062
06.02.21 PLATER, PRINTED CIRCUIT BOARD PANELS (electronics), 500.684-026
06.02.22 BRAZER, ASSEMBLER (welding), 813.684-010
06.02.22 CABINET ASSEMBLER (furn.), 763.684-014
06.02.22 ELECTRIC-SIGN ASSEMBLER (signs), 729.684-022
06.02.22 FURNITURE ASSEMBLER (furn.), 763.684-038
06.02.22 MOTORCYCLE ASSEMBLER (motor. & bicycles), 806.684-090
06.02.22 UTILITY WORKER (mfg. bldgs.), 869.684-074
06.02.23 ASSEMBLER, MUSICAL INSTRUMENTS (musical inst.), 730.684-010
06.02.23 ASSEMBLER, PRODUCTION LINE (photo. apparatus), 714.684-010
06.02.23 ASSEMBLER, SEMICONDUCTOR (electronics), 726.684-034
06.02.23 ASSEMBLER, SURGICAL GARMENT (per. protect. & med. device), 712.684-010
06.02.23 BITE-BLOCK MAKER (medical ser.), 712.684-014
06.02.23 CAPACITOR ASSEMBLER (elec. equip.), 729.684-014
06.02.23 CHAIN MAKER, MACHINE (jewelry), 700.684-022
06.02.23 ELECTRICAL-CONTROL ASSEMBLER (elec. equip.), 729.684-026
06.02.23 ELECTRONICS ASSEMBLER (electronics), 726.684-018
06.02.23 PRINTED CIRCUIT BOARD ASSEMBLER, HAND (electronics), 726.684-070
06.02.23 TUBE ASSEMBLER, CATHODE RAY (electronics), 725.684-022
06.02.23 WHEEL LACER AND TRUER (motor. & bicycles), 706.684-106
06.02.23 WIRER, SUBASSEMBLIES (office mach.), 729.684-062
06.02.24 ARMATURE BANDER (any ind.), 724.684-010
06.02.24 ASSEMBLER, METAL BONDING (aircraft-aerospace mfg.), 806.684-030
06.02.24 BOAT PATCHER, PLASTIC (ship bldg. & rep.), 807.684-014
06.02.24 BRIGHT CUTTER (jewelry), 700.684-018
06.02.24 GREASE BUFFER (silverware), 705.684-022
06.02.24 MESH CUTTER (jewelry), 700.684-050
06.02.24 PRESSURE SEALER-AND-TESTER (aircraft-aerospace mfg.), 806.684-110
06.02.24 REPAIRER, FINISHED METAL (any ind.), 809.684-034
06.02.24 RING STAMPER (jewelry), 700.684-066
06.02.24 SKI REPAIRER, PRODUCTION (sports equip.), 732.684-118
06.02.24 SPINNER (jewelry), 700.684-074
06.02.24 TROPHY ASSEMBLER (jewelry), 735.684-018
06.02.25 BOX MAKER, WOOD (wood. box), 760.684-014
06.02.26 PRESSER (print. & pub.), 977.684-018
06.02.27 BLOCKER, HAND 1 (hat & cap), 580.684-010
06.02.27 CUTTER, MACHINE 1 (any ind.), 781.684-014
06.02.27 LEATHER CUTTER (leather prod.), 783.684-022
06.02.27 LEATHER WORKER (leather prod.), 783.684-026
06.02.27 MATTRESS MAKER (matt. & bedspring), 780.684-074
06.02.27 MENDER (carpet & rug), 782.684-042
06.02.27 SPOTTER (laundry), 361.684-018
06.02.28 DOUGHNUT MAKER (bake. prod.), 526.684-010
06.02.29 RUBBER-GOODS REPAIRER (any ind.), 759.684-054
06.02.30 GLASS CUTTER (any ind.), 775.684-022
06.02.30 PLASTER MAKER (statue & art), 779.684-046
06.02.30 PLASTER-DIE MAKER (pottery & porc.), 774.684-026
06.02.32 BOW MAKER, PRODUCTION (sports equip.), 732.684-038
06.02.32 BRUSH MATERIAL PREPARER (brush & broom), 739.684-022
06.02.32 CABLE MAKER (elec. equip.), 728.684-010
06.02.32 ETCHED-CIRCUIT PROCESSOR (electronics), 590.684-018
06.02.32 OPAQUER (medical ser.), 712.684-030
06.02.32 RACKET STRINGER (sports equip.), 732.684-094
06.02.32 SKI MOLDER (sports equip.), 732.684-114

06.03.02 ELECTRONICS INSPECTOR II (electronics), 726.684-022

06.03.02 ELECTRONICS TESTER II (electronics), 726.684-026

06.03.02 INSPECTOR, INTEGRATED CIRCUITS (electronics), 726.684-058

06.03.02 INSPECTOR, PRINTED CIRCUIT BOARDS (electronics), 726.684-062

06.03.02 INSPECTOR, SEMICONDUCTOR WAFER (electronics), 726.684-066

06.04.08 CERAMIC CAPACITOR PROCESSOR (electronics), 590.684-010

06.04.19 ELECTRONIC-COMPONENT PROCESSOR (electronics), 590.684-014

06.04.19 PLATER, SEMICONDUCTOR WAFERS AND COMPONENTS (electronics), 500.684-030

06.04.19 POLYSILICON PREPARATION WORKER (electronics), 590.684-038

06.04.19 SEMICONDUCTOR PROCESSOR (electronics), 590.684-022

06.04.22 ASSEMBLER, AUTOMOBILE (auto. mfg.), 806.684-010

06.04.22 LAMINATOR, HAND (furn.), 763.684-050

06.04.22 NAILER, HAND (any ind.), 762.684-050

06.04.22 PLASTIC-TOP ASSEMBLER (furn.), 763.684-062

06.04.22 RIVETER, HAND (any ind.), 709.684-066

06.04.23 ASSEMBLER (jewelry), 700.684-014

06.04.23 ASSEMBLER (elec. equip.), 723.684-010

06.04.23 ASSEMBLER (sports equip.), 732.684-014

06.04.23 ASSEMBLER, MOLDED FRAMES (optical goods), 713.684-014

06.04.23 ASSEMBLER, SMALL PARTS (any ind.), 706.684-022

06.04.23 BENCH ASSEMBLER (agric. equip.), 706.684-042

06.04.23 COIL WINDER (elec. equip.), 724.684-026

06.04.23 EARRING MAKER (jewelry), 700.684-030

06.04.23 ELECTRIC-MOTOR ASSEMBLER (elec. equip.), 721.684-022

06.04.23 FILLER (house. furn.), 780.684-066

06.04.23 LOCK ASSEMBLER (hardware), 706.684-074

06.04.23 MULTIFOCAL-LENS ASSEMBLER (optical goods), 713.684-034

06.04.23 TIRE MOUNTER (fabric. prod. nec), 739.684-158

06.04.24 ARBORER (jewelry), 700.684-010

06.04.24 BENCH GRINDER (any ind.), 705.684-010

06.04.24 BENCH WORKER (optical goods), 713.684-018

06.04.24 BUFFER 1 (any ind.), 705.684-014

06.04.24 FILER (jewelry), 700.684-034

06.04.24 GRINDER 1 (any ind.), 705.684-026

06.04.24 GRINDER-CHIPPER 2 (any ind.), 809.684-026

06.04.24 JIGSAWYER (jewelry), 700.684-046

06.04.24 METAL FINISHER (any ind.), 705.684-034

06.04.24 MOLD DRESSER (any ind.), 519.684-018

06.04.24 OXIDIZER (silverware), 700.684-054

06.04.24 POLISHER (any ind.), 705.684-058

06.04.24 POLISHER, EYEGLASS FRAMES (optical goods), 713.684-038

06.04.24 REFINER (medical ser.), 712.684-038

06.04.24 SILK-SCREEN ETCHER (engraving), 704.684-014

06.04.24 STONER (jewelry), 735.684-014

06.04.24 STRETCHER (jewelry), 700.684-078

06.04.25 CANER 2 (furn.), 763.684-022

06.04.26 TRIM-STENCIL MAKER (any ind.), 781.684-058

06.04.27 BOW MAKER (any ind.), 789.684-010

06.04.27 CANVAS REPAIRER (any ind.), 782.684-010

06.04.27 SEWER, HAND (any ind.), 782.684-058

06.04.27 THREAD CUTTER (any ind.), 789.684-050

06.04.28 BONER, MEAT (slaught. & meat pack.), 525.684-010

06.04.28 CANDY DIPPER, HAND (confection.), 524.684-010

06.04.28 CIGAR MAKER (tobacco), 790.684-014

06.04.28 DECORATOR (bake. prod.), 524.684-014

06.04.28 FISH CLEANER (can. & preserv.), 525.684-030

06.04.28 TRIMMER, MEAT (slaught. & meat pack.), 525.684-054

06.04.29 FABRICATOR, FOAM RUBBER (any ind.), 780.684-062

06.04.30 GLASS FINISHER (glass prod.), 775.684-026

06.04.30 SAGGER MAKER (pottery & porc.), 774.684-030

06.04.30 TABLE-TOP TILE SETTER (brick & tile), 763.684-074

06.04.31 WELDER, PRODUCTION LINE (welding), 819.684-010

06.04.33 ENAMELER (plumb. supplies), 509.684-010

06.04.33 METAL SPRAYER, PRODUCTION (any ind.), 505.684-014

06.04.33 PAINTER, BRUSH (any ind.), 740.684-022

06.04.33 PUTTY GLAZER (any ind.), 749.684-042

06.04.33 TOUCH-UP PAINTER, HAND (any ind.), 740.684-026

06.04.34 ARTIFICIAL-FLOWER MAKER (artif. flower), 739.684-014

06.04.34 BROOMMAKER (brush & broom), 739.684-018

06.04.34 DECAL APPLIER (any ind.), 749.684-010

06.04.34 DRILLER, HAND (any ind.), 809.684-018

06.04.34 INSULATION-BLANKET MAKER (aircraft-aerospace mfg.), 806.684-078

06.04.34 MAT CUTTER (framing), 739.684-126

06.04.34 MOUNTER, HAND (photofinish.), 976.684-018

06.04.34 PAINT MIXER, HAND (any ind.), 550.684-018

06.04.34 PHOTO MASK CLEANER (electronics), 590.684-034

06.04.34 SCREEN PRINTER (any ind.), 979.684-034

06.04.34 WIREWORKER (elec. equip.), 728.684-022

06.04.35 LAUNDERER, HAND (laundry), 361.684-010

06.04.35 LAUNDRY OPERATOR (laundry), 369.684-014

06.04.35 PRESSER, HAND (any ind.), 363.684-018

06.04.38 PARACHUTE RIGGER (air trans.), 912.684-010

06.04.39 EQUIPMENT CLEANER (any ind.), 599.684-010

06.04.39 LABORER, GENERAL (mach. shop), 609.684-014

06.04.39 WASHER (optical goods), 713.684-042

685 Comparing, Taking Instructions — Helping, Tending

05.06.02 AIR-COMPRESSOR OPERATOR (any ind.), 950.685-010

05.10.05 TYPESETTING-MACHINE TENDER (print. & pub.), 650.685-010

05.11.04 DUMP OPERATOR (any ind.), 921.685-038

05.12.06 WATER TENDER (any ind.), 599.685-122

05.12.19 AUXILIARY-EQUIPMENT OPERATOR, DATA PROCESSING (clerical), 213.685-010

05.12.19 BRAILLE-DUPLICATING-MACHINE OPERATOR (print. & pub.), 207.685-010

05.12.19 BURSTING-MACHINE TENDER (clerical), 217.685-010

05.12.19 COLLATOR OPERATOR (clerical), 208.685-010

05.12.19 FOLDING-MACHINE OPERATOR (clerical), 208.685-014

05.12.19 INSERTING-MACHINE OPERATOR (clerical), 208.685-018

05.12.19 MICROFILM MOUNTER (clerical), 208.685-022

05.12.19 PHOTOCOPYING-MACHINE OPERATOR (clerical), 207.685-014

05.12.19 PHOTOGRAPHIC-MACHINE OPERATOR (clerical), 207.685-018

06.02.02 BRAKE OPERATOR 2 (any ind.), 619.685-026

06.02.06 SEAMLESS-HOSIERY KNITTER (hosiery), 684.685-010

06.02.18 STILL TENDER (any ind.), 552.685-026

06.03.01 CABLE STRETCHER AND TESTER (aircraft-aerospace mfg.), 806.685-010

06.04.02 BENDING-MACHINE OPERATOR 2 (any ind.), 617.685-010

06.04.02 DRILL-PRESS OPERATOR, PRODUCTION (mach. shop), 606.685-026

06.04.02 DRUM STRAIGHTENER 1 (any ind.), 619.685-034

06.04.02 EMBOSSER (any ind.), 583.685-030

06.04.02 LATHE OPERATOR, PRODUCTION (mach. shop), 604.685-026

06.04.02 MACHINE OPERATOR 2 (any ind.), 619.685-062

06.04.02 MAGNETIC-TAPE WINDER (electronics), 726.685-010

06.04.02 NIBBLER OPERATOR (any ind.), 615.685-026

06.04.02 POWER-PRESS TENDER (any ind.), 617.685-026

06.04.02 PUNCH-PRESS OPERATOR II (any ind.), 615.685-030

06.04.02 SCROLL-MACHINE OPERATOR (struct. & ornam. metalwork), 616.685-062

06.04.02 TURRET-PUNCH-PRESS OPERATOR, TAPE-CONTROL (any ind.), 615.685-042

06.04.02 WIRE-DRAWING-MACHINE TENDER (wire), 614.685-026

06.04.03 ARTIFICIAL-LOG-MACHINE OPERATOR (fuel briquettes), 569.685-010

06.04.03 BUZZSAW OPERATOR (any ind.), 667.685-026

06.04.04 BAG-MACHINE OPERATOR (paper goods), 649.685-014

06.04.04 BINDERY WORKER (print. & pub.), 653.685-010

06.04.04 CARTON-FORMING-MACHINE OPERATOR (any ind.), 641.685-022

06.04.04 CARTON-FORMING-MACHINE TENDER (paper goods), 641.685-026

06.04.05 ADHESIVE-BANDAGE-MACHINE OPERATOR (per. protect. & med. device), 692.685-014

06.04.05 BUTTONHOLE-AND-BUTTON-SEWING-MACHINE OPERATOR (garment), 786.685-042

06.04.05 EYELET-MACHINE OPERATOR (any ind.), 699.685-018

06.04.05 FASTENER-SEWING-MACHINE OPERATOR (any ind.), 787.685-010

06.04.05 FOLDER-SEAMER, AUTOMATIC (any ind.), 787.685-014

06.04.05 HEMMER, AUTOMATIC (house. furn.), 787.685-018

06.04.05 PLEATING-MACHINE OPERATOR (any ind.), 583.685-082

06.04.05 SEWING-MACHINE OPERATOR, SPECIAL EQUIPMENT (matt. & bedspring), 689.685-118

06.04.05 SPREADER, MACHINE (any ind.), 781.685-010

06.04.05 STRIP-CUTTING-MACHINE OPERATOR (any ind.), 686.685-066

06.04.05 SURGICAL-DRESSING MAKER (per. protect. & med. device), 689.685-130

06.04.05 TACKING-MACHINE OPERATOR (any ind.), 787.685-042

06.04.06 BEAM-WARPER TENDER, AUTOMATIC (asbestos prod.), 681.685-018

06.04.06 PICKING-MACHINE OPERATOR (any ind.), 680.685-082

06.04.06 YARN WINDER (any ind.), 681.685-154

06.04.07 DESIGN PRINTER, BALLOON (rubber goods), 651.685-014

06.04.07 RUBBER CUTTER (rubber goods), 559.685-158

06.04.08 COREMAKER, MACHINE 1 (foundry), 518.685-014

06.04.08 CRUSHER TENDER (any ind.), 570.685-022

06.04.08 LENS-FABRICATING-MACHINE TENDER (optical goods), 716.685-022

06.04.08 MILLER (cement), 570.685-046

06.04.09 CROWN-ASSEMBLY-MACHINE OPERATOR (any ind.), 692.685-062

06.04.09 CUTTER (photofinish.), 976.685-010

06.04.09 CUTTER, MACHINE 2 (any ind.), 699.685-014

06.04.09 CUTTING-MACHINE TENDER (any ind.), 690.685-122

06.04.09 EMBOSSING-PRESS OPERATOR (any ind.), 652.685-030

06.04.09 KEYMODULE-ASSEMBLY-MACHINE TENDER (office mach.), 692.685-274

06.04.09 PHOTORESIST LAMINATOR, PRINTED CIRCUIT BOARD (electronics), 699.685-042

06.04.09 SCRAP HANDLER (any ind.), 509.685-050

06.04.09 SPRAY-PAINTING-MACHINE OPERATOR (any ind.), 741.685-010

06.04.09 WAX MOLDER (foundry), 549.685-038

06.04.10 DIE-CASTING-MACHINE OPERATOR 2 (foundry), 514.685-018

06.04.10 INJECTION-MOLDING-MACHINE TENDER (fabric. plastic prod.), 556.685-038

06.04.10 MILL OPERATOR (any ind.), 599.685-058

06.04.10 OXIDIZED-FINISH PLATER (any ind.), 599.685-062

06.04.11 CENTRIFUGE OPERATOR, PLASMA PROCESSING (drug prep. & related), 599.685-018

06.04.11 CHEMICAL PREPARER 1 (chem.), 550.685-030

06.04.11 DRIER OPERATOR (chem.), 553.685-042

06.04.11 MIXER (paint & varn.), 550.685-078

06.04.13 BOWLING-BALL MOLDER (sports equip.), 556.685-018

06.04.13 COMPRESSION-MOLDING-MACHINE TENDER (fabric. plastic prod.), 556.685-022

06.04.13 CONTACT-LENS MOLDER (optical goods), 690.685-090

06.04.13 LENS HARDENER (optical goods), 573.685-030

06.04.13 RECORD-PRESS TENDER (phonograph), 556.685-070

06.04.13 TIRE MOLDER (rubber tire & tube), 553.685-102

06.04.15 BAND-SAW OPERATOR (slaught. & meat pack.), 525.685-010

06.04.15 BREWERY CELLAR WORKER (beer prod.), 522.685-014

06.04.15 CENTRIFUGE OPERATOR (dairy prod.), 521.685-042

06.04.15 CHOCOLATE MOLDER, MACHINE (choc. & cocoa), 529.685-054

06.04.15 COFFEE GRINDER (food prep nec), 521.685-078

06.04.15 COOK, FRY, DEEP FAT (can. & preserv.), 526.685-014

06.04.15 FLOUR BLENDER (grain & feed mill), 520.685-106

06.04.15 HONEY PROCESSOR (food prep nec), 522.685-070

06.04.15 MILL OPERATOR (corn prod.), 521.685-226

06.04.15 OVEN TENDER (bake. prod.), 526.685-030

06.04.15 PRESS OPERATOR, MEAT (slaught. & meat pack.), 520.685-182

06.04.16 EXTRACTOR OPERATOR (any ind.), 581.685-038

06.04.16 HARDENING-MACHINE OPERATOR (hat & cap), 586.685-026

06.04.17 AUXILIARY-EQUIPMENT TENDER (cement), 570.685-010

06.04.17 SHELL MOLDER (foundry), 518.685-026

06.04.19 COATING EQUIPMENT OPERATOR, PRINTED CIRCUIT BOARDS (electronics), 590.685-066

06.04.19 CREMATOR (per. ser.), 359.685-010

06.04.19 DEVELOPER, AUTOMATIC (photofinish.), 976.685-014

06.04.19 DISPLAY-SCREEN FABRICATOR (electronics), 725.685-010

06.04.19 ETCHER-STRIPPER, PRINTED CIRCUIT BOARDS (electronics), 590.685-082

06.04.19 FILTER OPERATOR (any ind.), 551.685-078

06.04.19 METALLIZATION EQUIPMENT OPERATOR, SEMICONDUCTOR WAFERS (electronics), 590.685-086

06.04.19 PRINT DEVELOPER, AUTOMATIC (photofinish.), 976.685-026

06.04.19 UTILITY WORKER, FILM PROCESSING (photofinish.), 976.685-030

06.04.20 ASSEMBLY-PRESS OPERATOR (any ind.), 690.685-014

06.04.20 CORRUGATED-FASTENER DRIVER (woodworking), 669.685-042

06.04.20 MOUNTER, AUTOMATIC (photofinish.), 976.685-022

06.04.20 STAPLING-MACHINE OPERATOR (any ind.), 692.685-202

06.04.21 CERAMIC COATER, MACHINE (any ind.), 509.685-022

06.04.21 DIPPER (any ind.), 599.685-026

06.04.21 DIPPER AND BAKER (any ind.), 599.685-030

06.04.21 ELECTROLESS PLATER, PRINTED CIRCUIT BOARD PANELS (electronics), 501.685-022

06.04.21 JEWELRY COATER (jewelry), 590.685-046

06.04.21 PAINTER, TUMBLING BARREL (any ind.), 599.685-070

06.04.21 PAINTING-MACHINE OPERATOR (any ind.), 599.685-074

06.04.21 PLATER, HOT DIP (galvanizing), 501.685-010

06.04.21 SEED PELLETER (agric.), 599.685-126

06.04.34 MACHINE SNELLER (sports equip.), 732.685-026

06.04.34 STUFFER (toys & games), 731.685-014

06.04.35 PRESS OPERATOR (laundry), 363.685-010

06.04.35 PRESSER, FORM (any ind.), 363.685-018

06.04.37 NAME-PLATE STAMPER (any ind.), 652.685-054

06.04.37 TICKETER (any ind.), 652.685-098

06.04.38 CARDER (any ind.), 920.685-034

06.04.38 PACKAGE SEALER, MACHINE (any ind.), 920.685-074

06.04.38 PACKAGER, MACHINE (any ind.), 920.685-078

06.04.39 WASHER, MACHINE (any ind.), 599.685-114

06.04.39 WASHING-MACHINE OPERATOR (any ind.), 599.685-118

06.04.40 CHAR-CONVEYOR TENDER (sugar), 529.685-050
06.04.40 CONVEYOR TENDER (any ind.), 921.685-026

686 Comparing, Taking Instructions — Helping, Feeding — Offbearing

05.12.03 PRESS BUCKER (any ind.), 920.686-042
05.12.19 COIN WRAPPER (clerical), 217.686-010
06.04.02 GRAINER, MACHINE (any ind.), 652.686-014
06.04.03 CHAIN OFFBEARER (planing mill), 669.686-018
06.04.03 LATHE SPOTTER (veneer & plywood), 663.686-022
06.04.04 FOLDING-MACHINE FEEDER (print. & pub.), 653.686-014
06.04.05 CEMENTER, MACHINE APPLICATOR (boot & shoe), 690.686-018
06.04.05 GLOVE TURNER AND FORMER, AUTOMATIC (glove & mitten), 583.686-018
06.04.09 MACHINE FEEDER (any ind.), 699.686-010
06.04.10 LABORER, GENERAL (nonfer. metal prod.), 519.686-010
06.04.13 FUSING-FURNACE LOADER (optical goods), 573.686-014
06.04.15 BAKER HELPER (bake. prod.), 526.686-010
06.04.15 CANNERY WORKER (can. & preserv.), 529.686-014
06.04.16 MACHINE FEEDER, RAW STOCK (felt goods), 680.686-018
06.04.18 DIGESTER-OPERATOR HELPER (build. board), 532.686-010
06.04.19 HEAT TREATER (electronics), 504.686-022
06.04.19 LABORER (drug prep. & related), 559.686-022
06.04.21 SPRAY-UNIT FEEDER (any ind.), 599.686-014
06.04.27 LABORER, GENERAL (leather mfg.), 589.686-026
06.04.35 WASHING-MACHINE LOADER-AND-PULLER (laundry), 361.686-010
06.04.38 BAKERY WORKER (bake. prod.), 929.686-010
06.04.40 CONVEYOR FEEDER-OFFBEARER (any ind.), 921.686-014
06.04.40 LABORER, CONCRETE PLANT (concrete prod.), 579.686-010
06.04.40 LABORER, GENERAL (iron & steel), 509.686-010
06.04.40 SAWMILL WORKER (sawmill), 667.686-014

687 Comparing, Taking Instructions — Helping, Handling

01.06.02 DISTRESSER (furn.), 763.687-018
02.04.02 LABORATORY ASSISTANT, BLOOD AND PLASMA (drug prep. & related), 078.687-010
03.04.01 CHRISTMAS-TREE FARM WORKER (forestry), 451.687-010
03.04.01 FARMWORKER, GENERAL 2 (agric.), 421.687-010
03.04.01 FARMWORKER, VEGETABLE 2 (agric.), 402.687-010
03.04.01 SORTER, AGRICULTURAL PRODUCE (agric.), 529.687-186
03.04.02 CHAINSAW OPERATOR (logging), 454.687-010
03.04.02 FOREST WORKER (forestry), 452.687-010
03.04.02 FOREST-FIRE FIGHTER (forestry), 452.687-014
03.04.04 GROUNDSKEEPER, PARKS AND GROUNDS (gov. ser.), 406.687-010
03.04.04 HORTICULTURAL WORKER 2 (agric.), 405.687-014
03.04.04 LABORER, LANDSCAPE (agric.), 408.687-014
05.08.04 DECKHAND (water trans.), 911.687-022
05.09.01 LABORER, STORES (any ind.), 922.687-058
05.09.01 SHIPPING CHECKER (clerical), 222.687-030
05.09.01 SUPPLY CLERK (per. ser.), 339.687-010
05.09.03 RECEIVING CHECKER (clerical), 222.687-018
05.10.01 CARPET-LAYER HELPER (ret. tr.), 864.687-010
05.12.03 BAGGAGE HANDLER (r.r. trans.), 910.687-010
05.12.03 CONSTRUCTION WORKER 2 (const.), 869.687-026
05.12.03 DOLLY PUSHER (radio & tv broad.), 962.687-010
05.12.03 ETCHER HELPER, HAND (print. & pub.), 971.687-010
05.12.03 GARBAGE COLLECTOR (motor trans.), 909.687-010
05.12.03 INSTALLER (museum), 922.687-050
05.12.03 LABORER (petrol. production), 939.687-018
05.12.03 LABORER, PETROLEUM REFINERY (petrol. refin.), 549.687-018

05.12.03 LABORER, SHIPYARD (ship bldg. & rep.), 809.687-022
05.12.03 MATERIAL HANDLER (any ind.), 929.687-030
05.12.03 YARD LABORER (paper & pulp), 922.687-102
05.12.04 CHOKE SETTER (logging), 921.687-014
05.12.04 GRIP (motion pic.), 962.687-022
05.12.06 LINE-SERVICE ATTENDANT (air trans.), 912.687-010
05.12.08 GARAGE SERVICER, INDUSTRIAL (any ind.), 915.687-014
05.12.08 LUBRICATION SERVICER (auto. ser.), 915.687-018
05.12.08 OILER (any ind.), 699.687-018
05.12.12 AUTOMOBILE-BODY-REPAIRER HELPER (auto. ser.), 807.687-010
05.12.12 DECORATOR, STREET AND BUILDING (any ind.), 899.687-010
05.12.17 COOK HELPER (hotel & rest.), 317.687-010
05.12.18 AUTOMOBILE DETAILER (auto. ser.), 915.687-034
05.12.18 BARTENDER HELPER (hotel & rest.), 312.687-010
05.12.18 CARETAKER (dom. ser.), 301.687-010
05.12.18 CENTRAL-SUPPLY WORKER (medical ser.), 381.687-010
05.12.18 CHANGE-HOUSE ATTENDANT (any ind.), 358.687-010
05.12.18 CHIMNEY SWEEP (any ind.), 891.687-010
05.12.18 CLEANER 2 (any ind.), 919.687-014
05.12.18 CLEANER, COMMERCIAL OR INSTITUTIONAL (any ind.), 381.687-014
05.12.18 CLEANER, HOSPITAL (medical ser.), 323.687-010
05.12.18 CLEANER, HOUSEKEEPING (any ind.), 323.687-014
05.12.18 CLEANER, INDUSTRIAL (any ind.), 381.687-018
05.12.18 CLEANER, LABORATORY EQUIPMENT (any ind.), 381.687-022
05.12.18 CLEANER, SIGNS (signs), 739.687-062
05.12.18 CLEANER, WINDOW (any ind.), 389.687-014
05.12.18 FURNACE CLEANER (any ind.), 891.687-014
05.12.18 KITCHEN HELPER (hotel & rest.), 318.687-010
05.12.18 LIGHT-FIXTURE SERVICER (any ind.), 389.687-018
05.12.18 ORDINARY SEAMAN (water trans.), 911.687-030
05.12.18 SANDBLASTER (any ind.), 503.687-010
05.12.18 SEWAGE-DISPOSAL WORKER (sanitary ser.), 955.687-010
05.12.18 STEAM CLEANER (auto. ser.), 915.687-026
05.12.18 STREET CLEANER (gov. ser.), 955.687-018
05.12.18 TANK CLEANER (any ind.), 891.687-022
05.12.18 TUBE CLEANER (any ind.), 891.687-030
05.12.18 VENETIAN-BLIND CLEANER AND REPAIRER (any ind.), 739.687-198
06.03.02 CALIBRATION CHECKER 2 (inst. & app.), 710.687-018
06.03.02 GARMENT INSPECTOR (any ind.), 789.687-070
06.03.02 GLASS INSPECTOR (any ind.), 579.687-022
06.03.02 HYDRO-PNEUMATIC TESTER (any ind.), 862.687-018
06.03.02 INSPECTOR (jewelry), 700.687-034
06.03.02 LENS EXAMINER (optical goods), 716.687-022
06.03.02 LUMBER SORTER (woodworking), 922.687-074
06.03.02 METAL-FINISH INSPECTOR (any ind.), 703.687-014
06.03.02 PAINT-SPRAY INSPECTOR (any ind.), 741.687-010
06.03.02 PHOTO CHECKER AND ASSEMBLER (photofinish.), 976.687-014
06.03.02 PHOTOFINISHING LABORATORY WORKER (photofinish.), 976.687-018
06.03.02 PRINT INSPECTOR (pottery & porc.), 774.687-018
06.04.17 KILN WORKER (pottery & porc.), 573.687-022
06.04.22 ASSEMBLER, BICYCLE 2 (motor. & bicycles), 806.687-010
06.04.22 ASSEMBLER, PRODUCTION (any ind.), 706.687-010
06.04.23 ASSEMBLER, SMALL PRODUCTS (any ind.), 739.687-030
06.04.23 TOY ASSEMBLER (toys & games), 731.687-034
06.04.24 CONTACT-LENS-FLASHING PUNCHER (optical goods), 713.687-014
06.04.24 LABORER, GOLD LEAF (gold leaf & foil), 700.687-038
06.04.24 MELTER (jewelry), 700.687-042
06.04.24 PREPARER (jewelry), 700.687-062
06.04.25 CROSSBAND LAYER (veneer & plywood), 762.687-026

06.04.25 WOODWORKING-SHOP HAND (woodworking), 769.687-054

06.04.27 CARPET CUTTER 2 (carpet & rug), 585.687-014

06.04.28 CANDY MOLDER, HAND (confection.), 520.687-018

06.04.28 POULTRY DRESSER (agric.), 525.687-070

06.04.33 PAINTER (jewelry), 735.687-018

06.04.33 PAINTER, SPRAY 2 (any ind.), 741.687-018

06.04.34 ELECTRONICS WORKER (electronics), 726.687-010

06.04.34 LABORER, GRINDING AND POLISHING (any ind.), 705.687-014

06.04.34 LEADER TIER (sports equip.), 732.687-038

06.04.34 MASKER (any ind.), 749.687-018

06.04.35 LAUNDRY LABORER (laundry), 361.687-018

06.04.37 MARKER 2 (any ind.), 920.687-126

06.04.37 STENCILER (any ind.), 920.687-178

06.04.38 ASSEMBLER, HOSPITAL SUPPLIES (inst. & app.), 712.687-010

06.04.38 FLOOR WORKER (chew. gum), 920.687-090

06.04.38 PACKING-LINE WORKER (rubber goods), 753.687-038

06.04.39 CLEANER AND POLISHER (any ind.), 709.687-010

06.04.39 DIPPER (jewelry), 735.687-010

06.04.40 CLAMP REMOVER (veneer & plywood), 569.687-010

06.04.40 DISTILLERY WORKER, GENERAL (distilled liquor), 529.687-066

06.04.40 GENERAL HELPER (oils & fats), 529.687-094

06.04.40 LABORER (slaught. & meat pack.), 529.687-130

06.04.40 LABORER, CHEMICAL PROCESSING (chem.), 559.687-050

06.04.40 LABORER, SALVAGE (any ind.), 929.687-022

06.04.40 MUNITIONS HANDLER (ammunition), 929.687-034

07.05.02 REVIEWER (insurance), 209.687-018

07.05.04 MAIL HANDLER (gov. ser.), 209.687-014

07.07.02 ADVERTISING-MATERIAL DISTRIBUTOR (any ind.), 230.687-010

07.07.02 CHECKER 1 (clerical), 222.687-010

07.07.02 CONTROL CLERK, DATA PROCESSING 2 (clerical), 221.687-010

07.07.02 PAGE (library), 249.687-014

07.07.02 SORTER (clerical), 209.687-022

07.07.03 COIN-MACHINE COLLECTOR (bus. ser.), 292.687-010

09.05.02 COUNTER-SUPPLY WORKER (hotel & rest.), 319.687-010

09.05.07 CLOTHES-ROOM WORKER (medical ser.), 355.687-010

Appendix F
Office of Employment Statistics (OES) Codes

These codes are used by the Office of Employment Statistics (OES) to categorize the occupations people work in when the census is taken each 10 years. These codes and occupational names are also used by each state to track employment statistics such as salaries paid and outlook for future openings. The numbers are useful in cross-referencing occupations listed in *The Enhanced Guide for Occupational Exploration* or with other occupational information systems and are arranged in numeric order.

13002	FINANCIAL MANAGERS
13005	PERSONNEL, TRAINING, AND LABOR RELATIONS MANAGERS
13008	PURCHASING MANAGERS
13011	MARKETING, ADVERTISING, AND PUBLIC RELATIONS MANAGERS
13014	ADMINISTRATIVE SERVICES MANAGERS
13017	ENGINEERING, MATH, AND NATURAL SCIENCE MANAGERS
15002	POSTMASTERS AND MAIL SUPERINTENDENTS
15005	EDUCATION ADMINISTRATORS
15008	MEDICINE AND HEALTH SERVICE MANAGERS
15011	PROPERTY AND REAL ESTATE MANAGERS
15014	INDUSTRIAL PRODUCTION MANAGERS
15017	CONSTRUCTION MANAGERS
15021	MINING AND RELATED MANAGERS
15023	COMMUNICATIONS, TRANSPORTATION, AND UTILITIES OPERATIONS MANAGERS
15026	FOOD SERVICE AND LODGING MANAGERS
19002	GOVERNMENT CHIEF EXECUTIVES AND LEGISLATORS
19005	GENERAL MANAGERS AND TOP EXECUTIVES
19999	ALL OTHER MANAGERS AND ADMINISTRATORS
21102	UNDERWRITERS
21105	CREDIT ANALYSTS
21108	LOAN OFFICERS AND COUNSELORS
21111	TAX PREPARERS
21114	ACCOUNTANTS AND AUDITORS
21117	BUDGET ANALYSTS
21199	ALL OTHER FINANCIAL SPECIALISTS
21302	WHOLESALE AND RETAIL BUYERS, EXCEPT FARM PRODUCTS
21305	PURCHASING AGENTS AND BUYERS, FARM
21308	PURCHASING AGENTS, EXCEPT WHOLESALE, RETAIL AND FARM PRODUCTS
21502	CLAIMS TAKERS, UNEMPLOYMENT BENEFITS
21505	SPECIAL AGENTS, INSURANCE
21508	EMPLOYMENT INTERVIEWERS, PRIVATE OR PUBLIC EMPLOYMENT SERVICE
21511	PERSONNEL, TRAINING, AND LABOR RELATIONS SPECIALISTS
21902	COST ESTIMATORS
21905	MANAGEMENT ANALYSTS
21908	CONSTRUCTION AND BUILDING INSPECTORS
21911	INSPECTORS AND COMPLIANCE OFFICERS, EXCEPT CONSTRUCTION
21914	TAX EXAMINERS, COLLECTORS, AND REVENUE AGENTS
21917	ASSESSORS
21921	CLAIMS EXAMINERS, PROPERTY AND CASUALTY INSURANCE
21999	ALL OTHER MANAGEMENT SUPPORT WORKERS
22102	AERONAUTICAL AND ASTRONAUTICAL ENGINEERS
22105	METALLURGISTS AND METALLURGICAL, CERAMIC AND MATERIALS ENGINEERS
22108	MINING ENGINEERS, INCLUDING MINE SAFETY ENGINEERS
22111	PETROLEUM ENGINEERS
22114	CHEMICAL ENGINEERS
22117	NUCLEAR ENGINEERS
22121	CIVIL ENGINEERS, INCLUDING TRAFFIC ENGINEERS
22123	AGRICULTURAL ENGINEERS
22126	ELECTRICAL AND ELECTRONICS ENGINEERS
22127	COMPUTER ENGINEERS
22128	INDUSTRIAL ENGINEERS, EXCEPT SAFETY ENGINEERS
22132	SAFETY ENGINEERS, EXCEPT MINING
22135	MECHANICAL ENGINEERS
22138	MARINE ENGINEERS
22199	ALL OTHER ENGINEERS
22302	ARCHITECTS, EXCEPT LAND AND MARINE
22305	MARINE ARCHITECTS
22308	LANDSCAPE ARCHITECTS
22311	SURVEYING AND MAPPING SCIENTISTS
22502	CIVIL ENGINEERING TECHNICIANS AND TECHNOLOGISTS
22505	ELECTRICAL AND ELECTRONIC TECHNICIANS AND TECHNOLOGISTS
22508	INDUSTRIAL ENGINEERING TECHNICIANS AND TECHNOLOGISTS
22511	MECHANICAL ENGINEERING TECHNICIANS AND TECHNOLOGISTS
22514	DRAFTERS
22517	ESTIMATORS AND DRAFTERS, UTILITIES
22521	SURVEYING AND MAPPING TECHNICIANS
22599	ALL OTHER ENGINEERING TECHNICIANS AND TECHNOLOGISTS

24102	PHYSICISTS AND ASTRONOMERS
24105	CHEMISTS
24108	METEOROLOGISTS
24111	GEOLOGISTS, GEOPHYSICISTS, AND OCEANOGRAPHERS
24199	ALL OTHER PHYSICAL SCIENTISTS
24302	FORESTERS AND CONSERVATION SCIENTISTS
24305	AGRICULTURAL AND FOOD SCIENTISTS
24308	BIOLOGICAL SCIENTISTS
24311	MEDICAL SCIENTISTS
24502	BIOLOGICAL AND AGRICULTURAL TECHNICIANS AND TECHNOLOGISTS
24505	CHEMICAL TECHNICIANS AND TECHNOLOGISTS, EXCEPT HEALTH
24508	NUCLEAR TECHNICIANS AND TECHNOLOGISTS
24511	PETROLEUM TECHNICIANS AND TECHNOLOGISTS
24599	ALL OTHER SCIENCE TECHNICIANS AND TECHNOLOGISTS
25102	COMPUTER SYSTEMS ANALYSTS
25105	COMPUTER PROGRAMMERS
25108	COMPUTER PROGRAMMER AIDES
25111	PROGRAMMERS, NUMERICAL, TOOL, AND PROCESS CONTROL
25302	OPERATIONS RESEARCH ANALYSTS
25312	STATISTICIANS
25313	ACTUARIES
25315	FINANCIAL ANALYSTS, STATISTICIANS
25319	MATHEMATICIANS AND ALL OTHER MATHEMATICAL SCIENTISTS
25323	MATHEMATICAL TECHNICIANS
27102	ECONOMISTS
27105	URBAN AND REGIONAL PLANNERS
27108	PSYCHOLOGISTS
27199	ALL OTHER SOCIAL SCIENTISTS
27302	SOCIAL WORKERS, MEDICAL AND PSYCHIATRIC
27305	SOCIAL WORKERS, EXCEPT MEDICAL AND PSYCHIATRIC
27307	RESIDENTIAL COUNSELORS
27308	HUMAN SERVICES WORKERS
27311	RECREATION WORKERS
27502	CLERGY
27505	DIRECTOR, RELIGIOUS ACTIVITIES AND EDUCATION
27599	ALL OTHER RELIGIOUS WORKERS
28102	JUDGES AND MAGISTRATES
28105	ADJUDICATORS, HEARING OFFICERS, AND JUDICIAL
28108	LAWYERS
28302	LAW CLERKS
28305	PARALEGALS
28308	TITLE SEARCHERS
28311	TITLE EXAMINERS AND ABSTRACTERS
28399	ALL OTHER LEGAL ASSISTANTS
31114	NURSING INSTRUCTORS
31117	GRADUATE ASSISTANTS, TEACHING
31202	LIFE SCIENCES TEACHERS
31204	CHEMISTRY TEACHERS
31206	PHYSICS TEACHERS
31209	ALL OTHER PHYSICAL SCIENCE TEACHERS
31210	SOCIAL SCIENCES TEACHERS
31212	HEALTH SPECIALTIES TEACHERS
31216	ENGLISH AND FOREIGN LANGUAGE TEACHERS-POST SECONDARY
31218	ART, DRAMA, AND MUSIC TEACHERS
31222	ENGINEERING TEACHERS
31224	MATHEMATICAL SCIENCES TEACHERS
31226	COMPUTER SCIENCE TEACHERS
31299	ALL OTHER POST SECONDARY TEACHERS
31302	TEACHERS,PRESCHOOL AND KINDERGARTEN
31305	TEACHERS, ELEMENTARY
31308	TEACHERS, SECONDARY SCHOOL
31311	TEACHERS, SPECIAL EDUCATION
31314	TEACHERS AND INSTRUCTORS, VOCATIONAL EDUCATION AND TRAINING

31317	TEACHERS, ADULT (NONVOCATIONAL) EDUCATION
31321	INSTRUCTORS AND COACHES, SPORTS AND PHYSICAL TRAINING
31323	FARM AND HOME MANAGEMENT ADVISORS
31399	ALL OTHER TEACHERS AND INSTRUCTORS
31502	LIBRARIANS, PROFESSIONAL
31505	TECHNICAL ASSISTANTS, LIBRARY
31508	AUDIO-VISUAL SPECIALISTS
31511	CURATORS, ARCHIVISTS, MUSEUM TECHNICIANS, AND RESTORERS
31514	COUNSELORS
31517	INSTRUCTIONAL COORDINATORS
31521	TEACHER AIDES, PARAPROFESSIONAL
32102	PHYSICIANS
32105	DENTISTS
32108	OPTOMETRISTS
32111	PODIATRISTS
32113	CHIROPRACTORS
32114	VETERINARIANS AND VETERINARY INSPECTORS
32199	ALL OTHER HEALTH PRACTITIONERS
32302	RESPIRATORY THERAPISTS
32305	OCCUPATIONAL THERAPISTS
32308	PHYSICAL THERAPISTS
32311	CORRECTIONAL AND MANUAL ARTS THERAPISTS
32314	SPEECH-LANGUAGE PATHOLOGISTS AND AUDIOLOGISTS
32317	RECREATIONAL THERAPISTS
32399	ALL OTHER THERAPISTS
32502	REGISTERED NURSES
32505	LICENSED PRACTICAL NURSES
32508	EMERGENCY MEDICAL TECHNICIANS
32511	PHYSICIAN ASSISTANTS
32514	OPTICIANS, DISPENSING AND MEASURING
32517	PHARMACISTS
32521	DIETITIANS AND NUTRITIONISTS
32523	DIETETIC TECHNICIANS
32902	MEDICAL AND CLINICAL LABORATORY TECHNOLOGISTS
32905	MEDICAL AND CLINICAL LABORATORY TECHNICIANS
32908	DENTAL HYGIENISTS
32911	MEDICAL RECORDS TECHNICIANS
32914	NUCLEAR MEDICINE TECHNOLOGISTS
32917	RADIOLOGIC TECHNOLOGISTS
32921	RADIOLOGIC TECHNICIANS
32923	EEG TECHNOLOGISTS
32925	CARDIOLOGY TECHNOLOGISTS
32926	EKG TECHNICIANS
32928	SURGICAL TECHNOLOGISTS
32931	PSYCHIATRIC TECHNICIANS
32999	ALL OTHER HEALTH PROFESSIONALS AND PARAPROFESSIONALS
34002	WRITERS AND EDITORS
34005	TECHNICAL WRITERS
34008	PUBLIC RELATIONS SPECIALISTS AND PUBLICITY WRITERS
34011	REPORTERS AND CORRESPONDENTS
34014	BROADCAST NEWS ANALYSTS
34017	ANNOUNCERS, RADIO AND TELEVISION
34021	ANNOUNCERS, OTHER
34023	PHOTOGRAPHERS
34026	CAMERA OPERATORS, TELEVISION, MOTION PICTURES, VIDEO
34028	BROADCAST TECHNICIANS
34032	FILM EDITORS
34035	ARTISTS AND RELATED WORKERS
34038	DESIGNERS, EXCEPT INTERIOR DESIGNERS
34041	INTERIOR DESIGNERS
34044	MERCHANDISE DISPLAYERS AND WINDOW DRESSERS
34047	MUSIC DIRECTORS, SINGERS, AND RELATED
34051	MUSICIANS, INSTRUMENTAL
34053	DANCERS AND CHOREOGRAPHERS

34056	PRODUCERS, DIRECTORS, ACTORS, AND ENTERTAINERS
34058	ATHLETES, COACHES, UMPIRES, AND RELATED
39002	AIR TRAFFIC CONTROLLERS
39005	TRAFFIC TECHNICIANS
39008	RADIO OPERATORS
39011	FUNERAL DIRECTORS AND MORTICIANS
39014	EMBALMERS
39999	ALL OTHER PROFESSIONAL, PARAPROFESSIONAL, AND TECHNICAL WORKERS
41002	FIRST LINE SUPERVISORS AND MANAGER/SUPERVISORS
43002	INSURANCE SALES WORKERS
43005	BROKERS, REAL ESTATE
43008	SALES AGENTS, REAL ESTATE
43011	REAL ESTATE APPRAISERS
43014	SECURITIES AND FINANCIAL SERVICES SALES WORKERS
43017	SALES AGENTS, SELECTED BUSINESS SERVICES
43021	TRAVEL AGENTS
43023	SALES AGENTS, ADVERTISING
43099	ALL OTHER SALES REPRESENTATIVES AND SALESPERSONS, SERVICE
49002	SALES ENGINEERS
49005	SALES REPRESENTATIVES SCIENTIFIC PRODUCTS AND SERVICES
49008	OTHER SALES REPRESENTATIVES, EXCEPT RETAIL
49011	SALESPERSONS, RETAIL
49014	SALESPERSONS, PARTS
49017	COUNTER AND RENTAL CLERKS
49021	STOCK CLERKS, SALES FLOOR
49023	CASHIERS
49026	VENDORS, SOLICITORS AND RELATED
49032	DEMONSTRATORS, PROMOTERS AND MODELS
49999	ALL OTHER SALES AND RELATED WORKERS
51002	CLERICAL SUPERVISORS AND MANAGERS
53102	BANK TELLERS
53105	NEW ACCOUNTS CLERKS, BANKING
53108	TRANSIT CLERKS
53111	LOAN INTERVIEWERS
53114	CREDIT AUTHORIZERS
53117	CREDIT CHECKERS
53121	LOAN AND CREDIT CLERKS
53123	ADJUSTMENT CLERKS
53126	STATEMENT CLERKS
53128	BROKERAGE CLERKS
53302	INSURANCE ADJUSTERS, EXAMINERS, AND INVESTIGATORS
53305	INSURANCE APPRAISERS, AUTO DAMAGE
53308	INSURANCE EXAMINING CLERKS
53311	INSURANCE CLAIMS CLERKS
53314	INSURANCE POLICY PROCESSING CLERKS
53502	WELFARE ELIGIBILITY WORKERS AND INTERVIEWERS
53505	INVESTIGATORS, CLERICAL
53508	BILL AND ACCOUNT COLLECTORS
53702	COURT CLERKS
53705	MUNICIPAL CLERKS
53708	LICENSE CLERKS
53802	TRAVEL CLERKS
53805	RESERVATION AND TRANSPORTATION TICKET AGENTS
53808	HOTEL DESK CLERKS
53902	LIBRARY ASSISTANTS AND BOOKMOBILE DRIVERS
53905	TEACHER AIDES AND EDUCATIONAL ASSISTANTS, CLERICAL
53908	ADVERTISING CLERKS
53911	PROOFREADERS AND COPY MARKERS
53914	REAL ESTATE CLERKS
55102	LEGAL SECRETARIES
55105	MEDICAL SECRETARIES
55108	SECRETARIES, EXCEPT LEGAL AND MEDICAL

55302	STENOGRAPHERS
55305	RECEPTIONISTS AND INFORMATION CLERKS
55308	TYPISTS
55311	TYPISTS, WORD PROCESSING EQUIPMENT
55314	PERSONNEL CLERKS, EXCEPT PAYROLL AND TIMEKEEPING
55317	CORRESPONDENCE CLERKS
55321	FILE CLERKS
55323	ORDER CLERKS, MATERIALS, MERCHANDISE, AND SERVICE
55326	PROCUREMENT CLERKS
55328	STATISTICAL CLERKS
55332	INTERVIEWING CLERKS, EXCEPT PERSONNEL AND WELFARE
55335	CUSTOMER SERVICE REPRESENTATIVES, UTILITIES
55338	BOOKKEEPING, ACCOUNTING, AND AUDITING CLERKS
55341	PAYROLL AND TIMEKEEPING CLERKS
55344	BILLING, COST, AND RATE CLERKS
55347	GENERAL OFFICE CLERKS
56002	BILLING, POSTING, AND CALCULATING MACHINE OPERATORS
56005	DUPLICATING MACHINE OPERATORS
56008	MAIL MACHINE OPERATORS, PREP HAND
56011	COMPUTER OPERATORS, EXCEPT PERIPHERAL EQUIPMENT
56014	PERIPHERAL EDP EQUIPMENT OPERATORS
56017	DATA ENTRY KEYERS, EXCEPT COMPOSING
56021	DATA ENTRY KEYERS, COMPOSING
56099	ALL OTHER OFFICE MACHINE OPERATORS
57102	SWITCHBOARD OPERATORS
57105	DIRECTORY ASSISTANCE OPERATORS
57108	CENTRAL OFFICE OPERATORS
57111	TELEGRAPH AND TELETYPE OPERATORS
57199	ALL OTHER COMMUNICATIONS EQUIPMENT OPERATORS
57302	MAIL CLERKS, EXCEPT MAIL MACHINE OPERATORS AND POSTAL SERVICE
57305	POSTAL MAIL CARRIERS
57308	POSTAL SERVICE CLERKS
57311	MESSENGERS
58002	DISPATCHERS, POLICE, FIRE, AND AMBULANCE
58005	DISPATCHERS, EXCEPT POLICE, FIRE, AND AMBULANCE
58008	PRODUCTION, PLANNING, AND EXPEDITING CLERKS
58011	TRANSPORTATION AGENTS
58014	METER READERS, UTILITIES
58017	WEIGHERS, MEASURERS, CHECKERS, AND SAMPLERS, RECORD KEEPING
58021	MARKING CLERKS
58023	STOCK CLERKS, STOCKROOM, WAREHOUSE, OR YARD
58026	ORDER FILLERS, WHOLESALE AND RETAIL SALES
58028	TRAFFIC, SHIPPING, AND RECEIVING CLERKS
58099	ALL OTHER MATERIAL RECORDS, SCHEDULING AND DISTRIBUTION WORKERS
59999	ALL OTHER CLERICAL AND ADMINISTRATIVE SUPPORT WORKERS
61002	FIRE FIGHTING AND PREVENTION SUPERVISORS
61005	POLICE AND DETECTIVE SUPERVISORS
61008	HOUSEKEEPERS, INSTITUTIONAL
61099	ALL OTHER SERVICE SUPERVISORS AND MANAGER SUPERVISORS
63002	FIRE INSPECTORS
63005	FOREST FIRE INSPECTORS AND PREVENTION SUPERVISORS
63008	FIRE FIGHTERS
63011	POLICE DETECTIVES
63014	POLICE PATROL OFFICERS
63017	CORRECTION OFFICERS AND JAILERS
63021	PARKING ENFORCEMENT OFFICERS'
63023	BAILIFFS
63026	U.S. MARSHALS

63028	CRIMINAL INVESTIGATORS, FEDERAL
63032	SHERIFFS AND DEPUTY SHERIFFS
63035	DETECTIVES AND INVESTIGATORS, EXCEPT PUBLIC
63038	RAILROAD AND TRANSIT POLICE
63041	FISH AND GAME WARDENS
63044	CROSSING GUARDS
63047	GUARDS
63099	ALL OTHER PROTECTIVE SERVICE WORKERS
65002	HOSTS AND HOSTESSES, RESTAURANT/LOUNGE/COFFEE SHOP
65005	BARTENDERS
65008	WAITERS AND WAITRESSES
65011	FOOD SERVERS
65014	DINING ROOM AND CAFETERIA ATTENDANTS AND BARTENDER HELPERS
65017	COUNTER ATTENDANTS, LUNCHROOM, CAFETERIA
65021	BAKERS, BREAD AND PASTRY
65023	BUTCHERS AND MEAT CUTTERS
65026	COOKS, RESTAURANT
65028	COOKS, INSTITUTION OR CAFETERIA
65032	COOKS, FAST FOOD
65035	COOKS, SHORT ORDER
65038	FOOD PREPARATION WORKERS
65041	FOOD PREPARATION AND SERVICE WORKERS, FAST FOOD
65099	ALL OTHER FOOD SERVICE WORKERS
66002	DENTAL ASSISTANTS
66005	MEDICAL ASSISTANTS
66008	NURSING AIDES, ORDERLIES, AND ATTENDANTS
66011	HOME HEALTH AIDES
66014	PSYCHIATRIC AIDES
66017	PHYSICAL AND CORRECTIVE THERAPY ASSISTANTS AND AIDES
66021	OCCUPATIONAL THERAPY ASSISTANTS AND AIDES
66023	AMBULANCE DRIVERS AND ATTENDANTS, EXCEPT EMT
66026	PHARMACY ASSISTANTS
66099	ALL OTHER HEALTH SERVICE WORKERS
67002	MAIDS AND HOUSEKEEPING CLEANERS
67005	JANITORS AND CLEANERS
67008	PEST CONTROLLERS AND ASSISTANTS
67011	ELEVATOR OPERATORS
67099	ALL OTHER CLEANING AND BUILDING SERVICE WORKERS
68002	BARBERS
68005	HAIRDRESSERS, HAIRSTYLISTS, AND COSMETOLOGISTS
68008	MANICURISTS
68011	SHAMPOOERS
68014	AMUSEMENT AND RECREATION ATTENDANTS
68017	GUIDES
68021	USHERS, LOBBY ATTENDANTS, AND TICKET TAKERS
68023	BAGGAGE PORTERS AND BELLHOPS
68026	FLIGHT ATTENDANTS
68028	TRANSPORTATION ATTENDANTS, OTHER
68032	WARDROBE AND DRESSING ROOM ATTENDANTS
68035	SOCIAL WELFARE SERVICE AIDES
68038	CHILD CARE WORKERS
68041	FUNERAL ATTENDANTS
69999	ALL OTHER SERVICE WORKERS
72002	FIRST LINE SUPERVISORS, AGRICULTURE, .
73002	FALLERS AND BUCKERS
73005	CHOKE SETTERS
73011	LOGGING TRACTOR OPERATORS
73099	ALL OTHER TIMBER CUTTING AND RELATED LOGGING WORKERS
79002	FOREST AND CONSERVATION WORKERS
79005	NURSERY WORKERS
79008	LOG GRADERS AND SCALERS
79011	GRADERS AND SORTERS, AGRICULTURAL PRODUCTS
79014	GARDENERS AND GROUNDSKEEPERS, EXCEPT FARM
79017	ANIMAL CARETAKERS, EXCEPT FARM
79021	FARM EQUIPMENT OPERATORS
79999	ALL OTHER AGRICULTURE, FORESTRY, FISHING, AND RELATED WORKERS
81002	FIRST LINE SUPERVISORS, MECHANICS AND REPAIRERS
81005	FIRST LINE SUPERVISORS, CONSTRUCTION AND RELATED
81008	FIRST LINE SUPERVISORS, PRODUCTION AND RELATED
81011	FIRST LINE SUPERVISORS, TRANSPORTATION AND RELATED
81017	FIRST LINE SUPERVISORS, HELPERS AND LABORERS
83002	INSPECTORS, TESTERS, AND GRADERS, PRECISION
83005	PRODUCTION INSPECTORS, TESTERS, ETC.
83008	TRANSPORTATION INSPECTORS
85112	MACHINERY MAINTENANCE MECHANICS, TEXTILE MACHINES
85113	MACHINERY MAINTENANCE MECHANICS, SEWING MACHINES
85116	MACHINERY MAINTENANCE MECHANICS, MARINE EQUIPMENT
85117	MINE MACHINERY MECHANICS
85118	MACHINERY MAINTENANCE MECHANICS, WATER/POWER
85119	ALL OTHER MACHINERY MAINTENANCE MECHANICS
85123	MILLWRIGHTS
85126	REFRACTORY MATERIAL REPAIRERS
85128	MACHINERY MAINTENANCE WORKERS
85132	MAINTENANCE REPAIRERS, GENERAL UTILITY
85302	AUTOMOTIVE MECHANICS
85305	AUTOMOTIVE BODY AND RELATED REPAIRERS
85308	MOTORCYCLE REPAIRERS
85311	BUS AND TRUCK MECHANICS AND DIESEL ENGINE SPECIALISTS
85314	MOBILE HEAVY EQUIPMENT MECHANICS
85317	RAIL CAR REPAIRERS
85321	FARM EQUIPMENT MECHANICS
85323	AIRCRAFT MECHANICS
85326	AIRCRAFT ENGINE SPECIALISTS
85328	SMALL ENGINE SPECIALISTS
85502	CENTRAL OFFICE AND PBX INSTALLERS AND REPAIRERS
85505	FRAME WIRERS, CENTRAL OFFICE
85508	TELEGRAPH AND TELETYPE INSTALLERS AND REPAIRERS
85511	SIGNAL OR TRACK SWITCH MAINTAINERS
85514	RADIO MECHANICS
85599	ALL OTHER COMMUNICATIONS EQUIPMENT MECHANICS, INSTALLERS, AND REPAIRERS
85702	TELEPHONE AND CABLE TV LINE INSTALLERS AND REPAIRERS
85705	DATA PROCESSING EQUIPMENT REPAIRERS
85708	ELECTRONIC HOME ENTERTAINMENT EQUIPMENT REPAIRERS
85711	ELECTRIC HOME APPLIANCE AND POWER TOOL REPAIRERS
85714	ELECTRIC MOTOR, TRANSFORMER, AND RELATED REPAIRERS
85717	ELECTRONICS REPAIRERS, COMMERCIAL AND INDUSTRIAL EQUIPMENT
85721	POWERHOUSE, SUBSTATION, AND RELATED ELECTRICAL
85723	ELECTRICAL POWERLINE INSTALLERS AND REPAIRERS
85726	STATION INSTALLERS AND REPAIRERS, TELEPHONE
85728	ELECTRICAL INSTALLERS AND REPAIRERS, TRANS. EQUIPMENT, MANUFACT.

85799	ALL OTHER ELECTRICAL AND ELECTRONIC EQUIP. MECHANICS, INSTALLERS, AND REPAIRERS	87921	ROUSTABOUTS
		87923	ROOF BOLTERS
		87941	CONTINUOUS MINING MACHINE OPERATORS
85902	HEATING, AIR CONDITIONING, AND REFRIGERATION MECHANICS AND INSTALLERS	87943	MINE CUTTING AND CHANNELING MACHINE OPERATORS
85905	PRECISION INSTRUMENT REPAIRERS	87949	ALL OTHER MINING MACHINE OPERATORS
85908	ELECTROMEDICAL AND BIOMEDICAL EQUIPMENT REPAIRERS	87999	ALL OTHER CONSTRUCTION AND EXTRACTIVE WORKERS
85911	ELECTRIC METER INSTALLERS AND REPAIRERS	89102	TOOL AND DIE MAKERS
85914	CAMERA AND PHOTOGRAPHIC EQUIPMENT REPAIRERS	89105	INSTRUMENT MAKERS, PRECISION
		89108	MACHINISTS
85917	WATCHMAKERS	89111	TOOL GRINDERS, FILERS, ETC.
85921	MUSICAL INSTRUMENT REPAIRERS AND TUNERS	89114	PATTERN AND MODEL MAKERS, METAL
85923	LOCKSMITHS AND SAFE REPAIRERS	89117	LAYOUT WORKERS, METAL, PRECISION
85926	OFFICE MACHINE AND CASH REGISTER SERVICERS	89121	SHIPFITTERS
		89123	JEWELERS AND SILVERSMITHS
85928	MECHANICAL CONTROL AND VALVE INSTALLERS AND REPAIRERS	89126	HAND WORKERS, JEWELRY AND RELATED PRODUCTS, PRECISION
85932	ELEVATOR INSTALLERS AND REPAIRERS	89128	ETCHERS AND ENGRAVERS, HAND OR MACHINE, PRECISION
85935	RIGGERS		
85938	MOBILE HOME REPAIRERS	89132	SHEET METAL WORKERS
85944	GAS APPLIANCE REPAIRERS	89135	BOILERMAKERS
85947	COIN AND VENDING MACHINE SERVICERS AND REPAIRERS	89199	ALL OTHER PRECISION METAL WORKERS
		89302	PATTERN AND MODEL MAKERS, WOOD
85951	BICYCLE REPAIRERS	89305	PATTERN MARKERS, WOOD
85953	TIRE REPAIRERS AND CHANGERS	89308	WOOD MACHINISTS
85956	MENDERS, GARMENTS, LINENS, AND RELATED	89311	CABINETMAKERS AND BENCH CARPENTERS
85999	ALL OTHER MECHANICS, INSTALLERS, AND REPAIRERS	89314	FURNITURE FINISHERS
		89399	ALL OTHER PRECISION WOODWORKERS
87102	CARPENTERS	89502	PATTERN MAKERS AND LAYOUT WORKERS, FABRIC AND APPAREL
87105	CEILING TILE INSTALLERS AND ACOUSTICAL CARPENTERS	89505	CUSTOM TAILORS AND SEWERS
87108	DRYWALL INSTALLERS	89508	UPHOLSTERERS
87111	TAPERS	89511	SHOE AND LEATHER WORKERS AND REPAIRERS, PRECISION
87114	LATHERS		
87121	BRATTICE BUILDERS	89514	SPOTTERS, DRY CLEANING
87202	ELECTRICIANS	89517	PRESSERS, DELICATE FABRICS
87302	BRICK MASONS	89521	DYERS, PRECISION
87305	STONE MASONS	89599	ALL OTHER PRECISION TEXTILE, APPAREL, AND FURNISHING WORKERS
87308	HARD TILE SETTERS		
87311	CONCRETE AND TERRAZZO FINISHERS	89702	COMPOSITORS AND TYPESETTERS, PRECISION
87314	REINFORCING METAL WORKERS	89705	JOB PRINTERS
87317	PLASTERERS	89706	PASTE-UP WORKERS
87402	PAINTERS AND PAPERHANGERS, CONSTRUCTION AND MAINTENANCE	89708	LITHOGRAPHY AND PHOTOENGRAVING WORKERS, PRECISION
87502	PLUMBERS, PIPEFITTERS, AND STEAMFITTERS	89712	PHOTOENGRAVERS
87505	PIPELAYING FITTERS	89713	CAMERA OPERATORS
87508	PIPELAYERS	89715	SCANNER OPERATORS
87511	SEPTIC TANK SERVICERS AND SEWER PIPE CLEANERS	89717	STRIPPERS
		89718	PLATEMAKERS
87602	CARPET INSTALLERS	89719	ALL OTHER LITHOGRAPHY AND PHOTOENGRAVING WORKERS
87605	FLOOR LAYERS, EXCEPT CARPET		
87608	FLOOR SANDING MACHINE OPERATORS	89721	BOOKBINDERS
87702	AIR HAMMER OPERATORS	89799	ALL OTHER PRECISION PRINTING WORKERS
87705	PILE DRIVING OPERATORS	89802	SLAUGHTERERS AND BUTCHERS
87708	PAVING, SURFACING, AND TAMPING EQUIPMENT OPERATORS	89805	BAKERS, MANUFACTURING
		89808	FOOD BATCHMAKERS
87711	HIGHWAY MAINTENANCE WORKERS	89899	ALL OTHER PRECISION FOOD AND TOBACCO WORKERS
87714	RAIL-TRACK LAYING AND MAINTENANCE EQUIPMENT OPERATORS		
		89902	FOUNDRY MOLD AND CORE MAKERS, PRECISION
87802	INSULATION WORKERS	89905	MOLDERS/SHAPERS, EXCEPT JEWELRY AND FOUNDRY, PRECISION
87805	SHEET METAL DUCT INSTALLERS		
87808	ROOFERS	89908	PATTERNMAKERS, MODEL MAKERS, AND RELATED WORKERS, PRECISION
87811	GLAZIERS		
87814	STRUCTURAL METAL WORKERS	89911	DETAIL DESIGN DECORATORS AND PAINTERS, PRECISION
87817	FENCE ERECTORS		
87899	ALL OTHER CONSTRUCTION TRADES WORKERS	89914	PHOTOGRAPHIC PROCESS WORKERS, PRECISION
87902	EARTH DRILLERS, EXCEPT OIL AND GAS	89917	OPTICAL GOODS WORKERS, PRECISION
87905	BLASTERS AND EXPLOSIVES WORKERS	89921	DENTAL LAB TECHNICIANS, PRECISION
87908	ROCK SPLITTERS, QUARRY	89923	MEDICAL APPLIANCE MAKERS
87911	ROTARY DRILL OPERATORS, OIL AND GAS EXTRACTION	89926	GEM AND DIAMOND WORKERS
		89999	ALL OTHER PRECISION WORKERS
87914	DERRICK OPERATORS, OIL AND GAS EXTRACTION	91102	SAWING MACHINE TOOL SETTERS AND SET-UP OPERATORS, METAL AND PLASTIC
87917	SERVICE UNIT OPERATORS		

91105	LATHE MACHINE TOOL SETTERS AND SET-UP OPERATORS, METAL AND PLASTIC
91108	DRILLING MACHINE TOOL SETTERS AND SET-UP OPERATORS, METAL AND PLASTIC
91111	MILLING MACHINE SETTERS AND SET-UP OPERATORS, METAL AND PLASTIC
91114	GRINDING MACHINE SETTERS AND SET-UP OPERATORS, METAL AND PLASTIC
91117	MACHINE TOOL CUTTING OPERATORS AND TENDERS, METAL AND PLASTIC
91302	PUNCHING MACHINE SETTERS AND SET-UP OPERATORS, METAL AND PLASTIC
91305	PRESS MACHINE SETTERS AND SET-UP OPERATORS, METAL AND PLASTIC
91308	SHEAR MACHINE SETTERS AND SET-UP OPERATORS, METAL AND PLASTIC
91311	EXTRUDING AND DRAWING MACHINE SETTERS AND SET-UP OPERATORS, METAL AND PLASTIC
91314	ROLLING MACHINE SETTERS AND SET-UP OPERATORS, METAL AND PLASTIC
91317	FORGING MACHINE SETTERS AND SET-UP OPERATORS, METAL AND PLASTIC
91321	MACHINE FORMING OPERATORS AND TENDERS, METAL AND PLASTIC
91502	NUMERICAL CONTROL MACHINE TOOL OPERATORS AND TENDERS, METAL AND PLASTIC
91505	COMBINATION MACHINE TOOL SETTERS AND SET-UP OPERATORS, METAL AND PLASTIC
91508	COMBINATION MACHINE TOOL OPERATORS AND TENDERS, METAL AND PLASTIC
91702	WELDING MACHINE SETTERS AND SET-UP OPERATORS
91705	WELDING MACHINE OPERATORS AND TENDERS
91708	SOLDERING AND BRAZING MACHINE SETTERS AND SET-UP OPERATORS
91711	SOLDERING AND BRAZING MACHINE OPERATORS AND TENDERS
91714	METAL FABRICATORS, STRUCTURAL METAL PRODUCTS
91902	PLASTIC MOLDING MACHINE SETTERS AND SET-UP OPERATORS
91905	PLASTIC MOLDING MACHINE OPERATORS AND TENDERS
91908	METAL MOLDING MACHINE SETTERS AND SET-UP OPERATORS
91911	METAL MOLDING MACHINE OPERATORS AND TENDERS
91914	FOUNDRY MOLD ASSEMBLY AND SHAKEOUT WORKERS
91917	ELECTROLYTIC PLATING MACHINE SETTERS AND SET-UP OPERATORS, METAL AND PLASTIC
91921	ELECTROLYTIC PLATING MACHINE OPERATORS AND TENDERS, METAL AND PLASTIC
91923	NONELECTROLYTIC PLATING MACHINE SETTERS AND SET-UP OPERATORS, METAL AND PLASTIC
91926	NONELECTROLYTIC PLATING MACHINE OPERATORS AND TENDERS, METAL AND PLASTIC
91928	HEATING EQUIPMENT SETTERS AND SET-UP OPERATORS, METAL AND PLASTIC
91932	HEAT TREATING MACHINE OPERATORS AND TENDERS, METAL AND PLASTIC
91935	FURNACE OPERATORS AND TENDERS
91938	HEATERS, METAL AND PLASTIC
92197	ALL OTHER METAL AND PLASTIC MACHINE SETTERS
92198	ALL OTHER METAL AND PLASTIC MACHINE OPERATORS
92302	SAWING MACHINE SETTERS AND SET-UP OPERATORS
92305	HEAD SAWYERS AND SAWING MACHINE OPERATORS AND TENDERS, SETTERS AND SET-UP OPERATORS
92308	SAWING MACHINE OPERATORS AND TENDERS
92311	WOODWORKING MACHINE SETTERS AND SET-UP OPERATORS
92314	WOODWORKING MACHINE OPERATORS AND TENDERS
92512	OFFSET LITHOGRAPHIC PRESS OPERATORS
92515	LETTERPRESS OPERATORS
92519	ALL OTHER PRINTING PRESS SETTERS AND SET-UP OPERATORS
92522	SPECIALTY MATERIALS PRINTING MACHINE SETTERS AND SET-UP OPERATORS
92524	SCREEN PRINTING MACHINE SETTERS AND SET-UP OPERATORS
92525	BINDERY MACHINE SETTERS AND SET-UP OPERATORS
92529	ALL OTHER PRINTING RELATED SETTERS AND SET-UP OPERATORS
92541	TYPESETTING AND COMPOSING MACHINE OPERATORS AND TENDERS
92543	PRINTING PRESS MACHINE OPERATORS AND TENDERS
92545	PHOTOENGRAVING AND LITHOGRAPHING MACHINE OPERATORS AND TENDERS
92546	BINDERY MACHINE OPERATORS
92549	ALL OTHER PRINTING, BINDERY AND RELATED WORKERS
92702	TEXTILE MACHINE SETTERS AND SET-UP OPERATORS
92705	TEXTILE MACHINE OPERATORS AND TENDERS, WINDING
92708	EXTRUDING AND FORMING MACHINE OPERATORS AND TENDERS, SYNTHETIC FIBERS
92711	TEXTILE DRAW-OUT MACHINE OPERATORS AND TENDERS
92714	TEXTILE BLEACHING AND DYEING MACHINE OPERATORS AND TENDERS
92717	SEWING MACHINE OPERATORS, GARMENT
92721	SEWING MACHINE OPERATORS, NON-GARMENT
92723	SHOE SEWING MACHINE OPERATORS AND TENDERS
92726	LAUNDERING AND DRYCLEANING MACHINE OPERATORS AND TENDERS, EXCEPT PRESS
92728	PRESSING MACHINE OPERATORS AND TENDERS, TEXTILE, GARMENT AND RELATED
92902	ELECTRONIC SEMICONDUCTOR PROCESSORS
92905	MOTION PICTURE PROJECTIONISTS
92908	PHOTOGRAPHIC PROCESSING MACHINE OPERATORS AND TENDERS
92911	TIRE BUILDING MACHINE OPERATORS
92914	PAPER GOODS MACHINE SETTERS AND SET-UP OPERATORS
92917	COOKING MACHINE OPERATORS AND TENDERS, FOOD AND TOBACCO
92921	ROASTING MACHINE OPERATORS AND TENDERS, FOOD AND TOBACCO
92923	FURNACE, KILN, OR KETTLE OPERATORS AND TENDERS
92926	BOILER OPERATORS AND TENDERS, LOW PRESSURE
92928	COOLING AND FREEZING EQUIPMENT OPERATORS AND TENDERS
92932	DAIRY PROCESSING EQUIPMENT OPERATORS, INCLUDING SETTERS
92935	CHEMICAL EQUIPMENT CONTROLLERS AND OPERATORS
92938	CHEMICAL EQUIPMENT TENDERS
92941	CUTTING AND SLICING MACHINE SETTERS
92944	CUTTING AND SLICING MACHINE OPERATORS AND TENDERS
92947	PAINTERS, TRANSPORTATION EQUIPMENT
92951	PAINTING MACHINE SETTERS AND SET-UP OPERATORS
92953	PAINTING MACHINE OPERATORS AND TENDERS
92956	CEMENTING AND GLUING MACHINE OPERATORS AND TENDERS

92958	CLEANING AND PICKLING EQUIPMENT OPERATORS AND TENDERS
92962	SEPARATING AND STILL MACHINE OPERATORS AND TENDERS
92965	CRUSHING AND MIXING MACHINE OPERATORS AND TENDERS
92968	EXTRUDING AND FORMING MACHINE SETTERS
92971	EXTRUDING AND FORMING MACHINE OPERATORS AND TENDERS
92974	PACKAGING AND FILLING MACHINE OPERATORS AND TENDERS
92997	ALL OTHER MACHINE SETTERS AND SET-UP OPERATORS
92998	ALL OTHER MACHINE OPERATORS AND TENDERS
93102	AIRCRAFT ASSEMBLERS, PRECISION
93105	MACHINE BUILDERS AND OTHER PRECISION MACHINE ASSEMBLERS
93108	FITTERS, STRUCTURAL METAL, PRECISION
93111	ELECTROMECHANICAL EQUIPMENT ASSEMBLERS, PRECISION
93114	ELECTRICAL AND ELECTRONIC EQUIPMENT ASSEMBLERS, PRECISION
93117	WATCH AND CLOCK ASSEMBLERS AND RELATED WORKERS, PRECISION
93197	ALL OTHER PRECISION ASSEMBLERS, METAL
93902	MACHINE ASSEMBLERS
93905	ELECTRICAL AND ELECTRONIC ASSEMBLERS
93908	COIL WINDERS, TAPERS, AND FINISHERS
93911	GLAZIERS, MANUFACTURING
93914	WELDERS AND CUTTERS
93917	SOLDERERS AND BRAZERS
93921	PRESSERS, HAND
93923	SEWERS, HAND
93926	CUTTERS AND TRIMMERS, HAND
93928	PORTABLE MACHINE CUTTERS
93932	CARPET CUTTERS, DIAGRAMMERS, AND SEAMERS
93935	CANNERY WORKERS
93938	MEAT, POULTRY, AND FISH CUTTERS AND TRIMMERS, HAND
93941	METAL POURERS AND CASTERS, BASIC SHAPES
93944	MOLDERS AND CASTERS, HAND
93947	PAINTING, COATING, AND DECORATING WORKERS, HAND
93951	ENGRAVING AND PRINTING WORKERS, HAND
93953	GRINDERS AND POLISHERS, HAND
93956	ALL OTHER ASSEMBLERS AND FABRICATORS
93999	ALL OTHER HAND WORKERS
95002	WATER AND LIQUID WASTE TREATMENT PLANT AND SYSTEM OPERATORS
95005	GAS PLANT OPERATORS
95008	CHEMICAL PLANT AND SYSTEM OPERATORS
95011	PETROLEUM PUMP SYSTEM OPERATORS
95014	PETROLEUM REFINERY AND CONTROL PANEL OPERATORS
95017	GAUGERS
95021	POWER GENERATING PLANT OPERATORS
95023	AUXILIARY EQUIPMENT OPERATORS, POWER
95026	POWER REACTOR OPERATORS
95028	POWER DISTRIBUTORS AND DISPATCHERS
95032	STATIONARY ENGINEERS
95099	ALL OTHER PLANT AND SYSTEM OPERATORS
97102	TRUCK DRIVERS, HEAVY
97105	TRUCK DRIVERS, LIGHT
97108	BUS DRIVERS
97111	BUS DRIVERS, SCHOOL
97114	TAXI DRIVERS AND CHAUFFEURS
97117	DRIVER/SALES WORKERS
97199	ALL OTHER MOTOR VEHICLE OPERATORS
97302	RAILROAD CONDUCTORS AND YARDMASTERS
97305	LOCOMOTIVE ENGINEERS
97308	RAILROAD YARD ENGINEERS, DINKY OPERATORS, AND HOSTLERS
97311	LOCOMOTIVE FIRERS
97314	SUBWAY AND STREETCAR OPERATORS
97317	RAILROAD BRAKE, SIGNAL, AND SWITCH OPERATORS
97399	ALL OTHER RAILROAD VEHICLE OPERATORS AND CONTROLLERS
97502	CAPTAIN
97505	MATES, SHIP, BOAT, AND BARGE
97508	PILOTS, SHIP
97511	MOTORBOAT OPERATORS
97514	ABLE SEAMEN
97517	ORDINARY SEAMEN AND MARINE OILERS
97521	SHIP ENGINEERS
97702	AIRCRAFT PILOTS AND FLIGHT ENGINEERS
97802	BRIDGE, LOCK, AND LIGHT HOUSE TENDERS
97805	SERVICE STATION ATTENDANTS
97808	PARKING LOT ATTENDANTS
97899	ALL OTHER TRANSPORTATION AND RELATED WORKERS
97902	LONGSHORE EQUIPMENT OPERATORS
97905	TANK CAR AND TRUCK LOADERS
97908	OIL PUMPERS, EXCEPT WELL HEAD
97911	WELL HEAD PUMPERS
97914	MAIN LINE STATION ENGINEERS
97917	GAS PUMPING STATION OPERATORS
97921	GAS COMPRESSOR OPERATORS
97923	EXCAVATION AND LOADING MACHINE OPERATORS
97926	DRAGLINE OPERATORS
97928	DREDGE OPERATORS AND DIPPER TENDERS
97932	LOADING MACHINE OPERATORS, UNDERGROUND MINE
97935	SHUTTLE CAR OPERATORS
97938	GRADER, DOZER, AND SCRAPER OPERATORS
97941	HOIST AND WINCH OPERATORS
97944	CRANE AND TOWER OPERATORS
97947	INDUSTRIAL TRUCK AND TRACTOR OPERATORS
97951	CONVEYOR OPERATORS AND TENDERS
97953	PUMP OPERATORS
97956	OPERATING ENGINEERS
97989	ALL OTHER MATERIAL MOVING EQUIPMENT OPERATORS
98102	MECHANIC AND REPAIRER HELPERS
98311	HELPERS, BRICK AND STONE MASON
98312	HELPERS, CARPENTERS AND RELATED
98313	HELPERS, ELECTRICIANS AND RELATED
98314	HELPERS, PAINTERS AND PAPERHANGERS
98315	HELPERS, PLUMBERS AND RELATED
98316	HELPERS, ROOFERS
98319	HELPERS, ALL OTHER CONSTRUCTION TRADES
98323	HELPERS, EXTRACTIVE WORKERS
98502	MACHINE FEEDERS AND OFFBEARERS
98702	STEVEDORES, EXCEPT EQUIPMENT OPERATORS
98705	REFUSE COLLECTORS
98799	ALL OTHER FREIGHT, STOCK, AND MATERIAL MOVERS, HAND
98902	HAND PACKERS AND PACKAGERS
98905	VEHICLE WASHERS AND EQUIPMENT CLEANERS
98999	ALL OTHER HELPERS, LABORERS, AND MATERIAL MOVERS, HAND

Appendix G
Materials, Products, Subject Matter, and Services (MPSMS) Codes

These codes tell you what materials (M), products (P), subject matter (SM), or services (S) are used or provided in each job listed in *The Enhanced Guide for Occupational Exploration*. These codes are derived from the *Standard Classification Manual* published by the U.S. Department of Commerce and consist of 580 codes. This list is updated from the one published earlier in the *Handbook for Analyzing Jobs*, published by the U.S. Department of Labor and is presented here in numeric order. The MPSMS codes begin with the number 300.

300 Plant Farm Crops
301 Grains
302 Field Crops, except Grain
303 Vegetables & Melons
304 Citrus Fruits
305 Fruits, except Citrus
306 Tree Nuts
309 Plant Farm Crops, n.e.c.
310 Horticultural Specialties, Forest Trees & Forest Products
311 Floricultural & Related Nursery Products
312 Ornamental Trees
313 Standing Timber
314 Forest Nursery Products
319 Horticultural Spec., Forest Trees, & Forest Products, n.e.c.
320 Animals
321 Cattle
322 Hogs
323 Sheep & Goats
324 Poultry & Other Fowl
325 Captive Fur-Bearing Animals
326 Game & Wildlife
327 Horses & Other Equines
329 Animals, n.e.c.
330 Marine Life
331 Finfish
332 Shellfish
339 Marine Life, n.e.c.
340 Raw Fuels & Nonmetallic Minerals
341 Coal & Lignite
342 Crude Petroleum & Natural Gas
343 Stone, Dimension
344 Stone, Crushed & Broken
345 Sand & Gravel
346 Clay
347 Chemical & Fertilizer Minerals
349 Raw Fuels & Nonmetallic Minerals, n.e.c.

350 Raw Metallic Minerals
351 Iron Ores
352 Copper Ores
353 Lead & Zinc Ores
354 Gold & Silver Ores
355 Bauxite & Other Aluminum Ores
356 Ferroalloy Ores, except Vanadium
357 Mercury Ores
358 Uranium, Radium & Vanadium Ores
359 Raw Metallic Minerals
360 Structures
361 Buildings, except Prefabricated
362 Highways & Streets
363 Bridges, Tunnels, Viaducts, & Elevated Highways
364 Water, Gas, & Sewer Mains
365 Marine Construction
366 Powerplant Projects
367 Railroads & Subways
368 Oil Refineries
369 Structures, n.e.c.
370 Ordnance
371 Guns, Howitzers, Mortars & Related Equipment
372 Ammunition, except Small Arms
373 Small Arms
374 Small Arms Ammunition
375 Guided Missiles
379 Ordnance & Accessories, n.e.c.
380 Food Staples & Related
381 Grain Mill Products
382 Meat Products, Processed
383 Dairy Products
384 Bakery Products
385 Oils & Fats, Edible
386 Seafood, Processed
387 Fruits & Vegetables, Processed
389 Food Staples & Related, n.e.c.
390 Food Specialties
391 Coffee, Tea, & Spices

392 Sugar & Syrup
393 Confectionery & Related Products
394 Flavoring Extracts & Flavoring Syrups
395 Beverages, Alcoholic
396 Soft Drinks & Carbonated Waters
397 Macaroni, Spaghetti, Vermicelli, Noodles
398 Vinegar & Cider
399 Food Specialties, n.e.c.
400 Tobacco Products
401 Cigarettes
402 Cigars
403 Tobacco, Chewing, Smoking, & Snuff
404 Tobacco, Stemmed & Redried
409 Tobacco Products, n.e.c.
410 Textile Fibers & Related
411 Yarn
412 Thread
413 Cordage & Twine
414 Fiber Stock
419 Textile Fibers & Related, n.e.c.
420 Fabrics & Related
421 Fabrics, Broad Woven Cotton
422 Fabrics, Broad Woven Wool
423 Narrow Fabrics & Related Smallwares
424 Fabrics, Knitted
425 Fabrics, Non-woven
429 Fabrics & Related, n.e.c.
430 Textile Products
431 Carpets & Rugs
432 Textiles, Fancy
433 Paddings & Upholstery Filling
434 Impregnated & Coated Fabrics
435 House furnishings
436 Canvas & Related Products
439 Textile Products, n.e.c.
440 Apparel

441 Men's & Boy's Suits, Coats, & Overcoats
442 Men's & Boys' Furnishings, Work Clothing
443 Women's, Girls' & Infants' Outwear
444 Women's, Girls' & Infants' Undergarments
445 Hats
446 Hosiery
447 Fur Goods
449 Apparel, n.e.c.
450 Lumber & Wood Products
451 Logs & Hewn Timber Products, Untreated
452 Sawmill, Planing Mill, & Treated Wood Products
453 Veneer & Plywood
454 Wood Containers
455 Prefabricated Wood Buildings, Mobile Homes
456 Particleboard
457 Wood Articles
459 Lumber & Wood Products, n.e.c.
460 Furniture & Fixtures
461 Wood Household Furniture, except Upholstered
462 Wood Household Furniture, Upholstered
463 Metal Household Furniture
464 Mattress, Bedsprings, & Sofa Beds
465 Wood Office, Public Building, & Related Furniture
466 Metal Office, Public Building, & Related Furniture
467 Wood & Metal Fixtures
468 Plastic, Glass, & Fiberglass Furniture & Fixtures
469 Furniture & Fixtures, n.e.c.
470 Paper & Allied Products
471 Pulp
472 Nonconverted Paper & Paperboard
473 Nonconverted Building Paper & Building Board
474 Converted Paper & Paperboard Products
475 Paperboard Containers & Boxes
479 Paper & Allied Products, n.e.c.
480 Printed & Published Products
481 Newspapers
482 Periodicals
483 Books & Pamphlets
484 Manifold Business Forms
485 Greeting Cards
486 Blankbooks, Looseleaf Binders, & Related Products
489 Miscellaneous Published & Printed Books
490 Chemical & Allied Products
491 Chemicals, Inorganic
492 Plastics Materials & Synthetic Resins & Fibers
493 Drugs
494 Cleaning Preparations, Perfumes, & Cosmetics
495 Paints, Enamels, & Allied Products
496 Chemicals, Organic
497 Agricultural Chemicals
499 Chemical & Allied Products, n.e.c.
500 Petroleum & Related Products
501 Petroleum Products
502 Paving Materials
503 Roofing Materials
504 Fuel Briquettes, Packaged Fuel, & Powdered Fuel
505 Coke

509 Petroleum & Related Products, n.e.c.
510 Rubber & Miscellaneous Plastic Products
511 Tires & Tubes
512 Rubber & Plastic Footwear
513 Reclaimed Rubber
514 Rubber & Plastic Hose & Belting
519 Rubber & Miscellaneous Plastic Products, n.e.c.
520 Leather & Leather Products
521 Hides, Skins,& Leather
522 Footwear, except Rubber
523 Leather Gloves & Mittens
524 Luggage of any Material
525 Handbags & Related Accessories of any Material
529 Leather & Leather Products, n.e.c.
530 Stone, Clay, & Glass Products
531 Flat, Pressed, or Blown Glass & Glassware
532 Glass Products Made of Purchased Glass
533 Cement, Hydraulic
534 Structural Clay Products
535 Pottery & Related Products
536 Concrete, Gypsum, & Plaster Products
537 Cut Stone & Stone Products
538 Abrasive, Asbestos, & Related Products
539 Stone, Clay, & Glass Products, n.e.c
540 Metal, Ferrous & Nonferrous
541 Blast Furnace, Steelworks
542 Metal Castings
543 Nonferrous Metals, Smelted & Refined
544 Nonferrous Metals, Rolled, Drawn, & Extruded
549 Metal, Ferrous & Nonferrous, n.e.c.
550 Fabricated Metal Products
551 Metal Cans & Containers
552 Cutlery, Handtools & General Hardware
553 Nonelectric Heating Equipment
554 Fabricated Structural Metal Products
555 Screw-Machine Products
556 Metal Forgings & Stampings
557 Fabricated Wire Products
559 Fabricated Metal Products, n.e.c.
560 Machinery & Equipment, except Electrical
561 Engines & Turbines
562 Farm & Garden Machinery & Equipment
563 Construction Machinery & Equipment
564 Mining & Oil-Field Machinery & Equipment
565 Materials-Handling Machinery & Equipment
566 Metalworking Machinery & Equipment
567 Special Industrial Machinery
568 General Industrial Machinery & Equipment
570 Machinery & Equipment, except Electrical
571 Office, Computing & Accounting Machines
572 Service-Industry Machinery
573 Refrigeration & Air-Conditioning Equipment
579 Machinery & Equipment, except Electrical, n.e.c.
580 Electrical & Electronic Machinery, Equipment & Supplies

581 Electrical Transmission & Distribution Equipment
582 Electrical Industrial Apparatus
583 Household Appliances
584 Electric Lighting & Wiring Equipment
585 Home-Entertainment Electric Equipment
586 Communication & Related Equipment
587 Electronic Components & Accessories
589 Electrical & Electronic Machinery, Equipment & Supplies, n.e.c.
590 Transportation Equipment
591 Motor Vehicles & Motor-Vehicle Equipment
592 Aircraft & Parts
593 Ships & Boats
594 Railroad Equipment
595 Motorcycles, Bicycles & Parts
596 Space Vehicles & Parts
597 Travel Trailers & Campers
598 Military Tanks & Tank Components
599 Transportation Equipment, n.e.c.
600 Measuring, Analyzing & Controlling Instruments
601 Engineering, Laboratory, Scientific Instruments
602 Measuring & Controlling Instruments
603 Optical Instruments & Lenses
604 Surgical, Medical & Dental Instruments & Supplies
605 Ophthalmic Goods
606 Photographic Equipment & Supplies
607 Watches, Clocks, Clockwork-Operated Devices
609 Measuring, Analyzing & Controlling Instruments, n.e.c.
610 Miscellaneous Fabricated Products
611 Jewelry, Precious Metal
612 Silverware, Plated Ware, & Stainless Steel Ware
613 Jewelers' Findings & Materials
614 Musical Instruments & Parts
615 Games & Toys
616 Sporting & Athletic Goods
617 Pens, Pencils, & Other Office & Artists' Materials
618 Costume Jewelry & Novelties
619 Miscellaneous Fabricated Products, n.e.c.
700 Architecture & Engineering
701 Architectural Engineering
702 Aeronautical Engineering
703 Electrical, Electronic Engineering
704 Civil Engineering
705 Ceramic Engineering
706 Mechanical Engineering
707 Chemical Engineering
708 Mining & Petroleum Engineering
710 Architecture & Engineering
711 Metallurgical Engineering
712 Industrial Engineering
713 Agricultural Engineering
714 Marine Engineering
715 Nuclear Engineering
716 Surveying, Cartographic Engineering
719 Architecture & Engineering, n.e.c.
720 Mathematics & Physical Sciences
721 Mathematics
722 Astronomy
723 Chemistry
724 Physics
725 Geology & Geophysics
729 Mathematics & Physical Sciences, n.e.c.
730 Life Sciences

731 Agriculture, Horticulture, & Forestry
732 Biological Sciences
733 Psychology
739 Life Sciences, n.e.c.
740 Social Sciences
741 Economics
742 Political Science
743 History
744 Sociology
745 Anthropology
749 Social Sciences, n.e.c.
750 Arts & Literature
751 Fine Arts
752 Graphic Arts
753 Photography
754 Dramatics
755 Rhythmics
756 Music
757 Literature & Journalism
759 Arts, n.e.c.
850 Transportation Services
851 Interurban Railroad Transportation
852 Local & Suburban Transit & Interurban Buses
853 Motor Freight Transportation & Warehousing
854 Water Transportation
855 Air Transportation
856 Pipeline Transportation
859 Transportation Services, n.e.c.
860 Communication Services
861 Telephone Communication
862 Telegraph Communication
863 Radio Broadcasting
864 Television Broadcasting
867 Blueprinting, Photocopying, and Photofinishing Services
869 Communication Services, n.e.c.
870 Electric, Gas, & Sanitary Services
871 Electric Services
872 Gas Production & Distribution
873 Water Supply & Irrigation Services

874 Sanitary Services
875 Steam Supply
879 Electric, Gas, & Sanitary Services, n.e.c.
880 Merchandising Services
881 Retail Trade
882 Wholesale Trade
883 Route Sales & Delivery Services
884 Auctioneering, Vending, & Rental Services
885 Sales Promotion Services
889 Merchandising Services, n.e.c.
890 General Business, Finance, Insurance, & Real Estate Services
891 Clerical Services, except Bookkeeping
892 Accounting, Auditing, & Bookkeeping Services
893 General Administration
894 Financial Services
895 Insurance & Real Estate
896 Advertising & Public Relations Services
897 Blueprinting, Photocopying, & Photofinishing Services
898 Production Services
899 General Business Services, n.e.c.
900 Domestic, Building, & Personal Services
901 Domestic Services
902 Lodging Services
903 Meal Services, except Domestic
904 Beauty & Barbering Services
905 Janitorial & Portering Services
906 Apparel & Furnishing Services
907 Funeral & Crematory Services
909 Domestic, Building, & Personal Services, n.e.c.
910 Amusement & Recreation Services
911 Motion Picture Services
912 Theater Services
913 Sports Participation
914 Sports Services

919 Amusement & Recreation Services, n.e.c.
920 Medical & Other Health Services
921 Physician Services
922 Dental Services
923 Optometric, Chiropractic, & Related Services
924 Nursing, Dietetic, & Therapeutic Services
925 Health Technological Services
926 Medical Assistant, Aide, & Attendant Services
929 Medical & Other Health Services, n.e.c.
930 Educational, Legal, Museum, Library & Archival Services
931 Educational Services
932 Legal Services
933 Museum, Library, & Archival Services
939 Educational, Legal, Museum, Library & Archival Services, n.e.c.
940 Social, Employment, & Spiritual Services
941 Social & Welfare Services
942 Child & Adult Residential & Day-Care Services
943 Employment Services
944 Spiritual Services
949 Social, Employment, & Spiritual Services, n.e.c.
950 Government & Related Services
951 Protective Services, except Military
952 Military Services
953 Regulatory Law Investigation & Control Services
954 Postal Services
959 Government & Related Services, n.e.c.
960 Miscellaneous Services
961 Motor-Vehicle Services
962 Deodorizing, Exterminating, & Decontaminating Services
969 Miscellaneous Services, n.e.c.

Appendix H
Work Fields

The numeric work field codes used in *The Enhanced Guide for Occupational Exploration* are listed in numeric below along with their related definitions. They indicate the most significant skills(s) used in an occupation. There are 100 such work fields and each job uses one or more of them. The codes listed here are those now used by the U.S. Department of Labor and have some differences from the older list originally published in the *Handbook for Analyzing Jobs*.

001 Hunting-Fishing
002 Animal Propagating
003 Plant Cultivating
004 Logging
005 Mining-Quarrying-Earth Boring
007 Excavating-Clearing-Foundation Building
011 Material Moving
013 Transporting
014 Pumping
021 Stationary Engineering
031 Cleaning
032 Surface Finishing
033 Lubricating
034 Butchering-Meat Cutting
041 Filling-Packing-Wrapping
051 Abrading
052 Chipping
053 Boring
054 Shearing-Shaving
055 Milling-Turning-Planing
056 Sawing
057 Machining
061 Fitting-Folding
062 Fastening
063 Gluing-Laminating
071 Bolting-Screwing
072 Nailing
073 Riveting
081 Welding
082 Flame Cutting-Arc Cutting-Beam Cutting
083 Soldering-Brazing
091 Masoning

092 Laying-Covering
094 Caulking
095 Paving
101 Upholstering
102 Structural Fabricating-Installing-Repairing
111 Electrical-Electronic Fabricating-Installing-Repairing
121 Mechanical Fabricating-Installing-Repairing
131 Melting
132 Casting
133 Heat Conditioning
134 Pressing-Forging
135 Die Sizing
136 Molding
141 Baking-Drying
142 Crushing-Grinding
143 Mixing
144 Distilling
145 Separating
146 Cooking-Food Preparing
147 Processing-Compounding
151 Immersing-Coating
152 Saturating
153 Brushing-Spraying
154 Electroplating
161 Combing-Napping
162 Spinning
163 Winding
164 Weaving
165 Knitting
166 Tufting
171 Sewing-Tailoring

182 Etching
183 Engraving
191 Printing
192 Imprinting
201 Photographing
202 Developing-Printing
211 Appraising
212 Inspecting-Measuring-Testing
221 Stock Checking
231 Verbal Recording-Recordkeeping
232 Numerical Recording-Recordkeeping
233 Data Processing
241 Laying Out
242 Drafting
243 Surveying
244 Engineering
251 Researching
261 Writing
262 Artistic Painting-Drawing
263 Composing-Choreographing
264 Styling
271 Investigating
272 Litigating
281 System Communicating
282 Information-Giving
291 Accommodating
292 Merchandising-Sales
293 Protecting
294 Health Caring-Medical
295 Administering
296 Teaching
297 Entertaining
298 Advising-Counseling

Other Titles Available from

jist the job search people

JIST publishes a variety of books on careers and job search topics. Please consider ordering one or more from your dealer, local bookstore, or directly from JIST.

Orders from Individuals: Please use the form below (or provide the same information) to order additional copies of this or other books listed on this page. You are also welcome to send us your order (please enclose money order, check, or credit card information), or simply call our toll free number at **1-800-648-JIST** or **1-317-264-3720**. Our FAX number is **1-317-264-3709. Qualified schools and organizations** may request our catalog and obtain information on quantity discounts (we have over 400 career-related books, videos, and other items). Our offices are open weekdays 8 a.m. to 5 p.m. local time and our address is:

JIST Works, Inc. • 720 North Park Avenue • Indianapolis, IN 46202-3431

QTY	BOOK TITLE	TOTAL ($)
_____	*Getting the Job You Really Want*, J. Michael Farr •ISBN: 0-942784-15-4 • **$9.95**	_____
_____	*The Very Quick Job Search: Get a Good Job in Less Time*, J. Michael Farr •ISBN: 0-942784-72-3 • **$9.95**	_____
_____	*America's 50 Fastest Growing Jobs: An Authoritative Information Source* • ISBN: 0-942784-61-8 • **$10.95**	_____
_____	*America's Top 300 Jobs: A Complete Career Handbook* (trade version of the *Occupational Outlook Handbook*) • ISBN 0-942784-45-6 • **$17.95**	_____
_____	*America's Federal Jobs: A Complete Directory of Federal Career Opportunities* • ISBN 0-942784-81-2 • **$14.95**	_____
_____	*The Resume Solution: How to Write and Use a Resume That Gets Results*, David Swanson • ISBN 0-942784-44-8 • **$10.95**	_____
_____	*The Job Doctor: Good Advice on Getting a Good Job*, Phillip Norris, Ed.D. • ISBN 0-942784-43-X • **$8.95**	_____
_____	*The Right Job for You: An Interactive Career Planning Guide*, J. Michael Farr • ISBN 0-942784-73-1 • **$9.95**	_____
_____	*Exploring Careers: A Young Person's Guide to over 300 Jobs* • ISBN 0-942784-27-8 • **$19.95**	_____
_____	*Work in the New Economy: Careers and Job Seeking into the 21st Century*, Robert Wegmann • ISBN 0-942784-19-78 • **$14.95**	_____
_____	*The Occupational Outlook Handbook* • ISBN 0-942784-38-3 • **$16.95**	_____
_____	*The Career Connection: Guide to College Majors and Their Related Careers*, Dr. Fred Rowe • ISBN 0-942784-82-0 • **$15.95**	_____
_____	*The Career Connection II: Guide to Technical Majors and Their Related Careers*, Dr. Fred Rowe • ISBN 0-942784-83-9 • **$13.95**	_____

Subtotal _____

Sales Tax _____

Shipping: ($3 for first book, $1 for each additional book.) _____

(U.S. Currency only) **TOTAL ENCLOSED WITH ORDER** _____

(Prices subject to change without notice)

❑ Check   ❑ Money order   Credit Card: ❑ MasterCard   ❑ VISA   ❑ AMEX

Card # (if applies)_____Exp. Date_____

Name (please print)_____

Name of Organization (if applies) _____

Address _____

City/State/Zip_____

Daytime Telephone (   ) _____ — _____

Thank-you for your order!